Harvard Encyclopedia of American Ethnic Groups

Harvard Encyclopedia of American Ethnic Groups

Stephan Thernstrom, *Editor*

Ann Orlov, *Managing Editor*
Oscar Handlin, *Consulting Editor*

The Belknap Press of
HARVARD UNIVERSITY PRESS
Cambridge, Massachusetts
and
London, England
1980

Library of Congress Cataloging in Publication Data
Main entry under title:

Harvard encyclopedia of American ethnic groups.

   Includes bibliographies.
1. Minorities—United States—Dictionaries.
2. United States—Ethnic relations—Dictionaries.
3. Ethnicity—Dictionaries. I. Thernstrom, Stephan.
E184.A1H35   973'.04   80-17756
ISBN 0-674-37512-2

Introduction

During the Great Depression of the 1930s, Louis Adamic, a popular writer and journalist, conceived of a project that he believed "would excite all America about herself." A "great Encyclopaedia of the Population of the United States, from the Indians down to the latest immigrant group," would demonstrate, "in as great detail as possible, of what sort of human stuff America is made." Such a work, he wrote, "might very well revolutionize American writing and affect all thinking about the United States." It "would be invaluable to thousands of . . . school principals and teachers . . . and to librarians and social workers. It would appeal not only to New Americans and their immigrant parents . . . but to America as a whole" (*My America*, 1938).

Adamic himself had emigrated from Slovenia (then a province of Austria-Hungary, now part of Yugoslavia) at the age of fourteen, and throughout his life displayed intense interest in the origins of the American people. But, unfortunately, he could not raise the funds he needed from the Federal Emergency Relief Administration and had to give up the idea of the encyclopedia.

Forty years later, this project was well under way when the editors first saw a copy of the Adamic proposal. We were intrigued by what Adamic had wanted to undertake. He had envisaged a work of five to twenty-five volumes, a huge budget, and a staff of hundreds. The enterprise of which this volume is a product was modest in comparison. However, it proceeded on the basis of the article of faith with which he concluded: "But eventually, I think, this job will have to be done—somehow."

The job has been done—somehow. It has been difficult, occasionally frustrating, and always fascinating. It began six years ago with the conviction that a reference work assembling the basic information about the multitude of peoples who make up the population of the United States would be exceedingly valuable and that nothing like it existed. Much of course was available in print about groups as large and prominent as the Afro-Americans, the Mexicans, the Irish, and the Jews—so much, indeed, that the interested reader might not know where to begin. A succinct, authoritative synthesis of the origins, history, and present situation of such familiar peoples, along with an up-to-date critical bibliography, would meet a real need. A good many distinctive and obscure groups, however, seemed not to have a history, certainly not a bibliography, although they frequently did have a newspaper or a journal in a language inaccessible to most Americans. In the case of some, research was already under way, stimulated in part by the ethnic consciousness of the late sixties and early seventies, but little of it was available to the general reader.

At a small planning conference in November 1974 we concluded that the project was feasible and discussed such questions as: how to define an ethnic group, what entries to include, what shape to give the articles, and whether to treat individual groups or to cut topically across them. The nature of the encyclopedia and its organization were debated. Authors like Nathan Glazer and Daniel Patrick Moynihan in *Beyond the Melting Pot* (1963) and Andrew Greeley in *Ethnicity in the United States* (1974) had already demonstrated the value of the comparative analysis of a few major American groups. It seemed appropriate now to broaden the frame of reference for future ethnic studies by surveying all the ethnic groups in the United States, not only the immigrants and refugees who had come voluntarily but also those already in the New World when the first Europeans arrived, those whose ancestors came involuntarily as slaves, and those who became part of the American population as a result of conquest or purchase and subsequent annexation. It would be illuminating to treat the familiar and the obscure in a single volume—to juxtapose the English and the Estonians, the Germans and the Gypsies, the Swedes and the Serbs, in a distillation of the available evidence, presented concisely, informatively, and interestingly.

The growth of popular and scholarly interest in ethnicity during the preceding decade made available a large corps of consultants and ethnic group specialists willing to help. Eventually some 120 contributors wrote the entries in this book, either on individual groups or on broad themes relating to many. Their efforts make possible the first comprehensive and systematic review of the many peoples who constitute the population of the United States. The articles, even those about relatively well-known groups, offer new material and fresh interpretations. The entries on less well-known groups are the product of intensive research in primary sources. Many of these provide the first objective, scholarly discussion to appear in English.

An encyclopedia of American ethnic groups required a definition of an ethnic group, no simple matter because there is as yet no consensus about the precise meaning of ethnicity (*see* Concepts of Ethnicity). A de-

scription of this project, written in August 1976 for general circulation, noted that "the definition of an ethnic group has been necessarily flexible and pragmatic. In some instances it seems obvious; in others there is a question whether or not a group of a certain size perceives itself as different or is perceived as different by those around it. Regional and small religious groups raise other issues."

Ethnicity is an immensely complex phenomenon. All the groups treated here are characterized by some of the following features, although in combinations that vary considerably:

(1) common geographic origin;
(2) migratory status;
(3) race;
(4) language or dialect;
(5) religious faith or faiths;
(6) ties that transcend kinship, neighborhood, and community boundaries;
(7) shared traditions, values, and symbols;
(8) literature, folklore, and music;
(9) food preferences;
(10) settlement and employment patterns;
(11) special interests in regard to politics in the homeland and in the United States;
(12) institutions that specifically serve and maintain the group;
(13) an internal sense of distinctiveness;
(14) an external perception of distinctiveness.

The degree to which these features characterize any group varies considerably with the size and specific history of the group, especially the length of time it has been in the United States. Ethnic groups persist over long periods, but they also change, merge, dissolve. New ones come into being through the process known as ethnogenesis; others disappear. Some groups in this book now exist almost exclusively in the recollections of their descendants—the Scotch-Irish, the Wends, and the Manx, for example. But they played a role in the American past and their history is of interest. On the other hand, some groups have not yet been in the United States long enough to establish generational continuity or to develop the array of institutions conventionally associated with ethnic groups; but they seem to be in the process of formation. The Assyrians, the Bangladeshi, the Copts, and the Zoroastrians are examples.

Assembling an encyclopedia required a working principle for deciding what to discuss under a broad designation and what to distinguish under a less inclusive heading. In addition we had to confront the question of regional variations—whether to run a separate entry on Sicilians or to include them in the Italian entry, whether to include the Frisians with the Dutch, the Kassubes with the Poles. We decided for the Frisians but against a separate entry for Sicilians or for Kassubes.

The Encyclopedia contains 106 group entries, as well as 29 thematic essays, 87 maps, and other supplementary material. This does not mean that there are precisely 106 ethnic groups in the United States; it does mean that according to the abovementioned criteria there are at least 106. A different set of decisions might have expanded the list. Each of the more than 170 American Indian groups, for example, could have been

the subject of a brief entry. It seemed more useful to combine them in a single one, long enough to examine intertribal differences in appropriate detail. The Encyclopedia also combines the Flemings and the Walloons in the entry on Belgians, and discusses related peoples in the entries on Pacific Islanders, Central and South Americans, and North Caucasians, Tatars, and Turkestanis. It separates the people of the Balkans, but unites the Arabs in a single entry, including not only the Syrians, here for two or three generations, but also the Palestinians, Jordanians, Muslim Egyptians, and others who began to come to the United States in significant numbers only after 1965. The category British on the other hand is too broad for that large segment of the American population; it is divided among entries on the English, Cornish, Manx, Scotch-Irish, Scots, Welsh, and British Canadians. There are also entries on Australians and New Zealanders, and South Africans.

Many groups were so obvious that very little thought or investigation was necessary. Among these were immigrants (and their descendants) from Germany, Sweden, Poland, Italy, Greece (including the Greeks from Turkey), China, and Japan. There might have been a question in 1850 as to how best to discuss Americans of German or Italian origin, for they came from countries not then unified politically or culturally, but there is almost no question today about the meaning of these terms. Although provincial ties and informal networks remain important in the context of the United States, most regional groups from these countries have merged —certainly in the public consciousness—except perhaps for the Pennsylvania Germans and the Germans from Russia, whose ties to other Germans have been affected by special circumstances. It is not difficult to treat separately a number of other peoples who did not possess their own nation-state in the Old World but who are unquestionably distinctive in language, religion, and culture—the Assyrians, Basques, Gypsies, and Jews among them.

Greater difficulties arose, however, with respect to several groups "Made in America." To equate "ethnic" with "foreign" is a mistake. The Mormons, for example, originated entirely within the United States; yet the fascinating account of their history in these pages explains why they belong in this volume. The Amish, the Hutterites, and now the Zoroastrians also have a distinctiveness and cohesiveness that justifies such a judgment. The American regional groups included in the Encyclopedia—Appalachians, Southerners, and Yankees—were also "Made in America." They are not the same in character as immigrant or racial groups, but possess a historical identity of their own.

But about some ethnic groups in the United States the Encyclopedia has little to say. At least a few people from every country in the world live in the United States today, and yet they are not discussed in individual entries—Nigerians, Malaysians, and Tibetans come to mind. In most such cases the numbers are very small; but that was not the governing consideration, for the Kurds, the Kalmyks, and the Azerbaijanis have been included. It was not possible to develop a useful entry when the information available about a particular group was too scanty.

After decades of restrictive legislation, the United States has again become a major immigrant-receiving

society. Three million legal immigrants entered the United States in the 1950s, 4 million in the 1960s, and another 4 million in the 1970s. Many of them are members of groups about which Americans generally know very little—Samoans, Guamanians, Tongans, Turkestanis, even Koreans and Filipinos, whose history in the United States goes back many years but whose numbers have grown since World War II. What is written here about the "new new immigrants" should stimulate attention and further inquiry.

The Encyclopedia's coverage is almost exhaustive, but one category of Americans is not included: those who identify themselves as "plain" Americans. There is no entry for "nonethnic" Americans, even though their number is undoubtedly large. Just how large is a matter of dispute since the question of origins and ancestry has become increasingly popular in the last two decades.

Some scholars estimate that a majority of the population of the United States belongs in this category; others claim that it is a large minority. The U.S. Bureau of the Census in its Current Population Surveys has been asking about ancestry since 1969, but its results are not helpful here. When a respondent answers "American" to the question of ancestry, that response is not recorded, and in fact the interviewer is instructed explicitly to follow up such a reply with a probe designed to elicit some other answer. Americans who do not specify a foreign ancestry in answer to the original question or to the subsequent probe are tabulated with others who lack information as "don't know."

All Americans who are not themselves immigrants have ancestors who came from elsewhere. (In the case of the American Indians, the Eskimos, and the Aleuts, they came thousands of years ago.) But ancestry alone does not automatically confer distinctive ethnic identity, even though ethnicity is often viewed as ascriptive, immutable, and primordial, on the grounds that "you can't change your grandfather." The assertion is accurate: you cannot change your grandparents. But you can forget them, and many Americans have. Furthermore, many have such mixed origin that they cannot choose any one identity or affiliation; they have fused into the new breed idealized in the famous play by Israel Zangwill, *The Melting Pot* (1908). Others of mixed ancestry identify with different elements of their heritage in different contexts. And ethnic allegiances need not be mutually exclusive; some people feel an affinity to two or even more groups (*see* Intermarriage; *see also* Appendix I).

Ethnic identification, even when ethnic heritage is unmixed or fully understood, is a matter of individual choice, ratified on a continuum from passive acquiescence to active participation, from denial through mild curiosity to passionate commitment. It may change over time and may vary from one situation to another. It is very difficult to freeze at any single moment. This is less true, to be sure, of racial groups with distinctive physical characteristics, but even in their case "passing" reveals the volitional nature of ethnic identification for at least some members. The fluid and situational nature of ethnicity makes precise estimates of the numbers of "ethnic" or "nonethnic" Americans impossible.

Although this book does not specify how many "plain" Americans there are, nor describe them as a group, it illuminates the processes by which they have evolved. The essays on Assimilation and Pluralism, on American Identity and Americanization, on Education, and on Pluralism: A Political Perspective are especially pertinent. The group entries, also, reveal the powerful cohesive forces that have made the United States a nation of nations, that restore luster to the motto on the seal of the United States: *E Pluribus Unum*. In 1782 when the motto was adopted it referred to the union forged from thirteen separate colonies; subsequently it has come to suggest the ties that bind the remarkable array of diverse peoples who have settled here. Philip Gleason makes an important point in his essay on American identity: "An American nationality does in fact exist . . . To affirm the existence of American nationality does not mean that all Americans are exactly alike or must become uniform in order to be real Americans. It simply means that a genuine national community does exist and that it has its own distinctive principle of unity, its own history, and its own appropriate sense of belongingness." The pages of this Encyclopedia say much about the peoples of the United States and about the character of the national community as well as the local communities created by these peoples.

The contributors are almost as varied as the entries; each was the most qualified individual available, located by searching the literature and consulting at length with advisers in the United States and abroad. We weighed the merits of a sociological work with historical strength against an historical work with sociological depth. Because the origins of each group were of critical importance, a large number of entries were written by historians, but among the contributors are also anthropologists, political scientists, geographers, economists, sociologists, and humanists. Most are second- or third-generation Americans, but some come from abroad, providing a subtle shift in perspective— that of the sending rather than the receiving society.

Very frequently it turned out that only a member of a particular group knew enough or had the necessary language skills and interest to deal with that group. But the editors do not believe that an entry is authentic only if written by a group member. A scholar does not have to be black to write about Afro-Americans or West Indians, or French Canadian to write about Poles. The advantages and disadvantages of affiliation cancel each other out.

Some entries are unsigned at the request of the contributor. Others have been written by members of the editorial staff.

The editors did not seek to obtain identical information for each entry, nor were they interested in complete uniformity of style. But the authors of group entries received a framework, a checklist/outline that was suggestive rather than prescriptive, not a straightjacket but a standard of comparability.

Instructions to contributors asked for essays of 3,000, 8,000, 15,000, and in one instance 40,000 words, not according to any precise formula but on a rough scale based on the estimated size of the group, the length and complexity of its history in the United States, and the availability and nature of source material. Ultimately,

This outline is designed to be suggestive but not prescriptive. It is assumed that each contributor will organize the data available to him or her in the way that works best. Furthermore, these questions and categories are not equally applicable or significant for all groups, but when they do apply they are meant to have both historical and contemporary relevance. Finally, this is a long list but it does not exhaust all possibilities or viewpoints.

ORIGINS:

—from where does group originate? nation-state? state of mind? region? ancient state, present province? new state? awakened nation? are group members exiles or refugees? national community? a people among peoples? a linguistic group? a remnant?

—what languages has (does) the group spoken, written?

—what is the racial composition of group? religious affiliations? majority or minority faith at point of origin?

MIGRATION:

—who migrated? why? how many? where? when? who stayed behind? what were the circumstances of the migration? how was it organized? what policies at point of origin affected migration? at point of arrival?

ARRIVAL:

—when did group first arrive? how? in one or several waves? over a short or long time? did immigrants come alone, one by one, in small groups, or in a stream?

—how did group take shape? was it forcibly incorporated by conquest or slavery? were immigrants voluntary or involuntary? exiles or refugees?

—what kind of society did group enter? colonial? frontier? rural and agricultural? urban? industrial?

—has group been continually or sporadically refreshed by new arrivals? what governs reinforcement? distance? transportation? borders? government policy? changes in place of origin? has there been return migration? re-immigration?

SETTLEMENT:

—where did group settle? what was pattern of distribution? rural/urban? scattered/concentrated? dispersed/segregated?

—what was pattern of geographical mobility? toward dispersion or segregation? from country to city? from city to city?

—what was ecology of settlement? relations among home, workplace, community?

ECONOMIC LIFE:

—what was entry employment? was there specialization in economic activity? among first and subsequent generations?

—what is the characteristic pattern of enterprise? service? entrepreneurial? special resources? characteristic organization of business? relationship to unions? civil service?

—what is economic base of community?

SOCIAL STRUCTURE:

—relation between class and ethnic group? stratification within ethnic group? how did it develop? parallel or incongruous with system of larger society? has it changed? what have been patterns and sources of social mobility?

SOCIAL ORGANIZATION:

—what have been patterns of association? voluntary associations? parochial schools? religious activities and institutions?

—what have been patterns of informal organization? are neighborhood and territory important dimensions of community? are there characteristic social and visiting patterns?

—who are group leaders? how have they emerged or been chosen? for what reasons? from the center or periphery of group? what is their relationship to larger society?

FAMILY AND KINSHIP:

—what is characteristic family form? what is importance of kinship ties? what are marriage patterns? intermarriage? with whom? why?

—how is transition from generation to generation organized? formal institutions? informal *rites de passage?*

BEHAVIOR AND PERSONAL/INDIVIDUAL CHARACTERISTICS:

—are there data on literacy, level of education, mental health, physical health, alcoholism, divorce, childrearing, leisure-time preferences, consumerism?

CULTURE:

—has group maintained its language? orally? in written form? everyday or ceremonial use? how has it been maintained and by whom?

—what are characteristic forms of expression? literary tradition? folklore? folk customs? music? dance? costume? gastronomy? art?

—are there or have there been journals, newspapers, theatres, radio programs, TV?

—does folk tradition survive? where? in what forms?

—are group writings, etc., directed to group alone or to general public?

—ethnic specialists and intellectuals? who have they been? how have they emerged? how have they maintained themselves?

RELIGION:

—what is the religious identity of the group? shaped in USA or continuous with place of origin?

—what are the characteristic patterns of belief or unbelief? has religion been consonant or dissonant with ethnic identity? does religion divide or unify?

—what features of religious practice have been important? high or low participation? generational differences? periodic revivals?

—what have been the characteristic forms of religious organization?

EDUCATION:

—how has group been educated, formally and informally, over the generations? significant changes? parochial vs. public education?

—what relations among culture, education, and religion?

POLITICS:

—when did group enter local and national political life?

—what political organizations are characteristic?

—what coalitions have taken shape? on what base?

—what patterns of participation and behavior have evolved?

—what motivates participation? ideology? interest?

INTERGROUP RELATIONS:

—what contacts has group had with the Anglo-Americans and other ethnic groups? what accommodation has been reached with the larger society? acculturation? assimilation? minority status? separation?

—what conflict/consensus marks interaction between specific group and American society? what experience of racism, prejudice, and discrimination?

GROUP MAINTENANCE:

—what resources have been utilized to maintain the boundaries of community? what informal agencies and what formal institutions?

—what role is played by kinship and marriage patterns? what role is played by educational and religious institutions? by peer pressure?

—what role have relations with the homeland played?

INDIVIDUAL ETHNIC COMMITMENT:

—what are the individual roots of commitment? has there been a change over time? a change with age or with the generations? is it persistent or intermittent? steady or subject to fashion?

BIBLIOGRAPHY:

—please list no more than ten important works— works that will be available to the encyclopedia reader in paperback or in a moderate-sized public or college library. Do not list highly specialized, highly technical, or difficult to obtain works.

the length of each entry is a factor of the initial assignment, of what the contributor provided, and of what the editorial process permitted. No invidious inferences are to be drawn from the brevity or length of any entry.

The group entries are the core of this volume. The Encyclopedia contains, in addition, 50 other substantive entries and brief identifications. A series of thematic essays illuminates the key facets of ethnicity. Some of these are comparative, some philosophical, some historical; others focus on current policy issues or relate ethnicity to major subjects such as education, religion, and literature. The remaining entries, most of them very short, define terms that require more than recourse to a dictionary, with special attention to the major characteristics and constituents of religious groups unfamiliar to Americans and bewildering in their historical complexity.

Eighty-seven maps designed and drawn especially for this volume illustrate the homelands or the regional origins of most of the groups. The size of each map and the amount of information it conveys correspond in most cases to the size and content of the entry it accompanies. Occasionally circumstances required that the map be larger than a relatively brief entry might otherwise warrant. All maps indicate present-day international boundaries and country names; some also show the historic boundaries of former countries or provinces. Shaded areas indicate regions where the group or groups in question live or where certain languages are generally spoken.

The standard for the spelling of place names is *Webster's New Geographical Dictionary* (1972), which generally accepts the dominant language of the present-day country. These forms often differ from those used by certain ethnic groups, but to spell names in the local language would have complicated the maps unduly. At the request of some contributors, however, alternative place names appear in the text in parenthesis on certain maps. When *Webster's* did not list a place name, as for countries that have come into being since 1972, and, in particular, for the historic provinces of former multinational empires in eastern Europe, the Encyclopedia uses the official language of the period treated. Thus, historic provinces within the former Russian Empire are in transliterated Russian, except for those within the Congress Kingdom, which are in Polish. Similarly, county names within the former Hungarian Kingdom are given in Hungarian, except on the map with the Slovak entry, where they appear in Slovak.

In Appendix I, Australian demographer Charles A. Price discusses the complex and controversial methods of estimating the size of groups. He explains why estimates for the same group in different sources vary so greatly. Appendix I offers guidance for readers attempting to sort out conflicting claims and to understand the limitations of the statistical data provided by the U.S. Census Bureau and other federal agencies. Examples of the data available are reproduced in facsimile in Appendix II. Table 4, from the Seventh U.S. Census in 1850, is the first survey of the foreign-born conducted in the United States. Tables from 1860 to 1976 demonstrate the nature and variety of existing statistical evidence. Not only the totals but the organization of the data are

interesting. Most tabulations first list persons from England, Scotland, and Wales. The results of the Twentieth U.S. Census, conducted in April 1980, which asked significant questions on ancestry and ethnic origins but unfortunately not on mother tongue, will not be published until 1982 or 1983.

Readers should be alert to biases characteristic of the ethnic literature. Few groups as described have rivals, much less enemies. Prejudice and discrimination typically seem always to emanate from "the dominant society," though tensions and conflicts among rival ethnic groups do receive some attention. Little is available about dislocation and disappointment. Poverty, crime, alcoholism, racism, anti-Semitism, mental illness, and social pathology are generally absent, although not entirely. Authors are eager to recount the achievements of the groups about which they write, but they provide little insight into the ethnic origins of the poor.

It is generally assumed that maintenance of ethnicity is desirable, that preservation of differences is healthy, and that loss of group identity is to be deplored. The view that ethnicity is a social good became fashionable during the 1970s. The Encyclopedia's underlying premise is that ethnicity, whether good or bad, has been and remains important in the American social fabric. The content of the following pages helps provide a sound basis for thinking through the complex value issues at stake in this emotionally and politically charged area.

The ethnic origins of the American people are incredibly diverse and new elements of diversity are still being added. The capacity of the United States to absorb so many different peoples and to forge binding ties among them is no less incredible. The complex interplay between assimilation and pluralism is one of the central themes of American history, and it will continue to be so long into the future. This volume sheds new light on both the variety and the unity of American civilization and reveals "of what sort of human stuff America is made."

A great many people have made this work possible. The staff, the contributors, and our advisers have been cooperative and diligent. Innumerable ethnic group informants have been willing to answer questions or provide important material. Officials at the U.S. Bureau of the Census and the Immigration and Naturalization Service have gone out of their way to be helpful. Two of our advisers, in particular, have been indispensable—Nathan Glazer and Harold J. Abramson. Over and over again we have depended upon them for sage advice and good judgment. Ann Louise McLaughlin has supervised the publication process for the Harvard University Press with great skill and tact. Judith Rogers has helped us out during several emergencies competently and cheerfully.

Finally, we are very grateful to the Ethnic Heritage Studies Program of the Office of Education for a pilot grant in 1974–1975, and to the National Endowment for the Humanities and the Rockefeller Foundation for their support of this work from 1976 to 1980.

May 1980   S.T.
Cambridge, Massachusetts   A.O.
                                                                       O.H.

Editorial Staff

Stephan Thernstrom, *Editor*
Ann Orlov, *Managing Editor*
Oscar Handlin, *Consulting Editor*

Research Editors

Josef J. Barton
Karen Johnson Freeze
Paul Robert Magocsi
Reed Ueda

Staff Assistant

Mary Bowen Wright

Map Editor

Paul Robert Magocsi

Cartographer

Robert Williams

Manuscript Editors

Margaret E. Anderson
Chase Duffy
Ann Hawthorne
Maria Kawecki
Margaret Sevcenko

Editorial Assistants

Tong-Soo Chung
Anna Kirsten Clark
Robin L. Johnston
Thomas Walsh

Project Assistant

Dorothy E. Beardsley

Contributors

ROGER D. ABRAHAMS
Scripps College
Claremont, California

HAROLD J. ABRAMSON
Department of Sociology
The University of Connecticut
Storrs, Connecticut

ARŪNAS ALIŠAUSKAS
Department of History
University of Prince Edward Island
Charlottetown, Prince Edward Island

NIKOLAY G. ALTANKOV
Santa Barbara, California

EDGAR ANDERSON
School of Social Sciences
San José State University
San Jose, California

ELLIOTT ROBERT BARKAN
School of Social and Behavioral Sciences
California State College
San Bernardino, California

ULF BEIJBOM
Emigrantinstitutet
Växjö, Sweden

PAULA BENKART
Department of History
Saint Joseph's College
Philadelphia, Pennsylvania

ALEXANDRE BENNIGSEN
Committee on Slavic Area Studies
The University of Chicago
Chicago, Illinois

WILLIAM S. BERNARD
Professor Emeritus, Department of Sociology
Brooklyn College
Brooklyn, New York

ROWLAND BERTHOFF
Department of History
Washington University
St. Louis, Missouri

DWIGHT BILLINGS
Department of Sociology
University of Kentucky
Lexington, Kentucky

THOMAS E. BIRD
Department of Slavic Languages

Queens College
Flushing, New York

VALDIMAR BJÖRNSON
State Treasurer Emeritus
Minneapolis, Minnesota

PATRICK J. BLESSING
Department of History
The University of Tulsa
Tulsa, Oklahoma

GERALD J. BOBANGO
Romanian-American Heritage Center
Grass Lake, Michigan

ARASH BORMANSHINOV
Department of Germanic and Slavic Languages and
Literatures
University of Maryland
College Park, Maryland

DAVID BRODY
Department of History
University of California, Davis
Davis, California

ALAN A. BROOKES
Department of History
University of Guelph
Guelph, Ontario

DAVID C. CHAMPAGNE
Center for Afghanistan Studies
University of Nebraska at Omaha
Omaha, Nebraska

NATHELA CHATARA
Springfield, Illinois

NOEL J. CHRISMAN
Department of Community Health Care Systems
School of Nursing
University of Washington
Seattle, Washington

KATHLEEN NEILS CONZEN
Department of History
The University of Chicago
Chicago, Illinois

CARLOS E. CORTÉS
Department of History
University of California, Riverside
Riverside, California

GORDON DONALDSON
Professor Emeritus, Department of Scottish History

University of Edinburgh
Edinburgh, Scotland

WILLIAM A. DOUGLASS
Basque Studies Program
The University of Nevada
Reno, Nevada

RICHARD A. EASTERLIN
Department of Economics
University of Pennsylvania
Philadelphia, Pennsylvania

CHARLOTTE J. ERICKSON
Department of Economic History
The London School of Economics and Political Science
London, England

JOSHUA A. FISHMAN
University Research Professor of Social Sciences
Yeshiva University
New York, New York

JOSEPH P. FITZPATRICK, S.J.
Department of Sociology and Anthropology
Fordham University
Bronx, New York

GEORGE M. FREDRICKSON
Department of History
Northwestern University
Evanston, Illinois

KAREN JOHNSON FREEZE
Russian Research Center
Harvard University
Cambridge, Massachusetts

ARIF GHAYUR
Department of Social and Community Services
Southern Illinois University
Carbondale, Illinois

NATHAN GLAZER
Graduate School of Education
Harvard University
Cambridge, Massachusetts

PHILIP GLEASON
Department of History
University of Notre Dame
Notre Dame, Indiana

ARTHUR A. GOREN
Department of American Studies
The Hebrew University
Jerusalem, Israel

VICTOR GREENE
Department of History
The University of Wisconsin–Milwaukee
Milwaukee, Wisconsin

TALAT SAIT HALMAN
Department of Near Eastern Studies
Princeton University
Princeton, New Jersey

JOEL HALPERN
Department of Anthropology
University of Massachusetts
Amherst, Massachusetts

IAN F. HANCOCK
Department of English

The University of Texas
Austin, Texas

OSCAR HANDLIN
University Librarian
Harvard University
Cambridge, Massachusetts

TAMARA K. HAREVEN
Department of History
Clark University
Worcester, Massachusetts

MONA HARRINGTON
Cambridge, Massachusetts

DAVID M. HEER
Department of Sociology
University of Southern California
Los Angeles, California

GLENN L. HENDRICKS
Department of Anthropology
University of Minnesota
Minneapolis, Minnesota

JOHN HIGHAM
Department of History
The Johns Hopkins University
Baltimore, Maryland

PATRICE LOUIS RENÉ HIGONNET
Department of History
Harvard University
Cambridge, Massachusetts

ARTHUR E. HIPPLER
Institute of Social and Economic Research
University of Alaska
Anchorage, Alaska

A. WILLIAM HOGLUND
Department of History
The University of Connecticut
Storrs, Connecticut

THOMAS C. HOLT
Department of History
The University of Michigan
Ann Arbor, Michigan

JOHN A. HOSTETLER
Department of Anthropology
Temple University
Philadelphia, Pennsylvania

ALAN HOWARD
Department of Anthropology
University of Hawaii at Manoa
Honolulu, Hawaii

ARIAN B. ISHAYA
Department of Anthropology
University of California, Los Angeles
Los Angeles, California

JOAN M. JENSEN
Department of History
New Mexico State University
Las Cruces, New Mexico

DOROTHY M. JONES
Institute of Social and Economic Research
University of Alaska
Anchorage, Alaska

MALDWYN A. JONES
Department of History
University College London
London, England

THOMAS F. JURAVICH
Department of Sociology
University of Massachusetts
Amherst, Massachusetts

MARGARET KAHN
Palo Alto, California

EDWARD R. KANTOWICZ
Department of History
Carleton University
Ottawa, Ontario

EDWARD KASINEC
Ukrainian Research Institute
Harvard University
Cambridge, Massachusetts

HYUNG-CHAN KIM
Department of Education
Western Washington University
Bellingham, Washington

HARRY H.L. KITANO
School of Social Welfare
University of California, Los Angeles
Los Angeles, California

ARTHUR M. KLEINMAN, M.D.
Division of Social and Cross-Cultural Psychiatry
School of Medicine
University of Washington
Seattle, Washington

DALE T. KNOBEL
Department of History
Texas A&M University
College Station, Texas

MICHEL S. LAGUERRE
Department of Afro-American Studies
University of California, Berkeley
Berkeley, California

H.M. LAI
San Francisco, California

PIERRE-HENRI LAURENT
Department of History
Tufts University
Medford, Massachusetts

MARVIN LAZERSON
Faculty of Education
The University of British Columbia
Vancouver, British Columbia

MARIETTA M. LeBRETON
Department of History
Northwestern State University of Louisiana
Natchitoches, Louisiana

WILLIAM G. LOCKWOOD
Department of Anthropology
The University of Michigan
Ann Arbor, Michigan

RICHARD A. LONG
Center for African and Afro-American Studies
Atlanta University
Atlanta, Georgia

JOHN H. LORENTZ
Middle East Studies Center
Portland State University
Portland, Oregon

FREDERICK C. LUEBKE
Department of History
The University of Nebraska–Lincoln
Lincoln, Nebraska

PAUL ROBERT MAGOCSI
Ukrainian Research Institute
Harvard University
Cambridge, Massachusetts

RAEF MARCUS, D.M.D
Levittown, Pennsylvania

DEAN L. MAY
Department of History
The University of Utah
Salt Lake City, Utah

H. BRETT MELENDY
San José State University
San Jose, California

ROBERT MIRAK
Winchester, Massachusetts

JOHN MODELL
Department of History
University of Minnesota
Minneapolis, Minnesota

STANLEY MOSS
Newton, Massachusetts

PETER A. MUNCH
Department of Sociology
Southern Illinois University
Carbondale, Illinois

EDEN NABY
Center for Middle Eastern Studies
Harvard University
Cambridge, Massachusetts

ALIXA NAFF
The National Center for Urban Ethnic Affairs
Washington, D.C.

HUMBERT S. NELLI
Department of History
University of Kentucky
Lexington, Kentucky

GEORGE R. NIELSEN
Concordia Teachers College
River Forest, Illinois

MICHAEL NOVAK
American Enterprise Institute
Washington, D.C.

MICHAEL OLNECK
Department of Educational Policy Studies
School of Education
University of Wisconsin–Madison
Madison, Wisconsin

ANN ORLOV
Langdon Associates, Inc.
Cambridge, Massachusetts

ANDREW PARKIN
Department of Politics

Flinders University of South Australia
Bedford Park, Australia

TONÜ PARMING
Department of Sociology
University of Maryland
College Park, Maryland

LISANDRO PÉREZ
Department of Sociology
Louisiana State University
Baton Rouge, Louisiana

WILLIAM PETERSEN
Professor Emeritus, Department of Sociology
The Ohio State University
Columbus, Ohio

MICHAEL B. PETROVICH
Department of History
University of Wisconsin—Madison
Madison, Wisconsin

THOMAS F. PETTIGREW
Department of Psychology and Social Relations
Harvard University
Cambridge, Massachusetts

THOMAS PHILIPP
Center for Middle Eastern Studies
Harvard University
Cambridge, Massachusetts

CHARLES A. PRICE
Department of Demography
Research School of Social Science
Australian National University
Canberra, Australia

FRANCES LEON QUINTANA
Aztec, New Mexico

ENAYETUR RAHIM
Department of History
Edgecliff College
Cincinnati, Ohio

JOHN SHELTON REED
Department of Sociology
The University of North Carolina
Chapel Hill, North Carolina

LA VERN J. RIPPLEY
Department of German
Saint Olaf College
Northfield, Minnesota

FRANCIS M. ROGERS
Department of Romance Languages and Literatures
Harvard University
Cambridge, Massachusetts

PETER H. ROSSI
Social and Demographic Research Institute
University of Massachusetts
Amherst, Massachusetts

JOHN ROWE
School of History
The University of Liverpool
Liverpool, England

THEODORE SALOUTOS
Department of History
University of California, Los Angeles
Los Angeles, California

LEO SCHELBERT
Department of History
University of Illinois at Chicago Circle
Chicago, Illinois

BRADD SHORE
Department of Anthropology
Sarah Lawrence College
Bronxville, New York

DOROTHY BURTON SKÅRDAL
American Institute
University of Oslo
Oslo, Norway

WERNER SOLLORS
Department of English and Comparative Literature
Columbia University
New York, New York

EDWARD H. SPICER
Professor Emeritus, Department of Anthropology
The University of Arizona
Tucson, Arizona

M. MARK STOLARIK
The Balch Institute for Ethnic Studies
Philadelphia, Pennsylvania

RUDOLPH M. SUSEL
Slovenian-American Heritage Foundation
Euclid, Ohio

ROBERT P. SWIERENGA
Department of History
Kent State University
Kent, Ohio

ABIGAIL M. THERNSTROM
Lexington, Massachusetts

REED UEDA
Department of History
Harvard University
Cambridge, Massachusetts

DAVID WALLS
Appalachian Center
University of Kentucky
Lexington, Kentucky

MICHAEL WALZER
Institute for Advanced Study
Princeton, New Jersey

DAVID WARD
Department of Geography
University of Wisconsin—Madison
Madison, Wisconsin

JOHN T. WERTIME
Arlington, Virginia

JAMES D. WRIGHT
Social and Demographic Research Institute
University of Massachusetts
Amherst, Massachusetts

MARY BOWEN WRIGHT
Williamsburg, Virginia

DON YODER
Folklore and Folklife
University of Pennsylvania
Philadelphia, Pennsylvania

Consultants

DANIEL AARON
Department of English
Harvard University
Cambridge, Massachusetts

ROGER D. ABRAHAMS
Scripps College
Claremont, California

HAROLD J. ABRAMSON
Department of Sociology
The University of Connecticut
Storrs, Connecticut

ARŪNAS ALIŠAUSKAS
Department of History
University of Prince Edward Island
Charlottetown, Prince Edward Island

BERNARD BAILYN
Department of History
Harvard University
Cambridge, Massachusetts

GUNTHER BARTH
Department of History
University of California, Berkeley
Berkeley, California

WILLIAM S. BERNARD
Professor Emeritus, Department of Sociology
Brooklyn College
Brooklyn, New York

ROWLAND BERTHOFF
Department of History
Washington University
St. Louis, Missouri

THOMAS E. BIRD
Department of Slavic Languages
Queens College
Flushing, New York

JOHN BODNAR
Pennsylvania Historical and Museum Commission
Harrisburg, Pennsylvania

KRINE BOELENS
Fryske Akademy
Leeuwarden, The Netherlands

FREDERICK BOHME
U.S. Bureau of the Census
Washington, D.C.

GERARD J. BRAULT
Department of French

Pennsylvania State University
University Park, Pennsylvania

JOHN W. BRIGGS
Department of History
University of Rochester
Rochester, New York

FAWN M. BRODIE
Department of History
University of California, Los Angeles
Los Angeles, California

RICHARD CHAMBERS
Oriental Institute
The University of Chicago
Chicago, Illinois

STEPAN CHEMYCH
Ukrainian Studies Fund
New York, New York

JAMES F. CLARKE
Department of History
University of Pittsburgh
Pittsburgh, Pennsylvania

BRANKO COLAKOVIC
Department of Geography
Mankato State University
Mankato, Minnesota

ALAN A. CONWAY
University of Canterbury
Christchurch, New Zealand

KATHLEEN NEILS CONZEN
Department of History
The University of Chicago
Chicago, Illinois

MICHAEL CONZEN
Department of Geography
The University of Chicago
Chicago, Illinois

FRANCESCO CORDASCO
Department of Sociology
Montclair State College
Montclair, New Jersey

CARLOS E. CORTÉS
Department of History
University of California, Riverside
Riverside, California

ARTHUR F. CORWIN
Milford, Iowa

LINDA DEGH
Folklore Institute
Indiana University
Bloomington, Indiana

JOHN DEMOS
Department of History
Brandeis University
Waltham, Massachusetts

REINHARD R. DOERRIES
Historisches Seminar
Universitaet Hamburg
Hamburg, West Germany

JORGE I. DOMÍNGUEZ
Center for International Affairs
Harvard University
Cambridge, Massachusetts

ROBERT DONIA
Department of History
The University of Michigan
Ann Arbor, Michigan

MARIO DUGO
Consulate of the Republic of Malta
New York, New York

JAMES TAYLOR DUNN
Minnesota Historical Society
St. Paul, Minnesota

FRANKLIN EDWARDS
Department of Sociology
Howard University
Washington, D.C.

STANLEY ENGERMAN
Department of Economics
University of Rochester
Rochester, New York

CHARLOTTE J. ERICKSON
Department of Economic History
The London School of Economics and Political Science
London, England

MICHAEL M.J. FISCHER
Department of Anthropology
Harvard University
Cambridge, Massachusetts

STEPHEN A. FISCHER-GALATI
Department of History
University of Colorado
Boulder, Colorado

FRANKLIN L. FORD
Department of History
Harvard University
Cambridge, Massachusetts

JOHN HOPE FRANKLIN
Department of History
The University of Chicago
Chicago, Illinois

BERNARD J. FRIDSMA, SR.
Frisian Information Bureau
Grand Rapids, Michigan

MICHAEL FRISCH
Department of History
State University of New York at Buffalo
Buffalo, New York

RICHARD N. FRYE
Department of Near Eastern Languages and
*   Civilization*
Harvard University
Cambridge, Massachusetts

LAWRENCE FUCHS
Department of American Studies
Brandeis University
Waltham, Massachusetts

BRUCE GARVER
Department of History
The University of Nebraska–Lincoln
Lincoln, Nebraska

WASILI G. GLASKOW
Cossack's Library
New York, New York

NATHAN GLAZER
Graduate School of Education
Harvard University
Cambridge, Massachusetts

PHILIP GLEASON
Department of History
University of Notre Dame
Notre Dame, Indiana

NANCIE L. GONZALEZ
University of Maryland
College Park, Maryland

MILTON GORDON
Department of Sociology
University of Massachusetts
Amherst, Massachusetts

VICTOR GREENE
Department of History
The University of Wisconsin–Milwaukee
Milwaukee, Wisconsin

ALAN HARWOOD
Department of Anthropology
University of Massachusetts, Boston
Boston, Massachusetts

EINAR HAUGEN
Professor Emeritus, Department of Germanic
*   Languages and Literatures*
Harvard University
Cambridge, Massachusetts

SIDNEY HEITMAN
Department of History
Colorado State University
Fort Collins, Colorado

JOHN HIGHAM
Department of History
The Johns Hopkins University
Baltimore, Maryland

PATRICE LOUIS RENÉ HIGONNET
Department of History
Harvard University
Cambridge, Massachusetts

RICHARD G. HOVANNISIAN
Department of History
University of California, Los Angeles
Los Angeles, California

NATHAN I. HUGGINS
Department of History

Columbia University
New York, New York

KRISTIAN HVIDT
Folketingets Bibliotek og Oplysiningst Jeneste
Copenhagen, Denmark

HAROLD ISAACS
Department of Political Science
Massachusetts Institute of Technology
Cambridge, Massachusetts

MALDWYN A. JONES
Department of History
University College London
London, England

TERRY G. JORDAN
Department of Geography
North Texas State University
Denton, Texas

DAVID E. KAISER
Department of History
Harvard University
Cambridge, Massachusetts

MICHAEL KARNI
Iron-Range Interpretive Center
Chisholm, Minnesota

MORTON KELLER
Department of History
Brandeis University
Waltham, Massachusetts

PHYLLIS KELLER
Harvard University
Cambridge, Massachusetts

GAIL P. KELLY
Department of Social Foundations
State University of New York at Buffalo
Buffalo, New York

THOMAS KESSNER
Department of History and Political Science
Kingsborough Community College
Brooklyn, New York

ROY C. KETELSEN
Frisian Roundtable
Bronx, New York

JAMES H. KETTNER
Department of History
University of California, Berkeley
Berkeley, California

NATHAN KEYFITZ
Department of Sociology
Harvard University
Cambridge, Massachusetts

MARION D. DE B. KILSON
The Mary Ingraham Bunting Institute
Radcliffe College
Cambridge, Massachusetts

MARTIN L. KILSON, JR.
Department of Government
Harvard University
Cambridge, Massachusetts

VITANT KIPEL
The Research Libraries
The New York Public Library
New York, New York

KLAUS-FRIEDRICH KOCH
Department of Anthropology
Northwestern University
Evanston, Illinois

JOHN I. KOLEHMAINEN
Professor Emeritus, Department of Politics and
   Government
Heidelberg College
Tiffin, Ohio

WILLIAM KORNBLUM
Department of Sociology
Graduate Center, City University of New York
New York, New York

ROGER KRIEPS
d'Letzeburger Land
Luxembourg

WILLIAM S. LAUGHLIN
Department of Biobehavioral Sciences
The University of Connecticut
Storrs, Connecticut

MARK LEONE
Department of Anthropology
University of Maryland
College Park, Maryland

RICHARD A. LONG
Center for African and Afro-American Studies
Atlanta University
Atlanta, Georgia

ADALBERTO LOPEZ
Latin American and Caribbean Area Studies Program
State University of New York at Binghamton
Binghamton, New York

JOSEPH LOPREATO
Department of Sociology
The University of Texas
Austin, Texas

FREDERICK C. LUEBKE
Department of History
The University of Nebraska–Lincoln
Lincoln, Nebraska

STANFORD LYMAN
Department of Sociology
New School for Social Research
New York, New York

RICHARD MAGAT
The Ford Foundation
New York, New York

MICHAEL E. MALONEY
Urban Appalachian Council
Cincinnati, Ohio

VICTOR S. MAMATEY
Department of History
University of Georgia
Athens, Georgia

ARTHUR MANN
Department of History
The University of Chicago
Chicago, Illinois

VASYL MARKUS
Department of Political Science
Loyola University
Chicago, Illinois

ERNEST R. MAY
Department of History
Harvard University
Cambridge, Massachusetts

JOHN MEYENDORFF
St. Vladimir Orthodox Theological Seminary
Crestwood, New York

T. SCOTT MIYAKAWA
Department of Sociology
Boston University
Boston, Massachusetts

JOHN MODELL
Department of History
University of Minnesota
Minneapolis, Minnesota

JOAN MOORE
Department of Sociology
The University of Wisconsin–Madison
Madison, Wisconsin

NURIA MOREY
Newton, Massachusetts

FRANÇOISE MORIN
Institut de Sciences Sociales
Université de Toulouse
Toulouse, France

PETER A. MUNCH
Department of Sociology
Southern Illinois University
Carbondale, Illinois

BASIM F. MUSALLAM
Department of History
University of Pennsylvania
Philadelphia, Pennsylvania

PETER NEW
Department of Behavioral Sciences
University of Toronto Medical School
Toronto, Ontario

MICHAEL NOVAK
American Enterprise Institute
Washington, D.C.

PHILLIP J. OBERMILLER
Urban Appalachian Council
Cincinnati, Ohio

TAMARA PACHMUSS
Department of Slavic Languages and Literatures
University of Illinois
Urbana, Illinois

SARAH PANARITY
Simmons College
Boston, Massachusetts

ORLANDO PATTERSON
Department of Sociology
Harvard University
Cambridge, Massachusetts

ROBERT S. PERRAULT
Association Canado-Americaine
Manchester, New Hampshire

WILLIAM PETERSEN
Professor Emeritus, Department of Sociology
The Ohio State University
Columbus, Ohio

JOHN A. PETROPULOS
Department of History
Amherst College
Amherst, Massachusetts

MICHAEL B. PETROVICH
Department of History
The University of Wisconsin–Madison
Madison, Wisconsin

THOMAS F. PETTIGREW
Department of Psychology and Social Relations
Harvard University
Cambridge, Massachusetts

THOMAS PHILLIP
Center for Middle Eastern Studies
Harvard University
Cambridge, Massachusetts

MICHAEL PIORE
Department of Economics
Massachusetts Institute of Technology
Cambridge, Massachusetts

Y. POORTINGA
Fryske Akademy
Leeuwarden, The Netherlands

CHARLES A. PRICE
Department of Demography
Research School of Social Science
Australian National University
Canberra, Australia

PETER R. PRIFTI
Department of Linguistics
University of California, San Diego
San Diego, California

OMELJAN PRITSAK
Ukrainian Research Institute
Harvard University
Cambridge, Massachusetts

BOHDAN PROCKO
Department of History
Villanova University
Villanova, Pennsylvania

GEORGE J. PRPIC
Department of History
John Carroll University
Cleveland, Ohio

F. PAUL PRUCHA, S.J.
Department of History
Marquette University
Milwaukee, Wisconsin

CARLTON C. QUALEY
Minnesota Historical Society
St. Paul, Minnesota

CLAIRE QUINTAL
Assumption College
Worcester, Massachusetts

MARC RAEFF
Department of History
Columbia University
New York, New York

LEE RAINWATER
Department of Sociology
Harvard University
Cambridge, Massachusetts

DIANE RAVITCH
Teachers College
Columbia University
New York, New York

JOHN SHELTON REED
Department of Sociology
The University of North Carolina
Chapel Hill, North Carolina

RICHARD RENOFF
Department of Sociology
Nassau County Community College
Garden City, New York

DAVID RIESMAN
Department of Sociology
Harvard University
Cambridge, Massachusetts

MOSES RISCHIN
Department of History
San Francisco State University
San Francisco, California

JOHN P. ROCHE
Fletcher School of Law and Diplomacy
Tufts University
Medford, Massachusetts

FRANCIS M. ROGERS
Department of Romance Languages and Literatures
Harvard University
Cambridge, Massachusetts

PETER ROSE
Department of Sociology
Smith College
Northampton, Massachusetts

ROGER ROSENBLATT
The New Republic
Washington, D.C.

PETER H. ROSSI
Social and Demographic Research Institute
University of Massachusetts
Amherst, Massachusetts

ROBERT I. ROTBERG
Department of Political Science
Massachusetts Institute of Technology
Cambridge, Massachusetts

PAULA RUBEL
Department of Anthropology
Barnard College
New York, New York

NORMAN RYDER
Office of Population Research
Princeton University
Princeton, New Jersey

NADAV SAFRAN
Department of Government
Harvard University
Cambridge, Massachusetts

JULIAN SAMORA
Department of Sociology
Notre Dame University
Notre Dame, Indiana

JEAN SCARPACCI
Department of History

Towson State University
Baltimore, Maryland

DAVID M. SCHNEIDER
Department of Anthropology
The University of Chicago
Chicago, Illinois

FRANKLIN D. SCOTT
The Honnold Library
Claremont, California

INGRID SEMMINGSEN
Historik Institut
University of Oslo
Oslo, Norway

ANNE SHERRILL
Mills College
Oakland, California

DAVID SILLS
The Social Sciences Research Council
New York, New York

ALEX SIMIRENKO
Department of Sociology
Pennsylvania State University
University Park, Pennsylvania

DOROTHY BURTON SKÅRDAL
American Institute
University of Oslo
Oslo, Norway

TIMOTHY L. SMITH
Department of History
The Johns Hopkins University
Baltimore, Maryland

WERNER SOLLORS
Department of English and Comparative Literature
Columbia University
New York, New York

RICHARD SORRELL
Department of American Civilization
Brookdale Community College
Lincroft, New Jersey

THOMAS SOWELL
Department of Economics
University of California, Los Angeles
Los Angeles, California

EDWARD H. SPICER
Professor Emeritus, Department of Anthropology
The University of Arizona
Tucson, Arizona

PETER STANLEY
Carleton College
Northfield, Minnesota

M. MARK STOLARIK
The Balch Institute for Ethnic Studies
Philadelphia, Pennsylvania

RUDOLPH M. SUSEL
Slovenian-American Heritage Foundation
Euclid, Ohio

ROBERT P. SWIERENGA
Department of History
Kent State University
Kent, Ohio

CHARLES TILLY
Department of Sociology
The University of Michigan
Ann Arbor, Michigan

GEORGE B. TINDALL
Department of History
The University of North Carolina
Chapel Hill, North Carolina

LYDIO F. TOMASI
Center for Migration Studies
Staten Island, New York

S.M. TOMASI
Center for Migration Studies
Staten Island, New York

DONALD M. TOPPING
Social Science Research Institute
University of Hawaii
Honolulu, Hawaii

VERNON VAN DYKE
Department of Political Science
University of Iowa
Ames, Iowa

RUDOLPH J. VECOLI
Immigration History Research Center
Minneapolis, Minnesota

BRANT L. VINER
Department of Romance Languages and Literatures
Harvard University
Cambridge, Massachusetts

MARIS VINOVSKIS
Department of History
The University of Michigan
Ann Arbor, Michigan

PRISCILLA WALTON
Davis, California

MICHAEL WALZER
Institute for Advanced Study
Princeton, New Jersey

DONALD P. WARWICK
Institute for International Development
Harvard University
Cambridge, Massachusetts

BRIAN WEINSTEIN
Department of Political Science
Howard University
Washington, D.C.

VLADIMIR WERTSMAN
The Brooklyn Public Library
Brooklyn, New York

STEPHEN WILLIAMS
Peabody Museum of Archaeology and Ethnology
Harvard University
Cambridge, Massachusetts

JOHN WOMACK, JR.
Department of History
Harvard University
Cambridge, Massachusetts

CONRAD E. WRIGHT
Institute of Early American History
Williamsburg, Virginia

LUBOMYR WYNAR
Program for the Study of Ethnic Publications
Kent State University
Kent, Ohio

JOSEPH ZACEK
Department of History
State University of New York at Albany
Albany, New York

Contents

THEMATIC ESSAYS

MAPS

TABLES

ABKHAZIANS: *see* NORTH CAUCASIANS

ACADIANS

More than 200 years after the British expelled the French Catholic Acadians from their farms in what are now the maritime provinces of Canada, Acadians still live in tightly knit communities in Louisiana and northern Maine. There are about 800,000 Acadians, popularly called Cajuns, in south central and south Louisiana, and another 20,000 living on the south side of Maine's St. John's River Valley, territory annexed by the United States following the 1842 Webster-Ashburton Treaty. In both areas the Acadians have clung tenaciously to their religion, language, and customs. Their original exile and suffering were immortalized by Henry Wadsworth Longfellow in the well-known poem *Evangeline* (1847).

ACADIA AND DIASPORA.

When France attempted to establish a North American colony in the early 17th century, families from northwest and central France, especially Normandy and Brittany, were recruited to settle the land called Acadie or Acadia, a region that then included Nova Scotia, New Brunswick, Prince Edward Island, and part of the state of Maine but that was generally restricted after 1713 to the present peninsula of Nova Scotia. They lived there as industrious colonials, producing most of their own necessities, farming, fishing, lumbering, and raising stock. Large families were common, and in isolation they held on to the traditions, speech, and customs of the French provinces from which they had come. Over time, just as English settlers and pioneers came to think of themselves as Americans, the Acadians began to consider themselves as a people distinct and apart from their fellow Frenchmen. They were not only a long way from Quebec but had come under English rule in 1713 as a result of the Treaty of Utrecht that ended one of several French-English wars. At the time they were directed to withdraw into French territory or to swear unconditional loyalty to the English monarch, but apparently they did neither and continued to prosper as before. The issue was raised again in 1730 when the Acadians finally agreed to an oath which they understood would exempt them from bearing arms against their own countrymen and their Indian allies. They were known as the "French Neutrals" and enjoyed another period of steady development until 1755 when the English authorities, for reasons still obscure, forced 6,000 to 8,000 Acadians at bayonet point to abandon their homes and flee for their lives. This mass displacement became known as *Le Grand Dérangement*. The exiles underwent great hardships as they were scattered by sea to other parts of British America, where they lived in extreme poverty and were persecuted because of their Roman Catholicism. It was only after the Treaty of Paris was signed in 1763, ending the last Anglo-French war in North America, that the refugees and exiles began to return to Canada or to relocate in France, Louisiana, and other French dominions. (*See also* French Canadians.)

THE ACADIANS IN LOUISIANA

As early as 1756 some Acadians probably reached the French colony of Louisiana from Maryland, the Carolinas, and Georgia. Louisiana was widely viewed as a hospitable place to begin life anew, and despite the fact that by secret treaty in 1762 (not made public for two years) it had become a Spanish possession, Acadians continued to migrate to the area. Many followed the rivers and streams that flow westward into the Mississippi and then traveled south to New Orleans.

Among the first Acadians to be noted in official government records were 193 refugees who had taken temporary refuge in Santo Domingo; they arrived in Louisiana in February 1765. Hundreds more came in 1765 and 1766 from the West Indies and the British colonies; they settled chiefly on the wide, fertile, and undeveloped plains of southwest and south central Louisiana. The Spanish officials who had arrived in New Orleans in 1766 were eager to aid the French exiles; they donated small parcels of land and provided food, seed, tools, and other necessities to the industrious Acadians, who chose to settle in the Attakapas and Opelousas regions. Areas settled later included Bayous Teche and Lafourche, the land bordering the Mississippi River south of New Orleans, and what eventually came to be known as the Acadian districts—St. James and Ascension.

The early Acadian migrants were joined, in the next twenty years, by others who had tried unsuccessfully to settle in France or the West Indies. Three thousand Acadian exiles left France between 1777 and 1788. They fanned out over southern Louisiana and established the villages of St. Martinville, Delcambre, Lafayette, Broussard, St. Landry, and Abbeville, the heart of Acadian Louisiana. Others continued to settle along the Mississippi River so that by 1788 St. James numbered 1,559 persons and Ascension 1,164. In the late 1780s Acadians moved into the lower Bayou Lafourche area; other groups migrated westward and settled around Lake Charles near the Texas border.

The Acadian settlers of the Louisiana frontier set to work raising livestock; they also planted sweet potatoes and sugar cane. The more prosperous bought slaves and expanded their land holdings. The inventory of Pierre Arceneaux's estate in St. Martinville taken in 1793 indicates the wealth accumulated by the more successful. At the time of his death, his estate was valued at $5,530, a sizable amount in the currency of that time. He owned several large buildings, 400 head of cattle, 15 horses, and numerous slaves.

Although Napoleon repossessed Louisiana in 1800 and then negotiated its sale to the United States in the famous Louisiana Purchase of 1803, the growth of the Acadian settlements was undisturbed. By 1810 St. James parish reported a population of 3,995 and Ascension more than 2,219. A second generation made its appearance, and the makeshift cabins of the exiles were

gradually replaced with more substantial homes. More than 2,500 slaves worked for the wealthy families in St. James and Ascension parishes; the 36-mile strip of the Mississippi that flowed through the two parishes became known as the "Golden Coast" of Louisiana. The majority of Acadians, however, continued to live as they had in Acadia; they were *petits habitants* (small land proprietors). On their modest plots, in some cases protected by levees from overflowing streams, they grew or raised their basic necessities. Some also gathered moss, fished, or trapped.

Those who had settled in the Opelousas and Attakapas regions concentrated on raising and selling cattle. From their neighbors the Spanish they learned to care for livestock. Soon they established *vacheries*, or ranches, on the prairies and began to supply cattle to the markets of New Orleans. The cattle industry served as the central support of the Acadian economy in southwest Louisiana until the early 20th century. Subsequently many ranches were converted into farms for growing rice, cotton, sugar cane, and corn.

SOCIAL AND FAMILY LIFE

By and large the Acadian communities existed in isolation; often living in rural and inaccessible areas, the inhabitants were self-sufficient and kept very much to themselves. They became known colloquially as "Cajuns" (a corruption of the word Acadians), and many outsiders noted their extreme insularity, buttressed by the use of Acadian French, their maintenance of Acadian folk customs, and their tendency to marry only other Acadians. Their Roman Catholic religion separated them from others, yet strongly bound them together as a group. They considered education a function of the church and viewed formal schooling as unnecessary; most Acadian parents taught their children the skills of farming and domestic arts at home. Even the establishment of a public school system in 1845 did not alter the Acadian view of education. They continued to rely on a practical, secular education bolstered by religious training, and thus many Cajuns never learned to read or write. In everyday life they used one of a number of different variants of Cajun French, variants fostered by the isolation of the individual settlements.

Cajun women occasionally married outsiders—Germans, Spanish, English, and others. By the early 20th century there were Cajun families by the name of Schneider, Lopez, Kibbe, Higginbotham, Hoffpauir, Smith, and Hernandez. In almost all such instances, however, the outsiders were completely absorbed into the Cajun culture and community; they learned to speak French and adopted the local customs. Family ties were very strong, and Cajun women generally raised their children in the Cajun way of life.

Up until the early 20th century these children were usually part of large households. They lived with their aunts, uncles, and grandparents as well as with their parents. Extended-family households were economic units. The whole family would work on the farm and fish in the bayous, and every adult would participate in making decisions that affected the welfare of the group as a whole. Acadian families expected and welcomed numerous offspring and it was not uncommon for women to have 10 or 12 children. Between 1815 and

1880 the Acadian population rose from 35,000 to 270,000.

Non-Cajun neighbors tended to regard the Cajuns as fun-loving backwoods provincials. The numerous Cajun celebrations—the Mardi Gras, the *fais-dodo* or public country dance, the *boucherie de campagne* or hog-killing gathering—were all important features of early Cajun life. The Cajuns' resistance to change, their reluctance to use English, and their determination to preserve French customs were viewed by others, especially their Anglo-Saxon Protestant neighbors and the Creoles, as the marks of a separate and backward social existence. (*See* Creoles.)

Nonetheless, the Cajuns were unable to hold out against change forever. Advances in transportation, communications, and education began to penetrate Acadian Louisiana after World War I. Mechanization modified the three traditional occupations: farming, fishing, and herding. By the early 20th century the ranching economy was largely supplanted by intensive production of sugar, cotton, rice, and corn. New roads and bridges, many of which were constructed under the administration of Governor Huey P. Long, linked isolated settlements to each other and to the larger towns and cities of Louisiana. Radio, motion pictures, and television were gradually introduced to Cajun country, altering values and culture, especially of the young. Public education was promoted more actively once the Cajuns realized it was needed in order to improve their standard of living. Compulsory school attendance through age 15 was introduced in Louisiana in 1916 but not effectively enforced until 1944. In 1940 the rural-farm population of Louisiana (which included nearly all the Acadians) aged 25 and older had received an average of 6.3 years of schooling. Presently, Acadian children are literate but their parents and more often their grandparents are not. Many still attend parochial schools. Beginning in the 1950s the discovery of large oil and gas deposits brought hundreds of outsiders to Cajun communities. Further alterations of traditional Cajun culture resulted from the new economic activity.

The use of Cajun French gradually declined until it was finally prohibited in the public schools by the 1921 state constitution. Cajun children were even forbidden to speak French on school grounds outside of the classroom. As a result, many younger Cajuns today cannot speak or understand French. Recently the Council for the Development of French in Louisiana succeeded in reintroducing French into many public and parochial elementary schools as a second language, but many feel this will further threaten Cajun French because it is standard French that is taught in the schools. Louisiana law now requires school boards to establish programs of French instruction in all grades upon petition of 25 percent of the parents concerned. Approximately 38,000 children participate in the elementary French-language instruction programs.

GROUP MAINTENANCE

The modernization of Louisiana has brought major social and cultural changes to Cajun communities. The average family itself is smaller as an increasing number of couples decide to limit the size of their families. There is more marriage outside of the community and

less dominance of the Cajun in such unions. The extended-family household and economic unit has undoubtedly changed, but Cajuns retain strong emotional and physical ties to their families. The Roman Catholic Church still occupies an extremely important place in Cajun life. To counter this, some of the Protestant churches have begun to offer services in French. Like other Americans, Cajuns have experienced occupational and geographical mobility. Since World War II, fewer live in rural areas. Many Cajuns are employed in the oil and gas industries of Louisiana and Texas. Cajun celebrations, such as the Crawfish, Rice, and Yam festivals, are no longer simply local community activities; they attract many outsiders and wide publicity to Acadiana. Cajun culture and Cajun communities thrived in rural isolation; in the 20th century they have become partially Americanized. It is not clear what the future holds.

In both Louisiana and northern Maine, the ethnic revival of the 1970s has brought increased self-awareness to Acadian communities. The Madawaska Historical Society, established in 1968, promotes local historical projects and celebrates key events in the history of the Maine Acadians. The French language, although not generally used by the younger generation, is receiving greater emphasis in some New England schools. The New England–Atlantic Provinces–Quebec Center of the University of Maine has developed Franco-American programs, which include the study of Acadians, and sponsors conferences on the French and Acadians living in Canada and New England. In 1960 Acadian and other French-speaking proponents of bilingualism succeeded in repealing the Maine law that had made English the sole language of instruction in the state's schools. In 1970 two St. John's River Valley school systems—Van Buren, Madawaska and St. Agatha, Frenchville—received a developmental grant under Title VII of the Elementary and Secondary Education Act of 1967 to promote bilingual programs in public schools. Valley high schools have since begun to offer courses in Acadian and French history.

In Louisiana several organizations dedicated to the preservation of Acadian history and traditions have been founded. The University of Southwestern Louisiana in Lafayette (*Université des Acadiens*) has established a Center for Acadian Folklore and Culture and maintains a general policy of encouraging Acadian studies. The Council for the Development of French in Louisiana enthusiastically supports and promotes the renewed study of French culture, history, and language in Louisiana elementary and high schools. The state of Louisiana has designated 22 parishes as "Acadiana." There is renewed interest in Cajun music, humor, and celebrations. Today, an increasing number of Acadians from Maine and Louisiana are taking pride in their heritage and resolving to sustain the unique Acadian culture.

Bibliography
An excellent account of the society and environment of Acadia is Andrew Hill Clark, *Acadia: The Geography of Early Nova Scotia to 1760* (Madison, Wis., 1968). General treatments of the Acadian diaspora and resettlement are found in Bona Arsenault, *History of the Acadians* (Quebec, 1966), and Dudley J. LeBlanc, *The Acadian Miracle* (Lafayette, La., 1966).

The most informative works on the Acadians of Louisiana are Sidney A. Marchand, *Acadian Exiles in the Golden Coast of Louisiana* (Don-aldsonville, La., 1943); T. Lynn Smith and Homer L. Hitt, *The People of Louisiana* (Baton Rouge, La., 1952); Lauren C. Post, *Cajun Sketches: From the Prairies of Southwest Louisiana* (Baton Rouge, La., 1962); Steven L. Del Sesto and Jon L. Gibson, eds., *The Culture of Acadiana: Tradition and Change in South Louisiana* (Lafayette, La., 1975); Glenn R. Conrad, ed., *The Cajuns: Essays on Their History and Culture* (Lafayette, La., 1978). The most useful work on New England Acadians is Edward Schriver, ed., *The French in New England, Acadia, and Quebec* (Orono, Me., 1972).

Descriptive studies of the Acadian French language are Joseph LeSage Tisch, *French in Louisiana: A Study of the Historical Development of the French Language in Louisiana* (New Orleans, 1959), and Marilyn C. Conwell and Alphonse Juilland, *Louisiana French Grammar* (The Hague, 1963).

MARIETTA M. LEBRETON

ADYGHE: *see* NORTH CAUCASIANS

AFGHANS

Immigration to the United States from Afghanistan has been sporadic. There are approximately 2,500 Afghans in the country. Many of the recent immigrants from Afghanistan entered the United States as students and stayed; others were trained in the United States under various developmental programs, returned to Afghanistan, and later came back to the United States for political or economic reasons. The majority of Afghans residing in the United States are well educated and able to find employment and economic security. They represent many of the linguistic, religious, and ethnic groups of the nation-state of Afghanistan.

The name Afghanistan is of relatively recent origin. In its earliest usage, it did not refer to any organized political entity, but was first used by the Safavid dynasty of Iran and the Moghul dynasty of India to refer to the geographical areas of their empires populated and controlled by Pushtun (Pathan) tribal peoples.

Since 1747 some of the lands controlled by the Pushtuns have been united into a recognizable social-political unit. In that year Pushtun tribal elders chose Ahmad Khan Saduzay as the head of a new confederation of Pushtun tribes, establishing the first independent Push-

Afghanistan

tun-controlled kingdom in central Asia. Ahmad Shah Saduzay took the title "Durrani" and his kingdom became known as the Durrani Sultanate. Today he is looked upon as the father of Afghanistan. The sultanate became an empire stretching from the Indus River to the Dasht-i Lut (desert) and from the Oxus River to the Indian Ocean. The simultaneous decline of the Safavid Empire of Iran and the Moghul Empire of India, and the growth of proto-nationalism among some of the western Pushtun tribes, were largely responsible for the emergence of this new state. Modern landlocked Afghanistan is located within a portion of this vast area.

The area that became the Durrani kingdom had a long history of its own; it had been the crossroads for the central Asian invaders of India and the western Islamic world. Numerous pre-Islamic and Islamic states had formed here, including those of the Kushans, Bactrians, Ghaznavids, and Ghorids. Afghanistan's heterogeneous population reflects the various groups who conquered and passed through it.

At the end of the 18th century the empire dissolved, but the central core remained. For most of the 19th century Afghanistan was the arena for Anglo-Russian rivalry in central Asia, acting as a buffer zone between Russian Central Asia and the British Empire in India. In the 1880s, after a long period of internal conflict and external pressures, Afghanistan was reunited under Amir Abdul Rahman. Only then did the name Afghanistan become widely accepted by the inhabitants as the official name of their country.

A strict ethnographic definition of the word "Afghan" refers to native speakers of Pashto (Pushtu), many of whom live outside present-day Afghanistan in the northwest part of Pakistan. But in the broadest sense, Afghan signifies all current citizens of the nation-state of Afghanistan.

A divisive factor in Afghan society is the persistence of intense extended-family and tribal loyalties among the people. The strongest loyalty is to the extended family, then to tribe and religious sect, and lastly to the nation-state. Only among the literate and younger generation does the concept of identity with and loyalty to the nation-state outweigh responsibility to the extended family, tribe, or religion. For this reason, tribal groups have always dominated Afghan politics and nepotism is common.

There are 12 to 15 million people in modern Afghanistan. At least two million of them are nomads, but there has never been any comprehensive census. It is estimated that the population is comprised of approximately 60 percent Pushtuns, 15 percent Tadzhiks, and the remaining 25 percent a mixture of Turkomans, Uzbeks, Hazarahs, Baluchi, Kirghiz, Nuristanis, and others. Various dialects of Dari (Afghan Persian), another Indo-European language, are spoken by over 85 percent of the people as either a first or second language. At the present time both Pashto and Dari are among the official languages of Afghanistan. Numerous other languages and dialects are spoken, including Turki, Uzbeki, Kirghizi, and Baluchi.

The introduction of Islam by Arab invaders during the 8th and 9th centuries was one of the most important events in the area. Today 99 percent of the population is Muslim—80 percent Sunni, 19 percent Shiite. Hindus, Sikhs, Zoroastrians, and a few Jewish families make up the remaining 1 percent. Hindus and Sikhs play important roles in the cities of Kabul (the capital), Jalalabad, and Kandahar, in the textile, spice, and import-export trades.

Determining the proportion of the various Afghan ethnic groups among those who have immigrated to the United States is difficult. Before 1953 statistics are virtually nonexistent. Those that do exist group Afghans and others in a category entitled "other Asians," with no specific mention of country of origin. A group of 200 Pushtuns came to the United States in 1920. Although they came from the North-West Frontier Province of what was then British India (now a province of Pakistan), some of them were probably Afghan citizens. During the 1930s and 1940s immigration from Afghanistan was minimal. Those who did immigrate came alone or in small family units. These early immigrants were members of the Afghan elite—highly educated people from the diplomatic, medical, engineering, and business professions, some of whom were married to Europeans. The immigrants of the 1930s and 1940s tended to locate on the East and West coasts and around Washington, D.C.

Between 1953 and 1963, according to the U.S. Immigration and Naturalization Service, only 78 people from Afghanistan became American citizens. In the next ten-year period an additional 155 Afghans were naturalized, a marked increase reflecting foreign travel and educational opportunities resulting from Western ties.

Emigration from Afghanistan between 1953 and 1963 was still on an individual and extended-family member basis. During the 1950s and 1960s Afghan males came to the United States usually to obtain a college education and then stayed, later sending for their wives and families. In the late 1950s and 1960s Afghan women also began to travel to the United States for higher education. Some stayed, though the percentage of women remaining in the United States was much lower than that of men.

The period between 1973 and 1977 saw a large increase in the number of Afghans naturalized, perhaps as a result of political upheavals in Afghanistan. In total, between 1953 and 1977, 343 Afghans became American citizens.

In addition to those Afghans who opted to become citizens, several thousand since 1953 obtained resident alien status; 575 Afghan nationals in the United States at present have this designation. Some 300 others are in the country on various government-sponsored educational and cultural exchange programs.

Most Afghans who live in the United States maintain close ties with their extended families in Afghanistan, although they live in nuclear families. Though they have adapted well to their new country they have retained Islam as their religion, and tend to observe its tenets.

There are Afghans in almost every state of the Union. The largest concentrations of them are in the cities of Los Angeles, Washington, D.C., and New York. Afghans are attracted to these and other large metropolitan areas by employment opportunities. As a group, the Afghans in the United States still represent the social and economic elite of their native society. Now, however, members of other groups of Afghan peoples have gained the opportunity to study abroad because of

their intellectual abilities. A higher percentage of the smaller Afghan minority groups, including Uzbeks, Turkomans, Hazarahs, Nuristanis, and Baluchi are present among the more recent immigrants.

Overall, Afghans in the United States tend to be well-educated members of the academic and business communities. Medicine, engineering, education, anthropology, languages, and various scientific fields are their most common professions. Numerous Afghans hold high positions at universities throughout the United States. Many have gone into private business, from solar energy development to carpet cleaning. Afghans have established restaurants in Washington, D.C., New York, Los Angeles, Denver, Minneapolis, and Oakland, Calif.

The institution of a Marxist regime in Afghanistan in 1978 and subsequent turmoil have caused a recent influx of immigrants to the United States. The number of Afghans applying for extensions of student visas and for resident alien status has substantially increased.

A small group of second-generation Afghan Americans does exist. Where both parents are Afghan, the children usually are bicultural and bilingual. The children of mixed marriages tend to be bicultural, but speak only English. Afghan Americans continue to give their children Afghan or Islamic names. In so doing they maintain a measure of cultural continuity and help to preserve ties with their extended families in Afghanistan.

Bibliography
There are no published studies on Afghans living in the United States. The most comprehensive volume on Afghanistan and Afghans is Louis Dupree, *Afghanistan* (Princeton, N.J., 1973). Mountstuart Elphinstone, *An Account of the Kingdom of Caubul* (1815; reprint, Karachi, 1972), is a basic work on Afghan tribal society. For a history of the Pushtuns see Olaf Caroe, *The Pathans, 550 B.C.–A.D. 1957* (New York, 1968).

For political developments in Afghanistan, see Ludwig Adamec, *Afghanistan, 1900–1923* (Berkeley, 1967); Leon Poullada, *Reform and Rebellion in Afghanistan, 1919–1929* (Ithaca, N.Y., 1973); Rhea Talley Stuart, *Fire in Afghanistan, 1914–1929* (New York, 1973); and Hasan Kakar, *Government and Society in Afghanistan: The Reign of Amir 'abd al-Rahman* (Austin, Tex., 1979).

The two major organizations in the United States involved with Afghanistan are the Afghanistan Council of the Asia Society, in New York City, and the Afghanistan Studies Association based at the Center for Afghanistan Studies, in Omaha, Nebr.

DAVID C. CHAMPAGNE

AFRICANS

Africa is the source of one of the principal American ethnic groups. The vast majority of the 25 million Afro-Americans in the United States are descendants of the 400,000 black Africans who were transported to North America against their will before the United States banned the slave trade in the first decade of the 19th century. (*See* Afro-Americans; *see also* Central and South Americans; Dominicans; Haitians; West Indians.) That was not the end, however, of the movement of people from Africa to the United States. Voluntary migration has brought a good many others since.

In the 19th century only a few came, on the average less than 30 per year, according to U.S. immigration records, which until the 1960s never recorded the country of origin of immigrants from the African continent. By World War I the average was closer to 1,000 a year; following the war the number dropped sharply as a result of the restrictive legislation of the 1920s and the Great

Depression. The numbers began to climb again after World War II. Approximately 14,000 Africans entered the United States between 1951 and 1960; 29,000 between 1961 and 1970; and in the 1970s the total probably reached 60,000. This last figure includes Egyptians, who alone among immigrants from Africa have been separately tabulated since 1967. (*See* Copts; *see also* Arabs.)

Until very recently, however, few of the immigrants from Africa, as distinguished from the students who entered on student visas, were indigenous African blacks. In the 1910, 1930, and 1960 U.S. Censuses, 88 or 89 percent of the African-born people were recorded as white. A large number of these came from Britain's colonies. In 1930, 42 percent of the African-born whites claimed English as their mother tongue; 8 percent came from homes in which Italian was spoken; 7 percent French; 6 percent Yiddish; 4 percent Dutch; and 3 percent Armenian. Only 30 percent had spoken a non-European language as a child.

Since World War II the greatest increase in the U.S. African-born population has resulted from the collapse of colonial regimes. There are no data available about the ethnic ties or associations of these white African immigrants, but insofar as they clustered at all, it probably has been not with other Africans but with other Americans of English, Italian, French, or Jewish background. The South Africans may be an exception. (*See* South Africans.)

Black Africans—Nigerians, Kenyans, Ghanians, Ethiopians, and others—are identifiable on some college campuses and in a few cities, especially Washington, D.C. Most of them have not entered the United States as immigrants and do not plan to settle permanently, although their plans are occasionally affected by political unrest in their homelands. In the 1960s the number of African-born blacks in the United States increased sixfold—from 2,192 in 1960 to 13,442 in 1970. In earlier censuses they accounted for only 12 percent of the African-born immigrants; by 1970 their proportion was 22 percent. It undoubtedly rose higher in the 1970s.

For the most part, the small numbers of African blacks in the United States seem to have blended into the Afro-American community at large. They have come from a large number of independent nations and an even larger number of separate African ethnic groups, and there is no evidence that they consider themselves or will evolve into a cohesive American ethnic group.

AFRIKANERS: *see* SOUTH AFRICANS

AFRO-AMERICANS

There were an estimated 24 million Afro-Americans in the United States in the mid-1970s, a figure making them not only the largest ethnic group in America, but second only to Afro-Brazilians in the Western Hemisphere and larger than any single ethnic subgroup in Africa. However, not their tremendous number but their minority status has governed the position of blacks in America. Not since 1880 have Afro-Americans composed more than 12 percent of the nation, and in only three states have they ever constituted a majority. Yet black Americans have had an importance in

the nation's growth and development much beyond their numbers.

The patterns of population distribution contributed to the disjunction between size and significance. During the 19th century, when sectional tensions formed the context for policy discussions and decisions, more than half—often up to 90 percent—of the blacks lived in the South and composed a large share of the populations of southern states. More recently, as urban problems have become crucial, blacks have clustered in the inner cities. In 1970 more than half lived there (compared with 26 percent of the whites), and in cities with populations over a million almost three of every ten residents were black.

The black presence has been a troublesome and critical one, posing a continuous paradox at the heart of American nationality. In the same pages in which Hector St. John de Crèvecoeur posed his famous query about who was an American, he also expressed dismay at having come across a slave left hanging in a cage to die in the forest. Nor was this an isolated vignette: Nathaniel Hawthorne described a similar trauma in his *Journals*, as did Mark Twain in his fiction, and Thomas Jefferson in his description of Virginia. Contradictions in the national vision have persisted. On the eve of America's bicentennial, its black citizens still earned little more than half the income of whites and were more than twice as likely to be below the national poverty level. Furthermore, blacks were only 80 percent as likely to finish high school as whites, 70 percent as likely to go to college, and 50 percent as likely to be in the professional, entrepreneurial, or managerial class. The black male infant had only half the chance of the white one of reaching its first birthday, and could expect six years less of life thereafter.

Yet the paradox of the black presence in America has been more than a problem of aligning ideals with realities and more complex than the unequal distribution of material resources. Paradox and ambivalence have shaped Afro-American perceptions and reactions as well. More than a hundred years after Crèvecoeur formulated his question about American nationality, W.E.B. Du Bois (1868–1963) posed the problem of black nationality in terms not entirely dissimilar: "It is a peculiar sensation, this double-consciousness, this sense of always looking at one's self through the eyes of others . . . One ever feels his twoness—an American, a Negro, two souls, two thoughts, two unreconciled strivings; two warring ideals in one dark body, whose dogged strength alone keeps it from being torn asunder. The history of the American Negro is the history of this strife—this longing to attain self-conscious manhood, to merge his double self into a better and truer self." Du Bois touched on a dominant theme of the Afro-American experience, the continuing paradox of acculturation and alienation, of being so intimately a part of and yet so starkly apart from the majority. It is not a problem black Americans faced alone, but their particular group experience has been as distinctive as the color of their skins and as old as America itself.

AFRICAN ORIGINS: A CULTURAL BASELINE

The Diaspora Africans accompanied the earliest European voyagers to North America. Some, like Estevanico, a 16th-century explorer of the Southwest, left an imprint on the historical record; others, like the slaves accompanying the abortive Spanish settlement in the Carolinas in 1526, remained anonymous. The permanent settlement of Africans in North America began in 1619 when a Dutch frigate sold 20 blacks to English colonists at Jamestown, a year before the *Mayflower* landed Pilgrims at Plymouth and more than a century after the first African slaves had been brought to Hispaniola in the West Indies in 1501. African peoples were thus involved in the formative stages of American development, and their ties to the soil antedate those of most other ethnic groups in the United States. On the other hand, slavery in the North American colonies developed more than a century later than in the Southern Hemisphere.

According to recent estimates, approximately 10 million slaves landed in the Western Hemisphere. About 60 percent of them arrived in the 18th century and were destined for the sugar plantations of Brazil and the Caribbean. British North America and French Louisiana received fewer than 1 of every 20 slaves, or about 427,000 altogether. Some of the earliest slaves were brought from the West Indies, but most came directly from Africa. The majority of the slaves bound for North American colonies arrived during a relatively short span of 70 years, between 1741 and 1810. The economic, social, and political consequences of these trade patterns would be far-reaching. One in every 5 inhabitants who witnessed the inauguration of the new American nation in 1789 was black and only about 1 in 5 of those had been born in Africa. Thus most were creoles, born in America but no more than three generations removed from their African origins. Furthermore, the peak of the U.S. slave trade (over 5,000 per year from 1741 to 1760) preceded by four decades the full development of the crop most closely associated with the U.S. slave economy, short-staple cotton; and the abolition of slavery in 1865 lagged nearly sixty years behind the importation of the last legal slave in 1807. In each of these respects the United States differed radically from its counterparts to the south.

Latin American and Caribbean slave societies had proportionately larger black populations, a shorter interval between the closing of the slave trade and the abolition of slavery, and consequently, a larger number of African-born freedmen. In contrast, no overwhelming black population majority emerged in either the U.S. North or South. In addition, the early closing of the slave trade relative to emancipation compelled Afro-Americans to develop indigenous cultural reserves, so that ultimately they diverged more sharply from their African roots than Caribbean or Latin American blacks. The first generation to live in freedom in the United States would be almost entirely creole—that is, third- and fourth-generation natives of the American soil.

The African Past The process by which African influences merged with the evolving creole culture of the slave involved a welding of diverse African cultures as well as an adjustment to the strange white and red peoples encountered in the American wilderness. Only in the Americas did "black" take on ethnic as well as physical significance for Africans—inhabitants of a continent that encompassed a vast array of humankind who differed physically and culturally among themselves.

Africa

1 SENEGAL
2 GAMBIA
3 GUINEA-BISSAU
4 SIERRA LEONE
5 LIBERIA
6 TOGO
7 BENIN
8 EQUATORIAL GUINEA
9 RWANDA
10 BURUNDI
11 MALAWI

1000   Km.   Miles

The origins of Afro-Americans cannot be determined accurately. European record-keepers were unperceptive about the subtler differences among Africans, and their records often referred to the general place of embarkation, not to the specific groups within that area. Nevertheless, most of the slaves brought to British North America appear to have come from a narrow strip of the West African coast, along with a significant minority who came from central Africa. About half appear to have been taken from areas presently occupied by Angola and southern Nigeria, about one-eighth each from Ghana, Senegal and Gambia, and Sierra Leone, and

smaller proportions from the Benin area and Mozambique.

Military and diplomatic conditions among West African suppliers and European traders rather than the preferences of New World planters determined the ethnic origins of American slaves. However, planters' preferences did influence the distribution among the colonies. South Carolinians expressed a strong preference for Senegambians, especially the Bambara and Malinké, but they had a decided aversion to the shorter and allegedly more suicide-prone Ibo of Biafra. These prejudices together with conditions of supply produced a Carolina

slave population that was about 40 percent Angolan, 20 percent Senegambian, and only 2 percent Biafran. Virginians were less particular and consequently ended up with a larger proportion of Biafrans, who made up a bit less than 40 percent of their total imports.

It took years before these different groups identified themselves as "African" or "black" rather than as Ibo, Malinké, or Yoruba. They had not had extensive experience in developing national identities across ethnic boundaries. Even their religions, which shared many common features, were particularistic. One was born into a religion and absorbed its tenets with mother's milk; conversion to any religion but Islam was unlikely. But the shock of enslavement, the degradation of the middle passage, and the brutalities of the American plantation forced Africans to seek out common cultural elements. Although a minority of the slaves may have had primarily pastoral backgrounds, most came from settled agricultural societies where the primary political and social unit was a small rural village. Although some owed allegiance and paid tribute to relatively large imperial polities and most sold surplus produce in thriving market cities and towns, these institutions had limited influence on their daily lives. Their crops, their social systems, and religious beliefs differed, but they shared common ways of looking at the world and common understandings of their relation to it. Kinship ties—both by blood and by marriage—were the essential social cement, providing the basis for social cohesion, political behavior, economic organization, and psychological attitudes. Kinship pervaded and shaped relations to the land, jurisdiction over community disputes, economic obligations and privileges, and attitudes toward death. Those cultural elements which entailed specific social arrangements or material prerequisites were most likely to be suppressed or starved in America, but general psychological and sociological orientations were more resistant; indeed, in some perverse way the latter might be reinforced by the very disorientation of slavery.

The physical environment that shaped the ancestors of Afro-American slaves was harsh and demanding. Much of West Africa is subject to semiannual climatic shifts from drought to flooding, which affect the supply and the storage of food. The tsetse fly restricts areas habitable by cattle and horses. Shallow soils of low fertility necessitate frequent shifts of farm sites to preserve the productivity of the land. Malaria, yellow fever, and a host of diseases and parasites stalk African villages, allowing only one of every two children to reach adolescence.

Perhaps these harsh environmental conditions fostered the characteristic African stoicism—that willingness to celebrate life in the face of extreme suffering—which European observers so frequently mistook for docile accommodation or mindless hedonism. The African societies of scarcity required a social discipline and world view in which the individual existed for the benefit of the vulnerable community and his life gained its highest meaning only through and within the group. A wide variety of African social systems reinforced a belief in custom, convention, and conformity that would be anathema to a competitive, individualistic society. Thus, a Lozi proverb: "Go the way that many people go; if you go alone you will have reason to la-

ment." For the Kongo a man without his clan was like a grasshopper that had lost its wings. Among the Kanuri of Nigeria, the man who lived alone was *ngudi*, or unfortunate. And among the Douala the word for alien, *bakom*, was the same as that for slave.

Freedom was not synonymous with personal autonomy or solitude, but the opposite, and was achieved by meeting obligations to the group. Procreation was therefore a primary social objective, the family a primary social institution, and the ties among the individual, the family, and the larger society "a seamless web." Because the community's survival depended on growth, infertility was a just and sufficient cause for divorce, the unmarried and childless did not receive full ceremonial honors upon their deaths, and polygamy was sanctioned and encouraged.

In such a society a child belonged not merely to the parents, but to the larger kinship group of uncles, aunts, grandparents, and cousins. Through this network one gained the right to work the land, which one could use but not own. The resolution of disputes and trial and compensation for crimes involved not only the individual offenders and victims, but their entire families as well. And the only immortality African traditional religions recognized was achieved by living in the memory of one's descendants.

This world view heightened the horror and terror of slavery, which tore the African from land and family and cast him among strangers black and white. Some had already experienced the terrors of slavery in their own land at the hands of other black men—as prisoners captured in intertribal wars, as children surrendered as compensation for crimes committed by other family members, as pawns to secure or work off unpaid debts, or as family members sold in times of famine to allow the survival of the group. The key differences between enslavement in Africa and in America were economic and racial. There was not an economic system in precolonial Africa producing staples for the world market and emphasizing the exploitation of labor for profit, nor was there a major indigenous commercial market for slaves. Although ethnic and sometimes religious differences existed between African master and slave, they were not developed into racist ideologies that would permanently stigmatize the enslaved and their descendants. In any case most of the slaves brought to America were not the surplus slaves of African societies; they were captured and enslaved specifically for the purpose of exportation.

BLACKS AND THE AMERICAN FRONTIER

The emergence of a black man more American than African occurred more quickly and completely in the Northern Hemisphere than in the Southern. The major factors associated with this rapid acculturation of Afro-American slaves were a small black population relative to whites, small plantation labor forces that permitted cultural contact between races, and the closing of the slave trade many years before the achievement of abolition, which together with lower mortality encouraged the early growth of a creole population. All these phenomena mark 1807, the year the legal slave trade ended, as a watershed in Afro-American history. As long as the trade continued, critical demographic imbalances in the slave communities occurred. Since male imports out-

numbered females two to one and young adults were preferred, sex and age structures in the slave quarters were distorted. Furthermore, the infusion of fresh African immigrants increased the potential for rebellion, as in New York City in 1712 and South Carolina in 1739.

Planters encouraged acculturation, not only to develop more manageable and efficient workers but also to establish a more comfortable presence. The Africans' strange languages, ritually scarified bodies, and filed teeth were visible reminders of alien and threatening natures. The tendency of colonial Virginians to refer to their creole "servants" in contrast to their African "slaves" may reflect the extent to which planters were unnerved by the difference. Many Virginians who owned vast tracts of land scattered their slaves over a number of work sites, separating their holdings into "home" plantations and less accessible, backcountry "quarters." The quarters were inhabited by as few as 8 to 30 slaves, almost all newly imported Africans, while the more acculturated and creole slaves were taken to the home plantations. In other areas African laborers were mixed with white indentured servants and Indians on relatively small holdings. Such devices were probably more effective in the subversion of cultural identities than deliberately mixing different African ethnic groups, especially given the North American planters' low level of demand and limited control over supplies. Although they resisted it at first, colonial planters also permitted religious proselytizing among their slaves after they had been satisfied by legislation ensuring that Christian conversion would not lead to manumission and persuaded that the gospels did not encourage rebellion. However, neither the Anglican South nor the Puritan North succeeded in converting many slaves in the colonial period. Only in the latter half of the 18th century, with the emergence of antislavery religious sects and a large creole slave community, did Christian conversion become significant among blacks.

African resistance to acculturation ultimately produced that compromise between Africa and America that is Afro-American culture. For example, Africans retained their traditional modes of reckoning time and distance and their traditional ethnic identities. During the first six months of captivity they were most likely to escape and try to return to Africa or, failing that, to try to recreate African-style maroon colonies in the backcountry. Depending on age and the nature and extent of their contacts with English speakers, the Africans generally became fluent over a period of two or three years. But the nature of the language that emerged depended on which elements were reinforced and which were discouraged or suppressed in the new cultural environment. For example, in the South Carolina Sea Islands among the Gullah a dialect developed in which slaves tended to give their children African daynames. But the names and words that survived tended to be those with European phonetic or semantic equivalents; thus "Quaco," an African name for a male child born on Wednesday, became Jack; "Cudjoe" (Monday) became Joe; "Phiba" (Friday) became Phoebe; "Cubena" (Tuesday) became Benah; and the African "sasi" merged with the Englishman's "saucy."

Acculturation was not a one-way process: the master influenced the slave, but was also influenced by him. A frontier society confronting the problems of survival

undoubtedly permitted more open interchange with and borrowing from Africans than would occur later in more settled times. For example, colonial planters readily used African skills in cattle raising and rice culture. In Virginia and the Carolinas blacks were the pioneers, woodsmen, watermen, and craftsmen who carved the early colonial societies out of the southern wilderness.

The African was also the conduit for cultural transfers between white and red men. American Indian culture contained many elements familiar to Africans, including matrilineal descent among the Iroquois, the naming ceremony for newborn infants among the Cherokee, and the relations among kinsfolk. From the Indians blacks gained knowledge of the woods and waterways and soon supplanted them as guides and messengers. They learned to adapt African medicinal knowledge to the vast and strange flora of the New World from the red men, whose pharmacopoeia and medical practices were not entirely dissimilar. And the fact that African folk tales became common among the Creek, Cherokee, Seminole, and others demonstrates a significant and intimate cultural interaction.

The colonial whites feared this intimacy and encouraged—with considerable success—hostility in its stead. From the Iroquois in the North to the Seminole in the South, Indian villages had been a haven for runaway slaves, who often intermarried with the villagers and fought with them against white rule. Colonial authorities made treaties with many of the same Indians to capture and return fugitives and to assist in suppressing insurrections; and blacks often were used to put down Indian uprisings, a practice that would be revived in the West in the 1870s and 1880s.

Slavery and Racism Slavery was brutal, but frontier conditions did not permit the complete and consistent degradation of blacks as the lowest form of labor. In the early days blacks labored beside Indian slaves and white indentured servants whose material circumstances were little better than their own. Although the absence at that time of oppressive legal codes does not mean the absence of racist ideas or oppression, it does suggest that oppression and ideas were not uniform, and that therefore a wider range of practices was possible. Rough frontier conditions necessitated a rational use of all available resources rather than strict adherence to a racial division of labor. Thus, the Dutch in New Amsterdam instituted an arrangement that allowed slaves to work on plots assigned to them and simply pay an annual tribute to the owner. Slaves in colonial South Carolina were permitted freedom of movement and economic initiatives that were to be unthinkable to later generations. Some blacks held as indentured servants rather than as slaves were able to amass considerable property after serving their terms. In South Carolina and Virginia free blacks were allowed to vote until the second decade of the 18th century. Laws to prohibit intermarriage between whites and blacks indicate not only the growth and codification of racist fears, but also the existence of considerable interracial contact.

Gradually the black slave's status was clearly differentiated from the indentured servant's when colonial laws prescribed that the slave's condition was for his lifetime and that it was transferred to his children through the mother. Furthermore, in 1656 Virginia laws restricted the status of slave to non-Christians brought

10

to the colony by water—that is, to Africans and not Indians. New York had done the same in 1649. Later the fact of Christian conversion was made irrelevant. Between 1640 and the 1660s laws and judicial interpretations in Virginia and Maryland made "slave" and "black" synonymous and clearly marked the black slave for harsher, more brutal control than other laborers. The very fact that options for control were increasingly limited—a slave could not be given more time or further degraded—may have encouraged more brutal physical tortures. It was in this condition that Afro-Americans greeted the "new birth of freedom" in America at the end of the 18th century.

Slavery: The Ante-Bellum Era The first half of the 19th century was an era of nation-building for the United States. In the South among blacks and whites, both of whom were creole dominated, cohesive group identities slowly took shape. Among the whites the dominant group in influence, though not in number, were the planters. There were striking contradictions and ambiguities in the planters' character: noblesse oblige and incredible brutality, paternalism and unrestrained exploitation, grace and charm and boorish manners, lavish hospitality and the quick-tempered anger that made dueling endemic, and a chivalric code that placed white women on a pedestal yet allowed the prostitution of black females.

Large planters were a minority among the 385,000 slave owners in 1860, but they controlled the lives and destinies of most of the slaves. The other major factor shaping the slave's life and culture was cotton, followed in order of importance by tobacco, sugar, rice, and hemp. Nevertheless, large numbers of slaves worked in urban areas, two-thirds of them as craftsmen, stevedores, draymen, barbers, house and hotel servants, and common laborers. And although the South was still overwhelmingly rural and agricultural, a growing number—about 5 percent of the total—were employed in factories, mines, and other industrial occupations. They made the hemp bags used to haul cotton from the fields, mined coal and iron in Appalachia, gold in the Piedmont, lead in Virginia and Missouri, and salt in western Virginia, Kentucky, and Arkansas. They extracted turpentine in North Carolina, provided half the labor force at the Tredegar Iron Company in Richmond, Va., and built railroads throughout the South. The infant southern cotton industry used them, and the tobacco factories were totally dependent on them. About 20 percent of these industrial slaves were hired from urban and plantation owners by the month or year, and the rest were owned by the companies that employed them. Conditions for these slaves were probably worse than on the plantation. Most of them were men who were often housed in barracks away from families; they were generally worked for longer hours and had less leisure than their rural counterparts.

The conditions of plantation slaves were not enviable, however. The quantity of the slave's clothing issue varied, but it did little more than protect against the elements and preserve a sense of modesty. Indeed, a regular northern and European-based industry grew up to supply drab, uncomfortable clothing "for slaves only." Their shelter was probably more inadequate than their clothing, and they had few options to improve upon what the planter provided. Although by the 1850s reforms in slave housing were being urged, most slaves continued to live in windowless one-room huts about 10 to 15 feet square, with dirt floors.

The standard weekly ration for most slaves was 3.5 to 4.0 pounds of salt pork and a peck of corn for a young male adult, with women, children, and older adults receiving various smaller portions. Rice might be substituted for corn where it was the staple, and in other areas salt fish and molasses might be supplemental items. To this basic diet some planters added greens, sweet potatoes, beans, cowpeas, wheat flour, or milk, depending on the season and the size and diversity of the plantation crops. The vegetables were often from the slaves' own garden plots, but the practice of allowing gardens was not universal. Primitive techniques of food preservation added another element of uncertainty; there were frequent descriptions of spoiled and wormy meat.

The average life expectancy of slaves was at least 12 percent below that of white Americans in 1850, and the mortality of infants under a year old was at least 25 percent above the rate for southern whites. Many of the diseases common among slaves can be linked to deficiencies of niacin, thiamine, and riboflavin which a pork and corn diet would foster. Beriberi, pellagra, and a condition ante-bellum doctors called "sore mouth" (associated with deficiencies of riboflavin and Vitamin A) were widespread. Furthermore, the slaves' general material condition and work situation increased their susceptibility to infectious diseases which ravaged the ante-bellum South: malaria, yellow fever, cholera, and pneumonia.

Slave Family and Community The mortality of Afro-American slaves—appalling as it was compared to that of whites—was mild compared to that of slaves on Caribbean sugar plantations. Afro-American slaves not only survived; they were fruitful and multiplied, increasing by natural means even before the cutoff of the slave trade. That event helped equalize the male-female ratio by 1850, a condition that encouraged nuclear mating patterns. During the ante-bellum era, slaves tended overwhelmingly to live in two-parent households. A sample of slave families in a recent study shows that fewer than one in four families were without a male parent, and female family heads were mostly age 40 or older, suggesting that many were widows.

The end of the slave trade also had a negative effect on black family life. The dramatic growth of cotton production and the opening of the Southwest shifted at least 835,000 slaves from the economically declining eastern states (Virginia, Maryland, the Carolinas) to the booming western ones (Mississippi, Louisiana, Alabama, Texas), with more than 40 percent of this migration occurring in the two decades before the Civil War. This westward movement, together with intrastate and intraregional sales caused by the bankruptcy or death of the master and the practice of hiring out slaves for long periods, had one inevitable by-product: the dissolution of slave marriages and families. One sample of slave marriages during the Civil War revealed that one of four included members previously separated from a spouse by force. Clearly the threat of family separation loomed over every human relationship in the slave quarters.

Planters sought to diminish the authority of the black male in the family, possibly to reinforce their self-images as plantation patriarchs, but they had to allow a

certain amount of male assertiveness and responsibility in order to maintain order and morale. Many slave husbands and fathers did assert themselves in these roles, despite their restricted capacity to provide for and protect their families. Similarly, slave families, though subject to severe shocks and strains, resisted being torn asunder because they valued ties of marriage and kinship. Most slaves sought to maintain stable two-parent households, and many marriages lasted for ten years or more, suggesting that marriage and family were internalized cultural values.

Despite forced migrations and separations slaves carefully passed on the surnames of their black family of origin and declined to take the names of their various subsequent owners. The large percentage of sons named for their fathers suggests the important status of the male parent. Naming practices also indicate the resilience of African concepts of kin: children were named for grandparents, uncles, and aunts; and the practice of addressing elders as "auntie" and "uncle" was quite likely a slave invention to show respect. The terrible strains on the nuclear family highlighted the role of this extended kinship network in protecting children and fulfilling the supportive functions of family should the nuclear unit be broken. There were few black orphans either before or after emancipation; the black community automatically took in and raised orphaned children.

The family—indeed the whole slave community—functioned to socialize its children, to foster acceptable values, and to shape the Afro-American culture it passed on to its posterity. The family was generally able to perform its emotional and supportive functions despite the instability and brutalities of slave life. The length of many slave marriages, the remarriage ceremonies, and widespread searches for spouses and children immediately after the Civil War suggest that black family members cared for each other and were held together by strong bonds of affection. Like their African ancestors Afro-American communities developed their own ways of surviving in a hostile environment.

FREEDOM: EMANCIPATION AND POST-EMANCIPATION

The plantation system left gaps which allowed the development of quasi-independent cultural institutions such as the slave family, the black church, music, and folklore. Within these institutions the slave fostered emotional supports, community interaction, and vision that were alternative to the planter's; within them he could socialize his children to comprehend an alternative world view.

However, the choices available to individual slaves or to the slave community were terribly abbreviated and lay within the narrow range between violent resistance and accommodation to the status quo. Accommodation consisted of deciding to survive, to raise a family, to protect it where possible, and to maintain as strong a sense of self-worth as family, religion, and individual skills would permit. These decisions might also involve accepting the racist ideology of the white society and the legitimacy of white hegemony, but not necessarily. The slave who remained a slave necessarily had a conservative outlook: he was content to change what in his view could be changed and to accept as given what could not. Such behavior is explained less by the inter-

nalizing of racist values than by the unavailability of opportunities to act otherwise. Thus few slaves were completely accommodationist or completely rebellious; time and circumstance made them first one and then the other, or both simultaneously.

Slave resistance took the form of violent revolt more frequently in the colonial and early national periods than later. White hegemony was then less solidly established and less geographically complete. The ratio of blacks to whites was higher, especially in the South, and there were still significant external military threats from Europeans and Indians. Furthermore, the ratio of Africans to creoles was still high; the revolts in New York in 1712 and Stono, S.C., in 1739 suggest that slaves with fresh memories of Africa were more likely to rebel than those born into slavery. The last major revolt, Nat Turner's in 1831, occurred 30 years before the general emancipation. Nonviolent, individualistic forms of resistance were more common than open revolt; the creole slaves attacked the labor regime through slowdowns and various subtle methods of disruption. When they could stand their lot no longer, they ran away to whatever haven was reachable—to friendly Indian villages, to northern and southern cities, to Canada.

Few systems of slavery, in the New World or the Old, among blacks or whites, have been toppled by the slaves themselves. Emancipation in America was framed by the American Revolution and the Civil War. From Crispus Attucks (c. 1723–1770) in the Boston Massacre to Peter Salem (d. 1816) at Bunker Hill to Salem Poor at Valley Forge, Afro-Americans—free and slave—seemed to understand the import of the Revolution. While white patriots were vacillating about the role of black men in the struggle against Britain, the blacks acted. In the winter of 1775, several hundred joined the British when promised their freedom; others joined colonial forces for similar pledges. Before the conflict ended, 4,000 had served with the Continental Army and thousands more in the state militias. Whatever interpretations whites applied to these events, the slaves clearly revealed their perceptions by the surnames they took upon enlistment: Jeff Liberty, Ned Freedom, Juperter Free.

The military necessity that required the whites to accept the enlistment and liberation of black soldiers did not undermine the institution of slavery as a whole. Indeed, 90 percent of the slaves—those residing in the five southern states—were barely touched by the war. The Deep South states refused to enlist slaves under any circumstances and only those 5,000 or so who left Charleston, S.C., with the British at war's end benefited from the conflict.

Even in the North the direct effect of the war was limited. Increasing public opposition to slavery was reflected in more frequent manumissions and newspaper attacks on the institution. The constitutions of several New England states incorporated the rhetoric of the Declaration of Independence on human equality, and these words were soon applied by courts and legislators to free the slaves. Thus by 1790 there were only 3,763 slaves among the 16,882 blacks in New England, and these slaves were less than 1 percent of the region's population. Nevertheless, most northern slaves lived in New York, New Jersey, and in Pennsylvania; and only

Pennsylvania began to abolish slavery before the end of the war in 1783. The strong Quaker influence that was part of the traditional political and economic establishment of Pennsylvania contributed vitally to early abolition there. In New York and New Jersey the dramatic rise of slave prices in the postwar era, the increasing numbers of cheaper, free white laborers, and the diminished political hegemony of the slave-holding class contributed to the success of abolition in their legislatures in 1799 and 1804 respectively. The Revolution may have contributed to abolition indirectly through the economic dispossession and political disgrace of Loyalists, among whom land-ownership and slave-holding tended to be concentrated. In any case, abolition in these three states was a gradual process and slave-owners were compensated by being permitted to hold former slaves in apprenticeship well into their adult years.

By the beginning of the 19th century, most northern blacks were at least technically free. The Northwest Ordinance, passed the same year the Constitution was written, prohibited slavery in what was to become the upper Midwest, and the Missouri Compromise of 1820 kept it out of the North altogether.

Until 1860 the dynamic westward expansion of the country kept reopening the issues of statehood, representation, and citizenship, and with them the festering sore of slavery itself. Very soon the moral issue was joined—imperfectly—with the political issues of representation and the balance of power; this marriage of issues ultimately broke open the whole system of compromise and precipitated America's most devastating war in 1861.

There was no unanimity among northern whites about war objectives or about the future status of blacks, slave or free. Ironically this lack of unanimity, together with the protracted and costly nature of the struggle, soon made it necessary to recruit black troops and to liberate the slaves held by rebels. Black troops filled gaps created by white opposition to enlistment or conscription; emancipation was required not by wholehearted northern support for the ideal of freedom, but by the diplomatic necessity of branding the South's cause in European capitals as the preservation of slavery and by manpower needs. Before the war ended, there were about 180,000 black troops in the Union armies; they had fought 39 major battles against Confederate forces, and 17 soldiers and 4 sailors had received the Congressional Medal of Honor. Their sacrifices contributed in no small measure to the liberties and rights gained by black people after the war. The limited and contingent freedom offered in President Abraham Lincoln's Emancipation Proclamation in 1863 was supplanted by the general, unconditioned emancipation of the Thirteenth Amendment in 1865. Three years later black citizenship was guaranteed by the Fourteenth Amendment, and in 1870, the right to vote by the Fifteenth.

The Problem of Freedom However, freedom was not without serious qualifications. Both before and after the Civil War free blacks found themselves with a generally limited and deteriorating occupational base, except in cities in the Deep South where they continued to dominate the skilled crafts. In cities elsewhere they faced increased job competition from immigrants and exclusion by protests from organized white workers. In some places there was already a perceptible development of ghettos in city centers or on semi-industrial fringes, and the basis for an institutional ghetto was already evident in law and custom.

When abolition was debated in northern legislatures in the 1790s, it was not social justice but social control that most concerned the lawmakers. In almost every state emancipation was either accompanied or soon followed by laws banning racial intermarriage, voting, or the immigration of free blacks. When Fort Sumter was fired on in 1861, blacks could vote in only five New England states and in New York only if they owned $250 in debt-free property, a requirement not applied to whites. In states where slavery was barred by the Northwest Ordinance or the Missouri Compromise, blacks could not vote or serve in the militia. They were excluded from juries in Iowa, Ohio, and Illinois. They were barred from settling in Indiana, Illinois, and Iowa, and were required to post a $500 bond to live in Ohio. They were forced to attend segregated schools in Ohio after 1850 and had no public schools at all in Illinois and Indiana.

Some of these laws were impossible to enforce, but they defined the racial boundaries as northern whites perceived them and the racial climate blacks confronted. These laws had been rationalized as necessary to prevent inundation by hordes of escaped or freed southern slaves seeking a northern refuge. However, there was no mass migration north in the 19th century, and race relations distinctly improved in northern states after the Civil War.

Leaders in northern communities of free blacks perceived the subtle connection between the conditions of southern slaves and freedmen and their own plight. Northern blacks contributed directly to the southern leadership cadre during Reconstruction, and the antebellum free Negro institutions were models for southern freedmen.

One of the most important of these institutions, the church, influenced the political as well as the social life of the larger black community. It was the one institution available to both slaves and free men during the ante-bellum period, and it helped bridge the gap between their experiences. The freedmen of the revolutionary era charted the course that those of 1865 would follow. Two months after the U.S. Constitution was completed at Independence Hall, the Reverends Richard Allen (1760–1831) and Absalom Jones led a group of freed slaves out of Philadelphia's St. George's Methodist Church. Their action initiated a general exodus of free blacks from white churches during the next three decades and the establishment of black churches and ministries. The withdrawal from St. George's and many similar incidents were precipitated by segregation and insulting treatment during the services. But it was the congregation's desire for autonomy, for complete control over at least one important aspect of their corporeal and spiritual existence that brought about the formation of separate black religious institutions. The fact that Richard Allen had proposed separate services for the black members of St. George's before the withdrawal is evidence of the desire for autonomy. A completely separate church organization, the African Methodist Episcopal Church, was not organized until 1816.

During the intervening years Allen's group held services in a separate church but remained loosely under the authority of the Methodist church. Only the repeated efforts of white ministers to take over their church property and to control their services led the blacks to break completely with the white Methodists. They did not object to worshiping separately from the whites, but they did object to white control of their worship.

The fact that the most prominent leaders of the independent black churches were former slaves implies some continuities between slave religion and the free black church. Although the black slave had been converted to Euro-American religious doctrines and beliefs, there were subtle differences in emphasis and style of worship between whites and blacks. Afro-American slave religion, like its African precursors, was less concerned with individual sin and more with social order and community. Its form drew more from ritual than from meditation. Black spirituality was preeminently social, drawing more on the communion of the group and less on the one-to-one relationship with God, less still the individual introspection characteristic of Protestantism. It was for this reason that Allen and his followers, soon after leaving St. George's, abandoned the Free African Society's Quaker-style services and formed a Methodist congregation. Like the improvisational, call-response patterns of Afro-American music, the black preaching style tended to be extemporaneous within set patterns and to blend the speaker's inspiration with the congregation's reaction. Rather than expostulate on a theological proposition, the black preacher chose to persuade, to seize upon immediate situations and events, to create an emotional atmosphere conducive to acceptance and giving.

Allen's organization, Mother Bethel, was a model for the social role of the institutional church. Within it were a multitude of social benefit and mutual-aid associations, schools, and havens for runaway slaves. While Allen's sermons emphasized the power of God's love and personal salvation, they were not entirely otherworldly, but dealt with problems in this world. Indeed, a great deal of church business involved regulating the conduct and behavior of members, including domestic feuds, sexual misbehavior, stealing, and indebtedness. Church membership contributed strongly to class status and community prestige. With punishments ranging from temporary suspension to expulsion, the black church was an effective instrument of social control.

Not surprisingly, it was from the church that much of the post–Civil War leadership was drawn. In Reconstruction South Carolina, for example, about 20 percent of black officeholders whose occupations are known were ministers, the majority Methodists and Baptists. It was less a matter of the churches themselves being a base for organizing a constituency than simply the attractiveness of the church for black men of ambition and leadership potential.

Ante-bellum free blacks generally provided a disproportionate share of the leadership in southern black communities immediately after the war. Some came from the North as ministers, missionaries, and soldiers; others emerged from among the artisans and petty bourgeoisie of southern cities. Free Negroes were fewer than 1 in 40 of the total black population of South Carolina in 1860, but they constituted one-fourth of the blacks elected to federal or state office after the war. More than 97 percent of the local black political infrastructure of postwar New Orleans had been born free. And while the proportions were lower in states with smaller ante-bellum free black populations, their impact was considerable nevertheless; nearly all of the 16 Negroes elected to the U.S. Congress during Reconstruction had been free before the war.

Before the Civil War ended, these men spearheaded a nationwide drive for civil and political rights. Black delegates from 18 states met in Syracuse, N.Y., in October 1864 to form the National Equal Rights League and push for the right to vote. Chapters were formed in northern states to pressure state governments. Conventions organized in the South demanded black suffrage as a precondition for readmitting the ex-Confederate states. In both southern and northern cities (Philadelphia, Charleston, Richmond, New Orleans) free blacks led successful boycotts against segregated streetcars. In New Orleans they led a campaign against segregated public schools which brought about the integration of 19 schools and the mixing of about 1,000 white students and an equal number of blacks for a seven-year period. Freeborn legislators in South Carolina and Louisiana led struggles to pass civil rights laws opening public accommodations and travel to blacks.

Successful assaults on southern segregation were short-lived and limited in extent, however. The Louisiana civil rights laws of 1869 and 1873 were easily evaded; blacks in integrated bars found exorbitant prices and cayenne pepper in their drinks. Nominally desegregated hospitals had segregated wards; outside New Orleans the public school system continued to be segregated despite the state constitutional provision to the contrary. With the end of Republican political control in 1877, the initiatives in race relations begun during Reconstruction were reversed. The late 19th century was characterized by increasing legal and extra-legal proscription and persecution of black citizens which culminated by the turn of the century in their complete disfranchisement and segregation. Between 1889 and 1902 four southern state legislatures passed laws to disfranchise blacks; between 1890 and 1910 seven others amended their constitutions for the same purpose. Between 1873 and 1896 the U.S. Supreme Court whittled away the protections afforded by the Thirteenth, Fourteenth, and Fifteenth Amendments, and in *Plessy* v. *Ferguson* (1896) endorsed apartheid with the rationalization "separate but equal."

The Failure of Freedom   The immediate concern of the ex-slave was not the freedom to ride first-class on trains, sit in theaters, or attend integrated schools, but the control of his labor and the land he worked. On this issue freeborn leadership was less adequate and the consequences more devastating than in the battle against segregation. Governmental responses to the land hunger of the freedmen ranged from simple inadequacy to outright hostility. During the war the federal government settled freed slaves on conquered plantations in South Carolina, Virginia, Mississippi, and Louisiana. On many of these the blacks simply toiled as laborers for a white lessee or government manager, but on several they were allowed to work as families and on their own account. In the South Carolina Sea Islands, land

belonging to rebel planters was sold for tax defaults; and although the bulk of it went to white northern speculators in 320 acre sections, about 16,000 acres were purchased by blacks under a special financial arrangement.

The most promising prospect for land reform during the war was the confiscation of coastal plantations in South Carolina and Georgia which General William T. Sherman's Field Order No. 15 set aside for the thousands of freedmen who followed his army on its march to the sea. About 40,000 heads of households were to receive 40-acre plots which they would farm until Congress validated their titles; but the plan was aborted when President Andrew Johnson pardoned the ex-Confederate planters and ordered his generals to remove black settlers from the confiscated plantations.

The Southern Homestead Act of 1866 opened public lands in Alabama, Florida, Arkansas, Louisiana, and Mississippi to purchase on installments by settlers. Much of the land was of poor quality, and all of it was undeveloped, thus requiring more venture capital than most freed slaves possessed; despite these handicaps about 4,000 blacks settled on these 80-acre plots by 1870. Several hundred blacks in South Carolina obtained land through a commission created by the Republican government to purchase and subdivide plantations for sale on easy credit terms. Other state governments resorted to such indirect devices as raising taxes on uncultivated land and limiting the acreage of sections sold at tax auctions.

By 1900 a substantial minority—25 percent—of black farmers in the South owned their own farms, mostly through private initiatives such as the numerous black land cooperatives organized in the postwar years. These purchases were less a matter of dismantling the large plantations than of simply extending small-farm cultivation. By far the greater proportion of owners were in the upper South and Southeast: in Virginia 60 percent of the black farmers owned their own land, in North Carolina 33 percent, in South Carolina 20 percent, in Georgia 14 percent, and in Mississippi 11 percent. Therefore, in the Deep South, postwar plantation ownership passed not to blacks but to northern capitalists seeking to take advantage of the high postwar prices of cotton and sugar.

Without land of his own the freedman had little choice but to work for the white planter. However, blacks resisted working in gangs and insisted upon controlling the labor demands made upon their wives and children. The cotton planter accommodated these demands by subdividing his acreage and allocating plots to freed families. Unable or unwilling to meet a weekly payroll, he furnished the worker shelter, rations, seed, tools, and stock and feed in return for one-half to two-thirds of the crop. The goal of the sharecropper was eventually to become a cash tenant, renting the farm for a specified amount and providing seed, tools, and stock himself. However, he still had to mortgage the crop to landowner or storekeeper in exchange for food, clothing, and supplies.

The system was open to abuse. The landlords' greed and dishonesty, the tenants' illiteracy and subservience, high interest rates, a general decline in the agricultural economy—all could plunge tenants or sharecroppers into a perpetual cycle of poverty. Although the postwar recovery of cotton production was rapid, the average price of cotton fell by more than 50 percent between 1874 and 1890. Thus the tenants became enmeshed in debts from which their share of the crop never seemed enough to extricate them.

To make their workers "stand in fear," the system of southern law maximized labor control by convict lease and peonage. The leasing of convicts to private employers, begun in some areas before the Civil War, became widespread in the 1880s and 1890s. Blacks convicted of minor offenses, such as vagrancy and disorderly conduct, were hired out by state and county courts to planters and other employers for a small fee. Peonage, a related practice, continued in the South well into the 20th century and legally forced the laborer to work to satisfy debts incurred under the crop-lien and advance system. If he left the plantation he was subject not to civil suit for breach of contract, but to criminal penalties and, upon conviction, leased to the same or another employer. Despite a Supreme Court decision in 1911 declaring that the practice violated the Thirteenth Amendment, cases were uncovered in Georgia and Florida in the 1940s.

The 10 to 20 percent of the black population living in urban areas in the late 19th century also faced economic difficulties. Throughout the 19th century, three-fourths or more of the urban black male work force had been relegated to menial and unskilled jobs, but in many cities there had been a significant core of skilled artisans. After the Civil War there was a general and precipitous decline in the numbers of skilled and semi-skilled laborers. This decline was more extreme in northern and midwestern cities where between the Civil War and World War I skilled blacks lost ground to foreign-born workers, on the one hand, and to the changing structure of the job market on the other. In Cleveland, for example, 32 percent of the black labor force had been engaged in skilled trades in 1870; only 11 percent were so employed by 1910. In 1890 the percentage of black males in skilled work was down to under 5 percent in New York City, under 10 in Boston, and under 8 in Chicago.

The decline of the black artisan may be traceable in part to his inability to upgrade his skills in a new industrial era. The black artisan tended to be a jack-of-all-trades rather than a specialist. But the primary cause of the postwar decline was racial prejudice. Whites began to prefer white barbers and waiters to black; craft unions excluded black workers, and new manufacturing plants did not hire them. For example, in 1890 there were only three blacks employed in the entire Cleveland steel industry, none in a host of new occupations —typesetters, electricians, cabinetmakers—and only five plumbers in 1910. Radical changes in retail merchandising, greater advertising, and an emphasis on public image discouraged white employers from hiring black women as clerks in the new department stores or as telephone operators.

There was regional variation among the cities of the North, upper South, and lower South. Southern black males had a stronger grip on skilled trades than their northern brothers, stronger still in the lower than in the upper South. Black predominance in skilled labor and property-holding increased in the post-bellum period in cities like Savannah, Ga., and New Orleans, in contrast

to the national pattern of decline in the face of competition with foreign-born workers. In New Orleans, blacks remained strong in the building trades well into the 20th century, and in Savannah between 1870 and 1880 they doubled their representation in several trades. The cities of the lower South were exceptional, however, owing to the relative absence of immigrant competition.

For the first half-century after emancipation most southern blacks worked as sharecroppers on plantations under a legal and economic bondage that rivaled slavery. Twenty years after emancipation their material circumstances had not substantially improved. Toward the end of the century Booker T. Washington (1856–1915) and W.E.B. Du Bois described conditions of the most abject poverty in rural Alabama and Tennessee, respectively. In Georgia in the 1930s a survey of the diet, clothing, and housing of black farmers revealed conditions similar to those of their enslaved ancestors.

Black southerners began the 20th century with an increasingly circumscribed range of choices. Despite the sudden reversal of political fortunes in 1877 and the violence, fraud, and intimidation of the 1880s, they had continued to vote in substantial numbers and to send black representatives to the state legislatures and to Congress. Six blacks served in Congress between 1877 and 1901, 46 sat in the South Carolina General Assembly between 1878 and 1895, and six were still in the Mississippi legislature the year its Jim Crow constitution was written. This was not introduced without resistance. Eighteen black Louisiana legislators protested the passage of that state's Jim Crow transportation statute in 1890. Black communities in 30 southern cities boycotted segregated streetcars and tested segregation laws in the courts. One such test in Louisiana led eventually to the *Plessy* v. *Ferguson* decision of 1896 by which the U.S. Supreme Court upheld state laws requiring separation of the races.

The Great Migration Given the triumph of segregation, political disfranchisement, and economic bondage, only one option remained: migration. The economic depression beginning in the 1890s, aggravated by drought and an infestation of boll weevils in the early 20th century, spurred a major shift from farm to city, and eventually from the South to the North. This was not the first sizable migration by blacks. Throughout the 19th century there had been a small but fairly constant trickle to Liberia and West Africa. In 1879 there had been an explosive exodus out of Louisiana, Mississippi, and Texas into Kansas. Smaller movements from Kansas to Oklahoma later had established all-black towns.

But the movement from countryside to city had always been larger than all the other migrations combined. During the ante-bellum period far more slaves escaped to southern cities than to northern states and Canada. After emancipation there was an even more dramatic rise in the urban black population. Between 1860 and 1880 the black population of Savannah increased almost 100 percent. The freed blacks of Alabama moved from its predominantly white counties into the southwestern region; by 1870 the black populations of its four largest cities—Mobile, Montgomery, Selma, and Huntsville—had increased almost 58 percent. There was also a minor northern migration from

the border states and upper South, and a substantial movement from rural areas within some northern states in response to declining agricultural opportunities.

However, the Great Northern Migration during and after World War I permanently transformed Afro-Americans into a predominantly urban people and profoundly affected both their destinations in the North and the communities they left in the South. The southern migrant came North to fill jobs made available to him through the virtual cessation of foreign immigration after 1914. The movement continued through the 1920s, diminished briefly during the Great Depression, resumed during World War II, and continued for three decades more.

The demographic impact on northern black communities was immense; 554,000 blacks left the South, followed by 902,000 more during the next decade. The black population of the eastern north-central states increased 71 percent and of the Middle Atlantic states 43 percent compared with an increase of less than 7 percent in the nation as a whole. Black communities in Pittsburgh and New York absorbed substantial increases of 47 and 66 percent, and Chicago, Cleveland, and Detroit, jumped 148, 307, and 611 percent, respectively.

The migrants' motives were primarily economic, but southern racial relations and educational inadequacies also urged them North. Although labor recruiters attracted many southerners to the North, most were probably convinced by relatives and friends who already resided there. For example, a mass exodus from Caswell County, N.C., to Xenia, Ohio, followed the homecoming of a young woman who painted an attractive picture of her new life. Chain migration patterns were illustrated by a survey of Greene County, Ga., in the 1930s. Young unattached males left first, followed by young couples with no children or very few, then unattached females, and finally families with children. In the case of families, the husband left first, and after he had settled, wife and children followed. Other surveys show that the migrants were usually skilled or semi-skilled workers from southern cities and towns. The dramatic increase of the black population in southern cities during the decade preceding the Great Northern Migration also suggests a two-stage movement—rural South to urban South, urban South to urban North. The wage laborers and share tenants who left the countryside were the youngest and best educated, leaving behind the very old and the very young and giving urban areas a disproportionate number of the young adults.

The migrants confronted severe problems in the northern cities. They paid excessive rents, for example, in Cleveland as much as 65 percent more than whites. Many black households had to take in lodgers in order to make ends meet. Overcrowding added to already serious health problems; tuberculosis was three times as prevalent among blacks as among whites. In every city, blacks found themselves confined not only to separate residential areas but also to separate institutions. Access to public places and predominantly white institutions had always been uncertain despite the civil rights laws passed in the North during the 1880s. In most northern states, white restaurants, hotels, and public schools were closed to blacks, although the line

was never hard and fast. The mass migration of southern blacks revived fears among northern whites similar to those of the Civil War era, and integrated institutions were quickly segregated. Admission to theaters, restaurants, hotels, hospitals, schools, YMCAs was increasingly "for whites only."

The migration also encouraged the development of black institutions to serve a greatly expanded population denied services by the larger society. Suddenly there was a market that made a number of business and professional ventures more viable than ever before—real estate, retailing, banking and insurance, medical and legal services. There was increasing demand within the black community for the establishment of black hospitals and social service organizations.

Clearly there were psychological as well as economic advantages in the developing urban ghetto. Whatever the problems in the North, the migrant was better off in terms of his income, the chance to educate his children, and the intellectual and spiritual stimulation of the urban environment than he had been in the South. He lived in the midst of a black cultural awakening in music, theater, and literature. The old paternalistic bonds were finally broken. Prosperity was possible despite the obvious difficulties. Many black intellectuals in Chicago, Cleveland, or Washington agreed with the observations of Alain Locke (1886–1954) about Harlem; they saw as he did a "spiritual emancipation," "the laboratory of a great race-welding," a first chance for "group expression and self-determination," a chance "to repair a damaged group psychology and reshape a warped social perspective," a chance "to convert a defensive into an offensive position, a handicap into an incentive." What they saw was not a dark ghetto, but a black metropolis.

The Literary Renaissance For Alain Locke, as for many other young intellectuals, a by-product of the unprecedented urban migration was an explosion of artistic creativity. This was a new era, and it belonged to a "New Negro." Of course, Locke and his generation were not the first new Negroes; practically every generation since Appomattox had claimed as much. Nevertheless, the generation of the 1920s was more urban, better educated, and had greater access to the media—black as well as white—than any of its predecessors.

The northern migration provided visibility and an economic basis for cultural activities as well as for black business enterprises. Cleveland, Chicago, Washington, and especially New York were the centers for creative contacts and media attention. Urbanization was accompanied by a significant expansion of the black media: the number of newspapers increased 30 percent between 1890 and 1940. *The Pittsburgh Courier* (f. 1910) and *The Chicago Defender* (f. 1905) attained national circulation. The NAACP's *Crisis* magazine (f. 1910) and the National Urban League's *Opportunity* (f. 1923) provided space for poets and storytellers.

Perhaps most important of all to the literary renaissance was the dramatic expansion of black education during the decade after World War I. After Reconstruction indifferent or hostile southern legislatures had stifled public education for blacks. But northern missionary societies continued to support the 47 private black colleges and normal schools established during the 1870s and 1880s; and by the turn of the century the

phenomenal success of conservative educators like Booker T. Washington in fostering vocational education had assuaged the fears many southerners harbored of educated blacks. With the encouragement of northern philanthropic organizations like John D. Rockefeller's General Education Board and the Julius Rosenwald Fund, and substantial contributions from black citizens, schools were constructed, teachers trained, and books and supplies provided in thousands of rural communities. In 1912 less than 6 out of 10 southern school-age blacks attended elementary classes, but by 1930 almost 9 out of 10 were in school. In 1916 there were only 64 public high schools for blacks in the southern and border states; by 1930 there were 1,200. During this same period the black illiteracy rate was almost halved, decreasing from almost 31 percent to 16 percent, and the number of college and professional graduates more than doubled. The writers of the renaissance era were heirs to this progress: most had attended college, most were the sons and daughters of professional parents.

The creative output of the 1920s easily surpassed that of any previous era. Afro-Americans had published only 31 novels in the 70 years before 1920, beginning with William Wells Brown's (1816–1884) *Clotel, or the President's Daughter* (1853); 28 of these were published after 1890. In contrast, between 1920 and 1940 black writers published 37 novels. Because the works of Jupiter Hammon (1720–1800), Phillis Wheatley (c. 1753–1784), and George Moses Horton (1797–1883) are of little more than antiquarian interest to the 20th-century reader, the reputation of early black poetry rests primarily on the works of Paul Laurence Dunbar (1872–1906), published between 1893 and his untimely death from tuberculosis. Black poets published more volumes during the decade after World War I than during the half-century before it. A century after Ira Aldridge (1805–1867) and James Hewlett performed Shakespeare before the raucous audiences of New York's Grove Street Theater, black theater came to Broadway with Willis Richardson's one-act *The Chipwoman's Fortune* (1923), Garland Anderson's (1886–1939) full-length *Appearances* (1925), and Wallace Thurman's (1902–1934) melodrama *Harlem* (1929). In the intervening years blacks had performed in minstrel shows and in the musical comedies and revues of Will Marion Cook (1870–1947), Bob Cole (1863–1911), Noble Sissle (1889–1975), and Eubie Blake (1883–), but not in dramatic productions. In 1926 the Harmon Foundation offered annual awards to encourage the activities of young sculptors and painters.

Other claims of the renaissance generation were more problematic. Their elders lacked "self-understanding," wrote Locke, and consequently blacks had been "almost as much of a problem to ourselves as we still are to others." Self-conscious and defensive, "the elder generation of Negro writers expressed itself in cautious moralisms and guarded idealizations; the trammels of Puritanism were on its mind because the repressions of prejudice were heavy on its heart." They always sought to "put the better foot foremost." In contrast, the New Negroes regarded themselves as unselfconscious, unapologetic; they shared a "lusty vigorous realism"; they had "broken with the old epoch of philanthropic guidance, sentimental appeal and protest." They no longer spoke for the Negro but as Negroes;

they spoke to their own rather than try to interpret their people for whites. They were independent and would continue to sing even "if America were deaf." "They have stopped posing, being nearer the attainment of poise."

Locke's unflattering assessment of his literary elders contained some truth. More often than not the works of the previous century had been addressed to a white audience either in protest or supplication. The slave narratives popular in the 1840s and 1850s were written to serve the abolitionist cause. After the turn of the century the resurgence of racist propaganda like Thomas Dixon's *The Clansman* (filmed as *The Birth of a Nation*, 1915) called forth novels of protest. One response to racist attacks, popular in the early 20th century but with ante-bellum antecedents, was insistence upon the Negroes' innate capacity for civilization and bourgeois respectability; they were after all only white men in black skins.

But the new generation had its own identity problems despite its bold claims of self-confidence and independence. The historical works of Carter G. Woodson (1875–1950), founder of the Association for the Study of Negro Life and History in 1915; Arthur Schomburg, the great bibliophile; and W.E.B. Du Bois, together with the political excitement of Marcus Garvey's (1887–1940) back-to-Africa movement, inspired renewed interest in an African heritage. Yet, much of their artistic work revealed only a shallow knowledge or abstract rendering of African culture. Jazz and blues flourished in the 1920s, but only a few black writers—Langston Hughes (1902–1967), Sterling Brown (1901–), and Zora Neale Hurston (1903–1960)—were genuinely at home with the black American's rural and urban folk culture; so the dichotomy between the literary and folk arts remained.

These artists shared the cultural ambivalence of the rising black middle class, who blushed at Langston Hughes's portraits of Harlem cabarets and street life. They also shared the ambivalence of white Americans who found in the black urban life-style a foil to materialism and conventional morality. The prevailing cultural milieu reinforced the excessively atavistic and exotic tendencies of the renaissance. And although black writers were not blind to the terrible problems festering in Harlem and other northern ghettos, they still emphasized the urban excitement and energy. Not until Richard Wright's (1908–1960) *Native Son* in 1940, James Baldwin's (1924–) *Go Tell It on the Mountain* in 1953, and Ralph Ellison's (1914–) *Invisible Man*, winner of the National Book Award in 1953, would the harsher features of the northern ghetto dominate Afro-American literature.

The shock of the Great Depression disabused the New Negro intellectuals. Business enterprise, employment, and cultural activity all suffered severely. The decade before had already witnessed a dramatic increase in racial tensions that made a mockery of the North's reputation as a "promised land." Open violence exploded when blacks and whites competed for employment and housing, reaching a peak in the summer of 1919 when a wave of terror swept black urban communities. Nevertheless, the spatial and cultural self-consciousness of the urban ghetto encouraged a political self-consciousness which revitalized black political

life. By the end of World War II other changes were in motion that would revolutionize American race relations.

FREEDOM NOW: A SECOND RECONSTRUCTION

"There can be no question but that the relations between American Negroes and the balance of the population in the United States have improved during the last generation." That was how W.E.B. Du Bois began a review in 1948 of the previous 30 years of race relations. He pointed to increases in public employment, favorable Supreme Court decisions, increases in university education, the hiring of black faculty by white universities, and increased cooperation between black leaders and southern moderates through interracial organizations like the Southern Regional Council formed in 1944. Du Bois attributed these changes to the growth of the kind of scientific predisposition and scholarship he had championed at the turn of the century—"the increasing willingness and indeed, compulsion among observers of social phenomena to depend upon some kind of social measurement for their judgments rather than upon individual observations." He was pleased to see the growing participation of philanthropic institutions such as the Carnegie Corporation, the Rockefeller Foundation, and the Julius Rosenwald Fund in the study and treatment of the race problem. Indeed, he felt confident enough to state that "science and the general public have attacked the concept of ineradicable race differences with devastating success."

Du Bois's optimism was naive but not entirely groundless. Blacks came out of World War II in a much stronger position than they held at its beginning, and their progress continued in the postwar period. Nonwhite income had been only 41 percent of white income in 1939 but rose to 54 percent in 1947 and 60 percent by 1960. Just under 12 percent of the black labor force was classified as semiskilled operatives in 1940, but increased to 21 percent in 1950 and 24 percent in 1960. The percentage of black males in agricultural work declined from 41 in 1930 to 12 by 1960. The black share of government employment rose from 6 percent in 1940 to 11 percent by 1960. The number of blacks employed by the federal government alone increased from 50,000 in 1933 to 200,000 in 1946.

In addition, the number of blacks enrolled in college increased from 124,000 in 1947 to 233,000 in 1961. This was no mean accomplishment when one considers that in 1930 the average southern black youth had a school year 20 days shorter than his white counterpart, had only 30 percent as much money spent on his education by the state, and was instructed by teachers who received only 61 percent of white teachers' salaries.

The year 1948 was a critical one for American race relations. On July 26 President Harry S Truman issued Executive Order 9981 which eventually desegregated the armed forces, and in September he appointed a special advisory committee to implement that order. In May the U.S. Supreme Court's decision in *Shelley* v. *Kraemer* made residential segregation more difficult by invalidating the court enforcement of restrictive covenants. Later that summer the Democratic party adopted its strongest civil rights plank, sparking a southern walkout and third-party movement. These events merely brought into focus changes that had been in

progress since the late 1930s and that would reach a peak in the mid-1950s. The migration of blacks to the critical industrial cities of the North made them politically visible, and the close election of 1948 demonstrated their importance to the Democratic coalition. Furthermore, given the tremendous expansion of the power of the federal bureaucracy during the depression and World War II and the inaction of a southern-dominated Congress, the federal executive and judiciary assumed the more active role in formulating racial policy. Appointments by Presidents Roosevelt and Truman altered the composition of the Supreme Court, which between 1937 and 1954 gradually dismantled the existing precedents for racial policy in force since 1896. The exclusion of blacks from juries, the white primary, school segregation, and Jim Crow transportation all fell as the court expanded the coverage of the Fourteenth Amendment from the narrow interpretation allowed by *Plessy* v. *Ferguson.*

In 1954 and 1955 these legal, political, and social developments became clear in *Brown* v. *Board of Education* and the Montgomery, Ala., bus boycott. In the Brown decision the Supreme Court reversed the 58-year-old doctrine of separate but equal, and the Montgomery boycott attracted national attention to the renewed militancy of southern black leadership. Neither of these dramatic developments was entirely unprecedented. In 1947 President Truman's Civil Rights Commission had declared invalid the doctrine of separate but equal. In June 1950 the Supreme Court decided almost as much, in *Sweatt* v. *Painter;* the court saw clearly that Herman Sweatt's education in a newly created black law school could not equal "those qualities which are intangible of objective measurement but which make for greatness in a law school," such as the prestige, faculty reputation, and alumni influence which were available to whites in the University of Texas Law School.

But Chief Justice Fred Vinson's opinion did not extend far enough to invalidate the *Plessy* decision; Earl Warren's declaration four years later, that separate was inherently unequal simply by virtue of its invidious distinction and the ramifications of those distinctions on the individual's self-concept, was a far from inevitable consequence of judicial reasoning or history. Significantly, the decisive argument in the justices' minds was the very fact that the times had changed so drastically as to render segregated education an anachronism. The justices were impressed with the vast metamorphosis in race relations over the past generation and were encouraged that further change was possible. They were also aware of the necessity for such change in the national interest. Justice Robert Jackson referred in a private memorandum to the horror of Nazism which had revealed "the awful consequences of racial prejudice." Justice Stanley Reed—who was persuaded to concur with the majority only at the last moment—was urged by his law clerk to consider the effects of segregation on America's position in international affairs. There was no need to add that agitation for the decolonization of Africa was beginning and that competition between the United States and Russia for the allegiance of the emerging unaligned world had already begun. Indeed, the Justice Department had made this point explicitly in its *amicus curiae* brief in the restrictive covenant

cases of 1948: racial segregation and discrimination had an adverse impact on the country's ability to formulate and implement foreign policy. The State Department's interest in the *Brown* decision is suggested by the fact that within one hour after it was announced, the Voice of America had broadcast the news in 34 languages around the world.

And finally there was the notion that vast social changes were already in motion and the times were ripe. Felix Frankfurter, the court's strongest advocate of judicial restraint, wrote in a private memorandum on the *Brown* case: "The effect of changes in men's feelings for what is right and just is equally relevant in determining whether a discrimination denies the equal protection of the laws." He too was convinced that "experience happily shows that contacts tend to mitigate antagonisms and engender mutual respect." Reflecting the general perceptions of change that prevailed among blacks themselves, Chief Justice Warren noted in the majority opinion that "many Negroes have achieved outstanding success in the arts and sciences as well as in the business and professional world."

Like the *Brown* decision, the Civil Rights Movement that followed also grew out of developments within the black community immediately before and after World War II. The great migration to northern cities and the expansion of the black professional class had had a profound effect on the character of community leadership. The greatly increased black population and its concentration in centralized ghettos spurred the growth of business and professional services for the segregated market. A new middle-class elite emerged to seize these advantages, eventually developing intellectual rationalizations for their monopolies; by the 1930s the slogan "Buy Black" had come into wide usage by the black business and professional sectors. The Great Depression dealt a crippling blow to black businessmen and to the professional elite. But it did not reverse the tendency for the college-educated—doctors, lawyers, and educators—to expand their leadership in the black community. Doctors joined the NAACP to fight segregated medical facilities. Black lawyers like Charles H. Houston (1895–1950), Thurgood Marshall (1908–), and William Hastie (1904–) had taken control of the NAACP's legal apparatus and were fashioning a broad-based attack on inequality in education. Young black faculty and students at Howard and Fisk universities voiced increasingly militant criticism of both American society and the traditional protest leadership, especially the NAACP.

Perhaps the militancy of this group, many of whom contributed to his monumental research on the race issue, *An American Dilemma* (1944), led Gunnar Myrdal to expect a movement for racial change to emerge in the North. Instead it began in the urban South. On December 1, 1955, six months after the *Brown* decision, Rosa Parks (1915–), a black seamstress, refused to surrender her seat to a white man on a Montgomery bus. Her subsequent arrest sparked a year-long boycott and brought national attention to direct action as a militant and effective weapon against American apartheid. The decade that followed Rosa Park's arrest was one of increasing protest which came to be known collectively as The Movement. Sit-in demonstrations in 1960, freedom rides in 1961, and mass street demonstrations

from 1962 through 1966 shook not only the white South but the traditional black leadership as well.

These tactics were not unprecedented in the black community. There had been boycotts and sit-ins over segregated transportation in the 1870s and again in the 1890s. In the 1940s Irene Morgan had refused to move to the back of a Greyhound bus traveling from Virginia to Baltimore and won her case before the U.S. Supreme Court, which ruled in *Morgan* v. *Commonwealth of Virginia* (1946) that segregation in interstate commerce was illegal. During the following years the Congress of Racial Equality (CORE) sought to test this ruling by sponsoring a freedom ride, or "Journey of Reconciliation," through Virginia and North Carolina on Trailways and Greyhound buses. Many of the same CORE activists participated in sit-ins in Chicago's Loop in 1942 and stand-ins at New Jersey's segregated Palisades Amusement Park in 1947. A. Philip Randolph (1889–1978), the militant head of the Brotherhood of Sleeping Car Porters, organized the March on Washington Movement in 1941 and threatened to bring 100,000 protesters to the nation's capitol if job discrimination in defense industries was not ended and the military services desegregated. Although the march was canceled after President Franklin Roosevelt issued Executive Order 8802 establishing the Fair Employment Practices Commission in 1941, the march organization continued to press for an integrated armed service and expanded federal job opportunities in the postwar period. Randolph's threat in the spring of 1948 to counsel black youth to resist the draft and engage in civil disobedience may have hastened President Truman's executive order the following summer creating a commission to promote desegregation of the military services.

Despite these tactical precedents, however, the new movement of the 1950s and 1960s was a visible break with the traditional leadership. The National Association for the Advancement of Colored People (NAACP), founded by white and black progressives in 1909 in response to the Springfield, Ill., riot of 1908, was the most prominent and best-known traditional civil rights organization. For almost half a century it had lobbied Congress for favorable legislation, sponsored legal suits against segregation, and provided legal aid for black defendants in racially inspired litigation. Although its campaign to get a federal antilynching bill had failed, the NAACP had been successful in the courts. Various disfranchisement devices, unequal pay for teachers, legislative and judicial enforcement of residential segregation, and school segregation had all fallen beneath its judicial onslaught. But as young militant intellectuals like Ralph Bunche (1904–1971) and E. Franklin Frazier (1894–1962) had pointed out during the 1930s, these victories did not touch the problems of the majority of black citizens, nor did they involve them directly in the struggle.

The National Urban League, founded in 1911, had an even more conservative reputation. Like the NAACP it was a child of the progressive movement, but its founders also shared many of Booker T. Washington's ideas about industrial education, economic development, and accommodation to the status quo. The league tried to assist southern migrants in adjusting to conditions in the urban North and provided aid in securing housing and jobs. Although for a brief period in the 1930s it

sought to develop a relationship with the CIO and organized scores of black worker councils, it generally identified with and sought to accommodate employers and managers rather than unions and workers. Indeed, both the NAACP and the National Urban League were heavily dependent on white philanthropists, especially Julius Rosenwald and John D. Rockefeller. By the postwar period, however, the NAACP's expanded membership had become its main source of financial support.

CORE was born in 1942 out of direct action campaigns in the North and upper South. Its biracial leadership was ideologically committed to pacifism and socialism. But the group's early efforts neither involved nor organized significant sectors of the black communities as did the sit-ins and mass demonstrations of the 1960s. When those actions began CORE veterans moved quickly to lend leadership and direction, and during the following year they sponsored the freedom rides into the Deep South. But CORE acquired a reputation for militant, direct action only as a younger generation of black activists gradually supplanted the older veterans.

The success of the Montgomery boycott led to the organization in 1957 of the Southern Christian Leadership Conference, a loosely federated alliance of ministers under the leadership of the Reverend Dr. Martin Luther King, Jr. (1929–1968). Born of Atlanta's middle class and educated at Boston University, King was strongly influenced by the writings of Henry David Thoreau and Mohandas K. Gandhi, which he skillfully wove into a philosophy of nonviolent direct action that appealed to his Southern Baptist constituency. But although there were isolated bus boycotts in other southern cities, no major campaign followed the Montgomery victory. And although the Supreme Court ban on segregated public transportation that grew out of Montgomery brought compliance in much of the urban South, voter registration and school desegregation proved more difficult to achieve.

Two civil rights laws in 1957 and 1960 aimed at ensuring the right to vote in federal elections were largely ineffective in the face of growing southern resistance and evasion. Indeed, many Deep South states moved to reduce the numbers of blacks already registered. New black registrants faced intimidation, as did the sharecroppers in Fayette County, Tenn., who were evicted for daring to register. A provision to allow the Justice Department to bring suits to integrate schools had been stricken from the 1957 Civil Rights Act, so the burden of litigation remained with the black plaintiffs. Federal executive power was used only grudgingly to enforce the law, as in Little Rock, Ark., in 1957, when President Dwight D. Eisenhower federalized the National Guard to enforce court-ordered school desegregation. Meanwhile southern whites taxed their ingenuity to evade desegregation. Schools were boycotted in Arkansas, closed down in Prince Edward County, Va., and bombed in Clinton, Tenn. The White Citizens' Council was born and the Ku Klux Klan revived. In 1964, ten years after the *Brown* decision, less than 2 percent of the South's black students attended integrated schools.

Black civil disobedience emerged with revolutionary force in the early 1960s in reaction to official and private lawlessness and national indifference. As with Rosa Parks, individuals seized the initiative and the tra-

ditional leaders and organizations scrambled to catch up. College students in Greensboro, N.C., in February 1960 launched the sit-in movement that spread quickly to Nashville and Chattanooga, Tenn., San Antonio, and Jacksonville, Fla. By October four national chain stores had integrated lunch counters in about 150 stores in 112 cities. With the assistance of Martin Luther King, Jr., the student leaders met in Raleigh, N.C., in April 1960 to form a new protest organization, the Student Nonviolent Coordinating Committee (SNCC). A few months later the students joined CORE to conduct freedom rides into Alabama and Mississippi. But unlike the CORE-sponsored Journey of Reconciliation in 1947, some of the participants returned to organize the local communities along the route. Thus in Albany, Ga., a new form of direct action appeared in 1961–1962 when the black community was mobilized for a broad-based attack on the racial system with sit-ins, mass street demonstrations, and jail-ins. The Albany movement failed, but a similar strategy in Birmingham, Ala., was partially successful in the spring of 1963.

The civil disobedience phase of the movement peaked in the summer of 1963. Southern blacks filled local jails from Cambridge, Md., to Plaquemines Parish, La., and from Greenville, Miss., to St. Augustine, Fla. On June 19, when President John F. Kennedy sent an omnibus civil rights bill to Congress, plans were being made to carry the civil disobedience campaign to the nation's capitol. The march that took place on August 28 was a polite demonstration, by approximately 200,000 whites and blacks, of broadly based support for the proposed legislation.

During the summers of 1964 and 1965 President Lyndon B. Johnson signed into law the third and fourth civil rights bills of the decade. Unlike the measures passed in 1957 and 1960, these acts had a tremendous impact on American race relations. They reopened public accommodations and facilities and voting booths to black southerners for the first time since the 1890s. Furthermore, the Voting Rights Act of 1965 laid the groundwork for a dramatic change in the South's balance of political power.

But as the pace of change quickened so did the violence of southern reactionaries. On June 12, 1963, just days after the victory in Birmingham, NAACP leader Medgar Evers was assassinated outside his home in Jackson, Miss. Within weeks of the March on Washington, in September 1963, four children were killed in a bomb explosion in the 16th Street Baptist Church in Birmingham. While President Johnson signed the 1964 Civil Rights Bill on July 2, the FBI searched the swamps and rivers of Mississippi for the bodies of civil rights workers James Chaney, Michael Schwerner, and Andrew Goodman. With each legislative victory, the list of martyrs grew longer.

For southern blacks the bitterness aroused by these atrocities was partially offset by the tangible gains and renewed self-respect they derived from their ability to change the system. But for northern blacks the southern outrages heightened tensions that the new legislation could not assuage because it was largely irrelevant to their conditions and merely exposed more difficult problems of poverty and inequality. The brutalities and viciousness of southern sheriffs Eugene "Bull" O'Connor of Birmingham, James Clarke of Selma, Ala., and

Lawrence Rainey of Meridian, Miss., resonated with the impersonal atrocities of ghetto life and in the daily conflict with local police. Thus the riots in Harlem in 1964, Watts in 1965, Cleveland in 1967, and Detroit in 1968 all began with police incidents—often minor, isolated, and inconsequential in themselves but exemplifying the frustrations of a whole people. Following the assassination on April 4, 1968, of Martin Luther King, Jr., 125 cities erupted in violence that required 70,000 troops to quell. These were not places in which King and the movement had been active and successful, but rather northern communities resentful that the celebrated progress had touched them so lightly. This was and remained the nation's unfinished business.

Progress and Poverty   The northern riots perplexed most Americans because they occurred during a period of unparalleled racial and economic progress: a revolution had reversed attitudes and practices, and federal programs had expanded educational opportunities, reduced poverty and hunger, and addressed the decay of urban neighborhoods. The typical rioter was not an irresponsible, uneducable, unemployable southern immigrant unassimilated to the urban environment, but northern-born, better educated, and more likely to have been employed (though temporarily) than his nonrioting neighbors. He was also more likely to be alienated from the values of the nation, resentful of whites, and to perceive racial discrimination as the primary obstacle to a decent life.

Black Americans shared the rioters' frustrations and alienation more than many of their leaders realized. There was ample evidence of great changes in the living conditions of blacks, but there was also evidence of persistent poverty and continued degradation. The proportion of blacks earning less than a poverty level income dropped from 56 percent in 1960 to 31 percent in 1975, but the rate for blacks was still 3 times that for whites, just as it had been in 1960. Moreover, the number of female-headed households—an indicator of poverty because most such households were poor—continued to rise. Unemployment for blacks was twice the rate for whites during good times and bad. On the other hand, optimists hailed the growth of a new black middle class and the greater parity between black and white incomes. The median family income for blacks had been only 37 percent of the white median in 1939, but was 61 percent by 1974. No doubt this change resulted largely from the vast shift from low-paid agricultural labor into nonfarm occupations. However, almost half (47 percent) of the postdepression shift had occurred between 1940 and 1950 (see Table 1). Indeed, more change toward income parity had occurred in the decade 1939–1949 (37 to 53 percent) than in 1961–1971 (53 to 60 percent). There was significant growth at the upper occupational level. Over 12 percent of the black work force was employed in professional or managerial jobs in the mid-1970s, more than 3 times the proportion in 1940. But it was still only half the percentage for whites as a whole, or indeed, for white ethnic groups such as the Poles (27 percent), Italians (25 percent), and Irish (24 percent).

The lowering of barriers to collegiate and professional education offered hope of even more rapid equalization in the future. There was more than an 85 percent increase in black college enrollment between 1964 and

Table 1. Occupational distribution of Afro-Americans, 1890–1974 (in percentages).

Occupation	1890	1900	1910	1920	1930	1940	1950	1960	1965	1970	1974
Professional, technical, and administrative	1.1	1.2	1.3	1.7	2.5	3.8	5.1	6.1	9.3	10.6	12.2
Clerical and sales	0.9[a]	0.6[a]	0.4[a]	0.8	0.7	1.8	4.6	7.3	9.4	16.0	16.7
Manufacturing and mechanical	6.8	6.9	10.6	18.7	18.6	13.1	24.1	25.7	29.7	27.0	27.1
Trade, transportation, and communication	3.8[a]	4.6[a]	6.0[a]	9.4	10.5	—	—	6.3	—	5.7	5.7
Personal service	18.0	21.2	14.2 ⎫	23.0	19.3	11.7	15.2	16.9 ⎫	33.5	20.0	20.6
Domestic service	13.1	11.8	11.9 ⎭		9.3	22.4	15.1	15.0 ⎭		8.3	5.6
Nonfarm labor	—	—	—	2.2[b]	2.0[b]	14.2	15.5	12.6	13.1	9.4	9.4
Agricultural	56.2	53.7	54.6	44.2	36.1	32.3	18.5	8.1	5.0	3.0	2.7

Source: U.S. Bureau of the Census, U.S. Census Reports, 1890, 1900, 1910, 1940, 1950, 1960; U.S. Bureau of the Census, *Negroes in the United States, 1920–1932* (Washington, D.C., 1935); U.S. Bureau of the Census, *Social and Economic Status of the Negro, 1974* (Washington, D.C., 1976). Because of errors in reporting, not all columns total 100 percent.
 a. Reaggregated for comparability.
 b. Forestry, fishing, and mining only.

1968, most of it attributable to the 144 percent expansion of black enrollment in white colleges; indeed, for the first time more blacks were being educated in white colleges than in black. Paradoxically, this expansion came precisely at a time when the utility of college education in raising income and security was being increasingly questioned. Moreover, the programs of financial aid upon which most of the new black student population depended could no longer be taken for granted.

The clearest and most visible result of the Civil Rights movement was the expanded participation in the political process by blacks in both the South and North. Five black congressmen witnessed the March on Washington in 1963; within a decade their number tripled. Following passage of the Voting Rights Act in August 1965, 2 million new black voters registered in the South. In Mississippi black registration increased tenfold by 1978. Areas like Lowndes and Greene counties in Alabama and McComb, Miss., where law enforcement officials had ignored and encouraged violence against civil rights workers, now had black sheriffs and police officers. In the South as a whole in 1968 only 250 blacks held elective office; ten years later more than 2,000 were officeholders. In the decade after 1965 there were dramatic political changes in the North as well, as several major cities (Cleveland, Gary, Detroit, Newark) elected black mayors and greatly augmented representation in state and local offices. But in neither section did black political power reach its potential during the 1970s. In 1978 black officeholders were still only 3 percent of the South's elected officials, and 66 predominantly black southern counties (out of a total of 100) were still without a single black elected official. On the other hand, a few blacks were elected by predominantly white constituencies in western and northern states.

Evidence of changing racial attitudes was also difficult to evaluate. After 1942, surveys showed a fairly consistent softening of white expressions of hostility to interracial contacts and political and economic equality; this development was very rapid from 1964 to 1970. Desegregation of education and improved economic opportunities brought greater interracial contact; and the people most likely to experience such contacts—the younger, better educated, more urbanized—consistently expressed less hostility toward blacks. Nevertheless, stubborn differences between the life experiences and perceptions of blacks and whites remained, and

they had policy implications. For example, in a 1977 survey a large majority of whites (85 percent) and blacks (92 percent) favored integrated schools, but an equally large majority of whites opposed busing to achieve it, while better than 4 out of 10 blacks favored that solution. Meanwhile a 1974 survey revealed that most whites thought there had been and would continue to be great progress in race relations, but blacks were much more skeptical. Almost a quarter-century after the *Brown* decision, most black children still attended predominantly black schools—50 percent in the South and 66 percent in the North; continued separation in education reflected continued residential separation. By the 1970s a significant legal counterattack was in progress which made the future of the second Reconstruction as problematic as the first.

THE GIFTS OF BLACK FOLK: AMERICAN RACISM AND BLACK ACHIEVEMENT

In the last half of the 20th century the black presence in the United States still posed a paradox for national unity and a dilemma for American ideals. If Crèvecoeur's disturbing specter of a hanged slave in the new American forest was still pertinent, so too was W.E.B. Du Bois's double-consciousness. In his 1903 collection of essays, *The Souls of Black Folks*, Du Bois lamented not only the denial of social justice and the exclusion of blacks from the material richness of America, but also the "sense of always looking at one's self through the eyes of others" and the malaise "of measuring one's soul by the tape of a world that looks on in amused contempt and pity." Du Bois was proud of his Afro-American heritage: "there is no true American music but the wild-sweet melodies of the Negro slave; the American fairy tales and folklore are Indian and African; and, all in all, we black men seem the sole oasis of simple faith and reverence in a dusty desert of dollars and smartness." Black Americans came bearing three gifts: the gift of story and song, the gift of sweat and brawn, and the gift of spirit.

But these artistic, physical, and emotional contributions of Afro-Americans shared a common characteristic: they were not intellectual. In the context of a racist tradition of black inferiority and incapacity, this special black pride frequently turned ambivalent and these unique gifts were often viewed with a peculiar combination of envy and condescension. For some, the

sources of the Afro-American's special talents were the unique experience of slavery and its impact on their African heritage. As the black writer Ralph Ellison put it: "For the art—the blues, the spiritual, the jazz, the dance—was what we had in place of freedom." More often these special talents of song and dance were identified, whether overtly or implicitly, as inherent "racial" traits. Many whites took them as evidence of an unbridgeable cultural chasm between the races and further justification for separation and discrimination; some blacks proudly seized upon these reputedly inherent talents as possessions which they alone controlled. In either case black achievement was always evaluated in the context of the prevailing American racial ideology.

Thomas Jefferson was one of America's first public figures to address the question of racial differences in intelligence, and it is interesting that in his *Notes on the State of Virginia* (1785) he linked that discussion with observations on black artistic abilities. It was Jefferson's "suspicion . . . that the blacks . . . are inferior to the whites in the endowments both of body and mind." He granted that blacks were musically gifted, but doubted that they could compose anything beyond "a small catch." Because he distinguished between that part of intelligence that was merely imitative and that which was cognitive and rational, Jefferson was confused and noncommittal upon receiving six years later an *Almanac* (1791) by the black amateur astronomer Benjamin Banneker (1731–1806). Here was evidence of sophisticated mathematical thinking by a free black man, and it raised anew the possibility that "that want of talents observed in them is merely the effect of their degraded condition, and not proceeding from any difference in the structure of the parts on which intellect depends."

Jefferson's confusion was characteristic of American thought. In the 19th century prominent scientists lent their talents to developing theories of inherent racial inferiority. In the 1840s Louis Agassiz, the Harvard biologist, supported the idea that blacks were created separately from other races. During the late 19th century social Darwinian theories supported the notion that blacks were on a different evolutionary track and that their oppression was justified as the outcome of the "survival of the fittest." During the first half of the 20th century most social and natural scientists retreated from theories of inherent racial inferiority, but others resurrected them in the 1970s.

Frequently, white Americans sympathetic to black aspirations also emphasized their spiritual and nonintellectual capacities, although in these they found blacks superior to whites. Thus the abolitionist Charles Sumner told a Faneuil Hall audience in 1862: "The African is not cruel, vindictive, or harsh, but gentle, forgiving and kind." And after the Civil War the American Freedmen's Inquiry Commission characterized blacks as "a knowing rather than a thinking race." Perhaps the most radical statement of such notions was made by the Reverend Increase Tarbox; arguing against the deportation of blacks after the Civil War, he urged that whites had much to learn from them: "We want them, that our harsh and grasping spirit, as a race, may be tempered by the sight of their more simple-hearted and forgiving natures. We want them that our anxious and giving natures. We want them that our anxious and never-resting lust for gain may be shamed and softened by their more joyous and holiday feeling." Before the Civil War Harriet Beecher Stowe's *Uncle Tom's Cabin* had expressed similar stereotypes. This juxtaposition of cold, intellectual, rational, Puritan, masculine white cultural virtues against tropical, spiritual, emotional, pagan, feminine virtues of black culture has received wide expression in American thought. The novels of Mark Twain, Ernest Hemingway, William Faulkner, and the plays of Eugene O'Neill express such themes. The Lost Generation of the 1920s, the Beat Generation of the 1950s, and the Hippie Generation of the 1960s reflected it. Americans found in the black cultural presence a scapegoat for their anxieties and a reassurance of their own uncertain cultural identities.

As with many stereotypes there was some truth in the characterization of black talent. Black performers in sports and music achieved successes—often against great personal odds and in a racially hostile environment—that could scarcely be ignored. At one time or other blacks were excluded from professional boxing, baseball, basketball, and football, but by the 1960s black athletes were the most prominent, in some cases the numerically dominant, performers in each of these sports. As late as the 1950s black popular music could be heard infrequently, if at all, on most American radio stations; two decades later the roots of most American popular music were in the black musical tradition of blues or jazz. By the mid-20th century white American youth spoke in black "ghetto" idioms and danced to black rhythms, while white athletes used the street dude's "hand slap" rather than the handshake to congratulate a teammate for a good play.

But the celebration of black popular culture overshadowed the accomplishments of Afro-American intellectuals, scientists, and inventors. Given that widespread literacy and education were 20th-century phenomena for Afro-Americans, the contributions of black scientists and the more than 300 patents awarded to black inventors before 1900 are impressive. During the 19th century Norbert Rillieux (1806–1894) invented the vacuum-cup evaporation process which revolutionized sugar refining, Jan E. Matzeliger (1852–1889) developed the shoe-lasting machine, Lewis H. Latimer (1848–1928) patented an improved carbon-filament electric lamp, and Andrew J. Beard (c. 1850–1910) invented the automatic coupler for railroads. In the early 20th century Garrett A. Morgan (1877–1963) patented the automatic traffic light, and Elbert R. Robertson (d. 1925) won the patent for the "chilled groove wheel" and the "third rail," both important to railroads. Ernest Everett Just (1883–1941), an expert on cellular theory, William A. Hinton (1883–1959), an authority on venereal diseases, and Charles R. Drew (1904–1950), developer of the system for blood banks, made significant contributions to medical science. Discoveries by chemist Percy Julian (b. 1898) aided the treatment of glaucoma and arthritis.

Although these contributions argue strongly against the traditional stereotypes of Afro-Americans, the stereotypes have had greater force in defining black identity and have stimulated the alienation of which Du Bois wrote so eloquently in 1903. Du Bois's ultimate resolution of his divergent national identities was to seek asylum in the emerging African nation of

Ghana, to which he moved in 1960. The same poignant sense of alienation within one's native land led other Afro-Americans in the 1960s to follow Du Bois's lead and to embrace physical and institutional separation as positive goods as well as defenses against racial oppression. In the process of seeking a tradition that would provide a rationale for their political faith, they helped revive the study of black history, literature, and culture.

And, of course, a venerable tradition was there: in Paul Cuffee's (1759–1817) voyage to Sierra Leone in 1816, in Martin R. Delany's (1812–1885) exploration of the Niger River in 1859, in Henry McNeal Turner's (1834–1915) campaign for federal aid for African repatriation in 1890, in the efforts of Henry Sylvester Williams (c. 1869–1911) and Du Bois to halt colonialism and create a Pan-African movement in 1900 and 1919, and in Marcus Garvey's Back-to-Africa campaign in the 1920s. In the mid-20th century there was the effort to build a separate society within the United States by the Black Muslims and the biting rhetoric of Malcolm X (1925–1965). A less radical tradition, understandably neglected by the 20th-century nationalists but intimately related nevertheless, was to be found in the Baptist and Methodist missionaries of the ante-bellum and post-bellum eras who traveled to western and southern Africa to educate and Christianize the Africans. In 1912 the secular phases of their efforts were taken up by Booker T. Washington's Tuskegee Institute (f. 1881), which sent educators and agriculturalists to Liberia. In 1953 Africanist William Leo Hansberry (1894–1965) founded the African-American Institute, which began the Operation Crossroads Africa program of cultural exchanges in 1957 and greatly expanded them in the 1960s. Significantly, in 1976 the first black U.S. Ambassador to the United Nations, Andrew Young (1932–), made the nationalist ambitions of Africa's peoples his special concern.

Thus while the United States celebrated its bicentennial, Afro-Americans—like their ancestors on slave ships 300 years before—sought to reach across the boundaries of time and place to sublimate their cultural identity and merge their dual consciousness. Yet the testimony of Afro-American expatriates suggests that in Africa they found they were aliens still. It was not their country, not their culture. For better or worse they would have to nurture their special gifts honed by centuries of oppression and be at ease with their unique, hyphenated American culture. They were as American as the Mayflower Compact and as much a part of the national heritage as the Mississippi River. Ultimately they would have to find their "better and truer selves" in America—just as their ancestors had done almost a third of a millennium before.

Bibliography
The most comprehensive general survey is John Hope Franklin, *From Slavery to Freedom: A History of Negro Americans*, 4th ed. (New York, 1974). August Meier and Elliott Rudwick, *From Plantation to Ghetto: An Interpretive History of American Negroes*, 3d ed. (New York, 1976), though shorter, includes some materials not available to Franklin. Basil Davidson, *The African Genius: An Introduction to African Cultural and Social History* (Boston, 1969), is a general introduction to African culture and character; John S. Mbiti, *African Religions and Philosophy* (New York, 1969), provides a more comprehensive survey of African thought. Philip Curtin, *The Atlantic Slave Trade: A Census* (Madison, Wis., 1969), remains the only detailed quantitative survey of the diaspora. The impact of American slavery on African culture is described by Peter H. Wood in *Black Majority: Negroes in Colonial South Carolina from 1670 through the Stono Rebellion* (New York, 1974). The evolution of Afro-American culture is demonstrated from different perspectives by John W. Blassingame, *The Slave Community* (New York, 1972); Eugene Genovese, *Roll, Jordan, Roll: The World the Slaves Made* (New York, 1974); Herbert G. Gutman, *The Black Family in Slavery and Freedom, 1750–1925* (New York, 1976); and Lawrence Levine, *Black Culture and Black Consciousness* (New York, 1977). On the material conditions of slavery, see Leslie Owens, *This Species of Property* (New York, 1976).

Comprehensive studies of free blacks are Leon F. Litwack, *North of Slavery: The Negro in the Free States, 1790–1860* (Chicago, 1961), and Ira Berlin, *Slaves without Masters: The Free Negro in the Antebellum South* (New York, 1974). Roger Ransom and Richard Sutch describe the evolution of sharecropping and crop liens in *One Kind of Freedom* (Cambridge, Mass., 1977). Thomas Holt, *Black over White: Negro Political Leadership in South Carolina during Reconstruction* (Urbana, Ill., 1977), examines political developments in one state. J. Morgan Kousser, *The Shaping of Southern Politics: Suffrage Restrictions and the Establishment of the One Party South, 1880–1910* (New Haven, Conn., 1974), tells how black voters were disfranchised. C. Vann Woodward, *The Strange Career of Jim Crow*, 3d rev. ed. (New York, 1974), and Joel Williamson, *The Origins of Segregation* (Boston, 1968), debate the origins of Jim Crow. For life in the early 20th-century rural South, see Theodore Rosengarten, *All God's Dangers: The Life of Nate Shaw* (New York, 1974), and Charles S. Johnson, *Shadow of the Plantation* (Chicago, 1934). An illuminating study of the rise of urban ghettos is Kenneth L. Kusmer, *A Ghetto Takes Shape: Black Cleveland, 1870–1930* (Urbana, 1976).

On the literary renaissance of the 1920s, see Nathan Huggins, *Harlem Renaissance* (New York, 1973). Various aspects of the post–World War II civil rights movement are covered by Richard Kluger, *Simple Justice: The History of Brown v. Board of Education* (New York, 1975), and August Meier and Elliott Rudwick, *CORE: A Study in the Civil Rights Movement, 1942–1968* (New York, 1973). There are no comprehensive social and cultural histories of Afro-Americans, but access to various subtopics can be gained through Reynolds Farley, *Growth of the Black Population: A Study of Demographic Trends* (Chicago, 1970); Norman E. Whitten, Jr., and John F. Szwed, eds., *Afro-American Anthropology: Contemporary Perspectives* (New York, 1970); Henry A. Bullock, *A History of Negro Education in the South from 1619 to the Present* (Cambridge, Mass., 1967); and Margaret Just Butcher, *The Negro in American Culture*, 2d ed. (New York, 1971).

For more extensive, annotated bibliography, see James M. McPherson et al., *Blacks in America: Bibliographical Essays* (New York, 1971), and Elizabeth W. Miller, *The Negro in America: A Bibliography*, 2d ed. (Cambridge, Mass., 1970). Useful compilations of factual data are John P. Davis, ed., *The American Negro Reference Book* (Englewood Cliffs, N.J., 1966); and *The Chronological History of the Negro in America* (New York, 1969), compiled by Peter M. and Mort N. Bergman. Among major repositories of materials on black Americans are the Schomburg Collection in the New York Public Library, the Moorland-Spingarn Collection at Howard University, the Amistad Collection at Dillard University, the Southern Historical Collection at the University of North Carolina at Chapel Hill, and the Archives of the Fisk University Library.

THOMAS C. HOLT

ALABAMAS: *see* AMERICAN INDIANS

ALBANIANS

Albanians first came in large numbers to the United States at the beginning of the 20th century. At present there are an estimated 70,000 Albanian Americans, including the original immigrants and their descendants.

ORIGINS

The Albanian homeland is located in a rugged, mountainous region of the Balkan Peninsula. Almost 2.5 million Albanians (95 percent of the country's population) live in Albania; another 1.5 million live in the adjacent Yugoslav territories of Kosovo, Montenegro, and Macedonia; in addition, there are more than 300,000 in Greece, southern Italy, and Sicily, and almost as many in Turkey and other Balkan countries.

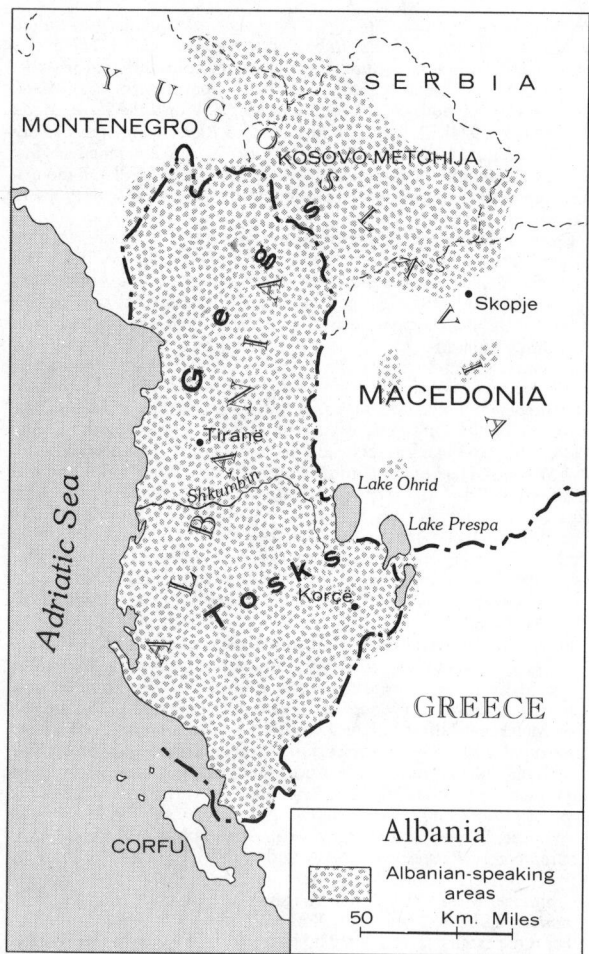

Albania

Albanian-speaking areas

50   Km. Miles

The Albanians are made up of two distinct groups, the Gegs and the Tosks, who are roughly divided by the Shkumbin River which cuts across the center of Albania. The Gegs, who account for approximately half of the population, lived largely in isolation until recently. The mountainous terrain in which they lived made it possible for them to maintain their traditional way of life until World War II. The Tosks, who live in less rugged southern Albania, have been subjected to a greater degree of foreign control and influence than the Gegs. Since 1945, however, both groups have experienced vast changes in their lives as a result of the nation's new social order. One of the most important changes has been a growing interaction between southern and northern Albanians which has served to lessen the differences between them.

This change is reflected in the language. Albanian is an Indo-European language, although it shows no close affinity to any other language in that group. Most speakers of the two main dialects, Geg and Tosk, are able to understand one another. Each of the dialects has served at different times as the basis for the standard written language. At present, a uniform literary language featuring elements of both is in use, though the Tosk dialect has more weight than the Geg.

In 1967, 73 percent of the population of Albania was Muslim, 17 percent Eastern Orthodox, and 10 percent Roman Catholic. Almost all the Albanians in Yugosla-

via (Gegs) are Muslim and, like the Gegs in Albania, largely of the orthodox Sunni sect. In the past their almost fanatical regard for Islam dominated their way of life. A small minority of Gegs in Albania (10 percent) is Roman Catholic. Among the Tosks religious feeling is less pronounced. About 70 percent are Muslim, equally divided between the Sunni and more liberal Bektashi sects; the remainder are Orthodox Christians. In 1967 the government of Albania outlawed religion, making that country officially the only atheist state in the world.

The Albanians are descendants of the Illyrians, who inhabited the Balkan Peninsula as early as the second millennium B.C. During the past two thousand years Albania was controlled by a succession of Roman, Bulgar, Serb, Venetian, Byzantine, and Ottoman Turkish rulers. From time to time native feudal lords arose, the most famous being the national hero, Scanderbeg (Gjergj Kastrioti [George Castriota]; 1405–1468), who in the mid-15th century successfully resisted Ottoman Turkish rule. In the centuries that followed many Albanians entered the bureaucracy and military in the Ottoman Empire, and some rose to the highest positions in that state. During the final decades of the 19th century a nationalist movement developed (prompted to a considerable extent by Albanians living abroad), and after several revolts against the Ottoman Turks, Albanian independence was declared in 1912. The following year the western European powers recognized the new nation within borders almost the same as those of present-day Albania. The country was occupied by foreign armies during World War I and it was annexed by Italy in 1939. Local guerrillas, led by the Communist Enver Hoxha, established a socialist republic in 1946. The rigidly orthodox Marxist Albanian regime allied itself successively with Yugoslavia, the Soviet Union, and the People's Republic of China. Since 1978, however, it has stood aloof from all its former Communist allies.

ARRIVAL, SETTLEMENT, AND ECONOMIC LIFE

The first Albanian on record to settle in the United States was Kole Kristofor (Nicholas Christopher), who landed in Boston in the 1880s and is still remembered by Albanian Americans as the pioneer of their ethnic group. It was not until the first decade of the 20th century, however, that Albanians began to arrive in substantial numbers. Almost all of them were Orthodox Christian Tosks from the south—young bachelors or married men seeking means to support the families they had left behind. They did not intend to settle permanently, and after World War I an estimated 10,000 returned to Albania. A new group of Albanian Tosks arrived after World War I; most of these immigrants intended to stay and either brought their families or married after settling in the New World. A rather different group of Albanians came after World War II. Most were political exiles from Communist-ruled Albania and Yugoslavia, of whom a substantial number were Gegs, either Muslims or members of the Roman Catholic minority in Albania.

It is not possible to know the precise number of Albanians who came to the United States, for the early immigrants did not often identify themselves as Albanians. In 1920 some 6,000 people reported Albanian as their mother tongue—the language spoken in their

homes when they were growing up. In 1970 the figure was 17,382. Allowing for families that abandoned their native tongue, it is reasonable to estimate that approximately 70,000 Albanian immigrants and their descendants live in the United States today.

The earliest arrivals settled in Boston and spread from there into other parts of New England: Worcester, Natick, and Southbridge, Mass.; Manchester, N.H.; Biddeford-Saco, Me.; Bridgeport and Waterbury, Conn. Others went to live in New York City (in particular the Bronx), as well as Jamestown and Rochester, N.Y., Philadelphia, Pittsburgh, Cleveland, Detroit, and Chicago—and as far west as St. Louis. Later immigrants were drawn to the same cities, with the result that the geographic distribution of Albanian Americans today is essentially what it was at the turn of the century.

The early Albanian immigrants were mainly peasants. Most were illiterate, partly because education in the Albanian language was strictly forbidden by the Turkish government. Eventually many were taught—by their better-educated fellows and the immigrant press—to read and write English and Albanian. As peasant farmers they did not have the kind of experience needed for skilled work in industrial America, and they were forced to take jobs as unskilled laborers in textile and shoe factories, mills, foundries, and shipyards, or to perform menial tasks in restaurants and hotels. A few were peddlers.

The pioneers worked hard and led a spartan existence. They considered entertainment and sports frivolous and remained aloof from both the larger American society and other ethnic groups. To save money they crowded together in tenements, 10 or 15 to a single apartment in a living arrangement they called a *konak*. Existence in the konak was drab, especially for peasants accustomed to outdoor life. They kept house by taking turns at cleaning and cooking, washing their own clothes and mending their own shoes. They endured the impersonal urban life of America's sprawling industrial centers because they saw a way to make money and to escape the cycle of poverty into which they otherwise seemed permanently trapped.

The Albanian workers alleviated their miseries by organizing social institutions: in Boston—always the capital of Albanian Americans—were the Kafene Vatra (Hearth Coffeehouse) and the Hotel Skënderbeu, named after Scanderbeg. Societies were also formed to aid villages in the homeland by providing money to build schools and roads, or even a dowry for some destitute girl. Some of these societies still exist: in the Greater Boston area the Katundi Society and the Panarity Society, named after the villages where the members originated, continue to hold periodic meetings and an annual banquet.

The socioeconomic status of the Albanian group changed over time. Some of the immigrants set up small businesses, sent their children to school, and began to adopt American middle-class ways. The postwar immigrants included a number of intellectuals, former government officials, political leaders, and professionals, bringing greater diversity to the community. The overwhelming majority of Albanians today continue to live in the city and hold jobs in industry, business, government, and education; a few are wealthy. A substantial number own small businesses,

most often restaurants, but also groceries, tailor and flower shops, and the like. Many of the most recent immigrants remain in menial jobs, however, as custodians, window washers, and general handymen, especially among the 12,000 Bronx Albanians who make up one of New York's newest ethnic communities.

SOCIAL AND FAMILY LIFE

Albanian-American social and family life is a fusion—sometimes a confusion—of two value systems: the old, tradition-bound, male-dominated Albanian one; and the new, flexible, future-oriented American one. In accordance with Albanian tradition, the husband is still the head of the family, even though he no longer wields the nearly absolute authority he once had. The wife's place used to be at home, for it was considered demeaning for her to work outside; but that is no longer the case, especially among the second and later generations.

Until the 1950s nothing pained Albanian parents more than the thought that their son or daughter might marry a non-Albanian, but when, despite their bitter protests, it happened, they usually resigned themselves to the change. Albanian parents also used to think that a high-school diploma was already more than was required for a girl's education: her moral purity and strength of character might be damaged by exposure to too much learning. This attitude also has changed in recent years, except in the communities of postwar immigrants where the stern moral code of the Albanian mountains is still alive; there, the efforts of church and social organizations are needed to keep girls in school past the age of 13.

Albanians maintain close contact with their relatives and continue to observe many traditional greetings and rituals when they visit and entertain one another. They enjoy cooking Albanian dishes and are especially proud of their vegetable pies. At communal celebrations of national and religious holidays they still sing Albanian songs and dance Albanian dances, sometimes in native costume. Picnics draw them from widely scattered towns—sometimes hundreds of miles from the picnic site—and attract entire families, from elderly grandmothers to infants. For a time Albanians in Manchester, N.H., owned their own picnic ground, where they gathered to eat olives and feta cheese, chicken and roast lamb, spinach-, leek-, or squash-filled pies (*lakror*), and pastries called *kurabie, brushtull,* and *baklava.* They still sometimes celebrate name days instead of birthdays; they observe Albanian Independence Day; the Orthodox Christians among them honor Easter above all other religious holidays; the Muslims observe *Bairam* and other holidays.

Albanians are for the most part law-abiding citizens. The exceptions have been mostly among the postwar Gegs, who brought traditional blood feuds with them to the United States—to the Bronx especially, but also to Detroit and to Los Angeles, where a community of several hundred Albanians came into existence in the 1970s. In the Bronx, many Albanians moved in alongside the Italians south of Fordham Road (presumably because they learned to speak Italian in refugee camps in Italy before coming to America; they also share their Roman Catholic faith). Incidents of retribution have become rare, however, as the newcomers learn to bring

their ideas of personal honor, justice, and ethnic pride into better harmony with American law and to settle differences through mediators rather than with weapons.

RELIGION

Albanian-American life still centers upon religious institutions: for Albanians as for other eastern Europeans, religion and ethnic identity have traditionally been inextricably intertwined. Most of the first immigrants were Orthodox Christians from the Korçë region in southeastern Albania, the principal center of Tosk culture. This Orthodox community was under the jurisdiction of the Greek Orthodox Patriarch, who from his seat in the Turkish capital of Istanbul tried to maintain strict control over the faithful in Albania as well as those who left the country. In the United States, however, where the constraints of Turkish rule were nonexistent, the Albanians rebelled. In the early 1900s when a Greek Orthodox priest in Hudson, Mass., refused to officiate at a funeral for a young Albanian on the grounds that he had been a nationalist and was therefore excommunicated, the Albanians of Massachusetts called a meeting and decided to obtain their own priest. They invited Fan S. Noli (1882–1965), who was subsequently ordained by the Russian Orthodox archbishop of New York on March 8, 1908. This date marks the beginning of the Albanian Orthodox Church of America, the first of its kind anywhere in the world. Initially under the jurisdiction of the Russian Orthodox Church, in 1919 it was reorganized as an independent diocese.

The success of the Albanian Orthodox Church was due largely to Fan Noli, a Harvard-educated writer, composer, and politician who had come to the United States in 1906 with the express intention of organizing immigrants to work for the Albanian national cause. Noli introduced Albanian into the liturgy, and after returning from Europe in 1932 he served as Metropolitan of the Albanian Orthodox Archdiocese in America until his death in 1965. Today the archdiocese, with its mother church in Boston, has 13 parishes and is part of the Orthodox Church in America. (See Eastern Orthodox.)

The Albanian Orthodox Diocese of America, headed since 1949 by Bishop Mark Lipa, is a splinter organization with only two parishes, one in Boston, the other in Chicago. The diocese was formed during the cold war, when Bishop Lipa and his followers accused Bishop Noli of being a Communist sympathizer and therefore unfit to preside over the Albanian Church. Noli's supporters in turn charged Lipa with being an agent of the Greek Orthodox patriarchate in Istanbul, sent to the United States to further Greek nationalist aims. The conflict raged for several years, but Bishop Lipa was unable to undermine the church of Bishop Noli, whose past achievements were still respected by the majority of the Orthodox community.

The Albanian Muslims founded their first society in 1915 in Biddeford, Me. In 1949 Imam Vehbi Ismail organized the Albanian-American Muslim Society in Detroit. Since then other Muslim religious centers have been established in Waterbury, Chicago, and Brooklyn, N.Y. The New York center (f. 1972) is known as the Albanian-American Islamic Center for the states of New York and New Jersey, and is the most active of the four. The Bektashi Muslim sect, which is mystic in character and inclines toward pantheism, has its own *tekke* (monastery) in Detroit (f. 1954) under the leadership of Baba Rexhep (1901–). The Bektashis have played a significant role in Albanian national life, and since 1925 the world headquarters of the sect has been in Albania. At their Detroit monastery the Bektashis have recreated something of their Old World agrarian monastic life by growing vegetables and raising poultry.

Albanian Catholics are the most recent arrivals and consequently the last to establish organized religious life. There are Albanian Catholic parishes in the Bronx and Detroit. The Bronx parish, Our Lady of Good Counsel (f. 1962), is led by Monsignor Zef Oroshi (1916–); since 1969 it has operated an Albanian Catholic Center to serve approximately 3,500 first-generation Albanian Catholics throughout Greater New York.

POLITICAL LIFE

Albanian Americans have not played an active role in American political life; for them politics most often means concern with the fate of the homeland. The Albanian struggle for independence during the first decade of the 20th century coincided with the initial large-scale immigration of Albanians to the United States. In an environment free from Turkish political or Greek religious pressure, Albanian leaders, notably Fan Noli, Faik Konitza (1876–1942), Christo Dako, and Constantine Chekrezi (1892–1959), were able to aid the cause of Albanian independence. In April 1912 they formed the Pan-Albanian Federation of America, popularly known as Vatra (The Hearth). Based in Boston, Vatra at the height of its power had 72 branches throughout the United States. Its publications infused immigrants with a sense of the Albanian national purpose, while its leaders brought the Albanian issue to the attention of the western powers. This resulted in the recognition of an independent Albania (albeit without Kosovo and other Albanian ethnic lands) by the London Conference in 1913. When Albanian independence was threatened by foreign occupation during World War I, Vatra raised $150,000 in 1917, began to publish an English-language monthly, *Adriatic Review* (Boston, 1918–1919), and through the mediation of Fan Noli won a pledge from President Woodrow Wilson to defend Albanian interests at the Versailles Peace Conference. Even after the country's independence was assured, Albanian Americans continued to play a role in homeland politics. Bishop Noli returned to Albania after World War I where he became Primate of the newly formed Albanian Autocephalous Orthodox Church and the leader of western-oriented liberal politicians intent upon modernizing the country. Noli was appointed Minister of Foreign Affairs in 1922; then he led a successful revolt in June 1924 and became prime minister. After six months he was forced into exile, eventually returning to the United States in 1932. Noli was succeeded by a conservative landowner, Ahmed Zog (1895–1961), who later declared himself king. Another Albanian-American activist, Faik Konitza, served the new monarchy as its minister plenipotentiary in Washington, D.C.

A serious split developed between the Noli and Konitza forces within Vatra in the mid-1920s, when Konitza switched his political allegiance from Vatra's anti-

Zog platform to open support of Zog. As a result, the society was weakened and a vacuum developed in Albanian-American political life.

But the Italian occupation of Albania during World War II prompted renewed political activity. Constantine Chekrezi, a founding member of Vatra, set up a rival organization, Shqipëria e Lirë (Free Albanian Organization), in South Boston in 1941. It brought together nationalists, antimonarchists, anti-Fascists, radicals, and disillusioned Vatra members, and soon had branches in a number of American cities.

After World War II both Vatra and the Free Albania Organization tried to adopt a realistic platform; in essence, this meant the adoption of a sympathetic attitude toward the Communist-ruled homeland. Because of this, the new anti-Communist political exiles were excluded from the ranks of these organizations. Only after 1957 did Vatra begin to modify its position toward Communist Albania and accept the new immigrants as members, becoming somewhat revitalized as a result. Since 1960 Vatra has organized several seminars on Albanian studies; and through its student fund it has awarded scholarships to several dozen college students of Albanian descent.

Despite Vatra's change of policy, most postwar Albanian immigrants have remained loyal to the over one dozen Albanian political parties that have been recreated or established in the West. Among the most influential are the Agrarian-Democratic party, heir to Balli Kombëtar (National Front), which has a republican and middle-class platform; the Organizata Kombëtare Lëvizja e Legalitetit (National Organization of the Legality Movement), a conservative party that champions the politics of the late King Zog; the Blloku Kombëtar Indipendent (National Independent Bloc), a Catholic party that has attracted people disenchanted with the policies of the World War II "historical parties"—the National Front and the Legality party; and the Bashkimi Demokrat Shqiptar (Albanian Democratic Union), an anti-Communist nationalist umbrella group that strives to unite the existing parties, intellectuals, and other elements. The large number of inhabitants from Albanian-inhabited regions of Yugoslavia also have their own Lidhja Kosovare (Union of Kosovars), a militant organization with strong support in Michigan, Illinois, and New York advocating the creation of a "democratic ethnic Albania" that would include the Kosovo and other Albanian-populated areas in present-day Yugoslavia. A number of these organizations and groups hold periodic meetings and publish newspapers or journals, but none appears to have a perceptible influence on American politics.

In reaction to chronic factionalism and general ineffectiveness, in 1946 a group of young Albanian Americans established in New York the Albanian-American National Organization (AANO) to help its members adjust to the realities of American life. AANO has met with a modicum of success; like Vatra, it awards annual scholarships to students of Albanian descent.

CULTURAL LIFE

From the earliest days of the Albanian-American community, the press has played an important informative and educational role. Coming from a Turkish-ruled province where the teaching of Albanian was forbidden, many immigrants learned to read their native language only in the United States. The first Albanian newspaper was *Kombi* (The Nation; Boston, 1906–1909). This was succeeded by *Dielli/The Sun* (Boston, f. 1909), which was founded by the Besa-Besën (The Pledge) society and in 1912 became the official Vatra organ. The most influential Albanian newspaper in the United States, *Dielli* was edited from 1944 to 1963 by G.M. Panarity (1892–1976). *Dielli* also published school textbooks that were used in the Albanian homeland as well as in the United States.

There were several short-lived political and educational reviews, such as the monthly *Albanian Era* (Denver, Colo., 1915–1916), the semimonthly *Illyria* (Boston, 1916), and the monthly *Ylli i Mëngjezit/The Morning Star* (Boston, 1917–1919); the liberal newspaper *Republika* (Boston, 1930–1932), the biweekly *Lajmëtari Shqipëtar* (The Albanian Messenger; Worcester, Mass., 1934–1937), and the leftwing radical newspaper, *Demokratia* (Democracy; Boston, 1938). The *Shërbestari* (The Serviceman; New York, 1950–1961) of the Agrarian Democratic Youth and *Shqiptari i Lirë* (The Free Albanian; New York, f. 1957) of the Free Albanian Committee have appeared since World War II.

More successful is *Liria/Liberty* (South Boston, f. 1941), the weekly organ of the Free Albania Organization, begun by that group's founder, Constantine Chekrezi, and edited for another three decades by Dhimitri R. Nikolla. In more recent years each of the Albanian religious communities has had its own periodical: the Muslim *Jeta Musilmane Shqiptare* (Albanian Muslim Life, 1953–1961) and *Përpjekja e Jonë* (Our Effort; New York, f. 1974); the Bektashi Muslim *Zëri i Bektashizmés* (The Voice of Bektashism; Taylor, Mich., f. 1954); the Orthodox *Drita e Vërtetë* (The True Light; Jamaica Plain, Mass., f. 1958); and the Catholic *Jeta Katolike Shqiptare* (Catholic Albanian Life; Bronx, N.Y., f. 1966). The total annual circulation of all Albanian and Albanian-English periodicals is approximately 10,000.

Albanian language and culture have been transmitted through schools as well as the press. Christo Dako started to teach Albanian in Natick, Mass., in 1908. Since then numerous attempts, usually by churches, have been made to teach the language to young Albanian Americans. The results have not been encouraging, for very few third- or fourth-generation Albanians understand—much less speak—the language. Nevertheless, efforts persist. During the 1960s Vatra sponsored the publication of an Albanian-language textbook by Fehime Pipa, and the Albanian-American Islamic Center in New York established an Albanian language program in Manhattan. Classes in Albanian are also offered in Brooklyn, the Bronx, and Worcester. Radio broadcasts in Albanian have also been popular and have contributed to language maintenance in the United States. The oldest such program is *Zëri i Shqipërisë* (The Voice of Albania) which began in Boston in 1938; Albanian radio programs are also broadcast from New York, Detroit, and Worcester.

Although there are no centers for Albanian studies at a university level, the language has been taught at several universities. Courses were given during the 1950s and 1960s at Indiana University, Columbia University, and the University of California at Berkeley. In the late 1970s only the University of Chicago taught Albanian.

The U.S. Army Defense Language Institute in Monterey, Calif., maintains the most active language program. Nelo Drizari (1902–1978), author of Albanian-English dictionaries, grammars, and other teaching aids, served as its chairman for many years.

Albanians were far more active culturally in the early days than at present. Theater groups were particularly popular, and in the Boston area amateur performances of plays by Albanian authors like Sami Frashëri, Foqion Postoli, Kristo Floqi, and Mihal Grameno were quite common. Albanian-American musical life was dominated by Thomas Nassi (1892–1964). In 1915 he organized the Boston Albanian Mandolin Club and the Albanian String Orchestra, and the following year he formed the Vatra band which after World War I toured Albania and stayed on to become the Royal Band at King Zog's court. In later years Nassi returned to Massachusetts to conduct the Cape Cod Philharmonic Society.

Albanian-American newspapers were often filled with literary works by immigrant authors. The first significant Albanian-American writer was the master of Tosk prose, Faik Konitza, who also founded the magazine *Albania* (Brussels and London, 1897–1909), which stimulated nationalist fervor and served as a repository of Albanian folklore, history, and literature. Albanian-American poetry was enriched by Fan Noli and, more recently, by Arshi Pipa, each of whom has published several volumes.

Albanian Americans have long recognized the need to prepare scholarly works which would preserve the culture of the homeland as well as present it to the larger American public. The leading scholar was Bishop Fan Noli, who, in addition to his poetry, musicology, religious studies, and translations into Albanian of Shakespeare and other literary classics, wrote a biography (1950) of the national hero Scanderbeg.

The Albanians have a reputation as a brave, loyal, hospitable, proud, and fiercely independent people—and also as a martial, headstrong, and feuding people. Albanian Americans share the cultural heritage of their rugged ancestors. They preserve the tradition of hospitality; they are proud of their customs, manners, and morals, in spite of some questioning of their value by their children and grandchildren. And they have a certain relish for controversy and factionalism within their community, as if those were necessary ingredients for a meaningful, zestful, and productive communal life.

Decades of life in the United States have had an impact on them, as a group and as individuals. The community has been changing steadily. The clannish, feuding consciousness is weakening, perhaps even dying out. The martial tradition, no longer needed to defend the group or personal and family honor, has given way to more practical interests and goals, such as advancement in business and the professions, respect for books and learning, and personal expression in sports. Like other Americans, most Albanians pursue material success: making money, accumulating property and possessions, and seeking social recognition. In short, they share the American dream.

Bibliography
The basic work on Albanians in the United States is *The Albanian Struggle in the Old World and New* (Boston, 1939), prepared by the Federal Writers' Project of Massachusetts. A personalized account of the pioneer immigrants is found in a booklet by Constantine A. Demo, *The Albanians in America: The First Arrivals* (Boston, 1960). For the history of Albanian Orthodoxy, see Fan S. Noli, *Fiftieth Anniversary Book of the Albanian Orthodox Church in America, 1908–1958* (Boston, 1960). The activity of the Vatra organization and its newspaper *Dielli* is treated in several essays in *Seminari Ndërkombëtar i Federates Panshqiptare "Vatra,"* ed. H.H. Oruci (Rome, 1971).

For an introduction to Albania itself, see Stavro Skendi, ed., *Albania* (New York, 1956), and Stavro Skendi, *The Albanian National Awakening, 1878–1912* (Princeton, N.J., 1967). See also A. Logoreci, *The Albanians: Europe's Forgotten Survivors* (London, 1977), and R. Marmullaku, *Albania and the Albanians* (London, 1975). More recent developments are treated in Peter R. Prifti, *Socialist Albania Since 1944* (Cambridge, Mass., 1978), and Nicholas C. Pano, *The People's Republic of Albania* (Baltimore, 1968).

The richest repository of archival materials on Albanian Americans is the Fan S. Noli Library at St. George Albanian Orthodox Cathedral in South Boston. Besides the papers of this prominent leader, the library contains several Albanian-American newspapers and other related publications.

ALEUTS

The Aleuts' first contact with western civilization occurred in the mid-18th century when Russian fur hunters occupied their territory. At the time of contact, the Aleuts numbered between 12,000 and 16,000 and inhabited several hundred villages along the Aleutian Archipelago and the western end of the Alaska Peninsula. Today only about 1,800 Aleuts still live in the Aleutian area, and the number of villages has been reduced to 12—St. Paul, the largest, had a population of 437 in 1977; Squaw Harbor, the smallest, 15.

The Aleuts have occupied the Aleutian area for about 9,000 years, having crossed the Bering land bridge from Asia. This ancient people has a distinctive language, culture, and racial composition, although the Aleuts are closely related to the Eskimos. Living on the edge of the sea, they have relied for subsistence primarily on marine products. They are noted for their outstanding seamanship and sea hunting skills, and at one time they provided the main labor force for the Russian fur companies.

Most Aleuts live in small households. About 20 percent of the households include grandparents and other relatives, but fully half consist of nuclear families (the remainder are incomplete families and single adults). The population is young, with a mean age of 21 years; men slightly outnumber women, probably because more women than men leave the villages. Because of intensive and extensive Russian and later, American, contact, the Aleuts are one of the most acculturated native groups in Alaska. Many of their traditions have either disappeared or been greatly altered as they have incorporated Russian and American cultural elements.

In former times, coastal Aleuts hunted in skin boats called *bidarkas*, very similar to the Eskimo kayaks. Using darts, spears, and throwing boards, they killed whales, sea lions, sea otters, seals, and birds. With bone hooks, they fished for halibut, cod, greenling, sculpin, mackerel, herring, and salmon. These traditional activities are receding in importance. Many Aleuts now live in commercially developed villages with a money economy; those who do not are still dependent to some extent on fishing and hunting, but they usually spend part of each year working for wages outside their villages. Almost all Aleuts work for cash at least part of the year, laboring in the fur-seal, shellfish, or finfish industries; trapping fur-bearing animals; or working in Aleut vil-

lage and regional corporations, the tourist industry, retail trade, or community service. Most are unskilled or semiskilled laborers. A recent survey revealed that only 25 percent of the Aleuts in the labor force work full time year-round; 64 percent work less than full time year-round; and 11 percent are unemployed. Annual household income varies considerably according to the availability of local jobs.

Traditional Aleut society was essentially egalitarian and communal. Hunters shared their catches with the entire village, and a system of mutual obligations assured the welfare of every village member. Today Aleuts still share their fish and game, though generally just with friends and relatives rather than the entire village. The old system of mutual aid, however, survives, as the Aleuts continue to feed the hungry and shelter the homeless.

The Aleuts' former political system consisted of chiefs and elders. The village chief was responsible for organizing war parties and communal activities as well as arbitrating disputes; along with other village notables, the chief sat in judgment in cases involving serious crime. Crime and violence, however, were infrequent, and formal authority was rarely invoked. The Aleuts have had a highly developed system of informal social controls directed at avoiding conflict and maintaining village harmony through the use of third-party intermediaries and subtle, indirect modes of communication.

Remnants of this system of social control can still be found in Aleut villages. The formal system has disappeared from all but one village, but other leaders have taken over the chief's functions. In many villages, however, the former system competes with a modern political form—the municipal councils run by both Caucasians and Aleuts. In addition to municipal councils, the Aleuts have organized regional and village corporations under the Alaska Native Claims Settlement Act to operate private profit and nonprofit enterprises.

In earlier times, child rearing involved the entire village. Women, under the supervision of maternal uncles, raised the infants and girls. The uncles trained boys in the discipline of seafaring and inducted them into the adult community through religious ceremonies; the elders transmitted the heritage of the people through myths and stories.

In the late 18th and early 19th centuries, Russian missionaries introduced the Russian Orthodox religion to the Aleuts. Previously, they had had no formal religion, although a belief in spirits pervaded all areas of their life. The Aleuts quickly adopted the Russian Orthodox faith, and today it is an integral part of their cultural identity.

Russian missionaries also established the first schools in the Aleutians. Father Ioann Veniaminov, an early missionary and an authority on Aleut ethnography, codified the language, constructed an Aleut alphabet, and translated primers, liturgical texts, and other literature into Aleut. Along with their own language, many Aleuts learned to read and speak Russian and, later, English.

In 1890 the first American school was founded in the Aleutians, on the island of Unalaska. Currently all but one of the Aleutian villages have an elementary school; three have secondary schools of two or more grades.

The Aleut language has three major dialects, all related to the Eskimo language, although Eskimo and Aleut are no longer mutually intelligible. Aleut is more commonly used in the traditional villages. In Atka, for example, it is spoken in nearly every home; in the more modern village of Sand Point, it is spoken in only a few households. Educators and native organizations interested in preserving the language have now established bilingual programs, however, and for the first time in many decades Aleut children are receiving instruction in their own tongue.

The Aleuts are noted for their intricately designed, tightly woven grass baskets. They also carve tools, toys, and other implements from wood and ivory. They are fond of music and dancing and have enthusiastically adopted modern musical instruments; some villages have their own bands.

Planes are the main means of transportation in the Aleutians, and by now almost every village has an airport, as well as a post office; electricity for heating, lighting, and refrigeration; washing machines and freezers; grocery stores; indoor plumbing and running water; and citizen-band radios. Some villagers enjoy television by satellite or from cassette tapes.

Health care within the villages is provided by health aides and nurses, and emergency care is provided by the Indian Health Service located in Anchorage, 500 to 1,000 miles distant from most of the villages. Some of the more modern villages show signs of social disorganization, mostly in the form of family problems and alcoholism. The Alaska Division of Social Services sends itinerant social-welfare workers once or twice a year, but contact with social service agencies is more apt to be by mail. The villages handle many social service problems themselves. For example, Unalaska has developed a model health and social service program that employs local people to deal with child and family welfare problems.

Bibliography
Useful sources are *Aleutian/Pribilof Islands Regional Study and Five-Year Health Plan* (Anchorage, Alaska, 1977); Dorothy M. Jones, *A Study of Social and Economic Problems in Unalaska, an Aleut Village* (Ann Arbor, Mich., 1969), and *Aleuts in Transition: A Comparison of Two Villages* (Seattle, 1976).
Also consult Vladimir Jochelson, *History, Ethnology and Anthropology of the Aleut* (1933; reprint, Atlantic Highlands, N.J., 1969); William S. Laughlin, "Eskimos and Aleuts: Their Origins and Evolution," *Science* 142 (1963): 633-645; Aleš Hrdlička, *The Aleutian and Commander Islands and Their Inhabitants* (Philadelphia: Wistar Institute, 1945).

DOROTHY M. JONES

ALGERIANS: *see* ARABS

ALSATIANS

Immigrants from Alsace, a French province between the Vosges Mountains on the west and the Rhine River on the east, have been coming to North America since the early 18th century. Occupied by Germanic tribes in the 5th century, Alsace became a land of predominantly German language and culture. After the Thirty Years' War, France under Louis XIV gradually extended its rule over the area, completing the process in 1681. Since then the province has remained French, except for the years between the Franco-Prussian War (1871) and the end of World War I, when Alsace and the neighboring

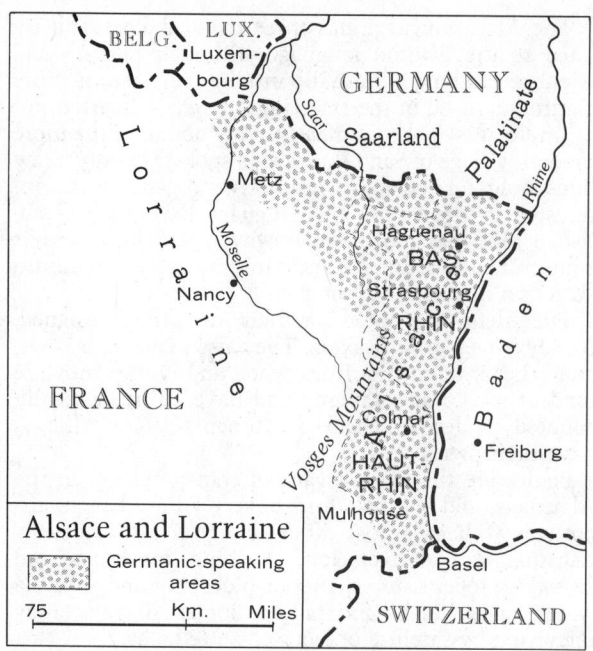

Alsace and Lorraine

Germanic-speaking areas

75   Km.   Miles

province of Lorraine were incorporated into the German Empire. After the return of Alsace to France, the French government sponsored vigorous programs to Gallicize the population. French became the language of the schools and is now commonly used throughout the province, though most communities continue to be bilingual.

Cultural diversity has been characteristic of Alsace throughout its modern history. Although more than 90 percent of Alsatians have Germanic roots, there are communities that have always used the French language. The German-speaking Alsatians, however, are not all alike. Those who live in the northern part of the province speak a Franconian dialect, whereas southern Alsatians speak an Alemannic dialect related to that of their Swiss and Swabian cousins to the south and east. The linguistic pattern is complicated further by religion. During the Reformation, Strasbourg, the capital of Alsace, became a center of Protestant activity, and its schools were famous for humanist learning. As a consequence of the Counter Reformation, however, Catholicism was resurgent, especially in Upper Alsace. Today there are pockets of Protestantism in Alsace, but most Alsatians are Roman Catholic.

Alsatian emigration is best understood historically as a part of the great exodus from the southwestern German states, including Baden, Württemberg, Hesse-Darmstadt, and the Palatinate. Collectively known as Palatines in colonial America, these emigrants, almost all Protestants, fled economic distress intensified by the devastation of frequent wars. Alsatians mingled with other Germans as they journeyed down the Rhine and sailed to America.

It is not possible to determine precisely how many Alsatians came before 1775. Rosters of Palatine immigrants often list persons as coming from Alsace or from individual Alsatian cities or villages. Most of them settled in eastern Pennsylvania, but some were scattered in other areas, including a few who in 1719 founded a colony on the Mississippi River a few miles upstream

from New Orleans, called the German Coast. The Louisiana settlers were supplemented by a contingent of Lutheran Alsatians in the 1750s. Victims of religious persecution in France, this group was exiled to Louisiana by the French government. Invariably, however, the 18th-century Alsatian immigrants in Louisiana, as elsewhere, blended into the larger German group and lost their distinctive characteristics.

From 1775 to 1825 few emigrants from Europe entered the United States. But thereafter the flow from the southwestern German states increased significantly and by the 1850s had reached the proportion of a flood. German-speaking Alsatians were a part of this movement, and Alsace became a leading area of emigration from France. In Louisiana, for example, the overwhelming majority of French immigrants in the decade before the Civil War were Alsatians. As in the colonial period, most Alsatian immigrants settled in German enclaves. Inevitably there was a high level of intermarriage, especially among persons of the same religious beliefs.

By the 1830s a few distinctively Alsatian settlements developed, usually as a result of chain migration. A small community in McHenry County, Ill., illustrates the process. In 1838 three families from Drachenbronn in Lower Alsace, who had lived for a short time in New York, started an agricultural settlement on the Illinois frontier. In response to their letters to relatives and friends, other Alsatians joined them during the next several years. In 1845 one person returned to France and recruited an additional 45 settlers, most of them from the same village in Alsace. By the end of the decade, more than a hundred Drachenbronners had settled in McHenry County. Several similar concentrations developed on the midwestern frontier in Ohio and Indiana.

Formal colonization efforts were less common than chain migrations. Perhaps the most important was a colony organized on the Texas frontier in 1844 by Henri Castro, who brought several thousand emigrants from France to settle on a grant in Medina County west of San Antonio. In 1848 a visitor reported that Alsatians were the most numerous group in the colony and that Alsatian speech was more commonly heard than French. The colony also included many emigrants from Württemberg, Baden, and Switzerland, as well as from Lorraine.

The majority of Castro's colonists were Roman Catholics, as were most 19th-century Alsatian immigrants; some were Lutheran, and a few were Amish or Mennonite. According to one estimate, as many as 3,000 Amish from Alsace and the southwestern German states settled in Ohio, Indiana, and Illinois between 1825 and 1870.

After 1871, when Alsace became part of the German Empire, people who wished to retain French citizenship and not live under German rule migrated to Paris and other parts of France, but few came to the United States. During the entire period of German control, Alsatian emigration generally was very low compared to that from other German districts. The largest movement occurred from 1885 to 1889, when an average of 52 people per 100,000 emigrated. Even this figure was only a quarter of the national average for Germany at that time.

Throughout much of the 19th century many Alsa-

tians settled in American cities, both large and small. Manuscript census data for Winona, Minn., disclose a typical pattern. In 1800 approximately 3,000 of the town's 10,200 inhabitants were of German stock. In addition, of 33 adults listed as having been born in either Alsace or France, all but 5 had distinctively German names. Most were employed as craftsmen and shop-keepers; 4 were classified as laborers, one as a banker, and another as a manufacturer.

In the 20th century, migration from Alsace has been negligible, and the few Alsatians who came to the United States are difficult to trace. The census of 1920 reported 22,000 German-speaking, French-born persons in this country; they accounted for 14.4 percent of the total French immigration. Most were from Alsace.

Because they have lacked sufficient numbers to organize their own social, cultural, and economic institutions, Alsatians have usually joined existing German or French organizations. Even in the decade preceding World War I, when German-American voluntary associations were enjoying their fullest development, there were few specifically Alsatian societies in the United States. Nevertheless, some Alsatians have retained separate traditions, especially the wealthier and better-educated immigrants who had had a rich and meaningful exposure to French culture. In general, immigrants from Alsace have assimilated rapidly into American society.

Bibliography
There are no readily accessible monographs or articles on Alsatians in the United States. The most comprehensive is an article by Heinrich Neu, "Elsässer und Lothringer als Ansiedler in Nordamerika," *Elsäss-Lothringische Wissenschaftliche Gessellschaft zu Strassburg. Jahrbuch* 3 (Heidelberg, Germany, 1930): 98-129. See also Glenn R. Conrad, "L'Immigration alsacienne en Louisiane, 1753–59," *Revue d'histoire d'Amérique française* 28 (March 1975): 565–577, and Lorenzo Castro, *Immigration from Alsace and Lorraine: A Brief Sketch of Castro's Colony in Western Texas* (San Antonio, Tex., 1871).

FREDERICK C. LUEBKE

ALTAMAHA: *see* AMERICAN INDIANS

AMERICAN IDENTITY AND AMERICANIZATION

The term "identity" has become indispensable in the discussion of ethnic affairs. Yet it was hardly used at all until the 1950s. The father of the concept, Erik H. Erikson, remarked on its novelty in his widely read book *Childhood and Society* (1950): "We begin to conceptualize matters of identity at the very time in history when they become a problem. For we do so in a country which attempts to make a super-identity out of all the identities imported by its constituent immigrants." In an autobiographical account published 20 years later, Erikson, himself an immigrant, quoted this passage and added that the terms "identity" and "identity crisis" seemed to grow out of "the experience of emigration, immigration, and Americanization."

The relationship between ethnicity and American identity—or super-identity, as Erikson called it—is complex and elusive. The difficulty of talking about it is compounded because the terms we must use are inescapably multivalent and can be understood in many different senses. For this reason, it is desirable to be as explicit as possible about the terms at the outset.

First, "American identity" will be employed here interchangeably with "American nationality" and "American character." It is true that these are vague expressions, and that distinctions could be introduced among them, but their imprecision accurately reflects the indeterminacy of the phenomena to which they refer, and in common usage these expressions are more or less synonymous. Even Erikson, whose definition of psychological identity is highly specific, writes as though national identity and national character were pretty much the same thing. It should also be noted that "identity" as used here is not intended to convey specifically Eriksonian psychological connotations but is to be understood in a looser, more informal sense.

Second, the aim of this essay is the relatively modest one of reviewing historically the place of ethnicity in the tradition of thinking and writing about American identity. My intention, in other words, is not to establish what the relationship of ethnicity to American identity actually is or was, but to ascertain the relative *salience* that issues we now think of as ethnic have had when Americans have debated among themselves about what it means to be an American.

THE IDEOLOGICAL ORIGINS OF AMERICAN IDENTITY (1776–1815)

Although there were glimmerings of a sense of American distinctiveness in the late colonial period, it was the separation of the colonies from Great Britain by the Declaration of Independence and the Revolution that created the need for a national consciousness as the spiritual counterpart of the political entity that had come into being. The revolutionary generation was quite cognizant of the fact that nation building required not just fashioning viable political institutions but also nurturing an American nationality in keeping with the values, philosophy, and outlook embodied in the Constitution and the laws. The fact that the American people were of diverse ethnic strains was not overlooked in discussions of nationality, but because of the nature of the events that brought the nation to birth, the American identity was conceived primarily in abstract ideological terms. Ethnic considerations were subsidiary.

More than two decades ago, Hans Kohn emphasized the ideological nature of American nationalism. A sense of distinctive peoplehood could be founded only on ideas, he pointed out, because the great majority of Americans shared language, literature, religion, and other cultural traditions with the nation against which they had successfully rebelled and from which they were most determined to establish their spiritual as well as political independence. The non-British minority did not offer a language, religion, or common culture upon which the national identity could be based. The foundation of nationality had to be laid on the same bedrock of political principle that justified separation from the mother country and underlay the constitutional framework. The United States defined itself as a nation by commitment to the principles of liberty, equality, and government on the basis of consent, and the nationality of its people derived from their identification with those principles.

Two elements can be distinguished in the structure of ideas underlying American national identity. First, there was the English tradition of liberty that stressed self-government, institutional limitations on the power

of the sovereign, and procedural safeguards in law for the person accused of a crime. The earliest protests against the imperial policies of the British in the 1760s appealed to this tradition, for although the rights of Englishmen were prescriptive and not doctrinaire, the American colonists considered themselves participants in the tradition and entitled by birthright to the privileges and protection that were their heritage. Only when Parliament and the king rejected their interpretation of the traditional rights of Englishmen did Americans turn to a second, more abstract and theoretical line of argument. Here they were able to draw upon the thinkers of the Enlightenment, who had been inspired by the example of English liberties but who had transformed those lessons into universal principles. Thus, as Kohn puts it, "The historical birthright of Englishmen became in America, under the influence of eighteenth-century ideas, the natural right of man, a universal message, the birthright of mankind." Each of these elements was necessary. If it had not been rooted in the empirical English institutional and procedural tradition, American liberty might have destroyed itself in utopian extremism, but without the additional dimension of Enlightenment universalism, America could not have become the "asylum of liberty" for all people, regardless of national origin.

This formulation requires some modification today in the light of the work done on republican ideology. As a number of scholars have shown, the American patriots drew heavily on a tradition of British political writing that went back to the middle of the 17th century and linked there with classical republican thought, which had been revived in the Renaissance, particularly in Machiavelli's *Discourses* on Livy's history of Rome. This scholarship suggests that the theoretical dimension of American ideology is less dependent on the continental writers of the 18th century than Kohn believed. However, it does not shake his central insight that American nationality rests on a structure of ideas about freedom, equality, and self-government and that this ideology combines abstract, universalist elements with a historically grounded appreciation of the practical machinery for self-government and protection of individual liberties.

Besides uncovering different sources for revolutionary political ideas, scholars of the republican school have shown that these ideas carried the deepest kind of moral significance. A republic demanded virtue of its citizens, for only a people willing to subordinate private gain to the good of the polity could govern itself. The citizenry must be vigilant in guarding against corruption in its rulers and in the community at large. Simplicity and self-reliance were the most effectual guarantees, for the former preserved the people from the enervating effects of luxury, and the latter removed them from dependence on the good will and largess of others, which made them subject to corruption. The "cultivators of the earth" lovingly described by Jefferson in his *Notes on Virginia* were God's chosen people precisely because the life of the yeoman farmer accorded so well with the prescriptions of simplicity, self-reliance, and virtue imposed by the republican ideology.

Jefferson believed that the safety of the American republic was secure so long as the nation was composed primarily of independent yeoman farmers, but he trembled at the prospect that the servile masses of Europe might overwhelm the nation by immigration. Others used the republican ideology to argue in favor of building up commerce and manufacturing, even if that required inducing skilled European mechanics to emigrate to the United States. How could the nation remain self-reliant and virtuous if it was completely dependent upon other states for its manufactured goods? Thus republicanism did not provide unambiguous guidelines to policy, and it was not without competing theories about the relation between private behavior and civic well-being. The rising current of utilitarian thought was based on the assumption that there was such a thing as legitimate self-love, that actions dictated by self-interest might be perfectly compatible with general social benefit, and that civic virtue did not always require Spartan self-denial.

Insofar as republicanism was an element in the ideological basis of American identity, it added to the moral intensity and precariousness of the American experiment. The republican emphasis on virtue invested politics with religious seriousness and encouraged men to look upon policy disagreements as the reflection of fundamental qualities of good or evil in personal character. This line of thinking, which blended easily with what has been called "civil millennialism," helps explain why the 1790s were a period of superheated controversy, in which partisanship reached levels of utter frenzy, and charges of treason, corruption, and moral depravity became staples of political discourse. Because it made the success of republican government contingent upon an almost heroic kind of disinterestedness and civic vigilance, the republican ideology added to the difficulties of establishing a political order that would realize in practice the high principles proclaimed as the foundation of national existence.

But the very precariousness of their experiment made Americans highly self-conscious about their national identity. One could collect many references to the national character, from Thomas Paine's plea in 1783 for unity among the states as a basis for American nationality to Henry Clay's remark in 1815 that the just-concluded war with England had achieved one of its principal objects, "the firm establishment of the national character." Erik Erikson expressed the surprise modern readers feel on encountering this degree of self-consciousness: "It is hard for us to believe . . . how conscious these early Americans were of the job of developing American character out of the regional and generational polarities and contradictions of a nation of immigrants and migrants." Three marks of the developing idea of nationality are especially significant.

First, the ideological quality of American national identity was of decisive importance vis-à-vis the question of immigration and ethnicity. To be or to become an American, a person did not have to be of any particular national, linguistic, religious, or ethnic background. All he had to do was to commit himself to the political ideology centered on the abstract ideals of liberty, equality, and republicanism. Thus the universalist ideological character of American nationality meant that it was open to anyone who willed to become an American.

About eight out of ten white Americans were actually of British derivation in 1790, and there was a la-

tent predisposition toward an ethnically defined concept of nationality. Indeed, universalism had its limits from the beginning, because it did not include either blacks or Indians, and in time other racial and cultural groups were regarded as falling outside of the range of American nationality. Yet such exclusiveness ran contrary to the logic of the defining principles, and the official commitment to those principles has worked historically to overcome exclusions and to make the practical boundaries of American identity more congruent with its theoretical universalism.

Newness was the second significant mark of American nationality. Despite a long colonial past, the origin of the American nation could be definitively assigned to the Revolution and the establishment of a unified government in the 1780s, events that constituted a decisive break with the past. America had turned its back on Europe and proclaimed itself the new order of the ages, the model for the future. The heroes in the national pantheon were the men who had brought this new order into being, the founding fathers. Other symbols of national identity—such as Independence Day, the Declaration, and the Constitution and Bill of Rights —were all associated with the classic time when the new nation had been formed.

The third mark of American nationality, future orientation, is closely related to the second, for the great accomplishments of the revolutionary generation were but a founding, a beginning. What they had created was handed on not only as a glorious heritage but also as a task, a sacred trust. To be true to their national identity, Americans had to make good the aspiration expressed in the founding documents. The differences of opinion that arose almost immediately when the federal system was set in motion made clear how arduous this struggle would be. Americans quickly realized they were far from realizing the abstract excellence of their system. Joel Barlow put it neatly in 1809: "As a nation, we are not up to our circumstance." The full realization of national identity lay in the future.

Compared to the ideological quality, emphasis on newness, and future orientation, the ethnic element in American nationality was quite recessive in the first years of the republic. This may be seen by looking briefly at a classic statement made in 1782 about ethnicity and nationality and by considering some of the practical questions related to naturalization and political controversy in the 1790s.

The classic statement is Michel-Guillaume Jean de Crèvecoeur's *Letters from an American Farmer*, first published in London in 1782 but largely written in the decade before the revolution. A landmark in American literature, Crèvecoeur's *Letters* is equally famous for its formulation of yeoman-farmer agrarianism and for the enunciation of the so-called melting-pot idea of immigrant assimilation and American nationality. In a passage that has probably been quoted more often than any other in the literature of immigration, Crèvecoeur highlighted the elements of newness and future orientation in stating the assimilationist view:

What then is the American, this new man? He is either a European or the descendant of a European, hence that strange mixture of blood, which you will find in no other country. I could point out to you a family whose grandfa-

ther was an Englishman, whose wife was Dutch, whose son married a French woman, and whose present four sons have four wives of different nations. *He* is an American, who, leaving behind him all his ancient prejudices and manners, receives new ones from the new mode of life he has embraced, the new government he obeys, and the new rank he holds. He becomes an American by being received into the broad lap of our great *Alma Mater*. Here individuals are melted into a new race of men, whose labours and posterity will one day cause great changes in the world.

Here and elsewhere Crèvecoeur stressed the ethnic and religious diversity of the American population, but he was actually far less interested in what the American people had been than in what they were becoming and would be in the future. Ethnic diversity, though notable, was not so much an essential feature of the national identity as a condition that America transformed in the process of creating a new nationality. Americans would still be a new people, although probably not the same kind of new people, even if all of them had been purely English in background.

Although he stressed the elements of newness and future orientation, Crèvecoeur was less explicit about the ideological dimension, perhaps because the work was written before independence was an accomplished fact and because Crèvecoeur tended toward loyalism in his political sympathies. Yet his discussion implicitly endorsed the American ideology by its heavy emphasis on the importance of social equality and mobility in "regenerating" the poor of Europe and making them into freemen. By following his own self-interest, Crèvecoeur affirmed, a man could be transformed into an American, improve his material situation, and live a life of simplicity and virtue. The elements of the American dream were all there, not expounded as theory but asserted as practical facts and illustrated in the story of Andrew the Hebridean, whose rise from oppression to freedom, "from obscurity . . . to some degree of consequence," concluded Crèvecoeur's treatment of the question, "What is an American?"

Turning to the place of immigration and naturalization in the politics of the 1790s, we find again that the ideological dimension was more prominent than the ethnic. There is no question that the perception of linguistic and cultural differences, as well as traditional suspicions and animosities, played a role in the controversies over naturalization and the political activities of aliens and immigrants, but these considerations were definitely secondary. Moreover, the policy on naturalization that ultimately emerged from these controversies and remained in force until the early 20th century bespoke great confidence in the power of American principles, institutions, and environment to transform foreigners into acceptable Americans within a brief period and without systematic indoctrination. (*See* Naturalization and Citizenship.)

The question of how foreigners could be admitted to citizenship and thus officially become Americans was taken up in the first Congress that met under the federal Constitution. There were differences of view when it was debated, with New Englanders showing a greater spirit of exclusiveness than men from the middle colonies, but the naturalization law of 1790 was extremely liberal. Even so, some republicans considered the two-year waiting period before an immigrant could become

a citizen a requirement lacking in "general philanthropy."

When naturalization was brought up again in the closing days of 1794, the political climate was more highly charged. Divisions over domestic issues, such as Alexander Hamilton's fiscal program, overlapped with sharp disagreements on foreign policy, while the ideological passions aroused by the French Revolution and the outbreak of war in Europe linked these internal quarrels to the clash of irreconcilable principles across the seas. The two incipient political parties—the Federalists, centered in New England, and the Republicans, led by Thomas Jefferson and James Madison—differed in their sympathies toward the French Revolution and in their approach to domestic and foreign policy issues, but each had reason to be uneasy about some of the immigrants coming into the country as a result of the revolutionary upheavals. The Federalists were most concerned about the prominence of radical refugees from the British Isles in the ranks of their Republican opponents. They therefore pushed for an extension of the waiting period for naturalization and wanted two credible witnesses to swear to the good character of an applicant for citizenship. The Republicans, although opposed to the measure, had their own suspicions of royalist émigrés from the Revolution and succeeded in attaching to the naturalization law of 1795 a provision requiring an applicant to give up any hereditary title before he could become a U.S. citizen.

Although the law of 1795 extended the waiting period to five years, it did not provide the safeguards the Federalists considered necessary in the political crisis that arose over the XYZ Affair and the quasi-war with France. Fear of immigrant radicals and alien activists of a Jacobin hue prompted the passage of the notorious Alien and Sedition Acts of 1798, which provided for the deportation of potentially dangerous aliens and for the imprisonment of anyone making false or malicious statements about the incumbent administration or Congress. These acts also included the naturalization law of 1798, which marked a sharp departure from the previously established policy by requiring 14 years of residence before an immigrant could be admitted to citizenship, thus effectively disfranchising adult immigrants for a very extended period.

The Alien and Sedition Acts were so obviously a political weapon against the Republicans and were enforced in so partisan a manner that they backfired against the Federalists; the widespread reaction damaged the party badly in the 1800 election and contributed to Jefferson's victory. With the Republicans in office, the naturalization requirements were restored by an act of 1802 to those prevailing before the alien and sedition crisis. No major changes in the procedure were made until 1906, when the whole process of naturalization was overhauled. Thus during a century of massive immigration, any free white immigrant could become a U.S. citizen simply by swearing that he had lived in the United States for five years, that he renounced all hereditary titles and political allegiance to any other state, and that he would support the U.S. Constitution.

As these simple requirements make clear, acquisition in law of an American identity was a matter of adherence to the political values embodied in the Constitution and repudiation of all other political loyalties. The ease with which these standards could be met and the absence of adequate machinery to check the applicant's statements testified to confidence that a free, white person could become an American no matter what his national background or language. Both the character of the requirements for naturalization and the fact that the immigration controversies in the 1790s revolved around political issues support the contention that— except in the area of race—American national identity was conceived in the earliest days in abstract ideological terms much more than in ethnic terms.

A negative factor helping to make possible this concentration on the ideological aspect was the low immigration of the period. The best estimate is that only about 250,000 immigrants came to the United States in the quarter-century after the inauguration of the federal government. Without steady reinforcement from abroad, the non-English-speaking population became palpably Americanized in language. The next century, however, showed that greater immigration would bring more distinctively ethnic elements to the forefront.

RELIGION IN AMERICAN IDENTITY, 1815–1860

The years between the end of the War of 1812 and the outbreak of the Civil War were marked by extremely rapid growth, both in territory and in population, and by dizzying social and economic change. Intensified nationalism accompanied westward expansion, giving rise in the 1840s to the bombastic doctrine of Manifest Destiny, yet expansion also heightened sectional tension by intensifying the opposition of North and South over the question of slavery in the territories. The sectional issue was by far the more important in regard to national identity; ultimately it exploded in violence, testing the Union by a four-year war. Yet the massive immigration that began in the 1830s also had clear implications for American identity, especially because so many of the newcomers were Catholics. Anti-Catholic and anti-immigrant feeling coalesced in the 1840s and 1850s in bitter outbursts of nativism. In comparison to the earlier period, ethnically rooted cultural (or, in this case, religious) differences became more prominent in the effort to define American identity. Yet the ideological emphasis continued strong and was closely connected with the religious issue. At the same time, the question of how religious and civic identities should interact became matters of debate within the Catholic community.

The sheer increase of immigration and the sudden growth of the Catholic population were basic to these developments. After being largely cut off for a generation, immigration picked up gradually after the restoration of peace in 1815. Although observers in the 1820s were impressed by the size of immigration, the flood did not set in till after 1830. Between that date and 1845 more than a million immigrants poured into the country, and in the next ten years (1846–1855) the figure almost tripled as a result of the mass exodus set off by crop failures, famine, and other economic and political disturbances in Ireland and on the continent. By 1860 the 25 principal cities had a higher percentage of the foreign-born than they have had at any time since.

Because one-third to one-half of the immigrants were Catholics, the tremendous influx made Catholics the largest religious denomination in the country. In 1790

there were perhaps 35,000 in a total white population of 3.2 million. By 1830 their numbers had increased to something more than 300,000; in the next 30 years the Catholic population shot up three-and-a-half times faster than the total population, reaching a figure of 1.6 million in 1850 and 3.1 million in 1860. Paralleling this growth was a tremendous elaboration of Catholic institutions. By 1852, when the first Plenary Council of Baltimore brought together all the Catholic bishops in the country, there were over 30 of them (only 8 of whom were American-born), presiding over ecclesiastical jurisdictions from New England to California. The Catholic population was served by more than 1,400 priests; religious communities were multiplying rapidly, as were colleges, seminaries, parochial schools, newspapers, and Catholic societies.

Growth of this magnitude could hardly be expected to occur without creating friction in a country that had been so strongly Protestant and bitterly hostile to Catholics in the 17th and 18th centuries. Despite an improvement in feeling as a result of the alliance with Catholic France in the Revolution, the situation worsened after 1830 because the period of rapid Catholic growth coincided with a terrific burst of Protestant evangelicalism. Many revivalists saw an intimate connection between Protestantism and the national destiny, which was routinely portrayed in millennial colors. To the aroused evangelicals the existence of Catholicism was utterly incompatible with the millennial promise, so the obviously increasing strength of the Catholic church in the United States appeared to be the work of the Evil One and had to be combated vigorously. Seen in this light, the campaign against Catholicism was as much a reform drive as was the temperance crusade; both were intended to eliminate evils that militated against the coming 1,000-year reign of Christ's love.

The first episodes of anti-Catholicism in the 1830s were closely connected to the evangelical revival. A series of sermons delivered by the evangelical leader, Lyman Beecher, was widely regarded as having sparked the riotous attack that led to the burning of the Ursuline convent in Charlestown, Mass., in 1834. Anti-Catholicism springing from this source could draw on the accumulated fears and hatreds of centuries of religious strife, and it often sank to the lowest levels of vilification, as exemplified in the salacious slanders of Catholic priests and nuns in works such as Maria Monk's *Awful Disclosures of the Hotel Dieu Nunnery of Montreal* (1836).

Anti-Catholic nativism expanded from these beginnings to a climax in 1844 when the "Native American" phase of the movement erupted in Philadelphia in two episodes of rioting, each lasting several days, which cost more than a dozen lives and resulted in the burning of two Catholic churches. A temporary lull followed these frightening outbursts, but after 1850 the anti-Catholic form of nativism reached its historic high point in what was called Know-Nothingism. The Know-Nothings, a political party officially known as the American party, developed as an offshoot of a secret patriotic society, the Order of the Star-Spangled Banner. Dedicated to extending the naturalization requirement to 21 years and excluding Catholics and the foreign-born from holding office, the Know-Nothings reached

the peak of their influence in 1855 when they controlled 6 states (Massachusetts, Connecticut, Rhode Island, New Hampshire, Maryland, and Kentucky) and sent some 75 representatives to Congress. The movement, accompanied by sporadic episodes of violence, declined quickly after 1856 as sectional tension over slavery overshadowed all other issues.

Anti-Catholicism was basic to these developments, but ante-bellum nativism also reflected a fundamental concern with national identity. The question that bothered the Native Americans and Know-Nothings might be expressed in colloquial terms as, "Whose country is this, anyhow?" They were disturbed and angry because the vast influx of Catholic foreigners not only challenged the hegemony of Protestantism, but seemed to threaten republican principles, the political process, the educational system, and prevailing cultural and behavioral norms.

Three widely circulated works of the mid-1830s played a key role in linking anti-Catholicism with fear of immigration and in highlighting the ideological threat represented by the growing strength of the Catholic church. In his *Foreign Conspiracy against the Liberties of the United States* (1834) and its sequel, *Imminent Dangers to the Free Institutions of the United States through Foreign Immigration* (1835), Samuel F.B. Morse argued that Catholic immigration was being deliberately stimulated and guided to the United States by the reactionary powers of Europe, especially Austria, as part of a calculated design to weaken republicanism and thereby frustrate "the onward march of the world to liberty." Morse singled out the Catholic mission-aid societies in Europe as evidence of such a plot, laying particular stress on the Leopoldine Society, founded in Vienna in 1829 and named after the daughter of the Austrian emperor. Lyman Beecher's *A Plea for the West* (1835) developed the same general line of argument, except that he stressed the Ohio Valley, rapidly filling with immigrants, as the crucial area of competition between Protestant republicanism and Catholic-immigrant despotism.

Although the contention that Catholicism was despotic was not new, it became more timely and urgent, not only because of the swelling numbers of American Catholics, but also because of the spectacular resurgence of European Catholicism that accompanied the Romantic movement and the restoration of legitimist regimes after the downfall of Napoleon. In the polarization between liberalism and republicanism, on the one hand, and conservatism and royalism, on the other, the Catholic church in Europe was definitely aligned with the latter. The prospects for rapprochement were worsened by the revolutions of 1848, which transformed Pope Pius IX from a moderate progressive into a rigorous reactionary. Hence the uprisings of 1848, which Americans generally approved of, tended to confirm their view that Catholics were dangerously antirepublican. The clash was dramatized by the reception accorded Louis Kossuth when the Hungarian revolutionary leader visited the United States in 1851: he was lionized by American liberals, but denounced by Catholic spokesmen as a "Red Republican" symbol of atheism and anarchy. The passions associated with 1848 also inflamed the visit in 1853–1854 of the papal nuncio, Gaetano Bedini, who was defamed, hung in effigy,

and physically endangered by mobs in several American cities for his alleged role in putting down the revolution in Bologna.

One aim of Bedini's visit had been to settle the worst of the old disputes over "trusteeism" in Catholic congregations, the conflicts between bishops and lay trustees over control of church property. Rebellious trustees usually claimed to be trying to introduce a more republican system of internal administration to the Catholic church, and they often welcomed the aid of nativists. By involving himself in this issue Bedini lent plausibility to the charge that Catholics were dominated by foreign princes. Thus, though trusteeism was an internal issue of church discipline, it touched on republican values in a manner that fed nativist suspicions.

In politics the conduct of Catholics and immigrants also gave serious offense; although Germans came in for their share of suspicion, the Irish were regarded as the chief offenders. They were the most numerous and conspicuous of the Catholic immigrants; they were concentrated in the great eastern cities; they spoke English and were already politicized to some extent before emigrating; they were extremely active in party politics, usually as Democrats; and they were associated with some of the worst political abuses of the day. Because of their lack of habituation in republican virtues, it was said, the immigrants were easily manipulated; they voted in blocs at the behest of their priests or political bosses and were involved in all manner of fraudulent practices. Immigrants were sworn in as citizens before meeting the residence requirement; they were "colonized," sent to vote in districts where reinforcements were needed although they did not live there; and they were believed to be responsible for much of the physical intimidation and violence at polling places. For all these reasons, the nativists concluded that U.S. politics could never be restored to true republican purity until the immigrants were eliminated by extension of the waiting period for naturalization to 21 years and restriction of office holding to the native-born.

Irish immigrants also aroused misgivings because of their noisy agitation on behalf of homeland causes like Daniel O'Connell's Repeal Movement or, a few years later, Fenianism. But this type of political activism, although it suggested to nativists an undue attachment to the homeland, was not nearly so repugnant as the organized political efforts by Catholics to get public funds for their schools. Education was perhaps the most highly charged issue of all, bringing together in a single focus all the passions associated with religious belief, moral theory, ideological conviction, political sensitivity, parental affection, and concern for future generations.

The development of the common school paralleled the massive ante-bellum immigration and the striking growth of the Catholic church. The parallelism was not wholly fortuitous, for the common school was intended, among other things, to meet and overcome the potentially disintegrative influences flowing from immigration and Catholic growth. The developing public schools, in other words, were supposed to serve an Americanizing function, and the version of Americanism they symbolized integrated a nondenominational Protestant outlook in religion and morality with a re-

publican viewpoint in political principle and practice. Evangelical leaders like Calvin Stowe (the son-in-law of Lyman Beecher) played a crucial role in promoting the common schools, and a Protestant consensus in education was widely regarded as essential to the preservation of genuine Americanism. Seen against this background, the establishment of separate Catholic schools was bound to arouse hostility, and Catholic efforts to gain public funds seemed a form of lèse majesté. (See also Education.)

Catholic schools were objectionable in themselves, because they were looked upon as perpetuating religious error and inculcating an antirepublican mentality, but the first major battle in a tradition of controversy that has continued to the present day was set off in 1840 when Bishop John Hughes of New York tried to win public funds for Catholic schools. Although it was Governor William Seward who first broached the matter of public support for Catholic schools, Hughes's campaign of lobbying, political pressure, and mobilization of Catholic voters outraged Protestants and confirmed nativists in the conviction that Catholicism was intolerable politically as well as educationally. Additional bitter controversy arose over Catholic objections to the reading of the King James version of the Bible in the common schools, an issue deeply involved in the anti-Catholic riots in Philadelphia in 1844. And a concerted effort by Catholics in several states for a share of the school fund was part of the immediate background to the emergence of Know-Nothingism in the early 1850s.

Besides being objectionable on religious and political grounds, parochial schools reflected a Catholic clannishness and separatism that aroused resentment among the Protestant majority. Similarly the strangeness of the immigrants' costume, language, accent, and manners struck the natives unfavorably. The poverty of many immigrants, especially those fleeing from Ireland in the famine years, the squalid, overcrowded quarters in which many of them had to live, and the debauchery and drunkenness that flourished in such surroundings also contributed to the impression that immigration was degrading American character and morals. The weakness of the Irish for drink, associated as it was with riotously boisterous "Paddy funerals" and all manner of brawls, was particularly damning because the temperance movement had early taken on symbolic importance as a crusade to preserve the moral character of American society.

The flood of immigration thus raised questions about the national identity from the perspectives of religion, ideology, politics, education, and general culture. It was the presence of vast numbers of Catholic immigrants, more than anything else, that brought religious and ethnic considerations into the discussion of what it meant to be an American. The full proscriptive program of the Know-Nothings, a coalition hung precariously around anti-Catholicism and antiforeignism, was nowhere enacted, but the fear of and hostility toward Catholicism that it mobilized remained active in American politics for the next century.

Besides creating external opposition, the Know-Nothings also precipitated an internal debate among Catholics over how the church should adjust to the novel environment of the United States. The first ex-

plicit intra-Catholic controversy over Americanization occurred in the middle 1850s, although Catholic interest in this question dated back to the earliest days of the new republic. John Carroll, the first Catholic bishop, came from an old Maryland family and was keenly sensitive to the need to bring the church into line with American institutions. Later Catholic leaders shared Carroll's approval of the American system of separation of church and state and of governmental noninterference in religious affairs. Catholics took pride in the role played by their coreligionists in the exploration and settlement of the country, especially in the pioneering example of religious toleration furnished by the Catholic colony of Maryland. Formal commemoration of the landing of the Maryland colonists began in the 1840s in order to highlight the Catholic contribution to American religious freedom.

Official statements by churchmen inculcated civic loyalty and devotion to the Constitution. On occasion, Catholic spokesmen also took note of the dangers of isolating themselves from the rest of the community, especially in nationalistic, rather than religious, societies. The Boston *Pilot*, an Irish Catholic paper, spoke out in 1854 against the kind of groups that gave the impression that the Irish were "a community and army *encamped* merely upon a foreign ground." Bishop Hughes in New York publicly opposed Irish colonization projects for similar reasons. Nor did church leaders fail to criticize immigrant customs that attracted unfavorable notice from natives, for example, boisterous wakes and funerals, of which the *Pilot* said in 1849: "The old habits of Ireland will not answer here."

But despite the earlier history of concern over these issues, the relationship of Americanism and Catholicism assumed a new level of self-consciousness and importance in the 1850s. The first reason was obviously nativism, which Catholics could not ignore even if they wanted to. Second, the overwhelming immigration of the 1840s and 1850s brought in a multitude of Catholics who tended to identify their religion with their former nationality. This was as true of the Germans as of the Irish, but because the latter were more numerous and conspicuous, the chief practical result was a tendency to equate Catholicism with being Irish and Protestantism with being American.

The unwisdom of any such association was clear to most church leaders on the theoretical level, but it was personally offensive to Orestes A. Brownson, the most prominent of a group of notable American converts to Catholicism. A Vermont Yankee by birth, Brownson was affronted by immigrant Catholic sneers at "Natyvism" and by what he perceived as an active dislike of the American people and character on the part of many Catholic leaders. He also felt a strong aversion for the Irish on social and cultural grounds, referring to them in his private correspondence in very unflattering terms. What troubled him most, however, was the implicit assumption that Irish and Catholic were interchangeable terms. Brownson was very sympathetic to the view of his friend and fellow-convert, Isaac Hecker, that Americans were a deeply religious people who would respond eagerly to Catholicism if it were presented to them in a congenial manner.

These factors prompted the appearance of two articles in the July 1854 issue of *Brownson's Quarterly Review*, "Schools and Education" and "Native Americanism," which opened the first Catholic debate on Americanization. Brownson followed up in October with "The Know Nothings," in which he defended himself against the criticism called forth by the previous articles. Related pieces appeared from time to time over the next several years, one of which contained the first use of the word "Americanization," according to *A Dictionary of American English on Historical Principles*.

Brownson's position in the controversy was strongly assimilationist. Although he admitted that the two had become intermixed, Brownson insisted that nativism was not the same as anti-Catholicism. He rejected the latter, of course, but said that nativism should be understood as a legitimate expression of nationality on the part of Americans who loved their homeland. A people with as much national pride as the Irish, he remarked, ought to be able to understand the same feeling in Americans. They would also have to accept the fact that the American nationality had already been formed in a basically Anglo-Saxon mold, and that the immigrants must conform to it because no deliberate perpetuation of foreign nationalities on American soil would be tolerated. Because this kind of Americanism was the appropriate nationality for the country and because it would prevail, it would clearly be suicidal for the Catholic religion to allow itself to be identified with any foreign nationality. Hence it was imperative to distinguish between nationality and Catholicity, so that immigrants would not abandon their faith in the process of Americanizing, and Americans would understand that to become a Catholic one did not have to give up his nationality.

In politics the real immigrant threat, in Brownson's view, came not from Catholics but from the radical extremists who had fled from the unsuccessful European uprisings of 1848. Nevertheless he agreed that naturalization was a "boon" rather than a natural right and that the franchise should be reserved to the American-born. He also warned Irish nationalists against mobilizing in the United States for homeland causes. In education Brownson regretted that anti-Catholicism made it necessary to maintain a system of separate schools and argued that Catholics could gain much from the public schools because of their Americanizing tendency and because the faith of Catholic children would be strengthened by early contact with Protestants, provided their parents and pastors took pains to instruct them outside the school. Later Brownson also criticized Catholic colleges and seminaries for reflecting an Old-World mentality and failing to prepare their students for the kind of problems they would face in the United States.

Many Irish and Catholic spokesmen were outraged by Brownson's blast, and others regarded it as ill-timed. The reaction led him to clarify his position and to emphasize the essential point that Catholicism was not to be identified with *any* nationality; he believed that an emphatic statement was needed to bring this home both to immigrant Catholics and to Protestant Americans. This rhetorical need, along with Brownson's personal antipathy for the Irish, accounted for the harshness of his 1854 statement. In other contexts he emphasized different aspects of the subject. But Brownson did not retreat from his contention that Catholi-

cism in the United States must cut itself free from identification with the Old World and be brought into line with American norms and values wherever that could be done without threat to the faith. If the church were to be true to its universal mission, it had to be at home in all cultures. Brownson's perception that this required a kind of Americanization set off a brief flurry in the 1850s, anticipating the controversies that rocked the American Catholic community 30 years later over the German nationality question, education, and theological Americanism. Thus the relationship of religion to nationality became an explosive issue among American Catholics just as it was between Catholics and the larger community.

ETHNICITY IN AMERICAN IDENTITY (1860–1924)

Although the religious element in ethnicity emerged as an issue in the first half of the 19th century, other cultural, or what used to be called "racial," elements did not become central to the discussion of American nationality until the latter decades of the century. The Civil War reawakened nationalism and solidified the identification between the Union and liberty, but immigration and ethnic differentiation played very little part in this. The participation of immigrants in the Union armies reduced suspicion of the foreign-born, and although anti-Catholicism flared up more than once after the war, it was never again the primary focus for a general nativist movement. Other issues, such as Reconstruction policy and economic expansion, took center stage after Appomattox, and immigrants were welcomed to fill the labor needs of a rapidly industrializing nation. The volume of immigration mounted in the later decades of the century and rose to unprecedented heights after 1900, but by this time, immigration had again become controversial. It was associated with a variety of social problems and regarded as undesirable in itself. Unlike the Civil War, World War I fueled ethnic animosities, with the result that soon after peace returned, a series of restrictionist laws cut back immigration sharply.

The reversal of the nation's historic policy of free immigration was the most important result of the debate carried on from the 1890s to the 1920s. There was also a theoretical legacy, because several of the terms in which subsequent discussion of ethnicity and national identity has been carried on emerged in this era.

The Melting Pot This term, which remains the most popular symbol for ethnic interaction and the society in which it takes place, was launched by Israel Zangwill's play *The Melting-Pot*, which had a long run in New York in 1909. Zangwill was an English Jew who adopted the expression "melting pot" from its conventional usage in England as a metaphor for the process of fundamental transformation. Before Zangwill's play the expression was not common in the United States; since then it has been used almost exclusively to refer to ethnicity and intergroup relations.

Zangwill's play tells of an idealistic young Jewish immigrant who believes that Old-World nationalities should be forgotten in the United States and that all elements should fuse together in the creation of a new and superior American nationality. These ideas were very old; in one sense all Zangwill did was furnish a new symbol for a set of loose, informal notions (which had

long been associated with terms like "melting," "blending," "fusing," and the like) about America's great powers of assimilation, powers that had traditionally been thought of as operating automatically. At the same time the symbol of the melting pot invited an interpretation of assimilation as a purposeful process of burning off impurities and molding immigrants to a predetermined type.

The best-known early statement of the traditional view is that of Crèvecoeur, the key passage of which has already been quoted. Although he did not use the expression "melting pot," Crèvecoeur did speak of persons from many nations being "melted into a new race of men," and it is quite appropriate to regard his discussion as the classic formulation of what might be called the cosmopolitan-nationality version of the melting-pot theme. As John Higham has pointed out, the motto *"E pluribus unum"* summed up "the essence of America's cosmopolitan faith—a conviction that this new land would bring unity out of diversity as a matter of course." This was the majority view through the 19th century, reaffirmed against the nativists of the 1840s and 1850s by Ralph Waldo Emerson and others; when it appeared in Zangwill's play, audiences responded to what one critic called a drama "touched with the fire of democracy, and lighted radiantly with the national vision."

The critic's language was legitimate, because of the close congruence between the cosmopolitan-nationality version of the melting-pot idea and the national ideology, with its abstract universalism, its emphasis on newness, and its orientation toward the future. The melting pot paralleled these points in its undiscriminating acceptance of newcomers who were willing to identify themselves with American principles, commit themselves to a new life in the new land, and labor for a better future for their children and grandchildren. It was minimalist in what it asked the immigrant to do in order to become an American and optimistic in the expectation that his experience in the new homeland would solidify his commitment to the principles of American democracy. This version of the melting pot also assumed that the conditions of American life, particularly egalitarianism and the opportunity for material improvement, would automatically transform foreigners into Americans—with some help from the common schools. Another thread in this complex of ideas was the belief that the emerging American nationality would be enriched by the diversity of the ethnic elements that composed it. By the 1850s scientific arguments of a Spencerian or Darwinian sort were occasionally offered in support of the theory that mixed peoples were superior to those of a single strain.

Yet with all its liberality and tolerance, the cosmopolitan version of the melting pot was still a theory of assimilation. The idea that the immigrants must change was basic; they were to become new people. The American identity might not be fully formed, but it was far from indeterminate. Some of its features were established by the basic political ideology; others were more vague, deriving in a tacit manner from the majority culture and the evolving experience of the national community. This was the nationality into which the immigrants and their children were expected to merge. In doing so they would enrich it, refine it, or modify it in

detail, but no one anticipated fundamental revision. And of course there were racial limitations: blacks and Indians were excluded from the outset, and Asiatics after 1882, when a new law banned the immigration of Chinese laborers.

From Crèvecoeur's time until late in the 19th century, most Americans supported this version of melting-pot thinking, and even the growing Anglo-Saxonism of the post-Civil War years at first reinforced it. The Anglo-Saxons were touted as a people distinguished by their capacity to assimilate others, absorbing their desirable qualities without being basically changed themselves. But confidence in America's absorptive capacities was essential to the continued viability of this laissez-faire melting-pot thinking. From the 1880s on, increasing numbers of Americans came to doubt that the mysterious alembic of American society was actually functioning as it was supposed to—too many immigrants were coming into the country; they were coming too fast; they were too different from the American national type to be assimilated painlessly or even, many felt, to be assimilated at all.

When Zangwill's play appeared, a minority of Americans still retained their confidence in the nation's absorptive powers, but they were soon swamped by those who believed that the situation required, at the very least, a more active policy of purposeful Americanization. The title of the play supplied a perfect symbol, not only for the traditional cosmopolitan-nationalists, but also for those who wanted to intervene more actively in the processes of assimilation. Did not a melting pot require watching? Might it not become overheated? What was to be done about the dross and slag that were waste products of its operation? Metaphorical elaboration along these lines and the use of the melting-pot symbol by the fervid 100-percent Americanizers of the World War I epoch tended to submerge the earlier strain of tolerant cosmopolitanism; especially among liberals, the melting pot came to be associated with a repugnant, forced-assimilation approach.

In the 1920s the symbol of the melting pot was discredited, not only among liberals, but also among ultranationalists, who decided that even its superheated version had not worked. Although still popular in journalistic usage, the term did not figure prominently in serious discussions of intergroup relations for a number of years. It was to some degree revived and rehabilitated by Will Herberg's *Protestant-Catholic-Jew* (1955), which popularized the notion that the "three great faiths of democracy" constituted a "triple melting pot." But the symbol was subjected to a barrage of unfavorable commentary in the ethnic revival of the 1960s and 1970s. Nathan Glazer and Daniel Moynihan's *Beyond the Melting Pot* (1963), an early landmark, set the tone for much later usage in announcing that "The point about the melting pot is that it did not happen." Later spokesmen for the new ethnicity treated the melting pot as a symbol of everything hateful in the nation's record on immigration and intergroup relations.

However, these writers seem unable to talk about the subject without using the expression melting pot. They have thus given it a more central place in discussions of ethnicity and nationality than it has had at any time since World War I. Their unrelievedly negative and hostile interpretation of the symbol has also reproduced

the set of relationships that developed in that era when the melting pot was identified with forced Americanization and contrasted with cultural pluralism.

Americanization This term, in its generic sense roughly equivalent to assimilation, became attached to a specific movement in the first two decades of the 20th century; its meaning since then has been colored to some extent by identification with the movement. The words "Americanize," "Americanizing," and "Americanization," were all in common usage during the antebellum nativist controversies, clearly referring to the immigrants' becoming assimilated into American life. However, there was disagreement as to precisely what the process required. The Irish, who were being urged by Brownson to Americanize, inquired of him what pattern of Americanism they were to conform to—that of New England, Virginia, or Kentucky. They also insisted that some forms of Americanization, such as heedless materialism and mammon-worship, were unwholesome.

Just what it means to become or to be an American is the central question concerning the national identity. Some have interpreted true Americanism as requiring close conformity to the cultural majority in language, religion, and manners, while others have adopted a more relaxed position about the range of variation that could be accommodated within the national identity. In the late 19th century, along with the shift in thinking about the melting pot, the balance swung toward the former view, as more Americans began to feel the nation required a higher level of cohesion and solidarity.

In part the shift resulted from the increasingly visible presence of the new immigrants crowding into the cities from eastern and southern Europe. These Italians, Slavs, and Jews not only seemed more alien than earlier immigrants in their language and culture, they were also linked in the public mind with strikes, social unrest, and urban problems such as crime and slum housing. Also involved was the development of a more ethnically restrictive, Anglo-Saxon version of American nationality. As Anglo-Saxon racialism waxed, it became easier to persuade Americans that other groups needed more systematic assistance in emulating the virtues of the older stock.

These two considerations operated powerfully in the minds of those who interpreted Americanism in narrow terms and who believed that Americanization was needed to protect the national character from the dangers posed by the immense immigration of the times. Other Americanizers, however, were animated by a more positive desire to assist the immigrants in adjusting to the strange and often harsh conditions of life they encountered in the United States. This group represented a continuation of the older tradition of cosmopolitan nationalism. The Americanization movement included both of these orientations, but as it developed from about 1900 to the early 1920s the former emphasis became more dominant, eventually giving the whole movement a repressive and nativistic tone.

The Americanization movement passed through three phases: the first extended from around the turn of the century to 1914; the second covered the years of World War I; the third, the immediate postwar years. In the first phase, the nervously nationalistic strain was represented by such patriotic groups as the Daughters of

the American Revolution (DAR) and by the Boston-based North American Civic League for Immigrants, founded in 1908. On the other hand, settlement-house workers, advocates of the social gospel, and others committed to progressivism stressed the need for protective legislation for immigrants and took a positive view of the cultural contributions they could make to American life. Both groups sought a more harmoniously integrated society.

Differences in approach and shifts in emphasis were particularly evident in the area of education. The importance of the public school in bringing together the children of diverse ethnic strains and teaching them the responsibilities of U.S. citizenship had been recognized from the earliest days. What was new in the Progressive period was heightened self-consciousness and a greater sense of urgency about these matters. But agreement that the schools played a vital role did not imply agreement about how they should go about it or the spirit in which it should be undertaken. To a racialist like Elwood P. Cubberly, a well-known educational historian, the task was "to implant in their [the immigrants'] children, so far as can be done, the Anglo-Saxon conception of righteousness, law and order, and popular government; and to awaken in them a reverence for our democratic institutions and for those things in our national life which we as a people hold to be of abiding worth." At the other extreme John Dewey prescribed cosmopolitanism as the correct "nationalizing" policy for the public schools. It was the responsibility of the schools, he told the National Education Association in 1916, to "teach each [ethnic] factor to respect every other, and . . . to enlighten all as to the great contributions of every strain in our composite make-up."

Instruction in hygiene, domestic science, and industrial arts was also linked to Americanization at the level of practical school programs, but the principal new departure was in adult education for immigrants. Special classes were offered both by settlement houses and by patriotic groups; the YMCA entered the field in 1907 with evening courses in English and civics, the two subjects most heavily stressed.

The ethnic reverberation set off in the United States by the outbreak of the European war in 1914 marked the opening of a far more intense phase of the Americanization movement. The return to Europe of thousands of immigrants who were reservists in the armies of the belligerents and the eruption of ethnic nationalism on the part of immigrant groups with close ties to the warring powers came as a shock to many Americans, who had not realized just how "foreign" the sentiments and attachments of the foreign-born population actually were. Sensational exposés of German propaganda and sabotage efforts in the United States, coming on the heels of the *Lusitania* crisis, reinforced anti-German sentiment and gave rise to a formidable campaign against "hyphenation." The hyphen in such compounds as German-American was regarded as symbolizing divided loyalties, and "100 percent Americanism" became the goal of Americanization programs. (*See* Loyalties: Dual and Divided.)

The wartime Americanization campaign reached its climax during the years of U.S. involvement in the fighting, but several significant changes were evident by 1915. First, the number of agencies and organiza-tions supporting the movement expanded greatly, as did the frequency and visibility of its activities and the level of mass support they received. By 1915 the U.S. Bureau of Education and the U.S. Bureau of Naturalization were actively involved; after 1917 the Committee on Public Information also took part. State and local governmental bodies pitched in, joined by innumerable private groups, chambers of commerce, advocates of "preparedness," and special organizations, the most important of which was the National Americanization Committe (NAC).

The NAC, which evolved out of earlier organizations dedicated to a cosmopolitan-nationalist, reform-oriented approach, illustrates the second significant change in this phase of the movement. Its director, Frances A. Kellor, had a background in social work and strong progressive commitments. Aptly described as "half reformer, half nationalist," by 1915 Kellor had allowed her national inclinations to take charge, although they were still integrated with a Rooseveltian, progressive belief in efficiency, scientific planning, and rational control. Under her leadership the NAC moved clearly in the direction of forced assimilation, and Kellor's 1916 book, *Straight America*, argued that military preparedness, industrial mobilization, universal service, and Americanization were all essential to a more vital nationalism.

Kellor and the NAC were also deeply involved in a third significant feature of wartime Americanization, the widespread participation in the movement of manufacturers who employed immigrants. Usually courses in English and citizenship were grafted on to existing programs of welfare work or industrial betterment, which had been gaining ground since the turn of the century. They were products of the emerging subprofession of personnel management, and though an expression of enlightened self-interest on the part of employers, the health and safety education programs and the general improvement of working conditions in the plant also benefited workers. The addition of Americanization classes may be thought of as bringing to a new level of self-consciousness the linkage between assimilation to American culture and the acclimation of preindustrial immigrants to factory discipline, which has been a recurrent feature of American social history.

Americanization reached its most feverish level in the third phase of the movement, which occurred in the context of postwar fear of social revolution. While antiradicalism reached panic level in the Red Scare, patriotic groups intensified their Americanization programs to inoculate the great mass of the immigrants against the revolutionary contagion being spread by the radical few. Businessmen were deeply involved in these programs, and Americanization became closely identified with welfare capitalism and antiunionism. But business leaders were generally more moderate than groups such as the National Security League and the American Legion. Strongly nativistic, they called for the deportation of alien radicals and resorted to high-pressure propaganda tactics. Many state and local authorities stepped up their efforts by restricting the use of languages other than English in the schools, by requiring public school teachers to be American citizens, and (in an Oregon law declared unconstitutional in

1925) by compelling all elementary-age children to attend public schools.

The relatively few liberals who had taken the sympathetic "immigrant gifts" approach to Americanization withdrew in disgust at the reactionary chauvinism of the movement in the postwar years. Immigrant spokesmen likewise openly expressed their resentment of cultural aggression against their language and customs in the name of Americanization, which in its last phase was thought of almost exclusively in narrow and nativistic terms. The Ku Klux Klan's appropriation of the term Americanism reinforced the same association and further discredited the whole idea.

The major legacy of the movement was to make Americanization a bad word, even in its generic sense of assimilation. Although this development was understandable, it created a problem in respect to national identity, because it made the national name disreputable. It also gave rise to a situation in which those who resisted Americanization on the practical level (as assimilation) and reviled it as an idea could claim to be the truest Americanists of all. This is roughly what happened after the introduction of the idea of cultural pluralism, which implied resistance in practice and rejection in principle of Americanization as assimilation. One reason that cultural pluralism seemed so attractive by contrast was that Americanization had been closely linked to Anglo-Saxon racialism and was therefore adversely affected by the reaction against racism that took root among intellectuals in the 1920s and spread to broader strata of the population in the next decades.

Anglo-Saxon Racialism Anglo-Saxonism began as a form of ethnic pride; eventually it became, or was absorbed into, a much harsher form of racism understood as a scientific doctrine linking the qualitative status of different peoples (that is, whether they placed high or low on an absolute scale of civilization) to biologically determined factors that were passed on genetically from one generation to the next. As used here, the term "racialism" embraces both the earlier, prescientific Anglo-Saxonism and the rigid, naturalistic racism that reached a climax in the first quarter of the 20th century. Throughout its development, Anglo-Saxon racialism was intimately related to ideas of American nationality, but significant changes took place in the way the relationship was understood and the implications it was thought to have for immigration policy and intergroup relations.

The roots of Anglo-Saxonism go back to the political controversies of the English Civil War in the mid-17th century. The champions of Parliament portrayed their struggle with Charles I as a defense of the immemorial liberties of the English people against the tendencies toward royal absolutism implanted by the introduction of feudal law at the time of the Norman conquest. The contrast between the despotic "Norman yoke" and the "Gothic liberties" of Anglo-Saxon times were elaborated during the Commonwealth period and kept alive after the Stuart Restoration; this contrast became one of the elements of the "true Whig" or "country" ideology of 18th-century republicanism, both in England and in the American colonies.

Anglo-Saxonism was thus closely identified from the first with love of freedom, dedication to republicanism, and a commitment to law and limited government. Al-

lied to these political qualities were such domestic and personal virtues as respect for womanhood, honesty, simplicity, and bravery. This ensemble remained the substantive core of Anglo-Saxonism, but it came to be understood in more distinctively racial terms; that is, a commitment to liberty and republicanism was no longer regarded merely as the political heritage of the Anglo-Saxons, but as their native genius, the form of social life and organization toward which they were innately disposed and for which they were peculiarly well suited.

Romanticism accounted for the new racial stress in Anglo-Saxonism; races or nations were thought of as collective entities with lives of their own, each having characteristic qualities—its *Volksgeist* or national soul. Romantic fascination with these matters was reflected in early-19th-century historical studies, the study of languages and folklore, and ethnological curiosity about the races and cultures of man. The romantic view of the Anglo-Saxons as a simple, upright, freedom-loving race was popularized by Sharon Turner's *History of the Anglo-Saxons* (1799–1805) and by Walter Scott's portrayal of the clash between Saxons and Normans in *Ivanhoe* (1817). By mid-century, Anglo-Saxonism in England had developed into a full-blooded racialist version of nationalism, which exalted the special virtues of the Saxons and contrasted them to the inadequacies of other races, particularly the Celts of Ireland.

This kind of thinking was slower to develop in the United States, an Anglo-Saxon country at one remove from the homeland. Another possible handicap to its development was that the most race-conscious group in America—southern slaveholders—identified themselves with the Norman elite of post-Conquest England, rather than with the subjugated Saxons. Yet the mounting Anglo-Saxon enthusiasm in England found echoes in the United States. An American edition of Sharon Turner's history was published in 1841, and a decade later a writer in *North American Review* observed that "of late years, we have come to call ourselves Anglo-Saxons in common parlance." In 1843 George Perkins Marsh traced the origins of New England institutions back to the forests of Germany in his *Goths in New England*, combining anti-Celticism and militant anti-Catholicism with his Gothic passion. It was generally accepted that Protestantism was the natural religious expression of the freedom-loving, independent-thinking Anglo-Saxons, while Catholicism was best suited to the more servile peoples who lived under Latin forms of despotism. Even Brownson, the Catholic convert, distinguished between "Romanic" and "Germanic" traditions, the former identified with submission to the ruler, while the latter provided for a freer kind of cooperation in self-government. And as we have seen, Brownson believed that the American nationality was already set in a fundamentally Anglo-Saxon mold.

Ante-bellum Anglo-Saxonism was more closely linked with the expansionist version of American nationalism than with its nativist version. Fundamentally it was an expression of ethnic pride by the American cultural majority, those of English background who gloried in the heroic virtues and splendid achievements of their ancestors and who associated their own national accomplishments with this virile heritage.

Anglo-Saxonism was interwoven with the ideological and religious aspects of the national identity. Although racial, it had more to do with a romantically understood racial "character" than with the biological transmission of fixed physical attributes. It was inclusive rather than exclusive, as the *North American Review* asserted in 1851. "We are the most mixed race that ever existed; and yet the admixture has never been such as to weaken or impoverish the original Saxon stock; on the contrary, it has infused into it new life and energy."

After the Civil War, those who were most conscious of springing from "old American stock" continued to promulgate Anglo-Saxonism as their version of ethnic nationalism. The connection between Anglo-Saxonism and the nation's free institutions was reinforced by the historical works of Edward A. Freeman, whose enthusiastic Teutonism was almost as popular in the United States as in his native England; by John Fiske, who interpreted the federal system as America's distinctive addition to the Saxon tradition of self-government; and by Herbert Baxter Adams, who made the "germ theory" of Teutonic origins the orthodox paradigm for historical investigations at Johns Hopkins University. Josiah Strong's widely read *Our Country* (1886) appealed to the Anglo-Saxon heritage as part of his effort to arouse Americans to meet their religious and patriotic responsibilities in a rapidly changing world. The association of Anglo-Saxonism with America's mission to extend the blessings of free institutions to other peoples reached a climax in turn-of-the-century imperialism.

There was in all this a clear continuity with ante-bellum Anglo-Saxonism and confidence that the incomparably vigorous Saxon race would go on extending its beneficent influence. But in the 1880s and 1890s another and more ominous strain of thought developed, which called attention to the threats to Anglo-Saxon predominance and the national identity rooted in that racial heritage. This modulation toward a defensive and hostile version of racialism, useful not merely to enhance the pride of its adherents but even more to measure the inferiority and undesirability of others, was one of two major shifts that took place in Anglo-Saxon race-thinking between the Gilded Age and World War I. In a second, closely related development, Anglo-Saxonism was linked to scientific racism, which was understood as a matter of biological and physical-anthropological determinism.

New England was the earliest center of the defensive form of racial Anglo-Saxonism, and its patrician class was at the forefront of the transition. Anxieties stemming from the economic and cultural decline of the region and the slippage in status of the Brahmin elite contributed to a growing hostility toward immigrants, whose increasing numbers, growing political influence, and discordant foreign ways made the race-proud Anglo-Saxon aristocrats feel like aliens in their own homeland. In the 1890s racialist opposition focused on the new immigrants from eastern and southern Europe. The Immigration Restriction League, founded in Boston in 1894, dedicated itself to reducing the stream of new immigrants by pushing for the enactment of a literacy test.

Although some promoters of the literacy test frankly avowed their intention to protect the Anglo-Saxon basis of American nationality from dilution by lesser breeds, it is significant that the restrictive mechanism itself—

the literacy test—was not explicitly racial. Openly racial restrictive criteria were not incorporated into legislation until the 1920s; the rapid dissemination of scientific racism, coupled with the blending of race-thinking and panicky xenophobia in the early 1920s, made possible the enactment of the national-origins quota system in 1924. Racial ideas had taken on scientific coloring earlier through association with notions of evolutionary progress, especially with the Spencerian version of social Darwinism, understood as a competitive struggle among different social groups for survival and dominance. After 1900, however, scientific racism became notably more precise and stringent through the popularization of Mendelian genetics in biology and the physiographic measurement and classification of races carried out by anthropologists.

William Z. Ripley's *Races of Europe* (1899) synthesized the anthropological studies and supplied a threefold classification of European peoples into the Teutonic, Alpine, and Mediterranean races. Ripley himself was only a mild Teutonist and stressed environmental, rather than hereditary, factors in accounting for differences between races. But his typology accorded nicely with the traditional distinctions used by those who preached a stark Teutonic supremacy, and it fitted the needs of restrictionists who wished to protect Anglo-Saxon culture from the contamination of inferior Alpine and Mediterranean stocks. It was commonly assumed at the time that cultural traits were inherited along with physical attributes, and the restrictionists drew impressive support from the new science of eugenics for their view that the indiscriminate mixing of races was more likely to result in cultural debasement than cultural improvement.

Racialist doctrine was given its most systematic and influential statement in Madison Grant's *The Passing of the Great Race*, published in 1916. For Grant, "race pure and simple, the physical and psychical structures of man" lay at the basis of every manifestation of human creativity, and the Nordic was "the master race" that had led humanity upward since the dawn of civilization. He flatly denied the traditional American premise of equality, characterized the idea of the melting pot as "folly," and warned Americans that "this generation must completely repudiate the proud boast of our fathers that they acknowledged no distinction in "'race, creed, or color.'" Grant made no effort to conceal his hatred and contempt for the "human flotsam" of the new immigration. He regarded as "pathetic and fatuous" the belief that such miserable human materials could be transformed into acceptable citizens through the influence of American institutions and environment. Racial self-preservation clearly demanded restriction of immigration, and in the introduction to the fourth edition of his book in 1921 Grant observed with satisfaction that "one of the most far-reaching effects of the doctrines enunciated in this volume and in the discussions that followed its publication was the decision . . . to adopt discriminatory and restrictive measures against the immigration of undesirable races and peoples."

The racism preached by Grant and by popularizers like Lothrop Stoddard did play a decisive role in shaping the restrictive laws of the 1920s. Indeed, the principle of racial selectivity remained in force until the immigration law of 1965 abandoned the national-origins quota

system. But as a scientific doctrine and a popular intellectual force, racism began to recede almost as soon as the national-origins system was enacted, and by the end of the decade the tide was clearly running against racism. Psychologists who had earlier interpreted the results of World War I army intelligence tests as confirming inborn racial differences shifted to an environmental explanation of the differences, and in anthropology the critique of racism mounted by Franz Boas and his students carried the day. Observation of the grotesque extremes of Nazi racism in the next decade and the revelation of its ghastly consequences during World War II utterly discredited racism as an idea and filled most Americans with repugnance for a theory so inhuman and opposed to democratic values.

Because of its identification with nativistic racialism, Anglo-Saxonism was also discredited. Although it had earlier been associated with liberal values, after 1930 Anglo-Saxonism seemed to intellectuals and social scientists the paradigm of narrow ethnocentrism. The term was not rehabilitated even by "consensus" writers of the 1950s who interpreted the American tradition more benignly than their "progressive" predecessors, and in the 1960s the acronymic WASP (white Anglo-Saxon Protestant) became the only ethnic slur permissible in enlightened circles. Like "melting pot" and "Americanization," the term "Anglo-Saxon" symbolized ideas and values that were contrasted unfavorably to "cultural pluralism."

Cultural Pluralism The interpretation of ethnicity and American identity that came to be known as cultural pluralism was first presented in an article entitled "Democracy versus the Melting Pot: A Study of American Nationality," by Horace M. Kallen, which appeared in *The Nation* in February 1915. The article was reprinted in a collection of Kallen's essays (one of which was a passionate attack on the Americanization movement) called *Culture and Democracy in the United States* (1924), in which Kallen introduced the term cultural pluralism to designate his radically anti-assimilationist viewpoint. An early commentator, Isaac B. Berkson, writing before the term cultural pluralism was coined, in *Theories of Americanization* (1920) characterized Kallen as calling for a "federation of nationalities" in the United States, which is a fairly accurate expression of Kallen's position. He held that ethnic nationalities neither should nor could be transformed into any generic American nationality. Indeed, he affirmed that although there had been a unitary American nationality, it had been dissipated by the great waves of immigration, with the result that by 1915, America was not a nation with its own distinctive nationality but a political state within which dwelt a number of different nationalities. In these circumstances Kallen saw but two policy options: to work for unison or for harmony. He believed that the first option—the attempt to enforce conformity to a common pattern—would violate America's democratic ideals and the spirit of its institutions. Hence he recommended the goal of harmony, holding out the vision of "a possible great and truly democratic commonwealth."

Its form would be that of the federal republic; its substance a democracy of nationalities, cooperating voluntarily and autonomously through common institutions in the enterprise of self-realization through the perfection of men ac-

cording to their kind. The common language of the commonwealth, the language of its great tradition, would be English, but each nationality would have for its emotional and involuntary life its own peculiar dialect or speech, its own individual and inevitable esthetic and intellectual forms. The political and economic life of the commonwealth is a single unit and serves as the foundation and background for the realization of the distinctive individuality of each *natio* that composes it and of the pooling of these in a harmony above them all. Thus "American civilization" may come to mean the perfection of the cooperative harmonies of "European civilization"—the waste, the squalor and the distress of Europe being eliminated—a multiplicity in a unity, an orchestration of mankind.

This passage is the closest Kallen ever came to operationalizing the concept of cultural pluralism or to describing in practical terms the kind of situation its application would produce. Its extreme sketchiness and the obscurity of the language help explain why the idea is so hard to pin down and why the term was later used in so many different ways. It has always been more a vision than a rigorous theory.

Despite the vagueness and generality of Kallen's vision, several points are clear from the quoted passage and the discussion that preceded it. First, Kallen regarded his prescription as being more authentically American than the program of the Americanizers. Indeed, he saw cultural pluralism as the next logical stage of true Americanism, while forced-assimilation programs actually contravened American principles. According to Kallen, Americans were beginning to understand that "the political autonomy of the individual has presaged and is beginning to realize in these United States the spiritual autonomy of his group." But while there was growing appreciation of the fact that individual rights are fulfilled in group rights, this was by no means universally accepted by Americans. There was a real choice to be made between the two goals of unison or harmony. Kallen believed that unison could be achieved, but that to do so would require regimentation and controls that were incompatible with the basic law of the land and the traditional understanding of democratic procedures. The goal of harmony, on the contrary, was in line with realization that groups as well as individuals have rights and could usher in a "truly democratic" social order. While Kallen thus disagreed with the kind of program the 100-percent Americanizers espoused, he shared their convictions that the nation needed a positive policy in the area of ethnicity and national identity and that such a policy should be based upon the principles of the national ideology.

The second point to be underscored is that although Kallen envisioned a "democracy of nationalities" interacting within the same "federal republic," he was talking about cultural, not political, entities. Thus he spoke of the political autonomy of the individual giving rise to the spiritual (not political) autonomy of the group, and he portrayed the common political and economic system as furnishing the unitary foundation and background for the cultural realization of each distinctive *natio*. Kallen's pluralism was cultural because it dealt with such matters as the "emotional and involuntary life" of each group and the "peculiar dialect or speech . . . [the] individual and inevitable esthetic and intellectual forms" through which that life expressed itself. In 1924 Kallen dismissed critics who

were disturbed about what he called "the irrelevant political suggestion of the word 'nationality.'"

But Kallen could not justly complain if people misinterpreted his position on the political status of "nationalities," because he left the entire political dimension woefully underdeveloped from the theoretical standpoint. He said nothing about why American principles did not demand the same respect for an ethnic nationality's political and economic autonomy as for its spiritual autonomy. He gave no hint as to how the legitimate cultural claims of a natio were to be distinguished from any inadmissible political claims, nor what political means a natio might employ in trying to obtain or protect its cultural rights. Kallen likewise failed to specify any concrete features of the political program that would be required to put his pluralistic vision on the road to realization, much less bring it to the multicultural perfection of an orchestration of mankind.

The failure to take up these obvious theoretical problems seems particularly puzzling in a man who was a professional philosopher and a disciple of the great pragmatist, William James. The best explanation for this curious deficiency is that Kallen was in this respect an optimistic idealist rather than a pragmatist. He simply assumed that these problems would take care of themselves if all efforts at cultural regimentation were abandoned by Americanizers and other melting-pot enthusiasts. Contemplating the world "with the benign gaze of a romantic," John Higham observes, "Kallen lifted his eyes above the strife that swirled around him to an ideal realm where diversity and harmony eternally coexist."

Besides being a romantic in the sense that he prized diversity and assumed that differences would automatically blend into cooperative harmonies, Kallen was also a romantic in his racialism. Because cultural pluralism came to be understood as liberal, anti-Anglo-Saxon, and antiracialist, it comes as a surprise to discover that Kallen shared the kind of romantic racialism represented by Anglo-Saxonism before it was absorbed into biological racism. Kallen's racialism was romantic in that he valued diversity as such and did not attempt to rank human groups as superior or inferior according to any absolute scale of racial merit. But he also resembled the romantics in attributing the distinctive characteristics of peoples to inborn racial qualities whose origin and nature were obscure. He did not discuss them in clearcut biological or physical-anthropological terms, but "ancestry" played a crucial role, and even more central was a *Volksgeist*-like element of "inwardness."

In his 1915 essay Kallen spoke of respect for ancestors and pride of race as "primary and ultimate standards" and of a like-mindedness that was "inward, corporate and inevitable" because it sprang from "a homogeneity of heritage, mentality and interest." This like-mindedness, Kallen believed, was the necessary ground for the development of true freedom and equality, but it could not be generated by external conditions. Rather its "prepotent cause" was "a prevailing intrinsic similarity." Of the nationality of the immigrant Kallen wrote: "Behind him in time and tremendously in him in quality, are his ancestors; around him in space are his relatives and kin, carrying in common with him the inherited organic set from a remoter common ancestry. In all these he lives and moves and has his being. They constitute

his, literally, *natio*, the inwardness of his nativity." Because the immigrant "cannot change his grandfather," his nationality could never change. Kallen concluded that "What is inalienable in the life of mankind is its intrinsic positive quality—its psycho-physical inheritance." This was a crucial point, for it was the inward and inevitable nature of immigrant nationalities that required their having full pluralistic scope for development.

Chided by Isaac Berkson for the emphasis on race in his 1915 article, Kallen was quite unrepentant in his 1924 book. He characterized his critics as laboring "to prove over again the well-known anthropological commonplace that race is a concept the underlying facts of which are contradictory," but at the same time he commended those who recognized the persistence and influence of heredity, and he insisted that "intermarriage or no intermarriage, racial quality persists, and is identifiable . . . to the end of generations." In 300 years intermarriage among white peoples in America had not produced a new race; rather the "older types" persisted, despite a superficial uniformity among all Americans accounted for by the school system, the mass media, and so on.

Race, culture, family socialization, and nationality were all blurred together in Kallen's discussion. Concerning the "great tradition of Europe," he wrote: "Race, in its setting, is at best what individualizes the common [cultural] heritage, imparting to it presence, personality, and force." In some "vague . . . not well analyzed, and much misrepresented [way], race reacts selectively to culture"; hence, despite their other artistic accomplishments, the British were deficient in music, the Germans in architecture, the French in poetry. How were these temperamental differences between races perpetuated? Kallen seemed here to invoke a nonhereditary, family-socialization explanation. "Birth, which we do not choose," he wrote, "carries with it simultaneously certain cultural acquirements of a nature so basic, so primary, as to be indistinguishable from inheritance. The acquirements are, in fact, the infant's immediate social inheritance. They are the aboriginal impressions from the familial *milieu*." But Kallen did not systematically develop the distinction between biological and cultural inheritance, and his concluding statement brought physical inheritance again into prominence and linked race with nationality. All human associations, he stated, "have constituted communities tending to preserve and to sustain the continuity of the physical stock. Empirically, race is nothing more than this continuity confirmed and enchanneled in basic social inheritances. It is hardly distinguishable from nationality."

I have discussed at some length the racialist dimension of Kallen's original statement of cultural pluralism and his additional commentary in 1924 for several reasons. In the first place it is not widely known that racialism played any positive role in the tradition of cultural pluralism. Although Berkson drew critical attention to the racialist assumptions of Kallen's original formulation, cultural pluralism received very little attention of any kind for a number of years thereafter, and when it did begin to gain some currency in the late 1930s it was regarded simply as an attractively liberal and tolerant alternative to the melting pot or forced

Americanization and was not associated in any way with racialism, which by that time had become much more disreputable.

Second, the racialist element was central to Kallen's argument that true democracy required cultural pluralism. Kallen believed that "the enterprise of self-realization," which it was the responsibility of democratic government to facilitate, could be successfully carried out only among groups whose members were inwardly like-minded, whose "inalienable selfhood" derived from common racial inheritance. From this it followed that democratic policy should "seek to provide conditions under which each [group] might attain the cultural perfection that is *proper to its kind.*"

Third, Kallen's racialism was also central to his conviction that ethnic nationalities would perpetuate themselves indefinitely. In this regard, he fully agreed with Anglo-Saxon nativists like Edward A. Ross, whose *The Old World in the New* (1914) apparently prompted Kallen's original article, and Henry Pratt Fairchild, who called the melting pot a "mistake" because "races" do not blend but go on being what they are despite the American environment. Kallen's conviction may also account for his failure to discuss the problem of *how* ethnic nationalities were to protect themselves from the inroads of assimilation, which had long been a danger to the integrity of ethnic cultures. This whole area is ambiguous, however, because although Kallen's language in the long passage quoted earlier indicates that he anticipated the indefinite perpetuation of ethnic phenomena, such as the mother tongue and societies, in another place he speaks of a group's undergoing changes but not losing its continuity, "even if it loses its memory." This seems to suggest that group identity would persist even after the loss of the cultural forms in which it expresses itself.

The fourth point to be emphasized is that Kallen's whole handling of race was extremely ambiguous. He was certainly not a strict biological racist like Madison Grant, but neither did he systematically distinguish between biological and cultural elements in the manner of Franz Boas. On the contrary, Kallen's discussion blurred the distinction Boas was trying to establish between a group's cultural heritage and its biological "continuity of physical stock." Moreover, Kallen talked about "nationalities" as embodying this undifferentiated inheritance in such a way as to make it virtually impossible to determine which elements of an ethnic group's identity were genetically determined and which were culturally transmitted.

Kallen never clarified these issues, and those who came after him in the pluralist tradition apparently failed to recognize them (except for Milton Gordon) and certainly failed to address them. Therefore the crucial role of Kallen's ambiguous racialist assumptions still constitutes a major theoretical problem in the cultural pluralist interpretation of ethnicity and American identity.

Kallen's assumption of automatic harmony among dozens of ethnic nationalities, each encouraged to develop its "spiritual autonomy" to the fullest, constitutes a second major theoretical ambiguity in cultural pluralism. Kallen himself simply postulated the elimination of the hatred and conflict that had historically marked the coexistence of different nationalities in Europe. He said nothing about how this happy circumstance was to be attained, and although later commentators denied that cultural pluralism would produce Balkanization and a clash of ethnic nationalities in the United States, none explained just what feature of the theory was to forestall such an eventuality.

Perhaps one reason these conceptual weaknesses have been so persistently overlooked is that Kallen's formulation did not attract wide attention for some time, and when the term cultural pluralism did gain currency, it was used very loosely and with small regard for what Kallen meant by it. The most significant early notice came from Randolph Bourne, who acknowledged his debt to Kallen in a 1916 *Atlantic Monthly* article on "Trans-National America," and from Isaac Berkson and Julius Drachsler, who dealt more critically with Kallen's ideas in studies of assimilation published in 1920. These matters seemed less pressing, however, after the 1924 national-origins law virtually cut off the flow of European immigration. Thus, interest in assimilation and related issues began to wane almost precisely at the moment that Kallen introduced the term cultural pluralism. Those who did discuss cultural pluralism generally equated it with a liberal approach to Americanization—one that encouraged immigrants to retain their distinctive cultures during a period of initial adjustment, but anticipated eventual assimilation and the emergence of cultural unity.

By the late 1930s growing concern about prejudice and intergroup relations was reflected in Francis J. Brown and Joseph S. Roucek's compendious *Our Racial and National Minorities,* first published in 1937, reprinted in 1939, and revised in two later editions. Part IV was headed "The Trend toward Cultural Pluralism," but none of the authors in that section referred to Kallen, nor did his name appear in the 66-page bibliography. The section on cultural pluralism stressed the contributions made by Indians, Negroes, and immigrants to American culture, urged preservation of "the best that each group has brought," and noted the desirability of preserving "the fundamentals of [immigrant] heritages . . . for generations." Yet the writer who treated these matters most explicitly, E. George Payne, a prominent educational theorist at New York University, also denied that cultural pluralism meant "the ultimate preservation of different cultural streams in our civilization." Although he could see "no harm" in such a result, he regarded some degree of acculturation as inevitable and was confident that "a new and superior culture will emerge." Cultural pluralism, Payne concluded, "does not imply that the special cultures will continue unchanged in the general stream for all time. The theory involves essentially a technique of social adjustment which will make possible the preservation of the best of all cultures . . ."

World War II added urgency to the task of improving intergroup relations. Cultural pluralism came into its own as a term designating both the actual existence of social diversity and the belief that such diversity was good, provided it was not accompanied by ethnocentrism, prejudice, or discrimination among the diverse groups. As it gained in popularity, however, cultural pluralism lost all semblance of conceptual rigor, becoming ever more vacuous and bland. Ostensibly it was an alternative to assimilation, but it implicitly assumed

a degree of consensus sufficient to rule out serious tensions among groups. At the same time the growing tendency to employ the word pluralism (and derivatives such as pluralistic) without the modifier "cultural" made the concept all the more generalized and indeterminate.

Thus by the 1950s, cultural pluralism had become very popular and at the same time quite problematic as to content and meaning. I shall return to this matter in discussing the most recent period.

The most important point about the period 1860–1924 is that ethnicity assumed greater salience as an element in the national identity than it has had at any other time before or since. Especially during the first quarter of the 20th century, the ethnic factors of "race," nationality, language, and so on were the issues that sprang immediately to mind when Americans asked themselves, "What does it mean to be an American? What kind of Americanism do we want?" The four interpretations reviewed—the melting pot, Americanization, Anglo-Saxon racialism, and cultural pluralism—represent different ways of articulating the national self-understanding so as to answer those questions and at the same time indicate the general lines of policy that should be followed to realize the goals.

There were significant differences among the four perspectives, but they also overlapped with each other, which was inevitable in view of the elusive quality of matters relating to national identity. The four perspectives were subject to different interpretation because they had to be broad and multivalent in order to function as symbols for the processes and goals they represented. It should not be too surprising that the melting pot has been both equated with and contrasted to Americanization, or that some of the post-Kallen versions of cultural pluralism have been characterized as liberal Americanization and closely resemble a relaxed and tolerant version of the melting pot.

The four perspectives can be most usefully distinguished according to whether their inherent tendency is toward unity or multiplicity, whether they place greater stress on the *unum* or the *pluribus* in the national motto. The melting pot and cultural pluralism aspire to encompass both, but the former is assimilationist in tendency and assigns priority to unity, while the latter is antiassimilationist and, as originally articulated, looks to the preservation of a multiplicity of distinct ethnic nationalities. The melting pot envisions an overarching national culture and a distinctive American identity to which various ethnic cultures and identities would contribute, but into which they would be integrated as constituents, disappearing as separate cultural entities. *Pluribus* is thus taken into account, but is subordinated to and assimilated into *unum*. By contrast, Kallen's cultural pluralism leaves *unum* to take care of itself, so to speak, while making specific provision for *pluribus*, for the preservation of ethnic-cultural entities, not as contributors to a single distinctive national identity, but as equal partners in a pluralized, harmonious national identity.

Both Americanization and Anglo-Saxon racialism focused more exclusively on unity than did the melting pot. They had earlier been interpreted in a more liberal manner, but they came to mean that there was only one kind of acceptable American. Conformity to that version of cultural unity was required of all immigrants, who were not regarded as having anything valuable of their own to contribute to the national culture or identity. Americanization was more optimistic, because it assumed the immigrants could be systematically brought into conformity with the minimal requirements of Americanism; Anglo-Saxon racialism, however, finally denied that this was possible unless the immigrants were the right kind of racial material to start with. Americanization implied forced assimilation to one cultural pattern; racialism implied exclusion of all who did not already fit that pattern.

Just as these approaches may be ranged abstractly along a unity–multiplicity spectrum, their popularity or dominance can be aligned with the concern for unity at different times. Generally speaking, tolerant and inclusive versions of the melting pot, Americanization, and Anglo-Saxonism dominated during most of the 19th century, when national unity did not seem threatened by ethnic diversity. Uneasiness grew in the 1890s, however, as the flood of new immigration was coupled in the public mind with various forms of social, economic, and political unrest; during the crisis of World War I uneasiness became deep concern and was specifically linked with the dangers posed to national unity by the divided loyalties of "hyphenated Americans." In these circumstances faith in the automatic processes of the melting pot gave way, first to an active commitment to Americanization and then to a racialist-tinged despair over the nation's capacity to integrate the immigrants. Once restriction had been accomplished, Americans could afford to relax about national unity. They even became a little embarrassed about their former anxiety-induced narrowness and took a more benign view of cultural differences still existing. At this point, cultural pluralism began to gain general acceptance, but in a hazy form that differentiated it from assimilation much less sharply than when it was introduced by Horace Kallen.

Kallen's defense of multiplicity may also be understood as a response to the crisis of national unity in World War I. It seems clear that he was prompted to publish his pluralistic theory because of the extreme forms that the drive for unity was taking. At a time when members of ethnic minorities were being told, in effect, that they could not be good Americans if they continued to be who they were, it was fitting to articulate a philosophy of minority rights that justified their resistance to such campaigns and taught them that American principles could be marshaled in their defense. And perhaps cultural pluralism became less sharply differentiated from assimilation a generation later, not only because of *de facto* acculturation, but also because members of ethnic minorities were not subject to the same sort of insulting external pressures.

A final point about the salience of ethnicity as a dimension of American identity in this era concerns the central role played by Jewish immigration and Jewish intellectuals. The coming of about 2 million eastern European Jews between 1870 and 1914 made the Jews a numerically very significant element in the new immigration; their visibility and impact was heightened by their concentration in New York City; in 1915 they numbered about 1.4 million and constituted 28 percent of the city's population. Antisemitism developed along

with nativism and lent a special edge to the cultural pessimism of a patrician like Henry Adams or a racialist aristocrat like Madison Grant, both of whom despised Jews, while E.A. Ross lamented in *The Old World in the New* that Jews could not be made into good Boy Scouts! In the xenophobic 1920s, popular anti-semitism was reflected in the Ku Klux Klan and fed by the calumnies circulated in Henry Ford's newspaper, the *Dearborn Independent.*

But far more important than the negative reaction against Jews was the positive role played by Jewish intellectuals who dealt with the question of ethnicity and American identity. Israel Zangwill and Horace Kallen were both Jews. Zangwill was English; Kallen, though German-born, had lived in the United States since early childhood. Both were highly self-conscious about their Jewishness: Kallen was a Zionist, and Zangwill, who was one of the founders of Zionism, broke with the majority in 1905 and founded the variant form known as "territorialism." Berkson and Julius Drachsler, early commentators on the melting pot and pluralism, were also Jewish and were specifically concerned with problems of Jewish survival and assimilation. Franz Boas, who did more than any other individual to refute racialism as a scientific doctrine, was also Jewish. And Randolph Bourne's adaptation of Kallen's ideas was an early milestone in the formation of the cosmopolitan, but heavily Jewish, New York intelligentsia.

In short, Jews played the same central role in the emergence of ethnicity as a salient element in the understanding of American identity that Catholics had earlier played in the emergence of religion as a prominent element. Blacks were to play a somewhat similar role in the next phase of the story.

ETHNICITY RECESSIVE AND RESURGENT (1924–1979)

Several of the terms and concepts reviewed in the previous section have continued in use to the present day, but their persistence is not the most notable feature of the era since the closing of massive overseas immigration. When considered as a unit, what is most striking about the past half-century is the ebbing and resurgence of ethnicity as a dimension of American identity. Two major themes interact; the first is the powerful reaffirmation of American ideology as the basis of national identity, which dominated the scene from World War II to the mid-1960s, and whose crests and troughs are inversely related to those of the ethnic impulse. The second is the issue of the status and condition of black Americans, which became increasingly central in the 1950s and 1960s, and whose evolution reveals most clearly the modulation from an ideological to an ethnic emphasis. Other features of the period that deserve attention are the explicit interest in the "American character" in the 1940s and early 1950s, and the growing involvement of social scientists (and to a lesser extent historians) in national-character studies and the resurgence of ethnicity, as well as in studies of blacks and the racial question.

Intense concern with ethnicity began to ebb in 1924. The national-origins law not only removed the issue from center stage politically, it also inaugurated an era in which the processes of assimilation gave the whole immigrant-derived population a more "Americanized" aspect. Ethnocultural passions played a prominent role in Al Smith's 1928 presidential campaign, but that contest proved to be a kind of epilogue to the period. The crash of 1929 and the Depression turned people's attention from cultural issues to elemental bread-and-butter concerns. National self-confidence rallied under Franklin D. Roosevelt, but neither New Dealers nor ordinary citizens gave much thought to ethnicity or national identity during the Depression decade.

The atmosphere of liberalism that prevailed under the New Deal did, however, encourage interest in intergroup relations in the later 1930s. The appearance of Brown and Roucek's 1937 book has already been noted; much other social science research was synthesized in William C. Smith's *Americans in the Making* (1939), significantly subtitled "The Natural History of the Assimilation of Immigrants." In history a cluster of outstanding works published between 1938 and 1941— Ray Allen Billington's *The Protestant Crusade,* Carl Wittke's *We Who Built America,* Marcus Hansen's *The Atlantic Migration* and *The Immigrant in American History,* and Oscar Handlin's *Boston's Immigrants*— marked a new level of visibility and sophistication for immigration historiography.

These historical works were sympathetic to the immigrant, but none of them claimed that ethnic groups had preserved their cultural identity in the pluralistic manner described by Kallen two decades earlier, nor did any of them imply that ethnic groups should do so. Insofar as they dealt with the matter at all, and allowing for differences of emphasis, these authors held to something like the classical version of the melting pot—that is, their accounts portrayed immigrant groups coming to the United States, meeting with various vicissitudes (including nativistic hostility), interacting with the host society, and eventually becoming part of that society, while at the same time contributing to it something distinctive from their own heritage. Like the subtitle of William Smith's book, the subtitle of another excellent historical work, Theodore Blegen's *Norwegian Immigration to America: The American Transition* (1940), epitomized the assumption of scholars of that era that they were describing a process of Americanization, the gradual blending of many diverse elements into one people.

All tendencies to underscore Americanism and national unity were massively reinforced by the entry of the United States into World War II. Indeed it would be difficult to exaggerate the importance of the war as the central event in shaping Americans' understanding of their national identity for the next generation.

On the level of practical social reality, the war was a great common experience, especially for the 12 million young men and women who served in the armed forces, but also for the whole population, which shared "for the duration" anxieties, privations, losses, hopes, and in the end, exhilaration. The feeling that "we're all in this together" was strong, inconceivably so to the Vietnam War generation. The typical war movie featured an Italian, a Jew, an Irishman, a Pole, and assorted "old American" types from the Far West, the hills of Tennessee, and so on, and this motif was not confined to Hollywood. The same image of military life as a kind of melting pot appeared in the winter 1942 issue of *Common Ground,* a journal put out by the Common Council for American Unity, which was dedicated to strengthening

national cohesiveness by improving mutual understanding among the diverse groups in the population.
Participation in the war effort gave even the newest immigrants a livelier sense of belonging to the national
community. Howard Stein and Robert Hill in *The Ethnic Imperative* (1977), emphasize the significance of
wartime experiences in broadening the horizons and
hastening the assimilation of second- and third-generation immigrants in the Pittsburgh area.

Even more important was the accentuation of the
ideological basis of American identity that accompanied the wartime crisis. This development was perfectly understandable in view of the challenge posed by
the rise of totalitarianism and the frightening spectacle
of Nazi arms sweeping across Europe. As Carl Becker
acknowledged in vindicating "some generalities that
still glitter" in 1940, it was Nazism that "brought into
strong relief [democracy's] essential virtues," even for
those, like Becker himself, who had previously found
much to criticize in American democracy. In these circumstances, Americans were sensitized to ideology, as
noted in 1943 by one of the keenest students of intergroup relations, Robert E. Park. They became highly
self-conscious affirmers of their own system of values,
having been galvanized to a fresh appreciation of freedom, equality, and the other principles of American democracy by the monstrous contrast of Nazism.

The implications of this ideological reawakening for
ethnicity and its relation to national identity were
brought out clearly in the statement of purposes on the
inside cover of *Common Ground*, edited in its first year
and a half by Louis Adamic. The Common Council for
American Unity (known earlier as the Foreign Language
Information Service) listed the first of its purposes as:

> To help create among the American people the unity and
> mutual understanding resulting from a common citizen-
> ship, a common belief in democracy and the ideals of lib-
> erty, the placing of the common good before the interests
> of any group, and the acceptance, in fact as well as in law,
> of all citizens, whatever their national or racial origins, as
> equal partners in American society.

The statement called for appreciation of the contributions of each group, for tolerance of diversity, for the
creation of an American culture "truly representative"
of all the people, for an end to racial or ethnic prejudice,
and for assistance to immigrants or their children who
encountered difficulties in adjusting to American life.

Here ethnicity and pluralism of a sort were taken
seriously into account. But although they were portrayed as important features, they were not the basic
elements of the national identity. Rather it was identification with a set of universal ideas and values that
made Americans what they were, despite differences of
race, religion, or national background. Acceptance of all
groups on an equal basis and tolerance of ethnic diversity derived as corollaries from "a common belief in democracy and the ideals of liberty." They were crucial
corollaries, to be sure, but they were derivative from,
not constitutive of, the essence of Americanism.

The need to emphasize both the ideological core and
the ethnic-tolerance corollary was particularly pressing
when *Common Ground* began publication in the fall of
1940. An "Editorial Aside" in the first issue explained
the reasons: "We begin in difficult times. Never has it

been more important that we become intelligently
aware of the ground Americans of various strains have
in common . . . that we reawaken the old American
Dream, the dream which, in its powerful emphasis on
the fundamental worth and dignity of every human
being, can be a bond of unity no totalitarian attack can
break." American entry into the war made unity all the
more imperative, further heightening the stress on the
commitment to freedom and democracy that bound all
Americans together. And despite the prominence given
to the "from-many-lands" motif, ethnicity was in fact
compromised as a legitimate principle of group cohesiveness because of its kinship to the racialism and *volk-
isch* nationalism of the Nazis. The term ethnicity had
not yet come into use as a designation for group belongingness or a "sense of peoplehood," but ethnocentrism
was very widely used and its connotations were wholly
negative; it meant the kind of group consciousness that
expressed itself in feelings of superiority toward others
and inspired prejudice and discrimination. The urgent
wartime need was to eliminate this kind of ethnic consciousness on the basis of the democratic ideology.

The prefatory remarks to the second and third editions of Brown and Roucek's volume bear witness to
the predominance of the ideological theme. Both of
these editions, published in 1946 and 1952, respectively, carry the main title *One America* as a testimony
to the authors' conviction that "in the crucible of war
we are moving toward a cultural democracy. We have
become and will remain One America." The substitution of the term "cultural democracy" for "cultural pluralism" made explicit the ideological basis of the appeal
for unity and ethnic tolerance. In 1952 Brown and Roucek insisted that deeper understanding of the roots of
America's heterogeneity was required if ethnocentrism
was to be avoided and "if democracy is to be a living reality for each of the 150,000,000 people who make up
our population." The third edition also showed that the
cold war continued, indeed sharpened, the ideological
accent. Because "the problems of America's minorities
[were] problems of world minorities," the nation's performance took on new significance. "The degree to
which we achieve equality of opportunity for each
American is of international consequence for it is a
basic propaganda weapon in the struggle between democracy and communism. Ideals, no matter how effectively portrayed, are counteracted even by isolated
manifestations of prejudice and discrimination." Race
relations was the crucial area in this respect.

The growth of interest in "the American character"
in the 1940s and 1950s had two sources, both associated
with World War II. Generically it was part of the intense curiosity about the United States and American
culture that resulted from the nation's new role as one
of two global superpowers and as the bastion of the
values of Western civilization. In this sense, American
character studies may be thought as part of the broader
American studies movement that grew up in the postwar years, not only in the United States but also in Europe and elsewhere.

More specifically, studies of the American character
were inspired by, and represented one variety of, investigations of national character by social scientists working for the U.S. government during the war. Margaret
Mead, author of one of the best-known examples of the

genre, *And Keep Your Powder Dry* (1942), later explained that she and other anthropologists were called upon by defense agencies to apply their skills to such questions as how civilian morale might be maintained under various conditions, such as bombing attacks, how friction between the British people and American troops could be minimized, what policies were best calculated to persuade the German or Japanese people to accept surrender, and so on.

In dealing with inquiries like these, Mead and her colleagues attempted to apply "at a distance" (without direct observation of the peoples involved) the techniques worked out in the 1930s by the culture-and-personality school of anthropology. Mead was one of the leaders of this school, which combined psychoanalytic assumptions about the crucial importance of infantile and childhood experience with ethnographic studies of child rearing and socialization patterns to identify the "basic personality structure" produced by the social needs and cultural norms of particular groups. "By the end of the war," Mead wrote in 1961, "the term 'national character' was being applied to studies that used anthropological methods from the field of culture and personality, psychiatric models from psychoanalysis, statistical analysis of attitude tests, and experimental models of small-group process."

The development of national-character studies is relevant to our concern with American identity for several reasons. Most obviously, it stimulated interest in the subject and made that interest more explicit. Before 1940 most commentary on national character was a by-product of discussions on history, religion, literature, or some other subject, written, for the most part, by humanistically inclined writers. When social scientists took up the question of national character during the war, it became an object of "scientific" study, and its lingering disreputability because of the previous connection with racial theories was removed. Now the national character was associated with a method of investigation that was regarded as the best hope of solving the problems confronting society.

It is of particular interest that Erik Erikson was associated with the social scientists engaged in wartime national character studies. His book *Childhood and Society* (1950) appeared at the height of the enthusiasm for such studies, and a chapter entitled "Reflections on the American Identity" was perhaps the first example of the use of the term identity in such a context. In the same book Erikson explicitly connected ethnicity with identity in the passage quoted at the beginning of this essay.

Erikson was not alone in associating ethnicity and identity. The immigrant experience also figured prominently in Mead's *And Keep Your Powder Dry* and Geoffrey Gorer's *The American People* (1948). Both writers employed an assimilationist perspective in that they obviously assumed that in the lives of immigrants Americanization had been a much more significant reality than preservation of ancestral cultures. Indeed, both writers focused on assimilation as the paradigmatic dimension of immigrant experience for understanding the American character. For Gorer the immigrant's rejection of the European past was paradigmatic; for Mead it was the ambiguities of third-generation status.

Gorer's first chapter, "Europe and the Rejected Father," opened with the immigrants' being required to give up their past and transform themselves into Americans. Those who immigrated as adults were unable fully to do so and hence became objects of disdain to their American-born children, who rejected them as role models and authority figures. "It is this break of continuity between the immigrants of the first generation and their children of the second generation which is . . . of major importance in the development of the modern American character," according to Gorer, who generalized along Freudian lines to account for Americans' rejection of authority, the minimal familial role of fathers as compared to mothers, and so on.

Much of this had been anticipated by Mead, although she did not stress the Freudian implications so strongly. References to the immigrant experience recurred throughout her book, and its ruling interpretive metaphor was developed in a chapter entitled "We Are All Third Generation." Mead's point was not so much that many Americans actually were third-generation immigrants, but that "most of us—whatever our origins—[are] third-generation in character structure . . . [because] we have been reared in an atmosphere which is most like that which I have described for the third generation." Mead summed up the third-generation mentality as follows:

Father is to be outdistanced and outmoded, but not because he is a strong representative of another culture, well entrenched, [and] not because he is a weak and ineffectual attempt to imitate a new culture; he did very well in his way, but he is out of date. He, like us, was moving forwards, moving away from something symbolized by his own ancestors, moving towards something symbolized by other people's ancestors . . . And to pass him it is only necessary to keep on going and to see that one buys a new model every year. Only if one slackens, loses one's interest in the race towards success, does one slip back. Otherwise, it is onward and upward, *towards* the world of Washington and Lincoln; a world in which we don't fully belong, but which we feel, if we work at it, we some time may achieve.

The ideological note, as in the reference to Washington and Lincoln, was strong, because Mead's aim was to marshal scientific self-understanding for the tasks of winning the war and building a better world. She was sensitive to the tensions between democracy and a social-engineering approach, but concluded that the two were compatible. "Those social behaviors which automatically preclude the building of a democratic world must go," she stated categorically; social science could contribute to this effort, it seemed, by showing how antidemocratic attitudes and institutions could be changed with the greatest possible tolerance and humanity.

The ideological dimension of the book is of considerable interest, especially because Mead recognized and dealt explicitly with the problem of the limits of tolerance. But the point that is most pertinent here is that for her, as for Gorer, the person of immigrant derivation was a prototypically American figure, not because of any distinctiveness of cultural heritage, but for exactly the opposite reason, because the ethnic exhibited in extreme degree the "character structure" produced by the American experience of change, mobility, and loss of

contact with the past. This interpretation was consistent with the picture of the immigrant experience portrayed in Oscar Handlin's *The Uprooted* (1951), doubtless the most widely read and influential book on immigration history. Published at the height of interest in the American character, *The Uprooted* began with the author's assertion that "the immigrants *were* American history," and the central metaphor of uprootedness could be applied to Americans generally. Handlin made the point explicit in his last chapter: "The newcomers were on the way toward being Americans almost before they stepped off the boat, because their own experience of displacement had already introduced them to what was essential in the situation of Americans."

Although it ended on the positive note that migration meant liberation and that uprootedness had called forth new creative energies, Handlin's moving portrayal of the immigrant's alienation and his elegiac tone gave *The Uprooted* a place in the literature of existentialist and mass-culture criticism of American society. Existentialist criticism dwelt on the rootlessness and alienation of modern man, his irrational fears and anxieties. The mass-culture theme, which often overlapped the existentialist, focused on the shallowness and superficiality of an "other-directed" people who were unduly preoccupied with material success and status symbols, conformist in attitude and thought, and easily aroused to hysterical outbursts of nativism, anti-intellectualism, or anti-Communism. Both types of criticism flourished mightily at mid-century.

All these themes—the ideological revival, the belief that immigrants were the archetypical Americans, and the existential and mass-culture critiques—interacted in shaping the highly elusive and contradictory understanding of pluralism and diversity that obtained in the 1950s. That understanding seemed to be that although Americans were a pluralistic people, they did not have much real diversity; they therefore needed more, but this diversity must never be divisive.

The first two assumptions reflected the belief that although immigrants came from many lands, the later generations were not only Americans all but had Americanized so thoroughly that they were fast becoming an indistinguishable part of a bland, homogenized, and conformist society. The conviction that America needed more diversity followed from the cultural critique as a remedial prescription and also grew out of the democratic commitment to tolerance; if diversity disappeared, would that not imply that we had been untrue to the principle of tolerance? But the diversity so much desired could not be of the sort that divided Americans against each other in any serious way. In respect to ideology, the limits of permissible diversity were sharply demarcated. Un-Americanism in the 1940s and 1950s was ideological rather than religious or ethnic. But religion too was an area where diversity had limits: one of the standard arguments in the controversy over public aid to parochial schools was that such schools were "divisive." It was an argument that carried weight even with liberals who bemoaned the homogenization of American life and regarded the anti-Communist crusade as a betrayal of American principles.

It is within this context that we can best approach

two significant books of the period, Horace Kallen's *Cultural Pluralism and the American Idea* (1956) and Will Herberg's *Protestant-Catholic-Jew* (1955).

Kallen's book, consisting of three lectures by the author, overwhelmingly favorable comments by nine other scholars, and a reprise by Kallen, was his first important statement on the subject since the 1920s. The volume, intended as the first in a series of studies in human relations to be published by the University of Pennsylvania, symbolized the degree to which cultural pluralism had become the conventional touchstone of enlightened wisdom. The fact that Kallen was invited to initiate the series also indicated that he had been rediscovered as the father of cultural pluralism. But Kallen's 1950s cultural pluralism was very different from what it had been 30 years before. All hint of racialism had disappeared, but so had the specifically ethnic quality of cultural pluralism, which now embraced the "diverse utterances of diversities—regional, local, religious, ethnic, esthetic, industrial, sporting and political . . ." And Americanization, which had been a movement to be resisted in the 1920s, had been replaced by an "Americanization, supporting, cultivating a cultural pluralism, grounded on and consummated in the American Idea."

Kallen's extremely diffuse notion of cultural pluralism implied a specific philosophical understanding of democracy, which he called "the American Idea." The longest essay in the collection was devoted to a Whitmanesque roll call of its prophets, symbols, doctrines, and the documents that constituted "the Bible of America." In replying to R.J. Henle, a Roman Catholic critic who challenged Kallen's tendency "to regard Americanism as an ultimate ideology, to make it a surrogate religion, and to identify it with cultural relativism," Kallen's language revealed how much his thinking had been affected by the ideological revival of World War II:

> Of course, then, the [American] Idea isn't a "surrogate" to any religion. Nor is it a substitute for all. It is that apprehension of human nature and human relations, which every sort and condition of Protestant, Catholic, Judaist, Moslem, Buddhist, and every other communion must agree upon, be converted to and convinced of, if they mean to live freely and peacefully together as equals, none penalizing the other for his otherness and all insuring each the equal protection of the law. And this is how the American Idea is, literally, religion.

In the 50s Kallen was as insistent as ever on pluralism, but it was pluralism bounded by a universally required commitment to Americanism, understood in quasi-religious terms.

Will Herberg, a "Judaist," approached the matter from a diametrically opposite position in his book. He meant to repudiate the tendency to erect "the American Idea" into what came to be called a civil religion in the 1960s. The situation needed unmasking, in Herberg's view, because traditional religionists had been misled by the contemporary revival of religion into thinking that their churches were gaining strength and influence, whereas they were in fact being reduced to the status of functionally useful supporters of "the American Way of Life,"—the *real* religion of Americans.

Herberg began with the paradox that America was

simultaneously experiencing a great revival of religion and a continuing growth of secularism. To explain this, he turned to the social psychology of an immigrant-derived people, suggesting that the resurgence of the churches resulted from the desire of third-generation immigrants to reestablish contact with their ancestral heritage. This inclination had first been noted by Marcus L. Hansen, and Herberg gave the name "Hansen's Law" to the formulation, "What the second generation wants to forget, the third generation wants to remember." According to Herberg, the religious dimension of an ethnic heritage was best suited for third-generation remembering for several reasons. First, it had persisted more successfully than other dimensions of immigrant culture, such as language, which had been almost completely eroded by assimilation. Second, the religious traditions had been Americanized and now suited the mentality of the third generation. Third, religion provided an effective vehicle of social identity by providing an answer to the question, "Who am I?" Finally, religion, which was much prized in American society, offered an attractive linkage to the past, whereas foreign "nationality" was not only fading away but was also suspect as a form of ethnocentrism.

Herberg thus portrayed the religious revival as deriving largely from the fact that religion served as a kind of residuary legatee of ethnic feeling. But why did the view that religion was good enjoy such widespread support in American society? Why did leading public figures like President Eisenhower insist so strongly that religion was indispensable to national well-being? The reason, Herberg said, was that the American ideology itself was a spiritual construct embodying such values as freedom and individual dignity, as well as more mundane elements associated with material progress, and it had always been closely associated with religion. In the early days it had been intertwined with Protestantism, but with the coming of the immigrants and the adjustment of their religious traditions to the new environment, Catholicism and Judaism took their places beside Protestantism as "the three great faiths of democracy." Hence Protestantism, Catholicism, and Judaism were socially praiseworthy because they constituted three equally acceptable ways for the individual to manifest his commitment to the "spiritual values" underlying the American way of life. Herberg greatly admired the American ideology, but he steadfastly opposed the tendency to erect it into a civil religion. No traditionally believing Christian or Jew, he said, could acquiesce in the view that religion was a good thing primarily because it furnished the spiritual underpinnings for a secular ideology.

Herberg's critique is particularly interesting as a contrast to Kallen's elevation of the American idea to religious status. Even more pertinent here is that both writers placed ideological consensus at the center of American identity, even though Kallen was considered the prophet of cultural pluralism, and Herberg stressed an ethnic explanation for the religious revival and drew attention to the fact that American religion had actually been pluralized, or at least trinitized.

The ideological element was equally prominent with respect to race relations, and what has already been said about the influence of World War II applies in this area too. Systematic study of race relations was hardly a dec-

ade old when the Carnegie Corporation in 1937 commissioned a massive investigation of the situation and prospects of the American Negro and selected the Swedish social scientist, Gunnar Myrdal, to direct the project. The enormous collaborative effort was completed the year after Pearl Harbor and appeared in 1944 as *An American Dilemma*. The dilemma was that the treatment of blacks in the United States was in direct contradiction to what Myrdal called "the American Creed," to which he believed Americans were genuinely committed, despite their sorry record of racial prejudice and discrimination.

Myrdal's concluding chapter, "America Again at the Crossroads," drew together several strands of argument and analyzed with remarkable prescience the forces that were to revolutionize race relations in the next generation. After stating that the war was crucial for Negroes and was bound to bring about a redefinition of their status, Myrdal reviewed the social trends that had brought the racial situation to the point that the war would have that effect. The most important was the gradual destruction of the theoretical basis for race prejudice, which was now regarded as a mark of ignorance. This development robbed white people of confidence and troubled their conscience, but it heartened black Americans, who were becoming better educated, more self-conscious, and more assertive. Myrdal summed up the state of affairs on the eve of World War II as follows:

> *America can never more regard its Negroes as a patient, submissive minority.* They will continually become less well "accommodated." They will organize for defense and offense. They will be more and more vociferous . . . They will have a powerful tool in the caste struggle against white America: the glorious American ideals of democracy, liberty, and equality to which America is pledged not only by its political Constitution but also by the sincere devotion of its citizens. The Negroes are a minority, and they are poor and suppressed, but they have the advantage that they can fight wholeheartedly. The whites have all the power, but they are split in their moral personality. Their better selves are with the insurgents. The Negroes do not need any other allies.

This was the shape of things when World War II broke out. Myrdal's assessment of its effect on the situation also deserves quotation:

> This War is an ideological war fought in defense of democracy. The totalitarian dictatorships in the enemy countries had even made the ideological issue much sharper . . . than it was in the First World War. Moreover, in this War the principle of democracy had to be applied more explicitly to race. Fascism and nazism are based on a racial superiority dogma—not unlike the old hackneyed American caste theory—and they came to power by means of racial persecution and oppression. In fighting fascism and nazism, America had to stand before the whole world in favor of racial tolerance and cooperation and of racial equality . . . It had to proclaim universal brotherhood and the inalienable human freedoms.

The war thus accelerated "an ideological process which was well under way," stimulated Negroes to exert greater pressure for change, and redoubled the discomfiture of white Americans at their failure to abide by the principles of freedom and equality in the area of race.

In the midst of this "dramatic stage of the American

caste struggle," Myrdal unerringly identified "a strategic fact of utmost importance . . . that the entire caste order is extra-legal if not actually illegal and unconstitutional." The Jim Crow laws of the South were only a partial exception, because "even they are written upon the fiction of equality" in the form of separate but equal treatment. The idea of legalizing a color-caste system on a national basis was never entertained, Myrdal declared, because that would be too radical a repudiation of the American creed.

> Caste may exist, but it cannot be recognized. Instead, the stamp of public disapproval is set upon it, and this undermines still more the caste theory by which the whites have to try to explain and justify their behavior. And *the Negroes are awarded the law as a weapon in the caste struggle.* Here we see in high relief how the Negroes in their fight for equality have their allies in the white man's own conscience. The white man can humiliate the Negro; he can thwart his ambitions; he can starve him; he can press him down into vice and crime; he can occasionally beat him and even kill him; but he does not have the moral stamina to make the Negro's subjugation legal and approved by society. Against that stands not only the Constitution and the laws which could be changed, but also the American Creed which is firmly rooted in the Americans' hearts.

On the basis of this analysis of the situation, Myrdal urged Americans to seize the opportunity presented for reform, for the principal conclusion of his study was that *"not since Reconstruction has there been more reason to anticipate fundamental changes in American race relations, changes which will involve a development toward the American ideals."* Developments in race relations over the next generation testify to the astonishing acuity of Myrdal's insight in apprehending the imminence of change, in identifying the factors that would bear upon it, in singling out the resort to law as a key weapon in the struggle, and above all in insisting that the ideological issue was uppermost and that stressing it would win the conscience of white society as an ally in the cause. Without depreciating other factors or glossing over the ugly resistance engendered, it seems indisputably clear that growing consciousness of the flagrant discrepancy between American ideals and American racial practice was the crucial point of leverage in the civil rights phase of the black movement, from World War II through the mid-1960s. During these years the ending of separate-but-equal and the drive for desegregation of schools and public accommodations brought the democratic ideals of freedom and equality together with the goal of an integrated society in which black and white might intermingle freely on the basis of common citizenship and mutual adherence to the values of the American creed. There were great differences between the situation of blacks and that of "national" minorities, but blacks too were embraced within the vision of One America, a nation made up of diverse peoples who were tolerant of each other and united around a set of universalist values.

Because race was the most important issue in American domestic life in the early 1960s, any shift in the relative weight of ethnic, as distinguished from ideological, considerations in this area was bound to have a profoundly influential effect on national thinking. Such a shift occurred in the mid-1960s and presaged a much wider revival of ethnicity that was clearly noticeable by the end of the decade.

No specific dates can be confidently assigned to changes of this nature, but two events in 1965 and one in 1966 may be taken as symbolic indications of the reorientation that was under way. Two pieces of legislation passed in 1965—the civil rights act of that year and the immigration law that eliminated national origins as a principle of selectivity—stand as climactic achievements of the approach that had emphasized universalist principles to improve intergroup relations and create a better social order. By contrast Stokely Carmichael's dramatic introduction of the slogan "Black Power" in 1966 symbolized the emergence of a much greater emphasis on particularistic group consciousness, pride, cohesiveness, and assertiveness, which is associated with the enhanced salience of ethnicity in American public life both as an issue in debates about social policy and as a dimension of our national self-understanding.

Ethnicity had been a factor in these matters before 1966, and ideology continued to make itself felt after that date. What changed was the relative weight given to these two elements. From the mid-1960s there was not only a much greater positive stress on ethnicity, but also a passionate critique of the national ideology that discredited the older Americanist emphasis. Against the background of the Vietnam War and the racial crisis, Myrdal's language about the American creed or Kallen's about the American idea seemed inappropriate, to say the least. The revival of ethnicity thus was part of a deep crisis of confidence and self-respect among the American people. In reviewing this most recent phase of the interplay between ethnicity and American identity, we must therefore consider not only the growth of ethnic consciousness but also the weakening of the ideological element.

Social scientists were calling attention to the development of stronger ethnic feeling among blacks by the early 1960s. Reviewing race relations in the 20 years since the publication of *An American Dilemma*, Robin Williams reported in 1965 that "a stronger sense of common fate, of shared values, beliefs and interests and of collectivity obligations" had undoubtedly emerged among blacks since 1944. Three years earlier another sociologist had described the process of "ethnogenesis" at work among blacks since emancipation, especially in the 20th century. As these studies were published, whites were being eliminated from leadership positions in the civil rights movement, and increasing black militance was fueled by the successes already won and by the solidarity engendered by the violent outbursts of urban rioting. After 1965 pride of race manifested itself not only in a new self-designation—"black" instead of "Negro"—but also in the purposeful promotion of black power, black pride, black history, black studies, and black consciousness, with black separatism and the paramilitary Black Panthers representing the extreme positions. The great mass of American blacks never supported the more extreme versions of militance, clinging instead to the ideals of equality and integration that had been emphasized in the earlier civil rights phase. However, they welcomed the new sense of group

pride and dignity, for they had never regarded integration as a process that required them to deny their own identity.

The effects of this shift toward an "ethnic" emphasis by blacks were enormous. The first of three distinguishable effects was that it legitimated the reality of ethnocentrism, although it did not legitimate the term. "Ethnocentrism" had been used pejoratively for so long that it was irredeemable as a label, which may be why the new term "ethnicity" gained popularity so rapidly in the late 1960s and early 1970s. But the new attitude pioneered and legitimated by blacks was ethnocentric in the literal sense that it was strongly centered on group membership, group solidarity, and group interests, and in the further sense that it made these dimensions of group existence normative; a thing was judged to be good or bad according to whether it strengthened or weakened the group, furthered or hindered its interests. The claims of the group were equated with the requirements of abstract justice, and hostility to outsiders was justified on the grounds of this coincidence between group interests and universal justice.

American blacks could argue with a good deal of plausibility that justice sustained their group claims, but the legitimation of ethnocentric assertion of group claims could not be restricted to blacks. And because blacks seemed to be getting a great deal by the militant statement of such claims, backed up by group pressure and even by violence or the threat of violence, other groups naturally followed suit. This widespread imitation may be thought of as the second way in which the ethnic revival among blacks affected the general social scene. Chicanos and American Indians could also make strong claims on the national conscience, and they soon emulated the blacks with Brown Power and Red Power movements.

The "white ethnic" movement was conditioned by both of the factors already mentioned, but it also reflected a third effect of the black movement: it was systematically promoted as a way of defusing white backlash. The danger that white working-class resentment of black pressures would intensify racial strife had been recognized as early as 1964. But not until 1968, *after* the black legitimatization of ethnicity, was there the beginning of a movement to depolarize the situation by attending sympathetically to the complaints of the white working class and by encouraging their sense of ethnic identity and expression of ethnic aspirations. The connection was made quite explicit at a Consultation on Ethnic America held in New York in June 1968 and at a similar gathering two weeks later in Philadelphia. The American Jewish Committee was the principal organizer of these events and remained actively engaged in the white ethnic movement. In 1970 its ongoing National Project on Ethnic America was announced and designated a Depolarization Project. The same intention to persuade white ethnics that blacks were their allies was observable in the community-organization aspect of the white ethnic movement. The fact that it was promoted as an effort to reduce racial tensions helped to make foundation support available.

Although the influence of the black assertion of ethnicity was very great, it could not have had such an effect if there had not been a pool of latent ethnic consciousness among other groups. In other words, the revival of ethnicity represented a positive development by other segments of the population, as well as an imitation of, and reaction to, developments among American blacks. The positive quality of the ethnic affirmation was especially notable among Mexican Americans and other Hispanics because these groups are large, still strongly attached to their language and culture, and heavily reinforced by the continuing arrival of first-generation immigrants. But the work of historians and sociologists who dealt with older groups is also instructive because it reflected growing interest in the subject of ethnicity and showed that ethnicity was persisting much more tenaciously than earlier students had assumed it would.

The most important institutional center for immigration history in the 1950s was Harvard University, where Oscar Handlin guided a number of able scholars into the field. John Higham, who did his doctoral work at Wisconsin, published his rich study of American nativism in 1955, and in 1961 the Cornell-trained Lee Benson pioneered in "ethnocultural political analysis" in *The Concept of Jacksonian Democracy*, a critique based on close study of New York State. The ethnocultural approach in political history was carried further in the 1960s by scholars like Frederick Luebke, Richard Jensen, and Paul Kleppner, while Stephan Thernstrom, a Handlin student, introduced a new approach to the quantitative study of immigrant social mobility in *Poverty and Progress* (1964). In 1965 the first steps were taken toward organization of the Immigration History Society, and Timothy L. Smith set up an archive for materials relating to immigration at the University of Minnesota. At about the same time Rudolph J. Vecoli (who later became the director of the Minnesota Immigration History Research Center) published the first widely noted essay by a historian challenging the assumption that immigrants had been radically uprooted from their ancestral culture, suggesting by implication that they had preserved much more of their ethnic heritage than scholars had previously believed.

The same point had been made with greater impact in two books by social scientists: Nathan Glazer and Daniel Moynihan's *Beyond the Melting Pot* (1963) and Milton Gordon's *Assimilation in American Life* (1964). The former analyzed the persistence of group self-awareness and distinctive patterns of group culture among the Negroes, Puerto Ricans, Jews, Italians, and Irish of New York City and showed how this kind of ethnicity influenced upward social mobility and the political life of the city at large. Glazer and Moynihan's title and the statement that the melting pot "did not happen" implied that the authors denied the reality of assimilation, but their point was actually more subtle. Assimilation was real, and cultural pluralism in the federation-of-nationalities sense was "as unlikely as the hope of a 'melting pot.'" But "the assimilating power of American society and culture operated on immigrant groups in different ways, to make them . . . something they had not been, but still something distinct and identifiable." In their view, stated in italics, *"The ethnic group in American society became not a survival from the age of mass immigration but a new social*

form." Ethnicity, then, persisted, but it was transformed in the process.

Like Glazer and Moynihan's book, Gordon's study is too complex and nuanced to be adequately characterized in a few lines. From the viewpoint of later developments in the ethnic revival, however, two features stand out. First, Gordon's lengthy and knowledgeable review of earlier assimilation theories became the standard treatment of the subject. Second, he clarified and elaborated an important distinction between cultural pluralism and structural pluralism. Although he and other writers had outlined this distinction in the 1950s, *Assimilation in American Life* established its significance more fully. According to the distinction, cultural pluralism meant that an ethnic group maintained distinctive cultural features, such as language and customs, whereas structural pluralism meant merely that the members of the group interacted socially with each other more than they did with outsiders. Gordon believed structural pluralism was replacing cultural pluralism; although ethnic languages and customs were disappearing, the members of groups that had earlier been distinguished by these cultural markers still interacted with each other more frequently than they did with persons who did not belong to the group.

Gordon's work appeared too soon after Glazer and Moynihan's to permit him to comment on their assertion that ethnicity persisted but was transformed. His notion of structural pluralism was quite compatible with their argument, however; in fact, the two interpretations reinforced and illuminated each other. Both were also compatible with the influential suggestion by Fredrik Barth in 1969 that in studying ethnic groups the primary focus should be on "the ethnic *boundary* that defines the group, not the cultural stuff that it encloses." Thus by 1970, when the ethnic revival was getting under way, scholars had refined their earlier conceptions of assimilation and acculturation; they were coming around to the view that ethnicity was a more durable quality than they had previously supposed, and they were prepared to credit the possibility of its expression in novel or unexpected forms.

The themes of ethnic persistence *and* transformation are present in the work of the sociologist Andrew M. Greeley, a Roman Catholic priest and director of the Center for the Study of American Pluralism at the National Opinion Research Center, who has been prominently associated with the new ethnicity on the academic and scholarly front. The same is true of Michael Novak, a Roman Catholic layman of Slovak descent who approaches the subject of ethnicity in a more personal manner. Novak's *Rise of the Unmeltable Ethnics* (1972) remains the major manifesto of the movement.

These spokesmen sometimes stress that the new ethnicity really is *new* and not a carryover from immigrant nationalities of the past, but that is not the impression conveyed by the movement as a whole or by the rhetoric employed by its advocates. In fact, quite the opposite impression is conveyed by the constant reiteration that the melting pot never happened, that assimilation was a myth, that Americanization was a repugnant but futile effort to force everyone into the mold of "Anglo-conformity," that the nation was in the beginning, is now, and ever shall be "unmeltably" ethnic, and that

those who called themselves the Americans were only another ethnic group—the WASPs—who lorded it over everyone else for far too long, but who have finally been unmasked.

This brings us to the other dimension of the ethnic revival, the fact that it is dialectically related to the weakening of the ideological element in American identity, which was so dominant in the epoch of World War II. There is a paradox here, for the advocates of the new ethnicity have not, of course, repudiated the principles of freedom, equality, and democracy. Indeed, they insist that their position conforms to the requirements of these principles more adequately than does the assimilationist mentality that they assail. Nonetheless, their approach implicitly denies that there can be a unitary *American* identity based upon common assent to universalist principles, an identity that makes Americans *one people* despite differences of ethnic derivation. And to treat terms like Americanization, assimilation, and melting pot as hateful labels for reprehensible policies—as the spokesmen for the new ethnicity consistently do—inevitably implies that the nation never represented values and ideals that immigrants could reasonably accept, identify with, and defend.

Although Americanization and the melting pot acquired unfavorable connotations around World War I, that is not the principal source for the intensely negative usage of these terms in the revival of ethnicity. As we have seen, even Horace Kallen spoke favorably of Americanization in the 1950s, and Will Herberg's popularization of the "triple melting pot" almost restored that much-maligned symbol to respectability. Rather, it was the events of the 1960s that discredited Americanism and made it possible, even fashionable, for ethnic spokesmen to treat these terms as wholly opprobrious.

The racial crisis and the Vietnam War, which had the opposite effect of World War II, were clearly the two most important forces that called American values and institutions into question. Closely related were revolutionary New Left radicalism and the counterculture that repudiated virtually all the values traditionally associated with American life. Radical feminism reinforced the tendency to reject traditional values. And in the Watergate scandal of the early 1970s, those who had cast themselves as true patriots and defenders of the old-fashioned virtues further weakened public confidence in American institutions and severely damaged national self-respect. No brief review could do justice to these tangled developments; it will be sufficient simply to highlight a fundamental shift of assumptions about America and to show how this shift is related to the subject of ethnicity and national identity.

The traditional position was that the American system was good and that Americans were committed to it, even though they did not fully live up to its ideals. Myrdal had elaborated the critique implied by this set of assumptions as it related to race relations, and the civil rights movement incorporated the same assumptions. For although they charged that the American people were hypocrites, the leaders of the civil rights movement acted on the premise that the nation really believed in equality and that its legal and political system offered the means that would, in the end, bring about racial justice. Outside the racial area, President

Kennedy was able to appeal to patriotism without embarrassment and mobilized youthful idealism for service to the world through the Peace Corps.

A decade later the situation had changed drastically. The view that America was systemically oppressive and immoral was not the majority view, but it had been advanced so vehemently by numerous partisans and acquiesced in so tamely by authoritative figures that national confidence and self-respect were severely shaken. Both domestic and foreign policy were castigated, not merely as wrong, but as evil and obscene, not as the results of incompetence or human error, but as the inevitable products of a fundamentally vicious system. Although the critics differed over whether the root of the evil was racism, imperialism, militarism, fascism, or simply capitalism, they concurred in the view that "AmeriKKKa," as the most extreme radicals phrased it, was built upon oppression. The American creed, according to this interpretation, had never been anything but a sham; the American dream had always been a nightmare; democratic procedures were but a smokescreen, and the ideal of law and order merely a code term for the preservation of a system of exploitation manipulated by the establishment.

Although sketched here in fairly drastic form, a critique along these lines found wide acceptance among an intelligentsia that was particularly sensitive to the racial issue and historically susceptible to the appeal of romantic anticapitalism as proclaimed by the neo-Marxist New Left and by certain apolitical elements of the counterculture. Anti-Americanism of this intensity was always a minority position, but it represented in grotesque caricature the self-doubt and self-disgust Americans felt as they beheld the nation mired down in an ignoble foreign war and torn apart by racial violence, political assassinations, gunplay and riotous confrontation on college campuses, as well as scandal in the highest reaches of government. The decade 1965–1974 thus witnessed a severe weakening of confidence in the American system—in the principles on which it was based, in the integrity of those who espoused such principles, and in the efficacy of its institutions.

This crisis of confidence was more than just the background against which the revival of ethnicity took place. It was also an indispensable element in the revival, for ethnic identities would never have been so vigorously affirmed if the ideological version of American identity had not been so tarnished. In these circumstances, it was highly functional for people to remember that they were really ethnic, simultaneously dissociating themselves from responsibility for the defects of the American system and establishing a claim against those who were responsible—the WASP establishment. In many cases, the claim was basically for emotional restitution, but that was no small matter. And as national policy moved toward what Nathan Glazer has called "affirmative discrimination," ethnicity seemed on its way to becoming a criterion for the receipt of more tangible benefits. In the view of many observers, this development was well calculated to stimulate the ethnic revival even more by raising the stakes—that is, by rewarding those who successfully established a group claim for special treatment and punishing those who failed to establish such claims.

Like practically everything else associated with the new ethnicity, the point just mentioned is controversial, not merely in the sense that disagreements naturally arise over what ethnic groups, if any, are entitled to benefits, but also in that it implies what has been called an "optionalist" interpretation of ethnicity, which is at odds with the more traditional "primordialist" understanding. According to the latter view, ethnicity is a basic element in one's personal identity that is simply there as an inheritance from the past, one of the primordial qualities that enable an individual to situate himself in the world and that remain part of him no matter what. The contrasting optionalist view holds that ethnicity "may be shed, resurrected, or adopted as the situation warrants," because it is not some indelible stamp impressed on the psyche, but a dimension of individual and group existence that can be consciously emphasized or deemphasized as the situation dictates.

The conflict between these two interpretations goes to the heart of the relation between ethnicity and group identity, but I cannot attempt to evaluate it here, and I cannot pursue the development of the new ethnicity in greater detail. The revival of ethnicity is still too new, too much in process, to permit summary treatment, and any effort to provide an adequate description of the views of its advocates and critics would prolong the discussion unduly. Having reviewed the factors involved in the emergence of the new ethnicity and having shown how it contrasts with the ideological version of American identity, I will conclude with a few brief reflections on the evolution of American thinking about national identity.

Conclusion

Milton Gordon's definition of ethnicity as a sense of peoplehood is the simplest and most satisfactory yet proposed. It is compatible with both of the interpretations of ethnicity mentioned above, because a sense of peoplehood may be conceived as either primordially given or optionally cultivated. But the way the term ethnicity is used has given rise to a serious misunderstanding of the relationship between ethnicity and American identity. The problem derives from the fact that although Gordon's definition is theoretically generic (that is, it applies to any and all forms of the sense of peoplehood), in practice the term is restricted to the sense of peoplehood felt by subgroups within American society. Because ethnicity has become so closely associated with the particularistic identities that differentiate the population internally, it has come to be regarded as qualitatively different from American identity. This impression, which has established itself more or less inadvertently, is mistaken. If ethnicity is defined as sense of peoplehood, then the sense of peoplehood shared by all Americans is *not* different in kind from the sense of peoplehood shared by those Americans who trace their ancestry to Italy, for example.

American identity and ethnic identity, then, are not two different kinds of identity, although conventional usage implies that they are—and further implies that the latter is a good deal more real and natural because it is a matter of grandfathers and intimate personal associations. But while it is generically the same, American identity differs from ethnic identity, as commonly un-

derstood, in two ways. First, the sense of peoplehood that characterizes the national community is more inclusive than the peoplehood of ethnic groups. Secondly, and precisely because it must be more inclusive, American identity has a more generalized formal principle (namely, commitment to the universalist ideals of Americanism) than those that form the bases of belongingness among ethnic groups. But the abstract quality of the American ideology does not mean that American identity is without what might be called the grandfather effect. In the eight generations since independence, many series of grandfathers have revered the symbols of national loyalty, fought to uphold them, and thought of themselves as full-fledged Americans. Even for descendants of more recent immigrants, what Abraham Lincoln called the mystic chords of memory are intertwined with homes, and graveyards, in the new land, as well as with traditions from beyond the seas.

The generation of the founding fathers understood very well that building a new nation required the development of a national sense of peoplehood. They were quite self-consciously concerned over the establishment of what they called the national character. Because four out of five whites were of British derivation, because virtually all were Protestant, and because blacks and Indians were not considered part of the national community, Americans of that era may be considered highly homogeneous in culture. Dedication to freedom and self-government was an integral element in their British heritage and in their recent American experience, so there was naturally a close correspondence between the sense of peoplehood of the cultural majority (the founders, or core group, or WASPs) and the national sense of peoplehood they projected for the nascent republic. Yet American nationality was not simply "WASP ethnicity" writ large. On the contrary, it was regarded as something novel and distinctive; it was oriented toward the future rather than the past; and, most important, it rested on a commitment to universalist political and social principles rather than on particularist cultural features such as language, religion, or country of origin. Thus the ethnic consciousness of kind of the American core group was closely related to, but not identical with, the American nationality that was to be formed.

As the years went by, American nationality became more a reality and less a project for the future simply because of the accumulation of lived experience by people who thought of themselves as Americans. If the original mix in the population had continued without change, if there had not been massive immigration of culturally variant peoples, the original consciousness of kind of the core group would presumably have coalesced with American nationality in an unproblematic way—with the very large exception, of course, of the problem of where blacks and Indians fit in, which already existed at the founding and was not materially affected by immigration. But the coming of floods of immigrants who differed significantly from the cultural majority in language, religion, and country of origin raised intricate problems about the relation between American nationality and ethnicity. These problems were created, not just for the immigrating peoples, but also for the descendants of the founders, who had to articulate their tacit assumptions about the relation of American nationality to their own particularistic group sense.

This latter group—the WASPs in today's demeaning tag—could legitimately claim overwhelming credit for the establishment of the nation and the creation of its distinctive institutions, including its legal and political institutions. Not unnaturally, they had a proprietary sense about the nation and regarded themselves as the appropriate arbiters of what it meant to be an American. Yet spokesmen for the immigrating peoples could just as legitimately point out that becoming an American did not require one to become an Anglo-Saxon or even to be like an Anglo-Saxon, except in adhering to the principles of freedom, equality, and republican government and in repudiating all former political allegiance, accepting the Constitution, and obeying the laws.

In establishing American nationality on the basis of abstract social and political ideas, Protestant Americans of British background had in fact committed the nation to a principle that made it inconsistent to erect particularist ethnic criteria into tests of true Americanism, but they did not fully realize this at the outset. The growth of a large and culturally divergent immigrant population brought out into the open the tension between the universalist criteria of Americanism and the core group's natural desire to perpetuate the cultural hegemony of its own way of life. Hence the coming of the immigrants made the nature of American nationality problematic and required a rethinking of what it meant to be an American. Periods of intense concern over these issues, which generally took the form of nativism, may be understood as crises of nationality. This essay has shown that a difference in religion became the central issue in the first of these crises, while the crisis of the late 19th and early 20th centuries focused on so-called racial qualities. The drastic reduction of mass immigration in the 1920s ended that crisis, and the emphasis on democratic tolerance during World War II made nativism seem un-American, thus helping to pave the way for the positive valuation of ethnicity that emerged in the late 1960s.

It would overstate the case to call the contemporary revival of ethnicity a crisis of American nationality, yet it has made the question of what it means to be an American more prominent than it has been since the 1920s. Moreover, in the tradition of national debate on these matters, this is the first time that the affirmers of ethnicity have taken the offensive. The traditional Americanist position has not only been placed on the defensive, it has been left virtually undefended. However, it is by no means indefensible, and without deprecating the real gains in national self-understanding that we owe to the new ethnicity, that position is presently in greater need of a critique than is the traditional Americanist position. Such a critique might include two or three important points.

The first is simply that an American nationality does in fact exist. That it seems necessary to make such a statement indicates the degree to which the rhetorical imbalance of the recent discussion of ethnicity has created a situation in which very basic matters related to American identity appear questionable. For that reason it may not be redundant to add that American nationality is not Anglo-Saxonism or WASP ethnicity,

nor is it a Kallenesque collocation of subgroup ethnicities taken together. Rather it is a distinctive sense of peoplehood, not different in essence from the peoplehood-sense of ethnic groups, which furnishes what Justice Felix Frankfurter once called "the binding tie of cohesive sentiment" underlying the "continuity of treasured common life" of the national community.

To affirm the existence of American nationality does not mean that all Americans are exactly alike or must become uniform in order to be real Americans. It simply means that a genuine national community does exist and that it has its own distinctive principle of unity, its own history, and its own appropriate sense of belongingness by virtue of which individuals identify with the symbols that represent and embody that community's evolving consciousness of itself. American nationality, so understood, does not preclude the existence of ethnicity in the subgroup peoplehood-sense, but neither does the existence of the latter preclude the former; nor should subgroup ethnicities be regarded as more privileged, as having some sort of existential priority over American nationality.

In the past, many ethnic nationalists explicitly denied that there was any such thing as American nationality, and Horace Kallen's original version of cultural pluralism rested on the assumption that, although at one time a distinctive American nationality did exist, it had been dissipated by the great waves of immigration. At present, however, the existence of an American nationality has been made questionable, not by flat denials of its existence, but more indirectly, as the result of rhetoric employed by spokesmen for the new ethnicity. One feature is the claim that the American people are simply a collection of ethnic groups, one of which—the WASPs—have oppressively dominated all the others and tried to impose Anglo-conformity. Harold Cruse, for example, has stated: "America is a nation that lies to itself about who and what it is. It is a nation of minorities ruled by a minority of one—it thinks and acts as if it were a nation of white Anglo-Saxon Protestants." And Michael Novak reported that Americanization "was really WASPification." Similarly, the repeated insistence that the melting pot "never happened" and that assimilation is a myth implies the non-existence of American nationality, because that was what the melting pot was expected to produce and what immigrants were supposed to be assimilated to.

The standard rhetoric of the ethnic revival has also contributed to the erosion of confidence in the ideological principles upon which that nationality is based. That is not the intention of the ethnic spokesmen, to be sure, but respect for American principles cannot help but be weakened when the very words Americanism and Americanization are treated as terms of abuse and when earlier efforts to articulate the nation's values and to give them symbolic expression are dismissed as hypocrisy or worse. Polemical excesses were committed in the past by crusaders for 100-percent Americanism, but some contemporary champions of the new ethnicity are guilty of equal but opposite excesses. These excesses are potentially more destructive, however, because by undercutting respect for American values and institutions, immoderate criticism simultaneously erodes the ideological basis for the critics' claim for a fuller measure of justice. Claims for tolerance, equality, and justice must be based on the democratic principles of the national ideology, not on ethnicity as such. Spokesmen for the new ethnicity seem somehow to have forgotten that the particularistic sense of membership in a specific race, religion, or ethnic nationality in itself creates no claim on others for tolerance, respect, equality, or anything else.

To judge from current usage, one might infer that cultural pluralism meets all the points of the critique so far advanced. As customarily invoked, it seems to be regarded as a democratic principle of nationality that supplies a warrant in justice for all particularist ethnic demands and guarantees that these multitudinous claims will not conflict with each other, but will automatically promote the common good and produce a harmonious and richer culture. Perhaps a theory of pluralism will eventually be worked out that will do all this—or that will at least provide an analytical perspective and conceptual tools to identify and deal with the real problems involved in maintaining unity and diversity, in reconciling the conflicting claims of the one and the many. Unfortunately, cultural pluralism today is not such a theory. It was filled with theoretical ambiguities when introduced by Kallen in the 1920s; as popularized in the 1940s and 1950s, it meant something quite different (even in Kallen's usage), and the ambiguities were multiplied. Against that background, the vicissitudes of the past 15 years or so have emptied cultural pluralism of theoretical coherence. Today it is not so much a theory as an incantatory expression that enables people to avoid confronting the need for a theory.

But the very popularity of the term, as well as the vigorous assertion of ethnic claims, bespeaks a real change in the Americans' sense of who they are and who they want to be. We need a better theory to deal with this than is presently available. What the new ethnicity and all the talk of pluralism signify is that the perennially problematic issue of American nationality is taking on a new configuration. It is a continuing task to make a reality out of the ideal proposed in the national motto—E Pluribus Unum. We cannot hope to settle the issue definitively, to finish the task once and for all. But we cannot even begin to do justice to the problem as it is posed in our own time unless we grant the same kind of recognition to the imperative of unity that we give to the reality of diversity.

Bibliography

The brief section headed "Ethnicity and Identity" in *Ethnic Identity in Society*, Arnold Dashefsky, ed. (Chicago, 1976), provides a few hints toward a much needed history of the term "identity." Of Erik Erikson's writings on identity, the most relevant to this subject are: "Reflections on the American Identity," in *Childhood and Society* (New York, 1950); "Identity and Uprootedness in Our Time," in *Insight and Responsibility* (New York, 1964); "Autobiographic Notes on the Identity Crisis," *Daedalus* (Fall 1970); and *Dimensions of a New Identity* (New York, 1974). Michael McGiffert, ed., *The Character of Americans*, rev. ed. (Homewood, Ill., 1970), is a collection of readings on the closely related concept of American character, and Thomas L. Hartshorne, *The Distorted Image* (Cleveland, 1968), traces the historical evolution of the concept of American character from the 1880s through the 1950s.

Hans Kohn, *American Nationalism* (New York, 1957), is basic for the ideological origins of American identity. Also very useful are: Paul Nagel, *This Sacred Trust* (New York, 1971); Michael Kammen, *A Season of Youth* (New York, 1978); Benjamin T. Spencer, *The Quest for Nationality* (Syracuse, N.Y., 1957); and Merle Curti, *The Roots of American Loyalty* (New York, 1946). Robert A. Shalhope, "Toward a Republican Synthesis: The Emergence of an Understanding of Republicanism in American Historiography," *William and Mary Quarterly*

(January 1972) is an excellent introduction to the recent scholarship on republicanism, and Lance Banning, *The Jeffersonian Persuasion* (Ithaca, N.Y., 1978), shows how republicanism influenced the political and ideological struggles of the early national period. For "civil millennialism," see Nathan O. Hatch, *The Sacred Cause of Liberty* (New Haven, Conn., 1977).

Thomas T. McAvoy, *A History of the Catholic Church in the United States* (Notre Dame, Ind., 1969), provides a general account of Catholic developments, 1815–1865; Jay P. Dolan, *The Immigrant Church: New York's Irish and German Catholics, 1815–1865* (Baltimore, Md., 1975), is a valuable social history. Ray Allen Billington, *The Protestant Crusade 1800–1860* (New York, 1938), the standard account of ante-bellum nativism, is nicely supplemented by Robert F. Hueston, *The Catholic Press and Nativism 1840–1860* (New York, 1976), which concentrates on the Catholic reaction. Oscar Handlin's landmark study, *Boston's Immigrants*, rev. ed. (Cambridge, Mass., 1959), illuminates the special quality of Catholic–Protestant tensions in Boston. On the school issue, see Vincent P. Lannie, *Public Money and Parochial Education: Bishop Hughes, Governor Seward, and the New York School Controversy* (Cleveland, 1968), and Timothy L. Smith, "Protestant Schooling and American Nationality, 1800–1850," *Journal of American History* (March 1967). Philip Gleason, "Coming to Terms with American Catholic History," *Societas* (Autumn 1973), is a more wide-ranging review of Americanism and Americanization as issues in Catholic history.

John Higham's classic *Strangers in the Land* (New Brunswick, N.J., 1955) is indispensable for understanding the melting pot, Americanization, and Anglo-Saxon racialism; his *Send These to Me* (New York, 1975), chaps. 10 and 11, are crucial for cultural pluralism. Milton M. Gordon, *Assimilation in American Life* (New York, 1964) is also enlightening on these matters. Philip Gleason, "The Melting Pot: Symbol of Fusion or Confusion?" *American Quarterly* (Spring 1964), and "Confusion Compounded: The Melting Pot in the 1960s and 1970s," *Ethnicity* (March 1979), deal primarily with semantic issues. Maurice Wohlgelernter, *Israel Zangwill* (New York, 1964), places *The Melting Pot* in the context of Zangwill's other writings.

On Americanization, see Edward G. Hartmann, *The Movement to Americanize the Immigrant* (New York, 1948); Daniel Weinberg, "The Ethnic Technician and the Foreign-born: Another Look at Americanization Ideology and Goals," *Societas* (Summer 1977); and John F. McClymer, "The Federal Government and the Americanization Movement, 1915–24," *Prologue* (Spring 1978). Lawrence A. Cremin, *The Transformation of the School* (New York, 1961), chap. 3, sets Americanization against the background of progressivism in education. For the involvement of employers, see Gerd Korman, *Industrialization, Immigrants and Americanization* (Madison, Wis., 1967).

Higham, *Strangers*, chap. 6, is the best short discussion of racism, but Reginald Horsman, "Origins of Racial Anglo-Saxonism in Great Britain before 1850," *Journal of the History of Ideas* (July/September 1976), is also extremely valuable, not only for its substantive content, but for its comprehensive citation of primary and secondary literature. Barbara M. Solomon, *Ancestors and Immigrants* (Cambridge, Mass., 1956), traces the rise of Anglo-Saxon racialism and nativism in New England. Thomas F. Gossett, *Race: The History of an Idea in America* (Dallas, Tex., 1963), is a useful general account. For eugenics and race, see Mark H. Haller, *Eugenics* (New Brunswick, N.J., 1963); for the critical work of Franz Boas, see George W. Stocking, Jr., *Race, Culture, and Evolution* (New York, 1968).

Critical commentaries on Kallen are few; the best are: Higham, *Send These to Me*, chap. 10; Gordon, *Assimilation in American Life*, chap. 6; and James H. Powell, "The Concept of Cultural Pluralism in American Social Thought, 1915–1965," Ph.D. dissertation, University of Notre Dame, 1971 (University Microfilms, Ann Arbor, Mich.). Moses Rischin, *The Promised City: New York's Jews 1870–1914* (Cambridge, Mass., 1962), is excellent for the social and cultural background of Jewish thinking on ethnicity and identity.

American thinking on ethnicity and identity in the period 1924–1979 has been little studied as a distinct subject. A number of works that constitute primary evidence of shifting views in this area are mentioned in the text and will not be listed here. Fred H. Matthews, *Quest for an American Sociology* (Montreal, 1977), makes a valuable contribution by focusing on the pioneering work of Robert E. Park and the "Chicago School." Park, *Race and Culture* (Glencoe, Ill., 1950), is a collection of his essays on these themes. Peter I. Rose, *The Subject Is Race* (New York, 1968), is helpful, as is Everett C. Hughes and Helen M. Hughes, *Where Peoples Meet* (Glencoe, Ill., 1952). Stanford M. Lyman, *The Black American in Sociological Thought* (New York, 1972), is also relevant here, especially for its chapter on Gunnar Myrdal and *The American Dilemma*.

Although Howard F. Stein and Robert F. Hill, *The Ethnic Imperative* (University Park, Pa., 1977), is primarily a critique of the new ethnicity,

it also contains valuable evidence on the impact of World War II. For the war-related boom in studies of the national character, see the relevant chapters of Hartshorne, *Distorted Image*, and Margaret Mead's contributions to Daniel Lerner and Harold D. Lasswell, eds., *The Policy Sciences* (Stanford, Cal., 1951), and to Seymour M. Lipset and Leo Lowenthal, eds., *Culture and Social Character* (New York, 1961). Daniel Bell, "Modernity and Mass Society: On the Varieties of Cultural Experience," in *Paths of American Thought*, Arthur M. Schlesinger, Jr., and Morton White, eds. (Boston, 1963), offers a convenient entry to the cultural critique of the 1950s.

For perceptions by social scientists of changes among American blacks in the early 1960s, see L. Singer, "Ethnogenesis and Negro-Americans Today," *Social Research* (Winter 1962); and Robin M. Williams, Jr., "Social Change and Social Conflict: Race Relations in the United States, 1944–1964," *Sociological Inquiry* (Winter, 1965). Rudolph J. Vecoli, "European Americans: From Immigrants to Ethnics," in *The Reinterpretation of American History and Culture*, William H. Cartwright and Richard L. Watson, Jr., eds. (Washington, D.C., 1973), is a comprehensive review of shifting emphases in historical scholarship on ethnicity. See also Richard L. McCormick, "Ethno-Cultural Interpretations of Nineteenth-Century American Voting Behavior," *Political Science Quarterly* (June 1974). Perry L. Weed, *The White Ethnic Movement and Ethnic Politics* (New York, 1973), is informative on the organizational development of the new ethnicity; Maxine Seller, *To Seek America; A History of Ethnic Life in the United States* (Englewood, N.J., 1977), chap. 13, offers a brief interpretive overview; and *America and the New Ethnicity*, David R. Colburn and George E. Pozzetta, eds. (Port Washington, N.Y., 1979), is a useful collection of readings. For more theoretical discussions, see William L. Yancey, Eugene Ericksen, and Richard N. Juliani, "Emergent Ethnicity: A Review and Reformulation," *American Sociological Review* (June 1976), and Peter K. Eisinger, "Ethnicity as a Strategic Option: An Emerging View," *Public Administration Review* (January/February 1978), which discusses several recent works and suggests the distinction between the primordialist and optionalist views of ethnicity.

PHILIP GLEASON

AMERICAN INDIANS

In the 1970s there were 173 American Indian groups, variously called tribes, nations, bands, peoples, and ethnic groups. The largest of these—the Navajos of Arizona and New Mexico—numbered more than 160,000, the smallest—such as the Chumash of California and the Modocs of Oklahoma—fewer than a hundred. Nearly as many Indian tribes exist in the 20th century as when Europeans first encountered them in the 1600s.

It is not known precisely how many different nations (as they were then called by Europeans) existed at the time of first contact. A widely accepted rough estimate is that there were, in the late 1600s, upward of 200. If so, it can be said that the number of groups has declined by only about 30, or perhaps 16 percent. But these figures do not tell the whole story. Fifty or more groups are known to have become extinct as a result of disease, massacre by whites, absorption into other groups, or harsh conditions during the early phase of contact with Europeans. It is safe to say that one-fourth suffered extinction.

On the other hand, groups with a new sense of identity have been formed as a result of nations being separated into two or more groups and having different experiences in the course of their later history. The Cherokees of Oklahoma and the Eastern Band of Cherokees in North Carolina, the Citizen Potawatomis of Oklahoma and the Forest Potawatomis of Michigan are two of many examples. Also several remnant groups have sometimes consolidated into a single new one, such as the Brothertons and the Stockbridge Indians, once of New Jersey and New England, respectively, and now of Michigan.

The important fact is that American Indians have maintained a high degree of diversity and continue to develop in a variety of ways. They were not and have not become a single undifferentiated people justifying the single label—the American Indian—as most Americans believe. They comprise at least 170 peoples with different cultural backgrounds, different historical experiences, and, as a result, different senses of identity.

Nor are Indians, as popular belief portrays them, a vanishing people. Expert estimates of precisely how many Indians there were within the territory of the United States when the white man arrived range from a conservative and widely accepted figure of 850,000 up to more than a million. The United States Census count for 1970 was 791,839. Although this suggests a decline in population, if we look more deeply into the figures, a different view emerges. The Indian population did indeed decline rapidly from the 1600s through the 1800s. In 1900 it was recorded as 237,196, indicating a nearly 75 percent decline during the previous 200 years. The greatest reduction took place during the 19th century, and undoubtedly it is that period of deep decline that gave rise to the stereotype of the Indians as a vanishing race.

However, from 1900 the trend has been toward a continuing increase, especially in the 20-year period from 1950 to 1970, when there was an increase of 100 percent. It appears that the Indian population in the 1980s will considerably exceed what it was in the early years of European contact.

In respect to both numbers of individuals and numbers of distinct ethnic groups, Indians have held their own over the past 300 years, and recently the rate of growth has accelerated greatly. These facts are significant for understanding the place of Indians in the American system of ethnic relations, as is their distribution in the general population and the historical events that account for that distribution.

Nearly 700,000 Indians—the overwhelming majority —live west of the Mississippi River. In 1970 almost half of this population lived in three western states: Oklahoma, with 97,731; Arizona, with 95,812; and California, with 91,018. In contrast, 25 states east of the Mississippi (not including Michigan and Wisconsin) had an Indian population of only 128,525, or about one-fifth of the total.

These figures reflect fairly closely the historical circumstances that have powerfully affected Indian life during the past two centuries. To some extent the relatively small number of Indians throughout the East is a result of early decimation by disease (which hit Indians hardest during their initial European contacts), warfare, and massacre. However, the primary cause for depopulation was the government policy of systematically forced migration, as white Americans put heavy pressure on Indians to move out of their way, that is, westward. They usually paid something for Indian land but forced the sale whenever Indians were slow or refused to move. The most extensive program of removal and deportation began about 1830, when the Five Civilized Tribes—to be defined later—of the Southeast were forced into agreements to move to Indian Territory. At least 70,000, of whom some 20,000 died en route, were thus removed from the southeastern states. Similarly, the Indians of the Ohio Valley were pushed west,

leaving some of the best farmland in the United States. By the late 1800s only tiny Indian enclaves remained east of the Mississippi, such as the Wampanoags in Massachusetts and the Catawbas in South Carolina, except for a few larger remaining groups: in New York, where most of the Iroquois somehow withstood the pressures; in the states bordering the three western Great Lakes; and in North Carolina, where unusual circumstances resulted in the creation of an entirely new tribe of 40,000—the Lumbees.

The present concentration of the Indian population in three western states also reflects important historical developments. Oklahoma, with the largest Indian population in 1970, was once Indian Territory, to which the Five Civilized Tribes were deported, as were many other eastern, midwestern, and Plains tribes. Oklahoma represents the major monument to the removal policy.

The second-largest concentration of Indian population is in Arizona, for quite different reasons. First, the Pueblos and the Piman-speaking peoples, who were already settled as farmers there when the Spaniards began their colonization from New Spain in 1598, were not removed from their lands by either Spanish or American conquerors, although there was much encroachment by whites. However, the high population figure in the Arizona–New Mexico region is mainly a result of the spectacular growth of the Navajo Indians, who in Arizona, New Mexico, and Utah came to occupy the largest of all Indian reservations. They increased from fewer than 9,000 during early Spanish colonization to more than 160,000 in 1975, becoming the largest Indian nation in the United States. Their relative freedom to develop in their own way as sheepherders in sparsely settled country for most of a century (between 1868 and the 1930s), with little or no government interference, played a part in their population explosion. In the Southwest, then, a considerable segment of Indian population has experienced a minimum of dislocation, has expanded in numbers, and has developed distinctive ways of life.

The third-largest Indian concentration is in California. Although some portion of this population consists of rural native California Indians for whom federal reserves were never created, by far the greater part is the result of large-scale voluntary migration from reservations to San Francisco and the Bay region, Los Angeles, and San Diego during and after World War II.

Thus the present distribution of Indians reflects the forced migrations of the 19th century, the relative isolation of some groups, especially in the West, and the more recent migration from the rural reservations to the cities.

During the early period of European settlement, Indians were distributed in a very different pattern across the continent. The East was more heavily populated over most of its breadth than was the West. There were also areas of relatively high density: for example, southern New England, where the Massachusetts and Connecticut Indians lived; tidewater Virginia, where the Powhatan Confederacy arose; and the coastal areas of the Carolinas. Other relatively dense populations existed in the country of the Choctaws, Creeks, and Cherokees. All these areas were almost devoid of Indians by the 19th century. In the vast expanse of the West, which was relatively sparsely populated by In-

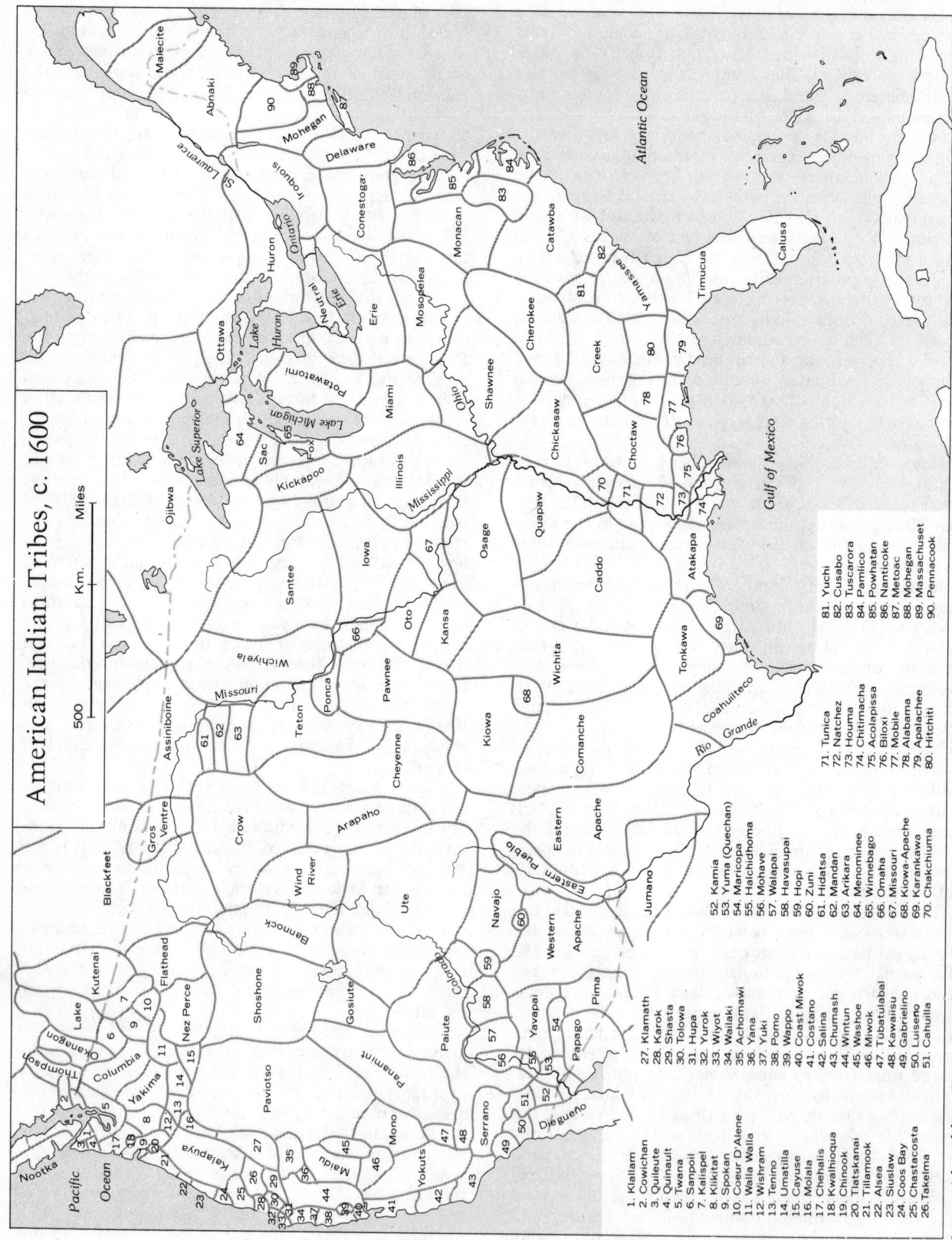

American Indian Tribes, c. 1600

Source: Adapted from George Peter Murdock, *Ethnographic Bibliography of North America*, 3d ed. (New Haven, 1960).

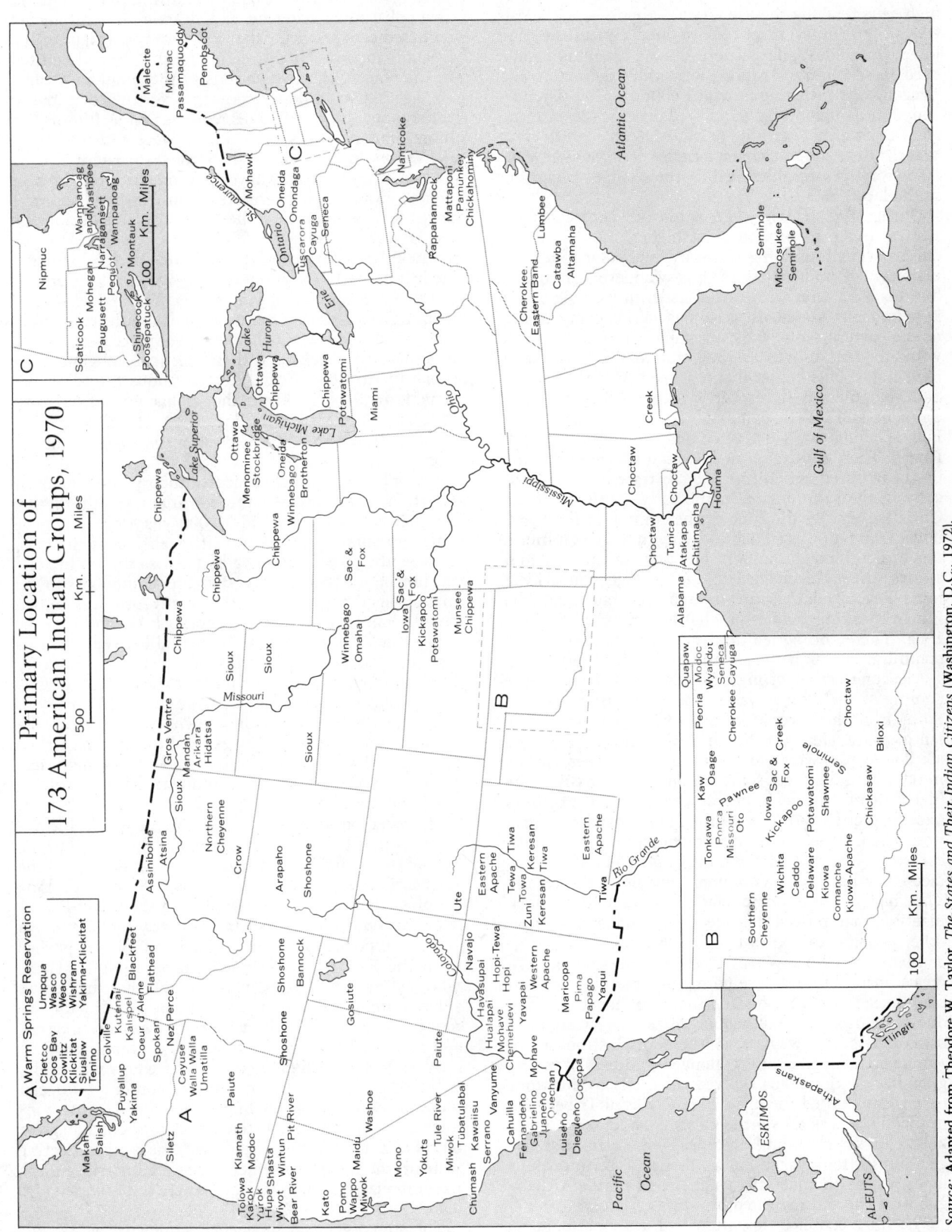

Primary Location of 173 American Indian Groups, 1970

Source: Adapted from Theodore W. Taylor, *The States and Their Indian Citizens* (Washington, D.C., 1972).

dians, there were also areas of higher density: the Southwest Pueblo country to a limited extent but with high density along the Rio Grande; the lower Gila Valley, where Pimas practiced irrigated agriculture; the lower Colorado Valley, where Yuman-speaking people used flood-water irrigation; western Washington and Oregon, where fishing provided abundant subsistence; and, surprisingly, large parts of California, despite the absence of either farming or abundant fish. It is clear that the demographic characteristics of all but a few Indians were greatly disrupted by the changes beginning in the late 1700s.

During the 1600s, when intensive contacts with whites began, three centers of higher, more complex culture were flourishing. Contrary to popular belief, the majority of Indians were not wandering nomadic hunters but rather farmers and fishermen, living either in permanent, stable villages or, as among many groups of the eastern woodlands, in stable communities but with frequent moves as they shifted the location of their fields. One center that reached the highest levels of development with respect to religious life, local government, and artistic expression was that of the Pueblo Indians along the Rio Grande and the Little Colorado Rivers. Their cultural growth, which was based on the use of irrigated agriculture, can be traced archaeologically in the same region to the early centuries of the Christian era. By the time of the coming of the Spaniards, who found the Pueblos living in large communities of contiguous, masonry buildings of three or four stories, their culture had reached a high point. Even more developed irrigation systems characterized the Piman-speaking peoples in what became southern Arizona. There the agricultural developments and large communities can be traced back to the 3rd century B.C.

A second center of high cultural growth before the coming of the whites was in the southeastern United States from the lower Mississippi Valley east to the Atlantic coast. Here the Natchez, Choctaw, Creek, and similar peoples were prominent, the Cherokees sharing in the cultural growth somewhat later. The basis of the high culture was again effective agricultural practices and distinctive forms of political and social organization. The Creeks' town government lent itself to political expansion, and with the impetus of European contacts they became the dominant people of the region. They had a basically democratic form of political organization that proved capable of absorbing numerous other peoples. In contrast to the Pueblos, the Creeks, and later the Choctaws and Cherokees, demonstrated a great capacity for creative borrowing, not only in their ready utilization of tools and means of economic production, but also in political organization. Fusing their own democratic ways with the formal structure of American democracy, they, along with others of the region, had by the 1830s evolved culturally to the point that whites called them the Five Civilized Tribes. Yet ironically, it was they—the Creeks, Choctaws, Cherokees, Chickasaws, and Seminoles—who were first singled out for removal to Indian Territory, because their lands, which included the goldfields of northern Georgia, were the most coveted by whites.

The third center of important cultural development was among the Iroquois in what became New York State. About the time that the French made first contact with Iroquoian-speaking peoples in the 1500s, and possibly before that, the Iroquois had initiated a remarkable political confederacy, and although it was founded on hereditary privilege, the form that the League of the Iroquois took was highly democratic. Politically united in the league, the five nations of the Iroquois became an aggressive military power, exerting dominance throughout the Great Lakes region as far as Illinois; for more than a century the Iroquois were a force that all the European nations and the strongest eastern Indians had to reckon with. However, under the stresses of French, British, and American military and cultural pressures, by the end of the American Revolution the league was in a shambles.

The origins of these and other cultural developments are lost in the 10,000 or more years without written record that preceded European contact. The archaeological record gives only the main outline of cultural growth but does not tell us much about the predecessors of the Iroquois and Creeks and their political, religious, and social institutions. Even the continuous record of material growth from 300 B.C. that archaeologists have uncovered in the Southwest does not go far in supplying the details we normally expect in the histories of nations.

According to a widely accepted theory, the Indians of North America reached the continent via the Bering Strait between 10,000 and 20,000 years ago. There is much to support this view, although recent findings, such as the possibility of sailing across the Pacific and the northern Atlantic, suggest greater complexity in the migrations that gave rise to the North American Indian population. However, these theories leave an immense gap in the record—that is, the period between the earliest arrivals and the coming of the Europeans. Very little of importance is known about the cultural origins of the League of the Iroquois before the 16th century or about the Creek and Natchez towns or even about the high cultures of the Southwest earlier than the Christian era. None of the theories provides a historical account comparable to what is known about the origins of the European nations.

However, something is known about important migrations that began about the time of the arrival of the Europeans. From the region of the Great Lakes and the northern Mississippi Valley, groups of Siouan-speaking peoples were moving westward onto the Great Plains. This movement was accelerated greatly by Chippewas who in response to the French demand for furs pushed from the East for additional hunting grounds. Those who had moved onto the plains found that they could subsist almost wholly on buffalo meat by using the European horse to hunt the vast herds. As horses, guns, and metal knives came into wide use among the new arrivals in the northern plains, a whole new way of life developed rapidly. It was not a diffusion of a European mode of living, but a new Indian creation. The most influential of all American stereotypes of the Indian grew out of this: the feathered headdress, the scalp-collecting warrior, the fabled horsemen of the Plains tribes came to symbolize that nonexistent being, "the American Indian."

The stereotype was broadened somewhat as a result of the settlers' experience with Apaches in the Southwest. A century or more before the Spaniards made

their way from Mexico into the Pueblo country, the ancestors of the Apaches of Arizona and New Mexico, who spoke Athapaskan languages, migrated south from Canada. They developed raiding as a way of life and preyed on the Spaniards' villages in New Mexico and farther south. Among the last of the western Indians to be conquered by the U.S. Cavalry, the Apaches, like the Plains Indians, left a tremendous impression on the American imagination, embodied in the thousands of pages written about Cochise and Geronimo. Until they were dominated by whites, Indians like the Apaches and the Sioux were making dynamic adaptations.

The diversity in ways of life before the Europeans arrived was very great, ranging from simple bands of food-gatherers to farmers living in city-states (as the Pueblos have been characterized) and highly organized political confederacies. The diversity is no longer so extreme; common ways of making a living have been adopted, the American legal and political systems have been accepted, and the English language learned by nearly all Indians. Diversity has not, however, disappeared, as the maintenance of 173 different identities indicates.

Aside from distinct histories and experiences, one of the elements of this identification is the continued use of native languages in addition to English. Perhaps half the persisting groups still use the Indian language in the home to some degree, and many others use selected words of an Indian language when referring to things that are part of their cultural heritage. Some languages of each of the 14 major Indian linguistic families are still spoken: Hopi, Pima, Paiute, and others of the far-flung Uto-Aztecan family; Seneca, Cherokee, Onondaga, Tuscarora, and others of the Iroquoian family; Mohave, Quechan, Hualapai, and others of Yuman; Choctaw, Creek, and others of Muskogean—to mention only a few. These major families are as distinct from one another as are the great language families of Europe and Asia. Moreover, the languages of a family such as the Algonkian—Delaware (Lenni Lenape), Narragansett, and Chickahominy—or the Uto-Aztecan—Hopi, Pima, and Yaqui—are mutually unintelligible. Some of this great diversity of language has been lost, as slightly less than one-half of the Indian languages have become extinct, and more are certainly on the way out.

However, a majority of Indians continue to speak an Indian language as well as English. In view of the widespread, violent dislocations of Indian groups and the determined efforts of the Bureau of Indian Affairs (BIA) to root out the Indian languages through formal schooling, it is surprising that so many are still vigorously in use. There are new influences that tend to keep the language diversity alive, among them the development of practical ways of writing. Seven orthographies are in use, for Cherokee, Cree, Creek, Crow, Navajo, Ojibwa, and Lakota (Teton), and others are in process. Interest in writing their languages is high among, for example, Papago, White Mountain Apache, and a dozen others. Indian languages are being taught in the state universities of Arizona, Minnesota, and New Mexico; Northern Arizona University; Navajo Community College; Pima Community College; and others.

Far more than in language, Indians remain as varied in religious belief and practice as they were when Europeans arrived. Due to the unremitting efforts of missionaries to replace the native religions with Christian denominations, the great majority of Indians profess Roman Catholicism or one of the varieties of Protestantism. But many who profess some form of Christianity also participate in one of the dozen or more native Indian religions that have grown up during the centuries of contact.

The Handsome Lake (or Longhouse) religion among the Iroquois, which came into existence in 1800, is particularly notable, having developed texts in the Seneca language and thousands of adherents among the Six Nations of New York and Canada. More widespread among Indians of different tribes is the Native American church, which in the late 19th century diffused from Mexican Indians among the Kiowas, Delawares, and others in Indian Territory. It has spread to many Oklahoma, Plains, and Midwest groups and more recently to the Navajos, and it maintains a national organization. A central ritual makes use of the hallucinogenic fruit of the peyote cactus and combines Christian with native American belief and ritual. Other religions that have developed during the past century include the Indian Shaker religion of the Northwest; the Drum Dance cult (using sacred songs and dances selected from traditional religions), common in the Midwest among Menominees, Potawatomis, and others; the Silas John cult of the Southwest, which uses giant ground paintings; a variety of modified Medicine Bundle religions, revolving around sacred fetishes owned by clans; and the sacred fire ceremonialism associated with the Keetoowah beliefs of eastern Oklahoma.

Some native religions have maintained with only minor changes their traditional orientations, concepts, and rituals, such as those of the Hopis of Arizona, the Rio Grande Pueblos, the Navajos, the Potawatomis, and the Sioux. Indians in many communities across the country, and particularly in the Southwest, participate only in their native American religions, consciously rejecting Christian beliefs and judging them unfavorably in relation to the Indian ways.

The long-standing diversity in ways of life manifests itself in other respects as well—in preferred house types, such as the Navajo hogan, the Kickapoo wigwam, the Sioux tipi, the Pima sandwich house (walls of earth packed between sticks of desert shrubs), and others; in the use of distinctive dress and footwear; in modes of fishing; in dance and song; and in family values.

Nevertheless, adoption of white ways has been the dominant process over the centuries. At first, borrowing of traits took place through trade and simple proximity. Then the active programs of missionaries, followed by dependence on whites resulting from the destruction of traditional ways of making a living (such as the Plains tribes suffered when the buffalo became extinct) and the imposition of BIA programs to replace Indian ways fostered the loss of Indian and the adoption of white ways. From the 1880s into the 20th century the government programs of forced assimilation were the strongest influence.

It must be emphasized that while forced cultural assimilation brought about replacement of a wide range of Indian ways, it also resulted in extensive alienation of Indians from whites. As Indians borrowed white modes of behavior, belief, and organization, they did not necessarily come to admire whites or identify with them. Rather they identified themselves more intensely as In-

dians and developed symbols of their identity in the form of religious beliefs, music, dance, selected items of dress like headbands and moccasins, particular ceremonies, and their own heroes and heroines, many of whom were admired because they fought for Indian independence. Each tribe emphasizes symbols associated with events in their historical experience. This vital process has counterbalanced the extensive replacement of cultural elements in Indian life and blocked their absorption by the dominant society.

A question of some importance to Indians is what their group entities should be called. During the century or two of early European contact, the term nation was in general use for those Indian groups that were land-controlling entities and that had enough internal cohesion to oppose whites or make treaties with them. A nation was made up of Indians who spoke a common language or a set of mutually intelligible dialects and maintained a common set of customs. Such units were regarded by whites as similar to those that were recognized in Europe as nations. However, during the early 19th century Americans began to speak of Indians as "tribes," and this term eventually replaced nation. It had some connotation of inferiority, or in Rudyard Kipling's phrase, a "lesser breed without the Law," and as Indians sensed that, especially by the middle of the 20th century, they rejected the term, and many began to speak again of their groups as nations. The official title of the Navajos and of numerous other Indian entities is now nation, even though the Bureau of Indian Affairs continues to use the term tribe and has officially designated the political bodies it has encouraged as tribal councils. Usage is therefore not consistent and involves political considerations.

To avoid the confusion involved in a general application of either the U.S. government usage or the self-conscious Indian usage, a neutral term such as "ethnic group" is the most useful. By ethnic group is meant a number of people who share a particular Indian group name and other symbols of a common historical experience unique to those who use the group name. Such an identity unit often makes use of a common Indian language and customs and beliefs of Indian origin. However, because of assimilation processes, it may be that the language is replaced and only the historical experience, as symbolized, and the group name remain of the Indian heritage. Nevertheless, the sense of identity among members of culturally assimilated groups may be very intense as a result of alienation from whites. The ethnic group in this sense is of very great importance in understanding developments in Indian–white relations during the 20th century. The 173 entities mentioned at the beginning of this entry are considered ethnic groups of this kind.

Eighty years ago the great majority of Indians lived on government reservations, that is, on land owned collectively by Indians but held in trust for them by the Secretary of the Interior. A small minority of Indians lived on state reservations, chiefly in the eastern United States, and others, as in North Carolina, Michigan, Montana, and California, lived in communities that had no special relationship to state or national government. In Oklahoma, where federal reservations were abolished at the end of the 19th century, federal Indian agencies nevertheless were maintained to take care of various land, business, and other interests of Indians. Nowhere was their mobility restricted; Indians were not required by law to live on any of the several kinds of reservations that had been established for them. While there were small towns around agencies on the reservations, and a few Indians had adapted to city life, until World War II nearly all lived under essentially rural conditions on the reservations or in off-reservation communities.

With the possible exception of some of the northern Athapaskan ones in Alaska, all the Indian communities were composed of genetically mixed peoples. Intermixture with Europeans, blacks, and other Indians had been taking place since colonial times and continued in the 20th century. Among some groups, such as the Nanticokes, Chickahominies, Rappahannocks, Mattaponis, Amherst County, Haliwas, Persons County, Houmas, and Seminoles, intermixture with blacks was especially important. Among Pueblos and Indians of southern California, a major genetic element was Mexican, and in other regions the various European strains predominated. By the 1970s, as Indians moved in large numbers to the cities, a new intensified phase of genetic blending had begun.

Even during the rural phase, Indians began to move into the general occupational structure of the United States. On the reservations, opportunities were limited; most Indians on the western reservations were farmers, stock raisers, laborers, or clerical workers in government jobs. In Oklahoma, as the reservations were abolished, Indians began to enter the whole range of American occupations, from business executives, university professors, politicians, and lawyers to the lower-paid white- and blue-collar positions. Only a very few distinctive Indian occupations developed, such as basket- and pottery-making, blanket-weaving, and high steel construction work.

Movement into American occupations depended heavily on formal schooling. Until the 1930s relatively few Indians were educated for occupations outside the reservations. Indian schools were developed first by the various Christian missions, which reached only a small percentage of Indians during the 19th century. The mission schools were supplemented by schools organized by the Five Civilized Tribes as soon as they became settled in Indian Territory. Until the local tribal governments were abolished by the U.S. government, these were the most advanced school systems west of the Mississippi, and they succeeded in laying a foundation of literacy and elementary education.

The Bureau of Indian Affairs, which assumed responsibility toward the end of the 19th century, relied heavily on boarding schools off the reservations to spearhead the cultural assimilation program. The boarding schools did bring many more Indians into close contact with off-reservation life, but in general they succeeded in orienting only a very few Indians toward the wide range of American occupations. During the 1930s the bureau concentrated on schools on the reservations and also on paying the tuition of Indian children in nearby public schools. These efforts established more and more effective foundations for formal schooling comparable to that of non-Indians. Some tribal councils, such as the Navajo, which began to derive income from oil and gas leasing, provided scholarship funds beginning in the 1940s and 1950s. These, supplemented

by BIA scholarship funds, opened up new opportunities in higher education. In 1970 there were 14,191 young Indians in institutions of higher learning, an increase of nearly 300 percent over 1960. Two Indian junior colleges, established during the 1960s among the Navajos and the Sioux, indicated a trend toward placing Indian and non-Indian education on an equal basis.

The next sections are devoted to the Indian ethnic groups as they exist in the 1970s in 12 regions of the United States. In each region the historical experience and cultural background of the groups have distinctive common elements. A few groups have been selected as illustrative of the range of historical experience and current conditions and have been presented in some detail. The selection is not based on any conception of more or less important groups, but rather on the basis of representativeness. In addition, all of the Indian groups living in each region are listed.

Bibliography
The standard reference for all tribes and their locations is J.R. Swanton, *The Indian Tribes of North America* (1952; reprint, Washington, D.C., 1969). Uniquely useful for recent populations both on and off reservations is Sol Tax, Samuel Stanley, and Robert K. Thomas, *The North American Indians, Distribution of the Descendants of the Aboriginal Population of Alaska, Canada, and the United States* (Chicago, 1961). For aboriginal populations, although it is currently questioned, A.L. Kroeber, *Cultural and Natural Areas of Native North America* (1939; reprint, Berkeley, 1963) is still the most useful. Of the several histories that attempt to cover the whole range of time and cultural variety, Ruth Underhill, *Red Man's America: A History of the Indians of the United States* (1953; reprint, Chicago, 1971), focuses on cultural traits, and E.H. Spicer, *A Short History of the Indians of the United States* (New York, 1969), focuses on Indian–white relations. Robert K. Thomas, "Pan-Indianism," in Stuart Levine and N.O. Lurie, eds., *The American Indian Today* (Deland, Fla., 1968), and *Red Power: The American Indian's Fight for Freedom* compiled by A.M. Josephy, Jr. (New York, 1970), sketch political movements and other cultural processes of the mid-20th century.

PEOPLES OF THE ATLANTIC COAST

In the early 1600s at least 75,000 American Indians lived along the coast from Maine to North Carolina. Divided into approximately 40 groups, they differed from one another in language, customs, and sense of collective identity. However, all of their languages belonged to one linguistic family—Algonkian—and they shared many basic cultural traits, such as the small-scale cultivation of corn, beans, and squash; a religious belief centered on the acquisition of supernatural power through shamans; and a strong tradition of absolutist and hereditary political authority with tribute payments to a principal headman.

In 1970 there were 16 distinct Indian groups in the same area along the Atlantic coast, with a total population of under 10,000. Only two or three of the languages were still in use, although many Algonkian words, such as *pow-wow, wigwam, wampum,* and *quahog,* have entered the English language. In general, their cultural characteristics do not readily distinguish them from the surrounding American culture, but each group has a sense of distinctive identity, which in fact has intensified during the past 50 years. Less than 10 percent of the Indian population live on state reservations and none on federal reservations. The great majority live in communities without a special relationship to the government, and many are scattered among the general population.

In New England, there are Indian communities in Maine, Massachusetts, Connecticut, and Rhode Island. Most populous and prominent are the Wampanoag-Mashpees of Massachusetts, the Narragansetts of Rhode Island, and the Penobscots and Passamaquoddies of Maine, in addition to a small cluster of Pequots and Mohegans in Connecticut.

WAMPANOAG-MASHPEES

In 1960 about 1,200 persons in Massachusetts identified themselves as Wampanoags or Wampanoag-Mashpees. They lived in eight communities in the southeastern part of the state—near Mashpee on Cape Cod; at Gay Head and Christian Town on Martha's Vineyard; near Plymouth, Fall River, Dartmouth, New Bedford, and south of Middleboro, all places where Indians had lived at the time of the first English settlement. Claiming descent from some of the reported 20 groups of Algonkian speakers who formed the Wampanoag-dominated federation of tribes during the 1600s, they are genetically much mixed also with whites and blacks. They all speak English, except for the use of Algonkian in ceremonial songs. Their formerly characteristic bark and pole houses, called wigwams, have not been used since the early 1700s. Their clothing, occupations, religious affiliations, and other customs are also not dissimilar from those of the other people in the area.

Their persisting sense of common identity rests in part on two kinds of distinctive organization. First, Wampanoag tribal councils exist in several communities, such as Mashpee and Gay Head. These representative elected bodies, formally organized in 1972 or earlier from a base of informal leadership groups, are revivals of organizations that existed during the 1940s, the 1860s, and earlier. During the 1970s the Mashpee tribe and the Wampanoag Tribal Council of Gay Head, with the assistance of the Native American Rights Fund, brought suit against the towns of Mashpee and Gay Head for the restoration of land that they claimed had been taken from them illegally. The Wampanoag tribal councils also send delegates to meetings of an organization called the Coalition of Eastern Native Americans.

In addition to this distinctive political organization, the Wampanoag-Mashpees since the 1920s have held an annual pow-wow focusing on intertribal dances, music, and ritual and providing a point of contact with other Indian groups, especially those from the Great Lakes and plains regions. This event has grown in scope and participation, especially during the 1960s. Since 1940 the pow-wow organizers have fostered pageants that portray scenes from Wampanoag history, such as the last stands of Moshup, the Gay Head sachem, and Pometacom (King Philip, d. 1676), leader of the Wampanoag federation and son of Massasoit (d. 1661), who was the first Wampanoag sachem to receive the English, in 1621.

For the modern Wampanoags, Pometacom symbolizes what is most important in their history. Although the period between the arrival of the Pilgrims in 1621 and Massasoit's death was for the most part peaceful under Massasoit's policy of friendly cooperation, the Indians suffered progressive land losses and encroachment, aggressive evangelism, and gradual political subordination. By 1675 Pometacom had quietly organized

all the Indians of southeastern Massachusetts for active resistance, and in a bitter two-year war (King Philip's War) most of the Wampanoag leaders were killed, including Pometacom, whose head was cut off and his body quartered (the parts were exhibited at Plymouth for 24 years). Not only was Wampanoag leadership broken, but Indian community life was destroyed, as the English took over the land. King Philip's greatness has become a legend for both parties to the struggle.

Another series of historical events has gained new significance in today's Wampanoag communities. In 1870 Massachusetts passed legislation that resulted in the loss of the land remaining to the Wampanoag-Mashpees; the last community of Indians at Troy, near Fall River, was dispossessed in 1907. A state senate investigation begun in 1861 decided that the Indians had become self-sufficient economically, having adopted the occupations of surrounding peoples. It also found that there had been much intermixture with blacks and others, although the Indians had tried unsuccessfully to prohibit intermixture. On this basis, sentiment developed in the legislature for abolishing the reservations established by the state in the 1700s and eliminating state aid for schooling and welfare. Despite the fact that the Indian majority voted against the breakup of the reservations (their consent was required by previous agreement), the legislature proceeded to dissolve them. In 1976 these state actions came under legal review with the filing of the suits by the Mashpee and Gay Head councils. A jury decision in 1977 went against the Indians on the grounds that they were not a tribe, but the case was appealed and awaits final decision.

NARRAGANSETTS

The Narragansetts in 1970 numbered approximately 400 persons who lived for the most part in a community at Charlestown, R.I. Every August there is a pow-wow in Charlestown, where ceremonial dances are an important activity. The present-day dances, music, and costumes, like those of the Wampanoags, bear little resemblance to 17th-century practice; they are strongly influenced by plains and other western Indians, as well as by Iroquois. Before the 1970s periodic efforts were made to revive Narragansett ceremonialism.

The Narragansetts maintain a community house, called a longhouse, where tribal meetings and annual elections of councilmen are held. The council deals with internal affairs and relations with other Indian tribes concerning the annual pow-wow, and for two years it published a newspaper called *The Narragansett Dawn*. The group maintains a Methodist church with a Narragansett minister and a committee that manages church affairs. In 1926 the Narragansetts organized a local chapter of the Algonquin Council of Indian Tribes, which gave impetus to the pow-wows, held on the church grounds, and turned them toward an intertribal emphasis.

The Indian Reorganization Act of 1934 (IRA) stimulated tribal organization, although because the Narragansetts do not live on federal trust land, they were not required to have a tribal council. Their church and community organizations provide a channel of communication and a means for maintaining their strong sense of Narragansett identity, which has been sustained for 370 years.

The Narragansetts are completely assimilated culturally in housing, dress, and almost all other aspects of culture. They have not spoken the Narragansett language for at least a hundred years and do not, in contrast with the Wampanoags, have ceremonial songs that preserve the language. They are much mixed genetically with whites, blacks, and some other Indians and have absorbed several other Indian groups, most notably the Niantics.

The Narragansetts were rivals of the Wampanoags and kept themselves distinct, but they joined them in the 1675 war against the English, who had executed their most respected leader, Miantonomo, in 1643. Because of this long-standing grievance and a growing sense of helplessness in the face of English encroachments, the Narragansetts welcomed King Philip's War. They maintained their own separate command but joined actively in support of the Wampanoags; as a result they were nearly exterminated even before Pometacom was defeated. After the war the Narragansetts became increasingly subject to supervision by the English, as their few remaining younger sagamores, or hereditary chiefs, sold one piece of land after another.

By 1709 they held only one very small parcel, which was made into a reservation, where their population very slowly increased over the next century. The Indians built a Methodist church there and maintained a community government. In 1776, the hereditary chiefs having grown irresponsible, the system of sagamore leadership was changed to the elected representative council form (as it remains today). From 1792 the state regulated the election of council members and arranged for a commissioner to represent Narragansett interests before the state legislature.

In 1879 the community voted to abolish its tribal status. Two years later the state confirmed their action and proceeded to break into individual allotments the 1,000 acres that had been held jointly since colonial times. Thus the state reservation was eliminated, but the community organization continued, adopting the designation Narragansett Tribe. It was this organization that brought suit in 1976 for recovery of Narragansett lands on the grounds that the state of Rhode Island had acted illegally in breaking up the reservation and dispossessing the Indians of other lands as well. In 1978 the case was settled out of court with the award of 1,900 acres to the Narragansetts in trust.

PENOBSCOTS

In Maine there are two state reservations inhabited by peoples who preceded whites into the area. In addition there are more than a thousand Malecite and Micmac Indians, who over many years have migrated from Canada. They have no reservations and no special relationship with the U.S. government. In 1970 the Penobscots numbered between 600 and 700, living chiefly in one major community on a reservation near Old Town on the Penobscot River, an area where they have concentrated since 1669. The state-supervised, 4,481-acre reservation is a portion of the land in which they formerly lived and hunted.

Within the community the Penobscots maintain a political system of their own devising and speak of themselves as the Penobscot Nation. The government consists of the Old Party and the New Party, which take

turns every two years controlling the community government. The party in power, served by a single council house, elects a governor, a council, and a representative to the Maine state legislature. In 1975 the Penobscot Nation sued the state for recovery of some 10 million acres that it claimed had been taken from them without the approval of the U.S. Congress, as required by the Indian Nonintercourse Act of 1790. During 1978 the Penobscot attorneys, the state of Maine, and representatives of the federal government negotiated a settlement.

The Penobscots are for the most part bilingual, speaking an Indian language and English. A few families speak Penobscot, but most use Malecite, the language of Indians of northern Maine and Canada who have intermarried extensively with Penobscots. In contrast with Massachusetts Indians, a high proportion of Penobscots are of purely Indian descent, chiefly Penobscot-Malecite or Penobscot-Passamaquoddy mixtures. Most Penobscot cultural traits have been replaced, but much hunting, fishing, forest, and sea lore has been retained and is vital to the important occupation of guiding people through the Maine woods. Another major source of employment is a woolen mill that was built near the Penobscot settlements in 1889.

During colonial times the Penobscots were the largest group of northern Algonkian speakers in their region. They were active in a confederation of Indian nations formed to combat Iroquois expansion; this confederation, however, was dominated by Abnakis and bore their name, despite the numerical importance of Penobscots. They were involved with the French and other Indians against the English, who in the 1740s offered bounties for Penobscot scalps. In 1749, however, a general peace was made between the English and the Penobscots. After the French and Indian War in the late 1700s, when most tribes of western Maine migrated to Canada, land cessions reduced their former large territory to disconnected bits, including islands in the Penobscot River and the community near Old Town. From a reported 1,000 individuals in 1736, the Penobscot population declined to 387 by 1900. Their numbers had almost doubled by 1970.

PASSAMAQUODDIES

In 1970 approximately 700 Passamaquoddies lived in two communities on a state reservation in southeastern Maine near Passamaquoddy Bay. Each community has a local governing body: the Indian Township Tribal Council and the Pleasant Point Tribal Council; in addition there are a Passamaquoddy tribal council and a governor elected by popular vote. While the Passamaquoddy language is spoken by some families, all of these Indians speak English, and many speak Malecite and Micmac. They participate regularly in pow-wows of other eastern Indian groups. They are culturally assimilated to the ways of neighboring whites to about the same degree as the Penobscots.

The Passamaquoddies were not involved in much warfare during the colonial period, although some fought in the Revolution on the side of the Americans. A treaty with the United States in 1777 included a guarantee of their lands in perpetuity, but this treaty was never ratified by Congress. Beginning in 1794, individual chiefs began signing agreements with Maine and Massachusetts to cede all of their extensive hunting ter-

ritory for no compensation whatever. Ultimately the Indians controlled only an 18,000-acre tract, which, when the state of Maine was formed, was recognized as a state reservation. In 1971, working with the Native American Rights Fund, the Passamaquoddy Tribe initiated a suit against the state for recovery of the land that had been signed away without the approval of Congress. In 1975 the U.S. Department of Justice supported the suit and arranged to give assistance in prosecution or negotiation. The case influenced other Indian groups of the eastern United States to bring suits on a similar basis. In 1978 a compromise on the land claim was reached with the state.

NANTICOKES

During the 18th and early 19th centuries the Indians of the Middle Atlantic states—the Mahicans, the large Lenni Lenape (Delaware) Nation, and the Conestoga, for example—were almost entirely eliminated. By the 1970s only three small groups remained in these states—the Poosepatuck and Shinnecock, numbering less than 150 each on tiny state reservations on Long Island, N.Y., and the Nanticokes of southern Delaware.

The Nanticokes in the 1970s numbered between 400 and 500. They live along the Indian River in an area they had occupied at the coming of the Europeans. Their land is individually owned, and they have worked for many years in the local occupations, chiefly farming, chicken raising, and various kinds of wage work. The Nanticokes, who no longer speak the Nanticoke language, have intermarried with both whites and blacks. Some native customs survive, especially among those engaged in fishing, chiefly the customary law regarding use rights along the rivers and a belief in dreams as a mode of establishing relations with the wildlife of the area. Other traditions, such as matrilineal descent of social status and property, have entirely disappeared. All of the Nanticokes are nominal Christians. Generally classed by local whites as colored and on that basis excluded from white schools until the 1950s, some Nanticokes formed the Nanticoke Indian Association, which was successful in eliminating segregation. However, a segment of the community preferred to identify with blacks, and a division along those lines continues to exist in the community.

The Nanticokes were one of the Algonkian-speaking coastal groups of the Chesapeake Bay that were strongly hostile to the early white settlers. Their hostilities culminated in war in 1742 when they, along with the Choptanks and the Conoys, were defeated, and Maryland established a reservation for them. The Nanticokes split into three bands; one group joined the Delawares and went with them during their westward migrations to Texas and Indian Territory. Another group, associated primarily with the Conoys, moved north, establishing temporary settlements (sometimes still known as "Nanticoke Towns") in Pennsylvania and New York. By 1781 this band was at Fort Niagara, N.Y., where they lived under the protection of the Iroquois. Shortly after, they moved into Canada and were merged among the Iroquois in the Six Nations Reserve. The third group returned from the Maryland reservation to their traditional territory in southern Delaware and settled as fishermen and tenant farmers. After 1865, when the plantations were broken up, they bought land,

which they still own. Culturally they have steadily assimilated into the rural life of the area, but they preserve a strong sense of Indian identity in their daily lives.

CHICKAHOMINIES

Five different, formerly Algonkian-speaking peoples lived in Virginia in the 1970s. In 1960 more than 3,000 persons were recorded as identifying as Indians, but the 1970 census estimated barely 2,000. The great majority live in independent communities outside the two state reservations.

The most numerous of the Virginia Indians in 1970 were the Chickahominies, of whom there were about 500, the same population as in 1923, living southeast of Richmond. The people, much mixed with blacks, whites, and other local Indian groups, made a determined effort in the late 19th century to avoid being categorized as Negro by the state and were successful, with the assistance of their Baptist church connection and the county government, in having themselves classified as Indians. They maintain a tribal organization with elected representatives. During the past 75 to 80 years they have become increasingly culturally assimilated, ceasing to speak their Algonkian language and generally adopting white ways. Only with respect to fishing, hunting, and some farming practices have traditional ways of thought and practice been retained. Since the 1920s they have engaged in pow-wows of eastern Indians and through such activities have revived an interest in native dances, music, and ceremonial costume.

At the time of European settlement, the Chickahominies lived on the southern margin of the settlements controlled by the chief Powhatan (c. 1550–1618). However, they maintained their own separate tribal organization and in the early 1600s were probably the largest Indian nation in Virginia. Renouncing ties with Powhatan in 1613, they made a treaty with the English in which they agreed to be "forever called Englishmen." When a new English governor tried to exact more tribute from them, however, they resisted and became involved in hostilities between the English and Powhatan's people, under the leadership of Opechancanough of the Pamunkeys. The major settlement of the Chickahominies was destroyed by the British, Openchancanough was disastrously defeated, and the Pamunkeys made a treaty ceding all the lands of the Powhatan Confederacy to the English. The Chickahominies withdrew from further contact, but settlers moving into the interior overwhelmed them, and by 1660 they were almost landless. The English gave them a grant of land not in their traditional territory, but to the north in former Pamunkey territory, and placed them under the domination of the Pamunkeys. Their independent position deteriorated thereafter; by 1750 they had lost their reservation, their several towns had been reduced to one, and their population was apparently less than 300. By the end of the 1700s it seemed that the Chickahominy language, style of dress, and other ways were lost. They were landless, poverty-stricken wanderers, and yet through all their troubles they retained a tribal organization. Around 1800 all the remaining Chickahominies were converted by a Baptist evangelist, whose activities were stimulated by the second Great Awakening, which was then sweeping the American frontier.

During the last half of the 19th century the Chickahominies drifted back to their traditional territory and formed two communities, each with a Baptist church as the center of community life. Their traditional organization had disintegrated, but they organized themselves sufficiently to adopt measures that emphasized their Indian identity, such as wearing their hair long and barring intermarriage and social mingling with blacks. During the 1880s they began to revive the use of Indian given names. By the end of the 19th century the state of Virginia began to make certain distinctions in law between Indians and blacks, and a separate Indian school was established for them.

In the early 20th century, anthropologists James Mooney and Frank Speck encouraged them to reinstitute their traditional form of tribal organization. Further impetus in this direction came from the Algonquin Council of Indian Tribes, which was first organized in the 1920s by their neighbors, the Rappahannocks.

PAMUNKEYS

In any description of their history and present condition, the Pamunkeys cannot be readily separated from their immediate neighbors, the Rappahannocks and the Mattaponis. In 1970 these three groups numbered approximately 2,000 to 3,000. Fewer than a hundred each of Pamunkeys and Mattaponis live on the two state reservations established for them. The others are scattered through tidewater Virginia between Richmond and the coast from the James River to the Rappahannock. Five distinct communities exist, organized as tribes and affiliated with Baptist churches. The reservation-dwelling Pamunkeys and Mattaponis each speak of themselves as a tribe and maintain organizations that in some features resemble the organization that existed in the 1600s when the Pamunkeys were politically dominant. Most of the reservation dwellers, who are accorded higher status than the scattered families, are farmers, and some are in small business; all engage in fishing. Their housing and other traits are like those of the surrounding American culture. English is the only language used.

The Pamunkeys were the heirs of the Powhatan Confederacy, which was reported by the early English settlers as consisting of some 30 nations whose population was estimated as high as 9,000 to 10,000. These nations were probably small groups of villages with local names that distinguished one group from another; they may have spoken different dialects. Powhatan, a hereditary leader, headed the confederacy at the time of the founding of Jamestown in 1607. He was regarded by the English as a king, and his family constituted a royal line. His relations with the English, at first hostile, improved after his niece, Pocahantas (1595?–1617), married John Rolfe. But an undercurrent of hostility was continually fed by small clashes between Indians and outposts of English settlers, usually over land encroachments. When Opechancanough succeeded Powhatan in 1618, the clashes intensified, and in 1622 Opechancanough unsuccessfully led some Pamunkeys in organized resistance. For the next 20 years the English regularly de-

stroyed Indian crops and laid waste their fields. Both sides were guilty of frequent killings.

In 1644, when the last Indian resistance was contained and Opechancanough was killed, the confederacy completely disintegrated, and the English introduced direct rule over them. The Indians still thought in terms of a Pamunkey royal line, with hegemony over all the Indians of Virginia, even though the English were wholly dominant. The Pamunkeys' status as the leading nation was emphasized by their successful defeats of the Iroquois, who raided Virginia in the late 17th century. In peace treaties signed by the British, the Iroquois, and other Indians in 1685 and 1722, the Pamunkeys were officially accorded this special status.

The English made vigorous efforts to culturally assimilate the Pamunkeys and associated Virginia peoples during the 18th century. In 1714 the Pamunkeys agreed to send 20 young men every year to study at William and Mary College. The Pamunkeys and others formally agreed to become Christians, and active proselytizing by various Protestant denominations continued through the century. By 1727 an official interpreter was regarded as no longer necessary in the courts and elsewhere, and the office was abolished, not because the Algonkian languages had disappeared, but because many Indians had become bilingual. The village groups had been displaced from their territories and were no longer in touch with one another. By the end of the century many Virginians believed that the Pamunkeys would disappear in a few years.

They did not disappear, however. Although the Pamunkeys and other Indians worked in many of the occupations common in the tidewater area, such as sailing, fishing, and various kinds of skilled work, the Pamunkeys and Rappahannocks especially continued to maintain a distinct Indian identity. This effort was powerfully stimulated by their desire not to be classified and treated as Negroes and, like that of the Chickahominies, it met with some success. They have retained their Indian identity and some degree of continuity in the traditional Algonkian political and community organization. The process has also been aided by the state's creation of reservations for Pamunkeys and Mattaponis, which, although few live on them, provide stable political centers. The Rappahannocks in the 1920s made a wider Indian identification, participating in the formation of the Algonquin Council of Indian Tribes, which brought the Virginia nations together again.

Other Atlantic coast Indians in the 1970s were the following: the Malecites and Micmacs of Maine; the Montauks, Poosepatucks, and Shinnecocks of New York; the Mattaponis and Rappahannocks of Virginia; the Nipmucs of Massachusetts; and the Paugusetts, Pequots, Mohegans, and Scaticooks of Connecticut.

Bibliography
The only introductory survey of history and cultural changes among the coastal Algonkians is T.J.C. Brasser, "The Coastal Algonkians: People of the First Frontiers," in Eleanor B. Leacock and Nancy O. Lurie, eds., *North American Indians in Historical Perspective* (New York, 1971). Two valuable cultural histories detailing processes of change and tribal persistence are T. Stern, *Chickahominy: The Changing Culture of a Virginia Indian Community* (Philadelphia, 1952), and E. Boissevain, "Narragansett Survival, A Study of Group Persistence through Adopted Traits," in Deward E. Walker, ed., *The Emergent Native Americans* (Boston, 1972). For the early history of Indian–white contacts, see Alden T. Vaughan, *New England Frontier: Puritans and Indians, 1620–1675* (Boston, 1965), and Francis Jennings, *The Invasion of America* (Chapel Hill, N.C., 1975). For an Indian viewpoint on the history and culture of once-important Massachusetts Indian groups, see Milton A. Travers, *The Wampanoag Indian Federation: Indian Neighbors of the Pilgrims* (Boston, 1961).

THE DEPOPULATED SOUTHEAST

In 1970 in the area extending from the Atlantic coast to the Mississippi River and, excluding Virginia, from the Ohio River south to the Gulf of Mexico, there were eight distinct Indian groups with a total population of less than 40,000. One of them—the Lumbees—numbered almost 30,000; the population of the other groups was about 6,500–7,000. This large region is one of small Indian population, in sharp contrast to the early years of contact with Europeans. During the 17th and 18th centuries it was one of the most heavily populated Indian regions, with as many as 23 distinct Indian peoples at the time of the beginning of the European invasions. Two-thirds of the groups apparently have been eliminated, and a population estimated at more than 150,000 reduced by more than two-thirds. If, because of their peculiar circumstances, we set aside the Lumbees for the moment, the Indian population may be said to have declined by about 90 percent.

This great contrast between conditions in the late 17th and the mid-20th centuries came about largely because the southeastern states were the scene in the 19th century of the most thoroughgoing application of the removal policy. These states were President Andrew Jackson's home territory, and it was he who set out to clear the region of Indians. His policy was popular with the whites, because of the tremendous land boom in the 1830s, stimulated by cotton production. Although not totally successful, the policy did remove the region's largest and most "civilized" tribes. By 1970 Kentucky, Tennessee, Georgia, and West Virginia had no Indian communities; Alabama had only a scattered few, and South Carolina had but one small community. Only three states—North Carolina, Florida, and Mississippi—had numbers comparable to those of the surviving Indian groups in the coastal states of the Northeast.

EASTERN BAND OF CHEROKEES

In 1960, in the mountainous southwest corner of North Carolina, there were 4,266 Cherokees living on a federal reservation of 44,000 acres. Residents of this reservation constitute a small minority of the former Cherokee nation; the great majority was deported in the 1830s to Indian Territory. The official name of the North Carolina group is Eastern Band of Cherokees.

The Eastern Band was organized in the manner of most Indians on federal reservations who formed tribal councils under the regulations of the IRA in the 1930s. The Eastern Band has a constitution and a tribal council whose primary function is the regulation of land usage. Elected for terms of two years by popular vote of reservation residents, council members represent the six towns into which the reservation is divided. All who can prove one-thirty-second Cherokee descent are eligible to vote. There are also Free Labor Companies, based on the traditional *gadugi*, social units that

cooperate with each other in labor exchange. A chief and a vice-chief are elected every four years.

One of the chief's functions is to serve as president of the Fair Association, which sponsors an annual fair designed to encourage the Cherokee farmers in agricultural pursuits and to revive some traditional entertainments, such as the stickball game. A Cherokee Historical Association maintains a museum that presents exhibits on Cherokee history and culture and sponsors a summer production of *Unto These Hills*, a historical drama that attracts millions of tourists every year. Many ceremonial dances have been revived.

Most Cherokees are members of Baptist churches, and some are Holiness, Methodist, or Episcopal church members, but many also participate in traditional religious dances and ceremonies. Cherokee religion as an integrated whole has disappeared. The Cherokee language is used in the home by perhaps 50 percent of the families, although many of them also speak English. The syllabary devised by the leader Sequoyah (1770?–1843) is used by some individuals, even though an effort to teach it along with the Cherokee language in the schools has failed. Bibles written in the syllabary are used by many older people.

When the main body of Cherokees was forcibly removed from their territory in northern Georgia during 1833–1838, about 1,000 fugitives scattered into North Carolina and were never deported. Many of these were followers of Yonahguski, a conservative peace leader who, yielding to the intense pressures that had built up for Indian land cessions by 1819, had signed a treaty ceding a large amount of land to Georgia. Yonahguski was awarded a personal holding of 640 acres at the important ancient town site of Kituhwa, which became the nucleus of the area in which the fugitives settled.

When Yonahguski died in 1839, a white trader named William Thomas, who had lived among the Cherokees for some 20 years, undertook to legalize the fugitives' residence in North Carolina and to secure more land for them. Five towns of the traditional Cherokee type were established in the vicinity of what became the federal reservation, but there was no formal organization until 1861. In 1870 Cherokee efforts to organize the five towns resulted in a tribal government, which was incorporated in 1889. Meanwhile, the U.S. commissioner of Indian affairs had taken note of the Eastern Band and had become trustee for their lands, which were all secured by individual deeds.

In 1881 the Society of Friends established schools, and a majority of Cherokees became bilingual. Most became small-scale farmers, raising cattle and hogs, but by the 1920s conditions for this kind of farming had deteriorated, and the Cherokee standard of living steadily declined. It was not until the early 1950s that the tourist business resulted in relative economic prosperity. By this time their houses and general lifestyle closely approximated that of rural whites of the region.

The reservation is by no means culturally homogeneous, however. Lifestyles and world views range from that of the full-bloods, who constitute about one-fourth of the population, to that of what some observers call middle-class Indians. The latter, a very small part of the population, are employed in nonfarming business and in the reservation offices of the Bureau of Indian Affairs. The majority are oriented to both sets of values,

expressing one or the other extreme in different circumstances at different times. Some think of themselves as Indians and attend Indian pow-wows across the United States, but are not fully at ease with the ways of the full-bloods. Some identify with Indians at times but are more fully oriented toward the local rural white way of life.

LUMBEES

In 1970 about 31,000 Lumbees lived in southeastern North Carolina, constituting the principal element in the population of Robeson County, where they live in small towns and as scattered rural families. The major concentration is in and around the town of Pembroke. About 600–700 live immediately over the state line in South Carolina, and another 2,000 recent emigrants from Robeson County live in Baltimore.

The Lumbees are a nearly unique group of Indians in the United States. Although they identify themselves very definitely as Indians, no vestige of an Indian language is spoken among them, nor is there any conclusive historical or ethnological evidence that they have ever spoken an Indian language. One supposition is that their ancestors spoke a Siouan language, and another that the ancient language was Algonkian. The name Lumbee itself is of unknown origin and has never been attributed to any tribal group on record. The major river flowing through Robeson County is officially named the Lumber River, although the Indians call it the Lumbee, leading to speculation that they derived their name from the river. Investigators during the 19th century became convinced that the Lumbees were derived from the "Croatan Indians" of the Cape Hatteras area and persuaded the North Carolina legislature in 1885 to officially name them the "Croatans." The Indians rejected the designation, because there never was such an Indian group. In 1911 the legislature also rejected the name Croatan and officially named them Indians of Robeson County.

The Lumbees maintain that they are of mixed origin, combining an unknown Indian element with that of the lost colony founded in Roanoke Island in 1587 by John White, which was never definitely identified thereafter. The first records that clearly cite the Lumbees are land grants to individuals beginning in 1732. There was no indication that they used any other language than English at that time. Their physical appearance ranges from clearly European to a dark-skinned type classified as Indian, which led to their suffering the same disabilities as Negroes during the 19th century. In the 20th century they have been the victims of discrimination in some places, and the Ku Klux Klan has burned crosses in their communities.

A notable characteristic of the Lumbees has been a strong sense of solidarity. This became especially apparent after 1835, when the North Carolina Constitutional Convention, responding to fears generated by slave insurrections and abolitionist activities, excluded nonwhites from political participation and the benefits of citizenship. For the next 50 years Lumbees were disfranchised and denied schools. Tensions mounted in Robeson County, culminating during the 1860s in what became known as the Lowrie War. The hero of this series of conflicts, from the Lumbee perspective, was Henry Berry Lowrie, who led a band of Lumbees in guer-

rilla warfare in the county until he mysteriously disappeared in 1872.

It was not until 1885 that the status of Lumbees as Indians began to receive attention. Funds were made available for the development of a school, first called the Croatan Normal School and later renamed Pembroke State College. As the college improved and became the major educational influence in the area, Lumbees gradually took the important roles in its faculty and administration. In the meantime they regained the right to vote, and in the 1880s they began to organize the Christian religious life that they had carried on, without benefit of churches, for more than a century. In 1880 what became the Burnt Swamp Baptist Association, the major Lumbee church organization, was organized to unite the Baptist communities in Robeson County. By the 1970s there were also Methodist, Assembly of God, Holiness, and other churches. There seems never to have been any form of native Indian religion or ceremony.

In the 1950s some Lumbees began to believe that the group was descended from the Tuscaroras, who had migrated from eastern North Carolina to join the Iroquois Confederacy. They held that some Tuscaroras had stayed behind, moved west, and become the ancestors of the Lumbees. Mad Bear, a well-known militant leader of the New York Tuscaroras, visited the Lumbees in 1954, encouraged them in this belief, and urged more vigorous efforts to establish their status as Indians through federal recognition. The Lumbees of the 1970s, who by then had a relatively high level of formal education, campaigned for recognition by the federal government which, in the late 1970s had not been conferred.

CATAWBAS

The population of the Catawbas, the only group of Indians in South Carolina, except for scattered Lumbee families, was listed in 1970 as 631, but the tribal roll that year carried 1,334 individuals. Most live on individually owned land near Rock Hill in the northern part of the state, but some live on a 640-acre tract that was once a state reservation and is now collectively owned. Since 1900 no one has spoken the original Siouan language. The Catawbas are almost wholly culturally assimilated, working in industry or engaged in farming, small business, or clerical work. Nearly all are Mormons, having been converted by missionaries in the 1880s. Their political organization consists of the Catawba Nation Executive Tribal Committee and a popularly elected general assembly. Elections are held once a year, but the chairman, vice-chairman, and two councilors serve staggered terms of one, three, and four years. They hold no pow-wow of their own and, except for attendance at the Eastern Cherokee Fall Festival each year, rarely participate in other Indian pow-wows.

During the late 17th century they were reputed to have been a nation of 6,000 and were rated by the English as one of the four great nations of the region. They increased rapidly in numbers and prestige during the early 1700s, and they took into a confederacy and ultimately absorbed a number of Siouan-speaking peoples from the Atlantic coast to the mountains. They supported the English against the Tuscaroras in 1711 but joined with the Creeks and others in the Yamassee War against the English in 1715, which involved all the In-

dians from North Carolina down the coast to St. Augustine, Fla. The Catawbas extricated themselves before a crushing defeat of the other Indians and thereafter supported the English. Although distinguished fighters, they suffered serious defeats by the Senecas in 1737 and, as smallpox epidemics hit them, lost population heavily. During the next 25 years they declined to barely 400 people, who were dependent on the English and sought their protection in Virginia.

In 1763, at the close of the French and Indian War, they made a treaty with the colony of South Carolina, which assured them of 144,000 carefully bounded acres containing the site of the former capital of their six towns. They maintained a tribal government on this land, and two of their headmen, Young Warrior and "King" Hagler, became well known. Their numbers continued to decline; they leased most of their land to whites and became increasingly dependent on the state. In 1840, after years of pressure for Indian removal, they made a treaty with South Carolina, which provided that the state would pay them $5,000 for their 144,000 acres if they would leave the state. The Catawbas were anxious to join the Five Civilized Tribes in their move to Indian Territory, but the Cherokees rejected them, although a few Catawbas settled among the Eastern Band. The Choctaws accepted a few, who moved west with them. Some very small groups on their own initiative moved to Colorado and Utah, where they still preserve their identity, their number being less than 100. The fewer than 100 who remained in South Carolina were ultimately given a state reservation of 640 acres of very poor land, but no assistance of any kind for nearly 50 years. Throughout their ordeals they maintained the office of chief and an elected council.

In 1941 the Bureau of Indian Affairs took over their jurisdiction. It secured 2,500 acres of better land, over which it assumed trusteeship and introduced a constitution and tribal government but supplied no services. In 1959 the Catawba Tribal Committee asked that tribal assets be divided among the individuals but that federal recognition be maintained. In 1961 the newly acquired land was distributed, and the BIA withdrew from jurisdiction, but the tribe retained ownership of the 640-acre reservation.

In 1904 the Catawba Nation advanced a claim against the state for the 144,000 acres taken as a result of the treaty of 1840. In 1972 this claim was renewed, with the aid of the Native American Rights Fund, in the form of a suit for restoration of the land or compensation. In the late 1970s the suit was still unresolved.

SEMINOLES AND MICCOSUKEES

In 1967 there were 1,350 Indians in Florida, 1,000 identifying as Seminoles and 350 as Miccosukees. Most of the Seminoles live on three federal reservations, one at the western edge of Lake Okeechobee and two near the Big Cypress Swamp in southern Florida. The Miccosukees live on several parcels of land near the Everglades under a single BIA administration. A state reservation exists, but it is not much used. In addition, some 400 Indians live along the Tamiami Trail and elsewhere in independent communities.

Both the Seminoles and Miccosukees are organized under the IRA with constitutions and tribal councils. Their lands are held by tribal titles under federal trust.

The Seminoles speak a Muskogean language related to Creek, the Miccosukees a language of the Hitchiti family. Many are nominal members of Southern Baptist congregations, but native religious participation is common, especially in the all-night dance-ground ceremony derived from the Creek religion. Traditional dress and palm thatch houses (called *chikee* by many whites) are common. A return to native crafts has been encouraged since the 1960s, such as basketry, beadwork, leather goods, and patchwork. As an important tourist attraction, exhibition villages in aboriginal style have been established both on and off the reservation. Since 1959 there has been much interest in pan-Indian pow-wows. Although they often live near one another, the Seminoles and Miccosukees maintain separate identities, reinforced by the use of different languages.

Neither the Seminoles nor the Miccosukees are native to the area. At the time of the European invasions, Florida was occupied by tribes that became extinct from disease, enslavement, deportation to the West Indies, and warfare. Beginning in the late 1600s, members of the Creek Confederacy began to raid from the north and then settle in the region that the Spaniards controlled and called Florida. The Creek settlement continued through the 18th century, first in the north around Tallahassee and what is now Gainesville but steadily extending southward into central Florida. Among the Creek-affiliated settlers were some speakers of Hitchiti languages, the ancestors of the Miccosukees. The Muskogean-speaking pioneers among the Creeks were the forebears of the reservation-dwelling Seminoles. The term Seminole was not an aboriginal tribal name but came from the Spanish word *cimarrón*, perhaps with the broad meaning of frontiersmen or pioneers, as used by the Creeks.

These Indians from the north retained their languages and way of life with a minimum of European influence until well into the 19th century. In 1814, after Andrew Jackson's defeat of the conservative Redstick faction of the Creeks, several hundred refugees made their way south to join the Florida Indians. The U.S. government turned its attention in this direction, both because the Americans wished to eliminate the Spaniards from their southern border and also because the region had become a haven for escaped slaves. These concerns sparked what was called the First Seminole War in 1817–1818, in which U.S. troops destroyed the Muskogean-speaking towns from the coast west to Tallahassee. After the United States acquired Florida in 1819, the federal government made an agreement with the Seminoles. Although the Indians had no central governing body, the United States forced them to cede all claims to land in Florida in return for a reservation in the central swampland. However, the reservation was never established.

According to the government, the situation in Florida had not improved: the Indians were accused of harboring slaves and there were some raids, which eventually led to the Second Seminole War in 1835. The war lasted seven years and was extremely costly to the government because of the very great difficulties imposed by the terrain. By 1842 U.S. troops had rounded up 4,420 Indians, along with many blacks, and deported them to Indian Territory in accord with Jackson's policy of forced removal, where they became known as one of the Five Civilized Tribes. Only 500 Indians remained in the vicinity of the Big Cypress Swamp in extreme southwestern Florida. In 1860 the Third Seminole War resulted in the deportation of 240 more Indians and blacks, leaving 200–300 in the most impenetrable region of all—the Everglades.

The Bureau of Indian Affairs in 1891 began to seek land for the remnant of Florida Indians and ultimately established three reservations, but as late as 1930 only 10 percent had accepted bureau supervision. Even in 1970 more than a quarter of the Indians preferred to live off the reservations.

Other Indians of the Southeast in the 1970s were the Altamahas of Georgia, some Creeks of Alabama, and the Choctaws of Mississippi.

Bibliography
Most useful on the few surviving tribes in the Southeast are John Gulick, *Cherokees at the Crossroads* (Chapel Hill, N.C., 1960); W.C. Sturtevant, "Creek into Seminole," in E.B. Leacock and N.O. Lurie, eds., *North American Indians in Historical Perspective* (New York, 1971); and Charles M. Hudson, *The Catawba Nation* (Athens, Ga., 1970). Adolph L. Dial and David K. Eliades, *The Only Land I Know: A History of the Lumbee Indians* (San Francisco, 1975), gives an Indian view of the history of this controversial tribe.

THE IROQUOIS OF THE EASTERN GREAT LAKES COUNTRY

On the U.S. side of Lakes Ontario and Erie in the 1970s there were Indians only in the state of New York; the Conestogas, Eries, Neutrals, and other Indians of Pennsylvania and Ohio had disappeared from the region. Those who live in New York are Iroquoian-speaking peoples; numbering at least 10,300, they live on eight state-supervised reservations and in widely scattered families throughout the state and in Brooklyn. They identify broadly as Iroquois (descendants of the League of the Iroquois) but primarily as belonging to one of six distinct tribal groups—Mohawk, Onondaga, Cayuga, Oneida, Seneca, and Tuscarora—as had their ancestors at least since the 1500s. The six groups are officially designated as nations in New York State.

The total Iroquois population in the 1970s was between 20,000 and 25,000. Besides those in New York, somewhat fewer than 10,000 live in Canada, 3,500 in Wisconsin, and 900–1,000 in Oklahoma. Although the history and present life of the Canadian and New York Iroquois are not separable, the following discussion is confined mainly to those in New York. Of the six distinct national or tribal identities, the Mohawks, Onondagas, Tuscaroras, and Senecas have their own reservations; the Cayugas have no reservation, but the 303 listed members of that nation in 1970 lived on one of the Senecas' reservations; the Oneidas have no reservation in New York but do have some tax-exempt land on which 129 individuals live, while 470 others live on the Onondagas' reservation. Another 3,500 Oneidas live in Wisconsin on their own reservation.

Until recently the Senecas were the largest of the six nations, with a population of 4,600 on three reservations in western New York. The Mohawks were the second largest, with an official population of 2,229 on a single reservation along the St. Lawrence River; they call themselves the St. Regis Band of Mohawks. Some 800 Mohawks from the Caughnawaga Reservation in Canada live in Brooklyn. The Onondagas numbered 900

on one reservation, and the Tuscaroras, about 700 on their reservation. The progressive loss of their once-vast hunting territories after early contact with whites has been a major theme of Iroquois life. However, only the Tuscaroras have been completely displaced from their former homeland in eastern North Carolina.

The Iroquoian languages are spoken in some homes in all of the groups, including the Brooklyn community of Mohawks, with the highest proportion of Iroquoian-speakers among the Senecas and the Mohawks. Probably most adult Iroquois are bilingual, and many know two or three Indian languages as well as English.

Their lifestyle has changed profoundly since the time of the fur trade in the 18th century, and there has been a great deal of cultural assimilation. Twentieth-century ranch-style and suburban houses mingle with earlier 19th-century frame farmhouses. Incomes vary widely, as Iroquois have moved into a wide range of occupations as professionals, white-collar workers, and skilled and unskilled labor in various businesses. Their most distinctive specialty is high-steel construction work on bridges and skyscrapers. Iroquois belong to many different Christian churches, the Mohawks being predominantly Catholic. However, more than half of the New York Iroquois, including many members of Christian churches, are active participants in the Handsome Lake religion, sometimes called the New, or the Longhouse, religion. Members are found on all the reservations, with the heaviest concentrations among the Senecas and the Onondagas. There are ten Longhouses, or religious centers, in the New York and Canadian Iroquois communities. A single organization brings together annually the members of all six nations for extended ceremonies.

Political organization also links the people of the various reservation communities. One form of organization recognizes the authority of hereditary leaders and preserves the traditions of the aboriginal League of the Iroquois, but this concept is rejected by many Senecas and others, whose councils are composed of elected representatives. Usually both kinds of organization exist on a reservation, and each has its adherents. Whichever form is followed, there is a commonly held belief that the Iroquois are a sovereign people and not subject to the U.S. government, except with regard to land matters. In that respect the authority of Congress is recognized as paramount within the framework of treaties it has ratified.

During the 1950s and later, the Mohawks, Senecas, and Tuscaroras found themselves in conflict with the New York State Power Authority and the U.S. Army Corps of Engineers over proposed power and flood-control projects. The Indians sought injunctions and brought suits to stop the government from appropriating parts of the small amount of reservation land left to them. The power authority attempted, without consulting the Indians, to take the land. In one case the Tuscaroras succeeded in blocking their efforts; other projects were eventually carried out, but only after the fight had been carried to Congress. The Kinzua Dam controversy, in which the Senecas brought suit, gained national attention and enlisted the support of many whites.

These conflicts, together with the general conditions of ethnic group assertion during the 1950s and 1960s,

led to reinvigoration of the Iroquois sense of identity. In the 1960s boys and young men revived the old scalp-lock hairdo. Indian costume was revived, usually in the manner of the Sioux of the northern plains or of the Chippewa of the western Great Lakes. A cultural revival movement with a strong civil-rights orientation derived leadership chiefly from the more highly educated Iroquois. A Tuscarora named Mad Bear gained national attention in the struggle against the state power authority. Mad Bear visited widely among such Indians as the Catawba, the Miccosukee, and western tribes, demanding recognition of long-ignored Indian rights and calling attention to the federal government's mismanagement of Indian affairs. The militant movement also resulted in some new efforts to educate Iroquois adults and schoolchildren more fully in their history and cultural heritage and to project the Iroquois viewpoint on historical and current matters into the schools and before the public.

At the time of first contacts with Europeans, the Onondagas, Senecas, Mohawks, Oneidas, and Cayugas were organized into a confederacy, called by whites the League of the Iroquois, which unified the efforts of the Iroquois to take a leading role in the fur trade and to contain the French and the English. But the league had a deeper significance in Iroquois life. According to Iroquois legend, it was founded by two late-16th-century men, Deganawidah and Hiawatha, who conceived the idea of uniting the five peoples in a council of 50 sachems and proclaimed sacred principles of law unique among the Indians of the Great Lakes or of any other region. Imbued with faith in these laws, the Five Iroquois Nations became the most powerful of the Northeast Indians, destroying, absorbing, or becoming the protectors of all the tribes around them, including their Algonkian neighbors. Even large nations like the Delawares accepted their military and spiritual dominance.

Although the Iroquois became the enemies of the French and were generally supportive of the English, their real aim with respect to the Europeans was to be the dominant middlemen in the fur trade with the Indians of the North and West. In this they were successful during the early 1700s, but as friction developed between the British and their colonies, the pressures on the Iroquois from three sides became divisive. By the time of the American Revolution, the Six Nations (the Tuscaroras had joined the original five) were hopelessly split, and the league was no longer a power. During the Revolution the Oneidas and the Tuscaroras gave aid to the colonists, while the Cayugas, the Senecas, and many Mohawks were pro-British. When the English were defeated, the Americans destroyed the Seneca villages and fields and in 1783 took over the greater part of the land of the Cayugas, Mohawks, and Onondagas. Some fled to Canada when offered a large land grant there; this land became the Six Nations Reserve and served as a major center of Iroquois life into the 1970s. The New York Mohawks lost most of their population, which had dwindled to about 400, in the Canadian migration. After the Revolution the Americans sought to cultivate the able Seneca leader, Cornplanter, as leader of the New York Iroquois and gave him land grants in the old Seneca territory; these became the Allegany and the Cattaraugus reservations.

However, the spirit of the Senecas, as of the other Iro-

quois in New York State, had been broken. Their rebuilt villages became slums in the wilderness, disorganized and beset with drunken young men. New pressures came from the whites intent on acquiring land. In a treaty of 1797 most of the remaining Seneca land was ceded for a small sum. Without their hunting grounds, the Senecas sank into deep despair, a thoroughly disorganized society.

Meanwhile, a new force had developed within Seneca society. In 1800, Handsome Lake, one of the drunken young men of the 1790s, received a revelation that he believed pointed the way to a new life. The new way consisted of combining the old religious traditions with elements of white ways. By the time of his death in 1815, his sacred code of behavior had spread to all the Six Nations except the St. Regis Mohawks. Longhouses were built as centers for the new religion, which continues to be a major influence in Iroquois life.

As the new religion expanded, the state of New York, spurred on by land interests and missionaries, tried to remove the Indians to the west, to facilitate the purchase of their lands. Two Iroquois factions—the Christians and the Pagans—crystallized during the early 1800s. It was a period of deep disorganization, but eventually five small pieces of land were retained, and after 1840 the code of Handsome Lake and new concepts of political organization began to point out new directions. In 1848 the Seneca Nation was formed, with a republican form of government composed of a council of 18 members, a president, and three peacemakers or judges. This organization, chartered by the federal government, helped to revitalize Iroquois political life, although the hereditary chief system of the old league persisted in the other communities. Many Iroquois attended Carlisle Indian School in Pennsylvania, another important stimulus for encouraging new contacts among the Six Nations. In 1925 Iroquois leaders joined with other Indians and whites in organizing an Indian Defense League, which sought to redress long-standing grievances and give the American public a better understanding of what Indians regarded as government injustices. This league was a mild precursor of the more vigorous militancy of the 1950s and 1960s.

Bibliography
Edmund Wilson gives a penetrating description, together with relevant history, of 20th-century Iroquois life in *Apologies to the Iroquois* (New York, 1960). Anthony F. Wallace, *The Death and Rebirth of the Seneca* (New York, 1970), is a classic cultural history of one Iroquois tribe. More technical, but indispensable for basic understanding of Iroquois life, is A.A. Shimony, *Conservatism among the Iroquois at the Six Nations Reserve* (New Haven, Conn., 1961).

THE WESTERN GREAT LAKES COUNTRY

In the 1960s more than 33,000 Indians lived in the states (Michigan, Indiana, Illinois, Wisconsin, and Minnesota) adjacent to Lakes Huron, Michigan, and Superior. This figure represents about two-thirds of the number living there when the French began to arrive in the 1500s. While most of the groups have shrunk since then, and at least one large group—the Illinois—has become extinct, the Chippewa, or Ojibwa group is considerably larger than at the time of first European contact.

Since the 1500s the number of distinct Indian groups has decreased from 14 to 10. However, these figures mask the shifts in location of the Indian tribes of this region. Of the ten groups present in the 1960s, three—the Oneidas, the Stockbridges, and the Brothertons—were not descendants of original inhabitants of the region but had come from the east as a result of white pressures. Of the remaining seven, five represented only parts of earlier groups, larger segments having migrated or been forcibly removed from the region as a result of white settlement. Five groups had completely left the region through migration, which was voluntary only in the sense that the decision was made by Indians faced with white invasion. It is apparent, therefore, that the distribution of peoples in this region has changed radically and is a result of a history of conflict among Indians and between Indians and whites.

By states the distribution is very uneven. Illinois has no Indians outside of Chicago, and in Indiana there are only a few hundred Miamis living in scattered families. Minnesota has the largest number, with a rural population of 18,450 living outside of Minneapolis–St. Paul. Wisconsin has the second-largest Indian population with 13,927 in seven separate groups. Michigan has about 1,500 Indians.

CHIPPEWAS

As of the 1960s a total of about 36,000 Chippewas (often called Ojibwas) lived in the United States, mostly in Minnesota, and at least this many in Canada. Their distribution was as follows:

Minnesota	17,860
North Dakota	9,700
Wisconsin	4,800
Michigan	2,450
Montana	1,160

The modern U.S. total is about the same as the whole Chippewa population in 1650. By 1884 the number of Chippewas had declined to possibly 15,000, but since then it has steadily climbed, and the growth rate seemed in the 1960s to be increasing.

The Chippewas live on 15 federal reservations and in a half-dozen groups of nonreservation communities, as well as in urban neighborhoods and scattered residences in Minnesota, Illinois, and elsewhere. Most of the people on the reservations in five states, from central Montana to Michigan, identify themselves as Chippewas. The extent to which distinctions in identification are made by the people of different reservations or localities is not on record, although presumably distinctions are made, with varying degrees of importance. Separate identification within the common category of Chippewa is no doubt encouraged by their separate political organizations.

In Minnesota six of the eight reservation communities are organized into a single political-administrative unit called the Minnesota Chippewa Tribe, which maintains an elected tribal council as provided by the IRA. Other groups of communities and reservations are organized separately such as the Mississippi Band of Chippewas, which has a kind of traditional chieftainship; the Red Lake Chippewas and the reservation peoples in other states have their own tribal councils.

To some extent these separate organizations are linked through the Great Lakes Inter-Tribal Council.

Considerable variation exists in the degree and kind of replacement of native cultures. In general, it was impossible to maintain the older ways of subsistence, as game disappeared, timber stands were sold or logged off, and farming on the poor reservation land became a losing enterprise. Factions formed as tribal life became disorganized, and government employees managed what economic production was possible, favoring those Chippewas they regarded as "progressive." A high proportion of Indians were on relief from the 1940s through the 1970s. On the Minnesota reservation at Red Lake, which is closed—that is, not allotted individually and closed to white intrusion—some effective tribal organization has developed. In general, however, community life is characterized by disorganization and apathy. Traditional ceremonial organization exists to varying degrees, although most people are also Catholic or Episcopalian.

A steady migration to Minnesota cities began before World War II and accelerated afterward, so that many, perhaps most, families made some degree of urban adjustment. In Minneapolis, Chippewas and Sioux were active leaders in many community development programs. Out of these urban interests grew a militant organization called the American Indian Movement (AIM), with Chippewas active in the national leadership. AIM carried out demonstrations at the BIA office in Washington, D.C., in 1972 and occupied the town of Wounded Knee, S. Dak., in 1973. Underlying these spectacular demonstrations, aimed at publicizing Indian poverty, bad government management, and legal injustices, were some vigorous and constructive achievements in Minnesota. Among these were programs to improve police protection in low-income urban neighborhoods and the introduction of a successful Indian Studies program at the University of Minnesota.

Unlike most eastern and southern Indians, the Chippewas were not forcibly removed from their homeland by the government, although whites took the greater part of their lands and depleted most of the resources. In the earlier phase of European invasion the Chippewas had expanded their territory considerably and (considering Canadian and U.S. Chippewas together) doubled their population as they sought new trapping grounds for their increasing involvement in the fur trade with the French. For example, groups of Chippewas moved from their original Lake Huron area into western Minnesota and fought the eastern Sioux for their lands. By the end of the 1700s the Chippewas had essentially taken over the territory as far west as the eastern prairies, and their population increased in these new areas as the fur trade peaked during the early 1800s. They organized themselves in small roving bands, thus breaking up the large stable communities in which they had lived during their early participation in the fur trade.

The remarkable adaptation of the Chippewas to the forest and lake country as hunters and trappers was reported to Americans in the early 19th century and became a focus of romantic interest in the Indian. The ethnologist Henry Rowe Schoolcraft reported the idyllic aspects of their life, and the poet Henry W. Longfel-low, mistaking the Iroquois Hiawatha for a Chippewa, gave epic expression to the Chippewa way of life, with which a large audience in the United States and Europe became familiar.

During the 1830s, when the world fur market was suddenly curtailed, the Chippewas' economic base began to erode. In addition, the westward movement of whites put pressure on them, and in 1837 they began to make treaties, ceding large amounts of land in return for fixed annual payments over a limited time period. By the 1860s all the Chippewas were either living on very small parts of their old hunting territories or were landless wanderers within or near their old territories. The small areas to which the whites tried to confine the Chippewas were among the least usable parcels of land. As early as 1854 a treaty was forced on the Chippewas by which they agreed to assign 80 acres to each able-bodied male. In 1889, in line with national policy, the Minnesota legislature, in "an act for the relief and civilization of the Indians," provided for the division of all remaining Chippewa land into individual allotments. In 1904 arrangements were made for logging the reservation areas wherever timber remained. With little interest in farming the poor soil and without other resources, the Chippewas lived on their allotments in poverty and dependence until after World War II, when many began to move to cities.

MENOMINEES

Numbering about 3,000 in 1976, the Menominees live on approximately 275,000 acres in northeastern Wisconsin which are in the process of being changed back to an Indian reservation, which they were before 1954. The Menominee Restoration Committee was elected by the tribe in 1974 for the express purpose of restoring the tribe's special relationship with the federal government and the reservation status of the land, which had been abolished, in accord with President Dwight Eisenhower's policy, by the Menominee Termination Act of 1954. During the 19 years when this policy was in effect, the condition of the Menominees was one of transition, and their relations with the federal government were tumultuous. The tribal treasury of $3 million was completely dissipated; their reservation became a state county; the lumber industry, which had been built up over some 50 years, was on the verge of insolvency; and Menominee land held in federal trust for 100 years was being sold piece by piece. The controlling authority of Menominee Enterprises, which had been created by the termination act to manage the Menominee lumber industry, passed from Menominee hands. To keep the shaky business solvent, parcels of land were sold along the Wolf River, the heart of the old reservation. With the loss of their land, the Menominees organized DRUMS (Determination of Rights and Unity for Menominee Stockholders), revived the tribal council, and worked for the reversal of the termination act. Action by Congress in 1973 required the transition back to earlier conditions under the direction of the Menominee Restoration Committee.

The Menominees are unusual among American Indians in that by the 1920s they had developed a successful sawmill and logging business under reservation conditions, using the profits to pay for health and education services, to provide salaries for Bureau of In-

dian Affairs employees, to support telephone and electric utility companies, as well as distributing profits to some tribe members and building a tribal fund. The lumber business also provided jobs for most of the group. In many other respects the native culture had been replaced, as, for example, in housing, food, and clothing. The majority are Roman Catholic, but a segment of the tribe is devoted to the so-called Drum Dance religion (nimihetwan), or Dancing Rite, and a few are members of the Native American church, which uses peyote in its rituals. The Menominee Algonkian language is spoken by most non-Catholics and by many Catholics. It was apparently their high degree of cultural assimilation, especially as manifested in their business operation, that led the BIA to terminate the Menominees' federal services and trust relationship.

French explorers and traders first encountered the Menominees in the late 1600s near Sault Sainte Marie and the northern end of the Michigan peninsula. They were a relatively sedentary people, who regularly harvested wild rice; their name in fact means "wild rice gatherers." As they engaged in the fur trade and became more and more dependent on trade goods, they became, like their close cultural relatives the Chippewas, more nomadic. Although by 1740 most of the Algonkian-speaking groups had been pushed out of the region, the Menominees remained in the general area of Green Bay, Wis. Generally, they supported the French and later the British and were little disturbed in hunting and gathering activities in their native territory.

However, as the Americans moved into the Northwest Territory, the usual steady erosion of Indian hunting lands took place. By an 1854 treaty they were restricted to their present 250,000-acre reservation, having ceded 9 million acres. For 20 years or more they received some rations from the U.S. government along with annual payments for the land ceded. They regarded the 1854 treaty as a final guarantee of their security and sovereignty on the reservation. The Bureau of Indian Affairs tried to introduce them to farming, but instead the Menominees developed a small-scale lumber business. By 1872 they were involved in logging under BIA supervision and had already built up a small tribal fund.

During the 1870s they held out actively against selling their timber to the "pine ring" of large lumber companies and also managed to resist having their reservation broken up into individual allotments when U.S. policy moved in that direction. Theirs was the only remaining unallotted reservation in the Great Lakes region, except for the Chippewa Red Lake reservation in Minnesota.

By 1905 the authority of the traditional headmen had been so greatly weakened that when a business committee was formed to manage the lumber business it was dominated by government employees and outside business interests. A period of extreme mismanagement ensued, with BIA employees as much or more involved than the Menominee business committee. Despite bad management and rampant fraud, the BIA did institute a sustained-yield timber production system, and during the 1920s the business prospered under its supervision. Although it was recommended in 1928 that the enterprise be given some degree of independence from government supervision, no Indians were trained for upper-level management positions. As a result, much friction developed between the elected Menominee Advisory Council and the BIA-hired management. In 1934 the Menominee tribe brought suit against the bureau for many years of mismanagement, which was settled in 1951 for $7 million.

WINNEBAGOS

The population of the Winnebagos was between 5,000 and 6,000 in 1970. The majority, probably more than 3,000, live in Wisconsin; about 1,500 reside on a reservation in northeastern Nebraska. The remaining 1,500 are scattered in Ontario, Minnesota, and South Dakota. The two major centers of population are a large area of small communities extending from La Crosse to Wittenberg to Wisconsin Dells in central Wisconsin, and the Nebraska reservation area. There is constant visiting and communication among the widely dispersed Winnebago families.

The Wisconsin Winnebagos, who have never had a reservation in that state, live on bought or rented land; as squatters on land surrounding religious missions, as at Black River Falls; and on government land. Some are farmers, as in South Dakota and Nebraska, but the great majority are engaged in a wide range of other occupations, from local industry to seasonal harvesting of fruit and vegetables. There is some seasonal use of the traditional wigwams, which are usually covered with tarpaper rather than bark, but the majority in both Wisconsin and Nebraska live in frame houses built by the BIA. Men and women both wear ordinary American clothing, although women tend to use a distinctive style of ornament of generalized American Indian pattern.

The Winnebago language is generally spoken in the home, especially in Wisconsin. Winnebagos follow three different religious traditions—the modified traditional Medicine Lodge, or Medicine Dance, religion; the Native American church; and Christian denominations, chiefly evangelical Protestantism. The Medicine Lodge religion tends to be exclusive and its practitioners hostile to the Native American church in most communities; however, many individuals participate in all three types of religious observance. The traditional burial-house customs are practiced in many communities. Since 1969 the Winnebagos of Wisconsin have had a statewide organization under an IRA type of constitution. Their vigorous retention of traditional religion in its adapted forms, use of their language, and relatively limited cultural assimilation appear to be a result of the absence of BIA supervision. This is suggested by a comparison with the reservation people of Nebraska, where assimilation has been more extensive. It should be emphasized, however, that the Wisconsin Winnebagos were not isolated from white ways; rather, they had the opportunity to select from among white customs to a greater extent than the reservation Winnebagos. In general, they have maintained, with modifications, basic elements of their native world view and customs wherever they have lived.

The history of the Winnebagos might suggest that their contacts would have been conducive to breakdown and disorganization of their culture. A Siouan tribe in respect to language, they were wedged between

the Algonkian-speaking Menominees and the Sauk and Fox tribes when French explorers entering the central Great Lakes region encountered them about 1634. Through a corridor to the south, they maintained communication with the Siouan tribes of the Mississippi Valley region, such as the Iowa and Omaha. Fighting broke out in the 1670s and 1680s among the Chippewas, Foxes, Sauks, the French, and others in their vicinity, which was very disruptive to the Winnebago lifestyle. In 1671 they were seriously defeated by the Illinois and seem to have been reduced from about 4,000 to a single village. Their numbers increased greatly during the following century, and in 1806 they were reported to be living in seven large villages. Their numbers were reduced again during the early 19th century as a result of war with Chippewas and with the Americans. Some 40 Winnebagos died in the Shawnee chief Tecumseh's unsuccessful war against the Americans, after which the tribe sought peace with the Americans. Yielding to increasing American pressures, they made a series of treaties between 1816 and 1855 in which they ultimately ceded all their lands east of the Mississippi River and then those lands west of the river granted by the United States. They were shunted first to a neutral ground in Iowa, then successively to reservations in Minnesota, South Dakota, and finally Nebraska, where the United States bought for them half of the reservation guaranteed to the Omahas. With every shift of location, each of which broke the prior treaty, some Winnebagos were left behind. Soldiers tried to force them to stay on the Minnesota and South Dakota reservations, but with little success. By the time the Nebraska reservation was established in 1865, after 40 years of being moved about, 1,700 Winnebagos had settled in that state. There were still 860 in Wisconsin, as well as others scattered along the way.

In 1874 the government finally gave up in its efforts to keep them from returning to Wisconsin, but no reservation was established there. Instead, 40-acre homesteads, tax-free for 20 years, were granted to each family head who could be located among the 900 or so Winnebagos who had outlasted the government's 50-year effort to move them out of Wisconsin. Meanwhile, the government made individual allotments to the Winnebagos who remained on the Nebraska reservation; an Indian agent continued to supervise their affairs, even though the reservation was no longer owned collectively. Many farmed and proceeded generally on a path of cultural assimilation.

The Wisconsin Winnebagos remain a powerful influence on the reservation people. Besides vitalizing the Medicine Bundle religion of their ancient tradition and contributing to its continuation among some reservation Winnebagos, the Wisconsin group became prominent in the Peyote cult when it began to diffuse from the southern Plains Indians in 1908, and they encouraged the ritual among the Nebraska Winnebagos.

Other Indians of the western Great Lakes are the Forest Potawatomis and Ottawas of Michigan, the Brothertons, Stockbridges, Oneidas, and Potawatomis of Wisconsin, and the Miamis of Indiana.

Bibliography

Of the many studies of Great Lakes peoples, past and present, the following constitute an introduction to four major types of cultural development. Harold Hickerson, *The Southwestern Chippewa: An Ethno-*

historical Study (1962; reprint, New York, 1971), sketches the complex history of the most numerous people of the region, while Victor Barnouw, *Acculturation and Personality among the Wisconsin Chippewa* (1950; reprint, New York, 1971), gives an introduction to the changing Chippewa culture. Felix Keesing, *The Menominee Indians of Wisconsin, A Study of Three Centuries of Culture Contact and Change* (1939; reprint, New York, 1971), is an analysis of long-term cultural processes. Nancy O. Lurie, ed., *Mountain Wolf Woman, Sister of Crashing Thunder: The Autobiography of a Winnebago Indian* (Ann Arbor, Mich., 1961), interprets a culture through one individual's experience of it. The Oneidas, a transplanted Iroquois group, are described in R.E. Ritzenthaler, "The Oneida Indians of Wisconsin," *Bulletin of the Public Museum of the City of Milwaukee* 19 (1950): 1–52

THE MISSISSIPPI VALLEY

In the central and lower Mississippi Valley region, the original native peoples were almost entirely exterminated or driven out by invading whites and other Indians: Iowa, Missouri, Arkansas, and Mississippi were without Indians by the late 19th century. Only Louisiana retained some of the variety of original Indian inhabitants, although all except the Houma, much intermixed with French, were reduced to a tiny fraction of their former numbers; some groups were entirely extinguished.

During the 1900s the Fox and the Choctaws returned to Iowa and Mississippi, respectively, and became permanent residents. One group of Choctaws accepted a reservation, but others live in independent communities. A small Indian population, almost all on federal reservations, lives in Nebraska and Kansas. In the 1960s the total Indian population of this western edge of the Mississippi Valley, together with the Foxes of central Iowa, was between 6,000 and 7,000; the returned Choctaws in Mississippi numbered about 2,600, and the Indian population of Louisiana was 2,980. This total population for the region, about 11,750, is approximately one-fifth of the population that existed in about the same area at the time of initial contacts with whites. There were possibly about the same number of distinct groups—15 to 20—in the 1960s as during the early phases of contact, but not an exact correspondence. Five of the groups came from the western Great Lakes region, pushed out of their homeland by the pressures of European settlement and forced migration. The main bodies of two of these tribes—Chippewas and Winnebagos—are still in their Great Lakes homelands; the Kickapoos and the Sauks and Foxes were completely displaced. The Potawatomis of Kansas represent only one important division of that tribe, the others being located in Michigan, Wisconsin, and Oklahoma.

POTAWATOMIS

By the 1970s there were about 6,000 Potawatomis in the United States, distributed in four states as follows:

Michigan (3 communities)	450
Wisconsin (2 communities)	400
Kansas (1 U.S. reservation)	2,000
Oklahoma (former reservation)	3,000
	5,850

In addition, a few Potawatomis live in Ontario and in various urban centers. They regard themselves as three distinct groups: the Forest Potawatomis of Michigan and Wisconsin, the Prairie Band of Potawatomis of Kansas, and the Citizen Potawatomis of Oklahoma.

On the Kansas reservation a core of long-time, extremely conservative residents, the Prairie Band, successfully resisted having their land broken into allotments, rejected organizing under the IRA, and through a business committee won a $5 million claim before the Indian Claims Commission. As the money became available in the 1950s, the tribal roll increased from 500 to 2,000. Those who returned to the reservation, who had moved away and dissociated themselves from tribal affairs prior to the 1930s, engaged in a struggle for adoption of a constitution and a tribal council. They were finally successful in 1961, but their conflict with the conservatives continues to dominate local politics. Most of the conservative faction never became Christians, maintaining active participation in native religious life focused around the Dream Dance, the Medicine Dance, or the Native American church, and they continue to speak the Potawatomi language. The others on the Prairie Band tribal roll are Christian and in occupation, dress, and other ways are very much assimilated.

The 3,000 Citizen Potawatomis of Oklahoma are even more assimilated, whereas the descendants of the Forest Band in the Great Lakes region are generally less so. Most live under a tribal council government but are otherwise like rural whites of the area. The Prairie Potawatomis have been extremely active in pan-Indian pow-wows and in the militant Indian movements of the 1960s.

The Potawatomis claim as their homeland a region of the north shore of Lake Huron, where they were associated with Ottawas and Chippewas at the beginning of the white invasions. They then moved south and by the end of the 18th century dominated the Indians of the Illinois area. Their resistance to white encroachment was sporadic and not well organized, and they steadily ceded lands during the early 19th century. In the Treaty of Chicago of 1833, they ceded 5 million acres in Illinois and Indiana and moved across the Mississippi, where they settled first in Iowa, then Missouri, and later in Kansas. Some Potawatomis remained behind in scattered groups and became known as the Forest Band of Ontario, Wisconsin, and Michigan.

A federal reservation was established in northeastern Kansas where the Potawatomis of the United Band of Potawatomis, Chippewas, and Ottawas (the Prairie Band) were forced to settle, as were a group of very assimilated Potawatomis called the Mission Band. A serious schism developed in the 1860s over the issue of accepting individual allotments of land, a plan pushed by whites in an effort to break up the tribal organization and hasten individual cultural assimilation. When the General Allotment Act of 1887 was passed, a determined segment of Potawatomis continued to oppose allotment, and the majority of the Prairie Band were never forced to accept it. Descendants of the Mission Band and others, who were becoming white-oriented, accepted allotment and U.S. citizenship and became individual farmers. This group, calling themselves the Citizen Potawatomis, was anxious to separate from the conservatives, so they sold their allotments and established a reservation in Oklahoma. That reservation, too, was eventually broken up into allotments; they continue to live there, generally prospering as farmers and livestock raisers. In 1948 they organized as the Citizen Band of Potawatomi Indians of Oklahoma with a charter from the state.

About 1876 the Prairie Potawatomis began to share, along with the Forest Band, the Menominees, and the Winnebagos, in a new religious revelation. Brought by a Sioux woman, the Dream Dance, as it was called, offered an alternative to the many forms of Christianity. The chief spirits of the new religion were the traditional supernaturals in whom they had believed and some newer prophets, who spoke in the traditional Indian languages but met the Indians' changing needs with regard to health and the ordering of experience. The Dream Dance involved no sweeping changes but was part of a process of continuing vitalization of the traditional forms.

FOXES

In the 1970s there were between 500 and 600 Fox Indians living on 2,800 acres near Tama, Iowa. Their situation is unusual in that this land is not a reservation (it was purchased during the 19th century and held in federal trust), but the BIA does have some role in their lives. They lease another 520 acres to whites, the rent going toward payment of taxes on the main tract.

From the early 18th century the Foxes were closely associated with the Sauk, or Sac, Indians of the upper Great Lakes area, and by the 20th century the Foxes had largely absorbed their allies. There are 130 Sauk and Fox Indians living on a small reservation in eastern Nebraska and Kansas and another 1,000 on a reservation in central Oklahoma. The Oklahoma reservation, it is claimed, is inhabited chiefly by Sauk rather than Fox Indians, but the family lines are so mixed that no clear determination can be made. Since about the 1830s no separate listing of the two groups has been made.

The Foxes (Meskwaki in their own language) are the only Indian group now living in Iowa, which was the temporary residence of a dozen different tribes during the 18th and early 19th centuries. The Foxes are farmers, but they also work in industry and for non-Indian farmers. Frame houses have been used since 1902, when all the village dwellings were burned by order of Iowa health authorities in order to stop a raging smallpox epidemic. When they rebuilt, they dispersed in the manner of American farmers, and they continue to maintain this pattern today. They also use Algonkian wigwams and for certain religious ceremonies erect canvas-covered tipis. Most families have automobiles and many use tractors in their farming.

In the 1960s nearly one-third of the Tama community spoke only the Fox language, and some persons could read and write using the Algonkian syllabary. Two-thirds were bilingual in English and Fox. Very few Foxes participate in Christian religious churches, and nearly all are members of the medicine societies, whose religious rites revolve around sacred medicine bundles. Some are active in the Native American church, and others practice the Drum Dance rites introduced by Potawatomis, some of whom lived in the Fox community. In addition, there is another religion called the Singing-Around Society, introduced by Wisconsin Indians.

An elected council, organized somewhat along the lines of the IRA prescription, has been in existence since 1937. There are two recognized factions in the community, often thought of as antiwhite and prowhite, but this is an oversimplification. The community supports an elementary school with some aid from

the federal government and from non-Indian organiza- tions. Community effort is totally organized in the an- nual pow-wow, a public spectacle that draws thousands of whites, Indians, and tourists and makes use of the pan-Indian pageantry common at pow-wows, including the Hiawatha and Minnehaha symbols that are wide- spread throughout the eastern United States. Three sa- cred bundle feasts and four Drum Dance ceremonies take place each year.

During early French exploration of the Great Lakes area, the Foxes lived on the west side of Lake Michigan, and the Sauks lived immediately to the north of them, west of Green Bay. After a brief friendly traffic with French traders and missionaries, the Foxes became deeply hostile to the French and gained their enmity by interfering, somewhat successfully, with French trade with other Indians. By the late 1720s the French had launched a campaign to exterminate the Foxes, enlist- ing Winnebagos, Ottawas, Chippewas, and Menomi- nees against them, and in 1730 they almost succeeded. The remnant of the Foxes was befriended by the Sauks, and both groups allied with the Kickapoos in a confed- eracy with other tribes of the Great Lakes region. However, the fact that the Foxes were friendly with the Iroquois made them enemies of the northern Great Lakes tribes. Foxes played a small role in Ottawa chief Pontiac's 1763 uprising and later aided Tecumseh's great effort to unite the Algonkian-speaking nations against the Americans during the War of 1812. Their loyalty shifted several times, but by the beginning of the 19th century the Foxes had sided with Spain and Britain against the Americans. In 1804 some chiefs of the Sauk and Fox tribes made a treaty, not authorized by the responsible tribal authorities, ceding to the Americans all their lands on both sides of the Missis- sippi. The Americans held to the treaty, which became a point of serious conflict with the Foxes. As pressures for Indian removal grew, Black Hawk (1767–1838), an elderly Sauk war leader in Illinois, mounted a short- lived and unsuccessful resistance against the Illinois militia and other troops, called the Black Hawk War, in 1832. After the village was burned, the crops destroyed, and Black Hawk taken prisoner, leadership passed to another Sauk, Keokuk (c. 1790–1848), who sought to cooperate with the Americans.

Under his rule the Sauk and Fox Indians, like other Great Lakes tribes, were pushed from one place to an- other, and treaties with them were broken repeatedly. First they were put on a reservation in Iowa, then in Kansas, and then in Oklahoma. The main body went to Oklahoma, where in 1891 their land was individually allotted. Some Foxes returned to the Iowa area and bought 80 acres of land. They steadily added more land, paid for with the annuities from other land cessions. Their Iowa land was under state trust until 1895, when the federal government assumed responsibility. They became tax-paying citizens of Iowa, little interfered with by either missionary groups or federal employees. Their continuing interest in the Meskwaki language and the several native American religions in which they participate indicate their cultural independence.

The other branch of the Sauk and Fox Indians in Oklahoma moved toward cultural assimilation. Since allotment they have had no collectively owned land and have been supervised in various ways by the Bureau of Indian Affairs. A BIA boarding school was maintained

on their land after 1872. In 1885 they organized as the Sac and Fox Nation under a written constitution and es- tablished tribal courts. In 1936 they reorganized, retain- ing very much the old political structure but under the provisions of the Oklahoma Indian Welfare Act. Most are Methodists or Baptists. A very few still speak the Algonkian languages, as well as English.

KICKAPOOS

Kickapoo history is in many respects the most re- markable of all the Indian histories in the United States. Some of them have maintained the major ele- ments of their aboriginal way of life through 350 years of the most varied social and physical conditions expe- rienced by an Indian group. They moved from their woodland home near the Great Lakes in northern Wis- consin into the prairies and then to the progressively more arid regions from Indian Territory to Coahuila in northern Mexico. They have survived under successive conditions of nearly constant warfare, brief government supervision, and then complete independence. They have been subjected to removals and to reservation life. Yet even without a long-sustained and stable land base, many kept their traditional ways.

By the 1960s they were settled in three major loca- tions, the northernmost some 1,500 miles from the southernmost—in Kansas 400 live on a federal reserva- tion; in Oklahoma there are 300 in an independent vil- lage; and in Coahuila, Mexico, there are 400. The more than 1,100 Kickapoos of the 1960s were slightly more than one-half the number encountered by Europeans 300 years earlier. Their population declined from about 2,000 in the mid-19th century.

The way of life of the modern Kickapoos of Coahuila closely resembles that of the 17th century with respect to housing (wigwams), hunting ways, religion, Algon- kian language, community structure, and family life. On the other hand, the Kansas reservation community, called the Prairie Band, is like a community of Ameri- can farmers, with frame houses, modern, successful farming methods, and membership in the Baptist or Methodist church; however, most members of Chris- tian churches also follow the religious practices pre- scribed by the 19th-century prophet Kennekuk. They have a representative government modeled according to the IRA plan.

In Oklahoma the Kickapoos' ways vary from the ex- treme conservatism of the Mexican group, to those of the Kansas Kickapoos, but the majority are conserva- tive. Their houses are still built on the plan of the bark houses of the Great Lakes Algonkians but are now cov- ered with mats and canvas. In their farming they use the old hand tools along with recently adopted modern farm implements. Their religion is of the old Manitou type, centering around sacred bundles and requiring lengthy ceremonials at New Year and at the Green Corn rituals in the summer.

The Kickapoo cultural conservatism has been main- tained in spite of extreme changes in their conditions. When they were first known to whites in northern Wis- consin, they were a farming and hunting people. Their religious, family, and other customs were similar to those of the Foxes and Potawatomis. The Kickapoos' early contacts with the French led to permanent hostil- ity, as they held the French responsible for stimulating Sioux raids into their country from the west and Iro-

quois raids from the east. The Kickapoos turned to warfare as a major pursuit, organizing a confederacy with the Sauk, Fox, and Forest Potawatomi tribes. They supported Pontiac in his abortive effort to eliminate the whites in 1763 and later, in the early 1800s strongly supported the Shawnee prophet Tenskwatawa and Tecumseh. They thus established themselves as active opponents of the Americans.

The Kickapoos had begun to move westward, pushed by the tribes moving into the Great Lakes area, even before the defeats of 1811–1812. Some had been forced out of Wisconsin into Illinois and ranged farther west as early as the last quarter of the 18th century. Along with other displaced peoples, like the Delawares, the Shawnees, and some Mississippi Valley tribes, they became mercenary soldiers for the Spaniards. They protected the Spanish settlements from the Chickasaws and later from the Osages of the Missouri River region. Between 1819 and the 1880s the Kickapoos were referred to as "the lords of the middle border," an appellation that recognized their excellent fighting abilities.

At the end of the 18th century those who remained in the east participated in the near extermination of the Illinois and other tribes of the area, then established villages in the former Illinois territory. This occurred at the very time when Americans were moving in large numbers into the virgin farmland of the area, which resulted in constant clashes. After the defeat of Tecumseh and subsequent unsuccessful fighting by the Kickapoos, they signed a treaty in 1819. They agreed to cede all their land in Illinois and Indiana and to move across the Mississippi into what became Missouri. Many small bands resisted removal, but eventually all went to western Missouri, where villages had already been established by the mercenary Kickapoos and their relatives along the Osage River. By 1824 there were 2,200 Kickapoos reported there, most of the tribe. About this time a prophet appeared among the Kickapoos, a man named Kennekuk, who had been a war chief. His vision called for peace, a cessation of opposition to the Americans and peace with other Indians. His teaching was wholly inconsistent with the adopted lifestyle of the majority of Kickapoos, but he promptly gained several hundred adherents. He advocated settling down to a farming life while adhering to some of their traditional religious beliefs and rituals.

The majority continued their border warfare, and during the 1820s they redoubled their war activities; the passion for raiding that had characterized their early resistance to the French was renewed against the Osages of the Missouri basin and against the steadily advancing settlers. Another segment of the tribe had settled permanently in Spanish Territory, in what was shortly to become Texas. During 1815–1817 this group joined a Cherokee leader from Arkansas, Chief Bowles, who had made an arrangement with the Spaniards to settle on the Sabine River in Texas territory, where, along with Delawares and Shawnees, they became Spanish citizens. They were soon joined by Kickapoos from the north.

In 1832, Missouri Kickapoos, seeking land farther west, made a treaty with the Americans for a reservation in Kansas near Fort Leavenworth. Some 700 followers of Kennekuk, along with a strongly anti-American segment, moved to the Kansas reservation in 1833,

where the prophet and his followers settled down permanently. Some of the opposing faction left in 1837 to join the Texas Kickapoos. Meanwhile, the Republic of Texas had been established, and in 1839 the Texans, who were deeply hostile to Indians, forced the Texas Kickapoos out of the republic. Some went north into what had become Indian Territory; some Kickapoos and others moved south into Mexico, where they established a community on the Rio Grande. Although the Kickapoos who went north to Indian Territory had no formal relationship with the U.S. government, having lived outside the country for years, they established themselves west of the Chickasaw Nation and from there regularly raided the Texans, the Chickasaws, and other Indians. They numbered at this time about 1,200 and regarded themselves as being at war with the Republic of Texas, which had ousted them from villages they had established long before the republic was founded. Faced with the growing hostility of other Indians moving into Indian Territory, the Kickapoos accepted a friendly invitation to settle in the Creek Nation and provide protection from other raiding "wild tribes." In 1842 the Texans changed their approach and sought the protective assistance of the Kickapoos and invited them to return to Texas, where they reestablished their villages along the Brazos and the Canadian rivers, becoming specialized as hunters, traders, and soldiers defending the Creeks against attacks.

With the outbreak of the Civil War, the Kickapoos moved north into Kansas in an effort to escape the pressure to ally themselves with the Confederacy. Some went first to the Kansas reservation but found themselves unable to live in harmony with the steadily assimilating northern group descended from Kennekuk's disciples. In 1865 all the southern Kickapoos, after raiding the Cherokees, Creeks, and others who had gone over to the Confederacy, trekked to Mexico, taking up residence in Coahuila, at the invitation of the Mexican government. There in Nacimiento they acted as a buffer between the Mexicans and the constantly raiding Comanches and Lipan Apaches—a situation they enjoyed. However, between 1865 and 1872 they also raided Texas, making serious inroads into the southern settlements.

In an effort to make life safer for the Texans, the United States tried to force the Mexican Kickapoos to return across the border by, among other tactics, raiding into Coahuila, destroying the Kickapoo village, killing women and children, and taking 40 women and children hostage. Eventually, after much negotiation, 350, or about one-half the Mexican Kickapoo community agreed to follow their captive relatives to Indian Territory; 400 remained in Coahuila. From 1874 on, a community of some 450 Kickapoos existed in Indian Territory and remained after the state of Oklahoma was established.

The Kickapoos in Indian Territory maintained themselves very much as they had wherever they had lived before. In large measure they kept control of their own affairs. They chose their own location near the Sac and Fox, refusing to accept the location chosen for them by the BIA because it was next to their enemies, the Osages. They built their traditional bark or mat-covered houses, refused to send their children to school, maintained vigorously their old religious ceremonies and

beliefs, rejected white medical treatment, hunted (on Chickasaw lands) in their old destructive manner, spoke their own language, and devoted much time to visiting and to religious life. Each time BIA employees attempted to force cultural assimilation programs on them, the Kickapoos threatened to return to Mexico, but they accepted rations and farming tools as their due. When the government program for individual allotment reached its peak about 1895, nearly all the Kickapoos refused to accept it. When it was forced on them and surplus lands were opened to white settlement, some returned to Mexico, where the Coahuila settlement continued to thrive. Some aspects of allotment in Oklahoma were delayed until 1915 because of a complex case of fraud by an agent of the Kickapoos. Similarly, when allotment was pushed on the Kansas reservation, there was fraud involving the government Indian agents, as a railroad company sought to swindle the Indians out of a large portion of the reservation lands. Most Kansas Kickapoos nevertheless accepted the government program, continued to farm, and became culturally very much like their neighbors.

OMAHAS AND PONCAS

Besides the Winnebagos, two other surviving Indian groups—the Omahas and the Poncas—live along the Missouri River in Nebraska, on the western margin of the Mississippi Valley. Unlike the Winnebagos, who are of Great Lakes origin, the Omahas and Poncas are related to the southern Plains Indians in their way of life. During the previous centuries the two tribes were closely associated in the region of Nebraska where their 20th-century reservations were ultimately established. The main body of Poncas is in Oklahoma, but some 450 live intermingled with Santee Sioux on a reservation on the Missouri River in northeastern Nebraska. The remaining Omahas, about 2,000 in 1960, live on a reservation in eastern Nebraska that adjoins the Winnebago reservation on the south.

The Omahas live on individually held land among white farmers and stock raisers whose land was formerly part of the reservation. There is thus some intermingling of whites and Indians in the area, but the Omahas are separate from the white society in most ways. They are classified as Indians by the government and therefore receive medical and educational assistance for which whites are not eligible, and to some degree they are supervised by the BIA. Under the provisions of the IRA, the Omahas organized a tribal council that has some jurisdiction over the land they still hold in common (by tribal title) and that organizes the annual camp ceremony. The council has no taxation power or other governmental functions.

More than 90 percent of the Omahas under the age of 40 speak English. Many speak Omaha as well, but there is an apparent trend toward the loss of the Siouan language. They dress much like the surrounding whites, the men having adopted the cattlemen's large Stetson hats. Families live in frame houses, and the children attend public school. The men engage in a variety of occupations, but most residents derive a large part of their income from leasing farm or range lands to whites. Most profess to be Presbyterians, but few attend church with any regularity. Some families are active Mormons. Nearly all the Omahas participate to some degree in the

Native American church, and there is much interest in intertribal pow-wows, which Omaha dance groups attend.

The Omahas suffered relatively little displacement in the course of their contacts with whites, in contrast with most of the peoples east of the Mississippi. Their present location is a small portion of the land where they built villages before the invasion by whites. They were an agricultural people, who supplemented their intensive farming with annual buffalo hunts in the plains to the west and north. They lived in relatively dense village communities, where related families lived together in large earth lodges. The Omahas never developed coup-counting warfare or the total dependence on the buffalo that characterized other tribes farther west and north. They retained many woodland tribal traditions, such as the Medicine Bundle religion and the curing societies, including the Midewiwin, which was characteristic of the Indians to the northeast. They also sought visions for supernatural inspiration.

The Omahas had little contact with French fur traders, their earliest important contacts being with Anglo-Americans at the beginning of their push beyond the Mississippi River. They remained friendly to the Americans and, partly as a result, were never removed wholly from their aboriginal territory. In 1850 they ceded nearly all of their land to the United States and were assigned a reservation about twice the size of their modern land. By the 1890s half of it had been taken from them, despite the 1850 treaty, to provide a reservation for the Winnebagos, and their reservation was entirely allotted, with the surplus opened for white settlement.

From 1850 the Omahas were the object of cultural assimilation programs by both the Presbyterian church and the Bureau of Indian Affairs. They yielded with little overt resistance, settled down to live in the frame houses provided, began to wear "citizens' clothes," sent their children to school, became nominal Presbyterians, and gave up their council of hereditary chiefs for BIA supervision.

By the early 1900s they seemed on the verge of thorough social and cultural assimilation, but their special status as American Indians under government supervision encouraged other cultural processes. During the 20th century, instead of wholly becoming farmers, they found it possible to make a living by leasing their land to whites, which allowed them to nurture many other interests, such as ceremonial dances, singing, and gambling. Although they did some farming, they developed a certain degree of contempt for the daily labor involved. At the same time the new Native American church was introduced, probably by Potawatomis and Winnebagos, and filled important needs. This religious rite, focusing on the use of peyote and the visions it induced, embodied many traditional Indian concepts and rites and therefore appealed to people who were losing their traditional cultural ways under the pressures for assimilation. The peyote cult became the dominant religious interest of the Omahas. Through it, many of the traditional religious practices including curing societies and sacred bundles, were revived and integrated with new elements such as funeral rites.

A kind of reservation culture has developed. Even as the Native American church declined among them dur-

ing the 1930s, new cultural interests were fostered by increasing contact with other Indians. Various pan-Indian activities, as in the pow-wow circuits, have claimed their interest and consumed much time.

Other Indians living in the lower Mississippi Valley in the 1970s were: Alabamas, Atakapas, Biloxis, Chitamachas, Coushattas, Iowas, Munsee-Chippewas, and Tunicas.

Bibliography

Many histories of the tribes removed or native to the lands west of the Mississippi are now available, especially in the Civilization of the American Indian Series published by the University of Oklahoma Press. One of these is A.M. Gibson, *The Kickapoos: Lords of the Middle Border* (Norman, Okla., 1963). Two studies of another transplanted people of the Mississippi River Valley are N.F. Joffe, "The Fox Indians of Iowa," in Ralph Linton, ed., *Acculturation in Seven American Indian Tribes* (1940; reprint, Gloucester, Mass., 1963), and F.O. Gearing, *The Face of the Fox* (Chicago, 1970). Margaret Mead, *The Changing Culture of An Indian Tribe* (1932; reprint, New York, 1971) describes the Omahas.

THE CRUCIBLE OF OKLAHOMA

In the 1970s at least 39 different Indian ethnic groups lived in Oklahoma—the greatest number in any state of the United States. The reason for the large number of distinct peoples was the U.S. government's attempt during the mid-19th century to concentrate all Indians east of the Mississippi River and many from the Great Plains into the small compass of Indian Territory, which later became Oklahoma. Before that time, the area contained no more than four Indian tribes, which ranged widely beyond the limits of what became Indian Territory. The Indian population of the state is not easy to estimate, but it is somewhere in the neighborhood of 165,000, as contrasted with less than 10,000 before removal. Thus in Oklahoma there has been a sixteen-fold increase in the Indian population during about 150 years, and there are more than nine times as many tribes.

DELAWARES

In 1970 nearly 8,000 persons in the United States identified themselves as of Delaware descent, although perhaps less than 2,000 live in identifiable Delaware communities. Two Delaware communities in Oklahoma—one in the northeast near Bartlesville, with a population of about 1,350, and one in the southwest near Anadarko with no more than 200—constitute the main body of the tribe, which in 350 years has migrated across the country from the Atlantic coast to Texas and Oklahoma.

The Delawares of Oklahoma live like American white rural and urban people, using the same kinds of houses, clothing, tools, and farm implements. The Delaware language is not used in the home, although a few individuals have cultivated a knowledge of the tongue. Most Delawares are Christian, Baptists predominating, but some are members of the Native American church, especially in the Anadarko community. The native Delaware Big House religion has not been practiced for half a century, and the sacred carvings that characterized the Big House ceremonial building have been relegated to a museum. Although cultural replacement is far advanced, a strong sense of Delaware identity exists in both the Anadarko and the Bartlesville groups. The

latter have an elected Delaware Tribal Business Committee, which represents the group in all business dealings, including those with the Indian Claims Commission, and maintains a corporate existence for the tribe. A similar but separate organization exists among the Anadarko Delawares, consisting of a committee of six called the Delaware Tribe of Western Oklahoma.

There are other groups of Delaware descent in the United States. In Wisconsin a group calling themselves the Brothertons or Brotherton Indians, deriving their name from a town in New Jersey, numbers about 1,500. Although they do not usually call themselves Delawares, the nucleus from which they are descended had the same eastern United States origin as the Oklahoma Delawares. In Wisconsin there is another group of less than 500, known as the Stockbridge Indians, whose origin is more diverse than the Brothertons but includes some Delawares. Both the Brothertons and the Stockbridges have reservations. There is also a nonreservation community in Ontario of about 350 Delawares. Thus, there are 4,000 people living in Delaware communities in the United States, but less than half of these claim a simple Delaware identity. The figure of 8,000 mentioned above can best be clarified through a recounting of Delaware history.

The Delawares are descended from one of the largest Algonkian-speaking groups of the Atlantic coast. When the Dutch first settled in their country in 1642, there were between 8,000 and 12,000 speakers of their language. Their tribal name was Lenni Lenape, although they accepted their current designation from the name of the Englishman who administered their tribal area in the early colonial period. At that time they inhabited what is now New Jersey, southeastern Pennsylvania, northern and central Delaware, and northeastern Maryland. They did not live as a single organized tribe; rather they were groups of independent villages, each with a hereditary headman. As with the other Indians of the northern Atlantic seaboard, friendly relations with Europeans turned hostile as pressure on them increased. The Delawares were subordinated politically to the Iroquois, who exacted tribute from them and prohibited them from taking up arms. This made them especially easy to dominate and push from their lands, which the English did after 1664, when they took over political control of the region.

Immediately after the English takeover, the Delaware population began a steep decline, and by the end of the 1600s they were reduced by half. Much Delaware land was sold during the administration of William Penn, and by 1720 they were concentrated in three groups west of the Delaware River. In 1742 the Iroquois ordered the Delawares to move farther west to the Susquehanna Valley, where two large settlements of Shawnees and other displaced peoples under Iroquois domination were being established. For the Iroquois these communities served as a buffer against British settlement in the Southeast. The Delawares took up residence in the Wyoming Valley and vicinity in Pennsylvania, where they remained for some 25 years. Eventually, some Delawares began to drift westward, and two branches of the nation developed, an Ohio group under an hereditary chief named Shingas and a Susquehanna group under a nonhereditary chief named Teedyuscung. Both men supported the Iroquois effort to

stay neutral in the French-British rivalry for control of the fur trade. Ultimately in 1765 and the next few years, the Iroquois sold their allies' land in Pennsylvania, leaving the Delawares landless.

Three thousand moved west into Ohio and settled along the Muskingum River, while others went north through Iroquois country to Ontario. A small community in an area called Brotherton, N.J., was placed on a reservation and refused to go west at the urging of the Ohio Delawares. Much later, in 1802, the Brotherton Indians sold their reservation and moved to Wisconsin, where they now live.

When the Revolution broke out, the Delawares in Ohio consisted of two very distinct factions—the Christians and the non-Christians—who lived in separate communities but continued to identify and associate with each other. Moravian missionaries who were active in the settlements put their language in written form and encouraged the Indians to read and write. A Delaware leader called White Eyes sought to persuade the Americans to create a 14th state for all Indians. Another Delaware leader—Captain Pipe—opposed the Americans and influenced all the Delawares to fight against them. The result was a systematic massacre by American militia of the major Delaware Christian community in 1782. By treaties in 1785 and 1795, the Delawares lost all the land rights given to them by the Wyandot Indians in Ohio and were forced west.

The Miamis invited the Delawares to settle with them in their territory along the Wabash River, and by 1801 there were 11 Delaware villages near what is now Muncie, Ind. Some Delawares moved farther west to southeastern Missouri, then to Arkansas, and then Texas, where they became mercenaries for the Spaniards, fighting the Comanches.

Meanwhile, a nativist movement developed among the Delawares in Indiana. Reacting against the breaking of treaties by Americans, they rejected white ways by, for example, going back to bark houses and refusing to use plows. But the movement was short-lived. Yielding to the ever-mounting pressures, they ceded all rights to their Indiana land in 1818 and two years later moved across the Mississippi River into Missouri. Immediately they were thrown into conflict with the Osages, on whose land they and other eastern Indians had settled. After years of great difficulty, they made a new treaty with the United States in 1829, which granted them 2 million acres in Kansas along with an outlet corridor to the plains for buffalo hunting.

Here the Delawares lived for 38 years, most farming, but a few serving as mercenaries for the United States in the costly struggle to conquer the Seminoles in Florida. They formulated a constitution and a set of tribal laws in an effort to curb the lawlessness that had grown among them. In 1860 most of their land in Kansas was allotted; by 1866, after years of harassment by settlers, railroad company agents, and their own government agents, they left Kansas and settled down in Indian Territory on a tract of land on the eastern margin of the Cherokee Nation. In their treaty with the Cherokees, negotiated before they left Kansas, they had agreed to assume all the rights and obligations of Cherokee citizens. Delawares were elected to the Cherokee National Council. Two divisions developed, the so-called modernists, who were predominantly Baptists, and the tra-

ditionalists, who practiced the Big House native religion. There was a revival of native crafts and old ways of hunting.

When allotments in Indian Territory were forced in the 1890s, there were about 1,000 Delawares. Some were prominent in the founding of the Native American church, based on peyote ceremonialism, into which Delaware ritual was incorporated. When the Indian Claims Commission was created in 1946 the Delawares presented claims for land they had lost in Ohio, Indiana, Missouri, and Kansas and were awarded about $13 million in compensation. Eligibility to share in these benefits was based on relationship with persons listed on the tribal roll of 1867, when departures for Kansas had begun. With this incentive, 7,926 individuals had established eligibility by 1970. The new roll included hundreds of Delawares who no longer lived in Delaware communities, many of whom had remained in one of the areas through which the group had passed in its long journey.

CHEROKEES

Population estimates for the Cherokees in Oklahoma vary widely, indicating the considerable cultural diversity among them and the varying definitions of ethnic identity. The estimates during the period 1960–1970 ranged from 75,000 down to about 16,000. A figure for 1950 of about 47,000 is probably the best approximation in terms of the criterion employed here, namely, self-identification. The 1960 census figure was 25,600, while the much higher estimate of 75,000 that same year represents the total number having legal status as Cherokees through tribal roll eligibility. The low figure of 16,000 is a careful estimate of the culturally most conservative Cherokees in the area of heaviest rural concentration in northeastern Oklahoma, where they constitute a considerable percentage of the total population in six counties.

Most Cherokees live in Oklahoma, both in rural areas of the northeast and in cities and towns all over the state. They vary greatly in culture; for more than a century they have been in the vanguard of what most Americans call civilization in Indian Territory and Oklahoma, but they also live in isolated communities in the hilly eastern part of the state under circumstances most Americans would consider backward. By the 1970s they were established in a wide range of occupations, from business executives to fishermen and industrial workers.

Most Cherokees are Baptists or Methodists, but many also participate in forms of the native Cherokee religions as practiced by the United Keetoowah Band, the Keetoowah Society, the Nighthawk Keetoowahs, the Seven Clans Society, and the Four Mothers Society. These groups meet in rural areas and some towns and do not exclude members of Christian churches. The Native American church has very few adherents among Cherokees.

Tribal government consists of a principal chief appointed by the president of the United States and an advisory cabinet representing the Cherokee Nation and serving as the channel for various federal economic development programs. The tribal government maintains a Cherokee National Fund, has established a cultural center in Tahlequah that annually produces the drama,

The Trail of Tears, employs a legal staff to prosecute Cherokee claims before the Indian Claims Commission, and maintains an arts and crafts development program, a national archives, and a Cherokee National Museum. There is also a newspaper, the *Cherokee Nation News,* and other enterprises. An organization known as the Elected Community Representatives was established in the 1970s to democratize the tribal organization through popular elections.

During the early 19th century the Cherokees came to think of themselves as full-bloods and mixed-bloods. Although by 1970 the terms had no significance genetically, they did refer to meaningful cultural divisions. The term full-blood refers to rural dwellers, whose way of life is chiefly farming and hunting, whose attitude toward urban lifestyles is conservative and disapproving, and who maintain the Cherokee language as a functional part of their lives. The term is also sometimes applied to urbanized individuals whose interest in Cherokee native traditions intensified during the 1950s and 1960s, but who are not necessarily accepted as full-bloods by the other full-bloods.

The Cherokees are an Iroquoian-speaking tribe that was never anything but the enemy of the Iroquois. They helped drive the Tuscaroras out of North Carolina in 1711 when that tribe sought the protection of the Iroquois League. Europeans encountered the Cherokees when they were living in what became eastern Kentucky and Tennessee and western North and South Carolina. During the early period of English settlement, they were pushed southwest, and by the early 19th century, as a result of the pressure of American settlers, they had moved into northern Georgia as well. By this time they had divided into three groups: the most conservative group remained in the southern Appalachian Mountains and became the nucleus of the 20th-century Eastern Band of Cherokees; another group voluntarily moved west of the Mississippi, settled in Arkansas, and was spoken of as the Western Band; the main body of Cherokees concentrated in northern Georgia, moving their old town center of Echota there and calling it New Echota.

In the first third of the 19th century, the Georgia Cherokees initiated profound changes in their mode of life, including organizing a political structure similar to that of the United States, which led to their classification by whites as a civilized tribe. They wrote a constitution establishing them as the Cherokee Nation and a body of laws, making use of the syllabary for writing Cherokee; they set up a national capital; elected a national body of legislators; published a newspaper, the *Cherokee Phoenix* (New Echota, 1828–1835); took steps to eliminate the system of blood revenge that had been rife among them; and set up a judicial system and law-enforcement body. In the midst of this rapid development of an intense national consciousness, gold was discovered in northern Georgia.

As white settlers rushed to the goldfields, the state of Georgia began a systematic effort to get rid of the Cherokees and take over their land, which in 1785 had been guaranteed by federal treaty. Reaction to the removal policy caused the Cherokee Nation to split. One small faction under the leadership of The Ridge, a distinguished Cherokee who had earlier helped write a law calling for death to any Cherokee who signed away tribal land, urged acceptance of the removal policy. The great majority, under the leadership of John Ross (1790–1866), strongly opposed removal and began determined but unsuccessful efforts in Washington to maintain their land. When Congress approved a new treaty with the support of President Andrew Jackson, the Ross segment finally had to be forcibly removed by the army. The Trail of Tears, as the hardships of removal were recorded in their history, resulted in the death of some 4,000 Cherokees. The operation was not completed until 1839, when all except the Eastern Band were finally placed in Indian Territory. There the leaders of the party that had favored removal were promptly assassinated.

Once removal was accomplished, the Cherokees set themselves to build anew the sort of society they had established in Georgia, putting their constitution and national laws into effect, setting up a representative national council, passing legislation making the new land a collective holding for the benefit of all, and devoting special attention to organizing a public school system. By 1887, the Cherokees had excellent schools; they were largely literate in both Cherokee and English, had established a new newspaper the *Cherokee Advocate,* printed in both languages, and were on the way to political and economic development comparable to that of other Americans. They had weathered another split over the issue of supporting the Union in the Civil War, the majority seeking to remain neutral but ultimately yielding to pressures from the Confederacy.

Their uncompromising stand against allotting their land and giving up the surplus under the General Allotment Act of 1887 led to defeat. Not only was the land broken up into individual allotments against their protests, but also their reestablished government was dissolved. By 1907 the Cherokees no longer existed as a distinct political entity in the United States. They did exist, however, as a distinct people, as was demonstrated in many activities through the 20th century. New religious integration based on reinvigorating of traditional tribal concepts was manifested in the Redbird Smith movement. In 1944 Cherokees played a major role in organizing and leading the National Congress of American Indians. The Cherokee language continues to be spoken and the writing of it encouraged, and during the 1960s there was a burst of interest in the study and interpretation of Cherokee history.

CHOCTAWS

The Choctaws are the third largest of the Five Civilized Tribes, with a population in Oklahoma estimated in the 1960s between 20,000 and 40,000. There are also communities in Mississippi and Louisiana with a total population of about 3,000, some of whom are descendants of Choctaws who escaped removal. The only reservation is in Mississippi.

The approximately 30,000 in Oklahoma are concentrated in 13 counties in the southeastern part of the state, where the Choctaw Nation was once located. In the 1970s there were many small communities of full-blood people devoted to the rural way of life that characterized most Choctaws for nearly 200 years, culturally a combination of southern Anglo-American and native customs and techniques. However, Choctaws, like the Cherokees, are also widely dispersed in cities

throughout Oklahoma and elsewhere and vary considerably in occupation and income. Like the Cherokees, they are chiefly Baptists, Methodists, and Presbyterians, but some also participate in native forms of religious life in the "stomp grounds" and other ceremonial centers, probably to a lesser extent than Cherokees and Creeks. The Choctaw language is the language of the home in 30 percent or more of the rural families. They gave the state its name, *okla* meaning "people" and *homa*, "red" in their language.

The Choctaws' political organization consists of a principal chief appointed by the president of the United States and an advisory council elected annually by popular vote. This organization defends Choctaw interests before the Indian Claims Commission and, through a business committee, handles tribal affairs, such as maintaining a tribal roll based on the 1907 roll for the distribution of per capita payments resulting from claims cases.

The Choctaws, a Muskogean-speaking group, originally lived in the central portion of what became Mississippi and western Alabama. In this area is the sacred center of their country, preserved as a prehistoric mound site, called Nanih Waya. Like the other Civilized Tribes, the Choctaws were agricultural, village Indians; there were at least 115 villages or towns in the Mississippi area in the 18th century. They allied themselves with the French after 1699, a move that brought them into wars against the Chickasaws and the Natchez. During the early 1800s the Choctaws, under the leadership of able men such as Pushmataha, Apukshunnubbee, and Moshulatubbee, became steadily more committed to cooperation with the Americans and little inclined to support either military opposition, as urged by Tecumseh, or vigorous legal opposition, as pursued by the Cherokees. They were inclined to follow the ways of whites and allowed missionaries to establish schools. Many of them learned to use English, but they also developed a written form of Choctaw. In the late 19th century, converts to Methodism became influential in tribal affairs, and a systematic effort was begun to alter their governmental system along American lines. A national council of elected representatives from each of the traditional four districts was created, but the hereditary chieftainship through clan membership, instead of being abolished, was combined with new forms of representation. Before 1830 a code of laws was developed, alcohol was prohibited (although the ban was not well enforced), trials for persons accused of witchcraft were instituted, and a police force of "light horsemen" was created.

In 1820, as the desire of whites for the good cotton land in Alabama and Mississippi intensified, the Choctaws began to sign treaties ceding parts of their territory in return for land west of the Mississippi. In 1830 they signed the Treaty of Dancing Rabbit Creek, an agreement of vital importance in Choctaw history. It provided for a perpetual grant by the U.S. government of the southern half of Indian Territory if the Choctaws ceded their Mississippi lands. The government promised the usual annual payments, in this case $6,000 a year, in return for some 6 million acres. In the same year Mississippi passed laws giving Choctaws citizenship if they would relinquish tribally held land and accept individual allotments. A few did so, but 20,000

agreed to move to Indian Territory. Removal took place over three years, and a cholera epidemic and inadequate food and shelter en route took 5,000 lives. In 1833 the Choctaws became the first of the eastern tribes to settle in Indian Territory.

Establishing themselves as the Choctaw Nation on their 3 million acres, they proceeded to make a rapid new adaptation. The wealthiest Choctaws of Mississippi had brought their slaves with them, some families with as many as 500. They immediately began breaking and cultivating the new land and were soon raising cotton, corn, pecans, hogs, and cattle. They developed transportation systems both across country and along the navigable Arkansas River. A vigorous reaction against changing to new ways, headed by the able hereditary chief Moshulatubbee in the northern district was short-lived. In 1842 a school system was established, consisting of neighborhood day schools and boarding schools and was vigorously developed for the next 50 years; in 1853 a superintendent of public instruction for the whole nation was chosen. The Choctaws revamped their governmental system slowly and experimentally, in contrast with the Cherokees. By 1860 a constitution was accepted, and an elected principal chief, bicameral legislature and a court system were established. The Choctaws maintained great political solidarity; not even the Civil War split them. They allied themselves with the Confederacy but maintained an independent political position. Later, in a statesmanlike paper, their leaders pointed out that their support of the Confederacy had seemed the best way at the time to preserve their own distinct nationality. They made a separate peace with the Union. Deliberations of the council were always in the Choctaw language, although laws and actions were also translated into English. Choctaw names ceased to be used after the 1850s; families prominent in politics were the McCurtains, the Wrights, and the Joneses.

Pressures mounted in Indian Territory during the 1880s for the elimination of the Choctaw (and other Indian) governments and the breakup of the collectively held land into individual holdings. As with all the Civilized Tribes, factions arose as a result of these pressures, and although some violence did occur, the differences were eventually healed by political means. Ultimately, however, they were forced to yield to the implacable U.S. Congress. The Choctaw government was dissolved during the first decade of the 20th century, the land was divided, and the surplus sold. Choctaws, who had always segregated Negroes in schools and excluded them from voting or holding office in the Choctaw Nation, fought bitterly over whether Negroes should have equal assignment of allotments. Unlike the Chickasaws, they finally allowed equal division with Negro members of their nation.

CREEKS

Although the BIA agency in Okmulgee, Okla., listed only about 10,000 Creeks, conservative estimates of the number eligible for claims payments reached 45,000 in 1970. The Creeks therefore can probably be rated as the second largest of the Five Civilized Tribes.

They are concentrated in seven counties of east-central Oklahoma, north of the Choctaws and southwest of the Cherokees. The full-bloods in the tribe vigorously

maintain native religious ways and customs, but they also send their children to public schools and belong to the Methodist, Baptist, or Presbyterian churches. Since the formal dissolution of their national government in 1906, they have used the designation Creek Tribe of Oklahoma and have maintained a tribal organization consisting of a general council of elected representatives from each of what had been the tribe's basic political units for more than a hundred years; called towns, the modern settlements are based on the traditional Creek towns, which were composed of several villages. The council also includes members elected by Seminoles living west of the Creek region. The representatives meet regularly at their Oklahoma capital, Okmulgee, to deal with matters of education and welfare, chiefly through the Bureau of Indian Affairs. There is also an elected business committee and three credit associations, also organized on the town basis. There is, in addition, the nominal office of principal chief, appointed by the president of the United States.

Many of the Creek towns maintain another ancient institution, namely, the "square grounds" or "stomp grounds," where regular meetings are devoted to traditional dances, rites connected with the sacred fire, and annual ceremonies such as the Green Corn rites. The traditional ball games are also sometimes played.

The mixed-bloods, including many persons whose ancestry is white, black, and Indian, live in cities and towns of eastern Oklahoma, particularly Tulsa, Eufaula, and others in the territory of the old Creek Nation. They work in a wide range of occupations, whereas the majority of full-bloods are farmers living in the heart of the Upper Creek area of the old Creek Nation.

The Creeks, who lived in northern Georgia and a large part of Alabama along the Alabama, Chattahoochee, and Flint rivers, played a major role in the development of trade after the arrival of Europeans in the southeastern states. They spoke a Muskogean language and called themselves Maskoke. During the 17th and 18th centuries they formed what the whites called a confederacy, a loose organization of friendly and allied tribes, including the Alabamas, Apalachees, Hitchitis, Yuchis, Natchez, and a band of the Shawnees, for the purpose of maintaining peace. The confederacy was also notable for its absorption of lesser groups. Generally they conceived of themselves as having two major divisions, the Upper Creeks, with a principal town at Tukabatchee in eastern Alabama, and the Lower Creeks, with a major town at Coweta in northern Georgia. The Coweta Creeks, generally accepted as the dominant segment during the early 18th century, maintained an alliance with the British and against the Spaniards, although they favored a policy of neutrality concerning the Europeans and their struggles for power.

For about twenty years after the Revolution a prominent Upper Creek named Alexander McGillivray (c. 1759–1793) worked to unify the Creeks and align them with the United States. The unity he achieved was broken during the first quarter of the 19th century, the period of influence of William McIntosh (c. 1775–1825), a Lower Creek. One source of cleavage was the cession of lands to the United States, which went on constantly through lesser *mikos* (headmen), so that by 1811 the general Creek council imposed the death sentence on any Creek who signed land cession treaties with the Americans.

In 1811 and 1812 Tecumseh made a great effort to enlist the Creeks, as well as other southern Indians, in his pan-Indian resistance movement. This split the Creeks; most opposed him, under the leadership of Pushmataha, but one group called the Red Sticks favored his plans and during 1814 fought against the Americans and against the Creeks who opposed them. American troops under Andrew Jackson not only defeated the fighting Creeks but also forced them to conclude treaty ceding most of their land in Georgia, including that of the loyal majority. More land cessions were made in 1825, but the treaty was annulled. A new treaty in 1826 ceded most Creek land east of the Mississippi to the Americans and contained an agreement that all Creeks would move to Indian Territory.

Some Creeks were given the privilege of accepting land allotments in Mississippi and thereby becoming American citizens. Others, chiefly followers of William McIntosh, who had been executed for selling land, went to Indian Territory in 1828, where they were opposed by Osages and Delawares, who regarded them as encroaching on their lands. In 1832 a final treaty left the remaining Creeks with no land east of the Mississippi. In-fighting developed, and although a few Creeks joined the Seminoles in Florida who were fighting against removal, most refused to move. In 1836 General Winfield Scott was ordered to lead the forced migration, despite Creek opposition. Of the more than 17,000 Creeks who started the two-year trek on the Trail of Tears, only 15,000 safely arrived in Indian Territory. Within months after arrival 3,500 more died of disease or starvation.

Once in Indian Territory in 1839, the Creeks worked for unity, at first accepting the leadership of the McIntosh faction. They established an organization along the lines of their old confederacy, which was strongly democratic. The old town structure was at its base, with each town having a principal chief and an elected council. Their written code of laws was expanded and approved in 1840 by the whole council of what was called the Creek Nation. There was still a division between Lower Creeks, who tended to be receptive to newer ways, and Upper Creeks, who tended to be strongly conservative; the latter dominated, but differences were settled in council meetings rather than by violence.

The national council prohibited missionaries from preaching, but, like the Cherokees, did allow them to establish schools. Baptists, Presbyterians, and Methodists created neighborhood and boarding schools, which many Creeks attended. The national council also continued its traditional policy of welcoming other Indian peoples like the Delawares, Shawnees, Kickapoos, Quapaws, and Miamis, as well as the Seminoles, but only after the U.S. government purchased some Creek land on which to establish them. They were active in encouraging intertribal organization and cooperation among the tribes of Indian Territory. The Creeks were split by the Civil War, but in 1867 promulgated another constitution that helped reunite them. In this reorganization they designated Okmulgee as their capital and established a bicameral body composed of a House of Kings and a House of Warriors, based on the old traditions, which functioned effectively as an elected body.

The old conflicts, as well as some new ones, resulted in the Green Peach War of 1881, as a host of outside pressures for railroad rights of way and other land encroachments came to a head. The factions were led by Isparharcher, a full-blood who had favored the North, and Checote, a Confederate sympathizer. The new divisions were quieted by this outbreak, and the full-bloods reasserted dominance under Isparharcher as principal chief. He and most of the Creeks were adamant against accepting land allotment, with the inevitable result—the dissolution of the Creek government in 1906 under the Curtis Act. A later nativistic movement led by Chitto Harjo failed to obtain general Creek support for reestablishing the old laws, but the tradition of the sacred fire and other religious rites continue to be the basis for the traditional square-grounds ceremonial activities.

CHICKASAWS

By the 1970s there were more Chickasaws in Oklahoma than had ever been reported in the course of their history; estimates ran from 5,500 to 9,000, the differing figures resulting from the same factors as in the case of the other Five Civilized Tribes—that is, varying degrees of cultural assimilation and wide dispersal of the population. The Chickasaws, more than the other five peoples, had lost their full-blood conservative segment by the 1970s. The mixed-bloods are in the great majority and have been for several generations.

Chickasaws are prominent in the professions, as cattlemen, and in various other occupations. They are scattered through Oklahoma but are to some extent concentrated in several south-central counties, where they were assigned land in the 1830s and 1840s. The majority are Methodists, and some are Baptists. There are no organized forms of native religion. They maintain a political organization consisting of a federally appointed governor, an elected tribal council, and the Chickasaw Tribal Protective Association. These organizations deal with claims cases and other business matters and ceremonial-symbolic functions. The Chickasaws show considerable interest in maintaining a symbol of their nationhood through the annual election of a tribal princess, who appears in the American Indian Exposition at Anadarko.

At the time of Hernando de Soto's expedition in the 1540s into what are now the southeastern states, there were approximately 4,000 Chickasaws, who occupied the area of northwestern Alabama, northern Mississippi, western Tennessee and Kentucky, with a corridor to the hunting grounds of the Ohio Valley. During the colonial period they were concentrated in large villages in northern Mississippi along the Tombigbee River. They were strongly agricultural. Their overall tribal organization was headed by a man the whites called a king, whose office was hereditary, and who was advised by a council. They exhibited a capacity for military effectiveness and strongly resisted domination by any other people: they defeated de Soto in 1541 when he ordered them to supply him with carriers, they remained independent of French domination—even absorbing remnants of the Natchez tribe after their devastating defeat by the French—and they resisted domination by the Creeks who invaded their territory in 1795.

During the 18th century they became well known as traders; after 1763 the Chickasaws tended to ally themselves with the British in the three-way European power struggle for control of American territory. Until late in the American Revolution they favored the British, but a pro-American faction grew among them and by 1786, when the Hopewell Treaty was signed with other tribes, they were cooperating with the new government. Between 1800 and 1818 they made treaties with the Americans, ceding large portions of their territory, and in 1813–1814 they fought the Creek Red Sticks on the side of the Americans.

A small mixed-blood group dominated their internal politics, using the traditional king and council form of government to rule the trading empire they controlled. By 1829 they had formulated a body of laws. During the 1830s they negotiated but did not resist strongly the removal pressures that were impinging on all the Civilized Tribes, in which they were included because of the extent to which they had adopted European-derived ways. They signed a treaty in 1833 agreeing to move to Indian Territory, to pay the Choctaws $53,000 for rights as citizens in the Choctaw Nation in Indian Territory, and to sell their 6 million acres of land in Mississippi.

Their removal took place over 13 years, not being completed until 1850. Like the others who traveled the Trail of Tears, they suffered many hardships and perhaps 1,000 died en route. Until 1854 the Chickasaws did little to reestablish their tribe as it had been in Mississippi. Instead they were content to live on the annuities they received for their eastern lands and to drift within the new location as citizens of the Choctaw Nation. Gradually, however, their spirit returned. In 1855 they made an agreement to separate from the Choctaws, whom they accused (probably unjustly) of tyrannical controls over them. They moved to the lands they had originally paid the Choctaws for, along the Canadian River, and reorganized their political and economic life. They wrote a constitution; set up an elected governor, a legislative body composed of a senate and house of representatives, and a court system; elected a superintendent of public instruction; and began to build a school system comparable to that of the other Civilized Tribes. The Civil War, which they entered on the side of the Confederacy, interrupted their political and educational development. When it resumed, the invasion of settlers into Indian Territory profoundly interfered with their progress.

Pressures began for the formation, bitterly opposed by the Chickasaws, of a territorial government that would supersede the Indian national governments. When the General Allotment Act was passed in 1887, it became clear that the whites were determined to break up the Indians' collective land holdings and, if necessary, the local governments that the Chickasaws and the other peoples had built; in 1893 the allotment policy began to be applied to the Five Civilized Tribes. To overcome Chickasaw opposition, the Curtis Act was passed in 1898, dissolving the Chickasaw government and instituting individual allotment. From that time their cultural assimilation proceeded more rapidly than among the other Civilized Tribes.

COMANCHES AND KIOWAS

In the 1960s there were about 2,700 Comanches and the same number of Kiowas, as well as some 400

Kiowa-Apaches, in Oklahoma. They live in southwestern Oklahoma on individually owned tracts of land; four tracts of collectively owned land are held in trust by the U.S. government. Some whites are interspersed among them on this land, which was bought from the U.S. government or from Indians to whom it had been allotted. A BIA agency at Anadarko provides some federal services and attends to property trust matters. The population of the Comanches is about what it was during initial contact with whites in the southern plains country; the Kiowas' population is probably 1,000 greater than it was.

Comanches, Kiowas, and Kiowa-Apaches are organized as a business corporation through the Kiowa-Comanche-Apache Business Committee, on which Comanches and Kiowas are equally represented, with members elected for four-year terms. The purpose of the committee is to take care of various tribal interests in accord with the Oklahoma Indian Welfare Act of 1936 and in conjunction with the BIA agency. The Indians live on scattered homesteads as farmers or stock raisers, but many have moved to cities in other states or to the larger cities in Oklahoma. Methodists and Dutch Reformed church members predominate among the Comanches, while Kiowas belong to the Catholic, Methodist, Episcopal, and Baptist churches. A considerable number in each group are members of the Native American church, and some profess the native tribal religions. All participate actively in the annual American Indian Exposition at Anadarko, one of the most heavily attended and best-known expressions of pan-Indian ceremonialism and pageantry in the United States. Kiowas especially have become well known for artistic endeavors, particularly painting, which has been encouraged by the University of Oklahoma since 1927. The writer N. Scott Momaday, a Kiowa and professor of English literature at Stanford University, won the Pulitzer prize in 1969 for the novel *House Made of Dawn*.

The Comanche and Kiowa languages belong to different linguistic stocks—Comanche being Uto-Aztecan and Kiowa being Tanoan—but the two tribes have been closely associated for more than 100 years, and their recent histories are similar. They both lived originally in the eastern Rocky Mountains, the Comanches probably in the Wyoming area and the Kiowas in Montana. Both moved eastward beginning in the late 1600s, the Comanches into the country of the North Platte River in Nebraska and the Kiowas into South Dakota. In these new locations they acquired horses and became more nomadic and warlike. The Sioux and the Cheyennes pushed them south, and they in turn fought with the Eastern Apaches and the New Mexico Spaniards. In these raids the Comanches, especially, took many Spanish prisoners and became mixed genetically with them as well as with other Indian foes. Both tribes were established by the late 1700s in what became western Kansas, Oklahoma, and eastern Texas, the Kiowas along the Arkansas River and its tributaries, the Comanches along the Canadian River. From these locations in the southern buffalo country, they raided New Mexico, Texas, and as far south as Chihuahua, Mexico. Their adaptation to the horse and buffalo culture was as thoroughgoing as that of any Plains Indians, and for nearly 100 years they were the terror of the Spaniards and later the Mexicans and Texans. The Texans were so fearful of their raiding that they estimated the Comanche population at 20,000 when there were barely more than 2,000.

In 1790, after many years of mutual raiding, the Kiowas and the Comanches made peace with each other, but they remained at war with the Cheyennes and Osages for another 50 years. As Americans came into their territory, hostilities developed. Numerous efforts were made by the Americans to make peace treaties, but these failed, especially after Texans in 1840 murdered a group of ten Comanche headmen who had come to a peace conference. Americans moving west were constantly infiltrating the territory of the two tribes. In 1853 a coalition of resisting tribes, consisting of Comanches, Kiowas, Cheyennes, Osages, Arapahos, and others attempted to wipe out the encroaching whites once and for all but were defeated by an alliance of Sauks and Foxes and other settled Indians fighting for the whites in Indian Territory.

From this time the whites redoubled their treaty-making efforts, but they had little success until the Treaty of Medicine Lodge in 1867. The Comanches and Kiowas were to settle on 3 million acres in southwestern Indian Territory, which the government had forced the Choctaws and Chickasaws to cede. A small minority of both groups went to live there and to receive the meager rations promised in the treaty. About 1,000 Comanches and fewer Kiowas lived on the new reservation, a tiny portion of the land over which they had formerly ranged.

Most of the Indians still lived in their old territory and continued, along with the reservation residents, to raid into Texas and Mexico. The federal government, after unsuccessfully trying President Ulysses S. Grant's peace policy, brought in more troops. In the resulting clashes 26 Kiowa leaders, including their most respected men, were sent to Florida for imprisonment, where several died. At the same time the Comanches moved in a different direction. During 1873–1874 a messiah named Ishatai persuaded the young warriors that they could wipe out the whites and bring back the buffalo. The first uprising stimulated by the preacher ended in miserable defeat, and his influence waned.

During the 1880s the last holdout bands came onto the reservation, including one headed by the distinguished Comanche, Quanah, who became known as Quanah Parker. By then 50 percent of the people were living on rations and did so until 1901. During the 1890s the Comanches and Kiowas began to farm and raise cattle, but to a large extent they lived by leasing grazing rights to whites, who were pushing hard on all sides for land. During the 1880s the Comanches through their Mexican contacts played an important role in spreading the Native American church, which Quanah Parker helped found.

PAWNEES

From a population of 10,000 in the 1830s, the Pawnees were reduced to about 700 in 1900 and seemed destined for extinction. By the 1960s, however, their population had increased to a reported figure of about 1,200. The Pawnees live in Pawnee and Payne counties in north-central Oklahoma, at the southern edge of the earliest known range of one of their bands.

They live on individual allotments on some 28,000

acres, about one-tenth of what had been their federal reservation in 1892. They are for the most part small farmers and stock raisers on not very productive land, making as much of their living from leasing grazing- and farm-land to whites as from their own activities. They are organized as the Pawnee Indian Tribe of Oklahoma under a constitution and bylaws chartered by the state under the Indian Welfare Act of 1936. The tribal organization includes the four distinct bands that have always characterized the Pawnees. The band chiefs make up what is called the Nasharo Council, which meets regularly and contributes to the Pawnee sense of common identity. There is also a business council with eight elected members. Most Pawnees are at least nominally Methodists, some are members of the Native American church, and a large number participate to some degree in traditional religious ceremonials. They are active in the annual American Indian Convention at Anadarko and in pan-Indian activities around the United States.

The Pawnee language belongs to the Caddoan linguistic family, to which the Caddos and the Wichitas of Oklahoma also belong. Before the European invasions began, the Pawnees and linguistically related groups were probably concentrated chiefly in the lower Mississippi Valley. Their culture was based on intensive agriculture, and they lived in settled villages of closely clustered, elaborately built earth lodges. Their religion made use of sacred medicine bundles, visions, and organized ceremonial societies. The annual sacrifice of a young woman captive to the morning-star deity was an important ceremonial.

In 1720, when the Spaniards first made contact with them, the Skidi Band of the Pawnees was living in what became eastern Nebraska and Kansas. This band, which had become active buffalo hunters on foot, pioneered the westward movement of the Pawnees, stimulated first by their interest in buffalo hunting and later by pressure from eastern Indians who were displaced by the early white settlers. The Pawnees made increasing use of horses as they moved west and made contact with the developing nomad cultures of the plains—the Kiowas, Comanches, Arikaras, and Sioux.

By the end of the 17th century some Pawnees had already settled in what is now central Nebraska, and some eight villages on the Republican River reportedly had a population of more than 10,000 about 1700. Throughout the 1700s more Pawnees (such as the group called the Black Pawnees) moved west and were in touch with French traders prior to 1750. They never made war on the United States; on the contrary, they were allied with the Americans in their efforts to control the raiding of Sioux, Osages, and Comanches. In 1818 they made a treaty of peace with the U.S. government and then from 1833 through 1857 made treaties ceding all their territory except for a small reservation along the Loup River in east-central Nebraska. As they settled on this reservation, they engaged in warfare with the Sioux, allied with the U.S. cavalry as effective scouts.

All during the 19th century the Pawnees suffered a succession of devastating misfortunes. Shortly after 1800 a severe smallpox epidemic reduced their many villages to one. Smallpox continued to afflict them through the 1830s, with 5,000 reported dying during that decade. At the same time their numbers were further reduced in raids by the Sioux and other nomadic tribes contending for the buffalos. By 1893 there were only 821 Pawnees left. In that year, after acquiring a reservation in Oklahoma in return for giving up their land in Nebraska, they were immediately forced to break up the reservation into individual allotments, with the surplus land opened to settlement by whites. Rations were cut by the government in order to force more farming, but this had the reverse effect, leading the Pawnees to depend on lease money from white cattlemen and farmers.

In 1891–1892, as forced allotment became imminent, the Pawnees actively adopted the Ghost Dance religion, but its leader was imprisoned and the movement forced underground. Whites then suggested that if allotments went through, the Pawnees would no longer be under federal government supervision and could freely practice the Ghost Dance. During these years the peyote cult spread among the Pawnees. The Ghost Dance died out, but the Native American church continued.

During the 20th century Pawnees increasingly adapted to Anglo-American ways. In 1962, in a suit against the federal government for illegally taken land, the Indian Claims Commission awarded the Pawnees $7 million, which was administered by their tribal organization to improve their economic condition.

SHAWNEES

In 1970 about 2,250 Shawnees lived in Oklahoma. The tribe is divided into three fairly distinct groups living in different parts of the state, with the largest number, some 1,100 individuals, living among Cherokees and whites in northeastern Oklahoma. A group of 450 living in the extreme northeastern corner of the state are known as the Eastern Shawnees; intermixed with Senecas and some other groups, their history has been rather separate from that of the other Shawnees for more than a century. In central Oklahoma near the town of Shawnee are another 700, who were long known as the Absentee Shawnees.

The Shawnees maintain two tribal organizations. Those in the vicinity of Shawnee are organized as the Absentee Shawnee Tribe of Indians of Oklahoma and have an elected council and principal chief. Those in the northeastern part of the state are organized as the Eastern Shawnee Tribe of Oklahoma in accord with the Oklahoma Indian Welfare Act of 1936. Both tribal organizations maintain business committees that handle land and other matters in conjunction with agencies of the Bureau of Indian Affairs.

Shawnees are farmers and stock raisers and work in a variety of occupations like those of the whites in the region. Some are Christian, belonging to congregations of Methodists, Baptists, or the Society of Friends, and a large percentage follow traditional religious ways. The Big Kim Band of the Absentee Shawnees is the most active community in the annual Thanksgiving and War ceremonials. Few know the Shawnee language, which belongs to the Algonkian linguistic family.

In the 1600s there may have been no more than 3,000 Shawnees, apparently living in the Ohio River Valley. Their known migrations began before 1690, when they were driven from their settlements by the west-ranging

Iroquois. From that time until the 1870s they moved about more than any other Indian group except the Delawares and the Kickapoos. In their moves they separated into distinct groups that lived apart for many years at a time.

Most of the Shawnees first migrated southwest as far as South Carolina and Georgia, and one village became established among the Creeks in Alabama. Later they separated into two groups, one moving north to join the Delawares, with whom they had friendly relations, in the Susquehanna Valley in Pennsylvania, another group moving northwest into Tennessee along the Cumberland River. Others ranged into Florida in small units during the 1700s. The Tennessee group was then pushed northward by attacks from Cherokees and Chickasaws and by 1730 had moved as far north as Ohio. In 1755, as a result of the pressures of whites in Pennsylvania and of the Iroquois ordering the Delawares to leave eastern Pennsylvania, the Shawnees of the east also moved to Ohio, so that for a time they were joined again with the other bands of Shawnees. Despite this fragmentation, they maintained the Shawnee language, and many remained devoted to their religious traditions. They produced one of the ablest Indian leaders, who worked for unity among all the Indians east of the Mississippi—Tecumseh (c. 1768–1813).

The Shawnees generally assisted the French against the British in the struggle for control of the fur trade and the land west of the Appalachians. Their Ohio settlements were allied with other Algonkians who were opposing the westward advance of the English. Under these conditions a movement for Indian unity arose at the end of the 18th century. The political aim of this movement, for which Tecumseh was spokesman, was to prevent any further cessions of land to whites. Culturally, it was a nativistic religious movement spearheaded by the prophet Tenskwatawa, Tecumseh's brother, who preached rejection of white man's ways and a return to Indian customs. The religious movement took hold among the Algonkian peoples who had been displaced into and those native to the Ohio-Indiana region. Tecumseh, noted as a war leader, made a great effort to bring the strong southeastern tribes such as the Creeks into his resistance movement, but failed. In 1811 the Prophet's Town in Indiana where Tenskwatawa's followers had settled in large numbers was destroyed by U.S. military action, and in 1813 Tecumseh was killed while fighting with the British against the Americans.

With the end of British support after the War of 1812, the embattled Algonkians began to give way, selling their lands in Ohio and Indiana and moving west in 1831 to a reservation in eastern Kansas, where they began to farm. Other Shawnees had moved to Missouri before 1800 and then southwest to Arkansas, Indian Territory, and to Texas on the Brazos River. Eventually, the Shawnees in Kansas were forced to give up their reservation and buy land in Oklahoma with the proceeds. Later all the Shawnees moved to their three present locations in Oklahoma. The Eastern Shawnees, mixed with Senecas, had settled in what became northeastern Oklahoma as early as 1832. The Shawnees who had moved before 1800 to Texas and were pushed out 50 years later were moved to central Oklahoma; they became the nucleus of the Absentee Shawnee community. Like many other Indian Territory peoples, their lands were allotted during the period 1891–1893, and they became individual property owners or promptly lost their land to whites.

OSAGES

The approximately 1,100 Osages living in Oklahoma in the 1920s were described by some as the wealthiest people in the world. Every individual in 1925 was receiving $13,200 a year as a headright to oil and gas lease proceeds. The headright is still the main source of income of those identifying themselves as Osages. From 1920 to about 1970 the group received some $500 million. Their income per person was reduced by the 1970s, but it was still substantial. One reason for reduction was that in 1970 nearly eight times as many people —8,244—were listed as Osages. The right to receive income from the Osage oilfield led many to identify as tribal members who were not interested earlier.

Although a majority of Osages still make their homes in Osage County, nearly as many live in southern California, and others are scattered through 36 different states in some 300 different U.S. communities. They work in a variety of occupations; among those who have distinguished themselves are the Tallchief sisters, Maria and Marjorie, both ballet dancers, and Major General Clarence L. Tinker (1887–1942).

The Osages in Oklahoma are still organized under the provisions of the special act of Congress of 1906, without constitution or corporate charter. A principal chief, assistant chief, and council of eight, elected every four years, are chiefly concerned with leasing the oilfield and using tribal funds. The tribe pays for the expenses of the BIA agency at Pawhuska and has established a health clinic and other services for Osages in Oklahoma. Osages are predominantly Catholic, but some are Baptist, Methodist, or members of the Society of Friends. In 1918 there were 25 congregations of the Native American church, but the participants declined in numbers through subsequent years. In some homes a Siouan language is still spoken.

Before the entry of the English into Virginia, the Osages lived in the Piedmont area and also along the Ohio River in what became Kentucky. By 1673 they had encountered Europeans along the Osage River in western Missouri. They were strongly agricultural but also hunted buffalo. They lived in circular skin-covered lodges or in tipis when hunting buffalo.

The Osages allied themselves with the French traders and military from about 1712, but by 1790 they had become opposed to the French and then to the Spanish. They remained largely independent of all alliances with other tribes or with Europeans and resisted various efforts of the Spaniards to control their trade with and military action against other Indians. They began ceding land to the United States in 1808 and by 1825 had been given a reservation in Kansas, which many refused to settle on for some time. In these decades there was fighting between Osages and Cherokees on land that the Osages claimed. By 1839 most of them had moved to the Kansas reservation, where they continued to hunt buffalo and to raid and be raided by Plains tribes. During their residence in Kansas from 1839 until 1871, the Osages established military alliances with Comanches, Kiowas, and Apaches and prospered

through trade. By 1847 the pressures of invading white settlers began. The government forced the Osages to cede part of the reservation, but that did not slow down the invaders. In 1868 they were forced to sell the rest of the reservation to a railroad company and to buy land in Indian Territory. By 1872, 4,000 Osages with 12,000 horses were settled south of Pawhuska. In 1881 they approved a constitution modeled on the Cherokees'; law and order were kept through a court and police system. By 1893 half of the reservation was leased to white farmers and cattlemen. Under the leadership of Bigheart, the Osages resisted allotment, and the process was suspended until 1906. When they were forced to accept allotment, they arranged to retain subsurface rights to minerals and oil in the name of the tribe and managed to have all land allotted to Osages, with no surplus for whites. Thus each Osage received 658 acres and a $3,819 share of the tribal fund. Eventually Osage County became a reservation—the only present-day reservation in Oklahoma—with the subsurface rights held as tribal trust.

Other Indians living in Oklahoma in the 1970s were the following: the Arapahos, Biloxis, Caddos, Cayugas, Southern Cheyennes, Iowas, Kaws, Miamis, Missouris, Modocs, Otoes, Ottawas, Peorias, Poncas, Quapaws, Senecas, Tonkawas, Wichitas, and Wyandots.

Bibliography
A most useful introduction to the mélange of peoples now living in Oklahoma is Muriel H. Wright, *A Guide to the Indian Tribes of Oklahoma* (1951; reprint, Norman, Okla., 1965). Outstanding in its employment of documents and direct observations to unravel the complex history of a modern Oklahoma group is C.A. Weslager, *The Delaware Indians: A History* (New Brunswick, N.J., 1972). Angie Debo, *The Road to Disappearance: A History of the Creek Indians* (1941; reprint, Norman, Okla., 1967), is one of several fine histories by this author of the Five Civilized Tribes. Marion I. Starkey, *The Cherokee Nation* (1946; reprint, New York, 1972), is a highly readable account of this important and influential eastern Oklahoma tribe. Ernest Wallace and E.A. Hoebel, *The Comanches, Lords of the South Plains* (Norman, Okla., 1952), combine the techniques of historian and ethnologist in an account of the history and culture of a western Oklahoma tribe. Two very different accounts of the Pawnees are valuable: Gene Weltfish, *The Lost Universe* (New York, 1965), and "The Pawnee: Horsemen and Farmers of the Prairies," in Wendell Oswalt, *This Land Was Theirs: A Study of the North American Indian* (New York, 1973).

THE NORTHERN PLAINS

The upper Missouri Valley region, including the Yellowstone and North Platte drainages and the headwaters of the Snake, may be called the northern plains. A region of prairie and high plains, it includes the states of North and South Dakota, Montana, and Wyoming. Formerly this was the major part of the buffalo's habitat; now it is an area of ranching and dry farming. The northern plains contain some 16 distinct Indian groups, although these can be counted in several ways, so that if all the varieties of Sioux and others were listed separately, for example, the number could be as high as 29. The population of Indians in the whole region in 1960 was over 80,000, the bulk of whom lived on federal reservations, mostly small fractions of the lands claimed by the Indians before their first contacts with whites. Both the population and the number of Indian ethnic groups are about the same as they have been for the past 200 years. In fact, according to one estimate, the Indian population has increased by a few thousand since first contacts. Possibly four more groups identify separately

from one another than was the case during the precontact period, resulting from placement on separate reservations. The state most heavily populated by Indians was Montana, with some 40,000; South Dakota was close behind with 33,150; North Dakota had 5,800; and Wyoming, about 3,300.

Some 250 years before the arrival of white settlers, Indian groups moved freely through the northern plains. The area was occupied by tribes moving west from the Great Lakes, by others moving from the Southeast, and by tribes moving east from the Rocky Mountains. Later movements were stimulated by opportunities for a new kind of life using guns and horses, as well as by the pressures generated by European settlement in the East. Some of the newcomers who began to arrive about the end of the 17th century relied almost entirely on buffalo hunting, others made a dual adjustment by hunting buffalo part of the year and living the rest of the year by farming. The eastern Sioux never wholly deserted their former forest-based life for the nomadism of buffalo-hunting. Some purely farming groups lived along the larger rivers in permanent, densely populated villages. A number of such peoples, the Mandans and Pawnees especially, never turned to the nomadic life but continued to be sedentary, with buffalo hunting as a secondary source of subsistence.

A second characteristic of the newly mobile peoples of the northern plains was that they became especially concerned with and adept in warfare. The competition for hunting grounds was intense as more and more Indians moved into the region. Thus for survival they developed fighting techniques, and warfare became a major orientation of their cultures.

It is important to note that the Indians of this region have been characterized by their vigorous maintenance of cultural values and identity; despite extremely adverse circumstances they have not only maintained their groups without exception, but have also exerted a profound and continuing cultural influence on nearly all the other tribes of the United States. Their way of life also became the stereotype of the Indian way for whites, so they have played a special role in white history and culture as well.

SIOUX

It does some violence to the realities of Sioux life to describe them as a whole, for there were in the 1960s at least ten distinct subgroups among the Sioux, the largest single group among the northern plains peoples. These groups all speak languages belonging to the Dakota family of the Siouan language stock. Their sense of identity as separate bands has to some extent been brought about or intensified by their placement on 13 different reservations.

In South Dakota in 1960 between 33,000 and 35,000 Siouan- or Dakota-speaking peoples lived on seven reservations under federal supervision. The largest of these reservations, on which the greatest number of Sioux are concentrated, are in southwestern South Dakota—the Pine Ridge and Rosebud reservations, the first with a population of 10,648, and the second with 8,183. The population of the other five reservations ranged from 4,307 to 705. In addition 289 Sioux live in a group of independent communities that do not constitute a reservation. In North Dakota there are two Sioux reserva-

tions with a population of 5,800. There are smaller reservations of Sioux in Montana, Minnesota, and Nebraska.

Nearly all of the Sioux of South and North Dakota live according to what seems superficially to be the white man's way; they live in frame houses like other rural Dakotans or in the dilapidated remains of log cabins that were built when they first relocated on the reservations. Nowhere do the traditional tipis appear as regular living quarters, although they are in evidence during summer ceremonials and in connection with other religious rites, such as the Peyote cult. About one-fifth raise cattle, and a much smaller number dry farm some land. The majority, some 60 percent, work for wages in nearby towns, for neighboring white farmers and Sioux stock raisers, or in BIA operations. The land on most reservations is checkerboarded, that is, partly occupied by whites who bought allotments from Indians or homesteaded the land when it was open for settlement after allotment. Thus Indians and whites are interspersed, and there is much mutual hostility.

As many as half the people on most reservations claim unmixed descent, but among the Sioux there is a well-recognized distinction between mixed-bloods and full-bloods, with mixed-bloods outnumbering full-bloods. As among the Cherokees, the distinction is primarily a matter of cultural differences. The term mixed-blood refers in ordinary usage to persons who follow the ways of non-Indians, speak English at home, strive to amass property, furnish their houses in white style, and either actively reject Sioux religious ways and values or rarely if ever participate in them. However, they do identify themselves as Indians, although full-bloods may regard them as less Sioux than themselves. Full-bloods speak one of the Dakota languages and encourage their children to do so, respect elements of traditional Sioux religion, participate in some of the surviving dances and other rituals, and in other ways pursue an Indian lifestyle. The distinction is obviously not a hard and fast one dividing the Sioux of any reservation community into sharply bounded segments, but it is a strong and important distinction in their thinking. Full-blood and mixed-blood are more fluid categories than the general distinction between Indians and whites.

Nearly all Dakotas are nominally members of Christian congregations—usually Episcopalian, Roman Catholic, Church of God, or an evangelical sect, and most participate to some degree in the organization and services of these churches. At the same time the Native American church has many practicing members, as does the Yuwipi cult, which is the chief surviving active tradition of the native Dakota religion. The two types of religion, Christian and traditional, are not regarded as mutually exclusive, although there is a strong tendency for members of the Native American church to ignore their Christian affiliations. The pow-wow gatherings, which stress traditional Dakota music and dance and portions of some ceremonials, are important in the lives of nearly all Dakotas on the reservations, and they present opportunities to maintain contacts with other Indians across the United States.

On most of the federal reservations tribal councils are organized under the provisions of the Indian Reorganization Act of 1934. These political bodies assume various functions related to the provision by the BIA of school, economic, law and order, and welfare services. These councils are the focus of active political interest and give rise to strong factional divisions, despite the fact that their political power is limited by the BIA supervisory role. There are also tribal courts with elected judges, which decide domestic and other cases. Most groups of Dakotas take an active part in the affairs of the National Congress of American Indians, and some are members of the militant American Indian Movement (AIM).

In 1973 the Dakotas won national attention when leaders of AIM occupied the town of Wounded Knee, S. Dak., the name of which gave prominence (as the leaders of AIM wished it to do) to one of the important symbols of Dakota collective identity. Indeed, many of the most important symbols of the troubled relations between whites and Indians—Sitting Bull, Red Cloud, the Ghost Dance, Wounded Knee, General Custer—derive from events in Sioux history of the late 19th century.

About 1680 all of the Dakota-speaking peoples, consisting of three major divisons—the Santees, the Wichiyelas (sometimes called Yankton), and the Tetons—were living around the headwaters of the Mississippi River in the Mille Lacs area of Minnesota. They were under pressure from the Chippewas moving west from the central Great Lakes, who had acquired guns from the French and other Europeans. As the Chippewas sought control of the hunting areas of the upper Mississippi, the Dakotas steadily moved westward, the Teton division moving first and prevailing against more westerly Indians, such as the Cheyennes and the Kiowas, in what became western South and North Dakota. In doing this the Tetons gave up entirely their forest way of life. They were followed by the Wichiyelas, who established themselves to the east and south and became primarily hunters. The Santees remained at the eastern edge of the prairie country bordering on the forest lands and maintained a mixed way of subsistence. As the Dakotas established themselves in new areas (the Tetons and Wichiyelas completely revolutionizing their way of life), they became the dominant peoples of the northern plains and the most thoroughly adapted as horse-riding buffalo hunters.

The Teton and Wichiyela Dakotas were at the height of their prosperity and military power during the first half of the 19th century. It was they who offered the most formidable resistance to the thousands of white immigrants who began to move across the plains after 1849. Their raids, along with those of the Cheyennes and Arapahos, in 1849 and 1850 led to strong efforts by the U.S. government to keep the wagon trains moving freely westward. In treaties, such as the Fort Laramie Treaty of 1851, the Indians agreed not to molest the settlers, in return for annuities and guarantees of peace. But the treaties were ineffective, and hostilities became more intense. Neither the Dakotas nor the U.S. cavalry were disciplined to follow the agreements, and conflicts continued.

Sitting Bull (c. 1834–1890), Red Cloud (1822–1909), and Crazy Horse (c. 1877) were formidable figures who attracted national attention. Red Cloud became a famil-

iar figure to the U.S. officers, signing treaties, accepting their invitations to travel to Washington, making a speech at Cooperstown, N.Y., that caught the attention of the whole country, and moving back and forth between hostile and peaceful stances. The implacable Crazy Horse was a great war leader, winning his most famous victory against Custer and his men in the Black Hills of South Dakota in 1876. The superior weapons of the U.S. Army and their mobility, because of the newly built railroad, proved decisive in the long run. What had been set aside in 1868 as the Great Sioux Reservation (comprising most of what became North and South Dakota) was broken up, and the Dakotas began to settle into new, small reservations scattered across the northern plains. Red Cloud had to make peace, and the Dakotas were forced to accept the supervision of the BIA on nine reservations. The BIA prohibited the Sun Dance, the major expression of Dakota religious and community life, and the forced scattering of Indians into very small settlements or isolated homesteads began. The buffalo was soon wiped out by white hunters, and the Dakotas became dependent on government rations. American-style schools and churches were established, and by 1889 the authority of the chiefs was being undermined in a variety of ways by the Indian agents.

The Dakotas turned in 1889 to a new religion, the Ghost Dance, which originated among the Paiutes farther west. At Pine Ridge Reservation, when the Oglalas (a division of the Sioux) began enthusiastic dancing, the BIA representative and the cavalry officers misunderstood the nature of the new religious expression, regarding the rites as a signal for attacks on the whites. The result was the massacre of 128 Dakotas at Wounded Knee Creek. The event became known across the United States and symbolized what many whites had come to regard as the tragedy of the Indians and the injustice and incompetence of the government in dealing with them. Wounded Knee underlined the message of an influential book published a few years before, Helen Hunt Jackson's *A Century of Dishonor* (1881), an eloquent denunciation of injustices done to the Indians.

The government had begun to issue cattle to the Dakotas in 1885, and slowly they turned to cattle raising, with some success. By 1912, on the Pine Ridge Reservation alone, there were 40,000 head of cattle, and the situation was similar on other Sioux reservations. When World War I brought high prices for cattle, they sold nearly all their stock and leased their land to whites, who offered to pay high rents because of the chance to make great profits during the war boom. By 1918, as a result of the sale of cattle and the allotment and subsequent sale of land, most Dakotas on the reservations were living in poverty, which was aggravated when the Depression wiped out the leaseholders. By 1939 most of the employed Dakotas were working for wages or had moved away from the reservations to larger cities throughout the United States. The federal government made efforts during the 1940s to help reestablish the cattle industry, but by the 1960s not more than 7 or 8 percent of Dakotas were cattle owners, and the majority of these were barely making a living. Their depressed economic condition continued into the 1970s.

CROWS

The Crows, whose name for themselves is Absaroka, have occupied a federal reservation in southern Montana since about 1868. They are the westernmost of the Siouan-speakers. In 1970, 4,992 Crows were listed as residents of the reservation, although 1,242 of these were not actually living there. The Crows hold 50 percent of the reservation in private ownership, as a result of allotment about 1900, but they lease most of this land to non-Indians. About 25 percent of the land is owned by whites, and another 13 percent is held in common title by the Crow tribe. Most resident Crows raise cattle on their own land or work for wages in BIA or tribal operations; 40 percent live largely by leasing their land to whites. The Crows maintained their aboriginal tribal organization after taking up residence on the reservation but reorganized in 1935 under the IRA. Their tribal council is unusually strong and independent. The majority of Crows are nominal Christians but are also active in the Native American church and regularly hold Sun Dance gatherings.

Like the Dakotas, the Crows completely adapted to the horse-riding, buffalo-hunting way of life, although it is likely that they were sedentary village-dwelling people before horses were introduced about 1740. They became active traders in the late 1700s, trading guns for horses with the Shoshones to their southwest. During the first half of the 19th century they developed the highly organized buffalo-hunting culture characteristic of the Dakotas and other northern Plains tribes. They fought other Indians to retain their territory east of the Rocky Mountains, and they claimed land as far east as the Black Hills. Their Plains culture traits included the vision quest for guardian spirits, the Sun Dance, and the war complex, including the counting of coups and the eagle-feather war bonnet. In contrast with the Dakotas, they were organized into clans with descent through the female line. In addition to men's age-graded societies there was the Tobacco Society, which treated tobacco as a sacred plant and managed ceremonies honoring the morning star.

Like other Plains tribes, the Crows suffered great population losses as a result of smallpox and cholera epidemics during the first half of the 19th century. From 4,000 to 5,000 when first recorded about 1780, their population declined by nearly half. By the 1960s their numbers had climbed again to about 5,000.

The experience of the Crows on the reservation has been much like that of the Dakotas, but they are less disorganized and their political organization is stronger. Like the Dakotas, they are active in intertribal powwows in which their costumes, ceremonials, dances, and music are influential.

OTHER NORTHERN PLAINS PEOPLES

Before the invasion of the northern plains area by the Dakota-speaking peoples, Siouan tribes lived along several of the rivers, including the upper Missouri, as sedentary agricultural villagers. Notable among these were the Mandans, who lived in what became North and South Dakota. Together with a similar group of farmers, the Hidatsas, their population numbered more than 6,000. Their villages were composed of large earth

lodges, built closely together in communities of as many as 1,000 to 1,500 people. Their complex culture resembled somewhat that of the Arikaras and Pawnees farther south, the Caddoan-speaking sedentary people of the southern plains. The Mandans lost population on a large scale during the epidemics of the early 1800s and were reduced to a handful of people. The Hidatsas were somewhat less hard hit. The remnant of the Mandans merged with the Hidatsas, and the resulting mixed small groups in the 1960s were living with the Gros Ventres, an Algonkian-speaking group formerly closely associated with the Arapaho, on the Fort Berthold Reservation in northwestern North Dakota.

The Assiniboines, reputed to have branched off from the Yankton Dakotas at about the time they moved west onto the plains, lived farther north in Canada, but portions of the tribe moved south in the 1860s and agreed to live on the Fort Peck and Fort Belknap reservations in northern Montana.

BLACKFEET, CHEYENNES, AND ARAPAHO

In 1960 there were about 5,000 Blackfeet living on a reservation in northwestern Montana. Greatly reduced after a century of smallpox and cholera epidemics from 1781 on, the Blackfeet may have numbered as many as 15,000 in 1780, when whites first recorded their population. In 1960 about 2,000 Cheyennes lived on a reservation adjoining that of the Crows in southern Montana, and about 1,100 northern Arapaho, sometimes called Gros Ventres, lived on the the Fort Berthold Reservation in North Dakota.

The history of these Algonkian-speaking peoples is generally similar to that of the dominant Siouan-speaking groups of the region. There is no indication that the Blackfeet moved into the plains from the east, but the Cheyennes were first encountered by Europeans in western Minnesota, where they lived as sedentary farming people until the early 1800s. They obtained horses by the last quarter of the 18th century but did not start hunting buffalo on horseback until the 1840s. Along with the Crows, they engaged in constant warfare with whites, suffered well-known massacres at the hands of U.S. Cavalry at Sand Creek and Ash Hollow in Colorado, and participated with the Sioux in the defeat of Custer. Finally, in 1877–1878 they suffered defeats and were sent south to Oklahoma. Even though guarded by cavalry, they refused to remain in the state and marched north to their Wyoming-Montana homeland. They were forced again to the south, and when they resisted many were killed. In the 1880s they were reestablished beside the Crow Reservation in Montana, where they now live.

The Cheyenne, Blackfeet, and Arapaho experience on the reservations in Montana is similar to that of the other northern plains tribes—rations, slow adaptation to cattle raising, forced assimilation through schools, and regulations against their native religious practices. After the change in U.S. policy in 1930s, they organized a tribal council under the IRA, revived the annual Sun Dance, and became vigorous participants in the peyote rites of the Native American church.

Other Indians living in the northern plains in the 1970s were the Arikaras, Atsinas, Chippewas, Crees, and Kutenais.

Bibliography
Gordon Macgregor, *Warriors without Weapons: A Study of the Society and Personality Development of the Pine Ridge Sioux* (Chicago, 1946), is a classic study of the most numerous and most famous people of the northern plains. Ethel Nurge, ed., *The Modern Sioux: Social Systems and Reservation Culture* (Lincoln, Nebr., 1970), expands the view of the Sioux to all the tribes and recounts more recent developments. Vine Deloria, Jr., *Custer Died for Your Sins: An Indian Manifesto* (New York, 1969), presents a modern Sioux's view of Indian affairs. John C. Ewers, *The Blackfeet: Raiders of the Northwestern Plains* (1958; reprint, Norman, Okla., 1967), relates the cultural history of another important northern plains group.

THE WESTERN BORDER OF THE PLAINS

Living in the eastern Rocky Mountains and their margins in the plains and also in the Great Basin are Indians who speak five distinct languages. Their communities are chiefly in Idaho, Colorado, Utah, Nevada, and northern Arizona. In the 1960s a population of about 12,000 lived on 22 federal reservations and 6 colonies. For the most part these peoples lack the large-scale cohesive organization and complex religious and social life of the northern plains peoples. Two of the groups—the Paiutes and the Shoshones—are widely scattered in small communities, both on and off reservations, and probably do not share a common sense of identity. Their history and their situation in the 1960s are rather different from those of any of the plains peoples. The Nez Perce and the Utes living on federal reservations are more concentrated. The Utes are on three different reservations and maintain the largest Indian communities of the region.

NEZ PERCES

The Nez Perces continue to bear the name given them by French fur traders, referring to the custom of piercing their noses for the insertion of ornaments. They belong to the Sahaptin language family, in contrast to the other peoples of the region, who speak languages of the Shoshonean branch of the Uto-Aztecan stock. The Nez Perces number more than 1,500, a reduction of about 2,500 since their first contact with whites. The great majority live on a reservation in northern Idaho; less than a hundred live on the Colville Reservation in Washington.

The Nez Perces, despite their distinctive language, are culturally typical of the northern Rocky Mountains region. Before being forced into reservation life, they lived in small independent bands and subsisted by hunting, gathering, and salmon fishing. By the 1730s they had obtained horses from their former enemies, the Shoshones, a development that enhanced their traditional nomadism and made them partly reliant on buffalo hunting in the plains. They alone among Indians developed selective breeding of horses, resulting in the Appaloosa. The Nez Perce adopted many traits of the northern Plains Indians, although not the more complex religious ceremonials or the strong political organization.

Having heard something of Christianity from their early contacts with the French, in 1831 the Nez Perce sent a delegation to St. Louis to request books and teachers. Presbyterian and later Catholic missionaries arrived, and most of the tribe became Christians, chiefly Presbyterians, but in the late 1840s, as white

settlers moved into their area, they became disaffected with the missionaries, who nevertheless remained active. In 1852 the Union Pacific Railroad was surveyed through Nez Perce country, and the Indians were divested of their land in the usual way. In 1855 a treaty was signed by separate Nez Perce headmen, ceding a large part of their land, and the main body of the tribe was forced into a portion of its former hunting territory, from which a reservation was formed in central Idaho.

One group in the Wallowa Valley of northeastern Oregon, whose headmen had not signed the treaty, refused to move. At first the federal government allowed this, but pressures from white settlers resulted in conflict, and eventually the government decision was reversed. Finally military action was taken against the group, and Nez Perce, settlers, and cavalrymen were killed. Forcible removal of all Nez Perces to the Idaho reservation was attempted, but the Wallowa group resisted and tried to escape to Canada. Their retreat of more than 1,000 miles—in its last phase under the leadership of Heinmot Tooyalakekt, or, as the whites called him, Chief Joseph (c. 1840–1904)—became famous all over the United States. Chief Joseph's speech, when he was finally captured in 1877, gave currency to the concept of the "vanishing American" and was very widely quoted. As the bulk of Nez Perces settled into reservation life in Idaho, Chief Joseph and some 400 followers were shipped to Fort Leavenworth, Kans., and then to Indian Territory, where many died. Settlers near the Nez Perce reservation in Idaho were so strongly opposed to Chief Joseph's return that the government decided to send him instead to the Colville Reservation in Washington territory, where a miscellaneous group of Indians was assembling.

The Nez Perces on the reservation were furnished rations for a time and turned to stock raising and some farming. The BIA agent required them to cut their traditionally long hair and to wear conventional American-style clothing. The agent appointed a tribal chief and subchiefs, who were paid salaries until 1880. From 1875 to 1895 the Presbyterians were the most powerful force on the reservation. They opposed all aspects of traditional life—ceremonies, gambling games, dances, and curing rites—and made a deliberate effort to curb the authority of the traditional headmen and the ordaining of native ministers, of which there were a dozen by 1893. They also put the Sahaptin language into written form and published all their religious literature in that language. The BIA agent worked closely only with the Presbyterians, so an opposition Catholic group supported a Catholic chief, and the foundations of a strong factional split were laid.

Between 1890 and 1895 the reservation was allotted, despite the opposition of the Nez Perces; more than two-thirds of the land was declared surplus and promptly went into white hands. In 1892, through the efforts of the BIA agent, a nine-man committee of Presbyterians was formed to solve the problems caused by allotment. By 1923 one-half of the remaining land had been sold, with the result that the majority of the Nez Perces were forced into wage labor for white farmers and ranchers or in the towns of the region.

By the 1960s their way of life had become barely distinguishable from that of white neighbors. Most Indian children attend public schools, and there has been much intermarriage, so few Nez Perces claimed to be full-bloods. Most of the mixture is with whites, but there are some intertribal marriages, chiefly with other plateau tribes. By 1963 more than 25 percent of the Nez Perces lived off the reservation, many in the immediate vicinity.

Since 1940 there has been considerable participation in two evangelical denominations—the Assembly of God and the Church of God. After the introduction of these white-controlled churches, three independent evangelical sects arose that were managed entirely by Nez Perces. The independent evangelicals are especially interested in the second coming and the millennial doctrines of these denominations. The tendency to religious schism, begun by the Nez Perce Presbyterians, has continued strongly.

The Nez Perce tribe continues to exist as a distinct political entity. The rival Presbyterian and Catholic chieftainships of the 1870s showed a strong interest in organized leadership and a capacity for political organization, which continued into the 20th century. The committee on allotment was revived in 1923—this time with one Catholic member—when the BIA instituted a five-year economic development plan. The committee functioned in conjunction with an all-male general assembly. A constitution was written and approved by the BIA, which established the committee as the official body for handling leasing and other business matters. With this organization functioning, the Nez Perces rejected reorganization under the IRA in 1934.

However, many young men returning from the armed services in 1948 regarded the committee as too much dominated by the BIA and wrote a new constitution, which established the Nez Perce Tribal Executive Committee as the dominant political body. The former general assembly no longer functioned. The NPTEC has remained a focus of vigorous political interest and has stimulated the formation of political parties. In the 1950s the Warriors, a group favoring the revival of traditional ceremonies and gaming activities and opposing the 1948 constitution, was active. In the 1960s that group disappeared, but a new organization, the Nez Perce Indian Association, composed of off-reservation Indians, continued to oppose the constitution. Its rival is another new organization, largely of reservation-dwellers, called the Loyal Nez Perces, which actively supports the constitution and also the revival of traditional ways.

UTES

In their history and present situation, the Utes somewhat resemble the Nez Perces. The Utes lived in the eastern Rocky Mountain area and acquired horses before 1675, somewhat earlier than the Nez Perces because the Utes were closer to the supply in New Mexico. They also hunted the buffalo, but to a lesser degree than did the Nez Perces, because they were kept out of the plains region by Comanches and then by Cheyennes and Arapahos. The Utes engaged in little warfare with whites, although in 1855, under pressure of the advancing settlers, they joined with the Jicarilla Apaches in brief opposition and were defeated. From that time they did not organize for warfare but lived either in isolation

or at the edges of white settlements in New Mexico, Colorado, and Utah. Their numbers were reduced from perhaps 4,500 in the early 19th century to about 2,500 in 1960.

Originally inhabiting central and western Colorado, eastern Utah, and northeastern New Mexico, they were reduced to the Uintah and Ouray reservation in northeastern Utah and the Southern Ute and Ute Mountain reservations in southwestern Colorado. Like many of the tribes of the Rockies area, they were not forced onto reservations until the 1880s.

The contrasts among the different groups are exemplified on the Colorado reservations, on each of which there are about 500 Utes. The Ute Mountain Band has an unallotted, closed reservation held in common under federal trust. They are somewhat nomadic, many following their sheep to different locations and living in tents or intermittently in cabins. Most are members of the Native American church and all practice the traditional ceremonial Bear Dance. Few of the older people speak English; the Ute language is spoken in most homes. The Ute Mountain Utes lived largely on rations until 1931. After that they supported themselves largely by raising sheep or working for wages at the BIA agency. They had no tribal council under the IRA, instead living by the traditional headman authority system.

In contrast, Utes on the Southern Ute Reservation live on individually held land and are largely small-scale farmers. English is generally spoken, and their houses are like those of neighboring whites, but both hair styles and clothing are traditional. They have a tribal council organized under the provisions of the IRA. The Peyote rites have been strong since 1917, although probably most Utes also belong to Christian churches. The tribal Bear Dance is an important annual event.

SHOSHONES AND PAIUTES

Small communities of Shoshones and Paiutes are scattered through Utah, Nevada, southern Idaho, and northwestern Arizona. In addition, Shoshones live on two large reservations, one in Wyoming and one in southeastern Idaho, and Paiutes live on a reservation in Nevada. The Shoshones in Idaho share the Fort Hall Reservation with the Bannocks, another Shoshonean-speaking people; and the Shoshones of the Wind River Reservation in Wyoming share theirs with the northern Arapahos. About 4,000, or more than 40 percent of the Shoshones and Paiutes, live in the region but off the reservations; some of these groups are called colonies and have arrangements for services, such as health care, with the federal government. The population on the larger reservations of both Shoshones and Paiutes is about 5,000.

The situation of the reservation Shoshones is little different from that of the Nez Perces and Utes on the allotted reservations. The adoption of white ways is well advanced, especially with regard to occupations, housing, clothing, and other aspects of material culture; most are Christians. Tribal councils under IRA provisions govern the reservations. A distinct sense of Indian identity has been fostered by the possession of some land under tribal trust and the prosecution of claims through the Indian Claims Commission. The sense of

tribal identity is perhaps strongest among the Wind River Shoshones, the Fort Hall Northern Shoshones, and the White Knife Shoshones of the Duck Valley Reservation in Idaho and Nevada. They are also active in intertribal pow-wows and have adopted much of the ceremonial symbolism of those circuits.

The thousands of other Paiutes and Western Shoshones of Nevada, Utah, and Arizona have a history either of peaceful relations with whites as they advanced into this inhospitable region or of occasional attacks on wagon trains. Because of their lack of overt hostility and the widely scattered and never centrally organized character of their life, they were largely ignored by the whites, except for an occasional massacre in retaliation for pilfering. Most of the scattered Paiutes, Utes, and Shoshones became laborers in the towns or domestics and ranch hands on the ranches that slowly grew up in the region.

In the late 1880s Wovoka (c. 1856–1932), the originator and messiah of the Ghost Dance religion, became widely influential. He was a Walker River Paiute of a very peaceful group, but his vision of the disappearance of the whites was clearly indicative of the underlying resistance to white culture, which was probably as strong among individual Paiutes as among any organized groups that fought against white domination. Wovoka's tradition of leadership continued among the Walker River Paiutes into the 1960s. For example, the National Indian Youth Council, organized by "young Turks" within the National Congress of American Indians in the 1960s, derived its leadership from Paiutes as well as from Oklahoma Poncas.

Bibliography
Robert Emmitt, *The Last War Trail: The Utes and the Settlement of Colorado* (1954; reprint, Norman, Okla., 1972), is an effective portrayal of the impact of whites on Utes in the frontier period. Jack S. Harris, "The White Knife Shoshoni," in Ralph Linton, ed., *Acculturation in Seven American Indian Tribes* (1940; reprint, Gloucester, Mass., 1963), describes a group of the widely scattered Great Basin people. Edward Dorn, *The Shoshoneans: The People of the Basin-Plateau* (New York, 1966), is useful as a broader view of the simple culture of these people. Deward E. Walker, *Conflict and Schism in Nez Perce Acculturation* (Pullman, Wash., 1968), analyzes the processes of cultural change under reservation conditions.

THE SOUTHWEST

The Indian population of New Mexico and Arizona is unique in a number of respects. During the 1960s the Southwest had the largest number of Indians of any region in the United States, although this has not always been true. The population of approximately 217,000 in these two states is nearly three times what it was during the period of Spanish conquest in the 1500s and 1600s. The increase has been especially rapid during the 20th century because of the growth of a single tribal group, the Navajos. The other groups are either below or only slightly above their numbers at the time of first contact with Europeans.

The Southwest is also characterized by a large number of Indian ethnic groups, more than there are in any other geographic area. There were in the 1960s about 40 groups that regarded themselves as distinct from one another. Some tribal extinctions have occurred—three tribes that lived along the lower Colorado River, per-

haps three that lived in the Rio Grande Valley, and two or three others. These extinctions are balanced by increases resulting from the creation of new identities through the establishment of separate reservations for groups that were formerly unified and the arrival of Indian groups new to the area.

To a far greater extent than anywhere else in the United States, the Indian groups in the Southwest have maintained their own customs, ways and fundamental values and have selectively borrowed cultural elements from Europeans and others. This does not mean that the Indian cultures have not changed but rather that the government programs of forced assimilation have not worked so effectively here and that the Indian communities have been less penetrated by whites than elsewhere. Indian ways of life are more readily recognizable as such in this region, and their cultural orientations remain more clearly distinctive.

Several circumstances have contributed to this situation. One of great importance is that the native peoples here were not forced to move as much from their home areas nor were they forced to cede vast territory. Not until the late 20th century did the pressures for appropriation of Indian land, water, and mineral resources become as intense as they had been 150 years earlier in the rest of the country. By that time federal Indian policy had changed radically, and Indian organization had developed to the point that it is possible that the experience of other Indians will not be repeated in this part of the United States. The phase of wholesale expropriation of Indian lands may have passed.

THE EASTERN PUEBLOS

In the 1960s there were about 8,500 people along the Rio Grande in New Mexico whom whites lumped together as Pueblos, a collective term that these people have also adopted. This population is made up of 16 distinct groups that live in communities quite separate from one another, maintaining their own very distinct identities. Each uses as the language of the home one or another dialect of four different language groups—Tewa, Tiwa, Keresan, and Towa. The communities in which they live consist of contiguous masonry or adobe houses built around plazas in very much the same plan as when the Spaniards first saw them in 1540. Some houses are built in stepped two-, three-, or even four-story arrangements, following a regional apartment-house style that is at least 700 years old. The houses also have window glass, hinged doors, and other such additions from white culture, representing a selective borrowing characteristic of the Pueblos in most aspects of life. Each community practices its own native religious ceremonies, which are centered in partially underground buildings called *kivas*. Nearly every community also has a Catholic church, supplementing the elaborate ceremonies of the native religion. The Native American church has members in only one village.

All the Pueblo communities are characterized by a local governmental organization that combines the traditional hereditary offices with some offices introduced by the Spanish. This local government operates in conjunction with a general assembly. Three of the Pueblo communities, in addition, have IRA-based tribal councils that cooperate with the BIA agency in Albuquerque. Also the communities elect representatives to an all-Pueblo council that deliberates regularly on matters of collective concern.

The religious ceremonies are vigorously maintained, and nearly everyone in a village participates. The economic life combines farming and some stock raising, and most villages have active workers in pottery, textiles, and other crafts. There are a number of painters and some sculptors who combine native traditional subject matter with Western artistic traditions, and whose works are bought by the general public.

In 1540 the Eastern Pueblos accepted Spanish political control and Franciscan missionaries reluctantly after some resistance; they remained peaceful until 1680, when they united in a revolt against the Spaniards, resulting in the killing or ousting of all Spaniards from their country. They were reconquered in 1695–1697, but they succeeded in keeping the Christian missionaries at arm's length by allowing them to build churches at the edges of their communities, while continuing their own religion in secrecy. They integrated elements of the administration required by the Spaniards with their own community organization. From the time of the reconquest they remained peaceful and found effective ways to limit the efforts of both Spaniards and Americans to alter their way of life.

The Rio Grande Pueblo people joined with the Spaniards during the 1700s and early 1800s in military resistance to raids by the surrounding nomadic tribes, such as the Navajos and Apaches. There was an intricate interweaving of Indian and European culture traits in most aspects of life, but never cultural dominance by the Spaniards. The Spanish and Mexican colonists also assimilated many Indian cultural traits. During the 1920s the Pueblos successfully withstood legal efforts by New Mexicans to reduce their land, a result of concerted effort by an all-Pueblo council, the first common organization since 1680.

The Pueblos suffered less loss of land than most other western Indians and also succeeded in blocking to some extent the efforts of the BIA to assimilate them culturally. Nevertheless, they send their children to schools and have steadily became bilingual. During the post-IRA period one of their languages, Tewa, was given written form by the Bureau of Indian Affairs and was used for a time in the federal schools serving the Tewa-speakers. Also the BIA instituted a special school to train Indians in Indian arts, which encouraged new creative developments and national recognition of Indian artists. During the 1960s the Pueblos, with federal aid, instituted programs for the development of native arts and built museums to encourage interest in their traditions.

WESTERN PUEBLOS

Five groups, the Hopis, Hopi-Tewas, Zunis, Acomas, and Lagunas, whose way of life is generally similar to that of the Rio Grande Pueblos, live in western New Mexico and northeastern Arizona; they numbered about 12,000 in the 1960s. Each group lives in masonry Pueblo-type towns or groups of towns, including smaller satellite communities. The Acoma and Hopi villages are situated on the tops of mesas.

The Hopis, the largest of the western Pueblos in Arizona, with about 5,000 population, almost entirely escaped lasting influence by the Spanish and the early

missionaries. Some of their present villages are dated by tree rings as having been built at least as early as the 14th century. According to their myths they emerged from the ground at a place called Sipapu on the Little Colorado River. They then wandered in the region for centuries before settling in their present locations. They joined in the 1680 revolt against the Spaniards and following that were successful in keeping Franciscan and other missionaries out of their villages by, for example, destroying one Hopi community that favored the return of the Spaniards. Thus the culture that they have preserved into the 20th century lacks the strong Spanish influence apparent among the Rio Grande Pueblos.

During the late 19th and 20th centuries Mennonite and Baptist missionaries gained converts among the Hopis, while the Zunis, along with the Acomas and Lagunas, came under Catholic and Dutch Reformed influences. Most of the western Pueblos practice the native religion, centering on the kivas and emphasizing belief in the *kachinas*, ancestral spirits who are represented in masked dances during the spring and summer. The religion requires an exacting round of ceremonial observances for most villagers. Religious leadership is along hereditary lines in certain clans, and all adult males are initiated into the kachina society.

All of the western Pueblos have tribal councils according to IRA regulations. Among the Hopis the institution of the council gave rise to vigorous opposition from residents of the two western groups of villages, who believed that such organization was contrary to sacred prophecy. However, the council has continued to grow in acceptance and influence and has won favorable settlements before the Indian Claims Commission.

APACHES

In the 1960s four groups bore the name of Apache, two on New Mexico and two on Arizona reservations. Together they numbered 9,229, some 3,000 to 4,000 more than in the 1600s when they were first encountered by the Spaniards. Some cultural traits of the Jicarillas in northern New Mexico, such as their use of tipis, reflect their life on the plains during the 17th and early 18th centuries. But in most respects all the Apaches are similar: they live in frame houses and wear American-style clothing and are for the most part stock raisers; the Western Apaches of Arizona occupy some of the finest cattle-grazing land in the state. Their native religion, which has not been highly organized, persists in the form of curing rituals and rites for adolescent girls and as elements in new religions that they have adopted. Most are nominally Catholics, Lutherans, or members of evangelical Protestant denominations. Beginning in the 1950s the Mormons and the Assembly of God gained Apache converts. The Assembly of God has been especially successful among the Western Apaches, as among the Nez Perces and some Plains peoples. There are also some independent Protestant denominations that seceded from Lutheran and other denominations over the issue of Apache control of the ministry. In addition there is a synthetic new religion that follows the ideas of a Western Apache called Silas John, which combines Catholic, Protestant, and, above all, native Apache rituals. Apaches are active in

pan-Indian pow-wows and in the National Congress of American Indians.

The use of the Apache language in the home is widespread. In the 1960s a movement developed among the Western Apaches for reviving the language and reducing it to writing; that had already been done by Lutheran missionaries, but the new effort was conceived and carried out by Apaches. In their religious life, especially in the Assembly of God and the Silas John movement, Apaches have sought to manage their own affairs and reject white controls. Apaches are active in the arts, particularly in sculpture and painting. Alan Hauser was nationally prominent as a painter.

All the Apaches organized tribal councils under the provisions of the IRA and have actively participated in the resulting political organization. Through their councils they prosecute suits before the Indian Claims Commission and manage cattle industries and other tribal economic enterprises.

Their tribal history is important to the Apaches, and they generally hold that it has not been written correctly, despite the large number of publications on the subject. The Apache point of view is usually omitted, they believe, or misrepresented. For example, they do not accept the well-known Apache leader Geronimo (1829–1909) as an adequate symbol of their recent past, but regard his reputation as a white invention.

The Apaches came into the Southwest probably not before the 15th or 16th century, having been pushed into the region from farther north and east by Comanches, Kiowas, and Eastern Apaches. The Western Apaches, consisting of the ancestors of the San Carlos, White Mountain, and Chiricahua groups, moved in first, followed by the Mescaleros and Jicarillas. One incentive was the opportunity to obtain horses from the Spanish settlers who were invading New Mexico and what became Arizona and Sonora, Mexico. The Apaches developed a way of life that depended heavily on raiding for horses and provisions. They never bred horses but used them for greater mobility in raiding, and often they ate their flesh. They became well adapted to a life of periodic raiding and participated in the slave trade stimulated by the Spaniards during the 1700s. Between 1685 and the late 1700s the Apaches were successful in slowing down the Spanish occupation of the region. The Spaniards were unable to control Apache raiding, and in desperation they offered bounties for their scalps. They also tried to attract the Apaches to settle peacefully in the vicinity of presidios, or forts, giving them liquor, food, and clothing, but most Apaches remained hostile and were never converted to Christianity.

When the United States, under the stimulus of the Texans, invaded northern Mexico in 1845 and ultimately obtained New Mexico, Arizona, and California by conquest, it regarded the Apaches as conquered subjects; however, the Apaches regarded themselves as allies of the United States in a common war against the Mexicans and therefore resisted being forced on to reservations. The result was a long period of uncontrolled hostilities between them and the American settlers and miners of southwestern New Mexico and central and southeastern Arizona. The campaign to assemble all the Apaches on three reservations in southern Arizona

and New Mexico was costly and went on for 20 years, from 1866 to 1886, under different commanders of the U.S. Cavalry. Nearly all the Apaches had begun to settle on the reservations and to allow themselves to be divided up into tag-bands or ration-receiving groups by the time Geronimo and some other individuals became prominent through their breakaways from the reservations. By 1887 all the Apaches were finally gathered on the reservations, the raiding ceased, and they began a total reorganization of their lives. Geronimo and his Chiricahua followers were sent to Indian Territory.

The BIA was unwilling to allow the Apaches sufficient freedom to hunt and gather food in their accustomed ways. Rations were issued for more than 20 years as Apaches were forced into the new concentrations of population. Slowly some farming and stock raising were introduced; others did wage work on the large irrigation dams, such as the Roosevelt Dam in Arizona. It was not until the 1940s, when land was placed back in Apache hands after years of the BIA leasing it to white cattle companies, that the basic new Apache economy began to take hold. By the 1950s Apaches were well established in the cattle industry and did not experience the setbacks suffered by the northern Plains tribes. The Apache reservations have never been allotted but are held in common under trust with the federal government.

Western Apaches did not pay much attention to the Ghost Dance religion, and new religious ways did not arise among them until the 1930s. In the late 1920s they began to be interested in the teachings of Silas John, a White Mountain Apache who had been a Roman Catholic. The Silas John movement continued to grow for the next 50 years, despite the jailing of the prophet, and was maintained along with the developing independent Protestant churches managed by Apaches.

NAVAJOS

More than any tribe in the United States, the Navajos have increased their numbers since first contacts with whites. In 1868, when a treaty was made between the Navajos and the U.S. government, there were between 8,000 and 9,000 Navajos; by 1975 the estimate had risen to about 160,000, making them by far the largest single tribe in the country. The great majority live on the largest reservation in the United States, which is chiefly in Arizona but overlaps into New Mexico and Utah.

The Navajos also have the largest tribal income in the United States—approximately $50 million in 1970, largely from oil and gas leases and royalties and returns from other mineral and forest resources. The tribe as a business corporation is engaged in various enterprises, ranging from the manufacture and sale of arts and crafts to the production of lumber. However, many Navajos live far below the poverty level. These economic contrasts indicate the great variations that characterize Navajo life generally.

The Navajo Nation, as it is officially designated, has a democratically elected tribal council, which existed before the passage of the IRA in 1934, but has never been reorganized in accord with that act. The Navajo Nation has never ratified a constitution, but its political organization functions essentially like those of

tribes organized under the IRA and has progressively taken over governmental functions from the BIA during the 1970s.

Navajos work in a variety of occupations, with wage work both on and off the reservation the source of the greater part of individual income. Sheep raising and construction work are important, and several kinds of industries have moved onto the reservation, while the tribal administration manages a sawmill and the manufacture of other forest products. Irrigation farming is important on several parts of the reservation, as is coal mining. The tribe manages a tribal park service and a fish and game department. In many respects the tribal government functions like a state government, always with the special assistance of federal aid, especially in the maintenance of schools and in medical services.

The Navajo Nation during the 1960s started, with the help of governmental and private foundation funds, a special experimental school on the reservation. The aim of the Rough Rock Demonstration School is to bring Navajo cultural traditions into school programs so that they can play an important role in childhood learning and development. The Navajo language is used in instruction, and tribal information is gathered from older Navajo-speaking men and women for instructional purposes. In addition the tribal council inaugurated with private and public funds the Navajo Community College, a junior college in which Navajo Studies, including the language, tribal history, and elements of their culture, are the core of the curriculum.

Navajos are members of a wide variety of churches—Roman Catholic, Episcopal, Baptist, Assembly of God, Mormon, Church of the Nazarene, Native American church (Peyote cult), and many others. The Peyote cult gained adherents rapidly during the 1960s and 1970s, although the tribal council passed legislation against the use of peyote. The native Navajo religion continues to be strong among a majority, with curing aspects the special focus of interest. The Navajos speak an Athapaskan language, very close to that of the Western Apaches. It is spoken as the language of the home by probably a majority on the reservation.

The Navajos probably separated from the plains-dwelling Athapaskans as early as the 12th century and came into contact with Pueblo Indians in the region of the upper Rio Grande drainage. Traditional Navajo belief holds that they originated in the region in which they were living when Europeans first encountered them in the 1600s; the traditional region of origin is marked by four mountain peaks in Arizona, New Mexico, Colorado, and Utah. During the Pueblo revolt against the Spaniards in 1680 many Pueblos came to live with them, and the Navajos borrowed much from the Pueblos culturally, especially religious beliefs and rituals. They also borrowed important elements of material life from the Spaniards, although only a tiny percentage of Navajos ever came into close contact with them. Through trading and raiding they borrowed the techniques of silver-making and weaving, as well as the use of sheep and horses, and as a result of these resources the Navajos became a herding culture during the 17th and 18th centuries. They remained at the periphery of Spanish society in New Mexico, unlike the Rio Grande Pueblos, who were in the center of it.

When the United States invaded New Mexico and the area to the west during the Mexican War, the Navajos did not accept U.S. control. In 1864 nearly every Navajo was rounded up and made to walk, under the direction of the U.S. Army, 800 miles northeast to Fort Sumner, N.Mex., where the government proposed to make farmers out of the herders and hunters. The plan failed completely, many Navajos died, and ultimately the government agreed to allow the 8,000 Navajos to walk back to their old territory, where a reservation was set up and a treaty was made in which the Navajos agreed to be peaceful and the U.S. government promised to set up schools and provide other services and means of livelihood. The march to and from Fort Sumner, in the course of which there was much suffering, became known in Navajo tradition as the Long Walk.

Once back in Arizona Territory, they engaged in sheepherding, which steadily became their major means of livelihood; the blankets they wove from the wool began to be known across the United States. In the 1930s, however, the technicians of the Soil Conservation Service decided that the range on the reservation was being seriously depleted and that in order to save it, Navajo stock—sheep, horses, and goats—would have to be drastically reduced. Stock reduction was carried out amid Navajo pleas that their sole means of livelihood was being destroyed. Deep hostility and distrust of government resulted, and this event, like the Long Walk, assumed a prominent place in Navajo history.

During the 1960s the Office of Economic Opportunity instituted a large-scale training program in community development techniques, which gave thousands of Navajos a chance to participate in government on a scale they had not practiced before. Prior to this, the Bureau of Indian Affairs had encouraged local community organizations known as chapters. By the 1970s the foundation was laid for widespread individual participation in Navajo government at the local group level, as well as at the level of the tribal council. The Navajos by 1975 were participating in American society in a great variety of ways and were at the same time placing a high value on their own language and tribal traditions.

PAIS

The Pais consist of several bands of people who speak closely related dialects of a Yuman language and live at the southwestern edge of the Colorado Plateau in what is now northwestern Arizona. By the 1970s the Pais had been divided into four different groups and placed on six reservations. Their population was about 1,800; the largest groups, the Hualapai, numbered about 800. A smaller group of about 400 have come to be known as the Havasupai and live on a separate reservation at the bottom of Cataract Canyon, immediately west of the Grand Canyon, on the Colorado River. These two, constituting the majority of Pai-speaking peoples, were very closely associated until the late 19th century, but the creation of reservations in the 1880s led to the development of somewhat separate identities by the 1970s, and whites regarded them as entirely distinct peoples.

Most of the Hualapais (or Walapais) live near Peach Springs in northwestern Arizona, where the BIA has established an agency. The Hualapai Indian Nation has a nine-member tribal council and a tribal court system organized in 1939 under the regulations of the IRA. Like most other southwestern Indian peoples, the Hualapai Tribe manages a number of enterprises, including a thriving herd of cattle, a doll manufacturing business, a trading company, a housing authority, and a wildlife department. In addition to cattle raising, many men work on the railroad. They belong to various Christian churches but also maintain interest in older Hualapai ceremonial dances and songs and participate annually in pow-wows and intertribal ceremonials. Most speak Hualapai in the home, but interest is declining on the part of young people, who speak English as a result of their schooling. Frame, masonry, or concrete-block houses have entirely replaced the former frame wickiups. Clothing is of the western ranch type, except for long full dresses worn by many middle-aged and older women.

The Havasupais, who live on a reservation 60 miles northeast of the Peach Springs agency, developed in somewhat different ways from the Hualapais. Until the 1950s they lived in what had been a relatively inaccessible area, at the bottom of a steep-walled canyon. Their location contrasts with that of the Hualapais at Peach Springs, through which have been built the Santa Fe Railroad in the 1880s and the most traveled highway across the United States. As a result of their inaccessibility, the Havasupais were better able to fend off the efforts of the BIA and others seeking to change their way of life. Various churches, from Mormon to Episcopal and Baptist, tried but failed to establish themselves among the Havasupais. Although efforts were made to introduce frame houses, the Havasupais used them for storage and continued to live in their traditional brush wickiups most of the year. However, during the 1970s they began to use the ranch-style houses built by the BIA. All families speak the Pai language at home, and most are bilingual. At one time Havasupai life was divided between the canyon, where they farmed by irrigation and maintained peach orchards, and the plateau 5,000 feet above, where they raised cattle and horses. During the 20th century Havasupais learned to make their living through tourism, first at the Grand Canyon and later by conducting tours into their own highly scenic canyon. They organized a tribal council and adopted a constitution in 1938, under IRA regulations, through which they manage a tribal cafe, store, and tourist enterprise. The tribe also manages the Native American Education Program and a tribal library and archive. Tourist-related jobs are probably the chief source of livelihood, except for farming on the canyon bottom and raising some livestock on the plateau.

Pai contacts with Spaniards and Mexicans were for the most part indirect. They were not conquered by the Spanish, but through them, via the Hopis, they became familiar with metal, cattle, horses, peaches, apricots, and melon production, and woolen blankets and clothing. The Pais had practiced irrigated agriculture before the coming of the Europeans. Intensive contacts with whites did not begin before the mid-19th century and were at first chiefly clashes with military exploring parties. As miners and then cattlemen made encroachments on their land, all bands of Pais resisted, and fighting began. The Havasupais, however, gradually retired from the conflict to their canyon and figured very little

in the hostilities. The Hualapais, however, fought hard and gained a reputation for courage and fighting ability. By 1866 the U.S. government, freed of the military demands of the Civil War, sent cavalry in considerable numbers into Arizona Territory to protect the many miners and ranchers who had moved into the Indian country without treaty or arrangement. What was called the Walapai War was fought against both the Hualapais and the Yavapais to the south between 1866 and 1869. When Hualapais were ultimately subdued, they joined the Americans against their traditional enemies, the Yavapais. In 1874 the government decided to eliminate completely the Hualapais from the mountain country by sending all they could round up to La Paz on the east side of the Colorado River in the lowland desert country, where they would be more manageable. During the relocation, many died or became sick; they tried to escape and were brought back. Eventually, in 1875, after being moved again, the Hualapais broke away and returned in small groups to their old hunting territories. The Havasupais had been overlooked entirely, remaining undisturbed in their vast canyon.

Having to accept rations from the government on their now-restricted territories, the Hualapais steadily lost hope as they lost independence. In 1889 they embraced the Ghost Dance, with its promise of a future life of the old free kind, but when the whites did not disappear in a few years, they turned to cooperation with them and accepted reservation life as cattlemen.

Reservations were created in the 1880s for all the Pai people, the Havasupais and Hualapais being located in very small parts of their former territories, the Yavapais on a tiny acreage at Camp Verde, Ariz., on another small reservation at Fort McDowell near Phoenix, and with Apaches on the San Carlos Apache Reservation farther east. One small group of Yavapais maintained residence at Prescott, but had no federal recognition or trust land until the 1960s.

PIMAS AND PAPAGOS

Like the Pais, the Piman-speaking peoples of southern Arizona are another group whose political organization and distribution on reservations does not reflect their original affiliations. Although they all speak dialects of the same Uto-Aztecan language, whites have come to think of them as two distinct peoples—Pimas and Papagos—because of the naming of the reservations that were carved out of their land. In the valley of the Gila River south of Phoenix is the Gila River Reservation, where the Indians were called Pimas or Pimos by the white immigrants who encountered them in the mid-19th century. Farther south are three very small reservations—the Akchin, the Gila Bend, and the San Xavier—and one very large one, the Sells, all of which are the homes of people regarded by whites as Papagos. Other Piman-speakers also live there, and all, along with the Pimas of the Gila River Reservation, speak mutually intelligible dialects of the widely distributed language that the Spaniards called Pima.

In 1970 the Papagos on their four reservations numbered somewhat less than 15,000, the Pimas on their two reservations about 11,000. In addition at least another 2,500, who identify themselves as Papagos, are scattered in communities of southern Arizona. Thus the total Pima-speaking population of Arizona on and off reservations is in the neighborhood of 29,000–30,000—currently one of the larger tribes of the United States and probably more than three times the population of the area at the beginning of European contacts.

Three of the Papago reservations, although 60 and 75 miles apart, are organized into a single political structure—the Papago Tribe—and participate in the Papago Tribal Council with a constitution approved by the BIA under the IRA. The council, with funds from various government sources and with tribal income from cattle sales and mining royalties, manages some 30 enterprises, ranging from a tribal herd to a comprehensive employment training program. The council also sponsors an annual rodeo and fair and a Miss Papago contest and manages an arts and crafts production and sales center and a utility authority. In some of these enterprises the administrative responsibilities are shared with the BIA.

Papagos are members of Catholic, Presbyterian, Baptist, Methodist, or Assembly of God churches. The largest number belong to the Catholic church, which has maintained Franciscan missionaries among the Pima-speaking people since the late 1700s and Jesuits before that for nearly a century. Most of the more than 70 villages in which Papagos live maintain their own small churches, with a style of worship sometimes called Sonoran Catholic, which is a folk version of Catholicism oriented around St. Francis Xavier, the patron of the Jesuits. In 1970 only a minority of families spoke Papago in their homes, but at least 80 percent of Papagos were bilingual in English and Papago.

The Papagos have maintained a tribal organization embracing the whole group only since the IRA. Groups of villages had organized in 1695 and again in 1750 to resist the Spaniards and their program of military and missionary domination. The 1750 revolt led by Oacpicagigua was a serious threat to the Spaniards for a year, but after that, resistance gave way to an extended period of peaceful cooperation with Spaniards, Mexicans, and finally Anglo-Americans. When the Western Apaches raided Spanish and Mexican ranches, the Papagos fought with Spaniards and later the white settlers against them. But their cooperativeness did not help the Papagos in combating the intensified white encroachments as mines and ranches were opened up during the last years of the 19th century.

It was not until 1917 that the large Papago reservation was established, covering much of the land the desert Papagos had ranged over; in contrast, the river Papagos, living where whites began to concentrate after 1900, were forced to accept only a tiny portion of their territory around the Spanish mission of St. Francis Xavier. Marked rural-urban contrasts exist between Papagos living in the many villages scattered over the desert country and those living in the major concentration at Sells. Government-planned housing near Sells, resembling the suburban tracts in Arizona cities, contrasts with the small adobe houses and shade structures in the villages. As the Papago population has grown, thousands have found jobs in Arizona cities, and a permanent city group has formed; the city-dwellers, however, are linked through kinship and regular visiting with the reservation communities.

The Papagos after World War II became preeminent in basket-making, developing new forms and patterns

of decoration based on the traditional styles. Their baskets have gained a national market and are exhibited and sold at intertribal gatherings everywhere in the United States. In their music and art, in contrast, they tend to borrow from rather than influence other Indian groups.

The Pima situation is basically similar to that of the Papagos. They have had an effectively functioning tribal council with an elected governor and representatives since the 1930s. The tribe as a business corporation is similarly engaged in numerous business and industrial enterprises, manages a tribal farm and herd of cattle, and sponsors a tribal museum, a regionally well-known arts and crafts center, and other activities. Pimas are chiefly Presbyterians and Catholics and to a greater extent than the Papagos have lost traditional forms of religious expression. However, there is some revival of traditional crafts, pottery, and basket-making, and ceremonial dance.

Like the Papagos, they maintained mostly friendly relations with the Spaniards and Anglo-Americans. Under the peaceful leadership of Antonio Azul, they sold food to the wagon trains that began to pass through their country in the mid-19th century. Despite their friendly assistance, Anglo-American settlers, from the 1880s into the 20th century, appropriated almost all the water from the Gila River, which their villages had relied on for 2,000 years. They still use to some extent the system of irrigation canals that their ancestors had laid out beginning in 300 B.C. By the 1950s the Pimas were unable to subsist by farming, at which time they brought a claim against the United States through the Indian Claims Commission. As water storage facilities were developed there was some relief, but only small-scale agriculture was possible.

MOHAVES, CHEMEHUEVIS, AND CUCHANS

In the 1960s three groups of Yuman-speaking peoples —Mohaves, Chemehuevis, and Cuchans—lived on reservations in the lower Colorado River Valley. Their total population of about 2,350 represents a considerable reduction from about 150 years ago, when there were seven Yuman-speaking groups with a population of at least 13,000. Three groups have become extinct, and one—the Maricopas—was forced to take refuge on the Gila River Reservation. In 1970 about 200 Maricopas preserved their identity distinct from the Pimas in a single community.

Of the surviving groups, the Cuchans, commonly called Yumas, number 1,150 and live on one reservation at Fort Yuma in extreme southeastern California. They are organized as a business corporation and a tribe, farm much of their reservation, maintain important native ceremonials, and participate regularly in southwestern and other intertribal gatherings. Next largest are the Mohaves, who number about 900 and live on two reservations, one at Parker, Ariz., the other in Arizona and California, near Needles, Calif. Both groups of Mohaves, who identify separately, have tribal councils. The Parker political–administrative organization is known as the Colorado River Tribes. The Needles, or Fort Mohave, people live chiefly by wage work on the railroad. The Parker Mohaves possess excellent irrigated farmland, most of which they rent to non-Mohave farmers. They share the reservation land with some 300

Chemehuevis, a Shoshonean-speaking group, former residents of the desert lands to the west, and colonies of Navajos and Hopis who have been assigned land on the reservation.

YAQUIS

Four major communities of Yaquis exist in Arizona —Guadalupe near Phoenix with 700, Old Pascua in Tucson with 500–600, New Pascua Pueblo near Tucson with 1,000–1,200, and Barrio Libre in South Tucson with an unestimated population. Scattered in the vicinity of these concentrations and elsewhere in southern Arizona are an estimated 2,500–3,000 Yaquis, making a total of between 5,000 and 6,000. Yaquis work in a wide variety of urban occupations and professions and to a lesser extent as agricultural laborers. Their houses and dress are like those of the urban dwellers among whom they live. All those who identify as Yaquis participate in distinctive Catholic-derived religious ceremonies in churches that the Yaquis maintain independently from Catholic church administration. The ceremonies are strongly Roman Catholic in character, but they are also strongly native American, especially with respect to two forms of ceremony—that of the Pascolas and the Deer Dancer, widely known in the region and in Mexico as distinctively Yaqui.

New Pascua Pueblo consists of communally owned land and is governed by a popularly elected tribal council. In 1978 New Pascua was formally recognized by the federal government, and the 200-acre tract on which the village is located became a reservation. Guadalupe was organized as an Arizona municipality, its city council having Yaqui as well as other representation. Old Pascua has an informal governing council, whose members are primarily holders of ceremonial offices, but the community also belongs to a neighborhood council organization. Barrio Libre, which has been divided by a freeway, has only a church-focused committee.

Yaquis in small numbers have lived in the southern Arizona region since the 1700s. In the 1890s their numbers were greatly increased when the regime of Porfirio Diaz forced hundreds of Yaquis from their traditional Mexican territory to the United States, where they were accorded the status of political refugees. Most Yaquis in Arizona in the 1970s were descendants of those refugees. Arizona and Mexican Yaquis communicate freely about their developments and problems.

Other Indians living in the Southwest in the 1970s were Paiutes and Utes.

Bibliography
Edward P. Dozier, *The Pueblo Indians of North America* (New York, 1970), is the most succinct and useful introduction to the complex cultures and historical background of all the Pueblo Indians. Laura Thompson, *Culture in Crisis: A Study of the Hopi Indians* (1950; reprint, New York, 1972), gives a detailed view of the past and present situation of a single Pueblo group. The standard introduction to the largest American Indian tribe is Clyde Kluckhohn and Dorothea Leighton, *The Navaho* (1946; reprint, Cambridge, Mass., 1974), which should be supplemented with David F. Aberle, *The Peyote Religion among the Navajo* (Chicago, 1966). Lesser-known peoples of the Southwest are the Yuman-speaking Pai tribes described in Henry F. Dobyns and Robert C. Euler, *Wauba Yuma's People: The Comparative Socio-Political Structure of the Pai Indians of Arizona* (Prescott, Ariz., 1970), and the Piman-speaking Papagos treated in Alice Joseph, Rosamond B. Spicer, and Jane Chesky, *The Desert People: A Study of the Papago Indians* (Chicago, 1949). The literature on the Apaches, especially on their 19th-century warfare with whites, is very extensive, but there is no general introduction to all the

Apache groups or their present situation. Morris E. Opler, *An Apache Life Way: The Economic, Social and Religious Institutions of the Chiricahua Indians* (1941; reprint, New York, 1965), is a useful starting point.

CALIFORNIA

In the 1960s California had about 13,000 Indians, exclusive of those who lived in the large cities. The modern population may be considered survivors of early contacts with Europeans in the 17th and 18th centuries. Probably the most reasonable estimate of the total Indian population at the beginning of contact is 133,000, indicating a steady decline to less than one-tenth of the original population. From the founding of Spanish missions along the coast of southern California, beginning in 1769, to 1846, when California declared itself independent of Mexico, the Indian population declined rapidly by possibly one-half; this was a result of disease and poor living conditions in the mission communities of the south where they were forced to live. By the late 1840s the Indian population may have fallen to approximately 70,000. Then, as Anglo-Americans came for gold and land, a further precipitous drop took place: indiscriminate murder by whites, new epidemics, and displacement of whole communities resulted in a decline within 40 years to about 17,000.

Despite the precipitous decline in total population during the first 200 years, probably no more than one-quarter of the different groups became extinct. Possibly there were 40 language-culture groups among the original 133,000 population, and in the 1960s the number of groups was 29. This figure must not be taken as indicating the maintenance of strong Indian identity throughout the 200 years of intensive contact. The Gabrielinos, who formerly occupied the area that is now downtown Los Angeles, were completely dispersed, maintained no communities anywhere, and had totally lost their language and all distinctive cultural elements; thus they could have been called extinct as a cultural group before the middle of the 20th century or earlier. Yet when a claims case began to be developed in the 1950s, 1,500 individuals presented genealogical credentials to qualify for a share of the settlement. By the standard of sustaining a common community life, the Gabrielinos could be regarded as extinct, but in terms of self-identification they are not. Of the 29 mentioned above as distinct Indian ethnic groups, 9 number fewer than 100. To assume that groups so small are necessarily on the verge of extinction has been demonstrated many times to be unjustified; there have been instances in which very small groups have intensified their sense of identity and built new community structures rather than moved toward disintegration.

The situation of the Indians in California is unique. Although the population density of the region's aboriginal cultures was perhaps the highest north of Mexico, no political organization had developed beyond the level of the local community. There were no strongly centralized tribal groups capable of effective military organization or any intertribal confederacies exercising control over large regions, such as those Europeans encountered in the East and in the plains. California Indians lived in small villages that were not linked with even their nearest neighbors for any common purposes

except in some cases ceremonials or games. Consequently, the incoming Europeans were faced with no need for diplomatic maneuvers or military campaigns to establish political control. The result for the California natives was chaos and destruction from the first.

The Spaniards began with Christian missions on the coast of southern California in 1769. What began as voluntary individual conversion of the Indians ended as forced labor and forced cultural assimilation. The mission communities were built into large agricultural and industrial establishments into which Indians were forcibly recruited and kept under strict dormitory discipline. By the time Mexico won its independence (1821), tens of thousands of coastal Indians had been stripped of their culture and reoriented as lower-class laborers in Spanish society. The secularization of the missions that occurred under Mexican rule brought to the Indians not land and independence but more extreme dependence under the Mexican landlords who took over.

The coming of the Anglo-Americans in 1848–1849 after the U.S. war with Mexico extended the Indians' condition of absolute subordination to the whole state. The newcomers were the extreme in frontiersmen, without respect for any law other than what they made themselves. The idea of Indian rights to land or to anything else was wholly foreign. Indians were murdered, plundered, pushed from what land they held, and then ignored in the constitutional government ultimately established (except for specific denial of the right to testify in court). The result was not only death and loss of property, but 75 years of social limbo, which no other Indians in the United States experienced. Despite efforts by a few reformers on behalf of white–Indian relations during the early 1850s, neither the federal government nor the state recognized the Indians' existence. They were not citizens, but neither were they wards of the state. The state appointed a superintendent of Indian affairs whose office did nothing, and the federal Bureau of Indian Affairs took no responsibility. The result was steady separation of Indians from nearly all their land, and frequent starvation. Some whites hunted Indians for sport and rounded up children and sold them.

It was not until the 1920s that the situation improved markedly. In 1928, after the federal government declared Indians to be citizens of the United States, California passed the California Indian Jurisdictional Act, which, as the forerunner of the legislation that brought the U.S. Indian Claims Commission into existence, enabled Indians of California to sue the federal government for damages suffered as a result of loss of land and resources. This led to a slow but steady assumption of responsibility by both state and federal government until 1954, when the U.S. Congress voted to withdraw from any responsibilities to Indians. In 1958 the United States began a slow withdrawal by giving land titles to all California Indians who asked for them. Legal complexities developed, but the process continued into the 1970s.

By 1960 there were 117 reservations and rancherias in California that belonged to Indians under trust arrangement with the federal government. Twenty-eight of these are reservations created at different times since the 1850s, most being very small, the largest consisting of 87,000 acres in the Hoopa Valley in the northwestern part of the state. The rancherias are sometimes less

than an acre and usually are the sites of houses that Indians had occupied from the mission period. The residents of the rancherias often have little sense of identity as Indians but consider themselves ethnically distinct from both Anglos and Mexican Americans, which they express in terms of locality.

LUISEÑOS

From San Diego north to Santa Barbara, Franciscan missionaries with Spanish troops established five mission settlements, which gave their names to coastal-dwelling Indians—Diegueño, Luiseño, Juaneño, Gabrielino, and Fernandeño. These Indians and another group culturally similar to them to their north—the Chumash—numbered possibly as many as 25,000 when the first missions were established in 1769. By 1960 this population had been reduced to about 2,000, the largest being the Luiseño, with 1,200–1,300. No communities of Fernandeños, Gabrielinos, or Juaneños have been recorded, but individuals scattered through the highly urbanized region of coastal southern California still identify themselves in those terms.

The Luiseños, like the other Mission Indians, were first recruited on a voluntary basis by the Spanish missionaries. They built the mission of San Luis Rey, a massive stone building, and worked the large acreage surrounding it, doing all the manual labor to establish orchards, vineyards, and fields for wheat, corn, and a variety of other crops. The Luiseño territory included not only a strip on the coast but also an extensive inland area for hunting and gathering. At first their work at the mission establishment was seasonal, but very soon they were forced to remain permanently, send their children to school at the mission, and abide by a rigid schedule of workdays. Men and women lived separately in dormitories, which became more and more crowded. The simply organized Luiseño communities largely broke down as the people were forced to live under missionary rule. Cultural assimilation was rapid, and language and traditions were lost. By the time of the Mexican War for independence in the 1820s, most Luiseños lived under Spanish rule, although a few small communities still existed inland from the mission.

In 1834, under Mexican rule, the management of the missions was taken from the priests. The Indian workers were dismissed, and the land was taken over by politicians and landlords. Serrano and other Indians of the interior raided the Mexican settlements. The Luiseños scattered, some joining the inland Cahuillas, others moving to Los Angeles or wherever they could get work. Many Diegueños also moved from the south to Los Angeles. The coastal communities were broken up, and Spanish replaced the Indian languages.

Poverty-stricken Indians were paid the lowest possible wages. Drunken at payday, many were herded into open corrals and their labor sold on Monday mornings to the highest bidder. Some built huts near the old missions or on parts of their former territories and fell under the rule of other Indians who were recognized as captains, who acted as go-betweens with white employers. Under these circumstances the Gabrielinos, Fernandeños, and Juaneños disappeared from white notice, but some communities of Diegueños and Luiseños survived into the 20th century and began to receive some state and federal aid and land protection. An unor-

ganized group of 87 Chumash survived as separate families in a rancheria near their former mission. Most of the 28 reservations placed under trust during the 20th century are in southern California in the former mission back country, where the Luiseños now live.

CAHUILLAS

In the 1970s some Cahuilla Indians possessed one of the most valuable reservations in the United States. Partially located in Palm Springs, where land values have risen tremendously, the Palm Springs Reservation houses 96 residents. Other Cahuillas lived on four small reservations in the surrounding mountains. The total Cahuilla population is about 530, about 2,000 fewer than in the 18th century, when they roamed over the San Jacinto Mountains and the desert north of Imperial Valley.

The affairs of the Palm Springs Reservation are managed by a tribal council, which during the 1950s was composed of five women. The Cahuillas are completely assimilated culturally, living like other well-to-do citizens of Palm Springs. Their cohesion as a group rests entirely on their kinship relations and their common interest in the valuable land, the management of which they are negotiating with the BIA.

The Cahuillas, like the coastal mission Indians, speak a Shoshonean (Uto-Aztecan) language. At the time of first contact with Europeans, they had adapted to the extremely arid conditions of the Coachella Valley and vicinity, living in small clusters of brush shelters around deep hand-dug wells. Mesquite beans were their major source of subsistence, or if they lived higher up in the mountains, acorns. They hunted and gathered seeds and were the only Indians of southern California to make pottery. In other respects their culture and social organization matched the simplicity of other tribes.

Cahuillas were not involved in the mission system of forced labor. They were generally friendly with Anglo-Americans and acted as a bulwark against raiding tribes from farther east. One of their headmen, Juan Antonio, was well known during the late 19th century and much relied on by whites for assistance. After the secularization of the missions, the Cahuillas sheltered Luiseños, Diegueños, and other Indians.

Like many other California peoples, they negotiated a treaty with the government in 1852, which guaranteed the areas later to become their reservations. However, this treaty was never ratified, and during the 75 years after 1852 they steadily lost land to encroaching whites. Moreover, neither the state nor the federal government assumed any active responsibility for aiding them. As their situation deteriorated, the writer Helen Hunt Jackson (1830–1885) was asked by the Interior Department to make a report on the condition of southern California Indians preparatory to providing some kind of assistance. When her report was ignored, she decided to write a novel to draw attention to what she regarded as inexcusable neglect. She chose as her subject a Cahuilla woman known as Ramona and named the novel for her. It became a best seller and probably influenced the passage of the Mission Indian Relief Act by the California legislature. The act resulted in no immediate aid for California Indians, but by 1962 portions of the old Cahuilla territory were put in trust status and thus the valuable Palm Springs land stayed in Cahuilla hands. The

Cahuillas never organized under the provisions of the IRA but did develop an effective tribal council.

POMOS

In northern California, Indians did not have early intensive contacts with Europeans. It was not until the middle of the 19th century, when Anglo-Americans discovered gold in their territory and began to arrive by the thousands, that contacts began. A group that is typical of the Indians of central and northern California is the Pomos, who live in a deep, mountain-ringed valley near Ukiah. There were 900 Pomos in the 1960s, a reduction of perhaps 10,000 from their number in the 17th century. They are intermixed with whites, other Indians, and Filipinos, so it is not possible to identify a Pomo as Indian unless his or her family connections are known. Their houses and clothing are like those of their neighbors. They belong to Mormon and Pentecostal churches and work in a variety of occupations. Other Pomos live in cities, where they hold many different types of jobs. There is a Pomo Tribal Council, organized under the IRA in the 1940s. Pomo crafts, especially baskets, are well known for their fine quality and are sold at intertribal functions and in craft stores throughout the United States. There has been a revival of interest in their native ceremonial dances during the 1960s.

The Pomos and their neighbors in Ukiah have not always been on good terms. In their early contacts with Spaniards, some Pomos were captured for the slave trade, but relatively few. Small-scale clashes occurred with early Anglo-American miners crossing or prospecting in their country, but there was never any organized warfare by the Pomos. They lived like most native Californians in small villages that were not organized politically beyond the local community and not at all for war. They lived by gathering acorns and horse chestnuts and by hunting game. Their first extended contacts with white men were with settlers taking up land for cattle and sheep raising. When white women joined these men, they immediately cut off intimate contacts with Indians; they refused to hire Pomo women as servants and generally established a segregated community. Their land having been appropriated, the Indians were squeezed out of town and into migratory labor, picking fruit and hops. It was from contacts with other migrant workers rather than from the people of segregated Ukiah that they learned white ways.

By 1939 the Pomos began to take action against the segregation and discriminatory employment practices in the town of Ukiah. The women organized a Pomo Mothers' Club, which sponsored craft shows and made fine baskets. They held intertribal dances and revived the elaborate dance costumes of earlier days. They hired a lawyer who successfully combated segregation, so that by 1946 the Pomos were living on an equal basis with other residents.

Other Indians living in California are the Bear Rivers, Chemehuevis, Fort Mohaves, Hupas, Karoks, Katos, Kawaiisus, Maidus, Miwoks, Monos, Paiutes, Pit Rivers, Shastas, Shoshones, Tolowas, Tübatulabal, Tule Rivers, Vanyumes, Wappos, Washoes, Wintuns, Wiyots, Yokuts, and Yuroks.

Bibliography
The best brief introduction to the past and present of the many Indians of California is J.F. Downs, "California," in E.B. Leacock and N.O. Lurie, eds., *North American Indians in Historical Perspective* (New York, 1971). Two publications that give some understanding of the processes at work in the decimation of the California Indians are J.H. Bushnell, "From American Indian to Indian American: The Changing Identity of the Hupa," *American Anthropologist* 70 (1968): 1108–1116; and "The Cahuilla," in Wendell H. Oswalt, *This Land Was Theirs* (New York, 1973). Theodora T. Kroeber, *Ishi in Two Worlds: A Biography of the Last Wild Indian in North America* (Berkeley, Calif., 1961) is also useful.

THE NORTHWEST

In 1960 there were approximately 28,000 Indians in Oregon and Washington, about one-quarter of the population at the time of initial contact with Europeans. The great decrease in population was a result of many factors, including introduced diseases, forced change in their ways of life, and absorption into the general population, all under largely peaceful conditions. The reduction in the number of distinct ethnic groups was also fairly substantial. About 1960 there were 40 groups; at the beginning of contact there were 55 or more. The figures on numbers of groups, however, even more than in other regions, should be taken as only suggestive. The nature of ethnic identification before contact remains largely unknown, but it does appear that ethnic boundaries between groups remained rather indistinct.

The placement of several different groups on a single reservation, with consequent important influences on Indian identity patterns, is one of the distinguishing characteristics of the region, especially in eastern Oregon. Groups that had been separate before reservation days merged. The former Klamath reservation included not only Klamaths but also Modocs, Paiutes, and others. The Colville Reservation of northeastern Washington was set aside expressly for groups that had no treaty arrangements with the federal government: some 14 tribes are represented by small bands, some consisting of only a few families. The Warm Springs Reservation in northern Oregon has some ten different tribes represented.

In western Washington the various Salish- and Nootkan-speaking peoples, numerous but all small in population, were placed on small reservations within their former hunting and fishing territories; in contrast with many tribes farther east, they were not moved about repeatedly.

During the 1960s the Indians of western Washington became especially interested in the assertion of fishing rights along the rivers, inlets, and coasts where they had traditionally lived, and they initiated numerous lawsuits to reestablish these rights, claiming they had not specifically been taken away by the numerous land treaties. In general, as key cases came to court, the Indian rights were affirmed, and rivers that white commercial and sports fishermen had been exploiting came again under partial control of the Indians, some of whom were on reservations that no longer included fishing areas.

KLAMATHS

The largest Indian group in Oregon during the 1960s was the Klamaths, with a population reported as 1,717. The Klamaths had a reservation until 1955, but the federal government withdrew from its trust relationship over the land in 1954, and the Klamath Tribal Council, which had been organized under the provisions of the

IRA, was disbanded. These actions were a result of the policy known as termination, eliminating all special relationships between the Klamaths and the federal government. More than 70 percent of the members of the tribal body had voted for withdrawal of federal trust over the reservation land, with the understanding that the government would buy the extensive timberland owned in common by the tribe, make it into a national forest, and distribute per capita payments of $43,500 to the tribe's members. However, by the late 1960s only about 570 of the former tribal members had been judged competent, had received the per capita payments, and thus severed ties with the federal government. Approximately 250 of these continued to live on what had been the reservation.

Of the other 1,200 or so, the great majority were judged by the federal government as not fully competent to manage their own affairs and were continued under protective management. Thus, for only about one-third of the tribe there was new status as wholly independent United States citizens; for the great majority this had not taken place. For them the most decisive element in the new situation was the destruction of the tribal political structure. They chose an executive committee from among their ranks to handle business matters with the bank, but other than that their political life had merged with non-Indians.

As many Klamaths live outside the former reservation area as on it. They are scattered through the immediate rural area, in Klamath Falls, and in other towns and cities of Oregon and the West Coast. Most are members of Methodist or Four Square Gospel congregations. The Klamath language is spoken in very few homes, although it is frequently used in public meetings and has been, as much as English, the language of the tribal council. Klamaths are businessmen, cattlemen, farmers, and wage workers in a wide range of the regional occupations.

The 1,200–2,000 Klamaths aboriginally were of the Plateau culture, hunting and gathering, living in earth lodges in small villages, with no political organization beyond the local community, except sporadically for war-making. Penutian-language speakers, they had some contacts with Plains Indians. They ranged over southeastern and central Oregon and were associated with the Modocs to their southwest. They did not obtain horses and firearms until the 1820s. It was not until the 1840s that they began to figure in white history, first as raiders of the Pit River Indians and later, after a serious epidemic had reduced their numbers to a few hundred, as providers and guides for the expeditions led by John Charles Frémont in the 1840s. For the most part they avoided warfare with whites, and after 1859 a peace party headed by a prominent headman named Lileks fairly consistently sought peace, even though white encroachments often gave rise also to hostile leadership. A treaty signed by Klamath leaders in 1864 resulted in establishment of a reservation in 1870 and an agency; a farmer was assigned to teach them.

The Klamaths adapted rapidly and easily to new ways, abandoning their hunting and gathering economy for farming, stock raising, and logging. They accepted the administrative structure of the agency and the leadership of a strong superintendent, who managed the tribal police and courts. Even forced reduction in the activity of shamans was accepted, and many joined the Methodist church. Nevertheless, the Ghost Dance religion took hold for a short time, and aspects of native religion continue in the form of the Earth Lodge cult and the Dream Dance.

Allotment of land began in 1895 and was completed in 1910, but it resulted not in opening the reservation to white settlement, but rather in tribal ownership of the reservation's valuable timber resources. The timber was harvested under BIA management, and by 1950 every Klamath (along with Modocs and Paiutes) was receiving an annual payment of $800, which kept many from taking up regular employment. For others the income provided economic security as they raised cattle, farmed, or worked off the reservation. The Klamath tribal council, organized in 1908, clashed with the BIA superintendent regarding the basis for tribal membership; the superintendent favored membership according to percentage of Klamath Indian descent, while the Indian leadership favored membership according to degree of participation in reservation community life. Bitter factionalism developed in tribal council affairs and characterized Klamath life until the council was dissolved in 1955. Different constitutions were adopted, the last in 1950. Shortly after the disbanding of the tribal council, the Klamaths joined the National Congress of American Indians and became very active in pan-Indian activities.

Planning for individual distribution of the tribal resources began in 1910, and over the years various plans were presented and became the focus of political conflicts. Seldon Kirk, active in the Committee for the Perpetuation of the Tribe, led the faction for maintenance of the tribe in some form. During the early 1950s the two major factions agreed on formation of a tribal corporation as the means for eliminating government supervision, but Congress implemented its plan for termination, although tribal members generally had a very inadequate understanding of the alternatives.

WASCOS

The two largest among the ten Indian groups on the Warm Springs Reservation (now the largest reservation in Oregon) are the Sahaptin-speaking Warm Springs people and the Chinookan-speaking Wascos. There were about 500 Wascos during the 1960s. The Wascos are much mixed genetically with the Chinookan-speaking Wishrams, who live on the Yakima Reservation in Washington, some other Indians, and whites; most Wascos, in fact, are married to non-Wascos. The Wascos are nearly surrounded by peoples of the Plateau-type culture (Yakimas, Klikitats, Teninos) and live in scattered camps with no overall tribal organization. The Indian language most Wasco children learn on the reservation is the Sahaptin of the Warm Springs tribe.

In most respects the Wascos are much more assimilated culturally than the other Indians of the reservation; their houses, clothing, and occupations are like those of whites. They raise some cattle and horses, and a few farm. They depend considerably on income from the sale of timber, cattle, and grain produced on the reservation. Until 1950, when a dam was built on the Columbia River, they fished seasonally for salmon, which is typical of the Chinookan culture. In 1938 the Indians

of the reservation joined to form an IRA-type tribal council, in which the Wascos held the most offices and took the most vigorous interest. The tribal council was very successful in developing income-producing business enterprises with the aid of expert professional advice. Wascos are members of the Presbyterian and Indian Shaker churches, but most also participate in the Indian Longhouse religion. Occasionally they stage a complex traditional ceremony called the Wasco Dance, but there is more interest in rodeos and various traditional gambling games. The Plains craft of beadwork on buckskin is prominent among the women.

The Wascos and other Chinookans—in contrast with Sahaptin-speakers—responded peacefully to white pressures, readily signing treaties for removal to reservations beginning in 1855. By 1858 the Wascos had moved to the Warm Springs Reservation and immediately began farming and spreading out in individual homesteads. They even gave up their fishing rights with no conflict in 1865. They maintained their concept of a stratified society, including a lowest stratum of slaves, until the 1870s. Traces of the concept survived into the 20th century.

MAKAHS

In the 1960s there were between 500 and 600 Makah Indians in Washington, most of whom live on a reservation that includes the town of Neah Bay near the tip of Cape Flattery. The Makah occupy the same coastal territory they have lived in since the birth of their traditions. They are in most respects like the whites who live within the reservation area, which includes not only the coastal strip but also a large timber acreage to the south. Makah houses, dress, and occupations are like those of the surrounding peoples; they fish for salmon and halibut, work in the logging industry on their reservation and in other forms of wage work, and provide services for tourists who visit the reservation. They also receive some income from timber sales on land allotted to tribal members. Their tribal council, organized in 1936 and chartered by the federal government a year later, maintains a tribal fund from sales of timber from reservation land held under tribal title.

The Makahs are either bilingual in English and their Nootkan language or speak only English. Many are multilingual in the various Indian languages of the region, like Quinault and Quileute. They are genetically mixed and not readily distinguishable physically from other residents of the region.

A majority are members of the Presbyterian or Apostolic church, and a few belong to the Indian Shaker church. Many call themselves heathens and practice traditional rituals connected with supernatural power-seeking and the spirits of the dead. The Makahs make use of Plains Indian headdresses and other pan-Indian elements of costume in secular ceremonial dances and participate in such dances with other Indians in Washington and elsewhere.

The traditional Makah way of life has been replaced in most of its fundamentals as well as in particular customs, although they have never been relocated from their homeland. Their present area of concentration around Neah Bay is the holy land of their legends, their mythical place of origin, and continues to have much of that meaning for them. Their subsistence still rests heavily on the traditional fishing, although they use mostly new techniques, despite the fact that the fishing banks have been seriously depleted.

The Makahs were one of many Nootkan-speaking groups who lived along the North Pacific coast when whites first arrived. Like the others of the region, they lived in autonomous villages with no tribal organization above the local level. The large plank houses were shared by many family groups. The society was stratified, consisting of a chiefly, or titled, class and a commoner class, as well as a slave class. They practiced the potlatch, a ceremonial feast in which social status was displayed by giving away possessions.

In the course of contact with whites they experienced no important dislocation or large-scale infiltration and invasion, probably because of their location. They ceded to the United States their property rights in a treaty of 1863 and were given a reservation that remained nearly intact for more than a hundred years. They were never put on rations and suffered no conflicts with white settlers.

However, from 1863 until the 1930s aggressive Indian agents dominated their life on the reservation, vigorously pursuing the general BIA assimilation policy. The potlatch, major religious ceremonials, and traditional gambling games were prohibited. The communal houses were torn down and American-style frame houses put up. Long hair was cut and native clothing was replaced forcibly by "citizens' dress." Women were jailed for keeping their houses in a condition the agent regarded as unclean. The agent attempted to force the men to farm, apparently not regarding commercial fishing as a proper economic pursuit for development. From 1874 the children were required to go to boarding schools, where the Makah language was prohibited and Christian religious instruction was required.

The result of these measures during a hundred years was fairly complete cultural replacement and a definite alienation from whites. A strong self-identification as Makahs resulted and, during the 20th century, a broader identification with other Indians in the United States and Canada. This was intensified especially during World War II, when a few white civic leaders attempted to segregate the women's Red Cross groups. The Makahs' continued exclusive possession of their land as a reservation, the resources of which they manage partly through their tribal council, also contributes to the separate identification as Indians. They have learned to shield their concept of social stratification, as well as certain religious practices, from white interference.

PUYALLUPS

Among the many Salish-speaking groups living along the coast of Puget Sound and its tributaries in Washington are the Puyallups. In 1960, 354 Puyallups were living on a reservation in the immediate vicinity of Tacoma. The reservation, however, was in uncertain status and by 1970 was not listed as a reservation by the BIA. As many as 20 families now live on what had been that reservation. Some have small farms; others, including some lawyers and businessmen, work in the city; most are clerical or wage workers. The majority of Puyallups are scattered and separate from one another in northwestern Washington, and a number of families

live on Warm Springs Reservation in Oregon. They are culturally indistinguishable from other ethnic groups of the region, and none seem to know anything of the Salish language, which they had formerly spoken.

One group of Puyallups insists that it constitutes an organized tribal group; it maintains a representative tribal council that has made a claim against the U.S. government for the former reservation land. The legal status of this land has been in question for some time, and the legal existence of the tribal council depends on whether the land belongs to the Puyallups. Although the scattered Puyallups maintain no common community or religious life, the land case has increased their awareness of their history.

The Puyallups traditionally ranged along the southern margin of Puget Sound and its tributary, the Puyallup River. Their first contacts with whites came in 1792, but intensive contacts did not begin until 1832, when the Hudson's Bay Company built a post among the Nisqually Indians immediately west of Puyallup territory. The purpose of the post was to oversee the settlement of farm homesteads for Hudson's Bay Company retirees in the prairie land over which Puyallups and Nisquallies ranged. As settlement spread, there was some resistance by the Indians, but it was quickly controlled, and a treaty was prepared.

The Treaty of Medicine Creek in 1854 was a major turning point in Puyallup life. All the Indians of the southern Puget Sound area ceded their territories and agreed to the creation of three reservations—for Nisquallies, Squaksons, and Puyallups—on Squaxin Island. The Puyallups and others refused to go there, and after a short war the reservation was enlarged, and the Puyallups settled on their portion of the island.

For 30 years relations between Indians and whites in the region were amicable. Many white men married Indian women, and there were many mixed households. There had been no organized tribal life, so the whites made no aggressive efforts to reorganize Indian society, nor did Presbyterian and Catholic missionaries push to replace the Indian religion. The traditional ways of fishing were maintained, and both Indians and whites used the Chinook jargon for communication. By 1874, however, the Bureau of Indian Affairs broke up the communal dwellings and made allotments to individuals, which were inalienable and could not be sold. By this time there had been a great deal of cultural assimilation: nearly all Puyallups spoke some English and dressed and lived largely like whites. They continued to be self-supporting in very much their old patterns of work.

When Tacoma began to be important as a major railroad terminus in the mid-1880s, railroad companies tried to put a major line through the reservation. The Puyallups resisted, but after litigation and Congressional intervention, the allotments needed by the railroad were sold and tracks were built across the reservation. The immediate result of the conflict was increased disorganization in Puyallup society and the murder of individuals who had attempted to provide leadership. More allotments were sold, and Puyallup society became steadily more disorganized. During the 20th century it ceased to exist as an organized unit. It was only with the passage of the IRA in 1934 that new efforts were made to vitalize the tribe. Land was secured for a reser-

vation, but its legality remained questionable, and the struggle over it continued into the 1970s.

Other Indians living in the Northwest in the 1970s were the Coast Salish—including the Chehalis, Clallams, Lummis, Nooksacks, Quileutes, Quinaults, Skagits, Skokomishes, Swinomishes, and Tulalips; other tribes were the Cayuses, Chetcos, Colvilles (Salish), Coos Bays, Cowlitzes, Kalispels, Klickitats, Siletzes, Siuslaws, Spokans, Teninos, Umatillas, Upper Umpquas, Walla Wallas, Warm Springs, Weacos, and Yakimas.

Bibliography
Homer G. Barnett, *Indian Shakers: A Messianic Cult of the Pacific Northwest* (1957; reprint, Carbondale, Ill., 1972), gives an introduction to the situation of all Indians of the Northwest Coast. One of the best studies of a single tribe in this region is Elizabeth Colson, *The Makah Indians: A Study of an Indian Tribe in Modern American Society* (1953; reprint, New York, 1971). Theodore Stern, *The Klamath Tribe: A People and Their Reservation* (Seattle, 1965), is an excellent tribal account, as is D. French, "Wasco-Wishram," in E.H. Spicer, ed., *Perspectives in American Indian Culture Change* (Chicago, 1962).

ALASKA

The Indian population in Alaska in the 1960s was about 16,000 and was about evenly divided between coastal dwellers, chiefly Tlingits, and interior Athapaskan-speaking peoples, such as the Tananas, the Kutchins, and the Koyukons. Although there are no estimates for all the interior peoples at the time of first European contacts, there is little reason to believe that the Indian population for the whole of Alaska in the 1960s was substantially different from what it was at the beginning of contact. The Indians are, of course, to be distinguished from the other Alaskan natives, the Eskimos and the Aleuts, whose population in the 1960s was twice that of the Indians.

The experience of the Alaskan Indians since first contact differed in very important respects from that of all other Indians of the United States. For example, there was practically no warfare between whites and Indians; no treaties were made between the United States or Russian government and the Indian tribes; neither government assumed the kind of close control over Indian lives that took place in all other parts of the United States; and there were no reservations. It is also notable that there was no change in the number of distinct Indian ethnic groups from the beginning of contact until the 1970s.

The Alaskan Indians' early contacts were with Russians, whose government made no legal distinctions between Indians and Russians, although missionaries of the Russian Orthodox church were sent to make converts. When the United States bought Alaska in 1867, it assumed no responsibility for what were designated in the treaty of cession as the "uncivilized tribes," who did not live in the Russian settlements. Thus, there was no special relationship between the Alaskan Indians and the government until the passage of the IRA in 1934. A 1936 amendment to that act defined Indian political status in terms of village rights to manage land in common and also opened the way for villages to become reservations, but the villages were generally distrustful of the government and did not ask for reservation status. During the 1940s and 1950s business interests in Alaska repeatedly sought to extinguish all

Indian and Eskimo rights to land, a matter that was not settled until 1971, when 40 million acres were declared in native possession, and compensation for other lands acquired by whites was set at $500 million, plus royalties from oil income. The administration of the native lands was placed in the hands of an all-native board of management.

TLINGITS

In the 1960s the Tlingits lived in some 25 locations along the Pacific Coast and coastal islands from Yakutat Bay to Ketchikan in the southeastern extension of Alaska. Several of these sites are identical to those where they lived before European contact. Apparently the Tlingits have inhabited the area for several millennia, although some of their traditions come from the south and the east. Tlingits also occupy former white settlements that whites abandoned after the gold rush of the 1890s. Still others live scattered in Juneau, Anchorage, and other coastal towns. They work in the fish canneries, at various kinds of wage work, and in traditional subsistence fishing and hunting. Most are Presbyterians, Roman Catholics, Anglicans, or Salvation Army members, and traditional ceremonies are carried out only for secular celebrations or for the benefit of tourists. Most speak English, only a few retaining any use of the Tlingit language, which belongs to the Nadene linguistic family. Clothes and houses are like those of neighboring whites.

Most Tlingit villages have chapters of the Alaska Native Brotherhood and the Alaska Native Sisterhood, affiliates of the Tlingit tribewide organization, which was set up in 1912 by two Presbyterian converts. Strongly advocating full cultural assimilation, including the replacement of the Tlingit language with English, the organization played an important role in securing voting rights, which were denied Indians and Eskimos until 1922, and has been quite effective in combating the segregation and widespread discrimination that have characterized white–Indian relationships since the late 19th century. After the territorial government passed the Jurisdictional Claims Act in 1935, the organization began to push land and other claims and in 1971 secured recognition of native rights to the land and its resources. In 1966 the brotherhood expanded to include Eskimos and Athapaskan Indians and became the nucleus of the Alaska Federation of Natives.

The Tlingits were a maritime people who lived by fishing and by hunting sea mammals and forest game when Russians first made contact with them in 1741. Their culture was one of the most complex ever evolved by a nonagricultural people, but they did not have tribal government or other large-scale organization. The village, or the clan within the village, was the highest unit of loyalty and cooperation, except occasionally during time of war.

Although the Tlingits traded furs with the Russians, they kept their villages clear of any political domination, demonstrating a readiness to fight off any encroachments. They successfully blockaded extension of the fur trade to inland Athapaskan peoples during the late 19th century. They accepted a Russian Orthodox priest, but few converts were made. Later in 1877, after the U.S. purchase of Alaska, Presbyterians came, set up schools, and were active in conversion. Their influence resulted in much cultural replacement and a strong tendency toward assimilation. They opposed cremation, multiple wives, the custom of maintaining slaves, the practices of shamans, and the potlatch, which was highly important in the Tlingit social system. The potlatch and the use of totem poles, which were significant in Tlingit culture, were eliminated by about 1904. Since the 1960s there has been a considerable revival of traditional arts, including the carving of totem poles, which Tlingits continue to use in their social ranking system, rather than for purchase by tourists or museums.

ATHAPASKANS

Very different from the coastal Tlingits, the seven groups of Athapaskan speakers live in inland Alaska. Although they were never removed from their land and continue to use their traditional hunting territories, profound changes have occurred. Once hunters and fishermen living in simply organized nomadic bands, they ceased to be nomadic in the course of contacts with Europeans and were concentrated into more or less stabilized villages of as many as 600 inhabitants. In the 1960s there were between 50 and 60 villages, each separate in its organization. While they continue to speak the seven different languages they used at the time of contact, there are some English-speakers in every village, especially since the 1930s, when the U.S. government began to build village schools. Nearly all have become Christians, either Roman Catholic or Presbyterian.

The Athapaskans still trap much as they did in the late 1700s, when the Russians and the English vigorously brought them into the fur trade. However, because of the depletion of fur-bearing animals, a steep decline in fur prices, and their own inclination to remain close to the stores, schools, baseball diamonds, and nursing stations in their villages, trapping has assumed a steadily more minor role in their lives. They support themselves chiefly by wage work for BIA or U.S. Army installations, logging, or other sources and through government welfare. They remain isolated, seeing few whites in their relatively remote villages, but a few have been active in the expanded Alaska Federation of Natives.

Bibliography
For the coastal Indians of Alaska, "The Tlingit: Salmon Fishermen of the Northwest," in Wendell H. Oswalt, *This Land Was Theirs* (New York, 1973), is a good short introduction. It may be supplemented with Philip Drucker, *The Native Brotherhoods: Modern Intertribal Organizations of the Northwest* (Washington, D.C., 1958), and Fredericka de Laguna, *The Story of a Tlingit Community* (Washington, D.C., 1960). For the inland Athapaskan-speaking peoples, James W. Van Stone, *Athapaskan Adaptations: Hunters and Fishermen of the Subarctic Forests* (Chicago, 1974), is a useful introduction.

URBAN INDIANS

In 1970 the United States Census listed the total Indian population of the United States at 791,839. Of this total, 340,367—about 43 percent—were listed as urban, that is, living in cities and towns. About one-fourth of the total Indian population—192,316—lived in cities of 100,000 or more. Most projections indicated that by 1980 more than half the Indian population would be urban.

The increase in urban-dwelling Indians was quite dif-

ferent from that of U.S. city dwellers in general. There was no steady increment in the urban Indian population through the late 19th and early 20th centuries, corresponding to the growing urbanization of the population as a whole. On the contrary, the Indians were almost exclusively a rural population until the 1890s, when they began slowly to join in the mainstream movement to the cities. The urban movement was not marked until the 1940s, and the greatest increase has taken place since 1950.

The factors resulting in the urbanization, or lack of it, of Indians also were notably different from those of the general population. First of all, government policies of removing whole tribes westward and concentrating them on reservations increased their segregation. Except for a few remnants of the peoples of the northeastern states who were absorbed into towns in Massachusetts, Rhode Island, Connecticut, and New York, Indians continued to live in separate communities from whites through the first three-quarters of the 19th century. Here and there individual Iroquois and others found their way into the growing towns of the East, such as Albany and New York, but these few (who often were strikingly successful in the white man's world, such as Ely S. Parker, who became a commissioner of Indian affairs) were rarities.

The appreciable movement of Indians into towns after 1890 is also related to the General Allotment Act of 1887. The 30-year period following the passage of the act was one of profound upheaval for most Indians. Tens of thousands suddenly became landless people, as the newly allotted acres slipped out of their grasp. Whites acquired land on what had been reservations, moved in, and established towns in the midst of the disrupted Indian communities. Indians found their only means of subsistence either in the white towns near the reservations or farther away in the cities. The process of moving into more urban ways of life, usually as wage workers, was aided to some extent by the boarding-school program of the BIA. Small numbers of young people in the boarding schools, as at Riverside, Calif., Albuquerque, N.Mex., Phoenix, Ariz., and Chilocco, Okla., took jobs as domestics or in other capacities in those cities where the schools were located and, at least for a time, stayed away from their homes in Indian country. A few settled permanently in these cities or nearby. Some accepted jobs in the Wild West Shows of the period and traveled widely, often settling permanently in larger cities, like New York or Los Angeles.

By the 1920s perhaps several thousand Indians lived in towns near reservations and in half a dozen large cities throughout the country. Although the number of Indians who began to live off reservations in this period is not known, it seems probable that there were relatively very few compared with the total Indian population. They were for the most part poor and working in unskilled occupations. The Meriam Report published in 1928 pointed them out as a serious problem for which the BIA was not taking adequate responsibility. Most of the off-reservation Indians lived in what the report called colonies, that is, in small clusters. They uniformly reported that they had left the reservations because of lack of work there and criticized the BIA for having leased land on reservations to whites, who did not provide Indians with jobs.

During the 1930s the numbers of town- and city-dwelling Indians declined, and the population of the reservations increased. The reasons for the return to the reservations were the growing scarcity of jobs in the cities because of the Depression and an increase in jobs on the reservations under the administration of Commissioner John Collier. This was the New Deal period in American political life, and many public works programs on and near reservations were undertaken, the most notable, with respect to influence on Indian life, being those carried out by the Civilian Conservation Corps (CCC). Hundreds of Indians were taken into the corps and employed in a wide variety of jobs, ranging from construction of small check dams for erosion control to extensive water storage and irrigation projects. As a result of these latter projects, many reservations underwent new agricultural development, and the various conservation measures salvaged and improved large range areas. The CCC, which had a special Indian division, may be regarded as the first effort on the part of the government to bring Indians systematically into the national work force on a par with other Americans. A generation of young Indians gained the experience of regular work at standard wages both on and off the reservation. The Depression years resulted, on many reservations, in economic stabilization for Indian families whose lives had been disrupted by land loss and unsuccessful adjustment to white town life. Many individuals gained new abilities to cope with the white man's economic ways.

World War II also helped create a sizable new urban Indian population. During the war some 25,000 Indians volunteered or were drafted into the armed services, where they learned to use English, as few had been forced to previously. A team of Navajo servicemen made a distinguished record in Army Intelligence by using their own language in lieu of code, which enemy code experts found unbreakable. Another 40,000 Indians were estimated to have left reservations for work in war industries, chiefly in West Coast cities. By the end of World War II there were nearly 80,000 urban-dwelling Indians.

Although many Indians returned to reservations when the war ended, the BIA made a special effort to encourage movement to the cities. Lack of employment opportunities and poor social environment on the reservations were given as reasons for the new program, which began at about the same time Congress was preparing legislation to terminate the special relationship between Indian tribes and the federal government. To spearhead the program, Dillon S. Myer was appointed commissioner of Indian affairs in 1948. During the war he had been director of the War Relocation Authority program for resettling the 110,000 Japanese Americans who had been evacuated from their homes and placed in relocation centers; before the end of the war the authority had found jobs for about one-fourth. Myer's achievement in directing this relocation and a multifaceted program for reintegrating evacuees promptly into American life led to his appointment as commissioner.

Modeling policy to some extent on the earlier resettlement program, Myer and his associates established a Relocation Division of the BIA to stimulate movement from the reservations into American cities. The new ef-

fort was named the Employment Assistance Program in order to avoid the implication that it was attempting to liquidate the bureau and force all Indians off the reservations. The program became the major influence in the large migration of Indians to the cities during the 1950s and 1960s.

Through offices established in Chicago, San Francisco, Los Angeles, Denver, Minneapolis, and other large cities, the BIA assisted Indians who left the reservation in finding employment, housing, welfare aid, and other services. By 1968 the bureau reported that it had assisted at least 50,000 individuals to settle in major cities, chiefly in Los Angeles, San Francisco–Oakland, and Chicago, although it was also reported that some 35 percent of those relocated during the 1960s returned to reservations. There is no doubt that the BIA relocation program was a major influence in the sudden new shift from an almost exclusively rural population to a high proportion of urban residents.

By 1970 the largest concentrations of urban Indians were in the following states:

California	60,000–65,000
Oklahoma	27,000–32,000
Arizona	18,000–20,000
Minnesota	10,000–15,000
Illinois	10,000–12,000
Washington	9,000–9,500
Texas	8,000–8,500
New Mexico	5,000–6,000
Michigan	5,000–6,000
Wisconsin	4,000–4,500
Oregon	4,000–4,500
Massachusetts	3,500–4,000
Arkansas	3,500–3,800
Pennsylvania	3,000–3,600

The cities with the largest Indian populations were the following:

Los Angeles	47,000
San Francisco–Oakland	18,000
Tulsa, Okla.	15,000
Minneapolis–St. Paul	13,000
Oklahoma City	12,000
Chicago	12,000
Phoenix, Ariz.	10,000

Urbanization of American Indians was also taking place in cities and towns close to reservations, especially near the largest ones, and it was apparent that different processes were at work in these locales. In some areas, such as western New York State, New Mexico, and the Dakotas, this kind of urbanization had been going on for many years prior to World War II, and it increased and intensified after the war. With the tremendous growth in the Navajo population during the 20th century, the reservation population spilled over into towns like Gallup and Farmington, N.Mex., and within the reservation, urban concentrations developed around Shiprock and Window Rock. Rapid City in the Black Hills country of South Dakota attracted Sioux from the nearby Pine Ridge and Rosebud reservations. Similarly, the urbanization of the Salish-, Sahaptin-, and Chinookan-speaking peoples of western Washington began

early as Seattle and Tacoma expanded. Buffalo, N.Y., and other cities in the vicinity of the Seneca and other Iroquois reservations became the residence of Iroquois families early in the 19th century. However, the processes by which Indians moved into cities near the reservations differed substantially from those in the largest United States cities, the most important way being an intensification of Indian identity in the large cities, which was not usually apparent in the towns near reservations.

The experience of some urban enclaves, founded by Indians long before the BIA began relocation efforts, illustrates this point. For example, in 1970 there were 800 Mohawks in the North Gowanus section of Brooklyn, N.Y., who had lived there since the 1920s. They had come in response to a demand for their skills as high steel workers on bridges and skyscrapers, such as Rockefeller Center in New York City. The Brooklyn enclave constituted a well-defined neighborhood served by a Presbyterian church where the minister preached in the Mohawk language. Although they have made a satisfactory adaptation to urban life, the Mohawks do not regard the urban settlement as their home. Most remain Catholic, as they were on their home reservation of Caughnawaga in Quebec; they often send their children to the reservation to be educated, and most spend long summer vacations there, where each family owns land and where most plan to retire. The urban settlement is the scene of only one phase in each family cycle, but it is a stable element in which Mohawk Indian identity receives emphatic expression through the use of the Mohawk language, participation in the Iroquois Longhouse religion, and active interest in various pan-Indian pow-wow activities.

Indians in other large cities, however, do not live in such sharply defined enclaves. In Los Angeles there are groups of Cherokees and Creeks from Oklahoma who first came to the city in the 1930s during the dustbowl migrations from Arkansas and Oklahoma. In Minneapolis, as employment opportunities on the Minnesota and Dakota reservations declined even before the Depression, a small, steady trickle of Indian families established themselves in that city. These Indian migrants, unlike the Mohawks, had no distinctive occupational specialties, nor were they able to cluster in the same neighborhood. They nevertheless maintained consciousness of their Indian identity to a greater or lesser degree and were vitalized in this respect during the 1950s and 1960s with the new influx of Indian migrants. This sense of identity emphasizes participation in pan-Indian symbols and activities more than tribal distinctiveness.

Where there are the heaviest concentrations of reservation population, Indians have moved out somewhat beyond the reservation borders into the neighboring towns, where the tendency to lose their cultural distinctiveness and sense of Indian identity seems stronger than in the large cities. Certain segments of such groups, however, seem to develop a capacity for behaving acceptably in both Indian and non-Indian cultures.

Rapid City, S.Dak., one near-reservation community, is an example of this phenomenon. Some Sioux families have lived there since before World War II and have become strongly oriented toward middle-class white ways. They live like their non-Indian neighbors

and are concerned with getting ahead economically and rising in the class system. They identify with Indians only for very special purposes and generally dissociate themselves actively from Indians arriving from reservations. In Rapid City, as elsewhere, there was a large increase in the number of Indians during and after World War II. By 1955 in this town of 50,000, there were 5,000 Sioux, and their numbers have continued to grow. The new arrivals are usually desperately seeking work, often remain unemployed, and speak both substandard English and substandard Dakota. For the most part, they live in tents and shacks and contrast with the older Indian residents in their adoption of lower-class rather than middle-class ways. The longer-settled Indians pride themselves on being mixed-bloods. A fairly sharp distinction is maintained between the older and the newer Indian migrants. Similar processes of cultural reorientation of earlier Indian migrants are apparent in Albuquerque, Phoenix, and other near-reservation cities, as well as their separation from those who came later, during the 1950s and 1960s.

By 1970, 47,000 Indians lived in Los Angeles County, including members of 101 tribes from all over the United States. Most numerous are Navajos from the Southwest and Sioux from the northern plains; next in numbers are Pueblos from New Mexico and Cherokees, Creeks, and Choctaws from Oklahoma. The list also includes Chickahominies, Mohicans, Potawatomis, Nanticokes, Mandans, Delawares, Iroquois, and Kiowas. Beginning with handfuls of the original displaced natives of the area, such as the Gabrielinos and Dieguenos, the Indian population was slightly increased during the late 1800s by other remnants of small California Indian groups dispersed by the new immigrant miners and ranchers. A substantial addition resulted from the dustbowl migrations of the 1930s, chiefly Cherokees, Creeks, Choctaws, and Seminoles from Oklahoma. Some 6,000 of these took up residence in the Los Angeles area during the Depression and constituted, by the 1950s, the major Indian population.

Meanwhile, the industries of World War II had begun to draw Indians from all over the United States. During the 1950s the majority were from Arizona, New Mexico, the Dakotas, and Montana. As the BIA relocation program came into full operation in the early 1950s, the rapid increase in number of Indians led to a wholly new situation. In the late 1950s as many as 1,300 Indians a year arrived in Los Angeles. The newcomers had no special preparation for urban living, although some had served in the armed forces. All were from reservations where they had been unable to find employment, and none had special skills to offer. Some 86 percent spoke an Indian language and used English imperfectly. Those who succeeded in getting work went into low-paying unskilled jobs or service occupations that did not require a good speaking knowledge of English. Eventually 37 percent returned to their reservations. Despite the high rate of failure at adaptation, it must be emphasized that the great majority of those who came stayed, and some moved permanently into jobs and situations that they found satisfactory. The reservation life no longer attracted them, and they became established urban Indians.

The very great majority of the Navajos in Los Angeles are essentially rural people from areas of the reservation where contacts with whites were at a minimum, where urban occupations were unknown, and where the language of daily life was Navajo. Consequently, those who remain in the city through the initial period of difficult adjustment associate with one another rather than with whites or with other Indians. This seems largely true of Pueblos also, even though their background is that of town-dwelling people.

The situation of the next largest group of migrants, from the several Sioux reservations of the Dakotas, contrasted markedly with that of the Navajos. They had experienced much disorganization in their native society largely as a result of the infiltration of whites on their reservations after land allotment. They, therefore, had had some association with whites, and many were a little better prepared as a result of occupational experience in the towns of their region. They were somewhat better able to use English than the Navajos. These factors have led to a different adjustment pattern from that of the Navajos, and the Sioux are able to associate with persons other than fellow Sioux. This has not led to a loss of their Indian identity, but rather to a wider association with other tribes and to an intensification of pan-Indian identity. This kind of adaptation is also characteristic of many others, such as Kiowas, Iroquois, and Omahas.

Few Indian families in Los Angeles live very close to one another, and Indian neighborhoods have not developed. The most important, or at least most widely attended, organizations are the churches. More Indians are Catholic than any other denomination, and 70 percent attend church more or less regularly, 27 percent being involved in all-Indian congregations. There are nine fundamentalist Protestant churches composed chiefly of Indians, and one Mormon (Latter-day Saints) congregation. The largest Indian church, composed largely of Navajos, is an Assembly of God group.

More is known about Indians in the San Francisco Bay area than about any other urban Indian population. In 1970 the U.S. Census counted about 12,000 concentrated in the vicinity of San Francisco and Oakland and another 4,000 near San Jose. These figures are probably an undercount; it might be safer to assume that there are nearly 20,000 Indians living in this region. Like the movement of Indians into the Los Angeles area, the migration into the San Francisco Bay area tremendously accelerated after the 1940s. Similarly, there are no contiguous-residence Indian neighborhoods, and, as in Los Angeles, 100 tribes are represented.

The Intertribal Friendship House, founded and maintained by the Society of Friends, plays an important role in bringing Indians together. It is managed by a non-Indian board of directors and provides various services for assistance in adapting to city life, such as vocational training and welfare aid. Most important in Indian life, it sponsors social dances, classes of verious kinds, and athletic events and provides a meeting place for a ladies' club, a young peoples' club, and a Navajo club, among others.

The Bay Area American Indian Council, managed by an all-Indian board of directors, formed in opposition to Friendship House to bring about more Indian participation in policy making. Its functions are very similar to those of Friendship House, but it also encourages interest in political issues and Indian participation in politi-

cal activities. Many associations, both formal and informal, meet at the council center, which sponsors both social and ceremonial dance groups. Certain tribes have organized associations among themselves, such as the Navajos, the Pueblos, the Tlingit, the Haida, and the Pomo; other associations focus on pan-Indian activities, with members from many different tribes. They engage actively in pan-Indian dance and music and use pan-Indian symbolism, each tribal group making its own distinctive contribution within this context. Pan-Indian-oriented associations have been formed by the Oklahoma peoples, such as the Cherokees and Creeks, and by the Chippewas from Montana and Minnesota. The intensification of a pan-Indian sense of identity is fostered by these associations.

A third major concentration of urban Indians is in the Chicago area, where much the same patterns obtain as in the California cities: great acceleration in migration during and immediately after World War II, and 90 to 100 tribes in the total population, but with the heaviest representation from Sioux, Chippewa, and Winnebago and other western Great Lakes peoples. In Chicago, however, clubs limited to a single tribe are less important than the pan-Indian associations. As in San Francisco, Indian centers play a prominent role in bringing Indians together, as well as in giving varied assistance in the urban adjustment process. There are two such institutions—the Chicago American Indian Center, managed by an all-Indian board of directors, and the St. Augustine's Center, managed by the Episcopal church. The American Indian Center is an important meeting place for a variety of organizations, ranging from Boy Scouts and Alcoholics Anonymous to the Sioux and Winnebago clubs, which, despite their names, are pan-Indian in orientation.

The movement of Indians into the cities has proceeded on a quite different basis from the urbanization of European or Asian immigrants. It is not characterized by the growth of extensive contiguous neighborhoods in which thousands of persons of similar cultural backgrounds live in subcultural enclaves. The urbanization of Indians in the United States has been a relatively small-scale movement of individuals and small family groups from quite different tribal cultural backgrounds. Nevertheless, a sense of common interest and problems was fostered by the Employment Assistance Program, which applied the common category of Indian to all the migrants, thereby reinforcing preexisting reservation attitudes. The most characteristic cultural process has been the stimulation of a sense of pan-Indian identity transcending tribal identities. The expression of pan-Indianism takes many forms in athletic clubs, dance groups, and councils that embrace, or purport to represent, all the Indians of a given city. Important among these are the strongly politically oriented organizations that arose during the late 1960s, such as the American Indian Movement, which adopted a militant program first formulated by the urban Indians of Minneapolis.

Urban Indian organizations, often actively supported by Indian students on university campuses, sought to give leadership to Indians on reservations during the late 1960s and 1970s, but with little success. While considerable numbers of urban Indians maintain contact with their families on reservations, close personal relations had not by the mid-1970s brought about acceptance by reservation Indians of the politically militant organizations. There developed a division between the reservation leadership generally and the urban leadership. The leaders of tribal councils on the reservations represent a conservative position, including cooperation with the BIA, and an easy-going leadership, which had grown up since the 1930s under the conditions of the IRA.

On the other hand, the urban and student leaders view themselves as having much in common with minority groups in the United States generally; they espouse civil rights causes and have been influenced by the viewpoints of blacks and Mexican Americans. Such a conception of themselves was foreign to the reservation residents. Militant movement activities carried to reservations have received either very little support or, most frequently, active opposition. Nevertheless, a new set of ideas about their place in the United States was injected into Indian life as a result of the rise of the urban leadership.

By the 1970s an urban segment of the Indian population had become permanently established. While nearly half of all Indians were listed as residing in urban areas, the number that could be regarded as permanent urban-dwellers was not known; for many, movement between the reservations and the cities was constant. The Indian population of New York City exhibits perhaps the extremes in adaptation: of the 2,000 Indian residents of New York, only the 800 Mohawks maintain strong, definite ties with their reservation. The other 1,200 are largely second-generation city dwellers from 30 to 40 different tribes. Born in New York of parents who for the most part settled there many years earlier, they are permanently established as New Yorkers and have broken their reservation ties. However, they pursue an active interest in Indian traditions and maintain an extremely vigorous organization—the Thunderbird American Indian Dancers—that covers many social and civic functions. In Minneapolis–St. Paul there are also long-established, clearly permanent families who nevertheless have maintained close family relations with reservation people in Wisconsin and Minnesota. In the large West Coast cities, as well as in cities closer to reservations elsewhere in the West, movement in and out of urban life is more fluid. It is clear, however, that in all major urban localities there are growing cores of permanently settled Indian families that continue to help Indians from the reservations gain more or less permanent places in city life.

The growing segment of settled city dwellers often regard themselves as members of the various reservation tribes, and in fact they are, by the established criteria. They not only maintain family ties and seek advice from elders on the reservations in regard to the technicalities of the traditional dances and music, but they also vote in the reservation communities and promote their political interests in tribal affairs. When tribes have won their claims before the Indian Claims Commission, the urban people have often clashed with reservation residents. Usually they have opposed using the funds for reservation development, as urged by the BIA and many tribal majorities on reservations; instead, they vote for per capita payments. On other issues there are also differences between urban and reservation people, and sometimes there have been protracted

struggles for political power between factions on and off reservations, as among the Potawatomis. In this respect, as in the matter of militancy and civil rights, a new element has been injected into reservation life as a result of the steady growth of the urban segment.

These differences extend also to the relationship with the federal government. In 1972 an organization called the National American Indian Council was founded by Indians representing Indian centers in San Francisco. The council took a strong position in urging the government to assume responsibilities for off-reservation Indians comparable to those it maintains for reservation residents. There were also court cases supporting extension of specific services. Thus, the federal government–Indian relationship was in process of change during the 1970s, a direct result of the rapid urban shift in the Indian population.

Bibliography
No general survey of the urban Indians brings the situation beyond the mid-1970s. Useful as an introduction is the brief treatment in Murray Wax, *Indian Americans: Unity and Diversity* (Englewood Cliffs, N.J., 1971). The articles in Jack O. Waddell and O. Michael Watson, eds., *The American Indian in Urban Society* (Boston, 1971), provide a somewhat uneven survey through the 1960s. Joan Ablon, "Relocated American Indians in the San Francisco Bay Area: Social Interaction and Indian Identity," in *Native Americans Today: Sociological Perspectives*, compiled by Howard M. Bahr, Bruce A. Chadwick, and Robert C. Day (New York, 1972), an early survey, gives the best-integrated view of Indians in one city. An excellent study of the role of pan-Indianism in urban Indian life is James Hirabayashi, William Willard, and Luis Kemnitzer, "Pan-Indianism in the Urban Setting," in Thomas Weaver and Douglas White, eds., *The Anthropology of Urban Environments* (Washington, D.C., 1972). A useful short demographic study is Henry F. Dobyns, Richard W. Stoffle, and Kristine Joes, "Native American Urbanization and Socio-Economic Integration in the Southwestern United States," *Ethnohistory* 22 (Spring 1975): 155–179.

EDWARD H. SPICER

AMERICAN INDIANS, FEDERAL POLICY TOWARD

The policy of the U.S. government toward American Indians can be separated into five distinct periods, reflecting shifting views of Indians specifically and of the place of ethnic groups generally in American life. These periods may be summarized as follows: (1) separation, during which the prime objective was to remove Indians from the land that whites desired and draw boundaries between the two peoples; (2) coercive assimilation, during which whites sought to replace Indian ways with their own ways and to help them become self-sufficient farmers and artisans, under conditions dictated by whites; (3) tribal restoration, phase I, during which whites made an about-face and encouraged Indians to maintain their corporate tribal existence if they chose to do so; (4) termination, during which the objective was to break off all relationships of protection and assistance with the federal government; and (5) tribal restoration, phase II, during which tribal corporate adaptation to American society was again encouraged and cultural choice was reaffirmed. The long second period of cultural assimilation and the short fourth period of termination are related and must be understood as expressions of a persistent tendency in American society.

During the first century of U.S. independence, the idea prevailed that Indians were a separate, not an integral, part of the political society. Apparently not considered in the Declaration of Independence among "all men . . . created equal," Indians were only once mentioned in the Constitution (in connection with the regulation of commerce with foreign countries), and Indians were not admitted to citizenship, except a few by special treaty provision, until after 1887. The principle of separation was enunciated by President James Monroe in 1825 and embodied in the Indian Removal Act of 1830.

By the 1880s a different view was evolving, that Indians should be incorporated rapidly into American society whether they wished it or not. The Dawes Act of 1887 and the Curtis Act of 1898 defined the means for achieving this and were supplemented by directives of the Bureau of Indian Affairs (BIA), beginning as early as 1873, aimed at the complete replacement of Indian cultures. This policy prevailed into the 1920s, and in 1924 Congress granted citizenship to all Indians.

However, a view emerged during the 1920s that Indians should not be coerced into discarding their cultural traditions, a position embodied in the Indian Reorganization Act (IRA), passed in 1934, which recognized the right of Indians to their own local government on the reservations. Also, the BIA encouraged freedom of choice in religion and other aspects of life. This new approach was based on the concept that distinctive Indian ways could be expected to exist indefinitely, reversing the view that Indian cultures were dying out.

In the 1950s a reaction set in against the policy inaugurated by the IRA. Actions of Congress, beginning with a House Resolution in 1953, defined a new approach, which sought to eliminate reservations and end the special relationship between Indians and the federal government through the BIA. The policy, labeled termination, was vigorously opposed by almost all Indians. It also aroused strong negative reactions both within and outside of Congress.

In 1961 the new administration repudiated the termination program, as did each successive administration into the 1970s. In 1973 Congress restored the working relationship between the BIA and the Menominee Tribe, one of the few that had been terminated. The trend through the 1970s was to affirm and develop further the provisions of the IRA. A major landmark in the reinstituted policy came in 1975 with the passage of what became known as the Indian Self-Determination Act.

The general trend of Indian policy has been toward increasing acceptance of Indians as part of the body politic, but during the 20th century there have been sharply differing views as to how their role should be defined. These striking shifts of policy cannot be understood apart from general trends in the United States and the Western world. The political exclusion of Indians, their subjection to a powerfully implemented cultural assimilation program, the restoration of local government and freedom of cultural choice, the effort to place integration on an individual rather than a group basis in the termination program, with subsequent reaffirmation of ethnic group existence—each of these policies respecting integration into the nation-state has parallels in attitudes toward black, European immigrant, and other ethnic groups in the United States. From a still broader viewpoint, U.S. Indian policy has unquestionably been influenced by ethnic group policies in Great Britain,

Spain, France, and other Western nations, especially during the 19th and 20th centuries.

SEPARATION

The roots of the earliest U.S. policy lay in the British colonial experience and grew out of the struggle for land that immediately developed between Indians and the English. Some of the early invaders bought land, thus recognizing the Indians as rightful possessors, while others merely squatted where they landed and continued to expand their holdings, ignoring prior Indian possession. Once the Europeans gained a foothold, a fairly consistent official policy emerged in various agreements between Indians and colonists in Virginia, Pennsylvania, New England, and elsewhere. It was most clearly embodied in the Proclamation of 1763, at the close of the French and Indian War. Two principles were implicit: the Indian peoples, or nations, as they were usually called, were political entities to be dealt with as the British customarily dealt with territory-controlling nations in Europe, that is, by diplomacy, warfare, and treaty; and conflict would be prevented if there were clear boundaries between colonists and Indians that the central government would control. The proclamation set a boundary along the crest of the Appalachians, west of which Indians could enjoy their lands in peace. The statement also affirmed by implication the legality of British possession of the lands east of the line as a *fait accompli*.

The cornerstone of British policy was thus the idea of defined and respected boundaries, adjusted when necessary by treaties. It established an honorable tradition of discussion and mutual agreement. After the United States won its independence, Secretary of War Henry Knox was given the responsibility for developing Indian policy. He conscientiously sought to establish a policy of "liberal justice" in dealing with Indians, basing his efforts on the British separation principle. In the Indian trade and intercourse acts that Congress passed between 1790 and 1796 as their first significant policy statements, the concept of "Indian country" was established, and congressional regulation of Indian–white relations affirmed. The paradoxical concept of a people within the territory of the new nation and yet outside the processes of its political life was beginning to take form.

This troublesome principle was expressed by the Supreme Court in 1831. During the previous decade friction and what amounted to border warfare had developed between the Cherokees and the other residents of Georgia. The Indians' territory was demarcated by treaties, but the Georgians refused to recognize Indian jurisdiction over the land and claimed the right to enter the territory and administer their own laws. Invasions of the Cherokee territory became increasingly frequent when gold was discovered there in 1828. The Cherokee Nation brought suit against the state, asking for an injunction to restrain Georgians from attempting to apply the laws of the state within Cherokee territory. The case reached the U.S. Supreme Court, which ruled that the Cherokee Nation had "an unquestioned right to the lands they occupy" but denied the injunction on the ground that the court could not "control the legislature of Georgia." However, this equivocal decision included Chief Justice John Marshall's definition of the tribes as

"dependent domestic nations" within the United States, a definition that became a source of ideas about the legal status of the Indians.

In an 1833 decision, in a case of a missionary living within the Cherokee Nation who was abducted by officers of Georgia and sentenced to hard labor under the laws of that state, Marshall made his concept of "dependent domestic nation" much clearer. He wrote in the court's decision: "The very term 'nation,' so generally applied to them [the Indians], means 'a people distinct from other.' The constitution by declaring treaties already made, as well as those to be made, to be the supreme law of the land, had adopted and sanctioned the previous treaties with the Indian nations, and, consequently, admits their rank among those Powers who are capable of making treaties." Marshall also specifically affirmed certain rights of Indians within their bounded territories: "These articles [asserted in treaties] are associated with others, recognizing their title to self government. The very fact of repeated treaties with them recognized it; and the settled doctrine of the law of nations is, that a weaker power does not surrender its independence—its right to self government —by associating with a stronger, and taking its protection." The decision nullified Georgia's action against the missionary and in so doing affirmed principles of policy that have not been superseded by later decisions.

Thus, by the 1830s American policy toward the Indians had been defined in some detail. Its ultimate legislative expression may be taken to be the Indian Removal Act of 1830, which in the tradition of the Proclamation of 1763 proposed to remove Indians to the sparsely populated country west of the Mississippi River for their own protection and the welfare of the United States. However, this was not to be done without the Indians' consent. There were to be negotiations and land exchanges. Appropriate payments were to be made, and the Indians were to be free to continue or set up local governments as they saw fit in the new lands assigned to them. Every removal was to be based on a mutual agreement, the conditions of which were to be duly recorded in a treaty signed by both the Indians and the federal government. In fact, though, tribes reluctant to move west were subjected to heavy pressures to do so. By the 1850s the removal policy had been applied in such a way as to move the Indian–white frontier west beyond the tier of new states on the west bank of the Mississippi. The old frontier problems had not been eliminated but merely moved to new locations.

Separation continued to be the guiding principle for another quarter of a century, although it was becoming clear that the sweeping approach of the Proclamation of 1763 as embodied in the Indian Removal Act would have to be abandoned. The vision of a distant Indian country, sufficiently remote so that border clashes could be avoided by drawing boundaries, was no longer realistic. There were Indians and white settlers everywhere in the West. True enough, there was Indian Territory, established in 1825, resulting from removal of the Five Civilized Tribes (as whites referred to the Cherokees, Choctaws, Creeks, Chickasaws, and Seminoles) and many other Indian groups. But it was recognized that the concentration in Indian Territory could not increase much more, and white settlers were pushing in there as well.

The principle of separation was now applied piecemeal in the form of the reservation system, which spelled out specific boundaries for each newly conquered tribe. A separate treaty with each of the scores of tribes brought under U.S. control was necessary to designate their new reservation, usually a portion of the territory they had roamed or had settled on. Although the idea of reservations was not new, having been used from colonial times, what was new was the realization that the hope of an "Indian country" truly separate geographically from white society had become impossible to sustain. White society had to reckon with Indian tribes within its midst, and dependent domestic nations scattered widely throughout the United States began to seem anomalous. Moreover, the Indians were now powerless, as the U.S. Cavalry supervised the settling of once-formidable tribes into the reservations. The result of the new conditions was a radical change in policy. By 1887 the tradition of negotiation with Indian tribes was dead, and unilateral government action had come to be regarded as perfectly appropriate. Even at the time Chief Justice Marshall was formulating a policy of negotiation, an opposite, unilateral approach was developing.

President Andrew Jackson undertook the administration of the Removal Act after 1830. He had earlier declared that he believed treaty-making with Indians to be absurd. A frontiersman and experienced Indian fighter who held that only military power worked, he proceeded to follow the letter but not the spirit of the law in furthering Indian removal. Anxious to remove the Cherokees and the other Civilized Tribes of the southern states, he sought out any handful of Indians who would sign a removal treaty without considering whether the signers represented the tribe as a whole. In this respect, Jackson was a precursor of the new era in Indian affairs. The viewpoint was reinforced in 1871, when Congress voted to abandon the policy of making any treaties with Indians. In 1872 Secretary of the Interior Columbus Delano formulated the view that had by then become dominant: "In our intercourse with the Indians it must always be borne in mind that we are the most powerful party . . . we assume that it is our duty to coerce them, if necessary, into the adoption and practice of our habits and customs." From a policy of recognition of Indians as near equals, with whom negotiation respecting their affairs was important and necessary, the U.S. government moved to a position from which Indians were seen as subordinate and indeed no more to be consulted with than children.

COERCIVE ASSIMILATION

Faced with tens of thousands of Indians on large areas of highly coveted land, who were rendered dependent both legally and physically, as their former means of subsistence were much reduced or wholly destroyed, Congress began during the 1880s to formulate new policy objectives within the framework of "coercion if necessary." To this end Congress was strongly influenced, not by consultations with Indians as to their needs, but rather by the views of various well-meaning religious groups. Most of the Christian denominations had had some experience with Indians. In colonial times missionaries had spent years in efforts to convert them, to reduce their languages to writing, and to provide schools. Many religious groups had received specific government sanction to work on particular reservations during President Ulysses S. Grant's peace policy of the 1860s, which was designed to encourage persuasion rather than military force in the effort to get Indians to settle on reservations. During the 1880s many religious persons with concern for Indians met annually at Lake Mohonk in New York State. Ideas from these and similar conferences crystallized into a coherent set of policy objectives, which were translated into the General Allotment, or Dawes, Act of 1887. This legislation, together with subsequent acts of Congress and regulations of the BIA, initiated the second phase of U.S. Indian policy.

In contrast with the separation policy that had prevailed until then, the predominant idea became assimilation or, as it was often phrased, the civilizing of the Indians. The General Allotment Act, drawn up specifically to make the Indians into white men, culturally speaking, assigned title to 160 acres to each family head. It was believed that individual responsibility for the land and for a family's welfare on it would promptly result in each Indian becoming a hard-working, economically motivated person like the thousands of white settlers who had spread across the land. At the same time, other Americans would profit; after all the Indian family heads had been assigned land, the United States could distribute the surplus to non-Indians, who were ready to take it up. The plan would solve at one stroke the problem of how to bring about the maximum utilization of the land, which had been a concern ever since the time of Jefferson.

Thus, one major policy objective was seen as the assimilation of Indians to white economic ways through redistribution of the land. A secondary, related goal was the elimination of Indian community and political organization. Most whites assumed that Indians were incapable of governing themselves or that they maintained corrupt and highly inefficient local governments, as had been developed, they believed, by the Five Civilized Tribes in Indian Territory. Whites understood that all Indian organization rested on collective, tribal holding of the land, which was regarded as a serious obstacle to their becoming civilized. Breaking up the land into individual parcels would bring about not only individual responsibility in economic affairs but also the elimination of the land base for tribal organization.

Land allotment was carried out by agents of the BIA, who treated Indian political organization as nonexistent, except in the cases of the Five Civilized Tribes, a few others of Indian Territory, and the Senecas of New York. The governments of these tribes were expected to negotiate with government officials to carry out allotment. When it became apparent that the Cherokees and Choctaws would not allow allotment and in fact brought suit in federal courts, Congress passed the Curtis Act of 1898, which dissolved those tribal governments as legal institutions. That legislation made it clear that the federal government was determined to act unilaterally and that no Indian governing bodies would be allowed to continue unless they obeyed the federal administrators.

The third objective of this second phase, although not embodied in either the Dawes or the Curtis acts, was based on stipulations in the Dawes Act that all Indians

who received titles to their allotted land were to be granted U.S. citizenship, conditional on having "adopted the habits of civilized life." These habits apparently were assumed to be obvious, as they were not further defined in the act or in other federal legislation, and they probably were obvious to the white employees of the BIA; civilized habits were their own ways of behaving, that is, speaking English, wearing hair and clothing in the fashion of the period, working six days a week, going to a Christian church on Sunday, and so on. Coercing Indian children if necessary into these ways was the ultimate objective of the assimilation program.

From 1887 to 1934 the efforts of the BIA, supplemented by those of Christian churches, which were active on most reservations, were directed energetically to assimilation. Although the three objectives—replacing collective by individual landholding, eliminating Indian self-governing institutions, and replacing Indian cultural ways—were never fully realized, the effects on Indian lives were very great. This policy phase engendered the deepest distrust of the federal government and the maximum hostility toward whites.

During the first 25 to 30 years of the allotment program, Indians lost at least two-thirds of all their landholdings, not only through the sale to the United States of the surplus on each reservation after allotment, as provided for by law, but also through purchase and fraudulent deals by whites, who devised a great variety of means for acquiring the allotted land. In this way Indian ownership was reduced in many areas to small fractions of the land they had once held. In addition, many reservations were checkerboarded, that is, they became areas in which whites and Indians lived side by side, a circumstance that effectively interfered with Indian community life but rarely resulted in cooperative relations among Indians and whites. Eventually, after some 30 years of administrative complexities, the whole allotment program was abandoned, and large reservations in many parts of the West were never, or only to a limited extent, allotted. The northern plains and the Southwest, particularly, escaped allotment. By the 1920s it was clear that tens of thousands of Indians had not become farmers or ranchers according to the white model and that collective tribal ownership of land (with titles held in trust by the government in order to control the sale and prevent the loss of land) remained an important framework for the majority of Indians in the United States.

The Bureau of Indian Affairs, by creating an institution of its own—the superintendency—was much more successful in destroying local Indian institutions than in allotting all the land. Although agents of the government had been assigned to various administrative tasks among Indians ever since colonial times, during the coercive phase of Indian policy the field agents, called superintendents, sought to undermine their local governments and inhibit any autonomous community organization. The superintendent of a reservation or area of a former reservation, as in Oklahoma (formerly Indian Territory), ordinarily became the most powerful influence on local Indian affairs, even though he was a government employee, not responsible to the Indians but to his superiors in Washington. Through him came the assistance that the Indians needed for any kind of development, and through him usually were channeled

all important relations with outsiders. Indians who cooperated with him received favors.

Thus, the administration of reservation affairs was carried out by a government employee surrounded by his Indian allies. In all but a few cases the superintendents despised the Indian local governments, as in the case of a superintendent among the Pueblos, who characterized their ancient institutions as "opera bouffé." Under these conditions, some once-flourishing tribal governments, like those of the Five Civilized Tribes, disappeared, and some, like the complex Pueblo institutions, operated in almost an underground status, or at least without an effective relationship with the federal government. In 1910 a commissioner of Indian affairs, voicing the viewpoint of the government policymakers of the time, wrote: "The Indian problem has now reached a stage where its solution is almost wholly a matter of administration." In other words, benevolent agents would now manage the affairs of Indians in accord with government regulations. Under the assimilation policy, Indian tribal government had been replaced, not with American representative democracy, but with administrative bureaucracy.

To an observer it might have appeared that the third objective of policy—the replacement of Indian ways by "the habits of civilized life"—had been largely successful from the 1880s to the early 1930s. During this half-century the changes in Indian lifestyles were certainly considerable. The majority of Indians in every part of the nation learned to speak English and adopted clothing and houses basically similar to those of neighboring whites; only a few tribes, such as the Pueblos and Navajos of the Southwest, maintained some traditional features of dress and housing. The most distinctive ways of making a living, such as buffalo hunting, raiding Mexican ranches, wild food gathering, or small-scale floodwater farming, were no longer possible and were replaced by wage work and other occupations of the industrial age. A closer look at Indian ways of life, however, reveals that fewer than a dozen of the Indian languages died out, many forms of Indian religious life and ceremonialism were vigorous, and Indians everywhere asserted that they lived by values distinct from and preferable to those of the majority of Americans.

These mixed results may be better understood in the light of the methods used to replace Indian cultures. Federally administered schools, supplemented to some extent by schools managed by the various religious denominations, were considered the chief tool for achieving assimilation. Even before the 1880s the boarding schools began to be regarded as playing a key role, because they separated children from the influence of their parents and of the Indian communities. According to BIA regulations, an important duty of superintendents was to keep the boarding schools full by any feasible means, such as withholding rations from parents if they refused to send their children voluntarily. Parents did resist, and there was coercion. The boarding schools were kept more or less full for nearly 50 years, and the children were often placed in white households during the summer in a determined effort to keep children in contact with white culture and out of contact with Indian culture. The techniques employed were indicated in 1908 by Richard H. Pratt, who founded Carlisle Indian School in Pennsylvania and who was called by

whites the "Red Man's Moses": "The multiplicity of tribes represented enabled a mixing of tribes in dormitory rooms. The rooms held three to four each and it was arranged that no two of the same tribe were placed in the same room. This not only helped in the acquirement of English but broke up tribal and race clannishness, a most important victory in getting the Indian toward real citizenship." Such techniques were effective in diffusing knowledge of English and white ways among Indians as well as in broadening the horizons of Indian children beyond their own tribal boundaries. Many intertribal marriages resulted, and boarding-school Indians sometimes settled in white communities for many years. However, the major complaint of the federal educators during the early 20th century and before was that Indians everywhere were "going back to the blanket." By this they meant that despite the considerable experience of "civilized ways," Indians were choosing to live in Indian communities, that is, on reservations.

In general, it may be said that formal education away from home resulted more frequently in new problems of cultural conflict on reservations than in a steady flow of Indians out of the reservations into white society. The return to reservations with widened outlook often resulted in individual personality problems and in factional strife within Indian communities, as well as in acceptance of many features of white civilization. In addition, new hostilities developed toward whites and white ways, and it may be said that the policy of off-reservation education had many unanticipated consequences that the proponents themselves rated as undesirable.

Another element in the program for "civilizing" Indians consisted of encouraging Christian missionaries and suppressing the native religions. The missionaries were strikingly successful everywhere in gaining adherents to their many different churches, so that by the 1930s the great majority of Indians professed Christian church affiliation. However, certain of the native religions were still vigorous in the 1930s, such as those of the Pueblo Indians of New Mexico and the Navajos. In addition, new religions sprang up, especially during the period of most intensive suppression. The Native American church, which employs some Christian concepts and symbols along with the use of peyote, became well established from Oklahoma through the plains and ultimately in the Southwest. The Redbird Smith movement revitalized traditional Cherokee beliefs and became an important influence in eastern Oklahoma. The Indian Shaker church integrated traditional and Christian beliefs among thousands of Indians of different tribes in the Northwest. The Longhouse religion of the Iroquois continued its vigorous growth from its beginnings in 1800. In every region, Indians developed new religions, increasing the number of sects of the reservations.

In the mid-1920s the primarily destructive effects of the coercive assimilation policy attracted the attention of new policymakers in government and of private organizations concerned with Indian rights. The result was an extensive study of the condition of Indians on all reservations, undertaken not by the BIA or any other branch of government but by the Brookings Institution, an impartial private organization devoted to research into government operations and policies. Published in 1928, the study, entitled *The Problem of Indian Administration*, reported that on all fronts the assimilation program had failed to realize its objectives and that Indians lived in conditions of extreme poverty, with poor health and inadequate education. The report recommended that the BIA recast entirely its approach to education and adapt its inadequate school system to the needs of Indians as members of U.S. society. The report, along with other, more specialized analyses, influenced the government to develop a radically different approach to Indian affairs.

THE INDIAN REORGANIZATION ACT

During the early 1930s congressional committees worked on drafting new legislation to replace the policy of the 1880s. In 1934, under the innovative administration of Franklin D. Roosevelt, Congress passed the Indian Reorganization Act (IRA), defining a new framework for Indian policy. It aimed at reversing the effects of the General Allotment Act, the Curtis Act, and the succession of BIA regulations designed to force cultural assimilation. In some respects the new act reaffirmed the viewpoint of the Supreme Court in its decisions of the early 1830s.

The cultural distinctness of Indian communities was recognized as a fact, and no effort to alter that distinctness was made. The act provided for the restoration of some Indian lands and proposed means for recovery of some more, thus repudiating allotment, the basis of Indian policy since 1887. The IRA not only affirmed the importance of the reservations as a continuing land base but also reasserted the rights of Indians to govern themselves locally. Reversing the policy trend since 1871 of eliminating Indian political organization, the IRA made specific provision for tribal adoption of constitutions and election of representative councils.

This change represented a return to the Marshall doctrine that Indians had an inherent right to govern themselves within their own territory—but with a significant difference. The Marshall viewpoint was simply that Indians had the right to maintain their own governing institutions, which already existed at that time. The new legislation specifically proposed that the tribes adopt new institutions modeled on those of constitutional representative democracies. This was an advocacy of cultural assimilation with respect to political organization, but it was not coercive, in that Indians were not required to adopt the proposed form of government. The new policy also authorized Indian communities to organize as corporations for the management of tribal business enterprises. The new policy strove to relate reservation societies dynamically to the economic life of the nation.

These features of the IRA constituted a rejection of the Indian policy that had guided the U.S. government for more than half a century. They encouraged Indian communities to engage in landholding, politics, and economic development. The legislation resulted in immediate enlargement of some reservations and gave legal sanction to tribal landholding, officially recognizing the Indian land system as an existing institution rather than a disappearing phenomenon. These provisions of the IRA were far-reaching in their implications regarding the place of Indians as an ethnic group in American

society. John Collier, the commissioner of Indian affairs who was appointed in 1932, wrote in a memorandum: "I see the broad function of Indian policy . . . to be the development of Indian democracy . . . The most significant clue to achieving full Indian democracy . . . is the continued survival, through all historical change and disaster, of the Indian tribal group, both as a reality and a legal entity." Such a view was at the opposite pole of opinion from that of nearly every Indian commissioner since the 1870s. Collier, who had been active in organizations working to define and protect Indian rights and to improve economic and other conditions on the reservations, regarded the new tribal councils, which nearly every tribe voted to organize during the 1930s and early 1940s, as training grounds for Indians to assume leadership and management of their own communities.

His administration also sought to define new goals for the federally administered school system. Day schools on the reservations were emphasized over boarding schools, although the latter continued to be the most important in the governmental education program. In both kinds of schools an effort was made to change the content of teaching so that Indian cultures were dealt with positively rather than ignored or disparaged. The new administration even introduced the teaching of Indian languages and prepared primers in three major tongues—the Navajo, a Pueblo, and a Siouan language. But these programs for a new orientation in the schools were not popular in Congress and in some respects turned out to be impracticable. Because of the inertia of the BIA and the hostility in Congress to spending government funds for teaching any language other than English and any history other than that of white Americans, there was little change in the schools by 1945, when Collier resigned in frustration.

Under the influence of the IRA, the effects of the hundred years of forced assimilation were not erased, of course, but important changes did begin. The superintendency as the arm of the BIA in reservation life continued, as did many constructive programs begun in the previous policy phase, such as the building of irrigation systems, the development of Indian-owned cattle herds, the expansion of crafts production, and the exploitation of oil, natural gas, and other minerals on reservations. However, Indians began to participate in planning and management through tribal councils and council committees. The BIA retained control because of its annual appropriations from Congress and its trained personnel, but many tribal councils began to act with some degree of independent leadership and forced the BIA to take them into account. Some superintendents believed in the new policy and tried to bring Indians increasingly into management and policymaking at the reservation level. The effects of the IRA were mixed with respect to the degree of Indian participation in shaping their destiny, but there was no doubt that immediately after 1934 new political processes were stimulated, which had not been true during the long period of coercive policy. There was a tendency toward growth of the representative democracy that Commissioner Collier envisioned.

In addition, political action by Indians outside the purely local sphere revived intertribal organizations in a way that had not been apparent since before the General Allotment Act had gone into operation in Indian Territory. With the Collier administration's encouragement, Indian leaders in 1944 founded the National Congress of American Indians (NCAI), an intertribal association whose varied program included lobbying in Congress and correcting misleading stereotypes of Indians. The NCAI, beginning with leadership by Cherokees and other groups from eastern Oklahoma, steadily increased in size and influence to become an important political force among all tribes of the United States.

Consistent with these developments, Congress in 1946 established an Indian Claims Commission. This was a product of the deep and widespread sentiment among Americans generally that Indians had been dealt with unjustly throughout American history, especially with respect to their land. The commission was empowered to hear cases brought by a tribe and to provide compensation for proven illegal or unjust losses. During the next 30 years the commission judged many cases and awarded millions of dollars. The common effort to prepare claims cases brought new solidarity in many tribes but also new factionalism, arising in some cases from the distribution of compensation funds. Cases before the commission were still being settled in the 1970s.

In the first phase of this new policy, during which tribal restoration was the dominant principle, organized corporations developed widely among Indian tribes. New forms of organization within and among tribes grew and became instruments for economic and political initiatives. The Indians' economic and health conditions continued at very low levels as compared with the general U.S. population, but the level of formal education rose somewhat, and the Indian population, which had reached an all-time low in the late 19th century, was on the increase in nearly all groups.

TERMINATION

Support for the earlier policy of coercive assimilation did not disappear with the passage of the IRA, however. In most sessions of Congress bills to abolish the reservations were proposed. A good many Americans thought that reservations were a species of concentration camp, and that the Indians should be set free. Conflicts of jurisdiction between tribal councils and county governments and between the BIA and the states embodied the contradictions built into Indian policy. During the early 1950s these viewpoints began to dominate in Congress, and policy was formulated that opposed the IRA and its associated programs. During President Dwight Eisenhower's administration there was an attempt to get the federal government "out of the Indian business." In 1953 the House and Senate approved a resolution calling for an end to the Indians' "status as wards of the United States" and specifying that certain tribes "should be freed from Federal supervision." Among these were two large tribes whose reservations contained important stands of timber—the Menominees in Wisconsin and the Klamaths in Oregon. Paying lip service to Indian consent, as in the 1830s, the federal government proceeded to sever its connection with the designated tribes under a policy that came to be called termination.

The Indians, when pushed to vote on termination,

were split into factions. The majority did not understand the issues, as became apparent later. When they realized what the results of termination would be, namely, loss of control of their timber lands, some groups sought to reverse the action. The Menominees in 1973 were ultimately successful in reestablishing their federal relationship, whereas the Klamaths remained terminated. The policy of termination, which was rejected when the administration in Washington changed after the 1960 election, aroused strong, widespread negative reaction in the United States among non-Indians as well as almost universal, active opposition by Indians.

TRIBAL RESTORATION

After that, policy again moved in the new-old directions pointed by the IRA. The most notable addition—community action programs—emerged during President Lyndon Johnson's administration in the 1960s. The community action programs on the reservations, administered by the Indian Desk of the Office of Economic Opportunity (OEO), introduced new organizations that supplemented the tribal councils, which in many cases had become merely administrative arms of the superintendencies. The new programs introduced three features: the training of Indian citizens in action programs; the creation of responsible committees for making decisions about the use of federal funds; and in some instances, contracts between Indian communities and the OEO for the administration of development programs. These provisions were in the spirit of the IRA goal of reestablishing effective community organization among Indians, for they tended to transfer decision making from the BIA to the Indian communities. The new arrangements often challenged those tribal councils that had been overwhelmed by the superintendency and had not worked for maximum independence. The making of contracts specifically opened the way to a new approach by encouraging participation of Indians in the management of their reservations, which the BIA had not been capable of doing.

The OEO and its community action committees were liquidated during the early 1970s, but the spirit in which they had been formulated continued. In 1970 the administration of President Richard Nixon announced its Indian policy: "Self-determination among the Indian people can and must be encouraged without the threat of eventual termination . . . This is the only way that self-determination can effectively be fostered . . . This, then, must be the goal of any new national policy toward the Indian people: to strengthen the Indians' sense of autonomy without threatening the sense of community . . . we must assure the Indian that he can assume control of his own life without being separated involuntarily from the tribal group. And we must make it clear that Indians can become independent of Federal control without being cut off from Federal concern and Federal support." In the spirit of this presidential message, Congress in 1975 passed the Indian Self-determination Act. It appeared that the change in Indian policy marked by the IRA in 1934 had inaugurated a long-term trend and that the termination legislation of the 1950s was but a brief interlude.

By the 1970s two opposing views existed, one that saw Indians as "just like everybody else" and therefore to be "melted" into American society as individuals, and another that saw Indian group distinctiveness within the whole of the United States as of high value and therefore to be nurtured. The general public was ambivalent and confused, and opinion tended to swing successively in different directions. Indian policy was a dynamic political issue that certainly was not stabilized by the 1970s.

INDIAN INITIATIVES

During the various changes in government policy, Indians did not stand by passively; they also developed policy of their own. In the early separation period under the British, the major reaction of the Indians was to build confederations of tribes. The Iroquois and, on a smaller scale, the Abnakis, the Wampanoags, and some others formed political confederacies in the Northeast and resisted white pressures to acquire their land. The Creeks and the Pamunkeys in the Southeast acted similarly, but none of these, not even the powerful Iroquois League, was able to stand against the military power of the whites. By the time of American independence, all the confederations had broken down.

Nevertheless, as the Americans vigorously pursued separation and removal, the policy of Indian unity reached an even broader expression than during British dominance. The Shawnee leader Tecumseh (1768–1813) by 1811 conceived of unity among all the tribes of the North and South. He preached personally to all the many displaced groups of the Northwest Territory to cease selling their land, to hold on to it, and to resist all pressures. Tecumseh urged his policy goals on his own Algonkian-speaking peoples, and he traveled south to influence the once-powerful Creeks and the rising Cherokees. He was eloquent, and his policy was clearly formulated and strongly presented, but he was not successful; only one small faction of the Creeks joined the Northwestern tribes. In the war between Tecumseh's supporters and the federal government that began with the battle of Tippecanoe, the Indians were crushed and Tecumseh was killed.

Military resistance by confederacies was not the only policy that guided Indians faced with the determined separation and removal policy. As President Andrew Jackson moved under the authority of the Removal Act to push the Civilized Tribes of the Southeast out of the white man's way, some of the Cherokee leaders decided to resist by lobbying in Washington, by appealing for justice to the general American public, and by appealing to the federal courts. This policy, vigorously pursued by John Ross (1790–1866) and other Cherokee leaders, also failed. All of the Five Civilized Tribes were forced by U.S. troops to abandon their peaceful program of resistance.

By the time the forced assimilation policy had crystallized in the 1880s, Indians everywhere had capitulated to white military power and were in various stages of adaptation to life on the reservations. Their struggle for control of the land had been lost, and white power was being employed to divest them of still more land. Indian hopes reached a low, and Indian political leadership lost momentum; only the Cherokees, Creeks, and Choctaws maintained some vision and strength.

For the most part, Indian leadership now appeared in

religious life; it was the religious prophets who set their goals. Among the Indians removed from the Great Lakes area, among the newly demobilized Plains Indians, among the Northwest Coast people, prophets arose, telling of promised lands where the old ways could be renewed without white domination. Wovoka (c. 1856–1932), the Messiah of the Paiutes in Nevada, spread the Ghost Dance across the West; the power of that religion frightened the whites into the massacre at Wounded Knee, S.Dak., which became a burning symbol for both Indians and whites. The peyote cult and, in the Northwest, Smohalla's vision were typical responses in this period of declining hopes in the material world. Policy was ritualized and dealt with the spiritual world instead. Many of these visionary religions became permanent and continued to give guidance, as in the Native American church. However, even the religious spirit was overwhelmed in the assimilation phase. White control was so well established that not only was military resistance impossible, but the spiritual world itself seemed conquered.

It was under these conditions that whites offered the new policy of tribal restoration. The Indians' acquiescence to the tribal council system may be regarded as the beginning of a new policy era for them, in which they generally accepted their assigned role within the American social system. No longer socially and politically separate, no longer able to take refuge in visionary worlds, the Indians set goals within the white-dominated society and utilized the institutions of that society to realize them. The limits of policy were somewhat expanded, both within and outside of the reservations. This kind of widespread involvement in the dominant institutions had been foreshadowed more than a hundred years earlier by the Cherokees just prior to removal to Indian Territory, when they built political institutions modeled on those of the whites.

The termination phase was too short for much Indian-formulated policy to develop, although they generally opposed it. Despite long-standing resentment of BIA methods, they viewed the bureau as their only bulwark against what they believed to be the continuing desire of their immediate neighbors to acquire Indian land and wipe out their cultural differences. Moreover, the feeling was strong among Indians generally that the U.S. government owed them a great deal for taking nearly all their land and for failing to live up to the many treaties as settlers moved across the continent. Thus, termination was strongly opposed on the ground that the federal government had not equipped the Indians to resist successfully the ever-present pressures for eliminating them as a people. If termination policy had continued longer, many different tribes undoubtedly would have organized the kind of action that resulted in Congress rescinding the Menominee termination program.

When the tribal restoration policy resumed after 1960, the Indians pursued some distinctive new policies. For tens of thousands on reservations, there was no essential change, but since World War II there were also tens of thousands of Indians who no longer lived permanently on reservations, who had migrated to cities in every part of the country. A considerable number of off-reservation dwellers were or had been college students. These people, removed from the more conservative in-

fluences of the tribal council communities, developed new ideas about the place of Indians in American society. Political militancy grew during the 1960s, and younger Indian leaders in California, Minnesota, and elsewhere organized demonstrations to acquaint the American public with conditions on and off the reservations. An early action consisted of an attempt in 1969 to take over Alcatraz Island, the former federal prison in San Francisco Bay; claims that it was legitimate Indian land were advanced, and short-lived efforts were made to establish a training school for Indians on the island. The young and militant Indian leadership then organized more demonstrations, including a march on Washington in 1972, called the Trail of Broken Treaties, and the occupation of the BIA building in Washington the same year. In 1973 leaders of the American Indian Movement (AIM) took over the small community of Wounded Knee, where violence erupted between federal officials and Indians. The Indians' militancy paralleled that of blacks and Mexican Americans during the 1960s.

Other forms of action during the late 1960s and 1970s included a kind of cultural renaissance and new legal actions, both guided by new, specialized, nonpolitical associations. A group of Indians in San Francisco organized an Indian Historical Society for the purpose of writing and publishing history from the Indian, rather than the white, point of view. They published a journal called *The Indian Historian*, encouraged Indians to write for it, and printed articles about Indian history that contrasted greatly with those published in the usual scholarly journals. An Indian Press Association released to newspapers and magazines news about Indian affairs that often varied considerably from news of the same events disseminated by the wire services. These and other activities that flourished during the 1960s and 1970s were initiated with funds from various private foundations and individuals; they constituted an area of Indian life in which the federal government played no role at all, in sharp contrast to the reservations, where the government's role was still very prominent.

With private funds the Native American Rights Fund was founded in Colorado. Among other activities, it researched legal aspects of the many land cessions made by Indians since colonial times and discovered that a number of such cessions were apparently illegal. When East Coast states such as Maine and Massachusetts had pushed through cessions of land from the Passamaquoddy, Wampanoag-Mashpee, Narragansett, and other groups, they had bypassed Congress, the only body that had the legal power to carry out such negotiations. With legal guidance from the Native American Rights Fund, tribes brought suits against the states, and during the 1970s a number of such cases were being adjudicated. One in Massachusetts involved the very small group of Mashpee Indians, which a jury decided had not been constituted as a tribe at the time the state took over their land; the court suspended judgment, and the case was then appealed. It appeared that in the future the policy of the Indians would be to avoid jury trial. Instead, their strategy would be negotiation by lawyers with specialized knowledge. The fact that these cases were taken to court rather than to the Indian Claims Commission indicated a new role for Indians, much

freer from control by the administrative arm of the government.

The fullest understanding of U.S. Indian policy comes through comparison with the policies of other modern nation-states for dealing with ethnic groups in their territories. To some degree, governments of the West went through similar developments in ethnic policy from the 1600s to the 1970s. A not-uncommon policy before the 19th century was separation of a conquering group and the conquered natives. This policy was practiced by the English after their conquest of the Irish, when a pale of settlement was established at the River Shannon in 1653, and all English-speaking persons who behaved like Englishmen and rejected Irish ways were enjoined to live east of the Shannon; those who spoke Gaelic and clung to Irish modes of dress and other customs were required to live west of the line. Earlier the Romans had set patterns in this regard in Britain and in the Iberian peninsula. The Romans and Romanized persons lived in the cities, while the barbarians lived beyond the cities' bounds. European countries during the Middle Ages had clearly bounded ghettos for Jews, and Russia had a well-established rural pale of settlement in the 19th century. Separation policy was not universal, but some form of it appeared in most European states as an accepted means for keeping apart the conquered natives or immigrants, regarded as below the cultural level of the dominant group that controlled the state apparatus.

Again we can turn to English policy in Ireland for a parallel with the U.S. policy. The pale of settlement kept "civilized" peoples and barbarians from mingling, but it did not necessarily keep English and Irish apart; many Irish men and women took on English ways, from language and dress to religion and world view. Nevertheless, a hundred years after the pale was set up, a majority of Irish continued to reject the English language, the Anglican church, and most other English ways. The English response was ultimately to take vigorous steps to assimilate the Irish culturally. Many legal devices were tried, but in the 19th century something like the U.S. government's Indian school policy was adopted— not boarding schools separating parents and children, but national schools in which the Gaelic language and Irish history were ignored; the schools were wholly English in language and outlook. Irish Catholicism came under fire, and an organized effort to Anglicize the religion was instituted. It was indeed a coercive assimilation policy, if not so drastic in method as that in the United States, and proceeded on the same assumption, namely, that English culture was superior in all respects to Irish culture and had to be adopted for the good of the Irish. In many European countries during the 19th century assimilation programs were instituted, often using less drastic means than the English or Americans, but with the same goals. Efforts to introduce a standard language and to teach a national history were essentially aimed at replacing the many languages and cultural identities of European peoples who did not belong to the dominant ethnic group controlling the government. Catalan, Basque, Flemish, various Germanic and Slavic languages were labeled as inferior and not officially recognized, although they were spoken by millions of people. The assimilation policies promulgated by the ethnic groups in power grew out of the idea that the nation-state should be culturally homogeneous and were part of Europe's colonial expansion phase, which rested strongly on the concept of racial and cultural superiority.

The tribal restoration policy in the United States was instituted in the aftermath of World War I and it may be regarded as related to the influence of discussions about the Versailles Peace Treaty, in which President Woodrow Wilson became the spokesman for the rights of minorities and for self-determination of European ethnic groups. The restoration of independence and the expansion of self-determination were in the air in the Western world. Ireland won independence; it was seen that Europe's colonies would inevitably become new nations. President Wilson maintained a blind spot with reference to the self-determination of American Indians, but the Indian policy of the 1930s formulated by others was in the spirit of his proposed changes in the map of Europe.

However, the United States was an integrationist rather than a pluralist state; that is to say, its political structure was wholly individualistic. In contrast with some other Western states, such as Switzerland, it had never given political recognition to any ethnic group as such within its borders (except for the Indians). The United States was ready by 1924 to grant full citizenship to Indians, but on an exclusively individual basis. Its basic law could not be construed as sanctioning any role for ethnic groups in its political structure. It was this political standpoint that was the foundation of the termination policy.

Nevertheless, Indians had been recognized as distinct ethnic groups holding land collectively, and in the 1934 legislation Congress formalized these groups as having a kind of political existence under the tribal councils. In its tribal restoration policy, the government was consistently moving with one strong trend of the times, an important tendency of post-World War I Europe and the former colonial world. Following the brief interlude of termination in 1954, the U.S. Congress continued vigorously the tribal restoration policy, a major action being the Indian Self-Determination Act of 1975.

Bibliography
Of the two most comprehensive accounts of American Indian policy, the one by S. Lyman Tyler, *A History of Indian Policy* (Washington, D.C., 1973), is written from a government administrator's point of view; it includes useful lists of sources, especially for published and unpublished government documents. D'Arcy McNickle, *Native American Tribalism: Indian Survivals and Renewals* (New York, 1973), analyzes policy from an Indian point of view and is more selective. Different phases of policy development are described in two books by F.P. Prucha, *American Indian Policy in the Formative Years: The Indian Trade and Intercourse Acts, 1790–1834* (Lincoln, Nebr., 1970), and *Americanizing the American Indian: Writings by the "Friends of the Indian," 1880–1900* (Cambridge, Mass., 1973). See also Loring B. Priest, *Uncle Sam's Stepchildren: The Reformation of United States Indian Policy, 1865–1887* (1942; reprint, New York, 1969).

EDWARD H. SPICER

AMISH

Old-Order Amish Mennonites are a Germanic people who stem from the Swiss Anabaptist movement that emerged during the Reformation in the 16th century. Anabaptists were radical groups holding unorthodox beliefs, and those that have endured, including the

Amish, the Mennonites, and the Hutterites, evolved from the original movement that developed between 1525 and 1536. These groups are characterized by the maintenance of a voluntary and disciplined community, pacifism, separation from the world, adult rather than infant baptism, and emphasis on simple living.

The Amish originated between 1693 and 1697 as a dissenting orthodox faction of the Swiss Anabaptists (also at that time called Mennonites, after their founder, Menno Simons). The leader of the Amish, Jacob Ammann, introduced shunning (the social avoidance of members who were excommunicated), footwashing as a ceremonial part of communion service, and simplicity of dress and grooming styles. The Amish continue to this day to abide by the rules established by Jacob Ammann as interpreted by each local community.

Like other Anabaptist groups in Europe, the Amish were severely persecuted and imprisoned. Later they were allowed to leave the countries where they lived, but if they remained, they were forbidden citizenship and could not own land. Therefore they were unable to establish permanent settlements in Europe in which to develop their distinctive social structure, although by settling in mountainous areas and by becoming farmers they developed techniques of self-reliance. Their livelihood, place of residence, and population growth were subject to the policy of local rulers and neighbors. During their years in Europe the Amish lived in Switzerland, Alsace-Lorraine, the Palatinate (in what is now West Germany), France, and Holland.

With other Germanic peoples, the Amish began settling in Pennsylvania from 1727 to 1790. About 500 came to America during this period. A second wave of 3,000 Amish immigrated from 1815 to 1865 and settled in Ohio, New York, Indiana, and Illinois. Those who stayed in Europe have since been assimilated into the prevailing religious bodies there. (See also Hutterites; Pennsylvania Germans.)

About 80,000 Amish people now live in 20 states and one Canadian province (Ontario); of these, 75 percent live in three states—Pennsylvania, Ohio, and Indiana. Their annual population increase is about 3 percent, which means a doubling of the population every 23 years. This growth results from large families—seven or eight children are typical.

The Amish have no central office. In the regions where they live, families are grouped into "church districts" (congregations), which serve as the governing units. Each district is governed by its own local leaders —usually a group of three or four men selected from the members and ordained to the offices of bishop, preacher, and deacon. A district consists of from 25 to 35 married couples and their children. The districts are bonded together by respect for common customs and by the bishops, who meet informally to share concerns.

The Amish are distinguished by their simple traditional ways of living, nonconformist attitudes, ingroup marriage patterns, and resistance to modernization. By living in rural areas, speaking the Pennsylvania German dialect, using horses for farming, and dressing in "plain" clothing resembling that of Europeans two centuries ago, they have maintained socially distinct communities even though they are neighbors to non-Amish people. Biblical High German is used in religious ser-

vices, but all Amish people also speak English. They meet for worship in their farmhouses, usually every two weeks on a Sunday for three or four hours. Their rules forbid members from having more than a practical elementary education and prohibit the latest products of technology and convenience, including the ownership of automobiles and telephones and the use of electricity. Such practices distinguish them from more progressive Mennonite groups.

This striking nonconformism within the larger society is grounded in religious and cosmic perceptions not uncommon to monastic groups in earlier centuries. The Amish view of reality is conditioned by Christian dualism that distinguishes between evil and goodness, carnality and spirituality, and pride and humility, but it does not set matter in opposition to spirit. The account of the creation in Genesis, encompassing a garden with animals, plants, and marine life, is accepted as good, with men and women as caretakers or stewards. The Amish accept marriage, family, children, and a disciplined life expressed in a brotherhood. They also accept personal property expressed in farms and family dwellings as a form of stewardship, but they carefully avoid any ostentatious display of wealth.

The Amish rejection of worldly value structures is based upon their rejection of carnal or worldly loyalties. Their own cosmos includes the creation of a community of Christian believers who "have truly repented, who are rightly baptized," who are "a chosen people," who live separate and apart from the "blind, perverted world." Living in such a church-community (Gemeinde) is viewed by them as essential for redemptive purposes. The "charter" of Amish society includes, in addition to separation, voluntary commitment to membership (by baptism), conformity to the consensual rules (Ordnung), the practice of excluding and avoiding obdurate members, simple living, and an agricultural way of life.

For two and a half centuries the Amish have formed unique farming communities in the United States. They are excellent farmers and usually live on productive soils, most notably in Lancaster County, Pa. The young are given rewarding and meaningful roles of responsibility in family and farm work. Amish children help their parents on the farm until they themselves get married, and then the parents try to secure farms for their children. Influenced by their self-reliant experiences in Europe, the Amish combine family labor and management with an integrated agricultural way of life. The Amish and Mennonites were among the first to practice rotation of crops, stable feeding, and the use of natural fertilizers. The Amish resist large-scale and single-crop farming, and prefer to maintain a "small-scale" farm with a diversity of crops and livestock, and one that is manageable with family labor and horse-drawn equipment. Their charter prohibits the use of tractors and more highly mechanized farm implements in the interests of simplicity and the use of family labor.

Amish communities today are located in regions compatible with their style of community and farm life; the most populated areas include Pennsylvania, Ohio, and Indiana. The Amish attempted to form communities on the Great Plains as early as 1871 and at various times since then. These efforts were not successful, as the soils were suited to specialized rather

than diversified farming and to large acreages rather than intensive small-scale farming.

Although the Amish people are hard workers and generally good managers of farms, they have not been pioneers in the sense of being the first to possess new lands or territory. As pacifists, they were ill-equipped to cope with frontier situations requiring the use of force and coercion. They are builders and conservators. They have generally followed other pioneers, improving and gardening the soil after others have moved on, and in recent decades they have successfully farmed in areas where the soil has been depleted by their non-Amish predecessors.

As a multibonded group with many ethnic ties, Amish society has many features of a small commonwealth—but not a territorial commonwealth, for the Amish forbid participation in politics or public office-holding. Members are bound by social, economic, ceremonial, kinship, linguistic, and moral ties. The many social rules for living constitute a way of life that is set off by explicit social boundaries and by signs and symbols that delineate the culture. With few exceptions, only the children of members of the Amish church, through instruction and baptism, become members themselves. There are occasional converts to the Amish community, but they must first demonstrate their ability to follow the Amish way of life. The Amish do not proselytize. Of the 126 family names current among the Amish today, one-third are of American origin. The 45 most typical family names derive from the 18th-century immigrants. In Lancaster County five family names—Stoltzfus, King, Fisher, Beiler, and Lapp—account for about 70 percent of the population. In Ohio the most common Amish surnames are Miller, Yoder, Troyer, Raber, and Hershberger.

The Amish appear not to marry close relatives, and marriages between second cousins are rare. However, there has been considerable inbreeding for generations. Several recessive genetic disorders have a relatively high occurrence, among them phenylketonuria, a rare type of anemia; hemophilia; and six-fingered dwarfism. Because the Amish are a well-defined population and have kept good genealogical records, it is possible to trace many of the cases to a common ancestor.

The Amish rely upon mutual aid in many ways, but not to the point of complete self-sufficiency. They emphasize hard work, thrift, mutual aid (barn raisings), and rejection of city ways. Family organization has always been strictly monogamous and patriarchal. The husband is allocated overall authority, but there are many areas of cooperation between spouses; the husband is the farmer or provider and the wife is manager of the household and garden. Amish married couples devote much time to rearing and caring for their children. Parents do not have individual rights, but they have responsibilities and obligations for the correct nurture of their children. Amish women are not employed away from home. Divorce is not permitted. Both men and women vote as individuals in church councils.

The Amish have large families; infant mortality is low, birth-control measures are prohibited, and life expectancy is long. The majority of babies are born in a hospital, though the Amish prefer home deliveries when they can find physicians and midwives to perform them. Amish women do not view birth as threatening, but as status-enhancing.

The continual growth of the population and the moral directive to till the soil have created economic problems, such as the high price and scarcity of land. The Amish have resolved these problems by dividing their farms to accommodate the younger generation and by allowing the younger men to work in woodworking, repair, and construction shops. In recent years many Amish families have moved to less developed areas to form new settlements where land is available at more reasonable prices.

Not all Amish children when they reach the appropriate age (usually 18 to 22) formally declare their intention of becoming members of the Amish church. There is an overall dropout rate of approximately 25 percent, although dropouts do not occur at random, but are clustered in certain families. They are usually the children of family heads who only marginally conform to the rules, of parents who themselves were not farming, and of parents who could not help their young with the economic burden of setting up a farm. In spite of this attrition rate, the Amish growth rate is stable. Most dropouts from the Old-Order Amish join a more progressive Amish or Mennonite church. Differences over the interpretation of Ordnung (rules) and the influence of proselytizing fundamentalist groups have fragmented some of the Amish into progressive and orthodox factions.

The destruction of natural isolation by industrialization and rapid social changes has greatly affected the Amish, as it has other rural communities. The Amish response to rapid change has been further withdrawal from the mainstream culture. Their desire is not to be more different from non-Amish neighbors, but simply not to change so rapidly. They foresaw that their family and church communities could be overwhelmed by wholesale technological changes, large-scale enterprises, and concentrations of power for reasons of convenience and efficiency. Compulsory conscription, federal old-age insurance programs, consolidation of elementary schools, and the extension of compulsory attendance into the high school years all posed specific threats to their communities. Although these threats have been tempered or resolved in recent years, in every instance some of the Amish suffered the consequences by paying fines, serving time in prison, or moving to other localities. The Amish will support the state with their taxes, rarely with their vote, and never with their lives. They hold that Christian brotherhood requires members to care for their own. Their rules forbid them to serve in the military, accept any government subsidy or old-age insurance, or attend schools that do not teach the cultivation of humility, simplicity, and the fear of God.

When the population in the United States was primarily rural and the major occupation was farming, the Amish had no real objections to public schooling, and considered some mixing with non-Amish children desirable. The method of learning (by oral means and by example) was consistent with Amish culture, and the basic skills—singing, memory work, and Bible reading—were relevant to their way of life. Amish schools originated in response to state consolidation of public schools, for the most part since 1940. Today the Amish have over 425 one- and two-room schools that emphasize the basic skills, shared rather than individual knowledge, and the dignity of tradition rather than the

importance of progress. Amish schools do not formally teach religious doctrine but support a style of living taught in the home and community. In 1972 the U.S. Supreme Court ruled in *Wisconsin* v. *Yoder* that compulsory school-attendance laws that compelled Amish children to attend school beyond the elementary grades violated their religious rights. The court held that the Amish did not pose a threat to the public safety, peace, or order and that their way of life did not materially detract from the welfare of society.

Most theories of survival have assumed that once the peasantlike energy of the Amish tradition was exhausted, the society would be absorbed. This has not occurred. The Amish have increased from approximately 5,000 in 1900 to about 80,000 today. Aside from a high rate of fertility and a tradition that is voluntarily accepted by the members, there are certain adaptive strategies that serve them well. The notion that the Amish do not change or unilaterally resist changes from the outside is not true. The Amish will gradually accept changes that do not threaten the social bond, but they will not permit technology and convenience to dictate their family and community life. Their solution is one of balance between convenience and old-fashioned work, between technology and community self-realization. They see no inconsistency in using magic markers for writing but driving a horse and buggy, in using a pay telephone but not having telephones in their homes, or riding in but not owning an automobile. The rules that forbid members from having electricity mean that electrical conveniences from clothes dryers to toasters are not available to them. In many ways the Amish culture is oral rather than literary, which helps to explain why they maintain limited isolation is spite of mass communication systems. The Amish forbid radio and television in their homes and schools. Their way of life is so far outside the mainstream of American culture that shared knowledge with outsiders is limited.

In some regions, notably in Lancaster County, the Amish have become the unwilling attraction of a multi-million-dollar tourist industry. Tourist enterprises offer the Amish landscape to travelers as a scarce commodity, a living museum, and a quaint sideshow. This activity, together with a change of mood in the larger society whereby the Amish are romanticized and given celebrity status, poses a new problem but apparently no threat to their survival.

Bibliography
For general treatments see John A. Hostetler, *Amish Society* (Baltimore, 1968); and Calvin G. Bachman, *The Old Order Amish of Lancaster County* (Norristown, Pa., 1961). For an account of child training and family life, see John A. Hostetler and Gertrude E. Huntington, *Children in Amish Society* (New York, 1971). Other aspects of Amish society and culture are treated in Albert Keim, *Compulsory Education and the Amish* (Boston, 1975); Phyllis Haders, *Amish Quilt Designs and Patterns* (Clinton, N.J., 1976); and Victor A. McKusick, *Medical-Genetic Studies of the Amish* (Baltimore, 1978).

JOHN A. HOSTETLER

ANGLO-AMERICAN

This term commonly refers to Americans of British ancestry or background. Occasionally it is applied to any American who is not black, Asian, or Spanish-speaking. In areas of the United States where there are large numbers of American Indians or Spanish-speaking persons the term Anglo is often used to designate inhab-itants who speak English and are not black, Indian, mestizo, or mulatto. The meaning of the term tends to vary somewhat, depending on the context in which it is employed.

ANGLO-SAXON

Anglo-Saxon originally designated the descendants of the three Germanic tribal groups that invaded and won control of England in the 5th and 6th centuries—the Angles, the Saxons, and the Jutes. Now the term is used more broadly to describe any person of English ancestry.

In Great Britain and the United States in the 19th century, theories about the unique capacity of the "Anglo-Saxon race" for self-government gained widespread currency—a loose concept depending on national character rather than on genetically derived traits. By the end of the century, however, the notion of a genetically distinct and superior Anglo-Saxon race was widely accepted in American scientific circles and became an important weapon in the arsenal of those who fought to restrict immigration; earlier immigrants, it was argued, had blended smoothly into American society because they were predominantly Anglo-Saxon, Nordic, or Teutonic. The new immigrants from eastern and southern Europe were regarded as unassimilable because they were of Alpine or Mediterranean stock. In recent decades these racial theories have lost all scientific respectability, and the term Anglo-Saxon has fallen into general disuse except as part of the epithet WASP (White Anglo-Saxon Protestant).

APACHES, EASTERN: *see* AMERICAN INDIANS

APACHES, WESTERN: *see* AMERICAN INDIANS

APPALACHIANS

In recent decades several million migrants from rural Appalachia have made their way to urban centers, mainly in the Midwest and the South. In adjusting to urban life they have had problems similar to those of earlier immigrants from other lands. The city people among whom they have come to live have to some extent imposed a group identity upon them. Many are regarded as "hillbillies" or "briars." Appalachians lack the church organizations, distinct language, and racial characteristics that often define an ethnic group. What group consciousness they have comes from their distinctive kinship system, religion, dialect, and music. Their group identity is only partial, but they are very often perceived as a group.

The Appalachian Mountains stretch from Quebec to Georgia; the Appalachian Regional Development Act of 1965, as amended, established the boundaries of the Appalachian Region as including 397 counties in 13 states from New York to Mississippi, with an estimated population in 1975 of about 19 million people. But only the central and southern highlands, extending more than 600 miles diagonally across Maryland, West Virginia, Virginia, Kentucky, North and South Carolina, Tennessee, Georgia, and Alabama, are commonly meant by the term Appalachia.

Southern Appalachia was initially colonized by English, Scotch-Irish, and German immigrants or their de-

scendants from Pennsylvania, the Carolinas, and eastern Virginia, who settled among small groups of Cherokees and other American Indians. Slaves, though few, were present, and a number of small groups of mixed origin, called Melungeons or Guineas, lived in isolated areas. Although the region has been romanticized by missionaries and local-color writers as an "arrested frontier," it has never been as isolated as is popularly believed. Subsistence agriculture supported a rural culture that stressed freedom, democratic values, and fundamentalist Protestantism, as was the case throughout the nonplantation South, but race was less of an issue. The nation's first abolitionist newspaper, Elihu Embree's *Emancipator*, was founded in the Tennessee mountains in 1819. There were considerable abolitionist and, during the Civil War, Union sympathies throughout the mountains, which survive in many areas today as a strong Republican tradition. The family was the most important social unit and remains so among the rural population despite the changes wrought by industrialization.

Religion remains an important component of Appalachian culture. Fundamentalist Protestant beliefs are widely held, although church membership is below national norms. The largest denomination by far is the Southern Baptists (around 40 percent of church members), followed by Methodists (some 20 percent), and Presbyterians as a distant third (around 5 percent). In the more isolated rural areas, small sects, including various Holiness and old-time Baptist groups, flourish.

Appalachia can be viewed as a heterogeneous set of rural fringes peripheral to such cities as Pittsburgh and Atlanta, where the economic decisions affecting its population and resources are made. The region has also been treated as something of an internal colony, whose resources are exploited with little benefit to the local population. Railroads opened up the mountains for extraction of timber, oil, and gas in the late 19th century, and chemical and textile production became important industries, but coal mining in the Allegheny and Cumberland plateaus had the greatest impact. Between 1870 and 1930 mining led to the concentration of much of the rural population in company towns, created a class-conscious industrial work force, intensified social stratification, and attracted new ethnic groups into the mountains. Although the region is commonly described as a reservoir of homogeneous Anglo-Americans, one study revealed that 34,400 of 53,000 new jobs in West Virginia mines between 1890 and 1910 were filled by immigrants from southern and eastern Europe. Later southern blacks also augmented the labor force: in southern West Virginia they constituted nearly a quarter of the mine workers in the 1920s.

In the 1930s the United Mine Workers of America succeeded in organizing the coalfields of southern Appalachia. Led by John L. Lewis, that union played a vital role in the creation of the Congress of Industrial Organization and of unions in the auto, steel, and rubber industries. Many of the emigrants from Appalachia brought with them a strong commitment to unions as they moved to industrial cities north of the Ohio River in the 1940s and 1950s.

The decline of the coal industry in the 1950s, resulting from the use of diesel fuel for the railroads and the growing popularity of other fuels for home heating, led to mechanization and to the layoff of nearly 250,000 miners. Unemployment forced a huge emigration from Appalachia. West Virginia, for example, lost 75,000 mining jobs in the 1950s and nearly a half-million people. Although the population of some portions of Appalachia, such as the Georgia mountains near Atlanta, continued to grow, heavy emigration from other parts of the region (totaling some 1.6 million net loss through migration in the 1950s—16 percent of the 1950 population) kept the Appalachian population almost stationary in spite of considerable natural increase. Nearly half that total loss was accounted for by emigration from 26 coal-mining counties in the Allegheny and Cumberland plateaus. In the 1960s net migration loss fell to about 600,000, but natural increase also declined sharply, so the Appalachian population grew only 4.3 percent. Emigration from 1950 to 1970, then, had a profound impact both on the composition of the Appalachian population and on the cities to which the migrants moved.

MIGRATION AND RESETTLEMENT

Migration from the Appalachians is not a recent phenomenon. At various periods in the 19th century, people left the mountains of Kentucky, Tennessee, and the Carolinas and made their way to the Ozarks, southern Illinois, Texas, and Oklahoma. Another migration stream of long standing led from two sources in the southern Appalachians to areas of settlement in western Washington State, some 2,000 miles away. It began around 1880 in conjunction with the growth of the western timber industry, hit a peak between 1900 and 1917, and continues on a more moderate scale to this day. Except for the coal counties and urban areas, the southern Appalachians had a net emigration during the 1920s. During the Depression more people returned to the land than left it, and the region had a net immigration. The great emigration took place in the 1940s, 1950s, and to a lesser extent, the 1960s. During the 1970s the overall population in some counties grew for the first time in decades.

Millions of people from southern Appalachia (not less than 3 million, perhaps 6 to 8 million) now live outside the mountain region, mostly in the same cities chosen by the migrants during the last five or six decades. Atlanta, where 20 percent of all immigrants are white Appalachians from Georgia and Tennessee, has recently received the most, but the migrants to midwestern cities attract more attention. There the immigrants from the coal-mining counties of the Allegheny and Cumberland plateaus are sometimes the largest single source of new population. Migrants from eastern Kentucky gravitated to the Miami River Valley from Cincinnati to Dayton, Ohio. Approximately 80,000 first- and second-generation Appalachians live in Cincinnati, one of the first midwestern cities to attract an Appalachian population; they now constitute about 17 percent of the city's inhabitants. Industrial towns in the Miami Valley have received large numbers of Kentucky mountain people. In Middletown, Hamilton, and South Lebanon, Ohio, Appalachian migrants probably make up as much as 50, 60, and 95 percent, respectively, of the population. Migratory streams from northern West Virginia lead to Pittsburgh; other West Virginia Appalachians migrate to Cleveland (where they are 13 percent of the

population) and Columbus, Ohio (where they are 33 percent); smaller groups go to Washington, D.C., Baltimore, Indianapolis, Ind., Detroit, Chicago, and Los Angeles.

All these migratory streams have been sustained by kinship networks that produce a uniform settlement pattern. Often entire families migrate to the same city, neighborhood, and street where former neighbors and kin already live. These kinship networks link rural mountain communities with a variety of urban communities and are consequently a primary source of information and stability for Appalachian migrants. Family ties not only provide housing and jobs, but assist new arrivals in less tangible ways. Urban Appalachians are less apt to depend on welfare or voluntary organizations than are other low-income groups, because the extended family provides many of the necessary social services and bears much of the cost of relocation.

Social class origin affects residential location and many other aspects of the process of migration. Many higher-status Appalachians left the mountains a long time ago, taking their families with them and settling in small industrial towns and working-class suburbs, where they rather easily and quickly assimilated. The less-well-off frequently settled first with kin in urban slums such as Chicago's Uptown, Cleveland's Near West Side, East Dayton, or Cincinnati's Over-the-Rhine. Because many of them were literally economic refugees, forced to leave because of depression in the coal regions and subsistence farming areas, they arrived with no relevant vocational skills and have been especially vulnerable to economic recession. Many are still dependent on casual day labor, and perhaps one-third of the migrants still live in the slums. In Cincinnati, for example, Appalachians make up 65 percent of the slum population and 50 percent of the total unemployed, and they are reported to have the highest school dropout rate in the city. But the majority of urban Appalachians have achieved stable employment in industry, for the most part in unskilled and semiskilled jobs. In some manufacturing plants in the Cincinnati area, 75 percent of the work force is mountain born. Here also the family has cushioned the adjustment of inexperienced rural migrants to industrial work. Frequently, family members are employed at the same plant, and employers have found that kinship networks ensure a steady labor supply and that family sponsorship encourages labor discipline. Many of these workers were laid off in the 1950s and 1960s, but most of them subsequently acquired stable employment and promotions. Workers typically move from slum to working-class neighborhoods and then to often predominantly Appalachian suburbs. In recent years many Appalachians have completed college either in the mountains or in the cities; a sizable number are in white-collar occupations such as teaching.

ETHNIC COMMITMENT

Appalachia was simply a physiographic term until after the Civil War. Little distinguished the way of life there from frontier life generally. Southern Appalachia as a distinctive cultural region was invented in the mid-1870s by local-color writers who began to use the mountains as a setting for fiction and travel sketches published in popular magazines. Prolific writers on such mountain themes as conflicting Civil War loyalties, moonshining, and feuding included Mary N. Murfree, James Lane Allen, and John Fox, Jr. Educators and social reformers, in the meantime, described the southern Appalachian cultural region as a problem area deserving the attention of church home-mission boards and private philanthropic foundations. Leaders of this middle-class "uplift" movement, including William G. Frost, president of Berea College, and John C. Campbell, founder of the Conference of Southern Mountain Workers (later the Council of the Southern Mountains), were more interested in influencing private and public policy than in developing the people's identity as southern highlanders or Appalachian mountaineers.

Appalachians lack the characteristics of distinctive race, nationality, or religion that typically set apart ethnic groups in urban environments. Most are Anglo-Americans, but they remain in identifiable communities in many northern cities. Residential segregation determined by poverty and sustained by kinship-based settlement patterns encourages isolation. Hillbilly bars, restaurants, and tiny storefront Pentacostal churches dot the neighborhoods where they live. Although it is questionable whether the traditional Appalachian culture should be viewed as in any way distinct from that of the rest of the upland South extending through the Ozarks, a recognizable sociolinguistic pattern and shared folk traditions help to sustain a mountain identity, which is reinforced by frequent trips "down home." Participation in the kinship structure means that to some extent lower-class migrants are members simultaneously of a rural and an urban community. One study found that 20 percent of the city-dwelling mountain people who were interviewed would give up one-fifth of their current income if they could find jobs in Appalachia.

Hillbilly stereotypes cause some migrants to disavow their Appalachian origins, but they also function to pull the group together. Many Appalachians have felt the influence of such stereotypes, probably more often from public-service agencies than from employers. Appalachian migrants are also often assumed to be antisocial and delinquent by police and the courts.

A number of cities now have organizations to encourage the Appalachian population to participate more effectively in urban life. One of the most successful of these is the Urban Appalachian Council in Cincinnati, which approaches Appalachian problems as those of a minority ethnic group. It cooperates with organizations inside Appalachia, such as the Council of the Southern Mountains, on "down home" projects and with black groups on voter registration and community–police problems. The Appalachian Identity Center in Cincinnati tries to improve the Appalachians' self-image and to combat prejudice against hillbillies in the schools. Appalachians are becoming recognized as a distinct ethnic community in midwestern cities and are beginning to be felt as a political bloc.

Appalachian advocates build their programs on the work of John C. Campbell, who founded the Council of the Southern Mountains and its magazine, *Mountain Life & Work*, which began publication in 1925, to counteract stereotyped characters like Snuffy Smith, Li'l Abner, and the Beverly Hillbillies. Since the white Appalachian migrant with a steady job probably encoun-

ters few barriers to assimilation into the American mainstream, it is probably easier for him or her to assimilate than to maintain the Appalachian identity and struggle against the stereotypes it involves. For the majority of the region's people, Appalachian has never been as important a symbol of identity as family, community, county, or even state and nation. Still, the kinship system means that events down home as well as events in the cities may foster a sense of Appalachian ethnicity. Whether Appalachian ethnicity will become more important depends on its significance to Appalachians both in the southern mountains and in the cities.

Bibliography

The classic study of the Appalachian region is John C. Campbell, *The Southern Highlander and His Homeland* (1921; reprint, Lexington, Ky., 1969). A comprehensive academic treatment is Thomas R. Ford, ed., *The Southern Appalachian Region: A Survey* (Lexington, Ky., 1962). Harry M. Caudill, *Night Comes to the Cumberlands* (Boston, 1963), is a popular social history of eastern Kentucky. Interviews with Appalachians in the mountains and in the cities are found in Robert Coles, *Migrants, Sharecroppers, Mountaineers* (Boston, 1971), and *The South Goes North* (Boston, 1972); Kathy Kahn, *Hillbilly Women* (New York, 1972); Guy and Candie Carawan, *Voices from the Mountains* (New York, 1975); and Todd Gitlin and Nanci Hollander, *Uptown: Poor Whites in Chicago* (New York, 1970). A study over a 30-year period of the adaptation of migrants from a small community in eastern Kentucky to cities in Ohio is Harry K. Schwarzweller, James S. Brown, and J.J. Mangalam, *Mountain Families in Transition: A Case Study in Mountain Migration* (University Park, Pa., 1971).

The *Bibliography of Southern Appalachia*, compiled by Charlotte T. Ross (Boone, N.C., 1976), is a comprehensive listing of books and monographs. The best collection of materials on social and economic aspects of the region is in Morgantown at the West Virginia University Library, which also publishes a periodic *Appalachian Bibliography*, covering books, articles, and theses. The Berea College Library in Berea, Ky., has the best collection on regional literature and folk arts. The library of the Urban Appalachian Council in Cincinnati has a collection of material on Appalachian migrants in the cities. The best source of current demographic information is the Appalachian Regional Commission in Washington, D.C., which publishes the journal *Appalachia*.

DWIGHT BILLINGS AND DAVID WALLS

ARABS

Slightly more than 1 million Arabs—90 percent Christian and 10 percent Muslim—over half of them well assimilated third- and fourth-generation descendants of immigrants who arrived between 1875 and 1948, live in the United States. This estimate may be too high or too low, but it is reasonable in the absence of accurate data. It is known, however, that most of the Muslim Arabs, perhaps 90,000, have come to the United States since 1948.

Most of the original Arab immigrants were Christians from the Syrian province of the Ottoman Empire that included the semiautonomous administrative district of Mt. Lebanon, the coastal mountain range between the Syrian port cities of Beirut and Tripoli. They were likely to call themselves Syrians (the independent parliamentary republic of Lebanon was not established until 1946) and tended to identify themselves in terms of their region, village of origin, or religious preference. They were not called Arabs, a term that has become familiar only in recent years. Most of the more recent Arab immigrants are Muslims from independent and often rival Arab states; in contrast to the earlier immigrants, they are frequently ardent Arab nationalists.

Christian and Muslim Arabs share a common heritage, but they are far from unified. Deeply rooted religious and sectarian beliefs as well as politics divide them in the United States as they do in their homelands, but at the same time an overarching Arab-American identity has begun to take shape. The Arab-American movement is little more than a decade old. Before the mid-1960s, and even now in some households, pre–World War II immigrants and their descendants were more comfortable with the designation Syrian or Lebanese American. Interest in their Arab heritage has been awakened by the presence of Arab nationalists, indignation over U.S. foreign policy in the Middle East, objections to the unfavorable Arab image in the U.S. press, and the general contemporary interest in ethnicity.

Nomenclature is one problem; statistics is another. Official statistics are clearly distorted. In immigration records until 1899 and in census records until 1920, all Arabs were recorded, together with Turks, Armenians, and others, under "Turkey in Asia." After 1920 the increase in their numbers warranted the separate classification "Syria," but religious differences were not noted. Official records have been slow to keep up with political changes; until relatively recently, for example, non-Syrian Arabs might be counted as "other Asian" and North African Arabs as "other African." Since 1948 the Palestinians, who account for much of the post–World War II Arab immigration, have been designated simply as refugees, or as from Palestine or Israel, or as nationals of the country of their last residence.

HISTORICAL BACKGROUND

Propelled by the fervor of a new religion, Arabs rode out of their homeland in the 7th century and in about 100 years conquered territory from Central Asia through North Africa to Spain. These Arabs were Muslim; their religion, Islam, meaning submission to one God, was revealed to the Arab prophet Mohammed in the Arabian peninsula. His revelations provided the believers with the *Quran* (Koran), a text that became one of the bases for the immutable holy law that governs every activity in the lives of its adherents. In Islam as in Judaism (and in Christianity before the Reformation), religion, politics, and society were inseparably linked. Many of its basic tenets also resemble those of Judaism and Christianity, to which it is loosely tied. But the unity of religion and society as it was envisioned by the Prophet was short-lived. Thirty years after Mohammed's death, schism resulted from a problem of succession. The Muslims first split into two sects—Sunnis and Shiites; other heterodoxies developed subsequently.

Relations between the ruling Muslim majority and religious minorities among the indigenous populations of the lands they conquered were based upon the belief that Mohammed was the last in a long line of messengers of God that included both Moses and Jesus. As followers of these honored, if lesser, prophets, Christians and Jews enjoyed a wide measure of toleration under the jurisdiction of their own religious hierarchies, although their communities were more heavily taxed as the price they paid for protection by the Muslim army.

One of the great civilizations, Islam in the Middle Ages exerted an intellectual ascendancy unmatched in

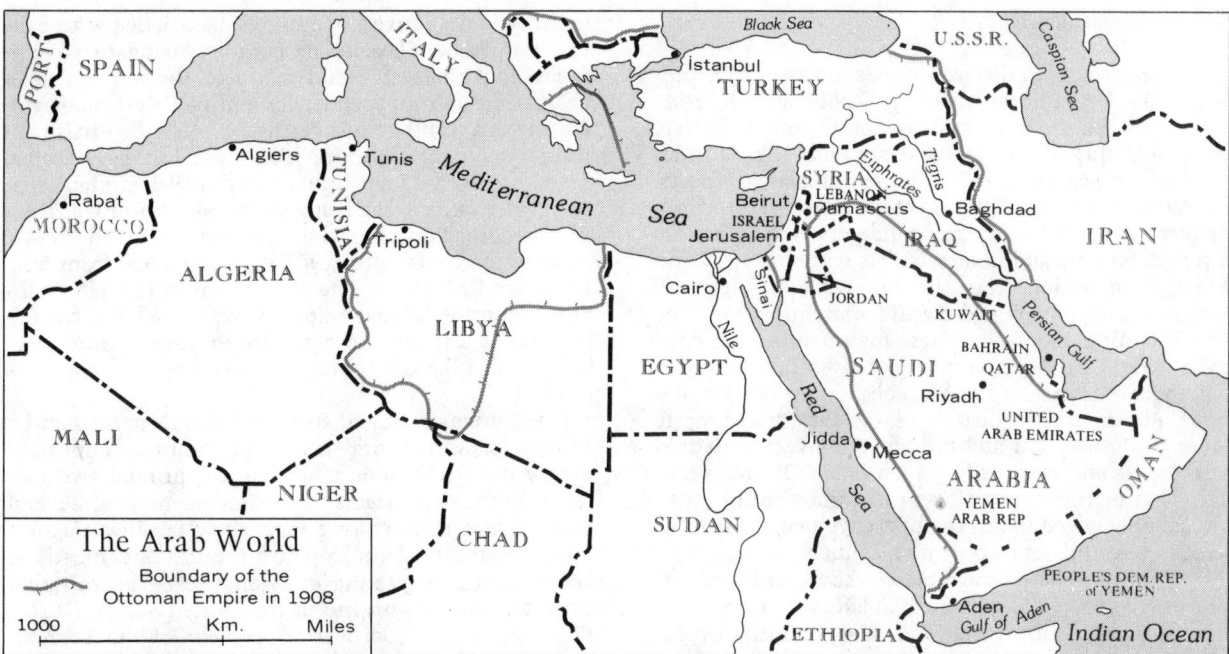

The Arab World

Boundary of the Ottoman Empire in 1908

1000   Km.   Miles

Europe until the Renaissance. Its decline in subsequent centuries followed cycles of conquest, internal disintegration, and regeneration. The last Islamic empire was ruled by Ottoman Turks for 400 years before its fall in 1918.

The modern Arab world encompasses Algeria, Bahrain, Egypt, Iraq, Jordan, Kuwait, Lebanon, Libya, Morocco, Oman, Palestine, the People's Democratic Republic of Yemen, Qatar, Saudi Arabia, Syria, Tunisia, the United Arab Emirates, and the Yemen Arab Republic. Although most Arab Americans are descendants of Syrian immigrants, all these countries are represented in the Arab-American population, including several thousand who are in the diaspora from Palestine, now the State of Israel.

To speak of the Arab world, however, implies a cultural unity that ignores a number of cleavages created by differences in geography and history. Mountains and deserts have contributed to the perpetuation of particularisms and parochialisms, particularly in Mt. Lebanon where oppressed heterodoxies had historically sought refuge during periods of religious conflict. The Arab lands lie at the crossroads of major trade routes between East and West and their great commercial cities have been conquered by imperial armies since biblical times. The discovery in the Middle East in the 20th century of the world's largest reserves of oil added another dimension both to Arab politics and to the strategic importance of Arab lands.

Christian sects abound in the Arab world. Conquering Muslims found several rival sects around the Mediterranean; still other sects, differing in both doctrine and rite, came later. Most of these are in Syria and Lebanon; there is a sizable Coptic Christian minority in Egypt. Relations are further complicated by the affiliation of Maronites, Melkites, and Syrian (Jacobite) and Chaldean Catholics with the Roman Catholic Church and by the antipathy of the scattered Eastern Orthodox community and the small Protestant group to Rome.

(See also Copts; Eastern Catholics; Eastern Orthodox; Muslims.)

When Arabs today discuss the golden age of Arab culture, Muslims tend to emphasize its Islamic content, Christians its Arab. Both date the eclipse of Arab power to the period of Ottoman Turkish rule, but Muslims are apt to attribute it to Western Christian influences inimical to Islam, while Christians may explain it in terms of the poverty and stagnation that centuries of Muslim Ottoman domination produced.

The tradition of accommodation between Muslims and Christians was severely disrupted in the 19th century. European powers competed for influence in the tottering Ottoman Empire by exploiting the loyalties and interests of the various Christian sects. In Syria the French supported the Maronites and the Melkites; the Russians supported the Eastern Orthodox; and England vacillated between the Christians and the semi-Islamic Druses as its interests dictated. France encouraged a Maronite dream of political dominance in Lebanon and alienated Muslims, Druses, and the Orthodox Christians who tended, then as now, to support the Muslims in politics. In Egypt, England's support of the Copts antagonized the Muslim majority. European interference generated hostility between Muslim and Christian and exacerbated factionalism among the rival Christian sects. Their higher social and economic status led the Western-supported Christians to treat the already embittered Muslims with arrogance.

American influence during this period was solely educational. American Protestants opened numerous schools in Mt. Lebanon and Syria where they taught at least the rudiments of Arabic and English to a significant number of boys and girls and provided food and medical assistance in periods of strife. Of most lasting importance, they established the Syrian Protestant College (later the American University in Beirut) whose numerous graduates went on to make valuable contributions to modern Arab life and thought.

EARLY IMMIGRATION

The first Arabs to discover the economic opportunities in the United States were probably the Christian tradesmen who, encouraged by the Ottoman Sultan, came to exhibit Syrian wares at the Philadelphia International Exposition in 1876. Their enthusiastic reports, the activities of steamship agents recruiting labor from all over the world for American industry, and the efforts of native brokers and moneylenders combined to begin a chain emigration from the Mt. Lebanon area, the source of most pre–World War II Syrian migration. The overwhelming majority of these mountain-village emigrants were Christians pursuing economic interests.

In the late 19th century, Mt. Lebanon was an autonomous administrative district of the Ottoman Empire under the protection and influence of Western Christian powers and governed by a Christian Ottoman official. This district, according to historian Philip Hitti, was acknowledged to be "the best governed, most prosperous, peaceful and contented country in the Near East." Some residents migrated to escape military service which after 1908 became mandatory for Christians as well as Muslims under the new Turkish revolutionary government. Fear that they would be unable to maintain their Islamic traditions in a Western Christian society discouraged a mass migration of Muslims to the United States. Fragmentary data suggest that only a few hundred young Muslim men joined the Christian emigrants between 1900 and 1914, most of them after 1908.

The pioneers reported their success in letters home and demonstrated it in the amount of money they sent or in their ostentatious behavior if they went back to visit. The evidence attracted so many emigrants that before the turn of the century an entrepreneurial network of independent services developed to assist villagers along the stages of their journey. The operation of the network throughout most of the early period encouraged still more migration.

Adventurous bachelors were soon followed by married men and families. Some were small tradesmen, artisans, and skilled laborers, but most were off the land—owners of small, scattered holdings, tenant farmers, or laborers. Only a handful were intellectuals or professionals. With few exceptions, they came hoping to make a quick profit and return home to enjoy the status and privileges that money would bring; they were not leaving to escape religious or political persecution or economic oppression. Most of them were poor but not destitute. Emigration was generally a family venture and was financed by family resources. It was considered an investment whose return would be both wealth and prestige when the emigrant returned to his native village. Later, relatives already in the United States often paid for the trip.

Despite their unreliability, official immigration records are useful in revealing trends and characteristics of the Syrian migration. Immigration increased dramatically each year, from a few hundred in 1887 to over 4,000 in 1898; it rose to over 9,000 in 1913, but dropped sharply as a result of World War I. Immigration rose again briefly, partly in anticipation of the restrictive Immigration Act of 1924; the threat of restriction hastened the migration or reentry of Syrians with their families and relatives, of émigrés dissatisfied with British and French League of Nations mandate governments that had been established after the war instead of promised Arab independence, and of Palestinians migrating as a result of bitter struggles with the British authority over the influx of Jews from Europe who had been promised a Jewish homeland in Palestinian territory. Restrictions, the Depression, and World War II severely curbed immigration between 1925 and 1948. Arab immigration after 1945 included a few from Iraq, Egypt, and Morocco. The records show 115,535 Arabs arriving in the United States through 1948, but the figure is only a rough approximation resulting from inaccurate recordkeeping, illegal entries, and other sources of error.

Few Syrians returned to their villages permanently. Family commitments, economic failures, and temporary dissatisfactions produced a continual two-way traffic, though villagers sometimes remained several years before reemigrating with their families. Figures for 1908–1910 show a 25-percent return rate, mostly of single males, suggesting individual restlessness rather than discontent with life in the United States. During the depressed 1930s over 60 percent of the approximately 1,500 arrivals left for home or elsewhere.

From 1899 to 1915 women composed about 47 percent of the Arab total; they, too, came to acquire wealth, join spouses, or increase their chances for marriage as villages emptied of single men. Despite their arrival, family, sect, and village traditions still compelled many men to seek wives in the homeland. In the twenties, when a sense of permanence set in, the women immigrants outnumbered the men. Throughout the period of immigration, up to 75 percent of the Syrian immigrants were between the ages of 15 and 45. The 44-percent illiteracy rate before 1910 reflected their humble origins; by the twenties it had dropped to 21 percent.

Arab traits and values hinge on the central position held by the extended family in Arab society. The enhancement of family honor and status is an inviolable trust for its members; in return for protection, identity, and status, the family demands conformity and the subordination of individual will and interests. The honor or dishonor of an individual reflects on the entire family.

Noble ancestry, a claim few families can credibly make, has been supplanted in the United States by wealth as the basis for status and honor. Although money alone does not confer distinction on a family, it increases the ability of family members to manifest values—magnanimity, munificence, generosity, and hospitality—which even the poorest families cherish. Since in the structure of Arab society family honor is intricately entwined with loyalty to religion, sect, village, and even quarter, individual loyalty must extend to those as well. This system of values breeds family and group ties with strong clannish and factional tendencies. The determination to elevate and defend family honor and status produces a competitive spirit and an ethic of hard work, thrift, perseverance, shrewdness, and conservatism. The fear of shame restrains crime and indigence. Given the economic opportunities and the system of values in the United States, Syrians readily became success-oriented free-enterprisers. No two

more dissimilar molds could have produced more similar products.

ECONOMIC LIFE

Peddling was not a common occupation for Syrian Arabs; in the homeland it was left to minorities like Greeks, Armenians, and Jews. But before 1914 at least 90 percent of the immigrants, including women and children, took up the trade in the United States, if only for a short time. Peddling yielded good profits and required little training, capital, or English. The immigrants were not deluded about its hardships, but they preferred its independence to the drudgery of the factory and the isolation of the farm. Peddling drew young men and women from villages in groups of up to 60 or more, allowing the network of transit services to be formed and stimulating a Syrian industry of manufacturers, importers, and wholesalers to supply their needs. Those who did not peddle, or who tried and found its hardships intolerable, turned to work in mills and factories. A very few farmed or homesteaded in the West.

The transit network began in the homeland, but had its base in the new country in a peddling settlement clustered around a supplier, usually an enterprising veteran peddler. The port community of New York was the mother of peddling communities and their major supplier, but by 1900 Syrian peddlers had penetrated the remotest parts of the nation, from where suppliers, sometimes two or more in a town, recruited fellow villagers or attracted others. This proliferation of peddling settlements distributed Syrians throughout the United States; it also spared new arrivals the anxiety of finding work, since they could immediately be absorbed somewhere in the constantly expanding system.

Peddling was initially a trade in rosaries, jewelry, and notions that would fit into a small case. It soon expanded into suitcases filled with a wide range of dry goods from bed linens to lace—almost anything that an isolated farmer's wife or housebound city dweller might want to buy. Horses, wagons, and later automobiles allowed some peddlers to sell imported rugs and linens supplied by international traders in New York's Syrian community. By frugality, resourcefulness, long hours of work, and charging all that the market would bear, peddlers commonly calculated earnings into the thousands annually. Relatively few failed.

Syrian peddlers developed a network of routes from New York to California and from Maine to Texas. The more enterprising and determined, including a few women, remained on the road for weeks or months at a time, covering several states. Others concentrated on a single area. Most women, children, and old people remained within range of the settlement to which they returned in the evening. In addition to peddling, many women crocheted, embroidered, and sewed goods at home for their menfolk to sell, or worked in kimono or garment factories, sometimes also owned by Syrians. They generally continued this economic partnership through the various stages along the family's route to prosperity.

Suppliers were important figures in the early period. As businessman, leader, and often founder of a settlement, a supplier served many functions. He attracted and sometimes recruited peddlers, supplied them (frequently on credit), organized their routes, banked their savings, mediated between them and local authorities, rented them the crowded and poorly furnished quarters suited to their itinerancy, frugality, and temporary status, and involved himself in their social life and communal welfare. Supplier and peddler formed an interdependent relationship firmly based on canons of tradition that validated the supplier's leadership and limited his excesses. No special title attached to him nor was abject obedience demanded. If the peddler disagreed with him the supplier's prestige and income were both at risk, and he frequently made concessions. The supplier's territory was the peddler's economic base and a refuge made up of relatives and friends. Since the peddler joined the group voluntarily, he could also leave when his personal and material objectives were better served elsewhere. He might join other villagers in more lucrative areas or establish his own supply store or other business.

Peddling hastened acculturation and in the process contributed to its own obsolescence. Peddlers accumulated capital, learned English quickly, and through constant contact with native-born Americans acquired new values, including the notion of settling permanently in the United States. When Syrians settled down the majority opened family businesses in cities or smaller towns. Dry goods and grocery stores were the most common, but businesses ran the gamut. Numerous Syrian publications reflect the pride Syrians still take in "being in business."

Meanwhile, Muslim Arabs were also arriving, though in far smaller numbers. Higher industrial wages in the United States after 1910 attracted them to such industrial cities as Chicago, Toledo, and Dearborn, Mich., although industrial labor usually proved to be a transitory occupation for the Muslims as well as for the Christians. When adjustment and capital were sufficient they generally turned to other pursuits.

SETTLEMENTS

From 1910 through 1930, according to census records, over 88 percent of the Syrians lived in or near urban centers, almost half of them on the East Coast. Of the remainder, about 2 percent farmed and the rest were businessmen in small towns or rural areas. New York, the first and the leading business, cultural, and intellectual center for Syrians until well after 1948, sheltered about 2,600 in Manhattan and Brooklyn in 1904; 7,631 in 1930. Only Boston's 3,150 Syrians came close to this number in the early years, but Detroit's colony increased from 417 in 1910 to 5,520 in 1930. Today Greater Detroit, with over 70,000 Arabs, is the largest Arab-American community in the United States.

Syrian-American settlements were modeled on community life in the homeland and reflected the traditional, relatively homogeneous grouping by religion, sect, or village. Its leaders were more apt to be drawn from the most experienced and enterprising than from the high-born. The community served in the first place to ease the adjustment for newcomers; migrants subsequently moved in and out of it as their interests required. In both the cities and the remoter settlements, Syrian village life and values were maintained to some extent. The large communities were often noisy and congested; coffeehouses, stores, and restaurants sup-

plied from New York provided traditional fare. Celebrations and quarrels alike often spilled into the streets.

Unlike the post-1948 Arabs, the Syrians had relatively smooth relations with other Americans. Hostility toward them was neither specific nor sustained and Syrians were only dimly aware of it. They were more sectarian than nationalistic and their population small and dispersed, and this also made them inconspicuous. Driven by economic ambition, they also began rather early to imitate their neighbors and to seek their approval. They became citizens, bought homes, and followed the middle-class course out of old neighborhoods into better ones and ultimately into the suburbs. The process was slower among the few Arab industrial laborers and other wage earners.

RELIGIOUS INSTITUTIONS

A sense of permanence in the Syrian community was signaled first by the establishment of communal institutions—places of worship, newspapers, and associations. Leadership in founding these institutions was assumed by the more enterprising and prosperous men and women in both Christian and Muslim communities.

The first Syrian migration had not included clergy. Their passage was arranged by lay leaders who had already organized the churches and mosques; thus the clergy's dependence on and answerability to these leaders was conditioned even before they arrived. Often overzealous and poorly educated, the immigrant clergy helped transplant sectarian and religious factionalism to the New World.

Founding Eastern-rite churches whose masses would be conducted in Arabic or Syriac was the first concern of the Christian Syrians. The first churches—one Melkite, one Maronite, and one Orthodox—were built in New York between 1890 and 1895. By the early 1920s approximately 75 churches of one or another of the three sects were scattered through 28 states. But more than half of them were in the East, leaving vast areas unserved by a Syrian Eastern-rite church; many communities went more than a generation without one. Some regularly attended other churches; some awaited the sporadic visits of itinerant priests for important ceremonies; some succumbed to the temptation of belonging to churches they considered American—both Roman Catholic and Protestant—draining away adherents of each sect in sufficient numbers to alarm its leaders. They responded by Americanizing several aspects of the service and in the process inadvertently promoted assimilation by diluting the distinction between themselves and the "American" churches.

Defending their traditions against acculturation pressures was much more difficult for the Muslims than for the Christians. Although Muslims have no priesthood and can pray in any ritually uncontaminated space, the mosque and its prayer leader (imam) are central to Muslim religious practice and a symbol of community unity. A Muslim working and living in a non-Muslim society has to make essential religious compromises: it is not usually possible to observe the Sabbath on Friday, pray five times a day, and fast during the sunlight hours of the holy month of Ramadan. Clues to the effect of American society on a Muslim group are provided by

a small community established near Ross, N.Dak., around 1900. Before a mosque was built in the 1920s, prayer and ritual were conducted in private houses and led by the best informed among the group. Without a mosque for almost 30 years and without any cultural reinforcement from newcomers, the Muslims rapidly lost the use of Arabic, assumed Christian names, and married non-Muslims. The community dwindled as children moved away, and the mosque was abandoned by 1948. Elsewhere the sparse and scattered Muslim communities rarely even built mosques; only three are known to have been constructed in the twenties.

THE PRESS, CULTURE, AND ETHNIC ORGANIZATIONS

The first Arabic newspaper was published in New York in 1892; by 1907 there were seven daily or weekly competitors; by 1920 that number doubled, and numerous other periodicals were in circulation as well. The impetus was provided by a few Syrian immigrant intellectuals influenced by a literary revival led by Syrians in Egypt. Competition was keen, the quality mixed, and the papers often short-lived. The most durable and influential was *al-Hoda* (The Enlightener), which began in 1898 and was the organ of the Maronites, followed by the Orthodox *Mirat al-Gharb* (Mirror of the West) in 1899 and the Druse *al-Bayan* (The News) in 1910. Established from the start on a sectarian basis, the Arabic press did nothing to discourage community fragmentation. Its editors published news and opinion on events in the homeland and in the United States, social news, literature and literary criticism, and encouraged good citizenship. Textbooks for learning English, American customs, and procedures for naturalization were also published.

The decline in both the number and quality of Arabic publications between the wars reflected the ignorance of Arabic language among the descendants of Syrian immigrants. Attempts to teach Arabic to children at home and in private schools competed unsuccessfully with the Americanization process. The number of Arabic readers was also diminished by restrictive immigration laws and political stability in the homeland. Too few immigrants came, and the Syrian Americans turned their attention to domestic news. Arabic newspapers also lost their intellectual quality. They had to compete in style and technology with the American press and simplify their language for readers whose lack of facility in Arabic required an easy, clear journalistic style.

By the mid-1920s the editors who had earlier contributed to the acceleration of Americanization began pressing for a revival of the community's ethnic consciousness, but with little success. The all-English journal *Syrian World*, founded by *al-Hoda* in 1926 for that purpose, lasted about six years. English predominated in the ethnic press, whose content and transience both indicated a diminished awareness of the Arab heritage.

The Syrian literati influenced by European and American free verse, who were active in New York before 1914 had little influence on Syrians in the United States, notwithstanding the revolutionary effect they had on literature in the Arab world. Syrian Americans had little appreciation for Arabic literature. Its content was so alien to their experience that hardly a single name from this prolific literary group is known to them. Gibran Khalil Gibran (1883–1931) is the only

exception, and even his works were introduced to most Syrians by the non-Arab Americans who popularized them. Concerned primarily with the impact of their innovations on general Arab literature, this literary elite failed in the United States to preserve or transmit any work of lasting ethnic social or cultural significance. The works of a few talented American authors of Syrian descent such as William Blatty (1928–) and Vance Bourjaily (1922–) reflect little or no influence either of their Arab predecessors or of their ethnic origins.

Early ethnic organizations formed around the religious sects. They built places of worship, buried the dead, and helped the needy. In time, others were formed to maintain sectarian solidarity, promote American patriotic ideals and citizenship, further understanding between Syrians and other Americans, and make philanthropic contributions to benefit their respective ancestral villages. With the exception of an influential Maronite group founded just before World War I to support a French-backed Maronite-dominated Lebanon, homeland politics were not reflected in Syrian-American organizations until after 1948. Whatever their other aims, the paramount objective of all these societies was perpetuation of the group, mainly through in-group marriage. To arrest the growing drift of youth away from it, parents and priests sponsored local, and later regional, family, village, and sectarian organizations.

Syrians had such a propensity for organizing that at any given time the number of organizations was out of all proportion to the number of Syrians in the population. Their fondness for organization reflected their factional tendencies and slowed the erosion of group solidarity and traditional values in the United States. Their contributions made possible the building of numerous churches, orphanages, hospitals, and schools in the homeland. They did not establish comparable charitable or educational institutions in the United States, although individual Arabs have contributed generously to American philanthropic causes.

The early Syrian organizations were not political in purpose but neither were they immune to political vicissitudes in the homeland. When in 1920 Greater Lebanon was created by the pro-Maronite French mandatory government from Mt. Lebanon and land belonging to Syria proper, many non-Maronite immigrants from the incorporated Syrian areas refused to use the term Lebanese. The controversy over whether organizations should be called Syrian-American, Lebanese-American, or both, subsided only when Lebanon and Syria achieved full independence after World War II.

Unification of the Syrian community was attempted in 1932 when a regional federation of local organizations was formed in Boston. By that time leadership had passed to the American-born, English-speaking generation who were less sectarian in their interests and who hoped to transcend the divisions perpetuated by their elders. Although hampered by the depression and by internal conflicts, the Eastern Federation was successful enough to inspire other regional federations. They sponsored social activities, provided scholarships, and sought to improve relations between Syrian Americans and others. Aside from some interest in Arabic food, music, and dance, little Arab ethnic heritage was apparent in these organizations. The degree to which Americanization had overtaken their institutions ex-

plains in part why Syrian Americans were so slow to comprehend the significance of the Arab political and social issues that so preoccupied the post-1948 arrivals. Even when they did, it was primarily as Americans and only secondarily as Arabs.

GROUP MAINTENANCE

The breakdown of the patriarchal, extended family into nuclear units and the reduction in the father's authority were the first effects of immigration on Arab family life. Long hours, even days, away from home, peddling or minding the store, and the participation of wives in the family business weakened the paternal authority. The father lost ground as a disciplinarian, although he retained the respect due him as head of the family. American influence, education, and economic opportunities might impel sons to establish their own households when they married, but sentimental attachments and concern for the welfare of the family still tied the various units together.

The energy that women devoted to the economic goals of the family gradually freed them from some Old World customs. Muslim women usually abandoned the veil when they emigrated. Covering the head, a custom common to both Christian and Muslim women, was also soon abandoned except by the most traditional-minded. Working wives and mothers did not relinquish their domestic roles, but they adjusted to necessity by having fewer children, cooking fewer time-consuming Arabic meals, and gradually adopting the custom of prearranged social visits.

Their labors helped build and support churches and kept the youth within the group. Their independence ended some time-honored traditions: by World War II the segregation of sexes at social gatherings in homes and churches had vanished except in mosques and among the most traditional Muslims. Later marriages and unarranged ones became the rule; daughters were allowed to remain single if they wished, and the preference for male children lost much of its force.

Any hope for keeping marriage within the ethnic, religious, sectarian, or regional group was thwarted in the earliest years by a shortage of Syrian women, attendance at non-Syrian churches, and desire for acceptance in the larger American society. Interethnic, though not interreligious, marriages were sufficiently common to elicit admonitions against them in the Arabic press before 1914. An increase in the number of immigrant Syrian women, churches, and associations slowed the trend but did not entirely reverse it. Both convention and religion allowed men greater latitude than women in the choice of spouses. Until World War II unmarried women usually remained under the surveillance of the family, and their choices were carefully controlled and arranged to serve its interests. Women were expected to adhere to the faith of their husbands; if they married outside the sect they and their children would be lost to it. Marriage was consequently a frequent source of conflict between the immigrant and the next generation. The children yearned for the aspects of American middle-class life that they had been exposed to through school, movies, radio, and military service. Marriage was for many an escape from parental authority; a non-Arab marriage presented itself as a solution to the dilemma of living in two cultures. Only occasionally did

interethnic marriage result in permanent rupture in family relationships, however, and by the 1950s it was in any case so commonplace, especially among returning servicemen, that it ceased to be a major source of contention.

Marriage for the few Muslim Arabs posed more serious problems. In the early years women were few, and departure from custom, which had the force of holy law behind it, was attended with greater concern. The traditional-minded initially sought spouses in the homeland, but eventually the rate of interethnic (which for Muslims also meant interfaith) marriages among them increased as well. Beginning in the mid-sixties it soared among the professional and educated classes of both religious groups.

The attempts of the immigrant generation to maintain Arab culture ran afoul of their eagerness to succeed in the United States; the requirements of success relegated tradition to second place. Immigration restrictions after 1924 encouraged assimilation and prepared the way for the gap that developed between the descendants of the early immigrants and the culture-conscious Arabs of more recent times. The participation of the early immigrants in American life was somewhat cursory; coupled with their prosperity, however, it was nevertheless sufficient to allow their children to enter the larger American society with relatively little psychological stress.

The family, the keystone of Arab identity and social organization, had already been modified in the first generation to a degree determined by the family's economic status, the number of Syrians in the community, and the family's own inclinations regarding its cultural heritage. Hardly a family was unaffected at least to some extent to the assimilation process. The second generation maintained those elements of their parents' culture that were not incompatible with an American household. They raised their children according to local practices; they still relished ethnic food, but usually only on special occasions; if they did not attend church regularly, they at least observed religious holidays. They maintained family bonds but also developed relations with non-Syrian Americans of their own class.

The third and fourth generations are considerably more remote from the culture of the first. A recent awakening to their ethnicity has caused them to turn to their parents for cultural pegs on which to hang their identity; but parental knowledge is often superficial, based only on being Syrians of one religious sect or another. Grandparents add little more than nostalgic reminiscences of an outdated past. If political and economic events had not reactivated Arab immigration and an interest in Arab culture, Syrian Americans might have Americanized themselves out of existence.

THE POSTWAR IMMIGRATION

For more than a century the West altered both social relations and political boundaries within the Arab world. By 1920 France ruled Morocco, Algeria, Tunisia, and Syria, including Mt. Lebanon. England governed Egypt, Sudan, Palestine, Transjordan, Iraq, and the eastern and southern shores of the Arabian peninsula, and exerted considerable influence in Libya. Only Saudi Arabia and Yemen remained independent. Greater Syria, which was supposed to be the basis for an inde-

pendent, unified Arab nation promised by the West in return for Arab military aid to the Allies in World War I, was artificially divided in 1920 into a truncated Syria, a Maronite-dominated Greater Lebanon (incorporating the Syrian port cities of Sidon, Tyre, Beirut, and Tripoli), Transjordan, and a promised homeland in Palestine for the Jews. Lingering separatist feelings hardened and new ones developed. Arab nationalist ideology was born out of resentment and frustration over broken promises and thwarted aspirations. Arab nationalists set about building up Arab self-esteem and encouraging unity to counter foreign rule. The Arab nations gradually won their independence after World War II, but Arab unity foundered on separatist nationalist ideologies and sentiments that were reinforced by religious differences.

Between the wars Western influence had led the upper and middle classes to send their sons, and some daughters, to be educated in Europe. After independence, governments committed to modernization subsidized education abroad, particularly in the United States. The rate of modernization lagged well behind the rate of education, however, as competing revolutionary ideologies, military coups, and wars with Israel sapped economies and career opportunities. As a result, despite the emigration restrictions imposed by several Arab governments and the dedication to the development of their countries of the individuals involved, hundreds of Muslim and Christian students sent to the United States for training simply remained there. Many professionals also emigrated, entering the United States under the terms of the professional-preference clause in the Immigration and Nationality Act of 1965. This Arab "brain drain" reached its highest point between 1968 and 1971, but from 1965 through 1976 "professional, technical, and kindred workers" averaged about 15 percent of Arab immigrants—Egypt alone lost nearly 7,000. A high percentage of immigrants from Jordan, Lebanon, and Syria are undoubtedly Palestinians; other Palestinians were admitted as refugees or under Israeli passports.

This immigration wave began in 1948, but it accelerated greatly after the Arab defeat in the Arab-Israeli war of 1967. From 1949 through 1976 arrivals totaled approximately 154,000, about 104,000 of whom came after 1967. More than 35,000 came from Egypt; Jordan, Lebanon, Iraq, and Syria together provided about 87,000, most of them Palestinians; 8,000 entered from Palestine; the rest came from North African countries, aside from a few from the Arabian Peninsula. Some, like the stateless Palestinians, were pushed by political events; some by economic uncertainties. But most of them came to improve their prospects. In this group Muslims exceeded Christians by about 60 percent. About 45 percent were women, and over 50 percent were between 20 and 49 years old. From 1965 to 1976 skilled workers averaged 15 percent and unskilled workers 10 percent of Arab immigration; wives, children, and others reporting "no occupation" averaged over 50 percent. Recent arrivals under these classifications include Palestinians and Lebanese displaced by civil war in Lebanon.

Settlement and adjustment have been considerably easier for these Arabs. They have the advantages of education, language, special skills, and the communities

and precedents already established by the Syrians. Most of them intended to return home eventually, and were simply awaiting a change in the circumstances that had precipitated their migration. Few actually go back. Some, like the unskilled Yemeni farmers and factory laborers, travel back and forth several times before finally deciding to settle.

The immigrants preferred to live among their own kind, but where they actually settled was necessarily determined by employment opportunities. With the exception of the 0.6 percent (mostly Yemeni) listed in the 1970 U.S. Census as farm laborers and the 1.0 percent as farmers and farm managers, they are predominantly city dwellers. If they came to join relatives, they generally found them in mixed neighborhoods, for by the postwar period few urban Arab communities remained. Some, like the Egyptian Copts and the Yemenites have formed new communities. They have already experienced considerable upward mobility. The professionals, best equipped to deal with the problems of settlement and adjustment, have already become almost indistinguishable from other Americans of their class.

The few communities of Arab industrial workers are more unified. In South Dearborn, Mich., a predominantly Muslim community dating from about 1916 has received a steady stream of Palestinians, Yemenis, and refugees from Lebanon since the mid-1960s. The residents have organized to house, guide, instruct, and generally serve the needs of the newcomers.

The recent immigrants are considerably less sectarian, a trend that parallels declining sectarian allegiance among the American-born. Wherever they settle, postwar immigrants find American-born Arabs. Before the Arab-Israeli war of 1967 the two groups had difficulty understanding each other's concerns and tended to associate mainly with those Arabs who did not seriously challenge their views on Arab issues. After 1967 what they perceived as general American hostility toward Arabs drew the two groups closer together.

Arabs of the recent immigration are nationalistic and are eager to maintain their traditions. Their efforts harmonize with those of the newly ethnicized American-born Arabs. One result has been a sharp increase in the number of mosques in the United States. Since its use is essential to the Muslim faith, Arabic is also being revived. Mostly immigrant imams are trying to revive religious discipline and knowledge both of Arabic and of modern Islamic thought. Many Christian Arab churches have also begun to offer classes in Arabic language, history, and culture. Social events feature modern Arab food, songs, and dances; discussions at the parish level consider ways of encouraging a sense of community.

Outside the religious institutions a growing number of Syrian Americans are also showing an interest in their ethnicity, learning about their culture, and taking at least some colloquial Arabic at college or doing research on Arabs and Arab Americans in graduate school. One group in concert with the recent arrivals is trying to improve the quality of the teaching of Arab history and culture in high school. The long-term effects of all this activity remain to be seen, for in the meanwhile the children of the immigrants again experience the temptations of assimilation.

The Arab-American press reached its nadir in the for-

ties. After 1950 several new newspapers in Arabic appeared, along with several journals in English. They stress the politics and economics of the Arab world, although they do not entirely neglect social and cultural items. Editorials interpret events in terms of the publisher's attitude toward American involvement in Arab-Israeli affairs. Competition for a limited audience still results in constant turnover. None of these papers enjoys the national success of the earlier Arab publications.

The formation of associations by the new immigrants coincided with important changes in those established earlier by the Syrian community. The Eastern Federation of American Syrian-Lebanese Clubs, under a younger, more educated leadership, attempted to influence American foreign policy toward the emerging Arab nations and inform American public opinion. In 1950 regional federations coalesced into a more politicized National Association of Federations. Editorials in its monthly publication, however, revealed conformity to American political attitudes and fear of condemnation from other Americans. In the decade of McCarthyism its Syrian readership was particularly sensitive to Syria's sharp swing to the political left. The national organization had all but dissolved by the sixties, its leadership claiming in its waning days that integration into American life had rendered ethnic organizations obsolete. As it turned out, its attempts to become a national ethnic interest group had simply been premature. The Syrian community was too disunited to pursue a common goal.

In the fifties the loyalties of the new Arabs in America were confounded by the intensity of competing Arab ideologies in the Arab world, by U.S. refusal to sell arms to the pro-Western revolutionary government in Egypt, by President Gamal Abdul Nasser's consequent arms deal with the Soviet bloc, withdrawal of U.S. funds for the Aswam Dam, nationalization of the Suez Canal, and the Suez War of 1956. Yet in their diffuse and confused way these organizations initiated the consciousness-raising process in the United States that would accelerate after the 1967 Arab-Israel war. The unexpected Israeli victory, followed by hostility toward the Arabs in the American press, brought the two Arab-American communities together. The Association of Arab-American University Graduates held its first convention in 1968. It proposed to unify the Arab-American community, influence American Middle East policy, and correct misinformation about Arabs in general and the image of Arab Americans in particular through a public information program and publications by its members. Dominated by post-1948 immigrants, it takes a militant stand on solutions to the Arab-Israeli conflict. The National Association of Arab Americans founded in 1972 in Washington, D.C., and dominated by American-born Arab businessmen and professionals, also has among its aims the improvement of the Arab image in the United States and the involvement of Arab Americans in the American political process and in questions of domestic concern such as job discrimination. It also registered as a lobby on behalf of Arab Americans to influence U.S. Middle East policy. Both these national organizations are potentially more viable than their predecessors.

Before 1948 Arab Americans did not feel the need to

gain influence as a group in American life, although individuals attained positions of prominence in party politics, labor unions, entertainment, education, and the press. Emphasis on individual achievement required neither unions nor political parties, and the general satisfaction of Syrian Americans with their way of life obviated their participation.

A sizable percentage of Arab Americans today are professional and semiprofessional people in practically all fields. Their rate of achievement is high; Arabs have a long roster of public personalities in law, consumerism, finance, medicine, politics, government, journalism, the sciences, education, show business, and literature.

POLITICS

Syrians became naturalized, voted at least as faithfully as the rest of the population, and joined Rotary and Kiwanis clubs, if only because these were the "American" things to do. If city machines thought them too few to court, small-town ward bosses did not. One or two Syrians in the United States aspired to public office as early as 1910. Later, Syrians won election as mayors, city councilmen, and state legislators, and were appointed to public office. In 1958 the first Syrian won a seat in Congress; in 1978 a U.S. senator from South Dakota and congressmen from Texas, South Dakota, Connecticut, Ohio, and West Virginia were all descendants of early Syrian immigrants. However, Arabs are more likely to win elective office in small towns where their families have been prominent and where their ethnic origins play little or no part in their political success. They are too individualistic and scattered to be relied on as a political bloc.

On domestic matters Arabs vote their private interests. Although five of the six Arabs in Congress are Democrats, the majority of Arab Americans are conservative and generally Republican, in part because most Syrians began moving up the economic ladder in the twenties when the Republican party was ascendant. Arab Democrats generally adhere to the party's social and economic platform, conservative in the South, more liberal in the North; they are rarely radicals.

Likewise, in national elections the Arab vote does not seem to have been significantly affected by U.S. policy in the Middle East, which in any case was neutral or nonexistent before President Harry S. Truman's recognition of the State of Israel in 1948. Despite ethnic awakening and the outspoken criticism by Arab-American leaders of America's Middle East policy since 1948, the situation has not perceptibly altered.

Recent Arab immigrants have succeeded in arousing ethnic loyalty among the Americanized generations and have also taught them what their parents had not—that the label Arab includes both Muslims and Christians. They have precipitated a movement toward Arab cohesion; it is frequently superficial and still meets with resistance from many quarters, but that any cohesion at all could be generated among the descendants of the early immigrants is itself remarkable. The elements of Arab culture that survived, fostered in churches, mosques, and the family, have proved to be tenacious.

The relations between Arabs and other Americans have generally been amicable, marred only by occasional anger and disillusionment in recent years. The problem for the second generation was to avoid assimilating to the point of becoming invisible. The task for Arab Americans today is to breach factional divisions and form a cohesive Arab-American community.

Bibliography
Louise Seymour Houghton's four-part study, "The Syrians in the United States," *Survey* 26 nos. 1 (July 1911): 480–495; 2 (August 1911); 647–665; 3 (September 1911): 786–802; and 4 (October 1911): 957–968, provides detailed data not found elsewhere. It is based on visits to the various communities discussed. See also Philip Hitti, *Syrians in America* (New York, 1924). Hitti was a Syrian immigrant and a prominent Arab scholar, but much of his study is now outdated. Philip and Joseph Kayal's *Syrian Lebanese in America: A Study in Religion and Assimilation* (Boston, 1975) provides some insight into the general Syrian experience despite its Catholic emphasis. Sociological studies on Arab-American communities include several published dissertations: Abdo Elkholy provides a comparison of two Muslim communities, Detroit and Toledo, in his *Arab Moslems in the United States: Religion and Assimilation* (New Haven, Conn., 1966); Atif A. Wasfi concentrates on the Dearborn, Mich., Muslims in his *Islamic-Lebanese Community in the U.S.A.: A Study in Cultural Anthropology* (Beirut, Lebanon, 1971); Ibrahim Othman, *Arabs in the United States: A Study of an Arab-American Community* (Beirut, 1974) examines the Christian community of Springfield, Mass.

Articles on the Syrians published in newspapers and journals before World War II tend to be descriptive; later articles are more apt to be sociological. Two collections are Elaine C. Hagopian and Ann Paden, eds., *The Arab-Americans: Studies in Assimilation* (Wilmette, Ill., 1969); and Barbara Aswad, ed., *Arabic-Speaking Communities in American Cities* (Staten Island, N.Y., 1974). The focus of the latter is on Dearborn, Mich.

The following articles provide data on groups and subgroups not discussed elsewhere: Afif Tannous, "Acculturation of an Arab-Syrian Community in the Deep South," *American Sociological Review* 8 (1942): 264–271; E.D. Benyon, "The Near East in Flint, Michigan: Assyrians and Druse and Their Antecedents," *Geographic Review* 24 (1944): 234–274; Mary Sengstock, "Telkeif, Baghdad, Detroit: Chaldeans Blend Three Cultures," *Michigan History* 54 (1970): 293–310; Mary Bisharat, "Yemeni Farmworkers in California," *Middle East Research and Information Reports* (January 1975): 22–26; L. Jaafari, "The Brain Drain to the United States: The Migration of Jordanians and Palestinian Professionals and Students," *Journal of Palestine Studies* 3 (Autumn 1973): 119–131.

The Immigration History Research Center at the University of Minnesota has a growing collection of source materials on Arab Americans.

ALIXA NAFF

ARAPAHOS: *see* AMERICAN INDIANS

ARGENTINIANS: *see* CENTRAL AND SOUTH AMERICANS

ARIKARAS: *see* AMERICAN INDIANS

ARMENIANS

The Armenians are one of the many groups who immigrated to the United States in the late 19th and the early 20th century. By 1924 nearly 100,000, for the most part from Turkey and Russia, had made their way to America. By the mid-1970s the Armenian-American community numbered between 350,000 and 450,000. Approximately 45 percent of its members live in New England and the Mid-Atlantic states, 15 percent in Michigan, Illinois, Ohio, and Wisconsin, and 25 percent in California. Today most of the world's Armenians live in the Soviet Union: about 2.2 million in Soviet Armenia, another million in the rest of the U.S.S.R. There are also large Armenian communities in Lebanon, Syria, Iran, Turkey, France, Canada, Argentina, Uruguay, and Brazil.

The ancestors of all Armenians lived in northeast

Asia Minor around the first millennium before Christ. Because they were never a very numerous people and because their territories were crossed by the trade routes to the East, they were often attacked and sometimes subjugated by more powerful neighbors. Nonetheless they managed to create a high civilization, particularly notable for its literary and artistic achievements, and for their early adoption of Christianity as the national religion. A period of invasion that lasted from A.D. 1000 to 1500 finally destroyed the kingdom. First a succession of Asiatic hordes—Seljuk Turks, Turkomans, Tatars, and Mongols—overran and pillaged fields and cities. Many Armenians fled to Cilicia —an area on the Mediterranean coast of what is now south-central Turkey, far from their original homeland —and established an Armenian kingdom there that lasted from 1080 to 1375. Others fled to Constantinople (modern İstanbul), which was until 1453 the capital of Eastern Christianity, or to Smyrna (modern İzmir) on the Aegean Sea; still others went to Poland or the Crimea.

The conquest of Armenia by the Ottoman Turks in the 16th century proved to be the last of these Asian incursions. Though parts of historic Armenia were ruled by Russia and Persia, Armenia remained chiefly under Ottoman Turkish rule until World War I. In this Muslim Turkish society, some Armenians assumed a role somewhat akin to that of the Jews in predominantly Christian Europe: they became bankers, skilled artisans, bureaucrats, and businessmen; some were advisers to the sultans. But these remained a small and elite group. Unlike the Jews of Europe, the Armenians of Turkey were allowed to own land, and the majority were farmers, peasants, or craftsmen. Regardless of occupation, however, the Armenians, like all other non-Muslim Ottoman subjects, were regarded with contempt by the Turks as *rayah,* or unwashed infidels. Although the 19th-century Westernization of the Turkish Empire led to reforms that alleviated some of the more onerous prohibitions against them, the Armenians remained second-class citizens of the empire until the virtual elimination of the Armenian population in 1915 and the empire's collapse shortly thereafter.

In the 19th century the Armenians awoke to the nationalist and socialist ideas current in Europe, and an intellectual and political revival swept through the Armenian communities in both Turkey and the Russian Empire. Armenian schools, hospitals, charitable organizations, presses, libraries, and colleges were founded. In Turkish Armenia the people learned about the New World from American Protestant missionaries and began to rebel against the poverty, oppression, and degradation that had long bound them. This rebellious spirit, coupled with the deterioration of the Ottoman Empire, destroyed the centuries-old relationship with the Turkish government that had ensured the Armenians' survival. In 1894–1896 and again in 1909 hundreds of thousands of Armenians were deprived of their property and either forced into exile or killed. In 1915 the Turks, alleging treason among their Armenian subjects, exploited religious, economic, and political tensions to exterminate over a million of them. The Armenians, whose hopes for survival as a people and a nation had since 1878 been tied, in vain, to Western intervention, were helpless to resist. The memories of the massacres and of the West's unfulfilled promises of aid have never been erased. Neither has the hope of someday establishing a free Armenian nation.

The attempted genocide reduced the Armenian homeland in Turkey to a wasteland inhabited by a

Armenia

～～～ Border of historic Armenia

－ － － Border of Turkish Armenia

· · · · · Border of Cilician Armenia

Major concentrations of Armenians

200   Km.   Miles

small but determined group of survivors. Taking advantage of the collapse of the Ottoman government in Turkey and the tsarist government in Russia, this small remnant managed to create a tiny republic in 1918. In barely two years, however, it had become the victim of Allied duplicity and Turko-Soviet enmity and was absorbed by the Soviet system, which from then has formed from it the modern industrial and agricultural Armenian Soviet Socialist Republic. Though many Armenians regard the U.S.S.R. as their protector against the Turkish menace, they still look upon the Armenian Republic as far short of their dream of full nationhood.

Throughout the period of Ottoman Turkish rule, the Armenians maintained their Christian faith. The Armenian Apostolic Church, to which the vast majority of Armenians still belong, was given the status of *millet*, or nation, by the Ottoman regime, which meant that it was an officially recognized religious community with some degree of autonomy. At the head of the millet was an Armenian patriarch, whose seat was in Constantinople, the Turkish capital. The head of the church itself was the *catholicos* in Russia.

The Armenian Apostolic Church derives its name from the apostles Thaddeus and Bartholomew, who according to tradition began the conversion of the Armenians to Christianity between A.D. 43 and A.D. 68. Armenia adopted Christianity as the official state religion in 301—that it was the first state to do so is still a source of great pride to Armenians. In 506 the church declared itself independent of both Constantinople and Rome, and it remains autonomous to this day.

Although much weakened by centuries of Turkish domination, the Apostolic church remained the church of the vast majority of Armenians in both Turkey and Russia. Before World War I it claimed the allegiance of perhaps as many as 95 percent of the 4 million Armenians who lived there. The remainder were either Eastern-rite Catholics or members of the Protestant Armenian Evangelical Church. The Eastern-rite Armeno-Catholic Church was established in the 16th century, although it did not seriously begin to proselytize until the 18th century. The 200,000 Armeno-Catholics in 1910 lived in the Turkish-Armenian communities of Constantinople, Ankara, Aleppo, and Mardin. The Armeno-Catholics, whose ultimate allegiance was to Rome, were led by the Armeno-Catholic Patriarch of Constantinople, whose see was transferred to Beirut in 1925. (*See* Eastern Catholics.)

The smaller Armenian Evangelical Church was a result of American missionary efforts originally directed toward the Muslim Turks. When these efforts were thwarted, the missionaries turned their attention to the Armenians and organized their first Armenian mission in 1831; by 1847 it had also been recognized as a millet. But despite this and despite the enormous contribution of the American missionaries to the Armenian national awakening, the Protestants had made barely more than 50,000 converts by 1914.

Along with the Armenian Apostolic Church, the Armenian language has helped to maintain unity among the Armenians scattered throughout the world. Armenian is an Indo-European language that did not acquire its alphabet until A.D. 406; called Krapar, it was the literary language until the 19th century and is still used today as the liturgical language of the Apostolic church.

Classical and modern Armenian (Ashkharapar) share the same 38-character alphabet. Armenian has two dialects: Russian and Iranian Armenians use an eastern variant, Turkish Armenians a western one; regional variations are numerous. Certain Armenian communities of Cilicia that had large Turkish majorities were the only ones whose first language was Turkish.

MIGRATION AND ARRIVAL

The London Company of Virginia included among its colonists one "Martin the Armenian," who arrived in 1618 or 1619; some other Armenians followed him to the New World in 1653 to raise silk, but these were isolated cases, and they formed no New World Armenian community.

The first systematic movement of Armenians to the United States began in the early 19th century when American missionaries, who had gone to Turkey to establish churches, missions, schools, and hospitals, encouraged students to go to the United States for their education so that they could return to serve as clergy, doctors, and engineers. Simultaneously a few adventurous businessmen with missionary-school educations emigrated to seek their fortunes in America; perhaps 60 had come by 1870. More significant in number were the artisans and laborers from the Turkish interior who began emigrating in the 1870s and 1880s, chiefly from the densely populated plain around Kharpert in the province of Mamuret-Ul-Aziz. By the late 1880s perhaps 1,500 Armenians had arrived in the United States, most of them looking for better jobs.

After 1890 the emigration of Armenians from Turkey escalated in direct correlation with the deteriorating state of Armeno-Turkish relations. In 1894 Sultan Abdul Hamid II, "the Damned," quelled what had started as a minor Armenian uprising in mountainous Sasun by massacring 10,000 Armenians. Beginning in September 1895, Armenians were massacred in every major Turkish Armenian settlement from the Bosphorus to the Caspian Sea. In all, more than 100,000 were slain. Refugees fortunate enough to escape from Turkey to the United States rapidly increased the Armenian immigration rate, until it reached 2,500 annually in the middle and late 1890s. Then the migration subsided, as many more thousands who sought to escape were deterred by troubled political conditions, strict travel restrictions, and the inability to pay the exorbitant bribes required to obtain official permission.

After 1900 a new and still larger migration took shape; over 50,000 Armenians had made their way to the United States by 1914, most of them fleeing the Turkish government's continuing policy of economic and political repression. Until 1908, for example, Turkish officials forbade Armenians to conduct business in the interior or even to travel there; at the same time tax collectors were remorselessly squeezing taxes from their often impoverished Armenian subjects. Some Armenians feared a repetition of the massacres, especially after an uprising of Macedonian Christian nationalists in 1903. Newly established immigrants in the United States encouraged friends and relatives to come, producing the familiar process known as chain migration. After 1905 the lowering of the price of passage from Black Sea and Mediterranean ports to New York City also made migration easier.

In 1908 a revolution led by the reformist Young Turk movement, in which Armenians participated, overthrew the Sultan Abdul Hamid and at first appeared to usher in a new order. But in 1909, 15,000 to 20,000 Armenians were massacred in the district of Adana on the Cilician Plain. In September the Young Turks passed conscription decrees that reversed the Ottoman policy of exempting non-Muslims from military service and allowed them to begin inducting Christian subjects into the Turkish army. The massacre and the possibility of perishing in the service of the Turks convinced many young Armenian men to escape and go to America; the outbreak of war in the Balkans and the continuing economic paralysis of eastern Turkey encouraged others. Over 5,500 Armenians fled to the United States in 1910. The highest number for a single year, 9,355, entered in 1913.

In the meantime emigration from Russian Armenia to the United States had also begun. In 1898 the Russian Dukhobors and Molokans, two Protestant pacificist sects who lived among the Russian Armenians and were victims of severe persecution by the tsarist government, began to emigrate to the New World. The letters they sent back encouraged the Armenians to follow them to Canada, but a few found it not to their liking and moved on. They ended up in southern California, and soon their communications home were encouraging yet another group to come. The Russian Armenian settlement in California was established between 1908 and 1914, when emigration was cut off by the outbreak of World War I.

Altogether perhaps 2,500 Russian Armenians migrated to the New World between 1898 and 1914. The Russian Armenian immigration was so much smaller than the Turkish probably because political persecution had taken less violent forms in the Russian Empire; there were no Protestant missionaries to encourage emigration as there had been in the Ottoman Empire; and Russian Armenia's level of economic development, while low, was still somewhat higher than Turkey's. The migration also started much later, and was soon cut off by the war.

In 1910 the U.S. Immigration Commission surveyed the character of the migration from southern and eastern Europe and the Middle East. Compared with other immigrant groups, the number of Armenians was small; the 51,950 Armenians (1899–1910) represented less than 5 per 10,000 of the total Old World Armenian population—minimal compared with the eastern European Jews (100 per 10,000), southern Italians (79 per 10,000), and the Poles (42 per 10,000). As was often the case with immigrants at the time, the overwhelming majority were young adult single men. They outnumbered women four to one (a somewhat higher ratio than the average of seven to three for all immigrant groups combined, though still low compared to some other groups). Only 9 percent of the Armenian immigrants were under 14 years old, 87 percent fell into the 14–45 category; only 4 percent were over 45.

But the Armenian immigrants had some untypical socioeconomic characteristics as well. In contrast to much of the eastern European migration, some 35 percent had skills (most were tailors, shoemakers, carpenters, or clerks), 4 percent had been in business, 2 percent could be categorized as professionals, and the vast ma-

jority were literate; 40 percent were town dwellers, a proportion far exceeding that of most other southern and eastern European immigrant groups of the time. This was partly because urban Armenians were more likely to be prosperous and thus able to pay the price of emigrating, partly because businessmen and professionals accounted for a sizable proportion of the Armenian population in Turkey to begin with, and partly because that group was most likely to be exposed to the idea of emigration through the Protestant missionary schools. Finally, the Turks had seen to it that they had good reason to want to depart.

The migration that had been halted by World War I resumed in 1919, as wartime refugees, many of them maimed or orphaned survivors of the massacres and deportations, came to America. In contrast to the earlier migration, this was an exodus mainly of women (52 percent) and children (21 percent). Armenian charities, American and European missionaries, and family members brought Armenian children from Turkish homes or orphanages and settlement camps in Syria, Greece, and Egypt. In 1920, according to the report of the commissioner general of immigration, 10,212 survivors entered the country, the largest single annual migration in the history of the movement. Between 1920 and 1924, 20,559 more arrived, while many other thousands fled to the Middle East and western Europe.

The imposition of the restrictive national-quota system after 1924 ended the migration to the United States. A bill to exempt Armenian orphans and refugees from the quotas imposed by the immigration legislation was introduced, but it was not enacted. A few more Armenians entered on the League of Nations refugee documents known as Nansen passports, but by 1925 the Armenian immigration had for the most part come to a halt.

In the more than 50 years since the imposition of restrictive U.S. immigration quotas, only two periods show exceptional numbers of Armenians arriving in the United States. The first of these, just after World War II, followed the passage of the Displaced Persons Act (1948), which authorized exemptions to the quota system that would permit wartime refugees to find asylum in the United States. Approximately 4,500 Armenians, many from the Soviet Union, who had been interned in German and Italian settlement camps during the war, entered the United States under this act. The American National Committee for Homeless Armenians (ANCHA) was instrumental in resettling them when they arrived. Between 1951 and 1965 ANCHA also helped to resettle an additional 8,500 Armenians, including those displaced from Palestine by Arab-Israeli conflicts in the 1950s.

The Displaced Persons Act was a temporary measure. Longer lasting in its effects has been the Immigration and Nationality Act of 1965, which ended the national-quota system altogether; countries with large Armenian populations (Lebanon, Syria, and Greece) had previously been limited to a quota of a few hundred annually. The first to take advantage of the new regulations were people from the approximately 50,000-member Armenian-Egyptian community who were unhappy with the various extreme anti-business measures that had been implemented by Egypt's first president, Abdul Gamal Nasser. Military rule and the Arab-Israeli con-

flict uprooted Armenians from Aleppo in Syria. The Armenian Turkish community, most of it in İstanbul, shrank considerably after the mid-1960s because of the emigration to western Europe, Canada, and the United States, which had resulted from increasing economic, political, and cultural harassment. By 1960 handfuls were leaving Soviet Armenia; 9,000 others soon followed, many of them people who had gone back to Soviet Armenia from Europe, the Middle East, and the United States after World War II but had found it impossible to adjust to conditions there.

Others left from Iran, Iraq, and Bulgaria, but by far the largest group fled the civil wars in Lebanon. Well organized and prosperous, the Lebanese Armenian community, although it had maintained its neutrality in the conflict, suffered heavy losses in the crossfire. Large sections of the Armenian quarter in Beirut were damaged or destroyed, and casualties were numerous. Perhaps 30,000 of its 160,000 population fled, most of them to the United States.

About 2,000 Armenians are still entering the United States from these and other countries each year. Most are well educated, ambitious, and young. The continuing migration out of Soviet Armenia and the Middle East is seen as an ominous sign by Armenians everywhere. For them it represents a drain of Armenian manpower in precisely those communities that are nearest the homeland and consequently are seen as bastions of the Armenian cultural traditions. If they disappear, they will take with them the foundation upon which some future sovereign Armenia might be established.

Although the desire to return to the homeland has been a cohesive force in the community's history, few Armenian Americans have actually been willing to repatriate themselves, partly because of the tragic experiences of the few who have tried. Under the rule of Sultan Abdul Hamid, immigrants returning to Turkey, whether naturalized American citizens or not, were harassed by the authorities; suspected Armenian nationalists were arrested, jailed, or thrown out of the country for seditious activity. As a result those who had come to the United States as sojourners, hoping to amass wealth and then return to live in comfort in the old country, rarely in fact returned. The Young Turk movement that began in 1908 did encourage some overseas Armenians, including some leading political figures in the United States, to return. Even after the 1909 Adana massacre the Armenian Revolutionary Federation, the leading Armenian political organization, was still encouraging Armenians to come home and rebuild the shattered nation. Rallied by the call of *tebi yergir* (to the nation), about 4,500 sold their American homes and possessions and departed for Turkey between 1908 and 1914. Many were old or unskilled, however; the young, able-bodied, and skilled were clearly reluctant to leave the United States. During the period of the Armenian Republic (1918–1920), a few more went back; between 1920 and 1932, when data cease, about 120 departed annually for the homeland.

The end of World War II revived hopes for a massive repatriation to Soviet Armenia, which had been left by the war short of manpower, capital, and material goods. In 1946 a call from Soviet Armenia for 400,000 repatriates was apparently enthusiastically received by Armenians worldwide, though the contingent of Armenian

Americans who actually went numbered only 152, most of them between 50 and 60 years of age, and about 40 of them minors. They sailed on the Soviet ship *Rossia* in November 1947. Automobiles, refrigerators, and tools worth around $60,000 were shipped along with them free of charge. All of them renounced their American citizenship: the prosperous expected to become leaders in Armenia, while the poor hoped simply to do better than they had been able to in the United States. Another 171 followed in subsequent years, but the Armenian Americans remained a tiny portion of the 100,000 who returned.

The repatriates were soon bitterly disappointed. They found no housing accommodations; they lived in the open air or in tents, even during the winter. Their possessions were confiscated by the Soviet police. Soon many were trying to return to the United States. As late as 1971, after 22 years in Armenia, one Armenian American was still seeking permission to go back. Only in recent years have the original repatriates finally been granted permission to return to America if they wish.

SETTLEMENT

The first Armenian communities grew up in the metropolitan areas of the Northeast and the Mid-Atlantic states; 60 percent of the Armenians settled in Massachusetts, New York, Rhode Island, Connecticut, New Jersey, or Pennsylvania. In 1910 New York City claimed the largest number of foreign-born Armenians (2,616), with Providence, R.I. (1,970), Worcester, Mass. (1,584), and Boston (1,189) following closely. Significantly smaller Armenian settlements in the Midwest were in Chicago, Cleveland, Detroit, Racine, Wis., Waukegan, and East St. Louis, Ill., the Chicago suburb of Pullman, and Grand Rapids, Mich. Immigrants shunned the rural areas—the single exception being the large agricultural colony in Fresno County, Calif.—and rarely ventured into the Rocky Mountain states or the deep South. They remained an overwhelmingly urban population. They went where plentiful unskilled jobs, cheap housing, and public transportation were readily available. Worcester's wire mills, New York's shirt and garment industries, and New Jersey's silk mills provided them with jobs.

Settlement followed a regular pattern. First the bachelors or married men who had left their families behind arrived and moved into the communal boarding houses and tenements near the factories or mills. There they put up with severe overcrowding, poor sanitation, and insufficient food to save their meager funds. The living quarters of the 120 Armenian textile workers in Lawrence, Mass., in 1913 were located in two of the most densely populated blocks in the entire state. In time women and children began to arrive from the old country, alleviating the worst of these urban living conditions by providing some domestic amenities and eliminating the necessity of sending money to Armenia. As the neighborhoods filled up with families, the unmarried men moved on to the Midwest, where there was less competition for jobs, and reestablished the boarding house system.

In Fresno the proportion of immigrants coming in family units was high from the beginning. In 1920 California accounted for 16 percent of the Armenian for-

eign-born in the United States and for 27 percent of the native-born children. Of the California immigrants, according to one study, 86 percent had first labored from five to ten years in eastern mills or factories to save money. They then moved on to Fresno to invest in vineyards, raise their families (children were needed to help in the vineyards), and build their homes.

Beginning in 1920 the immigrant families who had remained in the East also began to move out of the central cities; economic success, the availability of interurban transportation, and the arrival in their neighborhoods of new and unwelcome immigrant groups prompted their departure. In New York the congested tenement district along Manhattan's Third Avenue was abandoned in favor of upper Manhattan, Queens, Brooklyn, and the Bronx. Boston's South Cove was abandoned for Dorchester, Jamaica Plain, and the western suburbs of Watertown, Somerville, and Malden. In Worcester the original Armenian quarter moved from the Gold and Assonet Street slums westward toward Bell Pond and Clark University. A few were too poor or too attached to the "Little Armenias" to abandon them, however, so the old Armenian neighborhoods, while considerably diminished, did remain.

Jobs beckoned many more to the Midwest, especially to Detroit. There, according to the U.S. Census, the 1910 foreign-born Armenian population of 337 had expanded to 1,692 by 1920, chiefly as a result of Henry Ford's guarantee in 1914 of a $5 workday; by 1930 Detroit's Armenian population (3,508) ranked second only to New York City's (6,919).

California, especially Fresno County, had the most rapid growth until the 1930s, expanding from about 10,000 in 1919 to 18,000 a decade later. Despite, or perhaps because of, their increasing numbers, Fresno Armenians were kept from spreading out of their original neighborhoods by restrictive covenants against Armenians, Japanese, Chinese, blacks, and Mexicans. Meanwhile the small, sleepy towns surrounding Fresno—Parlier, Fowler, Yettem (Eden in Armenian, the only town in the United States exclusively settled by Armenians), and Dinuba—were rapidly populated by Armenian farmers. This phase ended temporarily with the Great Depression, which was ruinous to California's agriculture. Many young Armenians joined the unemployed in San Francisco or Los Angeles.

After World War II new highway systems, suburban housing developments, and greater affluence encouraged Armenians to leave the old settlements for new ones farther outside the city. But communal roots persisted. Some of the easterners again looked to Fresno and Los Angeles as the new paradise; in Fresno the outlawing of restrictive codes in 1948 finally permitted Armenians to move into the middle-class neighborhoods there.

The approximately 2,000 immigrants who now come annually from Soviet Armenia, the Middle East, and Europe are also bypassing the older settlements for suburban ethnic neighborhoods. Haverhill, Mass., closed its Protestant Armenian church in 1977 for lack of parishioners. Watertown, Mass., remains an active center of Armenian community life, and New York City attracts some newcomers, but more are going on to California, especially to the San Francisco Bay area and Los Angeles County. According to one newspaper report,

one section of downtown Hollywood, Calif., houses fully 5,000 new Armenian immigrants.

ECONOMIC LIFE

The members of the first immigrant generation of Armenian Americans were generally very successful in their adjustment to the economic life of the adopted country. They had arrived with a number of advantages: many had skills or backgrounds in business. The literacy rate was exceptionally high. Their long experience as a minority group in their native land had taught them the techniques of survival in an alien environment. Finally the devastation of Turkish Armenia in 1915 had compelled the vast majority to regard their move to the United States as a permanent break with the homeland, and not simply a temporary, money-making sojourn.

In the beginning, nonetheless, the Armenians joined the other new arrivals as unskilled labor in the factories and mills. They arrived without capital or any knowledge of English, which prevented their entering immediately into business. Statistics from the Massachusetts State Census in 1915, which are typical for the period, show two-thirds of the labor force of 4,239 Armenians employed in manufacturing industries, chiefly iron, steel, and metal foundries, textile mills, boot and shoe factories, and rubber manufacturing. The need for money also forced immigrant women into the factories: of 98 Armenian laborers' families listed in the 1910 U.S. Immigration Commission survey, one-quarter reported earnings from the wife. In Troy, N.Y., three-quarters of the Armenian women were employed, all of them in the city's shirt and collar industries.

As newcomers to the "satanic mills," the immigrants endured 60-hour workweeks of hard, monotonous, and dangerous labor, foul working conditions, and low wages—when they had work at all. Sometimes, as in 1907, 1913, and 1919, there was no work. Desperation led them to strikebreaking in Middleboro, Mass., in 1892, in Paterson, N.J., in 1902, and in Bridgewater, Mass., in 1907, and to undercutting the wages of Irish immigrant and native American labor (Worcester, 1893). Jobs were often obtained by bribing English-speaking Armenian foremen. Although two-thirds of the 500-man Armenian labor force in Lawrence, Mass., took part in the 1912 Lawrence textile strike, and labor-conscious journals like the *Hairenik* (Fatherland) blacklisted scabs and promoted the cause of the American Socialist movement, before 1915 Old World Armenians did not generally support the U.S. labor movement, partly because they did not understand American labor practices, partly because they needed jobs, partly because they did not want to be identified as "working-class."

Most Armenians regarded their factory employment as only a stepping stone to a career in business, although some spent their entire lives in the Worcester foundries, in the Hood Rubber Company of Watertown, or in the Riverside Cement Works in California. But many others soon moved out of the factories into small businesses or into farming. The U.S. Immigration Commission survey remarked that Armenians in Lowell, Lawrence, and Chelsea, Mass., and in West Hoboken, N.J., were ambitious and "disliking the wage relation, quickly moved out of the factories." Other data confirm

that they were able to endure the monotony, long hours, and toil of the mills only long enough to save money and escape working-class life.

Judging from the Boston and New York City directories of 1910 and 1920, which listed residences and types of jobs, the Armenians were most likely to establish tailors' shops, grocery stores, meat markets, shoemakers' shops, and similar small retail trades. Among the skilled were some pioneers in photoengraving and photography. A small shop provided a better living than a factory job and was physically less punishing. It was also more dignified and allowed the immigrants to join —or in some cases rejoin—the middle class. A few were exceptionally successful, but most remained small storekeepers, working 14 hours a day, 7 days a week. Some became clergymen or doctors. Most notable among the latter was Dr. Varaztad Kazanjian (1879–1974), a pioneer in plastic surgery who was knighted by Britain's George V for his remarkable battlefront operations during World War I. He went on to have a distinguished career in writing, teaching, and surgery at the Harvard Medical School.

In Fresno the Armenian farmers took one of two courses. Some went directly from the old country to Fresno, where they began to set aside money by working as field hands or fruit packers. Others went to the eastern factories first and came West only after they had saved the $2,000 to $10,000 needed to buy vineyards or ranches. Either way, every penny went into land. They started out with large mortgages and deeply in debt; the whole family worked on the ranch, economized, and saved. Money was rarely sent abroad or used for anything but necessities, so that any profits could be used to pay off the mortgage or improve or buy more land. Others ventured successfully into the packing industry and real estate, and, as in the East, into small business. Armenian farmers introduced the casaba melon and some other types of produce to the American market.

In almost every large city Armenians could soon be found in the Oriental-rug trade. In New England, New York, and elsewhere they virtually monopolized both the trade and the rug-cleaning business. The Karagheusian family of New York made significant inroads into the domestic-rug trade, in both production and distribution, and pioneered the manufacture of the "domestic Oriental." Two factors help to explain this penchant for the rug business. First, Victorian tastes in the late 19th century included a vogue for Oriental decoration. It was a time, noted the 1896 *Ladies' Home Journal*, of the "Oriental nook, with its hookah, ottomans, and profusely scattered Oriental rugs." Also, the Oriental-rug trade in the Old World was often in the hands of Armenian merchants, and many of the more successful Armenian-American businessmen were sons of Old World rug merchants who supplied them with goods, funds, and the benefit of their experience.

Although immigrants occasionally acquired some education in the United States, mainly through special citizenship classes, the vast majority concentrated on getting established so they could educate their children. In 1921 Armenians were said to have the most students in college in proportion to their numbers of any immigrant group. Children forced to leave school during the Depression pooled family resources so that younger siblings could attend high school and college in their stead.

Evidence confirms that these efforts were rewarded with white-collar and professional occupations in the second generation. A study made in 1946 noted that the children of Oriental-rug merchants were leaving the trade for more prestigious professions. Oral-history interviews of 60 Armenian survivors of the 1915 massacre revealed that their most common occupations were in unskilled or semiskilled labor, but that their children were largely in medicine, engineering, or teaching. This upward mobility was further accelerated in the third generation. A 1976 study noted that there were 1,252 Armenians in academic life in the United States, 31 per 10,000 of the total U.S. Armenian population, compared to only 21 academics for every 10,000 in the U.S. population as a whole.

Yet the attraction of business remained strong. The sons and grandsons of the original California farmers in time established a flourishing agricultural community in central and southern California, and a study of the second generation in Whitinsville, Mass., noted a powerful inclination toward business and property-holding. Kirk Kerkorian (1917–), a Fresno-born Las Vegas entrepreneur and chief stockholder of Metro-Goldwyn-Mayer, is something of a hero in the Armenian-American press. Called a "Croesus in the desert," Kerkorian built a gambling and hotel empire second only to that of Howard Hughes. A bicentennial study of Armenian Americans devoted more space to "commerce and industry" than to any other field of endeavor.

The recent immigration is more heterogeneous in both interests and background, for it includes Armenians from Iran, Iraq, Lebanon, Egypt, and the Soviet Union. Scattered data suggest that Iranian Armenians were able to bring considerable financial resources with them. The Soviet Armenians, on the other hand, are poor but well-educated professionals and artists disenchanted with the Soviet regime. Armenians from Arab countries come from a variety of backgrounds—the Iraqi Armenians, for example, range all the way from the Hovnanian brothers, the sons of Iraq's largest road builder, to others of distinctly modest means; the Lebanese Armenians are similarly mixed.

Again, these newcomers often depend at first on menial work. According to a 1974 survey, the largest proportion were semiskilled blue-collar workers (27 percent), followed by unskilled service workers (19 percent), and white-collar professionals (14 percent). But the transition to higher social class apparently occurred more quickly for these newcomers. ANCHA could soon report that the majority of those they assisted had repaid their loans (which totaled thousands of dollars) within a brief time, often by establishing the traditional Armenian small store.

Covert discrimination against Armenians was common in the first part of the century; they were often made to feel unwanted and inferior, in part a result of late-19th- and early-20th-century nativist hostility against all newcomers from the Mediterranean basin. The Armenians were grouped with the Syrians and Lebanese as the "scum of the Levant," and pseudoscientific racist opinion categorized them as "Asiatics." This animosity grew more bitter in the early 1900s when Armenians hired themselves out as strikebreakers in Massachusetts, New Hampshire, and Pennsylvania, which made them unpopular with local labor. In Worcester,

Mass., gang fights erupted when the Irish Catholics taunted the Armenians by calling them "Turks."

Discriminatory acts against Armenians were common in Fresno. Restrictive covenants against landholding, discrimination in employment, prohibitions against membership in lodges and clubs, including the YMCA and veterans' organizations, were enforced. The Armenians were called "Fresno Indians" and "lower-class Jews." In 1894 a group of Armenian parishioners was ousted from the First Congregational Church, despite the fact that they had been among its founding members, because others felt uncomfortable with them as church members. Discrimination in housing persisted until the U.S. Supreme Court in *Shelley* v. *Kraemer* (1948) struck down restrictive covenants against "undesirables." Informal restrictions persisted until the 1960s.

Attempts were also made to abridge their legal rights. In 1909 and again in 1913 the California State Assembly proposed legislation that would deprive certain aliens of the right to lease or own land. The legislation sought to prevent the Japanese and the "cheap labor of southern Europe" from taking "possession of our soil" and driving out the "American people," and the threat to the Armenians and their extensive agricultural investments caused widespread apprehension. In 1909 federal authorities prevented Armenians from obtaining American citizenship briefly, contending that the Armenians were "Asiatics" and therefore did not fulfill the "free white" qualification required for naturalization. But the same year Judge Francis Cabot Lowell, in a U.S. circuit court of appeals ruling, declared in *In re Halladjian* that the appearance, ethnography, and history of the Armenians classified them as Caucasian, not Asiatic, and hence eligible. Thus when a California law forbidding "aliens ineligible for citizenship" from owning land was passed in 1913 it did not affect the Armenians. In 1924 in the *Tateos Cartozian* case a U.S. district court upheld the Halladjian ruling.

The discrimination in Fresno resulted from hostility toward an unusually large and successful group of immigrants who had overwhelmed a small-town farming community. Elsewhere, Armenians were too few to appear as a threat, and as refugees they benefited from the humanitarian efforts of Americans as well. By the end of World War II, hostility began to abate even in Fresno, and by the 70s the Armenian community has been able to turn its attention to other problems.

FAMILY AND SOCIETY

The most useful adaptive institution for any immigrant group is very often the family. This was very much the case with the Armenians. The typical Armenian immigrant family was usually limited to husband, wife, and children, although occasionally more distant relatives (usually of the husband), boarders, and sometimes children orphaned by the massacres were added to the household. Though in the earliest years most immigrants were bachelors, after the 1894–1896 massacres women began to join the exodus, and after World War I women and children composed two-thirds of the Armenian immigrants. Men long outnumbered the women, however, and in the early years this made it difficult to marry within the group. According to one study of approximately 18,000 Armenian immigrants of

marriageable age in the years 1910–1917, males outnumbered females by 668 to 100. Still, intermarriage was extremely rare. A statistical study of intermarriage in New York City in the years from 1908 to 1912 revealed that in 91 marriages involving Armenians, only 16 men married outside the group. Armenian women married only Armenian men.

The low incidence of intermarriage stemmed from intense feelings that marriage to an *odar* (non-Armenian) would be unhappy and would lead to divorce, that it occurs only among undesirables, weakens "ethnic purity," and leads to the eventual extinction of Armenian culture. Prejudice against Armenians, especially in Fresno, discouraged it as well.

Elaborate stratagems were employed to perpetuate these Armenian unions. In the early days the paucity of females led many prospective bridegrooms to return to Europe to find wives—in Turkey before World War I, and in Marseilles, a populous Armenian community, or Beirut after the war. Immigrant men also imported wives from abroad after no more introduction than an exchange of photographs. The more liberated young in Fresno bewailed the immigrant matchmaking.

The question of intermarriage sharply divided many families. In preference to marriage arranged by the parents, the American-born children, influenced by the movies and popular magazines, gave wholehearted allegiance to the American notion of romantic love. Parental censure prevented women, particularly, from marrying non-Armenians, and as a result not a few remained unmarried for life. But in spite of this opposition, intermarriage continued to rise.

Armenians took pride in their family cohesiveness, discipline, and strict moral standards. Symptoms of family and social disintegration such as divorce (although allowed by the church), desertion, alcoholism, pauperism, crime, and juvenile delinquency were rare among Armenians in the early part of the century. But the sons and daughters of the immigrants soon faced the conflicting demands of their parents' Armenian world and of the world outside. Their upbringing in the 1920s and 1930s emphasized the importance of remaining faithful to Armenian traditions and its language and honoring the family; their experiences outside the family circle taught them that perpetuating the immigrant culture was un-American and that their Armenian names, dress, foods, and their parents' accents were odd. Parents did not ease their children's problems when they ruled out sports and other extracurricular activities because they interfered with afternoon or Saturday Armenian-language schools or with home and family-business chores. Finally, their strict moral discipline forbade unchaperoned social activities between the sexes, the wearing of cosmetics, and American ballroom dancing.

Greater affluence, mass culture, and almost universal education as far as college in the years after World War II sharply transformed the Armenian family ethos. The next generation adopted middle- and upper-middle-class American values. The Californians were generally more thoroughly assimilated than the easterners, but studies of individual parishes indicated that 60 to 70 percent of all third-generation Armenian Americans intermarried—raising troubling prospects for future ethnic preservation. Few were learning the language. Col-

lege-educated offspring replaced the tradition of ingrained respect for their elders with egalitarianism and meritocracy. Only a minority of ethnically conscious professionals, intellectuals, or community workers persisted in adhering to traditional family values.

The incidence of divorce, desertion, alcoholism, and the like among third-generation Armenians has not been studied, but there is evidence that divorce is on the increase, although the rate of divorce is still far below the national average. Crime and juvenile delinquency, though still minimal, are also increasing, especially among children of affluent parents. Brushes with the law among the children of immigrants from Soviet Armenia and the Middle East indicate the possible presence of severe generational problems among the newest arrivals.

The conflict between the old, prewar immigration and the new, postwar immigration from the Middle East, Bulgaria, and Soviet Armenia is a problem in the community today. Although the newcomers have been generously welcomed and some older immigrants enjoy the "Armenianness" they have injected into the community, tensions are obvious. Many of the newcomers are better educated than the older population, and they are equally ambitious. They appear to be taking over the leadership of established community institutions such as charity organizations and church boards. Behavioral differences arising from diverse backgrounds also create misunderstandings. Some newcomers, for whom churchgoing is routine, do not dress up for Sunday services, shocking the sense of propriety of the older Armenians. The newcomers' children play on the church grounds—unthinkable behavior to the older generation. In Los Angeles the alleged involvement of the newcomers' children in petty larceny and juvenile delinquency has brought dishonor to the entire community, according to the older generation. The Soviet Armenian immigrants have a reputation for perennially trying to outwit the government, imperiling generations of effort to establish a respectable place in American society.

On their side, the newcomers charge the earlier immigrants with being less Armenian and less patriotic than themselves, chiefly because they no longer have a good command of the language. To the immigrants and their children, whose many sacrifices built Armenian churches, supported Saturday schools, and assisted later arrivals, the charge of being "bad Armenians" is calumny. The newcomers feel degraded by the patronizing attitude of the older generation, are shocked that Armenian is not spoken in Armenian-American homes and disappointed that not all Armenian Americans are rich.

SOCIAL ORGANIZATION

The earliest and most numerous social organizations were the fraternal societies. A common feature of most immigrant groups, these societies brought together immigrants from the same villages, towns, and regions of the old country to raise funds for projects in their birthplace and to renew communal ties. At their peak in the 1920s and 1930s there were hundreds of them, with chapters in every large Armenian-American community. They organized reading rooms and at annual conventions voted funds for churches, schools, orphanages, and hospitals in Soviet Armenia and the Middle East. In contrast to the organizations of other immigrant groups, however, sickness or burial insurance was conspicuously absent; families were regarded as solely responsible for dealing with those contingencies.

Some of the organizations cut across regional affiliations. The Armenian General Benevolent Union (AGBU), founded in Cairo in 1906 and established in the United States in 1908, became the largest and most important of them. Its motto is, "An Armenian must not open his hand before an *odar*." Organized to provide relief for Turkish and Russian Armenians, the AGBU grew from a membership of 8,500 in 1913 to 18,700 in 1976; it now has an endowment of $32 million. Until 1960 its primary function lay in dealing with the material and educational needs of Armenian refugees throughout the Middle East. In the past 20 years it has also embarked on projects in the United States, especially the sponsoring of day schools in Massachusetts and Michigan; educational summer camps; relief, counseling, and job assistance to newcomers; and cultural activities, especially in dance and literature. An English-language quarterly, *Ararat* (1960), and a semimonthly in English and Armenian, *Hoosharar* (The Awakener; New York, f. 1913) are its major publications.

A second international philanthropic institution is the Armenian Relief Society, founded in 1910 as the Armenian Red Cross. The only Armenian organization limiting its membership to women, it now has about 16,000 members in 85 chapters in North America. Like the AGBU, it is involved chiefly in providing assistance and filling educational needs in Turkey, Cyprus, and the Middle East, although it has also embarked on major educational efforts in the United States, including a day school in Detroit and thirty-five Saturday schools in the United States and Canada, with a total enrollment of 1,000. The Armenian Relief Society remains separate from the AGBU because of the different political leanings of its members.

The AGBU and the Armenian Missionary Association of America (1918–) have established centers for the education of Armenian newcomers in the English language and in American customs and law in an attempt to bridge the gap between the old immigrant group and the new. The newcomers have also brought with them their own cultural institutions, among them the Homenetmen (a youth and athletic group), the Hamazkaine (International) Cultural Association, and the Tekeyan Cultural Association.

In addition to these organizations, informal social activities maintained regional and kinship ties during the immigrant generation. Visits between members of families, often unannounced, took place every Sunday. At these often-large gatherings, the women cooked Armenian meals (based on considerable advance preparation "just in case"); Armenian music on the *oud* (lute) and *doumbeg* (hand drum), children's singing, and recitations followed. Picnics were also extremely popular, and continue to be today. Sponsored by religious, political, or social groups, Sunday picnics in the early days could draw as many as 5,000 people to a nearby grove, park, or lake. They included speeches, marching-society drills, dancing, and athletic events. Beginning in 1909, Armenians participated in annual Raisin Day parades that celebrated the grape harvest in Fresno. In

fall and winter the major social events were the *hantes* (festivals) sponsored by a variety of community groups, often for fund-raising purposes. Some of them commemorated historic events—one large celebration in 1906 marked the 1,500th anniversary of the Armenian alphabet. A flourishing immigrant theater and athletic events, particularly boxing and wrestling, always found appreciative audiences.

The only exclusively male social institution was the coffeehouse (*srjaran*). There, in the early days, lonely workingmen could find Turkish coffee or strong drink, companionship, old-country foods, and a spirited backgammon game, garner the latest news, gossip about the homeland, and even occasionally pick up leads on jobs. A few immigrants began business careers as coffeehouse proprietors. The crowded coffeehouses served as indispensable social centers for a lonely male clientele, although in the process they often earned unsavory reputations as hangouts for gamblers and drunkards.

The adoption by the Armenian community of social activities more typical of the local culture did not really begin until the second generation. In the 1920s American-born Armenians played college football at Harvard, Brown, and Williams. In the 1930s the Armenian Olympics, sponsored by the Armenian Youth Federation, an offshoot of the Armenian Revolutionary Federation, each year brought Armenian youth together to compete in track and field, tennis, golf, swimming, and basketball. The Armenian Olympics are still held, and other games of the same type are also sponsored by the Western Armenian Athletic Association and the Homenetmen.

Social activities among the third generation include debutante cotillions, charity balls, and fund-raising banquets featuring celebrated stage, opera, and television performers. In California Armenians support Triple X, an Armenian athletic and charitable fraternity. Country clubs and tennis centers have multiplied, and in the 1970s the AGBU initiated annual fund-raising Armenian open golf tournaments at various country clubs.

The newcomers from the Middle East, the Soviet Union, and Europe are now reviving some of the older social forms, especially picnics and the ethnic theater.

POLITICS AND THE PRESS

The Armenian question in international politics arose with the Treaty of Berlin (1878). After the terrible atrocities of the 1877–1878 Russo-Turkish War, the European nations—England, France, Germany, Italy, Austria, and Russia—promised in that treaty to relieve the plight of the Armenian minority in Turkey. But European power rivalries and indifference soon led them to break the promise, just as rising nationalism and the example of the statehood of Greece and of the Balkan peoples inspired the Russian Armenians to attempt to liberate Turkish Armenia. By the early 1890s political parties were organizing to oppose Ottoman rule and form an independent nation.

The Armenian question first entered American politics during the massacres of 1894–1896, when outrage at the slaughter of 100,000 Christian Armenians and the threat to American missionaries and U.S. property in Turkey stirred up a national protest. In Washington surprisingly strong demands by members of Congress included gunboat diplomacy, the severance of diplomatic relations with Turkey, and the partition of Turkey between Russia and the West. However, the isolationist mood of the nation, President Grover Cleveland's conservatism, and the brewing Spanish-American War limited the administration to an appeal to the Treaty of Berlin signatories to effect reforms. Private humanitarian relief efforts were numerous, however. Armenophile organizations led by Alice Stone Blackwell and Julia Ward Howe joined others to dispatch the American Red Cross to Turkey. Schools, colleges, hospitals, and industries were rebuilt through American and Armenian philanthropy.

World War I summoned forth America's hitherto greatest humanitarian crusade. Organized through Near East Relief, the sole agency incorporated by Congress for aid to refugees in Biblical lands, and Armenian philanthropic organizations, American contributions to the "starving Armenians" enabled the building of refugee camps and hospitals and distribution of food and clothing to hundreds of thousands of Armenian refugees and orphans. Fund raising for them became so universal that American schoolchildren, said President Woodrow Wilson, knew as much about Armenia as they knew about England. Many first-generation Armenian Americans owe their lives to Near East Relief.

World War I saw the apogee of American involvement. In 1918 President Wilson, cognizant of the great sufferings of the Armenians and the bankruptcy of the Ottoman rule, called for an American mandate over the embattled Armenian Republic, and the geographical boundaries of Wilson's Armenia became the basis for Armenian national aspirations. Although the United States recognized the republic in 1920, conservative opposition to the League of Nations and the rejection of Wilsonian internationalism soon doomed the mandate and the cause.

The first Armenian nationalist group formed to further the cause of Armenian independence was the Social Democratic Hnchagian party, founded in Geneva in 1887 and in New York City and Providence, R.I., in 1891. In 1895 a second group, the Armenian Revolutionary Federation (Tashnagtsutiun, or the Tashnag party, or ARF), founded in Tiflis in 1890, established its first New World cadres. In 1898 the Hnchags split into two rival factions, opening the field to the Tashnags. In 1908 a new conservative organization, the Armenian Democratic Liberal party (the Ramgavars), formed by schismatic Hnchags and other groups, was organized first in Cairo and then throughout the diaspora. Another significant political organization was the Armenian Progressive party, a pro-Communist group founded in the United States in the 1930s. The combined membership of all these parties never exceeded 10,000 and is today about 5,000. Each of these parties is controlled by a central committee operating from Europe or the Middle East.

The function of each party was to organize émigré political support for its own solution to the Armenian question and to recruit men and collect supplies for political and military warfare in the Old World. Each founded journals to propagandize its effort. They established youth groups, reading rooms, and women's organizations to preserve Armenian identity in the diaspora until repatriation in a free Armenia became possible.

They also held public meetings and fund-raising rallies. Operationally each party's power rested with its *gomide* (cell) and the central committee.

Tactical and ideological issues sharply divided all the parties. In the early 1890s conservatives battled the revolutionary committees over the dangers involved in armed opposition to Sultan Abdul Hamid's regime. In the conservatives' view, help could come only through reliance on the European nations and the Treaty of Berlin. After the 1894–1896 massacres the nationalist Hnchag and Tashnag committees were suspected not only of having precipitated the massacres but even of having deliberately provoked the Ottoman regime into staging them as a way of forcing European intervention, a charge that envenomed the debate. This version is often accepted without criticism in Western writing on the Armenian question.

Since the Armenian Republic's absorption by Soviet Russia in 1920, the major political lines have been drawn in terms of attitude toward the U.S.S.R. For the Tashnags, who espouse a nationalist and irredentist cause, the destiny of the Armenians lies in a free and independent Armenia; under the Soviets, they believe, the will to be independent can only be weakened, perverted, and eventually destroyed, along with the Armenian Apostolic church, whose catholicos in Echmiadzin is seen as simply a tool of the Soviet Union. Although the Tashnag party briefly supported the post–World War II repatriation campaign of diaspora Armenians to Soviet Armenia, it remains staunchly anti-Soviet and anti-Communist; it found sustenance for the movement during the height of the cold war.

By contrast, the conservative Ramgavars accepted Soviet rule as an inevitable and beneficial step toward ensuring eventual independence by providing a great-power mandate over the beleaguered Armenians. In their view Soviet rule is infinitely preferable to an independence threatened by annihilation through Turkish massacres. The dramatic, though painful, social and economic progress of the Armenians under Soviet rule helps to support the Ramgavars' position. The pro-Communist Armenian Progressive party follows the international Communist party line with respect to Soviet Armenia and has no interest in liberation.

The immigrant press grew out of this party formation. The first Armenian-language papers in the United States actually predated the parties, but they were all short-lived, unable to attract outside support. The first long-lasting political journal was *Hairenik* (Fatherland), established by the Tashnag party in New York City in 1899, later moving to Boston. A daily since the pre–World War I period, *Hairenik* remains an important Armenian-language paper. The daily *Baikar* (Struggle), published in Watertown, dates from 1923 and is the organ of the Ramgavar party. Both major parties publish an English-language weekly: the Tashnag organ is the *Armenian Weekly* (Boston, f. 1934); and the Ramgavar, the *Armenian Mirror Spectator* (Watertown, f. 1932). Other Armenian-language newspapers include the Armenian Progressive *Lraper* (Messenger; New York, f. 1937), and the Hnchag *Eridasart Hayastan* (Young Armenia; Boston, f. 1903). The recent appearance of the weekly English-language *California Courier* (Fresno, f. 1958), *Armenian Observer* (Los Angeles, f. 1971), and *Armenian Reporter* (New York, f. 1967) suggests that nonpolitical journals may now be able to survive.

Unquestionably political parties nurtured Armenian national consciousness and interest in the Armenian question through their clubs and newspaper offices, which often became the center of the immigrants' political and intellectual life. However, the political divisions also fostered discord and disaffection. Since 1914 all but a few Armenian institutions and organizations have had a party affiliation—Hnchag, Tashnag, or Ramgavar. The parties' often-obsessive absorption in sterile issues has discouraged many younger people from becoming involved in Armenian community politics at all.

At the present time political tensions are waning, and the prospects for unity more encouraging. Every April 24 the three major political parties join together to commemorate Martyrs' Day in honor of the million victims of the 1915 massacre. The parties jointly support a variety of causes—the adoption by the U.S. Senate of the International Genocide Convention; the admission by the Turkish government that genocide did occur; demands for reparations; protection of Armenian monuments in Turkish lands, restoration of the historic Armenian lands to the nation, and justice for the sizable Armenian minority in Turkish Cyprus. The newest tool in this effort to achieve unity is the Armenian Assembly, formed in 1972 with headquarters and a professional staff in Washington, D.C., which encourages collaboration among all groups on a host of political and cultural endeavors.

Rising interest in Armenian political concerns today derives from a newly mobilized Armenian-American community, supported by national organizations and political representation. The first Armenian American to gain prominence in U.S. politics was Steven Derounian (1918–), a congressman from New York from 1952 to 1964. Since then substantial numbers have held local, state, and national office, especially in California, where in the 1970s George Deukmejian (1928–), minority leader of the California Senate, and assemblyman Walter Karabian (1938–) represented Armenian interests. Paul Ignateus (1920–) served as secretary of the navy under President Lyndon B. Johnson. The Armenian Assembly (1972) has encouraged Armenians to run for Congress.

On non-Armenian issues, the majority of the community leans to the Republican party, upholds conservative, middle-class attitudes about crime (Senator Deukmejian, for example, is a powerful advocate of reinstating capital punishment), taxes, education, and American foreign policy. For all the Armenians' conservatism, however, presidents Wilson and Franklin Delano Roosevelt remain heroes to the immigrants and still stand among the community's most revered political figures.

RELIGIOUS LIFE

The first parish of the Armenian Apostolic church in America was established in Worcester in 1891 under the pastorship of the Reverend Joseph Sarajian (1852–1913), who became the first bishop of the diocese in 1898. The first diocesan assembly was convened in Worcester in 1902. Despite severe financial and political problems and the dearth of educated clergy, the Armenian-American community was supporting 10

churches and 17 priests by 1916. Women and lay boards of trustees were particularly active in this early work. Communities that had no church worshiped in rented halls with lay or itinerant priests, or in nearby Protestant Episcopal churches, toward which, for a variety of emotional and historical reasons, the Armenians felt a particular affinity.

Over the next six decades the church grew substantially. In all the two Apostolic organizations now support 92 parishes in 52 communities. The establishment in 1962 of the St. Nerses Theological School in Evanston, Ill., which in 1966 became affiliated with St. Vladimir's Orthodox Theological Seminary in Crestwood, N.Y., alleviated the church's dependence on foreign-educated priests to serve their often almost entirely American-born congregations.

The church suffered a grievous constitutional split in 1933 over the attitude Armenians should take toward the Soviet regime in control of the Armenian church in Echmiadzin. The irredentist, nationalist Tashnags militantly refused to accept Soviet control. Their opponents, the pro-Echmiadzin church community and the Ramgavars, recognized Soviet control as a necessary accommodation. The schism was precipitated by the assassination of Archbishop Levon Tourian while he was celebrating the divine liturgy on December 24, 1933, in Holy Cross Church in New York City. Nine Tashnags were convicted of the crime. The "Tourian episode," as it was referred to, split the Armenian church; communities, parishes, and even families were arrayed against each other. Although the Tashnags steadfastly deny any official role in the crime and maintain that their party members were wrongly convicted, the Tashnag party is still held responsible for the assassination and is anathematized by many older Armenians.

The Ramgavars and others recognizing the Armenian catholicos in Echmiadzin remain under the jurisdiction either of an archbishop whose diocesan headquarters are in New York City or of one in California. The Tashnag group organized its own prelacy in 1958 and in 1965 successfully petitioned to be taken under the jurisdiction of the Cilician catholicate in Antelias, Lebanon, which recognizes the spiritual leadership of Echmiadzin, but remains, as it has in the past, administratively independent of it. The pro-Echmiadzin church asserts that the Apostolic community is split 80 percent Echmiadzin and 20 percent Antelias, but the pro-Antelias church claims 55 percent Echmiadzin and 45 percent Antelias. There are no doctrinal differences between the two groups, and attempts at rapprochement are actively under way.

Today the church remains the single most important institution in the Armenian-American community. The people revere it as a means of preserving the community's culture and identity. Although regular attendance at services is low, an estimated 70 percent of the group have been baptized into the church, and Christmas and Easter services still draw overflow crowds. The steady proliferation of churches and cultural centers, of which the St. Vartan Armenian Cathedral and Cultural Center in New York City (1968) is the most imposing, is evidence that the church remains strong.

Priests in the United States are elected by the laity and ordained by bishops; ultimate authority rests with the catholicos in conjunction with lay and clerical councils. Holding to tradition, the *kahanas* (lower-order priests) may marry, but *vartabeds* (doctors of theology), from whom the episcopacy is drawn, are under vows of celibacy. The three-hour service remains intact, with the liturgy in classical Armenian; the sermon, however, is often in both English and Armenian.

One of the church's major accommodations to the New World culture is the diminution of religious life. The emphasis on saints' days, the 160 fast days, the kissing of church walls, and daily visits to matins and vespers disappeared very early. Even Sunday attendance had lapsed by 1914. To keep its communicants, the contemporary church has had to adopt such modern innovations as youth groups, athletic groups, bazaars, bingo games, parents' associations, men's societies, and women's clubs. But to survive, the church must resolve the problems of a diminishing priesthood, of ever-growing financial demands, of language, of waning attendance, especially among younger communicants, and above all, of schism between the two communities.

The most significant religious minority in the Armenian-American community are the Armenian Protestants. Of the 19 Protestant churches, 17 are Congregational and 2 are Presbyterian; together they have an estimated 4,000 communicants and another 4,000 supporting members, about 2 percent of the community. In 1971 the Protestant Evangelical Union of Eastern States (f. 1901) and the Armenian Union of California (f. 1908) united into the Armenian Evangelical Union of North America. There is also a handful of Armenian Spiritualist churches scattered among the various communities. The Protestants faced far fewer challenges in the early years than did the Apostolic church members. Local missionary societies, many of whose personnel were former missionaries in Turkey, supported the tiny congregations with funds, Armenian-language prayer books, and accommodations for prayer meetings in Congregational churches.

The Protestants laid less stress on preserving their Armenian culture and identity, although they did emphasize that they were "good Armenians" and belonged to an Armenian church. Services were first held in Armenian and Turkish, but quickly shifted to English. Armenian heroes and historical events were not such frequent subjects of sermons; the injunction to speak Armenian in the home was not imposed as sternly as it was among the Apostolic Armenians; and rates of intermarriage were significantly higher. The clergy were soon more assimilated and are now more liberal than their Apostolic counterparts are apt to be (the only Armenian cleric to march in a civil-rights demonstration in the 1960s was a Protestant).

Nonetheless, ethnic revival among the Protestants has also been noticeable in recent years. Ties with the mother church are closer—a result of the recent immigration and the ecumenical movement. In 1970 the Protestant churches sponsored a committee of rapprochement with the Apostolic church, which was welcomed by the Armenian catholicos in Echmiadzin. Retreats for clergy of both faiths have been held. Protestant churches have begun to incorporate Armenian hymns, historical themes, and ceremonial practices, such as the use of candles in the church and wine instead of grape juice in the Eucharist into their services. They have also participated in community-wide commemorations of the 1915 massacre. In return, Ar-

menian cleric to march in a civil-rights demonstration bers of the Armenian-American community.

A third religious community is the Armeno-Catholics. Their first congregation was established in New York City around 1910; five more have since been added. Of the six churches, those in Cambridge, Mass., and Los Angeles are of the Armenian Mkhitarist Order of Vienna, while those in Detroit, New York City, Philadelphia, and Paterson, N.J., are under the authority of the Armenian Catholic patriarchate in Beirut, and ultimately of the Pope in Rome; the community numbers about 7,000. The Eastern-rite mass and liturgy are in Armenian, although sermons are commonly in English. The Holy Cross Armenian Catholic Church in Cambridge supports St. Gregory's Armenian Language School and a camp on Cape Cod and produces Armenian-language phonograph records. In 1976, on the 300th anniversary of the birth of the order's founder, Abbot Mkhitar of Sivas, planning began for a *vank* (monastery) in Cambridge.

CULTURE AND GROUP MAINTENANCE

The immigrant generation found time to establish a rich cultural life out of the traditions they brought with them from the Old World. Armenian food stores, Turkish Armenian music and cuisine, Armenian dance, theater, language, and newspapers lent an unmistakable Old World flavor to the larger colonies. But changes were soon apparent. Most dramatic was the diminished use of the Armenian language, whose maintenance had long been regarded as essential to preserving Armenian identity. Factory laborers early learned American slang; second-generation children whose parents addressed them in Armenian responded in a hybrid, kitchen Armenian and used only English outside the home. Until recently the third generation was almost totally ignorant of the ancestral language. The written language fared even worse, and immigrant men of letters writing in the mother tongue soon lacked both a ready audience in America and contact with Armenia. Political journals like *Hairenik Amsakir* (Hairenik Monthly; Boston, f. 1922) and the *Baikar Patsarig* (Baikar Annual; Boston, f. 1941) provided outlets for writers in Armenian, but generally the United States did not support writers in the old language, and the community even begrudged them sustenance as teachers, editors, or party organizers.

Although literature was not a common pursuit among the second generation, there were a few notable writers, among them William Saroyan (1908–), born and raised in Fresno. Saroyan's *Daring Young Man on the Flying Trapeze* was published in 1934; his play, *The Time of Your Life*, won a Pulitzer Prize in 1939; by the early forties he was a popular new voice in American letters, often writing about the Fresno Armenians of his boyhood. Leon Surmelian's (1905–) autobiographical *I Ask You, Ladies and Gentlemen* (1945) was well received; Michael Arlen (Dikran Kouyoumjian, 1895–1956) was a popular British novelist of the twenties; his son, Michael J. Arlen (1930–) is known for *Exiles* (1970), *Passage to Ararat* (1975, National Book Award), and as the television critic for the *New Yorker* magazine. Diana Der Hovanessian (1924–) is a noted poet.

The appearance in 1960 of *Ararat*, an English-language quarterly sponsored by the AGBU, has created a forum for young Armenian-American writers, but its circulation (currently 800) testifies to the limitations of the community's present literary commitment.

Armenian music enjoys continuous and widespread popularity. Folk and liturgical music, compiled in part by the 19th-century composer Gomidas Vartabed (1869–1935), expressed the Armenians' religious, national, and cultural yearnings. Armenian operas were produced by popular touring companies in the 1920s. The most celebrated singer was Armen Shah Mouradian (1878–1939), whose recordings had a place in every Armenian home. Since the 1950s professionally led choral groups like the Gomidas Male Choir (New York) and the Erevan Choral Society (Boston) have enjoyed widespread success. Armand Tokatyan (1899–1960), Lucine Amara (1927–), Paolo Ananian, and Lily Chookasian (1925–) have had careers in opera. Composers whose works often draw on Armenian inspiration are Richard Yardumian (1917–) and Alan Hovhaness (1911–). Dance also remains extremely popular, both in small informal groups and in professionally led troupes like the Antranig and Nayiri dance groups in New York City. Visiting dance troupes from Soviet Armenia draw capacity crowds everywhere. Church groups often provide scholarships for promising musicians and composers. The newest popular music derives its inspiration from the modernized, Western idiom of Lebanon, the homeland of the current wave of immigrants, in contrast to the more traditional styles of the older immigrant-generation music, although a new movement toward ethnic purism has led to criticism of the inclusion of Turkish dances and songs in Armenian repertories.

Distinguished cultural contributions have also been made by Rouben Nakian (1897–), Haig Patigian (1876–1950), Arshile Gorky (born Vostanig Adoian, 1905–1948), and Hovsep Pushman (1877–1966) in art; Yosuf Karsh (1908–) in photography; Rouben Mamoulian (1897–) in the theater; and Ben Bagdikian (1920–) in journalism.

The Friends of Armenian Culture encourage appreciation of Armenian arts among non-Armenians. They have sponsored 17 annual Armenian Nights in Boston, featuring premières of works by Armenian composers. For years the Friends have also sponsored a weekly radio program of classical Armenian music.

On a popular level, Armenian cooking has gained many adherents. Armenian foods such as *lavash* and *dun hatz* (breads) and bulghur (cracked wheat) pilaf, as well as the more generally Middle Eastern foods, shish kebab, yalanchi dolma, madzoon (yogurt, allegedly introduced into the United States by Armenians), losh kebab, and baklava, are increasingly familiar items everywhere.

The community has been a conduit for study of Middle Eastern civilizations, especially during World War I, when books about the massacres, written by Armenian Americans and American missionaries in Turkey, and Alice Stone Blackwell's widely disseminated translation of *Armenian Poems* (1896) were widely read. Armenians are aware that Americans know little about Armenia; they call the massacre of 1915 the "unremembered genocide." Films, ethnic-heritage publica-

tions, and institutions like the Armenian Library and Museum of America and the Armenian Cultural Foundation, both in Boston, seek to end this neglect.

In the past decade a powerful effort has been made to revive Armenian-American cultural awareness, emphasizing language and heritage maintenance and the active pursuit of Old World political claims. As cultural interpenetration, intermarriage, and other evidence of acculturation increase, vigorous conservative forces are seeking to preserve the threatened ethnic heritage. The first step in this effort was the Armenian studies movement. In 1959 the Armenian-American community, through the National Association for Armenian Studies and Research, established a chair in Armenian studies at Harvard University. The $300,000 donation by the Armenians indicated both their commitment to learning and their apprehension over the possibility that, unsupported by a political state, their culture would eventually disappear. This and subsequent endowments at the University of California at Los Angeles and the University of Pennsylvania ensure the recognition and study of their heritage. Programs at Wayne State University in Detroit, Boston University, Columbia University, Fresno State College, and the Armenian-International College (f. 1976) in LaVerne, Calif., also now promote the study of the Armenian past.

The rapid growth in the period since 1960 of an Armenian primary and secondary parochial-school system reveals the new stress on language and cultural maintenance. The afternoon and Saturday schools had operated vigorously but on limited resources; meager funding, old-fashioned materials, and competition with other activities limited their success. In the 1960s a more prosperous community, expanded by the newcomers from the Middle East and buoyed by the more general revival of ethnic studies, established full-day, professionally staffed, and well-financed schools with Armenian and non-Armenian curricula. To some Armenians ethnic survival is inextricably tied to the survival of the language. To others it is obvious that the flourishing community is already being led by many non-Armenian-speaking sons and daughters and that a renaissance of the language would in any case not revive Armenian letters. Nonetheless, in addition to the currently bolstered Saturday language-school system, with 62 schools and 3,800 students, there are 13 full-time schools with a total enrollment of 1,950 and every prospect of expanding.

Another support for group maintenance has come from the contacts between Armenian Americans and Soviet Armenia, especially since the end of the Stalinist regime. In 1959 Armenian-American travel agencies began scheduling group tours to the homeland, and by now 1,200 Armenian Americans annually spend two to three weeks in Yerevan, Echmiadzin, and the Armenian countryside. In the same period, dance and music groups, monthly English- and Armenian-language magazines and newspapers, and other cultural imports from Soviet Armenia, many sponsored by the Committee for Cultural Relations with Armenians Abroad, have been enthusiastically received in the United States.

The future of the ethnic revival is uncertain. Assimilation will continue with increasing intermarriage and with the adoption of English and of middle-class mores by the most recent arrivals. It is the almost unavoidable result of exposure to the public school system, the press, and television, of geographic mobility as well as the tolerance toward different cultures that exists in the United States. The depletion of the Armenian community in the Middle East, long the bastion of Armenian nationalism, is also a cause for concern. On the other hand, the growing unity of the churches and political parties, the existence of the Armenian Assembly, pride in the achievements of their fellows in Soviet Armenia, and visits to the homeland are sources of ethnic strength. The common memory of a tragic past and the quest for recognition of past injustices will stimulate further political mobilization, and the fear of ultimate national extinction will foster ethnic cohesion. The prospect for the Armenian Americans in the next generation is for continued ethnic vitality amid growing acculturative forces.

Bibliography
A useful introduction to the Old World background is David Marshall Lang, *Armenia: Cradle of Civilization* (London, 1970); Sirarpie Der Nersessian, *The Armenians* (New York, 1970), on the ancient and medieval periods, is more scholarly. A superb study of political backgrounds, by Richard G. Hovannisian, an authority on the modern period, is *Armenia on the Road to Independence, 1918* (Berkeley, Calif., 1967).

A modern comprehensive study of the Armenian Americans has not been published. M. Vartan Malcom, *Armenians in America* (1919; reprint, San Francisco, 1969), was the first English-language work on the subject. "Armenians in America," a special Bicentennial issue of *Ararat* 18 (Winter 1977), contains articles on the community's history, culture, and achievements. Useful studies of important Armenian-American communities are W.P.A. Writers' Project, *The Armenians in Massachusetts* (Boston, 1937); Charles Mahakian, *History of the Armenians in California* (San Francisco, 1974); and Wilson D. Wallis, *Fresno Armenians, to 1919* (Lawrence, Kans., 1965). Sarkis Atamian, *Armenian Community: The Historical Development of a Social and Ideological Conflict* (New York, 1955), covers the internal political conflicts from a Tashnag point of view. Other studies are Mary Bosworth Treudley's stimulating "Ethnic Group's View of the American Middle Class," *American Sociological Review* 11 (1946): 715–724; and Robert Mirak, "On New Soil: The Armenian Orthodox and Armenian Protestant Churches in the New World to 1915," in *Immigrants and Religion in Urban America*, ed. Randall Miller and Thomas Marzik (Philadelphia, 1977).

The best introduction to William Saroyan is *The Saroyan Special* (1949; reprint, Freeport, N.Y., 1970), which includes sparkling descriptions of early Fresno. A brilliant account of one Armenian American's discovery of his heritage is Michael J. Arlen, *Passage to Ararat* (New York, 1975).

The most important collections of primary materials on Armenian Americans are in Greater Boston at the Armenian Cultural Foundation (on the immigrant press), the Armenian Library and Museum of America (a collection of oral-history tapes and artifacts), and the archives of the Armenian Revolutionary Federation (on politics).

ROBERT MIRAK

ARYAN

Aryan refers to the Indo-European-speaking people who occupied the Iranian plateau and the Indian subcontinent in prehistoric times. These people, who amalgamated with the non-Aryans already living in this area, spoke a language from which all Indo-European languages subsequently evolved. In more modern times the term Aryan has been used as a synonym for Nordic or Gentile. The Nazis used it in the racist literature of the 1920s and 1930s to distinguish the ideal German from the Jews, Gypsies, Slavs, and other peoples whom they considered inferior and expendable. Except in linguistics, the term is now in general disfavor.

ASIAN

The term Asian, as it is commonly used in the United States, refers to people of East Asian ancestry, most often to the Chinese, Filipinos, Koreans, and Japanese, as well as to Southeast Asians—Burmese, Indochinese, Indonesians, and Thai. In some contexts the Kalmyks and the Tatars are described as Asian.

Asian Americans currently prefer the term Asian to Oriental, which has almost the same meaning. Earlier in the history of the United States, almost all people from geographic Asia—Turkey, Persia, India, and Asia—were referred to as Asians, Asiatics, or Orientals.

ASSIMILATION AND PLURALISM

The historical and contemporary reality of the United States as a society composed of different ethnic groups and backgrounds has encouraged many interpretations of diversity and change. From its inception as a new, unique political system and society to the present day, the United States has been acknowledged to be a blend of numerous people of different origins. Accordingly, we have long been confronted with a major question: what happens to the groups and individuals who make up this diversity? What has happened in the past, and how can we describe what is happening in the present?

Popular characterizations of American society generalize the product of diversity in such metaphors as melting pot, salad bowl, mosaic, transmuting pot, stewing pot, crucible, and symphonic orchestration. These intriguing symbols are matched by more scholarly terms describing the processes and consequences of diversity: accommodation, acculturation, adaptation, amalgamation, Americanization, ethnocentrism, ethnogenesis, homogenization, integration, miscegenation, nativism, naturalization, racism, segmentation, and segregation. Centripetal and centrifugal forces are complements in the American experience.

The many different ideas and terms fall into two broader categories: those of *assimilation*, the processes that lead to greater homogeneity in society, and those of *pluralism*, conditions that produce sustained ethnic differentiation and continued heterogeneity. In both categories, however, there are variations that make it all the more difficult to describe the reality. Assimilation, for example, involves fundamental social change, but it has many levels and stages; individuals and groups may be partially, as well as completely, assimilated over the course of lifetimes and generations in the United States. More important, the question arises of assimilation to what? The three possibilities, all discussed subsequently, are further specifications of ethnic change: individuals and/or groups of a particular ethnic background may assimilate to some form of the dominant Anglo-Saxon Protestant ethnicity; there may be assimilation to another ethnic collectivity, perhaps one that is a minority in terms of size and power; and last, a group or individual may assimilate to a truly mixed subculture, either one that becomes a "new ethnicity" itself, as in the ethnogenesis of the Appalachians or the Mormons, or perhaps to a less structured and more diffuse subculture, such as that of the mixed-background Americans who do indeed constitute the "new breed" of the melting pot.

Pluralism, too, is a complex and dynamic category. The heterogeneity of the American people is not necessarily limited to static sources of traditionalism, past affiliations to race, religion, and national origin. Diversity may evolve, not only through the transplantation of ethnic communities in immigration but through the development of neotraditionalism, the emergence of differentiated regional ethnic cultures, the rise of religioethnic sectarianism, different forms of political ethnicity, and new syntheses, as in ethnogenesis. That both assimilation and pluralism, the phenomena of greater homogeneity and greater heterogeneity, are linked with the idea of change in a culturally diverse society is not always appreciated. Each has its own dynamic evolutionary nature, but each has a correspondence to the other. It is in this sense that the assimilationist and pluralist perspectives resemble the image of the glass of water that is either half full or half empty.

Assimilation and pluralism share another characteristic, that of group belonging and group boundaries. On the question of ethnic diversity in the United States, anthropology, history, sociology, and the popular media have generally emphasized group behavior as opposed to that of individuals or social types. A remarkable number of terms, ideas, and concepts have been developed to describe or predict the changing nature of group life in the United States or to document persisting ethnic forms. The words quoted in the second paragraph of this essay, for example, have usually been used to describe either the whole society or a particular ethnic group; the nature of ethnic change for the individual has been relatively neglected.

Assimilation and pluralism apply in some way to the majority of Americans. For the individuals involved, the tug between the forces that urge absorption into some other ethnic background and the constraints that affirm distinctive attachments creates pressure and a dilemma. In either case, however, whether representing a form of assimilation or an aspect of pluralism, the individual is part of a group; for the first, one is changing from one group to another, and for the second, one is remaining or changing within the group. Both ideas involve group relationships. There are other possibilities as well, particularly in an ethnically diverse society that is experiencing social upheaval and widespread change. These possibilities concern individuals more than groups, and the ethnic factor is central to their stories.

GROUP EXPERIENCE AND CHANGE

Concepts of American diversity can be considered in three general stages. In the years before 1900 diversity was often discussed with respect to the ethnic variety of the population, both in the later years of the 18th century and throughout the old immigration of the 19th century. The new immigration, mainly from southern and eastern Europe at the beginning of the 20th century, stimulated even more debate and had different nuances. The third stage coincided with the beginnings of American sociology in the 20th century, when scholars began to study the changes of ethnic life in the United States systematically from sociological and political perspectives.

These three stages—the first two expressed in reports

by travelers, journalists, foreign visitors, educators, and social philosophers; and the third, in studies by social scientists—all generally regard ethnicity as a group phenomenon. Change was described and predicted for those many Americans who belonged to the more visible ethnic backgrounds that may not have been white or Anglo-Saxon or familiarly Protestant. These writers assumed that adaptation to life in the United States meant some form of assimilation or of pluralism and thus some adjustments in a group's ethnicity, and indeed in the very meaning of ethnicity.

The word *ethnicity* is of recent usage, but the idea is old. The less precise definitions in the early social science literature convey the same interpretation as that used by the popular media: groups of distinctive national origin or language viewed as foreign minorities, such as the Irish, the Hungarians, or the Italians. Ethnicity was not an attribute of the native-born Protestant Yankees or of the dominant majority group in any community. Ethnicity, furthermore, did not have a racial (meaning physical) component, so Afro-Americans and American Indians were not considered to be ethnic groups. (Here one must deal with the confusions in the past usage of the word *race*, which was often used to mean ethnicity, as in the Irish race or the Jewish race.)

Ethnicity did not generally apply to religious distinctiveness either, so the Mormons and the Amish were not typically seen as ethnic groups, although the Jews were variously described as racial, ethnic, or religious, depending often on the context. And finally, ethnicity did not extend to regional distinctiveness, so New England Yankees, Texans, and Southerners were not regarded as ethnic groups. While the words ethnic and ethnicity were not commonly used before the turn of this century, the idea was conveyed implicitly and in a general way through the use of such terms as immigrant group, foreign stock, language group, race, and national background. Interestingly, the three major sources of ethnicity are located quite explicitly in the celebrated threefold qualification of the egalitarian American ethic—"regardless of race, creed, or national origin."

A more modern and encompassing definition of ethnicity would emphasize group criteria without reference to any specific content or form. Questions of assimilation and pluralism, then, would apply to any group of people that had a common historical origin, some conception of cultural and social distinctiveness, a role as a unit in a larger and diverse system of social relations, a manifest or latent network of associations beyond kinship and locality, some acknowledgment of its own diversity in different settings and for different individuals, and some attachment to a set of historically derived group symbols. With total assimilation one would expect the formerly specific content of these six attributes to change over time. The historical meaning of the ethnic culture and the corresponding network and group identity would ultimately disappear, and the change could be said to be complete.

Directions of Assimilation   There are three paths to complete assimilation, and the question of direction is critical. A group's attachment to its origins and to its cultural and social distinctiveness could yield to attachment to the dominant culture, as in the possibility of German Lutherans or Dutch Calvinists or French Huguenots becoming English Protestants, in group terms. The different ethnic groups would become a part of the English Protestants in culture, structure, and identity. Complete assimilation would mean that the formerly different would now be integral parts of English ethnicity; there would be a change from minority ethnicity to dominant ethnicity. The dominant group, in this case, would not change but would be large enough to receive others into the ethnic background. This is one meaning of Anglo-conformity or Americanization.

Theoretically, this kind of assimilation would mean that every formerly distinctive ethnic group would change and become part of the Anglo-Saxon ethnic majority, which is viewed as dominant. All Americans would possess the ethnicity of the English, there would be complete homogenization and cultural uniformity, and the traditional meaning of ethnicity would disappear in the United States, along with the notion of diversity. This phenomenon was anticipated by a number of past writers.

A second possibility, that of assimilating into another nondominant ethnic background or group, is considerably less likely to have been described historically. Under these terms, individuals who share a distinctive ethnic culture, structure, and identity would alter those aspects of their group life and assume the identity of another ethnic collectivity in the United States. This possibility is suggested in Ruby Jo Reeves Kennedy's theory of the "triple melting pot," in which nationality groups merge through intermarriage and acculturation into their larger respective religious backgrounds: Swedish, German, and English Protestants, for example, as one pool; Italian, Irish, and Polish Catholics as another; and Spanish, German, and Eastern European Jews as a third.

Will Herberg anticipated this development in his vision of tripartite religion in the United States; he went even further, arguing that this kind of assimilation could result in the dominance of a single ethnicity in each religious blend. Italian Catholics might be said to become "Irish" as they merged into the Irish model of Catholicism in their American experience. Analogously, Sephardic and German Jews, despite their earlier arrival in America, might lose their respective distinctiveness in the face of the much more numerous East European Ashkenazim, as all Jews underwent assimilation in the United States. Scandinavian and Dutch Protestants, similarly, would evolve into an English or Anglo-Saxon ethnicity through intermarriage and amalgamation. The melting of backgrounds might result in the merger of the Catholic and the Jewish groups into related but different minority ethnicities, while the various European Protestant groups would be assimilated into Anglo-conformity, the first direction discussed above. In this assimilation process, the relative similarity of ethnic background is the key. Related phenomena include the expected absorption of West Indian blacks into the larger Afro-American community through marriage and acculturation, the integration of some of the smaller Spanish-speaking ethnic groups into the larger Mexican or Puerto Rican collectivities, and even the reception of interracial children into the black subculture. These all suggest assimilation from one minority background to another.

The third possibility, assimilation of truly mixed backgrounds in a new ethnicity or character, is the meaning of the melting pot per se in most of the literature. In this development no one dominant ethnicity or past ethnic contribution stands out more than any other. Unlike the other two possibilities, in this case the ethnic group's culture, structure, and identity are not incorporated into the dominant background, as in Anglo-conformity, or into another ethnic minority, as in the Catholic fusion. Instead all ethnic backgrounds, including the dominant Anglo-Saxons as well as the various minority ethnic groups, are integrated into a new creation, a new breed of humanity, presumably with its own ethnic culture, structure, and identity in a still diverse world. Ethnogenesis, the evolution of and assimilation to a new ethnicity rather than to a preexisting culture, is a relatively unexplored idea in modern times. In the United States the Creoles of color, or on a smaller scale the Nanticoke Indians, correspond to this development. In other parts of the world, there are comparable fusions of diverse ethnic backgrounds, all culminating in something new out of something marginal, as with some Israelis, the Cape Coloureds of South Africa, the Anglo-Indians of India, the mixed people of Hawaii, the Eurasians of Indonesia, or what Everett Hughes has called "new peoples."

Anglo-conformity versus the Melting Pot The writings of the earliest commentators on American diversity, in the 18th and 19th centuries, emphasized assimilation over pluralism for many different ethnic groups and backgrounds, but they did not generally include America's blacks and Indians. Nor did they foresee an ethnic group's absorption into another minority ethnic category. The debate was largely between those who prophesied the amalgamation of diverse cultures, mostly of northern and western European origin, under the hegemony of the English or Anglo-Americans, and those who saw the incorporation of such diversity into a uniquely American national character.

The Anglo-conformity view prevailed. John Jay expressed it this way in *The Federalist* papers (1787): "Providence had been pleased to give this one connected country, to one united people, a people descended from the same ancestors, speaking the same language, professing the same religion, attached to the same principles of government, very similar in their manners and customs." Many other writers also perceived the development of the American people, with the inevitable exclusion of blacks and Indians, as an assimilation to the ethnicity of the English, transplanted to America. The process would evolve over time, changing Anglo-Saxons and other Europeans and their descendants into what Winthrop Jordan terms "non-English Englishmen."

A good many advocates of Anglo-conformity championed the cause vigorously throughout the 19th century. Writing on immigration to the United States, Jesse Chickering in 1848 acknowledged the great diversity of the white population but emphasized its growing assimilation to Englishness. In his view of the American people, "The English language is almost wholly used; the English manners, modified to be sure, predominate, and the spirit of English liberty and enterprise animates the energies of the whole people. English laws and institutions, adapted to the circumstances of the country,

have been adopted here . . . The tendency of things is to mould the whole into one people, whose leading characteristics are English, formed on American soil." The same perceptions, speculations, and wishes were expressed by many others in succeeding decades, some with dispassionate objectivity, others displaying the emotions represented by nativism, Know-Nothingism, Anglo-Saxonism, and the Ku Klux Klan.

Like Anglo-conformity, the melting pot idea had early beginnings. Fewer people envisioned the society as a new synthesis, however, and they did not always agree on terms and details. The idea of the "new humanity" may have seemed too innovative, too overwhelming, and too romantic. In *Common Sense* (1776), Thomas Paine declared that "Europe, and not England, is the parent country of America." Other descriptions of the United States as a nation free of English dominance, emphasized the idea of a blend. Jean de Crèvecoeur, in his *Letters from an American Farmer* of 1782, asked the famous question, "What, then, is the American, this new man?" and answered by referring to the many European ingredients in the biological and cultural amalgam, resulting in a national character that transcended Europe. "Here individuals of all nations are melted into a new race of men, whose labours and posterity will one day cause great changes in the world."

In stressing the European rather than the narrowly English origins of American civilization, such commentators did not take adequate account of the presence of the blacks from Africa and the native American Indians. Crèvecoeur ignored the blacks, and in another letter he predicted that the Indians would eventually disappear from the colonized settlements of the United States. Another emphasis on European exclusivity was offered by Jedidiah Morse in *The American Geography* (1789):

> Intermingled with the Anglo-Americans, are the Dutch, Scotch, Irish, French, Germans, Swedes and Jews; all these, except the Scotch and Irish, retain, in a greater or less degree, their native language, in which they perform their public worship, converse and transact their business with each other. The time, however, is anticipated . . . when the language, manners, customs, political and religious sentiments of the mixed mass of people who inhabit the United States, shall have become so assimilated, as that all nominal distinctions shall be lost in the general and honourable name of Americans.

Less political and more poetic figures did include the native Indians and the blacks in the idea of a complete merger. Writing in 1845, Ralph Waldo Emerson may have been the first to employ the metaphor of the melting down and fusing together of different metals to create a new compound. As with the development of Corinthian brass, he wrote of the Americans, "so in this continent,—asylum of all nations,—the energy of Irish, Germans, Swedes, Poles, and Cossacks, and all the European tribes,—of the Africans, and of the Polynesians, —will construct a new race, a new religion, a new state, a new literature, which will be as vigorous as the new Europe which came out of the smelting-pot of the Dark Ages, or that which earlier emerged from the Pelasgic and Etruscan barbarism. *La Nature aime les croisements.*"

One early commentator on diversity, Alexis de Tocqueville, saw several distinct possibilities. In *De-*

mocracy in America, written in 1835, Tocqueville wrote a lengthy chapter on "The Present and Probable Future Condition of the Three Races That Inhabit the Territory of the United States." Discussing the Indians, Negroes, and Europeans in an arrangement of tense pluralism, he wrote that "fortune has brought them together on the same soil, where, although they are mixed, they do not amalgamate, and each race fulfills its destiny apart." Not optimistic about these interethnic relations, Tocqueville nevertheless saw persisting cultural differences and a kind of pluralism and diversity as a basic condition in American society. He predicted, however, that the Indian nations were ultimately "doomed to perish" with extensive European settlement, and that the blacks "must either wholly part or wholly mingle" in order to avoid continued subordination, even after emancipation. Parting was either difficult or impossible, but mingling, to Tocqueville, represented a "true bond of union" between the different races. Although not frequent, there had been enough amalgamation of races in Tocqueville's America to convince him, not only of the possibility, but also of the uniqueness of assimilation. Writing of European and African mulattos, he said, "the two races may really be said to be combined, or, rather, to have been absorbed in a third race, which is connected with both without being identical with either." Tocqueville saw the solution to racial antipathies in a new, distinctive ethnicity. As for the European presence in the United States, he predicted a continuing assimilation to Anglo-American life, with some exceptions and qualifications. Homogenization seemed inevitable. "If this tendency to assimilation brings foreign nations closer to each other," he argued, "it must *a fortiori* prevent the descendants of the same people from becoming aliens to one another. The time will therefore come when one hundred and fifty million men will be living in North America, equal in condition, all belonging to one family, owing their origin to the same cause, and preserving the same civilization, the same language, the same religion, the same habits, the same manners, and imbued with the same opinions, propagated under the same forms."

Tocqueville, like others in the early 19th century, was viewing a relatively homogeneous white immigrant population, mainly from northern and western Europe. Much greater diversity came later in the century. The sources of mass immigration shifted to eastern and southern Europe. By 1900 alternatives to complete ethnic change, transition, and assimilation, began to be discussed; the time had come for an explicit philosophy of cultural pluralism.

With the more evident diversity of the 20th century, particularly in the most heavily populated sections and in the large cities, social thought on the ethnic question began to divide three ways. The melting pot ideal took on renewed vigor with the production of a play of that name in 1908, written by an English Jew, Israel Zangwill. The phrase became established in the popular mind as a prophecy for America's many ethnic constituencies. Zangwill's ideas were romantic, but like Emerson's words in 1845, they were egalitarian and universal. Everyone was to be involved in the merger, not just minorities, but the dominant cultures as well. It was not just for diverse white European groups but em-

braced the African and Asian cultures as well. The crucible of America would solve *all* conflicts among different races, religions, and nationalities by eliminating their historic origins and creating a new identity instead. The Zangwill romance acknowledged no English or Anglo-Saxon hegemony; no "real" American had emerged at the time of the play, for the process of assimilation was not yet complete.

The Pluralist Alternative The overall response to Zangwill's play demonstrated both the persistence of Anglo-conformity and the beginnings of cultural pluralism. Many groups, dominant and minority, were apprehensive, anticipating the loss of cultural distinctiveness. Anglo-conformity, now called Americanization, took more precise shape. There was still some tolerance, but nervousness and hostility were increasing. Critics of the new immigrants compared them unfavorably with model Anglo-Americans. The new immigrants were usually poor, visibly different, mainly non-Protestants; they came from southern and eastern Europe; they were Roman Catholics, Jews, or members of various Orthodox churches. Their critics viewed Anglo-conformity as the best "solution" to what they saw as crime, poverty, and deprivation among the immigrant masses.

During the years of the movement to restrict immigration in the United States, and in the build-up of emotions that preceded the 1921 trial and conviction of Nicola Sacco and Bartolomeo Vanzetti, Anglo-conformity included variants of the threat "shape up or ship out." A popular song written in 1915 symbolized the anti-immigrant mood. The title, "Don't Bite the Hand That's Feeding You," compared the new immigrant to an angry and ungrateful dog, and the words were quite specific: "If you don't like your Uncle Sammy, Then go back to your home o'er the sea, To the land from where you came, Whatever be its name, But don't be ungrateful to me!" Gratefulness came to mean not only loyalty to the nation but cultural imitation of Anglo-Americans. Still, Anglo-conformity was broadly conceived and could mean anything from out-and-out conversion to Anglo-Saxon cultural symbols, relationships, and ethnic identity, to sharing some of the extrinsic symbols of the United States and avoiding any accented criticism.

Responses to Anglo-conformity resembled those to the melting pot, since both goals required assimilation and the presumed loss of former ethnic distinctiveness. The question of becoming an American was minimally an issue of naturalization and citizenship, and advocates of cultural pluralism could insist that it was possible to take on American citizenship without losing one's ethnic heritage. In answer to the melting pot, for example, a German-American writer argued that it was not at all necessary or valuable "for us to permit ourselves to be twisted and reformed into Americans, for we are Americans in the political sense—and only in this—as soon as we swear allegiance and unite ourselves to the common body of our German-American people." In response to Anglo-conformity, a Polish-American priest protested the common equation of "Americans" with the native-born of Anglo-Saxon background. "You English constantly speak," he objected, "as if you were the only Americans, or more Americans than others . . . There is no reason for the

English to usurp the name of American. They should be called Yankees if anything. That is the name of English-Americans. There is no such thing as an American nation. Poles form a nation, but the United States is a country, under one government, inhabited by representatives of different nations."

For some, Americanization permitted cultural diversity, the kind of pluralism advocated by Jane Addams and Jacob Riis, who recognized the importance of past histories as a foundation for American citizenship. Randolph Bourne in 1916 and Horace Kallen in 1924 went even further, viewing America as a "unique sociological fabric" woven of different but persisting ethnic communities and contributions. For the first time it was seen that the specific ethnic components did not necessarily have to disappear and assimilate. Instead, the differentiated lifestyles were seen as vital in a federation of peoples, a "trans-national America," a mosaic of different, harmoniously coexisting cultures. As the American social and political system evolved, the cultural pluralists argued that diversity could persist, with many distinctive subcultures, substructures, and ethnic identities, all in the philosophical spirit underlying William James's A Pluralistic Universe (1908).

These concepts—the melting pot, Anglo-conformity, and cultural pluralism—were fairly well established in American social thought by the second decade of the 20th century. It was then that the social scientists, particularly the sociologists, began to assess the extent of assimilation and differentiation among different ethnic groups and to recognize varied nuances in American diversity.

Studies of Group Life The scholarly approach was not always free of racism and ethnocentrism, of attacks on the lifestyle and behavior of other ethnic groups, or of arguments for the cultural superiority of one's own background. Indeed, social scientists were among the vocal and intemperate advocates of racist policies in eugenics, immigration restriction, and Anglo-Saxonism. A leading voice of bigotry was that of Edward Ross, a sociologist from Wisconsin, whose The Old World in the New (1914) was a scholarly counterpart to the Ku Klux Klan. His descriptions of ethnic group life showed such bias and prejudice that it was impossible to infer any kind of future for diversity, save that of dire perils and national subversion. The book was published seven years after the peak year of the new immigration, with its millions from the countries and empires of southern, central, and eastern Europe.

More dispassionate and thoughtful studies of ethnic group life and of the future began at the same time. Among the earliest works to make a substantive, empirical contribution was Emily Greene Balch's Our Slavic Fellow Citizens (1910). Since World War I a number of essentially sociological studies, variously descriptive, empirical, and predictive, have been published, on the extent of and changes in ethnicity in various parts of the United States. Some of the more consequential, with relation to assimilation and ethnicity, include the work of Julius Drachsler on ethnic marriages in New York City (1920); Robert E. Park and Ernest W. Burgess on a model of assimilation (1921); Park with Herbert A. Miller on transplanting group customs and lifestyles (1921); Park on the foreign-language press (1922); W.I. Thomas and Florian Znaniecki

on the adjustment of Polish immigrants (1927); Louis Wirth on the nature of the ghetto (1928); Bessie B. Wessel on ethnic groups in Rhode Island (1931); Caroline F. Ware on ethnic communities in New York (1935); Everett V. Stonequist on ethnic marginality (1937); Elin L. Anderson on ethnic groups in Vermont (1937); Marcus Lee Hansen on the meaning of generations among American ethnic groups (1938); Oscar Handlin on Boston's immigrants (1941); Ruby Jo Reeves Kennedy on the "triple melting pot" in New Haven (1944); St. Clair Drake and Horace R. Cayton on the blacks of Chicago (1945); W. Lloyd Warner and Leo Srole on ethnic group differences in Massachusetts (1945); E.K. Francis on the meaning of the concept of the ethnic group (1947); Oscar Handlin on the nature of the immigrant community (1951); Nathan Glazer on ethnic group experience in the American environment (1954); and Will Herberg on religion and ethnicity (1955). Since the 1960s, particularly with the publication of Beyond the Melting Pot by Nathan Glazer and Daniel Patrick Moynihan in 1963, and Assimilation in American Life by Milton Gordon in 1964, there has been a steady stream of historical, political, anthropological, and sociological research on the questions of ethnic change and ethnic persistence in the United States.

The greater part of all this sociological attention, with the noted exception of the 1937 Stonequist work on marginality and isolation, discussed ethnicity as a group phenomenon. In this connection, Louis Wirth in 1945, writing about those ethnic groups that were also minority and subordinate groups, provided a classification of ethnic group goals. In the larger context of the world, he wrote, ethnic minorities in different political and social systems can be seen to pursue four possible group goals, all theoretically different, but all of which can be followed by different members of a group at the same time. All four goals apply to the complex experience of minority American ethnic groups. The Wirth classification covers most of the terms, expectations, and realities of ethnic group life in the United States.

The goal of assimilation represents loss of group identity, typically through complete acceptance by the dominant ethnic group and through intermarriage. Wirth assumed that assimilation would be one-sided, meaning absorption into the dominant ethnicity, as in Anglo-conformity. Assimilation could also mean the loss of all former ethnic identities, as in the ideal of the melting pot. Wirth did not distinguish among different kinds of assimilation; it was Milton Gordon in 1964 who differentiated cultural assimilation (often termed acculturation), or the change in ethnic values, customs, and cultural forms, from structural assimilation, or the change in one's primary and institutional relationships. The key to complete assimilation, Gordon said, lies in structural change.

Wirth's other three group goals all refer to ethnic group persistence in some form. The most familiar of these goals is termed pluralism, the preservation of ethnic differentiation within the larger society. Pluralism assumes that some ethnic categories will be more clearcut than others, but the goal itself represents the hope for tolerance of different ethnic cultures coexisting in the larger framework. Pluralism operates within the existing political arrangement of the society, but the last two group goals seek to alter the status quo. Secession,

the third goal, is a movement for separatism, not pluralistically within the established order but culturally and politically outside the existing society. Secession as a goal includes the different forms of political nationalism, ethnic movements for independence, and efforts for separate statehood. Thus it would include the ethnic developments within the Ottoman and Austro-Hungarian empires, as well as the separatist movements among the French-Canadians in Quebec, the Basques in Spain, and the Puerto Ricans in the United States.

In American history one can look at various expressions of ethnic group withdrawal from the larger American political boundaries, movements that were never that widespread or successful, as additional illustrations of the secessionist goal. The Mormon trek to the West, the efforts among some leaders for a "New Germany" in Missouri and Texas in the 19th century, Marcus Garvey's back-to-Africa movement and the demand of the black Nation of Islam for black states, and even the withdrawal of the white South in the Civil War to retain its regional ethnic distinctiveness, may all be seen as counterparts to the more classic forms of ethnic nationalism.

The fourth goal in Wirth's classification, militancy, is the least frequent in the American experience. Militancy is taken to mean seizure of political power by the ethnic minority within the existing social system. The ethnic minority and the ethnic dominant group exchange political and social roles: the minority becomes dominant, and the formerly dominant group becomes the minority. Power changes hands. Because minorities usually lack power, this goal is not likely to be realized, unless the minority population grows much larger and, most important, there is some assistance from a foreign ally. Wirth's example is that of the Sudeten Germans becoming dominant over the Czechs in the years just after the Munich settlement (1938) with the aid of Nazi Germany.

Because of the fluidity and diffusiveness that characterize American diversity, the shift of ethnic minority and dominant groups has not taken place at the federal and societal level. But there are some instances of militancy at the local and community levels in terms of political and economic change. Different ethnic groups may compete for power, but these exchanges of roles and levels of power are more appropriately seen as examples of pluralism than of militancy, as Wirth defines them. The goal of militancy requires a complete transition of all cultural assumptions from one group to another, a change that has not taken place in American life.

Individual Experience and Change

The individual ethnic experience in the United States does not always correspond to the group experience of assimilation and pluralism, because the presumably ethnic individual may or may not be connected to a given group. An individual's attachment to ethnicity stems from the extent of his or her affiliation to a given ethnic culture and structure. Every ethnic group is characterized by distinctive values, customs, beliefs, language or dialect, heritage, and history—its culture—and by distinctive primary and secondary relationships, networks, bonds, social circles—its structure. These may be entirely or partially self-contained and enclosed, and they may be voluntarily or involuntarily designed, but in all cases there are manifest and latent expressions of group identity and belonging that result from the symbols of the ethnic culture and from the relations of the ethnic structure.

Existentially a person derives ethnicity from a particular culture and structure in a diverse world. That individual knows who he is because of what he believes and what he responds to (symbolic ethnicity), and with whom he relates (relational ethnicity). But the American experience is noted for its widespread change and social upheavals, much of it involved with the ethnic factor, whether through external forces of racism, slavery, genocide, and international migration or through the internal flux of shifting frontiers, geographic mobility, economic change, and urban and rural displacement. These factors result in realignments of symbolic and relational ethnicity. The most dramatic evidence for transitions of ethnicity is found in the alternating presence or absence, certainty or ambiguity, of ethnic symbols and relationships in the lives of individual Americans.

Theoretically, there are four social and cultural conditions of ethnicity for the individual. The first, the most common constellation, is that of presence and certainty of both ethnic symbols and relationships. Forms of ethnic traditionalism, regionalism, religioethnic movements, and even syntheses of new ethnicities all fulfill this condition, because they consist of ties to a given ethnic culture and structure, with shared awareness of a somewhat distinctive origin and way of life. Relationships with one's contemporaries make up some, if not all, of the subsystem, which is larger than kinship or locality but smaller than the society. Membership becomes part of one's group identity. Traditional ethnicity is not necessarily static, provincial, and conservative, because symbols adapt and evolve, as do their interpretations, and some forms of traditional ethnicity can provide the basis for a more universalistic impulse.

The second condition, probably the next most frequent, is that of beginning ethnic change, away from the anchors of traditionalism. Broadly expressed, the second condition can be viewed as certainty of ethnic structure but ambiguity of ethnic culture. This defines quite explicitly the convert who has assimilated and been received into a group that differs from the one into which he or she was born. Converted ethnicity is emphatically relational, for the individual derives a sense of ethnic belonging primarily from the networks and bonds of the people he has joined. This is the meaning of structural assimilation, the merging with another culture and structure on the primary level of close sentiments. What is different for the convert is the uncertainty of the symbols of the new culture. There is always some degree of confusion between the old and the new, between the ethnic culture taken for granted by those born and raised in it, and the assumptions about that culture made by those who come to it from outside. As with religious change, the convert has probably learned the extrinsic aspects of the new culture, but the intrinsic forms may pose some problems. The distinction between the traditionalist and the convert is the difference between *being* and *becoming*.

The reverse of this is the third condition, less common among Americans but the basis of much drama in literature. In this case the memories and symbols of an ethnic culture exist, but there are no primary networks and structural attachments. This is the condition of social and cultural exile, of isolation with a past identification and a memory of belonging. Unlike the collective exile of refugees, émigrés, and displaced people, this exilic ethnicity is notable for the isolation of the individual. He is not a member of a community by virtue of primary connections; his ethnicity in exile is reflected from the past and from allusions to the past. There is no living meaning to this ethnicity, for its distinctive culture cannot be made part of an ongoing structure. If the convert's ethnicity represents the odd-man-in, the exile's situation represents a kind of odd-man-out.

The fourth condition, the most infrequent and the most extreme possibility, involves a lack or ambiguity of both ethnic culture and ethnic structure. The symbols and relationships that provide the individual with some kind of group identification are missing or deficient. This condition is the antithesis of the ethnic traditionalist. Personal and societal vicissitudes may bring about such a condition for children wrenched away from the group's upbringing and the family's enculturation, with nothing provided to replace them. The lack of sustained group identity becomes the paramount characteristic of the individual's persona, for there are no memories of a history and no ongoing personal relationships. These deficiencies may border on the pathological, as the illustrations from American literature will suggest, for ambiguity of symbolic and relational ethnicity isolates an individual all the more severely. The ethnic exile may be able to "go home again" or at least convert and assimilate, the ethnic convert is able to reciprocate group connections, and the ethnic traditionalist is moored to an entity of belonging. But without symbols and group relations, there is little for the isolated individual to build on.

Looking at the United States as a culturally diverse society characterized by upheavals and vicissitudes, one can view the four conditions just described as the voluntary or involuntary responses of survivors. From the perspective of ethnicity, Americans have indeed responded to social change in numerous ways. Some, even many, have managed to preserve in one fashion or another their connections to ethnic symbols and relationships. Change takes place even within the context of ethnicity; surviving in the mass society requires volition and ingenuity, and there are many forms and examples of persisting pluralistic ethnicities.

Patterns of Tradition   The best-known form is the traditional ethnic community, as seen among transplanted immigrant groups. Visible residential enclaves, ghettos, ethnic districts, and national parishes are the most familiar forms of such persistence—Chinatown, Little Italy, Polonia, Greektown, and Bronzeville. Less appreciated in this light are the ethnic connotations of Beacon Hill, the Lower East Side, Maxwell Street, and Shantytown. Groups in these areas may persist or relocate because of physical destruction and urban renewal, past the first generation and into the second and even later generations. They may survive not as anachronisms but as viable communities, despite extrinsic ac-

culturation and successful accommodation to the general American lifestyle.

Social mobility, rural and agricultural change, and urban dislocation may all cause the physical dispersion of ethnic neighborhoods. Ethnicity, however, may transcend locality, immediate kinship, and face-to-face interaction. Thus, there often develops what can be called neotraditionalism. This variant of ethnicity in the United States accounts for the term "hyphenate" to describe a person undergoing some greater degree of change and adaptation to American life.

The hyphenate can be said to have accommodated somewhat to the Anglo-American culture in terms of language, clothes, manners, and other extrinsic values. Individual Finnish Americans, Armenian Americans, or Japanese Americans may be different from the first-generation immigrants in these respects and may not reside with other members of their ethnic group. But this does not mean that they have become invisible or have assimilated structurally to other identities; their cultural and relational lives may still be traditionally ethnic to the extent that they retain their symbolic ties and their attachments to networks. The hyphenate synthesizes a larger loyalty to America with a historic loyalty to the ethnic past. For many, the synthesis is successful.

During World War II the many pressures concerning loyalty, identity, and national commitment caused many Americans to affirm their particular ethnic existence. In *Mount Allegro* (1942), Jerre Mangione wrote, "Separated though I was from my Sicilian relatives, my bond with them grew stronger through the years. The older I became and the more I appreciated them, the less desire I had to cut myself off from them. The memory of my life in Rochester gave me a *root* feeling, a sense of the past which I seemed to need to make the present more bearable." Rabbi Milton Steinberg in 1941 put it quite explicitly: "The history of America is my history . . . But Jewish history is my background, too. Lincoln and Jefferson are my heroes together with Rabbi Akiba and Moses Maimonides. The four get along in my imagination most companionably." For many, there is no inconsistency in being American and something else. Indeed, one might argue that there really is no meaning to being just American, given the scope and diversity of ethnic backgrounds.

Another broad adaptation to the pressures of the American experience is found in religioethnic sectarianism. Forces for modernism and the shock of cultural and economic change often lie behind social movements, which are expressions of status discontent for both the poor and the affluent, of the upheavals of communities, and of group assertion. As H. Richard Niebuhr wrote of it, religious denominationalism has many social sources. An individual may seek to reaffirm a prior ethnic bond, as in those who are "born again"; or he may seek to reinterpret the ethnic past in a more modern or more American light, as in Unitarianism, Mormonism, and Reform Judaism; or he may assert sectarian differences, as in the many religious movements emerging from the "Burned-over District" in upstate New York during the first half of the 19th century.

Tolerance of religious diversity and the separation of church and state have facilitated innumerable efforts at religioethnic differentiation in the United States. The regional distinctions among white and black Baptists,

the religious leadership of Daddy Grace, Father Divine, and Elijah Muhammad, the generational and ethnic differences within the Jewish community, the ideological conflicts between Polish Roman Catholics and Polish National Catholics, the middle-class white Protestant interest in Christian Science, and the messianic or revivalistic movements among American Indians—all are collective ethnic responses to the forces of widespread change. Individuals may respond to perceived assaults on their economic status and their ethnicity through sectarianism.

Regionalism, too, offers the possibilities of differentiated ethnic or quasi-ethnic cultures and structures. The more isolated and remote a region, it is often proposed, the more likely it is to develop a distinctive way of life and even an original interpretation of history. The work of Harry Caudill, Jack Weller, and Kai Erikson illuminates the ethnicity of the Appalachians. White Appalachian migrant neighborhoods in major cities, such as Uptown on Chicago's North Side, bear evidence of the ability of ethnic traditionalism to transcend geographic relocation. Recent portraits of the white South, in the work of Carl Degler, Lewis Killian, John Shelton Reed, and George Brown Tindall, all reveal the South as a locus of American ethnicity.

Related arguments have been made or can be developed for the ethnicity (in sociological terms of culture, structure, and identity) of New England, the towns of the Midwest, Texas, and the states of the Far West and the Pacific Coast, certainly historically if not always for the present. Homogenization across regions may be increasing, particularly as measured by external forms, but this does not necessarily eliminate the meaning of already formed regional ethnicity. This kind of regional identity, which is often taken for granted, can be articulated quite nicely, as by Senator Sam Ervin on his retirement from Washington politics and return to Morganton, N.C., or by Senator George Aiken's return to Vermont.

Forms of Changing Attachments Vicissitudes may influence an individual's choosing to reaffirm a given ethnic background, but social change also brings about fundamental transitions in ethnic attachment. Cultural conversion and structural assimilation include different examples of individual change in America. Name-changing, physical and cosmetic alterations, and learning English suggest aspects of assimilation, but it may well be only partial, a form of adjustment to what is seen as the dominant Anglo-American style. Individuals who change their names are not necessarily changing their larger ethnic allegiance, for life in the United States may be viewed as requiring some extrinsic alterations from the ethnic past.

Modifications in language, name, gestures, and other personal symbolism, may or may not take place, but it is voluntary or involuntary change in personal relationships that is the key to ethnic conversion. Such structural assimilation includes, when physically possible, the phenomenon of passing, movement out of one ethnic background and into another. A minimum of cultural change is required for such a movement, but there will always be some ambiguity and confusion in the experiences. The "black" American who decides to pass as "white" and, perhaps, as "Anglo-Saxon," takes a certain risk because, although it may not be apparent to others, he was raised and acculturated to a black subculture and may feel not entirely comfortable in white, Anglo-Saxon ways. It was personal history that caused the society to label him as a black in the first place, and after making the change, there will doubtless be moments when he is confronted with his marginality, despite the fact that he is accepted structurally in the new ethnicity. St. Clair Drake and Horace Cayton describe precisely these dilemmas of passing in *Black Metropolis*. Racial passing is not limited to the minority member becoming a member of a more dominant group; cultural conversion includes the reverse phenomenon as well. The white who becomes a cultural black, the Frenchman who goes native in the South Seas, and the Anglo-Saxon who joins the Indians on the frontier are all illustrations of structural assimilation and ethnic change. There have been and will continue to be many such individual instances.

The cultural transition of passing carries the same sociological meaning as the kind of religious conversion that involves a change from one specific religion to another quite different one. This is not the conversion of those who reaffirm a past culture, it is the change from being Catholic to becoming Jewish, from Hindu to Episcopalian, from Greek Orthodox to Mormon. Such conversions mean not only a change in religious beliefs, which are aspects of culture, but disconnections in personal and primary relationships. The change in beliefs is ongoing and apprenticelike, but the change in networks and spheres of participation is immediate, reciprocated, and indicative of a new group boundary. As with those who pass racially, the individual who alters religious ethnicity is likely to experience ambiguity and marginality. The religious convert, though accepted, still encounters a qualified membership. He may be pointed out as different, for he is either "better" because he has joined the group voluntarily and has learned so much more about the religion, or he is "worse" because he was not born into the community and is apt at times to make a gaffe. In both cases, the convert is seen as different, at times a source of pride and at other times a source of embarrassment. It is this marginality that explains the convert who is "holier than thou," more Chinese, more Jewish, or more Baptist than everyone else.

The most familiar American conversion phenomenon, however, is emancipation from the ghetto and the shift away from the immigrant background for children and grandchildren of non-Protestant, non-Anglo-Saxon Europeans. Pressures of social mobility, visibility, alienness, prejudice, and discrimination have influenced Americans not only to change their names (discussed at length by Louis Adamic in the 1942 book, *What's Your Name?*), their accents, and their manners, but to alter their claimed origins as well. The individual tries to pass, convert, and become someone else, Protestant and Anglo-Saxon, for example. Many German Americans in World War I either changed all the way, from Schmidt to Smith, or withdrew into a more exclusively German world.

Some Irish, Italian, Greek, Jewish, and Slavic individuals also chose to discard their pasts and "turn Yankee." Turning in this sense meant changing partners and associates; it was an act of conversion rather than gradual acculturation. As with some religious converts,

there was a tendency at times to be more fervent than those born to the culture; some of the new Yankees became flag wavers, superpatriots, and true believers. The ethnic convert denies and rejects his origins while the ethnic traditionalist either passively or actively retains them. Conversion represents structural change; traditionalism represents persisting differentiation and cultural pluralism.

Intermarriage, or exogamy between different races, religions, or national origins, is often said to accompany structural change, but intermarriage per se does not necessarily mean social and cultural conversion. The white man who joins the Indian community, marries an Indian woman, and is accepted into the larger Indian society, provides an example of exogamy as an aspect of structural and cultural conversion. Similarly, the Polish or Italian Catholic woman who marries a Jewish man, converts to Judaism, and is included in the Jewish community, can be said to have structurally assimilated to another ethnic background. There are, however, alternative possibilities. Marriage between two people of diverse backgrounds, under certain circumstances, may result in both partners becoming ethnic exiles, treated as outcasts by their respective ethnic groups. Under more tolerant conditions intermarriage may mean the coexistence of both ethnic worlds, with no conversion by either spouse and the preservation of group relationships for both. Indeed, if there are enough cases of intermarriage, whether treated benignly by the society or scorned and rejected, a new ethnic identity may emerge from the fusion of cultural ingredients, as in the Anglo-Indians of India and the Mormons of the United States.

American history offers numerous examples of social and cultural change, both of traditionalism and of conversion. The individual has many ways in which to handle ethnicity. Ethnic traditionalism and ethnic conversion are, however, group-connected; the individual either remains with past group ties or changes those attachments. There are dramatic illustrations of the remaining two ethnic conditions as well, but the focus is much more on the individual.

Survivors as Exiles The ethnic exile, like the prototypical stranger, is removed from the supports and constraints of group membership. What he does possess is limited to past antecedents and former identity. As a phenomenon, exile usually has political and ideological dimensions. The exiled person may be "the man without a country," a Robinson Crusoe in some remote place, a hermit, a defector, or a refugee. Cultural isolation stems from the fact that the individual is unconnected to any old or new ethnic group boundaries. As with all civilizations and polities, America has had many such exiles. In the history of migrations, frontier movements, slavery, lynchings, genocide, forced evacuations, and the entire range of fluctuating populations, a certain number of people have been more or less involuntarily removed from their ethnic past. The removal may well result in the condition of individual exile.

Racism and slavery have certainly brought about the separation of some blacks from their communities, causing a dispersal in which some individuals flee and end their lives as the only black American in some homogeneous, northern white town. Although the waves of immigrants predominantly settled collectively in various ethnic neighborhoods and communities, there have been cases of the only Hungarian family or the only Lebanese Druse in some small town. Exilic conditions invariably produce some loss of identity, for there is no group to sustain a sense of belonging. There is a major difference between the only Chinese person in a community who lives alone and apart and the one Chinese who preserves his connections with the Chinese outside through visits, correspondence, and the retention of far-flung networks. In the latter situation there is no continuous isolation, but instead the management of trading and extrafamilial connections that has long characterized ethnic peoples in diaspora.

As biography and fiction show, the ethnic exile is sequestered. Joanna Burden, as the only Northener in the small Mississippi town in William Faulkner's *Light in August* (1932), in residence but apart, is an illustration: "She lives in the big house alone, a woman of middle-age. She has lived in the house since she was born, yet she is still a stranger, a foreigner whose people moved in from the North during Reconstruction. A Yankee, a lover of negroes . . ."

The Jewish survivor of the Nazi Holocaust in Edward Lewis Wallant's novel, *The Pawnbroker* (1961), adapts to life in New York, not in a rejoined community of Jews or in a new beginning with some other group, but in lonely, uncommunicative exile. Sol Nazerman is 45, tortured by the memories of the extermination of his family, unable to relate to the present, and stirred only at times by escape into memories of Poland and of river trips on the Vistula. The former instructor at the University of Kraków has become the cynical trader "in other people's sorrows." There are many references in American literature to those immigrants whose shock at being uprooted and relocated is so great that they cannot join an existing ethnic community. Instead, they withdraw into themselves, avoid primary ties with those who are around them, and live alone with their memories. Such is the condition of exile.

American writing, viewed through the lens of ethnicity, assimilation, and pluralism, is heavily weighted with the drama of these individuals whose humanity is evident to the reader but whose lives are isolated from the surrounding community because of an ethnic stigma. Separated from their own culture and social circle, the ethnic exiles are variously shunned and deprived of their humanity, often in willful as well as involuntary isolation. The ethnic traditionalist in a circumscribed minority group may well be treated as a pariah, with the important difference that he retains his group, his community, and his identity, even—or especially—while subject to prejudice and discrimination. The group sustains his ethnicity. The ethnic exile, on the other hand, has no community, and if he is alone for the rest of his life, his ethnicity dies with him. There is no continuity to individual exile.

Exile may result in conversion under more tolerant circumstances. The individual Ukrainian or Norwegian, finding himself in a strange world with no connections to a former ethnic background may not experience impermeable boundaries. If the outsider wants, he may be welcomed into a proximate community. Marriage, friendship, and participation in the networks of the larger receiving group may take place over

time. In this development, the individual shifts from exile to conversion, and his marginality changes to another kind.

The Isolation of Detachment One kind of cultural alienness goes beyond the stigma of particular ethnicity, beyond pluralism and assimilation. Exile, at least, means the retention of memory, of the cultural past, of the symbolism of one's province, people, and Weltanschauung. The fourth possibility is that of the individual who is deprived not only of group relations, but also of a cultural history and ethnic past. This is the stigma of having no ethnicity at all in a world where some form of ethnicity is taken for granted. Some societies and political systems throughout history have institutionalized this condition quite deliberately, in order to have a number of outsiders as slaves without the distraction of competing loyalties. American democracy has not formed such institutions, but the vicissitudes of the society and the accidents of personal misfortune have resulted at times in precisely this form of loss.

Because the basis of assimilation and pluralism is ethnicity, an individual's formation of ethnic belonging is critical. Americans in general may be said to possess ethnicity, because as children they were socialized to a given way of life through family, relatives, neighborhood, community, and social institutions. This is the meaning of early enculturation, the essence of ethnic traditionalism in a diverse society. Further, some adults may be said to possess ethnicity because they willed it through socialization to another way of life that is culturally different from that in which they were raised. This is the meaning of ethnic conversion. Finally, some possess ethnicity because they are thought of as being culturally different because of their personal attributes, their cultural inheritance, and what they remember from their youth. This is the meaning of ethnic exile.

The more extreme condition of ethnicity manqué is unusual, because as a child the person received neither enculturation to a group mind and group ethos nor attachment to a network of primary relations. Unlike the adult torn from his province or people, who may become an ethnic exile, this uprooted person is generally a child who was never given a sustained opportunity to develop a sense of group ethnicity. For the child it is the tragedy of homelessness, where the home means the symbols and relationships of continuity.

Lack of ethnicity stands out as unique in a nation of diverse ethnic backgrounds, and other people tend to misread the situation. Individuals who lack an ethnic identity seem ambiguous to those around them and may be labeled as foreign or different or be assigned some quite specific background where none really exists. The allegation is meaningless, for the individual may be called something he knows nothing about. In the confusion of identity and its sources, the isolate is given an empty name. The ethnic exile may be called Jewish or Afro-American or East Indian, but that person remembers what it means to be that. The ethnic isolate, however, when identified as something, has no understanding of what he is.

This kind of ethnic isolation with no foundation of memory or background is found in some American fiction that is concerned with the dynamics of marginal-ity. Also, some orphans and foundlings, deprived of community, reflect this ambiguity. Bernard Malamud's novel, *The Assistant* (1957), tells of an encounter between a poorly subsisting grocer in New York, the Jewish traditionalist Morris Bober, and Frank Alpine, an alien young man, a wanderer who was brought up in an orphanage and raised in no ethnicity. He is called an Italian, but being Italian is as meaningless to him as his life. With the death of Bober at the end of the novel, Alpine attempts the impossible, the simulation of becoming Jewish. He endures a circumcision, but his amorality, a result of his isolation, inhibits his becoming anything.

More extreme is the condition of Joe Christmas in *Light in August*. Faulkner has created the complete alien, brought up ambiguously in an orphanage in Memphis and in foster homes and accorded no ties with humanity. In the rigid race relations of the South, Joe Christmas is denied by everyone, for the white traditionalists think him a strange sort of black, and the black traditionalists consider him a strange sort of white. He looks white but acts like nobody. Stigmatized like some social and cultural eunuch, Joe Christmas has been called by one critic "the loneliest man in American fiction." His loneliness and apartness create his amorality, and his amorality induces tragedy; he is lynched by a mob, turned ultimately into the eunuch he had been figuratively all his life.

Malamud and Faulkner suggest the drama of the rootless individual in a changing society. The social and cultural vicissitudes of a frontier society may have set the tone for the extremes of ethnic change and for the ethnic upheaval that has characterized the two centuries of American growth. American Indian children in a white world and white children in an Indian world, for example, point to contrasting ethnic contacts from the very beginnings of America. Children in an alien environment could acculturate successfully if the host culture ensured a meaningful socialization. If so, these children grow up either as traditionalists or as converts, depending on their age when their life changed. On the other hand, acceptance and reciprocity are not always guaranteed, and the Indian child among whites might experience little real integration. A child who is continually treated as "not one of us," as an outsider, may grow up to have little or no group identity.

The racism of slavery matches the genocide and subhuman treatment accorded Indians, and both racism and slavery have produced, though in unequal distribution, all four conditions of ethnic change. Black Americans, like all other ethnic groups, only more so, responded to widespread stress and pressure. Most blacks, subject to racism and segregation, developed their own neotraditionalist ethnicity on American soil, an ethnogenic movement and an elaboration over time of distinctive black symbols and relationships. Other black Americans may be said to have converted to Anglo-American ways, to have structurally assimilated in relationships, either through racial passing or through more figurative symbolism. Still other blacks have become exiles from their ethnic past. Regarded as the only "nigger" or "Negro" or "colored" in a town, the black individual is cut off from meaningful relationships, tolerated only as a kind of resident stranger.

Finally there have been those blacks whose early lives were so disconnected that they could not understand the meaning of blackness or Negritude and would be unable to respond to it. One common phenomenon that may produce this cultural confusion is mixed mating and marriage. The child of such a marriage, rejected by the families and communities of both parents, may grow up knowing neither and having nothing else. He receives no link to history, no connection to any group. The terms of this cultural isolation are not unlike those governing the feral child raised in the wilderness, the ostracized physically deformed person in past times, and socially and culturally untutored foundlings. In earlier periods, mixed-racial children, as with the Creoles of color and the first mestizos, endured some such isolation. With greater numbers of such offspring, the idea of mixed background becomes more prevalent, more customary, and may even lead to a new sense of ethnicity.

American society, through history and fiction, is revealed as a composite not only of many ethnic backgrounds but also of many different ethnic responses. The United States has not only been a society of "many countries," as Harriet Martineau envisioned it, but also a country with many associational styles. Tocqueville emphasized voluntary and involuntary association as a key to understanding American democracy. The fluidity of American life has meant social change and dislocation; however, fluidity has resulted not in the disappearance of ethnic diversity, but in the persistence of group cultures and structures; not in total assimilation and homogenization of a mass society, but in the variants of assimilation; not in the tyranny of pluralistic group life, but in change and diversity within distinctiveness. There is no one single response or adaptation. The variety of styles in pluralism and assimilation suggest that ethnicity is as complex as life itself.

Bibliography
There is an enormous body of social science literature on the subject, which tends to be divided between the processes of assimilation in the United States and the conditions and forms of American pluralism. Among the many provocative works on assimilation are Julius Drachsler, *Democracy and Assimilation: The Blending of Immigrant Heritages in America* (New York, 1920); Robert E. Park and Ernest W. Burgess, *Introduction to the Science of Sociology* (Chicago, 1921); Ruby Jo Reeves Kennedy, "Single or Triple Melting-Pot? Intermarriage Trends in New Haven, 1870–1940," *American Journal of Sociology* 49 (January 1944): 331–339; and the influential work of Milton M. Gordon, *Assimilation in American Life: The Role of Race, Religion, and National Origins* (New York, 1964). Many recent studies address the issues of assimilation in contemporary America; a good conceptual approach is provided by L. Paul Metzger, "American Sociology and Black Assimilation: Conflicting Perspectives," *American Journal of Sociology* 76 (January 1971): 627–647; and an empirical assessment is offered by Richard D. Alba, "Social Assimilation among American Catholic National-Origin Groups," *American Sociological Review* 41 (December 1976): 1030–1046.

In contrast to this focus on the melting pot and other forms of assimilation, fewer studies examine the meaning and expressions of pluralism. One of the first serious statements is Horace M. Kallen, *Culture and Democracy in the United States* (New York, 1924); more recent debate on the issue is provided in Horace M. Kallen, *Cultural Pluralism and the American Idea: An Essay in Social Philosophy* (Philadelphia, 1956).

During the 1970s a number of authors have offered views on ethnic pluralism. Michael Novak affirms "the new ethnicity" in *The Rise of the Unmeltable Ethnics: Politics and Culture in the Seventies* (New York, 1972); Edward O. Laumann, *Bonds of Pluralism: The Form and Substance of Urban Social Networks* (New York, 1973), contributes substantive and empirical analyses of patterns of ethnicity in Detroit; William M. Newman, *American Pluralism* (New York, 1973), links minority groups to social theory; and Andrew M. Greeley integrates a wide range of issues, both conceptual and empirical, in *Ethnicity in the United States: A Preliminary Reconnaissance* (New York, 1974).

Most of the literature relates to the group level of assimilationist and pluralist behavior. Studies that give some attention to the individual in interethnic contact and that consider American as well as other societal experiences include Robert E. Park, "Human Migration and the Marginal Man," *American Journal of Sociology* 33 (May 1928): 881–893; Everett V. Stonequist, *The Marginal Man: A Study in Personality and Culture Conflict* (New York, 1937); Everett C. Hughes and Helen M. Hughes, *Where Peoples Meet: Racial and Ethnic Frontiers* (Glencoe, Ill., 1952); and Harold J. Abramson, "On the Sociology of Ethnicity and Social Change: A Model of Rootedness and Rootlessness," *Economic and Social Review* 8 (October 1976): 43–59.

A large number of works in the field relate to both assimilation and pluralism in the more specific context of ethnic diversity. Some of the most important studies are: Louis Wirth, "The Problem of Minority Groups," *The Science of Man in the World Crisis*, Ralph Linton, ed. (New York, 1945), pp. 347–372; Joshua A. Fishman et al., *Language Loyalty in the United States* (The Hague, 1966); Nathan Glazer and Daniel Patrick Moynihan, *Beyond the Melting Pot: The Negroes, Puerto Ricans, Jews, Italians, and Irish of New York City*, 2nd ed. (Cambridge, Mass., 1970); and Andrew M. Greeley, *Why Can't They Be Like Us?* (New York, 1971).

In this encyclopedia, see also American Identity and Americanization; Concepts of Ethnicity; Education; Pluralism: A Humanistic Perspective; and Pluralism: A Political Perspective for further discussion of the substantive issues.

HAROLD J. ABRAMSON

ASSINIBOINES: *see* AMERICAN INDIANS

ASSYRIANS

Assyrian immigrants have come to the United States from regions in the Middle East that are at present part of Iran, Iraq, Turkey, Syria, and Lebanon. Some have come directly; some have lived for varying periods of time in other parts of the world. It is not possible to estimate their numbers precisely. Neither the U.S. Census nor the U.S. Immigration and Naturalization Service has ever used Assyrian as a designation, but Assyrian leaders believe that there are 1 million Assyrians scattered over the world at present. There are approximately 150,000 in the United States, concentrated primarily in California, Illinois (especially around Chicago), Michigan, New Jersey, New York, Connecticut, and Massachusetts.

ORIGINS

Modern Assyrians claim descent from the inhabitants of the ancient Assyrian empire, and their different dialects have developed from ancient Aramaic, a language widely used in that empire. Many also call their language Assyrian, although scholars, reserving the terms Assyrian and Babylonian for the cuneiform writing of the ancient empire, generally refer to the modern tongue as neo-Aramaic, Chaldean, or Syriac. Whether written in cuneiform or in an alphabet, these languages all belong to the Semitic family of languages.

The Assyrian Nestorians and the Assyrian Jacobites, some of whom prefer to be known as Syrian Arameans, form the core of the Assyrian community. They refer to themselves as *surayi*, an Assyrian word that can be translated into English as either Assyrian or Syrian. Scattered among Assyrians in the Middle East are some Jews and Armenians who speak the same language as the Assyrians, but are not considered Assyrian. Neither

Assyrian
Homelands

150   Km.   Miles

are the East Indians who belong to Assyrian Christian churches, although their religious leaders participate fully in the worldwide activities of the denominations.

A full understanding of Assyrian ethnicity is only now developing in the United States and Canada. Until recently in the Middle East relatively few Assyrian Nestorians knew very much about Assyrian Jacobites, and vice versa, because religious rivalries have divided the community for centuries. However, as a result of the massacres that accompanied World War I, and the subsequent dispersal of their people, Assyrians—easterners and westerners—are beginning to come into closer contact and to understand their common heritage. In their homelands, the Nestorians have been the easterners and the Jacobites the westerners.

Both the Nestorians, who supported the Church of the East, and the Jacobites, who maintained the Church of Antioch, have been considered schismatic by Western church authorities since the 5th century. The term Nestorian, which some consider pejorative, comes from Nestorius, patriarch of Constantinople (428–431), deposed and considered a heretic when he disputed decisions taken at the Council of Ephesus (A.D. 431). The Jacobites are named for Jacobus Baradeus and his followers, also considered heretical when they defended the monophysite position at the Council of Chalcedon 20 years later.

The ancient split between the Church of the East and the Church of Antioch, and between these two and the rest of eastern and western Christianity, continues into the present. However, beginning in the 16th century, Jesuit missionaries, followed by Eastern Orthodox and eventually Protestants of various denominations, made their way to the Middle East to convert the indigenous Christians. To some extent they were all successful in winning converts from the Church of the East and the Church of Antioch. This has led to a bewildering variety of Christian denominations and patriarchs in the Middle East. Some Nestorians have continued to support the Church of the East; the Nestorians who converted to Roman Catholicism are known as Chaldeans. Most Jacobites remained with the Church of Antioch; those who converted to Catholicism are called Syrian Catholics. All four of these groups support a church hierarchy or patriarchy in the homeland. Since World War I there have been shifts occasioned by political strife but in the late 1970s the Nestorian patriarchate was temporarily in Teheran, the Jacobite seat in Damascus, the Syrian Catholic in Beirut, and the Chaldean in Baghdad.

In the United States about one-half of the Assyrians are either Nestorians or Jacobites; that is, they belong either to the Church of the East or to the Church of Antioch; one-fourth of them are either Roman or Eastern Catholic; about 20 percent are Presbyterian; and 5 percent belong to Eastern Orthodox, Baptist, Methodist, and other groups. Assyrian group life continues to reflect ancient religious as well as relatively new political divisions. The Syrian Arameans of New Jersey are Jacobites, but they prefer to call themselves Syrian rather than Assyrian in order to avoid political implications with which they disagree. Some Assyrians are in favor of the establishment of an Assyrian homeland; others are not and do not wish to offend the present Syrian and Iraqi governments; still others have no interest at all in the politics of the Middle East. Since the Syrian Arameans are sometimes referred to as Syrian Orthodox, it may be useful to point out that they should not be confused with the Syrian Arabs who are Greek Orthodox. (See Eastern Orthodox; Oriental Orthodox; see also Eastern Catholics.)

From the 3rd century to the 20th the Assyrians lived under both Persian and Ottoman rule, usually as religious minorities governed by their own ecclesiastical representatives. In 1900 the great majority were rural peasants (tribal and nontribal); only a few artisans and intellectuals among them lived in towns.

When World War I broke out, the Assyrians fought on the Allied side against the Turks. They had been heavily influenced by European and American missionaries to support the "Christian powers," and led to believe that their efforts on behalf of the Allies would win them the homeland they had wanted for so long. This alliance led directly to their massacre and expulsion by Turkish and other Muslim neighbors. About 10,000 were able to find shelter in Russian Transcaucasia while many others were herded by British authorities into refugee camps in Baquba (Iraq) where they suffered heavy losses. In 1924 the Mosul Commission appointed by the League of Nations to investigate the plight of the Assyrian refugees advised that they be settled en bloc in the Iraqi district of Mosul with a measure of local autonomy under the Nestorian patriarch. However, the recommendations of the commission were ignored; the Assyrians were further dispersed throughout the Middle East; some have made their way to Europe, to Australia, and to North and South America.

ARRIVAL AND SETTLEMENT

The first Assyrians in the United States were young men sent by American missionaries in the 1880s to be trained for further missionary work in their homeland.

They were followed shortly afterward by immigrants who had heard stories about fabulous opportunities in the United States. Opportunities may have been less than fabulous but letters home brought more immigrants, and eventually family groups and distant relatives, as the original pioneers became established. The chain migration is still in process.

The most recent Assyrian immigrants are refugees dislocated by the Kurdo-Iraqi war of the 1960s and 1970s. Caught between two opposing forces in a war zone, the Assyrians of northern Iraq found it impossible to remain neutral. They eventually joined the Muslim Kurds to oppose the policies of the Baathist government that was harassing non-Arab groups in Iraq. Two thousand Assyrians left homeless by the war fled to Lebanon and Greece, and from there many were brought to Chicago through the efforts of the Assyrian American National Federation (AANF) and its affiliate, the Assyrian National Aid Society. The Assyrian community in Chicago has worked vigorously to help the newcomers find housing and employment, but efforts to forge group unity so far have failed to overcome the historic factionalism that has divided tribally oriented Iraqi-mountaineer Assyrians from those who lived on the Iranian plains.

In the past, kin groups and Assyrians of common denominational background or regional origin have tended to settle close to each other. At present, Jacobite Assyrians are found predominantly in New York and Massachusetts, Chaldeans in Michigan. Villagers from Gogtapa and Taka Ardishay in northwestern Iran live in Connecticut while Assyrians from other villages in northwestern Iran have been attracted to Turlock in Stanislaus County, Calif., where the climate favors their traditional skills with orchards and vineyards.

The early immigrants settled in the industrial cities of the East and Midwest where they found factory jobs. Many went to work in the automobile industry; others who had more skills initially found jobs as bricklayers, carpenters, tailors, and farmers. Most of their descendants today have entered the middle class. The children and grandchildren of the immigrants have become professionals—physicians, attorneys, and engineers. Thus far, Adam Benjamin, a congressman from Michigan, has attained the highest national elective office to be held by an Assyrian American.

Other Assyrian Americans who have achieved renown are George Lamsa (1893–1975), translator of the very early *Peshitta* manuscript from Aramaic into English; William Daniel (1909–), a poet and composer who has modernized the rules of Assyrian grammar, spelling, and syntax; and M. Yonan-Malik (1904–) who invented a widely used process for converting rice and is now working to promote fortified adobe as an inexpensive replacement for cement in developing countries. Among Daniel's important contributions to Assyrian literature is his epic, *Kateeni Gabara* (Kateeni the mighty; vol. 1, Teheran, 1961; vol. 2, Chicago, 1974).

Assyrians have founded a number of national organizations. The AANF (formerly AAF) was forged from smaller regional groups in response to the 1933 massacre of a large number of Assyrian families in Simail, Iraq, after an incident that resulted in the expulsion of the Nestorian patriarch from his ancestral see. About 40 affiliated organizations are located throughout the United States and Canada. AANF conventions, held in different states each year, draw Assyrians from all over North America. The AANF is affiliated with the Assyrian Universal Alliance (AUA), an international umbrella organization with chapters in the United States, Europe, the Middle East, Australia and Latin America. Since 1952 the AANF has published a bimonthly magazine *Kokhva-d Atour* (The Assyrian Star), written in English, Assyrian, and Arabic. *The Assyrian Sentinel* serves as the organ of the AUA and has been circulating from Hartford since 1976.

During the past decade both the publications and institutions of Assyrians in the United States have multiplied, reflecting the renewed ethnic vigor of the community and its diversity of political and cultural opinion. A political activist group, the Bet Nahrain Democratic Party (BNDP) was established in 1976; in 1977 it organized the International Confederation of the Assyrian Nation (ICAN), as a framework for a provisional government of an Assyrian state. ICAN headquarters are located in Washington, D.C., at the Assyrian Chancery. The primary objective of the BNDP/ICAN organizations is the establishment of a semiautonomous Assyrian state in the ancestral homelands of the Assyrians, which would include parts of eastern Turkey, northwestern Iran and northern Iraq. The BNDP point of view is expressed in the bilingual (English-Assyrian) magazine, *Bet Nahrain* (land between the two rivers), and in the English-language newspaper, *The Assyrian Quest*, both established in 1974 and issued from California and Chicago respectively. A rapprochement between the older AANF which promotes "cultural Assyrianism" and the BNDP which is a partisan nationalist group has met with limited success. Additional organizations and publications in recent years include the Assyrian Foundation of America and its publication, *Nineveh* (Berkeley, 1978). These periodicals, supplemented by publications of Assyrian groups in the Middle East and Europe, provide the community with a variety of political, social, and cultural materials.

The Assyrian American Educational Association, founded in 1949, supports Assyrian schools teaching the Assyrian language and other efforts to preserve Assyrian culture and heritage, ancient and modern. The "Assyrian Voice," an ethnic radio program is broadcast in Chicago and in Ceres, Calif. An Assyrian television program is produced in the Modesto-Ceres-Turlock region of California.

But it is the Assyrian denominational churches in the United States that retain a traditional role as the locus of community activities. Many ancient rituals have survived, although they are somewhat modified. The *shahra* (fiesta), the traditional village festival held on various Saints' days, is celebrated. So is the *doukhrana* (sacrifice) ceremony, in which a lamb is sacrificed at the church. Traditional folk tunes and ring dances are a vital part of Assyrian-American festivities.

Assyrian Americans are inclined to socialize with members of their own group and to marry within their group, although interethnic marriage is on the increase. Of all the other Middle Eastern groups with whom they come in contact they are perhaps closest to the Armenians, with whom they share a historical and religious background. Nonetheless, there is a continuing erosion

of traditional culture and values. Command of the language has declined sharply among second-generation immigrants, even more thereafter. Many Assyrians have westernized their names and ties with kinfolk have become attenuated.

To counteract these trends some Assyrian Americans have organized language and heritage classes in cities with large Assyrian populations. It is not clear whether or not Assyrians will be able to maintain a distinct ethnic identity in the next generation, but currently the rise of nationalist politics and the renewed quest for a homeland are contributing to diverse cultural, religious, and linguistic activities.

Bibliography

For a well-documented history of the contemporary Assyrians in the Middle East, see John Joseph, *The Nestorians and Their Muslim Neighbors* (Princeton, N.J., 1961). Material on the Assyrian immigrant colonies in the United States is scanty. S. Jackson and V. Nevils, "The Assyrians: Settlers from the Near East," in Helen A. Hohenthal, *Streams in a Thirsty Land: A History of the Turlock Region* (Turlock, Calif., 1972), is a charming account of the settlement of the first Assyrian colony in the San Joaquin Valley. See also William Saroyan's poignant "Seventy Thousand Assyrians," in *The Daring Young Man on the Flying Trapeze* (New York, 1934). A brief ethnographic sketch of a Chaldean colony in Detroit, Mich., is found in Mary C. Sengstock, "Telkaif, Baghdad, Detroit: Chaldeans Blend Three Cultures," *Michigan History* 54 (1970): 293–310; and ethnographic data on the Assyrian immigrant colonies in Canada and the United States are found in Arian Ishaya, *The Role of Minorities in the State: History of the Assyrian Experience*, Anthropology Papers, No. 19 (Winnipeg, Canada, 1979). The chapter by George Marogi on Syrian Arameans in *The New Jersey Ethnic Experience*, ed. Barbara Cunningham (Union City, N.J., 1977), provides a Syrian Orthodox (Jacobite) perspective.

ARIAN ISHAYA AND EDEN NABY

ATAKAPAS: *see* AMERICAN INDIANS

ATHAPASKANS: *see* AMERICAN INDIANS

ATSINAS: *see* AMERICAN INDIANS

AUSTRALIANS AND NEW ZEALANDERS

Australians and New Zealanders are treated together in this entry mainly for convenience, since published immigration statistics usually do not differentiate between the two countries. However, little distortion is introduced by the combination. Although New Zealand did not join the six British colonies that federated in 1901 to form the Commonwealth of Australia, and although the two countries remain independent sovereign nations with quite distinct national self-images, they have much in common. Most obviously, the populations of both countries are overwhelmingly of English, Irish, and Scottish background. Australia and New Zealand are noteworthy more as competitors for, than as providers of, immigrants to the United States. According to the 1970 U.S. Census, 82,000 persons of Australian or New Zealand stock (born or with at least one parent born in either country) resided in the United States, a figure representing a minimal 0.25 percent of all foreign stock. The 2,693 immigrants who came from Australia and New Zealand in 1970 were just 0.7 percent of the American immigration for that year. In the preceding 100 years, from 1871 to 1970, around 99,000 people were recorded as immigrating to the U.S. from

the two countries, again a minute 0.3 percent of all immigrants. Reliable figures for the years prior to 1870 are not available for the Pacific region.

Australians and New Zealanders have thus made only a small numerical contribution to the U.S. population profile. Their annual rate of immigration has, however, fluctuated considerably, peaking in the first two decades of the 20th century, declining for the next three, and steadily increasing from a low of 460 in 1950 to a recent rate of over 2,000 per year.

Within this largely uneventful history, two unusual immigration peaks, a century apart, are particularly interesting. In the 1945–1948 period over 11,650 immigrants came from Australia and New Zealand and in 1946 alone over 6,000, representing in that year a full 5.5 percent of the United States total. A large proportion of these immigrants were war brides, resulting from the presence of American armed forces in the South Pacific during World War II. Another major influx had occurred 100 years earlier, in 1849–1850, this time in response to news of the discovery of gold in California, which reached Sydney and Auckland before it reached much of the U.S. East Coast. One source contends that "by the end of 1850 more than ten percent of Sydney's population of 60,000 were digging in the California mines," while another has uncovered records of 212 sailings between Australia or New Zealand and California in 1849–1850, carrying up to 8,000 people to the goldfields. Among them were a large number of ex-convicts who had been deported from Britain to provide the original colonists for Australia. Even as lawless a frontier town as San Francisco in 1850 apparently lived in fear of these "Sydney Ducks," who introduced organized crime into the waterfront neighborhood. Consider this flamboyant account:

> There, in particular, gathered the ruffianly larrikins from the frontier towns of Australia, and the escaped convicts and ticket-of-leave men from the British penal settlements at Sydney, in New South Wales, and on the island of Tasmania, then called Van Diemen's Land. This wave of undesirable immigration, which to all intents and purposes was one hundred per cent criminal, began to wash against the shores of California about the middle of 1849 . . . By the early autumn of 1849 the arrivals from Australia had become so numerous, and so thoroughly dominated the underworld, that the district in which they congregated began to be known as Sydney-Town, and it was so called for some ten years. It was this area that later became notorious throughout the world as the Barbary Coast . . . Unquestionably, these foreign felons gave San Francisco's underworld its initial flavor; they were pioneers in the viciousness and depravity for which the Barbary Coast became famous . . . The more commercial spirits among the Sydney Ducks opened lodging-houses, dance-halls, groggeries, and taverns . . . Drunkenness, robbery, and all manner of strife and lewdness went on in these places . . . He was a fortunate man who could visit a resort in Sydney-Town and escape without being slugged and robbed.

Although recent scholarship suggests that only 12 percent of the emigrants from Sydney were actually ex-convicts, the impact of the Sydney Ducks was dramatic. The California legislature tried in vain to prohibit the entry of ex-convicts. More effective was the action of a Committee of Vigilance, comprising at its height some "400 influential men," who lynched three

or four Australians, banished others, and screened ships from the South Pacific for possible criminal elements.

The immigration tide reversed completely in 1851 when gold was discovered in eastern Australia. Most of the Australians and New Zealanders returned home (accompanied by many Californians), thereby terminating a brief period in which people from Down Under probably had their biggest impact on American society.

The California connection persisted, however. In 1970 California accounted for 10 percent of the American population but was the location of 30 percent of the foreign stock of Australian or New Zealand heritage. California is, of course, the closest mainland state to the South Pacific and has a long history of trans-Pacific trade. It also possesses in its climate, lifestyle, and sprawling suburbia much that is familiar to people from Down Under. Among the notable California Australians has been Harry Bridges (1901–), whose activities as a radical union organizer on the San Francisco waterfront in the 1920s and 1930s led the Immigration and Naturalization Service (INS) and the Congress, through special legislation, to attempt his deportation (the Supreme Court ruled in his favor in 1941). Part of Bridges's problem, concluded Harvard Law School Dean James Landis (the INS trial examiner in one deportation hearing), was that his "conceptions as to the place of trade-unionism derive considerably from his Australian experience and upbringing." Organized labor has always been prominent in Australia in both the industrial and the political arenas: the Australian Labor party had become the first working-class party to govern a nation in the decade before Bridges arrived in San Francisco.

Bridges is one of the few Australians and New Zealand immigrants whose national background remains visible: others in this category include professional sportsmen (such as the Australian tennis players who appear to monopolize the tennis-camp business in the South and Southwest, plus assorted golfers and professional football players), entertainers, and writers. But for every Rupert Murdoch, whose publishing exploits in New York provoked *Time* to splash across its cover "Aussie Press Lord Terrifies Gotham," there are a legion whose origins go unnoticed. It is not widely known, for example, that Elton Mayo, designer of the classic "Hawthorne experiments" in human relations conducted at the Harvard Business School, was Australian.

Most Australians and New Zealanders in the United States assimilate quickly with minimal difficulty, owing both to their small numbers and to their transfer from advanced, industrial English-speaking countries similar to the United States in social structure and culture. That those from Down Under are not immune to congregating in an ethnic neighborhood is demonstrated by their presence, perhaps somewhat transiently and diffusely, in the Earl's Court area of London, but there is no comparable area in the United States. London, as the mother city of the British Commonwealth, no doubt provides the focus for that concentration. Still, it is also possible, if some comparative studies of social values are to be believed, that Australians find themselves culturally more similar to Americans than to Britons, and hence assimilate in America more readily than in the mother land.

No particular occupational group appears to predominate. Around 18 percent of the Australians and 20 percent of the New Zealanders admitted in 1969 were "professional, technical, and kindred workers," figures comparable to those for the United Kingdom (20 percent) and Canada (16.5 percent), but much less than those for countries like India (48 percent) and the Philippines (35 percent). There are some organizations of Australians and New Zealanders in the United States, but they are loose regional bodies with many American and transient members. The Australian and New Zealand Society of New York, for example, is based in the Qantas Airways building, and its primary attraction seems to be the provision of charter packages for trans-Pacific air travel.

Since Australia, New Zealand, and the United States are all "immigrant societies," some people from other source countries have sampled the immigrant experience on both sides of the Pacific. Particularly after Australia began encouraging and subsidizing non-British European immigration in 1945, Europeans later moved on to the United States, a process labeled "transilient migration." A rough estimate of some 1,150 such transilient migrants from non-British Europe through Australia to the United States can be made for the year 1966. Almost certainly recorded as immigrants under their own nationality, it is probable that those permanently settling in the United States could not be distinguished from other ethnic Americans by their Australian experience.

Australia and New Zealand are not likely to become significant providers of immigrants to the United States. Those who have migrated from Down Under have generally dispersed and assimilated into the dominant culture of the United States, and thus do not constitute a visible ethnic group in the associational and behavioral senses of that term.

Bibliography
The only direct studies of Australian and New Zealand immigration to the United States relate to the California gold-rush influx of 1849–1850: Charles Bateson, *Gold Fleet for California: Forty-Niners from Australia and New Zealand* (Sydney, 1963), and Jay Monaghan, *Australians and the Gold Rush: California and Down Under 1849–1854* (Berkeley, Calif., 1966). The reaction of San Franciscans to the Sydney Ducks is documented in George R. Stewart, *Committee of Vigilance: Revolution in San Francisco, 1851* (Boston, 1964), and in Mary Floyd Williams, *History of the San Francisco Committee of Vigilance of 1851* (1921; reprint, New York, 1969). The story of Harry Bridges is colorfully told by Charles P. Larrowe in *Harry Bridges: The Rise and Fall of Radical Labor in the United States* (New York, 1972). The parallel experiences of Australasia and the United States as immigrant societies are discussed from two different perspectives in Charles A. Price, *The Great White Walls Are Built: Restrictive Immigration to North America and Australasia 1836–1888* (Canberra, 1974), and Andrew Parkin, "Ethnic Politics: A Comparative Study of Two Immigrant Societies, Australia and the United States," *Journal of Commonwealth and Comparative Politics* 15 (March 1977): 22–38.

ANDREW PARKIN

AUSTRIANS

To be Austrian in the United States has no consistent or uniform meaning for persons of Austrian birth or parentage. This is a result of the complex history of Austria during the past two centuries and of the fact that many different ethnic groups were governed by the Austrian state until 1918, when the Republic of Austria came into existence. A spirit of nationalism never developed among Austrians as it did among other Euro-

pean groups. Austrian immigrants therefore have tended to deemphasize their national origin and instead to identify themselves as having come from Vienna, Styria, Burgenland, or some other province of the republic. Although they are a people of Germanic language and culture, they generally have wanted to maintain an identity distinct from the German.

This was not always the case. Before 1867, the year in which the Dual Monarchy of Austria-Hungary was created, the term "Austrian" applied to all subjects of the Hapsburg monarchs without regard to their ethnic background; after 1867, however, a distinction was ordinarily made between the residents of the Austrian and Hungarian parts of the empire. Occasionally Germans who lived anywhere within the borders of Austria-Hungary were called Austrians; the term then included not only the people of Austria proper, but also such groups as the Sudetenland Germans of Bohemia and Moravia, the Siebenburger Saxons of Transylvania, and Danube Swabians of the Banat. When the multiethnic Dual Monarchy collapsed at the end of World War I, Austria was reduced to a remnant of the empire—the German-speaking core region, including the provinces of Upper and Lower Austria, Styria, Carinthia, Tirol, Vorarlberg, Salzburg, Vienna, and in 1921 Burgenland. Had the Allied powers permitted the Austrians to express their wishes at that time, they probably would have preferred annexation to Germany to independence.

Because of these profound territorial and political changes, the statistics on Austrian immigration are inconsistent and confused. The Austrian government kept no records of emigration in the 19th century, so statistical information has had to be gathered from materials found at ports of embarkation, such as Hamburg, Bremen, and Antwerp. U.S. Census data are lacking in consistency, because census takers listed the country of birth according to the political status of that country at the time the census was taken. It is possible, for example, that German-speaking people born in Transylvania before 1918 might have reported to the census taker of 1920 that they were born in Austria, Austria-Hungary, Hungary, Romania, or Transylvania. This confusion has resulted in inaccurate data on Austrian emigration for the 19th and early 20th centuries. Nor are the data for the years since 1920 entirely reliable. Both before and after World War II unknown numbers of Austrians emigrated or fled to other countries and eventually entered the United States from Canada, Britain, France, and other countries, where sometimes they had already acquired new citizenship. Similarly, many persons listed as Austrian immigrants in the post–World War II period were actually non-Austrian refugees, often of German ethnicity, from Hungary, Yugoslavia, and other Central European countries, who had fled westward as the armies of the Soviet Union swept across Eastern Europe in 1945.

EARLY ARRIVAL AND SETTLEMENT

Despite this lack of reliable data, we know that a small number of Austrians came to the United States before the Civil War, although very few arrived during the colonial period. Of the latter, the most important were the Protestants from Salzburg who found new homes in Georgia in 1734, after the Catholic bishop-

prince of Salzburg had initiated a program to suppress Protestantism in the lands under his jurisdiction (1728). Of the approximately 30,000 Protestants forced into exile by 1731, most found refuge in the various German Protestant states, but about 50 families immigrated to the newly founded American colony of Georgia. They were granted free passage and land near Savannah, where they established a settlement named Ebenezer. Poor soil, disease, and lack of agricultural skills made life extremely difficult, and two years later the Salzburgers relocated on better, higher ground nearby. There they prospered until the revolutionary war, when their homes and farms were ravaged and their settlements scattered. One of them, Johann Adam Treutlen, was the first elected governor of the state of Georgia.

Only a few thousand Austrians came to the United States in the first half of the 19th century. Clusters settled here and there, such as at Korntal, Ill., and New Wien, Iowa, but most were attracted to large cities, and by 1860 both St. Louis and New York had well over a thousand each. As German-speaking people, they associated readily with immigrants from the south German states. They had no special identity as Austrians at that time, and they thought of themselves as Germans in much the same way that Bavarians or Rhinelanders did. For the census they would ordinarily list for their birthplaces cities such as Vienna or Linz, provinces such as Tirol, or even the "German empire," by which they meant the Hapsburg realm.

Catholic priests were an important element in the early Austrian immigration. Sent by the Leopoldine Society, which was founded in Vienna in 1829, they served Catholic immigrants from Germany as well as Austria. Eventually 100 to 200 priests were commissioned for this work. They were particularly active in the development of German-language parochial schools in midwestern states and in large eastern cities.

Another small but influential group of Austrians came to the United States as political refugees following the revolutions of 1848. As radical reformers, these well-educated, middle-class people hoped to remake the world according to liberal principles. When they failed in Vienna, a few of them fled to America, where they loudly proclaimed their anticlerical and antislavery sentiments. Although some of these so-called forty-eighters, like their fellow reformers from the German states, had difficulty adjusting to American life, as a group they left their mark on the politics, journalism, music, and medicine of their adopted country.

According to official data there were fewer than a thousand Austrian residents in the United States in 1850. Although the actual number was no doubt larger than that, it was nonetheless minute compared with the numbers that were soon to arrive. During the next decades, emigration from the Hapsburg empire vastly increased. Most who came were non-Germanic ethnic groups living in Austria-Hungary (Czechs, Slovaks, Hungarians), but according to one generous estimate the number of German-speaking Austrians in the United States had risen to 275,000 by 1900.

A variety of causes impelled this great movement. In the second half of the 19th century Austria-Hungary began to experience the same overpopulation and land hunger that had earlier affected other European countries. Some Austrian emigrants were impoverished

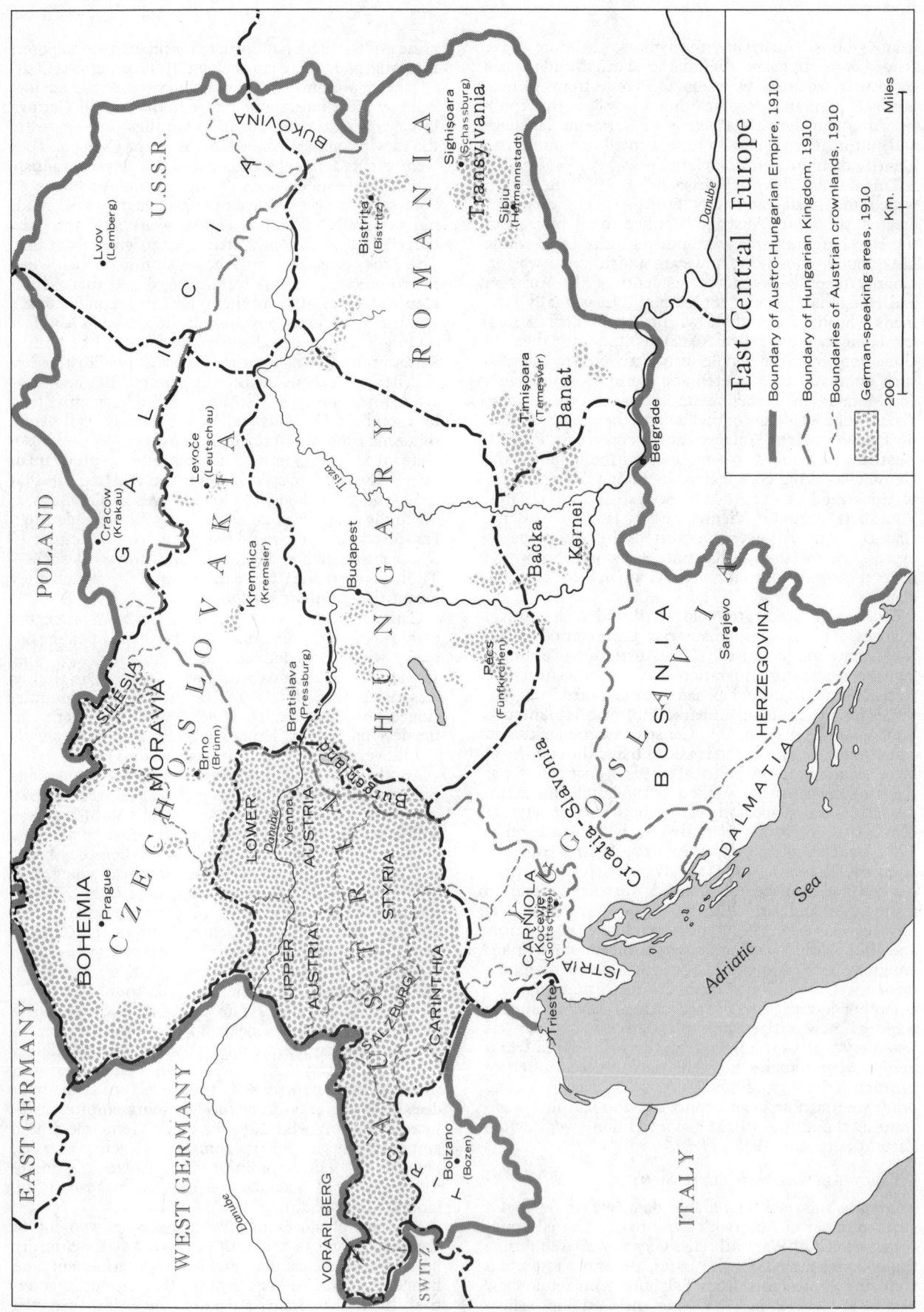

East Central Europe

— Boundary of Austro-Hungarian Empire, 1910

— Boundary of Hungarian Kingdom, 1910

–– Boundaries of Austrian crownlands, 1910

▒ German-speaking areas, 1910

POLAND

U.S.S.R.

Lvov
(Lemberg)

Cracow
(Krakau)

G A L I C I A

BUKOVINA

ROMANIA

Bistriţa
(Bistritz)

Sighişoara
(Schässburg)

Sibiu
(Hermannstadt)

Transylvania

Timişoara
(Temesvar)

Banat

Levoče
(Leutschau)

Kremnica
(Kremsier)

C Z E C H O S L O V A K I A

Tisza

H U N G A R Y

Budapest

Kernei

Bačka

Danube

Belgrade

EAST GERMANY

WEST GERMANY

BOHEMIA

Prague

SILESIA

MORAVIA

Brno
(Brünn)

Bratislava
(Pressburg)

Danube

LOWER
AUSTRIA

Vienna

Burgenland

Pécs
(Fünfkirchen)

Croatia-Slavonia

Y U G O S L A V I A

BOSNIA

Sarajevo

HERZEGOVINA

DALMATIA

Adriatic
Sea

UPPER
AUSTRIA

SALZBURG

S T Y R I A

TIROL

CARINTHIA

CARNIOLA

Kočevje
(Gottschee)

ISTRIA

Trieste

VORARLBERG

SWITZ.

Danube

Bolzano
(Bozen)

ITALY

Danube

Miles

Km.

200

peasants and unemployed village laborers whose problems stemmed in part from patterns of landholding. In some cases the land was owned in huge tracts and was worked seasonally by day laborers. In many other instances tracts had become so small, as a result of generations of divisions made in accordance with inheritance laws, that they could no longer support the families that lived on them. Rural workers had to seek employment nearby as hired hands and domestic servants. Later they went to Vienna and to the provincial cities of Austria and Hungary, where they found employment mostly in construction and in factories. Gradually the search for work extended to the United States. What had been merely a seasonal migration for many became a permanent migration for thousands of others.

Emigration as a solution to economic distress increased steadily until a peak was reached early in the 20th century. Like thousands of Germans who had preceded them, many Austrian peasants established themselves on American farms, in tiny rural colonies in the Midwest, and on the agricultural frontier of the Great Plains. But as industrialization developed in the United States a growing proportion sought work in the manufacturing cities of the Northeast.

Overpopulation was also a reason for emigration. In the late 19th century improved sanitation dramatically lowered the death rate in Austria. At the same time, the birthrate continued at the high levels typical of preindustrial societies, resulting in a burgeoning population too large for the agrarian economy of Austria-Hungary to support. Nevertheless, the rate of emigration among German-speaking Austrians was low compared to that for other ethnic groups in the Dual Monarchy: in 1912, for example, the Polish rate was 711 per 100,000, compared to 182 per 100,000 for the Austro-Germans.

Wisconsin, the most German of American states, provides an example of the pattern of Austrian settlement at the beginning of the 20th century. The 1905 state census revealed that of 2,319 heads of families born in Austria proper (as distinguished from Galicia, Bohemia, and other Austrian lands), almost exactly half lived in cities, including 732 in Milwaukee alone. Although these families were widely distributed across the city, they were most numerous in Ward Six, a strongly German district. Another significant urban concentration of Austrians was in Sheboygan, also a strongly German city. Outside the cities Austrian families lived in small towns and rural areas scattered across the state; only in Pepin County did they constitute a major foreign-born group. The colony consisted mostly of farmers, Catholic in religion, who had emigrated from Lower Austria in the 1870s. Eighty-two families resided in rural Lime Township; another 30 lived in the county seat of Durand.

In the later part of the 19th century, several other groups settled along the agricultural frontier of the Great Plains. Although they identified themselves as Austrians for the census, ordinarily they did not come from Austria proper. Several settlements in Kansas illustrate this pattern. Two groups of German-speaking Moravians arrived in Barton County, near the center of the state, in 1875; at the end of 20 years their numbers had increased to more than 1,200. Another group from Bukovina, the easternmost Hapsburg province, now part of the Soviet Union, settled in Ellis County in 1877. In the same year, a colony of German speakers from Hungary settled still farther west in Rawlins County; by 1895 the group had grown to more than 900 persons. This group had emigrated from western Hungary, probably from the region that later became the Austrian province of Burgenland. Similar colonies of farmers, most of them Protestants, settled in other parts of the Great Plains in the late 19th century.

By the end of the 19th century the agricultural frontier had largely disappeared, and mechanized agriculture was taking over in the American Midwest. Few new immigrants came with the financial resources necessary to set up such large-scale farming efforts, so the family emigration of the earlier period gave way in the 20th century to a migration predominantly made up of young males. They came intending to stay only a few years, then to return home and establish themselves with the money they had earned. In the first decade of the 20th century, this new emigration from Austria-Hungary assumed the proportions of a mass movement. German-speaking Austrians constituted approximately 12 percent of the total and averaged about 28,000 per year. Of these, two-thirds came from the Hungarian half of the empire, chiefly from Burgenland, the Banat, and Transylvania. Most of the remainder came from Bukovina, Moravia, and Carniola, where German speakers were a minority group, and from the city of Vienna. Few emigrated from Tirol, Salzburg, Vorarlberg, and Upper Austria, where virtually everyone was German.

Of all the provinces of Austria and Hungary, Burgenland provided the largest number of German-speaking emigrants bound for America. This long and narrow border province, located south of Vienna, had been part of Hungary for over 900 years. Because its people were 85 percent German (15 percent Croat and Hungarian), Burgenlanders elected to become part of Austria in a 1919 plebiscite. Formal transfer from Hungary to Austria occurred in 1921 with the approval of the Allied powers. Mass emigration began in the northern part of Burgenland where the proportion of agricultural wage laborers was especially high. It moved like an epidemic southward to districts where small landholding was common and where an extensive viniculture had been ruined by disease. Military conscription also stimulated the flight to America, especially when war threatened. In some districts, so many men emigrated that houses stood empty and fields were left untilled. Wives and children remained behind as husbands and fathers left to work in the stockyards of Chicago, the breweries of New York, or the cement factories of Allentown, Pa. America seemed to be a land of hope—or at least a source of money to bring back home. During those years the rate at which emigrants returned approached 35 percent.

When World War I erupted in 1914, Austrian immigration dropped sharply and then ceased entirely. After the war, when the Austrian Republic was created out of the German-speaking fragment of the empire, political, economic, and social conditions were at best uncertain, and flight to America resumed. Between 1919 and 1924, 18,000 Austrians sought the relative security of life in the United States.

As in the decade before the war, Burgenland was again the center of the movement; 70 percent of the emigration originated in this former part of the Hungar-

ian kingdom, attaining a peak of 6,700 persons in 1923. Its emigration rate was more than twice that for Vienna; neighboring Styria and Lower Austria accounted for most of the rest. In several Burgenland communities, the people who left for America were in the majority. Burgenlanders in the United States sent so much money home that in some areas two currencies were commonly in use—Austrian shillings were used for petty transactions, while larger purchases, especially of real estate, were made in United States dollars.

Then, in 1924, the U.S. Congress passed a highly restrictive immigration act that established a quota system based on national origin. The Austrian quota was first reduced to 785 persons per year, then raised to 1,413 by legislation in 1929. These restrictions had the effect of deflecting some Austrian emigration to Canada, Argentina, and Brazil.

During the 1920s Austrian immigrants continued to concentrate in certain industrial cities, as they had before the war. New York, as the major port of entry, retained a large proportion, sometimes over 50 percent of those coming from particular towns and villages. Other major communities of Austrian immigrants, such as those in Chicago and Detroit, increased greatly, as did those in several smaller cities in Pennsylvania and New Jersey. According to one estimate, by 1930 Allentown, Pa. had 6,500 Austrian-born inhabitants, easily constituting the largest foreign-born group in the city. Large Burgenlander colonies developed in Coplay and Northampton, Pa., two nearby towns of only a few thousand persons each.

WORLD WAR II AND THE POSTWAR IMMIGRATION

The flow of Austrian immigration to the United States diminished to a mere trickle during the depression of the 1930s. When it resumed toward the end of the decade, it was of a different character from the earlier mass movements. These had usually consisted of peasants and unskilled workers from the provinces, while the emigration of 1938 and 1939 was made up mostly of well-educated, middle-class Jews from Vienna, who were fleeing the anti-Semitism that had engulfed the country even before its annexation by Germany (the Anschluss) in March 1938. Although these fugitives were not the first Jewish Austrians to emigrate—a large proportion of the pre–World War I emigration had been Jewish (some from Vienna, but more from Bohemia, Moravia, and Galicia)—they were a group that was especially distinguished in business, the professions, and the arts.

About 80 percent of the Austrians who fled the Nazis were Jews; according to one estimate, nearly 29,000 Jewish Austrians emigrated between the Anschluss and the entry of the United States into the war in December 1941. They left voluntarily only in a technical sense, seeking safety in France, England, Portugal, and eventually the United States. Some entered the United States under the quotas of other countries; others had to wait until after the war was over. Flight was for them a drastic, unwelcome step that meant the abandonment of property, position, and often family. Accustomed to the comfortable security of the middle-class in a moderately stratified society, they faced an uncertain future in the fluidity and competitiveness of American life.

They often had to accept menial, tedious jobs until more appropriate employment became available, or until they could meet the requirements for the practice of their professions—medicine, architecture, and law—in the United States. Although the resulting loss of social and economic status was psychologically difficult, ultimately the skills and experience that the majority brought with them allowed them to adjust successfully. Physicians did especially well. Lawyers, by contrast, trained in a different kind of law, found it almost impossible to practice their profession and shifted to other fields, often to teaching. The majority of these Austrian émigrés settled in New York; a few returned to Austria after the war.

These exceptional people adjusted easily, learned English readily, and were soon enriching American cultural life. Among them were the celebrated pianist Artur Schnabel (1882–1951), the composers Arnold Schönberg (1874–1951) and Erich Korngold (1897–1957), conductor Bruno Walter (1876–1962), author Franz Werfel (1890–1945), economist Ludwig von Mises (1881–1973), producers and directors Max Reinhardt (1873–1943) and Otto Preminger (1906–), psychoanalysts Theodor Reik (1888–1969) and Bruno Bettelheim (1903–), and Nobel Prize-winning scientist Viktor Hess (1883–1964).

Developments during World War II laid the foundation for a large postwar movement of Austrians to the United States. A few were originally from South Tirol, a district that had been taken from Austria-Hungary after World War I and made into the Italian province of Alto Adige. Most of the province's German-speaking inhabitants had remained, however, until in 1939 Benito Mussolini, following the German-Italian accord of that year, attempted to Italianize the population. He gave ethnic Germans living in Alto Adige the opportunity to resettle in Austria, and subsequently approximately 60,000 moved to Tirol, Vorarlberg, and Carinthia, at that time parts of Hitler's Germany. Approximately 13,500 Gottschee Germans, residents of a district in northern Yugoslavia that had once been part of Austria-Hungary, were also allowed to migrate to Austria when Mussolini annexed the area in 1941. Members of both groups eventually settled in the United States after the war.

Many more ethnic Germans—refugees from Russia, Romania, Hungary, and Yugoslavia—fled westward before the advancing Soviet army as World War II drew to a close. In the postwar period Austria functioned as a refuge for over 1.6 million people, at least half of whom were ethnically German. One-third of the total became Austrian citizens; a sixth went to Germany.

The experiences of the Kernei Germans of Yugoslavia illustrate what happened to many of the isolated clusters of ethnic Germans in the Banat, Transylvania, and elsewhere in the former Hapsburg empire. Numbering about 6,000 persons in 1945, the Kerneier were the descendants of Germans who in the 18th century had been brought by their Hapsburg rulers to settle a depopulated district between the Danube and Tisza rivers. When the region fell to the Communists at the end of World War II, about half of the Kerneier escaped to Austria and Germany. Eventually more than 3,000 settled in the United States and Canada, chiefly in Chicago and Toronto. In 1948, the U.S. Congress facilitated the immigration of refugees through passage of the Displaced

Persons Act, which remained in force until 1952. Under its terms 2,500 Austrians were admitted, and nearly 25,000 other ethnic Germans came from former Hapsburg lands in Yugoslavia, Hungary, and Romania. Other special legislation allowed for the admission of war brides of American soldiers stationed in Austria and other countries.

During the 15-year period following the war nearly 40,000 Austrian immigrants were admitted into the United States, almost 60 percent of them under the quota provisions. Most were highly educated or had technical training or specialized experience, as required by postwar immigration legislation. However, the Austrian quota, which remained at about 1,400 per year, could accommodate only part of those who hoped to escape the disorganization of the postwar period and to make a new start elsewhere. As a result, many more Austrians chose instead to go to Canada and Australia. This was especially true of the Burgenlanders, who again formed a major part of the Austrian emigration. In 1951, for example, only 382 Burgenlanders were admitted into the United States while 2,529 went to Canada, chiefly to the Toronto area.

In recent years Austrian immigration to the United States has dropped off sharply, even though Congress finally abandoned quotas based on national origin with the passage of the Immigration Act of 1965. From 1966 to 1975, nearly 20,000 immigrants listed Austria as the country of last permanent residence, but only 7,768 gave Austria as their country of birth. This discrepancy indicates that Austria continues to serve as a temporary home for many Eastern Europeans who have fled the land of their birth. During the 1970s an average of only 515 Austrian-born immigrants have entered the United States per year.

Geographic and Occupational Distribution

In general, the geographic distribution of Austrians in the United States has not changed much in the 20th century. Austrians have been less widely dispersed than Germans, chiefly because a greater proportion of them are Jews who tend to settle in New York City. Austrian immigrants are most numerous (in proportion to the total population) in the Middle Atlantic states of New York, New Jersey, and Pennsylvania, and in Connecticut. They are next most numerous in the midwestern states, with Illinois in the lead, followed by Wisconsin and Ohio. Austrians are actually less widely dispersed today than they were 50 years ago. Concentrations have become greater in New York, New Jersey, and Florida and smaller in the Midwest and in the mining states of the West.

Data on the occupations of Austrians in the United States, like data on geographic distribution, are limited in usefulness because consistent distinctions were not made between the various ethnic groups from the Austro-Hungarian Empire. Statistics for 1900 show that, compared to the total white male population, immigrants from Austria-Hungary were 10.5 times more likely to be tailors, 7.5 times more likely to be miners, and 4.3 times more likely to be hucksters and peddlers. Jews largely accounted for the first and third categories, non-Jews for the second. Very few Jewish Austrians went into agriculture, making the frequency of Aus-

trians in agricultural employment one of the lowest for any immigrant people, even though German-speaking Austrian farmers were not unusual in the midwestern and Great Plains states. Immigrants from Austria-Hungary were also disproportionately numerous among iron and steel workers, saloonkeepers, waiters, and common laborers, but the breakdown by ethnic group is not always clear.

Fifty years later the Austrians remained strongly represented in some of the same occupations. Among tailors the proportion of Austrians was eight times higher than among the adult white population of the United States; employment of Austrians in clothes manufacturing was even higher at 8.4 to 1. Many continued to be employed in food-related occupations—as bakers, waiters, bartenders, and slaughterhouse and meat-packing workers; miners and service occupations also ranked high. More recently acquired occupations are those of medicine and dentistry and managerial positions of various kinds.

According to the 1970 census, Austrian immigrants in the United States number 214,014; another 761,311 are reported as being of Austrian parentage. The Austrian-born are now a very old population, with a median age of 68.3 years; nearly two-thirds of them immigrated before 1925. The census category "born in Austria" still includes large numbers of Poles, Ukrainians, Slovaks, Italians, Croats, and others who were born in the Hapsburg crownlands before 1919, an ethnic heterogeneity confirmed by the fact that only 56 percent gave German as their mother tongue and an additional 12 percent indicated Yiddish. The remainder were divided up among the other language groups represented in the old Austro-Hungarian Empire. The older the age group of the Austrian-born, the lower the proportion of German speakers: only 44 percent of those 75 years or older gave German as their mother tongue compared to 85 percent of the 25-to-44 age group.

Austrian immigrants in the United States are overwhelmingly city dwellers. In 1970 by far the largest number—one-fourth of the total—were living in New York, the second largest in Chicago, the third in the Los Angeles–Long Beach area. The younger German-speaking Austrians are much more numerous in Chicago, Los Angeles, and the Paterson-Clifton-Passaic area of northeastern New Jersey (where Burgenlanders have tended to congregate); the older non-Germans are more numerous in New York, Miami, and Pittsburgh: 71 percent of Chicago Austrians gave German as their mother tongue, compared to 38 percent in Miami; another 38 percent of the Miami group indicated Yiddish as their native tongue, compared with 3 percent of the Chicagoans. Pittsburgh, much like Miami, reported a very old male population with a median age of 77.9 years, and only 33 percent listed German as their mother tongue. Very few Pittsburgh Austrians were Jews, however, whereas 25 percent of them were Slovak. Among New York Austrians the male median age was 57.3 years; 48 percent reported German, and 30 percent Yiddish, as their mother tongue.

The 1970 Census also reveals that German speakers have continued to form a substantial proportion of the immigrants coming from those countries that before 1919 formed part of the Hapsburg Empire but were outside Austria proper. In Philadelphia 43 percent of the

Yugoslavs and 27 percent of the Hungarian immigrants gave German as their mother tongue, and in Chicago 30 percent of each. Percentages ranging from 10 to 30 percent were recorded for the same groups in Los Angeles, Miami, New York, and the Paterson-Clifton-Passaic area.

ORGANIZATIONS

All European ethnic groups have tended to form voluntary associations that will help them assimilate, and Austrians have been no exception; they have not been strongly attracted to these organizations, however, and only a small fraction are active members. German-speaking Austrians often join German societies, just as they ordinarily read German newspapers, and many, especially among the recent immigrants, are well educated and skilled; they feel no need for the social and psychological support such societies offer. Because Austrian Americans are a heterogeneous people, no national organization can effectively unite their interests. German Austrians have tended to prefer small, intimate clubs to large national organizations.

The majority of Austrian-American organizations are organized by province of origin. Burgenlander societies are the most numerous (Chicago is the headquarters for the Burgenland Society founded in 1956, a national organization with 5,000 members), but in some cities Styrians, Carinthians, and Tirolians have organized their own clubs. New York has the largest number and variety, including two or three dozen mutual-benefit associations, athletic clubs, and social and cultural societies devoted to card playing, singing, folk dancing, and bowling. Most centers of Austrian-American population have local societies to support Austrian culture: Chicago, for example, has the American-Austrian Society of the Midwest, and similar organizations can be found in Minneapolis, Buffalo, and other cities. Such organizations typically combine social, educational, and cultural goals in their programs and have memberships of one or two hundred, many of them American-born persons interested in Austrian culture. Although some organizations display strongly anti-Communist leanings, political clubs are rare. Sometimes the appeal narrows, perhaps unintentionally, to specific elements within the Austrian population. The Austrian-American Association of Miami Beach (f. 1954), for example, consists chiefly of persons who fled Austrian Nazism before World War II. They share a lively interest in Austrian music and hold regularly scheduled dinner meetings.

The most vigorous of the societies are those that draw their membership from the post–World War II immigration, which includes large numbers of German-speaking refugees from Romania, Hungary, and Yugoslavia who resided in Austria and acquired Austrian citizenship before coming to America. Many join appropriate provincial societies, such as those for Transylvanian Saxons, Danube Swabians, Gottscheer, and Banaters. The National Union of Danube Swabians is located in New York; a union of German-Hungarians in Philadelphia; and a Gottscheer bowling club, relief society, and health-insurance association can all be found in Ridgewood, N.Y. Transylvanian (or Siebenburger) Saxon organizations are especially numerous in Detroit and in Cleveland—where the Alliance of Transylvania

Saxons, a life-insurance association with nearly 10,000 members, has its headquarters.

Because Austrians read German newspapers, a separate German-language Austrian-American press has not emerged, but a few of the national organizations publish monthly journals, for example, *Burgenland Society* and *Nachrichten der Donauschwaben in Amerika* (News of the Danube Swabians in America; f. 1955), both published in Chicago, and the *Siebenburgisch-Amerikanisches Volksblatt* (Siebenburg-American People's Press; f. 1905) a Detroit weekly with a circulation of 3,850.

In their church affiliation, Austrians in America continue to reflect the religious composition of their ancestral provinces. The great majority are either Roman Catholic or Jewish. Of the Austrian provinces, only Burgenland has a significant Protestant minority— about 14 percent—most of them German Lutherans. A large proportion of German speakers from Transylvania and other parts of the former Kingdom of Hungary are also Protestant. In America, German Austrians constitute the majority of members in a few Catholic parishes, such as Trinity Church in Passaic, N.J. Protestants have almost all joined congregations that are not distinctively Austrian.

GROUP MAINTENANCE

The ease with which Austrians have been assimilated into American society is reflected in their generally high naturalization rates, especially after World War II, but some immigrants retain Austrian citizenship despite long residence in this country. In 1975 a total of 17,568 Austrian aliens were living in the United States, mainly in New York, California, Illinois, Pennsylvania, and New Jersey.

Austrians in the United States usually think of themselves as a distinct German-speaking group that differs in many respects from immigrants from Germany in much the same way that Americans of English ancestry think of themselves as having traits that distinguish them from the English. They see themselves as being more amiable, tolerant, and sophisticated, and less intense and nationalistic, than the Germans. While this attitude may apply to educated, middle-class immigrants from Vienna, the cosmopolitan capital of a former multinational empire, and even to the rural Burgenlanders, it is less appropriate for the more strongly nationalist immigrants from the German-speaking minority enclaves in the Hungarian half of the former Dual Monarchy.

The Austrian immigrants have been, on the whole, rather quiet invaders. They have not attracted much attention as an ethnic group, although they have contributed a great deal to American culture. The working-class immigrants of the early 20th century were often lumped together with other groups from Austria-Hungary, and the later German speakers with immigrants from Germany. The writers, musicians, and dramatists among them have been dedicated to the international world of art rather than to their country of origin.

Bibliography

Historians have studied German-Austrian immigration only incidentally; the two surveys on the subject, both published in Austria, are E. Wilder Spaulding, *The Quiet Invaders: The Story of the Austrian Impact upon America* (Vienna, 1968), and Wilhelm Schlag, "A Survey of

Austrian Emigration to the United States," in *Österreich und die angelsächsische Welt*, ed. Otto von Hietsch, 2 vols. (Vienna and Stuttgart, 1961), II, 139–196. Spaulding is the more useful; Schlag provides a good introduction. See also Franz Goldner, *Austrian Emigration: 1936–1945*, trans. Edith Simons (New York, 1979). Other useful materials are almost all in German. Walter Dujmovits, *Die Amerikawanderung der Burgenländer* (Stegersbach, Austria, 1975), is essential for understanding the Burgenlanders in Austria and the United States. An excellent essay by Johan Chmelar, "The Austrian Emigration, 1900–1914," *Perspectives in American History* 7 (1973): 275–378, treats the European scene only. Benjamin Blied, *Austrian Aid to American Catholics 1830–1860* (Milwaukee, Wis., 1944), is restricted to only a minor aspect of the Austrian experience in America.

FREDERICK C. LUEBKE

AZERBAIJANIS

The Azerbaijanis in the United States are a small group of recent immigrants numbering perhaps 200 families. In their homeland the Azerbaijanis, or Azeri Turks as they are sometimes called, number between 8 and 9 million people, half of whom live in the Azerbaijan Soviet Socialist Republic, the remainder in the northwestern regions of Iran. Their language is Azeri Turkic, which differs only slightly from the Turkish used in neighboring Turkey. First written in Arabic script, but since 1939 written in Cyrillic letters, Azeri Turkic is the official literary language of the Azerbaijan S.S.R. The Azerbaijanis are Muslim; about 80 percent are Shiite; the remainder are Sunni. (*See also* Muslims; Turks.)

Since ancient times the lands of the Azerbaijanis have been invaded repeatedly. In the late 7th century, Arabs subjugated the territory and converted its inhabitants to Islam; between the 10th and 12th centuries several Turkic tribes arrived and mixed with the local inhabitants, creating a new Turkic language, Azerbaijani. However, because most of the Azerbaijanis have been Shiites, they have felt closer to the Persians (Iranians), who are also largely Shiite, than to other Turkic-speaking peoples. In the early 18th century Russia briefly challenged Persian political control in the area, but it was not until the 1820s that the region was finally wrested from Persia as a result of tsarist expansion in the Caucasus. After the 1917 Russian Revolution, Azerbaijan became an independent republic. In 1920 it was taken over by Soviet Bolshevik forces, and together with Georgia and Armenia it was part of the Transcaucasian Soviet Republic until 1936, when a separate Azerbaijan Soviet Socialist Republic was established.

Most of the Azerbaijani immigrants in the United States were German prisoners of war during World War II who left the western zones of Germany for the United States in the early 1950s. There is also a small number of surviving refugees who fled their homeland in 1920 after the demise of the independent republic of Azerbaijan. The post-1920 refugees first settled in Turkey and Iran, then came to the United States for economic reasons in the 1950s and 1960s. Both groups settled in New York City, northern New Jersey, and Massachusetts, and more recently in Florida and California. Generally, the former prisoners of war found blue-collar jobs; the immigrants from Turkey and Iran were able to

Azerbaijan
Areas inhabited by Azerbaijanis
200   Km.   Miles

reestablish themselves in their old occupations as merchants, artisans, and clerks.

Religious differences persist between the Shiite and Sunni Azerbaijani communities. The larger Shiite community observes its own religious festivals and maintains two prayer houses and social centers in Paterson and Newark, N.J., the latter known as the Azerbaijan Society of America (Azerbaijan Türkleri Dernegi). The Sunni Azerbaijanis join forces with the Tatars and the North Caucasians in their prayer houses in Brooklyn. (*See* North Caucasians; Tatars.)

These sectarian differences are important, but in spite of them an ethnic solidarity, especially a sense of unity with other Turkic peoples, exists. On some occasions the Azerbaijanis participate in Turkish-American activities; they are members of the Federation of Turkish American Societies. Both the Sunnis and the Shiites use Turkish as a common written language and speak Azeri Turkic among themselves. Perhaps as many as 80 percent have married within the Azerbaijani community, but this is not likely to continue, because the flow of Azerbaijani immigrants has ceased and the group is not very large.

Bibliography
There is no published study of Azerbaijani immigrants. Among the few works in English on the homeland is the article by Frank Huddle, Jr., "Azerbaidzhan and the Azerbaidzhanis," in Zev Katz, ed., *Handbook of Major Soviet Nationalities* (New York, 1975).

ALEXANDRE BENNIGSEN

AZERI TURKS: *see* AZERBAIJANIS

AZOREANS: *see* PORTUGUESE

BAHRAINI: *see* ARABS

BALKAN PEOPLES: *see* ALBANIANS; BOSNIAN MUSLIMS; BULGARIANS; CROATS; GREEKS; MACEDONIANS; ROMANIANS; SERBS; SLOVENES

BALKARS: *see* NORTH CAUCASIANS

BALTIC PEOPLES: *see* ESTONIANS; LATVIANS; LITHUANIANS

BALUCHI: *see* AFGHANS; PAKISTANIS

BANGLADESHI

There are approximately 3,500 Bangladeshi in the United States, about 200 of whom have become U.S. citizens. Their country came into being in December 1971 when the eastern portion of the historic Indian province of Bengal and the former Sylhet district of Assam became the People's Republic of Bangladesh (land of Bengal). This area of the former Indian subcontinent, more than 1,000 miles from West Pakistan, was originally known as East Bengal and then as East Pakistan. Tied to the Indian state of West Bengal by language and history but separated by religious faith, East Bengal became part of Pakistan in 1947 and achieved sovereign independence following the Pakistan-Bangladesh civil war. (*See* Pakistanis.)

The 81 million Bangladeshi are overwhelmingly Muslim, of whom, except for a small sprinkling of Shiites, the majority are Sunni. Approximately 15 percent are Hindu, Buddhist, or Christian. Less than half a

Bangladesh
Areas inhabited by Bengalis
200   Km.   Miles

million are Urdu-speaking Bihari. Among the Bangladeshi population in the United States, these groups are represented in about the same proportions.

Aside from the tribes in the Chittagong Hill Tracts and some scattered aborigines, the Bangladeshi are descended from a mixture of several Australoid, Mongoloid, and Aryan groups. They are distinguished from other South Asians not by any physical characteristics but by their language and culture.

The spoken and written language of the Bangladeshi is Bengali or Bangla. It belongs to the Indo-Aryan group of languages and is spoken in a variety of dialects. The written form has a distinct phonetic alphabet that is more than a thousand years old. Bengali history and culture have been enhanced over the centuries by a rich literary tradition, and the maintenance of their language in the United States is a primary concern for the Bengalis who value ethnic cohesiveness.

The first Bengalis or immigrants from East Pakistan came to the United States for a variety of personal reasons, usually seeking enhanced economic opportunity. Once the independence movement got under way in 1970 others began to emigrate to escape the political turmoil at home, or, if they were members of religious minorities, to avoid discrimination or conflict. Since independence was achieved in 1971 the flow of Bangladeshi immigrants has increased almost steadily. There were 154 in 1973; 147 in 1974; 404 in 1975; and 590 in 1976. Many entered as refugees from the civil war and eventually won permanent resident status. More recently immigration to the United States has been spurred by endemic political and economic tensions in Bangladesh, by the extremely high population density and continuing rate of population growth, and by the loss of economic opportunities formerly available in Pakistan.

By now there are a few Bangladeshi settlers in nearly every state and in Puerto Rico, the largest number of whom are found in New York, New Jersey, California, Massachusetts, Illinois, and Texas. Employment opportunities, rather than ethnic affiliation, determine settlement patterns. A third of the Bangladeshi are professionals, and the rest with few exceptions white-collar workers; most are city dwellers. Occupational advancement is often more important than group cohesion, and the Bangladeshi are willing to move about a good deal. At least a third of them have professional training and almost all the rest have various marketable skills. As a result, most have been able to obtain good jobs, frequently in the field for which they were trained. The rest have adapted well to new occupations. The attraction of greater professional rewards and higher incomes in the United States, and the uncertain socioeconomic conditions in Bangladesh, have caused a substantial "brain drain."

The majority of Bangladeshi immigrants are between 10 and 39 years of age; 62 percent are men. More men than women have come to the United States because relatively few opportunities for education and employ-

ment are available for the women of Bangladesh, and custom discourages single women from venturing abroad for jobs or education.

Approximately 50 percent of the men and 60 percent of the women are married when they arrive; the rate of divorce among Bangladeshi has thus far been exceedingly low. Most marriages are arranged by families and are confined to the ethnic group; some immigrants even travel back home to select their spouses. Less than 5 percent of all marriages are outside the group, and most of those involve Bangladeshi men and non-Bangladeshi women, since Bangladeshi women, bound by tradition, usually agree to negotiated marriages within their community.

Extended-family establishments are not uncommon, since many immigrants aid the adjustment of newly arrived relatives by taking them in as lodgers. Families of more than two children are rare.

A group of Bangladeshi living in the same area is likely to form a civic association. There are now perhaps 15 of these, many of them founded during the independence movement in 1971. They provide a focus for social activities, mutual support, and cultural preservation.

Most Bangladeshi Americans appear to lean toward the Democratic party, an attachment strengthened by the Republican administration's support of Pakistan during the Bangladesh independence movement.

Bibliography
Nothing has been published as yet on Bangladeshi Americans, because Bangladesh is a very new nation and the Bangladeshi community in the United States is recent and small. Some useful statistical data are available from the U.S. Immigration and Naturalization Service. For background information on the origin of Bangladesh consult: John H. Broomfield, *Elite Conflict in a Plural Society: Twentieth-Century Bengal* (Berkeley, Calif., 1968); Suniti Kumar Chatterji, *The Origin and Development of the Bengali Language* (Calcutta, 1926); and Subrata Roy Chowdhury, *The Genesis of Bangladesh* (New York, 1972).

ENAYETUR RAHIM

BANNOCKS: *see* AMERICAN INDIANS

BARBADIANS: *see* WEST INDIANS

BASHKIRS: *see* TATARS

BASQUES

The Basque homeland is small, scarcely 100 miles across on either a north-south or east-west tangent. It lies in southwestern France and north-central Spain where the western ridges of the Pyrenees meet the Cantabrian seacoast, and encompasses the French regions of Labourd, Basse Navarre, and Soule and the Spanish provinces of Navarra, Alava, Guipuzcoa, and Vizcaya. Six-sevenths of the total land area is on the Spanish side of the frontier; of about 2.5 million inhabitants, only 200,000 are French nationals. Not all inhabitants of the area are culturally Basque, however. The Spanish Basque provinces are among the most heavily industrialized regions of Iberia and therefore attract migrants from throughout Spain.

Basques refer to themselves as *Euskaldunak* or "speakers of *Euskera*" (the Basque language). There are approximately 700,000 Basque speakers in the entire Basque country, about 27 percent of the total popula-

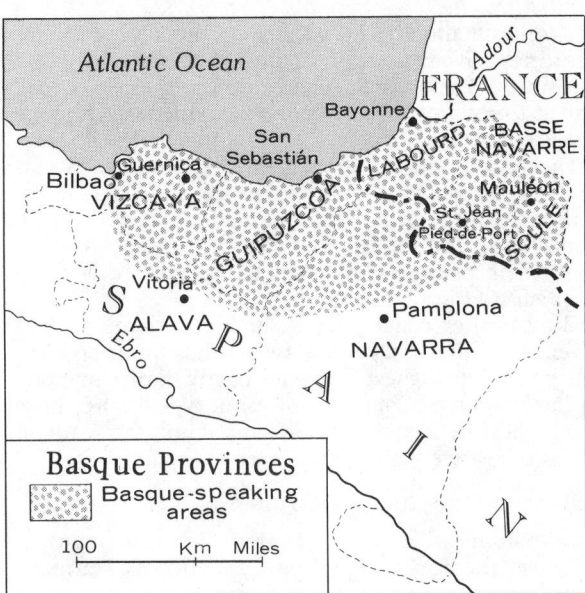

Basque Provinces
Basque-speaking areas
100 Km Miles

tion. Most rural areas of the French Basque provinces are Basque-speaking; on the Spanish side of the frontier Basque-speakers are concentrated in northern Navarra, Guipuzcoa, and rural Vizcaya.

In recent years there has been a resurgence in the use of the language. *Ikastolak,* or Basque-language schools, have proliferated even in urban centers like Bilbao, San Sebastian, Pamplona, and Bayonne—places where a few years ago Basque was rarely heard. In the late 1970s, in the Spanish area alone, about 40,000 children and 35,000 adults were enrolled in special Basque-language courses. With the new emphasis upon formal language instruction, the incidence of literacy in Basque is increasing and several publishing houses specialize in Basque-language materials, from scientific treatises to literature and children's books. As recently as the turn of the present century Basque-language publications were limited almost exclusively to such religious items as bibles, missals, and catechisms.

The Basque language is strong evidence of the uniqueness of its speakers. Despite five centuries of effort, philologists and linguists remain unable to demonstrate a relationship between Basque and any other human tongue. Consequently, it remains the only known representative of its own language family. It is reputed to be extremely difficult to learn. A Basque legend contends that the devil once came to the Basque country to study the language in order to ensnare the inhabitants, but after seven years abandoned the effort having learned only two words, *ez* and *bai* (no and yes). Basque surnames are striking; they derive from the names of ancient dwellings and are usually descriptive of a house site. A common one is Etxeberria (new house); and the longest is said to be Iturriberrigorrigoikoerrotakoetxea, which means "the new red house near the upper mill spring."

The Basques are perhaps the oldest surviving ethnic group in Europe and occupied their Pyrenean homeland prior to the invasions of Indo-European tribes during the second millennium B.C. They may be directly descended from the prehistoric people who left the famous cave paintings at Lascaux and Altamira.

Basques maintain a keen sense of ethnic pride and for centuries have resisted the political control of Madrid and Paris. They sustain one of Europe's most robust, and at times violent, nationalist movements. Although the Basques do not possess a nation in a political sense, their claim to ethnic uniqueness is irrefutable. A current slogan, *zazpiak bat* (the seven are one), refers to the unity of the traditional Basque regions of both Spain and France, and reflects the attitude of many Basques that their common interests transcend the French-Spanish frontier.

Biological evidence likewise underscores the distinctiveness of the Basques vis-à-vis neighboring peoples. They have the highest frequency of any European group of the blood type O and the lowest of type B. They have the highest incidence of any population in the world of the Rh negative blood factor.

BACKGROUND TO EMIGRATION

Migration is a long-standing Basque tradition. Through the ages, Basques have excelled as mariners. They were Europe's earliest whalers, and their whaling and codfishing fleets plying the North Atlantic may well have visited the coasts of the New World before the first voyage of Columbus. Basques formed the largest ethnic contingent in Columbus's crew. Elcano, Magellan's first mate, was a Basque and became the first man to circumnavigate the globe. Basque maritime and commercial interests were key factors in Spain's overseas colonial ventures. During much of the 16th century 80 percent of the shipping on the American run depended upon Basque vessels and crews.

As inhabitants of a region that had never been conquered by the Arabs, the Spanish Crown accorded Basques the status of *hidalgos* or noblemen. Such collective nobility allowed people of even modest background to enter the civil and ecclesiastical hierarchies. Consequently, throughout the Spanish colonial era there was considerable emigration of a Basque elite who came to occupy key administrative posts throughout Latin America and in Spain's Asian colonies. The subsequent return of people, capital, and ideas affected almost every community in the Basque country and helped sustain their tradition of overseas emigration.

Other factors that stimulated emigration included the scarcity of arable land in the mountainous Basque country and inheritance practices that were closely attuned to it. The peasant farmstead, rarely more than ten hectares in size, was transmitted intact in each generation to a single heir. The heir's siblings were provided with dowries, but were then expected to leave.

In the late 18th and early 19th centuries the Basque country suffered considerably from political and military developments. French Basques opposed the centralist policies of the victorious revolutionary government and paid a high price in loss of life and property. During the Napoleonic campaigns the Basque region served as the corridor for the French army's invasion of the Iberian peninsula; both sides inflicted damage and suffering upon the Basques. Again, between 1833 and 1839 Spanish Basques were on the losing side in a civil war. The defeated Carlist forces and sympathizers were forced to flee from Spain, and many of these dispossessed political refugees emigrated to the New World.

The early period of Basque settlement in the United States often followed and was conditioned by prior emigration to South America. Independence movements in Spain's former colonies curtailed the emigration of Basque administrators to Latin America during the early 19th century. But after an initial period of anti-European xenophobia, the Rio de la Plata nations, faced with the task of settling vast interiors, welcomed immigration. A trickle of Basques arrived at Montevideo in the late 1820s and either went on to the interior of Uruguay or entered Argentina clandestinely, thereby circumventing the anti-immigration measures of the Rosas regime (1830–1852). In the 1830s and 1840s Basque emigrants to southern South America numbered several thousand annually. Most of these new immigrants were people of modest background and means.

In the Rio de la Plata nations the Basques were quick to seize upon opportunity. Vast areas were either unused or underused by the cattle-oriented *estancieros* or ranchers. The Basques secured rangeland for the purpose of raising sheep. By the 1840s several thousand of them were engaged in sheep ranching under frontier conditions in southern Buenos Aires Province. To the Argentines, Basques were the stereotypic sheepmen of the pampas.

The discovery of gold in California in 1848 attracted fortune seekers throughout the world. Excitement was particularly keen in South America, which was closer by sea to the goldfields than either Europe or the eastern United States. Many European-born Basques entered California as a part of the "Chilean" contingent, as the South Americans were called. French Basques in considerable numbers migrated directly to the area from Europe.

It is impossible to determine the exact numbers involved, for Basques entered the United States as Spanish, French, Chilean, Uruguayan, and Argentine nationals. However, from such fragmentary sources as passenger lists it is clear that several hundred Basques came to California during the first year of the gold rush. As early as 1850 a German traveler commented upon the large numbers of Basques living in Murphy's Camp.

SHEEPMEN AND CATTLEMEN

Few, if any, Basques were successful in mining. By the early 1850s some of them settled in southern California, where conditions would have been familiar to those with prior experience in South America. The southern California *dons* owned enormous cattle ranches. Although the mining camps created considerable demand for meat, the dons were in grave financial difficulty: a combination of unwillingness to upgrade livestock strains, reluctance to raise sheep, a flamboyant and costly lifestyle, and political setbacks experienced under the new American administration had all but immobilized the area's ranching industry.

As early as 1854 one Basque with previous South American experience signed a sheep-range lease agreement with a southern California rancher. By the late 1850s and early 1860s such arrangements were common, and Basques were becoming established as the area's sheepmen. These operators gained a competitive advantage when, in the late 1850s, cattle prices plummeted while sheep values remained relatively stable. Furthermore, sheep proved to be more resilient than cattle during the severe flooding followed by drought

that plagued the area between 1861 and 1864. Whereas the number of cattle in Los Angeles County declined by 71 percent between 1860 and 1870, sheep tripled to more than 3 million animals.

Although not all California sheepmen were Basques, many were. As their operations grew, the Basque sheepmen summoned relatives and fellow villagers from Europe to serve as herders. They developed a distinctive pattern of sheep husbandry based on transhumance (the seasonal movement of the bands in search of pasturage). The animals were wintered on leased or purchased range in the lowlands of southern California and the San Joaquin Valley and trail-driven in the summer to the high Sierra Nevada mountains, where they were grazed on the public lands. In some cases this annual trek covered a distance of more than 500 miles.

It was a difficult existence for the sheepherder, who had to forgo the pleasures of family life and most of the comforts of civilization. However, for the young Basque immigrant there were many attractions as well. The solitary nature of the occupation meant that his lack of English did not handicap him unduly. He had job security: sheep were generally disparaged in the region's cattle-oriented society, so few non-Basques were motivated to compete for such jobs. Because transhumant sheepmen were constantly on the move and therefore had little need to invest in a home base, the enterprising herder could quickly capitalize his own operation by working for three or four years while taking his wages in ewes. When he possessed enough animals (about 1,000) to form a band, he could strike out on his own, seeking feed on the public lands. If his luck held, within a few years he could sell out and return to Europe with his profits.

In this fashion itinerant Basque sheep operations proliferated, and the Basque sheepherder became a ubiquitous figure even in outfits owned by non-Basques. By the 1870s the California ranges were overcrowded with literally thousands of these small-scale bands. Since transhumance proved highly adaptable to much of the American West, many operators moved inland in search of new range. In the 1870s and 1880s Basque sheepmen spread across northern Nevada and northeastern California; in the 1890s they entered southeastern Oregon and southern Idaho. By 1910 Basque sheepmen were present in all the western open-range districts, with the largest concentrations in California, Nevada, and Idaho, and smaller colonies in Washington, Oregon, Arizona, New Mexico, Texas, Utah, Colorado, Wyoming, and Montana.

By this time the image of Basques was ambiguous in the wider society. On the one hand, the Basque sheepherder was a yeoman figure loyal to his charges and his employer. Basques were esteemed for their propensity for hard work and dedication to thrift and free enterprise. In some communities a few Basques had acquired large ranch properties and were leading citizens. On the other hand, the itinerant sheepmen—"tramps" to their detractors—were embroiled in a major confrontation with the settled livestock interests. Although grazing on public lands theoretically was available to all on a first-come basis, the settled ranchers (both cattlemen and sheepmen) regarded the public range contiguous to their holdings as their private domain. The itinerant sheepmen by their very presence challenged such an in-terpretation. Mary Austin reflected the sentiment of the settled ranchers in *The Flock* (1906): "The best days of shepherding in California were before the Frenchmen [Basques] began to appear on the mesas. Owners then had, by occupancy, the rights to certain range, rights respected by their neighbors. Then suddenly the land was overrun by little dark men who fed where the feed was, kept to their own kind, turned money quickly, and went back to France to spend it."

Again, in 1909 the *Caldwell Tribune* (Idaho) reported that the sheepmen of Owyhee County were "sorely beset by Biscayans, Bascos as they are commonly called." The report continued: "These Bascos are coming in great numbers and are driving the other sheepmen from the range . . . The scale of living and the methods of doing business of the Bascos are on a par with those of the Chinamen. However, they have some undesirable characteristics that the Chinese are free from. They are filthy, treacherous, and meddlesome. However, they work and save their money. They are clannish and undesirable but they have a foothold and unless something is done will make life impossible for the whiteman."

In their frustration the ranchers pressured the itinerant herders with many tactics, including intimidation and occasional violence. The resulting confrontations provided copy for the newspapers and litigation for the courts. The most concerted efforts, however, were legislative. Ranchers lobbied for local laws designed to restrict the movements of the itinerants or tax them unfairly. Most of those that were enacted were later declared unconstitutional.

The settled livestockmen were more successful at the federal level. Western ranchers joined with eastern conservationists to support the creation of the national forest system. Testimony surrounding the enabling legislation reflects considerable anti-Basque and anti-itinerant sentiment. During the first decade of the 20th century most of the mountain ranges of the western United States were subsumed into the national forest, where grazing, though still permitted, was to be strictly regulated by local boards of settled stockmen. Moreover, aliens and persons without ranch property were to be denied access to the grazing areas.

Headlines in the regional newspapers approvingly proclaimed, "Basque sheepmen are excluded from reserve." However, the verdict that the itinerant sheepmen were through proved to be premature. In several areas mountains with suitable summer sheep range were insufficiently timbered to qualify as forestland. The new law forced itinerants to concentrate within these more marginal districts, where consequent overgrazing and erosion heightened the competition for range use. The situation culminated in 1934 in the passage of new federal legislation sponsored by Senator Edward Taylor of Colorado. Under the provisions of the Taylor Grazing Act portions of the public domain not incorporated into the national forest system were organized into grazing districts administered by an agency that ultimately became known as the Bureau of Land Management. Again range use was to be determined by a local board of ranchers and was reserved for U.S. citizens who owned ranch property.

There were other sources of anti-Basque sentiment. During the Spanish-American War Basques were (at

times erroneously) thought to be sympathetic to the Spanish cause. They also felt the sting of rising anti-immigration attitudes. The quota limitations based on national origins placed upon immigration in the 1920s were particularly deleterious to Basque interests. The annual quota for Spanish nationals was set in 1924 at only 131, which virtually interdicted Spanish Basque emigration to the United States. (See also Spaniards.)

By the 1930s, then, there was ample reason for Basques to maintain a low group profile. They had experienced considerable economic and political discrimination in their dealings with non-Basques. To say "Basque" was to say "sheepherder" and evoke the image of one of the least esteemed roles in local society. Basque parents, accustomed to the epithet "black Bascos," encouraged their children to assimilate.

THE CHANGING IMAGE

It was at this time that the image of the Basques began to change. The Taylor Grazing Act, painful as it was for many Basque sheepmen, effectively terminated unbridled competition for the range and hence removed a major source of irritation between Basques and their neighbors. The cumulative effect of the immigration quotas took a toll upon the sheep industry: as older Basque herders died, retired, or returned to Europe, younger ones were no longer available to take their places, and few non-Basques would accept the work. The Basque sheepherder therefore became a scarce and esteemed figure in the region's labor force. The shortage became so acute during World War II that representatives of the western states brought a series of unusual bills before the Congress. Each of the Sheepherder Laws, as they were called, accorded permanent residency to one or more Basques who had managed to enter the United States illegally, make his way west, and get a job herding sheep. Between 1942 and 1961 some 383 men thus secured permanent residency.

However, this mechanism was cumbersome and the labor shortage continued to accelerate. Desperate sheep ranchers banded together to bring pressure upon the Congress. During the early 1950s Senator Patrick McCarran of Nevada, himself an ex-sheepman, sponsored legislation that established a program exempting from immigration quotas herders recruited in Europe by representatives of the California Range Association (rechristened the Western Range Association in 1960). The recruits had to sign three-year labor contracts that required them to remain in herding. They could renew the agreement only after sojourning outside the United States, and thus were kept ineligible for U.S. citizenship after five continuous years of residence.

Between 1957 and 1970 the range association processed 5,495 sheepherder applications. Although the program continues to function, few Basques have entered under its provisions since the early 1970s when rising wages in the Basque country reduced the incentive to emigrate. Contract herders are now more likely to come from Peru, Mexico, or southern Spain. After more than 125 years Basque immigration to the western United States may have ended.

GROUP CHARACTERISTICS

There are several ways in which the Basques are unique among American ethnic groups. No other people became as closely identified with a single economic activity as did the Basques with sheepherding. Because of the nature of the sheep business Basque immigration consisted almost entirely of single males between the ages of 16 and 30. Few entered the United States with the thought of remaining; rather, most were obsessed with the desire to make enough money to return home and buy a farm or start a small business. Some changed their minds, of course. These were generally men who, after at least ten years in the West, were in a position to hire herders for their bands and settle on a ranch property or in a town residence. Most of them either sent or went back to the Basque country in search of brides. Subsequent generations, however, have commonly made non-Basque marriages.

It is impossible to document with precision either the magnitude of Basque emigration to the United States or the size of the group at any given time, since both immigration and census records list Basques as Spanish or French. Also, after more than a century of immigration and a considerable amount of intermarriage, there are no clear criteria for defining the group. Basques themselves will not contest the claim of anyone with a single Basque ancestor: in this sense being a Basque is as much a state of mind as a genealogical fact. Few Basque Americans know the ancestral language; the 1970 Census recorded that only 8,108 Americans had grown up in households in which Basque was spoken. But a reasonable guess would place the current population of Basque descent in the American West somewhere between 50,000 and 100,000.

Basque emigration to the United States tended to follow Old World regional distinctions. Thus, the Basques of California, central Nevada, Arizona, New Mexico, Colorado, Wyoming, and Montana are in the main of French Basque and Navarrese origin. Those of northern Nevada, Oregon, and Idaho are primarily Vizcayan. Until recently these two distinct colonies were scarcely aware of each other's existence.

Another of the group's unique characteristics is that Basques historically have been scattered lightly over an enormous geographic area. Most Basque Americans were brought up either on isolated ranches or in small towns in the region's sheep-raising districts. In no western community or county have they ever been in the majority. Those residing in towns have shown little tendency to create ethnic neighborhoods or, with one notable exception (the Basque hotel), ethnic businesses.

The occupational identification and settlement pattern of Basque Americans have conditioned their collective experience in other respects. Most are politically conservative in line with the Republicanism of the rural western United States. Socioeconomic mobility essentially has meant progression from sheepherder to owner within the industry. Most Basque Americans continue to be involved in some aspect of animal husbandry or are small businessmen in rural communities or regional centers like Boise, Idaho, and Reno, Nev. However, because Basques have acquired a reputation for hard work, loyalty, and honesty, they are in demand as employees in mining companies, construction firms, and sawmills. In San Francisco several hundred are engaged in gardening, and in the greater Los Angeles area many are employed as milkers in dairies.

Although Basques have enjoyed considerable economic success both as entrepreneurs and manual la-

borers, few have entered the professions. Today there are only a handful of Basque doctors and lawyers. This small showing may be attributable partly to the intellectual climate of the rural American West, but their European background has contributed an added selective factor: most Basques came to the United States from rural areas where schooling was poor; furthermore, they came from an Old World culture that valued hard physical labor over intellectual activity.

Only recently have Basque Americans begun to enter politics. Paul Laxalt (1922–), Nevada's former governor and current U.S. senator, is the only Basque to have held federal office. A few others have served at the state level: Peter T. Cenarrusa (1917–) as secretary of state of Idaho; Anthony Yturri (1914–) as a leading figure in the Oregon senate for many years; Peter Echeverria (1918–) as a Nevada legislator and, more recently, chairman of the Nevada Gaming Commission.

ETHNIC PUBLICATIONS

The fact that Basque Americans lack an intelligentsia has seriously hampered the development of an ethnic press. In 1885 a Basque American founded a Basque-language newspaper, *Escualdun Gazeta*, in Los Angeles, but it lasted for only three issues. Interestingly, it was the first Basque-language newspaper published anywhere in the world. Another Los Angeles–based newspaper, *California'ko Eskual Herria*, struggled for survival from 1893 to 1898. The group remained without a newspaper until 1974, when the monthly *Voice of the Basques*, published almost entirely in English, was founded in Boise. With the exception of the novelist Robert Laxalt (brother of Paul), Basque Americans have not produced literary spokesmen.

Basque Americans curious about their heritage have had few scholarly or literary sources to inform them. Most scholarship on the Basques is published in either Spanish or French and is unavailable in American libraries. Until recently there were few English-language books and articles on the Basques, no Basque-English grammars and dictionaries, and no formal instruction in the Basque language anywhere in the United States. Thus, although many Basque Americans know some Basque, few are literate in the language and few Basque-language publications reach Basque-American homes.

The small numbers of Basques and their dispersion have limited the development of ethnic institutions. Basques tend to reserve expressions of their ethnicity for home celebrations or the company of fellow ethnics. Most of them have remained Roman Catholics. On occasion, the diocese of Boise has imported a Vizcayan chaplain. The French Basques of California support their own chaplain (based in Fresno), who ministers widely as far east as Montana. With these minor exceptions, the sparsely settled Basques have made no effort to establish an ethnic church.

THE BASQUE HOTEL

There is, however, one ethnic institution common to the group—the Basque hotels or boarding houses that were operated throughout the western sheep-raising districts. The sheepherders depended upon them for a wide range of services, including information regarding employment opportunities. They served as a permanent address for the herders' mail as well as a place to store their personal effects while they were out on the range. During the winter months when sheep bands were combined and the need for herders declined sharply, almost half the herders in any one area faced annual layoffs lasting several months. The hotels provided an ethnic haven during such periods. The hotelkeeper was always a European-born Basque with herding experience, fluency in English, and a working familiarity with western ways. He served as adviser and interpreter for the herders in their dealings with storekeepers, bankers, and lawyers. The hotel also served as a marriage market, since the owners regularly sent back to Europe for Basque serving girls. The turnover in the ranks of the young women was formidable.

The hotels provided other services as well. Wives living on isolated ranches would spend the last months of their pregnancies in a Basque hotel and frequently gave birth there. When ranch children reached school age, it was common for them to board at a hotel and attend classes at a local school. The hotels were also the scene of dances, family celebrations, and wakes. For Basque Americans the hotels were the only place outside the home where they might meet with foreign-born Basques and practice waning language skills.

The Basque hotel also served as a liaison between the Basques and their non-Basque neighbors. Although the establishments rarely advertised, and a few even refused to serve non-Basques, the majority welcomed a tourist trade. For some westerners, frequenting the little-known Basque hotels became a kind of insiders' experience. The fame of their hearty cuisine and relaxed family-style atmosphere spread by word of mouth. Consequently, each evening the boarders had an opportunity to mingle with a few non-Basque guests; many immigrants received their initial impressions of other Americans in the congenial setting of a Basque boarding house. Conversely, Basques acquired a group reputation as fun-loving people fond of good food and drink.

GROUP MAINTENANCE AND ETHNIC IDENTITY

Basque Americans have been slow to form ethnic associations. In 1907 the Basques of Stockton, Calif., made an abortive attempt at founding a social club. Such an organization existed in San Francisco in 1924, but was disbanded ten years later. In 1938 the Basques of Kern County, Calif., formed a club that still functions. Shortly thereafter two small clubs were established in La Puente and Chino, Calif. In 1949 the Basques of Boise formed Euskaldunak, Inc., which constructed its own meeting hall and banquet facility. All these organizations had limited membership and their scope and goals were largely social. They sponsored dinners, possibly a summer picnic, and occasionally a charity ball. Some clubs periodically formed children's folk-dance groups which performed at the organization's activities.

In June of 1959 the Western Basque Festival was held in Sparks, Nev., a suburb of Reno. It attracted more than 5,000 participants and included sheepdog trials, weightlifting (popular in Vizcaya), woodchopping (a Navarrese favorite), folk singing, and folk dancing. There was also a public dance and a huge western-style barbecue featuring favorite dishes from the Basque hotel cuisine. The event had no analogue in Old World Basque society and was in large measure an invention of

its organizers. Nevertheless, it gave Basque Americans a renewed sense of ethnic pride. Stimulated by the festival, the Basques of several communities founded social clubs. The clubs in Reno, Ely, and Elko, Nev., initiated annual festivals of their own, modeled after the original event. The Elko festival, since 1964 celebrated annually on the Fourth of July, is called the "National Basque Festival."

Today Basque Americans are among the most visible ethnic groups in the western United States. The highly publicized and well attended festivals provide the context in which Basques periodically stage and display aspects of their ethnicity, for themselves and for non-Basques. They are increasingly the subject of television specials, documentary films, and popular magazine articles. Groups like the Oinkari dancers of Boise and the musical band or *klika* of the San Francisco Basque Club perform widely. Basque Americans have been well represented at the Seattle, New York, and Spokane world's fairs, Expo 70 in Montreal, and the Bicentennial Festival of American Folklore in Washington, D.C.

The 1960s and 1970s therefore represent a high-water mark of ethnic pride and activity among Basque Americans. In the late 1970s social clubs functioned in San Francisco, Redwood City, Los Banos, Kern County, Chino, and La Puente, Calif.; Winnemucca, Reno, Fallon, Elko, and Ely, Nev.; Caldwell, Boise, and Mountain Home, Idaho; Ontario, Ore.; Salt Lake City, Utah; and Grand Junction, Colo. In 1972 the majority of Basque clubs in the West federated as North American Basque Organizations, Incorporated (NABO), in order to foster regional interaction among the Basques of the American West and to initiate contacts with the Basque country in Europe. NABO has sponsored handball and *mus* (a Basque card game) tournaments for contestants drawn from its member clubs. It has arranged the American tours of Old World Basque musicians. It has also developed materials for public presentations of both Old World and New World Basque culture.

This resurgence in ethnicity is attributable to a number of factors. The Basques' propensity for hard work, honesty, and thrift is esteemed within the American value system. Recent interest in native and rural life in America has cast the sheepherder in the role of a romantic figure leading a rustic life amid spectacular scenery. Renewed positive interest in ethnic pluralism in America has encouraged Basque Americans to display their ethnic characteristics.

The strong interest of Basque Americans in their heritage has not, however, translated into much sympathy for the Basque nationalist cause in Europe. Most people of French Basque descent are either ambivalent or indifferent, since the issue is much more explosive in Spain than in France. Even among the Vizcayan Basque Americans, however, Basque nationalism gets a mixed reaction. In recent years some Idaho groups and individuals have publicly denounced the Spanish government's methods of dealing with the nationalists and have raised money to help political refugees. However, many Idaho Basques remain indifferent or even hostile to the nationalist cause, partly because until recently Basque nationalism was largely an urban, middle-class phenomenon and the majority of Basque immigrants came from unpolitical rural origins. The relative lack of

support for Basque nationalism by Basque Americans is in marked contrast to the attitude of Basques in such places as Mexico City, Caracas, Buenos Aires, Montevideo, and Santiago de Chile, where a substantial number of middle-class and professional persons support the movement.

In recent years the Basques of the American West have attracted the attention of some of the region's universities. The library of the University of Idaho at Moscow has developed a fine collection of Basque-related items. Boise State University has periodically offered classes in the language and occasionally sponsored a year abroad in the Basque country. The University of Nevada, which possesses the finest Basque library outside Europe, instituted a Basque Studies Program in 1967, offering courses in the language as well as Basque history, literature, linguistics, and social anthropology. It also publishes a Basque book series and periodically sponsors a Basque summer session in Europe.

Although the majority of Basque Americans live in the western United States, there are three concentrations in the East. New York City has a port-of-entry colony that dates at least from the turn of the century and may at one time have numbered several thousand. Most of these were manual laborers in the area, although some eventually found employment in Pennsylvania mines and on New Jersey docks. In 1913 the New York City Basques founded an association which in 1925 acquired its own meeting hall. In 1926 the community split over the issue of Basque nationalism, and an activist splinter group formed its own club in Brooklyn, which ceased operations in 1938. The original association continues to function.

The Greater Miami area has a small concentration of Basques. Jai alai is a Basque game, and the majority of players for the Miami courts are recruited in the Basque country. During the season young Basque players from Europe swell the ranks of former jai alai players who have married and settled in the Miami area. The Cuban refugee community in Miami is another source of Basques, who were prominent in Cuba's business elite prior to Castro's victory.

The newest Basque concentration in the United States is in Connecticut and Rhode Island. In 1976 jai alai facilities were established in Bridgeport, Hartford, and Newport. Approximately 250 Basques (players and their families) have settled in each city.

Bibliography
The best English-language source on Old World Basque society is Rodney Gallop, *A Book of the Basques* (Reno, Nev., 1970). Robert Laxalt, *In a Hundred Graves: A Basque Portrait* (Reno, 1972), is a Basque American's impressionistic description of the Basque country; his *Sweet Promised Land* (New York, 1957) is a lyrical biography of his father, a sheepman of the American West. Also by Laxalt, "Lonely Sentinels of the American West: Basque Sheepherders," *National Geographic Magazine* 129 (1966): 870–888, describes the herders' way of life. Pat Bieter, "Reluctant Shepherds: The Basques of Idaho," *Idaho Yesterdays* 1 (Summer 1957): 10–15, dispels myths about Basque sheepherding. William A. Douglass, "Lonely Lives under the Big Sky," *Natural History* 82 (March 1973): 28–39, describes the psychological stresses produced by the herder's social isolation. Adrien Gachitéguy, *Les Basques dans l'Ouest Americain* (Bordeaux, 1955), is the first general study of Basque Americans; *Amerikanuak: Basques in the New World* (Reno, 1975), by William A. Douglass and Jon Bilbao, is more comprehensive and compares emigration to the United States with the movement to Latin America.
The largest U.S. collection of Basque materials belongs to the Basque Studies Program, University of Nevada, Reno. Other centers with sign-

ficant holdings include the University of Idaho (Moscow), the Newberry Library in Chicago (primarily linguistic texts), and the New York Public Library.

WILLIAM A. DOUGLASS

BEAR RIVERS: *see* AMERICAN INDIANS

BELGIANS

Approximately 200,000 Belgians came to the United States between 1830 and 1975: about 63,000 arrived before 1900; some 75,000 came during the next two decades; and another 62,000 have arrived since 1920. Almost all of these immigrants were seeking better economic opportunities, although the largely rural 19th-century newcomers sought fertile land, and the more recent middle-class and urban professionals, career advancement. There were also some refugees among those arriving after both world wars.

Belgians at home and in the United States form not one ethnic group but two: the Dutch-speaking Flemings of the northern provinces, generally known as Flanders, and the French-speaking Walloons of the southern provinces. The long-standing conflicts between these two groups have motivated some to emigrate. Most of the Belgians who came to the United States before the 1930s were Flemish; the more recent immigrants have been largely Walloons. What national identity they have as Belgians reflects for the most part a response to the suffering that followed the German invasion and occupation of Belgium in the two world wars.

HISTORICAL BACKGROUND

The major divisions in Belgium today can be traced back to the northward expansion of the Roman Empire, which reached its limits along a frontier that runs across the middle of present-day Belgium. Latin culture

and language were established south of the frontier, and Germanic culture and language to the north. The Germanic Belgians were ruled successively by Franks, Burgundians, Spaniards, Austrians, French, and Dutch. When the southern provinces of the Netherlands rebelled and cast off Dutch rule in 1830, the major European nations met and created the Belgian state to maintain the balance of power.

The Flemings speak a Germanic language that is almost indistinguishable from Dutch; the Walloons speak French. The population is approximately 56 percent Flemish and 32 percent Walloon, with a small German-speaking minority on the eastern border. In contrast to the sharp linguistic division, the majority of both Flemings and Walloons are Roman Catholics. Belgium's capital, Brussels, is bicultural and bilingual, but except for the German element the rest of the country remains distinctly either Walloon or Flemish. The Walloons dominated Belgian politics and society in the 19th century until Flemish nationalism emerged to challenge their supremacy.

MIGRATION AND ARRIVAL

Inhabitants of the southern Lowlands played a significant role in the early history of North America. In the 16th century Pierre de Mura accompanied Spanish missionaries into the western reaches of Oregon and California to convert the Indians. French-speaking Walloons from Hainaut were among the first to settle the Hudson River Valley and Manhattan Island between 1620 and 1626. Eight Belgian Protestant families fleeing Catholic Spanish religious persecution joined Dutch settlers in 1624 to settle what became New Amsterdam, and Peter Minuit (1580–1638), a Walloon, was prominent in the colony. Father Louis Hennepin (1640?–1701) accompanied the La Salle expedition along the Mississippi River in 1675. In the 19th century the Jesuit Pierre de Smet and J.-C. Houzeau de Lahaie were prominent figures in exploration, Indian pacification, and colonization.

Between 1840 and 1884 the land shortage in Belgium made emigration a virtual necessity for the approximately 22,000 who came to the United States. This number represented only 17 percent of the people who left Belgium during that period; the majority moved to neighboring European states. The Belgian government encouraged emigration with a plan, attributed to King Leopold I, for sending Flemish paupers to colonies in Algeria and Guatemala, as well as in Texas, Pennsylvania, and Missouri. The scheme was not successful, however; New Flanders, Pa., the longest lived of these settlements, lasted only ten years.

After the Walloon-dominated, bourgeois, and predominantly Catholic Belgian state was formed in the 1830s, many Flemish and some Walloon Protestants emigrated for political and religious reasons. Then, as a result of dislocations stemming from the onset of industrialization, rural dwellers and artisans left for what they hoped would be a brighter future in the United States. But it was the agricultural crises, particularly the continuing aftereffects of the potato blight in the 1840s, that spurred the great exodus from the villages and countryside. Until 1900 at least, most were from the agrarian north and northwest. The emigrants departed from the port of Antwerp on the newly inau-

North Sea

NETHERLANDS

Rhine

Brugge

WEST FLANDERS

Ghent

EAST FLANDERS

ANTWERP

Antwerp

LIMBURG

WEST GERMANY

B E L G I

Louvain

Brussels

BRABANT

Liège

LIEGE

HAINAULT

Namur

NAMUR

LUXEMBOURG

LUX.

F R A N C E

Belgium

Areas inhabited by Flemings

Areas inhabited by Walloons

50   Km. Miles

gurated Antwerp–New York steamship line. Until the 1860s poor emigrants were subsidized by the Belgian government or aided by midwestern land promoters and American labor recruiters.

By 1900 Belgium's cities had absorbed the surplus population, and a sharp decline in the birthrate alleviated population pressure. Craftsmen and tradesmen replaced rural laborers in the pursuit of better opportunities in America. The records of the port of Antwerp show that before 1888 almost 80 percent of the Belgian emigrants came from rural provinces; afterward, less than 60 percent. Less than 10 percent of the emigrants were tradesmen and artisans in the 1880s, compared to about 30 percent between the 1890s and 1924. Industrial workers were rare in this movement, in part because of government welfare measures and passage of universal male suffrage in 1893.

A small majority of Belgian immigrants were from rural regions in the peak period 1900–1920, but artisans, craftsmen, and small entrepreneurs from towns and cities made up 40 percent of those who entered the United States. Semiskilled and skilled craftsmen in the building trades and allied occupations constituted the largest group of Belgians in the Michigan and Illinois population centers at the turn of the century. The hardships of World War I and the interwar period accelerated the urban-commercial migration to Canada and the United States, and by 1936 most of the newcomers were from the bilingual area around Brussels and Flemish Antwerp.

SETTLEMENT

In the 19th century, economic motives far outweighed political or religious factors in the Belgian emigration. The illiterate Flemish and Walloon farmers anticipated prosperity, which in their experience went hand in hand with abundant arable soil. Once they arrived in the United States, their reports widely published in Belgian newspapers of available fertile land encouraged others to leave, and passage money sent by the immigrants to relatives and friends at home further stimulated emigration. Some went first to Canada, but it is not possible to establish the exact number. Perhaps as many as 18,000 Walloons moved across the unguarded frontier between 1870 and 1924.

Between 1850 and 1924 the majority of Belgian immigrants made their homes in the states around Lake Michigan—Illinois, Wisconsin, Indiana, and especially Michigan—and remained there. Most of the others went to Iowa, Pennsylvania, New York, and Massachusetts. In the Lowell-Lawrence area of Massachusetts they were quickly absorbed by the larger immigrant communities, especially by the French Canadians.

Before the Civil War many Flemish peasants settled in the northern Michigan counties of Delta and Marquette, and after 1865, in Detroit; between 1870 and 1928 Flemings and Walloons helped settle more than a hundred rural Michigan towns. Walloons moved farther west to northern Illinois and to the eastern Wisconsin counties of Door, Brown, Kewaunee, and Ozaukee. Many settled in the Green Bay area, and some then moved north to Michigan's Upper Penninsula or to the eastern side of Lake Michigan. By 1880 a few Belgians had settled in Moline, Rock Island, and Danville, Ill. Settlements were rarely mixed; Walloons and Flemings

settled in different communities. Belgians avoided the American cities; like many Scandinavian immigrants, they had left the homeland not to become industrial workers, but to exchange a poor farm for a better one.

CULTURE AND LANGUAGE

Those Belgians who established or joined small, semiisolated communities were generally able to maintain their Old World culture. Those who chose urban areas were less successful. The geographic isolation of the Green Bay, Wis., region and the Upper Peninsula of Michigan retarded assimilation, though industrial society brought about changes that struck deep into even those remote regions, as the cities beckoned the young from their rural labors. Belgians with occupational skills could easily find work in the furniture, automobile, and machinery industries of Michigan and in the factories of Green Bay, Milwaukee, and Chicago. The second generation began to take white-collar jobs, and their quest for status became a source of intergenerational conflict, particularly among the farmers. Marriage outside the ethnic community was not uncommon in the Walloon dairy-farming communities of Wisconsin by 1920.

The efforts of both Flemings and Walloons to maintain their languages were more successful than the latter group's attempts to maintain the French Walloon dialect or patois of southeastern Belgium, which died with the first generation. Parochial education maintained religious teaching with linguistic and ethnic traditions, but only for a minority. According to the foreign-language press, the first generation spoke the mother tongue almost exclusively until World War I, but very few among the young attempted to learn it.

The Flemish language, fortified by the large Dutch press in Michigan and Illinois, endured longer than French. Two Flemish publications, the *Gazette van Moline* (1907–1921) in Illinois and the *Gazette van Detroit* (f. 1914) in Michigan, flourished for a short time then quickly declined. The Detroit paper attained a circulation of almost 10,000 in the late 1920s but shrank to less than 5,000 in the 1960s. Walloons supported French-language newspapers in Wisconsin and Illinois.

Interaction and assimilation between Flemings and Dutch and among Walloons, French, and French-Canadians began early. Belgian cultural activities were often integrated into Franco-American or Dutch-American organizations, and in many areas Walloons mixed with French speakers and Flemings with Dutch. As a result, few communities had a distinctly Belgian group identity until World War I. The one Walloon-Flemish settlement was Mishawaka, Ind., a small South Bend suburb that grew from a population of 5,000 in the 1890s to 25,000 by the 1930s. It had a number of Belgian cultural organizations, mainly choral societies and cycling clubs. There and in Michigan City, Ind., Belgian food specialties were still obtainable in recent times.

ORGANIZATIONS

Between 1889 and 1907 a number of Roman Catholic Flemish parishes and parochial schools were established in Illinois and Iowa. Many Walloons were secularized before their arrival, however, and participated little in any religious activities. Protestants joined local churches in smaller towns. In Wisconsin and Michigan

there were few distinctly Flemish or Walloon parishes; the Belgians simply joined French- or Dutch-speaking congregations. The Roman Catholic parishes in Escanaba, Mich., Dearborn, Ill., and Door County, Wis., were probably established by Belgians.

The Flemings who settled in lower Michigan were largely Catholics; the Dutch, whose language they shared, were Protestants, and the Dutch Reformed church was bitterly anti-Catholic. The Flemings therefore often gravitated to the larger communities, where Catholic churches had already been founded by German or Irish immigrants. The Flemings quickly learned that Dutch strongholds like Holland, Mich., would not accept them. Walloon Catholics sought out French and French-Canadian Catholics in Wisconsin; Walloon Protestants searched for congenial midwestern towns in northern Illinois and Indiana.

The American College in Louvain, Belgium, erected in 1857 alongside the famous Catholic University, produced 7 Belgian-American archbishops, 20 bishops, and more than 300 clergy in 80 years, but few of them were directly associated with the Belgian immigrant communities; Belgian religious orders were active in 16 states in 1900. One of the more ambitious and successful groups was the Sisters of Notre Dame of Namur, a Walloon teaching order. Beginning in 1885 they opened bilingual schools in 14 American cities in less than 40 years. Belgian Benedictines followed the railroad builders from Atchison, Kans., into Wyoming. St. Louis University, which was established by Jesuits in 1818, received Belgian money and talent after 1860.

In the 20th century business groups, then social and recreational associations, took the place of the 19th-century religious organizations. Historical clubs appeared but were replaced by less formal activities like the elaborate *kermesse* (fairs) and singing and carrier-pigeon-racing societies. Some groups, like the Center for Belgian Culture of Western Illinois, sponsored lectures and published books and other ethnic-heritage materials, but they had a steadily declining membership after World War II. Groups promoting social activities and sports, like the B.K. (avoiding the use of Flemish or French for Kingdom of Belgium) and the Belgian-American Chamber of Commerce of New York City, enjoyed more consistent support. The best-known organization is the Belgian-American Educational Foundation, an outgrowth of the Commission for the Relief of Belgium established during World War I. It administers exchanges and fellowships between the academic, artistic, and scientific communities of the two nations.

Group Maintenance

Very few of the immigrants went back to Belgium. Most were reasonably successful in the New World and were virtually never the targets for ridicule, criticism, or organized discrimination. Catholic Belgians sometimes suffered from anti-Catholic attitudes in the rural regions of the Midwest in the 1890s, but not as Belgians, let alone as Walloons or Flemings. The history of the disastrous Peshtigo, Wis., fire in 1871 and its aftermath, when a Walloon community was rebuilt by non-Belgian neighbors and competitors, testifies to the good will the Belgians experienced.

Before World War I many Belgians in the United States were identified as Dutch, French, or Canadian, but Belgium's tragic experience in the war and the courage shown by its people aroused the sympathy of Americans and led both Flemings and Walloons in America to stress their Belgian origins and culture. The Flemings made a strong effort to dissociate themselves from the Germans. As a result, the war simultaneously hastened assimilation and encouraged the growth of Belgian ethnic consciousness. Most Belgian organizations that exist today date from that time.

Belgians brought to the United States outstanding talents and skills, especially in music, science, medicine, education, and business. Belgian carillon masters have been the foremost practitioners of that art in the United States. Many Belgian Americans have made scientific and technological contributions: among them the engineer-builder of the Panama Canal, George Goethals (1858–1928); the pioneer of modern plastics, Leo Baekeland (1863–1944); and the contemporary father of the Atlas missile, Karel Bossart (1904–). Other notable Belgian Americans include George Sarton (1884–1956) a major figure in the history of science; economist Robert Triffin (1911–); economic historian Raymond de Roover (1904–1972); and Charles Schepens (1912–), an ophthalmologist.

Many of those who fled Belgium in the face of World War II, like the immigrants of the first postwar epoch, were professionals. After 1945 Belgians seeking jobs in American universities, laboratories, and businesses became a major "brain drain" for the tiny European state. But these men and women were a noteworthy addition to American society.

Bibliography
Historical background is provided in Henry G. Bayer, *The Belgians: First Settlers in New York* (New York, 1925), Antoine de Smet, *Voyageurs Belges aux États-Unis de XVIIe Siècle à 1900* (Brussels, 1959), and the essays in "Belgians in the United States," *Memo from Belgium* (Belgian Ministry of National Education, 1976): pp. 3–90. Carlo Bronne, *Des Andes au Kremlin: Les Belges dans le Monde* (Brussels, 1956), has useful information. On the Flemings, see Henry Lucas, *Netherlanders in America* (Ann Arbor, Mich., 1955), and Melvin Holli, *Detroit* (New York, 1976). The only available English treatment of the Walloons is Philemon D. Sabbe, *Belgians in America* (Thiel, Belgium, 1960). Various issues of the Belgian Government Information Center publication, *News from Belgium*, 1940–1945; *Wisconsin Magazine of History*, 1921–1936; and *Michigan History Magazine*, 1917–1934, contain articles on individual communities. The University of Wisconsin at Green Bay houses the Belgian-American Resources Collection.

PIERRE-HENRI LAURENT

BELORUSSIANS

The Belorussians are one of several Slavic peoples from the Russian Empire who first came to the United States in significant numbers between 1880 and World War I. At that time, they had little sense of national group identity and associated themselves with either existing Russian or Polish communities. In contrast, the Belorussians who arrived after World War I were more aware of a distinct identity. Hence, only since the early 1920s has a specifically Belorussian-American community emerged, and it is this group, which numbers between 175,000 and 200,000, that is discussed here.

The Belorussians speak an East Slavic language. They were converted to Christianity in the 10th century and were Orthodox until their incorporation into the territories of the Polish-Lithuanian Commonwealth in the

Belorussia

Boundaries of pre-1917
Russian guberniyas
Boundary between Poland
and Belorussian S.S.R.
1921-1939
Areas inhabited by
Belorussians

300   Km.   Miles

16th century when some converted to Catholicism. By the late 19th century about 80 percent of the population was Orthodox and the remainder Roman Catholic, a ratio that still holds for the Belorussian community in the United States today.

Belorussian (also spelled Byelorussian) is the name most commonly in use today, but the group has also been called Kryvian (from Krivichi, one of several Slavic tribes from whom they are descended) or Lithuanian (from Licviny, the name of the state in which they lived for several centuries). In English they are sometimes referred to as White Ruthenians or White Russians, a literal translation of *Belarusy*, not to be confused with the term applied to the so-called "White Russians" who opposed the "Red" Bolsheviks.

Belorussia was part of the Grand Duchy of Lithuania in the Middle Ages. The Duchy stretched from the Baltic to the Black Sea, bordered by Poland to the west and Muscovy (the original principality that became Russia) to the east. Its official language and dominant culture were Belorussian. In 1569 the Grand Duchy of Lithuania joined with the kingdom of Poland to form a commonwealth that lasted until the second half of the 18th century, when a series of partitions (1772, 1793, 1795) destroyed the commonwealth and eliminated Poland from the map of Europe. In 1840 the name Belorussia was formally prohibited, and by the end of the 19th century the Belorussian homeland was designated by the tsarist government as the Northwestern Region, later divided into the administrative provinces (guberniyas) of Vilna, Vitebsk, Minsk, Mogilev, Kovno, Grodno, and Smolensk. This administrative division of Belorussian territories lasted until the end of World War I.

Until the late 19th century most of the inhabitants of the Northwestern Region did not call themselves Belorussians. When asked, they identified themselves only in terms of their religion—*pravaslaŭnyia* (Ortho-

dox) or *katoliky* (Catholics)—or as *tuteishyia* or *tutashniia* (natives or local residents). If they were educated at all they usually called themselves Russians or Poles.

After the collapse of the Russian Empire in 1917 Belorussian patriots proclaimed a short-lived independent republic in March 1918. For the next three years, civil conflict and a war between Poland and the Soviet Union devastated the Belorussian homeland until a treaty was signed in March 1921, splitting the Belorussians among four new states: the U.S.S.R. (part in the Belorussian Soviet Socialist Republic, part in the Russian Soviet Federated Socialist Republic), Poland, Lithuania, and Latvia. During the 1920s a national renaissance took place in both Poland and the Belorussian S.S.R. which was to assure the future of Belorussian national identity. Poland lost its Belorussian territories after World War II and today there is a Belorussian S.S.R. that includes 75 percent of the total Belorussian population of 11 million. Twenty-five percent live as minorities in other parts of the Soviet Union and in Poland.

In the late 19th century many Belorussians emigrated as a result of poor economic conditions, rapid population growth, a shortage of land, a slow rate of industrialization, and religious discrimination against Catholics and Jews. Perhaps as many as 100,000 Belorussians came to the United States between 1861 and 1914; precise figures are not available because U.S. immigration and census officials did not distinguish Belorussians from Russians or Poles. Between the wars emigration was greatly limited by the U.S. national quota system, by the Soviet government, and then by the Great Depression.

During World War II, more than half a million Belorussians fled their Soviet-ruled homeland, while others were deported by Hitler's armies to forced-labor camps in Germany. These refugees wound up with many other groups from the Soviet Union in postwar camps for displaced persons in Germany and Austria. From there, tens of thousands of Belorussians emigrated to the United States. The earlier immigrants had been chiefly peasants unaware of their Belorussian heritage, but the post-1945 immigrants were predominantly professionals, artisans, and skilled workers. Moreover, because these new immigrants had been educated during the national renaissance in both Soviet Belorussia and Poland, they were fully aware of their Belorussian identity.

Both the original and the newer immigrants settled in the industrial regions of the northeastern United States. In the early years, many held unskilled jobs in the mills and factories of New York, New Jersey, Pennsylvania, Ohio, and Illinois. Several industrial cities in northern New Jersey, New York, Michigan, Ohio, and Maryland still contain concentrations of Belorussians. Some also settled in farming communities on Long Island, in southern New Jersey, and in Maine.

Before World War II, Belorussian Americans did not have their own churches. Orthodox Belorussians would join one of the Russian Orthodox churches and, as a result, were often absorbed into the Russian-American community. The Russian Orthodox Church was an instrument for propagating Russian culture and identity, not only among immigrants who were ethnically Great Russians, but among the largest number of its pa-

rishioners who were either Belorussian, Carpatho-Rusyn, or Ukrainian. Likewise, Belorussian Catholics joined parishes with many Poles and often became part of the Polish-American community.

Organized religious life changed with the arrival of the post-1945 immigrants. In an attempt to preserve their ethnic identity, one group joined the newly constituted Belorussian Autocephalic Orthodox Church. This church was first established in the homeland in 1922, then destroyed, and revived in 1942 and 1949, after which its hierarchy came to the United States and established its seat in Cleveland. Although this church has not yet been able to attract large numbers of Belorussians (in the 1970s it had only five parishes totaling about 1,800 families), the parishes actively propagate Belorussian culture by sponsoring Saturday and Sunday Belorussian-language schools, and by publishing the most widely circulated Belorussian periodical, *Holas tsarkvy/Voice of the Church* (Brooklyn, N.Y., f. 1954). Three other Belorussian Orthodox parishes (with about 300 families) are under the jurisdiction of the Greek Orthodox patriarch of Constantinople. This group also supports Belorussian Sunday schools and has its own periodical, *Tsarkoŭny svietach* (Church's Light; South River, N.J., f. 1951). Belorussian Roman Catholics do not have their own churches, but belong to ethnically-mixed parishes wherever they live. Belorussian Eastern Rite Catholics do have their own church in Chicago, although most have joined other Byzantine Rite churches, usually in the Carpatho-Rusyn and Ukrainian jurisdictions.

Besides Belorussian-language schools held in Orthodox churches, other aspects of religious life have fostered group identity among all Belorussian Americans, regardless of their religious affiliation. These aspects include baptisms, weddings, and funerals, and most especially the observances associated with Christmas, Easter, and other saints' days which are often celebrated in the traditional Belorussian manner.

The earliest secular associations of Belorussian immigrants before 1914 consisted of informal social gatherings of people from the same town, region, or province who met to exchange information about the homeland, to celebrate a religious holiday, or just to share common social interests. None of these organizations had a specific Belorussian character, and prior to the late 1940s only two formal Belorussian organizations existed: the Belaruski Kamitet (Belorussian Committee) founded in the 1920s and the Belorussian National Council (f. 1941). Both were based in Chicago and both sponsored lectures, publications, dances, and picnics.

Early Belorussian immigrants did not organize separate fraternal societies either. When they needed the financial and psychological support provided by such brotherhoods, they joined organizations like the Russian Consolidated Mutual Aid Society (ROOVA) and the Russian National Mutual Aid Society (RNOV). The latter has accommodated its Belorussian members since the 1940s by providing Belorussian cultural programs, sponsoring trips to the homeland, and hosting Soviet Belorussian writers and literary evenings.

However, the post-1945 immigrants set up a number of distinctly Belorussian organizations. In 1951 a group of scholars founded the Francis Skaryna Kryvian Society (later the Leu Sapieha Greatlitvan Bielarus Foundation), which published the scholarly journal *Veda* (Knowledge; New York, 1951–1953). About the same time, the Belorussian Institute of Arts and Sciences was also established in New York City. The institute sponsors lectures and conferences on Belorussian culture and maintains a reference library for Belorussian materials. It has also published several issues of a literary journal, *Konadni* (Vigils; Bronx, N.Y., 1955–1963), and an annual scholarly journal, *Zapisy* (Annals; New York and Jamaica, N.Y., f. 1952). A Belorussian Youth Association was founded in 1950. Based in New York City, the group was later renamed the Belorussian-American Youth Organization (BAYO); at the present time it has branches in seven states. Almost all the branches have folk-dance ensembles and sports groups, and sponsor lectures and seminars on Belorussian culture. The BAYO also publishes a bilingual quarterly, *Byelorussian Youth/Belaruskaia moladz'* (Brooklyn, N.Y., 1959–1967; Jamaica, N.Y., f. 1972), which has become a forum for young Belorussian writers.

Belorussian politics in the United States are dominated by the post-1945 immigrants, who are active in criticizing the Soviet government through publications and rallies, marches, and protests on U.S. and Belorussian national holidays, especially Belorussian Independence Day (March 25) and the annual commemoration of the uprising in the Slutsk region against Soviet rule in 1920. These celebrations include speeches by Belorussian-American leaders and often feature proclamations by state governors or mayors in cities where Belorussians reside. Group members are also active in both the Republican and Democratic parties, and try to influence public opinion in the United States through the Belorussian Republican Federation, which is affiliated with the National Republican Heritage Groups Council in Washington, D.C. Most of these political activities are coordinated by two New York City–based national organizations: the Belorussian-American Association (BAZA; f. 1949), and the Belorussian Congress Committee of America (f. 1951).

An important vehicle for expressing and preserving Belorussian culture in the United States is language, and the role of the post-1945 immigration is again crucial. At present, there are ten Belorussian and two Belorussian-English bilingual serial publications with a total circulation of 10,000. The oldest and largest of these is the monthly *Bielarus* (Jamaica, N.Y., f. 1950), which prints news about the homeland and information on the Belorussian-American community.

Belorussian is still spoken by the pre-1914 immigrants who survive and by those who came after 1945. The children and grandchildren of the earlier immigrants have either forgotten or never knew the language of their forebears; on the other hand, children of the nationally conscious recent immigrants are encouraged to use the language and make an effort to become fluent in it. Most churches run Saturday schools in Belorussian, and bilingual textbooks for grades one through five are available. The meetings and programs of the Belorussian American Youth Organization are often conducted in Belorussian, but the major journal for young people, *Belorussian Youth*, is now published largely in English.

The Belorussian-American community has produced a small group of writers, who publish in periodicals

such as *Konadni* and *Byelorussian Thought*, in the newspaper *Bielarus*, in anthologies, and in individual volumes. Among the better-known are the poets Natalla Arsiennieva (1904–), Ryhor Kazak, Mikhas Kavyl' (1915–), Ianka Zolak, Siarhej Iasien' (1926–), Ian Iukhnaviec, and the critics and prose writers Vasyl Birych (1909–), Iurka Vits'bich (1905–), Uladzimir Hlybinny (1910–), Masiej Siadniou, S. Braha, and S. Stankievich.

Several choirs are run by Belorussian parishes, and youth groups have organized dance ensembles such as Vasiliok in Highland Park, N.J., Lanok in South River, N.J., Matylki in Somerset, N.J., Miaselitsa in Queens, N.Y., and Kryzhanchok in Cleveland, Ohio.

The Belorussian community is still divided into two distinct groups in the United States: the immigrants who came before 1914 and their descendants, and those who came after 1945. Although the first group is much larger, it contains few self-consciously ethnic Belorussians. The older immigrants usually regard themselves as Russian, and their children and grandchildren either do so as well, or are vague about their ethnic heritage. Members of the second group generally have a clear Belorussian ethnic sense and are passing it on to their children. Nonetheless, the second group faces several challenges: it must continue to urge members, even of the post-1945 group, to be active participants in the Belorussian-American community; it must try to broaden its membership by convincing descendants of the earlier immigration that they should be loyal to their Belorussian heritage; and it must preserve in its own children the willingness to think of themselves as Belorussian Americans. Success or failure in these areas will determine the future of the Belorussian-American community.

Bibliography

There are only two studies of Belorussians in the United States: the comprehensive work by Vitaut Kipel, "Byelorussians in New Jersey," in *The New Jersey Ethnic Experience*, ed. Barbara Cunningham (Union City, N.J., 1977), and the short essay, "The Byelorussian Community of Cleveland," in *Ethnic Communities of Cleveland*, ed. Michael S. Pap (Cleveland, 1973).

The best studies of the homeland include a history by Nicholas Vakar, *Belorussia: The Making of a Nation* (Cambridge, Mass., 1956), and the analysis of more recent developments by Jan Zaprudnik, "Belorussia and the Belorussians," in *Handbook of Major Soviet Nationalities*, ed. Zev Katz (New York, 1975).

PAUL ROBERT MAGOCSI

BENGALIS: *see* BANGLADESHI; EAST INDIANS

BILINGUAL EDUCATION: *see* LANGUAGE: ISSUES AND LEGISLATION; *see also* EDUCATION; LANGUAGE MAINTENANCE

BILOXI: *see* AMERICAN INDIANS

BLACK SEA GERMANS: *see* GERMANS FROM RUSSIA

BLACKFEET: *see* AMERICAN INDIANS

BLACKS: *see* AFRO-AMERICANS

BOHEMIANS: *see* CZECHS

BOLIVIANS: *see* CENTRAL AND SOUTH AMERICANS

BOSNIAN MUSLIMS

Bosnian Muslims are Serbo-Croatian-speaking Muslims whose homeland is now the republic of Bosnia-Herzegovina in Yugoslavia. Known colloquially as "Muslims," they appear in the Yugoslav census under the category *Muslimani u smislu narodnosti* (Muslims in the ethnic sense). An estimated 10,000 to 12,000 Bosnian Muslims, including both foreign-born and their descendants, now live in the United States.

ORIGINS

Bosnia-Herzegovina is the most central republic of the six that constitute modern Yugoslavia and the only one not associated with a particular nationality. According to the 1971 Yugoslav census, Bosnian Muslims constitute 40 percent of the population of Bosnia-Herzegovina; Serbs and Croats together account for nearly 60 percent. All three groups speak dialects of Serbo-Croatian; they are distinguished by their adherence to Islam, Orthodoxy, or Catholicism. Nine percent of Yugoslav Bosnian Muslims live in the adjacent republic of Serbia, and 4 percent in Montenegro. The census lists 1,729,923 Bosnian Muslims in all, 8 percent of the total population of Yugoslavia. Outside Yugoslavia there is a large group (possibly 100,000) in Turkey, whose ancestors moved there after the Ottomans lost Bosnia-Herzegovina in 1878. They are still known there as Bošnjaci (the Turkish word for Bosnian), as they were during the Ottoman Empire.

The ethnic affiliation of Bosnian Muslims is somewhat ambiguous and is not wholly agreed upon even within the group. This ambiguity reflects the complex political history of the region and the purposeful manipulation of religious and ethnic affiliation by various interest groups both within and outside the area. Because of selective factors involved in the immigration, this is particularly true of those Bosnian Muslims now living in North America.

In 1463 the Bosnian kingdom and in 1482 the Herzegovinian duchy fell to the Ottoman Empire. Over the

Central Yugoslavia

next four centuries the Ottomans ruled Bosnia-Herzegovina, and there were mass conversions to Sunni Islam. The situation that developed as a result was unique in the Balkans. The ruling landowners were indigenous but Islamicized Slavs; the serfs were predominantly Christian, although there were a few Muslims among them as well. The free peasantry was predominantly Muslim. This sharp class division was maintained throughout the periods of Austro-Hungarian colonialism (1878–1918) and the Serbian-dominated Kingdom of Yugoslavia (1918–1940). Eradication of the economic basis of differentiation and increased social mobility and communication finally led to an amalgamation of the two classes of Bosnian Muslims. By now they have come to think and act as a single people.

Fragmentation of the Bosnian Muslim group was intensified in the period between the two world wars. Both Serbian and Croatian nationalists claimed national kinship with Bosnian Muslims and advanced historical arguments to prove their contention, in the process claiming the areas of mixed settlement for their own group. Certain Bosnian Muslims, nearly all belonging to the urban elite, declared themselves Muslim Serbs or Muslim Croats, depending upon where they thought their interests lay, in effect becoming a religious minority of either Serbia or Croatia.

But the great majority, particularly the Muslim peasantry, declined affiliation with either. They evolved over the years into a distinct ethnic community with its own interests and identity.

ARRIVAL AND SETTLEMENT

The immigration of Bosnian Muslims to North America began around 1900 when the first Muslim immigrants arrived from Bosnia-Herzegovina, looking for jobs; they came from Herzegovina, for the most part, the least productive and most desolate of all areas of Bosnian Muslim settlement in Yugoslavia. All were peasants, and most were young, unmarried men who did not plan to stay in the United States; those few who were married had left their wives and families behind.

Just after World War II another large number of Bosnian Muslims arrived. These were displaced persons, refugees, and self-imposed exiles who left largely for political reasons. The majority had joined or been forced onto the side of the Fascist Croatian puppet government during the war and afterward had to flee to escape retribution. A few had affiliated with the Chetniks, the Serbian forces who had sought to reimpose the monarchy.

This early postwar group of immigrants was much more heterogeneous than the prewar group: they came from the whole area of Muslim settlement, mostly from urban but some from rural communities, and represented all classes, including wealthy landowners whose holdings had been confiscated by the new Communist regime. Although men were in the majority, families were brought whenever possible. Many of these immigrants had spent a number of years in western Europe after leaving Yugoslavia. On the whole they were better educated than the prewar arrivals.

The refugees have been followed by still another wave of immigrants seeking economic improvement. As Yugoslavia lifted restrictions on emigration, Muslims began to come to North America in search of opportunity, while others joined the even larger migration to northern Europe. They continue to come from a variety of backgrounds, both regionally and socially, but they are less educated than the refugees and more likely to be from rural areas. There are more women than before; successful male immigrants soon send for their families or visit Yugoslavia to marry and bring their wives back with them.

ORGANIZATION AND SOCIAL LIFE

By far the largest Bosnian Muslim community in the United States has been and remains in Chicago. Early immigrants from Herzegovina settled in a neighborhood on the Near North Side and concentrated their social life in the several coffeehouses that were the primary social institutions of the period. Chain migration led to concentrations from particular Herzegovinian villages (especially Gacko and Trebinje), each of which had its own coffeehouse. Most of these early immigrants were employed as common laborers, especially in construction and tunnel building; surviving members of this generation take special pride in their conviction that Bosnians dug the Chicago subway. A lodge, Džemijetul Hajrije (Beneficent Society), was formed in 1906; it had both social and mutual-assistance functions, but its primary purpose was to provide medical insurance and to establish two Muslim cemeteries, one for bachelors and one for married members and their wives. There was no mosque, but families sometimes joined for Friday evening prayer in private homes. Bosnian Muslims formed a very close-knit community, although there was some interaction and intermarriage with other Muslims in Chicago, especially with the Turks. Bosnian Muslims sometimes married Christians, especially other Slavs (including Ukrainians, Slovaks, and Croats). A large percentage remained bachelors, however. Before World War II the Chicago community never totaled more than a few hundred.

During this period two smaller communities were closely linked to Chicago. One developed early in Gary, Ind., where some Bosnian Muslims had found employment in the steel mills. Chicago and Gary can be regarded as almost a single Bosnian Muslim community; the Gary Muslims belonged to the lodge centered in Chicago, but had their own coffeehouse. Another small community took shape in Butte, Mont., where Bosnian Muslim men from the Chicago area regularly went to work in the copper mines. Most of the early immigrants worked in Butte at one time or another, but there were never more than about 50 Bosnian Muslims there at any one time. The Butte community no longer exists.

The World War II refugees produced a significant change in the Bosnian Muslim community. In Chicago the original immigrants were dying, their children were moving to other cities, especially to Los Angeles and elsewhere in the West, and those who remained had little in common with the new immigrants except their religion. More numerous and more politically active, the new immigrants soon came to dominate the Chicago community.

In 1956 the last Bosnian coffeehouse in Chicago closed. Their residential area was gradually abandoned as members of the original community died or moved to the suburbs or the West Coast and as the newer immigrants chose to live elsewhere in the city. A number

of Bosnian Muslims now live in the suburbs north of Chicago, but no real neighborhood has developed.

The organizing skills of the refugee immigrants led to a number of new institutions. The membership of Džemijetul Hajrije dwindled, as elderly members died and few new members joined. But another organization, the Bosnian American Cultural Association (originally called the Moslem Religious and Cultural Home), formed in 1955, better serves the needs of the new immigrants. Its membership includes Bosnian Muslims in Gary and in Milwaukee, Wis., and even a few elsewhere in the country. It is now the central Bosnian Muslim organization in the United States. In the late 1950s it sponsored the only periodical (*Glasnik Muslimana*) published specifically for Bosnian Muslims in the United States, although the paper survived only a few years. A Bosnian mosque, together with a social center and Islamic school, was established in 1955 in the original Chicago neighborhood. Later it was sold, and in 1976 a large, new Islamic center was built in the Chicago suburb of Northbrook with substantial financial aid from Saudi Arabia and Kuwait. Sixty percent of the new center is owned by the Bosnian American Cultural Association, and Bosnian members and leaders are in the overwhelming majority, although there are a few Turkish, Arab, and Pakistani members.

About three-quarters of the Bosnian Muslims live in the Chicago-Milwaukee-Gary area. Chain migration is again in evidence; in Chicago there are groups of recent immigrants from the villages of Gračanica (in western Bosnia) and Bar (on the Montenegrin coast). There are also small Bosnian communities in Cleveland, Detroit, New York, Toronto, and elsewhere. Toronto is now the second-largest community and has the only Bosnian Islamic Center outside of the Chicago area.

The majority of those who migrated immediately after World War II are white-collar workers. Those who have come more recently are less educated and are likely to be employed as skilled or semiskilled workers, machinists, or carpenters. Others first find work as janitors, then as building superintendents, then eventually buy an apartment house of their own, usually in a working-class neighborhood. Several postwar immigrants, despite their rural background and lack of training, have done well in business. The largest Bosnian Muslim-owned business is the Precision Carbide Tool Company in Chicago, which employs approximately 300 workers, many of them fellow Bosnian Muslims. It may well be the largest firm in North America to give all employees paid vacations on the major Islamic holidays.

Nearly all of the immigrants who came during the refugee phase call themselves Muslim Croats; a very small number identify themselves as Muslim Serbs. The number of both these groups in North America is disproportionately large, a result of the self-selecting factors in the immigration process. But the vast majority both of the prewar immigrants and their descendants and of the most recent immigrants consider themselves a distinct ethnic group: the prewar immigrants because they came prior to the intensification of Serbian-Croatian conflict, the most recent immigrants because they have been affected by the official recognition of Bosnian Muslim nationality in postwar Yugoslavia. Most Bosnian Muslim Americans refer to themselves by the regional term in either Serbo-Croatian (Bosanci) or Turkish (Bošnjaci). (*See also* Croats; Serbs.)

Bibliography
Virtually no publications deal specifically with Bosnian Muslims in America. Gerald G. Govorchin, *Americans from Yugoslavia* (Gainesville, Fla., 1961), and George J. Prpic, *The Croatian Immigrants in America* (New York, 1971), contain useful data on immigration from Yugoslavia, and both mention Bosnian Muslims, the latter from a strongly Croatian perspective. Lois Rankin, "Detroit Nationality Groups," *Michigan History Magazine* 23 (1939): 129–205, has a brief description of the prewar community in Detroit. Two booklets, one by S. Karić, *Otvorenje Džamije i Škole Muslimanskog Kulturnog Doma u Chicagu* (Opening of the Mosque and School of the Muslim Cultural Home in Chicago; Chicago, 1957), and another entitled *The Islamic Cultural Center of Greater Chicago: Inauguration of the First Phase* (Chicago, 1976), contain limited but helpful information.

WILLIAM G. LOCKWOOD

BOYASH: *see* GYPSIES

BRAVAS: *see* CAPE VERDEANS; *see also* PORTUGUESE

BRAZILIANS: *see* CENTRAL AND SOUTH AMERICANS

BRITISH: *see* CORNISH; ENGLISH; MANX; SCOTCH-IRISH; SCOTS; WELSH; *see also* CANADIANS, BRITISH

BRITISH HONDURANS: *see* WEST INDIANS

BROTHERTONS: *see* AMERICAN INDIANS

BULGARIANS

Bulgarian Americans originated in present-day Bulgaria and in surrounding areas in the Balkans, most especially the historic region of Macedonia, located today primarily in southern Yugoslavia and northern Greece. Their ultimate source is a subject of dispute. But whether Asian or Slavic, Bulgar tribes had developed an independent state by the early 8th century, and their empire covered a large part of the Balkans. They

accepted Christianity in the 9th century and the liturgical language, Old Church Slavonic, was very close to Old Bulgarian, a distinct South Slavic language written in the Cyrillic alphabet.

After several decades of intermittent domination by the Byzantine Empire, Bulgaria lost its independence in the late 14th century and was absorbed into the Ottoman Empire. Turkish rule lasted until a Bulgarian national renaissance in the early 19th century. This led to a series of uprisings (crushed by the Turks) and the eventual attainment of independence in 1878, largely through the intervention of Russia. For a few months the new Bulgarian principality included most of historic Macedonia, but this territory was restored to the Ottoman state by the Western powers at the Congress of Berlin in June 1878. Bulgaria became a kingdom in 1908; its borders expanded and then contracted during the two Balkan wars (1912–1913). The desire to regain lost territory, especially Macedonia, prompted the Bulgarian government to ally with the Central powers during World War I and again with the Axis powers in World War II. In 1946 Bulgaria became a republic, and since that time has been dominated by a Communist government closely allied with the Soviet Union.

MIGRATION AND ARRIVAL

Bulgarian Americans are composed of two groups: the majority who came from Macedonia and those who came from Bulgaria proper. For the most part, Macedonian Bulgarians arrived in the United States before World War I, at a time when the idea of a distinct Macedonian nationality had not yet developed. This group of people continue to refer to themselves as Macedonians, but only in the sense of identifying themselves with a geographic region; as for nationality or ethnic descent, they consider themselves Bulgarian. (*See also* Macedonians.)

Those Bulgarians who came from "the kingdom" (as the independent Bulgarian state was called) emigrated mainly from areas that suffered from overpopulation and economic hardship. As a result, these regions traditionally had been suppliers of seasonal and migrant labor. Conditions at that time in Macedonia (still under Ottoman rule) were similar, but inhabitants there left for an additional reason: the Macedonians revolted against the Turks in 1903 but were unsuccessful, and many people fled in the face of mass reprisals by the Turkish army.

The first period of Bulgarian immigration to the United States began around 1900 and lasted until 1910. An estimated 50,000 came during these years; the vast majority were single men—peasants or unskilled laborers with little or no education who came with the intention of earning enough money so that they could return home and buy land or open a small business. The U.S. restrictions on immigration that went into effect in 1924 limited to only 100 the number of Bulgarians who could be admitted in any one year. Between 1924 and 1965, when the national origin quota restrictions were abolished, official statistics state that 7,660 Bulgarians came to the United States, but there were many more who entered illegally or with non-Bulgarian passports. During the interwar years (1919 to 1939), the immigrants were largely women and children joining husbands and fathers who had decided to remain permanently in the New World. The last period of immigration began after World War II and continues to the present.

The most recent immigrants are likely to be political refugees and opponents of the Communist regime in Bulgaria. Among them are a large number of educated and professional people who come with little prospect of ever returning home.

In contrast, the earlier immigrants showed a very high rate of reemigration; between 1910 and 1929 the number of returnees exceeded the number of new immigrants. Some left in order to join the Bulgarian army during the two Balkan wars and World War I, while others were dissatisfied with their life in the United States.

It is not possible to determine the exact number of Bulgarians who came to the United States or who live here now. U.S. immigration statistics have classified Bulgarians with Serbs and Montenegrins; in 1950 and 1960 they were not listed at all, but the 1910 Census shows 19,380. In 1970 the Bulgarian language does not appear in the mother-tongue table but the table on the origin of the foreign stock in the United States records 20,553 Bulgarians. Unofficial estimates place the number of immigrants and their descendants as high as 100,000, however, and it seems reasonable to assume that the figure is about 70,000. The discrepancies can be explained in several ways: many Bulgarians arrived illegally via Canada or Mexico; others came at different times with Turkish, Greek, Serbian, Romanian, Russian, or Yugoslav passports; some are recorded by the country of last residence rather than by country of birth.

SETTLEMENT AND ECONOMIC LIFE

Most of the early immigrants headed for the Midwest. Towns like Granite City and Madison, Ill., may have had as many as 8,000 Bulgarians in 1907. Eventually they settled all over the United States, although many were attracted to the Northeast by the growth of American industry. Because they were peasants with practically no capital or marketable industrial skills, Bulgarians had to accept low-paying unskilled jobs in the mines and steel mills of Pennsylvania and in the factories of several midwestern states. Out west they worked in railroad construction. At present the majority of Bulgarian Americans live and work in industrial centers, although a growing number have been able to start small businesses such as restaurants, grocery stores, taverns, bakeries, and construction firms.

The settlement patterns of Bulgarian Americans have changed little. The largest number still live in Michigan—as many as 10,000. There are smaller concentrations in Ohio, Indiana, Illinois, New York, New Jersey, Pennsylvania, Missouri, and California. The cities with the greatest concentrations of Bulgarian immigrants are Detroit, Mich.; Gary, Fort Wayne, and Indianapolis, Ind.; Lorain, Toledo, Cleveland, Youngstown, and Akron, Ohio; New York City; and Los Angeles. At one time Pittsburgh was a leading center for Bulgarians, but it has declined in importance in recent years.

SOCIAL AND FAMILY LIFE

The earliest Bulgarian immigrants were concerned primarily with their jobs and with overcoming the diffi-

culties of adjusting to the new environment. Nonetheless, in response to social needs they established in the United States two institutions: the *boort* (a Bulgarian-American version of the English boarding house) and the *kafené* (coffeehouse). Both were very popular in the first three decades of the immigration.

The boort was a simplified boarding house, usually run by a Bulgarian, sometimes with the help of his wife and family. Typically he would let two big rooms to a group of as many as 12 immigrants, who would use one room as sleeping quarters and the other as a combination living room, kitchen, dining, and recreation area. Often the immigrants would work at the same factory, would come from the same place in the old country, or would be relatives or close friends. Sometimes they would work in different shifts at the mill, using the same beds at different times. Since many steel mills functioned 24 hours a day, 7 days a week, there was not much opportunity for the two groups to meet. One of the shifts would prepare meals, the other would do housekeeping and other chores. Sometimes, the boort owner would also provide meals, but in most cases the boarders, to save money, preferred just to rent two big rooms and to divide their other expenses among themselves.

The kafené was a place for recreation and a social club on days free from work. It would usually be owned and run by a Bulgarian, but he was likely to be better educated or more experienced than the boort owner. In order to succeed he probably would have had to have been in the United States for a few years, to be familiar with the English language and local customs; he would act as an interpreter, counselor, and attorney, and as an insurance, job, and real-estate broker; he would enjoy considerable prestige among his clientele, for whom he would stock traditional Bulgarian drinks and snacks. Often he would also run a supplementary business, such as a grocery store, restaurant, hotel, boarding house, or even a banking establishment.

Family life among Bulgarian Americans generally followed a traditional pattern. The father had the dominant role in family affairs and the second generation lived with or near their parents. Initially, of course, there were not many Bulgarian families because the great majority of early immigrants were single men. Those who decided to settle in the United States often acquired brides from the homeland, either directly during a visit home or by prearranged plan through friends and relatives. These so-called mail brides were not unusual, and because of the similarity in background and the careful groundwork done by the parents of both parties, such arrangements often resulted in happy and sound marriages. Few Bulgarians married outside the group, and whenever intermarriages took place someone with at least a Balkan background was preferred.

The family was usually closely knit, and parents tried to instill in their children the ethical principles and customs they themselves had learned. Members of the second generation, however, were often eager to become Americanized. Children wanted to shed the vestiges of a past which they thought had prevented their parents' (and might similarly threaten their own) acceptance in the United States. Nonetheless, even among the second generation there are numerous instances where love

and respect for one's family and ethnic heritage have been stronger than the desire to assimilate or to deny one's background. In the case of the third generation, there is even more interest in the heritage of the homeland.

RELIGION

The majority of Bulgarian Americans are Eastern Orthodox. The first Bulgarian Orthodox church was founded in 1909 at Granite City, Ill., and thereafter 30 more were established, although many have since closed. After World War I, the ruling Holy Synod of the Autocephalous Orthodox Church in Bulgaria created a Bulgarian Eastern Orthodox Mission for the United States and Canada. In 1938 the mission was raised to the status of a diocese, headed by Bishop Andrey Velichki (d. 1972). However, jurisdictional and political controversies developed between the Bulgarian-American diocese and the mother church, disputes that were exacerbated after World War II when Bulgaria came under Communist rule. In 1963 several parishes formally broke relations with the Holy Synod in Bulgaria. They now have an independent diocese comprising eight churches with its own bishop, Kyril Yoncheff, and in 1976 they joined the Orthodox Church in America. Eight other Bulgarian Orthodox churches in the United States remain under the jurisdiction of the Bulgarian hierarchy, while two are independent. (*See* Eastern Orthodox.)

Despite jurisdictional controversies, Bulgarian Orthodox churches remain at the center of community life. Social events are often held in churches and many parishes sponsor schools where Bulgarian and English are taught. A small minority of Bulgarian immigrants joined Protestant sects, but the influence of Protestantism among Bulgarians has declined substantially since World War II. In 1907 a Bulgarian Evangelical Mission was established with branches in several Bulgarian settlements. These missions performed not only religious but also valuable non-religious functions, assisting newly arrived immigrants to find houses and jobs and conducting courses in English and civics.

SOCIAL ORGANIZATION AND POLITICS

Bulgarian immigrants organized voluntary associations, most of them consisting of former inhabitants of a village or region in the homeland, and they formed fraternal or mutual-benefit societies in order to provide assistance to members in need. There were also societies with a nationwide appeal, but these were mostly concerned with organizing and coordinating immigrant efforts to assist the homeland in times of crisis, such as during the Balkan wars of 1912–1913 and the two world wars.

Since the majority of the early immigrants came from Macedonia, the first societies, such as the Macedo-Odrin (Adrianople) Club (Chicago, f. 1902), had a decidedly regional profile. In an attempt to attract all Bulgarian Americans, a Bulgarian People's Union and a women's society, Bulgarkata v Amerika (Bulgarian Woman in America), were established in 1913. The largest and most successful group was and continues to be the Macedonian Political Organization (Fort Wayne,

Ind., f. 1922), which in 1952 changed its name to the Macedonian Patriotic Organization (MPO). It has branches in most cities where Bulgarians live. The MPO, which publishes the weekly *Makedonska tribuna/Macedonian tribune* (Indianapolis, Ind., f. 1927), claims that all Macedonians are Bulgarians and supports the idea of a united and independent Macedonia made up of parts of present-day Yugoslavia, Bulgaria, and Greece.

From the very beginning, Bulgarian immigrants also showed an interest in American and international politics, most especially of the left-wing variety. Some joined the Industrial Workers of the World, the American Socialist party, or the Communist party. In 1910 they even founded their own Bulgarian Socialist Labor Federation, which for several years published *Rabotnicheska Prosveta* (Workers' Enlightenment) in Madison, Ill. In 1917 the federation joined the Socialist Labor party, and after the group split in 1919 some Bulgarian members joined the Communist party, others the Socialist Labor party (DeLeon branch).

Several new leftist and radical groups emerged during the 1920s and 1930s. These activities were especially pronounced during World War II when the joint American-Soviet military effort encouraged so-called All-Slav fronts, the most prominent being the American Slav Congress. Many of that group's founders, including the general secretary, George Pirinsky (1901–), were Bulgarians. After the war the U.S. Attorney General declared many of these organizations to be subversive and some of their officials were deported.

The post-1945 immigrants have also established political organizations, such as the anti-Communist Bulgarian National Committee—Free and Independent Bulgaria (Washington, D.C., f. 1949). Led by the former Bulgarian politician, Georgi M. Dimitrov (1903–1972), the committee claimed to represent all Bulgarian Americans. This claim has been successfully challenged by royalist and other right-wing anti-Communist refugees who have set up the Bulgarian National Front (New York, f. 1958). Both groups hope to see political changes that would result in a non-Communist Bulgarian homeland.

There also have been several attempts to create umbrella groups to unite the divergent political and regional trends among Bulgarian-American organizations. One was the anti-Communist American Bulgarian League (New York, f. 1944), which published the *American-Bulgarian Review* (Pittsburgh and New York, 1952–1962) in order to present the Bulgarian cause before the American public. Another was the Bulgarian National Council (New York, f. 1960) which for five years included representatives of twenty Bulgarian-American organizations.

In recent years, a few Bulgarians have been successful in American politics. The author Stoyan Christowe (1897–) was elected a state senator in Vermont and served on various federal boards. Also, several officials and elected representatives in other states, especially Indiana, have been Bulgarian Americans.

CULTURE AND ETHNIC COMMITMENT

The history of the Bulgarian-American press reflects both the cultural achievements of the group and its ability to sustain itself. More than 50 Bulgarian newspapers and magazines have appeared in the United States, although most of them have been short-lived. The most important was *Naroden glas* (National Herald; Granite City, Ill., 1907–1950). During its height, between 1913 and 1926, this newspaper appeared in a daily edition of 8,000 copies; it also sponsored the publication of almanacs (until 1933) and books in both Bulgarian and English. These materials provided news of the homeland and the immigrant community, and also fostered knowledge and pride in the native culture. The oldest Bulgarian-language publication still in existence is the weekly published by the Macedonian Patriotic Organization. In addition there are 6 other publications, 4 Bulgarian and 2 Bulgarian-English; their total circulation is in the vicinity of 7,000.

The decline of the press reflects the decreasing use of the Bulgarian language among the Bulgarian-American community. The language survives (though Americanized through the incorporation of many English words) in family conversations, in church services, and in social gatherings such as picnics and *vecherinkas*—typical Bulgarian meetings with literary-musical programs and dances. Yet while language maintenance has declined, there has been a recent surge of interest in Bulgarian music and folk dances, especially among the younger generation. More and more young people are participating in Bulgarian gatherings, which, coupled with Easter, Christmas, and other national holidays, provide occasions on which immigrants and their offspring can get together—an important factor in the preservation of Bulgarian culture and traditions.

Bibliography
A comprehensive study of the group has recently been published by Nikolay Altankov, *The Bulgarian-Americans* (San Carlos, Calif., 1979). Several articles by social and charity workers describing the life of the early immigrants were published between 1908 and 1914 in *Charities and the Commons* and *Survey*. The sociological study by Margaret Byington, *Homestead: The Households of a Mill Town* (1910; reprint, Pittsburgh, 1974), discusses Bulgarians in Pennsylvania. Joseph Roucek, "The American-Bulgarians," *Orientator* (1937), is an early scholarly account.

The almanacs of *Naroden glas* (Granite City, Ill., 1908–1933), especially the 25th anniversary issue, *25-godishen iubileen almanah na vestnik Naroden glas i Bulgarite v Amerika*, present a rich mine of information on the life and activities of the immigrants. Also useful are *Makedonski Almanah, 1940* (Indianapolis, 1940) and the *American-Bulgarian Review* (New York, 1952–1962).

Autobiographical accounts of life in Bulgaria and in the new world are Peter D. Yankoff, *Peter Menikoff, The Story of a Bulgarian Boy in the Great American Melting Pot* (Nashville, Tenn., 1928); Boris George Petroff, *Son of the Danube* (New York, 1940); and three by Stoyan Christowe: *This is My Country* (New York, 1938); *My American Pilgrimage* (Boston, 1947), and *The Eagle and the Stork, An American Memoir* (New York, 1976).

There is a small collection of materials on the Bulgarian-Americans at the Southern Illinois University, Edwardsville, Ill.

NIKOLAY ALTANKOV

BULGARS: *see* TATARS

BURGENLANDERS: *see* AUSTRIANS

BURIATS: *see* KALMYKS

BURMESE

It is not known whether there are any well-established Burmese communities in the United States. In 1975 sizable numbers of immigrants from Burma lived in California, Illinois, Maryland, Massachusetts, New York, Ohio, Pennsylvania, and Texas.

Burmese immigrants began to enter the United States in the early 1960s. By 1965 there were approximately 500; by 1971 approximately 6,000. Since then only about 500 a year have been admitted as immigrants; there are no data on their return migration. Most Burmese immigrants, at the time of arrival, have been between the ages of 20 to 40; very few have been 50 or older. Family units seem to predominate; the men are largely professional, technical, and white-collar workers. The number of skilled craftsmen and engineers has been especially large; the number of agricultural or unskilled workers has been very small.

BYELORUSSIANS: *see* BELORUSSIANS

BYZANTINE-RITE CATHOLICS: *see* EASTERN CATHOLICS

C

CADDOS: *see* AMERICAN INDIANS

CAHUILLAS: *see* AMERICAN INDIANS

CAJUNS: *see* ACADIANS

CAMBODIANS: *see* INDOCHINESE

CANADIANS, BRITISH

During the past 200 years English-speaking Canadians have contributed much to the growth and development of the United States. Despite the commonly accepted view that British Canadians migrated in a random and widespread fashion and assimilated easily, the fact is that they often moved in clearly defined streams, determined by social and economic characteristics and family relationships. Moreover, their migrations took place during specific periods, most notably the second half of the 19th century, and certain first-generation Canadian immigrants remained as distinctly foreign elements in the United States.

In the century between the conquest of New France by the British (1763) and the establishment of the Dominion of Canada (1867), the populations of the British North American colonies of Nova Scotia, New Brunswick, Prince Edward Island, Newfoundland, and present-day Ontario and Quebec expanded sufficiently to fill in much of the accessible land. During the 1760s and 1770s small but influential numbers of colonists from New England and New York—most of them of British descent—moved northward to take up land in Nova Scotia or commercial positions in Quebec. They were joined in 1783 by some 40,000 Loyalists from the 13 colonies, who, for a variety of reasons, had been opposed to the American Revolution. The Loyalists and those who followed during the next 25 years (often re-ferred to as late Loyalists) to acquire free farms were from diverse religious and ethnic backgrounds. They were joined by sizable numbers of newcomers from the British Isles. Protestants from the west of England and Catholics from Ireland followed the trade of the cod fisheries into Newfoundland, while Catholics from the Highlands of Scotland moved into eastern Nova Scotia and Prince Edward Island. The largest number of immigrants from Britain, however, arrived after the Napoleonic wars ended in 1815. Thousands of Presbyterians from Ulster and the Scottish Lowlands; Anglicans, Methodists, and Baptists from England; and Irish Catholics fleeing from famine swelled the population of the British North American colonies to approximately 3.25 million by 1861.

From 1850 to 1896 economic change, stagnation, and depression in Canada reversed the trend and stimulated a mass movement southward to the growing cities and expanding western frontier of the United States. By the 1880s the migration had reached such vast proportions that the story of the new Dominion of Canada, according to political wags, "began in Lamentations and ended in Exodus." English-speaking Canadian emigrants of these years, from diverse social and economic backgrounds, overwhelmingly chose the United States as their destination. On the eve of the Civil War, they formed approximately 6 percent of America's foreign-born population, and 40 years later, 8 percent. Despite a second major outpouring during the 1920s, their proportion of the foreign-born fell to 6 percent in 1930 and remained at 6 percent in 1970.

BACKGROUND TO EMIGRATION

Although almost exclusively of British origin, English-speaking Canadians (or British North Americans as they were known prior to 1867) displayed strongly diversified social characteristics during the 19th century. In 1871 the population of the area then making up British Canada was approximately one-third Irish in origin,

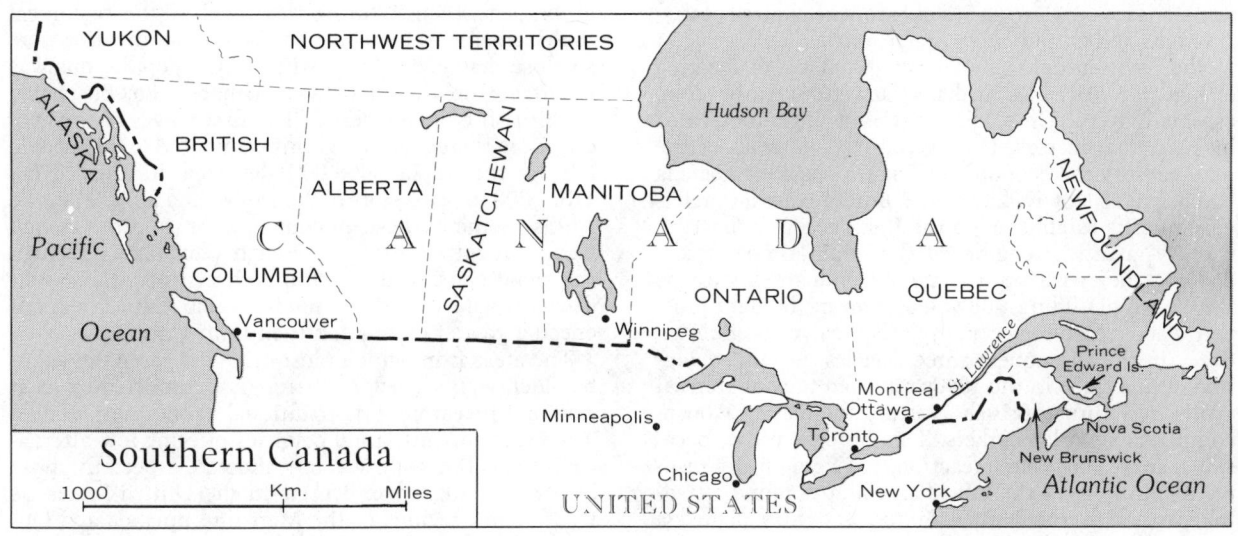

Southern Canada

one-fourth English, one-fifth Scots, and one-fifth a mixture of others. In religion roughly one-quarter were Methodists; Presbyterians, Catholics, and Anglicans were each one-fifth; Baptists and others the remaining 15 percent. Frequently such divisions were reinforced by socioeconomic distinctions or heightened by geographical separation, both among and within regions. English-speaking Canadians had a strong sense of localism centered on the family and an extended network of other kin and friends. An observer writing of Nova Scotian society in 1960 noted, "A blending had not taken place a century ago and is far from complete today. It is going on, and most rapidly in the metropolitan areas. But large parts of the countryside and the smaller towns still bear the hallmarks of the original settlers—traditions, beliefs, prejudices, and habits of life and work." His observations apply to other areas of Canada as well.

Economic activities and employment were diversified in 19th-century English-speaking Canada, though almost everywhere a system of farming combined with other employment was common. Dominated by the export of natural products, the Canadian economy provided seasonal opportunities in a variety of industries. In 1901 only 24 communities had more than 10,000 inhabitants, so it is apparent that many people lived in rural areas. Yet prior to the 1870s, with the exception of pockets such as the wheat counties of southern Ontario, agriculture was rarely developed to much more than a subsistence level. Even during the mid-century Ontario wheat boom, farmers used wasteful techniques characteristic of frontier husbandry rather than of highly developed commercial farming. In the Maritime Provinces (Nova Scotia, New Brunswick, and Prince Edward Island), farmers and their sons engaged in fishing, lumbering, shipbuilding, or sailing for several months of the year to earn supplementary income. In Ontario, lumbering, canal and railway construction, and Great Lakes shipping offered similar opportunities. Increasingly after 1850 young people from rural areas moved to nearby towns and cities for work as well as the chance for some adventure. There was an urban minority of British Canadians accustomed to congested living and factory work, and a large majority more familiar with farming, fishing, lumbering, sailing, and a variety of traditional crafts. These experiences counted heavily in decisions to emigrate and in subsequent choices of destinations and employment opportunities.

The 19th century was an era of abrupt and dislocating change for British Canadians, and their emigration, especially to the United States, was strongly motivated by economic factors. During the last 40 years of the 18th century the economy of English-speaking Canada had begun to slowly take shape. British colonial preferential tariffs established in the first decade of the 19th century greatly strengthened the infant timber trade, and together with other emerging industries such as fishing, shipbuilding, and wheat farming, brought prosperity and a thriving economy, despite cyclical fluctuations, in the subsequent three decades. Britain's adoption of free trade in the 1840s removed the preferential tariffs and thrust British North America into open, competitive world markets. This brought panic, occasional angry and violent reaction, and a groping for readjustment. By 1854 the Canadian colonies found a trading partner in the United States, and they signed a treaty allowing for the duty-free exchange of natural products. Its commerce strengthened by increased American demand during the Civil War, English-speaking Canada in the 1860s emerged from the crudeness and chronic poverty of a frontier society to the golden age of its traditional, preindustrial economy.

Even at the height of the unprecedented prosperity, however, elements of disruption and change were apparent. The wheat economy received a severe blow in 1859–1860, and throughout the 1860s new, long-distance railways began to centralize the economy and transform the countryside. Profits from the Civil War came to an end in 1865, and the following year the United States terminated the reciprocity agreement. In 1867 the political union of most of the British North American provinces under the British North America Act gave a major thrust to interregional economic and social integration, breaking down old Atlantic and local ties. The National Policy, a plan to stimulate industrial and urban growth through protective tariffs, transcontinental railways, and development of the west, also had an effect in many areas. The panic of 1873, which triggered a major depression in the United States, had an even more severe and lasting impact in Canada. All the while, technological advances and increasing integration were undermining the supremacy of the Maritime Provinces' wooden sailing ships and Ontario's wheat crops. Moreover, the urban and industrial growth of the last third of the 19th century was concentrated in a few places and was insufficient to provide livelihoods for the population of the dispersed small towns and rural areas.

EMIGRATION

A certain amount of emigration had always taken place from English-speaking Canada, mainly to the United States. In the closing decade of the 18th century, disenchanted Loyalists had slowly filtered back across the border. Many of the British emigrants who took advantage of the cheaper fares to Canadian ports in the period after 1815 moved on to American destinations, either immediately or after a temporary sojourn to earn enough money to reach eastern cities or, by the 1830s and 1840s, the expanding Ohio country. On occasion they probably enticed other British North Americans to accompany them. During the years of the reciprocal trade agreement, Canadian and U.S. economic ties were so close that a certain mingling of the populations was inevitable; in the 1850s approximately 86,000 people left British North America. The first waves of the exodus more than quadrupled this number; 376,000 people left in the 1860s; 438,000 departed in the 1870s; 1,108,000 in peak years of the 1880s; and 507,000 in the 1890s. (Some of these, of course, were from the French Canadian community; see French Canadians.) Though the trend continued into the 20th century, those four decades were the only ones in which Canada experienced a greater emigration than immigration.

The areas from which most migrants came tended to be older, well settled, and strongly committed by location and investment to traditional economic pursuits. The predominantly rural counties offering few alternatives to decline were severely affected, especially those near expanding urban centers in the United States, as were poorer regions of the Maritime uplands and Ontario. The causes were clear: the replacing of traditional

local industries by urban factories; the by-passing of many districts by the railways; and the movement of manufacturing establishments to larger centers as improved transportation extended the influence of the bigger cities and towns.

The emigrants reflected the diversity of the nation. Farmers and their children appear to have been well represented in the migration, yet the loss of rural nonfarm workers, the traditional craftsmen, was undoubtedly greater. They were joined by lumbermen from New Brunswick, the Ottawa Valley, and the Ottawa-Huron tract of northwest Ontario; by fishermen from Cape Breton and the shores of western Nova Scotia, New Brunswick, and Prince Edward Island; and by clerical and professional workers made redundant by a rapidly diminishing clientele. In addition to the thousands who departed for essentially negative reasons, forced out by change and dislocation, were younger people who had served apprenticeships in new manufacturing industries or received an education qualifying them for white-collar occupations. They perceived the greater possibility for advancement in the rapidly expanding U.S. cities after 1865 and moved because they desired a better future than Canada offered.

During the early years of the exodus many of the migrants were young, single males, who often moved southward on a seasonal basis. As opportunities for part-time supplementary employment declined in English-speaking Canada, the traditional, short-distance seasonal migrations to the woods, the sea, or the cities were gradually extended—to New England for the Maritimers and the Midwest for Ontario youth. The newspapers of the day continually bemoaned the fact that Canada was being drained of its youth, the "bone and sinew" of the population on which future development depended. By the late 1860s young men were being joined by single women and young married couples. By the 1870s and 1880s a significant proportion of the movement consisted of older migrants, whole families, and even the aged, who accepted invitations of support from successful offspring who had emigrated earlier. In these years the emigrants tended to settle in the United States permanently.

During the first two decades of the 20th century, movement from Canada was somewhat diminished because of increased industrial opportunities in eastern Canada and the dynamic expansion of the wheat economy in the west. In the 1920s, however, there was another major outpouring of the population, especially from the Maritime Provinces, stimulated by the familiar causes of rural decline, combined with industrial collapse in Nova Scotia. Canadian blue-collar workers found wages higher in American cities and left their lower-paid positions in Canada for recently arrived immigrants to fill. The Great Depression of the 1930s brought a substantial return migration, as the unemployed moved back to the farms to sit out the hard times. Since World War II, changing economic demands and immigration policy in the United States have considerably altered the nature of Canadian emigration. Rather than providing escape and better opportunities for skilled craftsmen, laborers, and domestics, the United States has selectively attracted increasing proportions of well-trained professional workers.

Although there were already 250,000 British North Americans in the United States by 1860, their numbers and proportion among the foreign-born grew significantly in the following decades. Twenty years later some 610,000 English- and French-speaking Canadians from Ontario and Quebec, 51,000 Nova Scotians, 42,000 New Brunswickers, and 7,500 Prince Edward Islanders were living in the United States. By 1900 a total of nearly 788,000 English-speaking Canadians made up 8 percent of America's foreign-born, compared to 26 percent for the Germans, 16 percent for the Irish, 5 percent for the Italians, and 4 percent for the Poles.

DISTRIBUTION AND EMPLOYMENT PATTERNS

Canadians lived in every state of the union after the Civil War but tended to concentrate in certain regions, particularly the border states. They also tended to move to areas with many job opportunities and high per capita income. As Table 1 shows, in 1880, immigrants from the Maritimes were overwhelmingly clustered in New England, the closest region to their places of origin. Smaller groups of Prince Edward Islanders and New Brunswickers lived in the East Central and West Central areas, and Maritimers generally were thinly scattered through other sections. British Canadians from Ontario were somewhat less clustered in their settlement patterns, though the picture is blurred by the failure of the U.S. Tenth Census to differentiate between French and British Canadians. Well over one-third of the Ontario and Quebec Canadians listed by the census were located in the East Central section, the nearest region to Ontario, and most of these probably were Eng-

Table 1. Percentages of Canadians in U.S. regions, 1880.

| Region | Provinces of birth | | | |
	Nova Scotia	New Brunswick	Prince Edward Island	Other provinces[a]
New England	70	65	57	28
Mid-Atlantic	7	5	5	15
East Central	6	11	16	37
West Central	7	9	11	14
West	10	9	9	5
South	1	1	1	1

Source: U.S. Census Office, *Statistics of the Population of the United States at the Tenth Census, 1880* (Washington, D.C., 1883).
a. Includes both English- and French-speaking immigrants from Ontario and Quebec.

Table 2. Occupational distribution of British Canadians, 10 years and older, in the United States, 1880 and 1930 (in percentages).

| Occupation | 1880 | 1930 | |
	Both Sexes	Male	Female
Agriculture	21	20	3
Mining		1	0
Manufacturing and mechanical	44	39	25
Transportation	9	10	1
Trade		13	7
Professional		5	14
Domestic and personal service	26	4	41
Public service		2	0
Clerical		5	9
Total number	351,103	326,547	94,361

Source: U.S. Census Office, *Statistics of the Population of the United States at the Tenth Census, 1880* (Washington, D.C., 1883); Leon E. Truesdell, *The Canadian-Born in the United States* (New Haven, Conn., 1943).

lish-speaking—just as the majority of Canadians in New England were most likely French-speaking. British Ontarians also settled in New York State and the West Central region. Fewer British Canadians settled in the Far West, though their numbers in that region increased during the 20th century. The proximity of New England for Maritimers and the Midwest for Ontarians was the most important factor in the choice of destination, and these regions were made increasingly accessible after 1850 by regular and inexpensive steamer and railroad service.

British Canadians were drawn to these sections of the United States not only by the prospect of a short journey to a well-paid job, but also by the expectation of employment in a familiar occupation, especially for those trained in traditional crafts. Table 2 shows that the largest share (44 percent) of the Canadian work force in the United States in 1880 was engaged in manufacturing, mechanical, or mining industries. There were more than 15,000 carpenters, which accounted for over 4 percent of employed Canadians, a proportion substantially higher than that among the Irish, Scandinavians, British, or Germans. The second largest portion (26 percent) of employed Canadians in 1880 were in the professional and personal sector, including over 22,000 domestic servants (6 percent of the work force); 21 percent were in agriculture and 9 percent in trade and transportation.

This pattern of employment altered only slightly in the following half-century. At the end of the second great wave of Canadian immigration in 1930, the largest share of Canadian working men still were in manufacturing and mechanical industries, with carpenters 6 percent of the total. Domestic service was still the most important form of work for Canadian women; 17,700 females were domestics in 1930. An increasing number of women were working in factories, in the professions, especially nursing, and in clerical positions. Though white-collar jobs gained in importance, particularly for women, the number of British Canadians employed in skilled crafts, domestic work, and agriculture in the United States remained fairly constant from 1860 to World War II.

This preference for certain jobs, as well as for short-distance travel and high wages, helps explain the distribution of English-speaking Canadians in particular states and communities. Prince Edward Islanders, to whom farming and land ownership were important, were the only Maritime group with a noticeable representation in Iowa (6 percent) in 1880. Lumbering dominated the economy and lives of New Brunswickers, and in 1880 a third of the New Brunswickers in the United States lived in Maine, with smaller proportions in the lumbering areas of Minnesota, Wisconsin, and Michigan. The forest industry was much less important to Nova Scotians and Prince Edward Islanders, and in 1880 only small percentages of their total number in the United States were located in Maine. Fishing was the most important industry in Nova Scotia, and by the 1880s Nova Scotians were 12 percent of the population of Gloucester, Mass., and a large proportion of the Gloucester fishing fleet. Because of the problems facing agriculture and an increasing shortage of good land in their native province, Ontario farmers moved to farms in upstate New York, the Midwest, and the home-

steading areas of the plains. Like their New Brunswick counterparts, Ottawa Valley lumbermen migrated to the woods of Michigan, Wisconsin, and Minnesota. In places such as the Dakotas, where frontier-type farming in the summer was often combined with winter sojourns to the logging camps of Minnesota, British Canadians maintained their traditional pattern of part-time and seasonal employment.

OCCUPATIONAL AND SOCIAL CHARACTERISTICS

In addition to occupational training and the desire to maintain or improve personal fortunes in familiar jobs, the social differentials of age, sex, and marital status were important in determining British Canadian migration patterns to the United States. After the Civil War the prospective Canadian emigrant was faced with a large choice of destinations. Young, single males predominated in the lumbering and mining frontiers of the Far West, as well as the cities of California. Young, single women, in contrast, tended to move to the nearest American cities. There were more women than men among Canadian immigrants in Boston, Detroit, and Chicago. Young families and single males were likely to relocate in the midwestern farming regions. Older, married men and women with larger families found short rural-to-urban moves easier and cheaper than more distant migration. Similarly widows and widowers with offspring probably found life easier in American cities than in rural Canada. In the cities older children could be sent out to work, and the fortunate widow with some capital could purchase a boarding house and earn enough to keep the family together.

Though cities were always the major magnets for Canadians moving to the United States, they became even more important following the closing of the American frontier in the 1890s. In 1880, 57 percent of Nova Scotians, 50 percent of Prince Edward Islanders, and 29 percent of New Brunswickers in the United States were living in Massachusetts, and a fifth of both the Islanders and the Nova Scotians lived in Boston. There Maritimers formed 15 percent of the foreign-born population, a proportion second only to that of the Irish. By 1900 their numbers in Boston had risen to over 47,000 and their proportion of the foreign-born to 22 percent. Many more lived in suburban towns and cities, such as Cambridge (1,680; 11 percent of the foreign-born in 1880) and Lynn (1,568; 22 percent of the foreign-born). What Boston was to the Maritimers—the nearest, expanding English-speaking metropolis—the towns and cities of the Midwest and New York State were to the Ontarians. In 1880 in Chicago Canadians, predominantly British Ontarians, formed 6 percent of the foreign-born population; in Detroit, 23 percent; in Buffalo, N.Y., 12 percent; and in Rochester, N.Y., 14 percent. Ontarians were one of the largest immigrant groups in most of these cities, which continued to attract Ontarians well into the 20th century.

The diversity of the occupational groups that left Canada after 1850 was reflected in the wide variety of positions they assumed in American urban centers. Maritimers in Boston, for example, worked as laborers, domestic servants, police officers, politicians, physicians, and lawyers. But men from agricultural backgrounds tended to become laborers or teamsters. Those

with crafts experience came to dominate the house- and shipbuilding industries in Boston prior to World War I and earned the nickname of "Nova Scotia hatchet and saw men." By 1880 they constituted over 20 percent of the carpenters in the city and formed a similar proportion of building-trades workers in Worcester, Mass. Approximately one-quarter of the Maritimers living in Boston were concentrated in the "streetcar suburbs" of Roxbury, West Roxbury, and Dorchester up to about 1910. Another one-quarter, many of whom were shipbuilders, lived in East Boston. There the yard of Donald McKay (1810–1880), a native of Nova Scotia, produced such famous clippers as the *Sovereign of the Seas,* the *Flying Cloud,* and the *Great Republic* and undoubtedly served as a beacon; the district continued to attract skilled craftsmen from the Maritimes long after McKay's bankruptcy in the 1860s.

At home many young Canadian women had labored at domestic chores on the farm with little financial recompense. In Boston they could earn wages for performing similar tasks; thus women from the countryside and small towns of Canada engaged in service in the homes of Beacon Hill, the Back Bay, or the less affluent establishments of the suburbs and the South End. In the latter district, single men and women lodged in boarding houses, close to sales and clerical jobs in the downtown area. Lesser numbers of industrial workers with Canadian apprenticeships or factory experience to their credit, such as machinists and ironworkers, found opportunities for advancement in various manufacturing establishments around the city. Another small but significant group of professionals and factory owners settled in Boston's suburbs.

English-speaking Ontarians followed similar locational patterns in the Midwest. Certain rural craft workers preferred the smaller border towns of Massena and Ogdensburg, N.Y., and Port Huron and Sault Sainte Marie, Mich., to the larger cities, but many more moved to Detroit, Chicago, Buffalo, or Rochester, where they engaged in a wide variety of occupations. Again, their settlement was dispersed, though they preferred the less densely populated outlying areas. This trend was still discernible among Maritimers and Ontarians in American cities in 1930.

Once occupational and social differentials had placed British Canadians within certain clearly defined migration streams to American farms, forests, towns, and cities, their cultural origins tended to determine their place of residence and subsequent patterns of adjustment, advancement, and persistence. In contrast to the homogeneity of French Canadians, many of whom worked together in the same factories and lived in the same urban neighborhoods, Canadians of British origin tended to display little more unity abroad than they had at home. Differences in ethnic and religious background reinforced the pattern of dispersed and fragmentary settlement initially dictated by their different occupations. In Boston, for example, New Brunswick Irish Catholics tended to live in South Boston with first-generation Irish Catholics; Nova Scotia Presbyterians mixed with Scots Presbyterians in East Boston; Baptists from the Maritimes often settled among rural or small-town coreligionists in northern New England. This pattern of association extended to membership by the various Canadian subgroups in English, Scots, and Irish charitable societies, as well as to intermarriage. Similar trends were evident among Ontarians in Detroit and Chicago. Those who were of Loyalist or late Loyalist origin readily moved into the districts, clubs, societies, and families of the native-born. The comparatively small number of black British Canadians, who were segregated at home, settled in northern U.S. cities among black migrants from the South.

ETHNIC AND SOCIAL INSTITUTIONS

Cultural fragmentation and dispersed employment severely restricted the formation of distinct ethnic institutions. Presbyterian churches in the U.S. border cities during the late 19th and early 20th centuries were likely to have predominantly Canadian congregations, and expatriate followers of the Reverend Donald Macdonald of Prince Edward Island built a Macdonaldite church in Cambridge, Mass., but in most cases Canadians constituted smaller elements in established American Methodist, Episcopal, or Baptist congregations. One weekly newspaper, the *American Canadian* (East Boston, f. 1874), adopted a deliberately nonpolitical, noncontroversial policy in order to unite the Canadian immigrant reading population, but it failed within two years. A magazine, the *Maple Leaf* (f. 1906) begun by the small Canadian enclave in Oakland, Calif., managed to survive into the early 1940s; it appealed to Canadians throughout the United States with nonpolitical news on "Departed Friends," individual success stories, and occasional descriptive pieces on the "old country." The *Canadian-American* (Minneapolis and Chicago) served British Ontarian newspaper readers in the Midwest from 1883 to 1934. These and a few other fugitive publications hardly amounted to a flourishing immigrant press. The fact that Canadian papers of the desired political, religious, ethnic, and local persuasion could probably be procured easily through the mail or on the newsstands in larger American cities most likely impeded any such development.

British Canadian social institutions in the United States were also rare, the more durable ones owing their success to specialized appeals to fragments of the Canadian immigrant population rather than to the group as a whole. The famous Canadian Club of New York City and the Intercolonial Club of Boston, for example, were both founded early in the 20th century as havens for expatriate gentlemen, scholars, and businessmen. The Sons and Daughters of the Maritime Provinces enthusiastically announced its formation in 1893 in Brockton, Mass.; it reported on two subsequent meetings and then apparently disappeared. Four other lodges of the society had similarly short lives in Boston, East and North Attleboro, and Fall River, Mass., during 1892 and 1893. Even smaller subgroups, such as the St. Croix Valley Association (Boston, 1903–1905), the Prescott Committee (Chicago, f. 1914), or the Stratford Old Boys (Chicago, 1907–1914), were founded on the local loyalties of Maritimers or Ontarians. The members met occasionally for picnics and Sunday afternoon strolls or to organize return visits to their native districts for "old home week."

ASSIMILATION AND PAST LOYALTIES

The lack of national cohesion was conducive to the apparently easy assimilation of British Canadian immi-

grants into the larger society. They were of the same British stock as many Americans and often held similar values and beliefs. The American and Canadian educational systems were similar, and both groups read the same periodicals and popular novels. Nevertheless, certain British Canadians of the first generation did not integrate completely, as can be readily discerned from naturalization figures. In 1875, 65 percent of the Canadian males of voting age in Boston, most of them English-speaking, were classified as aliens, meaning that they were not citizens and did not possess first papers. This was only slightly less than the proportion of aliens among the unassimilative French Canadians in Lawrence and Lowell (78 and 85 percent, respectively). In time, more Canadians became naturalized, but the differences between English-and French-speaking immigrants became smaller. By 1930, 29 percent of British Canadian males over 21 years old in the United States were aliens, compared to 36 percent of French Canadians. In the same year, only 17 percent of the Irish-born adult male population in America were aliens, and 14 percent of the Germans.

The question remains whether the failure of British Canadians to participate fully in United States politics and life was a result of their own reluctance or of native-American prejudice. One authority has suggested that the Canadians were so similar that their coming was hardly noticed. Nevertheless, it is possible to find evidence of occasional native-born prejudice. Canadian Protestants were welcomed to swell the ranks of such anti-Catholic organizations as the American Protective Association or the Orange Order, which had formed to counteract the growing influence of Irish Catholics in U.S. cities during the second half of the 19th century; Irish Canadian "Papists" clearly were not welcome. One of the major riots involving APA supporters during 1895, in which a man was killed and 40 others injured, occurred in East Boston, where many Maritimers lived. During the prolonged strike for the eight-hour day in Boston in 1886, angry workers stormed to the wharf to dissuade scab labor from disembarking from Yarmouth and Saint John steamers. The *New York Herald* reacted in equally hostile tones to British Canadians in 1893, describing them as "ignorant and poverty-stricken scrubbers" who had "an odor distinctively their own." This "motley crowd," the *Herald* warned its readers, constituted a great danger, a menace to "the interests of legitimate labor." Such differential acceptance and occasional native reaction in times of economic depression, high unemployment, and labor unrest, however, did not match the pattern of hostility and rejection experienced by many other immigrants in the United States.

It is most likely that the persistent failure of certain British Canadians to obtain citizenship or become completely assimilated was a result of their own personal reluctance. Occasional perceptive remarks by contemporary Americans accused them of "hypernationalism," of being "personally selfish" and "clannish" both at work and in native social institutions. Some seemingly refused to join any societies or clubs. During their leisure hours they gathered together in "sets," and some Canadians of Loyalist origin were even observed to instruct their children in anti-Americanism, prompting them to ask "distressing historical questions" of schoolteachers.

Much of this reluctance to assimilate may be explained in terms of motives for migration. Those who left Canada with the intention of working a while and returning had no reason to acquire real estate, take out citizenship, or join unions or clubs. They had no intention of seeking anything more than money to take home, which might also account for the occasional comments about British Canadian "stinginess." The nearness and cheap accessibility of their Canadian homes contributed to the belief prevalent among a large proportion of the migrants that they would return home some day. That as many as 40 or 50 percent did not return testifies to an important transition during their lives and careers in the United States. Economic success in America, the worsening of prospects in rural Canada, and the assimilation of the second generation undoubtedly contributed to the permanent relocation of substantial proportions of the immigrants. Some procrastinated about obtaining citizenship until old age, while others never quite made the transition, choosing to have their bodies shipped back to the graveyards of small Canadian villages and towns, where they might rest among familiar surroundings, old friends, and relatives. Such posthumous return migration is strong evidence of the ultimate loyalties of certain British Canadians, even after decades of life in the United States.

The family and its extensive kinship network was, in fact, the central focus of British Canadian experience in the United States, just as it had been in Canada, where ties were strongly localized. Loyalty to the family rather than to occupational or cultural group often determined the routes and destinations of Canadian emigrants, perpetuated migration flows, and assisted in the adjustment process in new surroundings. When he came of age (18), Harris Hudson left his native village of Scotts Bay, Nova Scotia, and moved to Boston. In 1888 his 19-year-old brother James and sister Eunice (17) departed for the towns of Lynn and East Walpole, Mass. Four years later, the rest of the Hudson family, the parents and seven children, moved to the Boston area to join Harris. Similarly six members of the Meek family left the town of Canning, Nova Scotia, at intervals between 1876 and 1890. In 1892 five of them were living in Denver, and the other was not too far away in South Dakota.

In the United States, as at home, the family was an essential unit in both economic and social activities. For example, in 1861 Arthur McArthur was living with his Scots Presbyterian farming family at Hammond, New Brunswick. Twenty years later, at the age of 38, he was still in the parental household, but living at 156 Lexington Street, East Boston. In 1878 he had married Louise Chaloner, a native of the adjacent parish of Sussex, New Brunswick, where Arthur's mother, Emma Freeze, had been born and raised. Louise's father, a carpenter, and his mother were living on nearby Putnam Street, East Boston, in 1880. Arthur had entered the furniture business, and by 1885 he had formed a partnership with Willard McLeod, also from Sussex; the arrangement lasted into the 20th century, even though McLeod moved to suburban Malden in 1890. Charles H. Lincoln, a carpenter from Fredericton, New Brunswick, moved to Boston with his parents in 1860 at the age of 23. Lincoln wrote to his former workmates describing his location in the city (169 Ruggles Street), his woodworking job in an organ factory, and other employment

opportunities. During the next 20 years at least two other carpenters from the same small shop in Fredericton moved to Boston. Lincoln's father, a shoemaker, worked in Boston until his death in 1905; Charles married a Massachusetts woman and set up home at 171 Ruggles Street; sister Annie married Charles Sutherland, the son of another Fredericton shoemaker, and remained in the parental household next door. These examples were undoubtedly duplicated by many British Canadians during the late 19th-century exodus and the second wave of emigration in the 1920s. They provide considerable evidence for the importance of family and local ties in a gradual process of migration; for the easy absorption of British Canadians into the American economy; and also for a certain resistance to complete social integration among the first generation.

After World War II the pattern of Canadian emigration to the United States changed considerably, owing to shifts in economic opportunities in both countries. Increasingly, during the 1950s and 1960s, Canadian emigrants were from highly skilled or professional backgrounds. The "brain drain" migration was smaller than that of the mass waves of blue-collar, crafts, and unskilled labor during the century after 1850. The United States had turned to other nations for its supply of such workers. Nevertheless, these new Canadians, including such well-known figures as actor Raymond Burr (1917–), economist John Kenneth Galbraith (1908–), and hockey players Gordie Howe (1928–) and Bobby Orr (1948–), as well as the less visible academics, physicians, lawyers, and businessmen, continue to have an impact, albeit on a different section of U.S. society. Because of their more specialized occupations, these immigrants have been less influenced by distance in deciding where to settle in the United States and are less likely to live among other Canadians. Temporary moves are still important, as they must be in an international migration that for over 100 years has displayed characteristics more typical of the internal, rural-to-urban movement common on the North American continent. The fact that in 1900 there were over 1.7 million persons of British Canadian birth or parentage south of the 49th parallel, which increased to well over 2.2 million by 1930 and remained over 2.0 million in 1970 is adequate testimony of the extent of their contribution to the economic growth and cultural development of the United States.

Bibliography

Marcus Lee Hansen and John Bartlett Brebner, *The Mingling of the Canadian and American Peoples* (New Haven, Conn., 1940), and Leon E. Truesdell, *The Canadian-Born in the United States* (New Haven, 1943), are the only studies of English-speaking Canadians in the United States. While both are useful, the former occasionally suffers from overgeneralization in an attempt to cover the period from 1604 to 1938 and from strained efforts to portray Canadians and Americans as being culturally homogeneous or completely intermingled. More specialized recent essays include R.K. Vedder and L.E. Gallaway, "Settlement Patterns of Canadian Emigrants to the U.S., 1850–1960," *Canadian Journal of Economics* 3 (1970): 476–486; Albert J. Kennedy, "The Provincials," *Acadiensis* 4 (1975): 85–101; and two essays by Alan A. Brookes, "Out-Migration from the Maritime Provinces, 1860–1900: Some Preliminary Considerations," *Acadiensis* 5 (1976): 26–55, and "Islanders in the Boston States," *Island Magazine* 2 (1977): 11–15. For more recent trends see T.J. Samuel, "Migration of Canadians to the U.S.A.: The Causes," *International Migration* 7 (1969): 106–116, and L.W. St. John-Jones, "The Exchange of Population between the U.S.A. and Canada in the 1960s," *International Migration* 11 (1973): 32–51.

ALAN A. BROOKES

CANADIANS, FRENCH: *see* FRENCH CANADIANS

CANARY ISLANDERS: *see* SPANIARDS

CAPE VERDEANS

The Cape Verde Islands were a Portuguese dependency until July 5, 1975, when the inhabitants won their independence and inaugurated the Republic of Cape Verde. In the years prior to independence, Cape Verdeans coming to the United States were considered as Portuguese. Since 1975, however, many Cape Verdean Americans prefer to think of themselves as a separate ethnic group. (*See also* Portuguese.)

THE ISLANDS OF ORIGIN

The Republic of Cape Verde is the largest of the three Portuguese island clusters in the North Atlantic. Its area (1,557 square miles) is greater than that of the Azores (902 square miles) and the Madeiras (307 square miles) combined. The Azores and the Madeiras still belong to Portugal. Furthermore, the islands of São Tiago or Santiago (383 square miles), on which stands the capital city of Praia, and Santo Antão (301 square miles) are the largest of all the Portuguese and formerly Portuguese islands. In 1970 the Portuguese government reported that the population of the islands was 272,072, an increase of 35 percent over the 1960 census.

The islands form two distinct groups. The northern group is known as the Barlavento (Windward Islands) because it is exposed directly to the northeast trade winds; it includes Santo Antão; São Vicente, with the spacious bay called the Porto Grande on which the city of Mindelo is located; São Nicolau; Sal, on which is located a large international airport originally built by the Italians in 1939 for their South American land plane service; and Boa Vista. The southern group is the Sotavento (Leeward Islands), which is protected by the Barlavento; in addition to large São Tiago, it includes spectacular Fogo, with a volcanic cone towering to 9,281 feet; Maio; and tiny Brava, the size of Manhattan. So many have emigrated from or through Brava that Cape Verdeans have often been called Bravas.

Cape Verde Islands

The population of the Cape Verde Islands is said to be 1 percent European, 28 percent African, and 71 percent *mestiços* (mixed European and African ancestry). Africans were brought in as wives, free laborers, and slaves by the Portuguese, who were responsible for revealing the archipelago to Europe in the mid-15th century.

For some Cape Verdeans, racial divisions have been important, but the vast majority view their society as basically homogeneous. In Crioulo, the Creole language spoken by most Cape Verdeans, although it varies from island to island, the word *mulato* is used to describe this mixed group.

There are mulattos on all the islands, but the largest number of Africans is on São Tiago, which was an important 17th-century slave emporium, especially during the decades when the Spanish kings ruled Portugal (1580–1640). The people of Brava tend to have light complexions, in part because Azorean and Madeiran Portuguese migrated there in centuries past. For years Cape Verdeans were distributed on the socioeconomic scale according to the color of their skin. The blacker one's skin the more likely one was to be poor and underprivileged, the less likely to be able to emigrate to the United States. The situation is humorously expressed in a well-known Crioulo verse translated as follows:

> The white man dwells above the shop,
> The mulatto dwells in the shop,
> The black man dwells in a shack,
> Sancho [the monkey] dwells on a rock.
>
> The day will come when
> Mr. Trasco Lambasco [Sancho],
> His face all wrinkled,
> His tail lengthened,
> Will run the black man out of the shack,
> The black man will run the mulatto out of the shop,
> The mulatto the white man out of his dwelling,
> The white man will go to the rock, and fall off.

The Cape Verde Islands are in general very arid and are exposed to hot dry winds from the Sahara that often bring sand with them. Along with chronic drought go high mortality and constant suffering. Whether the islands were always so infertile is not known; some historians believe that the continental Portuguese in early colonial days exploited not only the inhabitants but also the land, depleting the soil by excessive cultivation of crops and use of domestic animals. As early as 1778, when long-range whaling ships from the United States began to frequent Cape Verdean waters, the men seized the opportunity to leave home in search of a better life.

LIFE IN AMERICA

Like the Azoreans, many of the Cape Verdeans eagerly filled any vacant berths, often ending up in New Bedford, Mass., where they settled, sending for the other members of their family. Here they continued to eat their *cachupa*, drink their *grogue*, sing their *mornas*, and cultivate their rich folklore.

Cape Verdeans remained in the whaling industry and also worked in specialized factories such as New Bedford's cordage plant (once known as Brava College); some became highly appreciated cooks both ashore and on local fishing vessels. Eventually the Cape Verdeans fanned out in several directions. They found employ-

ment in the cranberry bogs of southeastern Massachusetts, in Wareham, Onset, Carver, and Plymouth. Other Cape Verdeans became gardeners around Scituate, Mass., and recent arrivals from Fogo in the 1950s followed in their footsteps as laborers as well as gardeners. Still others went to work in the jewelry factories of Attleboro, Mass., on the docks of Providence, R.I., and in the Navy Yard in Brooklyn, N.Y. As early as 1906, Cape Verdeans from Brava made their way to California, where they assisted in reconstruction after the San Francisco earthquake. In turn they attracted others, who worked as farmers, dairy ranchers, gardeners, and railroad hands in Sacramento, San Francisco, Alameda, and the Napa Valley. The major concentration, however, has always been in eastern Massachusetts.

By the time the whaling era ended, Cape Verdean seamen had established regular sailing-ship service between the islands and the United States, chiefly New Bedford and Providence. The "Brava packets" even brought seasonal workers on a contract basis to the cranberry bogs. The round trip was facilitated by a relatively mild wind and current pattern: northwest from Fogo or Brava to the Gulf Stream, then north to New England, east and southeast past the Azores to the northeast trades, then south to home: 35 days to America, 45 days return, with variation in track and time according to the season.

Before immigration was severely restricted in the 1920s, Cape Verdeans entered the United States freely with other Portuguese from the Azores, the Madeiras, and the mainland; following the restrictive legislation, they had to share the limited Portuguese quota. In 1965, however, the new immigration law, which eased the way for a great many people who wanted to come to the United States, made things difficult for the Cape Verdeans. The new law provided that any immigrant born in a colony or dependent area of a foreign state was chargeable to that foreign state up to a limit of 1 percent of the maximum number of immigrant visas available to that foreign state. This restricted the Cape Verdeans to 200 visas a year, and this situation prevailed for 10 years, until the Republic of Cape Verde was established. On independence day, the United States recognized the Cape Verde Islands as a sovereign nation, and the U.S. Department of State notified the Department of Justice that the Cape Verdean quota was to be increased from 200 to 20,000.

It is virtually impossible to calculate the number of Cape Verdeans who have immigrated, for they were almost always included in the U.S. Immigration and Naturalization Service's totals for Portugal. A reasonable guess might be 10 to 20 percent of the Portuguese, or from 43,000 to 85,000 over the years 1820–1976, not including illegal immigrants.

It is equally difficult to estimate the size of the total Cape Verdean–American community, including immigrants and descendants of immigrants. The U.S. Bureau of the Census has in the past included them under its totals for Portugal or for the even more ambiguous "Other Atlantic Islands." The Department of State in its *Background Notes—Cape Verde* issued in October 1976, however, accepts the estimate of ethnic leaders that "about 300,000 persons of Cape Verdean descent live in the United States, mainly in Massachusetts, Rhode Island, and Connecticut."

Most Cape Verdeans settled originally in southeastern Massachusetts, and many became successful in business and the professions, for example, the late Alfred J. Gomes, a lawyer for whom a public school in New Bedford is now named. Some later moved from there to Greater Boston and melted into the broader society of the state's capital city. A number of these became prominent in the law and academic life, for example Fogo-born lawyers Roy F. Teixeira (1893–1978) and Antonio de J. Cardozo (1904–) and Professor Norman Araujo of the faculty of Boston College. Beginning in the 1950s, some immigrants from Cape Verde began to settle in black districts of Boston such as Roxbury, Mattapan, and Dorchester, where they tended to join forces with the Afro-American community. As more and more arrived in this area—some 10,000 to 15,000, it is believed—these new Cape Verdean Americans formed their own distinctive community. Their Catholicism tended to keep them apart from the U.S. blacks, who are largely Protestant; the Archdiocese of Boston established a special mission for them in 1970. Here, in Roxbury's St. Patrick's Church, an elegant structure in a formerly Irish neighborhood, priests from the islands who know Crioulo as well as Portuguese minister to the flock.

Cape Verdean Americans had experienced segregation by color earlier. American racist attitudes had been absorbed quickly by the other Portuguese and, although the Cape Verdeans were never formally excluded, they were never truly welcomed in the de facto Portuguese national parishes of southern New England. By 1905 the Diocese of Fall River had established a special parish for Cape Verdeans in New Bedford. Known as Our Lady of the Assumption, the parish was staffed by the Belgian Sacred Hearts Fathers. It continues to flourish in a modest but beautiful church built after World War II. As in Roxbury, the language of the service is Portuguese (or English) rather than Crioulo. After the use of the vernacular was approved by the Second Vatican Council, authorities in Lisbon insisted that the Cape Verdean vernacular had to be Portuguese, just as they had insisted that standard Portuguese be taught in the island schools. Crioulo was not to be used in either school or church.

Crioulo, although based on Portuguese, is more than a dialect; it is a separate, creolized or pidginized language like the Papiamento of the Netherlands Antilles or the Patois of St. Lucia. It manifests certain simplifications of Portuguese grammar introduced in the early contact between the dominant Portuguese traders and the exploited Africans, and it includes certain African features, such as nouns that describe the geographical milieu of the islands. Crioulo today is the everyday language of an isolated archipelago whose national and international language is and will certainly continue to be standard European Portuguese.

Language is intimately tied to national identity, however, and Cape Verdeans have been seeking their own identity for many decades. When independence came in 1975, it heightened long-standing conflicts for Cape Verdean Americans. The substantial number who were no longer content to be regarded as Portuguese demanded that their children be provided with schooling in Crioulo under the provisions of the Massachusetts Transitional Bilingual Education Act of 1971 in spite of an insufficient number of teachers and teaching materials. Classes in Crioulo were organized in New Bedford, Scituate, and Boston, and also in Brockton, Mass., where a relatively recent Cape Verdean community had sprung up. A school census for 1977–1978 revealed that in these communities Cape Verdean children of limited English-speaking ability numbered respectively 135, 80, 376, and 109. The census in addition listed 61 in Falmouth, Mass., which had no Crioulo program in 1978–1979. Harvard University's Commission on Extension Courses in the fall of 1978 for the first time offered a course in Cape Verdean Crioulo. The demand for Crioulo-English bilingual education has important political implications and typifies the strong Cape Verdean interest in education. Even under Portuguese rule in the 1960s and 1970s, 100 percent of the children in the Cape Verde Islands were said to be attending elementary school, conducted in Portuguese, not Crioulo. However, secondary education, as in continental Portugal, was limited to schools in the cities of Praia and Mindelo.

It seems likely that Crioulo will replace Portuguese as the vernacular language at Catholic services attended by a large number of Cape Verdeans. If this does not happen, many more Cape Verdeans will turn to the Protestant sects, which have long been active in the islands in translating the Gospels into Crioulo. Many revere the colorful Charles Manuel "Sweet Daddy" Grace (1881–1960), who established the House of Prayer for All People in America and, following in the footsteps of Father Divine, became a bishop and spiritual leader for a number of Cape Verdean Americans and innumerable southern blacks.

CONFLICTS WITHIN THE GROUP

In the past the Catholic Cape Verdean Americans of mixed European and African ancestry, language, and general culture—but with family and given names indistinguishable from those of Portuguese Americans—did not choose to identify with American blacks. The Cape Verdeans had not shared the American slave experience, and for the most part they followed a different religious tradition. Moreover, to have identified with blacks in a racist society would have limited their upward social and economic mobility, already threatened by their inadequate English. At the same time, although they considered themselves more or less Portuguese and aspired to join the mainstream of U.S. society, they found that the United States did not permit this option either. The American color spectrum, they quickly learned, had a very narrow white and a very broad black band, but no center band corresponding to their reality. Today the new ethnicity, with its emphasis on roots and distinct ethnic groups, is even more discouraging to those Cape Verdeans who want to assimilate to what they perceive as the mainstream of American life. Other Cape Verdeans want to be as distinct as possible, and as a result the community is badly split.

Relations with the Portuguese-American community is one issue; another is whether or not Cape Verdeans should join the black movement in the United States. Some Cape Verdeans who observed the realities of military service during World War II are inclined to feel that the community would be best served if it explicitly

joined forces with other blacks. This issue, of course, has also split the Puerto Ricans and the Cubans. Now that the Cape Verdeans have their own national identity and can claim to be a wholly distinct ethnic group, the option of joining forces with other blacks to win specific local objectives appears increasingly attractive. It brings with it certain legal and financial advantages and seems to appeal primarily to the young and native-born whose ties with the islands are tenuous.

The older and more conservative, more established Cape Verdean Americans are not interested in such adventures. They prefer to remain within the Portuguese community, even if they are a subgroup and not fully accepted. Beginning in the 1960s they tended to emphasize their cultural and, on occasion, political identity with other Portuguese Americans; however, the logic of this choice was destroyed by Cape Verdean independence in 1975.

In the late 1970s the majority of Cape Verdean Americans seem to prefer a compromise. They consider themselves Americans of Cape Verdean origin, a separate ethnic group with minority status yet without rigid identification with either blacks or Spanish-surnamed Americans. These Cape Verdeans have bilingual education programs in Massachusetts and also, in Boston, an increasingly active organization, Tchuba, the American Committee for Cape Verde, under the leadership of Raymond A. Almeida. Tchuba and its newsletter of the same name are reminders of the desperate plight of Cape Verdeans in their native islands. In Crioulo, *tchuba* means "rain," a metaphor or symbol for hope.

Although there have been ephemeral Cape Verdean-American newspapers over the years, in Portuguese and in English, members of the group have tended to read the Portuguese-American press, in the past, *Diário de Notícias*. Today the *Portuguese Times* of New Bedford, in particular, provides them with considerable information about their community in the United States and about the islands, especially Cape Verde politics. Over the past decade they have also been reading *Cape Verdean*, issued monthly primarily in English by Manuel T. Neves in Lynn, Mass., and proclaimed the only Cape Verdean newspaper in America.

Cape Verdean Americans seem hopelessly divided concerning the political direction that the Republic of Cape Verde should take, and as a result no single organization or individual can claim to speak for all of them. Indeed, they have no national or even interstate association, although local groups have long existed, for example, the Cape Verdean Ultramarine Band Club of New Bedford.

Independence for the Cape Verde Islands was won by a left-wing organization known as PAIGC, Partido Africano da Independência da Guiné e Cabo Verde (African Party for the Independence of Portuguese Guinea and the Cape Verde Islands), whose leadership was chiefly Cape Verdean. (Portuguese Guinea became independent Guinea-Bissau on September 10, 1974.) There are now two independent republics with a single dominant party. Some Cape Verdean Americans wish to see the Republic of Cape Verde totally divorced from African mainland politics and oriented toward Portugal or at least participating in a Portuguese-Atlantic commonwealth. Others prefer the African connection. Ironically, the U.S. Ambassador to Cape Verde is also accredited to, and resident at, Bissau, Guinea-Bissau.

Bibliography
Because Cape Verdeans until 1975 were legally Portuguese, information concerning them is included in studies of Portuguese Americans, for example, Leo Pap, *The Portuguese in the United States: A Bibliography* (Staten Island, N.Y., 1976), and Francis M. Rogers, *Americans of Portuguese Descent: A Lesson in Differentiation* (Beverly Hills, Calif., 1974). A basic study not listed by Pap, available only in manuscript, but widely used by students interested in Cape Verdeans in the United States is David Bruce Tyack, "Capeverdean Immigration to the United States" (senior honors thesis, Harvard University, 1952). Other useful studies are José Gonçalves, "A Presença Caboverdiana na Califórnia," in Eduardo Mayone Dias, ed., *Report: First Symposium on Portuguese Presence in California, June 8 and 9, 1974* (San Francisco and San Leandro, 1975), pp. 18–19, which discusses frankly the racial problem posed for the Cape Verdeans in the United States, and Raymond A. Almeida and Patricia Nyhan, *Cape Verde and Its People: A Short History*, pt. I (Boston, 1976), a brief synopsis with maps, photographs, and bibliography, published by the American Committee for Cape Verde.

There is valuable background information in Norman Araujo, *A Study of Cape Verdean Literature* (Chestnut Hill, Mass., 1966), originally a Harvard University doctoral dissertation, written by a New Bedford native whose parents came from São Nicolau in the Cape Verde Islands.

FRANCIS M. ROGERS

CARPATHO-RUSYNS

Most Carpatho-Rusyns in the United States stem from the group that arrived as part of the great immigration from southern and eastern Europe which took place from 1880 to 1914; today the surviving original immigrants and their descendants number over 600,000 people.

The Carpatho-Rusyns have never had their own state; they have always lived as a minority in a region ruled by one or another foreign power. Their name indicates both the geographic location of their original homeland (along the upper slopes and in the valleys of the Carpathian Mountains) and their ethnoreligious affiliation ("Rusyn" suggests both their ethnic origins and their adherence to Eastern Christianity). The term Rusyn (or Rusin) derives from the word Rus', a name applied to all Eastern Slavs in the Middle Ages before they became differentiated as Russians, Belorussians, and Ukrainians. Only in the Carpathian region did the name Rusyn persist. It remained in general use until World War II, and in some places is even used today. In both Europe and the United States the Rusyns also have been known as Rusnaks, Ruthenians, Uhro-Rusyns, Carpatho-Russians, or Carpatho-Ukrainians.

Until 1918 the Carpatho-Rusyn homeland, known as Carpatho-Ruthenia or Subcarpathian Rus', was part of the Kingdom of Hungary, which in turn was part of the Hapsburg-ruled, multinational Austro-Hungarian Empire. During the second half of the 19th century, a Rusyn national movement was initiated by a small group of leaders, most of them clergymen, but nationalism had little impact on the population as a whole. Many of the emigrants who left before 1914 did not have a clear sense of any national identity.

After the dissolution of the Hapsburg empire in late 1918, the Carpatho-Rusyns, then numbering about 460,000, were incorporated into the newly formed state of Czechoslovakia; 80 percent of them lived in the province of Carpatho-Ruthenia (Podkarpatská Rus), the remainder in northeastern Slovakia, an area popularly known as the Prešov Region. After Nazi Germany forced the breakup of Czechoslovakia in early 1939, the province of Carpatho-Ruthenia was taken over by Hungary, while the Prešov Region remained part of a semi-

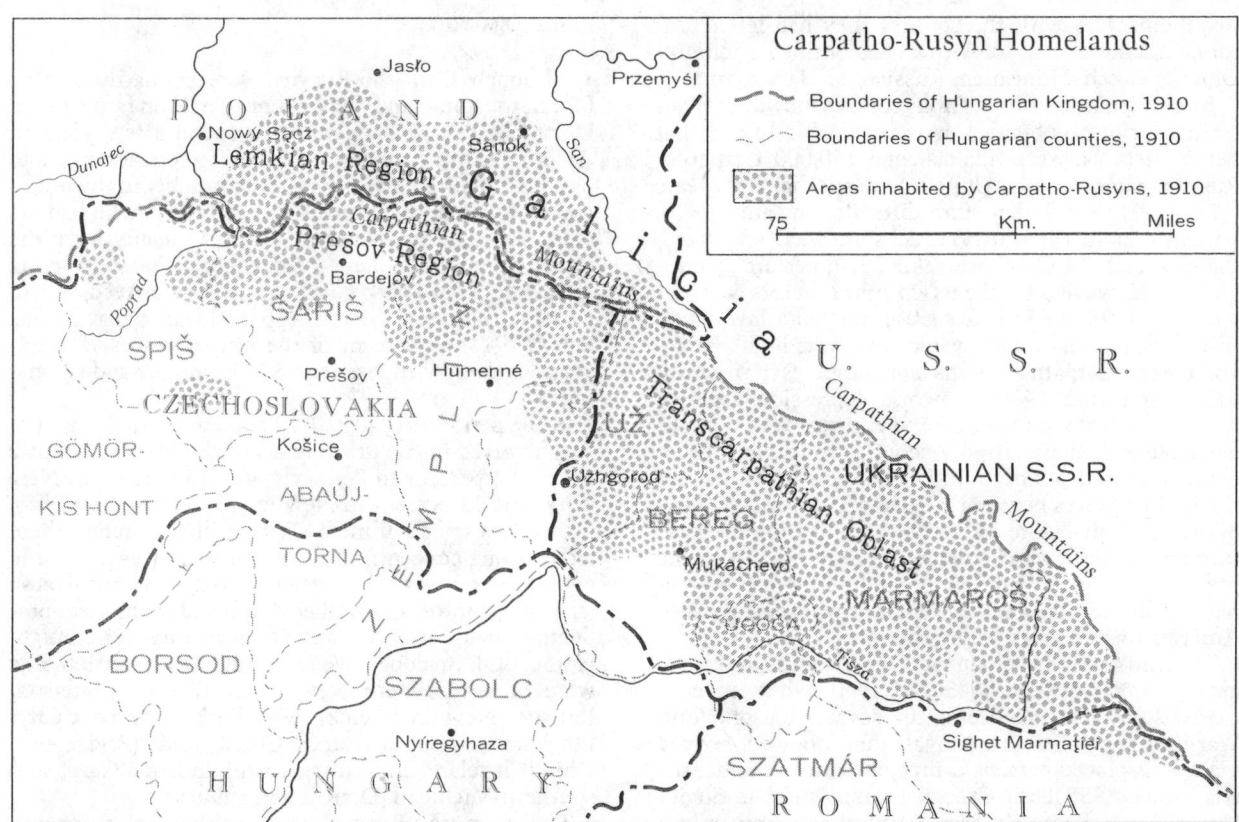

independent Slovak state. As a result of World War II, the borders of the Soviet Union expanded westward, and since 1945 Carpatho-Rusyns have been divided between two countries: former Carpatho-Ruthenia is now the Transcarpathian Oblast of the Ukrainian Soviet Socialist Republic; the Prešov Region is part of the Slovak Socialist Republic within Czechoslovakia.

Carpatho-Rusyns are an Eastern Slavic people who speak several dialects, all classified with the Ukrainian language. Since 1945 most Carpatho-Rusyns in the homeland have gradually given up their separate identity and call themselves Ukrainians, but Carpatho-Rusyn immigrants and their descendants in the United States maintain themselves as a distinct ethnic group.

MIGRATION AND ARRIVAL

At the time of the major Carpatho-Rusyn migration, the Hungarian Kingdom was basically an underdeveloped agrarian country with little industry. Carpatho-Rusyns were peasants, and the area they inhabited was one of the poorest in all Hungary. Ninety percent of them tilled small plots or were agricultural day laborers; 80 percent lived in villages of less than 2,000 inhabitants. Social and geographic mobility was virtually nil; 97 percent of the Carpatho-Rusyns in rural areas married someone of their own religion and died in their native village. The priesthood was one of the few escapes from this agrarian existence; ordination was the highest attainable goal for the bright and ambitious sons of peasants.

As is typical in traditional peasant societies, the Carpatho-Rusyns had a strong attachment to the land. Acquiring land was often an economic necessity, but it

was also a symbol of success—an attitude that persisted among immigrants to the United States, where owning one's own house and yard was and still is an important goal. It was precisely the lack of land at home, caused in part by an increase in population and in part by inefficient agricultural practices, combined with the fear of induction into the imperial army, that prompted young Carpatho-Rusyn men to emigrate during the late 19th and early 20th century. At that time, industry in the United States was expanding rapidly and needed cheap labor. Industrialists and shipowners not only welcomed immigrants, they actively sought them by sending recruiting agents to the Austro-Hungarian Empire. After the first Carpatho-Rusyns arrived and worked for a while in the United States, their letters to relatives and friends at home describing high wages (by old-country standards) prompted others to join them. Emigration continued even after the Hungarian government, facing the depopulation of some areas, imposed legal restrictions to control departures. Of all the regions in the Hungarian kingdom, those counties where Carpatho-Rusyns lived—Spiš, Šariš, Zemplin, Už, and Bereg—had the highest emigration rate.

It is difficult to determine the exact number of Carpatho-Rusyns who came to the United States, because Hungarian statistics recorded only legal departures and U.S. authorities listed immigrants only by country of origin until 1899. After that date immigrants were classified by "race or people" in addition, but it is still impossible to determine from the rubric "Ruthenian/Russniak" who came from Hungary and who from neighboring Galicia or Bukovina. Adding to the confusion, many Carpatho-Rusyn immigrants tended to iden-

tify themselves with the country they had left (Hungary, Czechoslovakia) or with a neighboring nationality (Slovak, Czech, Hungarian, Russian, or Ukrainian).

By extrapolating from various sources, however, a fair estimate can be obtained. It is reasonable to say that before 1914 between 125,000 and 150,000 Carpatho-Rusyns came to the United States. The war years (1914–1918) made departure difficult, but after 1920, when the political situation had somewhat stabilized, the new state of Czechoslovakia again permitted emigration. However, by then two other factors were at work: in 1924 the U.S. Congress enacted a law establishing a national quota system that was highly unfavorable to Carpatho-Rusyns and other eastern Europeans; and after 1930 the world depression severely reduced both the number able to emigrate and the jobs available once they arrived. According to official Czechoslovak statistics, only 7,500 Carpatho-Rusyns left for the United States between 1920 and 1938, and of these 87 percent left before 1931. The composition of these immigrants differed at least in the beginning from the pre-1914 group in that women and children predominated, joining husbands and fathers who had gone to America to find work before the war.

The most recent group of Carpatho-Rusyn immigrants came between 1945 and 1950, when an estimated 2,000 refugees fleeing the devastation of World War II or the political upheavals that followed, arrived via the displaced-persons camps of Germany and Austria. Since 1950 both Czechoslovakia and the Soviet Union have effectively barred emigration, and only a few hundred Carpatho-Rusyns have managed to reach the United States, most of them during a brief period of liberal travel policies in effect in Czechoslovakia in 1968–1969.

The only way it is possible to obtain a reasonable estimate of the number of Carpatho-Rusyns and their descendants in the United States today is to consider church membership, since even after three or four generations Carpatho-Rusyns remain members, if not always active communicants, of certain religious denominations. On the basis of the figures in Table 1, it is possible to estimate that 618,000 Carpatho-Rusyns, both foreign-born and their descendants, were living in the United States in the 1970s.

SETTLEMENT

Although Carpatho-Rusyns were primarily a rural folk in the homeland, they did not settle on farms in the United States. Most planned to spend a few years in America earning money, and then to return home and buy land. This could be done most quickly in the mines and factories of the Northeast. Even those who had decided to settle permanently did not usually have the funds to purchase land near the northeastern ports (especially New York City) where they arrived, nor to travel farther west where cheap land was still available. Before 1914, 65 percent of the Carpatho-Rusyn immigrants arrived with less than $30 in money and belongings.

In the period 1910–1920, 78 percent of the Carpatho-Rusyns lived in the urban areas of the Middle Atlantic states: 54 percent in Pennsylvania, 13 percent in New York, and 12 percent in New Jersey, followed by Ohio, Connecticut, and Illinois. Within these states, there were strong concentrations of Carpatho-Rusyns in the anthracite-mining districts of eastern Pennsylvania (around Scranton and Wilkes-Barre) and in the steel-producing areas of western Pennsylvania (Pittsburgh, Homestead, Braddock, McKeesport). Other settlements were in northeastern New Jersey (Passaic, Paterson, Rahway, New Brunswick), New York (New York City, Binghamton), southwestern Connecticut (Bridgeport), Ohio (Cleveland and Youngstown), Indiana (Gary), and southern Michigan (Detroit and suburbs).

The Carpatho-Rusyns first settled in company-owned houses and tenements near the mines or factories. When they had saved enough money they bought houses that were usually close to their job sites. The second and third generations moved away from these neighborhoods and settled in nearby suburbs, such as the northeastern New Jersey towns near New York City and in Parma, Ohio, outside Cleveland. Beginning in the 1960s some Carpatho-Rusyns, usually the elderly, began to move to scattered settlements in Florida and California. However, the majority of Carpatho-Rusyns and their organizations remain within the industrial cities of the northeastern and north-central states, as can be seen by the distribution of parishes in two of the largest Carpatho-Rusyn church organizations. Of the

Table 1. Carpatho-Rusyn church membership.

Church	Diocesan seat	Membership	Carpatho-Rusyn membership (estimate)
Byzantine Rite Catholic Metropolitan Archdiocese	Pittsburgh, Pa. Passaic, N.J. Parma, Ohio	281,000[a]	225,000
American Carpatho-Russian Orthodox Greek Catholic Church	Johnstown, Pa.	108,400[b]	105,000
Orthodox Church in America (formerly Russian Orthodox Greek Catholic Church of America—the Metropolia)	New York	1,000,000[b]	200,000
Russian Orthodox Church in the U.S.A.—the Patriarchal Exarchate	New York	50,000[b]	18,000
Other Orthodox, Roman Catholic, and Protestant denominations	—	—	70,000

Source: Official Catholic Directory for 1978 (New York, 1978); Yearbook of American and Canadian Churches (Nashville, Tenn., and New York, 1974).
a. 1978 figure.
b. 1972 figure.

296 parishes in the Byzantine Rite Catholic Church and the American Carpatho-Russian Orthodox Greek Catholic Church, 80.5 percent are located in four states: Pennsylvania (50 percent), Ohio (13.5 percent), New Jersey (11 percent), and New York (6 percent).

ECONOMIC LIFE AND SOCIAL STRUCTURE

By now at least four generations can be distinguished among Carpatho-Rusyn Americans, from survivors of the original pre-1914 immigrants through their great-grandchildren. With each generation the proportion of unskilled workers has decreased and the proportion employed as skilled or white collar workers has risen.

The Carpatho-Rusyn peasant arrived in industrial America with few skills and almost invariably had to begin as an unskilled laborer. Data are scarce but a study of the Carpatho-Rusyn community in Minneapolis (see Table 2) shows that over the generations the proportion in unskilled occupations decreased markedly and the fraction holding managerial, semiprofessional, and professional jobs increased sharply. A Minneapolis occupational profile for 1910 and 1930 also reveals marked upward mobility: in 1910, 58 percent of the Rusyns were unskilled laborers; by 1930, 67 percent had become skilled and semiskilled workers, foremen, or clerical workers. A similar study in Bridgeport in 1936, however, still reported a large majority (78 percent) in semiskilled or unskilled occupations during the depression decade.

Since the earliest years some Carpatho-Rusyns also have been small shop owners—butchers, grocers, tavernkeepers, travel and package-sending agents—but in the main they have not shown much inclination for business ownership, preferring the security of working for an established company and the opportunity to rise though the ranks.

RELIGION

Religion has always been an essential part of Carpatho-Rusyn life, both in the homeland and in the United States. In the Carpatho-Rusyn villages of eastern Europe, at least until the advent of Communist-dominated governments after 1945, the life cycle was governed by the precepts of the church. Numerous religious holidays, with their feasts and fasts, were strictly observed; baptisms, marriages, funerals, and family celebrations took place in strict accordance with the guidelines of the church. The immigrants soon set about creating a similar community in the United States. Even after three or four generations, U.S. Car-

patho-Rusyn community life and ethnic identity continue to depend in large part on the individual's relation to the church.

Carpatho-Rusyns are almost all Eastern Christians. They belong either to the Byzantine Rite Catholic Church or to one of the several Orthodox churches listed in Table 1. Those who came during the peak years of immigration (1880–1914) were Byzantine-rite, or Greek, Catholics. Since then, the group's religious history in the United States has been marked basically by two developments: the attempt to maintain the traditions of the Byzantine Slavic rite, usually in the face of an antagonistic U.S. Catholic hierarchy, or to convert to Eastern Orthodoxy whenever that proved impossible. The struggle to maintain the old religion was energetically fought, for the traditions at issue were perceived by Carpatho-Rusyns as not only essential to their religion, but symbolic of their whole historical and cultural past. (*See* Eastern Catholics; Eastern Orthodox.)

Until 1916 all Greek (Eastern-rite) Catholics in the United States, whether Carpatho-Rusyn, Ukrainian, Slovak, Hungarian, or Croat, belonged to the same church. The immigrants who came in the 1880s at first were obliged to attend Roman Catholic parishes until at their request a few Greek Catholic priests were sent from Europe. The first parishes were established in eastern Pennsylvania; during this early period the initiative for founding churches came from the immigrants themselves. Often led by a successful Carpatho-Rusyn shop or tavern owner, they would form a committee, buy a piece of land, build a church, and pay to bring a priest from the homeland. These laymen often owned the church property outright, in sharp contrast to general Catholic practice in the United States. Eventually this led to difficulties with the U.S. Catholic hierarchy.

The Roman Catholic hierarchy had jurisdiction over Greek Catholics but regarded them with suspicion. The married priesthood was an especially difficult issue. Although anathema to Latin-rite Catholics, marriage is canonically acceptable for Eastern-rite priests, both Catholic and Orthodox. Some American Catholic bishops, such as John Ireland of St. Paul, Minn., and Patrick J. Ryan of Philadelphia, simply refused to accept married priests regardless of their canonical legality. In an attempt to avoid conflict, the Vatican between 1890 and 1907 issued three decrees designed to regulate relations between the groups; more often than not they placed restrictions on the Eastern-rite churches. Carpatho-Rusyns considered the decrees insulting to both their church and their culture, and responded either by protesting to Rome or by converting to Eastern Orthodoxy.

Many of the protests included the demand for a Greek Catholic bishop. In 1907 Rome appointed the Reverend Soter Ortynsky (1866–1916) to serve as the first bishop for Greek Catholics in the United States, although he was not given full episcopal power until 1913. A new Vatican decree issued in 1914 finally guaranteed the right to worship according to the Greek Catholic rite, but this accommodation was to last barely fifteen years. Bishop Ortynsky's appointment also sharpened the already existing differences between the various ethnic groups within the Greek Catholic Church, in particular between immigrants from Galicia, many of whom began to identify themselves as Ukrainians, and those

Table 2. Occupations of Carpatho-Rusyn males in Minneapolis, 1890–1960, by generation (percentages).

Occupation	First generation	Second generation	Third generation
Unskilled	55.2	9.5	2.9
Skilled and semiskilled	34.5	57.1	35.3
Clerical and sales	10.3	16.7	8.9
Managerial, semiprofessional, and professional	0.0	16.7	52.9

Source: Alex Simirenko, *Pilgrims, Colonists, and Frontiersmen* (New York, 1964), p. 96.

from the Hungarian kingdom, led by the Carpatho-Rusyns, who opposed anything associated with Ukrainianism. Ortynsky was a Ukrainian from Galicia, so many Carpatho-Rusyns from Hungary refused to recognize him as their bishop. These conflicts continued until his death in 1916, when the Vatican established two separate administrations, one for Greek Catholic immigrants from Galicia (Ukrainians), the other for those from Hungary (Carpatho-Rusyns, Slovaks, Magyars, and Croats). In 1924 both administrations were given the status of dioceses: a Carpatho-Rusyn, the Reverend Basil Takach (1879–1948), was appointed bishop of the Pittsburgh diocese, which eventually came to be known as the Byzantine Ruthenian Rite Catholic Church. In this context Ruthenian meant Greek Catholic; besides Carpatho-Rusyns the diocese included Slovaks, Hungarians, and Croats.

At last Carpatho-Rusyns had their own Greek Catholic diocese and bishop, and their own priests conducting services according to the Eastern rite, but peace did not prevail for long. In 1929 Rome issued a new decree, *Cum data fuerit*, which called for the enforcement of celibacy and attacked the practice by which lay trustees controlled church property. The community was again aroused, and several priests and thousands of parishioners defected to Russian Orthodox parishes and eventually established a distinct Carpatho-Rusyn Orthodox church. Only since World War II has the Byzantine Rite Catholic Church been able to consolidate and prevent further large-scale defections. To strengthen its bases within the American Catholic community, it was transformed in 1969 into the Byzantine Ruthenian Metropolitan Province with its seat in Pittsburgh and sister dioceses in Passaic, N.J., and Parma, Ohio.

From the earliest days, Carpatho-Rusyn Greek Catholic immigrants have always been able to turn to the Orthodox church whenever they felt their religious or national traditions threatened. Since their rites are similar, they felt they were not abandoning their religion but rather preserving it when they joined an Orthodox community. Moreover, there was historical justification: before 1649 Carpatho-Rusyns were all Orthodox.

The first important convert to Orthodoxy was the Reverend Alexis G. Toth (1853–1909), who had been sent to the United States in 1889 to serve the Greek Catholic parish in Minneapolis. Rejected by the Roman Catholic Archbishop John Ireland because he had once been married, Toth converted to Orthodoxy and in March 1891 was accepted into the Russian Orthodox Diocese of Alaska and the Aleutian Islands, which then had its seat in San Francisco. He was sent to Pennsylvania and other places on the East Coast to convert Greek Catholic communities to the Orthodox church. By the time of his death he had made 25,000 converts, most of them Rusyn immigrants from Hungary and Galicia.

Toth's work coincided with a period of intense Russian Orthodox missionary activity in both Europe and the United States, an effort that was one aspect of the foreign policy of tsarist Russia in the three decades prior to the outbreak of World War I. The Russian government hoped to undermine the power of the Hapsburg empire by converting Greek Catholic peasants within Austria-Hungary and its emigrants in the United States

to Orthodoxy; conversion to the Russian Orthodox Church was thought to foster loyalty to the tsar and to all things Russian. The growth of the Russian Orthodox Church in the United States was directly related to this policy. As a result of its missionary activity, an estimated 250,000 Greek Catholics (Carpatho-Rusyns, Ukrainians, Belorussians) joined the Orthodox church by 1914. In 1903 the seat of the diocese was transferred from San Francisco to New York, and in 1924 it was renamed the Russian Orthodox Greek Catholic Church in America. Since 1970 it has been part of the Orthodox Church of America.

Those Carpatho-Rusyns who converted, however, still tried to obtain their own bishops and administrative autonomy. In 1916 a Carpatho-Russian eparchy was set up within the Russian Orthodox Greek Catholic Church and at various times it was administered by Bishop Stefan Dzubay (1857–1933), Bishop Adam Philippovsky (1881–1956), and the Reverend Andrew Slepecky (1894–1976); but this administration was never transformed into a self-governing diocese. Later defectors from Greek Catholicism, realizing that conversion to Russian Orthodoxy would mean subordination to a larger church dominated by Russians, decided instead to establish their own Orthodox church. As a result of the Vatican's *Cum data fuerit* decree of 1929, which enforced celibacy and reinstated episcopal ownership of church property, a group of Greek Catholic priests led by Orestes Chornock (1883–1977) established an independent American Carpatho-Russian Orthodox Greek Catholic Church (f. 1937) in Bridgeport, Conn. This church, whose seat is now in Johnstown, Pa., remains the only church in which the members are almost exclusively of Carpatho-Rusyn extraction.

Despite these bewildering conflicts, the churches, whether Byzantine Rite Catholic or Eastern Orthodox, have remained at the center of Carpatho-Rusyn immigrant life. The church was usually the first public edifice to be built in early immigrant settlements; it was there that wedding parties, dances, and cultural and social events were held, and the first schools and reading rooms housed. Churches still sponsor activities of this sort. Even if many third- and fourth-generation descendants of Carpatho-Rusyn immigrants are unsure of their ethnic identity, they preserve the heritage of their ancestors by some church-related activity, whether it be participation in processions, attendance at Christmas or Easter services, or the preparation of family recipes on religious holidays.

Nonetheless, the church itself has not always made the most of its opportunity to preserve the integrity of the Carpatho-Rusyn community. Although the large majority of those who left the Byzantine Rite Catholic Church were not lost to the Eastern rite when they adopted Orthodoxy, they often began to think of themselves as Russians rather than Rusyns. Moreover, some Rusyns became Roman Catholics, especially during the early years when there were not very many Orthodox or Byzantine Rite Catholic churches. A few Carpatho-Rusyns even joined Baptist or other fundamentalist Bible-reading communities. The often protracted controversies among the various factions have also caused dissension within the community and sometimes even within families; during the 1930s and

1940s disputes over who owned the church's property often ended up in court. This embarrassed and alienated many young people especially.

The churches have always been committed to preserving their rights and traditions, but these have not always coincided with the idea of a Carpatho-Rusyn cultural identity. All the bishops and other leaders of the Byzantine Rite Catholic Church have been of Carpatho-Rusyn background, but they try to avoid alienating the other groups in the church like the Hungarians and especially the Slovaks. At least until World War II the Byzantine-rite church had an influential Hungarian faction which generally scorned Slavic culture. Then during the 1950s and early 1960s the church underwent an Americanization process which entailed a greater use of English and reduced the distinctions between it and the Roman Catholic Church. Only since the American Bicentennial and the recent ethnic revival has the Byzantine Rite Catholic Church under Metropolitan Stephen J. Kocisko (1915–) cautiously initiated a policy of emphasizing the Carpatho-Rusyn origins of the church and most of its members. The restitution of iconostases (icon screens), many of which were removed during the 1950s, is an example of this reversion to Eastern-rite tradition.

The Orthodox reaction to Carpatho-Rusyn identity has been mixed. Many of those who joined the Russian Orthodox Church before 1914 were lost to the community. The Russian-dominated hierarchy viewed Carpatho-Rusyn language and culture as suitable only for peasants and encouraged the Rusyns to regard themselves as Russians. From time to time, token gestures were made to appoint Carpatho-Rusyn administrators but they had little practical effect. Still, within the Orthodox family there remains one full-fledged ethnic church, the American Carpatho-Russian Orthodox Greek Catholic Church, and it continues to instill in its young priests and parishioners some awareness that they are the bearers of a distinct Carpatho-Rusyn culture.

SOCIAL ORGANIZATION

Aside from the church, the most important organizations among Carpatho-Rusyn immigrants have been fraternal societies and brotherhoods. In a foreign land where most immigrant workers had no resources to fall back on in case of accidents or mishaps, the fraternal organizations provided a minimal, but nonetheless important, source of financial help. They also published newspapers, organized youth and athletic clubs, and sponsored social gatherings, all of which provided some modicum of psychological security and sociability during the few leisure hours available. The fraternal societies also saw themselves as defenders of Carpatho-Rusyn culture and religion; they played an active and aggressive role whenever they thought the group's interests were being threatened.

Each faction of the community, whether religious, political, or regional, has had its own fraternal society. They began as local lodges, but later united into national organizations. The oldest and still the largest of these is the Sojedinenije Greko-Kaftoličeskich Russkich Bratstv (Greek Catholic Union of Rusyn Brotherhoods), founded in Wilkes-Barre, Pa., in 1892. At its

height in 1928, the Greek Catholic Union had 120,000 members in 1,328 lodges. By 1977 it claimed 50,000 members in 1,093 lodges.

In addition to providing insurance coverage, the Greek Catholic Union had as its original goal the achievement of unity among the majority of "Greek Catholics who speak Rusyn," as well as the encouragement of education, the construction of churches and schools, and the protection of widows, orphans, and the indigent. The society was perhaps least successful in its effort to maintain unity. Through its influential weekly newspaper, the *Amerikansky Russky Viestnik*, later the *Greek Catholic Union Messenger* (first published in 1892 in Mahoney City, then successively in Scranton, New York City, Pittsburgh, and Homestead, Pa.), its editors and columnists, among them Pavel J. Žatkovich (1852–1916), Peter I. Zeedick (1891–1970), Adalbert M. Smor, and the Reverend Stephen Varzaly (1880–1957), spoke out against what they saw as threats to the survival of the Carpatho-Rusyn community. Until the late 1930s the Greek Catholic Union was almost invariably opposed to the policies of the Greek Catholic Church: it opposed the appointment of Ukrainian Bishop Soter Ortynsky and continued to attack him between 1907 and 1916, and it led the struggle for the married clergy during the 1930s when it established a Committee for the Defense of Our Faith (1932), which proposed secession from the Catholic church. These developments resulted in friction between members of the Greek Catholic Union and the Byzantine Rite Catholic Church it ostensibly served.

The Greek Catholic Union has been more successful in achieving some of its other goals. It has helped to build several churches and contributed to the construction and maintenance of both the St. Nicholas Orphanage at Elmhurst, Pa. (1922–1955), and the Byzantine Ruthenian Rite Catholic Seminary of SS. Cyril and Methodius, which opened in 1951 in Pittsburgh. It also sponsors youth and athletic groups.

Other Carpatho-Rusyn fraternal societies grew out of the ideological, regional, or personal rivalries that arose within the Greek Catholic Union. In 1903 members who felt the attacks on the Greek Catholic hierarchy to be unwarranted founded the United Societies of the Greek Catholic Religion in McKeesport, Pa. Those who joined the Orthodox church formed the Greek Catholic (later United) Russian Orthodox Brotherhood (UROBA) in Monessen, Pa., in 1915. Unhappy with the disproportionate number of benefits being paid to Greek Catholic Union lodge members who lived in Pennsylvania, a group in New York and New Jersey founded the Greek Catholic Carpatho-Russian Benevolent Association Liberty in Perth Amboy, N.J., in 1915. Later this organization supported the American Carpatho-Russian Orthodox Greek Catholic Church in Bridgeport, Conn. (now in Johnstown, Pa.). All these organizations, as well as a few minor ones, published their own newspapers and almanacs and organized youth groups and social affairs. None ever rivaled the influence of the Greek Catholic Union, however, and since World War II their function has been reduced primarily to the payment of insurance benefits to their ever-decreasing membership.

The Carpatho-Rusyn community also founded a few

cultural organizations. One of the earliest was the Rusin Elite Society, established in 1927 in Cleveland, Ohio, at the initiative of the Reverend Joseph Hanulya (1874–1962). The society set up ten branches in Ohio and western Pennsylvania, published an English- and Rusyn-language monthly, *Vožd/The Leader* (Cleveland, 1929–1930), and sponsored a Rusyn exhibition at Cleveland's All Nations Exhibition in 1928.

After World War II, older Greek Catholic immigrants founded the Bishop Basil Takach Carpatho-Russian Society, which published a few books about the homeland. More recent immigrants with a Ukrainian national orientation established the Carpathian Alliance and the Carpathian Research Center in New York City. Both groups publish periodicals and books and sponsor conferences dealing with the history and culture of Carpatho-Ruthenia, but because of their Ukrainian orientation they have had little, if any, impact on the majority of Carpatho-Rusyn Americans.

The Carpatho-Rusyn community also has established some youth organizations. The most important of these is the Sokol (f. 1910), an athletic organization sponsored by the Greek Catholic Union which supports baseball, volleyball, and basketball teams. For a time the Sokol had its own Rusyn-language newspaper, *Amerikansky Russky Sokol* (Homestead, Pa., 1917–1936), almanac, and journal for its youth branches, *Svit ditej/Children's World* (Homestead, 1917–1936). Other Carpatho-Rusyn fraternal societies also sponsored youth branches; the American Carpatho-Russian Orthodox Greek Catholic Church has fostered the American Carpatho-Russian Youth Association since 1937. Since 1976 several song and dance ensembles have been founded by young people—Slavjane (McKeesport, Pa.), Krajane (Dayton, Ohio), Karpaty (Ambridge, Pa.), Rusyny (McKeesport, Pa.), and the Carpathian Regional Culture Dancers (Monessen, Pa.).

CULTURE

In the mind of most immigrants, Carpatho-Rusyn culture is synonymous with the Eastern-rite liturgy and the attendant rituals and festive traditions associated with the church calendar. Church music is particularly important. In the homeland Carpatho-Rusyns had developed a form of liturgical plain chant, called *prostopinie*, which was distinguished from other Eastern-rite liturgical music by its liberal use of local folk melodies. Church choirs in the United States continue to maintain this Carpatho-Rusyn musical tradition in the church and in concert. Among the larger choral groups still in existence are the Byzantine Rite Catholic Metropolitan choirs of Philadelphia and New York.

Carpatho-Rusyn churches also reflect homeland models. Their gold onion domes and three-barred "Russian" crosses made Carpatho-Rusyn churches distinctive landmarks in many industrial urban centers of the eastern United States; inside, the iconostases remind the community of its Byzantine artistic heritage. In recent years churches have more often been constructed in a bland functional style although the Byzantine Rite Catholic Church of St. Mary in Manhattan (completed 1963) is a striking exception. It combines the functionalism of the international school with motifs from the Carpatho-Rusyn Eastern-rite heritage.

Language is an important tool for maintaining Carpatho-Rusyn culture. Members of the community describe their speech in a variety of ways: Rusyn (*rus'kyi*), which in English is often incorrectly rendered "Russian," Carpatho-Russian, Slavish (a meaningless designation) or *ponashemu,* the most frequently used term, which means simply "in our own manner." Linguists classify Carpatho-Rusyn dialects as belonging to the Ukrainian language, but, because the Rusyns lived along the extreme western boundaries of the Ukrainian linguistic area, their speech has a strong admixture of Slovak and Hungarian and as a result differs markedly from standard Ukrainian. In the United States, spoken Carpatho-Rusyn has acquired many Anglicisms in both syntax and lexicon.

Carpatho-Rusyn speech is by now the preserve of the few original immigrants who still survive, and even they often prefer to use broken English instead of their mother tongue. Their middle-aged children may understand Carpatho-Rusyn but are able to speak very little. Third- and fourth-generation descendants rarely know any Rusyn at all.

Few formal means have been available to preserve the language. During the 1940s and 1950s, radio stations in cities like New York, Pittsburgh, and Cleveland offered short programs in Carpatho-Rusyn and the churches gave brief sermons in the language until the 1940s (the liturgy was sung in Old Church Slavonic, a classical language that functioned as Latin did until recently in the Roman Catholic Church). Since World War II, English has become the only language except in a few services where Old Slavonic may still be used for the liturgy.

Until the 1940s many church schools offered some instruction in Carpatho-Rusyn, but there were never adequate textbooks. Since the 1950s the Byzantine Rite Catholic Seminary in Pittsburgh and the Carpatho-Russian Orthodox Greek Catholic Seminary in Johnstown, Pa., have offered instruction in Carpatho-Rusyn, but it has been largely ineffectual because of the lack of suitable texts and the restricted functional use of the language outside the classroom. A more serious attempt to teach Carpatho-Rusyn was a course offered at Duquesne University in Pittsburgh from 1975 to 1977.

In the past, the press was probably the most effective medium for preserving the language, because each fraternal or church member automatically received the newspaper and almanacs of his organization. But even here difficulties arose over the form of written language to be used, a problem that had prevailed in the European homeland as well. Some publications were printed in Carpatho-Rusyn vernacular (using the nonstandardized forms of the individual writers and editors), others in a peculiar variation of Russian with numerous local Carpatho-Rusyn (and English) additions. Examples of these languages are found in the daily newspaper *Den'* (New York, 1922–1927) and the weeklies *Prosvita* (McKeesport, f. 1917), *Russky viestnik* (Pittsburgh, f. 1916), and *Vostok* (Perth Amboy, 1920–1950). The immigrants who arrived after World War II printed periodicals either in standard Ukrainian (*Karpats'ka zoria* [New York, 1951–1953] and *Visnyk* [New York, 1970–1972]) or in standard Russian (*Svobodnoe slovo Karpatskoi Rusi* [Newark, N.J., f. 1959]).

The early Carpatho-Rusyn publications were printed

in the Cyrillic alphabet, but by the 1930s most had adopted a Latin alphabet basing the system of transliteration on Slovak orthography. Since the 1950s, almost all newspapers that serve the community have been printed in English; only a few, such as the *Greek Catholic Union Messenger* and the Carpatho-Russian Orthodox Greek Catholic *Church Messenger* (Pemberton, N.J., f. 1947) still reserve a few pages for a version of the native language.

The Carpatho-Rusyn immigration has produced some literature. Plays and poetry have been the most popular genres. Short plays describing village life in Europe or the United States were particularly popular because they provided a repertory for the adult and children's dramatic circles that functioned in most local parishes and fraternal lodges before World War II. The most talented and prolific author was the Reverend Emilij A. Kubek (1859–1940), who published short stories, poems, and a three-volume novel, *Marko Šoltys* (1923), treating the Carpatho-Rusyn immigration. The Reverend Sebastian Sabol (1909–), who used the pen name Zoreslav, had been a well-known poet in the homeland; he continued to publish poems and to contribute to several Ukrainian-language periodicals after his arrival in the United States in 1950.

Others like the Reverend Sigmund Brinsky (1881–1932), the Reverend Orestes Koman (1894–), the Reverend Ivan A. Ladižinsky (1905–1976), Peter J. Maczkov (1880–1965), the Reverend Jurion Thegze (1883–1962), and the Reverend Stefan Varzaly (1890–1957), have produced patriotic, religious, and sentimental books of limited literary value. Most Rusyn-American literature has appeared in newspapers, almanacs, or in the short-lived literary monthly *Niva* (Homestead, 1911–1912).

Several publishing houses were available to put out this literature. Until the 1950s, the Greek Catholic Union Typography (Homestead), Vostok Publishing Co. (Perth Amboy), and George Sabo, a book dealer and publisher formerly based in Nyack, N.Y., accounted for most of it. More recently, scholarly and popular books dealing with Carpatho-Rusyn culture are published and distributed by the Byzantine Seminary Press (Pittsburgh), Transworld Publishers (Englewood, N.J.), and the Carpatho-Rusyn Research Center (Fairview, N.J.), which also puts out a quarterly, the *Carpatho-Rusyn American* (f. 1978).

POLITICS AND INTERGROUP RELATIONS

Carpatho-Rusyns have for the most part avoided participation in American politics. At first many of the early immigrants thought they were in the United States only temporarily, and in any case they did not have the time, interest, linguistic skills, or political experience necessary to get involved in "American" matters. Even when it was clear that they would remain, their experience with politics in the homeland, where the fate of Carpatho-Rusyns was usually decided by foreign governments, had left them with a pessimistic view of how much influence they could have on the political process. Although their newspapers and almanacs frequently featured stories about American heroes like Washington and Lincoln, this did not seem to have much patriotic effect. An attempt was made to organize a Carpatho-Russian Club within the Democratic party,

but the group has never had any real influence, and no politician has ever had cause to refer to the Carpatho-Rusyn vote. Only in the 1970s were some state officials of Rusyn origin elected in Pennsylvania.

To most Carpatho-Rusyn immigrants, politics usually means the debates and controversies that surround national identity and relations with other ethnic groups, especially the Ukrainians and Slovaks, and to a lesser degree, the Russians and Hungarians. Until the early 1920s Carpatho-Rusyn organizations identified themselves as representing a distinct nationality and culture known as Uhro-Rusyn, or Rusyn. They did this after having established religious and lay organizations separate from those of the Ukrainian and Russophile immigrants from Galicia, and after having rid their own organizations of pro-Hungarian sympathizers. By the 1930s, however, many spokesmen began to call the group "Carpatho-Russian" in an attempt to associate it with Russian culture. This trend resulted largely from the incorrect translation of *Rusyn* as *Russian*. Those Carpatho-Rusyns who tried found it difficult or impossible to speak or write in Russian, while for its part, the Russian immigrant community usually ignored the Carpatho-Rusyns. Because Ukrainian and Slovak immigrants generally refuse to recognize Carpatho-Rusyns in the United States as a separate ethnic group, but call them Transcarpathian Ukrainians or Byzantine-rite Catholic Slovaks, friction often arises with these groups as well.

Carpatho-Rusyn immigrants have been able to play an influential and sometimes decisive role in the history of their homeland. Toward the end of World War I, realizing that the collapse of the Hapsburg empire was imminent, immigrant leaders formed several political organizations in an effort to organize a national movement. These were the League for the Liberation of Carpatho-Russia in New York City (July 1917), the American Russian National Defense in Pittsburgh, and the American National Council of Uhro-Rusyns in Homestead (July 1918). The basic question they all faced was what the political future of the homeland was to be. Did they want to form an independent state, to become an autonomous province of some other country, or to remain united with Hungary? Gregory I. Zsatkovich (1886–1967), acting as spokesman for the Homestead National Council, met with President Wilson and the Czech leader Tomáš Masaryk in October 1918 and reached an agreement stipulating that the Carpatho-Rusyns were to join the new state of Czechoslovakia as an autonomous province. A plebiscite was held among Carpatho-Rusyn immigrants in the United States in November 1918 and the positive American decision was greeted favorably by leaders in the homeland in May 1919. An agreement was pushed through the Paris Peace Conference (September 1919) by Czechoslovak statesmen, and the new Czechoslovak government appointed Zsatkovich to serve as the first governor of Carpatho-Ruthenia (Podkarpatská Rus) in April 1920.

Zsatkovich lasted less than a year in office. He resigned in protest when the Czechoslovak government refused to grant the autonomous status that had been promised the Carpatho-Rusyns by the Paris agreement. Carpatho-Rusyn immigrant organizations, including the Pittsburgh-based Rusyn Council for National Defense (f. 1922), led by Michael Yuhasz, Sr., and the Car-

patho-Russian Union (f. 1933), led by Aleksei Gerovsky (d. 1972), joined in the protest. Later, a few Carpatho-Rusyns led by the Reverend Emil Nevytsky (1878–1940) joined with Ukrainian immigrants to establish the Committee for the Defense of Carpatho-Ukraine; it raised money to support the pro-Ukrainian autonomous government during its few months of autonomy (October 1938–March 1939). After the Hungarians seized the province in early 1939, Zsatkovich and the Reverend Ivan A. Ladižinsky founded the American Carpatho-Russian Central Conference (1942). Reversing the previous stance of many of its members, this group came out in support of a Czechoslovakia that would again include an autonomous Carpatho-Ruthenia. When the Soviet Union annexed the province in 1945, a newly founded American Carpathian Russian Congress sent protests to the U.S. Department of State, while the Council of Free Podkarpatsky Rusins, set up in 1950 by Ladislav Fedinec (1890–), joined with other Czechoslovak émigré groups in protesting the Soviet presence. But none of these groups had any effect; aware of their inability to influence European developments they have largely abandoned their activity in the past two decades.

More significant has been the economic impact of the Rusyn-American community on Carpatho-Ruthenia. Between 1919 and 1938 immigrant workers sent thousands of dollars in cash and goods back to the homeland, money that had a perceptible impact on the welfare of Rusyn families in Europe; the immigrants were largely responsible for financing the Subcarpathian Bank (1920–1933) which operated in Uzhgorod, the administrative center of Carpatho-Ruthenia. After World War II, Americans could no longer send aid to Soviet-held territory, but food, medicine, and clothing distributed mainly by the United Nations Relief and Recovery Administration (UNRRA) reached Carpatho-Rusyns living in the Prešov Region of northeastern Slovakia. Some U.S. money is still going to Carpatho-Rusyn villages in Czechoslovakia in the form of social-security benefits paid to the widows of immigrants. These funds have given eastern Slovakia something of a reputation for affluence.

ETHNIC COMMITMENT AND GROUP MAINTENANCE

The majority of third- and fourth-generation descendants of Rusyn immigrants have little or no idea of their heritage and even less of an entity called Carpatho-Ruthenia. Very few know the language. Those children who did learn some Rusyn were told that they spoke "soft Russian" (as opposed to the "hard" or standard Russian) or Slavish, linguistically meaningless terms that led them to believe they were speaking Russian. As a result, younger Carpatho-Rusyn Americans, who now attend college in greater numbers, are often puzzled when language teachers refer ironically to the few dialectal words they may remember from home as "kitchen Russian." Even after the boom in area-studies programs in the 1960s, most U.S. colleges did not offer instruction in any Slavic language other than Russian, let alone provide even a rudimentary approach to Carpatho-Rusyn language and culture.

The young people also do not have a nation-state for reference. Carpatho-Ruthenia does not exist on any map, nor has much been written about it in English until very recently. Some older people also have experienced a sense of loss: those who visited the homeland in the 1970s returned home complaining that they could no longer understand the language—the younger generation now speak either Slovak (in Czechoslovakia) or Ukrainian (in the Transcarpathian Oblast). And in the United States their sense of identity is often restricted to their church affiliation or their association with other groups that do have a recognizable political referent, such as Russia, Slovakia, or sometimes the Ukraine. Their confusion, and sometimes embarrassment, often results in an inclination to call themselves almost anything but Carpatho-Rusyn, which until recently has not been perceived as a positive term.

In the 1930s the Byzantine Rite Catholic Church dropped the designation Greek Catholic and tried to de-emphasize Rusyn/Ruthenian or any other national name in an effort to end the quarrels among its members and to avoid alienating any further the Hungarians, Croats, and especially Slovaks among them who had come more and more to resent the name Ruthenian. By the 1950s, the Pittsburgh Metropolitanate generally referred to its communicants as "Byzantines," and in most of its church publications, at both the diocesan and the parish level, avoided any ethnic designations at all. This trend has been reversed in some ways recently. The current enthusiasm for roots has prompted the Byzantine Rite Catholic Church to revive an interest in its ethnic origins. It has established heritage museums in the Pittsburgh and Passaic dioceses, funded a project at the University of Minnesota for preserving the community's newspapers and journals, subsidized several major publications dealing with Carpatho-Rusyn culture, and supported several folk ensembles, most especially in the Pittsburgh area. It is doing more along these lines than the Greek Catholic Union, which has always prided itself on its role as preserver of the Carpatho-Rusyn ethnic heritage.

The traditional mechanisms that maintain ethnic awareness—newspapers, elementary schools, dramatic clubs, choirs, religious processions, and traditional social gatherings—either have disappeared altogether or have had their Carpatho-Rusyn content so diminished as to be meaningless. As a result of the ethnic revival of the mid-1970s, several folk ensembles, a few Carpatho-Rusyn language texts, a quarterly newsletter, and books on history and culture have appeared, but it is still too early to determine what effect, if any, they will have.

LEMKIANS

The Lemkians are a group of Carpatho-Rusyns who have developed their own organizational structure in the United States. Their name derives from Lemko, a term used to describe the westernmost group of Carpatho-Rusyn dialects, spoken in the territories located both north and south of the Carpathian Mountains, in what is today southeastern Poland or Lemkovshchyna (the Lemkian Region) and northeastern Slovakia (the Prešov Region). However, only people from the northern, Polish, side of the mountains call themselves Lemkian, and most members of Lemkian organizations in the United States have their origins in that area.

Lemkian immigrants share many characteristics

with other Carpatho-Rusyns; the majority of them also came in the period from the 1880s to 1914. They came from the mountainous regions of the then Austrian province of Galicia, in particular the districts of Nowy Sącz, Grybów, Gorlice, Jasło, Krosno, Sanok, and Lesko. Galicia had been part of Poland since the Middle Ages; in 1772 it was incorporated into the Austrian half of the Hapsburg empire. After 1919 the Lemkian territory was once again made part of Poland and, with the exception of the World War II years (1939–1945), has remained under Polish domination. Although most Lemkian immigrants were Greek Catholics upon arrival in the United States, by the early 1920s about half had converted to Orthodoxy. The remaining Greek Catholic adherents were placed under the jurisdiction of the Ukrainian Catholic administration (1916) and diocese (1924).

Some Lemkians joined Carpatho-Rusyn fraternal societies, others joined those founded by Russophile immigrants from Galicia. But they soon felt the need for their own organization, and in 1931 a group met in Cleveland to establish the Lemko Association. Its headquarters were later moved to Yonkers, N.Y., where in 1939 a large center for social and cultural activities was opened. It remains the largest of the Lemkian organizations, claiming 1,500 members in 1977. Since 1959 it has operated a resort in upstate New York called Lemko Park, with hotel facilities, a small museum, and an amphitheater that hosts a folk festival each summer.

For Lemkian immigrants, politics most often means debating the problem of national identity and trying to influence developments in the homeland. Its two main factions are the Russophiles, who regard Lemkians and all other Carpatho-Rusyns as Russians, and a smaller number of Ukrainophiles, who regard them as Ukrainians. These different orientations determine attitudes toward political developments in the homeland.

Toward the end of World War I, the Russophile organizations, such as the New York–based League for the Liberation of Carpatho-Russia, petitioned the U.S. government and its allies to have the Lemkian territory in Galicia joined with the Rusyns south of the Carpathians to form a unified province of Carpatho-Ruthenia (Karpatskaia Rus') within the new state of Czechoslovakia, but they were unsuccessful. By the 1930s, the Russophile Lemkian Association had become pro-Soviet, and in 1939 its members formed a Carpatho-Russian National Committee in New York which called for the unification of all Carpatho-Rusyn territory (parts of which were then ruled by Poland, Slovakia, and Hungary) and its incorporation into Soviet Russia. But it was only after World War II that the influence of Lemkian-American immigrants was felt in the homeland. Between 1946 and 1947 the Communist-dominated Polish government deported Lemkians from their villages, sending about 80 percent to the Soviet Ukraine and resettling the remainder in former German territories that had been annexed to Poland. A Lemko Relief Committee was organized in 1946; led by the wealthy Bridgeport, Conn., industrialist, Peter S. Hardy (1897–), it collected funds to help them. In 1957, Hardy signed an agreement with the Polish government in Warsaw allowing for money, food, and clothing to be sent to displaced Lemkians throughout Poland who wanted to return to their native villages.

The pro-Russian and pro-Soviet attitudes of the Russophile Lemkians prompted a smaller group of Ukrainophiles to found an Organization for the Defense of the Lemkian Land, to oppose the Polish government's policy during the 1930s of separating Lemkians from Ukrainians. The organization, founded in Philadelphia in 1936, was reorganized in Yonkers in 1958 by new Ukrainophile immigrants who protested the postwar deportations, the destruction of the Greek Catholic Church, and the Communist regime in Poland.

Lemkian immigrants have sponsored various cultural endeavors. In contrast to other Carpatho-Rusyn groups, the Lemkian press still publishes in some variety of the native language: either the local vernacular, as in the Lemkian Association's Lemko (Cleveland and New York, 1930–1938) and Karpatska Rus' (Yonkers, f. 1938); or standard Ukrainian, as in the organs of the Organization for the Defense of the Lemkian Land, Lemkivs'kyi dzvin (New York, 1936–1940) and Lemkivs'ki visti (New York and Toronto, f. 1958). They have also published histories of the homeland, almanacs, and language textbooks. In recent years ignorance of the language among descendants of earlier immigrants has forced the Lemko Association to issue English-language periodicals: the Lemko Youth Journal (Yonkers, 1960–1964) and the Carpatho-Russian American (Yonkers, 1968–1969). In 1973 a group of post–World War II Ukrainophile Lemkians founded a World Lemkos Federation which publishes the Annals, an annual scholarly journal in Ukrainian, English, and Polish (Camillus, N.Y., f. 1974). Lemkian writers have propagated the homeland culture through publication of histories, language texts, and short plays for amateur drama groups. Among the more prolific are the Reverend Ioann Borukh (1877–1961), Ivan F. Lemkin, Simeon Pysh (1894–1957), Stefan F. Telep (1882–1965), and Dmitrii Vislocky (1888–1968).

Bibliography
There is no general history of Carpatho-Rusyns in the United States. A survey by Walter C. Warzeski, *Byzantine Rite Rusins in Carpatho-Ruthenia and America* (Pittsburgh, Pa., 1971), and an excellent essay by Stephen C. Gulovich, "The Rusin Exarchate in the United States," *Eastern Churches Quarterly* 6 (1946): 459–485, deal primarily with the Byzantine Catholic community. The period before 1914 is best described in Iuliian Bachyns'kyi, *Ukraïns'ka immigratsiia v Z"iedynenykh Derzhavakh Ameryky* (Lvov, 1914), although Bachyns'kyi continually blames Carpatho-Rusyns for their anti-Ukrainian separatism. A valuable discussion with bibliographical and biographical data can be found in Richard Renoff and Stephen Reynolds, eds., *Proceedings of the Conference on Carpatho-Ruthenian Immigration, 8 June 1974* (Cambridge, Mass., 1975). The most comprehensive analysis of the Old World background and the immigrant role in European politics is Paul R. Magocsi, *The Shaping of a National Identity: Subcarpathian Rus', 1848–1948* (Cambridge, Mass., 1978).

The community's religious development has been the focus of attention in several works. On the Greek Catholic Church, see Athanasius Pekar, *Our Past and Present: Historical Outlines of the Byzantine Ruthenian Metropolitan Province* (Pittsburgh, 1974), and Bohdan P. Procko, "The Establishment of the Ruthenian Church in the United States, 1884–1907," *Pennsylvania History* 42 (1975): 137–154.

The only socioeconomic analyses are the general essay by Richard Renoff, "Carpatho-Ruthenian Resources and Assimilation, 1880–1924," *Review Journal of Philosophy and Social Science* 3 (Meerut, India, 1977): 53–78; and a case study of the Minneapolis community by Alex Simirenko, *Pilgrims, Colonists, and Frontiersmen: An Ethnic Community in Transition* (New York, 1964). General surveys of individual communities include Walter C. Warzeski, "The Rusin Community in Pennsylvania," in *The Ethnic Experience in Pennsylvania*, ed. John Bodnar (Lewisburg, Pa., 1973); and Paul R. Magocsi, "Immigrants from Eastern Europe: The Carpatho-Rusyn Community of Proctor, Ver-

mont," *Vermont History* 42 (1974): 48–52. The only discussion of cultural activity is found in Paul R. Magocsi, "Rusyn-American Ethnic Literature," in *Ethnic Literatures since 1776: The Many Voices of America,* vol. 2 (Lubbock, Tex., 1978).

The best repository of materials for the study of Carpatho-Rusyn immigrants is the Immigration History Research Center at the University of Minnesota, which holds microfilm copies of more than 60 immigrant newspapers and journals. Other important collections are at the library of the Holy Trinity Monastery, Butler, Pa.; the Byzantine Metropolitan Heritage Museum, Munhall, Pa.; and Harvard University.

PAUL ROBERT MAGOCSI

CASTILIANS: *see* SPANIARDS

CATALANS: *see* SPANIARDS

CATAWBAS: *see* AMERICAN INDIANS

CAUCASIANS: *see* NORTH CAUCASIANS

CAYUGAS: *see* AMERICAN INDIANS

CAYUSES: *see* AMERICAN INDIANS

CEBUANOS: *see* FILIPINOS

CELTS: *see* CORNISH; IRISH; MANX; SCOTCH-IRISH; SCOTS; WELSH

CENTRAL AND SOUTH AMERICANS

More than one million immigrants from Central and South America have settled in the United States since 1820, but their role in the development of American society remains uncharted. The U.S. Census Bureau did not tabulate separate statistics for individual Central and South American nations until 1960; in most discussions, they are not considered apart from other Spanish-surnamed people, although they are not at all a homogeneous group. They represent a variety of national and ethnic groups and number now more than 800,000 people from 18 different countries. Some speak languages other than Spanish. They have come from Costa Rica, El Salvador, Guatemala, Honduras, Nicaragua, and Panama in Central America; and from Argentina, Bolivia, Brazil (Portuguese-speaking), Chile, Colombia, Ecuador, French Guiana (French-speaking), Paraguay, Peru, Surinam (Dutch-speaking), Uruguay, and Venezuela in South America. Immigrants from Belize (formerly British Honduras) and Guyana (formerly British Guiana) are considered British West Indians. (*See* West Indians.)

In 1976 the U.S. Census Bureau estimated that Central and South Americans from Spanish-speaking countries accounted for 7 percent of the Spanish-origin population in the United States. Colombians and Ecuadorians are among the fastest-growing Hispanic groups in the United States, but it is not possible to estimate their numbers accurately, because some migrate repeatedly between the United States and their country of origin, and an unknown number are undocumented or illegal aliens. (See Table 1.)

Until 1960 the characteristics of the individual national groups were buried in aggregated immigration and census statistics. Moreover, it is still not possible to distinguish statistically Italian Argentinians from

Table 1. Central and South Americans in the United States.

Country	Arrivals 1967–1976	1970 Census Total	White	1976 alien registration
Central America				
Costa Rica	12,093	25,840	21,645	14,454
El Salvador	19,665	23,502	22,970	22,827
Guatemala	19,683	26,865	25,394	20,196
Honduras	13,604	31,150	23,020	16,039
Belize (British Honduras)	—	14,221	7,561	—
Nicaragua	7,455	28,620	27,104	13,439
Panama	16,963	38,196	19,807	14,596
Other	—	—	—	1,529
Total	89,463	188,394	/147,501	103,080
South America				
Argentina	26,221	67,364	66,874	29,970
Brazil	15,035	46,758	45,561	18,905
Chile	10,522	25,125	24,512	13,065
Colombia	62,135	84,921	82,505	67,627
Ecuador	44,489	49,491	47,287	43,967
Guyana	24,200	—	—	11,706
Peru	16,981	35,450	33,488	20,638
Paraguay	—	—	—	1,241
Uruguay	6,314	7,041	6,928	4,996
Surinam	—	—	—	230
French Guiana	—	—	—	—
Bolivia	—	10,187	9,916	5,068
Venezuela	5,868	17,321	16,292	11,641
Other	7,222	45,806	30,641	2,403
Total	218,987	389,464	/364,004	231,457

Source: U.S. Immigration and Naturalization Service, *Annual Report, 1976* (Washington, D.C., 1977), pp. 89, 142; U.S. Bureau of the Census, *Census of the Population, 1970,* vol. 1, *Characteristics of the Population,* pt. 1, *U.S. Summary* (Washington, D.C., 1973), I, p. 598, table 192.

German Argentinians, or Spanish Ecuadorians from mestizo Ecuadorians (those of mixed Spanish and Indian descent). Almost every Central and South American country has received slaves or immigrants from other parts of the world, who, in varying degrees, have intermarried with each other or with indigenous Indians. The number of mestizo Hondurans, mulatto Colombians, or African Panamanians, for example, can be inferred only from the count of nonwhites in the 1960 and the 1970 U.S. Census.

It is often assumed that Central and South Americans share a common culture, and the majority do have a Spanish or Portuguese heritage, but they represent very diverse peoples who have been incorporated into nation-states relatively recently. It is only in the context of immigration that we can refer tentatively to Bolivians or Brazilians or Colombians as ethnic groups, but even this may distort that already difficult concept beyond recognition.

Central and South American countries vary greatly in geography, history, language, size, and socioeconomic development. Brazil, the largest, occupies nearly half the continent of South America and in 1972 had a population of 100 million, over 80 percent of whom were mulatto, mestizo, or pure African in origin. Uruguay, on the other hand, is one-fiftieth the size of Brazil; it has only 3 million inhabitants, 95 percent of whom are white. Argentina, another nearly all-white nation, had an annual birthrate in 1972 of 22 per 1,000 persons; Honduras, 60 percent mestizo, had an annual birthrate of 49 per 1,000. Some countries, Argentina and Venezuela for example, are considerably industrialized, with a per capita gross national product (GNP) of over $1,000

MEXICO

BELIZE
Belmopan
GUATEMALA
Guatemala
HONDURAS
Tegucigalpa
San Salvador
EL SALVADOR
NICARAGUA
Managua

COSTA RICA
PANAMA
Panamá
San José

West Indies

Atlantic

Caribbean Sea

TRINIDAD &
TOBAGO

Ocean

Caracas
VENEZUELA

Magdalena

Bogotá
COLOMBIA

Orinoco

GUYANA

Georgetown
Paramaribo
FRENCH
GUIANA

SURINAM

Quito
ECUADOR

Guayaquil

Amazon

B R A Z I L

Pacific

PERU

Lima

La Paz
BOLIVIA

Brasília

Ocean

PARAGUAY

Asunción

Rio de Janeiro
São Paulo

Paraná

Valparaíso
Santiago

CHILE

Andes

ARGENTINA

URUGUAY

Buenos Aires
Montevideo

Atlantic

Ocean

FALKLAND IS. (Br.)

Central and
South America

1000   Kms.   Miles

in 1972; El Salvador and Bolivia reported a per capita GNP for the same period of only $290 and $160, respectively.

Central and South American immigrants also represent differing social strata, regional attachments, and ethnocultural backgrounds. The four major ethnocultural groups are: the descendants of the indigenous Indians, living for the most part in highland regions of Central America and the Andes Mountains of South America; blacks and people of mixed black and Indian descent, who live on the east coast of Central America and the northern coast of South America; people of European descent, predominantly Portuguese in Brazil, and Spanish, Italian, and German elsewhere; and mestizos of mixed European and Indian stock, who live throughout Central and South America. There are also some Asians and people from the Middle East, particularly in Argentina, Peru, and Brazil.

However, all ethnocultural groups in Central and South America have been deeply affected by Spanish and Portuguese traditions, which transcend national boundaries and ethnic origins. There are some Jews, Muslims, and Protestants, and a number of Buddhists and Hindus, but nearly all Central and South Americans are nominally Roman Catholic. All who speak Spanish understand each other but differ in dialect and in usage, and when asked, may say that they speak Argentinian or Peruvian rather than Spanish.

The immigrants to the United States include black middle-class *costeños* from the coast of Colombia; mestizos from Honduras or El Salvador, many employed as domestic servants in large U.S. cities; European Jews who fled to Argentina and Uruguay in the 1930s and 1940s; second-generation Jewish Chileans; and descendants of the Italians who migrated to South America in the early 20th century. There is also a small number of East Indian, Japanese, and Chinese migrants from Central and South America. The Japanese population of Brazil, for example, is about as large as the Japanese population of the United States, and some Japanese Brazilians have immigrated to the United States.

Social relations among Central and South American ethnic groups in the United States defy generalization. Their ties with other Hispanic groups (Cubans, Dominicans, Mexicans, Puerto Ricans, Spaniards) in the United States are not well developed, but similarity of religion, lifestyle, and language often draws them together irrespective of country of origin. Although their ethnic-group boundaries are permeable and flexible, they may be rigid with respect to class and race. White and nonwhite Colombians in Chicago appear to have little social contact with each other. But class, race, or religious differences may recede when Chilean, Argentinian, or Nicaraguan immigrants organize on a national basis in response to a political crisis or natural disaster in their homeland.

IMMIGRATION FROM CENTRAL AMERICA

The number of Central Americans in the United States increased slowly. In the 1830s only 44 arrivals were recorded, but by the early 20th century more than 1,000 came annually. After World War I, immigration tapered off. The 1940 census listed only 7,000 Central Americans; many apparently had died or returned home. After World War II, however, the number of immigrants increased rapidly, and by 1970 the Central Americans numbered 174,000.

The great majority of Central American immigrants live in cities, especially in the New England, Middle Atlantic, Great Lakes, Gulf Coast, and Pacific Coast states. They are densely clustered in New York City, Los Angeles, San Francisco, Miami, and Chicago, the groups in each city varying in size and ethnic composition. Costa Ricans, Salvadoreans, and Nicaraguans are most numerous in western cities: there were 7,000 Salvadoreans in San Francisco in 1970 and only 1,000 in New York City. Guatemalans favor Los Angeles, and Hondurans flock to the Gulf Coast and the cities of the Northeast, where Panamanians also tend to congregate. New York City contains the largest urban population of Hondurans and Panamanians; over 15,000 Panamanians lived in New York in 1970, and fewer than 600 in San Francisco. Mestizo, black, and Indian Central Americans of all nationalities are more numerous in New York than in any other U.S. city, numbering over 17,000 in 1970. But the forces that have led these groups to one locale or another—employment opportunities, the nucleus of an ethnic community, transportation links with the homeland—are not well understood.

It is paradoxical that the flow of immigrants from Central America was small for nearly the entire period in which there were no immigration restrictions on applicants from the Western Hemisphere, but increased dramatically after the 1965 Immigration Act, which imposed a ceiling of 120,000 admissions from the hemisphere. Since 1958, an average of 1,000 to 2,000 immigrants each year has come from the Central American countries. By 1970 the 38,000 Panamanians and 31,000 Hondurans constituted the largest of the Central American groups in the United States. In 1970 over 90 percent of all those from Costa Rica, Guatemala, El Salvador, and Nicaragua were whites; a substantial proportion of Panamanians and Hondurans were nonwhites. Women outnumber men among Central American immigrants by about one-third. The number of immigrant males per 100 females was very low in the late 1960s, falling to 60 for Nicaragua and 51 for Panama. The percentage of immigrants under 20 years of age has been higher for males than for females; most female immigrants have been between 20 and 49, many of them service, domestic, or low-paid white-collar workers who have come to earn money to send home.

The occupational characteristics of Central American immigrants have changed little in the last two decades: 30 to 40 percent are professionals and white-collar workers, and very few are agricultural or industrial laborers—usually no more than 5 percent each year from each country. Since 1962 the percentage of employed newcomers who are domestic servants has remained high, ranging between 15 and 28 percent from each country. The entry of housewives and children after 1968 was facilitated by the immigration preference system favoring family reunions.

IMMIGRATION FROM SOUTH AMERICA

In the 19th century almost ten times as many South Americans as Central Americans came to the United States, and from 1910 to 1930 over 4,000 South Americans entered annually. Thus the population of the United States includes a number of third- and fourth-

generation South Americans who probably have not maintained any ethnic ties; most have undoubtedly melted into the ranks of Americans who do not identify with any particular ethnic group. In 1970 first- and second-generation South Americans numbered over 350,000. The South Americans concentrated in the Northeast, especially the New York metropolitan area, and in Chicago, Los Angeles, and San Francisco.

The sex ratios among migrants from many South American countries were more balanced than those for newcomers from Central American countries. Women held a small majority over men among immigrants from Argentina, Ecuador, Colombia, Peru, and Venezuela from the 1950s to the mid-1960s, but men predominated among Venezuelan immigrants in 1959 and 1960; an average of 103 men per 100 women entered the United States from Peru between 1961 and 1965. In the 1970s the sex ratios remained almost even for all South American countries except Bolivia, Brazil, and Colombia. With the exception of Venezuelans, Brazilians, and Ecuadorians, the percentage of young males from South American countries has been larger than that from Central American countries.

Immigrants from South America have different occupational characteristics from Central Americans. From 1959 to 1975 a high percentage of employed immigrants from South American countries (except Uruguay and Ecuador) were professionals. Between 1968 and 1975 the proportion was as high as 35 percent for Chileans and 34 for Venezuelans. The highest percentages of professionals have come from Bolivia: from 36 percent in the early and mid-1960s to almost 38 percent from 1968 to 1975. Conversely, a much smaller proportion of employed South American immigrants were domestic workers; from 1968 to 1975, for example, such workers constituted only some 4 or 5 percent of the immigrants from Argentina and Venezuela.

The volume of South American immigration has varied greatly from country to country, and it does not seem to be related to the population of the sending country. By far the largest numbers have come from Colombia, Ecuador, and Argentina, but the return migration to Ecuador has also been extremely high. The immigration from certain countries has distinctive characteristics. Venezuelans entering the United States in the last 20 years have been much younger than those from any other South American country. Between 1959 and 1967, 61 percent of Venezuelan males and 52 percent of the females were under 20, whereas the percentage of male immigrants under 20 from every other country ranged from 30 to 40 percent, and the percentage of all such females, from 25 to 36 percent. This pronounced trend of young migrants from Venezuela continued into the 1970s. Housewives and children constitute a large proportion of Venezuelan immigrants —from 1959 to 1975 about 75 percent—indicating chain migration and family reunions. Bolivia and Venezuela have sent the highest percentages of clerical workers, and Argentina, Colombia, Ecuador, and Uruguay have sent the highest percentages of craftsmen and semiskilled workers, a growing share of the immigrants from these countries in the last decade.

The South and Central American immigrants have shared common patterns of migration, settlement, and social characteristics. Throughout the 19th and 20th centuries both groups congregated in urban areas, especially in very large metropolitan centers. In 1920, for example, when 49 percent of the U.S. population lived in rural areas, 87 percent of the Central and South Americans were living in cities. They gravitated to urban centers in northeastern, Pacific Coast, and Gulf Coast states because their education, occupational skills, and lifestyles were suited to urban society. In 1970 among the Argentinians, Bolivians, Colombians, Ecuadorians, Uruguayans, Venezuelans, Salvadoreans, and Guatemalans the first generation outnumbered the second generation by two to one, reflecting the recent arrival of large numbers of immigrants from those countries.

Two controversial issues related to immigration from Central and South America remain beyond precise analysis. For obvious reasons there are no hard data on undocumented migration, although there are indications that many thousands of immigrants have entered the United States illegally. Nor is there firm evidence about the extent of the "brain drain," the migration of highly skilled and educated persons to the United States. Professionals have arrived in striking numbers from some countries, and between 1959 and 1967 over 20 percent of the immigrants from every Central and South American nation except Argentina were clerical workers, so there has been a significant migration of highly trained and skilled persons from these countries.

COLOMBIAN IMMIGRANTS:
A CASE STUDY IN NEW YORK CITY

The Colombian experience reveals the complex problems that Central and South Americans have had to overcome in the United States. A few hundred highly educated Colombians arrived in New York City at the end of World War I. These newcomers, many of whom were accountants, nurses, pharmacists, or technicians, were drawn to the Jackson Heights area of the borough of Queens because it provided attractive housing, schools, and easy access to Manhattan. They formed the nucleus of a white, middle-class Colombian community that gradually absorbed later arrivals.

At the outbreak of World War II the Colombian population numbered 1,000 to 2,000. After the war, however, political and social disturbances at home sent larger groups of immigrants to New York. Rural unrest and political upheaval between 1948 and 1962 drove many Colombian peasants to urban areas, while the residents of smaller towns moved to the largest metropolitan centers. Many Colombians believe that "La Violencia," as the unrest was called, triggered the large-scale immigration: from 1945 to 1955, 8,000 Colombians entered the United States; they came from a wider range of social-class backgrounds than the immigrants who had preceded them.

By 1960 more than 3,000 Colombian immigrants were arriving each year. The movement was accelerated by the mechanization of agriculture and industry, which forced farmers, craftsmen, and mechanics out of their traditional places in the economy. In addition, the population of Colombia was growing at an average of 3 to 4 percent annually, and the development of the economy could not keep pace with the increasing numbers of young people who needed jobs. By the 1970s the estimated unemployment in Colombia ran as high as 20 to 25 percent.

The combination of unprecedented pressures on the middle and lower strata of Colombian society and of low-cost air transportation induced many people to emigrate to the United States. By 1970 some 27,000 first- or second-generation Colombians lived in New York City, 1,200 of them nonwhite. Most of these newcomers had lived in urban centers in Colombia for some time before they emigrated. Primarily they were seeking better jobs and education for their children. Many parents, concerned about the limited number of students who could attend Colombian universities, were interested in New York's city colleges and state universities.

Although they have dispersed across the five boroughs of New York City, Colombians continue to congregate in Jackson Heights, a neighborhood that also contains pockets of Irish, Italian, Jewish, and German Americans. Dominicans, Cubans, Argentinians, Ecuadorians, and Puerto Ricans have also moved into this area and into nearby Corona and Elmhurst. In these areas, which are the most cosmopolitan sections of Queens, the various ethnic groups prefer to live in separate neighborhoods. Enterprising South Americans have opened *bodegas* (grocery stores) to supply traditional and familiar foodstuffs. The new immigrants have opened Colombian and Ecuadorian restaurants; their native-born children are prominent in real estate and the travel business. Newspapers from Guayaquil, Ecuador; Bogotá, Colombia; and Buenos Aires, Argentina, appear on Jackson Heights newsstands within a day or two of publication.

The Colombians interact with Hispanics from other countries in offices, stores, and schools, but they remain very conscious of their separate ethnic identity and prefer to socialize with other Colombians. They call their Jackson Heights neighborhood "Chapinero" after one of Bogotá's middle-class suburbs. Deeply attached to their traditional values and practices, they make a vigorous effort to distinguish themselves from other Hispanics. One observer has remarked that "the first thing Colombians wish the outsider to understand is that they are not Puerto Ricans." Their sense of distinctiveness is based in part on their claim to speak the purest form of Spanish in the Western Hemisphere. They view Cubans as their chief economic and social competitors.

A 1970 study of the Colombians in New York City showed that they were younger on the average than the population of the city as a whole. Nearly 50 percent were between 25 and 44, whereas only 27 percent of the city's population was in this age range. Women outnumbered men three to two. They had a lower birthrate than the population at large, average levels of education, and slightly lower levels of income. Their families were slightly smaller—one or two children—than the two-child average for the city. Colombians had completed an average of just under 12 years of school, equal to the rest of the city's population, and earned $4,791, slightly less than the median wage of $5,049.

Although many single Colombians have immigrated, the majority have established family households. Single people who find a living place and employment are often joined by other family members. The husband is the usual source of authority in the family. Acculturation to the surrounding society, however, has produced major changes in the relations between men and women, as well as in roles and attitudes, chiefly because women have an opportunity to work, and men have trouble finding jobs that match the positions they held in Colombia. The men appear to accept the need for working wives, and they have assumed many untraditional domestic chores, such as shopping for groceries and doing laundry. "The *machismo* of the male is *frenado* (blocked) . . . the man tends to stay at home much more . . . he does not have the same opportunities to stray as in Colombia." The conventional *ama de casa*—the married woman who does no work outside her home—is virtually unknown among immigrant Colombian families in New York City. Husbands, obliged to take jobs that are less remunerative or less prestigious, lose both status and the advantage of their superior earning power. As a result, Colombian women have made modest but real gains in the power they wield in the family.

Many Colombian parents, worried that public-school education will erode their traditional religious and cultural values, enroll their children in parochial schools at a great financial sacrifice. In the early 1970s the New York archdiocese established the Spanish Apostolate, sponsored by the diocese of Brooklyn-Queens. The Reverend René Valero, a dynamic young priest of Venezuelan background, headed the program and recruited several Spanish-speaking priests. By 1973 the diocese had 30 Spanish-speaking priests. About 12 Colombian priests have settled in Queens without sponsorship or any formal affiliation with the diocese and work informally with individual parishes. Some parishes have made an effort to attract Colombians and other Central and South Americans by celebrating the liturgy as it is done in Colombia.

Outside of the church few institutions, clubs, or associations maintain ethnic ties and group consciousness. Recreational organizations, primarily soccer clubs such as the Club Medellín and the Club Cali, reflect the regional origins of their members. A few professional organizations have been founded, but political clubs and associations have failed to take root. Colombians are more concerned with politics at home than with American politics, because the homeland government allows Colombian residents of the United States to vote in national elections. The Colombian Liberal and Conservative parties campaign actively in Queens. An estimated 5,000 or more Colombians living in New York voted in the 1973 presidential election.

COLOMBIANS IN CHICAGO: THE COSTEÑOS

The Colombian community in Chicago is both similar to and different from the one in New York. The costeños, immigrants from the coastal region, where Afro-Caribbean culture is predominant, are of mixed African, Indian, and Spanish descent. At home the costeños hold themselves apart from the Spanish Colombians, who live in the interior cities of Bogotá, Medellín, and Cali. Spanish Colombians enjoy social and economic advantages because they are white and because they live in areas with the greatest opportunities for social mobility. Improvement of the educational system in the coastal districts has multiplied the number of highly skilled costeños who aspire to middle-

Table 2. Median earnings (in dollars) by years of schooling and sex of Spanish-origin groups, 1969.

	Schooling (years)	Mexican	Hispano	Puerto Rican	Cuban	Central and South American	Non-Spanish white
Men	Under 12	4,460	4,940	5,080	4,980	5,050	5,850
	12	6,070	6,610	5,960	5,810	6,530	7,730
	13–15	6,310	6,380	5,920	6,640	6,630	7,920
	16+	8,990	9,620	9,820	8,590	10,360	11,620
	Total	4,970	5,800	5,430	5,710	6,140	7,290
Women	Under 12	1,670	1,600	3,170	2,920	3,090	2,230
	12	2,930	2,950	3,880	3,470	3,960	3,400
	13–15	2,940	2,820	4,060	3,570	3,600	2,870
	16+	5,590	5,710	6,090	4,550	4,660	6,000
	Total	2,100	2,350	3,420	3,260	3,470	3,090

Source: A.J. Jaffe, Ruth M. Cullen, and Thomas D. Boswell, *Spanish Americans in the United States—Changing Demographic Characteristics* (New York, 1976), p. 64.

class status, but the sluggish rate of economic development has not produced enough jobs for them. Regional and racial disadvantages, combined with the structural limitations of the Colombian economy, have led ambitious costeños to emigrate to the United States.

In 1970 about 3,500 foreign-born Colombians lived in the Chicago area, in contrast to the 27,000 in New York. They are highly educated and middle-class—many of them doctors, engineers, accountants, and architects who have brought their families. Most come as young professionals in their 30s; they enter the United States at Miami and then move directly to Chicago. They settle first in apartments on the Far North Side until they are able to purchase homes in the suburbs of Skokie, Evanston, Arlington Heights, Glencoe, or Buffalo Grove.

The racial and regional cleavages of Colombian society have been reproduced in Chicago. The costeños socialize with one another and with Cubans, but not with Spanish Colombians. Regional, racial, and ethnocultural variations thus shape group consciousness, ethnic identity, and social interaction. The costeños are Catholics, and their families are small, usually no more than two or three children. They prefer to send their children to parochial schools to teach them traditional values and a basic knowledge of Spanish.

The two most important Colombian organizations in Chicago are the Cartagena Medical Alumni Association, established by costeño physicians in the late 1960s, and the Colombianos Unidos para Labor Activista. As membership of the former group expanded, it began to include other professionals, such as engineers and architects. Besides raising funds to support the medical school in Cartagena, from which many members graduated, the association helps Colombian newcomers establish themselves in Chicago. It functions as a mutual-benefit society and as a center for fund-raising dances and monthly dinners and meetings in the Club

Colombia, one of Chicago's oldest Colombian restaurants. The association is dominated by costeños. Some Spanish Colombians attend occasional social functions but decline to enroll as formal members.

The Colombianos Unidos para Labor Activista is a political club of students and permanent residents who hold monthly meetings to discuss social, political, and economic problems. They also sponsor guest lectures, movies, and social activities. Colombianos Unidos has members from all regions and ethnic backgrounds, including many costeños. Both it and the Cartagena Association function as conduits of information on conditions in the homeland and facilitate contact with newly arrived immigrants.

Like the Colombians in New York City, they have been slow to naturalize. In a 1975 sample of Chicago Colombians, nearly all of whom were costeños, less than one-fourth had taken out naturalization papers. Many families split their citizenship status; one spouse becomes a U.S. citizen, and the other retains Colombian citizenship to keep open the possibility of return migration and to secure their economic interests in Colombia. As in New York, the Colombians of Chicago eagerly keep abreast of politics at home. The costeños do not participate in either Chicago or national politics. They do not form political alliances with other Spanish-origin groups, nor do they identify with them explicitly. They tend to hold themselves aloof from American blacks, Mexicans, and Puerto Ricans.

The social adjustment of the costeños in Chicago closely resembles that of the chiefly white Colombians in New York City. The costeños have integrated into the middle-class economic stratum, retain enduring attachments to homeland culture and politics, and hope to return there in the future. This orientation has resulted in very limited efforts to form organizations for the maintenance of ethnic-group ties and advancement of Colombian interests.

Table 3. Number of earners per Spanish-origin family, 1970, in percentages; median income of Spanish-origin families, 1969.

Earners	Mexican	Hispano	Puerto Rican	Cuban	Central and South American	Non-Spanish white
0	7.7	8.9	20.7	6.0	6.3	8.7
1	41.4	42.3	43.1	33.0	39.5	40.3
2 or more	50.9	48.8	36.2	61.0	54.2	51.0
Median income	$6,960	$7,860	$6,230	$8,690	$8,920	$10,100

Source: A.J. Jaffe, Ruth M. Cullen, and Thomas D. Boswell, *Spanish Americans in the United States—Changing Demographic Characteristics* (New York, 1976), pp. 60, 421.

Table 4. Percentage of foreign-born Spanish-origin 12th year of school or higher completed, 1970.

	Age	Mexican	Puerto Rican[a]	Cuban	Central and South American
Men	20–24	38.3	37.1	70.3	65.7
	25–29	27.9	29.2	66.2	69.5
	30–34	21.9	23.0	47.7	
	35–44	15.3	21.5	45.3	64.1
	45–54	17.1	19.1	46.7	56.9
	55+	9.1	11.7	40.9	42.5
Women	20–24	32.1	37.1	65.5	40.9
	25–29	26.0	28.8	57.9	60.5
	30–34	19.4	23.1	43.4	
	35–44	16.7	19.4	46.4	55.0
	45–54	15.7	14.7	42.3	49.3
	55+	8.6	9.8	24.9	36.3

Source: A.J. Jaffe, Ruth M. Cullen, and Thomas D. Boswell, *Spanish Americans in the United States—Changing Demographic Characteristics* (New York, 1976), pp. 382–387.

a. Island-born Puerto Ricans.

COMPARISON WITH OTHER SPANISH-ORIGIN GROUPS

Central and South Americans in the United States, once a small and dispersed group, now have large settlements in several major urban centers, and more defined and coherent ethnic associations are emerging. There are opportunities to return home, and a stream of newcomers refreshes their contacts with the culture and society of their homelands.

In the United States they must adapt to other people of both Spanish and non-Spanish origin. Encounters with Mexicans, Puerto Ricans, Spaniards, Dominicans, and Cubans raise important social and political issues. Affirmative-action, bilingual, and multicultural programs for Spanish-origin groups have charged Central and South American ethnicity with new significance and new advantages and have raised the question of the utility of alliances with other Spanish-origin groups. The rise of a Hispanic political movement and interest group also adds new pressures that could shape and reinforce ethnic attachments.

Data from the 1970 Census allow some interesting comparisons. Central and South Americans have very high levels of income and education when compared to other Spanish-speaking groups. In these and other char-

acteristics they most clearly resemble the Cubans. The median annual incomes of Central and South American males, $6,140 (see Table 2), and of families, $8,920, are the highest of all Hispanic groups (Table 3). The proportion of foreign-born Central and South Americans who have finished the 12th grade is at least twice as large as the proportion for foreign-born Mexicans and Puerto Ricans in most age groups (Table 4). Most striking, the percentage of U.S.-born Central and South Americans of all age cohorts (except females 45–54) who have completed the 12th grade or more is higher than that of any other group, including non-Spanish, American-born whites (Table 5). Central and South Americans have the highest proportion of employed adult males (40.4 percent) working in professional, managerial, and other white-collar occupations, which is only a few percentage points lower than that for non-Spanish white males and about twice as great as the proportion for Mexican and Puerto Rican men (Table 6). The proportion of Central and South American men who are semiskilled or unskilled workers is the lowest for all Hispanic groups. The occupational distribution of Central and South American women, however, is very similar to that of women of other Spanish-origin groups. Over 45 percent are employed as white-collar workers—but mainly in low-status jobs—and the remainder are in blue-collar and service occupations. The distribution of Central and South American families according to the number of wage-earners is almost identical to that of the non-Spanish white group. Nearly 40 percent of all families had only one wage-earner, 54 percent had two, and only 6 percent had no income earners in 1970. Demographic data show that Central and South American families have two or three children.

Thus, more than any other Spanish-origin group, Central and South Americans exhibit middle-class characteristics. To a large degree, these features are the result of a recent migration dominated by highly trained and skilled immigrants. Concealed within these impressive aggregate statistics, however, are countless examples of husbands and wives working long hours in unfamiliar occupations, living in a frugal manner and sacrificing for future investments; blue-collar and domestic workers striving to establish a foothold so family members can join them or so they can send remit-

Table 5. Native-born persons of Spanish origin who have completed 12th year or higher of school, 1970 (in percentages).

	Age	Mexican	Hispano[a]	Puerto Rican[b]	Cuban	Central and South American	Non-Spanish white
Men	20–24	56.0	68.1	58.8	81.8	83.1	82.0
	25–29	49.8	61.5	54.3	77.3	76.3	77.8
	30–34	40.7	55.9	55.4	68.4		72.9
	35–44	30.2	43.9	45.9	66.7	72.0	64.7
	45–54	20.1	39.5	34.7	44.2	65.6	56.3
	55+	8.8	19.4	11.8	14.5	57.8	33.7
Women	20–24	53.3	66.8	64.3	81.2	83.9	82.4
	25–29	45.1	56.6	53.9	74.5	77.4	77.6
	30–34	38.2	50.7	52.0	65.8		73.2
	35–44	25.0	40.2	46.5	60.2	76.0	67.3
	45–54	16.2	32.7	36.4	39.6	53.4	59.3
	55+	9.3	23.2	15.8	20.3	51.2	37.4

Source: A.J. Jaffe, Ruth M. Cullen, and Thomas D. Boswell, *Spanish Americans in the United States—Changing Demographic Characteristics* (New York, 1976), pp. 382–387.

a. Hispanos are native of native parentage, most of whose ancestors have been in the United States for a number of generations.
b. Puerto Ricans born in the mainland United States.

Table 6. Spanish-origin persons 16 years of age and over, by broad occupational groups, 1970 (in percentages).

	Occupation	Mexican	Hispano	Puerto Rican	Cuban	Central and South American	Non-Spanish white
Men	White-collar	18.6	30.5	23.2	37.4	40.4	42.7
	upper	9.6	16.5	8.8	20.6	24.5	27.4
	lower	9.0	14.0	14.4	16.8	15.9	15.3
	Craftsmen	20.5	21.9	15.5	18.0	18.9	21.7
	All other	60.9	47.6	61.4	44.5	40.8	35.6
Women	White-collar	39.6	53.7	42.9	41.5	45.4	65.4
	upper	8.5	13.7	8.9	10.9	12.6	20.5
	lower	31.1	40.0	34.0	30.6	32.8	44.9
	Craftsmen	2.4	1.6	2.4	2.6	2.1	1.9
	All other	58.0	44.8	54.7	56.0	52.4	32.8

Source: A.J. Jaffe, Ruth M. Cullen, and Thomas D. Boswell, *Spanish Americans in the United States—Changing Demographic Characteristics* (New York, 1976), p. 66.

tances back home; and numbers of second- and third-generation Central and South Americans who have worked to achieve greater social mobility than their parents were able to attain.

The social and economic characteristics of Central and South Americans contrast sharply with those of immigrants from other Hispanic groups. A comparison establishes that the social and economic position of the South and Central Americans and, therefore, the problems and decisions they face in order to advance in society are extremely different from those confronting Cubans, Puerto Ricans, or Mexicans. *See* Cubans; Dominicans; Mexicans; Puerto Ricans; Spaniards; Spanish; West Indians. *See also* Cape Verdeans; Haitians; Portuguese.

Bibliography
The major statistical sources for the demographic and social history of Central and South American immigrants are the U.S. Census reports and the annual reports of the Immigration and Naturalization Service. Statistics on the current population are available in the U.S. Bureau of the Census, *Current Population Reports, Persons of Spanish Origin in the United States: March 1976*, Series P-20, no. 310 (Washington, D.C., 1977). An important comparative treatment of Central and South Americans from the Research Institute for the Study of Man is A.J. Jaffe, Ruth M. Cullen, Thomas D. Boswell, *Spanish Americans in the United States—Changing Demographic Characteristics* (New York, 1976). A brief, interesting analysis of early Chilean immigrants is Carlos U. Lopez, *Chilenos in California: A Study of the 1850, 1852, and 1860 Censuses* (San Francisco, 1973).

Among the general histories that supply useful background information are Hubert Herring, *A History of Latin America*, 3d ed. (New York, 1968), and Ronald Hilton, *The Latin Americans* (Philadelphia, 1973). Michael D. Olien, *Latin Americans: Contemporary Peoples and Their Cultural Traditions* (New York, 1973), is an interesting anthropological survey. P.M. Hauser, *Urbanization in Latin America* (New York, 1961), and Bruce Herrick, *Urban Migration and Economic Development in Chile* (Cambridge, Mass., 1965), are helpful studies of major economic and social changes.

A large body of literature has explored recent immigration, especially the migration of highly educated or skilled persons. On Colombian immigrants, the most informative studies are Inés Cruz and Juanita Castaño, "Colombian Migration to the United States," Part 1, and Elsa M. Chaney, "Colombian Migration to the United States," Part 2, in *The Dynamics of Migration: International Migration* (Washington, D.C., 1976). Other helpful works are Alejandro Portes, "Determinants of the Brain Drain," *International Migration Review* 10 (1976): 489–508, and Ian R.H. Rockett, "Immigration Legislation and the Flow of Specialized Human Capital from South America to the United States," *International Migration Review* 10 (1976): 47–61. A general work on the migration of human capital is Robert G. Myers, *Education and Emigration: Study Abroad and the Migration of Human Resources* (New York, 1972).

Studies and accounts of local Central and South American communities are sparse. The best are Paul Cowan and Rachel Cowan, "For Hispanos It's Still the Promised Land," *New York Times Magazine*, June 22, 1975; Karen De Witt, "Washington's Hispanic Community Growing Rapidly," *New York Times Magazine*, February 13, 1978; and David Lowenthal, "New York's New Hispanic Immigrants," *Geographical Record* 66 (1976): 90–92. An informative and extensive study of one national group is Priscilla Walton, "Colombians in Chicago," unpub. M.A. thesis, University of Texas at Austin (1973).

ANN ORLOV AND REED UEDA

CHALDEANS: *see* ASSYRIANS; EASTERN CATHOLICS

CHAMORROS: *see* PACIFIC ISLANDERS

CHECHEN: *see* NORTH CAUCASIANS

CHEMEHUEVIS: *see* AMERICAN INDIANS

CHERKESS: *see* NORTH CAUCASIANS

CHEROKEES: *see* AMERICAN INDIANS

CHETCOS: *see* AMERICAN INDIANS

CHEYENNES: *see* AMERICAN INDIANS

CHICANOS: *see* MEXICANS

CHICKAHOMINIES: *see* AMERICAN INDIANS

CHICKASAWS: *see* AMERICAN INDIANS

CHILEANS (CHILENOS): *see* CENTRAL AND SOUTH AMERICANS

CHINESE

The Chinese, with a population of 435,062 in the 1970 U.S. Census, were the second largest Asian-American ethnic group in the United States, ranking just below the Japanese. The number includes Chinese both on the U.S. mainland and in Hawaii. A slight majority—229,237—were American-born. However, the number of foreign-born has increased dramatically since 1965, when the United States changed its national-quota immigration system.

ARRIVAL AND SETTLEMENT ON THE MAINLAND

Chinese immigration to the U.S. mainland has a long history. Some Sinologists, basing their theory on a 7th-century Chinese source, believe that a Buddhist priest, Huishen, sailed east across the Pacific to North America in the 5th century after Christ; but little supports this claim. That Chinese were present on the

American continent soon after European settlement of the New World, however, has been established. There were Chinese among the servants of Spaniards aboard the galleons that sailed between the Philippines and Mexico after 1565. Chinese worked at shipbuilding and other trades in Acapulco, and as early as 1635 they had formed the beginnings of a Chinese colony in Mexico City. A few appear to have gone north to visit Los Angeles and Monterey during the 1780s, but the first Chinese name on record in California is Ah Nam (d. 1817), who came to Monterey in 1815 to work as a cook for the Spanish governor.

By the end of the 18th century Chinese were also aboard the ships of other Western nations engaged in the China trade. The first documented arrival of Chinese on the East Coast of the United States was in 1785, when the *Pallas* reached Baltimore from Canton with the Chinese seamen Ashing, Achun, and Accun on board. On the West Coast the settlement established at Nootka Sound on Vancouver Island in 1788 by an English captain, John Meares, included a number of Chinese carpenters and smiths. Subsequent ships brought other seamen, servants, students, and merchants throughout the first half of the 19th century. It was not until the second half of that century, however, that Chinese immigration was large enough to have a significant impact on U.S. society.

The discovery of gold in California in 1848 attracted thousands from all over the world including many Chinese. San Francisco, the main port of entry, came to be called among the Chinese immigrants Jinshan or, in Cantonese, Gam Saan—the Golden Mountain. Jinshan was also used to refer to California.

The Chinese in California represented only a small part of an extensive exodus from southeastern China to Southeast Asia, Oceania, and both Americas. During the latter half of the 19th century the Chinese empire was in decline. Land ownership had become more and more concentrated in the hands of the wealthy; the peasants' lot worsened, and corruption and oppressive rule frequently drove the peasants into revolt. During this same period England and other Western nations were aggressively seeking to open up China to foreign trade; they succeeded after the Opium War (1839–1842) in which England defeated China and ended its closed-door policy. In the following decades, continuous economic and political pressure exerted by the Western powers led to a rapid breakdown in China's economy and traditional society and brought still greater hardships to the masses. At mid-century the Taiping Rebellion (1851–1864) shook the empire to its foundations.

Although the Taiping Rebellion did not extend very far into the southeastern coastal provinces of Fukien and Kwangtung (the principal area of emigration to the United States), local anti-imperial secret societies, taking advantage of the unstable political situation, fomented a series of insurrections around Amoy in Fukien (1853) and in the Pearl River Delta and the West River Valley in Kwangtung (1854–1861). Civil war also broke out (1856–1867) between the Hakka and Cantonese dialect-group villages in the Sze Yap (Ssui or Four Districts: Hsinhui, Taishan [Hsinning until 1914], Kaiping, and Enping) area southwest of the Pearl River Delta. The consequent political chaos and economic dislocations in the southeast forced many people to leave.

Changes elsewhere in the world at mid-19th century affected the destinations of Chinese emigrants. The United States, developing its industries and frontier regions, required an abundant supply of cheap labor. Industrialization and colonial exploitation by western European nations created similar manpower needs which the impoverished Chinese peasants could fill. From 1840 to 1900 about 2.4 million laborers went abroad to Southeast Asia, Peru, Hawaii, the Caribbean islands, and North America.

From 1850 until 1882 when the Chinese Exclusion Act went into effect, more than 322,000 Chinese, including reentrants, entered the United States. Some of the immigrants were merchants and craftsmen but the overwhelming majority were unskilled laborers, peasants from the rural areas of Kwangtung and Fukien. Most of those who went to North America came from the Sze Yap, but a significant minority came from Chungshan (Hsiangshan until 1925) in the southern part of the delta; from the Sam Yap (Sani, or Three Districts: Nanhai, Panyu, and Shunteh) area surrounding Canton; and other districts adjacent to them. The vast majority were Cantonese speakers, although a number spoke the Hakka dialect, and those from certain areas of the Chungshan district spoke variants of the Southern Min dialect.

Many emigrants were able to raise the funds for passage; for those who could not two systems were available to finance the journey. In one, organized by Chinese middlemen, passage was advanced to an emigrant who agreed to work out his debt after arrival. This system was common among the emigrants to Southeast Asia, Australia, and North America. The other system, commonly used in Peru, Cuba, and Hawaii, required the emigrants to sign contracts agreeing to serve in a foreign land for a specified time in return for passage.

These arrangements were handled at the treaty ports by Chinese recruiters working for Western entrepreneurs. Under the latter system laborers were frequently tricked and coerced into going abroad, and upon arrival often forced to work under slavelike conditions. Labor contracting became known among the Chinese as "pig selling," and its practices became notorious. Some of the emigrants to California during the early 1850s came as contract laborers, but public opposition soon forced adoption of a system whereby passage was paid off through automatic wage deductions.

The Chinese were also among the first to stake claims to the fields after the discovery of gold in California, but they were not numerous in the early years; in 1850 only 500 of the 58,000 miners in California were Chinese. Their numbers quickly grew, however, and in reaction mining camps passed resolutions excluding them. In 1852 the state legislature reenacted the Foreign Miners' Tax law, directed first in 1850 against Mexican miners and this time against the Chinese. Chinese nevertheless soon spread throughout the West, following the new gold strikes in Nevada (mid-1850s), southwest Oregon (mid-1850s), British Columbia (late 1850s), the upper Columbia River basin (early 1860s), Idaho and northeast Oregon (mid-1860s), Montana (mid-1860s), Colorado (early 1870s), and as far east as the Black Hills of South Dakota (mid-1870s). They remained in these areas for many years, often extracting gold from lean claims and tailings after the other miners had left.

As the gold fever subsided in California, entrepreneurs began to exploit the state's other resources. To compete in the national market, however, they had first to link the West to the more populous East. An era of railroad building began.

Chinese workers had been employed to build some intrastate railroads in California as early as 1858, but the first large-scale use of Chinese labor—some 12,000 to 14,000 workers—was in the construction of the Central Pacific portion of the transcontinental railroad completed in 1869. They also constructed the western sections of the Southern Pacific and Northern Pacific, as well as a number of trunk and branch lines. As the railroads were finished, many Chinese workers settled in railroad towns from California to Utah and Texas, as well as in Washington, Oregon, and British Columbia. A few migrated to the Midwest and East, seeding new Chinatowns in metropolitan centers.

Completion of the transcontinental railroad opened up development of the rich resources of the West, especially of California. The Burlingame Treaty signed with China in 1868 ensured that emigration from the Far East would continue to supply the cheap labor needed. In the decade that followed, the number of Chinese in the United States grew steadily: immigration averaged more than 12,000 per year. By 1880 more than 105,000 were in the United States, most of them in California, where Chinese laborers had become an important factor in the economy. They converted the tule swamps of the Sacramento–San Joaquin River Delta in California into rich farm land; their skills in planting, cultivating, and harvesting were used extensively in vineyards, hopyards, orchards, and ranches. They raised such crops as sugar beets, citrus fruits, and celery. Some farmed as sharecroppers; others raised their own vegetables for the market. In 1880 they amounted to more than a third of California's truck gardeners, and Chinese vegetable peddlers had become a familiar sight in many towns. Most of their contributions have gone unrecorded, but their horticultural skills can be inferred from such legacies as the cherry named for by Ah Bing, a foreman working in Milwaukie, Ore., in the 1870s; and the orange developed by pomologist Lue Gim Gong (1860–1925) of De Land, Fla., in 1888.

Chinese factory workers were also important in the California industries that had grown up during the Civil War, especially woolen mills and the cigar, shoe, and garment industries of San Francisco. By the early 1870s they composed 70 to 80 percent of woolen-mill workers and 90 percent of the cigar makers in the city. By the mid-seventies they were a majority of the shoemakers and garment makers, producing almost all the undergarments on the market; they also manufactured brooms, slippers, and cigar boxes. As early as the 1860s Chinese entrepreneurs had started cigar, shoe, and garment factories that competed with Caucasian-owned firms. By the mid-1870s Chinese-owned enterprises had become numerous enough to absorb many of the workers discharged from Caucasian-owned factories as a result of pressure from anti-Chinese labor agitators. Although never more than a tenth of the California population, they formed about a quarter of the state's labor force because they were nearly all males of working age.

Chinese worked in the quicksilver mines in California, the coal mines in Utah, Wyoming, and Washington, and the borax deposits in California, Nevada, and Oregon. In the San Francisco Bay area and in Louisiana, Chinese entrepreneurs and laborers developed shrimp fisheries which by the 1880s were exporting a million pounds of dried shrimp and shell annually. They were also pioneers in developing California's abalone fisheries. Chinese workers were a mainstay of the canneries, especially the salmon canneries in the Pacific Northwest, British Columbia, and Alaska. Thousands more operated or worked in laundries and served as cooks or domestic servants.

Industries elsewhere in the United States also sought out Chinese labor. Contingents were recruited to construct the Alabama and Chattanooga and the Houston and Texas Central railroads. For a brief time Louisiana, Arkansas, and Mississippi planters used Chinese field hands to replace freed slaves. When the substitution proved unsuccessful, some stayed and established settlements in the South. Some eastern factory owners also imported workers from the Pacific Coast until the panic of 1873 created vast unemployment in the eastern cities and ended the need for Chinese labor.

Chinese workers were often supplied to Caucasian employers through a Chinese contractor or foreman who was paid a lump sum for the work. The contractor usually also held the concession for provisioning the workers he hired for a job. This was in essence the padrone system common among Italians and other immigrants who arrived without a grasp of English. It was particularly common in agriculture and other industries where the demand for workers was seasonal; the system lent itself well to supplying a large number of workers on a short-term basis.

Low wages and poor working conditions led to labor

unrest. In 1867 about 2,000 Chinese working on the Central Pacific Railroad struck to obtain terms equal to those for Caucasian workers, but the strike failed. California farmers complained about Chinese field hands who struck for high wages during the harvest. In the cities, labor guilds organized by Chinese factory workers tried to protect workers' interests. But Chinese laborers were a minority with limited power. They continued to be exploited as cheap labor by Caucasian and Chinese entrepreneurs alike.

The Chinese Exclusion Movement In the 19th century the western European nations continued their global expansion while the United States pressed steadily westward in accordance with its "manifest destiny." Both movements postulated the superiority of the white race and of Western civilization in order to justify territorial expansion; the resulting racism had serious consequences for the Chinese in the United States. The first Asian group to immigrate in large numbers, they soon became the target of attacks that established a pattern for the treatment of subsequent Asian immigrants. During the gold rush they were often victims not only of discriminatory legislation and unequal treatment but also of physical assaults. At first, hostility was limited and disorganized; but as their numbers increased and as employers began to hire them in place of Caucasian labor, antagonism grew and became more organized, particularly in California, which had the largest Chinese population and had been the center of anti-Chinese agitation since the arrival of the first immigrants.

In the late 1860s an intense struggle developed in the state between the railroads, the major corporations, and large landowners and their Chinese workers on one side, and a coalition of workers, small entrepreneurs, and small farmers on the other. Out of it grew the anti-Chinese movement, spearheaded by racist elements in the labor unions, supported by small entrepreneurs and small farmers, and vociferously advocated by demagogues and opportunistic politicians. Anti-Chinese spokesmen alleged that the Chinese were unassimilable and undesirable additions to American society: too servile and docile, they caused depressed wages, unemployment, and other economic and social ills. Anticoolie associations were formed in a number of cities. Discriminatory measures included an 1870 San Francisco city ordinance that prohibited the use of sidewalks to those carrying loads on a pole—the way Chinese customarily carried heavy objects. They were the victims of frequent pranks, torments, and demonstrations. In 1871 a riot in Los Angeles ended with the murder of 19 Chinese.

Hard times in the 1870s made matters worse. Employers were pressured into discharging Chinese workmen; anti-Chinese conventions passed resolutions urging total exclusion from the United States. "The Chinese must go!" was the slogan of Denis Kearney of the California Workingmen's party; politicians echoed this cry to win votes, and labor leaders exploited the issue to encourage union organization. In 1877 the California legislature appealed to Congress to limit Chinese immigration; in 1879 it adopted a new constitution containing a section with punitive anti-Chinese provisions.

The Chinese received no support from a homeland weakened by corruption and imperialist politics; they had to appeal instead, often unsuccessfully, to the U.S. courts. Some tried migrating to the Midwest and East— by 1890 they could be found in every state and territory of the Union—but they encountered anti-Chinese sentiment everywhere. The use of Chinese strikebreakers in North Adams, Mass. (1870), Belleville, N.J. (1870), and Beaver Falls, Pa. (1872), provided anti-Chinese forces with an opportunity to direct national attention to the "Chinese question."

Pressures to act mounted in Congress. In 1876 a joint congressional committee held hearings in San Francisco and issued a report recommending curtailment of emigration from China. As long as California remained short of labor, such action was resisted by the large employers. By the early 1880s, however, the influx of tens of thousands of new settlers had substantially decreased dependence on Chinese labor for development of the state's economy; only mild opposition greeted the congressional act of 1882 which excluded Chinese laborers for ten years. Officials, teachers, students, merchants, and those who "travelled for curiosity" were exempted from the act in accordance with an 1880 treaty with China. This law marked the end of the traditional free-immigration policy of the United States.

Exclusion of newcomers did not end discrimination against the Chinese already in America. Frequent riots continued to flare up throughout the West in the 1880s and 1890s. In one outbreak at Rock Springs, Wyo., in 1885, a mob killed 28 Chinese. Chinese were evicted from a number of western towns; in others those who stayed were subjected to harassment. Anti-Chinese groups continued to press for tighter restrictions, and Congress obliged: an 1884 amendment to the act of 1882 broadened the definition of "laborer"; an 1888 measure barred Chinese laborers from reentry unless they already had family or property in the United States; the Scott Act later that year prohibited reentry to laborers who had departed temporarily, immediately affecting some 20,000. In 1892 the Geary Act extended Chinese exclusion for another ten years and required laborers already in the country to obtain certificates of residence. In 1902 all Chinese exclusion laws were extended for yet another decade. In 1904 the Deficiency Act extended the laws to all U.S. possessions and barred Chinese laborers indefinitely.

Social Structure and Organization Chinatowns grew up wherever economic opportunities attracted a sufficient number of immigrants: mining camps, railroad towns, farming communities, and cities. They served as places where Chinese could transact business and enjoy the fellowship of their countrymen. In times of persecution they served as havens, for there was some safety in numbers. The oldest Chinatown is in San Francisco, the primary port of entry. It took shape soon after the gold rush began and is still one of the most important centers of activity for Chinese Americans.

The society the Chinese established in the United States mirrored the society of China in many ways. The immigrants maintained their native customs in food and dress: the men wore the shaven head and queue originally imposed as a badge of submission by the reigning Manchu dynasty in China; the women bound their feet as a sign of gentility. They brought with them many attitudes of their 19th-century homeland. Their

social conduct was conditioned in large part by Confucianism and the cult of ancestor worship which kept them attached to kin and native village. They revered the past, respected their elders, and obeyed their parents, for filial piety was particularly valued.

In China the society was male-dominated. Men and women did not mingle in public. The oldest male, in most cases the father, ruled the family; the mother and other females were subservient, and their place was at home. Sons were prized more highly than daughters. Polygamy, with a chief wife and concubines, was allowed but in practice was limited to the rich. A large family with several generations under one roof was regarded as ideal; it was not uncommon for married sons and their families to live with parents.

The dominant religion saw heaven, earth, and the underworld as basic reflections of a hierarchy of supernatural beings with power to determine the fate of man. For divine assistance in daily affairs the Chinese could appeal to a pantheon drawn from history, folk legends, and Taoist and Buddhist mythology. This folk religion did not have an elaborately structured priesthood; temples, or joss houses, with idols of deities for worship, were usually run by local individuals or institutions. Such temples are preserved in the California towns of Weaverville, Oroville, Marysville, Hanford, Mendocino, and Bakersfield.

Despite important similarities, Chinese-American communities differed from the homeland society in several respects. Their population in the United States was overwhelmingly male; there were few families. Most early immigrants considered themselves sojourners, accumulating savings to take back to their native village; these intentions reinforced their reluctance to abandon traditional ways. In observance of Confucian beliefs, most wives had been left behind in the homeland to serve the parents-in-law, to raise the children, and to tend the ancestral shrines. Their husbands sent them remittances from the United States and periodically visited them. Low wages, the high cost of living, and the temporary, seasonal nature of much of the work available to them also deterred them from forming family units. The few women who came were apt to be wives of merchants (or of other men with steady occupations), servants, or prostitutes. Because families were so rare in the Chinatowns, practices and institutions developed around the needs of an overwhelmingly bachelor society.

The immigrants observed all the major Chinese festivals: the New Year, the Dragon Boat—to commemorate the death of Qu Yuan (c. 277 B.C.), a patriotic statesman-poet—Mid-Autumn, and Winter Solstice. Annual offerings to all spirits were made at the *Shaoi* ("burning mock clothes") ceremony in summer, a Chinese version of All Souls' Day; graves of families, relatives, and friends were visited during the spring and fall. Religious beliefs also required that any dead buried in foreign lands must eventually be exhumed and returned to the native village for interment.

The Chinese store not only sold merchandise but also sometimes supplied workers to local Caucasian employers; in addition, it served as a bank for the immigrants' earnings, a depository for remittances to China, and a postal service. In most cases the owner and employees were related or had come from the same area in China, so the store also functioned as a social and communications center where men could exchange gossip, meet the latest arrivals from the native village, or keep track of the whereabouts of departed fellow villagers. A villager passing through town could drop into the store and expect a free meal or two and lodgings for the night. The store also frequently served as a clubhouse and an agency for community subscriptions for various causes. Each group of immigrants from a given area soon looked to the storeowner as the dominant figure.

The primary immigrant organizations derived their structure from traditions of loyalty to clan or region. Coming from regions of various dialects and customs, where in many cases a single lineage or clan comprised the total population of a village, the immigrants necessarily carried these local and clan ties to the New World. Fellow villagers banded together, helped each other find work, and patronized particularly stores owned by someone from the native locality. Merchants and contractors preferentially hired workers from their native area. Once immigrants from a given village established themselves, others from the same place tended to join them, producing a chain migration and concentrations from a specific locality or clan village in various U.S. towns and cities: people from the Panyu district dominated the Chinatown of Hanford, Calif.; the Teng (or Ong) clan from Kaiping that of Phoenix, Ariz. They also were likely to pursue the same occupations; most of the butcher shops of the San Francisco Bay area, for example, were run by people from Chiuchiang in the Nanhai district. Regional and clan loyalties led to the formation of a number of rival groups vying for influence in the community. A network of organizations based on geographic origin or surname evolved both to maintain order within each association and to protect it from rival groups.

The *huiguan,* or locality or district association, commonly called a "company" during the 19th century, was patterned upon similar organizations that had existed in China since the Ming dynasty (1368–1644). Membership was made up of immigrants from a given district, group of districts, or parts of a district. The companies were led by merchants, performed social and charitable services, and provided protection; company officers mediated and settled internal disputes. New arrivals from the company's district were greeted, temporarily fed and housed in the association's bachelor dormitories, and registered in the association's rolls. Any member returning to China had to have prior clearance from his district association certifying that he had settled his debts. This requirement ensured collection of funds advanced by the huiguan for passage to the United States. An individual refusing allegiance to his huiguan would find himself stripped of protection and aid and faced with social ostracism, a practice that guaranteed the loyalty of a huiguan's constituents.

The huiguan usually included one or more subordinate organizations, called *shantang,* which maintained the cemetery for its members and periodically sent the remains of the dead to China for burial. Each shantang had jurisdiction over people within a given area, and sometimes served essentially the same functions as the huiguan but at a lower level.

The first two huiguan were founded by the Sam Yap and Sze Yap communities in San Francisco around

1851; associations for other districts soon followed. Branches were established outside San Francisco as the need arose. Over the years the number of huiguan fluctuated in accordance with internal splits and combinations.

The huiguan acting in concert spoke for the community in its dealings with the non-Chinese society. In the 1870s there were six major huiguan in San Francisco, known collectively as the Six Chinese Companies. Around 1882 when anti-Chinese agitation was at its height, an umbrella organization, the Chunghua Huiguan (Chinese Consolidated Benevolent Association, CCBA), was established in San Francisco to deal more effectively with anti-Chinese activity and community problems. This organization acted as community spokesman for its constituents and also assumed leadership of the Chinatown power structure. It too was commonly referred to as the Chinese Six Companies. The number of member associations fluctuated over the years; today the CCBA has seven constituent huiguan.

As the communities in other cities grew, local CCBAs, with local clan and district associations and even secret societies as members, were founded (most of them during the early 20th century) with functions similar to those of the CCBA in San Francisco. These CCBAs formed a nationwide network; each remained spokesman for its local community, but all were subordinate to the CCBA in San Francisco, which spoke for all the Chinese in the United States.

The clan or family association was based on the concept of the lineage community commonly found in Kwangtung clan villages, but its membership included everyone bearing the same surname, regardless of lineage. Other clubs, called *fang*, included people from the same lineage and locality. The fang arose in the early days of immigration; the clan association was formed somewhat later, often of several constituent fang. Both the fang and clan association served the same functions—maintaining order and providing mutual aid and protection against external threats—as the huiguan but at a lower level.

The larger clans often formed their own associations. Clans with few immigrant members banded together into multi-clan associations to offset the numerical superiority of the larger clans; for example, the Liu (Lew, Lau, Low), Kuan (Quan), Chang (Cheung, Jeung), and Chao (Jue, Chew) clans banded together to form the Lung Kong Association.

The principal rivals of the clan and district associations in the Chinatowns were the secret societies, more familiarly known in the United States as tongs. The word *tong* means simply "meeting hall," but the notoriety of the secret societies soon gave it a sinister connotation to many non-Chinese. Membership in a tong was based on a fraternal principle that accorded the same treatment to every member and disregarded social status, clan ties, or locality of origin. Formed for mutual aid and protection, the tongs appealed especially to those who lacked money and influence, did not belong to a powerful clan, had some grievance, or were alienated from the established social system. Their rivalry with the clan and district associations included an element of rebellion against domination by affluent merchants.

The earliest secret societies in the United States derived from the Triad, or Heaven and Earth, Society, which was widespread in southeast China and was responsible for instigating a number of antidynastic insurrections. Many of its members emigrated overseas and by the early 1850s had established lodges in California. Additional lodges sprang up as the Chinese spread across the continent, and these later formed a loose nationwide confederation called the Chee Kung Tong. As the population grew, similar secret societies proliferated; others drew their membership from certain localities, clans, or combinations of clans. Many were involved in the gambling, prostitution, and opium traffic that flourished in this largely bachelor society.

Within this multitude of rival groups many clashes inevitably occurred, arising from private quarrels, alleged infringements on business or occupational rights, competition for control of gambling, prostitution, or opium, and the like. These feuds increased in both frequency and ferocity in the 1870s as the Chinese population grew. Assassinations were carried out by members known as hatchetmen or highbinders; anyone in the opposition was a potential target whether or not he had been involved in the original dispute. These so-called tong wars were widely publicized in the American press.

The guild was another organization modeled on those that had existed among craftsmen and merchants in China. As early as the 1850s merchants in San Francisco formed a guild to regulate prices of commodities. Later, laundrymen cooperated to prevent cutthroat competition. In some smaller communities the guilds often combined functions with those of the CCBA. As industries developed, workers organized guilds to protect their interests, using methods similar to those of American craft unions. Strong guilds existed among cigar makers, shoemakers, and garment workers, and were often in conflict with both Caucasian and Chinese employers. Because of the hostility of the Caucasian workers the guilds never became part of the American labor movement; when these specialized Chinese industries declined, their respective guilds faded with them.

In this early period only one American institution set about actively to influence the Chinese community; this was the Protestant church. Missionaries considered the conversion of Chinese in the United States the first step toward converting the 400 million in China to Christianity. In 1850 they organized to distribute Christian tracts to Chinese in San Francisco. By 1853 the Reverend William Speer had established a Presbyterian mission in the city, and soon the Methodists, Baptists, and Congregationalists joined the effort.

Although the missionaries made few converts—there were only 1,931 Christians among the approximately 110,000 Chinese in this country in 1892—for many years these Protestant missions were the only American institutions with which the Chinese people had amicable relations. They provided Sunday schools and English classes in which they promoted American middle-class values. They were among the earliest to advocate raising the status of Chinese women. Because of their vested interest in the missionary effort, they defended the Chinese against anti-Chinese agitators. But their attitude toward Chinese culture was often conde-

scending. Many missionaries were intolerant of Chinese tradition, and their attacks on ancient customs and practices as idolatrous and heathenish were resented by many.

Missionaries were instrumental in introducing Chinese newspapers; they thought they would be useful tools for spreading the gospel. In 1854 the weekly *Golden Hills' News* was established in San Francisco; the next year the Reverend Speer started the bilingual *Oriental;* in 1856 the first Chinese daily, the *Sacramento Daily News,* began publication. All these enterprises were short-lived, however; it was not until the 1870s that the literate community was large enough to support a journal.

THE EXCLUSION ERA, 1882–1943

The six decades of exclusion (1882–1943) sharply curtailed Chinese immigration to the United States. The population on the mainland declined from a high of 107,488 in 1890 to a low of 61,639 in 1920 as many in the bachelor society died or returned to China. After the 1920s, however, the growth in the number of families and some relaxation of immigration restrictions as a result of a series of favorable legal decisions produced a slow increase to 77,504 by 1940 (see Table 1).

The Chinese did not accept the discriminatory exclusion laws passively. Chinatown leaders frequently petitioned for more equitable treatment. Diplomats such as Wu Tingfang (1842–1922) and Liang Cheng (1864–1917), and prominent Chinese Americans such as Ng Poon Chew (1866–1931), the managing editor of the influential San Francisco Chinese newspaper, *Chung Sai Yat Po* (1900–1951), protested in numerous speeches and writings the draconian enforcement of the immigration laws. When the United States sought to revise the 1894 treaty with China in accordance with newly enacted exclusion provisions in the Deficiency Act of 1904, Chinese Americans called on their friends in China to pressure the United States into improving its treatment of immigrants. In 1905 China and a number

of overseas Chinese communities boycotted U.S. goods. These efforts brought about some improvement in the treatment of those seeking entry, but the exclusion laws remained in effect.

The Chinese took numerous cases to court to clarify and affirm their rights of entry. In the case *United States* v. *Gue Lim* (1900) the U.S. Supreme Court ruled that Chinese merchants had treaty rights to bring wives and minor children into the country. The right of an American-born Chinese to citizenship and hence to admission to the United States was affirmed by the Court in the case *United States* v. *Wong Kim Ark* (1898). Subsequent court decisions affirmed the right of derivative citizenship for foreign-born minor children of American-born Chinese, but the right to citizenship of foreign-born grandchildren was not affirmed until 1927 in the case of *Weedin* v. *Chin Bow.* The decisions made in these citizenship cases had significant consequences, for in the two decades from 1920 to 1940, 71,040 were admitted as U.S. citizens and only 66,039 as aliens.

When the right of derivative citizenship was affirmed, a slot system was devised whereby Chinese Americans returning from China would falsely report the birth of children, usually sons, to the authorities, thus creating eligibility slots for future immigrants. Prospective immigrants were then assigned or sold these slots or papers, adding the terms "paper son" and "paper father" to the Chinese-American vocabulary.

To block these fraudulent entries authorities introduced detailed and extensive interrogations. From 1910 to 1941 most applicants for admission were processed through the immigration station on Angel Island in San Francisco Bay. There they were detained in isolation, for as little as a few days or as much as a month, until immigration officials could rule on their admissibility. Those who had to appeal adverse rulings to higher authorities or the courts could find themselves confined there for as long as two years. Over the years, immigrants wrote or carved numerous poems on the wooden walls of the detention building, venting their worries, fears, frustrations, and anger; the inscriptions are visible there today.

Although the exclusion laws could bar only aliens from citizenship, Chinese Americans fared little better, for racial prejudice was a fact of life for all Chinese in the United States. Discrimination continued to be particularly virulent on the Pacific Coast. Chinese were segregated in schools and theaters, and were refused service in barber shops, hotels, restaurants, and other public places. Some towns barred them entirely; in others, restrictive covenants prohibited them from buying or moving into some neighborhoods. In a number of states aliens could not purchase land. Chinese could not marry Caucasians. These developments, combined with the group's intrinsic cohesiveness, induced their withdrawal and isolation from the mainstream of American life.

In the late 19th century the Chinese population centers began to shift as people migrated seeking better economic opportunities. There was a steady flow to eastern and midwestern cities as well as to some parts of the South. In 1880 only 3 percent of Chinese on the U.S. mainland lived east of the Rockies, but by 1910 the proportion had jumped to 27 percent and by 1940 to 40 percent of the total. California's percentage accordingly

Table 1. Chinese population in the continental United States, 1850–1975.

Year	Population	Males per 100 females	Percentage U.S.-born	Total Chinese immigrants in decade[a]
1850	4,018[b]	—	—	—
1860	34,933	1,858	—	41,397
1870	63,199	1,284	1	64,301
1880	105,465	2,107	1	123,201
1890	107,488	2,679	3	61,711
1900	89,863	1,887	10	14,799
1910	71,531	1,430	21	20,605
1920	61,639	696	30	21,278
1930	74,954	395	41	29,907
1940	77,504	285	52	4,928
1950	117,629	190	—	16,709
1960	198,958	139	54	9,657
1965	—	—	—	8,156
1970	383,023	112	48	97,987
1975	—	—	—	107,120

Source: U.S. Immigration and Naturalization Service, *Annual Report, 1975* (Washington, D.C., 1976); U.S. Bureau of the Census, Population Reports, 1860 to 1970. Figures are for people classified as of the Chinese "race," including the third and later generations.

   a. Includes Chinese immigrants to Hawaii after 1898. Post-1965 data are for immigrants born in mainland China, Taiwan, and Hong Kong.

   b. Estimated.

declined from 71 percent in 1880 to a scant majority of 51 percent in 1940. New York State acquired the second largest contingent: by 1940 about 18 percent lived there. In contrast, the population in the other western states dropped from 14 percent in 1880 to less than 4 percent in 1940. (These figures do not include the large Chinese group in Hawaii, discussed separately below.) Concurrent with this eastward shift was the increasing urbanization of the Chinese population. Many smaller Chinatowns disappeared as older people died or returned to China and the younger ones departed for the big cities where the newer immigrants also tended to settle: the percentage of urban dwellers rose from 76 percent in 1910 to 91 percent in 1940.

Economic Life The Chinese were excluded from many occupations, and had to seek employment in jobs where Caucasian labor did not compete, such as domestic service, laundries, and restaurants. In 1930, 61 percent of the work force were in these service occupations which restricted them to low wages and substandard working conditions and also ensured their continued efforts to organize. In 1918 the Mon Sang (People's Livelihood) Association was established by Chicago waiters; the syndicalist-led Gongyi Tongmeng (Unionist Guild) was formed among garment workers in the San Francisco Bay area and farm workers in Suisun City, Calif. Neither was very effective.

In the 1920s progressive elements within the American labor movement began to establish ties with some workers in the major Chinatowns and eventually helped place Chinese members in national unions. By the thirties even unions on the Pacific Coast were accepting some, chiefly service or unskilled workers; they were still barred from most craft unions. In 1937 the left-wing Jiasheng Huagong Hezuohui (Chinese Workers Mutual Aid Association) was organized in San Francisco to link workers with the American labor movement. The next year national unions penetrated Chinatown when workers at the National Dollar Stores' garment factory in San Francisco organized an affiliate of the International Ladies' Garment Workers Union (ILGWU), but the momentum slackened, and Chinatown workers remained largely ununionized.

From the middle of the 19th century enterprising Chinese were also going into business for themselves. Those who wanted to open a business often acquired the capital by means of a *hui,* or rotating credit association, an institution introduced from southern China. Members of a hui, often fellow villagers or clansmen, would pay a specified sum into a common pool. They would then compete by bid, election, or lot to win the right to use the entire sum; a month later the members would meet again, raise another sum, and those who had not yet had their turn at investing a sum would compete again. This continued until each member of the hui had had a chance to use the pool. In this way many could find at least enough capital to get started and sometimes quite a large sum if they belonged to several hui. Some forms of hui continued in use into the 1970s.

By the turn of the century enough small businessmen had met with success to begin investing in more ambitious ventures, such as oil wells, mines, and automotive plants. In the San Francisco Bay area, Chinese-American capital financed at least two canneries. In

1915 merchants pooled their resources to establish the China Mail Steamship Company for which they purchased three ocean-going vessels. The capital for these projects was supplied by the first Chinese-American bank, the Canton Bank of San Francisco, incorporated in 1907. The rise of this entrepreneurial class stimulated the establishment of Chinese-American chambers of commerce in New York in 1904 and in San Francisco in 1908, which promoted Chinese businesses and replaced the protective functions of the old mercantile guilds.

But in the end many of these large enterprises failed because of insufficient financial resources. They lacked both the capital and the managerial experience to compete with other U.S. corporations. Racial prejudice hindered them as well. In 1923 the China Mail Steamship Company filed for bankruptcy, pulling down with it the Canton Bank, whose closing in 1926 was precipitated by a run on its funds. By the 1930s Chinese owners had lost control of their canneries. The only two major enterprises that continued to prosper were the San Francisco-based National Dollar Stores (f. 1921), a department-store chain selling men's and women's wear, and the Wah Chang Corporation of New York (f. 1916), which traded and processed tungsten.

Until World War II most Chinese Americans remained single proprietors or partners in small businesses such as merchandising or in small concerns (particularly garment factories) which manufactured products that were labor intensive and required relatively low capital. Such enterprises could survive by long hours of operation, low profit margins, and low wages. By far the most numerous were laundries, which made the Chinese laundryman an American stereotype, and restaurants, which made chop suey and chow mein (American adaptations of Chinese dishes) and the fortune cookie almost as familiar as apple pie. These businesses were particularly common in the East and Midwest, where there had been fewer opportunities for diversification than in California.

In the Deep South, particularly in the region around Augusta, Ga., and the small towns along the Mississippi River from Memphis to Vicksburg, Chinese grocers served the rural black population that white shopkeepers turned away. The grocers were also successful in southwestern cities such as San Antonio, Tex., and Phoenix and Tucson, Ariz.

Most Chinese Americans maintained some kind of economic ties with the native land. The early immigrants had continued to send sizable sums of money to China, Hong Kong, and Macao for family support and investments in houses and land. When China began to modernize toward the end of the 19th century, overseas Chinese also sent money for other purposes. Until the depression reduced the flow in the 1930s, their money contributed to financial, merchandising, and manufacturing enterprises and to the establishment of educational and charitable institutions. U.S. and Canadian Chinese financed construction of the Sunning Railroad in the Sze Yap region; Chin Gee Hee (c. 1844–1929), a former Seattle merchant and labor contractor, promoted the project. When Chinese Americans learned specialized skills or acquired college degrees but found few opportunities in the American job market, many left to pursue their careers in China instead.

From 1900 to 1910 many contributed generously to Kang Yu-wei's effort to reform the Chinese empire and Sun Yat-sen's effort to overthrow the Manchu dynasty. During the civil wars that followed the 1911 Chinese Revolution, Chinese Americans supported various partisan groups whose diversity of opinion was apparent in the polemics of the Chinese newspapers in San Francisco, New York, and later Chicago. The best-organized faction was the Kuomintang (Chinese Nationalist Party), derived from Sun Yat-sen's revolutionary party. It had numerous branches abroad, including many in various U.S. Chinatowns; after it had established a national government in Nanking in 1927, the Kuomintang became the dominant voice in the Chinese-American communities.

Interest in Chinese politics was also sustained by the many threats to China's sovereignty. From the 1900s through the 1930s Chinese Americans frequently raised funds to support China's resistance to Japanese aggression and organized boycotts of Japanese goods. When Japan invaded China in 1937, communities in the United States poured millions of dollars into Chinese war bonds. They contributed more than $56 million toward refugee relief and supplies during the eight years of the war.

The Second Generation During the exclusion years many Chinese Americans adapted to American culture. Most of the early immigrants had resisted the pressures of assimilation and maintained their native ways. The small minority who married and had children in the United States were unwilling to see their offspring forsake tradition, and took steps to have them educated in the Chinese languages; private classes were common in the early years. Some even sent their children back to China to be educated. In 1888 San Francisco Chinese established the first community-supported Chinese school, and in subsequent years many other Chinatowns followed their example.

In the 20th century this situation began to change. The number of families and consequently of American-born children increased. In 1870 only 1 percent of the Chinese population was American-born. Although the Chinese Exclusion Act sharply curtailed immigration, the admittance of wives and families of exempt classes allowed the American-born proportion to reach 10 percent in 1900 and 52 percent in 1940. These children were influenced by the ways of the larger society, especially through the schools, the Protestant churches, the YMCA, YWCA, and the Boy Scouts. Because the Chinatown institutions had been established to serve the needs only of adult male bachelors, outside institutions in part filled the needs of the younger Chinese for social contacts and recreation. The children took up social dancing, dating, and competitive sports. They became more progressive and egalitarian in outlook than their elders. Their clan and regional loyalties were weak. Behavior between the sexes was more relaxed, although by Western standards still reserved. By the thirties many had an inadequate command of the language and dealt with their elders and each other in a mixture of Chinese and English. They abandoned many traditional customs. Choosing one's own marital partner gradually took the place of parental matchmaking, often not without some strain within the family circle. Some children attended college, although poverty and the un-

certainty of finding work afterward kept this number small. Women gradually emerged from the home to find jobs and add their wages to the family income; more girls were permitted to attend school and sometimes even college. The degree of Americanization was not uniform throughout the community, which reflected a wide variety of combinations of Chinese and Western ways.

One result of the growing independence and Americanization of the second generation was the formation of new organizations. The first of them was the Native Sons of the Golden State (NSGS), founded in 1895 in San Francisco and patterned after American social fraternal organizations common at the time; in 1915 it was renamed the Chinese-American Citizens Alliance (CACA) and for years remained the leading second-generation Chinese-American organization, with chapters ("parlors") in many cities. The CACA combated discriminatory immigration laws and segregation in the public schools, and encouraged Chinese Americans to participate actively in American political life. In 1924 CACA members established the *Chinese Times* in San Francisco, a Chinese-language newspaper that is still one of the most influential in the community in the West. By 1935 the second-generation community was large enough to justify founding the *Chinese Digest* (1935–1940) in San Francisco, the first Chinese-American newspaper in English.

The ambitions of the second generation, like those of their more traditional-minded parents, were frustrated by prejudice and discrimination; no matter how many American habits they might adopt, they were never fully accepted in the larger society. A number looked to China for their future, though that option was open to comparatively few: most lacked the education, specialized skills, social status, and connections necessary for success in the motherland. The United States had to remain their home.

Some Chinese Americans served as bridges between their ethnic group and the larger society in positions such as interpreters, heads of Chinese departments of banks, and agents for American firms. By the early decades of the 20th century some Chinese-American doctors and dentists were practicing in the Chinese communities. A few left the Chinatowns to work at clerical jobs, and a handful of teachers and professionals had positions in the larger society. For the great majority, however, racial prejudice was still a barrier.

A few became prominent, among them Yung Wing (1828–1912), the first Chinese graduate from an American college (Yale, 1854), whose lifelong work for the modernization of China spanned both the period of free immigration and the exclusion era. He lived many years in the eastern United States, where he eventually retired; he died in Hartford, Conn. Another was Dr. Ng Poon Chew, lecturer on China and the Chinese in America. In 1902 the name of a trusted servant was preserved for posterity when the Dean Lung chair of Chinese at Columbia University was established from donations by General H.W. Carpenter, his employer. A few Americanized Chinese became recognized performers on the vaudeville circuit. In the 1920s cinematographer James Wong Howe (1899–1976) and actress Anna May Wong (1907–1961) attained fame in Hollywood. In the 1930s Dong Kingman (1911–) gained na-

tional recognition as an artist, and Lin Yutang (1895–1976) began interpreting his version of Chinese culture to Americans.

The Changing Chinatowns Until the 20th century, Chinatowns were in continual turmoil from the gang fights and assassinations of the tongs. However, the growth in the number of families eventually took effect. Prostitution and opium dens slowly disappeared along with the bachelor society that had supported them; gambling operations were much reduced in scale. The fading of these activities eroded the economic base for the tong and removed many of the causes behind the tong conflicts. The diminished flow of immigrants limited the availability of recruits to replenish the ranks of aging hatchetmen. Desire for the law and order necessary for the well-being of family life and business resulted in growing public pressure to put a stop to tong strife. Tong wars gradually became less frequent, and by the 1930s were a thing of the past; the disputes that occasionally did break out were resolved without violence. The tong leaders joined forces with the merchant elite, and tongs frequently became components of local CCBAs.

The rising nationalism in China in the early 20th century brought with it modernization and Western ways that resulted in the abandonment of many traditional practices in the Chinatowns. The shaven head and queue, the bound feet, and the traditional male garb disappeared after the 1911 Chinese Revolution; folk religion and festivals were gradually abandoned; temples languished for lack of worshipers. Chinese sought to erase the notion that opium dens, slave girls, and bound feet were typical of their culture.

The traditional organizations lost many of their reasons for existence. Organizations representing new interest groups—the Chinese chambers of commerce, the Chinese Hand Laundry Alliance (founded in 1933 in New York City), the CACA, Chinese branches of the YMCA and YWCA, and local Kuomintang chapters—arose to challenge their power and to satisfy new demands. These organizations soon entered the power structure in many communities by joining the local CCBAs.

As long as Chinese Americans continued isolated from the national mainstream, however, traditional organizations led by the CCBA played an important role by establishing hospitals and schools and fighting for repeal of the restrictive immigration laws; in periods of economic distress their aid relieved the suffering of the unemployed and helped the Chinese to survive.

Many Chinatown organizations became involved in politics in China, particularly after the Kuomintang government was established in Nanking in 1927. Many influential organization leaders were supporters of the Kuomintang; some even became party members. During the Sino-Japanese War (1937–1945) this domination accelerated; by 1945 many organizations from the CCBA on down were controlled by elements sympathetic to the Kuomintang.

THE POST-EXCLUSION PERIOD, 1943 TO THE PRESENT

World War II was a turning point for the Chinese in America. The wartime manpower shortage opened up job opportunities to minorities; many Chinese found work in shipyards and other war-related industries or filled technical, professional, and white-collar positions. An estimated 8,000 of them served in the armed forces, and after discharge many of them furthered their education under the G.I. Bill.

To bolster China's morale during a critical period and to reduce the effectiveness of Japanese propaganda in Asia during World War II, the United States repealed the Chinese exclusion acts in 1943. China's resistance to Japanese imperialism, the partial assimilation of Chinese Americans, and their occupational specialization in noncompetitive fields had further combined to mitigate anti-Chinese feeling. Only a token immigration quota of 105 was given to the Chinese, but permanent-resident aliens were finally permitted to become naturalized. Even with this small quota the postwar years showed an increase in the number of Chinese women who came to America. They were admitted as nonquota immigrants under the provisions of the War Brides and G.I. Fiancées Act, and almost every year from 1943 until the 1970s female immigrants outnumbered the men; 4,126 women were admitted between 1945 and 1948 alone.

In the postwar years Chinese Americans benefited from a series of actions favorable to minority rights. The California and Oregon Alien Land Laws were judged unconstitutional by state supreme courts. In 1948 the U.S. Supreme Court barred racially restrictive covenants in housing. Gradually many Chinese moved out of the Chinatowns into other neighborhoods, though not always without incident. The California ban on racially mixed marriages was ruled unconstitutional by the state supreme court in 1948; the U.S. Supreme Court did not void antimiscegenation statutes throughout the nation until 1967. One by one other discriminatory laws and practices were eliminated, although social prejudice persisted in subtler forms.

After the Japanese surrender in 1945 the civil war dating from the late 1920s resumed between the Kuomintang and the Chinese Communist party. By 1949, despite U.S. support, Chiang Kai-shek's forces had been defeated on the mainland and had retreated to the island of Taiwan. On October 1, 1949, the victors proclaimed the People's Republic of China in Peking.

The civil war and its outcome resulted in new emigration from China. Many of the émigrés were members of the intelligentsia, and many were wealthy, including numerous former officials and supporters of the Kuomintang. Chinese students already in the United States applied for permanent-resident status. Because it was clear that most would probably not return to live in the homeland, earlier immigrants shed the last vestiges of their sojourner mentality and began to consider the United States their permanent home.

The People's Republic of China aligned itself with the Communist-bloc nations; the resulting Sino-American cold war sharply curtailed relations between the Chinese in the United States and those in mainland China. Federal agents investigated Chinese suspected of being sympathetic to the People's Republic. The Kuomintang took advantage of U.S. government sympathy and the anti-Communist climate to attract support in the Chinatowns and influence Chinatown institutions, especially traditionist organizations, chambers of commerce, Chinese schools, and the Chinese newspapers.

Anti-Communist leagues were organized, and cultural and economic ties with Taiwan were strengthened. The Kuomintang drew its supporters particularly from those who had suffered losses in the recent revolution, and it capitalized on the general anti-Communist sentiment that swept America in the late forties and early fifties.

In 1955 Everett F. Drumwright, the U.S. consul-general in Hong Kong, charged that many Chinese were entering the United States fraudulently and warned of Communist infiltration. Federal authorities began reports of immigration irregularities. In 1957 alarmed leaders in the CCBAs of various cities called a national conference of Chinese communities and formed a National Chinese Welfare Council to lobby against the massive prosecutions and deportations that threatened. The government, aware of the difficulties involved in deporting thousands and obliquely admitting the injustice of past immigration laws, encouraged confessions of fraud in return for the granting of proper immigration status. They charged these cases against the annual immigration quota. Some 22,000 such cases were processed by the San Francisco district immigration office alone.

These events made the Chinese apprehensive; they were particularly circumspect regarding political activities involving China until President Richard M. Nixon's visit to China in 1972 led to a relaxation of hostilities between the United States and the People's Republic.

Economic Progress Despite political problems, Chinese Americans shared in the prosperity of the postwar period. Their job horizons broadened; by 1970 about 20 percent of employed Chinese men were earning over $10,000 a year—fewer than the 25 percent national average for all Americans, but nonetheless a considerable improvement. Their percentage would have been far higher but for the concentration of so many in service work—25.2 percent, triple the national average. In professional and technical occupations they advanced spectacularly—from 3 percent in 1940 to 7 percent in 1950 to 26 percent in 1970, more than double the gain of the general population. Many chose careers in science, technology, engineering, education, and health, for competence in those fields could be gauged objectively, which tended to preclude discriminatory practices. In 1970 more than 84 percent of Chinese-American professionals were in these fields. Many of them were students who had come to attend college in the United States and had subsequently stayed. Their presence helped boost the proportion of Chinese men with four or more years of college to 26 percent in 1970, the highest in that year for any American ethnic group.

A number of the professionals became outstanding in their chosen fields. C.N. Yang (1922–) and T.D. Lee (1926–) won the Nobel Prize for Physics in 1957; C.H. Li (1913–) won the Albert Lasker Medical Research Award in 1962; Samuel Ting (1936–) won the Nobel Prize for Physics in 1976; T.Y. Lin (1911–) was known for his contributions in structural design using prestressed concrete; and I.M. Pei (1917–) is a noted architect. In sociology, American-born Rose Hum Lee (1904–1964) published pioneer studies on the Chinese in America.

A handful made their names in literature. Jade Snow Wong (1922–) is a successful ceramicist and decorator;

her autobiographical *Fifth Chinese Daughter* was a best seller. The novel *Flower Drum Song* by C.Y. Lee (1917–) was made into a Broadway musical and motion picture. *The Woman Warrior* by Maxine Hong Kingston was a best-selling autobiography. In the 1960s a group of young writers, typified by Frank Chin (1940–), began to explore the social problems of Chinese Americans. A few others were prominent in the performing arts, particularly music. Two nationally known artists are bass-baritone Yi-kwei Sze (1920–) and composer Wen-chung Chou (1923–).

Since civil-service positions ostensibly are filled on the basis of ability, many first sought jobs in the federal, state, and municipal government for the equal opportunity they offered. As private industry began to hire more Chinese in the 1960s the number entering civil service dropped somewhat, but even in 1970 one out of six Chinese Americans on the mainland worked in government.

The vast expansion of the government bureaucracy and financial institutions also provided low-level white-collar positions for large numbers of women. In 1970 one out of every three employed Chinese women was a clerical worker. A great number are American-born, but with the arrival of more immigrants already fluent in English, an increasing number of the foreign-born fill these positions.

There are still many Chinese in unskilled manual occupations (see Table 2). In 1970 the large proportion (25.2 percent) of Chinese men in service occupations included many recent immigrants working in laundries and restaurants; Chinese domestic servants, once so common in the West, had all but disappeared. Garment factories employed about 10,000 Chinese women, more than one-third of the foreign-born. These occupations absorbed a large percentage of non-English-speaking immigrants who, like their predecessors, were forced to endure low pay and poor working conditions, especially in the Chinatowns. They constitute most of the 23 percent of Chinese males 16 years old or over in the 1970 Census who had not gone beyond elementary school and the 43 percent who made $4,000 or less annually. The better-paid blue-collar industries employ few Chinese; the craft unions have continued to resist enrolling

Table 2. Occupational distribution of Chinese in the continental United States, 1970 (in percentages).

Occupation	Male	Female	Overall[a]
Professional and technical workers	29.9	19.4	26.0
Managers and administrators, except farm	11.1	3.5	8.3
Sales workers	4.1	4.4	4.2
Clerical workers	9.2	30.9	17.2
Craftsmen and foremen	5.7	1.1	4.0
Operatives, including transport	10.6	24.9	15.9
Laborers, except farm	3.1	0.8	2.2
Farmers and farm managers	0.4	0.2	0.3
Farm laborers and foremen	0.3	0.3	0.3
Service workers, except private household	25.2	12.1	20.4
Private household workers	0.5	2.2	1.1

Source: Betty Lee Sung, *Statistical Profile of the Chinese in the United States, 1970 Census* (Washington, D.C., 1975), table 6.

a. In 1970, 101,118 Chinese males and 59,368 Chinese females were in the U.S. work force.

minorities, although some began to admit token numbers in the 1950s.

Improved circumstances have enabled many to accumulate savings and make business, real estate, and other investments. By 1949 Chinese in the United States owned 10,232 laundries, 4,304 restaurants, and 2,047 grocery stores. During the 1950s rapid advances in U.S. technology created demands for new products, which provided opportunities for some. A number of Chinese enterprises were founded, and a few prospered; one of them is Wang Laboratories, Inc. (f. 1951), of Tewksbury, Mass., which manufactures minicomputers and word-processing equipment; its annual gross sales reached $97 million in the mid-1970s. Opportunities in international trade enabled some to begin successful shipping ventures such as the Sea King Corporation (f. 1959) based in New York. Several financiers became active on Wall Street; one of the better known is Gerald Tsai, Jr. (1928–), who organized the Manhattan Fund in 1966. Another large Chinese enterprise is the National Dollar Stores, which operates about 40 branches in five states. Increasingly, capital from Taiwan, Hong Kong, and Southeast Asia has also been invested in U.S. enterprises in Chinatowns and elsewhere.

Most Chinese businesses, however, can be classified as small or medium in size. Retail trade, especially in food stores and restaurants, is still the most common business venture. Chinese-run supermarkets dot California's Central Valley and the southeastern and southwestern states. In the 1970s the Farmer's Markets in Sacramento County, Calif., had 40 branches. More numerous are the small "mom and pop" groceries, although by the 1970s the retail food business had become less attractive because of competition from the large supermarket chains. Similarly, the advent of automatic laundry equipment and permanent-press fabrics has driven many Chinese laundries out of business.

Restaurants far outnumber other Chinese enterprises; one source in 1970 estimated them at about 9,400. Many outside the Chinatowns serve both Chinese and American dishes. Since the 1950s American tastes in Chinese cooking have become more sophisticated, so that in addition to establishments offering the familiar Cantonese fare, an increasing number of restaurants specialize in the cuisine of other regions in China, especially Peking, Shanghai, Hunan, and Szechwan.

Garment factories remain numerous in the Chinatowns of San Francisco, New York City, Los Angeles, Boston, Chicago, and Seattle. Nearly all are run by subcontractors operating on slender profit margins. The low pay of the workers, often recent immigrants, has periodically led to charges of sweatshop conditions from unions and social workers. Other Chinese businesses are the gift shops that sell Asian art goods and souvenirs to tourists, the importers and processors of Chinese food products, and the retailers of carry-out Chinese foods. Of the few who remain in agriculture, most raise Chinese vegetables for the Chinese market.

Increased entrepreneurial activity has stimulated growth of Chinese-American financial institutions with capital from both Chinese and non-Chinese sources. Besides the Bank of Canton of California (incorporated in 1937, the only Chinese-owned bank on the mainland remaining from the prewar period) there are the United Savings and Loan Association of Seattle (f. 1952), the Bank of Trade of San Francisco (f. 1961), Cathay Bank of Los Angeles (f. 1962), and the Chinese-American Bank of New York (f. 1967). Additional banks and savings-and-loan associations have been established in the 1970s.

The Postwar Immigrants In the 1950s and early 1960s the number of new immigrants and refugees was small, still restricted by immigration laws. A great increase occurred after the immigration act of 1965 ended the national-quota system. The newcomers breathed new life into the major Chinatowns.

Most immigrants embarked from Hong Kong or Taiwan. Political events in Cuba (1959), Burma (1964), South Vietnam (1975), and Indo-China (1979) brought overseas Chinese by the thousands. There was a steady flow from Southeast Asia, Africa, Japan, Korea, and other areas. Many students from Taiwan and Hong Kong again applied for permanent-resident status after completing their studies. Out of 15,959 Taiwanese students who came to the United States from 1962 through 1969, only about 3 percent ever returned to the island. Most of the rest settled on the U.S. mainland. The foreign-born constituted 52 percent of the mainland Chinese population in 1970.

The liberalized 1965 law allowed the reunion of many families long kept apart. Again a large proportion of the newcomers were women, bringing the male-to-female ratio close to parity by 1970. Many new immigrants came in family groups, especially after 1965. They differed from the pre–World War II immigrants in that most were city people and were generally better educated. Although the great majority were Cantonese, a significant number were from other regions of China, especially Shanghai and the surrounding region, Fukien, Taiwan, and North China. The latter accounted for 10 to 15 percent of the Chinese-American population in 1970, and the proportion is increasing.

The new influx of immigrants produced a corresponding new demand for goods and services provided by the Chinatowns; they became busy shopping areas not only for the various groups of Chinese but for other Asians as well. The newcomers brought with them the latest styles from Hong Kong and Taiwan—in food, fashions, literature, *kung fu*, and the performing arts—which in turn affected Chinatown ways. Folk religion enjoyed a revival, but instead of temples, the worshipers congregated in the premises of a number of newly formed Buddhist and Taoist associations.

The increased population, as well as technological advances in publishing, aided the proliferation of Chinese newspapers; at one point in San Francisco in the mid-1970s there were as many as nine dailies and ten semiweeklies and weeklies, only two of which were in English. These included several newspapers in Hong Kong and Taiwan which since the 1960s have published American editions which compete effectively with the locally owned press.

Most of the new immigrants settled in cities with major Chinatowns, especially in San Francisco, Los Angeles, and New York. These communities were not equipped to absorb such a large number of new arrivals, and housing facilities were inadequate; overcrowding and substandard conditions soon resulted. Those who

knew no English were easily exploited for low wages and reduced to less skilled occupations. Unemployment, underemployment, and underutilization of talents were serious problems.

Many immigrant families needed more than one wage earner to make ends meet. The absence of both parents at work (about half the wives in Chinese families worked in 1970 compared to 39 percent in the total population) weakened parental authority. As the younger children learned English at school and lost their facility in Chinese, communication between generations again became a problem. The adoption of American behavior and customs by the younger generation gave rise once more to cultural and generational conflicts. Some of the older immigrant children could not cope with their lessons; lacking encouragement from parents or teachers, they dropped out of school. As a result teenage unemployment was high, and juvenile delinquency and crime soon became serious problems. From the mid-1960s to the mid-1970s, crime among the young escalated from petty larceny to burglary, assault, gang warfare, armed robbery, extortion, and murder. Some tongs apparently tried to recruit from among these youths, but most of the criminal elements appear to have remained outside the control of the tongs.

The new immigration coincided with the inauguration of President Lyndon B. Johnson's War on Poverty. A number of social agencies, generally staffed by Chinese Americans or bilingual immigrants, were established in Chinatowns to help low-income groups and to help the immigrants adjust to American society. The services helped to alleviate but did not solve their multiple, complex social and economic problems. They did, however, help to lessen the isolation of the Chinese communities from the larger society. The influx of funds from outside sources also helped shape a new power structure that could act independently of the traditional organizations in the Chinatowns and offer services the latter could not render. This tended to undermine still further the influence of the traditionalist groups.

The clan and district associations and the tongs benefited little from the increase in the Chinese population. Designed for a predominantly bachelor society, they had long since outlived their time. Their activities were often of no interest to younger Chinese Americans nor could they recruit many of the new, urban immigrants whose clan and regional loyalties were apt to be weaker than those of the generation which had come from the countryside. The preponderance of families also reduced the need for societies organized mainly for bachelor companionship. The once crowded associations were now reduced to a small circle of older immigrants plus a few who joined to advance their economic or political interests, particularly Kuomintang adherents eager to demonstrate that the Chinese in the United States supported the Taiwan regime.

Some organizations tried to change to meet the practical requirements of modern life. The Lee Family Association established a national credit union for members; the Soo Yuen Association in San Francisco ran a program for the aged; others gave scholarships and prizes to the children of members to encourage outstanding scholastic work. Most associations, however, limited their activities to banquets and picnics, or, in the case of district associations, also to maintaining a cemetery for members.

Group Maintenance Radio, television, the press, the public schools, and the churches have augmented the cultural influence of the larger society on Chinese Americans since World War II. As discrimination eased, they moved to other areas and found work outside the ethnic communities. Chinatown has become a place chiefly for weekend shopping or occasional social gatherings, but removed from the day-to-day life of many. Sino-American hostility cut off cultural influence from mainland China for two decades, and until the 1960s the Taiwan regime was too concerned with its own survival to export culture.

The cultural impact of the larger society is most noticeable among the American-born and those who immigrated at an early age. This group includes most of the Christian minority (15–20 percent of the total population, almost two-thirds of whom are Protestants). Many people have accepted American middle-class ideals and customs, while clinging to at least some aspects of their Chinese heritage.

A great many have dropped traditional practices. Some still observe the major festivals of the Chinese New Year, the Dragon Boat, and Mid-Autumn. In spring at Chingming or Tomb-Sweeping Day, families still visit the cemeteries, but these observances have lost most of their religious significance and have become largely social occasions. In San Francisco and Los Angeles the Chinese New Year has become a public festival and tourist attraction, complete with parade and a contest for the queen.

Despite the availability of Chinese schools in most communities, knowledge of Chinese among many of the American-born is rudimentary or nonexistent. In many families English is the primary, often the only, language. Boys and girls are usually treated as equal family members, and the relationship between parents and children tends to be warmer and more intimate than it was in the traditional or earlier immigrant Chinese family, where the emphasis was always on reserve and respect reinforced by discipline.

Many Chinese Americans have extended their social circle beyond the ethnic group as they join lodges, clubs, and societies of their peers in the larger society. Intergroup marriage has increased, especially among the younger generation. In 1970, 30 percent of the men and 22 percent of the women in the 16-to-24 age group in California had non-Chinese spouses.

Some have become active in U.S. politics. In 1946 Wing F. Ong (1904–1977) of Arizona was the first Chinese American on the mainland to be elected to a state legislature. In California, March Fong Eu (1929–) became a local school-board member in 1956, went to the state assembly in 1966, and was elected secretary of state in 1974, the highest-ranking elected officeholder of Chinese descent in the continental United States. In 1977 Thomas Tang (1922–) was confirmed as judge for the ninth circuit court of appeals. Democratic and Republican clubs became active in major Chinatowns as many Chinese Americans began to use politics to advance their interests.

Although by the 1960s flagrant discrimination against them had become rare, Chinese commonly encountered it in more subtle forms when applying for

jobs or promotions. For the Americanized generation who grew up after World War II it often came as a shock to find that they were not fully accepted. In the 1960s when blacks led the demand for equal opportunities, they found support among the Chinese-American middle class. When government, businesses, and other institutions were forced to remedy past inequities and place minorities in responsible roles, many Chinese benefited by being promoted to supervisory and middle-managerial posts; others were appointed school principals, city-board members, and judges. Affirmative-action programs also helped them enter television, public relations, and accounting, where opportunities had previously been restricted.

The War on Poverty inspired a number of Chinese students to return to the Chinatowns, involve themselves in local issues, and participate in programs for the young and aged, health and child care, housing, employment, and recreational facilities.

Demands for equal opportunity also produced a heightened ethnic awareness, reflected in San Francisco in the formation of such groups as the Chinese Historical Society of America (f. 1963), the Chinese Culture Foundation (f. 1965), and the bilingual newspaper *East–West* (f. 1967). Many other communities also have ethnic clubs. Ethnic political action by Americanized middle-class Chinese led to the formation of the San Francisco–based Chinese for Affirmative Action (CAA, f. 1970) and the Organization of Chinese Americans (OCA, f. 1973) with headquarters in Washington, D.C.; both of these organizations use political and legal channels to safeguard the civil rights of Chinese Americans and to fight stereotyped images of Chinese in the media. Others brought to court the case of *Lau* v. *Nichols* by which in 1974 the U.S. Supreme Court ruled that the failure of the San Francisco School District to provide special assistance to non-English-speaking Chinese students violated the provisions of the Civil Rights Act of 1964. This decision had nationwide implications, for it established the principle of bilingual education not only for Chinese but also for other non-English-speaking minorities; it is still too early to gauge its results. (*See* Language: Issues and Legislation.)

The realization that their political effectiveness was limited by their comparatively small numbers led Chinese Americans to join with other people of Asian descent to work toward common objectives. Around 1968 under the influence of the Black Power movement, the concept of Asian-American identity gained currency on the West Coast, and Asian origin was declared the basis for political unity among Chinese, Japanese, Koreans, and Filipinos in the United States. Asian Americans have jointly founded periodicals such as *Bridge* (New York, f. 1971), *Amerasia Journal* (University of California at Los Angeles, f. 1971), *Asian American Review* (University of California at Berkeley, f. 1972), and *Jade* (Los Angeles, f. 1974), as well as a number of newspapers.

On the campuses Asian Americans joined forces with black students to demand ethnic-studies courses. After a student strike at San Francisco State University the first course in Chinese-American history and the first Asian-American Studies department were organized in 1969; they were followed by similar programs at other universities.

A number of Chinese Americans became politicized and radicalized by participation in the civil rights, student-power, and anti–Vietnam War movements. Asian-American political groups proliferated. During the early years the movement was characterized by frequent changes and splits. Some early organizations were the Red Guards (f. 1968) of San Francisco, the Asian American Political Alliance (AAPA, f. 1968) on the West Coast, and the Asian Americans for Action (AAA, f. 1969) on the East Coast. These were soon eclipsed by the I Wor Kuen (IWK), established in 1970 in New York and in 1971 in San Francisco, where it absorbed the Red Guards; it publishes a newspaper called *Getting Together* (f. 1971). Around 1974 the Workers' Viewpoint Organization was formed on the East Coast, and by 1976 it had spread to the West. Strong local groups, such as the Wei Min She (WMS, f. 1971) in San Francisco, cooperated closely with radical white and Third World political activists. These radical groups are generally small and mostly recruited from Americanized Asian students and young intellectuals. In 1975 the WMS joined the Revolutionary Communist party; in 1978 the IWK merged with the Chicano August 29th Movement to form the League of Revolutionary Struggle (M–L).

Also affected by these social movements were the hitherto politically apathetic students from Taiwan and Hong Kong. The territorial dispute in 1970 between Taiwan and Japan over the Tiaoyutai Islands sparked many demonstrations and protests against Japan. Most of the participants relapsed into inactivity, but some remained active in the Chinatowns and on campuses.

The resurgence of the left and the growth of middle-class liberal groups in the Chinatowns brought conflict with the conservative, CCBA-led Chinatown establishment. When the People's Republic of China began to emerge as a world power, the liberals were among the first in the Chinatowns to urge recognition of the realities and to advocate normalization of U.S. relations with the People's Republic. In this, of course, they came into conflict with the Kuomintang. Initially they were no match for the entrenched conservative forces, but their influence increased as the CCBA-led traditionalist organizations failed to attract members from the younger generation and new immigrants, integration into the larger society continued, and political ties developed with other social groups. The establishment of formal relations between the United States and the People's Republic of China helped as well. By the mid-1970s the liberals and the left had both become forces that could not be ignored in Chinatown power relations. This new political alignment is reflected in the newly established nationwide National Association of Chinese Americans (NACA, f. 1977).

Today the Chinese population in the United States is the largest in any nation outside Asia. The 1970 Census recorded 383,023 on the U.S. mainland; births and immigration had increased this number to well over a half-million a few years later. According to the 1970 Census they are predominantly city dwellers—97 percent of them were living in urban areas, up slightly from 96 percent in 1960. The San Francisco Bay area and New York have the largest concentrations with around 100,000 each, but Los Angeles is close behind.

In recent years the population centers have shifted

somewhat. Since 1960 more Chinese immigrants have settled in and around New York than in the San Francisco Bay area. Those living in New York rose from 19 percent of the mainland population in 1960 to 21 percent in 1970, while those in California dropped from 48 percent to 44 percent. San Francisco, however, retains the highest percentage of the total U.S. Chinese population (8.2 percent in 1970).

In the South many Chinese groceries have closed as a result of competition from blacks. The population in Houston has increased as Chinese move in from the rural South to join professionals and scientists employed by various technological enterprises in that area. Many professionals and educators are now settling in industrial or university towns, often far from the main centers of ethnic population.

Chinese occupational and social roles in the United States have changed with the development of the nation. Despite their small numbers relative to the total population (about 0.2 percent) and the full acculturation of many, they remain an identifiable group with a distinct, though by no means homogeneous, subculture: for some, Chinese customs are an integral part of daily life; for others they are practically foreign. Differences persist between Cantonese and non-Cantonese, between old immigrants and new, and between immigrants from urban and from rural backgrounds. But regardless of this diversity Chinese Americans form a distinctive part of the American ethnic mosaic.

THE CHINESE IN HAWAII

China's demand for sandalwood established the Hawaiian Islands as a primary port of call in the China trade. Chinese crewmen and craftsmen serving on board ships sailing between China and the northwest coast of North America stopped at the islands as early as 1788. When Captain George Vancouver visited Hawaii in 1794, he found a Chinese serving King Kamehameha I.

Arrival and Settlement A Chinese entrepreneur built the first commercial sugar mill in 1802 on Lanai. In the second quarter of the 19th century the sugar industry began to grow, and Caucasian planters soon found that their labor needs could not be satisfied by the declining native-Hawaiian population; they began to look to the more populous nations, such as China, for manpower. In 1852 the *Thetis* initiated the coolie trade in Hawaii, bringing a load of 175 field workers and 20 houseboys from Amoy. However, in the next decade only a few hundred contract laborers came to Hawaii, and the Chinese population remained small.

The ending of the American Civil War boosted the sugar market. In 1876 a reciprocal trade agreement between the United States and the Hawaiian kingdom permitted the duty-free importation of Hawaiian sugar and rice to the United States. The growth of Hawaiian agriculture increased the demand for Chinese labor, and both Chinese and Caucasian firms organized to transport workers from China. The first of these, including both contract laborers and free immigrants, formed the first permanent Chinese community. The majority were Cantonese speakers (called Punti in Hawaii) from the Chungshan district in the lower part of the Pearl River Delta. A significant percentage also originated from areas in Chungshan-speaking variants of the

southern Min dialect. About one-fourth were Hakkas, mostly from districts on both sides of the Pearl River estuary. There were also smaller numbers from Sze Yap and other districts. Just as on the U.S. mainland, there were many intergroup antagonisms, especially between the Punti and Hakka. Hostility and sometimes open violence marked their relations during the early period.

More than 90 percent of the laborers who immigrated to Hawaii from 1852 to 1878 were from China. Chinese immigration reached a high in the 1880s with 4,243 arrivals in 1883. They increased from 4 percent of Hawaii's population in 1872 to almost 25 percent in 1884, and of that number over 95 percent were male.

Before the 1880s Chinese constituted the main labor force on the sugar plantations. Working conditions were harsh and life austere in the camps where they lived. The laborers expressed their discontent frequently by protests to officials and at times, riots. But the most common response was simply to leave the plantation. Many changed to rice growing, an industry started and dominated by the Chinese. A growing number joined their fellow countrymen in Honolulu and other towns. Many became skilled workers, artisans, and small proprietors, competing with the haoles (Caucasians) and Hawaiians.

The large influx of Chinese became a heated political issue in the islands for many of the same reasons that it did on the U.S. mainland, and it pitted the planters against government officials and local labor. In 1882 Murray Gibson, premier and minister of foreign affairs, initiated a policy to curtail Chinese immigration and substitute laborers from other countries. In 1884 Hawaii tried to induce Hong Kong to prohibit further emigration to the islands. The Chinese, however, continued to come: 4,405 new arrivals were recorded between 1884 and 1886.

The restrictionists also attempted to limit intermarriage between the Chinese and others and in this way prevent their establishing permanent residence. Business became increasingly troubled by Chinese competition—of the 692 firms listed in the Honolulu business directory in 1886, 219 were Chinese-owned. In 1888 the Hawaiian government began to set limits on the number of agricultural laborers entering from China and shortened the length of stay for nonresidents to five years. The planters turned to the Japanese and other groups as alternatives. These restrictions and a high departure rate reduced the Chinese population from 18,254 in 1884 to 16,752 in 1890. Labor shortages con-

Table 3. Chinese population in Hawaii, 1900–1970.

Year	Chinese population	Males per 100 females	Percentage U.S.-born
1900	25,767	642	16
1910	21,674	379	33
1920	23,507	222	53
1930	27,179	156	72
1940	28,774	128	84
1950	32,376	111	89
1960	38,197	105	91
1970	52,039	101	91

Source: U.S. Bureau of the Census, *Census of the Population, 1950* (Washington, D.C., 1953), vol. 2, pt. 52, pp. 13, 18; U.S. Bureau of the Census, *Census of the Population, 1960* (Washington, D.C., 1963), vol. 1, pt. 13, p. 119; U.S. Bureau of the Census, *Census of the Population, 1970* (Washington, D.C., 1973), vol. 1, pt. 13, pp. 28, 201.

tinued, however, so the planters induced the government to ease the laws against Chinese entry. Between 1890 and 1896 the Chinese population increased 29 percent.

The United States annexed Hawaii in 1898, and as a result the U.S. Chinese exclusion laws applied to Hawaii as well: in 1896 some 5,000 Chinese entered Hawaii; in 1906, only 106. For the next four decades new arrivals were too few to play a major role in the development of Hawaii's Chinese community. The population remained between 21,000 and 29,000 until restrictions against Chinese immigration were lifted during World War II.

When the flow of newcomers ceased, the Chinese community gradually became more stable in structure. The foreign-born Chinese population shrank as older agricultural laborers died or returned to China. In 1900, two generations after the arrival of the first contract laborers, foreign-born Chinese still composed 84 percent of the Chinese population in Hawaii; by 1930 the proportion was down to 27 percent, and 74 percent of those had arrived before 1898. But of those employed in 1930, 50 percent were still foreign-born—either men who had been so successful they did not want to return to China or, inversely, those who had been so unsuccessful that they could not return home and had resigned themselves to staying in Hawaii permanently.

The color line was less rigid in the multiethnic society of Hawaii than on the U.S. mainland, and many Chinese men married local women; in 1913, for example, of 121 Chinese men who married in Hawaii, half took non-Chinese wives, most of them native Hawaiians. A declining number of bachelor immigrants and the increase in Chinese families of the exempted classes subsequently reduced the percentage of marriages between Chinese men and non-Chinese women from 42 percent (1912–1916) to 25 percent (1920–1930).

As the agricultural laborers of the late 19th century departed and those remaining turned to other occupations, the Chinese became a predominantly urban population. In 1900, 32 percent of Hawaii's Chinese lived in Honolulu; in 1930 the proportion was 71 percent. But Chinese involvement in agriculture during the early period left an impressive legacy. In addition to rice, Chinese were early growers of taro, pineapples, bananas, coffee, tobacco, and garden vegetables. They also introduced numerous Chinese flowers, fruits, and vegetables which flourished in the Hawaiian climate, so similar to that of the immigrants' native Kwangtung. Until the first years of the 20th century they also played major roles in hog and poultry raising, in bee culture, and in the fishing industry.

Social Structure and Organization As in the large Chinatowns on the U.S. mainland, so in Honolulu and even in the smaller towns Chinese stores performed many social functions for the immigrants. The Chinese in Honolulu, and to a lesser extent in smaller cities such as Hilo, also participated in a number of organizations. Societies sprang up to serve the largely male population; their organization and functions were similar to those on the mainland: to provide fellowship and some measure of social control, to arbitrate disputes, and to lend aid and protection. The locality associations played a particularly large role in the lives of new-

comers; the clan associations allowed permanent settlers and Hawaiian-born Chinese to expand their affiliations. Economic interests were protected by trade and craftsmen's guilds and such organizations as the Chinese Chamber of Commerce, founded in 1911. Secret societies also abounded, although in Hawaii they were all lodges of the Triads and did not split into the rival tongs whose feuds had made the term "tong war" so notorious on the mainland.

The first Chinese organization in Hawaii was the Lin Yee Wui Burial Society, established in 1854 to ensure all Chinese a proper burial should they die in Hawaii. An overall Chinese organization, the Chunghua Huiguan (United Chinese Society), was established in 1884. As more immigrants settled in Hawaii the Chinese began to differentiate among themselves, forming dialect and locality associations; the people of Lungtu (Loong Doo in Hawaii), a subdistrict in Chungshan, who were about 15 percent of the Chinese Hawaiian population, established the first subdistrict association in 1885. A number of even more localized societies based on village of origin were established during the 1920s.

By 1940 the foreign-born population had decreased further: 66 percent of the 5,884 foreign-born males of 1930 had either died or departed. In 1930 there were 156 males for every 100 females; by 1940 the ratio was down to 128 for every 100. The foreign-born population now consisted primarily of families who had come to settle permanently. The elaborate network of regional organizations has declined greatly in importance.

As on the mainland, Chinese immigrants maintained close economic, cultural, and political ties with their native land, and for many of the same reasons. Newspapers supporting rival political factions expressed interest in homeland politics in a diversity of opinions. The earliest newspaper was the *Hawaiian Chinese News*; it was founded in 1883 as a nonpolitical newspaper but by 1904 had begun to support Sun Yat-sen's revolutionary party.

Chinese schools were also established as early as 1899 in an attempt to preserve the Chinese heritage of the American-born generation. One of these early schools, Mun Lun, founded in 1910 in Honolulu, was the largest Chinese school in the Western Hemisphere in the mid-1930s with an enrollment of more than 1,340.

The Chinese, especially the native-born, used education as the first vehicle for assimilation and success in Hawaiian society. From 1910 to 1940 the Chinese had a higher percentage of 16- and 17-year-olds attending schools than any other ethnic group; in the mid-1920s almost 15 percent of schoolteachers in Hawaii were Chinese. By 1940 more than a third of gainfully employed Chinese were in professional or clerical work. Some became prominent in the cultural sphere—Dai Keong Lee (1915–), for example, was a nationally known composer in the 1940s.

The Chinese were also active in local political life. Their way had been paved by a number of Hawaiian Chinese who became prominent public servants both during the monarchy and after the annexation. In 1925 the Hawaii Civic Association was established to fight for the civil rights of American citizens of Chinese ancestry. In 1926 Dr. Dai Yen Chang and Yew Char be-

came the first Chinese to be elected Honolulu city and county supervisor, and representative to the state legislature, respectively. Chinese Americans have been active in Hawaiian politics ever since.

The Postwar Period The trend toward city living, the growing predominance of family groups, and the balancing of the sex ratio changed Chinese social life in Hawaii. Chinese immigration, which had remained steady throughout the 1940s and 1950s at about 100 a year, tripled after passage of the liberalizing 1965 immigration law and quadrupled by 1974. The 60-year decline in the population of foreign-born Chinese was reversed, although the native-born still predominated with 91 percent of the population in 1970.

The new immigrants embarked chiefly from Hong Kong. Generally they were better schooled than the early immigrants, and a number were cosmopolitan and well educated. Most newcomers joined the established group in the main city. By 1970, 48,288 out of 52,039 Chinese in Hawaii—representing 96 percent of the total group and 77 percent of its foreign-born members—lived in Honolulu or its mostly middle-class suburbs. By then they no longer regarded it necessary to settle in exclusively Chinese areas, and Honolulu's Chinatown began to decline. In 1900, 70 percent of all Honolulu Chinese lived in Chinatown; today only 20 percent live there.

The occupational profiles of Chinese Americans in Hawaii and on the U.S. mainland are similar but not identical. The proportion of professionals is slightly smaller, and that of managers and administrators slightly larger, in Hawaii than on the mainland. Only 6 percent of Chinese men on the mainland work as craftsmen or foremen, in contrast to 20 percent of Hawaiian Chinese. About 25 percent of employed Chinese men are service workers on the mainland; only 11 percent in Hawaii.

Chinese-American entrepreneurs have played a far larger role in the Hawaiian economy than in the mainland's. When the Chinese began leaving the plantations for the city, many sought economic independence by becoming small proprietors. Filling the vacuum in Hawaiian society caused by the lack of a well-established native middle class, a Chinese entrepreneurial class with substantial financial resources was firmly established before World War II. Its financing needs were met by the hui and the Chinese-owned Chinese-American Bank (f. 1916) and Liberty Bank (f. 1922). In 1939 Chinese Americans owned 56 of 275 manufacturing establishments in Hawaii. Particularly successful were the C.Q. Yee Hop interests, which by the late 1940s owned supermarkets and a slaughter house, dealt in real estate, and operated the American Brewing Company (f. 1933).

After World War II a new kind of entrepreneur—the Chinese tycoon—challenged the hegemony of the Big Five, the sugar magnates who controlled corporate business in the islands. Four notable examples are Chinn Ho, Hiram Fong (later the first Chinese to be elected to the U.S. Senate), and the brothers Hung Wo Ching and Hung Wai Ching. Hung Wo Ching resuscitated the bankrupt Trans-Pacific Company and turned it into the thriving Aloha Airlines. His brother Hung Wai established a financial empire that became a cornerstone of postwar Hawaiian economic development. Chinn Ho secured 9,000 acres of fallow sugar land in 1947 and converted them into a housing development; later he branched out into the hotel and newspaper-publishing businesses. Hiram Fong made a fortune in real estate and insurance operations. According to a survey conducted in the mid-1970s Fong was the wealthiest member of the U.S. Senate.

The enterprises initiated by these Chinese businessmen helped establish the conditions for diversification of the Hawaiian economy after statehood. They strengthened ties with businesses outside Hawaii and stimulated commerce and travel between the mainland and the islands.

But even apart from these exceptionally enterprising individuals, the Hawaiian Chinese are economically a notably successful ethnic group. In 1970 their average annual family income in the Honolulu metropolitan area was $16,568—about 40 percent higher than the comparable average for their counterparts in mainland cities with substantial Chinese populations—and only 5 percent had incomes below the poverty line. Chinese now constitute about 7 percent of the population of Hawaii, the highest for any American state or territory. Clearly the Chinese community plays a major role in the life of the Hawaiian Islands.

Table 4. Occupational distribution of Chinese, 15 years and older, in Hawaii, 1970 (in percentages).

Occupation	Male	Female	Overall
Professional and technical workers	21.6	19.0	20.5
Managers and administrators, except farm	14.1	5.5	10.4
Sales workers	6.6	9.2	7.7
Clerical workers	11.2	37.0	22.1
Craftsmen and foremen	19.5	1.9	12.1
Operatives, including transport	9.2	8.0	8.7
Laborers, except farm	5.3	1.0	3.5
Farmers	0.4	0.1	0.3
Farm laborers	0.7	0.5	0.6
Service workers	11.3	16.9	13.7
Private household	0.1	0.9	0.4

Source: U.S. Bureau of the Census, *Census of the Population, 1970,* Subject Report PC(2)-1G, *Japanese, Chinese, and Filipinos in the United States* (Washington, D.C., 1973), p. 94.

Bibliography
The classic study on the Chinese in America is Mary R. Coolidge, *Chinese Immigration* (1909; reprint, New York, 1969). Modern works providing a general introduction to the history and society are Thomas W. Chinn, H.M. Lai, and Philip P. Choy, *A History of the Chinese in California: A Syllabus* (San Francisco, 1969); Victor G. and Brett de Bary Nee, *Longtime Californ': A Documentary Study of an American Chinatown* (New York, 1973); and Stanford M. Lyman, *Chinese Americans* (New York, 1974). Pertinent facts and dates are presented in outline form in H.M. Lai and Philip P. Choy, *Outlines: History of the Chinese in America* (San Francisco, 1973), and W.L. Tung, *The Chinese in America 1820–1973: A Chronology and Fact Book* (Dobbs Ferry, N.Y., 1974). A book in a more popular vein for the general reader is Betty Lee Sung, *Mountain of Gold: The Story of the Chinese in America* (New York, 1967).

Rose Hum Lee, *The Chinese in the United States of America* (Hong Kong, 1960), is a pioneer sociological study. Other useful works are S.W. Kung, *Chinese in American Life: Some Aspects of Their History, Status, Problems and Contributions* (Seattle, 1962), and essays in Stanford M. Lyman, *The Asian in the West* (Reno, Nev., 1970).

Ping Chiu, *Chinese Labor in California, 1850–1880: An Economic Study* (Madison, Wis., 1963), is authoritative. The anti-Chinese movement is discussed in Stuart C. Miller, *The Unwelcome Immigrant: The American Image of the Chinese, 1785–1882* (Berkeley, Calif., 1969), and Alexander P. Saxton, *The Indispensable Enemy: Labor and the Anti-Chinese Movement in California* (Berkeley, 1971). Charles A.

Price, *The Great White Walls Are Built: Restrictive Immigration to North America and Australasia* (Canberra, Australia, 1974), is an illuminating comparative study of responses to Chinese immigration.

Pardee Lowe, *Father and Glorious Descendant* (Boston, 1943), Jade Snow Wong, *Fifth Chinese Daughter* (New York, 1950), and Maxine Hong Kingston, *The Woman Warrior: Memoirs of a Grilhood among Ghosts* (New York, 1976), are autobiographies relating experiences of Chinese Americans growing up in the United States.

Selections of Chinese-American creative writings are in Frank Chin et al., eds., *AIIIEEEE! An Anthology of Asian-American Writers* (Washington, D.C., 1974).

Reference materials on the Chinese in Hawaii are not as numerous as those for Chinese on the mainland. Tin-Yuke Char compiled and edited *The Sandalwood Mountains* (Honolulu, 1975), which includes selected readings on the early Chinese Hawaiians. By the same author, *The Bamboo Path* (Honolulu, 1977) includes a number of essays on Chinese-Hawaiian history. Information on the Chinese can also usually be found in scholarly books on Hawaii; for example, Lawrence H. Fuchs, *Hawaii Pono: A Social History* (New York, 1961), pp. 86–105, includes a chapter, "Success *Pake* Style."

Extensive holdings of materials, serials, books, and pamphlets are in the Asian-American Studies Libraries of the University of California at Berkeley and Los Angeles, and the Californiana Room of the San Francisco Public Library. Many 19th-century primary documents are in the Bancroft Library, University of California, Berkeley. The Chinese Historical Society of America has a number of 20th-century publications in English and Chinese as well as a museum collection of artifacts and photographs. Extensive archival materials are also available at the Federal Archives and Records Center, San Bruno, Calif.; the National Archives, Washington, D.C.; and the California State Archives in Sacramento.

For those interested in Chinese-language materials a good collection is in the East Asian Library, Hoover Institution on War, Revolution, and Peace, Stanford, Calif.

Primary documents on the Chinese in Hawaii can be found in the Archives of Hawaii Newspapers, and books are available at the Hawaiian and Pacific Collection, Hamilton Library, University of Hawaii. The Asian collection in the same library can be consulted for Chinese-language materials. The Hawaii Chinese History Center also has a number of publications in Chinese and English.

The section of this entry on the Chinese in Hawaii was written by Reed Ueda.

H. M. LAI

CHIPPEWAS: *see* AMERICAN INDIANS

CHITIMACHAS: *see* AMERICAN INDIANS

CHOCTAWS: *see* AMERICAN INDIANS

CHUMASHES: *see* AMERICAN INDIANS

CIRCASSIANS: *see* NORTH CAUCASIANS

COCOPAS: *see* AMERICAN INDIANS

COEUR D'ALENES (SALISH): *see* AMERICAN INDIANS

COLOMBIANS: *see* CENTRAL AND SOUTH AMERICANS

COLVILLE (SALISH): *see* AMERICAN INDIANS

COMANCHES: *see* AMERICAN INDIANS

CONCEPTS OF ETHNICITY

The English language has often been enriched by the incorporation of more or less synonymous words from two or more sources. The many terms used in the analysis of ethnicity or nationalism, however, have not generally contributed to greater clarity. With so complex and contentious a topic, all designations have remained more or less ambiguous, and commentators are often unable to agree on the precise meaning of any of them. It might be useful in a fully authoritative piece to stipulate the "correct" meaning of each term; more realistically, the intent here is to trace the meanings assigned to each, beginning with its etymology and continuing through the connotations associated with it in various contexts.

SEARCH FOR A TERMINOLOGY

The word "ethnic" derives via Latin from the Greek *ethnikos,* the adjectival form of *ethnos,* a nation or race. As originally used in English, ethnic signified "not Christian or Jewish, pagan, heathen"; for example, in *The Leviathan* Thomas Hobbes exhorted Christian converts to continue obeying their "ethnic" rulers. "Nation" comes from Latin via French; its ultimate source is *nasci,* "to be born," and the closer source is *natio,* meaning originally "birth," later one of the barbarian tribes outside the Roman world.

The physiological association suggested by these etymologies was long retained in English, as we can see especially from some currently obsolete or rare usages. Like dozens of other words (such as "barbarian," meaning "not Greek") both "ethnic" and "nation" were applied originally to outsiders as a class. With the lessening of what we now term ethnocentrism, the range of many such words was extended from alien peoples to any people, including that of the speaker. And from their originally biological context, the meaning of both terms broadened to include cultural characteristics and political structures. But neither of these shifts has been consistent or unidirectional.

"Ethnic" is an adjective, and English never adopted a noun from the Greek *ethnos.* The lack of a convenient substantive form has induced writers to coin a number of makeshifts, all of which have their drawbacks. Of these, the commonest (as suggested by the name of this encyclopedia) is "ethnic group." Unfortunately, users of this term too often forget the crucial distinction between a group, which by definition has some degree of coherence and solidarity, and a subpopulation, category, grouping, aggregate, bracket, or sector, which denote no more than a patterned differentiation. The connotation of ethnic "group" is that its members are at least latently aware of common interests. Despite the difficulty of determining at what point people become a group, that is, the point at which coherence is established, it is important to retain the fundamental distinction between a group and a category, because many of the processes analyzed in the study of ethnic relations consist of the interaction between the two. Assimilation, thus, can be defined as movement from group to category, the rise of nationalism as movement in the other direction.

As professional jargon, "minority group" is even less suitable, for both its elements are ill chosen. According to Louis Wirth, whose writings did much to popularize the term, it refers simply to victims of a subordination that he condemned; "the people whom we regard as a minority may actually, from a numerical standpoint, be a majority." But in most of history, as well as in most of the non-Western world today, the dominant social division has been between a small ruling elite and a vast ruled mass; what Tocqueville called "the tyranny of the majority" can arise only in the exceptional democratic

society. Wirth's term merely muddies, and thus facilitates a manipulation to fit the political occasion: in the British Isles the Irish are a widely dispersed minority; in all of Ireland the Protestants are a minority; in Northern Ireland the Catholics are a minority. Simply by drawing the appropriate boundary and stressing the self-serving portion of an area's history, partisans can almost always find a way to picture themselves as a victimized minority group.

In other works I have suggested the term "subnation," denoting simply a unit smaller than a nation but otherwise similar to it. A nation is a people linked by common descent from a putative ancestor and by its common territory, history, language, religion, and/or way of life. Obviously neither all nations nor all subnations conform to every element of this list, but the precise limits of subnations are often more difficult to fix because they are seldom directly associated with the counterpart of a boundary-protecting state. Hardly any other analysts have adopted "subnation" in place of the terms it was intended to supplant. One reason is that it also is ambiguous in suggesting that all of a nation's characteristics are typically shared by its ethnic parts.

The same difficulties are encountered in trying to fix the meanings of other derivatives from the word "nation." Originally "nationality" meant "national quality or character," then "a nation, frequently of a people potentially but not actually a nation." However, in the most common current usage in such multiethnic countries as the United States or the Soviet Union, it denotes a particular type of ethnic category. The words "nationalism" and "nationalist" can pertain to existent nations (in which case they are more or less equivalent to "patriotism" and "patriot"), but they are more likely to refer to ethnic sentiment with or without an implicit aspiration to establish an independent country: Polish nationalists want an independent Poland; Flemish nationalists want equal status with Walloons in a continuing Belgian state. It is unfortunate that we use the same word to designate both "black nationalism," most of whose advocates do not demand independence from the United States, and Canada's "French nationalism," whose leaders have demanded that the province of Quebec become a separate state. The term is especially imprecise in describing a shift from one level of group consciousness to another. In multiethnic Austria-Hungary, for instance, the creators of a new Slav awareness first demanded no more than greater group rights within the empire; only later did some of the Slav proponents begin to insist on independence for what eventually emerged as Czechoslovakia and Yugoslavia. And in such areas as black Africa today, it is less an analytic than a political judgment whether the surviving "tribalism" (or, in India, "communalism") expresses dissent within an essentially unified entity or the strivings of real nations to throw off the dominance of alien rulers.

Interpretation is likely to falter also when words in other languages are translated as "ethnicity" or "nationalism." This is the case even among the closely related western European languages. The French word *nation* has the same double meaning as its English derivative, either a community based on common characteristics or a political unit. A biological linkage is likely to be expressed by *peuple*, "people," and a territorial or sentimental one by *patrie*, "fatherland." The word *état*, "state," has the convenient derivatives *étatisme* and *étatisation*, which are rendered far less appropriately in English by "nationalism" (as in "economic nationalism") and "nationalization." Under the Nazi German program to delete all foreign words, *Nation*, which had usually implied a cultural rather than a political unit, was largely supplanted by *Volk*, very roughly, "people," but in fact untranslatable. The adjective *völkisch* denoted the essential, organic character of Germans, usually including more than those who were then living in the Reich. Since 1945 both *Volk* and *völkisch* have been used less, for they are considered tarnished by Nazism. French has a similar term, *ethnie*, to denote those bound by racial, cultural, and sentimental ties regardless of national boundaries; *l'ethnie française* thus comprises the French-speaking sectors not only of France but also of Belgium, Switzerland, Italy, and so on. According to Guy Héraud's *L'Europe des ethnies*, however, "each such population always represents, either actually or potentially, an *ethnie* also in the subjective sense—a nationality."

Ethnie is a neologism not yet included in general French dictionaries, and it may be that English will solve the terminological dilemma by adopting as a suitable noun either *ethnie* or the Greek *ethnos* or, most probably, "ethnic" itself. In recent popular writing it has been used as a substantive, usually applied only to certain categories: "white ethnics" are Italians and Poles, for example, but usually not Scots or Norwegians. If the meaning of the noun became comprehensive, like that of the adjective, and if the usage did not remain substandard, "ethnic" might be the most suitable term.

ETHNOS VERSUS RACE

Of the various criteria of ethnicity, race is in many respects the most significant; the characteristics of the body, that most palpable element of one's persona, have been used throughout history to define the most pervasive type of group identity. Since *ethnos* with its derivatives pertained originally to a biological grouping, it was close to our "race" (probably derived from *ratio*, which in medieval Latin was used to designate species). In its current usage a biological connotation sometimes adheres still to "ethnic," but not necessarily: some groupings are defined by their genetic heritage, others by their language or religion or some other criterion. Apart from poetry or metaphor, "race" in English has referred consistently to a biological unit, but its size has varied from a family line (as in Tennyson's "We were two daughters of one race") to the entire species (as in "the human race"). Indeed, as physical anthropologists use the term, the size of a race depends simply on the purpose of the particular investigator: it denotes a subpopulation that differs significantly from others in the frequency of one or more genes, with "significantly" specified according to the context. Its cognates in other European languages—French *race*, German *Rasse*, and so on—are still used with a seeming indifference to either the range of the unit or the amount of difference between it and other subpopulations. English, however, has shown a trend toward what would be a useful distinction, reserving "race" for mankind's major biological divisions and using another designation for smaller

groupings within it. Thus, many American writers now distinguish "racial" from "ethnic" minorities, the former being Negroes, Asians, and other "nonwhites," the latter the European nationalities.

The separation of the two terms has been inhibited, however, by the confusion in real life between physiological and cultural criteria. Very often a racial group is set off from the rest of the population by cultural characteristics as well; conversely, if the endogamy enjoined or at least encouraged by most religious faiths and other cultural groups continues for enough generations, it is likely to result in a perceptible physical differentiation. In a Mexican census enumeration, following that country's usual perception of its ethnic pattern, an "Indian" is one who speaks an Indian language and wears Indian clothing; if he learns to speak Spanish and shifts from huaraches to shoes, he becomes a "mestizo." The stereotype that an Indian is unable to perform industrial tasks is not only true but a truism: a factory worker is no longer an Indian.

In the aftermath of the Nazi program of genocide, a number of anthropologists have argued that we should delete "race" from our languages, not only because it is associated with racism but fundamentally because it is a vague category with imprecise and shifting boundaries. Whether the removal of a word would also eradicate group antipathies is doubtful; one suspects that with another classification Jews and Gypsies would have been murdered just as bestially. In any case, deleting the term does not remove the need for some designation. Ashley Montagu, who has argued the case most vociferously, suggested that "ethnic group" be substituted for "race," but the consequent confusion of biological and cultural characteristics, paradoxically, is the hallmark of racism. Whether Jews constitute the "race" (or, to use a common euphemism, "stock") that the Nazis asserted them to be depends on the context. In a discussion of religious or other cultural characteristics, genetic make-up is manifestly irrelevant, but in a study of dysautonomia, a genetic disease especially prevalent among Jews, the crucial factor is precisely their hereditary links. Moreover, the notion that only "pure" categories may be admitted to exist is bizarre; it follows from the theory of evolution itself that all biological divisions, from phylum through subspecies, are always in the process of change, so there is almost never a sharp and permanent boundary setting one off from the next.

CULTURALLY DEFINED GROUPINGS

If the demand for pure categories were to be extended to the indicators generally used in the social disciplines, acceding to it would bar most research. For the difference is also partly arbitrary, and thus more or less mutable, between, say, the rural and the urban, the employed and the unemployed, the literate and the illiterate, and so on. As Abraham Kaplan put it in his classic *The Conduct of Inquiry,* "It is the dogmatisms outside science that proliferate closed systems of meaning; the scientist is in no hurry for closure. Tolerance of ambiguity is as important for creativity in science as it is anywhere else."

The meaning of "language," probably the second most prevalent indicator of ethnicity, is as ambiguous as that of "race." Forms of speech known to be related constitute what is known as a "linguistic stock," made up of what are deemed to be languages and what are called dialects. But with the advance of knowledge, the Germanic stock, for example, was recognized as a subunit of the larger Indo-European stock. As Edward Sapir put it in his standard work on linguistics, the terms dialect, language, branch, and stock are all only relative, convertible as our perspective widens or contracts.

Often linguistic characteristics matter less in determining the designation than the cultural or political status of the subpopulation that uses a particular speech. Flemish was once the "dialect" of Dutch spoken in Belgium, but now, after the successful effort of Flemish nationalists to establish it as such, Flemish or "Southern Dutch" is one of the country's two official "languages." Romansch, comprising several dialects spoken by tiny remnants of some Roman legions, was elevated in 1938 to the fourth official language of Switzerland. Perhaps the strangest case is the recent acceptance of a second language, Landsmål, in Norway, a country with some 4 million inhabitants and one of the few in the world that until then had not manifested any significant ethnic differentiation. Because the standard speech used by the educated middle class was close to Danish, agitation for recognition of the new language was based in part on "patriotism"; and because Landsmål, an amalgam of several dialects, is spoken by peasants and fishermen, a second appeal could be made based on "democracy." After more than a century of accelerating agitation, the proponents of a second official Norwegian language achieved their purpose, and today the country's schoolchildren must learn both.

The meaning of "region," another ethnic indicator, is also far from clear-cut. Sometimes it is based on what is termed a "natural area," that is, a physiographic unit delineated by its topography, soil type, climate, or similar features. Particularly among primitive peoples, who have relatively little control over their physical environment, a natural area may overlap within what anthropologists call a "culture area," which approaches what we ordinarily think of as a region. The U.S. Bureau of the Census divides the United States into four regions (Northeast, North Central, South, and West), with each subdivided into "geographic divisions." These designations developed only gradually and remain somewhat arbitrary; whether there actually are subcultures associated with New England, the Midwest, and so on depends in large part on where one draws the boundaries and which indexes one uses to measure the supposed differences.

In short, none of the group characteristics—whether cultural or physical—that are used to denote ethnicity generally set off any subpopulation sharply. A great contrast is likely only when several indexes overlap. In Canada, for example, the French-speaking sector resides mostly in the province of Quebec, is Catholic rather than Protestant like most other Canadians, and—to add a nonethnic factor—was until recently concentrated in the lower and lower-middle classes in contrast with the English-speaking employers and professionals in the province. The world-famous amity of the Swiss, on the other hand, has been partly based on the happy accident that the lines of ethnic division have cut across one another. The main emotional issue in 19th-century Switzerland was religion; then it became

nationality, with each of the three main language communities speaking a tongue in common with a contiguous foreign country. But both the German- and French-speaking Swiss are both Catholic and Protestant; opposed in one arena, they have always been aware that they would be allies in another. Moreover, the proportions of German-, French-, and Italian-speaking Swiss were constant for more than a century, so that no one had to fear the day that a minority would reach the fateful 51 percent—when any modus vivendi that had been worked out would become obsolete.

OFFICIAL COUNTS OF ETHNIC GROUPS

The vagaries of ethnic classification are especially apparent in the several United Nations comparisons of the criteria used in the world's censuses. According to the first of these compilations, in 1957, 39 countries divided their populations by a geographical-ethnic criterion, 10 by race, 8 by culture, 22 by a combination of race and culture, 11 by a combination of culture and geography, one or two by origin as indicated by the language of the respondent's father, and several by "mode of life." Even when the same term was used, the meaning sometimes was different. Replies to questions on matters reflecting social prestige were probably often false. And the enumerations have not improved since this initial comparison.

If the subnations of any society are classified only partly according to their objective characteristics, how are the nonobjective criteria set? Most obviously, they are chosen to fit the view that the politically dominant grouping has of the whole, and invariably one of the principal dimensions divides "insiders," variously defined, from "outsiders." In the United States, for example, "English American" occasionally has been defined as one nationality among others, and the census bureau tabulates persons with English-born parents or grandparents as part of the "foreign stock"; more generally, those with English forebears have been regarded as the core population with which others have been compared. In other circumstances the dominant group may be given the most statistical attention. American whites are divided by nationality, but Americans of other races are considered single entities—though in a Negro community the distinction is just as significant between a southern and a West Indian background, or in a Japanese community between origin in the main islands and in Okinawa. On the other hand, American Indians are enumerated by tribe, including even very small ones, and in Hawaii a count has been made of the perhaps 2 percent of the population listed as pure Polynesian, though most in that category are actually part-Hawaiians who claimed unmixed ancestry in order to gain special access to schooling, homesteads, certain occupations, and other opportunities.

In the continuous interplay among groups, any answer to the question of how they shall be designated seldom remains fixed. The formal names of those low in an ethnic hierarchy, recurrently seen as derogatory, are repeatedly replaced with one synonym or another. When the National Association for the Advancement of Colored People (NAACP) was founded at the beginning of the 20th century, the only fully acceptable term for Negroes was "colored"; "negro," "Negro," "Afro-American," "black," and "Black"—terms that sectors of the Negro population have successively insisted on —were then regarded as insulting. Several groups of Negro-Indian-white ancestry in the southern Appalachians successfully demonstrated against their enumeration as "Negro" and were reclassified as "Indian." On the other hand, a decision *not* to classify a population along a particular dimension, though it is typically justified by an assertion that the differentiation is unimportant, may be based rather on a reluctance to publicize significant ethnic-class or ethnic-political correlations. For example, when the U.S. Bureau of the Census suggested including a question on religious affiliation in the 1960 schedule, the opposition from Jewish organizations was so strong that the proposal was dropped.

An important influence on any classificatory system, finally, is the convenience of the administrative agency that makes the count. The census bureau is under heavy and often conflicting pressures, and the choice between monetary or other costs and its assessment of national utility has varied from time to time. Since 1890, the first year that all Indians were counted, the inclusiveness of the definition has shifted from one census to the next, so that the total enumeration has fluctuated. The money-saving procedure of dividing printed tables into only two categories, "whites" and "nonwhites," makes sense for areas where nonwhite is virtually equivalent to Negro, but not in the Southwest or Hawaii, where substantial percentages are Chinese, Japanese, American Indian, or Polynesian. The trend from a *de jure* to a *de facto* definition of residence has also affected reported counts of particular areas. The decision, for instance, to include members of the armed forces and their dependents in the population of Hawaii —a choice no less arbitrary than to exclude them—substantially altered not only the state's racial proportions but also the reported age structure, mortality, fertility, income level, and so on through the whole range of demographic and social data.

In sum, ethnic differentiation is typically both important and imprecise. Paradoxically, an impressionistic account of how one ethnic sector is set off from others can be more accurate than one based on sharp divisions. In law and demography, however, an absolute demarcation is almost inescapable. If members of certain minorities are given preferential access to colleges and jobs through "affirmative action," precise criteria for eligibility are necessary. And a census that reports the race or nationality of every individual in the society leaves no place for miscellany. Like most other social indicators, ethnic ones are likely to transform the stupendous complexity of our world into a more comprehensible simplicity, and much of what we think we know about ethnicity derives from such statistics.

PROCESSES OF ASSIMILATION

The shorthand denotation of the prevailing belief early in this century was that America is a "melting pot." In later attacks on this symbol of total assimilation, it was often forgotten that the slogan derived from a play written by Israel Zangwill, paying homage to "the great Alchemist [who] melts and fuses them with his purging flame—Celt and Latin, Slav and Teuton, Greek and Syrian," and, as represented in the play's hero and heroine, Jew and Gentile. The melting pot was probably an accurate metaphor for the insecure first

generation's aspiration to disappear totally, to merge into indistinguishable sameness with "real" Americans.

At that time placing restrictions on immigration was a crucial political issue. If all immigrants were indeed developing into identical American citizens, then obviously the xenophobic demands of restrictionists were not well based. Academic leaders gave ideological support to this antirestrictionist argument. According to the most important social theorist of the 1920s, Professor Robert E. Park of the University of Chicago, all interethnic relations go through an invariable and irreversible four-stage succession of contact, competition, accommodation, and assimilation. Progress along this line is inevitable—except when some factor interferes with it temporarily. Once its premises are accepted, the schema is unassailable; the many ethnic groups that have remained distinct for decades (or centuries) can always be explained by special circumstances, and the dogma that full amalgamation will be attained "eventually" remains intact. In two respects Park went beyond even Zangwill's extravagantly utopian view. He generalized the vista to all peoples; as he wrote, "the melting pot is the world." And in the United States, Park was mainly concerned not with European nationalities but with races, whose differences were etched in law and in seemingly strong and unchanging sentiment.

This view of race relations in the United States was adopted in Gunnar Myrdal's An American Dilemma (1944), still the major synthesis of works on its topic. In a hundred contexts, Myrdal and his collaborators argued that all but the most superficial differences between whites and blacks derived from white prejudice and discriminatory institutions. As one example of a vicious circle leading to a pattern of mutually supporting elements, racially segregated schools derived from the whites' belief that Negroes are genetically of inferior intelligence, and products of the poorer Negro schools often validated the thesis that on the average Negroes are indeed more stupid. For the common phrase "vicious circle," Myrdal substituted his own term, the "principle of cumulation," for he wanted to emphasize that the process could work in either direction. If those who did not accept racist dogma demanded the desegregation of education (and the Brown decision of the Supreme Court was delivered only a decade after An American Dilemma was published), then the Negroes who consequently got a better schooling would erode the belief in genetic differences in intelligence, and gradually all significant distinctions between the races would disappear.

A high point in American views of acculturation was reached in Milton Gordon's Assimilation in American Life (1964), which incorporated the thesis of "cultural pluralism" developed by Horace Kallen and provided a much more cautious analysis than the academic version of the melting pot. Desegregation, Gordon held, need not lead "immediately" or "necessarily" to the integration of ethnic communities, but he made the point mainly in order to quell the fear of "die-hard segregationists" that the granting of civil rights would result in widespread intermarriage. To the "built-in tension between the goals of ethnic communality and desegregation" there seemed to be no solution except good will on the part of all.

With such works American sociologists gave an aura of verisimilitude to the vista of a future either without meaningful ethnicity or at least with little or no ethnic conflict. In spite of its now manifest faults, this American theory (as we might term it) has been influential in other countries whose history has been shaped by immigration, such as Australia. European analysts were more likely to be concerned about how to prevent assimilation—how language communities, for instance, could maintain their identity and prevent what the Nazis termed Gleichschaltung (which can be inadequately translated as "homogenization"). And social scientists everywhere have been influenced by Marx, reflecting both his lack of interest in nationalism and ethnicity and his certainty that these primordial sentiments, remnants of a past age, had survived beyond their term.

THE RISE OF ETHNICITY

To most analysts of ethnic relations, the worldwide rise of racial, religious, linguistic, or nationalist sentiment—and often violent opposition to it—came as a surprise. Why, contrary to almost every informed opinion, have recent years seen a reassertion of ethnicity? Only a few strands of the complex answer to this question can be offered here.

First, one should note that almost all the earlier doctrines—whether the melting pot or Marxism—typically evolved as support for a political position rather than as a purely objective analysis of the trend in interethnic relations. Even as ethnic identity was becoming more significant in the United States, attempts were being made, in conformance with national policy, to disguise the very existence of racial differences. Such pressure groups as the American Civil Liberties Union tried to have the question on race deleted from the 1960 census schedule, and for one year New Jersey actually did omit race and color from its birth and death certificates. Following the prestigious example of the New York Times, many newspapers left out racial identifications of all persons on whom they reported. Various states passed laws stipulating that applications for employment or for entrance to college and similar forms could not require an ethnic identification or a photograph, which was considered an approximate equivalent. These procedures were all based on the premise that an official recognition of ethnic (and particularly racial) differentiation facilitated discrimination, but even in the context in which they were proposed they were inept. It was hardly possible to evaluate the many experimental programs designed to raise the status of blacks, for example, without data on race. And the subsequent change to new imperatives came so quickly that universities, for example, were for a time simultaneously forbidden to record the race of their faculty and students and required to report what proportions of each were of specified minorities. One reason that rising ethnicity burst on us with such startling suddenness was the earlier effort to combat racism by omitting race, religion, and nationality from public records.

A parallel stance was common in the analysis of prejudice. Literally, "prejudice" means prejudgment, a judgment before knowledge. In Theodore Newcomb's Social Psychology (1950), then one of the dominant texts in the field, prejudice was defined as "an unfavorable at-

titude—a predisposition to perceive, act, think, and feel in ways that are 'against' rather than 'for' another person or group," contrasted with a "predisposition toward intimacy and/or helpfulness." In the authoritative *Handbook of Social Psychology* (1954), as another instance, the term was defined as "an ethnic attitude in which the reaction tendencies are predominantly negative . . . simply an unfavorable ethnic attitude." Ostensibly any hostile judgment concerning any group was denounced, but of course this was not the case. The substitution of adverse judgment for prejudgment was itself a political stand.

The negativism included blocking out scholarly works with a different point of view. Paradoxically, America's first outstanding analysis of ethnicity, William Graham Sumner's *Folkways* (1906), was in some respects the most perceptive. Terms that Sumner introduced—"folkways" itself, "mores," "ethnocentrism," "in-group," "out-group," and so on—became common usage in subsequent works, but no trace remained of his belief that group differences, because they are based on distinctions seen to be more or less immutable, are likely to persevere. One cannot change the mores, he wrote, "by any artifice or device, to a great extent, or suddenly, or in any essential element . . . Changes which are opposed to the mores require long and patient effort, if they are possible at all."

Second, the assumption that assimilation, however fast or slow, is a one-way process proved to be quite mistaken. Marcus Lee Hansen's hypothesis of "third-generation nationalism" showed an unusually shrewd appreciation of assimilation by picturing it as a cycle, with marked differences between immigrants, their children, and their grandchildren. The national churches, immigrant-aid societies, foreign-language newspapers, and other institutions that the first generation set up were not impediments to acculturation but generally the contrary. The manifest difficulties of the second generation derived from "the strange dualism into which they had been born," and they tried to solve it by escaping the stigma they saw attached to their alien lineage. The immigrants' sons "wanted to lose as many of the evidences of foreign origin as they could shuffle off." But what the son wanted to forget, the grandson wanted to remember. Approximately 60 years —that is, two generations—after the high point of each nationality's immigration, the ethnic group into which it evolved typically celebrated its origins in a succession of amateur historical and genealogical societies, folklore associations, and other organized efforts to maintain or revive specific elements of various overseas cultures. Hansen's thesis, as he remarked in one place in the essay, was "deliberately overdrawn," and subsequent scholars have challenged its application to particular nationalities, but it can be regarded not only as a largely valid analysis of acculturation but also as a special case of a far broader social change.

In the transformation to a modernist, bureaucratic society, much is given up that eventually is regarded as valuable. Personal identity is very thin unless it is enmeshed with what Harold Isaacs calls the "idols of the tribe," the symbolic meanings given to group differences in body, name, language, history, religion, and nationality. It was hardly surprising, after all, that once the more pressing demands had been met, many tried to escape the impersonality of metropolitan life and retrogressively to establish a fuller emotional environment for themselves. Of course, the cycle was not precisely three generations long in every case. Zangwill, whose play was a prominent symbol of the first step, became an ardent Zionist later in his life. But apart from such details, it seems to be generally true that attempts to acculturate to the dominant population arise from an initial insecurity, and that from later security there develops in turn a yearning to distinguish one's group from the mass.

Because of their special circumstances, American blacks took several generations more to reach the attitudes that Hansen associated with the grandchildren of immigrants. A generation or two ago, most of the Negroes who succeeded in moving up the social ladder— painfully, step by step—imitated the lifestyle of middle-class whites, moving both physically and spiritually as far from the black slum as possible. The standard of feminine beauty, as a crucial example, comprised mainly a light skin and "good" hair. Having achieved a middle-range income, in short, the "black bourgeoisie" (as the Negro sociologist Franklin Frazier opprobriously labeled them) generally tried to consolidate their new status through acculturation to the norms of the superordinate sector. With the federal government's accelerated legal attack on discrimination during the 1960s, the exceptional advance of individual Negroes became more general. A measurement of the rise of the whole black race averages two quite distinct subgroups: those Negroes who took full advantage of the expanded opportunities and those who, because of age, region, or family structure, found it difficult or impossible to do so. If we control for these three factors, the income of whites and blacks was close to parity by the early 1970s. Nothing in the whole assimilationist doctrine, from Park's race-relations cycle to Myrdal's principle of cumulation, prepared Americans for what happened. The response to an improvement in the economic and civil condition of Afro-Americans greater than at any time since Reconstruction was a massive resurgence of black separatism, led sometimes by the very men who had moved up farthest and fastest.

Third, it would be fanciful to suppose, however, that the rise of ethnicity in the United States and throughout most of the world was due solely to a postponed search for roots. Obviously more is at stake than sentiment.

Even when it was fashionable to deny the relevance of race, religion, and nationality in national politics, this myth could hardly be applied with even minimum plausibility to America's multiethnic cities. In their relation to the federal government, voters were supposed to act as ethnically undifferentiated Americans, but in a metropolitan context they obviously and unabashedly constituted ethnic units—partly, of course, because an openly double ethnic identity was seen as a sensitive issue in national politics. The principal reason for the contrast between nation and city, however, was that by their functions local governments could distribute jobs, contracts, licenses, access to facilities, and so on. In order to get preferential treatment from a ward boss, a person had to join with others into a smaller, less blunt wedge than the heterogeneous national political parties, and one obvious base for mustering such power lay

in the already existent, quasi-political, ethnically based clubs or churches.

With the New Deal there began a continuous, often accelerating, transfer to Washington of multitudinous local or private functions, all of them associated with special favors to particular sectors of the population. With its version of the welfare state, the United States moved closer to the European norm, which eventually was imitated everywhere. The worldwide rise of ethnicity is based, in other words, not only on what Robert Nisbet called the "quest for community" but also, and more importantly, on the wider functions of the state and thus the greater impetus to organize in order to get what the state is distributing—and to prevent others from getting it.

THE ORIGINS OF ETHNIC GROUPS

Even if we postulate the only half-effective melting pot that critics of Zangwill's original formulation seem to have substituted, we must ask how (rather than why) it is that ethnicity has become a more and more important organizing principle. The conventional American view of ethnic relations is that subnations come into being mainly—or even only—through migration, but relative to the world's population, generally only small proportions have migrated. The dilemma is similar to that faced by pre-Darwinian exponents of biology: all species had been brought into being only once, at the time of the world's creation; some had disappeared, as was known from their fossil remains, but the number of species in the world seemed to be growing. Darwin resolved the dilemma by describing how new species arise, and it is also necessary, on a more modest scale, to consider the origins of ethnic groups and the process by which they emerge—ethnogenesis. The examples are drawn from American society except when the types can be illustrated only from other parts of the world.

Migration In the long and often disputatious discussion of how immigrants relate to American culture, some interesting analytical points have been largely ignored. It is not true that one can judge the impact of Swedish immigrants, for example, by comparing the cultures of Sweden and the United States; migrants are almost never a random sample of the populations they leave and enter. In this instance, since most emigrants were neither urban nor upper-class, they took with them not the general culture of Sweden but rather a peasant variant, expressed in local dialects and comprising regional customs. Free migrants, moreover, are generally already half-assimilated even before leaving home; before someone left to go to a Swedish-American settlement, he started his acculturation in an American-Swedish milieu, made up of New World letters, photographs, mementos, knickknacks—all stimuli to what was termed "America fever." In order to understand fully the interaction between migrants and a host population, therefore, one should conduct research at both ends of the movement, but of the many scholars of migration to the United States, only two men in their generation manifestly satisfied this requirement—Marcus Lee Hansen for emigrants from northwestern Europe and Melville Herskovits for the movement of slaves from West Africa.

One characteristic of immigration that U.S. analysts often take for granted is that the receiving population is sufficiently large, powerful, and cultured to act as a "host" to newcomers. In contrast to this pattern, the Jewish population of Israel in the early 1970s included about half who had not been born in the country, and fewer than a tenth were natives with native-born fathers. During the decades following the establishment of the nation in 1948, acculturation was thus not to a host population but rather to the ideology of Zionism. As another example, immigration accounted for 58 percent of the population growth of Argentina over the century 1841–1940 (compared with 41 percent in the United States, 22 percent in Canada, and 19 percent in Brazil). More importantly, immigrants became Argentina's modernizing force, the major constituent of both the urban proletariat (as in the United States) and the urban middle class. The complexities of Argentina's politics, reflecting the rapid and anomalous shifts in the social structure, are related to the only partial integration of an unprecedentedly high proportion of the well-to-do foreign-born in the country's population.

Consolidation According to a compilation by the anthropologists Charles and Florence Voegelin, at the time of Columbus's voyages the Indians of North America spoke a total of 221 mutually unintelligible languages, not including some contiguous dialects that permitted a minimal communication. Such other basic cultural elements as means of subsistence, religion, and family organization also varied greatly, and the differences were aggravated by a long history of violent competition and institutionalized warfare. Not only the name "Indian" but also the concept of a single people was a product of white contact. Even so, Indians might have become a single ethnic minority in the American population except for various federal policies, in particular the Indian Reorganization Act of 1934, that reinforced the atomized structure by giving tribal leaders a much enhanced power. The intermittent efforts to establish an intertribal movement have been fostered mostly by young men alienated as much from tribal life as from the white middle class. Over the next generation or two, the aspirations of many—probably most—younger Indians to participate fully in the world beyond the reservation will probably be realized. The decline of tribal units is likely to promote the rise of a new ethnic group, based ostensibly on cultural remnants that its members half-recall, but more fundamentally on the benefits obtainable from today's ethnic politics.

Inhabitants of the Appalachian Mountains provide another example of consolidation-in-process. Like the American Indians, their past relations with one another have been hostile; residents of each hamlet, huddled in its narrow valley, perceived those from over the mountain as unwelcome strangers. Also as with Indians, the isolated pockets of humanity were first defined as a single entity from the outside, especially by those in federal agencies set up to combat the region's poverty. A wide range of organizations and institutions is now active in promoting the subculture of "the Mountain People," and the consequent consolidation may have been assisted by their increased contacts with others and their greater awareness that those who live in the Appalachian region are distinct. It is at least possible, as it is probable for Indians, that their further accultura-

tion to the general society will be by the circuitous route of uniting into a firmer and more self-conscious subculture.

Promotion As we have noted in the case of Norway, raising a dialect to the status of a language can shift a lower social class to parity on an ethnic scale. In the United States the rise of "black English" suggests a similar process, though at a far earlier stage. The trend has been to define the black subculture not as standard American culture truncated by educational deprivation but as an immigrant way of life with significant transfers from Africa, and accordingly some have now defined the speech of lower-class blacks as a genuine dialect. It is said to have derived in large part from the pidgin English developed along Africa's west coast (as with Swahili along the east coast) for the greater convenience of the slave traders. Some students of black English advocate merely that it be used in elementary grades as a convenient bridge to learning English, but others have proposed that clergymen, for instance, become "bilingual," preaching in the parishioners' language and communicating with the broader community in standard English. In other words, the typically long process has been collapsed: even before a lower-class argot has been generally recognized as a dialect, some have begun to insist that it is in fact a language. Afro-Americans constituted a distinct ethnic group earlier, of course, but the usual academic position a generation ago was to ascribe their cultural differences almost entirely to their lower-class status.

Schism In the alternation between sect and church —that is, between a small group espousing unadorned doctrine and the end product of its gradual embellishment with ritual and institutional form—there are repeated schisms. Sometimes the differentiation, though at first defined in religious terms, broadens to include a whole way of life, with the consequent formation of a new ethnic group. The Latter-day Saints, or Mormons, might be so regarded. In the 19th century dozens of new religions and secular communal settlements blossomed in New York, Pennsylvania, and Ohio, but almost all except the Mormons disappeared. The crucial difference may have been persecution, for nothing is so likely to nourish a new religion as the martyrdom of its leaders. The long trek to Utah (celebrated in partisan accounts as are those of the Boers in South Africa or of the Chinese Communists' "Long March") eventually brought about the Mormons' partial isolation, though not an end to hostility. Under two acts of Congress, polygamy was prohibited, the church lost its corporate status, with its property escheated to the nation, and men with more than one wife were disfranchised and imprisoned. This renewed martyrdom reinforced the devotion of the faithful, and even after polygamy was abandoned in 1890, relations with "Gentiles" did not improve greatly. Contrary to the constitutional principle of separation of powers, church and state for Mormons were joined in what outsiders saw as a theocracy. Suffrage in Utah meant that church members elected religious leaders, who also became the heads of civil government. In short, even after the issue of polygamy was long past, even after the isolation of their desert home was breached by greatly improved transportation, the Mormons remained a distinct group, now set apart less by their religious doctrine than by

the social-political organizations associated with the church.

Race Crossing In many works on ethnicity what is termed "amalgamation" is denoted as one major route to the formation of new groups. American history challenges the validity of this thesis in at least some instances. Afro-Americans have a high proportion of white forebears, but apart from the very few who have passed into the white population, the group as a whole has been defined in law and general perceptions as one race, regardless of the degree of admixture. As a second example, sociologists in Hawaii have retained the melting-pot theory as a guide to their thinking far longer than the rest of the country, and one reads again and again that a new composite race is developing on the islands. Even if this were so biologically, it is an unlikely social prognosis. The Chinese in Hawaii, for instance, have set up Chinese-language schools for their children and made other efforts to maintain their separate subculture, even though probably a majority carry a great many Polynesian and other non-Chinese genes.

The Cape Colored of South Africa, in contrast to American Negroes, do constitute a separate subnation that was brought into being by race crossing. They have no tribal homelands; they are not tribally organized; they speak mostly Afrikaans rather than a language of one of the black peoples. For many years they had a separate juridical status, different from that of both whites and blacks, and vestiges of their intermediate status remain in certain occupational or residential privileges. In other words, the Cape Colored became a separate ethnic group not by race crossing alone but by this combined with a number of sociopolitical institutions that set them apart.

By one or more of these processes—migration, consolidation, promotion, schism, and race crossing—new ethnic groups are continually coming into being. The development is generally through three stages—category, group, and community. A category consists of a subpopulation distinguished in a census count, say, but with no internal coherence. An example might be "Canadian Americans," people born in Canada and resident in the United States; the English-speaking ones, at least, are not organized along ethnic lines and probably have little knowledge even of one another's existence. From such a base, however, an ethnic group can arise, particularly at a time when the self-awareness of others leads to preferential treatment of various kinds. Often there is considerable difficulty in defining a nascent group's precise dimensions. The "Spanish-speaking" or "Hispanic" grouping includes immigrants from Spain and some of their descendants—Mexican Americans, Puerto Ricans, Cuban refugees, and contingents from other Central and South American countries. Whether such a conglomerate can merge to form a single, self-conscious group may depend on such extraneous factors as the quality of leadership, the advantages of corporate effort as against intercategory competition, and so on. But if a group coalesces and prospers, it often develops enough of an institutional structure to be deemed a community. Sometimes, however, the progression from category to group to community is blocked or reversed by the contrary process of assimilation. Neither differentiation nor its opposite is ordained, and we know too little even to say which is more likely under speci-

fied conditions. No one, however, will any longer challenge the generalization that ethnicity is here to stay for quite a number of years; and that, strangely, is a new datum.

Bibliography
Early American theories of ethnicity include Robert E. Park, *Race and Culture* (Glencoe, Ill., 1950); Louis Wirth, "The Problem of Minority Groups," in Ralph Linton, ed., *The Science of Man in the World Crisis* (New York, 1945); and William Graham Sumner, *Folkways* (1906; reprint, New York, 1940). Gunnar Myrdal, *An American Dilemma* (1944; reprint, New York, 1975), a massive two-volume composite of interwar beliefs about Negroes, applied the assimilation doctrine to that minority. The analysis of assimilation was raised to a higher level of sophistication in Milton Gordon, *Assimilation in American Life* (New York, 1964).

Among the specifically historical works, those by Marcus Lee Hansen are especially valuable—*The Problem of the Third Generation Immigrant* (Rock Island, Ill., 1938; reprinted in *Commentary*, November 1952); *The Immigrant in American History* (1948; reprint, New York, 1964), a series of stimulating essays; and *The Atlantic Migration, 1607–1860* (Cambridge, Mass., 1951), the first of a projected three-volume series, never completed because of his premature death. Among other excellent works are Oscar Handlin, *Boston's Immigrants*, rev. ed. (New York, 1972); John Higham, *Strangers in the Land* (New York, 1963); Melville J. Herskovits, *The Myth of the Negro Past* (Boston, 1958).

Among the rather few works commenting on the formal counts by ethnicity, see two papers by William Petersen: "Religious Statistics in the United States," *Journal for the Scientific Study of Religion* 1 (1962): 165–178; and "The Classification of Subnations in Hawaii: An Essay in the Sociology of Knowledge," *American Sociological Review* 34 (December 1969): 863–877. A fascinating paper on a similar topic is Fulmer Mood, "The Origin, Evolution, and Application of the Sectional Concept, 1750–1900," in *Regionalism in America*, 2nd ed., Merrill Jensen, ed. (Madison, Wis., 1965). The case for deleting "race" from the language is argued at length in Ashley Montagu, *Man's Most Dangerous Myth: The Fallacy of Race* (New York, 1964).

Of the recent flood of works on ethnicity, the following are recommended, partly for their excellence and partly because each represents a special emphasis lacking in blander texts: Brewton Berry, *Almost White* (New York, 1963); Nathan Glazer and Daniel P. Moynihan, *Beyond the Melting Pot: The Negroes, Puerto Ricans, Jews, Italians, and Irish of New York City*, 2nd ed. (Cambridge, Mass., 1970); Andrew M. Greeley, *Ethnicity in the United States: A Preliminary Reconnaissance* (New York, 1974); Einar Haugen, *Language Conflict and Language Planning: The Case of Modern Norwegian* (Cambridge, Mass., 1966); Harold R. Isaacs, *Idols of the Tribe: Group Identity and Political Change* (New York, 1975); Charles J. Levy, *Voluntary Servitude: Whites in the Negro Movement* (New York, 1968); and William Petersen, *Japanese Americans: Oppression and Success* (New York, 1971).

                                          WILLIAM PETERSEN

COOS BAYS: *see* AMERICAN INDIANS

COPTS

Since 1966 many Egyptian Christians have migrated to the United States. In the late 1970s community leaders offered estimates as high as 85,000 to 100,000. The U.S. Immigration and Naturalization Service, however, reports a total of less than 15,000 Egyptian immigrants for the decade 1967–1976, and some of these must have been of other religious persuasions. Just how large the group is now cannot be determined reliably.

Egyptian Christians belong to two distinct churches; a minority of 5 to 10 percent are members of the Coptic Catholic Church, which is in communion with Rome. The Copts described in this entry are members of the Coptic Orthodox Church, sometimes called Oriental Orthodox. (*See* Eastern Catholics; Oriental Orthodox.)

The Copts assert that Christianity was introduced to Egypt by Saint Mark in the first century. For the next five centuries the church at Alexandria was in the fore-

front of Christian scholarship, but in 451 the patriarch of Alexandria broke with Rome in a dispute over the nature of Christ. Since then Egyptian Christians have been known as Copts, a word derived from *Qubt* or *Quobt*, an Arabic word in turn taken from the Greek term "Aigyptos," also the source of "Egyptian."

The break with Rome removed the Copts from the center of Christian activity in Rome, but they did not become a small and isolated community until the 7th century when the Arabs conquered Egypt and converted many Egyptians to Islam. Except in church use, the Coptic language also gave way to Arabic, but Coptic faith and ritual survived in some quarters through 13 centuries of sporadic persecution. Napoleon's brief expedition to Egypt (1798–1801) was of major importance. The Copts, who were virtually the only educated group in Egypt, appealed to Napoleon to improve their position. He responded favorably and appointed educated Copts to key positions in the administration, in finance, taxation, justice, and the army. Since then, although they form less than a fourth of the population of Egypt, the Copts have dominated many professions, including medicine, engineering, law, and education. They have also been large landowners as well as active in banking and commerce.

On July 23, 1952, a group of army officers overthrew the government of King Farouk, and in 1954 Gamal Abdul Nasser came to power. In 1959 the government adopted a pan-Arabist policy, which significantly affected the Copts and other minorities in Egypt. Although the government was committed to protecting minority rights, the minorities began to feel the results of revolutionary zeal and pan-Islamic ideology; private business was nationalized and land redistributed. Many Copts suffered financial losses, but above all the pressure for an Islamic state made them uncomfortable.

In the 1960s the Copts began to consider emigration, and the 1965 U.S. immigration law made it possible for more Egyptians to enter the United States. Not only many young Copts but also Egyptian Jews and Muslims took advantage of the opportunity to seek economic security and a more agreeable political climate. Emigration accelerated after 1967 when the consequences of defeat in the Egyptian-Israeli war began to be felt. Ironically, in the United States the Copts have been widely assisted in resettlement by individual Jews and Jewish organizations.

Thirty to forty percent of the first Copts to arrive in the United States were single males in their twenties. There were very few single women at first, but gradually wives and children began to arrive. The Coptic immigrants come mainly from urban centers like Cairo and Alexandria, and they have settled for the most part in urban centers in the United States. There may be as many as 10,000 Copts in the New York metropolitan area, perhaps 5,000 in Los Angeles, and other, smaller concentrations in Chicago, San Francisco, Detroit, Philadelphia, Washington, D.C., and Houston. Most of the men are college or university trained. They have been able to relocate without too much difficulty and to establish themselves in their professions. The transition has been relatively smooth, although some report that they were not prepared for the long hours and pace of American offices and institutions. Transition and adjustment have been more difficult for the less well-edu-

cated. Copt immigration tapered off in the mid-1970s, a decline attributed by some authorities to the recession in the U.S. economy. The newest immigrants are often the wives, children, or other relatives of the men who came earlier and are now established.

The various Coptic communities and the Copts as a whole exhibit a considerable degree of cohesion. Ninety percent marry within the group, but it is too soon to know if this pattern will continue. Although divorce is forbidden in the Coptic Church, it is increasing among Copts in the United States.

Each Coptic settlement has established its own church, which is the center of the social and religious activities of the community. In the late 1970s there were 16 churches following the Coptic Orthodox rite of the Church of Alexandria, and several more were being planned. The Coptic clergy have been highly regarded by their congregations, who look to them for spiritual and political leadership; the clergy continue to serve as their spokesmen. It was a great occasion when Pope Shenouda III, the patriarch of Alexandria and leader of the Copts in Egypt, the Sudan, Ethiopia, and in Diaspora, came to the United States in the spring of 1977 for a month of consultations and celebrations.

In the 1970s four Copt newspapers were published briefly. *The Copts* (Jersey City, N.J.), a bilingual newspaper, has appeared quarterly since the mid-1970s; it serves as a news and opinion forum for the entire Coptic-American community, with particular attention to the treatment of Copts in Egypt. The Egyptian National Committee (f. 1972) and the American Coptic Association (f. 1973) maintain close touch with the homeland as well as support the interests of the U.S. Coptic community.

Bibliography
Very little has appeared in print about the Copts in the United States except in occasional issues of the *New York Times*. One overview is presented by the Reverend Gabriel Abdelsayed, "The Coptic-Americans: A Current African Contribution," in *The New Jersey Ethnic Experience*, ed. Barbara Cunningham (Union City, N.J., 1977). For background see A. Atiya, *History of Eastern Christianity* (Notre Dame, Ind., 1968); S.H. Leeder, *Modern Sons of the Pharaohs* (London, 1918); and Edward Wakin, *A Lonely Minority: The Modern Story of Egypt's Copts* (New York, 1963).

RAEF MARCUS

CORNISH

Cornish immigrants to the United States have come from the most southwestern county of England, an 80-mile-long peninsula with the Atlantic Ocean to its north and west, the English Channel to the south, and the Tamar River and the neighboring county of Devonshire to the east.

In 1971 the population of Cornwall reached 379,892 and for the first time in over a century exceeded the census figure of 369,390 recorded in 1861, a short time before the collapse of the local copper-mining industry caused the first large-scale emigration. By the end of the 19th century the Cornish population had declined from the level of 1861 by some 50,000, or 13 percent. The drop was due to large-scale migration overseas, principally to the United States but also to Australia, New Zealand, and the Witwatersrand goldfields in South Africa. Most migratory Cornish were classed as English or British in records of emigration or immigration, and

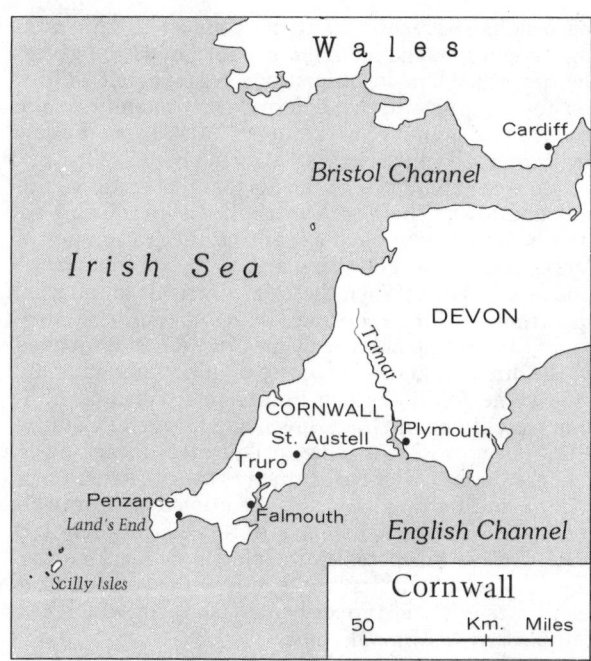

this fact together with extensive remigration makes it difficult to estimate the total numbers of those who came to and settled in the United States. The aggregate number of immigrants from Cornwall before World War I is estimated at 100,000.

To estimate the number of people now in the United States with claims to Cornish descent is far more difficult. The immigrants' constant mobility as they followed the shifting mining frontiers of the 19th century meant association and intermarriage with other English-speaking people and ultimately a loss of distinctly Cornish identity. There are still numerous groups in certain old mining areas, notably Grass Valley in California and Butte City in Montana, that remain predominantly Cornish, but the progressive exhaustion of the copper and iron deposits of the Lake Superior region has dispersed the once considerable concentration there.

Both geographic and historical factors distinguish the Cornish as an ethnic group. Although nowhere rising higher than 1,375 feet above sea level, Cornwall falls geographically within the western—and northern—highland zone of Great Britain. The presence of various metallic ores in its geologically ancient rocks afforded opportunities for mineral exploitation from very early times (Cornish tin seems to have been known to the Phoenicians); the rugged terrain and moist climate were suited to pastoral pursuits rather than to the agriculture favored by the topography and drier climate of southeastern England.

The Cornish were Brythonic-speaking Celts who came from the European mainland about the 1st century B.C., later than the Goidelic-speaking Celts who settled in Scotland and the islands, the Isle of Man, and Ireland. The Brythons occupied Wales, Cornwall, and Brittany. In the isolated southwest peninsula of England, Celtic racial customs and ways of life persisted, not coming under Anglo-Saxon dominance until the 10th century. The language itself survived until the 17th century; even afterward, linguistic traits, includ-

ing peculiar occupational terms connected with mining, agriculture, and fishing, continued in use long after the first considerable emigrations began, about 1830.

Those immigrants to America came mainly to the lead-mining country of the upper Mississippi Valley, the center of which was at Mineral Point, Wis., but whose area extended into the neighboring states of Illinois and Iowa. The first Cornishmen to reach this region had already worked a while in the iron mines of Pennsylvania and New Jersey or prospected in Maryland and Virginia. When these early arrivals found good opportunities for experienced hard-rock miners, they wrote to kinsmen and friends in Cornwall and touched off the direct migration of scores of miners annually. By 1850 some 6,000 Cornish immigrants and their children were living in Grant, Iowa, and Lafayette County, Wis., and up to 3,000 more in Dubuque, Iowa, and Jo Daviess County, Ill. Many turned to the combination of mining and farming that was traditional in Cornwall and by 1845 owned holdings of 40, 80, or even 100 acres. Others prospered as merchants or blacksmiths. They replaced their first crude huts with typically Cornish limestone and timber houses, some of which can still be seen in Mineral Point.

By mid-century the skilled miners had started to move from the lead mines to the Keweenaw copper country of upper Michigan and to the California gold fields. Particularly at Grass Valley, the Cornish were associated almost from the first with underground, hard-rock mining rather than with the exploitation of alluvial placer deposits. From California some Cornish moved on to other locations in the Pacific Coast area—wherever "keenlier lodes" were promised (but did not always materialize)—to the Washoe and then to the Comstock lodes in Nevada, or to even more distant regions whence had come news or rumors of gold strikes in British Columbia, Montana, Colorado, Dakota, and Arizona. Many miners who spent a few successful years in western gold camps returned not to Cornwall but to Wisconsin, where they bought holdings that equaled in size the estates of Cornish squires in the old country.

In 1866, when the devastating slump in Cornish copper mining caused a large-scale exodus, many emigrants came to upper Michigan; in the early 1880s rich copper finds in Butte drew many to western Montana. By mid-decade South African gold fields had become a counter-lure, although right up to the 1920s many, especially those with relatives already in the country, continued to come to the United States, where the Detroit automobile industry furnished employment in place of the worked-out Michigan copper mines.

On the early mining frontiers, life was often harder for Cornish women than for men. Women in the lead-mining region had a higher death rate than in Cornwall, but the proportion of men dying in their prime was lower; American mines were shallower than those in the old country, and in this respect were safer and placed less strain on the men working in them. When the men were mining or off hunting or prospecting for gold in California, full care of the farm and livestock fell to the women. Many women died in childbirth or were victims of epidemics of cholera or fever. Infant mortality was also high.

Women made up 27 percent of the Cornish population in Michigan's copper-mining region in 1854; a dec-

ade later they formed nearly 40 percent. Most were housewives who looked after their families and often several miner-boarders. In northern Michigan, Cornish families usually lived by mining alone, since soil and climate were unfavorable for farming beyond growing potatoes for home use and raising a few farm animals. A few Cornish women worked as dressmakers, milliners, and school teachers, and widows sometimes kept boarding houses.

It was fairly common for a single member of a Cornish family, usually a young man, to emigrate and discover just what opportunities the new country offered. If he was fortunate, he wrote home for other members of his family or close friends to come out and join him, and he sometimes sent money to help pay their passage. This practice affords one answer to speculation about the origin of the term "Cousin Jack," so widely applied to Cornishmen: on hearing of a job vacancy in the mine where he was working, a Cornishman would go to the manager or foreman, say that his "Cousin Jack" would fill the post admirably, and suggest sending for him straightway. The term, however, may have far more ancient origins.

Clannish ties were strong among the immigrants; many young unmarried men who came to the United States returned to Cornwall after two or three years for a brief visit, married a girl who had been left behind, and then returned to settle permanently in the new country. Those who married in America outside the Cornish group generally had religion in common. Children of first-generation immigrants were also likely to marry within the group, but the common English language accelerated intermarriage with other Americans of different origins, and soon it was no longer possible to quote the old rhyme, "By Tre-, Lan-, Ros-, Car-, Pol-, and Pen- / You may know the most of Cornishmen." These Celtic prefixes, meaning respectively "home-place," "church," "heath" or "moorland," "fort," "water," and "height" or "headland," were indicative of the way Cornish surnames were taken from place names. Few of these place names, however, were given to American locations, even to mines.

Modern American intonation or "twang" has often been described as being remarkably similar to present-day Cornish dialect, and possibly results from the survival of the West Country accent in both lands. Many early English settlers came from southwestern England, and the Cornish acquired and kept the same intonations from their English-speaking neighbors when they shifted into that language. Among the most pronounced features of Cornish dialect are longer vowel sounds, with a word like *now* phonetically becoming *naow*, the omission of the final g in present participles, and the omission of aspirate accompanied by the corollary intrusive h before vowels. A marked singsong intonation can be considered a Brythonic Celtic trait.

Some Cornish immigrants in the early 1860s felt that the Civil War was none of their concern, and evaded the draft by going to British Columbia or even to Australian mining camps, but most affiliated with the Republican party. Most, too, continued to show the same indifference if not actual antipathy toward labor unions that they had in Cornwall. The traditional tribute system, with usually three to six men bidding for a contract to work a "pitch," or section, of a mine for a percentage of

the yield, had established a tradition of individual competitiveness that belied the old-country motto "One and All" in industrial organization and relations. This system also provided free time during which Cornish miners developed and pursued other occupations, especially farming.

Individualism characterized Cornish religious life too. The majority were Methodists of one denomination or another. In the new mining camps in Michigan, Wisconsin, and on the Pacific Coast they were among the first to build their own churches; well into the present century a considerable proportion of Methodist ministers in California were of Cornish origin or descent. In these mining areas Cornish life centered around their chapels and included Sunday services with lengthy sermons, revival meetings, temperance rallies, sports events, and Sunday-school teas. The emphasis on singing in Methodist worship was continued by the immigrants and their descendants, especially in Grass Valley, where for over a century a Cornish carol choir went the rounds of local churches at Christmas, singing carols still remembered in America when they were all but forgotten in Cornwall. Near Central Mine, in the Keweenaw Peninsula of Michigan, a reunion or "homecoming" service continued to be held regularly in the Cornish chapel, on either the last Sunday in July or the first in August, long after the old Michigan Central Mine closed down in 1898 and the miners went to other mines or, later, to Detroit.

Social activities in connection with the churches included teas and suppers, sometimes picnics, at which traditional Cornish fare—pasties, saffron cake, and heavy cake—was served. The pasty was reputedly created as a method of providing a substantial meal for a miner on a long shift down in a deep mine; it was generally a mixture of meat and vegetables enclosed in a crimped crust of short pastry. Cornish housewives prided themselves on the neatness of their crimping. Saffron cake, like the spice and dye itself, was always something of a luxury and was rich in currants, raisins, and citrus peel; the more plebeian heavy cake had a high percentage of fat and sometimes a few currants. Chapel teas, of course, were just that. The temperance associations of many Cornish Methodist groups almost certainly contributed to the strength of the Prohibition movement in the United States, besides adding somewhat to the antagonism felt toward other, more bibulous immigrant groups—an antagonism which at times erupted into violence in upper Michigan, Virginia City, and Butte.

With the passing years, features of daily life both in the old country and the new have inevitably changed. Technology has ended hand rock-drilling contests; brass and silver bands struggle for survival; highly individualistic Cornish wrestling matches are only very intermittently revived as commemorations of a bygone time. In addition the Cornish brought the English game of cricket, although it was never as popular among Cornish immigrants in the United States as it was among those in Australia and South Africa.

Though three, four, or even more generations removed from their immigrant forebears, Cornish Americans are as genealogically conscious as any other immigrant group in the United States. Among them have survived family memories of the Cornwall they left long ago; and the predominant practical-mindedness that first motivated the Cornish to emigrate persists as a distinctive characteristic of their descendants today.

Bibliography
The predominance of miners among Cornish immigrants occasions discussion of them in works dealing with particular localities in America, notably in John B. Martin, *Call It North Country: The Story of Upper Michigan* (New York, 1944), and the WPA Writers' Program of Montana, *Copper Camp* (New York, 1943). More recently Arthur C. Todd, *The Cornish Miner in America* (Glendale, Calif., 1967); A.L. Rowse, *The Cousin Jacks: The Cornish in America* (New York, 1969); and John Rowe, *The Hard-Rock Men: Cornish Immigrants and the North American Mining Frontier* (New York, 1974), have surveyed Cornish immigrants throughout the United States. Newton G. Thomas's novel *The Long Winter Ends* (New York, 1941) provides insights into Cornish life in Michigan. A comprehensive survey of the Cornish in the homeland is Alfred K. Jenkin, *Cornwall and its People* (1945; reprint, Newton Abbot, England, 1970), while particular aspects are depicted in Kenneth C. Phillips, *Westcountry Words and Ways* (Newton Abbot, 1976), and Pamela Pascoe, *Cousin Jennie's Cook Book* (Padstow, England, 1976).

JOHN ROWE

COSSACKS

The ethnic distinctiveness of the Cossacks is based primarily on their particular mode of life and their geographic location. They were a military caste that settled along the frontier regions of the Russian Empire. Those living along the Don River may once have had their own language, but by the 19th century most of them spoke either Russian or Ukrainian. In the United States today there are approximately 3,500 to 4,000 Cossacks and their descendants.

In the homeland, the Cossacks were organized into several groups or "hosts," such as the Don, Kuban, and Terek, which emerged during the 15th and 16th centuries. The largest and the most powerful were the Don

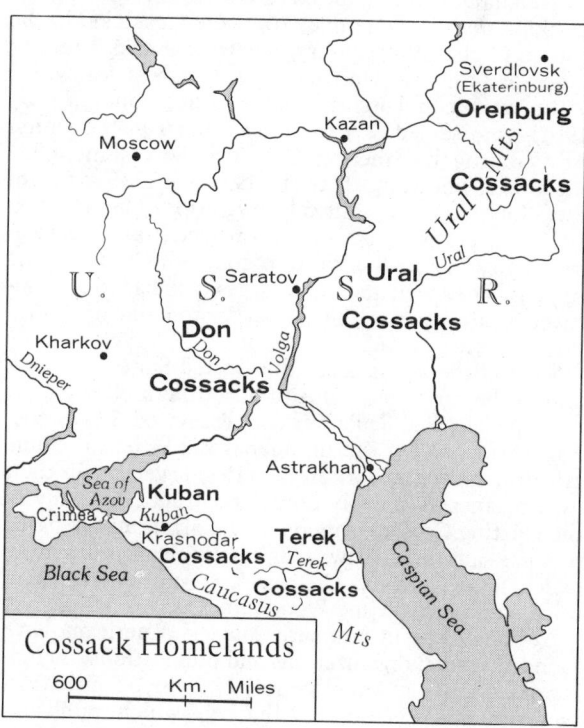

Cossack Homelands

Cossacks who settled along the banks of the lower Don River in the southeastern territories of European Russia. In return for certain privileges, all the Cossack hosts served the tsarist government both as settlers and protectors of the Russian Empire's expanding southern and eastern frontiers—from Turkey and the Caucasus Mountains in the west, across the Asian continent, and up to the Mongolian and Chinese borders in eastern Siberia. They led the eastern expansion of Russia and were among the first explorers and settlers of Russia's colony in Alaska during the 18th century. An important part of the tsarist army, they acquired an infamous reputation as oppressors or instigators of internal disturbances in Russia, such as revolutionary uprisings and anti-Jewish pogroms.

The primary concern of the Cossacks was to preserve the semiautonomous status of their territories within the Russian Empire. Whenever their privileges were threatened they responded in force, and some of Russia's greatest revolts were led by Cossack chieftains. During the Russian Revolution and civil war (1917–1921), the Don Cossacks at first supported the revolution and then opposed the victorious Bolshevik forces. In December 1917 they proclaimed an independent state, but it lasted only until 1920. This experience produced two attitudes which still dominate the perceptions of Cossacks in the United States: they remain violently opposed to the Soviet regime in the homeland and continue to glorify the Cossack Republic of 1917–1920, which is considered the modern equivalent of the Cossack autonomy of earlier times. Cossack opposition to Soviet rule persisted throughout the 1920s and 1930s. Government reprisals resulted in their cooperating with the Germans against the Red Army, after Hitler invaded the Soviet Union in 1941.

The earliest Cossacks came to the United States as part of the Russian colonization of Alaska. The total Russian population in the colony never exceeded 800; it is likely that no more than 100 were Cossacks. In the course of the 19th century, a few Cossacks came to other parts of the United States, the best known of whom was John Turchin (Ivan V. Turchaninov, 1822–1901), who served as a brigadier general in the Union Army during the American Civil War. Several more fled the new Soviet regime between 1920 and 1935 as part of the White Russian political emigration. Finally, after 1950, the last group of Cossacks arrived from displaced-persons camps in the Western zones of Germany and Austria. They were mostly refugees who had fought unsuccessfully against the Soviet Union during World War II.

Most of the Cossacks in the United States have settled in the rural communities of southern New Jersey: Farmingdale, Red Bank, Jackson, Freewood, Lakewood, Englishtown, New Kuban, Buena, and Vineland. Some are farmers, some work in factories, several own their own businesses (mostly home construction). Many of the existing Cossack-American organizations are based in these same small towns. Cossacks also live in Providence, R.I., Cleveland, Chicago, Los Angeles, San Francisco, and Portland and Woodburn, Ore.

Although few in number, Cossack Americans have founded several organizations and publications, including the Kazach'e Amerikanskii Narodnyi Soiuz (Cossack-American National Alliance), which publishes books about the homeland, and a periodical in Russian and Ukrainian, Kazach'ia zhizn'-Kozache zhyttia (Cossack Life, Providence, R.I., f. 1952); the Cossack-American Citizen's Committee, which publishes Free Cossackia/Svobodnaia Kazakiia (New York, f. 1976), and the Supreme Cossack Representation in New York City, which attempts to work for the liberation of the Cossack homeland by cooperating with other anti-Soviet ethnic groups in the United States. To preserve a sense of community life, the Cossacks have built several centers in New Jersey: the Cossack National Home in Freewood Acres; the Cossack National Home in Farmingdale; and the Monastery of the Virgin Mary in Vineland, where there is also a Cossack library and museum-archive.

Cossack religious life plays an important role in preserving a sense of community. The Cossacks are Eastern Orthodox, but they do not have their own church; they belong to either the Russian Orthodox Church Outside Russia (the Synod) or to the Orthodox Church in America (the former Russian Metropolia). A few Cossacks are Old Believers, a traditionalist Orthodox sect that has been persecuted in Russia since the 17th century. Cossack Old Believers first settled in New Jersey, but fearing that their children would succumb to the temptations of modern living moved to rural retreats in Woodburn, Ore., or Alaska.

Most Cossacks speak Russian, but they maintain a certain distance from the Russian-American community and rarely join Russian-American organizations. The Cossack heritage has been kept alive in the United States by writers like Sergei V. Boldyrev (1890–1957), Wasili G. Glaskow (1908–), Georgii V. Gubarov (1894–), and Aleksei I. Skrylov (1894–), who have published Cossack histories, anthologies, and language primers. Their most ambitious project is the three-volume Kazachii slovar'-spravochnik (Cossack Dictionary and Reference Book, 1966–1969), edited by Skrylov and Gubarov. Several Cossack almanacs and journals have also appeared: Obshchekazachii zhurnal (Pan-Cossack Journal, Farmingdale, N.J., 1947–1952), Kazachii istoricheskii kalendar' (Cossack Historical Almanac, Cleveland, 1951–1957), Kubanskii istoricheskii i literaturnyi sbornik (Kuban Historical and Literary Anthology, Orangeburg, N.Y., 1960–1968), The Cossack Quarterly (Cleveland, f. 1962), and Kazach'e slovo/The Cossack Word (Paterson, N.J., f. 1965). The group is known to the larger American public mainly through the concert performances of several Cossack choral groups, particularly the Don Cossack Choir of Serge Jaroff, which although based in western Europe has been giving concerts in the United States since the 1930s.

Bibliography

No studies have been published on Cossacks in the United States. A general introduction to life in the Don and Kuban Cossack homeland is given in Maurice Hindus, The Cossacks: The Study of a Warrior People (1945; reprint, Westport, Conn., 1970). The best general history is by Philip Longworth, The Cossacks (New York, 1970). A historical survey from earliest times written by a Cossack is published in Wasili G. Glaskow, History of the Cossacks (New York, 1972).

PAUL ROBERT MAGOCSI

COSTA RICANS: see CENTRAL AND SOUTH AMERICANS

COWLITZES: see AMERICAN INDIANS

CREEKS: *see* AMERICAN INDIANS

CREES: *see* AMERICAN INDIANS

CREOLE

Creole refers to people, to culture, to food and music, and to language. Originally from the Portuguese *crioulo*, the word for a slave brought up in the owner's household, which in turn probably derived from the Latin *creāre* (create), it became *criollo* in Spanish and *créole* in French. By the early 17th century the term distinguished Europeans born in Caribbean and Indian Ocean colonies from foreign-born colonists. Initially it seems to have had political implications; Creoles felt differently about the homeland than did the first generation. The 18th-century expression "as rich as a Creole" referred to the wealthy planters from Mauritius, the West Indies, and elsewhere. In Mexico the word *criollo* is reserved for someone of pure European ancestry; in the United States the term not only refers to Louisianans of French or Spanish descent but also was used to distinguish a native-born slave from an imported slave. (*See* Acadians; Afro-Americans; *see also* Cape Verdeans; Haitians.)

Creole is also applied to a variety of languages spoken in former and existing colonies around the world. In the 18th century a number of creole languages were known, among them those of the French-speaking islands of Saint-Domingue (Haiti) and Bourbon (La Réunion) and those of English and Portuguese origin. In the 1960s and 1970s the study of creole languages has begun to attract wide interest, and has provided insight for an understanding of human speech generally; international conferences and journals on the study of creole languages have become widespread. The so-called Gullah dialect of the southeastern United States is now recognized as a creole language. On the other hand, the creole (also known as gumbo) of Louisiana and adjacent states is virtually a dead language.

Louisianans of French and Spanish descent began referring to themselves as Creoles following the Louisiana Purchase (1803) in order to distinguish themselves from the Anglo-Americans who started to move into Louisiana at this time. The indigenous whites adopted the term, insisting, most unhistorically, that it be applied exclusively to them. The life of this dying group is depicted in George Washington Cable's *Old Creole Days* (1879) and in some of the works of Lafcadio Hearn.

In the United States in the 20th century, Creole most often refers to the Louisiana Creoles of color. Ranging in appearance from mulattos to northern European whites, the Creoles of color constitute a Caribbean phenomenon in the United States. The product of miscegenation in a seigneurial society, they achieved elite status in Louisiana, and in the early 19th century some were slaveholders. Many, educated in France, were patrons of the opera and of literary societies. A description of their lives is provided by Alice Dunbar-Nelson in the *Alice Dunbar-Nelson Reader* (1979) and by Rodolphe Lucien Desdunes, *Nos Hommes et Notre Histoire* (1911; English translation, 1978). Francis J. Woods tells the life story of one extended family in *Marginality and Identity: A Colored Creole Family Through Ten Generations* (1972).

Louisiana Creoles of color thus constitute a self-conscious group, who are perceived in their locale as different and separate. They live in New Orleans and in a number of other bayou towns. Historically they have been endogamous, and until late in the 19th century spoke mostly French. Perhaps the best-known Creole of color is the jazz musician Jelly Roll Morton, whose own social status must have been marginal in Creole society. Overwhelmingly Catholic, the New Orleans Creoles usually attend parochial schools; Xavier University is closely associated with them. Their ethnicity is exceedingly difficult to maintain outside the New Orleans area. Over time, a great many have passed into white groups in other parts of the country, and others have become integrated with blacks. This latter choice is not based wholly on appearance, for many Creoles who choose to identify as Afro-Americans are white in appearance.

RICHARD A. LONG

CREOLES OF COLOR: *see* CREOLE

CRIMEAN TATARS: *see* TATARS

CROATS

The Croats are one of the South Slav peoples who inhabit the Socialist Federal Republic of Yugoslavia. In 1971 they made up 22.1 percent of the Yugoslav population. Most Croats live in Croatia, one of the six constituent republics, but there are Croats in the other republics as well, especially in adjacent Bosnia and Herzegovina.

Related to two other large Yugoslav groups, the Serbs and the Slovenes (39.7 and 8.3 percent of the 1971 population), the Croats are distinguished from them mainly by their divergent history, which has been long and complex. Furthermore, the Croats have a strong Roman Catholic tradition, as have the Slovenes, while the Serbian tradition has been Eastern Orthodox. Religion, however, has had a diminished role in Yugoslavia since World War II. Language both binds and divides: the spoken language of Croat and Serb is virtually the same although some people in both groups assert that Croatian and Serbian are two different languages. Croatian is written in the Latin alphabet; Serbian uses the Cyrillic. The 1974 constitution of Yugoslavia accords official status to all languages of the peoples and nationalities of the country.

An independent kingdom in the 10th and 11th centuries, Croatia accepted union with the Kingdom of Hungary in 1102, a tie that endured until the end of World War I. In 1526 the crown of Croatia passed to the Hapsburg dynasty where it remained until the disintegration of the Austro-Hungarian Empire in 1918. Throughout these centuries Croatia was allowed a degree of local autonomy that helped preserve the dream of independent statehood. The Croatian region of Dalmatia, which adjoins the eastern shore of the Adriatic Sea, passed into the hands of the Venetian Republic in the 1400s. It was acquired by Austria at the Congress of Vienna (1814–1815) but was kept politically and administratively separate from the rest of Croatia. Bosnia-

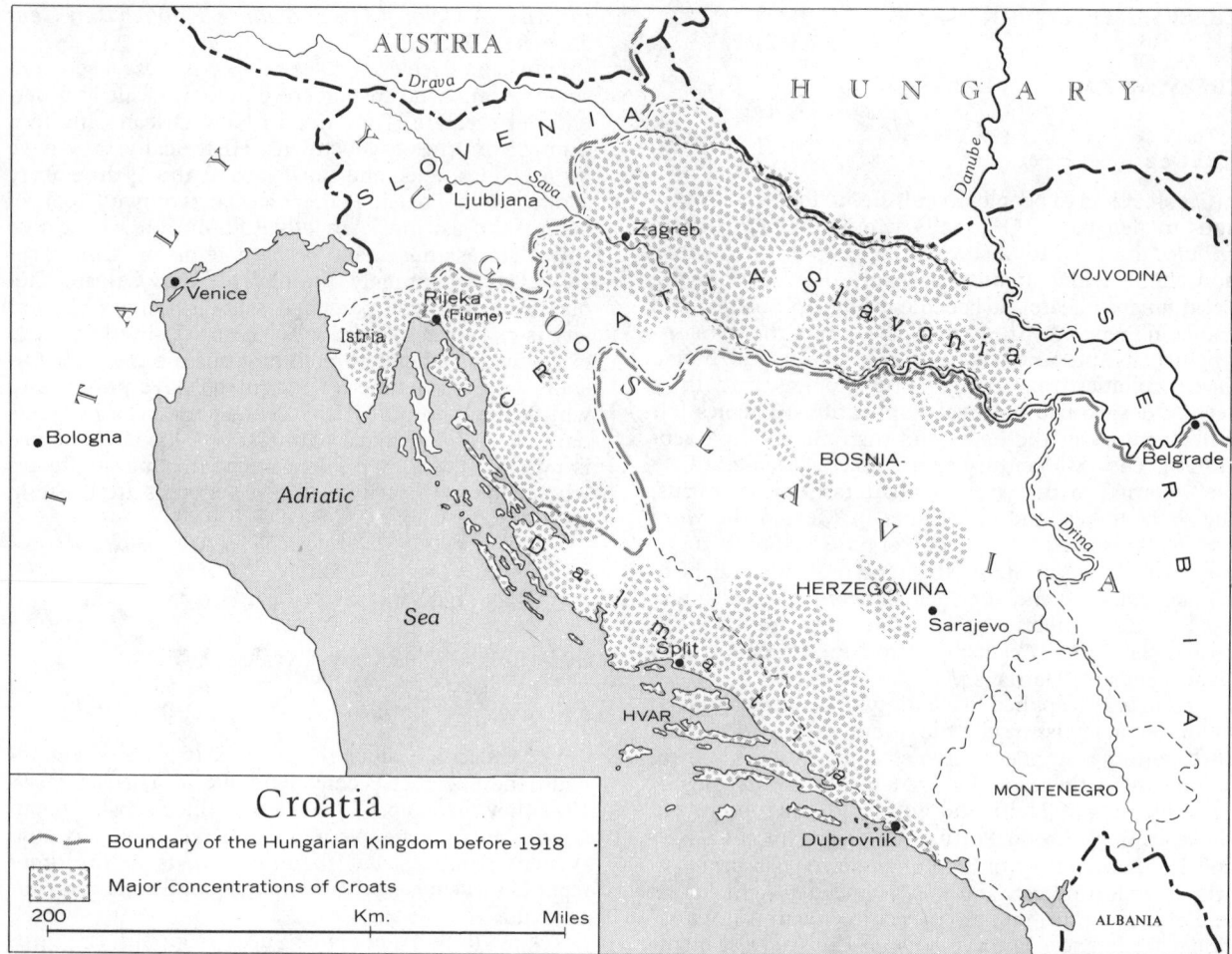

Croatia

〜 — Boundary of the Hungarian Kingdom before 1918

Major concentrations of Croats

200 Km. Miles

Herzegovina, another constituent republic of Yugoslavia, is claimed by both Croatian and Serbian nationalists.

The first independent Yugoslav state was formed at the end of World War I. Known officially as the Kingdom of Serbs, Croats, and Slovenes, its name was changed in 1929 to the Kingdom of Yugoslavia. Because the kingdom was dominated from the beginning by Serbs, the Croats were dissatisfied with their status. When the Axis powers overran and dismembered Yugoslavia in April 1941, they permitted the establishment of an independent Croatian state which was under Axis control. The 1945 victory of the Communist Partisan-led forces under Josip Broz Tito—Croat on his father's side, Slovene on his mother's—resulted in the reconstitution of a Yugoslav state with Croatia as one of its constituent republics.

PATTERNS AND CAUSES OF MIGRATION

Croats began coming to the United States in significant numbers about a century ago. By now there are between 500,000 and 750,000 Americans who are entirely or partially of Croatian descent, making the Croats the most numerous of the South Slav groups that have settled in the United States. Some authorities argue that the number is over a million. Precise figures cannot be obtained because in the 19th century Croa-

tian immigrants tended to identify themselves in terms of the region from which they had come—Slavonia, Dalmatia, Istria, Bosnia-Herzegovina, and so on—and until 1918 the U.S. Immigration Service did not distinguish Croatians from Slovenes or other immigrants from the Austro-Hungarian Empire. The U.S. Bureau of the Census added to the confusion by listing Croatian, Serbian, and Dalmatian as separate mother tongues from 1910 to 1940, but then treating Serbo-Croatian as one language and Yugoslavia as one country of origin in the 1970 Census.

A handful of sailors, merchants, craftsmen, adventurers, and missionaries, most of them from the Dalmatian coast, reached America in the 17th and 18th centuries. By the early 19th century ships manned by Dalmatian sailors were traveling regularly from Dubrovnik and other Adriatic ports to North American trading centers. Many of these sailors jumped ship in New Orleans and San Francisco. They found a temperate climate similar to that of the Adriatic and Mediterranean regions, and by 1860 some 16,000 to 20,000 Dalmatians had settled in the United States.

In the 1850s and 1860s some Croats began to arrive from inland as well as coastal regions, drawn by reports of gold in California and the expansion of copper and coal mining in a variety of states. The single largest wave of Croatian immigrants (perhaps as many as

400,000) came in the 24 years between 1890 and 1914—the peak year, 1907, brought an estimated 83,000. This exodus depleted the labor force in many parts of Croatia and provoked Croatian authorities to issue several ordinances and regulations to curb it, but they had little effect, largely because the imperial government did not support them, preferring that dissatisfied subjects leave.

In the years before and immediately after World War I, most Croatian immigrants were landless peasants or others adversely affected by rural overpopulation or by the phylloxera blight that destroyed many vineyards. Some were merchant seamen displaced by the demise of the sailing vessel, young men wishing to escape military conscription, or people fleeing political oppression. They were encouraged to cross the Atlantic by letters from the friends and relatives who had preceded them and wrote about the freedom, high wages, and comforts of living in the United States, a rosy picture that ignored gloomier realities. The most notable realistic account was *Preko Atlantika do Pacifika: život Hrvata u Sjevernoj Americi* (Across the Atlantic to the Pacific: The Life of the Croatians in North America) by the Croatian writer and political figure Ante Tresić-Pavičić. Tresić-Pavičić was shocked by the conditions under which his countrymen labored in the United States and described them fully in his book. Published in Zagreb in 1907, it did not accomplish the author's purpose but served to encourage thousands more to emigrate.

The pre–World War I Croatian immigration was as much as 85 percent male. They were often illiterate (28 percent in 1910, according to the U.S. Immigration Commission), and, from a peasant background, often without the skills needed in an industrial economy. As a result, 80 percent took jobs as unskilled laborers.

They lived for the most part in crowded boarding houses or in cooperative households, saving as much money as possible in order to bring their families to America or to buy passage back to Croatia. Some came with the hope of buying land in the United States, but few actually did so; a larger number came with the intention of returning to buy land in Croatia or to free existing landholdings from debt, and many more achieved that aim. Available data indicate that return migration to Croatia was high: between 1899 and 1924 one of every two Croatians and Slovenes returned to the homeland, at least for a while; between 1924 and 1943 the rate was 57 percent. The rest of these immigrants, however, settled down permanently, becoming part of America's industrial working class and establishing households and raising families.

During the late 1940s and early 1950s thousands of Croats emigrated to the United States as a result of the Communist revolution in Yugoslavia in 1945. These political émigrés were for the most part better educated than their predecessors, which seems to have eased their way, although they, too, often had to begin as common laborers because they had had to leave behind whatever wealth they possessed. During the 1960s and 1970s additional thousands of Croats came—and are still coming. As before, their main objective seems to be to better themselves financially.

Both groups of post–World War II Croatian immigrants have produced a significant number of political activists espousing the cause of an independent Croatia. Extremists from this group have initiated a number of terrorist incidents, some causing injury or death as well as considerable property damage. Few Croats are this extreme, although the concept of an independent Croatia enjoys considerable support in the Croatian-American community.

SETTLEMENT

The earliest Croatian settlements in the United States were on the Gulf of Mexico and in California. A number of Croats, many of them affiliated with Roman Catholic missionary orders, came as early as the 16th century to Spanish America. The most notable was the Jesuit Ferdinand Konšćak (1703–1759) from the north-Croatian town of Varaždin; he was known among the Spanish as Fernando Consag. Father Consag reached the San Ignacio Mission in 1733 and there was responsible for the baptism of many Indians. He undertook an exploration up the Gulf of California to the Colorado River in 1746 and proved that Baja California was not an island but a peninsula. His map of Baja California has been reproduced in many works dealing with that region.

It was in the warm coastal areas along the Gulf of Mexico that the first significant number of secular immigrants settled, beginning in the second half of the 18th century and extending into the later part of the 19th. By the late 1700s the Atlantic and Gulf coasts—and increasingly the Pacific—were well known among the seafaring people of the Dalmatian coast. The ships of Dubrovnik sailed regularly to England's American colonies and to other ports in the Caribbean and South America. There were individual Croatian settlers during this early period, but the records are fragmentary. Jerome Matulich was a successful merchant in Texas around 1760. Numerous Dalmatians from at least the 1780s onward were landowners, merchants, and ship captains in Louisiana, Alabama, Mississippi, and Florida.

A form of official recognition of the Croatian presence in the new American republic came in 1783, when U.S. officials in Paris assured Frano Favi, a representative of the Republic of Dubrovnik, that Dubrovnik's ships and subjects would be given protection while in the United States. During this early period the Croats from Dubrovnik and other parts of Dalmatia who resided in the United States often were called Venetians, because until 1797 most of the Dalmatian coast belonged to the Republic of Venice. In 1814–1815, after the Austrian empire was given control of the territories along the Adriatic coast from Venice to present-day Albania, immigrants and almost everyone else who arrived from this region in Austrian ships or other vessels were likely to be listed as Austrians by U.S. immigration authorities.

The haphazard pattern of immigration—including the many Dalmatian sailors who apparently jumped ship—resulted in a population of perhaps several thousand Croats in and around New Orleans and other Louisiana towns by the 1830s. Some of them moved up the Mississippi River and settled in the interior. Marco Maranovich, for example, was a prosperous plantation owner on the Cane River in north-central Louisiana; a nearby community was named Marco after him. By the 1850s many Croats in the South were permanent set-

tlers with wives and children. It is not clear how many brought their families from Croatia, but probably not many. The U.S. Censuses of 1850 and 1860 list hundreds of Croats engaged in various trades and businesses.

Luke Jurisich, a Dalmatian who settled first at Bayou Creek near New Orleans in the 1850s, stands out among this group of Mississippi Delta residents. Jurisich was a pioneer in establishing the large-scale cultivation and marketing of oysters in the area. By the late 19th century the Croats controlled the oyster business and had established a New Dalmatia on the Mississippi. A terrible hurricane in 1893 killed 2,000 people on the Delta and devastated entire communities, but the Croats rebuilt the oyster industry in a few years, and continued to dominate it.

More than 3,000 Croats lived in the South by the time of the Civil War, when the main flow of Croatian immigration shifted to California. They lived in New Orleans and adjacent Plaquemines Parish or in the coastal counties of Mississippi. Most were Dalmatians, but a significant minority were from Slavonia. Many Croats served in the Confederate army and navy; two Slavonian rifle companies and a unit known as the Austrian Guards were composed entirely of Croats; others fought in the Tenth Louisiana Infantry Regiment; they were also scattered among various units formed in Louisiana, Mississippi, Alabama, Georgia, and Texas.

In spite of their relatively concentrated settlement in the South, the Croats apparently were not very active organizers of ethnic societies. In 1874 a group of Croats and Serbs from the Adriatic coast founded the United Slavonian Benevolent Association, primarily a burial society, in New Orleans, but as its name implies its members were not exclusively Croatian; its first two presidents were Serbs. The absence of Croatian ethnic activity can be attributed partly to the small size of the community, partly to the absence of women and thus of Croatian families, and partly to a rather low level of national consciousness among the settlers. The organization formed in New Orleans in 1874 was typical of the great majority of the organizations formed by the immigrants in the late 19th and early 20th centuries: provincial or regional names, such as Dalmatian or Slavonian, were the rule, and some Croatian and Slovene organizations carried the word Austrian.

Beginning in the 1840s and continuing through the remainder of the century, a significant number of Croats settled in California. Matthew Ivancovich was present when gold was discovered at Sutter's Mill in January 1848. Thousands of Croats joined the gold rush that followed, some coming directly from the homeland and others from elsewhere in the United States. San Francisco became a permanent home for many Croatian forty-niners; some found fortunes easier to make there than in the gold fields, and over the years became prosperous as merchants, restaurant and saloon owners, and other kinds of businessmen.

In 1857, under the leadership of Dr. Vincent Gelcich, a Dalmatian from the island of Hvar, a group of Croats and Serbs established the Slavonian Illyrian Mutual Benevolent Society in San Francisco, the first Croatian-Serbian fraternal organization in the United States. The Slavonian Society was a burial and sick-benefit association that soon enrolled more than 700 members and is still in existence today.

In 1861 the Slavonian Society purchased a part of Calvary Cemetery and established the first Croatian-Serbian cemetery in the United States. The San Francisco Croats, in contrast to most other Slavic Roman Catholic groups and to Croats elsewhere in the United States, did not establish a national or ethnic parish but they did arrange to bury their dead in a separate section of the cemetery.

Information is unavailable about the marriage and family patterns of the Croatian immigrants in California before 1880. The number of female newcomers, however, was low, and most Croatian men consequently married women of Spanish, Mexican, Irish, or other ethnic origin. Only a handful went home for their brides. More, but still probably a minority, sent for wives they had left behind or had others arrange marriages for them in Croatia. Because it generally took immigrants a long time to establish themselves—particularly those who began as gold miners and prospectors—late marriage was fairly common.

As the decades passed, the Croats in California and adjacent states prospered, or at least the traces of those who failed generally disappeared. Some of the more successful Croats in the San Joaquin Valley became truck farmers or established ranches, orchards, and vineyards. One of the more striking examples of Croatian agricultural success in the Far West was the "New Dalmatia" in the Pajaro Valley, near the town of Watsonville south of San Francisco; shortly before World War I a group of Dalmatians started growing and selling apples in the domestic and foreign markets. They introduced new methods of packing, drying, and shipping, as well as ways to fight the diseases to which the apples and the apple trees were prone. In *Valley of the Moon* (1914) Jack London described the ingenuity and success of these "ragged Slavs" and how they managed to "squeeze out" the Yankees. One of them, Stephen N. Mitrovich, born in Dalmatia, arrived in Fresno in 1880. Later he imported fig cuttings from the Adriatic region and founded the California fig industry.

Two other California industries into which Croats moved in sizable numbers and with considerable success were fishing and mining. Many hundreds became fishermen along the Pacific as they had been along the Dalmatian coast; although most of them plied the southern coast from Los Angeles to San Diego, they could be found working in teams all the way from Alaska to Peru. A major place of settlement was San Pedro, the port of Los Angeles and still the largest Croatian fishing center in America. Some of the Pacific Coast Croats moved into the fishing-related industries of canning and marketing. Among the specifically ethnic organizations established by the Los Angeles area Croats in this early period were St. Anthony's Roman Catholic parish, the Croatian Zvonimir Society (1893), and the Croatian-Slavonian Benevolent Society (1895). A newspaper, *Dalmatinska Zora* (Dalmatian Dawn), was founded in 1892 but lasted for only a brief time.

Along with their fellow Slovene, Serbian, and Montenegrin South Slavs, the Croats also settled in all the major mining districts in the United States. A number worked in the California gold fields, especially around

Jackson, but they were less successful in gold mining than in agriculture and fishing. More found success in Nevada, where extensive silver deposits attracted many Croats to Carson City, Virginia City, Aurora, Austin, and Reno in the 1860s and 1870s.

In the 1890s Croats began to arrive in Gallup, N.Mex., to work in the coal mines; the thriving colony soon included several Croatian businessmen. The largest Croatian mining settlement between 1881 and 1914 was in the copper fields of Upper Michigan, centered in the town of Calumet. An ethnic parish was founded and a large church built; a variety of fraternal organizations, saloons, and other business enterprises, including cooperative stores and newspapers, were established. In the Calumet area the Croats were in close contact with the Slovenes and other South Slav groups. After 1900 Butte, Mont., with its huge ore deposits, had a major Croatian colony that included Slovenes and other Slavs; some of the Croats there moved into trades, ranching, and restaurant operations. Hundreds from the Lika region settled in the Minnesota Iron Range, in Utah, Wyoming, and other western states.

A few of the Croatian settlers were part of the old Wild West. Several died at the hands of Indians. Nikola Perasich was killed in a gunfight, as were several other Croats. Anton Mazzanovich was a particularly colorful character. He came to San Francisco with his parents in 1868, and is said to have enlisted at the age of ten as a musician in the U.S. Army, serving until 1873. Reenlisting in 1881, Mazzanovich joined the Sixth U.S. Cavalry and took part in the campaign against the Apache chief Geronimo. In 1885 he became a member of the New Mexico Rangers and fought Indians in that territory. In 1931 near the end of his life, he wrote a book of recollections called *Trailing Geronimo*.

By 1880 at least 20,000 Croatian immigrants were in the United States, most of them in the West. Quite a few were well established in business, and some were probably in the professions, though exactly how many will never be known since there are not any reliable statistics. From time to time they were subject to attacks from American nativists who asserted that the secret of Croatian economic success was their clannishness. In reality, for Croats as for other ethnic groups, success—when it came—was the result of ambition, luck, and years of hard work.

Croatian immigration changed after 1880 in several important ways. One of them was place of origin: Dalmatia no longer provided the great majority; they now came from the interior regions of Croatia proper (Inner Croatia), Slavonia, and Bosnia-Herzegovina. Social origin was another: the seafarers, merchants, and fishermen from towns or island communities gave way to people of peasant background. Place of settlement in the United States was a third: beginning as early as the 1860s, but mainly from the 1880s onward, huge numbers of Croatian immigrants began to settle in the East and Midwest. Eventually more Croats came to live in Pennsylvania than in any other state, most of them in Pittsburgh and surrounding Allegheny County. The first Croats arrived in the state in the 1860s; by the 1890s there were about 9,000, and by 1908 some 85,000. They worked at a variety of jobs, but the great majority were unskilled or semiskilled laborers in the coal mines, steel mills, iron foundries, factories, in building construction, or on the railroads. In addition to Pittsburgh, there were large Croatian settlements in Steelton, Johnstown, and Sharon. There were also many Croats in New York City and adjacent New Jersey towns. Some found jobs in the harbor area as tugboat crewmen and pilots, and as longshoremen; others worked as artisans and in factories. In Hoboken, N.J., a Slavonian Benevolent Society was founded in 1894, as was a newspaper, *Napredak* (Progress).

Beginning in the 1880s and 1890s numerous Croats settled in the metropolitan Chicago area. This colony eventually grew to approximately 50,000, the largest in the United States after Pittsburgh. By the beginning of World War I there were sizable settlements in Cleveland, Kansas City, Mo., and Gary, Ind. The previously established colonies in the Far West and the South also showed growth as thousands of new immigrants traveled to those areas, often to join family members already there.

SOCIAL ORGANIZATIONS

As a result of the predominantly agricultural economy in the homeland, the majority of Croatian immigrants to the United States from 1880 until World War II were from the peasant class. Only a tiny fraction had professional training or skills of the kind that would permit entry into the middle class, and as a result well over 80 percent of the first-generation immigrants remained unskilled or semiskilled industrial workers. In 1910 the Croats employed in Pennsylvania coal mines ranked among the lowest paid of all groups, and their unemployment rate was among the highest. Statistics from this period further reveal that only 34 percent of the Croats had steady year-round employment. Because unemployment compensation did not exist in the early 1900s, the lot of these Croats and their families (34 percent had wives and often other relatives in America by 1910) was harsh indeed. These conditions probably explain the high rate of return to the homeland.

Three institutions were especially important to the early Croatian immigrants—the fraternal association, the saloon, and the boarding house. The fraternal association was likely to be an insurance or burial society, as in San Francisco in 1857 and in New Orleans in 1874, but it had social functions as well. Its meetings were generally well attended, and debates were intense and frequently acrimonious. Although the two earliest organizations had both Serbian and Croatian members, the growth of nationalism among the Balkan peoples in the late 19th and early 20th centuries adversely affected the relations between these two groups both in the homeland and in the immigrant communities. Eventually the San Francisco and New Orleans societies became predominantly Croatian. The same split occurred elsewhere in the United States where Croats and Serbs were in close contact, and Croat-Serb animosity persists to the present time.

Croatian-owned and -operated saloons also appeared quickly in new settlements and were ways in which ambitious immigrants could join the entrepreneurial class. The saloon was a place where the immigrants could meet with friends in a convivial atmosphere, acquire the latest gossip and news from the homeland,

read Croatian-language newspapers, and attend to personal business. The saloon owner also often acted as a banker and advised his patrons on political and legal matters; he might even collect union dues and parish contributions, arrange to send money to the immigrant's family in Croatia, serve as an intermediary between the Croatian worker and his American employer, and perform a variety of other necessary tasks the immigrant did not feel competent to handle for himself. As with any group, the trustworthiness and ability of the saloonkeepers varied considerably, and many Croatian immigrants were victimized by unscrupulous operators. Nevertheless, the role of the saloon in the Croatian community was a significant one.

A third institution common in all Croatian settlements, especially during the first decades, was the boarding house, or a modified form of it, the cooperative household. As long as the immigration remained predominantly male, which it did until at least the early 20th century (in a study of 674 Croats and Serbs in New York City at that time, 573 were unattached men), most Croats lived in some such arrangement for a period of time. For the bachelors or the married men who had left their families behind, the boarding house was more than a place to eat and sleep; it was a surrogate home with a substitute family whose members had similar backgrounds and concerns and spoke the same language. Many of the boarding houses were operated by Croatian women whose husbands had saved enough money to buy or build a house with extra room and who also worked as saloonkeepers or laborers. The life of these women was hard. Their responsibilities extended beyond the care of their own families, which were often large, to that of ten or more boarders. Sixteen- or eighteen-hour days were by no means uncommon. Unfortunately, little information is available about the role of these women, or women in general, in the Croatian-American group.

Cooperative living arrangements varied, but they all represented an extension of collective family traditions and the old South Slav *zadruga* (a type of village commune). Some groups hired a male "boss" who cooked and ran the household; others divided chores and expenses equally. In most cases the household consisted of men from the same village or district who banded together to survive in an alien environment until they could make enough money to return home or to bring family members to the United States.

Like most immigrant groups, the Croats founded a wide range of fraternal organizations, especially in the large settlements that developed from the 1880s onward in the East and Midwest. Originally the organizations functioned only in a particular settlement, which left them vulnerable to collapse from a rapidly changing membership because of the high mobility of the early immigrants, or to major disasters that could deplete or liquidate accumulated funds. These independent societies soon strengthened their forces by merging into regional or national associations and thereby spreading the risk among a much broader membership. The Hrvatska Zajednica (Croatian Union) was the first of these national organizations. When it was established in Allegheny City (now part of Pittsburgh) in 1894 it provided health- and life-insurance benefits to about 600 members in a few lodges; ten years later, it was responsible for 22,384 members in 281 lodges. In 1896 it took over the publication of *Napredak* (Progress), a newspaper founded in 1891. In 1897 it changed its name to the National Croatian Society.

The Croatian League of Illinois was founded in Chicago in 1905, the Croatian Unity of the Pacific in 1910, with headquarters in San Francisco. A patriotic gymnastic organization established in 1908 was the Croatian Sokol (Falcon). For a brief time after 1910 it had chapters in most of the Croatian settlements in the United States, but it declined when interest waned rapidly after World War I. By 1912 most of the approximately 1,500 Croatian fraternal societies of all kinds throughout the country were affiliated with the National Croatian Society or the Croatian League of Illinois.

The Croatian Catholic Union was established in Gary in 1921. This organization was regarded by its founders, a number of whom were priests, as an alternative to what they perceived to be the increasingly leftward swing of the National Croatian Society. The principal publication of the CCU was *Naša Nada* (Our Hope), begun in 1921. By the 1970s the Croatian Catholic Union had about 11,000 members and the circulation of *Naši Nada* was around 6,000. The Croatian National Society, the Croatian League of Illinois, and several other large fraternal groups merged with the Croatian Fraternal Union in 1925. The CFU thus became, and remains, by far the largest Croatian-American organization; in the 1970s it retained a membership of 112,000, and its weekly newspaper, *Zajedničar* (The Fraternalist), had a circulation of approximately 40,000.

CULTURAL LIFE AND RELIGION

Vocal and instrumental music have always been popular in the Croatian settlements, especially folk music and dances originating in the homeland, where each region has its own distinctive style. The colorful costumes also varied according to region and indicated to knowledgeable observers the part of Croatia their wearer came from; these costumes are still worn on festive occasions by Croatian Americans. Two of the earliest musical groups were Zora (Dawn) in Chicago and Javor (Maple) in Pittsburgh. The instrument most closely associated with the Croats in America is the mandolin-shaped *tamburitza*. Croatian Americans have always been prominent in the ranks of Pittsburgh's Duquesne University Tamburitzans (f. 1937); an ensemble of predominantly South Slav Americans, it continues to perform throughout the United States and abroad. Duquesne University also maintains the Tamburitzan Institute of Folk Arts, with an associated museum and archives. The Junior Cultural Federation of the Croatian Fraternal Union comprises about 50 children's tamburitzan groups which meet at an annual festival and perform music, songs, and various dances, particularly the *kolo*, or circle dances. The tenth annual festival of this group was held in the Croatian capital of Zagreb in 1976 in commemoration of the American Bicentennial.

Father Joseph Kundek (1809–1857), a secular priest and one of the many missionaries the Leopoldine Society of Vienna sent to the United States, was an isolated but locally significant Croatian missionary in the

Midwest. He arrived in Jasper, Ind., in 1838, and spent most of the rest of his life ministering to the needs of the numerous German-speaking immigrants in the area; reportedly he helped more than 7,000 of them get settled in various parts of southern Indiana. In the early 1850s Kundek returned to Europe and found a number of other priests, including one Croat, willing to come to America; with them he founded the St. Meinrad Archabbey near Jasper.

Although the Roman Catholic Church had played a very important role in their homeland, the Croats were slower than other Slavs to found their own parishes. Well over 100,000 Croats were already in America before their first ethnic parish was established in Allegheny City in 1901; several hundred thousand Croats were served by only 12 parishes and 4 parochial schools in 1912. Within the next six years, however, 15 more appeared. Some of these eventually became elaborate cultural centers with schools, printing presses, and recreational facilities. Another half-dozen parishes were established in the interwar period and one after World War II in Monessen, Pa., in 1957. In the 1970s there were 33 Roman Catholic Croatian parishes; 10 of them in Pennsylvania (4 in Pittsburgh), 7 in Illinois (6 in Chicago). Ohio has 4 parishes and Indiana 3, with 2 each in New York, California, and Wisconsin. Settlements in Michigan, Oregon, and Missouri have 1 parish each.

Croats belong to several Catholic religious orders which maintain orphanages and hospitals in the United States. Croats are most numerous in the Franciscans; the Dominicans and Conventuals also have a number. In the early 1900s a number of nuns from various locations in Croatia came to the United States to work in parochial schools, orphanages, and hospitals. The Croatian Eastern-rite Catholics of Cleveland maintain two parishes; elsewhere Eastern-rite Croats usually attend Ukrainian or Carpatho-Rusyn churches. The few Croatian Protestants have customarily shared their churches with other South Slavs. The first known Croatian Lutheran minister in the United States was the Reverend Louis Serjak. Ordained in 1914, he is best known for *In Silence* (1938), an account of his American experiences.

In recent years several Roman Catholic churches have been built in the older Croatian settlements, and some parishes are thriving, largely because of the influence of the postwar immigrants. St. Raphael's in New York City boasts both a church and a Croatian center, and is the largest Croatian parish in the United States; it had 5,000 members in the late 1970s. St. Paul's in Cleveland ranks second with 3,500 members. Some of the Croats in Cleveland attend other Catholic churches; a significant number belong to St. Vitus's, a Slovene parish. This cross-ethnic pattern is common to all the Croatian colonies. Croatian priests still come from the homeland on occasion, and thereby sustain ties between the Croatian-American parishes and the Catholic Church in Yugoslavia. In the fall of 1970, for example, the chapel of Our Lady of Bistrica was dedicated by the Archbishop of Zagreb at the National Shrine of the Immaculate Conception in Washington, D.C.

POLITICS

Politics among Croatian Americans has centered almost exclusively on the homeland. This interest has not deterred Croats from acquiring U.S. citizenship, performing military service, or voting; yet, at the same time, Croats have strong feelings about their homeland, and not infrequently have demonstrated their feelings publicly. Their interest dates from the early 1900s, when both the National Croatian Society and the Croatian League of Illinois contributed funds to aid in the struggle against Hapsburg rule over Croatia. These activities provoked a split in the NCS, since its president, Frank Zotti, and his followers opposed the anti-Hapsburg campaign. Zotti was a prosperous banker and the publisher of the daily *Narodni List* (National Gazette) in New York. When Zotti's bank failed in 1908, however, and his depositors lost more than $800,000, he was removed as NCS president. At the organization's 11th convention in September 1912 a new political group called the Croatian National Alliance was founded. Its goal was to help overthrow the Hapsburg monarchy and establish a federal South Slav state in which Croats, Serbs, and Slovenes would be equal partners. A weekly published since 1901 in Chicago, *Hrvatska Zastava* (Croatian Flag), was the organ of the alliance.

The depth of the passion involved was revealed on August 18, 1913, when Ivan Dojčić, a young Croatian-American nationalist, tried to assassinate the Hungarian governor of Croatia, Baron Ivan Skerlecz. Skerlecz survived, but Dojčić was captured and sentenced to ten years in prison. He confessed he had come from the United States specifically to assassinate the governor. Although in some Croatian-American circles he was hailed as a hero, most Croats denounced his use of violence.

When Austria-Hungary attacked Serbia in July 1914 and thereby precipitated World War I, most Croatian Americans remained loyal to the Hapsburgs in spite of their continuing opposition to Hapsburg rule over Croatia. Given the claims advanced by both the nationalist Croats and Serbs over Bosnia-Herzegovina and other areas, the prospects for Croatia if the Hapsburgs lost and Serbia won were not encouraging. Frank Zotti's *Narodni List* remained pro-Hapsburg and gave its support to a group of Croatian and Slovene priests who advocated the formation of a Croatian-Slovene state within the Hapsburg framework. This program never received wide support in either the Croatian or the Slovene communities, however, and the rush of events soon made it unfeasible.

As the war continued into 1915 and the possibility increased that Austria-Hungary would be defeated and perhaps disappear altogether, Croatian-American leaders sought to exert some control over developments. Many saw the wisdom of coordinating their activities with those of Slovenes and even the Serbs. The first coherent expression of this activity was the establishment in the spring of 1915 of the South Slavic National Council of Chicago. The moving forces in this group were the Reverend Nikola Gršković of Cleveland; Joseph Marohnić, the president of the National Croatian Society; Dr. Ante Biankini, a noted Chicago physician; and several other men prominent in the Serbian and Slovene communities. The council had ties with the Yugoslav Committee in London, a group composed of exiles from the South Slavic areas of the Hapsburg monarchy and also founded in 1915. The goal of both organi-

zations was to promote the creation of a South Slav, or Yugoslav, state. The two most important Croatian-American newspapers supporting the council's activity were the Chicago *Hrvatska Zastava* and *Hrvatski Svijet* (Croatian World), a New York daily with a circulation of 10,000.

How much impact these and other activities had on the emergence of the Kingdom of Serbs, Croats, and Slovenes, which came into existence December 1, 1918, is debatable. But the Croatian Americans were soon profoundly disappointed in the resulting independent Yugoslav state and expressed their unhappiness in both word and deed during the next two decades. Several thousand Croatian immigrants did return to their homeland in the first few years after World War I, but far more—perhaps 35,000—came the other way in an influx that probably would have continued unabated had not the United States severely curtailed immigration beginning in 1924. Yugoslavia was given a quota of less than 1,000 per year. In the late 1920s and the 1930s a number of Croatian-American groups with an explicitly anti-Yugoslav orientation appeared; some of them supported the activities of the Fascist Ustashas led by Ante Pavelić (1889–1959). On the whole, however, Croatian Americans displayed less and less interest in their homeland as their absence from it lengthened and as the second and third generations—most of whom had no direct experience of Croatia—grew older. In the 1930s they were too preoccupied with surviving the Great Depression to involve themselves with distant politics.

The Axis attack on Yugoslavia in April 1941 somewhat altered this situation. After conquering Yugoslavia and taking what territory he wanted for the Third Reich, Hitler divided the rest among his various allies. Italy received the most generous share; Croatia was given independent status, and Pavelić, the founder of Ustasha, was placed at its head. Although it was an Axis satellite, Pavelić's Croatia had a degree of internal administrative autonomy. From then until the end of the war the Croatian people were divided into at least four factions: the Ustashas, the dominant minority; the passive non-Fascist and non-Communist majority, especially the adherents of the Croatian Peasant party and various other prewar parties; some Communists and many more non-Communists who joined the Partisans; and the very few who, mostly out of loyalty to their oath as Yugoslav army members, joined the predominantly Serbian Chetniks of Draža Mihailović. There were still others. Croatia was the scene of extraordinary bloodshed: the Ustasha massacred hundreds of thousands of Serbs, Jews, and others; the Partisans murdered Croats and others suspected of being Ustashas or enemies. In 1945, at the very end of the war, tens of thousands of Croats were massacred by Partisan forces for the same reasons, and tens of thousands of other Croats fled into exile to escape death or imprisonment.

The situation was almost beyond understanding to those experiencing the events in Croatia; the confusion in the Croatian-American community was even greater. Reliable information was impossible to obtain; competing stories of atrocities led to sharp antagonism between Serbs and Croats. To organize support for the victims of the conflict and to ensure that the Allied powers were aware of the needs and demands of the South Slavs, a number of Croatian leaders convoked a huge All-Slavic Congress in Detroit in 1942. Among the numerous groups that emerged were the Croatian War Aid Committee and the Yugoslav Relief Committee, each of which collected over $1 million in fund-raising campaigns to aid the victims of war. The U.S. decision to support the Partisan movement of Marshal Tito persuaded many Croats and other South Slavs in the United States to support or at least tolerate it.

But reports of the harsh and dictatorial Communist government established by Tito in postwar Yugoslavia, along with news of large-scale massacres of anti-Communists (stories that were eventually substantiated) united most Croatian Americans in opposition to the regime. Some, like Ivan D. Butkovich, the president of the Croatian Fraternal Union, who earlier had been pro-Tito, changed their views and expressed strong anti-Communist sentiments. In 1945 ten Croatian-American societies opposed to Communist rule in Yugoslavia founded an organization called the United Croatians of America and Canada (in 1966 renamed the United Croats). With a membership of about 5,000 in the late 1970s, the United Croats has continued to protest the Communist regime in Yugoslavia. Another group with similarly strong views is sponsored by the Croatian Franciscans in Chicago, who publish *Danica* (Morning Star); formerly known as *Hrvatski list i danica hrvatska*, this publication reaches 4,500 subscribers. These two groups and others have been buttressed by the thousands of Croatian political refugees who have settled in the United States and Canada.

This preoccupation with homeland politics has not kept some from achieving prominence in American political life and in the U.S. armed forces. Croatian Americans have served in the armed forces in all the conflicts of the 20th century. Thousands fought in World War I; several hundred were killed, others were wounded, and many received decorations for valor. At least four won the Congressional Medal of Honor. Tens of thousands served in World War II; more than 300 members of the Croatian Fraternal Union were killed in action. Many have served on the local level and in state legislatures, but only a few have reached the upper ranks of government. Mike Stepovich became governor of the Alaska Territory in 1957 and the first governor of the state in 1959. In Minnesota, Rudy Perpich (1928–), a miner's son, was elected lieutenant governor in 1970 and served as governor from 1976 to 1979. Michael A. Bilandic (1923–) became acting mayor of Chicago when Richard J. Daley died and served as mayor in his own right from 1977 to 1979. From 1977 to 1979 Dennis J. Kucinich (1946–) was mayor of Cleveland. Most Croatian-American politicians have been Democrats, as have Croatian Americans in general.

GROUP MAINTENANCE

When the Croats first settled in the United States in the 19th century, they found it difficult to maintain distinct communities. Few Croatian women came with them or followed them. Men, if they married, married outside the group, although often they chose other Catholic Slavs. Their children generally identified themselves in terms of the ethnic affiliation of their

mother. In the 20th century, however, large numbers of Croatian women began to migrate to America; their arrival helps explain the marked increase in organized Croatian ethnic activity, including the national Roman Catholic parishes. Compact Croatian working-class communities took shape in many of the large industrial centers of the East and Midwest. These enclaves made it easier for the Croats to preserve their customs, and especially in the case of women, the Croatian language. They avoided learning any more than the most rudimentary English.

However, the Croatian immigrant generation could hardly avoid acquiring at least a passive knowledge of English, and when it did, a Croatian-American dialect developed incorporating English words and Croatian endings—such as *kara* (car), *ronati* (run), and *šapa* (shop). Second-generation children attended public schools where they learned to speak and write English, but a strong extended-family tradition encouraged many to stay in the community, often as skilled workers in the same factories where their fathers were still employed as unskilled laborers.

By the 1930s and 1940s a substantial number of Croatian-American children had completed high school; some had gone on to college and even beyond. As the economic position of the Croats improved, especially after midcentury, many finally moved from the old ethnic enclaves to the suburbs, and the urban neighborhoods passed to the post–World War II newcomers. A few Croats left the cities altogether to establish farms, as their fathers had wanted to do; some of them still live in the area around Eagle River, Wis. The majority of the second generation did not use the Croatian language, although they continued to understand a little. Even the Croatian parochial schools shifted to English.

A number of immigrant and American-born Croats achieved success in a variety of professions. American-born Henry Suzzalo (1873–1933) was president of the University of Washington from 1915 to 1926. The violinist Zlatko Balokovic (1885–1965) arrived in the United States in 1924. Zinka Milanov (1906–), a native of Zagreb, was a Metropolitan Opera Company soprano between 1935 and 1966. Ivan Meštrović (1883–1962), one of the greatest sculptors of the 20th century, settled in the United States after World War II and taught at the University of Notre Dame. Nikola Tesla (1856–1943), born in Lika, Croatia, was an inventor of electric motors and other devices and an innovator in electronic theory. Although his parents were Serbs, many Croats like to regard him as one of their own.

The process of assimilation has been slowed by the post–World War II immigrants, who sought out Croatian enclaves in the United States and helped revive them, and by the ethnic revival in the United States since the late 1960s. Between the late 1940s and early 1970s an estimated 42,000 Croats arrived in the United States and an additional 2,000 to 3,000 came annually during the 1970s. The newcomers often were relatively well educated, with a degree of competence in English that made it easier for them to adapt to their new environment. Those who emigrated primarily for economic reasons were apt to keep in close touch with the homeland; some families visit Croatia every year or two, a practice that serves to preserve the Croatian language among their American-born children.

Because so many of the immediate postwar arrivals were intensely nationalistic and generally better educated than the earlier immigrants or their children, relations between them were not always cordial. There is no doubt, however, that the newcomers are responsible for much of the ethnic enthusiasm currently displayed by Croatian Americans. Also helpful has been the receptive attitude of the Yugoslav government, which encourages tourism and promotes the study of Croatian language and history. Even many strongly anti-Communist Croatian Americans take advantage of these opportunities, secure in their convictions and usually adept in avoiding difficulties with the Yugoslav authorities. Some older Croatian Americans have chosen to retire in Croatia, where their U.S. pensions go much further than they would in the United States.

Language study has increased in the 1970s, aided by Croatian-language newspapers and other publications. Assimilation of the Croatian Americans, especially the immigrant generation, would have been much more rapid and thorough, especially in language, had these publications not existed. Except at the major American universities, opportunities for formal language study are rare, although in this respect the Croats are better served than the Slovenes or Carpatho-Rusyns, for example. In the late 1970s there were 15 Croatian Roman Catholic parochial schools with an average enrollment of 200 pupils each. Instruction is in English, but some of the schools offer optional Croatian-language classes after regular school hours or on Saturday. In Croatia, the University of Zagreb offers special language programs geared to the needs of foreigners.

These factors—the small but continuous influx of newcomers from the homeland, the panoply of active organizations, the ability to maintain relatively close contact with Croatia and its contemporary culture and language, and the diminishing need to know Croatian in order to belong to the group—all point to the survival of the Croatian Americans as a cohesive ethnic group.

Bibliography
There are no modern analytical works on the Croats in the United States. George J. Prpic, *The Croatian Immigrants in America* (New York, 1971), is a traditional narrative and includes a 28-page bibliography. Gerald G. Govorchin, *Americans from Yugoslavia* (Gainesville, Fla., 1961), covers the Croats and their neighbors. Extensive and valuable information may be found in the issues of the annual *Journal of Croatian Studies* (New York, f. 1960) and the quarterly *Croatia Press* (New York, f. 1950).

For historical and cultural background see Francis Preveden, *A History of the Croatian People* (New York, 1955), and Francis H. Eterović and Christopher Spalatín, eds., *Croatia: Land, People, Culture,* 2 vols. (Toronto, 1970).

Emily G. Balch's classic *Our Slavic Fellow-Citizens* (1910 reprint, New York, 1969) gives a great deal of invaluable information (along with statistics and illustrations), and Louis Adamic, the Slovene author, wrote about the Croats in his many articles and books, notably *The Native's Return* (New York, 1934), *Cradle of Life* (New York, 1936), and "Manda Evanich from Croatia" in *From Many Lands* (New York, 1940). See also G.J. Prpic, *The South Slavic Immigration in America* (Boston, 1978).

Manuel P. Servin, ed., *The Apostolic Life of Fernando Consag, Explorer of Lower California* (Los Angeles, 1968); Dunstan McAndrews, *Father Joseph Kundek, 1810–1857* (St. Meinrad, Ind., 1954); and Lawrence Schmeckbier, *Meštrović, Sculptor and Patriot* (Syracuse, N.Y., 1959), deal with important figures in the Croatian immigration.

Two reference books of value are Vladimir Markotic, ed., *Biographical Directory of Americans and Canadians of Croatian Descent* (Calgary, Alberta, 1973); and G.J. and Hilda Prpic, *Croatian Books and Booklets Written in Exile* (Cleveland, 1973).

The Immigration History Research Center, University of Minnesota; Croatian Ethnic Institute, Chicago, Ill.; the archives of the Croatian Fraternal Union, Pittsburgh, Pa.; and Matica Iseljenika Hrvatske, Zagreb, Croatia, contain extensive collections of primary and secondary materials.

CROWS: *see* AMERICAN INDIANS

CUBANS

Cubans, for the most part, have come to the United States relatively recently; only in the 1970s did they begin to have a visible cultural and economic impact on the cities where they have settled in sizable numbers. The number of persons of Cuban origin or descent residing in the United States in 1977 was estimated at 681,000 by the U.S. Bureau of the Census. Less than 20 years earlier, there were probably not more than 50,000 Cubans in the United States, less than 8 percent of the 1977 estimate.

EARLY MIGRATION

Although most of the Cuban immigrants have lived in the United States for less than 20 years, Cuban immigration has a long history. As early as 1831 approximately 50 Cubans were living in Key West, Fla., where a small, Cuban-owned cigar factory employed about 16 craftsmen. Later, during the waning years of Spanish colonial rule of Cuba, some Cubans looked upon the United States as a likely place of refuge when the political or economic climate was unfavorable for them. There was substantial migration just before, during, and after the Cuban struggle for independence from Spain in the late 19th and early 20th centuries. Many of the emigrants then were also cigarmakers. From 1868 to 1878 the emigration of tobacco workers increased as the anti-Spanish struggles devastated many tobacco plantations, especially in the eastern part of the island. In response, a few Cuban cigar manufacturers, including Vicente Martínez Ibor and Eduardo Hidalgo Gato, relocated their factories in Key West or Tampa, Fla., or in New York City, taking with them many skilled workers who were seeking freedom and better wages. In the 1880s

and early 1890s José Martí (1853–1895), a towering figure in Cuban history, lived in exile in the United States, where he garnered substantial and crucial support from the cigar makers of Tampa, Key West, and New York for the Cuban independence movement. Martí spent much time in these communities and directed many of his speeches and writings to them. Tampa's modern cigar industry and its Ibor City section still show the impact of the 19th-century migration. In 1970 approximately 8 percent of Tampa's population identified themselves as being of Cuban origin or descent. (*See also* Spaniards.)

From the beginning of the 20th century until the revolution of 1959, immigration fluctuated according to the changing political and economic conditions on the island. In the late 1950s, during the last years of the turbulent dictatorship of Fulgencio Batista (1901–1976), Cubans migrated to the United States at an estimated rate of 10,000–15,000 annually. Those who immigrated prior to the revolution of 1959 were a heterogeneous group, including members of the ruling elite who were out of favor at the time, other politically or socially alienated persons, and unemployed workers seeking jobs.

MIGRATION AFTER THE REVOLUTION OF 1959

Immediately after the overthrow of Batista's government by the rebel forces led by Fidel Castro (1927–), some people who were closely associated with the Batista government fled to the United States. The emigration did not really start in earnest, however, until 1960, when the new government began to make it clear that Cuban society was to be completely restructured. This threatened various segments of the population, who looked for refuge to the United States. Although President Dwight Eisenhower's administration severed diplomatic relations with the Cuban government on January 3, 1961, commercial air traffic between the two countries was not suspended until the October 1962 missile crisis, when all direct contact between the United States and Cuba ceased. More than 155,000 Cubans immigrated to the United States between January 1959 and 1962. Their entry was facilitated by U.S. hostility toward Cuba; the U.S. government granted them refugee status, which allowed an unlimited number to enter outside the Cuban immigration quota. Some entered the country with immigrant visas granted by U.S. embassies in a third country or in Cuba prior to the severing of diplomatic relations, but most entered with temporary visas and had parolee status until 1966, when a procedure was established by which they could become permanent residents.

The suspension of direct flights from Cuba to the United States lasted more than three years. During that time the immigration was considerably slowed, because it was possible to leave Cuba only clandestinely, often on small boats, or through a third country, usually Spain or Mexico. One way or the other, 30,000 Cubans arrived in the United States during that period. The tempo of the immigration picked up considerably, however, after President Lyndon Johnson's administration signed a "memorandum of understanding" with the Cuban government in December 1965, which established an airlift between Varadero and Miami. These daily flights brought some 257,000 Cubans to the

United States between December 1, 1965 and December 31, 1972. The airlift ended in 1973, and since then immigration has slowed considerably, being limited to those who can manage to go somewhere else from Cuba and then apply for admission to the United States.

SOCIOECONOMIC CHARACTERISTICS

Cubans arriving after the 1959 revolution have been labeled exiles or political refugees because their emigration was a response to the profound changes instituted by a new government. The socioeconomic characteristics of such exiles are predictably different from those of migrants who have left their homeland in search of jobs and improved economic opportunities. The latter are usually drawn disproportionately from the less advantaged and skilled segments of their society, while exiles are almost always members of somewhat more privileged classes. Their specific socioeconomic composition depends largely on the nature of the political and economic changes that have led to their emigration.

In the case of Cuba between 1960 and 1962, a capitalist system was replaced by a socialist political and economic order, resulting in emigration of the upper and upper-middle classes—professional, managerial, entrepreneurial and commercial people and landowners. The degree of class selectivity should not be exaggerated, however. The American public tends to think that all the Cubans living in the United States are former government officials, bank presidents, large landowners, millionaires, military leaders, or aristocrats, compelled to leave the country when their power and wealth were threatened by Castro's revolutionary government. In fact, even before 1962, when the immigrants were disproportionately wealthy and powerful, they were not a homogeneous group. The revolution also alienated people without political or economic power who disapproved of or distrusted the new order. The Cubans who came to the United States later, after more than a decade of socialism, were noticeably different from the earlier immigrants: people of lower-middle-class and blue-collar backgrounds predominated. As a result the Cubans living in the United States have come more and more to reflect the Cuban population as a whole, although the upper levels are still overrepresented, and the rural poor, in particular, are underrepresented.

Because of the relationship between class and race in prerevolutionary Cuba, whites are also overrepresented in the immigrant population. In the Cuban census of 1953, approximately 72 percent of the population was classified as white; in the 1970 U.S. Census almost 95 percent of Cubans in the United States identified themselves as white. Socioeconomic selectivity explains most of this difference, but, in addition, black Cubans were probably less likely to emigrate because of their perception that race relations in the United States are less satisfactory than they are in socialist Cuba. Cuba's revolutionary leaders emphasize their achievements in assuring racial equality and describe the United States as oppressive and exploitative of black people. There is evidence that these claims are supported by the experiences of black Cubans in the United States. In Miami, black Cubans experience housing discrimination even in predominantly Cuban neighborhoods. Significantly, the majority of all Cubans in the United States live in the South, but the majority of black Cubans live in the Northeast. They are discriminated against both as a racial and as an ethnic minority; they are cut off from their ethnic group and at the same time isolated by a language and cultural barrier from other black Americans.

Asian Cubans, especially those of Chinese ancestry, constitute another racial minority. The 1953 Cuban census listed 16,657 people, or 0.3 percent of the population, as "unmixed persons of the yellow race." The 1970 U.S. Census indicated that about 2 percent of the U.S. Cuban population was of Asian extraction. This overrepresentation of Chinese Cubans is probably the result of their role in the economy of Cuba; most of them were either small entrepreneurs or engaged in service occupations, two categories that were eliminated or curtailed by the socialist government.

The Cuban population in the United States also includes a disproportionately large number of elderly people. During the early years of the revolution many members of the older generation were convinced that the new government would not survive and refused to leave the country, but in the late 1960s and early 1970s they finally gave up and came to join their children. The Cuban government encouraged the emigration of this largely dependent elderly population and readily granted them permission to leave. At present, nearly 10 percent of Cubans in the United States are over 65 years old, a proportion about three times larger than that for the rest of the Hispanic population.

GEOGRAPHIC DISTRIBUTION

The 1970 Census found Cubans living in every state except Wyoming and Vermont. Yet despite this apparently broad dispersal, Cubans, particularly those who immigrated after the 1959 revolution, are largely found in a few major U.S. cities; 99 percent were urban dwellers in 1970. Metropolitan Miami (Dade County, Fla.) is the undisputed center; in 1970 more than 40 percent of all the Cubans in the United States lived there. Most of the rest are in New York City, Jersey City and Newark, N.J., Los Angeles, and Chicago, all of which are large centers for other Spanish-speaking peoples.

Their distribution throughout the country has been influenced by the efforts of the U.S. Cuban Refugee Program. Since its creation in February 1961, the program has sought to minimize the impact of the Cuban influx on the Miami community by encouraging resettlement outside of southern Florida. The program provided sponsors, if the refugees had no family ties in the community, as well as job contacts and temporary assistance. Between January 1961 and December 1972, almost 300,000 Cubans were settled away from Miami, but many returned. As the number of new immigrants declined in the mid-1970s, the resettlement program tapered off until it ceased to be an important factor in the settlement of Cubans in the United States.

In the past few years a substantial number have returned to Miami after acquiring job skills, training, or work experience somewhere else. Because of the large Cuban community, the climate, and other considerations, most Cubans want to live in the Miami area. The skills they have acquired elsewhere, combined with the

growth of southern Florida, make it relatively easy for them to find employment. Those who resettle permanently in other areas of the country are likely to be in technical or professional occupations; the Cuban population elsewhere in the United States has more education and a higher average income than the Cuban population in Florida.

ECONOMIC LIFE

The economic achievements of Cubans in the United States have often been exaggerated because of the rags-to-riches success stories of a few individuals. In 1976 the median income of Cuban families in the United States was $11,773, more than $3,000 below the U.S. median; 15.4 percent of Cuban families earned less than $4,000 a year, a higher proportion than that of all Spanish-origin families. The figure for all U.S. families was 8.9 percent. Most Cubans hold clerical, semiskilled, or service jobs, and their unemployment rates are higher than for the total U.S. labor force. On the other hand, Cubans in the Miami area have helped to revitalize the economy there. They have created jobs through their countless business enterprises, and politicians and businessmen in Miami are aware that they are important producers and consumers.

In Cuba before 1959, social class standing was generally determined by family background; in the United States income and achievement are important social-class determinants. As a result, most of the exiled members of Cuba's aristocratic and traditionally wealthy families, although they retain a certain prestige among the immigrant group, have lost status as well as wealth. Some live in poverty, others are more comfortable, but virtually all have suffered a loss in social standing. Their position has been taken by Cubans whose origins may have been modest but who have been able to take advantage of opportunities in an expanding economy. Many Cuban immigrants have improved their economic status, some substantially.

Upwardly mobile families have attempted to adopt and preserve the trappings of upper-class life in prerevolutionary Cuba. A number of social registers are published annually; each one is larger than the volumes that used to be published in Havana, and each edition is longer than the last. Social clubs are patterned after the yacht, tennis, and country clubs of 25 and 30 years ago, except that the primary requirement for admission is a family's ability to pay a stiff membership fee rather than "appropriate" family background. The society pages of Miami's Hispanic newspapers are filled with descriptions and photographs of increasingly lavish social events. Weddings and birthdays (particularly the traditional 15th birthday party for girls) are occasions for successful families to display their new wealth.

CULTURAL LIFE

Cubans are relatively recent immigrants, and the first-generation foreign-born predominate. They are exiles who came to the United States not so much because they preferred the U.S. way of life, but because they felt compelled to leave their country. For these reasons most Cuban immigrants fiercely attempt to retain the culture and way of life they knew in prerevolutionary Cuba. Their effort is strongly nostalgic, because it invokes the way of life of another place and another time, without contact with the homeland. In short, they behave like most groups of exiles throughout history.

Those who live in large Cuban settlements, especially in Miami, obviously can retain more of their culture more easily than those who are scattered throughout the United States. In Miami the exiles can fulfill all their needs in all aspects of their lives within the ethnic community. They can work, shop, bank, and be entertained in establishments owned or managed by other Cubans, where only Spanish is spoken. The use of Spanish is perhaps the most tangible evidence of their cultural maintenance. Young Cubans educated in public schools are likely to be more proficient in English than in Spanish, but their parents and older relatives and friends tend to speak Spanish almost exclusively. In fact, the immigrants need not learn English, because Miami is now officially a bilingual city, and all public documents, notices, and forms must be in both languages. There are two Spanish-language television stations, a half-dozen radio stations, a Hispanic daily newspaper, a weekly magazine, and a number of weekly and biweekly tabloids, all owned and operated by Cubans for the Spanish-speaking community in Miami. Some Spanish-language broadcasts and newspapers are available to the Cuban communities in New York City and New Jersey.

There are numerous Cuban-owned neighborhood grocery stores in Miami, specializing in traditional foods that are usually not found in supermarkets. A modest but flourishing Cuban-owned industry imports, produces, processes, and distributes many of the staples of the Cuban diet. Most of the traditional vegetables and fruits are imported from Central America and the Dominican Republic.

Cuban nightclubs and restaurants serve the immigrant community and also add greatly to the tourist attractions of Miami. Many of these establishments, along with many Cuban retail businesses, are located on S.W. Eighth Street and on Flagler Street in the heart of "Little Havana," a predominantly Cuban section that is being refurbished by the municipal authorities to exploit its potential for tourism.

The various Spanish-language bookstores in Miami feature works by Cuban exiles. Much of this material is printed in Spain or in Latin America, but some comes from a Miami publishing house that publishes Cuban fiction, poetry, and literary criticism, as well as history, philosophy, and the social sciences for a predominantly Cuban audience.

A number of Cuban artists, especially painters, exhibit their works in Miami. In recent years theater and dance companies have staged original plays and musical productions in Spanish, acted by well-known Cuban performers, as well as traditional Cuban operettas and plays. There are also song recitals and presentations of classical works. A few young Cuban interpreters of classical music have become prominent musicians with major U.S. symphony orchestras. A fairly large number of entertainers and musical groups perform popular Cuban music on records produced and manufactured in Miami or New York. Renditions of traditional Cuban music and rhythms appeal to the older immigrants. Younger musicians mix Latin rhythms with contempo-

rary soul and rock in styles not very different from the Hispanic music popular in New York City.

MARRIAGE AND FAMILY PATTERNS

The Cuban household in the United States is likely to include at least one relative, most often a widowed and dependent grandparent, in addition to the nuclear family. The U.S. Bureau of the Census estimated in 1977 that the number of persons of Cuban origin or descent who were living as "other relatives" (other than wife or child) of the head of the household amounted to 8.8 percent of the Cuban population. The corresponding figure for the total U.S. population was 3.8 percent, for the Mexican-American population 5.9 percent, and for mainland Puerto Ricans, 4.0 percent. This situation is largely the result of the age selectivity of the emigration. When the elderly, particularly the widowed, arrived in the United States, their adult children, in keeping with traditional Cuban values, could not permit them to live alone or to be institutionalized. Because so many Cuban women work, the elderly also are important as housekeepers and babysitters. They have a considerable impact on the household because they are in a position to pass on language and culture to the new generation. Nonetheless, many of the elderly do have to live by themselves or in institutions. Their needs and their status as dependents are a major problem for the Cuban community in Miami.

The courtship patterns of prerevolutionary Cuba, especially the strict supervision of unmarried women, are undergoing change. After more than a decade of residence in the United States, the immigrants' customs have been noticeably liberalized. Requiring a chaperone is by no means an extinct practice, but many, if not most, young women are allowed to go out on unchaperoned dates or, more frequently, on double dates. Abstaining from premarital physical intimacy continues to be the norm for women. Although the extent of parental supervision varies greatly, depending on the family, the age of the young woman, and whether or not the family resides in a Cuban neighborhood, the norms and values surrounding courtship are still somewhat more conservative than those in U.S. society as a whole, a situation that tends to limit the range of potential mates largely to other Cubans. Parental pressure, intergenerational language barriers, and the institutional completeness of the ethnic community also keep marriages within the group. For young women, this situation may be changing; the Cuban law prohibiting the emigration of males of military-service age has resulted in an uneven distribution of the sexes among U.S. Cubans of marriageable age. In 1970 among U.S. Cubans between 20 and 29 years of age, there were 76 males for every 100 females. But at present, endogamy remains the norm, and unless this changes, approximately one-quarter of the young women will not be able to find appropriate marriage partners.

Cubans still place great value on family ties; the family is usually viewed as stable and strong, but there are also some signs of disintegration. The 1970 U.S. Census showed that among Cubans who immigrated between 1960 and 1970, there were 6.2 divorced persons for every 100 married persons. The corresponding figure for the total U.S. population in 1970 was 5.3, and for the rest of the foreign-born who immigrated in the same decade, 2.9.

RELIGION

Most Cubans in the United States are nominally Roman Catholics, and their arrival in Miami has led to a tremendous expansion of the local Catholic archdiocese. Virtually all Catholic churches in the Miami area now have at least one priest who offers mass, hears confession, and gives counsel in Spanish. Parishes in Cuban neighborhoods conduct all their services in Spanish. Church-related organizations are among the most important voluntary associations in the community.

Although little information is available on the immigrants' religious preferences or on postimmigration changes in religious affiliation, it is apparent that they are not any more theologically homogeneous than they were at home. There is a wide variety of Protestants, some Jews, and members of several nondenominational churches, along with a significant number who belong to various Afro-Cuban cults. Sometimes known as *santería*, these cults exhibit varying degrees of syncretism with Catholic practices and beliefs. Small stores specialize in selling or dispensing *santería* materials, and practitioners of the religion flourish in the principal Cuban and Puerto Rican communities in the United States.

EDUCATION

The U.S. Cubans are fairly well educated. More than 51 percent of those over 25 have completed four years of high school or more, and nearly 15 percent are college graduates, again reflecting the nature of the migration and the compulsory public education in the United States. The value that many Cubans attach to success leads them to encourage their children to attend college. This has been facilitated by the community colleges and public universities in the cities where many Cubans live, particularly in Miami and New York, and by the Cuban Student Loan Program instituted by the federal government to provide financial assistance for Cuban students.

A growing number of Cubans now teach in U.S. colleges and universities. Some of them received their training in Cuba prior to the revolution, but the majority received advanced training in the United States. Many of those in the social sciences and humanities contribute to the study of Cuban society, culture, and history, particularly the revolution, the migration to the United States, and related subject areas. The most important research journal among Cuban academicians in the United States is *Cuban Studies*, published by the Center for Latin American Studies at the University of Pittsburgh. The Institute of Cuban Studies, an independent organization based in Miami, brings together Cuban scholars from around the world.

The Cuban community of Miami also has its own private elementary and secondary schools. In the early years of the immigration, several Catholic religious orders established parochial schools for Cuban children in the Miami area; more recently, private secular schools have proliferated. Most are small, teach most of their classes in Spanish, emphasize Cuban history, ge-

ography, and culture, maintain strict discipline, and adhere to the traditional values. They flourish because many Cuban parents are greatly concerned with transmitting to their children their language and culture. They are also anxious about busing and alleged crime, immorality, and drugs in the public schools. When possible they prefer to avoid schools with a high percentage of blacks.

POLITICS

The politics of the Cuban exiles is two-dimensional: one dimension involves relations or contacts with Cuba, the other relates to participation in the U.S. political system. Interest, and sometimes participation, in counterrevolutionary activity has been common, particularly in the early 1960s when the Cuban government was much less stable than it is now. Many exiles anticipated the overthrow of the Castro regime and their return to their homeland. Under U.S. direction, Cuban exiles were involved in the unsuccessful Bay of Pigs invasion, and from time to time exiles undertake acts of terrorism and sabotage against Cuban officials or facilities outside Cuba, or against other exiles in the United States who oppose terrorism publicly or are known to favor conciliation with the present Cuban government. The number involved in terrorist activity is undoubtedly small, but their actions have become progressively more frequent and extreme, perhaps reflecting the growing futility of their cause.

Although most of the immigrants appear to be primarily concerned with making a successful adjustment to American life, they have demonstrated an increasing interest in at least two issues related to their homeland in the past few years: the release of political prisoners and the relaxation of travel restrictions to the island. In November and December 1978, the Cuban government invited 75 members of the Cuban exile community to participate in a series of discussions about those two issues. As a result of the talks, the government in December 1978 started to release most of the political prisoners and allowed them to emigrate. In addition, Cubans living in the United States were allowed to visit their relatives at home. In January 1979, the first month in which such visits were permitted, more than 3,500 Cubans visited their homeland. Since many refugees undoubtedly still disapprove of the present Cuban government, there are differences among them on the issue of conciliation with Castro's government. Overall, the greatest difference is between the older generation that suffered the dislocations of the revolution and the second generation, which tends to take a more dispassionate view. The young academicians in the United States are apt to be among the most liberal of the Cuban community; most of them favor a reconciliation between the United States and Cuba.

An increasing number of the immigrants have been naturalized or are applying for citizenship. With the right to vote, they are beginning to constitute an important political force in southern Florida, and some hold positions of leadership in Florida's Democratic and Republican party organizations. But on the whole, Cuban participation in the electoral process is not as great as its potential. Many who are eligible to vote do not exercise their right; they are apathetic about local and state politics, and as a result there are very few Cubans in local government. In the late 1970s there were none in state or federal legislative bodies. Cuban candidates tend to be handily defeated, even in districts with significant Cuban populations.

INTERGROUP RELATIONS

Acculturation and assimilation have been slow in Miami, as is to be expected in a community as self-sufficient as Little Havana. Furthermore, there appears to be a lack of social and cultural integration between Cubans and other Hispanic groups in U.S. cities with sizable and differentiated Spanish-speaking populations. Of the major Hispanic groups, only the Cubans have come as political exiles, and this has resulted in social, economic, and class differences. In the New York area, Cubans and Puerto Ricans maintain a distinct social distance. Many Cubans feel or perceive that they have little in common with Puerto Ricans, Mexicans, or Dominicans.

There is undoubtedly a political dimension to this apparent lack of communication. A number of Puerto Ricans and Mexicans in the United States have been involved in militant, antiestablishment, and leftist political activities—strikes, civil disobedience, demonstrations, and in some instances violence against symbols of authority. The politically conservative Cubans, wary of leftist or disruptive social movements, are bound to disapprove.

The younger Cubans, schooled in the United States, are more likely to regard themselves as immigrants than as exiles. They are also more likely to take advantage of programs for improving the status of Hispanic groups in the United States. Young Cubans who do not share their parents' conservative views can be found working side by side with Mexicans and Puerto Ricans in bilingual-education programs, community-advancement agencies, Hispanic political coalitions, and other action groups. By 1990, when second-generation Cuban Americans come to dominate the Cuban population in the United States, the structure and character of the communities will probably undergo many changes.

Bibliography

For background information consult Jorgé Dominguez, *Cuba: Order and Revolution* (Cambridge, Mass., 1978). Two reports by the Cuban Minority Study focus on the problems and needs of Cubans in the United States: Rafael J. Prohias and Lourdes Casal, *The Cuban Minority in the U.S.: Preliminary Report on Need Identification and Program Evaluation* (Boca Raton, Fla., 1973), and Andrés R. Hernández, ed., *The Cuban Minority in the U.S.: Final Report on Need Identification and Program Evaluation* (Washington, D.C., 1974). Richard R. Fagen, Richard A. Brody, and Thomas J. O'Leary, *Cubans in Exile: Disaffection and the Revolution* (Stanford, Calif., 1968), is the definitive work on the factors prompting emigration from Cuba during the early 1960s.

Eleanor Meyer Rogg, *The Assimilation of Cuban Exiles: The Role of Community and Class* (New York, 1974), analyzes the assimilation of Cubans into a specific community, as does Alejandro Portes, "Dilemmas of a Golden Exile: Integration of Cuban Refugee Families in Milwaukee," *American Sociological Review* 34 (1969): 505–518. The works of Raul Moncarz are the best source for the question of economic adjustment in the United States, especially *A Study of the Effect of Environmental Change on Human Capital among Selected Skilled Cubans* (Washington, D.C., 1976).

The racial selectivity in the migration is treated in Benigno Aguirre, "Differential Migration of Cuban Social Races," *Latin American Research Review* 11 (1976): 103–124. Other useful works are Michael G. Wenk, "Adjustment and Assimilation: The Cuban Refugee Experience," *International Migration Review* 3 (1968): 38–49, and Juan M. Clark, "The Cuban Escapees," *Latinamericanist* 1970, 1–4, which deals with clandestine emigration.

Cuban Studies, published by the Center for Latin American Studies

at the University of Pittsburgh, is the only journal that regularly publishes bibliographies of works about Cubans outside Cuba. For a comprehensive review of the literature, see Lourdes Casal and Andrés R. Hernández, "Cubans in the U.S.: A Survey of the Literature," *Cuban Studies* 5, pt. 2 (1975): 25–51.

LISANDRO PÉREZ

CZECHOSLOVAKS: *see* CARPATHO-RUSYNS; CZECHS; SLOVAKS

CZECHS

The Czechs have had a thousand years of experience in ethnic survival, since they live in a region of central Europe long coveted for its natural resources and subjected to continuing external pressures as a result. Under foreign rule for much of their history, they have learned to benefit from other cultures without relinquishing their own values. Altogether some 400,000 Czechs have come to America to seek prosperity or escape oppression; of these, at least 350,000 (nearly 1 in 16 Czechs in 1890) immigrated between 1848 and 1914. In 1970 the U.S. Census estimated that about 450,000 Americans had grown up in homes where Czech was spoken. Only 70,000 of them were immigrants; 150,000 were native-born of native parentage, whose parents or grandparents spoke Czech.

The Czechs are the most Western branch of the Slavs; their language, together with Slovak, Polish, and Sorbian, is classified as West Slavic. Their traditional homelands, Bohemia and Moravia, and Czech Silesia make up the Czech component of the Czechoslovak Socialist Republic. The first Slavs to reach America in significant numbers, the Czechs arrived when land was still cheap and plentiful and became the only large Slavic farming population in the United States. They came largely in family groups rather than as single immigrants. They were highly skilled, the consequence of a relatively advanced, industrialized Old World economy, and their

literacy rate was never less than 97 percent. Although skills, education, and values enabled them to adapt to their new environment quickly, the Czechs did not assimilate rapidly. Their language was unrelated to that of most of their neighbors, and while they could usually communicate in German, they found English difficult to learn. Wherever they congregated in sufficient numbers they remained aloof, preserving ethnic traditions longer than most groups of a similar socioeconomic background—even while considering themselves loyal Americans. As former Austrian subjects, they were accustomed to preserving their distinctiveness within a large state.

Because most Czechs came from Bohemia (Böhmen in German, Čechy in Czech), they were often called "Bohemians" before World War I—even though a Bohemian could also have been a German from Bohemia and not a Slav. By 1914, however, the Czechs preferred that foreigners use their unambiguous ethnic name, Čech. During World War I, Czech and Slovak leaders attempted to popularize the term "Czechoslovak" to denote a single nationality, thus justifying the political union of these two closely related but distinct groups. The term is widely used outside the country, but within it after 1939 the two groups referred to themselves emphatically as Czechs or Slovaks. (*See* Slovaks.)

HISTORY

By the time Columbus discovered America, the Bohemian state was already 500 years old, its history laced with the myths that would continue to nourish Czech thought and traditions. The Czech kingdom reached its height in the mid-14th century when the dynamic Charles I (1316–1378), as Holy Roman Emperor Charles IV, made Prague his residence and the heart of central Europe. He established the first university in central Europe in 1348 and graced the city with an expansive, regal architecture. In the early 15th century the great prelude to the Reformation in Europe, the Hussite Wars, rent Bohemia. Though church corruption had been attacked before, Jan Hus (John Huss, c. 1372), a priest and university professor in Prague, preached against it vigorously in vernacular Czech and created broad support for reform. He was executed for heresy in 1415, precipitating a half century of violent struggle between his followers and the Roman Catholic Church, and also between Czechs and Germans. When the Turks defeated Hungary in 1526, the Czech nobles, fearing a similar fate, elected a Catholic Hapsburg to the Bohemian throne. At first the Hapsburgs respected the Protestant beliefs of most of the population, but as the Counter Reformation gained strength in the early 17th century, the Hapsburg rulers began to close churches and otherwise antagonize the Protestants. In 1618 the enraged Czech nobles deposed their king, a gesture of defiance that sparked the Thirty Years' War. But only two years later the Protestant Czechs were defeated by the Hapsburg forces at the Battle of White Mountain. Their leaders were executed and some 36,000 families (virtually the whole Czech intelligentsia) emigrated to Protestant countries rather than convert to Catholicism. The Hapsburgs reduced the Bohemian kingdom to subordinate status, distributed the exiles' lands to court favorites, and forcibly Catholicized and Germanized the Czechs who remained.

Table 1. Czechs in the United States, 1870–1970.[a]

Year	Foreign-born	Native-born[b]	
		Foreign parentage	Native parentage
1870	40,289	—	—
1880	85,361	—	—
1890	118,106	—	—
1900	156,901	356,830	—
1910	228,738	310,654	—
1920	234,564	388,232	—
1930	201,138	—	—
1940	159,640	279,040	81,760
1950	—	—	—
1960	91,711	—	—
1970	70,703	233,165	148,944

Source: U.S. Bureau of the Census, *Twelfth Census of the United States, 1900,* I, *Population* (Washington, D.C., 1901), pt. 1, p. clxxi; U.S. Bureau of the Census, *Sixteenth Census of the United States, 1940, Population: Mother Tongue* (Washington, D.C., 1943), p. 7, table 1; U.S. Bureau of the Census, *Census of the Population, 1960,* Subject report 1E, *Mother Tongue of the Foreign Born* (Washington, D.C., 1963), p. 1, table 1; U.S. Bureau of the Census, *Census of the Population, 1970,* I, *Characteristics of the Population, U.S. Summary* (Washington, D.C., 1973), p. 599, table 193.

a. Figures for the years 1870–1900 are according to country of origin, Bohemia-Moravia; for the years 1910–1940 and 1960–1970 they are according to mother tongue; data distinguishing Czechs from Slovaks are not available for 1950.

b. Published census data do not include Bohemia as a country of origin in tables of the ethnic origins of the native-born until 1900; mother-tongue inquiries about the native-born were not made in 1930, 1950, and 1960.

Czech culture was suppressed, the language was preserved only among peasants, and Protestantism survived only as the underground faith of a devoted few.

By 1800 German romanticism and a growing sense of Bohemian identity inspired a movement to study the Czech language and past. By 1830 leaders of the Czech national revival could communicate in their native tongue to an increasingly literate populace. When revolution swept the Hapsburg lands in 1848, the Czechs failed to achieve self-rule in a federated empire, but they did help force emancipation of the peasants, who became free to move and emigrate.

PATTERNS OF MIGRATION

The immigration that built the Czech-American community consisted of a very small, partly religious immigration during the colonial period; the largely economic mass migration from the mid-19th century to World War I; and the smaller, predominantly political migrations of the mid-20th century.

The exodus of the Czech Protestant elite after the defeat at White Mountain in 1620 had repercussions across the Atlantic by the 1630s. Although the most illustrious member of the emigration, educator and bishop Jan Amos Komenský (Comenius, 1592–1670), declined the presidency of Harvard College to stay in Sweden, many other émigrés joined Swedish and Dutch trading companies and set sail for America. Though statistically insignificant, they are nevertheless important in the historical mythology of Czech Americans.

The first known Czech in the New World was Augustine Herman (c. 1605–1696), a surveyor and merchant who arrived in New Amsterdam in 1633 and established himself in tobacco cultivation and trade. On huge estates granted by Lord Baltimore of Maryland in exchange for cartographic services (20,000 acres alone in 1660), Herman founded Bohemia Manor and named

the Bohemia River of Maryland. The "Bohemian merchant prince" Frederick Philipse (1626–1701), arrived in Yonkers about 1647 and left his name to Philips Manor there; his granddaughter, Mary, is said to have spurned the attentions of George Washington. Several dozen less prominent Czechs appear in 17th- and 18th-century chronicles and church records; Czech was one of 18 languages spoken in mid-17th-century New York. The Moravian Brethren (Unitas Fratrum), descendants of Czech Protestant and German Protestant followers of Hus who went underground after 1620, have often been claimed as part of the Czech-American historical heritage, although they were thoroughly Germanized by the time they established the colonies of Bethlehem, Nazareth, and Lititz, Pa., about 1740. (See Germans; Pennsylvania Germans.)

The core of the Czech-American community derived from the mass immigration of the 19th and early 20th centuries (see Table 2). Probably no more than 500 Czechs arrived before 1850, but by 1890 some 170,000 persons, nearly one-half the total immigration, had arrived, and over 60 percent had come by 1900. As much a part of the "old immigration" as the new, the Czechs established their major ethnic institutions before 1890—fraternal and gymnastic societies, newspapers, churches, labor organizations, and Free Thought congregations.

The pathbreakers of the early 19th century included the first of the Czech doctors, professors, composers, and journalists to come to America and assorted scientists, farmers, and entrepreneurs. The first male American saint (canonized in 1977) was Bohemian-born Jan Nepomuk Neumann (1811–1860), who arrived in 1836; he was instrumental in the founding of the American parochial school system. Some 39 Czech soldiers escaped from their base in Mainz (in what is now West Germany) and reached American shores in 1847. And

Table 2. Czech immigration to the United States, 1850–1950.

Decade	Number of immigrants
1850–1860	23,009
1861–1870	33,123
1871–1880	52,079
1881–1890	62,050
1891–1900	42,711
1901–1910	94,516
1911–1920	41,995
1921–1930	27,296
1931–1940	1,682
1941–1950	14,969
Total	393,430

Source: Compiled from *Mitteilungen aus dem Gebiete der Statistik* (Vienna, 1870, 1872), vols. 17, 19; *Statistische Monatschrift* (Vienna, 1877, 1879, 1880, 1881, 1882, 1884), vols. 2, 3, 5, 6, 7, 8, 10; Annual Reports of the Superintendent of Immigration (Washington, D.C., 1892, 1893, 1894); Annual Reports of the Commissioner General of Immigration (Washington, D.C., 1895–1932); Annual Reports of the Secretary of Labor (Washington, D.C., 1933–1940); Annual Reports of the U.S. Immigration and Naturalization Service (Washington, D.C., 1941–1950).

by the end of 1848 revolutionaries fleeing the police began making their way to the United States.

Drought and crop failures in the 1840s caused many Czechs to think of leaving their homeland for better opportunities elsewhere, but the legal, social, and psychological barriers to emigration remained virtually insurmountable. The Revolution of 1848 knocked down those barriers, driving many intellectuals and craftsmen into exile and facilitating emigration for peasants. The movement westward began slowly, but rumors of gold, letters from America extolling freedom and abundance, newspaper articles praising democratic institutions, land agents' advertisements, and the ubiquitous shipping company agent impelled wavering artisans and peasants to emigrate. Neither disparagement from people who felt it was unpatriotic to leave, nor depressing letters from less successful relatives in America, nor government measures could stem the flow. By 1860, 23,000 persons had left legally—nearly half of them children under 17. The movement accelerated in response to the passage of the Homestead Act (1862) and reached a new peak in 1867. The increase also reflected the hardships inflicted by the Austro-Prussian war (1866) and the abolition of high passport taxes. Steamships now dominated the favored routes between Hamburg and Bremen to New York and Galveston. They shortened the two- or three-month sailing voyage to two or three weeks, dispelling fears generated by the horrors of the immigrant ships of the 1840s and 1850s.

A severe depression beginning in 1873 and particularly affecting sugar-beet growers was largely responsible for the next wave of Czech immigrants. In the 1880s and 1890s economics continued to play a primary role, as the small farmers, ruined by the world grain crisis, moved to the cities to seek employment. But Bohemian industry could not absorb the excess labor force. Emigration accelerated rapidly in 1890 and 1891, remained high for two more years, then dropped to an annual average of about 2,500 until 1903. Another surge peaked in 1907, when 13,544 Czechs left for America. Some now had a new motive: the desire to avoid military service.

During the six and a half decades of heavy migration the occupational background of the immigrants shifted from predominantly agricultural to skilled labor. Most of the earlier immigrants were cottagers who had sold their insufficient plots of land, mainly in southern Bohemia or Moravia, and set out for the Midwest or Texas. From the 1890s on, the cottagers were outnumbered by skilled workers; from 1900 to 1910 only 19 percent of the Czech newcomers had a farm background and 41 percent were skilled laborers. In the peak year of 1907, for example, 43 percent of all Czechs stating an occupational background were skilled, with tailors, miners, carpenters, and shoemakers in the lead. Masons, locksmiths, and butchers were close behind. Only 808 professionals arrived in the decade between 1899 and 1910; 277 were musicians and 143 engineers.

The Czechs brought more money to the United States than most immigrants. In 1902 their average declaration per person of $23.12 was considerably above the $14.84 average for all entrants. Though hardly riches, this money facilitated further transportation and settlement in the western United States. Moreover, Czech immigration was predominantly family immigration, especially in the earlier decades when the Czechs came primarily to farm; women and children accounted for over two-thirds of the immigrants at that time. The ratio of men to women was fairly constant; even after 1900, as the number of factory workers increased, the proportion of men rose only to 57 percent, and later many of the men who came alone sent for their wives or parents. Finally, the Czechs had a low rate of return immigration—only 11 percent between 1908 and 1910.

In 1920, when the census recorded the largest number of foreign-born Czechs in the United States, the second generation already composed 62 percent of Czech America, compared to 57 percent in 1910. This shift reflected a relatively high birth rate among first-generation Czech women, but also a decline in new immigration after World War I. After 1918 the Czechs and Slovaks formed an independent state, and as the dominant nationality, Czechs had less reason to leave. Nevertheless, over 17,000 Czechs—including many who had intended to leave before the war—immigrated before the annual immigration quota was imposed in 1924. In the late 1930s a few hundred Czechs, mostly Jews, left before the Nazi occupation, and a trickle of refugees arrived during and immediately after the war.

It was the Communist coup of 1948 in Czechoslovakia that produced a new immigrant wave, an exodus of professionals and highly skilled workers who felt threatened by the new regime. An estimated 25,000 eventually made their homes in American cities, assisted by the American Fund for Czechoslovak Refugees and other agencies. Soviet intervention in 1968 brought a new wave of perhaps 10,000 Czech immigrants over the ensuing decade.

SETTLEMENT AND ECONOMIC LIFE

By 1900 two settlement and occupational patterns had been firmly established: (1) 45 percent of foreign-born Czechs lived in New York, Cleveland, and especially Chicago, which had more Czech residents than the other two combined; and (2) well over half the first-generation Czechs were engaged in agriculture, with 71 percent of these clustered in the states of Nebraska, Wisconsin, Texas, Iowa, and Minnesota. These three

cities and five farm states accounted for 84 percent of the foreign-born Czech population in 1900; this portion was about evenly divided between urban and rural areas. The rest were scattered in small towns and villages in Kansas, Michigan, Missouri and the Dakotas, and in such cities as Baltimore and St. Louis.

Chicago became the leading Czech-American metropolis in the 1860s and by 1900, after Prague and Vienna, was the third largest Czech urban center in the world. In 1870, when Chicago had a Czech-born population of 6,300, only 1,500 lived in New York and a mere 800 in Cleveland. By the 1880s all three centers were drawing a steady stream of immigrants, who settled in well-defined neighborhoods with their own shops, taverns, national halls, Sokol halls (gymnastic societies), and churches. Chicago (with 41,000 first- and second-generation Czechs in 1890) had several such neighborhoods, including "Praha," "Pilsen," and "Czech California," each located successively farther west and south, where the Czechs could afford bigger lots and have room for small gardens. For the same reasons, Chicago suburbs Cicero and Berwyn became large Czech centers in the 1910s and 1920s. New York Czechs—numbering 11,868 of both generations in 1890—settled in the Lower East Side in the early years, but by the 1890s they had migrated uptown to Yorkville, later the fashionable East Seventies, where in 1896 they built a new national hall and a Sokol hall.

Czech farmers were first attracted to Wisconsin, where one-third of all Czech immigrants had settled by 1860. Most came for the cheap and plentiful land that could be claimed from virgin forests. Ironically, since more Czechs knew German than English, they tended to settle near their old enemies, the Germans. The rural immigration centers moved westward during the 1860s as thousands of Czechs claimed homesteads in Nebraska, Minnesota, and Iowa; during the next decade significant numbers settled in Kansas as well. Thousands of Czechs from Moravia who settled in Texas sailed from Germany directly to Galveston. Chain migration was common, but migration in large groups to a single settlement was virtually unknown—and unsuccessful when tried. In the 1880s and 1890s some Czechs who had been ruined by drought or locusts on the prairies bought abandoned farms in Virginia and elsewhere in the South; their principal settlement was in Petersburg, near Richmond, Va. Wherever they settled, towns and villages sprang up with a distinct Czech character; colorful and crowded garden plots of tall perennial blossoms occupied the space in front of the house instead of a bit of lawn. Each of these several hundred settlements had a Czech society of some kind, a church, and an amateur band. Some bore Czech names, some did not—for example, Wilber and Milligan, Nebr.; New Prague and Litomyšl, Minn.; and the Pilsens of Iowa. Kansas, and Wisconsin. Not all Czech farmers lived near a Czech settlement, however, as illustrated in Willa Cather's *My Ántonia* (a novel about a Czech woman in Nebraska).

By 1970 settlement patterns no longer revealed such sharp contrasts between rural and city Czechs. Nearly all Czech Americans had become part of the urban or rural nonfarm population, but they were no longer concentrated in the three traditional cities. Among the foreign-born (only 16 percent of those claiming Czech as their mother tongue) a third still lived in Chicago and New York; most lived elsewhere, including California (11.3 percent), which had not previously had a significant Czech population. The largest proportion of the first and second generations still lived in Illinois, but Texas, the home of nearly one-fourth of the third-generation Czechs who had spoken the language as children, outranked all states in the total number of Czech Americans. Another quarter of the third generation lived in Wisconsin, Nebraska, Iowa, and Minnesota; the Czech language apparently survived longer in rural and small-town environments than in the large cities.

Occupations In 1900 nearly 130,000 Czech men and women made up a large, highly skilled labor force. Only 14 percent of the foreign-born men and 8 percent of the second-generation men worked as unskilled laborers, mostly in Chicago and Cleveland. Most Czech men worked in agriculture (33 percent of the first generation, 42 percent of the second) and skilled manufacturing and mechanical jobs (40 percent of the first generation, 29 percent of the second). In the three main cities, over two-thirds of Czech workers were in manufacturing and mechanical jobs, especially in the tobacco and garment industries. Women were also prominent in domestic service, men (to a lesser extent) in trade and transportation. In New York the dominant occupation for both men and women was cigarmaking; in 1865 perhaps as many as 95 percent of Czech wage earners worked in cigar factories or (mostly women and children) did piecework at home. By 1900 the number of cigar workers had declined to 26 percent of the foreign-born Czech men and about 8 percent of the second-generation men, but two-thirds of the immigrant women and half their working daughters were still employed in the industry. By 1920 cigarmaking was no longer a Czech trade. Another Czech business in New York was the manufacture of pearl buttons; by 1920 Czech shops produced almost half the pearl buttons made in the United States. In Ohio, with slightly more Czech workers than New York, nearly 12 percent of the foreign-born and 9 percent of the second generation worked in iron and steel foundries.

In Chicago, where there were more Czech workers than in Cleveland and New York combined, both men and women concentrated in the garment industry, most as skilled tailors (13 percent of foreign-born men, 9 percent of their sons, and 33 percent of all the women). Chicago Czechs were prosperous: in 1900 they owned 565 of 697 dwellings in a single neighborhood. By 1924 they controlled 15 state and federal banks in Chicago, with half the capital of all the Czech banks in the country. Over half the assets of all Building and Loan Associations in Chicago were held by 104 Czech associations, reflecting the Czechs' preoccupation with property as a form of security.

Throughout the United States the share of Czech men and women in professional occupations was under 2 percent of the Czech work force, but they were a main source of leadership for Czech communities, urban or rural. Slightly more than half the men in professional positions worked in Chicago, New York, or Cleveland, but a smaller portion of professional women worked in these three centers (41 percent of the first-generation

professional women, 31 percent of the second). Of 979 immigrant male professionals recorded in 1900, nearly one-third were musicians or music teachers; the rest were clergymen, doctors, electricians, teachers, lawyers, journalists, artists, and actors. Fewer members of the second generation went into the arts and journalism; more took up teaching, electrical work, law, and architecture. There were 401 professional women in the second generation compared to 126 in the first; in both cases over three-fourths were teachers. Relatively few teachers lived in the large cities—35 of 92 immigrant teachers and only 89 of the 317 native-born.

About 55 percent of all immigrant workers were in agriculture, and 80 percent owned their farms. Of the second generation, 61 percent were on the farms, including sons working at home. Especially in Nebraska, Wisconsin, Texas, Iowa, and Minnesota, farming was the characteristic way of life for the vast majority of Czech Americans and their families. This life was not easy at first; many settlers wrote of the hardships they had to endure: living in damp, infested dugouts until they could build a log cabin or a sod house; subsisting on corn mush or potatoes until they could afford a cow and some chickens; losing their crops to drought, blight, or grasshoppers; fighting loneliness in the woods or on the prairies. But they usually came with their families, feather beds, cooking utensils, and a few tools to make a new home, and most persevered. Because of their success and prosperity, the Czechs were recruited to occupy frontier homesteads or to take over abandoned farms in the South. The Bohemians, it was said, could make crops grow where no one else could.

After World War I the native-born generation increasingly outnumbered the immigrants; by 1940 the foreign-born constituted only 31 percent of Czech Americans. As they became older, the immigrants began to leave the farms; whereas about 33 percent had been farmers in 1910, only 18 percent were on the farm in 1940. A larger portion of native-born Czech Americans worked in agriculture, however: 28 percent of the second generation, and 63 percent of the third and later generations from homes where Czech was spoken.

By 1970 the occupational distribution had changed dramatically. There were only 1,000 first-generation Czech farmers (about 2 percent of the employed Czechs); 7,800 second-generation farmers (5 percent), and 9,400 in subsequent generations (almost 9 percent). The strength of the farmers among the latter group again owes more to the ease of maintaining the mother tongue in a rural setting than to the occupational pattern of third-generation Americans of Czech descent. Far more important than farming in 1970 were white-collar jobs, held by 44 percent of the first generation of employed Czechs, 46 percent of the second, and 50 percent of later generations. Professional and technical workers were the largest group among the foreign-born employed (16 percent), while clerical workers led all native-born generations (18–21 percent). The number of white-collar workers among the foreign-born reflects the educational level of the two wartime refugee groups; among the native-born it indicates high mobility. Blue-collar occupations declined from 35 percent among combined first- and second-generation workers, to 29 percent in later generations. Service workers ac-

counted for 17 percent of the first-generation employed, 13 percent of the second, and 11 percent of later generations. Only 1.5–2.0 percent of workers of all generations worked as agricultural laborers.

CULTURE AND SOCIETY

Although rationalism had been a strong current in both European and American thought since the 18th century, nowhere in the 19th century did faith in reason, science, and the individual conscience—so-called Free Thought—become such a broad-based, organized movement, at times with religious overtones, as among the Czechs in America. A split between Catholics and Freethinkers, both urban and rural, generated antagonisms that pervaded Czech-American religious life, secular societies, the press, and schools until World War I. Only in the arts and business was cooperation possible; yet even these areas became strained in communities where anticlericalism from the local press and antirationalism from the pulpit were daily fare. Not until late in World War I did passions subside and permit Czechs to unite for a common goal; after 1918, religious and secular convictions increasingly gave way before a spirit of mutual toleration.

Religion and Free Thought According to Hapsburg statistics, Czechs in Bohemia and Moravia made up over 96 percent of the empire's most strongly Catholic subjects in the 19th century. Although a decree of 1781 granted religious freedom to Calvinists and Lutherans (but not to the heirs of the Hussite movement—the Czech Brethren and the Utraquists), only a small minority remained to benefit. The Counter Reformation had produced at least nominal Catholics among most educated Czechs and often faithful ones among the peasantry. Yet by the 19th century the majority of Czech Catholics were notoriously indifferent to their faith. From Jan Hus and his followers they inherited a tradition of dissent; from their Protestant ancestors of the 15th century to the Battle of White Mountain they claimed a national religion and literature; and from the zealous recatholicization carried out by the Hapsburgs and the Jesuits, they had bitter memories of the Catholic church as a militant arm of the state. Despite the church's contributions to Czech culture and scholarship in the early stages of the revival, most Czechs associated it and its representatives with the German language, German oppression, and German Hapsburg rulers.

Just how illusory the Austrian statistics on religion were became evident when the Czechs emigrated to the United States. Though the immigrants were often well educated and hence susceptible to secular influences, it is nevertheless striking that one-half to two-thirds of the predominantly rural 19th-century Czech immigrants left the Catholic church. In 19th-century America this was a shocking phenomenon, especially in the rural communities where Czech Free Thought prevailed. Even though their Protestant neighbors could not find fault with the hardworking Czechs' morality and deportment, they were aghast at the singing, dancing, and merrymaking in which the Czechs indulged on Sundays. Some observers, noting the high suicide rate among the Czechs (exceeded only by that of the Danes),

blamed it on irreligion; Protestant missionaries viewed the Freethinkers as a field ripe for their work. More important for the Czechs themselves was the behavior of their strong-minded leaders, whose acrimonious conflicts polarized their community into Freethinking and Catholic camps.

Most Czech Freethinkers were moderate liberals, favoring the separation of church and state but tolerant toward their Catholic compatriots—so long as the latter confined their religion to the parish. These moderates dominated most Czech-American newspapers and secular societies and provided leadership for the grassroots work of the Czech National Alliance during World War I. A militant minority of agnostics and atheists, however, were prominent in several Freethought institutions, including some newspapers whose editors repeatedly assailed the Catholic church and ridiculed the clergy. Beginning in 1870 the radicals organized into Free Congregations; in 1907 they united in the Svaz svobodomyslných (Free Thought Union). The elaborate rites for weddings and funerals (they had their own cemeteries) seemed to many a mere parody of the tradition they had rejected; their 14-point creed, published in 1871 for the Free Thought schools, reflected a deistic faith in natural law that had already become old-fashioned and did not survive World War I. After 1918, too, Free Thought lost its political raison d'être: the anti-Hapsburg struggle was irrelevant now that national liberation had been achieved. Although the foundations for a Czech-American culture laid by the Freethinking majority remained, the ideology of Free Thought faded. Liberalism and secularism among the native-born generations waned; by the 1940s the fraternal and benefit societies—the backbone of Czech Free Thought since the 1850s—had become generally conservative. Many lodge members now belonged to a variety of churches, joined through marriage or general acculturation to American patterns.

Given the readiness of most Czech Catholics to abandon their faith upon leaving their homeland, the task of the Czech clergy was to disassociate themselves from the Austrian hierarchy and to affirm the autonomy and Czech-American identity of their parishes. Wherever parishes had priests sensitive to the history and mentality of their people, Catholicism thrived and won the respect of the Czech community, even where the majority remained Freethinkers. The first Czech-American Catholic church, St. Jan Nepomuk, was built in St. Louis in 1854. After Father Josef Hessoun arrived from Bohemia in 1865 to become its pastor, the parish became a center of Czech Catholicism. In the 1860s and 1870s the Czechs established parishes in both rural and urban centers; Chicago's first church, built in 1864, was named after the Czech patron saint Václav, the "Good King Wenceslas" of the traditional carol. The Czech Benedictines arrived in 1885. They established the Czech Benedictine Press and founded near Chicago the College of St. Procopius (1887), soon the Catholics' intellectual center.

Czech Catholicism in America had its greatest growth in the 1920s, when about 350 priests served 268 Czech parishes and 156 mixed parishes shared by Czechs and other groups, such as the Irish or Germans. The greatest number of parishes (68) was in Texas, where Catholics from Moravia had always formed a majority of Czech settlers, and in Wisconsin, Nebraska, and Minnesota. Their urban center was Cleveland.

Protestant denominations also enjoyed some success among the Czechs by the 1920s. They often started their Czech congregations through non-Czech missionary activity and continued to assist them financially. By 1920 the most active were the Presbyterians, with 50 churches and 3,500 members. In Texas alone in 1920 the Unity of Bohemian-Moravian Brethren claimed 24 parishes with 1,500 members. Congregationalists, Methodists, and Baptists, who had begun work among the Czechs in the 1880s (especially in Cleveland and Chicago), could by 1930 claim 11, 23, and 20 churches respectively. In the 1920s these churches were all represented in a Czech interdenominational organization in Chicago, the Hus Union.

Social Organization Most Czech immigrants before World War I came from small towns or villages with an active community life that revolved around church, market, and tavern. On holidays and Sundays the local amateur band played lively music from the small pavilion in the village square, as peasants and townspeople strolled about in their Sunday best. Though eroded and threatened by industrialization and social change, this traditional community life still formed the core of immigrant memories. Life on the typically isolated midwestern farm was a stark contrast. It was sometimes many years before a Czech pioneer family heard their language from the lips of an outsider; when their numbers increased to form small communities, they eagerly joined the network of Czech-American organizations that had first taken shape in the cities.

Urban Czechs too had been accustomed to contact with their countrymen, especially after the constitutional reform of 1867 made it possible for them to enjoy the fellowship of dozens of cultural, educational, and social organizations. Many of these they would try to duplicate in their new home. In 1850 a small group of Freethinking intellectuals (mostly forty-eighters) and businessmen in New York City founded the first such organization, the Česká společnost (Czech Society). According to its librarian, Vojta Náprstek, the society's purpose was to provide aid and fellowship to incoming Czechs; however, it attracted only 42 members and disbanded after two years. But the pattern was set, and by 1920 an estimated 2,500 organizations were active—500 of them in Chicago alone.

The Czechs' earliest organizations were fraternal benevolent societies to provide death and sick benefits. The first emerged out of a discussion among a few Freethinkers in a St. Louis tavern in 1854. Called Československanská podporující společnost or ČSPS (Czech-Slavonic Benevolent Society), it soon had many branches sponsoring a variety of social and cultural activities, especially in small towns that could not support many separate Czech organizations. Where their membership was strong, the ČSPS lodges built national halls (often shared with other Czech societies) for concerts, dances, and plays. Since the ČSPS did not admit women (except wives of members) in their insurance programs, the women founded several major benefit societies of their own. The largest was the Jednota českých dám (Union of Czech Women) founded in 1870, with headquarters in Cleveland. Its membership reached 23,000 in 1920, more than all other Czech women's groups combined.

In 1897 two groups of western lodges seceded from the ČSPS because they wanted to admit women as equal members and to charge insurance premiums according to age. They formed the Západní česko-bratrská jednota (Western Bohemian Fraternal Association) which became the Western Fraternal Life Association in 1971, and the Slovanská podporující jednota státu Texasu (Slavonic Benevolent Order of the State of Texas). The ČSPS merged with several smaller societies in 1933 and became the Czechoslovak Society of America; it is the oldest existing fraternal benefit society in the United States. Most of its 200 lodges are in the traditional Czech metropolitan areas, while the other two societies continue to dominate in the farm states. Together they had a membership of 153,000 in the mid-1970s; none required Czech ancestry for membership.

Czech Catholics too had benefit societies, beginning in 1879. Ten major ones had a combined membership of 33,000 in 1920, slightly over one-fourth the size of the Free Thought societies. Katolický dělník (The Catholic Workman, 1891) and Česká-římsko-katolická jednota (Czech Catholic Union, 1879) had 19,000 and 6,000 members respectively in the late 1970s.

While the fraternal associations of the Freethinkers dominated organizational life, the educational and cultural associations were more characteristically Czech, often patterned after organizations in the homeland. The first was the Slovanská lípa (Slavic Linden; named after a political society of 1848), branches of which appeared in several communities after 1860 and sponsored libraries, reading circles, choral societies, theater productions, and language classes. Industrial workers organized their first workmen's club, Dělnický klub, in Chicago in 1866; others followed in Cleveland in 1869, and in New York in 1870. After World War I, Czechs formed a number of local or special-interest societies, some of which are still in existence: stamp-collecting clubs (the First Czechoslovak Philatelic Club of America, 1924; the Society of Czechoslovak Philately, 1939); local ethnic societies such as Czech Karlin Hall in Cleveland, 1936; and cultural or academic associations such as the Masaryk Institute, established in New York City in 1937.

Most popular before World War II were the gymnastic societies or Sokols. Established in Prague in 1862 to promote patriotic education through disciplined physical, moral, and intellectual development, the Sokol (falcon) had its first American branch as early as 1865 in St. Louis. When the National Sokol Union was formed in 1878 there were 13 local branches; by 1895 the number had risen to 48. The first gymnastics festival (slet)—with mass calisthenics characteristically set to music—was held in 1879. The socialists sponsored the first Workingman's Sokol in New York in 1893, and the Catholics organized gymnastics societies to combat the Freethinking atmosphere of the Sokols. The peak of Czech-American Sokol activity came in 1927 when 125 branches had 14,000 members, of whom 6,500 were active gymnasts. Their largest festival, in 1933, drew 2,556 participants. Before World War II, American Sokols attended the international festivals held every four years in Prague. By 1930, however, memberships were declining. Still, in 1970 the American Sokol Organization (formed in 1917 from a merger of the two leading national groups) had 7,750 adult members in 70 branches, with 9,000 children participating in gymnastics classes, cultural activities, summer camps, and festivals.

Education The Czech nation took great pride in its long tradition of education, a symbol of which was the University of Prague, established in 1348. More important for the masses, however, were the ideas of Comenius, whose proposed 17th-century reforms anticipated most modern educational movements, beginning with universal education. Czech immigrants were eager to educate their children, and wherever public schools were available they established high attendance records. They also wanted their children to preserve their ancestral language and to know the traditions their parents and grandparents cherished. The Catholics established the first formal Czech-language school in St. Louis in 1855; more parochial schools followed, primarily in Chicago, Cleveland, and Texas. By 1930 some 21,000 pupils attended 121 Catholic elementary schools and one high school; by then, however, most schools used English as the language of instruction. In 1970, only some 3,300 children from Czech-speaking families were attending parochial schools, few of which provided instruction in the Czech language.

The Freethinking majority preferred to send their children to public schools and to supplement their education with Czech language schools in the afternoons or on weekends. These so-called Free Schools, supported by various Freethought organizations, taught Czech culture and history as well. As a supplement to the Free School curriculum or as a substitute for such schools where none existed, the Freethinkers in Chicago in 1893 began the monthly *Svobodná škola* (The Free School), an illustrated magazine for Czech youth. The first Free School was established for 65 pupils in New York City in 1865; in the mid-1920s some 10,200 pupils were still attending 97 schools, but use of the Czech language declined in these schools too.

The Czechs established only one college, the Benedictines' College of St. Procopius at Lisle, Ill., the site of their abbey. Originally intended to prepare Czech and Slovak youths for the priesthood, it evolved into a liberal arts college that changed its name to Illinois Benedictine College and became coeducational in 1968.

Teachers, professors, and businessmen of Czech descent organized the Matice vyššího vzdělání (Council of Higher Education) in Cedar Rapids in 1902 to assist needy college students. By 1969, this organization had provided 571 students with interest-free loans. The council (which moved to Chicago in 1924) also supported the Komenský (Comenius) clubs at colleges and universities attended by students of Czech descent, the first appearing at the University of Nebraska in Lincoln. Most of these clubs closed at the outbreak of World War I; a few were revived in connection with Czech language study several decades later, but none sustained student interest.

Music and Arts The familiar saying, "Co Čech, to muzikant" (If he's a Czech, he's a musician) was scarcely an exaggeration. If an emigrating Czech took anything from home other than a feather quilt and food for the voyage, it was a musical instrument. A sociologist studying a Czech community in a particularly poor part of Virginia in the 1920s noted that even in the

barest, most sparsely furnished homes, musical instruments were in evidence. Those who did not have instruments improvised at first, at least for percussion effects. For many decades the amateur brass band or orchestra was ubiquitous and eased the lingering homesickness for the old country; indeed, music-making as a diversion from unrelenting labor is a common theme in pioneer memoirs. Outside of Czech settlements a Czech family might contribute their musical talents to an international gathering on the prairies, especially with German neighbors. Larger communities were able to support professional groups; in 1975 there were still 16 Czech bands in Nebraska, perpetuating the popular Czech polkas and waltzes.

But folk music was only part of the Czech tradition. In the 19th century professional musicians of Czech ancestry performed in every major American orchestra; a single local musicians' union in Cleveland had 179 Czech members in 1918. Many Czechs were teachers in major conservatories, especially in New York; others were bandmasters in the armed forces. One of the most successful Czech-American composers was Rudolf Friml (1879–1972), well known for operettas such as *The Vagabond King*, written in the 1920s. Czechs were fond of opera and built their first opera house as early as 1885 in Manitowok, Wis. Most famous among musicians visiting from the homeland was Antonín Dvořák (1841–1904), who directed the National Conservatory of Music in New York for three years (1892–1895) and incorporated in his compositions the spirit of American folk themes. His *New World Symphony* became a symbol for Czech Americans of the creative symbiosis between their old and adopted countries. Composer Bohuslav Martinů (1890–1959) sojourned in New York and Princeton, N.J., from 1941 to 1953.

The amateur theater was popular in Czech-American communities; at one time Chicago alone had six amateur troupes. The heavy concentration of Czechs in Chicago enabled them to support one professional company—Ludvík's Theatrical Troupe. František Ludvík (1842–1910) had come with 22 members on a tour from Prague in 1893 and ended up staying in Chicago until his death. His troupe continued to perform for two more decades. Another Czech who has become well known in the arts is film director Miloš Forman (1932–), who immigrated in 1969.

Press During the 1860s and 1870s the most powerful Czech Americans were journalists, especially newspaper editors. The editor and his paper monopolized public opinion; he was usually a man of many trades and talents—amateur actor, fundraiser, language teacher, political adviser. Whereas Freethinkers were not permitted to publish in the homeland, in America they could fully express their ideas in print, and often did so in such polemical form as to polarize the community and, more often than not, leave their enterprises virtually insolvent. From the late 1870s the Czech-American community was large enough to support publications other than the Free Thought press. More papers failed than succeeded, nonetheless; an estimated 326 papers were started between 1860 and 1910; 104 still existed in 1910. Of these about 13 percent were Catholic, 11 percent Protestant, and 76 percent nonsectarian (including some socialist papers). Though the number of publications declined, total circulation rose, reaching

a peak in 1920, when there were 8 dailies, 25 weeklies, 10 biweeklies, 31 monthlies, and 7 other periodicals. In 1976 some 30 periodicals were still being published, including the daily *Denní Hlasatel* (Daily Herald; Chicago, f. 1891) and a farmers' bimonthly, *Hospodář* (The Husbandman; Omaha, Nebr., f. 1891); over half the remainder were fraternal organs.

The first paper issued by a Czech was Vojta Náprstek's Milwaukee *Flugblätter* (Leaflets, 1852–1855), which, ironically, was published in German because Czech readers were so few. The first Czech-language papers were *Slowán Amerikanský* (American Slav; Racine, Wis., 1860) and *Národní Noviny* (National Gazette; St. Louis, 1860). Within a year, financial difficulties led to merger and the birth of *Slavie* (Racine and Chicago, 1861–1946), edited for many years by Charles Jonáš (1840–1896). Jonáš, who immigrated in 1863, was the archetypal Czech editorial power in the 1870s; a moderate Freethinker, he was later active in Wisconsin politics and the U.S. diplomatic service. Over the next two decades the Czechs established several major papers; all but one were Free Thought organs, a few intensely anticlerical. Most extreme was *Pokrok* (Progress; 1867–1878), which titillated its readers with stories of lecherous priests and fallen nuns. Its editor was Josef Pastor (b. 1841), who eventually left America to become a steamship agent in Hamburg, where he published in 1884 a useful periodical for prospective Czech emigrants. More sophisticated than Pastor's paper but equally anticlerical were the first Czech American daily, *Svornost* (Concord; Chicago, 1875–1957), and the weekly *Dennice novověku* (Morning Star of the New Era; Cleveland, 1877–1917), edited for 34 years by Václav Šnajdr (1847–1920). Most influential in the Midwest was Jan Rosický's *Pokrok západu* (Progress of the West; Omaha, 1871–1915). New York acquired its first daily in 1875, published intermittently as *New Yorské listy* until 1966, when it merged with the weekly *Americké listy* (American Gazette, f. 1966).

The Catholics' first response in print to the "godless" press was Father Joseph Molitor's *Katolické noviny* (Catholic News; Chicago, 1867), which folded after one year. More successful were Father Hessoun's *Hlas* (Voice; St. Louis, 1872–1950) and the Benedictines' popular *Katolík* and *Národ* (The Nation), both published in Chicago from 1893 to 1975. The newest Catholic journal is *Hlas národa* (Voice of the People; Chicago, f. 1976).

Some Czech-American journalism was socialist. Lev Palda (1847–1912), the father of Czech socialism in the United States, edited the first, short-lived socialist paper, *Národní noviny* (National News; Chicago, 1870), followed by *Dělnické listy* (Worker's Gazette; Cleveland, 1875–1883, 1893–1898). Later, moderate Czech socialists in Chicago founded the daily *Spravedlnost* (Justice, 1900–1930). Together with smaller socialist papers in Cleveland and New York, *Spravedlnost* had a circulation of over 15,000 in 1920. In the 1970s only one socialist publication remained, the organ of the Workingmen's Sokol in Cleveland, *Besídka sokolská* (Sokol News, f. 1892).

The Czech community also supported women's, satirical, agricultural, and other special interest papers. The feminist *Ženské listy* (Women's Gazette; Chicago, 1894–1947) was founded and edited until 1906 by Jo-

sefa Humbolt-Zeman (1870–1906), social worker, journalist, and suffragette. The agricultural *Hospodář* (Omaha, f. 1891) had a circulation of 30,000 in the 1920s; it moved to Texas in 1961 and had about 7,000 subscribers in 1975. The Czechs even had a monthly *Drůbežnické listy* (Poultry Gazette; Benson, Nebr., 1913–1918) for poultry farmers.

Perhaps 2,000 to 3,000 Czech books have been published in America, the great majority translations, reprints, or nonfiction—grammars, dictionaries, histories, cookbooks, songbooks, and travel guides. Original works of poetry and fiction have been few. Among Czech immigrants who began their writing careers in America were many who were at least part-time journalists. Their themes usually reflect sentimental homesickness or unrestrained praise or social criticism of American life; examples are essayist Bartoš Bittner (1861–1912), humorist Jan V. Čapek (1842–1909), and poet-socialist Josef Martínek (b. 1889). Another category consists of those Czech writers who only briefly sojourned in the United States but continued to draw upon that experience, such as Pavel Albieri (1861–1901) and Josef V. Sládek (1845–1912), who in the years 1868 to 1870 became captivated by Indian folkways. There are also writers who began their careers in the homeland and continued to write in the United States. Most of these were post-1948 or post-1968 political exiles; their works rarely reflect specifically American experiences. Perhaps the most well known is novelist Egon Hostovský (1908–1973). Others include Zdeněk Němeček (1894–) and Milada Součková (1901–). Among the post-1968 group are Jiří Hochman, Jan Beneš, Ota Ulč, Antonín Liehm, and Arnošt Lustig.

Czech Americans have been prominent in all fields of science and scholarship. Aleš Hrdlička (1869–1943) was the first curator of the Smithsonian Museum's division of physical anthropology and founded the *American Journal of Anthropology*. Those well known in the humanities include historians Otakar Odložilík (1887–1974), Francis Dvorník (1893–1975), and Robert Kerner (1887–1956); literary critic René Wellek (1908–); and philosopher Erazím Kohák (1933–).

POLITICS

In the old country the Czechs were accustomed to opposition politics. The nationalist movement whetted their desire for a bigger role in government and from the mid-19th century, as they read idealized accounts of American democratic institutions, some looked toward emigration as a way of obtaining such a role. Czech immigrants who settled in ethnic enclaves were active in local government, led at first by compatriots who had had previous political experience in the homeland and who held both nationalist and socialist convictions.

But beyond local politics the Czechs as a group were slow to take part in the political process. In the homeland they had come to expect little from the government, stressing instead self-reliance; typically, the Czechs were among the last to seek government assistance in times of crisis, even during the Great Depression. Language was another barrier. By the 1880s Czechs took their voting privilege seriously but, characteristically, never became a voting bloc. In some areas they voted Democratic because they believed the Democratic party was for the common man, or because the Republicans were in power and they were used to being in opposition. In others, they voted for Republicans as supporters of farm interests. Though Czech Americans were proud of their compatriots in high office, they could never claim responsibility as a voting bloc for their election. The first to reach a state legislature was Edward Rosewater, a Czech Jew and leading publisher in Omaha, elected in 1870. By 1920 there were dozens of Czechs in local and state offices, as well as four U.S. congressmen; one, Adolph Sabath of Chicago, served from 1907 to 1952. Anton Čermák was elected mayor of Chicago in 1931, but two years later was killed by an assassin's bullet intended for President Franklin Roosevelt.

The Czech socialists became an integral part of American politics from the moment they arrived. They formed their first club in 1866 and their first trade union—among New York cigarmakers—in 1872. The Czech-American socialist press also served socialists in the homeland when their press was stifled in the 1880s. Lev Palda, who immigrated in 1867, became only three years later the spokesman for the Czech branch of the American section in the First Socialist International. In 1878 the Czech labor movement had its first state legislator (Leo Meilbek, elected largely by Chicago Germans on the Workingman's party ticket). Dominated in the 1880s by Czech anarchists who had fled Austrian anti-socialist laws, the Czech movement reemerged in the 1890s in a more moderate form and quickly gained popularity, especially through the Czech press and the Sokols. Now Czech socialists were part of the Socialist Labor party in New York and the Debs Social Democratic party in Chicago. After 1900 they had regular contact with fellow socialists in the homeland; two who later served in Czechoslovak ministerial posts, Gustav Habrman and František Soukup, were prominent visitors. After World War I one of their activists, editor and poet Josef Martínek (b. 1889) returned briefly to Prague to edit the main Social Democratic newspaper.

Many Czech Americans who lived through World War I considered the creation of the Czechoslovak Republic a high point in their lives. Along with the Slovaks, they raised $675,000 for the Czechoslovak National Council in Europe to help convince the Allies of the reasons for establishing an independent Czechoslovak state. By 1917 the contentious factions of both nationalities in the United States had joined in the Czechoslovak National Council in America and carried on a public campaign throughout the country. The Czech National Alliance, one of the council's affiliates, strengthened their efforts by publishing an English-language monthly, *Bohemian Review* (Chicago, f. 1917) which became the *Czechoslovak Review* (Chicago, 1918–1924). Once the United States declared war in 1917, the Czechs eagerly volunteered to serve in the army and bought proportionately more war bonds than any other foreign-born group. Throughout the war an espionage service of some 80 Czech Americans, organized by Emanuel Voska, provided valuable information to the Allies on German and Austrian activity in the United States.

The final stage of Czech war efforts came in the spring and summer of 1918. In January, President

Woodrow Wilson published his peace plan, calling for reorganization of Austria-Hungary on ethnic lines, but not its dissolution. When Professor Tomáš Masaryk arrived in May of 1918 as leader of the Czechs in exile, President Wilson had already begun to modify his views; there remained the task of persuading him to recognize a Czechoslovak state. Masaryk, Eduard Beneš, and other leaders who traveled around the country were greeted everywhere with mass rallies organized by the American Czechs and Slovaks to draw attention to their cause. On May 30, in Pittsburgh, Americans from both ethnic groups signed a brief declaration as equal partners in support of a Czechoslovak republic. Later in the year Czech-American leaders reached similar agreements with Carpatho-Rusyn immigrants. This expression of unity, the rallies, and the arrival in America of the Czechoslovak legionnaires, who had fought the Bolsheviks across Russia to Siberia—all served to sway public opinion in favor of Czech and Slovak independence, while political activity by Czech-American congressmen and sympathizers in Washington influenced the president. Wilson finally met with Masaryk and in September 1918 publicly recognized the right of the Czech and Slovak people to their own state, which was established the following month.

During World War II, Czech and Slovak Americans (except for a few Communists and the Slovak Separatists) again united in a political effort to free their homeland from Nazi rule. They also aided the war effort through extensive propaganda work and involvement in the American Red Cross. After the war they raised several hundred thousand dollars for relief funds, which, along with $4 million from the American government, were distributed from 1945 to 1949 by the American Relief for Czechoslovakia.

Since the war Czech politics have been confined largely to a minority active in the anti-Communist movement. Their chief organization is the Czechoslovak National Council in America, which publishes two monthlies: *Věstník* (Herald, f. 1954) and *American Bulletin* (f. 1954). In American politics generally, many persons of Czech descent hold public office but do not represent an ethnic vote.

GROUP MAINTENANCE

In adversity or in the face of an enormous challenge Czechs were able to come together; otherwise, they were highly individualistic and divisive. Their contentious character was reflected in their institutions in the United States, which were unable to cooperate in any effort until the struggle for the Czechoslovak state during World War I. Yet this characteristic fragmentation did not hasten the acculturation and assimilation of Czech Americans. Indeed, diverse views may have served to delay assimilation.

Despite their affinity for American values, the Czechs were slower to assimilate than other groups with similar demographic and occupational profiles. One study of 500 Czech urban workers in 1900 found that only half of those who had been in the United States more than ten years could speak English. Intermarriage with other ethnic groups was uncommon; as late as 1900 some 92 percent of the men and 93 percent

of the women born in Bohemia had married within the group. Fewer than half the non-Czech spouses—2 percent of the brides, about 4 percent of the grooms—were "other foreign-born"; of these, three-fourths were Austrian or German, evidence that Old World enmity and ideologies were less important than a common language, German in this case. The remaining spouses may well have been second-generation Czech Americans. Marriage within the group continued to strengthen Czech family ties at least until World War I. In the city or on the farm, these families worked as economic units; children lived at home until marriage, working as "farm labor" in the countryside or contributing factory wages to the family income in the cities. A social worker in New York in 1904 noted exceptional self-reliance and maturity in the children of Czech working mothers, and a willingness among the men in the family to do housework. Another admired the independence and self-reliance of the women who could take over and run the family farm, as many did during the war.

Whenever a Czech settlement included several families, they joined in a fraternal or cultural society that formalized social ties and helped maintain traditions and language. Unlike the organizations of some other groups, theirs did not suffer perceptibly from the antiforeign hysteria of World War I, nor did their press. In the course of the campaign for Czechoslovak independence, the Czechs and Slovaks won support even in the nativist camp; hence their institutions emerged from the war years largely intact. For the next decade, language schools, churches, and fraternal societies enjoyed their heyday. Several communities and villages, such as Milligan, Nebr., and Petersburg, Va., were still solidly Czech in the 1920s.

The Czechs' obsession with their past also favored the survival and development of ethnic identity. Historian and national "awakener" František Palacký (1798–1876) laid the foundations of modern Czech historiography and by 1880 there was a respectable school of historians to unearth, celebrate, and explain the past. That historical consciousness was transferred to America, and as early as the 1890s Czechs in America began to explore the group's experience in the New World by analyzing decades of press archives, diaries, and letters; they also interviewed Czech pioneers. Primarily antiquarian or reportorial, their works preserved many memoirs and records intact. The first major work, *Dějiny Cechův Amerických* (History of American Czechs), was published in 1910 by Jan Habenicht, a physician who had published his own memoirs in 1897. Most prolific was lawyer-banker-journalist Thomas Čapek, who was the first to interpret his people to the American public in *The Čechs (Bohemians) in America* (1920). Immigrating in 1879, Čapek traveled throughout Czech America before beginning to document, in both English and Czech, its history. Other Czechs wrote local histories, such as Rose Rosicky's *Czechs in Nebraska* (1929; original Czech edition, 1928). The Czech American Press Bureau (Česko-Americká tisková kancelář), founded in 1909, was also active in collecting and transmitting information in both Czech and English about Czech history and culture. A highlight of its prewar activities was a lecture tour of American universities by Count Francis Lützow, a German count edu-

cated in England who wrote several studies in Czech history. A less heralded activity was the role the organization played in urging the U.S. Census Bureau to include questions about language use in the 1910 Census.

Direct ties with the homeland were important in maintaining ethnic identity, at least until World War I. In the 1880s and 1890s, the Czechs organized excursions to Prague; the first, the "theater ship" of 1885, took 177 Czech Americans to the opening of the National Theater in Prague; a second took 287 Sokol members to Bohemia in 1887 (a visit reciprocated by Czech Sokols in 1909). Politicians and journalists from Bohemia also visited the United States, lecturing to Czech-American audiences and writing about their experiences for compatriots at home. Most important was Professor Masaryk, future "president-liberator" of Czechoslovakia. In 1878 he married Charlotte Garrigue of Brooklyn, N.Y., and in 1902 and 1907 he returned to the United States for university lecture tours. Vojta Náprstek, the 1848 immigrant active in ethnic organizations and the press in the 1850s, returned to Prague in 1857 and became a one-man Czech-American culture service. His permanent legacy is the Náprstek Museum in Prague, which today contains one of the most extensive—and as yet largely untapped—archives of Czech-American publications, letters, and other documents.

Czech Americans maintained contact with the homeland in the period between the world wars as well. A few returned to Czechoslovakia after 1918 to serve in responsible positions; several returned to the United States as diplomatic representatives. The exchange of students and scholars, and tours by Czechoslovak performing artists, continued to strengthen ties between Czechs of both countries. To meet the needs of younger generations without enough knowledge of Czech to enjoy a Czech play, to read a Czech book, or to speak to relatives in the old country, the Czechoslovak National Council sponsored in 1920 the publication of *Progressive Czech*, a language textbook by Bohumil Mikula. In 1928 the Czechoslovak government established the Czechoslovak Foreign Institute to publish works favorable to Czechoslovakia in English and to encourage tourism to the old country by American-born Czechs.

The 1920s, although a zenith for the Czech-American community, also marked the onset of its decline. The first blow was the immigration quota established in 1924, which drastically reduced the influx of new immigrants. A quarter of a century would pass before a new group of Czechs came in the wake of the Communist coup of 1948, and they would form a distinctly separate community. A second blow was dealt by the Great Depression, which left many ethnic institutions insolvent and forced them to close, since members simply could not pay their dues. The quota and the Depression, however, did not cause the fading of Czech culture but merely accelerated it. Long-term processes had been at work ever since the Czechs had arrived. Even those who most resisted acculturation and stubbornly maintained the language considered themselves Americans, solidly and patriotically. Their values—democratic, pluralistic, imbued with an ethic of work and thrift—were compatible with those of their new homeland. Their naturalization rates reflected their attitude: in 1910 among a sample of urban Czech family heads who had been in the United States ten years or more, 80 percent

were naturalized citizens and 13 percent had their first papers. Moreover, the skills Czechs brought with them usually helped them to overcome linguistic handicaps and allowed them to integrate fairly rapidly into the American economy. And as if to make America their own in a tangible way, Czechs took out mortgages and bought their homes. This rootedness of the homeowner persisted less in the urban centers; like other Americans, Czechs moved to the suburbs as they became increasingly prosperous and acquired homes that reflected that prosperity.

Assimilationist tendencies were evident in still other ways: many Czechs changed their names after living in America for a time. Plch became Pelch; Pospišilová, Bosbyshell; Černý, Black; Křejčová, Taylor. By 1910 at least two-thirds of the first generation knew English; many Czechs observed that their American-born children insisted on using English if the parents understood, and after a few years in the public schools the children had all but forgotten their mother tongue. Some immigrants lamented this development, while others considered it inevitable; after all, they were Americans, and they believed in the melting pot. In the 1930s, with fewer institutions to transmit ethnic heritage, fewer language schools, fewer Czech church services, and fewer Czech newspapers, the American-born generations outside large urban centers or isolated rural communities lost interest in the culture and homeland of their parents and grandparents. They freely married other native-born citizens of various backgrounds and felt themselves thoroughly American. Only in March 1939 would they suddenly be jolted into remembering their Old World origin as their parents wept at the news of Hitler's triumphant march into Prague.

THE REFUGEES OF 1948 AND 1968

The arrival of the post-1948 refugees opened a new chapter in the story of Czechs in America. Those who fled the Communist regime were professional people and skilled craftsmen whose socioeconomic characteristics and recent European experience placed them for the most part outside the mainstream of Czech-American life. Though they were assisted in resettling and finding jobs by agencies such as the American Fund for Czechoslovak Refugees, they usually established social contacts with fellow professionals, rather than with their compatriots. Nevertheless, their very presence and activity has regenerated Czech ethnic culture in the United States. They established the Czechoslovak Society of Arts and Sciences in America (Československá společnost věd a umění v Americe, SVU) in 1960. A small organization of Czech, Slovak, and Rusyn intellectuals in all fields, it has sponsored publication of works in English on Czech and Slovak history and culture; it also publishes a literary journal, *Proměny* (Metamorphoses, f. 1964). The post-1948 refugees also founded anti-Communist organizations, parallel to those of other East European refugee groups, which continue to mobilize opposition to the present regime in Czechoslovakia.

The Soviet-led invasion of Czechoslovakia in 1968 produced a smaller influx of refugees similar in socioeconomic background to the 1948 group. In the increasingly cosmopolitan environment of American cities

and universities, they too found jobs and acceptance rapidly. At first, for essentially political reasons, they chose to remain apart from other Czech Americans, especially the 1948 group. A large gap separated immigrants who left before or because of the Communist takeover from those—especially young people—who had lived for two decades in a socialist Czechoslovakia. Many of the latter were socialist intellectuals, if disillusioned ones. They hoped to return to their homeland under an amnesty and carefully avoided association with anti-Communist factions among American Czechs. And the earlier immigrants, for their part, were often suspicious of the politics of the new arrivals. When perhaps half of the 1968 group claimed to be Catholics (now that the church's role in Czech history had been reversed to one of opposition to the government) their sincerity was questioned. Then too, the frankly economic motives of some of the 1968 group offended many of the earlier arrivals, even though economics had always been the dominant motive for all immigrants. Although the majority of the 1968 refugees eventually were assimilated, a minority—mainly from 1968, a few from 1948—continued to consider themselves exiles, or Czechs living abroad. The intellectual centers of the exiles are New York and Toronto, where Czech writers in exile, headed by Josef Škvorecký (1924–), have established a Czech publishing house.

ETHNIC REVIVAL

The ethnic revival of the 1970s was most intense in large cities, especially where ethnic enclaves had economic or cultural grievances. When the government sought to overcome discrimination against particular minorities by funding bilingual education and ethnic studies programs, other groups—including the Czechs—benefited as well. But the ethnic revival in Czech America has gone beyond politics and federal funding. Czechs in Nebraska, Iowa, and Texas have issued publications to document their history and explain their culture to younger generations. The Czech Heritage Foundation and a Czech Council for the Arts in Cedar Rapids, Iowa, have established a museum and archive, published Czech-English picture books for children, restored a Czech shopping district to 19th-century charm, sponsored several festivals, and issued a newsletter that prints excerpts from archival holdings. The Omaha Czech Culture Club (f. 1959) has functioned in a similar way throughout Nebraska, sponsoring (along with the Nebraska Czechs, Inc., of Wilber) "Czech Days," when everyone enjoys Czech food (especially the traditional pork and dumplings with sauerkraut and beer) and folk dancing. Several Texas communities have revived similar traditions and have reintroduced Czech language courses in high schools. In both Iowa and Texas, ethnic heritage studies funds have been used for language and culture courses and materials. The Czech fraternal insurance societies, with a membership of at least 190,000, are also active; though English is usually the language of business, they encourage the use of Czech (often sponsoring language classes) and issue at least part of their publications in Czech. The revival of the Sokol may be more precarious, however, since it must adapt to the interests of American children and young people. College students can study Czech at a dozen schools in the United States, or in Prague at the Summer School for Slavonic Studies at Charles University. In 1975 historians specializing in Czech and Slovak history formed the Czechoslovak History Conference, an affiliate of the American Historical Association.

Czech Americans are still a diverse group and as divided as they have ever been. Nonetheless, they still share the traditional bonds of a national culture and customs—the literature and cuisine, myths and folkways that nourish ethnic identity and pride.

Bibliography
General studies of Czech Americans are few, and no comprehensive modern work exists in any language. Thomas Čapek wrote the discursive Čechs (Bohemians) in America (1920; reprint, New York, 1969) and published with his wife, Anna Čapek, the still useful Bohemian (Čech) Bibliography: A Finding List of Writing in English Relating to the Čechs (New York, 1918). Emily Balch, Our Slavic Fellow Citizens (New York, 1910) includes valuable information. Protestant missionary Kenneth Miller interpreted the group to his fellow Americans in The Czecho-Slovaks in America (New York, 1922) and Joseph Rouček offered a sociological perspective in several articles, including "Czechoslovak Americans," in One America, ed. Francis J. Brown and J.S. Rouček (New York, 1945). More recent are Joseph Svoboda, "Czechs: The Love of Liberty," in Broken Hoops and Plains People: A Catalogue of Ethnic Resources in the Humanities: Nebraska and Surrounding Areas, Nebraska Curriculum Development Center (Lincoln, Nebr., 1976), and Vera Laska's chronology with selected documents and brief bibliography, The Czechs in America, 1633–1977 (Dobbs Ferry, N.Y., 1977). The Czechoslovak National Council and the Czechoslovak Society of Arts and Sciences in America have published a compendium of articles, Panorama: A Historical Review of Czechs and Slovaks in the United States of America (Cicero, Ill., 1970). A treatment of Czech culture and science can be found in Francis Dvornik, Czech Contributions to the Growth of the United States (Chicago, 1962). Specialized studies include Robert Kutak, The Story of a Bohemian American Village (1933; reprint, New York, 1970), a sociological analysis of Milligan, Nebr.; Josef Čada, Czech-American Catholics, 1850–1920 (Lisle, Ill., 1964); Guido Kisch, In Search of Freedom: A History of American Jews from Czechoslovakia, 1745–1945 (London, 1949); and Rose Rosicky, A History of the Czechs (Bohemians) in Nebraska (Omaha, Nebr., 1929). The best modern bibliography is Esther Jerabek, Czechs and Slovaks in North America (New York, 1977).

The largest archival collections are in the University of Chicago's Archives of Czechs and Slovaks Abroad and the University of Minnesota's Immigration Research Center. Important smaller collections are at Southern Illinois University, Edwardsville; the Western Reserve Historical Society, Cleveland; the Balch Institute, Philadelphia; and the Czech Heritage Collection at the University of Nebraska at Lincoln.

KAREN JOHNSON FREEZE

D

DAGESTANIS: *see* NORTH CAUCASIANS

DALMATIANS: *see* CROATS

DANES

On July 4, 1893, immigrants marched in Worcester, Mass., to celebrate the birthday of their adopted land. First came a magnificent green and gold float bearing an Irish harp, followed by about 10,000 Irishmen. Next came throngs of Swedes with a float in the form of a Viking ship and masses of Germans with a float bearing a Rhine maiden on an island. Then came the Danes: no float, no band, but all 62 of them—every Danish man in town—dressed in white sailor suits, proudly marching behind their red banner with its white cross. According to the local newspaper, the watching crowds gave them the biggest ovation of the day. As this incident symbolizes, there are not very many Danes compared to other ethnic groups in the United States, but the Danes have been welcomed and approved by almost everyone.

Compared with their fellow Scandinavians, the Swedes and Norwegians, the Danes were fewer in number, came to America later, dispersed more widely across the continent, and assimilated more rapidly. Yet a minority who have been interested in their ethnic heritage have founded and maintained distinctive institutions and organizations, some of which are experiencing new growth. According to the 1970 U.S. Census, the Danish-born residents of the United States and their children numbered 326,000, as against 806,000 Swedes and 615,000 Norwegians.

EARLY EXPLORERS AND SETTLERS

By the time the Danes set sail for North America in the early 17th century, Denmark had been a Christian kingdom for more than 600 years. It had contributed much to Viking lore, had briefly conquered England, and had ruled an extensive realm that for short periods included much or all of Scandinavia. Following the adoption of Lutheranism in the mid-16th century, Denmark experienced an intellectual and cultural renaissance. Its political power had already waned, however, and by the mid-17th century it had lost its bid for hegemony in the north. Only Norway and Iceland remained under Danish rule, the former until 1814 and the latter until 1918.

Jens Munk (1579–1628) was the first Dane to sail to America and the leader of the only Danish expedition to this continent. His two ships left Denmark in 1619 and explored Hudson Bay in an attempt to find the Northwest Passage. More than a century later Vitus Jonassen Bering (1681–1741) sailed west under the Russian flag; he discovered the Bering Strait in 1728 and Alaska in 1741.

The first Danish immigrants also reached America in the early 17th century and joined the Dutch in New Amsterdam. By 1675 about a hundred had come, including Jonas Bronck (d. 1643), who arrived in 1629 and bought from the Indians a large tract of land later

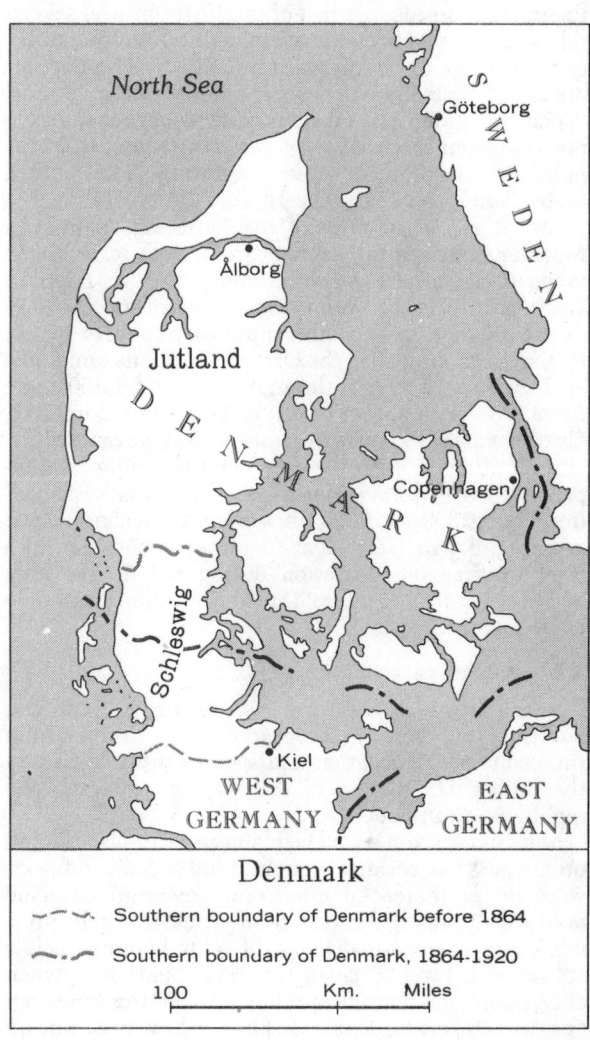

Denmark

~⌒~   Southern boundary of Denmark before 1864

~·⌒~   Southern boundary of Denmark, 1864-1920

100   Km.   Miles

known as the Bronx. In 1735 Danish converts to Moravian pietism established a mission at Bethlehem, Pa., and after 1750 many more Danes of that faith, traveling in organized companies, joined the predominantly German settlements in the same area. In addition, both before and after the American Revolution, a number of Danes migrated to America from the Danish West Indies (Virgin Islands), which Denmark sold to the United States in 1917.

From colonial times until after the Civil War, most Danish immigrants, with the exception of the Moravians, were single men who married women born in the United States and who rapidly assimilated. The best known of these immigrants was "Old Denmark," Hans Christian Febiger, or Fibiger (1749–1796), who became one of George Washington's most trusted officers. A few Danes are also recorded among the adventurers and pioneers who opened the American West. For example, Peter Lassen (1800–1859), a blacksmith from Copenhagen who settled in Missouri, led pioneers across the Rockies to California in 1839, blazing the trail later fol-

lowed by the forty-niners. Lassen Peak in California bears his name.

A century after the migration of the Moravians to Pennsylvania, religious repression caused more Danes to emigrate. In the first half of the 19th century, several religious sects gained ground in Denmark in spite of the opposition of the Lutheran state church. The Baptists organized their first congregation in Denmark in 1839. When this group and others formed later met with opposition from the authorities and harassment from the public, their members began emigrating to the United States, some as early as the 1840s.

The first missionaries of the Latter-day Saints, or Mormons, arrived in Denmark from Utah in 1850 and made their earliest converts among Danish Baptists. Until the 1890s the Mormons were more successful in Denmark than in any other European country except England. About half of the Danish Mormons emigrated —an estimated 17,000 through 1904, and 1,300 more from 1904 to 1930—and most of them settled in Utah. Until the 1880s this emigration was organized by church officials, with the emigrants traveling in companies, as the Moravians had done a hundred years earlier. From 1860 to 1930 Danes were the second largest ethnic group in Utah, next to the British. Then, in a brief upsurge of emigration during the decade after World War II, 900 more Danish Mormons came to Utah. (*See* Mormons.)

MASS EMIGRATION

In the late 18th and early 19th centuries Denmark, like the other western European nations, suffered from the economic dislocation and social unrest caused by the Industrial Revolution, the Napoleonic wars, and rapid growth in population.

Mass emigration developed later in Denmark than in other countries because economic and social conditions were better there. An intelligent governmental land policy encouraged the growth of efficient small farms while preventing subdivision of farm holdings below subsistence level. Even in the 1870s and after, when cheap grain was pouring into Europe from the American prairies, Danish farmers, aided by the growing cooperative movement, maintained economic viability by rapidly shifting from grain production to livestock and dairy products. Industrialization also developed rapidly in Denmark after 1850, supporting the growth of Copenhagen and the provincial towns, which attracted a large proportion of the surplus rural population.

Politically, the first half of the 19th century was a period of reform, culminating in the liberal constitution of 1849; this constitution established wide suffrage and personal freedom, including freedom of worship. The same period was also one of cultural awakening. Universal elementary education became compulsory in 1814. The dynamic folk-school movement inspired by Bishop N.F.S. Grundtvig (1783–1872) started in the middle of the century, providing general secondary education for rural youths. Literature and art flowered under the stimulus of national romanticism.

In the 1860s, however, conditions changed for the worse. Defeated by Prussia and Austria in the war of 1864, Denmark lost almost one-fourth of its territory. To escape from German military service and cultural repression in North Schleswig, Danes fled to the United

States in much larger numbers than to the homeland. National defeat and dismemberment plunged Denmark into economic and spiritual depression. In 1866 a conservative government revised the liberal constitution, an action that paralyzed reform and resulted in three decades of political struggle. Continued population growth swelled the numbers of laborers and servants beyond the capacity of the national economy to absorb them. The result was widespread unemployment, crowded slums, growing crime, increasing labor unrest —all compounded by rising expectations of social betterment, even among the poor.

Meanwhile the United States was becoming better known. The first Danish emigrant guidebooks were published in 1847, and letters from Danish pioneers appeared in newspapers. Rasmus Sørensen (1799–1865), a radical politician who served in the Danish parliament from 1849 to 1852, published a series of tracts about America based on letters from his son in Wisconsin. He urged all poor Danes to emigrate, and in 1852 he went to Wisconsin with his family. He continued to publish his pamphlets in Denmark, and in the 1860s he made three trips to the homeland to lecture on the United States and lead companies of Danes to the New World. An even more fiery radical, Mogens Abraham Somner (1829–1901), lifelong enemy of the Danish establishment, founded an emigration agency in Copenhagen in 1864 and personally escorted many large groups to the United States.

After the 1870s, agents promoting emigration, often hired by railroad, steamship, or land companies, grew in number and importance. Letters from friends and relatives in the new country were also a stimulus to prospective emigrants, especially when they contained money orders or prepaid tickets. In the last quarter of the century about one-fourth of all Danish emigrants traveled on tickets prepaid from the United States. Such agitation and publicity created an "America fever" in Denmark as elsewhere. Between 1850 and 1900, the number of emigrants totaled 245,000, or one-tenth of the population in 1900 (2.45 million).

Once the large-scale emigration got under way in the 1870s, it generally followed the same pattern as the Norwegian and Swedish emigration, though on a smaller scale, with the highest peaks in the periods 1881–1883 and 1903–1905. The all-time high came in 1882, when more than 11,000 Danes arrived in the United States. The numbers fluctuated with the economic ups and downs on both sides of the Atlantic. Danes continued to emigrate in considerable numbers after World War I, but when the United States established immigration quotas in the 1920s, a growing proportion went to Canada and other countries instead. About 1,000 Danes migrated to the United States annually between 1950 and 1970, and about half that number annually in the 1970s. American immigration figures for the 1820–1975 period totaled about 363,000 Danes, as compared with 1,270,000 Swedes and 855,000 Norwegians.

The striking difference in number between Denmark and the other Scandinavian countries was due to three factors: the earlier and more extensive urbanization and industrialization of Danish society, the fact that Danish mass emigration began a generation later than the Swedish and Norwegian, and the size of the homeland

populations. Sweden has always had the most inhabitants, while Denmark and Norway had roughly the same number until about 1900, when Denmark began to pull ahead.

American census figures show that the number of Danish-born immigrants in the United States increased rapidly from about 1,800 in 1850 to 189,000 in 1920. The number of Danish-born residents declined sharply thereafter; about 61,000 were reported in 1970. Of course, the number added by immigration in each decade was reduced by deaths and returning migrants. Between 1900 and 1910, for example, about 65,000 Danes immigrated, but the net increase in the Danish-born population was only 27,000. There are no Danish records of returned emigrants, and American remigration figures did not begin until 1908. From then to 1914, however, the average return rate to Denmark was almost 9 percent, which scholars believe to be too low for the entire emigration period.

By 1900 the children of immigrants, the second generation, outnumbered their parents. Americans with one or both parents born in Denmark numbered 320,410 in 1920 and increased by nearly 30,000 over the next decade, then began to decline slowly to 264,151 in 1970. In 1920, however, the two generations together totaled well over half a million.

SOCIAL COMPOSITION

In terms of sex and age groupings, Danish mass migration followed the same pattern as that of other western European nations. Until about 1890 a high proportion of emigrants traveled in family groups, with adults 25 to 39 years old and small children predominating. After 1890, however, the proportion of young single adults rose steadily, especially those 15 to 19 years old. The group aged 20 to 24 made up about a quarter of the total throughout the period of mass migration.

Males predominated, except among the Mormons. A downward trend in the proportion of men toward the end of the 19th century was reversed by a steep rise thereafter, and for many years women averaged only one-third of all departing adults. This fact noticeably affected the distribution of the sexes in the homeland, where the oversupply of women did not give way to normal equilibrium until 1950.

Mass emigration began in the islands of southeastern Denmark closest to Sweden and spread from there to the west and north. As in other countries, some provinces were affected much more than others. Central Jutland, for instance, lost comparatively little of its population, while northern Jutland lost heavily. In all, about two-fifths of Danish emigrants came from Jutland, one-fifth from Copenhagen, and the remaining two-fifths from other areas.

In the 1890s Scandinavian emigration shifted from a predominantly rural to a predominantly urban movement. The more advanced urbanization of Denmark meant that at all times a higher proportion of Danish emigrants were from the cities and towns than was the case in Norway and Sweden. In addition, Danish towns consistently sent a larger percentage of their inhabitants to the United States than rural areas did, though a considerable number of those leaving the towns had moved there earlier from the countryside.

Few Danish emigrants were of upper- or middle-class origin; of those few, a number were "black sheep" whose families sent them off to avoid the shame of alcoholism, bankruptcy, or marriage beneath their station. The police were known to have provided some criminals and paupers with one-way tickets to the New World, but the total number of undesirables was very small. The vast majority of Danish emigrants were law-abiding peasants and working-class people. Between 1869 and 1900, 69 percent of adult wage earners who emigrated were laborers and servants, mostly from rural areas, and over 18 percent were craftsmen and artisans, a total of 87 percent landless manual workers. After World War I, however, the proportion of more highly educated and skilled workers grew steadily and reached almost total dominance after World War II.

SETTLEMENT PATTERNS

Danish colonies began to appear in the United States in the 1870s, when small groups of Danes settled in East Coast cities from Pennsylvania to Maine. Later arrivals often worked in a business or factory run by their countrymen before moving west; in the early 20th century, for example, the terra-cotta works in Perth Amboy, N.J., employed 5,000 Danes out of a local population of 30,000.

Before 1845 there were too few Danes on the frontier to form exclusively Danish settlements, and they mingled with other groups, especially Norwegians. In that year, however, the first Danish farming settlement was founded near Hartland, Wis., followed shortly by others at New Denmark and Neenah. In the next two decades many more settlements sprang up in Wisconsin, as well as in Illinois and Michigan. These early rural colonies were populated mainly by people who had come in organized parties from a particular island or area in southeastern Denmark. By the 1870s the mingling of the old immigrants with new arrivals from many different parts of Denmark made the later western settlements more cosmopolitan.

In 1860 Utah, because of the Mormon migration, had more Danish residents than any other state. In 1870 Wisconsin took the lead, then Iowa between 1890 and 1920. In 1920 California became the state with the most Danish-born residents and has remained so ever since. In the peak years of immigration, 1880–1920, the heartland of Danish America extended from southern Wisconsin across northern Illinois into Iowa.

Iowa has been the most conspicuously Danish state. In 1910 over 10 percent of all the Danes in the United States lived in Iowa, although they made up barely 2 percent of the population of the state. In 1853 a party of 40 Norwegian and Danish families from Wisconsin founded St. Ansgar, Iowa, under the leadership of a Danish Lutheran minister, Claus Lauritsen Clausen (1820–1892). Mormon apostates who dropped off in Iowa on the trek west added to the Danish population, especially in the Council Bluffs area. Then in 1865 a company of Danish Baptists settled in Shelby County, where groups of Lutherans, Seventh-Day Adventists, and others built up what became known as the Elk Horn–Kimballton settlement, the most important of all Danish-American rural communities. In Elk Horn, the oldest predominantly Danish village in the state, a folk school was built in 1878, a Lutheran church in 1882, and an orphanage in 1890. By the 1890s there

were Danes in every county in the state. Most of them were farmers, but sizable groups also lived in the larger towns.

Rural and small-town Danish colonies grew up in the other midwestern states in the 1870s, but they remained smaller, fewer, and more mixed with other groups than comparable Swedish and Norwegian settlements. Between 1886 and 1935, in an effort to preserve Danish ethnicity, Lutheran ministers and other cultural leaders cooperated with private land companies in developing nearly two dozen rural settlements (including a few in Canada), in which land was sold only to Danes for a set number of years. The Dansk Folkesamfund (Danish Folk Society) sponsored a number of these settlements, the best known of which were founded at Tyler, Minn., in 1886; Danevang, Tex., 1894; Askov, Minn., 1905; Dagmar, Mont., 1906; and Solvang, Calif., 1911. Since World War II Solvang has become a flourishing tourist attraction with many buildings in the Danish style and shops and restaurants that specialize in Danish products.

Toward the end of the 19th century, Danish urban colonies began to grow rapidly. Though the first Dane was recorded in Chicago in 1819, a small community did not evolve there until 1870. Three distinctly Danish neighborhoods developed in Chicago over the next 70 years. By 1920 there were 12,000 Danish-born residents, though they were not a homogeneous group. Many Danes of upper-class origin gravitated to Chicago, where, along with successful businessmen, prosperous craftsmen, and intellectuals, they made up a small elite quite separate from the working-class majority. The rapidly growing middle class, however, helped bridge the social gap, and by World War II the last Danish neighborhood was dissolving as Danes moved to the suburbs. Over the years Chicago attracted about one-tenth of all Danish immigrants for various lengths of time and until the 1930s held the largest urban concentration of Danes outside Denmark.

Omaha, Nebr., and Council Bluffs, Iowa, on opposite sides of the Missouri River, had major colonies of Danes for many years. There were significant concentrations in other cities on the Great Lakes (especially in Racine, Wis., which for a long time had a larger proportion of Danes than any other U.S. city), as well as in the Northeast and on the West Coast. Danes, more than other Scandinavian immigrants, tended to settle in urban areas; before 1900 at least 33 percent of them lived in cities. The U.S. Census of 1910 recorded over 48 percent of the Danish-born population as urban residents. In the 1970s at least 80 percent of the Danish-born lived in cities, four-fifths of those in major metropolitan areas. The largest concentrations in 1970 were in the Los Angeles area (roughly 18,000) and in Chicago (17,000). Only 4 percent of the Danish-born still lived on farms.

Few ethnic groups have been so widely and thinly spread as the Danes. Since 1870 they have been present in every American state and territory. In 1916 a Danish-American almanac listed ethnic organizations in 31 of the 48 states. The regional distribution of Danes has changed noticeably during the past century, as the proportion of Danes living on the West and East coasts has increased, and the proportion in the Midwest has declined (see Table 1).

Table 1. Regional distribution of Danes in the United States, 1870 and 1970, in percentages.

Region	1870	1970
Northeast	12	25
South	3	8
Midwest	60	30
Rocky Mountains	18	7
West Coast	7	30

Source: "Hvor mange danske—og hvor?" (How many Danes—and where?), *Danmarksposten* 57 (May 1976): 28.

OCCUPATIONS

The substantial shift in occupations after the Danes arrived in the United States indicates their upward mobility. Table 2 shows the percentage of wage earners in each major occupational group before and after emigration.

The percentage of rural laborers fell sharply after emigration, while that of landowners rose, indicating that large numbers achieved the goal of owning their own farm. In addition, by 1900 the number in business and the professions doubled. The rising percentage of domestic servants probably reflected the growing number of single women who emigrated toward the end of the century. Like other European immigrant groups, Danes became increasingly skilled in the United States, though there continued to be considerable numbers of unskilled workers.

Although Danes entered a variety of occupations in the United States, they were most prominent in certain fields. Many in agriculture concentrated on gardening, raising livestock, and dairy farming. The dairy system launched by the farmers' cooperative movement in Denmark in the early 1880s remained technically superior to any other country's for many years. In 1890 the total number of dairymen in Denmark was 2,560, and 744 professional dairy farmers came to the United States before 1900. The first centrifuge separator in the United States was brought to Iowa by a Dane in 1882; thereafter the most advanced dairy equipment and techniques were regularly introduced by Danish-American dairymen, who became the leading experts in the country. Many served as professors in American agricultural colleges and as inspectors for the federal and state governments. Danes also led in founding scientific

Table 2. Occupations of Danes before and after emigration to the United States, 1868–1900, in percentages.

Occupation	Emigrants 1868–1900	Immigrants 1890	Immigrants 1900
Agriculture and fishing	48.1	39.2	39.1
Landowning farmers	3.4	24.8	28.4
Rural laborers	43.2	12.0	9.0
Manufacturing and mechanical	32.2	22.6	25.5
Domestic service	11.9	24.5	19.7
Business and professional	7.8	12.9	15.6

Source: Based on K. Hvidt, *Flight to America* (New York, 1975), p. 118; U.S. Census Office, *Compendium of the Eleventh Census, 1890* (Washington, D.C., 1892), pp. 532–539; *Report of the Immigration Commission* 28 (1911): 254–255, 344–345, as cited in P.S. Friedman, "The Danish Community of Chicago, 1860–1920" (unpub. diss., Northwestern University, 1976).

dairies and farmers' cooperatives throughout the Midwest.

Though generally not so well represented industrially as other groups, Danes were prominent in the manufacture and distribution of dairy equipment and products and in the lumber and construction industries. About 7 percent of Danish wage earners found employment in the building trades. Danish-American businessmen engaged in a variety of enterprises. Professionals were concentrated in the fields of art and architecture, but this group also included many schoolteachers and administrators. These concentrations should not be overemphasized, however, because Danish immigrants were distributed over the entire spectrum of American occupations.

CHURCHES AND SCHOOLS

The Scandinavian Lutheran churches long remained the central social organizations of their ethnic communities, and all of the Danish-American schools were church affiliated. Still, the Danes joined ethnic churches less frequently than did either the Norwegians or the Swedes, probably because of their greater urbanization and more recent emigration. In addition, because they were so few in number and so widely dispersed, the Danes often lacked the economic resources to support churches of their own, which caused many who were religiously inclined to join other faiths.

Before 1870 Danish Lutherans in America joined Norwegian, Swedish, or German congregations, because they had no churches of their own. A score of these mixed congregations were served by pastors of Danish birth, among whom Claus L. Clausen, the founder of St. Ansgar, Iowa, was particularly important. He established settlements and congregations with equal energy, served in county and state offices in Iowa, and helped found the Norwegian Evangelical Lutheran Church in America (1853) and the Norwegian-Danish Lutheran conference (1870), of which he was first president. Visiting Denmark in 1867, he helped awaken concern in church circles for Danish Lutherans in the United States. Two years later the Commission for the Furtherance of the Proclamation of the Gospel among Danes in America was established by a committee of ministers of the state church in Denmark. The commission sent four Danish pastors to the United States, and in 1872 they founded what became the Danish Lutheran Church in America. The commission continued to support this church for nearly a century, organizing a special training program for prospective emigrant ministers and sending advice and even money in the early years. But it failed to resolve the quarrels that eventually led to schism.

The four pastors who founded the Danish Lutheran Church in America were followers of Bishop Grundtvig. Working within the state church of Denmark, Grundtvig opposed both formalism and pietistic separatism, emphasized the Apostles' Creed and the sacraments against other Biblical authorities, and affirmed the importance of joy in Christian life and the significance of national heritage. The Grundtvigians in the United States actively encouraged the continuance of folk customs and formal culture from Denmark; tried to preserve the Danish language; and founded folk schools, societies, and colonies to enlarge and enrich the cultural life of their group. But this program was resisted by Danish pietists in America, who emphasized revivalism, literal interpretation of the Bible, and strict morality in an exclusive church. They argued that to spread the gospel they had to become Americanized and begin to use the English language as quickly as possible. These theological and cultural disputes were compounded by personal feuds between pastoral leaders.

A son of Bishop Grundtvig, Frederick Lange Grundtvig (1854–1903), led the ethnic-heritage faction. Although he originally came to Wisconsin in 1881 to study birds, he was ordained in 1883 and became a leading minister in Iowa. Four years later he founded the Danish Folk Society to unite all Danes in the effort to preserve their heritage for the benefit of their adopted land. Even though the society grew rapidly both in Denmark and in the United States, the pietistic faction within the Danish Lutheran Church in America demanded its dissolution.

Meanwhile in 1884, the Danish minority within the Norwegian-Danish Lutheran conference of 1870 withdrew from that organization to found their own Blair Synod with strong pietist leanings. This synod established Trinity Theological Seminary at Blair, Nebr., in the same year.

Disputes within the Danish Lutheran Church in America concerning the Danish Folk Society and the religious authority of the Bible culminated in schism in 1894. The pietist faction, known as the North Church, withdrew and two years later joined with the Blair Synod to form the United Evangelical Lutheran Church in America. This organization became the largest Danish synod, but it abandoned its ethnic identity. In 1930 it joined four other Lutheran synods in the American Lutheran Conference, which through a total merger in 1960 became the American Lutheran Church.

The Grundtvigian Danish Lutheran Church in America failed to grow as much as its Americanized rival. In 1952 it changed its name to the American Evangelical Lutheran Church, and in 1962 it merged with three other synods to form the Lutheran Church in America. At the same time, however, the surviving Grundtvigian ministers formed the Danish Special Interest Conference to preserve their ethnic heritage within the larger organization. This conference still publishes a biweekly periodical, *Kirke og Folk* (Church and People), sponsors cultural-religious conferences, and arranges speaking tours.

Despite the strong feelings of both groups of Danish Lutherans, the percentage of Danes who joined their own ethnic churches remained comparatively small. In 1910, for instance, the total number of members in the two Danish-American synods was 40,700—about 20 percent of the number of Danish-born Americans, or 8 percent of the immigrant generation plus the second generation. Statistics for Danish membership in most other churches are lacking, but it has been estimated that only 35 percent of the Danes in the United States were members of any church—not a high figure.

Even before the establishment of the Danish Lutheran Church in the 1870s, Baptists and Methodists had begun to recruit Danish Americans. The Baptists founded their earliest Danish-language congregation in Potter County, Pa., in 1854. A decade later there were ten Danish Baptist congregations in the Midwest, orga-

nized mainly by Lars Jørgensen Hauge (1837–1925). The Danish Baptist General Conference of America was organized in 1910. A Methodist minister, Christian B. Willerup (1815–1866), who had been converted as a young immigrant in Georgia, built the first Scandinavian Methodist church in Cambridge, Wis., in 1852. He was sent as a missionary to Norway in 1856 and introduced Methodism in Denmark two years later. After preliminary mergers with other bodies, the Scandinavian-American Methodists joined the United Methodist Church in 1968.

Danish immigrants were also recruited by the Latter-day Saints, Episcopalians, Seventh-Day Adventists, Salvation Army, and other denominations, in which they rapidly became assimilated. The comparatively large numbers of Danes among the Latter-day Saints in Utah enabled them to dominate the Scandinavian meetings that were organized within many congregations and that sponsored such ethnic activities as choral societies, holiday celebrations, and a Danish-language weekly, *Bikuben* (The Beehive, 1876–1935).

Some Lutheran ministers tried to found parochial schools because they considered American public schools irreligious, but most Danes soon turned to Sunday schools and summer religious instruction instead. The first Lutheran Bible camp in the United States was held by the United Evangelical Lutheran Church in 1924.

The first theological seminary of the Danish Lutheran Church in America opened at West Denmark, Wis., in 1887, but it closed five years later as a result of the quarrels that led to the 1894 schism. From then until the mergers of the 1960s, each synod maintained its own seminary—the Pietists in Blair, Nebr., and the Grundtvigians in Des Moines, Iowa. Both schools ultimately developed into liberal arts colleges: Dana College at Blair and Grand View College at Des Moines.

Danish folk schools in the Grundtvigian spirit were unique if impermanent contributions to American secondary education. All but one were founded by leaders of the Danish Lutheran Church in America. The exception was the Brorson Folk School, opened in Kenmare, N.Dak., in 1905 by a pastor of the United Evangelical Lutheran Church. The Danish Lutheran Church supported six folk schools in the United States, the first of which opened in Elk Horn, Iowa, in 1878 and the last in Solvang, Calif., in 1911. The others were at Grant, Mich. (1882), West Denmark, Wis. (1884), Nysted, Nebr. (1887), and Tyler, Minn. (1888). Their economic support was precarious, their size small, and their span of existence brief; but the two strongest, at Tyler and Nysted, flourished between 1900 and the Great Depression. The school buildings at Tyler were renovated in the 1940s and are still used for community activities and for short-term camps and conferences in the Grundtvigian spirit.

ETHNIC ORGANIZATIONS

Danish-American ethnic organizations, like those of other immigrants, grew out of the need for mutual help in an alien environment. As with their churches and newspapers, Danes at first cooperated with other Scandinavians. Dania, founded in Chicago in 1862, was a pan-Scandinavian society during its early years. Starting with a health insurance program, it developed a wide range of activities, many of which were taken over by separate clubs as the number of Danes in Chicago increased. The success of Dania and of the Dania Ladies Society of Chicago, both of which are still active, inspired the founding of similar local clubs in other urban centers, such as Racine, Wis. (1867), Oakland, Calif. (1879), and Brooklyn, N.Y. (1886). Dania of California, with its women's auxiliary, Dannebrog, has grown into a statewide organization with local lodges in nearly all the principal cities of the state and a branch in Reno, Nev.

Danish Americans have formed more than 100 different organizations in the United States and well over 300 local lodges of national societies. Some organizations have been purely local and others regional or even international. No survey has yet been made of all the local clubs and societies that have existed for shorter or longer periods wherever Danish communities have sprung up. They have been devoted to a wide variety of interests: culture, sports, charity, youth, social activities, and nostalgia for Denmark. Most of the purely local organizations flourished between the turn of the century and the Depression, but after a generation of decline, some have been experiencing new growth. Luncheon clubs and senior citizens' social groups were formed in a number of cities in the 1970s. Danish-American newspapers contain many reports and advertisements of the activities of local groups. In Chicago, for example, ten societies publicize their activities, including the Danish American Athletic Club (f. 1922), which advertises gymnastics, folk dancing, and Danish-language classes for all ages; the Harmonien Singing Society (f. 1886), which announces weekly rehearsals and occasional concerts; and the Danish National Committee (f. 1908), which works for cooperation among all the Danish groups in Chicago.

The Danish National Committee of Chicago grew from 26 members in 1908, each representing a different club, local lodge, or church, to 40 members in 1933. In 1909 it started annual celebrations of Danish Constitution Day on June 5, and through the years it has sponsored amateur dramatic productions, guest appearances of Danish artists, and banquets and receptions for visiting royalty and other important Danes. It has also supported ethnic charitable organizations and activities in Chicago, such as the Danish Relief Fund—founded in 1911 and reorganized in 1927 as the independent, nationwide Danish Relief Committee—which provided considerable aid to Denmark during both world wars. Coordinating committees similar to the Danish National Committee of Chicago were organized later in other cities. Especially in California, Florida, New York, and the Midwest, clusters of local clubs and activities continue to flourish side by side with the local lodges of regional and national organizations and church activities.

The oldest and largest nationwide fraternal order is Det Danske Brodersamfund (The Danish Brotherhood), founded in 1866 in Omaha as an insurance scheme limited to Danish war veterans. In 1882 it was reorganized and incorporated in its present form, with its purpose redefined to include the preservation of Danish culture. Its initiation ceremony, with religious overtones adopted in imitation of American secret lodges, led

Danish churchmen to oppose it and similar societies for many years, but it grew rapidly to incorporate more than 300 lodges, including Lodge No. 318 in Copenhagen for returned emigrants. The Danish Brotherhood began to decline during the Depression, but growth has resumed in recent years. In 1977 it reported 150 lodges in 26 states, Canada, and Denmark, and showed an increase of 2,000 members during the preceding two years. It now enrolls all members of a family, and in addition to its central insurance program offers such services as tapes, slide programs, and films for instruction in the Danish language, folk dance, and Danish traditions. It publishes the monthly *American Dane Magazine* and a newsletter called *Viking Adventures*. Its Viking clubs provide special activities for members under 16, who are also offered summer-camp stipends and college scholarships. A parallel organization for women, the Danish Sisterhood, was founded in Michigan in 1883 and still maintains a separate organization with headquarters in Chicago.

Many other kinds of ethnic societies have been organized. The youth clubs sponsored by Grundtvigian Lutheran churches formed a national organization in 1902; the Danish Singers' League united choral societies all over the country in 1920; the American Society of Danish Engineers was founded in New York City in 1930. Two veterans' organizations are affiliated with similar societies in Denmark: Den Danske Soldaterforening (Danish Veterans Society), whose members have served in the Danish, American, or Canadian armed forces; and the unique Garderforeningen (Royal Danish Guards Association outside Denmark), for men who have served in the King's Guard in Copenhagen. The latter was founded in New York in 1928 and has branches in several American and Canadian cities.

Danish lodges of American fraternal orders include Masons, Odd Fellows, Knights of Pythias, and Good Templars. In addition, Danes helped found and participate in Scandinavian organizations, such as the American Scandinavian Society.

In recent years many new Danish ethnic organizations have appeared in the United States. Business interests incorporated the Danish American Trade Council in 1964 to promote trade between the two countries and maintain a lobby in Washington. The Danish-American Chamber of Commerce was organized in Los Angeles in 1976 for business and social purposes. In the same year the Danish American Language Foundation was incorporated in Illinois to support existing publications in the Danish tongue. The Danish American Heritage Association was founded in 1977 with headquarters in Oregon to fill the long-felt need for a historical society. It puts out two special publications: a newsletter and *The Bridge*, a journal of historical and cultural articles.

It is impossible to tell how many Danish immigrants and their children have belonged to ethnic organizations, because the records of these societies, especially the local clubs, are either nonexistent or incomplete. But it is clear that many individuals have belonged to different societies simultaneously or successively. Most ethnic organizations have been small; in 1903, for instance, each of the 17 Danish organizations in New York City had fewer than 100 members. Ethnic clubs, which have often competed with the churches for members, have been a predominantly urban phenomenon, while Lutheran congregations have been undisputed centers of ethnic life in rural areas and small towns. And as the churches have lost their Danish identity, the secular societies, whose purpose is to preserve it, have grown in importance.

POLITICS

Unlike the Swedes and Norwegians, Danes have not been especially active in American politics. They were originally too few in number and too scattered to make up effective voting blocs, except for limited periods in some midwestern counties. With the votes of other Scandinavian Americans, however, they have managed to elect a fair share of Danes, most of them members of the Republican party, to Congress and to local and state offices. Danish-born politicians have served as governors of Minnesota, Wyoming, South Dakota, Iowa, and New Jersey, and at least two sons of Danish immigrants have also been governors: Culbert L. Olson (1876–1962) in California from 1939 to 1943, and Frederick Valdemar (Val) Peterson (1903–) in Nebraska from 1947 to 1953. Among the several members of Congress of Danish birth or ancestry, Ben Jensen (1892–1970) of Iowa served 27 years, and Lloyd M. Bentsen (1921–) of Texas served in the House from 1948 to 1954 and was elected to the Senate in 1970 and 1976.

CULTURE

In the field of journalism, Danes in the United States worked closely with Norwegians. The written language of the two groups was almost identical throughout the 19th century, and even after separate Danish and Norwegian periodicals began to flourish in the United States, writers of both nationalities continued to publish in each other's journals. The largest and longest-lived newspaper was *Den Danske Pioneer* (The Danish Pioneer), founded in Omaha in 1872 by Mark Hansen (1830–1908) and sold in 1887 to Sophus Neble (1858–1931). Since 1958 it has been published biweekly in Elmwood Park, Ill. Democratic in politics, the early *Pioneer* was strongly anticlerical and antiauthoritarian. From 1886 to 1898 it was banned from the Danish mails because of derogatory articles about the king and conservative government. Neble's lifelong egalitarian attitudes determined the *Pioneer*'s consistent attacks on American trusts and big business. By 1914 the *Pioneer* had a national circulation of nearly 40,000; no other Danish-American paper has had even a quarter as many subscribers. As a prominent ethnic leader, Neble practiced what he preached, combining nostalgic affection for the old country with practical achievement and patriotism for the new. In 1925 he was knighted by the Danish king as the major spokesman for Danish immigrants in the United States.

A more exclusively businesslike approach to journalism was taken by the "Danish Newspaper King," Christian Rasmussen (1852–1926). He ran a string of four weekly newspapers in Minnesota, Wisconsin, and Illinois; three magazines; and an advertising agency. He also published many Danish and Norwegian books at printing plants in Minneapolis and Chicago. Some of his magazines were long-lived. *Kvinden og Hjemmet* (The Woman and the Home; 1886–c. 1948) was edited

by two Norwegian sisters, one of whom was married to a Dane. It appeared in identical Dano-Norwegian and Swedish editions and attained a peak combined circulation of 80,000.

Danish-language newspapers, like all immigrant journalism, served three main functions: to teach newcomers about conditions in the United States, to maintain ties with the homeland by printing news from abroad, and to hold the ethnic group together by reporting its activities throughout the country. Until immigrants could read English, they needed general news in their own language.

The papers published by editors like Neble and Rasmussen were rurally oriented, quite different from the more sophisticated publications of the big cities. Representative of the city press, which was headed by journalists trained in Denmark and often from the upper class, was *Nordlyset* (The Northern Light; 1891–1953), published in New York. Another newspaper, *Bien* (The Bee), founded in San Francisco in 1882 and since 1975 published weekly in Los Angeles, illustrates the changes in content and function by the Danish press as its reading public became assimilated. General news and information about American conditions gave way to feature articles about Denmark, and finally the paper's main function became the reporting of ethnic group activities across the nation.

A total of 95 Danish, Dano-Norwegian, and Scandinavian newspapers have been published for and by Danes in the United States, 50 of which have used only the Danish language. In addition, 30 church periodicals have been published in Danish and 9 in English. These range from newsletters, children's magazines, and Christmas annuals to newspapers such as *Dannevirke* (Bulwark of Denmark; 1880–1951), oriented toward the Danish Lutheran Church in America. Besides newspapers and church periodicals, there have been 20 magazines in Danish and 17 in English, including journals of agriculture and dairying, humor magazines, almanacs, general family magazines, and journals about Denmark for the second generation. Among the English journals, *The American Dane Magazine* (circulation 9,500) has been published in Omaha since 1882, and *The Dana Review* (circulation 12,500) in Blair, Nebr., since 1945. *The Bridge*, a journal published by the Danish American Heritage Society, began publication in 1978.

Of the ethnic publications in Danish, only three survive: *Den Danske Pioneer* (circulation 3,800), *Bien* (circulation 3,598), and *Kirke og folk* (circulation 1,000). In 1976 the Danish American Language Foundation was incorporated in Illinois to administer a fund collected in Denmark during the American Bicentennial celebration to help maintain the three Danish-language publications.

Probably the best known Dane in the United States was Jacob Riis (1849–1914), muckraker, reformer, and author, who made his name not in ethnic but in American journalism. Called "New York's most useful citizen" by Theodore Roosevelt, Riis exposed the evils of the city's slums through his articles, pioneering photography, popular lectures, and books, the best known of which is *How the Other Half Lives* (1890).

Danish Americans contributed not only to journalism but also to belles-lettres. Danish-American literature began to appear in book form in the 1870s, reached full flower in the 1890s, and though declining in quantity after World War I, continued to appear in the 1930s. Danish Americans published fewer books than writers of the other Scandinavian groups, and the bulk of their fiction and poetry can be found only in periodical files. Little of it measures up to either American or Danish national literature in quality, but its quantity is impressive. The more serious Danish-American authors earned their living in professions that involved writing: the ministry, teaching, and journalism. A number of their works were also published in Denmark.

The three most effective writers in Danish were Adam Dan (1848–1931), Kristian Østergaard (1855–1931), and Carl Hansen (1860–1916). Anton Kvist (1878–1965), a Chicago bricklayer, was an outstanding poet. Both Dan and Østergaard were Gruntvigian ministers, and Dan was a founder of the Danish Lutheran Church in America. Regarded as the Grand Old Man of Danish-American culture, he wrote novels, short stories, poetry, travel accounts, and devotional literature throughout a long career. Østergaard founded and taught in Danish folk schools on both sides of the Atlantic, served in many churches, and wrote more books than any other Danish ethnic author. Hansen, a teacher, journalist, lecturer, and businessman, was a gifted writer of short stories.

The leading Danish-American author writing in English was Sophus Keith Winther. Born in Denmark in 1893, he grew up in Nebraska and became a professor of English. The first two novels in his trilogy (*Take All to Nebraska*, 1936; *Mortgage Your Heart*, 1937; and *This Passion Never Dies*, 1938) have recently been reissued. They portray the hard life of Danish tenant farmers in Nebraska.

FOLK CUSTOMS

In families that remain conscious of their Danish-American identity, some Old World customs have survived, especially those surrounding Christmas. The celebration on Christmas Eve includes a church service and a festive dinner, often with the traditional roast goose and red cabbage and always a rich rice pudding. Whoever finds the single whole almond in the pudding wins a marzipan prize. Gifts are opened after dinner. The custom of dancing or walking around the Christmas tree hand in hand while singing carols is followed not only at home but at Christmas programs in churches and lodges.

The other Danish holiday still widely celebrated is Constitution Day on June 5, although other dates in early summer may be substituted. The four Danish homes for old people in Chicago, Minneapolis, Minn., Croton, N.Y., and San Rafael, Calif., sponsor Constitution Day celebrations each year. A growing number of towns conscious of their Danish heritage also hold annual festivals that include folk dancing, gymnastics, traditional games, and booths that sell Danish pastries, especially *ebleskiver*, a sweet dumpling fried in a special pan. The oldest of these "Danish days," held in Solvang, Calif., has become a major tourist attraction since World War II.

TIES WITH THE HOMELAND

Danish emigrants in America established special ties with the homeland quite early. Shortly after the turn of

the century, Danish Americans purchased 200 acres of open moorland in northern Jutland for Denmark's first national park. The area, named Rebild National Park, was later greatly enlarged, and an emigrant museum was added in 1934. Since 1912, with the exception of the war years, thousands of Danes and Danish Americans have gathered there annually to celebrate the Fourth of July. The Rebild National Park Society in Ålborg, which organizes and finances these activities, has individual and group memberships in both countries, as well as a dozen local chapters in the United States. One of the first emigrant archives in the world, the Danes Worldwide Archives, was established at Ålborg in 1932.

The leading spirit behind Rebild was Dr. Max Henius (1859–1935), a native of Ålborg, who took his doctorate in Germany in 1881, then emigrated to Chicago, where he set up a laboratory specializing in the fermentation process and also a brewery school. In 1892 he proved that a recent typhoid epidemic had been caused by milk diluted with water from Lake Michigan, and the resultant outcry led to improved dairy standards and better public sanitation. Tireless in his efforts to build spiritual links between Denmark and the United States, Henius was for 30 years the undisputed leader of the Chicago Danish community.

Dansk Samvirke (The Association of Danes Abroad) was founded in Copenhagen in 1919. Well over 10 percent of its 7,000 worldwide members are in the United States and Canada. As the number of permanent emigrants has declined, the number of Danes temporarily residing abroad has increased. Dansk Samvirke provides both groups, as well as emigrants' descendants who know the language, with advice, information, and other services, such as the annual homecoming program for visiting Danes. Its publication, *Danmarksposten*, is issued eight times a year and is the only publication in Denmark exclusively for Danes overseas.

Charter flights and conducted tours to Denmark have become a frequent and popular activity of various Danish-interest organizations in the United States. Danish-American choruses still visit the homeland for concert tours, especially in connection with the Rebild festivals, and study groups hold short courses on folk-school campuses. A number of college students of Danish background spend their junior year abroad at Danish folk schools under the auspices of the Scandinavian Studies program, which in 1978 also opened a summer international study program at the Scandinavian Seminar College in Holte, a suburb of Copenhagen. The Dana College–Denmark Spring Semester at the University of Copenhagen offers courses, taught in English, in Scandinavian and Danish subjects.

ASSIMILATION

Danes adapted very rapidly to American life. Census figures on the parentage of immigrants' children show that Danes chose marriage partners outside their own group more frequently than did other Scandinavians. In 1910, for example, 72 percent of Swedish-American children had two Swedish-born parents, but only 57 percent of the Danish second generation had two Danish-born parents; 28 percent had one American parent, and 15 percent had one parent from another national group. Obviously, mixed marriages led to more rapid assimilation.

There is evidence that Danes also learned English more rapidly than many other immigrants. In 1911 a study of immigrants employed in mining and manufacturing reported that 97 percent of the Danes spoke English, as compared with 53 percent of all those polled. Yet the Danes had not been in the United States any longer than many of the newer immigrants, including those from southeastern Europe. English, however, is more closely related to Danish than to Slavic, Baltic, and the other languages of the recent arrivals, which helped the Danes learn it more quickly.

Danes assimilated more rapidly than other Scandinavians because they were fewer in number, arrived later, and were more thinly settled across the country. They formed only a handful of predominantly Danish settlements, had a low record of participation in the Danish Lutheran churches, and maintained fewer and smaller ethnic organizations. For a long time they lacked a historical society and still have no central archives in the United States. These characteristics inevitably led the majority of immigrants to lose their ethnic identification and to adapt quickly to American life.

Four other factors helped the Danes be readily accepted in the United States. They had a high rate of literacy, brought with them a Protestant faith and ethic, were familiar with a parliamentary political system, and were in general law-abiding. Since these are basic traits of American culture, Danish newcomers offered no threat to established Americans. On the contrary, they were welcomed wherever they went.

In spite of the loss of ethnicity by a majority of Danish Americans, a few ethnic organizations—churches, fraternities, and clubs—kept the heritage alive and maintained ties with the homeland. These organizations finally began to see the fruit of their labors in the 1970s, a decade of ethnic revival in the United States. More and more immigrants and their descendants were stimulated to claim and become familiar with the unique character of their Danish ancestry, resulting in an upsurge of activity and the formation of new organizations to cultivate their ethnic heritage.

Bibliography
Kristian Hvidt, *Flight to America: The Social Background of 300,000 Danish Emigrants* (New York, 1975), is a detailed and illuminating scholarly study of Danish emigration from 1868 to 1900. Hvidt, *Danes Go West: A Book about the Emigration to America* (Copenhagen, 1976), is a popularized account that includes the European background and statistics in *Flight to America* but revises some points of view and adds new information. Thomas Peter Christensen, *A History of the Danes in Iowa* (Solvang, Calif., 1952), contains an excellent summary of Danish immigrant history and is the definitive history of Danes in the most Danish of states.

The main studies of Danish-American Lutheranism are Paul C. Nyholm, *The Americanization of the Danish Lutheran Churches in America* (Copenhagen, 1963); John M. Jensen, *The United Evangelical Lutheran Church* (Minneapolis, Minn., 1964); and Enok Mortensen, *The Danish Lutheran Church in America: The History and Heritage of the American Evangelical Lutheran Church* (Philadelphia, 1967). Arlow W. Anderson, *The Salt of the Earth: A History of Norwegian-Danish Methodism in America* (Nashville, Tenn., 1962) treats another Scandinavian religious group.

The story of the two Danish-American colleges is told in William E. Christensen, *Saga of the Tower: A History of Dana College and Trinity Seminary* (Blair, Nebr., 1959), and Thorvald Hansen, *We Laid Foundation Here: The Early History of Grand View College* (Des Moines, 1972). Hansen, *School in the Woods* (Askov, Minn., 1977), recounts the troubled history of the first Danish-American Lutheran seminary, and Enok Mortensen, *Schools for Life: A Danish-American Experiment in Adult Education* (Askov, 1977) is the history of Grundtvigian folk schools in America. *Scandinavian Studies* 48 (Autumn 1976) contains

articles on Danish-American history, a survey of Danish-American literature, and a bibliography. The most complete bibliography is Enok Mortensen, *Danish-American Life and Letters* (Des Moines, Iowa, 1945).

The main U.S. archives are at Grand View College, Des Moines, Iowa, and Dana College, Blair, Nebr. Church materials are collected in the archives of the Lutheran Church in America at the Lutheran School of Theology, Chicago. Danish collections are in the Danes Worldwide Archives, Ålborg, and also at the Association of Danes Abroad, Copenhagen.

DOROTHY BURTON SKÅRDAL

DELAWARES: *see* AMERICAN INDIANS

DIEGUEÑOS: *see* AMERICAN INDIANS

DOMINICANS

Current estimates place the population of Dominicans in the United States at 300,000, of whom 200,000 are foreign-born and 100,000 are the descendants of immigrants. Illegal immigrants may account for several thousand more.

The homeland of these people is the Dominican Republic, a nation that, with Haiti, occupies the Caribbean island of Hispaniola. Its proximity to the United States (1,560 miles to New York City, 850 miles to Miami, and only 80 miles across the Mona Passage to Puerto Rico) has facilitated migration back and forth between the two nations.

The site of Columbus's first settlement, the Dominican Republic originated as a colony of the Spanish empire and was called Santo Domingo. The colonists attempted unsuccessfully to enslave the native Taino Indians, who were extinguished by disease and overwork within two generations of the Spaniards' arrival. Unlike many of the other Caribbean colonies, Santo Domingo did not initially develop a sugar-plantation economy; as a result, fewer African slaves were brought there than to adjacent island societies such as Haiti. Until the 20th century the Dominican Republic was relatively free from pressures of overpopulation.

Like many other Latin American nations, it was ruled until the early 19th century by Spain, and was peopled by migrants from a number of European countries, from various parts of Africa, and from the New World. When large-scale sugar production began late in the 19th century in the postemancipation period, black laborers were recruited from other Caribbean sugar-producing islands.

Hispaniola

Patterns of social stratification in the Dominican Republic are based on family, education, and economic status more than on race. In contrast to the United States, mulatto is an official category. A 1966 census showed that 77 percent of the population was mulatto, 12 percent white, and 11 percent black. Mulatto Dominicans often experience difficulty adjusting to what they perceive as sharper racial delineation in the United States, where they are considered black.

In the past half-century the population of the Dominican Republic has increased 450 percent. As the supply of available land was exhausted and meager industrial development created few opportunities, many Dominicans attempted to leave the island. Dominicans emigrated to the United States without restriction until the 30-year dictatorship (1930–1961) of Rafael Trujillo, when tightly controlled emigration permitted comparatively few Dominicans to leave. Following Trujillo's death and the subsequent political upheaval, the numbers arriving in the United States on immigrant visas soared. The volume of Dominican arrivals at five-year intervals from 1960 through 1975 demonstrates this increase. In 1960, 756 Dominicans entered the United States; 9,504 came in 1965; 10,807 in 1970; and 13,081 in 1975. In addition, a very large number of Dominican citizens have been admitted to U.S. territory as temporary visitors—57,704 in 1970 and 67,835 in 1975. Many Dominicans living in the United States overstay their visitors' visas and thus become illegal residents.

Although Dominicans are scattered throughout the United States, most have clustered in the urban areas of the Northeast, Florida, and Puerto Rico. Because of physical and linguistic similarities, on the mainland they are often mistaken for Puerto Ricans. This confusion often works to the advantage of both Dominicans and Puerto Ricans: illegal Dominican aliens frequently identify themselves as Puerto Ricans, who are U.S. citizens, thus facilitating their stay; the mainland Puerto Rican community gains greater political influence through greater numbers.

As among many groups of European immigrants, Dominican migration has occurred in a chainlike sequence, with one member of the family, usually a young male, beginning the process. After securing an economic foothold, he is able to obtain immigrant visas allowing family members to join him. Dominicans in the United States regularly send money to family members remaining in the Republic, a practice that strengthens ties to the homeland.

Dominicans have entered all occupational levels of American society. The fashion designer Oscar de la Renta is a Dominican immigrant, and a number of Dominican major-league baseball players have become well known to the public. The majority, however, hold lower-level service and manufacturing jobs in urban areas of the Northeast.

Dominican newcomers to the United States in the first half of the 20th century settled almost entirely in the New York City area in well-defined enclaves. In recent years many have resettled in other areas, moving along the northeastern seaboard into manufacturing cities as far north as Boston, and southward to Washington. As Miami's Spanish-speaking population has grown, increasing numbers of Dominicans have moved there.

During the early 1960s immigration characteristically occurred in a two-step process: Dominicans first moved from rural to urban areas—chiefly from the northern agricultural region of Cibao to the metropolis of Santo Domingo—and from there to the United States. Since then, as emigration became a central feature of the Dominican social process, the pattern has changed. Now a *campesino* (country person) is more likely to go directly from the farm to New York, and to originate from any region of the Republic. Dominicans in the United States—most of whom were raised in the home country—continue to perceive themselves as members of distinct social classes and regional groups.

Despite recent rapid urban growth, the population of the Dominican Republic remains primarily rural. Many of the present urban dwellers moved to the city only recently; consequently, the migrant population to the United States consists mainly of persons of rural origin. Educational levels are low; half the population in the Republic is illiterate. Many Dominicans, therefore, come to the United States with little education and few job skills. They enter the labor force as unskilled restaurant workers, machine operators in clothing manufacturing, assembly-line workers, and janitors. After long residence in the United States some have become owners of small stores and tourist agencies, subcontractors in the clothing industry, and nonunionized skilled workers. Because the burgeoning Spanish-speaking population in the United States has produced a need for bilingual white-collar workers, highly educated Dominicans increasingly are finding employment in local-government offices and businesses.

The recent migration of so many first-generation Dominicans has resulted in the transfer of the Republic's social patterns. In the New York City area many clubs and other kinds of associations appeal to the Dominican urban middle class. But they seldom include in their activities those who once were campesinos or working-class urban dwellers.

Dominicans in the United States maintain a strong interest in the political life of their homeland. A former president of the Republic is alleged to have plotted his political comeback in a Manhattan cafeteria. The party of his successor in office depended heavily on the support of Dominicans in the United States.

Modern forms of transportation and the proximity of the Dominican Republic to the United States allow for frequent return. The persistence of direct contact with the homeland, coupled with the growth of the Spanish-origin population in northeastern urban areas, have slowed acculturation to the dominant English-speaking society. Many immigrants assume that they will return to the Republic after accumulating sufficient capital to buy land, to establish a small business, or to retire; a large number have already gone back. Those who have adjusted to life in the United States and have made the decision to stay permanently are shaping a distinctive Dominican-American culture and are increasingly influenced by other Spanish-speaking groups.

The immigration laws facilitating family reunion permit the continuance of close ties characteristic of Dominican families, but in some ways they attenuate other family attachments. For example, American legal definitions of kinship relations are not always congruent with Dominican definitions: concubinage and po-

lygamy are acceptable forms of Dominican conjugal relations at all levels of society. Dominicans distinguish between *union libre* (free union), *matrimonio por la ley* (legal marriage), and *matrimonio por la iglesia* (ecclesiastical marriage); children born as a result of any of these unions are considered legitimate. The U.S. immigration law, however, does not recognize children of "free unions" as qualifying for visas, so they are often left behind. *Compadrazgo* or coparenthood relations further extend the kinship group. A Dominican couple may choose a *compadre* (fictive father) and *comadre* (fictive mother) for their child at a major occasion such as baptism. The rights and obligations resulting from the relationship between the real parents and the fictive parents are often regarded as more binding than those between siblings.

The extended family which includes compadrazgo relations has traditionally furnished the organizational unit for group activity in Dominican society. Political factionalism based on family ties and distrust of persons outside the family circle has impeded the formation of organizations such as labor unions, political parties, and cooperative marketing associations.

The extended family network also shapes the associational life of Dominicans in the United States and combines with regional attachments and class interests to limit membership in organizations. Although dozens of Dominican clubs, societies, and political organizations are active in New York City, no organization to this date has had a broad enough appeal to claim to represent the full spectrum of groups in the Dominican community.

The Catholic church is the one institution with which the majority of Dominicans identify, but there are no separate Dominican parishes. Moreover, a number of Dominicans are members of fundamentalist denominations. A few are adherents of cult religions that combine African and Christian religious elements, but they are far less numerous than among immigrants from Puerto Rico, Cuba, and other islands of the West Indies.

The feature of Dominican social life that has undergone the most dramatic change after migration is probably the position of women. Dominican women have taken advantage of new opportunities to work, with significant impact upon family relationships: the families of working women remain smaller than the average family in which the housewife is not employed, and the traditional authority of Dominican men has been undermined by the working wife's role as a much-needed wage-earner. Working women frequently influence their husbands to spend more time at home and to pay less attention to other women.

Dominican immigrants are eager to educate their children and often make economic sacrifices to send them to parochial schools, which they prefer to public institutions. Education for their children represents a key step toward the social and economic advancement these newcomers seek in the United States.

At present it appears that the Dominicans' assimilation into the mainstream of American society has not proceeded very far. However, in terms of the Hispanic-American culture emerging along the eastern U.S. seaboard, their adaptation has been considerable. On an individual basis, though, the degree to which each Do-

minican family assimilates is often a function of its socioeconomic status prior to migration, the degree of social mobility during residence in the United States, and the extent to which the physical features of its members are associated with American racial stereotypes.

Bibliography

There are few scholarly accounts of Dominicans in the United States. The most complete study is Glenn Hendricks, *The Dominican Diaspora* (New York, 1974), an anthropological look at Dominican villagers and their life in New York. A Spanish translation of this work with an added chapter on the effects of migration on one village is *Los Dominicanos Ausentes* (Santo Domingo, 1978). Nancie L. González, "Peasant's Progress: Dominicans in New York," *Caribbean Studies* 10 (October 1970): 154–171, examines immigration from the point of view of Dominican newcomers. Anthropologist Vivian Garrison has studied mental health and religious cults of Spanish-origin groups in the New York metropolitan area. She reports on the psychological and social effects of shifting male roles in "A Case of a Dominican Migrant," in Roy S. Bryce-LaPorte and Claudewell S. Thomas, eds., *Alienation in Contemporary Society* (New York, 1976). Changes in women's roles are treated in Nancie González, "Multiple Migratory Experiences of Dominican Women," *Anthropological Quarterly* 49 (January 1976): 36–44.

GLENN HENDRICKS

DUTCH

The Dutch presence in America dates from Henry Hudson's explorations in the *Half Moon* in 1609. Five years later the Dutch built Fort Nassau (later Fort Orange) near present-day Albany, N.Y. In 1624 this fur-trading post became part of the Dutch West India Company's colony of New Netherland and was joined in 1626 by the settlement of New Amsterdam on Manhattan Island. Despite the indifferent success of the col-

ony over the next few decades, the Dutch were firmly rooted in the Hudson and Delaware river valleys before the English took over the area in 1664. The first federal census of 1790 indicates that 100,000 people of Dutch birth or ancestry were then living in the United States, 80,000 of them within a 50-mile radius of New York City, where they formed one-sixth of the population.

Because of this clustering pattern, which has always characterized Dutch settlement in America, the Dutch have had a greater visibility than their numbers warrant. In 1970 they ranked only 18th in size among immigrant groups in America, with 110,000 members of the first generation and 273,000 members of the second generation. The Dutch-born and their descendants of all generations number an estimated 4 million. The primary settlement area is the northern Midwest, within a 50-mile semicircle around the shoreline of Lake Michigan from Muskegon to Green Bay. Secondary areas are New York and northern New Jersey, northwestern Iowa (and adjacent counties in southwestern Minnesota and southeastern South Dakota), and southern and central California.

Unlike other western European nations in the 19th century, Holland experienced no mass migration like the one that emptied a third to a half of the Irish countryside; group migration affected only a few villages and for only short periods. Few of the Dutch who emigrated were driven by a desperate struggle to survive. Most of them made a conscious calculation that the future promised more prosperity for them and their children in America than at home. Cultural and religious motives were secondary except among a few thousand Quakers and Mennonites in the 17th century and among several thousand dissenters from the national church in the 1840s. Nor did libertarian political ideals attract Dutchmen to America as they did German forty-eighters. "Family, faith, farming" were the Netherlanders' watchwords, not "liberty, fraternity, equality."

The nation of the Dutch—the Netherlands—is, together with Belgium and Luxembourg, one of the Low Countries on the northwestern coast of Europe. The Germanic peoples of this region remained on the fringes of Roman civilization until the Middle Ages. In the 15th and early 16th centuries the small principalities in the region were gradually consolidated under Catholic Hapsburg rule. This development was ended by the spread of Calvinist Protestantism after 1550 and the abdication a few years later of Charles V in favor of his militantly Catholic son, Philip II of Spain. Philip resorted to force to hold his northern possessions for the church and crown, but the seven provinces under Protestant rule north of the Scheldt River—led successively in the 16th and early 17th centuries by the able William the Silent, prince of Orange; Johan van Oldenbarneveldt; and William's son, Maurice of Nassau—successfully revolted and finally won independence from Spain. In 1648 the Dutch republic was officially established as a Protestant state linked with the privileged Dutch Reformed Church.

During the 17th century the Netherlands enjoyed its golden age, when Holland's merchant princes founded a worldwide commercial empire with colonies in Asia, Africa, and the Americas. Beginning in the 18th century, Dutch glory became tarnished by defeats at the

hands of more powerful neighbors—England, France, and much later, Germany. Napoleon controlled the nation from 1806 to 1813, but the Congress of Vienna (1815) reestablished an independent Dutch state and united it with the ten Belgian provinces. The Belgians rebelled in 1830, however, and won their independence, taking all but two of the Catholic provinces in the south, Limburg and North Brabant, which remain today the overwhelmingly Catholic part of the Netherlands. Dutch borders have remained unchanged since the 1830s. The original Protestant majority has gradually given way before growing Catholic and secularist minorities so that today Protestants, Catholics, and secularists are about equal in number.

The vast majority of the Dutch in America are Hollanders who speak the Dutch language. Next numerically are Frisians, who constitute a national minority in the Netherlands and Germany; their language is related to but distinct from Dutch. Two smaller subgroups in America are the Flemish-speaking Belgians from the southern Netherlands, whose language is virtually identical to Dutch; and the Dutch-speaking people of German background from Graafschap Bentheim and Ost Friesland. Although the Dutch language is a Low German linguistic form and the word "Dutch" is philologically the same as "Deutsch," the Dutch in America have always carefully maintained their separate identity, even to the point of calling Germans "Duitschers" and themselves "Hollanders" or "Netherlanders." U.S. Census reports and statistical compilations referring to the mother tongue have always followed the country-of-origin principle; that is, they include Dutch and Frisians born in the Netherlands, but exclude Flemings from Belgium and Dutch- and Frisian-speakers from Germany, even though the latter groups may associate and intermarry with Dutch Americans. (See also Frisians.)

MIGRATION

Dutch immigration to North America has been continuous since the early 17th century, but the rate and type of movement have differed over time. There were three distinct phases: the immigration occasioned by the commercial expansion of the 17th century, the free immigration of the 19th and 20th centuries, and the planned immigration following World War II.

Colonization of New Netherland began as an adjunct to the fur-trading ventures of the Dutch West India Company. Few families wished to migrate to North America, however, given the dangerous ocean passage, the harsh wilderness and Indian hostility, the company's economic restrictions, and a feudal land system dominated by all-powerful patroons, or proprietors. As a result, the colony primarily attracted religious refugees and the poverty-stricken—Belgian Walloons, French Huguenots, Italian Waldensians, Dutch soldiers and Jewish settlers from an aborted Brazilian colony, teenagers from Dutch poorhouses and orphan asylums, families of unemployed day laborers from Amsterdam, agricultural tenants from landed estates, and a few political visionaries. Even among these people, who emigrated under duress at company or government expense, hundreds remigrated. Thus by 1664, when the English seized control of the colony, fewer than 10,000

European settlers (of whom 30 percent were non-Dutch) were living in the inland valleys of the Hudson and Delaware rivers and on Manhattan and western Long Island.

The loss of New Netherland caused a hiatus in Dutch colonization until the 1830s and 1840s. A sporadic trickle of settlers continued during the colonial era, however: primarily working-class families, plus some merchants who opened offices in American port cities, and Dutch Reformed clergymen to serve the nearly 100 churches already established in America. William Penn attracted to his colony several groups of Dutch Quakers and Mennonites who were among the founders of Germantown. Labadists from West Friesland, members of a communitarian sect who were ostracized at home, found refuge in Maryland in 1684, but their community eventually failed.

Throughout the 18th century the original Dutch colonists in the New York area multiplied in accordance with the prevailing cultural pattern of large families. As farm land became scarce in the older settlements, young families and newlyweds pushed northward into virgin land along the Hudson tributaries—the Harlem, East, Mohawk, and Pocantico rivers. Others moved southward into New Jersey, following the Hackensack, Passaic, and Raritan river systems. Some families crossed the Delaware River into Bucks County, Pa., and later, in the 1760s, more than 150 families settled in the southeastern part of the state. In the 1780s Dutch families pushed into central New York, and a few went as far as the Kentucky frontier. By the early 19th century a few Dutchmen were starting farms in western New York and the Great Lakes area. Thus Dutch farmers were in the vanguard of the northern colonial frontier, although New York remained the nucleus of the community.

Unlike the minimal and commercial migration of the early colonial era, the great migration that began in the mid-19th century was a free movement that brought 250,000 Dutch peasants and rural artisans and their families to America. This migration reduced by approximately 5 to 8 percent the total population of the Netherlands, which increased from 3.1 million in 1850 to 5.1 million in 1900.

The migration began in the 1830s as a sporadic movement of a few venturesome individuals and families seeking economic betterment, probably in response to the pressures of population growth since the 1750s. In the mid-1840s the group phase began, influenced by the example of German mass migration and triggered by a potato crop failure and a pietistic revolt against the Dutch Reformed Church. Beginning in 1845 and continuing for a decade, neighborhood, kinship, and religious groups, numbering more than 20,000 people, emigrated en masse, including entire congregations of Seceders and Roman Catholics led by their pastors or dominies (Dutch dominee) and priests. Some 1,000 followers of Dominie Albertus C. Van Raalte (1811–1876) located in southwestern Michigan on the shores of Lake Michigan and called their settlement Holland. Dominie Hendrik Pieter Scholte (1805–1868) took his congregation of 900 to the prairies of central Iowa and founded the community of Pella. Father Theodorus Johannes Vanden Broek (1783–1851) led 350 to the Fox River Valley of Wisconsin where he created the major Catho-

lic Dutch colony in America, which soon grew to 40,000.

The U.S. economic panic of 1857 and the outbreak of the Civil War stemmed and altered the character of the Dutch exodus. In the Netherlands, too, economic improvement and the provision of protection for religious dissenters in the constitution of 1848 removed two major stimuli of emigration. During the American Civil War and increasingly in the postbellum decades, the composition of the emigration shifted to families and individuals rather than congregations or large neighborhood groups. Many of the later 19th-century emigrants left the same communities that had been touched previously by emigration fever. This chain migration, stimulated by letters from family and friends in America, continued to draw people from the areas first affected, mainly the Achterhoek (Backcorner) along the German border and the regions of sea-clay soil along the North Sea. Other areas remained unaffected.

After the Civil War the rate of emigration peaked and waned in response to a variety of factors. The major peaks were in the years 1880–1893, 1903–1914, and 1920–1928, and the major troughs came in periods of depression and war—the 1870s, 1890s, the World War I years, and the decade of the Great Depression. In the 1880s a serious agricultural crisis in the northern Netherlands caused nearly 75,000 people to emigrate to the United States before the panic of 1893 halted the flow. From 1900 to 1914 another 75,000 Dutch settlers passed through Ellis Island. In the 1920s about 35,000 Dutch aliens arrived. From 1931 to 1945 the Great Depression and World War II reduced the number of Dutch immigrants to a mere 7,500, half of whom fled the Nazi occupation. In the two decades after 1945 about 80,000 Dutch came to the United States. Since the late 1960s the migration has waned. Over the years comparatively few Dutch have remigrated: the estimated return rate was 15 percent for 1875–1913, and only 13 percent for 1944–1952.

Social characteristics of the 19th-century migration can be determined from the *Landverhuizers* (emigration) lists compiled by the Dutch government, which cover virtually all emigration before 1880, emigration to all lands, not just to the United States. Of more than 60,000 emigrants in the period 1835–1880, fewer than 5,000 lived in the major seaport cities of Amsterdam and Rotterdam and in the government center of The Hague; the remainder were from rural villages and the countryside. Farmers and day laborers made up 55 percent of the family heads or single individuals; 20 percent were village craftsmen. Less than 15 percent were professionals, businessmen, and white-collar commercial people. There was a vast exodus of the rural poor: nearly 25 percent of the emigrants were "without means," and many of these were on the public dole. Only 13 percent were well-to-do; moreover, 4 out of every 10 of these prosperous families or individuals migrated to Dutch colonies in Indonesia or South Africa. In contrast, 96 percent of those in average circumstances and 85 percent of the very poor chose the United States as their new home.

Religious forces may have prompted some of the Dutch to depart. More than 10 percent of all emigrants from the province of North Holland to New York City were Jews from Amsterdam. This group, which amounted to only 1 percent of all Dutch emigrants in the 19th century, had a larger proportion of poor (29 percent) than any other group. Roman Catholics and Seceders contributed 20 and 13 percent respectively to the total migration.

Economic reasons, however, motivated most of those emigrating. Rising birth rates and living costs, periodic food shortages, plant and livestock diseases, unequal and heavy taxation, and a generally gloomy prospect at home made American land and wage opportunities seem increasingly attractive—an impression reinforced by letters from Dutch immigrants to friends and relatives in the old country. Many such letters appeared in the Dutch press, accompanied by rebuttals and admonitions from Dutch officials, clergymen, and liberal intellectuals, all of whom viewed emigration as unpatriotic, economically detrimental, and morally and spiritually debilitating.

On the whole, official policy in the Netherlands neither hindered free migration nor attempted to control and supervise it. Some private and religious organizations tried to help the emigrants, such as the Utrecht Christian Association for Emigration and the New York–based Netherlands Society for the Protection of Emigrants from Holland. But ultimately relatives who had previously immigrated and Dutch-American church communities provided most of the necessary assistance to newcomers. The Old Dutch in the United States, prosperous and well established after many generations, had retained a strong religious and cultural identity with the homeland even though most had lost command of their native tongue. They warmly welcomed the new immigrants into their homes and churches and provided advice and financial assistance.

The third and final phase of Dutch immigration to the United States began after World War II, when free migration gave way to a planned migration. The Great Depression and the war had so weakened the Dutch economy that the nation could no longer provide for its people, especially since the Netherlands had had the highest birth rate in northwestern Europe: its population had doubled between 1900 and 1950. The war had brought six years of Nazi occupation, the massive bombing of Rotterdam, the deportation to Germany of 500,000 forced laborers, the mass killing of most Dutch Jews, the inundation by salt water of much farm land, and the loss of the Indonesian empire. As a result of these disasters and postwar Soviet expansion in Europe, the Dutch again became emigration-minded. Surveys in 1948 revealed that 33 percent of all Hollanders seriously considered leaving the homeland. In a major shift of policy in 1949, the Dutch government decided to encourage resettlement abroad by subsidizing transportation and negotiating agreements with receiving countries such as Canada and Australia. The United States remained the favored destination, but the immigration system based on quotas by national origin enacted in the 1920s now had a telling impact: the annual Dutch quota was only 3,136, and by 1952 the waiting list was 40,000. This dismal situation induced nearly a million postwar Dutch emigrants to settle in Canada, Australia, or elsewhere.

Congress, cognizant of Dutch difficulties, allowed several notable exceptions to the quota restriction. The Refugee Relief Act of 1953 authorized visas for 17,000

Netherlanders displaced from their homes, including refugees from the disastrous delta flood of 1953 and repatriates from Indonesia. Congressional acts of 1958 and 1960 allowed another 10,000 Dutch nationals displaced by Indonesian independence to enter the country above quota limits. This law created a significant breach in the national-origins quota system; it was the first instance in which "refugee" was defined in nonpolitical terms. Altogether 31,000 Dutch Indonesians resettled in the United States between 1958 and 1962. Unlike newcomers from the Netherlands, they did not congregate in Dutch communities, and have rapidly assimilated.

The 80,000 Dutch nationals who entered the United States between 1945 and 1965 were 19 percent of the total Dutch emigration in the postwar decades. Canada received 35 percent (152,000) and Australia 29 percent (125,000); South Africa and New Zealand accepted 8 and 6 percent respectively. In 1965 Congress replaced the national-origins system with quotas based on needed skills. When the law took effect in 1968, however, unprecedented economic prosperity in the Netherlands had brought large-scale emigration to a halt. Fewer than 1,000 Netherlanders per year have migrated to the United States since that date.

After the war the composition of Dutch immigration also changed. Among immigrants with church affiliations, orthodox Calvinists and Roman Catholics became more numerous than members of the state church. Orthodox Calvinists, who stood in the tradition of the 19th-century Seceders, predominated in the years 1948–1952, and many Roman Catholics immigrated in 1958–1962. Farmers and rural day laborers, long in the majority, gradually gave way to skilled industrial workers, engineers, technicians, and professionals. Farmers declined from 48 percent in 1948 to only 1 percent in the period 1966–1968.

This occupational shift led to different settlement patterns. In the 19th century more than 90 percent of Dutch immigrants entered via New York harbor and moved inland along the Erie Canal and Great Lakes to Michigan, Illinois, Iowa, and Wisconsin. In 1880, 41,000 of 58,000 Dutch-born inhabitants lived in the Great Lakes region, primarily in rural communities, and most of the remainder lived in the East. In contrast, in 1970 the postwar immigrants were overwhelmingly settled in coastal metropolitan areas such as Los Angeles and New York City and its New Jersey suburbs rather than in the traditional midwestern Dutch communities. The immigrant patterns thus reflected the evolution from rural to urban societies in both the Netherlands and the United States: the farming frontier of the mid-19th century had given way to commercial and corporate farming, and many of the rural towns and villages that formerly attracted the Dutch had grown into medium-sized cities or had been absorbed by expanding metropolitan areas.

SETTLEMENT PATTERNS

Although the Netherlands is a small country, its people are culturally diverse and unusually attached to their own localities. Dutch social scientists in the late 19th century identified nearly 100 distinct subregions based on variations in dialect, religion, soil type, and economic activity. A Netherlander's province or municipality often took pride of place over the nation.

Immigrants carried this localism to America and frequently tried to create segregated enclaves within the larger Dutch communities. This pattern was particularly evident in the colony of Holland, Mich. The central town, called simply *de stad*, was founded in 1847 largely by people from Gelderland and Overijssel provinces. Within two years, new arrivals founded villages within a 10-mile radius bearing the provincial names of Zeeland, Vriesland, Groningen, Overisel, North Holland, Drenthe, and Geldersche Buurt (Gelderland Neighborhood), or the municipal names Zutphen, Nordeloos, Hellendoorn, Harderwijk, and Staphorst. There was even a settlement called Graafschap, consisting of Dutch-speaking, Reformed Church Germans from Bentheim in Hanover. The majority of settlers in these villages originated in the place bearing the village name; they spoke the local dialect and perpetuated local customs of food and dress. The entire Michigan settlement was known as *de Kolonie*, but it required the passing of the first generation before the colony became a common community.

The Pella, Iowa, and Chicago settlements, also founded in 1847, similarly had particular regional origins. The majority of the Pella settlers came from the cities of Utrecht and Amsterdam. In Chicago, immigrants from the province of South Holland located their community in the Calumet district of south Chicago, calling their village first Lage (Low) Prairie and later South Holland. Meanwhile, other immigrants from the province of North Holland founded their settlement six miles north in Hooge (High) Prairie (later Roseland), while another group from Groningen Province established themselves slightly west of the center of Chicago in a neighborhood popularly known as the Groningsche Hoek (Groningen Quarter). As in the Kolonie in Michigan, this type of localism did not survive the first generation. Common struggles to adjust to the larger community forced the Dutch to abandon their particularism, except for festive, ritual occasions when local dress and foods appeared.

By World War I Dutch communities were thriving in every state along the northern tier from New York to the Rockies. Most settlements were rural, but Dutch neighborhoods also existed in major cities and developing industrial centers along the main transportation corridor from the port of New York to the Great Lakes—Paterson, N.J., Albany, Rochester, Buffalo, Cleveland, Detroit, Grand Rapids, Chicago, and Milwaukee. The Dutch urban ghettos, settled by the initial wave of immigrants at mid-century, expanded slowly compared to the growth in rural areas, where the majority of newly arriving immigrants chose to settle.

Dutch internal migration patterns differed in rural and urban communities, but movement was generally from one Dutch settlement to another. In rural areas parent colonies expanded by establishing daughter colonies some distance away. In the mid-19th century the primary colonies were Holland, Mich., and Pella and Orange City, Iowa. Within 30 years (1880) the Holland Kolonie in Ottawa County had expanded into five adjacent counties and one small settlement 100 miles north. By 1900 people from these areas had settled in the Upper Peninsula and also in or near Detroit. As a re-

sult of the subcolonization process the Dutch and their descendants today are the largest ethnic group in western Michigan, numbering at least 150,000. In Grand Rapids in 1959, after decades of industrial growth and heavy in-migration, one-quarter of the population was still of Dutch ancestry.

Pella also claims to be the "mother of colonies," but its brood compared to that of the Michigan Kolonie was small. At the close of the Civil War a local resident called Pella a "beehive ready for swarming." Farmland in Iowa at that time fetched $60 an acre and was scarce at that price. In 1870 some 50-odd families trekked in a wagon caravan to Sioux County in the northwest of the state, where they became homesteaders. Cheap land around the new colony of Orange City soon attracted settlers from overpopulated Dutch colonies in Wisconsin and Michigan as well as immigrants directly from the Netherlands. By 1900 almost every township in Sioux County was filled with Dutch settlers, and they spilled over into adjoining counties and also across the border into southwestern Minnesota (around Edgerton) and westward into South Dakota. Subsequently, the Orange City settlement played an important part in the Dutch movement to the Pacific Northwest in the first two decades of the 20th century. By 1920 at least 5,000 first- and second-generation Hollanders lived at Lynden in western Washington (the largest Dutch settlement on the Pacific Coast), on Whidbey Island, and in the Yakima River Valley. Several thousand Dutch also migrated to Montana and Utah at this period. The Utah settlers were Mormon proselytes from the Netherlands.

In rising metropolitan centers such as Chicago, Milwaukee, and Grand Rapids the Dutch immigration pattern differed from that of the rural areas. It was both centripetal and centrifugal. The cities initially served as magnets that attracted Dutch settlers from nearby rural villages and farms. Several pioneer Dutch communities near Milwaukee, for example, lost virtually all their families to the metropolis. Simultaneously, as the city cores became industrialized and densely populated, the Dutch tended to move outward in concentric circles. The more affluent moved into more comfortable and attractive suburbs, and those who preferred to continue truck gardening resettled beyond the suburban limits, moving repeatedly as the city expanded.

The Dutch Calvinists in Chicago and its environs exemplify this urban pattern. Initially, in the 1840s, Chicago Hollanders founded three core communities: the near–West Side settlement of Groningers, a working-class group of teamsters, peddlers, and day laborers employed in the central city; Roseland, a truck-gardening settlement 14 miles south of the city; and South Holland, a general farming settlement 20 miles southeast. These communities grew slowly but steadily until the 1880s and 1890s, when a new affluence, urban sprawl, and a renewed wave of immigration from the Netherlands created a mass uprooting. Land became scarce in the two farming communities; at the same time other ethnic groups, such as Italians and Greeks, began to encroach on the West Side settlement. Within a generation the entire West Side Dutch community sold their homes, churches, and Christian day-school building and moved two miles west along Roosevelt Road to the Douglas Park–Lawndale district. A few West Siders went seven miles south to the vegetable farms of En-

glewood, where they were joined by new immigrants— victims of the agricultural crisis of the 1880s—from the provinces of Groningen and Friesland. Other West Siders opened truck farms in the western suburbs of Bellwood and Maywood and the southwestern suburb of Summit.

The Roseland vegetable gardeners were invaded in the 1880s by such industrial firms as the Pullman Palace Car Company, International Harvester, Sherwin-Williams Paint Company, and the Illinois Central Railroad yards and shops—all of which attracted tens of thousands of Slavic and southern European laborers. Most of the Dutch farmers who had bought their land in 1849 for $5 per acre now sold it for $2,000 and more per acre. Many who chose to adapt to urban life remained in Roseland, but others bought farms in South Holland or in northern Indiana. A few moved a short distance north to Englewood where vegetable farming remained viable. Every location, of course, contained a Dutch Reformed community complete with churches, Christian day schools, and shops.

The second phase of Dutch resettlement in Chicago occurred from the 1920s through the 1940s in response to the continuing influx of new laboring groups from different ethnic backgrounds—the same pressure that had prompted the migration of the West Side community before World War I. The expansion of the South Side black community into West Side districts added new impetus to the removal. Within a generation the Douglas Park–Lawndale Dutch community, now numbering over 2,000, moved farther west to the adjoining suburbs of Cicero, Berwyn, and Oak Park; they purchased land and built six churches and a Christian day school. The Dutch shopkeepers, merchants, morticians, lawyers, and dentists from the old neighborhood eventually followed their customers and clients.

After World War II the inexorable flight to the suburbs continued as the rapidly expanding black community of the South Side and West Side pressed against the Dutch communities. Within barely 20 years, the Dutch enclaves in Englewood and Roseland and more than half the West Side group resettled. The Englewood Dutch, many of whom had immigrated from the Netherlands after World War I, moved a short distance into the southwest suburbs of Evergreen Park and Oak Lawn, and a few families pushed farther outward to Worth, Palos Heights, Orland Park, and Tinley Park. Roseland Hollanders joined the westward trek or went southeast to the South Holland–Lansing area or farther east into suburban Lake County, Ind. The West Side Dutch continued to move into the far western suburbs of Western Springs, Maywood, La Grange, Elmhurst, Lombard, Wheaton, and Des Plaines. Before World War II Des Plaines contained a small group of Dutch truck gardeners, but the expansion of nearby O'Hare International Airport and the concomitant industrial development drove the small farmers into blue-collar jobs or retirement. Professional and white-collar Dutch families from the West Side joined the farm remnant in Des Plaines after the war, and the Dutch community now seems stable.

Thus, in the course of 125 years the Protestant Hollanders of Chicago by a series of community migrations entirely abandoned the inner city for the suburbs. Although they number only 30,000 to 40,000 out of a pop-

ulation of several million in Greater Chicago, their religious solidarity, their practice of marrying within the group, and their clustering tendency have enabled them to retain their ethnic identity for four or five generations. Given the existence of churches and Christian day schools in each cluster area, the Chicago Dutch could choose the way of life they preferred—urban, suburban, or rural—without jeopardizing their ethnoreligious solidarity. Ethnic communities in that area, however, are breaking down more rapidly than ever before, and one cannot predict whether Dutch solidarity will survive one or two more generations.

ECONOMIC LIFE

Immigrant Hollanders typically were rural folk—farmers, laborers, and artisans—who brought to the United States an ethic of hard work, practical farming methods, and a strong desire for agricultural land. Their prosperous settlements throughout the Midwest and the northern plains states attest to this land hunger. Except for the Dutch Jews of New York City and the Protestant enclaves in Paterson, Passaic, Cleveland, Detroit, Chicago, Grand Rapids, and Milwaukee, most of the Dutch pursued farming. Those near metropolitan centers engaged in vegetable gardening, often after laboriously draining swampy lands that others had passed over. They supplied cauliflower, cabbage, onions, and especially celery to urban wholesale markets. Onions came from South Holland, celery from Kalamazoo and Hudsonville, Mich., and from Celeryville, Ohio, and tomatoes and melons from Des Plaines. Dairying was a natural specialty for Hollanders in Wisconsin, Michigan, New York, and Washington. In Iowa, Minnesota, the Dakotas, and elsewhere on the plains, however, the Dutch adopted American methods of mixed grain and livestock farming on extensive acreages. Fishing and bulb growing, although traditional in the homeland, attracted few immigrant practitioners, except for a Zeeland fishery at Sayville, N.Y., and bulb fields at Grand Rapids, Kankakee, Ill., and Puget Sound, Wash.

Between 1880 and 1920 the United States rapidly became urbanized, and the Dutch likewise moved to the cities. By the latter date 56 percent of Dutch first- and second-generation immigrants lived in urban areas. But compared to other foreign-born whites, the Dutch ranked forty-sixth among 50 nationalities in percentage of urban residents. Only the Norwegians, Finns, Danes, and Mexicans were more rural. Of the urban Dutch, only 36,000 lived in the 25 principal U.S. cities; the remainder were inhabitants of smaller towns.

Dutch immigrants in the 19th century were artisans and rural laborers who understood simple mechanics but not a factory system with sophisticated machinery. Those who settled in the cities, however, easily adjusted to industrial work, as did the sons of rural immigrants who gravitated from farms to cities. By 1880 the Grand Rapids furniture industry, largely Dutch owned and manned, was nationally known. The Pullman company in Roseland, the Paterson textile mills, and lumber mills in rural Michigan and Wisconsin also attracted an increasing number of Dutch workers in the late 19th century.

Most urban Dutch preferred to remain independent. They opened small shops to cater to an almost exclusively Dutch clientele, or they penetrated the service sector, becoming building contractors, general teamsters, and refuse haulers. Groningers of Chicago's West Side, for example, took advantage of their initial location near the downtown area to become refuse haulers and teamsters. By the mid-20th century they virtually monopolized the commercial refuse business in the city and both the residential and commercial business in many suburbs. After World War II the hard-driving and prosperous refuse haulers expanded to Denver, Dallas, Milwaukee, Phoenix, and elsewhere. Many of them incorporated and in the 1950s became subsidiaries of two rubbish conglomerates whose stocks are traded on the New York Stock Exchange: Waste Management, Inc., with headquarters in Oak Brook, Ill., and assets of over $200 million, and the even larger Houston-based Browning Ferris Industries.

As the third, fourth, and fifth generations attained higher levels of education, the Dutch moved increasingly into the professions, white-collar jobs in the civil service, and corporate management positions. An occupational survey in 1969 of all Christian Reformed household heads revealed that 41 percent held white-collar positions, 33 percent were blue-collar workers, and only 14 percent were farmers. For religious reasons, orthodox Calvinist Dutch workers traditionally opposed the secular American craft and industrial unions. Indeed, until as recently as 1950, holding a union card precluded members in some churches from being nominated for ecclesiastical offices. A 1959 survey of male members of three Christian Reformed churches in Grand Rapids found that 35 percent believed that lay church leaders ought not to hold membership in an AFL-CIO or other secular union, and 27 percent believed that no Christian should hold membership. Negative responses would have been much higher in rural areas. Wherever possible, Dutch workers have remained nonunion or formed independent locals based on Christian principles, such as the Christian Labor Association, which flourished for a time in the 1950s in Michigan and Illinois and remains strong in Ontario, Canada.

SOCIAL STRUCTURE

Dutch American economic and social life, at least among the Protestant majority, was heavily influenced by the religious nature of their social organization. Hollanders in America are notorious for their clannishness even among the fifth and sixth generations. The 19th-century immigrants and their kin settled in self-contained neighborhoods where they established formal and informal associations to maintain ethnic and religious ties. These associations permitted gradual acculturation but retarded assimilation. The goals of each community were ethnoreligious continuity and economic security. In stable agricultural communities and the small towns where for many decades 90 percent or more of the populace was Dutch, it was easier to maintain the group.

Dutch cohesiveness remained nearly as strong even in rapidly growing large cities. The West Side Chicago Dutch community, for example, included a full complement of Dutch-owned shops, professional offices, service businesses, a community newspaper, *Onze Toekomst* (Our Future, 1894–1952), and even a Dutch section, identified by a decorative windmill, in one of

the local cemeteries. The Chicago area Dutch Protestant community was further sustained by an institutional network of churches; by parent-owned Christian day schools, high schools, and a liberal arts college (Trinity Christian College, f. 1959); and by special associations providing residential and nursing homes for the aged and schooling for the handicapped and retarded. Thus it was (and to a lesser degree still is) possible for Dutch Americans to proceed from cradle to grave without leaving the primary associations of the ethnic community. Even secondary associations such as employment were a group responsibility, because it was customary and expected for the Dutch to employ compatriots.

Because of strong and close group ties, social stratification and economic inequality were not pronounced among the Dutch. Stratification often became apparent in little things such as possession of the newest household appliances or a luxury automobile. Home ownership was a mark of success achieved by most of the thrifty Dutch: in Grand Rapids a higher proportion of Hollanders than any other ethnic group owned their own homes. The suburban migration eventually offered greater opportunities for social advancement, but group cohesiveness persists.

The cement in community relationships in the new country, as in the old, was the church and its dominie. Often a man of superior education, the dominie in the earliest days served not only as spiritual adviser but also, especially in rural colonies, as promoter, realtor, banker, newspaper editor, and leading politician. As the pioneer settlements prospered and new colonies formed, successful businessmen and lawyers soon challenged the dominies' economic and political leadership; but in religious and cultural matters, the dominies set the tone of group life for generations. Only since World War II have lay leadership and influence become significant.

"The Dutch immigrant's home was his castle," declared historian Henry Lucas; "the world and its cares rarely crossed its threshold." Family life was closely knit, warm, and strongly patriarchal, although women sometimes managed the family and often shared in its business affairs. Families were large—in the 19th century a dozen children were not unusual and six were common. There are no early statistics on family size, but a 1963 survey of married couples in the Christian Reformed Church found that white-collar families averaged 3.0 children, blue-collar families 3.2, and farm families 3.5. Young children shared in household chores, and teenagers sought outside jobs to supplement family income. Immigrant girls and young women were especially popular as domestics and young men as unskilled laborers. The family diet was monotonous but adequate, with a heavy emphasis on bread, potatoes, vegetables, and dairy and poultry products. Salt pork and bacon added flavor to the potatoes, but until recently beef was seldom eaten.

Family ties remain strong and are nurtured by weekly coffee klatches in homes following Sunday morning and evening worship services and by family picnics and annual reunions of the larger kinship groups. Among Dutch Calvinists, marriage within the group has always been the norm. In Wisconsin between 1850 and 1905, for example, only 8 percent of the first generation married non-Dutch-born partners, usually Germans or Dutch Americans. In comparison, 25 percent of first-generation Dutch Catholics and 41 percent of the second generation married other than Dutch-born partners. Since World War II the rate of Dutch Reformed intermarriages has risen slowly, but non-Dutch partners usually share similar religious beliefs. Increasingly, religious affiliation is becoming a stronger bond than ethnicity. Divorce is rare among Dutch Calvinists, but the incidence has risen rapidly in the 1970s. A Christian Reformed Church membership survey in 1969 revealed that only 2 percent had been divorced; among former members, however, the figure was 7 percent. The implication that divorced persons may have resigned from the deonomination is understandable, because they are sometimes subject to social ostracism and church discipline, although excommunication is no longer automatic when remarriage occurs.

The Dutch in America have almost always retained family ownership of farms and businesses; a married son or son-in-law usually assumes ownership when the father retires or dies. If no member of the immediate family is available, a distant relative or fellow church member customarily purchases ownership.

Dutch lifestyle has moved from privation to abundance, if not affluence, during the past 100 years. Frugality, thriftiness, and self-help are qualities that have been much esteemed. Only recently has consumerism made inroads. The Dutch spend comparatively little on popular entertainment and still generally eschew theaters, dancing, lotteries, night clubs, and liquor establishments. Since the 1950s, however, the taboo against "worldly amusements" such as motion pictures and social dancing has largely disappeared among the younger generation. In rural areas, however, the Prinsburg, Minn., lifestyle may not be atypical. In 1978 this small community of Dutch Calvinists had no saloons, liquor stores, dance halls, or billiard parlors. Use of alcoholic beverages, especially beer and wine, within the home is common, however; the Dutch, like their German neighbors, have never been teetotalers. Many orthodox Calvinists influenced by American fundamentalists have nevertheless become abstainers.

Social problems such as alcoholism, malnutrition, neglect of the aged, poverty, illegitimacy, and crime have been minimal. The Dutch Reformed community nationally maintains three mental health facilities. The most notable is Pine Rest Christian Hospital in Grand Rapids, the largest private, church-related hospital of its kind in the nation. There are also an alcoholic rehabilitation center in Phoenix, Ariz., several residential centers and schools for mentally retarded and physically handicapped youngsters, residential centers and nursing homes for the aged, and an agency for unwed mothers and for adoptive and foster-care placement. Staff in these private institutions are largely Dutch Reformed, and all employees are expected to subscribe to Calvinist theology.

RELIGIOUS AND CULTURAL LIFE

Dutch-American religious identity is a product of the homeland, because religious disputes and traditions were invariably carried to the New World. The two most significant events in Dutch religious history were the triumph of Calvinism during the Reformation,

which led to the creation of the national Dutch Reformed Church, and the influence of the rationalist ideas of the 18th-century Enlightenment. The great majority of Dutch immigrants to America were members of the Reformed Church; less than 20 percent were Roman Catholics, Mennonites, or Jews. The Catholics were the largest minority group.

In 1834, however, the first of several major secessions from the national church created additional minority groups, known as Seceders or *Afgescheidenen*. These separatists objected to the doctrinal heterodoxy and the government-imposed reorganization of the Reformed Church, which they felt was succumbing to the theological liberalism of the Enlightenment and to the Erastianism of the House of Orange. Their opposition struck a responsive chord in rural areas of the Netherlands, and increasing numbers joined them. Dutch ecclesiastical and political authorities viewed the Afscheiding as a civil threat that could not be tolerated; their leaders were arrested and heavily fined, and Seceders sometimes lost their jobs. This persecution, coupled with the effects of the potato blight and the economic depression of 1845 and 1846, caused 5,000 Seceders to emigrate to the United States before 1850. They formed the nucleus of the Holland, Zeeland, and Pella colonies. Their orthodoxy, individualistic beliefs, and cultural conservatism and clannishness gave form and substance to their community life for generations.

The Reformed churches in the United States were further influenced by a second secession (known as the *Doleantie*) from the national church in the Netherlands. This break occurred in 1886 under the leadership of Abraham Kuyper (1837–1920), founder of the Free University of Amsterdam (1880) and head of the Christian Anti-Revolutionary party. This ardently Calvinist party won control of the government in 1892. Prime Minister Kuyper reshaped social institutions along religious lines, notably by providing tax support for sectarian schools and eventually universities. Immigrants to the United States from the Doleantie group (often identified as Kuyperians) were imbued with a Calvinist world view and sought to organize their social, economic, and educational life around Reformed principles. Although Kuyperians were a small minority among Dutch Americans, it was their impetus in the pre–World War I decades that led to the establishment of the church-supported schools and social agencies described earlier.

Religious life among the Dutch Calvinists in the United States since the mid-19th century has been influenced largely by the Afscheiding and Doleantie heritages with their differing emphases. The Calvinists are divided into two major and several minor denominations. The major two are the Reformed Church in America, founded in New Netherland in 1628 (and thus one of the oldest denominations in the United States), and its daughter church, the Christian Reformed Church, which originated in an 1857 schism in western Michigan. People of the Afscheiding tradition joined both American denominations, but Doleantie immigrants affiliated almost exclusively with the Christian Reformed Church, where they composed the leadership and dominated the denominational seminary faculty. In the Canadian branch of the Christian Reformed Church, which grew rapidly after World War II, the Kuyperian followers have been even more influential. This influence has strengthened the radical cultural activism of the Doleantie wing in the Christian Reformed Church, but it also has exacerbated tensions with the majority group, the individualistic Afscheiding.

The Reformed Church in America grew slowly throughout the colonial era. The meager Dutch immigration to New York virtually ceased after 1650, and the church clung tenaciously to the Dutch language in the midst of the predominant English culture. Ecclesiastically the colonial church remained under the jurisdiction of the Classis of Amsterdam, the governing body of the church, but after 1750 rising American nationalism and then the Revolution fundamentally changed the colonial Dutch church into an American church. In 1772 the colonial church broke with the Amsterdam Classis and in 1792 adopted the present form of ecclesiastical government. Rutgers College (f. 1766) and the affiliated New Brunswick Seminary (f. 1784) were also founded during this era to provide American pastors. English became the official language of the Reformed Church in 1794; services in Dutch generally ceased after 1800, and were entirely discontinued by the early 1840s at the onset of the second Dutch immigration. At this turning point the Reformed Church had 33,000 communicants in 274 churches, almost all in the New York area. The denomination was unified, closely knit, and fully aware of its Dutch Calvinist heritage yet proudly American.

When the new wave of Dutch immigrants began arriving in the 1840s, Dutch Americans in New York generously assisted them economically and soon invited the newly founded midwestern Seceder churches to join their denomination. Attracted by ethnic loyalties and the warm fellowship and acts of kindness, the Holland and Zeeland churches joined the Reformed Church in 1850, and the Pella church followed in 1856. In the next half-century the Board of Domestic Missions of the Reformed Church organized more than 100 Dutch-language churches in the communities that spread throughout the Midwest and in immigrant communities in Passaic, Albany, and Rochester. During the same period another 100 English-language Reformed churches were established among Dutch Americans in the East.

In 1916 the Reformed Church in America numbered 150,000 members and 715 churches, two-thirds of which were located in the East and used English exclusively in services. The remainder were in the north-central region and used a foreign language alone or in conjunction with English. The effect of the great migration, therefore, was to create within the Reformed Church an English-speaking, largely native-born, eastern majority and an orthodox, Dutch-speaking western minority. This diversity was a source of strength as well as of conflict, providing a blend of pragmatic American Christianity and orthodox Reformed tradition. In the 20th century the Reformed Church has deliberately suppressed its Dutch image and sought to move into the mainstream of American Protestantism. Many new congregations of the period 1950–1975 have a small Dutch-American nucleus but are largely non-Dutch in composition; but on issues of ecumenism, doctrinal revision, and ordination of women, the theologically and culturally conservative midwestern wing has slowed the Americanization process within the denomination.

The other major Dutch Reformed denomination, the Christian Reformed Church, originated in western Michigan in 1857 when four congregations and two pastors rejected, on doctrinal, cultural, and idiosyncratic grounds, the ecclesiastical union of 1850 with the Reformed Church. For six years the fledgling sect of 250 members had only one pastor; after the Civil War, however, the Christian Reformed Church expanded steadily through an effective home mission program that attracted the increasing numbers of Dutch immigrants moving into the Midwest. In the decades prior to World War I this attraction was particularly pronounced among the followers of Kuyper. The church also gained strength from two accessions, one in 1884 of 6 churches and pastors and 300 families in Michigan who left the Reformed Church, and another in 1890 consisting of the entire True Reformed Church in New York and New Jersey, an English-speaking remnant of an 1822 secession from the Reformed Church. By 1916 the Christian Reformed Church consisted of 226 churches with 39,000 members, all but 5,000 living in the Midwest. The eastern churches held services exclusively in English; the others, except for 52 mainly urban congregations, clung to the mother tongue.

A variety of theological and cultural reasons explains the initial growth of the Christian Reformed Church, but the salient issue was the agitation over Masonry, which surfaced in the 1850s and came to a head in the 1880s. European Masonry was strongly deistic, following the spirit of the Enlightenment, in contrast to the more tolerant "Christian" American lodges. European churches, both Protestant and Roman Catholic, had banned Masonic membership; immigrant Hollanders consequently arrived in the Midwest with antagonistic feelings toward Masonry. In 1880 four regional church assemblies declared it and all other oath-bound societies to be "(1) anti-Republican, (2) anti-Christian; and (3) anti-Reformed." The largely immigrant congregations, knowing that church members in the East, including some clergymen and elders, belonged to Masonic lodges, demanded that the Reformed Church in America take a definite stand and bar lodge members from church membership. When the General Synod equivocated and refused to condemn oath-bound secret societies in its 1880 meetings, four congregations in the Midwest and a substantial number of members elsewhere seceded and joined the young Christian Reformed Church, which had already taken an anti-Masonic stand. More important, in 1885 the Seceder Church in the Netherlands, for whom American Masonry had also become an issue, after repeated admonitions to the Reformed Church in America, advised its emigrating members not to affiliate with that denomination. Most immigrants obeyed, for cultural if not doctrinal reasons. Newcomers probably experienced less social tension in the splinter denomination, since by the 1880s the Reformed Church was much more Americanized than the Christian Reformed Church; as a result, the latter received most of the flood of immigrants in the decades before World War I.

The second factor that encouraged growth and cohesiveness in the Christian Reformed Church was its commitment to Christian day schools embodying Dutch Calvinist theology in the curriculum. Such schools have provided the institutional cohesive that sets the newer denomination apart from the Reformed Church, whose children have mainly attended public schools. Thus, although the two denominations are theologically similar, especially in the Midwest, their contrasting educational patterns have created pronounced cultural and behaviorial differences. The Christian Reformed community has maintained its ethnic identity through at least four generations, while the Reformed community, with fewer institutional bulwarks and little leadership from the Netherlands, has largely been assimilated. Both denominations have remained small: in 1976 the total baptized membership of the Reformed Church in America was 356,000; the Christian Reformed Church, 288,000.

The only viable Dutch Catholic parish was at Little Chute in the Fox River region of southern Wisconsin, where in 1850 a succession of Dutch missionary priests from the Order of Crusade Fathers in Uden, North Brabant, began serving the struggling churches. This frontier parish was multiethnic, and services were conducted in English, French, and Dutch. In 1879, after the community was well established, the Crusade Fathers discontinued their work in Wisconsin; in 1910 they founded a new Dutch immigrant settlement in Onamia, Minn. In 1893, a new order, the Premonstratensians (or Norbertines), began a lasting ministry in Green Bay, Wis., and later in St. Willibrord's parish in Chicago. Although the Dutch were a minority in these parishes, their language was one of those used in the confessional until at least 1955. Nevertheless, the religious life of Catholic Hollanders has led to their rapid assimilation.

Church life was a key factor in language retention among the Dutch in America. In multiethnic Catholic and Jewish parishes and in urban areas where immigrants mingled with coreligionists of other nationalities, the Dutch soon lost their language and culture. By contrast, the midwestern Calvinists who created isolated ethnic communities generally retained the Dutch and Frisian languages in all their varied dialects for two or three generations. The strong community life and constant arrival of new immigrants also encouraged language retention. The first generation spoke Dutch exclusively within their homes and churches but learned rudimentary English for business and political affairs. Among the second and third generations, conversational Dutch gave way to Yankee Dutch, a corrupted blend of Dutch dialects and English words, although the dominies retained purer forms in preaching and teaching the catechism. Dutch-language services were usual in midwestern Reformed churches (and also in the few eastern immigrant churches) until World War I. In the next decades English made steady gains, and by the 1960s few services were held in the Dutch language. As recently as 1940, however, nearly one-fourth of the grandchildren of foreign-born Hollanders reported Dutch as the principal language spoken in their childhood homes. That proportion was exceeded only among Spanish- and French-speaking Americans.

A strong literary and folk tradition has also perpetuated the language. Imported books of a popular or theological nature adorned the bookshelves of most immigrant families. Protestant church periodicals such as *De Hope* (1862–1933) of the Reformed Church and *De Wachter* (The Watchman, f. 1868) of the Christian Re-

formed Church, and newspapers such as *De Grondwet* (The Constitution, 1860–1930) of Holland, Mich., *De Standaard* (1875–1943) of Grand Rapids, the Orange City *Volksvriend* (People's Friend, 1874–1951), and the Pella *Weekblad* (Weekly, 1861–1942) also had a continuing impact. The several dozen newspapers and periodicals introduced the American political scene to the immigrants and informed them of news and developments in both Holland and the United States. The two most influential papers, *De Grondwet* and *De Volksvriend,* enjoyed nationwide circulation. In contrast to the flourishing Protestant press, the widely scattered Dutch Catholic settlements never mustered support for more than a few short-lived newspapers in Wisconsin, such as the De Pere *De Volksstem* (Voice of the People, 1886–1919). Both Catholic and Protestant groups have maintained annual folk festivals that perpetuate traditional costumes, foods, and dances. The Hollandtown, Wis., Dutch Catholic festival, *Schut,* has been celebrated since 1850, and the tulip festivals of Holland, Pella, and Orange City have grown in popularity since the last century. Originally primary agents of cultural preservation and group maintenance, these festivals, however, have become tourist attractions.

EDUCATION

Elementary education was commonplace in the Netherlands by the 17th century; thus, few emigrants were illiterate. In America the Dutch stressed education informally in church catechism programs and formally through public and Christian day schools. Education was considered an integral part of salvation because of the necessity for each Calvinist to read and understand the Bible. Wherever the Dutch predominated, as in some New York towns in the colonial period and in several midwestern towns in the mid-19th century, church consistories supervised the tax-supported schools. They selected the schoolmasters, mandated Dutch-language instruction, incorporated a Reformed or Catholic attitude into the curriculum, and required doctrinal instruction after school hours. Gradually, as the communities and public schools became multiethnic, the people of Seceder background in the Christian Reformed Church developed congregational or parent-owned day schools. In 1916 there were 65 Calvinist schools with 10,000 students. Today there are more than 200 schools, including about 40 at the secondary level, scattered among both urban and rural Dutch communities in 28 states, plus many more in Canada. In 1969, 80 percent of all Christian Reformed families sent their children to these Calvinist schools. In that year also, 50 percent of the household heads of this denomination had graduated from high school, 27 percent had a college education, and 1 percent held Ph.D. degrees.

Although Christian day schools are the special concern of the Christian Reformed followers of Kuyper, all the Dutch Reformed in the United States have a history of commitment to higher education, owing to the need for an indigenous and educated clergy. The Old Dutch established Queens College (Rutgers) for this purpose in 1766; the Dutch in the Midwest founded Hope College (1866) in Holland as the preparatory and theological school of the Reformed Church in America, and Calvin College (1876) in Grand Rapids as the sister institution of the Christian Reformed Church. These colleges and their seminaries made western Michigan the intellectual and religious center of all the Reformed Dutch settlements in North America. Subsequently the Reformed Church established Northwestern College (1882) in Orange City and assumed control of Central College (1916) in Pella—a college originally founded by Dominie Scholte in 1853 under Baptist auspices. Also in Iowa the Christian Reformed Church founded Grundy Center College (1916) which became defunct in the 1930s and Dordt College (1955) in Sioux Center. Both denominations cooperated to launch Trinity Christian College in Chicago in 1959. As yet there is no Dutch Reformed university. Dutch Catholics founded St. Norbert College at De Pere, Wis., in 1898 and Crosier Seminary at Onamia, Minn., in 1922, but because of the diversity and international scope of the Catholic church these institutions did not long remain ethnically distinct.

Among the ethnically homogeneous Dutch Protestants, the commitment to Christian education, more than any other institutional factor, has slowed the process of assimilation. The schools sustain ethnic consciousness, marriage and family patterns, and inculcate a systematic Calvinist philosophy and theology that graduates carry into their churches, homes, occupations, professions, and politics.

POLITICS

Although the Dutch have been politically active in America, their small numbers and their cultural isolation have generally limited their influence to the local level. Little is known of the political behavior of the colonial Dutch. Most were disfranchised, except for wealthy patroon families such as the Van Cortlandts, Van Rensselaers, Schuylers, Roosevelts, and Stuyvesants. Three presidents of the United States, Theodore Roosevelt (1858–1919), Franklin D. Roosevelt (1882–1945), and Martin Van Buren (1782–1862), a Kinderhook, N.Y., farmer and tavernkeeper's son, were of colonial Dutch ancestry.

Immigrants who arrived after the Jacksonian democratic revolution of the 1830s valued citizenship and the ballot box. A few espoused ideals of political liberalism in Europe and had chafed under the suffrage restrictions of the Netherlands. But, for most, self-interest dictated political involvement. The Dutch in America wanted schools, roads, and public projects such as harbor improvements at the Black Lake inlet of Lake Michigan at Holland City and dredging to make the Des Moines River in Iowa navigable for steamboats and thus benefit Pella residents. National issues held little interest unless they impinged upon local lifestyles or future economic opportunities, as did naturalization laws, slavery in the territories, and Prohibition.

Initially, in the 1840s and early 1850s, both rural and urban Dutch in the Midwest affiliated with the Democratic party and rejected Whig nativism and Know-Nothingism. But the political revolution of the mid-1850s, sparked by the Kansas-Nebraska Act and growing southern dominance of the Democratic party, drove the Protestant Dutch into the Republican camp, where they have remained solidly entrenched until the present. The Civil War placed a stigma on the Democrats for decades, and postbellum Dutch Protestant im-

migrants increasingly voted Republican. Almost the entire Dutch press carried Republican mastheads during the 19th century. The Democrats made slight gains in the 1890s among Dutch settlers in the central plains, largely owing to the Populist movement and President William McKinley's policy of neutrality toward England and Dutch South Africans in the Boer War (1899–1902). During World War I, while the Netherlands government proclaimed neutrality, Dutch Americans supported the war effort, but some Boer War activists remained anti-British if not pro-German. During World War I, Congressmen Gerrit J. Diekema (1859–1930) of Holland, Mich., and Dow H. Drukker (1872–1963) of Passaic, N.J., stirred patriotism among Dutch Americans, as Michigan's Senator Arthur H. Vandenberg (1884–1951) did in World War II.

In the 20th century the Democratic party's alliance with the labor unions has alienated Protestant Hollanders, just as the slavery issue and the Civil War did earlier. Exceptions to the Republican sway among Dutch Americans are few, though defections to the Democrats, especially among intellectuals, have been growing since the 1950s. Gerald Ford's Republicanism was fairly representative of the group. Apart from the Dutch Catholics, who were always Democrats, only one Calvinist community, Pella, has consistently voted Democratic. In 1859 their leader, the Reverend Hendrik P. Scholte, joined the Republicans and in 1860 actively campaigned for Abraham Lincoln, but the people had felt the sting of nativist attacks in the mid-1850s and refused to follow him into the party that included Whig and Know-Nothing nativists.

GROUP MAINTENANCE

The high point of Dutch ethnic consciousness in America was the period 1900–1920, bracketed by the Boer War and World War I. Throughout the last half of the 19th century the Dutch strove for economic security and cultural space in a host society. But their political activism during the Boer War gives evidence that by then they felt sufficiently secure to move boldly into the public arena. In 1903 a group of Christian Reformed ministers and laymen formed a political club in Grand Rapids to work for a Christian political party modeled after Kuyper's Anti-Revolutionary Party. This movement was stillborn, but Dutch-American politicians—Drukker, Diekema, Vandenberg, and Richard Vander Veen of Grand Rapids (1922–)—have tinctured their politics with ethnic and religious allusions.

The events of World War I shattered Dutch ethnic ascendancy and solidarity. Dutch Americans fell victim to the strident nativism of the time, particularly because the public often confused them with Germans. Use of the Dutch language in schools and churches aroused suspicions of lack of patriotism; ardent patriots burned a Dutch church and school building near Pella. The governor of Iowa issued a proclamation requiring the use of English in all public assemblies, including church services and church schools. The Dutch were generally put on the defensive. War-generated nativism contributed to the push for restrictions against foreigners and helped bring about the quota system of the 1920s, which greatly reduced the rate of immigration and cut off the language- and culture-sustaining support

the Dutch communities derived from new arrivals. Finally, the war hastened the process of cultural change and assimilation.

World War I was thus the turning point in the acculturation of Dutch Americans. Immigrant leaders encouraged the Americanization movement in their churches and schools. As a result, between World Wars I and II Dutch-language preaching virtually disappeared, as did most Dutch newspapers and periodicals. Out of some 25 Dutch-language publications in 1918, only one newspaper, *De Volksvriend*, and one periodical, *De Wachter*, survived to serve Dutch Americans. The number of foreign-stock Dutch also stabilized in 1920 at 132,000, peaking in 1930 at only 133,000. So rapid was acculturation that in 1939 third- and fourth-generation Dutch Americans reportedly showed little more resentment about the Nazi invasion of the Netherlands than they had about the fall of Norway and Denmark a month earlier. The wartime service of tens of thousands of Dutch-American G.I.s also broke down ethnic homogeneity and led to a marked increase in intermarriage.

Dutch cultural awareness among the third and fourth generations had a marked, if temporary, revival after World War II because of the resurgence of Dutch immigration and the new ethnic consciousness among all Americans. Membership is still growing in the old and prestigious Holland Society of New York (f. 1855) and there are many newer cultural organizations throughout the United States, such as the Dutch Immigrant Society (DIS) of Grand Rapids and the Dutch Club AVIO of La Habra, Calif., each of which now has 10,000 to 15,000 members. Individual and group travel to the homeland is increasing. Study programs on the Netherlands are now part of the regular curricula of the Dutch Reformed colleges. Several colleges have established historical archives, and in 1963 Calvin and Hope colleges, in conjunction with the Holland, Mich., Netherlands Museum (f. 1937), formed the Dutch-American Historical Commission to foster archival and research work, sponsor symposia, and support publication. Professional organizations and newsletters are thriving, such as the Netherlands Language and Literature Group of the Modern Language Association, the American and Canadian associations for Netherlandic Studies, and the Association for the Advancement of Dutch-American Studies. The Dutch language is taught in at least 25 colleges and universities. There are special professorships in Dutch history, literature, language, and culture —Columbia University's Queen Wilhelmina Chair (f. 1913), Calvin College's Queen Juliana Chair (f. 1953), and the University of California at Berkeley's Princess Beatrix Lectureship (f. 1971). The University of Texas offers a Ph.D degree in Dutch studies, and both Harvard and the University of Michigan regularly sponsor guest lectureships for Dutch professors. In addition to these efforts in the United States, there is a free flow of ideas across the Atlantic. Calvinist theology and philosophy as articulated in the Free University of Amsterdam, from which a number of Dutch-American professors and pastors hold advanced degrees, continues to influence the Dutch Americans. Bolstered by this activity, Dutch ethnic identity will probably survive the pressures of social conformity and the loss of the ancestral language.

Bibliography

The best general histories are Henry S. Lucas, *Netherlanders in America: Dutch Immigration to the United States and Canada, 1789–1950* (Ann Arbor, Mich., 1955), based on Dutch-language primary sources; and Gerald F. De Jong, *The Dutch in America, 1609–1974* (Boston, 1975), an interpretive history that is especially strong on the colonial Dutch. A popular account that stresses Dutch-American "contributions" is Arnold Mulder, *Americans from Holland* (New York, 1947). An excellent source of primary documents in English is Henry S. Lucas, ed., *Dutch Immigrant Memoirs and Related Writings,* 2 vols. (Assen, Netherlands, 1955).

Studies of religious life and ethnic leaders are Albert Hyma's scholarly biography, *Albertus C. Van Raalte and His Dutch Settlements in the United States* (Grand Rapids, Mich., 1947); Elton J. Bruins, *The Americanization of a Congregation* (Grand Rapids, 1970), a study of the Third Reformed Church of Holland, Mich., from 1867 to 1967; Henry Zwaanstra, *Reformed Thought and Experience in the New World: A Study of the Christian Reformed Church and Its American Environment, 1890–1918* (Kampen, Netherlands, 1973), an analysis of Americanization in this denomination; and eight historical essays edited by James W. Van Hoeven, *Piety and Patriotism: Bicentennial Studies of the Reformed Church in America, 1776–1976* (Grand Rapids, 1976).

Regional histories include Jacob Vander Zee's pioneer work *The Hollanders of Iowa* (Iowa City, 1912), and Alice P. Kenney, *The Gansevoorts of Albany: Dutch Patricians in the Upper Hudson Valley* (Syracuse, N.Y., 1969). A more specialized work is William Petersen, *Some Factors Influencing Postwar Emigration from the Netherlands* (The Hague, Netherlands, 1952). Studies based on Dutch emigration lists are Robert P. Swierenga and Harry S. Stout, "Dutch Immigration in the Nineteenth Century, 1820–1877: A Quantitative Overview," *Indiana Social Studies Quarterly* 28 (1975): 7–34; and "Socio-Economic Patterns of Migration from the Netherlands in the Nineteenth Century," in *Research in Economic History: An Annual Compilation of Research,* vol. 1, ed. Paul Uselding (Greenwich, Conn., 1976), pp. 298–333. Robert P. Swierenga, "The Ethnic Voter and the First Lincoln Election," *Civil War History* 11 (1965): 27–43, treats Dutch political behavior in frontier Iowa.

Manuscripts and other materials are collected in The Netherlands Museum in Holland, Mich.; the Heritage Hall Colonial Origins Collection at Calvin College and Seminary, Grand Rapids; Beardslee Library of Western Theological Seminary and Hope College, Holland; and Herrick Public Library, Holland. The Scholte Collection in the Central College Library, Pella, Iowa, is also extensive. There is no central repository of Dutch Catholic materials.

ROBERT P. SWIERENGA

E

EAST INDIANS

The East Indians in the United States, who sometimes refer to themselves as Asian Indians or Indo-Americans, are largely South Asian Indians from the present-day Republic of India or their descendants; few emigrated before 1965 from the areas that are now Pakistan, Bangladesh, and Sri Lanka. Since the late 19th century East Indians have been leaving their country either as refugees or in search of better jobs. They began to leave while Great Britain ruled India, and eventually settled in more than 50 countries, but the United States was the destination of only a few of these migrants. (See also Bangladeshi; Pakistanis.)

Between 1820 and 1976 a total of over 130,000 East Indian immigrants entered the United States; fewer than 17,000 of these came before 1965 (see Table 1). Only 700 scattered adventurers, merchants, monks, and professional men—mainly from northern India—came during the 19th century. Punjabi agricultural workers composed the majority of the 7,000 who entered between 1904 and 1923; their arrival on the West Coast during a period of general hostility toward Asians provoked executive exclusion orders in 1910 and congressional exclusion laws in 1917 and 1923 that virtually halted East Indian immigration. In the next two decades perhaps 3,000 workers entered surreptitiously through Mexico, and several thousand students and merchants entered legally. Almost 1,500 East Indians returned to India between 1911 and 1920; in the next decade another 3,000 left the United States. This return migration together with the restrictive U.S. immigration laws and the predominantly male population caused the community to dwindle to fewer than 1,500 by 1946. Relaxation of the Asian quota in 1946 allowed limited immigration; approximately 6,000 East Indians were admitted to the United States between 1947 and 1965.

The second phase of East Indian immigration began when the 1965 immigration law eliminated national quotas, dramatically increasing the number of Asians eligible to enter the country. In 1970 the U.S. Census recorded 51,000 foreign-born and almost 25,000 native-born Americans of East Indian descent in the United States; within five years there were another 72,000; by 1980 the East Indian population may well exceed 200,000 people.

The largest concentration of East Indians is in the New York metropolitan area; at least 30,000 live within 50 miles of the city: about 5,000 reside in Flushing, Queens; 1,200 in Jersey City; and 600 in Westchester County. At least 30,000 are settled in California, mainly in and around San Francisco and Los Angeles, with smaller communities in Sutter and Yuba counties and the Central and Imperial valleys. In Illinois there are over 10,000, most of them in Chicago; communities numbering several thousand can be found in Pennsylvania, Ohio, Michigan, Maryland, Massachusetts, and Texas. The remaining East Indians are scattered across the country, often in college or university centers.

India, the second most populous nation in the world, has a diverse racial, regional, and linguistic population politically divided into 30 territories and states. This heterogeneity is reflected in the variety of East Indian peoples who have entered the United States. At least 85 percent are Caucasian. Most have come from the Indo-Gangetic Plain of northern India, from Gujarat in western India, or from the Dravidian region of southern India, but every state in India is represented in the community as are Indians from Fiji, Hong Kong, England, Sri Lanka, and Africa—areas where East Indians have lived and maintained a cultural identity for generations. More than 2,000 East Indians sought refuge in the United States after they were expelled from Uganda in 1972.

Language is the primary distinction among East Indians from various regions. The Indian government recognizes 15 national languages, of which Hindi, Bengali, Punjabi, Urdu and Gujarati of the Indo-Aryan family and Tamil of the Dravidian language family are the main languages spoken by East Indian immigrants. English, also an official language in India, is often their common medium of communication. Each of the Indian languages has its own extensive literature, and some of the languages are written in more than one script. Punjabi, for example, may be written in the Gurmuki, Persian, or Devanagari script.

Religion is another important distinction. Hindus are a majority both in India and among the American immigrants. Sikhs are only 2 percent in the homeland but between 30 and 40 percent of the East Indian population in California. Muslims make up 5 percent of the population of India, but are probably a smaller proportion in the United States. The Jains from the area of Gujarat and the Zoroastrians from Bombay are small groups in both countries (see Zoroastrians).

In the early 20th century nearly 90 percent of the immigrants were agricultural workers from the Doab and Malwa regions of the Punjab. The increasing division of agricultural land in the Punjab led the younger sons of

Table 1. East Indian immigration to the United States, 1820–1976.

Period	Number of immigrants
1820	1
1821–1830	8
1831–1840	39
1841–1850	36
1851–1860	43
1861–1870	69
1871–1880	163
1881–1890	269
1891–1900	68
1901–1910	4,713
1911–1920	2,082
1921–1930	1,886
1931–1940	496
1941–1950	1,761
1951–1960	1,973
1961–1970	30,461
1971–1976	90,399

Source: U.S. Immigration and Naturalization Service, *Annual Report, 1976* (Washington, D.C., 1977), pp. 86–88.

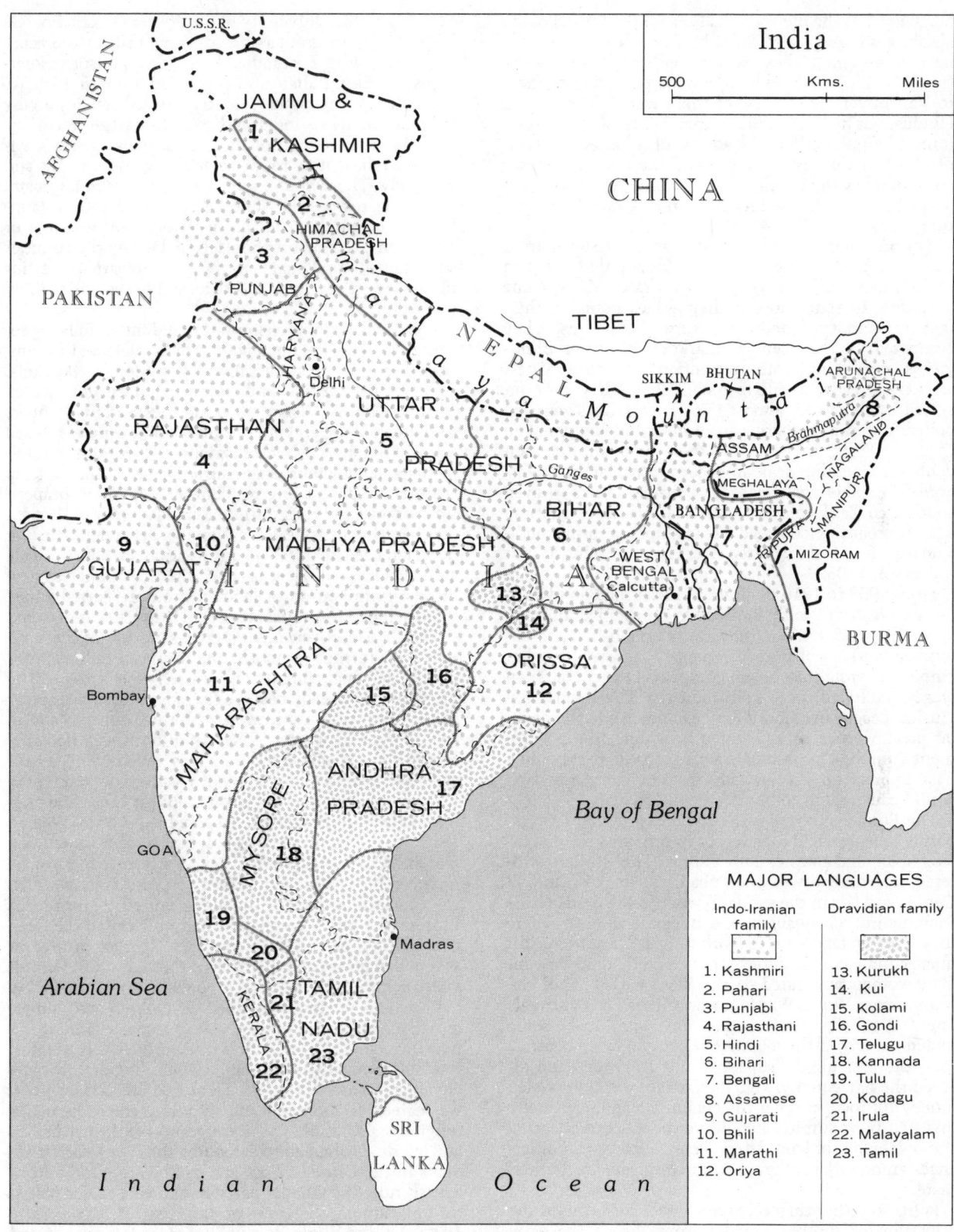

India

500   Kms.   Miles

MAJOR LANGUAGES

Indo-Iranian family   Dravidian family

1. Kashmiri   13. Kurukh
2. Pahari   14. Kui
3. Punjabi   15. Kolami
4. Rajasthani   16. Gondi
5. Hindi   17. Telugu
6. Bihari   18. Kannada
7. Bengali   19. Tulu
8. Assamese   20. Kodagu
9. Gujarati   21. Irula
10. Bhili   22. Malayalam
11. Marathi   23. Tamil
12. Oriya

some families to leave India for North America, where they were expected to earn money to pay family debts or to buy extra land. Veterans of the British Indian army or British police in Hong Kong, Singapore, or Shanghai provided leadership for the small village and kinship groups that responded to the solicitations of Canadian employers and steamship company agents in northern India. Few of the Punjabis could read or write their own

language, but the men who had served the British could speak, read, and write English, a crucial skill for the new immigrants. These young men left the Punjab by train for Calcutta, by ship to Hong Kong, and from there to Vancouver, B.C. A few of them were Muslims and Hindus, but most were Sikhs (members of a militant reform religion). Earlier Sikh adventurers had set up temple hostels throughout Asia, and there were support communities in cities like Hong Kong. As a result the Sikhs had a particular advantage in this early immigration.

The immigrants followed the railroads south from Canada into the United States seeking employment in the lumber mills of Washington State. Many came intending to send most of their wages home to their families and eventually to return themselves. They competed on the open job market with other immigrants, provoking a strong reaction from West Coast workers already hostile to Asian labor. They were insulted and harassed; almost 1,000 East Indians were expelled from the lumbering areas around Bellingham and Everett, Wash., in 1907, and there were similar incidents on a smaller scale in other northwestern towns. Some Punjabis fled back to Canada; others moved south into California to work in railroad construction. The railroads encouraged steamships to bring additional men to San Francisco after Canada excluded East Indians in 1908.

From 1908 to 1910 thousands of East Indians worked on the Western Pacific Railroad in northern California. When the work ran out, the already established and unionized workers of European ancestry, suspecting that employers would use Asian competition to drive down wages, excluded them from industry. The Asiatic Exclusion League demanded total exclusion and the popular press warned of a "Hindoo invasion"; the government complied by issuing a series of rulings excluding East Indians on the grounds that job discrimination would cause them to become public charges.

The Punjabis moved into rural areas, taking farm laboring jobs that had been left to immigrants from Mexico, Japan, and southeastern Europe. The workers wintered in farming towns like Yuba City, Stockton, and El Centro and left in the spring to work in the fields of the Sacramento, San Joaquin, and Imperial valleys, where they lived on farms and in work camps. These were still mostly male communities—not more than 30 East Indian women emigrated to the West Coast in all the years before World War I. Fewer of these later arrivals knew English; those who did and had some understanding of the job market became labor contractors; the rest hired themselves out in groups and divided the pay equally. Punjabi day laborers also pooled money for food in order to economize, and eventually invested their surplus income in the collective leasing and ownership of land. There were no real social differences among them: they all came from the *Jat* (farmer) caste.

Political rather than economic conditions caused the migration of another, smaller group during the early 20th century. These were northern Indians, educated men either looking for technical, political, or military training or escaping British repression brought about by their nationalist political activities. Within a few years East Indian students at the University of Washington in

Seattle and the University of California at Berkeley had formed support groups and had arranged for the more successful of the East Indian farmers to sponsor scholarships for East Indian students. The *Modern Review,* published in English in Calcutta, printed articles urging students to leave India and explaining the necessary procedures. Other nationalist newspapers similarly encouraged dissenters to go where they could speak and act freely. These young men settled in urban areas and university towns and worked at part-time jobs in laundries or hospitals, or at an occasional job teaching or translating, to support themselves. During the summer some joined the Punjabis in the fields to earn money for the winter. They lived in boarding houses with fellow countrymen.

Legal and social discrimination did much to bring together the educated but poor intellectuals and the uneducated but economically self-sufficient Punjabis. Campus fraternities and other organizations denied membership to Asian students; restaurants, hotels, rooming houses, and public amusement centers refused service to Asians, whether agricultural workers or intellectuals; landowners used restrictive covenants to keep them from purchasing residential property. Competition for jobs and the continued involvement of East Indians in the struggle for national independence in the homeland led to legal discrimination in both Canada and the United States. In 1917 the U.S. Congress prohibited immigration of laborers from a "barred zone" that included India and nearly all other Asian nations.

The British government's tacit sanction of these restrictions further cemented the union of Indians from diverse regional, linguistic, and religious groups. The Punjabis had already begun a literacy campaign in order to maintain communication with their families and to defend their rights in the New World through newsletters and periodicals. Taraknath Das (1884–1959), a Bengali student at the University of Washington, attempted to organize a political group on the West Coast and published the *Free Hindusthan* sporadically from 1908 to 1910. In 1914 a number of political refugees including Das and Har Dayal (1887–1939), a student who had renounced his Oxford scholarship in protest against British educational policies in India, united the scattered immigrants into a single political unit called the Ghadar (Mutiny) party. The newspaper *Ghadar*, printed in several languages and distributed throughout the immigrant community, became a powerful force for Indian nationalism. Poetry published in *Ghadar* and subsequently set to music evoked a deep response among the new immigrants. For the first time in the United States, Punjabis, Bengalis, and other regional linguistic groups developed a broader Indian identity. The Ghadar party was careful to include leadership from the three major religious affiliations of immigrants—Sikh, Muslim, and Hindu. Dedicated to defending the rights of East Indians in the United States and to liberating India from British rule, the Ghadar party remained a major political force among the group on the West Coast until the 1930s. During World War I, Ghadar leaders encouraged immigrants to return to India to start an armed revolution. In 1918 the U.S. government prosecuted 29 East Indians for conspiracy to violate neutrality laws in connection with their Ghadar activities; 14 men were convicted and imprisoned.

A more moderate group, the Home Rule League, was based in New York where a small East Indian community had developed after 1910. Lala Lajpat Rai (1865–1928) supported the Indian National Congress movement for constitutional home rule, edited the periodical *Young India*, and led the league after its formation in 1917. The league lacked the broad community support that the Ghadar party enjoyed. By the time Rai returned to India in 1920, its role was already being challenged by the newly formed Friends for the Freedom of India, which was based in New York, supported the Ghadar party, and was composed mainly of Americans, not East Indians, who advocated complete independence for India. This group organized a successful campaign against federal efforts to deport the 14 Indians who had been convicted of conspiracy and imprisoned. Both the Friends and the Home Rule League disappeared in the early 1920s as American interest in India waned and East Indian communities faced with still other forms of legal discrimination declined in number.

Beginning in 1906, East Indians were refused U.S. citizenship. Inspired by anti-Asian hostility in the West, the 1790 naturalization law—which stipulated that only "free white" people could become citizens—was interpreted to mean that declared Asian groups were nonwhite and therefore ineligible for citizenship. East Indians were in a legally anomalous situation: they were brown-skinned and from Asia but anthropologically Caucasian. On the latter grounds they were first declared eligible for citizenship in 1910 (*United States* v. *Balsara*) and in 1913 (*in re Akhoy Kumar Mazumdar*), and more than 100 were consequently naturalized. In 1923 the Supreme Court in *United States* v. *Bhagat Singh Thind* declared them ineligible after all, whereupon federal officials argued that East Indians naturalized earlier had received their papers fraudulently and should be denaturalized. About 50 were denaturalized before a case involving an East Indian attorney in *United States* v. *Sakharam Ganesh Pandit* reversed the ruling. Further naturalization was halted, however, and East Indians in California were notified that they must also dispose of their California landholdings because the state's Alien Land Law (1913) prohibited aliens ineligible for citizenship from owning or leasing land. Escheat proceedings were never completed, partly as a result of British protests on behalf of Indian owners as imperial subjects, but many Indians had already sold their holdings; those who did not sell lived in fear of confiscation. (*See* Naturalization and Citizenship.)

In response to this hostile activity many East Indians gave up and left the United States. A number of those who remained had married non-Asian-American women; almost half the agricultural laborers had married Mexican Americans. The majority of East Indians in California remained in small, aging communities, aided by the Sikh Pacific Coast Khalsa Diwan Society, the Muslim Association of America, and the Hindustani Welfare Reform Society. The Ghadar party, dominated by Sikhs and under continued attack by state and federal officials for its prorevolutionary activities, gradually disintegrated.

After 1937 several moderate East Coast–based groups organized to reverse discriminatory immigration and naturalization laws. The India League, the National Committee for India's Freedom, the India Welfare League, and the All-India Muslim League worked with federal officials who expected that an independent India would some day become a major power in Asian affairs. In 1946 Congress passed a bill that established a token quota for East Indian immigration and restored naturalization rights. A California Punjabi Sikh, Dalip Singh Saund (1899–1973), was the first East Indian to use these restored rights to gain high public office. Saund had come to the United States in 1919 as a student and had become a successful Imperial Valley rancher before his naturalization in 1949. He then joined the Democratic party, won election as the first East Indian congressman in 1956, and served for three terms.

With immigration from India still restricted but at least possible after 1946, many relatives joined the East Indians on the West Coast. In the Punjabi culture, brothers and their families traditionally lived together in extended households, and in a few rural immigrant households this pattern was reestablished. Most families were now urban, however, and remained small. Sikh *gurdwara* (temples) remained the centers of communal and political activities.

The 1965 immigration law phased out the national-quota system and for the first time made it possible for large numbers of East Indians to immigrate. The law also determined the composition of arrivals by giving preference to highly trained professionals and their families at a time when Indian professionals were looking elsewhere for work. Almost 46,000 engineers, physicians, scientists, professors, teachers, and businessmen entered the United States during the next ten years along with almost 47,000 wives and children. These families became the basis for the new East Indian communities.

Urban, educated, and English-speaking, these families experienced a relatively smooth transition from life in India to life in America. In New York, both families and bachelors lived conveniently and inexpensively in residential hotels until they could find permanent homes. The professionals, mostly male college graduates between 20 and 40 years of age, found well-paid employment in hospitals, corporations, and academic institutions. Wives with some college education often found clerical work in business or public-service institutions. Adults returned to college for additional training; children adjusted well to public schools. Families were small, usually with 3 to 5 members, and able to save and invest in land, houses, and shops. Over 8,000 became citizens between 1966 and 1975.

The rapid transition to American life was not without its costs, however. Professionals commuted long hours to work; jobs were highly competitive and relatively impersonal; the most successful felt discriminated against when they attempted to move into administrative positions. Tension was more common in the United States than in India. The economic independence of some women concerned their husbands; working wives were not able to provide traditional care and services. Most wives were committed to marriage and their families and attempted to fulfill their traditional roles, but the strong support of relatives upon which they could have counted in India was not available. Parents were concerned about the erosion of traditional family authority, and the effect it would have on their children as they grew up. They worried about the

lack of respect for the elderly. Daughters, whose occupation and marriage could be closely controlled in India by the family, asserted their right to choose work and husband or to remain single. Sons did not feel the responsibility toward the family that was expected of them. Children found it difficult to maintain their East Indian identity and values. Fewer wives (2,000) than husbands became U.S. citizens, perhaps from reluctance to close the family's option of returning to India at some future time.

Regardless of future plans, most East Indian adults try to maintain their heritage and to resist assimilation. They have established ambitious cultural programs to offset the isolation of their children from the ancestral culture and to make East Indian culture more widely known. Community schools teach regional languages as well as music and dances from the homeland. Monthly lectures on Indian subjects, films (shown at commercial theaters in New York, at rented halls, or on college campuses elsewhere), television and radio shows, and annual festivals have all become ways of maintaining cultural heritage and ethnic identity. Groups have sponsored summer festivals in Central Park, a Durga-puja (festival of the goddess Durga), a ceremony to celebrate Saraswati (the Hindu goddess of learning), annual India days, and musical festivals. In New York alone there are at least 25 centers providing cultural and social events. *India Abroad,* a New York weekly established in 1970, and the California *Sikh Sansar,* established in 1972, print English-language educational articles and information on community activities for almost 20,000 subscribers.

Several national organizations and some of the more than 100 East Indian organizations in New York concern themselves with political issues. The largest and most influential of these groups, with over 20,000 members, is the Association of Indians in America, which mounted a campaign to classify East Indians as Asian Americans in the 1980 U.S. Census in order to establish their eligibility for affirmative-action programs. Smaller groups like the Indians for Democracy and the Indian People's Association in North America were active in protesting the restriction of civil liberties in India in 1976.

Religion has acquired greater importance in the recent immigration because it is a way of maintaining Indian culture. Sikhism has always been an influence in the East Indian community, but Hinduism is now much more visible than it once was. The first Hindu immigrants used pictures, prayers, and incense in their worship and often read the *Bhagavad Gita* as a religious text, but they had few religious institutions. What some people took to be Indian religious institutions were in fact organizations for non-Indians interested in learning about Indian religions. The Vedanta Society, established by Swami Vivekananda in 1894 in New York, the Ramakrishna-Vivekananda Center, founded in New York in 1933, and the Self-Realization Fellowship, founded in 1920 and based in Los Angeles, all maintained temples which East Indians attended on occasion but whose membership came principally from outside the group. The Agni Yoga Society, the Himalayan International Institute of Yoga Science and Philosophy, the Hindustan Bible Institute, the International Society for Krishna Consciousness, and the Sikh 3H Foundation

(Healthy, Happy, Holy Way of Life)—all established since 1946—also attract primarily outsiders to their teachings and religious communities. Now, however, Hindus maintain at least six temples in New York where large numbers of East Indians go for group services on Sundays.

Muslims, too, have always read the Koran, held *Namaz* or evening prayer meetings and Friday evening prayer services, and celebrated the fast of Ramadan, but for them religion has become a more public social institution. Even Jains, who practice those principles of nonviolence and asceticism that so deeply influenced Mohandas Gandhi, and Zoroastrians, whose religion emphasizes a reverence for nature and a struggle between good and evil on earth, have become visible as established religious groups.

East Indian foods traditionally associated with religions and regions have also been retained. Although Punjabi Sikhs prefer a largely vegetarian diet, they have no religious prohibitions against eating meat and thus have little difficulty in combining an American diet with their native one. Muslims, who eat no pork or pork products, find the availability of kosher and Black Muslim food helpful in observing traditional religious prohibitions. Hindus, some of whom practice the doctrine of *ahimsa* and abstain from killing living creatures for food, find eating eggs, fish, or even occasionally meat almost a necessity in modern urban American life. Most East Indians eat American-style meals for breakfast and lunch, but a large number of Indian grocery shops, spice shops, and restaurants provide them access to their traditional cuisine at dinner. Unleavened wheat bread (*chapati* or *roti*), vegetables, fruits, yogurt-based food, and curries remain important in the diets of all East Indians.

Of all the aspects of their culture, perhaps the most difficult to maintain has been East Indian medicine. India has a great variety of medical systems of which Western medicine is only one. Muslim practices (called *unani tibbi*) which borrow extensively from Arabic medicine, homeopathic systems, and regional and local health practices are a part of the medical heritage of East Indians. While most doctors have been trained in Western medicine, ayurvedic medicine is still an integral part of Indian culture. *Ayurveda,* the science of health, is a highly complex medical system that emphasizes a physical, mental, and spiritual balance. Prevention includes a regulated daily life, rejuvenating measures, and the practice of yoga. According to this system, disease is caused by an imbalance of the bodily humors and cured by a restoration of the balance through medication and diet. Depending on the type of ailment, East Indians may consult a doctor familiar with ayurvedic concepts before they will turn to a doctor trained only in Western medicine. East Indians have worked with American hospital personnel to bring dietary and procedural practices into greater harmony with religious and medical beliefs. (*See* Health Beliefs and Practices.)

The post-1965 immigration coincided with a new interest and involvement by many Americans in East Indian philosophy, religion, music, and politics; this coincidence has served to decrease the amount of discrimination and to provide a basis for greater cultural pluralism. The *Bhagavad Gita,* the sitar and tabla,

the guru, and the principle of nonviolence have all become familiar to large numbers of Americans. The new immigrants, better educated and trained than the early pioneers, are also now coming from an independent country rather than a colonial outpost and are better able to provide for continuity in their culture. Americans from other groups are in a better position to appreciate the contributions of East Indians to American life.

Bibliography
Gary Hess, "The Forgotten Asian Americans: The East Indian Community in the United States," in Norris Hundley, ed. *The Asian American* (Santa Barbara, Calif., 1976), pp. 157–178, is the only general overview of East Indians available. For the early nationalist movement, see L.P. Mathur, *Indian Revolutionary Movement in the United States of America* (Delhi, India, 1970); Emily C. Brown, *Har Dayal: Hindu Revolutionary and Rationalist* (Tucson, Ariz., 1975); Don K. Dignan, "The Hindu Conspiracy in Anglo-American Relations During World War I," *Pacific Historical Review* 40 (1971): 57–76; and Joan M. Jensen, "The 'Hindu Conspiracy': A Reassessment," *Pacific Historical Review* 48 (1979): 65–83.

Other groups are discussed by Lawrence A. Wenzel, "The Rural Punjabis of California: A Religio-Ethnic Group," *Phylon* 29 (1968): 245–256; and George V. Coelho, *Changing Images of America: A Study of Indian Students' Perceptions* (Glencoe, Ill., 1968). See also D.S. Saund's autobiography, *Congressman From India* (New York, 1960).

For the post-1965 period, see Parmatma Saran, "Cosmopolitans from India," *Society* 14 (September/October 1977): 65–69. Issues of the *Sikh Sansar, India Abroad,* the *Directory of Indian Immigrants* (New York, 1975), and *India Guide* (New York, 1975) are useful sources of information on recent immigrants.

Sohan Singh Josh, *Hindustan Gadar Party,* 2 vols. (Delhi, 1977–1978), has a detailed bibliography on the party. The South and Southeast Asia Library Service at the University of California at Berkeley has a large collection of published and unpublished material relating to the Ghadar movement.

JOAN M. JENSEN

EASTERN CATHOLICS

Eastern Catholics, the majority of whom are Byzantine or Greek Catholics, belong to churches that developed in the eastern half of the Roman Empire or in lands culturally dependent on the Byzantine Empire. They give allegiance to Rome but at the same time maintain a number of their traditional Eastern religious customs. Some Eastern Catholic churches were founded in the early centuries of the Christian era, others after the 11th-century split between Roman Catholicism and Eastern Orthodoxy.

In the United States there are an estimated 630,000 Eastern Catholics, representing at least 13 ethnic groups. They worship in accordance with the Antiochene, Armenian, Byzantine, or Chaldean rites rather than the Latin rite of Rome. There are also a few Egyptian Coptic Catholics.

By far the largest group are Slavic immigrants and their descendants. They are listed in *The Official Catholic Directory* as Ruthenians (an old-fashioned term that includes such distinct groups as Carpatho-Rusyns, Croats, Hungarians, and Slovaks) and Ukrainians. The Ruthenians collectively number 280,000; the Ukrainians, 263,000.

Some Ukrainians became Catholic after 1595. In that year a number of Orthodox bishops from the Rus' (later Ukrainian) population, living in what was then the eastern region of the Polish-Lithuanian Commonwealth, met at Brest-Litovsk and swore allegiance to the pope in Rome. A second act of union took place 50 years later at Uzhgorod (Hungarian: Ungvár) in 1646

Table 1. Eastern Catholics in the United States.

Rite	Ethnic group	Estimated members	Estimated parishes
Antiochene	Arabs (Maronite jurisdiction)	36,000	49
	Syrians	3,000	1
Armenian	Armenians	5,000	6
Byzantine	Belorussians	1,000	1
	Italo-Albanians	10,000	1
	Arabs (Melkite jurisdiction)	22,300	26
	Romanians	8,000	17
	Russians	1,000	3
	Ruthenians (Carpatho-Rusyns, Croats, Hungarians, Slovaks)	280,000	223
	Ukrainians	263,000	196
Chaldean	Assyrians	2,500	3
Total		631,800	526

Source: Adapted from *The Official Catholic Directory* (New York, 1979).

when several Orthodox bishops of the Rus' (Carpatho-Rusyn) population in northeastern Hungary united with Rome. Initially, the church and its members were known as Uniate. This term, still occasionally used for Eastern Catholics, carries derogatory connotations. In the late 18th century, at the request of the hierarchy, the church came to be known as the Greek Catholic Church—Greek referring to the rite (actually Byzantine or Byzantine-Slavonic), Catholic signifying unity with Rome.

When these groups first came in large numbers to the United States at the end of the 19th century, they were all united as Greek Catholics; after 1907 they came under the jurisdiction of their own bishop. Political and regional conflict between Ukrainian and Carpatho-Rusyn immigrants, however, led the Roman Catholic authorities to set up two separate administrations (1916) and later two dioceses (1924). One diocese was based in Philadelphia to administer the affairs of the Ukrainian Byzantine-rite Catholics from the former Austro-Hungarian province of Galicia. The other was a "Ruthenian" diocese in Pittsburgh for the Carpatho-Rusyn, Slovak, Hungarian, and Croatian Byzantine-rite Catholics from the former kingdom of Hungary. This division has survived, but both the Philadelphia and Pittsburgh sees have been elevated to metropolitanates, and each is now divided into three dioceses.

The Melkites constitute the third largest group of Byzantine-rite Eastern Catholics. The early Melkites were Arab Christians who lived in Syria, Palestine, and Egypt and supported the christological doctrine at the Council of Chalcedon (A.D. 451). After the Catholic-Orthodox split in 1054, the Melkites sided with the Orthodox. But after the Ottoman authorities replaced native hierarchs with Greeks, some Arab Orthodox turned to the Vatican for support, and in 1724 two bishops, including Patriarch Cyril Tanis, succeeded in uniting with Rome to form the Melkite Catholic Church headed by its own patriarch. The structure of the Melkite liturgy is similar to that of other Byzantine-rite churches, although the languages used are Arabic, Greek, or English. In the United States from the 1890s to the 1960s the Melkites were under the jurisdiction of the local Roman Catholic bishop; in 1966 they received their own bishop; and in 1976 a Melkite-Greek Catholic eparchy was established with a seat in Newton, Mass.

Like the Melkites, the Maronites, who number an estimated 36,000, are Levantine Arabs, but the Maronites observe the Antiochene rite. They are spiritual descendants of the hermit Maron (d. A.D. 410), who lived on a mountain top in northern Syria. Maronite tradition claims that the group has always been Eastern Catholic in union with Rome, although this is disputed. Definitive consolidation took place in the 16th century. Today the vast majority of Maronites, many of them from Lebanon, live in the Western Hemisphere. Their liturgical languages are Syriac, Arabic, and English. For decades they were under the jurisdiction of local Roman Catholic bishops, but in 1962 they received their own bishop and in 1971 a diocese with a seat in Detroit, since transferred to Brooklyn, N.Y.

The other groups of Eastern Catholics—Syrians (Antiochene rite); Armenians (Armenian rite); Belorussians, Albanians, Romanians, and Russians (Byzantine rite); and Assyrians (Chaldean rite)—maintain a few parishes in the United States. However, they do not have their own bishops and are under the jurisdiction of the local Latin-rite ordinary.

Traditionally, Eastern Catholics have been distinguished from Roman Catholics by their maintenance of ancient Eastern rites and usages guaranteed to them when they united with Rome. Historically these features have included singing the liturgy in some language other than Latin; the separation of the altar from the rest of the church by high screens (iconostases) adorned with icons; both a married and a celibate priesthood; the administration of communion to the laity in both kinds (bread and wine); observance of the Julian calendar (in which holidays are usually one or two weeks later than in the Gregorian); and the rendering of the cross with three bars, the bottom one placed diagonally. The Melkites have been the most successful in preserving Byzantine traditions; other groups have been forced by pressure from Rome and the U.S. Roman Catholic hierarchy to abandon their distinctive practices, enforce celibacy, and adopt the Gregorian calendar. In recent years, however, the ethnic revival has permitted a return to traditional altar configurations and the use of vernacular languages.

Bibliography
Donald Attwater, *The Christian Churches of the East*, vol. 1, *Churches in Communion with Rome* (Milwaukee, Wis., 1961), provides a good general introduction. See also the official Vatican publication *La Sacra Congregazione per le Chiese Orientali nel Cinquantesimo della Fondazione 1917–1967* (Rome, 1969), and *The Official Catholic Directory* (New York, 1979).

PAUL ROBERT MAGOCSI

EASTERN ORTHODOX

Eastern Orthodox Christians stem from four ancient patriarchates, five newer patriarchates, and several autocephalous or autonomous Orthodox churches in Europe and Japan. Informed estimates place the total number of Eastern Orthodox in the United States at between 5 and 5.5 million. Organized jurisdictions (dioceses or archdioceses) exist for Albanians, Bulgarians, Belorussians, Carpatho-Rusyns, Greeks, Macedonians, Romanians, Russians, Serbians, Syrians, and Ukrainians. There are, in addition, separate parishes without the rank of diocese for small groups of Estonians and Finns and, for political reasons, for particular groups of Belorussians, Russians, and Ukrainians.

The Greek Orthodox Archdiocese of North and South America and the Orthodox Church in America (formerly the Russian Orthodox Greek Catholic Metropolia in North America) account for probably three-fourths of the Orthodox Christians in the United States —between them approximately 3.5 million.

It is not easy to distinguish neatly the Eastern Orthodox communities in America because of overlapping criteria: ethnic origin, geographic distribution, liturgical language, and political orientation. Culturally, however, Eastern Orthodoxy can be divided into Slavic, Hellenic, and Arab expressions. The Oriental Orthodox are a fourth, and more distinct, group. (*See* Oriental Orthodox.)

Orthodoxy came to the United States in 1794 when a group of Russian monks from the monastery of Valaamo began missionary work among the Aleuts, Eskimos, and Tlingit Indians of Alaska. After Alaska was sold to the United States in 1867, the missionary diocese of New Archangel (Sitka) was transformed into an independent diocese (1870). The cathedral was transferred to San Francisco in 1872 and to New York City in 1905.

Parochial organization in the continental United States, frequently including several ethnic groups within a single parish, was initiated in the 1860s. The first period of significant growth took place toward the end of the 19th century, at the time of the mass immigration from eastern and southern Europe. During this period the jurisdiction of the Russian episcopate was acknowledged by all Orthodox parishes in the United States on the basis of the Second Canon of Carthage, which stipulates that canonical jurisdiction belongs to the church that initiates missionary work in a new area. After 1891 several hundred Eastern Catholic parishes, consisting largely of Carpatho-Rusyn and Galician immigrants, joined the Russian Orthodox Church. The descendants of these former Eastern Catholics constitute a large percentage of the membership of the Orthodox Church in America and the Carpatho-Rusyn and Ukrainian Orthodox jurisdictions. (*See* Carpatho-Rusyns; Eastern Catholics; Russians; Ukrainians.)

Following the political upheaval in Russia in 1917, the cessation of material support by the imperial Russian government and the interruption of normal canonical direction resulted in the formation of other U.S. dioceses, subject to mother churches abroad: Albanian (1918), Ukrainian (1919), Serbian (1921), Greek (1922), Romanian (1930), Antiochian (Syrian) (1936), Bulgarian (1938), Carpatho-Rusyn (1938), Belorussian (1951), and Macedonian (1960). Although this pattern of multiple episcopates with overlapping geographic areas of jurisdiction was alien to traditional Orthodox practice and contrary to canon law, by 1940 it had become an accepted fact of church life.

This centrifugal trend was arrested in 1960 when a dozen Orthodox hierarchs formed the Standing Conference of Canonical Orthodox Bishops of America (SCOBA) in order to provide for cooperation among the member jurisdictions and to establish norms of relations with non-Orthodox groups. This consultative

body is made up of the heads of the ten Orthodox bodies in communion with the patriarchs of Antioch, Bulgaria, Constantinople, Moscow, and Serbia, and with each other.

During the 1970s five events dramatically shifted the direction and development of the Eastern Orthodox communities in the United States.

(1) On April 10, 1970, Patriarch Alexis of Moscow, together with the Holy Synod, confirmed and proclaimed the Russian Orthodox Greek Catholic Church in North America to be independent and self-governing (autocephalous) and named it the Autocephalous Orthodox Church in America. This body consists today of eight regional dioceses plus the Albanian Diocese, the Bulgarian Diocese, and the Romanian Episcopate in the United States; a diocese of Canada; a diocese of South America; a mission in Mexico; and a mission in Australia.

(2) By decree of Patriarch Demetrios I of Constantinople, together with the Holy Synod, the Greek Orthodox Archdiocese of North and South America was reorganized on March 15, 1979. This body consists today of eight regional dioceses in the United States, a diocese of Canada, and a diocese of South America.

(3) On June 24, 1975, Patriarch Elias IV announced the signing of a document of agreement between Archbishop Philip Saliba and Archbishop Michael Shaheen, ending 40 years of division of the Antiochian Orthodox faithful in North America.

(4) On October 18, 1978, the First National Conference of Orthodox Bishops in America was held in Johnstown, Pa., under the chairmanship of Archbishop Iakovos, chairman of SCOBA, who initiated the call for the conference. All Orthodox bishops in the United States were invited. A committee was appointed to develop concrete proposals for further cooperation.

(5) On February 11, 1979, it was announced that the Inter-Orthodox Commission for Dialogue with the Oriental Orthodox Churches had decided to request that an official dialogue between the two church families begin. Representatives of virtually all the national church bodies involved in this dialogue are in the United States.

These events underline the trend toward the development of an indigenous Orthodox church in the United States. The action of the Moscow Patriarchate in 1970 and the response of the Ecumenical Patriarchate in 1979 have slowed intramural relations within American Orthodoxy at the same time that dialogue increased with both the Oriental Orthodox and Roman Catholic churches.

Bibliography
Basic works are: Demetrios J. Constantelos, ed., *Encyclicals and Documents of the Greek Orthodox Archdiocese of North and South America Relating to Its Thought and Activity: The First Fifty Years (1922–1972)* (Thessalonica, Greece, 1976); Arthur C. Piepkorn, *Profiles in Belief: The Religious Bodies of the United States and Canada,* vol. 1, *Roman Catholic, Old Catholic, Eastern Orthodox* (New York, 1977); Archimandrite Serafim (Surrency), *The Quest for Orthodoxy in America: A History of the Orthodox Church in North America* (New York, 1973), and Constance J. Tarasar and John H. Erickson, eds., *Orthodox America 1794–1976: Development of the Orthodox Church in America* (Syosset, N.Y., 1975).

THOMAS E. BIRD

ECUADORIANS: *see* CENTRAL AND SOUTH AMERICANS

EDUCATION

Schooling is a dominant motif in American imagery. The little red schoolhouse of the 19th century is immortalized in paintings and sketches; the high school is at the center of 1930s murals adorning public buildings. Abraham Lincoln's struggle to gain an education is almost as important in the Lincoln legend as his emancipation of the slaves. The school is central to the immigrant epic, and the school bus today symbolizes the persisting conflict between white and black Americans. When the U.S. government declared war on poverty in the 1960s, it first sought to give poor children a head start on school success.

Shaping character and promoting collective and individual material progress have been acclaimed as the two principal accomplishments of schooling. Nineteenth-century crusaders advertised public schools as the means to national unity and prosperity. Twentieth-century educators have been assigned the burden of integrating foreign, minority, and rural newcomers into the cities. Religious, racial, and ethnic leaders have promoted alternative private schools to preserve the faith and raise group consciousness.

The aims and accomplishments of American education have also received a large share of criticism. Schooling, recent "revisionists" claim, has not provided economic opportunity so much as it has implemented cultural domination and the exploitation of some groups at the expense of others. Public education, they argue, has imposed cultural homogeneity on the ethnic mosaic of America. Private schools have preserved a special class and ethnic position for certain white Americans, while nationality and religious schools have had to blur their distinctiveness in order to survive. Other critics hold that schools are actually irrelevant to the economic achievements and cultural values of America's ethnic groups, that schools are, in effect, socially marginal institutions.

These conflicting interpretations of the relationship of ethnicity to education raise complex issues. American beliefs about the centrality of education account for the passion involved in creating, maintaining, criticizing, and interminably reforming the schools. Education touches deep and enduring concerns for individuals and groups; it has an important role in shaping American national consciousness.

Nowhere do these issues emerge more forcefully than in the historical relationships between schools and ethnic and religious diversity. The common school did not produce the harmony its promoters proclaimed for it; it did not eliminate all differences rooted in race, religion, or national origin. But it did embody a vision of cultural integration that revealed the anxieties, aspirations, and expectations of Americans. Debates about the public schools' exclusive claim to public funding allowed individuals and groups to articulate alternative visions of the ideal American community and establish alternatives to the common school. Although factories, unions, and the small businesses in which ethnic groups participated were at least as important as the schools in shaping a national identity, it is in the educational programs that were designed to create Americans that the meaning of Americanization becomes most clear. Also, in the development of alternative or supple-

mentary ethnic schools we can see how different groups defined their own identities and how such schooling was designed to strengthen both ethnic affiliation and American identity. The forms of supplemental schooling suggest the terms on which ethnic voluntarism was acceptable to and compatible with the competing demands of being an American.

The relations between white and nonwhite Americans can also be examined through analysis of educational developments. Obviously, territorial conquest, slavery, and economic discrimination were more central to white domination of nonwhite Americans than was schooling; yet where nonwhites went to school, as well as the extent and content of their education, tells a great deal about the place the white majority assigned them as well as about nonwhites' aspirations and achievements.

During the 1970s a new educational theme emerged, the "new pluralism" or "new ethnicity," which brought curricular reforms along multicultural and bilingual lines. These programs may ultimately have little significant effect on school achievement or on how ethnic groups view themselves; they may be more important as a reflection of changing alliances and conflicts among America's ethnic groups. Or the new ethnicity may bring about a change in how Americans view themselves and in how they treat one another. The eventual effect on the schools is not clear; whether intense and aggressive assertions of ethnic cultural autonomy and self-determination can be absorbed into the present system of public education is an open question. Ethnic-heritage programs may prove insufficient for groups seeking cohesion, cultural reconstruction, or new forms of community. Ethnic groups will also undoubtedly differ on how much multiculturalism they want in the schools. Understanding these issues provides significant insights into the broader changes that the United States is experiencing.

FROM COMMON SCHOOL TO AMERICANIZATION

Sensitive to their former dependent status and to the fragility of republican governments, anxious about the less noble impulses of human beings, and concerned about the uniqueness of the American experiment, in the decades after the Revolution, Americans self-consciously sought to forge a unified nation and a peculiarly American identity. "We have changed our forms of government," wrote Benjamin Rush, a signer of the Declaration of Independence, "but it remains yet to effect a revolution in principles, opinions, and manners so as to accommodate them to the forms of government we have adopted."

Rush exaggerated the change in governmental form represented by the adoption of the Constitution; through their colonial and state legislatures, Americans were already experienced in representative government. The major change represented by the Constitution was the uniting of the states, and the major change required of the populace was to extend the boundaries of personal identification and loyalty. Given the wide range in national origins that came to characterize the U.S. population, an appeal to common principles of government and conduct as the means of achieving common peoplehood made sense, much as an appeal to Commu-

nist ideology provides a common force for shaping a Soviet nation out of diverse peoples.

Revolutions and schooling both represent intentional efforts to shape the future. How to educate the young in post-Revolutionary America was, not surprisingly, a topic of concern. To further the "accommodations" of which Rush wrote, revisions of the traditionally limited and fairly lax system of schooling were proposed. A prize-winning essay sponsored by the American Philosophical Society in 1795 on a national system of education concluded that a national curriculum was required, with uniform texts, lessons, fees, and administrative procedures. George Washington's last annual message to Congress a year later called for the creation of a federally sponsored national university to train the nation's leaders. Noah Webster, the country's first great textbook author, urged a uniform national language as the basis for a permanent national identity, calling upon Americans to discard Old World books which "stamp the wrinkles of decrepit age upon the bloom of youth and . . . plant the seeds of decay in a vigorous constitution."

Proposals for a national school system never reached fruition. Americans were suspicious of centralized authority and ambivalent about the claims of national loyalty. Moreover, what it meant to be an American citizen and how a common national identity was to be established were not clear. Indeed, the great problem for education was to define a common set of institutional goals for a heterogeneous population—and to provide rationales for the status of those people, such as black slaves, who were considered deviations from the standard.

One means of establishing commonality was to minimize or ignore differences among Americans, focusing instead on the differences between them and outsiders. Throughout the 19th century, a constant theme of school textbooks was national unity rather than diversity of origins, cultures, or ideals. Despite occasional dissent, and even the Civil War, the textbooks proclaimed that Americans, unlike ever-warring Europeans, stood together on moral, political, and economic issues. The country's heroes were no mere mortals. Washington was portrayed on occasion as resembling Christ, and one text advised, "Begin with the infant in his cradle/Let the first word he lisps be WASHINGTON." Continuing a tradition of the New England Puritans, whose own errand into the wilderness was conceived as placing a city upon a hill for the whole world to take note of, post-Revolution Americans portrayed their experiment as directed by God. One 19th-century book about the making of the nation concluded, "We cannot but feel that God has worked in a mysterious way to bring good out of evil. It was He, and not man, who saw and directed the end from the beginning."

The problem of relating the story of the American people was more difficult, because it was not a tale of common origins. One way to cope with that was to tell only the story of the English settlers, as if the founding of the Republic proceeded from their experience alone. Non-English settlers were treated as peripheral to understanding the colonial period; in later periods this simplification allowed newcomers to be portrayed as groups having no inherent claims on citizenship, and their welcome was contingent on their acceptance of an

already established way of life. In short, Americans reconciled the conflict between a sense of different origins and their commitment to open immigration by making membership a matter of converting to what later became known as "the American way of life." Newcomers were expected to abandon practices and traits associated with their groups in the Old World.

Textbooks taught what values and characteristics were to be abandoned through stereotypical portrayals of racial, religious, and nationality groups. The negative traits associated with various groups stood as warnings to newcomers, but Americans were ambivalent about the capacity of newcomers to conform. On the one hand, they believed the United States represented a unique environment that promised a new beginning, transcending history. On the other hand, in the 19th century old ideas about superior and inferior peoples expanded into full-blown racist theories, seemingly sanctioned by Darwinian evolutionism.

By the end of the century, mankind was portrayed as divided into separate, immutable races with inherent characteristics, and distinctions among the criteria of color, religion, and national origin were blurred in the hierarchy of peoples. Blacks were the most degraded group: mindlessly happy, stupid, and subject to violent passions. Catholics were portrayed as sheep paying heedless allegiance to a church that undermined the state, secretly fostered immorality, and promoted tyranny, superstition, and greed. Jews were viewed as a racial group whose quest for material goods had taken on sinister overtones, as people afflicted with urban vices offensive to rural morality.

The national identity of residents of other countries was similarly seen as a product of racial characteristics. The Irish were impulsive, quick-tempered, violent, fond of drink, and prone to pauperism. The French posed complications: frivolous and Catholic, they were still the people of Lafayette and Napoleon. Italy was seen as a vast ruin ruled by superstition and the pope; Spain and Portugal were hopelessly bigoted and premodern, the home of the Inquisition. Some nations, especially England and Germany, received more generous treatment, but as the 19th century progressed, textbooks increasingly portrayed newcomers in harsh stereotypes. The message was ambiguous: immigrants could become Americans by adopting the values associated with white, Anglo-Saxon Protestants, but it was not certain that they could do so successfully.

The views of textbook writers about national identity and the fears they expressed about cultural disunity were widespread and played an important part in shaping the establishment, expansion, and systemization of tax-supported public education. In New York City, for instance, there was a generally benign attitude toward the various ethnic and religious groups before 1830. These groups provided whatever schooling existed; state funds for education went to a host of ethnic and denominational schools. After 1830, however, the increasing size of the immigrant population undermined the existing consensus, which favored public tax support to all groups maintaining schools. The Public School Society, a nondenominational organization that supervised and supported the schools until the 1850s, denied appeals from the Catholic hierarchy for school funds, first opened and then abolished a school for German children, and rejected appeals for one for Italians. "When foreigners are in the habit of congregating together they retain their national customs, prejudices and feelings," the society reported, and thus are "not as good members of society as they would otherwise be." Children in the German school, the report noted, "retain their national costume, manners, and feelings, while those German children who mingle promiscuously lose all trace of nationality." Whether German children who lost the visible traces of their nationality would be viewed as full-fledged Americans, the society did not say. Indeed, commentators even into the 20th century, while voicing trepidation about foreigners congregating, were vague about the effects of dispersal.

Though they posed as opponents of sectarianism and factionalism, the early public school advocates clearly tied ideals of citizenship and national identity to Protestantism. Although the United States had no established state church, many people expected their society to be religious and Protestant and their public institutions to reflect that expectation. In schooling the young, the question was how to inculcate religious values when the state was committed to nonsectarianism. In answer, Americans made a distinction between particular Protestant denominations and allegiance to generalized moral values deriving from a belief in the Diety. This distinction allowed for the adoption of Protestantism as a common denominator within public institutions.

That the denominator appeared more Protestant than common to some can be seen in debates during the 1840s between New York's Roman Catholic bishop, John Hughes, and representatives of the Public School Society. Speaking against the common school system, Bishop Hughes argued that the society's ideas of divinely inspired but commonly understood moral values were rooted in Protestant doctrine; that while the "professed charm" of a system of common school education was "the expulsion of sectarianism, there was in it, and inseparable from it, a sectarianism of another kind, which was sapping the young minds of the Catholic children." The Catholic church, he continued, "never recognized the principles of leaving the mind of a child without religious culture until it grew up." The common school system was therefore Protestant, "but it was not the system Catholics could adopt with their children, because they gave religious instruction to their children as a duty which was imperative, while Protestants were independent of religious education, and were of opinion that it was best to have religion to come at some uncertain period, when a change of heart would occur, and a person was to 'join the Church.'"

The society's representatives refused to concede any sectarian motivation and continued the identification of common Protestantism with a national consensus by treating what was to the Catholics inherently Protestant as simply shared morality sanctioned by the Bible. One representative explained that "when the term 'moral' education was used, it only means that education which instructs the children in those fundamental tenets of duty which are the basis of all religion; it does not mean that sectarian or dogmatic teaching which constitutes what is more properly termed a 'religious' education. It has been thought that, for the purposes of moral teaching, the Bible contains that in which all

sects can agree . . . If the whole Bible cannot be used, cannot such extracts from it be compiled as will satisfy all parties?" Another put it succinctly: "And yet, gentlemen, we don't teach anything that is disputed among Christians."

The evolving connection between Protestantism and national identity was highlighted in the mid-19th century by the enthusiastic participation of Protestant ministers, who were often the most educated men in their communities, in the crusade for common schools. Ministers petitioned state legislatures for funds to establish public schools. In many areas, they were themselves the teachers, superintendents, and textbook authors. On a larger scale, the American Home and Baptist Missionary societies crossed denominational lines to organize Sunday schools and distribute Bibles. Protestant colleges in the Midwest stressed the training of teachers for the common schools. Because the colleges drew primarily from local areas and needed whatever tuition-paying students they could find, they frequently muted their particular denominational bases. In establishing and controlling public and private schools, churchmen forged an interdenominational Protestant ideology that was essential to the expansion of common schooling. The Reverend Lyman Beecher, a Congregationalist, called for "a Bible for every family, a school for every district, and a pastor for every thousand souls."

The generalized moral values and patriotism offered by nondenominational Protestantism failed to satisfy those who were more committed to particular Protestant doctrines. The German Lutheran and Dutch Reformed churches, for example, established separate schools to keep their national and religious heritages alive. Nor did the common schools make Protestants out of Catholics and Jews or eliminate commitments to Irish or German identity. Indeed, the decentralized structure of American education throughout most of the century gave ethnic groups an influence over the schools they would not possess in the 20th century.

The emerging definitions of Americanism, however, did order the values of the nation so that allegiance to generalized moral, as opposed to strong doctrinal, beliefs became central to the national identity, along with white skin and an Anglo-Saxon background. These standards meant that incoming groups were expected to partake of a culture and heritage not of their own making. This pattern persisted in the 20th century, as the children and grandchildren of eastern European immigrants learned to say "we" when speaking of the Pilgrim settlers ("our" first Thanksgiving), and "they" when speaking of their own parents and grandparents ("they" came looking for work).

Although concerns for national identity and unity were present throughout the 19th century, and conflicts periodically flared up between native-born Americans (white and black) and immigrants, it was not until the last decades that systematic national efforts of Americanization were directed specifically at the foreign-born and their children. Until that time, public schooling was decentralized and voluntary. The curriculum was essentially the same for all students, because Americans assumed that schooling should provide basic literacy and shared moral values. They relied on these and on the open environment to assimilate newcomers. For

those, such as Asians, who were viewed as immune to these laissez-faire influences, there was exclusion, or in the case of blacks, first slavery and then segregation.

Commitment to more formal means to protect the country from outsiders intensified in the last decades of the 19th century, partly in response to economic depressions in the 1870s and 1890s. Attempts were made to impose a literacy test for immigrants. The Supreme Court in 1896 pronounced segregation of blacks legal with its decision in *Plessy* v. *Ferguson* that "separate but equal" facilities were constitutional. In education many of these protective concerns coalesced around Americanization.

The movement to Americanize immigrants through public schooling reflected a belief in the need for coercion combined with optimism that sufficient zeal on the part of educators and employers could transform immigrant cultures, eliminate dual identity, ensure loyalty to the nation, and bring industrial peace. The first targets were young foreign-born workers not in school. Legislation in a number of states required minors between 14 and 21 who were illiterate in English to attend school part-time. These laws increased attendance at public night schools and often changed the composition of the student body from an English-speaking to a non-English-speaking majority. Publicly funded night schools were expanded to include adults, whose attendance was voluntary but strongly encouraged by employers and civic organizations. The goal of the evening school was not merely English literacy but direct instruction in "proper" home economics, personal hygiene, political participation, and behavior on the job.

The position of the night school in the education of immigrants is ambiguous. On the one hand, immigrant associations themselves started many evening programs to help newcomers learn about America, learn English, and meet in convivial setting. After these classes were incorporated into the public schools, they continued to be a way of acquiring useful knowledge. Immigrants, especially women, saw it as a means of enlarging their sphere of contact in the New World. On the other hand, the night-school movement expanded because of perceptions that immigrants and their cultures were a threat, that it was necessary for the state to require non-English-speaking people to attend school. Attendance was often embarrassing, with little effort made to make classrooms regularly used by young children appropriate to adults. The extent to which evening schools actually touched the lives of immigrant families is uncertain. Many adults at some point in their lives enrolled in evening classes, but rates of attendance and completion of programs lagged well behind enrollment. Some ethnic groups disapproved of the mixing of the sexes at night away from family supervision. The night school was thus no certain or frequent route out of the ghetto, although it served that purpose for some.

The best-organized Americanization efforts focused on adult immigrants, because they were perceived as posing the greatest threat to national stability. Children in school did not foment industrial unrest and socialist agitation, nor did they require direct instruction in the proper ways of factory life. The desirability of learning American ways and language to improve job prospects made such programs acceptable, and the less extreme

ones were supported by immigrant leaders. Business and social-service elites as well as school personnel participated in the effort to Americanize adults. Often the movement combined nationalist goals with those of industrial discipline. Factory schools taught work rules along with English, as an early 20th-century lesson from a Milwaukee factory illustrates:

I hear the whistle. I must hurry.
I hear the five minute whistle.
It is time to go into the shop . . .
I change my clothes and get ready to work.
The starting whistle blows.
I eat my lunch.
It is forbidden to eat until then . . .
I work until the whistle blows to quit.
I leave my place nice and clean . . .

The Americanization of immigrant children through the schools was a more ongoing but less coordinated effort, although World War I did stimulate some intensive, usually short-lived, programs. Broadly speaking, Americanization in the schools attempted to provide patriotic indoctrination and to exclude foreign influences. The daily flag salute and observation of national holidays became widespread. By 1919, because of fears stimulated by the war against Germany, 15 states (many of them with large German settlements) had made English the sole language of instruction in all public and private elementary schools. Foreign languages as subjects of study were removed from the curriculum in many areas. New York and other states required public school teachers to be citizens. In American history courses the connections between present conditions and a hallowed past were stressed, and civics was introduced, to teach not only governmental structures but political behavior as well.

By stressing behavior—language use, patriotism, American ways, on-the-job performance—the Americanization movement tried to submerge the complex relationship between ethnic background and national identity. The movement assumed there was an American identity to which all should aspire, but expressed doubts whether all ethnic groups could ever fully assimilate. These doubts received their strongest support after World War I under the impact of the mental testing movement. Lewis Terman, a pioneer in this field, expressed widely held views about ethnic differences:

The intelligence of the average negro is vastly inferior to that of the average white man. The available data indicate that the average mulatto occupies about a mid-position between pure negro and pure white. The intelligence of the American Indian has also been overrated, for mental tests indicate that it is not greatly superior to that of the average negro. Our Mexican population, which is largely of Indian extraction, makes little if any better showing. The immigrants who have recently come to us in such large numbers from Southern and Southeastern Europe are distinctly inferior mentally to the Nordic and Alpine strains we have received from Scandinavia, Germany, Great Britain, and France.

Thus the period of most intense Americanization efforts ended with a commitment to an American way of life, but without answering the question of what exactly that constituted. During the 1920s discriminatory immigration quotas emphasized the belief that some foreigners made better Americans than others. But it had become clear that the schools were where youth and, if necessary, adults, would learn the requirements of being an American.

ETHNIC RESPONSES AND ALTERNATIVES

Most educators sought to promote cultural homogeneity and the work ethic of industrial capitalism. But some, like Julia Richman in New York and Chicago settlement-house worker Jane Addams, recognized that both the possibility and the desirability of quickly remaking the immigrants were questionable. They feared that the more extreme forms of Americanization would demoralize immigrant families, disorganize ethnic communities, and stimulate further generational cleavage between immigrant parents and their children. They sought to keep the immigrants' personality and self-respect intact by stressing the "contributions" of immigrant "gifts" to American culture. To some extent, these more moderate Americanizers were suggesting a different view of the United States, a view that accepted cultural pluralism as a basis upon which to build a nation. More often, however, they simply expected to use milder methods over a longer period to achieve assimilation and cultural homogeneity.

The moderate wing was not the only factor impeding the Americanization movement from reaching its most extreme goals. While educational programs in any period represent the dominant ideology, the actual outcomes depend on the interaction between the educators and the populations with whom they deal. In both the 19th and 20th centuries, ethnic groups varied, and individuals within groups differed, in their responses to the opportunities and demands of public education. Furthermore, the diversity of American life, the democratic political structure, and the importance of voluntarism, even with increasing state involvement, produced tensions and conflicts that had an impact on education. The decentralized structure of most school systems during the 19th century left schools open to ethnic and political pressures, and minority groups could often successfully secure at least some recognition of their special needs. Groups that were strong enough and sufficiently disaffected shunned the public schools altogether and established their own alternatives, and groups that embraced public schooling but were anxious to preserve or formulate their ethnic identities turned to supplemental schooling.

Most ethnic groups sought acceptance as Americans and were willing to identify with and support public institutions. Few groups came to the United States to build particularistic communities, and some, such as the eastern European Jews, were fleeing from state-imposed separatism. But ethnic groups and individuals also desired some continuity with their past. Many sought public recognition of their ethnic cultures, both as a way of solidifying generational continuity between parents and children and as a way of commanding acknowledgment from the wider community. They opposed educational programs that denigrated their groups, even as they desired to become Americans, and they resisted demands that made educational achievement depend on rejection of familial and group values.

The clearest examples of ethnic resistance to denigration were protests against biased textbooks. Catholics and Jews frequently opposed anti-Catholic and anti-Semitic books and teaching materials, and Irish and Italian organizations forced revisions in materials that denigrated their groups. Blacks pressured school systems to reject textbooks that portrayed them as satisfied with being slaves, violent by nature, and incapable of participating in democratic government. Although the effectiveness of such protests have varied, numerous minorities at one time or another have lobbied for fairer treatment in learning materials.

Language Instruction In addition to opposing blatant examples of cultural denigration, groups attempted to have some of their own traditions incorporated into the schools, usually through language instruction or the teaching of a group's history. During the 19th century some non-English-speaking groups that were heavily concentrated in an area were able to get their languages introduced into elementary and secondary schools, either as courses of study or as languages of instruction. In California during the mid-19th century large numbers of Spanish-speaking children were taught in their own language, owing to the initial constitutional recognition of both English and Spanish as essential languages and to state funding of denominational schools. During the same period Texas reimbursed parents for each child enrolled in a recognized school, thereby allowing some Mexican children access to Spanish schools, and the territory of New Mexico officially recognized public Spanish-language schools until the 1890s. Scandinavians, Italians, Czechs, Dutch, and other European groups similarly pressured school systems to at least allow the study of their language as an option and demanded the hiring of teachers from their group.

The Germans in a number of states and cities, especially in the Midwest, managed to make German a regular part of the school curriculum. In Cincinnati during the last decades of the 19th century, children in the first four grades could split their school week between English and German teachers. St. Louis's superintendent of schools, William Torrey Harris, defended his city's bilingual program by claiming that "national memories and aspirations, family traditions, customs, and habits, moral and religious observances—cannot be suddenly removed or changed without disastrously weakening the personality." Although Germans were unusually successful in this effort, the restriction of bilingualism to the early grades reveals that their aspirations, and others', were limited to ensuring ethnic continuity without socializing their children into separatist enclaves and that educators were committed to furthering Americanization, albeit by cushioned and gradual means.

Other European groups in urban areas were not so successful as the Germans, but ethnic enclaves in rural areas made small schoolhouses virtual extensions of the ethnic community. In these areas European languages, ethnic holidays, and religious traditions were an integral part of schooling for the children of immigrants well into the 20th century. In the cities the incorporation of these cultural values was more problematic. Eastern European immigrants at the turn of the century were viewed with distrust, often hostility, and did not command the cultural admiration that the late-19th-century Germans did. The mixture of eastern European immigrant groups also made it difficult for any one group to organize sufficient political pressure for recognition of its ethnic heritage in the schools.

Concessions to ethnic culture were frequently short-lived, as pressures developed against "special status." Often the elimination of a foreign language or ethnic studies was an example of blatant discrimination, as occurred in attacks upon Spanish in the Southwest. The ethnic groups themselves were ambivalent about the extent to which their language and culture should be a feature of the public schools. Although the use of German in the St. Louis schools was initially highly attractive to German parents, the commitment of these parents and especially their children to assimilation was also strong. When German-language instruction was terminated in the public schools 25 years after its introduction, there was little protest from the German community.

Parochial Schools Ethnic groups resisted assaults on their culture but were wary of too forceful assertions of their distinctiveness in public institutions; they were uncertain of how much to demand and of what was best for their children, but in most cases they were committed to public schooling and had little intention of separation. Despite frequent attacks on their cultural and class behavior, immigrant groups never construed ethnic preservation as inimical to American citizenship and loyalty. Only when they were directly threatened or excluded did groups turn away from the public system. But their alternative educational arrangements did not fundamentally challenge the dominant ideas of public education. Even parochial schools, which were highly responsive to ethnic variations, became exercises in religious, not ethnic, diversity. However powerful the role of ethnicity in shaping alternatives to public schooling, the formal justification of most nonpublic schooling has not been to legitimate ethnic differences.

Most ethnic groups at one time or another established their own day schools, but these did not develop into the full-fledged system that the Catholic parochial schools became. The relationship of this system to the public system and the patterns of internal differentiation shed light on the limits of both ethnic aspiration and majority tolerance. The parochial system emerged out of struggle and ambivalence; its growth was conditioned by the development of the Protestant-oriented public school system and by tensions within and among Catholic groups of differing national origins. Its persistence in the 20th century lay in good measure in its ability to blur the sharp differences that initially separated it from the public system.

In the early 19th century, when there was little distinction between sectarian and common schooling, most denominations supported schools under their own auspices and received state aid. The systematization of public education after 1840 replaced this pattern with tax-supported, universally available free schooling. Many Catholics, however, without regarding their action as separatist or antipublic, rejected the new common school system. They protested the transfer of education from parental and church auspices to the state and the imposition of a barely disguised Protestant sectarianism on Catholic children.

Until the end of the century, when public officials finally rejected all efforts to keep the Catholic schools within the system, there were repeated examples of local cooperation between public and Catholic educators. In some communities public funds were allocated directly to parish schools. Catholics in other communities sent their children to public schools with the assurance that Protestant observances would be eliminated. Some Catholic schools were placed under the administration of the public school system, and teachers were drawn from religious orders; religious instruction was provided outside regular class hours. Although not numerous, some arrangements of this sort were in effect as late as 1898. Their termination reflected the upsurge of anti-Catholicism in the late 19th century and a number of court decisions that restricted state support for religious institutions. And Catholics themselves were uneasy about cooperation with public education.

The development of Catholic education was related to more than Protestant–Catholic differences over the role of the state in education. In large measure, the dramatic growth of Catholic schools between 1880 and 1920 was a result of ethnic heterogeneity within the church. For Catholics the American environment was unique in that it broke long-standing ties of territory, nationality, and church practice. In Europe geographic boundaries had traditionally permitted distinctive patterns of religious worship within national and regional lines. In the urban United States, however, different nationality groups lived in close proximity, and conflicts flared over language differences, saints to be honored, church architecture, piety, and the relationship between clergy and laity. Such difference generated the national parishes that became the hallmark of 19th-century American Catholicism. Irish and German groups before the Civil War, and later Polish, French Canadian, and other groups established separate hospitals, orphanages, benevolent societies, and schools. Each group organized its parish along its own lines, and the bishops frequently, if reluctantly, acquiesced in appointing priests of the respective nationalities. In city after city, the number of foreign-language parishes increased, often overlapping with the "official" territorial parish, which was usually Irish. For example, the proportion of foreign-language parishes among all parishes in Chicago went from 26 percent in 1869 to 47 percent in 1889 and 54 percent by 1899.

While the episcopate stressed parochial schools as an obligating alternative to the Protestant-based, "godless" public schools, it was the interplay and competition among nationality groups and between national-origins communities and the hierarchy that influenced the rapid growth of the Catholic school system. Irish and German Catholics established competing schools side by side; later nationality groups did the same. Lithuanians in Chicago successfully ousted Polish sisters teaching in their parish schools. Within the parish the school was believed to assure the permanence of the faith and to shield Catholic children from the hostility and temptation of outsiders. Indeed, the parish school became the center of the ethnic Catholic's associational life.

Different immigrant groups had different expectations for their parishes and schools, based on the history of the church in the old country. Just as there was no single immigrant experience in the public schools, there was no uniform pattern of experience with parochial schooling. Among eastern European Catholics, the Poles were most committed to segregated national parishes and schools. Their intense demands for autonomy within the church's federated structure even led to the establishment of the schismatic Polish National Church. Italian Catholics, in contrast, had little concern for nationality-based religious institutions and were the only foreign-language group within the church that did not demand more and more parish facilities. Opposed in many ways by the Irish-dominated Catholic hierarchy, the Italians were singularly inactive in establishing national parish schools. Although in 1930 the Poles in Chicago outnumbered Italians by 2 to 1, they sent 13 times as many children to Catholic schools. Only with the entrance of Italian Catholics into the middle class, residential mobility, and the development of a modern parochial school system did Italian Americans send large numbers of their children to church-sponsored schools.

The intensity of interethnic relationships within the Catholic church also sharpened the hierarchy's fear of fragmentation. The struggle to maintain harmony and establish lines of authority led to a series of moves to centralize decision making. Coinciding with these efforts were the systematization and modernization of parochial education, resulting in a system which, save for its religiosity, was explicitly based on public school norms. In retrospect, there was probably little alternative. State certification requirements for schools and teachers, as well as pressure to make parochial education comparable to public schooling so that children could move between the two systems, required a similar curriculum and structures.

After the 1920s nationality differences within the church tended to weaken although they by no means disappeared. Despite its development based on ethnic differences, the Catholic parochial system thus matured into a system serving a community defined principally by religious affiliation, not national origins. Parochial schooling continued to play an important role in shaping Catholic-American identity even beyond the second generation.

Attempts by other groups to establish explicitly ethnic-based schooling—for example, the system established by the German Lutherans of the Missouri Synod, the second-largest separate school system in the United States—showed the same pattern of evolving into religious-based schooling. Although ethnic diversity has by no means been transformed into simply religious distinctions—Protestant, Catholic, Jew—ethnically rooted activity has tended to be institutionalized within a framework of religious activity. Religion and ethnicity are inherently difficult to separate, but religious organization has historically been accorded a legitimacy that ethnic organization has not, and therefore it provided acceptable opportunities for satisfying ethnic needs. The development of ethnic schooling within a religious framework that diminished the differences between ethnic groups, illuminated in the history of Catholic separate schools, is similar to the development of supplemental schooling.

Jewish Education For no other group, except perhaps individual American Indian tribes, are religious and

ethnic identity more complexly linked than for Jewish Americans. Despite variations and even intense conflict in religious expression, political outlook, and national background, Jews share a sense of common peoplehood that is more than religious affiliation. Under segregated conditions in eastern Europe, they developed traditions of communal organization and self-government; in the United States these traditions evolved into extensive networks of voluntaristic organizations to meet the needs of immigrants. One might have expected that a group whose identity incorporated an enduring component of separateness, whose members were skilled in institution building and had often suffered from government policies, would enthusiastically develop alternatives to public schooling. Instead Jews embraced the public schools and placed group schooling in a clearly secondary position, assigning to it the delicate task of preserving group identity while not impeding social and economic integration. To a great extent, supplemental schooling for Jews, as for most other ethnic groups, has been an instrument of ambivalent self-preservation and defense.

The predominantly German 19th-century American Jewish community was committed to supplemental schooling that imparted a sense of Jewish identity without developing characteristics that would noticeably distinguish the students from other Americans. The German Jews were more dispersed throughout the country than the later eastern European Jewish immigrants were, they were economically successful, and in the spirit of Reform Judaism, they deemphasized traditional authority and communal ties. They tended to view themselves as German Americans, distinguished only by the practice of a different religion. Almost all Jewish schooling was supplemental, assumed attendance at public day schools, and rarely included Hebrew-language instruction.

The characterization of Jews as simply another religious group was tested severely at the end of the 19th century, as anti-Semitism grew and massive immigration from eastern Europe altered the composition of American Jewry. The newcomers, though by no means a homogeneous group, represented a dramatically different type of Jewish community and brought a different approach to Judaism. In eastern Europe, where they were legally excluded from participation in non-Jewish and economic life, Jews nourished their religious and cultural practices in isolation and evolved their own communal and institutional structures. They held little hope of becoming full citizens of the new national states in eastern Europe; unlike Jews in western Europe, most of them did not even speak the national language. Their use of Yiddish reinforced their sense of segregation, and the practices of Orthodox Judaism regulated home and community life.

Relations between the established German Jewish community and the newer immigrants were tense. German Jews often viewed the newcomers as ignorant, poverty-ridden, and anarchistic. After first trying to discourage immigration and encourage the dispersal of immigrants to agricultural areas, German Jews turned to educational activities. Paralleling the efforts of settlement houses, Jewish organizations promoted Americanization and "uplift" through clubs, reading and discussion groups, lectures, English-language and civics classes, and essay contests along the lines of "Why I Wish to Become a Citizen." In this effort they were joined by groups within the eastern European community.

The success of these efforts cannot be measured. Attendance at the various activities was good, but the eastern Europeans, unwilling to be molded along the lines set down by the German Jewish community, reshaped the programs to reflect their own concerns. Even more revealing were the choices the new immigrants made in schooling their children, which suggest that German Jews, and other Americans as well, had little reason to worry about their assimilation.

In eastern Europe the girls received no formal schooling; boys from about 5 to 15 years of age attended *heder* in the home of a teacher (*melamed*) for 11 to 12 hours daily, where they were immersed in Jewish religion and tradition and learned Hebrew. In the United States, Jewish education was voluntarily transformed from the Old World form, into congregationally based supplemental schools that prepared both boys and girls for specific rites of passage and for participation in the life of the wider community. American Jews rarely schooled their children for a life apart from the mainstream, though they briefly experimented with communally based schooling and attempted to reinfuse a sense of peoplehood into American Judaism. The heder changed drastically from a communally sanctioned, well-established enterprise to a second-class and almost desperate after-school effort to transmit something of the traditional knowledge to children already fatigued by their day in public school. Until 1910 economic pressures, the difficulties of establishing community consensus in metropolitan areas, and the universal opportunity to attend public school undermined all except minimal standards of Jewish education.

The most important fact about the fate of traditional Jewish education in the United States is not that an Old World form degenerated, but that it was abandoned voluntarily for the public schools rather than transformed into a parochial system. Whatever cultural preservation meant to Jews, it did not mean transferring the system of ghetto education to America. That system had been a product of exclusion by Gentiles, the futility of integrationist aspirations, and strict Orthodoxy, whose most loyal adherents remained in Europe. In the absence of social imperatives to continue a system that obstructed assimilation and mobility, immigrant Jews found scant reason to reinstitute such practices. Unlike Catholics, Jews associated separation with stigma, feared the opprobrium of Gentiles, and did not have a clerical hierarchy to urge and legitimize parochial education.

Parents were nevertheless eager to prevent their children from abandoning their Jewish identity and the essential practices of Judaism. While many Jews had minimal expectations of Jewish schooling, however, community leaders and Jewish educators elaborated institutional structures, rationales, and a curriculum for a modernized Jewish education. In New York City during the 1920s, a citywide Bureau of Jewish Education tried to develop professional educational programs for Jewish schools by providing financial assistance in return for the adoption of uniform standards and curricula. The bureau's establishment of model schools in which to train teachers and experiment with curricula stimu-

lated the development of a Jewish education profession. The bureau also sponsored weekly lectures and slide shows in the immigrant community. The aim of Jewish schooling, the bureau believed, in a society in which Jewish identity seemed to be waning and the risks of social atomization were high, was to convince youth of their Jewishness, not to impart a corpus of traditional knowledge.

The bureaus of Jewish education in New York, Chicago, Philadelphia, and other cities assumed that Jewish schools would be supported by the whole community. Because the Jews were "a people," their schooling would be communally sponsored. This view, however, ran counter not only to that of the established German Jews, but also to the demography of the Jewish community. The immigrants moved rapidly out of the areas of initial settlement. New synagogues could be built relatively easily to serve new neighborhoods, but schools based on communal expectations could not so easily be moved, nor could new ones easily be established. Along with other roles geared to serving more than the needs of worship and observance, the new synagogues took on the task of Jewish schooling. In 1917 over three-fifths of the children attending Jewish schools were in Talmud Torahs—schools supported by tuition and donations, governed by boards of trustees, and not affiliated with synagogues. By 1929 the figure was less than a third, and by 1934, it was only 28 percent. By 1936 three-quarters of the Jewish schools outside New York were congregational, and in later decades the provision of Jewish schooling became a main attraction of suburban synagogues.

The transformation from communal to congregation-based education does not mean that American Jews returned to 19th-century Reform definitions of Judaism. Especially since World War II, the curriculum has stressed the peoplehood of Jews as much as it has preparation for synagogue or home worship. But congregational schooling is evidence of the predominance of religious organization over other possible forms of ethnic and national expression.

Jewish supplementary schooling and Catholic parochial schooling, while in some ways representing conflicting visions of assimilation and accommodation, both suggest that the aspirations of immigrant groups were quite compatible with all but the most extreme demands of the native-born. Many, if not most, Catholics would probably have preferred to remain within the public system if satisfactory compromises had been possible, and the system they evolved mirrors the public system in many ways. Jews stress their peoplehood, but not as a group apart, and have always been among the strongest supporters of public schooling. The fragmentation feared by nativistic Americanizers was never on the ideological or institutional agendas of the newcomers.

Protestant Boarding Schools The parochial day schools and the afternoon supplementary schools were, on the whole, attempts to integrate ethnic culture with American life. They thus tended to originate among minorities, the less powerful, the poor and working class —those who in important ways were outsiders. Another group, however, which included the most powerful people in the country—the social elite and those seeking access to it—also used education to confirm group identity and ensure economic and social success. They established, especially in the three decades after 1880, a succession of private boarding and day schools to provide special, segregated learning environments for their children.

The most prestigious of the elite boarding schools— Andover, Exeter, St. Paul's, Choate, Groton, among others—were located in the eastern states. Often associated with the Protestant Episcopal church and frequently modeled on what were the presumed best aspects of elite English public schools, these preparatory schools were specifically for wealthy white Protestant boys although there were analogues for girls and for Catholic and Jewish elites. The schools expanded in the late 19th century because of a growing self-consciousness among America's wealthy as to proper aristocratic lifestyles in a democracy, a resurgent Anglophilia, and the emergence of urban political leadership in the European immigrant communities. The elite schools were the other side of the democratization of public secondary education; as the proportion of middle- and working-class youth in public high schools increased at the turn of the century, the wealthy withdrew to their own segregated facilities.

These schools mixed academic preparation for entry into colleges—Harvard, Yale, and Princeton especially —with reinforcement of the socialization befitting Christian gentlemen. The lessons were not those of a European aristocracy; in important respects they replicated the accepted wisdom regarding success in the United States: a belief in meritocracy, public service, replenishment of family income, and high ethical standards, ideas as easily found in the rags-to-respectability stories of Horatio Alger. What distinguished the elite Protestant schools was the intimate relationship between these codes of conduct and social and economic power. Yet like the ethnic schools of the less powerful, the elite schools were a group attempt to balance familial and community standards, to preserve a certain way of life, with the requirement that no American be too different from any other American.

SCHOOLING AND NONWHITE AMERICANS

For nonwhite Americans the choices of how to school their children and expectations of that schooling were more limited and complicated than they were for whites, and the benefits of schooling less tangible. Like other ethnic groups, nonwhites looked to education to enhance their children's opportunity, but they often had to fight for the right just to attend school; if they were not denied access, they had to cope with inferior settings under the "separate but equal" rule. The educational provisions that lower-class communities could make for themselves depended upon limited resources, aided by support from some members of the white community. Educational opportunities for Japanese and Chinese were shaped by the ebb and flow of discrimination, economic conditions, and international politics. Mexican Americans and other Hispanic groups found themselves legally white but not "Anglo" and were sometimes segregated on racial grounds. Racial antagonism and discrimination forced black Americans to depend heavily upon their own community efforts in the form of elementary schools, manual-training pro-

grams, and the black colleges established in the post-Reconstruction period. American Indians suffered most, for the white man's educational agenda for them was the most explicitly oppressive.

For people of color, then, the promise of education as the ultimate opportunity to join the American mainstream was often hollow. Though the ideology of public education required that as many children as possible be brought into the public schools, nonwhite Americans were frequently excluded and regularly segregated. The specifics varied by group, region, city, and town, as did group responses and the interplay among groups. No ethnic group was simply a passive victim of other people's decisions; each drew upon its resources and traditions to shape educational opportunities.

American Indians White policy toward Indians can broadly be divided into two phases: expulsion from tribal lands during most of the 19th century and Jim Crow-like exclusion from economic and social opportunities for the period since. Before the 1870s most federal treaties with Indian tribes included provisions for public services, including education and apprentice-style instruction in manual trades. Often the treaties were phrased in terms of religious uplift or social reform; they were, an 1819 Congressional enactment declared, "for the purpose of introducing among them the habits and arts of civilization." (*See* American Indians, Federal Policy Toward.)

Although white proposals to educate Indians had a rhetorical similarity to the broader appeals of the 19th-century common school movement for whites, sharing the claim that education would improve social and economic opportunities and bring allegiance to properly constituted authority, the notion of civilizing the natives always stood in tension with the white desire for rapid westward expansion. Education and the land were in essential conflict, and white policy was soon dominated by forced removal of the Indians.

During the final decades of the 19th century the success of the westward movement, the economic costs of Indian wars, and public outrage led to revisions in Indian policy. With the introduction of measures to wean Indians away from their tribes through land allotments to individuals, new educational policies were adopted to alienate the Indians from tribal and group loyalties and promote assimilation. After 1871 bilingual mission schools were replaced by English-only government schools, and tribally run schools, like those of the Cherokees, were undermined. Government-sponsored boarding schools were especially important, the U.S. Commissioner of Indian Affairs wrote in 1885, because "the barbarian child of the barbarian parent spends possibly six of the twenty-four hours of the day in a school room. He returns, at the close of his day-school, to eat and play and sleep after the savage fashion of his race." Loyalty to native language and dress was viewed as the preeminent evil. Pupils in government schools were not allowed to study in any language other than English. Samuel Chapman Armstrong, founder of Hampton Institute, regarded with "unambivalent triumph" the letters in which Indian students promised to shun Indian ways and to "walk the white man's road."

In the Indian schools militarylike discipline, corporal punishment, and kidnapings to assure attendance were common. Since federal funds depended upon enroll-

ments, a premium was placed on getting children into the schools and keeping them there. Teachers of Indian children were paid less than public school teachers, and poor facilities, geographic isolation, and primitive living conditions compounded recruitment problems. Conditions were worst at the boarding schools, but conditions at day schools on or near reservations—a growing trend after 1900—were also bad. After 1885 operational procedures were centralized, and curriculum, examinations, grading, and rates of financing were made uniform. Enrollments and attendance were low. Frequently Indian children, caught between totally inadequate reservation and boarding schools, tried to attend local public schools, where they were usually unwanted.

Government educational policy for Indians before the 1920s was thus explicitly directed at detribalization. It resulted in both divisiveness and resistance. Some Indians refused to send their children to the federal schools, leading Congress in 1893 to authorize withholding federal support from Indian families who did so. Among the Hopis, a sharp split developed over attending white schools. Some tribes used tribal funds to contract with missionary groups to provide more culturally balanced programs. Given the option of government schooling exclusively on white terms, many Indian children either never attended school or dropped out after a short period.

The 1920 Census reported that 36 percent of the Indians were illiterate, compared to 6 percent of the total U.S. population. Findings like these were at the basis of sharp criticism in a 1928 Brookings Institution report rejecting government policies that tried to "crush out all that is Indian." Federal policy changed and began to stress the strengthening of tribal social structure and culture as a more effective, less alienating means of assimilation. Legislation strengthened tribal government, classes began using native languages, and attendance at local public schools began to replace the boarding and day schools. In 1934 the Johnson-O'Malley Act provided financial assistance to the states for Indians living on or near federal trust lands who attended public schools. State responses varied, in part because states with large Indian populations had already established their own procedures; often federal funds were used for non-Indian children.

In California small financial incentives offered to school districts that enrolled Indian children were unsuccessful; community prejudice kept Indians out of the public schools. Until the mid-1920s California law had allowed Indians to be excluded from public schools on the ground that they had access to federal schools. California modified its approach during the 1920s, and when federal funds became available, the state quickly channeled Indians into local public school districts. But even then, in California and elsewhere, the "New Deal" in Indian education was barely fulfilled. Prejudice and discrimination continued, conflicts over which public agencies were responsible for Indian schooling abounded, and segregation was common even after exclusion ended. In the 1940s and 1950s the federal government began to cut back its already limited commitments to educational quality. However, the situation has improved substantially in the past two decades.

Asians For immigrants from Asia the politics of ra-

cial exclusion, America's labor needs, questions about who could become citizens, and restrictions on such fundamental rights as land ownership affected educational opportunities. During the 1870s and 1880s racial antagonism was sufficiently high to exclude Chinese children from San Francisco's public schools entirely, in order to protect California's white children "from this invasion of Mongolian barbarians." On the West Coast especially this kind of hostility toward Chinese and Japanese was a recurring phenomenon. The growing expectation that all children, even those of disreputable background, should be socialized in the public schools, however, soon undermined the policy of exclusion from the schools. A California state court ruled in 1885 that Chinese children had to be admitted to public schools, but the court did not deny the state's right to segregate on the basis of race.

Exclusionist, followed by segregationist, policies directed at Asian students strengthened the position of missionary and language schools in the Chinese and Japanese communities. During the late 19th and early 20th centuries, a number of denominations held English-language classes to Christianize newcomers from Asia in return for teaching them enough English to gain employment. More important were the association-run language schools that emphasized traditional culture and values under the assumption that most youngsters would soon return to their homeland. Among the Japanese, whose migration was less oriented toward an eventual return, such classes were more assimilationist.

Though the language schools were important among the Chinese and Japanese, both communities had become strongly committed to the public schools by the first decades of the 20th century. But they resisted the forced enrollment of their children in inadequate, segregated facilities. One Chinese mother whose children were admitted to San Francisco's public schools protested against their being "compelled to attend a school set apart exclusively for Chinese."

The most important protest against segregation, however, occurred in 1905–1907 when the Japanese resisted a San Francisco school board requirement that all Asian children attend segregated schools. The board's action precipitated a major diplomatic controversy and the most serious school-segregation conflict prior to the 1950s.

Between 1890 and 1910 the number of Japanese residents in the United States grew from roughly 2,000 to 72,000; more than half lived in California. In the first years of the century attempts were made to extend to them the immigration exclusion legislation directed against the Chinese. Complaints abounded that Japanese children were "over aged and diseased" and were, unlike the Chinese, attending integrated neighborhood schools. In May 1905 the San Francisco school board called for separate schools for Japanese children so "that our children should not be placed in any position where their youthful impression may be affected by associations with pupils of the Mongolian race." The following fall, with anti-Japanese sentiment hardening, the school board moved to require that "all Chinese, Japanese, and Korean children" be sent to the "Oriental Public School."

Reaction in the Japanese community was immedi-

ate. Parents overwhelmingly refused to send their children, held protest meetings, and complained to the Japanese consul. Tokyo newspapers declared that their countrymen "have been humiliated." The American ambassador in Tokyo informed Washington that a diplomatic crisis was brewing. President Theodore Roosevelt, concerned about upsetting friendly relations with a powerful nation, condemned the San Francisco action as a violation of treaty agreements on the rights of Japanese residents in the United States and sent Secretary of Commerce and Labor Victor Metcalf to California to negotiate a settlement. Metcalf's report criticized the school board's decision. Only 93 of the city's 28,000 students were Japanese, and the teachers he interviewed claimed their Japanese students were among the best behaved, cleanest, and brightest they had. Other than racial hostility, there appeared to be little justification for the policy of segregation.

The outcome of the controversy neither ended segregation in California nor settled issues involving the relationship of the federal government to state and local education authorities. The compromise arranged by Roosevelt rescinded the segregation policy in return for a "gentlemen's agreement" that ended the immigration of Japanese laborers to the United States. The Japanese, though, continued to face outbursts of racial hostility for another generation.

The territory of Hawaii was more open to providing educational opportunities to its Asian population, but attacks were also made upon Asians there, especially over the Japanese supplementary schools. Effective political organization among the Hawaiian Japanese, however, coupled with a supporting U.S. Supreme Court decision, limited the right of public authorities to intervene in private foreign-language schools. In general, despite outbreaks of anti-Asian feeling, the cosmopolitan nature of Hawaii's population allowed groups like the Chinese and Japanese to take advantage of expanding educational opportunities.

The strong commitment of Chinese and Japanese families to public education had a major effect on their private language schools. As the number of American-born children increased, Chinese and Japanese parents became concerned about their children losing contact with the ancestral culture. The Chinese-language schools, which initially tried to replicate the traditional schools of the homeland, eventually provided only minimal levels of contact with traditional ways. For the Japanese the language schools had similar aims, although they were also supposed to help second- and third-generation children communicate American values to their parents and to introduce small children to the English language. There is little evidence, however, that either the Japanese- or Chinese-language schools, which were often haphazardly attended, had a substantial effect in inculcating traditional language and culture. Once accessibility to public education was assured, the Asians centered their aspirations for the young in the public schools.

Spanish-Speaking Groups America's Spanish-speaking peoples have been placed in a particularly difficult position with regard to ethnicity and education. Although rarely reported as nonwhite by federal and state authorities, they have often been treated as a separate racial group by officials, especially in states along the

Mexican border. Concern for the education of Hispanic Americans mounted in the decades around World War I, when American labor shortages and social and economic unrest in Mexico markedly increased migration to the United States. In addition, the immigration shifted from primarily single young men to increasing numbers of families. The growth of the school-age population was striking. In 1922, 1.5 percent of Texas's student-age population were of Mexican descent; by 1929, 13 percent. In southern California two years earlier, about 10 percent of the public-school population were Mexican.

The new immigrants spoke little English, maintained close ties to their nearby homeland, were poor, and were highly transient, often working as migrant laborers. In sheer numbers they overwhelmed existing and sometimes long-established Spanish-speaking communities. Their circumstances made enrollment and attendance at school a major educational problem. In 1928 all but a small fraction of the Texas Anglo students were enrolled in school, but only about half the Mexican children, a quarter of them in the first grade. Mexicans, like other groups living in poverty, regarded education as a means of social mobility, but acquiring it substantially reduced the family's immediate earnings.

School attendance often exposed Spanish-speaking children to open hostility and inferior facilities. Legislation in Texas, originally passed in 1918 to limit the use of German, was soon applied to the Spanish-speaking, who were forbidden to use their native language on school grounds, a restriction enforced in other states as well. The Texas superintendent of public instruction warned Mexican parents in 1923 that their private schools should also come under this language restriction. Even under the aegis of Americanization, however, investment in schooling for the Spanish-speaking was low. In Texas educational funds were siphoned off to the Anglo schools, leaving the teachers of Spanish-speaking children underpaid, and housing and equipment grossly inadequate.

Growing segregation further complicated the education of Mexican Americans. Because the Spanish-speaking were rarely named in state legislation that allowed separation of the races, direct *de jure* segregation was considered unconstitutional. What emerged, as part of a broader movement during the 1920s, was a system of segregation ostensibly based on instructional needs rather than race; segregation of Mexican children was held to be essential to their progress. The expectation, a California superintendent of schools declared in 1928, was that "pupils should not be put into Mexican classes because they are Mexican, they should be put there because they can profit most by instruction offered in such classes." Segregated schools were also declared necessary to limit the disruptive effects of a transient student body on regular Anglo school programs. IQ and other tests were interpreted to show the inherent inferiority of Hispanic children and to justify separate and inadequate facilities.

Although segregation was widespread, it was never universal. A small number of Spanish-speaking Americans, especially if they were middle class and well assimilated, could enter high school, which facilitated a degree of integration into the mainstream. The general segregation of Hispanic children came under attack in

the 1930s and 1940s as racist theories were discredited. Findings that Mexican children learned English better in mixed than in segregated classes, and growing attention to the environmental basis of low test scores and poor school achievement challenged the belief that Spanish-speaking children benefited from their enforced isolation. But most important were the protests waged by Mexican Americans themselves. Protests against inadequate facilities in local school districts were initially led with sporadic success by assimilated middle-class parents during the 1920s and 1930s. Not until World War II, however, were the protests large or consistent enough to have much impact. In 1947 a U.S. court of appeals declared that the segregation of Spanish-speaking children violated California law; during the next three years, federal courts similarly ruled against *de jure* segregation of Mexican-American children in Texas and Arizona. Yet segregation and inadequate education opportunities continued and in many ways may have worsened as the urban Hispanic population has continued to grow. Under the impact of pressures to achieve racial integration, a number of school districts in the Southwest classified Mexicans as white and integrated them with blacks to avoid integration of Anglos and blacks. By the early 1970s Spanish-speaking children were even more likely to be segregated from Anglo children than they had been in 1945. Recent federal support for bilingual education, paradoxically, may perpetuate such segregation.

Blacks More than any other group, black Americans have experienced exclusion and segregation in education. In the South restrictions on slave education became even more severe in the decades before the Civil War. Yet as oppressive as slavery was, southern blacks, free and slave, nonetheless organized to transmit knowledge among themselves and across the generations. Communal and family ties were strong, their religion drew upon oral traditions, vocational skills were learned on the job, and in countless ways traditional African and white mores and behavior were adapted to the realities of black life to create an indigenous Afro-American society.

Free blacks in the North before the Civil War were either excluded from common schools or forced into segregated schools, often no more than basements in church buildings. Black public schools were extremely underfinanced in comparison with those for whites. The proportion of black to white children in New York's public schools was 1 to 40; the proportion of expenditures, 1 to 1,600. Urban blacks organized in a number of states to provide their own educational and social services. They opened and attended nonpublic schools as alternatives to exclusion and racially hostile environments. What they negotiated and fought for often depended on the local situation; in Boston they sought separate black public schools to avoid harsh treatment in mixed schools, but later in the 1840s they joined with white abolitionists to attack the city's policy of segregated schools. A Massachusetts court declared in 1850, in a case that after the Civil War set the legal precedent for Jim Crow, that separate but equal school facilities were legal—a decision the state legislature overturned in 1855. Philadelphia's blacks opened private schools and pressed to place teachers in the segregated public schools. Whatever the approach, ante-

bellum blacks received little support from whites in improving their schools or gaining access to white institutions. One black complained in 1839 that when "a colored man comes to the door of our institutions of learning" with a desire for education and improvement, "the lords of these institutions rise up and shut the door; and then you say we have not the desire nor the ability to acquire education."

These difficulties did not eradicate their commitment to schooling. Black voluntary societies provided places for the young and adults to become literate; other self-help agencies offered vocational training. After the Civil War, emancipated slaves were, in Booker T. Washington's words, a "whole race trying to go to school." Black parents called for greater public expenditures on schooling. White missionary societies, ambivalent about their goals, combined paternalistic settings and methods with commitments to equal citizenship through education. Appeals were made to the southern whites' economic interest in having a trained and docile labor force now that slavery no longer existed. Blacks themselves combined faith in the economic rewards of education with notions that literacy could result in increased political participation. And they pressed to expand their education beyond the official tolerance of southern whites.

The period after 1865 thus saw growing faith in educational opportunity among blacks in conflict with a begrudging acceptance of black schooling by whites. The returns blacks actually received from schooling were limited. In St. Louis their lack of economic and political power and the hostility from whites prevented blacks from gaining access to the public schools before the Civil War. When black children gained entitlement to public funds in 1865, their schools were segregated and poorly financed. The black community built its own facilities, boycotted the public schools until they could get black teachers, and organized unsuccessfully to have black public schools named for black heroes. But they also attended school in striking numbers; black enrollment equaled or exceeded that of white working-class students. This commitment, however, did not translate into social mobility. The overwhelming proportion of blacks (97 percent in 1891) held unskilled or semiskilled jobs. Going to school was neither encouraged nor rewarded by the white community. As a New York City educator suggested early in the 20th century, it was hard to tell a black student to stay in school when he "must face the bold fact that he must enter business as a boy and wind up as a boy."

At the turn of the century blacks were being excluded from educational opportunities or were legally segregated by the expansion of Jim Crow legislation, sanctioned in the 1896 *Plessy* v. *Ferguson* decision. In the South public school funds were distributed unequally to white and black school systems; indeed, despite their poverty, the unequitable use of tax funds meant that blacks carried the financial weight of their own schools. School terms for blacks were shorter and more irregular than for whites; when educational funds ran short, black schools were the first closed. Facilities were overcrowded and often in deteriorating condition, and transportation to school was provided for rural whites but not for rural blacks.

Large-scale migration of blacks to southern and northern cities meant that black children enrolled in once all-white schools. The resulting tension and conflict over the expansion of black residential areas, explosively revealed in race riots in East St. Louis and Chicago, Ill., and elsewhere during the first two decades of the century, led many cities to institutionalize school segregation and related practices. White groups in Chicago tried to get the school board to require segregation, then settled for redistricting and school-construction practices that took advantage of residential segregation to keep the schools segregated, a pattern visible in other cities as well.

Legal segregation was reinforced by more subtle discrimination. A rhetoric of special education for those of limited abilities effectively undercut access to educational opportunity. The funds diverted from black to white schools were sanctioned as in the "best interest of the school district." Atlanta's dual school system was typical: grammar schools for whites had access to the city's centralized high schools, but black elementary schools, partly funded by philanthropy, were not tied to any secondary schooling. Industrial education was justified as a means of overcoming alleged black indolence and to meet the realities of low-skilled jobs available to blacks. Whites excused such practices as resulting from the low mental abilities shown by black children in educational tests and from the effects of the immoral atmosphere in which they grew up.

Blacks countered the denials of educational opportunity in varied ways, by pressuring public authorities to establish integrated schools or by demanding more funds and black teachers for segregated schools. In Gary, Ind.; Alton and Chicago, Ill.; East Orange, N.J.; and Springfield and Dayton, Ohio, black parents boycotted segregated and inadequately funded schools. The protests were complicated by the fact that many parents recognized that segregation protected their children from white hostility and provided them with black teachers, many of whom were prominent members of the community. For many the issue was not integration, but improving segregated facilities. Some black schools became centers of academic excellence; Frederick Douglass High School in Baltimore, Dunbar High School in the District of Columbia, and McDonough 35 High School in New Orleans were training grounds for an emerging black middle class. Segregated schools became the basis for a growing number of black teachers, around 50,000 in 1930—the largest professional group, except for ministers, in the black community.

The growth of higher education for blacks was funded initially through philanthropic agencies such as the American Missionary Society and the Peabody Fund, then later with funds provided by the Morrill Act of 1890 and tuition fees paid by students. Black public and private colleges provided education in basic literacy, teacher training, and, much more infrequently, graduate programs. Howard University and Meharry Medical College prepared most of the country's black physicians, while Lincoln University in Pennsylvania was a center of black undergraduate education. But as was true for elementary and secondary schools, when black colleges depended upon white funding, they were invariably shortchanged and discriminated against. White funds were heavily targeted to Tuskegee and Hampton Institutes, both of which played down black political

and social rights. In the 1930s, per-student expenditures for Negro land grant colleges in the Southeast were 55 to 65 percent of those for parallel white institutions. Nonetheless, the black colleges were of major importance in the development of black consciousness and the emergence of an economically viable middle class.

ETHNICITY AND SCHOOL SUCCESS

Among the more popular legends about American schools is the story that children of the poor and minorities eagerly seized the opportunity to attend school, studied hard, and as a consequence rose rapidly into the middle class. The widespread belief that the white immigrant poor in particular rose quickly, in large measure because of schooling, explains some of the fascination of contemporary policymakers for combating poverty with nursery schools, kindergartens, and compensatory education. Perhaps because the story of school success emphasizes American opportunities and aspirations, the actual extent of school success has not received close attention from historians. The relationship between ethnicity and schooling is in fact a great deal more complicated than customarily believed. Although school was an avenue of success for many, especially second- and third-generation children of immigrants, educational achievement was neither uniform across groups nor the only route to economic success.

Whereas our common memory recalls the early 20th-century urban school as the avenue out of poverty for the masses, the perceived failure of those urban schools baffled and preoccupied school administrators at the time. The complaints were common: the schools were being overwhelmed with large numbers of pupils who had neither aptitude nor taste for formal schooling; children came to school from homes where English was unknown; the progress of pupils from immigrant and nonwhite homes was slow; and the eagerness with which children dropped out of school was far more evident than the eagerness with which they pursued their studies. Numerous cities commissioned large-scale studies to document the problems. Surveys with titles like *Laggards in Our Schools* were common in the first two decades of the century. And those seeking to restrict immigration and expand Jim Crow legislation against nonwhites cited "data" showing the inability of immigrant or nonwhite children to succeed in school.

The perceptions of the early 20th century educators reflected the prevailing fears and anxieties, as well as their own aspirations to extend schooling to larger populations and over longer periods. On closer inspection it does not appear that immigrant children contributed disproportionately to school failure or that the failings of nonwhite children were caused by inherent deficiencies. More important than the comparability of immigrant children to children whose parents were American-born were the differences among nationality groups in educational progress and school retention. The ethnic experience in schools as in other spheres was varied and conditioned significantly by specific backgrounds and forms of discrimination.

Even though schoolmen exaggerated the failings of immigrant and nonwhite children, some differences from children with white native-born parents were marked; for example, they were more likely to leave school when legally permitted to do so. In 1910, 1920, and 1930 the proportion of 7- to 13-year-olds attending school in the United States did not differ appreciably among native-born children of native parentage, native children with foreign parents, and foreign-born children; until 1930, however, foreign-born 14- and 15-year-olds were much less likely to be in school than others. Significantly, as early as 1910 native-born 14- and 15-year-olds with foreign-born parents were almost as likely to be in school as children of native parentage, but until 1930, 16- and 17-year-olds with native parents were much more likely to be in school than others of that age.

Comparisons for the nation as a whole exaggerate the similarity of school attendance for immigrant children and others, because they include children of native parentage in nonurban areas, where overall attendance was low. The United States Immigration Commission Report (1911) suggested that in major cities children with native-born parents who finished grammar school were much more likely to go on to high school than were children with foreign-born parents, while blacks fell somewhere in the middle. Nationwide attendance data obscured this finding. Immigrant children and blacks who began high school in major cities, however, were as likely as others to graduate.

Although immigrant children were less likely to continue in school, they do not seem to have done markedly worse there than their counterparts with native-born parents. In fact, both groups seem to have had substantial difficulty in keeping up the pace set by the schools. In 12 cities studied by the Immigration Commission, 41 percent of children 10, 11, and 12 years old with native-born white parents were two or more years behind the appropriate age-grade level in 1908. The percentage was almost twice as high for native-born blacks, while 46 percent of children with foreign-born parents were behind. A substantial proportion of the rather small discrepancy between children of immigrants and children of native-born whites may have been caused by the fact that the former were more likely to begin school late. Urban schools struggled with large segments of their student population, regardless of parentage, and large segments of that population remained in school only as long as was legally required. School retention was always a problem, especially for blacks, but the distinction schoolmen often drew between the progress of immigrant children and others was tenuous at best.

Differences among ethnic groups were more striking than differences between immigrant and nonwhite children in general and children with native-born parents. For example, children with Swedish and German parents in Boston, Chicago, and New York in 1908 were about as likely to be behind in school as children of native-born white parents. Children of English, Irish, and Russian-Jewish parents tended to fall in a middle range, and southern Italian, Polish, and native-born black children were the most likely to be behind. Persistence in school, particularly entrance into high school, also varied significantly among ethnic groups.

It is tempting to explain such differences as the result of a variety of measurable factors or of outright discrimination. For example, some groups were more likely to already know or use English, some entered their chil-

dren in school earlier, some had lived longer in the United States, and some had more advantageous occupations and higher incomes. Although these factors contributed to differential responses to schooling, they do not entirely explain the differences among at least five groups—southern Italians, Russian Jews, eastern European Slavs, Romanians, and Japanese—whose different cultures shaped different responses to schooling.

These groups differed in their views of book learning, schooling, teachers, and the ends of education. Commentators have frequently noted, for example, the strong commitment of Jewish Americans to schooling. (Less often noted are the significant variations among German, eastern European, and Sephardic Jews.) Jewish commitment to formal schooling derived from their traditional stress on both the intrinsic value of learning and the utility of education as an avenue of upward social mobility. In contrast, the *contadino* or agricultural laboring class, from which most southern Italian immigrants came, viewed educational institutions with distrust because in Italy they had represented the heavy hand of the government and had rarely proved of benefit. Formal schooling was not reinforced by religious style; for the southern Italians both religious and secular knowledge was rooted in community folklore, not written texts as it was for eastern European Jews. Nor did the southern Italian tradition encourage debate and textual interpretation, as the Jewish Talmudic tradition did. And unlike Jews, for whom the material success of children brought pleasure and honor, the pursuit of upward mobility stressed by the schools threatened traditional Italian conceptions of family solidarity.

Among Slavic immigrants still another pattern was apparent. They felt education per se to be important, but in terms of cultural continuity and the retention of familial, linguistic, and religious values. Many Slavs viewed the Americanization goals of the public schools as similar to the Magyarization policies of the Austro-Hungarian Empire—the repression of their group culture by the politically and economically dominant Magyars. Searching in part for an alternative to the perceived materialism and individualism of the American public schools, they established religiously based ethnic schools in which language and religion, familial and ethnic continuities could be maintained. Among unskilled Slavs schooling was frequently seen not as preparation for work but as its competitor, restricting the amount of income brought into the family.

For Romanians and Japanese, school achievement appears to have been related to group values and prior acquaintance with public schooling. Romanian parents in Cleveland showed strong commitments to upward mobility, positive associations toward schooling as an avenue of mobility for their children, and a willingness to limit family size, which may have helped them pay for their children's extended education. The Japanese who arrived in the United States in the first two decades of the 20th century came from a rapidly modernizing country with an extensive school system. The Japanese may have been America's best-educated immigrant group; over 90 percent of arriving immigrants were literate in Japanese and averaged eight years of schooling, considerably above the educational attainment of the average American at the time. The Japanese believed that education promoted economic and social well-

being, and they passed these values on to their children. Reinforced by familial and group codes that stressed discipline, respect for authority, obedience, and responsibility, Japanese children, despite the continuing social discrimination against them, were among the highest school achievers.

Distinctive views of education go a long way toward explaining why groups responded so differently to schooling and why even in succeeding generations ethnic variations persisted, albeit in attenuated form. This emphasis on cultural values, however, should not obscure other processes of differentiation that had little to do with ethnic values and much to do with discrimination and exclusion in education and occupations. For black Americans and Mexicans, school achievement was rarely translated into economic rewards commensurate with those gained by whites with equivalent schooling. Studies through the 19th and 20th centuries revealed the same story: that school attainment had less to do with the type of work later pursued than did race, and that student aspirations and educational attainments were not matched by significantly better jobs, save for the small number of college-educated middle-class blacks and Hispanics who provided professional services within their communities or the relatively few who found jobs in the civil service.

THE NEW ETHNICITY AND THE LEGACY OF HISTORY

The issues of ethnic identity and education were not resolved when mass European immigration was halted in the 1920s, or even later, when racial integration was legally mandated. Some would argue that the 1970s have witnessed a resurgence of ethnicity. Although the dimensions and consequences of such a resurgence are uncertain, the forms that a new ethnicity or a new pluralism might take in education are shaped and constrained by the past. One is struck less by what is new than by what is old and less by what is novel than by what is persistent. While expressions of ethnic attachment may intensify, most educational programs appear to continue older understandings about the proper relationships among ethnicity and public institutions.

This does not mean, however, that nothing new of importance has occurred. It seems conceivable that, symbolically at least, American ethnic groups are being accorded parity and that the tension between diversity and the effort to fashion a core people is being resolved in favor of diversity. Whether this resolution comes because of the political and economic power that diverse groups have attained, or because social acculturation has proceeded to such a degree that no radical changes are threatened, is unclear. Certainly the socioeconomic differences that divided white ethnic groups before World War II have narrowed or disappeared, but the groups in the forefront of movements for cultural diversity—blacks, Hispanics, and Indians—remain disproportionately poor. Acculturation to a single norm is by no means the case. But while ethnic differences persist in critical areas of private life and public behavior, few groups are demanding radical reformulations of their relationships with public institutions.

For example, black demands for community control of and participation in the schools in the 1960s were

predicated more on desires for fair treatment and inclusion in the political power system than on a vision of racial separation. Advocates of community control stressed the low quality of ghetto schools; white resistance to desegregation; the lack of responsiveness, innovation, and accountability on the part of educational bureaucracies; and the principle of participating in decisions affecting their lives. Their demands were couched in terms well established and accepted in American political discourse.

No doubt both the political assertions of specific ethnic groups and the limited nature of the demands represented by the new ethnicity play a role in the acceptability of the movement. So, too, may the attractiveness of substituting symbolic parity for economic equality. But another factor may be the essential continuity throughout this century of educational thought about diversity.

The problem lingering from the 19th century was the formation of an American peoplehood. Nineteenth-century common schooling did not address the problem head-on but concentrated instead on cultivating morality and civic conscience. Similarly the Americanization efforts of the 1885–1920 period concentrated on securing loyalty, patriotism, and a common language. But the movement was ambivalent about both the wisdom and the possibility of creating a common people. The principal aim of Americanization was to ensure that newcomers fit in on terms acceptable to the native-born. It was not to obliterate lines of ethnic division—if only because to do so would invite social mixing, which was an anathema to many.

During the 1930s reactions against the excesses of the 1920s and against the blatant racism of Nazi Germany produced a more tolerant view of ethnic differences. By the 1940s educators clearly anticipated the continuation of ethnic diversity and sought ways to temper conflicts they attributed to ignorance, misunderstanding, and even exploitation. Fair and peaceable relationships among groups was the stated goal of educators developing "intergroup" or "intercultural" education. They claimed to teach principles of citizenship that all could share and appeared to be committed to teaching the traditional virtue of tolerance by calling on the understanding of dominant groups.

Textbooks for intercultural education reflected an American population divided into those who were somehow central and established and those who were peripheral and required understanding. One text began by speaking of "the majority (or dominant) culture group, or of minority (or less privileged) culture groups in the community" and later, identifying various groups of interest, noted that "these people are usually referred to as nationality groups." Instructing students of the majority group in the reasons why "these people" were different but still worthy of respect, the text continued: "The minority traits to which the majority most seriously objects are more often traceable to the poverty, ignorance, and ill-will resulting from economic and social discrimination than they are survivals of old-world values, traditions, and folkways."

Educators of this persuasion were ambivalent about the persistence of cultural differences, tending to explain them away, as the language above illustrates, rather than appreciating or encouraging them. They

conceded that the persistence of cultural variety might be "desirable and necessary," that it could "prevent cultural stagnation and deterioration," but warned that while "there is room in America for many cultural subgroups and wide cultural variation . . . there is no place for group isolation." Still, the vision they advanced was not aggressively assimilationist, and while they stressed "respect for others," their work suggests both the possibilities for and limits of education for pluralism; differences are expected to endure, but group withdrawal or separatism cannot be condoned.

The recent movement for multicultural education views cultural differences more positively, but its expectations about the bases of public participation and identification are not significantly different. Competition between groups and isolation in ethnically based institutions continue to be bugaboos to educators; multicultural education is more often viewed as an instrument to prevent such occurrences than as an instrument of autonomous group self-definition. In this, contemporary multicultural education is traditional, both in its objectives and methods. Reminiscent of the "immigrant gifts" ideology and the warnings of gradualist Americanizers, it stresses the need for individuals to have positive ties to their backgrounds and, continuing the intergroup education tradition, aims at building tolerance through mutual understanding.

"We have polarization now simply because of the lack of knowledge of each other," explained Representative Roman Pucinski, a sponsor of bills to provide federal funding for ethnic studies, "and so people distrust each other because of the religious, cultural, and ethnic conflicts, simply because they don't know much about each other." The idea that intergroup conflict arises from ignorance has a long history and is favored by educators and laymen alike. Few symposia on multicultural education fail to stress the objective of enhanced harmony through learning.

Concomitantly, little in the multicultural education movement has stressed ethnic group cohesion, autonomy, or assertion. The federal Ethnic Heritage Studies Program Act of 1972 explicitly rejected funding resource centers that might invite political activism. Mindful of the highly politicized black-studies centers, Pucinski explained the emphasis on university-based curriculum development: "If we tried to leave this in sources other than universities, it could become an instrument of political infeuding and various things . . . We are not talking about a political instrument here. We are talking about a resource instrumentality: knowledge, information, not political activism." In the final version of the legislation, resource centers were abandoned, and funds were eventually provided solely for curriculum development projects and other special, one-time efforts. (See Ethnic Heritage Studies Program.)

Nor do multicultural educators themselves claim goals that lie outside the mainstream of American educational ideology. James Banks, a leading figure in the field, identifies the goals of multicultural education as helping "students to become more ethnically literate and consequently more tolerant of cultural differences" and helping them "develop the ability to make reflective decisions so that they can resolve personal problems, and through social action, influence public policy and develop a sense of political efficacy."

It is the very popularity and acceptability of multicultural education, at least at a rhetorical level, that call into question claims that it represents an appreciable change in the status quo. Andrew Greeley, whose name is prominently associated with the new pluralism, characterized the purposes of multiculturalism as "legitimation, encouragement, respect, some scholarship" and added: "that does not seem to be an irrational or unreasonable set of requests. We do not want . . . to go on an ethnic binge." Greeley has identified the key sociological indicators of resurgence of ethnicity as renewed interest in the high culture of a group, visits to ancestral homelands, increased use of ethnic names, and increased use of languages other than English in the home. None of these requires or even suggests revision of existing relationships between private identity and public policy. And little in the movement suggests reformulating public schooling, whose bases were laid well in the past and command the allegiance of most Americans.

That no ideological revision appears to be in the offing does not mean that nothing is new, different, or significant. The language of multicultural education stresses parity among ethnic groups. The board of the American Association of Colleges for Teacher Education explains, "To endorse cultural pluralism is to endorse the principle that there is not one model American." The hullabaloo over cultural pluralism may well signal that ethnic attachment is not viewed as socially pathological. This would be no small achievement, but it would fall well within the logic of early American understandings.

Bilingual education, which represents a second major commitment to pluralism in education, is also formulated well within traditional values. Its programs are intended for the most part to extend equal educational opportunity to students whose competence in English is limited. Bilingual education usually aims at a "transition" or "language shift" from the mother tongue to English and is viewed as a compensatory measure, limited to especially needy clientele and dispensed with when English competence is achieved. In these terms bilingual instruction is in the tradition of the gradualist Americanizers and does not aim at language or cultural preservation or at the cultivation of strong ethnic attachments. (For a somewhat different view, see Language: Issues and Legislation.)

Milton Yinger observed some time ago that the religious revival of the 1950s came at the time when secularization of church practices was at a height, and he noted that "what one returns to is often an institution that makes few creedal demands." He also noted, "the decline of distinctiveness in the standards of a group may be accompanied by an increase in the sense of identity with it." The new ethnicity may well be similar to the return to religion: an important intensification of sentiment and identification that poses no threat to accepted patterns of conduct and participation.

Unfortunately, the cultural parity represented by multicultural and bilingual education may be illusory. As anthropologists remind us, cultures are not just collections of facts, common memories, or vocabularies. When these aspects of culture are taken out of their original context and then reassembled into packaged curricula, they are unlikely to provide the sense of belonging and self-esteem that come from a culturally intact community that enjoys the respect of other communities. Reduced to curricula in the hands of professional educators, they may represent an ironic victory of dominant cultural forms. Nor can cultures be easily reduced to optional lifestyles. When educators suggest that black or American Indian "ways of behaving" are alternatives that Anglos can freely embrace, they trivialize cultural continuity and community survival and ignore long-standing connections between ascription and tradition. The characteristic American emphasis on individual choice may thus preclude any fundamental reshaping of ethnicity, community, and education.

Bibliography
Few single works focus primarily on ethnicity and American educational history, but a number of interpretive histories place ethnicity in a larger social and economic context. Carl F. Kaestle, *The Evolution of an Urban System: New York City, 1750–1850* (Cambridge, Mass., 1973), treats the ante-bellum period; Marvin F. Lazerson, *Origins of the Urban School: Public Education in Massachusetts, 1870–1915* (Cambridge, Mass., 1971), examines the impact of large-scale immigration on educational practice and pedagogy; and David B. Tyack, *The One Best System: A History of American Urban Education* (Cambridge, Mass., 1974), assesses the influence of race and ethnicity on education from after the Civil War to the present. Diane Ravitch, *The Great School Wars: New York City, 1805–1973* (New York, 1974), discusses controversies involving race, ethnicity, and education.

For connections between 19th-century schooling and Protestant hegemony, see Timothy L. Smith, "Protestant Schooling and American Nationality, 1800–1850," *Journal of American History* 53 (March 1967): 679–695. Ruth M. Elson, *Guardians of Tradition: American Schoolbooks of the 19th Century* (Lincoln, Nebr., 1964), connects nationalism and schooling.

James W. Sanders, *The Education of an Urban Minority: Catholics in Chicago, 1833–1965* (New York, 1976), discusses one type of nonpublic schooling. The best source for Jewish schooling, at least the early 20th-century phase, is Alexander M. Dushkin, *Jewish Education in New York City* (New York, 1918).

The most comprehensive account of nonwhite education is Meyer Weinberg, *A Chance to Learn: A History of Race and Education in the United States* (Cambridge, Mass., 1977).

The performance of immigrant groups in the public schools is assessed in Michael R. Olneck and Marvin F. Lazerson, "The School Achievement of Immigrant Children, 1900–1930," *History of Education Quarterly* 14 (Winter 1974): 453–482, and by David K. Cohen, "Immigrants and the Schools," *Review of Educational Research* 40 (February 1970): 13–28.

There is no single scholarly analysis of contemporary movements tied to educational pluralism. Most materials concerning community control, bilingualism, and multicultural education originate within the movements with which they deal and are, in effect, primary sources.

MICHAEL R. OLNECK AND MARVIN LAZERSON

EGYPTIANS: *see* ARABS; COPTS

ENGLISH

In 1607 people from England began settling permanently in the part of North America that became the United States. From then until the American Revolution, the dominance of English trade and capital, of English language and literature, of the English system of law and law-making, reinforced by arrival of clergymen, lawyers, and public officials reared or trained in England, produced a culture unmistakably English, in spite of the inevitable modifications caused by distance and dispersion.

By the time of independence these English people and their descendants constituted about half the population, but the Revolution reduced migration from Eng-

land to a trickle between 1776 and 1815. Thereafter new arrivals encountered an American nationalism fueled by denunciations of British wickedness. Relations between the two countries disintegrated into war only once, in 1812, but diplomatic strain persisted throughout the 19th century. The predominance of English influence on American literary and artistic culture also nourished feelings of ill will, and English investments in American railways, land, cattle, or mining companies met a certain hostility.

However, in spite of the many public manifestations of Anglophobia, English immigrants were welcome in the United States. They found familiar institutions: the common law, representative government, and the Christian religion divided into numerous Protestant denominations, including the Episcopalians, a direct offshoot of the Church of England. As at home, Roman Catholics were a minority, though a growing one. Immigrants from England found a common written language that they generally understood when spoken. They also encountered significant differences: republican institutions, a wider suffrage, and no established church. In New England and the South Atlantic states, an influential portion of the population retained a sense of admiration for England and nourished the desire to emulate its culture and way of life.

English immigrants regarded themselves as belonging to the same ethnic stock as a majority of the native-born whites, and they met few obstacles to participation in the same social and institutional life. Their sense of group identity and their ethnic institutions rarely endured beyond the second generation. Though the English shared with non-English immigrants the experience of changed physical environment, settlement among strangers, differences in cultural life, and nostalgia for the homeland, their organizations were usually swamped by the native-born and other immigrants. They could never be sure, therefore, whether they were a separate group or not.

In the first half of the 20th century, immigration from England declined. The majority of those who left Britain went to British Commonwealth countries, especially to Canada, Australia, and New Zealand. The minority who came to the United States were more likely to be skilled workers and professional people. An English background acquired a renewed value in the United States, particularly when the diplomatic rapprochement achieved between 1898 and 1904 was reinforced by alliance in two world wars. A spate of high-society marriages at the turn of the century and academic exchanges such as the Rhodes (1902) and Commonwealth (1925) scholarships further strengthened bonds among the academic, business, and government elites of the two countries. Although 20th-century immigrants from England have probably received a warmer welcome in certain circles than did working-class immigrants in the 19th century, prominent Englishmen even then were often lionized by a people supposedly committed to twisting the lion's tail. Nineteenth-century county histories throughout the United States devoted much space to the lineage of Americans who traced their descent to English settlers of the colonial period.

Americans of English descent today, insofar as they are conscious of their heritage, are perhaps less likely to proclaim it in the face of the upsurge of ethnic pride and loyalties by blacks, Mexicans, and other ethnic groups. Indeed, after centuries of intermarriage and internal geographic mobility, many are unable to determine a specific English origin. For these reasons, perhaps no other part of the pluralist American society is so difficult to describe as a separate entity as the English. The task is compounded by the nature of the historical raw materials.

HISTORICAL BACKGROUND

English migrants to the United States come from a nation that has been united under a fairly stable monarchy since 1485. Three waves of invasion and conquest—the Saxon in the 4th century, the Danish in the 9th, and the Norman in the 11th—had pushed the indigenous Celts back to the north and east and to Ireland. These people include the Scots, Welsh, Manx, and Cornish, all subjects of separate entries in this volume.

Historical records did not always keep these groups separate. Because the English government ruled Wales after 1485, most demographic data did not distinguish the English from the Welsh. Scotland was united with England in 1707, and some of their people thereafter mingled. American sources frequently grouped the English, Welsh, and Cornish together. Thus, for want of separate data, occasional reference must be made to the British or to Great Britain, which includes England, Scotland, and Wales. England is, and has been, by far the most populous part of Great Britain and consequently has contributed far more immigrants to the United States than has Scotland or Wales.

Also, the arrival in the United States over the past two centuries of people from Canada and, to a lesser extent, from Australia, makes it difficult to measure the numerical influx of English-born people or their descendants. Immigrants from Canada in the 19th century were not accurately counted, and Canadians of English stock were not distinguished from those of Irish or French descent. (See Canadians, British.) In short, the English were often invisible immigrants, and their children largely indistinguishable from the native-born white population.

17TH-CENTURY SETTLEMENT

Except for the very earliest settlers, the people arriving in the 17th century did not have to accommodate themselves to another society, for they quickly shouldered the Indians aside. Nevertheless, like other immigrants, migration subjected them to forces that converted them or their children into Americans.

During the great migration of 1628–1642, approximately 80,000 English people, an estimated 2 percent of the entire population, departed from the British Isles. Of this number, 58,000 crossed the Atlantic to the mainland of North America or to the Caribbean Islands. Those traveling to the mainland went either to Virginia (founded in 1607) and Maryland (1632) or to Plymouth (1620), Massachusetts Bay (1630), Connecticut (1635–1636), and Rhode Island (1636).

Disease and the shortage of food nearly liquidated the settlement at Jamestown, Va. Vain hopes of finding gold led to terrible hardships until the settlers began to grow their own food along with tobacco for export. The to-

England

County boundaries
prior to 1974

bacco boom created an acute labor shortage and led to strenuous efforts to recruit additional settlers. Offers of land attracted some self-financing settlers, but they were a minority among the migrants to Virginia. Indentured service, based upon the familiar English system, was introduced by 1620 and became the principal means by which the colonies south of New England obtained British and Irish farm labor, domestic servants, and skilled artisans. Prospective emigrants covered the cost of their passage by an agreement or indenture to enter into service for a term of years, during which period they received board and lodging but normally no

wages. At the end of their term, in the early years at least, they might obtain grants of land in addition to clothing and sometimes tools. Black slaves did not become a significant part of the colonial labor force until the close of the century. Apart from them, one-half to two-thirds of the migrants to colonial America south of New England arrived as unfree labor.

The settlers thus recruited have been described as "mostly miserable poor people," but also as "neither menials nor criminals," though there was "a certain proportion of undesirables" among them. Only 120 to 180 convicted felons are known to have been shipped to Virginia before the English Civil War. Most of the servants recruited as indentured labor were young; on some ships sailing in 1635, nine-tenths of the passengers were aged 14 to 30. In spite of the effort to secure more women, the passengers were also predominantly male, mostly single rather than in family groups. Although economic motives were of prime importance —the prospect of independence and a better livelihood at the end of the period of service—settlers in Virginia, like those in New England, were "Bible readers, psalm singers . . . and great attenders at sermons" before they left England. However, the new environments of Virginia and Maryland, which severed them from families and congregations, were not likely to nourish these religious practices.

By contrast the contemporaneous migration of over 20,000 people into New England consisted chiefly of families and congregations and included far more women and children. Most of the men were middle-aged, many of them in their declining years. Both sexes and all ages were far better represented than among the migrants to Virginia and Maryland.

The Massachusetts Bay colony attracted clergymen, lawyers, merchants, and others with comfortable estates. The settlers represented very nearly a vertical cross section of the English people, including all ranks except the highest and lowest. Over two-thirds were from East Anglia, the West Country, and the London area. However, every county except Westmorland and Monmouth was represented; a sizable group came from Yorkshire and many from Lincolnshire and the Midlands. Four-fifths of the New England colonists of the 1630s came from south of a line from the Wash to Bristol Channel—the most populous, as well as the most Puritan, part of the country.

Few arrived in New England as indentured servants. Prospective migrants considered suitable by the leaders but unable to finance themselves had their way paid from a company fund or by well-to-do ministers, or they were brought as servants by wealthier colonists. A large number of the settlers were religiously motivated, which explains the distinctive features of the migration to New England.

When Parliament overthrew and finally executed Charles I and the Puritan Commonwealth seemed capable of realization in England, emigration virtually ceased. Between 1640 and the restoration of the monarchy in 1660, more university-trained men returned to England than left it. This return migration, often of potentially unemployed and dissident intellectuals, may have enhanced the social cohesion of early Massachusetts. Unlike the original settlers, newcomers after that

time, even from England, were immigrants to tightly knit communities.

Indentured service continued to be the chief means of emigration to the southern colonies, at least until the 1680s, when the increased importation of Negro slaves gave planters an even more profitable source of labor. On average, between 1,500 and 2,000 indentured servants reached Virginia annually between 1635 and 1705. Maryland received perhaps 500 a year.

In the late 17th century some of the male servants departing for the colonies were unskilled laborers, but indenture agreements suggest that most of the emigrants were farmers or skilled craftsmen and tradesmen. The bound migrants came from much the same occupational background as the paying passengers, though the latter were somewhat older and were more likely to be married. Most of the indentured servants were still young and single, but there were a few more women than formerly. Many of the servants going to the new colony of Pennsylvania between 1682 and 1687 were listed with the men who brought them out, not sold as servants to strangers on arrival.

In the third quarter of the 17th century, religious nonconformity and economic hardship motivated cloth workers from the West Country to leave England, but among the poor and unskilled, only the very ambitious sought to emigrate. Even among farmers and skilled workers, emigration was highly selective. Religion may not often have been the primary motive, but it did provide a network of traveling companions and an attitude of mind that enabled people to take the risks of a 3,000-mile voyage to a strange place under difficult conditions.

Migration to the colonies diminished for nearly two decades after 1689. By granting freedom of worship to all Protestants, the English Act of Toleration in that year removed a substantial incentive to emigration. The trade in indentured servants also suffered reverses after the 1660s as planters came to prefer slaves as field hands. Merchants and their recruiting agents encountered obstacles in obtaining cargoes of British servants, and the increasing difficulty of gaining land in Virginia and Maryland diminished the attractiveness of voluntary service there.

18TH-CENTURY IMMIGRATION

When migration to the American colonies revived early in the 18th century, the English no longer dominated the movement. French, Germans, Scotch-Irish, and Scots arrived in numbers that together outweighed the English contribution. This influx was notable in the middle colonies, particularly Pennsylvania, whose population grew rapidly in the 18th century. By the end of the colonial period, settlers of English birth or descent no longer formed a majority of that colony's population. Peaks of relatively heavy immigration in the 1720s, the early 1750s, and above all, from the end of the 1760s to the beginning of the American Revolution were determined in large part by the breaks in warfare among the European powers.

The trade in English servants was smaller in the 18th century than it had been, but the trade in convict labor reached significant numbers. After 1655 a felon could be released on pardon if he agreed to leave the country.

Although 4,500 such pardons were granted between 1655 and 1699, probably not many criminals actually arrived in the mainland colonies. However, a statute of 1717 authorized the treasury to pay contractors to transport convicts sentenced to 7 years' transportation for mild offenses and 14 years' transportation for the many felonies punishable by death. Efforts of colonial legislatures to resist receiving transported criminals were overridden as contrary to parliamentary statute. Apart from a brief experiment in Georgia in 1732, no penal colonies were established in America. Instead, convicts were sold as servants and intermingled with the population without special supervision.

Approximately 30,000 convicts were shipped from Great Britain during the 18th century, but allowing for deaths at sea and for some who may have gone to the West Indies, about 20,000 actually landed in the mainland colonies. Contractors in convict labor found their market chiefly among tobacco planters in Virginia and Maryland. In Maryland convicts probably accounted for half the indentured servants imported during the 18th century.

In the early 1770s emigration reached such an unprecedented peak that Parliament ordered customs officials to keep a record of the departures. From December 1773 to April 1775 over 6,000 emigrants sailed to the New World from Liverpool, Bristol, London, Hull, and six other ports. Virginia and Maryland took 76 percent of them and Pennsylvania 21 percent. Fifty-five percent were indentured servants; 6 percent were redemptioners (similar to indentured servants but allowed on arrival to seek "redeemers" to pay off their indebtedness); about 5 percent, convicts; and the remaining 34 percent paid their own fares. The ratio of women to men remained low (149 per 1,000), the majority were between 20 and 25 years old, and children were only 8 percent of the total. Some 5,500 adults reported 258 different occupations. About 60 percent were craftsmen and tradespeople, and only 16 percent had worked in agriculture. A mere 11 percent of the men were unskilled laborers, and another 5 percent were clerical workers and schoolmasters. Most of these 18th-century newcomers settled in towns.

There was a considerable shift in geographic origins after the 17th century. The largest number of emigrants now came from London, and the second largest from the north, both of which were areas of economic and urban growth. It was not so much hard times and increased rents as it was "the spirit of progress and improvement" that proved unsettling to the farmers of the Yorkshire uplands and moors. The 150 adults who sailed from Hull in 1774–1775 did not include any of the poor people in Leeds being fed by public subscription that winter; rather, they were men of considerable property from 30 different trades who took along their families and sometimes one or two servants.

THE IMPACT OF INDEPENDENCE

In 1690, 90 percent of the mainland colonists were of English birth or descent. At the end of the colonial period, this share had been reduced to 60 percent of the white population or 49 percent of the entire population, according to a study of distinctive surnames recorded in the 1790 Census.

Region	% English in white population
New England:	
Massachusetts	82
Rhode Island	71
Connecticut	67
Maine	60
New Hampshire	61
Vermont	76
Middle Atlantic:	
New York	52
New Jersey	47
Pennsylvania	35
Delaware	60
South:	
Virginia	69
Maryland	65
North Carolina	66
South Carolina	60
Georgia	57
West:	
Kentucky and Tennessee	58
Northwest Territory	30

In Pennsylvania, where immigrants of other nationalities were arriving in considerable numbers in the 18th century, the English too were occasionally looked upon as immigrants. A Philadelphia mechanic in 1772 complained that in a Philadelphia shop one might find a "vintner from London, a shoemaker from Bristol, or a schoolmaster from France," and the competition of these skilled immigrants reduced the natives to want. English immigrants also came in for a share of the criticism that strangers in port towns were living off public or private charity. Residents of Philadelphia established the first Society of Sons of St. George in 1772 "for the Advice and Assistance of Englishmen in Distress," 13 years after the Irish, 23 years after the Scots, and 8 years after the Germans there had founded similar organizations to aid needy immigrants.

English settlers and their descendants retained their dominance in the New England colonies throughout the colonial period. After taking hesitant steps to encourage immigration during the labor shortage just after 1700, the town of Boston ruled in 1708 that all strangers must post bond or leave town. In 1718 ships carrying indentured servants were turned away. In the 1720s Boston instituted a system of registration and required immigrants to post a bond of £100 to remain. This system was relaxed in the 1730s, as the colony took over from the town part of the burden of caring for paupers. Immigrants who were able-bodied tradesmen or indentured servants and those who possessed £50 were permitted to stay.

In the southern colonies, contacts with the old country through trade were much greater than in New England. Yet one immigrant of 1759 from Cumberland, a tutor on a Virginia plantation, later recalled that he had felt "in every sense of the word in a new world. The people, in their persons, manners, pursuits and modes of life were as new and strange to me as their country

and climate were." However, he accommodated easily until the revolutionary crisis of the 1770s.

When war broke out in 1776 the percentage of British-born colonists who claimed compensation for losses on account of their loyalty to the Crown was larger than their share of the total population. Roughly 60 percent of these claimants had arrived after 1763. Most lived in towns and cities and were somewhat wealthier than the average; many were officeholders, Anglican clergymen, and merchants. But English-born residents divided over the issue of independence in much the same fashion as other groups, and at least two signed the Declaration of Independence. While Loyalists in some places, in addition to losing their property, were subjected to persecution, torture, and even death, the English-born as such were not persecuted as a minority.

Nevertheless, for many years after the war, English immigrants could not express affection for England without incurring considerable hostility. In any case, for the next 30 years, newcomers from England were few in number. The St. George's Society of New York City enabled some of them "to obtain among themselves that social relaxation and enjoyment which was denied them by other members of the community." In 1805 the English in Charleston founded a St. George's Society to join the struggling associations in New York and Philadelphia, which during these years were short of both funds and members.

The English government discouraged emigration during the generation after independence. It made serious efforts to tighten and enforce long-standing prohibitions on the departure of skilled artisans in textiles and more recent restrictions on workers in iron, steel, and coal. From 1795 masters of foreign vessels were required to submit musters of all their passengers, giving their ages, occupations, and nationalities. Emigrating artisans and manufacturers discovered by these means were to be arrested; the former risked loss of citizenship and property; the latter, fines and imprisonment. These regulations may have deterred the faint-hearted, but they were easy to evade if a man was set on emigrating.

The Passenger Act passed by Parliament in 1803 was more effective in preventing the emigration of craftsmen and industrial workers with limited means, so many of whom had indentured themselves in the previous century. This act allowed British vessels to carry only one passenger for each two tons of unladen capacity, and though ostensibly passed for humanitarian reasons, it so raised the cost of passage that it discouraged emigration, particularly of the poor. Whatever the reason—war, legislation, or cumbersome administration—the number of English emigrants during these years was small.

A bulge in immigration right after the American Revolution included people who were sympathetic with the former colonists. One of these sympathizers, who was typical also in his attraction to the land and agriculture, was George Courtauld (1759–1824). Courtauld sold an unprofitable silk mill and left for America in 1785 "fill'd with an ardent love of Liberty" and "pleas'd with ye idea that he had form'd of ye simple life of an American farmer." He bought 100 acres in Montgomery County, N.Y., but became so involved in the movement for the adoption of the Constitution that he impaired his economic prospects. In 1793 he returned to England and emigrated again some years later.

The French Revolution and the persecution of suspected Jacobins in England brought a renewed immigration of political radicals in the early 1790s. Some of them tried to establish English colonies, encouraged by land promotion activities in the United States as well as by a desire to keep their own traditions and beliefs. The best-known was the colony started on the banks of the Susquehanna River in Pennsylvania in 1794 under the leadership of Dr. Joseph Priestley (1733–1804) of Birmingham and another well-known French sympathizer, Thomas Cooper, M.D. (1759–1840), although this small band of intellectuals soon abandoned their attempt to clear the wilderness. A colony of English Quakers sponsored by William Knox of Philadelphia at Ceres in northwestern Pennsylvania survived but had little influence beyond its isolated situation and made little contribution toward the hoped-for "transplantation of institutions and customs as well as of individuals." Nevertheless, the English continued to found separate colonies in the United States throughout the 19th century.

During the War of 1812 British aliens were regarded as potential enemies, and all males over 14 years old were immediately ordered to register with the nearest U.S. marshal. At least 10,000 did so. Sixteen percent of those who registered in 1812 gave their occupations as merchants, clerks, bookkeepers, or professional people. These groups included not only employees, partners, and agents of British merchant houses but also young bachelors, many of them from Yorkshire, sent to the United States to find markets for their families' manufacturing firms.

In March 1813 certain categories of aliens, principally those engaged in maritime trade and those who had arrived after war commenced, were ordered interned in centers at least 40 miles from the coast. This requirement was applied most severely in New York City and in Charleston, S.C., where there were substantial communities of English merchants. Englishmen from New York City were relocated at Fishkill, N.Y., without their usual means of livelihood and with nothing provided for them. English industrial workers and manufacturers, on the other hand, were permitted to continue their work. Immigrants who had declared their intention of becoming naturalized citizens before the outbreak of war, had married Americans, or owned real property could secure waivers. In all, British subjects found their freedom of movement restricted by federal authorities, and they suffered from legal disabilities for the duration.

19TH-CENTURY IMMIGRATION

The close of the long period of hostilities between the United States and England in 1815 brought the beginning of an unprecedented immigration of English people. Although the U.S. government reported the arrival of only 61,036 English immigrants between 1820 and 1849—a serious underestimate—278,678 natives of England were enumerated in the 1850 Census. If one assumes that about 20 percent of the passengers leaving for the United States from English ports between 1825 and 1840 were Irish and that about 75

percent were Irish thereafter, the number of English and Welsh immigrants to the United States between 1825 and 1850 would come to about 410,000—a reasonable estimate in light of the census figure.

The English immigrants of this period were almost entirely self-financed. Peaks in the flow of passengers from English ports to the United States, each larger than the previous one, were reached in 1818, 1827, 1832, and 1842. Before the middle of the century these highpoints occurred in the years of social unrest and depression in England; later in the century, they occurred in years of peak business activity in the United States. Even so, those affected most directly and severely by adverse circumstances did not swell the ranks of emigrants during these periods of poor harvests, high unemployment, and high prices. In spite of local and temporary hardship for some, industrialization in England dampened the overseas movement. Many of those who lost their jobs because of mechanization sought improvement by moving within England, where cities were growing at an unprecedented rate.

From the time of the potato famine of 1845–1847, English emigration, although it did not rival that of the Irish and Germans, also grew. Whereas the increase in English-born inhabitants of the United States from 1810 to 1850 was probably about 225,000, the increase from 1850 to 1890, a firmer figure based on census returns, was 631,000—more than two-thirds the increase of the Irish-born population of the United States during the same period. Census data make it clear that the average rate of emigration from England to the United States must have been nearly three times as high after 1850 as it had been before that date. It continued to reach new peaks after 1870 when Irish emigration slowed down. Between 1870 and 1890 the number of English- and Welsh-born inhabitants of the United States increased by some 375,000, slightly more than during the previous 20 years.

English emigration rose in three waves, paralleling the flow of people from other parts of Europe. The first began in the late 1840s and peaked in 1854. The second started before the end of the U.S. Civil War and reached a high point of 75,000 in the fiscal year ending June 30, 1873. The largest movement of English immigrants ever to enter the United States began in 1879, reached peaks of 82,000 or more annually in 1882 and 1888, and did not drop significantly until the financial panic of 1893. In contrast with immigration before the Civil War, arrivals in the last third of the century coincided with changing levels of economic activity in the United States. When American business activity rose, immigrants responded within a surprisingly short time. During the ebb tides of migration, after the panics of 1873 and 1893, potential emigrants may have had positive inducements to remain at home; in those periods building construction and investment in England increased, providing more jobs.

Social and Geographic Origins In the 1820s, 1830s, and 1840s the heaviest flow of emigrants in relation to population was from the more rural and less developed southern and western areas, the traditional regions of emigration. Yet just as in the colonial period, some emigration was reported from every county.

Emigrants from the agricultural sector were mainly farmers rather than the more numerous farm laborers.

Preindustrial craftsmen of all kinds made up a larger share of English immigrants than did either farmers or laborers. In 1831 they constituted 35 percent of male immigrants over 19 years old, as compared to 25 percent who were farmers and 10 percent who were laborers. A further 16 percent came from the modernizing sectors of English industry, such as textiles, metal working, and engineering. Skilled industrial workers probably outnumbered agricultural workers even more in the peak years of 1827 and 1841–1842. The passenger lists of 1827 showed that 28 percent were industrial workers, many of them weavers.

The 19th-century emigrants' occupations and regions of origin were similar to those of the emigration just before the American Revolution, when industrial and agricultural change was quickening in England. Extinction of the trade in indentured servants, however, may have made it more difficult for poorer people to emigrate. The cost of the trip, which the migrant now had to pay, included not only fare and provisions but also earnings forgone during an ocean voyage of 4 to 10 weeks. Very occasionally English landlords assisted prospective emigrants; poor-law authorities also made such grants, encouraged by the act of 1834. Emigrants to British colonies were given preference, however, in funds contributed; they were rarely granted to prospective emigrants to the United States. The expense of the journey favored those who were better off, who could finance their voyage by selling their assets.

As emigration to the United States became self-financed, families became the most important source of travel directions and information about prospects after arrival, especially among those emigrants who expected to take up land for farming. A high proportion of English immigrants made the journey with other family members—in 1831, for instance, over 75 percent arrived in family parties. Farmers, laborers, and craftsmen, including handloom weavers, were more likely to travel in family groups than were workers from modernizing industries. Family immigration suggests an intention to settle permanently in America and underlines the fact that those without resources were in a minority, because lower fares for children made it far cheaper to take a family to Canada.

Nearly all those traveling without families were males. Industrial workers who did not intend to farm or were unable to do so immediately on arrival were more likely to travel unencumbered as they sought work, especially skilled workers from the newer industries, such as engineers and cotton spinners. Some may not have decided to make their immigration permanent. These men sometimes carried introductions to employers, or at least names and addresses. They frequently relied on former workmates for information and assistance.

Occupational Background In the last half of the 19th century the increased emigration from England lost the features of a family movement. Economic motivations gradually replaced the earlier ideal of becoming an independent American farmer; emigrants instead sought improved material standards and were less committed to the United States as a permanent home.

Whereas a variety of occupations characterized English immigrants early in the century, laborers, miners, and workers in the building trades (21 percent in 1831)

accounted for 56 percent of the arrivals in the late 1880s. The share of farmers had fallen below 10 percent by the 1880s, and other skilled industrial workers formed a smaller percentage than earlier in the century. The most significant change was a higher proportion of unskilled laborers than ever before. The percentage of laborers increased whenever the American business cycle turned upward; it reached 50 percent in 1882.

The number of building-trades workers and miners may have been increasing as early as the 1850s. In the 1880s both groups were overrepresented relative to their proportion in the English labor force, in spite of their being, on average, among the best paid. Appreciation of the value of the dollar relative to the pound after the Civil War stimulated a significant seasonal and temporary migration of these workers, whose skills were readily transferable to the growing cities and mines of the United States. By the 1880s about 15 percent of New York State's construction force consisted of seasonal workers from Britain. Thus the large numbers recorded in the passenger lists of the 1880s exaggerate the amount of permanent immigration, since many passengers were repeaters counted as immigrants each time they arrived. Many did not intend to stay in the United States but sought the best return for their labor in an international market, a relatively new feature of transatlantic migration.

The number of clerks apparently also increased proportionately among English emigrants in the 1880s. Their work, like that of laborers, building-trades workers, and miners, was as yet largely unmechanized. Professional people, on the other hand, rarely came. In the 1880s England was not losing to the United States exceptional numbers of workers with specialized and sophisticated skills in the industrial, professional, or transport sectors.

The immigrants of the 1880s were far more likely to come from principal towns than their counterparts earlier in the century. Of the English emigrants of 1885–1888 who gave their last place of residence on passenger lists, 78 percent came from towns of 20,000 or more inhabitants, whereas only 50 percent of England's population lived in such towns. The most industrialized counties with the highest wage levels contributed more than their share of emigrant Englishmen in the late 1880s. There were fewer children among the emigrants of the last third of the century; only 21 percent were under 15. The share of emigrants in the main productive age group, 15–39, increased to 67 percent, and in the late 1880s males traveling alone or with friends outnumbered those in family groups by eight to one. Females in the emigration of 1871–1891 numbered 641 per 1,000 males.

These changes in composition—particularly the increased share of unskilled workers, the greater incidence of seasonal and temporary immigrants, and the greater tendency of males to emigrate alone—occurred because of improved transport and sources of information. By 1867 over 90 percent of the passengers arriving in the United States from English ports, even those traveling steerage or third class, came on steamships. Although steamer fares were 30 to 50 percent higher than fares on sailing vessels, the advantages of a ten-day crossing and the superior accommodation on vessels built especially for the passenger trade made the jour-

ney less costly in earnings forgone as well as less daunting.

By the 1880s emigration was reaching the poorer levels of English society, but even so the really poor rarely went to the United States. Remittances from already-established immigrants, a means by which the poor of other countries managed to pay for the voyage, were not common among the English.

SETTLEMENT AND DISTRIBUTION

The distribution of English immigrants proceeded largely according to informal networks of family and friendship gradually built up during the 19th century. By 1812 more than half the English-born males who registered as aliens lived in the mid-Atlantic states of Pennsylvania and New York. The concentration in this region was still pronounced when the first complete census of the foreign-born was taken in 1850: 48 percent of the English-born then lived in the mid-Atlantic states, a proportion which declined over the rest of the century (see Table 1). New England, with only 11 percent of the English-born inhabitants in 1850, had also receded in importance as a destination. In 1850 nearly a third of the natives of England were living west of the Appalachians and north of the Ohio River. After New York with 92,402 and Pennsylvania with 46,968, Illinois, Wisconsin, and Ohio had more English-born residents than any other states.

The English made special efforts at colonization in the Midwest between 1815 and 1850. The earliest were entrepreneurial ventures, led by a few individuals of considerable means who tried to persuade others to follow. The prototype was Morris Birkbeck (1764–1825), a farmer from Surrey, who with George Flower (1788–1862), a native of Hertford, founded settlements on prairie lands at Wanborough and Albion in Edwards County, Ill., in 1818. These colonies became well known in England through the publications and promotional efforts of Birkbeck, Flower, and his father, Richard Flower (1761–1829), as well as through the reports of the many travelers who visited them. After Birkbeck died in 1825, his family left the United States. Flower and his family remained in Albion for many years; he eventually moved to New Harmony, Ind.

In 1818 Saunders Hornbrook, a woolen manufacturer and iron founder from Devon who was influenced by Birkbeck's writings, inaugurated a short-lived English

Table 1. Regional distribution of the English-born in the United States, 1850–1890, in percentages.[a]

Region	1850	1860	1870	1880	1890
Mid-Atlantic	48.4	39.0	37.5	34.3	34.4
East north-central	28.5	32.4	29.7	26.7	23.3
New England	11.2	10.6	11.7	12.8	14.7
South and Southwest	7.0	6.6	5.0	5.3	5.1
West north-central	3.3	6.5	8.5	10.8	11.1
Mountain and Pacific	1.6	4.9	7.6	10.1	11.4

Source: U.S. Census Office, *Seventh Census of the United States, 1850* (Washington, D.C., 1853), pp. xxxvi–xxxvii; *Population of the United States in 1860, from the Eighth Census* (Washington, D.C., 1864), pp. 620–621; *Ninth Census: The Statistics of the Population of the United States, 1870* (Washington, D.C., 1872), pp. 340–341; *Statistics of the Population of the United States at the Tenth Census, 1880* (Washington, D.C., 1883), p. 493; *Compendium of the Eleventh Census, 1890*, II, *Misc. Doc.* (Washington, D.C., 1894), p. 493.

a. The census enumerated 278,675 English-born in 1850; 431,692 in 1860; 550,924 in 1870; 662,676 in 1880; and 908,741 in 1890.

colony on the banks of the Wabash River in Vanderburgh County, Ind. George Courtauld returned to the United States in 1818, purchased land in Athens County, Ohio, and tried similarly to attract immigrants to take up these lands. However, he died within a few years, and his family dispersed.

The English also participated in a number of experiments in communitarian living. One of the earliest of these, and ultimately the most successful, illustrates how English institutions made an impact on the native-born in such a way that in time the institutions ceased to be either immigrant or English. A small group of dissenters known as Shaking Quakers arrived in America from Manchester in 1774 under the leadership of Ann Lee (d. 1784). The Shakers formed a religious colony in upper New York and flourished; when Mother Ann died, she was succeeded by an English-born follower named James Whittaker. The Shakers' missionary efforts in New Hampshire, Connecticut, and Massachusetts went so well that on Whittaker's death in 1787, both leadership and membership became largely native-born. Unlike other English communitarian efforts, the Shakers persisted into modern times and are only now dying out.

The founder of one of the earliest secular communitarian colonies in America, social reformer Robert Owen (1771–1858), studied the successful Shaker colony. In 1825, through the mediation of Richard Flower, Owen purchased 30,000 acres and a number of buildings from the German Rappites on the Wabash River at New Harmony, Ind. Extensive publicity attracted more native-born Americans than immigrants. This experiment in a self-sufficient community, ill-planned as to practical details, soon expired—as did other Owenite communities at Bloomfield, Mich., and at North Prairie, Wis. It is possible 150 years later to visit more than 30 buildings and sites at New Harmony, some of which have been restored to their original uses.

Efforts to revive the joint-stock method of colonization in the 1840s included the British Temperance Emigration Society, founded in Liverpool in 1842 by a Methodist preacher with the support of a wealthy philanthropist. Under its auspices about 700 people, many of them factory workers, went to Dane County, Wis., between 1843 and 1850. The Potters Emigration Society, initiated by William Evans in the 1840s, also used the joint-stock method but ended in recriminations, although it deposited a few English families in Columbia and Marquette counties in Wisconsin.

Traces of less-publicized clusters of English settlement also survived. A group of 40 families arrived in Nelsonville, Ohio, in 1832, all of them from Wisborough Green in Sussex, where James Knight had been a maltster and shopkeeper before he emigrated in 1821. A colony of Wesleyan Methodists, most of them born in Lincolnshire, settled in New Albany, Ind., between 1841 and 1851. On the shores of Sand Lake in Cambridge Township, Mich., a small colony of English and Irish immigrants "distinguished for learning and culture" settled in 1831. In Illinois former industrial workers clustered near the Illinois River at Peoria, Canton, and Jacksonville.

More successful than any of these groups were the Mormons, an American sect with a communal economy, who conducted missions in the industrial cities of the North and Midlands in England in the 1840s. Some of the immigrants, induced to come to Illinois before their leader Joseph Smith was lynched there in 1844, remained behind at Nauvoo when the Mormons sought a new home farther west. Many others made the trek to Utah; in 1850 immigrants from England and Wales constituted over 70 percent of the foreign-born inhabitants of the territory. (See Mormons.)

Although the communitarian efforts attracted only a minority of English immigrants, and most of the colonies failed, they were one indication of the part the American frontier played in the lives and imaginations of some English people. Such immigrants consciously fled from the industrialization going on around them in an attempt to return to an older, simpler way of life, often without recognizing the sacrifices in standard of living that frontier living required.

Patterns of English settlement in the United States shifted markedly after 1860. The eastern north-central area lost some of its attraction when land was no longer cheap, and the share of the English-born population living in that region declined. The English-born populations of Michigan, Illinois, and Ohio increased less rapidly than the English population as a whole. Between 1870 and 1890 most of the rural midwestern counties where the English had been prominent failed to attract new immigrants, and the English communities eroded over time. In Illinois, for example, the number of English-born inhabitants actually increased in only a few counties near Chicago, along the Rock Island Railroad Line, and in the northern coal-mining region. Although the number of English-born residents in Chicago increased the most of any city, only 6 percent of Chicago's foreign-born inhabitants were English in 1890 (see Table 2). This urbanizing tendency was also evident among the English-born in Ohio and Michigan, yet in no other major midwestern town in the late 19th century were the English increasing as a share of the foreign-born.

Most of the new arrivals from England went to one of two main regions: either the new mining, farming, and cattle-raising areas west of the Mississippi River, or some of the nation's oldest mining and industrial areas in southern Massachusetts, Rhode Island, Pennsylvania, New Jersey, and the upper Ohio River Valley. An increasing share of the English immigrants settled in the farming states of the Great Plains, although the actual numbers were smaller than in older areas of settlement. The English-born population of Kansas reached 20,568 in 1890 and that of Iowa 29,806. In those two states, which the settlers favored over other plains states, the English had less impact on urban counties; the prospect of farm ownership continued to attract them.

During the late 19th century there were attempts to establish English agricultural colonies, for the most part in the plains states, where land bargains still existed. These colonies were all entrepreneurial, organized either to sell railway lands or to develop the considerable holdings of English investors. The colony founded in 1869 as Wakefield in Clay County, Kans., was at first projected as a cooperative venture. On the advice of the Reverend Richard Wake, a Methodist minister and naturalized citizen, settlers were allowed instead to purchase land as individuals and conduct their

Table 2. English-born inhabitants of selected cities, 1890.

City	Number	Increase since 1870[a]	Percentage of foreign-born	Percentage of population
Major cities:				
Philadelphia	38,926	16,892	14.4	3.7
New York City	35,907	11,465	5.5	2.4
Chicago	28,337	18,310	6.3	2.6
Brooklyn	26,493	7,650	10.1	3.1
Boston	13,454	7,476	8.5	3.0
Cleveland	10,950	6,417	11.3	4.2
Pittsburgh	10,143	7,305	13.8	4.3
San Francisco	9,828	4,656	7.8	3.3
Detroit	7,168	3,884	8.8	3.5
Smaller cities:				
Paterson, N.J.	6,548	3,201	21.0	8.4
Trenton, N.J.	3,882	—	27.6	6.8
Scranton, Pa.	3,065	1,621	12.0	4.1
Wilkes-Barre, Pa.	1,579	—	15.5	4.2
Camden, N.J.	1,747	—	22.6	3.0
Fall River, Mass.	11,002	6,959	29.2	14.8
Providence, R.I.	8,143	5,716	20.2	6.2
Lawrence, Mass.	4,985	2,529	24.3	11.1
New Bedford, Mass.	3,507	—	24.3	8.6
Pawtucket, R.I.	2,689	—	28.7	9.7
Youngstown, Ohio	2,451	—	23.3	7.4
Salt Lake City, Utah	5,982	—	48.9	13.3

Source: U.S. Census Office, *Ninth Census, The Statistics of the Population of the United States, 1870* (Washington, D.C., 1872), I, table VIII, pp. 386 ff.; U.S. Census Office, *Compendium of the Eleventh Census, 1890* (Washington, D.C., 1894), I, 370 ff., 670 ff.

a. For some cities information not available.

own enterprises. The settlers, from Shropshire, Oxfordshire, and elsewhere, bought their land from the Union Pacific and Kansas Pacific railroads, but they were not prepared for the blizzards, the tornado, the drought, and the grasshoppers that plagued them between 1870 and 1874.

Men of considerable means who had invested in western lands directed other attempts at colonization that catered to upper-class immigrants rather than working people, though the organizers usually brought out laborers to assist the settlers. Landed and even aristocratic families sent their sons on allowances; the organizers sometimes offered to train them as apprentices in agriculture and stock raising. These colonies all disappeared virtually without a trace within a few years, because the colonists were unprepared for frontier life and often had no farming experience.

Such a colony was started near Decorah, Iowa, in 1868 by former East Indies government officials, who took to farming with results, according to the reminiscences of a retired officer, "distressing in the extreme." The settlement at Le Mars, Iowa, was begun by the Close brothers, former Cambridge University crewmen, who from 1878 onward invested in tens of thousands of acres of land in Iowa and Minnesota. Le Mars was advertised in the London *Times* and the *Manchester Guardian* as affording English country gentlemen the means to recover their rents and provide for younger sons. Other residents of the area looked askance on the farm-pupil system and objected to the noisy drinking habits of the young men. The colony made no lasting impression on the region.

Kansas became the site of three or four such colonies

promoted to attract wealthy Englishmen and their sons. In 1873 a self-made London draper, George Grant, put his fortune into a settlement designed for the younger sons of the aristocracy. He bought 60,000 acres of Kansas Pacific Railway land at Victoria in Ellis County and hired a London architect, R.W. Eades, to lay out the town. The houses were all to be built of stone and to have curved driveways and well-trimmed hedges. The drought and grasshopper plague of 1873–1874, however, caused the English laborers to forsake the settlement. The few colonists who stayed benefited from the labor of Volga German immigrants (*see* Germans from Russia), who began coming to the north of the town in 1876 and who stayed to buy up the English farms. By 1878 Grant's purebred Aberdeen Angus cattle were "wandering away to mix with lesser breeds."

The founder of Runnymede, on the border of Harper and Klingman counties, Kans., in 1886 offered to train the sons of English gentlemen and help them acquire estates. By 1891 Runnymede's 50 recreation-oriented inhabitants, mainly young men, had established a race course, steeplechase, polo field, billiard parlor, bowling alley, and tennis courts, but by that time more settlers were leaving than arriving. Only the Episcopal church, founded in 1889, remained; it was moved to nearby Harper in 1892 and later housed a museum. Another party of "young bucks who believed in enjoying life" settled at Helper and Walnut, Crawford County, Kans., in the 1870s; Sir James Stuart Hogg started a similar colony at Manhattan, Kans., in the 1880s. Minnesota also had at least one colony of gentlemen at Fairmont in Martin County. Deserters from these colonies sometimes joined other settlements of English immigrants.

The percentage of English immigrants settling in the mountain and Pacific states also increased between 1850 and 1890. Mining counties such as Silver Bow, Mont.; Gilpin, Colo.; and Nevada, Calif., had some of the highest relative concentrations of the English-born in the country, as did Uinta County, Wyo., colonized by Mormons from Utah. In 1890 no other city in the United States was as English as Salt Lake City.

Another, much larger, contingent of English immigrants remained in the Northeast. The share of the English-born settling in New England, after declining in the 1850s, began to rise slowly after the Civil War. A major region of English immigration was Bristol County in southern Massachusetts, with its old textile towns of Fall River and New Bedford. Although two other Massachusetts counties had more English settlers, Bristol was the only county in which their concentration in the immigrant population equaled that of certain western farming and mining counties.

A marked redistribution in the settlement of English immigrants also took place in the mid-Atlantic states. Their share of the English-born declined from 48 percent in 1850 to 34 percent in 1890, largely because fewer immigrants remained in New York State than formerly. As American heavy industry expanded after the Civil War, Pennsylvania and New Jersey drew proportionately more of the new arrivals from England. In the anthracite mining counties of northeastern Pennsylvania, the English formed 12 to 14 percent of the immigrant population in 1890, and in the bituminous mining regions in Clearfield, Fayette, Westmoreland, and Washington counties, they formed more than 20

percent of the foreign-born population. The English-born inhabitants of Pittsburgh and Philadelphia, Pennsylvania's major industrial cities, increased between 1870 and 1890 as a percentage both of the foreign-born and of the total population.

While the English-born population of New York State increased by two-thirds between 1850 and 1890, that of New Jersey rose nearly four times. Most were concentrated in the old industrial towns of northern New Jersey, but the English-born population in nearly every county increased between 1870 and 1890.

ECONOMIC ROLE

In the first half of the 19th century many English immigrants settled on farms. Farmers, professional people, and manufacturers brought savings that they put into land and farms almost immediately. Though they were not immensely wealthy, some were able to lend money locally at an early stage and to build notable houses on the midwestern frontiers. Others began in jobs on canals or in lumber camps, or they paid the rent of a farm in a share of the crops. The largest group, those with preindustrial crafts, bartered their work for land, labor, or materials and managed to remain on their farms by continuing to work part-time at their trades. English people of an astonishing variety of occupations and background attempted to settle on American farms. Land speculators and entrepreneurial developers aside, a great many were influenced by notions of the virtues of farming life—Jeffersonians in spirit before they arrived. Many, unsettled by changes in English society, were rejecting industrial civilization, thus moving directly counter to the main trend of 19th-century overseas migration, which brought rural dwellers from Europe into urban and industrial occupations in America.

Not all of them remained on the farms. Some, particularly those accustomed to comfort and servants, fled back home when faced with the tasks of farm making and cultivation. Others either combined their trades or professions with farming, sometimes leasing out a part of their land, or moved into midwestern towns. The colonists in Vanderburgh County, Ind., moved to the nearby town of Evansville. By 1840 their original village of Saundersville had disappeared, as had Englishtown in Athens County, Ohio. Weavers were perhaps the least successful in returning to their former trade in the West; carpenters and builders, the most successful.

Throughout the 19th century some English immigrants continued to settle in regions where agricultural lands were still being opened up. In 1890 20 percent of the English-born men in the United States were in farming (see Table 3)—almost exactly the same percentage as among the British-born males who registered in 1812. England was more heavily urbanized and industrialized than any other country then sending immigrants to the United States, but a surprisingly large fraction of the English sought opportunity in the countryside.

In mining and manufacturing, English immigrants found the most numerous opportunities and had the greatest impact. The British who registered as aliens in 1812 were already highly concentrated in industrial occupations: 17 percent were textile workers or machine makers. They constituted 20 percent of the early textile labor force in Rhode Island. Approximately 700 British (9 percent of the total) registered as building and wood workers. Another 5 percent were metal workers of all kinds, and a similar percentage were tanners and shoemakers. A great variety of other trades was listed, from food processors and retailers to glass blowers, piano makers, printers, booksellers, and the manager of a paper mill.

Some of the immigrants from England during the period 1783–1812 are of a particular interest because of the changes in methods of manufacture in England—changes that form part of the transformation of English manufacturing, transport, agriculture, and society customarily termed the Industrial Revolution. English immigrants of this period transmitted the new technology to the United States, particularly in textile manufacture and machinery for the "perpetual" or continuous production of cotton and woolen cloth.

Most of the skills required for adapting steam or water power to textile manufacturing were available in the infant United States. Spindles and looms were customary features of household industry, and town and village workshops, especially in New England, furnished carpenters, blacksmiths, wheelwrights, and clockmakers, like those who became the metallurgical and mechanical workers for England's innovating textile industries. England did not prohibit the emigration of steam-engine builders, but signally wanting in the 1780s were persons capable of designing, assembling, and adjusting the new machinery—people who could make it work commercially without excessive breakages. In addition, people were needed with sufficient knowledge to oversee and manage textile processes, workmen whose experience and training enabled them

Table 3. Occupational distribution of English- and Welsh-born males, 10 years and older, in the U.S. labor force, 1890.

Occupation	Number	Percentage in sector	Concentration ratio/ foreign-born[a]	Concentration ratio/male labor force[b]
Agriculture and fisheries	100,346	20.6	83	49
Mining and quarrying	56,745	11.6	264	552
Manufacturing and mechanical industries	173,562	35.6	114	165
Trade and transport	76,284	15.6	101	95
Domestic and personal service	63,310	13.0	59	91
Professional	17,198	3.6	163	105
Total	487,445			

Source: U.S. Census Office, *Compendium of the Eleventh Census, 1890* (Washington, D.C., 1894), II, table 78, pp. 304 ff.; table 109. pp. 484 ff.
a. Percentage of English-born divided by percentage of foreign-born in each field.
b. Percentage of English-born divided by percentage of total male labor force in each field.

to judge and mix raw materials, make decisions about product types, and supervise unskilled operatives, many of whom were women and children.

Machine builders and managers from Britain were important in shortening the time involved in the transfer of technology to the United States. No designs of textile machinery were published before 1812; searching English patents was tedious, costly, and not always sufficiently informative. Until the early 1840s England prohibited the export of most textile machinery. A smuggled crate of parts was little use without a man who could assemble them to make the resulting machine function efficiently.

In the years 1783–1793 and 1807–1812, when diminished transatlantic trading opportunities heightened economic as well as patriotic reasons to reduce imports, American merchants and public leaders interested in stimulating manufacturing recruited British workers with the requisite skills. American manufacturers sent abroad for this purpose, occasionally offering inducements ranging from partnerships to advances of transport cost. They encouraged those recruited to invite friends and relatives to follow them, and they enticed the workers away from each other.

A number of English immigrants successfully established their own machine-building shops or managed or owned cotton or woolen manufacturing firms that survived, at least for a time. The best-known of the immigrants of this period, Samuel Slater (1768–1835) of Rhode Island and John (1758–1820) and Arthur Scholfield (1757–1827) of Pittsfield, Mass., enjoyed long careers in the New England textile industries. They brought with them knowledge of the best contemporary English practice in their fields, settled in, and adapted to the new culture. Slater married an American woman, and the Scholfields eventually brought over five brothers and their families.

Even after 1815 American employers from time to time actively sought English skills for the mechanization of cotton printing and in metalworking industries, where American practice was much behind the British. In the Connecticut brass industry, Israel Holmes (1800–1874) made three trips to England for labor between 1822 and 1834, and James Croft (1774–1837) was sent seven times by Benedicts of Waterbury for tools and workmen. In the late 1820s English and Welsh miners were imported for the new anthracite coal mines of Schuylkill County, Pa., though many of them left the area almost immediately.

Staffordshire immigrants started the pottery industries of East Liverpool, Ohio (1841) and Trenton, N.J. (1832). The American iron industry in the 1830s and 1840s was as backward compared to the English as cotton manufacture had been at the turn of the century. Although the Welsh and Scots were probably as important in this industry as English workers, the latter contributed the skills for constructing the first iron rolling mill in Pittsburgh in 1812; for introducing the boiling method of puddling in 1837; for pioneering early coal-burning blast furnaces; for building the first coke ovens in the Connellsville region of Pennsylvania in the 1830s; for producing the first blister steel and crucible steel west of the Alleghenies; and for assisting in developing rail making.

Thus, although England tried to keep its new technology to itself, Englishmen assisted in transferring it to the United States. However, industrial workers did not come in vast numbers to American industry. Of those states where English immigrants were principally employed in manufacturing, Massachusetts had only 16,-900 English-born inhabitants in 1850, Connecticut 5,-200, Rhode Island 4,500, and New Jersey 11,500. In some instances the English workers were too specialized in skills and experience to fit easily into the American industrial scene, where division of labor had not proceeded so far.

Unless an English workman had an all-around training that enabled him to go into business for himself or become a manager, there was often not much inducement to emigrate. Many workers who left England during the first half of the century did so hoping to earn enough through their trade eventually to buy land. A fair number managed to achieve this goal, not only textile and metal workers from new industries but also traditional craftsmen such as blacksmiths, carpenters, tailors, and shoemakers.

Facing no discrimination or language barriers, English industrial workers found opportunities in both eastern and western towns for employment commensurate with their skills. A study of Buffalo, Kingston, and Poughkeepsie, N.Y., drawn from data for 1855–1865, found that household heads of English and Scots birth clustered in the construction trades, in metal and apparel manufacture, and in the individual occupations of machinist, carpenter, baker, and tailor. In Milwaukee in 1850, 54 percent of the British held skilled jobs as compared with only 36 percent of the entire labor force. In South Bend, Ind., only 27 percent of the English were so employed in 1850, but this share rose sharply to 53 percent in 1860. The British were also well represented in some places in the ranks of proprietors and managers. In the locomotive, iron, and machinery industries of Paterson, N.J., from 1840 to 1880, almost all of the leading entrepreneurs were Englishmen from the centers of early industrialization in Lancashire and Cheshire who had risen from the ranks of skilled workers or even from lower in the occupational hierarchy. A smaller share of the British than of other groups were employed as unskilled, semiskilled, and service workers.

Table 3 shows that in 1890, English-born males were still more concentrated in manufacturing and mining than either the immigrant labor force as a whole or the native-born work force. They were twice as likely as other immigrants to work in the textile industries and also in primary and secondary metal manufacture, especially of iron and steel. Tool and cutlery making, model and pattern making, and boiler making also attracted relatively more of the English, as did pottery, glass making, and printing.

In contrast, a smaller share of the English, as compared with other immigrant groups, were employed in 1890 in the large preindustrial crafts and trades. The English were less likely to be butchers, bakers, shoemakers, tailors, cabinetmakers, and coopers, and were well represented only among millers and blacksmiths. However, they were conspicuous in every branch of the building trades except as carpenters and joiners.

The U.S. Immigration Commission of 1907–1910 found that English (and other British) immigrants were more frequently employed in the same industry as they had been at home than was the case with other immigrants. Eighty-three percent of English bituminous

miners, 48 percent of iron and steelworkers, 70 percent of male mule spinners, 56 percent of woolen mill operatives, and 68 percent of silk workers had experience in their respective industries before coming to the United States. Those without such experience may have been recruited from the unskilled laborers who made up about 30 percent of the new arrivals from England in the years 1875–1890 but only 11 percent of the English and Welsh workers in the United States in 1890. In the manufacturing industries to which they gravitated, English and other British workers held many of the most highly paid and skilled jobs, as foremen, overseers, managers, and except in coal mining and primary iron and steel, even as owners.

The manufacture of worsted was introduced into Lawrence, Mass., in the 1860s with English equipment and operatives; and Paterson's infant silk industry, as well as lace making in Philadelphia, Brooklyn, and parts of Connecticut, also depended heavily upon English workers. But ultimately their skills were displaced by changing technology. When their skills were no longer needed, employers were not sorry to get rid of English workmen, who had gained a reputation for being sticklers for high wages and trade unions, as well as for being prone to drink and absenteeism.

As American technology diverged from that of the early Industrial Revolution, English workers began to gain a reputation for conservatism. In iron and steel works and in machine shops, they were said to be too attached to old-country methods. English carpet weavers in the Philadelphia area clung to hand weaving into the 1880s, in spite of the availability of power looms long before. Framework knitters from Nottingham and Leicester continued to work in their homes in the Kensington and Germantown districts of Philadelphia till the end of the century, and master silk weavers from Macclesfield set up archaic looms in Paterson. Although many emigrants came from England seeking to maximize their incomes and gravitated toward places where wages were highest, a sizable number in this period still emigrated to avoid change in their ways of work and fields of work, a counterpart to the agrarian ideal that attracted so many industrial workers to the United States in the early part of the century.

The English did not provide proportionately more wholesale or retail traders than other immigrant groups of this period. A larger share as compared with other immigrants were employed as locomotive engineers and firemen, the better paid positions in rail transport, though few railroad workers emigrated from England. They were less likely than other immigrants to work in other railway jobs and as teamsters.

The English were more successful than other groups in securing jobs as clerks and bookkeepers and in the professions. Those in the professions were probably English-born children whose parents brought them to the United States when they were still young enough to train in American institutions. Such cases appear frequently in county histories. More English succeeded in becoming clergymen, engineers, lawyers, and doctors than did the foreign-born as a whole.

SOCIAL ADAPTATION

The attitudes of the receiving society were not unequivocally favorable to English immigrants. One of the most influential critics of England and the English was Hezekiah Niles (1777–1839), the editor of *Niles' Weekly Register* (f. 1811) of Baltimore. Welcoming the industrious Germans arriving in Philadelphia and Baltimore in the early 1830s, he contrasted them with the "loads of English paupers which are sometimes shovelled upon us." He conceded that efficient workmen from England were welcome if they maintained "a decent and orderly deportment, free from *assumed* superiority, and respect for the laws, freely admitting also, that Lakes Superior and Huron, are about as large as the pools in Cumberland, and that the course of the Mississippi, or rather Missouri, is quite as long as even that of the Thames." Such banter typified the tensions between the English and the native-born. But the English were disconcerted or wounded at times by the brash American nationalism. After the War of 1812 immigrants in Baltimore felt that to be an Englishman in that town "was an offence to both pride and patriotism, and all such were considered public and perfidious enemies."

By enlisting in the Union Army during the Civil War, English immigrants in the North offset the renewed anti-English sentiment caused by the evident Southern sympathies of many in authority in England as well as of many Lancashire cotton operatives. Some immigrants were first able to identify with the United States as their own country during the Civil War. Even so, a Yorkshire textile worker, who had returned to Philadelphia after serving in the federal army in Virginia, wrote: "The streets and houses gets familiar, but the inhabitants look on you as though you was infirier to the native born."

Although English immigrants confined ordinary relations to their own countrymen and even to people from their own shire, their children assimilated more easily, and with less tension between generations, than those of most ethnic groups. The clannishness and group consciousness of first-generation English immigrants were not so evident in residence patterns, intermarriage, and institutional separateness as in the letters they wrote home.

Studies of residence patterns among city dwellers almost invariably find that British immigrants were less segregated than other groups. The native-born and the British inhabitants of Milwaukee sought each other out. In 1860 the English in Boston lived near one another less frequently than did Irish, Scots, or Canadians; the British in Philadelphia in 1860 were less segregated than the Irish or Germans. There were no clusters of English families on streets in South Bend, Ind., in 1850.

Yet where ordinary English workers formed a considerable nucleus of the factory population in industrial towns, they may have lived in segregated residential areas, partly along occupational lines. The calico printers from Lancashire occupied English Row in Lowell, Mass., and the Sheffield cutlers in Waterbury, Conn., also lived near one another, as did English workers in Waltham, Mass. English kettlemen in Walcottville, Conn., demanded a separate building in which to work, which no Yankee was permitted to enter. The relatively modest number of English immigrants and their attraction to land in less settled regions, from which they continually dispersed, may have had more to do with their lack of residential segregation than any desire by first-generation English to mix with others.

Intermarriage with other groups was a function of age at arrival, the size of the immigrant community, and religious affiliation. Although 20th-century studies show high rates of intermarriage for the English, no statistics on the degree of intermarriage exist for 19th-century English immigrants. Only 45 percent of English-born males and females in New York City in the early 20th century had married within the group, and a mere 17 percent of the second generation had done so. Yet letter writers of an earlier period sought spouses among other English immigrants whenever possible. English-born parents complained about the American influence when their children moved away, apologized when their children married other immigrants or natives, and presumed to choose their sons' careers.

American Protestant churches were perhaps the most frequent meeting places, outside their places of employment, for the English and the native-born. The English found familiar denominations wherever they went, except along the thinly populated frontier. There, accustomed to congregational organization, they usually attempted to secure the services of a minister, at least occasionally, and to build a church. In such outlying areas schools were also begun in connection with churches, although there was no resistance to state-supported schools when they were introduced. The first Episcopal parish in Illinois started when the board of directors of the Domestic and Foreign Missionary Society of the Protestant Episcopal Church sent a minister to Jacksonville because a large English settlement a few miles to the west wanted his services. The Episcopal church in the West was so understaffed that Philander Chase (1775–1852), who was successively bishop of Ohio and of Illinois, raised money in the East and in England to establish seminaries to train clergy: Kenyon College (1824) in Gambier, Ohio, and Jubilee College (1839) in Peoria, Ill.

The Protestant Episcopal church in Massachusetts and Rhode Island benefited from the immigration of English mill workers, especially in textile towns. No other diocese enjoyed such "goodly accessions" in the late 19th century. In Fall River, Mass., a congregation of a distinctively English sect, Primitive Methodism, introduced into American coal- and ore-mining villages by English miners, was incorporated in 1874.

Perhaps no other migrants came so well prepared psychologically as the large numbers of English who were attracted to American agriculture. Many were skilled workers and farmers who were able to retain or raise their incomes and social rank in the United States. The strong family element in early-19th-century immigration enhanced the acceptability and the relative contentment of the English immigrants among strangers. The immigrants of this period approved of and were attracted by democratic institutions, as well as by low taxes, frugal government, and the atmosphere of social equality. Letters from immigrants also indicate that they were influenced by the opportunity for their children to receive a public education and to gain access to skilled trades. Many made sacrifices to secure and prolong the education of their children. The minority who found life without servants unacceptable or who were offended by the brashness of American ways usually could afford to return home.

Even so, the first generation found solace and society among other English immigrants. We have glimpses of literary or musical gatherings, of meetings to discuss agricultural matters, and of the founding of libraries in some English settlements in the West. Elsewhere immigrants met at each other's houses for reading aloud, singing, or conversation; they had parties, also, to which married folk as well as young people were invited, a custom for which they were criticized, in Wisconsin, by the American-born residents.

Some of the early-19th-century rural settlements of English immigrants in the Midwest were reinforced 20 years or so later by a second wave of immigrants from the same places and the same family networks in England. Very few reached sufficient maturity to spawn a St. George's Society, as did Madison and Janesville, Wis., and Clinton, Iowa. After the 1850s the story most often was one of assimilation in those English communities that lacked distinctive ethnic organizations and were unreplenished by new arrivals from England or the East. Thus a culture of institutions separate from those of native-born Americans never fully matured and disappeared almost without a trace in the rural West and Midwest.

However, English-speaking foreign-born residents of these regions were somewhat less likely to move on to other areas than either the native-born or other immigrant groups. This may well have been because of their age on arrival and the capital they brought with them, since the young and propertyless were most likely to move elsewhere. From the 1860s onward, the number of inhabitants born in England declined in county after county. Sometimes new arrivals displaced a former English settlement, as when Cambridge, Wis., was renamed Christiana, and Waterloo, Ill., became New Hanover. In other seats of early English settlement, such as Edwards County, Ill., or Athens County, Ohio, the English-born constituted a substantial share of the foreign-born as late as 1890.

In a few places a consciousness of the English origins of early settlement either survived or was revived in the 20th century. When Queen Victoria died in 1901, her portrait, draped in black, was placed over the high altar of St. Paul's Church in Clay Center, Kans.; 40 days of mourning were declared, and the congregation provided the rector with a new black suit. In October 1929, when a memorial plaque was dedicated to Morris Birkbeck in the town of Albion, Ill., the governor of the state and others praised the English colony for setting standards of citizenship and for keeping Illinois free of slavery. Two years earlier, 225 people had gathered in Racine County, Wis., to commemorate the 80th anniversary of the laying of the cornerstone of an English immigrant church and to listen to addresses by descendants of Edward Bottomley and other early English settlers.

Outside of the midwestern rural settlements, the English experience varied according to the timing of earliest settlement, the absolute size of the English population, as well as its size in relation to the foreign-born and total populations, and the social structure of the immigrant population.

Substantial numbers of English immigrants arrived in the nation's largest cities, where they formed a small and often declining share of the population. In New York City in 1885 there were English-born residents at most levels of society. A larger percentage there fol-

lowed mercantile and professional occupations than in other cities. They were represented, if weakly, among laborers and servants, and as elsewhere, large numbers were employed in heavy metal and building trades. The English concentrated in a few parts of the city: the better-off in places like Greenwich Village, while the laborers who worked in stables, slaughterhouses, and factories lived farther north.

The English immigrant social institutions were weak. The St. George's societies, one of which had appeared in New York as in other East Coast ports in the late 18th and early 19th centuries, served a social function for the elite but were not so successful in their aim of aiding recent immigrants. The St. George's Society in New York widened its membership to include descendants of the English-born, immigrants from the empire, and British officers and their sons wherever born; but it still remained a small organization of merchants and professional people. Insufficient funds limited its work among the needy. It did not succeed in keeping a labor bureau going or in securing representation among the state's immigrant commissioners.

In 1844 an effort by a group of English mechanics, with the approval of the British consul, to establish a labor bureau resulted in the formation of the British Protective Emigration Society; but it too suffered from indifference and lack of funds, and after a brief merger with the St. George's Society, expired in 1853. Ironically, the most substantial aid the latter was able to offer between 1859 and 1909 consisted of cheap passages back to England, supplied by the White Star and Cunard lines to deserving migrants upon the society's recommendation. The annual dinners of the St. George's Society were social events of an elite who were not in touch with the larger immigrant community. Artisans who wanted to join an ethnic provident institution created the Sons of St. George, which secured the help of the St. George's Society in opening an employment bureau for a brief period between 1884 and 1886.

Immigrants in some smaller cities never constituted a significant share of the labor force or of the foreign-born inhabitants. The British share of the population of South Bend, Ind., fell from 20 percent in 1850 to 5 percent in 1860 and remained there during the next two decades, while the town's population more than trebled. By 1880 the 500 English immigrants of South Bend had not organized any societies of their own.

West of the Mississippi the new immigration from England produced few rural colonies as long lived as those in the Great Lakes regions. All the counties that had as many as 1,000 English-born inhabitants by 1890 were either mining districts or urban areas such as Des Moines, Iowa, Omaha, Nebr., Topeka, Kans., Minneapolis, Minn., Seattle, Wash., Portland, Ore., and Los Angeles, San Francisco, San Diego, and San Jose, Calif. In California the English-born belonged to the elite out of proportion to their numbers. New and fast-growing western cities afforded them opportunities for social mobility and influence, which explains their failure to organize as a group.

The English most successfully developed an institutional life in the industrial and mining communities where they formed a substantial part of the immigrant population and where they clustered in particular occupations and industries. In textile towns such as Pawtucket, R.I., and Fall River, Lowell, and Lynn, Mass., the English constituted a homogeneous social body, largely of skilled manual workers, many of whom worked in the same factories. This was true also of the skilled miners and bosses in the mining communities of Pennsylvania. In Paterson, N.J., Philadelphia, and East Liverpool, Ohio, where the English tended to be entrepreneurs and worked in a wider variety of industries, they were less well organized. Rivalry with the Irish stimulated organization in some places, helped develop English group identity, and eventually led to attempts at fusion of the entire British-American population. Whatever the explanation, associations among English immigrants reached their peak in a few towns in the last part of the 19th century.

In Lawrence, Mass., created as a factory village in the late 1840s, the English organized immigrant societies in roughly the same order and at the same pace as the other nationalities, although they relied on the American churches. They were quicker than the Scots or Germans to set up benefit associations, but much slower than the Germans to organize celebrations of old-country events. The English started cultural and literary societies earlier than the Germans and experimented with a newspaper before either the Germans or the Irish, but trailed them when it came to political organizations.

English institutional life, where it flourished in the United States, reproduced the self-help associations of the working class at home: workingmen's clubs, trade unions, friendly societies, and cooperatives. It was difficult to keep such working-class institutions English, since their orientation was not so much ethnic as class.

Although English immigrants contributed to the American labor movement, their leaders were as likely to be Scots or Welsh or Irish. Even among the textile workers of Fall River and New Bedford—where the Lancashire element was very strong and where mill owners blamed the English particularly for their labor troubles—Robert Howard, head of the National Mule Spinners Union (f. 1885) and James Tansey, his successor, were Lancashire-born of Irish parents. English immigrants organized the first American miners' unions: in 1849 John Bates created a short-lived union in the anthracite region, and in 1861 Daniel Weaver and Thomas Lloyd from Staffordshire began the American Miners' Association based in the Belleville district in Illinois. When English immigrants were present in significant numbers, the trade unions they helped organize merged into the core culture from which other ethnic groups felt excluded. Their participation in the unions probably weakened rather than strengthened their group ties.

The cooperative movement in the United States developed independently, but English immigrants did introduce in some communities the ideas of Rochdale cooperators, of consumer cooperatives based on one vote per shareholder and dividends on purchases. Lancashire mill hands organized one of the first as the Fall River Workingman's Cooperative Association in 1867. The Arlington Association, founded by English workers in Lawrence the year before, with 3,440 members, became for a while the largest in New England. The cooperatives did not survive as a focus of English community life. Only three of the many founded in New England

manufacturing towns lasted into the 20th century, and the miners' cooperatives were also short-lived.

Working-class immigrants from England also founded fraternal lodges but failed to retain control of them. The search for companionship led to the organization of such lodges among newly arrived artisans and tradesmen early in the 19th century. The first fraternal group to survive was an Odd Fellows lodge founded in Baltimore in 1819 by Thomas Wildey (1782–1861), a coach-spring maker from London, and John Welch, an English-born house and ship painter. Nativist sentiment, as well as the desire of these immigrants for the familiar companionship of the English ale houses, led them to "separate themselves from a community in which they were . . . condemned by a national prejudice." Quite independently, after a diligent search for other Odd Fellows in Boston, James B. Barnes (b. 1790), a tinsmith who had been associated with a lodge in London, formed the first one in Massachusetts in 1820. In due course Odd Fellows lodges appeared among English factory workers in many towns. Membership in Pleasant Valley, N.Y., was limited to operatives in a cotton mill. Many of the members of the lodge in Taunton, Mass., worked in the local factory. The Merrimack Lodge in Lowell was started in 1829.

The Odd Fellows suffered from the antimasonic movement of the 1820s and 1830s, but many lodges were resuscitated in the 1840s. Thomas Wildey devoted most of his life to the movement after securing an independent charter for the American order from Manchester Unity, the emerging English national organization, in 1826. In 1889 there were 29 Odd Fellows lodges in Massachusetts and Rhode Island with 1,600 members, both English and Scots. The native-born seem to have been recruited from an early date, so that in spite of their origins, the lodges did not remain English or purely working-class institutions. The Sons of St. George was established by Scranton miners in 1870 precisely because Americans had not been excluded from the established fraternal lodges. The Sons of St. George limited its membership to Englishmen, although it imitated the social, secret, and insurance functions of the older bodies. By 1914 it had 292 lodges with 31,680 members of English birth or descent.

Other recreational activities among English workers were particularly evident in mill towns. Paterson silk weavers had Macclesfield wakes, or festivals, and Fall River cotton workers, Ashton wakes. English mill workers enjoyed entertainments modeled on the early English music halls at drinking places in the New England textile towns. Cricket clubs were organized in Philadelphia in the early 1830s and among mill workers in New York City, Brooklyn, Boston, Lawrence, and Lowell in the 1840s and 1850s.

Newspapers for English immigrant readers always had trouble surviving. The first appeared in New York. *Albion, or the British Colonial and Foreign Gazette* (1827–1863) and the *Anglo-American* (1843–1847) appealed to educated merchants and professional people. The *Old Countryman*, started in 1830 to cater to the tastes of workingmen and critical of *Albion*, merged with the *Emigrant* in 1835 or 1836 but proved short-lived. By the 1840s English workingmen in the United States were receiving newspapers from home, as the provincial press in England expanded after the reduction of stamp duties in 1836.

The vigor of the English provincial press until the rise of national dailies explained the abortiveness of the next generation's efforts. A New York *English American* (f. 1884), an *Anglo-American* in Lawrence in the 1870s, and one in Boston about 1899 lasted only briefly. Weeklies and monthlies aimed at British rather than purely English readers were somewhat more successful. The most important, the *British-American Citizen* (Boston, 1887–1913), the *Western British American* (Chicago, 1888–1922), and the *British-American* (New York and Philadelphia, 1887–1919), were part of the unsuccessful conscious effort to unite the three British nationalities into a political force.

Many English immigrants who settled west of the Alleghenies expressed a positive distaste for politics and public life. Some were too fastidious to enter the rough and tumble of American politics; some turned to political activity only after they lost family or friends. Though they held many local offices, the English apparently showed no interest in organizing a bloc of voters and lagged behind other groups in seeking American citizenship.

In the 1870s and 1880s political clubs appeared among English immigrants in the same cities where other societies had developed. Jersey City's British-American Club assisted the Republican campaign in 1874. The Lancashire workers in Fall River organized an English-American Club to secure more influence in city government in 1876. Similar organizations appeared in Worcester, Mass., in 1883, Philadelphia in 1886, in Lawrence the same year, and in Sanford, Me., a town that also had a successful cooperative among English woolen workers.

One of the main purposes of these clubs was to encourage naturalization by the reluctant English immigrants. By the time the first comparative statistics on naturalization rates were compiled in 1900, these efforts had already borne fruit, but even so, somewhat fewer English and Scottish immigrants had become citizens than had members of most other early immigrant groups.

The success of the Irish in American politics sometimes goaded English leaders into trying to mobilize the English vote. In 1887, when 400 members of English and Scottish societies held a grand banquet in Boston's Faneuil Hall to celebrate Victoria's Jubilee, 15,000 angry Irishmen tried to prevent their entry, and all politicians except the British-born stayed away. Within a few months British-American societies and newspapers had been launched in the major cities. By 1888 there were 60 branches of a national federation of these societies in Massachusetts, 11 in Rhode Island, 6 in Connecticut, 17 in New York, 15 in Pennsylvania, 18 in Illinois, and smaller numbers in New Hampshire, New Jersey, Ohio, Michigan, Iowa, and California.

This flurry of activity did not result in the formation of a British-American political bloc to offset that of the Irish. By 1892 the anti-Catholic American Protective Association (APA) largely absorbed the British-American clubs, and the national federation collapsed. APA members in the Midwest were "common folk, inarticulate, and perhaps frustrated by lack of identification with the major elements of American society." The association's support derived largely from hostility between British (often Scotch-Irish) and Irish immigrants, and it was burnt out by 1895.

This singular and unsuccessful effort to weld a British-American political force failed. Politicians were unwilling to seek the votes of British-American immigrants even in Fall River with its large English constituency. In South Bend the leading English-born politician did not rise to prominence through leadership in ethnic organizations as did German and Polish politicians. English politicians were reluctant to appear as ethnic leaders because of the difficulties of disciplining English voters and the unwillingness of either major party to risk alienating Irish voters. To some extent, at least, the degree of adherence to the Republican party reflected the strength of British-Irish hostility in a particular community. In Wisconsin, for instance, English constituencies polled lower Republican majorities than in Michigan, where bitter conflicts with the Irish in mining communities apparently stimulated the English-born to vote Republican.

At the end of the 19th century, the English had nowhere developed so extensive an institutional life as the Irish or Germans. The English lacked churches or schools of their own. The other organizations in which they participated—lodges, trade unions, and cooperatives—were not exclusively immigrant in membership and therefore did not reinforce social clubs and sports activities of either the working class in the mill towns or the elite in large cities.

One consequence may have been isolation and frustration among scattered immigrants who arrived without families and lived in places where no English community life provided the fellowship, warmth, and security that the Lancashire operatives found in Fall River or Lawrence, the Macclesfield immigrants in Paterson, or even the miners in the strife-torn coal fields of Pennsylvania. But the isolation was not reflected in excessive crime, insanity, or pauperism.

The incomplete English community life, even where it did emerge, failed to cross class barriers. The social mobility of the second-generation English immigrants undermined continued adherence to working-class institutions and customs. One study of a small sample of British Americans born in Boston between 1860 and 1897 showed that nearly half the sons of manual workers entered and remained in white-collar jobs. The social mobility of the second generation, as well as the absence of overt barriers to assimilation, weakened adherence to the typical organizations of workers.

Other developments after 1890 further reduced the need for separate English protective organizations. The diplomatic rapprochement between the United States and Britain after 1895, which culminated in the enduring alliance begun in World War I, removed fears of divided loyalties.

THE 20TH CENTURY

The pattern of English immigration after 1893 offered no further impetus to join British-American associations. The reduction of immigration during the depression of 1893–1897 proved to be the beginning of a long-run decline (see Table 4). Though prosperity returned in the decade after 1900, when the great influx of immigrants from southern and eastern Europe occurred, the annual average English immigration reached only 63,700, one-third lower than the level for the 1880s. English immigrants were 1.4 percent in 1890, only 0.7 percent in 1930. (See Table 5.)

Table 4. Immigration from England to the United States, 1881–1973.

Years	Arrivals	Percentage of arrivals from Europe	Percentage of arrivals from all countries
1881–1890	644,480	13.6	12.3
1891–1900	216,726	6.1	5.9
1901–1910	388,017	4.8	4.4
1911–1920	249,944	5.8	4.4
1921–1930	157,420	6.4	3.8
1931–1940	21,756	6.3	4.1
1941–1950	112,252	18.1	10.8
1951–1960	156,171	11.8	6.2
1961–1970	174,452	15.5	10.7
1971	11,125	12.2	3.0
1972	10,036	11.6	2.6
1973	10,450	11.5	2.6

Source: Based on U.S. Immigration and Naturalization Service, *Annual Report, 1973,* adapted from summary in Leonard Dinnerstein and David Reimers, *Ethnic Americans: A History of Immigration and Assimilation* (New York, 1975), pp. 164 ff.

Overseas emigration from England did not decline between 1900 and 1910, but each year from 1905 on, emigration to Canada exceeded that to the United States. By 1913 and 1914 only 18 percent of the emigrants leaving England and Wales gave the United States as a destination. Within a few years the era that began in the 17th century, when the colonies of North America were the favored destination for English emigrants, came to an end.

Immigration from England revived after World War I, though not to prewar levels. The English did not use all of the generous quota allotted to them in the immigration act of 1924. An average of about 11,000 English and Welsh emigrants left for the United States each year from 1925 to 1929, but with allowance for those returning home, the net figure was about 7,000 a year, fewer than in the 1830s. During the Great Depression the balance turned negative, and in every year from 1931 to 1938, more people returned to England than came as immigrants.

The English-born share of the American population continued to decline to 0.2 percent in 1970. The number living in the United States fell from over 840,000 in 1900 to 458,000 in 1970. As a share of the foreign-born population, the English tended to hold their own after the restrictive legislation of the 1920s discriminated against southern and eastern Europeans. The ending of national quotas in 1965 again reduced the English share of the foreign-born to only 4.8 percent in 1970.

The social characteristics of English immigration in the 20th century have changed, although the decline in common laborers began long before the quota laws. The

Table 5. Number of English-born as percentage of foreign-born and of total population of the United States, selected census dates.

Year	Number	Percentage of foreign-born	Percentage of total population
1850	278,675	12.4	1.2
1870	555,046	10.0	1.4
1890	909,092	9.8	1.4
1910	877,719	6.5	1.1
1930	809,563	5.7	0.7
1960	528,205	5.4	0.3
1970	458,114	4.8	0.2

Source: U.S. Bureau of the Census, *Historical Statistics of the United States, Colonial Times to 1970* (Washington, D.C., 1975), I, 117.

percentage of immigrants from England listed as laborers never fell below 40 percent in the 1880s, but the percentage was down to 12 in the immigration peak of 1907, and was less than 12 in every year during the 1920s except 1924. The share of farmers also fell from over 7 percent in 1882 to less than 2 percent in 1907. At the same time skilled workers again rose as a share of total, and the proportion of professional people increased from less than 2 percent of the 1882 influx to about 9 percent in 1907. From 1914 to 1930 more than 10 percent of the adult male English immigrants in almost every year were people with professional qualifications. The pattern has persisted. From 1957 to 1964 England sent more physicians and surgeons to the United States than did any other country.

The British, and especially the English, contribution to certain occupations, commonly referred to as the "brain drain," continued in the 1970s. Over half of the immigrant workers admitted from the United Kingdom in 1974–1975 were professional, technical, and kindred workers, managers, and administrators, as compared with only 32 percent of all immigrants in these categories. While the British by then constituted only 3 percent of all immigrants admitted permanently, they formed 8 to 9 percent of the temporary visitors. The United Kingdom contributed 14 percent of those temporary visitors allowed into the country because they were "workers of distinguished merit and ability." Residents of Massachusetts, California, and New York may be most conscious of this small but specialized immigration because almost two out of five recent immigrants from Britain have settled in those three states. Recent British visitors and immigrants include not only academics, doctors, and other professional people, but also nurses, secretaries, and nannies.

Shifts in sex ratios and marital status of English immigrants were also apparent after 1893. The number of women per 1,000 male adults rose from 557 in the 1880s to 658 in the years 1900–1907. By the 1920s women exceeded men—a feature of a waning immigrant movement. During the years 1946–1948, war brides arriving from the United Kingdom temporarily brought the ratio of females to 4,395 per 1,000 males. The share of married persons, both male and female, tended to rise, though in the decade after 1900 they still accounted for less than 42 percent of the adult English immigrants to the United States (32 percent in the 1880s). The share of children was lower from the 1890s to the end of the 1930s than it had been in the 1870s and 1880s.

English immigration in the 20th century was not a family migration. The proportion of immigrants bringing human capital embodied in skills was higher than in early days. But immigrants arriving in the 20th century were less likely to have dependent children and perhaps more often were single.

The waning numbers, the failure of immigration to continue in the old centers where the English labor force was overwhelmed by new arrivals from other parts of Europe, and the ending of any advantage for their old empirical industrial skills—all these factors eroded the base for any further development of the incomplete institutional life observed in textile and mining communities of the 1880s and 1890s. Some of the poets, professors, and journalists who sojourned in the

United States for some time or became permanent residents expressed their reactions in writing, as did travelers and writers in the 19th century. On the whole, however, the 20th-century immigrants from England have remained as invisible as their predecessors. The study of such immigrants, who rarely had the protection afforded by an ethnic community life from material or psychological pain, is important both for understanding the experience of immigration itself at various periods in the United States, but also as part of a spectrum of various responses, each of which helps illuminate the others.

Bibliography
There is no comprehensive work on English emigration or on English immigrants in the United States. For the colonial period, see the two articles by Mildred Campbell: "Social Origins of Some Early Americans," in James Morton Smith, ed., *Seventeeth Century America* (Chapel Hill, N.C., 1959), and "English Emigration on the Eve of the American Revolution," in *American Historical Review* 61 (1955): 1–20. David Galenson has challenged Campbell's conclusions in a number of articles; see, for example, "'Middling People' or 'Common Sort'? The Social Origins of Some Early Americans Reexamined," *William and Mary Quarterly*, 3rd ser., 35 (1978): 499–540. Abbott Emerson Smith, *Colonists in Bondage* (1947; reprint, New York, 1971), deals with indentured servants and convict labor, 1607–1776. On the Loyalists, see Wallace Brown, *The King's Friends* (Providence, R.I., 1965). Other studies of American attitudes toward England and the English are Harry C. Allen, *Conflict and Concord: The Anglo-American Relationship since 1783* (New York, 1959), and Edward P. Crapol, *America for Americans: Economic Nationalism and Anglophobia in the Late 19th Century* (Westport, Conn., 1973). For the 19th century, see Maldwyn A. Jones, "The Background to Emigration from Great Britain in the Nineteenth Century," *Perspectives in American History* 7 (1973): 3–92; the pioneer study by Stanley C. Johnson, *A History of Emigration from the United Kingdom to North America, 1762–1912* (1913; reprint, New York, 1966); and Wilbur S. Shepperson, *British Emigration to North America* (Oxford, 1957). Recruitment of Mormons is the subject of Philip A.M. Taylor, *Expectations Westward* (Edinburgh, 1965), and immigrant labor is the subject of Charlotte Erickson, *American Industry and the European Immigrant, 1860–1885* (1957; reprint, New York, 1967). For the British in industry, see the useful survey by Rowland T. Berthoff, *British Immigrants in Industrial America, 1790–1950* (1953; reprint, New York, 1968). David J. Jeremy probes the transfer of technology more deeply in, for example, "British Technology Transmission to the United States, the Philadelphia Region Experience, 1770–1820," *Business History Review* 47 (1973): 24–52. The social and economic adaptation of English immigrants is examined through their letters in Charlotte Erickson, *Invisible Immigrants* (London, 1972). Ray Boston, *British Chartists in America, 1830–1900* (Totowa, N.J., 1971), and Clifton K. Yearley, *Britons in American Labor* (Baltimore, 1957), deal with some interesting immigrants, and Wilbur Shepperson discusses some who returned home in *Emigration and Disenchantment* (Norman, Okla., 1965).

Collections of letters of English immigrants are deposited in the Collection of Regional History at Cornell University, Ithaca, N.Y., and in the British Library of Political and Economic Science in London. Others are scattered in county archives in England and state historical society collections in the United States.

Charlotte J. Erickson

ESKIMOS

The 35,000 Eskimos of Alaska form a group related linguistically and culturally to people who dwell along the North American Arctic littoral as far east as Greenland and as far west as Siberia. Probably deriving from north-central Asian migrants, Eskimos have been in the New World for at least 4,000 years.

Eskimo has a number of dialects, but most Alaska Eskimos are either Inupiaq speakers (in an arc from Unalakleet on the coast of Norton Sound around to the Canadian border) or Yupik speakers (from south of Unalakleet around to Prince William Sound in the Gulf of

Alaska). Siberian Yupik speakers inhabit St. Lawrence Island off the coast of West Alaska.

The character of Alaska Eskimo settlements traditionally has been determined by their means of livelihood. The Tareamiut were sea-mammal hunters and lived in large, permanent communities; the Nunamiut were island caribou hunters, lived in small camps, and moved seasonally to fish and hunt. To the south the distinction between the groups was less pronounced. The legendary igloo was never a major dwelling for any of the Alaska Eskimos. Caught in winter storms away from shelter, they would cut and stack blocks of snow to form a temporary shelter, but permanent dwellings were typically dugouts in winter and animal-skin tents in summer.

The appearance of Eskimos varies. Some are tall and slim and have sharp features; others are stocky with round smooth features. Most share the high cheekbones, skin, and hair coloring of the American Indians, and the epicanthic eye folds of Asian populations.

The earliest contacts of Eskimos with western Europeans were with Spanish, Russian, and English explorers in the 1770s; these explorers reported the Eskimos as being everything from friendly to hostile, but they were unanimous about one thing: Eskimos were extremely efficient exploiters of their environment when it came to gathering food. Before the arrival of the explorers the Eskimos were unaware that any other people existed, except for the subarctic Athapascans with whom they had sporadic—sometimes violent, sometimes trading—contact.

Aside from occasional conflicts with Russian colonists Alaska Eskimos never fought with settlers from outside and were not conquered by force or otherwise mistreated as so many American Indians were. In 1867 the United States purchased Alaska from Russia, and in subsequent years the Eskimos experienced at first a slow and then more rapid exposure to Western society. In 1971 the U.S. Congress settled Eskimo and Indian claims on Alaska's land with a compensation of $1 billion and over 40 million acres. This settlement allowed the creation of a series of Eskimo village and regional profit and nonprofit corporations and provided for village, regional, and individual land entitlements and individual cash payments. The compensation was to be paid over a 20-year period to allow the Eskimos time to absorb this massive sum and ensure that control over it would remain securely in Eskimo hands.

Today Alaska Eskimos live in some 100 villages ranging in size from 100 to 600 people, with most around 300. In addition, there are 4 small towns averaging 2,500–3,000 inhabitants. A sizable number also live in the major cities of Fairbanks (3,000) and Anchorage (3,500).

Most Alaska Eskimo villages have, or will soon acquire, electricity and hence household appliances (including freezers, useful for preserving food gathered in season) and lighting; all villages are accessible by air and have regularly scheduled mail and passenger flights. All the small towns—Barrow, Bethel, Kotzebue, and Nome—have U.S. Public Health Service medical facilities and a variety of other government agencies and projects. Increasing access to education and an abundance of jobs generated in part by the land-claims settlement have produced a labor shortage in the larger communities, for the new Eskimo businesses in the villages staff their offices with local Eskimos. All this development has come about in so short a time that most communities have changed unrecognizably in the past decade or so. Culture changes more slowly, however, and Eskimo life is now largely a reflection of the discontinuities that have resulted.

ECONOMIC LIFE

Some Eskimo villages still rely at least in part on hunting and fishing for survival; others have a totally commercial cash economy. Modern technology (rifles, snowmobiles, outboard motors, short-wave radios) makes traditional activities less dangerous and more productive, allowing even hunting villages to have a substantial cash economy. Commercial fishing, fur dealing, ivory carving, tourism, local retail establishments, state and local government positions, government transfer payments, Eskimo construction and commercial corporations, and forest-fire fighting in the summer all contribute to a substantial involvement in the larger economy. Only a few of the most isolated communities are not fully attuned to the contemporary economic system, and even these are not untouched by it.

In addition to the businessmen who administer the Eskimo corporations, a few Eskimos have acquired some kind of professional training, although there are as yet no full-blooded Eskimo physicians or lawyers. Many more are training as paraprofessionals or working in service and construction industries. These developments already have had an impact on Alaska politics.

SOCIAL STRUCTURE AND ORGANIZATION

Eskimo social organization was originally based on family, kin, and friendship ties. Devoid of social control mechanisms beyond the pressures of village gossip, Eskimo behavior was constrained only by the limits of what an individual felt he could get away with. Feuds and other forms of violence were ubiquitous. Eskimos developed circumlocutions, a smiling demeanor, and a tendency to interpret even the most antisocial behavior in neutral terms in order to avoid confrontations or violence that could disrupt the small community.

Cooperative behavior was necessary for hunting large land and sea mammals, and typically involved very complex arrangements, again often indirectly organized. This indirection, distrust of formal leadership, and constant effort to avoid conflict remain central features of modern Eskimo life. A typical conversation between a respected older hunter to other hunters might be: "One hears that seals have been seen." The others nod. He continues, "One wonders if it is time to hunt them." The others agree. Then he says, "Perhaps someone will hunt them tomorrow." No further conversation ensues. Translated, the message is, "I know there are seals, and I'm going hunting. If you want to come with me, do so; you know where my boat is and when I will leave." No one has been put into the position of having to say yes or no; no one even has to admit that communication has taken place.

Even with these methods, however, there have always been opposing factions in the village, and there still are. Relations between leadership in village coun-

cils, in corporation board membership, and in all areas of corporate existence are fragile. Leadership changes hands rapidly, alliances shift dramatically; close blood relations are the only source of stability. Very few Eskimos have mastered organizational and administrative skills, and the goals of any single unit are unclear and subject to almost whimsical fluctuations.

The most capable leaders tend to be part Caucasian, because they are most apt to have been exposed as children to contemporary Western ideas and greater concern for achievement. They are often the descendants of the strong-minded and ambitious whaling captains and entrepreneurs who around the turn of the century came to Alaska and later married Eskimo women. Their descendants had greater educational and other advantages than those of their full-blooded contemporaries. Through them the earlier pattern of vague and indirect leadership vested in older, skilled men with a sizable kinship group has given way to a leadership of younger, better educated, somewhat more aggressive men and women.

Almost all Eskimos under the age of 15 are at least minimally literate, but the proportion declines as the age group rises until perhaps only half or two-thirds of 50-year-olds and a much smaller percentage of those over 65 can read and write. In 1965 Eskimos showed a 30 percent dropout rate in grade school, 50 to 80 percent in high school, and 97 percent among the few who attended college. By 1975 the rates had decreased to a negligible grade-school dropout, 25 percent high-school dropout, and around 50 percent college dropout (the available figures are rough estimates). This change is so recent and so dramatic that its full effects are impossible to predict.

Mental health problems are endemic. The data are imperfect, but the incidence of psychiatric problems appears to be about twice that of the non-Eskimo population. Child care is sometimes neglectful and sporadic. Many children are given away by their parents or neglected as subsequent children are born (infant mortality rates have been dramatically reduced). Not surprisingly, children are poorly prepared for school and often grow up to be troubled adults. Alcoholism is the most serious problem. Difficulty in controlling their impulses and in communicating emotions leads to a great deal of violence—murder, child abuse, and vandalism. Murder is actually the leading cause of death in one of the larger Eskimo communities, and in nearly all of them there is a high incidence of drowning, freezing to death, or risk-taking while drunk. Suicide rates are also very high.

These forms of pathology may not all be attributable to pressures created by cultural change. What the rates were before Western contacts is unknown, but suicide, murder, infanticide, child abandonment, and difficulty in expressing emotion seem to have been characteristic of Eskimo culture before the explorers arrived. The introduction of alcohol, reduction in infant mortality, and stresses induced by change have exacerbated the problems, but they did not cause them.

Culture

Perhaps 50 percent or more of the Yupik still speak the original language, but fewer of the Inupiaq do. Nearly all Eskimo adults, including those fluent in the original tongue, are fluent in English. There have been efforts to devise a written Eskimo language, but the orthographies were idiosyncratic and their use limited. University of Alaska linguists recently have worked out a more viable system, but it is not in general use. Because there is no Eskimo literature and use of the spoken language is restricted to the home, occasional public meetings, and nonceremonial recreational activity, survival of the language is doubtful although it may live on for a while in some communities. Some political pressure is exerted locally to maintain the language, but nearly all ordinary communication is in English.

Most Eskimo folk art consisted of carved masks, labrets (plugs for holes made in the cheeks, face, and lips), and fans (used in dancing). Ceremonial dances expressed mythological, hunting, and everyday interests and routines, and often were accompanied by communal singing in the men's house (which was also used as a sauna). The most common musical instrument was a flat, one-sided drum made of walrus intestine or other thin animal material stretched over a wooden frame and beaten with a wand. These ceremonies are now rarely presented, and then only in attenuated form. Shamanism has been replaced by contemporary medicine and Christianity; marriages are no longer arranged, but some barter—for example, skins for seal oil—still goes on.

Several of the larger villages publish newspapers; the most important is the English-language *Tundra Times*, published in Anchorage. Other publications are occasionally issued by regional and village corporations. Some Eskimo poetry is published in English by the University of Alaska and occasionally by private or public service agencies, but neither the output nor the demand is substantial enough to support a full-time publication effort.

One major exception to the general disappearance of Eskimo customs is the whale hunt organized at Point Barrow. Although whale hunting is no longer an important source of subsistence, it retains traditional and recreational importance, particularly for local Eskimo enterpreneurs. Its continuation has provoked criticism from ecological groups.

Religion

The Eskimo religion was essentially animistic, using sympathetic and homeopathic magic to drive away evil spirits. Eskimo cosmology was not very well defined, but it involved a general magical connection between all things—when a whale was killed, for example, it was symbolically offered a drink of fresh water after it was beached so that its spirit would not be offended and drive away other whales. As in many such cosmologies all babies were thought to be reincarnations of recently deceased relatives. Supernatural and natural were not clearly distinguished; the afterlife was simply something vague and disquieting. Ghosts of the departed and part-human, part-monster creatures inhabited the tundra and were equally feared; even so, rituals for warding them off were never well developed.

The Eskimos rapidly abandoned their traditional religions when the Westerners came. Given the chance to abandon a religion with many taboos and few consolations for one with few requirements (going to church, not eating meat on Friday) and a positive and achievable

afterlife, they accepted Christianity with alacrity. The version they adopted retained a great deal that was Eskimo—they held onto some of their spirits and monsters. Still, Christianity offered an ordering perspective that stressed social control and peaceful behavior; on balance, it has probably been a positive influence. The suppression by missionaries of Eskimo dancing was Christianity's most substantial negative effect.

The Christian missionaries carved Alaska into spheres of influence, the Presbyterians taking the north coast, the Catholics the Yukon River area, the Moravians the Bethel region, and so on. But religious practice was fairly uniform regardless of official affiliation. Eskimos remain uncertain about proper sexual behavior: Christian puritanism vies with traditional sexual freedom, and some rigidity of behavior is still apparent. Dogma and theology appear to be completely irrelevant to contemporary Eskimo religious beliefs.

Participation in religious life is most common among the middle-aged, far less so among the young and the elderly. In villages where the church is strong it is able to perform the important function of prohibiting, or at least curbing, alcohol consumption. In recent times fundamentalist Christian sects have also made inroads in established church communities, probably because their stress on emotional release in religious expression appeals to Eskimos.

INTERGROUP RELATIONS AND ETHNIC COMMITMENT

Eskimos did not become active in local or state politics until after World War II, and have not yet entered the national political scene. In the 1960s a few were elected to seats in the state legislature previously held by Caucasians, and many more joined them after the land-claims settlement. By now no Eskimo community is politically controlled by non-Eskimos; although some technical jobs still are held by Caucasians, political and elective offices are all in Eskimo hands in areas where they are in the majority. Local, regional, and statewide coalitions are transitory; they are usually formed in the legislature to defend "bush" (village) against urban interests, but they have yet to become stable political organizations with statewide power. The increasing economic effectiveness of the regional corporations, however, offers an alternative basis for substantial community strength.

The political and economic activities of corporations are dominated by the better educated, usually part-Caucasian, Eskimos. Local electorates are poorly informed and vote on the basis of kinship ties or friendship or as their leaders instruct them. Ideological issues of a narrow sort have begun to dominate rhetoric in some of the larger villages. In its more extreme forms this rhetoric is separatist and hostile to non-Eskimos, who are portrayed as oppressing and exploiting the Eskimos, a view that to some extent reflects pressure from Caucasian teachers upon students to abandon Eskimo in favor of English. This pressure was largely halted by the bilingual education movement of the 1970s, however, and the accusations are in other respects somewhat exaggerated. The United States did not conquer Alaska, and it has provided substantial social services for the Eskimos. The Eskimos have suffered little from racial prejudice, especially compared to other American Indian groups. Most Eskimos in any case live in areas so remote that until recently contact with the outside has been minimal except for a few health, social service, police, government, and commercial representatives.

Prejudice, however, has existed. In Nome, where contact with a large non-Eskimo population is by now at least three generations old, substantial anti-Eskimo prejudice once could be found; for example, until the 1940s Eskimos were barred from movie theaters. But Alaskan law made such practices illegal long before the civil rights movement did so in the rest of the United States. Today preferential hiring gives Eskimos distinct advantages, and anti-Eskimo remarks are regarded as in poor taste by most Alaskans, who seem to have a positive, if somewhat romantic, attitude toward the group.

Prosperity, increased travel from village to city, and the sizable number of Eskimos living in Anchorage and Fairbanks have increased contacts between Eskimo and Caucasian and reduced prejudice still further. On the other hand, alcoholism and limited skills in Western technology still create some feelings of inferiority. Because there are few institutional and attitudinal barriers to Eskimo entry into the mainstream society, the group probably will assimilate into the dominant culture, though perhaps retaining certain folkways and customs. They show no self-conscious determination to remain a distinctive group, and intermarriage with non-Eskimos is common.

Some lip service is given to Eskimo culture, but because the content of that culture is limited mostly to family ties and traditional foods, it does not provide much of a base for retaining a separate identity. The schools take a value-free approach to cultural differences, so there are few clashes of values that might encourage ethnic maintenance. The older the Eskimo, the more likely he or she will be to wear animal-skin clothing, eat fish or caribou, speak an Eskimo language, and believe in spirits and ghosts; the younger the Eskimo, the more likely he or she will be oriented toward and involved in contemporary issues.

Bibliography
There is no single best source for studying contemporary Eskimo life. Robert Spencer, *The North Alaskan Eskimo* (Washington, D.C., 1959), and Nicholas J. Gubser, *The Nunamiut Eskimos: Hunters of Caribou* (New Haven, Conn., 1965), are useful and complementary studies of recent changes. James W. Van Stone, *Point Hope: An Eskimo Village in Transition* (Seattle, 1962); Wendell H. Oswalt, *Napaskiak, An Alaskan Eskimo Community* (Tucson, Ariz., 1970); Charles C. Hughes, *An Eskimo Village in the Modern World* (Ithaca, N.Y., 1960); and Norman Chance, *The Eskimo of North Alaska* (New York, 1966), together provide some idea of the range of change in Alaska Eskimo communities. Arthur E. Hippler, "The North Alaska Eskimo: A Culture and Personality Perspective," *American Ethnologist* 1 (1974): 449–470, is an introductory study of Eskimo behavior.

Excellent general collections of archival material are available at the Arctic Institute of North America in Montreal and the University of Alaska, Fairbanks.

ARTHUR E. HIPPLER

ESTONIANS

Estonians come from a country situated at the northeast corner of the Baltic Sea, south of Finland and west of Russia. Estonia presently is a part of the Soviet Union. Closely related linguistically to the Finns and more distantly to the Hungarians, the Estonians are physically, culturally, religiously, and socially more similar to Scandinavians than to Slavs.

Estonia was conquered in the 13th century by Germans, whose descendants became an entrenched upper class. From 1561 to 1700 Estonia was ruled by Sweden, and during this period the position of the Estonian peasants improved appreciably. However, Sweden lost control of Estonia to Russia in the Great Northern War (1700–1721), during which the Estonian population declined sharply from famine and disease. Afterward, the Baltic German nobility regained much of its earlier power.

Toward the middle of the 19th century, growing population pressures and economic changes impelled Estonians to emigrate eastward to inner Russia in order to take advantage of homesteading opportunities. However, when the pressures of Russification—the effort to suppress Estonian religion and culture—became too great, Estonians sought another refuge, and a number left for North America, where they were joined later by Estonian political refugees who fled the Russian Empire after the suppression of the 1905 revolution.

Estonia proclaimed its independence from Russia in 1918. The Baltic German nobility lost its power, and radical land reform helped reduce emigration to a very low level between World War I and World War II. But in response to Soviet annexation of Estonia in 1940, German occupation from 1941 to 1944, and Soviet reentry in 1944, there was a sizable flight westward. Although both Soviet and German authorities officially prohibited departure, about 10 percent of the population left Estonia. After a few years in refugee camps in Western Europe, the Estonian émigrés were resettled in Sweden, Canada, the United States, Australia, Great Britain, and West Germany.

ARRIVAL AND SETTLEMENT

A few people from Estonia arrived in North America as early as the mid-17th century, but the organizational structure of the Estonian-American community did not begin to emerge until the 1890s. How many Estonians came to the United States before 1922 cannot be determined with any accuracy because U.S. immigration officials have always kept records on the basis of country

of birth; many of the first Estonian immigrants were descendants of the Estonians who had gone to Russia more than a century before. Their exact number and fate are yet to be ascertained, but upon entry to the United States they were listed as Russians. In the 1920s congressional calculations numbered Americans of Estonian descent at 5,100 in 1890 and 69,200 in 1920; a contemporary specialist on immigration, however, estimated the number to be about 200,000.

From 1923 to 1939 the United States admitted about 3,000 Estonians, and from 1940 to 1965 about 15,000. Few have arrived since; the 1970 U.S. Census showed only 20,000 first- and second-generation Estonians in the United States.

Since the turn of the century most Estonian Americans have resided in the major metropolitan areas of the industrial states. However, the first organization founded by the Estonians in the United States was a Lutheran congregation near Fort Pierre, S.Dak., in 1897; the first church was erected in another rural settlement, Bloomville, Wis.; and the first community hall and school belonged to yet a third settlement near Chester, Mont. But the rural villages in the Dakotas, Wisconsin, Montana, Colorado, Wyoming, Washington, and Oregon—only a few with over 100 people—did not play a significant role in the larger Estonian-American community. In 1970 about 52 percent of the group lived in the Washington-Boston corridor, 15 percent in the Great Lakes region, and 19 percent on the West Coast.

ORGANIZATIONS

An early attempt at forging a sense of Estonian ethnic community along religious lines was made by the Reverend Hans Rebane, who came to the United States in 1896 at the invitation of the Lutheran Missouri Synod to minister to both Latvian and Estonian immigrants. Rebane crisscrossed the continent in missionary work until his death in 1911. Lutheran congregations were founded on his initiative in South Dakota, Wisconsin, New York, Philadelphia, and Boston. Rebane also published the first Estonian-American newspaper, the *Amerika-Eesti Postimees* (Estonian-American Courier, 1897–1911). But the urban congregations were small, reflecting Rebane's very pietistic orientation and the socialist leanings of most of the urban Estonians, who had already been anticlerical in Estonia, where the Lutheran Church was a Baltic German institution until 1918.

Estonians established informal groups before the 1890s in San Francisco and Astoria, Ore.; the first formal lay organization, the Amerika Eesti Heategew Selts (Estonian-American Beneficial Society), was founded in 1898 in New York as a mutual-benefit society; it also sponsored social and cultural events. In 1905 some of the members resigned to form a second organization, but the two merged again in 1910 to form the New Yorgi Eesti Selts (New York Estonian Society). Other lay organizations appeared early in the 1900s in San Francisco, Philadelphia, and Portland, Ore. The main functions of these early urban societies were to aid newcomers and to provide a social and cultural outlet.

During the period 1906–1919 the best-organized element in the Estonian-American community was the urban workers' movement. A number of Estonian socialist activists had come to the United States after the failure of the 1905 revolution in Russia, and most urban

Estonian Americans at that time were in the working class. Workers' societies were founded in 1906 and 1907, respectively, in New York and San Francisco, the main centers of the movement. Societies also appeared in 11 other localities from Portland to New London, Conn. By 1908 the movement had a national central committee, and in 1909 in New York it began to publish the weekly *Uus Ilm* (New World), which today is the oldest continually published periodical in the Estonian-American community.

The workers' societies appear to have been to the far left of the American socialist movement of the time, but they were ethnically important because in many localities they were the only Estonian organization. The larger ones provided mutual aid and sponsored social events, reading rooms, choruses, and theater groups. But the years 1917–1919 saw a fateful schism both in the Estonian-American community as a whole and specifically within the workers' movement, in reaction to developments in Russia and Estonia. Almost all Estonians welcomed the Russian Revolution, but they were divided over the future of Estonia. Both in Estonia and in the Estonian-American community the majority, including most socialists, favored a sovereign Estonian state. However, the most radical leftists cast their lot with the Bolsheviks and favored the inclusion of their homeland in the U.S.S.R.

By 1917 the radical leadership of the workers' movement had achieved editorial control of *Uus Ilm*, then the only newspaper in the community, and its increasingly Communist viewpoint caused serious strain. The radicals had also managed to gain control of several previously apolitical ethnic organizations and to use their assets in part to finance the return of some radicals to Europe. As a result, the New York Estonian Society, for example, ceased to exist. Yet, for several reasons, the radical-controlled workers' movement itself slowly declined beginning in 1919. First, the moderate socialists were alienated during the 1917–1919 conflict and joined competing organizations. Second, the most able radical leaders left to join the Russian Revolution, leaving the American movement without effective leadership. Third, the newly founded U.S. Communist party in the 1920s abolished the earlier structure of the socialist movement which had developed along ethnic lines; when the postwar workers' clubs became more Communist than Estonian, they lost much of their appeal. Finally, many of the postwar immigrants had fought in the Estonian War of Independence against Soviet Russia (1918–1920) and were ardent nationalists and often openly anti-Communist. The workers' clubs remained significant throughout the 1920s, but the organizational initiative continued to shift to non-Communists, and the Communists eventually ceased to be part of the mainstream Estonian-American community. The rejection was mutual.

When the old New York Estonian Society became defunct after the Communist takeover in 1918, nationalist activists formed the Ameerika-Eesti Ühisus (Estonian-American Union), which solicited aid for war-torn Estonia, sought diplomatic recognition for the newly proclaimed republic (by sending a special delegation to President Warren G. Harding), sponsored political rallies, advocated trade relations, and issued a monthly journal. After achieving its goals, it, too, temporarily

disbanded, leaving New York's Estonian-American community in organizational disarray.

The Lutheran congregations remained active in New York and several other places, but they lacked effective pastoral leadership after the death of the Reverend Rebane in 1911. The most active Estonian-American religious group after World War I was the Baptist Church. Persecuted in preindependence Estonia, a number of Baptists emigrated to the United States and established a congregation in New York City in 1919. Nationally one of the largest Estonian organizations, it sponsored musical and Christmas gatherings in addition to its regular services. The Baptists' Sunday School was the first functionally ethnic school in New York (a lay school had existed in the Estonian settlement in Montana and a Sunday school and confirmation class in Wisconsin more than a decade earlier). The Baptists also published an important monthly, *Ameerika Teekäija* (American Journeyer, 1918–1923), and a pamphlet series, *Ameerika Rändur* (American Wanderer, 1930–1932). A Pentecostal congregation in New York dates back to 1928. However, almost 80 percent of Estonia's population had been Lutheran, and most Estonian Americans are Lutherans as well. There are presently 28 Estonian-American Lutheran congregations.

The Estonian-American community that emerged in the 1920s was composed of the religious groups and many new lay organizations. By mid-decade the New York Estonians had recovered from their earlier conflicts and enjoyed new vitality. The latest immigrants had a strong ethnic consciousness. Also, New York City now had an Estonian diplomatic mission with close ties to the community. And the new Välis-Eesti Ühing (Estonia Abroad Society) founded in Estonia began to promote a global sense of ethnic unity. It sent books, periodicals, and information about the new sovereign republic to Estonian-American organizations, published an internationally circulated periodical, and encouraged visits to the homeland. Among the important lay organizations were the Estonian-American Athletic Club; the Estonian-American Music Club; the apolitical society, Edu (Progress); the socialist society, Kiir (Ray); and a Communist workers' club. New non-Communist societies also appeared in Cleveland (1925), Detroit (1926), and Los Angeles (1928).

In 1929 the New York groups (excluding the Communists) merged to form the United Estonian Society, partly because circumstances were threatening the financial survival of the many small and competing organizations. The new organization, soon renamed the Estonian Educational Society, quickly emerged as the largest national lay group. Today, with about 1,000 members, it continues to sponsor an array of ethnic social, cultural, youth, athletic, and leisure activities. It also operates a children's summer camp on Long Island and Estonian House, a community center dedicated in 1947, in New York City. During the postwar period Estonian centers were also opened in Lakewood and Seabrook, N.J., Baltimore, Miami, Chicago, Minneapolis, and Los Angeles.

In 1931 the Estonian Educational Society launched the monthly *Meie Tee* (Our Path), which is still published. New lay societies were formed in Chicago (1930), San Francisco (1930), Boston (1936), Baltimore (1936), and Washington (1937). An attempt at organiza-

tional centralization on a national scale was made at an Estonian-American Congress in New York in 1933. Immigration from Estonia was minimal during the 1930s, but contacts with the ancestral homeland were closer than ever, thanks both to the work of the Estonia Abroad Society and to improved transportation and communication. Estonian Americans were also active in introducing their culture to the larger society.

When Estonia was occupied by Soviet forces in 1940, a small group of Communists supported the move and promoted the Soviet viewpoint, but they found few listeners in the American press or government. Indeed, the United States has never formally recognized the Soviet annexation of Estonia. The majority of Estonian-Americans attempted to aid the republic and to mobilize public opinion on its behalf. A World Association of Estonians was founded in New York in 1940 to coordinate the struggle against the Soviet occupation, and in 1941 an Estonian Relief Committee came into being. Through public opinion and political pressure, Estonian Americans also helped Estonian refugees in Germany to avoid forced repatriation to the U.S.S.R. after the war was over. The community further helped to resettle many refugees in the United States by providing or obtaining job guarantees.

GROUP MAINTENANCE

The resettlement of the refugees—who had both a strong sense of identity and a determination to free Estonia from Soviet domination—revitalized the existing communities and inspired the formation of new ones. Organizations proliferated; according to one estimate, in 1970 there was an ethnic organization for every 65 first- and second-generation Estonian Americans.

In addition to the increase in the number of local organizations, the 1950s and 1960s also witnessed three additional important trends in the Estonian-American community, which may be called regionalization, national centralization, and internationalization. The Estonian communities began to organize ethnic activities with regional participation, and new regional umbrella organizations were created. On the East Coast, the main centers of New York City and Lakewood, N.J., are the sites of frequent large music and folk festivals, athletic competitions, and conventions. In the Midwest, a major folk festival was held in Minneapolis in 1967 and a song festival in Chicago in 1971. Annual midwestern youth gatherings have been held in several cities since 1957. On the West Coast, large biennial folk festivals and athletic competitions have rotated among San Francisco, Los Angeles, Portland, and Vancouver, B.C., since 1953. A very active and effective Estonian League of the West Coast was founded in 1954.

During the postwar decades national centralization of the community has come about in several different ways. National parent organizations have been created for specialized activities. By the early 1950s almost every Estonian community had a Lutheran congregation, a chorus or two, a supplementary ethnic school, scouting units, a veterans' chapter, and a women's club. Estonian-American Boy Scouts were united into a national council in 1949 and the Girl Scouts in 1952; scoutmasters' and scouting-related youth booster leagues soon followed. The Lutheran congregations banded together into two synods in 1954 under the Estonian Evangelical Lutheran Church in Exile, with headquarters in Sweden. The Association of Estonian Teachers and the Estonian Schools Center coordinated the network of supplementary schools. The veterans' chapters formed a national league, the women's clubs a national federation, and the choruses an association of singers. All these national bodies maintain contacts with comparable Estonian groups in other Western countries; some belong to an international parent organization.

The Eesti Rahvuskomitee Ühendriikides (Estonian-American National Council) was founded in 1952. Members are elected every three years by popular vote, and the council effectively represents the community to the larger society and the U.S. government. Like most national Estonian organizations, its headquarters are in New York City, the largest single Estonian-American community. And at three-year intervals since 1951 a national Congress of Estonian Organization has been convened.

In addition, many new organizations founded in the 1950s and 1960s with headquarters in New York are in principle national; they include the Estonian Learned Society, the Foundation for Estonian Arts and Letters, the Estonian Music Center, the Estonian Amateur Athletic Union, the Estonian Schools Fund, and the Estonian Students Fund. A weekly newspaper, *Vaba Eesti Sôna* (Free Estonian Word), was founded in New York in 1949, and a biweekly, *Eesti Postimes* (Estonian Courier), in 1964; both have nationwide circulations.

Estonian ethnicity also has an important international dimension. The postwar refugees have a common political goal that unifies Estonians throughout the world. The Estonian World Council, founded in New York in 1954, is designed to coordinate on a worldwide basis the struggle to free Estonia from Soviet rule. Two Estonian world congresses, the first in Toronto in 1972 and the second in Baltimore in 1976, brought together organizational representatives to discuss key ethnic issues. Younger activists held an international meeting in Pennsylvania's Pocono Mountains in 1976. Many aspects of cultural life are international as well. Choruses, folk-dancing groups, performers, and scholars often participate in ethnic events in other countries. Periodicals and books printed in one country are often circulated in the others. The Estonian Students' Fund in the United States sends students to Finland for post-graduate work; it is difficult to study Estonian in the United States, but every Finnish university has an Estonian department.

Estonian Americans maintain especially close ties with Estonians in Canada. In the early 1950s choruses traveled in both directions for concerts and song festivals, and scouts visited each other's camps. Estonians also sponsor scouting jamborees that are held in rotation in Canada, the United States, West Germany, and Sweden. The 1967 jamboree, Koguja, brought 1,000 scouts from around the world to the Estonian Scouting Reservation near Lakewood, N.J. The first North American Estonian Festival was held in Toronto in 1957 with 9,000 participants; it featured cultural events, pageants, social gatherings, specialized meetings, and political rallies; the second and fourth have since been held in New York (1960 and 1968) and the third again in Toronto (1964). A ten-day annual sympo-

sium, Metsaülikool, has been held in Canada since 1967 and a weekend cultural symposium, Kultuuripäevad, in the United States since 1970; these further unite the youth and younger intellectuals. In 1972 some 20,000 Estonians from western countries gathered in Toronto for the weeklong First Estonian World Festival; the second was held in Baltimore in 1976 and the third in Stockholm in 1980.

INTERGROUP RELATIONS

In pursuit of their goals Estonian Americans frequently cooperate with other groups, especially those from Eastern Europe. The Vaba Eesti Komitee (Committee for a Free Estonia) played an especially important role in this during the 1950s and 1960s. At the local, regional, national, and international levels, Estonians frequently work with Latvians and Lithuanians; in 1961 the three groups founded a committee of Americans for Congressional Action to Free the Baltic States as well as the Joint Baltic-American National Committee. In 1966 they established the Baltic Appeal to the United Nations and in 1972 the Baltic World Council. The Baltic communities also sponsor joint concerts, social events, athletic competitions, and scholarly associations.

By the 1960s most Estonian Americans had achieved middle-class status. Their rapid socioeconomic upward mobility reflects both a very strong emphasis on educational achievement and a very high rate of employment among women, even when they are married. Estonian Americans also are active in various civic activities and have acquired citizenship quickly. Politically, most Estonian Americans tend to affiliate with the Republican party; the Democratic party is perceived by many as the party of Franklin D. Roosevelt, who concluded the Yalta agreement with the Soviet Union, a particularly detestable act in the eyes of eastern European refugees. Even today, Republican positions on foreign policy appear to be more in line with the political goals of the Estonians than those of the Democrats.

In spite of organizational strength, cultural vitality, and strong, politically motivated social mobilization, the community has a very high rate of intermarriage and a decreasing rate of Estonian-language fluency among its children—trends not surprising for a numerically small, widely scattered, and middle-class group. Recent attempts to integrate the intermarried and their families into the community's structure have been pioneered in the Chicago area. Although losses to the community through intermarriage and general assimilatory drift have been quite noticeable among the younger adults, the activist core of the group has not decreased very much, although it is rapidly aging as a result of a low birth rate and the absence of immigrant reinforcement. The survival of the smaller centers is threatened by both these trends, but population relocation has also created new centers, and the older people still remain at the organizational base of the group, helping to create new clubs and societies and acting as a full-time ethnic cadre in many localities. The organizational centennial of the group in 1997 may well still be celebrated by an active Estonian-American community.

Bibliography
There are very few English-language sources on the Estonians in America. A brief chronological overview of the community and a bibli-ography are provided by Jaan Pennar, Tōnu Parming, and P. Peter Rebane, eds., *The Estonians in America, 1627–1975: A Chronology and Fact Book* (Dobbs Ferry, N.Y., 1975). The Estonian Learned Society in America is preparing a series entitled *The Estonian Heritage in America*; its first two volumes, edited by Tōnu Parming and Imre Lipping, are entitled *Early History and the Emergence of an Organized Estonian-American Community* (New York, 1979) and *Aspects of Cultural Life. Sources for the Study of the Estonians in America* (New York, 1979), compiled by Kersti Tannberg and Tōnu Parming and also published by the Estonian Learned Society, lists all known articles, pamphlets, books, and periodicals on the group through 1976.

The best work on the Estonian heritage in the old country is still Evald Uustalu, *History of Estonian People* (London, 1952). *A Bibliography of English-Language Sources on Estonia* (New York, 1974), compiled by Marju Rink Parming and Tōnu Parming, is a valuable reference aid for periodicals, bibliographies, pamphlets, and books. Archival materials and publications on the group can be found in the Estonian Archives in the United States in Lakewood, N.J., and in smaller collections at the Estonian House in New York City, the Immigration History Research Center at the University of Minnesota, and at Kent State University in Ohio.

TŌNU PARMING

ETHNIC HERITAGE STUDIES PROGRAM

The Ethnic Heritage Studies Program was established in 1972 as an amendment to the Elementary and Secondary Education Act of 1965 (Title IX). The authorizing act reads:

SEC. 901. In recognition of the heterogeneous composition of the Nation and of the fact that in a multiethnic society a greater understanding of the contributions of one's own heritage and those of one's fellow citizens can contribute to a more harmonious, patriotic, and committed populace, and in recognition of the principle that all persons in the educational institutions of the Nation should have an opportunity to learn about the differing and unique contributions to the national heritage made by each ethnic group, it is the purpose of this title to provide assistance designed to afford to students opportunities to learn about the nature of their own cultural heritage, and to study the contributions of the cultural heritages of the other ethnic groups of the Nation.

SEC. 902. The Commissioner is authorized to make grants to, and contracts with, public and private nonprofit educational agencies, institutions, and organizations to assist them in planning, developing, establishing, and operating ethnic heritage studies programs, as provided in this title.

SEC. 903. Each program assisted under this title shall—
(1) develop curriculum materials for use in elementary and secondary schools and institutions of higher education relating to the history, geography, society, economy, literature, art, music, drama, language, and general culture of the group or groups with which the program is concerned, and the contributions of that ethnic group or groups to the American heritage;
(2) disseminate curriculum materials to permit their use in elementary and secondary schools and institutions of higher education throughout the Nation;
(3) provide training for persons using, or preparing to use, curriculum materials developed under this title; and
(4) cooperate with persons and organizations with a special interest in the ethnic group or groups with which the program is concerned to assist them in promoting, encouraging, developing, or producing programs or other activities which relate to the history, culture, or traditions of that ethnic group or groups.

SEC. 905. (a) In carrying out this title, the Commissioner shall make arrangements which will utilize (1) the research

facilities and personnel of institutions of higher education, (2) the special knowledge of ethnic groups in local communities and of foreign students pursuing their education in this country, (3) the expertise of teachers in elementary and secondary schools and institutions of higher education, and (4) the talents and experience of any other groups such as foundations, civic groups, and fraternal organizations which would further the goals of the programs.

(b) Funds appropriated to carry out this title may be used to cover all or part of the cost of establishing and carrying out the programs, including the cost of research materials and resources, academic consultants, and the cost of training of staff for the purpose of carrying out the purposes of this title. Such funds may also be used to provide stipends (in such amounts as may be determined in accordance with regulations of the Commissioner) to individuals receiving training as part of such programs, including allowances for dependents.

Funding for the act has hovered consistently at around $2,000,000. The appropriation for fiscal year 1974, despite an initial congressional authorization of $15,000,000, was $2,375,000; in 1975 and 1976 it dropped to $1,800,000; in 1977 and 1978 it rose again to $2,300,000.

Organizations eligible for funds include ethnic, community, and professional organizations, as well as local educational agencies and institutions of higher learning. Until 1977 most of the money went into curriculum development; that year the focus shifted to the training of teachers.

The majority of projects funded have been multiethnic; rather than focusing on the experience of a single group, they either explore the heritage of several or concentrate on issues relevant to all. The program has also supported the development of ethnic studies courses, the preparation of ethnic reading materials, studies of neighborhoods, and collections of oral histories. Projects are often not only multiethnic, but multimedia as well, using films, videotapes, slides, and records.

The initial planning for the *Harvard Encyclopedia of American Ethnic Groups* was supported by the Ethnic Heritage Studies Program in 1974–1975. A complete list of the projects funded to date is available from the Office of Education of the U.S. Department of Health, Education, and Welfare and from the Ethnic Heritage Studies Clearinghouse, a division of the Social Science Education Consortium, Inc., Boulder, Colo. 80302.

F

FAMILY PATTERNS

In American society the family has always been regarded as sacred. Its significance as a private retreat from the outside world, as the guardian of tradition and barometer of social change, has been elevated to mythic proportions in American culture. Along with this idealization of the family's role, a stereotype of "the ideal family" has emerged. Although the stereotype emphasizes a uniform family ideal, diverse family patterns brought to this country by different ethnic groups have survived in the United States; within these families diverse values have been taught and learned which shape the most important aspects of the behavior of American ethnic groups.

The ties of affection and obligation that sanction distinctively "ethnic" behavior are exercised primarily within the family. Because the variety of values and mechanisms that operate within the "ethnic family" is enormous, this discussion attempts only to relate some aspects of the family within American society to some of the social processes that characterize the history of ethnicity in America. Four elements are emphasized: the emergence of ethnic families in the process of migration and settlement; demographic and structural variations in ethnic family behaviors; the family economy; and the family and cultural change.

Both the family and ethnicity are processes rather than static conditions. Over the past two centuries American families and the society around them have been changing simultaneously and affecting each other. Tabular data will provide an indication of the incidence and degree of change. This discussion of ethnic family patterns focuses on the first and second generations, with some reference to later generations. Because of the paucity of systematic evidence for earlier periods, 20th-century immigrants will receive most attention.

Since the 17th century the family has been considered the linchpin of the American social order, the agent most responsible for basic socialization and for the preservation and continuation of societal values. The condition of the family has therefore been considered a barometer of the stability of the social order. The recurring complaint that the American family is "breaking down" is a manifestation of concern over society's survival during periods of rapid and unsettling change.

Despite major changes in American family behavior over the past three centuries, there are some important continuities. First and foremost has been the prevalence of the nuclear family as a self-contained domestic and economic unit, consisting of parents and their children, in contrast to the more elaborate formalized kin networks of many other cultures. Although at times American households have included other relatives, the basic residential unit has been the nuclear rather than the extended family, as has also been the case throughout western Europe.

Related to the autonomy of the nuclear family is the persistence of boundaries between the conjugal couple and their own married children, manifested in the separation between the family of procreation and the family of orientation. In the United States, marriage has generally meant the establishment of an autonomous family unit, usually a separate household, economic independence of new couples, and exclusive parental responsibility for childrearing. This arrangement is consistent with privacy inside the family, but also permits generation-to-generation change in response to developments in the society outside. It does not, of course, preclude intensive interaction between the nuclear family and extended kin living outside the household. But relations between husbands and wives and the obligations of parents and their minor children to one another have been legally defined, while relations between adult children and their parents and other relatives have been primarily voluntary.

In colonial days the family was perceived not only as a barometer of the social order but also as an instrument of the state. In addition to caring for its own members, the family served as the arm of the commonwealth responsible for the welfare and social control of dependent members in society. The erosion of the family's traditional public functions of social control and social welfare in the 19th century coincided with the enormous increase of European immigration to the United States. At the same time, in urbanizing communities, households were ceasing to be major sites of production, as jobs shifted to specialized work places: shops, factories, and offices. These developments effected changes both in family organization and in society's expectations of family behavior. During this period, while the majority of the population was still living in rural settings in which the family continued to function as a work unit and as the major agent of social welfare, the urban middle class began to define "ideal" family life in new terms.

Privacy and domesticity emerged as crucial family values, distinguishing middle-class family ways from those of other social groups. The middle-class family increasingly withdrew from the public arena, turning the domestic sphere into a private retreat from the daily rigors outside. The role of women came to be restricted to custody of the domestic world; men were in charge of the world of work outside the home. The recognition of childhood as a special stage of life focused familial and particularly maternal attention on children as subjects for care, affection, and nurture. Even though these family ways were restricted to a minority of the population, they nevertheless became enshrined in the culture as the style of the normative American family.

There was an essential conflict between this newly emerging urban middle-class family type and the distinctive family forms that immigrants brought with them. The process of migration itself challenged settled family behaviors, sometimes making traditional patterns seem inappropriate, sometimes reinforcing such practices or modifying them to meet new conditions. Migration and resettlement were carried out in a variety of familial and quasifamilial forms and configurations, which together constituted the gradual adaptation to a new culture and new set of opportunities.

Distinctive ethnic behaviors—including aspects of family behavior—were not simply products of inertia, but developed and persisted where they served the practical needs of group members, notably in the economic realm.

The family behavior which characterized newly arrived immigrants resembled in some ways that of American families in the 17th and 18th centuries. They had in common high fertility, family integration as a work unit (including reliance upon child labor), and kin assistance as the basis of economic security. Thus, immigrant family patterns were likely to clash with the newer, 19th-century middle-class family ideals and values, most notably in the sentimentalization of family roles and in ideas about the appropriate nurture for children and the importance of privacy.

Changes in family patterns and the pace at which they occurred varied significantly among different ethnic groups and among different waves of immigration. The process was not linear; nor did change and adaptation mean simply the shedding of traditional patterns for new ones. The successive influxes of new immigrants into American society resulted in the regular infusion of traditional elements from a foreign land into a society undergoing constant change. The process was thus multilayered: native-born families, old immigrant families, second-generation families, and new immigrants all adapted to change at different paces. This is why a variety of patterns of family behavior persists in American society.

MIGRATION, SETTLEMENT, AND THE EMERGENCE OF "ETHNIC" FAMILIES

The family composition of the immigrants who reached the United States varied tremendously. Three types, defined by the nature of the critical population movement, may be singled out. No period was homogeneous: at all times, migration, as a goal-directed behavior, attracted different kinds of people according to the opportunities perceived and the means available to achieve them.

Of the three types, permanent families most nearly represent the carrying to a new place of an older family system; the families of married immigrants who left wives behind were subjected to distinctive strains; whereas unmarried immigrants established new family units in a new environment. The ethnic context to which each of these immigrant types came further determined the process by which distinctive ethnic families emerged.

The great 17th-century English Puritan emigration to New England was mainly a family migration; on the other hand, mostly young unmarried English men settled the Chesapeake and Middle Colonies at about the same time. Although unmarried immigrants generally outnumbered family groups among the English, Scots, Welsh, Irish, and Germans who immigrated in the first half of the 19th century, family migration was common. Each phase of immigration contained both young, unmarried, and propertyless persons—mostly males—and those who had the means to bring along their families. The latter included those who intended to farm, and who needed to bring their family members to help in that enterprise.

Demographic pressures in Europe in the 1840s and 1850s precipitated a huge immigration that contained unusually large components of families, mainly Irish, German, or English. This movement coincided with the beginnings of rapid urbanization and the Industrial Revolution in the United States, which offered a variety of nonagricultural jobs to members of propertyless immigrant families. As opportunities in American agriculture narrowed during the 19th century, immigration became more responsive to the demands of the rapidly growing industrial sector of the economy. The shift of opportunity from field to factory, from farm to city, also altered the family composition of immigration.

Population pressures during the later 19th and early 20th centuries affected western Europe first, then radiated east, northeast, and southeast. Simultaneously, the U.S. economy grew in scale. These developments produced the shift from the so-called old immigration to the "new" one from southern and eastern Europe. The new immigration included more unmarried males who intended only temporary stays. In 1879–1881, toward the end of the old immigration, there were 162 males per 100 females arriving from abroad. Twenty years later, during the new immigration, the ratio was 203 to 100. Almost 20 percent of the newcomers in 1880 were under 15 years of age and likely to be accompanying their parents; the proportion was down to 12 percent by the end of the century.

Short-term migration to the United States was, in effect, a more dramatic continuation of seasonal migration to the industrial areas of eastern and central Europe. This labor migration affected the family context variously. For example, the several Scandinavian migrations of the late 19th and early 20th centuries all had in common an initial preponderance of conjugal families, followed by a labor migration in which single males were a majority. These young men traveled abroad with the idea of making money to serve family goals back home; but they came with the planning, assistance, and continuing association of older kinsmen who had earlier migrated in family groups. Post–World War II immigration has been preeminently a movement of families, to a large extent because of shifts in the U.S. economy. Differing from both, the northward migration of southern blacks and whites began as a movement of individual migrants to fill narrow job categories (female servants among blacks, industrial labor for whites) but has become more substantially a family migration as economic demand has modified.

The variety of immigrant family arrangements is apparent from data on immigration and emigration compiled annually by the U.S. Commissioner of Immigration, presented in Table 1. These data from the peak of the "new" immigration offer several indicators of the link between the decision to migrate with an associated goal of creating or maintaining a family somewhere. The first is the departure rate, based on estimates of the proportions of all immigrant males during this period who left the United States (usually to return home) within two and a half years of arrival. The proportion of permanent families within the immigration may be gauged by sex ratios, percentages of children and of married men, and by the tendencies of females once in the United States to remain (usually in families). Finally, in the ratio of married men to married women in each

Table 1. Family characteristics of major immigrant groups, 1909–1914.[a]

Group	Estimated percent of departures of male arrivals within period	Number of males per 1,000 females	Percentage under age 14	Percentage married males ages 14–44	Estimated percent of departures of female arrivals	Number of married males per 1,000 married females
Czechs	5	1,329	19	36	10	1,453
English	6	1,358	16	35	13	1,157
Finnish	7	1,812	8	25	15	1,882
Germans	7	1,318	18	35	16	1,312
Greeks	16	11,696	4	29	12	8,643
Hebrews	2	1,172	25	36	3	1,258
Hungarians (Magyars)	22	1,406	16	63	38	1,968
Italians, South	17	3,200	12	46	15	3,181
Poles	13	1,876	10	38	16	2,695
Slovaks	19	1,622	12	55	27	2,659

Source: U.S. Bureau of Immigration and Naturalization, *Annual Reports*, 1910–1914 (Washington, D.C., 1910–1914).
a. Median annual observation except for estimated departure rate.

group, there is an indication of how many married male immigrants left their wives behind.

The variation among groups is enormous, suggesting just how diverse were the paths by which ethnic families evolved in the United States. About 1 in 5 of the transient Hungarians (Magyars) and Slovaks left within the two and one-half year period, but fewer than 1 in 40 of the highly stable Jews and Czechs. The sex ratio among Greeks indicates that only 1 Greek woman immigrated for every 11 Greek men, setting obvious limits to the possibility of Greek family life during these years. Aside from this extreme, the sex ratio ranged from more than 3 males per woman to nearly even. Children formed only 4 percent of the Greek immigration, but 25 percent of the Jewish. Among immigrant Jews, the most family-oriented of the groups under discussion, only about 1 woman in 30 subsequently left, in contrast to a quarter or more of the Hungarians and Slovaks. Such differences must reflect variations in the receptiveness of these families to the American scene. Magyars and Slovaks included in their migration substantially more married men than women: their wives apparently remained at home, subjecting both partners to distinctive stresses. By contrast, the Finnish immigration, which included few wives, also included relatively few young men with wives at home.

The emergence of the ethnic family must be examined as a product of two cultures interacting in extremely varied ways according to circumstances. Differences in opportunity and setting produced markedly different family arrangements from the moment of arrival.

The private conjugal family provided the arena within which distinctive "ethnic" behavior patterns emerged. Immigrants who arrived in family units were more subject to the effects of shock and displacement than those who arrived individually, for their moral as well as legal and economic bases were subjected to change. Despite these challenges, few marriages broke down as a result of immigration.

Men whose wives remained at home risked temptation and frustration as they strove to accumulate money so that the separation might be ended. Stories of wives forgotten are common; even more common must have been marriages whose traditional bases were un-

dermined by the separation and were different although faithfully reassembled and maintained. For unmarried immigrants who did not soon return home, the most common pattern was marriage in the United States, sometimes to brides first encountered here (most often in the ethnic milieu), but sometimes to brides known abroad by the immigrant or his family, with marriages arranged with family assistance. Postmigration marriage would seem to be most conducive to changes in the nature of marriage, for the parties involved were under less parental influence than were those marrying in the home country. They may more deliberately have addressed the matter of coming to terms with their American surroundings.

The setting to which families or individuals immigrated had an important effect on the modes of family adaptation. The economically and ethnically homogeneous rural settings common in 18th- and 19th-century America facilitated adaptations far less divergent from family patterns in the homeland. There were many instances of almost wholesale translation to American settings, usually rural, of village/kinship groupings which reconstituted in the New World their characteristic home and family patterns. Although many of these ethnic communities changed as American agricultural areas became integrated more closely with the commercial economy, many initial traits endured. The Germans from Russia (a distinctive group who had resided in Russia for generations) provide one example. This group settled in isolated sections of the American agricultural West at the end of the 19th century and long carried on distinctive family practices, including very early marriage and exceptionally high fertility, near universal remarriage after widowhood, and a highly cooperative family economy ruled by the family patriarch and operating in part through kin connections created by high fertility and strict norms of intermarriage. Hutterites also migrated to isolated rural areas in order to sustain their distinctive family patterns in a homogeneous, isolated setting. Immigrants' commitment to marriage and a family for themselves almost always outweighed the commitment to any particular set of family traditions. Isolated groups could maintain themselves over time partly because members tended to find marriage partners within the group. Isolated in-

Table 2. Percentages of New York City marriages outside ethnic group, by generation for selected groups of men, 1908–1912.

Group	First generation (immigrant)	Second generation
English	61	82
Irish	10	30
Germans	20	26
Jews	1	6
Poles	9	17

Source: Julius Drachsler, *Intermarriage in New York City* (New York, 1921).

Table 3. Percentages of women ever married, by age at time of marriage and nativity or race, 1910.

Group	Age groups			
	15–19	20–24	25–29	45–54
Immigrant groups				
Canada (French)	8	46	73	94
Eire	2	18	46	85
Germany	10	49	77	96
Great Britain	6	44	71	92
Italy	29	74	93	99
Japan[a]	51	85	87	93
Poland[b]	15	66	89	99
Russia	7	55	90	99
American-born groups				
Urban Negroes	16	57	—	94[c]
Whites of foreign or mixed parentage	6	37	64	87
Whites of native parentage	13	53	77	91

Source: U.S. Bureau of the Census, *Sixteenth Census of the United States: 1940. Population: Differential Fertility, 1940 and 1910. Women by Number of Children Ever Born* (Washington, D.C., 1945).

a. This is a racial, not a national, designation; however, almost all Japanese women age 15 or over in the United States in 1910 had been born in Japan.

b. Immigrant females who reported Polish as their mother tongue.

c. For age group 45–64. Few single women marry above age 54.

dividuals, on the other hand, typically had to marry outside the group. For sizable groups in regular contact with many different people (as in a city), the question of intermarriage was a critical one facing all within the emerging ethnic culture, for it was a mechanism that challenged current ethnic self-definitions.

Marriage within the ethnic group enabled immigrants to transmit their values to their children, whereas intermarriage was an agent of change. Most studies show that rates of marriage within each ethnic group were somewhat lower in the second generation than in the first; but virtually all studies reveal a marked tendency toward ethnic endogamy among nearly all groups. A classic study of the matter treats the period 1908–1912 in that most polyglot of places, New York City. Here the workings of intermarriage as an agent of change in family traditions can best be seen. Table 2 indicates the proportions of marriages that immigrant and second-generation men contracted outside the group, for selected groups. In the immigrant generation, only the English displayed little sense of ethnic solidarity. Overwhelming majorities of Irish, Polish, and Jewish men took wives from the same ethnic background. Although intermarriage was considerably more common for every group by the second generation, only among the English might we conclude that the family had not passed along a valued sense of ethnic distinctiveness. The remarkable strength of the Jewish family (no doubt intensified by anti-Semitism) is especially striking: no more than 1 in 17 second-generation men married non-Jews. (*See* Intermarriage.)

DEMOGRAPHIC PATTERNS AND STRUCTURAL VARIATIONS

Immigrant families had distinctive patterns of marriage, family formation, and fertility. These patterns reflect extensive differences among families from different national backgrounds. The timing of marriage and the pace and duration of childbearing had consequences both for individual families and for the shape of the second- and third-generation ethnic communities. Both the rapidity with which new ethnic generations would be created and the structure of existing ethnic households were related closely to characteristic patterns of age at marriage.

Tabulations from the 1910 Census indicate the age at which women of different backgrounds married, and the proportion who, unmarried at ages 45 to 54, were spinsters beyond the childbearing stage. Table 3 shows that most women married before the age of 45, and this was truer for most immigrant—except the Irish—and urban black women than for American-born whites.

The timing of marriage for women varied considerably: substantial percentages of blacks and of Italian and Polish immigrant women married in their teens; English, Irish, and second-generation American women married later. Large numbers of young Japanese women were brought as brides to Japanese men in the United States; thus their exceptionally high rate of teenage marriage.

The varied marriage patterns among different ethnic groups cannot be explained solely by economic causes; the Irish immigrants were poor and married late, but the blacks, Italians, and Poles were poor, too, yet married early. The Russians, Germans, and English were relatively prosperous groups at the time these data were collected, yet were different in pace of marriage, presumably reflecting distinctive cultural preferences. Second-generation American women married later and were somewhat less likely to marry at all than either whites of native parentage or most of the immigrant groups detailed here.

Distinctive ethnic marriage patterns generally attenuated by the second generation. Other census data indicate that, for instance, second-generation Irish-American women born in 1906–1915 married on average two years later than did Italian-American women born in the same period; but the difference for their parents' generation had been fully five years. The modification of cultural preferences resulted in increased similarity of behavior among different ethnic groups; it probably reflected increasing similarity in the conditions under which members of the several groups had been raised rather than an effort to emulate what were seen as American ways of marriage.

Variations in immigrant fertility patterns also reflected the impact of the American context on family-building preferences and social and economic factors characteristic of their place of origin. Social scientists as well as popular writers alleged that the birth rate of the new immigration was so high that old-stock Americans were in danger of being swamped. The story was more complex. It is true that most immigrant families

who settled in U.S. cities were larger than American-born families living there. But the immigrant-group fertility patterns were not uniformly high. Most rural migrants to cities, native Americans as well as foreign-born, had higher birth rates than the urban-born; southern blacks were an exception, for reasons that are still debated.

Census data for 1900 indicate the range of immigrant fertility preferences, how this range was modified by the local context, and how these two forces affected the behavior of the second generation. The figures reveal the lifetime fertility of married women in 1900 who had at that date been married between 10 and 19 years. Table 4 compares fertile immigrant and second-generation women from eight ethnic groups in four distinct settings. The figures show the percentage of child-bearing women with small families—that is, with only one or two children in 10 to 19 years of marriage. Such a small number of children was relatively uncommon among immigrant families at this time, in all settings. But the marked fertility differentials among the groups shown in Table 4 reveal how large the differences in taste and practice were. For example, although Irish immigrants married late, as we have seen, they had relatively large numbers of children thereafter. The "new" immigrant groups, despite other differences, had the largest families by this measure, and English immigrants the smallest.

Urban birth rates were generally lower than rural; this was truer for the second generation than for the first, and for the low-fertility groups than for those with generally high fertility. These patterns suggest intentional fertility regulation, with distinctive levels for different ethnic groups. As with age at marriage, conditions influenced second-generation families more than their parents' generation. The demographic decisions of immigrant parents resulted in the formation of distinctive ethnic families varying in size, age configuration, and structure. These families, in turn, transmitted their parents' cultural traditions, but with modifications.

The trend to acculturation and lessened fertility was not invariable, however. Data from selected Boston neighborhoods and Massachusetts cities in 1880 indicate that second-generation immigrants, largely Irish, had higher birth rates than the first generation. In this case it appears that dismal urban conditions led the first generation to produce fewer surviving children than traditional values would have dictated, the second generation learned the cultural preferences of the first and,

having achieved a more secure subsistence, was better able to achieve them.

HOUSEHOLD STRUCTURE

Household composition is jointly a product of demographic forces and customs governing admission to and exit from the household. We have seen that ethnic groups differed considerably in their demographic patterns, and also that the patterns varied with time and location. Likewise, the disparate circumstances in which ethnic families found themselves affected the degree to which customary preferences operated. Some patterns seem to have been persistent and distinctive. Black families have shown a tendency to lack adult male heads-of-household and to include—in semifamilial roles like "guest" or "subtenant"—kin and friends. Such arrangements are attributable in part to the effects of poverty, illness, and housing discrimination. But these practices also reflect different customs of family organization. A balanced account of the family life of this ethnic group would treat such departures from typical American behavior not as deviant but as aspects of a distinctive, adaptive strategy.

Regardless of whether they arrived in family units, reconstituted separated families, or formed new ones in the United States, immigrants usually organized their households in ways similar to those of native-born Americans, except during periods of temporary stress such as an influx of new immigration. The majority of households in American society were nuclear, and most ethnic families conformed to that pattern. Rarely did more than 10 to 15 percent of American households have other kin residing with the nuclear family. The exceptions tended to be when aging parents, especially widowed mothers, moved in with a married child. Nuclear households also became extended during periods of housing shortage, when newly married couples temporarily moved in with their parents. In general, both immigrants and native-born Americans lived in nuclear households and retained their independence for as long as they were able.

On the other hand, a greater proportion of immigrant families took in boarders and lodgers, or boarded with other people. Among immigrants, as among the American-born, the typical boarders were young men and women in a transitional stage between leaving the parents' household and entering into marriage and setting up their own household. In most groups this stage

Table 4. Percentage of women in 1900 currently married 10–19 years who had borne only one or two children, by national origin, generation, and place of residence.

	First generation				Second generation			
National origin	Rural Ohio	Cleveland	Rural Minnesota	Minneapolis	Rural Ohio	Cleveland	Rural Minnesota	Minneapolis
French Canadian	—	—	5	15	—	—	5	25
German	15	15	9	22	25	33	16	32
Swedish	24	25	12	20	—	—	16	33
Irish	17	12	15	17	25	22	11	23
English	24	29	16	31	39	42	27	43
Russian	—	8	—	8	—	—	—	—
Polish	—	5	—	5	—	—	—	—

Source: U.S. Immigration Commission, *The Fecundity of Immigrant Women* Reports, vol. 28 (Washington, D.C., 1911), pp. 762–767, 776–783.

corresponded closely with the time of immigration to cities. For immigrants, boarding or lodging provided a solution to the shortage of housing and the need for temporary quarters and furnished hard-pressed families with a source of ready cash. Similar functions would be served by kin who lived in the household, as was not unusual; often, kin considered their stay in others' households to be "boarding."

Industrial-immigrant families thus sometimes incorporated other adults—occasionally relatives—sometimes in large enough numbers that American-born middle-class reformers were alarmed, although the practice was by no means introduced into the United States by immigrants. The frequency of such arrangements declined markedly with length of residence in the United States. In areas where the demand for working-class housing was great, such arrangements were accommodations to particular circumstances rather than a matter of unconstrained choice, and in these areas they were formative experiences for the emerging "ethnic" family. Moreover, even if such boarding ventures were temporary, some of the flavor, say, of the South Slav Zadruga helped define the quality of life in South Slav boarding groups (which often contained relatives).

Most ethnic groups, as well as native-born families generally, tended to take strangers into the household rather than their own extended kin. However, kinship ties persisted outside the household and pervaded ethnic neighborhoods. Relatives followed and joined one another in the migration process, often settling in clusters in the same neighborhood. Through chain migration, kin who had pioneered the migration route often sent funds for tickets back to other relatives and acted as housing agents for them on arrival. Even individual immigration was not necessarily isolated; most individuals arriving were part of a chain joining kin already there and preparing the way for others to follow. Relatives who remained behind provided a potential source of support if family members failed in the United States, and assumed responsibility for taking care of aging relatives or keeping a family farm, especially if the owner had migrated on only a temporary basis.

Kin also performed important functions in finding employment for their newly arrived relatives and in facilitating their adaptation to industrial work. Large industrial corporations as well as smaller manufacturers and businesses used relatives for the recruitment and placement of newly arrived workers. Conversely, immigrants relied on kin already working in such establishments to place them in preferred jobs, to teach them the appropriate technology and new skills, and to assist them in their initial adaptation to new working conditions. A study of French Canadian factory workers in Manchester, N.H., shows that kinship networks were able to infiltrate bureaucratized industrial enterprises and thus to influence collectively the pace of work and to protect the members of the group from abuse and exploitation. Kinship ties not only survived the migration process but helped in the adaptation to new conditions and in the preservation of traditions, giving immigrant life a coherence often overlooked by outside observers. Kin also provided sociability, and through social gatherings and family rituals helped to transmit cultural traditions.

Premigration kinship patterns were not, however, transmitted to industrial America intact. The process was selective and involved adaptation to new conditions. French Canadians, for example, retained a tight kinship system after they migrated to New England textile communities, not out of blind traditionalism but because they could adjust some of their premigration kinship patterns to modern modes of production and organization of work, which required familiarity with bureaucratic structures and organizations, adherence to industrial work schedules and responsiveness to the rhythms of industrial employment, specialization in trade tasks, and technological skill. The use of kinship ties to meet these different challenges represented the creative use of traditional structures and relationships to meet new conditions and requirements.

THE FAMILY ECONOMY

The 19th-century American ideal that fathers' incomes were to support their entire families was at variance with the realities of life for working and peasant classes in the places from which most immigrants came; nor was it characteristic of native-born rural and working-class families in the United States. Immigrants from agricultural backgrounds practiced cooperative family economies. Working-class families in Europe, too, had learned that multiple incomes were required to meet the high cost of urban living. Many immigrants came from a setting in which both agricultural tasks and some household manufacturing were carried out cooperatively, with a division of labor among family members. Immigrant families frequently brought to the United States a view of the family's collective work responsibilities. The notion that men were to work, women to tend the home, and children to attend school was new to them.

This discrepancy did not pose great problems of adjustment until the late 19th century, when the American ideal was fully developed and to some extent mandated by law. Then, compulsory school-attendance laws and legal limitations on child labor challenged the complex family economy that had been characteristic of both European and American industrial settings. These restraints were especially disturbing to newcomers because of the economic insecurity caused by frequent fluctuations of the economy and by the absence of social insurance. Even under relatively stable economic conditions families were vulnerable, especially during the phase in the family life cycle when there were many mouths to feed but few potential earners.

How did such families cope with economic deprivation and vulnerability? Immigrant families shared several values as part of their cultural heritage. Foremost was the commitment to autonomy—to maintaining their own family unit, heading their own household, raising their children at home. Despite pressures of poverty and insecurity, most immigrant husbands, like their native U.S. counterparts, tried to keep their wives out of the labor force, especially if they had children, although the degree of commitment to keeping women at home varied in accordance with families' economic needs and the availability of employment for women. Even if married immigrant women did not work regularly or continuously on a full-time basis outside the

home, many spent at least some portion of their time working for pay, often by taking in laundry, sewing, or by housing a boarder. Whenever possible, immigrant women followed traditional patterns, trying to select those occupations that were least in conflict with their premigration practices and viewing necessary outside work as inseparable from their duties at home.

Although taking in a boarder or lodger eased economic pressures somewhat, most immigrant families depended on the wages of their children, either simply to survive or to lay aside savings to buy a house. Reformers concerned with the child-labor issue viewed immigrant families' dependence on the labor of their children as a form of exploitation and as a product of indifference or even hostility to formal education. In their view, child labor was not a solution to poverty, but instead a cause of future poverty. Reformers proposed that instead of sending children out to work, immigrant families should economize by confining their consumption to newly devised model family budgets. The U.S. Bureau of Labor Statistics, launching a massive collection of individual family budgets of working men in 1889, hoped to foster frugality and the proper allocation of resources among working-class, particularly immigrant, families.

At the peak of immigration, the extent to which families were dependent upon the work of several members is apparent from the labor-force participation rates of children 10 to 15 years of age in 1900 (see Table 5). These children were rarely living on their own; in a great majority of cases they were contributing to a complex family income. A comparison of children's labor-force participation in four cities, correlated with nativity within cities, indicates that the wage and occupational structures encouraged child labor more in some cities than in others, but that in all cities foreign-born children formed a larger percentage of the child-labor force than did any other group; in Boston and Fall River, Mass., both foreign-born boys and girls outnumbered the other two white groups combined. The tendency was less pronounced but still visible in immigrant families whose children had been born in the United States. Black children were not as likely to work as immigrant children, although in other respects—notably the outstandingly high employment rate of married women, including those who had husbands present—the black family economy was distinctive.

Local industrial conditions provided immigrant children with different kinds of choices (say, between school and work). Manufacturing, especially low-capitalization, low-wage, large-shop industry, offered fewer economic rewards to skilled operatives but extensive work opportunities for young children. Child labor was a common recourse in cases of need, which varied greatly according to time, place, and stage in the family cycle. Most such arrangements competed with formal schooling in a practical but not ideological sense. Heavy dependence upon child labor among immigrant families at the expense of schooling seemed, however, to middle-class contemporaries, to be an excessive price for occupational mobility.

Studies of mobility patterns since the mid-19th century reveal substantial variation in the occupational mobility rates of ethnic groups, but tell little of the part that individual family economic strategies may have played in creating the ethnic differentials. In many cases these strategies appear to have flouted those assimilationist American ideals that celebrated long-term "success" in careers. Such goals were not always compatible with demanding ethnic family ties. It is a strongly held assumption in American society that diligent attendance at school varies by ethnic group, and in such a way that it explains differences in group mobility rates.

A certain degree of economic advancement has always been possible for all nonblack minorities in the United States, including those most identified as "foreign," even in the first generation but more surely for their children. In at least some instances ethnicity did not hinder but rather benefited its members economically. For first- and second-generation Japanese Americans (particularly in their areas of heavy concentration in the Pacific Coast states) before their internment during World War II, a distinct ethnic economy existed, in which the availability of relatively cheap labor, often from family and kin, and community superintendence of business practices, encouraged the growth of a remarkably if precariously specialized economy. In Los Angeles the Japanese-American ethnic economy spread from truck farming into a vertically and horizontally integrated concentration in the produce business, which by 1941 was beginning to move into supermarket industry. Early on, the Japanese Americans had found that hard work could be most quickly translated into income through entrepreneurial activity, especially given two characteristics: the ability to practice extreme fam-

Table 5. Percentage of children ages 10–15 in the labor force in selected cities, by sex, nativity or race, and selected characteristics of manufacturing, 1900.

Group	Fall River, Mass.	Philadelphia	Boston	Pittsburgh
Boys				
Native of native parents	13	20	7	20
Native of foreign or mixed parents	20	24	8	20
Foreign-born	38	39	19	30
Negro, Indian, and Mongolian[a]	—	17	10	19
Girls				
Native of native parents	10	12	3	5
Native of foreign or mixed parents	19	18	6	8
Foreign-born	37	39	13	18
Negro, Indian, and Mongolian[a]	—	14	4	7
Manufacturing				
Mfg. hands per 100 population	31	19	13	22
Mfg. hands per establishment	42	16	10	36
Capitalization	$1,786	$1,934	$1,987	$2,760
Average annual wage per mfg. hand	$ 358	$ 454	$ 543	$ 524

Source: U.S. Bureau of the Census, *Twelfth Census of the United States: 1900,* vol. 8, *Manufactures,* pt. 2 (Washington, D.C., 1902); U.S. Bureau of the Census, *Child Labor in the United States, Based on Unpublished Information Derived from the Schedules of the Twelfth Census, 1900,* Census Bulletin 69 (Washington, D.C., 1907).

a. Almost all Negro in these cities.

ily thrift in behalf of economic enterprise, and community cooperation. Parallel though not identical instances of an economic advantage developing from the interpenetration of ethnic and family loyalties are seen in the Jews in the garment industry, the Mississippi Chinese in groceries, and the urban Irish in construction and city politics. Many similar patterns can be found among such recent immigrant groups as the Koreans, who have commonly devoted themselves to commerce.

However, economic mobility may well not have been the only economic goal sought by ethnic families. A study of South Slav immigrants suggests that when faced with choices between security and mobility —between regular, dependable employment and a job with chances for advancement, or between education for their children and jobs that increased the chances of family economic stability through children's wages —they intentionally chose to forgo chances for occupational advancement. The choice was not blind traditionalism, but a reflection of what they most wanted (once they had decided to remain in the United States at all) from the American economic system. French Canadians in Manchester, N.H., are a parallel instance. Here the immigrants accepted low-paying textile jobs with only slight opportunities for upward mobility within the factory, because the factory's rapid labor turnover and its willingness to hire on the recommendation of trusted employees permitted families to support a close kinship network that extended back to Quebec. This kind of kin influence on hiring differed in type but not in value from the kind of security the South Slavs sought. Each represented an interaction of traditional preferences and the contexts in which the families found themselves.

The huge influx of immigrants into American cities in the middle of the 19th century gave poverty a new visibility and led many Americans to see it as an immigrant phenomenon. In response, a host of new private and state agencies for the care of the poor, the sick, and the delinquent were created. Immigrant families were the major recipients of assistance from the newly founded associations for the Improvement of the Poor, as well as their major targets for discipline and reformation. Families unable to support themselves were removed to almshouses or were auctioned off to work as servants. Ironically, at the very time when middle-class urban families were glorifying an individualistic ideal of domesticity, institutionalization was emerging as the panacea for the families of the poor and the dependent. Children, including both orphans and those whose families were not self-supporting, were the major targets of the charity reform effort, both because they were in most urgent need of salvation, and because they could be used as agents of Americanization within their own families.

Later in the 19th century poverty came to be regarded less as the result of personal depravity and more as the result of environmental circumstances; the social-justice movement that peaked in the Progressive era thus aimed to reform the living and working environments rather than directly to change the ways of life of immigrant families. The movements for tenement-house reform, workmen's compensation, the abolition of child labor, and the protection of women and children in industry were directed toward improvement of the social and economic environment rather than toward intervention in the affairs of immigrant families. Such environmentalist reform was rarely in this period extended to the growing urban black ghettos, where families were practicing a variety of adaptive devices, some (like boarding) typical, others less so.

CULTURAL CHANGE AND ADAPTATION

Americanization was an overt goal of teachers, charity workers, social-care workers, and social reformers. It involved everything from teaching language and civics to inculcating "American" ways of life, habits of cleanliness, good housekeeping, nutrition, and social graces.

Settlement-house workers, as exemplified by Jane Addams, recognized some of the internal needs and distinct cultural values of immigrant families and managed to teach them to cope with poverty and improve their standard of living with slight offense to traditional family values. Even so, when settlement-house or charity-case workers aided immigrant men in finding jobs, they hoped also to supervise the disbursement of their salaries; when they gave assistance to immigrant housewives, they tried to inculcate cleanliness and modern methods of home economics and housekeeping. Social workers assisting families attempted to supervise school attendance and observance of child-labor laws; visiting nurses brought health care and middle-class American child-rearing methods. Many of the social reform and betterment movements and institutions that eventually were addressed to the entire population had been initially designed specifically for immigrants. Kindergartens and playgrounds, visiting nurses, boys' clubs, and the home economics movement are all cases in point.

Despite the challenge these agencies posed to cherished family traditions, immigrant parents generally cooperated with them, both because of the assistance they offered and because of the advantages their teaching and assistance promised for their children. Yet whenever possible, immigrant families continued to exercise their own choices in response to the cultural pressures. Middle-class contemporaries often found it difficult to accept the facts that immigrant families insisted on their freedom to exercise such choices and that preserving traditional family ways was often more important to them than the promise of social and economic advancement.

Sociologists of the Chicago School, like Progressive reformers, misunderstood traditional immigrant-family patterns of adaptation as deviant. The classic expression of this thesis is William I. Thomas and Florian Znaniecki's *The Polish Peasant in Europe and America*, written early in the 20th century, in part as an attempt to provide a nonracialist understanding of the high recorded incidence of delinquency in Polish immigrant families in the industrial cities of the United States. "There is a large proportion of immigrant children—particularly in large cities—whose home and community conditions are such that their behavior is never socially regulated, no life-organization worthy of the name is ever imposed on them." This familiar thesis has formed the core of much of the conventional wisdom about the immigrant family.

Thomas and Znaniecki proposed an essentially linear, evolutionary account of the immigrant family, one wholly at odds with more modern interpretations that stress adaptations informed by culturally determined preferences. "Formerly the individual counted mainly as a member of the family; now he counts by himself, and still more than formerly. The family ceases to be necessary at all. The unequal rate at which the process of individualization and the modification of traditional attitudes takes place in different family members leads often to a disintegration of both the familial and the personal life." Peasant wisdom was supposedly rejected abruptly on the streets of U.S. cities, where Polish-American children were exposed to alien values that seemed more appropriate to American life than did inflexible parental ways. Such an interpretation, however sympathetic, justified the optimistic, interventionist policies of progressive "Americanizers." In their view, immigrant families were what slowed the eventual transition to an assimilated population; to hasten the process these families had to be educated as well as granted the necessary assistance to enable them to hold together.

The cultural politics of the family is by no means a remote issue. Learned family behavior is still subject both to the occasional efforts of the larger society to impose its own values on ethnic families and to the varied social and economic context in which they live, as the Moynihan Report and the widespread academic response to it demonstrate. In the mid-1960s Daniel Patrick Moynihan proposed that structural weaknesses in the black family system were among the important causes of contemporary black urban poverty. Specifically, Moynihan pointed to the father-absent family as a legacy of slavery, a product of the inability of adult slave men to provide sustenance and protection for their families, pathological today because father-absent families fail to provide adequate motivation and training for the occupational attainment of subsequent generations. (The report was actually ambiguous and could be interpreted in a quite different light, but this is at least what many took its thesis to be.) The lively controversy that has arisen over this interpretation points to the imperfect triumph of cultural pluralism in the United States, and to at least one instance in which "pathological" behaviors are still thought to justify intervention in the privacy of the American family. Concrete instances (which are not to be attributed to Moynihan) are the numerous attempts by various jurisdictions to penalize "welfare mothers" for what are considered to be immoral family arrangements supported at the public expense. Recent scholarship, however, has been more inclined than either Thomas and Znaniecki or Moynihan to stress that even superficially deviant family behaviors contain large adaptive elements, and express group values.

To present ethnic family variation solely as a product of immigration, modified by elements of cultural convergence among subsequent generations, omits an important element of the current scene, one often associated with the notion of a third-generation return to ethnicity as a freely chosen value system. This theory holds that, on the whole, second-generation families have provided their children with a less culturally conflicted upbringing than their parents had afforded them.

At the same time, the third-generation child grows up in a somewhat "ethnic" context, though much attenuated. A combination of cultural confidence and a touch of ethnic upbringing often leads not to rejection of ethnicity but instead to its cultivation as a valued "heritage," and presumably to its translation into family processes.

The regeneration of ethnicity is recognizable in many families today. However, rediscovery of the ethnic past by third-generation families does not necessarily involve a recapitulation of the behavior of the immigrant generation. Members of the third generation do not really resemble their grandparents more nearly than they do their parents, for ethnicity is a set of somewhat distinctive behaviors and identities that evolve continuously out of a learned background within concrete contexts. Those who experience a "third-generation return" have incorporated the experience and style of the second generation and have then been led to improve their knowledge and increase their identification with an ethnic heritage. These "roots" are often a politically and self-consciously created product of family- or ethnic-group memory. Family ethnicity emerges, no less now than two generations ago, from the interaction of tradition and immediate context. For the third generation, that context is radically different from the one their immigrant grandparents knew.

CONCLUSION

The United States is still a nation of immigrants. Immigration is not the outstanding fact of American life that it was two generations ago, but it remains substantial. In 1970, 7 percent of all families in the United States were headed by immigrants, while in 1900, near the height of the new immigration, about 25 percent of all U.S. families were headed by persons of foreign birth. Recently, distinct signs have suggested that the long-dominant rural-to-urban internal migrations—the northbound movement of southern blacks and Appalachian whites—have slowed or reversed; the same is true of the Puerto Rican migration. Regional economic shifts continue, however, as do changes in the international economic areas. Internal migration is perhaps as likely as international immigration to produce new "ethnic" family types in the United States.

Recent changes in immigration legislation assure a heavy family component; half of all immigrants currently admitted to the United States are married. Most single newcomers marry soon after arrival, even members of groups—like the Greeks and Chinese—that once formed the predominantly unmarried migrant-labor stream. Among the nationalities increasing their representation within the U.S. population are groups that previously were not present in large numbers—such as Cubans, Koreans, and Vietnamese—as well as those long well-represented in the American population—including Chinese, Mexicans, Italians, and English. Each group of immigrants in its own way renews the cycle of the establishment of ethnic families on American soil.

Ethnic families and the concept of ethnicity have survived in American society. But ethnic families today (except for newly arriving immigrants) are by no means the equivalent of immigrant families. Both native and immigrant families have changed significantly.

The family exists as one institution among many. It is incontestable that corporate society and the growth of governmental and nongovernmental agencies—such as schools and the mass-communications industry—have constricted the domains of private families. Because family behavior is learned not only from the family itself but also from competing sources in the larger society, the growth and centralization of schools and the mass media must appear at least to challenge the plurality of family forms.

Even so, disagreement over proper family behavior persists, and thus provides evidence of persisting variation in family behavior per se. Ethnicity, though, is only one possible source of this variation; it may be minimal compared with class differences or with distinctive family behaviors emerging more or less directly from the objective facts of poverty, unmediated by cultural traditions. No final answer is yet available.

Two seemingly contradictory processes are at work—convergence and emergent ethnicity. For instance, ethnic influences upon marriage patterns continue, but to a lesser degree. In a study of college graduates, William McCready confirms some predicted ethnic differences in attitudes toward family and concludes that *some part* of the current variation in family attitudes must be attributed to ethnicity: "It is clearly as important as religion, [parents'] education (a proxy for socioeconomic background), and region."

The processes by which ethnic families were created are part of the fabric of U.S. history. Families' interactions with these processes and institutions and their degree of success in adapting to change have varied in accordance with ethnic background, recency of migration, and economic status. Both the nature of their response and their style of adaptation have been selective compromises between the dictates of external forces and internal traditions. Under certain conditions, the family has been affected by social change; under others, it has initiated change or innovation. In either case, immigrant families have not been merely victims or passive recipients of acculturation.

Bibliography
General treatments of the family and ethnicity are rare. The collection by Charles H. Mindel and Robert W. Habenstein, eds., *Ethnic Families in America: Patterns and Variations* (New York, 1976), is uneven. Oscar Handlin, *The Uprooted* (Boston, 1951), is a classic depiction of immigrant family life in its process of adaptation to American society Two compilations of statistics are indispensable: U.S. Immigration Commission, *Immigrants in Cities* (Reports, vols. 26 and 27, Washington, D.C., 1911); and U.S. Bureau of the Census, *Fifteenth Census of the United States: 1930*, vol. 6, *Special Report on Foreign-Born White Families* (Washington, D.C., 1933).
Recent studies that pay special attention to the family are: Herbert G. Gutman, *The Black Family in Slavery and Freedom: 1750–1925* (New York, 1976); Tamara K. Hareven, "The Dynamics of Kin in an Industrial Community," *American Journal of Sociology* (October 1978), which examines the interaction between kinship and industrial work among French Canadian workers; Tamara K. Hareven and Randolph Langenbach, *Amoskeag: Life and Work in an American Factory City* (New York, 1978), which recreates the experience of three generations of immigrant families; and Virginia Yans-McLaughlin, *Family and Community: Italian Immigrants in Buffalo, 1880–1930* (Ithaca, N.Y., 1977).
Robert E. Kennedy, Jr., *The Irish: Emigration, Marriage, and Fertility* (Berkeley, 1973); and Simon Kuznets, "Immigration of Russian Jews to the United States: Background and Structure," *Perspectives in American History* 9 (1975): 35–126, examine the importance of family concerns. The classic account of the clash of cultures in the ethnic family is William I. Thomas and Florian Znaniecki, *The Polish Peasant in Europe and America* (Boston, 1918–1920).

Three studies of the ways in which ethnic families have attempted to raise their children are: Arnold Green, "The Middle Class Male Child and Neurosis," *American Sociological Review* 11 (1946): 31–41; Timothy L. Smith, "Immigrant Social Aspirations and American Education," *American Quarterly* 21 (1969): 523–543; and John Bodnar, "Materialism and Morality: Slavic American Immigrants and Education, 1890–1940," *Journal of Ethnic Studies* 3 (1975): 1–20. See also William C. McCready, "The Persistence of Ethnic Variation in American Families," in *Ethnicity in the United States: A Preliminary Reconnaissance,* ed. Andrew N. Greeley (New York, 1974); and Calvin Goldschneider and Peter R. Uhlenberg, "Minority Group Status and Fertility," *American Journal of Sociology* 74 (1969): 361–372.

TAMARA K. HAREVEN AND JOHN MODELL

FERNANDEÑOS: *see* AMERICAN INDIANS

FIJIANS: *see* PACIFIC ISLANDERS

FILIPINOS

Although Filipinos have been coming to the mainland United States, to Hawaii, and even to Alaska since the beginning of the 20th century, the group has grown to its present size, between 400,000 and 500,000, relatively recently. At least half the Filipinos now living in the United States were born abroad.

The earliest immigrants came as American nationals, after the Treaty of Paris (1899) ended the Spanish-American War and gave possession of the Philippine Islands to the United States. Under American rule Filipinos had the right to travel on U.S. passports and to enter the United States freely; most other U.S. constitutional guarantees were extended to them as well, but not the right to trial by jury or the right to bear arms. This arrangement remained in effect until 1934 when the Tydings-McDuffie Independence Act conferred commonwealth status on the islands. The legislation was inspired in part by the independence movement in the Philippines and in part by the mood of a depression-ridden United States. In order to reduce unemployment some interest groups wished to exclude immigrant labor; a strong farm lobby wanted to exclude imports like copra, sugar, and hemp from the Philippines. Once the act was passed, Filipinos became aliens for immigration purposes; their quota was set at 50 persons per year. Twelve years later, on July 4, 1946, President Harry S Truman proclaimed Philippine independence and raised the quota to 100—the minimum permitted to any country by the immigration act of 1924. There were, however, a good many admissions outside the quota—as many as 1,100 in 1948 and about 3,000 annually in the early 1960s. In 1965 the Hart-Cellar Immigration Act abolished the national-origins quota system altogether, and opened the way for the 276,000 Filipino immigrants who entered the United States between 1966 and 1976.

ORIGINS

The Filipino homeland is an archipelago of about 7,000 islands which can be divided into three main areas. Luzon is the large northern island on which Quezon City, the capital, and Manila, the largest city, are located. Mindanao, an even larger island at the southern extreme of the archipelago, is the historical center of Muslim influence. Between these two islands lies a cluster of smaller ones known as the Visayan Islands. Parts of the Visayas, especially the island of Cebu, are

the most densely populated regions of the archipelago. They and the heavily populated Ilocos provinces of northwestern Luzon are the home regions of the majority of the immigrants to the United States. The next most numerous group are the Tagalogs, natives of the provinces surrounding Manila in central Luzon.

The people of the Philippines speak over 80 different dialects. The 8 or 9 most prevalent languages belong to the Malayo-Polynesian group and share characteristics that make it easy for members of different regional groups to communicate with one another. Most Filipinos in the United States speak either Visayan, Tagalog (Pilipino), or Ilocano. Visayan is spoken by about 44 percent of the total population of the Philippines, and the Visayans in the United States most often speak the dialect known as Cebuano. Tagalog, renamed Pilipino (pronounced Filipino) when it was proclaimed the national language in 1946, is the language of central Luzon. Its study is now required in all Filipino public schools, but at the time of independence it was spoken by about 25 percent of the population. Ilocano, spoken by only 15 percent of the Filipino population, is the language most commonly spoken by Filipinos on the U.S. mainland and in Hawaii.

Language is and has been the principal basis of association among Filipino immigrants; overseas, the Ilocanos, Tagalogs, and Cebuanos form separate community groups. Local and regional identification are more important to members of these groups than the notion of being a Filipino; for some, a national identity is not even relevant: too often, such an identity has been superimposed on the Filipinos' other loyalties by outsiders unaware of linguistic and other ties among groups.

The diverse ethnic origins of 20th-century Filipinos are the result of earlier migrations from Asia and Indonesia. The Negritos, distinguished by their small stature, were the earliest arrivals, probably crossing by land bridges more than 25,000 years ago. The most numerous migrants were various groups of Malays, the earliest of whom were ancestors of primitive tribes such as the Bontoks and Igorots. The later migration of culturally more advanced Malays reached a peak in the 13th century; the majority of modern-day Filipinos, including the Visayans, Ilocanos, and Cebuanos, are descendants of these people. During the 14th century Arab traders from the Malay archipelago brought Islam to the southern islands of the Philippines; their descendants, the Moros, remain militant Muslims.

European contacts began when Ferdinand Magellan reached the island of Samar in 1521, but European influence remained minimal until 1565 during the reign of the Spanish king, Philip II, for whom the islands were named. His governors successfully established a colonial rule that lasted for more than three centuries. Although few of the Spanish colonials sent to the islands had any intention of remaining there, some did settle down and marry Filipinos. Some of their descendants, known in the Philippines as *mestizos*, inherited vast tracts of land in the 19th century and controlled the islands' economy. Other powerful mestizos were descendants of marriages between Filipinos and Chinese settlers who came to the islands as merchants. They, too, belonged to the dominant political and economic class during both the Spanish and the American colo-

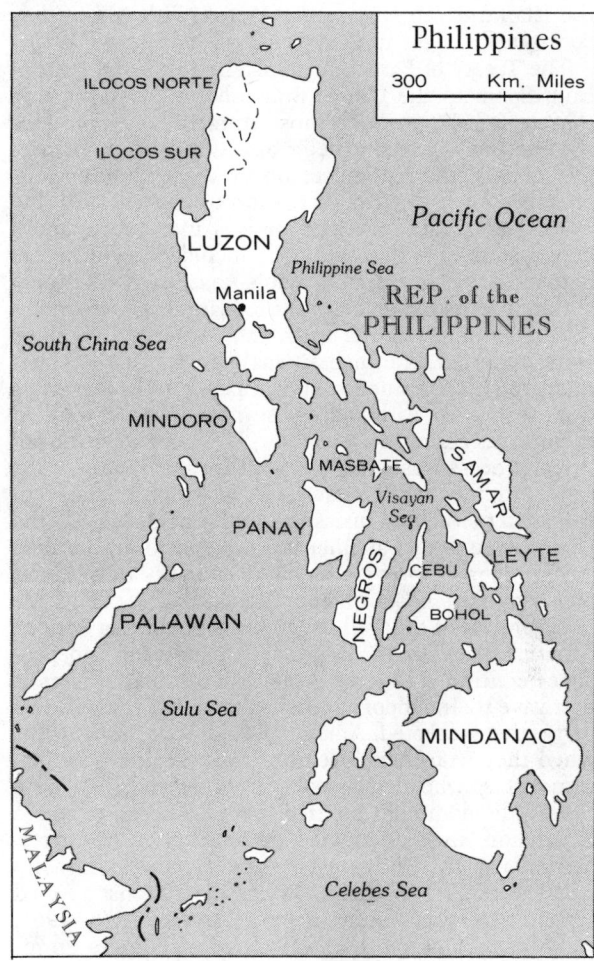

nial periods. Regardless of their backgrounds, the whiter their skin the easier it was for mestizos to enter the European and American island society. Throughout the Spanish colonial period the Roman Catholic Church was another important political and economic power, both as a large landowner and as controller of the educational system.

Imperialism implanted a Spanish culture that many Filipinos sought to emulate; it left a strong imprint on the language and customs of the elite and gave most of the Filipinos their religion—in 1946 almost 80 percent of the population was Roman Catholic. Virtually all the U.S. immigrants were at least nominally Catholic, but unlike many European immigrants with Catholic backgrounds, the young, single Filipino men who were the overwhelming majority before World War II did not attend church with any regularity. Only when whole families began to come in the 1970s did the church start to play a significant role in developing Filipino communities and neighborhoods.

The Filipinos resented colonial rule, regardless of its influence on their culture. During the last half of the 19th century, revolutionaries and reformers persistently protested imperial corruption and racial inequity. When the Philippines were handed over to the United States at the end of the Spanish-American War, rebellion continued against the new colonial power. U.S. troops eventually quelled opposition throughout

the islands except among the Moros, with whom they continued to fight in the southern islands until 1913.

The Treaty of Paris that transferred imperial control from Spain to the United States began a relationship that lasted 47 years. Almost immediately two U.S. commissions arrived to determine how to Americanize the islands; the regime set up by these commissions probably made its strongest impact between 1901 and 1913. Democratic government was introduced, and a new system of public education included a widespread network of elementary schools that taught Filipino children ideas about being American similar to those taught children on the mainland. American teachers were imported and English was required in the classroom, but the influence upon many rural youngsters was negligible. Although these new schools were in themselves enormously popular, U.S. control of the political process was not. After centuries of Spanish rule, some Filipinos simply assumed that the right to govern belonged to foreign Caucasians; but others regarded the U.S. regime as just another form of control by an alien government, however much it might talk about preparing Filipinos for home rule.

Regardless of the well-intentioned policies of various American governors, Filipino demands for independence continued to grow. American colonial officers at first gave their support to the Federalistas, the political party that accepted American rule; but from 1907, when they won their first municipal election, the Nacionalistas, who demanded early independence, were clearly the dominant political force. With no effective opposition, they dominated national elective offices, particularly the Philippine Assembly, and eventually won American backing. Political factions formed around two strong figures, Sergio Osmeña (1878–1961) and Manuel Quezon (1878–1944). Most Filipino immigrants to the United States and Hawaii were Nacionalistas, and they remained partisan. During World War II, when President Quezon and his staff formed a government-in-exile in Washington, D.C., they drew support from the Filipinos who labored in American cities and West Coast fields. Filipino immigrants, although generally banding together in linguistic groups, readily identified with and rallied to the independence movement and, in the 1940s, to the support of Quezon and the United States in ridding the home islands of the Japanese invaders.

The Jones Act of 1916 committed the United States to Philippine independence as soon as "stable" government could be established, but in practice the independence movement made little headway until 1932. Then the widening effects of the Great Depression in the United States and continuing pressures from the Philippines and from American groups, caused the U.S. Congress to pass the Hare-Hawes-Cutting Act, a measure that would have made the islands an independent republic. But the plan fell through, primarily because of domestic political rivalries in the Philippines which Quezon was unable to resolve. Finally in 1934 the U.S. Congress enacted, and the Philippine legislature accepted, the Tydings-McDuffie Independence Act, which provided for commonwealth status for a period of ten years. The commonwealth, established in 1935 with Quezon as president and Osmeña as vice president, lasted until 1946.

In 1946, after the war, Philippine independence was declared. The new nation survived some peasant uprisings and appeared to be a model democracy until the end of the second term of President Ferdinand E. Marcos (1917–). Elected for the first time in 1965, Marcos moved in 1972 to acquire dictatorial powers and to suspend civil rights. His repressive actions coincided with the newly liberalized immigration law in the United States; many of his political opponents found it expedient to depart, contributing to a sudden increase in Philippine immigration.

Poverty also continued to motivate emigration. To this day the Philippines maintain a socially stratified society which ranges from wealthy cosmopolites to landless peasants. Because a very large number of Filipinos were tenant farmers, owning a plot of land outright was their measure of wealth; the desire to earn money in order to buy or keep land was most often what motivated their migration.

The family, including both paternal and maternal relatives, was at the center of Filipino life; it provided economic sustenance, social connections, and the basis for political affiliation. The social structure also included neighbors, fellow workers, and those ritual or honorary kinsmen known as compadres. The compadrazgo system, based on the selection of godparents by the parents of a newborn child, established a close, lifelong relationship among the adults and rigidly excluded everyone outside it. In the islands the small integrated villages or barrios inhabited by members of these interlocking alliances assumed obligations that included sharing food, money, and labor. The system required an individual's strong sense of identity with and acceptance by the group, and served to promote beliefs that kin relationships tolerate no disagreement; that an individual should maintain his proper station in society, neither reaching above nor falling below it; and that a person's acts should contribute to his self-esteem but not cause embarrassment to others.

Village festivals and celebrations were frequent, to offset the daily routine of hard labor. The barrio commemorated religious holidays or annual events such as the harvest with celebrations that included not only the usual holiday fare but also a good deal of gambling. Betting on cockfights—a nationwide pastime on weekends—was particularly popular. The Ilocanos, Tagalogs, and Visayans who came to the United States brought these traditions and customs with them.

ARRIVAL AND EARLY SETTLEMENT

The first Filipinos to come to the United States were not peasants but students. The first U.S. civil governor, William Howard Taft, inspired a plan whereby the colonial government sent young men to attend college or university in the United States. These students, known as pensionados, were taken into American homes; after they finished their studies in such fields as education, engineering, agriculture, and medicine, they were supposed to return as disciples of democracy to teach the American way to their people. The program was started in 1903 with 100 students selected from 20,000 applicants; in 1907, 183 were enrolled in 47 schools and colleges. By 1910 all the pensionados had returned to the islands. At first they were received with jealousy by other Filipinos, who saw them as ambitious and over-

bearing, and with hostility by American colonials, who thought they no longer "knew their place." But they eventually assumed prominent roles in the economic and political life of the country, and their success encouraged other—though this time self-supporting—students to follow.

According to one estimate, only 300 to 400 Filipinos studied in American schools through 1924, but the number increased sharply thereafter. Altogether some 14,000 Filipinos had enrolled in various U.S. colleges and universities by 1938. Aside from the University of the Philippines, chartered in 1908 to be the capstone of the Americanized educational system, most colleges in the islands had remained under the administration of the Catholic church, and were largely traditional in curriculum. Young men looking for careers in technology, science, or social science generally sought training elsewhere, and the most obvious place was the United States.

According to the reminiscences of those who studied in the United States, the democratic ideals they learned in the islands hardly prepared them for the realities that greeted them on the mainland, particularly prejudice and discrimination. Many students also underestimated their expenses, ran out of money, and drifted into unskilled work. Still, some managed to finish their studies and return to the Philippines to join the pensionados as rising provincial and national leaders, and a few continued to bridge the two worlds of the Philippines and the United States by living in both places.

This student group was a small minority; the overwhelming number of emigrants were peasants, men under the age of 30 who sought employment as unskilled laborers. Their appearance in Hawaii and along the Pacific Coast was economically conditioned on both sides. Growing hostility toward the Chinese and then the Japanese in the Hawaiian Islands and in California had led the agricultural industries that depended upon a large pool of cheap labor to look elsewhere for their supply. They employed Koreans until Korea's absorption by Japan in the early 1900s, and by 1910 they turned to young Filipinos. Enticed by recruiting agents and steamship companies with promises of good wages and housing, the Filipinos first went to Hawaii to work in the sugar-cane mills and fields and on the pineapple plantations. Most signed up for three years and then returned to their barrios with their savings; others stayed longer and wrote home of their successes, sending money along as evidence; still others failed and were rarely heard from again.

Whether they sent money or brought it, the impact of these workers and their American dollars on the rural barrios was tremendous. When a Hawaiiano—a term applied to any returning Ilocano whether from Hawaii or, later, from the U.S. mainland—came home, he bought land, forgot the hard labor in the plantations, and became a person of great influence in his own village. Those who remained overseas sent dollars that could be used for purchasing land, paying taxes, financing the education of brothers or nephews, or fulfilling other obligations to the family system of alliances; the number of these obligations may well have been one reason why so many Filipinos stayed long beyond their original contract period—some never returned at all.

Although official records were not kept, it is clear that a large number eventually returned to the Philippines. The records of the Waialua Plantation on Oahu's north shore, for example, show that of over 1,000 Filipinos assigned to that sugar company at the rate of about 100 a year between 1909 and 1920, only 9 were still in the plantation town in 1948. According to the plantation records, most of them had returned to their barrios by the outbreak of World War II.

IMMIGRATION TO HAWAII, 1906–1946

In 1906 Albert F. Judd arrived in the Philippines to recruit plantation and mill workers for the Hawaiian Sugar Planters' Association (HSPA) in its continual worldwide search for workers. He found only 15 workers willing to accompany him back to Honolulu, and although his agent sent more workers during 1907, the HSPA concluded that Judd's experiment had failed. In 1909, however, Hawaii's Territorial Board of Immigration, always quick to respond to the needs of the plantations, reported that the Philippines had the only pool of cheap labor that could be tapped, since the immigration of Chinese, Japanese, and Koreans had been curtailed. In April the HSPA launched another larger-scale recruiting effort around Manila and on the island of Cebu. Its two agents transported 803 Filipinos, mostly Tagalogs and Visayans, in 1909 and another 4,173 workers the next year. After 1915 recruiting shifted to the Ilocano barrios, partly because plantation owners found the rural Ilocanos to be the "best workers," partly because economic hardship was acute in those provinces and they were most willing to come. By the late 1930s Filipinos, the majority of them still young single Ilocanos, constituted the largest ethnic group working in Hawaiian fields.

Filipinos coming to Honolulu through the HSPA's Manila office reached a high point of 11,621 in Honolulu in 1925. At that point the HSPA stopped active recruiting; the great number of voluntary enlistments made it unnecessary. For six more years, several thousand Filipinos arrived annually; in 1931 nearly 4,800 arrived. Altogether about 113,000 emigrated to Hawaii from 1909 through 1931; of these, over 55,000 remained in Hawaii, 39,000 returned to their home islands, and 18,600 moved on to the West Coast of the United States.

The HSPA recruits who arrived in Honolulu were assigned either to one of the sugar plantations on Hawaii's four major islands or to the Pineapple Growers' Association. Each worker signed a three-year contract in Manila that guaranteed free transportation to Hawaii, wages, free housing, water, fuel, and medical attention. After 1915 workers who completed the contract were transported back to the Philippines without charge. The HSPA was bound to the contract, recruits were not; but if a worker left his plantation job he forfeited all guarantees, including return passage. Filipinos in Hawaii today, if they came on an original contract, are still eligible for free transportation home.

Sugar plantations required the field hands who planted, cultivated, and harvested the cane to work a 10-hour day and a six-day week; mill hands worked a 12-hour day. Both types of workers carried out limited special assignments under close supervision. In 1915 workers received $1.00 a day and contractual benefits; by 1925 male workers averaged $2.25 to $2.50 a day

with the same contractual benefits and some additional bonus incentives. At first, recruiters in the Philippines received bonuses for signing up families, but later they were told to give preference to single Ilocano men. The few wives, mostly Tagalogs and Visayans, who came to Hawaii were paid substantially less than the male workers; in 1915 they averaged about 70 cents a day. Filipinos who later wrote or talked about their experiences agreed that their work in Hawaii was the hardest they had ever undertaken.

The regimented life of the plantations differed greatly from life in the barrios. In both Hawaii and the Philippines the peasants worked for someone else, but at home they were tenant farmers for a generally paternalistic landlord, growing crops that they consumed themselves or sold in the market. In Hawaii they were wage earners in a "factory in the field," governed throughout the workday by company regulations. Plantation life forced major cultural adjustments upon the Filipinos and other ethnic groups who worked in Hawaii.

The social life of the workers was restricted. A clubhouse was usually provided for social activities, movies, dances, and celebrations. Athletic activities were also organized within each of the national groups found on every plantation; the Filipinos were particularly fond of baseball, boxing, volley ball, and billiards, and were as enthusiastic about cockfights and gambling on the plantation as they had been at home. Within the larger community they tended to cluster in language groups—Tagalogs, Visayans, or Ilocanos together. In Honolulu's River District near the railroad station and the inter-island terminal, separate bars, barbershops, and poolrooms catered to each of these groups.

The immigrant society remained overwhelmingly male: in 1910 the ratio was 10 males to 1 female; in 1940 it had improved but was still only 3.5 to 1. Few women had the cost of ship's passage; it was more expensive for them because they were not allowed to travel in steerage. To make up for the absence of wives and other close kin, Filipino workers searched out friends and relatives from the barrio, and bunked and cooked and ate their meals together, producing the *compang,* a surrogate family of sorts, with the eldest person acting as head of household. The few women from Luzon and Cebu who migrated were much sought after and were often the cause of fights and brawling, or sometimes *coboy-coboy* (wife abduction). Some men married Hawaiian, Portuguese, or Puerto Rican women, whose cultural backgrounds and value systems were closest to their own; women in the islands' *haole* society were in any case largely inaccessible to them.

For the few who did marry, the traditional pattern had to be modified; the large family weddings customary in the Philippines could not be duplicated. When a child was born, the compadrazgo system became a means, both on the Hawaiian Islands and on the mainland, of maintaining close contact with relatives and others from the same barrio and of giving single males a role in the society by making them honorary kinsmen. It was not unusual for 50 to 200 sponsors to attend a child's baptism, although they might seldom acknowledge any obligation thereafter, unlike the homeland compadres whose relations to the child—and even more to the parents—were of lifelong importance. The

feasts that celebrated marriage and baptism were equaled by the funeral feast when a Filipino immigrant died, for this was also an occasion for Filipinos to come together and renew their customs and barrio ties.

In order to discourage the formation of labor organizations on the plantations and in the mills, the various national groups of workers were isolated from one another. For a long time the young Filipinos, separated from more militant groups and already indoctrinated to submission by the barrio political system known as *caciquismo,* made no attempt to rebel against the plantation system. As temporary residents they had no power in the system and little motivation to change it. The populations in the camps, although relatively settled by California migrant-worker standards, were by no means permanent; men moved from plantation to plantation to be near relatives or close to the Filipino colony in Honolulu.

Eventually, however, Filipinos began to join the struggle of other workers to organize, partly to ameliorate working conditions, but more importantly to increase wages—the more they earned, the sooner they could go home. In the 1920s Filipino plantation hands joined Japanese workers to demand better conditions and pay, but the strikes they called led only to retaliation by planters and territorial authorities. During a 1924 strike, 16 Filipinos and 4 policemen died in a labor-camp riot on the island of Kauai. Success did not come until federal legislation in the 1930s provided for collective bargaining: the first union contract for sugar workers was signed at the McBryde Sugar Company on Kauai in 1940. The International Longshoremen's and Warehousemen's Union (ILWU) began a major organizational drive in 1944 and unionized all plantation workers in 1946, securing job classification and tenure, seniority benefits, pension plans, and promotion and employment rules. By 1950 plantation workers in Hawaii were the highest-paid agricultural workers in the world.

For about 20 years young Filipinos migrated freely to the Hawaiian Islands. Then, as the depression of the 1930s created a surplus of plantation workers, emigration from the Philippines abruptly declined: only 462 new arrivals were recorded between 1932 and 1936. In 1932 the HSPA began serving as the sole agent for steerage passage on the Dollar Lines and limited ticket sales to 24 males each month. Clearly it was no longer interested in establishing a long-range Filipino community in Hawaii, although it still aimed at a continual turnover of its labor force. In the course of the 1930s about 22,000 Filipinos returned to their barrios as their labor contracts expired, but in both numbers and percentage they continued to make up the majority of plantation labor. According to the 1940 U.S. Census, about 46,000 Filipinos still lived on plantations, and only 6,800 remained in Honolulu.

The 1934 Tydings-McDuffie Independence Act provided that if the need existed the Hawaiian Islands could request exemption from the annual Philippine immigration quota of 50, and in 1945 the HSPA and the Pineapple Growers' Association of Hawaii sought permission to recruit workers again from the Philippines. World War II had created new and better employment opportunities which Filipinos already in Hawaii had seized; it was obvious that these workers would not re-

turn to the fields. Hawaii's territorial governor authorized the importation of 6,000 additional male Filipino agricultural workers and their families. In 1946 over 7,300 men, 450 women, and 900 children arrived; of these 5,800 were Ilocanos, fewer than 200 were Tagalogs from the environs of Manila, and only 1 worker was enlisted from Cebu. The composition of the group reflected not only the HSPA's longstanding preference for Ilocanos over the allegedly too carefree Visayans and too urbanized Tagalogs, but also the continued economic attraction that the Hawaiian Islands had for young men.

IMMIGRATION TO THE MAINLAND, 1903–1941

Immigration of Filipino laborers to the continental United States started somewhat later than in Hawaii, for there were no comparable recruiting efforts by agricultural interests in California. Most of the first arrivals were young men who had tired of Hawaiian plantation life and were lured to the West Coast by expectations of adventure and American life implanted by school teachers in the Philippines. Otherwise, the movement paralleled the migration to Hawaii: it reached its peak in the 1920s and declined with the onset of depression and the quota limitations imposed by the Tydings-McDuffie Act.

In addition to sojourners from Hawaii and the student pensionados and their successors, the earliest arrivals included a contingent of island carpenters sent in 1903 to build a Philippine village at the St. Louis Exposition. Immigration agents detained them in San Francisco because they lacked funds to pay the required head tax; their release was finally arranged by the U.S. War Department, and the Commissioner General of Immigration subsequently ruled that, as nationals, Filipinos were henceforth exempted from the tax. An unfortunate result of the Philippine venture at the St. Louis Exposition was that the demonstration of Philippine tribal customs left Americans with the impression that their new island possessions were populated by savages, and this notion influenced American attitudes toward the Filipinos who followed.

In 1910 the U.S. Bureau of the Census estimated that 2,767 Filipinos lived within the territories of the United States, outside the Philippines. Of these, 2,361 lived in Hawaii, 246 in Alaska, 109 in New Orleans, 17 in Washington State, and only 5 in California. The New Orleans community originated in Reconstruction days when a group of Filipino sailors left their ships, married local girls, found work, and settled down.

The restrictions placed on Japanese immigration in 1908 produced a concomitant increase in Filipino immigration, again as an alternative form of cheap labor: in 1920 the U.S. Census counted 5,603 Filipinos living in the United States and Alaska. The major increase was in California with a total of 2,674. Before 1930 another 45,000 came, most of them agricultural workers who lived in California; some settled elsewhere on the Pacific Coast and a few went on to Chicago, Detroit, New York, and Philadelphia. The Filipinos in Chicago found civil-service jobs in the post office or joined the navy and were based at the Great Lakes Naval Training Station. Another group was attached to the navy yard at Philadelphia. Filipinos in Detroit, New York, and Washington were mostly drifters, taking temporary jobs in hotels and restaurants or as domestic servants.

Another group, some of them former navy men, settled in New Jersey during World War I and on into the 1940s. There they raised families and worked in metal and chemical manufacturing and as chefs, truck drivers, musicians, railroad men, mechanics, accountants, and teachers. Miguel Macaoay, for instance, a leader in the state's Filipino-American community, started as a fireman and became a senior laboratory technician for the chemical company where he worked for 39 years. Some of the children of these immigrants became white-collar workers and professionals.

The immigrants who settled along the Pacific Coast were funneled into a limited range of occupations as soon as they arrived at one of the seaports. During the winter they stayed in the city and worked in hotels and restaurants or as domestic servants. In March they left the cities to follow the crops until the harvest, and then returned to the city. Californian, like Hawaiian, agriculture could always use cheap labor; Filipinos cut asparagus, picked lettuce and strawberries, and harvested sugar beets and potatoes. In the 1950s and the early 1960s they and the Mexicans constituted the backbone of California's agricultural work force.

In the 1920s both the Filipinos and the Japanese operated under a labor contract system whereby a contractor, or *padrone*, provided the workers for a specified job for an agreed-upon sum; he in turn paid the workers. The padrone supplied his crew with food and other necessities, charging those expenses against their wages. California's ranchers liked the padrone system, and became disenchanted with Filipino labor only when the workers started organizing to bargain for higher wages. The California Federation of Labor—also a leading force in the movement to exclude immigrant labor, especially Asians—opposed every effort to unionize the workers; as the Great Depression wore on, Filipino workers began to organize among themselves to fight wage cuts.

California agriculture resisted the unionization of its field workers until the 1960s. In 1959 the Agricultural Workers' Organizing Committee (AWOC), led by Larry Itlion (1914–), a Filipino, and the National Farm Workers Organization, led by César Chavez (1927–), a Mexican American, began recruiting union members in the fields. In 1965 AWOC struck against 31 grape growers near Delano in the lower San Joaquin Valley; eight days later, Chavez's union joined the strike. They were successful in their negotiations with Schenley Industries, which represented the major wine-producing interests in the area. The subsequent merger of the two unions as the United Farm Workers Organizing Committee (UFWOC) marked a turning point in California agriculture's labor relations. Working together, Filipinos and Chicanos have notably improved both wages and working conditions for California's farm labor.

Unskilled Filipino labor was not confined to the fields. Some found employment in the salmon canneries of Puget Sound and Alaska. Although most of them returned to San Francisco at the end of the salmon season, some stayed behind in the fishing villages: in 1936, 403 Filipinos lived in Alaska; in 1960, 814; and in 1970, 1,297.

On average, from 5,500 to 5,800 Filipinos were em-

ployed in the merchant marine annually between 1925 and 1932; in 1930 there were 7,869. Shipowners liked Filipino crewmen because they would work for low wages; other seamen disliked them for the same reason. In 1936 the Seamen's Union successfully lobbied through the Merchant Marine Act, which required that 90 percent of the crews on American ships be U.S. citizens, and thus eliminated jobs for most Filipinos. The U.S. Navy also provided employment on the seas for some 4,000 Filipinos, although for several decades they were allowed to work only as mess stewards. In 1970 many of the 14,000 Filipinos in the navy were still mess stewards, but some had been given other ratings. The base pay for a new mess steward was $1,500 a year in 1970, a salary commensurate with that of a lieutenant colonel in the Philippine army.

The Filipinos, confronted with prejudice both in Hawaii and on the West Coast, divided their world even more sharply than formerly into compadres and enemies. The alliance system that evolved in most California towns was based upon Filipino traditions of reciprocity, obligation, loyalty, and unity; those outside the group were suspect. As in Hawaii, compang groups developed in camps and cities. In the evenings and on weekends these provincial clans partied together and fought others in the local pool hall, bar, gambling house, or dance hall; most of the drunken battles were over women. In contrast to the plantation Filipinos, the West Coast single men moved around constantly seeking work; there was little semblance of permanent community. But associations based on home barrios formed from time to time to sponsor special occasions or collect money to finance some minor project in the barrio. The immigrants turned the traditional fiestas that at home marked annual events such as the harvest into purely social gatherings and celebrated Philippine holidays such as Commonwealth Day (November 15) and Rizal Day (December 30), in honor of the reformer José Rizal, with beauty contests, parades, banquets, dances, and speeches.

Unlike other American immigrant groups, particularly those from Europe, the young Filipino men who migrated prior to World War II generally did not form lasting social, religious, or political institutions. Frequent social efforts provided various short-term mutual benefits in West Coast cities, but these attempts usually disappeared with the coming of the new agricultural season. Because they were Asians ineligible for naturalization, political participation was impossible. Laws in many states kept Filipinos from practicing law or medicine. The few who managed to attend professional schools usually found they could not pursue careers in the United States. These circumstances promoted the continued transience of the Filipino population in urban areas.

One measure of community permanence is the presence of ethnic newspapers. Prior to the influx of Filipino immigrants in the late 1960s, only about a half-dozen Filipino newspapers existed in the United States for any length of time, and of those only the *Philippine Mail* of San Francisco predated World War II. Greater numbers and the changing character of immigration in the 1970s encouraged a greater sense of community and brought a marked increase in the number of newspapers—by 1975 there were about 20. About half strongly opposed the Marcos regime, reflecting the political motivation for emigration in recent years.

Until World War II, Filipino immigrants were plagued by problems of social adaptation and of unemployment. Handicapped by lack of education, adequate skills, and the ability to speak English well, they were also troubled by the racial prejudice that was directed at that time against any visibly different minority. The fact that they were transients also affected their social and economic status. Working long hours as unskilled agricultural labor or in urban service jobs dulled their enthusiasm for life; color and language separated them from the American majority. As the expense of living in the United States consumed what had appeared from the perspective of the Philippines to be an enormous wage, some of these young men began to regret ever having come. Without wives and families and—because of anti-miscegenation laws in California and elsewhere—without hope of obtaining them, they turned in their leisure time to prostitutes, taxi-dance halls, and gambling dens. Many managed to save the money they had come to earn and to return home; a few eventually acquired skills in the trades or professions; but many others remained transient laborers in the United States for the rest of their lives.

West Coast and Hawaiian employers who relied on cheap labor saw the Filipinos—as earlier they had seen other Asian groups—as necessary to their economic welfare. But people in other occupations, especially those who felt themselves threatened by the presence of this cheap-labor pool, soon demonstrated the same hostility toward Filipinos that they had toward other Asians. Many people persisted in believing that all Filipinos were savages; others were afraid they would lose their jobs to them, because the Filipinos were willing to work at wages unacceptable to American workers. They were attacked for their substandard living conditions, for posing a public health problem, and for crime. Because until 1946, in spite of the 1935 Repatriation Act, the Filipinos came from an American territorial possession, they could not be excluded as easily as the other Asian groups; but as "nonwhites" they could be denied citizenship and could be subjected to the humiliations of being refused service in restaurants and barbershops, swimming pools, movie houses, and other recreational facilities.

Because the Filipino population on the mainland was overwhelmingly male—in 1930 the ratio in California was 14 to 1—the right to marry outside the group was also an important issue. Before laws against interracial marriage were declared unconstitutional in 1948, Filipinos were targets of antimiscegenation legislation that prevented many of them from marrying at all. In 1910 California passed a law that prohibited Caucasians from marrying blacks, "Mongolians," or mulattos. In the late 1920s, when a marriage license was denied to Salvador Roldan, a Filipino, on the ground that he was a "Mongolian," he sued and won his case in the lower courts. In 1933 Los Angeles County appealed the case to the California Supreme Court, which ruled in favor of Roldan on the grounds that the legislature had not specifically forbidden marriages between "whites" and Filipinos. As a result the civil code was amended in

1935 to include the "Malay race" among those whom California "whites" could not marry, and other Pacific Coast states enacted similar restrictive laws.

On the West Coast any interest shown by Filipino men toward Caucasian women could easily create an explosive situation. Vigilante groups formed to terrorize Filipinos, often on the ground that they were leading local girls astray. They attacked Filipinos in Washington's Yakima Valley in 1928 and at Exeter, in California's San Joaquin Valley, in 1929. A vigilante committee roamed the region near Watsonville, Calif., for several days in January 1930, after a group of Filipinos leased a dance hall and hired some Caucasian women for partners. The ensuing fight left one young Filipino worker dead and several others wounded. There were other anti-Filipino incidents as well.

Following precedents used against other Asians, Californians next turned to legislation to get the Filipinos out of the country. To some extent these measures also had humanitarian motives, especially during the depression; as noncitizens, Filipinos were unable to qualify for work relief or welfare and were often jobless and destitute. The idea of sending them back home at government expense was advanced by Filipino groups, by some church groups and social workers, and by some people with nativist views.

In response to pressure from the exclusionists and other groups, the U.S. Congress passed the Repatriation Act of 1935. It provided free transportation back to the Philippine Islands; once back, the repatriates were subject to the same annual immigration quota of 50 as everyone else in the islands. The quota restriction eliminated the possibility of Filipino support for the repatriation program, so that from the exclusionists' point of view the law proved ineffective: only 2,190 of the 45,000 Filipinos in the United States agreed to return. By 1937, according to the U.S. Immigration Service, only about 7,400 Filipinos had gone back, including both government-sponsored and privately sponsored returnees. Either the depression and unemployment had not deprived many of the hope of achieving their economic goal, or perhaps some could not face returning home precisely because of their failure. In any case the exclusionists' efforts slowed down; many Filipinos remained, but the Tydings-McDuffie quota had provided an effective brake on further immigration.

As U.S. nationals, the Filipinos were in an ambiguous legal position which was not resolved until 1946 when they were declared eligible for citizenship. In 1902 Congress had declared that all Philippine residents who had been Spanish subjects and their progeny were citizens of the Philippine Islands; in 1906 it passed an act indicating that any citizen of a territory owing allegiance to the United States might under certain circumstances apply for U.S. citizenship. Opinions differed over the interpretation of a 1790 statute stating that "free white persons" were eligible for citizenship; this statute had become the basis for legislation depriving Asians of the right to be naturalized. Which Filipinos, if any, were "white" was disputed in several court cases, and in all of them the Filipino seeking naturalization lost the case. At the end of World War I, Filipinos who had enlisted and served three years in the U.S. Navy or Marines could petition for U.S. citizenship, and several did so. Filipinos in general, however, remained in an ambiguous status as nationals.

Although until 1934 Filipinos could enter the United States without restriction, almost all the advantages of being a national ended there. The U.S. Civil Service Commission allowed them to take examinations to qualify for federal jobs, but each state had its own rules pertaining to professional licensing. Most states did not allow them to practice law, medicine, and other professions. As noncitizens Filipinos also did not qualify for federal relief funds, until in 1937 Harry Hopkins, head of the Works Progress Administration, made them eligible to work for WPA projects on a nonpreferential basis.

At the outbreak of World War II, Filipinos were unable either to volunteer for, or be drafted into, the armed forces: their status as nationals exempted them. The U.S. Congress began to move toward granting citizenship to Filipinos during the war, since it made little sense for the United States to fight for Philippine freedom while denying Filipinos the rights of citizenship within its borders. Draft boards were eventually notified that nationals who were citizens of the Philippines could be "reclassified in the same manner as citizens of the United States." Some immigrants enlisted to form the First Filipino Regiment. Provisions were made to swear its members in as American citizens before they went overseas, but other Filipinos had to wait for the Naturalization Act of 1946.

POSTWAR IMMIGRATION

New arrivals from the Philippines after World War II and into the 1950s steadily increased; between 1950 and 1970 the number of Filipinos residing in the United States almost doubled. When the Philippines achieved independence in 1946, earlier immigrants sought to fill the annual quota of 100 with wives, children, and other kin, or with Filipino women they could marry. Their efforts were successful enough to produce a substantial number of second-generation Filipino Americans. In the immediate postwar period both the old-timers and the new arrivals still found themselves largely restricted to jobs as unskilled or semiskilled laborers, especially in agriculture. Only a few found their way into industrial and construction jobs, partly because California's trade unions remained closed to them and other Asians. Hawaii's unions were integrated much earlier, making it easier for them to enter the skilled labor force on the islands.

The 1965 Immigration Act dramatically changed the composition and increased the number of Filipino immigrants. The first immigrants had been peasants who had left a colonial society that had barely begun to enter the Western industrial world. Although many of the newer immigrants still came for the old reasons—Ilocanos were still looking for money to buy land—an increasing number had different motives. Arriving with wives and children, this new group clearly intended to settle down and remain. Women and men, most of whom were between 20 and 40 years old, came in about equal numbers; many came precisely because they had children and were looking for better opportunities than the Philippines seemed to offer them.

Table 1. Filipino immigration to the United States, 1966–1976.

Year	Number
1966	6,093
1967	10,865
1968	16,731
1969	20,744
1970	31,203
1971	28,471
1972	29,376
1973	30,799
1974	32,857
1975	31,751
1976	37,281

Source: U.S. Immigration and Naturalization Service, *Annual Report, 1976* (Washington, D.C., 1977), pp. 88–89.

More than two-thirds of the new arrivals qualified for immigration under the 1965 immigration act as "professional, technical, and kindred workers" whose skills were needed in the United States. Since the civil-rights movement had eliminated many of the discriminatory practices that would have denied them such employment earlier, most Filipinos encountered few of the problems of their predecessors. They did have to face other barriers, however, particularly the licensing problems of any alien not trained in an American professional school. Many newly arrived dentists, doctors, and pharmacists were forced to work at least temporarily in unskilled or semiskilled jobs to care for their families and fulfill the expectations of barrio kin until they could be properly licensed. Nurses fared much better because of several levels of licensing for which they could qualify. In 1968 one-third of all licenses in the United States issued to foreign nurses were granted to Filipinos fluent in English, primarily because they had been trained by a curriculum similar to that used in the United States.

Most of the new immigrants flocked to the big cities —Los Angeles, Chicago, New York, or Honolulu. They frequently sent for relatives in the Philippines to join them as soon as they could help finance the trip, provide housing, and assist them in finding jobs. Typical in this process was the immigrant to Hawaii who paid the airfare for his three brothers to join him; they in turn sent for their families, and before long more of the kin lived in Hawaii and California than in the Philippines. Large numbers of Filipinos continue to arrive each year, and the Filipino communities remain in a state of flux.

The recent immigrants brought with them the same kinship and alliance system as the earlier immigrants, but they have found it easier to maintain. Cheap airfares and incentives by the Philippine government encourage Filipinos in Hawaii and on the mainland to make visits home. The visits provide opportunities to pass on first-hand information about life in the United States and to bring home the dollars that help to pay taxes, buy land, send relatives to school, and support hometown organizations and churches. In the barrio, these dollars are viewed as common funds available to the immigrant's family and honorary kin as a part of the earner's social obligations. In the 1970s the mayors of several Ilocos Norte towns reported that $35,000 a month was being received in the form of remittances from recent emigrants and pension checks for old Hawaiianos.

When one Filipino meets another in the United States the first step is to establish place of origin: this determines linguistic background and consequently the language to be used—a common regional language or Tagalog. Although most immigrants know both English and Tagalog, the use of English is frowned upon. Strong feelings still divide Ilocano from Visayan from Tagalog, and each group still seeks out its own kin for social and business relationships, and lives in the same neighborhood.

Filipino loyalty to family and regional group has militated against their achieving success in American politics. They see no clear reason to form a Filipino political organization, and their tendency to group exclusiveness makes it difficult for any one Filipino to gain widespread support from the others. They also regard as unacceptable behavior any attempt by a member to seek and win office, because it sets him above the others. Provincial allegiances and personality clashes lead Filipino organizations to multiply rather than coalesce. But change in the political arena is becoming evident as the first large group of American-born Filipinos reaches adulthood. Some spokesmen now see the future of the Filipinos in the United States as fairly bright. Like many immigrants, they continue to be interested in the welfare of their homeland, but a large number of them will begin to have a greater impact on American affairs as the group becomes more settled and its children mature.

Bibliography
Studies on recent immigrants remain tentative and are not comparable to those for the earlier arrivals. The classic study on the first migration remains Bruno Lasker, *Filipino Immigration to Continental United States and to Hawaii* (Chicago, 1931). A more recent general study is H. Brett Melendy, *Asians in America: Filipinos, Koreans and East Indians* (Boston, 1977). J.M. Saniel, ed., *The Filipino Exclusion Movement, 1927–1935* (Quezon City, Philippines, 1967), includes essays on both Hawaii and California. Two anthologies compiled by the Asian American Studies Center, University of California, Los Angeles, are pertinent: *Letters in Exile: An Introductory Reader on the History of Pilipinos in America* (Los Angeles, 1976), and Emma Gee, ed., *Counterpoint: Perspectives on Asian America* (Los Angeles, 1976).

Two famous autobiographical accounts are Manuel Buaken, *I Have Lived with the American People* (Caldwell, Idaho, 1948), and Carlos Bulosan, *America Is in the Heart: A Personal History* (1946; reprint, Seattle, 1973). Roman P. Cariaga, *The Filipinos in Hawaii: Economic and Social Conditions, 1906–1936* (Honolulu, 1937), describes plantation life and includes some idealized biographical sketches. For Filipinos in New Jersey, see the essay by Gonzalo A. Velez in *The New Jersey Ethnic Experience,* ed. Barbara Cunningham (Union City, N.J., 1977).

During the anti-Filipino agitation of the 1930s, Emory S. Bogardus wrote *Anti-Filipino Race Riots: A Report Made to the Ingram Institute of Social Studies of San Diego* (San Diego, Calif., 1930). The California State Department of Industrial Relations, *Facts about Filipino Immigration into California* (Sacramento, 1930), is a classic expression of fear and hostility.

Statistical data on immigration and socioeconomic conditions appear in Andrew W. Lind, *Hawaii's People,* 3d ed. (Honolulu, 1967), and Charles B. Keely, "Philippine Migration: Internal Movements and Emigration to the United States," *International Migration Review* 7 (1973): 177–187. The most comprehensive bibliography is Shiro Saito, *Filipinos Overseas: A Bibliography* (New York, 1977). The largest collections of materials are at the University of Hawaii library and in the holdings of the Asian American Studies Center, University of California, Los Angeles.

H. BRETT MELENDY

FINNS

Although Finns settled in America as early as the 1630s and 1640s, large-scale immigration from their

part of Europe began only after the middle of the 19th century. Thousands of Norwegians and Swedes led the way, and after the Civil War, Finns and Danes came in greater numbers than before. The immigration from Finland to the United States reached its peak between 1899 and World War I, after which most Finnish emigrants settled elsewhere, chiefly Sweden, Canada, and Australia. In 1970 the first- and second-generation Finns in the United States numbered some 204,000, a much smaller group than the comparable populations of Swedes (806,000) and Norwegians (614,000), but not much smaller than the Danes (325,000).

HISTORY

The origins of the Finnish people remain relatively obscure. Before the beginning of the Christian era, migrants belonging to the Finno-Ugric language group began to settle in Finland. Probably originating in the middle Volga region, they dispersed from there into the Baltic and other areas. By the 11th century Swedish settlers were also arriving in the southwest part of Finland. Thus the population of Finland was divided between the Finnish-speaking majority and the Swedish-speaking minority, which constituted about 14 percent of the population in 1880.

In the 12th and 13th centuries Sweden sent many military and missionary expeditions to Finland to gain new fiefs for Swedish nobles and to Christianize the Finns. Finally, in the 14th century, Sweden completed the process of acquiring Finland. Two centuries later King Gustavus Vasa, intent on centralizing his authority, seized the Swedish fiefs in Finland, which was given the status of a grand duchy, and introduced the Protestant Reformation. Eventually Lutheranism became the state religion. By the early 1600s the population of the Duchy of Finland had increased to about 400,000. During the reign of Gustavus Adolphus (1611–1632), Sweden became a European power and tightened its control over Finland. Swedish nobles and military officials acquired more land; by the 1650s the nobles owned about half the settled area of Finland.

Sweden's rise in status under Gustavus Adolphus awakened mercantilist ambitions that, a few years after his death, inspired the Swedes to colonize in the New World. In 1638 a trading company formed by private investors, including Klaus Fleming (a Finnish-born noble and vice admiral in the Swedish navy), established New Sweden on a 35-mile stretch of land along the Delaware River. When settlers were difficult to recruit, the company made efforts to send Finns from the Värmland region of Sweden, where for several decades Swedish officials had encouraged Finns to settle and clear land by burning trees and brush. By the 1630s such practices were banned as wasteful, and violators were punished. Convicted "burnbeaters" were permitted to emigrate, however, instead of serving prison sentences. In 1655 at least a third of the more than 300 settlers of New Sweden were Finns. Ironically, shortly after the Swedes lost the colony to the Dutch in 1656, the company's twelfth expedition, including almost 100 Finns, arrived in America.

During 17 years of Swedish rule the colony developed other settlements besides Fort Christina (present-day Wilmington, Del.), such as Wicacoa near Philadelphia and, on the New Jersey side of the Delaware River, Rac-

coon (Swedesboro) and Finns Point, which is now the name of a Finnish cemetery near Salem. When the Dutch seized the colony in 1656, Finns and Swedes who were unwilling to accept the new rulers crossed into New Jersey and established farms under the English.

In spite of intermingling with the Dutch, English, and other nationalities, the Finns and Swedes managed to maintain their group identity for some decades. A group of them left their early churches and established a new one at Raccoon, and in 1669 a settler known as "Long Finn" led an uprising against the English, who had taken New Sweden from the Dutch in 1664. When William Penn arrived in Pennsylvania in 1682, he acknowledged the Swedish and Finnish role in developing the colony's agriculture, as did another Englishman, Thomas Paskell, who described the two groups as "ingeneous people." The settlers and their descendants learned to speak English and began to forget Finnish and Swedish. Eventually their churches were taken over by English-speaking Episcopalians, place names were changed, and family names became Anglicized, obscur-

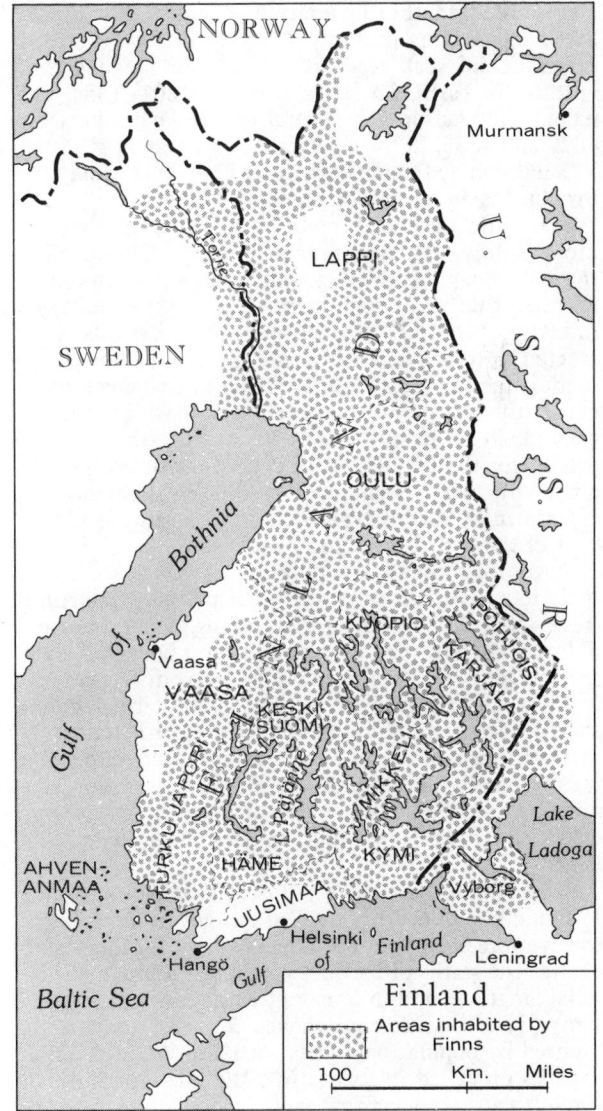

ing their origin. By the end of the 18th century few traces remained of the Delaware Finns.

For nearly a century and a half after the end of the colonizing venture along the Delaware River, Finland remained a duchy of Sweden. During a famine in the 1690s one-third of its population died of starvation or disease. In the early 1700s Russia, at war with Sweden, occupied Finland for 13 years. From 1750 to 1810, a period of peaceful growth, the population of Finland doubled. Both agriculture and commerce slowly expanded, and Finland became a major exporter of tar, made in the province of Vaasa. Finnish society was increasingly dominated by the "Swedicized" middle and upper classes, who were separated from the masses by wealth, position, and privilege, as well as language.

In 1808 Russia, again at war with Sweden, conquered Finland, and in 1809 Sweden formally transferred the duchy to Russia. During more than a century of Russian rule, the Grand Duchy of Finland was autonomous in internal affairs. The first decades of this period were associated with growing religious and political unrest. The rural revivalist followers of Lars Levi Laestadius resisted the duchy's state church, and Finnish nationalists challenged the domination of public life by the Swedish-speaking minority. They encouraged Finns to organize and seek recognition for their language and culture. In particular, Elias Lönnrot (1802–1884) collected and transcribed the oral epic *Kalevala* between 1829 and 1835. In the 1860s another nationalist, Johan V. Snellman, led the fight to make Finnish coequal with Swedish as an official language.

Economic and social conditions also began to change more rapidly. The government of the duchy continued the policy of consolidating land holdings, begun during Swedish rule, and lifted restrictions on commerce and industry. New textile factories and sawmills were erected in towns and cities, and there the labor movement gained a foothold. These economic changes accelerated the growth of the urban sector, which had expanded slowly until about 1850. At that time about 6 percent of the population of over 1.6 million lived in cities. By 1900 the number of city dwellers had increased more than 200 percent and constituted 12 percent of the over 2.6 million population.

By contrast, the rural population had increased only a little more than 60 percent in that period. Opportunities in the rural sector were shrinking. The proportion of landowners among the heads of rural households decreased from over 50 percent in 1815 to only 23 percent in 1901, and the number of tenants and farm laborers soared correspondingly. By the end of the century a third of those on the land were tenants, and 43 percent were laborers. Both groups were under mounting economic pressure to abandon the country for the growing cities and towns—whether in Finland or in another land.

There were unwelcome political developments too. In the late 19th century the Russian government began to pay more heed to its developing duchy. It proposed to change the status of the duchy, to make Russian the official language, and to conscript Finns into the Russian army. The Russification movement was temporarily blunted by popular opposition in 1905. When the Bolsheviks prevailed in Russia in 1917, the Finnish Diet established an independent republic, which the new So-

viet government was the first to recognize. Immediately afterward, in January 1918, a civil war erupted between the eventually victorious bourgeois nationalists and the socialists. The Republic of Finland was plagued by political instability in the 1920s and 1930s and was forced to cede part of its territory to the U.S.S.R. after the Russo-Finnish War of 1939–1940. It retained its independence, however, and since then has pursued generally neutralist foreign policies.

FINNISH EMIGRATION

Although Finnish cities and towns attracted most of the rural migrants before the 1860s, a few of these displaced people left Finland altogether. During the 1830s and 1840s Norway lured hundreds of the followers of Laestadius to engage in fishing, agriculture, and copper mining. In the same era about 200 Finns went to work in Alaska, which then belonged to Russia. One of the Finnish-born newcomers, Arvid A. Etholén, served as governor there in the early 1840s.

The other emigrants from Finland before 1860 were mostly sailors who deserted their ships to work in American ports such as Boston and New York. One, Charles Linn, went to Alabama in 1838 and became one of the richest men in the South. The California gold rush of 1849 lured more sailors from their ships, and in 1854 still others who wanted to avoid service in the Crimean War deserted Russian ships to remain in the United States. After the outbreak of the Civil War in 1861, the Union navy recruited some of them. Although they numbered only a few hundred, the sailors circulated news about the United States to friends and relatives at home.

In the mid-1860s Finnish immigration to the United States began to accelerate. Because of the need for laborers to develop the copper mines of the Keweenaw Peninsula of northern Michigan, companies sent agents to recruit miners from northern Norway, where the Finns had settled earlier. In 1864 about 20 Finns came with Norwegians to work for the Quincy Mining Company near Hancock, Mich. Other Finns who were not satisfied with life in Norway left with Norwegians who were seeking land in Saint Peter and Red Wing, Minn. Although only some 700 to 1,000 Norwegian Finns immigrated from 1864 to 1885, they introduced Michigan and Minnesota to the thousands from Finland who followed later. In 1866 the first immigrants arrived from the province of Vaasa. Probably only a few hundred came directly from Finland during the 1860s.

An estimated 3,000 more emigrants left Finland in the 1870s, and thereafter the exodus increased rapidly. About 21,000 emigrated between 1880 and 1886, and 40,000 from 1887 through 1892. In 1893, when over 9,000 Finns received passports to go overseas, mainly to the United States, the Finnish government began to collect statistics on emigration more systematically. Whereas nearly 16,000 applicants secured passports between 1894 and 1898, in 1899 alone the total was over 12,000. During the next two decades, largely before World War I, almost 237,000 Finns received passports. The largest number issued in any one year was 23,152 for 1902. Between 1893 and 1920 nearly 274,000 persons obtained passports to travel to the United States and elsewhere. While the mother tongue of most emi-

grants was Finnish, a minority, mostly from western and southwestern Finland, spoke Swedish.

Of the applicants receiving passports between 1893 and 1920, the vast majority were from rural areas. Almost 8 percent were landowners or agricultural tenants (*torpparit*) and 34 percent were their children; while 25 percent were cottagers or agricultural laborers; 12 percent were without fixed occupations; 6 percent were domestic servants; and 9 percent, skilled craftsmen or factory workers. Although represented in growing numbers toward the end of the period, city dwellers accounted for only 13 percent of the total.

Throughout, the majority of applicants for passports were young unmarried adults. Three-fourths of those who applied between 1901 and 1920 were unmarried. Over two-thirds were between 16 and 30 years old; persons between 31 and 40 were the next largest group. The majority thus came from the most mobile sector of society and were of prime working age.

Because emigration was largely a by-product of the forces that created rural dislocation, the main reasons for leaving Finland were economic. Neither agriculture nor industry provided adequate employment for the surplus rural population. Over 60 percent of the emigrants came from Vaasa and Oulu, which were among the least industrialized provinces. Between 1882 and 1902 some 2,000 migrants left Vaasa to work in Helsinki, but no less than 103,000 emigrated from Vaasa to the United States. Most Finnish migrants complained of rural exploitation and their inability to obtain land, and they sought better economic opportunities in the United States. Some undoubtedly wished to escape family tensions exacerbated by rural change and looked forward to the excitement of new experiences. Young men also fled to avoid conscription, and political refugees left to escape harassment. Unable to appreciate these reasons for leaving, the upper classes generally condemned the emigrants, accusing them of lack of patriotism and will to work. In an unsuccessful attempt to halt the exodus, clergymen and journalists warned of the moral danger and economic hardships in America. But only the economic depressions of 1893 and 1907 in the United States and the coming of World War I slowed the exodus.

Finns often journeyed to the United States by way of other European countries. In the earlier years of heavy emigration, they usually traveled first to Sweden, sailed from there to English North Sea ports like Hull, and transferred by train to Liverpool, which was their point of departure on transatlantic liners for New York. A German company also transported Finnish travelers by ship and train to Bremerhaven, where they boarded oceangoing liners. After 1891 the Finland Steamship Company began carrying most passengers to England from the Finnish port of Hangö (Hanko). Between 1891 and 1914, 70 percent of the travelers paid for their own passage. The rest—usually women and children and the very poor—received prepaid tickets from friends and relatives in the United States. Overseas travel was at its peak during the spring and summer months.

Most Finns headed for the tier of 13 northern states stretching from the Northeast through the Midwest to the Pacific Coast. In 1900 almost 47 percent of the nearly 63,000 Finns in the United States resided in Michigan and Minnesota. Another 15 percent lived in Massachusetts and New York. About 27 percent lived in the following states, each of which reported at least 2,000 Finns: Washington, Oregon, California, Montana, Wisconsin, Illinois, Ohio, Pennsylvania, and New Jersey. The rest were scattered, with the fewest in the South and the Southwest. By 1910 the Finnish-born residents of the United States numbered about 130,000, and 10 years later, nearly 150,000. In 1920, although more Finns continued to live in Michigan and Minnesota than in any other states, the Finnish populations of New York, Massachusetts, and some other states were growing more rapidly in response to employment opportunities. The Swedish-speaking Finns lived in many areas settled by Finnish-speaking immigrants, especially Washington, Minnesota, Michigan, New York, and Massachusetts. They represented almost 12 percent of all Finnish-born persons enumerated in 1920, about their share of the population in the homeland.

Finnish immigrants often moved one or more times to find better job opportunities, because few were content with their first place of employment. Many worked in dangerous mines like the one in Hanna, Wyo., where 96 Finns were killed by an explosion in 1903. They also suffered wage reductions and periodic unemployment. No line of work seemed to bring economic security. Whatever the reasons for leaving jobs, their search for employment created a continuing turnover in the population of immigrant communities. Until World War I, workers moved from mine to mine. The copper mines of Hancock, Mich., and Butte, Mont., periodically expanded their labor forces, and after the early 1890s the opening of iron mines drew men to northern Minnesota.

Salmon fishing provided jobs at Astoria, Ore., as did lumbering in Washington and California. Lake ports such as Ashtabula and Conneaut in Ohio employed Finns to unload iron-ore boats, and steel mills in Monessen, Pa., opened up new jobs. Carpenters were employed in new construction projects, especially in New York City. Finns worked in textile mills in Fitchburg, Mass., and in the granite quarries of Cape Ann in the same state. Some became shopkeepers and salesmen. Even more became farmers. By 1920 almost 15,000 Finns were operating farms, about two-thirds in Michigan, Wisconsin, and Minnesota. Although women sometimes worked in mills, they were most commonly employed as domestic servants. Often they were the real farm operators, as the men were likely to hold part-time jobs in addition to farming. Because of the vagaries of American employment and perhaps for other reasons, close to 30 percent of the Finns who entered the United States in the first quarter of the 20th century eventually returned to the homeland.

Only a minority of the newly arrived immigrants were married, and most had no family life. Unmarried men lived in rooming and boarding houses, and single women working as domestic servants usually resided in their employers' homes. Married men either came with their wives and children or sent for them after finding employment. Finnish immigrants usually did not intermarry with other groups, despite an imbalance in the sex ratio. In 1900 there were 182 males for every 100 females, though by 1920 the ratio had dropped to 132:100. The sexes were most balanced in New England and most imbalanced in the lumbering and mining

areas of the West, which in the earlier years generally attracted only males. In the Middle Atlantic states, however, women outnumbered men because of employment opportunities for female domestic servants in the larger cities. In 1910 over 90 percent of the 81,357 American-born children of Finns had two Finnish-born parents. Ten years later the percentage was only slightly less for 145,506 children, almost equal the number of foreign-born Finns.

ORGANIZATIONS IN THE UNITED STATES

Most of the immigrants generally had had little or no organizational experience at home, but immigration seems to have released their associative spirit. New experiences and the need for mutual assistance inspired them to organize. Because there was no state church to serve them, they had to form their own congregations. Their isolation from existing American organizations further impelled them to establish their own. Nor was there just one association of a kind, for dissidents—inspired perhaps by the lack of restraints in the new country—often organized rival groups. The increasing numbers of Finnish halls and churches testified to their enthusiasm for associative activities.

In 1867 the first organized groups were started by the Norwegian Finns who had emigrated from rural districts swept by the Laestadian revivalism in northern Norway and the neighboring part of Finland. Until the 1880s most Finns in the United States came from that area, so the Laestadians were the largest religious group among the newcomers. Because they believed in the personal confession of sin and absolution, they had no need for ordained clergymen or for liturgy in religious services. In 1867 Finnish Laestadians in Hancock, Mich., joined Swedish and Norwegian Lutherans in establishing a Lutheran congregation, but four years later, displeased with the Norwegian pastor's attempt to discipline them, the Laestadians formed their own church in nearby Calumet under the leadership of Salomon Korteniemi (1854–1919). In 1879 they began calling themselves Apostolic Lutherans, a name that was often used thereafter to identify other Laestadians. In 1888 the Calumet congregation split into two factions over doctrinal and other matters. In 1890 Arthur L. Heideman (1862–1928) arrived from Finland to serve as pastor for the faction that retained the church; the losers formed a new congregation. As believers in strong congregational autonomy, they had no central church body to define doctrines and polity, and later controversies further divided the Apostolic Lutherans. Their congregations were particularly strong in rural areas of Michigan, Minnesota, and some western states.

Adherents of the Lutheran state church of Finland also organized. After the Apostolic Lutherans withdrew or were expelled from the first Hancock church, other Finns acquired it. Their fellow believers also established two nearby congregations, securing as their pastor Alfred E. Backman (1844–1909), who arrived from Finland in 1876 and stayed seven years. His successor, Juho Kustaa Nikander (1855–1919), arrived in Hancock early in 1885 and insisted on the need for a trained clergy and a proper Lutheran ritual. During his leadership of more than 30 years, his supporters established new congregations. In 1890, rejecting a proposal for a national church body with a bishop, Nikander and his associates established the Suomi Synod, or the Finnish Evangelical Lutheran Church of America. In 1890 the Suomi Synod had 9 congregations with 2,100 members; eight years later its 43 congregations had 9,600 members. Relying in part on trained clergymen from Finland, the synod gained supporters throughout the major Finnish communities.

The announcement of the Suomi Synod aroused a wave of opposition, especially against the clergy, that lasted into the 20th century. Critics argued that the synod would copy the state church of Finland by introducing clerical authoritarianism and exacting financial contributions. In Calumet the Lutheran pastor excommunicated about 500 disaffected church members. The dissidents established an independent "people's" church, which later was active in forming a new religious body. Other independent Lutheran congregations were also organized by critics of the synod. In 1898 Kalle A.A. Koski, pastor of an independent congregation in Rock Springs, Wyo., issued a call to unite the people's congregations and received the support of Kalle Haapakoski (1867–1917), an editor opposed to clerical authority. The representatives of seven congregations met with Koski that year at Rock Springs and established the Finnish–American Evangelical Lutheran National Church. The founders were more preoccupied with church polity and the rights of laymen than with theology, but later the new church subscribed to the theology of the Gospel Society of Finland, which emphasized conversion. By 1900 the National Lutherans had 6,210 members in the Midwest and other regions.

In addition, Finns established churches under the leadership of American Congregationalists, who began their missionary work in 1889. The Congregationalists' chief centers of activity among Finns were in Massachusetts and New York. Methodists who had been converted by a mission school in Finland were active in Minnesota. By 1900 these various congregations, along with those of the Apostolic, National, and Synod Lutherans, numbered about 100.

Although the churches provided social activities, all kinds of local, state, and national secular societies complemented them. The temperance movement was strong in late-19th-century Finland, and the Finns promoted its goals in the United States as well. By the 1880s temperance societies appeared in Hancock and Ashtabula. The Synod Lutherans, who were particularly active in promoting them, united their societies into the Finnish National Temperance Brotherhood in 1888. Rival groups, disliking the brotherhood because of its clerical ties and ban on dancing, a year later formed the Finnish Friends of Temperance. Other independent temperance societies were also established. The temperance hall was a prominent feature of many Finnish communities.

Another type of society was the mutual-aid association, which assisted the destitute and provided sickness, accident, and funeral benefits. In 1898 the Knights of Kaleva was established as a fraternal society to promote the preservation of Finnish culture and to encourage harmony within the immigrant community. The Finns also started a few literary groups, although most community libraries were maintained by temperance and fraternal societies. In the 1890s workingmen began

forming special associations, such as the Saima Aid Society in Fitchburg, Mass., and the Imatra Society in Brooklyn, N.Y. The membership of all these organizations fluctuated, because immigrants moved around in search of work.

Reinforcing the sense of collective self-consciousness, immigrant publishers offered a variety of Finnish-language newspapers and other publications. In 1876 Anders Johan Muikku (1846–1877) of Hancock issued the first newspaper, which lasted only a few months. Other early publishers were equally hard pressed financially and lacked editorial talent to sustain their journalistic ventures. One of the first successful publishers was August Nylund (1836–1892), who began printing the *Uusi Kotimaa* (New Homeland) at Minneapolis in 1881. Later his newspaper, which lasted until 1931, was located at New York Mills, Minn. In 1891 the predecessor of *Siirtolainen* (Immigrant) was established; five years later the Finnish American Publishing Company acquired the newspaper (1893–1937) and published it in Brooklyn and elsewhere. Another well-known newspaper, the *Amerikan Sanomat* (American Tidings, 1897–1913) was published by August Edwards in Ashtabula, Ohio. Other early papers, such as the *Amerikan Uutiset* (American News), published by Kalle Haapakoski in Calumet, Mich., during the mid-1890s, were short-lived. Religious, temperance, and labor groups also published periodicals, though rarely newspapers. These pioneer publications were the first of over 350 newspapers and periodicals eventually initiated by the Finns. They were supplemented by a variety of annual calendars or yearbooks, festival journals, religious tracts, music books, and romantic novels. In 1892 Andrew Langila, himself an immigrant, published a novel about Finnish experiences in the United States. Although most publishers were primarily interested in profit, they shared the immigrants' interest in organized activities. The number of newspapers and other publications can be considered an index of growth of ethnic cohesiveness.

The Swedish-speaking Finns who came to the United States remained apart and established their own associations. Active in at least three Lutheran congregations during the 1890s, they organized new ones in the next decade at Gardner, Mass., Duluth, Minn., and Metropolitan and Thompson, Mich. Most of these churches became members of the Augustana Synod formed by Swedish Lutherans. In 1889 the first mutual-aid society for Swedish-speaking Finns and three years later the first temperance society were established in Worcester, Mass., and were followed by others. Also the *Finska Amerikanaren* (Finnish American, f. 1897), which first appeared in Worcester and later moved to Brooklyn, became the main newspaper of the Swedish-speaking Finns. In addition, particularly in areas where their numbers were small, they participated in organizations formed by Swedish immigrants, and if they were bilingual, also in those sponsored by their Finnish-speaking countrymen.

COMMUNITY LIFE, 1899–1920

Efforts to organize the Finnish community continued in the opening decades of the 20th century. By 1916 the three Lutheran groups had at least 245 congregations with over 33,000 first- and second-generation members.

In 1904 the largest group, the Suomi Synod, had established a seminary at Suomi College in Hancock because there were not enough clergymen from Finland to meet their needs. The Apostolic Lutherans experienced new doctrinal conflicts, while the National Lutherans and others were challenged by socialist members. The three Lutheran groups together probably represented five-sixths of the immigrant churchgoers.

Although competing groups drew members from it, the temperance movement still had about 200 societies with over 11,000 members in 1908. Mutual-benefit societies and consumer cooperatives were organized, and the Knights of Kaleva organized a ladies' auxiliary in 1904. Most organizations sponsored evening entertainments, concerts, picnics, and other activities. While relying on commercial publishers of papers like the *Päivälehti* (Daily Journal, 1901–1948), the major organizations also began to publish their own newspapers. In 1899 the Synod Lutherans led this new trend by starting the *Amerikan Suometar* (American Finn, 1899–1962), and eventually the organizations overshadowed the commercial publishers. Indeed, the period between 1899 and World War I was the golden age of competing organizations.

This organized community life was invigorated by the labor movement. In 1899 Antero F. Tanner (1868–1917) established a short-lived socialist club at Rockport, Mass. One of his followers, Martin Hendrickson, joined him in publishing a socialist newspaper for a few months in 1900. Their cause was further publicized by Matti Kurikka (1863–1915), the promoter of a utopian socialist community in British Columbia, which failed disastrously. In 1902 the Imatra Society of Brooklyn began to combine 32 workingmen's societies into the American-Finnish Workers' League Imatra, but by 1906 most of these societies had withdrawn to form the 2,000-member Finnish Socialist Federation, which joined the American Socialist party. The Imatra Society, however, remained outside the socialist movement, and its members employed Kurikka to edit their newly founded newspaper, *New Yorkin Uutiset* (New York News, f. 1906).

In the meantime the Finnish Socialist Federation recruited members among liberal churchmen and temperance supporters as well as newly arrived immigrants. By 1913 the federation had 260 local chapters with 12,651 members. Its chapters owned or rented halls for dramatic, musical, literary, athletic, social, and other activities. The socialists established the newspaper *Työmies* (Workingman, f. 1903) in Worcester, Mass., then moved it to Hancock, Mich. Next they began *Raivaaja* (Pioneer, f. 1905) in Fitchburg, Mass., and two years later, *Toveri* (Comrade, 1907–1930) in Astoria, Ore. In 1907 supporters of the federation took control of the Work People's College, near Duluth, Minn., from the National Lutherans. The school was used partly to train functionaries for socialist organizations. Prominent in the Minnesota iron strike of 1907 and the Michigan copper strike of 1913–1914, the socialists also established consumers' cooperatives to aid the class struggle against capitalism.

Although troubled by internal strife even before 1910, the Finnish Socialist Federation managed to maintain the momentum of its growth until World War I. Its chapters continued to debate the relative merits of

political action and industrial organization. The industrial unionists backed the Industrial Workers of the World. They believed that workers in all industries should unite into one giant organization and rely on economic rather than political power to topple capitalism. In 1914 between 3,000 and 4,000 industrial unionists withdrew from or were expelled by the federation. They proceeded to take control of the Work People's College as well as socialist halls, especially in Minnesota, and to establish the paper *Industrialisti* (Industrialist, 1917–1975), which cut into the circulation of *Työmies*.

This confrontation occurred while *Työmies* was being boycotted by advertisers and antisocialists dismayed by its support for striking copper workers in 1913–1914. The paper recovered, however, after being moved to Superior, Wis., and eventually attracted over 20,000 subscribers, a record probably never matched by any other Finnish newspaper. Meanwhile, socialists were establishing more cooperative stores, and in 1917 they organized the Central Cooperative Wholesale (CCW) to unite and serve their enterprises.

During World War I the labor movement suffered new blows. Industrial unionist leaders and the socialist editors of *Toveri* were arrested for opposing the war. Next the Bolshevik Revolution further divided the movement between supporters and opponents of Leninism. The left wing captured the Finnish Socialist Federation, which withdrew from the American Socialist party. From then on the labor movement remained bitterly divided into leftist and rightest factions.

The continuing arrival of more Swedish-speaking Finns reinforced their community life. The Swedish-speaking Finns established about 25 new Lutheran congregations, which had some 4,000 members by 1920. In addition they organized Baptist and Covenant churches. By 1920 the sick-benefit societies, which had formed a league in 1900, numbered about 50 chapters with approximately 3,500 members. The temperance societies, which likewise united into a league in 1902, had 60 chapters with about 2,500 members in 1920. The two leagues merged into a new organization, the Order of Runeberg, in 1920. On the eve of World War I the *Finska Amerikanaren* reached its peak of about 6,000 subscribers.

The Finns retained their ethnic ties. The new immigrants who kept arriving until World War I helped keep alive the use of the Finnish and Swedish languages. Except for those who came as young children and learned English readily, most immigrants never gave up their mother tongue for the new language. Nor did they forget other aspects of their cultural legacy, particularly familiar folk tunes and poetry. They practiced folk medicine, such as bloodletting, at times, and they built hay barns out of logs in the distinctive style used in Finland. Of all the old cultural practices, the use of the sauna for bathing was undoubtedly the most common. The cultural identity of the immigrants was further reinforced by nationalistic groups that proclaimed the need for ethnic unity, advocated the preservation of their heritage, and organized Finnish-language classes for children. The socialists, on the other hand, affirmed the need to unite workers of different ethnic backgrounds. Finnish immigrant communities in isolated rural areas probably preserved more cultural traditions than Finns living in urban centers, where they had to contend with the larger society.

Nevertheless, the new environment, whether rural or urban, was bound to alter the old cultural traditions and ways of thinking. It forced Finns to define their goals in "modern" ways, adopt new work styles, and eat unfamiliar foods. It also sharpened their self-awareness, which inspired them to undertake all kinds of collective efforts. Newspaper editors further reoriented their thinking through stories translated from American publications. Virtually all immigrants learned to use "Finglish," a blending of English words with Finnish case endings. Thus "farmer" became "farmari," and "to pick" became "pikata." Moreover, by 1920, 39 percent of the immigrant men had qualified for naturalization, which required knowledge of a certain amount of English. Most of these new citizens, though not the socialists, supported the Republican party, believing that the GOP was more likely to bring prosperity. The public schools also introduced immigrants and their children to new cultural influences. Whatever the degree and rate of acculturation, both the first and second generations were becoming Finnish Americans.

COMMUNITY LIFE AFTER 1920

World War I virtually ended Finnish immigration, and after the war other developments kept the influx low. Finnish Americans began a new stage in the process of acculturation. Immigration quotas enacted in the 1920s permitted only 471 Finns to enter the country annually between 1925 and 1929, and 566 thereafter; but except in 1928 this quota was never filled. Land reform and industrial development at home had by then reduced the pressures that had impelled the earlier exodus. In the Depression decade of the 1930s, only 1,538 Finns applied to enter the United States. Indeed, thousands already there left for Finland or Soviet Karelia, whose government, with the support of left-wing groups like the Finnish Workers Federation, was actively recruiting settlers to help develop its economy.

Death further reduced the ranks of immigrants. The Finnish-born population of the United States dropped almost 23 percent between 1920 and 1940, from almost 150,000 to just over 117,000. By 1940 the ratio of men to women was almost equal, and the decreasing number of unmarried men was hastening the disappearance of boarding and rooming houses in immigrant communities. Concurrently, American-born children of immigrants increased about 18 percent to 179,000 by 1930; the aging first generation was by then outnumbered by second-generation children who had never seen Finland.

Although land agents kept attempting to lure Finns to American farms after World War I, the majority pursued nonagricultural occupations and lived in urban areas. Still, in 1920 almost 47 percent resided in rural areas, and at least half of this rural group lived on farms. Two-thirds of the farmers were in Michigan, Wisconsin, and Minnesota, mainly on cutover land from which lumber companies had cleared the timber. A smaller number of Finnish farmers bought similar land in Oregon and Washington, and others secured old farms in Ohio, New York, and New England. In 1920 the average value of the farms owned by Finns was $5,275, in con-

trast to the $13,484 average value reported for all nationalities. Thus Finnish farmers often needed part-time employment to augment their farm income, which was further reduced by the agricultural crisis that began in the early 1920s. Their economic difficulties increased still more during the Great Depression of the 1930s.

Other Finns also faced economic difficulties, especially in the mining and lumbering areas. Automobile factories and steel mills created new job opportunities for some in the 1920s, but the Depression caused thousands to lose their jobs and seek public assistance. Except for a momentary, Depression-inspired movement from industry into agriculture, no major change occurred in the immigrants' occupational patterns. In 1940 a majority of Finns were still in urban areas, and half the rural residents resided on farms.

Because of the unstable economic conditions and the sharp drop in numbers of newcomers from Finland during the 1920s and 1930s, the supporters of churches, temperance societies, and similar groups could not easily maintain the level of their organized activities. The Depression made it especially difficult for them to support their organizations financially. The temperance movement, after recovering a little in the postwar period, was particularly hard hit and by 1934 had declined to about 50 societies. The Lutheran churches, too, ceased to expand. The Suomi Synod Lutherans continued to lose members from the mid-1920s until the end of the 1930s, and the National and Apostolic Lutherans also suffered losses. Between 1926 and 1936 these three Lutheran groups lost 31 percent of their membership, so that by 1936 they had only 340 congregations with about 44,000 members, including second-generation Finnish Americans. Swedish-speaking Finn groups, notably the Order of Runeberg, had similar losses.

The labor movement also lost momentum and splintered into factions. The industrial unionists, after achieving a peak of about 10,000 subscribers for their newspaper in the 1920s, declined in the next decade, losing some of their members to the Finnish Socialist Federation, which had withdrawn from the Socialist party and joined the American Workers' party. Four years later the federation was reorganized separately as the Finnish Workers Federation, and in 1941 it became a unit of the International Workers Order. During the 1930s its members supported the reviving trade-union movement. But their left-wing proletarian internationalism and support of the Russian Revolution antagonized right-wing socialists, who retained the newspaper *Raivaaja* and established a new federation within the Socialist party. In 1937 the right-wing federation withdrew from the party, and a few years later became the Finnish American League for Democracy. Although these groups were at times unable to retain ownership of their halls and suffered other setbacks during the Depression, most were able to continue functioning in the communities in which they had been active in the 1920s.

Despite all these difficulties the level of organized activities remained relatively high in the interwar period. In order to offset their losses of members, church, temperance, labor, and other groups made more strenuous efforts to raise funds and to enlist the services of their

supporters, and they also had some success in recruiting among the second generation. The success of the new consumer cooperatives was impressive. Promoted mainly by socialists during the decade of World War I, in the 1920s the cooperative movement, under the leadership of the Central Cooperative Wholesale of Superior, Wis., attracted many farmers. The CCW, which was close to the left-wing labor movement, at first regarded cooperatives as instruments of the class struggle. In the 1930s, however, after rejecting a request to aid Communists, the CCW repudiated the class struggle. By 1940 it had over 100 member societies in the Midwest, dominated largely by Finns. The spirit of activism was also sustained by other cooperative societies and by various clubs and societies as well as newspaper publishing houses.

Meanwhile the process of acculturation continued to reshape the immigrants and their children, who learned to rely less on the Finnish language. By 1930, according to the judgment of census enumerators, almost 90 percent of all Finnish immigrants who were 10 or older could speak English. Those who did not speak English were mainly people over 44, especially farm women. Men had always had more opportunities than women to learn English because of their contacts at places of employment and business. Partly because of the increasing number of children unable or unwilling to speak Finnish, the immigrants also gradually began to use English in their group activities. Although ethnic nationalists resisted the shift, in 1926 the Suomi Synod Lutherans conceded that English might be used in conducting their young people's meetings. By the 1930s more churches were conducting English-language activities. Other groups, such as the Central Cooperative Wholesale and the Order of Runeberg, introduced the use of English along with Finnish.

Another sign of acculturation was political involvement by immigrants and their children. The first—and in the late 1970s still the only—naturalized Finn to be sent to Congress, Oscar J. Larson (1871–1957), was elected in 1920. Finnish Americans also served in the state legislatures of Oregon and Montana, while others were elected to local offices in Hancock, Mich., and elsewhere. Others became local officials in their communities. Blaming the Republicans for the Depression, thousands of Finnish Americans shifted their political allegiance to the Democrats during the 1930s. In 1938 the major Finnish-American groups helped celebrate the 300th anniversary of New Sweden, thus associating their forebears with the origin of the modern United States. But the nationalistic groups continued to be proud of their cultural ties with the Republic of Finland, especially after war broke out between the Finns and the Soviet Union in 1939.

THE FADING IMMIGRANT COMMUNITY

After 1940 the total number of Finnish immigrants decreased, because few newcomers arrived from Europe to replace those who died. By 1960 half of the immigrants were 66 years old or more. Thousands of those who reached retirement age after World War II settled around Lantana, Lake Worth, and New Port Richey, Fla. Between 1940 and 1970 the number of immigrants decreased by more than 60 percent; they numbered only 45,449 by 1970. Their American-born children num-

bered 158,327 in that year. During World War II, thousands of Finnish Americans left their communities to serve with the armed forces or to work in industry. Others quit rural areas in the copper country of Michigan and elsewhere, especially during the 1950s.

These demographic developments lessened the role of immigrants in Finnish-American communities after World War II. Organized community life received only a momentary spurt as Finns formed new societies to aid the homeland and to commemorate the immigrant role in America. In addition, retired Finns in Florida were able to sustain a high level of organized activity as long as newcomers joined them from other communities. But the temperance societies, lacking new members to replace old ones, closed most of their halls, and the labor groups did the same. In the 1950s the left-wing labor movement was weakened by repressive measures taken by federal and state agencies. Organizations and commercial publishers suspended newspaper publication because of lack of readers. By 1980 only *Raivaaja*, *New Yorkin Uutiset*, and the *Työmies-Eteenpäin* survived, along with the newest paper, the *Amerikan Uutiset* (American News), founded under another name in 1932. The Swedish-speaking Finns still published *Norden* (North), the new name adopted by *Finska Amerikanaren* in 1935.

Some cooperatives had to close their stores during the 1950s. As the Finnish-born leaders of the cooperative societies declined in number, American-born Finns began to dominate the societies belonging to the CCW. Second-generation Finns were also active in churches, increasing the membership of the Suomi Synod congregations in particular. Fraternal societies, too, prolonged their existence by attracting the American-born.

The Finns have maintained strong community institutions since the late 1860s, but they and their children have not reproduced their cultural legacy intact from the Old World. The second generation's increased rate of intermarriage with non-Finns and their use of English have noticeably reduced their involvement with Finnish culture. That involvement has also been affected by external forces that have periodically reinforced or weakened interest in labor, temperance, and religious movements. When English-speaking Finnish Americans increasingly took control of immigrant societies after World War II, the process of acculturation was hastened. The CCW merged with the Midlands Cooperatives, a Minnesota-based organization, in 1963. About the same time, the Suomi Synod Lutherans joined non-Finns to establish the Lutheran Church in America, and the National Lutherans united with the Missouri Synod. American-born Finns also joined trade unions, business groups, and other organizations that had not been established by immigrants from Finland.

Yet not all of them forgot their Finnish ties. Perhaps for reasons of status, middle- and upper-class Finnish Americans were especially interested in historical societies and other organizations that celebrated their ethnic heritage. Cultural ties were affirmed by those who used "Finglish," read the *Kalevala*, and bathed in the sauna. But Finnish Americans did not primarily create the postwar vogue for saunas and Finnish imports, and this commercial promotion of Finland's culture was no measure of their own ethnic identity. By the late 1970s, in fact, it could not be claimed that the lives of most

Finnish Americans still revolved around the preservation of their ethnicity.

Bibliography
The major guide to printed primary and secondary materials is still John I. Kolehmainen, *The Finns in America: A Bibliographical Guide to Their History* (Hancock, Mich., 1947). A. William Hoglund, *Finnish Immigrants in America, 1880–1920* (Madison, 1960), is an overall account emphasizing organizational activities and providing bibliographical references. See also Anders Mattson Myhrman, *Finlandssvenskar i Amerika: The Finland-Swedes in America* (Helsinki, 1972).

The 17th-century immigration is examined in John Henry Wuorinen, *The Finns on the Delaware, 1638–1655: An Essay in American Colonial History* (1938; reprint, New York, 1966), and Federal Writers' Project, New Jersey, *The Swedes and Finns in New Jersey* (Bayonne, N.J., 1938).

The background of 19th- and 20th-century immigration is analyzed in Reino Kero, *Migration from Finland to North America in the Years between the United States Civil War and the First World War* (Turku, Finland, 1974). Other historical literature, exploring usually church, labor, and other organized activities include Ralph J. Jalkanen, ed., *The Faith of the Finns: Historical Perspectives on the Finnish Lutheran Church in America* (East Lansing, Mich., 1972), and *The Finns in North America: A Social Symposium* (Hancock, Mich., 1969); Michael G. Karni et al., eds., *The Finnish Experience in the Western Great Lakes Region* (Vammala, Finland, 1972); and Michael G. Karni and Douglas J. Ollila, Jr., eds., *For the Common Good: Finnish Immigrants and the Radical Response to Industrial America* (Superior, Wis., 1977). See also John I. Kolehmainen and George W. Hill, *Haven in the Woods: The Story of the Finns in Wisconsin* (Madison, 1965); Hans R. Wasastjerna, ed., *History of the Finns in Minnesota* (Duluth, Minn., 1957); and John I. Kolehmainen, *From Lake Erie's Shores to the Mahoning and Monongahela Valleys: A History of the Finns in Ohio, Western Pennsylvania and West Virginia* (New York Mills, Minn., 1977).

The major collection of printed and manuscript sources on Finnish immigration is at the Finnish American Historical Library, Suomi College, Hancock, Mich. Another significant collection is at the Immigration History Research Center of the University of Minnesota.

A. WILLIAM HOGLUND

FLATHEADS (Salish of Montana): *see* AMERICAN INDIANS

FLEMINGS: *see* BELGIANS

FOLKLORE

All groups inherit and develop ways of entertaining and instructing each other, ways that can be described as folklore. These become self-consciously enacted and practiced when the sense of family and community comes under question; this is the situation that commonly arises upon group movement, for migration and resettlement seem to engender cultural dislocation even under the best of circumstances. In these conditions folklore plays an important role in the lives of ethnic groups insofar as group members maintain connection with each other or with their homeland. To be sure, there are usually strong pressures to adopt the language and lore of the receiving culture. These pressures may raise the question of whether or not the most public and distinctive ways of displaying and celebrating one's cultural heritage should be maintained. Consequently, the study of the folklore of ethnic groups involves an analysis of traditional means of expression as they undergo self-conscious scrutiny both from group members and from outsiders.

The term folklore commonly refers to ways of talking, interacting, and performing, including traditional types of everyday expression such as proverbs, prayers, curses, jokes, riddles, superstitions (or, to use the more neutral term, statements of belief), tales, and songs. The

term also embraces the numerous types of story—anecdotes, testimonies, reminiscences—that emerge on both casual and ceremonial occasions. Folklore forms thus range from the short and economical devices employed in everyday interactions to the larger expressive genres, like songs and sermons, which are commonly called forth on special occasions.

However, folklore refers also to games, rituals, festivals, foods, health practices and beliefs, traditional crafts, and occupations. It encompasses work forms, serious as well as recreational, and draws from material as well as expressive culture. In the United States a distinction is often made between *folklore* and *folklife*. The former refers primarily to traditional ways of playing and performing, and the latter to the means and manner of work.

The study of folklore began with a special focus on country people and country ways and folklorists continue to favor the study of small communities, populated by those who interact regularly on a face-to-face basis. However, this emphasis on rural groups did not totally determine the perspective of American folklorists; in the charter of the American Folklore Society in 1888, not only were relics of past agrarian societies mentioned as an appropriate source of data, but also the traditions of American Indian tribes, blacks, and other ethnically distinct communities. The underlying principle bringing together such disparate groups is based on the sense of community they supposedly shared because of their social or geographical isolation, and on the relative intimacy between makers and users, performers and audience.

To the extent that verbal lore both instructs and entertains, it puts into words the most important shared values of group life; folklore in this way reveals attitudes that remind us of how life ought to be lived, cautioning us about the consequences of not following these precepts. Thus, folklore often provides the main patterns for the expression and enactment of group values and ideals.

To see the folk arts only from this instructive perspective, however, is to reduce such verbal formulations to the category of "kernels of wisdom," or worse, to clichés. However, on those occasions on which such playful forms as riddles, parodies, lampoons, jokes, and jibes are performed, the world view of the group may be given voice and tested—even turned upside down. Thus, the study of the folklore of a group opens the possibility of revealing the deepest feelings of its members at the same time as it may address their ways of playing, joking, testing the boundaries of the community from within.

In giving voice to values and entering into the celebration of ethnicity, oral traditions are a major component in establishing the boundaries of an ethnic group. A cultural performance may be a means of articulating boundaries in order to include members and exclude nonmembers; but it also may operate as means of distinguishing separate and even antagonistic segments within the community. Further, the same item of performance may on one occasion be drawn upon as a way of excluding a person or a group by designating them as nonpersons (devils, animals, crazies), and on another may publicly proclaim the community open to view and even membership. Surely this publicizing of otherwise private ethnic ways is the primary thrust of the many recent "folk festivals," in which a self-conscious attempt is made to celebrate cultural diversity by displaying different culinary, singing, dancing, and craft styles as *styles*, not really as alternative ways of life. The difference may simply be a matter of translating and explaining what is going on to outsiders, but in sociological terms that is a crucial difference.

Verbal lore is primarily tied to inherited patterns of language use. As linguistic acculturation to mainstream American English norms has occurred, foreign oral traditions have been undermined. Thus, collecting ethnic lore until relatively recently has been a retrieval project—collections established before the lore dies out with those tradition-bearers who have somehow survived the disruption of being put on a reservation, in a ghetto, or in an immigrant community or neighborhood. Collecting ethnic lore often proceeds on the assumption that the songs, stories, proverbs, superstitions, and other practices of the homeland will somehow be lost as soon as linguistic acculturation has taken place—an assumption not without foundation, even with English-speaking immigrants who are simply adapting to the American varieties of their tongue. But recent studies of the expressive dimension of ethnicity, based on more developmental principles, have been especially useful in understanding the various perceptible stages of Americanization. These are stages that are actually definable by the oral traditions that are maintained, modified, forgotten, or newly developed as a means of coping with new and more complex cultural situations.

Further, there is accumulating evidence that acculturation to the "mainstream" is far from unilinear and that social assimilation must be distinguished from acculturation because it represents a different process and obeys a different timetable. Again and again, groups that have begun to assimilate within the political and economic spheres continue or strive to maintain culturally distinct forms and prefer to live in separate communities or neighborhoods. Further, as this distinctiveness has become a political asset, rewarded by access to affirmative action and political leverage, the ethnic differences have to be self-consciously maintained as a means of making common cause politically or economically. This does not, in fact, demand radical stylistic alternatives as much as it requires a display that carries a minimal message of cultural uniqueness—even as superficial as drinking green beer on St. Patrick's Day. Such practices often draw upon an ethnic stereotype and turn it into a kind of self-conscious performance; that is, one's identity changes with the role and the relationships one takes on (whether willingly or not). In such a case, asserting one's ethnic heritage (whether real or derived from a stereotype) simply becomes a role which has become available because of the circumstance of one's ancestry and upbringing.

The dynamic of typing is one of the most important forces in the development of ethnic consciousness. Whether an ethnic group decides self-consciously to assimilate, or to attempt to maintain its separateness, the lore that develops in the new situation will reflect the social situation in which the group members find themselves. Thus, if exclusion is a constant problem, a concern with segregation is certain to be the subject of a

good deal of the lore shared by the members of the group. But even in those groups that have not encountered segregation, many traditional stories are told that relate the funny embarrassments that repeatedly arise with a strange language and a new culture. There are the problems, shared by most groups, that arise out of repeated linguistic misunderstanding or differences in manners—how close individuals stand when conversing, for instance, or the embarrassments resulting from a first encounter with an unfamiliar object or process.

An example of this, often recounted by Texas Chicanos, concerns the problems of a newcomer in dealing with his first paycheck. Wishing to buy some socks, he goes to a department store and asks for *calcetines*. The clerk doesn't understand, so the buyer repeats his request a few decibles higher. The clerk becomes nervous, as does the customer; the latter repeats his needs in an even louder voice, the former begins flying around holding things up to see if it is what the customer needs. Finally he holds up some socks, and the customer relievedly says, "*Eso, si que es.*" To which the clerk replies, "Well, if you could spell it, why in hell didn't you say so?" This kind of interlingual misunderstanding is frequently a source of common amusement, for both the immigrants and those with whom they regularly come in contact. Thus, one often hears the same story told by individuals in both groups, though seldom in interactions with each other.

It is precisely this private, in-group dimension of ethnic lore that demonstrates the way in which orally transmitted expression can dramatize the ethnic experience for those who are going through it. However, because such lore is amusing and instructive to those attempting to adjust or adapt, and because it lends itself to negative stereotyping, such lore or a discussion of its meaning is seldom found in serious discussions of ethnicity.

Such ethnic lore develops from a self-consciousness about language and cultural difference as it is experienced in the everyday world by the immigrant or refugee. Thus it is not just the life in the old country that is remembered but the shared experience of the newcomers. There are not only stories about the recurrent embarrassments of the new land and its ways but the deeper confusions sometimes labeled *culture shock*. Leaving home, even for "the promised land," involves great psychological dislocation, compounded by inevitable failures of expectation. Out of this experience comes a kind of private lore, stories of personal experience that one shares only with one's shipmates, others of that generation, and perhaps on rare occasions with younger members of one's family. Immigrants will commonly have formulaic hardship stories, or remembrances of the funny or awful experiences going through the port of entry.

As Barbara Kirshenblatt-Gimblett argues with great common sense, culture shock places the migrant or the refugee in the temporary position of a cultureless being, analogous to a child. The newcomer is forced to adapt to demands and to assume the role of one who doesn't know how to perform the most basic life tasks. The first experiences may thus operate in a manner not unlike that of the child, or even more the initiate—but without the careful and extensive preparation that commonly goes into the traditional initiation ritual. The culture broker—the appointed (or self-appointed) member of the ethnic community who leads the new arrivals through the worst spots—is a fascinating, insufficiently explored feature of the lore of all "minority" groups, including not only immigrants, but Indians, ethnic country folk who find themselves in strange environments, especially cities, and so on. As in other migratory situations, the newcomers look for the "home-boys"—the relatives, acquaintances, coreligionists, or whomever they can find who speak their language and who have found a place in the new society. When it is a family that has migrated, the brokers, too, are often families, husbands and wives who have already made the transition. Such brokers, in addition to providing help in finding housing and work, are commonly bilingual, often literate, and most important, have learned what is essential in order to get along in the new environment. As a way of dramatizing and humanizing this transition for newcomers, the broker often has developed a repertoire of stories, illustrative anecdotes of common embarrassment and crisis situations that provide lessons in getting through such situations with one's self-respect intact. These stories often float from one ethnic group to another, demonstrating that the sense of embarrassment is shared by many who come to a new country and have to learn new codes and languages.

A story, which appears in many forms in many communities, tells of the attempts of a newly arrived relative to get something to eat during the lunch break at his new job. His relative carefully coaches him to say, "I want a piece of pie and a glass of milk." On the first day, he successfully negotiates the purchase and is immensely proud of doing so. He repeats the order each day for several weeks thereafter. But one night he says that he would like to eat something else for lunch once in a while. Accepting the new task, his benefactor teaches him to say, "I want a ham sandwich and a cup of coffee." The newcomer, after practicing, walks boldly into the restaurant and renders his order. "I want a ham sandwich and a cup of coffee." "White or rye?" is the response, which is answered after a long pause, "Gimme a piece of pie and a glass of milk."

In such a situation of enforced acculturation, the individual who has become accustomed to the new language, new foods, new patterns of living, and new ways becomes something of a hero or heroine. The ability to switch codes (whether linguistic or behavioral) provides the clever immigrant with the power to resolve inadvertent dilemmas and conflicts. Add to this the message that the resolution may be learned and carried out with good humor, and it becomes self-evident why this role remains important in both adapting to the new situation and in remaining the central character in stories that recapitulate the embarrassments long after coming into the new social situation.

The collection and presentation-in-context of ethnic folklores has proceeded from three often overlapping strategies: first, using the devices of tradition to maintain a sense of continuity with Old World life and establishing a new sense of community in the alien New World setting; second, looking closely at the content of the lore—the reaction to displacement and to the attendant social problems (such as being marginalized, stereotyped, or ghettoized); and third, collecting and an-

alyzing the lore that emerges from the new environment, with special focus on the stages of acculturation and the manner in which lore is used, first as a device for surviving and then as a way of achieving a new sense of ethnic identification within a self-consciously pluralistic population.

FOLKLORE COLLECTIONS:
MEMORY CULTURE TO EMERGENT TRADITIONS

It is hardly surprising that studies of ethnic lore have followed the value preferences of the host culture. Early collections of folklore were carried out, moreover, in an antiquarian spirit, as a means of collecting lore before it died out, a practice typical of folklore collecting in general. From this perspective, texts are collected as a gauge of the extent of ethnic persistence and as a test of the culture-wave theory, which argues that international items in diffusion are often to be found at the peripheries of a culture area long after they have been lost at the center. Thus, folklorists have often been concerned with such lore collected within culturally conservative communities. Collections are made of texts of oral literature deriving from ethnic enclaves that self-consciously preserve their distinctiveness, commonly by maintaining a separate town or neighborhood or by clinging to an ethnic religious or social organization. These collections grow out of a desire to collect Old World rural items of wisdom and performance before the language and its remembered culture dies out. In such studies, the baseline against which the material is placed and judged is the Old World repertoire. Indeed, this is true of the many forms that have made up the mainstream of American folklore studies: British ballads, songs, and folktales. The "relics" of British countryside traditions have been actively sought in every area in the United States. Especially rich areas have been discovered throughout the upland South, in New England, and in the Ozarks. A hierarchy of forms and even items was established in the late 19th and early 20th centuries, but actual collection of such items in North America was not carried out extensively until the 1920s and 1930s. The research tools that document this collecting effort focus on the oldest and most widespread texts of ballads and folktales, illustrating, through bibliographical annotation, how widely the item has been found and in what range of versions and variants. Thus, when the local and regional collections are carried out, they, too, show the historical and geographical spread of the item through comparative annotation.

A number of Old World verbal traditions have been widely and deeply collected employing this essentially antiquarian approach. Especially notable in this regard are studies of Pennsylvania German, Louisiana French, and southwestern Mexican-American lore. These are commonly presented as evidence of the continuity in these culturally (and linguistically) conservative areas, a continuity emerging from living in isolated agrarian areas.

Such studies of immigrant and ethnic folklore are still being carried out using the body of Old World traditions as a point of departure. The point of these studies, however, is no longer antiquarian; rather, they attempt to epitomize, in the content of the lore, the complementary processes of tradition maintenance and change. Such community studies are aimed not only at understanding more fully the sociocultural dynamic of transmission, but at drawing upon folklore as a gauge of acculturation and community stability. These works underscore the selective maintenance of traditional forms and practices, those that enter actively into the adaptation of newly located groups. The pressures faced upon entering the new environment emerge from the need not only to learn occupational skills but a new language and system of manners. On the other hand, these needs are counteracted by a desire to maintain a sense of family, church, and community through keeping up some of the old practices.

The most important variables here seem to be the extent of the population movement that has taken place, the type of friend and family network that can be maintained, and the degree of development of the ethnic enclave into which the newcomer will enter. The ethnic farming community is susceptible to a high degree of language and culture maintenance, as is the intensive city neighborhood. The same situation of tradition-maintenance may hold when the newcomer is received into an occupational community—into mining, lumbering, or the cattle trade, for example.

Here we have some instructive accounts of ethnic persistence: Robert Georges' studies of the Tarpon Springs, Fla., Greek community, in which the traditional employment is sponge diving, may be usefully compared to the analysis of the urban Greek community in Philadelphia carried out by Gregory Gizelis. Both of these folklorists examine the narrative lore of a Greek-speaking population. But Georges' interests are, in the main, tied to the way in which both traditional and personal-experience stories maintain the belief and practice system revolving around the sea and the sponge-fishing trade. Though the folklife reported shows a range of responses to the pressures encountered in being surrounded by non-Greek-speaking American peoples, Georges is generally able to draw upon the Old World cultural baseline much more fully than can Gizelis, who collected from the more economically and geographically diverse Greeks in Philadelphia. Gizelis interviewed a great number of Greek Americans on the ways in which home traditions combine with ethnic awareness in a new environment where the newcomer is both establishing a sense of community and pursuing his individual identity. In contrast to the Tarpon Springs community, the urban Greeks had changed their occupations and lifestyles almost completely in making a place for themselves in the urban environment of Philadelphia. In the main, the character and forms of familiar verbal art displayed by Greek Americans correspond to those of most other groups in the process of acculturation. These forms, perhaps because of their ubiquity, have seldom been noted by folklorists or sociologists, and can thus only be found in joke books and immigrant autobiographies. For instance, Gizelis reports on the stories told about Greeks who have been successful in American life, each told with a strong note of what it is in Greek "character" that has made it possible for them to succeed. Similarly, he analyzes stories that present their perceived stereotype of themselves by Americans, and provide folk rationalization for why these stereotypes, these "misunderstandings," have arisen in the first place. Gizelis includes

many stories, both personal and jocular, about the various cultural and linguistic misunderstandings that the immigrants encountered. He underscores the variety of ways in which these narratives are used: recounting common anxiety situations; making jokes about newcomers, sometimes to share their anxiety; and offering reminiscences by those who needed to make a statement about how hard times had been. Clearly, this is emergent New World lore about an Old World group, lore in which Greek tradition has become subordinate to Greek-American lore.

A number of factors govern the selective maintenance or rejection of traditional practices. Different considerations are brought to bear if, for example, one is examining culinary traditions, in which case availability of foods and fuels might be crucial; or the existence of institutions outside the family that encourage festive gathering; or the health maintenance system, in which the role of healer and protector might or might not be challenged by the dominant medically trained personnel, and traditional remedies (like herbs) might or might not be available. Sometimes an investigator finds that parameters like age and sex are central to such a study. Carla Bianco, for instance, found in her study of the storytelling events in Rosetto, Italy, and Rosetto, Pennsylvania, that among the very old and the young, traditional tales remain important forms of entertainment.

Collections that take into account the persistence or adaptation of Old World traditions in mestizo or creole cultures—that is, when languages and ways of life are mixed in an alien environment—pose problems that are very different from those of studies of immigrant-to-ethnic lore. Some strange academic biases enter into the study of the culturally different communities that have emerged in the wake of the plantation and the *hacienda*, or the ghetto and the *barrio*. Studies of both Afro-American and Mexican-American folklore emerge in reaction to many of the same conditions of social segregation and subordination as do the sociological and historical accounts of the same ethnic groups. And though the folklore studies do underscore the creative process that seems to occur in reaction to these conditions, it is nonetheless the conditions and the exploitation that command our attention.

Moreover, in the attempt to relate the social conditions to the cultural bases of creativity, the investigator-collector has commonly accepted the argument that such folklore emerges in response to these conditions. Somehow, the African or the American Indian repertories or styles have supposedly been eliminated in the process of colonialization. Where specific items or practices have been reported elsewhere, it is presumed that they were learned by "imitation" from the European or Euro-American "masters." To a certain extent, this bias occurs simply because folklorists have collected and organized the Indo-European traditions much more fully than African or American Indian lore. But the assimilationist bias of the commentators has certainly had an effect on the way they present their position. Such arguments emanate from the notion that all culture rests on the superstructure of the institutions of community life: family structure, economic and governmental systems, and religion. The maintenance of African and American Indian institutions was, indeed, discouraged by the dominant European and Euro-American societies. By extension, it was assumed that all other features of culture would be undermined and replaced through imitating the culture of the dominant society, or through a shared creative reaction against their domination. This deculturation view is most identified with the Afro-Americanists E. Franklin Frazier and Robert Park, and was maintained by collectors of black life and lore until relatively recently. (The great exception is the work of Melville Herskovits and his students.) One of the earliest and best informed of these scholar-collectors, Richard Dorson, maintains this Europeanist point of view, with special reference to black folktales. He argues that the great bulk of Afro-American narrative lore in the United States, where it exhibits Old World antecedents at all, demonstrates a derivation from European rather than African antecedents.

In rebuttal, a number of commentators have noted that this defies both common sense and the evidence of the data: distributional studies of specific stories, especially of the Uncle Remus variety so widely collected in the United States, demonstrate a strong maintenance of African narrative lore; and morphological analyses of a variety of expressive forms—tales, dance, song, practices of worship—indicate that even when specific items are derivable from non-African sources, the deeper learned patterns of both construction and performance are demonstrably African or pan-Afro-American. Herskovits presents a model of acculturation that distinguishes three modes of continuity and adaptation: straight *retention*; *reinterpretation*, in which forms are maintained in new environments with new uses and meanings; and *syncretism*, in which similar elements of two or more cultures merge.

What Herskovits describes are a number of possible ways in which cultural forms and practices change. Those who have continued to study expressive culture in Afro-American communities generally analyze their data not only on the level of traits and practices, in which attributions of specified points of origin in Africa or Europe or the New World are asserted, but also on the deeper level of aesthetic and cosmological organization, or on the microbehavioral level (walking, running, and dancing styles, ways of greeting, eye-contact patterns). In these areas of culture, the deculturation argument goes against both common sense and the most casual observation. Thus, it is not in the areas of texts or traits that the most fruitful discussion of African retentions has been carried out but in the practices in which these deeper patterns may be observed most clearly—as in, say, hand-clapping and drumming, dance patterns, sermons and religious practices, and so on.

The cultural dynamic in which such deeper structures of organization and attitude operate is severely complicated in cases like Afro-American lore because of the constant possibility of introducing cultural elements from contemporary African or from Afro-American communities outside the United States. For instance, Afro-American dance in the United States has produced a great number of indigenous styles from "Jump Jim Crow," the "Buzzard Lope," and the "Turkey Trot" to the "Charleston," "jitterbug," and various kinds of "the boogie." But equally important have been the Afro-Latin dance crazes: Mambo, Limbo, Samba, Congo, Bossa Nova.

During the 1960s, when such practices became entwined with the "soul movement," a number of such display forms took on special meaning. *Dashiki* shirts and love beads came into the black American repertory through the Cuban Yoruba community newly moved to New York and Miami from Havana and the Oriente in eastern Cuba. The Cubans from this community had never lost contact with their Nigerian cousins—their religious leaders were often sent back for training, for instance. Thus, when they moved from Cuba they found fertile ground to grow in, and many of their practices came into wider fashion. In addition to the dashiki and beads, the multi-unit handshake and the emphasis on plaited hair decoration were reemphasized. The *corn-row* (or *cane-row*), for instance, had been one of many traditional styles in the American South as well as the West Indies. Rejected as a reminder of slavery times in favor of hair-straightening techniques (also found, incidentally, in many parts of traditional Africa), plaiting reemerged in this era of self-conscious cultural revitalization. Perhaps even more important is the fact that through all of the evolving history the importance of hair-styling, and especially of having a family member or friend to do the hair in public, remained constant. Perhaps the most potent way of dramatizing the point is to refer to the widespread African saying (also found in the West Indies): "Nothing is sadder to think about than a person with no one to take care of his hair."

THE INDIGENOUS AND BOUNDARY-MAKING STATEMENTS OF VERBAL ART

The concern with the maintenance and elaboration of relics of the past has become somewhat less central to the study of the folklore of American ethnic groups in the post–World War II era. The indigenous forms have assumed ever greater importance. Thus, more studies have been carried out that concentrate on the lore in which strong attitudes and images of self and other are explored. Here one can reasonably make a distinction between the *lore* that dramatizes one's stereotypes of one's own group and of contiguous cultures, and the *forms* and *styles* of traditional practice that are unique to the group. In both cases the lore is of an esoteric sort. The lore of self-typing and stereotyping projects and reinforces intragroup and intergroup conflicts. With such stereotypical material, its in-group character derives from highly biased content features that reveal the attitudes held by one group about another. In the case of the developing form and styles, the expression is so idiomatic to the group, so full of slang, jargon, or other special vocabulary, that it is virtually unintelligible to nonmembers. Perhaps more to the point, such esoteric lore is subject to constant intercultural misunderstanding, thus increasing the sense of in-groupness as well as intensifying the sense of exclusion felt by nonmembers.

This complex of ways in which ethnic lore explores the subject of social and cultural differences has been an especially productive way of drawing on folklore as an index to the intensity of social stratification and the dynamic of intergroup relations. This lore about self and others has been analyzed in terms suggested by William Hugh Jansen and expanded upon by Richard Bauman and numerous others. The esoteric-exoteric (or *s-x*) complex of factors concerns the techniques of boundary-making and the dynamic arising between the bounded groups as it is revealed within the corpus of an oral literature. These boundaries arise not only from the integrity and sense of shared experience, language, and values within the group, but from that group's image of the degree to which it is regarded as distinctive by nonmembers and how these differences are, in fact, regarded. Thus, the s-x factor would include not only the stereotypical depictions of self and other, but also the ways in which the lore points to cultural means of fighting against the negative effects of stereotyping.

Many of the more recent studies of both Afro-American and Mexican-American lore underscore this dynamic of stereotyping. For example, Américo Paredes has explored the relationship between "gringos" and "greasers" in the joke-lore of Mexican Americans, underscoring the impact of the antagonism between Chicanos and Anglos as recorded in real events in which social inequities are dramatized. The dynamic of recent Mexican-American lore, especially in-group jokes, provides a way in which the Anglo stereotype of Chicanos is drawn on to establish counter-boundaries, directing both laughter and derision at those who would otherwise be regarded as socially superordinate. This, too, involves the inversion of stereotype traits in which laziness as well as virility become devices of manipulation in encounters and in which supposed animality becomes a resource of sexual superiority. This same process of stereotypical inversion is emphasized in the many studies of urban Afro-American lore.

The expressive forms that arise within these ethnic enclaves, especially Hispanic-American and Afro-American, have received more critical commentary than virtually any other area of folklore and expressive culture in general. Characteristic of this interest in the in-group lore of these groups are many studies of blues—classic, country, and city. Such analyses often focus on the role of the bluesman as a social representative—even culture hero—of the blacks during the post-Reconstruction period.

These studies arise in great part not just from social concerns of the (predominantly white) commentators, but from a fascination with emergent and creative forms. In a similar manner, other emergent black forms of verbal art have received a great deal of commentary: the *sermon*, the *spiritual*, *jiving*, *playing the dozens* (*mother rapping*), and the *toast*. In all cases, attempts have been made to relate these forms, the nature of these performances, and their subject matter to the sociocultural condition of contemporary Afro-American life.

All of the social sciences might be enriched by the exploration of the content and performance of oral traditions. This becomes especially significant as the thrust of folklore studies has changed from an emphasis on texts to one on performance, play, and enactment. Traditional practices in new environments become a useful way to get to the core of the cultural dynamic of the community. Esoteric lore permits insights into the features of shared identity as perceived in different ways and intensities by individuals within the community under analysis. This extension of the s-x argument underscores the centrality of folklore in performance entering into the "typing" of self and others. This approach underscores features like age-grading, regional identification, occupational roles, kinship, and per-

ceived ethnic identity as means of entering more fully into this discussion of the way in which culture operates within social structures.

In essence, this shift in approach calls for an altered status for ethnic enclaves. The assumption of the analysis of ethnic communities has been that as "minorities" or "subcultures" their separation occurs only so long as power is unequally distributed. With the elimination of inequalities, the very existence of these minorities would be questioned. Assimilation and acculturation are inevitable, then, so long as access to power and responsibility are assured. Such a unilinear developmental approach does not recognize that there are cultural as well as economic exchange relationships that arise out of the cultural coming-together process, even when the exchanges are not actually reciprocal. The reliance of mainstream American culture on the alternative expressive forms and styles provided by Afro-Americans, for instance, resulted in these Afro-American performances achieving a life of their own—a life that is always ethnically acknowledged, but which may or may not reflect the maintenance of these traditions within Afro-American communities. Due to a combination of active imitation by Euro-Americans and the recording of the performance at some point within black communities (in books, phonograph recordings, or movies), which makes it possible for the imitators to return to the "originals" without returning to the communities, such forms as blues, tap-dancing, skiffle-music, and many others have endured. Though they are now popular rather than folk forms, inasmuch as their audience extends far beyond the ethnic community, their folk "roots" are widely acknowledged by their new audience.

Indeed, these dynamic community analyses of folklore often demonstrate precisely the ways in which certain enclaves resist assimilation because of differences in ethos, world view, and secular and religious practice. A self-consciously different religious community, especially, may maintain its deep sense of separation not only through a persistence of traditional religious practices, but also in language-maintenance and in recapitulating a sociocultural sense of community in which the old stories and songs are performed and transmitted because they continue to be employed in the traditional fashion. Though most such studies employ the ethnographic method in describing the group and therefore are not primarily concerned with the processes of oral transmission and dissemination, the lore reported often undercuts the assumption of the inevitability of assimilation in the contemporary world. Not insensitive to certain changes dictated by their new situation, the uses of the lore and the folkloric items themselves must be regarded not only as relics of past practices but as examples of a lively culturally emergent tradition as well. Such a process of tradition-maintenance and revitalization has been widely observed not only in immigrant communities but among American Indians and mestizos.

FOLKLORE AND THE CONCEPT OF CREOLE CULTURE

The same questions are asked of ethnic enclaves as are asked about regional cultures: to what extent are their ways unique, and how much is really shared with other communities within the American polity? This becomes even more problematic as the most marked features of regional or ethnic culture become part of popular iconography and, by extension, part of mass culture—the general expressive and symbolic vocabulary of the United States. We witness just such a process in the development of various regional and ethnic cuisines into national franchise operations. Going public in such a way often means needing to draw upon the very stereotypes that have operated as exclusionary techniques in other times and other intercultural situations. The way in which the masters of popular culture manipulate the images of the sleepy, sombrero-wearing Mexicans to sell tacos and burritos, or the white-suited Southern Colonels, or the pearly-toothed Uncle Bens, is fascinating—if a little fearsome—to behold.

Considering culture from such a perspective places emphasis on the interaction between cultures, especially on the importance of a coming-together of the expressive elements from a range of traditional backgrounds. The most common and in many ways the most productive way of studying such a synthesizing process would underscore the privileged status of those forms shared by the larger society, and would therefore involve a study of lore and language as it gravitates toward national norms and forms.

From a sociolinguistic point of view, individuals in ethnic groups in multiethnic settings often draw upon a range of codes or varieties of talking, ranging from the most archaic or ceremonial to the most recent slang or jargon. Each speaker within an ethnic enclave, then, might be studied in terms of the range of codes and varieties of speech in which he or she has developed a receptive (understanding) or productive (speaking) competence. In the language-contact situation arising from the mass movements of peoples, one language and one range of codes within that language are commonly accorded high prestige (H), often because they are the forms employed on literary occasions or in radio broadcasts. Other codes are given lower status (L), especially when they represent the language of old and often illiterate, backward, or defeated and enslaved people. Individuals are judged on the one hand by an ability to control the prestige form, or alternatively to switch at will between different varieties. Some seek to gain a place of importance in the community by enacting the widest range of speaking styles and codes; others will make their name by their total mastery of one form, such as oratorical English (one kind of H) or talk that demonstrates quick wit and a control of slang or jargon (forms of L).

This range of interactive and expressive codes has been called the *creole continuum* because in cultural contact situations new codes are produced during the earliest stages of the process of coming together. When these codes are predominantly organized around exchange (or trade) relationships between heretofore discrete language communities, the product is commonly referred to as *pidgin*. When social and familial situations draw on this in-between way of talking and broaden its expressive capacities, it is referred to as a *creole* language. But it remains a low-status means of interacting unless it develops a literature (as with the Anglo-Norman Middle English) or some other means of being adopted by a prestige group. If it remains an L

code, then, it will constantly be compared with H and will tend to be affected by such a comparison. But one cannot assume that this will produce a change in the lower-status varieties in the direction of the higher. The relationships, in fact, go both ways.

The first folklore collectors to actively employ the idea of the creole continuum worked in Afro-American communities in the United States and elsewhere in the New World. "Talking bad" or "broken" has become part of the apparatus of identity management of some blacks (especially males) in conflict and in festive entertainment situations. Such ways of performing even in casual streetcorner situations are regarded as a contest between the "good" or *respectability* norms and ideals of the community and the more hilarious "bad" *reputation*-seeking means of expression. As the linguistic varieties employed in such bad-talk are furthest away from so-called Standard English in the speech continuum, these ways of talking are maintained as an alternative means to respectability of achieving status within the community. Further, the ability to employ such varieties in performance forms like the epic *toasts* or in blues enables the performer to assume a kind of leadership over the reputation-seeking segment of the community. Conversely, speaking well (especially in oratorical or philosophical standard forms) places one at the potential center of the respect-seeking segment of the community. Thus we find a good deal of actual discussion within the community about the bluesman with regard to the preacher, and about the different ways of talking and performing in general. A very wide range of codes and varieties may be maintained within the same community as a means of continually dramatizing the (usually playful) opposition between these two value systems. And the person who can control all of these codes in their appropriate place is given very high status, indeed.

From the perspective of the history of codes and varieties, this situation in which a number of historically distinct forms are maintained for expressive purposes runs counter to the usual way in which the language and lore of ethnic communities are studied. More commonly, of course, immigrant groups have been observed and judged with regard to how quickly and effectively they acculturate from the Old World language to American English. But in social situations in which the ethnic group and alternative languages have been in this country for some time, as with Afro-Americans, Mexican Americans, and American Indians, this immigrant model of change does not pertain. Rather the concern of the sociolinguistically oriented folklorist has been to document the language situation as it maintains a number of codes or varieties as expressive resources.

In the only work of folklore scholarship that explicitly focuses on a native language as it gravitates toward English, Barbara Kirshenblatt-Gimblett brings together a corpus of materials from Toronto's eastern European Jewish community. She demonstrates that in the midst of the common acculturation situation, a complex of verbal traditions arose which calls for a variable control of both Yiddish and English and which develops an intermediate code which she names "Yinglish." Not only were Old World verbal forms kept alive while new ones were emerging from the immigration experience, but a large body of lore arose which turns on the active and usually witty commingling of these languages and cultural forms. Primary forms in such a situation are the stories told in English with Yiddish punchlines, and vice versa. Kirshenblatt-Gimblett demonstrates that learning a new language is a more complicated process than is generally recognized, because the very situation of change engenders verbal artistic forms as a means of displaying the centrality of a range of performance competencies. This emergent lore is, in the main, metacommunicative—made up of lore focusing on the character of communicating in a new sociocultural environment. The concept of being multicultural, then, becomes not so much a matter of shedding one culture and donning another, but of acquiring new cultural and linguistic resources which, by their very quality of newness, are "foregrounded" as flexible and functional devices of communication. There is an automatic foregrounding effect in such a transitional situation; through cultural contact the verbal lore becomes increasingly self-conscious as it draws upon an ever-widening range of expressive resources. Narrative lore especially comes to be employed as the means of asserting and testing (and later rehearsing) the newly learned competencies. In this situation, the multilingual narrator becomes the model for successful acculturation. Capitalizing on the otherwise dying language resources, the narrator maintains the usefulness of the old vocabulary, the old sayings, even if they serve only as a resource for humorous effects.

GOING PUBLIC

The idea of employing the creole continuum to understand the processes affecting ethnic folklores arises from the need to recognize what alternative expressive resources exist for a community at any time in its history. By underscoring such alternatives, we become conscious of the ways in which verbal creativity may operate in situations otherwise described as ones of alienation, marginalization, and exploitation. Furthermore, it is important to recognize that ethnicity is often a dimension of the performing self, a choice made individually of a role to be played, made possible by the persistence of these older ways of expression.

Looking at the coexistence of the many ethnic groups in the United States from outside these groups, however, presents a very different perspective, for the outsider is made especially aware of his nonstatus within the community, and of the difference between his or her traditions and those of the group. When there is any kind of defensiveness or social strain between such outside observers and the group being observed, the result is often a stereotypical one. "Different" comes to mean chaotic, acting like children or even animals; expressing another culture, then, signals having no culture—no style, no taste. But when such differences are dramatized in an environment of good will, the lack of understanding may be translated into willingness to learn about such cultural alternatives and even to enjoy them. Thus, outsiders are invited in to witness how life is lived, traditions carried on within the ethnic group. Naturally, the activities most available for observation and even participation are those in which the group is on its "best behavior"—as in rites

and ceremonies and festive meals—or when performing is in progress. In a shrinking world, the activities that attract the attention of outsiders will be those which have a strong sense of style and decorum. Indeed, it is such traditional forms and styles as dance, clowning, acrobatics, song (and music in general), ceremony, the decorative arts, crafts, and cooking that are the most easily understood and that transcend language differences. Consequently, it is in these realms that we witness traditional ethnic expression going public. Within any cultural enclave some genres of traditional lore and some situations of performance will be more private and family oriented, and some will be more public. Scenes or events carried on within the family or peer group are obviously more private and more topical in references and thus more limited in audience than the larger gatherings. With the growing value placed on ethnic diversity, some of these more private forms of aesthetic encounters are increasingly being developed into public presentations. We find this acceptance operating especially in those folk festivals employing professional folklorists, which were greatly accelerated by political demands to be part of the 1976 Bicentennial celebrations.

Typical of this drift has been the use of festivals or fairs or some other kind of announced public event as a means of dramatizing ethnic persistence in a community or neighborhood, church or social group. What has been *immigrant folklore* and then *ethnic folklore* becomes the *folklore of ethnicity*. Essentially this calls for the employment of the already public, community-wide events as a means of gaining an even wider public of noncommunity member participation. Events which at one point in the history of the community were employed as a means of asserting and maintaining ethnic boundaries become the very instrument by which the boundary is opened up—at least for the moment. Similarly, the more private forms become available for greater public exposure. Thus, for instance, the most in-group of black verbal contests became the focus of the staged street celebration in the African Diaspora presentations in the Festival of American Folklife at the Smithsonian Institution in the summers of 1976 and 1977, while nearby, surrounded by an audience, bartenders and cab-drivers sat in a tent telling stories that they usually reserve for their customers or for each other.

The concept of the *living-museum* or *folk-museum* increasingly attempts not only to reconstruct home behaviors like cottage-industry-style work and cooking; in addition, performances or reports of performances of the games, riddles, stories, and songs which are associated with the hearth or the dining-room are imported into these essentially tourist presentations. It is just these public demonstrations that make distinctive ethnic behaviors available for performance by anyone who chooses to learn them. Thus, ethnic style as well as items of performance become detached from the folk communities that gave rise to them and are employed for entirely different popular effects. (In fact, this has characterized American shows since the development of the blackface minstrel show, which drew originally on Afro-American traditions.) Rather than being employed within essentially homogeneous communities in which members meet face-to-face to entertain and

instruct each other, these ways of performing are employed in groups that come together only for the occasion of entertainment. Media of record (such as print, movies, and recordings) as well as the microphone vastly increase the audience, and individuals perform to others not known personally. Folk traditions provide the materials for a celebration of stylistic diversity that has little to do with the ethnic community out of which it emerges; the performance of ethnicity, far from becoming a statement of cultural continuity and rootedness, rather emerges as a way of entering the marketplace economy by those carrying on the ethnic style of performance or presentation. Everyone, at this point, can learn how to play a banjo or even a Japanese *koto*, just as they can take lessons in how to cook (or at least eat properly) grits or *sukiyaki*.

This process of making public the private also often means dramatizing what heretofore has not been dramatic, performing acts which are not inherently performative. For instance, in the development of folklife festivals, the problem of how to present crafts and work techniques has arisen constantly. It early became evident that folk festival audiences are as interested in the process of craftmaking and other work as they are in music and dance. Consequently, illustrating these crafts on the spot develops into performances as much as demonstrations. At such a point, the intermediacy of *presenters* is called for, individuals who can explain the process while it is being carried out. Such a figure often employs traditional narratives such as jokes, hero tales, and personal anecdotes as an important feature of the framing performance. At such a point, though items of verbal art are essentially the same as those found within the folk community, their context and thus their meaning is substantially changed. With the tremendous growth of ethnic-based folk festivals, the figure of the presenter begins to take its place beside the costumed tour guide and the folksinger as a popular culture role in the business of purveying ethnic folk culture.

In such presentations, the folklore of an ethnic group is no longer a means of keeping the family and community together, nor even a way of maintaining the old practices. Rather, folklore becomes part of the vocabulary of communicating across cultures in a situation in which the old stereotypes and boundary-making mechanisms are rejected as inappropriate. Ironically then, in such public presentations, both ethnic differences and the old folkways are kept alive but in a cultural setting as far away as one can imagine from the small face-to-face group in which they persisted. Yet the very event which most opens up family and community to outside observation and participation has elevated the tradition-bearer to eminence, and has brought generations within families to perform or demonstrate together in ways that seem to have been dying when carried on only within the home. It now seems easier, in other words, to get members of younger generations to enact ethnically in public than in private. It has been a working proposition in the folk festival movement, in fact, to bring public approval to these old-fashioned ways so that the younger members of the community will find more than family reinforcement to learn the traditional performances and practices. Moreover, such festivals, in seeking out traditional performers, often find them-

selves dealing with individuals who have been regarded as eccentric or even deviant within their home locale.

These public occasions in which demonstrations and performances are carried out in a real sense run contrary to ethnic persistence, for they become events aimed in the main at a popular audience. This tendency undermines the actual social base of ethnic persistence and relegates the fact of ethnic identification into that strange place in the possible repertory of roles in which to be "an ethnic" is to be a conveyor of stylistic alternatives, interesting ones no doubt, but with little of the sense of alternatives held in opposition to each other. In such popular displays, the esoteric-exoteric factor no longer is terribly important in the operation of the lore, for who is now being included and excluded? Something like this dislocation of boundaries seems to underly the Polack-cycle and other such recent jokelore. This cycle is just the latest rendering of the "noodle" or "moron" principle, the derogation of a class of people because of their semihuman character, their strange eating and sexual habits, their ugliness and lack of intelligence, and so on. Though on the surface the Polack joke turns on traits imputed to Poles in general, it becomes clear that those who tell these stories are not really directing them at the Polish people nor even implying that Poles exhibit such traits. Rather, they are like the elephant jokes that find elephants wearing tennis shoes, climbing and jumping from trees, and taking baths—a background of what-if suppositions against which generally absurd behavior can be projected and laughed at. These jokes are not tendentious, directed at a specific social problem. They maintain the language and the witty techniques of derision and exclusion, but on a supposed group that has little to do with the lives of those who tell the jokes. Ethnic behavior and, in this case, invented ethnic behavior has become a matter of depicting cultural differences as eccentric rather than deviant. The result is a strange kind of bonding rather than the exclusionary motive contained in the older kind of ethnically directed humor, such as dialect jokes. Thus, the Polack joke seems to operate within a popular culture environment—one which, like the "ethnic" programs on radio and now television, attempts to use stereotyping as a path to social acceptance. The Polack joke, like "Abie's Irish Rose," and the folk festival, like the earlier fairs and world expositions, operate on the principal of the acceptability of cultural pluralism.

Bibliography
Large-scale studies of folklore and ethnicity in America are a comparatively recent phenomenon, and most of them are not yet available in book form. Many of those written prior to 1970 are conveniently listed in Alan Dundes, *Folklore Theses and Dissertations in the United States* (Austin, Tex., 1976). More recent studies are referred to *passim* in the special issue of *Western Folklore* 36 (1977): 1–108, ed. Larry Danielson, which includes not only an important introductory essay by the editor, but Stephen Stern's groundbreaking article, "Ethnic Folklore and the Folklore of Ethnicity," 7–32. One doctoral dissertation, that of Barbara Kirshenblatt-Gimblett, "Traditional Storytelling in the Toronto Jewish Community" (University Microfilms: Ann Arbor, Mich., 1972) is of enormous importance.

Representative monographs on the folklore of specific ethnic communities are: Jerome Mintz, *Legends of the Hasidim: An Introduction in the New World* (Chicago, 1968); Robert Georges, "Matiasma: Living Folk Belief," *Midwest Folklore* 12 (1962): 69–74; Gregory Gizelis, *Narrative Rhetorical Devices of Persuasion* (Athens, Greece, 1976); Carla Bianco, *The Two Rosetos* (Bloomington, Ind., 1974); Américo Paredes, *With His Pistol in His Hand* (Austin, 1959); and Bruce A. Rosenberg, *The Art of the American Negro Folk Preacher* (New York, 1970). Richard Dorson's unique study *Bloodstoppers and Bearwalkers* (Cambridge, Mass., 1952; reprint, 1972), surveys the lore of a multiethnic region, the Upper Peninsula of Michigan.

In Roger D. Abrahams, *Positively Black* (Englewood Cliffs, N.J., 1970), the narrative lore of Afro-Americans is surveyed with regard to the ways in which it reflects stereotypes of self and others. The roles of bluesmen and preachers are explored in Charles Kiel, *Urban Blues* (Chicago, 1966) and John Szwed, "Musical Adaptation Among Afro-Americans" *Journal of American Folklore* 82 (1969): 112–121. A number of other works are surveyed in John Szwed and Roger D. Abrahams, *An Annotated Bibliography: Afro-American Folklore and Culture* (Philadelphia, 1978).

The authority on African communities in the New World remains Melville Herskovits; see *The Myth of the Negro Past* (Boston, 1941). The argument goes on between the deculturizationists and the Africanists; the most recent summary of the latter point of view may be found in Daniel Crowley, ed., *African Folklore in the New World* (Austin, 1977).

The developmental model is derived, in part, from the work of Herskovits, as well as Fredrik Barth, *Ethnic Groups and Boundaries* (Boston, 1969). Other valuable studies are: Linda Dégh, "Survival and Revival of European Folk Cultures in America," *Ethnologia Europaea* 2–3 (1968–1969): 97–108; William Hugh Jansen, "The Esoteric-Exoteric Factor in Folklore," *Fabula: Journal of Folktale Studies* 2 (1959): 205–211; Robert Klymasz, "From Immigrant to Ethnic Folklore," *Journal of the Folklore Institute* 10 (1973): 133–137; and Richard Bauman, "Differential Identity and the Social Base of Folklore," *Journal of American Folklore* 84 (1971): 31–41. A recent textbook which covers American traditions from the perspective of the performance of culture and ethnicity is Barre Toelken, *The Dynamics of Folklore* (Boston, 1979). See also the sociolinguistic work of Dell Hymes, especially his *Foundations in Sociolinguistics* (Philadelphia, 1974). Charles Ferguson discusses the distinction between *H* (High) and *L* (Low) in "Diglossia," *Word* 15 (1959): 325–340.

ROGER D. ABRAHAMS

FOREIGN STOCK

The term foreign stock was adopted by the U.S. Bureau of the Census in 1870 to refer to first- and second-generation Americans. Since then the Census has counted as foreign stock all people living in the United States who were born abroad and all those whose parents (one or both) were foreign-born. Third-, fourth-, and fifth-generation Americans have been considered old stock unless they are Afro-Americans, Asians, Hispanics, or American Indians. (*See* Appendix II.)

FOXES: *see* AMERICAN INDIANS

FRANCO-AMERICANS: *see* FRENCH CANADIANS

FRENCH

The question of French immigration to the United States, and in earlier times to the English-speaking colonies, is a scholarly *terra incognita*. No serious overall study of emigration from France has ever been written, and nothing whatsoever about immigration to the United States. Americans, no doubt, have considered the subject too minor; and Frenchmen, too distasteful. This indifference is regrettable. French immigration deserves to be studied because it is a revealing facet of both French and American life. The migratory propensities of the French have been suggestively distinctive: French immigration has been the smallest and most stable of that of any European country, and the rate of return home has been very high, even though the French have been extremely successful in the United States. The situation of the French in America has been highly paradoxical, and very different from that of the French Canadians or the Louisiana Acadians. Unlike

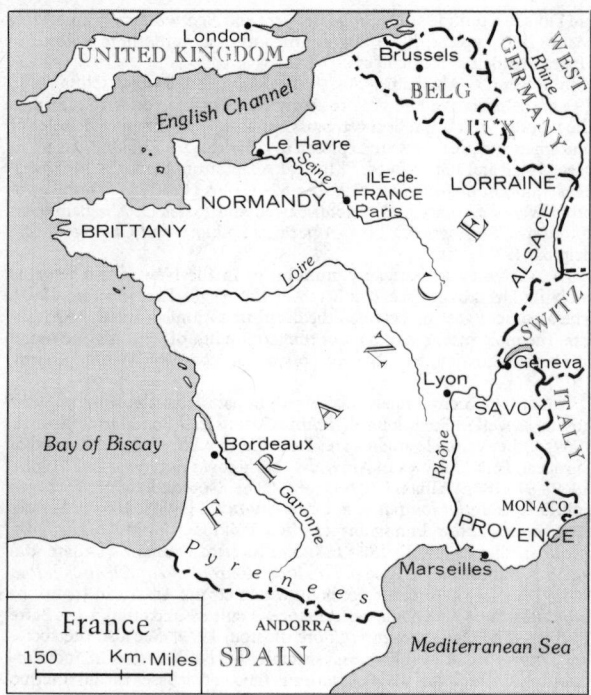

France
150 Km.Miles

their Francophone cousins, French migrants to the United States have been middle-class, urban, antitraditionalist, and incapable of sustaining their ethnic identity. (*See also* Acadians; French Canadians.)

SIZE OF THE IMMIGRATION

The precise extent of immigration for any national group is impossible to ascertain, but this is especially true for the French. Official U.S. immigration surveys estimate that 740,000 French nationals have come to settle in this country since 1820. Some 30,000 or 40,000 may have come before that. All figures are approximate.

For the 17th and 18th centuries, there are no statistics at all; for the 19th and 20th, American estimates are too high. Before 1869, visitors—like Alexis de Tocqueville—or merchants on tour were included in the tally. After this, U.S. immigration authorities based their count on the country of last domicile, a practice that caused considerable error because many so-called French migrants were not French at all. Some of them were East Europeans who had temporarily settled in France, which, like the United States, has had a large immigrant population in modern times. Others were Germans who had acquired false papers in France: it had been easy for them to cross the Rhine where border controls were lax, but the more rigorous police regulations that prevailed in French seaports made it advisable for them to claim French nationality en route. American authorities counted such people as French citizens, and this practice must be taken into account.

French statisticians have estimated that only 75 percent of individuals listed as French by U.S. immigration authorities were in fact born in France; but their sources are equally confused. The inspection of emigration instituted by the French in the 1860s, partly in response to Prussian pressure, was lackadaisical and biased. All third-class passengers leaving France with a one-way ticket were called emigrants, others not.

In theory, all French citizens who wished to leave their country were required to obtain a passport for that purpose. This regulation should have made the size of emigration crystal clear. In fact, French tabulations underestimated migration by half, because the French state was eager to downplay the outflow of its citizens. It even did what it could in the 1850s and 1860s to make departure more difficult: emigration agencies were thwarted, and emigrants were urged to move to French colonies instead, especially to Algeria.

In addition, the rate of return to France of French migrants has always been high. The number of French people who actually decided to make their home in the United States may therefore be no more than half of what official U.S. figures indicate, even if the total includes the natives of two regions that sent many immigrants to America: Savoy, which was Italian before 1861, and Alsace-Lorraine, which was under German rule from 1871 to 1918 (in 1920 one out of five Frenchborn Americans was an Alsatian). (*See* Alsatians.)

This statistical imprecision is regrettable; it blurs important nuances and makes more opaque the characteristic trait of French immigration to the United States, which is best described as a delicately balanced agglomerate of *individual* cases. But the figures, however they are interpreted, do bear out the important fact that very few French people have come to live in the United States; although more have come to the United States than to other countries in the Americas (like Canada, Mexico, or Argentina), the number has remained, in absolute terms, quite small. In modern times, approximately one Frenchman in a hundred has decided to settle in the United States. Norway, with one-tenth the population of France, has sent more migrants across the ocean—an especially striking comparison, in view of the fact that France was in 1815 the most populous country of Europe after Russia.

Another particularity of these relatively minute movements of population is that they have been very stable. In recent times, of all national immigrations, that of the French has fluctuated least. Since the French Revolution, with the exception of the Depression years of the 1930s, the numbers per decade have ranged from a cellar of 39,000 in the 1940s to a ceiling of 77,000 in the 1840s. The yearly maximum has ranged from a few hundred in the 17th and 18th centuries to an all-time high of 20,000 during the Gold Rush, in 1851. This unusual stability has meant, incidentally, that the desire of the French to emigrate was not thwarted by the quota laws in force from the 1920s to the 1960s, which set limits based on earlier levels of immigration. For the Italians such a ruling made an enormous difference, but for the French it had little importance.

By virtue of its small size, French immigration has unique features. For instance, in some years (1915, 1918, 1919, 1931–1935) more Frenchmen have left America than have come to it. And in 1930 the proportion of French-born residents to the total population of the United States was precisely equal to that of Americans in France to the French population: one in a thousand. Like Americans in Paris, the French in America have been a culturally important but numerically insignificant group.

A MIGRATION OF INDIVIDUALS

French migration to the United States has never been a mass movement. This is not to say that economic factors have been irrelevant; they have mattered, but in a particular way.

To begin with, migration from France to America has sometimes been an inverse extension of migrations within France itself. Since the 1840s especially, but beginning in the 18th century, the French have in good times moved out of overpopulated rural areas to the cities. But when internal migration became less feasible, as it did in the 1870s, French emigration grew.

The ups and downs of U.S. economic life have also been important. Although it has been relatively stable, French migration has not been wholly constant. It declined in the 1930s, as it had previously in the late 1830s, and for the same reason: French public opinion has always been impressed by the booms and busts of U.S. economic life. When conditions were good in France, or bad in America, would-be emigrants postponed their departure.

Economic concerns have been of some consequence for all French migrants, and they have been of great importance for some of them. In a few provinces of France, in Alsace, Savoy, and the Pyrénées, emigration has come much closer to being an economically motivated mass movement. Many Americans of French ancestry have their origins in these places, and the institutional focuses of French life in Los Angeles during the 1870s were the appropriately named Café des Alpes and the Hôtel des Pyrénées.

Nevertheless, it should be remembered that the parts of France where emigration was close to being a collective phenomenon were in some ways atypical. The Basque country, Alsace, and Savoy were mountainous or peripheral areas, incompletely integrated economically or culturally. Whereas the inhabitants of the Ile-de-France might naturally follow established local economic networks by moving to Paris, Basques in 1900 would, with equal ease, move to South or North America, as they had to Spain in previous centuries. (*See also* Basques.)

In this respect, it is also worth noticing that the Pays de Caux (near Le Havre) and the Basque country, two emigrant-producing areas, were characterized by their particular customs of inheritance. In France, partible inheritance is generally the rule: all children share more or less equally. But in these two areas, impartible inheritance prevailed. Younger children were left to fend for themselves, and as a consequence were more likely to emigrate. Ordinary Frenchmen stayed home.

In earlier times, it is true, French emigration had been a more collective phenomenon: in the 17th and 18th centuries, many Frenchmen did migrate from poverty, but to Spain, Germany, and Hungary rather than to America. When the redirection of French migration from Europe to the United States took place about 1846, it coincided with a downward turn in French population growth, the beginning of a secular rise in the standard of living, and the end of mass migrations out of France.

For the French, then, the "new" mass migration came, so to speak, before the old one. The pattern differs from that which took place, let us say, in Poland or Italy. There, the migration of individual nobles, intellectuals, or merchants in the 18th century preceded the mass migrations of peasants and refugees in the late 19th century. French migration followed an inverse historical evolution, and probably was more middle-class in 1920 than it had ever been before.

As a rule, Frenchmen have come to America in small numbers, as individuals, and for that reason efforts to organize departures from France have always failed. Some isolated instances of group departures can be found, many of them arranged by clerics; in the 1880s some 300 Breton families were thus settled in Pittsburgh. But these are exceptions. In the 19th century immigration companies met with no more success in France than the land-settlement schemes that had been funded in the late 18th and early 19th centuries by prominent Americans and Frenchmen like Robert and Gouverneur Morris, Jacques Necker, and Mme. de Staël, or by French Americans like James Le Ray de Chaumont (1760–1840).

The key factor here has been the tempo of population growth. The French in modern times have not left their country in large numbers, partly because their society has been relatively prosperous and humane, but principally because the level of population in France has been so stable. Total population in France rose from 36 million in 1850 to only 40 million in 1940. Indeed, the population of France would have declined had it not been for the fact that, in some decades, France has absorbed more immigrants in proportion to its size than has the United States. This stability was accompanied by an unobtrusive rate of industrial growth which did not dislocate French society, as happened in late 19th-century Germany. There was no overwhelming reason for the French to leave their homeland, and it is hardly surprising that few of them did so.

RELIGIOUS REFUGEES

French migration to the United States must be seen as a sum of private decisions, made by isolated individuals who voluntarily chose to exclude themselves from the mainstream of French life. These decisions can (as in all things French) be divided into three categories: religious, political, and economic-ideological.

Of the French who have migrated for ostensibly religious reasons, the best known are the Huguenots. Some 14,000 of them came to the United States, a relatively large number; by comparison, French Canada drew only 12,000 Catholic settlers from the mother country. Huguenots began to leave France in 1538, at first for Germany, but eventually for North America. Their first hope was to establish independent, French-speaking settlements, one of them in Florida. This they did not achieve, but they had great success as settlers in the English-speaking colonies. Most of the Huguenots who came did so shortly before or after the revocation of the Edict of Nantes in 1685, which made Protestantism illegal in France. But Protestants continued to arrive in sizable groups during the 1760s.

French Protestants were active in all 13 colonies. The first child born in New York City, Jean Vigné, was of French stock. Harlem and Staten Island, N.Y., were French enclaves, as were New Rochelle and especially New Pfalz (now New Paltz), which despite its German name was a homogeneously French settlement. The

governor of New York described Huguenots in 1700 as "a good sort of people," and Pennsylvanians made a determined effort to attract them. Many also settled in Virginia, and especially in South Carolina, which of all the original colonies had in 1790 the highest proportion of inhabitants of French origin (4 percent). Finally, French Huguenots were particularly conspicuous in Massachusetts, since in the 18th century that colony attracted no other non-British immigrant group of any size.

With the French Revolution came Roman Catholic refugees, among them 100 priests, who were to form a critical mass in a country that had a Catholic clerical establishment of only 25 in 1789. The first American seminary was founded at Baltimore in 1791 by French Sulpicians, and the flow did not dry up when the French Revolution ended. In the 19th century, hundreds of French priests, monks, and nuns came to the United States, many of them settling in areas that had been French in colonial times, such as Louisiana, St. Louis, the Ohio River Valley, and upstate Michigan. The first Catholic cleric elected to Congress was a French-born priest, Father Gabriel Richard (1767–1832), a native of La Ville-des-Saints and the cofounder of the University of Michigan. Many French priests were also sent to minister to French-speaking Americans of Canadian or Acadian origin, especially in New England. In 1833, 6 of the 12 American bishops were French-born; 35 French priests have been named to American sees.

The presence of the French in the United States has had an important effect on the personnel of the U.S. Catholic Church, and has had varying doctrinal consequences for the country as a whole.

In a first colonial phase, the arrival of French Protestants served to sharpen anti-Catholic feelings. Although Huguenots were often taken to be Jesuits in disguise, they were in fact extreme in their antipopery, and in the late 17th century they reinforced English Protestant suspicions of the Roman Catholic Church.

During the American Revolution, however, this same feeling was defused by the presence of Catholic (but unmistakably aristocratic and liberal) French army officers, some of whom settled in America. A similar effect was achieved after 1789 by the arrival of urbane and elegant clerics like Médéric Louis Elie Moreau de St. Méry (1750–1815), who thought that Irish priests were "fanatics," and Msgr. Jean Louis Lefebvre de Cheverus (1768–1836)—the first bishop of Boston, the first cardinal to have been entrusted with the care of American souls, a founding member of the Boston Athenaeum, and a man much appreciated by John Adams and the Boston establishment.

Then, in the second quarter of the 19th century, a shift in French presence once again exacerbated anti-Romanism in the United States. Nativist reactions were fueled in this third phase by the annexation of Louisiana with its concentrated Catholic population and by the arrival of French missionaries in the western territories. Anti-Catholic feeling ran high and led to acts of mob violence, such as the destruction in 1834 of a French Ursuline convent in Charlestown, Mass.

Finally, the United States has also been a land of freedom and refuge for French Jews, many of whom came to America after the fall of France to the Germans in 1940. The most famous of them—André Maurois (1885–1967), Jacques Lipchitz (1891–1973), Darius Milhaud (1892–1974), Pierre Mendès-France (1907–)—returned to France in 1945, but some did decide to remain.

As early as 1871 many Alsatian Jews had come to America, after the Franco-Prussian War had put Alsace-Lorraine under German control. It would, of course, be inaccurate to describe these Alsatians simply as religious refugees. At the same time, their migration to America did have something to do with their Jewishness. Like Captain Alfred Dreyfus (the most famous Alsatian Jew of all), the Alsatians were fiercely French and refused to become German after 1871. But having few material ties to French society, Alsatian Jews could more easily envisage migration to America, and to Los Angeles in particular, where the French community in 1870 already counted among its most prominent members Constant Meyer, Leon Loeb, P.N. Roth, and Eugene Meyer, the president of the French Benevolent Society.

POLITICAL REFUGEES

In addition to religious refugees, many political exiles have come from France to America. All of the great political debates that have racked France since the 17th century have had repercussions across the Atlantic. French people already in America were quick to take sides for or against what was taking place at home. During the French Revolution, for example, the bête noire of the pro-royalist paper *Etoile Américaine* was none other than a pro-Convention sheet entitled the *Courrier Français*. This was the beginning of a long tradition. In 1873, for example, the majority of the French community in California extended their congratulations to Adolphe Thiers, then president of the republic, but in 1874 its more progressively minded members fêted a leader of the revolutionary Paris Commune, who had escaped from a penal colony to which he had been confined by the Thiers government. And in May 1941 a fistfight nearly broke out at a service in the Huguenot Church of New York between Vichy's ambassador to the United States and the Gaullist spokesman for the French Americans.

At least 10,000 refugees came during the French Revolution. Many arrived from France, but most of them had lived in the French Caribbean islands, which explains the settlement in America of about 3,000 people of mixed French and black descent. Of these, the best known at the time may well have been a young woman who, to the outrage of Philadelphia society, lived with the statesman Talleyrand during his years of refuge in the United States. Others were Pierre Toussaint (1766–1853), who achieved some prominence among Catholics in New York, and Louise Noël, a former slave who became mother superior of the Oblate Sisters of Baltimore, an order which a number of black Santo Domingans also joined. Philadelphia was the émigrés' favored place of residence. Both the municipality and the state voted them financial aid, and for some years the city of Benjamin Franklin (a cult figure in France among the ultraleft) was ironically a haven for exiled French monarchists.

The fall of Napoleon in 1815 brought an altogether different group of a few hundred Republican farmers, ex-soldiers of the emperor, who set up three unsuccessful communities, in Texas, in Ohio, and at Tombigbee

River in Alabama. Indeed, Napoleon himself thought of settling here, and some of his relatives actually did so in Pennsylvania. Jérôme, the emperor's scalawag young brother, created by his first marriage an American Bonapartist branch which grafted itself onto the Baltimore *beau monde,* as did a Murat who later befriended Ralph Waldo Emerson. Many of the American Bonapartes have attended Harvard College, and their most prominent scion, Charles J. Bonaparte (1851–1921), was secretary of the navy in 1905. As a politically useful southern Republican, a reformer who was kind to his Negro retainers, and a Catholic who was a gentleman, Charles Bonaparte symbolized the ambiguous position of established French Americans at the turn of the century, eminently respectable though still faintly foreign.

Mid-19th-century politics brought yet more dissidents. Oddly enough, the city of St. Louis in 1848 welcomed both defeated French socialists and anxious French planters from the Caribbean islands whose slaves had once again been freed. Some Communards came here as well after their defeat in 1871, among them Eugène Pottier (1816–1887) who composed the radicals' anthem "L'Internationale" in Hoboken, N.J., shortly after 1871. World War II and the fall of France brought a last contingent of political refugees, some of whom like Yves Tanguy (1900–1955), Alexis Léger (also known as St.-John Perse, 1887–1975), and Marcel Duchamp (1887–1968), stayed in America after the war.

IMMIGRANTS OF THE MIDDLE CLASS

More common, however, than either religious or political refugees were those Frenchmen who came to the United States from a blend of economic and ideological motives. Traditionally, these French émigrés prospered in America, since they were as a rule more skilled than immigrants from other countries.

In the 18th century Huguenots were often artisans, like Paul Revere's father, or specially skilled farmers who could work with vines or mulberry trees. Many others were merchants like Philip English (Langlais), one of the richest men in Salem, who was accused of witchcraft in 1692 by the farmers of Salem village and fled to New York. No less prosperous in the following century were the three Faneuil brothers, one of whom, Peter, a slave trader, became the second richest merchant in Boston and gave his name to Faneuil Hall, the "Cradle of Liberty." In 1738 his coffin was followed to the grave by 1,100 mourners, the largest assembly of this sort the colony had ever seen. French Huguenots were also among the most affluent rice planters of South Carolina.

In the 19th and 20th centuries many French immigrants were bourgeois members of the professions. While Paris was until the 1850s a mecca for American doctors, many French doctors came to America from the late 18th century onward, like Dr. Porchier at Charlestown, Mass.; Laurent Clerc (1785–1869), who with Thomas Gallaudet (1787–1851) founded at Hartford, Conn., a school for the deaf and dumb modeled on the Paris establishment of Abbé Sicard; and in 1848 Edouard Seguin (1812–1880), a pioneer in the education of the mentally retarded. French engineers have also been prominent here, as have French architects, economists, geographers, ornithologists, army officers, journalists, chemists, and so on.

Not surprisingly, a profile sketch based on the census figures for 1910 showed that the 70,000 Americans of French birth were better off, more literate, more likely to be married, had fewer children, more living space, fewer boarders, and were more concentrated in the liberal professions even than immigrants from Britain. Very revealing of their modern bourgeois character was the large proportion of French-born women who were employed (1 in 3, as against 1 in 14 for immigrants as a whole). Even working-class French immigration was at its own level skilled. In New York alone, in 1930, 3,000 Frenchmen worked in the restaurant business. French women have more often worked in shops retailing than in manufacturing.

THE FRENCH BACKGROUND

Clearly, the French in the United States have been an atypical immigrant group. That many of them should have left France for political and religious reasons is hardly surprising, but that French immigration should have been so consistently middle class and skilled needs to be explained.

In some respects, this was because France itself was more modern and prosperous than, let us say, Ireland, Italy, or the Slavic countries. But the problem is more complex, since French migrants have also been an unrepresentative cross section of the French nation itself. In 1931 a comparison of the entire population of France with the number of French abroad showed that the proportion of industrial workers and domestics was similar for the two groups, but two seemingly contradictory tendencies stood out very vividly. Although France was then still a predominantly rural nation, only 11 percent of French migrants were farmers. A precisely inverse ratio held for the mercantile interest and for the professions, which accounted for a proportion of migrants eight times greater than for the country as a whole. This baffling discrepancy lies at the heart of the question of French migration and explains the strong assimilationist propensities of French immigrants and their descendants in the United States. In order to understand the unusual characteristics of French immigration, one must step back and consider briefly the particular evolution of France as a modern society since the 17th century, when migration to America began.

France has always occupied an ambiguous place in the spectrum of modernization. Until very recent times, the French have been a peasant nation: Catholic, rural, hierarchical. But unlike other such countries, France has been at the same time a modern state, and in some ways the most modern of all: anticlerical, Cartesian, centralized, bourgeois, and technologically advanced. French history has been uniquely shaped by continual efforts to integrate these contrasting elements—by four centuries of debate between modernizers and traditionalists.

In the late 16th century, France might well have split in two if the monarchy had sided with the Protestants and had fallen into a northern Anglo-Dutch orbit. The crown chose instead to remain Catholic, and thus retarded the course of economic and institutional modernization. The state, though increasingly rational and

economically interventionist, remained tolerant of feudal anachronism and exiled its Protestant subjects to the four corners of the northern European world and to America.

Then, in the 18th century, France once again reached for supremacy in a world economy that was based at the time on the importation of American raw materials and the exportation to eastern and southern Europe of manufactured goods in exchange for foodstuffs. French trade increased tenfold between 1715 and 1789. But the French Revolution broke the back of this world-oriented economy, and France in the 19th century was again, as it had been two centuries before, an incompletely modern state.

To be sure, in this more tolerant age, engineers and technocrats were not pushed out as Protestants had been. Indeed, placed at the middle of a political system which included extreme antiparliamentary traditionalists on the right and revolutionary Marxists on the left, the centrists often ruled. The Orleanists—believers in constitutional monarchy—were in this tradition, as was in the 1920s André Tardieu, a prime minister known to the masses as Tardieu l'Américain.

Nonetheless, until the 1950s the modernizers in France were never more than a tolerated minority, removed from the dominant culture of the nation which remained statist, static, rural, and hierarchical. Their spiritual home was elsewhere, in Britain during the 18th century and after the 1870s in America, which was secular, stateless, gigantic, wildly innovative, and classless (or so they thought). The French birthrate was low. French industries were inefficient, whereas the United States in the modernizers' eyes represented efficiency par excellence, a country whose guiding economic principle, outside the neofeudal southern states, was "la méthode Taylor" (the scientific management schemes of Frederick W. Taylor). The United States was New York, and New York, in Louis Ferdinand Céline's words, was "une ville debout"—a city standing up.

Those who stayed home included the rentier class, obviously, but also the French peasantry, who had no cause to leave: although 1789 had not been their revolution, they could not be ignored by the elite, and the political system responded to their needs. Tariffs after 1892 protected peasants from foreign competition and French industrial growth remained sufficient to absorb surplus rural labor. French peasants did not come to the United States, and the very few who did leave France moved elsewhere—to Canada, at Saint Brieuc-en-Saskachewan, for example, which was settled by Bretons under Catholic aegis in 1901. It was the modernizers who crossed first the Channel and then the Atlantic.

Such is the secular context in which French immigration to the United States must be understood. Other causes such as religion may appear more immediate, but the heart of the issue of French immigration lies in the ambivalent attitude of the French nation to modernization, and in the migrants' vision of America as the land of the future. On the face of it, for example, the Huguenots were Protestant refugees who had sought refuge in a Protestant haven. In fact, the Huguenots were enterprising artisans and merchants, and colonial America was a place where such people might expect to do well.

It is quite true, of course, that America in the 1680s was hardly at the center of the world economy. Britain and Holland were at the hub of things, and it was in these places that most French Protestant exiles chose to live. But neither was America excluded from world trade. On the contrary, it was a crucial if dependent part of it, and French Protestants naturally fitted into the circuit. In South Carolina they developed the technique of rice growing, a key staple of international commerce. In Boston, Protestants made use of their contacts with the Calvinist French diaspora that was scattered from the Caribbean to northern Europe and, covertly, in France itself. The career of Gabriel Bernon was typical: a native of La Rochelle, where his brother was a banker, Bernon developed connections in the Caribbean islands; went to Canada; returned; smuggled funds out of France into Holland; arrived in Boston in 1688; went into the naval goods business; traveled twice to London in 1693 and 1696; and died in Providence in 1736, a model of civic virtue, having sired four children by his second wife, whom he married at the age of 67.

A more or less similar pattern underlies later French immigration to America, when the locus of economic opportunity shifted away from commerce. To be sure, after 1800 many French immigrants came here as merchants in wines or as artisans in luxury trades; at Paterson, N.J., for example, they played an important role in the making of silk. But in a more technical and industrial age, the significant participants were in the professions: doctors, architects, engineers, professors, and the like.

To what extent such immigrants have been modernizers estranged from the dominant aspects of a tradition-bound, classic French culture, we will never know. But it is significant that so many of those Frenchmen who have come here appear to have been ill at ease at home. America for them was often the last stop in a peripatetic career of worldwide peregrination. A number of Protestants came here after having settled elsewhere, in the Caribbean especially; French miners who came to California and Basque shepherds had often resided first in South America. As many as a fifth of the French people arriving in the United States in the 1900s had migrated to some other place before: the sculptor Augustus Saint-Gaudens (1848–1907), for example, was French, but in a special way, since he was born in Dublin to a French cobbler who had temporarily settled there. Even more symbolic of the modernizing temperament and its estrangement from France is the career of Eleuthère Irénée Dupont de Nemours (1772–1834), an avid modernizer, a physiocratic free trader, a friend of the statesman Jacques Turgot and of Mme. de Staël, and the apologist par excellence of modern bourgeois values (self-reliance, thrift, industry). Dupont was disgusted by the French Revolution and came to the United States to create in 1802 what would in his descendants' care become the largest industrial concern in history—the Dupont Chemical–General Motors complex.

ASSIMILATION

From at least the 18th century, Frenchmen, at times with enthusiasm but usually with horror, have imagined the United States to embody in an outré but somehow operative form the corrosive forces that were at play in their own society. In the 18th century, America

was considered more natural and free. In the first half of the 19th century, it was judged more democratic and more materialist. Today, America is thought more unstable, more drug and crime ridden, and its inhabitants sexually more perverse—a complete reversal, incidentally, of Tocqueville's view of American women. It is to find these "scenes of future life" that French immigrants have come to this country.

Most Europeans have crossed the ocean to find a better present or to escape the past, but French immigrants have been resolute futurists, and never more so than during the decadent years of their national history, from 1870 to 1950, when French population growth was low and industry declined. American society has always seemed dynamic and forward-looking in comparison. "How can we explain the superiority of the Anglo-Saxons?" Edmond Desmolins asked in his best seller of 1902. French immigrants came here to find out.

Given this background of alienation and yearning, it is hardly surprising that French immigrants, self-selecting and at odds with the national ethos, should have been assimilationists. The French authorities (reported the *Literary Digest* in 1920) say "that it is not instinctive among the French to segregate themselves. They differ from some other races in not having social and cultural societies that hold them together as separate units." This is certainly true.

Two different explanations can be offered for this absence of group spirit among French migrants. First, French people in any one place were very few and could not sustain a lasting communal life. Second, all French people, traditionalists and modernizers alike, have a notoriously low capacity for group action. It is no surprise that the philosophe Comte de Volney, while visiting Indiana, should have nodded wisely when told that the French "understand nothing of political civil or domestic affairs . . . Their first demand was for a commanding officer, and it was the most difficult thing possible to make them comprehend anything of a municipal administration chosen by and among themselves." Neither should we reject the judgment of the last Russian commander at Fort Ross, who said of the French forty-niners that they were particularly disordered, "as they form no associations."

More important, however, is the fact that the French who came to the United States were thirsting for new forms of society and culture. They may not have come in order to be Americans, but they did intend to find the cultural ambience they had not found at home. They melted into the mass of American life because they wanted to. So-called Frenchtowns inhabited principally by French settlers have existed: one such was founded in Rhode Island in 1686, and others were later created in Maine, Michigan, and Pennsylvania. But city-born French who determined for some transient ideological reason to create rural communities as asylums removed from urban life were invariably unsuccessful. Of these, the best known was the Icarian community (f. 1848) of Etienne Cabet (1788–1856) on the Red River in Texas, which failed dramatically. Such picaresque ventures have had very little to do with the desires of most French immigrants to America, whose goal has been to live in metropolitan cities where they might fuse with the dominant elements of U.S. life.

Strikingly, the pattern in this regard was set at once

by the Huguenots, whose single most salient cultural decision wherever they settled in the colonies was to become Anglican. In France they had been unrepentant Calvinists because this stern doctrine best expressed their distance from the mainstream of French life. In America, where they wished to blend, Anglicanism seemed a better option, and it is easy to conclude that their adherence to this neopopish doctrine was a reflected social option, especially since many enterprising Puritan merchants were undergoing a similar conversion at the time. Gabriel Bernon typifies this conversion: at the age of 81 he traveled to London and asked the Society for the Propagation of the Gospel in Foreign Lands to assign an Anglican priest to the French community in Providence, where a church still bears his name. Most Boston Huguenots, with their minister Pierre Daillé, were similarly inclined. In South Carolina the French had converted by 1706; so did their brethren in New York, and the last surviving Huguenot Temple in that city was reconsecrated in 1804 by the local Episcopal bishop as the Church of the Holy Spirit. The French Calvinist minorities who remained adamant were at once more cohesively French, more rural, and less well off than their Anglicanized and assimilated compatriots.

The sequels of assimilationism in more recent times have been of the same sort. In France, cultural nationalism has been more acute than in any other European country, but the French in the United States have steadfastly rejected this example. The rate of exogamous intermarriage of French immigrants, for example, has been higher than that of any other non-English-speaking group.

French immigrants have always espoused local mores and have therefore become loyal supporters of the American establishment, regardless of its hue. When General John Charles Frémont led the Bear Flag revolt in California, some of the officers in the opposing Mexican army were acculturated French migrants who had settled in early Los Angeles. Later, during the Civil War, many French Americans and French-Canadian Americans in the North were enrolled in a special unit —the New York 55th Regiment. Officers of French descent were even more conspicuous in the Confederate army, one of them, the 68-year-old Benjamin Buisson, a veteran of Napoleonic wars. And when Admiral David G. Farragut, of French Huguenot ancestry, sailed up the Mississippi in 1862, he met with fierce resistance from the French-speaking Louisiana Zouave battalion, a martial outfit, but doctrinally confused, since it resisted the Union bombardment to the strains of the *Marseillaise*.

GEOGRAPHIC DISTRIBUTION

On the whole, the French who have come here have been eager to assimilate, and this is borne out by their geographic distribution in the United States. Traditionally, the French have not gone where other French were already living, but where new opportunities might be found. Their settlement in Louisiana bears this out. In 1860 the state counted 15,000 French-born residents, most of them in New Orleans. But when the Mississippi lost ground to the northern railways as a path to the West, and when the city ceased to be the great emporium that it had once been, French settlement

dropped off, regardless of sentimental ties, to 10,000 in 1880 and 7,300 in 1930. Conversely, the French population of California has risen steadily (with a slight drop in the 1930s) from 8,000 in 1860 to 22,000 in 1970. The vicissitudes of New York's French population are also revealing. In proportion to the total population of the city, the French-born community peaked in 1688. But in absolute numbers it rose until 1930 to 23,300 and has since steadily declined to 15,500. Very curious also is the sudden jump in the French-born population of the Southern sun belt. In 1940 it had fallen to an all-time low. But by 1970 it had doubled, a curious lead-indicator of economic growth in the United States. French immigrants have looked for a chance to rise, and this has meant by implication that the French from France have not had much to say to other Franco-Americans of more ancient vintage—to the Louisiana French of the stagnant South, or to the devout, tradition-minded French Canadians in decaying New England textile towns.

The destination of French immigrants was conditioned by their cultural outlook, and so was their place of origin in France. Although many French came from peripheral areas of the nation, the more representative migrant came from whatever part of France was at that time most closely integrated into modern economic life. In the 17th and 18th centuries when French northern and Atlantic ports were heavily involved in world trade, most migrants, both Catholics going to Canada and Protestants to the 13 colonies, came from Normandy, Poitou, Saintonge, and Bordeaux. But in the 19th century the geographic origins of the migrants shifted. Henceforth, they came from eastern France and the Paris basin—that is, east of the celebrated Le Havre–Marseilles line which separates modern France from the "désert français." Their homes in France were in regions where literacy was higher, the economy more dynamic, and the population more oriented to the principles of the market.

ORGANIZATIONS

The average French immigrant has been an unaverage sort of French person, eager to do well and eager to be integrated into the dominant strands of American life. This is not to say that the French in America have methodically denied their origins. Some such cases of apostasy do exist: John Jay of Jay's Treaty was bitterly anti-Catholic and therefore anti-French. Similarly, Charles Joseph Bonaparte "did not like the French and was not proud of his French ancestry." Having left under a cloud, many Americans of French origin, and their descendants, have naturally enough felt somewhat removed from the Grande Nation. The more usual pattern, however, has been one of distant loyalty.

Institutions designed to preserve French culture have always existed, and the first French newspaper in America was founded in Philadelphia back in 1784. French-speaking groups of more distant French origins have supported various publications (the *Moniteur de la Louisiane* was founded in 1794, and the French-Canadian *Le Patriote* was set up in Burlington, Vt., in 1834), but the French from France have also had publications of their own: *Le Courrier des Etats-Unis*, founded in 1840 by Frédéric Gaillardet (1808–1882), had a national audience, as does today *France-Amérique*, a New York weekly set up in 1943 by prominent French refugees.

Eighteenth-century fixtures such as the South Carolina Huguenot Benevolent Society (f. 1736) have also had 19th-century echoes in organizations like the Californian French Benevolent Association.

But many national French groups, such as the American Association of French Engineers or the American Association of the French Legion of Honor, have been elitist or assimilationist and have been principally concerned with bringing together prominent French Americans with prominent Americans interested in things French. The Society of the Cincinnati, founded immediately after the American Revolution to bring together bourgeois American and noble French officers, is typical: French-American institutions are seldom exclusively French.

Within French-American communities it is difficult to find many traces of continuity. Some links have existed. In 1756, for example, André Bénézet, a French Huguenot, took especial care of the hapless Acadians who had been dumped in Pennsylvania by British order. In the early 19th century, Stephen Girard (1750–1831) and James Le Ray, two French-born financiers, also had close contacts with French refugees of the right in the 1790s, and of the left after 1815. Many families in St. Louis have gone out of their way to welcome arrivals and to maintain contact with their French relations. Not too much, however, should be made of such connections, which were on the whole marginal to the lives of those involved. Though French immigrants have as a rule been eager to maintain some connection with the motherland, they have never made a fetish of their French "ethnicity."

FRENCH CULTURE IN AMERICAN LIFE

Most French immigrants have blended into American life. One important reason for their success has been the particular relation of the French culture to that in the United States. Ordinarily, ethnic cultures have been a brake on assimilation, but for the French, the reverse has been true. Culturally and metaphorically speaking, it has always been a shorter step from Paris to New York than from Palermo, Dublin, or Lublin. The brand of French culture to which French immigrants have subscribed has placed them squarely in the mainstream of American life. Because they represented the modernizing side of France, they more easily became "American"—that is, enterprising, progressive, secular, and upward bound.

It is also of great importance that Frenchness has always been in America a "most favored" foreign culture. Archibald MacLeish, for example, explained in 1941 that "if America had something to offer to French poets, artists and musicians exiled by the Nazis . . . it is the ability to find in America their own strength and purpose without having to sacrifice their French character or their artistic integrity"; this could hardly have been said in the same way, by an American, for any other foreign culture.

Of course, many Americans have held the French in very low esteem as small, dark, excitable, atheistic, immoral, and none too virile—Arsène Lupin at their best, Lucky Pierre at their worst. But this view of France has never been the rule, especially in the upper strata of American society. French culture has in fact been for many Americans an entrée into world culture. French

cooking, manners, fashions, music, books and plays, and for that matter the French language itself have always had a wide audience in the United States. Quintessentially American authors like James Fenimore Cooper, Mark Twain, and Ernest Hemingway lived for years in France, and Francophilia has been since the 1770s the expression of some deep longing in the American psyche.

The cultures of the two republics though quite different are also very close, and symbolically the great emblems of American life have all had some French dimension: the White House is a copy of a French château, the bald eagle is Major l'Enfant's less well-known gift to his adopted land, and the Statue of Liberty (on Bedloe's Island, a Huguenot settlement) is the work of a French sculptor—an ironic choice for the United States to have made, in a way, for if more impoverished French had joined Europe's teeming, huddled masses, America might well have turned to some other country to find the symbol that was for immigrants the promise of a more decent life. For the members of most American ethnic groups, to be "ethnic" is an act of mild defiance; for French Americans it is, paradoxically, an act of compliance.

FRENCH CONTRIBUTIONS TO AMERICAN LIFE

The contributions of the French to American life have been varied and on the whole positive. The principal role of French Americans has been to act less in their own right than as conveyors for the American bourgeoisie of French culture generally, and it can safely be said that the influence of France on America has far outstripped that of French Americans. The Marquis de Lafayette and Tocqueville have mattered more to Americans than the Faneuils or the Duponts. The French have been of primary consequence as disseminators in America of the message of the Grande Nation—as professors, minor practitioners of French-taught skills, architects of the Beaux Arts school, teachers of literature, draftsmen, musicians, and painters. In the same way, French immigrants have provided the kernel of an audience in America for French artists, writers, and performers ever since 1790, when a French troupe staged in Baltimore the first American performance of an opera, Giovanni Battista Pergolesi's *La Serva Padrona*.

That theirs should have been a minor creative role could hardly be avoided, given the minute scale of French immigration. But French immigrants have mattered in their own right. Their most distinctive function has been to introduce elements of Mediterranean culture into the mainstream of Protestant middle-class American life. Rather improbably, the Huguenots themselves did this. Regarded in France as dour and unbending, they were well known in America for their stylish way of life. French-Protestant vintners thrived in the colonies nearly two centuries before French-Catholic vintners arrived in California. Huguenot homes were decorated with better furniture, mirrors, and carpets; silversmiths of French origin like Paul Revere were the most skilled practitioners of their art in America, as they were in 18th-century Britain as well.

Standard American cooking is vastly superior to its British counterpart, and the French have had a great deal to do with this. It was the Huguenots who introduced yeast, buns, okra, artichokes, and tomatoes. A French émigré named Julien, the king of soups and consommés, was a well-known fixture in Boston, where he also made popular the cheese omelet. French fashions, shops, hairdressers, and ladies' maids come under the same general rubric of improvements in the quality of life.

No one could object to better food and wine. The political effect of French immigration, however, can be more varyingly interpreted. Baldly stated, the impact of immigration in America has been to accentuate the material reality of class differences and at the same time to weaken our awareness of them. Immigrants have traditionally been among the poorest in the land, and the myth of social advancement within a single generation has been for them a cruel hoax. And yet the poor in America have been far less class conscious than the poor in Europe. One reason for this is that ethnic and racial divisions in the United States have made the development of class consciousness much more problematic. The French have contributed to this syndrome in a roundabout way. By reinforcing the middle classes they have served to widen class differences, but their success has weakened the perception of class barriers in American life.

On the face of it, the success of French immigrants attests to the fluidity of American social life. In truth, it merely says that immigrants, like flowing water, will find their own social level. Class consciousness may not be able to leap over national borders, but practical class distinctions do so with ease. If French immigrants have managed to become bourgeois Americans, it is primarily because they were bourgeois in France. American social structure has had little to do with their success, but this has not been the general perception of their case.

FAILURE OR SUCCESS?

The nature of immigration from France to the United States has many interesting implications for the history of both countries. But its principal interest may be in what it tells us about the meaning of "success" for immigrants.

In an immediate sense, the French have been extremely successful in the United States. It was estimated in the 1930s that one entry in ten in the *Dictionary of American Biography* had some French connection. In addition to well-known signers of the Constitution and to presidents with French ancestors (like George Washington, John Tyler, James A. Garfield, Theodore and Franklin Roosevelt), one could add less prominent military figures like Admirals Stephen Decatur and George Dewey (Douay); Generals Benjamin Bonneville and John J. Pershing (of Alsatian descent); politicians like Robert La Follette and Gifford Pinchot; bankers like Girard, Le Ray, and J. Pierpont Morgan; businessmen like E.I. Dupont and Paul Tulane; sculptors like Augustus Saint-Gaudens and Gaston Lachaise (1882–1935); musicians like Pierre Boulez (1925–) and Pierre Monteux (1875–1964); and educators like Gallaudet, Matthew Vassar (1792–1868), and Henry Fowle Durant (1822–1881), the founder of Wellesley College.

Indeed, the French have often been perceived as "honorary Anglo-Saxons"; the founding of the Huguenot Society of America in 1883, of the Huguenot Society of

South Carolina in 1885, and of the Huguenot Historical Society in 1894 were ironically facets of a nativist, anti-immigrant mood. It is suggestive also that so many French names should have been successfully Anglicized (Revere from Rivoire, Bullitt from Boulez, Bowdoin from Baudouin, Bumpy from Bon Pas, Drinkwater from Boileau, Fauconnier to Faulkner, Chamois to Shanway, Tiphaine to Tiffany, and so on.)

But what is success for an immigrant? In a sketch of his life, Henry David Thoreau began with "I am of French extract," yet never alludes to this fact again. There are Jewish writers in America, but are there French writers? Although the list of American authors of French origin is considerable—including Philip Freneau, Henry Wadsworth Longfellow, John Greenleaf (Feuillevert) Whittier, Richard Henry Dana, Sidney Lanier, and Edna St. Vincent Millay—it would be absurd to speak of a Franco-American literary school. The term Franco-American is itself faintly ridiculous and utterly imprecise, since there has never been a Franco-American culture. French immigrants came here as individuals; succeeded as such, and in so doing, ceased to be French, without for that matter becoming really American, since the America they embraced was a figment of their own imagination. Punning on the double meaning of the term *naturalisé*, which in the French of taxidermists also means "stuffed," the naturalized Marcel Duchamp liked to paint himself as a *citoyen naturalisé*, stuffed and disembodied. He had become, in his own words, an "approximation."

The cost of assimilation has been high both for those who succeeded and "passed" into American life, and for those who failed to do so. The number of French immigrants who have returned to France has been unusually high, and in recent years, only one-third of registered French immigrants have decided to become American citizens. Of course, French immigrants, who are often middle-class, can afford to go back home, and being skilled, can find a place at home if they return. It is also true that the French, who feel their culture to be a superior one, have often been reluctant to integrate with native cultures—in Mexico or Argentina, for example. But it is harder to apply this concept to French people in America.

The overall picture is paradoxical. Few French people have chosen to come to the United States; of those who did, many were unusually successful. But many French immigrants also decided to return; in California, for example, the French community had a special fund to help those who wished to go home.

The conjunction of a high rate of success with a high rate of failure goes back to the particular nature of the French immigrant's vision of himself, of his homeland, and of the United States. The hopes of the French in America have run high, and consequently their disappointment has often been profound. This contrast characterizes the entire French immigration in the United States, and no better example of it can be found than that of French immigration to California between the years 1849 and 1851—the greatest single migration from France to the United States. A wave of 30,000 French immigrants broke on California's shores. "Everyone has rushed here," wrote a French journalist, "merchants, workmen, clerks, women, old men, children, everyone, from the peasant to the man of the

world and even (who would believe it?) the rentier, who hoped to triple his income and who is eating it up: all wanted to share this wealth which they would find so easily in this corner of the New World, but what they found, let us say it, is misery." Great expectations are difficult to sustain.

In some measure, the French have been better placed to resolve the classic dilemma of all immigrants, who must learn somehow to cope with two different and often conflicting ethics. French culture, in France, has characteristically been structured around a blend of public conformity and privatist, individual withdrawal. Because of this innately learned double standard, French immigrants were instinctively better able to be at once thoroughly assimilationist in their business life and intensely French in their private life; though they might not live in French quarters, they would go some distance to buy French bread. But even in this context, their success may not always bear close scrutiny. The French for all their well known malice are perhaps the most urbane and civilized of all western peoples. Theirs is a pessimistic culture—ordered, measured, balanced. That of the United States, for all its life and optimism, is full of sound and fury and violence. To pass from one to the other, even for modernizers eager to compete, is to pay a high cost for success.

Bibliography
The best thematic introduction to the question of French immigration to the United States is L. Chevalier's "L'Emigration française au XIXe siècle" in *Etudes d'Histoire moderne et contemporaine* vol. 1 (Paris, 1947). Henri Bunle's "L'Immigration française aux Etats Unis," in *Bulletin de la Statistique générale de la France*, vol. 14 (January 1925), contains interesting facts, figures, and charts, as do reports of the U.S. Bureau of the Census.

Gilbert Chinard's *Les Réfugiés Huguenots en Amérique* (Paris, 1925) is a learned account of the place of French Protestants in American life during the 17th and 18th centuries. Frances S. Child, *French Refugee Life in the United States, 1790–1800* (Baltimore, 1940), is a thorough study of the complexities of French-American relations during the French Revolution. Leo F. Ruskowski, *French Emigré Priests in the United States, 1791–1815* (Washington, D.C., 1940), carries the story into the 19th century, as does Howard Mumford Jones's sympathetic and intelligent account of *America and French Culture, 1750–1843* (Chapel Hill, N.C., 1927).

Particular aspects of French immigration are successfully treated in Abraham P. Nasatir, *A French Journalist in the California Gold Rush* (Georgetown, 1964), and Heinrich Neu, "Elsässer und Lothringer als Ansiedler in Nord-Amerika," *Elsass-Lothringische Wissenschaftliche Gesellschaft zu Strassburg: Jahrbuch* 3 (Heidelberg, 1930).

Henri Peyre, "Deux Cents Ans de relations franco-américaines," *The French Review*, vol. 49 (May 1976), and René Rémond, *Les Etats-Unis devant l'opinion française, 1815–1852* (Paris, 1962), have a different focus; they are more concerned with the United States as it was perceived in France than with French immigrants, but even their incidental remarks are enlightening and useful. Finally, Henry Blumenthal, *American and French Culture, 1800–1900* (Baton Rouge, La., 1976), is a recent survey of the question.

PATRICE LOUIS RENÉ HIGONNET

FRENCH CANADIANS

The French Canadians are the descendants of the explorers and settlers who came from France during the 17th century to establish New France in what is today Canada. Although some migrated southward from New France to the English colonies before the American Revolution and during the half-century after, the majority came to the United States between 1845 and 1895. Nearly two-thirds of the latter migrants settled in the six New England states; the rest spread across the

country as far west as Montana. However, their numbers fluctuated owing to extensive return migration. By 1950, in the last federal census to enumerate them separately, there were 238,400 foreign-born and 519,500 second-generation French Canadian Americans in the United States, over 70 percent of them in New England. In the 1970 Census, which distinguished Canadians only on the basis of the language spoken at home when they were children, 200,000 Canadian-born residents gave French as their mother tongue, as did nearly 495,000 second-generation Canadian Americans. Although the census does not provide information on later generations, it is reasonable to estimate that there are over 1.5 million people of French Canadian descent in the United States.

In 1970 foreign-born, French-speaking Canadians made up only 49 percent of the foreign-born whose mother tongue was French; among second-generation Americans, French Canadians accounted for 68 percent of those reporting French as their mother tongue. In other words, French Canadian Americans are one part of a larger group, sometimes called Franco-Americans. That term first appeared among French Canadians at the end of the last century and was adopted by all those whose families traditionally used French and who traced their ancestry to France. Despite that common background, historical experiences in America fostered significant differences among the French-speaking in terms of culture, customs, and dialect. For instance, French settlers in Acadia (today Nova Scotia, New Brunswick, and other nearby areas) were expelled by the British in 1755. Some came to live in northern Maine and are still known as Acadians, while other Acadians migrated to Louisiana, where their name eventually was corrupted to Cajun. In contrast, the French Canadians remained isolated in their settlements along the St. Lawrence River after the British defeated France in the French and Indian War (1754–1763) and acquired New France. In addition to Cajuns, Acadians, and French Canadians, other Americans of French background are those who came—or whose families came—directly from France. (See also Acadians; Alsatians; French.)

French Canadians, like the Cajuns and Acadians (but more so than the French from France), have struggled to preserve their ancestral language, Catholic faith, and distinct traditions. Proximity to Quebec province (as the populated region of New France was renamed) enabled them to keep their subculture intact longer than many other groups have been able to do.

FRENCH CANADIAN ORIGINS AND EARLY DEVELOPMENT

French Canadians have always regarded Quebec in the period preceding the British conquest as the root of their culture and identity. For them it was a lost para-

dise, peopled by an extraordinary group of explorers, Catholic missionaries, fur traders (*coureurs de bois*), and farmers (*habitants*). Only after the fall of New France and the American Revolution had curtailed the activities of the explorers, missionaries, and fur traders outside of Canada did the rural, parish-centered lifestyle come to dominate the French Canadian world. When that shift occurred, the survival of the French Canadian language, faith, and customs became the object of great devotion. It is the combination of the mystique surrounding the early groups and the legacy of the rural milieu, with its profound ethnic loyalty, that accounts for much of the pride and tenacity in the French Canadian subculture.

Samuel de Champlain (1567?–1635), the father of New France, established the colony of Quebec in 1608 at the narrows of the St. Lawrence River, under the sponsorship of a fur trading company. Hundreds of early French Canadians established settlements and trading posts, from Maine and Vermont as far west as the Great Lakes, Louisiana, the Rocky Mountains, and beyond. As late as the 1700s the adventures and successes of the fur traders lured farmers off the land and into the forests. Even in the United States, some 3,000 French place names, from Maine and Vermont to Oregon, testify to the dynamism of the early French Canadians. Their achievements remained an important source of inspiration long after the era of expansion had passed.

From the early years the spirit of the French Canadians was also intensely religious. The Recollects, ascetic Franciscans, came in 1615 to convert the Indians. The Jesuits followed a decade later and were soon joined by Capuchins, Ursulines, Sulpicians, and others. The royal charter for New France in 1627 stated that the king's goal was to convert Indians, and indeed that religious objective—along with the preservation of the faith of the colonists—shaped the life of New France. In fact, many Quebecois came to believe that they were a chosen people, a missionary people. François Xavier de Laval (1623–1708), vicar apostolic of New France (1659–1674) and the first bishop of Quebec (1674–1684), did much to shape that image. He established a powerful church structure more loyal to Rome than to the French monarchy and equal with the civil government of New France. He made Quebec a stronghold of clericalism and missionary zeal. The many missionaries who accompanied the explorers—when they were not traveling by themselves—added to the overall religious commitment urged by Bishop Laval. French Canadians never lost this commitment.

In 1663 Louis XIV and his minister, Jean-Baptiste Colbert, established a royal government in New France. They were determined to settle the colony with farmers. And farmers came, first from Brittany and Normandy and later from Perche, Poitou, Picardy, and elsewhere, increasing the population of New France from 2,500 in 1660 to 37,700 by 1734. In 1765, two years after the Treaty of Paris ended a century of war between France and England and changed New France into British Canada, between 60,000 and 70,000 French Canadians inhabited the area.

Despite this relatively small population, the French government had made an effort to enlarge its colony. Primarily, it had resorted to the seigneurial system, making grants of land along the St. Lawrence River on the condition that the recipients transport settlers to farm the land or forfeit their grants. As a way to transplant French feudalism, the effort failed, but as the foundation of rural French Canadian society, it succeeded. Many seigneurs found, contrary to their expectations, that they could not survive without working themselves. Conditions in the New World also profoundly affected the attitudes of their tenants. The settlers transported by the seigneurs rejected the traditional name of *censitaires* because of its servile connotations and insisted on being referred to simply as habitants. They paid few feudal taxes to the landowners, defied customs, and only occasionally, when not running off to trade in furs, farmed the land they had been brought to till. The farmers never acquired any role in government, however. Printing presses were forbidden; education and political consciousness were not encouraged. Obedience, humility, chastity, and religiosity were the ideals repeatedly stressed by church and government leaders. The result was a two-level society, with great concentrations of civil and ecclesiastical power at the top and below an uneducated people who possessed little civic consciousness but had a strong attachment to their church.

Although the Treaty of Paris ended the royal government of New France, it left the ecclesiastical structure intact. More importantly, the Quebecois were cut off from France and forced back upon themselves—upon their families, their land, their parish, their priests, their language, their law and customs, and upon their memories. The philosophy of *survivance* then emerged in the parishes along the St. Lawrence. Surrounded by an Anglo-Protestant—which for them was synonymous with "pagan"—nation, the French Canadians came to view themselves as abandoned, not conquered: they symbolically portrayed themselves as Esau and the English as Jacob, depriving them of their birthright.

The American Revolution brought about the first extensive contact between inhabitants of the 13 colonies and the Quebecois, for the revolutionary forces invaded the province of Quebec in September 1775. While many Quebecois were hostile toward the revolutionists because of their long-standing anti-French, anti-Catholic attitudes, others were stirred by their ideas of individual freedom, natural rights, and representative government. As a result, many Quebecois refused to take up arms against the invading forces. Approximately 500 *congressistes* actually joined the revolutionary side and were organized into companies by Moses Hazen and James Livingston. Another 125 or so French Canadians from Vincennes, Ind., and Kankakee, Ill., supported George Rogers Clark in the West. When the American armies retreated early in 1776, some 125 to 150 French Canadians accompanied them. These men and those who fought under Clark subsequently were rewarded with grants of land adjacent to Lake Champlain, known thereafter as "The Refugees' Tract," and in the Western Reserve.

THE ERAS OF FRENCH CANADIAN MIGRATION

Prewar and wartime patterns of contact with Americans continued, for feelings of wanderlust and discontent did not disappear among French Canadians after 1783. The land could not support all their children, nor were all content with a harsh life that revolved around a

bare three-month growing season. Many had had more or less regular trade relations with the English colonies and wanted to renew them with the new American states. This trade and the outlying settlements and trading posts established by the Quebecois were harbingers of developments that soon began in earnest: the drift of French Canadians south and southwestward to the timber- and farmlands of Maine, Vermont, New Hampshire, and New York and to the dense forests and the more open regions south of the three western Great Lakes. Thus the geographic and economic bonds of the colonial and revolutionary eras foreshadowed later ties between Quebec and the United States.

During the half-century before 1830, a number of French Canadians continued to explore, trade, and settle in the vast Louisiana Territory, even after the United States purchased it in 1803. Among these settlers were Julien Dubuque (Dubuque, Iowa, 1796), Joseph Robidou (St. Joseph, Mo., 1812), Jean-Baptiste Beaubien (Chicago, 1813), and Laurent Salomon Juneau (Milwaukee, 1818). There were approximately 6,000 French Canadians in the West in 1790 (although there may have been many more before 1763), including 3,100 in Michigan alone. By 1820 the Michigan group had increased to 6,000 people, three-fourths of whom lived in the Detroit area. Meanwhile in the East, French Canadians from the Quebec counties of Témiscouata, Kamouraska, and L'Islet had begun to join Acadians in the Madawaska-Aroostook (upper St. John River) region, which would become part of Maine in 1842. The first U.S. Census in 1790 listed about 350 Quebecois in Vermont, some 1,200 in Maine, and 1,000 in New Hampshire. During the first third of the 19th century, economic and political conditions pushed groups of families to Vermont and then farther south and east to Woonsocket, R.I., Worcester, Mass., Manchester, N.H., and Lewiston, Me., all of which later became major French Canadian centers.

The same economic and political conditions converged more forcefully in the years after 1830. First came an uprising against the British in 1838 which, though short-lived, remained an inspiration to French Canadians in their determined efforts to maintain their heritage. It climaxed years of mounting resentment over British Canadian intolerance, increasing religious and cultural conflict, and outright clashes. The economic threat of the nearby Erie Canal, England's drift toward free trade (with its adverse effect on its colony in Canada), and the oligarchic practices of the governor and his council compounded the dissatisfaction of the Quebecois. Coinciding with William Mackenzie's revolt in Upper Canada in 1838, there was a clash between habitants and British Canadian soldiers. This nascent nationalist movement aborted after some of the leaders fled to northern New York and Vermont. Others were caught and imprisoned, exiled, or executed. Another uprising the same year found few supporters returning from the United States and little military aid from that source. In the aftermath, many disheartened and discontented French Canadians migrated to New England, Illinois, Wisconsin, and even to California and Louisiana. However, many of them returned within a few years, when a general amnesty bill was passed.

In terms of numbers, the revolt produced no great migration. The French Canadian population of New Eng-

land in 1840, for example, has been estimated at only 8,200 (8,000 of them in Maine and Vermont). It did result in the six-month publication in 1839–1840 of the first French-Canadian newspaper in New England, *Le Patriote Canadien*. The revolt also had a definite impact on the ideas the Quebecois carried to the United States, because the political settlement afterward generally thwarted the full development of Quebec nationalism until after the great waves of migration began rolling southward—until, that is, the last decades of the 19th century and the rise of the French Canadian leader Henri Bourassa. Thus the French Canadians who migrated soon after the revolt carried with them not a well-developed sense of nationalism but rather a commitment to a definite lifestyle and set of beliefs, which formed the heart and soul of the French Canadian subculture. They and their children adhered to both, even as their attachment to Quebec itself weakened.

The peoples who carried that subculture to the United States did not migrate all at once, nor did they leave readily. What began as a temporary movement in the 1840s became more permanent as conditions in Quebec failed to improve. The tightly woven fabric of Quebec life could not stretch indefinitely. Increasing difficulties eroded the ability of the habitants to adapt to and remain in their family parish or even in the vicinity. French Canadian emigration to the United States continued irregularly up to a peak between 1880 and 1895, gradually tapered off, then surged again between 1923 and 1929. The migration was a response to six overlapping developments:

1. The shortage of desirable land in Quebec became acute during the 19th century, and population pressure became too great for the outmoded agricultural technology. Canada's economic maladies, slow industrial development, generally inhospitable western lands, and apathetic land policy left few alternatives once the land near the St. Lawrence could no longer contain the Quebecois. Those who already lived in cities and were unable to find work were the most numerous of the emigrants prior to 1860. After the Civil War those from the countryside constituted an ever-increasing proportion of the emigrants, more and more of whom took their families.

2. The geographical proximity of Quebec to the centers of U.S. development eliminated many of the customary obstacles facing emigrants. "Going to America" was a relatively short journey for the Quebecois, whether by lumber wagon, baker's cart, stagecoach, or foot. The opening of railroad lines between Quebec and Boston (1851), Portland, Me. (1853), and New York (1854), and between Toronto and Chicago via Detroit (1855), tightened the bond between the two North American countries and heightened the importance of proximity.

3. Canada, as a colony of Great Britain, had been shielded by the British Corn Laws from unlimited dumping of American grain on its markets. But in the 1820s Great Britain began moving toward a free-trade policy and in 1846 finally repealed its protective tariffs entirely, thereby placing Canadian farmers in direct competition with the more aggressive and technically more advanced American farmers. This action also crippled the Canadian milling and lumber industries.

4. Canadians plagued by economic uncertainties and

land shortages were attracted by opportunities that arose from American industrialization in the East and later in the Midwest and from the opening of vast agricultural lands in the midwestern states.

5. It has been argued that French Canadians did not displace the Yankees from New England, they replaced them. By 1880 over 3 million native-born Americans from Maine to Pennsylvania had moved to other states, mostly in the Midwest. That shift, occurring before the influx of East Europeans began, reduced the industrial labor force and compelled New England entrepreneurs to turn elsewhere for workers, particularly to nearby Quebec.

6. Finally, in the years between 1846 and 1914 some 60 million Europeans emigrated to other parts of the world, 60 percent of them to the United States. Quebec was caught up in this onrushing tide, for thousands of Europeans arrived in Canada on their way to the United States. In the century after 1851, 7.1 million people came to Canada, but 6.6 million emigrated from it, mostly to the United States. Many French (and British) Canadians caught the migration fever from those Europeans who stopped in Canada before continuing south.

Thus the massive French Canadian exodus was neither unique among Canadians nor different from contemporary European population movements. While its magnitude in relation to the population of Quebec constituted "a veritable trauma in the collective conscience of the Quebecois," its timing, reaching a crest well before that of the East Europeans, facilitated the social, economic, and political development of French Canadian communities in the United States.

The U.S. government only sporadically kept statistics on Canadians arriving before 1900 and never distinguished their ethnic origins. Although before 1860 more French Canadians migrated temporarily than permanently, the balance changed dramatically after 1870. In the next 60 years approximately 693,000 left; Quebec's greatest net losses came between 1871 and 1901, especially during the 1880s. Between 1851 and 1951 an estimated 1.2 million out of 6.6 million Canadian emigrants were of French descent. (*See also* Canadians, British.)

However, these figures do not separate the numbers of French Canadians who came and, having saved enough money, went back, or those who returned to Canada because of depressions in the United States or upswings in the Canadian economy. The fluctuations in migration, first visible before 1860, continued and served to some extent as a barometer of economic conditions in North America. For example, following the panic of 1873–1874 in the United States, over 23,000 French Canadians returned to Quebec. During the 1880s unstable conditions in the United States and new opportunities in Canada prompted more than 26,000 to remigrate to Quebec and another 5,000 to return to other provinces. Between 1900 and 1920 a combination of American recessions, Canadian prosperity, and the outbreak of World War I resulted in a fall of 22 percent in the foreign-born French Canadian population in the United States (to 307,790). Even the second generation declined slightly between 1910 and 1920 (to 562,360). Then from 1923 to 1929, with the curtailment of European immigration and a great upsurge in the American

economy, the tide reversed once more, and the number of foreign-born and second-generation French Canadians rose substantially. The 1930 Census revealed that 45 percent of all French Canadian immigrants then living in the United States had arrived after 1900 and 25 percent had come after 1920. The Great Depression set in motion still another decline in French Canadian immigration, which lasted more than 30 years. Large numbers of Quebecois left the United States with their American-born children. In 1931, 55,630 people born in the United States of French Canadian descent were living in Canada.

Although French Canadian communities had long existed in many parts of the United States, 62 percent of the first and second generation by 1890 lived in New England. That figure rose to a peak of 73 percent in 1920 and then leveled off. Outside New England, the leading state to which the Quebecois migrated had always been Michigan, followed by New York, Minnesota, Illinois, Wisconsin, and, more recently, California. In 1950, aside from New England, Michigan had the largest French Canadian foreign-stock population, and Detroit had more French Canadians than any other large city in the country. In 1970 first- and second-generation French-speaking Canadians were most prominent in the census regions encompassing Providence, R.I., Boston, Detroit, and Los Angeles. However, a number of smaller cities in New England, such as Lewiston, Biddeford, and Sanford, Maine; Manchester and Berlin, N.H.; and Woonsocket, R.I., remained quite French because of their many third- and later-generation French Canadians.

19TH-CENTURY FRENCH CANADIAN CULTURE

It has been said that the church was the soul of the French Canadian parish as the mother was the heart of the family. The church and family formed a union, with family and parish, father and curé working together. The church was "within the bosom of the family just as the family was in the bosom of the church." This union also included language, for, as one authority put it, the Quebecois believed that "a people whose territory is invaded is only conquered, but if they allow their language to be invaded they are finished." Three attributes represented the central trilogy of French Canadian culture: it was defined by language, determined by faith, and dedicated to the family. Conquest by England and isolation from France had led the Quebecois to nurture and sustain these elements.

The Faith Historian Josaphat Benoit observed that "the parish is not only the mother of the Franco-American soul, it is furthermore the most beautiful poem of faith, of hope and of devotion to *survivance catholique et française* in the United States"; moreover, "without the priests . . . the Franco-American ethnic group would never have existed." In Quebec the rural parishes—from which most emigrants came—were essentially homogeneous communities whose religious and civil needs revolved around the church, with the priest as the nucleus.

For the Quebecois the sacred and the secular were interwoven in the customs and celebrations that marked off each part of the year. For example, marriages were most frequent after the planting of the crops in July,

after the harvest in October, and during the festive month of the New Year in January. Among specific holidays in the yearly cycle the *fête-Dieu* of late May or early June was a time for blessing the crops; June 24 was the day to honor their patron saint, St. Jean-Baptiste (the symbol of great missionary work on behalf of the church); November 1 was All Saints' Day, followed by the solemn Day of the Dead; December 24 remained a fast day until the midnight mass, which was followed by a *réveillon* (feast); January 1 was the most joyous day of the year, with parties, visiting, gift giving, and especially, the blessing of the children by the father; and January 6 concluded the Christmas period with the celebration of Epiphany. Then came Mardi Gras, Lent, Holy Week, and Easter. Interspersed at many times during the year were dances, baptisms, marriages, and wakes that kept alive the joys of life, the collective memory of the epic of New France, and the regard due the spirit of one's ancestors.

The Family The French Canadian family in Quebec was more nuclear and autonomous than its peasant counterpart in France. Women had higher status and more authority, and there was a positive economic incentive to having many children, whose status and independence were also enhanced in the North American environment. Large families averaging nine to ten births promoted parish growth and furnished parents with needed helping hands, but they also created demands on land resources that could not be met. By the mid-19th century fewer children were able to acquire or inherit land. Those without land could join the priesthood or a religious order or, in some instances, attend the university in preparation for a profession (French Canadians did not hold business in such high esteem). Others in search of work migrated to the cities, where about one-quarter of French Canadians lived. By the 1840s the alternative of going to the United States, even temporarily, had become more appealing. To counterbalance the dispersal of the children, families made systematic efforts to maintain kinship ties (extending even to third cousins), to foster loyalty among immediate household members, and to encourage frequent visiting and mutual assistance among relatives.

The Language The French Canadians, both in the United States and in Canada, were convinced that their language embodied the uniqueness of their faith, family, and tradition. English was the language of the conqueror and, worse, of Protestantism. Preserving French would keep alien ideas from undermining their culture. "Let us worship in peace and in our own tongue. Let us read and write in our tongue. All else may disappear, but this must remain our badge." French Canadians on both sides of the border repeatedly resisted efforts to subvert their language and compel the use of English, especially in the schools. Ironically, however, given the emphasis in Quebec before the 1820s on French as "the carrier of tradition," there was no commensurate effort to provide education. Few people in the rural parishes were literate. And yet, migration into a non-French environment spurred campaigns to establish French-language parochial schools. For over half a century such schools had the unqualified support of many communities of transplanted habitants and became a bulwark of French Canadian society in the United States.

THE EVOLUTION OF FRENCH CANADIAN COMMUNITIES

In the complex process of settlement and community building, the primary tasks of most immigrants were to find jobs and housing. Soon they banded together for mutual protection, then sought to establish churches and to attract their own clergy. As the community became more stable and families grew, parents wanted to shield their children from "alien" influences through the formation of special schools. Newspapers and other publications were started to promote community solidarity. To protect the community and its interests, individuals naturalized and began taking part in political processes.

Despite all of the efforts of the newcomers to perpetuate their culture, their children and grandchildren did acculturate, some even assimilated, and gradually they abandoned one after another of their parents' cherished customs and traditions. The French Canadians became French Canadian Americans and then Franco-Americans, Americans of French Canadian descent, and some just plain Americans.

Employment Prior to the Civil War, French Canadians came to northern New England during the harvest and haying seasons and to work in the lumber trade, brickyards, or the few textile mills already in operation. Others were drawn by the lumber and copper booms in Michigan, the newly opened farming regions of the Midwest, and the gold fields of California. Besides those lured into the Union armies during the Civil War, many responded to the call for workers in wartime industries. Some worked as contract laborers—groups of men hired for specific jobs and brought into the United States by train.

The Civil War hastened changes in earlier patterns; afterward, fewer French Canadians sought farmlands, and increasing numbers sold their lands in Quebec and brought their families to work in the woolen and cotton mills, foundries, quarries, and boot factories in such places as Worcester, Fall River, and New Bedford, Mass.; Lewiston and Waterville, Me.; Manchester and Nashua, N.H.; and Woonsocket, R.I. (and after 1880, in particular, Fitchburg, Mass., and Central Falls, R.I.). Soon men in the professions followed to minister to the needs of the transplanted habitants. Eventually the immigrant men and women (and children—often employed by the age of eight) moved into an ever-wider array of jobs, but their role in New England's industries remains the most notable. By 1870, 67 percent of the textile-mill workers in 18 New England communities were French Canadian; in 1885, 60 percent of the workers in the boot and shoe industry in 15 Massachusetts towns were from Quebec. During the 1880s between 20 and 50 percent of New England's cotton mill workers, brick and tile makers, furniture workers, and sawmill employees were still of French Canadian stock (first or second generation). In 1890, 70 percent of the first- and second-generation French Canadians in New England were employed in manufacturing and mechanical industries. As late as 1950 over 40 percent of both the first- and second-generation French Canadians in New England remained in factory work. The shift both to more skilled and to white-collar jobs came only gradu-

ally to the first two generations. In 1950, only 16 percent of first-generation French Canadians held white-collar jobs in New England; 25 percent of the second generation did so. French Canadians were not merely more blue-collar than all other immigrant groups combined, both generations also earned significantly less than other groups. The native-born French Canadians lagged noticeably in education as well.

Many of the early factory workers, who came from rural backgrounds and intended to remain only a few years, were unfamiliar with the labor movement, to which the clergy were violently opposed. Consequently, they shunned union membership and at times worked as strike breakers. The unions responded with a prolonged anti–French Canadian campaign that climaxed in 1881 with the report by Carroll Wright, chief of the Massachusetts Bureau of Statistics of Labor, which declared that the Quebecois were "the Chinese of the Eastern States," uninterested in remaining or becoming citizens but only in earning money (partly through the labor of their children) and leaving. In reply, the French Canadians presented Wright with ample evidence that this description was invalid. The episode did not hasten their attachment to unions, although some joined the Knights of Labor in the 1880s. By 1900 the church's opposition to unions subsided, and workers were also more responsive. Since then French Canadian participation in unions and strikes has increased.

Secular Societies Both parishes and secular societies dealt with the immediate needs of immigrants, but the latter could be established independently, with little preparation and with smaller numbers of people. They were invaluable to newcomers seeking companionship, assistance, and a familiar environment. Mutual-aid societies sprang up quickly, offering sick and death benefits and charitable aid, among other services. Other types of organizations emerged to help maintain the traditional culture, provide a community structure, and facilitate the adjustment of newcomers. Some eventually sponsored publications, classes, and lectures; supported efforts to present the history of French Canadians in the United States; and fought prejudice and discrimination. There were Quebec-oriented political associations, a militia group—the New Hampshire Garde Lafayette (1887)—and literary, dramatic, musical, naturalization, civic, athletic, professional, and labor clubs.

In 1848 French Canadians in the East and Midwest established their first secular societies: the Société La Fayette in Detroit and the Société Jacques Cartier in St. Albans, Vt. Two years later the Société St. Jean-Baptiste was formed in New York City. Modeled after the society established in Montreal in 1834, it was the first chapter of one of the most important and enduring organizations among French Canadians in the United States. In September 1865 the first general convention of French Canadians met in New York and reconvened annually until 1876 and biennially thereafter. Although there were such societies in Michigan, Illinois, Wisconsin, and Minnesota, all but two of the conventions were held in New England or New York State. These meetings were national in scope, but other associations soon held regional, state, and local conventions.

During the 1890s the different societies began to show interest in federating. Among the federated organizations were the Association de Secours Mutuel des Canadiens Français Américains (Mutual Aid Association of French Canadian Americans), uniting all the Michigan and Illinois societies; the Association Canado-Américaine (ACA), which later became virtually the only U.S.-based group with chapters in Canada; and the Union St. Jean-Baptiste d'Amérique (USJB), which was the largest. Other secular, federated organizations that later played key roles in Franco-American communities were the Société des Artisans Canadiens Français (from Canada), the Société Historique Franco Américaine, and the Acadians' Société de Assomption. When the Ordre des Forestiers Franco Américains broke away from the Order of Foresters in 1906, the major French Canadian organizational structure was completed for some time, although fusions and absorptions of several societies continued to take place.

In the next phase, specialized groups emerged for young people, students, women, and professionals. But first came the effort to federate the federations. In 1902 the first congress of federated societies met, but only in 1916 did 23 groups establish an umbrella organization, the Fédération Catholique Franco Américaine (FCFA). A decade later, however, the FCFA was gradually undermined by the clash over the *Sentinelle* affair (1922–1929), described below. That episode pitted the president of the ACA against the secretary general of the USJB, generated bitter strife in both the United States and Canada, and temporarily divided and reduced USJB membership. As a result the FCFA broke apart by 1933. Nevertheless, most of the federations of societies survived those trying years of conflict and financial depression, and four major ones are still operating (USJB, ACA, Artisans, and Assomption). In 1960 the four were estimated to have altogether 197,000 members (many undoubtedly the same people holding multiple memberships). In 1975 the USJB itself had assets of $85 million and, with the ACA, had about 100,000 members.

While French Canadians generally avoided as assimilative such associations as the Masons, Odd Fellows, and Knights of Columbus, they did organize similar groups of their own, beginning in the early 1900s, including St. Mary's Cooperative Association (1908), the first *caisse populaire*, or people's bank, modeled after the one begun in Quebec in 1900. Of those groups still in existence, some are local only, such as Le Cercle des Dames Françaises and the Franco American Resource Opportunity Group, which began in 1972. There are regional associations, notably La Fédération Féminine Franco Américaine and Le Comité de Vie Franco Américaine (The Committee on Franco-American Life). In addition, international organizations have branches here, specifically Les Clubs Richelieu and Le Conseil de la Vie Française en Amérique (The Council on French Life in America). Finally, professional associations of Franco-American dentists, journalists, and radio broadcasters, among others, have existed for many years.

Priests and Parishes In mill towns and farm towns, wherever there were "Frenchvilles" or *Les petits Canadas,* French Canadians needed a church and a French-speaking priest if the community were to be viable. The practice of sending missionaries to care for the far-flung Quebecois began long before the American Revolution and continued for more than half a century after it. The need for more stable institutions than the missionaries

provided became apparent in the 1840s, when the growth of the French Canadian population in Vermont led to clashes with the Catholic Irish. Those incidents prompted some 300 Quebecois to meet with the Reverend Pierre-Marie Mignault in Burlington in April 1850 and lay the groundwork for the first French Canadian parish in New England. The parish of St. Joseph in Burlington opened in June 1851 with the Reverend Joseph Quévillon the first priest. Two years later the French-born Reverend Louis de Goësbriand, vicar general of Cleveland, became the first bishop of Vermont and the first bishop in New England actively to recruit numerous French-speaking priests.

The exact number of Quebecois parishes is unknown because some were national parishes (in which they, as the numerically dominant group, had a French Canadian priest) and others were mixed territorial ones (where there were many, sometimes a majority of, French Canadian parishioners and often bilingual services, but no French priest). The number of national parishes rose from about a dozen throughout New England in 1870 to nearly 90 in 1890 and to 138 in 1911 plus 82 mixed ones. After World War II there were still 178 national parishes, 107 mixed ones, and 142 more that were English-speaking yet contained a sizable number of French Canadians. For nearly three decades after the war that distribution remained largely unchanged.

Even though the parish often was established after other secular societies had been created, the many priests, brothers, and nuns working in the parish and other religious-based institutions provided the nucleus for the French Canadian community, gave it stability and direction, and helped preserve the language and traditions of the people. Many parish priests were instrumental in establishing parishes, newspapers, and schools, as well as social, athletic, and mutual benefit groups. Members of several dozen religious orders also labored to establish schools, hospitals, almshouses, orphanages, and convents. By the early 1900s over 400 priests and 2,000 nuns were active in New England. In the 1960s over 600 priests and 2,000 nuns and brothers were still involved in the Franco-American communities of New England.

Aside from periodic waves of anti-Catholicism, the greatest obstacle to their efforts to set up French national parishes and companion institutions was the series of increasingly acrimonious clashes with the predominantly Irish-American church hierarchy. Although contact with Irish newcomers had not generated much strife in Quebec, the intense ethnocentrism and economic competition of the two groups in the United States compounded their strong differences concerning assimilation and church practices. Among other factors, the Irish, having arrived in large numbers earlier, adopted American church practices in an effort to achieve rapid acceptance. They supported English-speaking priests in territorial parishes, choir singing in lieu of French Gregorian chants, and central (bishopric) control of parish finances rather than the local control that was traditional in Quebec.

For over three-quarters of a century the French Canadians resisted the Irish hierarchy's campaigns against national parishes and the teaching of French. They also fought discrimination that forced them either to stand during "Irish services" or to sit in segregated balconies. Notwithstanding, the priests insisted that the Quebecois make contributions to the church. Often they responded by simply not attending mass. This fiercely ethnic, internal struggle went on amid recurring periods of strident anti-Catholic activity by American Protestants, particularly by the Know Nothings in the 1850s, by the American Protective Association (APA) and others during the 1890s, and by the Ku Klux Klan in the 1920s. Despite a common external enemy, the Irish and French Canadian Catholics could not unite to pool their energies and resources. The French Canadians faced two sets of adversaries with no allies.

Thus, the Quebecois withdrew from their parish in Fall River when their priest died in 1884 and the bishop appointed an Irish replacement, although French Canadians outnumbered the Irish in the parish by more than seven to one. They were interdicted, but Rome interceded in 1886 to remove the interdiction and urge the appointment of a French Canadian. Between 1894 and 1896, the 1,800 French Canadians in Danielson, Conn., who far exceeded the 300 Irish there, refused to contribute to the construction of the parish school because an agreement to teach French had been withdrawn; they resisted until a French Canadian vicar was appointed. Three years later a similar struggle occurred in North Brookfield, Mass.

The strife escalated in Maine after Bishop Louis S. Walsh took over the Portland diocese in 1906. His efforts to control parish funds and other actions aroused the bitter opposition of Franco-Americans. In 1911 Franco-Americans supported an effort to place control over church property in the hands of lay trustees as a substitute for an earlier arrangement that made the bishop the sole proprietor of church property. Bishop Walsh interdicted the Franco-Americans who urged the change, and despite a massive gathering that included representatives from Quebec, they failed to revise the system.

The climax of the French Canadian struggle with the Catholic hierarchy came a decade later, after the Most Reverend William Hickey became bishop of Providence in 1921. His efforts to centralize control of parish funds and to Americanize the parochial schools, including a shift to teaching in English, came during a period of sustained xenophobia and legislative assaults, against parochial and foreign-language schools from Oregon to Rhode Island. Bishop Hickey called for several campaigns to raise money—voluntarily if possible and by levy if necessary—to support schools and other programs. The Franco-American community—lay and religious—became sharply divided in response to the campaign, with the opposition following Elphège Daignault, president of the ACA, and the bishop's supporters rallying behind Elie Vézina, secretary general of the USJB.

La Sentinelle became the mouthpiece of the Daignault faction in April 1924 and called for the inviolability of parish property and for more national parishes and bilingual schools; it opposed the Americanization policies of Bishop Hickey and the National Catholic Welfare Conference. The bishop opposed lay control and local parish control of church funds and of parochial high schools. Daignault's appeals to Rome failed, and in 1927 he asked the courts to curtail the bishop's

authority, but the Superior Court of Rhode Island held that the bishop's levies were legitimate. On April 15, 1928, Bishop Hickey called for the banning of *La Sentinelle* and the excommunication of over 60 members of the Sentinellist faction. Extensive public support, even from Quebec, failed to help the beleaguered group, and by February 1929 virtually all, including Daignault, had capitulated.

Although the rift has never quite healed among older French Canadians, the *Sentinelle* affair was the last significant challenge to church authority. The campaigns for French-language schools and French-speaking priests had nevertheless borne some fruit. Not only did the Franco-Americans' parochial schools survive, but in addition to their French priests, they secured the first French Canadian bishop, the Reverend Georges-Albert Guertin, who presided in Manchester, N.H., from 1907 to 1931. Not until 1960, however, was another Franco-American bishop chosen, and again for Manchester, the Most Reverend Ernest J. Primeau. By 1975 three more bishops had been appointed: the Reverend Odore-J. Gendron (Manchester), Louis E. Gélineau (Providence, R.I.), and Amédée-W. Proulx (auxiliary bishop, Portland, Me.).

Parochial Schools Although French Canadians in Quebec were relatively slow to begin an extensive system of education, in the United States they quickly came to see the importance of French-language parochial schools in maintaining their heritage. "A parish without a church is preferable to a parish without a Catholic school," stated an editorial in 1925, "for the excellent reason that where the second is lacking, the first often becomes useless." Precisely because the priests stressed instruction in French rather than English, their parochial schools became one of the chief sources of conflict between the French Canadians and English-speaking Catholics.

The first such school opened in Rutland, Vt., in 1869. By 1891, 53 French-language parochial schools in New England were attended by 25,000 French Canadian children. Eighteen years later the enormous increase in the second generation was reflected in a total of 133 schools (41 percent of the parochial schools in New England) with 55,000 pupils. A half-century later, 179 parochial elementary schools and 28 high schools were still teaching in French, together with 46 private schools, including Assumption College (1904) in Worcester, Mass., the first college with classes conducted in French. But the pressures of acculturation and the all-English environment began to take their toll.

By the time the French Canadians won their struggles to preserve their traditional schools, they had already begun to modify their instructional practices to accommodate the increasing number of Franco-American children who could not speak French. Gradually the use of French decreased, first to half a day and then in most places to an hour a day. Thus, according to the statistics, the schools appeared to have been saved, but their curriculum had radically changed. What is more, an analysis in 1972 of 33 schools in three Massachusetts dioceses found that 11 schools had closed between 1958 and 1971 (8 of them between 1968 and 1971), leaving only half the number of pupils that had been enrolled in 1956. Recent efforts to revive French instruction have

not stemmed the tide, although several colleges have stimulated a new interest in the study of French.

The Media Another long-lasting bulwark of French Canadian ethnicity was the press. Seven French-language newspapers had appeared between 1780 and 1834 in the East, the Midwest, and Louisiana, but the first among the French Canadians of New England did not appear until 1839, when Ludger Duvernay started *Le Patriote Canadien* in Burlington, Vt. It was short-lived, however, and many years passed before others appeared. Eventually, though, the press blossomed. Nearly 250 Franco-American newspapers were published between 1885 and 1935 alone and more than 300 altogether.

In 1868 the newspaper *Le Protecteur Canadien* was established in St. Albans. Soon thereafter Ferdinand Gagnon (d. 1888) began his short but important career as the foremost spokesman for French Canadians in the United States with the appearance of *Le Travailleur* in Worcester in 1874. Prior to Gagnon, many editors were more preoccupied with Canadian issues than with the needs of the émigrés, and consequently their journals had lacked mass appeal. By the 1880s their emphasis had shifted, and the leading newspapers began to appear: *Le Messager* (Lewiston, 1880), *L'Independant* (Fall River, 1885), *L'Etoile* (Lowell, Mass., 1886), *Le National* (Lowell, 1890; in March 1891 it became one of the first French Canadian dailies), *L'Opinion Publique* (Worcester, 1893), *L'Avenir National* (Manchester, 1894), and *La Tribune* (Woonsocket, 1895; the first French Canadian paper to start as a daily).

By 1910, 7 dailies and over 20 other publications, mostly monthlies, were published in the communities of New England; others appeared in the Midwest, notably *L'Echo de L'Ouest* (Minneapolis, 1883) and *Le Courrier Franco Américain* (Chicago, 1910). The period 1910–1930 marked the peak of French Canadian newspaper publishing. A combination of the Great Depression and return migration to Canada forced many of them to close down. By the end of World War II a new generation of Franco-Americans, exposed to English-language movies and radio programs and ready to move to the suburbs, were uninterested in supporting the French-language press. In 1950 only 2 dailies, 11 weeklies, and 2 monthlies survived in New England and 5 publications elsewhere, none daily.

By 1960 *L'Independant* of Fall River was the only daily. It became a weekly in November 1962 and ended entirely two months later, leaving only five weeklies in the country. One of the five remaining monthlies, *Le Travailleur*, founded as a weekly by Wilfrid Beaulieu in 1931 in Worcester, ended publication in 1979. Several organizations continue to publish monthly or quarterly newsletters in French or French and English, among them *Le Bulletin* of La Fédération Féminine Franco Américaine, *L'Union* of the USJB, and *Le Canado-Américain* of the ACA. Finally, a bilingual monthly publication begun in 1973 at the University of Maine at Orono, *Le FAROG Forum*, has become an important vehicle for those interested in preserving the Franco-American ethnic heritage. The few persisting efforts to publish in French cannot hide the reality that even among those reared in French-speaking homes, the ever-increasing tendency has been to use English.

One substitute for the declining French press has

been French-language radio broadcasts. Approximately 40 stations in New England (and possibly twice that many nationwide) aired French-language programs in 1960. In the 1970s a few New England stations continued to air weekly programs, usually with music from Quebec and France. Television programs launched in the 1970s include *La Machine Magique* and *La Bonne Aventure* (a Franco-American Children's Television Series—Project FACTS) by Maine Public Broadcasting, *Chez Nos Gens* by Rhode Island's public television station, and a French talk show, *Fenêtre Ouverte*, in Maine. A few Bicentennial specials were aired in New England, among them *Soirée Franco Américaine*, but the most extensive French programming appears to be in Chicago, possibly because of the large number of French Canadians now working in that area, many of whom commute from Canada.

Literature Particularly in the early years, the press was more than just "the midwife of the Franco-American parish," and its editors were more than community leaders; their papers initially were the community's major literary expression. Even as late as the 1940s they were the sole source of French culture for many Franco-Americans. Although not many literary figures migrated from Quebec, those who did, such as Louis Fréchette (1839–1908) and Honoré Beaugrand (1849–1906), combined journalism and other writing forms, and many early writings first appeared in the press.

Between the appearance of the first Franco-American novel, Beaugrand's *Jeanne la Fileuse*, in 1878, and World War II, French Canadian literature was uneven in content and quality and was almost exclusively directed to the French-speaking communities. In fact, one of its most common early themes was the history of a local parish. Much of the poetry, like the folklore and novels, revealed the influence of Quebec and a considerable nostalgia for and idealization of the province. Among the more prominent writers before 1945 were the Reverend Adrien Verrette (history and biography), Henri D'Arles (pseudonym for the Reverend Henri Beaudé, who wrote social commentary, history, and literary criticism), Anna Duval Thibault (poetry and novel), Rémi Tremblay (travelogues, poetry, novels, and history), Louis Dantin (pseudonym of Eugene Seers, who wrote novels, literary criticism, and poetry), Rosaire Dion-Lévesque (poetry), and Camille Lessard (fiction).

A new stage of sophistication in Franco-American literature was represented by Jacques Ducharme's episodic account of the history of French Canadians in the United States (1943), Alberic Archambault's novel of the migration (1943), Sister Mary-Carmel Therriault's literary history of New England Franco-Americans (1946), Robert Rumilly's extensive history of them (1958), and Gerard Robichaud's popular novel *Papa Martel* (1961). There were also theses and dissertations and the poetry and other works of Claire Quintal and Paul Chassé in 1964 and 1968. Another important aspect was literature in English that now reached the general public. Jack Kerouac (Jean-Louis Lefris de Kérouac, 1922–1969)—spokesman for the beat generation of the 1950s—and Grace (née Repentigny) Metalious, author of *Peyton Place*, both wrote novels based on their French Canadian background: Kerouac's *The Town and the City* (1950) and Metalious's *No Adam in Eden* (1963).

Naturalization and Politics Ties to the parish, culture, and tradition of Quebec were so strong and the return there so easy that French Canadians were reluctant to give up their original citizenship. What is more, their limited involvement in Canadian politics made it difficult for them to appreciate the benefits of political participation in their new country. That participation, not surprisingly, began in the Midwest, where they had been settled longer. Thus, Pierre Menard (1766–1844) was elected the first lieutenant governor of Illinois in 1818, and two other Quebecois were members of North Dakota's first legislature in 1852. In 1850 John Charles Frémont (1813–1890), illegitimate son of a Quebecois, became California's first senator and the first U.S. senator of French Canadian background. In 1873 Louis Vital Baugy (Bogy) of Missouri became the second French-Canadian U.S. senator.

The French Canadian political role in New England began in Maine in 1845 with Joseph Cyr's election to the state legislature. It then lapsed until 1874, when S.P. Merion was elected councilman in Lowell and Frank Côté sheriff in Fall River. The instability of the early New England communities, the substantial return migration (estimated at one-fourth of all newcomers), and the belief of many that converting their citizenship was treasonous to their ethnic group slowed the pace of naturalization and political activity until the 1880s.

By 1873, however, French Canadians had begun campaigns promoting American citizenship, and thereafter national conventions and newspaper editors continually urged the formation of naturalization clubs, but with limited success. The first accurate assessment by the U.S. Census Bureau, in 1910, indicated that only 45 percent of French Canadian males over 21 were naturalized (37 percent in New England), a substantially smaller proportion than among British Canadian, Irish, English, German, and Scandinavian immigrants. Twenty years later only 47 percent of all French Canadian immigrants were naturalized, and the gap was wider between them and the European groups. Even Italians, Poles, and Russians—relative newcomers—surpassed the French Canadians. By 1940 rising mortality rates and remigration to Canada lowered the foreign-born French Canadian population and left a higher net figure of 56 percent naturalized, which was still lower than every other enumerated group except Mexicans and Lithuanians. In the last recorded figures for French Canadians, in 1950, 72 percent were naturalized—less than almost every other major group.

With a gradually increasing body of foreign-born and second-generation voters, more French Canadians sought public office. Among other reasons, some understood that only in this way could they influence legislation concerning their French-language schools and offset Yankee and Irish political power. By 1890 a total of 13 French Canadians sat in New England state houses, and 5 in the midwestern legislatures. Forty more were city councilors in manufacturing centers such as Winooski, Vt., Holyoke, Mass., Woonsocket, and Manchester. In this period, as later, Franco-Americans did not adhere overwhelmingly to either political party. They organized both Democratic and Republican clubs,

a fact attributed by many to their lack of cohesion beyond the individual parish, by others to their inexperience and lack of leadership. Communities were also divided because they experienced rejection by both Yankee Republicans and Irish Democrats; some were inclined to follow the Republicanism of the mill owners, while others were drawn to the Democratic party because of the Catholicism of many of its supporters.

Meanwhile, their concentration in urban centers enabled French Canadians to elect 5 state senators and 35 assemblymen by 1907, and Aram-J. Pothier (1854–1928) as Republican governor of Rhode Island in 1908. Pothier won two more terms in 1910 and 1912 and a third in 1924, when he defeated another Franco-American candidate and replaced an incumbent Franco-American governor, Emery San Souci (1857–1936). French Canadians in Rhode Island also elected Louis Monast to the U.S. House of Representatives in 1926 and Felix Hébert as New England's first Franco-American U.S. senator in 1928. By the end of the decade there were Franco-American judges, governors, lieutenant governors, state legislators, mayors, sheriffs, city councilors, and French Canadians served as ambassadors and consuls abroad. The trend continued; the number of French Canadian state legislators in New England alone rose from 118 in 1932 to 159 in 1938.

Democratic presidential candidate Al Smith won 57 percent of the Franco-American vote in 1928, and Franklin D. Roosevelt received 67 percent in 1936. The economic and religious factors pulling French Canadians toward the Democratic party from 1928 to 1948 waned thereafter, and increasingly they returned to their Republican voting pattern of 1896–1912. The Democratic vote fell to 47 percent by 1956 but rose again when John F. Kennedy ran in 1960. Although Franco-Americans have remained strongly Democratic since 1960, they, like other groups, tend to divide along class lines and now prefer to register as independents rather than as Republicans. Despite the apathy of some Franco-American voters, men of French Canadian background, such as Senator Mike Gravel (1930–) of Alaska, Governor Philip Noel of Rhode Island, and Congressmen Fernand Saint Germain of Rhode Island and Norman D'Amours (1937–) of New Hampshire, held state or federal office in the 1970s.

PATTERNS OF INTEGRATION

Before the Civil War most French Canadians either returned frequently to Quebec or maintained such close ties with their homeland that they had little desire to acculturate. Clearly, the anticipation of returning home reinforced the isolation of the Little Canadas through the years. Moreover, the self-imposed isolation among those who expected to go back carried over to their American-born children. Observers often found people living in Quebec towns who had been born in New England during a family sojourn there but who spoke no English. A few of those who returned had acquired a taste for American conveniences, but most had changed very little. Some came to the United States only to earn extra money; others could not adjust or experienced economic adversity; some went back to Canada when World War I broke out, others to take over the family farm, still others for personal reasons—such as the new

wives of those Quebecois who had come south seeking spouses.

In contrast to those who returned permanently, many discovered that they missed the speed, novelty, comfort, and wages of the United States, and many of these people remigrated. Others came and went several times, gradually acculturating in the process. Most of the repatriation efforts launched by Canada and Quebec beginning in the 1870s failed to draw those who had found more prosperity in the United States and had begun to adapt. Even the great fêtes in 1874 in Montreal and in Quebec City in 1880 and 1889 had little effect. In fact, the prosperous appearance of the French Canadians who visited Quebec may have had the effect of luring others to the United States. Whatever the motive and/or the ultimate destination, the relative ease of repatriation, return, and remigration affected the French Canadians' rate of integration.

Other links that slowed integration in the United States were frequent correspondence with and visits to and by relatives and friends in Quebec; associational bonds, such as the ACA and the Société des Artisans Canadiens-Français, which had international memberships; and the extraordinary number of political and ecclesiastical bonds, which remained firm until the late 1920s. French Canadians on both sides were involved in them, along with people sent south by teaching and charitable religious orders in Quebec. In addition, from the time of Bishop de Goësbriand's efforts, Franco-American parishes sought priests in Quebec. During the controversies over the appointment of French Canadian priests and the control of parish funds, Franco-Americans appealed for and often received support from Quebec, most openly during the *Sentinelle* affair. Daignault was welcomed as a hero by both clergy and laity in Quebec and Montreal.

Many French Canadians in the United States during the 1870s and early 1880s strongly endorsed Louis Riel (1844–1885), the rebel leader of the métis in Manitoba, who had been sporadically fighting with the Canadian government since 1869 in defense of French rights. He visited Worcester, Mass., twice in 1874 to advance his cause and thank his New England supporters. At the Canadian reunions in 1874 and 1880, the representatives from the United States were more committed to him than were those from north of the border. When Riel was executed in 1885, protest meetings were held in Michigan and in at least nine New England communities. Eight years later Honoré Mercier (1840–1894), a noted French-Canadian nationalist and a hero in New England, spoke in Boston and Worcester, praising the achievements of French Canadians in the United States and urging the annexation of Quebec to the United States. The same year, another prominent nationalist, Henri Bourassa (1868–1952), urged Quebec to seek independence, using American financial support. In January 1902 he visited Lowell and Worcester and urged French Canadians to adapt to the United States and to maintain ties with Quebec. In 1914 and 1915 Bourassa again visited the major Franco-American centers of New England and urged preservation of ties with Canada, but he also encouraged French Canadians to end their exile mentality, to naturalize, and to learn English. They received him as "the interpreter, the champion, the incarnation of French Canada."

Divergent attitudes toward participation in World War I soured the Franco-American rapport with Quebec, which refused to conscript its men while Franco-Americans contributed many lives and dollars to the war effort. That issue was followed by the Americanization campaigns in the United States, the bitter aftermath of the *Sentinelle* affair, the U.S. immigration laws of the 1920s, and the growing indifference of younger Franco-Americans to Canada. A prominent observer wrote in 1924 that members of the younger generation "do not feel quite at home with those living north of the 45th parallel." When the option of reentry diminished because of the immigration laws and the onset of the Depression in 1929, the flow of newcomers to the United States virtually ceased, and that in turn quickened the pace of Franco-American assimilation.

These developments brought an end to many of the ties that had bound French Canadians to Quebec. The bonds of the past were maintained for the most part only by those Franco-Americans who attended the Second Congress of the French Language in Quebec in June 1937, participated subsequently in Le Comité Permanent du Congres de la Langue Française, and then involved themselves in the Third Congress in 1952—presided over by a New Englander, the Reverend Adrien Verrette. The committee later changed its name to include the phrase "la survivance française en Amérique" and is now called the Conseil de la Vie Française en Amérique. Several efforts in the mid-1970s to revive such links have attracted a growing number of Franco-American college students.

Thus the process of integration and assimilation was slow and fitful but eventually unavoidable. In certain cases, the lack of schools and French parishes and the nativist pressure of Know Nothing groups in the 1850s had prompted some French Canadians to form English-language classes, change their names (such as Boisvert to Greenwood, Lamontagne to Mountain, and Dubois to Wood), and even to accept Protestantism. In the Midwest and West, in particular, the scattered and soon outnumbered French Canadian communities did not long withstand their Anglo-American environment. Their organizations, schools, newspapers, and parishes succumbed to the English language well before those in New England. Elie Vézina wrote in 1907 that the children in the Midwest were learning only English, that intermarriage was "devouring us," and that the French Canadian college in Kankakee, Ill., had only Irish instructors. Even the communities in New York State, so close to Quebec, could not maintain their ethnicity, or even their language, for they lacked reinforcements, since most Quebecois were drawn to the mills of New England.

But the challenge to *survivance* was great even in New England. Many migrants, notably those from urban areas, were already somewhat familiar with American ways when they arrived in the United States. There was a shared North American milieu among people on both sides of the 45th parallel, which facilitated the French Canadians' acculturation after they reached the cities of New England. On the other hand, the French Canadians isolated themselves in the Little Canadas of the mill towns. There, proximity to Quebec, the strong attachment to language, faith, and customs, and their traditionalism, conservatism, spiritualism,

and particularism all contributed to French-Canadian ethnocentrism. In the end the French Canadians succeeded in maintaining their French-language parishes, presses, schools, and societies, only to lose their 20th-century children and grandchildren to wartime changes and the inescapable American influence of the radio, phonograph, automobile, comic books, television, English-speaking peer groups, and monolingual English-speaking teachers.

INDICES OF ASSIMILATION

The eventual Americanization of the French Canadian people can be seen in the rising rates of intermarriage, the perceptible shift in language usage, and the gradual transformation of the identification of young Franco-Americans.

Intermarriage During the 19th century, while immigration from Quebec was at its peak, the fact of intermarriage was remote because the mere idea was held to be "a crime against God and a national abomination." But even the worst crimes occur, and the U.S. Census of 1890 gave some of the first statistics. Nearly 66 percent of the second-generation French Canadians had parents who both were born in Quebec, but over 3 percent (7,742) had a Quebecois father and a foreign-born mother who was not Quebecois. (Most were English Canadian, Irish, French, British, or German.) Another 8,875 children with a Quebecois mother and a foreign-born father of another nationality were categorized by the father's country of origin, predominantly the same countries as those of the women who wed French Canadian men. The rest had one Quebecois parent and one native-born parent, in most cases probably a second-generation Canadian.

In 1900 only 58 percent of the second generation had two parents born in Quebec, and over 4 percent had one foreign-born non-Quebecois parent. These patterns continued in succeeding years. French Canadians who intermarried tended to wed other Canadians or English (usually Protestants), or Irish, French, or German Catholics.

A study in 1926 showed that only 11 percent of French Canadian parents in Woonsocket had married outside the group and that the majority of these had chosen Irish spouses. Of course, marriage within the group was relatively more feasable in a heavily populated, homogeneous area such as Woonsocket, "the Quebec of New England." The concentration of French Canadians in New England significantly lowered their rates of intermarriage compared to those living elsewhere in the United States. In New York City, for instance, between 1908 and 1912, 66 percent of 96 first-generation and 90 percent of 68 second-generation French Canadian men and women intermarried. Other cities outside New England with small French Canadian populations had similar patterns. In time intermarriage increased both in New England and elsewhere. In Fall River, for instance, 14 percent in 1880, 30 percent in 1912, 50 percent in 1937, and by 1961 fully 80 percent had married outside the group, and one-fifth had wed non-Catholics. Not even in that self-styled "third French city in America" could the tide be halted.

As the third generation of Franco-Americans matured in the 1930s and 1940s, the confluence of disruptive forces broke down first the taboos against wedding non-

Franco-Americans and, more recently, those against marrying non-Catholics. The shift is portentous because French Canadians invested so much importance in the family as the vehicle for ethnic survival. Intermarriage also undermined the group's ability to maintain their language, parishes, and parochial schools. Nevertheless, the recent process of ethnic redefinition in the French Canadian community suggests that intermarriage and even the loss of language need not lead to the loss of Franco-American identification; assimilation, intermarriage, and ethnic revitalization have been occurring simultaneously—but not in equal measure.

Language Usage Language patterns paralleled those of intermarriage. On the eve of World War I there were public complaints that Franco-American youth were singing American songs and speaking English among themselves. Thirty percent of French Canadian families in Woonsocket in 1926 were using English at home. Even 15 percent of the first-generation families used either English alone or both English and French, a figure that doubled when one parent was of the second generation and increased even more among couples of the second or of the second and third generations. By the mid-1920s these shifts were becoming commonplace, for well over one-third of French parochial schools in New England had reduced instruction in French to half a day.

In the 1930s complaints were common that children were not being taught French, that many were mixing English and French into "Franglais," and that Franco-Americans in general were becoming increasingly indifferent to the French-language press, possibly owing in part to a negative reaction to the *Sentinelle* affair. During World War II many French Canadians were ridiculed for their inadequate English, and their experience further hastened the decline of French. Although the rate of decline was slower in major centers such as Manchester, Woonsocket, Fall River, and Lewiston (and even in smaller cities such as Biddeford, Me.; Berlin, N.H.; and Southbridge, Mass.), in many other communities the percentage of French-speakers was too small, and the children learned only English. The lack of institutions and businesses using French made English necessary for job mobility. The impact of rising intermarriage rates, public pressure, and the lure of the wider cultural milieu also gave English a communication advantage over French.

Curiously enough, at the same time that Franco-American writers in the 1930s and early 1940s were lamenting that the outside world was blowing "English into every nook and cranny . . . and the wall of the home could no longer keep out the flood," a defensiveness appeared in the frequent insistence that their dialect, their *joual*, though characterized by minor variations and 17th-century idioms, was not inferior to standard French. Although the percentage of children whose mother tongue was French continued to fall, campaigns defending French and urging its usage continued into the 1970s, in part because self-consciousness about the quality of their French prompted Franco-American children to avoid speaking it altogether. That in turn led them to shun French-language parochial schools; French was no longer the "keeper of the faith."

During the 1960s several conferences were held in an attempt to deal with the crisis of French-language parochial schools and English-speaking Franco-American

children. In 1977, the struggle for linguistic (and cultural) survival took still another twist, when French Canadians campaigned for recognition as an ethnic group eligible for bilingual education funds under the Emergency School Aid Act. They supported their appeal with data from a 1975 federal census survey showing that French is the second language of 2 million Americans and the primary language of communication of 285,000 others, over a third of whom live in New England. Statistics also reveal high rates of school dropouts and low socioeconomic achievement among Franco-Americans. Franco-Americans of Acadian and Quebec descent have increased their cooperation in support of the bilingual-education legislation introduced by New England legislators. They also held the first joint conference on bilingualism with French-speaking Louisianians in March 1978 in Lafayette, La.

Identification French Canadians have sought to maintain their group identity for well over a century in the face of indifference from their old homeland and strong acculturative pressures in their new one. Ferdinand Gagnon lamented in 1880 that "the province of Quebec forgets its children in exile." And yet, symbolically enough, this former Canadian repatriation agent was naturalized. French Canadians in the United States struggled to reconcile their ethnicity and identity with their leaders began to acknowledge the changes that had Gradually they recognized that they had become members of the broader American society; the passage of time solved much of the problem. After World War I, their leaders began to acknowledge the changes that had been occurring and the need to adapt realistically in order to keep their identity and community viable. In the years of the Depression, it has been stated, "Franco-Americans became Americans." Among the young, "the land across the border is just that—the land across the border whence our parents came. A place we will visit, but not a place where we would care to live. All that is French is our cultural heritage, but all our life is here—in New England."

Visiting across the border has declined since the 1930s, as has interest in events in Quebec. A Franco-American writer noted in 1977 that most Franco-Americans seem "resigned to a slow decline in their French culture"; the liturgy in the Franco-American parishes is mostly in English, and the young "reportedly care less and less about maintaining the traditions and the language." Nevertheless, there are ardent French Canadians who have worked to preserve their community by keeping alive ethnic associations. Others, younger, have in recent years pressed for a revival of customs and language and of ties with Quebec. Numerous organizations and groups have worked within New England to establish ties with Canada and France; to focus attention on the issues of Franco-American women, workers, young school children, and the aged; and to stir pride in their ethnic identity and heritage. Franco-Americans in Lewiston, Me., began holding a festive Franco-American Week in 1976, and the first Franco-American Dance Night was held in Waterville, Me., in January 1978. Tours, courses, and festivals relating to Quebec have mushroomed. Despite the growing response to such activities, however, most Franco-Americans will probably remain organizationally uninvolved, politically conservative, low-key, blue-collar New Englanders pre-

occupied with the daily struggles to survive. That is clearly not the survivance espoused by the early French Canadians.

French Canadian identity may sometimes waver; its course may be uncertain, but sincere sentiments remain—in large part generated from within the group but to some degree spurred by the proximity of Quebec. The stream of events among Franco-Americans bears a striking resemblance to that among other ethnic groups: from nationality to ideology, from ethnic loyalty to group action, from mass participation to a combination of a dedicated few ethnic loyalists and some young members seeking to reaffirm their own identity. The processes of change and redefinition are taking longer for French Canadians than for many others because they have successfully created linguistically, religiously, and socially insulated communities, because they have maintained extensive ties with their nearby homeland, and because, as immigrants and the children of immigrants, they have had a fiercely proud attachment to their language, culture, and history.

Bibliography

Two comprehensive histories of French Canada provide excellent background: Jean Hamelin et al., *Histoire du Quebec* (St. Hyacinthe, Quebec, 1976), and Mason Wade, *The French Canadians, 1760–1967*, 2 vols., rev. ed. (New York, 1968). Sigmund Diamond, "An Experiment in 'Feudalism': French Canada in the 17th Century," *William and Mary Quarterly* 18 (January 1961): 3–34, explores the early years of Quebec.

Two articles analyzing the migration are found in *Recherches Sociographiques* 5 (September 1964): Albert Faucher, "L'Émigration des Canadiens Français au XIXᵉ Siècle: Position du Problème et Perspectives," 277–317, and Gilles Paquet, "L'Émigration des Canadiens Français vers la Nouvelle Angleterre, 1870–1910: Prises de Vue Quantitatives," 319–370. The more recent study by Yolande Lavoie, *L'Émigration des Canadiens aux États Unis avant 1930* (Montreal, 1972) is also valuable.

The best history of Franco-Americans is still Robert Rumilly, *Histoire des Franco Américains* (Montreal, 1958), published under the auspices of the Union St. Jean-Baptiste d'Amérique. Josaphat Benoit, *Catéchisme d'Histoire Franco Américaine* (Manchester, N.H., 1939), was sponsored by the Société Historique Franco Américaine. Robert Perreault, "One Piece in the Great American Mosaic: The Franco Americans of New England," *Le Canado-Américain* 2 (April 1976): 9–51, contains useful information, as does the series of articles edited by Gustave Lanctôt, *Les Canadiens Français et Leurs Voisins du Sud* (Montreal, 1941). See also the data gathered by Leon Truesdell, *The Canadian Born in the United States, 1850 to 1930* (Toronto, 1943).

Useful works on cultural aspects include: Jacques Ducharme, *The Shadows of the Trees: The Story of French Canadians in New England* (New York, 1943); Josaphat Benoit, *L'Âme Franco Américaine* (Montreal, 1935); Hervé-B. Lemaire, "Franco-American Efforts on Behalf of the French Language in New England," *Language Loyalty in the United States*, ed. Joshua Fishman (The Hague, 1966); and Sister Mary-Carmel Therrialt, *La Littérature Française de Nouvelle Angleterre* (Montreal, 1946). A publication begun in the 1970s provides information on current developments: *Le FAROG Forum* (University of Maine, Orono).

Archives are maintained by the Association Canado-Américaine in Manchester, N.H., and the Union St. Jean-Baptiste d'Amérique in Woonsocket, R.I.

ELLIOTT ROBERT BARKAN

FRENCH GUIANANS: *see* CENTRAL AND SOUTH AMERICANS

FRISIANS

Frisians have been coming to the New World since the early 17th century; yet despite their continued presence in the United States, where they have established their own ethnic organizations, they are virtually unknown to the American public. This lack of recognition results in part from their having been classified as Germans, Danes, and especially Dutch, as, indeed, they often identify themselves. (*See also* Dutch.)

The Frisian homeland lies along the coast and adjacent islands of the North Sea and stretches from the province of Friesland in the Netherlands through West Germany up to the border with Denmark. The Frisians were already known in 200 B.C. as herders and fishermen in this region. They were conquered by the Romans, who raised them to the status of allies. Between the 5th and 9th centuries, they became a leading maritime power. At this time, when the Frisians dominated trade and commerce from Rouen in southern France to Finland, the North Sea came to be known as the Frisian Sea (Mare Frisicum). The Frisians continued to be active traders through the Middle Ages but gradually came under the influence of neighboring states: the Netherlands, Germany, and Denmark. These areas later came to be known respectively as West or Mid-Friesland (after 1579 a province of the Netherlands); East Friesland, lying between the Ems and Weser rivers in Germany; and North Friesland, near the Danish border in northern Germany. The number of Frisians in Germany has progressively diminished, largely through assimilation.

Frisian belongs to the Germanic group of Indo-European languages and is closely related to English. Old Frisian was used in the Middle Ages for literary, legal, and administrative purposes, but it fell into disuse after Frisian political influence declined in the 15th century. In West Friesland, a literary renaissance occurred in the 17th century, but it was not until the 20th century that Frisian was revived as a viable literary language. A national revival has become especially pronounced since World War II, and at least recently has been supported by the Netherlands government. The area boasts its own research academy, several Frisian newspapers and journals, and elementary schools with instruction in Frisian. At present approximately 400,000 persons speak Frisian in the Netherlands. In Germany, the number of Frisian-speakers is much smaller—2,000 in

Frisian Homelands

the Saterland area of East Friesland and 10,000 along the coast and islands of North Friesland. North Friesland also has a research institute and several Frisian cultural societies.

Frisians were converted to Christianity in the late 8th century but the Roman Catholic presence was almost entirely eliminated during the Reformation. Today Protestantism predominates: in Netherlandish Friesland about 85 percent of the population belong to the Calvinist Dutch Reformed or Reformed churches and another 5 percent are Mennonites. In North Friesland Lutheranism prevails, while the small group of Frisians in the Saterland area of East Friesland are largely Roman Catholic. Immigrants and their descendants in the United States reflect this religious make-up.

Because Frisians are not distinguished from the Dutch or Germans in American, Dutch, or German statistical compilations, the exact number of those who came to the United States cannot be determined. The earliest Frisian immigrants came as part of the colonial settlement of New Netherlands (1624–1664) in the Hudson River Valley of New York and northeastern New Jersey. It is reported that a good many Frisians came from North Friesland at this time. The first and last governors of the colony, Bastiaen Jansz Krol (1595–1654) and Peter Stuyvesant (1592–1672), were both natives of West Friesland. Later in the century some Frisian Mennonites sought refuge in Germantown, Pa., and the utopian commune of Labadists in Maryland was founded in 1684 by members of the movement with roots in Friesland.

The next wave of Frisian immigrants arrived between 1847 and 1855. As in the previous century, their motivations were sometimes religious or political, sometimes economic. Discontent with the state-established Dutch Reformed Church forced several groups, known as Seceders, to emigrate. Seceders of Frisian background were among those who in 1847 founded Vriesland, Mich., and Pella, Iowa. Several years later a group of conservative Frisian Mennonites founded a settlement called New Paris near Goshen, Ind. Discontent with the Dutch monarchy prompted another group of Frisians to settle in Lancaster, N.Y., where they specialized in dairy farming.

Throughout the rest of the 19th century Frisians continued to come to the United States. The majority settled in the Midwest, especially Iowa. They pursued farming and farm-related work in small communities like Holland, Mich.; Friesland, Wis.; Pella and Orange City, Iowa; Lafayette, Ind.; and Emden and Pease, Minn.; or worked in industrial centers like Chicago, Minneapolis, and Grand Rapids, Mich. Other isolated farming and dairy communities where Frisians settled and still make up a large percentage of the population, are Whitinsville, Mass., and Bellflower, Hynes, and Petaluma, Calif. Frisians were also attracted to work in New York City, Cincinnati, and the manufacturing plants of Paterson and Passaic, N.J. Frisian immigrants who were successful in the business world include Frank Cooper (Folkert Kuipers, 1843–1904), Chicago department store owner; John Dykstra (1898–1972), for several years president of Ford Motor Company; and William S. Hofstra (1860–1932), lumber entrepreneur and benefactor of Hofstra College on Long Island.

The high point in Frisian immigration came during the first decades of the 20th century; afterward, U.S. restrictions on immigration and especially the economic crises of the 1930s discouraged new arrivals. After 1945, when economic hardship caused by the destruction of World War II forced Frisians to emigrate, most found new homes in Canada.

The first organizational efforts of the Frisian immigrants grew out of individual church parishes. Most of the Frisians were descended from the Seceder movement, which in this country was represented by the Reformed Church in America and the Christian Reformed Church. However, the churches were from the beginning primarily Dutch institutions and never provided a strong basis for a distinctly Frisian community life. The Bible and liturgical manuals were not translated into Frisian until the 20th century; Dutch was used in services, and later, English. Similarly, among North Frisians who attended Lutheran churches, German and English were the only practical languages. Despite the general non-Frisian nature of organized religious life, in recent decades an increasing number of church services have been conducted in Frisian in both Reformed and Christian Reformed churches. The first Frisian sermon was delivered in Grand Rapids in 1935 by the Reverend Broer D. Dykstra (1872–1955), who continued to preach in Frisian to several communities throughout the United States. Since 1959 it has become a tradition to have an annual sermon delivered in Frisian at one of the Christian Reformed churches in Grand Rapids.

Of more importance to the maintenance of Frisian ethnicity have been the *selskippen,* or Frisian social and cultural societies. The first of these was the Utspanning troch Ynspanning (Recreation through Effort) founded in Paterson, N.J., in 1893. At the height of its strength between 1910 and 1930 this organization had 350 members and its own meeting hall and library. Before its demise in 1969 the Utspanning troch Ynspanning sponsored a Frisian dance group, a dramatic club that put on plays in Frisian, and most popular, a group of players that competed in an annual Frisian handball (*keatsen*) tournament. Other Frisian societies include Friso (f. 1909) and Gysbert Japiks (f. 1933), both in Grand Rapids; Nij Fryslân (f. 1910) in Rochester, N.Y.; Ut en Thús (f. 1923) and Nocht en Wille (f. 1926) in Chicago; It Heitelân (f. 1936) in Orange City, Iowa; and Fier fan Hûs (f. 1940) in Springfield, S.Dak. Although most of these organizations are basically social clubs, the Gysbert Japiks of Grand Rapids is active in political affairs, especially with regard to developments in the homeland. Since 1943 this society, sometimes in cooperation with others, has submitted memorandums to the Dutch government demanding Frisian-language instruction and greater autonomy for Friesland. At the end of World War II it also campaigned successfully to put a halt to Britain's heavy bombing and evacuation of the North Frisian island of Heligoland.

With the exception of a few writings in Frisian by the Reverend Dykstra and Wybe Jelles van der Meer (1884–1948), Frisian Americans have had neither publications nor a press in their native language. As a result, Frisian is used mainly in its spoken form, and even that use is limited to older immigrants and some of their descendants. Frisian immigrant writers have used English, and several have become successful in American literary

circles. Among these are the novelists Frederick Manfred (Feike Feikema, 1912–), Henry K. Pasma (1881–1948), and David C. de Jong (1901–1967); the poet Frederick ten Hoor (1893–); the philosopher Marten ten Hoor (1890–1967); and the award-winning author of several children's books, Meindert de Jong (1906–). Most have used Frisian themes in their work.

A Frisian Information Bureau was founded in 1943 in Grand Rapids to preserve and promote a sense of Frisian culture and identity. Headed by Bernard J. Fridsma (1905–), the bureau publishes the monthly *Frisian News Items* (Grand Rapids, f. 1944), which includes a variety of information on the homeland and on Frisian life in the United States. A group of East Frisians led by L. Hundling and Richard B. Aden (1881–1972) attempted to preserve their heritage through the German-language *Ostfriesische Nachrichten*, later renamed *Ostfriesen-Zeitung* (Breda, Iowa, 1882–1972); more recently North Frisians from New York City and California have begun to issue a bulletin entitled *Frisian Roundtable* (Bronx, N.Y., f. 1975).

Despite these efforts, Frisian immigrants and especially their descendants have a weak sense of group identity. Since their arrival in the United States they have lived among Dutch or Germans, and in the early period were absorbed within the communities and religious structures dominated by those groups; moreover, they are usually classified as Dutch or German by American officials. The lack of a Frisian-language press, the small number of new Frisian immigrants, and the limited activity of most of the remaining societies are offset only slightly by the appearance of a few newsletters in English, the promotion and distribution of books about Frisians, and the occasional preaching of sermons in Frisian. On the other hand, the fact that in the homeland some Frisians think of themselves as a cultural minority gradually regaining national consciousness suggests that remnants of Frisian-American identity may persist.

Bibliography

The only general study in English is a short essay by Martin ten Hoor, "Frisians in the United States," *Michigan Alumnus Quarterly Review* 58 (1951). See also Geart B. Droege, "Frisians, Ethnicity and America in Twelve Questions and Answers," *Europa Ethnica* 36 (1979), pp. 28–42. For details on the early settlement patterns of immigrants from West Friesland, see Y. Poortinga, "Emigraesje út Westerlauwersk Fryslân nei en festiging yn'e Foriene Steaten (oant likernôch 1900 ta)," *Frysk Jierboek* 32 (Drachten, Netherlands, 1958). George Schnücker, *Die Ostfriesen in Amerika* (Cleveland, 1917), provides similar information on East Frisians. Valuable material about Frisian-American life is found in *Frisian News Items* (Grand Rapids, Mich., f. 1944). The best introduction to the history and contemporary situation in the homeland is provided in the sections on West Frisians and North Frisians in Meic Stephens, *Linguistic Minorities in Western Europe* (Llandysul, Wales, 1976).

G

GABRIELINOS: *see* AMERICAN INDIANS

GENTILE

The term Gentile most often means Christian, sometimes Aryan. For Jews a Gentile is anyone who is not a member of the Jewish nation; for Mormons a Gentile is anyone who is not a Mormon.

GEORGIANS

The number of Georgians who have immigrated to the United States is small. Since the end of the 19th century, approximately 750 people from Georgia, now one of the republics of the Soviet Union, have resettled in America permanently. Today there are only 1,000 to 1,200 Georgian Americans, but despite its small size, the community manages to support a variety of cultural associations, political organizations, and publications.

ORIGINS

The history of Georgia stretches back more than 3,000 years. The origins of its people are unknown, but they are thought to be descended from the earliest inhabitants of the Caucasus, tribes that wandered into that area from Asia Minor in ancient times. They were converted to Christianity in A.D. 337 by St. Nino of Cappadocia. The Georgian Orthodox Church is autocephalous within the Eastern Orthodox community and has its own patriarch.

From its earliest days, Georgia was invaded repeatedly. Romans, Persians, Arabs, Turks, and others besieged it at various times, but its culture nonetheless flourished, and in the 12th century, under the Bagration dynasty, it evolved from a loose confederation of autonomous states into a powerful and unified kingdom. Georgia reached its pinnacle of glory and power under Queen Thamara (1184–1213), with territories extending to what is now eastern Turkey. After her death, the

kingdom was plunged into war against a seemingly endless stream of Mongol invaders and was eventually compelled to turn to Russia, its nearest Christian neighbor, for protection. The treaty signed by the two countries in 1783 guaranteed Georgia's independence and territorial integrity, but its terms were violated by Tsar Paul I in 1801, and Georgia lost its autonomy until 1918. Then, taking advantage of the collapse of the Russian Empire, it declared itself a democratic republic, but its independence was short-lived. In February 1921 Georgia was incorporated into the Soviet Union.

Today the Georgian S.S.R. covers an area of 26,911 square miles and has a population of 5 million. It includes two autonomous republics, Abkhazia and Adzharia, and one autonomous region, Southern Ossetia. Sixty-four percent of its population is Georgian, 11 percent Armenian, 10 percent Russian, and 15 percent is divided among several small minorities.

The Georgian tongue belongs to the Kartvelian group of Caucasian languages, which are distinct from the Indo-European, Slavic, Oriental, and Semitic families. The oldest inscriptions in that language date from the first half of the 5th century A.D., and the 33-letter alphabet in use today dates from the 11th century.

ARRIVAL AND SETTLEMENT

Because U.S. immigration statistics classify Georgians as Russians, the number of Georgian immigrants who have come to America can only be estimated from the recollections of early émigrés and from whatever documentation exists. The first Georgians to come to the United States were probably the 15 men brought over by Buffalo Bill Cody for his Wild West Congress of Rough Riders in the 1890s to tour the United States and Europe as champion horseback riders. After 1900 another 30 men and women were signed by the Ringling Brothers Circus, also as horseback riders, and at about the same time 50 Georgian laborers contracted to come to the West Coast to work on the railroads. About 50 people from these two groups remained in the United States; the rest returned to Georgia.

Another group of 150 Georgians, largely military, political, and aristocratic exiles, arrived in the 1920s via Europe or China, after the Georgian republic collapsed. Two hundred and fifty more immigrated after World War II. Many of them had been prisoners of war who chose to remain in the West rather than face reprisals by the Soviet government; a number were Georgians who had been living in other parts of Europe since the Soviet invasion of Georgia in 1921. They were admitted to the United States under either the Displaced Persons Act of 1948 or the Refugee Relief Act of 1953. The Church World Service, the Tolstoy Foundation, and the Georgian Association were the agencies principally responsible for their resettlement.

Three hundred Georgian Jews, who arrived between 1971 and 1976 via Rome, Vienna, and Israel, are the most recent immigrants. These people, whole families for the most part, left Georgia voluntarily. The Hebrew Immigrant Aid Society, a worldwide Jewish migration

Georgia

Major concentrations of Georgians

250 Km. Miles

RUSSIAN U. S.

Caucasus

S. F. S. R.

Sukhumi 1

GEORGIAN S.S.R.

Black Sea

Batumi 2 3 Tbilisi

Mountains

Caspian

Sea

Kura

S. R.

TURKEY

ARMENIAN S.S.R.

AZERBAIJAN

S.S.R.

Baku

IRAN

1 Abkhazian A.S.S.R.
2 Adzhar A.S.S.R.
3 South Ossetian A.O.

agency, and the New York Association for New Americans assisted in their resettlement. The Georgian Jews have established ties with the older Georgian-American community and participate in the cultural and social events of the Georgian Association.

When Georgians first came to the United States, they congregated in a few major cities for mutual support. The largest settlement was and still is in New York City, the main port of entry. Other Georgians settled in Los Angeles, Washington, D.C., Chicago, Philadelphia, Seattle, and in smaller towns.

Cultural and Organizational Life   The Georgian community has never been large enough to support its own Orthodox churches or bilingual schools. Georgians attend Russian or Greek Orthodox churches and maintain their language, where possible, through individual effort and contact within the community. Georgians had their own foreign-language newspaper, *Kartuli Azri* (Georgian Opinion), between 1955 and the death of its publisher in 1975. It was supported by voluntary contributions and distributed to universities, libraries, and congressmen, as well as to the members of the Georgian community.

The educational level of Georgian immigrants, at least since World War I, has been high. Most newcomers have had the equivalent of at least a high-school education, and many have had higher degrees. Because few of the immigrants spoke English when they came, they often had to work as unskilled laborers at first. Georgians today are employed in a variety of professions—business, engineering, medicine, government, teaching, and the arts.

The first known Georgian organization in the United States was formed in San Francisco in 1924. Called Kartuli Sazogadoeba (Georgian Society), it was established by the handful of Georgians newly arrived from China, for the purpose of preserving Georgian culture in the United States. It lasted only a few years, since most of the Georgians moved to the larger community in New York City, where a second association was founded. The Caucasian Society Allaverdy (f. 1930), a coalition of North Caucasian nationalities—Georgians, Circassians, Kabardins, and Ossetians—promotes closer social and cultural relations among the various ethnic groups from the Caucasus region and with American society.

In 1931 a group of Georgians formed a more purely Georgian organization, Kartuli Sazogadoeba Amerikis Sheertebul Shtatebshi (Georgian Association in the United States), which was formally incorporated on December 1, 1931, with headquarters in New York City. The main goals of the association are to provide cultural, material, and moral support to its members and needy Georgians over the world and to spread information in the United States about Georgian issues. The association currently has about 200 members. The president, elected every two years by the membership, speaks for the entire Georgian community.

Soon after its founding, the Georgian Association purchased a building to house newcomers and to serve as a meeting place. Funds were established to provide scholarships for Georgian students. At the end of World War II, the association sent hundreds of relief packages to Georgians stranded in Europe and provided entry affidavits, loans, and jobs to Georgians able to immigrate to the United States. The association, in conjunction with the Harvard College Library, is raising funds to preserve the archives of the Georgian Republic, which were brought to Paris with the government in exile and are now temporarily deposited at Harvard, where the documents are being catalogued and microfilmed.

POLITICS AND GROUP MAINTENANCE

The Georgians who arrived at the end of World War II had strong political convictions. Three groups were organized in the 1950s—Kartul-Amerikuli Liga (Georgian-American League), Kartuli Erovnuli Kavshiri (Georgian National Alliance), and Sakartvelos Damoukideblobis Amerikuli Sapcho (American Council for Independent Georgia). There were some ideological differences between these organizations, but their major goals were the same: to oppose Communism, to keep the issue of Georgian independence alive in the United States, and to continue the struggle for liberation. The Georgian-American League published an English-language journal, the *Voice of Free Georgia* (1953–1958), and the American Council for Independent Georgia published *Chveni Gza* (Our Path; f. 1953) in Georgian with English summaries. With the changing political climate and the relaxation of tensions between the United States and the Soviet Union, these groups lost much of their fervor, and by the mid-1960s they had all dissolved.

Georgians have long been noted for their nationalistic spirit, their deep sense of kinship, and their gregariousness and hospitality. In order to perpetuate and publicize their traditions and their culture, the Georgian Association annually celebrates January 26, St. Nino's Day, commemorating the conversion of Georgia to Christianity; May 26, the declaration of Georgian independence; and August 29, 1924, the date of the Georgian uprising against the Soviet Union. Détente has enabled some Georgians to visit their homeland and renew contacts with friends and relatives.

The Georgian community is tiny, and there is little prospect that many newcomers will be added to its ranks. Georgians and their descendants are rapidly being assimilated into American society, but they still remain committed to at least some part of their heritage and their ethnic identity.

Bibliography

There is no literature dealing specifically with Georgians in the United States, but several good books are available on the homeland. W.E.D. Allen, *A History of the Georgian People* (1932; reprint, New York, 1971), and David Marshall Lang, *The Georgians* (London, 1966), treat the origins of Georgian civilization, the development of social organization, customs, and trade relations from ancient times to the Russian occupation in 1801. Lang, *A Modern History of Soviet Georgia* (1962; reprint, Westport, Conn., 1975), is a well-researched, concise account of the political events from 1801 to 1960.

NATHELA CHATARA

GERMAN RUSSIANS: *see* GERMANS FROM RUSSIA

GERMANS

For almost three centuries Germans have been one of the most significant elements in the American population. For statistical purposes, this entry treats as Germans all immigrants born in Imperial Germany, the various states that coalesced to form it in 1871 and the

governments that succeeded it after 1918. German-speaking Swiss, Austrians, and others often shared in German-American culture, however, while some German-born remained ethnically distinct because of religion or time of arrival.

Germans began emigrating to America in the 17th century and in the postcolonial period contributed more immigrants than did any other country: over 6.9 million between 1820 and 1970, or some 15 percent of the total immigration. During most of the latter half of the 19th century and for much of the period between 1923 and 1963, annual arrivals from Germany outnumbered those from any other single country. Between 1850 and 1900, Germans were never less than a quarter of all the foreign-born in the United States, and between 1880 and 1920 they were the largest single element among first-generation immigrants. Their actual numbers peaked in 1890 (see Table 1); in that year and in 1870 they reached their highest proportional share of the population and constituted over 4 percent of all U.S. residents. Together with the second generation, they accounted for over 10 percent of the population in 1900. As late as 1950 the Germans were more numerous than any other group of first- and second-generation Americans and thereafter were second only to Italians. By 1972, a census survey estimated that some 25.5 million people, or about 12 percent of all Americans, identified themselves as of German descent. Only Britain could claim more offspring (14 percent); the Irish (8 percent), Italians (4 percent) and other groups trailed further behind.

Despite such numerical strength, the Germans in the 1970s were among the least visible of American ethnic groups. Theirs was the first immigrant tide to ebb, with a sharp drop in numbers of annual arrivals (relative to the total immigration) in the 1890s. By 1972 most American residents calling themselves German were of third or subsequent generations. They differed little from national norms demographically or economically. Only their slightly greater tendencies toward marriage, male-headed households, higher education, lower unemployment, and greater than average proportions of farmers in their ranks suggested the last remnants of historically distinctive values and behavior. In surveys

they emerged moderately high in economic achievement; in attitudinal ratings they showed themselves generally conservative.

By and large, however, the distinctiveness of German Americans has been a consequence of complex patterns of family behavior and inherited influences of region, religion, and class, rather than of a consciously cultivated ethnicity focused in ethnic organizations and cultural activity. The "Little Germanies" of the cities are gone, their former presence marked at most by restaurants, sausage shops, or cafes. Only a tiny fraction of the once great German-American press clings to life, and organizations claiming to represent ethnic interests on the national level number their membership in the thousands rather than the scores of thousands they once claimed.

In the 19th century the German group in America seemed likely to persist. Its leaders could toy with the idea of creating a separate state; numbers and cultural consciousness enabled it to dominate large areas, and by the early 20th century, a single, massive organization represented its interests nationally. Other Americans admired the skills, diligence, thrift, and family strength that seemed to make the Germans ideal candidates for Americanization, but deplored the clannishness and cultural traits that kept them stubbornly apart. Nevertheless, the very size of the German immigration, its religious, socioeconomic, and cultural heterogeneity, its skills, time of arrival, and settlement patterns all combined to ensure a gradual process of acculturation and assimilation. The trauma of World War I only hastened the submergence of German ethnicity into religious, regional, class, or simply American self-identity.

COLONIAL ORIGINS

Scattered Germans found their way to the colonies during the 17th century, often under Dutch auspices as a result of the traditional seasonal migration of German laborers to the Netherlands. The earliest specifically German settlement began in 1683. William Penn, who had proselytized among pietistic dissenters from the established Protestant churches in the Rhine Valley, in-

Table 1. Germans in the U.S. population, 1850–1970.

| Year | German-born | | | Second-generation[b] | German stock[a] | |
	Number	Percent of foreign-born	Percent of total		Percent of foreign stock	Percent of population
1850	583,774	26.0	2.5	—	—	—
1860	1,276,075	30.8	4.1	—	—	—
1870	1,690,533	30.4	4.2	—	—	—
1880	1,966,742	29.4	3.9	—	—	—
1890	2,784,894	30.1	4.4	—	—	—
1900	2,663,418	25.8	3.5	5,340,147	30.8	10.5
1910	2,311,237	17.1	2.5	5,670,611	24.6	8.7
1920	1,686,108	12.1	1.6	5,346,004	19.2	6.7
1930	1,608,814	11.3	1.3	5,264,289	17.1	5.6
1940	1,237,772	10.7	0.9	3,998,840	15.1	4.0
1950	991,321	9.5	0.7	3,742,615	13.9	3.1
1960	989,815	10.2	0.6	3,330,849	12.7	2.4
1970	832,965	8.7	0.4	2,789,070	10.8	1.8

Source: U.S. Bureau of the Census, *Historical Statistics of the United States, From Colonial Times to 1970* (Washington, D.C., 1975), series C, pp. 195–227, 288–295; E.P. Hutchinson, *Immigrants and their Children, 1850–1950* (New York, 1956), table 3.

a. German stock includes first- and second-generation German Americans.
b. In this case, second-generation refers to native-born Americans with German-born fathers.

vited German sympathizers to settle in the Quaker colony that he established in 1681. He found a receptive audience among those already accustomed to migration from state to state in search of toleration. The result was the founding of Germantown, Pa., by 13 Quaker and Mennonite families from Krefeld, many of them actually Dutch, under the leadership of Francis Daniel Pastorius (1651–c. 1720). (See also Pennsylvania Germans.)

In 1709 large-scale emigration began when some 13,000 persons from the area of the Palatinate in southwestern Germany traveled down the Rhine River and across the North Sea to England. They left because of overpopulation in the wine-growing regions, devastation during the wars of Louis XIV, heavy taxation, and the exceptionally harsh winter of 1708–1709. A year earlier the Reverend Josua von Kocherthal (1669–1719), author of a 1706 pamphlet on the Carolinas, had led 41 Palatines to England. A petition to Queen Anne as refugees of war led to their settlement at Newburgh, N.Y., and provided a precedent for what followed. The British finally sent about 2,800 of the refugee Palatines to New York to manufacture naval stores along the Hudson River. Perhaps a seventh of them died en route or shortly after arrival, and the naval stores plan failed. Some Germans remained along the Hudson, others drifted to the Schoharie and then the Mohawk valleys, but most ultimately found their way to the freer land of Pennsylvania.

The migration thus begun swelled with the reports of the successful and with advertisements by proprietors in need of settlers. Each year America-seekers crowded into Rotterdam, Holland, many already penniless from the expense of the four- to six-week trip down the Rhine. To pay for the transatlantic voyage, many emigrants became redemptioners under a system that allowed them either to pay for their voyage within a certain time (usually two weeks) after arrival or be sold into servitude for a fixed period to cover the cost of their passage; four years was a common term. Perhaps half to two-thirds of the colonial Germans found their way to America as redemptioners; in time, increasing proportions of their purchasers were also Germans.

Most were from southwestern Germany—though they were called Palatines regardless of their origin—and traveled in family and even village groups. Many were landless farmers and rural laborers persuaded to leave by agents called "newlanders," who were commissioned by shippers to arrange cargoes for their waiting hulls. Groups of sectarians seeking tolerance also continued to arrive—Swiss Mennonites in 1710, Baptist Dunkers in 1719, Schwenkfelders in 1734, Moravian Brethren after 1735—but the increasing majority were members of the established Lutheran and Reformed churches. The Protestant colonies attracted few Catholics, who tended rather to move south and east to the new farmlands of the Austrian and Russian empires.

Philadelphia was the chief port of arrival, though New York, Baltimore, and Charleston, S.C., received smaller numbers. In 1717 the arrival in Philadelphia of three ships carrying 363 Palatines heralded the coming scale of the migration; between 1727, when Pennsylvania began recording the immigration, and 1740, 80 ships carrying immigrants arrived, followed by 159

more over the next 15 years. After a virtual halt during the Seven Years' War (1756–1763), 88 more ships arrived during the last 15 years before the Revolution. Estimates of the total numbers of Germans who arrived in the colonies range from 65,000 to 75,000 or even 100,-000. Benjamin Franklin estimated that perhaps one-third of Pennsylvania's colonial population was German. Estimates derived from the 1790 Census suggest that about 8.6 percent of the population of the new nation was of German descent. Pennsylvania remained the center of German concentration (33 percent of its population), but Maryland (almost 12 percent), New Jersey (9 percent), and New York (8 percent) also had significant elements, as did the more southern states and the new settlements west of the Alleghenies.

This pattern resulted from massive migration westward and then south along the mountain valleys after 1760. The French attempted to colonize Louisiana with Germans, and by 1721 almost 250 Germans were settled in three villages along the German Coast of the Mississippi, north of New Orleans, where they and their descendants remained a German-speaking enclave of small farmers in the midst of a plantation economy until their gradual submergence into Creole culture. The Revolution added further to the German element when perhaps 5,000 Hessian soldiers remained behind at the end of the hostilities.

The first Germantown settlers had been weavers, and artisans and merchants continued to find opportunity in the market towns and cities of the region. Perhaps 10 percent of Baltimore's adult males were German in 1796, most of them craftsmen. But like the other colonists, the majority of Germans were farmers. The sectarians settled close to Philadelphia, while Lutheran and Reformed immigrants who came later carved out farms farther north and west. They sought the frontier as readily as other groups, and their numbers and early arrival allowed them to get good land. Traveling in groups encouraged ethnic concentration, but there was also a good deal of ethnically mixed settlement. The agricultural villages of Germany were not duplicated.

Germans enjoyed a reputation as industrious, frugal, and skilled farmers who cared more for their land and livestock than for their own comfort, but during the colonial period they were not noticeably more wealthy than other farmers; their discipline and mutual aid, however, brought greater than average prosperity to the sectarians. After the Revolution, Germans paid more attention to improved farming methods. Their concern to keep the land within the family, often at the price of subsidizing the westward movement of some children and the purchase of land locally for others, ensured continued farm investment, stability and expansion of core areas of German settlement, and a steady westward migration.

Religion was central to the German identity in the New World, though this had not been so at first. There were few ministers among the early immigrants, but by 1734 this lack attracted Moravian missionaries, followers of the ecumenical pietistic movement of Count Nikolaus Ludwig von Zinzendorf (1700–1760). Based in communities at Bethlehem, Nazareth, and Lititz, Pa., the Moravians received such a warm reception from German settlers that the established German churches felt forced to respond. The pietistic Lutheran Halle Mis-

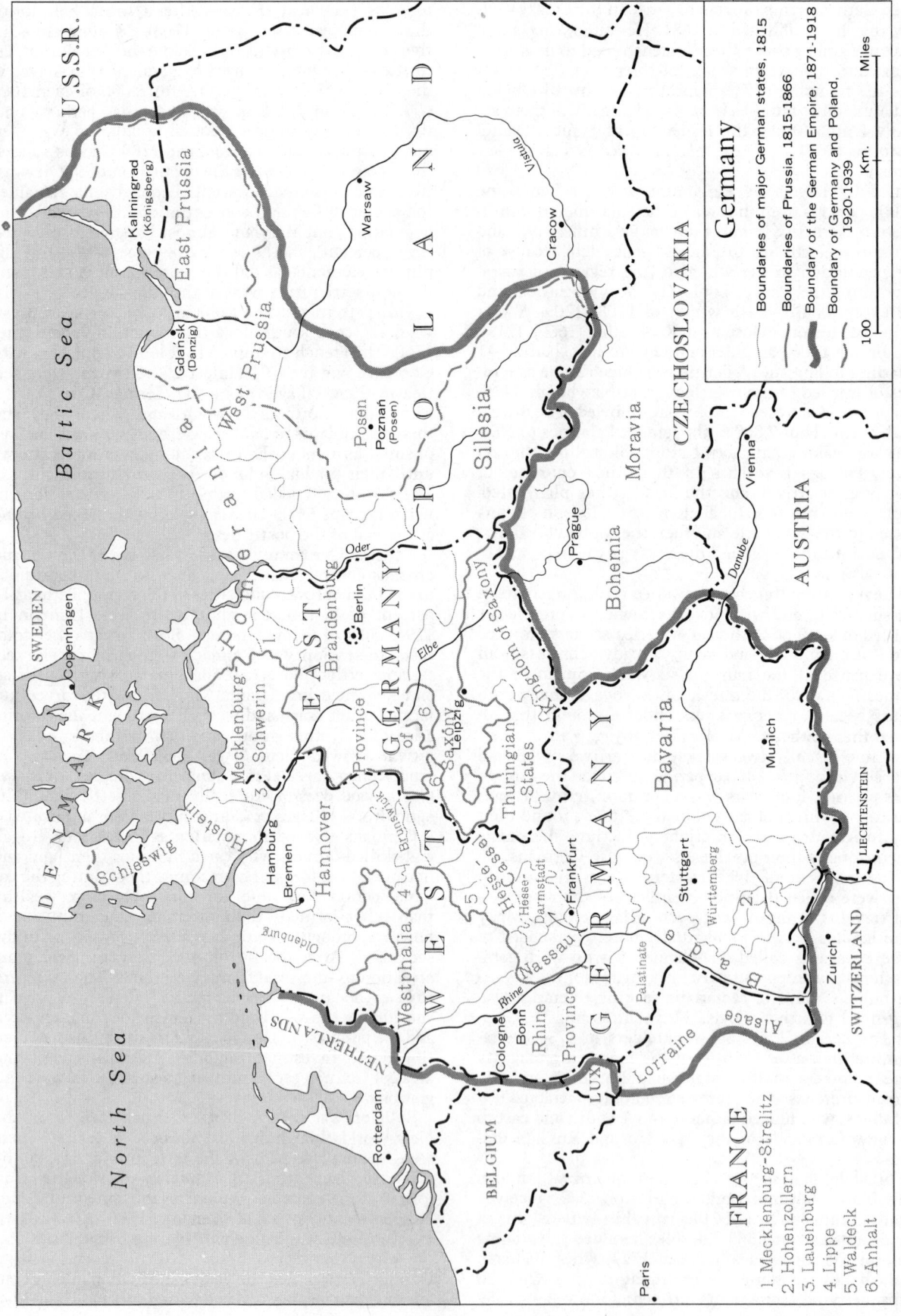

Germany

Boundaries of major German states, 1815
Boundaries of Prussia, 1815-1866
Boundary of the German Empire, 1871-1918
Boundary of Germany and Poland, 1920-1939

Km.
Miles
100

1. Mecklenburg-Strelitz
2. Hohenzollern
3. Lauenburg
4. Lippe
5. Waldeck
6. Anhalt

sionary Society sent over Henry Melchior Mühlenberg (1711–1787) in 1742, the Reformed church sent Michael Schlatter (1716–1790) in 1746, and the sectarians consolidated their organizational structure. In 1741 there had been only four ordained ministers for some 15,000 Reformed colonists, and only three for perhaps an equal number of Lutherans, but by 1765 about 15 Reformed ministers served some 40 congregations, and at least 40 Lutheran congregations throughout the colonies were associated with the synod established by Mühlenberg. Although the churches thus emphatically rejected the ecumenism of the Moravians (whose own denominational character soon emerged), cooperation often continued in union congregations sharing a building but served by separate ministers.

The religious revival, paralleling a similar awakening among English-speaking colonists, stimulated group identity not only by buttressing the German language but also by laying the groundwork for an ethnic school system. Mennonites and Moravians were early patrons of education, and by 1775, Reformed churches were supporting 63 schools, Lutherans perhaps 40. Large numbers were still left unschooled, but Germans strongly resisted mid-18th-century attempts by the British Society for the Propagation of Christian Knowledge to establish free charity schools among the Germans with instruction in English. Similar fears of language loss, secularization, compulsory attendance (and heavier taxation) later led Pennsylvania Germans to conduct a 30-year struggle to maintain their parochial systems after Pennsylvania introduced public schools in 1834.

A growing German press fed ethnic consciousness. German literacy was high enough to support 38 German newspapers at one time or another between 1732 and 1800. Foremost was the paper published in Germantown from 1739 on by Christopher Sauer (1693–1758, also publisher of the first Bible in America), which furnished a mixture of religious and practical advice, political commentary, and notices to some 4,000 German readers throughout the colonies. Almanacs, religious books, and political tracts were printed and widely disseminated by a variety of German presses.

After mid-century the increasingly self-conscious, diverse, informed, and prosperous Germans played a strong political role, though seldom a unified one. In Pennsylvania, issues of frontier defense divided Quakers against non-Quakers; pacifist German sectarians found themselves on the Quaker side, while church Germans, who settled more frequently on the frontier, joined the Quakers' opponents in support of military spending during and after the French and Indian War. The same pattern continued in the Revolution. Sectarians attempted to remain neutral, and the remainder threw their support to the revolutionaries. Many of the pacifist Mennonites migrated to Ontario.

German immigration on a large scale virtually halted with the Revolution and did not recover for almost 50 years, as warfare on both continents barred transatlantic movement. During the interval, acculturation and assimilation proceeded rapidly, both in the cities and in frontier areas. Even before the Revolution, the Germans of Germantown were Anglicizing their names, adopting English-style handwriting, using English in business and even in church records, and intermarrying at in-creasing rates. A desire to protect German immigrants from exploitation by shipping firms led to the founding of the first nonreligious organizations among the Germans—the German Society of Philadelphia, founded in 1764, in Charleston in 1766, in Baltimore in 1783, and in New York, in 1784. But the subsequent acceptance of non-German members by these organizations and their use of English suggests the rapid Americanization of their membership, largely drawn from the mercantile elite. Urban churches cut missionary ties with Germany and abandoned the use of German in services. Even Lancaster, Pa., in the middle of rural German settlements, introduced English services in 1815, although occasional use of German continued to 1851. A similar but slower process took place in the rural settlements outside Pennsylvania from New York to Georgia, so that by the Civil War integration was virtually complete. Only in rural Pennsylvania, where Germans were the original settlers and their communities expanded as other settlers moved away, did a more stable ethnic culture evolve.

Assimilation and mobility dispersed most of the older urban and frontier communities before the renewed onset of immigration after 1820. The well-settled and expensive farmlands of the Pennsylvania heartland had little attraction for newcomers. But the German societies of the cities survived to serve new immigrants after 1820, and descendants of colonial Germans mingled with them and provided leadership. In its origins, motives for emigration, the kinds of persons, patterns of settlement, and process of adaptation, the colonial immigration pattern was repeated by those who came later. It also bequeathed an important psychological claim for German participation in the formative experience of nationhood.

19TH- AND 20TH-CENTURY IMMIGRATION

Small numbers of Germans made their way to the United States in the intervals of peace between 1775 and 1815, but not until 1816–1817 did disastrous harvests and economic dislocation after the Napoleonic wars stimulate large-scale migration. Some 20,000 Germans, mainly from southwestern Germany, then reopened the old pathway. Despite sharp annual fluctuations, the trend moved generally upward in the late 1820s, peaking in 1854 at 215,009, and again in 1882, when over a quarter of a million Germans entered the United States. Decadal migration rose from under 6,000 in the 1820s to over 950,000 in the 1850s and to a high of 1,445,181 in the 1880s. After dropping off sharply in the 1890s, it continued at a much reduced level into the 20th century, with minimal arrivals during the two world wars and the Great Depression and minor peaks at levels far below those of the 19th century in each postwar decade (see Table 2).

Until the 1890s German trends were similar to and a major component of general immigration trends. In no decade between 1830 and 1890 did Germans constitute less than a quarter of all arrivals; in the 1850s and 1860s they made up over a third. However, the steep German decline at the end of the century coincided with the greatest periods of mass immigration from southern and eastern Europe. The German element dropped well below one-twentieth in the first two decades of the 20th

Table 2. German immigration by decade.

Decade	Total immigration	German immigration	German as percentage of total immigration
1820–29	128,502	5,753	4.5
1830–39	538,381	124,726	23.2
1840–49	1,427,337	385,434	27.0
1850–59	2,814,554	976,072	34.7
1860–69	2,081,261	723,734	34.8
1870–79	2,742,137	751,769	27.4
1880–89	5,248,568	1,445,181	27.5
1890–99	3,694,294	579,072	15.7
1900–09	8,202,388	328,722	4.0
1910–19	6,347,380	174,227	2.7
1920–29	4,295,510	386,634	9.0
1930–39	699,375	119,107	17.0
1940–49	856,608	117,506	14.0
1950–59	2,499,268	576,905	23.1
1960–69	3,213,749	209,616	6.5
1970	373,326	10,632	2.8
Total	45,162,638	6,917,090	15.3

Source: U.S. Bureau of the Census, *Historical Statistics of the United States: Colonial Times to 1970* (Washington, D.C., 1975), p. 105.

century before returning to higher if fluctuating proportions under the quotas of the 1920s, which favored old immigrants and severely restricted new arrivals from southern and eastern Europe. In the middle 1950s there was a significant downward shift in both numbers and proportions of German newcomers.

The interaction of conditions in the homeland and in the United States explained the volume and timing of German immigration. After the Napoleonic wars (1792–1815) Russia and eastern Europe were also favored destinations; many descendants of these settlers migrated to the United States later in the century. (*See* Germans from Russia.) In the 1820s Brazil and Argentina attracted perhaps half of the small flow of emigrants, and some Germans continued to find their way thereafter to Latin America and to Canada, South Africa, and Australia. But political freedom and economic promise made the United States more enticing to most. Some 90 percent of all registered German emigrants between 1835 and 1910 were bound for the United States. When depressions or war dampened that opportunity, as occurred periodically—after 1837, 1857, 1861, 1873, and 1893—German immigration lessened.

Some religiously motivated immigration continued, particularly during the earlier part of the 19th century: the Old Lutherans' trek in the late 1830s and early 1840s was partially in protest against Prussia's forced unification of the Lutheran and Reformed churches in 1837; Saxon followers of Martin Stephan came in 1839 to distance themselves from the wickedness of the Old World; pietists founded such communal societies as Harmony (1805) and Economy (1825), Pa., Zoar, Ohio (1817), and Amana, Iowa (1843 migration, 1854 founding); a communistic Catholic society settled at St. Nazianz, Wis., in 1854. German chancellor Bismarck's *Kulturkampf* against German Catholics in the 1870s also influenced decisions to emigrate, particularly among clergy and religious.

Few emigrated for purely political reasons. Certainly the reactionary Carlsbad Decrees of 1819, aimed particularly against students, and the repression of German liberals in the early 1830s sent some refugees to the United States, where they provided a distinguished core of educated leadership. Fugitives from the abortive democratic revolutions of 1848 were more numerous and more significant, but the "forty-eighters" numbered no more than several thousand of the almost three-quarters of a million Germans who arrived in America in the following six years. The uncertainty and disillusionment of the revolutionary years undoubtedly provided the final catalyst for many emigrants, but those who fled actual reprisals were few.

The Jews—perhaps 10,000 from Bavaria alone by 1839—who fled economic and social discrimination in the southern and eastern German states, were also refugees of a sort. The desire to escape military service influenced some immigrants, and the antisocialist laws in force from 1878 to 1890 stimulated others. Finally, a few emigrants—less than 1 percent of the total—were paupers and criminals whose passage was paid if they left the country, a practice halted by mid-century in the face of American objections and the concern of German ports to maintain the emigrants' good repute.

But the vast majority in the 19th century, as in the 18th, emigrated in response to social and economic changes that made it harder to maintain old ways of life and heightened the attraction of America. The slow diffusion of the Industrial Revolution into Germany, agricultural reform, and rural overpopulation made emigration for many farmers, traditional craftsmen, and small shopkeepers the most reasonable, even conservative way of sustaining familiar habits.

Increasing literacy and the spread of information about the United States converted discontent into decision. Until mid-century, emigration agents remained sufficiently effective that the German states frequently regulated their activities. The 10 guidebooks written for emigrants between 1816 and 1830 increased to something like 17 in the next decade and 58 in the 1840s, before their pace of production slowed. In the 1840s newspapers aimed directly at prospective emigrants appeared up to three times a week in editions of 500 to 1,000. Eight such papers at various times in the second half of the century offered advice on travel and information about America and reprinted letters from those already there. Numerous associations were formed to advise or direct emigrants, which occasionally resulted in attempts at group migration. Among the most noted were the Giessener Auswanderungs-Gesellschaft (1833), a group of young liberals who hoped to settle in Missouri in the manner advocated by Gottfried Duden in his immensely popular book (1829) about his experiences as a settler in Missouri between 1824 and 1827; and the Adelsverein, promoted by prominent noblemen in 1843, which attempted to settle several thousand Germans in Texas. But private letters undoubtedly remained the most important fund of advice and stimulus to emigration, particularly when they enclosed passage money from friends or relatives already in America.

Transportation improvements were also significant. The first areas of emigration bordered the Rhine, Germany's traditional artery for international communication. The gradual unification of the country, culminating in the creation of the German Empire in 1871, along with the spread of steamboats in the 1830s and of railroads in the 1850s simplified internal travel and made it

speedier. More frequent transatlantic sailings, larger ships, lower fares, and the gradual transition from sail to steam greatly relieved the previous hardships of the crossing. Finally, emigration was eased as German governments lifted 18th-century restrictions.

The preindustrial phase of emigration lasted to about 1865. During this period the impulse spread from the southwest—the Palatinate, Württemberg, Baden—north and east first to Hesse-Darmstadt, Hesse-Cassel, Franconia, Westphalia, Hannover, and Oldenburg by the 1840s, and then into Mecklenburg and Pomerania east of the Elbe by the mid-1850s. Emigration rose and fell with the cycles of bad weather, poor harvest (especially from the potato rot in the mid-1840s), and high grain prices that plagued Germany in these decades. Emigrants increased from about 1.0 per 1,000 population in the affected areas in the 1820s to about 2.5 by the 1830s, 3.5 in the 1840s, 5.5 by 1850, to an all-time peak of 14.1 in 1854.

Small farmers predominated in the migration from the southwest; artisans and household manufacturers were prominent among those from the more central regions; and day laborers and servants were predominant among emigrants from the northeast, where the spread of estate-based commercial agriculture barred young men from the secure employment needed to found their own families. Families dominated the first phase— two-thirds to three-quarters traveled in family groups. They were not the poorest but those who still had something to lose and with property or expectations of inheritance sufficient to finance their voyages.

American economic problems in the mid-1850s, industrial expansion in Germany, and then civil war in the United States brought this phase to an end. In the second phase, which lasted until about 1895, families continued to constitute perhaps two-thirds of the emigration. The numbers of independent farmers and artisans declined while those of agricultural laborers from the north and east increased; these were rural workers dislocated not by hard times but by the expansion of the German economy.

But when overpopulation reached East Prussia in the 1890s, the results were different. Depression and the closing frontier in the United States coincided with large-scale German industrialization, so that internal migration replaced emigration as Germans moved from country to city and from the east westward to Berlin, to the industrial areas of central Germany and Silesia, and to the Ruhr Valley. The emigration impulse in Germany spent itself sooner than in any other European country.

Emigrants in this third, mature industrial phase tended to be industrial workers seeking higher pay, many of whom planned to return. By the 1920s only 33 percent were arriving in family groups. Postwar economic chaos swelled the emigrant ranks in the 1920s, but American quotas (Germans had an annual quota of 25,957), the Great Depression, and the optimism of the early Hitler years in Germany meant that returning citizens outnumbered emigrants in the early 1930s. By the middle of the decade, political and Jewish refugees began to swell the statistics until World War II again halted transatlantic movement. Displaced persons of non-German origin accounted for most of the immediate postwar arrivals. Free immigration of Germans

again became possible in the early 1950s, when relatives of American servicemen and East German refugees made up the last sizable German group to settle in the United States. Prosperity held German immigration well below its yearly quotas after 1962, and return migration rates were high. The refugees of the 1920s and 1930s, generally educated, professional, and liberal, presented a strong contrast to the industrial immigrants who preceded them; post-World War II immigrants were a more random cross section.

Nineteenth-century emigration undoubtedly relieved overpopulation; its effectiveness as a safety valve ultimately outweighed contemporary fears concerning the drain of manpower, skills, and capital. For the United States, it brought industrious farmers during the period of greatest westward expansion and trained artisans when American cities were experiencing explosive growth. Most immigrants were not transients but stable settlers bound by family ties: up until World War I the proportion of males hovered near 60 percent (only the Irish and the English had so even a sex ratio), and return migration rates were low. The variety of occupational, regional, and religious backgrounds also gave the German immigrants a great degree of heterogeneity.

GEOGRAPHICAL DISTRIBUTION IN THE UNITED STATES

Where the Germans settled depended on time of arrival, changing occupational goals, shifting locations of economic opportunity, transportation routes, and the historical accident of settlement promotions, advertising, and reputation. Early-19th-century emigrants continued to use the Rhine route to Dutch ports, but the end of the redemptioner trade in 1819 was a hard blow to Dutch shippers who lacked regular commercial products to exchange with the United States. The slack was taken up first by Le Havre in France, the main port of entry for cotton destined for Alsatian mills, and then by Bremen, Germany's main port for American tobacco. These routes brought Germans to New Orleans in cotton ships and to Baltimore in tobacco ships, and from there they made their way inland to settlements along the Mississippi, Ohio, and Missouri valleys. Others sailed from Hamburg to Hull, transferred by rail to Liverpool, and then sailed to New York, though shipping lines like North German Lloyd and Hamburg-America, which specialized in the emigrant trade, soon established direct links with New York. From there the newcomers made their way to other eastern cities or westward by the Erie Canal and the Great Lakes or, after 1840, by railroad to the Midwest.

Emigrant guides publicized areas that their authors considered suitable for settlement (and in which they themselves often had an economic stake). Duden's tract sent large numbers to Missouri in the 1830s, while Wisconsin was favored in the following decade. States vied with one another to advertise their opportunities. Wisconsin established a commissioner of emigration in 1852, and other states followed suit. Private businesses in various cities supported emigration agents at East Coast ports and in Germany, and western railroads like the Northern Pacific engaged in vigorous promotion to lure settlers to populate their land grants. German churches attempted to direct their members to areas

where ministers were available. Wisconsin attracted attention when a German-speaking Swiss became Milwaukee's first Catholic bishop, and publicizing by a missionary priest helped create a Catholic concentration in central Minnesota.

In general, however, German settlement patterns mirrored the locations of greatest opportunity. The result was a widely dispersed but stable distribution, usually avoiding New England and the South in favor of the middle Atlantic, east north-central, and west north-central states (see Table 3). German immigrants after 1950 concentrated in the middle Atlantic region, and along with the second generation have participated in the national movement toward the southern and western states. New York has always claimed more German residents than any other state—18 percent of the national total in 1880, 17 percent in 1920, 22 percent by 1970. In 1880 Illinois (12 percent) followed, then Ohio (10 percent), Wisconsin (9.4 percent), and Pennsylvania (8.6 percent). The ranking remained similar in 1920, but by 1970 California (13 percent) had displaced Illinois (8.2 percent), and New Jersey (8.0 percent) had overtaken Pennsylvania (5.0 percent).

Wisconsin has always had the greatest proportion of Germans in its population. In 1920 they were well over three times more numerous in that state than their share of the total national population would have suggested. Minnesota followed, but all of the middle Atlantic, east north-central, and west north-central states (except for Pennsylvania and Kansas), along with Maryland, had German proportions greater than the national average. By 1970 New York and New Jersey, with over twice the national proportion, had the most disproportionate concentrations of German-born, but with both first and second generations counted, Wisconsin (with almost three times the national proportion) and Minnesota (with twice) remained the most German.

In the South, Germans, many of them Jews, responded to mercantile and manufacturing opportunities. But the lack of readily available land, unfamiliar climate and agriculture, limited urbanization, and fear of competition with black labor combined to keep most Germans away from the South, despite occasional colonizing efforts like that at Cullman, Ala., in 1872. Outside New Orleans, only Texas had extensive German settlements, the result of colonization schemes, favorable climate and soil, and generous land policies of the Mexican and Texas governments. Core setlements once established attracted later-comers, and a large agricultural area along the Brazos River, centered on New Braunfels and Fredericksburg, remained heavily German.

But most ante-bellum German immigrants perceived greater opportunity in the newly opened farmland and frontier cities of the Midwest. Many of the earliest immigrants followed the native-born Americans (many of whom were of colonial German extraction) to Ohio and Indiana farms and to towns like Pittsburgh, Cincinnati, and Louisville. In the 1830s Duden's enthusiasm attracted many of the best educated to Missouri; the communities of "Latin Farmers" (as contemporaries termed the well-educated settlers who knew more about Cicero and Virgil than they did about farming) around St. Louis and across the river in Belleville, Ill., acted as magnets that then drew German settlement west along the Missouri River valley, northeast into central Illinois, and north into Iowa. When immigration increased dramatically in the 1840s, the Erie Canal and Great Lakes route pointed to northern Illinois, southeastern and central Wisconsin, and Michigan, which became the areas of heaviest German concentration. By the Civil War this migration joined that from Missouri and Iowa moving into the river valleys of Minnesota. A chain of urban German communities stretched from Albany to Buffalo, N.Y., and along the Great Lakes from Cleveland, Toledo, and Detroit to Chicago and Milwaukee. The gold rushes of 1849 and 1858 provided a base for later concentrations in central California and the Denver area.

The second phase of immigration, after the Civil War, contained a smaller agricultural component. Germans still moved with the agricultural frontier to the prairies of eastern Kansas and Nebraska and into the Dakotas, but the drier high plains farther west proved less attractive, except to the German colonists from Russia.

German settlement reached its greatest extent by 1890. Few of the immigrants of the third phase came seeking farmland, and there were no new farming frontiers to be opened. Germans were found on almost every free-state frontier during the years of their heavy immigration. Frequently, however, they were not persons fresh from the old country but those with some American experience. Many of Milwaukee's earliest German settlers came from Buffalo or Detroit; Wisconsin's pioneers of the 1840s blazed trails to Minnesota for other Germans in the 1850s, from where others went forth to pioneer in the Dakotas a generation later. Once the experienced settlers established the nucleus of a community, greenhorns could safely fill it in. The hope of forming extensive ethnic communities encouraged settlement on the frontier, where Germans could hope to take over large areas. Migration chains frequently linked newer frontiers with older ones and with villages in Germany, easing the rigors of adjustment for newcomers and preserving the customs and dialect of particular old-country regions. Settlements large enough to support a German church were more likely to expand over time and intensify their ethnic character than were communities without the cultural

Table 3. Geographical distribution of German-born Americans, by region.

Region	Percentage of German-born			
	1850	1880	1920	1960
New England	1.2	1.8	3.0	3.9
Middle Atlantic	36.0	30.0	30.1	38.5
East North-Central	39.1	39.8	35.1	25.3
West North-Central	9.0	16.6	17.4	7.1
South Atlantic	6.6	3.6	2.4	5.8
East South-Central	3.0	2.0	1.0	0.9
West South-Central	4.6	2.9	2.8	2.2
Mountain	—	0.8	2.0	2.9
Pacific	0.6	2.5	6.1	13.2

Source: U.S. Census Office, *Seventh Census of the United States, 1850, Compendium* (Washington, D.C., 1853), p. 117; U.S. Census Office, *Statistics of Population of the United States at the Tenth Census, 1880, Compendium* (Washington, D.C., 1883), p. 434; Niles Carpenter, *Immigrants and Their Children, 1920* (Washington, D.C., 1927), p. 353; U.S. Bureau of the Census, *Census of the Population, 1960, Characteristics of the Population*, pt. 1, *U.S. Summary* (Washington, D.C., 1963), pp. 1–255.

reinforcement of religion. But the German rural frontier was seldom extensive in any particular region, although in Wisconsin the census in 1910 did disclose a range of ten nearly contiguous counties with populations at least 35 percent first- and second-generation German. Minnesota, Iowa, Nebraska, and Texas each had one county with such a concentration.

Most of the third-phase immigrants joined growing numbers of second- and third-generation Germans in the cities. As early as 1860 some 37 percent of the German-born resided in cities of over 25,000; by 1890 they were about 40 percent, more than double the percent of native-born urban Americans. In 1920 over 54 percent of the Germans were urban by this definition, and over 67 percent lived in cities of all size categories; this increased to 79 percent by 1950. Only in Minnesota, Iowa, and several states to the west were a majority of Germans still rural by 1930.

New York City, the port of entry for most immigrants, always contained the largest urban German concentration. Many simply found jobs after disembarking and remained there; its very size and heterogeneity proved irresistible to those seeking to reproduce the cultural excitement of German cities. New York's heavy industry employed many later immigrants and generated spillover communities in Hoboken, Newark, and Jersey City, N.J. New York's German population peaked in 1900 and fell relatively slowly thereafter.

The other major ports also had early German communities of some size. New Orleans's German element declined abruptly after 1860, when the Civil War irrevocably destroyed its position as a port of arrival. German numbers in Philadelphia and Baltimore peaked in 1890, and in San Francisco in 1900.

The large cities of the Midwest became the most characteristically German urban environments. Milwaukee and St. Louis, with slightly over 30 percent German-born, were the nation's most German cities in 1850. Ten years later Milwaukee moved decisively into the leading position, which it has since maintained. Cincinnati, Ohio, Louisville, Ky., and St. Louis reached their peak German populations relatively early, attracted fewer later German immigrants, and failed to acquire large numbers of other immigrants. But Chicago, Milwaukee, Detroit, Cleveland, and Toledo were sufficiently central to national urban-industrial growth to maintain vital German communities for a longer period while also attracting a broader ethnic mix.

Germans in the Erie Canal cities of New York State —Albany, Syracuse, Rochester, and Buffalo—never were as numerous nor proportionately as significant as in the midwestern cities, and their daily life was shared with a greater variety of other ethnic groups. Los Angeles was the one city in which the number of German-born residents continued to increase as late as 1930— undoubtedly older persons moving to California.

OCCUPATIONS

The stereotypical 19th-century German American was a skilled practitioner of a traditional craft—baker, carpenter, brewer—putting to good use a trade painstakingly learned in the Old World. But Germans were also merchants, farmers, musicians, and laborers. Almost a third of those reporting an occupation on arrival in 1875 claimed to be skilled craftsmen, almost one-quarter were farmers, and close to another quarter were common laborers. During the following years the skilled and agricultural components declined, and the proportion of the unskilled rose; by 1890 some 45 percent were laborers or servants. With the later transition to mature industrial immigration, the proportion of skilled workers again became more significant.

The occupational niches they found in the United States mirrored these backgrounds. In 1870 some 37 percent of the gainfully employed Germans had skilled jobs, 27 percent were in agriculture, 23 percent in professional and personal service, and 13 percent in trade and transportation. Compared with all American workers, they were considerably underrepresented in agriculture and overrepresented in industry: they made up 6.7 percent of the work force but only 3.8 percent of agri-

Table 4. Numbers of German-born in selected U.S. cities, 1850–1950.

City	1850	1860	1870	1880	1890	1900	1910	1920	1930	1940	1950
New York	56,141	119,984	151,203	163,482	210,723	324,224	278,137	194,155	237,588	224,749	185,467
Chicago	5,035	22,230	52,316	75,205	161,039	203,733	182,289	112,288	111,366	83,424	56,635
Philadelphia	23,020	43,643	50,746	55,769	74,974	73,047	61,480	39,766	37,923	27,286	19,736
Milwaukee	7,271	15,981	22,509	31,483	54,776	68,969	64,816	39,771	40,787	28,085	18,259
Los Angeles	—	—	—	—	2,707	4,032	9,684	10,563	18,094	17,528	17,302
Detroit	2,838	7,220	12,647	17,292	35,481	42,730	44,675	30,238	32,716	23,785	17,046
San Francisco	—	6,346	13,602	19,928	26,422	35,303	24,137	18,514	18,608	14,977	12,394
Cleveland	—	9,078	15,855	23,170	39,893	44,225	41,408	26,476	22,532	15,427	9,629
Saint Louis	22,571	50,510	50,040	54,901	66,000	59,973	47,766	30,089	22,315	14,120	8,112
Buffalo, N.Y.	—	18,233	22,249	25,543	42,660	49,812	43,815	20,898	18,816	12,483	7,775
Baltimore	19,274	32,613	35,276	34,051	40,709	33,941	26,024	17,461	13,568	9,744	6,943
Cincinnati	33,374	43,931	49,446	46,157	49,415	38,308	28,426	17,833	13,944	8,856	6,013
Pittsburgh	—	6,049	8,703	15,957	25,363	36,838	29,438	16,028	14,409	9,805	5,898
Rochester, N.Y.	—	6,451	7,730	11,004	17,330	15,685	14,624	10,735	10,287	7,302	5,012
Newark, N.J.	3,822	10,595	15,873	17,628	26,520	25,251	22,177	14,041	12,508	7,813	4,977
Jersey City, N.J.	—	1,605	7,151	10,151	16,086	17,838	16,131	11,113	9,631	6,206	3,681
Boston	1,777	3,202	5,606	7,396	10,362	10,739	8,701	5,915	5,381	3,851	3,289
Columbus, Ohio	—	—	3,982	4,416	6,882	6,296	5,722	4,098	3,582	2,422	—
Louisville, Ky.	7,357	13,374	14,380	13,463	14,094	12,383	8,471	4,748	3,219	1,953	—
Albany, N.Y.	2,875	3,877	5,168	6,648	7,605	5,963	4,620	3,068	2,513	1,687	—
New Orleans	11,425	19,752	15,224	13,944	11,338	8,743	6,122	3,418	2,159	1,403	—

Source: U.S. Census Reports, 1850, 1860, 1870, 1880, 1890, 1910, 1920, 1930, 1940, 1950.

cultural workers and 11.4 percent of those engaged in manufacturing, mechanical trades, and mining. Areas of German economic specialization included retailing of all kinds; food-related trades such as baking, butchering, brewing, and distilling; and skilled crafts like cigar making, cabinetmaking, and tailoring. Germans were prominent as artists, musicians, restaurant keepers, barbers, dairymen, and nurserymen, but were underrepresented among doctors, lawyers, clerks, teachers, and certain kinds of factory laborers.

According to census figures of 1880, women were a smaller proportion of the German work force than was the case for other immigrant groups or for the nation as a whole. Those German women who entered the labor market took service jobs as janitors, laundresses, nurses, servants, saloon and hotel keepers, peddlers, shopkeepers, bakers, and tailors, while avoiding factory work and the kinds of sales and clerical jobs that required education or a knowledge of English. These patterns generally were maintained in the following decades.

By the turn of the century, the second generation was taking a different course. Sons, not as concentrated in service and manufacturing as their fathers, were finding their way into white-collar employment in increasing proportions, as were their sisters. By 1950 the second generation had left the original German patterns of occupational concentration and had become notable for their above-average representation in farming. The first generation still gravitated toward certain crafts and service occupations but also reflected the highly professional orientation of the latest refugee immigration.

Regional differences can be attributed to variations in local economies and to the German position relative to that of other ethnic groups. Before 1860 the specialized markets of eastern port cities attracted skilled and commercially oriented Germans, while competition from Irish laborers sent unskilled German job hunters to the newer midwestern cities. In the 1850s, for example, the unskilled were perhaps an eighth of the German work force in New York or Boston, but a third or more in St. Louis or Detroit. Similar rough differentials persisted after the Civil War. First-generation job choices thus reflected a selective integration into those sectors of the expanding American economy most suited to German skills and migration goals. Their occupational diversity inevitably influenced both the reception they received from American society and their ability to create a cohesive ethnic identity. Above all, it helped determine their own and their children's career paths and rates of social mobility.

Germans and their descendants generally advanced at moderate rates; surveys in the 1970s found persons of German descent near the national economic norm. Their median family income in 1972 was higher than the national median, though lower than that of the Russians, Poles, Italians, British, and Irish; they showed similar intermediate status with regard to years of education and occupations. In the 1970 census, second-generation Germans reported lower median incomes, a lower median number of school years completed, and a smaller proportion of professional and managerial occupations than average for second-generation Americans, while first-generation Germans did significantly better by such measures than the foreign-born population as a whole.

Spectacular success rewarded the exceptional few. Several—John Jacob Astor (1763–1848), a butcher's son who made a fortune in the fur trade and invested in real estate; sugar king Claus Spreckels (1828–1908); and lumber baron Frederick Weyerhaeuser (1834–1914)—made dramatic rags-to-riches climbs, while Henry Villard (born Ferdinand Heinrich Hilgard, 1835–1900) used a good education and connections to reach the ranks of leading finance capitalists. Germans often brought significant skills, nest eggs, or business training, and they frequently were supported by other family members. But like other immigrant groups, they faced language problems, strange legal and business customs, and alien methods of production. Many clung to a conservative, defensive business mentality that was out of step with the speculative march of American economic life. Cautious with their savings and apt to invest in real estate, Germans achieved early security but were perhaps less inclined to risk all for spectacular success.

Economic prominence came most readily to those who had the technical advantages of German education, as in the case of John A. Roebling (1806–1869), wire rope manufacturer and designer of the Brooklyn Bridge; to those who had superior craft skills in growing demand, as in the case of piano manufacturer Henry E. Steinway (1797–1871); and to those who could combine these advantages with an assured German-American market, as did the brewers. A 1908 compendium of "160 successful German-Americans and their descendants" in one city included 16 export-import merchants, 16 brewers and distillers, 13 in food-related manufacturing and distribution, 10 in chemistry and drugs, 6 in musical instrument manufacture, 10 in metal goods and machinery, 5 in tobacco-related areas, 4 in leather goods, 4 in construction, and 9 in insurance and real estate. Such lists for other cities showed similar distributions.

Few Germans entered the top management of the nation's leading businesses in the late 19th and early 20th centuries, because a new phase of industrial development made obsolescent many advantages of the early immigrants. Poorly capitalized entrepreneurs, artisans, and farmers found it increasingly difficult to achieve independence or prosperity. The momentum of German social mobility was therefore steady rather than increasing from generation to generation.

The realization that even in the United States the chances for becoming an independent craftsman or businessman were diminishing spurred a variety of organizational efforts among German-American workers. Reform associations and labor unions were a prominent feature of German urban life from the 1840s onward. The early activity was sporadic and ephemeral, as immigrant workingmen, like their native-born counterparts, struggled to resolve ideological issues concerning appropriate goals and forms of organization. They founded a series of short-lived unions and citywide trades assemblies, and as early as 1853 attempted to organize nationally.

Language alone encouraged Germans to form separate organizations, but ideology also differentiated them from other workers. Wilhelm Weitling (1808–1871) and Joseph Weydemeyer (1818–1866) introduced competing forms of communism in the late 1840s and early 1850s and stimulated the first waves of agitation for social and economic reform on a base wider than

that of the local union. After the Civil War, Germans provided the impetus for and the bulk of membership of the International Workingmen's Association in America, established in 1869 as the American branch of the First Communist International, and of the Lassallean splinter groups and the Socialist Labor party that succeeded it. Germans also formed the membership core of the anarchist labor movement that was held responsible for the Haymarket bombing in Chicago during the great wave of strikes in 1886; five of the seven men convicted of the bombing were German. Despite their relatively small membership, such groups provided a vocal core of leaders, injected alternative solutions into the debate about the course of organized labor, and were direct antecedents of 20th-century American socialist movements.

As late as 1887 there was an abortive attempt to form a national confederation of German trade unions, and effective central bodies of German trade unions coordinated activities in New York, Brooklyn, Buffalo, Philadelphia, Cleveland, Baltimore, and other cities. But the need for workers to unite against employers spurred affiliation with non-German labor organizations, and the American Federation of Labor's (AFL) "pure and simple" unionism weaned many from socialist to more pragmatic principles. In Milwaukee, St. Louis, and Chicago, Germans dominated union membership and federated councils through the end of the century, and the AFL even permitted the use of German in its deliberations until 1890. Labor organization for many Germans thus was not only a way of improving personal and class status, it was an important vehicle for integration into American life, first through fellowship with other Germans and then through solidarity with workers regardless of ethnicity.

AGRICULTURE

Although Germans in 1870 were only 4 percent of all American farm workers, slightly over a quarter of all employed Germans were in agriculture, constituting over 33 percent of all foreign-born farmers. By 1900 Germans owned nearly 11 percent of American farms and accounted for almost 10 percent of the country's agricultural employment. Fifty years later, the German-born and their children were still the single most numerous immigrant group in agriculture.

The stereotypical 19th-century German farmer was regarded by contemporaries as stable, hard-working, dependable, and thrifty—some even said penurious. His land was a permanent home for his family and not a speculative investment; choosing it well, he endowed it with his own and his family's hard labor, methodically cultivating it with careful Old World techniques, and persisting and prospering while more restless neighbors moved on. Where Germans settled among non-Germans, such stereotypical behavior proved short-lived, as local norms prevailed. But where fellow countrymen reinforced familiar patterns of life and work, the traditional mind-set of the German peasant endured far longer, lending some truth to the stereotype and creating the only German-American ethnic cultures to persist into the middle of the 20th century.

German clustering of sufficient size to influence cultural persistence occurred in most midwestern states and in Texas. The logic of clustered settlement was per-

suasive. A nucleus established in an area not yet fully settled could support German churches, schools, local governments, and familiar social patterns and lured other Germans to fill in the remaining land. When other settlers moved on, their land was taken up by German newcomers or children of the pioneers; community norms discouraged sales to outsiders. America's wealth of land allowed farmers to fulfill the old-country goal of aiding their sons in acquiring farms, often in the immediate neighborhood. Intrafamily assistance and transfer of land to children during the parents' lifetime adapted German goals to American circumstances and fostered an unusual degree of persistence and expansion in many rural ethnic communities. Once established, such clusters usually endured, intensified, and expanded over time in Wisconsin, Minnesota, Missouri, and Texas.

Farmers relied upon family labor, avoided mortgage debts whenever possible, and exhibited relatively low rates of tenancy. Contrary to stereotype, Germans were not especially gifted in their choice of land. They settled on what was available, valuing access to market and to nearby German urban settlements and showing less willingness than many Yankees to gamble on future transportation improvements. Where they chose woodland over prairie, it was for the cheap housing, fencing, and fuel it afforded their labor-rich, cash-poor families. Their perception of the farm as property held in trust for succeeding generations encouraged intensive investment in buildings and soil conservation practices. Even in clustered settlements, Germans planted the locally prevailing crops, and almost everywhere they abandoned Old World village settlement patterns for the dispersed farmsteads of America. Differences in degree, not in kind, distinguished these from other rural communities.

Nevertheless, the persistence of distinctive attitudes and social patterns revealed the strength of the ethnic culture, which was encouraged by isolation and frequently centered around the local church. In many rural areas the German language has persisted to the fourth and even fifth generations, although improved roads, mass communication, consolidated school systems and longer attendance, and modern farming practices have all tended to break down the isolation of such communities. Yet family orientation, religiosity, and social and political conservatism, nurtured in rural self-containment and widely diffused by the migrations of numerous offspring, remained traits attributable to German ethnicity in the 1970s.

URBAN COMMUNITIES AND ETHNIC CULTURE

Urban Germans proved ultimately unable—and perhaps unwilling—to isolate themselves like the farmers. In 1900 the 15 cities with German populations of 15,000 or more contained over 36 percent of the total German-born population of the United States. A further 13 percent lived in the 94 cities with 1,000–15,000 German-born residents. Such numerical concentrations permitted urban Germans to create virtually self-sufficient neighborhood communities based on shared activities, voluntary associations, and formal institutions. Yet the very success of the first generation in creating a complex urban ethnic culture paradoxically drew the second generation all the more inexorably into the

American mainstream and made the community's survival dependent upon continuing immigration.

In the newer cities of the Midwest, Germans arrived early enough in sufficient numbers to dominate entire neighborhoods. Even in older cities like New York, Philadelphia, and Baltimore, certain areas took on a distinctively German cast as immigrants sought the convenience and comfort of neighbors who spoke the same language and patronized the same shops, churches, and social activities. "Little Germany" was a familiar and colorful feature of 19th- and early 20th-century American cities. Here were "German houses, German inscriptions over the doors or signs, German physiognomies," noted a Danish visitor to Milwaukee in the 1850s; "many Germans live here who never learn English, and seldom go beyond the German town."

Not all Germans lived in the "Over the Rhines," "Little Saxonies," and "Nord-Seites" that dotted American cities. In Saint Louis in 1860, only about 36 percent of the German population lived in the two wards with a German majority, and this pattern was probably typical. In the era before urban mass transit, the need to live near their work dispersed many Germans across the city, and the later appearance of the streetcar encouraged the upwardly mobile to scatter throughout the suburbs. Often several separate nuclei developed, and even heavily German areas included a number of non-German residents. But Germans were more successful in carving out such enclaves than many other 19th-century immigrants. Moreover, Little Germanies served important functions even for those outside its bounds, gathering together in convenient locations the institutions that served an ethnic lifestyle and vigorously symbolized the group's presence.

The German quarters sheltered large numbers of impoverished newcomers but were not defined solely by shared poverty. Reflecting the social and economic heterogeneity of the German immigration, they were microcosms of an urban society, not just a segment of it. The workers' cottages and tenements usually adjoined streets of solid houses owned by merchants and professional men. Because of their numbers and diverse backgrounds, Germans transferred to America much of Old World urban life, including its divisions. In the cities of the New World, Catholics rubbed shoulders with Lutherans and atheists, Bavarians with Prussians, university graduates with peasants. No single set of associations and institutions could embrace such diversity. German Americans frequently complained of the disunity that kept them from presenting a strong front against other groups, but it was also a strength: they established within the community a range of activities sufficiently broad to shield even the most urbanized and successful from the blandishments of Americanization.

To 19th-century contemporaries the greatest gulf was that between church and club Germans. The former were pious Protestants and Catholics, often former peasants or small craftsmen, who focused their lives around their church and took relatively little interest in the broader affairs of the community. Overwhelmingly predominant among rural residents, church Germans were numerically significant in the cities as well. But club Germans came to define, for themselves and for outsiders, the characteristic ethnic culture.

The club Germans themselves were a diverse lot. The liberal refugees of 1830 and 1848 provided educated, cultured leadership, but even they were frequently split by conflicts between the "grays," as contemporaries called the earlier, older immigrants, and the "greens," the more radical, more recently arrived forty-eighters. Joining them at mid-century were secularized, often free thinking or atheistic workingmen and entrepreneurs, as well as more conservative nationalists later in the century. Their organizations were modeled on the rich variety of activities that had grown up among the middle and working classes in German cities by the mid-19th century. Informal neighborly gatherings quickly gave way to organized coffee circles, convivial imbibers coalesced into formal singing societies, and the club life so characteristic of German America was born.

Many of the first clubs served practical needs: volunteer fire and militia companies combined opportunities for marching, music, and public show with demonstrations of newly acquired American patriotism, community service, and defense against nativist bullying. Weekly contributions to mutual-benefit associations provided a primitive form of insurance against sickness and death. By 1892 there was a national federation of benefit societies, which soon became the largest of the secular German associations. German mutual fire-insurance societies and building societies had their roots in similar needs.

Societies with other purposes frequently derived strength from their affiliated mutual-benefit sections, as in various workers' associations, compatriotic societies of persons from the same homeland region, and fraternal orders. German-speaking lodges of American orders began with a Philadelphia Masonic lodge in 1810. By 1871 over 300 of the 4,800 Odd Fellows lodges in the United States were German, and Germans also formed their own orders, most notably the Sons of Hermann (1840) and the German Order of the Harugari (1847). Lodge membership provided useful business and social contacts and gave secularized Germans some of the brotherhood and ritual of the churches within which they had been raised.

Educational, conversational, and debating societies, often linked to political activity and modeled on similar societies in Germany were important in the 1840s and 1850s. Many were socialistic reform groups; others were freethinking societies in search of a rational alternative to organized religion. The Turners, followers of the German patriot Friedrich Ludwig Jahn (1778–1852), stressed a mixture of physical culture and liberal nationalism that played an important role in the German revolutionary period. Exiled followers of Jahn brought gymnastics to the United States in 1824, but not until the arrival of the forty-eighters were Turnvereine (Gymnastics Associations) organized and a national federation formed. Building upon the prestige earned by the outstanding service of the Turners in the Civil War, the Turnerbund for a time acted as the main spokesman for German America. It supported a national gymnastics teachers' seminary after 1860, first in New York, then in Milwaukee, and organized large-scale competitions.

Music also brought Germans together. Singing societies were popular at all levels of society. Philadelphia's

Männerchor dated from 1835, Baltimore's Liederkranz from 1836. Soon casual gatherings of such groups grew to formal organizations sponsoring periodic competitions; the first Sängerfest held in Cincinnati in 1849 encouraged the formation of several regional federations whose Sängerfeste became massive public events, trumpeting to the nation the cultural achievements of its German residents. In Brooklyn in 1900, for example, 174 associations with 6,000 singers competed for the musical laurels. Germans also supported numerous societies devoted to chamber and symphonic music and opera; countless bands, both amateur and professional, enlivened community occasions.

From the amateur dramatic societies of the 1840s came the actors and audiences for the professional German theater of the 1850s. Most cities with significant German populations gave sporadic support to one or more such theaters until World War I, though few achieved the durability or reputation of New York's Germania, Philadelphia's Deutsches, or Milwaukee's Pabst theaters. German companies were continually trapped between their desire for quality drama and their audience's less sophisticated tastes. Chicago, for example, supported four or five German theaters and numerous amateur performances in the last decades of the 19th century, but an 1892 attempt to house a permanent company in a magnificent Adler and Sullivan building quickly collapsed. Chicago's German Theater continued to perform even during World War I but finally fell victim to competition from the movies in 1931.

A single organization, such as a militia company, a theatrical society, a reform club, or a Turnverein, might periodically emerge as the central focus for the organized German life of a city. But as the 19th century advanced, even that superficial unity became less common, with the increasing tendency of the elite to withdraw into their own clubs. Charities and the private schools founded to preserve the language and the German concept of education provided some sense of common enterprise. German societies modeled after those of Philadelphia, New York, and Baltimore appeared in other cities after 1834. Their purpose remained primarily to protect and aid newly arriving immigrants through information, advocacy, employment referrals, and direct relief. Pre-Lenten carnivals, outdoor Volksfeste, and annual German Day celebrations created other common bonds from the 1850s onward. But not until late in the century did attempts to unite all the German clubs in a city under a single umbrella organization have any lasting results. In 1915 a national roster of German-American associations listed 4 cities with more than 200 clubs (New York, Chicago, Philadelphia, and Milwaukee), 10 with between 51 and 200 clubs, and 26 with between 21 and 50. Such variety represented not just choice but replication, as urban Germans divided into ever-greater numbers of social cells.

Shared values and lifestyle created an identifiably ethnic culture, of which the family was a central focus. The stolid, uncommunicative, work-obsessed farm family of Ruth Suckow's novel, *Country People* (1924), and the cultivated, protective, and sentimental atmosphere of an upper-middle-class childhood evoked by Hermann Hagedorn's memoir, *The Hyphenated Family: An American Saga* (1960) are extremes reflecting the diversity of family styles transplanted from Germany. Many farm people brought to the United States the conception of the family, with numerous children, as a joint economic enterprise; wives and daughters worked alongside their menfolk, youngsters left school early, and mutual support obligations were recognized. The survival of such ideals in American cities led immigrant women to work in small-scale family enterprises and resulted in relatively early school-leaving ages, high rates of domestic employment among girls and of apprenticeship among boys, and frequent family-operated businesses. By contrast, the newer middle-class family norm freed both mothers and children from the need to work, stressing the role of the small, closed family circle, held together by bonds of love, in nurturing the developing child.

All of these family styles had in common an insistence on the dominant authority of the father and the subordinate status of wives and children. German immigrants were often aghast at the easy relationships between Yankee fathers and their children and the seeming deference and freedom given Yankee women. Rates of home ownership were usually higher among Germans than among other groups of similar status, more of them lived within nuclear families and fewer of the women worked outside the home once married. The spread of bourgeois values and of a sentimentalized conception of the home, family, and patriarchal authority, central to the emerging German national identity in the 19th century, also provided self-definition and unity among German Americans.

Other, more public components also came to define a German lifestyle in American cities. Immigrants brought with them a delight in relaxation, a love of nature and Sunday strolls, comfortable picnics and boisterous public feasts, songs, dances, and family visits, all enjoyed over a glass of beer, wine, or schnapps. The tavern became the center of social activity in every German neighborhood, the meeting place for clubs and for men after work. Milwaukee in 1860 boasted approximately one German tavern for every 30 German households. The summer beer garden with its music and pleasant landscaping offered distractions to the entire family. In a country devoted to Sunday blue laws and increasingly legislated temperance and prohibition, common commitment to a convivial lifestyle gave further coherence and content to German-American ethnic identity.

CHURCHES, SCHOOLS, AND THE PRESS

Ethnicity so defined was sufficiently broad and neutral to contain church as well as club Germans. However, religion was the primary force in the lives of many church members. Approximately a third of all German immigrants may have been of Roman Catholic background, with most of the remainder divided among the Lutheran, Reformed, or Evangelical churches; also included were smaller numbers of Methodists, Unitarians, Pietists, and Jews. But rationalism and anticlericalism had made deep inroads in the religious life of 19th-century Germany. Many immigrants lapsed in practice before arriving in the United States; once arrived, others took advantage of religious freedom to do the same.

German-American churches had to adapt to a competitive, voluntaristic religious environment. Protestant and Catholic alike, agreeing for different reasons that "language saves the faith," strove to retain the use of German as long as possible. For many Protestants, this was a way of preserving access to a rich doctrinal and liturgical tradition that was without parallel in English, while retaining members who might otherwise stray into related American denominations. For the Catholics, use of German was necessary to retain members who might otherwise leave their hierarchically organized international church for the familiarity of German-speaking Protestant or secular groups. Religion thus nurtured and was nurtured by ethnic consciousness; the least Americanized communities tended to be those with the strongest religious ties. Yet the church itself became an assimilating agent: to attend church was to act like an American, and defense of church interests often drew members into the public arena. The churches offered emotional continuity and communal support, and as their need to retain members forced adaptations to American circumstances, their conservative members were pulled along with it.

The struggles of German Catholics shaped the policy of the church toward later immigrant groups. The provision of Catholic services for the early immigrants was eased by the church's internationally centralized organization; donations from mission societies in German-speaking countries, including the Society for the Propagation of the Faith (founded in France in 1822 but with numerous German members), Austria's Leopoldinenstiftung (1829), and Bavaria's Ludwig-Missionsverein (1838), supported the emigration of the German religious. Their contributions also aided the construction of countless schools and churches. Secular priests often emigrated with their congregations and presented their credentials to the local bishop upon arrival. Individual members of religious orders volunteered for American mission work—often intending to work among the Indians, later transferring their ministry to newly arriving countrymen. Certain orders established their own American foundations, including most notably, the Redemptorists (arrived 1832), who staffed German parishes and conducted parish missions to revive the immigrants' flagging zeal, and the Benedictines (1846) whose abbeys and priories across the country became spiritual and physical nuclei for numerous rural settlements. Other orders of priests and brothers included the Fathers of the Most Precious Blood (1843), German Franciscans (1839), Capuchins (1856), and the Society of Mary (1849). German orders of nuns staffed parish schools and hospitals, including the various branches of the Sisters of the Most Precious Blood (1844), the School Sisters of Notre Dame (1847), Benedictines (1852), and Poor Sisters of St. Francis (1858). By 1869, 1,160 priests, about a third of the Catholic priests in America, were German-speaking, of whom at least 827 (71 percent) were German-born; by 1892 the number of German-speaking priests had increased to 2,882.

The normal system of territorial parishes, which included all communicants within given geographical boundaries, would have permitted German services only in areas of solid German settlement; few urban areas met such criteria. When Philadelphia's German Catholics first established their own cemetery in 1768 and then seceded from their Irish-dominated congregation to found their own parish in 1789, they pointed the way to the church's solution to the problem posed by the diversity of its immigrant members—national parishes, in which membership was personal rather than residential and based upon language rather than territory. By 1869 there were 705 purely German parishes and by 1916, 1,890, or 11 percent of all parishes in the United States.

Nevertheless, German Catholics were a minority in a church dominated by the Irish. Control of bishoprics seemed crucial. The first German-born bishop, Fredderick Rese (1791–1871) of Detroit, was appointed in 1833 but soon resigned under pressure. It was only with the appointment of Swiss-born John Martin Henni (1805–1881) to the newly created see of Milwaukee in 1844 that Germans really entered the episcopate. Three other German-born bishops joined him by 1860; by 1892 there were 19. But each episcopal appointment to an area with large numbers of Germans raised the ethnic controversy anew. An 1886 memorial sent to Rome by the archbishop of Milwaukee, requesting a more independent role for German Catholics, provoked a crisis that climaxed in 1890 when European members of the St. Raphaelsverein—a lay society for the protection of German Catholic immigrants, founded in 1871 by a German merchant, Peter Paul Cahensly (1838–1923)— petitioned Rome for more German bishops in the United States. Germans took the resulting condemnation of "Americanism" by Pope Leo XIII in 1899 as a condemnation of the liberal policies of Americanizing bishops, but only the ultimate decline of the German national parishes healed the rift that Cahenslyism symbolized.

Many of the national parishes were founded through the initiative of lay people. Conflict between pastors and lay trustees was frequent in pioneer German-American parishes, and more than one church found itself under interdict for refusing to accept a pastor or for disobeying him on issues like the support of parish schools. Such independence reflected the wish to shape religion to other needs, as did the desire for national parishes. The German churches had an elaborate and ritualistic liturgy richly embellished with music, and their parishes contained a wide array of confraternities and associations, ranging from mutual-benefit societies to prayer sodalities to shooting clubs, which were more closely related to secular German clubs than to Irish parish organizations. These societies and numerous church-operated orphanages, hospitals, and other institutions served the needs of German-speaking communicants and guarded them against anti-Catholic proselytizers. Parochial schools were even more central in preserving the faith and ethnicity of future generations. Laymen found a unifying focus in the Central-Verein, founded in 1855 as a national union of parish mutual-benefit associations, and in a vigorous press which, beginning in Cincinnati in 1837 with Martin Henni's *Wahrheits-Freund*, by 1900 had produced 61 dailies and weeklies.

But the edifice of German-American Catholicism rested upon self-destructing foundations. By the turn of the 20th century, upward mobility sent numerous German Americans to mixed suburban parishes; their old churches either became bilingual or were relinquished

to newer immigrant groups. In rural German clusters, the spread of mass culture, declining isolation, World War I anti-Germanism, laws requiring English in the schools, and school consolidation slowly encouraged the transition to English in services and, to a lesser extent, transformation of ethnoreligious cultural patterns. As early as 1916 only 11 percent of the German-speaking parishes used the mother tongue exclusively. Even so peculiarly German an organization as the Central-Verein found a new and more purely American role in the pursuit of social justice, thus retaining its Americanized membership. German Catholic gradually became simply Catholic.

German Protestants found coreligionists, offspring of the colonial immigrants, already established in the United States. But attempts by the German Evangelical Lutheran Synod of Pennsylvania or the West Pennsylvania Classis of the Reformed Church to draw newcomers into their fold met little success. Americanized in language, doctrine, and ritual, they did not offer the immigrants a familiar spiritual or cultural haven, and they lacked the resources for major missionary efforts. Only where the institutions were reshaped by the newcomers, as the Ohio Synod was in the 1840s, was adaptation successful.

Nor did German parent organizations play directing roles. European missionary societies were important sources of funds and of ministerial candidates, but the religious bodies founded by immigrants themselves were far more important. By 1906 the immigrant-founded synods loosely confederated in the Lutheran Synodical Conference had a larger membership than either of the major old-stock Lutheran associations, and over four-fifths of all Lutheran members in German-speaking congregations belonged to synods founded by the 19th-century immigration. Religion and ethnicity tightly bonded in such bodies produced some of the most enduringly German communities in the rural Midwest and molded the distinctive character of those denominations.

The conservative Lutheran synods, particularly the Missouri Synod (the name refers rather to its origin than to the location of member congregations), proved most successful in gathering in Protestant settlers whose denominational loyalties had often been blurred before emigration, first by rationalism, then by pietistic evangelism and unionism. By 1906 about two-thirds of those belonging to German-speaking Protestant congregations were Lutheran, over half of whom affiliated with the Missouri-dominated Synodical Conference.

Much of the Missouri Synod's strength lay in the confessional conservatism and ethnic exclusivism derived from its origin in the 1839 immigration of more than 600 devout, well-organized Saxons who were at odds with state authorities over religious practices. Shortly after the group arrived in Missouri, they expelled their charismatic leader, Martin Stephan (1777–1846), for immorality and misuse of funds. But under the guidance of C.F.W. Walther (1811–1887), they evolved a loose congregational organization and, finding existing American synods too liberal, in 1847 founded the Missouri Synod. To preserve their faith from outside contamination, they bound it tightly to the German language, proselytized only among German immigrants, and protected their members with a press, a publishing

house, and a school system that ultimately included not only elementary schools in about four-fifths of all congregations but also two large seminaries, two teachers' colleges, and six preparatory schools. Prohibition of lodge membership promoted further isolation. Fellowship was denied even with other conservative Lutheran synods, such as the Buffalo Synod of the Prussian Old Lutheran emigration of 1839.

Having initially enlisted ethnicity as a prop for doctrinal purity, the Missouri Synod increasingly championed German interests. However, the decline of immigration and the urbanization of the younger generation by 1920 forced the synod to Americanize in order to survive. The patriarchal authority of the pastor gave way to greater lay participation on the American model, Sunday schools gradually replaced parochial schools (though the synod retained the largest program of full-time education in American Protestantism), and voluntary associations multiplied. By 1925 only half the synod's congregations still used German in church services. By gradually, if often painfully, discarding an ethnic identity no longer capable of "saving the faith," the faith survived with its distinctive conservatism intact.

In the absence of doctrinal distinctiveness in other groups, such as the German Evangelical Synod, the American analogue of the Prussian state church, the use of German neither endured nor prevented later merger with other, more American bodies. The Evangelical Synod, which by 1906 claimed about 9 percent of the membership of German-speaking congregations, originated in the Kirchenverein des Westens, a loose association formed in 1840 by pietistic missionaries from Basel and Barmen (now Wuppertal). Establishment of a press and a seminary by 1850 and of a formal synodical organization by 1866 affirmed their distinctiveness from related American denominations, as did parochial schools and associations. Yet modifications of European polity and worship soon set in—congregationalism, traveling preachers, regeneration (spiritual rebirth) as a condition of membership, and insistence upon liberty of conscience in areas of doubtful scriptural interpretation. Because of increasing Americanization, however, its parochial school system went into irreversible decline during the 1890s, and its first English-language newspaper appeared in 1902. The Evangelical Synod's decision, after World War I, to concentrate on urban missions to persons of all national backgrounds foreshadowed the 1934 merger with the Reformed Church in the United States.

American Protestant groups in general were concerned for the spiritual welfare of German immigrants, whose social customs challenged their ideal of a sober and moralistic way of life. The Ohio Methodist Conference commissioned Wilhelm Nast (1807–1899), a well-educated, recently arrived convert, as its first German missionary in 1835; in the following decade Presbyterians, Baptists, and Congregationalists also commissioned German-trained ministers. All found it necessary to organize special German associations within their ranks—the General Conference of German Baptist Churches and the Convention of German Presbyters in the West in 1859, the Congregational German Association of Iowa in 1862, the first German Methodist conference in 1864—and to establish newspapers

and seminaries to train German ministers. But membership remained relatively low. German Methodism, for example, peaked with 60,344 members in 1917; membership gains dropped rapidly as early as the 1890s, ministers aged with their congregations, and by 1924 the German conferences began to reintegrate into mainstream Methodism.

Despite impressive educational efforts, no Protestant denomination was able ultimately to retard linguistic, social, and cultural assimilation and to retain a purely ethnic character. The end of immigration made denominational survival possible only for those whose separate identity was more than ethnic.

Even secular Germans frequently enshrined their beliefs in denominational form. Independent, nonaffiliated, unitarian, or rationalist congregations early expressed anticlerical religious impulses. The movement for "free congregations" that appeared in Germany in the early 1840s took firm root in the United States with the coming of the forty-eighters. By 1852 some 30 free congregations existed in Wisconsin alone, and in 1859 a national League of Free Congregations was organized by Friedrich Schuenemann-Pott (1826–1888), "speaker" of a Philadelphia congregation and for 21 years editor of an important freethinking journal. The educated elite tended to dominate the freethinking societies, few of which outlived the founding generation. Some merged into Turner or socialist groups, others ultimately affiliated with denominations like the Unitarians, and a few survived well into the 20th century.

Nonbelievers frequently sent their children to Lutheran or Catholic parochial schools when no other German schooling was available, but the arrival of educated immigrants after 1840 provided both teachers and a large demand for private secular institutions. The German schools, often aggressively freethinking, transmitted the ethnic cultural heritage and also reflected a negative judgment of current American pedagogy. It was largely through German efforts that music, gymnastics, kindergarten, manual training, and high schools were later incorporated into the American educational system. Baltimore's Knapp-Schule and Milwaukee's German-English Academy survived into the 20th century, but many schools failed when immigration declined and when German language instruction found a place in the public school curriculum.

Beginning with Pennsylvania and Ohio in 1839, numerous states permitted and several (Ohio, Wisconsin, Indiana) mandated German instruction in the public schools when local demand warranted it. Usually, as in Chicago and New York, this meant simply language classes, but some cities, such as Cleveland, Baltimore, and Indianapolis, established truly bilingual systems. Voter pressure and a desire to lure German children into the assimilating influence of the public school explained this trend. In Saint Louis in 1860 perhaps four out of five children of German stock were in private schools; 20 years later, after the introduction of bilingual instruction, four out of five were in public schools. According to an 1886 estimate, there were about 430,-000 children nationwide in schools with German instruction, 38 percent of them in Catholic schools, 23 percent in Protestant, 35 percent in public, and 3.7 percent in secular private. Comparative percentages for the turn of the century were 35, 19, 42, and 3.4. German instruction in the public schools was always precarious, however. Only the Catholic and Lutheran parochial systems and exclusively German rural school districts were able to use education to keep the second generation within the cultural fold.

Nor did German Americans establish higher educational facilities to perpetuate more sophisticated forms of ethnic culture beyond the first generation. Periodic proposals for a secular German university came to nothing. In 1878 the National German-American Teachers Association (formed in 1870) sponsored a seminary in Milwaukee, near the German-English Academy and the normal school for gymnastics of the American Turnerbund. Never very well supported, the seminary nevertheless trained some 335 graduates before it closed in 1919. The church Germans early established seminaries for clergymen and normal schools for teachers, but few of these institutions had aspirations beyond the practical; the training they offered seldom met the standards even of the secondary-level German *gymnasium*. However, by the turn of the century, some of these institutions provided the basis for a denominational college system that reinforced religious if not ethnic identity.

The press was used by the various subgroups of German Americans to define, transmit, and defend their versions of ethnic culture, and like the schools, it ultimately encouraged assimilation by informing readers about American life and their place in it. The German press was the largest, perhaps best edited, and most influential foreign-language press in the United States, tracing its origins to Benjamin Franklin's *Philadelphische Zeitung* (1732) and Christopher Sauer's longer-lasting Germantown newspaper, founded in 1739. By 1800, 38 different German newspapers had appeared at one time or another in Pennsylvania, and some had spread to other states. The new wave of immigrants after 1830 provided educated readers and skilled editors for numerous liberal, generally Democratic newspapers in all the cities of German settlement. In 1843, Cincinnati's *Volksblatt* (f. 1836) was still the only German daily in the United States; by 1850 there were 20, including 4 in New York, 3 each in Cincinnati and Milwaukee, and 2 each in Philadelphia, Baltimore, and Chicago. German journals numbered over 250 by 1860, and expansion in the ante-bellum decades continued to keep pace with immigration. Although growth lagged behind that of the nation's press as a whole, until the 1880s German publications constituted about 80 percent of the foreign-language press. The total number peaked at almost 800 in 1893–1894.

Between 1850 and 1875 publications represented all shades of opinion; green forty-eighters clashed with more conservative grays, Republicans challenged Democrats, and freethinking polemics provoked denominational ripostes. By the 1870s personal journalism gave way to a more business-oriented press on the emerging American model. When the older editors left the scene, neither the second generation nor the newer immigrants filled their places. The large dailies became essentially American newspapers printed in German. With the decline of immigration and the consolidation trends after 1890, German-language publications declined to 613 in 1900 and 554 in 1910, when they made

up only 53 percent of the foreign-language press; the 70 dailies constituted just under 13 percent of the German publications (though a far larger share of the circulation), weeklies 78 percent, and less frequent publications a further 9 percent. World War I accelerated an ongoing decline.

POLITICS, ASSIMILATION, AND ETHNIC UNIFICATION

The fragmentation reflected in the press, the schools, and the social lives of Germans and their children was one of the strengths of German ethnic culture. Duplicating the class, religious, and regional divisions of the fatherland, it assured persons of varied backgrounds the comfort of kindred spirits while supporting an ethnic culture sufficiently diverse to contain rather than expel even the educated and upwardly mobile. But the very cultural bonds that provided a sense of unity were those that most aroused conflict with non-Germans, which pointed up the political weakness inherent in diversity.

German Americans early won a reputation for political apathy. They failed to produce officeholders commensurate with their numbers and seldom performed as reliable cogs in the political machine. Even the most chauvinistic enumeration of prominent German politicians virtually began and ended with Carl Schurz (1829–1906), the forty-eighter who served as senator from Missouri and secretary of the interior under President Rutherford B. Hayes. Language difficulty, lack of familiarity with democratic practices, and the narrowly economic motivation of their immigration were some reasons for German political impotence. But more significant was the disunity that prevented overwhelming numbers from rallying behind a single party. Not even in defense of their status as equal citizens and of their right to their own lifestyle—the two related issues that periodically provoked massive German public action in the 19th and early 20th centuries—did they remain united for long.

Status was the main issue of the 1830s, as liberal refugees, conservative church members, and descendants of colonial settlers united to press for a German state in the West, German as an official language in Pennsylvania and Ohio, and German higher education. But little direct political action resulted. Germans generally found their way into the Democratic party, attracted by its egalitarian rhetoric and its welcome to the foreign-born. The ante-bellum reform impulse, of which nativism was a part, struck at German status and culture in efforts to restrict the influence of immigrants in public life and to legislate temperance, Sabbatarianism, and uniform public schooling. The moralistic evangelism of the reformers was unpalatable to many Germans, and the increasing centrality of abolition in reform agitation seemed irrelevant and sometimes even repellent to immigrant workers who were worried about competition from free blacks. The result by the 1840s was a strong German link to the Democrats in opposition to the Whigs and any other party that included a strong reform element.

That political solidarity dissolved in the following decade. The forty-eighters sought to realize the radical and utopian ideals of their failed revolution with programs ranging from cooperatives to socialism to the catchall reformism of Karl Heinzen's 1854 "Louisville Platform," a proposed foundation for a German reform party with planks covering everything from abolition of the federal system to antislavery, anticlericalism, female suffrage, and eased citizenship requirements. They succeeded only in polarizing the German communities, particularly with their bitter campaigns against organized religion.

Increasing numbers of Germans came to view the fight against slavery as an extension of their European struggle for liberty and abandoned the Democrats for the new Republican party. The Republicans assiduously courted them from 1856 on, and the 1860 Republican convention accepted a "Dutch plank" condemning nativism. But many Germans still did not view the Republicans as an acceptable alternative. The presence of too many nativists, "temperance fanatics," and anticlerical Germans kept many Catholics and Lutherans out of the Republican fold. Only in states like Illinois, Missouri, and Minnesota, where the Republicans dissociated themselves from nativism, did the Germans roll up significant majorities for Abraham Lincoln. Elsewhere, in Michigan, Wisconsin, Indiana, Ohio, the German vote stayed with the Stephen Douglas Democrats. Least apt to move into the Republican column were those who felt most threatened by nativism, the Catholics and to a lesser extent the Lutherans.

Geography placed the majority of Germans on the side of the Union in the Civil War. With over 176,000 soldiers in the Union army, according to an 1869 estimate, Germans contributed more than their share to the Northern victory—the result not only of patriotism but of enlistment bounties, inability to pay substitutes, hopes for rapid citizenship, and a demographic structure weighted with young males. Militia units and singing societies sometimes enlisted en masse; 50 to 60 percent of all Turners in 1861 served the Union. All-German regiments were common in the early years of the war, and forty-eighters like Schurz, Franz Sigel (1824–1902), and Ludwig Blenker (1812–1863) held prominent commands. The record of the German units was mixed. Incidents like the rout of the "flying Dutchmen" at Chancellorsville fueled nativism within army ranks, but by the war's end the German service record had won the group an unquestioned place in the nation's regard. The Confederacy also had German soldiers. Many Germans who could afford to do so owned slaves, and they enlisted or were drafted like other Southerners. There were antidraft riots among Texas Germans, but there were among Germans in Wisconsin as well.

Political loyalties formed before the Civil War tended to persist. Radical forty-eighters, meeting in convention in 1863 and 1864, criticized Lincoln for his foot-dragging on total emancipation and his leniency toward the South, and they deserted Andrew Johnson on similar grounds. But by 1872, under the leadership of Schurz, they took an active role in the Liberal Republican bolt from Ulysses S. Grant as a protest against governmental corruption, thereby initiating a reconciliation with those Germans who had remained faithful to the Democrats. Civil-service reform remained an important issue among liberal Germans; sound money became another. But their public influence waned after 1872, and for the rank and file, the visceral issues of the last dec-

ades of the century were the familiar ones of temperance and nativism, never absent for long in 19th-century America, with opposition to Sunday observance laws, woman suffrage, American imperialism, and particularly school language legislation also periodically arousing German votes.

When German bloc voting increased, particularly in areas of dense concentration, the Democrats were generally the gainers. Revived agitation for prohibition in Ohio and Wisconsin in the early 1870s, Iowa's attempt to enforce antiliquor legislation ten years later, the temperance-linked campaign for woman suffrage in Nebraska in 1882, all encouraged German unity and Democratic surges. With the revival of an organized national anti-immigrant movement in the mid-1880s, the use of German in public schools and the "un-American" education in parochial schools became an issue; Wisconsin's 1889 Bennett Law, which stipulated that only schools in which the basic subjects were taught in English met legal attendance requirements, provoked well-organized German protests with Lutherans in the lead. Both parties wooed Germans with patronage and with positions on the ticket. Only when the national political stalemate broke down during the depression of the 1890s did this pattern shift; the fusion of Democrats and Populists under William Jennings Bryan, a moralistic soft-money advocate, sent large numbers of Germans into the new national Republican majority.

These voting trends reflected growing assertiveness and self-confidence, fueled both by the group's size and success in the United States and by the reflected glory of the newly established German Empire. But they also revealed insecurity in the face of a reawakened nativism that often seemed aimed directly at Germans, despite the fact that they came to be viewed as desirable "old immigrants" when the larger numbers of eastern and southern Europeans poured into the country. Even the Cahensly controversy within the Catholic church took on the overtones of a German fight against nativism. At the same time, assimilation of the younger generations and slackening immigration were thinning the ranks of organized German America. The older liberal middle-class leaders were not replaced by persons of similar background.

The Catholic Central-Verein met this crisis of cultural and institutional continuity by shifting to a social reform orientation to attract both the progressive-minded second generation and recent working-class immigrants. Socialist appeal among a similar constituency peaked in the early 20th century, as exemplified in still heavily German Milwaukee under the leadership of the Austrian-born journalist and congressman, Victor L. Berger (1860–1929) and of the second-generation mayor Emil Seidel (1864–1947).

But not all German associations could fall back on a noncultural identity. For many, the combined assertiveness and insecurity of the turn of the century held out for the first time the hope of achieving long-sought organizational unification to make German culture and influence felt nationally. The founding of the National German-American Alliance (1901–1918) under the leadership of Charles J. Hexamer (1861–1921) of Philadelphia culminated a local federation movement and a series of abortive national efforts, often provoked by the school issue. The Alliance was a federation of existing organizations and claimed more than 2 million members by 1914, though perhaps no more than one-tenth were active. Leaders were mainly middle-class businessmen, journalists, clergymen, and professors. Most church organizations remained outside the Alliance, along with many socialists and intellectuals. Prohibited by its charter from direct political action, the Alliance sought to promote cultural interests, particularly the teaching of German; to encourage citizenship and participation in public affairs; to promote amicable relations between the United States and Germany; and to fend off nativist attacks. It did play a political role, though, in defending "personal liberty" and opposing the Prohibition campaign. By 1914 German America confronted the war in Europe with a strong organization, well financed by brewing and liquor interests and with high public visibility and assurance.

WORLD WAR I AND AFTER

With the outbreak of war, the organizational machinery crafted to defend German interests in America stood ready to take up the cause of the fatherland in the battle for American public opinion. Indeed, the heightened ethnic consciousness of the war years was a boon to German newspapers and organizations previously dependent upon a constituency that was rapidly assimilating. The German-American press was virtually unanimous in its pro-Germanism and its insistence on strict American neutrality. The Alliance and other German organizations sponsored press bureaus, mass demonstrations, collections for war relief, lobbying for arms and loan embargos, and, as Woodrow Wilson's pro-British bias strengthened, a massive campaign for his defeat in the 1916 presidential election. For most Germans, such activity was a confirmation rather than a betrayal of their status as full American citizens. Only a few, like the poet and journalist George Sylvester Viereck (1884–1962), editor of the vehemently pro-German English-language *The Fatherland*, received direct support from the German propaganda organization.

Despite general unanimity of aims, Germans even in this crisis were unable to agree on how best to influence American policy. To many Americans, pro-German agitation and even ethnic identification constituted unpatriotic attitudes. Woodrow Wilson's 1916 campaign fanned the growing anti-Germanism. Although more Germans voted Republican than was true of the electorate as a whole, local issues and internal divisions confused the pattern, and Germans did not form a solidly anti-Wilson bloc.

The real purgatory followed U.S. entry into the war in April 1917. Most German-American newspapers and associations quickly declared their loyalty; there was minimal protest against conscription or Liberty bond campaigns. Nevertheless, a storm of anti-Germanism raged between the fall of 1917 and spring 1918. A government-sponsored structure of local defense committees, the national propaganda machine of George Creel's Committee on Public Information, and the civilian watchdogs of the American Protective League all fostered a climate of harassment, including a ban on German-composed music, the renaming of persons, foods, and towns, vandalism, tarring and feathering, arrests for unpatriotic utterances, and even a lynching in

Collinsville, Ill., in April 1918. Public burnings of German books were frequent. By summer 1918 about half of the states had restricted or eliminated German-language instruction, and several had curtailed freedom to speak German in public. The German press suffered under the censorship powers of local postmasters, and pacifist Mennonites endured harsh attempts to force conscription on them.

One German-American response was a decided shift to the Republican party in the elections of 1918 and 1920, but far more significant was the rapid dismantling of the associational structure of German America. The total number of German-language publications declined from 554 in 1910 to 234 in 1920; daily newspaper circulation in 1920 was only about a quarter of its 1910 level. Language shift accelerated rapidly in the churches as elsewhere; in 1917 only one-sixth of the Missouri Synod Lutheran churches held at least one English service a month, while at the end of the war, three-quarters were doing so. The National German-American Alliance dissolved in April 1918 under Senate investigation.

Large-scale collections for relief of suffering in Germany gave purpose to a postwar revival of club life, but Prohibition compounded the destructive effects of persecution, and the associations never returned to prewar levels. The Steuben Society, founded in 1919 as an English-speaking organization of individual members (not a federation) and devoted to the public defense of German Americans rather than to cultural maintenance, never attracted more than 20,000 members, and Viereck's 1918 federation, the German-American Citizens League, remained even smaller. For most German Americans, ethnic culture had been a means to social, religious, or economic ends and was not valued for its own sake. When it jeopardized their status as Americans, their otherwise rapid assimilation permitted most to abandon its formal trappings with minimal difficulty. Even the revenge Republican vote faded by 1922, as German Americans largely reverted to prewar issues and allegiances, with the only reminder of past scars a tendency in some areas toward isolationist conservatism.

Consequently, Nazi party efforts to attract support among German Americans met with little success. Recruiting began as early as 1924, but the first large-scale organization was the Friends of New Germany, organized in July 1933 after orders from Berlin dissolved the existing Nazi cells. That organization collapsed in late 1935 when its activities brought it to the attention of the House Committee on Immigration and Naturalization and was succeeded by the German-American People's League, or German-American Bund, organized in March 1936 by Fritz Julius Kuhn (1896–1951), a German-born chemical engineer and former head of the Detroit local of the Friends. The Bund's organizational structure, pageantry, and propaganda line mimicked those of the party in Germany; although a frequent embarrassment to Nazi foreign-policy makers, it received support through several official and unofficial German agencies. Membership reached at the very most 25,000. The Bund's strength was concentrated in the industrial cities of the Northeast, especially New York, where postwar immigrants tended to congregate. Only about 10 percent of the members were second generation or pre-1900 immigrants; most were German nationals and recently naturalized southern Germans who had arrived in the 1920s as unmarried skilled workers and who were unemployed in the Depression. Their spectacular rallies, like those in Madison Square Garden in 1936 and 1939, and their blatantly racist program provoked public attention and investigation by the House Un-American Activities Committee, chaired by Martin Dies, in 1938. Following Kuhn's conviction and imprisonment for embezzling Bund funds in 1939, the organization fell apart under the pressure of adverse publicity and internal dissension; it formally disbanded when the United States entered the war.

The leadership of organized German America was slow to condemn either the Bund or Nazi Germany until 1938. Apolitical efforts at cultural maintenance of the sort represented by the Carl Schurz Foundation, organized in 1930, and the Congress of Americans of German Descent, meeting from 1932 to 1934, received greater attention but were unable to reverse the erosion of German ethnic identity. The arrival of some 130,000 German and Austrian refugees between 1933 and 1945 had little effect. Overwhelmingly Jewish, they formed their own organizations and were unusually assimilation-minded. World War II neither reawakened German-American ethnicity nor provoked a repetition of World War I repression; German America was fast fading, and even the arrival of a new wave of displaced persons and other immigrants after the war offered only temporary reinforcement of ethnic services and clubs in a few large cities.

In the 1970s only the Steuben Society (with members concentrated in the New York area) and the Chicago-based German-American National Congress (DANK; founded in 1958 and claiming a membership of about 20,000) were still devoted to improving the German image in the United States. Chicago's Germans still celebrate German Day and honor the Revolutionary general von Steuben with a parade down State Street; there are perhaps 100 social clubs, as compared with 452 in 1935. The city's more than 200 singing societies of 1900 dwindled to 95 by 1935 and only 10 by 1974. The number of German daily and weekly publications has steadily dropped from 201 in 1920 to 128 in 1930, 81 in 1940, 42 in 1950, 33 in 1960, and only 24 in 1976. By the last third of the 20th century, the end of immigration, the shock of the two world wars, and high loss of ethnic self-identification, encouraged by diverse occupational paths, movement away from German neighborhoods, and frequent intermarriage, made the United States' largest immigrant group one of its least distinctive.

GERMAN CULTURAL EXPRESSIONS

Germans brought to the United States all the cultural variety of the homeland. Diverse folk customs mingled in rural settlements, and it was rarely possible to transfer the full pattern of folk life intact. Heavily German areas in Texas, Missouri, Minnesota, and Wisconsin could generate an indigenous German-influenced folk culture, but even that was vulnerable to improved roads and the automobile.

In these communities some customs, such as the wedding dance and the feast at the home of the deceased after the funeral, marked family milestones.

Others, like the festivals celebrating the anniversary of the church dedication (Kirchweih) or the patron saint (Kirmes), affirmed communal values. The feast of Corpus Christi in Catholic communities often brought an outdoor procession to flower-decked altars, and Epiphany meant house-to-house visits, with singing and begging for treats, by young men wearing paper crowns. In Stearns County, Minn., a chapel erected in thanksgiving for deliverance from a grasshopper plague became the focus for pilgrimages of a kind familiar from Germany. Harvest processions, Kinderfeste (children's feasts, celebrated with parades and picnics), Schützenfeste (shooting matches), and Sängerfeste (singing festivals) were common wherever Germans gathered, and even the Fourth of July was celebrated with German heartiness. Universal, and copied by other Americans, was the German Christmas, with its family focus, its gift-giving and decorated tree, as well as the child-oriented Easter with its colored eggs and Easter rabbit. December 6 meant the visit of St. Nicholas and Knecht Ruprecht; New Year's was welcomed by groups of young men riding through the neighborhood saluting their neighbors with shotgun bursts. "Second Christmas" and "Second Easter" were times for public festivities after the family closeness of the first day of the holiday. The southern German pre-Lenten Karneval or Fasching, with parades and masked balls, found its way into urban German settlements as early as the 1850s.

In some areas it was the custom for a beribboned young rider to deliver wedding invitations in verse, and the wedding itself was often followed by a raucous charivari. Plentiful food, drink, and music were central to any celebration. Card-playing—skat, schafskopf, pinochle—was ubiquitous, and card parties frequently raised money even for religious organizations. When Prohibition aimed a deathblow at a lifestyle centered on the tavern and its meeting room, home brew permitted familiar habits to endure in less public form until repeal and engendered its own traditions.

The folk customs of 19th-century German immigrants also found expression in structures and household crafts. Initially, rural immigrants built with whatever came to hand—log cabins, lean-tos, dugouts—but for permanent shelter, they frequently adapted Old World construction methods and materials, though styles and room arrangements were similar to those of their American neighbors. Some customary elements, like the attached barn and the indoor smokehouse-kitchen, were abandoned quickly, but predilections for solid stone or brick construction and for half-timber framing survived considerably longer. When the immigrant was his own builder and there were few American neighbors to copy, he reproduced a range of German regional and historical styles, heterogeneity of background thereby ensuring considerable architectural variety within a small area. In Missouri and western Illinois, the "German cottage," built up to the street line and with a garden in back, remained a familiar house type. Distinctive brickwork traditions emerged in cities with German architects and craftsmen; the post–Civil War years also saw a rather self-conscious revival of medieval styles among the middle class, echoing the ethnic assertiveness of the period. Churches tended to preserve the old-country imagery most distinctly. By the late 19th century, however, the

later German immigrants were unable to maintain their folk building and crafts traditions when more general conventions and standardized products began to penetrate solidly German areas.

Heterogeneity of background also affected the language spoken by the immigrants and their children. Rural areas of dense German settlement—in Texas, Missouri, Minnesota, and Wisconsin—harbored fifth- or even sixth-generation German-speakers, but knowledge of the language rapidly disappeared among 20th-century generations. Spoken Geman tended to be a variant of high German; few settlements were sufficiently homogeneous to maintain German regional dialects, and churches, schools, and newspapers all reinforced the standard form, although with some specifically American usages.

German high culture was even more evanescent than folk culture. The institutions of German America were less and less able to compete with the maturing mass culture and the ever more sophisticated high culture of English-speaking America. Secular German-American culture suffered particularly from the inability to support institutions of higher learning. The literature, drama, music, and art that enriched the lives of urban German Americans often appeared derivative and sterile to European contemporaries, reflecting the culture at the time of emigration but unable to evolve under its own momentum.

German Americans produced a large body of literature written in their own language, but little was of exceptional quality. The strong colonial tradition of pious writing and hymns, supplemented by travel literature and political tracts, continued into the early 19th century. The 1830 and 1848 immigrations brought both the interest and the creativity to support literary periodicals and a German-language book publishing industry, which peaked at the end of the century; it specialized in reprinting classics but also printed immigrant works. Imaginative and lyrical literature flowered, but almost 90 percent of it was written by persons born and educated in Germany, and much of it either interpreted the immigrants' experience or evoked nostalgia for the homeland.

Several immigrant authors (most of whom ultimately returned to Europe) of romantic adventure novels set in the United States enjoyed great vogue among German readers on both sides of the Atlantic, including Friedrich Gerstäcker (1816–1872), Heinrich Balduin Möllhausen (1825–1905), Otto Ruppius (1819–1864), Emil Kaulprecht (1815–1896), and Reinhold Solger (1817–1866); the best known, Charles Sealsfield (Karl Anton Postl, 1793–1864), a runaway Bohemian monk who arrived in New Orleans in 1823, had some influence on English-language letters. Emigration stimulated poetic outpourings; lyric, epic, and some social-protest poetry flowed through the pages of German journals, the best of it by Konrad Krez (1828–1897), Niklas Müller (1809–1875), Robert Reitzel (1849–1898), and the prolific and sentimental H.A. Rattermann (1832–1923) in the 19th century, and later poets Konrad Nies (1861–1921), George Sylvester Viereck, and particularly Kurt Baum (1876–1962). Political controversies gave rise to essays and polemics, and immigrants wrote histories, memoirs, translations of some English-language works, and even an 11-volume encyclopedia: Alexander J. Schem, *Deutsch-Amerikanisches Conversations-Lexikon*,

1869–1874. In the last decades of the 19th century, religious publishing houses in midwestern cities—Concordia, Eden, and Herder in Saint Louis, and Wartburg in Dubuque, Iowa—published children's books, inspirational literature, apologetics, catechisms, and almanacs for church-oriented readers. German-American dime novels also appeared in profusion.

German-born American artists like the historical romantic painter Emanuel Leutze (1816–1868), the landscape artist Albert Bierstadt (1830–1902), and Leutze's pupil, Karl Ferdinand Wimar (1828–1862), noted for his studies of American Indians, brought to the United States the influence of the Düsseldorf romantic school. The introduction of high-quality lithography by Louis Prang (1824–1909) and Julius Bien (1826–1909) was probably a more important contribution to American artistic awareness; in 1907, 90 percent of the 240 lithography firms in the United States were owned by persons of German descent, and 70 percent of the employees were German-born.

In drama and music, German-American creativity was far inferior to performance and patronage. Love of drama stimulated immigrant playwrights, whose works were performed in German communities in the hope of swelling local ticket sales. But few such plays survived many performances or displaced the imported classical dramas, comedies, and operettas that were the staple of the German-American stage. But through their patronage the immigrants helped introduce new dramas and high performance standards, and despite the language barrier, influenced other Americans. Most directors and performers of chamber, orchestral, and choral music in mid-19th-century America were German, and they founded and staffed most of the leading conservatories of music. In 1842, 22 of the 52 performers of the New York Philharmonic Society were German; they were 70 of 81 by 1865 and 89 of 94 by 1890. German-born conductors like Theodore Thomas (1835–1905) in New York and Chicago, Carl Zerrahn (1826–1909) and Wilhelm Gericke (1845–1925) in Boston, and Anton Seidl (1850–1898) and Leopold Damrosch (1832–1885) in New York set the major American symphony orchestras on a solid artistic footing and spread appreciation for the classical music tradition far beyond the German community.

Support for German high culture began to decline in most German-American communities after the turn of the century. The arrival of the refugees in the 1930s created a new and more productive cultural ferment, but as an exile culture with a strongly Jewish character, it drew less on American experience than had the earlier German-American culture.

American culture in the century after 1880 moved in fits and starts toward the values cherished by German Americans. A love of music and drama and liberal attitudes about card playing, drinking, and Sunday relaxation ceased to be regarded as foreign imports. Much of the logic of German-American chauvinism was already eroding when the wars in Europe placed the homeland in an unfavorable light. Recent arrivals still support German clubs and services, but even the conservative descendants of church-oriented forefathers have channeled their dissent from contemporary American values into religious rather than ethnic forms. More than 30 years after the end of World War II, an occasional *Maifest* revival or lecture series on German-American culture signifies that the offspring of immigrants have joined to some extent in the national search for an ethnic heritage, but there is little to suggest the renewal of a viable German-American culture.

Bibliography

Works on 19th- and 20th-century German Americans include relatively few attempts at scholarly synthesis. The fullest and best recent general history is LaVern J. Rippley, *The German-Americans* (Boston, 1976). Albert B. Faust, *The German Element in the United States*, 2 vols. (1909; reprint, New York, 1969), remains an indispensable compendium; Richard O'Connor, *The German-Americans* (New York, 1968), is a lively popular history. John A. Hawgood, *The Tragedy of German-America* (1940; reprint, New York, 1970), offers a dated interpretation that should be supplemented by Guido A. Dobbert, "German-Americans between New and Old Fatherland, 1870–1914," *American Quarterly* 19 (1967): 663–680, and Frederick C. Luebke, *Bonds of Loyalty: German-Americans and World War I* (De Kalb, Ill., 1974).

The best summary of German emigration is Wolfgang Köllmann and Peter Marschalck, "German Emigration to the United States," *Perspectives in American History* 7 (1973): 499–557; see also Mack Walker, *Germany and the Emigration, 1816–1885* (Cambridge, Mass., 1964). For the distribution of Germans in the United States, consult Heinz Kloss, *Atlas of 19th and Early 20th Century German-American Settlements* (Marburg, W. Germany, 1974). The best state histories are Dieter Cunz, *The Maryland Germans* (Princeton, N.J., 1948) and Klaus Wust, *The Virginia Germans* (Charlottesville, Va., 1969). Terry G. Jordan, *German Seed in Texas Soil* (Austin, Tex., 1966), and Russell L. Gerlach, *Immigrants in the Ozarks* (Columbia, Mo., 1976), are excellent analyses of rural German settlements. For urban communities, see Kathleen Neils Conzen, *Immigrant Milwaukee, 1836–1860* (Cambridge, Mass., 1976); Robert Ernst, *Immigrant Life in New York City, 1825–1863* (New York, 1965); and Dean R. Esslinger, *Immigrants and the City* (Port Washington, N.Y., 1975).

Carl Wittke, *Refugees of Revolution: The German Forty-eighters in America* (Philadelphia, 1952) is an overview of the liberal immigration. Emmet H. Rothan, *The German Catholic Immigrant in the United States (1830–1860)* (Washington, D.C., 1946); Colman J. Barry, *The Catholic Church and German Americans* (Milwaukee, 1953); and Philip Gleason, *The Conservative Reformers: German-American Catholics and the Social Order* (Notre Dame, Ind., 1968), discuss the Catholic immigration. Protestant denominational studies include Carl E. Schneider, *The German Church on the American Frontier* (St. Louis, 1939); Walter O. Forster, *Zion on the Mississippi: The Settlement of the Saxon Lutherans in Missouri, 1839–1841* (St. Louis, 1953); and Paul F. Douglas, *The Story of German Methodism* (New York, 1939).

For the German-American press, see Carl Wittke, *The German Language Press in America* (Lexington, Ky., 1957), and Karl J.R. Arndt and May E. Olson, eds., *German-American Newspapers and Periodicals 1732–1955: History and Bibliography* (Heidelberg, W. Germany, 1961). Sander A. Diamond, *The Nazi Movement in the United States, 1924–1941* (Ithaca, N.Y., 1974), is the best account of that episode.

Except for Charles Van Ravenswaay's magnificent *The Arts and Architecture of German Settlements in Missouri* (Columbia, Mo., 1977), German folk culture has received little attention. For attempts to transplant German literary culture and language, see the essays in Gerhard K. Friesen and Walter Schatzberg, eds., *The German Contribution to the Building of the Americas* (Hanover, N.H., 1977); Don Heinrich Tolzmann, ed., *German-American Literature* (Metuchen, N.J., 1977); and Glenn C. Gilbert, ed., *The German Language in America* (Austin, Tex., 1971). Finally, Don Heinrich Tolzmann, *German-Americana* (Metuchen, N.J., 1975), offers a comprehensive recent bibliography of most aspects of German-American history and life, as well as a listing of archives containing material on German Americans.

There is no single central archive for research in German-American history. Much material can be found in state and local historical societies in areas of German settlement; examples of other important collections include Philadelphia's German Society of Pennsylvania and the Balch Institute, the Catholic Central-Verein of America and the Concordia Historical Institute in Saint Louis, and the Max Kade German-American Research and Document Center at the University of Kansas.

KATHLEEN NEILS CONZEN

GERMANS FROM RUSSIA

The Germans from Russia and their descendants in the United States, now estimated to number over one million, have had a long history of experience as immigrants. The group had been in Russia for a century

before the first immigrants began to come to the United States in the second half of the 19th century. In Russia they had lived in separate German communities, and in the United States at first they remained aloof from the larger society, relying on themselves and restricting their contacts with people outside their group, even with other German-speaking immigrants. It was not until the 1920s that they began to mix easily with other peoples.

ORIGINS

For centuries Germans tried to improve their lot by settling in Russia. In the early 16th century there was a colony of Germans in Moscow; two centuries later, under Peter the Great, the Moscow group numbered 20,000, and another 50,000 Germans lived in St. Petersburg. But it was not until the second half of the 18th century that there was a large-scale migration to Russia. It began when the German-born tsarina, Catherine II (1729–1796), sought to strengthen her empire by settling the vast steppe regions of southern Russia and the Ukraine with people willing to exploit its potential agricultural wealth and to defend the area against foreign intrusion. Early in her reign, in 1763, she issued a manifesto inviting foreigners to settle in her country, guaranteeing colonists and their descendants free land, exemption from military service in perpetuity, freedom of religion, local self-government, the use of their own languages, and other incentives. She hoped to attract able-bodied individuals to advance the interests of the Russian state; Swedes, Czechs, Swiss, Dutch, and many Germans responded. Her appeal was particularly inviting to German peasants in the southwest provinces of Hesse, Baden, Württemberg, Alsace, and the Palatinate, who had suffered religious persecution and wartime devastation during the Seven Years' War (1756–1763).

Between 1764 and 1768 approximately 20,000 German Protestants and Catholics established more than 100 colonies on both banks of the Volga River. They were followed by German Mennonites, who were attracted by the military exemptions and religious tolerance, which exceeded anything the Russian government offered its own people. In 1789 the Mennonites established Khortitsa on the Dnieper River in the eastern Ukraine, and in 1802 they initiated the Molochna colony. Other Mennonites later founded villages in both the Black Sea and Volga River regions. A group of Hutterites settled south of the Mennonites on the Molochna River near Melitopol. A century later, over 1.5 million Germans were living in approximately 3,000 colonies in Russia. Those who emigrated to the United States were only a small proportion of the Germans living in Russia, and although some came from the St. Petersburg area, the Crimea, the Caucasus region, and from Volhynia, then part of Poland, they are primarily differentiated as Volga Germans or Black Sea Germans, after their principal areas of settlement.

The German villages in Russia were not interdenominational; religious affiliation was of primary importance. Each village was Mennonite, Catholic, Evangelical Lutheran, or some other Protestant denomination. The majority were Protestant, 14 percent were Roman Catholic, and approximately 4 percent were Mennonite. Not only geographical but also religious distinctions continued to be important in the United States.

Traditionally the Germans in Russia had little to do with their Russian, Ukrainian, and Tatar neighbors. They lived totally apart, and their way of life was not threatened until the great reform period that began when the Russian serfs were freed in 1862. In the following decades, despite the original guarantees, attempts were made to Russify the Germans' schools and to introduce compulsory military service. The loss of their privileges, combined with economic hardships and a growing hunger for land, prompted many German Russians to emigrate again—this time to the United States, Canada, or South America. Their migration to the United States began in the 1870s, reached a peak in 1912, and almost came to an end after the outbreak of World War I. Only a few Germans from Russia entered the United States in the 1920s; a few others came after World War II. There was virtually no return migration to Russia, but a few made their way back to Germany. In 1920 the U.S. Census reported over 303,500 German-speaking Russians, of whom over 116,500 were foreign-born, figures that probably underestimate the total number of Germans from Russia in the United States at that time. Anti-German feeling during World War I led many to change their names and conceal their German origins.

Those Germans who remained in Russia experienced a very great change. As a result of the Bolshevik Revolution of 1917, the new Soviet state abolished all private landholdings, much to the distress of the German farmers. On the other hand, the process of Russification that had begun earlier was held in check, especially for the Volga Germans, who in 1924 were given their own republic, the Volga German Autonomous Soviet Socialist Republic. Other German-inhabited areas also received a measure of cultural autonomy.

All this ended after Hitler's invasion of the Soviet Union in June 1941. By August of that year, a Soviet

South Russia and the Ukraine

Areas inhabited by Germans, 1870

Boundary of the Volga German A.S.S.R., 1924-1941

400   Km.   Miles

government decree had abolished the Volga German A.S.S.R., and Soviet authorities began the forcible deportation of the entire German population of the republic eastward to Soviet Central Asia and Siberia. Deportation of Black Sea and Caucasus Germans followed. Many who were living in areas occupied by the German army fled to Germany, but about 45,000 of them were returned to the Soviet Union by the Allied powers in 1945. Over 1.6 million Germans in Siberia and the Central Asian republics of the Soviet Union were forbidden to leave their new areas of settlement until the late 1950s. Since then more liberal government policies have allowed freedom of movement within the Soviet Union, some cultural autonomy, and even emigration to West Germany. Nonetheless, in the traditional homelands of the Germans from Russia—the lower Volga and Black Sea regions—there are now very few Germans.

ARRIVAL AND SETTLEMENT

There is no precise count of the Germans from Russia who emigrated to the United States. They came from all areas of Russia where Germans had settled, and the majority were Evangelical Lutherans. Of the Volga German immigrants, approximately 65 percent were Evangelicals and 35 percent Roman Catholics; of the Black Sea Germans, approximately 45 percent were Evangelicals, 35 percent Roman Catholics, and 20 percent Mennonites with some Baptists. For the most part the Germans from Russia settled on the midwestern plains of the United States in regions that were geographically similar to the steppes where they had been living.

The first immigrants were 21 Black Sea German families who arrived in New York City in 1849 and moved on to Sandusky, Ohio, and Burlington, Iowa. Among them was Ludwig Bette (Lewis Beaty, 1821–1892), who soon became wealthy and was able to return to Russia in 1872 to visit relatives. His visit coincided with the government decrees that had nullified the privileges the Germans believed had been granted in perpetuity. Bette was expelled for adding to the unrest, and when he returned to the United States, many German families followed him; the large-scale exodus of Germans from Russia was under way.

Traveling overland to Hamburg and other North Sea ports, Germans from Black Sea villages like Johannestal, Rohrbach, and Worms eventually settled on farmland around Yankton, S.Dak. (the so-called Odessa settlement), and Sutton, Nebr. The Mennonites from the Black Sea region, who came in large numbers in the early 1870s (6,000 in 1874 alone), settled in Marion and Harvey counties in central Kansas, where to this day Mennonite influence is strong. Other Black Sea immigrants—Protestant, Catholic, and Mennonite—who followed during the 1880s and 1890s settled primarily in north-central South Dakota and in southern North Dakota.

Volga Germans, especially Catholics, began to come in large numbers after 1875. Attracted by agents of the Kansas Pacific Railroad, they settled in the central Kansas counties of Ellis and Rush, where they founded towns named after places along the Volga River—Munjor, Catherine, Herzog, Pfeifer, Schoenchen, and Liebenthal.

Beginning in the 1880s, distinct communities of Black Sea or Volga Germans were established in Oklahoma, Texas, Washington, Oregon, and the San Joaquin Valley of California, as well as in several of the north-central states and central New York State. The greater Denver area became the center of a belt of Volga German Protestant settlements extending northeastward to Sterling, Colo. In 1920, 45 percent of the Germans from Russia lived in North Dakota, South Dakota, Nebraska, and Colorado. Significant concentrations were in Michigan, Wisconsin, Oklahoma, Washington, and California. Most settled in rural areas, although some lived in cities such as Denver, Chicago, and Portland, Ore.

ECONOMIC LIFE

Most Germans from Russia were farmers or worked in farm-related industries. Many of the early immigrants had been able to sell their holdings in Russia, and with those funds they homesteaded or purchased land on the still sparsely settled Great Plains and in the Midwest. They had had decades of experience farming the steppe regions of southern Russia, and as early as 1874, Mennonites imported to Kansas the hard Turkey-red winter wheat that helped transform America's ocean of grass into the granary of the world. The Mennonites also developed and used modern agricultural machinery, and in Hesston, Kans., they still own a company that manufactures farm equipment.

Raising wheat was a specialty of the Black Sea Germans. At one time 95 percent of them engaged in wheat farming, and today many of their descendants still do. The Volga Germans, on the other hand, especially those who immigrated in the late 19th century, arrived too late for homesteading or for the land booms of the 1880s. Since they lacked sufficient funds to purchase land, many Volga Germans initially found employment in the cities and in railroad construction. But they had a strong desire to return to the land, and by the early 20th century 50 percent were engaged in farming or in farm-related activities. Many worked in the sugar-beet industry, first as stoop laborers recruited by the large sugar factories, then as owners of the beet-producing farms.

Some communities of Germans from Russia specialized in certain occupations: in New York State they raised onions; in the southwest corner of Michigan, peppermint. In California, they were prominent in horticulture and raising grapes; the Black Sea Germans settled around Lodi, and the Volga Germans in the San Joaquin Valley around Fresno. They became cement workers in Chicago and street-department laborers in Portland, Ore. Some urban communities grew out of winter camp sites connected with the sugar-beet industry, as in Lincoln, Nebr., and Racine and Milwaukee, Wis. Today Germans from Russia have entered the professions, notably law and banking, and enjoy careers in a wide range of civil-service occupations and in education.

The rural-dwelling Germans from Russia maintained with some success the traditional way of life they brought to the United States. The family continued to be the most important social unit, and the group's ideal was early marriage and many children. Families with 8 to 12 children were common; single or divorced men and women were rare. A patriarchial system prevailed, with the father hiring out his sons for wages then helping them establish farms of their own. Daughters

helped with the farm work and received dowries in return; their partners were chosen for them according to exacting traditions. Usually their husbands had to come not only from the group of Germans from Russia but from the same religious and regional subgroup. Decades passed before intergroup marriages were possible, and interfaith marriages within the group of Germans from Russia did not become acceptable until the 1950s. These attitudes resulted from the experience in Russia, where Germans staunchly resisted marriage with the "natives" for fear of losing family and cultural solidarity. Today, however, little effort is consciously made to forestall marriages with individuals of a different ethnic or religious background.

RELIGION

Religion has been a cornerstone of group identity both in Russia and in the United States. In 1920 the leading denominations among the Germans from Russia were Protestant (59 percent), Catholic (19 percent), and Mennonite (10 percent). Both Catholics and Mennonites maintained religious traditions brought from the homeland; the tenets of both faiths forbade amalgamation with other religions. Most communities in the United States were originally made up exclusively of Catholics or Mennonites, as they had been in Russia, and even in the present this pattern prevails.

This pattern was not so prevalent among the Evangelical Lutherans, however. Even before they immigrated to the United States, movements such as the Pietistic Brotherhood had become popular on the Volga, and Baptist missionaries were making headway in the Black Sea region. Upon their arrival in the United States, Protestant Germans from Russia found as many as 21 synods and conferences within the American Lutheran church alone. Because they settled in remote rural areas usually served only by transient pastors, it is not surprising that the Evangelical Germans from Russia joined a variety of existing American Protestant churches. Some affiliated with new denominations, for instance the German Congregational church; others joined the Brotherhood movement or became Baptists. Some small towns had as many as five Protestant churches for the Germans from Russia. By the 1930s some 45 percent of the Protestant group belonged to various synods of the Lutheran Church, 30 percent to the German division of the Congregational Church, 10 percent to the Baptist Church, 10 percent to the Methodist and Adventist faiths, and 5 percent to the German Reformed Church.

Despite these denominational divisions, religion played a positive role in creating group solidarity and maintaining ethnic traditions. No community was complete until it had constructed at least one church; the white wood-frame churches of Colorado, the Dakotas, and Nebraska and the imposing, spired limestone structures in western Kansas still stand as monuments to the architectural tradition of the Germans from Russia. Roman Catholic churches, as in Ellis County, Kans., were complemented by cemeteries with elaborate steel crosses, reflecting their folk art.

The most important events in the lives of the Germans from Russia were associated with religious customs. The confirmation of young people was recorded for posterity in church yearbooks with page after page of photographs of finely dressed boys and girls. Wedding ceremonies were even more elaborate, and here the Old World customs seem to have been preserved the longest. Two examples are the medieval German betrothal tradition of the groom's family calling on the bride's family with ribboned canes and the tradition of pinning money on the bride's dress as one danced with her. In the earlier decades of the 20th century, wedding celebrations usually lasted two or three days, but in modern times they have been shortened considerably. Ethnic music and dances, particularly waltzes and polkas, are still common at weddings and prenuptial showers. Bandleader Lawrence Welk (1903–) began his career playing the accordion at the celebrations of his kinfolk in the German-Russian community of Strasburg, N.Dak.

Germans from Russia had few secular organizations; the church was the predominant social as well as religious center. Moreover, church leaders, whether Protestant pastors and their wives and children or Catholic priests, monks, and nuns, formed the only real intelligentsia. From their ranks the communities drew most of the chroniclers whose articles and books preserved the history of the group. Not infrequently a community would send for a European German to teach their children and especially to edit their newspapers.

SOCIAL ORGANIZATION AND CULTURE

The Germans from Russia failed to develop strong secular organizations, in sharp contrast to German immigrants from the empire and many other groups. The few exceptions included the *Schützengilde* (Rifleman's Guild, 1877–1880), a self-protection society of Volga German settlers in Catherine, Kans., and the mutual fire and hail insurance companies, such as the Northwest German Farmers Mutual Insurance Company of Eureka, S.Dak. (1897). Since 1920 the company's policies have been written in English instead of German, and "German" has now been dropped from its name. In the same spirit of self-help, the American Volga Relief Society was organized to funnel monies and goods to victims of the great 1920–1923 famine in Russia, but even this society had to draw on the churches for support and leadership.

The Volga Germans who came to the United States via Germany after World War I began to found clubs similar to mutual-aid societies in 1924–1925 in their settlements in Chicago, Wisconsin, and Michigan. Today, with commercial insurance companies and municipal fire departments, there is little need for these societies, though a few persist in the form of fraternal or mutual insurance companies and as strictly social organizations.

During the final decades of the 19th century, communities of Germans from Russia established their own schools with German as the language of instruction. Young children were taught the German literary language (*Hochdeutsch*), but among friends and family they continued to use one of the regional or village dialects brought from Russia. In the often self-contained rural communities, dialectal characteristics were preserved longer than would have been the case in urban areas. Many of the city-dwelling Germans from Russia were exposed to people from Germany or Austria-Hungary who often disparaged the "ignorant Russians" who

could not speak "high German." Sensitive about their language, some turned inward and became more clannish, excluding not only their non-German-speaking neighbors, but also non-Russian Germans—as, for example, in Oshkosh, Wis., and in Lincoln, Nebr., where the lines between the German-speaking communities were very clearly drawn. Sometimes, however, the Germans from Russia who were made to feel ashamed of their "inferior" German dialect abandoned it and spoke only English.

The greatest decline in language maintenance among the Germans from Russia came as a result of outside pressure. As the frontier areas where they lived became more settled, state and county governments began to provide public schools in which English was used routinely, and teachers who did not know German were often brought in from outside the community. German-language instruction was then in the haphazard care of the churches. The Mennonites and Catholics maintained German-language schools for many decades, but most Evangelical church schools were soon converted to Sunday schools giving German-language catechism instruction. During the week the children attended English-language public schools. During the general anti-German hysteria of the World War I period, many states passed laws banning German-language instruction in the schools. These actions dealt a death blow to the efforts of the Germans from Russia to maintain the language among their youth. German continued to be used in Sunday schools until the 1940s, and on an alternating schedule with English, in church services until the 1960s; since then German has been used only for occasional special feasts. In the 1920s parents commonly spoke German to their children, who tended to respond in English. Adults who were children in the 1930s, however, still are able to carry on a simple conversation in German.

The Germans from Russia established their own press, which contributed both to language maintenance and to cohesiveness among members of the community. The oldest and most influential newspaper was the weekly *Dakota Freie Presse* (Yankton and Aberdeen, S.Dak., New Ulm and Winona, Minn., 1874–1954), which, though it was not always owned by Germans from Russia, was devoted exclusively to the group. Through its correspondence columns, it provided information about family members and relatives living as far apart as Russia, the United States, Canada, and Argentina. From time to time it also published local historical essays by readers in various communities. At its height, roughly from 1900 to 1930, the paper was owned and managed by F.W. Sallet (1859–1932), an immigrant from East Prussia; in this period it was sent to 1,150 post offices in 32 states as well as abroad.

Like the *Dakota Freie Presse,* other newspapers often were begun to serve a particular segment of the group, whether Black Sea or Volga Germans, Catholics, Evangelical Lutherans, or Mennonites; in time, however, each paper expanded its readership to include the whole group. Among the newspapers were the *Staats-Anzeiger* (Rugby and Bismarck, N.Dak., Omaha, Nebr., 1906–1954), which served Black Sea Germans initially; the *Welt-Post* (Lincoln and Omaha, Nebr., 1913–1954), which was the primary organ of the Evangelical Volga Germans; the *California Vorwärts* (Fresno, 1921–

1942), published for the Volga Germans and popular for its reporting of Bolshevik crimes in the homeland; and the *Ashley Tribune* (Ashley, N.Dak., 1900–1955) a local paper that switched to publishing half in German, half in English after World War I and changed to English altogether in the 1950s.

POLITICS AND INTERGROUP RELATIONS

Germans from Russia assumed an active political role once they became fluent in the English language and were elected to town, county, and state offices, especially in Kansas and in North and South Dakota. By 1885 South Dakota had a state senator who was a Black Sea German. By 1912 Germans from Russia in South Dakota were running for a variety of state offices, and in 1919 they held several state offices in North Dakota. In the nation's capital the Germans from Russia were considered a political force. In April 1917 Senator Asle J. Gronna (1853–1922) of North Dakota and Representative Royal C. Johnson (1882–1939) from South Dakota were among the few who voted against the declaration of war with Germany.

As conservative, rural folk, Germans from Russia and their descendants have retained a tendency to vote Republican. However, it is the Evangelical Germans who make up the Republican majority; the Catholics as a rule have identified as Democrats, along with the Irish and other German Catholics. A clear exception occurred in the presidential election of 1924 when the Germans from Russia warmly supported the Progressive candidate, Robert M. La Follette, the senator from Wisconsin who had fought for fair treatment of German Americans during World War I.

In their former Russian homeland, the Germans had not concerned themselves with politics, perhaps because they felt that their true homeland was Germany. Thus during the first three years of World War I, the Germans from Russia in the United States collected funds for German war widows and orphans and purchased German war bonds. In 1920 and 1921, a group of Black Sea Germans organized a Central Relief Committee, which sent money, clothing, and food to Berlin; the *Dakota Freie Presse* funded a program to send undernourished children from East Prussia to Baltic Sea resorts to regain their health; and Black Sea Germans from Kansas and the Dakotas sent three shiploads of cows to replace those taken from Germany by provisions of the Versailles treaty.

It was only later, between 1921 and 1924, that a Black Sea Marion Relief Committee and an American Volga Relief Society were founded to help German victims of famine in Russia. In general, however, the Germans from Russia did not concern themselves with affairs in their former homeland. All were opposed to the abolition of private landholdings under the new Soviet regime, and while some immigrants looked with favor on the autonomous Volga German A.S.S.R., their hopes were shattered after its destruction in 1941 and the wholesale deportation of Germans to Siberia and Soviet Central Asia.

The relationship of Germans from Russia with other Germans in the United States is an ambiguous one. Though the Germans from Russia feel their cultural roots to be German and have interacted with other Ger-

man immigrants, especially in the Protestant churches and the press, they nonetheless continue to feel distinct from other German Americans. Their Russian experience, their dialectal speech patterns, and the independent and frugal spirit developed on the Russian steppes and the American prairie, combined with their resentment of the condescension shown them by many German Americans, have preserved their feeling of separate identity.

ETHNIC COMMITMENT

Lacking German-language churches, schools, and a large-circulation press, all of which had served their needs before World War II, the group has continued to maintain itself primarily through the family and informal structures. More recently, as part of the general ethnic revival in the United States, historical organizations have been founded to preserve and propagate the Old World heritage and its manifestations in the United States. The most important of these is the American Historical Society of Germans from Russia (1968) founded at Greeley, Colo., but with headquarters in Lincoln, Nebr.; it has 32 chapters and members in many states. Not as large but equally significant is the Heritage Society of Germans from Russia (1971), with its headquarters in Bismarck, it has chapters in many counties of the state and members across the country. Both groups hold annual conventions, publish books and articles, and collect manuscripts, photographs, and keepsakes from older immigrants. The AHSGR maintains archives in Greeley and a museum in Lincoln. The GRHS has a museum in Rugby, N.Dak.; both museums display clothing, furniture, farm tools, kitchen equipment, books, passports, and the like. Both societies publish English-language periodicals, the *Journal* (formerly *Workpaper*) of the AHSGR (Lincoln, f. 1969) and the *Heritage Review* (Bismarck, f. 1971); and also newsletters. In their modest way, the newsletters replace the older German-language press in keeping readers informed and conscious of their heritage. In a few states this heritage has benefited from systematic analysis in an academic setting, such as the Germans from Russia in Colorado Study Project established at Colorado State University in Fort Collins in 1976 and the courses on the Germans from Russia offered at North Dakota State University at Fargo.

Bibliography

Basic orientation is provided by Richard Sallet, *Russian-German Settlements in the United States* (Fargo, N.Dak., 1974), and Henry C. Smith, *The Coming of the Russian Mennonites* (Berne, Ind., 1927). A pioneering work written in the early 20th century is Hattie Plum Williams, *The Czar's Germans*, Emma S. Haynes, Phillip B. Leger, and Gerda S. Walker eds. (Lincoln, Nebr., 1975); it focuses on the Volga Germans. George Rath, *The Black Sea Germans in the Dakotas* (Freeman, S.Dak., 1977), covers the subject but is marred by minor errors. The volume of essays edited by Sidney Heitman, *Germans From Russia in Colorado* (Ann Arbor, Mich., 1978), in the Western Social Science Association Series, touches upon the groups in the Soviet Union and South America as well as in Colorado.

The most comprehensive description of the group in Russia is Adam Giesinger, *From Catherine to Khrushchev* (Battleford, Saskatchewan, 1974). Fred Koch, *The Volga Germans* (University Park, Pa., 1977), deals exclusively with that subgroup, while Joseph S. Height, *Paradise on the Steppe* (Bismarck, N.Dak., 1972) and *Homesteaders on the Steppe* (Bismarck, 1975), treat the Black Sea Germans. Karl Stumpp, *The German Russians: Two Centuries of Pioneering* (Bonn, West Germany, 1967), and *The Emigration from Germany to Russia in the Years 1763 to 1862*

(Tübingen, West Germany, 1973) are excellent. His maps are indispensable for serious scholars.

The archives of the American Historical Society of the Germans from Russia are in the Greeley, Colo., public library and contain over 1,000 books and articles on German groups from Russia: Mennonites, Black Sea Germans, Volhynian, and Volga Germans. They also retain on microfilm many of the newspapers published in the United States and some published in Odessa and Saratov, Russia, before World War I. Other collections are in the Mennonite archives and libraries in North Newton, Kans.; Goshen, Ind.; and Freeman, S.Dak.

LA VERN J. RIPPLEY

GOSIUTES: *see* AMERICAN INDIANS

GREEK CATHOLICS: *see* EASTERN CATHOLICS

GREEK ORTHODOX: *see* EASTERN ORTHODOX

GREEKS

Greeks have been coming to the New World since colonial times—as sailors, explorers, students, cotton merchants, gold miners, and occasionally as settlers—but they did not arrive in numbers sufficient to establish permanent communities until the 1890s.

More Greeks lived outside Greece than in it during the peak years of emigration—mainly in territories that remained part of the Ottoman Empire when Greece won its independence in the 19th century, in the surrounding Balkan countries, or in Egypt—but the majority of the immigrants to the United States nonetheless came from Greece itself. Most of them came either between the early 1890s and the passage of the national-quota act of 1921 and the further immigration restrictions in 1924, or in the 1960s and 1970s after restrictions had been modified by the Immigration and Nationality Act of 1965. Although the numbers arriving in the most recent period were greater than they had been at any time since the early 1920s, they never equaled the numbers that came in the first two decades of the century.

The 1970 U.S. Census placed the Greek-American population at about 435,000, a number contested by Greek Americans primarily on the grounds that it includes only the first two generations, fails to include those born in countries such as Turkey, Romania, and Egypt who consider themselves to be Greeks, and excludes illegal immigrants. Greek Americans prefer to give the number for all generations, which some scholars place at between 1.3 million and 1.5 million; others, particularly political and church leaders, at closer to 3 million—a number that population experts regard with considerable skepticism. In 1976 the U.S. Immigration and Naturalization Service listed the total number of Greeks who had emigrated to the United States since 1820 at about 640,000, but many Greek Americans believe that this official immigration figure, too, underrepresents them (see Table 1).

Accurate statistics are admittedly difficult to obtain. In determining nationality the United States uses country of birth, rather than the "blood concept" of European countries, and many arriving Greeks were, of course, born outside of Greece. But some idea of their numbers can be gained by studying the U.S. statistics for immigration from Asian Turkey, the area from which most expatriated Greeks originated. Of the approximately 382,000 people admitted from Asian Tur-

Greece

Boundaries of Greece and the
Ottoman Empire, 1881-1912

Boundaries of Greece, 1913-1919

100   Km.   Miles

key between 1820 and 1975, more than 291,000, or
roughly three-fourths, arrived between 1901 and 1920,
when Greeks, Armenians, and Assyrians were fleeing
the persecutions of the Turkish government. It is likely,
therefore, that many of these "Turkish" immigrants
were in fact Greek. But it cannot be proved, though it is
often claimed, that the number of Greeks who came
from Turkey and elsewhere was higher than the number who came from Greece itself. The increase in immigration from Turkey during the 1960s and 1970s may
well be attributable also to anti-Greek activities in Tur-

key, especially the riots in Istanbul in 1955 and their aftermath, and the growing tensions between Greece and
Turkey over Cyprus.

Economic need, however, not political persecution,
has been the main stimulus behind the departure of
most Greeks. The population of Greece began to grow
rapidly in the late 19th century. By 1931 the country
had 870 inhabitants per square mile of cultivated land
(compared with 470 in Yugoslavia, 380 in Hungary, 365
in Bulgaria, and 380 in Romania); by 1940 the total population was 7.3 million, and in spite of the death and

Table 1. Immigrants to the United States from Greece and Asian Turkey, 1871–1975.

Period	Turkey	Greece
1871–1880	404	210
1881–1890	3,782	2,308
1891–1900	30,425	15,979
1901–1910	157,369	167,519
1911–1920	134,066	184,201
1921–1930	33,824	51,201
1931–1940	1,065	9,119
1941–1950	798	8,973
1951–1960	3,519	47,608
1961–1970	10,142	85,969
1971–1975	6,629	56,191

Source: U.S. Immigration and Naturalization Service, *Annual Report, 1975* (Washington, D.C., 1976), pp. 86–88.

destruction of the war years, it rose to 7.6 million by 1951. In subsequent years births continued to exceed deaths—for the period 1949–1971 by as much as 2 to 1. From the end of the 19th century to today Greece has been unable to provide sufficient food or jobs for all its people, forcing many of its inhabitants to move elsewhere.

Men sometimes left to avoid compulsory military service as well; women, especially those who were poor and those who came after World War I, hoped to find husbands in a country where Greek women were in short supply and dowries not required. Greeks born in other countries often emigrated because, in addition to internal pressures, the international situation made it possible that they would be impressed into a foreign army and might have to fight other Greeks.

Although the reasons for emigration throughout the years remained constant, the districts from which the immigrants came, their occupations, and the general character of the migration differed between the two groups. From 1900 through the 1920s the majority were unskilled males from villages mainly in the Peloponnesus but also elsewhere in Greece. The Greeks who came from Turkey in the same period tended to be more urbane and better educated. Frequently they were businessmen (and thus not trusted by the homeland Greek emigrants). The post–World War II emigrants included a larger number of women; they also included a great many well-educated, professionally and technically trained people from Greece itself, especially from Athens and central Greece. Peloponnesians and other villagers continued to emigrate to the United States, but in smaller numbers than in the earlier years. Emigrants before World War I expected to return to Greece with money saved in the United States, and eventually almost half did so; few emigrants left Greece after World War II with clear intentions of returning. Most came with their families, and were less inclined to think in terms of repatriation.

Emigration first picked up momentum after the United States began to work its way out of the mid-1890s depression; it was abetted by recurrent crop failures in Greece and reports of job opportunities in America. The Spartans came first, then the Arcadians, who eventually outnumbered them, then Greeks from central Greece, Crete, the Aegean and Ionian islands, the Dodecanese islands, Asian and European Turkey, Cyprus, the Balkan countries, and Egypt. By 1910 an es-

timated one-quarter to one-fifth of the total labor force of Greece had left. Drained of its young men, stripped of its military manpower in a period of growing tensions, the Greek government was alarmed, but did not take action. By the time they realized what was happening they could no longer bar emigration because Greece had become dependent upon the flow of money that Greeks abroad were sending back to their relatives.

To buy their passage the Greek emigrants sold their land or borrowed money, either by mortgaging family property or, if an agent or prospective employer agreed, by using future wages as collateral. A few fortunate ones had the cost of passage supplied by relatives or friends already established in the United States.

Before they left, most of the earliest immigrants had probably never ventured very far beyond their native villages, knew little about the country to which they were heading, and did not speak English. Few had gone beyond grammar school; a *gymnaseion* graduate was rare, rarer still the university graduate; women with any schooling whatever were the exception. Greeks seeking higher education, along with those already well educated or professionally trained, traditionally went to England, France, Germany, or some other European country, but even if they had chosen the United States instead, their futures would have been doubtful. A doctor with a limited command of English might have been able to build a practice among his immigrant compatriots, but a Greek-trained lawyer, for example, would have been totally at a loss.

EARLY SETTLEMENTS AND ECONOMIC LIFE

The Greeks looked upon city life as preferable to life on the soil, for they associated farming with hard times, saw no future on the land, needed the companionship of compatriots, and relied on the steady wages that urban industrial jobs offered. The isolated farm life of the United States was vastly different from village life in Greece, where small nearby plots were tilled by day and the farmer returned to his village home at night. It was no surprise, therefore, that most of the Greeks settled in the cities of the northeastern and north-central states, the one major exception being California (which by 1970 had the third largest Greek-American community, outnumbered only by New York and Illinois). They began by working in the textile mills, tanneries, slaughterhouses, coal mines, steel mills, and on railroad-construction gangs, or often in Greek-owned shoeshine parlors, restaurants, fruit and vegetable stands, confectionaries, and florists. Many islanders settled in Florida where they fished and dove for sponges.

A good many Greeks sought economic independence by establishing a small business. They would begin as pushcart peddlers or sidewalk merchants, or they would go to work for a countryman or relative who had already set himself up in business. The shoeshine parlor provided an ideal opening for someone with entrepreneurial ambitions; the capital outlay required was small and the necessary skills were minimal. Although as an occupation shoeshining was held in low esteem in the Greek community, it often served as the entering wedge for an enterprising immigrant who could soon branch off into his own restaurant, candy store, or florist shop. In rare cases, if his English was sufficient, he might go into real estate.

The restaurant business, however, was the favorite route for Greeks. No one knows why so many Greeks became prominent as restaurant owners and cooks, activities for which they brought no special talents from the homeland. Some probably began by preparing Greek food for themselves because they found the American cuisine unappetizing, and then found themselves serving homesick compatriots as well. Since many restaurants were—and still are—family enterprises, they could afford to stay open long hours. The Greeks did not necessarily excel in cooking, but the quality of their food was adequate, their prices low, and the bill of fare imaginative. Most made out well, although some were driven out of the restaurant business in the wave of xenophobia that swept the country during and after World War I. When failure occurred, it was often the result of poor management by owners who were incapable of distinguishing between operating expenses and profits. Dishonesty at the cash register, poor service, incompetent management, the acceptance of underweight merchandise, and the raiding of supplies by employees also took their toll.

Candy-store owners who catered to the general public instead of to their fellow immigrants tended to be more successful. The more venturesome set up shop in downtown areas where the flow of pedestrian traffic was heavy. Chicago was an early major center of the trade; many small-town confectioners served their apprenticeships and acquired capital and supplies there. During the Great Depression, however, heavy debts incurred from the purchase of equipment and supplies and competition from drugstore soda-fountains drove many corner candy stores out of business.

CHURCH ESTABLISHMENT

When the Greeks first arrived in this country, before they were able to organize their own churches it was common for them to attend Eastern-rite services at whatever Eastern Orthodox churches were already established in the cities in which they found themselves. (See Eastern Orthodox.) But when the numbers of Greek immigrants began to increase substantially, so did pressures to build parish churches in which both the priest and the service would be not only Eastern but Greek Orthodox. Since the church authorities in Greece did not send missionary priests to the United States, the concerned laity in each neighborhood had to take the initiative to start a local parish. When they had raised enough money or obtained enough pledges, they would appeal to the ecumenical patriarchate or the Holy Synod of Greece to staff their parish.

The lay tradition was strong among Greek immigrants, and it was consistent with the democratic principles of their new country. Laymen, often directed by prominent businessmen, would work hard to build and finance their churches. Having left their ancestral homes, anxious that they might never see them again, might lose their ethnic identity, and die in a strange land, many immigrants embraced their faith with new tenacity. At the same time, the immigrants were pragmatists and individualists who were not easily intimidated by priests or other church authorities. Their commitment to a strong lay parish government eventually led to conflict with the church hierarchy.

The first Orthodox church organized by Greeks in the United States was an outgrowth of lay activity, though it preceded the mass migrations by some years. It was established by Greek cotton merchants in New Orleans in 1864 as a place of worship for themselves, their employees, and others of Orthodox persuasion in the vicinity. Although establishing a church was a fairly common practice among Greek businessmen overseas, the New Orleans church was an isolated establishment in the United States, and it did not influence the pattern of the immigrant churches founded in the 1890s in New York, Chicago, and Lowell, Mass., and after 1900 in Philadelphia, Birmingham, and Boston.

The formation of parishes followed fairly closely upon the heels of the earliest large immigration. By 1909 services were already being conducted in a number of the smaller towns and cities of New England, such as Lynn, Ipswich, Peabody, Springfield, Haverhill, and Lowell in Massachusetts, and Manchester and Dover in New Hampshire; and in a number of midwestern cities, including Chicago, Milwaukee, Saint Louis, Indianapolis, and Omaha. Elsewhere, priests were officiating in Galveston, Tex., in Pueblo and Denver, Colo., in Salt Lake City, San Francisco, Los Angeles, and Portland, Ore.; in Atlanta and Savannah, Ga., Birmingham, Ala., Tarpon Springs, Fla., Louisville, Ky., and New Orleans.

Because the tempo of life in the United States was faster than in Greece, the customs and language so different, and the temptations, strains, and stresses of everyday living so much greater, both priests and parishioners faced problems that seemed insurmountable. Parishioners who looked to the priests for guidance often found them equally overwhelmed by the new environment.

As the first American-born generation began to make its appearance, so did the Greek-language school. These schools were often an adjunct of the parish church and were a means both of maintaining communication between parent and child and of preserving the Greek heritage in the new land. They emphasized the demotic, that is, the commonly spoken Greek, not the literary or classical language. Classes usually were held in an improvised classroom in a church basement, rented hall, or vacant store after the public-school day had ended.

As a rule the Greek parish priest did the teaching; sometimes he had been the classroom teacher in his native village or town. His educational training was probably limited, however, and his new teaching assignment could be a burdensome chore. Learning was by rote, the disciplinary methods stern, and the climate for learning stultifying. When the Greek neighborhoods began to break up, as the Greeks scattered to other parts of the city, only the persistent exhortation of parish leaders and cultural nationalists sustained the schools, though in later life many of their pupils came to appreciate the morsels of Greek they had acquired in them.

ORGANIZATIONS AND SOCIAL LIFE

The Greeks formed societies for a variety of purposes: to organize churches and schools, provide medical and death benefits for members, collect money for charitable and humanitarian causes in the villages and provinces from which their members had come, preserve and perpetuate Hellenism, and aid the national-defense

effort of Greece. This mania for forming societies, clubs, and associations has sometimes been attributed to the fact that Greece is a land of small valleys and plains shut off by mountains, a terrain likely to breed provincialism and make its inhabitants put greater trust in others from the same village and province than in their compatriots at large. People from one particular village, Arahova in Laconia, eventually formed a national, if not a worldwide, organization to which people from the village and their descendants still belong. The organization remains active and holds an annual reunion for all its members in Gastonia, N.C.

The first mutual-benefit societies were founded on this village level and were usually named after a local revolutionary hero, patron saint, or provincial benefactor. But they often came to an early end because village cohesion also bred village rivalry, unreasonable expectations, arbitrary acts, and general dissatisfaction. Provincial societies—the Pan-Arcadian, the Pan-Messinian, the Pan-Cretan, the Pan-Icarian federations—tended to last longer. Both types of organization were committed to the payment of health and death benefits and collected money for public improvements in the home village or province, such as building or repairing schools, churches, roads, and water-supply systems.

Another kind of organization, confined for the most part to the pre-World War I years when ethnic feelings ran high, was the Panhellenic Union, whose patriotic mission was to keep Greeks aware of their common heritage and of their obligations to the mother country. Branches were formed in all cities with substantial Greek communities. The Panhellenic Union played a conspicuous role in mobilizing the physical resources of the immigrants for the Balkan wars, which ended in victories for Greece. Under its influence an estimated 42,000 men returned to Greece in 1912 and 1913, most of them from the United States, to defend the country against its enemies; many eventually came back to the United States, bringing back Greek wives and families. After World War I, thoughts of repatriation for most had been vanquished by the military disasters that had overtaken Greece and her ambitions in Asia Minor in the early 1920s and the burning of Smyrna (İzmir), a Turkish city with a large Greek population. Rising xenophobia in the United States made ethnic assertiveness seem dangerous. Interest in the Panhellenic Union languished, for the community now needed an organization with functions more consistent with the requirements of a people intending to remain permanently in the United States.

The coffee house was an informal institution with an important role in Greek-American life. An exclusively male gathering place for after-work hours, weekends, and holidays, it was to Greeks what the saloon was to the Germans and the pub to the English. All an enterprising Greek had to do to open a coffee house was to rent a vacant store, assemble the requisite tables, chairs, decks of playing cards, cups, saucers, dishes, sweets, narghiles (water pipes), tobacco, lithographed portraits of political favorites and would-be patrons, and he was ready for business. Coffee-house proprietors often became well known in their communities and were repositories of gossip and information on community affairs. Patrons sipped black coffee, read Greek newspapers, played cards, and assessed the merits and demerits of the parish priest, the Greek schoolteacher,

or anyone else in the community. Political discussions were heated and bewildering to anyone who was not Greek. Despite the notoriety some achieved as gambling dens, the coffee houses served for many immigrants as a place to come for companionship, to while away lonely hours, to obtain job information, and to collect their mail.

The Greek-language press, which featured news especially of political events and personalities from Greece, also carried items about the immigrants' home provinces, towns, and villages. News of more general interest was translated from the American press. If circulation was large enough, the newspapers provided special correspondents and more comprehensive coverage of important events in Greece. Some papers, despite their ethnic emphasis, encouraged their readers to become better acquainted with American customs and institutions and with citizens of the United States. The Greek-language press was often charged with fomenting rivalries and feuds as a means of increasing its circulation.

ETHNIC POLITICS

Ethnic loyalties were always strong among the Greeks. From childhood days they were told how their ancestors had suffered under the Turkish yoke and heard patriotic folksongs, poetry, and stirring tales of how the greatly outnumbered Greeks courageously fought Turks in the hills and mountains of Greece in order to preserve their language and religion. The custom of celebrating March 25, 1821, as Greek Independence Day was soon transplanted to the United States.

The first major wave of emigration had coincided with a period of mounting tensions between Greece and Turkey, resulting from the revival of the imperial dream that envisaged the restoration of the glories of ancient Greece and the establishment of a new Greek Byzantine empire with its capital in Constantinople. This goal appeared within reach after Greece twice emerged victorious from the Balkan wars of 1912–1913 with minimal losses and a territory almost twice its former size, but in the early 1920s the renewed effort to regain formerly Greek territory from Turkey was to result in a national disaster.

After the Balkan victories, rivalry grew up in Greece between King Constantine I (1868–1923) and Eleutherios Venizelos (1864–1936), the energetic head of the Greek Liberal party. The resulting factionalism soon spread to Greek communities in the United States. Following the outbreak of World War I, the Liberals wanted to support Great Britain and France, because Britain had offered to give Cyprus to Greece in return for its joining the Allies. King Constantine, however, had been schooled in the German tradition, was married to the German kaiser's sister, and believed that Greece's interests would be better served if the country remained neutral. Venizelos and his Liberal followers claimed that Constantine was not neutral but sympathetic toward Germany, an accusation that many in the United States found easy to believe.

The *Atlantis* (1894–1973), the major American Greek-language daily, went unchallenged in advocating the royalist position until the appearance in 1915 of the *Ethnikos Kyrix* (National Herald), edited by Demetrios Callimachos (1879–1963). Callimachos, a fervent nationalist and fiery soldier-priest, had served as a chap-

lain in the Balkan wars and as secretary of the archdiocese of the Greek Orthodox Church in Alexandria, Egypt, before coming to the United States in 1914 as an agent of the Panhellenic Union. He was an uncompromising Liberal, as were most of the so-called unredeemed Greeks—that is, Greeks whose origins lay in once-Greek territories that were now outside the borders of the homeland—and he fought the *Atlantis* and its policies relentlessly.

Since the Greek Orthodox Church was the state church of Greece, it was often embroiled in political quarrels. The schism between Constantine and Venizelos soon affected the church both in Greece and abroad—especially churches in the United States, over which the Greek synod then still had jurisdiction. Most priests in the United States were immigrants and violently nationalistic, and the unredeemed-Greek priests more so than the rest. In the absence of a higher ecclesiastical authority in America, the priests were at the mercy of local church boards, who hired and fired them at will. In the end, the controversy probably had a more devastating effect on the Greek-Orthodox church in the United States than it had in Greece, although this did not become immediately apparent.

CHURCH GOVERNANCE

A major problem facing the church in the early part of the 20th century was the absence of an effective, central, coordinating agency to guide it. Authority over the Orthodox churches in the New World had originally been vested in the ecumenical patriarchate in Constantinople (İstanbul). But because the Russian Orthodox Church had a head start in establishing its version of Orthodoxy in the New World and had been aggressive in establishing new churches, pressure was exerted on the patriarchate in Constantinople to transfer jurisdiction over all Eastern Orthodox churches in the Americas to the Russian patriarch in Moscow—much to the distress of ethnocentric Greeks. In fact, so many immigrants of the Eastern Orthodox faith who had come to the United States were Greeks that allegiance to a non-Greek ecclesiastical authority had become unacceptable. The patriarchate therefore transferred authority over Greek-American churches from Constantinople to the Holy Synod of the Church of Greece, an arrangement that lasted from 1908 to 1922.

The Greek churches in the Americas were also in need of central direction, but differences between church and lay authorities delayed the establishment of a central administration. Finally, in 1918, the metropolitan of Athens, Meletios Metaxakis (d. 1935) named a trusted assistant, Bishop Alexander of Rodostolou, to the American bishopric. Alexander from the first faced insurmountable difficulties. The church's involvement in the Liberal-royalist controversy in Greece got his administration off to a turbulent start. Metropolitan Metaxakis had been appointed head of the Greek synod by Prime Minister Venizelos, who took office in 1917 when King Constantine was forced to abdicate in favor of one of his sons. In 1920, however, Venizelos fell from power and Constantine regained the throne. Metaxakis was dismissed as metropolitan and Bishop Alexander was summoned to Athens.

Alexander refused the summons, however, and sought support among priests in American parishes to negotiate with the Ecumenical Patriarchate in Constantinople rather than with the Holy Synod in Greece. He was joined in America by the deposed Metaxakis, and the two men continued to exercise jurisdiction over the parishes that supported their leadership. The situation became more complicated when a representative of the Holy Synod in Greece, Bishop Germanos Troianos of Sparta, also came to the United States to exert authority over the churches. Germanos proceeded to fire and hire priests as he pleased, staffing the churches whenever possible with priests who favored the new national and ecclesiastical regimes in Athens.

The Greek-American churches were soon in chaos. Dissenters who objected to the politics of those in control of their parishes seceded and formed rival parishes in communities that could not afford them. Litigation over church properties became common and disrupted social, business, family, and community relations. The presence in the United States of a deposed metropolitan of Athens cooperating with an American bishop who had defied the instructions of his superiors, both locked in battle with the exarch of the Church of Greece, was an exhibition of ecclesiastical politics at its worst.

Metaxakis meanwhile worked hard to strengthen and organize the churches that remained loyal to him and Alexander. He traveled extensively, became knowledgeable about Greek-American affairs, maintained contact with Venizelos, and built up good relations with Protestant leaders. It was not an undeserved honor, therefore, when in 1921 the ousted metropolitan of Athens was named to the ecumenical throne by the Holy Synod of Constantinople—the most prestigious office in the Eastern Orthodox Church—and ironically became the spiritual head of the Holy Synod of Greece which had deposed him. Metaxakis departed for his enthronement with the good wishes of his compatriots and of his American friends and admirers, and with a more realistic appreciation of the effects of political schism on all facets of Greek life. His appointment, combined with the humiliating defeat of the Greeks in Asia Minor in 1921–1922, seemed to mark the beginning of a new era of reconciliation and unity. One of the first acts of Metaxakis as patriarch in 1922 was to restore to the ecumenical patriarchate jurisdiction over the American Greek Orthodox churches.

Unfortunately, the new era proved short-lived. In 1923 Vasileos Komvopoulos arrived to serve as the archbishop for all the churches loyal to Constantine. The personal indiscretions of Alexander, who in 1922 had become archbishop of the newly established Archdiocese of North and South America, combined with the presence of Komvopoulos to prolong the feuding through the 1920s. In 1930, after much behind-the-scenes negotiating both in the United States and in Greece, Damaskinos, the metropolitan of Corinth, was sent to the United States as the representative of the ecumenical patriarchate and the Holy Synod of Greece. He worked out an agreement that resulted in the recall of the rival archbishops and two of the three bishops, and the designation of Athenagoras I of Corinth as the new archbishop for the Americas.

REPATRIATION AND ASSIMILATION

Almost half the Greeks who arrived in the United States during the peak years of emigration eventually returned to Greece. Some went home because they had

planned to all along, others to discharge their military obligations, especially during the Balkan wars. Precise figures on the number of permanent repatriates are unavailable, because many who repatriated returned again, sometimes making the trip back and forth several times before finally making up their minds where they would stay. In the period 1899–1924 the number of Greeks who departed from the United States amounted to 48 percent of those arriving.

The lot of the returning Greeks was not always a happy one. The butt of jokes and objects of ridicule, often brought on by their own indiscretions and by the envy of those they had left behind, they were viewed as neither Greek nor American. On the other hand, the repatriates could not help but bring to Greece some of the material and tangible qualities of American life.

More than half the immigrants ended up staying in the United States. As political, economic, and social disasters overtook Greece after World War I and following the defeats in Asia Minor, the Greeks began to realize that there was no returning. Although as aliens they could claim exemption from military service in the U.S. armed forces, many volunteered during World War I and even those who remained civilian, despite the wartime xenophobia that swept the country, increasingly came to regard the United States as their permanent home. They were encouraged by local groups, some Greek but mostly non-Greek, urging the foreign-born to learn English, become citizens, and involve themselves in American community affairs. The acculturation of their American-born children and restrictions on immigration that made a return to the United States more difficult once they had left added further to this tendency to look to America as a permanent home.

The result was a conflict best reflected in the rival philosophies of two organizations: the American Hellenic Educational Progressive Assocationn (AHEPA), founded in Atlanta in 1922, and the Greek American Progressive Association (GAPA), organized in East Pittsburgh in 1923. The AHEPA was a secret organization that preached a doctrine of Americanization and nonsectarianism, while the GAPA urged its members, and Greek Americans generally, to cling to their language and the faith of their ancestors and to eschew those who would have them turn their backs on their Greek heritage. In the 1920s this controversy was drawn along the same lines that had marked the royalist-Liberal battles.

AHEPA was accommodationist in philosophy and middle class in orientation, and it won the support of many members of the rising small-business and professional classes who subscribed to its principles. Membership in an organization that was secret and "exclusive," as the AHEPA was, also had its attractions. At its chapter meetings and social functions local and state politicians, aspiring office seekers, judges, lawyers, and educators spoke on subjects ranging from Americanism to the wonders of ancient Greece. Some took a dim view of AHEPA. Much of the furor against it arose over its alleged efforts to force Greek Americans to deny their roots, the designation of English instead of Greek as its official language, and the requirement that a member need only believe in a Supreme Being, and need not adhere to Greek Orthodoxy.

To the GAPA any slight to the Greek faith, the Greek language, Greek customs, and Greek traditions was anathema. Its membership was idealistic, if not romantic, in its philosophy, and out of step with the American realities of the 1920s. It considered nonsectarianism and mixed marriages as being equivalent to a renunciation of the Greek heritage, a view openly endorsed by the Greek church. Although the GAPA never mustered the strength of the AHEPA in its peak years, it was resolute in refusing to assimilate.

After the tempestuous 1920s the parish and Greek-American affairs faded in importance. The first generation were becoming naturalized citizens and were more interested in American than Greek-American affairs. They concerned themselves with rearing children and coping with hardship. Older Greek neighborhoods lost population as families moved out to ethnically mixed areas. More and more of their children were going to colleges and professional schools. Intermarriage with other groups was clearly on the rise.

Interest in the politics of Greece was also fading. The elevation of George II to the Greek throne in 1935 and the seizure of power by John Metaxas in 1936 elicited only passing interest. What eventually attracted more notice was the threat that Greece, whose dictator, Metaxas, was an admirer of Germany, might find itself aligned with Germany and Italy in the impending World War II; the Greeks speculated about what might then happen to their progress in the United States.

They need not have worried. Greece did not join the Axis powers. By 1941, when the United States officially went to war, prosperity and success in the world of small business, prominence in neighborhood affairs, commitment to the work ethic, and the success of the homeland in resisting the invading forces of Mussolini and the accomplishments of Greek guerrillas in the mountains of Albania all served to make them more acceptable than they had been during World War I. In addition, instead of again becoming embroiled in the political battles of Greece, they closed ranks and wholeheartedly threw themselves into the effort to aid its civilian population. There were no conflicting loyalties: the question was only whether they could coordinate the efforts of their widely scattered clubs, societies, and national organizations to help rescue Greece from starvation after it was invaded first by Italy and then by Germany.

Within two weeks after the invasion, the Greek War Relief Association (GWRA), headed by theater magnate Spyros Skouras (1893–1971), came into existence. Chapters of the AHEPA, GAPA, church parishes, the church hierarchy, and others lent their support, but the most effective leadership and assistance were provided by the AHEPA, which had a local and regional membership and leadership that were more conversant in English and better attuned to American ways of doing things. The parish priests and central church authority were too isolated from the American mainstream to be very helpful. The Greek War Relief effort continued unabated throughout the war and the immediate postwar years.

Once the Nazis had withdrawn from Athens in 1944, overtones of the political differences brewing within war-ravaged Greece among the monarchists, Liberals, and radicals again began filtering back into Greek-American communities. In the larger cities some Greek

Americans became involved in the widening rift, and for a time the names of some who were prominent in Greek-American affairs appeared on the letterheads of the Greek American Committee for National Unity, later called the Greek American Council (GAC), in a crusade to win support for a democratic Greece. The more active members of the GAC turned out to be better known in Greece than in the United States, however. Most Greek Americans remained indifferent to the GAC, many simply assuming that it was a Communist-front organization.

Still, the GAC was more conspicuous in the United States than its rival faction on the left, the National Popular Liberation Army (Ethnikos Laikos Apelefthero-tikos Stratos, or ELAS). The ELAS brought the program of the Ethnikon Apeleutheritikon Metopon (EAM) before the American public, labeled the government-in-exile of King George II pro-Fascist, urged a policy of close cooperation among the United States, Great Britain, and the Soviet Union, and organized delegations representing American trade unions and other Greek-American groups to visit the State Department and the embassies of Greece and Great Britain to plead the cause of the EAM. Conspicuous by their absence in these delegations were the leaders of the AHEPA, GAPA, and other Greek-American organizations whose voices had in the past been heard loudly and repeatedly whenever the interests of Greece were at stake.

Problems of American postwar readjustment rated a higher priority among Greek Americans than the problems of Greece—nor had the Greek community forgotten the bitter lessons of the royalist-Liberal controversy of earlier years. When the Truman Doctrine was announced in 1947 it became clear that the United States had agreed to assume responsibilities in Greece that Great Britain was no longer able to afford, instead of following the advice of the GAC and EAM which warned the United States not to follow in the footsteps of Britain.

By the postwar years few Greek Americans were contemplating returning to Greece to live. By then, the American-born outnumbered the Greek-born generation, and both felt closely attached to the United States. War veterans were taking advantage of the G.I. Bill by attending colleges, universities, professional and technical schools. New Greek Orthodox parishes were beginning to appear in the suburbs, indicating the degree to which Greek Americans were becoming prosperous and leaving the city. Although interest in Greece remained, Greek Americans were little inclined to become involved in its politics. While new immigrants helped to modify this indifference, their influence did not become manifest until the 1960s, when a military junta seized power in Greece, and the 1970s, when Turkey invaded Cyprus (1974).

One interest of Greek Americans after the war allied them with other ethnic groups: this was the move to force changes in the U.S. immigration laws so that more of their kin could enter the United States. The effort was temporarily distracted by the proclamation of the Truman Doctrine, which singled out Greece and Turkey for military and economic assistance, thus ironically pairing these archenemies, and by the designation in 1948 of Athenagoras, the archbishop of North and South America since 1931, as the new ecumenical pa-

triarch in Constantinople. The elevation of a churchman of strong pro-American sentiments to the ecumenical throne was hailed as a sign of the importance that the Greek-American churches had acquired in the Eastern Orthodox world.

The campaign to change the immigration laws of the country was soon resumed by AHEPA, still the most influential of the Greek-American organizations. After all its efforts, the McCarran-Walter Act of 1952 came as a cruel disappointment. Although President Truman's veto may have been of some comfort, the fact that the Greek quota remained at 308 people each year was not. Most Greeks entering the United States throughout the 1950s still had to enter as nonquota immigrants. The quota system was, however, at least somewhat attenuated by the passage of the Displaced Persons Act of 1948 and other special legislative enactments that permitted many more to enter the country than the quota allowed.

THE POSTWAR IMMIGRATION

Most of the immigrants of the postwar period came to the United States as a result of the 1965 immigration act that ended the national-quota system and gave preference to newcomers joining other family members in America. Pushed by low wages, unemployment, and the country's political instability, some 46,000 Greeks entered the United States between 1946 and 1960 and more than 142,000 between 1961 and 1975—the largest number to arrive in any 15-year period since before World War I. A much larger number of professionals and skilled workers were among these immigrants than had been the case in earlier periods. The new immigrants soon found jobs in food-service industries or as craftsmen, operatives, foremen, salesworkers, and clerks. The unskilled earned their living as domestic workers, farmers, and, especially in New York City, as cab drivers, a new occupation for Greeks.

Relations were strained, especially in the larger cities, between the new arrivals on the one hand and the earlier immigrants and their children on the other. In the years following World War II the American-born generation had conspicuously ascended the socioeconomic ladder. Whether or not they qualified for G.I. educational benefits, they found their way to colleges, universities, and professional schools, in the belief that higher education was a sure road to success. Urged on by immigrant parents who usually had had little schooling themselves, second-generation Greeks became doctors, lawyers, dentists, journalists, and businessmen and ranked among the highest second-generation ethnic groups in educational attainment. The median incomes of American-born Greeks were exceeded only by those of people whose parents had come from Lithuania, Japan, and Russia. Greek-American self-employment rates were among the highest and the proportion in laboring jobs among the lowest of any group.

In spite of this, and perhaps because of the humble origins of the earlier generation, the new immigrants tended to regard their predecessors as socially and intellectually beneath them. The earlier immigrants found the new arrivals to be arrogant, pretentious, boisterous, and overly demanding; nonetheless, they made an effort

to help the newcomers become established. In the Greek-American community, the American-born generation continues to occupy most positions of leadership, though conditions vary from place to place and the more recent immigrants are slowly moving in. Relations among professionals are improving. The common heritage will probably overcome temporary rivalries and bring about more amicable relations between the two groups.

The largest number of newcomers settled in New York City and experienced many of the problems common to recently arrived immigrants. To aid them, the Hellenic American Neighborhood Action Committee (HANAC), which beginning in 1972 was subsidized with municipal funds, pressed for bilingual legal services, an immigrant-orientation service, a job-placement and job-development center, expansion of the teaching of English as a second language; day care for children, civil-service employment, and economic-development assistance for small business enterprises. According to HANAC some 96 percent of the children of the new immigration still did not know English in the early 1970s. To remedy this, HANAC recommended the appointment of a citywide coordinator of Greek bilingual education and of a task force concerned with the education of the Greek child, the formation of parents' organizations, the extensive recruitment of Greek bilingual teachers, and the development of bilingual materials. Other recommendations included expanded offerings in Greek subjects at the secondary level of education, the creation of health-care and mental-health programs, welfare provisions for Greek senior citizens, and other social services provided to the elderly of the city.

Bilingual education was also encouraged in Chicago for the large numbers of young Greek people there who had little knowledge of English; there, as in New York, ethnic spokesmen were prompted to request their share of bilingual education funds when they became aware of the large outlays being made on behalf of other ethnic groups. In Chicago the inauguration of a voluntary bilingual program, which was designed primarily for children born in Greece, met with opposition from the American-born generation, at least in the beginning, and from others who feared that such a program would contribute to the creation of a Greek "ghetto," bring down property values in Greek neighborhoods, and compete with the Greek-language program of the parish church.

GROUP MAINTENANCE

The family, which in Greece was a tightly knit unit that included uncles, aunts, cousins, and godparents, has changed in the United States over the years, even in New York and Chicago where large colonies of Greek Americans dwell together. Respect for marriage within the group and for family traditions remain strong, and many members of the second and even the third generation have abided by them and married within the Greek Orthodox Church. Even before World War II, however, when women of Greek background were in short supply in America, intermarriage was by no means uncommon among members of the first generation; and in the postwar years mixed marriages have become frequent. The Orthodox church has had to modify its strict stand

against such marriages to avoid decimating its membership, and some parish priests openly admit that the non-Greek converted wives of their parishioners are even more willing workers on behalf of the church than the wives of Greek background. These intermarriages, coupled with the inability of many members of the second and third generation to speak much, if any, Greek, has necessitated more extensive use of the English language in the church services.

The Greek father no longer wields the patriarchial powers he once enjoyed. The Greek language is used less and less within the family, but Greek cooking and folk dancing persist. Visits to Greece have also become commonplace among members of the second and third generations, even among those who have taken non-Greek spouses. The birthday has replaced the name day, or the day of the saint after which a person is named, as a day of celebration, except in the case of the new immigrants among whom name-day celebrations remain common.

THE MODERN CHURCH

The direction the Greek Orthodox Church has taken since World War II has been dictated by the growing affluence of its parishioners, who want their success to be reflected in their parish church. New parishes have been built and old ones relocated in areas far removed from the immigrant neighborhoods of old. In Los Angeles, Milwaukee, Oakland, Atlanta, and San Francisco the new Greek churches have become tourist attractions. The American-born generation has assumed leadership of the parish councils. At social functions the successful Greek-American businessman or professional man—the well-tailored, cigar-smoking owner of a Cadillac or Lincoln Continental, often accompanied by an equally fashionable wife—has become a common sight. Although deference is paid to the teachings of the church fathers and the scriptures, the social occasions and the desire to be in the company of compatriots may be among the primary attractions of the local churches.

After World War II results from the founding of a school to train American-born sons for the priesthood were beginning to be felt. The Holy Cross Seminary was established in Pomfret, Conn., in 1937 and later moved to Brookline, Mass. The priests born and trained in America eventually outnumbered the foreign-born clergy, but their numbers did not increase fast enough to meet the needs of the newly formed parishes and the expanding old ones. If the American-born generation preferred the American-born and American-educated over the foreign-born and foreign-educated priests, the same could not be said of the newer immigrants, whose needs were different and whose knowledge of English was limited. Greek-born and Greek-educated clergy continue to come to the United States to serve the latter, but they come in smaller numbers.

When Athenagoras became archbishop in 1931, he set about centralizing authority over the Greek-American churches in the archdiocese, a policy continued by his successors. It met serious resistance. Some of the earlier priests had little formal education and feared for their future in the face of Athenagoras's reforms. The Reverend Christopher Contogeorge (1894–1950) of Lowell, Mass., was a steadfast foe of centralization and the leader of the traditionalists who vigorously opposed

the archbishop. At the heart of the establishment of this centralized authority was acceptance by member parishes of uniform archdiocesan bylaws. For a parish to retain its good standing, the bylaws required among other things the levying of annual dues or fees from each member or member family and the forwarding to the archdiocese of a fixed portion of the sums collected. At first the levies were set at one dollar per person, then at ten dollars, finally at amounts that varied from parish to parish, and then on a "fair-share" basis.

On the surface this plan seemed fair and appropriate for a church whose operations were expanding and financial needs increasing. But the requirements did not necessarily seem appropriate or fair to many old-timers who still were villagers at heart and to many others who believed in local autonomy. As a consequence, payments to the archdiocese lagged and various devices were used to get parishes to meet their obligations. On one occasion a parish was not given a replacement for a reassigned priest until it had paid the archdiocese what it owed. The failure or unwillingness of the archdiocese to release a satisfactory accounting of its receipts and disbursements and the persistence of rumors of the misuse of such funds exacerbated the problem. Critics protested the travels of the archbishop, whose frequent junkets to distant places were regarded as an unnecessary drain on the limited resources of the church and as interfering with his effectiveness as an administrator.

Members in good standing with the archdiocese—that is, those who pay their annual parish dues—usually number between 80,000 and 90,000 yearly and seldom reach 100,000 or more, a far cry from the 3 million that the church was claiming as its potential American congregation in the mid-1970s.

The newer immigrants, who were often less church oriented than the earlier arrivals, were even less inclined to pay church dues. A few were to the left of center in their political and economic thinking and distrusted organized religion in general. Most, however, were political moderates or conservatives, but were just as suspicious of the church. In Greece the only people who attended church were said to be children and the very old; the church was viewed as a wealthy, mercenary, tax-exempt landowner, insensitive to the needs of the people in a poverty-stricken land. It was easy for newcomers to transfer that attitude to the church in the United States, where they were bombarded with pleas to become dues-paying members—dues which they had to pay before they could participate in the sacraments—and if they became members, with an endless procession of money drives to meet parish mortgage payments and operating expenses. The newcomers also resented the indifference and aloofness of the American-born members and the widespread use of the English language, which many had not mastered and which in any case they considered a violation of the spirit of the Greek Orthodox Church, tantamount to de-Hellenization, and an effort to rob them of their Greek heritage. Finally they felt that the parish priest or the parish council, or both, did not show sufficient compassion for the needs of the homeland.

Although most parishes continue to have Greek-language schools of one kind or another, all-day parochial schools exist largely in the four cities with the most substantial Greek populations: New York, Chicago,

Washington, and Lowell, Mass. Archdiocesan statistics pertaining to these schools are impressive, but their effectiveness in teaching the Greek language varies considerably and most have trouble obtaining qualified teachers and overcoming transportation problems. The parochial schools also have the financial difficulties common to all private schools, and the attitudinal problems of all late-afternoon and Saturday-morning classes. The zeal of the parents, priests, and ethnically oriented parishioners keeps these schools alive, in some instances at the insistence of the church hierarchy and the clergy and in spite of the financial burdens imposed upon both parish and parents.

NEWSPAPERS AND RADIO

The immigrants early had available a fairly active Greek-language press. The *Atlantis* was founded in 1894 in New York and appeared daily from 1904 until 1973. The *Ethnikos Kyrix* (National Herald; 1915–) was founded in New York as a counterbalance to the royalist *Atlantis* and is now owned by a former Greek-American football star turned lawyer. The *Hellenikos Astir* (Greek Star) began in 1903–1904 in Chicago as a Greek-language paper but is now published in English; the *California* of San Francisco, founded in 1907, appeared regularly until the late 1940s or early 1950s, then ceased publication and has been twice revived. Both the *Atlantis* and the *National Herald* also published illustrated monthly periodicals: the *Atlantis's* began earlier, but the *Herald's* lasted longer—until 1939. For a brief time after World War II the *Atlantis* again published a monthly. The longest-lived independently owned quarterly, originally a monthly, *Athene* (1940–1967), was published in Chicago until its publisher died in 1967.

Although one English-language newspaper, a weekly, appeared before World War II, the growth of the Greek-American English-language press came mainly in the postwar years. The leading paper is the weekly *Hellenic Chronicle* (1950–), published in Boston, which specializes in local news and features Greek Americans in public life; it claims the largest circulation among newspapers catering to a Greek-American audience. Any crisis in Greece is apt to trigger the appearance of a number of short-lived newspapers that rarely last beyond the crisis that inspired them. After Turkey invaded Cyprus in 1974, for example, many papers were started but only two weeklies survived: the *Hellenic Times* of New York and the *Hellenic Journal* of San Francisco.

Greek radio programs proliferated after World War II. Hardly a city with a sizable Greek population is without a Greek radio hour that specializes in the playing of recorded modern Greek music and the airing of news about events in the Greek community. In New York City several programs are scheduled seven days a week, while listeners in the greater Chicago metropolitan area can hear some 16 or 17 radio programs.

POLITICAL PARTICIPATION

Greeks in the United States no less than in Greece have an ethusiasm for politics. Few of the earliest immigrants ventured far into American politics, however, owing to the language barrier and their unfamiliarity with the American political process. Those who did sel-

dom rose beyond the level of the state legislature. Entry into public service and politics became more common after World War II, when the second generation had reached maturity. Greek Americans became judges in some of the larger metropolitan areas. State legislators with Greek names, sometimes in Anglicized versions, became more common. Several of the smaller cities and towns of New England and elsewhere, as well as larger cities such as San Francisco, St. Paul, Minn., Hartford, Conn., Syracuse, N.Y., and Savannah, Ga., have chosen mayors of Greek background. Since, with the possible exception of Lowell, few if any of these elected officials have governed cities with significant blocs of Greek-American voters, it must be presumed that they were elected for reasons other than loyalty of an ethnic constituency.

Among the more politically conspicuous Greek Americans have been several congressmen who have served in the U.S. House of Representatives since 1959. The two most prominent are John Brademas (1927–) of Indiana and Paul Sarbannes (1933–) of Maryland, both Harvard graduates and former Rhodes scholars. Brademas, whose Greek ancestry is limited to his father's side, has been the Democratic whip in the House of Representatives since 1977, while Sarbannes, both of whose parents were Greek-born, distinguished himself as a member of the House Judiciary Committee in the hearings involving Richard Nixon in 1974, before becoming the first Greek American to be elected a United States senator in 1976. Spiro Agnew (1918–), whose father was Greek, became the first Greek American to be elected governor of a state, and the first to be elected Vice President of the United States, though he was forced to resign because of unethical conduct in high office. Michael Dukakis (1923–), both of whose parents were Greeks, one from Asia Minor and the other from Thessaly, served as governor of Massachusetts (1975–1978) and was the second Greek American to be elected a state governor. In 1978 Paul Tsongas was elected to the U.S. Senate from Massachusetts.

Some Greek Americans still limit their political activities to the annual conventions of the AHEPA and the election of the officers of the supreme lodge of the order. Rival parties set up rival slates of candidates, raise enormous sums of money, engage hotel rooms for delegates committed to their slate, and wine and dine the delegates after the fashion of the major American political parties. The benefits derived from these activities have never been clear, but they seem to satisfy the political appetites of the most active Ahepans, for relatively few of them have political careers outside the confines of the order.

Greek Americans presently constitute the largest Greek community outside Greece itself. Although they still maintain strong sentimental attachments to Greece, their attachment to the United States is becoming stronger with each passing year. Most Greek Americans by now belong to the middle class, a surprising number to the upper middle class, and many have taken their place among the notables in many fields of endeavor. Greeks are prominent in science, music, the fine arts, sports, and entertainment. In medicine they are represented by Dr. George Papanicolaou (1883–1962), who invented the Pap test for cancer, and Dr. George Kotzias (1918–1977), who developed l-dopa to combat Parkinson's disease; in music by Dimitri Mitropoulos (1890–1960), the conductor, and Maria Callas (1923–1977), the Brooklyn-born soprano; in wrestling by Jimmy Londos (d. 1975), the "golden Greek" and a world champion in his prime; in football by Harry Agganis (1930–1955) and Alex Karras (1935–); in baseball by Alex Grammas (1928–) and Milt Pappas (1939–); in theater and film by Elia Kazan (1909–) and John Cassavetes (1929–); in entertainment by Telly Savalas (1924–) and George Chakiris (1934–); in the fine arts by William Baziotes (1912–1963); in the fashion world by James Galanos (1924–). Indications are that Greek Americans are and will remain a vigorous force in American life.

Bibliography
The best of the earliest works are the unsympathetic but helpful study by Henry Pratt Fairchild, *Greek Immigration to the United States* (New Haven, Conn., 1911), and the more sympathetic but less scholarly work of Thomas Burgess, *Greeks in America* (1913; reprint, New York, 1970). Later studies include Theodore Saloutos, *Greeks in the United States* (Cambridge, Mass., 1964), and Michael N. Cutsumbis, *A Bibliographic Guide to Materials on Greeks in the United States, 1890–1960* (New York, 1970). See also Charles C. Moskos, Jr., *Greek Americans: Struggle and Success* (Englewood Cliffs, N.J., 1980).

Material on the Greek Orthodox Church appears in Demetrios J. Constantelos, ed., *Encyclicals and Documents of the Greek Orthodox Archdiocese of North and South America . . . 1922–1972* (Salonika, 1976), and George Papaioannou, *From Mars to Manhattan: The Greek Orthodox Church in America under Patriarch Athenagoras I* (Minneapolis, 1976). Local studies include Helen Z. Papanikolas, "The Exiled Greeks" in *The Peoples of Utah*, ed. Helen Z. Papanikolas (Salt Lake City, 1976), pp. 409–435; James Patterson, "The Unassimilated Greeks of Denver," *Anthropological Review* 43 (October 1970): 243–253; and Theodore Saloutos, "The Greeks of Milwaukee," *Wisconsin Magazine of History* 53 (Spring 1970): 175–193. See Theodore Saloutos, *They Remember America* (Berkeley, Calif., 1956), on the repatriated Greeks, and Nicholas Tavuchis, *Family and Mobility among Greek Americans* (Athens, 1972), on the Greek family. George Leber, *History of the Order of Ahepa, 1922–1972* (Washington, D.C., 1972), is a detailed compilation of activities taken from the order's official records.

Except for the Greek archives at the University of Utah, which are in the initial stages of organization, no serious effort has been made to compile Greek-immigrant materials in the United States. The Balch Institute in Philadelphia has back files of the *Atlantis* (New York, 1894–1973) and incomplete files of its archrival, the *National Herald* (New York, 1915–). The University of Chicago Library has the earlier years of the *Greek Star* (Chicago, 1904–) on microfilm, and the library of the University of California at Los Angeles has microfilm copies of *California* (San Francisco, 1907–) up to the early 1940s. The Houghton Library at Harvard University has the scrapbooks of Nicholas Culolias, a longtime resident of Boston and other eastern cities. The most useful collection for the study of Greek immigrants is in the New York Public Library.

                                                                    THEODORE SALOUTOS

GROS VENTRES: *see* AMERICAN INDIANS

GUAMANIANS: *see* PACIFIC ISLANDERS

GUATEMALANS: *see* CENTRAL AND SOUTH AMERICANS

GUJERATIS: *see* EAST INDIANS; ZOROASTRIANS

GUYANANS: *see* WEST INDIANS

GYPSIES

At the present time there are probably more than half a million Gypsies living in the United States and Canada. Gypsy communities are also found throughout

Europe, the Middle East, northern Africa, and South America.

Gypsies have figured in literature and folklore for hundreds of years, but not until the 19th century did scholars attempt to understand their origin and characteristics. Sebastian Munster in 1552 was the first European writer to allude to the Indian origin of the Gypsies; in 1760 the Hungarian theologian Stefan Valyi was the first to recognize that the Gypsy language, Romani (Romanés), had its roots in India. Earlier writers thought that the Gypsies were descended variously from the Jews, Egyptians, Arabs, "Atlantians," and even the same prehistoric race as the American Indians. Today, none of these theories is taken seriously, and scholars generally agree that their origins lie in fact in northern India.

The fundamental differences evident in the modern Gypsy populations may be the result of three distinct migrations out of the Indian subcontinent. In the 5th century after Christ, 12,000 Indian prisoners of war, thought to have been Gypsies and referred to as Zotts and Luri, were brought to Persia. Actual evidence linking this group with the modern Gypsies is lacking, but whatever the circumstances under which the earliest groups left India they did settle in Persia and Syria, and were later brought by the Byzantines to Anatolia. The precise record of their wanderings during these centuries is confused, but they seem to have moved farther and farther west as a result of wars in the Middle East.

The name Gypsy derives from the earlier 'Gypcian, a misnomer resulting from a confusion of Egypt proper with Ægyptus Minor (Little Egypt) or Epirus, in the western Byzantine Empire, the first place the Gypsies reached upon their arrival in Europe. Nonetheless, belief in an Egyptian origin is very widespread, even among the Gypsies themselves, who have evolved a folklore based upon that assumption. In the case of the Gitanos of Spain, it is likely that their ancestors did in fact pass through Egypt, entering the Iberian Peninsula via North Africa.

The earliest groups entered Balkan Europe on the tide of Ottoman expansion into that area in the early 14th century. By 1370 some groups had been enslaved, but others moved farther on into Europe. Documents show their presence in Serbia by 1340, Hungary by 1383, Germany by 1407, Switzerland by 1414, France by 1419, Denmark by 1420, Belgium by 1421, Italy by 1422, Spain by 1447, and finally Poland (1501), Russia (1501), and Scotland (1505). Initially, Gypsies were welcomed in many countries, and some even carried charters of protection from 14th-century leaders such as Pope Martin V and the Holy Roman Emperor Sigismund. But their way of life soon alienated them from the rest of the European population, and they were subjected to persecution for several centuries. These harsh attacks subsided in the 19th century, but were brutally revived between 1939 and 1945, when over 250,000 Gypsies were murdered during Hitler's attempt to exterminate the entire people along with the Jews.

In Europe the Gypsy population is broadly divided into the Gitanos of Spain, the Manouche of France, the Sinte of Germany and Italy, the Romnichals in Britain, the Rom in eastern and southern Europe, and the Boyash in Romania. The Rom, Romnichals, and Boyash have the largest representation in the United States; there are also smaller numbers of Xoraxaya (Turkish Gypsies), Afrikaya (Algerian Manouche), and some others.

ARRIVAL AND SETTLEMENT

From the earliest times Gypsy migration has been largely involuntary. Although in the late Middle Ages Gypsies carried letters throughout Europe indicating that they were Christian, the apparent oddness of their nomadic existence, their streetcorner entertaining and fortunetelling, and other unfamiliar practices did not endear them to the superstitious European peasantry. In addition, the closed and aloof nature of Gypsy society, which discourages prolonged social contact with non-Gypsies, must have antagonized many people and reinforced their suspicions that these practitioners of magic were up to no good. The result was a general anti-Gypsyism throughout Europe that often resulted in hangings or banishment.

England began deporting Gypsies in 1544, and it was from there and elsewhere in Europe that they first came to the New World. In 1655 a group was transported as slaves to the English colonies of Barbados and Jamaica. The English also sent large numbers to Virginia (1695), to the penal settlements in Georgia, and later to southern Australia. Similarly, the Portuguese had transported Gypsies to Brazil and Angola by 1591, the Spanish to the West Indies by 1580, the French to Louisiana by 1600, the Dutch to New Jersey by 1650, and the Germans to Pennsylvania by 1758. The fate of the Gypsies who have been in America since the 17th and 18th centuries is not documented. Certain communities, such as those in Pennsylvania and Louisiana, have remained distinct, and it has been suggested that the Melungeons of Tennessee may be of Romani ancestry. The largest group are the descendants of the Balkan Gypsy population who came en masse to the United States between about 1855 and 1885, when legal immigration became difficult if not impossible for them. Since then, Gypsies have continued to enter the country by way of Mexico and Canada.

It is not possible to determine the exact number of Gypsies in the United States. Estimates range from 20,000 to 1,000,000 and there are surely more than the 1,588 persons listed in the 1970 Census who claimed Romani as their mother tongue. Taking into account data from several studies, it is reasonable to assume that there are approximately 500,000 Gypsies in the United States. Many of the earliest arrivals led a nomadic existence, either to escape labor on the plantations, or later (especially in the case of the groups from the Balkans) in order to pursue traditional occupations. But after the Depression in the 1930s the Gypsies began to settle in the cities and are now found there in large concentrations. Surveys have indicated that the Rom Gypsy population alone accounts for about 15,000 in Los Angeles and 10,000 in Chicago. Gypsies are most numerous in New York, Virginia, Illinois, Texas, Massachusetts, and the three Pacific Coast states.

ECONOMIC LIFE

Most Gypsy families in the United States now live in houses or mobile homes; the tent-dwellers, still in evidence in the 1920s, are no longer common. In larger

cities a family may rent a store, the front serving as an *ofisa* (fortunetelling parlor), the family living in the rear. Sometimes a family rents an apartment above a store, since many groups have cultural prohibitions against living below other people, especially women. In the main, Gypsies rent or own houses which are, on the outside, indistinguishable from those around them, except perhaps for a sign bearing a picture of a hand, an Indian's head, or a deck of cards, indicating the presence of an *ofisa* within. Reading and advising (fortunetelling) are most commonly women's work, although the husband may perform those functions if the need arises. Usually the client will come to the *ofisa*, but the reader may also visit the client's home, or solicit readings in such places as theater lobbies, restaurants, and even public toilets.

Male occupations differ from group to group. Among the Romnichals, used-car dealing, carnival work, metal salvaging, and factory employment are common; the Rom sell cars, jewelry, clothing, small machinery, and firearms, or they repair and refinish restaurant and factory machines, stoves, boilers, and the like. The Boyash can be found in carnival work, blacktopping, and roofing. Other activities traditionally engaged in by Gypsies include skilled and unskilled artisan work such as auto body repair, metal plating, and spray painting. A growing number of Gypsies are also to be found in such pursuits as real estate, office work, acting, teaching, and the management of apartment buildings.

Among the Boyash and Rom, loose working alliances known as *kumpaniyi* are often formed among men living in a specific area; they function as a kind of union organizing the available labor force and dispersing to its members the jobs that may be available nearby. Smaller and more permanent partnerships known as *wortacha* (partners) are formed between friends, a father and son(s), or a husband and wife.

SOCIAL STRUCTURE

The most clearly defined structure for Gypsies is simply the fact that they are Gypsies and everyone else is not. All non-Gypsies, regardless of racial or ethnic affiliation, are known as *gazhé* (or *gawjas* among the Romnichals). Within the Gypsy community itself, of course, the social structure differs from group to group.

The Rom are divided into *natsiyi* (or *tabori*, depending on dialect), meaning "nations." All these nations came from the Balkans at some time in the past, but they are clearly distinguishable by the dialect of Romani each uses. The principal nations among the Rom are the Machwaya, the Kalderasha, the Churara, and the Lowara. Each of them was originally identified either by its traditional profession (*kalderasha*, for example, means coppersmiths) or by its traditional place of origin (the Machwaya supposedly came from Mačva in Serbia). Each nation has cultural and even physical features peculiar to itself. Among the Rom in America there exists a social hierarchy of "quality," the Machwaya generally being considered the most elite nation among them. This hierarchy is reflected in occupation, style of living, and attitudes toward intermarriage with members of other nations.

Each nation is divided into clans (*witsi* or *tseri*, depending on dialect). A clan is an alliance of families united by ancestral, professional, or historical ties. Clan distinctions are more evident among some nations than others: the Kalderasha, for instance, attach more significance to them than do the Machwaya. A clan may include several hundred individuals, but it is not uncommon for large ones to subdivide into smaller clans whenever increasing size leads to loss of individual contact. Although one or more families in a clan may live together under a single roof, the Gypsies prefer each family to have its own home. A family may consist of grandparents, parents, their children and spouses, or simply—though rarely—of a young and still childless couple.

Each clan has a leader, and if the group is a large one and the leader powerful enough, he or she might adopt the title "king" or "queen," though such self-styled assertions are most common when Gypsy leaders come into contact with reporters from the non-Gypsy world. Within Gypsy culture there is no royalty, and such titles are used only jocularly.

The social structure among the Romnichals is less complex; they are divided only into clans and families. This group has in the past been strongly matrilineal, but there are indications that this tradition is now weakening. The family name is that of the mother; after marriage the wife retains ownership of her property, and it is returned to her own family when she dies. Jointly owned property is not inherited by the husband's relatives, but by the men in the wife's family. The Romnichals are further distinguished from Vlach (originally Wallachian or Balkan) groups in that they have adopted English surnames such as Cooper, Cook, Palmer, Smith, Stanley, Pinfold. The Rom, who speak Vlach dialects and like the Romnichals use English surnames such as Adams, Evans, Marks, Johns, nonetheless maintain patronymics within the group: for example, a man might be known in the community as *o Wosho le Zurkosko*, Wosho, son of Zurka.

Boyash social structure is similar in many respects to that of the Rom, since both groups originated from the same area in Europe and share the same early history. Religious festivals, for instance, and the maintenance of saints' days are the same. Nonetheless the Boyash have less social contact with the Rom than with the Romnichals, who have similar occupations. Moreover, because the Boyash, like the Romnichals, do not know the Vlach dialects, this effectively excludes them from participation in the affairs of the Rom.

Among both Rom and Romnichals, marriages are usually arranged by the parents, sometimes even before birth. The groom's family is expected to provide a dowry. Intermarriage with other families and even with other Gypsy nations is increasing, but traditionally marriages are restricted to relatives, sometimes as close as first cousins. As a result, a certain amount of inbreeding occurs. There is also evidence that marriage with non-Gypsies, although still rare, is becoming more common.

SOCIAL LIFE AND RELIGIOUS BELIEF

Gypsies have generally adopted the religion of the countries in which they have lived; thus the Rom and Boyash are Roman Catholic or most especially Orthodox, while the Romnichals are Protestant. Evangelists in the United States have also succeeded in obtaining a number of converts from among the Rom and Romni-

chals (a National Gypsy Evangelical Conference was held in Arkansas in 1977). Because of the restrictions placed upon socializing with non-Gypsies, and even with Gypsy groups other than one's own, social life exists almost wholly among related families, who regularly get together for social, religious, or other functions. The most popular festivals among the Rom and Boyash include baptisms (called *bolimata* by the Rom, and *botezizmi* by the Boyash), weddings (*abiyawa; nunte*), and funerals and wakes (*gropimata* and *pomani; funeralyi* and *pomani*), as well as the major holidays: Christmas (*Krichuno; Krakyun*) and Easter (*Patradzhi; Pashti*) and various saints' days (*swuntsi dzhes; zilé de sfintsi*). Since most Romnichals are Protestant, they celebrate only the major holidays: Christmas (*Moldivus*) and Easter (*Yorradivus*), and family events such as weddings (*rummerins*), baptisms (*bollerins*), and funerals (*possabens*).

Among the Rom, a relative or other visitor (*streyino Rom*) may be welcomed with a *paichiu* or dinner given in his honor. Families in the same locality regularly visit and eat together to reinforce ethnic unity at the clan level and to counterbalance the detrimental effects of being among gazhé for too long a time.

If there was ever a particularly Gypsy religion, it no longer survives anywhere in any obvious form. The various Christian faiths most Gypsies adhere to were acquired during the centuries after their stay in the Byzantine Empire. Certain practices may be traced to non-Christian origins, however; stories explaining the creation of the universe common among some groups have parallels in Zoroastrianism, and notions about ritual cleanliness may stem from Hindu custom, or from contact with Zoroastrianism and Islam in Persia. Zealous attempts have been made by modern East Indian scholars to trace Gypsy religious, spiritual, and occult beliefs to Hinduism, but while some Indian cultural retentions are undeniable, the evidence provided for many of these theories is not conclusive.

THE GYPSY WAY OF LIFE

There is no single word in Romani for Gypsy. Each group has its own name by which it is known to other Gypsy groups, and its own understanding of what a Gypsy is, criteria which often result in the exclusion of other groups. Being surrounded by gazhé, Gypsies are very conscious of their own way of life and world view. The Rom call this *romaniya*. Existence and identification as a Rom are based upon the strict maintenance of all that the name stands for. Romaniya includes whatever is considered right and acceptable: diet, health, human contact, morality, and ritual. The opposite of romaniya is *marimos*. Marimos means both "defilement" and "banishment"; something is *marimé* if it goes against the concepts of romaniya. There is no corresponding word for romaniya among the Romnichals, but their equivalent of marimé is *mokadi*. For example, the lower, but not upper, part of the body and anything associated with it, is marimé. Thus, a woman's legs must be covered, but no shame is attached to exposing the breasts if, for example, it is necessary to feed a child in public. The feet and, above all, the genitals are especially marimé. Certain foods and animals are avoided on similar grounds. A person might be declared marimé

for transgression of romaniya. In order to purify himself and become once again undefiled (*wuzherdo* or, among the Romnichals, *yuser'd*), he may have to pay a fine, finance a banquet, or even remove himself from the community for a time. Since exile means living exclusively in a non-Gypsy society—much of which is considered marimé—this is regarded as being a particularly strict punishment.

Decisions dealing with marimos and other important issues, such as assault or divorce, are made at the *kris*, loosely translated as tribunal, a solemn gathering presided over by a group of arbitrators. A kris can go on for several days, during which time drinking and socializing are forbidden. One of its main functions is to reaffirm and reenforce the concepts of romaniya, and on occasion to adapt them to the changing times. Gypsies from other states are sometimes invited to serve as impartial participants. Less serious issues are dealt with in more informal discussions called *diwanurya*. Neither the kris nor diwanurya survive among the Romnichals.

CULTURE

Gypsy culture has been traditionally expressed through their language, called Romani (Romany, Romanés). Its structure is basically similar to Sanskrit, reinforcing the rationale of an Indian origin for the people. Through the centuries, this language has acquired numerous loanwords and grammatical features from those languages dominant in the areas in which Gypsies have lived. The language of present-day European Gypsies may very broadly be divided into Vlach and non-Vlach dialects. The Rom in the United States speak mainly the Kalderash and Machwaya varieties of Vlach dialects, and although these may contain many lexical and grammatical features from Romanian and Slavic languages, most of the grammar is unchanged, and may be traced back to Sanskrit. On the other hand, the Romnichals speak an uninflected language consisting of non-Vlach words and following English grammatical structure and pronunciation. The Boyash, who descended from linguistically acculturated Balkan house-slaves, long ago lost their original language and speak instead a dialect of northern Romanian with heavy Slavic and Romani lexical influences. Knowledge of inflected Romani is a very powerful criterion for group membership, and it is largely because of this that the Rom, the Romnichals, and the Boyash, and other groups do not mix with each other.

Music is central to Gypsy culture. Many learn to play musical instruments, especially the guitar and accordion. Some nations, such as the Lowara, have many professional musicians among their number, but usually talent in music and song is kept within the community. The Rom circulate 8-track cartridges or cassette tapes of music from family to family, sometimes recorded in studios rented for the purpose. A kind of Gypsy "hit parade" of these tapes exists, and a kind of copyright may even be attached in the form of a spoken warning at the beginning of the tape, threatening bad luck to anyone who copies it. Sometimes the tape is in the form of a radio show, with a Romani-speaking disc jockey joking and wishing the listeners well between songs. The songs are often adaptations of American compositions, sung in Romani in characteristic Gypsy style. Particularly popular are Gypsy versions of "If I Were a

Rich Man" (*Te barwalo simas-me*) and "Strangers in the Night" (*Streyinurya and'e ryat*).

Gypsy attitudes toward education vary. Children of more assimilated families may attend public schools for a while in the neighborhoods where they reside. But many Gypsy parents believe that all the education necessary for a Gypsy can be acquired within the Gypsy community itself, and that public schools not only ignore Gypsy values, but teach gazhé ones. Even more disturbing is the requirement that Romani youngsters be kept uncomfortably close to the gazhé for hours at a time. Rom who attend school do so only intermittently, though an increasing number of them are beginning to realize that some skills, particularly reading, are becoming more and more necessary in the modern world.

The problems arising from contact with the outside have eased somewhat in recent years, at least in those areas where government-funded Romani schools now exist. Schools whose course content is designed specifically for Gypsies have been established in Richmond, Calif., Washington, D.C., Seattle, Wash., and Chicago. So far, the failures have outnumbered the successes, to some extent because of lack of experience and to some extent because the schools necessarily rely on non-Gypsy teachers who, however well-intentioned, are not usually sufficiently knowledgeable about the Gypsies and the Gypsy way of life. The majority of Gypsies remain opposed to schooling of any kind.

INTERGROUP RELATIONS

In the English dialect of the American Rom, the word "public" means "within the Gypsy community." The more common meaning has its equivalent in *gazhengo pleyso* (place of the gazhé). This distinction reflects the persistent separation between the two worlds, a separation whose maintenance is fundamental to the preservation of Gypsy values, though its extent may vary from group to group and from time to time. One of the functions of the kris among the Rom is to approve or disapprove any change from the traditional way of life.

Not all the rationale behind separation from the gazhé can be sought in pre-diaspora India, because the first accounts of Gypsy-gazhé relationships indicate closer contact between the two in earlier centuries. Self-imposed cultural restrictions on fraternizing with non-Gypsies may have developed as a protective reaction against anti-Gypsy attitudes. Even the 1969 edition of the *Encyclopaedia Britannica* could still refer to Gypsies as "verminous, dirty wastrels," and the word is denied a proper-noun's initial capital letter in many publications. Scientific interest in Gypsies has been in existence only during the past two centuries; by that time marimos and avoidance of the gazhé were already well entrenched traditions. To insulate themselves from surrounding cultures, Gypsies would often provide false and fanciful information about their life, language, and customs, a tactic that they still employ. While it serves the purpose of protecting the group, it also contributes to the perpetuation of the inaccurate, and sometimes even harmful, popular stereotypes.

Such a negative image has resulted in government policies that discriminated against Gypsies in the United States. As early as 1891 a federal law was passed barring persons likely to become public charges and persons convicted of moral turpitude, a law which led to the exclusion and the deportation of those who arrived on immigrant ships. Although the immigration law was liberalized in 1965, their eligibility for admission remains uncertain. Various states have also directed laws against Gypsies. As recently as 1976 a family was expelled from the state of Maryland, where the law requires Gypsies to pay a licensing fee of $1,000 before establishing homes or engaging in business, and there is a bounty of $10 on the head of any Gypsy arrested who has not paid this fee. In New Hampshire in 1977 two families were legally evicted from the state without being charged with any crime by the police, solely for reasons of their ethnic identity. The June 1975 issue of *The Police Chief* includes an article advising police departments on how to keep their precincts free of Gypsies.

POLITICAL AWARENESS AND ETHNIC COMMITMENT

In recent years Gypsies in the United States have begun to organize in reaction to these discriminatory policies. Their new-found activism in many ways reflects developments in Europe, where Gypsy involvement in the struggle for minority rights has a history going back to the 19th century.

In the early 1970s, branches of the Paris-based Comité International Rom were set up in the United States and Canada, as the International Gypsy Committee (Komitia Lumiaki Romani and'e Amerika) or IGC. From offices in Quebec and Texas the committee provides accurate information to educational organizations, arranges legal advice for Gypsies needing it, and monitors and often protests the portrayal of Gypsies in the media. It also acts as a clearing-house for news from overseas and coordinates a number of otherwise unconnected Gypsy organizations throughout the country. Related to this development has been the participation of American Gypsies at international meetings, such as the International Roma Festival in 1976 in Chandigarh, India, where many Gypsies journeyed to the ancestral homeland to be greeted by Prime Minister Indira Gandhi, and the Second World Romani Congress, held in Geneva in the spring of 1978 and sponsored by the government of India and the World Council of Churches.

Gypsy activism in the United States has in large measure been the result of reaction to the wide publicity given two serialized stories and a novel by Peter Maas, *King of the Gypsies,* published in 1975. Based on the embellished exploits of a particular family of New York Rom, this book, which infuriated many Gypsies, resulted in the revival of many old anti-Gypsy laws across the country, and an increase in police harassment. Letters poured into the American press, and, as a result, individual Gypsies learned of each other's grievances and of the existence of the International Gypsy Committee. Since then, several new political and cultural groups have been founded, such as the American Gypsy Organization (E Organizatsia Romani Amerikani) in Indiana, the Gypsy Cultural Program (E Programa Romani Kulturalni) in Washington State, and the Pennsylvania Gypsy Alliance (O Kidinimos Romano Pennsylvaniako) in Philadelphia. For the first time in the United States, Rom, Boyash, and Romnichals are working together as members of the same organizations—the Gypsy Society of Chicago (E Komitia Ro-

mani and'e Shikaga) for example—and a common sense of identity seems to some extent to be reemerging. The rise of these and similar organizations reveals a new attempt on the part of the groups to present a more accurate picture of Gypsy life, while at the same time preserving the integrity of the groups and resisting cultural loss through assimilation into the larger American society.

Bibliography
The best introduction to the subject is Anne Sutherland, *Gypsies: The Hidden Americans* (London, 1975). This work focuses on the Rom, while the pioneering and still useful study by Irving Brown, *Gypsy Fires in America* (New York, 1923), considers all groups. The concept of defilement has been completely described in Carol Miller, "American Rom and the Ideology of Defilement," in *Gypsies, Tinkers, and Other Travelers*, ed. Farnham Rehfisch (New York, 1975), and Thomas A. Acton, "The Functions and Avoidance of Moxadi Covels," *Journal of the Gypsy Lore Society*, vol. 50, nos. 3–4 (1971). A general and somewhat popular account of religious and spiritual beliefs is found in Elwood B. Trigg, *Gypsy Demons and Divinities* (Secaucus, N.J., 1973). There are several sociolinguistic studies that not only describe various dialects but also discuss the Gypsy migration to North America, its social composition, and education: Ronald Lee, "Gypsies in Canada [and the U.S.]," *Journal of the Gypsy Lore Society*, vol. 46, nos. 1–2 (1967); vol. 47, nos. 1–2 (1968); vol. 48, nos. 3–4 (1969); Ian F. Hancock, *Problems in the Creation of a Standard Dialect of Romanés*, Social Science Research Council Working Paper in Sociolinguistics, no. 25 (Austin, Tex., 1975); and *Romani Sociolinguistics*, ed. Ian Hancock (The Hague, 1979).
The best treatments of the European historical background and development of anti-Gypsyism are George C. Soulis, "The Gypsies in the Byzantine Empire and the Balkans in the Late Middle Ages," *Dumbarton Oaks Papers*, vol. 15 (Cambridge, Mass., 1961); and Donald Kenrick and Grattan Puxon, *The Destiny of Europe's Gypsies* (London, 1971). Ion Calota, "Observatii asupra graiului unei familii de Rudari," *Acts of the 12th International Congress on Romance Linguistics and Philology* (Bucharest), 2 (1971): 343–350, deals with the phonology of the Romanian Boyash dialect and mentions several further sources. Nothing has so far appeared in English on the dialect, though work is in progress.

IAN F. HANCOCK

H

HAITIANS

Estimates of the number of Haitians living in the United States vary widely. Prior to 1965 the group was small; since then the Haitians have become one of the largest West Indian groups in America, distinguished from black British West Indians by language, culture, and often religion.

In 1970 the U.S. Census listed 37,469 Haitians, and according to the Immigration and Naturalization Service, about 35,000 Haitian immigrants were admitted to the country in the period from 1971 to 1976. However, community leaders estimated that there were more than 300,000 Haitians in the United States by the end of the 1970s. There are Haitian communities throughout the country, with major concentrations in New York City, Chicago, Miami, Washington, D.C., and the Boston area. Most of the immigrants are refugees from the governments of François "Papa Doc" Duvalier, who held power from 1957 to 1971, and his son, Jean-Claude Duvalier, who came to power in 1971. Haitians came to the United States for political security and improved economic opportunities.

From different regions of Haiti and from different social strata, the Haitians, especially in New York City, maintain their diverse cultural traditions through Protestant, Catholic, and Voodoo churches, a variety of folkloric and artistic groups (Ibo dancers, Troupe Kouidor), community newspapers (*Haiti-Observateur, Haiti Tribune, Unité*), and weekly radio programs such as Heure Haitienne, Mai-Amé, and Eddy Publicité. The immigrants concerned with the changing political situation in Haiti continue to display strong national loyalties.

The Home Country

The national development of Haiti is unique in the history of the West Indies. It is distinguished by a relatively short period of colonial subjection—from the arrival of Columbus in 1492 to independence in 1804. During the 18th century, French colonists in Haiti developed a plantation economy based on the intensive

Hispaniola

use of slave labor. Many thousands of Africans were imported from the coast along the Bight of Benin, and from what are now Angola, Senegal, Benin (formerly Dahomey), the Ivory Coast, and the Congo. A bloody revolutionary struggle led by slaves against French colonists led to the establishment of the Republic of Haiti in 1804. Other Caribbean islands remained under colonial rule for another century. The Haitian Revolution was the only slave revolt in history to lead to the permanent establishment of a new nation.

Today, Haiti has a population of approximately 5,500,000. Ninety percent of them are black, and they live for the most part in the countryside. A mulatto minority is concentrated in the cities such as Port-au-Prince, the capital, Cap Haitien, and Gonaïves. The mulatto elite and urban middle class are Roman Catholic and speak standard French; the black peasantry and urban workers believe in *Vodun* (Voodoo) along with some Catholicism, and speak Creole. Eighty-six percent of the Haitian population is illiterate. Haiti is one of the poorest nations in the world; its annual per capita income is $130 and its daily per capita food consumption is 1,700 calories.

History of Immigration

There are four main periods of Haitian immigration to the United States: the period of French colonization, the Haitian Revolution (1791–1803), the U.S. occupation of Haiti (1915–1934), and the administrations of the Duvaliers (1957–).

The first group of Haitian migrants to the United States were probably the French colonists and their slaves who arrived in Charleston County, S.C., in the mid-1600s to work the rice plantations. In 1772 Jean Baptiste Point du Sable, a mulatto Haitian fur trader who had married an Indian woman of the local Potawatomi tribe, became the first permanent settler and the founder of the city of Chicago. At the Battle of Savannah in 1779 a troop of 800 "men of color" from Haiti fought on behalf of American independence.

During the turbulence of the Haitian Revolution more than 50,000 white planters, free blacks, and slaves left for the United States. They settled in New York, Philadelphia, Boston, New Orleans, Norfolk, Va., and Charleston. The émigrés were attracted especially to Philadelphia, which became a cultural capital for Haitians. In Philadelphia, Médéric Louis Elie Moreau de Saint Méry (1750–1819), a former Haitian government official, ran a printing press and opened a bookstore that soon became a meeting place for concerned émigrés. There they read about the latest developments of the Haitian Revolution in *Le Courrier de la France et des Colonies*, a newspaper printed by Moreau de Saint Méry and published by Louis Gâtereau, another émigré. Moreau de Saint Méry wrote his outstanding two-volume work, *Description Topographique, Physique, Civile, Politique et Historique de la Partie Française de L'Isle de St. Domingue*, in Philadelphia. John James Audubon (1785–1851), the naturalist and illustrator of

birds, was born in Haiti and came to the United States in the summer of 1803. Another émigré, Joseph Savary, headed the Second Battalion of free men of color who fought in 1814–1815 under the command of General Andrew Jackson. He became the first black to hold the rank of major in the U.S. Army. New Orleans received more than 10,000 refugees in these years.

During the 19th century, small groups of American blacks left the United States to settle in Haiti. One of these was the grandfather of the scholar W.E.B. Du Bois; Du Bois's father was born in Haiti in 1825. However, most of the Afro-American settlers did not remain in Haiti; they returned to America with their French- and Creole-speaking wives and children.

The third wave of Haitians arrived during the period 1915–1934 when the United States occupied the Republic of Haiti to put an end to the political instability that threatened U.S. investments there. These migrants, well educated and deeply involved in opposition politics, came chiefly from Port-au-Prince. About 500 of them resided in Harlem in 1925. Those with leftist political views played an active role in the cultural movement known as the Harlem Renaissance, the African repatriation movement of Marcus Garvey, and the Harlem branch of the Communist party.

Haitian immigrants in Harlem developed import businesses, traded in fur, and worked in the garment industry. They ran retail stores which sold such Haitian products as honey, coffee, and rum. Some Haitians who had proper credentials were hired to teach French and Spanish in the public schools of New York. Educated and proud, the newcomers gradually improved their economic conditions and moved out of Harlem.

After World War II hundreds of Haitian women were recruited to work as domestic help, particularly as sleep-in maids in Washington, D.C., Evanston, Ill., Los Angeles, and upstate New York. Some brought relatives with them to the United States. The women did not plan to settle permanently in the United States but few ever returned to Haiti.

The fourth major period of Haitian emigration started in 1957 when François "Papa Doc" Duvalier was elected President of Haiti. By that time, Duvalier's two predecessors in office, Paul Eugène Magloire and Daniel Fignolé had settled in Queens and Brooklyn with some of their followers. Other politicians who hoped for a return to power remained on the island until "Papa Doc" was elected president for life through a manipulation of the vote in 1964. During his term in office, political persecution caused Haitian professionals, politicians, and students to leave the island in large numbers. Many came individually to the United States, but once here they sent for their immediate families, relatives, and friends.

From 1957 to 1964 many upper- and middle-class Haitians entered the United States. In the early 1960s about 50 percent of gainfully employed Haitian immigrants were professional or white-collar workers. From 1964 to 1971, when Papa Doc died and his son Jean-Claude replaced him, also as president for life, the volume of urban middle-class immigrants grew, stimulated by a liberal American policy promoting family reunion. In the 1970s the Haitian occupational profile changed as a greater number of semiskilled and domestic workers arrived.

In the early 1970s the "boat people" began reaching the shores of Florida after dangerous voyages in small craft. Most of them were peasants fleeing extreme rural poverty, who in some cases had been harassed by the Tontons Macoutes, the secret police force of the Duvalier government. Florida and U.S. officials apprehended many of these Creole-speaking illegal migrants, interrogated them in English which they did not understand, and sent them to jail to await eventual deportation; many of these cases are still pending appeal. Political and economic conditions in Haiti continue to drive more boat people seeking political asylum to Florida and other states along the Gulf Coast.

Rural poverty has been a constant factor spurring emigration from Haiti. Subsistence plots cultivated with the most rudimentary techniques cannot sustain a rapidly growing population. Rural Haitians flock to Port-au-Prince, where unemployment and the high cost of living impel further migration. Some travel directly to the United States; others come by way of Puerto Rico and the Bahamas, where the tourist industry offers a chance for interim employment.

The decaying position of the middle class, caused by declining productivity, decreasing overseas trade, and shrinkage of the private sector, has stimulated the departure of white-collar workers, educators, and professionals. Disagreement with the political policies of the Duvaliers also swells the number of Haitians arriving in the United States.

SETTLEMENT PATTERNS IN NEW YORK CITY

The Haitians in New York City live chiefly in three boroughs: 30 percent live in Manhattan, between West 86th Street and Cathedral Parkway from Columbus Avenue to the Hudson River; 50 percent live in Brooklyn, particularly in Crown Heights, Park Slope, Bedford-Stuyvesant, Brownsville, and East New York; and 20 percent are in Queens in Corona, Jamaica, Elmhurst, Jackson Heights, and Cambria Heights. These concentrations reflect not only the desire of Haitians to live near relatives and countrymen, but also their need to find cheap housing. Manhattan functions as a way station where newly arrived immigrants may spend several years before moving to Brooklyn or Queens. In the view of Haitians, Brooklyn, Manhattan, and Queens reproduce in New York the social stratification of Port-au-Prince: Brooklyn is referred to by Haitians as "La Saline," a slum district of Port-au-Prince; Manhattan is called "Bois Verna," Port-au-Prince's residential district; Queens is known as "Petionville," the fashionable quarter of the light-skinned class.

SOCIAL ADJUSTMENT AND PROBLEMS

Speaking only Creole, often illiterate, and accustomed to rural life, the lower-class immigrants who arrive in Manhattan are abruptly transplanted into a radically different urban world. At a time of considerable unemployment, they experience great difficulty in finding well-paying jobs. Many have to hold two jobs; unskilled factory work during the day is often supplemented by an unskilled evening job. They have to save to repay debts incurred before emigration, to help relatives in Haiti, to defray the legal expenses of obtaining a visa, and finally, to pay the passage of a spouse, children, or grandparents to the United States. Several im-

migrants often share a single room or stay with relatives who are already established. When their families finally join them they usually settle in the poorest quarters of Brooklyn.

The language barrier and their illegal immigrant status are major problems that confront both the professional and the peasant. Many Haitians take night courses in "English as a second language," but these are designed primarily for Spanish-speakers and are of little help to speakers of French or Creole. A Haitian professional who has mastered English sometimes enrolls in evening courses to obtain equivalent American diplomas. Some seek assistance from the American Council for Émigrés in the Professions, but most are wary of official agencies; many are exploited by dishonest lawyers who demand large sums of money in advance. In order to legalize their status, some young Haitian women pay for an arranged marriage with a U.S. citizen.

The younger generation assimilates more quickly, so that the lack of communication and misunderstanding between parents and children create a new set of tensions. Haitian children go to American schools, learn English, and acquire English-speaking friends, but their parents prefer to follow Haitian traditional culture, speak Creole and French at home, and maintain their friendships with the people whom they knew in Haiti.

Haitian women of all classes are gainfully employed; often they earn more than their husbands, which causes further tension in the family.

Many Haitian families in the United States lack some family members who are still in Haiti waiting for the chance to migrate. But despite the slow process of family reunion, the Haitian family in the United States is a strong and adaptive unit. Family members supply economic and emotional support to one another; links with relatives in Haiti are sustained by remittances and letters. Young children are often sent to the home island to be raised by their maternal grandmothers.

ECONOMIC LIFE

Legal immigrant status and educational qualifications are key determinants of Haitians' economic position in the United States. The average annual family income of educated, legal immigrants was $13,000 in the late 1970s; that of illegal immigrants was around $8,000.

In New York City the majority of Haitians are employed in low-paying factory and maintenance jobs. However, a number of Haitian entrepreneurs have established family-run restaurants, record shops, groceries, laundromats, dry cleaners, garages, and travel and real-estate agencies.

Many Haitian factory workers participate in *Sann,* a rotating credit association. Sann serves as an informal savings and loan agency for the illegal immigrant; those with legal status also use it as a quick source of capital for investment purposes. Haitians often play the numbers game, which they call *borlette* after the legal lottery in Haiti. Numbers are sold in Haitian restaurants, retail stores, bookstores, and record shops.

To help ease the adjustment of Haitian immigrants, the City of New York in 1967 funded a Haitian Neighborhood Service Center, directed by a Haitian; it offers instruction in English, legal advice, and a job placement service. Each year 6,000 Haitians have used the services of this facility. In 1969 a Haitian Community Center opened in Brooklyn to assist less educated, Creole-speaking Haitians to learn English and obtain skilled training. Other organizations have been established to help ease the process of adjusting to life in New York. The Diocese of Brooklyn has created the Haitian Apostolate to provide information and advice to immigrants; 12 Haitian Catholic priests are available to provide assistance in Brooklyn, Queens, and Manhattan.

Although the problems of employment and acculturation are similar for professionals and peasants, their responses to these problems differ. Peasant or working-class immigrants in New York find their new life scarcely easier than their old. They are sustained, however, by the prospect of upward mobility in American society, and especially by the opportunity to educate their children. Hard work, frugal habits, and the postal money order sent monthly to relatives back home express a steadfast determination to achieve economic progress and to establish their families securely in American society.

Middle-class Haitians, in contrast, do not appear as eager for full assimilation. Transplantation to a new environment inflicts upon them a loss of social and economic status; they take refuge in the New York Haitian subculture and the dream of returning home one day. Even those immigrants who manage to obtain U.S. credentials and practice their chosen profession suffer a profound disorientation: the proud citizens of the first black republic, the descendants of Toussaint L'Ouverture, have become a racial minority group in the United States. Some Haitian mulattos declare themselves "white" on census schedules; black middle-class Haitians speak French or Creole to each other in public places, or when speaking English may exaggerate their French accent to make sure that they are not mistaken for American blacks.

For both middle-class and working-class Haitians, language and culture inhibit understanding between themselves and black Americans, who find Haitian customs unusual and the accent puzzling. Haitian newcomers often feel segregated from whites by their color, and cut off from American blacks by their culture.

Although many middle-class Haitians tend to cling tightly to their French traditions as guideposts during a difficult period of transition, some are prompted by the difficulties of adaptation to reexamine their heritage. Some Haitians have developed the view that the French language and culture are "excess baggage" in New York, a mere vestige of colonialism serving no useful purpose. Radical émigré political groups denounce the "white soul and the black mask" of the Haitian personality.

POLITICAL LIFE

In recent years New York City has become a major base for Haitian opposition politics. From 1957 when François Duvalier was elected president of Haiti until 1964 when he became President for Life, New York Haitians were divided into three major political groups: supporters of traditional democracy and the ex-President Paul E. Magloire; the Jeune Haiti group that espoused a technocratic democracy; and the MOP

(Mouvement Ouvrier-Paysan) that sought to establish a populist democracy headed by ex-provisional President Daniel Fignolé.

In 1964 the exiles (except the Fignolé supporters) decided to unite under one leader, Paul E. Magloire, and to create La Coalition Haitienne. This organization published a weekly newsletter, *Le Combattant Haitien* for about five years and broadcast a morning radio program "Vonvon." In 1970 the coalition was dismantled to form La Résistance Haitienne which attracted a broader base of popular support.

When Duvalier died in 1971 a number of Haitian presidential candidates presented themselves in New York. Antoine Colas, Henry Vixamar, Emmanuel Fordes, and Ernst Fénélon campaigned actively among the New York Haitian population. At that time various Marxist-Leninist and Maoist political groups emerged from underground activities; today they number more than thirty.

Also in 1971, a progressivist coalition, the Comité de Mobilisation, was formed to overthrow the administration of Jean-Claude Duvalier. Before the end of that year, because of internal dissent within the Comité de Mobilisation, a new coalition, Le Mouvement Haitien d'Action Patriotique, was founded on an anti-imperialist and anti-dictatorial platform. The most recent, Le Regroupement des Forces Démocratiques Haitiennes, was formed in 1977 to force Jean-Claude Duvalier out of office after he completed his six-year term.

While émigré politicians have agitated for the overthrow of the Duvalier administration, other Haitians have become eager participants in American politics. In 1968 Haitian Americans formed the Haitian American Political Organization, a group of activist Democratic party members. Haitian-American candidates for elective offices in Brooklyn and Queens have had little success; in 1977, however, during the campaign for mayor in New York City, black candidate and Manhattan Borough President Percy E. Sutton appointed a Haitian, Louis A. Brun, chairman of his "election committee on the nationalities."

Bibliography

Helpful surveys of the historical development of Haitian society are found in Sidney W. Mintz, *Caribbean Transformations* (Chicago, 1974) and James G. Leyburn, *The Haitian People*, rev. ed. (New Haven, 1966).

Articles in popular periodicals provide the most current information on the changing community of Haitian Americans in New York City. The most useful come from the daily papers in New York City. Jervis Anderson, "The Haitians of New York," *The New Yorker* (March 31, 1975), is very informative.

The first systematic study of the Haitian population in New York is an unpublished dissertation by Nina Barnett Glick, "The Formation of a Haitian Ethnic Group" (Department of Anthropology, Columbia University, 1975). It deals with institutional factors that have shaped the Haitian-American community in New York City. Also useful is Michel S. Laguerre, *Ethnicity as Dependence: The Haitian Community in New York City* (New York, 1978). Pierre-Michel Fontaine, "Haitian Immigrants in Boston: A Commentary," in Roy Bryce-Laporte and Delores Mortimer, eds., *Caribbean Immigration to the United States* (Washington, D.C., 1976), provides an overview of Haitian emigration to Boston and discusses their adaptation. *Migration Today* 7 (September 1979): 9–46, is a special issue on Haitians.

The situation of the Haitian family in the United States is discussed in Michel S. Laguerre, "The Impact of Migration on Haitian Family and Household Organization," in *Family and Kinship in Middle America and the Caribbean*, ed. Arnaud F. Marks and René A. Römer (Van Gorcum, Netherlands, 1978); and K.H. Rey, *The Haitian Family* (New York, 1970).

The status of Haitian refugees who have sought political asylum in the United States is examined in *Haitian Emigration: Report of the* Subcommittee on Immigration, Citizenship, and International Law of the Committee on the Juciciary, House of Representatives, 94th Congress (Washington, D.C., 1976).

MICHEL S. LAGUERRE

HAVASUPAIS: *see* AMERICAN INDIANS

HAWAIIANS

The ethnic designation "Hawaiian" is generally reserved for the descendants of the original Polynesian inhabitants of the Hawaiian Islands. A combination of circumstances has rendered the term ambiguous and variable in current usage, however, and it is far from clear precisely who is a Hawaiian in the contemporary world. The situation has been greatly complicated by Hawaii's history of immigration, which has produced a cosmopolitan population that includes substantial numbers of people with Polynesian, European, Chinese, Japanese, Filipino, Korean, Portuguese, or Puerto Rican ancestry as well as their various intermixed offspring. A particularly high rate of intermarriage between native Polynesian Hawaiians and immigrants has resulted in an increasing proportion of people whose ethnicity can be described as problematic. Some people regarded as Hawaiian may have only one great-grandparent of Hawaiian ancestry, while others may have nearly all Hawaiian ancestors. One person of mixed background may identify himself as Hawaiian; another of equal or greater genealogical purity may consider himself or herself something else. Some with a low proportion of Hawaiian ancestry may have had far greater exposure to traditional cultural knowledge and practices than others with a higher proportion. Furthermore, within Hawaii's multiethnic community, people of mixed ancestry tend to change their ethnicity according to circumstances. For these reasons the boundaries of the group are unclear, and official statistics pertaining to the Hawaiian population must be regarded as questionable.

A recent estimate of persons of Hawaiian or part-Hawaiian ancestry in the islands, based on a state Department of Health survey conducted in 1974–1976, is 151,-652, making them the third largest ethnic group in the state following the Caucasians (*haoles*) and Japanese Americans. In this case the criterion for inclusion was reporting one or more native Hawaiian great-grandparent. In addition, according to 1970 Census data, approximately 27,000 people of Hawaiian ancestry reside on the mainland, more than half of them in California. This article discusses only Hawaiians and part-Hawaiians living in Hawaii. (For those on the mainland, *see* Pacific Islanders.) It is not clear how ethnic ties and ethnic identity have changed among Hawaiian migrants to California. Having a greater familiarity with the American way of life to begin with, they have had an easier adjustment than the Samoans and Tongans with whom they are sometimes confused.

The initial colonization of the Hawaiian Islands took place some 1,500 years ago by Polynesian voyagers, mostly from the Marquesas Islands more than 2,000 miles to the south. A subsequent immigration from Tahiti is believed by archaeologists to have contributed to their cultural development. The settlers thrived in the benign environment; by the time Captain James Cook

discovered the islands for Europe in 1778 the population had grown to approximately 300,000.

The Hawaiian language is a branch of Eastern Polynesian, which includes among other tongues Tahitian, Marquesan, Easter, and New Zealand Maori. In the absence of a written language, oral traditions played a great role in perpetuating cultural tradition and practices. At the time of the first European contact the Hawaiian social system was highly stratified, with a sanctified class of chieftains (alii); a class of specialists (kahuna) who controlled vital knowledge in arts and crafts, medicine, and religion; and a class of commoners (makaainana) who made up the bulk of the population. There was also a small pariah group (kauwa) of individuals who were regarded as ritually impure and degraded. The religious concepts of mana and kapu supported the status system. Mana refers to potency; it is power derived from the gods and genealogically inherited. The concept of kapu (taboo) refers to ritual avoidances, on the one hand, and the requirement for obeisance to persons possessing mana on the other. Failure to comply with taboos resulted in the imposition of supernatural as well as secular sanctions.

Among chiefs primogeniture was the principle for determining status, with first-born children of first-born parents taking precedence. Respect for rank based on genealogical seniority permeated the entire social system and was fundamental for ordering social relations. Even within families children were required to be deferential to their elder siblings. Among commoners, however, the importance of rank was complemented by a strong emphasis on affiliation and the maintenance of interpersonal harmony. Reciprocity between kinsmen was basic to the functioning of the extended family (ohana), which depended on a continual exchange of goods and services for its well-being. Chiefs functioned as redistributive agents within the economic structure, drawing from their subjects food and other commodities that they returned in the form of favors and ceremonial feasts. In general, the value of material goods was subordinate to the significance of social relationships; transactions were aimed primarily at affirming existing relationships and consolidating new ones. Generosity —the willingness to share what one had—was a primary virtue.

The extended family was rooted in the land (aina) of a particular locality and functioned as a corporate group for many purposes. It was the responsibility of the senior male to supervise the affairs of the group. He presided over family councils and exercised authority in such matters as worship, communal work, entertaining strangers, welcoming visiting chiefs, and other activities involving member households. The socialization of children was largely a concern of the extended family rather than the individual household, with all available elders taking responsibility for teaching children basic skills such as fishing, weaving, farming, and building. Adoption of related children was a common practice. Social harmony among family members was reinforced by a variety of customs and symbols, while conflicts were deterred by the threat of supernatural intervention.

The arrival of Europeans and the opening of the previously isolated islands to the outer world had disastrous effects on the Polynesians and the society they had evolved. In 1819, a year before the arrival of the first Congregational missionaries from New England, the traditional religious system was dramatically overturned when Liholiho, son of the recently deceased Kamehameha and heir to the position of premier chief, or king, of the islands, broke some sacred taboos at a public feast. Along with the traders who swarmed to the islands, the missionaries wrought further great changes. They vigorously attacked many traditional Hawaiian practices and attempted to replace them with Yankee beliefs and customs. Commercialization of the economy led the chiefs to engage in trading and to claim rights in land, fishing grounds, and other valuable property that went well beyond traditional prerogatives. Pressure to make land available to aliens resulted in a redefinition and reallocation of land rights in 1848, in which less than 30,000 out of some 4 million acres were awarded to native tenants. The remainder were set aside for approximately 250 chiefs, designated as crown lands of the Hawaiian monarch, or placed in the public domain. By sale and lease, crown and public lands increasingly came under the control of foreigners, and many Hawaiians were enticed into disposing of their land for trivial sums. Combined with the demoralizing effects of depopulation from European diseases and other wrenching changes, this had a shattering effect on Hawaiian society, particularly on the welfare of the common people.

Like most Pacific Islanders who had been isolated for centuries and lacked immunity to newly introduced diseases, the Hawaiians suffered a tragic decline in population following contact with the West. The first official census of the islands in 1853 reported a total of 71,019 native Hawaiians, less than a quarter of the number who dwelt there before the Europeans came. The decline continued until 1910 when the total Hawaiian population, including those of mixed ancestry, dropped to 38,547. As a result of depopulation and the massive immigration of aliens brought to work on the sugar plantations that were established in the mid-19th century, Hawaiians became a minority group in their own land, and by 1900 Hawaiians and part-Hawaiians constituted altogether only 24.4 percent of the population. The proportion continued to decline despite the fact that absolute numbers began to increase at a rapid rate after 1910.

A high rate of intermarriage between Hawaiians and immigrants resulted in an increasing proportion of people with mixed ancestry. As early as 1853 nearly 1,000 people were listed in the census as "part native." By the close of the century the number of Hawaiians of mixed ancestry recorded in the census had increased to nearly 10,000, constituting more than a quarter of all Hawaiians in the islands, and by 1930 they exceeded those claiming to be "pure" Hawaiians. From 1930 through 1960 the U.S. Bureau of the Census classified those with any Hawaiian ancestry as part-Hawaiian. The category therefore had a residual quality, inasmuch as persons with any degree of Hawaiian ancestry not eligible for inclusion in other groups were so classified. The 1960 Census showed 10,502 Hawaiians and 91,597 part-Hawaiians resident in the state of Hawaii, composing 1.7 and 14.5 percent of the population respectively. In 1970, however, people of mixed ancestry were classified either by self-identification or by race of father, and

the part-Hawaiian category was dropped. The census report for 1970 is therefore not comparable with previous ones; it shows 71,274 Hawaiians forming 9.3 percent of the state's population. This compares with a health department estimate for the same year of 135,152, or 18.3 percent of the population, using the criterion of one or more native Hawaiian great-grandparents. A count based on language other than English spoken in the home during a person's childhood (but not necessarily by the respondent) yielded an estimate of 18,700.

Demographic data compiled according to ethnic designation in Hawaii for 1970 show the Hawaiians to have an exceptionally high fertility rate, more than double the state average; their median age was 20.8 years. Despite a drift to the city of Honolulu over the years, the strongholds of Hawaiian ethnicity remain in non-plantation rural and semirural areas, especially in relatively remote subsistence communities, on cattle ranches, and in Hawaiian homestead communities.

Contrary to its avowed purpose of rehabilitating Hawaiians by returning them to the soil, the Hawaiian Homes Commission Act of 1920 promoted movement to urban areas, partly because the areas allocated for homesteading were marginal lands unsuitable for farming; as a result most have been leased by wage-earners for house sites. Over half the lessees now reside on the island of Oahu within commuting distance of Honolulu. Within Honolulu itself, Hawaiians have always been the most widely and evenly distributed of all the ethnic groups.

A 1976 needs-assessment study of the Hawaiian people revealed that, although the population as a whole is not a depressed one, segments of it are. The findings showed considerable economic differences between the Hawaiian population and other groups in the state. The percentage of non-Hawaiians in professional and managerial occupations was almost twice that of Hawaiians (18 percent compared to 10 percent). Median family income for Hawaiians was some 15 percent below the state average. Approximately one-fifth of the families had incomes below the poverty line, and 22.0 percent received welfare aid in 1975 compared to 13.5 percent for the state as a whole. Nor did Hawaiians fare as well as other groups on most health indicators. Death rates at all ages were higher than rates for the general population. Hawaiians also have higher rates of specific conditions such as cancer, diabetes, coronary heart disease, prematurity, infant mortality, and congenital malformations. Other problems were noted in housing, education, and the law.

As a consequence of their overrepresentation on indexes categorized as social problems, Hawaiians have been a prime target population for various health, education, and welfare programs. Implementation of these programs has raised issues over the viability of Hawaiian traditions and customs. On the one hand, some commentators assert that Hawaiian culture is dead and that these social problems are the consequences solely of economic impoverishment. They point to the demise of the Hawaiian language (which is spoken only in isolated rural enclaves) and the disappearance of most other formal cultural practices. They advocate providing Hawaiians with better educational and economic opportunities so that they can more rapidly assimilate into the local middle-class society. On the other hand,

some see in the Hawaiian people a uniqueness that derives from their Polynesian past. Despite the loss of much of their cultural heritage and the acknowledged corruption of Hawaiian art and music displayed to tourists in Waikiki, many important values that formed the underpinnings of traditional Hawaiian life still show considerable vigor. Those of this persuasion advocate a revitalization of Hawaiian ethnicity and a unification of the Hawaiian community for the purpose of preserving the Hawaiian lifestyle.

A three-year study of a working-class Hawaiian homestead community on Oahu revealed that traditional principles guide the behavior of many contemporary Hawaiians. These researchers found that the people they studied placed a strong emphasis on affiliative values and deemphasized individual achievement. One manifestation of this commitment was a tendency among the residents to choose to invest resources in social relations rather than in the accumulation of material wealth. The more money people had at their disposal, the more they tended to expand the number of people in their households and personal networks. Extended families were prevalent in the community, and nearly one-third of the households contained children who were adopted, usually in accordance with traditional practices. Exchanges of food, labor, and other commodities between households were common. The researchers also documented the persistence of traditional supernatural beliefs and the practices associated with them.

Although the traditional social structure based on genealogical priority completely disappeared following the overthrow of the Hawaiian monarchy in 1893, seniority remains an important principle for allocating privileges and responsibilities, particularly among kinsmen. At the community level, however, leadership has been fluid and increasingly has been based on accomplishment. For some time following annexation to the United States in 1898, Hawaiian politicians, in alliance with the Caucasian elite, were a prominent force in the islands. This changed after World War II when political control of the islands shifted to Asian Americans; for most of the 1950s and 1960s Hawaiians as a group were politically passive.

The 1975 state legislature included seven representatives and three senators of Hawaiian background, and in 1976 the first Hawaiian representative, Dan Akaka, was elected to the United States Congress.

Sparked by a number of political issues and encouraged by the rise of ethnic militancy on the mainland, a revitalization movement developed among Hawaiians in the 1970s. Led by the younger, relatively well-educated segment of the population, several organizations have taken root that champion Hawaiian social, political, economic, and cultural causes. Interest in traditional art and musical forms, in the Hawaiian language, and other aspects of the cultural heritage amounts to a genuine renaissance and has become the focus of a revitalized ethnic identity.

But the central theme for militant Hawaiians has been the alienation of land and its abuse. In the mid-1970s Kahoolawe, an uninhabited island, but a place of social significance for many Hawaiians, became a symbol of the Hawaiian cause. The island is used by the U.S. Navy for target practice. In defiance of legal orders,

groups of young militants led by Walter Ritte and Emmett Aluli, occupied Kahoolawe for brief periods, forcing the navy to halt the practice bombing and in the process drawing national attention to their cause. They are leaders of an organization known as the Protect Kahoolawe Ohana, an outgrowth of a group founded in 1973 on the island of Molokai to fight for more public beaches. The organization has spread throughout the islands and is concerned with redressing the political, economic, and cultural grievances of the native Hawaiians.

At a conference in 1976 sponsored by the Council of Hawaiian Organizations, five common goals were defined and given priority: to achieve self-determination through establishing and maintaining political influence in the state of Hawaii; to establish a land base for use by native Hawaiians; to ensure that the educational system adequately provides for what the Hawaiian people define as their needs; to achieve economic self-sufficiency; and to strengthen the spirit of *ohana* (family) and *puwalu* (cooperation) through the establishment of a communication system. The first edition of the *Native Hawaiian*, a newsletter reporting on issues concerning the Hawaiian people, was published in Honolulu in June 1977.

From the very beginning Hawaiians were receptive to outsiders and assimilated them through marriage, adoption, and neighborliness. The values placed upon generosity and *aloha* were extended to all, with the result that group boundaries were not clearly marked—by race, by language, or by culture. This has posed a serious problem for those who are attempting to mobilize the Hawaiian community for political purposes. As a rallying point some incipient leaders have encouraged antagonism toward groups in power, particularly the haoles, who have come to the islands in increasing numbers since Hawaii became a state in 1959. These leaders perceive mainland haole immigration as the primary cause of social, political, and economic changes that have disrupted their lifestyle, and they direct their anger accordingly. The critical problem for Hawaiians today appears to be the need to define what is central to their ethnic identity, so that they can mobilize effectively to pursue their common goals. Once this has been determined, it is likely that commitment to those goals will become a mechanism for preserving Hawaiian ethnicity.

Bibliography
For an account of traditional Hawaiian society, see E.S. Handy and Mary Kawena Pukui, *The Polynesian Family System in Ka'u, Hawaii* (Wellington, New Zealand, 1958). The social history of Hawaii following discovery is well told by Francine Gray in *Hawaii: The Sugar-Coated Fortress* (New York, 1972); Andrew Lind, *Hawaii's People* (Honolulu, 1967), provides useful sociological and demographic data. The effects of acculturation are explored in Ernest Beaglehole, *Some Modern Hawaiians* (Honolulu, 1939). Three more recent studies, Ronald Gallimore, Joan Boggs, and Cathie Jordan, *Culture, Behavior and Education: A Study of Hawaiian-Americans* (Beverly Hills, Calif., 1974); Ronald Gallimore and Alan Howard, eds., *Studies in a Hawaiian Community* (Honolulu, 1968); and Alan Howard, *Ain't No Big Thing: Coping Strategies in a Hawaiian-American Community* (Honolulu, 1974), treat various aspects of the contemporary scene.

ALAN HOWARD

HEALTH BELIEFS AND PRACTICES

Beliefs about maintaining health and curing sickness are part of the culture of any group. They stem from the world view, symbols, values, and patterns of social conduct that together constitute the essence of the life of the group, its ethnic identity, and its adaptations to one of life's major concerns—health, along with its corollaries, sickness, mental illness, and death. Health beliefs are integral to virtually every person's daily life. They merge with, and are often difficult to differentiate from, other beliefs that govern behavior in such areas as religion, ritual, and relations among kin. Routine principles, usually unexamined, guide therapeutic activities and make up the practical strategies used to manage health problems effectively.

A few important distinctions will be helpful in the discussion that follows. First, beliefs and practices vary widely. People have all sorts of ideas about the nature of health and sickness—for example, that colds are caused by "germs" or an imbalance of "hot" and "cold" qualities in the body. They also have beliefs about how healthy they are and how best to stay that way, and about how to label and categorize various symptoms. When people decide they are sick, yet another set of beliefs determines how they will act and the choices they will make among the various remedies or nostrums available to them. Finally, beliefs help determine how people evaluate the efficacy of the treatment they choose.

Health beliefs fall generally into two categories: those concerned with preventing sickness, and those involved in treating sickness when it occurs. Cures can involve both technologic treatments (such as massage, herbs, drugs, or surgery) and symbolic treatments (such as rituals or talk therapies) or frequently both. All social groups for whom there are adequate medical ethnographic data have ways of controlling, and culturally approved ways of explaining, both dysfunctional behavior and ill health.

Most important, what is known about the health beliefs and practices of American ethnic groups parallels knowledge about the historical experiences of the groups themselves. Although similarities among group beliefs abound, in most cases a result of the widespread influence of the scientific medical system and its success in curing disease, the impact of scientific medicine has been restricted to the last 60–70 years. There are still many differences among groups, closely linked to the maintenance of other cultural traditions within these groups. Two factors in particular contribute to the diversity of American health beliefs and practices: the homeland medical cultures of immigrant groups, and American folk medicine—an amalgam of medical traditions existing in the United States prior to the 20th century.

Members of American ethnic groups who come into contact with orthodox medicine that differs significantly from their traditional practices will often react by ignoring the treatment prescribed, or misusing it, or complaining about the quality of the care they are getting. The results are generally poor. Nevertheless, almost everyone eventually does come into contact with the medical profession, and in the process acquires still other beliefs and practices which are then added to the ethnic and popular store of health notions. The results are considerably less coherent than those in a traditional cultural setting; they often diverge across family and individual lines, even within the same local ethnic group. A general description of ethnic health beliefs is

possible, although one must realize that, in practice, they cannot be categorized so neatly.

It is important to distinguish between immigrants and their U.S.-born descendants. Migrants who come as adults arrive already equipped with a full set of values, beliefs, and cures learned in their native land. Chinese immigrants, for example, bring with them a well-developed medical system based on internal balance, and migrants from Latin America continue to treat ailments according to "hot-cold" health beliefs which derive from medieval European humoral pathology. Although they may adopt some of the precepts of scientific medicine, their basic perspective may never change and may continue to influence their behavior. Home remedies based on these ethnic medical theories are the most likely to be retained; many of these persist even into the second and later generations, especially those practices pertaining to common ailments that are not often subject to the scrutiny of a physician. As the later generations grow up they begin to rely more on the scientific medical system, but folk elements still persist in such matters as home remedies for "colds" and ways of treating minor injuries and burns. They may also persist in beliefs about the efficacy of local folk practitioners, and more generally in attitudes toward achieving the "good" life and maintaining health.

These beliefs are largely determined by the state of the medical system in the homeland. People whose ethnic heritage is non-European will be most apt to vary from mainstream American beliefs and will retain their differences even after many generations. Within the European immigrant groups, those from southern Europe are likely to retain folk notions, such as a belief in the evil eye. Variations between southern and northern Europe seem to originate in the different emphases the two regions have traditionally placed on scientific medicine, as well as differences in degree of exposure to scientific medicine in the United States. A strong agrarian peasant tradition lasted much longer in southern Europe, while the greater exposure of northern Europeans to the medical establishment has helped erode indigenous popular medical beliefs. Since the poor are usually the least likely to come into contact with professional medicine and the most likely to rely on family and ethnic remedies, they maintain their native theories much longer.

THE FOLK MEDICAL HERITAGE

Some of the complexity of America's folk medical heritage may be illustrated by examining historic changes among American Indians, blacks, and European whites. Changes in American Indian health practices must be spoken of in terms of Europeanization, or Westernization, rather than immigration and assimilation. Tribal diversity underlies a variety of health systems and beliefs, but tribal beliefs all have some points in common, and the isolated position of American Indians in the United States has led them to hold on to their belief systems. Virtually all Indian groups believe that the universe has a basic harmony. The human, the natural, and the supernatural worlds are interconnected; any disruption in this delicate balance can cause ill health and other misfortunes, while good health is maintained through their harmonious integration. This perspective is reflected in the Indians' belief in the importance of maintaining good relationships with their fellow men, with nature, and with the spiritual world. It is also a view at variance with the premises of medical science—namely, biological reductionism, mind-body dichotomy, and denial of the influence of any supernatural force.

American Indian groups in North America once had an extremely varied pharmacopeia, consisting mainly of potions made of ingredients from their natural environment. The Indians' skill made such a great impression on early settlers, both black and white, that until the rapid expansion of modern scientific medicine in the 20th century, Indian remedies were an important component in the treatment of illness throughout the United States. Some white doctors of the time even based their claims to competence on their studies with local Indians, and many of the remedies they learned are still common in the rural areas of the American Southeast.

The Afro-Americans arrived with their own distinctive health beliefs and practices, but the conditions they encountered and their forced dispersal under the slave system undermined their native therapeutic systems. Like the immigrant whites who surrounded them, blacks retained family health practices, borrowed new practices from the Indians, and relied in part on white doctors for their health care. African folk practices were more strongly retained on the Caribbean islands, and contact between island and mainland populations contributed to the persistence of the belief that malevolent magic may cause illness. Various forms of this magic, of which voodoo and rootwork are the best known, are still common among poor blacks in rural and inner-city settings.

Medical traditions among northern European settlers were based on the beliefs and practices current in Europe when the emigrants departed. They derive ultimately from Greek medicine as codified by Galen in the second century after Christ, which continued for centuries to form the basis for European folk and professional medicine. For example, sweating and blood-letting were considered effective methods for removing excess heat from the body; poultices were used to draw out impurities that might be causing a rash; and diet and exercise helped balance the "humors."

Combined with practices learned from the American Indians, an American folk medicine emerged that remained in common use until the late 19th century and that is the source of a large portion of the popular health beliefs that are still common today. From it derive the purgatives, "health foods," tonics, and other home remedies that form part of the medical repertory of many Americans. Attention to "signs" in nature—the belief that plants and other organisms symbolically reveal in their color or shape the kinds of disorders they can cure—comes from this source as well. Natural phenomena (for example, the configuration of the planets) are "read" to determine times that are propitious for undergoing medical or dental procedures. There is also a doctrine of maternal impressions, which holds that the mother's behavior determines the characteristics of the child—for example, the mother should visit museums, libraries, and the like to increase the intellectual powers of the baby or should not worry excessively about an ill person or the child might get sick. Faith healing and other religious practices are also part of the same tradition.

Beliefs and practices from American folk medicine have become mixed with and modified by scientific medicine, as it is understood by the layman. Exposure to scientific, or at least scientific-sounding, statements about medical "breakthroughs," new pills or therapeutic techniques, and various health-promoting practices through the popular press and television has provided a certain leveling of differences across ethnic-group lines. Mexican and Mexican-American migrant farm laborers might well use talcum powder poultices for "fallen fontanelle" (caída de la mollera) at home, but they will still demand penicillin from the doctor. The Amish, who eschew most modern conveniences in their daily lives, do not refuse the use of x-rays and modern surgical techniques in a hospital.

TYPES OF HEALTH SYSTEMS

The somewhat confusing array of medical ideas found in the contemporary United States can be categorized to some extent by identifying types of health systems. For example, conventional or legitimated medical care is part of the professional health-care system that is built upon scientific beliefs and practices related to health and illness. Sicknesses in this system are viewed as "diseases" that are classified and explained in Western biological and medical terms and confirmed by modern scientific methods. Treatment is delivered by orthodox health professionals such as doctors and nurses and by heterodox specialists such as chiropractors and osteopaths.

Another type is the cluster of folk health-care systems identified with particular cultural groups such as Hispanics or American Indians. The indigenous folk healers who are specialists know how to diagnose and treat "illnesses"—sickness as experienced, reacted to, and explained by the sick individual. The health beliefs and practices of folk healers such as curanderos (curer), rootworkers, espiritistas (spiritualist), herbalists, and faith healers tend to be more formal and systematic than those of the lay members of the ethnic group. The terms of their trade and the methods they use are often not understood by their clients, and this secrecy often adds to their potency. It is not uncommon to find folk healers of one ethnic group treating patients from another. The presence of folk healers can help to maintain ethnic beliefs and practices, and their absence can be associated with the loss of ethnic healing ways.

Knowledge about the professional and folk health-care systems is essential for understanding some of the health beliefs and practices of American ethnic groups. However, only 10 to 30 percent of all sicknesses in America are treated by formal medical practitioners, and folk healers are called in by only a portion of the people not seen by doctors. Thus, most sickness is taken care of in the popular health-care system: within family and neighborhood settings, using beliefs and practices handed down in families, learned from folk healers, and gleaned from popularizations of scientific medicine.

A combination of notions about the nature of sickness and its source determines the particular treatment chosen—diet, herbs, patent medicines, charms, incantations, healing rituals, or folk healers—and provides rough criteria for evaluating their results. The cultural perspective organizes each episode of sickness into a typical form that can be analyzed in terms of the beliefs and values of the particular group member involved.

Cultural beliefs about health and sickness have their own vocabulary for recognizing, labeling, and treating sickness. These special languages are found everywhere, but in the United States non-Western ones are most noticeable because they frequently diverge so sharply from the language of the medical scientist. Labeling sickness susto (fright) or "blues" reflects a range of popular ethnic beliefs regarding its source: "catching cold," the evil eye, witchcraft, spirit possession, a weak constitution, or exposure to "wind."

A wide range of social and cultural factors also influence how people take care of their health and respond to sickness. Sickness involves the popular beliefs and practices not only of the person afflicted but often of his family, neighbors, friends, coworkers, and community. At each of these levels socioeconomic and geographic differences can cut across ethnic similarities. Beliefs about illness may be influenced by past experience with sickness and its treatment, the degree of familiarity with biomedical and American folk-medical approaches, the availability of and proximity to resources, the nature and severity of the problems, and the family status and social role of the afflicted person. Factors such as the degree of assimilation, educational background, financial status, and occupation also influence reactions to illness.

While health beliefs and practices among all Americans are of interest, those identifiable as belonging to particular ethnic groups are especially significant because they are frequently so closely tied to people's lives that they can provide general insight into the nature of ethnicity in the United States. Maintenance of boundaries with respect to other ethnic groups may hinge in part on noticeable similarities or differences in health beliefs and practices. The processes of acculturation can be documented by tracing the changes in the health practices that people choose to follow.

HEALTH AND HEALTH MAINTENANCE

Health tends to be taken for granted, not only by individuals but also in the very fabric of society. Social roles are related to each other on the assumption that each person is well enough to play a part; health is usually called into question only in its absence. Yet most people conduct their daily lives in ways they hope will maintain and promote good health. Beliefs and practices relating to health maintenance can be seen in the most mundane but frequently the most telling ways, by looking at everyday situations: social relationships and activities, work, eating, rest, recreation, and so on.

The notion of the importance of balance or harmony that is common to American Indians, for example, influences their social behavior as well. They conceive of the universe as a harmonious whole and believe that health results from maintaining that harmony, by observing a number of taboos and by holding group ceremonies called "sings" each year. Failure to fulfill an obligation, or a personal rebuff in a relationship, can be the prelude to bad feelings that disrupt harmony and that are believed to be a potential cause of illness; maintaining good relations with others is thus another way of ensuring continued good health.

Other groups have similar beliefs about the connec-

tion between health and harmonious social relations. Sicilians and others from southern Europe take care to sustain respectful relations with people thought to have spiritual and occult powers and the ability to harm others; the curses of these people are believed to cause illness or death. Some Afro-Americans and Haitians also avoid trouble—and sickness—by maintaining their distance from strangers who may turn to "root doctors" or other witchcraft experts for retribution.

Food is a universal component of health maintenance and is used in a variety of ways. Traditional Asians and Mexican Americans, for example, believe that food has qualities that promote or upset the internal balance of the body. In Chinese medicine, Yin foods and Yang foods must be carefully balanced to retain a stable relationship between Yin and Yang elements in the body; imbalance can cause illness. A beef dish with "hot" or Yang qualities will include selected vegetables with Yin or "cold" qualities. Tea is neutral, and a balancing item is unnecessary. Mexican Americans pay similar attention to the "hot" and "cold" qualities in their diets in order to maintain a healthy balance in the body.

Certain foods can also be specifically prescribed or proscribed. Proscriptions often turn up in the form of the taboos found in ethnic sayings. Among Southern whites and blacks, for example, it is believed that eating red meat will give one high blood pressure; eating carrots will produce a clear skin; eating oysters will increase potency in men. Other beliefs are associated with pregnancy and the first few weeks following delivery. Southern whites who maintain ideas about "maternal impressions" believe that a pregnant woman with a craving for some particular food must not touch herself until the craving is satisfied or she will cause a birthmark on the baby. Pregnant Mexican-American women avoid "hot" foods such as chile or beans because these make the baby susceptible to diaper rash (chincual). After the child is born, the mother avoids "cold" foods such as tomatoes, citrus juices, pork, or cucumbers because they might cause varicose veins. Food taboos are supposed to prevent specific conditions. The effects attributed to prescribed foods are more generalized. Chicken soup among the Jews is a notable example of a food believed to possess general tonic, restorative, and therapeutic qualities. The herbal teas of Appalachian whites, Asians, and Mexican Americans fall into the same category.

Most people everywhere believe that eating the right foods is essential to good health, but what these "right foods" might be varies considerably from culture to culture. Common elements in a given diet—rice among Asians, corn and beans among Latin Americans, "soul foods" among blacks, and fish among Scandinavians—are thought to be essential to good health. Among blacks, collard greens, turnip greens, kale, and spinach are healthful; whites in the same area of the South will put carrots and potatoes on such a list and not even mention kale or greens. According to popular Chinese beliefs, rice is the basis for good health because it is neutral in terms of the Yin-Yang balance. In contrast, culturally proscribed foods are believed to have illness-producing effects, such as those attributed to non-Kosher foods by Orthodox Jews.

Many people—whether part of an ethnic community or not—believe that the body must be cleaned out regularly to prevent the build-up of impurities in the sys-

tem. Phlegm, another element of traditional European humoral pathology that underlies the "hot-cold" system, is identified by many Southerners, for example, as "slime." Slime ("germs" for some people) accumulates as a residue of normal digestive processes and must be cleaned out. Over-the-counter patent purgatives such as castor oil are used for the purpose; so are herbal teas. Northern Europeans tend to relate the importance of a "balanced" diet to their bowel regularity.

Impurities must also be carefully eliminated after childbirth. Filipinos stress the importance of postpartum vaginal bleeding as a way of cleaning out the uterus. Filipinos, Mexican Americans, and other Hispanics once customarily maintained the cuarentena (quarantine), a 40-day period of restricted activity during which the new mother had to rest and allow her body to return to normal. Many other ethnic groups have similar customs regarding a postpartum period of rest and special foods, such as "doing the month" among the Chinese or the nine-day confinement among rural southern whites. They are still practiced, though difficult to maintain, in American society. Some traditional Filipinos continue the practice of "roasting" the uterus for the first nine days. The woman sits in a slotted chair over a bed of coals, which "warms" the uterus and aids its return to normal shape. Mexican-American women avoid "cold" foods after giving birth; some have their backs rubbed with a mixture of warm olive oil and powdered sulphur to keep the lungs and chest clear, because during this period women are thought to be more vulnerable to sickness. Less striking postpartum practices are maintained by members of Scandinavian and German groups to assure that mothers are protected and restored to normal "strength" during this universally accepted period of high risk. European ethnic beliefs about vulnerability during the menstrual period relate to the same concern.

Numerous symbolic methods are believed to prevent illness, including prayer, rituals, charms, and amulets hung around the neck to ward off sickness. Italians hang a charm over an infant's bed to prevent the evil eye, and adults may wear a charm around the neck for the same purpose.

A notion common among the health systems of many European ethnic groups is moderation. Asian Americans, too, believe that good health is aided by avoiding extremes of Yin and Yang, as do Hispanic Americans whose "hot-cold" system is also based on the principle of healthy moderation.

People believe that their ethnic health practices work, whether they are symbolic or technological. Since these practices are well integrated into daily life they are also easy to maintain and are therefore likely to persist. Modern medicine is learning to work within the limits of these beliefs to promote the health of ethnic patients. Practitioners in clinics serving ethnic communities increasingly modify dietary requirements to meet the demands of notions such as "hot-cold," or, recognizing the stress-reducing effects of meditation techniques, prescribe rituals such as saying the rosary for patients with hypertension.

LABELING AND EXPLAINING SICKNESS

Cultural influences on perceiving, labeling, and communicating symptoms are well documented. A particular pain must be dealt with through a cultural haze of

custom and belief before it is acted upon. Among members of ethnic groups, there are great variations in responses to pain. Italian and Jewish Americans are more apt to complain than Americans of British or Irish extraction, who tend to be much more stoic. Jews and Italians differ, however, in the cultural meaning they ascribe to pain; Italian Americans are satisfied when their pain is relieved, but Jewish Americans require an explanation of the treatment because they suspect that the medication has simply masked the symptom and left the cause untreated. Irish Americans and Anglo-Americans are much more precise in describing their pain than Italians, in part because they have a great deal of faith in the skills of the medical team and want to play an active role in helping them as much as possible.

Culture can influence both the attitude toward and labeling of symptoms. For example, psychiatrists have found that Chinese patients, especially among the immigrant generation and those living in Chinatowns, typically deny any suggestion that they may be suffering from mental disorders. They prefer to attribute their illness to physiological malfunctions and to classify them according to Chinese medical tradition. One resident of Boston's Chinatown told a psychiatrist that the causes of his discomforts were "too much cold"—a humoral imbalance—and "not enough blood," conditions that were in turn caused by a "wind" disease acquired from sexual overindulgence with prostitutes. Wind disease, not enough blood, and cold are familiar and understandable illness terms in the Chinese tradition. As explanations they avoid the stigma of mental illness —a stigma that is very powerful in Chinese culture, in part because mental illness in the family reduces the marriage chances for other family members. As a result, the Chinese often insist on labeling as physical those symptoms that psychiatrists would be more inclined to call emotional or psychosomatic. Hysterical disorders, such as attacks of paralysis or blindness in the absence of organic pathology, which are nowadays found most commonly among southern whites, Puerto Ricans, rural blacks, and other impoverished and educationally disadvantaged ethnic groups who have only recently migrated to urban areas, provide another illustration of how cultural patterns of experiencing psychosocial stress conform with beliefs that do not sanction psychological explanations.

Common physical diseases can also be given very different explanations by various ethnic groups. Among the majority, who by now have integrated biomedical ideas into their popular health systems, diseases such as bronchitis, pneumonia, and gastroenteritis are labeled more or less as their doctors have directed, but some members of ethnic groups continue to see these conditions in traditional ways and to explain them in terms of folk ideas.

Anglo-Americans, for example, frequently maintain a belief that respiratory infections, such as colds, are caused by the entry of "coldness" and "dampness" into the body. Once damp coldness is established, it may move down to the nose or chest, for example, causing such symptoms as runny nose or chest congestion.

Among Hispanic Americans, hot and cold are qualities, applied seemingly without regard for temperature. Most respiratory problems are seen as "cold." When people catch cold they explain it by pointing to occa-

sions in the recent past when they have become chilled or have been exposed to a draft. Although such an explanation is common in the mainstream culture as well, the consequences for treatment are not the same. Mexican Americans or Puerto Ricans, for example, believe that their "cold" illness should be treated with "hot" foods. Another instance of superficial similarity between Hispanic Americans and northern Europeans is the explanation of stomach aches. People seek the cause in the foods they have recently eaten, but the explanations diverge after that. Northern Europeans will reflect on the possibility of spoiled or "undigestible" food or too many spices; Hispanic Americans will locate the cause in an excess of "hot" (such as beer) or "cold" (such as honey) substances in what had just been consumed.

Among ethnic groups who have maintained their traditional sickness labels, certain symptom patterns are given names. In Hispanic American culture susto is the name given to a combination of depression, anxiety, and fright; it includes culturally approved complaints that are learned by, and specific to, this ethnic group. Shrinking penis (koro) among Chinese Americans, Windigo psychosis among certain American Indian groups, Arctic hysteria among Eskimos, spirit possession among Puerto Ricans, hexing among rural blacks, and evil eye among Italians and Greek Americans are other examples of syndromes where specific customs determine both the symptoms and the way they are manifested in the course of the disorder.

Ethnic values also establish the criteria for determining the severity of a given sickness. Asian Americans tend to regard infectious diseases as more threatening than chronic ones, and they frequently still regard tuberculosis with great dread, although in the rest of society tuberculosis has long since lost its fearful reputation. Epidemiological reality obviously accounts in part for this difference: Asian Americans have more recently encountered high mortality rates attributable to tuberculosis and other infectious diseases than have most other American ethnic groups, and chronic disorders have much more recently taken over from infections as the major cause of mortality among Asian Americans. Changes in the prevalence and severity of disease over time can alter cultural beliefs, or, more usually, diminish their significance. Ethnic beliefs about leprosy, for example, are no longer so potent, since the disorder has become rare in the United States.

While the symptoms of an illness are the same for any ethnic group, the way they are expressed can vary. Patients with chronic schizophrenia suffer auditory hallucinations in all ethnic groups, but Chinese Americans complain of being possessed by ancestral ghosts or Buddhist gods; rural whites and blacks in the South who belong to fundamentalist religious sects are possessed by the devil; and many among the American middle class will elaborate on their hallucinations in terms of popular psychology.

Cultural categories can, then, exert influence on the symptoms and explanations of sickness. It is still to be discovered whether or not they influence its course. Research on mental disorders among ethnic groups has thus far failed to demonstrate conclusively that sociocultural factors can cause mental illnesses, though many believe that they can. It is certainly clear that re-

cent immigrants, whatever their origins, are prone to severe paranoid reactions; the normal suspicions that accompany immersion in an alien culture can lead to a full-blown psychotic state with paranoid delusions. But there is no evidence that one immigrant group is more vulnerable to this disorder than another.

Ethnic health beliefs and values also influence the nature of the role the sick patient plays and the behavior expected of him. Among city-dwelling European ethnic groups, the obligations and rights of the sick person are similar to those in the mainstream of American society. Recent immigrants from South American and Asian societies sanction a sick role that fails to include at least one important component of that in the American middle class: the expectation that the sick person will seek care from a bona fide physician. For these immigrants the sick role includes a requirement for self or family-based treatment or care from an indigenous healer, a difference that can easily cause difficulties in the relations between the professional medical establishment and members of these groups.

The labeling of sickness and its treatment among ethnic groups often involve the entire family, far more than does the similar process in middle-class American society, where, except in the care of children, the individual is left to diagnose the problem and determine its treatment by himself. These more highly developed family and social-network ties are particularly binding in certain ethnic groups (southern Europeans, Arabs, and Gypsies, for example), in which sickness and its treatment often provide an occasion for the recognition and resolution of tensions among kin or friends, becoming a social, or family, affair.

Seeking Help for Health Problems

Although Americans are inclined to say that a doctor should be consulted for health problems, only 10 to 30 percent actually do so when the occasion arises. The mental processes behind seeking help are often more complex than simply getting around to calling for an appointment. People whose ethnic identity is an important part of their daily lives will act in accordance with the traditional beliefs and practices of their ethnic heritage in determining which treatments do and do not make sense. The process begins with deciding whether or not a problem exists and, if it does, diagnosing what it might be; naming and categorizing the illness determine what cure will be used, whether a healer will be called, and if so what kind. During this process people depend upon their repertoire of popular cures and past successful treatments. If older family members are around, traditional diagnoses and remedies are even more likely to be used. Illnesses that are diagnosed as magical or spiritual usually involve popular or folk approaches. *Mal ojo* (evil eye) is one of these. In a traditional Mexican-American family, a child who has been sleeping fitfully, crying without much cause, perhaps suffering from diarrhea, vomiting, or fever will probably lead the family to diagnose a case of mal ojo, caused by the admiring gaze of an adult. The glance itself is not harmful; it is the normal reaction to a child. But illness is caused by the relatively greater spiritual power of the older person against which the spiritually less developed child has few defenses. To avoid causing the reaction the admirer must touch the child; this equalizes the difference in power and prevents the illness.

When the symptoms of mal ojo occur, people try to remember who had admired the child. Knowledgeable people, usually the mother, grandmother, and other female relatives, will be called together to examine the child and suggest a remedy. If relief is still not forthcoming, a specialized healer, the *curandero* or *curandera*, will be called in. A physician will usually not be consulted; if he is, the malady will be renamed because the family has learned to anticipate an adverse reaction to this "outdated superstition." Nor is mal ojo the only possible diagnosis for these symptoms. Another possibility is fallen fontenelle, which is diagnosed if a depression is found on the top of the head.

The joint action of women is common in ethnic neighborhoods in these circumstances. They are in charge of household and family matters, especially among Latin Americans, Greeks, Italians, and Middle Easterners, and they rapidly circulate information about sicknesses in general and illness in particular households. Categories of illness and suitable cures are kept alive through this constant interchange. Information from members of these networks is frequently sought and highly valued.

Whether or not help is sought outside the family is also determined by what people find satisfying and by how the illness is labeled. If everyone agrees that the symptoms fit a folk explanation, then folk remedies or folk practitioners must be tried. All ethnic groups have illnesses that are regarded as sicknesses appropriately cured by doctors, including some that are simply so novel and frightening that scientific medical help has to be sought. These decisions are determined by the fit between the illness and the supposed competence of lay healers, folk healers, or physicians.

Northern European ethnics behave very differently. Germans and Norwegians, for example, are self-reliant, discussing sickness, if at all, only within the immediate family and frequently only as a last resort, when they are forced to take to their beds. Folk remedies are used for "colds," aching muscles, and other minor maladies, but many health problems are more likely either to be discussed with a doctor or ignored. Indeed, among members of these groups, complaining about sickness may be seen as a sign of physical or moral weakness and sickness itself may be regarded as an expected and "natural" consequence of physical labor and a "hard" life.

If a physician is to be consulted, the self-reliant northern Europeans first look for advice about which doctor to use, but they ask very few people (this narrow referral system is generally found among the middle class, regardless of ethnic background). The poor, in contrast, will consult all sorts of people. Gypsies on the East Coast, who have few stable economic resources at their disposal and whose cultural beliefs encourage them to trust only each other, have a well-developed system of communication regarding acceptable practitioners. Doctors are partly chosen for their personal qualities. If a Gypsy has been successfully cured by a particular physician or clinic, he will recommend them to others. This can occasionally result in large numbers of Gypsies flocking to the same doctor, though if another Gypsy is somehow unsatisfied or offended, word spreads equally quickly and an alternative health pro-

fessional is promptly found. This system, reasonable enough to the Gypsies, is awkward for the doctor, who often finds it impossible to deliver any kind of follow-up care.

TYPES OF ETHNIC TREATMENT

Central to ethnic health beliefs and practices is the set of home remedies used before, during, and after a professional or folk practitioner is consulted. Although such cures are numerous and varied, similarities can be found among them, often because of the common use of American folk remedies and the easy availability of patent medicines. Even when the same substance is used, however, beliefs about its efficacy may vary. One product common in descriptions of popular treatments among many ethnic groups is Vicks VapoRub. Among European groups, this pungent ointment is used because it supplies heat to the chest and because the vapor helps clear nasal passages. Latin American ethnic groups, however, have categorized it as "hot" in their "hot-cold" system, and other groups use it in conjunction with prayer, ritual, or such culturally specified materials as red flannel. The same easily accessible substance is used in different ways according to the health perspectives of its users.

Within each particular popular or folk system there are both symbolic and technologic varieties of treatment. Technologic remedies result from experimentation with substances in the environment such as herbs, plants, or patent medicines. Once established, they can be passed from generation to generation as a customary family response to symptoms of illness: the combination of honey, whiskey, and lemon for a cold is an example.

Symbolic treatments, on the other hand, require a link with an explanatory system, because their efficacy as a treatment lies in the patient's belief in that basic system. The belief that the numbers three and nine have magical meaning has been common in European societies for centuries. These magic numbers have been integrated into American folk practices and are used in a number of ethnic-group remedies. Black practitioners light three or nine candles in conjunction with prayer to treat problems ranging all the way from weight loss to back pain and menstrual irregularity.

When the cause of illness is seen to lie in the spiritual realm, treatments must be found that will not only provide relief from symptoms, but also cure the underlying spiritual problem. Puerto Ricans in New York City seek help for their health problems from a variety of sources, such as neighborhood herb shops (botánicas) and doctors, but chronic or "spiritual" illnesses send them to seek the aid of a spiritualist. In either individual or group séances, the spirit medium must locate the spiritual agent causing the illness and identify the spiritual strengths of the patient. Once the cause has been found, one or a combination of treatments must be carried out to remove the negative spiritual influence, usually through exorcism, "working the cause" (convincing the spirit to leave the person alone), or prayer and ritual, sometimes accompanied by herb or medical treatment.

Illnesses caused by spiritual powers inherent in human beings also require symbolic treatments. Beliefs in these illnesses are found in a number of ethnic groups, particularly those of eastern European, Latin American, and Mediterranean origins. Evil eye, a widespread folk illness, may be cured by a knowledgeable family member, a curer, or a religious functionary. Among Mexican Americans, cure involves a variety of symbolic actions in addition to prayer. In some cases, the Mexicans pass a sanctified palm frond over the child's body, or move an egg over the child three times while making the sign of the cross; frequently, the egg is broken into a bowl placed under the child's bed, because it is believed that the egg can act to draw off the spiritual overload. Whether or not it has can be determined the next morning by examining the egg: a slightly cooked egg, especially one that has taken the form of an eye, is evidence (along with the better condition of the patient) that the treatment has been efficacious.

The connection between symbolic and technologic treatments in an ethnic health system can be illustrated by home treatments among Asian Americans. A large part of Chinese medicine involves the use of a great variety of herbs, which are available in grocery stores and herbal shops in all Chinese communities. Herbalists practice in virtually every large American Chinatown. These herbs in Chinese medicine are supposed to work within the cosmological system based on balance. Illnesses seen to result from an abundance of Yin elements, for example, will be treated by the use of "hot" Yang substances such as chili peppers, spices, or fatty meats. Particular exercises (kung fu or tai chi) and meditation may also be used to solve the problem, because they also help restore the body's balance. People discontinue one or another aspect of the regimen when they "feel different inside," for example, when the ch'i (vital essence) in the body is altered by engaging in exercise.

Herbs in Chinese medicine are supposed to help remove poisons from the body and clean out organs that have been clogged by a Yin-Yang imbalance. The notion is common, but the Chinese see these impurities in a somewhat different way. Filipinos, whose homeland system was influenced by Chinese medicine, are less apt to mention the concept of harmony, but they also have a number of remedies for flushing the body. When family members have colds mothers may apply vinegar to "sweat the sickness out." Herbal recipes are found in many American ethnic groups, and increasingly they are entering middle-class society through health food stores and publications on natural foods and self-care.

Modern medicine is one of the few outside influences that the Amish of Pennsylvania allow within their social order, but they also retain folk elements. Amish children are susceptible to an illness known as "liver-grown" (age-wachse), an ailment also known among the Pennsylvania Germans. The two causes of this condition are sudden changes in the environment (especially in temperature) and excessive shaking during a buggy ride, causes that have parallels in other medical belief systems. Some blacks, Hispanic Americans, and southern whites believe that the natural environment can influence health. Mexican Americans know about mal aire which is sometimes seen as a magical illness, sometimes as part of the "hot-cold" system. A person who goes from a hot shower to the cold outside can contract the condition. The influence of these conditions, directly on the body or indirectly by increasing the indi-

vidual's susceptibility, is common: witness the widespread beliefs about draft- or "wind"-induced health problems among Europeans as well as among Asian immigrants.

Amish families diagnose livergrown by attempting to bring together the left arm and right foot (or the reverse) of a child lying on his stomach; if it cannot be done the diagnosis is confirmed and treatment is started. *Brauche* (sympathy healing) is the only treatment for livergrown; a symbolic practice, it consists of the silent repetition of a secret ritual formula. An older member of the community who has learned the ritual from a knowledgeable person of the opposite sex will be called upon to perform the cure; the child need not be present. Like healers in many ethnic communities, the brauche specialist is not paid for his or her services.

Popular treatments can also reflect more general cultural features. Europeans tend to be stoic and pragmatic in the face of illness. Slovak Americans and other eastern and central Europeans place value on strength (physical and moral) and perseverance; they hesitate to "run to doctors," and rely on dosages of aspirin, Vicks, or other treatments. Children are taught to be strong, to bundle up, and avoid colds. If a child becomes sick, the mother rubs him down and sends him to bed. Only under severe conditions will a doctor be consulted. Adults behave the same way. They avoid taking aspirin as long as possible, preferring to "fight" the headache. In the case of more serious ailments, doctors' prescriptions may be taken, but only for a short period to demonstrate self-reliance, a view that is often unfortunate among older people because their rejection of the dependency that necessarily results from serious illness may preclude adequate medical care.

RELATIONS WITH PRACTITIONERS

Folk practitioners are more numerous and play a much more significant role in ethnic health care than is usually appreciated. Virtually every Chinatown in major American cities has practitioners of acupuncture, herbalism, traditional massage and exercise therapies, dispensers of traditional Chinese medicines, and, usually older, people believed to have secret knowledge about remedies. In urban black neighborhoods folk healers advertise on local radio programs and in newspapers. Herbalists, religious healers, and many other folk practitioners can be found there as well. In the Puerto Rican sections of New York, botanicas which sell herbal remedies and spiritualist centers which treat psychosocial troubles are major aspects of health care for the community. Much the same is true of Mexican-American communities in the Southwest, American Indians in the Far West, and immigrants from the West Indies. Recent immigrants from Southeast Asia do not appear to have included any significant numbers of folk specialists, but it may simply be too early to have identified their presence.

Folk healers, who are unlicensed and therefore illegal, practice fairly widely. They can be divided into two not always distinguishable categories: secular and sacred. Secular folk practitioners employ technologic interventions (herbs, massage, minor surgery) and frequently practice independent of folk religious settings. Sacred folk practitioners employ psychosocial methods and practice within some religious setting. Both have important extratherapeutic functions. They are sanctioned sources of traditional belief and interpreters of ethnic tradition. They have been described as brokers who mediate between the laity and the cultural norms that govern ethnic traditions. As such they function to preserve ethnic customs by giving culturally conservative advice, strengthening weakened family bonds or threatened cultural values, and resolving new social tensions. Folk healers are also potentially important sources for introducing change into ethnic groups and for easing the process of acculturation. They often provide traditional remedies and modern treatments, such as antibiotics, aspirin, and sedatives, and may even refer their patients to the professional medical system. Although there is a great deal of anecdotal evidence that they can and often do provide effective treatment, studies of the efficacy or potential toxicity of their practices have not been well evaluated, principally because their marginal status in the official health-care system makes such studies difficult, and medically trained researchers have been slow to take either their putative efficacy or toxicity seriously enough to try.

Ethnic patients and families seek folk healers under a variety of circumstances. They may consult them early in the course of sickness for diagnosis, or they may come to them with problems of health maintenance when no sickness is present. Most commonly they resort to folk practitioners well along in the course of a particular sickness, either after popular or professional treatments have been tried and found ineffective or when the chronic nature of a disorder or its unresponsiveness to home remedies and biomedical treatment suggests a culture-specific and often sacred cause. In cities it is typical to find ethnic patients consulting professional and folk practitioners simultaneously. Puerto Rican patients may take a child with fever and diarrhea to a pediatrician for an injection of antibiotics, to a botanica for herbs, and to a spiritualist for aid in treating some supernatural cause. The availability of a wide range of folk and unorthodox professional healers in the general culture has led to increasing use of indigenous healers from other cultural traditions. Middle-class whites with chronic diseases sometimes consult Chinese herbalists or acupuncturists. In Miami, a Cuban mother might try a Puerto Rican spiritualist if Cuban healers are unable to solve her child's problem.

European ethnic groups generally do not have folk healers. But even among groups who have lived in urban neighborhoods for several generations, there are always older people who are believed to possess special knowledge of therapeutic significance who may be called on as lay advisers, especially in the treatment of childhood illnesses and women's disorders. Women, children, and the elderly are most commonly clients of ethnic folk healers; the first and the last because they are apt to be culturally more conservative and children because they are sick most often and are thought to be most vulnerable to serious and potentially fatal diseases.

Healers may or may not provide effective treatments for any particular disease; their chief contribution is their recognition and management of the life problems that illness poses, including personal, marital, family, work, financial, and related difficulties that frequently accompany sickness. Mexican-American curanderos

and Puerto Rican spiritualists both provide explanations for suffering that have personal and social meaning, as well as cosmological or supernatural significance, and attempt to ameliorate anxiety, depression, and family troubles. Since folk healers are integrated into the network of ethnic social relationships, they are well known figures in the neighborhood and are usually trusted. They deliver care personally and their ways are familiar to their patients. They can provide services essential to their patients that are unavailable in the biomedical system. In this respect, ethnic patients may have an advantage over those who do not have alternative sources of care that are ready and available to treat the problems in daily living resulting from the psychosocial burden of sickness.

Relations between folk healers and the professional health-care system are for the most part nonexistent. The latter does not officially recognize the former and, with a few notable exceptions where community clinics use curanderos or other folk healers routinely, will not refer patients to or consult with a healer. The healers might refer patients with life-threatening or complicated medical problems to the orthodox professional system, but they do so haphazardly. The relationship is best described as hidden care—sometimes complementing, sometimes conflicting, often parallel. Even some middle- and upper-income people of northern European background are beginning to seek out ethnic healers such as naturopaths, herbalists, palm readers, astrologers, and lay psychotherapists when biomedical treatment does not satisfy them.

Orthodox professional practitioners are often frankly hostile to ethnic health practices, and as a result many ethnic patients have unhappy experiences in the professional health-care system. American Indian and Asian-American patients with cultural assumptions about psychosomatic and ecological interrelationships routinely encounter biomedical professionals who operate with concepts that separate mind from body and treat the latter as a machine unrelated to its social or physical context. The resulting clash of epistemologies, though rarely mentioned, often discourages ethnic patients from seeking professional care. Patients and professionals simply construct clinical reality differently. Ethnic patients in the clinics and wards of general hospitals who believe that "hot-cold" imbalance, or sorcery, witchcraft, or "possession," is the cause of their health problems often drop out of care or fail to comply with parts of their regimen. Navaho patients may break off chemotherapy for tuberculosis to participate in traditional healing sings in their ethnic community. Because professional biomedical institutions do not encourage discussion and management of illness in ethnomedical terms, the ethnic patients themselves assume the task of integrating professional, folk, and popular medical languages and treatments, and usually have to do so surreptitiously and haphazardly.

The case of Mr. Hsu illustrates this point. A 40-year-old, first-generation Chinese-American cook, Mr. Hsu had a history of "spells" consisting of palpitations, dizziness, and sweating. When they became worse he visited the internal medicine clinic at a large urban hospital, where repeated physical examinations and other tests disclosed no abnormalities. He was told by his doctor that he had no medical disease and that his problems were psychiatric. Referred to a clinic for psychotherapy, he refused to go and complained bitterly about all the expense with no treatment: in Taiwan, where he had lived before coming to the United States, doctors were paid, he said, solely for treatment. He angrily rejected the notion that it was all in his head, nor could he or his family and friends see the point of therapy that consisted entirely of talking. Mr. Hsu thought that he was suffering from a "cold" disorder owing to loss of Yang (male principle, and therefore "hot") from too frequent intercourse with his wife, whom he had married five months earlier and who was 14 years younger than himself. He was afraid that either he would not be able to fulfill his wife's sexual needs or that he would continue to get worse because of the continued diminution of Yang through loss of *ching* (semen).

Mr. Hsu and his doctors obviously held different views of his sickness and, partly as a result, conflicting notions about proper treatment. In Chinese culture the patient pays for treatment but not for the diagnosis, and psychotherapy is regarded as worthless. Although from a psychiatrist's point of view, Mr. Hsu was probably suffering from acute bouts of anxiety neurosis precipitated by his recent marriage, from his own perspective his problem was a disorder based on a system in which he knew his physicians did not believe.

Ethnic health beliefs and practices clearly influence the nature and consequences of clinical transactions between ethnic patients and both folk and professional practitioners. The reemergence of strong ethnic affiliations in American urban neighborhoods has not been associated with clearcut ethnic stands on folk healing, but it has brought forth increasingly severe criticism of professional health-care services. Transactions with the medical profession are hampered by differences in their ways of handling disease. The ethnic patient lacks a way of reconciling his own beliefs with the treatment he receives in an impersonal, scientifically minded setting. Moreover, his reliance on strong family and kinship ties, on patron-client social relations, and on lay networks for support, advice, and help challenges the "individual patient" orientation of biomedicine and its ethnocentric and medicocentric assumptions that the doctor is most responsible for making decisions about the patient's care.

When these conflicts occur, people do not know where to turn, especially since the impersonal attitude of many physicians contrasts so strikingly with the customarily warm and personal relations they have with folk practitioners. Even totally assimilated Americans can find the psychic cost of dealing with a physician too high for all but the most serious health problems. Recent attempts have been made to alleviate this problem by using professionals who share the client group's ethnic identity and language. For example, nurses in one urban Chinatown clinic, although they cannot always speak the dialect of their patients, do take the time to use sign language or to speak slowly and simply in order to assess and respond to the personal significance of illness. Health centers serving blacks often use street language. Rural migrant health clinics now contain Chicano physicians and mental health professionals who take their patients' beliefs seriously. In American Indian clinics, practitioners are now often knowledgeable about the nuances of Indian gesture and speech. Clinics

serving recent emigrants from Vietnam, Laos, and Cambodia include interpreters and health professionals who are interested in breaking down cultural barriers to acceptable and effective care.

Attempts are also being made to translate biomedical recommendations for diet, activity, and specific treatments into culturally acceptable terms. Hypertension therapies involving major change in diet, for example, can take into account beliefs about food traditionally eaten by ethnic patients. Medical personnel are learning to identify biomedical problems in terms of complaints as expressed in folk categories. Since attitudes among many ethnic group patients militate against seeking psychiatric help, people knowledgeable about folk illnesses can deal with it in other terms. Knowing that heavy bleeding following childbirth is seen by Filipino women as useful in flushing the body of impurities can lead professionals to help them avoid excessive hemorrhage.

CONCLUSION

This essay on the health beliefs and practices of American ethnic groups reflects what we know generally about ethnic diversity in this society: that ethnic differences persist, even among groups that are considered part of the mainstream culture, and that some groups possess highly variant perspectives on health and illness. The emphasis here, however, has not been on the groups themselves, but rather on types of health-related behaviors such as preventing, labeling, and seeking care for illness. This was done to demonstrate diversity but not to suggest that the behaviors and beliefs within individual groups are homogeneous. Similarities and differences among health beliefs and practices have been shown to relate to two major influences, one cultural and the other social. Culture influences the meanings of symptoms and the ways in which health problems are treated. The social aspect is involved with how families and kin or neighborhood groups influence people's health-related behaviors, and how ethnic social expectations influence practitioner-patient relationships.

Culturally influenced ideas about the prevention, causes, and cures of illness are derived from the traditional backgrounds of ethnic groups, from a heterogeneous American folk medical system, and from scientific medical knowledge. Members of each ethnic group draw upon these sources of information to express human distress (illness, family, and financial misfortune, personal troubles, and so on) from distinctive, but shared, perspectives. Traditional folk idioms frequently combine supernatural, magical, moral, and social components to explain how individual episodes of sickness are caused and how they should be treated. American folk medicine and scientific medicine are more secular and technical, and magical and supernatural beliefs are almost completely absent in the latter system.

The specifics of traditional idioms among ethnic groups vary significantly and many have become much more biomedical through acculturation. Perspectives on sickness among northern European ethnic groups are most similar to modern medicine. With greater education, upward social mobility, and the change in values from a traditional to a modern orientation, older illness beliefs and practices give way to biomedical ones. Problems that had once been defined by ancestors as moral, social, or spiritual are frequently redefined as medical or psychological. Problems formerly dealt with by family, kinsmen, clergy, or community leaders have come to be viewed as requiring expert attention from members of the health professions.

Historical changes in ethnic illness idioms have been neither uniform nor complete. Grandmothers' remedies, magical cures, and supernatural rituals persist in varying proportions among many groups, particularly those whose members are constantly increased through immigration, and others, such as blacks and Spanish-speaking Americans, whose assimilation experience has been most frustrated. These ethnic populations have tended to maintain higher proportions of traditional beliefs than the generally more acculturated and assimilated European groups. Traditional herbs and magical ceremonies may be no more than nostalgic memories for the latter, but they are the very stuff of medicine for the former.

What has been said about the cultural idioms of sickness needs to be understood as including many elements other than esoteric beliefs and treatment practices—elements such as distinctive values that color the seriousness with which given illnesses are perceived, the style of treatment expected from professionals, and whether or not pain and suffering are passively accepted as necessary consequences of the harshness of life or actively resisted as an unacceptable state for which the individual has the right to receive help. The ethnic idioms of sickness also refer to the way the psychosocial burden of physical disease is shaped as an intimate part of concrete daily life routines and kinship networks. These are the ingredients of the mundane experience of sickness that contribute to the varied health beliefs among Irish, Scandinavian, Jewish, black, Hispanic, and Asian Americans.

Significantly, a major influence upon the degree to which an ethnic group maintains traditional illness perspectives or uses modern medicine is the historical experience and societal position of the ethnic group in the United States. The factors that have tended to promote strong ethnic identities and integrated ethnic group structures also increase the possibility that distinctive ethnic health beliefs and practices will be retained.

Bibliography
The literature on the health beliefs and practices of American ethnic groups is scanty. The following items provide an introduction. Margaret Clark, *Health in the Mexican American Culture* (Berkeley, 1970), first published in 1959, is a classic ethnography of a Mexican-American community which includes many of the major traditional beliefs and practices. Wayland Hand, ed., *American Folk Medicine* (Berkeley, 1976) introduces the reader to the approach of folklorists. Alan Harwood, *Rx: Spiritist as Needed* (New York, 1977) examines illness and curing in a Puerto Rican context. Arthur Kleinman et al., eds., *Medicine in Chinese Cultures* (Washington, D.C., 1975) is a collection of reports from specialists working with Chinese cultures throughout the world. Loudell Snow provides an extensive and useful bibliography in her article on "Folk Medical Beliefs and Their Implications for Care of Patients," *Annals of Internal Medicine* 81 (1974): 82–96. Edward Spicer, ed., *Ethnic Medicine in the Southwest*, provides an excellent introductory essay and four case studies of blacks, Mexican Americans, American Indians, and low-income Anglo-Americans. Howard Stein, "A Dialectical Model of Health and Illness Attitudes and Behavior among Slovak Americans," *International Journal of Mental Health* 5 (1976): 117–137 provides a detailed examination of perspectives on illness and cures among an eastern European group. Virgil J. Vogel, *American Indian Medicine* (New York, 1970) presents a well documented view of American Indian beliefs and practices, including the use of medicinal plants.

Mark Zborowski, "Cultural Components in Responses to Pain," *Journal of Social Issues* 8 (1952) is the classic examination of responses to pain by Jews, Italians, Irish, and "Old Americans."

NOEL J. CHRISMAN AND ARTHUR KLEINMAN

HIDATSAS: *see* AMERICAN INDIANS

HISPANIC

The term Hispanic has been increasingly employed in the media and in general discussion as an easy way to refer collectively to a growing number of Spanish-origin or Spanish-speaking people in the United States. At one time it most often designated Mexican Americans in the Southwest and Puerto Ricans in the East. Later it was applied across the country to people whose connection to Spain or to a former Spanish possession was distant or recent. In local, national, and church politics it helped forge a common sense of purpose and unity among groups that differ widely among themselves. (*See* Central and South Americans; Cubans; Dominicans; Mexicans; Puerto Ricans; Spaniards; Spanish; *see also* Spanish-Surname.)

The term Hispanos, along with Tejanos and Californios, properly refers to the fourth- and fifth-generation descendants of the colonial Spanish largely concentrated in New Mexico and Texas.

HISPANOS: *see* SPANISH; *see also* MEXICANS

HONDURANS: *see* CENTRAL AND SOUTH AMERICANS

HOPI-TEWAS: *see* AMERICAN INDIANS

HOPIS: *see* AMERICAN INDIANS

HOUMAS: *see* AMERICAN INDIANS

HUALAPAIS (WALAPAIS): *see* AMERICAN INDIANS

HUGUENOTS: *see* FRENCH

HUNGARIANS

In 1970, according to the U.S. Census, there were over 650,000 Hungarian Americans in the United States. Census figures tend to underestimate the size of many American ethnic groups, however, and this number is probably low. Immigration officials and census takers have always had difficulty keeping accurate count of Hungarian immigrants. Before World War I, Hungary was the homeland of a variety of ethnic groups, of which the Magyars were only one; after the war Hungary's borders no longer included some areas where Magyars lived. However, within Hungary the Magyars were always the dominant group, and theirs was the official language of the country. In the Magyar language there is no clear distinction between the terms "Hungarian" and "Magyar," and as a result, when immigrants first began to arrive in the United States declaring themselves to be from Magyarország—that is, from Hungary—American officials often recorded them as Magyars, whether they were or not. Until the various groups from Hungary began to sort themselves out sufficiently to make their differences known to offi-cials, data on the newcomers remained jumbled and inconsistent. Eventually distinctions were made, and the term Hungarian American was restricted to the Magyar-speaking people from Hungary and their descendants. Most of these are ethnic Magyars, but they also include Magyarized Jews, Slavs, and others who had assimilated into the dominant culture before they left their homeland.

The population of Hungary before World War I was divided not only among ethnic groups, but also among several different religions. Approximately 60 percent were Catholic, most of whom observed the Roman or Latin Rite. Near Hungary's eastern borders, however, there were many formerly Orthodox Christians who had pledged their loyalty to Rome in the 17th century and in return had been allowed to retain their Eastern-rite traditions. Popularly called Byzantine or Greek Catholics, they accounted for perhaps one-sixth of the Catholics in Hungary. (*See* Eastern Catholics.) Close to 25 percent of the population were Protestants. Most of them were Calvinists who belonged to the Reformed Church of Hungary (Magyarországi Református Egyház), a number were Lutherans, a few were Unitarians or Baptists. Approximately 5 percent of the population were Jews. The remaining 10 percent belonged to one of the various Eastern Orthodox churches, though almost none of the Orthodox were Magyars. (*See* Eastern Orthodox.) In religious terms, then, the Hungarian immigrants left a country that was almost as diverse as the one they adopted, and they reflected that diversity to a large extent, except that they tended to come disproportionately from the more Protestant areas of the country.

ORIGINS

For over a thousand years the Magyar people have occupied the Danube basin of east-central Europe, the land other Europeans called Hungary after the federation of Magyar tribes (On-Ogur) who lived there. In 975 the Magyar chieftain Géza accepted Christianity, and after Géza's death his son Stephen (István) spread the Roman Catholic faith among his subjects. The pope welcomed Géza's and Stephen's advancement of the church and, according to tradition, furnished a golden crown for Stephen's coronation around the year 1000. Saint Stephen was canonized in 1083, and his crown has remained the state symbol of Hungary ever since.

Hungary served as western Christianity's outpost against the Turks from the middle of the 15th century until its defeat by the Ottoman army at Mohács on the Danube River in 1526. Hungary had also been a center of church reform, and under Turkish domination Hungarians turned to Protestant beliefs as a source of strength against their overlords. Because the Turkish presence effectively prevented the restoration of Catholicism in most of Hungary during the Counter Reformation, only those parts of western Hungary that escaped Turkish conquest continued to be Catholic. The people in that area relied upon the Austrian Hapsburg Catholic emperors for protection, so they were bound to remain loyal to that church.

Hungary again became a battleground as the Turks attempted to move westward into Europe. In 1683 Turkish armies reached Vienna, but finally the combined forces of the West drove them back, and in 1699

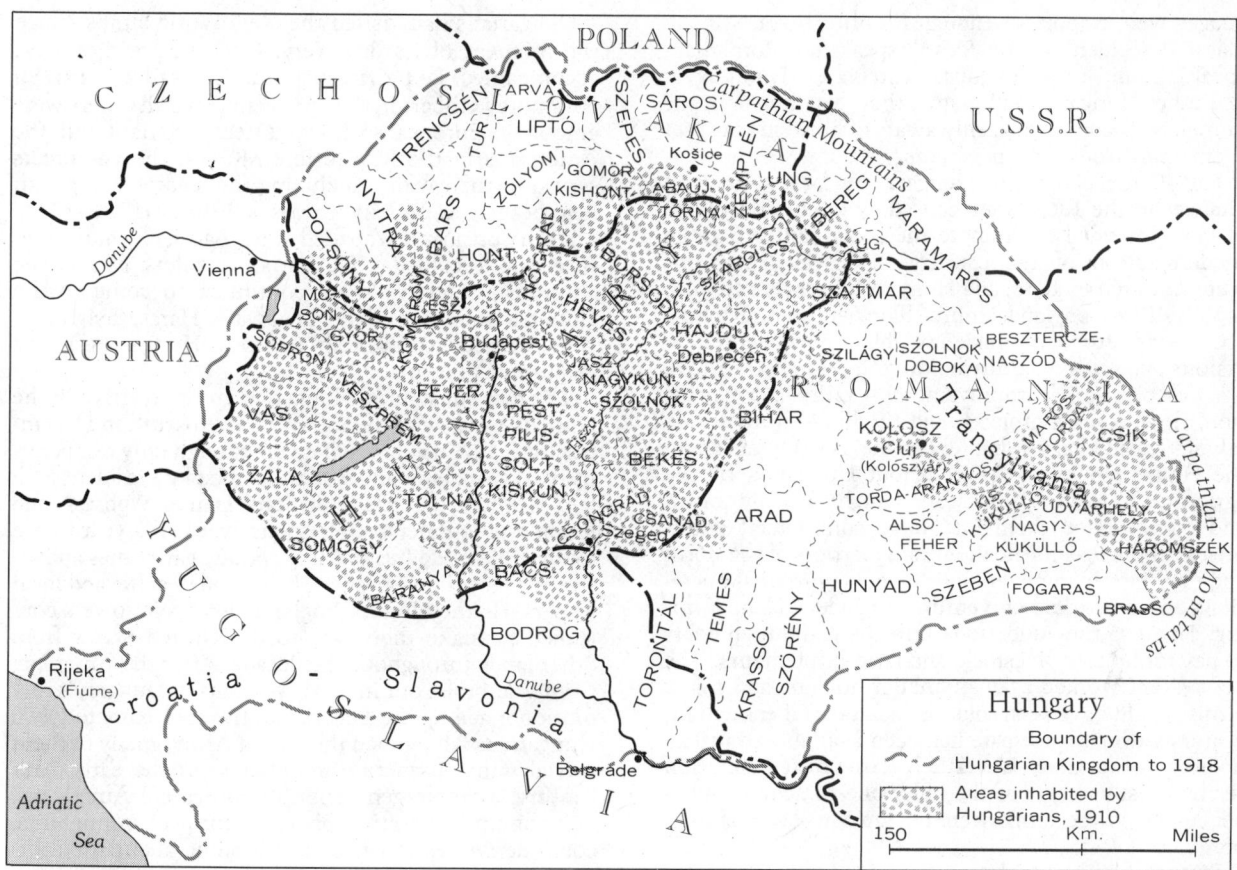

they ceded their claims over their Hungarian territories to the Austrian crown. To consolidate their claims, the Hapsburg emperors were determined to reimpose Catholicism in the rest of Hungary. In this they were not entirely successful, though they otherwise soon had a firm hold on the land; the wars of the previous two centuries had so devastated the country and so demoralized its people that they lacked the capacity to resist. The Magyar language fell into disuse as Latin became the language of the bureaucracy, German prevailed in commerce, and the imperial government encouraged its other subject peoples to settle on the lands of the depleted Magyar population.

In the early 1800s a new generation of Magyars, including Louis (Lajos) Kossuth (1802–1894), began championing both cultural revival and political autonomy for Hungary. When revolutions erupted throughout Europe, including the Austrian Empire, in 1848, the Magyar leaders seized the opportunity to seek reform. The Hapsburg government tried unsuccessfully to oust the reformers by turning the Slavic Croatian population against them, and Kossuth responded by proclaiming Hungary's independence. The Hapsburgs finally repressed the movement by calling in troops from Russia, and Kossuth fled the country in August 1849.

Ten years later Emperor Franz Joseph finally had to make some of the concessions to the Magyars that Kossuth and others had sought, because he needed Magyar support to bolster the Hapsburg empire's weakened defenses. After almost another decade of negotiations, the *Ausgleich* (Compromise) of 1867 established the so-

called Dual Monarchy, which gave Hungary independence in all internal matters but provided for shared ministries of defense and foreign affairs with Austria.

Because the Hapsburg government had been able to marshal aid from the Croats and Russians in suppressing the 1848 revolution, the Hungarians tended to look with suspicion on the mainly Slavic non-Magyar peoples who collectively made up a majority of Hungary's population. The Hungarian nationality act of 1868 recognized just one political nationality and one official language: Magyar. Both were required for entering the higher echelons of government and the upper level of the educational system. Hungary's minorities were to be accommodated only at the local political level and in the elementary schools. Concurrently the government attempted to promote assimilation into the Magyar group, often resorting to coercive methods to do so. The policy did encourage Magyarization, especially among the ambitious, but in some cases it simply provoked a stronger ethnic feeling among non-Magyar peoples.

As a result of these policies, ethnic identities in Hungary often centered on language rather than on nationality or religion. For example, many late-19th-century Hungarian Jews considered themselves Magyars of the Hebrew faith, and today ethnic partisans contend that some Hungarian heroes were actually Magyarized Slavs or Jews or that some Magyar Lutherans and Byzantine Rite Catholics were actually Germans or Rusyns. In any case, by 1900 speakers of Magyar did constitute 51 percent of the Hungarian population, though other lan-

guages were important enough for official statistics to classify residents into Slovak-speaking, Romanian-speaking, and other linguistic categories. For Magyar and other Hungarian emigrants, their experience in the homeland made them keenly aware of how language set them apart from their neighbors.

For all the peoples of Hungary, by far the greatest changes in the 1860s were caused by the promulgation of laws intended to promote the social and economic modernization of the country. Educational reforms were initiated in 1868, and Hungary's literacy rate rose rapidly. Laws on land tenure, likewise revised in the sixties and afterward, made possible unprecedented divisions and sales of family holdings. From 1860 to 1890 a series of internal improvements—railroad construction, flood-control projects, and the like—were undertaken. These changes had enormous consequences for the Hungarian people. Throughout Hungary's richest agricultural regions, investors bought up old farms and consolidated them into huge commercial enterprises. In the less-fertile mountain districts of the north and east, family members split up old communal operations and embarked on ventures in independent farming. To do so they undertook unrealistically high debts to pay for houses, livestock, and farm implements. The tax system worked against smaller holders, and many farms would have been sold for back taxes if enough investors with cash to spare had been available to justify holding tax auctions. Nevertheless, the next generation seemed just as eager as the older one to achieve independence, so the farms were cut up into even smaller plots.

Fortunately for residents struggling with mortgages and tax bills, railroad building and other transportation and flood-control programs required wage labor and offered comparatively good, if temporary, jobs. When a project was completed, the laborers could go on to a new building site or, in season, to the giant commercial farms. The railroads solved one problem but produced another: they brought into the countryside new manufactured goods, which destroyed the market for peasant handicrafts.

Efforts by political reformers to modernize the Hungarian economy touched even the remote northern and eastern areas, awakening aspirations, placing hopes ahead of traditions, and encouraging the notion that by moving out, a hard-working individual could move up in the world. People began migrating throughout Hungary as never before, but new opportunities could not keep up with the growing wants and needs of the population. Having already loosened their ties to their families and their birthplaces, Hungarians were ready to consider traveling even farther afield.

ARRIVAL AND SETTLEMENT

The people who came to the United States in the late 19th and early 20th centuries in search of new social and economic opportunities actually were the second of three groups of Hungarian immigrants. They had been preceded in the mid-19th century by an influx of political refugees and were followed around the middle of the 20th century by another such group. The three groups of immigrants account for the vast majority of Hungarians who came to the United States; the turn-of-the-century group was by far the largest.

Hungarians had visited the New World almost since the moment of its discovery. One is alleged to have accompanied Leif Ericsson; another sailed with Sir Humphrey Gilbert in the 16th century; still others were among the Europeans who volunteered to fight with the Americans in the Revolution. Most of the volunteers served in the cavalry, including the leading Hungarian hero of the war, Mihály Kováts de Fabricy (1724–1779), a cavalry organizer who died at the Battle of Charleston. After the Revolution, Hungarian travelers, merchants, naturalists, and explorers continued to come to the United States. One of them, Agoston Haraszthy (1821–1869), introduced the cultivation of Hungarian Tokay grapes in California.

The first substantial Hungarian group to arrive in the United States were the followers of Kossuth in December 1849. Kossuth himself came, though only temporarily, two years later and was welcomed by President Millard Fillmore, Secretary of State Daniel Webster, and Ralph Waldo Emerson. He spent over half a year in the United States, addressing large public gatherings and attending receptions arranged by national, state, and local leaders. He then left for England, but his followers continued to make their way to the United States from other lands throughout the decade. After the American Civil War broke out in 1861, veterans of Hungary's revolution made up the majority of the approximately 800 Hungarians who joined the Union Army; many of them served with distinction as officers. In the early 20th century, a whole generation of Hungarian Americans, growing up in an atmosphere scornful of immigrants, could derive reassurance from reading about the drillmaster of Washington's cavalry and Lincoln's Hungarian heroes.

Even without the example of the mid-19th-century intellectuals and activists, Hungarians would probably have eventually come to the United States, because of the social and economic changes taking place in Hungary and, for that matter, all over Europe. The United States was building railroads and developing its coal mines, steel mills, and factories in the years after the Civil War, and recruiters of labor for U.S. industries ranged over the European continent as the demand for workers grew. The first emigrants they enlisted prospered, which soon made further recruiting unnecessary. For increasing numbers of small farmers struggling to finance their independence, emigration became part of an overall plan. Instead of traveling around Hungary in search of temporary jobs, they would go to America, where wages were higher; they would do hard, dirty, dangerous, but well-paid work, live as cheaply as possible for a few years, then come back to Hungary to pay the bills, improve their farms, and satisfy their ambitions. Families would remain behind in the old country; only the youngest and strongest men would venture forth. Sociologists call emigrants such as these "sojourners," and almost all the Hungarian emigrants in this period started out in that category. In the end, however, many revised their plans and remained in the United States.

The year 1880 was a poor one for farmers in Hungary, especially for the non-Magyar Slavic peoples in the far northern mountains. They left their homes in Zemplén and other counties nearby and headed for America. Before long they started to send back money, and in

about five years some began to return, but in the meantime their letters and money encouraged others to venture forth. Soon a steady stream of returnees was transforming the local economy. They settled overdue tax bills, paid off mortgages, bought more land at top prices, and occasionally built new brick houses. Their habits of dress and diet were, by previous standards, luxurious. Their formerly more prosperous Magyar-speaking neighbors soon had to join the emigration just to keep up. By 1899 one in every four emigrants who left Hungary spoke Magyar, and by 1902 the proportion was one in three. By the next year, the Magyars were for the first time the largest single group of emigrants from Hungary.

Officials in the counties of Zemplén, Abauj-Torna, Szabolcs, Borsod, Veszprém, and Ung saw over a thousand of their Magyar-speaking constituents depart for America in 1902 alone. But according to the chief administrator of Abauj-Torna, the exodus was "an already solved riddle"; the emigrants wanted to become rich. Wherever there were examples of successful pioneers, the wish to emigrate spread. Hungarians overseas were sending home to each county hundreds of thousands of dollars annually. People in Veszprém received more than half a million dollars in 1903 alone.

It was soon common knowledge among Hungarians that diligent laborers in America could earn $2 a day and could save at least half that sum. By contrast, in Hungary the maximum daily wage was the equivalent of 60 cents, and then only at the peak season of the year; at other times it could be as little as 20 cents. Besides sending home money while they were gone, the sojourners were regularly bringing back anywhere from $80 to $400 in less than five years' time. The unsuccessful and the victims of industrial accidents rarely returned home to dampen enthusiasm.

From 1899, when great numbers of Magyar-speaking people started to leave Hungary, through 1914, when World War I cut off migration, about 458,000 Magyar-speaking immigrants came to the United States. Over two-thirds of them were men, and most were under 30. Nearly 89 percent were literate, although the literacy rate for all of Hungary at that time was only 59 percent.

The Hungarian Americans arrived during the great expansion of bituminous coal mining and the steel industry, so most of them found work in western Pennsylvania, eastern Ohio, West Virginia, and northern Illinois and Indiana. New York City had also attracted Hungarians since the days of Kossuth, and thousands of new immigrants settled there or moved into nearby New Jersey and Connecticut. Some cities and towns developed large Hungarian-American colonies that were much more noticeable than those in scattered mining camps; in particular, New York, Cleveland, Pittsburgh, and Chicago counted many thousands of Hungarians among their vast immigrant populations. Smaller Hungarian settlements formed in Bridgeport, Conn., New Brunswick and Passaic, N.J., South Bend, Ind., and Youngstown, Ohio.

New York and Cleveland were Hungarian centers before 1899, but the immigrants of the mass migration did not confine themselves to familiar places. They were men in motion, seeking temporary employment not permanent new homes. The unsteady nature of work in the mines did not disturb the sojourners, for when work ran out they simply moved on to other places where their labor was in demand; not only from one mine to another, but from mine to mill and from mill to factory. Hungarians flocked to Pittsburgh and to the newer industrial cities of Detroit and Akron, Ohio, though rarely directly from Europe. A few of the Hungarian immigrants departed from the sojourner pattern and brought their families to America, but even they remained mobile. Before World War I, Hungarian-American clergymen claimed that only one-third of the babies they baptized were still living in the same town at the age of confirmation. People moved in and out so rapidly that the annual turnover in some congregations was estimated by their pastors as being as high as 30 percent. These families planned to spend five years abroad, but widespread unemployment sometimes sent thousands home sooner. Such was the case in the fall of 1907 when the enrollment in one parochial school suddenly dropped from 1,000 to 700 pupils.

It is difficult to say exactly how many sojourners did go back. American officials began to list incoming Hungarian Americans under the heading "Magyar" in 1899, but the U.S. government did not begin to keep figures on migrants returning to their homelands until 1908; in both cases confusion in terminology probably led to confusion between non-Magyar and Magyar immigrants from Hungary. The U.S. Immigration Commission also calculated rates of return in a way that overestimated the percentage of Hungarian Americans leaving this country, and the errors were later repeated by others. Nevertheless, according to official American data on immigrant arrivals and departures, approximately 37 percent of the Hungarians who came before World War I went back home, although this percentage includes those who returned to Hungary just to visit. The U.S. Census of 1910 counted 74 percent of the Hungarians who had immigrated since 1899, and the Census of 1920 located 63 percent. Not long afterward, the Immigration Act of 1924 severely limited the entry of southern and eastern Europeans and ended altogether the era of the sojourner in American immigration. (See also Appendix I, Table 2.)

Hungarian immigration did not end entirely, however; from 1925 until World War II, close to 15,000 Hungarians entered the United States, most of them middle-class business and professional people. Among them were four internationally acclaimed scientists, John von Neumann (1903–1957), Leo Szilard (1898–1964), Edward Teller (1908–), and Nobel laureate Eugene Wigner (1902–), as well as four future conductors of American symphony orchestras, Antal Doráti (1906–), Eugene Ormandy (1899–), Fritz Reiner (1888–1963), and George Szell (1897–1970). Composer Béla Bartók (1881–1945) and author Ferenc Molnár (1878–1952) both arrived in 1940 protesting the policies of the Hungarian government. As in the mid-19th century, Hungarian immigration in the 20th again became a movement of political expatriates.

After World War II, 24,000 Hungarians waited years to gain admittance as displaced persons or as refugees from Hungary's Communist regime, part of a larger influx of central and eastern European refugees. Some were ardent nationalists, others were chiefly foes of Communism; but in either case the hardships they had suffered had only strengthened their convictions.

Within a decade their ranks were more than doubled by another group of refugees reminiscent of Kossuth's generation.

In October 1956 thousands of Hungarians rebelled against the Soviet Union's domination of their country, rallying around monuments to the 1848 revolution against Hapsburg rule. The Hungarian secret police fired on protesters marching to broadcast grievances over the radio, and for a week outraged Hungarians carried on a violent struggle with the secret police and Soviet troops. They raided prisons and freed, among others, József Cardinal Mindszenty (1892–1975), the Catholic primate of Hungary. In November 1956 Russian troops put down the Hungarian revolt. In the turmoil 200,000 Hungarians were able to flee the country, while Cardinal Mindszenty found sanctuary in the American legation in Budapest.

The Hungarian-American community's efforts to raise funds for the relief of these Freedom Fighters generated wide support, and Congress agreed to admit them to the United States—ultimately over 35,000 Hungarians came. With the help of the earlier immigrants and their progeny, they at first settled in the industrial towns the sojourners had favored. But many of them were professionals, and 3,000 were college students. They became impatient with unskilled work, soon learned English, and moved on to better jobs.

ECONOMIC LIFE

The 60,000 post–World War II Hungarian-American refugees were vastly outnumbered by the 250,000 Hungarian Americans already in the United States. By sheer weight of numbers, the remaining immigrants of the mass migration and their descendants have been the principal builders of the Hungarian-American community and still determine the shape of its economic life. While most of them came as unskilled workers, some gradually worked their way into skilled positions in American factories, after first becoming familiar with industrial routines in the mines and mills.

The few women in the early Hungarian settlements found work in partnership with their husbands as boarding house keepers. In 1910 about half of the Hungarian couples in the United States were taking in boarders. Sojourning laborers did not mind living temporarily in dilapidated, overcrowded quarters. The cheap rent allowed them to save more of their pay. They could move out on short notice when a better job beckoned elsewhere, and someone else had done the cooking and laundry when they returned exhausted from their work. Because the boarding house "boss" was often a laborer himself, his wife did the chores and served as manager, shopping for food and laundry supplies and keeping track of each boarder's account.

Opening any other small business in the United States required an investment the sojourners did not at first want to make. Yet every immigrant community needed grocers, undertakers, and tavern keepers, so Hungarians began to enter these typically ethnic businesses as they became distracted from their plans to go back home. They often opened meat markets and spice shops; the Hungarian diet favored those items over dairy products or fruit and vegetables, so they rarely ventured into the produce business so common among other immigrants. A few broke with the pattern of industrial labor in another Hungarian way, by working as part-time band and orchestra musicians, as the immigrants began to take time out for entertainment.

Eventually over 60 percent of the immigrants realized that they were never going back to their Hungarian farms. As a result they began to take a greater interest in union organization to improve working conditions and to protect job security. They also began to consider their children's future. Realistically, they could aspire to skilled trades for their sons. When they dreamed of seeing their children in the professions, they especially thought of engineering, a science in vogue among Hungarian aristocrats around the turn of the century. Hungarian-American parents in Detroit asked their church to sponsor mechanical-drawing classes on Saturday afternoons, and one Hungarian-American newspaper tried to attract readers with a scholarship contest for miners' sons seeking to become engineers. All in all, however, the economic life of the Hungarian Americans differed only in minor ways from that of other immigrants of the period. (*See*, for example, Poles; Serbs; Slovaks; Slovenes.)

SOCIAL ORGANIZATION

The Hungarian-American community reflected the religious composition of Hungary, where Protestantism was stronger than in any of the neighboring countries. On the other hand, Hungary had in common with its neighbors the division of its Catholic population between two different rites. In the late 19th century its Jews also identified closely with other Magyar-speaking citizens, in contrast to the Jews of the surrounding countries. The Hungarian Jews had emigrated earlier than the Magyar-speaking Hungarians, but once in the United States they were too poor to associate with the considerably more prosperous Jewish immigrants from Germany. For the most part ignorant of Yiddish, they could not easily communicate with fellow Jews from eastern Europe. Consequently, by the time the Magyars arrived, the Hungarian Jews had set up religious congregations that were somewhat isolated from the rest of the American Jewish population. Unlike the Magyar sojourners, the Jews had come to stay. They had begun to learn the English language and American political ways and to invest in small businesses, for which the Hungarian sojourners soon furnished a natural clientele. In industrial cities, large and small, Jewish pioneers acted for a time as middlemen between the Hungarians and the rest of society. In New York, organizers of the Hungarian Protestant church even elected a trusted Jewish adviser to their first council of officers. But the alliance lasted only so long as language was a barrier to the immigrants. As knowledge of English spread, contact between Magyars and Jews diminished.

In the long run, Protestant and Catholic Hungarians proved to have much more in common with each other than with their Jewish countrymen. They shared similar problems during their first years in the United States. The mutual-benefit society, an organization crucial to financial security in almost all immigrant groups, became the cornerstone of community life among the Hungarians as well. What all day laborers needed was a modicum of security: a small pool of money they could draw on to pay their room, board, and medical bills in case they were sick or injured on the

job. The first such Hungarian society was founded in Newark, N.J., in 1882, long before there were many Hungarians in the United States. By 1910 there were more than a thousand of these societies.

Although not all sick-benefit lodges had a religious affiliation, many acquired religious functions simply because sickness and injury often involved a need for spiritual comfort. At first the Hungarian Americans allowed the insurance societies to summon a clergyman only for funerals or special holidays; they were afraid any established religious organization would pressure them to invest their money in a pastor's salary, church, and parsonage, which they would leave behind when they went home. As a result many of the societies took on more and more of the functions of religious congregations. The longer the immigrants stayed, the more they needed someone to perform weddings, baptisms, and funerals, and to teach religion to their children. Almost all of the successful congregations grew out of insurance lodges; the early Hungarian Americans often felt it safer to finance their congregations with lodge funds than to rely on dues or the collection plate. They were not irreligious, but they did think that a less church-centered religious observance was better suited to their sojourn in the United States.

Churches did not begin to appear in Hungarian immigrant settlements until the 1890s, some ten years after the sick-benefit societies, and even then their progress was slow. In the year 1890 a mission board of the Reformed Church in the United States brought the Reverend Gusztav Juranyi from Hungary to Cleveland, but fewer than half the people who turned out for his first service were willing to found a congregation. Three other pastors struggled to keep that flock together before the last of them, Elek Csutoros (1870–1950), succeeded around 1898. By 1904 there were 16 Hungarian Protestant congregations in the United States, but 5 of them still had no regular pastor, and although they served Lutherans, Unitarians, and Reformed Protestants, few could claim more than a quarter of the local Hungarian Protestants as members. The Catholics were still slower to organize. Because Catholics did not stress scripture reading as Protestants did, Hungarian Catholics could easily worship in any Catholic church, for the liturgy was in Latin. One missionary priest met with little success among the Hungarian Catholic immigrants in the 1880s. Another, Father Károly Böhm, was able to organize the first Hungarian-American parish in Cleveland in 1892, but the second and third parishes did not follow until the end of the decade, at McKeesport, Pa., in 1897 and Bridgeport, Conn., in 1899. Meanwhile in 1892, the year of Böhm's breakthrough, an Eastern Catholic sick-benefit society in Cleveland requested a priest from their bishop in Hungary.

Hungarian-American congregations of all faiths struggled with debts. To solve the problem, they began to sponsor picnics, bazaars, and raffles, social events unknown to churches in Hungary. They also took over traditional Hungarian family and village festivals, such as the grape-harvest celebration and the pork-slaughter supper, but they now charged admission fees. Even so, they needed help from larger organizations. The Catholic church and its religious orders were accustomed to assisting newcomers, but the Protestant Hungarians often had to seek out the officials in charge of the American denominations' home missions when they needed help.

INSURANCE FEDERATIONS

About the time the religious congregations were beginning to grow, Hungarian Americans were preparing to expand their sick-benefit societies into nationwide federations. Like other immigrant groups, they realized that a larger body of members would give them greater security and would also be able to provide their families in Hungary or in the United States with death benefits. On Labor Day 1892, delegates of five societies in the Bridgeport, Conn., area organized the Betegsegélyző Egyletek Szövetség (Sick-Assisting Societies Association), popularly called the Bridgeport Association. Within three years it included groups from as far away as Pittsburgh, and a rival federation, eventually known as the Rákóczi Segélyző Egyesület (Rákóczi Aid Association), had begun, also with headquarters in Bridgeport. In 1896 another federation was formed when five Hungarian Reformed ministers tried to create a nationwide church body, or classis, by uniting the sick-benefit societies that were the backbone of their congregations. The classis failed, but the Amerikai Magyar Református Egyesület (Hungarian Reformed Federation of America) survived. Farther west, coal miners and steelworkers organized a fourth federation around the Verhovay Sick-Benefit Society, which a few pioneers had founded in Hazelton, Pa., in 1886.

In 1904 the Bridgeport Association claimed 4,600 members and the Rákóczi, 1,200. Four years later the Bridgeport Association reported that its ranks had doubled, but with 8,000 names on its rolls, the Verhovay was close behind. As of 1910 there were no fewer than nine Hungarian-American federations, the four named above plus several smaller ones, including one Roman Catholic and two Eastern Catholic organizations.

Of the four major associations, only the Reformed Federation had any religious affiliation. Local branches were sometimes identified with particular congregations, but Hungarians held too many different religious beliefs to build strong national organizations that way. The first convention of the Bridgeport Association drew Catholics, Protestants, and Jews while the Hungarian Reformed Federation admitted Jews at first and always enrolled Catholics. The practical appeal of insurance continued to outweigh religious and ideological considerations. Even the Hungarian-American socialists found they had to start insurance associations to hold their followers.

For Hungarians, as for other immigrants, the national federations enabled them to transfer their membership from place to place and so to develop a sense of community with their countrymen all over the United States. Because the insurance associations had to use newspapers to communicate with their scattered membership, their growth gave a boost to the struggling Hungarian-American press. In 1892 the Bridgeport Association named as its official paper one of the first Hungarian journals in the United States, *Amerikai Nemzetör* (American National Guardsman, 1883–1905), of New York. The Rákóczi Association established a similar arrangement with *Szabadság* (Liberty), a paper founded in Cleveland in 1891 and still published there. The Reformed Federation started its own publication, and as

insurance matters grew more complicated in the next century, other associations followed suit. Published reports from federation branches informed readers about working conditions, strikes, and accidents wherever Hungarians had settled and encouraged members to come to each other's aid. Eventually some of the papers devoted special columns to job information to help readers plan their many transfers more carefully.

When they arrived, Hungarian Americans saw the United States almost as an extension of the Hungarian economy. The overseas migration of so many young men had spread family ties across two continents and an ocean. Long before they began migrating around their own country or thinking of America, people regularly ventured beyond village bounds. A centrally located church often served scattered congregations in several outlying villages. For the immigrants dispersed throughout the United States, their earlier tradition of broadened horizons proved a useful heritage; interurban railways and other forms of transportation merely expanded the distances involved. Vineyard workers from Ashtabula County, Ohio, went some 30 miles to Cleveland for special religious occasions, and coal miners in southeastern Ohio similarly traveled 50 miles by train to Columbus. Hungarians from Duquesne, Pa., worshiped in Pittsburgh, 10 miles away, for several years, while a mother church at Johnstown, Pa., drew half its support from three congregations in Pennsylvania mining settlements. Hungarian-American community life was not made up of self-contained ethnic neighborhoods or isolated villages. Their insurance associations, newspapers, and churches served a widely dispersed community.

LITERATURE AND MUSIC

The newspapers were central to Hungarian-American literary life during the years of mass migration. The major poets, such as György Kemény (1875–1952) and László Pólya (1870–1950), were also journalists, and the works of Hungarian-American novelists often reached their readers as newspaper serials. József Reményi (1891–1956), perhaps the most famous of the immigrant novelists and short-story writers, came to the United States just before World War I and began his American writing career with *Szabadság* in Cleveland. He had earned his doctorate in Hungary and became a professor of comparative literature at Case Western Reserve University, but he continued to write fiction as well as scholarly books and articles.

The literature of the great immigration reached its peak in the 1920s, with 60 new Hungarian papers starting publication in cities and towns throughout the United States. The poets and novelists who had arrived before the war continued their work, and a number of playwrights enjoyed some popularity as amateur drama groups sprang up in local communities. A professional Hungarian-American theater company successfully toured the major cities. In the thirties, however, Hungarian literary activity in the United States steadily declined, along with interest in the mother tongue. Later refugees, addressing a more general audience, have produced well over half the books published by Hungarian-American authors.

The most important and most widely appreciated feature of Hungarian-American culture has been music. In the early 20th century almost every Hungarian settlement had its brass band; as the immigrant colonies grew larger, they organized orchestras and choruses as well. Even during the Depression of the thirties, there were enough Hungarians in Cleveland willing to spend an occasional quarter or half-dollar on a concert or a dance to support at least 17 musical groups. At the same troubled time, there were enough interested Hungarian parents in that city to sustain a number of music teachers and a continuous round of children's recitals. Not surprisingly, some 40 years later a list of famous Hungarian Americans included over 50 musicians and opera singers, and Hungarian-American conductors led 30 of the 500 U.S. symphony orchestras. In the quest for fortune, Hungarians may have sacrificed their native language to improve their children's chances for success, but they did not renounce their musical heritage.

TIES TO THE HOMELAND

Close political ties united Hungarians to their homeland at least from 1904 until the end of World War I. After four years of watching the dramatic rise in the emigration of its Magyar-speaking population, the Hungarian prime ministry decided that drastic steps were necessary. District officials in the areas of greatest emigration quickly convinced the national government that mere laws could not stop this great social and economic movement; the prime minister would be far wiser to let the sojourners go abroad and concentrate his efforts on making sure they came home again, rich and contented with their new earnings. By 1902 the ministry was at work on a plan to do just that. A secret conference in January 1903 laid groundwork for the "American Action," whose aims were first, to protect emigrants abroad from political pressure, apparently including pan-Slavism, Hungarian nationalism, and other movements, as well as from assimilation into American society, and second, to keep alive their desire to return to Hungary. The ministry would provide the funds, but the program was to be divided into Reformed and Catholic branches and operate mainly through the churches.

The entering wedge was to be help from home for the Hungarian-American churches, whose dependence on the American church hierarchies was creating problems. For instance, the Hungarians charged that an unsympathetic Irish-American bishop had reduced the Hungarian Roman Catholic parish in Youngstown, Ohio, to chaos by constantly changing its pastors. In not one of the Hungarian Catholic parochial schools did the teaching nuns speak Hungarian. There was turmoil among Protestants, too, for the governing bodies of American denominations did not know how to examine the credentials of clergymen from Hungary, and they had accepted some unqualified ministers who became embroiled in an ugly Presbyterian-Reformed competition for immigrant members. Church leaders in Hungary feared that the American churches would demand Americanization as the price for aiding the newcomers.

In 1904 the General Conventus of the Reformed Church of Hungary sent its second-ranking lay official to the United States to offer the immigrants a solution to their problems: join the homeland church. Each con-

gregation that united with the Conventus would receive yearly supplements of up to $450 toward the pastor's salary and up to $250 to hire a teacher (though these sums were intended as a subsidy, the congregations rarely came up with their full share, and the subsidy was sometimes all that the pastor received). The ministry had agreed to give the Conventus these funds and to refinance any mortgages that the American denominations held against the Hungarian immigrant churches. Six of the 16 Hungarian-American Protestant congregations promptly agreed to the plan and presented a total of almost $29,000 in property debts. By 1908 the annual salary budget of the Reformed Church branch of the American Action was nearly $12,000. Meanwhile as of 1906, writs from the ministry had authorized the Hungarian General Credit Bank to refinance over $300,000 in American church mortgages. By 1910 the Conventus held the allegiance of the largest single bloc of Hungarian-Protestant congregations, 23 in all. Further subsidies from home guaranteed the congregations their own denominational newspaper and almanac, as well as almost every other benefit enjoyed by Hungarians who stayed with the American denominations.

Hungarian-language schools were of great concern to the American Action. At first, Hungarian officials tried to start a daily Reformed Church parochial school in every settlement large enough to support one, and they furnished money and textbooks for that purpose. But by 1912 they had resigned themselves to simply requiring all congregations of the Hungarian Conventus to offer Hungarian language and culture classes during weekends and public-school vacations. The Conventus prescribed the curriculum and sent over the only permissible school supplies for the lessons. It also offered pastors of congregations with particularly well-attended schools a $50-a-year bonus.

The Catholic branch of the American Action was not as well organized as the Reformed, but Catholics received aid for their schools and for a newspaper too. The first Apostolic Visitator to the Byzantine Rite Catholics in America was a Magyar-speaking patriot who reported to the Hungarian prime minister. After he helped Hungarians in five cities separate themselves from Slavic parishes, each of the five resulting Hungarian congregations obtained a $300 annual subsidy from the homeland, and the parishes in Cleveland and South Lorain, Ohio, won additional sums for schools.

The secular Hungarian-American press also needed support, because the immigrants were not apt to take out long-term subscriptions. In 1903 the ministry began planning to supply funds and "inspiring" literary material to immigrant papers in the United States. After cautious surveys of the field, in 1907 the ministry approved dividing $5,200 among four Hungarian-American editors. The next year only one was judged sufficiently responsive to continue in the program, and even that editor ran into trouble with the government in 1911, when he encouraged his readers to become American citizens. The subsidy scheme backfired in Cleveland, where a publisher allegedly asked for more money than the government was willing to pay, then turned against the ministry when his application was rejected.

Authorities in the old country did not limit themselves merely to rescuing Hungarian-American churches, schools, and newspapers; the Austro-Hungarian foreign ministry financed a program aimed at protecting the health and lives of its emigrants in the United States. Consulates compiled dossiers on, and brought lawsuits against, companies that maintained unsafe working conditions. Cooperating with their Italian counterparts, the consuls tried to steer incoming workers away from notoriously irresponsible employers, such as the Colorado Fuel and Iron Company, where a number of Italian and Austro-Hungarian workers had lost their lives. They also lobbied for industrial-safety legislation and established contacts with state factory inspectors to ensure enforcement. Finally, if despite all these precautions an immigrant was hurt on the job, the nearest consulate hired lawyers to file damage suits on the victim's behalf.

Ties to Hungary helped bring the sojourners together as "children of one mother." Subsidized Roman Catholic and Hungarian Reformed congregations jointly celebrated Hungarian national holidays. If the Reformed congregation sponsored the only local language school, Catholic pupils attended it. In most places, Lutherans had to remain in Reformed congregations because the ministry would not help them organize separately.

COMMUNITY LIFE

By stressing the immigrants' Hungarian identity instead of their different religious loyalties and village or regional backgrounds, the American Action encouraged certain tendencies in Hungarian-American life. Because Hungarians rarely stayed anywhere for long, their settlements usually included people from any number of homeland regions. Hungarians in the United States rarely married someone from the same village or even from the same county. Religious intermarriage was not uncommon either; in some places anywhere from a quarter to a third of the Hungarian-American families had one Catholic and one Protestant parent.

The American Action also encouraged indifference to American politics, both by reminding the immigrants that they would be leaving the country soon and by making the homeland government as strong a presence in the Hungarian-American community as the government of the United States. Supporters of Americanization charged that the Hungarians were uncommonly slow to take out citizenship papers, and American Protestant leaders claimed that those Hungarians who joined the Conventus were the least likely of all to become citizens. In a few cases young men who wanted to run for office changed their last names, in the belief that an Irish name would help their chances of joining "America's political class."

Clearly, if any group was prepared to resist cultural and political assimilation, it was the Hungarians, but despite the heroic efforts of the Hungarian government to keep its emigrants Hungarian, the people overseas were changing. Young men came home with ambitions too lofty for authorities to understand, let alone satisfy. A Hungarian government study concluded that the returnees had picked up some "socialistic" philosophy that led them to demand "humane" treatment in hotels, train stations, or wherever they paid for service. The returnees told investigators that American public

officials called every man "sir," and most admitted they would rather be back in the United States.

But most of the immigrants never returned to Hungary at all. Instead, the number of women leaving for the United States gradually increased, and for whatever reason, women rarely went back. Many of them met and married young men from a different village, leaving the couple no single home to go back to. When they became parents, they thought of their children's future in terms of the United States. No matter what the ministry decreed, Hungarian Americans wanted the schools to teach their youngsters English first, and Hungarian only second. The parents prevailed. In 1914, after ten years of costly government efforts overseas, when church officials in Hungary suggested that the government sponsor trips to Hungary for the emigrants' American-born children, the Austro-Hungarian consuls unanimously vetoed the plan. Second-generation Hungarian Americans were too used to the conveniences and amusements of American urban life, the consuls said; a visit to their parents' rural birthplaces would only convince them that Hungary was not their homeland.

At the outset of World War I, many other immigrant groups moved swiftly to identify their national interests with those of the United States, but the Hungarians were too unfamiliar with American politics to act effectively in the crisis. The war ultimately transformed the Hungarian-American community. When the United States entered the war, Austria-Hungary was on the opposing, and eventually losing, side. Defeat ended the ministry's ability to carry on its American Action, and the terms of the Treaty of Trianon of 1920 drastically altered the Hungarian immigrants' prospects. Most of them had come from ethnically mixed areas of Hungary that after the treaty were part of Czechoslovakia, Romania, or Yugoslavia. If the immigrants were to return, it would not be to Hungary but to one of these new countries, where they would be in a minority group. Even if their homes were still within postwar Hungary's narrower boundaries there might be nothing left, for the war and its aftermath had devastated the nation.

When travel resumed after the war, about 32,000 Hungarian Americans, nearly three-fourths of them men, did go back to Europe, for a while at least. Weddings, baptisms, and funerals all declined in Hungarian churches across the United States. As American legislators prepared to restrict immigration from southern and eastern Europe, however, 29,000 Hungarians came to the United States, anxious to enter before the restrictions could take full effect. Over half of those postwar arrivals were women, a further indication that the days of temporary migration were over.

As permanent immigrants, Hungarians in the 1920s were more willing than they had been to invest in building an American ethnic community; cut off from the homeland, they could no longer take their religious and cultural heritage for granted. In addition, the postwar division of Hungary had left many feeling embattled and betrayed. As other Americans had organized Community Chests during the war, delegates from the Hungarian churches and societies in each city had often created a *nagybizottság* (grand committee). In the twenties these committees sponsored rallies to protest the treaty that had partitioned the homeland, raised money for Hungarian prisoners of war, and observed Hungarian national holidays. In 1929 a convention in Buffalo attempted, with only modest success, to create a nationwide organization to keep Hungary's cause alive.

At the same time, however, the immigrants began to combine concern for their homeland with a greater interest in American politics. Although in 1920 less than a third of the immigrant Hungarians were citizens of the United States, by the end of that decade a majority of them had been naturalized.

Similarly, there was a new commitment to support religious congregations in the United States. The Reformed Conventus in Hungary could no longer assist its believers overseas and had to dispose of its American properties. Hungarian church leaders twice negotiated agreements, first with the Presbyterian Church and then with the Reformed Church in the United States. But over ten years of competition had convinced many Hungarian immigrants that the American denominations were different from their own. They refused to join the Presbyterians, and although 28 of the Conventus's 32 former congregations voted to join the Reformed Church in the United States, a rebellion began in the financially stronger congregations. Preaching self-sufficiency and comparing the agreement with the Reformed Church to the Treaty of Trianon, a Free Magyar Reformed Church had organized 16 Hungarian-American congregations by 1929. Parents of all faiths similarly gave new support to Hungarian-language schools throughout the 1920s.

But Hungarian community life in the interwar years remained open to movement and change. Miners moved to the cities in greater numbers. One insurance federation averaged 70 transfers a month, mostly between old mining towns and new manufacturing centers such as Detroit. Hungarians in the cities were moving too; like so many other Americans, they had begun to buy automobiles. Hungarians in Bridgeport, Conn., began to desert the west end of town for neighborhoods as far west as Fairfield. Still, a Hungarian from Bridgeport would have been amazed at the dispersal occurring in the midwestern states. When the president of the Rákóczi Association visited Ohio in 1923, he complained that Youngstown's rapidly growing Hungarian-American population was so scattered it had been difficult even to locate all the potential Rákóczi members. In Cleveland during the twenties, Hungarians began moving to better residential areas, a trend that the Depression stalled only temporarily. The ethnic enclaves that appeared so colorful to other Americans often looked far different to an immigrant. By 1970 a decided majority of all Hungarian generations in metropolitan Detroit lived in the suburbs, and almost as many Hungarian Americans lived in California as in their former stronghold of Pennsylvania.

As the children grew up in the interwar years, the Hungarian-American community became more and more an English-speaking one. Insurance federations had to cater to the younger, English-speaking generation to remain solvent, and newspapers had to add English sections to attract younger readers. The Hungarian-language schools fell into disfavor in the thirties and regained enrollment only by becoming English-language vacation Bible schools. The organization of youth and young-adult groups led to the use of English in church

services. By World War II, attendance at the English services usually surpassed that at the Hungarian, even in the Free Magyar Reformed Church. Soon wartime-inspired patriotism led Hungarian congregations to begin holding classes in English and in citizenship for adults. For everyone the war hastened the adoption of American ways. Thousands of young Hungarians served in the armed forces—165 of them from a single congregation of 350. Their return to the community after the war speeded up the course of change.

After World War II the plight of Hungary, once again divided, stirred Hungarian Americans as it had in 1918, and concern mounted in the late forties as the Communists seized power. In 1956 the daring of the Hungarian revolutionaries was greeted with sympathy, although, like the other Western powers, the United States did nothing to support their fight. At mid-century the United States received two groups of refugees. The first émigrés, in the late 1940s and early 1950s, were heterogeneous in social background and political opinion. They included members of both the upper and middle classes and some former German sympathizers as well as more idealistic opponents of Communism. They were quite unlike the older generation of immigrants in their urban background and in the nature and intensity of their political concerns. The escapees who arrived after 1956 were also by and large well-educated urban dwellers. A majority considered themselves intellectuals. They were far younger than the postwar refugees and had been educated under the Communist regime. As a result they did not merge with the previous émigrés, and both sets of refugees stood apart from the older Hungarian-American community.

As relations between the Western powers and the Communist countries improved in the 1970s, political issues began to draw the three groups more closely together, but culturally and socially they continued to have little in common. First of all, the refugees found an American ethnic community that was still very much church-centered. Although clergymen were among the new arrivals both after the war and in 1956, most, especially the post-1956 group, were not religiously inclined at all. The émigrés soon learned English, but they and their children retained a native command of the Magyar tongue, and this made second- and third-generation Hungarian Americans feel awkward when they met. In 1951 when refugees organized the Hungarian Scout Association in Exile, only the children of new arrivals joined. For the most part the refugees joined educational and professional groups made up almost entirely of postwar immigrant members.

The church, the insurance lodge, and the daily or weekly newspaper had once been the pillars of the Hungarian-American communities, but they were all tottering by the time the refugees arrived. The newcomers were even less inclined to join the insurance federations than to join the churches, and they were much more likely to found new journals and magazines than to subscribe to the remaining old ones. Only in the late 1970s, with an awakening of ethnic interest among the grandchildren and great-grandchildren of the older immigrants, have the groups drawn closer together. The more recent arrivals are still able to teach the young the Hungarian language, literature, music, and dance. To be sure, the language is not one of the rural dialects the

youngsters' grandparents spoke; the literature avoids the popular sensationalism of the earlier immigrant press; and the music does not necessarily resemble that played by the popular Hungarian-American bands. But this more academic approach to cultural tradition may in fact be more appealing to the youth. To the extent that the survival of American ethnic groups depends on the recovery of a lost heritage, the presence of these recent refugees brightens the prospects for the Hungarian community. Much will depend, however, on the durability of the new ethnic interest, and this, of course, is impossible to foresee.

Bibliography

The patron of a moderate-sized public or college library will be fortunate to find even two books on its shelves specifically about Hungarian Americans. Joseph Széplaki, ed., *The Hungarians in America, 1583–1974: A Chronology and Fact Book* (Dobbs Ferry, N.Y., 1975), is the most up-to-date work. Emil Lengyel, *Americans from Hungary* (New York, 1948), and David Aaron Souders, *The Magyars in America* (1922; reprint, San Francisco, 1969), are outdated but commonly available general surveys. Rezsoe Gracza and Margaret Gracza, *The Hungarians in America* (Minneapolis, Minn., 1969), although intended for young readers, is also a good brief overview. Similarly, Laura Fermi, *Illustrious Immigrants: The Intellectual Migration from Europe 1930–41*, 2d ed. (Chicago, 1971), discusses "the mystery of Hungarian talent" at some length.

The most readable of the specialized scholarly studies is Joshua A. Fishman, *Hungarian Language Maintenance in the United States* (Bloomington, Ind., 1966), which treats many aspects of Hungarian-American life, though it underestimates the efforts of the Hungarian government to maintain the immigrants' language loyalty. George Bárány, "The Magyars," in *The Immigrant's Influence on Wilson's Peace Policy,* Joseph O'Grady, ed. (Lexington, Ky., 1967), describes the unique position of Hungarians in the United States during World War I. Two articles by Erdmann D. Beynon, "Occupational Succession of Hungarians in Detroit," *American Journal of Sociology* 39 (1934): 600–610, and "Social Mobility and Social Distance among Hungarian Immigrants in Detroit," *American Journal of Sociology* 41 (1936): 423–434, are among the few essays on Hungarian Americans to appear in a widely circulated scholarly journal.

The most significant collections of primary materials open to the public are at the Immigration History Research Center of the University of Minnesota in St. Paul and at the Hungarian Research Center of the American Hungarian Foundation in New Brunswick, N.J. Joseph Széplaki, ed., *Hungarians in the United States and Canada: A Bibliography* (Minneapolis, 1977), lists the holdings of the former, chiefly Hungarian-American publications and microfilms from archives in Hungary. The center at New Brunswick has papers and libraries of Hungarian-American individuals.

PAULA BENKART

HUPAS: *see* AMERICAN INDIANS

HUTTERITES

The Hutterite Brethren are the largest and most successful Christian communal group in the United States. Though fluent in English, they continue to speak German. They derive from the 16th-century Anabaptist movement, live in colonies, marry within their own group, have big families, wear traditional dress, practice pacifism, and operate large-scale mechanized farms on extensive tracts of land. Unlike other surviving Anabaptist groups—the Mennonites and the Amish—the Hutterites strictly adhere to common ownership of property and communal living patterns.

The main body of Hutterites first formed in Moravia in 1528, when a group of religious refugees from South Tirol decided to hold all their goods in common. They took their name from their principal leader, Jacob Hutter (burned at the stake in 1536), who organized them

into religious *Brüderhöfe* (common households, colonies) consisting of married couples and their offspring who shared all their possessions and practiced Christian communism in production as well as consumption. The Hutterites' absolute commitment to their communal pattern of living has made it necessary for them to migrate throughout their history. In the half-century from 1540 to 1590 Moravia accommodated an estimated 20,000 Hutterites, but between 1590 and 1621 the colonies were plundered and destroyed and the Hutterites driven from the country. They fled to Slovakia, Hungary, and Romania, and finally in 1770 to Russia. When the young men were threatened with conscription in the 1870s, the entire group emigrated from Russia to what is now South Dakota. Of the estimated 1,265 who came to the Dakota Territory, about 443 continued to live in colonies; the others bought their own farms and ceased to live communally. During World War I the young men were treated so severely because they were conscientious objectors that all but one of the Hutterite colonies moved to Canada. By 1974 the number of colonies increased to 229, of which 64 with about 6,000 inhabitants were located in the United States, principally in South Dakota and Montana, and the remainder in the prairie provinces of Canada.

A colony is a domestic unit, a religious community, a corporation, and a labor force, with strong ethnic ties to other Hutterite colonies. It provides for all the needs of the members, such as food, clothing, education, and economic support, and pays for professional medical and hospital care. The population of the colonies ranges from about 70 to 130 people, usually with four families living in separate apartments in a long house. Once a colony has reached an optimum size, it will seek a new location and divide into two groups, without regard to individuals or family units. A typical colony is run by a male council, elected by baptized men and consisting of a head preacher, his assistant, a steward, a farm manager, a German teacher, and one or two senior members. Women play a secondary role; their work is supervised by a female head cook. The members accept an ideological social order as an essential part of the colony's organization. Family and kinship groups are subordinate to the colony, and expectations for the individual are defined clearly by age and sex. Stable social patterns are strengthened by comprehensive socialization for all age groups, by the diffusion of authority within peer groups, by incentives for work without private gain, and by spiritual or mystical qualities generated by intense communal living.

Colonies are usually located away from small towns, but still near enough for the colonists to buy supplies and market their grain and livestock. Many are situated along rivers or other natural sources of water. A typical tract in South Dakota is 4,600 acres, but in more arid regions a colony may own up to 16,000 acres. The colonies are well adapted to farming large holdings, for they rapidly implemented advanced techniques of mechanization. Because they have capital and an eager labor force not available to the one-family farm, they tend to have more and better machinery than their non-Hutterite neighbors.

Hutterite kindergartens (formed in Moravia 270 years before those in Germany) are the backbone of their educational system. Although children go on to accredited public schools, taught with rare exceptions by non-Hutterites, these schools are so isolated that few outsiders attend. Classes in both written and spoken German are held before and after the public school day, and the Hutterites publish Bibles, hymnals, and curriculum materials in German. (They do not, however, publish any newspapers or periodicals.) Education stops before the high school level, for the colony provides adolescents with rigorous and meaningful work.

The viability of the Hutterites as an ethnic group has aroused interest in their population structure, genetic composition, and mental health. Studies by social scientists in the 1950s showed that completed family size was 9 children, the median age at marriage was 22 for women and 23 for men, and that few Hutterites remained unmarried. The Hutterites are strictly monogamous. There is no divorce. Extramarital affairs are strongly opposed, and any adult transgressions must be confessed by both male and female to the assembly of members. A high rate of natural increase (4 percent annually) and a very low rate of defection accounts for the group's phenomenal growth rate. Less than 2 percent of the members have left the colonies permanently; on the other hand, fewer than 50 people have joined as converts.

More often than not, married couples are closer than second cousins. In spite of increasing physical homogeneity and a tendency to heaviness, the group seems to have no more hereditary diseases than any other. Although members appear to have fewer financial problems and worries than other Americans, they are not free from mental illness; symptoms of schizophrenia are low, but manic-depressive reactions are high, especially among women. Personal violence among adults is uncommon; adultery, promiscuity, homosexuality, murder, and arson are unknown or extremely rare.

The Hutterites are not nationalistic, and with few exceptions do not vote. They generally comply with local civic, school, or tax laws, but their beliefs forbid payment of taxes levied for war purposes. They have incurred dislike because of their separatism, their markedly successful farming methods and consequent prosperity, and the constant threat of their unprecedented growth. Several states have attempted unsuccessfully to pass laws forbidding the sale of land to the colonies.

The Hutterites' ability to resist social assimilation is remarkable. They articulate uncompromising beliefs (vocalized as *Der Glaube*) that define and order their entire social system. These central beliefs provide the basis for supernatural authority and a view of the world that is hierarchical, separate from the social and carnal world; they provide for the use but not the ownership of material goods and property, and individual surrender (*Gelassenheit*) to the community. The Hutterites are uncompromising in their total commitment to and participation in a communal experience in which the spiritual nature is incarnated in the individual and rules over the sinful or lower nature. The deification of communal unity and the submission of the self minimize arguments, and the application of logical thought and reasoned solutions help resolve economic problems.

The Hutterites have been strikingly successful at adapting to natural, geographic, and agrarian environments. Their communal strategy and motivation have

permitted them to experiment with agricultural production and to develop capital equal to the challenge of prairie farming. Efficiency and reasoned technological innovation have been in their tradition since the 16th century, when they managed Moravian estates. Their mechanized agriculture and prosperity have permitted them to support a high rate of natural increase. Unlike the Amish, the Hutterites use electricity, motor vehicles, and telephones, but never allow them to become individual status-enhancing objects. Mechanization has altered neither the basic social institutions of the group nor its hierarchical authority patterns. When a colony is prosperous, all the individuals and families benefit equally. Neither wealth nor possessions confer social distinction.

A small communal movement, known as the Society of Brothers and founded in Germany in 1920, affiliated with the Hutterites after 1930. This affiliation, sometimes called the Bruderhof movement or the Hutterian Society of Brothers, has headquarters at Rifton, N.Y., and several nonagricultural communes in Pennsylvania, New York, and Connecticut.

Bibliography
For general descriptive treatments, see John A. Hostetler, *Hutterite Society* (Baltimore, 1974); John W. Bennett, *Hutterian Brethren: The Agricultural Economy and Social Organization of a Communal People* (Stanford, Calif., 1967); and Victor Peters, *All Things Common: The Hutterian Way of Life* (Minneapolis, Minn., 1965). Specialized studies are Joseph W. Eaton and Robert J. Weil, *Culture and Mental Disorders: A Comparative Study of the Hutterites and Other Populations* (Glencoe, Ill., 1955), and Joseph W. Eaton and Albert J. Mayer, *Man's Capacity to Reproduce: The Demography of a Unique Population* (Glencoe, 1954).

JOHN A. HOSTETLER

I

ICELANDERS

Iceland is an island on the edge of the Arctic Circle between Norway and Greenland. In spite of its name, it is as much an island of fire as of ice. Volcanically heated springs and the Gulf Stream provide warmth to mitigate both the cold of the northern latitude and of the glaciers that make much of the island uninhabitable. In 1970 the island's population was about 210,000.

Some 18,000 to 23,000 people of Icelandic birth or ancestry now live in the United States, about three-fourths of them in the region between the Mississippi River and the Pacific Ocean. Perhaps 1,000 of those born in America can speak Icelandic, a fusion of Old Norse and Celtic linguistic elements. Except for 200 or more Icelandic Mormons in Utah, the majority are Lutherans.

Origins, Migration, and Settlement

Iceland was first settled in A.D. 874 by Viking chieftains who wished to break away from the Norse king Harald Fairhair. They were joined later by Celts from Ireland. In 930 they established Europe's first national assembly, the Althing. In the year 1000 they adopted Christianity, about the same time that Leif Ericsson, who was born in Iceland, and a party of explorers discovered a continent they called Vinland. They remained several years somewhere on the North American coast before giving up the attempt to establish a permanent colony.

Icelanders and their culture flourished until about 1230, but were eventually weakened by internal feuding. The commonwealth submitted first to Norway's king in 1262 and then, along with Norway, to the Danish crown in 1397. It remained under Danish rule until 1918 when it became a separate kingdom, joined to Denmark only through recognition of the monarch. In

1944 Iceland broke with Denmark completely and became a republic.

Iceland's isolation from the rest of Europe during more than five centuries of Danish rule kept its language pure (modern Icelandic is almost the same as the language of the ancient sagas) but hurt the country's economy; in 1602 Denmark established a trade monopoly that crippled Icelandic commerce for over 250 years. By the early 1800s disease and the harsh climate had reduced the population to 45,000, and despite a slight economic recovery at mid-century, poverty remained widespread. Also by this time Icelanders who had been educated in Denmark had come under the spell of European romanticism, and their growing national consciousness led them to demand independence. Although Denmark granted Iceland a constitution and limited autonomy in 1874, many Icelanders remained dissatisfied. Political discontent and poverty were thus two causes of emigration in the 19th century.

It was, however, neither poverty nor politics, but religion that prompted the first emigration to America. In 1851 two Icelandic apprentices in Copenhagen, Thorarinn Haflidason Thorason and Gudmund Gudmundsson, were converted by Mormon missionaries, who had already drawn nearly 15,000 Danes into the fold of the Latter-day Saints. Thorason and Gudmundsson went home and converted some of their countrymen, 11 of whom left for America between 1854 and 1857. The first arrived in Utah in 1855, and a few years later 9 Icelanders settled among other Scandinavians in the town of Spanish Fork. Small groups of Icelanders, including a few Lutherans and Presbyterians, joined the settlement from time to time during the next 20 years.

A somewhat larger emigration from Iceland began in 1870, encouraged by the letters of William Wickmann, a Danish clerk who went to Milwaukee in 1865 after working for a time in Eyrarbakki on Iceland's southern coast. He wrote to his Icelandic friends about conditions of unlimited abundance—especially of coffee, the Icelanders' favorite drink—and his letters were widely circulated. In 1870 four Icelanders left for Milwaukee; they eventually settled on Washington Island, off the Green Bay Peninsula. Over the next few years Icelanders also settled in Minnesota. A colony called New Iceland was established in Canada, but harsh conditions, smallpox, and religious strife led 100 Icelanders —over half the settlement—to move south of the border in 1878. They joined newer Icelandic immigrants in the northeastern part of the Dakota Territory, now Pembina County, and with the generous help of the already established Norwegians and Germans, formed a settlement that was to become the largest Icelandic community in America.

In 1874 a few enterprising Icelanders, skeptical of succeeding in a climate and terrain so different from that of Iceland, proposed settling in Alaska. With the help of the U.S. government they were able to visit the newly acquired territory. Although they found Alaska

GREENLAND

Arctic Ocean

Iceland

200   Km.   Miles

Denmark Strait

Arctic Circle

ICELAND

To Denmark
1500 Km.

Reykjavik

Vestmannaeyjar
Islands
(Westman Is.)

Faeroe
Islands
(Denmark)

Atlantic Ocean

acceptable, the United States apparently lost interest in assisting the colony, and the plan was dropped.

Between 1870 and 1900 about 15,000 of Iceland's total population of some 75,000 emigrated to North America. Because until 1930 U.S. immigration and census officials counted Icelanders together with Danes, the exact number who entered the United States (as opposed to Canada) during this period is unknown; a cautious estimate is 5,000. In 1910 the U.S. Census reported that 5,105 residents of the United States had grown up in a home in which Icelandic was spoken. By 1900 new immigration virtually ceased, as a result of improved economic conditions in Iceland and the more liberal Danish rule begun in 1874. Iceland was beginning to prosper and its population tripled during the next 70 years. Most of the small number of Icelandic immigrants who came to the United States after the turn of the century were war brides, brought home by returning American soldiers who had been stationed on the island during World War II.

The early Icelandic immigrants, the Mormons, were largely skilled artisans, builders, or farmers. By the mid-1870s, however, economic depression in the United States had limited opportunities for employment, and newly arrived Icelandic artisans often found their skills useless for whatever jobs were available. Although many had at least a secondary education, few knew English well, and most had little money. When they first arrived, many worked on the docks in Milwaukee, as unskilled laborers in factories, or as woodcutters until they could accumulate some capital, learn American agricultural techniques, and establish farms of their own. The original Icelandic communities were predominantly agricultural, but second- and third-generation Icelanders moved quickly through the educational system and into white-collar or professional occupations. By 1970 well over half of the second and third generations were living in urban areas.

RELIGIOUS AND SOCIAL ORGANIZATION

Because Icelanders in the homeland traditionally associated the Lutheran Church with burdensome taxes, they were not dogmatically religious in their adopted country. Nevertheless, churches were important in their lives, providing community leadership and a focus for their social life. In Minnesota and North Dakota the Lutherans were led by Páll Thorlaksson and Jón Bjarnason, two of the earliest immigrants. The former had been trained in a Lutheran seminary in the United States and the latter had been an ordained pastor in Iceland. Their philosophies differed, and this soon resulted in a temporary split in the Icelandic-American Lutheran Church. In the 1880s the Unitarian movement gained a foothold in several Icelandic communities, but the competition only served to strengthen the Lutherans, who created an Icelandic Lutheran Synod in 1885.

During the early decades of Icelandic settlement the churches served as community centers, with young people's societies, ladies' aid societies, and Sunday schools. Their choirs performed classical European and Icelandic music. The Icelandic language was used in services until the 1930s, but since then English has made rapid gains.

Outside the church, Icelanders were active in the larger community, for they did not wish to isolate themselves from other Americans. They adopted local customs, but managed to retain most of their own traditions as well. After World War I the Americanization movement and ethnic feeling were both strong, and in 1919 Icelanders in America founded the Icelandic National League. The league had several branches devoted to preserving Icelandic language, traditions, and culture, though league activities eventually came to be conducted in English. Icelandic-American organizations in northern and southern California, Seattle, Chicago, Minneapolis, New York City, and Washington, D.C., along with one in Alaska, still provide social and cultural activities for their respective communities. Icelanders operate homes for the elderly in Blaine, Wash., and Mountain, N.Dak.

Even the poorest Icelandic immigrants were literate. In Iceland instruction took place in the home until schooling began at the age of ten. In the United States, home instruction was from the beginning supplemented by attendance at public schools. Icelanders in the Dakota Territory established their first school district in 1881, and several more soon followed. Through their children, the older Icelanders improved their English, learned American history, and absorbed the customs of the new land.

Icelandic immigrants preserved an unbroken literary tradition reaching back to the sagas of Eric the Red and his explorer son, Leif. The Icelanders brought books with them and later had them sent from the homeland. They organized reading circles to purchase books, and until the mid-20th century three presses in Winnipeg, Canada, and one in Minnesota published books in Icelandic. One of the largest collections of Icelandic works, the Willard Fiske collection at Cornell University, forms the core of a library for Icelandic studies. Other important collections are found at Brigham Young University in Utah and the universities of Wisconsin and North Dakota.

Reading aloud and discussing news, especially political items, from the Icelandic press were family pastimes. A number of Icelandic Americans became journalists and writers, including the poets Stephan G. Stephanson, Kristjan Niels Julius, and Richard Beck. There have been several Icelandic weeklies, most of them short-lived. *Lögberg-Heimskringla*, a merger of two newspapers founded in the late 1880s, is still published in English and Icelandic in Winnipeg and has a North American circulation of about 1,000, half in the United States, and another 1,000 in Iceland. Since the mid-1970s this paper has received an annual subsidy from the Icelandic government. Two local groups circulate news bulletins: the *Chicago Icelander Newsletter* and the *Icelandic Club of Greater Seattle Newsletter*.

Music was another traditional part of Icelandic life that was cultivated on the American frontier—in churches, in the community, and at home. Choirs and bands were particularly active during both Icelandic and American holidays. The most important of these is Christmas: for an Icelander the celebration lasts 13 days and marks not only the birth of Christ but also the return of the sun after the darkest days of winter. Until World War II the major national holiday celebrated among immigrants was August 2, 1874, which marked both the millennium of the island's settlement and the

granting of autonomy by the Danish king. Icelandic Independence Day, June 17, 1944, is celebrated in most of the larger Icelandic-American communities.

In the 1960s an ancient pagan festival called the *thorrablot* became popular; this was originally a midwinter sacrifice to Thorri, probably the Norse god Thor, but also the name of the winter month during which the festival is held. The custom died out when Iceland converted to Christianity, but was revived by Icelandic students in Copenhagen in 1873 and by a group of archaeologists in Reykjavik, who drank toasts from Viking horns in 1881.

ASSIMILATION AND GROUP MAINTENANCE

From the beginning, Icelanders in the United States felt secure enough in their own identity to adopt new ways and eagerly followed the advice of successful immigrants who had preceded them, especially the kindred Norwegians. They learned English, participated in community activities, and held public office in the frontier settlements. Many members of the second and third generations went to college and subsequently became active in state politics: in North Dakota alone they have produced 3 state attorneys general, 3 state supreme court judges, and 12 state legislators. Other Icelanders who have become prominent include Vilhjalmur Stefansson (1879–1962), the Arctic explorer, and Chester Hjortur Thordarson (1867–1945), an inventor and entrepreneur in the electrical field.

Although Icelanders have generally been quick to assimilate and become American citizens, they have not lost interest in their Icelandic past. In 1938 Kate Bearnson Carter of Utah, whose parents were Icelanders, sponsored the building of a lighthouse in Spanish Fork's Icelandic neighborhood as a monument to the first Icelandic settlers. Through the Icelandic-American Society and other contacts, this interest has been reciprocated. In 1930, when Iceland celebrated the millennial anniversary of the founding of their parliament, the Althing, the U.S. government presented it with a statue of Leif Ericsson. The centennial of Icelandic immigration in 1955 was celebrated at a three-day festival in Spanish Fork.

Icelandic Americans remain a successfully assimilated yet ethnically conscious group.

Bibliography
One of the few English-language sources on Icelandic settlements in the United States is Thorstina Jackson Walters, *Modern Sagas: The Story of the Icelanders in North America* (Fargo, N.Dak., 1953). See also Valdimar Björnson, "Icelanders in the United States," *Scandinavian Review* 64 (1976): 39–41. For an account of the Mormon immigrants from Iceland, consult "Icelandic Mission" and "Spanish Fork" in Andrew Jenson, *Encyclopedic History of the Church of Jesus Christ of Latter-day Saints* (Salt Lake City, 1941). Much more has been written about settlements in Canada. They are covered comprehensively, along with some U.S. settlements, in Thorsteinn Thorsteinsson and Tryggvi Oleson, *Saga Islendinga i Vesturheimi* (Saga of Icelanders in the Western World), 5 vols. (Winnipeg and Reykjavik, 1940–1953).

VALDIMAR BJÖRNSON

ILOCANOS: see FILIPINOS

IMMIGRATION: ECONOMIC AND SOCIAL CHARACTERISTICS

The magnitude of immigration to America is unmatched in the history of mankind. This article sketches the overall dimensions of the flow, its origins abroad and destinations within the United States, and the characteristics of the migrants. It also examines the causes of immigration and its effects on the increase in population, total economic output, and output per head.

DIMENSIONS

Trends and Fluctuations Since the settlement of Jamestown in 1607, well over 45 million people have immigrated to the present area of the United States. Not all of them stayed; for the period from 1810 onward, when the magnitude of the movement can be gauged more accurately, a rough estimate of the volume of net immigration, the excess of arriving immigrants over departing emigrants, is about 38 million.

Relatively few immigrants came to the United States in the first third of the 19th century (see Table 1). In the 1830s a notable increase began which, with some interruptions, persisted until the first decade of the 20th century, when more than 6 million newcomers arrived. World War I and the restrictive legislation of the 1920s brought this trend to a halt: immigration fell to 2 to 3 million people per decade between 1910 and 1930, and plummeted during the Great Depression; in the 1930s, for the first time in its history, the United States actually lost more people through migration than it gained. Since World War II a considerable net influx has resumed, amounting to about 3 million people in the 1950s and 4 million in both the 1960s and 1970s.

Although immigration to the United States has been of unprecedented size, its actual contribution to the total increase of population has been smaller, and often considerably smaller, than natural increase from the excess of births over deaths. Even in 1900–1910, the decade of peak immigration, immigration accounted for less than 40 percent of the total population increase. This appraisal is somewhat deceptive, however, for it fails to allow for the contribution to population growth

Table 1. Increase in U.S. population by component of change, 1810–1970 (thousands per decade).

Period	Total increase	Natural increase[a]	Net arrivals[b]
1810–1820	2,399	2,328	71
1821–1830	3,228	3,105	123
1831–1840	4,203	3,710	493
1841–1850	6,122	4,702	1,420
1851–1860	8,251	5,614	2,593
1861–1870	8,375	6,291	2,102
1871–1880	10,337	7,675	2,622
1881–1890	12,792	7,527	4,966
1891–1900	13,047	9,345	3,711
1901–1910	15,978	9,656	6,294
1911–1920	13,738	11,489	2,484
1921–1930	17,064	14,500	3,187
1931–1940	8,894	9,962	−85
1941–1950	19,028	17,666	1,362
1951–1960	28,626	25,446	3,180
1960–1970	23,912	19,894	4,018

Source: Conrad Taeuber and Irene Taeuber, *The Changing Population of the United States* (New York, 1958), p. 294, table 91; U.S. Bureau of the Census, *Historical Statistics of the United States: Colonial Times to 1970* (Washington, D.C., 1975), pp, 8, 49.
a. Excess of births over deaths.
b. Excess of immigrant arrivals over departures. Estimated natural increase and estimated net arrivals do not coincide precisely with total increase figures because of imperfect data for births, deaths, and immigration.

from the second and later generations, which is counted in the natural increase figures. Later an attempt will be made to provide a more accurate notion of the contribution of immigration to the increase of total population in the period since 1790.

Absolute numbers do not tell the whole story. An influx of 1 million newcomers obviously has quite different significance depending on whether they join a population of 2 million or 200 million. The rate of immigration is the number of immigrants relative to the number of people already living in the area. Figure 1 presents the annual rate of immigration, the number of immigrants in each year per 1,000 total population in the United States at that time. The rate of immigration, like the absolute number of immigrants, starts at low levels in the second and third decades of the 19th century, and then begins to rise noticeably in the 1830s. But from the 1840s through World War I the trend in the rate of immigration differs from that in numbers of immigrants. Whereas the number continues to rise, the rate of immigration stays at a fairly constant average level (though fluctuating), because the rise in the volume of immigration after the 1840s was no more rapid than the growth of the U.S. population as a whole. Moreover, the volume of 3 to 4 million people entering in each decade since 1950, though comparable in absolute numbers to the amount in the late 19th century, is much less significant relative to the current population of the United States. In that respect the restrictive legislation of the 1920s achieved its purpose.

Because the data plotted in Figure 1 are yearly, they reveal other features of the temporal pattern of immigration. First, there are noticeable year-to-year fluctuations which turn out to be associated with the business cycle. Economic expansions generated a rise in immigration, and contractions a decline, with a brief lag for the time it took information about new circumstances to cross the ocean. Second, these shorter-term fluctuations are dwarfed by a longer-term movement, usually of around 15 to 20 years' duration, which is apparent in the figures from around 1840 to 1940. Peak immigration periods in these "long swings" occur around 1851–1854, 1866–1873, 1881–1883, 1905–1907, and 1921–

1924. The dampening effect of restrictive legislation on both short- and long-term fluctuations is strikingly evident in the years after 1924.

In principle, the history of American immigration, together with that of the importation of slaves, dates from the founding of Jamestown, and is in a sense virtually coterminous with the history of the entire American population, except for the American Indians. It is customary, however, to distinguish colonial settlers and their descendants, the "colonial stock," from those who arrived after the establishment of an independent United States. Unfortunately, less is known of immigration in the colonial period. Records of immigration to the various colonies, to the extent that they exist at all, are uneven and spotty, and have yet to be systematically assembled and studied. For these reasons, this essay focuses on immigration after 1790, and especially during the period of free immigration, when the flow was at a maximum. Discussion will be confined to voluntary migration, and will not treat the enforced migration of slaves, an important but quite different subject.

Colonial Immigration A few general observations can be made regarding immigration in the colonial period. First, the absolute number of immigrants was much lower than in the 19th century: the cumulative total of immigrants over the 16 decades from 1630 to 1790 was well under 1 million. In contrast, in each decade between 1850 and 1930 net immigration ranged between 2 and over 6 million. Second, although the number of immigrants was substantially higher in the 18th than in the 17th century, most of the population in 1790 was native-born; natural increase was the principal source of its dramatically high growth rate. Third, the rate of immigration was high in the first half of the 17th century. By the 18th century the rate had fallen to an average level considerably lower than in the mid- and late 19th century: a reasonable contrast might be between, say, 2 per thousand and 10 per thousand. Finally, as in the later period, colonial migration was characterized by long-term swings—upsurges and declines—although more data are needed before these movements can be dated adequately.

Sex, Age, and Marital Status Although people came

Figure 1. Annual rate of immigration, 1820–1970 (per thousand total population).

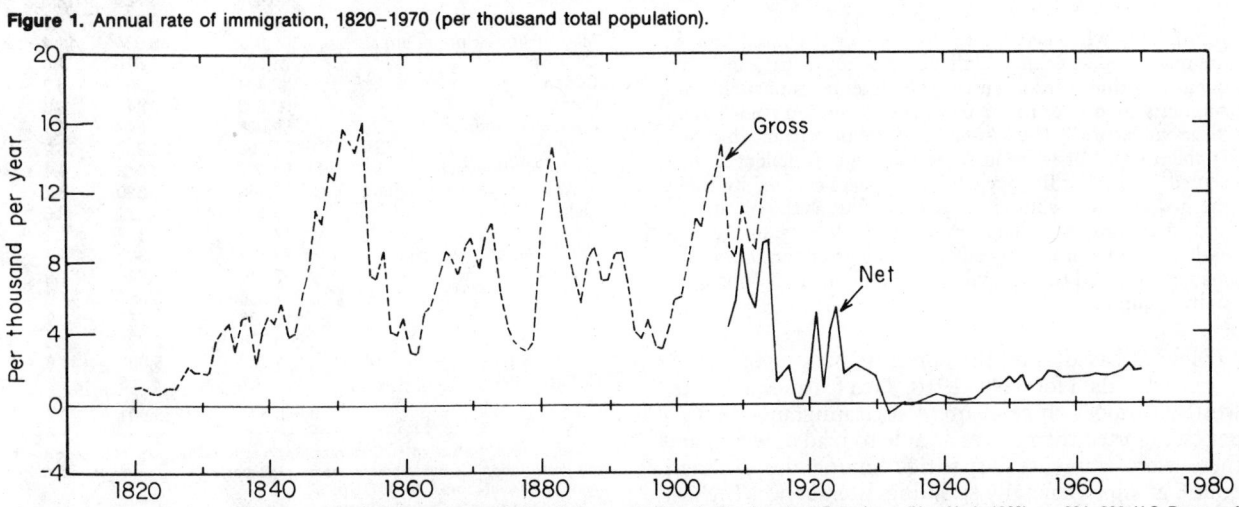

Source: Richard A. Easterlin, *Population, Labor Force, and Long Swings in Economic Growth: The American Experience* (New York, 1968), pp. 204–209; U.S. Bureau of the Census, *Historical Statistics of the United States, from Colonial Times to 1970* (Washington, D.C., 1975), pp. 8, 113.

to the United States for a variety of reasons, the primary impulse was for economic betterment. As a result, throughout the period of free immigration, a substantial majority of the newcomers were those whose services were most in demand, single males of prime working age. For most of the 19th century, males comprised about 60 percent of the total, and people aged 15–39, about two-thirds. In the two to three decades before World War I, the period of the "New Immigration" (see the discussion of national origins below), the dominance of prime working age males grew. The proportion male rose to around 67 percent and the proportion aged 15–39 climbed to about three-fourths.

Data are not available on the marital status of immigrants in the 19th century, but is seems likely that half or more were single. In the first decade of the 20th century the majority of immigrants—approximately 60 percent—were single.

The laws restricting immigration after World War I brought noticeable changes in the demographic characteristics of immigrants. Least affected was age composition; those of prime working age continued to predominate, although even their share in the total dropped, chiefly at the expense of younger persons: those aged 15–44 composed somewhat over 60 percent of the total in the 1960s. However, females became the dominant group for the first time in history, accounting for a majority of immigrants in every year since 1930. This trend reflects humanitarian concerns in the new laws —the priority given to family reunions as a criterion for immigration, and the importance of refugee or quasi-refugee movements. Closely related was a shift in marital status: married immigrants accounted for a slight majority in most years after 1930.

Literacy Immigrants have sometimes been characterized as a largely illiterate group, but the evidence available does not support this view. Information on literacy upon arrival in the United States began to be collected in 1899. Because these data cover the period of the "New Immigration," when illiteracy allegedly was highest, they are of particular interest. The concept of literacy is described in the 1910 report of the U.S. Immigration Commission, a special congressional committee established to investigate immigration problems, as follows:

Immigrants when seeking admission to the United States are not tested as to their ability to read and write, and the data upon this point represent the statements of such immigrants in answer to the inquiries, "Can you read?" and "Can you write?" The assurance of the immigrant that he is able to read or write in some language or dialect is accepted as proof of literacy. Of course, data secured by this method are not absolutely conclusive, but as the inquiries quoted are simple in character, and as the immigrant's educational status in no way affects his right to admission, it may be assumed that the information obtained is substantially accurate.

Table 2, based upon the commission's report, summarizes the data for 1899–1910. Two features are noteworthy: almost three-quarters of immigrants in this period reported themselves as able to read or write; and there were immense disparities among the different ethnic groups. Generally speaking, literacy was highest among people from northern and western Europe and lowest among those from southern and eastern Europe. Even for those from the latter areas, however, there were only a few groups among whom illiterates were a majority.

These data are consistent with those from another source, enumerations of the foreign-born obtained in the general census of the U.S. population taken every ten years. The census definition of literacy was essentially the same as that given above, but because the data do not refer to the date of immigration, they reflect improvements in the education of immigrants that occurred after their arrival. From the first census literacy count in 1880 over 85 percent of the foreign-born reported themselves as literate. Although literacy was slightly higher among the native-born, the difference

Table 2. Immigrants admitted to the United States, 14 years and older, who could neither read nor write, 1899–1910, by race or people.

Race or people	Number admitted	Persons who could neither read nor write	
		Number	Percent
Portuguese	55,930	38,122	68.2
Turkish	12,670	7,536	59.5
Mexican	32,721	18,717	57.2
Italian, South	1,690,376	911,566	53.9
Ruthenian (Russniak)[a]	140,775	75,165	53.4
Syrian	47,834	25,496	53.3
Lithuanian	161,441	79,001	48.9
East Indian	5,724	2,703	47.2
Bulgarian, Serbian, and Montenegrin	95,596	39,903	41.7
Dalmatian, Bosnian, and Herzegovinian	30,861	12,653	41.0
Russian	77,479	29,777	38.4
Korean	7,259	2,763	38.1
Croatian and Slovenian	320,977	115,785	36.1
Polish	861,303	304,675	35.4
Romanian	80,839	28,266	35.0
Greek	208,608	55,089	26.4
Hebrew	806,786	209,507	26.0
Pacific Islander	336	83	24.7
Japanese	146,172	35,956	24.6
Slovak	342,583	82,216	24.0
Armenian	23,523	5,624	23.9
African (black)	30,177	5,733	19.0
Spanish	46,418	6,724	14.5
Italian, North	339,301	38,897	11.5
Magyar (incl. Hungarian)	307,082	35,004	11.4
Chinese	21,584	1,516	7.0
Cuban	36,431	2,282	6.3
French	97,638	6,145	6.3
Spanish-American	9,008	547	6.1
German	625,793	32,236	5.2
Dutch and Flemish	68,907	3,043	4.4
West Indian (except Cuban)	9,983	320	3.2
Irish	416,640	10,721	2.6
Welsh	17,076	322	1.9
Bohemian and Moravian[b]	79,721	1,322	1.7
Finnish	137,916	1,745	1.3
English	347,458	3,647	1.0
Scots	115,788	767	0.7
Scandinavian	530,634	2,221	0.4
Other peoples	11,209	5,001	44.6
Not specified	67	5	7.5
Total	8,398,624	2,238,801	26.7

Source: U.S. Senate, 61st Congress, 3rd Session, Doc. No. 747, *Reports of the Immigration Commission, Abstracts of Reports of the Immigration Commission* (Washington, D.C., 1911), p. 99.
a. Ruthenians are Carpatho-Rusyns.
b. Bohemians and Moravians are from present-day Czechoslovakia.

was not very great. In considering the commission and census records it is useful to bear in mind that literacy could and probably often did refer to the native language of an immigrant, and that in many parts of northwestern Europe the development of formal school systems dated from the first part of the 19th century. It should also be remembered that a large share of the American-born population was from rural origins, and that schooling was less developed in rural than in urban areas.

The absolute number of immigrants in 1899–1910 who reported themselves illiterate—2.2 million—is sizable, and if, as was doubtless the case, they were largely concentrated in a few urban centers, it would have been easy for some native Americans to gain the impression that immigrants were generally illiterate. Moreover, even those who were literate at time of entry often did not speak English, and native Americans might well have thought of literacy in those terms. There are no figures on English-speaking ability at time of entry. The census data for 1890–1930, however, revealed the following percentages of foreign-born unable to speak English: 1890, 15.6; 1900, 12.2; 1910, 22.8; 1920, 11.0; 1930, 6.6. These data imply that even if a considerable number of immigrants did not know English at the time of entry, they acquired some knowledge in a fairly short time. Walter Willcox concluded that "the figures indicate that between seven-tenths and nine-tenths of the non-English-speaking immigrants had learned or claimed to have learned English between the time of arrival and a subsequent census."

The data do not mean that as a general matter most immigrants became highly fluent in English. They do suggest, however, that many immigrants had had some rudiments of formal education in their native land and picked up enough English to manage in the United States. Immigrants to the United States were not generally from the least literate ranks in their areas of origin. This makes sense, for immigrant families had to surmount the difficulties of travel and relocation to a foreign land, and a certain level of language competence was essential for this task.

Within the United States geographic differences in the extent of public schooling may account in part for the rapid linguistic assimilation of the immigrants. The South lagged noticeably behind the rest of the country. Estimates for whites in 1850 put school enrollment in the South at around six-tenths or less that in the rest of the United States, a differential that has persisted to the present, though in lesser magnitude. Schooling in urban areas has been significantly ahead of that in rural areas —data relating to literacy rates and educational attainment consistently show urban levels higher than rural. Immigrants generally avoided the South and were much more concentrated in urban areas than the American-born population. Consequently, their children, though not the immigrants themselves, generally acquired superior schooling to that available to the colonial stock.

NATIONAL ORIGINS

Where have the 45 million American immigrants come from? The answer varies depending on the time. In the colonial period virtually all immigrants were from northwestern Europe, the great majority of them from the British Isles. An estimate of the percentage distribution of the white population by nationality in 1790 shows:

British Isles		78.9
English	60.9	
Scottish	8.3	
Irish	9.7	
German		8.7
Dutch		3.4
French		1.7
Swedish		0.7
Unknown		6.6

These figures are based on a classification of surnames in the 1790 Census. Although most of this population had been born in the colonies, the impression the figures convey in regard to immigration is doubtless correct. English-speaking settlers were an overwhelming majority, with German and Dutch settlers, who accounted for most of the remaining immigration, a distant second.

The origins of immigrants from 1820 on are much better documented. As in the colonial period, throughout most of the 19th century northwestern Europe accounted for over two-thirds of U.S. immigration (see Table 3). However, the proportion of migrants from the British Isles, though sizable, was considerably reduced, and among them there was a much larger representation from Ireland (see Table 4). Germany and Scandinavia became increasingly important, together equaling or exceeding the British Isles in their contributions from the 1870s until World War I. In the 1890s southern and eastern Europe together became the major source of newcomers. To check this "New Immigration" was the central purpose of the restrictive quota laws of the 1920s. Earlier, immigration from Asia to the Pacific Coast had been effectively terminated by legislation and treaties which sought to stem the "yellow peril." Compared with other nations, the United States in the 19th century was indeed something of a "melting pot," though from an international, or even European, point of view the ingredients considered appropriate were rather narrowly defined.

The origins of immigrants from the 1920s on show clearly the impact of shifts in legislation restricting immigration. Through the 1940s there was considerable reversion toward the pattern in which northwestern Europe predominated as an area of origin—due to the national quotas of the 1920s legislation—and Canada also emerged as a strong contributor. (Data before 1900 on immigration from Canada do not permit satisfactory separation of Canadians from Europeans who were passing through.) More recently, however, in the Western Hemisphere, Mexico and the West Indies have become major sources—in 1961–1970 they surpassed Canada. Moreover, this does not take into account illegal immigration from Mexico, which is generally believed to have exceeded legal immigration in recent years. Also, in the same decade immigration from Asia accounted for the first time for over a tenth of the total, with substantial numbers of immigrants coming from the Philippines, Korea, India, Hong Kong, and Taiwan. Together, immigrants from Asia and areas in the Western Hemisphere other than Canada accounted for an unprecedented majority of the total in the 1960s.

Table 3. Distribution of total reported immigration, by continent, 1821–1970 (in percentages).[a]

| | | Distribution by area of origin | | | | | |
| | | Europe | | | | | |
Period	Total Europe	North and west[b]	East and central[c]	South and other[d]	Western hemisphere	Asia	All other
1821–1830	69.2	67.1	—	2.1	8.4	—	22.4
1831–1840	82.8	81.8	—	1.0	5.5	—	11.7
1841–1850	93.3	92.9	0.1	0.3	3.6	—	3.1
1851–1860	94.4	93.6	0.1	0.8	2.9	1.6	1.1
1861–1870	89.2	87.8	0.5	0.9	7.2	2.8	0.8
1871–1880	80.8	73.6	4.5	2.7	14.4	4.4	0.4
1881–1890	90.3	72.0	11.9	6.3	8.1	1.3	0.3
1891–1900	96.5	44.5	32.8	19.1	1.1	1.9	0.5
1901–1910	92.5	21.7	44.5	26.3	4.1	2.8	0.6
1911–1920	76.3	17.4	33.4	25.5	19.9	3.4	0.4
1921–1930	60.3	31.7	14.4	14.3	36.9	2.4	0.4
1931–1940	65.9	38.8	11.0	16.1	30.3	2.8	0.9
1941–1950	60.1	47.5	4.6	7.9	34.3	3.1	2.5
1951–1960	52.8	17.7	24.3	10.8	39.6	6.0	1.6
1961–1970	34.0	11.7	9.4	12.9	51.7	12.7	1.7

Source: Conrad Taeuber and Irene Taeuber, *The Changing Population of the United States* (New York, 1958), p. 53, table 11; U.S. Bureau of the Census, *Historical Statistics of the United States: Colonial Times to 1970* (Washington, D.C., 1975), pp. 105–109.
  a. Figures for 1821–1867 represent alien passengers arriving in steerage; 1868–1891 and 1895–1897, immigrant aliens arriving; 1892–1894 and 1898–1970, immigrant aliens admitted; 1819–1868, by nationality; 1869–1898, by country of origin or nationality; 1899–1970, by country of last permanent residence.
  b. Great Britain, Ireland, Norway, Sweden, Denmark, Iceland, Netherlands, Belgium, Luxembourg, Switzerland, France.
  c. Germany (Austria included, 1938–1945), Poland, Czechoslovakia (since 1920), Yugoslavia (since 1920), Hungary (since 1861), Austria (since 1861, except 1938–1945), U.S.S.R. (excludes Asian U.S.S.R. between 1931 and 1963), Latvia, Estonia, Lithuania, Finland, Romania, Bulgaria, Turkey (in Europe).
  d. Italy, Spain, Portugal, Greece, and other European countries not classified elsewhere.

Rates of Emigration from European Countries
Tables 3 and 4 present the relative importance of various areas in terms of the absolute number of U.S. immigrant arrivals. It is also of interest to consider migration in relation to the size of the population in the area of origin. A small country necessarily contributes a small absolute number of migrants; yet this number may be large in relation to the potential number of migrants. Table 5 presents the available data on the average annual rate of overseas emigration for the European countries per 1,000 population from 1821 to 1910. The data cover emigrants to all overseas areas, not just to the United States. However, because the United States absorbed the largest share of the migration (over two-

thirds in the period 1861–1910), the data furnish a reasonable indication of which countries sent migrants to the United States at the highest rate.

Ireland had by far the largest rate of emigration. Among other areas in northwestern Europe, Scandinavia and Great Britain are next in importance. Italy, Portugal, and (if sufficient data were available) probably Spain had considerably higher rates of emigration between 1861 and 1910 than did Germany, Austria-Hungary, or Switzerland, reflecting the very high levels of emigration from southern Europe. France and the Low Countries had the lowest rates of emigration, along with Russia and the Balkan area. In general, aside from the last two areas, which entered the movement

Table 4. Major sources of immigrants from Europe and Western Hemisphere, by country, 1821–1970 (thousands per decade).[a]

Period	Great Britain	Ireland	Denmark, Norway, Sweden	Germany	Austria-Hungary	Russia	Italy	Canada	Mexico	West Indies
1821–1830	25	51	—	7	—	—	—	—	—	—
1831–1840	76	207	2	152	—	—	2	—	—	—
1841–1850	267	781	14	435	—	—	2	—	—	—
1851–1860	424	914	25	952	—	—	9	—	—	—
1861–1870	607	436	126	787	8	3	12	—	—	—
1871–1880	548	437	243	718	73	39	56	—	—	—
1881–1890	807	655	656	1,453	354	213	307	—	—	—
1891–1900	272	388	372	505	593	505	652	—	—	—
1901–1910	526	339	505	341	2,145	1,597	2,046	179	50	108
1911–1920	341	146	203	144	896	921	1,110	742	219	123
1921–1930	330	221	198	412	64	62	455	925	459	75
1931–1940	29	13	11	114	11	1	68	109	22	16
1941–1950	132	27	26	226	28	1	57	172	61	50
1951–1960	192	57	57	478	—	6	185	378	300	123
1961–1970	206	40	43	191	—	8	214	413	454	470
Total	4,782	4,712	2,481	6,915	4,172	3,356	5,175	2,918	1,565	965

Source: Conrad Taeuber and Irene Taeuber, *The Changing Population of the United States* (New York, 1958), p. 56, table 13; U.S. Bureau of the Census, *Historical Statistics of the United States: Colonial Times to 1970* (Washington, D.C., 1975), pp. 105–109.
  a. Figures for 1821–1867 represent alien passengers arriving in steerage; 1868–1891 and 1895–1897, immigrant aliens arriving; 1892–1894 and 1898–1970, immigrant aliens admitted; 1819–1868 by nationality; 1869–1898, by country of origin or nationality; 1899–1970, by country of last permanent residence.

Table 5. Average annual rate of intercontinental emigration from Europe per decade, by country, 1821–1910.[a]

Country	1821–1830	1831–1840	1841–1850	1851–1860	1861–1870	1871–1880	1881–1890	1891–1900	1901–1910	Average 1861–1910[b]
Great Britain	0.7	1.5	2.8	3.8	3.1	4.1	5.9	3.7	6.5	4.6
Ireland	2.0	5.6	15.3	19.5	14.6	10.2	14.9	10.1	7.0	11.4
France	—	—	—	0.3	0.2	0.2	0.3	0.2	0.1	0.2
Belgium	—	—	—	0.1	0.2	0.2	0.6	0.3	0.6	0.3
Netherlands	—	—	—	0.5	0.6	0.5	1.2	0.5	0.5	0.7
Norway	—	—	—	2.4	5.8	4.7	9.6	4.5	8.3	6.6
Sweden	0.1	0.2	0.1	0.4	2.3	2.3	7.0	4.2	4.2	4.0
Denmark	—	—	—	0.2	1.1	2.0	3.9	2.2	2.8	2.4
Finland	—	—	—	—	—	0.3	1.2	2.4	5.4	2.1
Germany	—	—	1.7	2.6	1.7	1.5	2.9	1.0	0.4	1.5
Switzerland	—	—	—	1.0	1.4	1.3	3.1	1.4	1.4	1.7
Austria-Hungary	—	—	—	0.1	0.1	0.3	1.1	1.6	4.8	1.6
Portugal	—	—	—	—	1.9	2.9	3.8	5.1	5.7	3.8
Spain	—	—	—	—	—	—	2.2	2.1	5.7	—
Italy	—	—	—	—	1.0	1.0	3.2	4.9	10.8	4.1
Balkan states	—	—	—	—	—	—	0.1	0.2	1.6	—
Russia	—	—	—	—	0.0	0.1	0.3	0.5	1.6	0.5

Source: Walter F. Willcox, ed., *International Migrations*, I, *Statistics* (New York, 1929), pp. 229ff.; Gustav Sundbärg, *Apercus Statistiques Internationaux* (New York, 1908).

a. Number of emigrants per year per thousand of the resident population in that year. Figures before 1851 are approximate.
b. Averages for Spain and the Balkan states are not available because figures for the period are incomplete.

quite late, and Ireland, which experienced the catastrophic impact of the potato famine, rates of emigration tended to be higher the lower a country's level of economic development and the higher its rate of natural increase.

GEOGRAPHIC DISTRIBUTION

Two great geographic movements have dominated the distribution of the American population. One was the steady westward expansion associated with the process of farm settlement, which had largely run its course by the end of the 19th century. The other is urbanization, which began to gather momentum in the first half of the 19th century as industrialization took hold, and continues, somewhat modified, to the present.

In the 19th century, immigrants, American-born whites, and blacks participated differently in the spatial redistribution of the population. Westward expansion was accomplished primarily by native whites. But in urban growth after 1840, especially the growth of large cities, immigrants and their descendants played a disproportionate part (although American-born whites dominated the more influential urban occupations). Blacks remained concentrated in southern agriculture and participated in its westward expansion. In the 20th century, as urban concentration emerged as the dominant geographic movement, the location and economic function of the three population groups grew increasingly similar, although important differences continued to exist between whites and nonwhites (immigrant or native-born).

The trends are demonstrated most clearly when the white population is divided into native and foreign "stock." The foreign stock includes foreign-born (or first-generation) immigrants, and their children, that is, native-born people with at least one foreign parent. Native stock in the United States is defined as native-born persons of American parentage, and includes the grandchildren and subsequent descendants of immigrants. By these definitions 55 percent of the U.S. population in 1890 was native white stock; 33 percent, foreign white stock; and 12 percent, nonwhite.

The extent to which these groups participated in agricultural settlement is roughly indicated by the composition of the rural population toward the end of the 19th century in the areas settled subsequent to independence. As of 1890 in the north-central and western regions, 62 percent of the rural population was native white stock; 37 percent, foreign white stock; and 1 percent, nonwhite. In the south central region, 67 percent was native white stock; 2 percent, foreign white stock; and 31 percent, nonwhite. Thus in both areas the native white stock was disproportionately represented. But there was an interesting contrast between North and South in the roles of foreign white stock and nonwhites. Outside the South, the foreign white stock accounted for almost all of the remaining rural population; within the South, the nonwhites did.

When one turns to the figures on urban population the role of the foreign stock becomes prominent. Although the foreign stock represented only a third of the U.S. population in 1890, it made up 53 percent of the urban population. Again, as in the case of the rural population, there was a striking difference between the South and the rest of the country in the presence of foreign stock and nonwhites. Nonwhites accounted for only 2 percent of the urban population outside the South, but for 33 percent within it. The proportion of the foreign white stock in urban areas in the South was less, although it amounted to almost a quarter of the urban population in that region. Because of the varying roles the three groups played in the geographic redistribution of the population, they exhibited important differences in location as of 1890, differences which were germane to the development of their attitudes and subsequent behavior. The native white stock was still an essentially rural and small-town group both inside and outside the South. Three out of four people in this group lived in rural areas, and only 8 percent were in cities of 100,000 or more. In contrast, the foreign white stock was predominantly urban (58 percent), and a substantial proportion—one person in three—lived in large cities. As of 1890, nine out of ten blacks remained in the South, and four out of five were in rural areas.

The 20th century witnessed a major revolution in these patterns, as the frontier closed and urban concentration became the dominant force shaping population distribution. The result was a dramatic change in the distribution of both the native white stock and the nonwhites. By 1960 almost two out of three people of native white stock lived in urban areas; for nonwhites the proportion was a little higher.

The growing urban concentration of the population has vastly multiplied the contacts among groups from different backgrounds. In the late 19th century the problem of assimilation of immigrants, especially those from southern and eastern Europe, began to be felt with increasing urgency. Cutting off the supply of immigrants through legislation discriminating on the basis of national origin made the problem more manageable. At the same time, education of the children of immigrants made it possible for them to move up the occupational scale, and fostered their assimilation. But the curtailment of the immigrant labor supply had domestic repercussions. Immigrants and nonwhites were to some extent alternative sources of labor: where one group was large, the other was typically small. With the foreign labor supply largely cut off around World War I, periods of high labor demand in the North began increasingly to generate large movements of blacks out of the South. World War I and the 1920s were the first of these periods. After an interruption during the Depression of the 1930s, this process was resumed during World War II and afterward. With this shift in the sources of labor supply, the problem of assimilating immigrants was transformed into that of integrating blacks and, in the last three decades, Hispanics.

IMMIGRANTS BY OCCUPATION

Occupations in Area of Origin The impression that 19th-century immigrants were largely a displaced European peasantry finds only limited support in the data. Among those reporting occupations at time of entry, the dominant group by far is the unskilled category of general labor and domestic service, which accounted for about half of those reporting occupations in the period from 1851 through World War I (see Table 6). Those reporting an agricultural occupation accounted in most decades for around one-fourth or less of the total, not much more than those reporting occupations in industry and mining—a nonfarm manual labor group. Of course there were important differences by area of origin. For example, in 1899–1915 the proportion of non-Jewish immigrants from southern and eastern Europe reporting an agricultural occupation was one-third, while from northern and western Europe it was about one-seventh. Among Jews, who composed over one-tenth of the total immigration in this period, the proportion reporting an agricultural occupation was only 2.6 percent. It is also possible that some agricultural immigrants who anticipated urban employment may have responded in terms of their prospective urban occupations. Throughout the period of free immigration the highly skilled group in "liberal professions and public services" was a minuscule proportion of the total, averaging less than 2 percent.

A large proportion of immigrants reported no occupation. This group consisted largely of spouses and children, but in the period before 1890 it also included a substantial proportion of persons with "occupation unknown." It is difficult to judge whether omission of the latter group distorts the occupational distribution shown. Except for domestic service, the data for those with occupations refer mainly to male workers.

Immigration restrictions wrought a substantial change in the occupational makeup of immigrants, especially with the establishment after World War II of a system which gave preference to newcomers with special skills. The data on legal immigration show a major shift from an unskilled labor supply to a much more highly skilled one. In the 1960s, for example, the share of professionals had risen to close to one-fourth compared with a mere 1 percent in 1901–1910. In contrast, the share of farm and nonfarm laborers and domestic service workers had dropped to a little over 20 percent from a level exceeding 70 percent in 1901–1910.

Occupations in the United States The work taken up by U.S. immigrants was even less agricultural than one would have expected from their occupations in their countries of origin. This reflects partly the role of labor demands in the growing American economy in shaping the immigrants' occupational distribution. It is also partly due to the advantages in entering farming

Table 6. Immigrants by occupation at time of entry, 1821–1920.[a]

Period	Total (thousands)	Total reporting occupation (thousands)	Percent reporting occupation	Percent distribution of total reporting occupation				
				Agriculture	Industry and mining	Transport and commerce	Domestic service and general labor	Liberal professions and public service
1821–1830	166	66	39.8	21.4	22.3	36.3	16.8	3.2
1831–1840	640	272	42.6	32.3	27.1	18.5	20.4	1.6
1841–1850	1,703	766	45.0	32.4	21.8	6.7	38.2	0.9
1851–1860	2,940	1,355	46.1	30.5	17.2	10.2	41.5	0.5
1861–1870	2,660	1,241	46.6	17.5	21.0	11.0	49.3	1.2
1871–1880	2,812	1,382	49.1	18.9	21.5	6.6	51.5	1.5
1881–1890	5,247	2,602	49.6	14.5	18.3	5.2	61.0	1.0
1891–1900	3,844	2,147	55.8	11.9	17.4	6.1	63.5	1.0
1901–1910	8,795	6,478	73.6	26.7	17.8	4.7	49.4	1.5
1911–1920	5,736	3,924	68.4	29.8	18.3	6.7	42.5	2.7

Source: Walter F. Willcox, ed., *International Migrations*, I, *Statistics* (New York, 1929), pp. 399–400.
a. Figures for 1821–1867 represent alien passengers arriving in steerage; 1868–1891 and 1895–1897, immigrant aliens arriving; 1892–1894 and 1898–1920, immigrant aliens admitted.

Table 7. Distribution of U.S. labor force in major occupational groups by color, place of birth, and parentage, 1910.

Occupational group	Number (millions)	Distribution by percentage			
		Native whites of native parentage	Native-born whites of foreign or mixed parentage	Foreign-born whites	Nonwhite
Farm	11.5	61	12	9	18
Nonfarm	25.8	42	22	26	10
White Collar	8.0	56	27	17	1
Manual					
Craftsmen and operatives	9.8	40	24	30	6
Laborers	4.5	33	14	37	17
Service workers					
Private household workers	1.9	23	13	21	43
Others	1.7	35	19	26	20
All occupations	37.3	48	19	21	12

Source: D.L. Kaplan and M.C. Casey, *Occupational Trends in the United States, 1900 to 1950* (Washington, D.C., 1958); E.P. Hutchinson, *Immigrants and Their Children, 1850–1950* (New York, 1956).

that native whites had over immigrants because of greater capital and more pertinent farming experience.

Within the nonagricultural sector, immigrants played a distinctive role in filling the evolving occupational requirements of industrialization. Table 7 presents the number of workers in each major occupational group in 1910, the earliest date for which such data are readily available and each group's distribution by color, nativity, and parentage. Although each population group was represented in each occupational class, the native white stock was the predominant group filling white-collar jobs; the foreign stock, manual jobs; and the nonwhite, domestic service. In general, the native white stock predominated in higher-status occupations, the foreign stock occupied an intermediate position, and the nonwhites were at the bottom of the ladder. There is also an interesting difference between the first and second immigrant generations. The children of immigrants had a noticeably larger share than their parents in white-collar occupations and a noticeably lower share in the other, lower-status occupations.

The predominance of the native white stock in the higher-level occupations suggests that this group exerted disproportionate influence in decisions shaping the expansion of urban economic activity in the 19th century. That this is so is dramatically supported by studies of business leaders in the 1870s and from 1900 to 1910. The study for the latter period, for example, covered 190 members of the business elite—men who were either presidents or chairmen of the largest American corporations in manufacturing and mining, railroads, public utilities, and finance, or partners in the leading investment banking houses. In nonfarm occupations as a whole there were only four persons in ten of native white stock, but among the business elite there were eight out of ten. These men (there were no women in the group) were almost all from old American families and of British descent. The largest proportion came from the New England and Middle Atlantic states, and they had business family backgrounds. The poor 19th-century immigrant or poor farm boy who rose "from rags to riches" was a rare exception—only six people in the entire group fit this description. Thus, the descendants of the colonial white stock played a leading role not only in agricultural settlement but also in decisions

shaping urban development. Although the foreign stock were the majority in urban areas, they typically filled the manual occupations necessary for industrial growth. However, the 1910 distribution by occupation of second-generation whites is strikingly like that for those of native parentage. Although the rags-to-riches story is a gross exaggeration, significant economic improvement was possible for those of foreign origin, but the process typically required one generation or more.

CAUSES OF IMMIGRATION

Migration between different areas depends on many factors: differences in lifetime earning potentials; the costs of moving; nonmonetary factors such as language, religion, and political conditions; and the extent to which potential migrants possess relevant information. Although all these factors at one time or another affected the flow of persons to the United States, the most persistent and dominant force, especially in the great movements during the period of free immigration, was economic. Various types of data—such as comparative wage rates—make clear that in the 19th century economic opportunities in the United States were generally superior to those in Europe. But although this accounts for the direction of the flow of migrants, it is not sufficient to explain the noticeable variations in migration over time and by area of origin. Why is it that starting in the 1830s a pronounced and sustained increase occurred in the movement of Europeans to the United States? Why did this movement take a wavelike form? Why did the origins of the migrants shift increasingly from northern and western Europe to southern and eastern Europe?

Two developments seem primarily responsible for the continuous uptrend in European emigration throughout the 19th century. One was the industrialization process in the United States and the demands that it generated for manual labor in factories and construction work. Although industrial growth was taking place as early as the 1820s and 1830s, it was not until about 1850 that it reached a magnitude involving labor demands of substantial size. Confronted with the cost of native labor, which was being drained away by western agricultural opportunities, employers sought to re-

cruit cheaper foreign labor by publicizing opportunities in the United States and by other means.

The other principal factor in the increased volume of migration was the surge in population growth in Europe associated with the onset of modernization. When population was stable and sons could succeed to their fathers' positions, the inclination to move was low, especially in traditional societies. But under conditions of accelerated population growth, the opportunities available by virtue of the death or retirement of fathers were fewer than the number of individuals seeking them. A growing number of people were forced to seek new opportunities, including opportunities abroad. The population upsurge in 19th-century Europe placed increasing numbers of people in this position and thereby stimulated emigration. Safer means of travel and a decline in overseas transportation costs during the course of the century strengthened this tendency.

Another possible cause of the increase in European emigration was the occurrence of catastrophic events such as famines, wars, revolutions, epidemics, pogroms, and so on. Such events imply a deterioration in both income-earning prospects and the social advantages of the home country. It is doubtful that catastrophic events explain the continuous rise in emigration, because they occurred before as well as after that rise. But they did help determine which European countries responded most vigorously to opportunities in the United States, a point to be discussed below. And the overall volume of European emigration would have been less if there had been no such dislocations.

The 15–20-year swings in U.S. immigration appear to be due to major surges and declines in American economic conditions and thus in the growth of the demand for labor. A major economic boom or relapse tended to generate a corresponding movement in the flow of people from all the European countries. A tight American labor market offered the prospect of jobs at relatively attractive wage rates; a slack labor market meant great uncertainty about obtaining employment, whatever the wage rate.

Although conditions in the United States were chiefly responsible for immigration fluctuations over time, conditions in Europe were responsible for the distribution in the national origins of the arrivals. Given favorable conditions of labor demand in the United States, the countries that experienced more intense population pressure or catastrophic events typically responded most sensitively to that demand. The Irish exodus during the mid-19th-century potato famine is a case in point. Similarly, the shift in emigration from northern and western to southern and eastern Europe appears to be due to the shifting incidence of modern economic development with its attendant surge in population growth and associated dislocations. This process started in northern and western Europe and proceeded across the face of the continent in the course of the 19th century. Toward the end of the century, as population pressure grew in southern and eastern Europe, this area's overseas emigration rose correspondingly.

The continuing growth of European migration to the United States probably would have resumed after World War I, but it was forestalled by a change in U.S. policy.

EFFECT OF IMMIGRATION ON RATE OF POPULATION GROWTH

It would seem to be obvious that the free immigration to the United States increased total population growth. It has been argued, however, that immigration may merely have taken the place of native population growth which would otherwise have occurred. Some writers have asserted that the competition of immigrants exerted a negative effect on the fertility of the native population—that in the absence of immigration, native fertility would have been higher and population growth the same. The first president of the American Economic Association, Francis Amasa Walker, argued vigorously in an article entitled "Immigration and Degradation" that "the access of foreigners . . .constituted a shock to the principle of population among the native element" and "as the foreigners began to come in larger numbers, the native population more and more withheld their own increase." In Walker's view, "The American shrank from the industrial competition thus thrust upon him. He was unwilling himself to engage in the lowest kind of day labor with these new elements of the population; he was even more unwilling to bring sons and daughters into the world to enter into that competition."

The argument that immigration led to lower fertility is suspect because declines in American fertility are observed not only in times and places of high immigration but also in circumstances of little or no immigrant competition. Fertility became lower early in the 19th century, even before any substantial influx of immigrants occurred. Moreover, fertility declined not only in the areas of immigrant concentration but in others as well, notably the South. Fertility declines commonly set in in those areas where the land supply had been largely exhausted and the process of settlement completed, not as the result of competition from immigrants.

One must also consider the type of economic activity that the native population would have followed in the absence of immigration. It seems likely that in such circumstances the workers for American industrial expansion would have been drawn more from rural areas than was actually the case. This implies that over time, the native-born population would have been less involved in new settlement and more engaged in urban activities —that is, more exposed to an environment that encouraged low rather than high fertility. If there had been no immigration, then, fertility among the native stock might have been even lower than it was.

It is possible that the mortality of the native population might have been lower in the absence of immigration. It has been argued that immigrants sometimes transmitted epidemic or other contagious diseases to the native population The evidence suggests a higher life expectancy for native-born than for foreign-born whites: at the beginning of the 20th century, the native-born at age 20 had an edge of about 2.5 years. (The advantage of whites over nonwhites at that time was about 7 years.) By 1940 the differential between the native- and foreign-born white populations had virtually disappeared.

Thus, it is likely that in the absence of immigration both the fertility and mortality of the native white pop-

ulation might have been lower. Taking account of this one can make a rough estimate of the quantitative impact of immigration between 1790 and 1920 on the size of the population. If, in the absence of immigration, natural increase (the excess of fertility over mortality) of the colonial stock would have been the same as it was in the presence of immigration, then between 1790 and 1920 immigrants and their descendants contributed just as much to population growth as did the multiplication of the original colonial stock, white and nonwhite combined. In other words, the actual 1920 population was double that which would have resulted from increase of the colonial stock alone. By region, however, there were important variations. Little of the postcolonial immigration went to the South, and even in 1920 the population of this area was composed very largely of descendants of the colonial population.

EFFECT OF IMMIGRATION ON PRODUCTION GROWTH

What about the effect of immigration on the rate of growth of gross national product (GNP)? In considering this, a distinction between aggregate and per capita GNP is important. With regard to total GNP the effect of immigration is clear. If immigration had been substantially less, the growth of the labor force would have been less rapid and land would have come under cultivation more slowly. With fewer savers, capital accumulation would have been less. The slower growth of land, labor, and capital would in turn have implied a slower growth in aggregate output. Actual trends in the United States over the last century or so are roughly consonant with this reasoning: a continuous decline in the growth rate of population has been accompanied by a continuous decline in the growth rate of national product.

It is when one considers per capita output that the problem becomes most challenging. Between 1790 and 1840 immigration remained low, though it was rising. In the late 1840s, however, a major influx began which, if one includes descendants as well as immigrants, doubled the American population by 1920. Suppose that population growth had been kept much lower by curtailment of immigration. What then would have been the course of per capita output? Would the United States have reached a material standard of living comparable to that which it enjoys today? Or, as some argue, was immigration critically important to rapid growth in material well-being?

There are several ways in which immigration affected growth of per capita output. Immigration altered the age distribution of the population by raising the proportion of the working-age population to total population, and within the working-age population, by keeping the proportion aged 20 to 29 higher than it would otherwise have been. In terms of the effect on per capita product, both influences are favorable—the first because it raises the proportion of workers to dependents and the second because it increases the proportion of more vigorous, younger workers within the working group. However, the quantitative effect on the per capita output is small.

Offsetting these positive influences is the effect of immigration on the general health and educational levels of the labor force. Because the foreign-born had somewhat higher illiteracy rates and lower life expectancy than the native-born, in the absence of immigration the average health and education of the labor force would have shown more rapid improvement, and this would have made for somewhat faster growth in per capita production.

Did immigration add special skills or entrepreneurial abilities to the labor force? Certainly there were immigrants who succeeded as entrepreneurs and others who had special labor skills. The foreign-born, however, are underrepresented among the industrial leaders of the 19th century; the mass of immigrants filled manual jobs, and these could have been done by native workers.

What about economic motivation? Did immigration after 1790 provide a population group with an exceptional urge to get ahead? This seems dubious. A strong interest in material gain runs back to the earliest period of settlement. It was manifest in both towns and rural areas in the 17th century and was the despair of some early religious leaders. The story of land speculation seems much the same whether one is looking at Puritans in 17th-century New England or at their descendants in the 19th-century Midwest.

The principal impetus for rapid economic growth came from the burgeoning developments in modern technology that date from the Industrial Revolution in England toward the end of the 18th century. In the first half-century after 1790, a period in which U.S. immigration was relatively slight, the growth rate of per capita production in the United States rose to levels comparable to those of today, and the American system of manufacturing came into being, a system so distinctive that the world's leading industrial nation, Great Britain, sent a special commission in 1850 to study it. Thus, even before immigration rose markedly in the 19th century, the United States was well started on the transformation of its economy to modern technology.

It is important to note also that in Europe, and especially northwestern Europe, high emigration did not prevent the development of this new technology. In the United States between 1840 and 1957, the shift to modern technology led to a 460 percent increase in real per capita production. In the major European countries real per capita output grew as follows: United Kingdom, 1850s–1950s, 370 percent; West Germany, 1870s–1960s, 520 percent; France, 1840s–1960s, 520 percent. If U.S. growth in per capita production had been especially favored by immigration, the European countries of emigration should have been correspondingly disfavored; but there is little in the figures above to suggest that this was the case.

It seems reasonable to conclude, therefore, that while 19th-century immigration had a major impact on America's size—in terms of both total population and total output—it probably did not alter substantially the growth of output per capita. The major impetuses to the growth of per capita production were rapid innovation through the adoption of modern technology and an associated capital formation. These developments were fostered by a young, vigorous, relatively well-educated population with strong economic motivation operating under institutions which favored the pursuit of personal gain. All these conditions existed prior to the vast 19th-century immigration, and would have continued to operate even in the absence of that immigration.

A SMALLER AMERICA?

In other respects, however, 19th-century U.S. immigration was of considerable importance. Although per capita product growth might not have been much different in its absence, the economy would have grown much less in aggregate size. In addition, although many of the structural changes in the economy would still have occurred—for example, the proportion of urban concentration, the change in occupational structure, and the shifts in overall consumption patterns—there would have been differences in industrial structure, related in part to greater involvement in world trade. As for geographic expansion, it seems likely that some areas now being depopulated might never have been settled, and the reduction of the indigenous Indian population might not have been so drastic. Without 19th-century immigration, the American population would exhibit much less cultural variety than it does today. Conceivably, the role of women and of nonwhites would have been different. Economic assimilation of nonwhites might have proceeded more rapidly and problems of racial integration might have been posed and resolved sooner. Internationally, a smaller United States more dependent on world trade would have been a less important voice in world politics.

Bibliography

No single work covers the topic. Works with fairly general coverage include, by demographers, Warren S. Thompson and P.K. Whelpton, *Population Trends in the United States* (1933; reprint, New York, 1969), and Conrad Taeuber and Irene Taeuber, *The Changing Population of the United States* (New York, 1958), and, by historians, Marcus Lee Hansen, *The Atlantic Migration, 1607–1860* (Cambridge, Mass., 1940), and Oscar Handlin, ed., *Immigration as a Factor in American History* (Englewood Cliffs, N.J., 1959). More specific studies, focusing chiefly on the period from 1790 to 1950, or parts thereof, include Simon Kuznets and Ernest Rubin, *Immigration and the Foreign Born* (New York, 1954), on net versus gross immigration flows; Niles Carpenter, *Immigrants and Their Children, 1920* (Washington, 1927), on national origins; Stanley Lebergott, *Manpower in Economic Growth: The American Record Since 1800* (New York, 1964), and Edward P. Hutchinson, *Immigrants and Their Children, 1850–1950* (New York, 1956), on labor force and occupations; and Simon Kuznets et al., *Population Redistribution and Economic Growth, United States, 1870–1950*, 3 vols. (Philadelphia, 1957–1964), covering internal migration of the foreign born. Fluctuations in immigration are analyzed by Harry Jerome, *Migration and Business Cycles* (New York, 1926); Richard A. Easterlin, *Population, Labor Force, and Long Swings in Economic Growth: The American Experience* (New York, 1968); and Brinley Thomas, *Migration and Economic Growth*, 2d ed. (Cambridge, England, 1973). Brinley Thomas, ed., *Economics of International Migration* (London, 1958), focuses on economic causes and effects of migration. Two studies relating to the colonial period are J. Potter, "The Growth of Population in America, 1700–1860," in *Population in History*, eds. C.V. Glass and D.E.C. Eversley (Chicago, 1965); and P.M.G. Harris, "The Social Origins of American Leaders: The Demographic Foundations," *Perspectives in American History* 3 (1969): 159–344. Edward P. Hutchinson, ed., "The New Immigration," *The Annals of the American Academy of Political and Social Sciences* 367 (September 1966): 1–149, and Charles B. Keely, "Immigration Composition and Population Policy," in *Population: Dynamics, Ethics and Policy*, eds. Priscilla Reining and Irene Tinker (Washington, D.C., 1975), discuss recent immigration. The best works on immigration policy are Marion T. Bennett, *American Immigration Policies* (Washington, D.C., 1963), and Robert A. Divine, *American Immigration Policy, 1924–1952* (1957; reprint, New York, 1972). Major data sources are the U.S. Bureau of the Census, *Historical Statistics of the United States, Colonial Times to 1970* (Washington, D.C., 1975); U.S. Immigration and Naturalization Service, *Annual Reports* (Washington, D.C., 1819–); U.S. Senate, 61st Congress, 3rd Session, Doc. No. 747, *Reports of the Immigration Commission, Abstracts of Reports of the Immigration Commission* (Washington, D.C., 1911); and Walter F. Willcox, ed., *International Migrations* (New York, 1929).

RICHARD A. EASTERLIN

IMMIGRATION: HISTORY OF U.S. POLICY

In the nearly four centuries since the English first settled in Jamestown, over 45 million people have immigrated to the United States or to the colonies out of which the nation grew, and from the earliest years immigration has been of concern to the makers of public policy. Americans have sought to stimulate and regulate the flow of newcomers in a variety of ways. U.S. immigration policy has been a sensitive barometer both of the achievements and of the problems of national development, for it has been quick to respond to changing economic, political, social, and diplomatic circumstances. The history of American immigration policy falls into five distinct periods: the colonial era (1609–1775); the Open Door era (1776–1881); the era of regulation (1882–1916); the era of restriction (1917–1964); and the era of liberalization (1965 to the present).

THE COLONIAL PERIOD, 1609–1775

In the 17th century the English drive for overseas empire shaped the patterns of immigration and settlement in the North American colonies. The process of peopling the American continent was deliberate and organized, for population was needed to cultivate the virgin lands of the New World—population that would enable colonies to supply raw materials to the mother country and would consume its manufactured goods.

From the early 17th century to the American Revolution, colonial immigration policy was carried out on two levels: on one, the government of the empire—the Crown, Parliament, the Board of Trade—regulated the activities of the North American colonies; on the other, the colonial governments—legislatures, proprietors, and local officials—enacted and enforced laws within the imperial framework. On occasion the two levels came into conflict. In the 1660s, for example, when Parliament approved the transportation of convicted felons to the Chesapeake Bay area—considering that putting them to work in the labor-short colonies was more productive than executing or imprisoning them—the Virginia assembly, fearful of social disturbances, decreed that "no person trading with Virginia, either by land or sea, should bring in any 'jailbirds.'" Maryland in 1676 enacted a similar exclusionary law, but Parliament overruled the restrictions, and private contractors continued to arrange the transportation of convicts to those colonies into the 18th century.

On the whole, however, the consensus at both levels of government was that the goal of immigration policy was the recruitment of labor. It was left to colonial governments and entrepreneurs to devise schemes to attract people to the colonies and thereby increase property values, rents, and profits. To do this they advertised the opportunities of the New World to the people of the British Isles and Europe in a variety of ways. In 1609 the Virginia Company launched a publicity drive in London; its advertisements, preached from the pulpits, generated a flurry of gentry investment and volunteering for colonization. In the late 17th century, Anthony Ashley Cooper, the proprietor of the Carolinas, publicized throughout the West Indies and Europe the abundant land and the religious toleration that could be found there. William Penn made Pennsylvania the most widely advertised of all the colonies: he

himself went to Europe to supervise recruitment campaigns and distributed hundreds of pamphlets and advertisements in English, French, German, and Dutch announcing that Pennsylvania had given all males the right to vote, had enacted a humane penal code, and required no military service.

Colonial governments provided not only information about, but transportation to, the colonies and subsidized purchase of lands and tools for new settlers as well. The Puritans of Massachusetts Bay helped pay for the transportation, food, and equipment of recruits to their Holy Commonwealth. The Calverts of Maryland, Cooper of the Carolinas, and Penn dipped into family fortunes to stock the colonists with equipment and supplies, and sold land to new arrivals at low prices. By extending this helpful hand to enterprising immigrants, they provided them from the very beginning with a substantial stake in the settlement.

Colonies also offered "bounties" to recruiting agents who provided settlers. As early as 1678 South Carolina was paying bounties to importers of white servants, sometimes to the master of a vessel who brought the newcomers, and sometimes to immigration agents called "importers." These schemes for recruitment and transportation stimulated the first great wave of colonization in the Chesapeake Bay area. The Virginia Company pioneered the practice of indentured servitude, and in the 17th century brought an average of 1,500 bonded laborers each year to the Chesapeake Bay. An indentured servant bound himself to the company or to a planter for four to seven years; in return he received free passage, a year's provisions, a house and tools, and a share of the crops he produced. When his contract expired, he gained all the rights of a freeman and the opportunity to hold title to his own land. In 1619 the company established the "headright" system to promote still more immigration. The headright conferred upon a person a title to 50 acres of uncultivated land upon arrival in Virginia or, if he was already there, for paying the transportation costs of another settler who would discharge the obligation by working on his land.

Dedicated to reforming the English church and to building a regenerate society, the Puritans of the New England colonies limited their recruitment to fellow religious communicants of the gentry, yeoman, tradesman, and artisan classes of England. They sought family men with useful skills who could help build the community; they excluded or expelled itinerants, adventurers, Quakers, and members of other religious sects of which they did not approve. They spurned the mass advertising employed by the proprietary colonies and Virginia, relying for selection instead on the quiet working of religious inspiration. Since the Puritan polity tied civil government to ecclesiastical goals, full political and civil rights were granted only to the members of their church. The Puritan New England colonies were the most socially homogeneous settlements in America; religious orthodoxy functioned both as a process of selection and as a restriction on the numbers who came.

By 1700 nearly all the colonies were employing some combination of advertising, grants of land, employment incentives, transportation payment, and guarantee of rights and freedoms to increase the flow of immigrants; informal naturalization laws permitted aliens to secure freehold land (land without restrictions on transfer) once they had arrived. Like a giant magnet, the colonies drew farmers, workers, artisans, and tradesmen who had been dislodged by a changing European economy. Although the availability of work was the primary inducement, the religious policy of most of the colonies was an additional attraction. Outside New England's restrictive establishment, toleration of all Christian denominations, and even of Judaism, was gradually established. Some proprietors marked their colonies as havens for particular groups seeking protection from religious persecution: Lord Calvert made Maryland an asylum for England's Catholics; William Penn turned Pennsylvania into a sanctuary for Quakers and others; the strict orthodoxy of New England made its settlements the destination of those seeking an uncompromisingly reformed English church—though even in New England a degree of tolerance had been accorded to non-Congregationalists by 1700. Religious conformity itself declined throughout the 18th century. Without coercive authority, secure leadership, and state sanctions, religion became a matter of choice with little formal relevance to civil status, and religious tests for entry into any of the colonies soon fell into disuse.

The attraction of the New World for non-British groups was increased after 1740 by a major shift in policy toward arriving aliens. Until that year, colonial governments granted deeds of "denization," or naturalization, to aliens that bestowed civil and property-holding rights preliminary to full British citizenship. To speed up settlement, letters of naturalization were even issued to aliens in England. These deeds, however, were not binding upon the imperial government and were often not honored by the colonies. In 1740 Parliament cleared the ambiguous status of aliens by passing a universal naturalization act that made all aliens in the colonies fully naturalized British subjects as soon as they could prove that they had resided continuously on British territory for seven years.

Changes in the land-distribution policy of the colonies in the 18th century further stimulated the flow of newcomers. The headright system had concentrated an excessive amount of land in the hands of a few prosperous merchants and speculators, so in 1705 the Virginia legislature dismantled the program and introduced a system of direct government sale of land warrants to settlers at low prices; Maryland and the Carolinas soon followed the same course. In New England the practice of deeding land only to acceptable religious groups collapsed under the pressure of popular demand for new uncultivated areas. Land speculators obtained whole townships from the General Court of Massachusetts in the 1720s and, in the 1740s, held public auctions of New England land. The proprietors of the huge virgin-land tracts in the Northern Neck of Virginia, the hinterland of Pennsylvania, the Carolinas, and Maryland distributed freehold land at public sales and opened settlement unconditionally to all comers.

Three features of immigration policy that would shape 19th-century patterns were established in the colonial period. First, it was local government that exercised jurisdiction over immigration and settlement. Second, the central government left it to local governments and entrepreneurs to recruit immigrants from other countries. Finally, the increasing demands of eco-

nomic development led to a search for new sources of labor—a search that would spread in the 19th century into countries unimagined by Tudor Englishmen or colonial planters.

THE OPEN DOOR ERA, 1776–1881

The rejection by the British government of colonial demands for a more open immigration policy to attract newcomers was one of the many grievances that led colonists to take up arms against the British in 1775. The Declaration of Independence attacked the king and the Privy Council for endeavoring "to prevent the population of these states" by refusing to recognize general naturalization acts passed by colonial assemblies and by restricting westward settlement in the Proclamation of 1763 and the Quebec Act of 1774. As the Revolution progressed it also brought with it a new concept of national identity. In their struggle to separate themselves from Englishmen, Americans began to see themselves as a unique people bred from the frontier and from the mingling of several nationalities. The popular writer Tom Paine wrote in 1776, "Europe, and not England, is the parent country of America." By then more than a third of the country's white inhabitants were of non-English origin.

The Philadelphia convention that drafted the Constitution of the United States in 1787 debated the question of immigration. Alexander Hamilton, a West Indian by birth, argued that immigrants could make important contributions to the welfare of the nation and that they should be regarded as "on the level of the first citizens." George Mason of Virginia agreed, saying he "was for opening a wide door for emigrants," but hesitated "to let foreigners . . . make laws for us and govern us." Pierce Butler of South Carolina and Gouverneur Morris of Pennsylvania feared that immigrants would retain the political principles of the despotic countries they had left behind. Despite these reservations, however, the framers of the Constitution ended by making the foreign-born ineligible only for the presidency; senators had to be citizens for nine years or more, and representatives for seven. Congress was also empowered to establish a uniform naturalization law. (*See* Naturalization and Citizenship.)

Many leaders of the new republic clearly expected the immigrant to play a major role in the development of the nation. In the Northwest Ordinance of 1787, Congress guaranteed religious freedom in the Northwest Territories, hoping that this liberty would be an added attraction for immigrants. "That part of America which has encouraged [the foreigners] most, has advanced most rapidly in population, agriculture and the arts," observed James Madison, while Hamilton declared that "a perfect equality of religious privileges will probably cause [immigrants] to flock from Europe to the United States," and Assistant Secretary of State Tench Coxe composed notes for the information of the immigrant which endorsed the freedom of religion in the United States and promised that freedom to all.

The American Revolution and the Napoleonic wars hindered the flow of immigration until 1815. In the intervening period Congress passed (1790) the first federal laws loosely defining a uniform rule for the naturalization of aliens: any free white person who resided for two years "within the limits and under the jurisdiction of the United States" could acquire American citizenship. The review of naturalization applications was to be made by "any common law court of record in any one of the States." These generous terms for citizenship and open immigration laid the basis for the massive growth of population that was to follow in the next century.

But the political struggles of the new nation also led to the first, though ultimately unsuccessful, effort to impede the assimilation of newcomers. In 1798 the Federalist party secured the passage of the Alien Act designed to harass immigrants who they suspected might become Republicans, and to deny them the vote by raising the residency requirement for citizenship to 14 years. Three years later, after the Republican victory in the election of 1800, the act was repealed in favor of a 5-year residency requirement.

Authority over immigration continued to be exercised mainly by state governments and local officials until after the Civil War. In practice the regulation of immigrant traffic was assumed by those states having large ports, such as Massachusetts, New York, Pennsylvania, and Maryland. From 1820 to 1860 these states passed laws to reduce the social and financial costs of monitoring immigration. New York, where two-thirds of all newcomers landed, pioneered inspection and welfare laws and required shipmasters to report the name, occupation, birthplace, age, and physical condition of each passenger. On the basis of these reports, the infirm and the destitute who might become wards of the state could be identified and deported. Bond had to be posted for any immigrant suspected of being a potential charity case. New York also charged each shipmaster $1.50 for cabin passengers and $1.00 for those in steerage; the fees paid were used to maintain a marine hospital. Massachusetts ordered shipmasters transporting immigrants to pay $2.00 for each passenger to the city of Boston; those fees were used for support of those foreigners who, after admission, became paupers. To execute these laws the coastal states established immigration boards; run by social reformers and humanitarians who served without pay, their enforcement procedures tended to be casual.

New York's state laws requiring the screening of immigrants were challenged in a landmark U.S. Supreme Court case, *City of New York* v. *Milne* (1837), in which the defendant Milne, the master of a ship that transported immigrants, argued that the New York regulations were an obstruction of interstate and foreign commerce. The Supreme Court, however, found that the laws derived from the legitimate right of states to exercise police power within their boundaries: "We think it as competent for a State to provide precautionary measures against the moral pestilence of paupers, vagabonds, and possibly convicts, as it is to guard against the physical pestilence which may arise from unsound or infectious articles imported, or from a ship, the crew of which may be laboring under an infectious disease," the opinion read. This decision authorized state governments to set criteria for the suitability of immigrants for admission and to reject arrivals who did not meet their standards.

The processing of new arrivals in the mid-19th century was best exemplified by the procedures used at

Castle Garden, the immigration depot of New York City between 1855 and 1890. Converted from a former opera house at the southern tip of Manhattan, Castle Garden provided reception and orientation services, a hospital where sick passengers could recuperate before venturing forth, an inexpensive restaurant, free baths, baggage-carrying services, and a communal kitchen. The commissioners of Castle Garden served without pay, compiling employment listings, arranging for transportation, and even licensing numerous boarding houses to which they could direct immigrants who needed lodging. They gave a brief medical examination to all passengers, recorded names, ages, occupations, religions, and the value of the belongings they brought into the country. Castle Garden was run as if it were a protective charity foundation: it provided safety from swindlers and confidence men, a hospitable reception for the newcomers, practical advice, and social services. The spirit of benevolence guided the welfare workers on its all-volunteer staff.

During the first half of the 19th century the federal government did little to supervise, control, or promote immigration. Federal officials kept no records of immigrants until 1820, when the State Department first began to count the number of immigrant entrants each year. The tasks of recruiting immigrants and adjusting the newcomers to American life when they arrived were assumed by local governments and by entrepreneurs; the federal government simply relied on the open land market and other advantages and opportunities to attract immigrants.

The expanding frontier and industrializing cities continued to demand manpower. Several western states sent brochures and pamphlets overseas describing the opportunities to purchase public land at $1.25 an acre. In 1845 Michigan appointed an agent to recruit immigrants on the docks of New York City. Wisconsin followed suit, and also organized county committees to compile mailing lists of the settlers' friends and relatives still in Europe. Minnesota hired a clerk to draw up mailing lists and to send advertisements to Europe in English, Welsh, German, Dutch, Norwegian, and Swedish; it had a publicity agent covering Sweden and another stationed in Bremen, who visited shipping offices and emigrant boarding houses; and it awarded prizes for the essays that were judged best at describing opportunities in the state for the immigrant. These essays were published in seven languages and distributed in the appropriate countries of Europe.

In the second half of the 19th century, 33 state and territorial governments established immigration offices to attract newcomers. Their pamphlets extolled the virtues of the American frontier and of its allegedly salubrious climate. An Iowa pamphlet of 1870 described the beauty of an Iowan Indian summer; Minnesota pointed out that its death rate was only a fourth or a third of that in Europe. The theme most emphasized, however, was the contrast between American opportunity and European stagnation. The Iowa pamphlet declared that in the Midwest men could become prosperous and independent, while in Europe "the great majority . . . must live out their days as dependent labourers on the land of others." Minnesota's pamphlet proclaimed, "It is well to exchange the tyrannies and thankless toil of the old world for the freedom and independence of the new . . .

it is well for the hand of labour to bring forth the rich treasures hid in the bosom of the NEW EARTH." The competition for immigrants also inspired a fierce rivalry between states. Wisconsin charged that Minnesota was farther away, had fewer railroads, and more frequent natural disasters. Iowa and Minnesota disparaged the Dakotas, with their locusts, Indians, blizzards, and droughts.

As the flow of arriving immigrants increased, policy makers slowly began to realize that the federal government was going to have to devote greater attention to the new arrivals; in 1855 Congress directed officials of the U.S. Customs Service to compile both quarterly and annual immigration reports. In 1864 Congress passed a bill establishing a Bureau of Immigration, but in 1867 it transferred the job of keeping immigration records to the more technically capable Bureau of Statistics in the Treasury Department.

The first federal attempt at direct promotion of immigration was made in 1864, with a contract-labor law that authorized employers to finance the transportation of immigrant workers and to bind their services in advance, but the measure was repealed in 1868 in the face of protests from labor organizations.

The Republican party became the major advocate for a stronger federal immigration policy. The Republican platform of 1864 asserted: "Foreign immigration which in the past has added so much to the wealth, resources, and increase of power to this nation—the asylum of the oppressed of all nations—should be fostered and encouraged by a liberal and just policy"; in 1868 and 1872 the Republican party reaffirmed this plank.

A dispute in 1874 over the coming of Mennonite (Amish) immigrants nearly pushed Congress into an unprecedented policy, as congressmen debated a proposal to reserve a huge tract of western land for thousands of Mennonites as an inducement for them to come to the United States rather than to Canada. Opponents of the plan argued successfully that no group should receive preferential treatment on the basis of "a special right to compact themselves as an exclusive community." The controversy ended when three western states offered the Mennonites exemption from military duty and thereby lured most of them to the United States.

By the 1870s over 280,000 immigrants a year were disembarking at American ports. The highest levels of government could no longer afford to be diffident or to entrust to the states the management of the powerful force of immigration. In 1875, a United States Supreme Court decision inaugurated a major revision in national immigration policy. In *Henderson* v. *Mayor of New York*, a case raising issues identical to those in *New York* v. *Milne*, the Supreme Court reversed its 1837 decision: the justices now declared that all existing state laws regulating immigration were unconstitutional on the grounds that they usurped the exclusive power vested in Congress to regulate foreign commerce. The justices concluded by calling for federal supervision of immigration:

It is equally clear that the matter of these statutes may be, and ought to be, the subject of a uniform system or plan. The laws which govern the right to land passengers in the United States from other countries ought to be the same in New York, Boston, New Orleans, and San Fran-

cisco . . . We are of the opinion that this whole subject has been confided to Congress by the Constitution; that Congress can more appropriately and with more acceptance exercise it than any other body known to our law, state or national; that by providing a system of laws in these matters, applicable to all ports and to all vessels, a serious question, which has long been a matter of contest and complaint, may be effectually and satisfactorily settled.

This decision at first threw the burden of receiving foreigners and discouraging unfit immigrants onto private philanthropic organizations, because a federal agency to perform these functions had not yet been established. Overwhelmed by the growing volume of immigrants and the strain on their resources, charity workers soon petitioned Congress to authorize federal action. In the 1880s Congress enacted a series of statutes bringing immigration under direct federal control and—a measure that proved to be more significant—allowing the federal government to exercise its authority to restrict the entry of people thought to be undesirable.

THE ERA OF REGULATION, 1882–1916

In the late 19th century the federal government built the administrative and bureaucratic machinery that would operate this new federal immigration policy. Policy makers began to experiment with new ways of monitoring arrivals, so that only those thought to be most adaptable to American society would be admitted. As concern about social problems thought to be the result of immigration mounted, they gradually constructed regulations that admitted only those who were healthy and employable.

The drive for federal regulation of immigration originated in California, where Chinese immigrants had begun to arrive around the time of the gold rush of 1849; many more came to the West Coast in the ensuing years, largely as contract labor brought in to build the railroads. By 1869, 63,000 Chinese had come to the United States, and twice that number arrived in the course of the next decade. Public reaction to the mounting numbers led the government of California to experiment with laws that would cut down the rate of entry. As early as 1852 the governor and the state assembly were recommending restrictive measures; state courts declared the Chinese ineligible for naturalization on the grounds that they could not be categorized among the "free whites" stipulated by federal law. In 1855 California passed a law levying a $50 capitation tax on arriving passengers ineligible for citizenship. Two years later, however, the U.S. Supreme Court declared this act unconstitutional. In 1870 restrictionists, claiming that Asian prostitutes were being imported into the country, obtained a state law prohibiting the landing of any Mongolian, Japanese, or Chinese female who could not provide evidence of voluntary emigration and decent character. To curb the influx of contract labor, the law was subsequently extended to males.

Nearly all the Chinese who came were unskilled laborers who were willing to work for little pay and who therefore were thought to threaten the wages and working conditions of the locals. Labor organizations, led by the Mechanics State Council of California, decided that state regulation was not sufficient and appealed to the

U.S. Congress to place national limits on the immigration of Chinese workers. Republicans and Democrats alike in the far-western states agreed that federal action was required, but this placed the administration in an awkward position: Chinese immigration rights had been formally guaranteed by the Burlingame Treaty between the United States and China (1868), by which, in exchange for certain trade concessions, the U.S. government pledged that it would not restrict the numbers of Chinese workers coming into the country. But in 1879 Congress gave way to pressure from the western states, and in direct violation of that agreement enacted legislation banning from American ports any vessel carrying more than 15 Chinese passengers. President Rutherford B. Hayes vetoed the measure as a violation of international agreement. But the next year a new treaty was negotiated with China which permitted the United States to "regulate, limit, or suspend," but "not absolutely prohibit," the immigration of Chinese laborers, and in 1882 Congress took advantage of the provision to suspend the entry of Chinese workers for ten years. The Chinese Exclusion Act of 1882 stated that restrictions were needed because "in the opinion of the Government of the United States the coming of Chinese laborers to this country endangers the good order of certain localities."

The most radical provision of the law was the one that barred all foreign-born Chinese from acquiring citizenship. The basis for this statute was the Naturalization Act of 1790 in which acquisition of citizenship by naturalization had been limited to "free white persons"; an act of 1870 had subsequently extended the privilege to "aliens of African nativity and persons of African descent." Now, for the first time, a federal statute was designating a group as specifically ineligible on the grounds of race. Chinese immigration had aroused a national effort to identify an unassimilable alien race and to ban it from entry. Although in the 1880s the Chinese issue was kept distinct from the problems arising from European immigration, it nonetheless firmly established the prerogative of the federal government to raise restrictive barriers against specific national groups.

In 1882 Congress enacted the first comprehensive federal immigration law and delegated authority to the Treasury Department for enforcing it, but the states were still left with primary responsibility for the inspection of immigrants to see that all those excluded by law—convicts, lunatics, idiots, and incapacitated persons who might become public charges—were turned back. Carrying on another earlier state practice, immigrant welfare was paid for out of a federal fund raised by levying a charge of 50 cents on each entering alien.

In 1885 Congress passed the Foran Act, another exclusionary law, this time lobbied through Congress by the Knights of Labor. It prohibited the recruitment of unskilled labor by prepaid passage and advance contracting, but it did not affect skilled workers, artisans, or teachers. It was followed in 1888 by a supplemental law that ordered the deportation of alien contract laborers within one year of entry; by this measure the federal government was empowered to specify regulations that could lead to deportation.

At the same time as the groundwork was being laid for the imposition of federal controls, the character of

immigration also began to change, shifting in ways that aroused concern in some quarters and that led to demands for the government to find new solutions. Although immigrants from northern and western Europe remained in the vast majority in the 1880s, newcomers from southern and eastern Europe were becoming increasingly numerous. They were referred to as "new immigrants," a label that soon acquired invidious connotations.

By the 1890s the new immigrants were in the majority—and in most years it was a large majority. Many natives saw them as having peculiar habits and alien cultures. Some began to believe that the Slavs, Jews, Magyars, Sicilians, and others included in the group were innately inferior and racially unassimilable. Popular journals were filled with hostile references to the newcomers. A large foreign-born population only gradually being acculturated was filling the major urban centers. The demands for a more systematic public policy increased. State authorities were calling for federal assistance to process the multitude of immigrants and to facilitate their adjustment. They demanded that minimal health and competency standards be set for the welfare of native and immigrant communities alike. The Progressive movement, bent on the reform of government and industry and the improvement of social services, popularized the notion that government regulation of immigration would make its management more efficient.

In 1891 Congress finally established a permanent administration for the national control of immigration in the form of a superintendent of immigration within the Treasury Department. Minimum health qualifications for immigrants were formulated, as was an effective method for deporting immigrants rejected by U.S. inspectors: steamship companies were now compelled by law to return all unacceptable passengers to their country of origin. Aliens who landed illegally or became public charges within one year of arrival were subject to deportation. The law of 1891 also added new categories to those to be excluded: polygamists were banned, along with "persons suffering from a loathsome or dangerous contagious disease." The exclusion of contract labor was extended by prohibiting employers from advertising abroad for laborers and by preventing laborers responding to illegal advertisements from entering the country.

The law of 1891 ushered in full-scale federal control of immigration. Although the regulatory mechanisms operated only on overseas immigrants and did not affect people crossing U.S. borders by land, the state governments were at least no longer responsible for monitoring the stream of foreigners arriving from abroad. Overtaxed charity organizations were relieved of their burden as federal agents began to provide reception services to newcomers.

About three-quarters of the newcomers entered at the port of New York City. The old welcoming station, Castle Garden, was no longer sufficient, so a new federal facility, Ellis Island, was built to take its place. Constructed on the site of an old naval arsenal in 1892, Ellis Island was the gateway to America for millions of immigrants until 1932, when it was turned into a detention center; it was closed in 1954, but refurbished and reopened in 1965 as an immigration museum administered as part of the Statue of Liberty National Monument.

In contrast to the casual paternalism of Castle Garden, Ellis Island was efficient and impersonal. After quarantine and customs procedures immigrants were hustled past doctors, and a matron who examined pregnant women, on an assembly-line basis, each doctor assigned to looking for one specific disease; three special inspectors decided on the doubtful cases. As health regulations were added to the exclusion clauses, the examinations grew more complex and time-consuming. Those who passed were then interviewed by registry clerks who recorded vital statistics and other background information. Finally, the immigrants were sent to special offices housed in the federal station for currency exchange, rail tickets, baggage handling, and telegrams.

If Ellis Island was a symbol of hope and opportunity to millions of newcomers, it was also the symbol of rejection for many others. In the late 1890s, the more stringent examination system annually debarred over 3,000 applicants for admission; by 1910 the number exceeded 24,000. About 15 percent of those sent back were rejected as having contagious diseases, another 15 percent as constituting contract labor, and the remainder as potential charity cases. An organized movement to establish stricter controls over the massive influx of foreigners began to form at about the same time that Ellis Island opened. From 1891 to 1929 Congress erected a complex body of law designed to narrow the range of immigrants who qualified for admission. The course of this evolution of policy was, however, far from smooth. Well into the 20th century, generally speaking, the Democratic party was indifferent or strongly opposed to restriction. The urban electorate of the Northeast and Midwest pressured congressmen to keep immigration as open as possible. Steamship companies and industrialists lobbied for a liberal policy that would assure large cargoes of passengers and a steady supply of cheap labor. Several presidents, from Rutherford B. Hayes to Woodrow Wilson, vetoed congressional bills that would have tightened admissions standards or excluded whole national groups. The evolving immigration policies were the product neither of a coherent plan nor of a systematic philosophy. The total effect, however, was that step by step, requirements for entry were made more and more stringent.

By the turn of the century Congress had already begun to strengthen the administrative apparatus for controlling immigration. In 1893 boards of special inquiry were formed to handle immigration problems and to collect "a list or manifest of alien passengers" entering the United States. In 1906 authority over immigration was transferred from the overburdened Treasury Department to the newly created Department of Commerce and Labor, and a separate Bureau of Immigration and Naturalization was established within that department.

Further refinements and additions were made to the list of excluded. In part a reaction to the assassination of President William McKinley by an anarchist in 1901, but even more a reflection of a widespread fear of "radicals," Congress in 1903 barred anarchists and saboteurs from entry, along with epileptics and professional beggars. Repeated attempts were made to introduce liter-

acy as a requirement for entry, although it would be a long time before these met with any success. The Immigration Restriction League, founded in 1894 by a small group of young Harvard-educated Boston Brahmins, made the literacy requirement its goal for twenty years. In 1896 Massachusetts Senator Henry Cabot Lodge sponsored a bill in Congress that would have excluded any immigrant unable to read 40 words in some language. It was passed by Congress but vetoed by President Grover Cleveland on the grounds that it violated the traditional American policy of free immigration. Other attempts were made in 1898, 1902, and 1906, when the bills did not get through Congress, and in 1913 and 1915, when they did not receive a presidential signature.

The most thoroughgoing restrictions remained those placed on Asian immigration. In 1902 congressmen from the far-western states finally succeeded in having the Chinese Exclusion Act renewed indefinitely, but almost simultaneously the Japanese began arriving in California in numbers as great as those of the Chinese immigrants in their peak years. In reaction, leading businessmen and civic leaders organized the Japanese and Korean Exclusion League in San Francisco (1905), and the movement quickly spread. But again considerations of international diplomacy intervened; the result was the 1907–1908 Gentlemen's Agreement between Japan and the United States that called for voluntary regulation by the Japanese in exchange for the ending of the segregation of Japanese pupils in San Francisco's schools.

At the same time, elsewhere in the country restrictionists were becoming equally disturbed by the numbers of immigrants coming from southern and eastern Europe. In 1910 a congressionally appointed commission headed by a moderate restrictionist, Senator William P. Dillingham of Vermont, issued a 42-volume report on the alarming effects of immigration. It began with the assumption that the new immigrants were racially inferior to the old immigrants from northern and western Europe and manipulated mountains of statistics to provide a "scientific" rationale for restricting their entry. The evidence in fact contradicted the conclusions, but the Dillingham report nonetheless convinced many that southern and eastern Europeans were incapable of becoming Americans and that the best mechanism for restricting their numbers would be the imposition of a literacy test.

THE ERA OF RESTRICTION, 1917–1964

The Immigration Act of 1917 was the first in a series of severely restrictive statutes based on the findings of the Dillingham Commission. A literacy test was finally enacted; all newcomers over 16 years of age who could not pass it were turned back. No laborers were allowed from the so-called Asiatic Barred Zone, which included India, Indochina, Afghanistan, Arabia, the East Indies, and other, smaller Asian countries, but not China and Japan, which were covered by other legal provisions. The act was the first step in establishing a federal policy of restriction wholly based on a rank order of eligible immigrants that favored national groups thought to be most assimilable. Congress overrode the veto of President Wilson, who denounced the act as a violation of American ideals and the traditional Open Door policy.

The literacy test, it soon became clear, would not have its desired effect. In 1921 over 800,000 arrivals were recorded—a total only slightly below the prewar average—and the proportion of southern and eastern Europeans among them remained high. Congress then proceeded to the next step. By the Quota Act of 1921 (the Johnson Act) it limited the annual number of entrants of each admissible nationality to 3 percent of the foreign-born of that nationality as recorded in the U.S. Census of 1910. Quotas were established for countries in Europe, the Near East, and Africa, and for Australia and New Zealand. No limits were placed on immigration from nations in the Western Hemisphere. Congress continued to allow free immigration from its neighbors, partly to maintain good relations, partly yielding to pressure from southwestern agricultural lobbies interested in maintaining the flow of cheap farm labor from Mexico. Southern and eastern European immigration, however, was sharply curtailed; the annual quotas for southern and eastern European countries were in every case less than a quarter of the numbers admitted before World War I.

The principle of special preferences introduced in 1921 was greatly expanded in succeeding years. Preferences—but only within quota limits—were given to "the wives, parents, brothers, sisters, or children under eighteen years of age, and fiancées . . . of citizens of the United States, . . . of aliens now in the United States who have applied for citizenship in the manner provided by law, or . . . of persons eligible for United States citizenship who served in the military or naval forces of the United States [during World War I]." Establishing priorities in the interests of maintaining family unity represented yet another new principle of immigration policy.

The 1921 act also introduced a new class, later referred to as the "nonquota" category, which included aliens returning from visits abroad, professional actors, artists, lecturers, singers, nurses, ministers, and professors. After 1924 all wives and dependent children of U.S. citizens were allowed to enter as nonquota immigrants, as were aliens belonging to any recognized learned profession or employed as domestic servants. All these would be admissible over and above the quotas for the national groups to which they belonged. The nonquota list was extended by subsequent legislation, but the essential point of the original act was its principle that admission could be based on individual characteristics rather that on national quotas. It was to that extent, at least, a liberalizing provision in a law otherwise known only for its restrictionist features.

The law of 1921 was still not rigorous enough for many restrictionists, who, led by Senator Albert Johnson of the state of Washington, soon secured a more draconian measure. The Immigration Act of 1924 (Johnson-Reid Act) reduced the admissible annual total to 165,000, less than a fifth of the average prewar level (see Table 1), and the annual quota for each nation was set at 2 percent of the foreign-born of that nationality recorded by the 1890 Census. The choice of 1890 as the base year placed immigrants from southern and eastern Europe at a still greater disadvantage because few had come to the United States that early. The annual quotas for Italians, Greeks, Slavs, and others from that part of the world represented a mere 3 percent of their prewar

Table 1. The effects of the quota acts on the volume and sources of immigration.

Annual immigration	Immigrants from northern and western Europe	Other immigrants, chiefly from southern and eastern Europe
Average, 1907–1914	176,983	685,531
Under 1921 act	198,082	158,367
Under 1924 act	140,999	20,847
Under national-origins system[a]	127,266	23,235[b]

Source: Based on the annual reports of the Immigration and Naturalization Service.

a. The legal maximum of 150,000 has been exceeded slightly because the legal minimum per-country quota of 100 was in some cases a higher number than the strict application of the national origins formula would have allowed.

b. Southern and eastern Europeans only.

annual immigration average. The Immigration Act of 1924 also barred from entry all aliens ineligible for citizenship—that is, it reaffirmed Chinese exclusion and banned many Asians who were declared racially ineligible. For example, the Japanese who had been made racially ineligible for citizenship by a 1922 U.S. Supreme Court ruling were now prohibited from immigrating. Secretary of State Charles Evans Hughes vigorously protested Japanese exclusion because it violated the terms of the 1907–1908 Gentlemen's Agreement, but his protests were ignored.

All immigrants now had to procure a visa from an American consul in their country of origin, a system that provided an opportunity for initial screening, since the thrust of the 1924 act was not only to limit the number of immigrants, but also to select those considered best suited to American society.

Senator Johnson summed up the case for restriction and invoked its broad basis of popular support. The American people, he said,

have seen, patent and plain, the encroachments of the foreign-born flood upon their own lives. They have come to realize that such a flood, affecting as it does every individual of whatever race or origin, cannot fail likewise to affect the institutions which have made and preserved American liberties. It is no wonder, therefore, that the myth of the melting pot has been discredited. It is no wonder that Americans everywhere are insisting that their land no longer shall offer free and unrestricted asylum to the rest of the world . . .

The United States is our land. If it was not the land of our fathers, at least it may be, and it should be, the land of our children. We intend to maintain it so. The day of unalloyed welcome to all peoples, the day of indiscriminate acceptance of all races, has definitely ended.

Finally, the Immigration Act of 1924 provided for a "national origins" system favoring northern and western European groups which was to replace the formal quota system in 1927. The foundation of restrictionist policy until 1965, the national origins system was designed to prevent further changes in the ethnic composition of American society that might come from a new infusion of immigrants. The total annual immigrant quota from all nations was fixed at 150,000; each country received the percentage of that number that was equal to the percentage of people in the U.S. population of 1920 who could be counted as having derived

from that country by birth or descent. A minimum quota of 100 was allotted to every nation, but aliens ineligible for citizenship were barred from access even to these quotas; thus China and Japan theoretically received quotas of 100 each, but in practice the Chinese and Japanese people could not take advantage of them.

Since the U.S. Census did not classify Americans by descent beyond the second generation, national origins were determined by classifying and then counting surnames and by an intricate statistical analysis of the population since 1790 that was crudely adjusted for natural increase. For example, the surname "Smith" was assumed to indicate English ancestry, although it could as well be an Anglicized version of "Schmidt" or could belong to a black person. This dubious procedure gave Great Britain 57 percent of the total annual quota, whereas by using the 1890 Census, Britain would have received only 21 percent. Protests from Scandinavia and German-American civic groups caused the British figure to be recalculated and lowered in favor of other northern and western European countries, whose quotas were thus slightly increased. In the end, northern and western Europe (including the British Isles) received 82 percent of the total annual quota, southern and eastern Europe 16 percent, with 2 percent left to the remaining quota-receiving nations.

Whether the quota system was based on national origins or on the U.S. Census, however, it had the same conceptual weakness. The effort to assign quotas to encourage "assimilable" groups was thwarted by the ethnic diversity of the political units upon which apportioned quotas were based. Both systems assigned quotas to sovereign countries, ignoring the reality that within common political borders a variety of groups might dwell—Czechs, Poles, and others born in Germany, for example, were eligible for entry under the German quota—and that those boundaries might also change; for instance, as Poland's boundaries expanded and contracted, Austrian, Russian, German, and Baltic nationals sometimes qualified, and sometimes did not, under Poland's national quota.

By 1929 the national origins quota system was fully operative. But almost simultaneously immigration to the United States began to drop with the onset of the Great Depression and the series of events that led to World War II, and large portions of most quotas went unfilled. As unemployment rose in 1930, consular officials, acting on instructions from President Herbert Hoover, began vigorously to apply the clause excluding those likely to become public charges, so that all but the relatively well-to-do were prevented from obtaining visas. President Franklin D. Roosevelt subsequently revoked this order (1936), but the failure of the 1924 law to distinguish between immigrants and refugees in tallying annual quota counts still effectively limited the entry of Jewish émigrés who were then fleeing the fascist regimes in Europe. As a result, between 1933 and 1944 fewer than 250,000 refugees were admitted as immigrants, many of them on a nonquota basis. In that period, popularly regarded as the time of refugee immigration, the United States in fact received the smallest influx of newcomers since the 1830s. For the first time in its history, in the 1930s the number of people leaving the United States exceeded the number entering.

By the end of the thirties, when war again appeared

imminent, the federal government modified its immigration policy to meet what it defined as the security and defense needs of the nation. A 1941 law (the Smith Act) authorized American consuls to refuse visas to applicants who might endanger "the public safety" and empowered the president to deport any alien whose departure was "in the interest of the United States." The quest for Allied unity during the war resulted in a reversal of the government's hitherto restrictive policy toward the Chinese. On December 17, 1943, Congress repealed the Chinese Exclusion Act dating from 1882 and opened up citizenship to foreign-born Chinese. The salutary effects of the new law were in practice meager, however: the Chinese received only a token quota of 105 and remained the one exception to the policy that continued to exclude all other Asians.

The plight of millions of European refugees, uprooted by the ravages of the war, prompted the federal government to devise measures to help them migrate to the United States. Policy makers became concerned with this issue, in part from efforts to develop better relations with European national groups who might otherwise fall under Soviet influence. President Harry S. Truman issued an executive order in 1945 calling for the admission of 40,000 displaced persons to the United States, to be given priority under the regular quota system. In a more far-reaching move Congress passed the War Brides Act of 1946, which admitted on a nonquota basis some 120,000 alien wives and children and a few hundred husbands of armed-services personnel into the United States. Congress extended similar provisions to Chinese and Japanese spouses in 1947.

The first Displaced Persons Act (1948) provided for the admission for permanent settlement of more than 220,000 people over a two-year period, giving priority to applicants from the Baltic states and setting such an early date to qualify as a displaced person that Jewish and Catholic refugees from Poland, who came later, were largely excluded. Thirty percent of those admitted had to be farmers. Displaced persons were required to have sponsors who would guarantee their housing and employment; security screening was strictly mandated. The most controversial provision of the law—and a victory for moderate restrictionists—was the requirement that displaced persons were not to be admitted as nonquota immigrants. Instead, regular immigration quotas were to be "mortgaged" at 50 percent each year for as many years as it took to "pay back" the displaced persons allowed to enter under its terms. President Truman reluctantly signed the bill, but he found it "flagrantly discriminatory," criticized its restrictive clauses, especially the early cut-off date that "discriminated in callous fashion" against Jews and Catholics, and called for speedy and just amendment.

A revised Displaced Persons Act was passed in 1950 which liberalized the terms of admission and increased the annual quotas: the Baltic and agricultural preferences were removed and the technical provisions discriminating against Jews and Catholics eliminated. Other refugees created by the war's aftermath, such as Greeks and national minorities living inside German borders, were also given quotas. A new ceiling of 415,000 was set for a two-year period, but sponsorship requirements remained, and the mortgaging principle

was retained. The latter was dropped in the Refugee Relief Act of 1953, which admitted 205,000 refugees as nonquota immigrants.

The refugee acts showed that the exigencies of winning allies in the Cold War, combined with genuine humanitarian impulses, could loosen overall immigration policy. Annual quota limits were suspended, and in 1956 Congress allowed 20,000 refugees, mainly Hungarians, but also Chinese and Yugoslavs, to immigrate. In 1957 Dutch Indonesian refugees were admitted; in 1960 the World Refugee Year Law admitted displaced persons from Cuba and China. These were among the precedents for the recent program for the resettlement of refugees from Southeast Asia.

The Cold War also had its other side, however, bringing with it the Internal Security Act of 1950, which required the exclusion or deportation of all aliens who had been Communist party members or had belonged to so-called front organizations. National security was also given as the reason behind the need for a reevaluation of the whole body of immigration law. Both restrictionists and those wanting a more open policy agreed that the statutes passed in the early 20th century had to be recodified and updated.

In 1952 Congress approved the Immigration and Nationality (McCarran-Walter) Act, which assembled in a unified code all previous legislation that had been developed haphazardly for the past century and retained the exclusionary principle of national origins in fixing quotas. Once more, Congress had occasion to pass a restrictive immigration act over a presidential veto, as President Truman refused to sign the bill. Under the provisions of the McCarran-Walter Act, northern and western European nations received no less than 85 percent of the total annual quota. Tighter restrictions were placed on immigrants from the colonies of quota-receiving countries: their inhabitants could no longer qualify for admission under the quotas of the mother countries but were confined to a quota that was set for each colonial territory (a provision designed to cut the flow of black immigrants from the British West Indies, who had previously entered under the ample British quota).

Although the McCarran-Walter Act reaffirmed the old principle of national origins in its quotas, it abolished the category of aliens ineligible for citizenship and thereby loosened restrictions on immigration by Asians: Japan was given a quota of 185; China retained its quota of 105; and countries in an area designated the Asia-Pacific Triangle, including colonial areas such as Hong Kong, were given a quota of 100 each. Although these were small, token quotas, which lumped these people together with other "undesirable" groups, the practice of excluding Asian races and the ban on the naturalization of foreign-born Asians were at least ended.

The McCarran-Walter Act contained other liberalizing features. Special-preference categories were introduced into each quota for immigrants with extraordinary educational or technical training or other special abilities. The bill retained and enlarged the nonquota class, which included immediate relatives of citizens and of permanent-resident aliens. Thousands of wives from Europe and Asia were able to join their husbands

in the United States. A measure of equal treatment of the sexes was obtained by the granting of nonquota status to alien husbands of American wives.

In the late 1950s the national origins quota system was beginning to look more and more incompatible with mid-century international relations. The practice of restricting certain national groups had been eroded by refugee acts, the more liberal provisions of the McCarran-Walter Act, and, more generally, by changing public attitudes toward foreign peoples. The system seemed incongruous as the United States proclaimed itself the leader of the "free world" and emphasized its traditional role as an asylum for the oppressed. President John F. Kennedy attacked the system in 1963, charging that it had no "basis in either logic or reason. It neither satisfies a national need nor accomplishes an international purpose." After Kennedy's death, President Lyndon B. Johnson urged Congress to reform it.

The Era of Liberalization, 1965 to the Present

The movement to reform immigration policy culminated in the Hart-Celler Act of 1965 whose provisions took effect in 1968. Both cornerstones of restrictionist policy—the national origins quota system and the designation of the Asia-Pacific Triangle—were abolished. The ceiling on total annual immigration was raised to 290,000. The other countries of the Western Hemisphere had available 120,000 visas annually without limit for any one country; the Eastern Hemisphere had 170,000, of which no one country could use more than 20,000. Applicants were to be admitted on a first-come, first-served basis.

Nonquota admissions were retained in the 1965 act, as was the preferential treatment for certain quota immigrants, especially family members and individuals with particular skills, from the Eastern Hemisphere. No preferential system was provided for the Western Hemisphere. Refugees from both hemispheres were allotted only a small number of visas, but the new law allowed them to be admitted under parole with no numerical limitations.

The act of 1965 increased immigration from countries whose quota allocations had previously placed them at a disadvantage. In the decade before the Hart-Celler Act, China had sent a quota and nonquota total of 1,000 immigrants per year; in 1975 9,000 Chinese immigrants arrived. In 1965 India, Greece, and Portugal supplied 300 immigrants, 4,400 immigrants, and 2,200 immigrants, respectively; by 1975 these numbers had increased to 14,000; 9,800; and 11,000, respectively. Between 1920 and 1960, of all U.S. immigration, Europe as a whole accounted for 60 percent, South and Central America for 35 percent, and Asia for 3 percent. In 1975 Europe accounted for 19 percent, South and Central America for 43 percent, and Asia for 34 percent.

The lack of a preferential-treatment system for the Western Hemisphere nations was a source of complaint. Some immigrants seeking to join relatives who had already immigrated often had to wait a year or two before their numbers came up in the processing pattern that enabled their admission. A solution was reached in the Western Hemisphere Act of 1976 which distributed preferences equally to Eastern and Western Hemisphere

nations, and gave Western Hemisphere immigrants with special training, family ties, and skills priority over other immigrants. The 20,000-visa limit for countries in the Eastern Hemisphere was henceforth also applied to the West.

In recent years illegal immigration to the United States has become a controversial policy issue. The number of illegal aliens in the United States is unknown; estimates range between 1 and 8 million. The U.S. Immigration and Naturalization Service reports that it arrests and deports 500,000 people each year, most of them Mexican farm laborers and other unskilled workers. Advocates of restriction argue that these illegal immigrants are taking jobs from both American citizens and legally resident aliens; opponents maintain that they represent a useful supply of unskilled labor willing to perform tasks at low wages that no one else wants to do. Congressmen have sponsored legislation that would make willful employment of illegal aliens unlawful and punishable by imprisonment, but as of 1980 no implementing laws have been passed.

Since the colonial period American immigration policy has been determined by a variety of public institutions and governmental bodies—local until the late 19th century, and thereafter federal—as a result of a movement toward greater centralization of public policy. When the federal government assumed control over immigration, it began to establish criteria for admissions. Restrictive measures were installed and systematically enforced to ensure that only limited numbers and only those foreigners found acceptable by American society would be given entry. In the mid-20th century these exclusionary measures were gradually dismantled; the requirements of a diplomacy based on a closer international order and a growing tolerance for ethnic diversity eventually opened immigration on an equal basis to all national groups.

Bibliography

General works on the history of American immigration are Edith Abbot, ed., *Historical Aspects of the Immigration Problem* (1926; reprint, New York, 1969); Maurice R. Davie, *World Immigration, with Special Reference to the United States* (New York, 1936); Leonard Dinnerstein and David Reimers, *Ethnic Americans: A History of Immigration and Assimilation* (New York, 1975); Oscar Handlin, ed., *Immigration as a Factor in American History* (Englewood Cliffs, N.J., 1959), and, *The Uprooted*, 2d ed. (Boston, 1973); Marcus Lee Hansen, *The Atlantic Migration, 1607–1860* (1940; reprint, Cambridge, 1951); Maldwyn Jones, *American Immigration* (1960; reprint, Chicago, 1967); Philip Taylor, *The Distant Magnet* (London, 1971).

Interpretive studies of immigration policy are Marion T. Bennet, *American Immigration Policies* (Washington, D.C., 1963); William S. Bernard, ed., *American Immigration Policy: A Reappraisal* (New York, 1950); idem, "American Immigration Policy: Its Evolution and Sociology," *International Migration* 3:4 (Geneva, 1965); Robert A. Divine, *American Immigration Policy, 1924–1952* (1957; reprint, New York, 1972); Roy Garis, *Immigration Restriction* (New York, 1928); Charles Price, *The Great White Walls are Built* (Canberra, 1974); Emberson E. Proper, *Colonial Immigration Laws* (New York, 1900).

Informative discussions of the social and intellectual factors shaping American immigration policy are found in Ray A. Billington, *The Protestant Crusade, 1800–1860: A Study of the Origins of American Nativism* (1938; reprint, Chicago, 1964); Oscar Handlin, *Race and Nationality in American Life* (Boston, 1957); John Higham, *Strangers in the Land* (New York, 1963) and *Send These to Me* (New York, 1975); Barbara M. Solomon, *Ancestors and Immigrants* (1956; reprint, Chicago, 1972).

WILLIAM S. BERNARD

IMMIGRATION: SETTLEMENT PATTERNS AND SPATIAL DISTRIBUTION

The complex migrations of American Indians, Europeans, Africans, Asians, and Latin Americans to North America and their subsequent internal migrations have created striking differences in the spatial distribution, or geographic placement, of the various ethnic groups in the United States. Differences in economic advancement, social life, and political preferences among these groups are a recognized fact of American life and have become major preoccupations of public policies. That ethnic groups also exhibit distinctive locational patterns and that their uneven geographic distribution has helped perpetuate regionalism in the United States is less well understood.

Too often the social problems of particular ethnic groups have been related in a simplistic fashion to their segregated residential patterns. Not all segregation, however, is the involuntary consequence of poverty and prejudice. Many ethnic groups cluster in well-defined neighborhoods in an attempt to preserve their identity and community, and such voluntary segregation is not necessarily associated with material deprivation. Problems of ethnic unemployment may be an integral part of regional economic stagnation, but this predicament is caused not only by overrepresentation or segregation of a group but also by the depressed nature of the locale. School desegregation policies explicitly rely upon manipulations of the geographic boundaries of school districts, because such adjustments permit radical alterations in the ethnic composition of the student body. Although these measures certainly confront the problems of segregation, they may also obscure a more basic and persistent geographic element in the residential patterns of deprived ethnic groups: the fact that they live in those parts of the city defined by the poverty of their residents. The relationships between the identity and well-being of ethnic groups and their varied territorial arrangements are so complex that they require consideration at several levels: first, on the large or regional scale; second, on the intermediate or urban scale; and third, on the small or neighborhood scale.

ETHNICITY AND GEOGRAPHIC PLACEMENT

Few ethnic groups are evenly distributed throughout all regions of the United States; the tendency to concentrate in some areas and to avoid others reveals the close relation between ethnicity and territory. Of all the bases upon which human society is differentiated, ethnicity is perhaps the most sensitive to the relations between a group's identity and its past or present geographic placement. Ethnicity, like socioeconomic measures of class or status, defines human groups on the basis of specified traits, but unlike those measures, it groups people according to a common ancestry based upon a shared original homeland. Some ethnic identifications are explicitly locational and refer to a region, province, or nation, although ethnic groups may also be defined by dominant religion, language, or culture associated with the ancestral homeland.

Although complex migrations have radically altered the distribution of many ethnic groups, a group often keeps its ancestral locational identification for generations in a new homeland. In time, some of the ancestral identifications disappear, and at the same time the culture of a group may become so closely associated with its adopted location that during subsequent moves its ethnicity will be defined by reference to the most recent place of residence rather than to the original homeland. For example, English immigrants to New England and the southern colonies developed distinctive provincial subcultures. When these groups moved westward they were identified as New Englanders or Southerners rather than as English Americans. Similarly, French colonists to Quebec and Acadia (Nova Scotia) retained their North American labels in their subsequent movements to New England and Louisiana, respectively. The Mormons, an ethnic group originally defined by a set of religious beliefs, were formed in upstate New York, but today they are most closely identified with their adopted state, Utah. Other groups that have retained their original ethnic identification have become associated with the particular areas of the United States where they are concentrated, for example, the Japanese on the West Coast, Cubans in southern Florida, and Norwegians in the Northern Midwest. Even though many members of such groups live far removed from the region of greatest concentration, their ethnic identity continues to be associated with these regions.

The close relationship between ethnicity and place exists not only regionally but also in the larger cities of the United States. The Chinese and Jews, in particular, have settled in diversified metropolitan cities, and the various Slavic groups have gravitated to several large industrial cities. Because migration over the past century and a half has been largely a cityward movement, the presence of many different groups in one area is most evident in large cities. In spite of this pluralism, residential segregation and institutional differences have helped to maintain distinctive ethnic identities. "Chinatown" most graphically exemplifies the association of a group with a particular part of a city. Although such ethnic quarters are seldom occupied by only one group and usually do not house a majority of the dominant group, most large cities contain a mosaic of districts associated with particular ethnic populations.

Geographic concentration, however, is not a valid criterion for evaluating the social and economic conditions of ethnic groups, and the relationship between residential patterns and socioeconomic status must be evaluated with care. For some groups, concentration in particular regions or in urban neighborhoods is a source of local political power, a basis of economic advancement, and protection for ethnic distinctiveness. On the other hand, concentration may reflect a group's exclusion from full participation in the surrounding society and may therefore be a measure of relative deprivation. This paradox accounts in part for the ambiguity of the term "ghetto," which evocatively captures the synthesis of group identity and spatial concentration. Traditionally used to refer to the legally prescribed Jewish quarter of medieval cities, the word today often denotes the segregated quarters of any ethnic group. Hence, while concentration in a ghetto may imply an adverse and deprived material environment that obstructs economic advancement, it may also suggest a place with distinctive ethnic institutions that reinforce group solidarity and facilitate social well-being. Far more important to the socioeconomic position of an ethnic

group than the degree to which it is segregated is its specific location within a city or region, for example, a dilapidated section of the inner city or a region with high unemployment. Moreover, segregated residential patterns are but one geographic aspect of ethnic distribution, because substantial proportions of most American ethnic groups live outside their ghetto or area of greatest concentration.

ETHNIC COMPOSITION OF THE POPULATION

The discussion thus far has assumed that American ethnic groups are well defined and that regional and urban concentrations are readily identifiable. On the contrary, not only are data on ethnic groups limited and inconsistent, but rarely are these data presented for appropriate spatial units. Despite its many limitations, the 1970 Census is the most useful source from which to determine the present spatial distribution of American ethnic groups. Except for the fact that larger sections of the South are becoming destinations rather than sources of migrants, there is no evidence of major shifts in the distribution and composition of American ethnic groups since 1970.

In 1970 blacks accounted for 11.1 percent of the total population of the United States; people of Spanish heritage, 4.5 percent; people of Asian descent, 1.0 percent; American Indians, 0.4 percent; and people of European descent, 82.0 percent. The remaining 1.0 percent are grouped in a miscellaneous "other" category. The census also indicates the proportions of these ethnic groupings that were of "foreign stock," a classification that includes both first-generation immigrants (those born in a foreign country) and the second generation (those born in the United States of foreign or mixed parentage). Whereas 80 percent of the Asians and almost 38 percent of the people of Spanish heritage were of foreign stock, only 2 percent of the black population and a little more than 15 percent of the people of European origin fell into that classification.

Unfortunately it is not possible to break down accurately into its ethnic components the 85 percent of Americans of European descent but American-born parentage—to determine, for example, how many Scots or Swedes there are of the third or later generations. According to a 1971 Census Bureau inquiry, however, almost one-half of the people of European heritage who were questioned about their ancestry claimed one of the following seven national origins: English, Scottish, or Welsh (15.3 percent); German (12.6 percent); Irish (8.0 percent); Italian (4.3 percent); French (2.6 percent); Polish (2.4 percent); and Russian (1.1 percent). Had the list of origins been more inclusive, more people might have declared a specific ancestry. Although these responses do not necessarily indicate a well-defined ethnic identity, they do show that many Americans of European descent but American parentage are aware of their national origins.

National origins are not appropriate ethnic indicators for all groups. Religious affiliation is clearly a more sensitive measure for Jews, Mormons, and many smaller sectarian groups, such as the Mennonites. Unfortunately, statistical data on congregational membership are unreliable, but they do tend to confirm the impression of uneven distribution of religious groups. Ancestral language also remains a definitive trait for most

foreign-born immigrants, of whom only about 18 percent claim English as their mother tongue (the language spoken in the home when they were children). In the absence of continued immigration of an ethnic group, the persistence of the mother tongue after prolonged residence in the United States is quite rare: 82 percent of the American-born population claim English as their mother tongue. In most groups, persistence of the ancestral tongue is confined to a small minority.

REGIONAL PATTERNS

If the United States is divided into 12 regions, the geographic patterns of the major ethnic groups are very distinctive. This divisional scheme is a slight modification of the Census Bureau's groupings of states, which often combine regions with strikingly different migration histories into one unit. Specifically, the South Atlantic region has been subdivided into the Upper South Atlantic and the Southeast to distinguish those areas that are part of the northeastern metropolitan corridor from the southeastern areas. The eastern and western North Central states have been combined and then divided into three sections that are more consistent with the dominant paths of westward migration: the Eastern Midwest, Northern Midwest, and Southern Midwest. For similar reasons, the Mountain and Pacific regions have been altered to accommodate migratory distinctions between the Southwest and the Northwest.

In 1970 the most striking spatial patterns were those of some ethnic groups that were confined to extremely small areas of the United States. More than three-quarters of the population of Puerto Rican heritage were concentrated in the Mid-Atlantic states, primarily in the New York City area. Almost one-half of the population of Cuban origin were clustered in the Southeast, especially in and around Miami, and most of the other half were in the New York area. About one-half of the population of Mexican origin resided in California and the Southwest, and most of the remaining half lived in the adjacent West South Central region. These two adjacent regions also contained about one-half of the American Indian population; most of the other half were widely dispersed throughout all the western states. About one-third of both the Japanese and the Chinese were concentrated in California, but a second and equally large group of Chinese was clustered in the Mid-Atlantic region, and a large group of Japanese lived in Hawaii.

Similar patterns of concentration were visible among groups of European origin. In 1970 several first- and second-generation European ethnic groups were very heavily concentrated in New England, the Mid-Atlantic states, and the Eastern Midwest. Two-thirds of the first- and second-generation Irish and Italians lived in New England and the Mid-Atlantic states. Russians (mainly but not entirely Jewish) were also highly concentrated in the Northeast; almost 70 percent resided in the Mid-Atlantic states, primarily in the metropolitan areas of New York and Philadelphia. Two-thirds of the first and second generations of Poles, Czechs, Hungarians, and Yugoslavs, and more than half of the Greeks lived in the Mid-Atlantic and Eastern Midwest regions. The groups from northwestern Europe, particularly the Scandinavians, were more dispersed, but substantial proportions were concentrated in the Midwest and Pacific North-

west. The Southeast and the two South Central regions contained few people of foreign stock; they were populated mainly by blacks and whites of American parentage. These three southern regions, which in 1970 included about one-quarter of the total population of the United States, contained almost one-half of the black population. Most of the remainder lived in the Mid-Atlantic states and the Eastern Midwest. More than one-quarter of the French-speaking population resided in the Western South Central states, and more than one-third in New England. French Canadians from Quebec were concentrated in New England and the adjacent portions of New York, and almost all those of Acadian descent were in Louisiana.

Comparison of the proportion of each group living in a given region with the proportion of the total population living in that region reveals further spatial distinctions. Tables 1 and 2 indicate that the common practice of aggregating individual ethnic groups into larger units, such as the Spanish-speaking, the Slavs, or the Scandinavians, tends to obscure the spatial patterns of each constituent group. For example, the differences among the geographical patterns of the three major ethnic components of the Spanish-speaking group (Mexicans, Cubans, and Puerto Ricans) are far greater than the differences between these groups and many non-Spanish-speaking populations. As Table 1 shows, the one common element in the geographical patterns of all three Spanish-speaking components was their high level of overrepresentation in three distinct regions: the Mexicans in the Southwest, the Cubans in Florida, and the Puerto Ricans in New York. Asians were quite highly overrepresented in California and also to some extent in the Pacific Northwest. Japanese Americans were slightly overrepresented in the Mountain region but not in any of the southern, midwestern, or northeastern regions. The Chinese were underrepresented in all four of these areas but overrepresented in the Mid-Atlantic states. Like both the Mexicans and the Asians, American Indians were strikingly overrepresented in California and the Southwest, but they were also overrepresented in the Mountain region, the Pacific Northwest, the Northern Midwest, and to a lesser degree, in the Western South Central states. Blacks were overrepresented only in the four southern regions; their representation in the Mid-Atlantic and Eastern Midwest is approximately the same as in the nation as a whole.

Table 2 shows that although most European groups were overrepresented in the New England, Mid-Atlantic, and Midwest regions, the parameters for these ethnic groups varied considerably. Again the practice of grouping has obscured the regional distribution of each component group. Among the first- and second-generation Scandinavians, for instance, only the Swedes were overrepresented in New England and well represented throughout the Midwest; the Norwegians were highly overrepresented in the northern sections of the Midwest but underrepresented in the eastern and southern parts. Of Slavic Americans, only Poles were overrepresented in New England; in fact, their regional distribution was closer to that of the Greeks than to that of other Slavic groups. If, however, first- and second-generation Europeans are divided into four large groupings —those from northwestern Europe, those from Ireland, the Slavs, and those from Mediterranean countries —the most striking regional pattern evident in 1970 was the overrepresentation of northwestern Europeans in the three western regions of the United States. Especially prominent were the Norwegians in the Pacific Northwest and the Danes in the Mountain states. By contrast, the Irish, the Slavs (with the exception of the Yugoslavs), and people from the Mediterranean countries were underrepresented in these regions. The regional distribution of later generations of each ethnic group—the descendants of 19th-century immigrants— was probably very similar to that of the first and second generations. The geographical distributions of both first and second generations in 1970 certainly approximated the historic regional concentrations of earlier immigrants of the same ethnic group, whose patterns will be discussed later.

URBAN CONCENTRATIONS

Ethnic groups are also differentiated by their varying levels of concentration in cities. In 1970 some 73 percent of the total U.S. population lived in settlements of 2,500 inhabitants or more, and 58 percent resided in places, usually of more than 50,000 people, that are subdivided in the census into central city and fringe (largely suburban) areas. The residents of all the central

Table 1. Relative regional representation of non-European ethnic groups, 1970.[a]

Region	American Indian	Black	Mexican	Cuban	Puerto Rican	Chinese	Japanese
New England	0.2	0.3	*	0.4	0.8	0.7	0.2
Mid-Atlantic	0.3	1.0	*	1.6	4.2	1.2	0.3
Eastern Midwest	0.3	0.9	0.4	0.3	0.5	0.4	0.3
Northern Midwest	2.4	*	*		*	0.3	0.2
Southern Midwest	0.2	0.5	0.2	0.1	*	*	0.2
Upper South Atlantic	0.2	1.7	*	0.3	0.2	0.5	0.2
Southeast	0.8	2.0	*	5.0	0.3	0.1	0.2
Eastern South Central	0.2	1.8	*	0.1	0.1	0.2	0.1
Western South Central	1.6	1.4	3.8	0.3	0.1	0.3	0.2
California, Southwest	3.0	0.6	4.5	0.8	0.3	3.7	3.3
Mountain	3.1	*	1.2	*	*	0.4	1.1
Pacific Northwest	2.2	*	0.4	*	*	1.2	1.7

Source: U.S. Bureau of the Census, *Census of the Population, 1970,* vol. 1, *Characteristics of the Population,* pt. 1, *U.S. Summary* (Washington, D.C., 1973), I, p. 293, table 60; U.S. Bureau of the Census, *Census of the Population, 1970,* Subject Report PC(2)-1C, *Persons of Spanish Origin* (Washington, D.C., 1973), pp. 2–4, table 1.
a. The value of 1.0 indicates that the proportion of an ethnic group living in a given region equaled the proportion of the total national population living in that region. Values below 1.0 indicate underrepresentation, and values above 1.0 indicate overrepresentation.
*Values less than 0.1.

Table 2. Relative regional representation of European ethnic groups by country of origin, 1970.[a]

Country of origin	New England	Mid-Atlantic	Eastern Midwest	Northern Midwest	Southern Midwest	Upper South Atlantic	Southeast	Eastern South Central	Western South Central	California–Southwest	Mountain	Pacific Northwest
United Kingdom	2.0	1.6	0.9	0.6	0.5	0.7	0.6	0.2	0.3	1.5	1.3	1.3
Ireland	3.8	2.4	0.7	0.4	0.4	0.5	0.3	0.1	0.1	0.7	0.5	0.5
Germany	0.7	1.4	1.2	2.5	1.4	0.5	0.5	0.2	0.4	1.0	1.0	1.1
Norway	0.5	0.6	0.5	7.7	0.8	0.2	0.3	0.1	0.1	1.1	1.8	4.7
Sweden	1.6	0.6	1.1	4.2	1.2	0.2	0.4	0.1	0.2	1.3	1.7	2.9
Denmark	0.7	0.6	0.7	3.4	2.2	0.3	0.4	0.1	0.2	1.8	3.0	2.6
Netherlands	0.5	0.9	1.7	1.9	1.2	0.3	0.4	0.1	0.2	1.7	1.6	1.7
France	0.4	1.6	0.8	0.6	0.7	0.8	0.6	0.3	0.5	1.8	1.0	1.0
Switzerland	0.8	1.1	0.9	1.9	1.2	0.5	0.4	0.2	0.3	2.0	1.8	2.4
Austria	0.8	2.6	1.0	1.0	0.5	0.5	0.4	0.1	0.2	0.8	0.7	0.6
Hungary	0.8	2.2	1.6	0.6	0.3	0.5	0.5	0.1	0.1	0.9	0.3	0.4
Poland	1.8	2.3	1.6	0.9	0.2	0.5	0.3	0.1	0.1	0.5	0.2	0.2
U.S.S.R.	1.5	2.4	0.7	1.0	0.5	0.6	0.5	0.1	0.1	1.1	0.7	0.7
Czechoslovakia	0.6	1.9	1.7	1.4	1.0	0.5	0.3	0.1	0.5	0.6	0.5	0.5
Yugoslavia	0.2	1.4	2.3	1.6	0.6	0.3	0.2	0.1	0.1	1.2	1.1	0.9
Italy	2.5	3.0	0.7	0.2	0.2	0.4	0.2	0.1	0.2	0.8	0.4	0.3
Greece	2.4	1.8	1.3	0.4	0.3	0.9	0.5	0.2	0.2	1.0	0.8	0.6
Canada	5.3	0.7	1.0	0.8	0.3	0.4	0.5	0.3	0.2	1.4	0.9	2.3
French mother tongue[b]	6.0	0.6	0.4	0.5	0.2	0.4	0.3	0.2	2.7	0.8	0.4	0.5

Source: U.S. Bureau of the Census, *Census of the Population, 1970,* vol. 1, *Characteristics of the Population,* pt. 1, *U.S. Summary* (Washington, D.C., 1973), I, pp. 473–480, tables 144–147.

a. The value of 1.0 indicates that the proportion of an ethnic group living in a given region equaled the proportion of the total national population living in that region. Values below 1.0 indicate underrepresentation, and values above 1.0 indicate overrepresentation.

b. Primarily people of Quebec origin living in New England and those of Acadian origin living in Louisiana.

cities together accounted for about 31 percent of the population and those of the urban fringes for about 27 percent. Of the remaining 42 percent of the total population, about 15 percent lived in towns and about 27 percent in rural areas (settlements smaller than 2,500). Approximately half of the inhabitants of small urban centers lived in places of about 10,000 to 50,000 people, the other half in places with populations between 2,500 and 10,000. The remaining 27 percent of the population were classified as rural, but only 4 percent of the total were described as "rural farm." Because the vast majority of the total American population lived in cities and towns, and more than half lived in large cities, the varying levels of urban concentration among ethnic groups were less striking than their locations within the cities.

The distinction between central city and urban fringe is useful, even though central city does not always refer to the deprived inner-city slums, and urban fringe does not necessarily imply desirable living conditions. The proportionate representations of different ethnic groups in the central cities and urban fringes varied considerably in 1970. No less than 83 percent of Puerto Rican Americans were concentrated in the central cities, compared to 60 percent of the blacks and more than 50 percent of those of Hispanic and Asian origin. In contrast, 38 percent of first- and second-generation Europeans and 24 percent of later-generation Europeans lived in the central cities. The proportions of these latter two groups in the urban fringes were 37 and 28 percent, respectively. Thus one-quarter of first- and second-generation Americans of European origin lived in small towns and rural areas, and almost half of the later generations lived there.

Striking differences existed, however, among the individual ethnic groups of European, Spanish, and Asian heritage and also between the first and second generations of each group. Because the movement of groups from the central city to the urban fringe is often related to material advancement, differences in urban residential patterns between the first and second generations of several groups ought to reveal the selective nature of this process. Table 3 shows urban concentrations of the first and second generations of each group in 1970. More than 70 percent of first-generation Chinese immigrants and approximately 60 percent of first-generation immigrants from Greece, Russia, Poland, Ireland, and Cuba were clustered in the urban centers. Although half or less than half of the first-generation migrants from all other countries lived in central cities, their proportions on the urban fringes were even lower, with the exception of immigrants from Canada, the United Kingdom, Denmark, Holland, and Switzerland.

These ethnic differences among the first generation were roughly paralleled among their children. In the second generation, however, the dominance of the central city over the fringe was either reduced or eliminated. Again the same groups showed the largest percentages living in the central cities, but the percentages were decidedly lower. Among Czechs, Yugoslavs, and northwestern Europeans, higher proportions lived on the urban fringes than in the central cities. Indeed, the second generation of all ethnic groups from northwestern Europe, with the exception of Norwegians, were represented in higher proportions on the urban fringes

Table 3. Percentages of ethnic groups in central cities and urban fringes by country of origin and generation, 1970.

Country of origin	First generation		Second generation	
	Central cities	Urban fringes	Central cities	Urban fringes
United Kingdom	35.2	43.1	29.4	40.4
Ireland	58.2	31.9	43.0	40.0
Germany	40.1	36.1	30.8	31.5
Norway	38.0	27.8	26.9	23.4
Sweden	38.6	31.5	29.6	30.0
Denmark	32.8	34.4	26.8	28.8
Netherlands	30.0	40.1	24.2	34.6
France	44.8	35.7	33.9	36.8
Switzerland	33.4	36.6	27.2	30.1
Austria	51.4	31.5	37.7	40.0
Hungary	50.3	35.9	36.2	44.5
U.S.S.R.	61.1	28.3	46.5	38.2
Poland	60.4	28.6	43.5	39.0
Czechoslovakia	42.9	36.0	29.4	39.4
Yugoslavia	52.9	33.1	34.1	42.0
Italy	51.9	36.5	40.2	43.8
Greece	62.4	28.1	44.0	40.5
Canada	32.8	40.0	27.8	36.6
French mother tongue[a]	43.9	31.7	29.9[b]	24.5[b]
Cuba	57.7	39.0	52.0	39.2
Mexico	50.4	32.8	46.1	24.1
China	71.5	19.2	61.1	25.7
Japan	50.0	27.3	44.5	28.5

Source: U.S. Bureau of the Census, *Census of the Population, 1970,* vol. I, *Characteristics of the Population,* pt. 1, *U.S. Summary* (Washington, D.C., 1973), I, 103, table 97.

a. Primarily people of Quebec origin living in New England and those of Acadian origin living in Louisiana.

b. Applies to those of American-born parentage.

than was the population as a whole. Only one-half of the Norwegians, however, lived in urban areas. Overall about 27 percent of the total population lived on the urban fringes, compared to 30 to 40 percent of second-generation northwestern Europeans.

Representations of ethnic groups in small towns and rural areas also showed a good deal of variation, as Table 4 indicates. French Canadians, who predominated in New England and Louisiana, had the highest levels of representation in both towns and rural areas. Later-generation French-speaking Americans had the highest proportion (19 percent) of any group in towns—even higher than that of the population as a whole (15 percent), and they were represented in rural areas in the same proportion as the total population (27 percent). Other groups that were proportionately overrepresented in small towns and rural areas were second-generation Norwegians, Danish, Dutch, and Swiss; Swedes were represented in about the same proportions as was the population as a whole (42 percent). Of the groups underrepresented in towns and rural areas, Germans, Czechs, Yugoslavs, Japanese, and Mexicans, as well as blacks (with 30 percent) were better represented than were Italians, Greeks, Russians, and Cubans.

These noticeable ethnic differences in settlement resulted to some degree from the patterns of regional concentration, for the urban proportions of the population varied considerably from region to region. Groups concentrated in the Mid-Atlantic region, for instance, were far more likely to be living in large cities than groups that had settled in parts of the South. Nevertheless, even in the same region, the various groups differed in their proportionate distribution in central cities, urban fringes, small towns, and rural areas.

Table 4. Percentages of ethnic groups in small towns and rural areas, by country of origin and generation, 1970.

Country of origin	First generation			Second generation		
	Towns over 10,000	Towns 2,500 to 10,000	Rural areas (under 2,500)	Towns over 10,000	Towns 2,500 to 10,000	Rural areas
United Kingdom	5.0	4.4	12.2	6.6	6.0	17.6
Ireland	2.4	2.0	5.6	4.1	3.4	9.5
Germany	5.1	4.4	14.2	7.4	6.6	23.7
Norway	6.5	5.7	21.4	8.7	8.3	32.7
Sweden	6.5	5.6	17.7	8.1	7.5	24.9
Denmark	6.1	7.1	20.1	8.2	8.0	28.3
Netherlands	5.0	5.5	19.5	6.3	6.8	28.2
France	4.9	4.1	10.7	6.8	5.7	16.8
Switzerland	5.4	4.9	19.5	7.4	7.6	27.8
Austria	3.4	3.4	10.1	4.2	4.2	13.9
Hungary	2.7	2.1	8.9	3.3	3.0	12.9
U.S.S.R.	2.9	1.8	5.9	3.8	2.3	9.1
Poland	2.5	1.9	6.5	3.6	3.0	11.0
Czechoslovakia	3.2	3.9	13.7	4.9	5.8	20.5
Yugoslavia	3.0	2.6	8.8	4.9	4.4	14.3
Italy	3.6	2.6	5.3	4.2	3.4	8.4
Greece	4.0	2.2	3.4	4.9	3.0	7.4
Canada	6.9	5.3	14.9	8.2	6.6	20.8
French mother tongue	7.0	5.0	12.3	10.6[a]	8.7[a]	26.2[a]
Cuba	1.5	0.7	1.1	3.2	1.6	4.0
Mexico	6.7	6.4	12.5	8.0	7.8	13.7
China	4.2	1.6	2.9	5.1	2.5	5.3
Japan	6.6	5.2	10.8	8.4	6.1	12.5

Source: U.S. Bureau of the Census, *Census of the Population, 1970*, vol. I, *Characteristics of the Population*, pt. 1, *U.S. Summary* (Washington, D.C., 1973), I, 103, table 97.

a. Applies to those of American-born parentage.

Ghetto and Other Small-Scale Patterns

Large-scale regional and urban patterns obscure both the distinctive spatial patterns of many smaller groups and the degree to which different groups are segregated from one another within a larger area. Some of the most extreme examples of concentration are found among small religious groups that seek to maintain their identity and way of life through spatial and social isolation. Although the Mennonites, Hutterites, and other such groups are to some extent concentrated in specific regions, their most distinctive spatial patterns are the high concentration and ethnic exclusiveness of their settlements in any region. High levels of small-scale concentration also occur among rural American Indians both on and off reservations, as well as among rural blacks. Descendants of European immigrants may also be highly segregated. Many settlements in the Midwest are dominated by particular European ethnic groups, such as the extensive concentration of the Dutch in the Kalamazoo, Mich., area or the smaller clusters of Swiss in Wisconsin. Regardless of size, these ethnic concentrations are highly visible because they are unusual: normally, rural ethnic groups are interspersed with at least one or two other groups; they maintain their ethnic identity without depending on either exclusivity or propinquity.

Until recently, the typical urban immigrant experience was considered to be initial concentration in the least desirable sections of the inner city, followed by the second generation's socioeconomic advancement, assimilation, and dispersal to the suburbs. The suburbs, therefore, were presumed to house the assimilated descendants of ethnic migrants. Although observers have acknowledged the variable rates of suburbanization among different groups and also the persistence of ancestral religious loyalties, they have generally accepted the relationship between inner-city segregation and the maintenance of ethnic consciousness, on one hand, and the relationship between suburbanization and assimilation, on the other. Consequently, their efforts to explain the persisting inner-city segregation of blacks and certain other minorities presupposed a sharp contrast between these groups and an ethnically undifferentiated and assimilated suburban population of European origin.

Recent reinterpretations of the urban spatial patterns of European immigrants and their descendants suggest that while some ethnic groups have reconcentrated in suburban locations, others have maintained a strong presence in inner-city neighborhoods. To be sure, a varying proportion of each of these groups has dispersed into areas with no well-defined ethnic identity. Between 1930 and 1960 there was a greater reduction in residential segregation among first- and second-generation Americans of European origin than among blacks and Americans of Spanish heritage, but these reductions were not large. Considerable proportions of all groups lived in census tracts in which they were substantially overrepresented. For example, a recent survey of the New York–Northeastern New Jersey Consolidated Census Area revealed that blacks, Puerto Ricans, and first- and second-generation Europeans were indeed segregated, but that many individual European ethnic groups were just as highly segregated from one another as from blacks and Puerto Ricans. Norwegians, for example, were one of the most highly localized groups, and although their separation from blacks was especially marked, their separation from Russian Jews was even greater. Moreover, the patterns of segregation did not conform to the expected pattern; the longer-established groups from northwestern Europe were not less segregated than the more recent immigrants from southern and eastern Europe, nor were Protestant groups always more segregated from Catholic groups than from other Protestants. Consequently, earlier assertions that ethnic pluralism would gradually be simplified into religious pluralism, as individual ethnic groups merged into broader, religious-based groupings, are now open to question.

Conditions in the New York–New Jersey area are not necessarily replicated in other cities, but because the issue has been raised, ethnicity must be examined not only in social relations and political behavior but also in residential patterns. The familiar pattern of initial settlement in an inner-city ghetto followed by advancement, assimilation, and relocation in a suburb according to socioeconomic status is but one of many different paths. Although members of the same ethnic group have of course followed different paths, some general observations can be made about the residential patterns of particular groups.

First, the 19th-century northern European immigrants and their descendants did abandon their original locations to later arrivals, and in their new suburban neighborhoods they neglected or even rejected many of their Old World traits. Second, other groups—especially Jewish immigrants and their descendants—have

reconcentrated in well-defined suburban sections, and their new, affluent residential quarters, called "gilded ghettos" by one observer, are nearly as closely identified with the ethnicity of their residents as were their original inner-city ghettos. Third, Italians and Slavs have retained sections of their original inner-city quarters and experienced modest rates of suburbanization. Often the population distribution of these groups resembles a wedge, with its base in the inner-city or older suburban neighborhood and its apex in the newer outer suburbs, where representation decreases.

Finally, some ethnic groups, through a combination of poverty and prejudice, have remained heavily concentrated in the least desirable sections of the inner city. Blacks and Spanish-speaking groups belong to this category of involuntary segregation. When the housing supply of these groups is reduced by redevelopment, highway improvement, or simply physical deterioration, they have not always been able to relocate in adjacent areas. Some adjacent areas are occupied by other ethnic groups that are either at the ceiling of their own economic advancement or highly committed to their local ethnic institutions; such groups are unwilling to make room for new groups that attempt to infiltrate their neighborhood. These locational circumstances are often at the root of interethnic tension and conflict.

Not all ethnic groups display patterns of residential concentration. Perhaps the most obvious examples are immigrants from England and English-speaking Canada, who have often gained immediate access to the middle ranks of American society and have quickly merged into the neighborhoods of native-born Americans. Some more visible groups, notably Japanese and Koreans, have maintained a sense of group identity without the base of an ethnic neighborhood. Also, increasing numbers of almost all ethnic groups are far removed from their original quarters. Still, there is no reason to believe that less exclusive and less well-defined residential patterns will necessarily diminish the impact of ethnicity on social interaction or political behavior.

DEVELOPMENT OF REGIONAL PATTERNS

The distinctive spatial patterns of American ethnic groups have taken shape over several centuries of immigration and internal migration. Although the ethnic composition of the American population was already complex by the latter part of the 17th century, both the proportions of the various ethnic groups in the total population and the groups' geographical patterns have changed markedly. The most impressive changes have occurred in response to "push" factors in the countries or regions of origin, which altered the ethnic composition of the immigrant stream to the United States, and "pull" factors in different parts of the United States, which affected the immigrants' choices of destination. Once these combined influences had altered the composition and direction of migration, inertia often set in for a considerable period. The social groupings and information networks established by pioneering migrants influenced the destinations of those who followed, often long after the attraction of a destination had diminished. Thus the spatial differences established during the initial concentrations of each group persisted long after the flow of migration had ceased.

Major changes in the destinations of migrants to and within the United States occurred during the late 18th century, the fourth and eighth decades of the 19th century, and the second decade of the 20th century. Accordingly, the changes in the geography of migration that have most strongly influenced the present distribution of American ethnic groups fit into five historical periods: before 1775, 1775–1850, 1850–1890, 1890–1920, and 1920 to the present.

Before 1775 It is impossible to give an exact picture of the volume and composition of immigration to colonial America, because the available estimates either have been based upon fragmentary sources or have been inferred retrospectively from later data. But we do know that during the colonial period there were several well-defined peaks of immigration, the three highest in the 1720s, the 1740s, and the decade preceding the Revolution (1765–1775). Immigrants from Ulster and the German states dominated during the first two periods, and the Irish, both Protestant and Catholic, were predominant during the final surge. During the same century, immigration accounted for 15 to 20 percent of the growth of the white population, and the international slave trade accounted for 30 to 40 percent of the growth of the black.

The composition of the American population before 1775 must be inferred from data compiled for the first federal census in 1790. At that time, the population was composed of perhaps a half-million American Indians, about one million blacks, and almost four million people of European descent. As Table 5 shows, the English and Welsh accounted for about 50 percent of the total (not counting the Indians, whose numbers are quite uncertain) and Scots and Irish for an additional 14 percent. The Germans, the second largest European group, made up 7 percent of the population, but like the immigrants from the British Isles, they were from diverse provincial origins and religious groups. The Dutch, French, and Swedes accounted for most of the remaining population of European heritage.

With an overwhelming majority of the colonists from the British Isles, one might expect the population to have been fairly homogeneous, with little regional variation. On the contrary, the Old World differences within this large group were compounded and differentially altered in the New World. Distinct English subcultures appeared in New England, the Virginia and Maryland tidewater area, and the coastal Carolinas. Some of the differences among English colonists could be attributed to their regional origins, but their most obvious difference was religion. Nonconformists or dissenters, eventually regrouped as Congregationalists, predominated in New England, while Anglicans dominated the coastal South until about 1750. At that time these two denominations had the largest number of churches, but the Presbyterians and Baptists, as well as the German and Dutch ethnic churches, had grown more rapidly in the preceding half-century. Although the Congregationalists maintained their regional dominance into the 19th century, the Anglican church suffered large defections to the Baptists and Methodists.

Another factor contributing to the emergence or persistence of ethnic identities was the immigrants' uneven regional distribution. When blacks, who constituted about 20 percent of the population (almost twice

Table 5. Percentage of population and relative regional representation of ethnic groups, 1790.

Group	Proportion of total population	Relative regional representation[a]					
		New England	Mid-Atlantic	Delaware	Upper South Atlantic	Southeast	Eastern South Central
English and Welsh	49.2	1.4	0.8	0.9	0.8	0.9	1.0
Scots	6.6	0.6	1.1	0.9	0.9	1.5	1.3
Ulster Irish	4.8	0.7	1.6	1.0	0.8	1.0	1.2
Other Irish	2.9	0.6	1.1	1.5	1.2	1.1	1.5
Germans	7.0	—	2.7	0.1	0.7	0.5	1.7
Dutch	2.5	0.1	3.8	1.3	0.1	0.1	0.4
French	1.4	0.6	1.8	0.9	0.6	1.1	1.3
Swedish	0.5	—	2.2	9.5	0.6	0.3	0.9
Free black	1.5	0.9	1.0	4.4	1.3	0.7	0.6
Slave black	17.8	—	0.2	0.9	2.1	1.8	0.8
Unassigned	5.6	—					

Source: American Council of Learned Societies, "Report of the Committee on Linguistic and National Stocks in the Population of the United States," *Annual Report of the American Historical Association* 1 (Washington, D.C., 1932), table 13.

a. The value of 1.0 indicates that the proportion of an ethnic group living in a given region equaled the proportion of the total national population living in that region. Values below 1.0 indicate underrepresentation, and values above 1, overrepresentation.

their present proportion), are included in the computations of the regional representation of ethnic groups as given in Table 5, it can be seen that the English and Welsh were overrepresented only in the New England colonies. However, their underrepresentation in the other regions was very slight. Other groups had more striking patterns of concentration. Immigrants from Ulster and the Scots, Germans, Dutch, French, and Swedes were overrepresented in the Mid-Atlantic region, but the Scots were more overrepresented in the Southeast, especially in North Carolina. Table 5 devotes a separate column to Delaware, because it was the transitional colony (and later, state) between the Mid-Atlantic and Upper South Atlantic regions. Although the representation of black slaves in Delaware was close to that of the population as a whole and much greater than in the Mid-Atlantic region, it was far less than in the two southern regions. Free blacks, on the other hand, were greatly overrepresented in the Delaware population. Also overrepresented there were several of the non-English European groups that are usually associated with the Mid-Atlantic region, notably the descendants of the early Swedish colony.

In the two southern regions the proportion of blacks was twice as high as it was in the population at large. The non-British groups were greatly underrepresented, except for certain groups such as French Huguenots in South Carolina and German Protestants in North Carolina. The Eastern South Central region had less than 3 percent of the total population of the colonies, primarily in Kentucky and Tennessee; with the exception of the Dutch, the European ethnic groups were well represented there.

About 44,000 people lived in the French and Spanish territories of North America, which are not shown in Table 5. Almost all of the 20,000 persons in the Spanish holdings were of Spanish heritage, but only about 65 percent of the population under French control was of French heritage; the largest minorities were English and Germans. Most of the American Indians on the Atlantic seaboard during the colonial period were displaced by immigrants or ravaged by European epidemic diseases; the pattern of life of those in the interior was altered by the fur trade and related territorial rivalries of Britain, France, Spain, and the colonies themselves.

As the colonial period progressed, ethnic diversity became particularly evident in the Middle (Mid-Atlantic) Colonies and to a more limited degree in the South. Immigration to New England was limited after the Puritan migration of the 1630s. Instead, the greater economic potential and avowed religious toleration of Pennsylvania attracted the majority of new immigrants, who increasingly came from Ulster and the German states. Small-scale farming in the hinterland of Philadelphia appealed to an especially diverse population. Although some of the German pietist groups were highly concentrated, recent research suggests that other ethnic groups were intermixed; the level of ethnic pluralism in the Middle Colonies was unmatched in any of the small nation-states of Europe.

In the South—the tidewater Chesapeake area and coastal South Carolina—the emergence of large-scale plantation agriculture was responsible for the forced immigration of blacks from Africa and the West Indies. Only a minority of white Southerners owned large amounts of land and substantial numbers of slaves; most were small farmers, almost all from the British Isles.

1775–1850 Throughout the Revolutionary and Napoleonic wars, foreign immigration was slight. Although the flow of immigrants resumed in the 1820s, only in the 1840s did it begin to have a significant impact on the ethnic composition of the country. The period before 1850 was one of considerable internal migration, however. Even before the Revolution, New Englanders had moved northward, and Southerners and Middle Colonists had moved southwestward down the Great Valley of Virginia and through the Cumberland Gap into Kentucky and Tennessee. After the Revolution, the Mohawk Valley of upstate New York and the upper reaches of the Ohio River attracted New Englanders and Middle Colonists. New Englanders continued to dominate upstate New York, while the Southerners and Middle Colonists who had moved down the Shenandoah Valley merged with those who had pushed along the upper Ohio to create in the Ohio Valley a diverse population drawn from most of the original colonies. As cotton production expanded, Southerners also moved westward into the Lower Mississippi Valley, and the organization of an internal slave trade caused a

corresponding movement of blacks from their original concentrations in the Chesapeake tidewater area and coastal South Carolina to the cotton plantations of Georgia, Alabama, and Mississippi. The extension of the southern plantation system brought to these areas hosts of small farmers who were not slave owners but whose economic fortunes were tied to cotton production and whose social relationships were strongly influenced by the presence of large numbers of black slaves. Other Southerners settled in isolated areas of the Appalachians or Ozarks and maintained only loose connections with the market economy and with the southern and national cultures. Impoverished and isolated, these Southerners formed a distinct ethnic culture and tenaciously maintained the cultural patterns of their English or Scotch-Irish ancestors.

By the time the southern and Ohio Valley frontiers had reached the Mississippi Valley, New England pioneers had moved no farther west than upstate New York. Those who had looked beyond the Niagara River had found Upper Canada (western Ontario) more inviting than northern Ohio. The economic development of the Northern Midwest did not occur until export markets for wheat were developed, just as earlier settlement had been stimulated by the demand for cotton from the South and pork from the Ohio Valley. The Erie Canal, which linked upstate New York with the Atlantic seaboard, did not serve the Midwest until the 1840s, when New Englanders pushed on to the Great Lakes area in response to the improving market for wheat.

In 1820, as Table 6 indicates, about 14 percent of the total population of the United States was living in the two South Central regions and less than 9 percent had settled in the Midwest. By 1850 this situation had changed drastically. More than 18 percent lived in the Eastern Midwest alone, and another 5 percent in its southern and northern sections. The population of the South Central regions had increased slightly to about 19 percent, but this proportion declined thereafter. Because foreign immigration expanded only gradually in the 1820s and 1830s, the western populations were

drawn predominantly from the eastern states. Almost 80 percent of the American-born population of Wisconsin in 1850 had originated in New England or the Mid-Atlantic region, and almost 90 percent of the American-born in Mississippi had come from the Southeast and Eastern South Central regions. The people of Missouri, on the other hand, had come from more diverse sources: about 48 percent from the Eastern South Central region, nearly 19 percent from the Upper South Atlantic region, and about 15 percent from the Eastern Midwest.

The distinctive regional patterns of denominational affiliations are another indication of the selective latitudinal pattern of westward migration from the Atlantic Coast. The association of denomination and region was and is a marked trait in defining the different ethnic identities of the descendants of colonial migrants who selectively occupied the West and Southwest, although the absence of reliable data confine discussion of the subject to speculative observations. Baptists predominated throughout the newly settled South Central states, whereas Congregationalists, in keeping with the northerly trajectory of the Yankee movement westward, were prominent only in the northern sections of the Midwest. Religious affiliations in the southern sections of the Midwest and northern sections of the South Central region were extremely mixed, but the strong representation of Methodists and Presbyterians indicated the Mid-Atlantic and Upper South Atlantic origins of these populations.

1850–1890 Around the middle of the 19th century, the volume of foreign immigration increased sharply, as substantial numbers of western Europeans responded to famine or deteriorating economic conditions at home by crossing the Atlantic. Although the Catholic Irish and the Germans predominated, Scandinavians, Dutch, Swiss, and French immigrants, as well as British, entered the United States in large numbers. As early as 1850 the patterns of regional distribution established by the earlier immigrants attracted the majority of those who followed. The Irish were strongly overrepresented in New England and the Mid-Atlantic region, the Germans in the Mid-Atlantic and Midwest regions, and the Scandinavians, Dutch, and Swiss immigrants in the Midwest. The English and Scots were well represented in all those regions, but the Welsh, scarcely evident in New England, were more strongly represented than either the English or Scots in the Mid-Atlantic states.

Although very few foreign immigrants settled in the South, New Orleans as a major port attracted groups that added to the distinctive ethnic composition of the Western South Central region, already characterized by the considerable French-speaking population of Acadians (Nova Scotians). Spanish, French, Italian, and Portuguese immigrants were all overrepresented there. Across the continent, San Francisco also attracted substantial numbers of the same groups, thus accounting for the early overrepresentation of Latin Europeans in California and the Southwest. These patterns of overrepresentation were short-lived in the Western South Central region but persisted longer in California. Of this group of Latin-European nationalities, the Portuguese alone were overrepresented elsewhere, specifically in New England.

These distinctive distributional patterns record differences in Old World circumstances, in routes of mi-

Table 6. Regional distribution of the U.S. population, 1790–1970 (in percentages).

	1790	1820	1850	1890	1920	1970
East						
New England	25.8	17.3	11.8	7.4	7.0	5.8
Mid-Atlantic	24.2	28.0	25.4	20.3	21.1	18.3
Midwest						
Eastern	0.2	8.1	18.2	18.9	17.8	17.6
Northern	*	0.1	1.3	5.6	6.0	4.7
Southern	*	0.7	3.8	11.3	8.4	5.5
South						
Upper South Atlantic	28.6	16.4	9.8	6.2	6.0	5.7
Southeast	18.4	15.4	10.9	8.0	7.2	9.4
Eastern South						
Central	2.8	12.4	14.5	10.3	8.4	6.3
West						
Western South						
Central	*	1.7	4.1	7.3	9.7	9.5
California, Southwest	*	*	0.7	2.1	3.9	10.9
Mountain	*	*	*	1.5	2.5	2.7
Pacific Northwest	*	*	*	1.0	2.0	2.7

Source: U.S. Bureau of the Census, *Historical Statistics of the United States* (Washington, D.C., 1961), pp. 12–13.
* Not yet part of the U.S., unsettled, or less than 0.1 percent of population.

gration, and in the ability to respond to American opportunities. The commercial links of New Orleans and San Francisco with European ports accounted for their initially diverse populations. For example, the Portuguese settled in California and southern New England because of American trading connections with the Atlantic islands belonging to Portugal. Many Irish immigrants came as ballast on lumber ships returning to New Brunswick and then found their way to New England and New York by coastal packet or on foot. Somewhat less impoverished were those German and Scandinavian immigrants who had farmed small holdings at home but had been faced with stiff competition from larger landholders. They heard about the Midwest from agents of railroad companies offering land grants and from agents of states that needed more population. Thus many of the continental immigrants were attracted directly to the interior. Many Germans who had sailed on tobacco ships returning from Bremen to Baltimore or on cotton ships returning from Le Havre to New Orleans went straight to the Ohio and middle Mississippi valleys, but larger numbers concentrated in the newly settled Northern Midwest. Immigration from Scandinavia peaked somewhat later, when the settlement of the Northern Midwest was proceeding rapidly. The Scandinavian groups moved directly to the interior in even larger proportions than the Germans.

Europe was not the only source of immigration to the United States during this period: Canada, Mexico, and later Asia contributed substantially to the stream. Canadian immigrants were extremely diverse, comprising Newfoundlanders, French Canadians, and Maritimers; many of the last group were descendants of New Englanders who had moved north around the time of the Revolution. In addition, many Irish and British immigrants who had obtained cheap passage to British America moved down to the American republic. New England and, to a lesser degree, New York were the leading recipients of this migration. The Midwest also received Canadian immigrants, some of whom may have been the descendants of Americans who had preferred the northern to the southern shore of Lake Erie in their westward migration.

Mexican settlement in the Western South Central region proved to be more enduring than that of Latin-European immigrants. In this region, as well as in California and the Southwest, some of the Mexican population was obtained by annexation rather than migration. Only modest numbers of Asian immigrants had entered the United States by 1850, and they were concentrated almost exclusively on the Pacific Coast. Their overrepresentation diminished when other groups moved west and when Asian exclusion legislation in the 1880s curtailed their migration. The final stages of relocation of American Indians on western reservations also occurred in the 1880s, and their declining population began to stabilize. During the first six decades of the 19th century, the number of American Indians had dropped from a half to a quarter of a million; the rate of decline slowed thereafter, and the trend was reversed early in the 20th century.

Table 6 shows that between 1850 and 1890 the proportions of the population living in the Midwest and the West increased, and the proportion living in the Northeast and the South diminished. The regional des-

Table 7. Relative regional representation of Afro-Americans, 1850–1970.[a]

Region	1790	1850	1890	1920	1970
New England	0.1	*	*	0.1	0.3
Mid-Atlantic	0.3	0.1	0.2	0.3	1.0
Eastern Midwest	*	0.1	0.1	0.1	0.9
Northern Midwest	*	*	*	*	*
Southern Midwest	*	0.7	0.3	0.3	0.5
Upper South Atlantic	2.0	2.2	2.1	1.9	1.7
Southeast	1.8	2.9	3.8	4.2	2.0
Eastern South Central	0.8	2.1	2.7	2.9	1.8
Western South Central	*	2.5	2.5	2.0	1.4
California, Southwest	*	*	*	*	0.6

Source: U.S. Bureau of the Census, *Historical Statistics of the United States* (Washington, D.C., 1961), p. 12.

a. The value of 1.0 indicates that the proportion of an ethnic group living in a given region equaled the proportion of the total national population living in the region. Values below 1.0 indicate underrepresentation and values above 1.0 overrepresentation.

* Values less than 0.1.

tinations of immigrants strongly influenced these changes. In 1890 the blacks were as highly concentrated in the South as they had been in 1850, though they had been legally free to move since the end of the Civil War. As Table 7 reveals, their overrepresentation in the Southeast and Eastern South Central regions actually increased as a result of the westward movement of whites and the avoidance of the South by foreign immigrants.

1890–1920 As the first decade of the 20th century approached, the well-established sources of foreign immigration—the British Isles and continental northwestern Europe—continued to supply large numbers of newcomers. Their proportionate contribution, however, was greatly diminished by the rapid growth of immigration from southern and eastern Europe. Most but not all southern and eastern Europeans settled in fewer regions than did the earlier groups, except the Irish. After 1890 the highly industrialized cities of southern New England, the Mid-Atlantic region, and the Eastern Midwest were the chief destinations of the Italians and the various peoples of the Austro-Hungarian and Russian empires. By 1920 the portion of the total U.S. population living in the Mid-Atlantic region, which received most of these immigrants, had slightly increased after a century of decline (see Table 6). The census tabulations of the diverse ethnic groups coming from the Russian and Austro-Hungarian empires were rarely consistent, and it is difficult to obtain a precise determination of their regional concentrations. Nevertheless, data for 1890 reveal that, as was the case with the immigrants from northwestern Europe, the pioneering immigrants from southern and eastern Europe had already established enduring regional destinations. By that date the more dispersed patterns of Czech migrants and the secondary concentrations of Italians in New England and of Poles in the Midwest were apparent. In addition, both the South and the more rural sections of the Midwest were losing migrants to the more urbanized parts of the country.

After 1890 the population of the West continued to grow rapidly. While southern Europeans were well represented in California by 1920, most eastern European groups were underrepresented. Asian immigration, restricted in the 1880s, rose again after the turn of the

century and remained highly concentrated in California and the Pacific Northwest. The growth of substantial Chinese communities in the cities of the Northeast was already apparent, however, and the Chinese were overrepresented in the Mid-Atlantic region. Mexican immigration, which had never been large in the 19th century, increased sixfold in the decade of World War I, at least in part as a result of the diminished supply of European labor. During this decade also, black Americans moved to the Northeast and Midwest in large numbers. During earlier decades, and especially in the 1890s, small numbers of blacks had moved to northern cities, but these movements were swamped by the immensity of European immigration. By 1920 the Mid-Atlantic region and the Eastern Midwest contained over 10 percent of the black population; however, 85 percent of all blacks continued to live in the four southern regions. The regional patterns of Canadian migration were also maintained; the concentration in New England of more than 70 percent of French Canadians was the highest of any group in any one region.

Differences in dominant regional destinations of foreign immigrants before and after 1890 were among the criteria used by contemporary observers to distinguish the "old" immigration from the "new." Old immigrants were assumed to be from cultures similar to that of the United States, and their presumed rapid assimilation into American society was thought to have been facilitated by their widespread distribution and their settlement on the land as well as in the cities. These assumptions certainly did not apply to the Irish, the second largest immigrant group of the period before 1890, who were as highly concentrated in cities and in the Northeast as any of the new immigrants. Moreover, even though the Germans, the largest group of old immigrants, were more evenly distributed than the Irish between the Atlantic Coast and the Midwest, their group consciousness in the 19th century was as strong as that of any new ethnic group.

A large proportion of the new immigrants from southern and eastern Europe were indeed concentrated in northeastern industrial cities, where native-born Americans were a minority. That these immigrants settled primarily in cities is often attributed to their ignorance of opportunities elsewhere and their lack of occupational skills. In fact, it was the demand for unskilled labor, however poorly paid, that attracted most of them to urban centers. Although the unscrupulous promotional activities of transportation companies were a factor in the increased volume and distant sources of the new immigration, few immigrants were influenced primarily by corporate inducements. Most newcomers joined friends and relatives who were already established in the New World. The observers who made a distinction between new and old immigration did not understand the effects of length of residence in the United States on both the distribution and assimilation of immigrants, nor did they recognize the major differences in the locational characteristics of individual groups.

Table 8 shows the high proportions of urban residents among immigrants from southern and eastern Europe in 1920—over 80 percent for most. Among immigrant groups from northwestern Europe, the proportions were less than 75 percent, except for the Irish, who remained

Table 8. Urban concentration of first-generation white population, by country of origin, 1920 (by percentage).

Country of origin	Urban percentage of whole group	Percentage of total first-generation white urban population
Russian Empire	88.6	12.0
Ireland	86.9	8.7
Italy	84.4	13.1
Poland	84.4	9.3
Hungary	80.0	2.9
United Kingdom	75.0	8.4
Austria	75.0	4.2
Canada	74.5	8.1
Yugoslavia	69.3	1.1
Germany	67.5	12.3
Czechoslovakia	66.3	2.3
Scandinavia	54.6	7.7
Others	—	9.9

Source: Niles Carpenter, *Immigrants and Their Children*, U.S. Bureau of the Census Monograph No. 7 (Washington, D.C., 1927), p. 372, table 167.

one of the most highly urbanized immigrant groups throughout the entire period of mass immigration. Almost 87 percent of the people of Irish birth lived in cities, a proportion exceeded only by people born in the Russian Empire.

The contributions of several other old immigrant groups to the total immigrant population of all cities remained substantial in 1920. For example, only 67.5 percent of German immigrants lived in cities, but because the German group was so large it accounted for more than 12 percent of the total foreign-born white population in American cities. Only Italian immigrants, of whom more than 84 percent were urban residents, outnumbered Germans in the foreign-born urban population. Similarly, people from the United Kingdom, Canada, and Scandinavia together accounted for nearly 25 percent of the total number of urban immigrants. Thus, although many ethnic and national groups of the new immigration settled almost exclusively in cities, only those from Italy and the Russian Empire contributed substantially more people to American cities than did most of the groups of the old immigration.

1920–Present In the 1920s Congress enacted a series of laws designed to check the flow of immigrants to the United States, laws that openly discriminated against newcomers. The immigration quotas remained in effect, with some slight modifications, until 1965. They compounded the effects of declining population growth and improved living standards in those parts of Europe that had supplied the most immigrants before 1890. Because the countries with generous quotas were no longer major sources of emigration, the total volume of European migration to the United States was greatly reduced.

Despite the proverbial spatial mobility of Americans and the fading out of many overt ethnic traits in the children of immigrants, the regional patterns of most ethnic groups, often established early in the group's immigration, have been remarkably persistent. One striking exception to this stability of ethnic distributions over the past 50 years has been the reduced overrepresentation of northwestern Europeans in the Midwest and their increased representation on the Pacific coast. These groups have contributed greatly to the general migration to the West, especially the Pacific coast.

But by far the most conspicuous distributional change over the past half-century has been the movement of blacks to the Northeast and Midwest. In 1920 85 percent of all blacks were still concentrated in the South, but by 1970 the proportion had been reduced by half. More recently the Southwest and California have become leading destinations of black migrants, and an ebb tide of black movement back to the South may be beginning. Southern whites have also moved to the North and West in large numbers. Southern California has attracted numbers of people from the Eastern and Western South Central states as well as from the Midwest. In the past 15 years, too, the once isolated sections of Appalachia have become a source of white southern migration to the cities of the Midwest. The rate of Mexican immigration has also increased in the recent past, but their pattern of regional concentration has scarcely changed. Only recently has the immigration of Puerto Ricans and Cubans been substantial, with the resulting concentration of the former group in New York and the latter in Florida.

Thus the current regional ethnic group patterns are the result of an incremental process in which both the composition and destinations of migrants have changed. Each major immigrant group established an initial pattern of concentration, and subsequent migrants tended to choose the same destinations, attracted by networks of information and the sense of security generated by the presence of their compatriots. Often the intitial clusters represented new employment opportunities that happened to coincide with the arrival of a particular group, or, alternatively, the skills and enterprise of a newly arrived group were particularly appropriate to a growing sector of the economy. Not all immigrant groups, however, had the appropriate skills or arrived at the right time. Emigrants who left their homeland because of famine, acute agricultural distress, or repression probably had little control over their destination. Nevertheless, a rudimentary ethnic division of labor emerged, in which certain groups dominated certain kinds of employment and tended to cluster in certain regions or cities. Long after this ethnic division of labor had begun to lose its rigidity, group concentrations were maintained by institutional and family ties. In short, both social and economic factors encouraged the concentrations of ethnic groups in the United States, and the well-defined if overlapping regional clusters of most of these groups have persisted to this day.

Changing Urban Patterns

The large-scale regional distributions of American ethnic groups have been far more persistent than their urban residential patterns. By the late 19th century, the city had become the leading destination of all migrants, and the descendants of many people who had settled on the land in the middle decades of the century joined the cityward movement. The first observers of the urban experiences of migrants spoke of a kind of "elevator" of material advancement and assimilation, from initial residence in ethnically well-defined inner-city slums to suburbs with no obvious ethnic identification. This view acknowledged that the rate of advancement varied from group to group and that not all groups entered on the ground floor. Today we are aware, however, that the elevator generalization may not have applied to some groups, and further, that assimilation and suburbanization do not have a simple relationship. The elevator image was formulated during the early decades of the present century when large numbers of new immigrants were congregating in the inner cities and when some old immigrants and their descendants were moving to the suburbs. Although residence in an inner-city slum seemed to be a temporary part of the immigrant's experience in America, it was viewed as a symbol of the failure of the American dream, not only in regard to material conditions and opportunities but also because it spawned political corruption and threatened democracy.

More recent interpretations view the immigrants' urban experiences and their inner-city neighborhoods in a more positive light, emphasizing the value of ethnic institutions and family networks in helping immigrants adapt to their new country. Even 19th-century political corruption is seen as an informal and undemeaning welfare arrangement at a time when bureaucratic social services were undeveloped. The newer interpretations also reveal that there was a great range of inner-city social and material conditions and that although each ethnic quarter housed most of a group's institutions, it was not necessarily the dominant point of concentration for the group. In addition, the inner city, despite its congested housing, offered locational advantages to immigrants who were employed in an adjacent central business district. Because immigrant employment was often uncertain and seasonal or entailed awkward hours, even cheap local transportation was no substitute for the opportunity to walk or cycle to work. These reevaluations of the role of inner-city ethnic quarters, however, are appropriate only to the experiences of groups who moved to American cities in the late 19th and early 20th centuries. They are not generally applicable to (1) the masses of immigrants who arrived before the Civil War, (2) the South, or (3) those groups, mainly blacks, who dominate inner cities today.

In the first case, the conditions leading to urban segregation were lacking before the Civil War. The concentration of immigrants in central sections depended upon the abandonment of housing, or at least of space, by previous residents and upon locally available employment. Only during the 1870s and 1880s did the suburban movement reach such a scale that it released an adequate supply of centrally located housing to meet the needs of immigrant newcomers. Immigrants could be housed at increased densities, but before the 1870s they quickly filled the available central space, and many were forced to live on the edge of the city and on undesirable sites avoided by more prosperous residents. During the 1850s especially, when most eastern cities could not house the large numbers of newly arrived immigrants, many German and Irish newcomers were obliged to set up peripheral shantytowns similar to those common today in less-developed areas of the world. It was in the newer cities of the interior—where the number of immigrants often approached, equaled, or exceeded that of the native-born—that, in the absence of preexisting housing, large, contiguous inner-city concentrations could be established. In mid-19th-century cities, too, employment was characteristically

scattered and small in scale, and the still-developing manufacturing and commercial districts were not always the most important sources of jobs. Only toward the close of the century were the majority of immigrant groups and the leading sources of their employment concentrated in central urban locations.

Second, both before and after the Civil War cities in the South exhibited distinctive residential patterns, partly because the South attracted proportionately few foreign immigrants and partly because blacks were a major element in their populations. Extensive areas of segregation were rare; blacks often lived in the back alleys and rear lots of neighborhoods whose main streets were inhabited by whites. Thus clusters of blacks were dotted throughout southern cities, not concentrated in one well-defined black quarter. Even in border and northern cities, black populations often were widely scattered.

Third, when the blacks flooded northern cities during World War I, extensive and contiguous black quarters developed. Since most inner-city residential quarters in the North were already densely occupied by European immigrants, the expansion of black areas was limited to districts somewhat removed from the city center, where speculative overbuilding for middle-income people had created a supply of cheap dwellings suitable for subdivision. Boston's Roxbury, New York's Harlem, and Chicago's South Side are examples of urban areas that, though not the most centrally located, offered cheap housing to blacks. Subsequently, as other ethnic groups moved to the suburbs and as the black populations continued to grow, the initial black quarters expanded toward the inner city as well as outward. Yet even while larger sections of the inner city were becoming available to blacks, urban employment was becoming decentralized. Consequently, the black residential districts have remained well removed from the centers of employment.

The deprivation of blacks and other newcomers to American cities in recent decades is a result not only of their high levels of residential segregation but also of the timing of their arrival in relation to the changing locations of urban employment and changing employment opportunities. The persistence of distinctive regional and urban spatial patterns among groups is a record of the enduring effects of ethnicity in residential locations, but relative location in the city or region provides only a partial key to the material and social situation of each ethnic group.

Bibliography

The two most comprehensive overviews of the regional patterns of ethnic groups are Wilbur Zelinsky, *The Cultural Geography of the United States* (Englewood Cliffs, N.J., 1973), and Raymond D. Gastil, *Cultural Regions of the United States* (Seattle, 1975). Of several studies of individual ethnic groups, those by Donald W. Meinig, "The Mormon Culture Region: Strategies and Patterns in the Geography of the American West, 1847–1964," *Annals of the Association of American Geographers* 55 (1965): 191–220, and by Terry G. Jordan, "The Imprint of the Upper and Lower South on Mid-Nineteenth-Century Texas," *Annals of the A.A.G.* 57 (1967): 667–690, are exemplary. A fine collection of articles on the urban residential patterns of ethnic groups, including the study by Nathan Kantrovitz of segregation in the New York–New Jersey metropolitan area, have been edited by Ceri Peach, *Urban Social Segregation* (New York, 1975). Many of the controversial aspects of urban ethnicity are discussed in Nathan Glazer and Daniel P. Moynihan, *Beyond the Melting Pot*, rev. ed. (Cambridge, Mass., 1972), while a comparative review of several cities is found in Stanley Lieberson, *Ethnic Patterns in American Cities* (Glencoe, Ill., 1963).

A useful overview of the changing composition and circumstances of immigration is Leonard Dinnerstein and David M. Reimers, *Ethnic Americans: A History of Immigration and Assimilation* (New York, 1975). A more specifically geographic treatment of immigrant destinations is found in David Ward, *Cities and Immigrants: A Geography of Change in Nineteenth-Century America* (New York, 1971). For the colonial period, see James T. Lemon, *The Best Poor Man's Country* (Baltimore, 1972), a regional case study of the geography of ethnic pluralism in southeastern Pennsylvania. The changing distributions of blacks, Asians, American Indians, and Spanish-speaking groups are treated in Donald K. Fellows, *A Mosaic of America's Ethnic Minorities* (New York, 1972). Among the many case studies of the residential patterns of individual ethnic groups in specific cities, a recent classic is Kathleen N. Conzen, *Immigrant Milwaukee 1836–1860: Accommodation and Community in a Frontier City* (Cambridge, Mass., 1976). Other case studies are Paul A. Groves and Edward K. Muller, "The Evolution of Black Residential Areas in Late 19th-century Cities," *Journal of Historical Geography* 1 (1975): 169–191, and Caroline Golab, *Immigrant Destinations* (Philadelphia, 1977). Examinations of the residential patterns of southern cities in the 19th century are extremely rare; an exception is John P. Radford, "Race, Residence and Ideology: Charleston, South Carolina in the Mid-Nineteenth Century," *Journal of Historical Geography* 2 (1976): 329–346.

DAVID WARD

INDIANS: *see* AMERICAN INDIANS; EAST INDIANS; WEST INDIANS

INDOCHINESE

The Indochinese refugees in the United States come from lands intermittently torn apart by centuries of conflict. Of diverse origins, the Vietnamese, Cambodians, and Laotians are among the most recent groups to immigrate to the United States, and it is not at all clear how they will adjust or develop. The collapse of the South Vietnamese government in April 1975 and similar political upheavals in Cambodia and Laos led to the admission of more than 170,000 refugees to the United States. About 90 percent are Vietnamese; the remaining 10 percent are split almost equally between Laotians and Cambodians. Prior to this influx, the total number of Vietnamese immigrants for the decade between 1966 and 1975 was 20,038. There are no exact figures for Laotian and Cambodian arrivals before 1975, since they were too few to warrant a separate Immigration and Naturalization Service (INS) designation.

ORIGINS

Vietnam, Cambodia, and Laos today make up what was once known as the French Indochinese Union. Before French rule, each country came under a variety of cultural influences: Cambodia, by India, Siam, and Annam; Laos, by the Thai and Siam; and Vietnam, by China. Western penetration into the area began in the 16th century and culminated in the 19th-century colonization of the Indochinese peninsula by the French. In 1867, Cochin China, now part of Vietnam, became a French colony. France soon established protectorates over Cambodia (1863), Annam (1884), and Tonkin (1884), also part of present-day Vietnam. A union of these four states was formed in 1887 under the leadership of a French governor general. Laos joined this alliance in 1893. French rule continued until Japan occupied Indochina during World War II. Before the end of the war, the French announced a plan of reunion that allowed greater self-government to the member states. Although accepted by Cambodia and Laos, Vietnamese nationalists called for the complete independence of

Indochina

Boundaries of former
French Protectorates
Boundary of North and
South Vietnam, 1954-1975

500   Km.   Miles

caused thousands to flee their homelands and seek asylum in Thailand, Malaysia, Indonesia, Hong Kong, and Singapore.

The term Indochinese is a generic one that embraces the many Southeast Asian peoples who came under French colonial rule in the late 19th century. The peoples of Vietnam, Cambodia, and Laos are ethnically and linguistically diverse. The majority group in each country is ethnically homogeneous, however: 80 percent of those in Vietnam are Vietnamese; 85 percent of the Cambodian population are Khmers; and 50 percent of the population in Laos are Laotians, a people related to the Thai. Some of the minority groups include Chinese and Vietnamese in Cambodia; the Mon-Khmer, Yao, and Hmong in Laos; and Chinese, Thai, Muong, Nung, Hmong, and Montagnards in Vietnam. Theravāda Buddhism is the prevalent religion in both Cambodia and Laos. Until the Communist victory in 1975, Mahāyāna Buddhism was the official state religion in South Vietnam; Catholics made up a significant proportion of the non-Buddhist minority.

ARRIVAL

Before 1975 few Indochinese immigrated to the United States. Not until 1966 did "Vietnamese" become a separate designation in the Immigration and Naturalization Service statistics; before that the Vietnamese along with the Cambodians and Laotians had been included in the "Other Asia" category. There are no exact figures for the total number of Laotians and Cambodians in the United States before 1975 because the INS continued to count them together. The scanty information that is available suggests that these early immigrants were clustered in professional, technical, and other white-collar occupations. Between 1968 and 1971 Vietnamese wives and children of U.S. citizens—probably mostly American servicemen—comprised more than 75 percent of the total Vietnamese immigration to the United States. In 1965 the Vietnamese population was concentrated in California, New York, Washington, D.C., Illinois, and Texas. By 1975 sizable numbers were also reported in Florida, Massachusetts, Michigan, New Jersey, Ohio, Pennsylvania, Texas, and Connecticut. Before long, however, the ranks of the Indochinese in the United States would more than quadruple.

In April 1975, as the rebel forces moved closer and closer to Saigon, chaos prevailed throughout South Vietnam. Many Vietnamese began to fear a bloodbath. They anticipated reprisals by the Viet Cong against all who had been associated with the Thieu government or had been employed by the Americans in any capacity. Between April 21 and April 29 the American embassy helped arrange for the departure of more than 60,000 Vietnamese. The plans for evacuation were haphazard, and decisions concerning who left and who remained behind depended on the judgment of the American embassy workers who hastily processed exit visas. At the same time, an additional 70,000 Vietnamese arranged for their own transportation, often at great expense.

In all, about 130,000 people from Vietnam, Laos, and Cambodia arrived at American receiving stations in Guam and the Philippines. By the end of that summer, there were about 60,000 more in refugee camps in Hong Kong and Thailand. There the refugees awaited permis-

Cochin China, Annam, and Tonkin. Bitter fighting, which lasted for almost a decade, broke out in late 1946 between the French and a coalition of Vietnamese Communists and Nationalists known as the Viet Minh, led by Ho Chi Minh. Following the French defeat at Dien Bien Phu in 1954, an international conference at Geneva provided for the temporary partition of Vietnam along the 17th parallel, a division that created the Democratic Republic of Vietnam in the north and the Republic of Vietnam in the south. The conference mandated the withdrawal of all foreign troops from Cambodia and Laos and formulated a plan for the reunification of Vietnam to be achieved by elections in 1956. The partition was followed by refugee movement between borders and some reprisals on suspected enemies by each side. The elections which would have reunited the north and south were canceled in 1956 by South Vietnamese president Ngo Dinh Diem, with the support of the American government which sought to create an anti-Communist bastion in Southeast Asia. Shortly thereafter the National Liberation Front (Viet Cong) began a campaign of guerrilla warfare, backed by Ho Chi Minh, to topple the Diem regime and reunify the country. During the Kennedy, Johnson, and Nixon administrations the United States made an enormous commitment of American manpower and resources to preserve an independent South Vietnam, but to no avail. South Vietnam fell to the Communists in 1975. Cambodia and Laos, too, experienced disruptions from the war and internal political conflict. These upheavals

sion to move on to whatever countries would have them.

THE REFUGEE CAMPS

As the fall of Saigon seemed imminent, the U.S. government rapidly made plans to receive the refugees. On April 18, 1975, President Gerald R. Ford set up a special Interagency Task Force (IATF), representing 12 federal agencies "to coordinate . . . all U.S. Government activities concerning evacuation of U.S. citizens, Vietnamese citizens, and third country nationals from Vietnam and refugee and resettlement problems relating to the Vietnam conflict." A receiving station was established in Guam, and plans to open four resettlement camps in the United States were set in motion. The first mainland reception center opened at Camp Pendleton, Calif., on April 29, followed by centers at Fort Chaffee, Ark., Eglin Air Force Base, Fla., and Fort Indiantown Gap, Pa. The Indochina Migration and Refugee Assistance Act of 1975, enacted on May 24, provided funds for the resettlement program.

Upon arrival each refugee received bed linens, toiletries, a meal ticket, and a camp number. Living quarters afforded little privacy. At Camp Pendleton there were tents with wooden platforms, each housing 25 people; elsewhere, army barracks provided shelter. Low wooden partitions broke up the living space into cubicles, each accommodating approximately 15 people. The refugees shared bathrooms and ate together in mess halls.

Each refugee went through a rigorous "in-processing" procedure. Representatives from various U.S. agencies collected data on age, family size, occupation, education, skills, and religion. In order to complete security checks, officials took fingerprints and photographs. All refugees underwent medical examinations and received social-security and alien-registration numbers. Finally, each household head registered with one of nine private social service agencies, called VOLAGS (an acronym for voluntary agencies), which accepted the responsibility for the welfare and sponsorship of the refugees once they left the camps. The nine VOLAGS were the United States Catholic Conference, the International Rescue Committee, the Church World Service, the Lutheran Immigration and Refugee Service, the American Council for Nationalities Service, the United Hebrew Immigrant Aid Society, the Tolstoy Foundation, the American Fund for Czechoslovak Refugees, and the Travelers Aid International Social Service of America.

The camps were designed to facilitate the assimilation of the refugees into life in the United States as rapidly as possible. Since the Indochinese arrived at a time of economic recession, the resettlement workers made great efforts to find sponsors and jobs for them in order to keep them off the public welfare rolls. The camp administrators initiated special educational programs which they hoped would hasten the process of absorption.

A typical battery of programs included schooling for children from the ages of 6 to 18, language and vocational training for adults, and lessons on such skills as how to shop, apply for a job, and rent an apartment in an American community. Each camp also administered a number of recreational programs with such activities as nightly movies and volleyball games. Most camps had at least one newspaper, which explained camp rules and various facets of American life.

All elementary and secondary educational instruction was conducted in English, and students were forbidden to use their native tongue in the classroom. As a result, most students did not understand their instructors and appeared to be dumb or unresponsive. In a curious move, described at length by Gail P. Kelly, lists of slang words, including words current in the drug culture, were distributed to secondary school students. Apparently it was assumed that knowing these words would make it easier for students to adjust and to get along with their American peers. The programs stressed assertiveness and independence as basic American values, which clashed sharply with the tradition of respect for and submission to parental wishes. Many parents tried to keep their children out of school for this reason. Adult programs concentrated on preparing the refugees for jobs on the lowest rung of the occupational ladder, although concurrently urging them to aim for a suburban, middle-class existence.

The refugees felt they were being pressured into abandoning their traditional customs for "American" ones, and many resisted. Their resistance reached its height when it came time to find sponsors for each refugee family. The traditional Vietnamese family consists of grandparents, parents, children, and other relatives. It is not at all unusual for a single household to include 25 people or more. Most sponsors, however, whether individuals or groups, frequently drew the line at 5 to 7 people. As the resettlement period wore on, the agencies placed considerable pressure on family heads to split up their extended families into smaller units, with only partial success.

The statistics collected at the in-processing stage indicate some unexpected characteristics of Indochinese immigration. Of a sample of slightly over 123,000 individuals, approximately 55 percent of the 1975 arrivals were male. The vast majority were young: 82 percent under 35; 65 percent under 25. Of these, men between 18 and 25 comprised the largest segment. In that age group there were over 4,000 more men than women refugees. Many of the men had been members of the Vietnamese military—those most likely to be able to leave Vietnam without American assistance. But the great majority of the refugees had immigrated with their extended families.

Forty percent of those interviewed during in-processing indicated that they were Catholic, an unusually large proportion since Catholics in South Vietnam made up less than 10 percent of the population. This suggests that many who immigrated to the United States had also been part of the 1954 migration from North to South Vietnam, a hypothesis that was substantiated by a study based on interviews with refugees at Fort Indiantown Gap in the fall of 1975. Over 75 percent of those interviewed reported that they were Catholic and had been born in North Vietnam.

According to the initial INS profile, 20 percent of all the refugees over 18 years of age had at least some university education, 38 percent reported having some secondary schooling, 18 percent had some elementary schooling, 2 percent had none at all, and 23 percent did not report. Among the heads-of-household 27 percent had some university training, 48 percent some second-

ary education, 17 percent some elementary school education, 1 percent none at all, and 7 percent did not report.

Women in Indochina generally had less educational opportunity than men. Since less than 25 percent of the household heads were women, the predominantly male head-of-household group had a higher level of education. Older refugees were usually less well educated than younger ones, since under French colonial rule schooling was minimal in Cambodia and Laos. In Vietnam, educational opportunities were more extensive—a development related to the French insistence on Vietnam's cutting its ties with China. After 1954 school facilities were expanded, which accounts for the larger number of well-educated refugees among the young. Before the 1975 Communist takeover, most schools were in the cities and more than half of them charged tuition, suggesting that those refugees in the study came from an urban and relatively affluent sector of Vietnamese society.

SPONSORSHIP AND RESETTLEMENT

The transition from camp life to life in the United States often proved difficult for the refugees. The IATF planned to close all camps by December 31, 1975, and to facilitate this, all refugees had to be placed with sponsors as quickly as possible. As a result refugees were placed with sponsors too quickly, before they were ready to cope with American life.

The U.S. government strongly urged third-country resettlement. Despite IATF cooperation with the United Nations High Commissioner on Refugees and considerable urging on the part of camp officials, only 6,632 Indochinese refugees resettled in other countries. Such a small percentage of third-country placement was the result in great part of the unwillingness of other countries to admit refugees other than professionals such as doctors and engineers—the very people who were easiest to resettle in the United States. Canada accepted more than half of the 6,632; 1,877 went to France; 161 to Australia; 120 to Taiwan; and 115 to the Philippines. An even smaller number requested repatriation. Of these, 1,546 were repatriated to Vietnam in October 1975, but the over 400 refugees who have requested repatriation since then have been ignored by the Vietnamese government. In early 1976, 105 Cambodians returned to their homeland.

Of the almost 130,000 refugees who arrived in 1975, only a handful avoided the resettlement camps, all of them either former employees of large U.S. firms and their families or people who had $4,000 per family member in liquid assets. Finding sponsors for the rest proved an enormous task.

Sponsorship entailed a commitment to provide food, clothing, and shelter for a refugee family until it became self-supporting. Sponsors helped household heads find employment, enrolled the children in school, and provided advice and encouragement for the entire family. In addition, each sponsor accepted the financial responsibility for providing medical care when needed. Since sponsorship required a substantial monetary commitment, groups were usually better able to provide for the refugee household than were individuals.

Caseworkers at each voluntary agency matched sponsorship offers with refugees on the basis of English-language skills, job skills, and family size. Only rarely did sponsor and refugee meet before sponsorship arrangements were completed. The federal government provided a resettlement grant of $500 per refugee, administered through the individual voluntary agency. The agency retained all or part of this grant to help defray the administrative costs of sponsorship and resettlement. Sponsorship offers were frequently tied to offers of employment which were often exploitative. Fish and poultry processing firms and candy and machinery manufacturers both sponsored and employed refugees, often paying them the minimum wage or less. While the sponsorship offers had ostensibly included free room and board, some workers found deductions for this taken from their pay.

Until late August 1975 the refugees were free to reject any sponsorship offer they found unacceptable. Some cited unsuitable climate or isolation from other Indochinese families as reasons. Many declined offers that would have required the breakup of the family. Often Catholic refugees viewed offers from Protestant congregations as attempts to proselytize them. Some feared racial prejudice; others hesitated to leave the security of camp life. By September, however, it became the general policy to allow the refugees to turn down no more than two sponsorship offers.

Over 89,000 were settled by church-affiliated agencies, over 52,000 of them by the United States Catholic Conference; 27,199 refugees found sponsors in California; 9,130 in Texas; 7,159 in Pennsylvania; 5,322 in Florida; 4,182 in Washington; 3,696 in Illinois; 3,689 in New York; and 3,601 in Louisiana. Over half the refugees were settled in states where their total number would be less than 3,000, a practice encouraged by government officials who feared that large concentrations of refugees from Indochina in a single geographical area would cause economic and social problems.

In addition to the VOLAGS, five states agreed to undertake direct sponsorship of refugees. Washington, which sponsored 1,732, had the largest program. A temporary resettlement camp was opened at Camp Murray on the outskirts of Tacoma, where the refugees underwent orientation for several weeks before moving on to sponsors. Washington was one of the few states that used public-welfare funds to enable refugees to participate in English-language and job-training programs.

The state of Iowa sponsored 1,200 Tai Dam, a group who fled their native home in the North Vietnamese highlands for Laos following the French defeat at Dien Bien Phu in 1954. At last report, all heads-of-household held jobs, and none was receiving public assistance. New Mexico, Oklahoma, and Maine initiated similar programs to sponsor the remainder of the 4,000 refugees.

When the refugees found work it was usually at jobs that required little skill, paid low wages, and offered little chance for advancement. An IATF survey taken in 1975 indicated that 85 percent of those refugees who held white-collar jobs in Vietnam had blue-collar jobs in the United States, though by the summer of 1977 the proportion had fallen to 61 percent. The 1975 survey also indicated that 45 percent of the skilled blue-collar workers had joined the unskilled labor force because they could not find employment in the occupations for which they had been trained. Low wages and large fami-

lies combined to put many refugee households well below the poverty level, and this helped to drive refugee women into the job market. By August 1977, 50 percent of all female refugees over 16 years of age held either part-time or full-time jobs. This supplemental income seldom raised total family income above the poverty line, however. In the same survey, the task force reported that only 14 percent of employed refugees made more than $200 per week; 63 percent earned $100 to $199; 16 percent made $50 to $99; and 5 percent earned less than $50.

As the months passed, sponsors began to find that they could not provide the long-term supplemental support required even by those households with more than one wage earner, and responsibility began to shift from sponsors to the federal government. A November 1977 report by the U.S. Department of Health, Education, and Welfare (HEW) found that 33 percent of the U.S. refugee population received at least a portion of its support from federal cash assistance, even though 94.4 of the male and 92.5 percent of the female heads-of-household were in the labor force. The shift to welfare also indicates a change in attitude of many refugees toward their plight. Faced with low-paying dead-end employment, many found that public assistance provided as much support as the demeaning jobs they had been pressured into taking. A great many also supported themselves by public assistance while they acquired English-language skills and retrained for more lucrative jobs.

Within six months of the original resettlement, a significant regrouping of the refugee population had begun. Those in the scattered, rural settlements favored by the IATF began to move on their own initiative to urban centers, especially those with already established Indochinese, particularly Vietnamese, communities. Los Angeles, San Francisco, New Orleans, and Dallas drew significant numbers of immigrants. This regrouping can be seen as an attempt to end the isolation that accompanied many sponsorships and to create a supportive and viable community.

SOCIAL AND CULTURAL LIFE

From this conscious regrouping a variety of voluntary organizations have emerged. Sometimes short-lived, these societies run the gamut from purely social clubs to cultural and self-help organizations. Over 100 of them are Vietnamese, a dozen or more are Cambodian, and a few of them are Laotian. A typical example is the Boulder Vietnamese Alliance—a society in Boulder, Colo. whose weekly meetings often include volleyball and soccer games. The alliance publishes a bimonthly newsletter, maintains a telephone hot line, and aids members and their families in finding employment and housing. It also sponsors cultural events and an English-language tutoring program for school children.

The Cambodian Association of San Diego, Calif., founded by a former member of the Cambodian Foreign Ministry, has a membership of over 300. Its services include housing, emergency shelter, translation, and assistance in dealing with federal and state agencies. A Lao organization, APPLE, Inc.—an acronym for the Association for the Positive Promotion of Lao Ethnics—was founded in Des Moines, Iowa, in November 1976. APPLE's aims include developing educational materials for Laotians, establishing a network of communications

within the Lao ethnic group, and educating the American public about Lao culture. Other societies function under the sponsorship of American organizations, many of them church-related.

Since their arrival in the United States, the refugees have had at least some access to printed materials in their languages. Three of the refugee camps published their own papers: *Dat Lanh* (June 1975–December 1975) a bilingual daily in Vietnamese and English with occasional Cambodian language editions, printed at Fort Indiantown Gap; *Thong Bao* (May 1975–November 1975), another Vietnamese-English daily printed at Camp Pendleton; and *Ton Dan*, printed at Fort Chaffee. All were compiled and published by the camp administration; all conspicuously avoided news items about Vietnam. The exception, *Chan Troi Moi* (May 1975–August 1975), a Vietnamese daily, was edited and published by Vietnamese refugees on Guam and frequently included news of Vietnam.

In addition to a profusion of newsletters published by many of the voluntary societies, a multilingual monthly, *New Life*, is published by the Refugee Task Force division of the Social and Rehabilitation Service of the HEW. Its Vietnamese edition has a circulation of 35,000; 10,000 copies are published in Lao, and 5,000 in Cambodian. *New Life* presents a mélange of American and international news, self-help articles, and explanations of such American institutions as the tax system.

THE SECOND WAVE

An estimated quarter-million Vietnamese, Laotians, and Cambodians are now seeking temporary asylum throughout Southeast Asia—in Malaysia, Indonesia, Hong Kong, Singapore, and in a large number of refugee compounds in Thailand. Most fled their native lands to avoid forced relocation, religious persecution, or family separation. Refugees from Cambodia reported mass killings and other atrocities. Many escaped by boat from Vietnam in small unseaworthy vessels. It is estimated that only half of those who set out to sea make it safely back to shore—and many have been forced to wander from port to port before being granted asylum. The remainder came overland from Cambodia and Laos. The VOLAGS continue to make a concentrated effort to locate refugees who are waiting in camps in Hong Kong and Thailand and reunite them with their relatives in the United States.

Since the spring of 1975 the United States has authorized the admission of over 60,000 additional refugees, mostly Vietnamese, from Southeast Asia: 11,000 in 1976 at the request of President Ford; 15,000 in 1977 on President Jimmy Carter's initiative; and three separate contingents of 7,000, 25,000 and 2,500 in 1978 under the parole authority of the Attorney General. To supplement these special measures, a bill which places a total ceiling on U.S. immigration at 290,000 visas without respect for hemispheric limitations was introduced in 1978 to replace the 1965 legislation that limited yearly immigration to the United States at 170,000 from the Eastern Hemisphere and 120,000 from the Western Hemisphere. Regulations will then permit emigrants from the East to use any unused Western visas.

The most recent refugees are by and large less well educated than those who arrived at the resettlement

camps. Escapees from Communist governments, they are also more willing to accept hardship and to start at the bottom. The government has allocated considerably less for their resettlement. It pays their air fare, but they must sign a promissory note to repay a portion of it. There are no resettlement camps. Sponsors are found by private voluntary agencies which receive a government resettlement grant of $300 per refugee for the service.

The services provided by the Indochina Migration and Refugee Assistance Act of 1975 were extended in 1977 to allow each refugee to adjust his or her status from parolee to permanent resident following a two-year residency in the United States. All time spent in the United States after March 31, 1975 can be counted toward the five-year residency required for U.S. citizenship.

Like other refugee groups, the Indochinese in the United States continue to face a number of hardships. Uprooted from their war-torn homelands, they have to cope with language barriers, cultural differences, and isolation. In many cases, radical change in social status creates crises in self-esteem and makes adjustment even more difficult. Underemployment and unemployment plague the community, and have resulted in a steady rise in welfare recipients. Many refugees suffer from depression. On the other hand, a number of successful small businesses have been founded by Indochinese refugees; a restaurant cooperative, the WE (for West-East) Ethnic Restaurant in Pontiac, Mich. is among the most notable. After its first year of operation, the owner, Nguyen Huy Han, presented rebates totaling $10,000 to his 1,500 customers as a gesture of thanks and appreciation for their support.

The final outcome is uncertain. A vital and cohesive group is emerging, but only time will tell whether the refugees from Southeast Asia will achieve the same degree of success that other refugee groups in the United States have been able to experience.

Bibliography
For background information consult Nguyen Khac Khan, *An Introduction to Vietnamese Culture* (Tokyo, 1967), and *We the Vietnamese* (New York, 1971), ed. François Sully. Le-Thi-Que, A. Terry Rambo, and Gary D. Murfin, "Why They Fled: Refugee Movement During the Spring 1976 Communist Offensive in South Vietnam," *Asian Survey* 16 (September 1976): 855–863, covers the motives for emigration. The best surveys of the arrival and settlement process are Gail P. Kelly, *From Vietnam to America: A Chronicle of Vietnamese Immigration to the United States* (Boulder, Colo., 1977), and Darrel Moutero and Marsha I. Weber, *Vietnamese Americans: Patterns of Resettlement and Socioeconomic Adaptation in the United States* (Boulder, Colo., 1979). The annual reports to Congress of the HEW Refugee Task Force contain useful statistical information pertaining to the current status of Indochinese refugees in the United States. Consult individual issues of the *New York Times* for articles dealing with the refugees, especially during the spring and fall of 1975.

Primary materials can be found in the Vietnamese Immigration Collection at the State University of New York at Buffalo; taped interviews with refugees and camp officials, unpublished orientation materials, and copies of the camp newspapers are available there.

MARY BOWEN WRIGHT

INDONESIANS

There are about 10,000 Indonesians in the United States, half of whom are former Dutch colonials who left the islands in the early 1960s when Indonesia won independence from the Netherlands. Indonesia, the fifth most populous country in the world, has a multiethnic population of more than 130 million people, distributed over 3,000 large and small islands and largely Muslim. In the 1970s about 500 Indonesians a year were admitted to the United States, usually in family groups. Most of these immigrants were between 20 and 40 years of age at the time of arrival; the men were usually professional, technical, white-collar, or skilled workers.

INGUSH: *see* NORTH CAUCASIANS

INTERMARRIAGE

The elements that define ethnic groups usually include a common heredity, a common language, a common set of surnames, a common religion, a common geographic locale, and common behavioral norms. Primary social interaction is greater within the group than outside it, and as one of the most consequential forms of interaction, marriage tends to take place within the group as an effective means of maintaining its cultural distinctiveness and the only means by which common genetic inheritance can be maintained. Hence, groups that want to preserve their distinctiveness actively discourage marriage to outsiders.

Despite self-conscious attempts to preserve group integrity, group boundaries often blur or dissolve. For example, almost all members of the immigrant groups who have come to the United States speaking a language other than English have abandoned their native language in favor of English. This conversion eliminates a principal form of group distinctiveness and simultaneously reduces barriers to interaction between members of the particular ethnic group and all others. On the other hand, new ethnic boundaries can emerge, as they did between white Americans in the North and those in the South during the conflict over slavery and its expansion. This conflict shattered the religious unity of the nation many years before the Civil War broke out and divided the major Protestant churches into northern and southern branches which in several cases even now remain divided. Another 19th-century example was the establishment of the Mormon community in a white Anglo-Saxon Protestant milieu. Mormons today hold distinctive theological beliefs, follow different standards of social behavior, maintain a high degree of geographical segregation, and have a low rate of intermarriage.

Some ethnic groups are more distinctive than others. Residents of the Navajo Indian reservation, for example, who are differentiated from most other Americans by language, race, religion, customs, and geographic location, are highly distinctive, whereas Jews, who are differentiated from most other Americans only by religious belief, some customs, and to a certain extent by geographic segregation, are less distinctive. Ethnic groups characterized by racial differences are sharply differentiated from groups characterized only by differences in language, religion, or other aspects of culture; individuals can change their language, their surname, their religious belief, or other cultural habits, but they cannot change their skin color. Thus, if a Lutheran man marries a Catholic woman and himself converts to that faith, he can join the Catholic social group and many persons within that group will be unaware that he is a

newcomer. An American black interacting socially with American whites does not have the same freedom. The salience of race varies with the historical context, however, as the dramatic change in the social position of the Japanese and Chinese in the United States in recent decades makes clear.

The various ethnic groups also maintain varying amounts of social distance from one another, a phenomenon first examined in a 1928 study. Respondents were asked a variety of questions, such as whether they would work together with a person of some other ethnic group, whether they would agree to have a person of that group live in their neighborhood, whether they would invite a person of that group to their house, or whether they would marry a person of that group. A higher proportion of respondents said they would refuse to marry a person of a given ethnic group than said they would refuse to have other forms of contact with that group. Nevertheless, the reluctance to marry members of another ethnic group was found to relate to reluctance to have other forms of contact with that group. Thus, one can plot the social distance of one group from all other ethnic groups, and having done so, predict accurately the reluctance of its members to marry a member of each of the other ethnic groups. As a general rule, reluctance to intermarry is proportional to the number and degree of differences between the given outside group and one's own group. Thus, the theological difference between Protestants and Catholics in the United States is less than that between Catholics and Jews, and Catholic sanctions against marriage with a Jew are therefore stronger than those against marriage with a Protestant.

Finally, each ethnic group has a certain average social rank, so that members of a high-ranking group may wish to maintain more distance from members of a lower-ranking group than would be the case in reverse. The fact that white Americans prefer to keep more social distance between themselves and blacks than do black Americans with respect to whites is manifested by the greater approval whites have given laws prohibiting interracial marriage, which were only recently declared unconstitutional.

THE DETERMINANTS OF INTERMARRIAGE

Various factors are involved in an individual's decision whether or not to marry within the ethnic group. Among the most important are the relative availability of a suitable marriage partner from within or without the group; the barriers that the individual's group imposes upon marrying an outsider; the barriers that each of the other ethnic groups places upon outsiders wishing to marry into it; and the relative attractiveness of potential alternative partners, whether from the same group or not.

Sociological research has given most attention to the first of these factors—the availability of partners. With respect to marriage between Catholic and non-Catholic, Jew and non-Jew, black and nonblack it has been shown that the larger the proportion of all persons of opposite sex in the given area who are not of the individual's own group, the higher will be the proportion of outgroup marriages. The effect of this variable is powerful. For example, in the diocese of Raleigh, N.C., where Catholics were less than 2 percent of the total population, the percentage of Catholics involved in mixed valid marriages (that is, those performed by a Catholic priest) was 70 percent. In the diocese of Providence, R.I., where Catholics formed 50 to 70 percent of the population, only 18 percent were involved in mixed valid marriages. Similarly, in California the metropolitan counties showed very high positive correlations between the proportion of white grooms who married black brides and the proportion of all brides who were black and between the proportion of white brides who married black grooms and the proportion of all grooms who were black. However, a suitable marriage partner is also generally defined as being from a similar social class. Hence, the sheer numbers of ingroup and outgroup brides or grooms do not fully define the total of suitable and nonsuitable partners; the incidence of intermarriage is also inversely proportional to the degree to which ethnic boundaries coincide with class boundaries. Thus, Swedes will rarely marry Italians if the former are mainly middle class and the latter working class.

The barriers to intermarriage that each group imposes either on its own members or on outsiders may be classed as formal legal, formal religious, or informal. In the United States legal barriers to interracial marriage were enacted by white legislators in many states, particularly in the South and the West, until the Supreme Court deemed them unconstitutional in 1967. The first of these laws dates from the 18th century. By 1950, 30 states had laws prohibiting such marriage. Sentiment in favor of these laws then rapidly diminished, until by 1966 only 19 states, 17 of them in the South, continued to have laws against racial intermarriage. Unlike many European nations, none of the American states has ever had legislation restricting interreligious marriages.

Almost all religious bodies try to discourage or control marriage outside their respective memberships but vary in the extent of their opposition. Until relatively recently the Roman Catholic Church would not allow a priest to perform an interreligious marriage ceremony unless the non-Catholic partner promised to raise the children of the union as Catholics and the Catholic partner promised to encourage the non-Catholic to convert. However, in the late 1960s the Catholic church softened its policy, and since 1970 the pope has allowed local bishops to permit mixed marriages to be performed without a priest and also has eliminated the requirement that the non-Catholic partner promise to rear the children as Catholics; nevertheless, the Catholic partner must still promise to do all in his power to have the children raised as Catholic. Protestant denominations and sects also differ with regard to the barriers they place on the intermarriage of their members. At one extreme are the Mennonites, who excommunicate any member who marries outside the faith; on the other are numerous bodies that may wish their members to marry within the faith but provide no formal penalties for those who do not. Jewish religious bodies also differ in their degree of opposition to religious intermarriage, with Reform Jews more tolerant than either Conservative or Orthodox.

Informal controls are exercised primarily by the parents of potential brides and grooms and theoretically range from disinheritance and ostracism at one extreme to simple statements of disapproval at the other. For

contemporary parents the conflict between children choosing their own marriage partners and the expectation that marriage should be within the ethnic group has made parental controls less effective than in an earlier period.

Much of the existing literature on black-white interracial marriage focuses on the formal and informal barriers imposed by the white community on those of its members who consider marriage with blacks, and ignores any barriers that the black community may impose on its members. Such informal controls against interracial marriage operating within the black community have been real, however. In recent years the black community seems to have become increasingly able to invoke sanctions against black women who enter into social ties with white men.

The fourth determinant of intermarriage is the relative attractiveness of each potential marriage partner, some of whom may be ingroup members and some not. Attractiveness can be manifested as physical beauty, sensitivity to the needs of the partner, promise of high achievement, and so on. This factor has a special impact on marriages between whites and blacks in the United States, where the children of such marriages are generally considered to be black. Moreover, other things being equal, most white people have not wanted to have children whom other people would consider black. Therefore, it seems reasonable to suppose that white women marrying black men must receive something of extra value from their spouses in exchange for the privation of having children who may be considered socially "inferior." Accordingly, some scholars have postulated that the most frequent form of marriage between a black male and a white female is one in which the social class of the black husband is superior to that of the white wife, but a study based on 1960 Census data on relative educational levels of husbands and wives did not support this assumption. An analysis of data from the 1970 Census found the hypothesis to have some validity, provided the analysis instituted control for the availability of spouses of different educational level, which the previous study did not. However, the fact remains that white women who marry blacks do not in fact marry spouses of higher average educational attainment than those who marry whites. More must be involved in such marriages than the mere exchange of the two above-mentioned traits.

Definitions and Data Sources

The incidence of intermarriage is the number of intermarriages that take place during a given time period. The prevalence of intermarriage is the number of intermarriages that exist at a given point in time. Prevalence rates usually differ from incidence rates because of such factors as differentials in the mortality and divorce experience of couples, changes in incidence rates over time, and religious conversions. For example, the incidence of intermarriage for persons of religion A with persons of religion B might be 20 percent during 1978, but during that same year the prevalence of such marriages might be only 12 percent. The difference between the two might be explained by supposing that the greater number of marriages between persons of religion A and persons of religion B had taken place in recent years, that persons of religion A who had in previ-

ous years married into religion B might have had an unusually high propensity for divorce, or that a substantial proportion of adherents of religion A who had in previous years married persons of religion B either themselves converted to religion B or persuaded their spouses to convert to religion A.

Data on the incidence of intermarriage can be obtained from marriage licenses, and data on prevalence from the decennial censuses and from sample surveys. In the United States both types of data are far from adequate. Usually classifications in official publications are made in terms of national-origin group, religion, or race, but not in combinations of these three. Thus, data on an ethnic group such as Jews of Russian origin or Protestants of German origin may not be available at all. One is forced to work with data on the national-origin group independent of religion or on the religious group independent of nationality. Evidence on the incidence of intermarriage between national-origin groups is not usually found in official publications; instead data must be gathered by examining the surnames of bride and groom in marriage records. Moreover, marriage records in the United States do not contain data on a subject's actual identification with a national-origin group, and surnames can be highly misleading indicators. For many people of mixed national origin the surname may not indicate the preponderant national strain of the individual, much less his or her ethnic identification.

Data concerning the incidence of interreligious marriage are currently available only on marriage records from Indiana and from Iowa. Church sources include only the marriages performed by ministers of the given faith; hence, they do not provide a complete record of all marriages involving people of that faith. Fortunately, however, further inferences about the incidence of interfaith marriage in the United States can be made from the excellent data on the religion of bride and groom recorded by each Canadian province. Finally, data on interracial marriage in the United States are now available only from 32 states.

With respect to the prevalence of intermarriage, data for national-origin groups from the U.S. decennial census are (except for persons of Asian and Spanish origin) confined to the first and second generations. Only from the November 1969 Current Population Survey can one obtain official data on intermarriage among national-origin groups for all persons. Moreover, the census has never included a question on religion; data on married couples by religion of husband and religion of wife from the Bureau of the Census's Current Population Survey were gathered only during the year 1957. Fortunately, smaller nationwide surveys provide additional data on the prevalence of interfaith marriage and intermarriage among national-origin groups. Data on the prevalence of interracial marriage are available from the 1960 and 1970 censuses.

The validity of the data on the incidence and prevalence of interracial marriage—particularly that between whites and blacks—has been questioned. Since such marriages are only a tiny fraction of all marriages involving either racial group, a minute percentage of error in recording the race of husband or wife may prove large relative to the true number of such marriages. For example, among 485 cases of interracial mar-

riage in Philadelphia listed in the files of the Pennsylvania Health Department, actual marriage licenses from which the state files had been transcribed reveal that in 32 percent of the cases the marriage was not truly interracial.

Measuring either the incidence or prevalence of intermarriage is further complicated by the practices of researchers, some of whom measure the proportion of all marriages involving at least one member of the given ethnic group, whereas others measure the proportions of all individuals who marry outside that group. Unless either intermarriage or intramarriage is nonexistent, the former measure gives a higher rate than the latter. If group A, for instance, contains 50 brides and 50 grooms and 10 of each marry outside the group while the remainder marry within it, the number of marriages involving persons of group A will be 60 and the proportion of mixed marriages involving persons of group A will be 33 percent. On the other hand, the proportion of all persons of group A who intermarry will be only 20 percent. Fortunately, the former type of measurement can be translated into the latter, and vice versa, by means of a simple algebraic formula. In order to avoid confusion, this article will present quantitative results only concerning the intermarriage rates for individuals, and when possible will differentiate between the proportions of males and of females who marry outside their group.

INTERMARRIAGE BETWEEN NATIONAL-ORIGIN GROUPS

A pioneering study of trends in the incidence of intermarriage between national-origin groups examined marriages that occurred in New Haven, Conn., from 1870 to 1950. It revealed a marked decline in the proportion of all marriages in which brides and grooms were from the same surname group. The evidence showed little intermarriage between Protestants and Catholics or between Jews and Christians, which led the author to suggest that a "triple-melting-pot" was at work. This hypothesis, while perhaps true for New Haven, was not a very good description for the United States as a whole.

An analysis of data from the 1960 Census concerned the prevalence of intermarriages involving two partners of foreign stock (that is, born abroad or with at least one parent born abroad). The couples in which both husband and wife were of foreign stock were classified in seven major nationality groups (each according to birthplace of self, father, or the one foreign-born parent). For men and women with origins in the United Kingdom or Ireland the majority of marriages were intermarriages. For husbands and wives whose origins were in Canada, Germany, or Poland, 40 to 50 percent of all marriages were intermarriages. For husbands and wives with origins in the U.S.S.R. or Italy the proportion of intermarriage was 39 percent and 21 percent, respectively. The census data did not reveal to what extent people of foreign stock married people of the third or later generation of their own national-origin group in contrast to persons of similar generation of different national-origin groups. The 1960 analysis avoided this problem by considering only couples who were both of foreign stock, but the magnitude of the problem is indicated by

the fact that 38 percent of the husbands who were of foreign stock in 1960 married wives who were native-born of native parentage.

Inspection of tabulations from the 1970 Census identical to those from the 1960 Census reveal a further small increase in the prevalence of intermarriage for husbands of each of the seven national-origin groups. For example, for the group with the lowest percentage of intermarriage in 1960—that of Italian men of foreign stock married to a wife of foreign stock—the proportion of intermarriage increased from 21 percent in 1960 to 25 percent in 1970.

The 1970 Census provides a measure of national origin independent of generation for two groups, Mexicans and Puerto Ricans. According to the census, 16 percent of husbands of Mexican origin had wives not of Mexican origin and 19 percent of Puerto Rican husbands had wives not of Puerto Rican origin. Similar percentages of intermarriage were reported for the wives of the two groups. Data from the 1970 Census are also available to measure the difference in prevalence of intermarriage for husbands of the two groups dependent on decade of marriage. Among Mexican husbands married once and married in the period 1960–1970, 19 percent married outside the group in contrast to only 13 percent among those married once and married in the period 1950–1959. The corresponding percentages for husbands of Puerto Rican origin were 20 percent and 15 percent. These differences in prevalence by decade of first marriage may or may not indicate differences in incidence by decade of first marriage, since higher rates of marital dissolution for intermarriage than intramarriage could be a possible explanation.

The November 1969 Current Population Survey provides the best data for examining the prevalence of intermarriage among the various national-origin groups in the United States. Adult respondents were asked to give their national origin as Mexican, Puerto Rican, Cuban, Central or South American, Other Spanish, German, Irish, Italian, Polish, Russian, English, Negro, American Indian, Other, and Don't Know. Slightly more than 50 percent of the respondents answered either "Other" or "Don't Know," indicating that many Americans have such mixed ancestry that they do not identify with a particular national-origin group. For each of the six major groups of European descent tabulated in the survey, the percentage of husbands whose wives were not of the husband's national origin was as follows: English, 55 percent; German, 66 percent; Irish, 68 percent; Italian, 47 percent; Polish, 59 percent; Russian, 53 percent. The percentages of outgroup marriages include wives who did not state a specific origin, and would naturally have been lower if all respondents had been required to choose one origin from a preselected list. Nevertheless, the data are convincing as to the relatively high level of intermarriage for most of the national-origin groups in the United States today.

One of the best recent studies revealing a trend toward increased intermarriage among national-origin groups is based upon a 1964 nationwide area-probability sample of 1,575 white Catholics. Of those white Catholics then currently married to a Catholic spouse, only 55 percent were married to a spouse whose father was of the same main national-origin group as the respondent's own father. On the other hand, among 80

percent of the total respondents the main national-origin group of the father was identical to that of the mother.

INTERFAITH MARRIAGE

There can be a large discrepancy between the incidence and prevalence rates of interreligious marriage because religious conversion can change couples who were religiously heterogeneous at marriage into couples who are religiously homogeneous at time of interview. Furthermore, although the incidence of interreligious marriage is commonly calculated from the religion of bride and of groom at the time of marriage, the results might differ if the incidence were measured with respect to the childhood religion of bride and of groom, since people often change their religion prior to marriage in order to please the prospective spouse.

Iowa and Indiana are the only states that publish data on current religion of bride cross-indexed by religion of groom. An analysis of the Indiana data shows a rise from 1962–1964 to 1965–1967 in the percentage of brides and grooms in each major religious group who were in interfaith marriages. For Protestants the rise was from 6.6 to 7.6 percent, for Catholics from 38 to 42 percent, and for Jews from 31 to 37 percent. The rates for all three religious groups in Indiana are far from representative of the national average. The rate for Protestants is no doubt much lower than the national average and the rates for Catholics and Jews much higher, because Indiana contains a much higher proportion of Protestants and lower proportions of Catholics and Jews than does the nation as a whole, and the availability of partners of the same religion is an important factor in determining the intermarriage rate.

In contrast to the United States, each Canadian province provides tabulations of the current religion of groom and current religion of bride. From 1927 to 1972 the proportion of brides and grooms with an interfaith marriage increased substantially in each province for each of the three major religious groups. In Canada as a whole the proportions of brides and of grooms with an interfaith marriage in 1927 and 1972 were as follows: Protestants, 5.0 and 22.7 percent; Catholics, 7.2 and 20.5 percent; and Jews, 3.0 and 15.4 percent. The data for each religious group are affected by the availability of partners of same religion. Nevertheless, adjusting for this factor makes no difference to the trend. The 1972 data adjusted for the availability of partners of same religion indicate that Protestants and Catholics were about equally likely to marry outside their religion, while Jews were far less likely to do so than either Catholics or Protestants.

Nationwide data on the prevalence of interreligious marriage in the United States were collected only for the year 1957 from the Current Population Survey conducted by the Bureau of the Census. An analysis of these data confined to Protestants, Roman Catholics, and Jews married to a member of one of these three major groups showed that 4.5 percent of the Protestants, 12.1 percent of the Catholics, and 3.7 percent of the Jews had spouses of a different religious group. The study also showed that after adjustment was made for the availability of partners of the same major group, Catholics and Protestants were about equally likely to be married to a spouse outside their major religious group, whereas Jews were less likely to be so than either Catholics or Protestants. A more elaborate analysis of these data by sex, and by specific Protestant denomination for white persons only, showed the following proportions married outside their specific denomination: 17.5 percent of Protestant men, 19.3 percent of Protestant women, 11.9 percent of Roman Catholic men, 14.5 percent of Roman Catholic women, 5.2 percent of Jewish men and 2.7 percent of Jewish women. The proportion of members of each major Protestant denomination married to a spouse outside that specific denomination differed only slightly from the proportion of all Protestants married outside their specific Protestant denomination. For example, the proportion of Baptist men married to non-Baptist wives was 16 percent.

Two studies have shed light on the role of conversion in changing originally interreligious marriages into religiously homogeneous marriages. One study examined unbroken marriages among whites in a probability sample of the Detroit area and measured interreligious marriages in two ways: by current religious preference and by previous religious preference if the respondent indicated that his religious preference had changed. In a total of 91 couples one spouse originally had been Catholic and one Protestant, but at the time of interview there were only 39 couples for which this was the case. Thus, in 57 percent of the couples with an original religious difference, one or the other spouse changed religious preference to create a religiously homogeneous marriage.

Another analysis made use of a much larger nationwide sample of persons interviewed in 1968 who had graduated from college in 1961. It found a similarly high rate of religious conversion among the married alumni and their spouses. Among those whose 1968 affiliation was Catholic only 75 percent at time of marriage had been Catholics taking a Catholic spouse; however, 86 percent were currently married to a Catholic spouse. In 11 percent of the cases the non-Catholic spouse had converted to Catholicism. Similarly, among alumni whose 1968 affiliation was Methodist (the second largest group in the sample) only 30 percent at time of marriage had been Methodists espousing a Methodist; yet in 1968, 86 percent were married to a Methodist spouse.

INTERRACIAL MARRIAGE

The meaning of the word "race" is somewhat ambiguous when applied to individuals because of the large number of people who are of mixed biological race. A large proportion of "blacks" in the United States, for instance, have at least some white European ancestry, but legislation—following traditional social perceptions—has defined white persons as those whose ancestry was purely Caucasian and black persons as those having any mixture of Caucasian and Negro ancestry. Furthermore, since government statistical records have always used a social definition of race similar if not identical to the legal definition, this discussion of intermarriage must follow suit. The data on incidence of interracial marriage for each state are based on definitions peculiar to that state and may not necessarily be uniform across states. The data on prevalence of interracial marriage are derived from the decennial census of the United

States and thus, at least for any particular census, are uniform throughout the United States. However, the definition of race employed by a state government on its marriage records will not necessarily be identical to that employed by the U.S. Bureau of the Census.

Recent censuses have relied for the most part on self-definitions of race. For persons of mixed parentage who were in doubt as to their classification, the race of the father was used. However, the Bureau of the Census has classified as white those people who responded to the question on race with the answer of Mexican or Puerto Rican or with a category suggesting Indo-European stock. With respect to Mexicans, this represents a reversal of previous Census Bureau policy. In the 1930 Census persons of Mexican origin neither definitely white nor definitely Indian had been considered to be of "Mexican" race, presumed to be nonwhite. The 1970 Census tabulated separately each of the following racial groups: white, Negro (black), American Indian, Japanese, Chinese, and Filipino.

Although there may be considerable lack of agreement on definitions of race in official data on intermarriage, this is really not the case with respect to racial classifications for most persons. The overwhelming proportion of the American people considered white are unambiguously of European ancestry. The one principal exception to this rule is people of Mexican origin, who in 1970 constituted only 2.2 percent of the total population. On the other hand, quite consistently in all sources of data, people with any proportion of Negro ancestry are considered black. Moreover, since according to the 1970 Census only 1.4 percent of the population was of a race other than white or Negro (among which groups problems of racial classification may be more complicated), the race of most persons is likely to be classified in identical fashion by all statistical reporting systems.

For the most part, studies of the incidence of interracial marriage have relied on data from particular municipalities or states; only very recently have nationwide data become available. Since 1963 the National Center for Health Statistics has tabulated data on interracial marriage for whites, blacks, and all other races. For the period from 1963 to 1970 data were available for 35 of the 50 states, and these have been analyzed. For all the reporting states, the proportion of black brides or grooms who married a white person increased from 0.66 percent in 1963–1966 to 1.25 percent in 1967–1970. In the 12 southern states the percentage increased from 0.04 to 0.38 percent, and in the 23 northern states from 2.38 to 3.51 percent. Thus, the most dramatic percentage rise occurred in the 12 southern states, in none of which was black-white intermarriage legal prior to 1967. The reported incidence for the 1963–1966 period for these states thus reflects either a flouting of the law or errors in classification indicating the existence of a black-white marriage when there was none. For the most part, marriages between blacks and whites have involved a black male and a white female. For all 35 states the proportion of white-black marriages involving a black male increased from 72.4 percent in 1963–1966 to 77.6 percent in 1967–1970, for the southern states from 64.8 to 72.3 percent, and for the northern states from 72.6 to 79.1 percent.

The proportion of all brides and grooms of other race (that is, neither white nor black) marrying a bride or groom who was white was considerably higher than the proportion of black persons marrying whites. The proportion for the 35 states was 35.0 percent in 1963–1967 and 34.3 percent in 1967–1970. In marriages involving a white person and one of other race, in the 35 states 56.4 percent involved a white male in 1963–1967 and 55.4 percent in 1967–1970.

Data for Michigan for 1953 to 1963, after which the item of race was omitted from marriage licenses, show that the percentage of all black brides and grooms marrying whites increased from 0.75 to 1.56. Significantly, the largest increase was for black grooms marrying white brides: from 1.09 percent in 1953 to 2.34 percent in 1963. The proportion of black brides marrying white grooms increased only from 0.40 to 0.77 percent. Another area with a long-term series of data on interracial marriage, but which no longer collects such data, is New York State exclusive of New York City. Here the proportion of blacks intermarrying with whites increased from 1.2 percent in 1950–1954 to 2.0 percent in 1960–1964. However, the trend in black-white marriage in the United States has not always been upward. The proportion of blacks marrying whites declined in New York State (excluding New York City) from 1920–1924 to 1945–1949 and in Boston from 1900–1904 to 1914–1918.

Much research has been conducted to separate the factor of availability of partners from other factors that affect incidence of black-white marriage. Using the ratio of the number of persons actually in an intermarriage to the number who would be in an intermarriage if outgroup marriages occurred at random clearly shows that the relative availability of partners of a different race accounts for some but not all of the variation from state to state in the proportions of blacks marrying whites. Hawaii, in particular, has a very high ratio of actual to expected black-white marriage. An analysis of variations in the ratio of actual to expected black-white marriage for the metropolitan counties of California showed that this ratio varied negatively both with an index of residential segregation between blacks and whites and with the ratio of the proportion of whites in white-collar occupations to the proportion of blacks in white-collar occupations.

Extensive data on the prevalence of interracial marriage are available from the 1960 and 1970 censuses. Marriages counted in the census include both legal and consensual ones. This fact has great bearing on interracial marriage because of the existence in the South of a large number of consensual unions involving a white male and a black female. In many of these cases the white man may also have had a legal union with a white wife. It should also be reiterated that census data on the prevalence of black-white marriage may also contain a relatively high proportion of erroneously classified cases. According to the results of the 1960 and 1970 censuses the proportion of black males who were married to white females increased from 0.8 percent to 1.2 percent. Increases over the decade were recorded for all the regions of the United States except the South, where the proportion dropped from 0.5 percent to 0.4 percent. Since marriages between whites and blacks were not legal in the South in 1960, there are grounds for suspecting that the 1960 figure contains many in-

stances of intermarriage that are erroneous and, furthermore, given the increased incidence of legal marriage in the South involving black males and white females, that error in classification in the 1970 Census was less than in 1960. Nationwide the recorded proportion of black females married to white males decreased from 0.8 percent in 1960 to 0.7 percent in 1970. In the South the decrease was larger—from 0.7 percent in 1960 to 0.4 percent in 1970. This decline might be attributable to a decrease in the number of consensual unions or to a reduction in the cases of erroneous classification.

In summary, in the decade from 1960 to 1970 the reported proportion of black males married to white females increased substantially in the North and West but declined slightly in the South; the proportion of black females married to white males remained stable except in the South, where a substantial decline was reported. One commentator has pointed out that the reported decline in the South of marriages involving a white male and a black female, many of which are probably consensual unions, suggests a strengthening of barriers imposed by the black community on contact between black women and white men.

In contrast to the low prevalence of marriage between blacks and whites, the prevalence of intermarriage among the other nonwhite racial groups was high both in 1960 and 1970. The proportions of husbands who had a wife outside their own racial group in 1960 and 1970, respectively, were as follows: American Indian, 17.5 and 35.8 percent; Japanese, 6.1 and 11.4 percent; Chinese, 14.2 and 13.5 percent; Filipino, 46.9 and 33.5 percent. The proportions of wives who had a husband outside of their own racial group in 1960 and 1970, respectively, were as follows: American Indian, 24.2 and 39.0 percent; Japanese, 23.7 and 33.2 percent; Chinese, 10.8 and 12.2 percent; Filipino, 26.2 and 27.2 percent. The great discrepancy between the proportions of Japanese wives and Japanese husbands who married outside the group can be explained by the large number of white American servicemen who married a Japanese woman in Japan. Similarly, the large decline in the proportion of Filipino husbands marrying a non-Filipino wife can be explained by the sharp decline in the ratio of males to females in the Filipino population of the United States. The large increase in outgroup marriages among American Indians may possibly be related to an increased desire among persons with mixed white and Indian ancestry to identify themselves as American Indian. For all these racial groups, by far the greatest proportion of intermarriages were with persons of the white race.

CONSEQUENCES OF INTERMARRIAGE

Intermarriage affects the individual married couple, their children, the two ethnic groups involved, and the society as a whole. Two questions are pertinent with respect to consequences for the married couple. First, are intermarriages in general more or less successful than intramarriages? Second, for the individuals involved, is this marriage as good as or better than any other possible marriage each of them could have contracted? Considerable information has been accumulated concerning the answer to the first question, but to answer the second one would need data for each partner of each couple concerning the alternative partners

available at the time the marriage was contracted (or who would be available in the event the marriage were to be dissolved). The difficulties involved are so great that no social scientist has seriously attempted to answer the second question.

Several studies have attempted to estimate divorce rates for interfaith versus intrafaith marriages. A study of the parental marriages of 4,108 college students of the 1940s found that marriages involving a current Catholic and a current Protestant had a higher probability of having been disrupted by divorce or separation (14.1 percent) than either marriage involving two current Protestants (6.0 percent) or two current Catholics (4.4 percent). Currently religiously homogeneous but previously mixed Protestant-Catholic marriages had lower rates than currently mixed Protestant-Catholic marriages, but also higher rates than either homogeneous Catholic or homogeneous Protestant marriages. Marriages currently involving a Catholic husband and a Protestant wife had a higher probability of disruption by divorce or separation (20.6 percent) than those involving a Protestant husband and Catholic wife (6.7 percent). This study could be faulted because it was restricted only to marriages that resulted in children who later attended a particular college, and there was no control for other variables affecting the relationship between type of marriage and marital outcome. In addition, the sample was relatively small.

These methodological faults were corrected in a later study based on data for first-married white couples cross-classified by religion of bride and by religion of groom from the Iowa marriage records. The 72,485 marriages that took place in Iowa between 1953 and 1959 were classified according to religion of bride and religion of groom, and the divorce records for the same period were subdivided according to religion of bride and religion of groom at time of divorce. Probabilities of divorce were computed for each year of marriage duration for the first 6.5 years of marriage. The results were further subdivided according to age of the bride and occupational status of the husband, although these controls did not materially affect the results according to religion of bride and religion of groom. The calculated proportions of marriages disrupted by divorce at the end of 7.5 years were as follows: both spouses Catholic, 3.8 percent; both spouses Protestant, 13.8 percent; Protestant husband–Catholic wife, 20.2 percent; and Catholic husband–Protestant wife, 25.2 percent. This study, too, has a serious defect because it does not consider religious conversions. The divorce files recorded the religion at the time of divorce and not the religion at the time of marriage. Hence, if religious conversions reduce the probability of divorce, as the previous study implies, then the probabilities of divorce for the Iowa marriages in which originally one partner was Catholic and the other Protestant are artificially deflated, and the probabilities of divorce for the initially religiously homogeneous marriage are inflated

A third study avoided the methodological defect of the analysis of the Iowa marriages but suffered from a relatively smaller sample size; it dealt with 4,676 marriages that took place in 1960 in Marion County, Ind. (Indianapolis and its environs), classifying these according to religion of bride and religion of groom. The records of each of these marriages were matched to the file

of divorce certificates through 1964 to obtain a rate of early divorce for the marriages that were originally of each type. The following proportions of the various types of marriage ended in divorce: homogeneous Protestant, 9.2 percent; homogeneous Catholic, 1.8 percent; Protestant husband–Catholic wife, 9.3 percent; Catholic husband–Protestant wife, 7.6 percent. Thus, in Marion County in 1960 Protestant-Catholic marriages, although less enduring than homogeneously Catholic marriages, did not seem to have higher divorce rates than homogeneously Protestant marriages. Moreover, the finding of both previous studies that marriages between a Protestant husband and Catholic wife were less likely to end in divorce than marriages between a Catholic husband and a Protestant wife was not replicated.

Still another study to examine the relationship between interreligious marriage and marital stability was based on retrospective reports from the 1970 National Fertility Survey and is the first to provide nationwide data. It plotted divorce and separation rates for 5,442 women under age 45 who had been married at least once. It defined an interreligious marriage as one in which the religion that the wife grew up with differed from the religion of the first husband. The inclusion of women who were separated was valuable, since many women never obtain a divorce or obtain one only after several years' delay. A disadvantage of the methodology, in contrast to the type of study based on the matching of marriage and divorce records, was that some women might not tell the truth concerning whether a marriage had been disrupted. Moreover, the relatively small sample size made it impossible to pinpoint changes over time in the relationship between intermarriage and marriage stability. The procedure known as multiple classification analysis was employed to examine the relationship between interreligious marriage and marital stability while simultaneously controlling for other variables known to have an important influence on marital stability. The following proportion of women had a disruption of their first marriage: (1) Catholic married to Catholic husband, 11.6 percent, (2) Protestant married to Protestant husband, 14.2 percent, (3) Catholic married to Protestant husband, 20.8 percent, and (4) Protestant married to Catholic husband, 20.3 percent. This study also found a higher rate of marital disruption among Protestant husbands married to Catholic wives than among Catholic husbands married to Protestant wives. Evaluation of the differing results of the studies of interreligious marriage and marital stability should take into account that each study refers to marriages of a different period and that the difficulties associated with interfaith marriages may be changing over time.

The relative durability of black-white marriages as compared to homogeneously white or homogeneously black marriages can be estimated from data from the 1960 and 1970 censuses by comparing the number of each type of marriage reported in 1960 as having been contracted between 1950 and 1960 with the number reported in 1970 as having been contracted in that same decade. Although uncertainty about the reliability of the census count detracts from the validity of the results, the differences in durability are nevertheless striking, and the rank order of each marriage type with respect to stability of marriage is probably correctly determined. In brief, 89.8 percent of the homogeneously white marriages endured over the decade, 77.8 percent of the homogeneously black marriages, 63.4 percent of the marriages between a black husband and a white wife, and only 46.7 percent of the marriages between a white husband and a black wife. The low survival of the marriages between a white husband and a black wife may indicate that many of these marriages were consensual unions and that such unions were increasingly subject to condemnation by the black community.

Autobiographical information about the difficulties faced by children of mixed marriages is available, most of it concerning children of interfaith marriages. The problems for the children arise from their lack of a secure feeling of belonging to either religious group. A child of a Jewish father and a Catholic mother, for example, might be reared as a Catholic but treated by peers as Jewish because of a surname commonly identified as Jewish. There is agreement that the magnitude of the difficulties faced by children is determined by the importance each parent places upon his or her respective religion and of the degree of antagonism between adherents of the two religions in the wider society. The transformation of an originally religiously heterogeneous marriage to a religiously homogeneous marriage through the conversion of one of the parents clearly reduces the strains felt by the child.

More systematic evidence exists concerning children of black-white marriages. It is clear that such children are usually taught by their parents to regard themselves as black rather than white. It would be valuable to know more about the consequences of interracial marriage for the children of a black father and white mother in contrast to those for children of a white father and black mother.

Intermarriage has had an impact on the distinctive features of American ethnic groups, especially those of groups of European descent. A high proportion of Americans now have ancestors of so many different nationalities that they no longer consider themselves as belonging to any particular national-origin group, according to the 1969 Current Population Survey in which almost 50 percent of the adult population could not or would not identify themselves with a specific group. But this melding of ancestries does not mean that the cultures of the various European nationalities are in the process of dissolution. Italian festas are still being held but are being increasingly patronized by people with little or no Italian ancestry; lox and bagels are still being produced but are consumed by Jew and non-Jew alike. The distinctive elements of each European culture are being preserved in the United States by those people who appreciate them, who may or may not be those for whom the features form part of an ancestral heritage.

Religious intermarriage may already have contributed to a certain blurring of the distinctiveness of religious ritual between Protestants, Roman Catholics, and Jews in the United States, though these religions maintain clear-cut differences from each other. However, the relatively high frequency of interfaith marriages in the United States and the large proportion of subsequent religious conversions imply that leaders of each faith can no longer automatically count upon the continued fi-

delity of those brought up in that faith. On the other hand, such leaders can be assured of the possibility of many converts; they must now recognize the necessity of competing with each other to ensure that the membership of their faith continues to grow.

The relatively high intermarriage rate for the various Asian races in the United States in recent years, if it continues at the present level, will mean substantial biological amalgamation in the not too distant future. The same prediction can be made for the American Indians: in 1970 only 28 percent still remained on reservations. That segment of the Mexican group that is predominantly of American Indian descent will probably also experience biological amalgamation, although the process will be slower if large-scale immigration from Mexico continues. On the other hand, the relatively low rate of intermarriage between blacks and whites precludes biological amalgamation within the near future. One study has projected that under the most liberal assumptions, complete amalgamation between blacks and whites might occur within 12 generations; under the most conservative assumptions, it could take 1,000 generations. Thus, rather than describing the United States as a triple melting pot in which each of the three major religious groups maintains its identity through low rates of intermarriage, it would be more accurate to dub the United States a double melting pot in which the major barrier is that between blacks and all others. Nevertheless, the low rates of black-white intermarriage currently prevailing, which slowly increase the proportion of all "black" children with some white ancestry, may contribute to a lessening of status differences between blacks and whites.

Though knowledge of both the determinants and the consequences of intermarriage in the United States is incomplete, one fact stands out clearly: in recent years both the incidence and prevalence of intermarriage have risen sharply. Moreover, this rise appears to have occurred despite a waning of support for the melting pot ideal—which assumes that complete assimilation of all ethnic groups into one undifferentiated whole is desirable—and growing acceptance of the ideology of cultural pluralism, a belief that individuals will find a sense of community only by maintaining and strengthening the ties that bind them to their own ethnic group. This essay suggests that the ideals of cultural pluralism can be fulfilled; nevertheless, for white ethnic groups cultural pluralism can be maintained only if the leaders of each ethnic group begin to conceive of their following as united not so much by ancestral ties as by bonds of common interests and values.

Bibliography

Ruth Shonle Cavan's "Annotated Bibliography of Studies on Intermarriage in the United States, 1960–1970 Inclusive," *International Journal of Sociology of the Family* 1 (May 1971):157–165, is an excellent resource. Seven of the studies mentioned here are cited therein; accordingly, reference to them is not repeated. Two works that treat intermarriage in general are Milton L. Barron, "The Church, the State and Intermarriage," in *The Blending American: Patterns of Intermarriage,* ed. Milton L. Barron (Chicago, 1972), pp. 52–86, and Hugh Carter and Paul C. Glick, *Marriage and Divorce: A Social and Economic Study* (Cambridge, Mass., 1970). Studies primarily concerned with intermarriage between national-origin groups are Harold J. Abramson, *Ethnic Diversity in Catholic America* (New York, 1973), and Ruby Jo R. Kennedy, "Single or Triple Melting Pot: Intermarriage in New Haven, 1870–1950," *American Journal of Sociology* 58 (July 1952):56–59. Studies on interreligious marriage include: Larry L. Bumpass and James A. Sweet,
"Differentials in Marital Instability, 1970," *American Sociological Review* 37 (December 1972):754–766; Andrew M. Greeley, *The Denominational Society* (Glenview, Ill., 1972); David M. Heer and Charles A. Hubay, Jr., "The Trend of Interfaith Marriages in Canada, 1922 to 1972," in *Marriage, Family, and Society: Canadian Perspectives,* ed. S. Parvez Wakil (Toronto, 1975); Judson Landis, "Marriages of Mixed and Non-mixed Religious Faith," *American Sociological Review* 14 (June 1949):401–407; Thomas P. Monahan, "The Extent of Interdenominational Marriage in the United States," *Journal for the Scientific Study of Religion* 10 (Summer 1971):85–92 and, "Some Dimensions of Interreligious Marriages in Indiana, 1962–67," *Social Forces* 52 (December 1973):195–203; and John L. Thomas, "The Factor of Religion in the Selection of Marriage Mates," *American Sociological Review* 16 (August 1951):487–491. Studies on interracial marriage include David L. Brewer, "Black-White Marriage: A Norm-Conflict Theory," unpub. (1977); Kingsley Davis, "Intermarriage in Caste Societies," *American Anthropologist* 43 (July-September 1941):376–395; David M. Heer, "The Prevalence of Black-White Marriage in the United States, 1960 and 1970," *Journal of Marriage and the Family* 36 (May 1974):246–258; Robert K. Merton, "Intermarriage and the Social Structure: Fact and Theory," *Psychiatry* 4 (August 1941):361–374; and Thomas P. Monahan, "An Overview of Statistics on Interracial Marriage in the United States, with Data on its Extent from 1963–70," *Journal of Marriage and the Family* 38 (May 1976):223–231.

DAVID M. HEER

IOWAS: *see* AMERICAN INDIANS

IRANIANS

Immigration from Iran to the United States has become significant only in the past three decades. Most of it occurred before the Revolution of 1979, during a period of apparent political stability and economic prosperity in the homeland. Many of the immigrants entered the United States as students and then stayed on. Others were trained in Iran or elsewhere and came to the United States to take up or continue careers. On the whole, Iranians permanently residing in the United States are well educated and well off economically. They represent the ethnic, linguistic, and religious diversity that has long been characteristic of Iran.

The name Iran is derived from *aryana* (land of the

Aryans), which is what the invading Indo-European peoples called their new homeland in the first millennium B.C. Since the founding of the Persian Empire by Cyrus the Great in 559 B.C., Iran or Persia has enjoyed periods of great power and creativity, and at times has ruled over a vast number of lands and peoples (many of whom are no longer part of the Iranian state). Iran has also undergone long periods of subjugation to foreign rulers with customs, languages, and religions radically different from its own.

Prior to the impact of the modern West, the most significant outside influence on Iran came in the 7th century in the form of the Arab conquest and subsequent Islamization of the country. Invasions from central Asia in following centuries added important ingredients to the culture of modern Iran. Among other things, these bequeathed a large Turkish-speaking population to Iran and repeatedly called into play the adaptability and flexibility that have enabled Iranians to absorb and assimilate various foreign conquerors and to maintain the integrity of their own culture.

Iran today has a population of about 36 million, representing several linguistic groups. There are people who speak Arabic, Turkish, Kurdish, Baluchi, and a variety of Iranian languages and dialects. Most numerous are the native speakers of Persian, the official language of Iran that is known to a greater or lesser degree by most of its inhabitants.

What unites the overwhelming majority of Iranian citizens is their belief in Islam; about 90 percent of the population is Shiite and 8 percent is Sunni. Several minority groups, however, have maintained their separate religious identities while adapting in varying degrees to the dominant Persian-speaking Muslim culture. The most ancient of these minority groups is the Zoroastrians, whose religion was followed by a majority of Iranians before the coming of Islam. Zoroastrians speak a distinctive Persian dialect among themselves and use an ancient form of Persian for liturgical purposes. Also going back to ancient times are the Iranian Jews, who formed communities in various parts of Iran after being freed from the Babylonian captivity by Cyrus the Great in 538 B.C. They use Hebrew for religious purposes and Persian as their daily language. A small group of Nestorian and Chaldean Christians called Assyrians employ Aramaic, an ancient Semitic language, for both liturgical and social purposes. Armenian Christians, who came to Iran from Armenia in the 17th century, use the Armenian language in the same way. Finally, there are the Bahais who follow the teachings of their prophet, Bahaullah. Bahaism originated among Persian-speaking Shiites in Iran in the second half of the 19th century, and Iranian Bahais continue to use Persian for all occasions. (See Armenians; Assyrians; Jews; Zoroastrians.)

Confessional organization and consciousness are very strong among these minority groups and emphasize their differences with the Muslim majority, from whom they carefully distinguish themselves despite some common characteristics. This is seen in the use of the word *Irani* (Iranian) by the Christians and Jews. For many of them this term is synonymous with "Persian-speaking Muslim" and is not usually applied to themselves unless the frame of reference is allegiance to the Iranian state.

In its broadest sense, then, Iranian is a national designation, not an ethnic one. A more restricted meaning of the term would be "a person whose mother tongue is Persian," which would include Zoroastrians, Jews, and most Bahais, as well as Muslims, and exclude such Muslim peoples as Turks, Kurds, Baluchi, and Arabs. The narrowest use of the term would be confined to the largest and most important group in Iran, the Persian-speaking Muslims. With these distinctions in mind, the term Iranian is used here to designate any person originating within the borders of the modern nation-state of Iran. (*See also* Arabs; Kurds; North Caucasians; Turks.)

The proportions of the various religious and linguistic groups among immigrants to the United States from Iran are most difficult to determine. Figures from the groups themselves are nonexistent or exaggerated. The only breakdown available in official immigration and naturalization records relates to the years 1927–1932 and gives only a rough picture. Of the three minorities mentioned, Armenians constituted 47 percent, Assyrians 39.5 percent, and Jews 13.5 percent. Overall, it would appear that perhaps 45–50 percent of the immigrants born in Iran during the six years in question were from the religious minorities, and about 50–55 percent were Muslim. As one goes further back in time, the percentage of the minorities was probably higher. With the marked increase in immigration over the last decade, it is probable that the total percentage of minority groups has dropped substantially vis-à-vis the far larger Muslim population of Iran.

Immigrants from Iran have been predominantly individuals or individual families. During the peak decades of immigration to the United States, Iranian nationals were few: only 130 are known to have entered in the years 1842–1903, and from 1904 to 1924 Iranian arrivals were too few to warrant a separate breakdown in the immigration statistics. The annual reports of the Commissioner General of Immigration list 780 Iranian immigrants in the years 1925–1932; statistics are lacking for 1933–1944. In 1945 there were 82 immigrants. Annual arrivals in the Depression and war years probably were not more than this. However, starting in 1945 immigration from Iran rose steadily and in 1966 exceeded 1,000 per year. A peak was reached in 1972 with 3,059 immigrants. From 1945 to 1976, 30,262 persons born in Iran were admitted to the United States as permanent residents, including 2,259 in the 1947–1956 period; 6,019 between 1957 and 1966; and 21,984 from 1967 to 1976. If the maximum tenable estimates for the periods 1904–1924 and 1933–1944 are added to the available immigration statistics, total Iranian immigration into the United States from 1842 to 1976 amounts to about 34,000.

It is of particular note that 57 percent of all Iranian immigrants in the years 1958–1976 were granted permanent resident status after entering the United States in a temporary capacity. This reflects the dramatic growth in the number of nonimmigrant Iranians present in the United States. In 1952 there were 804; the number increased to 54,230 in 1976, 13,928 of whom were students and 23,037 tourists. Both these groups have figured prominently in recent immigration trends. In the period 1966–1976, 27 percent of Iranian immigrants were students who adjusted their status to per-

manent resident. Most did so by marrying U.S. citizens. Tourists who became permanent residents constituted 20 percent of all immigrants during the same period.

Ties of kinship have played a dominant role in recent Iranian immigration; over 60 percent of all immigrants were relatives of U.S. citizens or of permanent resident aliens. In contrast, occupational preferences have had a small part in admission of Iranians to the United States; only 9 percent of all immigrants (excluding spouses and children) from 1958 to 1976 were admitted specifically because they possessed skills in demand in the United States. This does not mean that the Iranian community is predominantly unskilled or poorly educated. On the contrary, immigration to the United States has consti- tuted a serious brain drain for Iran, as is clearly seen in the large number of students who have remained as per- manent residents. Another indication is that 54 percent of all immigrants between 1958 and 1976 who had an occupation fell into the category of "professional, tech- nical, and kindred workers." But the most dramatic in- dicator of a highly educated Iranian community in the United States is the large number of practicing Iranian physicians; in 1976 there were 2,373 physicians of Ira- nian origin on the rolls of the American Medical Asso- ciation.

At the end of the 1970s the total Iranian community in the United States probably numbered between 70,000 and 80,000, no more than a third of whom were permanent residents. Students make up most of the re- mainder. Their exact number is not known; however, an indicator of the magnitude of this group, the largest contingent of foreign students in America, is the num- ber admitted on student visas. In a three-year period from 1973 to 1976 there were 38,238. Others have en- tered as temporary visitors, but stayed on to study. The Iranian Embassy estimates that about 30,000 Iranian students were in the United States for the 1977–1978 academic year. Though unsubstantiated, figures as high as 50,000 have been cited by various sources for 1979.

The largest Iranian community in the United States is in California, where in 1977 a third of all permanent residents were located. Following California are New York with 15 percent; Illinois, 8 percent; Texas, 5 per- cent; New Jersey and Maryland, 4 percent each; Michi- gan and Virginia, 3 percent each; and Florida and Penn- sylvania, 2 percent each. The remaining permanent residents are scattered throughout the country. The dis- tribution of the temporary-resident population is simi- lar though not identical, and basically reflects the loca- tion of institutions of higher learning attended by Iranian students. California has double the number of any other state, followed by Texas, New York, Okla- homa, Illinois, Michigan, Massachusetts, Maryland, Ohio, and Florida.

Various factors have contributed to Iranian immigra- tion. Economic inducements perhaps have been the most important. Until recently, job opportunities and salaries were substantially higher in the United States than in Iran, which brought some Iranians and tempted others to remain. With the accelerated growth of the Iranian economy in the early 1970s this ceased to be the case. The relative rates of inflation were such during the 1970s that it was expedient to earn income in Iran and spend it in the United States, and many well-off Ira-

nians immigrated. Wealthy Iranians invested increas- ingly in American real estate and business whether or not they immigrated at the time.

Educational opportunities have also been a factor. A severe lack of educational facilities in Iran has led many students to attend U.S. universities. Others have sought a quality of education, or prestige, or economic advan- tage not associated with degrees from most Iranian in- stitutions of higher learning.

Politics is the third important factor influencing im- migration. The general political climate since the 1950s and the desire for greater political freedom and security led some Iranians to immigrate. More recently, the po- litical turmoil starting in early 1978 and leading a year later to the demise of the Pahlavi dynasty was responsi- ble for a large exodus of Iranians to the United States. Usually middle- and upper-class Iranians, most of these newer arrivals have come on temporary visas. Although many hope to remain permanently, it is probable that the majority of them will stay or return depending upon the outcome of the political situation in Iran. The num- ber of recent immigrants is unknown and no statistical breakdown is available. However, the vast majority of them are Muslim, although in earlier years a dispropor- tionate percentage were not.

The patterns of association characteristic of Iranians living in the United States are influenced to an important extent by religious affiliation. With the ex- ception of the Zoroastrians, the minority religious groups of Iran fit into long-established and well-orga- nized communities of American co-religionists. Their ties to these larger communities tend to outweigh, but by no means exclude, relations with Iranians of other faiths. For instance, there have been numerous at- tempts to establish social and cultural societies that emphasize Iranian rather than Islamic traditions and are open to all Iranians. Few of these have lasted long, mainly because of disrupting political issues. As a consequence, the institutional ties of minorities have tended to remain centered around confessionally ori- ented organizations.

In contrast, Iranian Muslims, especially the Persian- speaking ones, have come to the United States with a much less developed sense of religious cohesiveness. Their majority status and lack of formal political and religious organization in Iran are largely responsible for this. Not having had to organize as a community in order to preserve their identity, Iranian Muslims have tended to shun formal group gatherings in favor of small personalized get-togethers. But this does not imply an unawareness of fellow expatriates; they often know the names and backgrounds of many other Iranians through informal networks and family connections, and main- tain extensive contacts by means of these channels.

A significant exception to the general pattern of infor- mal contacts and lack of permanent institutions among Iranian Muslims has been the variety of political orga- nizations formed by Iranian students and former stu- dents. Membership in these organizations has included non-Muslim Iranians, though not to any great extent. The most important of these is the Iranian Students As- sociation (ISA), founded over 20 years ago in Europe and the United States. The American branch was originally apolitical, but soon became as politicized as the Euro-

pean ISA. Other student organizations have sprung up more recently, either as branches of the ISA or as reflections of differing political ideologies. Members of the permanent community of Iranians have participated increasingly in these organizations, though the most active members have always been students. The number and political activities of these groups greatly increased in the 1970s in conjunction with an increase in social and political unrest in Iran. Many Iranian students have remained in the United States as much for political as for educational reasons. The political and religious upheaval of the late 1970s in Iran and its eventual outcome will play a considerable role in determining both the number of Iranian students who come to the United States and their rate of return to Iran. To a lesser degree, the same circumstances will also determine whether members of the permanent Iranian community choose to remain in the United States.

The question remains as to whether there is, strictly speaking, an Iranian ethnic group in the United States. Excluding Iranian Armenians and Assyrians, Iranians in the United States do not exhibit a high degree of cohesiveness. Immigration of individuals rather than large groups, a lack of critical community size, the relatively recent arrival of most Iranians, the desire and ability to assimilate rapidly, prior lack of experience and trust in institutional forms, the prosperity of most immigrants, which enables them to get along on their own, and the lack of cohesiveness provided by a religious focus have all had an inhibiting effect on the formation of an ethnic group consciousness. However, the patterns of immigration have changed, the number of immigrants has increased dramatically in recent years, and there is continued devotion to Iranian culture among most Iranians, including those long resident in the United States. In addition, there is the recent emergence of instruments of group preservation, particularly the publication of several nationally distributed Persian periodicals aimed at the larger Iranian community. These factors suggest that a group consciousness is developing. As of the late 1970s Iranians in the United States are mostly a collection of individuals. However, most Iranians are new arrivals and it is too early to exclude the possibility that ethnic group consciousness will emerge.

Bibliography
Very little on Iranians in the United States has been published in books or journals. Hossein G. Askari and John Thomas Cummings, "The Middle East and the United States: A Problem of the 'Brain Drain,'" *International Journal of Middle East Studies* 8(1977): 65–90, is a useful secondary source. However, the information in this entry was derived from a variety of primary sources: conversations with the heads of various local organizations of Iranians around the country; a review and analysis of several newspapers aimed at the Iranian community abroad, the *Kayhan International*, published in Tehran, and the *Iran Times*, published in Washington, D.C.; discussions with Iranian and U.S. government officials, in particular those who have been involved in consular activities in Iran; and various statistical reports, especially the annual reports of the U.S. Immigration and Naturalization Service. For brief overviews of the history of Iran the reader is referred to Donald N. Wilber, *Iran: Past and Present* 8th ed. (Princeton, 1976), and A. Bausani, *The Persians* (London, 1971). Introductions to major periods of Iranian history may be found in R. Ghirshman, *Iran from the Earliest Times to the Islamic Conquest* (London, 1954); Richard N. Frye, *The Golden Age of Persia* (London, 1975); Joseph Upton, *The History of Modern Iran: An Interpretation* (Cambridge, Mass., 1960). An important work detailing the historical periods of Iran since

the advent of Islam is W. B. Fisher, ed., *The Cambridge History of Iran* (London, 1968–), although only three of the projected eight volumes are currently in print.

JOHN H. LORENTZ AND JOHN T. WERTIME

IRAQIS: *see* ARABS

IROQUOIS: *see* AMERICAN INDIANS

ISRAELIS: *see* JEWS

IRISH

For almost three centuries after the first settlement of the English colonies Ireland sent large groups of newcomers to America. In the first half of the 19th century the steady stream of travelers grew into the first of the great mass migrations to the United States. Irish immigrants provided the rapidly expanding nation with an army of unskilled laborers and much of the leadership of the Catholic church, big-city politics, and the labor unions. A decline in immigration from Ireland in the half-century after 1920 has combined with the successful assimilation of earlier arrivals and their descendants into the social mainstream to diminish the effect of the Irish presence on the American scene.

On the eve of English settlement in North America, Ireland was a country lightly populated by about a million people, the majority descended from early pre-Celtic tribes, followed in order of importance by men and women whose ancestors were Celts, Normans, English, Scots, and Vikings. The earliest semi-nomadic inhabitants of Ireland and more sophisticated agricultural settlers gave way to the Celts, whose arrival in about 250 B.C. stimulated a cultural blossoming in a land untroubled by invasion for over a thousand years. In the 5th century Christianity greatly enriched the native culture. In the 8th century Norse invaders laid the foundations of Ireland's first towns. In the 12th century Anglo-Norman invaders sought to conquer the country and were instead eventually absorbed by the earlier inhabitants. They built towns, manors, and abbeys, and established a feudal system under the English crown; but in many places the lower levels of society remained largely undisturbed. During the 14th century the Black Death and later conflicts between natives and settlers reduced Norman strength to the area around Dublin bounded by the Pale.

The countryside remained overwhelmingly rural, dominated by an Irish and Anglo-Norman aristocracy whose loyalty to the crown had become weak at best. After Tudor attempts to conciliate the Irish failed, Queen Elizabeth resorted to war and to plantation—the substitution of loyal English and Scottish colonists for disloyal Irish and Anglo-Irish landholders. The first plantation was unsuccessful, but after 1586 a more elaborate scheme in the southern province of Munster set a precedent for the transfer of large numbers of English and Scots to Ireland and created on that small island a medley of peoples, who in one province, Ulster, never learned to live in harmony. History had prepared the Irish to live among strangers and to deal with the problems of foreign rule.

IRELAND, 1600–1800

As Englishmen struggled to settle in the New World during the early 1600s, Ireland underwent a significant social transformation. The clearest index of this change was the transfer of land ownership: in 1603 Catholics owned the great bulk of land; by 1709 they held a mere 14 percent. In northern areas the collapse of Gaelic resistance in 1607 led to the resettlement of the province of Ulster, predominantly by Scottish Presbyterians. Many old Irish remained as tenants of the newcomers or in scattered clusters on less productive land. Movement into Ireland intensified in the 1650s, when Cromwell devastated the countryside and confiscated and distributed to his soldiers many of the Catholic lands outside the province of Connaught. These loyal Protestant immigrants, both Scots and Cromwellians, had a more profound impact on Ireland than earlier arrivals; they established an English administrative and legislative system that lasted into the 20th century.

The late 1600s and the early 1700s were years of consolidation. The established Anglican church, the Church of Ireland, successfully sought passage of penal laws directed against Catholics and dissenting Protestants. Catholics suffered the most severe restrictions: they were forbidden to acquire land from a Protestant by any means short of changing their religion, forbidden to lease land for more than 31 years, and forbidden to send children abroad to school. When the head of a family died, land could not pass to a single heir but had to be divided among all descendants—a striking contrast to the practice of primogeniture among non-Catholics.

Protestant dissenters suffered as a result of an act that compelled all in government service or in the legal profession to be communicants of the established church. Presbyterians in general were inconvenienced rather than persecuted, for the acts were rarely enforced against them. Quakers, however, because of their strong opposition to taking oaths and paying tithes to the established church, experienced severe persecution. But gradual abandonment of discriminatory laws against Protestant dissenters in the early 18th century left the important division in Ireland's population of 2 million that between Protestant and Catholic. The latter included most of the Gaelic-speaking descendants of the pre-Elizabethan settlers. Protestants composed about 25 percent of the total population and most were members of the established Church of Ireland. Presbyterians were the largest nonconformist group, followed by the Quakers. Antagonism between Protestants and Catholics on the lower levels of society intensified during the second half of the 18th century. By 1800 a wall of suspicion and antagonism separated them.

Sporadic gains in agriculture and industry tended to reinforce religious divisions. During the 17th century the country changed from a woodland to an agricultural economy and the woolen and linen industries expanded so rapidly as to provide unwelcome competition for English manufacturers. Parliament reacted by imposing restraints on Irish manufactures, beginning with woolen goods in 1699. In the 1720s depression created widespread hardship, and bad times recurred intermittently between 1740 and 1780. In industry, as in agriculture, the majority of men of wealth were Protestant.

In the two centuries after 1600 the Irish social struc-ture became increasingly complex. By 1775 predominantly Protestant landlords were at the top of the social pyramid in rural areas; only 5 percent of the land remained in Catholic hands. Next came tenants with leases; almost all Protestants held leases as did a small proportion of Catholics. Beneath them were overwhelmingly Catholic cottiers, who rented land from farmers, discharging their debt in labor. On the bottom of the social pyramid were rundale occupiers, groups of peasants who resided in cooperative clusters on patches of the less productive or more remote land that they held in common. Although most urban wealth was concentrated in the hands of Protestants, there were some wealthy Catholic merchants in the Irish cities.

IMMIGRATION IN THE COLONIAL PERIOD

Between 1600 and 1800 almost everyone in Ireland had reason to look beyond the island for a more favorable habitat. Presbyterians and members of the established church had economic grievances; Quakers and Catholics had both economic and religious problems. Catholics bore the heaviest burden of discrimination and were the first to leave in significant numbers. They were departing for the New World during the 17th century when Scottish and English immigrants, many of whose descendants were later to cross the Atlantic, moved into Ireland.

The Catholics, traditionally used to migration, showed little reluctance to travel overseas. Irish workers had moved about for centuries; some had crossed to work seasonally in England as far back as the Middle Ages. Irishmen traveled to the Newfoundland fisheries by 1650; and they readily served in continental armies; about 34,000 left for Europe during the 1650s and in the 19th century many European armies still boasted Irish contingents.

Some Irishmen therefore turned up in the New World from the earliest days of settlement. Edward Nugent, serving with Captain Ralph Lane in 1586, killed the Indian chief Pemispan in North Carolina. Among the Irish were both voluntary and involuntary migrants: bonded servants, convicts, prisoners of war, and paying passengers. In 1636 Thomas Anthony toured County Cork in a successful effort to raise a shipload of passengers interested in traveling to the American colonies as indentured servants—that is, willing to be sold into service for a period of years in lieu of paying for their passage. Under Cromwell in the mid-1640s the trickle of indentured servants developed into a tide as thousands of involuntary Catholic emigrants—political and military prisoners and their dependents—were sold into servitude. Many were sent to the West Indies; by the 1660s there were 12,000 Irish Catholics there, some of whom eventually journeyed to the mainland colonies.

In the 1620s the movement of Irish peasants and vagrants to Virginia was developing into a regular feature of commerce. Much of this traffic turned toward Maryland in the late 1630s, apparently because of the greater religious toleration there. Legislation restricting the entry of Irish "papists" as servants suggests that they were arriving in increasing numbers: South Carolina in 1698 and Maryland in 1699 passed laws specifically limiting immigration of Irish Catholic servants, while Virginia in 1699, by exempting the English and others

from restrictions on the importation of servants, obviously aimed its statute at Irish Catholics. Moreover, the restrictive laws in South Carolina applied to all Irish, suggesting that few if any servants from Ireland were Protestant.

Nor did high emigration decline in the 18th century. In 1703 the Anglo-Irish government authorized a sentence of transportation for a variety of offenses. Subsequent acts strengthened this law and provided bounties for shipowners engaged in transporting convicts, about 85 percent of them from provinces of overwhelmingly Catholic population. A variation of the indenture system appeared in the 18th century in the guise of "redemptioners." A redemptioner paid only part of his or his family's fare; if he failed within a certain period after arrival to find a "redeemer" (frequently a friend or relative) to pay the balance, he could be sold as an indentured servant. That a steady trade in servants and redemptioners continued until the decade after the American Revolution is suggested by the passage of laws prohibiting the importation of Irish Catholic servants, by frequent newspaper notices concerning fugitive Irish-speaking servants, and by growth in the numbers of Irish Catholics in colonial cities.

A small but significant number of affluent Irish Catholic migrants paid their own passage to the colonies. Sir Thomas Dongan (1634–1715) served from 1683 to 1686 as one of the ablest of New York's governors. Colonies of Irish, apparently Catholics from Tipperary and Waterford, settled in New Jersey as early as 1683. Maryland, established in 1634 as a refuge for Catholics, early attracted some Irish settlers, but they were vastly outnumbered by Protestant colonists, who during the 18th century expressed their hostility in a series of laws discriminating against Roman Catholics. After the crown confiscated his estates in Ireland, Charles Carroll moved to Maryland in 1681 and established an illustrious Catholic family. New York City had a contingent of prosperous Irish Catholics from about 1740, as did Philadelphia soon thereafter. The Protestant-formed Charitable Irish Society of Boston admitted Catholics after 1742, thereby acknowledging the presence of prosperous Irish Catholics in that city.

It is impossible to provide precise details regarding the age, sex, or occupation of the Irish Catholics who came to the New World before 1815. Few old people were among them: most were between the ages of 16 and 40 years and appear to have been accompanied by a relative or acquaintance from the home area. Men outnumbered women during the early years, but by the beginning of the 19th century the sexes were about equally represented. Artisans of all kinds, particularly tailors, were well represented, and the proportion of individuals who reported unskilled status, even among indentured servants, was small.

Despite sharp differences among denominations, particularly in the early years, bitter hatred of Catholicism united the Protestant settlers. In 1636 the arrival in Boston harbor of the Irish vessel *St. Patrick*, whose ensign depicted a cross, provoked an immediate reaction from colonists watchful for signs of a popish invasion. Labor shortages caused the colonists to overcome their antipathy and accept individual newcomers from the Church of Rome, but priests, particularly Jesuits, continued to be generally excluded. The overthrow of Charles I in England in 1640 precipitated several uprisings in the American colonies, all characterized by attempts to uncover "popish plots." Even after the American Revolution Catholics suffered from legal discrimination in some states.

The problems encountered by a Catholic indentured servant because of his lowly economic status were thus intensified by religious discrimination and prejudice. A Catholic bonded servant sold at dockside stood a far greater chance than a non-Catholic of spending the difficult period of "seasoning"—adjustment to the New World—working for an employer who did not share his religion and who detested him for his; these circumstances may well explain much of the poor performance of the Irish as servants in the colonies. Little is known of the fate of Catholic servants after completion of service.

Affluent Irish Catholic immigrants generally fared much better than their impoverished countrymen. While some of them changed their religion, others clung to their spiritual beliefs, and by going about their affairs quietly, avoided abuse. Although deprived of some civil rights, they were able in most areas to practice their religion in private and their economic activities were rarely hampered. By the time of the Revolution a number of affluent Catholics and ex-Catholics, either Irish-born or of Irish background, emerged among the outstanding men of the colonies. The most notable, and one of the wealthiest men in America, was Charles Carroll III (1737–1832) of Carrollton, Md., the only Catholic to sign the Declaration of Independence.

Catholics were not alone in the movement from Ireland to the American colonies. They were accompanied by many descendants of the Scots who had settled earlier in northern counties of Ireland, especially Ulster (*see* Scotch-Irish), some communicants of the established church, some Presbyterians; and a number of Quakers, predominantly English-born or converted settlers of English or Scots origin.

THE REVOLUTIONARY PERIOD

By the time of the American Revolution the Irish population of the American colonies was as heterogeneous as the population of Ireland. In the New World Catholics and Protestants who had regarded each other with enmity in Ireland coexisted without friction in the early years, perhaps because the groups had settled in different areas. In later years, most contacts between them occurred in the cities and towns where Presbyterians joined Catholics, Quakers, and Episcopal Irish in fraternal organizations to help impoverished compatriots.

The Revolution intensified this ecumenical spirit; Irishmen of all religions served together in military units, both loyalist and rebel. John Barry (1745–1803), a Catholic born in County Wexford, became the "Father of the United States Navy." The outstanding Catholic soldier of the Revolution, Irish-born Stephen Moylan (1734–1811), led successful units of largely Protestant membership. Protestant and Catholic Irishmen proved such fierce fighters for the rebels that in 1778 the British commander-in-chief, Sir Henry Clinton, proposed to augment his forces from that source "whence the rebels themselves drew most of their best soldiers—I mean the Irish." Subsequently, an Irish loyalist regi-

ment representing all religions, the Volunteers of Ireland, was raised in Philadelphia and served for the remainder of the war. Catholic and Protestant Irish could be found on the loyalist side in all areas, but most Irish backed the rebels. The French armies that aided the American forces had a large number of Irish Catholic soldiers. There was some justification for the accusation made in the Irish Parliament in 1784: "America was lost by Irish emigrants."

By 1800 Philadelphia, with about 6,000 newcomers from Ireland, was the most heavily Irish city in America and constituted a microcosm of urban immigrant society in the young nation. Irish Quakers, Presbyterians, and Episcopalians were important elements in the city, but Catholics were becoming increasingly numerous, as burial statistics showed. Between 1770 and 1775, 13 percent of the deceased who were buried in the city and whose religion could be discerned were Catholic; many were probably born in Ireland. The only Catholic signer of the U.S. Constitution, Irish-born merchant Thomas Fitzsimons (1741–1811), was a resident of Philadelphia. Despite their Catholic religion and Irish birth, Mathew Carey (1760–1839), Stephen Moylan, and John Barry were accepted members of the city's upper class. Most newcomers from Ireland, however, were at the other end of the city's social scale. Although they represented only about 7 percent of the city's population between 1794 and 1800, the Irish accounted for 36 percent of the criminals. Most Irish immigrants lived in proximity to Catholic churches and to taverns catering almost exclusively to their compatriots. By the turn of the century, the faint outline could be discerned of an "Irishtown" of the kind that was to appear in every major American city during the 19th century.

Since only a few local censuses gathered information about the national origins or the religion of the population during the colonial and early national periods, reliable figures on the number or religious affiliations of the Irish in America in these years are not available. The frequently cited study of the origins of the American population in 1790, the 1931 American Council of Learned Societies report on national stocks, is inconclusive. Probably the United States in 1790 contained about 400,000 people of Irish birth or descent—about half from an Ulster background, and the others from the remaining three provinces of Ireland. The Irish were the largest non-English group of immigrants during the colonial years. Presbyterians, who made up about 35 percent of the population of Ulster, dominated the movement from Ireland for most of the 18th century. Concentration on Presbyterians in the overall migration, however, has led to the neglect of the non-Presbyterians who dominated the movement in the 17th century and who continued to arrive in later years.

IRELAND TO 1845

Irish movement across the Atlantic during the 19th century and the first two decades of the 20th was part of a great dispersal of Europeans to all parts of the world. Newcomers from Ireland accounted for a significant proportion of all U.S. immigrants during that period. As Table 1 shows, about one in three immigrants between 1820 and 1840 were born in Ireland; during the 1840s the Irish accounted for 45 percent of all new arrivals. Despite an increase in actual numbers the Irish share of

Table 1. Irish immigration to the United States, 1820–1975.

Period	Number[a]	Percentage of total arrivals
1820–1830	54,338	35.8
1831–1840	207,381	34.6
1841–1850	780,719	45.6
1851–1860	914,119	35.2
1861–1870	435,778	18.8
1871–1880	436,871	15.5
1881–1890	655,482	12.5
1891–1900	388,416	10.5
1901–1910	339,065	3.9
1911–1920	146,181	2.5
1921–1930	220,591	5.4
1931–1940	13,167	2.5
1941–1950	26,967	2.6
1951–1960	57,332	2.3
1961–1970	37,461	1.1
1971–1975	6,559	—
Total	4,720,427	10.0

Source: U.S. Immigration and Naturalization Service, *Annual Report, 1975* (Washington, D.C., 1976), pp. 62–64.
a. Figures, especially those for the early decades, are not exact and should be used only as a rough guide.

the total immigration declined after 1850. By the second decade of the 20th century, the Irish made up only 2.5 percent of new arrivals in the United States.

During the century after 1820 about 4.7 million Irish crossed the Atlantic to the United States, a number exceeded only by the Germans. This impressive movement steadily expanded the Irish-born population of the United States until it peaked at 1.8 million in 1890 (see Table 2). Although Irish-born Americans declined by almost 45 percent in the three decades after 1890 to slightly over 1 million by the end of the period, the second generation exceeded 3.3 million by 1900 and remained above 3 million until the 1920s. This impressive increase in the population of Irish descent in the United States went hand in hand with a striking transformation of society in the homeland.

The years of the European wars, 1793–1815, were prosperous times in Ireland, whose farmers provided

Table 2. Irish stock in the United States, 1850–1970.

Year	Foreign-born	Native-born of foreign or mixed parentage
1850	961,719	—
1860	1,611,304	—
1870	1,855,827	—
1880	1,854,571	3,238,580
1890	1,871,509	2,924,172
1900	1,615,459	3,375,546
1910	1,352,251	3,304,015
1920	1,037,234	3,122,003
1930[a]	744,810	2,341,712
1940	572,031	1,838,920
1950	505,285	1,891,495
1960	338,722	1,434,590
1970	251,375	1,198,845

Source: U.S. Bureau of the Census, *Historical Statistics of the United States, Colonial Times to 1970* (Washington, D.C., 1975), I, 116–118; U.S. Bureau of the Census, *Census of the Population, 1950*, vol. 2, *Characteristics of the Population* (Washington, D.C., 1952–1953), table 24 in respective state volumes; U.S. Census Office, *Statistics of the Population of the United States at the Tenth Census, 1880* (Washington, D.C., 1883), pp. 674ff.; U.S. Census Office, *Report on the Population of the United States at the Eleventh Census, 1890*, pt. 1 (Washington, D.C., 1895), pp. 686ff.
a. Totals for 1930 and after are Eire only.

much of the food for the war and for an expanding English population. Cereal crops were in short supply and brought high prices, but the pressure of population and virtual lack of a police force prevented landlords intent on expanding production of grains from displacing tenants or enclosing land. The expansion was made possible within the existing agrarian structure by mixing cereal crops with the potato, which vastly increased the yield of the area under cultivation. The peasants were happy to plant potatoes on the landlords' estates in return for the use of a small patch of land to support themselves. The landlords thus enjoyed an increase in production and profits. A doubling of prices for farm products and a fourfold increase in rents between 1760 and 1816 further strengthened their economic position.

The peace of 1815 was an important turning point. War-inflated wheat prices dropped by as much as 50 percent. Less tillage and an expansion of grassland became desirable; the landlords now wanted to clear their estates of tenants. But the total Irish population grew from 6.8 million in 1821 to slightly over 8 million in 1841. The nonagricultural sector of the economy could not absorb the growing surplus of rural workers, for as population expanded, industry remained stagnant or declined. Thus at a time when it was economically advantageous for landlords to clear estates, agriculture remained the only means of subsistence for most of the growing population. The resulting conflict over the use of land was not resolved until the 20th century. Initially, depressions and bad harvests hampered the adjustment of both groups. Some landlords in 1816 and in 1826 succeeded in forcing passage of legislation to facilitate evictions, but the new laws ultimately failed to achieve their purpose. The area of land under tillage continued to expand until the Great Famine of 1845.

Whereas the number of tenants with large holdings and with small holdings remained about the same between 1831 and 1841, the population of agricultural laborers and farm servants doubled from 665,000 to 1.3 million, and their condition steadily deteriorated. The hardships of the partial potato crop failures of 1822, 1831, 1835–1837, 1839, and 1842 were confined almost entirely to the laboring population; some people on the middle and upper levels of society actually enjoyed an improvement in living conditions during this period.

Widespread emigration, permanent celibacy, and delayed marriage were the mechanisms of population adjustment. A significant movement of poor Irish had occurred during the 18th century to Great Britain as well as to North America. In 1800–1802 about 6,000 Irish left the country each year; then migration across the Atlantic slowed until the return of peace in 1815. In 1816, 6,000 Irish emigrated and the next year 9,000. In 1818 an extraordinary number, about 20,000, made the journey. The trend was clear; after 1825, with a few setbacks, departures grew steadily until they exceeded 92,000 in 1842. Between 1820 and 1845 more than 1.3 million Irish departed for America. Movement to the United States through Canada, typical for about a quarter-century after the Napoleonic wars, diminished rapidly during the 1840s, and by mid-century most Irish traveled directly to the United States.

The potato blight of late 1845 initially inspired no widespread fear. Rather quickly, however, it became apparent that this time the unprecedented destruction of the crop would have immense consequences: between 1845 and 1851 the population dropped by about 2 million. About half of the precipitous decline was due to death from starvation or disease, the other half to emigration. In 1845 some 77,000 people left Ireland; the following year, 106,000. The number of emigrants peaked at almost a quarter of a million in 1851. In all, between 1846 and 1851 over a million people sailed from Ireland.

From the end of the Great Famine until 1920 Ireland felt the continued impact of economic, social, and administrative forces that had been transforming the country since the Napoleonic wars. The British government's attempt to provide work on road-building projects for individuals left destitute by the disaster of the 1840s gave Ireland an advanced communications network. Along the new highways moved the products of England's expanding factories, driving out rural crafts and smothering industrial development. At the same time, increasing mechanization of agriculture depressed the demand for rural laborers and periodic famines made life precarious. Permanent celibacy and delayed marriage increased in western Ireland, and the urge to emigrate to the New World became general throughout the country.

SOCIAL CHARACTERISTICS

Movement across the Atlantic showed distinct patterns. Between 1869 and 1920 the sexes were in rough balance, although women outnumbered men in 25 of those years. Throughout the 19th century and into the 20th, the majority of Irish traveling to the United States were under 35 years old: 75 percent were in this category between 1803 and 1805 and 83 percent in the years 1901–1911. Although family ties were very important, most emigrants were unmarried.

The emigrants' areas of origin changed during the 19th century. In the early years most of them came from the north and east; by the 1840s the majority came from the midlands and the south; by the 1880s people were leaving the west in unprecedented numbers. Catholics, though well represented in earlier years, did not dominate the movement until the mid-1830s. By 1840 only about 10 percent of emigrants departing for the United States were Protestant, a proportion which remained steady until the 20th century.

The rate of literacy was high. From the earliest years of the 19th century unskilled rural peasants were common in the movement to the New World, and from 1850 to 1920 they accounted for about 80 percent of all departures. Nevertheless, at mid-century about 75 percent and by 1910, 97 percent of all the Irish admitted to the United States could read and write English.

After the Napoleonic wars population growth and social and economic change transformed the adaptive strategy of peasant families. It had been the custom for a father to provide a patch of land to each son upon his marriage, usually by subdividing the family's holding. As land grew scarcer, however, fathers could no longer thus provide for their sons. The offspring were forced either to join the expanding ranks of landless laborers or to leave the country.

The peasants' outlook changed. As communications improved and the power of the central government increased, the entire country felt the impact of adminis-

trators and police. Peasants had to pay taxes and rents in cash, earned by selling crops or farm animals, building roadways or railroads, working as seasonal migrants, or making and selling illicit poteen (whiskey). Education accelerated the changes. By 1820 almost 400,000 children were attending private schools where instruction was mostly in English, a language increasingly necessary for survival. After 1831 government-financed schools provided regular instruction in English, greatly expanding the proportion of peasants literate in the new language. Eventually a generation of peasants appeared whose knowledge of the world was no longer restricted to Irish Gaelic culture. Instruction in geography in schools, advertising campaigns by emigrant agents, the distribution of immigrants' letters from America, popular newspapers that provided information on the industrial societies of Great Britain and the United States all combined to expand the peasants' consciousness. By the time of the Great Famine a significant portion of this new generation of literate, English-speaking peasants had turned to emigration—some to Great Britain, but many more to the United States—as an alternative to the traditional pattern of marriage and land acquisition accepted by their fathers.

Irish kinship networks emerged to facilitate the movement. Most of the emigrants shared surnames with fellow passengers, suggesting a blood relationship, or traveled with individuals from the same place. But the most important function of such networks was the provision of money to pay fares. Relatives pooled resources to send out younger and more energetic family members who earned and remitted sufficient funds to pay the fares of those who remained behind. Poor families often moved in two stages: the husband or oldest son went out with friends or relatives and eventually sent home funds to finance the migration of the remainder of the family. Rare indeed was the peasant emigrant who tackled the Atlantic alone.

The enormous amounts of money sent from the United States to Ireland attest to the strength of family relationships. For the last half of the 19th century, remittances—over $8 million in some years—exceeded the amount required to pay all emigrant fares. This massive flow of cash helped ensure the survival of the smallest and most unproductive landholdings in traditional areas of Ireland. Large-scale Irish peasant movement to the New World, therefore, was not a mindless flight from intolerable conditions, but, within the limited range of alternatives, a deliberate departure of generally literate individuals who were very much concerned with the survival and well-being of family and friends remaining at home.

The more modern sector of Irish society made up about 20 percent of the total emigration from 1840 to 1920. Their departure, too, was the result of social and economic change. Few industries outside the Northeast competed successfully with England's factories, and as a result many urban artisans, merchants, and professionals found it impossible to make a living. Some non-peasant emigrants also had worked on managerial levels in rural occupations. The importance of their presence among the emigrants, however, lies in the difference in values between these segments of the "two cultures" of Ireland who between 1800 and 1920 trav-

eled to the New World. The peasant emphasized equality, disdained attempts to move up the occupational ladder, viewed land ownership as essential, and worked in cooperative units made up of family members. These criteria of success were at variance with values in the United States. The more modern group, with many urban members, was less influenced by tradition and more individualistic and oriented to change and the future; their values were similar to social values in the New World. These attitudes were important in the adaptation of the two groups to life in the United States.

SETTLEMENT PATTERNS

The majority of Irish immigrants remained in the Northeast, but a significant proportion, generally after spending some time in eastern cities, continued inland and some went on to the Pacific Coast states. In 1870 the Irish were the largest foreign-born group in California. By 1880 over a third of the Irish-born in the United States resided in areas other than the East Coast. The Irish at this time were among the three largest immigrant groups in all the western states or territories, with the exception of Utah. In the early 20th century, the proportion of Irish in the Northeast and in the Far West increased as the percentage in inland areas declined. Since the early 19th century, newcomers from Ireland had been as close to the cutting edge of the drive westward as any other immigrant group.

Irish settlement concentrated in urban areas. In 1850 almost 4 out of 5 newcomers settled in the more urbanized East coast states. Although some Irish immigrants had dispersed throughout the country by 1860, at that time 31 percent of the Irish-born population resided in 10 cities across the nation. Table 3 shows a decline in the number of Irish in those big cities after 1890, but since the total Irish-born population in the United States decreased even more, the proportion living in the cities actually grew during the period, from 39 to 44 percent. With 90 percent of all Irish Americans residing in urban areas by 1920, newcomers from Ireland were almost twice as likely to live in a city as the U.S. population as a whole.

Like other groups in the American population, these newcomers moved frequently within and outside the city. Some migrated from place to place in straitened circumstances seeking work; others traveled in comfort to join relatives or to take advantage of the prospect of better employment. Despite the predominance of the impoverished among Irish migrants in all parts of the country, movement away from the East Coast, and particularly across the entire continent, was selective of the young, skilled, literate, and generally more resourceful newcomers. Men vastly outnumbered women in the cross-country journey: in the 1860s there were about ten Irish men to every Irish woman in such West Coast cities as Sacramento and Los Angeles.

OCCUPATIONAL STRUCTURE

The selectivity in settlement patterns explains some regional differences in the occupations of newly arrived Irishmen. The likelihood of encountering a white-collar Irishman during the 19th century increased as one moved west across the continent. In 1850, 14 percent of Irish male immigrants in San Francisco and 12 percent

Table 3. Irish-born by number and percent of total population for selected years in ten cities of largest Irish population in 1890.

City	1860		1890		1900		1920		1970[a]
	Number	Percent	Number	Percent	Number	Percent	Number	Percent	Number
New York[b]	260,450	24	275,156	12	275,102	8	203,450	4	75,382
Philadelphia	95,548	16	110,935	11	98,427	8	64,590	4	8,076
Boston	45,991	26	71,441	16	70,147	13	57,011	8	12,894
Chicago	19,889	18	70,028	6	73,912	4	56,786	2	14,709
San Francisco	9,363	16	30,718	10	15,963	4	18,257	4	4,808
Pittsburgh	9,297	19	26,643	8	23,690	5	13,989	2	1,316
St. Louis	29,926	19	24,270	5	19,421	3	9,244	1	522
Jersey City	7,380	25	22,159	14	19,314	9	12,451	4	1,944
Providence	9,534	19	19,040	14	18,686	11	11,900	5	1,042
Cleveland	5,479	13	13,512	5	13,120	3	9,478	1	1,548
Total	492,857		663,902		626,882		457,156		122,241
Total Irish in the United States	1,611,304		1,871,509		1,615,459		1,037,234		292,212

Source: U.S. Census Office, *Population of the United States in 1860 from the 8th Census* (Washington, D.C., 1864), pp. 31–32; U.S. Bureau of the Census, *13th Census of the United States, 1910* (Washington, D.C., 1913), I, *Population*, pp. 854ff.; U.S. Bureau of the Census, *14th Census of the United States, 1920* (Washington, D.C., 1922), II, *Population*, pp. 729ff.; U.S. Bureau of the Census, *Census of the Population, 1970* (Washington, D.C., 1973), table 141 in respective state volumes.
a. Except for Boston, with 2 percent, all other cities had less than one percent.
b. New York for 1860 and 1890 includes Brooklyn.

in Los Angeles held white-collar positions compared to 6 percent in Boston. In 1880 these disparities between East and West still held: 20 percent of the Irish in San Francisco held white-collar positions as opposed to 13 percent in New York.

Irish male immigrants in urban areas throughout the country in 1850 worked in a relatively small number of occupations. The typical unskilled newcomer was a casual laborer who found it difficult to get steady work. Semiskilled newcomers were generally employed as bartenders, porters, or soldiers; skilled artisans as carpenters or blacksmiths; proprietors usually dealt in liquor or owned a boarding house. White-collar Irishmen generally worked as clerks, clergymen, or schoolteachers. By the turn of the century the Irish had scattered into a variety of jobs. The traditional source of employment for urban male immigrants—laboring—now engaged only one in five newcomers, and many of the unskilled had found steady employment as railroad or factory hands. The semiskilled included those Irish who made up 11 percent of America's policemen and longshoremen and 18 percent of the country's coachmen. The proportion of Irish owning their own businesses had increased steadily over the previous half-century and approached 6 percent. White-collar Irish were most often engaged as teachers, clergymen, or in politics. By 1920 the occupational distribution of Irish-born males reflected the diverse development of industrial America.

In rural areas during the 19th century Irishmen concentrated in a narrow range of occupations, all unskilled and, apart from farming, frequently dangerous. The small proportion of the group engaged as farmers (10 percent in 1870) were scattered throughout the United States. Some became farmers by joining Catholic or Irish colonization projects organized in the second half of the 19th century, but most had moved west in a series of steps, working along the way as laborers, railroad workers, miners, or soldiers—all occupations that attracted a transient population.

In 1870, 9 percent of Irish males in the United States were employed as farm laborers, generally at the most menial and exhausting tasks. After the Civil War the Irish—together with the Chinese—labored to place the

twin rails of iron that linked the continent in 1869. From California in 1849 to the Black Hills of Dakota in the 1870s, Irishmen mined gold and silver. By 1870 they were the largest foreign-born group in the Army of the West; 32 Irishmen were killed with Colonel George A. Custer in 1876 at the Battle of the Little Big Horn.

Irish-born women, overwhelmingly employed in urban areas, concentrated in an even narrower range of occupations than the men. In 1850 about 75 percent of employed women immigrants in New York worked as domestic servants, the remainder in mills and factories. At about the same time most unmarried Irish women in San Francisco found employment as servants. Throughout the last quarter of the 19th century, about 15 percent of all Irish-born females worked in factories, generally on the East Coast. There was a slight breakthrough into the upper levels of the occupational structure by 1900, when almost 2 percent worked as teachers; but in 1920 women born in Ireland still displayed little of the occupational diversity of the men: 81 percent of those employed worked as domestic servants, and factory work—usually textile and clothing manufacturing—remained the second most prevalent form of employment.

The poor preparation of most Irish newcomers for American urban life was reflected in their dismal record of movement up the occupational scale: they were the only immigrant group whose occupational mobility during the late 19th century appeared almost as small as that of American blacks. In Boston the native-born and all other major immigrant groups outperformed the Irish in job mobility. Everywhere as the Irish-born became older, they skidded down the occupational ladder more rapidly than the native-born. Those who experienced significant upward mobility were rarely from a peasant background; and Irishmen who moved from the East Coast were more likely than those who remained there to improve their employment status, generally by becoming farmers or proprietors of small businesses.

The children of Irish immigrants moved upward faster than their parents; in 1900 almost 5 percent of second-generation Irish males were in the professional ranks compared with only 2 percent of Irish-born males. In 1910 the priesthood was the leading professional

choice of second-generation men. The church and politics seem to have accounted for the upward mobility of most of the sons of Irish parents. Studies of the Irish male population in Boston, Poughkeepsie, N.Y., and Newburyport, Mass., confirm the pattern: the second generation moved ahead rather impressively, much faster than American blacks, although still lagging behind the native-born and major European immigrant groups. Second-generation Irish women abandoned domestic service and were likely to be found in trade, transportation, manufacturing, and the professions—particularly teaching. In 1900 daughters of Irish-born parents composed 10 percent of all female teachers of foreign-born parentage in the United States, exceeding the combined total of female teachers with English and German parents.

QUALITY OF LIFE

These achievements were made possible by the sacrifices of the first generation, who paid a heavy price for their decision to emigrate. Mortality statistics of Irish immigrants starkly reflect their concentration in the least desirable jobs, their poor living conditions, and their penchant for alcohol. Americans rarely saw a gray-haired Irishman during the mid-19th century. As early as 1850 death rates in Boston rose dramatically as the Irish arrived. Accidents and injuries were the primary cause of Irish male deaths throughout the country in 1880, particularly in the mining areas of the Appalachians and the Far West. Irish immigrants died from alcoholism and alcohol-related diseases far more frequently than others. Male death rates were generally much higher than those for females, but as late as 1920 Irish-born females were particularly susceptible to tuberculosis and problems of the circulatory system—diseases often caused by deprivation. Moreover, infant mortality—frequently related to poor living conditions—was higher than that in any other early immigrant group. In the early 20th century the Irish were the only immigrant group in the United States whose mortality rate was higher than in the homeland.

High death rates were offset by high fertility. In two Boston wards in 1880 Irish-born women as a group bore more children than other foreign-born women. By 1910 the Irish in the United States were second only to the immigrant French Canadians in rate of reproduction. The extraordinary Irish fertility was all the more remarkable in view of evidence indicating survival of pre-immigration patterns of permanent celibacy and late marriage. An extensive survey of female workers in 1910 found that more than one in four Irish-born women over 20 years of age remained unmarried, a proportion higher than that of any other old immigrant group.

The relatively balanced sex ratio among Irish immigrants crossing the Atlantic was a major factor in the impressive rate of marriage within the group. The famine generation in Boston had a higher rate of ingroup marriage than all other groups in the city. Records of Catholic marriages in Los Angeles between 1850 and 1870 show that Irish males made a real effort to marry Irish women. In Wisconsin in 1880 newcomers from Ireland were among the three foreign-born groups most likely to choose spouses of the same national back-

ground. In all regions Irishmen with non-Irish wives were generally on upper levels of the social structure and apparently from a nonpeasant background. In the four decades after 1880 the rate of endogamy dropped sharply in all areas of the country: by 1920 only 73 percent of Irish-born men in the United States were married to Irish-born women. But significantly, two out of three Irish newcomers who married outside their own group apparently married second-generation Irish. Thus while the decrease in endogamy may be viewed as assimilation, it represents assimilation of a decidedly limited kind.

HOUSEHOLD AND COMMUNITY

Households with an Irish-born head generally consisted of parents and children. Occasionally grandparents crossed the Atlantic to join immigrant families, usually ones residing on the East Coast. The proportion of female-headed families varied considerably according to locations and occupations, but the Irish had a higher rate of missing fathers than other major immigrant groups. This characteristic resulted from a combination of high male mortality and the selectivity of the western movement; many Irishmen wandering through the American West were household heads attempting to accumulate enough money to send for their families. Some families were augmented by boarders, usually individuals related to the household head or from the same place in Ireland. Families consisting of both parents who took in boarders generally did so after their own children were reared.

Economic adjustment and the relationship among family members during the mid-19th century show the imprint of life in the homeland. The father was the principal breadwinner, but children went to work at an early age, frequently as young as ten, often at the expense of their education. Yet even with most family members working, it is difficult to understand how they acquired the funds to support parochial schools or churches, or accumulated the impressive sums of money sent to relatives in Ireland. Mothers usually were reluctant to work outside the home for wages, and widows preferred to send their children to work rather than work themselves. But at home the mother was far from idle, for she played a vital role in solidifying ties with relatives and the community by doing washing, ironing, or sewing for the unmarried or disabled, often without payment. Families were large and children were viewed as a form of social insurance. Girls generally attended school as often as boys. According to the *Reports of the Immigration Commission*, by 1910 children of Irish immigrants not only attended school as frequently as other immigrant children but also were far more likely to be holding jobs at the same time. Despite the workload suggested by this finding, Irish children do not appear to have been overly eager to leave home. Apparently because of the combined effort of most members, the average Irish family income was then among the highest of any foreign-born group. By the turn of the century Irish families seem to have adjusted to industrial America, but it had been a slow and painful process, particularly for those from a peasant background.

The degree of order in Irish neighborhoods was

usually more impressive than the disorder. Newcomers from Ireland were among the least segregated groups in urban America: even in an area regarded as the archetypical Irish slum, the notorious Five Points of New York City, there was always a substantial non-Irish population (32 percent in 1855). Immigrant families from similar areas in Ireland generally lived in clusters of residences; despite the absence of a definite territorial base, a variety of familiar institutions drew these clusters together into distinctly Irish parishes and neighborhoods. Irish grocers and saloonkeepers acted as "cultural brokers" by extending credit and giving advice, particularly to recent arrivals. Fraternal, charitable, and religious organizations brought immigrants together. The number and variety of marching groups represented in a St. Patrick's Day parade were a useful index to the complexity of social institutions in an Irish community. By publicizing meetings and social events, the immigrant press made newcomers aware of secondary social agencies in the neighborhood and also helped maintain ties with the homeland by providing extensive news of Ireland.

The American perception of the Irish community changed during the first half of the 19th century. Initially other Americans could easily distinguish two groups of Irish immigrants: the educated and generally affluent newcomers, both Protestant and Catholic, who mingled with the native-born society; and the poor Catholics who clustered in the developing urban slums. But after the late 1830s, as peasants fled the famine in overwhelming numbers, Irish became synonymous with poverty, particularly along the Atlantic Coast. Soaring arrest rates, usually for disorderly conduct, gave the Irish a reputation for drunkenness and violence. At the same time, by becoming the most numerous national group in the Roman Catholic Church the Irish came to be permanently identified with it, intensifying the already strong anti-Catholicism in the host society. The burning of the Ursuline Convent in Charlestown, Mass., in 1834, began a series of violent incidents instigated by nativists against the Irish, who also experienced severe economic and social discrimination.

In the mid-19th century impoverished Irish immigrants were as estranged from other groups as they were from American Protestants. Competition for jobs led to deep hostility between blacks and Irish, a hostility intensified when blacks served as strikebreakers in the menial trades in which the Irish concentrated. As the Irish won control of Catholic schools and churches, they took steps to prevent blacks from attending. Relations with Germans were less embittered though not good; separation was intensified by the activities of German freethinkers who flocked to the Republican party. By the late 1850s most Irish immigrants in American cities were isolated from the rest of the population.

Emigrants from the more modern element of the home society reacted to these developments in a variety of ways. A few attempted to vanish into the larger society, a desire reflected in court petitions filed by Irishmen wanting to assume names not recognizably Hibernian. Some moved away from the Atlantic Coast to cities where Irish birth was less of a barrier to social or economic position. Ulster Presbyterians, heretofore

generally content to be called Irish, began to identify themselves as Scotch-Irish. But it was as officers of Irish immigrant organizations of all kinds or as writers for the immigrant press that most nonpeasant Irish newcomers embarked on an attempt, aided by the Catholic church, to improve the image of their impoverished peasant countrymen. The Irish nationalist movement in the United States was very much part of this impulse to counter the image of Irish immigrants as poor relatives of a conquered, and hence inferior, people. Such Catholic Irishmen as Andrew Carney (1794–1864) of Boston, Thomas O'Connor (1770–1855) of New York, Robert Elliott (1796–1841) of Detroit, Edward G. Ryan (1810–1880) of Wisconsin, Jasper O'Farrell (1817–1875) of San Francisco, and John G. Downey (1827–1894) of Los Angeles—the first Irish-born governor of a state, California—attempted to ease the adjustment of their peasant countrymen.

After 1860 these activities gradually improved relations between Irish newcomers and society in general. The demise of the Know-Nothing movement in the late 1850s, the waning of the issue of religious instruction in the public schools, the growth of contacts between Irish and native-born in schools, at work, in politics, and in public places had already somewhat mitigated earlier mutual hostility. The commitment of Irish immigrants to the Union during the Civil War made a favorable impact which remained undimmed by Irish participation in the New York draft riots of 1863.

Despite occasional setbacks in the decades after the Civil War, this gradual improvement in relations between the Irish and the larger society continued. During the 1870s and 1880s American cities, particularly on the East Coast, experienced numerous riots in which the Irish participated, thereby incurring the wrath of many. Yet during the same years the Irish image in literature and in the American press began to improve. The Hibernian became less threatening: newspapers and novels increasingly pictured him as an Uncle Sean—docile, comic, and childish. Concurrently, the Catholic press retreated from its aggressive stance of earlier years and avoided conflict with the larger society. Although the American Protective Association revived hostility in the 1890s, Irish immigrants and the rest of American society were slowly arriving at an accommodation.

Success in re-creating many of the communal patterns of rural Ireland in American cities eased the adjustment of peasant immigrants. The steady arrival of newcomers, contact with the homeland through the immigrant press, the regular exchange of letters, and frequent lecture tours by nationalists from Ireland perpetuated the inherited culture. Textbooks in Catholic schools provided children with stories about the history and culture of Ireland. When ocean travel became relatively easy around the turn of the century, more and more Irish visited home: between 1899 and 1910 over 18 percent of those arriving had previously resided in the United States.

The success of the impressive religious and political institutions built by the Irish in the United States during the 19th century rested on the parish and on the block and was made possible by the highly personal activities of the priest and the ward boss. The Irish

brought to America the ability to unite people on a neighborhood level and build a larger organization effective enough to make a significant impact. These talents were equally effective in Irish nationalist and trade union activities.

THE CATHOLIC CHURCH

The years of heaviest Irish immigration coincided with the most exciting and challenging period in the history of the American Catholic church. In 1800 the Roman church in the United States was in its infancy. Although of Irish ancestry, the only bishop, John Carroll (1725–1815), viewed himself as an American. But increasing numbers of priests from Ireland had been arriving in American ports since the Revolution to join English and French clergy already here. Not until the creation of new dioceses in 1808 was this Irish contribution to the church recognized. Irish-born bishop Luke Concanen (1747–1808) was appointed to New York, but died before he could assume his post. Two years later Michael Egan (1761–1814) was appointed to Philadelphia.

Thereafter the number of Irish priests steadily increased, and with it (despite the opposition of Catholics of other national backgrounds) the number of bishops of Irish birth or descent. Between 1840 and 1850 the number of priests in the United States jumped from 480 to over 1,500—about 35 percent of whom had Irish names—stimulating the impressive "first flowering" of American Catholicism. Many Irish clergymen came from the College of All Hallows in Dublin, which during the 60 years after its establishment in 1842 sent 1,500 priests to the New World. The selection in 1875 of John McCloskey (1810–1885), the son of Irish immigrants, instead of the Anglo-American James Bayley as the first cardinal in the United States signaled the hegemony of Irish churchmen in the American Catholic church. By the closing decades of the century about half the bishops were of Irish background and only 4 of 17 American cardinals had not been Irish. During the 19th century the American Catholic church had gradually assumed the self-confidence, and at times the aggressiveness, of Irish Catholicism, thereby arousing much resentment among outsiders but clearly strengthening the faith of American Catholics.

The cornerstone of Irish Catholic religious life in the United States was the parish. Until the time of the Civil War on the East Coast, and for a decade or two later on the frontier, Irish clergy were preoccupied with financial problems as they attempted to collect sufficient funds to maintain a church. A major problem in raising money was the tenuous bond between newcomers and the organized church: at best probably 50 percent of Irish Catholics attended church regularly in pre–Civil War New York. Nor was the situation better on the frontier: in the 1870s priests in the Wyoming Territory reported that their Irish parishioners rarely attended mass. Despite this imperfect attendance, the church, after the family, was the most important and familiar institution in the lives of the Catholic Irish, and its mission was both to preserve the faith and to convert nominal Catholics into regular churchgoers.

The ideal nun and priest were majestic figures who spared no effort to aid their flocks, particularly the sick and the poor. Irish nuns established schools, hospitals, and orphanages all across the country. From the slum of Five Points in New York City to the streets of Sacramento, Calif., they toiled to rescue homeless children of all nationalities and religions. During the Civil War, Irish nuns ministered to wounded on both sides. Irish priests went to similar heroic lengths; on the East Coast they labored day and night to help the poor and visit the ill; in the Far West they frequently made long and dangerous journeys to aid sick and dying soldiers and railroad workers. They also performed a vital role as cultural brokers, mediating contacts between the impoverished Irish masses and the host society. Parish clergy often provided political and economic advice, and some went so far as to establish savings clubs for newcomers. In times of stress in the homeland, priests collected funds to send to Ireland; they also helped prospective settlers find good land, sought out missing immigrants, and provided information on deaths to relatives. The concern of Irish nuns, priests, and bishops with aiding the social adjustment of their countrymen led to involvement in the Catholic Total Abstinence Union of America (f. 1872), the Irish Catholic Colonization Association (f. 1879), and the largest of all 19th-century immigrant charitable organizations, the Irish Catholic Benevolent Union (f. 1869), which attracted a peak membership of over 30,000 in 1876. A vast network of ancillary services—schools, hospitals, asylums, and orphanages—provided further evidence of concern for the general welfare of Catholic newcomers.

Of primary importance to Irish Catholic leaders was the establishment of a school for parish children, both to accommodate the parents' desire to safeguard the religion of their young and to comply with the intent of various church councils. The parish school during the early decades of the 19th century was relatively small and primitive; classes were frequently held in a church basement. In the mid-1830s in Boston and in 1840 in New York Catholics mounted campaigns to build their parochial school systems, funded largely by the pennies of working-class Irish. Increasingly these schools were staffed by nuns, many of them Irish, particularly after the introduction in 1843 of the Sisters of Mercy from Ireland. While the degree of commitment to founding parochial schools varied widely from place to place during the 19th century—New York and Chicago seem to have made a more intense effort than Boston—there were never enough church schools in any city to serve more than a small proportion of Catholic children. Moreover, many schools charged a small fee, thereby excluding children of the poorest families. In New York City, the center of parochial education, the Catholic education system in the late 1850s was valued at $2 million and could accommodate only about 35 percent of Catholic children.

Educational efforts gathered momentum after the Civil War in response to periodic decrees from the ecclesiastical hierarchy reminding Catholics of the necessity for establishing their own system. In many dioceses elementary schools were supplemented by high schools, producing an increasing number of students of Irish background qualified to take advantage of higher education. The growing number of Catholic colleges met this need. By 1900 an advanced education in Catholic institutions was within the reach of children of many Irish Catholic immigrants. Some immigrant chil-

dren nonetheless attended public schools, although bias in textbooks and required readings from the Protestant Bible were objectionable. After a bitter struggle, grudging compromises effected removal of the more biased books and made Protestant Bible readings optional. Despite an accommodation as early as the 1840s in New York and the 1860s in Boston, disagreements were common throughout the 19th century between Irish Catholics and the guardians of native tradition who ran the public schools.

Irish priests and bishops were actively involved in defining the position of the Catholic church on every major issue that arose during the 19th century. The controversy over "trusteeism" centered on the rights of laymen in parochial affairs, particularly of those who sought protection against the arbitrary decisions of immigrant bishops. Bishop Carroll initially favored the trustee system, which was supported by many Irish-born priests and laymen. When it began to interfere with church discipline, however, he initiated a long struggle to abolish it; this struggle culminated in 1829 in the first Provincial Council of Baltimore. The support of Irish bishops was crucial to the efforts of the Baltimore Council to limit the role of laymen. Moreover, the immediate enforcement of the decrees by Irish priests in English-speaking parishes was of the utmost importance in bringing about a solution.

Irish prelates were also important in defining the position of the American Catholic church on slavery. Cork-born Bishop John England (1786–1842), ignoring the advice of Irish abolitionists Daniel O'Connell and Father Theobald Mathew, became the spokesman for the Catholic view of slavery as a political problem outside the purview of religious doctrine. During the Civil War priests, bishops, and nuns from Ireland aided both Union and Confederate efforts, and a few engaged in diplomatic or propaganda work. Bishop Patrick N. Lynch (1817–1882) of Charleston toured Europe on behalf of the Confederacy while Archbishop John Hughes (1797–1864) of New York attempted to change the opinions of European supporters of the South.

For the remainder of the 19th century the Irish continued to play a prominent role in solving church problems. Donegal-born Bishop John J. Keane (1829–1918) succeeded in getting the Knights of Labor to drop their secret oath and thus avoid censure by the Pope, who opposed secret organizations. Toward the end of the century German and Italian Catholics challenged Irish dominance by petitioning the Vatican to give each ethnic group its own bishops, but the Irish-American Catholic hierarchy was able to prevent that. Although the Irish had been only one of several national groups providing leading churchmen during the 19th century, their early elevation to the most important posts in the church and their facility in English made them the leading spokesmen of American Catholicism.

POLITICS

Their experience in Ireland was a decided advantage in preparing the Irish for American politics. In the 1820s Daniel O'Connell's Catholic Association introduced Irish peasants to modern techniques of mass political organization. During the 1830s increasing literacy in English and the tithe war against the British government and the established church (marked by extensive rural campaigning) brought politics into the lives of the rural population. Entire districts became intensely involved in campaigns: voter and nonvoter alike turned up at the hustings to encourage their candidate and to intimidate political opponents.

The "Wild Irish" who supported Jefferson during the 1790s and their countrymen prominent on both sides in the presidential campaign of 1812 had little in common with the poorer immigrants of the 1820s. With the development of New York as the great Irish port of arrival and the enfranchisement of propertyless males in the city in 1822, the Hibernian voice in politics grew steadily louder and more Democratic, and American politicians witnessed the first assault of impoverished Irish on City Hall. The Society of the Sons of Tammany was forced in the 1820s to relax its prohibition against full membership for the foreign-born and include the Irish in the distribution of patronage. From then until the appearance of the first Irish-born political boss in 1873, "Honest John" Kelly (1822–1886), the Irish were content to accept their share of political favors from Tammany grand sachems.

The power of the Irish boss grew with the development of the city. New spatial divisions created neighborhoods that could be exploited politically, the most prominent being the Irish. The personal reciprocal relationships on which the power of the political machine was based and the respect for seniority and service that characterized the hierarchical power structure harked back to rural Ireland. The representative of the boss on the lowest level, the block captain, established a personal relationship with each immigrant, asking only a vote at election time—a small return for the support provided throughout the year: jobs, food, coal in winter, and help with the government or the law. At the same time the businessman provided the boss with bribes in return for a favorable court decision, the regulation of competitors, or the opportunity to provide essential services to urban residents. The activities of the boss had their seamy side, but the machine performed a vital service in bringing order to a fragmented city.

The Irish were not the first political bosses—William M. Tweed who preceded Kelly in New York City had Scottish ancestors—nor were they the last. But they brought an unprecedented degree of organization to the job, pioneering the development of modern American urban politics as the traditional aristocratic officeholders retreated from the disorder of city life.

The organizational talents of Irish politicians were most apparent in their response to changing population patterns. After 1890 declining immigration from Ireland reduced the proportion of voters of Irish ancestry in major cities; at the same time great numbers of other immigrant groups were arriving (see Table 3). This circumstance, however, did not destroy the power of Irish politicians, who made conscious efforts to win the votes of eastern and southern European immigrants. Their success in attracting voters varied from group to group and from place to place. Jewish suspicion of all politicians because of experiences in the Old World coupled with the interest of many Jews in socialist causes complicated alliances with them. Moreover, the political sophistication of the Jews and their elaborate network of social and charitable agencies rendered them less vulnerable than other immigrants to the ap-

peal of political bosses. But Irish bosses were forced to share power with the Jews: both groups united in the Democratic party. On the other hand Irish relations with the Italians were less amicable despite the common religious and peasant background; the very similarity of the two groups made them competitors for jobs, housing, and church authority and precluded political alliances. As a result, Italians frequently voted Republican.

After 1890 the progress of second-generation Irish and newer immigrants up the occupational ladder into the middle class and out to the developing suburbs broadened the spectrum of interest groups that a successful boss had to satisfy in order to retain power. The political support of many of these socially mobile ethnic voters aided the deadly enemy of the boss—the reformer. However, the machine eventually adjusted to the innovations introduced by the reformer—direct primaries, tightened registration requirements, and new city-management techniques. In the 20th century a new, more progressive boss of Irish ancestry emerged in many cities, the most notable of whom was probably Charles F. Murphy (1858–1924) of New York. But James M. Curley (1874–1958) of Boston was representative of an older type of Irish-American political leader that survived until World War II. By then the New Deal had created totally novel conditions—projecting the federal government into activities once the province of the boss; and forging a coalition of the minorities, within which the Irish had to work.

NATIONALISM AND THE CIVIL WAR

Involvement in American politics allowed the Irish to inject a deep concern for their native land into national affairs. As early as the 1790s the activities of the American Society of United Irishmen became so extensive in American cities that Federalists viewed them as a threat to the stability of the United States. During the 1820s various associations supported Daniel O'Connell's successful Catholic Emancipation struggle in Ireland. Almost two decades later the Irish in America again supported O'Connell, this time in an effort to win repeal of the Act of Union, which had abolished Ireland's parliament and made her part of Great Britain in 1801. In the 1840s Irish immigrants used the Oregon question to try to rupture Anglo-American relations. Feeble attempts at rebellion by the Young Irelanders inspired the formation of Irish Republican clubs in many American cities. The influx of refugees from the Great Famine resulted in the establishment of the first American organization appealing to the masses and dedicated to freeing Ireland militarily; it was named for a mythical band of Irish warriors, the Fenians.

The Irish Republican Brotherhood (as the Fenians were initially called) was founded in 1857 by two former Young Irelanders, John O'Mahony (1816–1877) of New York and James Stephens (1825–1901) of Dublin. Chief recruiter O'Mahony had scarcely begun his campaign to attract Irish members of state militia companies to the Fenians when the Civil War broke out. He and other zealots saw the war as an opportunity for Irishmen to gain military experience valuable in freeing Ireland at a later date, to win the respect of the U.S. government, and to strike a blow at England.

Although exact figures are not available on the total number of newcomers from Ireland who served in the Civil War, Ireland provided the largest proportion of foreign-born troops in the South and probably ranked equal with Germany as the source of the largest immigrant element in the Union armies. The overwhelming majority of Irishmen served the North: Irish regiments were raised in Pennsylvania, Ohio, Indiana, Illinois, and Iowa. At least eight Irishmen became generals in Union armies: Sweeny, Mulholland, Smyth, Shields, Kearney, Corcoran, Guiney, and Meagher. On the Confederate side, Alabama, Georgia, Missouri, North Carolina, South Carolina, Tennessee, Texas, and Virginia raised Irish units and five general officers were Irish-born: Cleburne, Finnegan, Hagan, Lane, and Moore. In both armies, most Irishmen served in units of mixed nationality. Both sides recognized that the Irish were fierce fighters. The courage of the Irish brigade in the Union forces at the battle of Fredericksburg, where two-thirds of the unit was lost, was admired even by the correspondent of the London *Times*.

The Irish related their involvement in the Civil War to their attachment to their homeland. They frequently went into battle with sprigs of green in their caps. Rarely was a speech made in an Irish unit of either Union or Confederate armies without reference to how "the (Irish) green would eventually flutter over the (British) red." But there the consensus ended, for neither side could understand the commitment of the other. Northern supporters were shocked at countrymen fighting against the Union whose liberty had been won from their ancestral enemies, the British; Confederate sympathizers failed to understand why any Irishman would fight against a people striving for independence.

Throughout the war the Fenians operated openly in the Union Army, publicly announcing their intent to wage war eventually with Britain; army sympathy for these activities was evident in 1863 when leave was granted to a great number of Irish soldiers to attend a Fenian convention in Chicago. After this meeting the pace of organization increased rapidly and funds came in at an unprecedented rate. The psychological awakening of Irish immigrants during the war gave them a growing awareness of the larger world. At the same time, Irish nationalism provided a cause that bridged the gap between the immigrant's concern for relatives in the homeland and his need to explain his low status to the host society. To win freedom for Ireland would improve conditions for those who remained there; at the same time it conferred dignity on the Celt in his struggle with the Saxon. Understandably, expressions of Irish nationalism took on American coloration: speakers at Irish gatherings invariably explained their interest in freedom for the homeland in terms of their appreciation for American values.

The direct Fenian attempts to free Ireland were anticlimactic, hampered by a split in the organization in 1865. One faction arranged a haphazard uprising in Ireland in 1867; the other attacked Canada—an undertaking which led to a few raids before the U.S. government stopped them. By 1870 the organization had receded into the background.

Even before the waning of Fenian power a new organization appeared to represent the cause of Irish freedom, Clan na Gael or United Brotherhood, founded in 1867 by Jerome H. Collins. An alliance between the clan and

the Irish Republican Brotherhood in the United Kingdom led to the formation of a joint revolutionary directory in 1877. Clan na Gael was very effective in attracting the sons of famine immigrants who had moved into the middle class, among them many doctors, lawyers, and journalists. Despite the strength of its membership, the clan in the 1870s merely attempted to form alliances with England's enemies and struggled over the control of finances.

Nationalist groups throughout the United States joined with Home Rulers and peasants in Ireland during the 1880s in one united front, the New Departure, under the leadership of Charles Stewart Parnell (1846–1891). Dedicated to freeing the homeland through political action, the coalition eventually helped break the control of the Anglo-Irish aristocracy in the homeland and set in motion the process that resulted in the creation of the present-day nation of small farmers. The concern for the poor at home and abroad on the part of one of the primary spokesmen of the movement, Michael Davitt (1846–1906), coupled with the nationalist instincts of Parnell, brought together for a time the issues of social justice and nationalism. Yet before the end of the decade the American branch of this united front divided over Clan na Gael's use of dynamite in England, the murder in Chicago of Dr. Patrick Cronin (1846–1889) during a struggle between different nationalist factions, and diverse views about American presidential candidates.

From 1890 until World War I, Irish nationalists in America tried unsuccessfully to restore the bond that had existed during the New Departure. The Irish National Federation of America, founded in 1891, entered into a series of improbable alliances in futile attempts to influence the U.S. government to break relations with Britain. Irish Americans led the pro-Boer faction in the United States; an Irish unit journeyed to South Africa to fight the British. But the continuing transfer of ownership of Irish land from landlord to peasant under the Ashbourne Act resulted in relative calm in the homeland and hampered Irish-American attempts to create problems there for England. Then in 1910 the Irish party under John Redmond (1856–1918) gained the balance of power in Parliament and Home Rule for Ireland again became a topic of serious discussion. Shortly thereafter Parliament passed a Home Rule bill but delayed its application until the end of World War I.

Most of the moderate Irish-American organizations and the Catholic church supported Home Rule, but they encountered opposition from radicals John Devoy (1842–1928) and Judge Daniel P. Cohalan, head of Clan na Gael. The moderates were buoyed by the activities of the Gaelic League, which was attempting to restore in Ireland the Gaelic language and literature, and believed that the Irish were attaining a new respectability. To them it was simply a matter of time before Ireland would have her freedom. The radicals were less optimistic. Clan na Gael and other groups still believed in physical force and reaffirmed an earlier pact with German Americans as Devoy perfected his plan to use the Germans to aid an Irish revolt. The subsequent Easter Rising of 1916 and the treason trial of Ulster-born Sir Roger Casement led to widespread attacks in the Irish-American press on President Woodrow Wilson, who refused to intervene decisively enough to prevent British executions of Irishmen. These attacks, spearheaded by Judge Cohalan and his Friends of Irish Freedom, drew a bitter reaction from Wilson. As war approached, the sympathies of Irish Americans appeared diametrically opposed to those of the president and most other Americans.

Yet the opposition of Irish-American leaders to the war policy of President Wilson had limited effect. Voting patterns in Irish wards of American cities during the 1916 election showed that the campaign against Wilson had little impact on the masses; the Irish voted for Wilson at least as heavily as they had voted for a Democratic president in the two previous presidential elections. As always, blue-collar Irish voters reacted to bread-and-butter issues: Wilsonian legislation such as the child labor and Adamson eight-hour acts, both signed into law during the campaign, had more influence than denunciations of Wilson as pro-British. Working-class support was doubtless supplemented by the pro-Wilson vote among many of the second generation who had moved up the occupational scale and shared middle-class approval of Wilson's efforts to keep the country out of war.

Irish Americans flocked into the army when the United States entered the war: the "Fighting Irish" Sixty-ninth Regiment from New York was one of the first units sent to France, where it joined Irishmen fighting for Great Britain: over 154,000 Irish served in the British forces during the first two years of war, many of them because of a promise of home rule for Ireland after the war. A few radical organizations in the United States, including the Friends of Irish Freedom, continued to criticize America's involvement in the war, and some were repressed by the government. But most Irish nationalists and all the church leaders actively supported the war. When peace was restored, Wilson's speeches emphasizing "justice to all peoples of all nationalities" raised hopes for a free Ireland. His failure, however, to pursue the case for Ireland at the Versailles Peace Conference in 1919, largely because of his fear of losing British support on other issues, led to the convening of an Irish Race Conference in Philadelphia. A strong lobbying effort by Irish Americans followed, but it failed to get Ireland placed on the agenda at Versailles prior to the end of the peace conference.

Disillusionment over Wilson's failure to plead the Irish cause at Versailles and fear that some of the clauses of the League of Nations treaty would result in American aid in suppressing dissent in Ireland led Irish-American Democrats to form an alliance with Republican isolationists in the Senate to deny Wilson the two-thirds majority required for participation in the new international organization. "Black and Tan" outrages in Ireland during the summer of 1920, coupled with the Democrats' apparent decision to write off the Irish during the presidential campaign of that year, led to mass defection of Irish voters in the large cities and the overwhelming defeat of the Democratic presidential candidate, James M. Cox. Just as it appeared that Irish Americans were about to re-create the old nationalist alliance of the 1880s, the one issue that kept them together was resolved. On June 11, 1921, hostilities in Ireland ceased. Shortly thereafter a treaty was signed that led to the partition of the country into the Irish Free State in the south with dominion status within the British Empire,

and six counties in the northeast that remained part of Britain. This division was eventually to create profound problems, and a half-century later, involved some Irish Americans in the conflict over Ulster's future.

THE LABOR MOVEMENT

Despite the absence of organized trade unions in rural Ireland in the 19th century, a tradition of peasant "combinations" carried over to the New World. In 1834 secret societies were credited with causing much of the fighting among Irish laborers working on the Chesapeake and Ohio Canal. In the 1850s rivalry among secret organizations similarly instigated battles among groups of Irish laborers working on the Illinois Central Railroad. Although a few skilled Irishmen headed associations which included both Irish and non-Irish tradesmen, by the 1850s most unskilled newcomers from Ireland joined associations and benevolent societies made up exclusively of their fellow countrymen.

In the 1860s and 1870s this situation changed drastically. Concern over poor wages, long hours, periodic unemployment, and the lack of protection against arbitrary decisions of employers was intensified by the necessity of many Irish workers not only to earn a living but also to send money to impoverished relatives in Ireland. By helping to establish in 1861 the American Miners Association, the first national organization of coal miners, Irish-born Martin Burke became the forerunner of a host of fellow countrymen involved in unionism. The talent for building organizations was evident in the leadership of William McLaughlin of the shoemakers' union, John Siney (1831–1880) of the anthracite miners' union, J.P. McDonnell (1841–1906) of the International Labor Union, and Denis Kearney (1847–1907) of the California Workingmen's party. The extent of Irish unionization became most evident in 1877: about one-third of the employees who struck against major East Coast railroad lines—and most workers in the Far West who smashed equipment in sympathy—were Irish. Many of those who used the boycott as an economic sanction in New York in the 1880s had experience with the weapon as a form of social ostracism at home. The son of a dispossessed Irish tenant, Terence V. Powderly (1849–1924), led the Knights of Labor; and Americans of Irish ancestry headed many other unions.

Some Irish miners in the Pennsylvania coal fields, reacting to frightful working conditions, banded together in a secret organization, the Molly Maguires. The enemy in Pennsylvania, as at home, was Protestant and British: the English, Welsh, or Scots overseer. A series of spectacular trials in the late 1870s revealed that the Mollies had murdered 9 men; 20 Irishmen were convicted and executed. The trials inflamed the public imagination, as Irish dynamite attacks in English cities had previously done, and the Mollies were credited with a far more extensive organization than they possessed—at no time did they have more than a few dozen members. The Phoenix Park murders in Dublin in 1882 and the murder of Dr. Cronin in Chicago in 1889 maintained in the popular mind the association between Irishmen and secret terrorist organizations into the early 20th century.

The labor violence of the 1870s and 1880s shocked prominent Irishmen, both secular and religious, into a new examination of social problems, an awareness reflected in the immigrant press. The *Irish World* (f. 1870) of New York promoted a more realistic understanding of labor and social problems, publishing the writings of such social theorists as Henry George (1839–1897), who believed private monopoly of land the major social evil—a thesis with obvious appeal for people one step removed from peasant Ireland. But the attitudes of the clergy were not nearly so clear-cut. An intense struggle developed between traditionalists, including Bishops Michael Corrigan (1839–1902) of New York City and Bernard J. McQuaid (1823–1909) of Rochester, N.Y., and progressives led by Archbishop (later Cardinal) James Gibbons (1834–1921), ably assisted by Bishop John Ireland (1838–1918) of St. Paul, Minn. The conflict was resolved in 1891 when the Vatican issued the encyclical *Rerum Novarum*, asserting the rights of private property but also sanctioning the relationship between capital and labor proposed by Irish-American progressives.

By the early 20th century, men and women of Irish birth or descent could be found across the entire spectrum of the American labor movement. On the left was Cork-born Mary Harris Jones (1830–1930), one of the foremost labor agitators in the United States. Jailed frequently for her activities, she spent much of her long life moving from place to place helping impoverished workers, particularly coal miners. In 1905 "Mother" Jones helped organize the Industrial Workers of the World (IWW). Also involved with the IWW was Irish-born "Big Jim" Larkin (1876–1947), who rallied workers to the organization and later helped found the American Communist party. Of Irish descent were Elizabeth Gurley Flynn (1890–1964), fiery IWW orator, and "Big Bill" Haywood (1869–1928), dynamic leader of the same organization. Irish Americans gained notoriety as members of the more radical labor groups through the bombings by the McNamara brothers in Los Angeles, the trial and unjustified conviction of Tom Mooney (1885–1942) on a murder charge in San Francisco, and the scathing speeches of Eddie "Bomb the Bosses" McLean in Philadelphia. But moderate Irish trade unionists, like Timothy Healy, leader of the International Brotherhood of Stationary Firemen, and James O'Connell (1858–1936), a vice president of the American Federation of Labor, were far more representative of their countrymen in labor organization. In 1892 Mary Kenney O'Sullivan (1864–1943), daughter of a railroad worker, became the first female general organizer for the American Federation of Labor; Leonora O'Reilly (1870–1926) was appointed to the board of the National Women's Trade Union League when it was founded in 1903. By 1900 Irish immigrants or their descendants held the presidencies of over 50 of the 110 unions in the AFL.

CULTURAL DEVELOPMENT

Much of the work of Irish-born writers in America was defensive. The earliest important works, William James MacNeven's *Pieces of Irish History* (1807) and Mathew Carey's *Ireland Vindicated* (1819), both attempted to refute Protestant accusations of Catholic inferiority. Of the historical apologies that continued to appear into the early 20th century, the most popular was *A History of Irish Settlers in North America* (1851)

by Thomas D'Arcy McGee (1825–1868), which contrasted the spiritual uncorrupted Celt with the mercenary Saxon. Other immigrant writers made extensive use of these stereotypes, notably Father Cornelius Herlihy in his racist *The Celt above the Saxon* (1890). Defensiveness characterized the Irish reaction to nativism after 1890. Numerous books and articles of doubtful merit emphasized the importance of the Catholic Irish in American history.

There were some notable exceptions. Mary Anne Sadlier (1820–1903), a native of Ulster's County Cavan, expressed satisfaction with the misfortunes of a lapsed Catholic in *The Blakes and the Flanagans* (1855), typical of many novels written for the Irish market at the time. Less bitter was the popular work by Donegal-born Father John Boyce (1810–1864, pseudonym, Paul Peppergrass), *Shandy McGuire* (1851), which attempted to make sense of the confusing changes in the peasant society of Ireland during the 1820s. Father Boyce was the first of a number of Irish writers who responded to the growing divisions in New England society after mid-century. Later contributions were the poems of Irish-born John Boyle O'Reilly (1844–1890), *Songs, Legends, and Ballads* (1878) and *The Statues in the Block* (1881). Less popular but influential were the collections of poetry and essays of two second-generation writers: *A Roadside Harp* (1893) and *Patrins* (1897) by Louise Imogen Guiney (1861–1920) and *On the Sunrise Slope* (1881) by Katherine Eleanor Conway (1803–1927). O'Reilly, Guiney, and Conway were important ambassadors from the Irish-American culture of Boston to the literate segment of Protestant society.

Much important Irish-American writing during the late 19th and early 20th centuries concentrated on social reform, almost all published as newspaper articles, apart from the classic *A Living Wage* (1906) by Father John A. Ryan (1869–1945). For 30 years, as editor of the Boston *Pilot*, poet John Boyle O'Reilly defended blacks, Jews, and immigrants. Yet he never overcame his suspicion of labor unions and on balance probably contributed more as a poet than as a reformer. Patrick Ford (1835–1913), both as a writer and as editor of the *Irish World*, began a debate that inspired new approaches to the problems of peasant immigrants trying to adjust to the expanding industrial system. The popular dialect columns of Peter Finley Dunne (1867–1936) made people think about social problems while making them laugh. These writings profoundly influenced Irish-American politicians and social planners of later generations.

Irish immigrants made their greatest contribution to American culture through the theater. As early as 1811, Irish concerts were being held in the larger cities and Irish characters were common. By 1850 Irish farces were a staple of the American stage; the plots were simple, the characters exaggerated, and comic personality traits emphasized. As audiences expanded, plays were mass produced to meet the demand. The best dramatist of Irish descent to emerge at mid-century was Dion Boucicault (1820–1890), whose plays added a chivalrous and sensitive dimension to the character of the stage Irishman. With their humorous portrayal of the New York Irish in the popular "Mulligan Series," Edward Harrigan (1844–1911) and Anthony Hart (1855–1891) made a major contribution to the development of the American musical. Irish-born Victor Herbert (1850–1924) became the most prominent composer of American light opera in the 1880s. By 1910 Irish plays and musicals were as popular as ever, but the stage Irishman was gone, the victim of an all-out campaign launched by the Ancient Order of Hibernians. The end of an era was clearly signaled in 1920 when an Irish American who was to have a profound impact on American theater, Eugene O'Neill (1888–1953), won the Pulitzer Prize for his play *Beyond the Horizon*.

Respect for physical endurance made sports popular with Irish Americans. Long before formal organizations fostered participation, every Irish neighborhood had its strong man and informal competitions. After the 1850s Irish-American sports became more organized and an American Irish Athletic Association was founded. St. Patrick's Day was frequently the occasion for football or hurling (similar to field hockey) matches. During the mid-19th century, the Irish played a prominent role in the boxing world. John Morrissey (1831–1878), a native of Tipperary who eventually became heavyweight champion of America, was the most notable of several Irish pugilists who began their careers as street-fighters for Tammany Hall in the 1840s. Irish-born Paddy Ryan, the only boxer ever to win the heavyweight championship in his first fight, was defeated in 1882 by John L. Sullivan (1858–1918), a second-generation Irish American who held the championship for ten years until defeated in turn by a San Franciscan of Irish parents, James J. Corbett (1866–1933). The names of these champions were household words in the late 19th century; indeed, Irish boxers were so popular that other immigrants assumed Hibernian names before embarking on a career in the ring. In baseball, players and managers of Irish ancestry contributed to the national sport. Later in the 20th century Catholic colleges with large Irish-American student bodies, such as Notre Dame, Fordham, Holy Cross, and Boston College, earned football fame.

ACCEPTANCE AND ACHIEVEMENTS

By the early decades of the 20th century the American Protestant fear of the Irish as a permanently depressed proletariat who owed allegiance to Rome had subsided. The grudging respect won by the Irish during the Civil War and the decades that followed was strengthened by a growing number of successful Americans of Irish descent. The surge of nativism during the 1890s, intensified by the depression of 1893, expressed itself in a number of anti-Catholic, anti-Irish organizations, the most powerful of which was the American Protective Association. But the movement had little permanent effect in slowing acceptance of the Irish by the larger society; by 1900 St. Patrick's Day was celebrated in American cities as a community festival as well as an Irish holiday.

By 1920 the evidence of Irish success was mixed, but in general modest. Many children of immigrants had moved up the occupational scale and into the developing suburbs—"lace-curtain Irish" they were contemptuously called by the "shanty Irish" who remained behind. There were some cases of spectacular achievement. In the Catholic church, men and women of Irish birth or descent held the highest offices. Although it

would be almost a decade before Al Smith knocked on the door of the White House, Irish-born members of Congress outnumbered by more than two to one all other foreign-born representatives. Joseph McKenna (1834–1926), a Catholic Irish American, served as U.S. Attorney General and became an Associate Justice of the Supreme Court. Many Irishmen or their sons had been very successful in the military services. General Philip Henry Sheridan (1831–1888), born a few months after his parents landed from Ireland, became Commander in Chief of the U.S. Army in 1884. More soldiers, sailors, and marines from Ireland won the Congressional Medal of Honor than members of any other foreign-born group. In business the Irish were represented by the Cudahy family of meatpacking fame and wealthy inventor Thomas E. Murray (1860–1929). As a member of the Wisconsin Woman Suffrage Association, Maria McCreery (1883–1938), whose grandparents were Irish immigrants, was a prominent fighter for the rights of women. Some Irish Americans had even entered high society.

But most newly arrived Irish immigrants were still strangers, with a culture significantly different from that of the general society. Peasant newcomers settled in the urban ghettos where the incidence of disease and death was still frightfully high; New York and Chicago had large Irish slums. Now, however, the Irish neighborhoods had a range of firmly established institutions that eased the trauma of adjustment. But the Irish-born population of the United States was declining sharply: by 1920 Americans of Irish parentage outnumbered the Irish-born by more than three to one (see Table 2). The story of the Irish in America was rapidly becoming the story of Americans of Irish descent.

IMMIGRATION AFTER 1920

Migration from Ireland to the United States, which had dropped significantly during and immediately after World War I, resumed its former intensity in 1920. After a strong surge during the early years of the decade, however, the destinations of Irish emigrants began to change. A steadily increasing number went to the United Kingdom; by 1930 about three to one preferred England to the United States as a destination. This pattern continued into the 1970s and had a profound impact on the Irish population in the United States.

The decline in U.S. Irish immigration in the mid-1920s resulted from increasing competition for unskilled jobs by blacks and new immigrant groups; the effects of the Great Depression discouraged immigration after 1929. At the same time a growing demand in England for workers, particularly servants, inspired movement to the sister isle, and more women than men left during the years 1926–1936. Thereafter the employment opportunities of an expanding British economy attracted more men, who predominated until the end of World War II. Accordingly, from the late 1920s until the late 1940s U.S. Irish immigration dropped to a trickle (see Table 1). It picked up and grew after World War II, particularly during the 1950s. In the early 1960s it again declined, dropping sharply after passage of the U.S. Immigration and Nationality Act of 1965.

Emigration patterns after 1920 reflected changing economic conditions in Ireland. A slump in agricultural prices from 1920 to 1927 spurred emigration. Improve-

ment in the Irish economy from 1927 until the mid-1930s coincided with the Great Depression in the United States and provided jobs at home for many; the population of Ireland stabilized for the first time since the Great Famine. But the Irish economy remained weak, and when it became stagnant during the 1950s emigration again soared. It declined as Irish industrial output rose from 1959 until the early 1970s. When the economic outlook dimmed later in the decade, the unemployed could look neither to Great Britain because of poor economic conditions there, nor to the United States because of the new immigrant admission requirements of the 1960s.

The occupational background, age, sex, and marital status of Irish immigrants to the New World remained close to traditional patterns. Most came from a rural background. After 1960, however, rural newcomers made up a decreasing proportion of the group (one out of four in the 1970s), largely because the Immigration and Nationality Act of 1965 severely restricted the immigration of unskilled workers. Immigrants continued to be in the younger age brackets, and the overwhelming majority were unmarried at the time of arrival. Until 1950 men and women were roughly balanced, but from 1951 women moved steadily ahead and by 1967 were in the majority by about two to one, apparently because of prosperity at home and the reluctance of Irish men to face the military draft in time of war. Afterward the sex ratio leveled off and in 1975 was again roughly equal.

Although the American population either born in Ireland or of Irish parentage declined steadily after 1920, the number of Americans of more distant Irish origin increased. A census survey in 1972 revealed that 16.4 million Americans claimed Irish descent. The 1970 Census recorded 1.5 million first- and second-generation Irish in the United States; therefore, Irish Americans of third and subsequent generations—approximately 15 million strong—outnumbered those of the first and second generations by ten to one.

The earlier concentration of Irish-born newcomers in American cities intensified somewhat during the 20th century, and they remain one of the most highly urbanized of all immigrant groups. Despite some redistribution to smaller cities from the major areas of 19th-century settlement, New York remains the city with the largest Irish population in the United States (see Table 3). By 1970 three out of four Irish immigrants resided along the East Coast, but there was a slight shift within the region to South Atlantic states. The only major change in the distribution of newcomers since 1920 has been the increasing proportion settling on the West Coast—a growth from 6 to 10 percent between 1920 and 1970. With the exception of a slightly larger proportion of Americans of Irish parentage residing inland, the distribution of second-generation Irish Americans corresponded to that of the Irish-born. Finally, the distribution of all Catholic Americans claiming Irish descent was roughly similar to the distribution of Americans of Irish parentage; Protestants of Irish background are slightly more concentrated in the South.

According to the 1970 Census, Irish immigrants on the West Coast were significantly better educated than their countrymen on the East Coast: in San Francisco and Los Angeles Irish-born males over 25 years old had a median education of 12 years as opposed to 9 years

among the same group in Boston, New York, and Chicago. At the same time a striking 1 in 4 Irishmen in Los Angeles were in the professional ranks compared with 1 in 18 in New York. The likelihood of encountering a white-collar Irishman generally increased with movement to the west. The age structure of Irish immigrants suggested that some of the drift to South Atlantic states was due to the movement of retirees: in 1970 Miami had a larger proportion of Irish immigrants over 65 years old than any other city in the country.

SOCIAL AND ECONOMIC TRANSFORMATION

Although generally lower on the occupational scale than any of the other older immigrant groups, the Irish had become well scattered throughout the occupational structure by 1950. Twenty-four percent of male newcomers born in Ireland were in the white-collar ranks (see Table 4). As in the past, the small proportion of Irishmen in the professional ranks were overrepresented as clergymen; at the managerial level they tended to be superintendents or managers of buildings. About 73 percent labored in blue-collar jobs, including 20 percent employed as craftsmen. Among semiskilled or service workers, the Irish were heavily represented as porters or cleaners, followed by firemen and policemen. Over 13 percent worked as laborers. Irish-born women retained their traditional representation in service work, predominantly in private households. Both men and women showed an aversion for agricultural employment.

Athough employment data on second-generation Irish (see Table 4) suggest considerable upward movement, their progress was rather sluggish compared with other major immigrant groups. Men with one or both parents born in Ireland, however, did move impressively into professional levels, generally as accountants, clergymen, or lawyers. Compared to other blue-collar workers of foreign parentage, males of Irish parentage were overrepresented as policemen and firemen. Second-generation women were fairly widely dispersed throughout the occupational structure and in white-collar fields were overrepresented in law, engineering, teaching, and clerical work. Like men of the second generation, the women specialized in the protective services.

The occupational structure of the entire male population of Irish descent regardless of generation differed from that of the general population (see Table 4). By 1969 males of Irish descent had moved impressively into white-collar ranks. But the male population of Jewish, English, and German descent outperformed men of Irish origin. Compared with the general working population, Irish Americans were overrepresented in law, medicine, and the sciences and slightly underrepresented in the social sciences and business. Clearly, the great majority of Americans of Irish descent did not inherit the disadvantages of the earlier immigrant generations.

Many characteristics of the Irish family in 19th-century America persisted into the 20th century. In 1960 the median age at first marriage for Irish immigrants or their children was higher than for any other major immigrant group. The Irish generally had larger families and fewer divorces than other foreign-born people. In 1960 Irish-born mothers were second in number of children only to women born in Mexico. In Rhode Island in the late 1960s, the number of children expected by married couples of Irish descent was higher than for any other ethnic group. The likelihood of Irish immigrants remaining permanently celibate by 1960 was also high, with about 15 percent of both sexes unmarried between the ages of 35 and 44. High fertility and celibacy rates appear characteristic of the entire population of Irish descent.

After 1920, when three out of four newcomers married within their own group, Irish immigrants and their children increasingly married outside the group. In New Haven in 1930, 74 percent of the Irish-born married spouses of a similar origin, a rate which dropped to 45 percent within a decade. National census data two decades later confirmed the continuation of this trend. By 1960 the first- and second-generation Irish population were actually more likely to marry outside their own group than within it.

Although in 20th-century Irish-American families the father was generally the principal breadwinner, the mother's position was a strong one. The overconcentration of Irish women in the professions and white-collar work suggests the continuing strength of traditional egalitarian attitudes toward sex roles. The sacrifices made to educate daughters were in many cases as great as those made for sons.

Mortality and disease rates for the Irish-born remained high in the United States in the 20th century for the same reasons as in earlier days—poverty and alcohol. In 1950 and 1960 Irish immigrants had the highest mortality rate among the foreign-born for all causes of death, particularly cardiovascular disease. Among all foreign-born or native whites in 1950, newcomers from Ireland had the highest rate of mental diseases, usually alcoholic psychoses. Although the children of Irish immigrants displayed significantly fewer psychological problems than their parents, they led all other second-generation Americans in rates of mental disorders. As in earlier years, mortality rates and the incidence of mental disorders were higher among the Irish in America than in Ireland.

Table 4. Occupational distribution of first- and second-generation Irish males, 1950, and males of Irish descent compared with the general male population, 1969 (in percentages).

| | 1950 | | 1969 | |
	First generation	Second generation	Irish descent	U.S. population
Professionals	4.2	9.5	14.1	13.6
Managers	7.6	11.6	19.1	17.0
Clerks	8.3	13.0	8.5	7.0
Salesmen	3.8	7.5	6.3	5.4
Craftsmen	20.6	19.3	20.8	20.1
Operatives	19.1	16.5	17.9	20.4
Service workers	18.8	11.0	6.0	6.7
Farm laborers	0.8	0.9	1.0	2.0
Laborers	13.7	5.9	6.1	7.5

Source: Data for 1950 are computed from a special sample of the 1950 Census reported in E.P. Hutchinson, *Immigrants and Their Children, 1850–1950* (New York, 1956), pp. 335ff.; for 1969 from the U.S. Bureau of the Census, *Current Population Report*, Series P–20, no. 221, *Characteristics of the Population by Ethnic Origin, November 1969* (Washington, D.C., 1971), table 15, p. 23; U.S. male sample for 1969 computed from U.S. Department of Labor, Bureau of Labor Statistics, *Handbook of Labor Statistics* (Washington, D.C., 1973), table 6, p. 39.

Group segregation declined after 1920, although the desire of newcomers from Ireland or their children to live close to one another did not completely disappear. In 1970 Irish immigrants in Detroit, Milwaukee, and Minneapolis showed a higher level of segregation than any other white foreign-born group. Moreover, in 15 major cities, newcomers from Ireland showed a strong propensity to reside in proximity to the second-generation Irish who, however, were far less segregated from native whites than their foreign-born parents.

Except in the largest cities, Irish neighborhoods disappeared after 1920. In the West and Midwest this transformation took place almost overnight. St. Louis, for example, at the turn of the century had a variety of Irish ethnic organizations: by 1930 the great majority were gone. The Irish-born population of that city dropped by almost 50 percent between 1900 and 1920 and continued to decrease rapidly thereafter; among second-generation Irish a similar decline occurred (see Table 3), intensified by a steady dispersal from the central city to the suburbs. Other cities with relatively small Irish-born populations experienced a similar rapid trend after 1920.

Meanwhile the structure of Irish communities changed. Prohibition destroyed the saloon, next to the family and the church the most important institution in Irish neighborhoods. Irish "beer barons" appeared during the Prohibition era, and immigrants were drawn into crime on an unprecedented scale. Neither the parish church nor secular clubs and organizations compensated for the loss of the saloon. During the 1920s the growth of popular culture widened the gap between the generations. Some Irish newspapers survived, but they were now delivered in suburban areas to the children of the immigrants. Radio increasingly supplanted newspapers as the source of information on the activities of the group.

Despite declining population and increasing pressure from newer immigrants and blacks, Irish neighborhoods in the larger cities such as Chicago, New York, Boston, and Philadelphia maintained their identity for some time. During the 1920s their presence expanded membership in the Ku Klux Klan all across the nation in its drive against Catholics, Jews, and other undesirables in cities. The incursion of outsiders into Irish neighborhoods occasionally caused violence. Regan's Colts, an Irish athletic club that reportedly enjoyed police protection, was typical of the groups that attacked blacks in Chicago after World War I. In the 1930s and 1940s serious street fighting took place between Irish and Jews in Dorchester, Mass., and in the Bronx and Brooklyn. Anti-Semitic organizations, notably Father Charles Coughlin's Christian Front, sparked much of the violence, as did a few Nazis of Irish ancestry, like Joseph E. McWilliams, head of the American Destiny party in New York. On the other hand, a retired American general of Irish descent headed the first anti-Nazi parade in New York and several Irish-American Catholic bishops declared themselves on the side of the Jews. After World War II the relationship between the inner-city population of Irish extraction and that of other origins was somewhat more peaceable. By 1970, except for enclaves in Chicago, Boston, New York, and Philadelphia, the Irish were no longer a major presence in urban areas.

CHURCH AND POLITICS AFTER 1920

The church membership of Catholics of Irish descent declined steadily after 1920; in the 1970s they accounted for only about 17 percent of the total. But they remained heavily overrepresented among the church's leaders: in 1970 over 50 percent of the bishops and 34 percent of the priests had an Irish background. Bishops of Irish extraction supported conservative causes ranging from backing General Franco in the Spanish Civil War to speaking in favor of the Vietnam War. On the other hand, progressive Irish-American bishops arranged the National Catholic Welfare Council meeting in late 1919, and a second-generation Irish-American priest, Monsignor John A. Ryan (1869–1945), director of its Social Action Department, developed guidelines during the 1920s far in advance of their time for dealing with unemployment, old-age insurance, and other social problems. Bishop James P. Shannon (1921–), later to resign from the church and marry, participated in a march through Selma, Ala., in 1965 with about 400 priests and nuns in an attempt to win social justice for blacks. Timothy Cardinal Manning (1909–) of Los Angeles, born in County Cork, supported the efforts of César Chavez to unionize Mexican-American agricultural workers of California in the late 1960s. However, other Irish-American bishops strenuously objected to the work of the activist prelates.

The majority of Catholic Irish Americans remain politically liberal. More of them favor governmental involvement in social reform programs than Americans of any other immigrant background except Jews. Catholics of Irish background also sympathize with black aspirations and civil rights. On religion, attitudes began to shift in the 1960s, and by 1974 for the first time there was a negative correlation between Irish-Americans' attendance at Catholic schools and support for a son's priestly vocation.

The Irish in America remained strong supporters of education, religious and otherwise. The number of years of schooling increased steadily with each generation: in 1960 the first generation had a median education of 9 years as opposed to 12 for their offspring. The proportion of college students of Irish descent grew steadily after 1920. The increase in college attendance was particularly noticeable after World War II, the result of increasing affluence and the educational benefits of the G.I. Bill. In overall educational attainment, descendants of Catholic Irish immigrants surpassed the general population, and once in college, they were twice as likely as other students to study law; they also tended to study the physical and biological sciences rather than sociology, history, or economics.

Irish bosses remained a powerful force in American urban politics after 1920. Among the most notable were Charles F. Murphy of New York, Frank Hague (1876–1956) of Jersey City, N.J., Thomas J. Pendergast (1872–1945) of Kansas City, Mo., Edward J. Kelly (1876–1950) of Chicago, David L. Lawrence (1889–1966) of Pittsburgh, Pa., and James M. Curley of Boston. Most of them took advantage of New Deal welfare legislation to strengthen their standing and emerged from the 1930s in a very powerful position. Within a few years of the disappearance of the last of the New Deal bosses, Chicago produced another powerful Irish-American boss,

Richard J. Daley (1902–1976), who served as mayor of the city from 1955 until his death.

Some characteristics underlying the political behavior of Irish-American politicians are based on traditional patterns of social interaction that have survived among people three or more generations removed from Ireland. Irish Americans scored consistently higher than all others on measures of sociability, localism, trust, and loyalty—talents vital to acquiring and keeping a political following. Irish-American politicians have used sophisticated forms of patronage to keep voters and businessmen within the party organization.

Despite their strength in urban politics, the Irish took more time to have a national impact. Only three Irish Catholics were appointed to important executive or judicial posts prior to the New Deal. Peter Finley Dunne's charge that native Protestant politicians willingly used Catholic Irish to do the dirty work in politics but forgot them when it came to important appointments was not without foundation.

In 1928 the Irish could support one of their own for president, Alfred Emanuel Smith (1873–1944). After a modest upbringing he had gone to work at an early age, for a time selling fish—he liked to call himself a graduate of the Fulton Fish Market. He entered politics and became a very competent public servant; he served four terms as governor of the state of New York. In 1928 he became the first Catholic ever nominated for president. Although the presidential campaign was marked by frequent outbursts of anti-Catholic bigotry, his candidacy was a turning point in American presidential politics, for it solidified the Democratic vote of millions of city residents, predominantly immigrants, and thus helped make possible the victory of Franklin Delano Roosevelt in 1932.

President Roosevelt did not forget the Irish when he moved into the White House. A brilliant corps of Irish Americans descended on Washington during the New Deal, among them Thomas G. Corcoran (1900–1977), James A. Farley (1888–1976), Frank Murphy (1890–1949), and Joseph P. Kennedy (1888–1969). They joined a growing number of Irish-American congressmen and senators who had benefited from the Depression backlash against Republicans, and who began a new era of Irish-American prominence in national politics culminating in the election of John Fitzgerald Kennedy (1917–1963) to the White House in 1960.

Two other Irish Americans had a profound impact on American society between the time of Al Smith and John F. Kennedy: Father Charles E. Coughlin (1891–1979) of the Shrine of the Little Flower in Royal Oak, Mich., and Senator Joseph R. McCarthy (1909–1957), Republican from Wisconsin. Early in the Depression, Father Coughlin became a national radio propagandist for many programs later initiated under the New Deal. But he grew more and more erratic; his attacks on Jews after 1938 catered to an anti-Semitic prejudice among the Irish in America that can be traced back to Patrick Ford and the *Irish World*. Coughlin's radio activities were finally ended in 1939 by lack of funds and the efforts of the Catholic hierarchy. McCarthy's anti-Communist campaign of the early 1950s appealed to elements of the Catholic Irish population caught up in the international effort to save coreligionists from Communist persecutions in Eastern Europe. McCarthy also

gave focus to suspicions harbored by many Irish-Americans about the patriotism of intellectuals. Before he finally met defeat in 1954, he had provoked a national crisis so profound that his name became part of the American language.

Coughlin and McCarthy shared a following among Irish Americans in the poorer districts of Boston, New York, and Chicago—areas that housed an aging Irish-born population. Coughlin was a practicing priest, and McCarthy was regularly applauded by priests; members of the Catholic hierarchy, including Francis Cardinal Spellman (1889–1967), whose parents were born in Ireland, refused to condemn his demagoguery. Irish Americans were very vulnerable to this kind of appeal; significantly, it coincided with some Irish defections to the Republican party. But the great majority of Irish remained Democrats, and Irish-American machine politicians generally avoided the controversy.

For the Irish in America, the 1950s were a turning point in a demographic as well as an intellectual sense. The first and second generations were rapidly disappearing: during the decade one-third of the Irish-born and one-quarter of the offspring of Irish immigrants recorded in the 1950 Census died. In the same period, the ratio of second- to first-generation immigrants grew to over four to one, while the median age of Irish-born Americans reached almost 60 years. The third and later generations of Irish Americans were becoming the representatives of the group.

The McCarthy episode caused acute personal anxiety among Irish Americans including Senator John F. Kennedy. Both his Irish Catholic constituents and his family were solidly behind McCarthy. Absent from the Senate when the vote was taken to censure McCarthy, he admitted later that had he not been ill at the time he would have faced a difficult choice. In 1960 he became the first Roman Catholic elected president of the United States after meeting the campaign issue of religion head-on. As a result Democratic gains in Catholic cities with large electoral votes outweighed Democratic losses in Protestant areas. Kennedy's administration committed the moral authority of the president to racial justice in an unprecedented manner.

Kennedy was a dramatic symbol of the distance traveled by the Irish in the United States. The great-grandson of a famine refugee who died 14 years after landing in Boston, he and the Kennedy family paradoxically achieved success in that part of the country where the Irish have experienced the most intense bigotry. Kennedy's political success came in the traditional Irish-American manner with the aid of Democratic party chairmen in the larger cities throughout the country.

Increasing Americanization diminished Irish involvement in events in the homeland after 1920. When elements of the Republican Army led by Eamon de Valera chose civil war rather than accept the Treaty of 1921, many Irish in the United States, satisfied with the limited freedom won by the homeland, became disillusioned with the continued violence. The *Gaelic American* criticized de Valera for fighting a civil war over a "quibble." Disillusionment was intensified during the 1930s by the appearance in Ireland of the fascistlike National Guard and by the bombing campaign in Britain sponsored by the Irish Republican Army. The Irish government's decision at the onset of World War II to

maintain neutrality, despite the plea of a delegation of prominent Irish Americans, further alienated some Irish Americans. (It did not prevent over 175,000 Irish from fighting in the British forces.) The increasing alienation between Irish Americans and their countrymen at home is evidenced in the subdued response to events in the North of Ireland during the 1970s. Despite intense reaction to the "Bloody Sunday" killings in Derry in 1972, and some successful fund raising by radical Irish organizations in the larger American cities, support for activities in Ireland fell short of that of the pre–World War II period.

LABOR LEADERS

Although Irish immigrants and their descendants moved up the occupational scale after 1920, they remained important as officers in American labor unions. Fiery Mike Quill (1905–1966) established the Transport Workers Union of America and became its first president. Burly Joe Curran, born in 1906 to an impoverished Irish family on New York's East Side, proved a skillful organizer of East Coast sailors during the 1930s and became the first president of the National Maritime Union in 1937.

The two most successful labor organizers of Irish descent after 1920 were Philip Murray (1886–1952), son of an Irish laborer, and William George Meany (1894–1979), grandson of a famine refugee. As president of the Congress of Industrial Organizations (CIO), Murray helped pave the way for the 1955 merger of the CIO with the American Federation of Labor (AFL). Meany, president of the combined AFL–CIO, was an important influence in American politics.

CULTURAL CONTRIBUTIONS

After 1920 Irish-American novelists and playwrights approached universal themes. In the work of three novelists, F. Scott Fitzgerald (1896–1940), John O'Hara (1905–1970), and James T. Farrell (1904–1979), and two playwrights, Eugene O'Neill (1888–1953) and Philip Barry (1896–1949), Irish-American literature came of age. Fitzgerald, a third-generation Irish American from a well-established St. Paul, Minn., family, attended Princeton and was accepted in the affluent Protestant world. He drew on his familiarity with upper-class life to create the novels that put him among the great writers of his era, *The Great Gatsby* (1925) and *Tender is the Night* (1934). O'Hara came from a wealthy Irish background in Pottsville, Pa., and was less successful in reaching the upper levels of society despite his fascination with those who did. His novel *Ten North Frederick* won the National Book Award in 1955. Reared in a tough Irish neighborhood on the South Side of Chicago, James T. Farrell, the son of a hard-working Irish-born teamster, drew upon his upbringing in both the trilogy *Studs Lonigan* (1932–1935) and the later pentalogy about Danny O'Neill. Farrell was preoccupied with the "scar of immigration" and with the spiritual deprivation of lower-class Irish life, which he blamed on the Catholic church. It was a message that many Irish Americans understood and one that made him exceedingly unpopular with the church. As late as 1948 efforts were still being made in Philadelphia to ban *Studs Lonigan.*

One figure towered over 20th-century American theater: Eugene O'Neill, the son of an Irish immigrant who fled the Great Famine in 1846 and prospered as an actor in the United States. O'Neill tried desperately to get away from his Irish background and the exaggerated humor of the early 20th-century American stage. For material he drew on his own experiences: his childhood, particularly his dealings with his father and the tormented relationships of other members of his family; the five years of drifting from job to job; his attempts to deal with alcoholism; and the uneasy relationship between Protestant Yankees and Catholic Irish. In 1936 O'Neill became the first and only American dramatist to win the Nobel Prize.

Less important than O'Neill but one of the most successful playwrights of the period was Philip Barry, son of a wealthy Irish-born businessman in Rochester, N.Y. Best known for his drawingroom comedies about the rich and well-born, notably *The Philadelphia Story* (1939), he also dealt with deeper subjects as in *Here Come the Clowns* (1938).

After World War II politics provided the material for Edwin O'Connor (1918–1968), *The Last Hurrah* (1956), and Wilfred Sheed (1930–), *People Will Always Be Kind* (1973). Family life was the subject of *House of Gold* (1970) by Elizabeth Cullinan (1933–) and *A Mass for the Dead* (1968) by William Gibson (1914–). Insights into church life appeared in Edwin O'Connor's *The Edge of Sadness* (1961) and in *The Prince of Darkness* (1947) and *Morte D'Urban* (1962) by J.F. Power (1917–). Tom McHale (1942–) illuminated the experiences of affluent Philadelphia Irish Americans in *Farragan's Retreat* (1971). Frank D. Gilroy (1925–), *The Subject Was Roses* (1965), and William Alfred (1922–) *Hogan's Goat* (1966), enjoyed wide success in the theater.

In the 1960s an economic boom in Ireland and the restrictions of the U.S. Immigration and Naturalization Act of 1965 caused a sharp drop in movement across the Atlantic. Meanwhile, the number of first-generation immigrants, the core group in maintaining Irish identity, rapidly dwindled: by 1970 almost 1 in 3 Irish-born Americans were over 70 years old. With few new arrivals to replace those who died, the rate of decline accelerated. Furthermore, the arriving Irish generally came from the more educated element of the home society and their adjustment to American society was more rapid than that of earlier newcomers.

Meanwhile the Irish became almost indistinguishable from others in those institutions which formerly had most set them apart from the larger society—the church and politics. During the 1960s the Irish in San Francisco lost all 7 seats that they had held on the city's 11-member governing board. After the death of Mayor Daley in Chicago in 1976, his efficient political machine passed to largely non-Irish Democrats. The most prominent Irish-born politician in New York City's government, Paul O'Dwyer (1907–), was defeated for reelection as City Council president in 1977. Irish political influence also declined in Massachusetts. There was, furthermore, a slight Irish shift to the Republican party. In 1963, 70 percent of Irish-American voters were Democrats; by 1972 the percentage had dropped to slightly over 60. But during the same period, the campaigns of Eugene J. McCarthy (1916–) and Robert F. Kennedy (1925–1968) for the Democratic presidential

nomination and the election of Governor Jerry Brown (1938–) of California and Senator Daniel P. Moynihan (1927–) of New York suggest that John F. Kennedy may have been the first of a new generation of Irish politicians.

Demographic studies show a progressive decline over the generations in the traditionally high rates of fertility and permanent celibacy, accompanied by the assumption of patterns of mobility, education, and marriage indistinguishable from the rest of American society. On the other hand, surveys of Irish-American attitudes indicate the persistence of distinct values; it is impossible, however, to gauge the relationship between imported culture and "ethnic values" in any but the most general terms.

The Irish experience in the United States was central to the country's social and economic development. The Irish were the first major immigrant group to threaten the stability of American society. Out of their interaction with the host society came a more diverse and tolerant America. Facility in the English language and familiarity with representative politics allowed the Irish to translate cultural and religious cohesion into organizations that profoundly influenced American politics, labor organizations, and the Catholic church while these institutions were in early stages of development. Irish immigrants and their descendants made important contributions to American literature and drama. They provided a cheap and willing labor force when the United States was making the transition from an agricultural society into the world's most powerful industrial nation. Despite the misery and suffering of the great "sorting out" of the 19th and 20th centuries, the small number of Irish immigrants who returned to the homeland attests to the general satisfaction of the rest with conditions in the United States. Movement to America allowed immigrants to aid destitute relatives at home, to support families, and to bring up their children in a world far more promising than the one they had known in Ireland. Their adjustment and that of their descendants to American society is today almost complete.

Bibliography
Irish migration to the American colonies has been adequately treated only in terms of religious groups. For Catholic movement, see Audrey Lockhart, *Some Aspects of Emigration from Ireland to the North American Colonies between 1660 and 1775* (New York, 1976); for Quakers, Albert Cook Myers, *Immigration of the Irish Quakers into Pennsylvania, 1687–1750* (1902; reprint, Baltimore, 1969). The early-19th-century migration is covered in the excellent but dated study by William F. Adams, *Ireland and Irish Emigration to the New World from 1815 to the Famine* (New Haven, Conn., 1932). For later years, see Carl Wittke, *The Irish in America* (1956; reprint, New York, 1970), and George W. Potter, *To the Golden Door* (1960; reprint, Westport, Conn., 1974). Experiences of Americans of Irish descent are emphasized by William V. Shannon, *The American Irish* (New York, 1966), and Andrew M. Greeley, *That Most Distressful Nation* (Chicago, 1973).

Population change in the area of origin is examined in detail by Robert E. Kennedy, *The Irish: Emigration, Marriage, and Fertility* (Berkeley, Calif., 1973). Peasant life in the 1930s is expertly explored by Conrad M. Arensberg and Solon T. Kimball, *Family and Community in Ireland*, 2d ed. (Cambridge, Mass., 1968). Arnold Schrier, *Ireland and the American Emigration, 1850–1900* (1958; reprint, New York, 1970), documents the impact of emigration on Irish society.

Works essential to understanding Irish adjustment to American urban areas are Oscar Handlin, *Boston's Immigrants* (1941; rev ed. Cambridge, Mass., 1959), and Stephan Thernstrom, *Poverty and Progress* (1964; reprint, New York, 1969) and *The Other Bostonians* (Cambridge, Mass., 1973). The Irish outside New England are treated by Robert Ernst, *Immigrant Life in New York City, 1825–1863* (New York, 1965); Dennis Clark, *The Irish in Philadelphia* (Philadelphia, 1974); Earl Niehaus, *The Irish in New Orleans, 1800–1860* (1965; reprint, New York, 1976); James Shannon, *Catholic Colonization on the Western Frontier* (1957; reprint, New York, 1976); and Sister Justille McDonald, *History of the Irish in Wisconsin in the 19th Century* (Washington, D.C., 1954).

For political activity see Terry N. Clark, "The Irish Ethnic and the Spirit of Patronage," *Ethnicity* 2 (1975): 305–359; and Edward M. Levine, *The Irish and Irish Politicians* (South Bend, Ind., 1966). Thomas N. Brown, *Irish-American Nationalism, 1870–1890* (Philadelphia, 1966), deals with the concern with events in the homeland. Jay Dolan, *The Immigrant Church* (Baltimore, 1977) provides insights into parish life in mid-19th-century New York.

The largest holding of materials on Irish immigrants and their descendants in the United States is that of the American Irish Historical Society, 991 Fifth Avenue, New York City. Most Catholic colleges throughout the United States, particularly in the Northeast, have impressive collections of manuscript materials on individual immigrants and their descendants.

PATRICK J. BLESSING

ITALIANS

More than 5 million Italians have settled in the United States since immigration records began to be compiled. The vast majority of them, almost 4 million, came between 1880 and 1920. They came for the most part from southern Italy—the provinces of Abruzzi, Campania, Apulia, Basilicata (Lucania), and Calabria—and from the island of Sicily. Italy as a nation did not inspire much loyalty from the majority of its emigrants, who continued to think of themselves in terms of native region, locality, or village. In the United States, however, 90 percent of them settled in the cities, where local ties proved difficult to maintain. Out of the necessity of joining forces with other Italian immigrants grew their first awareness that they shared a common Italian heritage.

The Italian immigrant communities that were formed from this massive influx of people thrived until immigration was cut off in the early 1920s. Then some of the neighborhoods that had once served the newcomers as places to learn American ideas and values languished. The children of the immigrants often regarded the old neighborhoods and their institutions with contempt, and it was left to the generation that came of age in the 1960s to revive interest in their ethnic origins.

Italy is a comparatively new nation. From the first centuries after Christ, when a succession of barbarian tribes from the north and east invaded and eventually overran the weakened Roman Empire, until the late 19th century, the Italian peninsula remained a collection of small and often warring states, many of them dominated, especially in the south, by one or another foreign power. As a result the development of northern, central, and southern Italy followed divergent courses, the effects of which persist to the present day. The rich and powerful city-states in the north were the source both of Italy's Renaissance and of its Risorgimento—the movement that ended in the unification of the entire peninsula in the 19th century. Rome and central Italy, comprising states under the secular control of the Catholic papacy, formed a dividing line. To the south a succession of foreign monarchs ruled the kingdoms of Naples and Sicily, exploiting the countryside without regard to the inhabitants. A feudal system persisted in which political power and social influence were based on hereditary possession of land.

Italy

Boundary of Italy and the
Hapsburg Empire, 1866-1919

100   Km.   Miles

SWITZERLAND

LIECHTENSTEIN

AUSTRIA

FRANCE

VALLE
d'AOSTA

TRENTINO-
ALTO ADIGE

FRIULI-
VENEZIA
GIULIA

LOMBARDY

VENETO

Milan

Venice

Turin

Po

PIEDMONT

Po

YUGOSLAVIA

Genoa

EMILIA-ROMAGNA

Bologna

LIGURIA

MONACO

Ligurian Sea

SAN MARINO

Florence

MARCHES

Ancona

I T A L Y

TUSCANY

Adriatic Sea

ELBA

UMBRIA

Tiber

ABRUZZI

CORSICA
(To France)

Ajaccio

L A T I U M

Rome

MOLISE

SARDINIA

CAMPANIA

APULIA

Naples

Bari

Cagliari

BASILICATA

Taranto

Tyrrhenian Sea

CALABRIA

Palermo

Messina

Reggio

SICILY

Catania

Ionian Sea

ALGERIA

TUNISIA

Mediterranean Sea

If the south Italian peasants had hoped to improve their lot through unification, they were soon disappointed. They found themselves in some ways worse off after 1860, when union was finally achieved, than they had been before. Foreign domination had ended, but exploitation continued, now by an efficient and ruthless northern-dominated government in Rome that treated the south like a colonial possession to further the industrial interests of the north. Discriminatory government policies in trade, industry, and education; infertile soil; an oppressive agricultural system; and an enormous growth in population guaranteed the southern peasant a dreary, marginal existence. While peasant life in northern Italy improved dramatically with the introduction of crop rotation, machinery, and fertilizers, few modern methods penetrated to the south, where large estates owned by absentee landlords and supervised by overseers were tilled by field workers with the same kinds of hand plows, hoes, and spades that had been used for centuries.

In 1900 in Europe only Belgium, the Netherlands, and England had higher population densities than Italy, and, unlike Italy, all three were already highly industrialized. The Italian population grew from 29 million in 1881 to 33 million in 1901 to over 35 million by 1911, in spite of the fact that mass migration had already begun.

The first 19th-century emigrants left from the north. They departed for a variety of reasons—to avoid military service or jail, to find religious freedom, political asylum, or greater economic opportunity—and the majority ventured no farther than central or western Europe. Comparatively few crossed the ocean, and for those who did, Latin America, especially Argentina or Brazil, was the most common destination. Although living conditions in southern Italy were certainly worse, emigration there began more slowly and much later. The southerners were less sophisticated, more conservative, and poorer; it was harder for them to think of departure. After unification, however, northern exploitation and population pressure gave them little choice. They went to North Africa at first, then to South America and to the United States as American industry expanded. In the 1890s southerners began to outnumber northerners on the transatlantic ships, but the destination of both was now the same: the passage to the United States was cheaper than to Latin America, and wages were better there. By World War I, Italy was losing population from emigration at a rate of more than half a million a year.

ARRIVAL AND SETTLEMENT

A few Italians, most of them northerners, had settled in North America as early as the 17th century—in New Amsterdam, Jamestown, Rhode Island, Connecticut, Pennsylvania, Maryland, and Georgia. Between 1820, when official immigration statistics were first compiled, and 1860, around 14,000 Italians were recorded, nearly three-quarters of them arriving in the 1850s. The discovery of gold in California in 1849 attracted a good many to the West; they stayed to work as merchants, shopkeepers, truck gardeners, dairy farmers, grape growers, and wine makers, and a few eventually became prominent local citizens. By 1860 at least a few Italians lived in almost every state. Among them were teachers and entertainers—actors, musicians, and ballet dancers—artists, stonecutters, and other craftsmen. California had the largest Italian population with 2,805; New York was next with 1,862.

Although there were some businessmen, professionals, and other successful Italians in New York City before the Civil War, most of the Italians there were poor. Many had used all their money to pay for their passage, and when they arrived in New York—the usual port of debarkation—they had no choice but to seek shelter in the neighboring slums, mainly a notorious area in lower Manhattan known as the Five Points district.

Unlike the earlier emigrants from the north, the people who left southern Italy after 1880 were men between the ages of 16 and 45 who hazarded the trip with the idea of remaining for a season or two in the United States, working at any available job, saving as much money as they could, and then returning to Italy. Between 1899 and 1910, 2,284,601 Italians came to the United States: 372,668 were northerners; 1,911,933 were from the south. By 1900 at least 100,000 were arriving every year; in 1907 the high point was reached with a total of 285,731. About half of them returned to the homeland, however—3.8 million Italians landed in the United States between 1899 and 1924, but some 2.1 million departed in the same interval. The departure rate for northerners was 48 percent; for the larger group from the south it was 56 percent. Some of the returnees simply stayed in Italy until they needed money again and then repeated the process; eventually many of these settled in the New World, although often not before they made the voyage back and forth several times and sometimes to both North and South America. After the turn of the century, immigration gradually became more stable as women and children joined the men who came seeking their fortunes. Table 1 shows the number of immigrants in each ten-year period after 1820.

Most of the immigrants of the late 19th and early 20th centuries settled in New York, New Jersey, Pennsylvania, and southern New England. The settlements in the large industrial cities toward which they gravitated followed the pattern set by the northern Italians

Table 1. Italian immigration to the United States, 1820–1975.

Years	Number of immigrants
1820–1830	439
1831–1840	2,253
1841–1850	1,870
1851–1860	9,231
1861–1870	11,725
1871–1880	55,759
1881–1890	307,309
1891–1900	651,893
1901–1910	2,045,877
1911–1920	1,109,524
1921–1930	455,315
1931–1940	68,028
1941–1950	57,661
1951–1960	185,491
1961–1970	214,111
1971–1975	93,151
Total	5,269,637

Source: U.S. Bureau of the Census, *Historical Statistics of the United States: Colonial Times to 1970* (Washington, D.C., 1975), I, 105–106, and U.S. Immigration and Naturalization Service, *Annual Reports,* 1971–1975.

Table 2. Population of Chicago's Near West Side Italian district in 1898, by precinct.

	Italians		Non-Italians		Total		
Precinct	Foreign-born	American-born	Foreign-born	American-born	Foreign-born	American-born	Principal non-Italian groups
1	239	121	379	663	618	784	Irish, German
2	1	5	297	600	298	605	Irish, German
3	10	2	430	483	440	485	Irish, German
14	10	12	377	671	387	683	Irish, Russian
15	349	306	276	361	625	667	Irish, German, Greek
16	706	450	346	387	1,052	837	Irish, German
17	850	614	178	221	1,028	835	Irish, German
18	730	482	182	186	912	668	Irish, German, Greek
19	544	365	376	575	920	940	German, Russian, Irish
20	202	239	664	671	866	910	Irish, Russian, German
29	124	150	825	1,005	949	1,155	Polish, Russian, German
30	9	3	1,283	1,044	1,292	1,047	Bohemian, Polish, German, Russian
31	66	92	491	546	557	638	Bohemian, Russian, Polish, German
32	202	162	759	844	961	1,006	Russian, German, Irish
33	—	12	994	894	994	906	Russian, Bohemian, German, Irish

Source: City of Chicago, Board of Education, *Proceedings, July 13, 1898, to June 28, 1899* (Chicago, 1899), pp. 187–189.

who had preceded them. The original enclave was always in or near the city's business area. As the newcomers got regular jobs, however, they tended to move out, making room for the new arrivals from overseas who continually swarmed into the older neighborhood. Their first housing had to be both cheap and close to work. All available structures, including warehouses and stables, were converted into living quarters, which returned handsome profits to their owners, who filled them with people and rarely laid out money for improving structures or facilities. New construction was limited to tenements designed to house the most people in the least space.

New York had both the largest and the most congested immigrant neighborhoods. Its walkup tenements rose to five or six stories and filled all but a narrow strip at the rear of the lot. In other cities tenements generally were lower—two or three stories—but flimsy, hastily constructed tenements were often tacked on to the back of the buildings, adding to the hazards of life in Chicago, St. Louis, and Philadelphia, just as the multistory firetraps threatened the health and safety of the immigrants in New York.

Newcomers from each locality tried to settle in the same street or tenement and to get jobs in the same factory but did not always succeed. They learned to meet and mingle with other Italians as well as with the Irish, Germans, Poles, and Scandinavians who lived and worked nearby. Aside from Boston's North End, New York's Mulberry Bend, and one or two others, few neighborhoods were inhabited exclusively by Italians. Between 1890 and 1920, for example, only limited sections of certain Chicago streets held a 50 percent or higher concentration of Italian immigrants and their children, and the proportion of Italians in most of the city's "Italian districts" was considerably below that (see Table 2). Even in the Near West Side community around Hull House, which between 1890 and 1920 had the heaviest concentration of Italians in the city, Italians constituted 50 to 80 percent of the inhabitants in only a few blocks and made up only one-third of the area's total population. Nonetheless the area was universally referred to as Italian, in large part because even though the Italian population had declined, their

churches, restaurants, stores, and other businesses remained, giving the area the appearance of ethnic cohesion. Italian businesses in the old neighborhoods have continued to prosper because, in addition to serving the dwindling number of residents who remain in the neighborhood, they also serve former residents who have moved to the suburbs but return on weekend shopping expeditions. These businesses also attract non-Italians who want to buy "authentic" ethnic products or eat in ethnic restaurants.

The location of Italian districts gradually shifted; one settlement worker reported in 1905 that the Italians in New York below Fourteenth Street hardly ever remained in one place more than two months before moving on to another building, another street, or another district of the city.

During the decades of large-scale immigration, 97 percent of the Italians entering the United States landed in New York. Although many moved on to other large cities, enough remained to give New York the largest Italian population of any American city, larger than the populations of Florence, Venice, and Genoa combined (see Table 3). By 1915 Italians had spread northward across Manhattan and into the Bronx, east into Brooklyn, and west across the Hudson River into Newark and other New Jersey cities (see Table 4). Still, despite the great size of the Italian population, the New York community did not differ significantly in character from those in Chicago, Boston, Baltimore, Philadelphia, Pittsburgh, Cleveland, Detroit, Milwaukee, Wis., Kansas City, Mo., and Denver. The only communities that

Table 3. Italian immigrants in selected cities, 1870–1910.

City	1870	1880	1890	1900	1910
Baltimore	146	385	824	2,042	5,043
Boston	264	1,277	4,718	13,738	31,380
Chicago	552	1,357	5,685	16,008	45,169
New Orleans	1,571	1,995	3,622	5,866	8,066
New York	2,794	12,223	39,951	145,433	340,765
Philadelphia	516	1,656	6,799	17,830	45,308
San Francisco	1,622	2,491	5,212	7,508	16,918

Source: U.S. Bureau of the Census, U.S. Census Reports, 1870, 1880, 1890 1900, 1910.

Table 4. Italian population in the boroughs of New York City, 1900–1920 (in percentages).

Borough	1900[a]	1910[a]	1920[a]
Manhattan	71.4[b]	58.6	47.2
Brooklyn	25.6	29.5	35.3
Bronx	—	7.4	10.1
Queens	2.1	3.3	5.1
Richmond	1.0	1.3	2.2

Source: Thomas Kessner, *The Golden Door: Italian and Jewish Immigrant Mobility in New York City, 1880–1915* (New York, 1977), p. 155. Data from the U.S. Census Report, 1900, 1910, and 1920.

a. Total Italian population for all five boroughs in 1900 was 145,433; in 1910, 340,765; and in 1920, 390,832.

b. In 1900, Bronx data were listed with Manhattan.

developed somewhat differently were in San Francisco and New Orleans, although the differences were more of degree than of kind. In contrast to other American cities, New Orleans attracted southern Italians from the beginning of the colony, while San Francisco remained northern Italian long after other cities were inundated with immigrants from the south. In both cities the Italian communities were wealthier than those in other urban centers, but the patterns of geographical mobility prevailed in San Francisco and New Orleans.

The Italians in San Francisco settled first near the city's business district, and then, as their numbers increased, they expanded toward Telegraph Hill, which by 1870 was the center of the colony, a convenient 15-minute walk to the waterfront and commercial district where most Italians worked. From there they spread down into the North Beach area and out to Russian Hill. Eventually the more prosperous moved into every part of the city, and new arrivals took their place. As late as 1930 San Francisco's Italian population was still predominantly northern.

New Orleans and the state of Louisiana had attracted Sicilians and other southern Italians even before the great immigrant wave. They had already trickled into Louisiana before the Civil War—in 1850 some 915 of them resided there, the largest number in any state at that time (835 lived in New York, 288 in California, and 196 in Massachusetts). By the 1890s Sicilian immigrants congregated along Ursulines, Chartres, Decatur, Royal, Barracks, and other streets in the French Quarter near the waterfront and the French Market; the neighborhood was soon dubbed Little Palermo. Little Palermo was both an area of settlement and a place for transients to stay until they moved on to jobs on the sugar, cotton, or rice plantations. In November 1905 the Louisiana Immigration Association estimated that 10,000 Italians would pass through New Orleans the following summer.

When the Italians in New Orleans began to move up the socioeconomic ladder, they were free to leave their ethnic enclaves if they wished; discrimination that prevented free residential movement by some immigrant groups in other cities did not operate in New Orleans, so long as the immigrants were white.

Well into the 1920s the populations of all the Italian communities continued to be transient. While movement was generally from one working-class neighborhood to another, it was typically from slums to more pleasant and less congested areas, especially after 1900 when improved and expanded cheap mass public trans-

portation made it possible to live beyond walking distance from work.

ECONOMIC LIFE

The overwhelming majority of Italian immigrants had been peasant farmers in Italy, and it seemed logical that they would want to settle on farms in America, as sympathetic observers encouraged them to do, in the expectation that they would be Americanized more rapidly in the isolation of the countryside than in the ethnic neighborhoods of a city. To assist them, the Italian and United States governments, some of the states, and some private agencies established agricultural colonies in Texas, Arkansas, Mississippi, Louisiana, and Alabama; despite some auspicious beginnings and official support, most of these ventures failed. In at least one of them—and it appears to have been typical of many—the settlers had to live in ramshackle houses unfit for winter habitation, and all the members of the colony slept together, several to a room, with no sanitation facilities. The farmers lacked capital and were perpetually in debt. In the South and Southwest a few Italians cultivated cotton, sugar cane, and tobacco for a time. But many had trouble because they did not understand traditional southern class and racial boundaries. Southerners were apt to regard Italian farmers as replacements for black tenant labor and to deal with their transgressions of southern custom by lynchings or public whippings. Some more extensive farming ventures, like the largely Sicilian colony in Bryan, Tex., founded in 1868, succeeded; most did not.

Italian city dwellers often raised vegetables and poultry for the market in vacant lots or on land abandoned by farmers who had moved West; they gardened in the summer months and worked in the city during the winter. This kind of farming did not require a large or a long-term investment, and it provided additional ready money. Since the plots were small, the immigrants were not isolated from their fellows as they would have been on large-scale farms.

Seasonal agricultural jobs were also common, because they required little skill and employed entire families; this was another source of supplementary income for immigrants who worked during the winter at industrial jobs. Seasonal laborers in the east could work from April to November, starting in the south and following the crops northward until the cranberry harvest in the fall. In Wisconsin Italians competed with Poles for jobs harvesting cranberries and beets.

By far the largest Italian agricultural settlements were in the West: in California primarily, but also near Portland, Ore., Tacoma and Seattle, Wash., and Denver, Colo. Farmers began as tenants and later bought the land they cultivated, often by forming partnerships. While those who farmed east of the Rocky Mountains were by and large southern Italians, northerners dominated Italian agriculture in the West. Many grew rich cultivating vineyards and making wine in the California counties of Sonoma, Mendocino, Napa, Fresno, and Madera. They grew vegetables on a large scale in the lands bordering the San Joaquin and Sacramento rivers. As in the East, truck farms were common near the larger towns and cities.

Unfamiliar customs and climate, squalid living conditions, the cost of land, and the isolation of farm life in

the New World, in contrast to the village-based agriculture of Europe, deterred the vast majority of Italian immigrants from turning to the land when they reached the United States. More important, most of them had not come all the way to America to go back to the farm. They had pulled up stakes to better their lot, and, especially after 1900, immigrants expected to find prosperity in the cities. In New York City in 1855 Italians worked as laborers, typically in skilled or semiskilled jobs or in service and trade occupations: in the building trades, the clothing industry, and as peddlers, plaster-statuette makers, and organ grinders. Children were sent out to the streets as bootblacks and organ-grinding performers.

According to the 1870 Census, Chicago's northern Italians were saloonkeepers and bartenders; fruit, candy, and ice-cream venders; confectioners; clerks; barbers; hairdressers; and restaurant owners and employees. Although a few had some money when they arrived, most, like the southerners who came after them, were poor and augmented their income by putting their children to work as peddlers or leaving them at home to keep house while their mothers took paying jobs.

The San Francisco Italian community contained the most prosperous group of Italians in the United States. They went into banking and small industry; they prospered as fishermen, fish brokers, commission merchants, horticulturalists, and food processors.

In New Orleans they took advantage of the many economic opportunities of the seaport. Sicilians found employment as fishermen, stevedores, and longshoremen. Others became importers, exporters, and retail merchants, fruit and vegetable peddlers and dealers. Italian capital and enterprise helped develop the fruit trade with Latin America. By 1880 Italians in New Orleans had established a stable, hardworking, and ambitious community.

A good deal of the late-19th-century social commentary dealt with southern Italians in the construction industry, in part because of the notoriety of the labor boss, or padrone. Southern Italian immigrants arrived knowing no English; they had no way of contacting employers, and they knew little about American life. They could only be grateful for an intermediary who spoke both languages, understood Old World traditions and New World business operations, and had contacts with local employers.

Some form of boss system was common among most non-English-speaking immigrant groups in industrial America from the 1860s into the 20th century. Before the Foran Act in 1885, which forbade the importation of contract labor, some padrones recruited men in Italy, paid for their passage, and arranged work for them in the United States, generally in construction. They usually brought over only adult men, although some recruited entire families, employing the men as laborers, forcing the women into prostitution and the children into the streets to shine shoes, play the mouth organ for pennies, or steal. After the Foran Act, padrones in the United States acted as local, unlicensed labor agents, as most had done even before the legislation.

Padrones hired men in New York, Chicago, and other cities, then shipped them wherever industries demanded a large supply of unskilled labor on short notice. Bosses sent Italian immigrant laborers all over the United States and into Canada to build railroads and work at other construction jobs. Because it was the principal port of immigrant entry, New York City was the first and largest padrone stronghold, and the methods used there were adopted by other large cities. Chicago soon became a padrone stronghold because of its position as a railroad center; it served as a clearinghouse for seasonal workers from the entire country.

San Francisco alone did not develop a padrone system. The high cost of transcontinental transportation was an effective barrier to the direct importation of laborers and precluded the coming of the poorest immigrants, and the fact that the Italians in that city were northerners, often city-bred, and comparatively skilled prevented the padrone system from becoming established.

The padrone (usually, though not always, of Italian birth or extraction) recruited immigrants at the docks by promising steady work at high wages. Those who did not sign up at once eventually succumbed when they needed ready money. To obtain employment through the padrone, immigrants paid him a commission (bossatura) varying from $1 to $15, depending in part on the length of employment and the amount of wages.

Not all bosses set out to cheat the laborers, but enough did to give them all a bad name. Many overcharged, shortchanged, or otherwise took advantage of the men from the moment they were hired until they were sent back to the city. But the padrones also performed a useful function by bringing together employers and laborers, who might otherwise have had no way of locating one another. The padrone also collected and paid out wages, wrote letters, acted as banker, supplied room and board, and handled other matters.

The heyday of the padrone system had already passed when Italian immigration reached its peak between 1900 and 1914. The padrones' decline was in part a result of the efforts of social workers and others who pressured state legislatures into passing restrictive laws and in part a result of the increasingly stable nature of the immigration after 1900. As early as 1897 the U.S. Bureau of Labor reported that the large numbers who were coming to join families no longer had to rely on the labor boss to find them work. The greater stability of the Italian community, increasing familiarity with American labor practices and with the English language, and prosperity eventually combined to end the padrone system entirely.

By the turn of the century Italians were working in a greater variety of trades and professions, and some had become successful merchants, manufacturers, and businessmen. A few were wealthy, such as Amadeo Obici, the "peanut king," who founded the multimillion-dollar Planter Peanut Company; Antonio Monteleone, who built a famous hotel in New Orleans's French Quarter, owned extensive property, and served as director of two banks; the Paterno brothers, Charles, Michael, Anthony, and Joseph, prominent New York builders and contractors, who constructed apartment buildings on Fifth Avenue, Sutton Place, Gracie Square, and West End Avenue. San Francisco's Raffaello and Amadeo Petri founded a cigar company as well as a large and successful winery. Others entered politics. Anthony Caminetti was elected to the California State Assembly in 1882, moved on to the U.S. House of Rep-

resentatives in 1890, and served as commissioner general of immigration in President Woodrow Wilson's administration.

Immigrant bankers flourished in every part of the United States where the newcomers from southern and eastern Europe had gathered. The original functions of these bankers were to receive deposits and send money abroad, but most also sold steamship tickets and performed other services. Such banks could be found in grocery stores, saloons, and similar gathering places. The typical immigrant banker had little experience in business methods. He ran his office with minimal capital and for the most part worked outside legal controls and without the restraints on investment practices that bound the state and national banks. The speculative ventures of these private bankers therefore often ended in disaster at the expense of immigrant depositors, who had no legal recourse and thus lost their savings. Immigrants transmitting money to Italy provided bankers with ample opportunities for fraud, either by investing the money with the intention of sending some of it overseas when the investment paid off or by keeping it outright.

Conditions for depositors improved somewhat after the turn of the century. Italy's Emigration Law of 1901 designated the Bank of Naples as the financial institution entrusted with transmission of savings to Italy from all parts of the world, including the United States. The bank forced many immigrant bankers to improve services for their clients, to modify rates of exchange, and to lower charges for transmitting money. States with large immigrant populations—Massachusetts, New York, New Jersey, Pennsylvania, and Ohio—enacted their own regulatory legislation to control immigrant-banking operations, but they were still far less stringent than the laws governing state and national banks.

Southern Italians early recognized the economic benefits of involvement in politics. Political machines in New York, Chicago, New Orleans, and other cities handed out patronage jobs to Italians (as they did to all immigrant groups) in exchange for support on election day. Public employment provided unskilled laborers with a relatively steady income and job security and convincing proof of the benefits to be derived from exercising one's right to vote. The numbers of Italians on the public payroll continued to increase, apparently unhampered by civil-service reforms in the last years of the 19th century.

In New York, Chicago, and other manufacturing cities, Italian women worked in the garment industry and in the manufacture of artificial flowers for millinery, and of silks, lace, candy, paper, and cigars. By 1910 Italian women represented the largest proportion (36 percent) of the female work force in the garment industry in New York City. They were 72 percent of the work force in the artificial-flower industry, a common occupation for women of the time because they could work at home and with little or no machinery, conditions that enabled young girls and women with small children to earn money. Whether at home or in the factory, Italian women worked long hours for low pay. By World War I they were also beginning to join labor unions.

Italian men moved into organized labor somewhat earlier than the women, although during the first years of immigration they were as likely to be strikebreakers as strike organizers. Southern Italian immigrants were brought into the Pennsylvania coalfields to break a strike in 1874; they helped break strikes by freight handlers on the New York docks and railroads in 1882 and by luggage makers in Chicago in 1912.

But in the same years some were joining unions in the stoneworking, garment, and building industries in the eastern United States. In addition to supplying rank-and-file support, they served as leaders of locals and even of national organizations. The International Hod Carriers' and Building Laborers' Union of America, formed in 1903 as part of the American Federation of Labor, issued its publication, the *Official Journal*, in Italian, German, and English, reflecting the nature of its membership. Domenico d'Alessandro of Boston became president of that union in 1908 and directed the organization from its early years until his death in 1926, when a Chicago Italian, Joseph V. Moreschi, took over. In the garment trades, Anzuino D. Marimpietri of Chicago was a founder of the Amalgamated Clothing Workers of America and served as its vice president. Led by Luigi Antonini, Salvatore Ninfo, and A. Baffa, Italians also joined the International Ladies Garment Workers Union and formed powerful ethnic locals in New York City.

Some of America's foremost radical labor leaders were Italians, among them Arturo Giovannitti and Giuseppe Ettor of the Industrial Workers of the World, who led southern Italian workers in the 1912 textile strike in Lawrence, Mass. But, when most southern Italians moved into organized labor, their actions were influenced more by practical grievances than by the philosophical tenets of radicalism or socialism. Successful organization depended on bargaining power—that is, some assurance that the union would be able to achieve its objectives, assurance that socialists and anarchists could seldom offer.

POLITICS

In exchange for a variety of services and favors, Italians provided some of the election-day support that kept ward and city political machines in power. In addition to jobs, a successful political boss obtained exemptions from city ordinances for businessmen; arranged bail and obtained pardons; and sponsored dances, parades, picnics, social and athletic affairs, bazaars, and church functions. He handed out free turkeys at Thanksgiving and Christmas, gave fuel and food to the needy, sent flowers to the sick, and added to the ranks of mourners at funerals. His patronage obligated the recipients to vote for his machine. Although they seldom formed a majority of a ward's eligible voters, they provided the machine's most loyal and disciplined following. Mobility kept most Italians and other immigrants from taking much interest in ward politics, but their apathy only increased the value of the votes that the boss controlled; they could determine an election's results.

Italian candidates could not depend on a bloc of countrymen large enough to determine the outcome of an election. The Italians who were registered generally voted the way the ethnic press and community leaders told them to—that is, they cast their ballots for fellow Italians, regardless of party affiliation. But there were not enough registered Italian voters in any large Ameri-

can city to guarantee an election except for local office. Italians, along with Greeks, Poles, and other recently arrived immigrant groups, had a low rate of naturalization. Between 1899 and 1910, according to the U.S. Immigration Commission, only 16 percent of the southern Italian immigrants in the country were naturalized. Many were—or considered themselves—sojourners; others were simply unaware of the advantages of citizenship.

In the Italian wards, the politcal bosses were most likely to be of Irish background. To organize the community they hired men who spoke Italian and knew Italian customs and prejudices. Often these functionaries first attracted the boss's attention by organizing a benefit society or a group of fellow workers, relatives, or friends, and leading them to the polls. Ambitious men turned control of votes to advantage, and their recommendations guaranteed jobs for supporters and friends. Now and then an Italian American gained elective office, but with a few notable exceptions, such as Fiorello H. La Guardia (1882–1947), success eluded these politicians until the 1930s. In the meantime they had ample opportunity to discover that political power did not come only from winning elections. Even later, some of the most influential politicians never sought office, or they settled for minor posts. The power of ward heelers like James March and Paul Kelly came solely from their ability to deliver the vote for others.

Born Antonio Maggio in southern Italy, James March arrived in the United States in 1873 at the age of 13. By 1880 he had settled in New York City and had gone to work for the Erie Railroad as a labor agent. He became a prosperous businessman, trustee of an Italian bank, owner of extensive property, and an influential politician. From 1894 to his death in 1910 March exerted political power as Republican party leader in the Lower East Side Italian colony.

March's Democratic party counterpart was a native of Naples, born Paolo Antonio Vaccarelli; he took the name of Paul Kelly during an early boxing career. By the turn of the century Kelly was an important cog in the local Democratic machine. The basis of his power was his position as leader of a gang of 1,500 largely Italian-American youths with a sprinkling of Jews, Irish, and others. On election day Kelly's forces would spread throughout the Lower East Side and herd voters to the polls to cast ballots for candidates endorsed by Tammany Hall, the Democratic machine. While maintaining his political power in the Lower East Side after 1908, Kelly turned his energies to organized labor, eventually becoming leader of a group of harbor unions and later a vice president of the International Longshoremen's Association.

It was not easy to go against the local machine, as the Chicago Italians discovered when they attempted to oust 19th Ward Alderman John Powers. In his nearly 40 years (1889–1927) as ward boss, Powers used his enormous political influence ruthlessly. Jane Addams, who challenged his control of the ward while she presided over Hull House, learned how he used his prominence in city politics and his influence over businessmen to get jobs for constituents, in addition to providing the usual benefits and services. In return he asked only for votes. But Powers also used force, fraud, and the promise of political office to buy off opponents, and out-

maneuvered every effort at local reform. He won the election of 1898 even though Hull House and the Italian community organized to fight him, and he continued to win elections until 1921. After 1920 his troublesome Italian opponents were silenced when reapportionment divided the huge West Side Italian community that had provided anti-Powers votes among four new wards, in each of which Italians were a minority.

SOCIAL ORGANIZATION

Italians who in Italy had never thought in terms of cooperation with other towns or provinces found in the United States that they could solve their problems only by joining together. They modified familiar institutions, such as the church, and adapted others that had scarcely touched their lives in Italy, such as the press and mutual-benefit societies, and still others that did not exist at all, such as the immigrant banks.

Native-born Americans often mistakenly assumed that the immigrant neighborhoods and their institutions attempted to reproduce the European environment, but these colonies in fact took important steps away from Old World patterns. The American cities did not allow for insularity; outside influences were unavoidable and the communities, far from being Italian in character, effected a transition from Old World to New World ways.

Mutual-Benefit Societies Mutual-benefit societies were certainly not transplanted institutions. In southern Italy the family provided all the aid in time of need; clubs were few, small, and strictly social. In the United States voluntary associations provided insurance and every welfare service, from aiding newly arrived immigrants to dealing with sickness, loneliness, and death. Such organizations had existed in the United States before the Italians arrived, apparently modeled on the English friendly societies. They became more social and fraternal in character, filling social and psychological needs for those uprooted from familiar surroundings and life patterns. The practice of passing the hat for members in trouble guaranteed help at minimum expense to all concerned.

Members contributed between 25 and 60 cents a month so that the benefit society would look after them when they were sick and bury them when they died. Regulations required members to attend funerals for fellow members or pay a fine—each member was thus assured not only proper burial but a well-attended service. Societies also paid stipends in the event of sickness or accident. To attract and hold members, they expanded their services from basic benefit functions to include recreational and social activities, picnics, dances, and religious celebrations as well.

At first, the societies recruited members on the basis of native town or province; these early groups were small, poor, and usually short-lived. New groups sprang into existence only to go bankrupt. At the turn of the century the Italians in Manhattan were supporting over 150 of them. In time small units combined or merged with larger ones, and Italian heritage rather than any specific town or region became the basis for membership. The largest and most influential Italian organization in the country, the Order of the Sons of Italy in America, started in New York City in June 1905. By

1921 the Sons of Italy had 125,000 members in 887 lodges all over the country.

Mutual-aid society membership was purely voluntary. The societies did not operate on sound actuarial principles and could not really be called insurance companies. They met their obligations by assessing their members the amount required for a given circumstance. When a death occurred and the society's cash on hand was inadequate, each member contributed a set amount to pay for the funeral. The same system served for sick benefits or other costs. For young, vigorous members this was an inexpensive way to provide insurance, but as the age structure moved upward and the mortality rate climbed, the societies had to either cut benefits or increase assessments. The Sons of Italy and other regional and national organizations eventually adopted the actuarial practices of insurance companies to solve the problem. The rest simply went out of business.

Press The immigrant press remained vital only so long as the Italian-American community needed its services. The newspapers saw themselves as an indispensable ally, offering newcomers, in the words of the journalist Luigi Carnovale, "Wise advice, moral and material assistance, true and ardent fraternal love—for their success and triumph" in a new world. Italian-language journals no doubt eased the first critical years of adjustment to the United States. News of events in Italy, especially the hometown and province, news of other immigrant communities and societies, and listings of collections for needy newcomers written in the native tongue helped Italian Americans feel more at home. Information about local and national events, emphasis on the importance of education and the benefits accruing from participation in politics, and advice about how to behave in a way acceptable to the native-born helped them fit into an American and urban world.

The first Italian-language newspaper in the United States was *L'Eco d'Italia* (f. 1849), a weekly printed in New York City. It lasted only a brief time, as was true of nearly all the Italian publishing ventures in New York and other cities before 1880. San Francisco's large and prosperous Italian colony supported the semiweekly *L'Eco della Patria* (f. 1859), which appears to have been the first Italian paper to sell advertising. In 1872 it was absorbed by *La Voce del Popolo* (f. 1867), which in 1943 was itself absorbed by *L'Italia* (f. 1889), which is still published in San Francisco.

After 1880 the expanding immigrant population encouraged the growth of the press. In Chicago alone at least 20 Italian-language newspapers appeared during the years between 1880 and 1921. The most popular and influential were *L'Italia* (f. 1886) and *La Tribuna Italiana Transatlantica* (f. 1898). By 1921 *L'Italia* had more than 38,000 subscribers; *La Tribuna*'s circulation was 25,000. The country's leading Italian-language newspaper was *Il Progresso Italo-Americano* (f. 1880) in New York City. Founded by a former padrone, Carlo Barsotti, *Il Progresso* soon expanded its influence and readership far beyond New York, and by 1921 it had 110,000 subscribers all over the country.

Small but nationwide in circulation and influential in their particular spheres were radical papers such as *Il Proletario* in New York (1896–1920) and newspapers published by religious groups, such as *La Fiaccola*

(f. 1898) founded by the Methodist Book Concern in New York City and converted to a monthly magazine in 1921.

The American press profoundly influenced the foreign-language papers with innovations such as large, bold headlines, brief articles, special features, photographs, and cartoons. Although successful Italian-language papers often started as journals in the European style, they soon began to adopt American fashions in content and format and to feature sensational news stories—often translated from the English-language press. Unsuccessful newspapers were generally those that did not adjust, or did not last long enough to adjust to the American style. The Italian-language press often suffered the disastrous effects of technological changes. The new equipment and high labor costs needed to compete forced small and generally unremunerative papers of the pre–World War I era to merge into larger units with greater purchasing power. Because they could not afford to pay good salaries, nearly all faced a shortage of competent reporters. Reporters for even the largest papers had to supplement meager wages with subsidies from the Italian consul, who expected them in return to print stories showing the policies of the Italian government in a favorable light.

Newspapers regularly lost readers as the immigrants were absorbed into the larger society. American-born children preferred to read English-language papers, and even the foreign-born turned to them for general news as soon as they learned enough English. The foreign-language papers, written simply and idiomatically in a mixture of Italian and English, unintentionally aided this adjustment to the profusely illustrated and simply written popular American papers.

The Italian-language press functioned as guide, coordinator, and promoter of Italian national pride. It served as an intermediary between the immigrant and his new homeland, between life in the Italian village and life in the cities of America. Within the Italian neighborhoods it provided a voice for people to make demands and raise complaints, but outside the immediate community it had no influence at all.

Church For Italians the Roman Catholic Church has always been an integral part of life, but in America they found it a cold, remote, puritanical institution, controlled and often staffed, even in Italian neighborhoods, by the Irish. Italians, whether devout Catholics or not, resented the Irish style and domination of the local church and early demanded their own priests and control of the churches in their communities. Some Italians were disaffected by the church's opposition to the unification of Italy and by its refusal to recognize the kingdom that had annexed the papal states. By 1900 disaffection was so intense that many Catholics doubted the church had any future at all among Italians in the United States.

The Protestants took advantage of the situation to seek converts. They openly supported the Italian kingdom and denounced papal intransigence. Methodists, Baptists, and Presbyterians financed 326 churches and missions in Italian neighborhoods with more than 200 pastors; they printed newspapers, books, articles, pamphlets, and leaflets in Italian and English. Protestant settlements and missions, evangelizing social workers, public-school teachers, and ministers lent

their assistance, but despite their costly and prodigious efforts, few Italians converted, and those who did usually joined congregations outside the ethnic neighborhoods.

Although most immigrants remained more or less loyal to Catholicism, the form it took differed from that of other Catholic groups. Irish and Polish Americans regarded Catholicism as an integral part of their nationalist cause; for Italians, at least until the concordat of 1929, nationalism and Catholicism were opposing forces. Nevertheless, although they raged against the church both in Italy and in the United States, they supported their Italian church against Irish usurpers and Protestants.

The images and superstitions, the festivals, processions, and feasts that were part of the daily religious life of an unlettered immigrant seemed to the sophisticated more pagan than Christian. The Italians saw these customs as basic to worship and to the maintenance of tradition. Some of the religious celebrations, like the Feast of San Gennaro on Manhattan's Lower East Side, are still held annually. What critics interpreted as a falling away from the church was in part simply an adaptation of old habits to new conditions and in part an effort to counteract the Irish influence that seemed to make the church impersonal and rigid.

To hold on to the immigrants and their children, the Catholic Church in the United States offered a variety of functions and services unknown to the homeland village, including missions, lay societies, and Sunday schools. The most significant manifestation of the effort to maintain the allegiance of its Slavic and Italian immigrants was the establishment of national parishes. The church intended these parishes to fill the needs of non-English-speaking newcomers and to aid the immigrants in adjusting to their new homeland. But in addition this system forced newcomers from different localities in Italy to forget or suppress Old World prejudices against people from other towns or provinces. They learned that Italians of any origin were closer to one another than to alien coreligionists.

Although each community institution or organization—press, mutual-aid society, church, immigrant bank, and labor agent—served vital functions during the early stage of immigrant adjustment, only the church escaped the decline that set in as the Italians and their children turned to newspapers, insurance companies, banks, and trade unions in the larger community. The national parish formed part of a larger international organization that was flexible enough to fill the needs both of the new immigrants and of long-time residents. When Italians moved, they simply left one national parish for another, often in the suburbs. Second- and third-generation Italian Americans regarded the church as the only remaining useful traditional institution. In the new neighborhoods it had much the same form as it had in the old. In the new neighborhoods, services were conducted in English instead of Italian, but in either case the liturgy was in Latin, and the ritual and vestments were as they always had been.

Some immigrants never expanded their loyalty or interest beyond their home village—even the kingdom of Italy remained outside their comprehension; others gradually joined the Italian-American group; still others, usually those who had arrived as children and

consciously cultivated the new habits and speech, used immigrant churches, journals, and societies as guides to American customs and ideas.

Education Italian immigrants had a reputation for denying their children adequate schooling. Although aware that their own lack of education kept them from getting better jobs, they still did not hesitate to send their offspring out to work at an early age. Between 1899 and 1910 southern Italians in the United States had among the highest illiteracy rates of all the southern and eastern European groups. Of a total of 1,690,376 who were 14 years of age or over when they came, 54 percent were illiterate, as compared with only 11 percent of northern Italians. When compulsory-education laws were passed, most Italians eventually complied with them, but they secured jobs for their children after school hours. In any case, the children could leave school by age 14 if they had a work permit. Just before World War I, less than 1 percent of Italian youth were enrolled in high school, although 73 percent of the children were enrolled in the primary grades. For an unsophisticated village family, the immediate advantages of a paying job were simply more obvious than the long-range profits of an education. Italian children, especially those whose families spoke English poorly or not at all, often left school because they were unhappy.

Most parents sent their children to public rather than parochial schools. The Italian-language press discouraged parochial education, as did Italian nationalists, who joined Protestant liberals and socialists in viewing it as a form of institutionalized thought control. But for the average immigrant, expense and inconvenience determined the choice. Although they may have preferred to have their children attend a parochial school, where they would receive religious training and learn the Italian language, they balked at paying tuition. Already convinced that the children should be out working and contributing their share to the family budget, an Italian parent was not eager to compound the loss by paying for their schooling. The parochial schools most often served parents who thought their children needed discipline—the sisters had a reputation for being able to control the incorrigible.

Eventually Italian parents began to recognize the value of an education. They took advantage of adult-education programs offered at the Young Men's Christian Association and the public schools. The settlement houses maintained all sorts of clubs, provided lessons in English and citizenship, and offered music lessons, gymnasium facilities, arts and crafts classes, concerts, lectures and forums, festivals, pageants, and dances. Many kept libraries and study rooms; the large ones had playgrounds, camps, and vacation resorts. The change in attitude toward education that resulted from these activities was sometimes apparent among the immigrants who went back to Italy: improving the village school was a typical project for returning expatriates. By 1920 the American public school was regarded as a vital link between the newcomer and his acceptance in the new land.

FAMILY AND KINSHIP

Most of the immigrants came from preindustrial, rural regions, and the problems they faced when they immigrated were essentially those of adjusting from

country to city life. Americans of many generations faced similar difficulties as they, too, left the farms and moved into the industrial cities.

In Italy the social structure of the rural village was founded on the family, whose interests and needs determined an individual's attitudes toward church, state, and school. Each family member was expected first of all to uphold family honor and to fulfill his or her particular duties and responsibilities. The father was the interpreter of all needs and interests and maintained his authority with strict discipline. The mother, although subordinate, had a voice in family decisions and mediated between the father and the often numerous children.

Children were given responsibility at an early age. Children, especially boys, were regarded as economic assets. Wages were turned over to the father, so the more sons, the more money was brought in. Daughters did not work, but prepared for marriage at home. Children were expected to accept the mates chosen by the parents from among the eligible young of the village, but once married they were allowed to establish separate households. Envy and suspicion often governed attitudes toward everyone outside the immediate family, including more distant relatives. One turned to relatives only in desperate need; it was not prudent to trust kinsmen completely. Most of the people in a southern Italian village might be related to one another, but still a sense of community did not exist.

In the United States parents wanted family life to continue in the traditional fashion, but the children wanted to behave in the American way. As the young became fluent in English, roles and relationships slowly began to alter. The children understood—or sometimes just thought they understood—the world in which they lived better than the parents, and this gave them a voice in family affairs. Dependence on the children was especially difficult for the father to accept, because it deposed him as head of the household. Gradually the children began to break entirely away from parental control.

Sons had always been allowed some freedom of action as befitted their role as future patriarchs, but daughters, too, acquired independence, largely out of economic necessity, and that troubled parents. A study in New York City in 1919 found that 91 percent of the girls over 14 years old in Italian families were working for wages. The pay envelope gave a girl an independence completely unknown to her counterparts in Italy.

The immigrants who came to the United States as children and raised their own families in the new land married somewhat later than in Italy and chose their own mates, although parental consent was sought. With rare exceptions, marriage remained within the Italian group, although of necessity the field was enlarged from native village or province to all of Italy.

Among the second generation, marriage to non-Italians and even to non-Catholics, was increasingly common, especially among the prosperous. Professionals, merchants, policemen, and others in public employment sometimes married women of Irish, German, Polish, Jewish, Scandinavian, or English background. Because of their more sheltered upbringing, Italian-American girls were less likely to meet and marry outsiders than their brothers, though work ex-

panded their range of choices as well. The majority of marriages, however, remained within the group.

Both generations adapted to the American urban experience in various ways. Some abandoned Old World ways entirely, intending to assimilate in as short a time as possible. They moved from the Italian neighborhood, learned English, and in many instances, changed the family name. This group was a minority in the first two generations—at most a quarter of the total—and tended to include the better educated and more ambitious. Others, who stuck tenaciously to Old World ways, were usually part of the working class and lived in an Italian neighborhood, with the children close to the parental home. They too represented a minority.

The vast majority represented a little of both. Although the second generation adjusted to American ways, they did not repudiate their past altogether. The children moved out of the old neighborhood and away from the parents and forgot most, but not all, of their Italian. Ignoring pressures from their parents to produce numerous grandchildren, they had small families. Though the family remained essentailly patriarchal, the second-generation husband was less rigidly authoritarian than his father and freer in his relations with his children, and the wife was less submissive and less dependent. She was also somewhat better educated and often had held a job before marriage. Her daughters enjoyed still greater freedom. Parents in the United States worried about the future of their offspring in ways quite unknown to families in southern Italy. They were no longer expected to select their children's marriage partners. The family had become subordinate to the interests and needs of its individual members.

CULTURE

The standard language of Italy is based on the Tuscan dialect, and by the end of the 19th century all educated and cultivated people spoke and wrote the standard language. The poor, however, knew only what they had learned at school, and most immigrants had had little education. Many arrived knowing only the dialect of their region. In the United States immigrants from one area of Italy could not understand their new neighbors from another area; they were reduced to speaking a mixture of the little standard Italian they knew, combined with words from one or another of the dialects and from English. The result was a new Italian-American language, with much of its vocabulary composed of Italianized English words. Some words had no Italian equivalent, or one that was unknown to the immigrants: thus they said *visci* for whiskey, *pichnicco* for picnic, *ghenga* for gang, *grosseria* for grocery, and *morgico* for mortgage. Some were common English words that simply drove out their Italian equivalents: *stritto* for street, *loya* for lawyer, *storo* for store, and *carro* for car. Some were Italian words whose meanings were corrupted by a smiliar-sounding English one: *rendita*, Italian for income, in Italian-American means rent; *sciabola* changed from saber to shovel, and *genitore* from parent to janitor. Over the decades Italian-American underwent changes as some words dropped away, the meanings of others altered, and new words came into use. This new Anglicized Italian was almost solely the language of the immigrant generation. The American-

born did not bother to learn it, and Italians in the homeland would not have understood it.

The Italian-language press used this dialect, but as immigration declined in the 1920s, so did the circulation of the newspapers. By the 1930s radio, which also used an Americanized Italian, was a successful competitor for providing news of the homeland and the local community for the small but steady stream of new immigrants to the United States, and it also had the advantage of providing other forms of entertainment: drama, comedy, and music. Arias and overtures from favorite Italian operas and popular folk songs took up approximately 70 percent of all Italian-language radio time.

For festivals and other special days, immigrants dressed in their colorful native costumes and danced the folk dances of southern Italy. But otherwise they adopted local dress, dancing, and behavior, and quickly learned to ridicule the recently arrived "foreigners." They remained more loyal to their cuisine. Although many Italian dishes later became American favorites, at the turn of the century Italians who insisted on eating macaroni and drinking red wine were regarded as not yet American. Their traditional kitchen withstood Americanization, however, and the production of or import from Italy of olive oil, spaghetti, artichokes, salami, and other foodstuffs provided an important part of the neighborhood economy. The immigrants craved their Old World dishes in part because it was only in the New World that they could begin to afford them. The traditional diet of the southern Italian peasants consisted largely of cornmeal, bread, pasta, a few vegetables, and some fruit. Only on special occasions could they afford meat or chicken. In America poor immigrants began to enjoy an Italian diet that was abundant, varied, and rich.

The urban culture of the new land offered Italian immigrants a wide variety of entertainment unknown to their rural past, including plays and vaudeville performances, puppet and marionette shows, and the opera. By the 1930s there was available a large and growing number of novels, poems, and other works describing and explaining their immigrant experience. Amateur theatrical clubs began in the 1880s, and their popularity encouraged professional actors to migrate to the United States. Antonio Maiori, the most important early figure in the Italian ethnic theater, came to New York in 1892 and was the star of the Italian-language theater from 1898 to the beginning of World War I. His specialty was Italianized adaptations of Shakespeare's plays; his two most successful roles were as Hamlet and Othello. Although legitimate theater had some first-rate performers, it was never as popular as vaudeville. The comedian Eduardo Migliacco, whose stage name was Farfariello, or Little Butterfly, specialized in character sketches, which he wrote as well as performed, drawn from life in New York's Little Italy. These acting troupes also went on tour. San Francisco had its own Italian theater, although it was never as successful as in New York. In other cities professional Italian theater generally appeared shortly after 1900, reached a peak of popularity around 1914, and dwindled in the postwar years along with the immigration from Italy. New York City continued to receive most of the new immigrants, and Italian theater remained active there into the 1950s.

Music halls had an even greater appeal for Italian Americans than the legitimate or popular theater. A theater ticket cost from 10 to 50 cents, but the music halls were free—their substantial profits came from the sale of liquor. Customers flocked to them for their Neapolitan songs and dances.

Opera, a popular art form in Italy, was popular with the immigrants as well, and unlike the music halls, it generated an appeal far beyond the Italian community. From the 1880s, when the Metropolitan Opera House opened in New York with Cleofante Campanini as its first conductor and director, until today, Italians have been prominent in opera in the United States and elsewhere in the world. Some artists came and went as visiting stars; others, like Giulio Gatti-Casazza (1869–1940), the general manager of the Metropolitan Opera from 1908 to 1934, and Ezio Pinza (1895–1957), an opera basso who in his last years started a new career as a Broadway musical star, stayed; still others, like the sopranos Anna Moffo and Rosa Ponselle (1897–) were American-born. Italians, most notably the conductor Arturo Toscanini (1867–1957), also made brilliant careers in serious music outside opera. Italian Americans, among them Russ Colombo, Frank Sinatra (1915–), Dean Martin (1917–), and Tony Bennett (1926–), have also enjoyed great success as entertainers.

Italian immigrants and their descendants have produced a sizable body of literature about the immigrant experience. Some books have been aimed at an exclusively Italian audience; others have reached a larger public. Arturo M. Giovannitti (1884–1959), who was born in southern Italy, won wide critical acclaim for his collected poems *Arrows in the Gale* (1914), written during a term in prison for his labor-organizing activities growing out of the Lawrence, Mass., textile strike of 1912. Jerre Mangione (1909–) expounded on the theme of Old and New World cultures in conflict in his portrait of Italian-American family life, *Mount Allegro* (1943). Pietro di Donato's (1911–) novel, *Christ in Concrete* (1939), became a best seller and later a motion picture; it described the suffering of an immigrant family in an American slum. The works of other talented writers, including Jo Pagano, John Fante (1909–), Guido d'Agostino, and Michael de Capite, did not enjoy the same wide audiences, and Mario Puzo's beautifully written and insightful *The Fortunate Pilgrim* was overshadowed by his popular novel, *The Godfather*, which became a bestseller and a profitable film.

THE POST-IMMIGRATION ERA

World War I cut sharply the numbers of newcomers from overseas. Italian immigration declined from 283,738 in 1914 to 49,688 in 1915 (the first full year of war) to 5,250 in 1918, ending the constant stream of newcomers into the Italian-American communities. The smaller supply of cheap labor, combined with wartime manpower demands, offered those already in the country wider job opportunities at higher wages than ever before. Large-scale Italian immigration resumed after the war, but it was almost immediately blocked again by restrictive legislation in the 1920s. The Immigration Act of 1924 assigned to Italians a yearly quota of only 3,845.

The case of Nicola Sacco (1891–1927) and Bartolomeo Vanzetti (1888–1927) illustrated the tensions that

had led to this legislation. Americans saw untrammeled immigration and the radicalism it was said to import from abroad as twin dangers, and the Sacco and Vanzetti case seemed to prove the point. The two immigrant anarchists, accused of robbing and killing the paymaster of a shoe factory and his guard in South Braintree, Mass., on April 15, 1920, were tried for murder and found guilty, a decision many believed was based more on their foreign birth and alleged anarchist beliefs than on the evidence. The presiding judge, Webster Thayer, boasted to his golfing companions that he had "done in" the "anarchist bastards," and during the trial he permitted the prosecuting attorney to make radicalism the cornerstone of his case. After numerous delays and despite the pleas of many concerned Americans, Sacco and Vanzetti were executed on August 23, 1927. Supporters of the two men never lost hope that they would be exonerated.

The Italians, along with more recently arrived immigrant groups, profited from the general prosperity bred by a wartime economy and the booming twenties, and this comparative affluence brought self-esteem to the Italian-American community. Combined with immigration restrictions, it also helped disperse the Italian neighborhoods. The comparatively modest economic gains of the 1920s were significant to the people involved. A comparison of occupations in New York City in 1916 and in 1931 showed Italians moving away from jobs as unskilled laborers. Fifty percent were employed as laborers in 1916; 31 percent just 15 years later. Increasing numbers of Italians worked as chauffeurs, clerks, mechanics, carpenters, salesmen, painters, and plasterers. Italian women dominated the garment industry; during the 1920s they displaced the Jews as the largest single group in the needle trades. By 1937, according to International Ladies Garment Workers Union president David Dubinsky, immigrant and second-generation Italians in the union numbered about 100,000 out of a total membership of 250,000 in the New York area.

Political patronage continued to provide benefits for loyal Italian voters, but organized crime became an even more lucrative source of income, thanks to the Eighteenth Amendment and the Prohibition Enforcement (Volstead) Act, which went into effect on January 16, 1920. Supporters of the Eighteenth Amendment had predicted that Prohibition would usher in a new era of "clean thinking and clean living," but the noble experiment instead provided quite different opportunities. The Capones, O'Banions, and Lanskys set about building the illegal liquor trade into a lucrative business.

The association of Italians with crime was not new. Long before Prohibition, the Italians had been plagued by their identification in the public mind with the Mafia. In southern Italy and Sicily secret criminal societies like the Mafia were part of the fabric of life, and like any other newcomers to the United States, the immigrant criminals were eager to re-create their familiar institutions and traditions in the new land. Transplanting the Mafia to the Italian districts of American cities proved not to be so simple. The constant and heavy turnover of residents prevented the formation of a stable community, and the Mafia and similar criminal societies could thrive only in a static environment. Mafia leaders had not even wanted to move to the

United States, but in the 1920s the Fascists forced many of them out of the country, and they headed for the United States for the same reason that everyone else did—they expected to get rich quicker there.

But while American awareness of Italian immigrant criminals was limited to the activities of Black Hand extortion gangs and tales of Mafia blood oaths, the bootleggers, whether Italian- or American-born, grew up as products of the American urban environment. They had little desire to associate with the immigrant criminals and were not averse to eliminating them when they got in the way. While the attention of the public was distracted by Black Hand bomb-throwers and the like, these young men quietly entered the world of illicit liquor, gambling, prostitution, narcotics, and extortion. The experience they gained and their contacts with politicians, the police, and fellow criminals served them well.

Although Prohibition had launched Italian Americans in entrepreneurial crime, repealing it did not reverse their fortunes. Gambling, narcotics, prostitution, and business and labor racketeering formed the basis of their profitable enterprises. Syndicate leaders loosely patterned their organizations on those of the legitimate business world and made entrepreneurial crime an avenue to prosperity for the American-born generation. Loyalty and cooperation were essential in the competitive world of American syndicate crime, and its leaders played an important role: Frank Costello, Charles "Lucky" Luciano, Frank Lazia, Al Capone, Joe Adonis, and John Torrio were in their way innovators and experimenters. The institutions and procedures they and their associates set up in cities throughout the country provided the framework within which criminal syndicates functioned thereafter.

Italians had few political successes comparable to their spectacular gains in syndicate crime. The most successful Italian-American politician was Fiorello H. La Guardia. Born in Greenwich Village of an Italian father and a Jewish mother, La Guardia was raised in Arizona. In 1914 he won his first elective office, a seat in the U.S. House of Representatives as a Republican from a traditionally Democratic district. He was elected in 1919 to the presidency of the Board of Aldermen of New York City, the most important elective position that any Italian had won in a major American city up to that time. Two years later La Guardia ran unsuccessfully for mayor, but the following year he regained the seat he had earlier held in Congress, which he kept from 1923 to 1933. Then he returned to New York and ran for mayor again—this time successfully—remaining in the post for the next twelve years. Two contemporary Italian Americans also served as mayors: in 1931 Angelo Rossi (1878–1948), son of Genoese immigrants, was elected in San Francisco and held office until 1944. Robert S. Maestri, son of an Italian father and a French mother, was mayor of New Orleans from 1936 to 1946.

A close and mutually beneficial alliance was formed between the urban political machines and the underworld organizations. In exchange for a free hand in operating houses of prostitution, saloons, and gambling halls, their operators helped get out the vote on election day and kept the opposition away from the polls by intimidation, bribery, violence, and trickery. A number of Italian politicians based their successes on connections

with organized crime, often controlled by men with whom they had grown up and gone to school. When they sought political office, their underworld friends could be useful contacts; gangster-controlled votes held the balance of power in many wards.

In the 1920s events in the homeland attracted the attention, and for some the admiration, of Italians in the United States; Benito Mussolini was a popular topic in the Italian-language press. Catholics approved of his efforts to bridge the chasm between the Vatican and the Italian government. The concordat known as the Lateran Treaty of February 11, 1929 (by which the Church recognized the Italian government and the occupation of Rome in exchange for acceptance of the sovereign status of Vatican City, indemnities, and recognition of Catholicism as the state religion) was greeted with wild enthusiasm by Italian Americans. Middle-class and working-class Italians differed on a number of issues, but Fascism was not one of them—they were united in their admiration for Mussolini, who seemed to have provided Italy with an ideal government. They also supported and glorified Fascist Italy, partly because they thought it was winning American admiration and partly because they took pride in Italy's position as an international power.

Enthusiasm waned, however, as the repressive aspects of the regime became more apparent. A group of distinguished Italians who arrived as exiles in the 1930s attested to increasingly repressive government methods. This group included, along with Toscanini, historians Gaetano Salvemini (1873–1957) and Giuseppe Borgese (1882–1952), former Italian foreign minister Carlo Sforza (1872–1952), virologist Salvador Luria (1912–), journalist Max Ascoli (1898–1978), literary historian Renato Poggioli (1907–1963), and physicists Enrico Fermi (1901–1954), Emilio Segre (1905–), and Bruno Rossi (1905–).

The thirties were a time of conflict within Italian-American communities between the loyal supporters and the growing number of opponents to Mussolini's Fascism. The battle raged in the press, on the radio, in the meetings of Italian organizations, and occasionally in the streets. But despite lavish outlays of money and extensive propaganda efforts by the Fascist government, after 1941 Italian Americans fully supported the American war effort against the Axis powers. Concern about the loyalty of alien Italians in the United States and a reluctance to employ them in war industries soon subsided, and by the fall of 1942 their enemy-alien status had been removed. Of more than 600,000 Italian aliens in the United States, only 228 were interned. An estimated 500,000 Italian Americans served in the armed forces; at least 12 received the Congressional Medal of Honor and 10 the Navy Cross.

GROUP MAINTENANCE

After World War II another half-million Italians entered the United States, about 228,000 of them in the decade following the passage of the 1965 immigration law that replaced the national-quota system. The 1970 U.S. Census counted over 4 million first- and second-generation Italian Americans, almost 70 percent in the heavily industrialized and urban Northeast (see Table 5). Italian immigrants and their offspring no longer nec-

Table 5. Regional distribution of Italian Americans, 1970.

Region	Foreign-born	Native-born of Italian or mixed parentage	Total Italian Americans
Northeast	706,940	2,196,732	2,903,672
North Central	150,873	473,026	623,899
South	53,501	228,244	281,745
West	97,219	334,244	431,463
Total	1,008,533	3,232,246	4,240,779

Source: U.S. Bureau of the Census, *Census of the Population, 1970, Characteristics of the Population* (Washington, D.C., 1973), vol. I, pt. 1, sec. 2, 1087–1088.

essarily lived in central-city districts, but they still tended to live in or around major cities. In 1970 nearly 2.3 million resided in only 12 metropolitan areas; 1 million of these in the New York metropolitan area, the rest in Boston, Providence, R.I., Buffalo and Rochester, N.Y., Philadelphia, Pittsburgh, Cleveland, Detroit, Chicago, San Francisco–Oakland, and Los Angeles–Long Beach.

The old immigrant-community institutions fell into disuse. Mutual-benefit societies and the Italian-language press had by the 1960s come on hard times. A survey of more than 300 Italian residents of Chicago's Near West Side found that none of the people interviewed belonged to an Italian fraternal organization and that none read a foreign-language newspaper, nor did anyone else in the family. Many were not even aware of the existence of the two largest Italian fraternal groups: the Sons of Italy and the Italo-American National Union. Only the Catholic Church continued to attract support: almost without exception, residents claimed membership in one of the three Catholic churches in the area, although religious observances appeared to be more common among the older generation than among their children.

The elderly in Chicago still obtained news of events in Italy from Italian-language radio broadcasts and from a monthly paper, *Fra Noi*, put out by a Catholic religious order, which regularly printed a summary page in Italian. During the mid-sixties *Fra Noi* was the only Chicago publication written about and for Italian Americans. Later a weekly, *L'Italia*, with a circulation in 1977 of 6,000, was started. The Italian-language press is somewhat stronger in the East, where Italian immigrants continue to arrive and congregate. Yet only New York's *Il Progresso Italo-Americano*, which has a national as well as a local edition, publishes daily. *Il Progresso*'s circulation in 1977 was 68,637; the next largest Italian-language paper had a circulation of only 14,500.

Italians remain loyal to the Catholic Church, though they do not exert leadership within it in proportion to their numbers. In 1972 more than half of an estimated 21 million Americans of Italian descent were still active Catholics (about 20 percent of the total Catholic population in the country), but there were only nine bishops of Italian background in the entire United States. In contrast, Irish Americans constituted 17 percent of the Catholic Church's membership and provided more than half its bishops. Italians have had to reconcile themselves to Irish domination over the U.S. Catholic Church.

Nonethnic parochial schools, parishes, and church-

sponsored social organizations have raised the incidence of intermarriage with non-Italian Catholics. Intermarriage by Italians in Buffalo, for example, increased from 12 percent in 1930 to 27 percent in 1950 and 50 percent in 1960. Intermarriage among third-generation Italian Americans in the United States was 58 percent in 1963–1964. Even when Italians marry outside the group, however, they tend to remain within the church and choose a mate of either Irish, German, or Polish Catholic background.

As La Guardia's success represented the coming of age of Italian Americans in city politics before World War II, the career success of John O. Pastore (1907–) indicated their acceptance on state and national levels. In 1946 Pastore, whose parents had migrated from southern Italy to Providence, became the first Italian American to be elected governor of a state (Rhode Island), although Charles Poletti and Louis W. Cappelli had been elected lieutenant governors before that time. Pastore was chosen as running mate for incumbent governor J. Howard McGrath in 1944, and within a year he had succeeded McGrath, who had resigned to become U.S. solicitor-general. In 1946 and 1948 Pastore was reelected governor, and in 1950 he was ready to seek national office. Although Italian Americans had served in the House of Representatives at least as early as 1887, when New York's Francis B. Spinola (1821–1892) began the first of his three terms, Pastore was the first Italian American to be elected senator. He remained in the senate from 1950 until his retirement in 1976. Pastore's victories, like La Guardia's, were based on his ability to appeal to Italians and non-Italians alike. As a result of their achievements, no city, state, or national office is beyond the reach of Italian politicians.

Italian Americans have shared fully in the general prosperity that the nation has enjoyed since World War II. Many veterans used the G.I. Bill to finance college educations and take professional training; they obtained jobs in industry or started businesses of their own. A 1963–1964 study of occupational patterns among Italian Americans found that 48 percent of the respondents were employed in white-collar jobs and 52 percent in blue-collar jobs. In contrast, 26 percent of the fathers of the respondents held white-collar positions, 71 percent were in blue-collar jobs, and 3 percent were employed as farmers. Furthermore, Italians in working-class occupations had shifted from unskilled to semiskilled and skilled jobs.

Movement out of the ethnic districts slowed during the 1930s because of the Depression, and during the 1940s because of wartime housing shortages, but by the 1950s the process had accelerated, and the formerly heavy concentration of Italians in immigrant neighborhoods has thinned out. Chicago's Near West Side had an Italian immigrant population of 12,955 in 1920; the same area contained 5,140 first- and second-generation Italians in 1960, and only 1,806 ten years later. The return migration from the suburbs of middle- and upper-income whites, especially young married couples, has played an important role in the breakup of some working-class Italian neighborhoods. In others the Italians have dispersed because of the influx of blacks, Puerto Ricans, and southern whites. Italians regarded these low-income newcomers with much the same apprehension that earlier residents had felt toward Italians; in the case of the blacks, however, prejudice has been tinged with envy and sometimes grudging respect for their effective use of political pressure to gain economic and other benefits.

Political demands by Italian Americans significantly did not include a return to the days of free immigration. The acrimony aroused by the 1924 restrictive quotas was directed against the attitude that Italians were somehow less acceptable citizens than others, as implied by their small quota (3,845), rather than against restrictive measures per se. Even the demands for a larger quota dwindled as the years wore on and finally ended altogether with the enactment of the 1965 law, which gave all nations the same access, with priority to immediate relatives of American citizens and alien residents.

Italian Americans now concentrate on campaigns to eliminate real or imagined social prejudice and ethnic slurs against them and on opening up areas of economic, political, or cultural activity hitherto closed to them. In the American system, benefits accrue through group pressure. During the era of the big-city machines, patronage jobs and other short-term benefits were the rewards of political power. Now that the Italian-American group is moving into the middle class, promises of pick-and-shovel jobs and neighborhood conveniences like bathhouses and small parks have long since lost their attraction.

Perhaps because Italian Americans are no longer subjected to the fierce hostility and prejudice that new immigrants encountered at the turn of the century, they feel free to proclaim their ethnicity and search for their roots. One result has been the formation, in various urban centers, of organizations that in the late 1960s and early 1970s directed rallies and demonstrations to protest the negative Italian-American image projected in television, movies, and newspapers.

Some Italian Americans, particularly in the East, firmly believe that group members are passed over in favor of blacks and Hispanics, who, they feel, are admitted to prestigious institutions or are given jobs for which Italian Americans are better qualified. Italian Americans by and large seem to feel that they have paid their dues and have earned their place in American society.

Bibliography

The most comprehensive general examination of the Italian immigrant experience is Alexander De Conde's *Half Bitter, Half Sweet: An Excursion into Italian-American History* (New York, 1971). Joseph Lopreato, *Italian Americans* (New York, 1970), is a sociological study, and Luciano J. Iorizzo and Salvatore Mondello, *The Italian-Americans* (New York, 1971), emphasizes the experience in small eastern cities. Humbert S. Nelli, "Italians in Urban America" in *The Italian Experience in the United States*, ed. S.M. Tomasi and M.H. Engel (Staten Island, N.Y., 1970), is an interpretive article that contains an extensive bibliographic essay. On Italians in various western states, see Andrew F. Rolle, *The Immigrant Upraised: Italian Adventurers and Colonists in an Expanding America* (Norman, Okla., 1968). Francesco Cordasco and Eugene Bucchioni, eds., *The Italians: Social Backgrounds of an American Group* (Clifton, N.J., 1974), is a selection of articles that focus on the era of large-scale immigration. Although badly out of date both in source material and conceptual framework, Robert F. Foerster, *The Italian Emigration of Our Times* (1919; reprint, New York, 1968), is still the only volume that examines the Old World background and the experience in the various countries to which Italians emigrated.

The more valuable Italian community studies are Thomas Kessner, *The Golden Door: Italian and Jewish Immigrant Mobility in New York City, 1880–1915* (New York, 1977); Federal Writers' Project, Works Progress Administration, *The Italians of New York: A Survey* (New York, 1938); Humbert S. Nelli, *Italians in Chicago, 1880–1930: A*

Study in Ethnic Mobility (New York, 1970); William Foote Whyte, *Street Corner Society: The Social Structure of an Italian Slum,* 2d ed. (Chicago, 1965); Herbert J. Gans, *The Urban Villagers: Group and Class in the Life of Italian-Americans* (New York, 1962); and Josef J. Barton, *Peasants and Strangers: Italians, Rumanians, and Slovaks in an American City* (Cambridge, Mass., 1975).

Topical studies include Silvano Tomasi, *Piety and Power: The Role of Italian Parishes in the New York Metropolitan Area, 1830–1930* (Staten Island, N.Y., 1975); Leonard Covello, *The Social Background of the Italo-American School Child* (Totowa, N.J., 1972); Paul J. Campisi, "Ethnic Family Patterns: The Italian Family in the United States," *American Journal of Sociology* 53 (1948): 443–449; Edwin Fenton, *Immigrants and Unions, a Case Study: Italians and American Labor, 1870–1920* (New York, 1975); Humbert S. Nelli, "The Italian Padrone System in the United States," *Labor History* 5 (1964): 153–167, and *The Business of Crime: Italians and Syndicate Crime in the United States* (New York, 1976); Francis A.J. Ianni, *A Family Business: Kinship and Social Control in Organized Crime* (New York, 1972). On Italians in politics, see Arthur Mann, *La Guardia: A Fighter against his Times, 1882–1933* (Philadelphia, 1959), and *La Guardia Comes to Power, 1933* (Philadelphia, 1965); Samuel Lubell, *The Future of American Politics* 3d ed. rev. (New York, 1965), chap. 4.

Although there is no archive devoted solely to the Italian-American experience, source materials can be found in research centers, historical societies, and libraries in cities where Italians settled in sizable numbers. Among these are the Center for Migration Studies, Staten Island, N.Y.; the Urban History Collection, University of Illinois at Chicago Circle; the Immigration History Research Center, University of Minnesota, Minneapolis; the Chicago Historical Society; the New Orleans Public Library; and the San Francisco Public Library.

HUMBERT S. NELLI

J

JAPANESE

In 1853 American ships under the command of Commodore Matthew G. Perry arrived in Japan seeking trade agreements on behalf of the United States and, in doing so, pierced the barriers that had isolated Japan from the Western world for well over two and a half centuries (1600–1868). These barriers were soon entirely destroyed. The Emperor Meiji, restored to the throne in 1868, reversed the earlier imperial policy of isolation and, in order to increase Japanese trade and consolidate his dynasty's political power, encouraged greater contacts with the West. Most of the earliest emigrants to take advantage of this new freedom of movement went to the Hawaiian Islands, but a handful managed to get as far as the West Coast of the United States. By 1890, 12,000 Japanese had settled in Hawaii and 3,000 on the American mainland, almost all of them in California.

A much greater immigration soon followed. In the next 30 years or so almost 300,000 Japanese emigrated across the Pacific, still primarily to Hawaii and Califor-

Japan

500   Km.   Miles

nia. Although many subsequently returned to Japan, the number remaining was large enough to form what would eventually become the largest Asian ethnic group in the United States. By 1970 the Japanese-American population numbered some 217,000 in Hawaii and 213,000 in California. Another 167,000 Japanese Americans also lived elsewhere on the mainland, but because Japanese have settled outside Hawaii and the West Coast states only in comparatively recent times—largely as a result of the displacements that followed the outbreak of World War II—the story of the Japanese settlement in the United States is largely confined to those two areas.

The earlier Japanese immigrants came from a feudal society that was crumbling under the strain of rapid industrialization, and they sensed that this change in the ancient order of things would bring a better life. At the same time they could not entirely shake off traditional ideas about the nature of society, and they continued to adhere to the Confucian prescriptions of exact, hierarchical social relations, to a rigid code of group cohesiveness, and to the blend of Buddhism and Shintoism developed since the 7th century that taught every Japanese the impermanence of worldly things and the importance of inner discipline.

Because the majority of the first generation arrived between the years 1890 and 1924, each successive generation has been comparatively homogeneous in age, culture, and sociohistorical experience. This homogeneity combined with the Japanese emphasis on filial piety has led Japanese Americans to identify themselves as well as their place in society by the generation to which they belong. They call *Issei* those in the immigrant or first generation; *Nisei*, those in the second; *Sansei*, those in the third; and *Yonsei*, those in the fourth generation.

HAWAII, 1868–1941

The need for laborers in the independent monarchy of Hawaii lay behind the first Japanese immigration to the islands. In 1868 the Hawaiian Trading Commissioner stationed in Tokyo recruited some 150 Japanese to work in Hawaii's sugar plantations, signing them up for a three-year contract. These first emigrants were called the *gannen-mono* or "first-year men," a reference to their departure during the first year of the Meiji era. Recruited from the streets of Tokyo and Yokohama, they were ill-suited for rural plantation life, and from the employer's point of view proved to be less than ideal immigrants. Japanese officials became involved when the workers turned to them with complaints about their living and working conditions, low wages, and the generally alien nature of Hawaiian life. The Japanese officials launched an investigation that did not significantly improve conditions, but it did establish the precedent of emigrants' calling upon the home government for protection. Eventually, most of the gannen-mono were returned to Japan at the planters' expense.

The problems that resulted from this first emigration alerted the Japanese government to the need to sort

through its prospective emigrants and send only those best suited for contract labor. Rather than recruiting vagrants from the streets of Tokyo and other large cities, the government turned to the hard-working laborers of the agricultural prefectures of Hiroshima, Yamaguchi, and Kumamoto. Japan hoped by this effort at "quality control" in issuing passports and visas to select only emigrants most suited for the job, and to avoid becoming the source of supply for cheap labor that China had been in the mid-19th century.

Between 1891 and 1920 the emigration to Hawaii increased enormously. The precise numbers are not known because the new arrivals were not very accurately monitored, nor did all who came stay, but by 1920 the Japanese population of the islands had reached 109,294 (Table 1).

Table 1. Japanese in Hawaii, 1900–1970.

Year	Total population	Percentage Japanese[a]	Number of Japanese[a]
1900	154,001	40	61,111
1910	191,909	42	79,675
1920	255,912	43	109,274
1930	368,336	38	139,631
1940	423,330	37	157,905
1950	499,794	37	184,611
1960	632,772	32	203,455
1970	768,561	28	217,175

Source: U.S. Bureau of the Census, *Census of the Population, 1970*, vol. I, *Characteristics of the Population* (Washington, D.C., 1973), pt. 13, *Hawaii*, table 17, pp. 18–19.

a. Figures are for persons of Japanese "race," including the third and later generations.

By the early 20th century the first objective for the Issei in Hawaii had become *dochyaku*—"to remain on the soil." Ethnic communities resembling Japanese villages by now adjoined the various plantations, community groups had controlled some of the problems of the first transient laborers, and the Japanese Benevolent Association had been established. The Japanese supported the planters' policy of maintaining separate areas for Japanese, Chinese, Portuguese, and Filipino laborers, and the resulting isolation helped to encourage the reproduction of Japanese village life in Hawaii. All social needs from birth to death were taken care of through village institutions and organizations, and Buddhist temples such as the Honpa Hongwanji—the principal Japanese Buddhist sect—had been established in the plantation camps by 1900.

Permanent settlement, the establishment of community institutions, and the increasing numbers of settlers soon made the Hawaii Issei a little bolder. Their leaders began to believe they could apply pressure upon the Hawaiian planters to improve working conditions, and this conviction was one factor that led in 1909 to the first major strike of Japanese sugar workers. The strike for higher wages and better conditions failed in part because the Japanese workers did not have the support of the non-Japanese workers, but it was at least an early experience in united community action. From it emerged the first Japanese-American community leaders, editor Fred Makino (1877–1953) of the Japanese-language newspaper, *Hawaii Hochi* (Hawaii Herald, f. 1912), and the Reverend Taki Okumura (1865–

1951) of the Makiki Christian Church. Makino was an outspoken civic leader and a fiery cultural nationalist. During the 1920s, when the Territory of Hawaii tried to outlaw all Japanese-language schools, Makino's *Hawaii Hochi* successfully protected them from being closed down. The Reverend Mr. Okumura's plan for Issei adaptation was more conciliatory. He urged them to forget Japan and things Japanese and, as a result, was labeled a traitor by some Issei, but his philosophy of accommodation was to have great influence on the thinking of the next generation.

CALIFORNIA, 1869–1941

The first 27 Japanese immigrants to California, later known as the Lost Colony of Wakamatsu (the name of their native prefecture), landed there in 1869 and, led by a European named Schnell, started a settlement just north of Sacramento. It ultimately collapsed as a result of crop failures and other problems, and the settlers left no trace except for a gravestone marked "Okei," a memorial to a 19-year-old girl who was possibly the first Japanese woman to die in this country. Japanese. travelers, students, and diplomats soon began visiting the United States, but these transients were few in number and had little impact.

Beginning in the 1890s, however, the numbers of immigrants grew rapidly. Between 1891 and 1924 a total of 295,820 Japanese immigrants was recorded; additional illegal and unrecorded Japanese filtered in from Canada and Mexico. Not everyone who came stayed, and some entered and left several times, so that the actual number of resident Japanese was somewhat lower than the recorded total. In 1920 the U.S. Census reported 111,010 Japanese-American residents, still mainly Issei, and in 1930, 138,834 (Table 2). West Coast nativists, alarmed by the influx of Japanese that had begun almost immediately after Chinese immigration had been halted, claimed that the country was being overrun by an Asian horde. In fact, however, the Japanese never comprised even as much as 1 percent of the population of California. The highest proportion of Japanese in Los Angeles County, recorded in 1920, was 2.1 percent.

A number of interrelated factors had stimulated this Japanese migration. The primary pull was the need for

Table 2. Japanese in the continental United States and Hawaii, 1870–1970.

Year	Mainland	Hawaii	Total
1870	55	—	—
1880	148	116[a]	264
1890	2,039	12,610	14,649
1900	24,326	61,111	85,437
1910	72,157	79,675	151,832
1920	111,010	109.274	220.284
1930	138,834	139,631	278,465
1940	126,947	157,905	284,852
1950	141,768	184,611	326,379
1960	260,059	203,455	463,514
1970	371,149	217,175	588,324

Source: Romanzo Adams, *The Peoples of Hawaii* (Honolulu, 1933), pp. 8–9; U.S. Bureau of the Census, *Census of the Population, 1960* (Washington, D.C., 1963), vol. 1, pt. 1, p. 145; U.S. Bureau of the Census, *Census of the Population, 1970* (Washington, D.C., 1973), vol. 1, pt. 13, p. 28; U.S. Bureau of the Census, *Census of the Population, 1970*, Subject Report PC(2)-1G, *Japanese, Chinese, and Filipinos in the United States* (Washington, D.C., 1973), p. 1. Figures include Japanese of all generations.

a. Figure for 1883.

cheap labor: on the railroads, in the canneries, in logging, mining, fishing, meatpacking, in the salt-refining industry, and in California's expanding agriculture. In 1909 approximately 30,000 Japanese were working on farms, often in collectives or in labor gangs managed by their own agents. Agriculture proved to be the best avenue for advancement: an individual could begin as an ordinary laborer, progress to contract farming, then to share tenancy and cash leasing, and finally to the outright purchase of land for his own truck farm.

Anti-Japanese Legislation The rapid penetration of the Japanese into the agricultural economy soon provoked legal efforts to curb their ambitions. The mechanism used to accomplish this, and the key to the unequal treatment of the Japanese (and other immigrants from Asia), was their designation as "aliens ineligible for citizenship." Because the law stated that only "free white persons" and those of African descent could be considered for citizenship, the U.S. Supreme Court chose to construe this, in the 1922 *Takao Ozawa* decision, as meaning that foreign-born Japanese should be kept in a permanent-alien status: no Issei was to be permitted ever to acquire U.S. citizenship.

In 1913 the California legislature passed the Alien Land (Webb-Heney) Act which made those aliens who were "ineligible for citizenship" also ineligible for ownership of agricultural property; simultaneously it limited any lease they might hold to three years. Although they could keep any land they already held, the act prevented them from bequeathing or selling it to one another (an amended California Alien Land Law in 1920 introduced still further restrictions). In practice, however, the amount of land owned by Japanese farmers dropped only slightly between 1920 and 1930 because many Issei registered deeds under the names of their children, who were, of course, citizens by birth.

In the towns and cities most Japanese were employed in domestic service—producing the popular image of the Japanese "houseboy"—or ran small curio shops, cafés, laundries, dry cleaners, rooming houses, grocery stores, and barbershops. An interdependent ethnic network connected these enterprises: Japanese rooming houses catered to Japanese customers, relied on Japanese suppliers, and were serviced by Japanese workmen. Restaurants, laundries, and other small businesses participated in similar economic networks. Many of these businesses also catered to other minority groups, especially other Asians. The small family-run business became a cornerstone of Japanese economic strength in urban areas.

The Japanese also employed financial systems such as the *tanomoshi* (literally, "to ask for help"), a mutual-aid group in which individuals would pool their money to form a common fund. Credit, regular savings, interest payments, and investments were all covered by the tanomoshi system. It fostered economic cooperation which in turn strengthened community cohesion. The tanomoshi served the early Japanese immigrants well when banks refused them loans, either outright or by setting prohibitive terms.

As the Japanese businesses began to grow, legislators contemplated other legal restrictions on Japanese enterprise. Legislation proposed by the state of California from 1910 to 1920 included provisions banning foreign-born Japanese from employing Caucasian women, making it illegal for them to inherit land, and making fishing-license fees higher for Asians than for others. In 1914 Attorney General Webb candidly stated the motives behind these measures: "The fundamental basis of all legislation has been, and is, race undesirability. It seeks to limit [the Japanese] presence by curtailing the privileges which they may enjoy here, for they will not come in large numbers and long abide with us if they may not acquire land. And it seeks to limit the numbers who will come by limiting the opportunities for activity here when they arrive." The ominous tangle of legal restrictions based on racial discrimination began to proliferate.

In 1906 a controversy over the segregation of Japanese students in San Francisco schools developed into a dispute of international significance. Although the actual number of segregated students was small, the Japanese government was affronted by the unequal treatment of Japanese in the United States. President Theodore Roosevelt finally had to intercede and convince the school board to rescind its segregation order to avoid an acrimonious confrontation. Japan had just won a war with Russia and was emerging as a world power not to be ignored. By the Gentlemen's Agreement reached late in 1907 between Japan and the United States, the Japanese government consented to use self-imposed quotas to limit its emigration; as a result, the number of Japanese coming to the United States had diminished by a third by 1914 (Table 3). Japanese emigrants began to turn instead to Brazil.

The U.S. Congress in 1924, responding to the public's view that uncontrolled immigration was a danger to social and economic stability, passed an exclusionary law fixing quotas for all immigrants based on their national origins. The Japanese and other aliens ineligible for citizenship were barred from entry altogether. This legislation was a major victory for nativist forces, and it was, not surprisingly, interpreted by Japan as an insult. Japan resented the implication that their emigrants could not be assimilated and the fact that Japanese nationals were denied the possibility of acquiring American citizenship. Japan pointed out also that the law violated the Gentlemen's Agreement, which contained a provision guaranteeing that the United States would not prohibit the immigration of the Japanese. The protest fell on deaf ears.

By the 1920s it was clear to the Issei that they would have to adjust to American life without the benefits and immunities that naturalization provided. Although many expected the Japanese government to negotiate a treaty providing them with civil protections, they soon

Table 3. Japanese immigration to the continental United States, 1861–1940.

Period	Number	Percentage of all immigrants
1861–1870	218	0.01
1871–1880	149	0.02
1881–1890	2,270	0.04
1891–1900	27,982	0.77
1901–1907	108,163	0.77
1908–1914	74,478	1.11
1915–1924	85,197	2.16
1925–1940	6,156	0.03

Source: William Petersen, *Japanese Americans* (New York, 1971), p. 15.

Table 4. Sex distribution of Japanese Americans, 1900–1970 (percentages).

Census year	Male	Female
1900	83	17
1910	78	22
1920	61	39
1930	56	44
1940	54	46
1950	52	48
1960[a]	48	52
1970[a]	46	54

Source: Adapted from "A Study of Selected Socio-Economic Characteristics of Ethnic Minorities Based on the 1970 Census," *Asian Americans,* HEW Publication no. (US) 75-121 (n.d.), 2:25.
a. Includes Hawaii.

found instead that Japanese officials were more concerned with the state of Japan's political and economic relations with the United States than they were with the well-being of its mostly laboring-class emigrants; thus, the Issei turned instead to developing their own resources and institutions.

Social Organization Between 1910 and 1924 the Japanese-American community began to assume a stable and permanent form. The mostly male Issei began to seek wives and raise families: sometimes they returned to Japan to fetch a waiting fiancee or to choose a bride, but more often they sent for "picture brides," so called because the only introduction the couple had before marriage was an exchange of photographs. As the Japanese family took root, the community began to form its network of extensive kinship ties and to raise the next generation of Japanese Americans—in sharp contrast to other Asian groups in California whose immigration until well into the twenties remained predominantly male.

The Japanese communities, realizing that complaints by individuals could easily be ignored but that concerted action by civic groups could be successful in attracting the attention of the public, then began to form their own local protective and educational associations. Because these local organizations had similar structures and functions, a member of a Japanese association in Pocatello, Idaho, who moved to San Francisco could easily fit into a Japanese association there. Association membership was restricted to men, and their leaders were usually those Issei who had achieved the greatest economic success in the community. Holding office was prestigious, and elections were fiercely competitive. The associations raised funds, sponsored picnics, provided interpreters, participated in American patriotic parades, cared for cemeteries, and supplied a variety of social-welfare services. They were especially concerned with upholding the reputation of Japanese as good and loyal citizens, and they functioned as an informal constabulary in the community.

In addition to the Japanese associations, the Issei formed ascriptive *ken* (prefecture) societies, such as the Hiroshima *Kenjinkai* (prefectural group), which included as members all immigrants from that particular region. They organized churches, both Buddhist and Christian, with all-Japanese congregations, religious youth clubs, and women's auxiliaries. They established Japanese-language schools. They formed study and hobby groups for activities such as flower arranging, cooking, martial arts, and fishing derbies.

The Japanese immigrants came to California with attitudes and values that were well suited for life in American society. Most of them were young; they tended to be hard working and efficient, to learn quickly, and to seize whatever opportunities presented themselves. These very qualities, however, were held against them: an editorial in the *San Francisco Chronicle* in 1910 declared that if the Japanese insisted on progressing beyond servile labor and competed with American workmen for better jobs and housing, they would no longer be considered acceptable members of American society. The ending of Japanese immigration and the prohibition on naturalization did little to reduce this antagonism on the West Coast: Japanese Americans continued to suffer discriminatory treatment. They were considered racially unassimilable, loyal only to imperialist Japan, hopelessly alien in religion and culture, and dangerously efficient economic competitors.

The Nisei But the Japanese-American community had reached a new stage. There were now wives and children and a developing ethnic society of great complexity and cohesiveness. All this meant a larger stake in American life. Moreover, the children—the Nisei—possessed one advantage that had been denied their parents: they were U.S. citizens by birth not "aliens ineligible for citizenship." Consequently, Issei parents invested heavily in the future of their offspring, hoping that the advantage of citizenship combined with the support the family could offer would ensure their children's success.

The Nisei used conventional methods for social advancement, and their achievements were solid and enduring. They were brought up to work hard, to conform to community standards, to do their best, to study diligently, and to respect authority. Most of them learned English well and acquired American habits. They were often excellent students: some went on to college, even to graduate school, and a few acquired professional training.

Nevertheless, they remained as much targets of prejudice as their parents before them. Elective and civil-service positions were virtually closed to them, teaching posts in public schools were difficult for them to obtain, and the professionals among them were generally confined in their practice to fellow Japanese. Even in the more tolerant climate of Hawaii, educated Nisei found few opportunities for advancement; on the mainland there were fewer yet. Farming, gardening, small businesses, and service jobs were the usual occupations for Issei and for many of their Nisei children as well, especially during the Depression when jobs were scarce. In the thirties many Nisei college graduates could be found working in fruit stands or as clerks in curio shops or grocery stores, often in the local Chinatown.

In 1929 concern for the limited employment opportunities of Japanese Americans that had been apparent even before the Depression prompted the Carnegie Corporation to fund a major study of educational and occupational opportunities offered to American citizens of Japanese extraction. The three monographs that resulted analyzed data from vocational-aptitude and psychological testing, delinquency and crime rates, demographic, occupational, and educational statistics collected from interviews with 9,690 Japanese living in California. They found that the Nisei themselves were

unsure about the causes of unemployment and their generally low place in American society, were anxious about the changing climate of relations between the United States and Japan, saw their future as insecure, and felt beset by dilemmas and painful choices. How would they make a living? Should they remain in the United States, return to Japan, or emigrate elsewhere? How would they overcome the discriminatory barriers they faced in the job market? The optimistic reported a determination to overcome all obstacles; others seemed to despair of any solution.

The objective findings of the study were encouraging, but they raised grave questions about the extent of discrimination faced by the Japanese. They showed the Nisei were as "bright" as Caucasians as measured by I.Q., their rates of crime and delinquency were low, and their records of achievement in school were extraordinary. The study found that race prejudice, not low achievement, was the fundamental cause of the Nisei's employment problems.

Japanese Americans, citizen and alien alike, faced a battery of hostile civic groups between 1920 and 1941, including special Asian-exclusion leagues, the American Legion, labor organizations, and the Native Sons and Daughters of the Golden West. The Hearst press revived fears of Japanese nationalism and of the "yellow peril" that was first ascribed to the Chinese immigration of the 1870s and 1880s. Japanese immigrants and their American-born children were both depicted as threats to the safety of the nation. Some Nisei, frustrated with their marginal position in the United States, returned to Japan permanently. There is little information about them, but it is probable that they faced many difficult years as aliens in their homeland, although some eventually rose to prominence.

The Nisei prior to World War II were in an untenable situation: they were not accepted by all as Americans and yet they were too thoroughly assimilated to feel themselves to be wholly Japanese. If they worked hard, they were seen as aggressive; if they did well in school, they were seen as too clever; if they attempted to join American organizations, they were accused of "not knowing their place," but if they lived in communities of their own, they were accused of being "clannish." To compensate for this social rejection they, as their parents before them, turned back to the community to develop a protective fabric of ethnic social life.

The Nisei developed organizations separate from the Issei because they had different interests growing out of their American upbringing and reflecting the diversity, acculturation, and complex value system of the group. Their common problems transcended divisions such as ken, religion, politics, and family. The Japanese-American Citizen's League (JACL), founded in the 1920s, was the most influential of the Nisei groups. The local Nisei organizations, whose names almost always included the words "loyalty league" or "citizen's league," were consolidated as the national JACL in 1930.

The Nisei were also active in Protestant, Buddhist, and, to a lesser extent, Catholic churches. But the churches served both generations: a typical Sunday's activities included Sunday school for the very young in English, a sermon for the older Nisei in English, and a service for the Issei in Japanese.

Athletic leagues for the Nisei children were sponsored by organizations such as the YMCA and YWCA, Boy and Girl Scouts, the churches, and other community groups. Since the Nisei were competing against each other rather than against Americans, who were of greater average stature, physical size was not a problem and a Nisei child, too, could become a sports hero. These leagues also gave the young players an opportunity to travel, to plan strategy, to be leaders, and to develop their social skills; dances, bazaars, and other fund-raising activities widened their audience. The Nisei had state and national championships for various sports, and in football the Rice Bowl was played in the San Francisco Bay Area between Chinese and Japanese teams. Although these activities reached their peak in the 1930s, Nisei athletic organizations again became popular in the immediate postwar period. By the 1960s, however, opportunities for participation in the larger society had opened up, and the next generations began to lose interest, though even today Japanese-American athletic leagues remain in California, now drawn mainly from the third and fourth generations.

Nisei organizations, recreation, and social activities were all patterned upon American rather than Japanese models. Although many children attended Japanese-language schools in the afternoons and on Saturdays, the vast majority never learned the Japanese language well. Many Issei parents complained that their children were truant, talked back to teachers, and behaved outrageously in the language schools, although they were models of good behavior in their American schools. A feeling developed among some Issei that the Nisei had rejected their Japanese heritage.

WARTIME EVACUATION, 1942–1945

The Japanese attack on Pearl Harbor on December 7, 1941, set into motion an extremist solution to the "Japanese problem" in California. The long history of anti-Japanese agitation had conditioned the public to believe that Japanese Americans had remained loyal to the Japanese government and were potential subversives. Congressmen, the press, farmers' associations, and patriotic organizations called for the evacuation of all Japanese from the West Coast. Government spokesmen, although they had access to information verifying the loyalty of Japanese Americans and knew that fears of an imminent Japanese invasion were unfounded, did little to allay the anxieties of the public. The Attorney General of California, Earl Warren, later Chief Justice of the Supreme Court, testified before the House of Representatives on February 21, 1942: "Many . . . are of the opinion that because we have had no sabotage . . . none [has] been planned for us. But I take the view that that is the most ominous sign in the whole situation." One congressman from southern California gave his criterion for determining the loyalty of Japanese Americans: any Japanese willing to go to a relocation camp, he said, was a patriot; those who refused proved their disloyalty.

Immediately after Pearl Harbor, a group of "enemy aliens," including over 2,000 Japanese, were arrested by the FBI, and curfew regulations and other restrictions were posted for Japanese-American neighborhoods. On January 19, 1942, the first series of orders by U.S. Attorney General Francis Biddle established security areas along the Pacific Coast from which all "enemy aliens" had to be removed. On February 13 a West Coast con-

gressional delegation wrote to President Franklin D. Roosevelt urging immediate evacuation of all Japanese, both citizens and aliens, from the Pacific Coast states. On February 19, 1942, the president signed Executive Order 9066, which empowered military commanders to remove "dangerous persons" from designated areas and authorized the construction of relocation camps to house them. By August 27 more than 110,000 West Coast Japanese, 64 percent of whom were American citizens, left their homes and were transported to temporary assembly centers, such as the Santa Anita racetrack near Los Angeles. They were then moved to permanent camps in the deserted and barren regions of Tule Lake and Manzanar in California; Poston and Gila River in Arizona; Minidoka in Idaho; Heart Mountain in Wyoming; Granada in Colorado; Topaz in Utah; and Rowher and Jerome in Arkansas, where they were detained behind barbed wire for four years. In 1944 the Supreme Court decision in *Endo* v. *United States* reversed the mass evacuation order, effective January 2, 1945. By the following December all the camps had been closed except Tule Lake which, because of special problems with militants, remained in operation until 1946.

It is impossible to pinpoint any single factor as the cause of the evacuation. Public outrage at the surprise attack on Pearl Harbor, subsequent Japanese advances in the Pacific, and fear of invasion were undoubtedly powerful forces. Farmers and businessmen who feared the competition of Japanese enterprises may have acted out of economic interest. The press and radio, which continuously harped on the Japanese menace, had an inflammatory effect. Political opportunists saw a strong anti-Japanese stand as a potent vote-getter. The federal government also played a crucial role: government agencies informed the public of the threat of a Japanese invasion; high-level administrative problems were left to minor officials to solve; secret meetings were held and untraceable decisions made. Although it is difficult to assess President Roosevelt's feelings about the evacuation, it was he who signed the executive order.

Another factor contributing to the evacuation was the absence of support for the Japanese. Liberals and civil-rights groups found the international effort to defeat Fascism more important than the civil rights of the Japanese American. Even those liberals who offered help seldom questioned the legitimacy of the evacuation; their offers of assistance were aimed at making the experience more humane and comfortable for the evacuated population.

The Japanese themselves were disorganized. They were comparatively few in number and had conflicting points of view concerning the war. Many Issei community leaders had already been incarcerated by the FBI. Most of the Nisei were still young. Their major civic organization, the JACL, eventually took the stand that they should cooperate with the authorities and have faith in the U.S. government, a decision that was unpopular with the more militant.

One element of the Japanese community that became important in the camps were the *Kibei*. The Kibei were also Nisei, but they had been sent to Japan at an early age to be reared by relatives and receive a Japanese education; they usually returned to the United States in their teens. This practice of sending at least one child to Japan for training was common between 1920 and 1941 and was inspired by a preference for the Japanese style of child-rearing and education, a desire to maintain communication with the home country, and pessimism about their children's future in the United States. When war came, 9 percent of the residents in the wartime evacuation centers, or about 9,000 individuals, were Kibei (many others were trapped in Japan when the war broke out). They had been exposed to the nationalism that permeated the Japanese education of the time and found that many of their ideas clashed with those of their Nisei brothers and sisters raised at home. Some of the conflicts in the wartime evacuation centers developed from these Kibei-Nisei quarrels. But the Kibei also influenced many Nisei who had decided that assimilation would never be possible. The pro-Japanese Kibei, along with some Issei and Nisei, deplored the policy of compliance adopted by the JACL, and in the relocation camps several JACL leaders were victims of violence.

Hawaii, despite its large population of Japanese Americans and greater geographical exposure to Japanese invasion, made no comparable effort to incarcerate its Japanese. Individuals suspected of cooperation with Japan were detained at Sand Island, and 900 Japanese aliens eventually ended up in mainland evacuation centers; Hawaii was placed under strict martial law, and ethnocultural institutions such as the Buddhist churches and Japanese-language schools were closed, but no massive relocation of Japanese Americans ever took place.

There were obvious practical reasons for this very different treatment of the Japanese in Hawaii. A proposal to send the 150,000 Japanese to the island of Molokai, then used as a leper colony, raised logistical problems; ships could not be spared to get them there, and neither the economy of Hawaii nor the war effort could have supported the evacuation of over a third of the population. In addition, many Hawaiians were racially mixed and much more accepting of ethnic diversity than Californians, and the commanding general had a more tolerant view of the Japanese than did his West Coast counterpart.

In the camps all Japanese, whether highly educated, wealthy, illiterate, or poor, were housed in barracks, ate mess-hall food, and received the same rates of pay for work—$16 a month for manual labor and $19 for professional work. They used communal toilets, took communal showers, waited patiently in line for everything; they wore identical clothes, and the sun, wind, and dust soon endowed them with the same concentration-camp complexion.

The most difficult problem proved to be the boredom and monotony of camp life; it exacerbated tensions and magnified irritations, resulting in fights, riots, strikes, and even homicides. Inmates complained constantly about the food, their neighbors, living conditions, and camp administrators. Conflicts between the Issei and Nisei added to the strain. Ideological arguments between those loyal to Japan and those who stood with the United States grew heated. The derogatory term *inu* (dog) was applied to those suspected of being spies or government collaborators, and some of the inu were the victims of severe beatings. Soldiers fired into striking crowds at Manzanar and Tule Lake. An Issei who wandered outside the gates at Topaz and apparently did not

understand when he was told to halt was shot dead by a soldier.

Family life was disrupted: the authority of the provider-father and the housekeeper-mother was undercut by government supervision; children ate in mess halls rather than in the family circle. They were stifled in an atmosphere of boredom and stagnation. Gambling became a problem, and petty family quarrels often escalated into violence.

From the beginning of the internment a policy of "resettlement" permitted individuals who passed governmental clearance to leave the camps and settle in areas outside the restricted zones. About 35,000, many of them older Nisei and those of college age, took advantage of this opportunity to move eastward and obtain employment or to enter college in the Midwest and East. Although there was some initial resistance—the liberal mayor of New York, Fiorella La Guardia, did not want Japanese in his area—the large midwestern cities such as Chicago, Cleveland, and Minneapolis were more hospitable.

Another route leading out of the camps was service in the armed forces. The Nisei felt the stinging irony of fighting against Nazi racism for the American way of life while their relatives were held behind barbed wire, and some Japanese refused to enlist in protest against the injustices of the evacuation. But others believed that they could prove their loyalty to the United States by enlisting and distinguishing themselves in war. The record of the 442nd Combat Team and the 100th Battalion composed of 33,000 Japanese Americans from Hawaii and the mainland was unparalleled. The most decorated units in American military history, they suffered more than 9,000 casualties and 600 dead.

The evacuation of over 110,000 West Coast Japanese showed that wartime exigency could be more compelling than constitutional guarantees: it was initially upheld by the Supreme Court in rulings in the *Hirabayashi, Yasui,* and *Korematsu* cases. By narrowly focusing on the issue of whether or not relocation was based on an official policy of racial discrimination, the Court avoided judgment on this massive invasion of civil rights. Finally, the Court found in 1944 in the case of *Endo* v. *United States* that the detention in relocation centers of persons whose loyalty was not at issue had in fact been unconstitutional. This decision heralded the end of the relocation program. The incarceration of an entire ethnic group without any hearing or any formal charge having been brought against a single member has been described as the worst assault on civil rights in American history.

POSTWAR RECOVERY, 1945 TO THE PRESENT

In the short span of three years, from 1942 to 1945, the patterns of Japanese-American social life were changed. In 1941 almost all Japanese lived along the Pacific; by 1945 they were residing anywhere but on the West Coast. The major questions facing all the Japanese, whether in or out of the camps, was the same: Where should they go? What kind of treatment awaited them? Decisions of where to settle involved practical questions about jobs and housing, as well as apprehension over how they would be received. In addition, because much of what the Issei had was leased, the evacuation had resulted in the loss of homes, farms, and businesses; many had nothing left to return to.

A few had adapted so completely to camp life that they wanted to remain; others were simply afraid to leave the protection that the camps provided; by May 1945, 24 incidents of terrorism against Japanese returning to the Pacific Coast had already been reported. Antagonism toward the returning Japanese also took other ugly forms. In Hood River, Ore., the local American Legion removed the names of 16 Nisei soldiers from the town's honor roll—4 of them had been killed in battle and 10 had been awarded the Purple Heart—and a headline advertisement in the Hood River *Sun* of February 2, 1945, in mocking imitation of the alleged comment of the Japanese envoy in Washington after the bombing of Pearl Harbor, read: "So sorry please, Japanese not wanted in Hood River." But in spite of the many fears and the elaborate plans for resettling in other parts of the country, in the end the overwhelming majority returned to the West Coast, particularly California. By 1950 approximately 85,000 of the 168,000 mainland Japanese had come back there, and by 1960, approximately 157,000 Japanese again lived in that state.

They came home to a different place. Thousands of people from the South and Midwest had been drawn West by the wartime industries, many had chosen to remain, and many more were soon to follow. New migrations of blacks from the South and an ever-increasing Mexican population had led to other kinds of racial tensions. Growing anxiety about the presence of blacks and Mexicans absorbed some of the antagonism formerly directed against the Japanese.

The transition from camp life to civilian life was aided by government relocation offices and by voluntary groups, especially churches. Large numbers of Nisei took advantage of the G.I. Bill to attend college. Gardeners were greatly in demand because of the postwar housing boom and the increasing affluence that allowed people to landscape their homes more elaborately. Young men starting their careers worked as gardeners to finance college educations or to gain supplementary income. Others became professional landscapers or branched out into the nursery business.

This opportunity structure for Japanese Americans was not at first dramatically different from what it had been in the prewar era. Jobs were still difficult to obtain, and civil-service positions were just beginning to open up. But change was nonetheless apparent. Californians voted down a ballot proposition in 1946 that would have permitted the state to take over lands bequeathed by Japanese aliens to their children; in 1952 the Alien Land Law was declared unconstitutional by the State Supreme Court. In the same year the Issei were allowed to become naturalized. Attitudes toward the Japanese American seemed to be more favorable. Their distinguished record in the U.S. armed forces during World War II was a contributing factor; feelings of regret and guilt over Japanese internment were another; that defeated Japan was no longer a military threat was a third. Japanese Americans themselves had changed. Many had lived in the East or Midwest for the first time and had worked in a variety of occupations. They were no longer content with jobs only in the ethnic community or with traditional service occupations.

Hawaii The first breakthrough for Japanese Ameri-

cans in politics occurred in Hawaii. The Japanese in Hawaii had become assimilated in a way very different from that of their countrymen on the mainland. Far from being a small scattered minority in a vast land, they were a numerically dominant group in a multiethnic island society (Table 2). Futhermore, the Japanese in Hawaii lived in a more racially tolerant culture and were geographically closer to Japan, which made homeland influences stronger. Although their early history was marked by discrimination similar to that faced by Japanese on the West Coast, the Hawaiian Japanese after World War II enjoyed a good deal of success and political power.

The postwar years brought unprecedented changes to Hawaii's politics and economy, and the Nisei sought to capitalize upon those changes. Many Nisei veterans in Hawaii took advantage of the G.I. Bill. The efforts of the International Longshoremen's and Warehousemen's Union (ILWU) led to the unionization of the plantations and the improvement of living conditions there. A growing tourist industry in the postwar years produced new jobs and stimulated business expansion. Nisei men and women began filling the ranks of the professions, becoming doctors, lawyers, dentists, teachers, and engineers. Japanese Americans saw their achievements as the reward for wartime sacrifices: they were proud of their dramatic economic progress, their record as law-abiding citizens, and their stable family life. Though some warned that the struggle was far from over, many Nisei took satisfaction in their reputation as a "model ethnic group."

The most dramatic advances for the Hawaiian Japanese came in the political arena. The large Japanese-American population, 37 percent of Hawaii's total in 1950, gave them a clear electoral advantage. By the McCarran-Walter Act of 1952 the Issei obtained the right to become naturalized, and citizenship brought with it the right to vote. This newly enfranchised group, supporting a growing multiethnic coalition of dissident Democrats, gave Nisei politicians an electoral majority. In 1954 the Democratic party, under the leadership of John Burns and a Nisei war veteran, Daniel Inouye, and composed largely of a young generation of Nisei politicians, vaulted into power by taking control of both houses of the territorial legislature. The victory marked the end of conservative, white Republican rule and the emergence of a modern Hawaii responsive to Japanese ethnic ambitions. The Nisei continued to play a major political role after statehood was attained in 1959. In 1962 Spark Matsunaga and Patsy Takemoto Mink were elected to the U.S. House of Representatives and Daniel Inouye to the U.S. Senate. In the next decade Matsunaga joined Inouye in the Senate. By 1974 the governor and the lieutenant governor of Hawaii, George Ariyoshi and Nelson Doi, were both Japanese Americans.

By the mid-1970s about 50 percent of the state representatives and the state senators were Japanese Americans; several Japanese Americans were head of important departments; and the state department of education had become something of a Japanese-American enclave.

The rise to power of the Hawaiian Japanese has caused some anxiety among other Hawaiians. They talk about a Japanese "takeover," an apprehension intensified by the recent flood of tourists and influx of capital from Japan: the purchase of some prominent Waikiki hotels by a Japanese businessman elicited protectionist protests. The success of Japanese-American politicians and the large Japanese vote they command have caused other groups to worry that they may achieve a monopoly on political power.

In the meantime, however, although homeland influences remain strong, the younger generations are forging a new version of ethnicity and cultural pluralism. The Sansei (third generation) and Yonsei (fourth generation) retain some allegiance to Japanese culture, but they more readily see themselves as Hawaiians. The Sansei enjoy Japanese foods, movies, television, and sports such as karate, as do other islanders. The Sansei life is first of all "local"—that is, the one adopted by most island residents. It is a combination of Polynesian, Asian, and Euro-American cultural forms. An international assortment of foods, games, entertainment, song, dance, folklore, beliefs, and daily habits, such as removing one's shoes at the door and eating with chopsticks, are shared by all Hawaii's residents. The Sansei life is a blend of Japanese tradition and cosmopolitan culture, and this removes much of the need for ethnic solidarity.

California Changes in California have proceeded at a slower pace. In the immediate postwar period the chief economic activity of Japanese Americans in urban areas continued to center in small businesses and in service jobs. Since the former evacuees needed homes, appliances, furniture, and practically everything else, real-estate offices, retail stores, and family groceries run by Japanese for Japanese did a lively business. Although many Japanese who returned to reclaim their farms found them run down, their determination to work long, hard hours paid off in rapid land improvement and high levels of productivity. As their earnings accumulated, many reinvested their profits in land.

By now the Japanese-American community includes several generations, extended families, and a variety of occupations and cultural values. The passage of time and the process of acculturation have produced diversity and paradox. It is not unusual to see an elderly Issei talking to her Sansei grandchildren or even her Yonsei great-grandchildren in a Japanese they can barely understand, while Nisei parents help to bridge the gap with a mixture of Japanese and English. Because the few surviving Issei have lived through a lifetime of patient struggle and because they retain some of the values of Meiji Japan, they are more conservative in their customs and behavior; the Nisei remember the difficult early years, but are now enjoying a period of relative affluence; the Sansei are often a product of economic security and have had fewer experiences of discriminatory treatment. Perhaps the most dramatic index of occupational mobility has been the increasing professionalization of the Japanese American. In 1940, 4 percent of Japanese males were classified by the U.S. Census as professionals; in 1960 the figure was 15 percent; and in 1970, 31 percent of U.S.-born Japanese males were in the professional-managerial category. Medicine, pharmacy, optometry, dentistry, and engineering are among the most common professions.

Although its social structure is by now more complex and pluralistic, the Japanese-American community still possesses a vital spirit. The community center in Gar-

dena, a suburb of Los Angeles, for example, serves as a focal point for social activities and civic affairs. At this center, classes are offered in kendo, judo, and other martial arts; all-Japanese Little League baseball and touch football are enthusiastically supported; the highly competitive fishing derbies remain popular; and regular gardening exhibitions are attended by professionals and amateurs alike. The center offers courses in the Japanese language which more and more Sansei are now beginning to attend, and sponsors welfare and counseling activities. Supported by the contributions of community members, the centers are symbols of ethnic pride and common endeavor. But the city of Gardena may be an exception, since most Japanese Americans no longer reside in concentrated ethnic areas.

The Postwar Immigrants Contacts with Japan have grown stronger with a more recent influx of Japanese immigrants. Japanese brides began to arrive from American-occupied Japan in the early fifties: an estimated 25,000 had come by the 1960s. Other Japanese came under nonquota immigration categories. The flow of students, businessmen, consular officials, United Nations representatives, and tourists increased steadily in the 1950s and 1960s. A total of 40,000 Japanese immigrants arrived between 1961 and 1970, and an additional 29,200 between 1971 and 1976.

Most of the recent immigrants have settled into American society without much difficulty. Friends, relatives, and the local Japanese community are often helpful in easing the process of adjustment. Since a small immigration has been spread over a relatively long span of time, community resources have not been unduly strained.

Gardening still serves some new immigrants as a starting point in the job market. The first generations of Issei and Nisei found that contract gardening required little knowledge of English and little social contact, and gardening still offers independence and good wages to newcomers who have no professional skills or capital. But now many new immigrants are professionals, white-collar workers, and skilled laborers.

Japanese businessmen representing Japanese companies form a large transient group, especially in New York and Los Angeles. Americans refer to them as the *Kai-sha*, or Japanese business, crowd. Their major contacts and social life are limited to other businessmen, and they can be seen at clubs, restaurants, and at golf courses, behaving very much as they do in Japan; their lives are classic examples of the sojourning businessman carrying out his temporary assignment in a foreign country. Although they have little contact with most Japanese Americans, their presence keeps the community aware of Japan's importance in world affairs. A growing number of Japanese Americans now also work in American branches of Japanese business firms, even though their chances of rising to the upper echelons are slim. Japanese-based firms seem to prefer to develop their own leadership, or to use Caucasians.

The arrival of people in closer touch with homeland culture has stimulated expansion of Japanese televison in the United States. Japanese-language television stations featuring programs imported from Japan are broadcast in Honolulu, Los Angeles, New York City, and San Francisco; watching them has become an increasingly popular pastime among Japanese Americans.

Group Maintenance The 1970 Census reported sizable groups of Japanese Americans residing in states such as New York (19,794) and Illinois (17,645). Japanese living outside California and Hawaii tend to be dispersed among other ethnic groups, however, and have become more quickly assimilated into the mainstream culture.

But even within the older regions of settlement homogeneity has given way to a bewildering diversity, reflected in a variety of political positions, interest groups, economic roles, and cultural styles. The heterogeneous nature of today's community can be illustrated by the Little Tokyo Redevelopment Project of Los Angeles, built in the early 1970s. The removal of Japanese businesses and the eviction of old people from Little Tokyo caused conflicting reactions among Japanese Americans. Young Japanese-American radicals opposed the project as destructive of an inner-city community. Meanwhile, Japanese-American business groups were vigorously bidding for redevelopment sites; Japanese-American government employees were trying to carry out federal housing policies; Japanese-American policemen and community officials were valiantly working to uphold law and order; and even Japanese businessmen from Japan were negotiating for choice parcels of the redeveloped sites. The traditional consensus of the Japanese-American community was nowhere to be found.

Although they lack electoral power because of their relatively small numbers and although they remain anxious about possible anti-Asian prejudice, Japanese Americans have been elected to high public office in California. Congressman Norman Mineta, the former mayor of San Jose, was first elected to the U.S. House of Representatives in 1972 and continues to serve. S.I. Hayakawa, a retired professor and college president, was elected to the U.S. Senate in 1976; Senator Hayakawa did not receive strong support from the Japanese-American community, however.

The aging Issei and Nisei population poses one of the most poignant social problems faced by the Japanese-American community. The younger generations have begun to abandon the customary practice of caring for elderly parents within the family unit. They have, however, had problems placing them in institutions. Not only do they have to contend with their own guilt and shame for resorting to such a solution, but they find that the elderly have language, food, and cultural preferences that create institutional difficulties. As a result, Japanese-American groups have established special retirement homes for elderly Japanese in areas with a Japanese population large enough to support them. Much of the financing has come from community funding drives, but in more recent times federal support has also been obtained.

Generational stratification is another major contemporary problem. The Sansei absorb the ever-changing mores of an American youth culture that estranges them from their parents. Marriage to a Japanese spouse, the honor of the family name, and filial obligations toward the family and community are not among their first concerns. They now tend to place a higher priority on individual satisfaction than they do on duty toward family or community.

One feature of Japanese adaptation to American life

that persists is the remarkably low incidence of crime, delinquency, and mental illness. Japanese arrest rates reported in FBI statistics were 347 per 100,000 in 1940, 202 in 1950, 187 in 1960, and 656 in 1970. By contrast, the national arrest rate was 462 per 100,000 in 1940, 524 in 1950, 1,951 in 1960, and 3,079 in 1970. Statistics on hospitalization for mental illness reveal that the Japanese also have extremely low rates of psychological disorder and suicide. Factors such as Japanese family authority, community control, group loyalty, and intragroup marriage may be important keys to these low rates of deviance and social disorganization. Although not as important as it once was, the family continues to play a major role in Japanese-American acculturation. Divorce among Japanese Americans is still rare; the U.S. Census shows that the divorce rate was 1.6 percent for both Issei and Nisei in both 1960 and 1970. Fragmentary evidence suggests that more divorces occur among the younger generations, since acculturation has eroded the emphasis on lifetime marriage and reduced the stigma attached to divorce that is so keenly felt by the Issei.

A picture of the modern Japanese-American family can be derived from the 1970 Census. Eighty-six percent of the families included both husband and wife, the same as the proportion for the country as a whole. The percentage of children under six years old (27 percent) was also at the national norm. The size of families was slightly above the national average (3.7 in comparison to 3.5) as was the proportion of extended families (16 percent compared to 12 percent). The mean family income was $13,511 in 1970, among the highest for all ethnic groups, and only 7.5 percent had incomes below the poverty level (compared to the national figure of 11 percent), with the preponderance of low incomes in the 65-years-or-older category. In Hawaii only 2.9 percent of Japanese families had incomes below the poverty level.

A dramatic change in family patterns has been the sharp rise in marriages outside the group since World War II. Antimiscegenation laws which prohibited Japanese and most other nonwhite groups from marrying Caucasians had been in effect in some states from the early years of the century until the late 1960s. Partly as a result, in the first half of the 20th century most Japanese married within their ethnic group. In the 1920s Los Angeles County records show that only 2 percent of marriages involving Japanese involved a non-Japanese spouse. Statistics for more recent years, however, show a rapidly rising rate of intermarriage. Twelve percent of marriages involving Japanese Americans were to non-Japanese spouses in 1948, 14 percent in 1952, 21 percent in 1955, and 23 percent in 1959. In 1971, 47 percent, and in 1972, 49 percent of Japanese-American marriages in Los Angeles were exogamous; data from San Francisco, Fresno, and Honolulu indicate that about 50 percent of recent Japanese-American marriages in those cities were to non-Japanese. While only Japanese females were marrying outside the group in the early 20th century, 45 percent of the intermarriages in 1972 involved Japanese men. The majority of intermarriages were to Caucasians.

These changes in marital patterns reflect increased opportunity for social contact, a weakening of the traditional Japanese family, acculturation, upward social mobility, and changing attitudes toward the Japanese. The trend toward more and more interethnic marriages will no doubt continue.

Social interaction among Japanese Americans is governed by behavioral norms such as *enryo* and *amae*. These derive from Confucian ideas about human relationships and define the dimensions of interaction and exchange between superior and inferior members of a social group. Although these forms of behavior were brought over by Issei immigrants, they still survive in attenuated form among the Nisei and even the Sansei.

Enryo prescribes the way in which a social inferior must show deference and self-abnegation before a superior. Hesitancy to speak out at meetings, the automatic refusal of a second helping, and selecting a less desired object are all manifestations of enryo. Japanese Americans often preface an invitation with "Now don't enryo" when they want the others to accept. Some use enryo as a warrant for insensitive and arrogant conduct toward those beneath them.

Amae behavior softens a power relationship through the acting out of dependency and weakness, and expresses the need for attention, recognition, acceptance, and nurture. A child displays amae to gain the sympathy and indulgence of a parent. A young, anxious-to-please employee in a business firm will act with exaggerated meekness and confusion to give his superior an opportunity to provide paternal advice and treat him as a protégé. Through the ritual display of weakness and dependency, reciprocal bonds of loyalty, devotion, and trust are formed. In this way amae creates strong emotional ties that strengthen cohesion within the family, business organization, and community.

Japanese Americans inherit an almost reverential attitude toward work. Their ancestors struggled for survival in a crowded island country with limited natural resources, and they placed great value on industry and self-discipline. Certain traditional attitudes encourage resilient behavior in the face of setbacks and complement the moral imperative to work hard. Many Japanese Americans are familiar with the common expressions *gaman* and *gambatte* which mean "don't let it bother you," "don't give up." These dicta, derived from Buddhist teachings, encourage Japanese people to conceal frustration or disappointment and to carry on. A tradition that places great value on work and persistence has helped many Japanese Americans to acquire good jobs and to get ahead.

The submerging of the individual to the interest of the group is another basic Japanese tradition, and one that produces strong social cohesion and an oblique style of behavior, one manifestation of which is the indirection or allusiveness of much communication between Japanese; another is the polite, consensual behavior expected in all social contacts. Both are common in Japan and are also visible among Japanese Americans. Today, even third- and fourth-generation Japanese Americans are apt to be seen by others as agreeable, unaggressive, willing to accept subordinate roles, and reluctant to put themselves forward.

There is a danger that the Japanese American may be becoming trapped in a "middleman minority" position. Their progress, if measured by their movement upward, is impressive, but if progress is measured by their distribution at the top, it is less so. Few are in the highest

leadership positions and many are overqualified for the jobs they hold. It may only be a matter of time before some break out of these middleman jobs, but the structural and cultural restraints may prove difficult to overcome.

The history of the Japanese Americans in the United States is one of both resilience and adaptation. Suffering from discriminatory laws and racial hostility in the first half of the 20th century, Japanese Americans were nonetheless able to create stable ethnic communities and separate, but vital, social institutions. Since the end of World War II, with the disappearance of legal discrimination and the weakening of social restrictions, they have assimilated more readily into American society and shown rapid economic progress. Scholars have searched for the key to their remarkable record of adaptation. Some have pointed to the Japanese family, others to a strong group orientation, and still others to Japanese moral training; all of these theories often tend to overemphasize the degree to which Japanese traditions have been maintained. Japanese Americans have displayed a pragmatic attitude toward American life, much as earlier Japanese in the homeland adopted elements of Chinese and Indian culture, reconciled Buddhist and Confucian tenets with their native Shintoism, and finally adopted Western ways. Rather than rigidly maintaining their traditions, Japanese Americans have woven American values and behavior into the fabric of their culture and have seized new social, cultural, and economic avenues as they have become available, extending the limits of ethnicity by striking a workable balance between ethnic cohesion and accommodation.

Bibliography
There are only a handful of general historical and sociological works on the Japanese population in the United States. Roger Daniels, *The Politics of Prejudice* (Berkeley, Calif., 1962), and Bill Hosokawa, *Nisei: The Quiet Americans* (New York, 1969), are useful historical accounts. The best sociological studies are Harry H.L. Kitano, *Japanese Americans: The Evolution of a Subculture*, 2d ed. (Englewood Cliffs, N.J., 1976), and William Petersen, *Japanese Americans* (New York, 1971).
The traditional culture and society of Japan is explored in the following: Robert N. Bellah, *Tokugawa Religion* (Glencoe, Ill., 1957); Tadashi Fukutake, *Japanese Rural Society* (New York, 1967); John W. Hall and Richard K. Beardsley, eds., *Twelve Doors to Japan* (New York, 1965); Chie Nakane, *Japanese Society* (Berkeley, Calif., 1970); and Robert J. Smith and Richard K. Beardsley, eds., *Japanese Culture: Its Development and Characteristics* (New York, 1962).
Useful monographs on particular aspects of Japanese immigration and adjustment in the early 20th century are Thomas A. Bailey, *Theodore Roosevelt and the Japanese American Crisis* (1934; reprint, Gloucester, Mass., 1964); Sydney L. Gulick, *The American Japanese Problem* (New York, 1914); Yamato Ichihashi, *Japanese in the United States* (1932; reprint, New York, 1969); Carey McWilliams, *Prejudice: Japanese Americans* (Boston, 1944); John Modell, *The Economics and Politics of Racial Accommodation: The Japanese of Los Angeles, 1900–1942* (Urbana, Ill., 1977); Bradford Smith, *Americans From Japan* (1948; reprint, Westport, Conn., 1974); and Edward K. Strong, *Japanese in California* (Palo Alto, Calif., 1933).
The internment of the Japanese in relocation camps has received much attention. The most perceptive studies of this painful episode are Leonard Broom and John I. Kitsuse, *The Managed Casualty: The Japanese American Family in World War II* (Berkeley, 1956); Audrie Girdner and Anne Loftis, *The Great Betrayal* (New York, 1969); Jacobus Tenbroek, Edward N. Barnhart, and Floyd W. Matson, *Prejudice, War and the Constitution* (Berkeley, 1970); and Michi Weglyn, *Years of Infamy: The Untold Story of America's Concentration Camps* (New York, 1976).
The Japanese population in Hawaii has not received as much attention as the Japanese on the mainland. Nevertheless, some helpful works are available: Hilary Conroy, *The Japanese Frontier in Hawaii, 1868–1898* (Berkeley, 1953); Andrew W. Lind, *Hawaii's Japanese* (Princeton, N.J., 1946); Dennis M. Ogawa, *Kodomo No Tame Ni: For the Sake of the Children* (Honolulu, 1978); and Robert C. Schmitt, *Demographic Statistics of Hawaii, 1778–1965* (Honolulu, 1968).

HARRY H.L. KITANO

JEWS

Since 1654, when the first group of 23 Jews arrived in New Amsterdam, Jewish migration to the United States has been nearly continuous. Meager during the colonial and early national periods, it increased substantially in the middle third of the 19th century; by 1880 approximately 180,000 Jews had come to the United States. From 2,000 in 1790, the estimated Jewish population rose to 6,000 by 1830, to 150,000 by 1860, and to 250,000 by 1880. Then the number soared. Beginning in 1882 and continuing for the next 42 years, some 2.3 million Jews entered the country. By 1924 the Jewish population stood at 4.2 million. The restrictive quotas that went into effect in 1924 reduced the immigration precipitously, and the Depression lowered it still further. It rose again just before and after World War II. Between 1925 and 1975 576,000 Jews entered the United States. In 1977 the Jewish population was an estimated 5.8 million.

The ebb and flow of immigration constituted one element in the social and ethnic configuration of the American Jewish population; its diverse origins constituted another. The successive migrations came from countries with disparate cultures and political systems, different social and economic conditions, separate policies regarding their Jewish minority, and variant ethnic traditions.

Language was one index of this diversity. Spanish- and Portuguese-speaking Jews (Sephardim), with roots in the Iberian Peninsula, established the earliest Jewish settlements in the New World. They were joined by Jews from the German-speaking areas of central Europe and from Poland (Ashkenazim) who spoke Yiddish, a language derived from Middle High German, with elements of Hebrew, Aramaic and whatever the language of the host culture happened to be. The mid-19th-century immigrants from Bavaria and Prussian Posen (now Polish Poznań) spoke Western Yiddish, Polish Yiddish, or, in the case of the more acculturated, German. Jews from Lithuania, Poland, the Ukraine, Galicia, Hungary, and Romania, who came in the great migration from eastern Europe beginning in the 1880s, were distinguishable by their regional Yiddish dialects. Jews arriving from the disintegrating Ottoman Empire in the early 1900s, from Nazi Germany before World War II, and from Europe, Latin America, and Israel after it spoke Ladino, Arabic, German, Yiddish, Hungarian, Spanish, Hebrew, and Russian.

Different times of arrival accentuated the disparities. The social and economic conditions prevailing in the United States at the time of entry largely determined the pattern of individual integration and influenced the evolving ethnic community. The arrival of the Jews spanned the colonial settlement, western expansion, and industrial and urban growth, changing conditions that corresponded in some degree with the changing origins of the immigrants. German Jews, who predominated in the years before the Civil War, spread out across the continent and filled mercantile roles in an

expanding economy. They acculturated rapidly and moved into the middle class with relative ease. Eastern European Jews, arriving a half-century or more later, joined the industrial labor force or became suppliers of consumer goods and services in the immigrant neighborhoods. The intense ethnic life in these enclaves underscored the cultural and class differences between the Americanized Jews and the newcomers.

The size and vitality of the large immigrant communities also intensified the divisions induced by old-country localism and religious-secular antagonisms, competing ideological movements, and conflicting approaches to communal needs. The refugees of the 1930s and 1940s, though far fewer, added a heterogeneous new stratum to the Jewish population. Those from Germany were largely middle-class professionals with deep roots in European culture. They had little in common with the ultra-Orthodox Jews arriving about the same time, who were bent on establishing closed sectarian communities. The German refugees had little rapport with the descendants of the earlier German immigration, and the ultra-Orthodox did not mix with the Americanized Orthodox Jewish community.

THE ETHNIC HERITAGE
AND THE EUROPEAN EXPERIENCE

Although the diversity of cultural and social backgrounds strained the ties of community, the countervailing force of a venerable heritage imposed a sense of group identity. Jews perceived their ethnic existence as part of an historic and religious continuum that extended back to Biblical times. Scripture not only conveyed the ritual and ethical teachings of Judaism but celebrated the origins of the nation, which was elaborated in the post-Biblical tradition of a people in exile awaiting redemption. The fusion of a universal faith with belief in national restoration found expression in a messianism that saw Israel as God's instrument for bringing salvation to the world. For the Jews, survival was a sacred obligation.

This notion of a consecrated people manifested itself in an exacting religious culture that permeated Jewish life until challenged by modern, secular influences. Although there were periods of fruitful interchange between Jews and non-Jews (in Spain from the 10th to 14th centuries), externally imposed and self-imposed barriers persisted. Increasing governmental repression, which reached a high point in the walled ghettos and expulsions of the late Middle Ages, turned the Jews inward and intensified their separatism, especially among the Ashkenazi Jews whose settlements, first in France and Germany and later in eastern Europe, became the centers of an austere but vigorous rabbinical Judaism. Revered rabbinical scholars, the interpreters and teachers of the tradition, exercised a decisive influence through their academies and as communal leaders. Religious study was required of every male child, urged upon every male adult, and rewarded by status in society. Scripture, ritual, Talmudic law (halacha), and customs, summarized in codes and homiletic tracts, regulated the moral, religious, and cultural life of the Jews.

A Jewish polity—the kehillah—provided the framework for group life. The halacha recognized the right of each Jewish settlement to form its own kehillah and adopt its own self-governing regulations. Secular rulers, for reasons of convenience, custom, and profit, treated the Jews as a corporate group accountable for the acts and obligations of its members. The Jewish community received a measure of autonomy in taxation, civil law, and administration, powers that the kehillah leadership, both lay and rabbinical, used to reinforce their authority over the private and public life of the Jews. In this way the community achieved the cohesion and discipline needed to face an alien and threatening society.

Christendom's hostility toward the Jews had been fed by inverting the Jewish notion that they were a people set apart; instead of an elect group, the Christians considered them pariahs. Stigmatized as "Christ killers," Jews lived a precarious existence beyond the pale of the social order and depended upon the uncertain protection of ruler or monarch. Prohibited from owning land or employing Gentiles and forced out of manufacture and handicrafts by the craft guilds, Jews gravitated to occupations that Christians considered risky, demeaning, or sinful. Their concentration in commerce, especially money-lending and tax-collecting, exposed them to exploitation by their protectors and to the fury of impoverished peasants and insolvent noblemen. This endemic antipathy erupted periodically in epidemics of violence. The First Crusade in 1096 set the pattern of pillage and massacre. In the Rhine Valley, a center of Jewish life, whole communities were destroyed, and secular and ecclesiastical authorities were powerless to contain the mobs. Contemporary Jewish and Gentile accounts recorded the acts of martyrdom of Jews who refused baptism and were slain. Martyrdom—"the sanctification of the Name [of God]"—became a dominant theme in the homiletic and pietistic literature of Ashkenazi Jewry.

The idea of the Jew as demon entered the folklore and literature of Europe and deepened the chasm separating Jews from Gentiles. Images of the Jew as sorcerer and "the devil incarnate" who mutilated the Host and used Christian blood for ritual purposes led to trials, executions, and expulsions; at the end of the 13th century, Jews were driven from England en masse, and at the end of the 14th century from France.

In 1492 the most massive expulsion took place in Spain, where the Jews were forced to choose between exile and conversion. Nearly 150,000 Jews left Spain, and about 50,000 converted, bringing to an end a communal history of 700 years. Most of them established themselves in the Muslim countries bordering the Mediterranean.

Ashkenazi Jews were moving eastward into Poland at about the same time, attracted by a relatively benign regime that needed their skills. They dominated the export-import trade, leased royal lands, and served as tax farmers; the great majority were tradesmen, artisans, or lessees of mills, distilleries, and similar occupations. By 1600 about 500,000 Jews were living in eastern Europe, perhaps twice as many as remained in the isolated Jewish pockets of central and western Europe. The Polish settlement was the heartland of European Jewry, its religious and cultural center.

Polish Jewry created a network of regional and national councils and courts that acted as a minority self-government. On the local level the kehillah combined a strong council of elected elders drawn from the wealthy

and learned and a wide-ranging network of voluntary associations. The council oversaw the communal government, assisted in the larger communities by paid officials: the town rabbi, rabbinical judges, an emissary to the Gentile authorities, teachers, administrators, clerks, and inspectors. The various voluntary associations interred the dead, ministered to the sick, cared for orphans, provided for paupers and wayfarers, maintained the free school for needy children, studied the Bible or Talmud, and performed similar functions. Artisans established guilds, and the synagogues had supporting societies. Social and religious activities were integral to these societies, and many provided welfare benefits for their members. In all, community life involved many of the residents and gave them considerable experience in communal government.

In the mid-17th century, eastern European Jewry entered a long, dark age of tribulation. Government oppression pauperized the group, and political convulsions such as the uprising of the Ukrainian Cossacks under Bogdan Chmielnicki in 1648 threatened its survival. In the anarchy that marked the disintegration of the Polish state in the 18th century, the Jews were decimated; many fled, and those who remained led a perilous existence that weakened community life. Hasidism, a pietistic religious revival and a disruptive force of another kind, found favor among the humbler folk because of its emphasis on spontaneity rather than knowledge, and on the role of charismatic leaders, or *zaddikim*. In time, these religious and social antagonisms abated, but they left behind bitter memories of schisms, which were later carried to the United States.

In the 19th century eastern European Jewry was divided among Prussia (the Posen region), Austria (the much larger Galician community), and Russia (most of Polish Jewry). The governments of all three viewed the Jews as an alien and backward element that ultimately was to be absorbed by the native population. The implementation of this goal varied from the relatively mild and partly successful tactics of Prussia to the enlightened despotism of the Hapsburgs and the draconian methods of tsarist Russia, which, aside from a brief interlude in the 1860s, maintained a systematic policy of oppression. The imperial ukase of 1827, for example, extended conscription to the Jews, with the proviso that their service last for 25 years. When quotas were not filled, children as young as 12 were conscripted or abducted. Conversion was the goal of Russian policy. Jewish folk songs, memoirs, and literature reflect the loneliness, brutal treatment, and martyrdom of those who were snatched away and the terror and despair of all Russia's Jews. Expulsion from the villages and exorbitant taxes were other methods used to reform the Jews; in 1844 the tsar abolished kehillah self-government, which it considered an obstacle to assimiliation.

In western Europe, the Enlightenment and the French Revolution altered the status of the Jews. Secular modes of thought opened the way for the emergence of a religiously neutral society. In the enlightened circles where a rationalist approach to religion, society, economics, and politics was current, Jews of similar persuasion found acceptance. Jewish emancipation, granted first by France in 1790, came slowly and uncertainly to the rest of western Europe: Prussia (1850), England (1858), and Austria-Hungary (1867). Even in the classic instance of France, citizenship was granted on condition that the Jews renounce the notion of Jewish nationality, discard their separate laws, and dissolve their self-governing institutions. Among the new nation-states, the prevailing assumption was that emancipation would bring assimilation.

The secularly educated, upper-class stratum of western Jewry responded with alacrity to the opportunity to be rid of the ancient disabilities and restrictions imposed by both the Gentile and traditional Jewish societies. Some embraced Christianity, others sought to retain their Jewish identity in ways that would not hinder their social and cultural integration. Religious services were substantially modernized—shortened and read in the vernacular with uncovered head and accompanied by the organ. Rituals and ceremonial laws that tended to segregate the Jews were ignored or altered. Germany, the center of Reform Judaism, was producing scholars and rabbis whose research and synods created a systematic theology to support the movement: Judaism, as an evolutionary and progressive religion, had freed itself from the restrictions of its more primitive, national past; its mission was now universal, to bring the message of social justice and brotherhood to mankind.

The breakup of traditional Jewish society was expressed in a variety of ways. Jewish modernists in Germany directed the poor youth of the cities and villages into vocational trades and agriculture. They sought to place communal organization on a voluntary basis and divest it of all its nonreligious functions. Among eastern European Jewry the new attitudes inspired a remarkable outpouring of political and cultural activity. Zionism (the movement to reestablish a Jewish homeland) and socialism, with their numerous factions, splits, and combinations, developed into full-grown organizations and challenged the bastions of traditional Judaism. A secular literature in Hebrew, Yiddish, and Russian found avid readers.

Some of those who emigrated to the United States embraced the new ideologies that were fragmenting the group in Europe. Nevertheless, until well into the 20th century the majority of the immigrants could recall, or had come directly from, a traditional Jewish society. The communal thrust of Judaism—the sense of being a community of fate, the discipline imposed by the halacha, and the obligation to brethren in distress—was still at the heart of their religio-ethnic outlook. Whatever their land of origin, American Jews saw themselves as part of Kelal Yisrael, the totality of Israel.

The younger and more adventurous, with fewer commitments to family and community, constituted a significant proportion of the immigrants; not many established leaders came. Freedom, tolerance, and the promise of material reward for the deserving individual struck a responsive chord among the immigrants and their descendants. From the start there was tension between individual integration in the larger society and group continuity, and questions of self-definition were important.

From a tiny outpost at the edge of the Jewish world, the United States became the largest Jewish population center in the world. In 1978 an estimated 40 percent of the world Jewish population resided in the United States, compared with 21 percent in Israel. The great migration movement from east to west explains this de-

velopment only in part. Six million of the 9 million Jews who lived in Europe on the eve of World War II perished in the Nazi holocaust. Suddenly and traumatically, American Jewry became the major center with the numbers and means to aid fellow Jews in peril.

THE COLONIAL AND EARLY NATIONAL PERIODS

The Sephardic Jews who settled on the North American continent during the colonial period were part of the Iberian-Jewish diaspora created by the 15th- and 16th-century expulsions from Spain and Portugal. One stream of Sephardim found havens in the rising commercial centers of Holland, England, and their colonies, where they were well prepared for a pioneering role. Being by necessity geographically mobile, they settled, migrated, and resettled along the colonial trade routes and adapted their mercantile skills to the needs of international trade and a frontier economy. Concentrated in urban centers, they succeeded in establishing small but viable Jewish communities. Their tradition also encouraged cultural flexibility. They retained pride in their civilization that had flourished during the golden age of Spain, when their forefathers had combined Hebraic and secular learning and had served both the state and their people with distinction.

In the New World, Sephardic influences dominated the five congregations established in the port cities of New York (1656), Newport (1677), Savannah (1733), Philadelphia (1745), and Charleston (1750), links in a chain of settlements extending to the Dutch and English West Indies and anchored in the parent community in Amsterdam and the smaller but increasingly important community in London. The first Jewish refugees to arrive in New Amsterdam were threatened with expulsion because of their religion. They petitioned their brethren in Amsterdam to intercede, and Jewish shareholders of the Dutch West India Company used their influence to establish a more tolerant immigration policy. The immigrants' questions of religious law were occasionally submitted to the rabbinical courts of London and Amsterdam. When the less affluent mainland communities wanted to build a synagogue, they turned for aid—in the words of the 1729 appeal of New York's Shearith Israel (Remnant of Israel) congregation —to "kindred Sephardi congregations in Central and South America and Europe." In 1750 Newport's Jews received contributions for that purpose from the congregations of Jamaica, Surinam, Curaçao, and London. But above all, trade and family ties reinforced the connections among the scattered Sephardi settlements of the colonial world. Merchant families such as the Lopezes, Gomezes, Hendrickses, Seixases, and Riveras were related through marriage with branches scattered from Newport to Savannah. Individual members went on business to London and to the Caribbean, and the few new arrivals who continued to reach the mainland colonies from Amsterdam and London by way of the Dutch or English West Indies sustained the bonds of religion, culture, and economic interests until well into the 18th century.

The Ashkenazi Jews who settled in colonial America came from widely dispersed points in central and eastern Europe, often with London as a way-station. Ashkenazi families sometimes settled in London and sent relatives to America in the interest of family business,

and immigrants, once established in the colonies, occasionally brought kinsmen from Europe, but chain migration did not develop. Those who crossed the ocean were by and large young, unmarried, and predisposed to adjust readily and individually to new conditions and join the Sephardi communities already there.

The fusion of the two groups in America was surprising. The Ashkenazi ritual differed from the Sephardi in style, pronunciation of the Hebrew, and liturgy. Furthermore, the first-generation Ashkenazim retained something of their own culture, reflected in a considerable body of correspondence in Yiddish. Nevertheless, Ashkenazim were among the leaders and main financial supporters of the colonial congregations. Moses Gomez, a Sephardi who presided over the Jewish community in New York in the first half of 1729, was followed by Jacob Franks (1688–1769), an Ashkenazi, in the second half. Two of the three trustees who acquired the site for the Newport synagogue in 1759 were Ashkenazim. The two groups intermarried with increasing frequency, despite occasional evidence of Sephardi hauteur. The sparseness of the Jewish population undoubtedly encouraged intermarriage, because for many the unacceptable alternative was to marry outside the faith. The occupational structure of the two groups was similar, and ethnic business ties quickly brought Ashkenazim and Sephardim together. The absence of authoritative religious leaders (the first ordained rabbis came to the United States in the 1840s) and the pace of Americanization also encouraged homogeneity.

The first small congregations met the full range of Jewish communal and religious needs. In addition to performing religious services, they maintained a school and a *mikveh* (ritual bath), supervised the supply of kosher meat, provided *matzot* (unleavened bread) for Passover, and either owned or cared for a cemetery. The synagogue accepted responsibility for the needy and supplied lodging for itinerants and medical care and burial services for the indigent.

The lay head of the synagogue (*parnass*) and the trustees endeavored to impose traditional norms of religious behavior upon their members with mixed success. Before a marriage could be performed, the approval of the parnass and sometimes of the trustees was needed. This was denied if one partner to the marriage was not Jewish. But sanctions such as fines, loss of synagogue honors, and denial of burial rights as a means of enforcing religious observance became less and less effective. In time both Shearith Israel and Philadelphia's Mikveh Israel (Hope of Israel) allowed the Jewish spouses of mixed marriages to be seatholders in the synagogue. Synagogue policy continued to be formally traditional and authoritarian but in practice it was indulgent toward the nonobservant.

Jewish identity was not a serious obstacle to participation in the larger society. As merchants and artisans, Jews provided necessary services. The decline of piety, the rise of deistic ideas, and the crystallization of American republicanism eased the way for Jews who wished to take part in public affairs. The Swedish naturalist Peter Kalm wrote as early as 1748 that Jews "enjoyed all the privileges common to other inhabitants." He also observed that they ate no pork, forbidden food for the observant Jew, but that "many of them (especially the young) when travelling did not make the least

difficulty about eating this or any other meat." Thirty years later a Hessian officer wrote that the Jews in Newport "enjoy all the rights of citizenship. But unlike our Jews they are not distinguishable by their beards and attire . . . while their women wear the same French finery as the women of other faiths." The wills of New York Jews reflected amicable relationships with non-Jews. Of the 41 extant wills, 23 are witnessed only by Gentiles, and 12 by both Jews and Gentiles. Jews were not denied honorific appointments. In 1768 Moses Michael Hays (1739–1805) of Newport was chosen deputy inspector general of masonry for North America. Myer Myers (1723–1795) of New York was elected president of the Silversmith's Society in 1776 and again in 1786. Gershom Mendes Seixas (1746–1816), minister of Shearith Israel, was appointed a trustee of Columbia College, then a Christian denominational institution, in 1784. In Philadelphia's grand procession to celebrate Pennsylvania's ratification of the United States Constitution, Benjamin Rush reported, "Pains were taken to connect Ministers of the most dissimilar religious principles together, thereby to show the influence of a free government in promoting Christian charity. The Rabbi of the Jews, locked in the arms of two ministers of the gospel, was a most delightful sight."

Although stereotypical anti-Jewish remarks occasionally appeared in the press and in public utterances, they reflected traditional prejudices rather than grave social mistreatment. Jews of standing joined clubs, charities, and private libraries along with their Christian peers and sent their children to the same schools. The daughter of the wealthy and observant Jacob Franks (1688–1769), pillar of Shearith Israel, married a DeLancey; his son married a Philadelphia Evans. In the 1790s Dr. David Nassy, a Philadelphia Jewish physician and scientist, replied to an accusation of Jewish self-segregation, "There are the Maraches, the Amrings, the Cohens, the Hombergs, the Wallachs, the Solises and several other families lawfully married to Christian women who go to their own churches, the men going to their synagogues, and who, when together, frequent the best society."

Jews did at first face civic and political disabilities derived from restrictions on religious dissenters, but even before the Revolution they had gradually acquired the privileges of domicile, trade, and religious organization. New York granted individual Jews citizenship: they voted and held minor appointive offices. Pennsylvania statutes that forbade Jews from holding public worship and restricted their commercial activities were not enforced.

Other colonies eager for commercial growth also allowed Jews to establish permanent settlements. The colonies either granted citizenship or ignored the question altogether. The growth of dissenting Christian denominations eased the way for the Jews as well. In 1740 Parliament recognized this reality by formally granting Jewish aliens in the colonies the right to be naturalized after seven years of residence and exempting them from taking the oath "upon the true faith of a Christian."

The American Revolution legitimized the set of rights and ad hoc privileges that individual Jews had won. Only minor disabilities remained in those states whose constitutions required religious tests for public office. Most of the Jewish population had taken part in

the struggle for independence; they had served in the army and distinguished themselves in battle. Jewish purveyors, merchant shippers, and financiers were in constant contact with government officials. Like the churches, the synagogues held special days of prayer and thanksgiving, issued petitions, and presented addresses to the political leaders and bodies of the republic. The Mikveh Israel Congregation petitioned the Commonwealth of Pennsylvania and the Constitutional Convention to remove religious restrictions on holding office and were gratified by the clause against religious tests and by the First Amendment's "no establishment of religion" proviso.

By the end of the century a largely native-born American Jewry participated in an increasingly open society. Even its Old Testament Hebraism formed part of the common American heritage. Biblical imagery reverberated equally in the congratulatory addresses sent by the Hebrew congregations to George Washington and in his replies. But by the first decades of the next century this high degree of integration began to raise a quite different question: would the American Jews be able to survive as a distinct entity? Of the five congregations that existed in 1776, one (Newport) had dissolved; fifty years later one new one (Richmond) had been established, and the two preeminent synagogues (Philadelphia and New York) had suffered secessions. When Shearith Israel's minister of 48 years, an energetic man of limited Hebraic learning, died in 1816 his place was assumed by a merchant who continued his own business activities and served as *hazzan* (reader) on a part-time basis.

Mordecai M. Noah (1785–1851), born in Philadelphia of mixed Sephardi-Ashkenazi stock (his maternal grandmother was Sephardi) was probably the best-known Jewish public figure in the first half of the 19th century. He settled in New York after serving from 1813 to 1815 as U.S. consul in Tunis, from where he was recalled by Secretary of State James Monroe because his religion formed an "obstacle to the exercise of [his] consular functions" and because of alleged mismanagement of funds. In 1818 when Shearith Israel rededicated its synagogue, Noah delivered the main address. He became a stormy figure in New York Democratic party politics, served for a time as editor of the *National Advocate*, and held the posts of sheriff (1822), grand sachem of Tammany (1824), and judge of the court of sessions (1841). In the 1830s, he edited and published the *Evening Star*, a Whig paper, and supported the anti-immigrant and anti-Catholic Native American party. He was a prolific playwright; five of his plays were produced between 1819 and 1822. For many years he also headed the most important Jewish charity, the Hebrew Benevolent Society.

Moved by the condition of North African Jewry, as well as by his own romanticism, Noah undertook to establish a "city of refuge for the Jews." In 1825, with the aid of friends, he purchased Grand Island in the Niagara River and renamed it Ararat. In an impressive dedication staged in the presence of militia, the Masons, local Indians (supposedly survivors of the ten lost tribes of Israel), and government officials, Noah proclaimed himself "Governor and Judge of Israel," offering the Jews of the world an asylum until "that great and final restoration to their ancient heritage." In 1844 he published his

Discourse on the Restoration of the Jews, which called on the free peoples of the world, particularly Americans, to aid in the restoration of Zion.

THE GERMAN MIGRATION, 1830–1880

Second synagogues, established in Philadelphia in 1802 and in New York in 1825, were a harbinger of changes to come in American Jewry. In both cities the recently arrived Ashkenazi immigrants regarded the American Sephardic ritual, the social distance between themselves and the native-born, and religious laxity as sufficient justification for establishing themselves in separate congregations. After that, consensual restraints no longer prevented the multiplication of synagogues. The stimulus for further diversity became apparent in the mid-1830s when more and more immigrants arrived in families and groups of families having common ties in particular Old World localities. Ten years after New York's initial secession, the two synagogues had grown to ten.

Jews spread across the continent, forming the map of Jewish communities essentially as it is today. By the Civil War, 160 places had a Jewish communal life. San Francisco had a Jewish population two-thirds the size of Philadelphia's. Most of these immigrants were from Bavaria, Baden, Württemberg, and Posen, who left because of repressive legislation and the disruption of the agricultural peasant economy. They came from small hamlets and market towns where they had been petty tradesmen and dealers in cattle and where they were burdened by humiliating taxes and severe limitations on their right to marry, find employment, and establish domiciles. Consequently most of the immigrants were young and unmarried. Records from Württemberg show that between 1848 and 1855 62 percent of the emigrants were between 11 and 20, and 70 percent were under 31. Though products of a traditional Jewish milieu, they had only a meager religious and secular education. Those from Posen came from sizable, compact Jewish communities with a more learned and rigorous religious leadership and an artisan class. Smaller, but influential, groups came from England, Holland, and Bohemia, where Jews had moved toward political and cultural integration by the 1840s. These groups supplied most of the small number of professionals and intellectuals.

Although entire families sometimes emigrated— Simon and Rachel Guggenheim and their 12 children provide a celebrated example—more often a family would send a single son, with the understanding that at the first opportunity he would arrange for the rest to follow. Joseph Seligman (1819–1880), the founder of one of the leading post–Civil War American investment houses, left Bavaria in 1837 at the age of 17, sent for his two oldest brothers in 1839, and for a fourth brother in 1841. By 1843 seven more brothers and sisters and a widowed father had been brought over. The Seligmans were more famous than the others, and there were more of them, but otherwise they were typical of this youth-led family chain migration.

The Jews were part of the German migration, and, despite religious differences and historic prejudices, were drawn into the German social and cultural milieu in the United States. But Jews from the same town or region often banded together and traveled as a group, sometimes taking with them the Torah scroll and other religious objects needed for the future congregation and making special arrangements for kosher food during the journey.

The age, family structure, ethnic ties, and European experience of the Jewish immigrants equipped them for successful integration into the expanding American economy. The rapidly growing cities of the East, particularly the ports of entry, provided opportunities for tradesmen and small merchants. New York City's population grew from 166,000 in 1825 to 805,000 in 1860, while its Jewish population rose from approximately 500 to 40,000. The Jews engaged in tailoring and shoe-making and dealt in second-hand clothes and dry goods —occupations brought from Europe. A New York merchant's reference guide for 1859 listed 141 wholesale firms with Jewish names, all connected with some branch of the garment industry. A quarter of the gainfully employed immigrants from Poland—mostly Posen Jews—were tailors.

Peddling, however, was the most frequent means of making a living. At a time when there were few retail stores outside of the large cities, peddling filled a vital function in bringing the city's goods to the countryside. Immigrants purchased their supplies in New York and left on rural routes for a week or more or faced the fierce competition of the city's neighborhoods. Better opportunities existed where the distribution network was less developed. In 1855, 59 percent of the gainfully employed Jews of Easton, Pa., were peddlers.

Peddlers needed little or no initial capital, because they began their business entirely on credit; when they accumulated enough money, they moved from pack peddler to wagon peddler and then to store owner. The nexus of peddler, supplier-creditor, dry-goods retailer, wholesaler, clothing manufacturer, and importer evolved quickly, with German Jews playing a central role. Because credit was crucial to the system, family ties were of paramount importance. Relatives in New York or Cincinnati sent goods to the South or Far West that they would not risk to strangers. The expanding distribution network required clerks, bookkeepers, and skilled factory workers, also drawn from among immigrant relatives or countrymen. By the 1850s Jews in Milwaukee, Wis., Chicago, and Cincinnati, Ohio, had entered the meat-packing industry, and the largest wholesale shoe firm in the country, with outlets in Boston, Memphis, Tenn., and St. Louis, Mo., was owned by the Friedmann family.

The growth of the distributive system shaped the map of Jewish settlement. The main transportation routes to the West became the sites of the new communities in the 1830s and 1840s. The first clusters of peddlers established themselves in inland cities like Albany (early 1830s) and Rochester, N.Y. (early 1840s), Cleveland (1839), Chicago (1845), Milwaukee (1844), and St. Louis (1837). Within three or four years the first Jewish retail stores or peddler-supply depots opened, additional family members and countrymen came, and a congregation was established. By the 1850s such centers had satellite communities.

Cincinnati, an early crossroads for westward-bound travelers, the most important inland river port serving the Ohio River system, and a region with a large German population, attracted many Jewish immigrants. Its Jewish population grew to 3,300 in 1850 and to 10,000 in 1860. Its most influential synagogue was founded by

peddlers, who by the 1850s had moved up to the retail clothing trade and had turned Cincinnati into a center for clothing manufacture. In 1855 its fifth synagogue was established, a Jewish hospital and benevolent-aid society had been founded, and two weeklies, one in English and one in German, went to subscribers throughout the region. Two of the preeminent rabbis in the country, Isaac Mayer Wise (1819–1900) and Max Lilienthal (1815–1882), held pulpits in the city. Cincinnati was the religious center for small communities throughout Indiana, Illinois, Tennessee, Kentucky, and Missouri. When Jewish merchants grew wealthy, they frequently sold their stores to younger brothers or relatives and moved to Cincinnati.

Jewish settlers also penetrated the South and the Far West, where regional differences affected the character of their economic and communal life. In the South, the path to success led from peddling to serving the commercial needs of the plantation economy as commission merchants and cotton brokers. New Orleans and Mobile and Montgomery, Ala., were representative of the small to medium-sized provincial communities. The structure of southern white society undoubtedly contributed to the survival of such isolated communities.

In the Far West, on the other hand, the boom that followed the discovery of gold in California resulted in the extraordinarily swift growth of San Francisco. By the mid-1850s the city had about 4,000 Jews, and by the end of the decade, a third more. Open and fluid social and economic conditions and the absence of an established elite provided the Jews with an opportunity to enter many more fields and to participate in civic life. In the first two decades, most Jews established themselves as merchants and wholesalers, often representing family concerns in the East. Jewish peddlers followed the prospectors into the mining towns of the Sierras, supplied them with clothes and tools, and established stores. Minuscule communities in towns such as Sacramento and Stockton established and maintained close ties with the Jewish community in San Francisco.

Congregation building and splitting were common in this period. As additional immigrants settled in a city, they strengthened the traditions of the initial group or introduced new ones. The original congregation, which generally included a bloc from Bavaria and Posen and a scattering of Bohemian, English, and Dutch Jews, usually divided into German and Polish congregations; then, if the population was large enough, as it was in New York, the proliferation continued. The splintering was largely social and cultural rather than doctrinal. The founders of the new congregations, laymen with a rudimentary religious background, simply wanted to maintain as best they could the cherished customs of home.

In the mid-1840s an additional factor contributed to fragmentation. In the more established synagogues, demands were made for minor innovations in the conduct of the services, although this did not imply a radical revision of traditional practice based on a new interpretation of Judaism. The changes, although rarely stated in those terms, reflected a desire to Americanize the synagogue with a more decorous service and an English sermon rather than a German one or none at all.

The arrival in the 1840s of the first ordained rabbis, by and large university-trained, added an ideological dimension. They brought the prestige of their religious station and their academic title, for ordination carried with it the authority to interpret religious law. For the traditionalists, this meant a rigorously conservative rendering of the halacha, but the immigrant rabbis, sympathizers or outright advocates of Reform Judaism, used their authority to legitimize the Reformist trends. They easily replaced or absorbed into their ranks the Jewish minister, a peculiarly American creation. The minister had evolved from the hazzan, who led the congregation in worship, a function any religiously observant Jew literate in Hebrew was allowed to fill. The professionalization of the hazzan had resulted in part from the paucity of qualified laymen, in part from the absence of rabbis. Influenced, too, by the Protestant model, he added preaching to his duties and assumed the title of minister.

One of these ministers, Isaac Leeser (1806–1868) became the spokesman for traditional Judaism and the first national leader in American Jewish life. Born in Westphalia, in Germany, where he received some Judaic and secular education, Leeser served as minister of Philadelphia's Congregation Mikveh Israel from 1829 to 1850. He founded the first American Jewish periodical, *The Occident,* in 1843, published a number of Jewish educational primers intended for a nationwide audience, and established a short-lived publishing house and rabbinical college.

Leeser's effort to create a "union of all Israelites in America" in 1841 was prompted by the accusation of ritual murder leveled against a group of Syrian Jews, which had become an international incident. For the first time American Jewry acted in concert, holding public meetings, enlisting the support of non-Jews, and calling on the U.S. government to intercede. Leeser emerged as the leading figure in the protest movement, but the momentum created by the collaborative effort was not enough to establish a permanent, representative organization. A central organization of sorts, the Board of Delegates of American Israelites, was founded in 1859, again using the impetus from protests over the violation of Jewish rights abroad, this time the case of a Jewish infant in Italy, who was baptized without the knowledge of his parents and abducted by papal guards to be raised as a Christian. Leeser tried to broaden both the constituency and the scope of the board, but the increasingly rancorous debate over religious reform absorbed the energies of its other leaders.

All through the 1850s and 1860s, efforts to establish a synod, issue a standard prayerbook, agree upon a set of guiding principles, create a federation of synagogues, and establish a theological seminary failed in the face of theological dispute and personal feuds. Cincinnati's Isaac Wise, a moderate Reform Jew, was a diligent compromiser and improviser in religious principles as well as in practice. Born in Bohemia, Wise received training in a Talmudic academy and probably also attended a university. After a brief ministry in a small provincial town, he emigrated to the United States, served as rabbi in Albany, N.Y., and was then called in 1854 to the wealthy B'nai Jeshurun in Cincinnati, which he turned into a base for his larger ambitions. To the theological left of Wise, David Einhorn (1809–1879) presented a radical and ideologically consistent view of Judaism. Einhorn arrived in the United States in 1855, already one of the established leaders of the radical Reform

wing in Germany. He had little patience with piece-meal efforts to modify old practices or with Wise's inconsistencies and compromises. No all-embracing framework could include the Leeser, Wise, and Einhorn factions.

Polemics and negotiations eventually resulted in the crystallization of a Reform denomination, although it was not the comprehensive liberal-traditional Judaism some had hoped for. On the congregational level, pragmatic laymen fitted their practices to the Reform style and paid little attention to theological controversies; Wise's flexibility and organizational ability gave the movement institutional form. In 1873 he established the Union of American Hebrew Congregations (UAHC), which soon absorbed the Board of Delegates of American Israelites. Two years later, the UAHC opened Hebrew Union College in Cincinnati, the first seminary established in the United States to train rabbis, with Wise as its president. By 1880 most American synagogues, aside from those established by the newly arriving east European immigrants, were Reform.

Ideological positions were also clarified. In 1885, Kaufmann Kohler (1843–1926), son-in-law and spiritual heir of Einhorn, convened a conference of rabbis and formulated a Reform platform that included the radical position that had been the source of contention twenty years earlier. The Jews were no longer a nation, the platform declared: they were a religious community. Judaism was a "progressive religion ever striving to be in accord with the postulates of reason." Of the "Mosaic legislation," only its moral laws and the ceremonials that "elevate and sanctify our lives" were binding. The rabbis called on all men of good will to establish "the reign of truth and righteousness among men."

The pronouncement indicated both the astonishingly rapid acculturation of the German Jews and the prompt acceptance by their ministers of advanced social theories. Scarcely a generation after their arrival, they had reformulated their Jewish identity in terms of the congenial model of late-19th-century liberal American Protestantism. Their congregations—now called temples—expressed their middle-class propriety. Elaborate structures and the distinguished and well-paid rabbis who preached from their pulpits bore witness to their affluence. Brief and decorous services, almost exclusively in English and accompanied by choir and organ, lightened the burden of attendance.

Some carried the radical teachings of Reform one step further. Felix Adler (1851–1933), trained for the rabbinate and son of an American Reform leader, concluding that Judaism was too confining in the pursuit of a universalistic humanism, founded the Ethical Culture Society in 1876. Charles Fleischer, rabbi of Boston's Temple Israel, severed his ties with his temple and began to preach a religion of democracy around 1900.

Philanthropy offered another avenue for expressing ethnic identity. The first relief societies had functioned under the auspices of the synagogue, then they became autonomous, then completely independent. Initially serving only the poor among the congregation, they later aided the Jewish poor of an entire city. Immigration increased the number of impoverished Jews, many of whom were not affiliated with synagogues, but the associations accepted members regardless of their affiliation. The same development took place among the women's charitable societies. By the 1870s the larger Jewish settlements had a variety of benevolent societies, some with broad community support and others based on old-country origin or on a particular philanthropic function. The wretched conditions of the public charitable institutions and the fact that most were sponsored by Christian denominations—raising the fear of proselytizing—led to the establishment of the first large welfare institutions: orphanages, hospitals, homes for the aged, and schools for the poor. Jewish hospitals were opened in Cincinnati (1850), in New York (1852), in Philadelphia (1865), and in Chicago (1868). Orphan asylums were founded in Charleston, S.C. (1801), in Philadelphia (1855), in New York (1859), and in Cleveland (1868). As the dimensions of the undertakings grew, so did the trend toward consolidation among some of the societies. In the larger communities "united Hebrew charities" came into existence in the 1860s and 1870s.

Mutual-aid societies underwent a similar process of dissociation from religious groups. Although synagogues retained control over some of them, most of the offshoots of the traditional sick-visitation and burial societies were able to survive the congregational splintering only by asserting their independence. That step also opened their doors to the growing numbers of Jews who were only casual attendants of the synagogue or no longer religiously observant.

Influenced by American models, the mutual-aid society developed into the lodge and fraternal order. Twenty-five years after its founding, the Order of B'nai B'rith was a national organization dedicated to "uniting Israelites in the work of promoting their highest interests and those of humanity," with a membership of over 20,000. Along with the other orders, it responded to the needs of Jews who had encountered discrimination in general orders like the Odd Fellows and the Masons.

The Jewish fraternal orders, with their secret rites, special regalia, and mottoes, offered an American aura denied them elsewhere and supplied the mutual aid and fellowship no longer provided by the factional synagogues. They also accepted communal responsibilities, sponsored charitable projects, and organized to fight prejudice. Social and literary societies mushroomed and in the 1870s acquired an institutional form in the Young Men's Hebrew Associations (YMHA), which began to appear in the larger cities. In all these activities the thrust of acculturation also led to social discrimination. The B'nai B'rith and YMHA in their early years did not welcome eastern European newcomers.

On the eve of the mass migration from eastern Europe, American Jewry was relatively homogeneous. The large German Jewish group had absorbed both the native-born community it found on arrival and the Posen, Bohemian, and other Jews, including the early arrivals from eastern Europe, who followed. Congregations established in the 1850s because the existing ones were too liberal or too German were, by the 1880s, affiliated with the Reform movement. Reform Judaism's prescriptive demands were minimal, and it offered no obstacles to a broad range of essentially secular associational activities. Thus diversity did not become divisive. The importance of German culture in the social and intellectual life of the group was an integrating

force of another kind. Jewish social clubs and literary societies reflected strong German influence. German Jews subscribed to and wrote for the German-language press and were patrons of the German-language theater. Some Jews completely identified with the German ethnic group, while others maintained a "triple loyalty," as expressed by the Chicago rabbi Bernhard Felsenthal (1822–1908): "Racially I am a Jew, for I have been born among the Jewish nation. Politically I am an American as patriotic, as enthusiastic, as devoted an American citizen as it is possible to be. But spiritually I am a German, for my inner life has been profoundly influenced by Schiller, Goethe, Kant, and other intellectual giants of Germany."

Between 1860 and 1880 a Jewish business elite appeared. Its leaders were the investment bankers, department-store innovators, clothing manufacturers, and metals, shoe-manufacturing, and meat-processing entrepreneurs. The family business pattern that had brought mercantile success in the 1850s had created large fortunes by the 1880s. The German Jewish patrician class in New York—closely knit by ethnic, social, and family bonds and by business dealings—was especially striking. It was also linked by social ties and business interests to its counterparts across the country.

As New York rose to financial preeminence, it attracted families who at first had local business outlets there and who then moved into finance or large-scale merchandising. Kuhn, Loeb and Company and Heidelbach, Ickelheimer and Company were run by Cincinnati merchant families who opened New York branches of their clothing and wholesale firms and then entered investment banking. The Lehman brothers—Emanuel (1827–1907), Henry (1821–1855), and Mayer (1830–1897)—who were originally cotton factors in the South, followed a similar path. By the 1850s their cotton brokerage firm required a New York branch; after the Civil War the brothers transferred their activities to New York, extended their commodity dealings, then entered investment banking. The Straus family—Lazarus (1809–1898) and his sons, Isidor (1845–1912), Nathan (1848–1931), and Oscar (1850–1926)—moved from Talbotton, Ga., to New York in 1866. By the 1880s Isidor and Nathan were partners in the dry-goods business of R.H. Macy and Company, which they turned into a giant department store.

The eight Seligman brothers moved from peddling to retailing, branched out from the South, and in 1847 opened an importing house in New York. The discovery of gold in California led Jesse (1827–1894) and Leopold (1831–1862) to set up a store in San Francisco in 1850. Two years later they began consigning gold, for reshipment to foreign markets, to the New York office headed by Joseph. During the Civil War the brothers underwrote U.S. bonds and supplied the Union Army with uniforms. When it ended, they turned from dry goods and clothing manufacture to international investment banking with branches in London, Paris, Frankfurt, San Francisco, and New Orleans, each branch headed by a brother.

In other cities men like Adam Gimbel (1817–1896), Louis Bamberger (1855–1944), Edward A. Filene (1860–1937), and Julius Rosenwald (1862–1932) revolutionized American retailing. German Jews held a commanding position in the clothing trades. In New York 80 per-cent of all retail and 90 percent of all wholesale clothing firms were owned by Jews; in the rest of the country the figure was only slightly less. A U.S. Census report in 1890 provides some notion of the general affluence of American Jews. Bankers, brokers, and wholesale merchants represented 15 percent; retail dealers, about 35 percent; accountants, bookkeepers, and clerks, 17 percent; salesmen, agents, and auctioneers, about 12 percent; professionals, 5 percent; skilled workers, about 12 percent; tailors, 3 percent; and peddlers, only 1 percent.

For the German Jews, all that remained was to achieve an acceptance in society commensurate with their economic and cultural success. But the appearance of impoverished, Yiddish-speaking immigrants from eastern Europe—about 30,000 of them between 1870 and 1880, and immensely larger numbers soon after—threatened the standing the American Jews had attained.

MIGRATION FROM EASTERN EUROPE, 1881–1924

In 1880 perhaps one-sixth of the 250,000 American Jews were immigrants from eastern Europe. Forty years later they and their children constituted about five-sixths of the 4 million Jews in the United States. One-third of eastern European Jewry left their homes during those decades, and over 90 percent of them came to the United States. This largest of Jewish population movements radically altered the demography, social structure, cultural life, and communal order of American Jewry.

Several factors combined to cause this mass exodus. A high birthrate and relatively low death rate increased the Jewish population of eastern Europe from approximately 1.5 million in 1800 to 6.8 million in 1900, all within the confining pales of Jewish settlement. Seventy-five percent of the immigrants were from the Russian Pale, which consisted of the 15 western provinces of European Russia and the 10 provinces of Congress (that is, Russian-held) Poland. The Pale constituted about 20 percent of the regions then within the borders of European Russia. All but a privileged few were forbidden to live outside the Pale, and within, restrictive laws further limited Jews to residence in towns and cities.

Another 18 percent of the immigrants came from Galicia, Bukovina, and Hungary, all regions of Austria-Hungary. The Hapsburg government had granted civil rights to the Jews in the 1860s, but local circumstances conspired to create a repressive situation, though it was less marked by the open violence that was common elsewhere. Only 4 percent of the immigrants were from Romania, where the proportion of emigrating Jews to Jewish population was as high as in Russia. The Jews in Romania lived under essentially the same conditions as in the Russian Pale: no civil rights, ruinous restrictions on trading, and periodic expulsion from towns and villages.

Economic and social changes upset the Jewish occupational structure and further stimulated departure. In the 1870s industrialization and modern agriculture began to displace the petty merchants, peddlers, artisans, teamsters, factors, and innkeepers. After the assassination of Tsar Alexander II in 1881, the new regime introduced policies that encouraged mob violence. Pogroms in 1881 and 1882 struck over 200 Jewish com-

Central Europe

Miles

Km.

500

Jewish Pale of Settlement in the Russian Empire

Boundary of the Congress Kingdom of Poland, 1815–1863

Boundary of the Hungarian Kingdom before 1918

North Sea

SWEDEN

Stockholm

Baltic Sea

DENMARK

Copenhagen

U.K.

London

NETHERLANDS

Amsterdam

BELGIUM

LUX.

Paris

FRANCE

EAST GERMANY

Berlin

Bremen

Hamburg

Hanover

WEST GERMANY

Leipzig

Elbe

Frankfurt

Nuremberg

Bavaria

Munich

Württemberg

Baden

Rhine

GERMANY

SWITZ.

German Empire

Milan

Genoa

Bologna

Rome

ITALY

Mediterranean Sea

Gdańsk (Danzig)

POLAND

Poznań (Posen)

Wrocław (Breslau)

Silesia

Prague

Bohemia

Moravia

CZECHOSLOVAKIA

Vienna

AUSTRIA

Bratislava (Pressburg)

Budapest

HUNGARY

Szeged

Austro-Hungarian Empire

Leningrad (St. Petersberg)

St. Petersberg

ESTONIAN S.S.R.

Estonia

LATVIAN S.S.R.

Riga

Livonia

Kurland

Kovno

LITHUANIAN S.S.R.

Vilnius

Vilna

Kovno

Grodno

Grodno

Vitebsk

Minsk

Minsk

BELORUSSIAN S.S.R.

Smolensk

Mogilev

Mogilev

Russian Empire

RUSSIAN S.F.S.R.

Moscow

U. S. S. R.

Volga

Don

Chernigov

Chernigov

Kiev

Kiev

Poltava

Poltava

Kharkov

UKRAINIAN S.S.R.

Volhynia

Podolia

Ekaterinoslav

Kherson

Kherson

Taurida

Sea of Azou

Crimea

Black Sea

Płock

Łomża

Vistula

Warsaw

Warsaw

Siedlce

Siedlce

Lublin

Lublin

Radom

Kielce

Kalisz

Piotrków

Cracow

Lvov (Lemberg)

Galicia

Dniester

Bukovina

Transcarpathia

MOLDAVIAN S.S.R.

Kishinev

Bessarabia

Dnieper

ROMANIA

Transylvania

Bucharest

Danube

Belgrade

YUGOSLAVIA

Adriatic Sea

ALBANIA

BULGARIA

GREECE

Istanbul

TURKEY

munities and ushered in three decades of anti-Jewish outbursts. An economic policy of pauperization—the infamous May Laws of 1882—included the expulsion of the Jews from villages and rural centers and severe restrictions on their trade in the cities. In 1900 no province in the Pale had less than 14 percent of its Jews on relief, and in Vilna, Kovno, and other cities, more than one in four Jews received some form of charitable aid from the Jewish community.

The banishment of 20,000 Jews from Moscow in 1891 was followed by similar actions in St. Petersburg and Kharkov, the Kishinev Pogrom of 1903, the Russo-Japanese War, more pogroms in 1905, and the 1905 Revolution, all of which accelerated emigration. In one year, 1882, the 13,000 who arrived in the United States following the pogroms of 1881–1882 amounted to almost half the number that had arrived in the entire decade of the 1870s. In 1891 the number of immigrants climbed above 50,000 and then rose by 50 percent the following year in the wake of new disturbances in Russia. Jewish immigration rose from over 200,000 in the 1880s to 300,000 in the 1890s. From 1900 to 1914 another 1.5 million arrived, many of them the wives and children of the earlier immigrants. In seven of the ten years preceding the outbreak of World War I, over 100,000 Jews arrived annually. The peak year was 1906, when 152,000 Jews entered the country, 14 percent of the total immigration for that year.

Data from 1899 to 1914 indicate that the immigrants were generally young people who intended to settle permanently; a high proportion were skilled workers, they were drawn overwhelmingly from cities and towns, and they were part of a family migration. The age group 14 to 40 formed 70 percent of the immigrating Jews, compared with 47 percent of the Jewish population of Russia in that age group. Females were 44 percent, children under 14, 24 percent, all of which indicates a young family migration. The Russian Jewish father in his twenties or thirties preceding his family was typical. The family character of the migration also indicated an intention to remain in America. Between 1908 and 1924, for every 100 Jews arriving in the United States, 5 returned to Europe, as compared to 33 returnees for every 100 in the total immigration.

The Jewish immigration deviated from the norm also in occupational distribution. Of the gainfully employed, 64 percent were skilled workers, compared with about 20 percent for immigrants as a whole. Less than 40 percent of the gainfully employed Jewish population in Russia were skilled workers. The data for mercantile occupations—31 percent of gainfully employed Jews in Russia and 5.5 percent among Jews emigrating from Russia—indicates the self-selecting factor of the immigration. Of the young, skilled workers who left Russia, 60 percent were in the clothing trades. The rise of a Jewish clothing industry in the Pale of the Settlement—a result of the economic forces restructuring the eastern European economy—provided an intermediate stage for many on the move to the United States. Overflowing cities like Łódź, Warsaw, Vilna, and Białystok drew uprooted villagers, artisans, and laborers but offered only a precarious existence.

Jews from southern Russia crossed into Austria-Hungary, often surreptitiously, reached Vienna or Berlin, and then proceeded to one of the transatlantic ports— Hamburg, Bremen, Rotterdam, Amsterdam, or Antwerp. From western Russia, the route crossed the German border to Berlin and thence to the ports. Jewish emigrant-aid societies in Europe tried to direct and control the exodus, but overwhelmed by numbers, they provided mainly emergency assistance at critical transfer points. At the ports of entry in the United States, local relief societies met the ships, guided the arrivals through landing procedures, and provided aid and shelter when necessary. New York, the preeminent port of entry, developed a model organization for the purpose, the Hebrew Immigrant Aid Society (HIAS).

The German Jews had spread out across the land, turning cities like Cincinnati and San Francisco into major Jewish centers. The eastern European, or "Russian" Jews, as they were commonly called, crowded into the great cities of the East and Midwest, especially New York. Of the nearly 1.5 million Jews who landed in New York between 1881 and 1911, about 70 percent remained there. In 1860, the city sheltered 25 percent of the total Jewish population of the United States. In 1880 its share rose to about 33 percent, and four decades later to 45 percent. New York and the cities with the next two largest Jewish populations—Chicago and Philadelphia—accounted for 58 percent of the Jewish population. Seven other cities, all in the East and Midwest, accounted for another 14 percent. Probably 60 percent of American Jews could be found in the northeast corridor from Boston to Baltimore, Md., another 30 percent in the main urban centers of the Midwest. The approximate proportion of Jews in the population of these cities in 1920 was New York (26 percent), Cleveland and Newark (13 percent each), Philadelphia (11 percent), Boston, Baltimore, and Pittsburgh (10 percent each), Chicago (9 percent), St. Louis (7 percent), and Detroit (6 percent).

Like other urban immigrants in the late 19th and early 20th centuries, Russian Jews crowded into ethnic enclaves. Chicago's West Side, Boston's North End, Philadelphia's downtown (South Philadelphia), and New York's Lower East Side were among the better known of these densely populated ghettos. Within the tight compass of the Jewish quarter, the immigrants found work, housing, and a network of familiar social and cultural institutions that offered continuity with the past and transition to the new life. In 1910, 540,000 Jews lived in the 1.5-square-mile area of the Lower East Side. In the typical five- or six-story tenement house, three- and four-room apartments housed families in which four or five children were common, and survival often required taking in a boarder as well. A 1908 survey of 250 East Side families showed that 50 percent slept three or four to a room; nearly 25 percent, five or more to a room; only 25 percent, two to a room. Though the Jews suffered a high rate of nervous disorders, suicides, and tuberculosis, they had a strikingly lower death rate than other immigrants.

A square block in the heart of any large ghetto held among its tenements the workshops of the garment trade, basement synagogues, saloons, and cafes. Workingmen, intellectuals, party functionaries and their followers, pious men, and an assortment of gamblers, prostitutes, *shtarke* (strong-arm men), and their clients rubbed shoulders.

Crime was of great concern to the immigrant com-

munity. *Noms de guerre,* such as Kid Twist, Yuski Nigger ("king of the horse poisoners"), Big Jack Zelig, Dopey Benny (a specialist in strike breaking), and Gyp the Blood, hid the identity of men like Max Zweibach, Joseph Toblinsky, William Albert, Benjamin Fein, and Harry Horowitz. These criminals operated almost exclusively in the Jewish quarter, extracting protection money from vulnerable Jewish merchants, gambling parlors, and houses of prostitution and supplying repeaters on election day and strikebreakers in industrial disputes.

Following every disclosure of vice or crime, the Yiddish press led the Jews in agonizing self-examination, playing on the theme that "the first generation to grow up under the free sky of America" had spawned the criminals. In 1902 German Jewish donors in New York City founded a Jewish Protectory and Aid Society to work with delinquents and prisoners. In 1912 the community established an investigatory bureau to collect evidence and cooperate with the authorities in combating crime in the Jewish neighborhoods. The number of Jewish felons was actually comparatively low, but they were very visible, and Jewish sensitivity made them even more so. In the 1920s, as conditions encouraged the growth of organized crime, criminals who had operated in the immigrant ghettos expanded their activities. Arnold Rothstein (1882–1928), son of a prominent member of New York's Orthodox Jewish community, became a leading underworld figure, and Louis "Lepke" Buchalter (1897–1944) headed the so-called Murder Inc. gang.

The associational strength of the immigrants was drawn from the clusters of fellow townsmen (*landsleit*) who sought one another out in the Jewish quarters. The landsleit met the immigrants' initial problems of adjustment through mutual aid. The vast majority of the 326 permanent congregations on the Lower East Side in 1907 were synagogues of landsleit, microcosms, so far as conditions permitted, of the old kehillahs. A 1917 study of the 365 Lower East Side congregations estimated that 90 percent owned cemetery plots, nearly half had free-loan societies, a third had sick-benefit societies, and nearly half sponsored traditional study groups. From the start, the landsleit also established separate societies or *landsmanshaftn,* which generally offered insurance, sick benefits, interest-free loans, and cemetery rights. They sent aid back to the home town and served as informal but effective employment agencies (contractors in the garment trades frequently recruited their workers from the landsleit). In 1917 about 1,000 such independent societies in New York had an aggregate membership of over 100,000.

Many of the landsmanshaftn found it financially advantageous to affiliate with a fraternal order. The Independent Order B'rith Abraham, one of a number, claimed a national membership of 182,000 in 1913. Regional groupings of landsmanshaftn into Polish, Galician, Romanian, and Sephardic confederations also formed to sponsor major philanthropic projects such as old-age homes, religious schools, hospitals, and orphan asylums. Through these sometimes complex undertakings, the landsmanshaftn introduced their members to American business practices and civic organization.

A newcomer's immediate need was a job. Most often he found it in one of the industries in the Jewish quarter, especially the clothing industry. In 1900 one out of every three Russian Jews employed in the major cities made his living in some branch of the garment trades. A high degree of specialization in production allowed the immigrant to quickly master a subspecialty commensurate with his experience and physical stamina. Small contractors and subcontractors recruited their own labor forces and organized production in the lofts and tenement flats of the Jewish quarter. Poverty and long workdays—until the turn of the century a 70-hour week was not uncommon—made proximity of shop and home imperative.

Other ghetto industries were the tobacco-and-cigar industry, which accounted for 7 percent of Jewish employment, and home construction (usually renovating ghetto property), which accounted for 6 percent in 1900. Many were bakers. The slaughtering and dressing of meat became Jewish industries because of the ritual requirements of *kashruth.*

But the apparel trade, with its 60-percent share of the 60 percent of Russian Jews in industry, was the backbone of the Jewish neighborhood economy in New York, Boston, Philadelphia, Baltimore, and Chicago. In New York in 1880 almost all of the almost 1,000 major clothing manufacturers were German Jews: they employed 64,669 people. By 1913 the industry's 16,552 factories were largely owned by Russian Jews and employed 312,245 people, about three-quarters of whom were also Russian Jews.

Jewish immigrant enclaves provided a range of entrepreneurial opportunities. In 1900 one-fifth of the gainfully employed Russian Jews were in mercantile trade; of these, a quarter were petty tradesmen and peddlers, and nearly half were proprietors of retail stores. A significant number acquired some measure of wealth. One reliable observer writing about New York in 1905 remarked: "Almost every newly arrived Russian Jewish laborer comes into contact with a Russian Jewish employer, almost every Russian tenement dweller must pay his exorbitant rent to a Jewish landlord." The Russian Jewish "fortunes" ranged between $25,000 and $200,000, he noted. Contracting in the apparel trades permitted the aspiring businessman to go into business with minimal capital by using family labor and a few hired workers. The chances of rising to manufacturer were slim, and the rate of business failures among manufacturers considerable, but it was an expanding industry, and the number of Russian Jewish clothing manufacturers nonetheless grew.

Real estate offered opportunities for those who had capital, access to credit, and willingness to invest in deteriorating property. The movement to newer neighborhoods after 1900 provided additional opportunities. By 1910 the class of retail merchants, proprietors of small businesses, white-collar workers, and professionals constituted a much larger share of the gainfully employed Jews than it had a decade before.

The newcomers who were religiously Orthodox—in all likelihood the majority of immigrants, at least when they arrived—transplanted their institutions and way of life with difficulty. In the towns they left, the traditional communal polity still exercised considerable control. Social movements and external pressures had weakened its consensual basis—a development more evident in the cities than in the towns—but the tradi-

tional structure was still intact. In education, charity, and religious needs, communal organization functioned well enough. In the United States, however, the very conditions of freedom and the absence of corporate group status, which the immigrants accepted gratefully, left only voluntary means for reestablishing their way of life. Various ideological movements competed freely for their loyalty, and fraternal orders, trade unions, cultural centers, and recreational enterprises offered alternatives to the synagogue community. A more direct confrontation to the Orthodox way of life was the economic necessity or opportunity of violating the Sabbath, so central to the Jewish religious culture.

The failure to re-create an authoritative religious leadership was a crucial element in the erosion of the Orthodox community, manifesting itself most critically in the decline of the rabbinate. In eastern Europe the rabbi's duties stemmed from his expertise in expounding the religious law that regulated Jewish civil life. He also served as arbitrator, overseer of public institutions, and scholar-teacher. In the United States his communal role atrophied. Supervising kashruth became a private, commercial undertaking, and the highly responsible function of adjudicating divorce cases now belonged to the state courts; granting a religious divorce, in fact, came perilously close to being a criminal act. At best, the rabbi found employment with a congregation that gave him no security, meager wages, and little authority. Most immigrant synagogues neither had the funds nor felt the need for a rabbi. Only rarely did a rabbi command the prestige and congregational support required to exert public authority in the religious life of the community.

Individual synagogues did develop broader constituencies during this period, drawing their members from a homeland region rather than from one particular town or city. They attracted larger, more acculturated, and more affluent memberships, acquired elaborate buildings, and called distinguished rabbis to their pulpits. Their lay leaders provided support for the few collaborative efforts mounted by the Orthodox community, of which religious education was the most difficult and perhaps the most important.

The conventional form of elementary schooling in eastern Europe was the *heder*, a class for boys of mixed ages, which met from early morning to dusk at the home of the teacher. Girls received no formal schooling, though some were instructed privately. The curriculum emphasized reading the prayerbook in Hebrew, studying the Pentateuch, and, for the more advanced, studying Biblical commentaries and the legal codes. Social constraints and parental concern ensured high standards. In the United States the heder became a supplementary school that children attended after public-school hours, and in the absence of communal restraints, it soon degenerated. A 1909 survey of Jewish education in New York described a heder as meeting "in a room or two, in the basement or upper floor of some old dilapidated building where the rent is at a minimum." The masters were ill equipped, their approach to education sterile, and their "sole purpose to eke out some kind of livelihood." Reports from Chicago and Philadelphia confirmed the survey's overall conclusion.

The enervating struggle for survival in part explained the acquiescence of immigrant parents to this system, but the alacrity with which they embraced the public school and relegated religious education to an ancillary position also indicated a new set of priorities. The free state school promised material and social betterment; the heder provided the minimum Jewish continuity. Parental exhortations to the young to find success in the secular world heightened the conflict between the traditional culture and the American way.

Traditionalists tried to remedy the inadequacy of the heder by establishing parochial schools, Talmudic academies, and communal supplementary education, but in 1910 there were only two parochial schools and a small nucleus of an academy, all in New York. Orthodoxy had neither the money, the leadership, nor the will to support more.

The afternoon communal school proved most promising. Its origin was the European Talmud Torah, a charity school for those unable to afford tuition for the heder. In the United States it retained its charitable and consequently communal character. Popular support, public accountability, and larger enrollments led to better pedagogy and more effective management. A New York survey in 1909 recorded 14,000 children attending 468 heders, and 10,000 attending 22 Talmud Torah schools. As their superiority to the heder became apparent, the Talmud Torahs began to lose their stigma as charity schools. By the decade after 1910, all large immigrant centers had them, usually supported by the lay leaders of the larger, community-minded synagogues.

Despite these signs of renewal, Orthodoxy as guardian and moderator of transplanted east European Jewry lost its hegemony in the passage to the United States. Most immigrants retained some allegiance to tradition —synagogues overflowed on the High Holy Days, and enterprising religious functionaries organized services in hundreds of halls. Most children received some religious training, for which parents preferred the old-country form of education to the modern schools established in the immigrant quarters by Americanized Jews. In the 1920s successful Americanized immigrants moved out of the ghettos and established synagogues that were still traditional but more lenient and moderately innovative, a compromise between their American middle-class desire for social integration and their ties to the traditional culture.

Socialism and Zionism, the secular ideologies from eastern Europe, opened new fissures within the communities, yet they also offered theories and programs that transcended ghetto parochialism. The ideologues and activists who were the pacesetters of these movements infused Yiddish culture with vitality and made it responsive to immigrant needs. The Yiddish press, theater, and literature were both polemical platforms and binding forces.

The Yiddish poets and prose writers—the "sweatshop school"—described the crushing, dehumanizing experience of industrial work. Morris Rosenfeld (1862–1923) wrote poems about the pain of never seeing his son awaken, of leaving for the shop while the child still slept and returning late at night. In 1907 a group of newly arrived immigrant writers dubbed the *Yunge* (young ones) launched another literary movement. More sophisticated than their predecessors and in-

fluenced by contemporary European trends, the poets Mani Leib (1884–1953) and H. Leivick (1886–1962) and the novelist Joseph Opatashu (1886–1954), wrote with an intimacy that reflected their weariness of high-flown rhetoric; they demanded art in place of propaganda. Other, still younger writers calling themselves the *In Zich* (introspectives) rebelled against the Yunge in the 1920s. Popular Yiddish novelists like Sholem Asch (1880–1957) and I.J. Singer (1893–1944), translated into English for American readers, achieved some popularity with their themes of Jewish life in eastern Europe and immigrant life in America.

Jacob Gordin (1853–1909) introduced serious drama to the Yiddish theater at the turn of the century and opened the way for others, such as David Pinski (1872–1959), whose works were produced by Max Rheinhardt in Germany, and Peretz Hirshbein (1880–1948). In the 1920s a revival of serious theater included experimental groups of merit. But the Yiddish theater was also recreation for the multitudes with its musicals and melodramatic potboilers—*White Slave, Love for Sale, Money, Love and Shame.* Benefit night, when organizations sold blocks of tickets, turned theater-going into a communal event. In New York in 1917 seven houses were presenting Yiddish plays, and Boston, Philadelphia, Baltimore, Chicago, and Los Angeles had Yiddish theaters. The spirited literary life of the Jewish quarter catered to all tastes and interests. Journals were launched and closed, literary feuds fought on the lecture circuit and in the newspapers, and, inevitably, politics and ideology left their imprint.

The immigrant community also developed a vigorous trade-union movement before World War I. Seasonal work, the decentralization into small plants and sweatshops, and continual turnover in manpower were long the bane of union organizers. Dual unionism and socialist factionalism further aggravated their difficulties. After 1900, however, increased immigration, experience, and a lessening of internal dissension provided a basis for expansion and consolidation of the unions. From 1909 to 1914 a series of massive strikes, often accompanied by brutality, in New York and Chicago transformed the unions into stable, aggressive organizations.

The "uprising of the twenty thousand" opened the union era. Young Jewish and Italian girls—many in their teens—in the shirtwaist branch of the garment industry held out on strike from November 1909 to February 1910, despite the blows of hired thugs and the abuses of the police and the courts. Progressives and feminists aided the strikers. Wealthy New York women raised bail for the arrested girls, and Columbia Law School dean George W. Kirchway (1885–1942), among others, helped defend them in court. The cloak makers struck half a year later, an event styled "the great revolt." The chairman of the strike committee, Abraham Rosenberg (1870–1935), saw the thousands leaving the shops in response to the strike order: "I could only picture to myself such a scene taking place when the Jews were led out of Egypt." Peacemakers from the settlement houses and from the Jewish elite interceded. Lillian Wald (1867–1940) of the Henry Street Settlement, Henry Moskowitz (1879–1936) of the Madison Street Settlement, and the two leading figures in Jewish communal affairs, Jacob H. Schiff (1847–1920), head of

Kuhn, Loeb and Company, and Louis Marshall (1856–1929) put pressure on the Russian Jewish manufacturers who refused to recognize the union. Through the efforts of Boston department store owner A. Lincoln Filene, Louis D. Brandeis (1856–1941), the lawyer and social reformer, entered the mediation effort and ended the strike. The 1910 Chicago strike in the men's clothing industry and others elsewhere followed a similar pattern.

Settlements modeled after the "protocol of peace" negotiated by Brandeis established the preferential union shop, lowered the workweek to an average of 50 hours, abolished contracting—the source of the "sweating system"—and provided permanent mediation machinery for settling grievances and overseeing working conditions. Both sides assigned officials to boards; under an impartial chairman and his staff of professional mediators, they dealt with every alleged infraction on all levels of the industry.

For men like Schiff and Marshall, class warfare in the Jewish quarter endangered the position of all Jews; to contain radicalism, they expected Jewish bosses to be reasonable. They also linked the labor problem to settling the newcomers; a more rational organization of the industry, therefore, was part of the Jewish community's responsibility to aid the immigrants. Enough Jewish manufacturers were concerned with their standing in the community to make them amenable to compromise. The union leaders—Morris Hillquit (1869–1933), Meyer London (1871–1926), Benjamin Schlesinger (1876–1932), Max Pine (1866–1928), and Sidney Hillman (1887–1946)—were all committed socialists, but they were bread-and-butter trade-union men at the bargaining table. They shared a Yiddish world with their adversaries and readily accepted the Jewish communal leaders as mediators.

The International Ladies Garment Workers Union (ILGWU), organized in 1900, and the Amalgamated Clothing Workers Union (ACWU), organized in 1914, were the main beneficiaries, but the smaller unions, such as the furriers and the hat and cap makers, expanded as well. In 1917, 250,000 Jews and many non-Jews belonged to these unions. The ILGWU started the first union health center, and its social unionism blossomed into programs of medical care, cooperative housing, unemployment and health insurance, recreational and vacation programs, and retirement benefits. Union economists studied the industry, and union negotiators recommended ways for improving productivity.

Until the New Deal, the union leaders and the rank and file retained much of their European radical heritage derived from the Bund, the Russian Jewish labor movement, many of whose supporters had emigrated after the abortive Russian Revolution of 1905. They considered trade unions as part of a crusade for socialist ideals. Though only a minority were actual members of the Socialist party or the affiliated Jewish Socialist Federation, the Jewish labor movement mobilized impressive support for the party's candidates in New York City elections. In 1914 the Socialist party achieved its greatest election success when Meyer London, a popular labor lawyer, was elected to Congress from the Lower East Side. London told his victory rally that he would show Washington "what the East Side Jew is." Ethnic pride counted for as much as Socialist party prin-

ciples in his position, and the district elected him twice more before it was gerrymandered out of existence. The party reached its peak in New York in 1917 when Morris Hillquit, a founding father of the Jewish trade-union movement, gained 22 percent of the mayoralty vote, and ten Socialist assemblymen, seven aldermen, and a municipal court judge were elected.

The Yiddish press contributed decisively to the collective identity of Jewish workingmen. The *Jewish Daily Forward* (f. 1897) with a daily circulation that climbed from 54,000 in 1908 to 175,000 a decade later, became the popularizer of radical ideas, the interpreter of the United States to the immigrant, and the forum for Yiddish men of letters. Under its influential editor, Abraham Cahan (1860–1951), the *Forward* served as the informal coordinating body of the movement. It reported union events daily, took strong positions on trade-union policy, and during strikes exhorted the workers and raised funds for the strikers. During the years 1908 to 1918 four other dailies were published: the radical *Warheit*, the Orthodox *Tageblat* and *Morgen Zhurnal*, and the liberal-nationalist *Tog*. A score of weeklies represented all socialist schools of thought.

Ambivalence characterized the relationship between the leaders of the labor movement (less so the rank and file) and the Jewish community. Radical leaders saw the struggle of Russian Jewish workingmen against Russian Jewish garment manufacturers as precluding communal collaboration; as assimilationists they also foresaw the amalgamation of all nationality groups into a "cosmopolitan American nation." Although the claims that Orthodoxy was reactionary became less strident as time passed, they remained part of the movement's European inheritance. Zionists were dangerous dreamers, diverting the attention of the masses from the class struggle to pipe dreams of rebuilding Palestine.

The tactics of the labor movement nevertheless took for granted a bedrock of ethnic unity. Striking unions appealed to the entire community for aid and good will; the *Forward* was alert to the ethnic sensibilities and interests of its readers. When the community mobilized all its resources to aid European Jewry during World War I, the Jewish labor movement lent its support. Influential intellectuals formulated a doctrine of secular ethnicity grounded in Yiddish culture and appropriate to America's pluralistic society. At the rank and file level, boundaries blurred. Many saw no conflict between remaining loyal to their landsmanshaft, attending synagogue, sending their children to the heder, sympathizing with Zionism, and belonging to a union.

The significance of the Zionist movement far exceeded its numbers; it had only 12,000 members in 1914. Although immigrants constituted most of its membership, it included an influential group of Americanized and native-born Jews. In the decade before World War I, its emphasis became cultural rather than political. American Zionism saw in the modern resettlement of Palestine (which had begun in 1881) a natural habitat for a renaissance of the Hebrew language and culture. The effort to support that undertaking and the effect of the revived center on the Jewish communities of the diaspora would contribute to the survival of Jews everywhere. Since assimilation loomed as the greatest danger, preservation of the Jewish collectivity transcended all particularist conceptions of Judaism, and

ethnic survival depended on the cooperation of all factions.

Established middle-class American Jews, well integrated into American life, saw the flood of Russian Jewish immigrants as a threat to their own status and as a burdensome problem. Throughout the 1880s and 1890s, leaders of the Jewish charities begged their European confreres to limit or stop the flow of immigration to the United States or at least exercise a rigorous selection. But organizations like the Alliance Israelite Universelle and the Hilfsverein der Deutschen Juden, which extended aid and eased the journey to the United States, were in no position to control the immigrant tide. As it swelled, American Jews were sensitive to the mounting anti-immigration and anti-Semitic feelings among American Gentiles. Their spokesmen criticized both the religious medievalism of the Orthodox Jews and the dangerous radicalism of the socialists.

After the Civil War, Jews had appeared with greater frequency in popular American literature as sinister and mercenary Shylocks demanding their pound of flesh. In 1862 General Ulysses S. Grant issued an order expelling "Jews as a class" from the Union lines for allegedly trading with the enemy. In the 1880s a pattern of social discrimination excluded upper-class Jews from the elite social clubs that 10 and 20 years before had accepted them. Summer resorts began turning them away, and the phrase "we prefer not to entertain Hebrews" commonly appeared in advertisements. Jacob Schiff, one of the most munificent philanthropists of the time, complained in 1898 of the "tacit understanding" that excluded Jews from the "trustee rooms of Columbia College, of the public museums, the public library, and many similar institutions."

By the end of the century, the stereotype of the Jews had become more specific and virulent; they were the money powers, manipulating international finance and involved in a giant conspiracy to dominate the world. Shylock had become Rothschild. The Boston Brahmin Henry Adams expressed his frustration and anger at his class's loss of place and power when he wrote in the 1890s of "a society of Jews and brokers" in which "I have no place. I detest it [the times], and everything that belongs to it, and live only in the wish to see the end of it, with all its infernal Jewry." Ignatius Donnelly, representing a western agrarian radicalism, published a utopian novel, *Caesar's Column* (1891), about a Jewish plot to take over the world. A bitter and defeated Populist leader, Tom Watson, became viciously anti-Semitic as well as anti-Catholic in his declining years in Georgia politics.

Racist and anti-Semitic theories imported from Europe—of Joseph Ernest Renan, Joseph Arthur de Gobineau, and Houston S. Chamberlain—merged with nativist notions. According to these views, clannishness, vulgarity, greed, physical inferiority, parasitism, and intellectualism were inherited traits that the Jews were incapable of shedding. The identification of the Russian Jews with the established American Jews as one racial group confounded and intimidated the Americanized Jewish community.

Notwithstanding the antipathy of the Americanized Jews to the Russian immigrants and the social and cultural distance between them, the older settlers accepted responsibility for the physical welfare and social adjust-

ment of the newcomers. In part their response was self-serving: expediting the integration of the new arrivals would remove the stigma the immigrants placed on all of them. However, American Jews also felt compassion for victims of oppression and recognized their common identity. While they complained of the continued flow of immigration, they opened their philanthropic institutions to the Russian Jews, raised funds to meet their needs, and fought efforts to limit immigration by law.

At first the community simply expanded its facilities and established new ones. Between 1878 and 1890, for example, some 90 new or reorganized YMHAs supplemented their cultural and recreational programs with specific services for young immigrants. Communities began to add vocational training schools, settlement houses, homes for delinquent youths, and agencies for assisting young women and the handicapped. The notions of scientific philanthropy guided the lay leaders and functionaries. The National Conference of Jewish Charities, formed in 1900, stimulated institutional reforms and encouraged clarification of issues and formulation of policy. National agencies were established to deal with family desertion and to divert immigrants to agriculture or to the interior cities.

In response to the rapid expansion of the older charitable societies and the mushrooming of new ones, 23 cities had organized local federations of Jewish charities by 1914. Their immediate purpose was joint fund-raising to increase income, but only institutions with modern standards and nonsectarian policies were eligible for such financing, so the federation tended to exclude the Orthodox institutions and those established by the immigrants. Thus the elite sought to maintain their control over the absorption of the immigrants and reduce to a minimum the detrimental effect of "inferior and alien" influences.

Americanization dominated the thought and the policy of the lay leadership. Jewish settlement houses in New York, Boston, Cleveland, Chicago, Milwaukee, and Cincinnati, such as the Educational Alliance, aimed to be of an "Americanizing, educational, social and humanizing character—for the moral and intellectual improvement of the inhabitants of the East Side." The Alliance offered a rich program in art, music appreciation, drama, physical education, English, civics, and domestic science. In its early years it prohibited the use of Yiddish in public programs, but after 1900 it softened its antipathy to Yiddish culture in an attempt to reach its constituents more effectively. Uptown philanthropists, including Jacob Schiff, Louis Marshall, and Daniel Guggenheim (1856–1930), financed the reorganization of the neo-Orthodox Jewish Theological Seminary (JTS), although they themselves were Reform Jews. To head it, they brought Solomon Schechter (1847–1915), reader in rabbinics at Cambridge University, a traditionalist of eastern European background with impeccable academic credentials. The JTS was to prepare young Russian Jews to be rabbis, faithful to tradition and at the same time leaders in Americanization. Young American-trained Russian Jews were appointed to administer the institutions of the established community.

A number of factors drew the old and new groups together. The Jewish labor movement and the Russian Jewish intellectuals won the attention of urban reformers. Brandeis's mediation of the cloak makers' strike in 1910 and his acceptance of the chairmanship of the board of arbitration renewed this assimilated German Jew's interest in his people; he became one of their outstanding leaders. American Jewish leaders were also influenced by the views of settlement workers, whose criticism of quick Americanization as socially disintegrative found wide support, for Jewish survivalists were at the same time elaborating these attitudes into theories of ethnic pluralism.

Between 1903 and 1914, crises at home and abroad interacted to spur communal undertakings on a new scale. The 1903 Kishinev pogrom and the two years of violence and bloodshed that followed elicited an unprecedented outburst of activity. Ad hoc committees and coordinating bodies raised emergency funds for relief work, organized mass protest meetings, and negotiated with the highest echelons of government to intercede on behalf of Russia's Jews. The experience provoked a public debate over the need for a permanent, central agency for American Jewry. The immigrant community demanded a representative body elected by all Jewish organizations. In response, the German Jewish elite in 1906 formed the American Jewish Committee (AJC) to defend Jewish interests. With men of the stature and means of Schiff, Marshall, Oscar Straus, Julius Rosenwald, Cyrus Adler (1863–1940), and Julian W. Mack (1866–1943), the AJC assumed the leadership of American Jewry on national issues.

The AJC, sensitive to accusations of elitism, coopted to its councils—though not to its inner circles—Zionists and immigrant leaders and supported an ambitious program for creating a new communal structure. Under its aegis, local community councils would coordinate all Jewish activities in their districts. The one major attempt to organize an all-embracing communal polity, the New York Kehillah, which was established in 1909, foundered in internal dissension and apathy a decade later. In national affairs, the AJC lobbied against immigration-restriction legislation and campaigned to abrogate the commercial treaty between Russia and the United States. Inspired by the need of the German Jewish leaders to reassert their hegemony, the AJC used its position to defend the rights of the Russian Jews, who, in return, accepted its leadership, although they resented the imperiousness of the notables and criticized their assimilationist philosophy.

The rapid Americanization of the second generation and their alienation from their ethnic heritage occupied the attention of communal leaders and young intellectuals during these years. Existing philosophies seemed unlikely to stem the tide of assimilation. Reform Judaism had removed all barriers to Americanization, and Orthodoxy survived only in the isolated immigrant synagogues and sterile heders of the Jewish quarter. Survivalists sought a broader interpretation of Judaism that would stress the possibility of creating a viable ethnic culture in America. Israel Friedlaender (1876–1920) a young professor of Bible at the JTS, and Judah L. Magnes (1877–1948), a Reform rabbi and Zionist, wrote, lectured, and used the small but influential Zionist organization to spread their ideas that Jewish survival depended on a synthesis of "religion plus nationalism." "In the great palace of American civilization," Friedlaender wrote in 1907, "we shall occupy our own corner, which we will decorate and beautify to the best of

our taste and ability, and make . . . an object of admiration for all the dwellers of the palace." Those who considered ethnic survival both desirable and compatible with American life rejected the melting-pot concept in favor of ethnic pluralism. In 1909 Magnes delivered a sermon entitled, "A Republic of Nationalities," in which he declared that a multiethnic society would enrich American culture and sustain the psychic health of the nation. Strong roots in one's ethnic heritage would avoid the social disorganization caused by immigration and assure a sound integration into American society.

Horace Kallen (1882–1974), a young professor of philosophy and a Zionist, offered a more secular interpretation. Hebraism, the total historical experience of the Jews, constituted the basis for Jewish survival and was a vital component of American civilization. Kallen's influential essay, "Democracy versus the Melting Pot," argued that ethnic self-realization was a part of democracy. Authentic America was a "democracy of nationalities."

Others elaborated on these theories. In 1915 before a Fourth of July audience in Boston's Faneuil Hall, Brandeis declared that "the new nationalism adopted by America" proclaimed the "right and the duty" of each "race or people" to develop and that such "differentiative development" was to the benefit of the United States. On another occasion Brandeis proclaimed, "To be good Americans, we must be better Jews, and to be better Jews, we must become Zionists."

Critical of the secular-nationalist emphasis and the ethnic separatism implied in the Kallen-Brandeis position, the young Jewish educator Isaac B. Berkson (1891–1975) enlarged upon the Friedlaender-Magnes approach. A protégé of Friedlaender and a staff member of the New York Kehillah's Bureau of Jewish Education, which was directed by Samson Benderly (1876–1944), Berkson presented a "community theory" of American life. He believed that Kallen's "federation of nationalities" assigned too powerful a place to ethnicity, which was inconsonant with the free play of democratic forces. The ethnic group was not self-perpetuating; one had to nurture it within a voluntaristic setting. Its survival depended on the education of the young. The community's ethnic school, which should be supplementary to the public school, was the primary agency of group maintenance.

All these theories of survivalism influenced communal policy. In the decade after 1910 the Friedlaender-Benderly-Berkson view prevailed in the movement to establish a modern Jewish educational system. Around the Kallen-Brandeis approach, with its strong ethnic and democratic motifs, the anti-elitists, anti-assimilationists, and secularists rallied to challenge the established leadership.

During World War I and the immediate postwar period, the attention of the American Jewish community shifted to events overseas. East European Jewry, trapped between the contending armies on the eastern front and then caught in the Russian civil wars, suffered famine, expulsion, and large-scale pogroms. Immigrants, fearful for their kinsmen, funneled aid and personal remittances to the homeland town and family through their societies and institutions. The sense of obligation in the community led to an unprecedented collaborative undertaking to provide relief. American Jewry was very aware of its new role as the one Jewish center of strength and influence unscathed by war. It bore the responsibility for carrying on the struggle for political equality and the right of self-determination.

The creation of the American Jewish Joint Distribution Committee (JDC), the leading agency for overseas relief, expressed this new temper. Although the German Jewish elite supplied the directors and the largest contributors—Felix Warburg (1871–1937), son-in-law of Schiff and senior partner in the firm of Kuhn, Loeb, was chairman—Orthodox and labor relief organizations were constituent members and, despite disputes over policy, the JDC remained united. Between 1914 and 1918 it raised slightly over $16.5 million, and in the first four postwar years, an additional $47.4 million.

A sophisticated and efficient organization gathered and distributed these funds. With extraordinary effectiveness, the JDC fund-raising apparatus reached all sectors of the Jewish population and became a unifying force. The transfer and distribution of aid entailed delicate diplomatic negotiations with the State Department and with governments at war as well as complex political dealings with local groups. By the early 1920s the JDC had established a vast relief network in Europe staffed by field workers and specialists. In addition to direct relief, it also developed programs of economic self-help, health and child care, and community reconstruction. At the height of its work, the JDC was aiding 700,000 Jews.

The cautious AJC, headed by the very able Louis Marshall, had preempted the area of diplomacy and politics. When the Zionists in early 1915 led a movement for a democratically elected central body, an American Jewish Congress, the AJC regarded the movement as a populist challenge to its hegemony and as a menace to the position of Jews in American society. The AJC notables viewed secularism—particularly secular Zionism, with its implied political loyalty to a foreign cause—with apprehension and the congress movement as an attempt to "consolidate the Jews of America into a separate nationalistic group." The leading spokesmen for the congress movement, Brandeis and Stephen S. Wise (1874–1949), a popular young Reform rabbi, social reformer, and Zionist, condemned the AJC as oligarchic and as misunderstanding American democracy and the Jewish collectivity. The Zionist organization they headed had increased tenfold during these years and had won to its ranks prominent figures like Julian Mack, Felix Frankfurter (1882–1965), Bernard Flexner (1865–1945), and Eugene Meyer (1875–1959).

Thus the immediate political issues became entangled with fundamental questions of the character of Jewish group identity and the nature of American society. The congress issue provoked an ardent debate that engaged all segments of American Jewry. America's entry into the war, the fall of the Russian tsar, and Britain's Balfour Declaration, supporting a Jewish homeland in Palestine, further intensified the conflict over principles and power, though by then a compromise had established a congress whose scope was narrowly defined.

In 1918 delegates representing the whole spectrum of Jewish organizational life, including some reluctant emissaries from the Jewish labor movement, met to select their representatives to the Paris Peace Conference.

Those chosen, a cross section of the American Jewish community, were instructed to support demands for Jewish civil and group rights in the new states to be recognized at Versailles and to support the cause of a Jewish home in Palestine. The diplomatic skills of Marshall, the dominant figure of the delegation, enabled him to balance a maze of conflicting views within his own group and among the European Jewish representatives and the Zionists. His lobbying was instrumental in winning guarantees of minority rights for Jews and other ethnic groups in the treaties of the eastern European nations.

The congress convened a second time in 1920 and, as previously agreed, received the delegation's report and disbanded. Those who favored a permanent organization remained to announce the immediate establishment of a new congress under Stephen Wise. It was politically more liberal, activist, and pro-Zionist than the AJC, whose preeminence it challenged, but the congress could no longer claim to speak in the name of all American Jewry.

American Jews found the path to cooperation easy when it came to overseas relief and philanthropy. On issues that touched on ideology, achieving a consensus proved more difficult. More elusive still was the goal of recasting American Jewry into a democratic communal polity. Nevertheless, by 1920 a functional pluralism existed; American Jews had become an interdependent community despite their diversity.

The near-cessation of immigration from 1915 to 1920 coincided with improved economic conditions that markedly raised the standard of living for the mass of Jewish workers. The average annual income of a garment worker in New York City nearly tripled between 1914 and 1919. Workingmen as well as merchants and white-collar workers moved out of the ghettos. The dichotomy between the German Jewish givers and the Russian Jewish receivers belonged to the past. America's entry into the war also contributed to acculturation. About 250,000 Jews served in the armed forces, the majority of them young immigrants. Jewish organizations fostered, and the Yiddish press publicized, citizenship and Americanization programs and civilian war-aid activities. Sensitivity to anti-Semitism and a need to demonstrate the patriotism of the group brought antagonists together in demonstrations of unity in which a newly self-confident Russian Jewish element and second-generation professionals and communal functionaries asserted themselves and were able to challenge or share leadership with the elite.

IMMIGRATION FROM 1924 TO THE END OF WORLD WAR II

In 1921 nearly 120,000 Jewish immigrants entered the United States, most of them joining families that had arrived earlier. After the passage of the Immigration Restriction Act of 1924, Jewish immigration fell to 10,000; thereafter new immigrants assumed a marginal place in American Jewish life, and rapid acculturation shaped the society.

Occupational change was a critical component. Within the span of one or two generations, eastern European Jews transformed themselves from a working-class population to a middle-class group in business,

white-collar jobs, and the professions. In 1900, 60 percent of the gainfully employed immigrant men were in industry. In the 1930s (according to data from a cluster of smaller cities and from Pittsburgh), the proportion had shrunk to 16.7 percent in the smaller cities and 24.2 percent in Pittsburgh. The proportion in industry of the general work force was two to three times that. In 1900 about 25 percent of the immigrant Jews were in trade or held clerical positions. By the 1930s the proportion had grown to 57 percent in the smaller cities and 63 percent in Pittsburgh, twice that of the general work force. In 1900 about 3 percent of the Russian Jews were in the professions; three decades later, Jewish professionals accounted for about 17 percent and 13 percent in the two surveys, significantly higher than the proportion for the general population. New York, because of its large Jewish population, higher ratio of immigrants, and the dominance of the garment trades, always had a higher proportion of Jews in industry. In the 1930s about 35 percent were in manufacturing, 34 percent in trade, and 11 percent in the professions.

A study comparing foreign- and native-born Jews in three localities during these years sheds some light on the mobility pattern of the second generation. Ten percent of the native-born compared to 18 percent of the foreign-born were in industry; 53 percent of the native-born compared to 62 percent of the foreign-born were in trade. In the professions the figures were 19 percent and 7 percent. In Boston "by 1930, the East European Jews were sufficiently established to give their sons as large a head start as the German Jews had in the late 19th century . . . The rate of initial white-collar jobholding" for Russian Jewish sons in 1930 was 71 percent; for German Jewish sons in the late 1890s it had been 73 percent.

Eastern European Jews became leaders in the motion-picture industry. Beginning as owners of storefront movie theaters in the immigrant neighborhoods (at a time when silent films offered no language barrier), they branched out into film distribution, chains of movie theaters, and then production itself. By the 1930s all but one of the major companies were managed and owned by Jews: Jesse Lasky, Adolph Zukor, and Barney Balaban (Paramount), Carl Laemmle (Universal), Samuel Goldfish (Goldwyn), Louis B. Mayer and Marcus Loew (Metro-Goldwyn-Mayer), Jack and Harry Cohn (Columbia), Sol Brill and William Fox (Twentieth-Century-Fox), Al Lichtman (United Artists) and Sam, Jack, Albert, and Harry Warner (Warner Brothers). Kuhn, Loeb and Company was the first bank to finance motion pictures. The men who entered the industry when it was still unstructured and financially risky shaped a powerful vehicle of mass culture.

The main route out of the working class remained trade. Jews became proprietors, salesmen, and providers of commercial services or white-collar workers such as bookkeepers and clerks. A professional career was a more difficult path and more accessible for the second generation. Professional status was highly esteemed by the group, and the material rewards and self-employment it promised were weighty considerations. Being a scholar carried great prestige in a culture that so revered learning. For immigrant parents, the discipline of learning was a social imperative they well understood, and the utilitarian nature of education in the United States

reinforced it. They encouraged their children to remain in school and go to college. The physicians, dentists, lawyers, and pharmacists serving the immigrant quarter confirmed the promised rewards.

Although accounting and pharmacy were popular, the number of Jews in medicine, dentistry, and law was even more notable. In New York City in 1937, Jews made up 25 percent of the population but 65 percent of its lawyers and judges, 64 percent of its dentists, and 55 percent of its physicians. In Cleveland in 1938, Jews constituted 7.7 percent of the population, 23 percent of the lawyers, 21 percent of the physicians, and 18 percent of the dentists.

The middle-class character of American Jews was also manifest during the 1920s and 1930s in their lowered birthrate. In the first two decades of the century, Jewish and Italian immigrant families were about the same size. By 1925 the Jews of New York showed a lower birthrate than the rest of the population, and it declined even further in the 1930s. Between 1920 and 1940, the decline was double that of the birthrate for the native white population as a whole.

In the interwar years the regional distribution of the Jewish population changed very little. The five cities that accounted for 63 percent of the Jewish population in 1918 maintained the same rank order 20 years later. Among the five cities that accounted for the next 9 percent, rank-order changes were minor. Los Angeles entered the list in the 1930s at seventh place.

Migration within the city accelerated, as the lower-middle-class and middle-class neighborhoods absorbed the young and newly prosperous. The older, poorer, and more religious Jews were left behind. In Harlem the rise and fall of the Jewish community was complete by 1930. Of 177,000 Jews living there in 1923, fewer than 5,000 remained in 1930. More commonly, however, neighborhoods that began receiving substantial numbers of Jews before World War I expanded rapidly during the war and the decade that followed, then remained stable until after World War II, restrained by the Depression and the war years.

In many of the new neighborhoods, the Jewish population was no less concentrated than in the ghettos it had left behind. Discriminatory housing practices and prejudice explain this in part, but the desire to remain in a Jewish environment was also important. By the end of the 1920s, a social hierarchy of neighborhoods reached to the suburbs, where the most acculturated and affluent of the Russian Jews were closing the gap with the old German Jewish families. In 1930 half the members of the Reform temples were of eastern European origin, and the most successful of the Americanized Russian Jews were elected as officers in philanthropic organizations and as members of the German Jewish clubs. A substantial segment of them were still Yiddish-speaking, however. Nearly half the Jewish population in 1920 declared Yiddish to be its mother tongue. In 1940 the proportion was somewhat more than a third. Even outside the ghetto they continued to be consumers of a flourishing Yiddish culture. In the mid-twenties, five Yiddish dailies were published in New York City and five more outside it.

Two institutions were found in almost every middle-class Jewish community; synagogues and community centers or YMHAs met traditional needs, represented group continuity, and satisfied social and recreational interests in a congenial setting.

In the 1920s over 1,000 synagogues were established in the new neighborhoods. Nearly all were sizable; some were elaborate structures with classrooms and recreational facilities. The old-town or regional organizing principle of the immigrant congregation had disappeared. Though many of the synagogues were Orthodox, they were meant to appeal to a modern, middle-class, Americanized public in a changed neighborhood. They overlooked the heterodoxy of many of their congregants and tried to win the indifferent back to Orthodoxy. They established schools to attract young families to the congregation and engaged "modern," English-speaking rabbis. The effort to revitalize American Orthodoxy included the founding of Yeshiva College in 1928 under the presidency of Bernard Revel (1865–1941). The goal of the college, which was linked to the Isaac Elchanan Theological Seminary, Orthodoxy's largest rabbinical school, was to educate lay as well as professional leaders.

Conservative Judaism also found a new following. With intellectual roots in 19th-century western Europe and the United States, the movement stressed "the maintenance of Jewish tradition in its historical continuity" but countenanced change in religious practice, provided it was done with reverence for "historical Judaism." Solomon Schechter, the president of the JTS from 1902 to his death in 1915, gave form and direction to this Conservative style, carefully eschewing doctrinal formulations. By the 1920s graduates of the JTS were entering the rabbinate, and the JTS was a prestigious center of Jewish scholarship. Schechter created a formal body, the United Synagogues of America, as an institutional framework. For Americanized Russian Jews and their offspring, elements of tradition coupled with innovations of convenience satisfied their desire for continuity and for accommodation to American middle-class norms. The Conservative synagogues were also centers for a great many civic, social, and cultural functions. By the end of World War II it had become the largest wing of Judaism.

The Jewish community center was a secular institution from the outset, Jewish but nonsectarian. An outgrowth of the YMHAs of the 19th century and the Jewish-sponsored settlement houses of the early 20th, it blended the two purposes of its predecessors: to give young Americanized Jews a place to pursue their essentially American interests and to hasten the Americanization of the immigrants. In the 1920s, when these centers were moved to the new neighborhoods, they continued to be supported by the federations, whose sponsorship was justified on the grounds that the second generation needed guidance and a suitable setting as they took their place in American society. Professionals, increasingly influential in the management of the centers, supplied the theory: character building and self-development through recreational programs and social group work—by definition nonsectarian—would imbue the young with democratic and humanistic values. The 300 centers, with nearly 400,000 members by the late 1930s, remained, ideologically at least, the domain of the nonsectarians. Financed by the Jewish community, staffed by Jewish volunteers and professionals, and serving a Jewish public at a time when so-

cial discrimination outside the neighborhood was common, the centers were an ethnic haven.

Synagogues and community centers reflected only in part the state of the American Jewish community. Only a third of the Jewish families in 1930 were affiliated with a synagogue, and only a quarter of the Jewish children attended religious schools. Many were satisfied with a superficial or peripheral identification with the community. For a considerable number, residing in a Jewish neighborhood was the sole manifestation of ethnic identity.

Mordecai M. Kaplan, a religious thinker associated with the Conservatives, was a founder of the Reconstructionist movement and influential in the JTS. His ideas found expression in his book *Judaism as a Civilization* (1934), in which he offered an overarching framework for the diversity and secularization of Jewish life. His theological formulations raised a storm of opposition among Conservative and Orthodox rabbis. Judaism, he wrote, embraced "language, folkways, patterns of social organization, social habits and standards, spiritual ideals, which give individuality to a people and differentiate it from other peoples." Jewish religion was the expression of group consciousness. Kaplan accorded a central place to Palestine in his program and called for an all-encompassing reconstruction of Jewish life and Jewish communal organization, although he acknowledged the priority that American life had on the individual's loyalty. The majority of American Jews agreed with Kaplan but were not prepared to make the commitments he felt were necessary to improve the quality and the efficacy of the community's institutions. Religiously skeptical or apathetic, they sought a Jewish identity that would be compatible with their Americanness and their liberal secular outlook.

The frenzied nativism of the 1920s intensified anti-Jewish agitation. The anti-Semitism that had taken shape the decade before made the Jews particularly vulnerable to the xenophobia of the times. During the Red Scare, the idea of the Jew as Bolshevik plotting to overthrow the state led government agents and journalists to search for revolutionaries among the Jewish radical movements. At congressional and legislative hearings, at public meetings, and in the organs of the Ku Klux Klan, immigrant Jews were portrayed as architects of the Russian Revolution and as agents of world Communism preparing to seize control of America. In 1920 Henry Ford added his powerful voice to the anti-Semitic campaign in his *Dearborn Independent*, a weekly he distributed through his thousands of dealerships, featuring accounts of cabals of Jewish bankers maneuvering to gain control of the economy. Especially pernicious was the wide publicity it gave to the notorious anti-Semitic tract, *The Protocols of the Elders of Zion*, which purported to be the report of a secret Jewish plan to establish a world dictatorship through financial machinations, war, and revolution.

The debate over immigration restriction from 1918 to 1924 provided a public platform for nativist racist theories. The notion of Nordic superiority, which became the justification for the national-origins quotas of the 1924 immigration law, was laced with anti-Jewish animus. One influential State Department report described the Jewish immigrants in transit to the United States as "of the usual ghetto type . . . filthy, un-

American and often dangerous in their habits . . . abnormally twisted, [their] dullness and stultification resulting from past years of oppression and abuse."

Although virulent anti-Semitism diminished in the mid-1920s, the prewar pattern of social discrimination continued. The barriers that affluent German Jews had met in seeking entrée to the elite clubs and resorts and, for their children, to the prestigious schools had widened to restrain the more modest ambitions of upwardly mobile Russian Jews. Housing restrictions in new areas of settlement and job discrimination in white-collar employment were common after 1910. A decade later the movement to the better neighborhoods encountered a well-developed system of restrictive real-estate covenants. The second generation met harsher barriers in the job market. Newspaper employment advertisements showed a sharp rise in discriminatory restrictions against Jews between 1920 and 1926, followed by a modest decline and then a renewed rise in the 1930s. Jewish stenographers, bookkeepers, and sales help found the large corporations and chain stores closed to them. Outside the large cities, Jews and Catholics rarely found employment in the public schools.

Discrimination in higher education particularly agitated the Jewish community. In the early 1920s the eastern universities, with large numbers of Jewish students, imposed quotas, which they defended as a means of correcting geographic and social imbalance of the student body or as a prophylactic measure against growing anti-Semitism. When Harvard's president, Lawrence Lowell, recommended a formal quota for the latter reason, Jewish leaders protested vigorously: "The only tests that we can recognize [for admission]," the AJC's Louis Marshall wrote, "are those of character and scholarship." The student body supported Lowell, but in the end the faculty defeated the proposal. Medical schools were most severe in their restrictive policies. The number of Jewish students enrolled in New York State medical schools dropped from 214 in 1920 to 108 in 1940. Marshall's dictum did not become university policy generally until after World War II.

Within the academic community, discrimnation was reflected in rare faculty appointment of Jews and in their exclusion from fraternities. Ludwig Lewisohn (1882–1955), already a man of literary attainments when he completed his graduate studies, nevertheless found all academic doors closed. Lionel Trilling (1905–1975), who began teaching literature at Columbia University in 1931, was the first Jew appointed to the English department. Thurman Arnold (1891–1969) of the Yale Law School, trying to place one of his graduates (Abe Fortas, 1910–, a future justice of the Supreme Court) in the mid-1930s, received a reply from the dean at Northwestern University that his colleagues had not once appointed a Jewish candidate during his tenure at the school. Another indication of social discrimination on the campuses was the rise in Jewish Greek-letter fraternities: 4 in 1908, 25 in 1926, and 37 ten years later.

In the 1920s personal and communal achievements in some measure offset distress over discrimination, but on both counts, the situation deteriorated in the 1930s. Hitler's accession to power, Nazi expansionism, and anti-Semitism at home struck a population already suffering from the debilitating effects of the Depression. The confluence of economic distress and anti-Semitism

provided a fertile field for demagogues preaching hate, while inadequate financial resources and discord among the Jewish community agencies over strategies for counteracting anti-Jewish attitudes impaired their ability to respond.

The German-American Bund represented a direct connection between Nazi Germany and rising domestic anti-Semitism; the bund received funds, organizational leadership, and propaganda material from the German government. Of greater concern was the influence of Charles E. Coughlin, a Roman Catholic priest whose nationwide broadcasts and newspaper, *Social Justice,* won an immense following. His anti-Communist crusade and his populist rhetoric relied on the old stereotypes of the Jews as Communist plotters and international bankers. By 1938 he was justifying the Nazi persecution of Jews as a defense against Communism. Important Catholic diocesan papers supported Coughlin's position and encouraged the Christian Front, an organization propagating anti-Semitism. Between 1939 and 1941, when the United States entered the war, some isolationists attacked the Jews as "the most dangerous force pushing the nation into war" and were echoed in Congress by Senators Burton K. Wheeler and Gerald Nye. During the war public opinion polls showed hostility toward the Jews rising substantially; soon after the war it disappeared almost entirely.

The refugees from Nazi Germany who began arriving in the middle 1930s—from 1935 through 1941 nearly 150,000 came—were for the most part middle-aged and middle-class: 74 percent were over 40; nearly 20 percent were professionals, another 60 percent were in commerce. Manhattan's West Side and Washington Heights, where about half the newcomers settled, became known as the "Fourth Reich." Chicago and San Francisco also had identifiable colonies. Arriving in the middle of the Depression, the refugees at first found it difficult to use their professional and entrepreneurial skills. For this highly educated, cosmopolitan group, cultural isolation and the loss of social and economic status made adjustment particularly painful. In 1941 a study was made to refute charges that the refugees were a burden on the economy; it reported that refugees had established 239 businesses in 82 cities and had created jobs for others.

Albert Einstein (1879–1955), the Nobel laureate in physics, was the best known of a brilliant army of refugee scientists, writers, artists, and scholars. Others like Otto Stern (1888–1969), Leo Szilard (1898–1964), Eugene P. Wigner (1902–), Emilio G. Segrè (1905–), Edward Teller (1908–), and Victor F. Weisskopf (1908–) contributed to atomic research. Psychoanalysis, a field in which Jews had played a dominant role in Europe, was enriched in the United States by outstanding refugees, including Helene Deutsch (1884–1973), Ernst Simmel (1882–1947), Heinz Hartmann (1894–1970), Hanns Sachs (1881–1947), Erich Fromm (1900–), Bruno Bettelheim (1903–), and Erik Erikson (1902–). Among the refugee social scientists were Hannah Arendt (1906–1975), Paul Lazarsfeld (1901–1976), Kurt Lewin (1890–1947), Herbert Marcuse (1898–1979), and Leo Strauss (1899–1973).

All efforts to ease the rigid immigration laws and increase the number of Jewish refugees failed. A bill that would have allowed 20,000 German Jewish children to enter the United States outside the quota was defeated in 1941. Other bills and appeals to the administration to permit refugees to enter by mortgaging future quotas and to open Alaska to them met the same fate. The State Department imposed even more complicated and time-consuming procedures on applications for visas. In mid-1940, when precious unused visas would have saved lives, the official in charge recommended putting "every obstacle in the way" and suggested various administrative devices that would "postpone and postpone and postpone the granting of visas." As reports from Europe described Nazi excesses against the Jews, American Zionists appealed to the administration to pressure Britain to alter its Palestine policy, but no action was taken. Jewish Palestine had been the most important haven for refugees during the 1930s, but Britain drastically reduced immigration in 1939 and deported Jews fleeing Europe who succeeded in reaching its shores. In late 1942 the State Department deliberately suppressed for months the first authoritative underground reports on the Nazi plan to systematically exterminate all Jews.

American Jewry was ill prepared to face the crisis. A conglomeration of institutions and agencies, reflecting different religious persuasions, conceptions of Jewish group life, and strategies of action, frequently competed with or duplicated each other's work. About 25 major organizations with national constituencies were in the field in the 1930s; representatives of 85 national organizations attended the American Jewish Conference in 1943. No less than four central agencies combated anti-Semitism and discrimination. The AJC, the oldest and most prestigious of them, had amassed an impressive record over the years by firmly but unobtrusively interceding in every serious instance of prejudice. It monitored state-church relations, cultivated ties with liberal church and civil-rights groups, litigated cases, and maintained relations with political and government figures. Its imgage continued to be one of conservative, moderate old German Jewish wealth. In keeping with this elitist cast, it eschewed public action, which it considered undignified and provocative. In the 1930s it clashed with the American Jewish Congress, which regarded itself as representing the mass of American Jews. Under Stephen Wise's aggressive leadership, the Congress organized demonstrations, boycotted German-made goods, and pursued the type of diplomatic activity that the AJC had considered its sphere. The Anti-Defamation League (ADL) of B'nai B'rith, established in 1913, and the Jewish Labor Committee, established in 1933 to represent the still substantial Jewish trade unions and the Jewish socialists, overlapped in their functions, but they were so genuinely different in outlook that any attempt at coordination or amalgamation was futile.

Raising funds for relief constituted the main collaborative effort, but even there the Zionists and non-Zionists could not agree. Nevertheless, between 1939 and 1945, the JDC sent close to $80 million to Europe, funneling funds when possible to Jewish groups in Nazi-occupied Europe and financing underground escape efforts.

In 1943 the American Jewish Conference attempted to establish a representative body to direct political and rescue efforts, but again, unity was not complete. The

conference was able to agree on a program, except on the issue of a declaration in support of a Jewish commonwealth to be established in Palestine at the end of the war. Over that question the Jewish Labor Committee and the AJC withdrew; a Zionist state ran counter to ideological positions long held by the labor committee, and the AJC regarded a sovereign Jewish state as fraught with danger for American Jews because of the specter of dual allegiance.

Thus, at a time when the intervention of the United States might have saved some from annihilation, the American Jewish community was unable to overcome internal differences and speak with a single voice. Some Jews feared that special pleading for Europe's Jews and for opening Palestine to refugees would make the war a Jewish war. The government viewed rescue efforts as a distraction from prosecution of the war and fended off Jewish pressure for action. The War Department rejected urgent requests in the summer of 1944 to bomb the gas chambers and crematoria at Auschwitz, though the U.S. Air Force was regularly bombing the area. To do so, it was argued, would divert military resources to nonmilitary objectives and extend the war. The dilemma was most poignant for those Jews with influence and with close ties to the Jewish community. Samuel I. Rosenman (1896–1973), Henry Morgenthau, Jr. (1891–1967), Benjamin V. Cohen, and Felix Frankfurter were among Roosevelt's trusted advisers, and Jews had supported Roosevelt and the Democratic party since 1932. Nonetheless Roosevelt did not take any action until 1944, when he created the War Refugee Board to seek ways to rescue Jews. In its brief tenure it showed the feasibility of such activity, but the main priority remained the defeat of the Axis powers.

About 550,000 Jews served in the armed forces. The shared struggle and sacrifices led to a firmer, more certain integration into American society, while the destruction of a third of world Jewry in the Nazi holocaust created a greater sense of group identity. Jews were thereafter both more at home in America and more aware of their ties to Jews in the rest of the world.

1945 TO THE PRESENT

Jews prospered in the postwar years. Those in commerce and the professions profited particularly from an expanding economy, with its rising demand for consumer goods and services. All Jews benefited from the decline in racial and religious discrimination and the resulting expansion of educational and occupational opportunities. The generation that came of age during those years was in the forefront of the civil-rights movement and in liberal and radical politics and was influential in the intellectual life of the country. Though relative newcomers, American Jewry compared with white Protestant society in educational attainments, income, and lifestyle. Largely native-born of Russian Jewish parentage in 1945, the population was third- and fourth-generation American by the 1970s. Although a high level of acculturation characterized a majority of its members, the organized community nevertheless maintained its stability and cohesion.

In the 40 years between 1937 and 1977, the population of the United States increased by over two-thirds, but American Jewry grew by only a fifth, so that the Jewish portion of the population decreased from a high of 3.7 percent in 1937 to 2.7 percent in 1977. The drastic drop in birthrate was arrested momentarily in the 1950s, but it remained among the lowest of all ethnic or religious groups. During these years immigration, though of qualitative importance, was too limited to have much effect on Jewish population growth.

Jews in the United States were also dispersed more widely across the nation in the 1970s. Los Angeles and Miami rose in the ranks of most populous Jewish communities, while Chicago, Cleveland, and Detroit fell. No less typically, Jews joined the flight of the white middle class from the city. By the late 1950s the urban Jewish neighborhoods of the interwar years had been abandoned except for pockets of mostly elderly and impoverished Jews. The rest settled in a ring of suburban settlements, often as distant from one another as from the city. Within these suburban belts, however, they continued to cluster together.

In New York some of the older neighborhoods showed considerable stability, reflecting the persistence of a Jewish working class, strong communal institutions, usually staunchly Orthodox, a concentration of postwar immigrants, and the elderly poor. A 1973 study classified 15 percent of the city's Jews as at or near the poverty level, two-thirds of them over the age of 60. The exodus from the Bronx (538,000 Jews in 1940 to 143,000 in 1977) and parts of Brooklyn (857,000 Jews in 1940 to

Table 1. Jewish population of selected cities,[a] 1948 and 1977.

	1948			1977	
	Number	Percentage of total Jewish population		Number	Percentage of total Jewish population
New York	2,000,000	40.0	New York	1,998,000	34.6
Chicago	300,000	6.0	Los Angeles	455,000	7.9
Philadelphia	245,000	4.9	Philadelphia	350,000	6.0
Los Angeles	225,000	4.5	Chicago	253,000	4.4
Boston	137,345	2.7	Miami	225,000	3.9
Detroit	90,000	1.8	Boston	170,000	2.9
Cleveland	80,000	1.6	Washington, D.C.	120,000	2.0
Baltimore	75,000	1.5	Bergen County, N.J.	100,000	1.7
Newark	56,800	1.1	Essex County, N.J.	95,000	1.6
Pittsburgh	54,000	1.8	Baltimore	92,000	1.6
Total	3,263,145	65.9		3,858,000	66.6

Source: *American Jewish Yearbook* 51 (1950): 71–73; 77 (1977): 275–278, 318; 78 (1978): 254–260.
a. Includes contiguous suburban areas; Bergen County includes Englewood; Essex County includes Newark.

514,000 in 1977) showed that New York Jews followed the general Jewish pattern, but at a slower rate and in a more selective fashion. Jewish poor could also be found in the old immigrant neighborhoods of Chicago, Philadelphia, Los Angeles, and Miami. One estimate placed the number at between 400,000 and 800,000, again mostly people aged 65 or over. Too poor to move, clinging to a small business or the comfort of an Orthodox synagogue, they have been frequent victims of crime, failing health, and isolation.

Prosperity, combined with the removal of educational and social barriers, opened up opportunities for the Jews of the postwar generation. Supported by the achievements of their parents, many of whom were independent businessmen, they entered the professions or, as white-collar workers, looked forward to becoming managers and executives. In 1971, 40 percent of a sample work force were employed as managers or administrators, a proportion three or four times that of the general population, and 29 percent of men and 24 percent of women were professionals. In 1963, 19 percent of the 45-to-64 age group in Detroit were professionals, compared to 42 percent of the 20-to-34 year age group. By the 1970s over 80 percent of college-age Jews were actually attending college, and 71 percent of all Jews between the ages of 25 and 29 had college degrees.

The numbers of Jewish workers in the clothing industry declined, but they remained heavily represented in management. Jewish businessmen were involved in real estate and in the construction of buildings and shopping centers connected with the move to the suburbs. They were prominent in communications: William Paley (1901–) of CBS and David Sarnoff (1891–1971) of NBC, pioneers of radio in the 1920s and 1930s, guided their networks into the television era; Leonard H. Goldenson (1905–) became president of ABC in the 1960s. The publishing houses of Alfred A. Knopf, Random House, and Simon and Schuster were all owned by Jews.

Jews were heavily represented in entertainment as entrepreneurs and artists, beginning in the 1920s. Florenz Ziegfeld, Lee Strasberg, and the Schubert brothers were prominent directors and producers. Composers for the musical theater were Irving Berlin, Jerome Kern, George Gershwin, and Richard Rodgers. The list of Jewish entertainers includes Fanny Brice, Eddie Cantor, Al Jolson, Groucho, Harpo, and Zeppo Marx, Milton Berle Danny Kaye, and Zero Mostel. Conductor-composer Leonard Bernstein and dramatist Arthur Miller were influential figures in the postwar period.

Though the professions that traditionally attracted Jews continued to do so, an enormous number also entered the academic world. The new prestige given scholarly pursuits and scientific research in the United States after the war provided new opportunities in the expanding universities and research institutes of the country. The still-potent, traditional reverence for the intellectual and the promises of greater rewards attracted young Jews to the universities. By 1970 over 10 percent of American professors were Jewish, and in the most prestigious universities the proportion reached 30 percent. Politically they were often liberal or radical, and their religious or ethnic ties were weaker than those of their fellow professors.

Intellectualism, radicalism, and assimilationism produced a number of creative writers, literary critics, and social commentators of Jewish origin. Though they addressed a general public, their work had common attributes that stemmed from their American Jewish milieu. Thoroughly acculturated and economically secure, they sympathized little with their parents' striving for middle-class respectability and the remnants of ethnic heritage. Nobel laureate Saul Bellow (1915–), Bernard Malamud (1914–), and Philip Roth (1933–) scorned the materialism and sterile ethnicity of their elders but also found American society wanting. The critical acclaim these writers received reflected the discontent shared by intellectuals in general. The themes of alienation and the anti-hero were depicted through Jewish characters and circumstances, but they struck a universal chord. These works also introduced the reader to a highly subjective depiction of the American Jewish subculture.

Other American Jewish novelists of distinction included J.D. Salinger, Herbert Gold, Wallace Markfeld, Isaac Rosenfeld, Joseph Heller, and Bruce Jay Friedman. Elie Wiesel's works on the holocaust and Nobel laureate Isaac Bashevis Singer's tales of eastern European Jewish life, translated from the Yiddish, re-created a vanished Jewish world. Among the poets of importance were Delmore Schwartz, Howard Nemerov, Karl Shapiro, and Babette Deutsch. Popular best sellers often dealt with Jewish themes, including Herman Wouk, *Marjorie Morningstar* (1955), Leon Uris, *Exodus* (1958), Chaim Potok, *The Chosen* (1967), and Gerald Green, *The Holocaust* (1978). Philip Rahv, Lionel Trilling, Alfred Kazin, Irving Howe, Susan Sontag, Leslie Fiedler, Irving Kristol, Norman Podhoretz, and Theodore Solotaroff dealt with literature in a broad social and cultural context and became social commentators for journals like *Partisan Review, Dissent, New York Review of Books, New American Review,* and *Commentary.* The proclivity of Jews for sociology drew upon reformist and radical traditions; psychiatry, the most humanistic medical field, continued to attract many.

The reformist-radical zeal that characterized the authentic political tradition of American Jews had its roots both in the Jewish immigrant settlements and in the *noblesse oblige* of the affluent German Jews. Democratic politicians early learned to take into account the issue-oriented Jewish immigrant voter. Al Smith (1873–1944), Tammany's most successful East Side politician, was elected governor with the support and influence of such Jewish liberals as Belle Moskowitz (1877–1933) and Joseph Proskauer (1877–1971). Louis Brandeis, Stephen Wise, and Henry Morgenthau (1856–1946), in their support of Woodrow Wilson, similarly represented the progressive commitment of the established Jews. Politicians who fought immigration restrictions such as Democrat James M. Curley of Boston received overwhelming support from the Jewish voters, and for two decades Tammany elected Henry F. Goldfogle (1856–1929) to the U.S. Congress from the Lower East Side. Republican Theodore Roosevelt's public criticism of anti-Jewish policy in Russia, his appointment of Oscar Straus as the first Jewish cabinet officer, and his praise of Jewish citizens made him a Jewish folk hero.

The reformist tradition of left-of-center liberalism ap-

peared in full form in Jewish support of the New Deal. Unlike others in the New Deal coalition, Jews tended to be equally liberal on political, social, and economic issues. In 1944 Roosevelt's popularity dwindled among many interest groups, but the pro-Roosevelt Jewish vote climbed to over 90 percent. This commitment to a comprehensive liberalism remained strong despite some erosion. In 1952 Democrat Adlai Stevenson received 44 percent of the popular vote but 75 percent of the Jewish vote when he ran for president against Dwight D. Eisenhower. Twenty years later Democrat George McGovern received only 38 percent of the popular vote but 60 to 70 percent of the Jewish vote. Other ethnic and religious groups became more conservative in their political outlook as they grew prosperous, but the Jews retained their essentially New Deal liberal views: legislation on behalf of underprivileged groups, defense of civil liberties and civil rights, and an internationalist foreign policy.

The radical tradition operated in tandem with Jewish liberalism and occasionally merged with it. The Jewish labor movement was involved in radical politics throughout the 1920s and was one of the largest contingents in the Socialist party, though its energy was dissipated in disputes over the unsuccessful efforts of Jewish Communists to dominate the garment workers' unions. Perhaps 15 percent of Communist party members during the 1920s were of Jewish origin. In the thirties, the Soviet Union appeared to some younger radicals to be the single power that was unequivocally opposed to Nazism and Fascism, and Communism seemed the only alternative to continued depression. Popular-front Communism attracted teachers, social workers, and intellectuals.

The New Deal provided an outlet for the political energies of the Jewish labor movement. Trade-union leaders Sidney Hillman and David Dubinsky (1892–), supported by Abe Cahan's socialist *Forward,* turned many away from immigrant radicalism toward Democratic party reform and provided Jewish liberalism with much of its earnestness and constancy. Liberal politics also provided an avenue into public life for those looking beyond the bounds of their ethnic group. Jews have been mainstays of the American Civil Liberties Union (ACLU) and the National Association for the Advancement of Colored People (NAACP) since their inception. The NAACP had two Jewish presidents: Joel E. Spingarn (1875–1939) from 1930 to 1939 and his brother, Arthur B. Spingarn (1878–1971), from 1940 to 1966. Felix Frankfurter, Louis Marshall, Samuel Leibowitz (1893–1978), and Jack Greenberg (1924–) are among the prominent Jewish lawyers who have fought major legal battles on behalf of civil liberties and equal rights. The AJC, the ADL, and the American Jewish Congress early broadened their concerns from anti-Semitism to discrimination in general and to civil rights and church-state questions. During the 1960s the large proportion of Jewish students in anti-Vietnam war activities, protest movements, and such New Left organizations as Students for a Democratic Society showed that the propensity for radical causes carried over to the third and fourth generation.

In the demonstrations, marches, sit-ins, and voter registration campaigns of the 1960s, Jewish students, professors, and rabbis were especially prominent. With the passage of the Civil Rights Acts of 1964 and 1965, American Jews acclaimed what appeared to be the attainment of equal rights for all. The dramatic change in black goals in the mid-sixties, however, generated hostility between the blacks and Jewish liberals, as blacks demanded compensatory measures to close the social and economic gap between themselves and whites. Their rhetoric affronted Jewish sensibilities, and their aggressive tactics, particularly the anti-Semitic slogans of extremists and the denunciations of Israel as racist and imperialist, collided with Jewish interests. Jewish merchants and landlords who had remained in or owned property in black, previously Jewish neighborhoods were victims of violence and vandalism. Jewish civil servants, social workers, and teachers felt threatened by black demands for community control and proportional representation in government service. In the Ocean Hill–Brownsville school district of New York in 1968 the traditional liberal notions of merit, union rights, and nondiscriminatory practices clashed head on with black demands.

Throughout the 1970s "affirmative action"—government enforcement of preferential treatment in hiring, promotion, and college admissions—became an issue of great concern to American Jews. Jewish organizations pressed hard for equality of opportunity but opposed quotas based on race and ethnicity, regarding government recognition of racial and ethnic categories as a dangerously retrogressive step. The same Jewish organizations that had submitted arguments for school desegregation in *Brown* v. *Board of Education* in 1954 and had fought for civil-rights legislation supported Allen Bakke's challenge to imposed quotas in university admissions, adjudicated by the Supreme Court in 1978.

In the 1960s and 1970s Jewish communal leaders began to fear that social integration was leading to complete assimilation and loss of Jewish identity. The response by those committed to group survival was to adapt older forms and to develop new strategies that would be more congruent with American life.

In the postwar years Jewish Americans were most likely to define themselves in terms of a religious community, and the synagogue gained in prestige and authority. The earlier Jewish ideological movements, specialized service organizations, Yiddish cultural milieu, and compact Jewish neighborhoods with their informal associational networks had provided secular alternatives to the synagogue. The decline of these alternatives coincided with a new religious emphasis that classified Jews as a religious denomination. Will Herberg (1902–1977), who had himself made the intellectual journey from Marxist theoretician to Jewish theologian, called Judaism one of "the three great religious communities." Protestant, Catholic, Jew constituted the three basic subdivisions of the American people, a view that dovetailed with a number of other developments: a religious revival that stimulated church and synagogue attendance, the interfaith movement that emphasized the Judeo-Christian tradition, and a search for consensus and tranquility.

The synagogue became the primary communal institution in the new suburban settlements, modeled on the synagogue center of the 1920s, but enlarged to meet more varied social and cultural requirements. The supplementary religious school was absorbed into the syn-

agogue, and membership in the congregation was the prerequisite for attending it. Transmitting Jewish identity to the young was the principal inducement for joining and supporting the synagogue; it assumed greater importance as the guarantor of ethnic continuity than it had as a house of worship. Few attended services regularly—about 15 percent in one poll—but nearly 50 percent of the Jewish population were members of a synagogue, and many more had been members at some previous time. The smaller the community, the higher the proportion of congregational membership.

Rabbis, educators, cantors, and administrators trained in the central institutions of the various religious wings of Judaism were the bearers of the cultural heritage. Jewish learning among laymen was common only in the most Orthodox synagogues. Vastly expanded theological seminaries, rabbinical associations, federations of congregations, and auxiliary agencies supported the scholarly endeavors, research, and professional training in those institutions, which served as resources for the transmission of the religious and cultural heritage. The influence of religious thinkers, such as Mordecai Kaplan, Louis Finkelstein (1895–), chancellor of the JTS, Abraham J. Heschel (1907–1972), professor of Jewish ethics and mysticism at the JTS, the Orthodox Joseph D. Soloveitchik (1903–), and Reform's Eugene B. Borowitz (1924–) and Emil L. Fackenheim (1916–), spread beyond professional circles.

Conservative Judaism continued to grow the most quickly, appealing as it did to the American-born descendants of the Russian immigrants, who retained sentimental attachments to traditional practice. The movement numbered 217 congregations in 1948, 832 congregations in 1970. In 1971, 40 percent of a national sample described themselves as Conservative, 30 percent as Reform, and 10 percent as Orthodox. Reform congregations increased from 360 in 1948 to 698 in 1970. Some Orthodox synagogues became Conservative, and some Conservatives adopted Reform as a result of merger or the move to the suburbs.

Orthodoxy, the most authoritative branch in religious observance, was institutionally the most fragmented. In 1964 many of its approximately 1,600 synagogues were located in the older neighborhoods and had few members, and some were conventicles serving small groups or sects. The Orthodox community included a federation of modern congregations, most of whose rabbis were trained at Yeshiva College, which was reorganized as a university in 1945. The seven additional Orthodox seminaries indicate the continuing strength of European regional and sectarian forces in Orthodox circles. One of the signal achievements of Orthodoxy was its parochial-school system, which grew from 17 schools with an enrollment of 4,600 in 1935, to 400 schools with an enrollment of 85,000 in 1976.

At the extreme end of the Orthodox spectrum were the sectarian communities that arrived in the United States during and after World War II, bringing their segregated, Old World traditions with them. Aaron Kotler (1892–1962), a rabbinical leader and Talmudic scholar, established communities built around the higher study of the Talmud, "the heartbeat of Judaism," choosing the isolation of Lakewood, N.J., for his center. By the 1970s branches existed in dozens of cities. Hasidic communities established their own self-contained neighborhoods. The larger Lubavitcher and Satmer sects, numbering an estimated 100,000, settled in sections of Crown Heights, Borough Park, and Williamsburg in Brooklyn, N.Y. Several groups established village enclaves in Monroe and New Square, N.Y.

The Sephardic Jews from the eastern Mediterranean formed another subgroup of American Jewry. In the wake of the Turkish revolt of 1908, the Balkan Wars of 1912–1913, and World War I, at least 25,000 immigrated from the Balkans, Turkey, and Syria. They spoke Judeo-Spanish (Ladino), Greek, or Arabic. Language, religious culture, and ethnic background set them apart from their Yiddish-speaking Ashkenazi neighbors. In New York City, where 90 percent made their home, the old Shearith Israel Synagogue took an interest in them, but the Sephardim maintained their separate communal institutions on the Lower East Side and Harlem. Differences among them in language and background made coordinated activity difficult. Smaller synagogue communities were established in Seattle, Los Angeles, and Atlanta. Levantine Sephardim numbered an estimated 100,000 in 1970; they still maintain separate synagogues and, in the case of Brooklyn's Syrian Jews, their own parochial schools. Although the third generation no longer speaks the ancestral languages, and intermarriage with the Ashkenazim is high, they have a great deal of ethnic pride. The descendants of one small group of Jews from the island of Rhodes continue to support synagogues separate from the other Sephardim in Seattle and Atlanta.

Secular societies and institutions were concerned with transmitting the cultural heritage as well. By the mid-1920s, six nonsectarian Hebrew teachers' colleges and a graduate school of Judaic studies, Dropsie College in Philadelphia, had been established. In addition to the Orthodox Yeshiva University, the Conservative JTS, and the Reform Hebrew Union College, American Jews established a nonsectarian liberal arts college in 1946, Brandeis University in Waltham, Mass., which has a full curriculum in the arts and sciences and an important graduate program in Jewish studies. By the 1970s several hundred universities offered courses and majors in Jewish subjects. B'nai B'rith, essentially a fraternal order in its earliest years, turned to combating anti-Semitism and then broadened its interests to human rights. In the 1920s it established a network of Jewish campus centers, the Hillel Foundations, and a nationwide youth program. These and an adult-education program were the principal activities of the organization. Community centers also had extensive educational programs in the 1950s.

The Jewish press reflected this heightened interest in preserving group continuity. About 30 monthly and quarterly journals of opinion, scholarship, and belles-lettres were being published in the late 1970s. Commentary, published by the AJC, is widely read and considered one of the more influential periodicals in the nation. Fifty communities published weekly newspapers in the late 70s, but the shrinking number of Yiddish readers were left with only one daily, the Forward, and eight periodicals.

The great majority of Jewish Americans depended upon the religious school to assure Jewish continuity. Second- and third-generation parents maintained few traditions in the home, and the neighborhood and ex-

tended family no longer supplied an ethnic setting. The burden of Judaizing the young was assigned to the congregational school. Since this entailed the study of the Hebrew language, the task of the religious school was a formidable one. Reform temples offered Sunday schools, and the Conservative synagogues, afternoon schools two to four times weekly. Schoolmen decried the limited time that children attended religious school (three to five years for most). Some sent their children to all-day parochial schools (nearly all of them sponsored by the Orthodox); nearly everyone else found the system acceptable. In 1970, 84 percent of the young men (15 to 19 years) and 72 percent of the young women received some Jewish education. Most Jewish Americans clearly wanted their children to identify as Jews and be conversant in the essentials of their tradition but preferred a way that would not hamper their integration in American society.

The struggle to survive as a communal entity and still achieve integration often involved the question of marriage to non-Jews. The dichotomy between Christian and Jewish society in pre-Enlightenment Europe and the prejudice that continued after it generally precluded close relations between Jew and Gentile. In those cases of marriage between Jew and Gentile, it was the Jew who converted. There was no secular society, and conversion to Judaism was not feasible. As a result, Jews associated intermarriage with apostasy, and parents severed their ties with the defecting child.

Colonial Jewry and the German Jews responded to the open, pluralistic, and less stratified American society by intermarrying in increasing numbers. But the massive Russian immigration, concentrated in ethnic neighborhoods and having a stronger separatist tradition, remained far more endogamous. The intermarriage rate between Jews and Gentiles was only 1.17 percent in New York in 1908, and it remained at about 3 percent until 1940. In the following 20 years it hovered around 6.5 percent, then nearly tripled to 17.4 percent between 1961 and 1965. Of every 100 Jews who married in the years between 1966 and 1972, 32 married non-Jews. Approximately one-fourth of the intermarrying non-Jewish females converted to Judaism, but few non-Jewish males did so.

The sharp increase in intermarriage reflected wider social acceptance and changing attitudes. The proportion of Jews opposed to intermarriage declined from about 80 percent in 1965 to about 50 percent a decade later. A modern, nontraditional generation subscribing to the notion of marriage based on romantic love found it difficult to oppose intermarriage, especially when that could be interpreted as reverse discrimination. The attitudes of the intermarried themselves showed a blurring of once-distinct boundaries. Jewish spouses continued to identify themselves as Jews, and a significant number of non-Jewish wives identified themselves as belonging to the Jewish community. In the 1960s and 1970s, especially in the academic world, tolerance, belief in universal values, emphasis on individual fulfillment, and the weakening of religious and family ties created a fluidity in relationships among individuals and groups, which, however desirable, deepened the dilemma of the survivalists.

Jewish Americans are profoundly affected by their ties to world Jewry. The mass murder of European Jewry, the plight of hundreds of thousands of survivors, only a small part of whom were able to find refuge in the free world, and the dramatic struggle of the Jews of Palestine to achieve independence and absorb the refugees have produced an outpouring of support. American Jews placed the creation and survival of the Jewish state at the center of their concerns. Except for small groups on the extremes of the religious spectrum, notably the American Council for Judaism, established in 1943, all the religious denominations, service organizations, and secular movements joined to extend aid to Israel.

The support of American Jewry was critical. Under the leadership of Rabbi Abba Hillel Silver (1893–1963), American Zionists mobilized public opinion and political support in favor of establishing a Jewish state in Palestine. To get the United States to support the United Nation's resolution for the partition of Palestine into Jewish and Arab states (approved by the U.N. in November 1947), it was first necessary to convince President Harry S Truman to override the State Department's position that support for partition would permanently alienate the oil-rich Arab countries. On May 14, 1948, hours after Israel proclaimed its independence and the neighboring Arab states launched their attack on the fledgling state, Truman extended de facto recognition to Israel.

The continuing needs of the new state in resettling the remnant of European Jewry and Jews forced to leave the Muslim countries, together with the threat from its neighbors, made activity on Israel's behalf a permanent part of the American Jewish community structure. The ties to Israel drew upon deep sentiments. The beleaguered state was associated with the fresh memory of the Nazi holocaust—American Jews had failed to come to the aid of their helpless brethren in Europe; they now had the opportunity to extend assistance to the embattled Jews of Israel, the "saving remnant." The themes of guilt and atonement and of martyrdom and redemption pervaded theological literature and public discourse.

The relationship was reciprocal. The remarkable activization of the Jewish community at moments of supreme crisis, as in 1948 when the state of Israel was proclaimed and in the 1967 and 1973 wars, when its destruction appeared possible, reflected the importance of its well-being for the self-esteem of American Jews and as an essential element in their group identity. Support of Israel served as a secular-ethnic replacement for, or reinforcement of, religion. As the center of Hebrew culture, Israel enriched American Jewry. To the religious, its scholars, Talmudic academies, and holy places were the living links with the Diaspora, as they had been for millennia.

The continual appeals for aid to Israel generated structural changes in the American Jewish community. Rising demands for overseas aid had encouraged the consolidation of fund-raising efforts in the 1930s; the dire situation in Europe and Israel in the 1940s and 1950s accelerated the trend. By the 1970s federations of Jewish philanthropies in 227 communities directed the raising and allocation of funds for local, national, and overseas needs. They also played an increasingly important role in organizing and planning local services such as family welfare, recreation, community relations, and care of the aged. About 60 percent of their funds was allocated to overseas needs, which after 1948

meant philanthropic and rehabilitation projects in Israel. About $6.9 billion was raised by the central Jewish community organizations between 1939 and 1976. The largest sum raised in a given year was nearly $600 million after the 1973 war; 82 percent of it was allocated to Israel. The Council of Jewish Federations and Welfare Funds, established in 1932, grew in influence as the local federations expanded. In 1955 the Conference of Presidents of Major American Jewish Organizations was formed as a consultative umbrella organization to deal with problems in the Middle East. Though these developments encouraged collaboration, only under the impact of the crises overseas did American Jewry achieve a modicum of organizational coherence. Even then, perhaps a third of the Jewish population remained outside the organized community.

New immigration underscored the complexity of the ties between Jewish Americans and world Jewry. The political and financial resources of the community were mobilized to help Jews who wished to leave the U.S.S.R. and others who were harassed for attempting to maintain their Jewish identity. But immigrants from Israel were often received with ambivalence and given no communal attention.

Spearheading the efforts on behalf of Russian Jews was the American Conference on Soviet Jewry. In addition to publicizing Soviet treatment of Jews, it and other Jewish organizations lobbied the U.S. government to intervene on the grounds that the Soviet government was violating human-rights agreements. The Jackson-Vanik Agreement, passed in 1973, linked the granting of most-favored-nation status to the U.S.S.R. to their adoption of a more liberal emigration policy. Between 1966 and 1977 about 130,000 Jews emigrated from Russia; some 15,000 of them came to the United States, and nearly half settled in New York City. Many were professionals and white-collar workers who had to accept lower-status employment; all found the transition to the free-market conditions of the United States difficult. Jewish organizations offered temporary financial support, aided the new immigrants in accommodating to American society, and integrated them into the Jewish community. Despite the experience of the organizations and an abundance of good will, the transition has often been distressing and difficult for the immigrants.

Since the founding of the Israeli state, as many as 300,000 Jews have emigrated from it to America. About half have settled in New York and another large contingent in the Los Angeles area. Some were Europeans or Levantines who lived in Israel only briefly and found adjustment to its austerities too difficult. Others were long-time residents who saw greater opportunities across the ocean. Still others left because of the wars, near-wars, and threats of more wars.

The Israeli immigrants pose a problem for the Jewish community: they have chosen to leave the land that every Jewish American has learned to regard as a haven, the guardian of Jewish survival, and the center of Hebraic culture. The ambiguity toward the *yordim* ("those who descend," the Hebrew term for these emigrants, which has connotations of abandoning the land of Israel) has expressed itself in the absence of formal recognition of the Israelis as a Jewish immigrant group. Individuals have successfully established themselves in the professional and cultural life of the greater society and

have contributed to the Jewish community as teachers and communal functionaries. Among themselves, the Israelis have almost no formal organization, though they have a lively informal social life. Many maintain close ties with the homeland, visit frequently, and in time of dire need have occasionally returned to fight in its defense.

Historical experience and religious culture fitted Jews for life in America. The intellectual discipline fostered by the Jewish religion, the social discipline required by life among hostile peoples, and urban mercantile skills facilitated their adaptation. Jews sought economic security in occupations with which they were familiar and which were least vulnerable to prejudice. Jews placed great store on deferring present rewards for future gains, and valued intellectual pursuit. In the 1970s the third and fourth generations of the great mass migration were a well-integrated body of citizens who accepted the values and mores of the United States and entered the public life of the nation with great vitality and few inhibitions. To that life they brought individual talents and a collective sensitivity toward the less fortunate.

Jews were no less well equipped for the task of maintaining their community. Their heritage and experience made them preoccupied with group survival. By the 1970s the bearers of this tradition could note a varied communal life that had evolved in response to freedom and equality: a multiplicity of religious outlooks, successful absorption of diverse subgroups, and a broad choice of ways to identify with the Jewish collectivity.

But for the survivalists, Jewish life in America was only a pale reflection of the rich cultural and religious tradition from which it had sprung. To some, the élan and the institutional strength of the community seemed to depend entirely on its responses to crises in Israel. When the peril passed, what would call forth a similar group commitment? The postwar generation, which had neither experienced the social prejudices of their parents nor witnessed the holocaust, was fully at home in the United States and at ease with its ethnic identity.

Having achieved prosperity and social integration as a result of a set of historical conditions, Jews now have the option of identifying with, or ignoring, the ethnic community nurtured by their collective experience.

Bibliography

Two broad-ranging surveys of the subject are Nathan Glazer, *American Judaism*, rev. ed. (Chicago, 1972), which stresses the religious and social aspects, and Henry Feingold, *Zion in America* (New York, 1974), the most recent and comprehensive study.

Jacob R. Marcus, *The Colonial American Jew, 1492–1776*, 3 vols. (Detroit, 1970), is a thorough study of the subject. Social and religious trends during the 19th century are treated in: Moshe Davis, *The Emergence of Conservative Judaism*, 2nd ed. (Philadelphia, 1965), and Leon A. Jick, *The Americanization of the Synagogue* (Hanover, N.H., 1976). Marshall Sklare, *Conservative Judaism* (1955; reprint, New York, 1972), places religious change in the 20th century within a sociological framework of the acculturation of American Jews; Charles S. Liebman, *Aspects of Religious Behavior of American Jews* (New York, 1974), includes important essays on the American rabbinate, Orthodoxy, and the Reconstructionist movement.

Irving Howe, *World of Our Fathers* (Philadelphia, 1976), is a massive and felicitous account of East European Jewry, focusing on New York and the Yiddish radical tradition; Hutchins Hapgood, *The Spirit of the Ghetto* (1902; reprint, Cambridge, Mass., 1967), is an evocative contemporary portrait; Charles S. Bernheimer, ed., *The Russian Jew in the United States* (1905; reprint, New York, 1970), contains valuable essays dealing with New York, Philadelphia, and Chicago. Moses Rischin, *The Promised City: New York's Jews, 1870–1914* (Cambridge, Mass., 1962),

is a thorough social and intellectual account of the eastern European Jewish settlement of New York. Will Herberg, "The Jewish Labor Movement in America," *American Jewish Yearbook* 53 (1952), is the best brief survey of the topic. Local, regional, and institutional histories provide valuable insights. Some representative studies are: Joseph Brandes, *Immigrants to Freedom: Jewish Communities in Rural New Jersey since 1882* (Philadelphia, 1971); Stuart E. Rosenberg, *The Jewish Community in Rochester, 1843–1925* (New York, 1954); Steven Hertzberg, *Strangers within the Gate City: The Jews of Atlanta, 1845–1915* (Philadelphia, 1979); Max Vorspan and Lloyd P. Gartner, *History of the Jews of Los Angeles* (San Marino, Calif., 1970); Naomi W. Cohen, *Not Free to Desist* (Philadelphia, 1972); Arthur A. Goren, *New York Jews and the Quest for Community* (New York, 1970); Melvin I. Urofsky, *American Zionism from Herzl to the Holocaust* (Garden City, N.Y., 1975). Henry L. Feingold, *The Politics of Rescue* (New Brunswick, N.J., 1970), discusses the refugee problem in the 1930s and 1940s.

Marshall Sklare, *America's Jews* (New York, 1971), is an important analysis and sociological profile; Sidney Goldstein and Calvin Goldscheider, *Jewish Americans* (Englewood Cliffs, N.J., 1968), treats generation change in the Jewish community of Providence, R.I., with special reference to intermarriage, culture, and religion. Solomon Poll, *The Hassidic Community of Williamsburg* (New York, 1962), is a socioeconomic analysis of an ultra-Orthodox group. The most comprehensive treatment of Jewish communal structure and its operation is Daniel Elazar, *Community and Polity* (Philadelphia, 1976). Marshall Sklare, ed., *The Jew in American Society* (New York, 1974), and David Sidorsky, ed., *The Future of the Jewish Community in America* (New York, 1973), are important collections dealing with contemporary American Jewish experience.

The *American Jewish Yearbook*, which has appeared annually since 1900, is the most complete record of American Jewish life. The *Encyclopedia Judaica* (New York, 1972) contains valuable entries. The *American Jewish Historical Quarterly, Judaism, Commentary*, and *Midstream* are among the important scholarly periodicals and journals of opinion. William W. Brickman, *The Jewish Community in America* (New York, 1977), is the most comprehensive annotated bibliographical guide of books, and Jacob R. Marcus, *An Index to Scientific Articles on American Jewish History* (Cincinnati, 1971), is a bibliography of scholarly articles.

The two most important depositories of archival material are the American Jewish Archives in Cincinnati, Ohio, and the American Jewish Historical Society in Waltham, Mass.

ARTHUR A. GOREN

JORDANIANS: *see* ARABS

JUANEÑOS: *see* AMERICAN INDIANS

K

KABARDIANS: *see* NORTH CAUCASIANS

KALISPELS: *see* AMERICAN INDIANS

KALMYKS

About 200 to 250 Kalmyk families arrived in the United States in the winter of 1951–1952. A few others came later, and the group now numbers around 300 families, approximately 900 people in all. The Kalmyks are Mongolian Buddhists, the only such group in the United States. Most of them live in New Jersey and Pennsylvania where they were first settled by representatives of the Church World Service and the Tolstoy Foundation.

The Kalmyks (also spelled Kalmucks and Kalmuks), who are closely related to all the Oirats of Inner Asia as well as to the Mongols and the Buriats, originally lived in Dzungaria, which is now the northern half of Sinkiang Province in northwestern China, north of Tibet. After the breakup of the great Mongolian Empire, the Kalmyks were forced from their homeland. They migrated westward and in the early 17th century settled on the steppes of the lower Volga, establishing a Kalmyk Khanate (kingdom) north of the Caspian Sea. The region was at the center of considerable trade and commerce and during this period Kalmyk economic and intellectual life reached its height.

This was also the period of Russian expansion, however, and the Russians brought an end to the Kalmyk Khanate. In 1771 the Kalmyks chose to return to

South Russia

Dzungaria rather than submit to imperial domination. In doing so they left behind about one-fifth of their number, the Kalmyks who lived on the west bank of the Volga River, because, it is said, the river did not freeze that winter, and so they were unable to join their brethren. For the next 150 years these western Kalmyks remained where they were, managing to get along with the Russian authorities and with the local non-Kalmyk population. After 1803 they were administered by a Russian "guardian of the Kalmyk people," continuing at the same time to obey and respect their few remaining *noyons* (princes). Along with the other ethnic minorities they greeted the Russian Revolution in February 1917 with a mixed reaction, eventually sustaining great losses in the Civil War when many of them joined in fighting the Bolsheviks. Some of the group fled to Turkey and from there went to France, Yugoslavia, Bulgaria, and Czechoslovakia. Those who remained in the Soviet Union experienced many vicissitudes as the Soviet policy toward minority groups evolved. In 1935 the Kalmyk Autonomous Oblast, in existence since November 1920, was elevated to the status of an Autonomous Soviet Socialist Republic. It had an estimated Kalmyk population of 140,000 in 1941.

When World War II broke out the Kalmyks fought with the Russians against the Germans, mainly in two special cavalry divisions. Eventually several thousand went over to the German side, others were taken prisoner by the Germans, and still others fled the advancing Red Army. After the war approximately 800 Kalmyks found themselves in displaced persons camps near Munich where they lived for more than six years. The political and economic uncertainties of postwar Europe led the Kalmyks to consider a move to any suitable country outside Europe, but several countries refused to admit them because they were Asians. In 1951 the International Refugee Organization (IRO) in Geneva allocated funds for transportation, and aided by several refugee organizations, approximately 650 Kalmyk refugees were admitted to the United States. Subsequently they were joined by a few other Kalmyks, mostly from France, and slowly began to adjust to the United States, learning English and improving their economic status.

From the very beginning of their life in the United States, the Kalmyks have lived in tight communities in the same neighborhoods where they are able to maintain close contact with each other. Only in the last decade have the increasing number of college and professionally trained Kalmyks begun to disperse to San Francisco, Los Angeles, Washington, D.C., and New York City. Common celebrations of ethnic and religious holidays are quite frequent, and a traditional Kalmyk wedding can draw together almost the entire community.

Most of them have achieved a degree of economic success. Like most refugees, when they arrived they had neither the language nor the skills necessary for a good job, and they entered the market as assembly-line workers and common laborers; most of the women went to work in the garment industry. In Freewood Acres, N.J.,

they quickly learned the construction trades, becoming contractors and subcontractors. By now many of the original immigrants have retired or reached retirement age and the American-born generation, educated in local schools, have acquired additional skills, professional training, and university degrees.

Shortly after their arrival the Kalmyks organized three associations, one in Philadelphia and two in New Jersey. The membership in the two New Jersey societies reflects the centuries-old tribal division of the Kalmyk people. The Torghuts, the Bagha (Little) Derbets, and the Iki (Great) Derbets, who came from the Astrakhan and Stavropol provinces of Russia, set up an organization in Freewood Acres, while the Buzava Kalmyks, who before the Russian Revolution inhabited the Salsk district of the Rostov Oblast, established their own society a couple of miles farther south. Their leaders, usually elected every two years, are frequently the sons of those who occupied the same positions 20 or so years ago.

The Society for the Promotion of Kalmyk Culture, founded in May 1954 as a nonprofit organization devoted to the study of the history and culture of the Kalmyk people and the kindred Oirats, and the Kalmyk Mongol Studies Council, founded in June 1975, are two examples of the intense concern with which the older Kalmyk community regards the preservation of its heritage. Most second-generation children speak Kalmyk poorly or not at all, and although most preschool children speak Kalmyk at home they soon give it up when they go to school. Efforts to counteract this trend have resulted in the establishment of Saturday and evening Kalmyk-language schools in all the Kalmyk communities.

The Kalmyks have always been and still are fervent Buddhists. Buddhism has become perhaps more important in their lives in the United States than it has been at any other time. They adhere to the Tibetan form of Buddhism, and for centuries have recognized the Dalai Lama as their highest spiritual leader. The more fortunate Kalmyks have been able to pay personal homage to the Dalai Lama either at his residence in Dharmsala, India, or during his visits to Switzerland and West Germany in 1974. The first Kalmyk Buddhist temple was built near Freewood Acres in 1955; three more temples have been built in the same area. The newest, dedicated in 1977, is a striking example of Kalmyk-Tibetan-Buddhist architecture, and an exotic and unusual addition to the New Jersey landscape.

These temples are the centers for the celebration of the three major religious festivals of the lunar year: Tsaghan Sar (the New Year), Ürüs-Ova (the Festival of Spring), and Zul (the Feast of Lights), as well as other religious holidays and ceremonial occasions. The marriage ceremony is one of the most traditional features of Kalmyk life. Kalmyk temples are staffed mainly by refugee Buddhist lamas from Inner Mongolia and Tibet; most of the Kalmyk monks who came with the refugees in 1951–1952 are no longer living.

The community remains solidly Buddhist. Conversion is unknown and intermarriage is infrequent, but this is bound to change in the second generation and to affect the Kalmyk family in many ways. Kinship and clan ties are very strong but marriage between young people of the same *yasun* (clan) and between distant cousins (up to the seventh generation) is being discouraged. This severely limits the possibilities for ingroup marriage. Divorce continues to be virtually nonexistent in cases of endogamous marriage, even after 30 years of living in the United States, but the divorce rate among couples where one partner is non-Kalmyk has become noticeable recently. Family customs may be a serious source of strain. Married sons are customarily expected to live with and to care for their aging parents, and when there are no married sons, married daughters are expected to assume this responsibility.

The Kalmyks are relatively prosperous and successful in the United States, but peace and prosperity have been costly. There has been rapid Americanization and alienation. Grandparents and their grandchildren experience a considerable cultural and linguistic gap; the gap is less severe between parents and children but it is still substantial. Most Kalmyk Americans below the age of 25 are monolingual in English, and speak English even with visiting Kalmyks from Europe. The customs and traditions of centuries are not faithfully followed by the second generation; they lack ethnic pride. The loss of the mother tongue, insufficient knowledge of Kalmyk customs and traditions, the inevitable increase in exogamous marriage, and adoption of the many-faceted culture of the United States all contribute toward alienation from Kalmyk culture. It is too soon to tell whether this process will be in any way reversed by the third generation. The Kalmyks have survived as an ethnic group over centuries in the face of extraordinary trials. Whether such a small group can continue to preserve a distinct identity in the United States is very uncertain.

Bibliography
Very little is available in English for the nonspecialized reader on the historical, religious, and cultural background of the Kalmyk people. The first six chapters of Arash Bormanshinov, *The Kalmyk Manual* (New York, 1961), provide historical and linguistic data. *The Kalmyk-Oirat Symposium,* eds. Arash Bormanshinov and John R. Krueger (Philadelphia, 1966), contains contributions in English, German, and Russian. David F. Aberle, *The Kinship System of the Kalmyk Mongols* (Albuquerque, N.Mex., 1953), Paula G. Rubel, *The Kalmyk Mongols: A Study in Continuity and Change* (Bloomington, Ind., 1967), and Fred Adelman, "Kalmyk Cultural Renewal" (unpub. diss., University of Pennsylvania, 1960), available on microfilm and xerox, are concerned with the early adjustment of the Kalmyks to the United States.

ARASH BORMANSHINOV

KARACHAIS: *see* NORTH CAUCASIANS

KARAKALPAK: *see* TURKESTANIS

KAROKS: *see* AMERICAN INDIANS

KASHUBES: *see* POLES

KATOS: *see* AMERICAN INDIANS

KAWAIISUS: *see* AMERICAN INDIANS

KAWS: *see* AMERICAN INDIANS

KAZAKHS: *see* AFGHANS; TURKESTANIS

KAZAN TATARS: *see* TATARS

KERESANS: *see* AMERICAN INDIANS

KICKAPOOS: *see* AMERICAN INDIANS

KIOWAS: *see* AMERICAN INDIANS

KIOWA-APACHES: *see* AMERICAN INDIANS

KIRGHIZ: *see* AFGHANS; TURKESTANIS

KLAMATHS: *see* AMERICAN INDIANS

KLICKITATS: *see* AMERICAN INDIANS

KOREANS

Although there were relatively few Korean immigrants or visitors to the United States until recently, Koreans are now one of the largest, fastest growing Asian groups; in the late 1970s authorities estimated the number of Koreans in America at between 250,000 and 300,000 including immigrants and their American-born children.

A handful of Koreans came to the U.S. mainland in the late 19th century and slightly more than 7,200 went to Hawaii to work for the Hawaiian Sugar Planters' Association between 1903 and 1905. The influx of Korean laborers ceased abruptly when Korea came under tighter Japanese control; in 1905 the Japanese closed the Korean emigration office that had opened only a few years before and forbade anyone to leave Korea. In addition, the U.S. government decided that its Gentlemen's Agreement with Japan, which severely restricted Japanese immigration, applied to Koreans as well. Later, Koreans were totally excluded by the laws curtailing all immigration from Asia.

As a result there were so few Koreans in the United States prior to the 1950s that a real community was never able to evolve. In Hawaii, however, a variety of institutions were established by 1905, and a distinct Korean community developed.

After World War II, with the surrender of Japan and the U.S. occupation of Korea, Korean emigration began to rise. It increased after the Korean War (1950–1953) and grew tremendously after the immigration law of 1965 repealed the old restrictions. Approximately 8,000 Korean refugees, war brides, and orphans were admitted in the years 1952–1960. In the next five years another 13,000 entered, 12,000 of them the wives or children of American servicemen. Several thousand students were admitted as well but they did not have very much effect upon the developing Korean-American community. Since 1973, however, more than 20,000 Koreans a year have entered the United States. According to the reports of the U.S. Immigration and Naturalization Service, more than 175,000 were admitted between 1965 and 1976.

BACKGROUND

Korea has a long and rich history. Korean society is built upon a complex of Confucian, Buddhist, and—more recently—Christian values and beliefs. The Korean language, although it has borrowed heavily over the centuries from Chinese and Japanese, is still a distinct tongue, of unknown origin; the modern language, known as Han'gul, is based on a 26-letter phonetic alphabet devised by a royal commission in 1446. It was

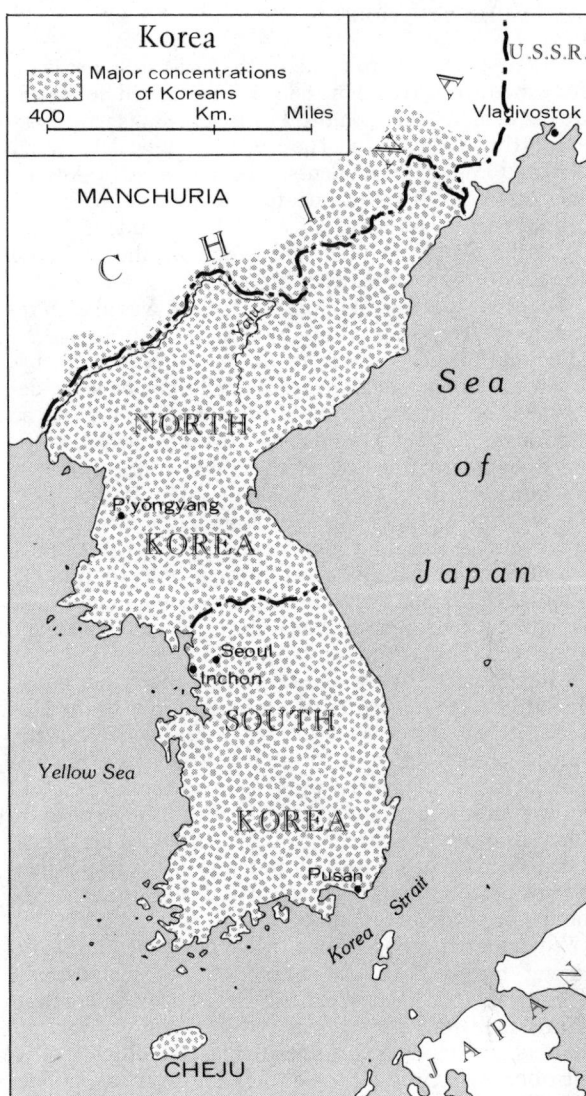

not widely used until it was officially adopted by the Korean government (in a 24-letter version) almost exactly 500 years later.

Korean emigration to any part of the world beyond neighboring China and Japan is a comparatively recent development. Under Chinese influence in the 17th century, Korea established an isolation so extreme that it was known as the Hermit Kingdom. A few Koreans managed small commercial enterprises on the Chinese coast, and some students and scholars traveled to China, Japan, and India to study, but the majority of Koreans had neither the opportunity nor the inclination to leave the homeland. It remained an isolated tributary state of China for 300 years.

In 1876 it was rudely jolted out of its self-imposed isolation by Japan when the Meiji government forced an unequal treaty upon Korea. The treaty of Kanghwa gave Korea a degree of autonomy, but in many ways simply put the Japanese in the dominant position the Chinese had previously held. Korea remained a bone of contention between China and Japan until China was defeated in the 1895 Sino-Japanese War. Finally, in 1905, Korea was made a Japanese protectorate.

EARLY IMMIGRATION

The first Koreans to come to the United States were three men who arrived in 1885. Two returned home but the third, a physician named Philip Jaisohn, spent most of his life in America. They were followed between 1890 and 1905 by 64 students, all encouraged by American missionaries to pursue further education in the United States. At least three of these students, Ahn Chang-ho, Pak Yong-man, and Syngman Rhee, became important figures in Korean history.

The first Korean emigration to Hawaii was also in response to recruiting efforts by Americans: Horace N. Allen and David W. Deshler. Allen had been a Presbyterian missionary in Korea since 1884 but he soon developed an interest in diplomacy and sought to be American minister to Korea. He was well qualified for the assignment but lacked the right connections in Washington until he met David Deshler. Deshler was the stepson of Judge George Nash, later governor of Ohio and a friend of President William McKinley. Through his stepfather Deshler was able to provide Allen with the political leverage he needed. Judge Nash recommended Allen to McKinley, and Allen was appointed to the post he wanted.

Allen became involved in Korean immigration to Hawaii after an encounter with a representative of the Hawaiian Sugar Planters' Association who was eager for Korean laborers to work on the Hawaiian sugar plantations. The idea appealed to Allen because he was interested in finding ways to involve the United States in Korea in order to counter Japanese influence and reassert Korean independence. In pursuit of this goal Allen did not hesitate to use both legal and illegal means, although he ultimately failed.

When he returned to Korea, Allen persuaded Emperor Kojong to establish the Yuminwon, a department of emigration. He also helped David Deshler obtain permission from the Korean government to recruit laborers, misrepresenting Deshler as an official of a fictitious "Territorial Bureau of Immigration." The recruiters were careful to claim that the Koreans were not being hired as contract labor, by then an illegal practice, but the system used to finance the laborers through an organization called the Deshler Bank amounted to the same thing.

Emperor Kojong had a personal as well as political interest in Korean emigration. He was proud to have Koreans welcome in a place that was by then forbidden to the Chinese. In addition, he saw a way to make money by issuing passports to the prospective emigrants. The emigration office, established within the royal secretariat, charged two *won* ($1) for a passport.

American missionaries in Korea also played a role in the emigration. By the turn of the century many Koreans had become Christians, and because their faith was largely the result of American missionary zeal they considered the United States the cradle of their religion. Two missionaries in particular, George Heber Jones and Homer B. Hulbert, encouraged this belief. Of the first shipload of Koreans to arrive in Hawaii—56 men, 21 women, and 25 children—half were members of Jones's church. He provided them with letters to influential friends in Hawaii, and the Reverend Mr. Hulbert promoted the emigration program in his popular magazine, the *Korea Review* (Seoul, January 1901–November 1906).

From 1903 to 1905, 65 ships carrying 7,226 Koreans (6,048 men, 637 women, and 541 children) set sail from Inchon for Honolulu. When each group arrived it was settled on a sugar plantation. However, in 1905 the Japanese barred all overseas emigration and closed the emigration office. In 1907 the U.S. government refused to recognize the Korean passports that had been issued from time to time in defiance of the Japanese government, and from then on any Korean entering the United States had to have a Japanese passport. These developments effectively ended almost all Korean immigration to Hawaii and the United States for 40 years.

After 1907 only the wives of already resident Korean aliens were allowed to enter the United States. The Gentlemen's Agreement with Japan, now extended to Korea, specified that picture brides, women who contracted marriages on the basis of an exchange of photographs, would be admitted. Between 1910 and 1924, when the practice was banned, almost 1,000 brides arrived in Hawaii and another 115 in California. The only other large group of Koreans to come to the United States in this period were 541 young political activists permitted to enter as "working students," although they were refugees from Japanese oppression. From their ranks came many of the leaders of the Korean Independence movement. Some other students continued to come to the mainland after 1924, but they were not permitted to stay in the United States after the completion of their studies.

In 1910 the U.S. Census reported 4,533 Koreans in Hawaii and 461 on the U.S. mainland. About 1,000 laborers eventually returned to Korea and others made their way to California. The figures for 1920 were 4,950 in Hawaii and 1,677 on the mainland; for 1930, 6,461 and 1,860; and for 1940, 6,851 and 1,711 respectively.

Early Institutions In both Hawaii and the United States the Korean immigrants began almost at once to organize their religious life. In contrast to immigrants from other Asian countries, they were overwhelmingly Christians, usually Protestants. The first Korean Christian service in the Hawaiian Islands was held on July 5, 1903; by 1905 the Methodists had organized churches; the first Episcopal services were held in Honolulu in the same year. A Korean Christian Church was also organized, though not until 1918.

In an effort to maintain their native language and culture, the immigrants also soon organized Korean-language schools, usually through the church, as a vehicle to promote national independence and in imitation of language schools already operated by the Japanese and Chinese. The schools also taught Korean history and culture. In Hawaii the church housed the school, partly because almost every work camp had a church and partly because, in a population that was 60 percent illiterate, often the only person qualified to teach was the pastor. There was a dearth of instructional material; the Bible and Christian hymnbooks were usually the only texts. The children also attended the local public schools; in time, the children became far more fluent in English than in Korean, and the generation gap characteristic of immigrant families began to develop.

The settlers on the mainland also organized churches and schools soon after their arrival. A Korean Methodist church was established in San Francisco by October 1905, and others were soon organized in Oakland and Los Angeles and as far east as Chicago and New York. Eventually there were language schools in Los Angeles, Sacramento, San Francisco, and several small towns in the San Joaquin Valley of California. As in Hawaii, however, it became increasingly difficult to keep the second generation interested in these language schools.

In Hawaii, the early settlement had some institutions peculiar to its plantation communities. The first of them was the *tonghoe* (council), created to maintain order in the work camps. Each plantation that housed a community of more than ten Korean families had its tonghoe. The *tongjang,* the village chief, was head of the council. He was elected once a year by an assembly of all the adult male Koreans on the plantation. The council was a law-enforcement agency authorized by its members to arrest, prosecute, and punish any Korean found guilty of violating the community's code of ethics. The chief was assisted by a *sach'al* (sergeant at arms), and the *kyongch'al* or police. Any Korean accused of having broken the law was brought before the village chief, who reviewed the case with the sergeant at arms. If the accused was found guilty, the offender was either fined or flogged, depending on the nature of the offense.

Another organization, the sworn brotherhood, was established for protection. Some Koreans had 50 or 60 sworn brothers, each tattooed to indicate his affiliation. Although the sworn brotherhood was initially designed to protect Koreans from outsiders, it eventually became a source of community conflict as rivalries arose and members of one brotherhood were pitted against those of another.

Most important to Korean life were political organizations, each of which represented some point of view as to how the Korean community should respond to the growing Japanese power at home. As early as 1903 the Shinmin-hoe (New People's Society) was established in Honolulu by Koreans concerned with ending Japanese domination. Between 1905, the year when Korea became a Japanese protectorate, and 1907, 20 more were established.

Political Activists Among the students who came to the United States before 1905 were three young men who were destined to play a large role in Korean life both in the immigration and in the homeland. One of these was Pak Yong-man (1881–1928). In 1910, starting with 27 students on a Nebraska farm, he began to organize the Korean military establishment he thought was necessary to free the homeland. In 1912 he left these military-training enterprises in other hands and went to Hawaii where he served as editor of the *United Korean Weekly,* published by the Korean National Association of Hawaii. In 1916 he departed for China to organize the independence movement from there, after an argument with the second of the three ex-missionary-school students, Syngman Rhee.

Rhee (1875–1965) was the first Korean to earn an American doctorate, granted to him by Princeton University in 1910. After his graduation he returned briefly to Korea but was soon back in the United States as a po-

litical refugee. He quickly became a leader in the national independence movement and dominated it after Pak left for China. When Korea won its independence after the defeat of the Japanese in 1945, he returned to become the first president of the Republic of Korea in 1948.

The third of these leaders was Ahn Chang-ho (1878–1938). Beginning in 1903 he organized students in California and soon found himself opposed to the methods of both Pak and Rhee. Much of the political history of Korea in its early years can be told in terms of the rivalry among these three men. At first there was a semblance of unity as all the Korean organizations joined to form the Hanin Hapsong Hyophoe (United Korean Society) in Hawaii and the Kongnip Hyophoe (Mutual Assistance Society) in California. These two consolidated organizations in turn merged on February 1, 1909, to create the Tae-Hanin Kungmin-hoe (Korean National Association). But the merger was short-lived; conflicts developed among its leaders over strategies and philosophies. On May 13, 1913, Ahn split off to found the Hungsa-dan (Corps for the Advancement of Individuals) in San Francisco. He and his followers saw achievement of Korean independence as a long process requiring the spiritual regeneration of each Korean citizen. Rhee founded the Tongji-hoe (Comrade Society) in Honolulu in 1921. His group believed that pressure from a sufficient number of major world powers could force Japan to give up Korea. Pak, whose Kun-dan (Military Corps) was supposed to be the basis for a military operation to regain Korean independence, believed that Japan would give up Korea only if it were militarily threatened or defeated.

Pak was assassinated in China in 1928 by a Korean, and the military corps soon dissolved. Ahn died from torture in a Japanese prison in 1938, but the Hungsa-dan and the Tongji-hoe continued to compete for allegiance and financial support. After 1948 these organizations became for the most part inactive, although they still maintain offices in Los Angeles and Honolulu.

The status of overseas Koreans took an ironic turn when war broke out between the United States and Japan in 1941. As Japanese subjects the Koreans were declared enemy aliens, subject to martial law; as anti-Japanese agitators they were leading pro-war patriots. One Korean leader in Hawaii went to California in 1942 to become a leading proponent of Japanese internment. On the mainland the Koreans eventually were declared not to be enemy aliens; in Hawaii they remained in that category but were not interned. In both places they took to wearing "I am Korean" badges and Korean native dress to distinguish themselves from the Japanese.

Economic Life Most of the Korean immigrants who came to the Hawaiian sugar plantations at the turn of the century were farmers, unemployed workers, or ex-soldiers of the disbanded Korean army. They toiled for meager wages under harsh conditions and were soon anxious to move on. It was a long time before they could do so, however: having borrowed the money for their steamship fare, they were indebted to the Deshler Bank, although that enterprise was not a bank at all, but an organization established specifically and illegally to finance the laborers in Hawaii. Normally an Asian under contract received $15 a month (a European

counterpart would receive $18). Living expenses varied but generally ranged between $6 and $10 a month, which made it difficult to save. Nor could a Korean get any money from the homeland, since for all practical purposes it had become a colony of Japan.

By 1910 a few Korean business enterprises had appeared, not only among the ex-sugar workers of Hawaii but also on the mainland. Ahn Sok-jung established the Hungop Chusik Hoesa (Prospering Business Company) in Redlands, Calif., issuing 60 stock certificates worth $50 each to invest in farming. The Korean National Association organized the T'aedong Sirop Chusik Hoesa (Great Eastern Industrial Company) to finance its political activities. One thousand $50 stock certificates were issued to purchase 2,430 acres of farmland in Manchuria, but as a result of mismanagement the initial investment was wasted, and the Korean National Association made no further entrepreneurial attempts. On a much more ambitious scale, members of the Comrade Society established the Tongji Siksan Hoesa (Comrade Investment Company) in 1924; organized by selling stocks to subscribers, it was incorporated for 25 years under the laws of the Territory of Hawaii. The company bought 930 acres of land and built a model village called Tongji-ch'on (Comrade Village). Syngman Rhee himself lived there and supervised the koa tree farm and vegetable fields, but again poor management led to losses, and the village site had to be sold.

Most of the early immigrants on the mainland worked as domestics or as California field hands, particularly in the cultivation of rice. By 1917 Kim Chong-nim was known among Koreans as the "rice king"; he cultivated 2,085 acres and amassed a considerable fortune. At one point one of Ahn's patriotic organizations also made money raising rice. Other Koreans ran successful orchards (one of which perfected a marketable nectarine) and nurseries or grew sugar beets.

Racial discrimination against Asians in California hindered the establishment of Korean businesses. Like the Chinese and Japanese, those born abroad were "aliens ineligible for citizenship" under prevailing law. However, by the 1930s Los Angeles sheltered about 60 Korean enterprises, all of them modest—vegetable stands, restaurants, and small stores. First-generation Koreans were barred from most professions as noncitizens; even their children, citizens by birth and frequently well educated, did not fare much better. The situation improved in the 1940s. A number of Koreans were active in the business and professional world in both Hawaii and the mainland, especially in medicine, dentistry, architecture, science, and technology.

IMMIGRATION SINCE 1965

Ninety percent of the Koreans presently living in the United States have been here for less than 15 years. The 1965 Immigration Act, which took effect on July 1, 1968, has been enormously important to all the Asian groups who were excluded by the earlier legislation. Now as many as 20,000 Koreans a year are able to enter the United States in pursuit of economic opportunity and a better life; in some years special exemptions have raised the total to over 30,000.

In contrast to the immigrants of the early 20th century, the majority since 1959 have been female. Seventy percent of those who arrived from 1959 to 1971 were women 20 to 39 years of age, many of them the wives of U.S. citizens. In the early 1960s wives and children made up nearly 90 percent of all Korean arrivals.

Since 1959 professionals have constituted the largest group of employed immigrants. From 1959 to 1965 they were 7 percent of all Korean immigrants; after 1965 professionals ranged from 15 to 25 percent of annual Korean arrivals. After 1965 the proportion of Koreans in managerial, clerical, private household, crafts, factory, and service occupations also grew gradually, while the percentage of housewives and other dependents decreased. In the 1970s the occupational backgrounds of Korean immigrants became increasingly diversified. Many were well educated and members of the middle class; a large number were politicians from the north or civil servants eased out of their jobs by the regime of Park Chung Hee, a southerner. The northerners, already uprooted once when they were forced to leave North Korea, again faced a painful relocation process. Koreans of means are continuing to leave their homeland for greater economic opportunity, out of opposition to the current regime, or to avoid another military conflict which they are convinced will soon break out between North and South.

The chief destination of the new Korean immigrants is Los Angeles. Only 10 years ago the Korean population of the city was 5,000; today it exceeds 150,000. Los Angeles is now the Korean capital of the United States. Half of these newcomers have settled in a residential and commercial area just west of downtown. Moving into what not long ago was a deteriorating neighborhood, they have revitalized it by establishing thriving small businesses and refurbishing old homes.

Perhaps half the Korean community has had a college education and has come from Korea's upper middle classes. Many were teachers, professionals, and administrators who were obliged to take lower-status occupations when they arrived in the United States. Some view these jobs as temporary and hope to pass the licensing examinations that will permit them to resume professional practice. Many others change their occupations entirely. A typical example is for a government administrator, having arrived with his wife and children, to secure employment first as a service station attendant. His wife works in a garment factory. After a few years, by working six or even seven days a week, they save enough capital to buy a retail store or restaurant. Eventually they are able to purchase a home, usually in the rapidly spreading Korean neighborhood. However, some immigrants are not as successful and return to Korea discouraged. Statistics on return migration are not available but experienced observers believe it to be substantial.

The new immigrants have revitalized existing community organizations, and in the major metropolitan centers where Korean immigrants tend to congregate new associations have sprung up. In the Los Angeles area alone, Korean residents support more than 50 nonprofit organizations, at least 80 churches, and over 50 Korean high school and college alumni associations. Of these new organizations the Korean Association of Southern California now enjoys the largest membership. In the many cities and towns across the United States where Korean residents have settled, the Korean Association is usually the largest community organiza-

tion, but the smaller church and alumni associations are functionally just as important: they may not attract a large membership, but their members tend to be very active.

The number of Korean Christian churches also has mushroomed. Virtually all of the new immigrants are Protestants. When they arrive they find themselves in an ethnic community isolated from the mainstream of American society by language and often by poverty, and they quickly turn to the churches for support. There are also many unemployed ministers among the immigrants, who lack other skills, and there is severe competition among them to attract congregations. There were said to be over 200 Korean ministers in the Los Angeles area alone in the 1970s, the majority of them unemployed.

The *tongch'ang'hoe* and *hakch'ang-hoe,* alumni associations, did not exist among the earlier Korean immigrants, but have emerged as one of the more vital institutions in the community. Popular also in Korea, these clubs are based on a kind of honorary, or fictive, kinship system determined by attendance at the same high school or college. Those who graduate earlier are regarded as older brothers/sisters to later graduates, and they can exercise authority over the more junior alumni. A senior member is called a *sonbae,* a junior member a *hupae.*

The number of small business firms has also increased dramatically. For all kinds of reasons—unfamiliarity with American life, inability to speak English, the need for mutual assistance and collective security in a strange environment, the need for access to public transportation, low-rental housing, and job opportunities—the newcomers have settled in urban areas. Many and varied small businesses have emerged to serve the ethnic neighborhoods.

A 1975 survey of 52 of these small businesses run by Korean immigrants in Chicago, Los Angeles, Honolulu, Seattle, and the San Francisco Bay area revealed some common characteristics: first, they were often operated by highly educated people—70 percent of the proprietors had been to college; second, a majority of them were started with capital of less than $15,000; third, most of their owners had been professional people who turned to business after immigration. The future of these small businesses is uncertain, however: one out of two new retail businesses in the United States fails within its first year of operation and two out of three fail within six years.

The community is plagued as well by various types of social discord. There is a pronounced conflict between recent immigrants and descendants of the earlier Korean immigrants. Some of the Korean Americans do not respect the newcomers on the ground that they do not understand American society but nonetheless insist on interfering with the social and cultural life of Koreans born in America. Others, bent on renewing their Korean identity, are irritated because their search is not appreciated by the newcomers. An uneasy, often even hostile, relationship also prevails between the Korean war brides of the 1950s and the rest of the people in the Korean community, who consider these women to be lower in social class, uneducated, and socially unacceptable. Some of the most recent political émigrés demand respect for the status they held in Korea regard-

less of their standing in America, not yet realizing that social standing in the United States depends upon present achievement rather than prior status. These tensions will probably diminish as the newcomers become more accustomed to American ways and as a large new group of American-born Koreans begins to appear.

In Hawaii most of the descendants of those Korean immigrants who came between 1903 and 1905 have achieved comfortable middle-class status. It has been argued that the cultural adjustment and upward social mobility of Koreans in Hawaii have been more rapid than for any other ethnic group in the islands. Several factors seem to have contributed to this success: on the average, second-generation Koreans stayed in school longer and achieved a higher rate of professionalism than some other groups; the Koreans mastered English faster than the Japanese and Chinese did; they left plantation work and went to the cities sooner; they more quickly abandoned their native diet, dress, and habits and exhibited the liberal and egalitarian attitudes approved by the surrounding society.

But the Koreans have paid dearly for their success with a high rate of divorce (the percentage of female-headed households in 1970 was 14.7, considerably higher than the national average of 10.8), mental illness, suicide, and juvenile delinquency. Both the socioeconomic success and the emotional problems have been attributed by some to the fact that, unlike most other groups, the Koreans did not maintain tight ethnic communities either on the plantations or in the cities; while their rapid dispersion no doubt hastened the process of assimilation, it also produced stress. But countervailing factors should also be taken into consideration. The immigrants were Christians; many had been taught by American missionaries; they were also in a certain sense nonconformists—it took some independence to ignore time-honored Confucian and Buddhist beliefs and remain one of only 100,000 Christians in a nation of 8 million people. The majority of the immigrants were city dwellers, and even before 1965 their ranks had included common laborers, ex-soldiers, government officials, students, policemen, miners, woodcutters, and household servants.

Politics in the Korean community is still largely governed by reaction to the internal affairs of the Korean peninsula. The various nationalist Korean liberation organizations have had very little influence over the foreign policy of the major world powers, but they nonetheless believed they could win Korea's freedom through international diplomacy. It is remarkable that these political organizations continued to receive substantial support from their countrymen throughout the entire four decades of Japanese colonial domination. But the cause of freedom did not unify the Koreans; instead, protracted ideological arguments pitted leaders of the Korean community against each other, encouraged factionalism, and produced personal rivalries.

This factionalism continues in post-liberation politics. When Syngman Rhee became the first president of the Republic of Korea in 1948, members of the Korean National Association openly opposed him and criticized his iron-fisted rule. Rhee acted swiftly to suppress the dissidents among Korean residents in the United States. Taking advantage of the Red Scare that was then sweeping America, he falsely accused some of them of

being Communists or Communist sympathizers, making it impossible for them to find employment or to obtain permanent-resident status.

Politics among the more recent immigrants from Korea is not very different. Organizations were established in recent years to support the regime of Park Chung Hee or to denounce it for its violation of political freedom and human rights. Voices opposing Park and his tactics became louder after the enactment of the Yushin Honbop (Reform Constitution), which virtually guarantee a lifetime dictatorship for him. Revelations of influence-peddling by Park Tong-son and of efforts by the Korean Central Intelligence Agency to bribe several U.S. congressmen produced other examples of the charges and countercharges that can be hurled in arguments about particular regimes. Opposition to the government in Korea often arises not so much from ideological differences as from some personal vendetta against the current leadership, or occasionally simply the need for recognition, especially when it comes from formerly important civic and political leaders in Korea who have neither status nor recognition in the new land.

The new Korean community with its large number of recent immigrants is not yet active in American politics because so few Koreans have been in residence long enough to have been naturalized and become eligible to vote. But because of its relatively small size the Korean community by itself probably cannot in any case become a political force; influence will come only through coalitions.

By now the functions of the social and religious associations in the Korean community have diversified. The original Korean-language schools of the earlier immigration disappeared when the children for whom they were intended became more and more Americanized and resisted being taught Korean language and culture. Comparable institutions today are more apt to provide youth-counseling centers, sports, activities, and summer camps than to teach language or culture. In spite of this, however, even American-born Koreans manage to retain a few of the old customs and habits. Dietary habits have changed considerably, but *kimch'i* (highly spiced and fermented pickled vegetables) remains a favorite dish, and *chanchi'i* (parties) are still held to celebrate the first and sixty-first birthdays (and sometimes other important events). The celebration of those particular milestones reflects a tradition of life in which survival through infancy was already rare and old age so uncommon that both were reasons for special celebration. Even a penniless immigrant will somehow manage to give a chanchi'i for his friends and relatives on these occasions.

Korean immigrants who do not understand English can listen to special programs televised for Korean audiences in Los Angeles. Radio stations broadcast in Korean in major urban centers where substantial numbers of immigrants live. Many newspapers circulate in Korean communities. In addition to *Shin-Han Minbo* (The New Korea, Los Angeles) which has been published intermittently since 1905, the *Ton-A Ilbo* (East Asian Daily, Los Angeles), *Choong-ang Ilbo* (Choong-ang Daily, Los Angeles), and *Hankook Ilbo* (Korea Times, Los Angeles) all combine news from Korea with articles reporting on the Korean community across the United States.

In literature and music several Korean immigrants have achieved international reputations. Younghill Kang (1903–1972), author of *The Grass Roof* and professor of literature at New York University in the 1930s, introduced American readers to the world of Korean childhood and adolescence by relating his experiences as a boy growing up in Korea. Richard Kim (1932–) has written successful novels: *The Martyred, Lost Names,* and *The Innocent.* Chong Myong-hun was appointed as assistant conductor of the Los Angeles Philharmonic in 1968 and his two sisters are among many in a new generation of Koreans who are rapidly achieving international reputations as musicians.

The Korean community in the United States is still in flux as immigrants arrive daily, and it is difficult to predict the changes that will result.

Bibliography
Koh Sŭng-che, *Han'guk iminsa yŏn'gu* [A Study on the History of Korean Emigration] (Seoul, 1973), treats Korean immigration to Manchuria, the Soviet Union, Japan, and the United States. For the history of the Koreans in the United States consult Hyung-chan Kim and Wayne Patterson, eds., *The Koreans in America, 1882–1974: A Chronology and Fact Book* (Dobbs Ferry, N.Y., 1974); Wŏn-yong Kim, *Chae-Mi Hanin osimnyŏn-sa* [A Fifty Year History of the Koreans in America] (Reedley, Calif., 1959); and No Jae-yon, *Chae-Mi Hanin saryak* [A Short History of Koreans in America], 2 vols. (Los Angeles, 1951 and 1963).

An analysis of Korean assimilation in America is presented in Hyung-chan Kim, ed., *The Korean Diaspora: Historical and Sociological Studies of Korean Immigration and Assimilation in North America* (Santa Barbara, Calif., 1977). For works on the Koreans in Hawaii consult Arthur L. Gardner, *The Koreans in Hawaii: An Annotated Bibliography* (Honolulu, 1970).

HYUNG-CHAN KIM

KUMYKS: *see* NORTH CAUCASIANS

KURDS

Although millions of Kurds (7 million according to standard reference works; 16 or 17 million according to the *New York Times*) live in the Middle East, only a very few have emigrated to the United States. Of these most come from Iraqi Kurdistan and see themselves as refugees from an intolerable political situation.

In 1975, only about 50 Kurds were living in the United States. Nearly all men, they had come individually as students and then stayed on, often marrying local women and finding employment as skilled professionals. They settled in various cities, mostly on the East Coast, getting together to celebrate the Kurdish New Year (*Newroz*) on March 21. Some of these students published a magazine, *The Kurdish Journal* in the sixties, but they were not very visible as a group. They assimilated easily, their English was excellent, and typically their children grew up without knowing Kurdish or practicing Islam. Still, these Kurds have remained in contact with each other about Middle Eastern politics. They are committed to supporting the fight for Kurdish political and cultural freedom in Iraq and, to a lesser extent, in Turkey and Iran. They collect money for newspaper advertisements, lobby at the United Nations, write letters, and organize small demonstrations.

Between 1975 and 1977 the number of Kurds in the United States increased more than tenfold. The U.S. State Department, through the United Nations High Commission on Refugees, agreed to allow two successive groups of approximately 350 Kurdish refugees to enter the United States in 1976 and 1977. These

Kurdish Homelands

refugees were among the thousands of Kurds who fled to Iran in 1974 and 1975, and were unwilling to return to Iraq following the collapse of the 1974 Kurdish Revolution. Although Kurds had been fighting Iraqis for decades, this was the first full-scale war and also the first time large numbers of Kurds had been forced to flee their homes. The U.S. government became indirectly involved in the fate of these Kurds through its support of Iran, and agreed to admit a small number of refugees to the United States. Sources involved in this refugee operation allege that political considerations by the U.S. government and the Kurdish Democratic Party (KDP) played a decisive role in determining which refugees were chosen for admission to the United States, where they were settled, and how much help they received. It is impossible to verify these allegations, but political factors are the key to understanding the current situation of these new immigrants.

In spite of the fact that the Kurds are a distinct national group, they have never had an autonomous homeland. For thousands of years, they have made their homes in and near the Zagros Mountains along the borders of the modern states of Iran, Iraq, Turkey, Syria, and the Soviet Union. Formerly pastoral nomads, until recently their political, social, and economic organization was mainly tribal. At various times in the past, Kurdistan has been divided and ruled by Kurdish *padishahs* (chiefs) and by governors sent from the Persian, Arab, or Turkish empires. Today Kurdistan is divided among five states, all of which have governments mainly hostile to Kurdish interests.

Salah Eddin Ayyubi (Saladin), the Muslim leader who repelled the Crusaders and regained Jerusalem in 1187, was actually a Kurd. Kurds, who were famous warriors, often fought for the empires that ruled them. Kurds, who are Sunni Muslim, see themselves as religiously aligned with Turks and Arabs, who are also Sunni, but culturally Kurds are closer to Persians.

The 750 Kurds now in the United States are not a representative sample of the millions of Kurds in the Middle East. In general, they are far wealthier, better educated, and more urban than most of the Kurds in Iraq, Iran, and Turkey, who reside in small villages. The literacy rate for Kurds in Iraq is presumed higher than that of Turkish or Iranian Kurdistan, but Kurdish estimates place it well below 50 percent of the population. Significantly, most of the refugees in the United States were not born in villages, but in Sulaimaniya, Mosul, Kirkuk, Erbil, Ruwandiz, and other cities located in the southern and more developed part of Iraqi Kurdistan. Nearly all the refugees are reported to be literate. About 75 percent have had high-school educations and approximately 10 percent were educated at the college level. Although this places them below the educational level of the earlier small group of 50 Kurdish emigrants, the new refugees still clearly come from the highest echelon of Kurdish society. This has made it extremely difficult for most of them to accept the sort of work they are able to find in the United States. In their own culture, manual labor is considerably more stigmatized than in the United States, and now many of the young men who once held prestigious administrative, military, or professional jobs in Iraq are forced to work as watchmen, waiters, and manual laborers. The main exceptions to this are those trained as doctors, if they are able to pass medical qualifying exams in the United States.

The refugees are unrepresentative also because there are very few women among them, perhaps 5 percent of the total. Many of the refugees approved for admission to the United States were young men with military backgrounds, only a few of whom were married. At the end of the war KDP officials and army officers were interned in special refugee camps in Iran where they were cut off from their families. Their mothers, sisters, and fiancees were inaccessible in Iraq; if the men chose to come to America they had to come alone. Women in Kurdish society are closely protected and supervised by fathers and husbands, and generally are not in a position to emigrate alone. One well-known refugee, the leader of the KDP, Mullah Mustafa Barzani (d. 1979), left his two wives in Iran when he came to the United States.

The refugees also differ from the general Kurdish population in religious observance. As Muslims, Kurds are required to pray five times a day, to fast during the month of Ramadan, to marry according to the precepts of the Koran, to avoid alcohol, and to observe laws proscribing ritually unclean foods (similar to Orthodox Jewish dietary laws). In Kurdistan, adherence to religious laws varies from one country to the next. Iraqi Kurds are said to be less religiously inclined than either Iranian or Turkish Kurds. In Iraq, educated urban Kurds, especially men, tend to be even less observant. The majority of the Kurdish refugees in the United States call themselves Muslim, but they are not dogmatic nor do they seem to identify with other Muslim groups currently in the United States. For a number of reasons (including Israel's support for the Kurds during the Kurdish-Iraqi war, the fact that large numbers of Jews once resided in Iraqi Kurdistan, and the interest Jewish groups have shown in Kurdish politics), Kurds seem favorably disposed toward American Jews. Only in sexual matters are Kurds as conservative as other Muslims. It is still difficult for some Kurdish men to allow their wives to be seen on the street in America, and single

men express considerable confusion about the role of women in American society.

If these Kurdish refugees are not practicing Muslims, if they have shed many of the identifiable Kurdish customs such as the distinctive clothing worn by inhabitants of Iraqi Kurdistan, if they are mostly male and can be expected to marry American women who will not know Kurdish, can one expect them to remain identifiable as Kurds? The religious organizations charged by the U.S. State Department with the settlement of the Kurds placed the refugees with sponsoring families in far-flung states like North Dakota and Florida, in cities like Chicago, San Diego, Calif., Dallas, Tex., Nashville, Tenn., and Washington, D.C. No community received more than 30 Kurds and most received fewer. Yet, the Kurds so far have remained in close contact with each other. Because the educated elite of Kurdish society is so small, and because almost all of these people participated in the revolution together, they know of each other even if they are not directly acquainted. A number of the older Kurdish immigrants have also been in touch with the newcomers and some Kurds have already moved from their original settlement to join other Kurds, notably in Washington, D.C.

The future of the Kurds as a group in the United States probably rests on their ability to resolve some of the arguments that currently divide the refugee community. Whatever the political means they espouse, all the refugees are strongly committed to the cause of Kurdish nationalism. On the basis of the experience of the earlier group of assimilated refugees, they will remain committed, but whether the Kurds will actually emerge as an identifiable ethnic group in the United States is still an open question.

Bibliography

There is no published work on Kurds in the United States. Derk Kinnane, *The Kurds and Kurdistan* (New York, 1964), gives a concise, accurate overview of Kurdish history, customs, and politics. More personal views of Kurdistan can be found in *Strange Lands and Friendly People* (New York, 1951), an account by William O. Douglas of his travels to the Middle East that includes chapters on his encounters with Kurdish villagers; and in *Journey Among Brave Men* (Boston, 1964), Dana Adams Schmidt's eyewitness account of the guerrilla fighting in Iraqi Kurdistan in the 1960s. For information about the role of the U.S. government in Kurdish affairs, see the *Village Voice* supplement (Feb. 16, 1976) on the Pike Papers.

MARGARET KAHN

KUTENAIS: *see* AMERICAN INDIANS

KUWAITIS: *see* ARABS

L

LABOR

Among the constants of industrialization, none seems more certain than the impulse toward collective action by workers. Essential uniformities underlying modern industrialism have given a common character to the labor movement of western nations. Even so, those movements have varied significantly, and none has departed more markedly from the norm than that of the United States. Nowhere else has the labor movement focused so militantly on narrow job interests, nowhere else has it so insisted on insulating labor's concerns from the political sector nor been so disinclined to question the standing order or to define its mission in class terms. No other movement has had quite so hard a struggle to establish its legitimacy and to organize its constituency. American trade unionism occupies a special place in the roster of working-class movements of the western world. Among the reasons for that distinctiveness, great weight must be given to the ethnic character of American working people.

For the half-century prior to World War I, the shaping years of the national labor movement, the foreign-born consistently made up roughly a seventh of the American population. Within the labor force, however, they were a much larger presence. In 1910 immigrants constituted 25 percent of the employees in transportation, 36 percent in manufacturing, and 45 percent in mining. If white-collar jobs are excluded, the concentration of foreign-born workers becomes still higher, running in many manual occupations from 50 to more than 75 percent. Immigrants made up nearly 58 percent of the wage earners in 20 principal mining and manufacturing industries in 1909. And when their American-born children are included, it becomes apparent that during the industrializing age the nation's working people were predominantly of recent origin.

The relative lack of an indigenous labor supply had distinguished the American industrial experience from the start. Unlike England, the United States could not draw on a numerous population of artisans and laborers to man its new factories. In the early days the giant cotton mills north of Boston recruited Yankee farm girls; textile producers in Rhode Island and elsewhere relied on family labor for mill work and on the putting-out system for weaving cloth. Some industries—such as the boot and shoe manufacture around Lynn, Mass., and the machine-tool production in the Connecticut Valley —were able to rely on chiefly local labor. In general, however, as industrialism gathered force, the need for hands far outran native sources of supply. More than any other force, it was this persistent shortage of labor that drew 35 million immigrants to the United States in the century ending with World War I. The Great Migration must be seen as primarily economic, ebbing and flowing along with the business cycle, drawing disproportionately on males of working age, and in its details, largely shaped by the changing needs of American industry for particular kinds of European workers.

The dependence on outside sources of labor did not end when the mass immigration from Europe was checked, first by World War I and then by the restrictive laws of 1921 and 1924. An exodus from settled farming areas had been under way throughout the 19th century, and while much of it went westward, the movement was also persistently cityward. The decline of immigration after 1914, however, made internal migration more decisively industrial in its direction. The half-million southern blacks who moved north during World War I, for example, boosted the black portion of the labor force in the Chicago packinghouses from 3 percent in 1909 to over 20 percent in 1918. By 1930 over 25 percent of the nation's black males were engaged in industrial occupations, compared to 7 percent in 1890. Similarly, Appalachian whites became a major source of labor for defense industries during World War I and for such growing manufacturing centers as Detroit, Mich., and Toledo and Akron, Ohio, during the 1920s.

These successive waves of newcomers did not enter the industrial system in a random way. Many of the western Europeans were seasoned artisans and industrial workers bringing applicable—and in the earlier years, essential—skills to American production. The more advanced British economy made an especially large contribution. Skills gave a distinctive ethnic stamp to the 19th-century occupational structure—the Welsh in anthracite mining and tin plate manufacture, the Scots in bituminous mining, Cornishmen in copper and lead mining, the English in iron, steel, and textiles, Germans in traditional crafts, Scandinavians on the Great Lakes boats, Russian Jews in the needle trades. Those who came without skills also found specific niches in the economic system. Rural Ireland was the main source of common labor in the pre–Civil War period. In Boston in 1850, for example, over 80 percent of the laborers were Irish. Starting as cartmen, longshoremen, and ditch diggers, the Irish moved into the factories and gradually up the scale of the expanding industrial economy. In 1855 they formed a substantial part of the skilled artisan class of New York City (40 percent of the carpenters, 50 percent of the blacksmiths, 60 percent of the masons and bricklayers). Similarly in industry and mining: by 1885 half the Irish involved in accidents in three Pennsylvania anthracite districts were classified as skilled miners, a proportion equal to that of the English and Welsh. As mechanization and mass-production techniques advanced in the late 19th century, dependence on European craft skills lessened, while the need for ordinary workers accelerated, which was one of the reasons for the remarkable shift of immigration from northern to southern and eastern Europe. In 1907 Slavs and Italians made up over 80 percent of the common labor in the Carnegie Steel Company. The low-paid, heavy work in northern industry and transportation became the virtual preserve of the "new" immigrants in the early 20th century.

Ethnicity cut deeply into American occupational patterns not only because of the varied skills of the immi-

grants. Within trades and industries, ethnic groups tended to cluster together in certain industrial locales and even within individual factories and mines. Settlement patterns worked to the same effect. French Canadians crossing the border did not normally venture beyond upper New England; Mexicans confined themselves to the fields and mines of the Southwest, the Chinese to the Pacific Coast. In a city such as Milwaukee, Wis., settled mainly by Germans, the trades were heavily German in composition (in 1860, 58 percent of the tradesmen were German, ranging from 42 percent of the machinists to 54 percent of the carpenters and 74 percent of the butchers). To some degree, ethnocultural characteristics, especially among preindustrial groups, determined the choices of occupation. The *padrone* system naturally led Italian peasants into construction and road work. Eastern European Jews flocked into the needle trades, not only because of prior experience but because the subcontracting and homework fitted (or could be made to fit) family, religious, and group needs in the tenement districts of the great cities.

There were, finally, persistent constraints imposed by the larger society on the job opportunities of particular groups. The blacks suffered most severely. Of all the ethnic groups in late-19th-century Boston, for example, blacks alone experienced no significant degree of upward mobility and remained confined, generation after generation, in menial and unskilled work (laborer, servant, porter, janitor). When blacks began to move into northern industry in much larger numbers after 1914, the experience was repeated: they were relegated to the most onerous and undesirable jobs. Although no other group (except the Asians in the West) was so completely handicapped, prejudice always played a part in pressing despised groups—from the Irish in the 1830s to the Chicanos in our own time—into the bleaker corners of the economic system.

Work in the United States was inscribed indelibly by ethnicity, and in consequence, so would be any American labor movement. How could such a movement capitalize on the strengths inherent in the ethnic groups and skirt the dangers of diversity and mutual antagonism? The answers to those central questions do not exhaust the subject, for the immigrant workers were not passive agents. They impressed the experiences from their own pasts on the American movement. This was most obvious among those who derived from a European working-class background and brought knowledge of European trade unionism and those who arrived dedicated to European radical ideologies, such as many of the Germans, Finns, and Russian Jews. But even those with no industrial past played an active part in shaping the labor movement. Why these immigrants joined and how they acted collectively were related to what they had known back home.

The origins of the American labor movement went back to the 1790s and possibly earlier. As the line became sharper between journeyman and employing craftsman, the cordwainers, printers, carpenters, and other artisans formed the first American trade unions. The basic unit of the labor movement—the local union of workers of the same trade—emerged. So did the basic economic thrust: protection of wage rates and labor standards, control of access to the trade, and exertion of economic power through the strike. During the 1830s the movement broadened into citywide organizations that united the local unions for purposes of mutual defense and political action. In the third stage of development 20 years later, national unions began to take root as local unions became aware that the transportation revolution was nationalizing the labor and product markets in their trades. After the Civil War the movement took the first tentative steps toward federation in order to define its larger purposes and cope with issues beyond the scope of city central bodies and national trade unions. This formative labor activity was inspired by economic forces within American society, and the basic tendencies of the movement sprang from the native environment. The participants themselves, however, were mostly European in origin.

In Illinois immigrants participated in the labor movement out of proportion to their numbers. Although foreign-born workers constituted 40 percent of the state's industrial labor force, they constituted over two-thirds of the union membership in 1886. Pondering this discovery, the Illinois Bureau of Labor Statistics stressed the immigrants' class-consciousness and craft identity: "The foreign workman . . . has no possibilities beyond a given sphere, and is trained and developed within it. Thus environed, his career and ambitions lie in the paths his fathers have trod, and his associations with his fellow craftsmen make the trade-union his natural and necessary place." Many of the industrial immigrants had been union men at home. It was, in fact, a regular practice of English unions to encourage unemployed members to emigrate by providing information and a ship ticket. A few English unions, such as the Amalgamated Society of Engineers, even set up American branches to serve their overseas members. "Everybody belonged to unions, it was taken for granted as a normal part of life," recalled John Brophy (1883–1963), an Anglo-American miner who later became an important 20th-century labor leader. His early success at organizing a miners' union in South Fork, Pa., he ascribed "to the fact that the miners were almost all of British origin . . . The British immigrants brought with them not only experience in British mines but also, like my father, the experience of British unions." There were regional variations, and probably greater native participation earlier in the 19th century, but in general American trade unionism was very much a movement of immigrant workers during the formative years.

Their presence helped surmount the organizational fragility of the movement. In every depression, unions that had been built up in prosperity foundered. As late as the 1870s economic crisis nearly put the labor movement out of business. Of some 30 national unions operating in 1873, fewer than 10 survived the depression, and even the strongest of these suffered severely from lost membership and defunct locals. Samuel Gompers (1850–1924) doubted that total membership exceeded 50,000 in 1878. It was not only their industrial past that made immigrant workers a stabilizing influence; ethnic bonds also served to cement labor organization. Wherever foreign-language immigrants clustered in a single trade, they tended to organize along ethnic lines. In New York City German artisans in the 1840s organized social clubs and mutual-aid societies, some of which evolved into trade unions. The New York German unions maintained their own central labor body, the Ar-

beiter Verein. The same kind of separate activity occurred in other cities with large German populations. The tendency to organize along ethnic lines eventually expressed itself formally in such bodies as the United Hebrew Trades, the United German Trades, and the Italian Chamber of Labor. From ethnic loyalties, too, roots were thrust down into the larger community. Through its large Irish membership, the Molders' Union of Troy, N.Y., had ties to the Irish fraternal orders, the Catholic church, and local politics. In its struggles with the stove manufacturers in the 1860s and 1870s, the Molders' Union could count on sympathy from the police (largely Irish) and public officials and on support from the Irish-American population. In an age when the vitality of trade unionism was still bound up in local community life, such ethnic linkages were an abiding source of strength to the labor movement.

The immigrant presence also exerted some force—subtle and immeasurable, to be sure—on the ultimate direction of the labor movement. From the 1830s through the 1880s the movement alternated between economic unionism and labor reform. It would be inaccurate to suggest any neat correspondence separating native and immigrant workers on this issue. For one thing, many of the utopian proposals—from land reform in the 1830s to cooperation later in the century—either derived from or closely paralleled European ideas, and the reform impulse that periodically took command always attracted a foreign-born following. Half the leading figures in the National Labor Union between 1862 and 1872 were British, as were 11 of 25 major leaders of the Knights of Labor at the peak of its power in 1886. And labor's ambivalence about its direction was genuinely internalized, existing within the minds of individuals as well as dividing organizations. Yet if one thinks of tendencies, the immigrants seemed less susceptible to the lure of broad reform than American workers. The goal of a cooperative commonwealth was grounded in notions of antimonopolism and of a producer society expressive of an American animus against industrialism. Such an appeal might reasonably be expected to exert its main force on native-born people who were experiencing a sense of loss and deprivation in the face of the economic changes then transforming American life.

That this was actually the case is suggested by the 1886 survey of the Illinois Bureau of Labor Statistics. Native-born participation was much stronger in the reformist Knights of Labor (43 percent) than in the trade unions (20 percent). Of nearly 35,000 Illinois residents who belonged to Knights assemblies, over 15,200 were native-born; of some 54,200 in trade unions, only 10,700 were native-born. This difference cannot be explained by the fact that the Knights of Labor was open to middle-class as well as manual occupations. Only 1,260 Illinois members (3.5 percent) fell into the former category, not enough to make any appreciable difference, even if all had been native-born. On the other hand, the inclusive recruiting policy of the Knights, especially during the wave of enthusiasm of 1885–1886, brought in large numbers of unskilled workers—over a quarter of the total in 1886—who were disproportionately of recent immigrant origin. The only two ethnic groups more heavily represented in the Knights than in the trade unions were Poles and Bohemians, al-

most entirely Chicago workers in the stockyards and heavy industry. The remaining membership of the Knights, representing the same occupations covered by the unions, thus was even more thoroughly American in composition.

Class-conscious by background and often trade-union by experience, industrial immigrants found comparatively uncongenial a reform philosophy that denied the significance of class and minimized those elements of militancy (including the strike) and craft identity that were at the heart of trade unionism. By the same token, the immigrants gave to American trade unionism much of the weight it needed to prevail over labor reform.

The industrial immigrants also helped set the ultimate direction of the labor movement by providing leadership. Of 77 American labor figures who were prominent between 1860 and 1875, 45, or 58 percent, had been born in Europe—13 in England, 11 in Ireland, 9 in Germany, 5 each in Scotland and Wales, 2 in France. A more comprehensive survey of 150 leaders prominent between 1870 and 1895 reveals that 48 percent of those with known birthplaces had been born abroad. Many of the immigrant leaders came as seasoned industrial workers and unionists. The Irish activists, for instance, generally arrived via English industry rather than, as most of their compatriots did, directly from the countryside. Of the foreign-born leaders of the 1870–1895 period, nearly two-thirds arrived in the United States after the age of 14, and as many as half of these had engaged in labor activities at home. Among this group were such pioneering figures as Thomas Phillips (1833–1916) of the Knights of St. Crispin and the Knights of Labor, John Siney (1831–1880) and Chris Evans (1841–1924) of the Miners, John Jarrett (1843–1918) of the Iron and Steel Workers, and Adolph Strasser (1844–1910) of the Cigar Makers. Equally notable was the preponderance of Britons among the 19th-century foreign-born leaders—two-thirds of them (not counting Canadians) for the 1870–1895 period, and an even higher proportion for the earlier group. Experience and predilection alike led them to put a particular stamp on American trade unionism.

"England has been the model," remarked French economist Pierre Émile Levasseur after surveying the American labor movement of the 1890s. "The ideas . . . cross the ocean with the tide of immigration." Britons figured prominently in the origins of at least 24 of the major national unions in the United States. When the Miners' National Association was formed in 1873, the Scotsman John James followed the constitution of Alexander Macdonald's Miners' National Association in Great Britain. English unions served as the models for, among others, the Boilermakers, Granite Cutters, and Carpenters and Joiners. Especially influential was the example of English "new model" unionism, with its stress on benefit systems, high dues, centralized control over local unions, and collective bargaining (a term the Americans borrowed from the British). The demonstration union for these policies in the American movement was the Cigar Makers, whose leaders boasted that they had "borrowed . . . most particularly from the English trade unions." Efforts at federation were similarly inspired. The Federation of Organized Trades and Labor Unions (FOTLU, f. 1881) was explicitly modeled on the British

Trades Union Congress, and so was its permanent successor, the American Federation of Labor (AFL, f. 1886). It was fitting that the temporary president of the FOTLU was a Welshman and that two Englishmen nominated a third, Samuel Gompers, for the presidency. Gompers himself honored Britain "as the cradle of our now universal movement."

But if structure and policy derived from British models, American trade-union philosophy traced its roots to quite different foreign sources. Ever since the 1840s, the Germans had been the principal bearers of European radicalism to the United States. The implanting of modern socialism after the Civil War was distinctly the handiwork of German immigrants, especially in New York City, where, for the four years until it expired in 1876, Karl Marx's International Workingmen's Association was based. Marx favored trade unionism as the means for building the class consciousness and economic power of the workers, while the followers of his rival, Ferdinand Lassalle, stressed political action. Although the issue was essentially tactical—should unions be the first step, or should all energy go into creation of a political party?—the debate was carried on furiously both in Europe and within the narrow confines of the German socialist community in the United States (but with some participation by others). The formation of the Socialist Labor Party in 1877 signaled the triumph of the Lassalleans and set the future course of American socialism toward politics.

As it happened, several key future unionists—Adolph Strasser, J.P. McDonnell (c. 1840–1906), P.J. McGuire (1852–1906), and Gompers—participated in the socialist controversy over politics and trade unionism. During that time they hammered out the philosophical position defining American pure-and-simple unionism (the term "pure-and-simplism" was used during the debate): first, a determined focus on concrete, short-term objectives; second, a reliance on economic power rather than politics; third, a membership limited to workers and organized on strictly occupational lines; finally, as Strasser said in 1883, a rejection of "ultimate ends . . . we are opposed to theorists." These ideas Gompers and his colleagues brought with them into the trade-union struggle and into the launching of the American Federation of Labor. Although it had been couched originally in Marxian terms of class struggle, pure-and-simple unionism cast off its radical moorings and, under Gompers's skillful hand, became the guiding philosophy of a profoundly conservative movement.

From a sectarian debate conducted mainly in German had come a set of ideas that would permanently distinguish American trade unionism from its European counterparts. Originating intellectually in a narrow corner of immigrant America, pure-and-simple unionism derived much of its compelling logic from labor's need to function within the wider world of immigrant workers. Central to Gompers's purpose was securing the common ground, narrow though it might be, on which workers of the most diverse persuasions and nationalities might unite.

The difficulty of building worker solidarity within an ethnically divided labor force had long been apparent. A half-century earlier, in the 1830s, Philadelphia workers had experienced a remarkable surge of militant organization. Not only the skilled trades but mill hands, laborers, and handloom weavers formed unions, which joined together to form the General Trades' Union of Philadelphia. After a general strike in 1835 secured the 10-hour day, the Trades' Union swelled to over 50 locals representing 10,000 members, and with its aid, Philadelphia workers won a series of stirring victories. The Panic of 1837, however, initiated a rapid decline in labor's strength and, within a year, the General Trades' Union collapsed. As the depression deepened, a religious revival swept through the distressed ranks of the Protestant artisans, who eagerly embraced the cause of temperance. Irish Catholic weavers and laborers, the target of this enthusiasm, angrily protested the intrusion on their personal liberty. Meanwhile desperate strikes, punctuated by violence and rioting, deepened ethnic tensions. A dispute over Bible reading in the schools brought matters to a head in May 1844. Triggered by Irish attempts to disrupt nativist meetings in their neighborhoods, an anti-Catholic riot swept through Kensington, leaving in its wake heavy casualties and burned houses. In politics the lines became sharply drawn, with the artisans in the nativist American Republican party, the Irish workers in the Democratic party. Catholic and Protestant gangs and fire companies fought pitched battles on the streets for years afterward. Class unity had fallen apart in an ugly shambles of nativism and bigotry.

The Kensington riots were a microcosm of the ethnic forces besetting working-class life in the 19th century. Fear of cheap competition almost invariably inspired settled workers to resent the next wave of immigrants, and when the newcomers entered as strikebreakers—a common event—job rivalries took on a murderous intensity. Mixed in with economic fears were ethnic tensions, which unions persistently complained were exploited by open-shop employers. An endless catalogue could be drawn up of conflict between Cornish and Irish hard-rock miners, Yankee and French Canadian textile workers, Irish and English anthracite miners, white and black locomotive firemen, Italian and native laborers, and so on.

Ethnicity also exerted a potent influence on political behavior. Recent studies of late-19th-century politics are consistent on this point: whether a man voted Democratic or Republican depended much less on whether he was a worker (even taking into account occupation and industry) than on whether he was a Catholic or an evangelical Protestant, an Irishman or a Yankee, a black or a southern white. Even the socialist parties, participating as they presumably were in an international class struggle against capitalism, actually were rooted in specific ethnic communities. In the 1880s, an uneventful political era by modern standards, electoral participation and party loyalty (as measured by voting behavior) stood at record levels because of the potent ethnocultural content of political life. Artfully aided by the major parties, this political mode proved highly resilient in the face of class interests activated by the depression of the 1890s.

Pure-and-simple unionism was strongly mindful of the ethnocultural realities of American working-class life. The AFL ruled "that party politics, whether they be democratic, republican, populistic, prohibition, or any other, should have no place" in its conventions. By rejecting any form of independent or partisan politics, the

Federation was abandoning a claim on its members' loyalties that it could not successfully have asserted in any case. At the same time, nonpartisanship would insulate the labor movement from the ethnocultural issues that divided American politics. Even if such an issue might unite workers politically, the result was hardly likely to be consonant with the purposes of the labor movement. Thus anti-Chinese sentiment in California spawned an independent labor politics in the 1870s, but it was so corrupt and opportunistic as to blight the California labor movement for years thereafter. This did not mean that organized labor stayed out of public life—that choice it never had—but that it pursued its necessary political objectives through lobbying and nonpartisan tactics that kept it free of the ethnocultural web of American politics.

Pure-and-simple unionism focused aggressively on the narrow job concerns of workers. The ruling principle, as Gompers always said, was that trade unions "should open their portals to all wage workers irrespective of creed, color, nationality, sex or politics." However these differences might divide them in the larger world, workers on the job were united by a common purpose: to maximize the return on their labor. And they were equally united by a common need: to act collectively to force fair treatment from employers. All questions of union structure and strategy were put to this economic test: will it enhance the bargaining position of workers? The ethnic basis of organization, frequently the essential first stage of unionization, normally gave way to more strictly economic units once collective bargaining began, either by a process of amalgamation or, as in the garment trades, by subordinating ethnic locals to the control of a joint board. Even such auxiliary bodies as the United Hebrew Trades were accepted only grudgingly by the AFL. To do so, Gompers remarked, was "theoretically bad but practically necessary." Relentlessly economic in its means and ends, pure-and-simple unionism negotiated a path through the tangle of conflicting loyalties inherent in American working-class life, asserting an absolute claim to what related to the job and excluding the rest. It goes without saying that Gompers was responding to other demands of 19th-century America, but clearly the genius of his formulation lay in its attack on the ethnic dilemmas facing the labor movement.

As it turned out, Gompers's success was more fully realized in theory than in practice. In 1888 the International Association of Machinists (IAM), a key union, sought affiliation with the AFL. Southern in origin, the IAM had a whites-only clause in its constitution. Gompers rejected the application.

Wage workers ought to bear in mind that unless they help to organize the colored man, they will of necessity compete with the white workmen and be antagonistic to them and their interests. The employers will certainly take advantage of this condition and . . . even stimulate race prejudice. View it in a common sense manner . . . not with the old prejudices . . . but study it in the light of the historical struggles of the peoples of all nations, and you will find that I am right.

This reasoning did not move the Machinists, however, and within a few years the AFL caved in. The IAM struck the offending clause from the constitution but not from the ritual, and blacks continued to be barred from the union. By 1900 even this sham collapsed. Anxious to bring in the railroad unions, which were notoriously antiblack, the AFL admitted the Order of Railroad Telegraphers and the Brotherhood of Railway Trackmen despite their constitutional racial bars. Then in 1902 the affiliated Stationary Engineers added an amendment excluding blacks. The Federation had already amended its constitution in 1900 to permit the chartering of federal unions for blacks who were not admitted into white unions. Whatever hopes Gompers might have harbored for future benefits from these accommodations, the harsh reality was that he was presiding over a virtually lily-white movement. In 1902 blacks constituted hardly 3 percent of the total union membership and were largely segregated in the ineffectual federal unions. Black organization in the coal mines and on the New Orleans docks stand out as lonely exceptions. Nearly two-thirds of all white unionists belonged to unions that had either no black members or negligible numbers.

The Federation's dismal record exposed underlying weaknesses in the pure-and-simple formulation. Issues, such as race, that stirred deep emotions could not be left outside the union hall. Nor were trade-union leaders, oriented as they were to economic interests, capable of meeting racism on a compelling moral plane. The vicious repression of blacks in the South in these years did not evoke official concern within the AFL. Gompers assured white workers who, "like many others may not care to socially meet colored people," that "there is no necessity to run counter to social distinctions." Organizing blacks, Gompers insisted, was "a proposition of the most eminent practicality . . . a bald business proposition." At the turn of the century, as it happened, the threat of black competition did not loom large. Ever since Reconstruction, relentless pressures had forced blacks out of their traditional southern jobs as artisans and down into menial and segregated work in both North and South. The New Orleans city directory of 1870 listed 3,460 blacks in a variety of skilled trades; not 10 percent remained in those occupations in 1904. By the time the AFL faced the issue, blacks were so confined economically as to pose no present danger to the trade unions, notwithstanding their use as strikebreakers. Ironically, racism and pure-and-simple tactics now tended to coincide rather than conflict. Craft unions had always tried to restrict access and control labor markets. What more efficacious way than along the color line?

Gompers may have perceived the longer-term dangers in this course, but he lacked the authority to counteract it. Because the national unions performed the key economic functions of the labor movement, they were conceded the rights of "trade autonomy." "To the union of the trade belongs absolute jurisdiction on all matters connected with that trade," Gompers admitted in his quarrel with the Machinists. "The recognition of this cardinal principle, however, did not deny us the right of expressing the sentiments of trade unionism against any matter involving the general interest of the labor movement." But if trade autonomy did not prevent Gompers from talking, it assuredly did deny him the capacity to act. In the end, Gompers justified his handling of the race issue (beyond an increasing tend-

ency to blame the blacks themselves) precisely on the grounds of trade autonomy: the AFL had no authority to instruct the national unions on the management of their affairs. The treatment of black workers would one day return to haunt the labor movement, but in the meantime, its failure could be taken as symptomatic of a larger incapacity to live up to the precepts of pure-and-simple unionism. Where ethnocultural divisions cut deeply, labor's economic focus and institutional structure proved unequal to, if not downright destructive of, the task of uniting workers.

At the turn of the century, labor faced no crisis from the excluded blacks. The same could not be said of the eastern and southern Europeans flocking into American industry. Contemporaries drew a sharp qualitative distinction between the old and the new immigration. Contempt for the Irish, virulent 75 years before, had long since died out, and the Irish now occupied a respectable place in the ranks of American workers. The other older immigrants had generally been treated with a good deal of respect all along—the Germans and Scandinavians for their skills and industrious habits, the Britons for those qualities and because they were regarded as compatriots. The new immigrants, on the other hand, seemed distinctly alien, ignorant of English, exotic in their habits, largely devoid of industrial skills, herding apart in crowded, noisome neighborhoods. It was a telling commentary that a Welsh miner, himself by no means certain that he would remain in America, referred derisively to Slavs and Italians entering the mines as "foreigners."

The perceived differences, moreover, were given an ominous permanence in the racist thought of the early 20th century. The prevailing belief, rooted in the "science" of eugenics and dignified in the writings of respected scholars, was that ethnic characteristics were inherited rather than culturally determined. The Dillingham Commission, established by Congress in 1907, undertook a vast survey of the new immigrants that was intended to document the various inferiorities making them undesirable additions to the American population. (That the data showed otherwise did not stop the commission from drawing the expected conclusions.) So the racist antipathies traditionally directed against blacks were now to some degree leveled at the new immigrants as well.

For the labor movement, the immigrants were different from the blacks in key ways. For one thing, immigration could be closed off at the source. The AFL already claimed much of the credit for the Chinese Exclusion Act of 1882, and during the 1890s, the Federation became a fervent advocate of a literacy test for entering immigrants. This, Gompers argued in 1902, "would exclude hardly any natives of Great Britain, Ireland, Germany, France, or Scandinavia. It will shut out a considerable number of South Italians and of Slavs and other[s] equally or more undesirable and injurious." When the Immigration Act of 1917, which imposed a simple literacy test, failed to have that effect, attention turned to the device of a quota system, and the AFL eagerly endorsed it.

There can be no question but that the labor movement was instrumental in bringing about the reversal of America's historic open-door immigration policy. Why labor favored restriction is less clear. The leading histo-

rian of the AFL, Philip Taft, has argued forcefully that the Federation was acting strictly—and properly—from economic motives. An overcrowded labor market, constantly replenished by outsiders eager to work at any price, was bound to undermine labor standards and the effectiveness of trade unionism. This was the incessant claim of AFL spokesmen. But there is no doubt about the racist coloration of their thinking. Unionists made no bones about their race animus toward the Chinese, and they were clearly intent not only on reducing the numbers of eastern and southern Europeans, but on eliminating "undesirable immigration." They applauded the distorted findings of the Dillingham Commission. (It should be pointed out, however, that the commission went out of its way to underscore the economic fears of the labor movement.) The AFL had no qualms about a quota system calculated on the blood mix of the population as it was in 1920. The racist assumptions behind this national policy were not objectionable to Gompers. As he wrote in his autobiography (published in the same year as the Johnson Immigration Restriction Act), it was about time that people understood "the principle that the maintenance of the nation depended upon the maintenance of racial purity and strength."

The flow of new immigrants ended, but millions had already entered the country. They were present in force in American industry. They confronted the labor movement with a challenge of far greater magnitude than did the blacks prior to World War I.

American trade unionism at the turn of the century was a movement of skilled workers. While efforts to organize the unskilled had not been lacking—the Knights of Labor and the American Railway Union were only the last in a string of failed experiments—those workers still remained beyond the bounds of trade unionism. The dominance of the craft unions, together with rules and structure designed to their specifications, rendered the AFL incapable for practical purposes of acting on its early promise to reach all workers. No place was likely to be made for the unskilled so long as the central premise of craft unionism remained intact: namely, the indispensability of the skilled, all-round worker. Industrial progress was relentlessly undercutting this worker's position, however. In field after field his importance was being eroded by the use of machinery, the subdivision of labor, and the techniques of scientific management. Some unions did devise effective defenses—the Typographers, for example, by asserting bargaining rights over the linotype machine, and the Carpenters by tight control over local labor markets and over machine-made wood products. But for the many unions incapable of such holding actions, craft exclusivity was called into question. They could not deny, as the Butchers' Union conceded after entering the Chicago stockyards in 1900, that technological change "places the skilled workman at the mercy of common labor and makes it necessary to organize all working in the large plants under one head."

By the time the crisis arrived, the mass of new immigrants had joined the unskilled ranks of American industry. In 1904 the AFL sent a team of organizers into the iron and steel industry, where only 15 years before, the once-proud Amalgamated Association of Iron and Steel Workers had been accounted the model craft

union. "We find on investigation that the number of skilled steel workers ha[s] been greatly reduced on account of improved machinery . . . On the other hand, a large number of the unskilled workers are foreigners, hardly able to speak or understand the English language, thereby complicating and retarding our efforts. All told, the field is not a promising one." This pessimism was not entirely misplaced. Nothing in their agricultural past had prepared the immigrants for trade unionism. Mostly intent on saving money and returning to the native village, green arrivals did not find the arguments of organizers persuasive. But with time and industrial experience, the immigrants disproved the stereotyped view that they were hopelessly docile. Their peasant origins, which stressed group decisions and communal approval, actually made them notably militant strikers and loyal unionists in coal mining. Similarly, the success of the garment unions after 1909 was rooted in the fact that it was a largely Jewish work force. The obtuseness of the trade unions on this point to some degree testified to the more deep-rooted problem: the ethnocultural chasm separating English-speaking workers—both leaders and rank and file—from the southern and eastern Europeans.

What this meant for trade-union policy cannot be separated out and given precise weight. For one thing, craft identity exerted a stubborn hold in its own right. Convention halls witnessed agonizing debates over the wisdom of broadening the membership. To admit specialists and helpers, IAM delegates protested, would "ruin" the machinists' trade and undermine "our dignity." Some unions—the Window Glass Workers and the Cigar Makers, for example—were so immobilized by craft sentiment as to fail utterly to respond to basic technological advances. Trade-union conservatism was fostered also by the institutional rigidities of trade autonomy and exclusive jurisdiction and by the vested interests of existing memberships and entrenched leaders. The results were often such cosmetic responses as the creation of second-class membership for the less skilled or formal broadening of jurisdiction unaccompanied by actual organizing programs. But these inherent tendencies within the labor movement were certainly nourished by the knowledge that the less skilled were mainly the eastern European immigrants.

There are enough instances to suggest that if trade-union logic clearly called for broader organization, prejudice might be thrust aside. In the coal mines, where immigrants entered easily and rose swiftly in the miners' ranks, the UMWA organized them (and blacks) and prospered thereby. The Mine Workers operated as a genuinely multilanguage, multiracial organization in the early 20th century. When the Butchers' Union concluded that the Chicago packinghouses could not be organized without the unskilled, it did not long hesitate to take them in, even though they were overwhelmingly of recent Slavic origin. And during World War I, a uniquely opportune time, the labor movement managed to mobilize very considerable resources and enthusiasm for organizing the unskilled in steel, meat packing, and other mass-production fields. Even if a union was faint-hearted or obstructive, this did not necessarily preclude the organization of immigrant workers. The men's clothing workers unionized themselves almost in spite of the old-guard United Garment Workers

and, finding themselves barred from influence there, split off in 1914 to form the Amalgamated Clothing Workers under the leadership of Sidney Hillman (1887–1946).

In the end, the governing factor was the trade-union calculation of profit and loss. The mass-production sector, in which the immigrant workers were heavily concentrated, proved nearly invulnerable to trade unionism. The employers not only had the technological advantage, they wielded enormous economic power by virtue of corporate business organization and strong trade associations, and they could normally rely on the support of the state and the courts. Most important was their ruthless determination to protect the open shop at any cost. The power balance shifted decisively to the side of management in the early 20th century and, in so doing, placed a deadly pall on the trade-union movement. Although labor shortages and government protection evoked a union resurgence during World War I, the crushing failures of the postwar period produced an abiding defeatism. Thereafter the labor movement effectively abandoned the immigrant industrial workers.

The wartime influx of southern blacks cut still another gap between workers that the trade unions could not bridge. New to the industrial scene and justifiably suspicious of organized labor, blacks largely resisted appeals to unionize. Terrible race riots in East St. Louis, Ill., in 1917 and in Chicago in 1919, plus a host of violent incidents elsewhere, etched in blood animosities that would not fade for a generation. Black workers generally stayed on the job during strikes and thereby contributed to labor's defeats in the postwar years.

The mark of pure-and-simple unionism had been its intention to bring together in job-conscious unity workers of the utmost ethnic diversity, but this unifying function was lost along with the capacity to organize the mass-production sector. Confined essentially to the skilled trades, American unionism took on a more fixed ethnocultural character. Fully a third of the union leadership after 1900 was Irish-born or of Irish descent, including the presidents of over 50 national unions and at least half the AFL vice presidents at any one time. The Catholic church, acting especially through the Militia of Christ, began to exert a marked influence on the AFL in these years. As the ethnically mixed United Mine Workers and clothing unions weakened during the 1920s, organized labor moved closer to cultural homogeneity. In the ethnically and racially diverse working-class world the labor movement lost its capacity to serve as a common ground and became instead an island for a minority of American-born northern European workers.

The American left exerted little counterforce on the trade unions. Since the 1890s, the main radical thrust had been into politics. The Socialist party did have a considerable trade-union following, mounting up to as high as a third of the delegate strength at the AFL convention of 1911 and including key national unions and central labor bodies. The Socialist trade-union program called for industrial unionism and militant organizing work. A strong resolution in 1912 urged the unions to begin "organizing the unorganized, especially the immigrants who stand in greatest need of organization." But this was more a symbolic than a real stance. The moderate Socialist leadership accepted the AFL as the

legitimate labor movement and minimized differences in the vain hope of winning over the Federation. Despite its own ethnic constituencies, moreover, the Socialist party did not take much interest in the immigrant industrial workers, and toward blacks and Asians its views were hardly more advanced than those of the AFL. Class-conscious rhetoric notwithstanding, Socialist trade unionists in practice acted like any other unionists. The persistent deterioration of their standing within the labor movement after 1912 ended any lingering prospects that the Socialists might revitalize American trade unionism.

For the left-wing minority that despaired of bringing about change from inside the Federation, the answer was a rival movement. In 1905 the Western Federation of Miners, Daniel DeLeon's (1852–1914) Socialist Labor party, and left-wingers from the Socialist party formed the Industrial Workers of the World (IWW), which proclaimed itself "an organization broad enough to take in all the working class." In a rampantly intolerant age, the IWW was singularly free of prejudice. Its doors were wide open to Asians as well as to eastern Europeans, and it held the AFL in contempt for "calling them 'undesirable' class[es] of immigrants, and . . . agitating for laws to bar them from America." Sensitive to their needs, the IWW employed foreign-language organizers, published materials in many languages, and aggressively asserted the worth of every worker, "no matter what his religion, fatherland, or trade." With its syndicalist philosophy, the IWW was more successful as a shock force to lead the immigrants when they rose in spontaneous strikes—for example, at McKees Rocks, Pa., in 1909, Lawrence, Mass., in 1912, Paterson, N.J., in 1913, and on the Mesabi Range, Minn., in 1916—than as a builder of permanent organization among immigrant workers. Beginning in 1913 the IWW shifted its attention to the harvest workers, miners, lumbermen, and itinerant construction workers of the West, far from the main centers of immigrant employment. Crushed by federal repression during World War I, the IWW left as its legacy not so much substantial success among minority workers as an ideal of working-class unity that still commands respect.

The Socialists and the IWW pursued alternative strategies for opening up the labor movement: the former by working within the AFL, the latter by starting up a separate movement. The Communist party, the principal vehicle of American radicalism from 1919 onward, tried both strategies, but with even less success. Partly because of the impact of the Bolshevik Revolution, the Communist following initially consisted very largely of recent immigrants—of the total membership in 1919, over 75 percent was eastern European, including 25 percent Russian. Although most of the Russians soon dropped out or left for home, the immigrant character of the membership persisted through the 1920s, when Finns, Jews, and eastern Europeans made up roughly 80 percent of the total. Ties to ethnic fraternal and cultural associations were a crucial source of support.

The Communists had been too disorganized and self-absorbed to play any part in the labor struggles of 1919–1920, but in 1921 they recruited William Z. Foster (1881–1961), who had been the key man in the AFL meat-packing and steel campaigns, and embarked on a program of boring-from-within the AFL. In 1925 the au-

tonomous language federations that the Communists had inherited from the Socialist party were abolished, and the basic party unit became the "shop nucleus" so as to focus organizational activity more directly on the economic struggle. Far from having a liberalizing effect on the labor movement, the Communists sparked bitter internal battles that decimated such unions as the International Ladies' Garment Workers and the United Mine Workers. The AFL, scarred by postwar losses and the Red Scare of the 1920s, reinforced its identification with "Americanism" (including ties with the American Legion and the anti-Bolshevik National Civic Federation). Linked in the public mind with the foreign-born ever since World War I, the Communist threat fortified the AFL in its growing inclination to steer clear of the immigrant workers. In 1928 the Communists abandoned their boring-from-within strategy and launched the rival Trade Union Unity League, which sought to hammer-from-without. Its efforts in mass-production fields were not notably successful but did not go wholly to waste; it provided a cadre of experienced organizers for the industrial-union drives of the later 1930s. But in the short run Communist rivalry only tended to confirm the private belief of conservative unionists that the labor movement ought to be reserved for the English-speaking workers in the skilled trades.

Great events intervened to confound that restricted view. The Depression injected a desperate militancy into the ranks of workers and reduced the resistant power even of corporate business. With the coming of the New Deal under President Franklin Roosevelt, labor found sympathetic allies and ultimately legal protection of the right to organize and to engage in collective bargaining. Life stirred in the old ideal of a labor movement for all workers. The AFL was actually hard pressed to break out of the encrustations of its own past —so much so as to force an impatient minority to launch the rival Committee for Industrial Organization (CIO). Embedded in the complex causes of the split were contrasting racial and ethnic attitudes. Throughout this period the AFL stubbornly rejected the pleas of black organizations for a liberal racial policy, even defeating their efforts to have antidiscrimination language written into the New Deal collective-bargaining legislation. The old-line leaders' reluctance to mount a strong organizing drive reflected their disdain for the mass-production workers—"rubbish," one craft official called them. On the other hand, the industrial-union minority consisted precisely of those unions— the Mine Workers and the garment unions—that traditionally had been multiracial and multinational. The cause they espoused called for structural reforms that would foster an open labor movement. As the Urban League rightly observed, there was "little hope for the black worker so long as the AFL remains structurally a craft organization." The industrial form of organization, said the CIO, had as its "basic principle . . . organization of all workers regardless of skill, race, nationality, religion or politics."

The CIO adroitly applied that precept in its organizing campaigns. The first CIO organizer sent into Detroit (a UMWA veteran) laid out a comprehensive plan to reach the immigrant auto workers: "Obtain information on the approximate location of the numerous nationalities . . . Approximate population, names and

addresses of the fraternal and social organizations maintained by these groups. Endeavor to contact such groups . . . By the use of organizers who speak foreign languages we will be able to reach the large foreign-speaking elements in our community." The CIO drive in steel was equally attentive to these considerations. At a CIO conference on October 25, 1936, delegates from 17 fraternal orders and several hundred lodges in the steel towns around Pittsburgh, Pa., pledged their support, including public endorsement, sponsorship of mass meetings, and enlistment of the foreign-language press in the CIO cause. For a rally of Jones and Laughlin steel workers in January 1937, the CIO was able to provide speakers in Polish, Lithuanian, Russian, Serbian, and Croatian and to list the endorsement of fraternal orders covering virtually every immigrant group in the industry.

The passage of time was meanwhile creating other changes. In the steel industry, European-born workers declined from 50 percent of the labor force in 1910 to 30 percent in 1930, and these workers were steadily rising from the bottom ranks; by 1930 less than half were in unskilled work, compared to two-thirds in 1910. In fact, European-born and native whites were equally numerous in the unskilled labor force in 1930. As the immigrants grew "to middle age in the industry" (in the words of one CIO publicist) and were joined by their sons, the distinction between "hunky" and "English-speaking" began to lose its corrosive force, and long-standing ethnic barriers to organization began to crumble.

Ethnic identity still exerted a powerful influence on unionization in mass-production industry. A detailed study of one Detroit auto-parts plant between 1936 and 1939 reveals this progression: the first to join were the young second-generation workers, who became militant unionists; then the older Polish and Ukrainian workers, initially hesitant, but ultimately intensely loyal; next, the scattered Appalachian workers, who tended to be strongly pro- or anti-union on moral grounds; and finally, the skilled workers of northern European descent, who had to be coerced into the union. The progression was not immutable; at the Detroit plant of Midland Steel, the skilled men of northern European extraction took the union lead between 1936 and 1939, only to be displaced in a factional battle by the second-generation semiskilled workers in 1940. However, there were certain underlying consistencies. For one thing, ethnic characteristics did exert continuing influence on labor organization. Thus the Appalachian leadership of President Homer Martin (1902–1968), who had once been an evangelical preacher, put a strong stamp on the early United Auto Workers. At the plant level ethnicity largely determined social groupings in which workers moved toward organization, and ethnic ties sometimes led to forms of ethnic unionism reminiscent of much earlier times. This happened, for example, among the copper miners of the Southwest, where Mexican-American fraternal orders, with links to unions across the border, persisted during the period of disorganization and served as the nucleus for the union revival in the early 1940s.

The black migrants to northern industry, like the eastern Europeans, had become seasoned workers by the 1930s, but racial barriers did not lessen so readily.

Black workers continued to be distrustful of white fellow workers and to feel a special reliance on the good will of employers. As with its approach to the immigrant workers, the CIO responded by hiring black organizers and seeking support from the larger black community. For the first time the National Association for the Advancement of Colored People (NAACP) and the National Urban League unequivocally endorsed trade unionism. Early in the steel drive, the CIO held a national conference in Pittsburgh that drew 200 representatives from black organizations and local unions to hear Philip Murray promise that the CIO would tolerate "no discrimination under any circumstances within its organization." Despite the range of support elicited by the CIO, its strategy was less successful among blacks than among immigrant workers. The organizational network reaching down to black workers was relatively weak, and the Negro churches, which had the strongest working-class following, remained on the whole unsympathetic to the union cause. But the balance between racial divisiveness and labor unity slowly shifted as the CIO scored collective-bargaining victories and demonstrated its genuine commitment to racial equality.

The evolution of trade unionism into a bastion of privileged labor was reversed by the industrial-union thrust. In 1938 the CIO proclaimed itself an independent movement—the Congress of Industrial Organizations—and proceeded to challenge the AFL on all fronts. The formidable competition provoked a remarkable revival throughout the labor movement. Such craft unions as the Machinists, Electrical Workers, Teamsters, and Meat Cutters began to organize vigorously on broad industrial lines and to reach a multiplicity of workers not easily accessible to the CIO unions. The AFL resurgence restored the basis for a single labor movement that was the defender of all workers. When the AFL-CIO was formed in 1955, it included millions of workers who 20 years earlier had found no place in organized labor. By the mid-1950s, the nativist force that had fostered exclusivity had largely exhausted itself, partly by the cycle of time and the passing of the immigrant generation, partly by the disrepute into which racist thought had fallen, especially since World War II. If the AFL-CIO applauded the excision of national-origins principles from American immigration policy in 1965, so did many other groups that had once decried the flood of "undesirable" immigrants.

Although ethnicity no longer constituted a real test of the egalitarianism of the labor movement, however, race still did. In its constitution the AFL-CIO pledged itself "to encourage all workers without regard to race, creed, color, national origin, or ancestry to share equally in the full benefits of union organization." Two black officials sat on the first executive council, and the administrative structure included a civil-rights section responsible for eliminating discriminatory practices "at the earliest possible date." But unlike corruption and Communism, discrimination was not designated as grounds for expulsion. And shortly the AFL-CIO proceeded to admit two railroad brotherhoods—Locomotive Firemen and Railroad Trainmen—despite racial bars in their constitutions.

This faltering start reflected the persisting constraints acting on the modern labor movement. Not

even the CIO in its most militant period had been immune to conventional trade-union calculations. Confronted by racism at the local level, industrial unions had generally moved cautiously, weighing the enforcement of principle against the cost in larger organizational interests, and not always coming down on the side of principle. The significant upgrading of black workers during the 1940s—the percentage employed as craftsmen and operators rose from 16.6 in 1940 to 28.8 in 1950—sprang much more from wartime labor shortages than from union activity. As employment conditions tightened, the CIO moderated its battle for full job equality, and it accepted the accommodations required to achieve a united labor movement. To one industrial-union president in 1958, the persistence of segregated southern locals constituted "practical problems" that had to be handled "in a realistic manner."

By the end of the 1950s the NAACP was attacking the AFL-CIO for failing "to eliminate the broad patterns of racial discrimination and segregation in many affiliated unions." After A. Philip Randolph (1889–1979) openly split with President George Meany (1894–1980) at the AFL-CIO convention in 1959, black unionists formed the Negro American Labor Council to exert continuing internal pressure on the labor movement. Black criticism of trade unionism was now directed at a laggard ally, not, as had been true prior to 1935, at an enemy of economic opportunity for black people. By contrast to those earlier years, organized labor now acted basically as a progressive force for racial equality. This tendency was much strengthened by the civil-rights revolution of the 1960s. But insofar as labor's thrust toward racial equality was rooted in internal changes, the main credit must go to the industrial unionists whose efforts opened the labor movement to all working people, irrespective of race, nationality, or creed.

That development, in turn, altered the political orientation of American trade unionism. Its nonpartisanship had been dictated by, among other things, the diversity of party loyalties among American working people. From the early 1920s onward, however, a major political realignment set in, especially among those ethnic groups that the CIO later reached. First by its identification with personal liberty during the intolerant 1920s and then by the enormous appeal of the New Deal, the Democratic party made heavy inroads among Catholics, recent immigrants, and, finally, even among the traditionally Republican blacks. So powerful was President Franklin Roosevelt's hold on these groups that the CIO exploited its ties to him in its organizing drive among steel, auto, and other industrial workers. The mass entry of such workers into the labor movement greatly weakened the logic of political nonpartisanship. Although the movement had been tilting toward the Democratic party ever since the Progressive Era, the events of the 1930s brought about the alliance that has lasted to the present day. And labor's eroding spirit of militant voluntarism was fatally undermined by the infusion of millions of workers favorable to New Deal social-welfare programs.

In this evolution, ethnicity acted as a remote influence, affecting the party preferences of union members and through them labor's political orientation. This probably characterizes the modern relation between ethnicity and the labor movement, although there are instances of direct interaction. The unionization of Chicano farm workers under Cesar Chavez offers a classic example of the power of ethnic identity as the basis for labor organization. In the South racial differences still can be made a barrier to unionization, and across the country in low-wage industries there are exploited ethnic groups—Mexicans, Puerto Ricans, Chinese, blacks—who replicate the organizing problems faced by the labor movement in the basic industries half a century ago. Nevertheless, as the great European migration to the United States grows more distant, so does the impact of ethnicity on the labor movement. So long as ethnic identity continues to be felt in American life —as social scientists believe it still does on succeeding generations—it will also act on the inner dynamics of the labor movement. But ethnicity derives its meaning today mainly in the form of a legacy: the enduring character of the American labor movement is rooted in the historical fact of a working class drawn from beyond the American industrial order. In the American ethnic experience, the significance of the labor movement likewise takes the form of a legacy: for the diverse, alien peoples flocking to this country, the trade unions in their imperfect way served as a primary vehicle for working-class unity and for entry into the American environment.

Bibliography

Of the general labor histories, Henry Pelling, *American Labor* (Chicago, 1960) is most attentive to the immigrant influence. Clifton K. Yearley, *Britons in American Labor, 1820–1914* (Baltimore, 1957), is a detailed account of the British impact on the American movement. Rowland T. Berthoff, *British Immigrants in Industrial America, 1790–1950* (1953; reprint, New York, 1968), treats the subject in the context of specific industries. Charlotte Erickson, *American Industry and the European Immigrant, 1860–1885* (Cambridge, Mass., 1957), describes the recruitment of immigrants and the reaction of the labor movement. The following are informative on the subject of this essay: Robert Ernst, *Immigrant Life in New York City, 1825–1863* (New York, 1949); Kathleen N. Conzen, *Immigrant Milwaukee, 1839–1860* (Cambridge, Mass., 1976); Gerd Korman, *Industrialization, Immigrants and Americanizers: The View from Milwaukee, 1866–1921* (Madison, Wis., 1967); Donald B. Cole, *Immigrant City, Lawrence, Massachusetts, 1845–1921* (Chapel Hill, N.C., 1963). Valuable contemporary accounts of the new immigration are Isaac A. Hourwich, *Immigration and Labor* (1912; reprint, New York, 1922), and William M. Leiserson, *Adjusting Immigrant and Industry* (New York, 1924). On coal mining, see especially Victor R. Greene, *The Slavic Community on Strike: Immigrant Labor in Pennsylvania Anthracite* (Notre Dame, Ind., 1968); on steel, David Brody, *Steelworkers in America: The Nonunion Era* (Cambridge, Mass., 1960); on the garment industries, Melvyn Dubofsky, *When Workers Organize: New York City in the Progressive Era* (Amherst, Mass., 1968). The most imaginative treatment of labor's response to the Chinese is Alexander Saxton, *The Indispensable Enemy* (Berkeley, Calif., 1971). On blacks and the labor movement, see Sterling D. Spero and Abram L. Harris, *The Black Worker* (1931; reprint, New York, 1968); Horace R. Cayton and George S. Mitchell, *Black Workers and the New Unions* (1939; reprint, College Park, Md., 1969); and F. Ray Marshall, *The Negro and Organized Labor* (New York, 1965). The fullest treatment of socialism, immigrants, and the labor movement is John M. Laslett, *Labor and the Left, 1881–1924* (New York, 1970). Warren R. Van Tine, *The Making of the Labor Bureaucrat, 1870–1920* (Amherst, Mass., 1973), is informative on the ethnic origins of union leaders. Peter Friedlander, *The Emergence of a UAW Local, 1936–1939* (Pittsburgh, 1975), analyzes ethnic influences on the organizing process. Herbert Gutman, "Work, Culture and Society in Industrializing America, 1815–1919," *American Historical Review*, 78 (June 1973), places immigration in a framework of working-class experience.

The sources for this subject are of necessity widely scattered. Many of the archives listed in the bibliographies of particular ethnic groups will yield materials. Of the labor collections, the most important are held by the Tamiment Institute in New York City, the Wisconsin State Historical Society in Madison, and the Walter Reuther Archives in Labor and Urban Affairs at Wayne State University, Detroit, Mich.

DAVID BRODY

LANGUAGE: ISSUES AND LEGISLATION

The United States, ethnically the most heterogeneous nation in the world, is one of the most linguistically homogeneous. Of course the process by which non-English-speaking immigrants acquired a command of the American language was neither easy nor uniformly successful, but in the past it generated remarkably little political controversy. Today, however, language and politics have become entwined to an unprecedented degree. A heightened consciousness of "the other Americans" has brought with it a new concern for the educational and political plight of the linguistically disadvantaged, and a widespread revolt against the homogenization of American culture brought into question the value of linguistic unity. "Every child is harmed if he loses full use of his mother tongue," the Chief of the Modern Language Section of the U.S. Office of Education argued in congressional hearings in 1967. "I rebel against a melting pot concept. I don't want to be melted down into a monolith," the Chairman of the House Subcommittee on Education exclaimed in 1970. We must "get rid of this melting pot theory and realize this country is really a salad bowl of all types of groups who all have a contribution to make," Representative Shirley Chisholm argued in urging the continuation of bilingual education in 1974.

The degree to which language and politics have become linked is apparent in the legislative and judicial record of the last dozen years. Bilingual education programs have been mandated by more than half the states. At least three important court decisions have enforced the right of children with limited English-speaking ability to compensatory education. And most important, amendments to two major federal acts recognize linguistic disadvantage: the 1968 amendments to the Elementary and Secondary Education Act of 1965, known as either Title VII or the Bilingual Education Act, and the 1975 amendments to the 1965 Voting Rights Act.

The Bilingual Education Act was ostensibly addressed to the problem of the educational handicaps faced by children with limited English proficiency—especially those of Hispanic background. Its aim, however, was not solely that of improving the school performance of Spanish-speaking and other linguistically disadvantaged children. The act must be seen as a product of its time and the expression of diverse goals, some educational and some political. Its authors were influenced by the black-power movement, translating its ideology into a respect for the culture of other ethnic groups. They were influenced, too, by the movement for local community control which reached its pinnacle in the Ocean Hill–Brownsville dispute. A Cold War concern about the state of foreign-language training played some part, as did a belief in the potentiality of psychological harm resulting from the forced assimilation of children into an alien culture.

The 1975 amendments to the Voting Rights Act for the first time officially recognized a limited capacity to speak English as a political liability. The aim of the original 1965 act had been the massive registration of the disfranchised southern blacks. The 1975 amendments equated racial discrimination with linguistic disadvantage, and not only made mandatory the provision of bilingual ballots in many jurisdictions, but also extended to certain designated linguistic groups the extraordinary federal protection formerly accorded primarily to blacks: protection against the drawing of district lines to their electoral disadvantage, against at-large elections (generally thought to dilute the vote of minorities), and against suburban annexations that add white voters to often heavily black or Chicano cities. Initially based on the Fifteenth Amendment and ostensibly protecting the right to vote, after 1975 the Voting Rights Act became a means of ensuring blacks, Filipinos, Japanese, Mexicans, and a host of other racially and linguistically "disadvantaged" groups maximum electoral effectiveness. The Voting Rights Act, to no less a degree than the Bilingual Education Act, made the use of one's mother tongue or native language a federally protected right.

THE BILINGUAL EDUCATION ACT

The Need for Legislation Although Congress specified that Title VII of the Elementary and Secondary Education Act (ESEA) might be cited as the "Bilingual Education Act," it is striking that in neither its summary of Findings nor its Declaration of Policy did the legislature refer specifically to bilingual instruction. Mention was made, instead, of "the special educational needs" of children of limited English-speaking ability and the desirability of "new and imaginative," "adequate and constructive," "forward-looking" elementary and secondary school programs. The problem was both political and definitional. In 1968, when the act was passed, nobody knew or had the authority to decide precisely what bilingual education meant. The commitment to "new and imaginative programs" left the definition of those programs largely in the hands of local school boards.

To the parents who demanded and obtained bilingual education for their children in Cincinnati in 1840, the meaning of that education was quite clear: instruction conducted in German as well as English. Not only in Cincinnati, but in many communities in the latter half of the 19th century, education using the native tongue of non-English-speaking immigrants flourished. But such education was always initiated and funded at the local level, and it was plagued by few of the politically explosive definitional problems that burden the more recent, federally sponsored legislation.

The Bilingual Education Act, like most congressional legislation, was passed in response to the demands of diverse interest groups and was, of necessity, sufficiently vaguely worded to satisfy advocates with conflicting views. It had no commonly agreed-on purpose. At a minimum it aimed to use the native tongue of non-English-speaking children for a limited number of years in order to ensure the acquisition of basic skills such as arithmetic and writing. At a maximum its goal was not only the provision of temporary help to children in the process of linguistic assimilation, but also linguistic and cultural maintenance—the preservation of the language and values of a foreign culture.

When Senator Ralph W. Yarborough in January 1967 introduced the bill that was to become the Bilingual Education Act, his main concern was with Mexican-American children in Texas. Discussion of Hispanics in general, but with particular emphasis on Mexican Americans, dominated congressional hearings on the bill. The school dropout rate of Hispanic children, it was argued, was appallingly high. Adult Mexican

Americans (those 25 years of age and older), Senator Yarborough said, had an average of 7.1 years of schooling, while the figure for Anglos was 12.1 and for non-whites 9. Those figures were also used by Harold Howe II, U.S. Commissioner of Education. The director of the University of Texas Inter-American Institute reported that the median years of schooling completed by Spanish-surnamed Texans 25 years and over was 6.1 in 1960. The county commissioner in Bexar County, Tex., used even lower figures: the average Mexican American would complete 5 years of schooling, he said. More than half the Spanish-surnamed men and almost half the women 14 years and older had not gone beyond 8th grade, Senator Thomas H. Kuchel of California stated. Many had had no schooling at all. "The fault lies with our educational system."

The fault did not lie entirely with the American educational system. A large proportion of the adults whose educational records were the basis of the statistics had been born and raised in Mexico. But sociological veracity was not the primary concern of the witnesses; political effectiveness was the aim, and for this purpose the figures relied upon served well.

Bilingual education, it was argued, would solve the special educational problems of Hispanic and other "limited English-speaking ability" (LESA) children. Two arguments were advanced. The first was that Hispanic LESA children dropped below the grade level of their peers largely because they missed the education in basic skills acquired by others in the first years of school. While other children learned their three Rs, these children were diverted by the task of acquiring English. Once behind, they stayed behind; the disadvantage they suffered in the early grades became permanent. A bilingual program, by allowing instruction in Spanish, would permit the simultaneous acquisition of English and those basic skills.

The second argument was less plausible. Spanish, it was said, was easier to learn than English; there was a closer correspondence between the written and the spoken word. For the Spanish-speaking child, then, the fastest route to English literacy was through Spanish. It was assumed that the ability to read transfers from one language to another.

The bilingual programs that were so strongly advocated did not, in fact, require any special legislation. But Senator Yarborough and others believed that if such education were really to take hold, federal promotion was essential. By the end of World War I all the programs that had arisen in the 19th century had died out. In the early 1960s, however, with the massive influx of Cuban refugees into Florida, interest in bilingual instruction began to revive. Bilingual programs were started in Dade County, Fla., and subsequently in Texas, Delaware, New Mexico, Arizona, and California. But these programs were on a limited scale and, more important, they fell into the traditional category of innovation at the local level.

Title I of the 1965 Elementary and Secondary Education Act had given financial assistance to local schools for the education of children from low-income families, and that assistance could be used for bilingual instruction. Faced with limited funds, however, local school boards were unlikely to place bilingual education high on their list of priorities. Senator Yarborough and his cosponsors were convinced that the establishment of such education would require separate and specific funding. More federal encouragement was necessary than Title I alone could provide.

A great deal of subsequent controversy over the Bilingual Education Act has centered on the accuracy of the initial assumptions behind it. Federal encouragement came at a price: intrusion into local education policy. Federal funds were used to force local educational authorities to make schools more responsive to the needs of the ethnic communities being served. The ESEA as a whole, by making educational content the concern of a federal agency, had constituted an important break in a long-standing American tradition, and Title VII—otherwise known as the BEA—was another and very important step in the controversial direction its parent legislation had set. Was such intrusion warranted by massive need? And how solid were the educational theories that suggested that bilingual instruction would meet that need?

Both questions remain unresolved. Neither at the time of the act's passage nor now do we have an accurate count of the number of LESA persons in the United States. Data have been gathered from a variety of sources: primarily from the Nationwide Survey of Income and Education conducted by the U.S. Bureau of the Census in 1976; from the Survey of Languages, a pilot study that formed part of the July 1975 *Current Population Reports* of the census bureau; and from a report by the National Center for Educational Statistics. But variety does not ensure accuracy. As the Library of Congress (an unimpeachably neutral source) put it in a 1978 report, "Currently there is no actual count of the number of persons in the United States that are of limited English-speaking ability and thus no valid estimates of the need for bilingual education programs."

Even with an accurate LESA count there would be controversy over the number of children requiring bilingual education. Some would argue that the necessity for such instruction is confined to children whose families are not in the process of assimilating to American culture. Children from Mexican-American families living close to the border and from Puerto Rican families in New York City fall most obviously into this category. The great majority of them come from homes with exceptionally strong ties to the native land. Members of the second and third generations often continue to speak Spanish and to move back and forth across the border—or, in the case of Puerto Ricans, between the island and the mainland. It is possible that the requirement of these children for bilingual education is unmatched by that of any other group—that the children of European immigrants, Asian Americans, other Latin Americans, and even other Mexican Americans have no comparable need.

Even the need of the "hard-core" Hispanics is debatable. It can be argued that the position of Mexican Americans in southwest Texas and of Puerto Ricans in New York City is comparable to that of the French Canadians in New England a century ago. The apparent cultural stability may be deceptive. Social isolation—and with it, cultural and linguistic loyalty—may be slowly breaking down. Predictions are hazardous, but any assessment of the magnitude of the need for bilingual education must rely upon them.

Dispute over the magnitude of this need is not confined to the question of the number of eligible ethnic groups or subgroups. Within any one group there is wide variation in income. Should economic disadvantage affect eligibility for federal aid? In 1967 it was the consensus of Congress that it should. The original act covered only children from low-income families, and in this respect was in keeping with the rest of the ESEA. Sponsors of Title VII assumed that English-only instruction would not adversely affect the careers of LESA children from middle-class homes. But in 1974 the link between linguistic and economic disadvantage was severed, and all LESA children became eligible for aid.

The legislative resolution did not close debate. A 1975 National Center for Educational Statistics graph comparing students two grades below modal grade by ethnic origin indicated that whereas Hispanic children began even more behind grade level than blacks, by ninth grade the records of the two groups looked identical. What role, then, does limited competence in English actually play in a record of academic failure? Can linguistic difficulties be isolated as a cause of that failure? Or is the multiplicity of socioeconomic causes such that bilingual education alone will not help?

An undisputed record of academic failure—even when coupled with an accurate LESA count—does not necessarily indicate the need for bilingual education. Causes equally important as linguistic disadvantage may lie behind the lack of scholastic success. Even if limited English is the main problem, is bilingual education the obvious answer? Proponents assume that the record of academic failure will be altered by a program which not only permits the acquisition of basic skills in the language to which the child is most accustomed but also (for the Hispanic child) promotes literacy by beginning with a language easier than English. But these are pedagogical assumptions that continue to be vociferously debated.

The Ideological Atmosphere Although the assumptions behind the passage of the 1968 act have been the source of considerable subsequent debate, at the time they were barely discussed. In congressional hearings on Title VII questions concerning the precise dimension of the need and the validity of the pedagogical theories were largely glossed over. This was due in part to the nature of the hearings themselves. The chairmen of the relevant House and Senate committees called not witnesses—in the sense of experts on the educational and political questions raised by the proposed legislation—but (with few exceptions) lobbyists. Ethnic activists, mostly Hispanics, came to testify on the bill's necessity. The hearings both began and ended with the committees convinced that there was a real need and that bilingual education would meet it.

In part, however, the proposed legislation sailed easily through committee hearings because forces other than concern over the educational fate of children were at work. The issue of bilingual education was raised in an atmosphere in which the goal of cultural unity and the concept of the melting pot were already under attack. As early as mid-1965 the left wing of the civil rights movement had begun to experience a growing sense of alienation from conventional American values, and the disenchantment that black militants felt spilled over and infected white liberal thought as well. To read

through the congressional hearings on bilingual education is to realize how profoundly the movement for black power and community control had come by 1967 to influence the thinking of white mainstream liberals as well.

At the center of the black-power argument was a psychological contention: that American racism had so damaged the self-esteem of blacks as to make a reawakening of racial pride the paramount task. It was a point built on the insights not of militants but of such moderates as Kenneth Clark, James Farmer, and Martin Luther King, Jr. "Human beings," Clark had written, "who are forced to live under ghetto conditions and whose daily experience tells them that almost nowhere in society are they respected . . . will, as a matter of course, begin to doubt their own self worth." "We must massively assert our dignity and worth," King had urged. "We must no longer be ashamed of being black. The job of arousing manhood within a people that have been taught for so many centuries that they are nobody is not easy."

The route to that newly aroused manhood, in the view of black-power advocates, was through the creation of institutions run by blacks. Black power would give blacks a new self-image—not only because it would demonstrate black capability but also because in schools taught and run by blacks, children could be taught racial pride. The control of the schools was considered crucial. "As long as the mind is enslaved, the body can never be free," King had asserted. Blacks must end the "cultural homicide" that had kept them down. Building on King, Stokely Carmichael and Charles Hamilton, in their manifesto *Black Power* (1968), went on to assert: "Our basic need is to reclaim our history and our destiny from what must be called cultural terrorism . . . We shall have to create our own terms through which to define ourselves . . . It is absolutely essential that black people know their history, that they know their roots . . . their cultural heritage."

Black control over schools and the building of a new curriculum emphasizing black history and culture required black schools. Advocates of black power were unanimous in rejecting the value of integration. The idea of the melting pot, in their view, had been ethnocentric—or, more accurately, *race*centric, since it demanded assimilation into the culture of another race. Black power "marks the end of an era in which black men devoted themselves to pathetic attempts to be white men," one spokesman said. "Millions of black parents have been confronted with the poignant agony of raising black, kinky-haired children in a society where the standard of beauty is a milk-white skin and long straight hair . . . This identity problem is not peculiar to the Negro . . . but for the Negro the problem has a special dimension, for in the American ethos a black man is not only 'different,' he is classed as ugly and inferior."

This crucial insight—that whatever the psychological damage done to other groups by white ethnocentrism, it could not be equal to that imposed on blacks, that no other group had experienced such prolonged and ubiquitous racism—was lost on congressional witnesses at the 1968 hearings on bilingual education. These witnesses transferred the argument for ethnic solidarity from blacks to other groups. American educa-

tion, they said, by forcing Hispanic children (especially) to accept an alien culture, encouraged them to reject themselves. "In its effort to 'assimilate' all its charges," a Mexican-American spokesman argued, "the American school assaulted . . . the cultural identity of the child . . . it developed in the child a haunting ambivalence of language, of culture, of ethnicity, and of personal self-affirmation." Congressman Claude A. Pepper from Florida warned: "Our general insistence on school instruction being given in English . . . may appear to the child a kind of rejection of himself." Several witnesses quoted a National Education Association report at length; the Mexican-American child, the report contended, finds himself in a school which wants him to grow up as another Anglo. "This he cannot do except by denying himself and his family and his forebears, a form of masochism which no society should demand of its children."

The liberals had adopted the black-power reversal of the Supreme Court's argument in *Brown* v. *Board of Education of Topeka, Kansas.* Children who are racially segregated suffer irreparable psychological damage, the Court had contended. "To separate [children] from others of similar age and qualifications solely because of their race," Chief Justice Warren wrote, "generates a feeling of inferiority as to their status in the community that may affect their hearts and minds in a way unlikely ever to be undone." Black militants and their liberal sympathizers turned this argument around. To *assimilate* children into an alien culture, they said, creates feelings of inferiority.

The argument was a compelling one with reference to blacks, yet much less so when applied to other groups. The essential element of the history of segregation was missing. It was not forced assimilation alone that had been so psychologically damaging to the Negro; the problem was assimilation to an unreceptive culture. Not the pressure to assimilate, but rejection by white society had led to black self-doubt. Neither the Hispanics nor any other group had suffered to the same degree from a combination of assimilationist pressure and ostracism.

Just as blacks had urged rejection of the assimilationist model, so witnesses at the congressional hearing advocated abandoning the notion of the melting pot. "I do not think we have ever measured the psychic cost of the melting pot," one witness remarked. Not only the healthy child but also the healthy polity were the objects of concern. Supporters of the bill believed in a pluralistic society and in cultural maintenance in part for their own sake. The U.S. Commissioner of Education called for the abandonment of the melting pot ideal: "perhaps a better image . . . is the image of the mosaic which has a great variety in it, and which gains its strength from variety," he said. "The United States should be big enough to allow us the freedom to be different without being oppressed," a former Texan schoolteacher remarked. "I think we have discarded the philosophy of the melting pot," Representative James H. Scheuer from New York said. "We have a new concept of the value of enhancing, fortifying, and protecting [people's] differences, the very differences that make our country such a vital country."

Congressional liberals had taken a point that was psychologically sound but culturally and politically problematic—that blacks could and should maintain separate institutions and distinct values—and by applying it to other groups had transformed it into a contention that was psychologically dubious but culturally and politically plausible. That is, although the psychological damage to blacks had been real, the maintenance of a distinct and segregated culture was difficult; assimilation had gone too far. But for certain pockets of the Hispanic community, the problem was reversed. The Mexican Americans in southwest Texas, for instance, had suffered no long-term psychic harm comparable to that experienced by blacks—at least there was no claim at the hearings that they had—but their relative isolation and the closeness of their ties to Mexico made cultural maintenance much more possible. The point applies to a lesser extent to other groups, such as Hispanics and Asian Americans.

The claim of psychic harm had been crucial to the black-power argument, upon which the case for ethnic solidarity rested. The sponsors of the Bilingual Education Act claimed that in the absence of bilingual and bicultural instruction, LESA children would suffer psychologically, but the point they made about such damage was different from that made by blacks. The blacks had argued that social rejection had led to self-rejection. Supporters of the bill asserted only that forced assimilation was traumatic; Anglo schools, witnesses contended, asked the Hispanic child to reject the values of his home, and took him, as Senator Yarborough put it, from the "warm, friendly environment of his family and friends" to a school where he would experience "profound shock" at the discovery that English was required.

Without the element of massive psychological harm resulting from unremitting racism, the argument for a rejection of mainstream American culture and for the maintenance of ethnic distinctiveness through the schools became quite different. Cultural nationalism no longer served the purpose of healing wounds, but instead was advocated as a means of circumventing either the pain or the pressure of assimilation. Not the provision of temporary shelter, but resistance to homogenizing forces became the primary goal. And the alteration in the problem's definition changed the logical solution. The new goal could not be met by short-term programs. Congressional supporters of the legislation spoke in terms of transitional bilingual programs—programs designed to cope with temporary problems of scholastic adjustment. But the arguments they employed, adopted from the civil rights rhetoric of the late 1960s, encouraged a quite different vision: building permanently protective ethnic enclaves within the schools.

The problem of the disparity between what the sponsors had hoped for and what they actually created did not become apparent until later. Few questions were raised at the hearings. Testimony was heard almost exclusively from ethnic lobbyists, and few committee members even bothered to attend. This was special-interest legislation, protected by the special status that all legislation related to civil rights had in the 1960s. Moreover, it was packaged well: images of needy children, discrimination, poverty, and potential psychological harm were floated before congressional eyes. The public was not watching; the expenditures envisioned

were relatively small; and most important, it was politically costly to oppose but potentially lucrative to support. Valuable political capital could be earned by backing the bill, but there was nothing to gain by opposing it. Few lobbyists campaigned against it; there were few organized groups against bilingual education. But there were plenty to conduct vociferous protest if its passage failed.

The Act   Title VII of the ESEA, otherwise known as the Bilingual Education Act, was signed into law in January 1968. It provided funds for the planning and implementation of programs "designed to meet the special educational needs of children of limited English-speaking ability in schools having a high concentration of such children from families (A) with incomes below $3,000 per year, or (B) receiving payments under a program of aid to families with dependent children." Such programs could be bilingual in nature; they could be "designed to impart to students a knowledge of the history and culture associated with their language"; they could consist of "efforts to establish closer cooperation between the school and the home"; and so forth.

The initial authorization for the fiscal year 1968 was $15 million. But authorizations set only ceilings. The important figure is the actual appropriation, and because the fiscal year 1968 ran from June 1967 to June 1968, by January it was too late to appropriate funds. Actual federal support for bilingual education thus began in June 1968 (fiscal year 1969). Although the authorization for that year was $30 million, the actual appropriation was only $7.5 million. Those funds were used to support 76 projects, serving 26,521 children.

The issue that lay in waiting and subsequently became the focal point of greatest controversy—the clash between the transitional programs Congress envisioned and the schools-within-schools that it encouraged—arose in the course of implementation. The actual design and administration of programs forced into the open the beliefs of those who supported linguistic and cultural pluralism. Supporters of the act thus broke into two more or less distinct camps: transition and maintenance. In the first were those who viewed bilingual education as a means of providing temporary shelter and a transition to competency in English; in the second were those who saw it as a way of resisting assimilation by keeping children within the linguistic and cultural fold of another culture.

1968–1974   In the years between the act's passage in 1968 and its renewal in 1974, administrators at the local level and in the Department of Health, Education, and Welfare (HEW), Division of Bilingual Education, generally supported maintenance programs, while those holding high positions in HEW and other executive agencies such as the Office of Management and Budget, if they supported the concept of bilingual education at all, favored a transitional approach. The alignment made sense. In local areas, those who came forward to design programs were those most concerned about the issue, and that concern was generally fueled by a commitment to cultural pluralism. The staffing of the Division of Bilingual Education by ethnic militants followed an administrative tradition: government programs aimed at a particular group are often run by militant members of that group. Politically aggressive veterans administer veterans' programs; civil rights enthusiasts staff the Office of Civil Rights in the Department of Justice; and so forth. Likewise, it was to be expected that the high-ranking Republican appointees in the Nixon administration who were responsible for a whole range of educational and budgetary policies would be more generally conservative.

In the contest of wills between the transition and maintenance advocates, the two sides were not evenly matched; the local authorities had all the advantages. In the first place, although united in opposition to maintenance programs, the Nixon appointees could not agree on a uniform policy. As one HEW official admitted in a 1973 internal memo, "All of us have been aware for some time now that we have not had a coherent and consistent policy for our Bilingual Education program." More important than the ideological dissension were the political realities. Congress had given the administration no mandate to impose such a policy, even if it had been formulated. On the contrary, the act had turned the task of defining bilingual education over to the local school.

In any case, the main weapon that the administration possessed against the ethnic pluralists in control of local programs was the power of the purse. But congressional authority over appropriations, combined with a steadily increasing suspicion of the Nixon administration, made it very difficult to pull those purse strings tight: Congress often doubled the appropriation that the president requested. It was not that the legislature positively favored cultural maintenance; its rhetoric had certainly encouraged such maintenance, but Congress had never committed itself to any one type of program, deliberately leaving the legislative language vague. Yet its opposition to the administration made it the ally of the ethnic pluralists: the enemy of its enemy became its friend.

In the years between 1968 and 1974, then, while the administration attempted to cut bilingual education funds, Congress made sure that the program steadily grew. The appropriation for fiscal year 1969 was $7.5 million; by fiscal year 1974 it was up to $58.3 million. The number of projects jumped from 76 to 383, and the number of children served from 26,251 to 339,595. The initial focus of the act had been on meeting the needs of LESA children from Spanish-speaking households, and that focus did not change. But by 1974 approximately 20 percent of the funds were going to 23 non-Hispanic groups.

In 1974 the act was renewed and altered to include a definition of bilingual education that distinctly favored maintenance. That inclusion was influenced by the decision in *Lau* v. *Nichols*, in which the Supreme Court ruled that LESA children were entitled to some sort of remedial instruction, and by pressure from the Commission on Civil Rights and various ethnic groups. The final form of the new act was the product of extended debate between Congress and the administration—and to a lesser extent within congressional committees themselves.

Senators Edward M. Kennedy and Alan Cranston were the prime movers behind the new legislation; their initial hope was for a bill whose wording would put the federal government unequivocally behind full-time bilingual and bicultural instruction as the means by which LESA children learn. The programs envi-

sioned would have been maintained through twelve years of elementary and secondary schooling. "When the United States is the fifth largest Spanish-speaking country in the world and when a near majority of people in this hemisphere speak Spanish," Senator Kennedy said, "surely our educational system should not be designed so that it destroys the language and the culture of children from Spanish-speaking backgrounds."

Yet although there was considerable support for the Kennedy-Cranston language bill in the education committees of both houses, there was also sufficient opposition and sufficient pressure from the administration to make modification necessary. In general the education committees are dominated by liberal congressmen; urban liberals gravitate toward the committees that deal with welfare issues. But in both the Senate and the House there were voices of moderation with considerable influence; and there was also the ultimate problem of a presidential veto. Despite some congressional unease, the Senate version written by Senators Kennedy and Cranston might have passed had not a veto by Nixon been a threat.

In the new act there were seven important changes.

(1) The poverty clause was eliminated. Eligibility was no longer confined to LESA children from low-income families.

(2) The emphasis on the experimental nature of bilingual education was replaced by a stress on the demonstrated efficacy of such instruction. The earlier act had declared it to be the policy of the United States to fund "new and imaginative" programs. In 1974 the policy became "to *encourage* the establishment and operation, where appropriate, of educational programs using bilingual practices." The act went on: "Large numbers of children of limited English-speaking ability have educational needs which *can* be met" by bilingual instruction (italics added). It should be noted that Senators Kennedy and Cranston initially opposed the inclusion of the modifying phrase "where appropriate" but became convinced that its addition would facilitate passage.

(3) The later legislation emphasized reliance on the use of the LESA child's native tongue to a degree the earlier one had not—again a reflection of augmented faith in the efficacy of bilingual instruction. The 1968 act had made vague reference to "the special educational needs" of the LESA child, but the 1974 legislation stated that "a primary means by which a child learns is through the use of such child's language and cultural heritage." Kennedy and Cranston had wanted the language to read "*the* means," rather than "a primary means," but again were forced to compromise.

(4) Bicultural instruction was now required. The definition of bilingual education was rewritten to include "instruction given with appreciation for the cultural heritage of such children."

(5) In order to foster cross-cultural appreciation, a limited number of children whose primary language was English could be enrolled on a voluntary basis in bilingual programs; but bilingual instruction could not be used to teach English-speaking children a foreign language.

(6) In an attempt to deal with the problem of the segregation of participating children, it was specified that such children should join their English-speaking peers for subjects such as art, music, and physical education.

(7) A special Office of Bilingual Education was created within the Office of Education.

1974–1978   The renewed and deepened commitment to bilingual and bicultural instruction was reflected in the continued growth of the program in the succeeding years. Between 1974 and 1978, when the act was once again renewed, appropriations jumped from $58.3 million to $135 million. The number of projects rose to 565, and the number of language groups served to 70. The expansion in the number of language groups included was due in great part to the *Lau* decision. Prior to 1974 HEW had not regarded groups such as Italians as sufficiently disadvantaged to warrant special bilingual instruction. But the *Lau* decision was widely interpreted as mandating some sort of remedial instruction for all children whose limited ability to understand English made them unable to "effectively participate" in the regular educational program.

Despite steadily increasing appropriations by 1978 the congressional mood had changed. The 1978 hearings had a quite different tone from those of 1968 and 1974. Spokesmen for bilingual-bicultural education were on the defensive. The idea of the melting pot was no longer in total disrepute—or at least there was heightened concern that children placed in bilingual programs learn English, and a notable absence of references to the costs of assimilation. Whereas attacks on the historic ethnocentrism of American education dominated the 1968 and 1974 hearings, the focus in 1978 was on the question of the educational efficacy of the programs. And the roster of witnesses was different in that professional experts by and large replaced ethnic lobbyists. The result was a serious debate about the value of bilingual education.

Over the decade the political mood had changed, and that change accounts in part for the shift in tone. The movement for civil rights had lost its moral clarity. Even the liberals had become budget-conscious. But equally important was the impact of several sobering evaluations of bilingual education, the most important of which was done by the American Institutes for Research (AIR), under contract from the U.S. Office of Education. The programs that had been so hastily and enthusiastically embraced now appeared to be full of flaws.

The four-year AIR study of 11,500 Hispanic students published in 1978 concluded that most of the children did not need to learn English; that those who did were not in fact acquiring it; that with few exceptions the programs aimed at linguistic and cultural maintenance; and that to the degree that the children were already alienated from school, they remained so.

The study found that in terms of English competency, the Hispanic LESA children in the program fared no better than those without. The only discernible difference between the two groups of students was that those enrolled in Title VII programs seemed slightly more proficient in mathematical skills, although by national standards they were still woefully behind.

The study revealed that in fact most programs were not designed to increase English competency. Bilingual students, able to speak English without an accent, had been enrolled. In one school all students were placed automatically in a bilingual project; the children of parents who objected were moved out of their district.

In fact, less than one-third of the students placed in Title VII classrooms were there because of their need for English instruction, and only 16 percent were monolingual in Spanish.

The programs served such a high percentage of English-competent students partly because transfers out of Title VII classrooms were rare: 86 percent of the project directors and teachers reported that students remained in the bilingual programs after they had mastered English. Another 9 percent said that students were transferred to English-only classrooms but with some Spanish language maintenance. Only 5 percent reported no effort to maintain either the Spanish language or culture.

Were the Title VII students happier in school? Did the programs—as it was initially hoped—whet their appetite for academic achievement? AIR found no evidence that they did. It was altogether a discouraging picture. As the director of the study told the House Subcommittee on Education, "There is no compelling evidence in the current data of the Impact Study that Title VII bilingual education as presently implemented is the most appropriate approach for these students."

The pall that the AIR study cast over the future of bilingual education was evident throughout the congressional hearings. Supporters of the act were on the defensive. In 1968 the chairman of the House subcommittee had announced that he was hopeful "that our action may ultimately become the forerunner of placing this Nation on a bilingual basis." But in 1978 when Congressman Albert H. Quie asked John C. Molina, Director of the Office of Bilingual Education, whether he thought the United States should become bilingual, he was forced to reply, "The idea is so far-fetched that I don't give it too much thought." Molina agreed that the first goal of a bilingual program should be to make students proficient in English, but those studies which indicated a lack of such proficiency did not trouble him. "You can't evaluate a bilingual education program," he attempted to argue. "It is a philosophy and management."

Molina had a point. The proposition that the preservation of native languages and cultures would produce healthy children and a healthy polity could not be tested. The social scientist could measure only the *educational* impact of the programs. AIR had based its work on a partially erroneous assumption: that better education—especially better English—was what Congress had had in mind. Congress had hoped, AIR assumed, that Hispanic and other LESA children would acquire the basic skills that lead to economic success. But the authors of the act had two conflicting goals in mind: they wanted both to enlarge the opportunity for individual mobility and at the same time increase the prospects for ethnic solidarity. And the latter was certainly as important as the former.

This basic point was missed by another critic of the legislation, Gary Orfield, a political scientist at the University of Illinois, Urbana. Orfield argued what certainly should have come as no surprise: that many of the bilingual programs "pursue not successful integration into American society but deeper cultural and linguistic identity and separation . . . There is nothing in the research to suggest that children can effectively learn English without continual interaction with other children who are native English speakers, yet the Federal money has supported programs with only about one-tenth Anglos in the average class. In a society where Spanish surname children are now more segregated than blacks . . . a program that tends to increase separation, raises very serious questions." It was a curious argument to make about bilingual education. Orfield was right, but his memory was short. In the 1968 congressional hearings "segregation" had been called ethnic integrity; and what Orfield championed—the integration of children into the dominant culture—in 1968 Congress had spurned.

The chastened congressional mood was reflected in the renewed but amended act of 1978. In the new legislation there were four important changes:

(1) A ceiling of 40 percent was placed on the number of English-speaking children who could be included in the program, and the primary purpose of such inclusion was no longer described as heightening cultural consciousness. The participation of "children whose language is English" was intended principally to help those with LESA improve their English language skills. Orfield's point about the necessity of integration to create "continual interaction" between English-speaking and LESA children had, in other words, been adopted. Yet the ceiling of 40 percent was a blow to advocates of linguistic and cultural maintenance; programs could no longer be composed mainly of English-competent ethnics, segregated into special classes for the purpose of maintaining ethnic solidarity.

(2) There was a new stress on the importance of parental involvement. Applications for federal assistance had to be developed in consultation with an advisory council "of which a majority shall be parents and other representatives of children with limited English proficiency"; parental consultations had to continue during the life of a program. In addition, periodic reports outlining the instructional goals of the program and the progress of the children in it were expected to be sent to parents. These provisions reflected a conviction expressed by several witnesses at the hearings, that although politically active ethnic leaders wanted maintenance programs, most parents did not. In fact, Dr. Malcolm Danoff, the director of the AIR study, described a forced reorientation of some programs in the face of parental demand that their children learn English.

(3) Local schools were instructed to use personnel proficient in both the language of instruction and English, and to provide measurable goals for serving those in need and determining when such need was exhausted. An individual evaluation establishing persistent linguistic disadvantage was necessary for any child kept in a program more than two years. The provision was another blow—or attempted blow—to the maintenance advocates; it created pressure on local schools to graduate from the bilingual programs those pupils who had become competent in English. But the definition of need was still in local hands, and the willingness and ability of the federal authorities to monitor compliance remained limited.

(4) The description of eligible participants was changed from those with limited English-speaking ability to those with limited English proficiency; thus, the meaning of linguistic deficiency was expanded to include reading and writing.

The 1978 modifications have not quieted the controversy that continues to surround the Bilingual Education Act. Due to expire in June 1983, its future remains uncertain. Budgetary considerations alone could result in its curtailment; AIR reported an average additional cost of 37 percent to educate a Title VII child, and at the present time that extra cost appears to bring no obvious educational benefit. The program could fall victim also to growing disillusion with the politics of ethnic entitlement. Political support for programs that tend to strengthen ethnic identity may entirely collapse. But whatever the fate of the act itself, bilingual instruction will not quickly disappear, for not only Title VII but also a variety of other federal and state legislative acts fund bilingual education.

OTHER FEDERAL AND STATE PROGRAMS

Several federal acts have a bilingual component. The Emergency School Aid Act (ESAA), enacted in 1972, provided local educational agencies with financial assistance to aid in the elimination of minority-group segregation and discrimination in elementary and secondary schools. Such assistance could take the form of funds for bilingual education. In order to qualify for a grant under the ESAA, however, a local education agency had to be implementing a desegregation plan as defined by the act. In 1978 the bilingual-education provisions of the ESAA were transferred to the Bilingual Education Act, but appropriations for ESAA programs remained separate. For fiscal year 1980 the authorization was $15 million.

Second, the Vocational Education Act contains bilingual provisions that were added in 1974. The legislation authorized the Commissioner of Education to provide grants to state and local education agencies, postsecondary institutions, private nonprofit vocational-training institutions, and other nonprofit institutions for the purpose of providing vocational training.

Third is the Adult Education Act. As of 1974, only those states providing special assistance to persons of LESA were eligible for federal adult-education grants.

Fourth, the provisions of the Higher Education Act which funded special programs for students from disadvantaged backgrounds were expanded in 1974. Students of LESA in institutions of higher education became eligible for participation.

In addition, in 1966 special provisions for the children of migratory workers were incorporated into Title I of the Elementary and Secondary Education Act. The Commissioner of Education was authorized to make grants to state education agencies to establish or improve programs designed to meet the special needs of migrant children.

Other federal programs with a bilingual component are: the Library Services and Construction Act (amendment, 1974), the National Reading Improvement Program (1974), the National Defense Education Act (amendment, 1967), the Indian Education Act (1972), and the Older Americans Comprehensive Services Amendments (1973).

Ten states have made bilingual education mandatory in districts which meet specified conditions, and 16 others have enacted legislation that generally authorizes the development of bilingual programs. A school district is thus often eligible for both federal and state bilingual aid. The federal funds go directly to the local education agency; the state has no control over their use.

LAU VERSUS NICHOLS

Bilingual education programs have come about partly in response to federal and state legislation, partly as a result of judicial action. Several court decisions have either required or been interpreted to require bilingual instruction, the most famous of which is *Lau* v. *Nichols*, decided by the U.S. Supreme Court in January 1974.

The case involved non-English-speaking Chinese students in San Francisco. At the time, there were approximately 2,800 such students in the San Francisco school district, roughly 1,000 of whom were receiving supplemental education in the English language. The remaining 1,800 brought suit in a class action, on the grounds that they had been denied equal educational opportunity. People similarly situated, they argued, should receive similar treatment; they, too, were entitled to the supplementary language courses.

Both the district court and the appeals court decided against them. In a restatement of the classic American doctrine of equality, the Court of Appeals said: "Every student brings to the starting line of his educational career different advantages and disadvantages caused in part by social, economic, and cultural backgrounds, created and continued completely apart from any contribution by the school."

But the Supreme Court reversed the decision. Avoiding the task of redefining the meaning of equal opportunity, it rejected the plaintiff's partial reliance on the Equal Protection Clause of the Fourteenth Amendment. It rested its opinion instead on statutory grounds —specifically on guidelines issued by HEW in order to clarify the meaning of Title VI, Section 601, of the Civil Rights Act of 1964. Title VI itself had banned discrimination based upon "race, color, or national origin" in "any program or activity receiving Federal financial assistance." The most pertinent guideline had gone on to state: "Where inability to speak and understand the English language excludes national origin–minority group children from effective participation in the educational programs offered by a school district, the district must take affirmative steps to rectify the language deficiency."

To the uninitiated, resting a judicial decision on a regulatory guideline might seem anomalous. As the Court pointed out, however, it had been done before; and in this case, Title VI itself had specifically directed HEW to secure compliance by "issuing rules, regulations, or orders." By this authorization the guidelines had, in effect, become part of the congressional act. In the Court's view, to violate them was to violate the legislation itself.

Although the students had brought suit to gain entrance to supplementary courses in English, and although the Court specified no particular remedy— leaving the question of an English immersion program or a bilingual one up to local authorities—*Lau* was nevertheless quickly interpreted by HEW as requiring both bilingual and bicultural instruction. Those who chose not to adopt such a program could propose an alternative but equally effective remedy. But, as one school administrator put it, it was difficult to prove that

something was as good as something else which nobody had proved the worth of. The HEW requirement that school districts provide bilingual education stuck.

The bilingual-bicultural programs that HEW imposes upon laggard school districts are funded through the Office of Bilingual Education. In theory, according to the language of the Civil Rights Act, school districts in violation of the law are faced with a cutoff of federal funds. In practice, however, a simpler and more efficacious sanction is applied: the school district is invited to apply for Title VII (Bilingual Education Act) funds. Thus, the line between the legislative and judicial action is largely dissolved. A school district with a significant number (over 20) of LESA children can choose not to apply for federal funds under Title VII; there is nothing mandatory about the programs authorized by the Bilingual Education Act. But that district then risks a finding by the HEW Office of Civil Rights of a violation of *Lau*, the remedy for which is precisely that application for funds which the school district had initially declined to make.

The 1975 Amendments to the Voting Rights Act

Language groups have acquired political rights as well as educational ones. The Bilingual Education Act and the *Lau* decision sought to protect LESA children against educational policies that penalized them for their linguistic disadvantage. The 1975 amendments to the Voting Rights Act of 1965 protect LESA adult citizens against state action in violation of their electoral rights.

The structure of the Voting Rights Act is both simple and clever. The original aim of the 1965 legislation had been the enfranchisement of southern blacks, the main obstacle to which had been the literacy test. Fraudulent tests, administered to southern blacks but never to whites, had kept all but the determined and lucky from the polls. The Voting Rights Act essentially eliminated the southern literacy test. A very effective formula was devised. On the assumption that discrimination had been practiced wherever the administration of a literacy test was accompanied by a low level of political participation, the act banned all such tests in every jurisdiction in which either the voting registration or turnout in the 1964 presidential election had been below 50 percent. Although it turned out that not all such jurisdictions were in the South, the great majority were. Seven southern states, in their entirety, fell under the purview of the act. The result was a revolution in black registration. In 1964, 7 percent of Mississippi's blacks had been registered to vote; by 1967 that figure had risen to almost 60 percent.

Although the original aim of the Voting Rights Act had been the registration of southern blacks, once that aim was met, the purpose changed. In order to ensure against the introduction of any new screening device— any new inventive and unprecedented form of literacy test—the act made federal approval the prerequisite for any change in the electoral law of a covered jurisdiction. In time, that provision came to be used for purposes its framers had never contemplated. Changes in electoral law subject to the approval of either the Attorney General or the District Court of the District of Columbia came to include a switch from ward to at-large voting, the annexation of a suburb, changes in district lines, and others. The new interpretation of the provision turned the act into an instrument whereby the federal government could monitor and adjust local electoral arrangements to augment the power of certain groups and diminish that of others.

In 1975 the tools that the framers and administrators of the act had so carefully designed to protect southern blacks against the disfranchising devices of the literacy test and the at-large election began to be used to protect the voting rights of a variety of language groups as well.

What accounted for this bewildering extension of legislation originally designed to protect Fifteenth Amendment rights against denial of the vote on the ground of race or color? Just as the aim of the Bilingual Education Act had been the closure of a gap left in the Elementary and Secondary Education Act, so the 1975 amendments to the Voting Rights Act were an attempt to complete a task left partially undone. In both cases the source of concern was the community of Mexican Americans in southwest Texas.

Mexican-American registration in Texas was low, and in the presidential election of 1972 only 38 percent voted. Texas, however, had no literacy test and was thus exempt from the provisions of the entire act. There was an additional problem: the Department of Justice, in administering the act, treated Mexican Americans as a racial group, and that designation rankled with congressional sponsors who thought it a mark of opprobrium to be classified nonwhite. A solution was needed that circumvented both the problem of the literacy test and that of race.

The one which was arrived at considerably altered the act. The 1975 amendments broadened the constitutional basis of the Voting Rights Act, making it rest on the Fourteenth as well as the Fifteenth Amendments so as to allow coverage of linguistic as well as racial groups. They also expanded the definition of a literacy test. For the LESA citizen, Congress reasoned, a ballot printed in English was equivalent to the conventional literacy test. Accordingly, in two different types of jurisdictions these English competency tests were replaced by bilingual ballots: jurisdictions in which more than 5 percent of the citizens of voting age were members of a linguistic group and in which either voting registration or turnout was below 50 percent, and jurisdictions in which the level of political participation was high but the literacy rate of the linguistic minority was low. In addition, in those places with a low level of political participation, all changes in electoral law— annexations, apportionments, and alterations in the method of filling public office—came under federal scrutiny.

Other problems remained, however. The first was the difficulty of identifying citizens illiterate in English but sufficiently literate in another conventional language to use a bilingual ballot. For such purposes of identification the mother-tongue data which the Department of Justice was forced to use are quite unreliable. (*See* Appendix II, Table 14.) The second and more serious problem was the inclusion, under the formula devised, of linguistic groups without any history of recent electoral discrimination. There was no necessity, in anybody's mind, of providing Italian immigrants with bilingual material, much less with protection against the dilu-

tion of their electoral strength by suburban annexations and at-large voting schemes. Nevertheless, according to census calculations, the number of Italians who did not regard their usual language as English was only slightly smaller than the number of Asians in identical circumstances, whom the sponsors of the legislation did want covered.

Congress adopted a brazen solution. The 1965 legislation protected all citizens denied the right to vote on account of race or color; the 1975 protection applied to four groups only: Alaskan Natives, American Indians, Asian Americans, and those of Spanish heritage. To cover its tracks, Congress labeled these groups linguistic minorities; the principle that determined inclusion thus became linguistic disadvantage.

Some such principle was needed. Equal protection demands that those who are similarly situated be similarly treated; no benefit can be conferred on one group to the exclusion of others with like needs. And some principle must be formulated to distinguish those who are similarly situated from those who are not—those eligible for federally conferred benefits from those ineligible. Otherwise the designation appears arbitrary and becomes constitutionally suspect.

The classification "linguistic disadvantage" thus solved the constitutional problem that would have arisen had the Mexican Americans alone been selected for additional protection. The level of their political participation in Texas had been the focus of the initial concern, but their plight was not unique. The concentration on blacks in 1965 had been defensible, for their history was indeed unparalleled by that of any other group. But once the Mexican Americans had been selected for inclusion, other groups qualified too.

Yet the formulation of the principle of linguistic disadvantage and the designation of four deserving groups did not solve all the problems. Some of the questions that have been raised with respect to the Bilingual Education Act can also be raised with respect to the 1975 amendments to the Voting Rights Act. There is no accurate count of LESA children or adults. Because "the linguistically disadvantaged" was too broad a category, Congress resorted to the designation of four groups. But it was a crude solution, prompted by political considerations, and the list includes one group—the Asian Americans—whose record of disadvantage in general is markedly different from that of the Mexican Americans. In addition, within the category of "citizens of Spanish heritage" there are many individuals whose level of English proficiency makes their protection on grounds of linguistic handicap inappropriate. Both the Bilingual Education Act and the Voting Rights Act are open to the charge of having provided too blunt an instrument for so fine a task.

Moreover, the designation of the four groups was a solution that came at a high price: further federal intrusion into areas normally the prerogative of local authorities. For the Voting Rights Act does more than make mandatory the provision of bilingual ballots; it authorizes federal monitoring of all electoral rearrangements in any jurisdiction with a sufficiently high concentration of one of the designated linguistic minorities and a sufficiently low level of political participation. As a result, for example, in the spring of 1979 all elections in the city of Houston, Tex., came to a halt. Annexations

had diluted the electoral strength of inner-city minority groups, and the Department of Justice was demanding the redrawing of district lines to the advantage of those groups.

Just as there may be very limited need for bilingual ballots, so there may actually be small need for the wider protection which the act affords. That need may be confined to those southern blacks, Mexican Americans, and members of other ethnic groups who are victims of racially directed political discrimination in such forms as gerrymandered district lines and annexations. It may be confined, in other words, to contexts of true racial polarization. Just as bilingual education may make sense only for those few groups who have resisted assimilation and can be predicted to continue to do so, so the Voting Rights Act may be appropriate only for that small number of minority subgroups that continue to be so victimized by racial prejudice as to make conventional efforts at political organization useless.

Bibliography

House and Senate subcommittee hearings in 1967, 1974, and 1977 provide the single most valuable source for understanding the Bilingual Education Act. Other helpful government publications include: the Annual Reports of the National Advisory Council on Bilingual Education; Office of Education, Department of Health, Education, and Welfare, *The Condition of Bilingual Education in the Nation: First Report by the U.S. Commissioner of Education to the President and Congress* (Washington, D.C., March 1977); U.S. Bureau of the Census, Department of Commerce, *Language Usage in the United States* (Washington, D.C., July 1976); U.S. Civil Rights Commission, *A Better Chance to Learn: Bilingual and Bicultural Education* (Washington, D.C., 1975); and U.S. Civil Rights Commission, *The Excluded Student,* Mexican American Education Study, Report III (Washington, D.C., 1972). In addition, the National Clearinghouse for Bilingual Education, established by the Office of Bilingual Education, HEW, is an invaluable source for up-to-date material. The explicit purpose of the clearinghouse is to provide the public with information on bilingual education.

Secondary source material on legislation as recent as the Bilingual Education Act is limited. For background a good starting point is Joshua A. Fishman's classic study, *Language Loyalty in the United States: The Maintenance and Perpetuation of Non-English Mother Tongues by American Ethnic and Religious Groups* (1966; reprint, New York, 1978). Also useful are: Malcolm N. Danoff, *Evaluation of the Impact of ESEA Title VII Spanish/English Bilingual Education Program: An Overview of Study and Findings* (Palo Alto, Calif., 1978); Noel Epstein, *Language, Ethnicity, and the Schools: Policy Alternatives for Bilingual Education* (Washington, D.C., 1977); Josue M. Gonzales, "Coming of Age in Bilingual/Bicultural Education: A Historical Perspective," *Inequality in Education,* no. 19, Harvard Center for Law and Education (Cambridge, Mass., 1975); Gary Orfield, *Must We Bus? Segregated Schools and National Policy* (Washington, D.C., 1978); Muriel Saville and Rudolph C. Troike, *A Handbook of Bilingual Education* (Washington, D.C., 1971); and Susan Gilbert Schneider, *Revolution, Reaction or Reform: The 1974 Bilingual Education Act* (New York, 1977).

On the Voting Rights Act, again the House and Senate subcommittee hearings of 1965, 1969, and 1975 are invaluable. Just as basic, however, are the judicial decisions interpreting the act and delineating voting rights guaranteed by the Fourteenth Amendment. Among the most important are: *Gaston County* v. *United States,* 288 F. Supp. 678 (1968), aff'd 395 U.S. 285 (1969); *South Carolina* v. *Katzenbach,* 383 U.S. 301 (1966); *Allen* v. *State Board of Education,* 393 U.S. 544 (1969); *Whitcomb* v. *Chavis,* 403 U.S. 124 (1971); *City of Petersburg, Virginia* v. *United States,* 354 F. Supp. 1021 (1972), aff'd 410 U.S. 962 (1973); *City of Richmond* v. *United States,* 376 F. Supp. 1344 (1974), vacated 422 U.S. 358 (1975); *United Jewish Organization of Williamsburg* v. *Carey,* 430 U.S. 144 (1977).

Useful secondary sources on voting rights include: Robert C. Dixon, Jr., *Democratic Representation: Reapportionment in Law and Politics* (New York, 1968); Ward E.Y. Elliott, *The Rise of Guardian Democracy: The Supreme Court's Role in Voting Rights Disputes, 1845–1969* (Cambridge, Mass., 1974); David H. Hunter, *Federal Review of Voting Changes: How to Use Section Five of the Voting Rights Act* (Washington, D.C., 1974); idem, "The 1975 Voting Rights Act and Language Minorities," *Catholic University Law Review* 25 (Winter 1976); Nelson Polsby, ed., *Reapportionment in the 1970s* (Berkeley, Calif., 1971); Abi-

gail M. Thernstrom, "The Odd Evolution of the Voting Rights Act," *The Public Interest* 55 (Spring 1979); and U.S. Civil Rights Commission, *The Voting Rights Act: Ten Years After* (Washington, D.C., 1975).

ABIGAIL M. THERNSTROM

LANGUAGE MAINTENANCE

In order to understand the impact of ethnicity upon language maintenance, it is necessary first to consider the process of language maintenance itself and then to examine a variety of bilingual contexts, including both those in which ethnicity and the possibility of ethnic transformation obtain, and others in which they do not. Indeed, whenever populations are in contact utilizing two or more languages the issue of language maintenance is of interest, for three long-range resolutions are possible: given two languages, A and B, initially utilized by two populations, it is conceivable (1) that both will be retained in use; (2) that A will displace B; or (3) that B will displace A. The basic problem is to determine what produces each of these outcomes and what role, if any, ethnicity plays in the process.

Linguistic minorities in the United States theoretically might provide examples of the interaction between language maintenance and ethnicity, but data from American ethnic groups have never been collected systematically. It is therefore necessary to refer to examples of bilingualism, language maintenance, and ethnicity elsewhere in the world as well, in order to understand their interaction and thereby to understand language maintenance and language loss in the United States itself.

Whether or not one considers the issue of ethnicity, either as a stimulus to language maintenance or as a possible by-product, the maintenance of a language is a subtle and complex phenomenon. The data pertaining to it, particularly the U.S. Census data, frequently involve little more than responses to questions about one's mother tongue. These data are suspect not only because they are based upon claims rather than upon actual proof of language use, but also because they relate to mother tongues rather than to current facility or, in the United States, to "the language most commonly used in your home during your childhood" (the working definition of mother tongue) rather than to that language actually first learned and used by the respondent. Other, equally serious, difficulties arise from attempts to measure actual language proficiency or use. Such data are almost impossible either to collect or to analyze on a nationwide basis. Even when gathered from a limited population in a particular locality, information will differ depending upon whether it refers to active or passive (listening or understanding) use; or if to active, whether speaking or literacy is being measured; or if to speaking, whether the frequency, the "correctness," or the context of speech (family, work, religion, government, and the like) is studied. The complexities involved in studying language maintenance make it doubly difficult to clarify its relationship to ethnicity. Nevertheless, some beginnings have been made in this connection.

LANGUAGE SHIFTS

Within language maintenance–language shift phenomena there is a basic distinction between contexts that involve two or more different ethnocultural groups and those that involve only one. In the former case a further distinction exists between contexts in which (im)migrant (or intruding) languages shift (as in Israel, the postcolonial United States, and Australia) and contexts in which indigenous languages shift (for instance, to Spanish in Latin America, to Russian in the Soviet Union, and to Arabic in the post-Islamic Near East). The shift of immigrant languages has been widely studied; least studied has been the course of language maintenance and language shift in stabilized diglossic settings, that is, in settings in which *one* ethnic group has incorporated and stabilized two languages (for example, both Yiddish and Hebrew in traditional Ashkenaz, Guaraní and Spanish in Paraguay, Swiss German and High German in German-speaking Switzerland, vernacular Arabic and classical Arabic in the Arab Near East, and so forth). As a result, most is known about language maintenance and ethnicity in those settings in which the greatest intergenerational change in ethnicity (transethnification) occurs, rather than about language maintenance and ethnicity in those settings in which there is the greatest ethnic stability. This imbalance necessarily colors our understanding of the total relationship between language maintenance and ethnicity.

The three major patterns of language shift can be summarized thus: (1) *shift of immigrant language* (from immigrant native tongue to the language of the host society); (2) *shift of indigenous language* in favor of intrusive language, accomplished through conquest or other severe dislocation of the original population; and (3) *disruption of former diglossia* through the reversal of intracommunal class, status, and power positions.

Shift of Immigrant Language Once it is realized that immigrant languages are not always the ones that are displaced, indeed that they sometimes are the displacers, it is useful to attempt to differentiate between the former and the latter situation.

Legal factors often have been examined first; recurringly they implicitly or explicitly penalize or weaken immigrant languages and therefore foster and/or require a shift to the indigenous or indigenized language(s). Legal restrictions or conventions have often barred or discouraged newcomers to the United States from using their native language in public or, at least, from using them with authorities or in institutions under governmental control. Except in the case of exceptionally authoritarian regimes, however, it is not clear that legal factors, prohibitions, or restrictions (encountered also in democratic regimes, such as Switzerland, that are committed to the territoriality principle of only one language in any one district) necessarily lead to a language shift at home or in intimate social settings since these are intragroup in nature, focused more upon spoken than written language, and the least governmentally encumbered or monitored. In addition, recent court actions in the United States have tended to weaken the earlier legal restrictions against the "official" use of languages other than English. The *Lau* v. *Nichols* (1973) ruling requires public school districts to provide educational equity for non-English-proficient children by educating them in their own mother tongues, while teaching them English as a second language, until such time as they can profit from education conducted in English. Similarly, *Mendoza* v. *New York City Depart-*

ment of Welfare (pending) would require public agencies to provide their services equitably by offering them in the dominant languages of their clients. Such legal considerations, as well as the Bilingual Education Act (1967, revised in 1974 and 1978), do not, however, directly affect the centers of language maintenance—the immigrant home, neighborhood, and community. They may, perhaps, ultimately influence attitudes there as well as in the larger Anglo-American community, but no such effect has yet been documented. (*See* Language: Issues and Legislation.)

A second factor often related to language maintenance in the United States is the degree of closure or self-sufficiency of the immigrant population. Immigrant self-sufficiency is most frequently looked at simply in terms of demographic indicators, to determine the extent to which even intragroup pursuits can be maintained in the immigrants' own language. Among the most commonly employed demographic indices have been: the number of immigrants, their concentration, their urbanization, the extent of their education via the host language, and their occupational concentration in service or other interactive pursuits. Generally speaking, and specifically in connection with immigrants to the United States, the fewer the immigrants, the greater their dispersion, the greater their urbanization and education in the host language and the greater their occupational interaction with the host society, the less likely it is that immigrants will be able to maintain intimate language and behavior networks in their own languages. Although none of these factors necessarily impinge on language maintenance in immigrant homes and communities, they all foster language shift, particularly among groups whose indigenous role and status systems tend to be dislocated by assimilation. When there is greater interaction with speakers of the host language, there is, correspondingly, a greater likelihood of intermarriage, friendship, and coworker ties, which, of course, do intrude on the domains of intimacy per se.

Such demographic indicators represent short cuts to the analysis of the social processes involved. Ultimately it is this type of analysis that is needed in order to fathom how and why immigrant tongues so commonly tend to be displaced and replaced. Among the factors that contribute to language shift are: the availability of countrymen who have previously shifted (for example, the availability of large numbers of Norwegian-American oldtimers who had shifted to English by the time newcomers arrived from Norway during this century), rapid and extensive social mobility, absence of religious or other formal institutional or ideological support for maintenance, and finally, the disruption of traditional home and family status/role relationships that result when children and women are gainfully employed outside the home and immigrant community. In all these cases speech networks that function in the host language develop within the immigrant groups themselves, so that language shift actually facilitates intragroup (and even intrafamily) functions as well as advancing social mobility in the host society.

Social mobility is a crucial element in language shift among American immigrant groups, not so much because it increases contact (even intimacy) with "outsiders," but primarily because it dislocates previous status and role relations in the immigrant family. As a result, social mobility (and to a lesser extent the other social processes mentioned above) invades and nullifies the last undisputed and indispensable domain of immigrant language use. When one no longer needs the immigrant language in order to be a member in good standing either of one's own family or of other intragroup institutions, then the immigrant language may linger on for metaphorical purposes (humor, insult, secretive identification), but its major vernacular role is gone. In the context of the powerful, participatory reward system that America has traditionally made available to so many of its inhabitants, few immigrant (or other minority) ethnicity reward systems have been able to remain aloof from or impervious to it. Those non-English-speaking populations who were outside the national system (for example, most American Indians, Mexican Americans, Puerto Ricans, and small, self-isolating groups such as the Hutterites or Amish) retained their non-English mother tongues. Their language remained part of their ethnicity owing to the absence of severe strains imposed by mobility opportunities.

Shift of Indigenous Language   In the United States as well as in the Soviet Union, Australia, Latin America, Ireland, and the Near East, many indigenous languages have been displaced by intrusive immigrant ones. In this connection it must be remembered that English itself (and Spanish) are immigrant languages in the United States vis-à-vis the American Indian languages. The factors involved in the displacement of indigenous languages are related to those already mentioned in conjunction with the displacement of immigrant languages. English in the United States—like Russian in much of the U.S.S.R.—although an intrusive language vis-à-vis others that preceded it, has had the benefit of legal protection at the expense of indigenous languages. Like Spanish in Latin America and Arabic in the Near East and North Africa, it has also had the benefit of numbers, concentration, and control of urban life, education, and entry into service occupations. Finally, although English in North America is an intrusive language vis-à-vis Navajo, it has dominated the avenues of social mobility, the ideological and organizational institutions of society (religion, government), and, perhaps most important, has been regarded as a model for home and family life as well.

Similar though the two processes may be, the shift from an indigenous to an intrusive language is usually indicative of far greater dislocation than is the shift from an intrusive (immigrant) to an indigenous language. Immigration itself is a dislocation. Therefore, regardless of the premigrational characteristics of hosts and newcomers, and regardless of the degree of consensus and similarity characterizing intergroup and intragroup values and overt behaviors, once immigration has occurred it is common to expect the immigrants to be more dislocated than their willing or unwilling hosts, if only in terms of the discontinuity of places, people, and pursuits and the language related to them. If and when an immigrant language displaces an indigenous one, it is rightly viewed as a somewhat unusual event. Such a state of affairs is usually brought about by conquest followed by punitive disruption of indigenous life (as in the case of the American Indians), and/or by

the wholesale transfer of populations so that immigrants literally swamp the locals and, in addition, bring with them a far higher level of technology and a complete society of their own. (Both of these circumstances applied in the massive resettlement of Russians and other Slavs throughout the U.S.S.R.) The remnants of dispossessed indigenous peoples in the American Southwest, in many parts of Latin America, in Soviet Central Asia and Siberia, in Australia and New Zealand, in various Pacific islands, and, to some extent, in minority pockets in Europe (in Ireland, Spain, France, Austria, Czechoslovakia, Poland, Romania, Turkey, and so forth) all attest to the displacement of indigenous populations as a worldwide phenomenon. Our own American experience (and mythology) of language maintenance concerns, in which the English host language has triumphed over immigrant tongues and in which immigrants and hosts often apparently became "one happy family," needs to be viewed in comparative perspective. It is not a pattern that immigrants either experience or seek everywhere (for example, the Dutch Boers in South Africa). However, whether the immigrant language triumphs or capitulates, ethnicity, considered apart from all other continuing social processes and developments, has played a relatively minor role.

One Population—Two Languages The one population–one language paradigm in the United States has often assumed overtones of moral, social, and psychological normalcy. Nevertheless, there are numerous historical examples of populations that function in a stable fashion in two or more languages. This has been true not only in Africa and Asia where superimposed political and religious systems have, in centuries past, added layers of society to preexisting ones, and, in the process, added languages of reading/writing and praying (and, more rarely, speaking) to the repertoires that were there before them. It has been equally true in the worlds of the Orthodox Jews (in the United States as well as in Israel and elsewhere), the Pennsylvania Germans, and in many supposedly shifted U.S. populations whose home and intimacy behaviors not only have escaped destruction (or undergone repair) but also have escaped the prying eyes and ears of neighbors, researchers, or authorities. Similarly, in Wales and Ireland (and perhaps in Scotland too), in Alsace, Provence, and Brittany, in Catalonia, Galicia, and the Basque country on the one hand, and in many immigrant settings on the other, the original languages are not only still there, at least among some speakers and for some purposes, but they have even experienced a recent revival. It is in this connection that ethnicity can be advanced as a support to language maintenance.

The expansion of education, political participation, and industrial involvement has provided most modern polities with single link-languages (often referred to as their official or national languages). In many cases these languages were themselves no more than peasant vernaculars a century or two ago, unrelated to reading, government, or technology and in many cases unused by their own territorial elites. Just as those elites often did not recognize the vernaculars of their own countrymen and/or subjects, so many of the latter today, in their own sociocultural ascendancy, may not recognize the vernaculars of some of their own ethnically different countrymen. This nonrecognition is abetted by na-

tional statistical agencies that ask about the frequency of movie attendance, radio listening, television viewing, and car ownership but tend to mask or ignore the multiplicity of home and neighborhood vernaculars. A degree of widespread and stable societal bilingualism continues to pervade much of modern life in many of the very same settings in which linguistic shift of one kind or another has occurred. Thus, in the United States, while a great deal of shift to English has doubtlessly transpired and unfamiliarity with English has become increasingly rare, according to the 1975 Current Population Survey about 8 million inhabitants continue to claim primary use of some language other than English. Another 17 million claim to use both English and another language in their daily life. In addition, according to the 1970 U.S. Census at least another 9.7 million and possibly as many as another 15 million claim a mother tongue other than English without professing to use it either primarily or regularly. Although these figures can serve only as rough estimates, they are not only far larger than their 1960 counterparts but they have grown much more rapidly since 1960 than has the U.S. population as a whole, and have generally done so in the absence of significant immigration for most of the language groups for which increases are reported. Obviously, there is considerably more language maintenance and/or language maintenance claiming in the United States than generally meets the ear. Many who claim non-English mother tongues appear to have worked out diglossic accommodations that merit close examination, for these accommodations, if actual, reveal greater stability and recovery potential than had been generally expected. On the other hand, their permanence also should be neither assumed nor expected.

Where it obtains today in the United States, diglossia is marked by some of the same more or less rigid distinctions that it possessed in premodern times: between formality and intimacy, between reading/writing and speaking, and between public (intergroup) and private (intragroup) communication. In each instance, the first-named alternative is of greater concern to the polity and its institutions (including official censuses and record keeping of all kinds), whereas the last-named become the preserve of apparently displaced ethnic mother tongues. The stability of this arrangement depends on the rigidity with which the distinctions between formality and intimacy are maintained. They become ever more difficult to maintain in modern days because of the very factors that lead to shift to begin with, but they also have supports that frequently are overlooked. Languages of narrowly ("in-group") focused, spoken, intimacy are commonly buttressed by unconscious (as well as by conscious) ethnicity; to the extent that this is so, diglossia patterns can be established that maintain a stable pattern of "one population, two languages." The pattern, however, not only faces strong external pressure from shift forces favoring the functional expansion of the language of formal, written, public communication; it also may come to face internal pressure from shift forces favoring functional expansion of the language of informal, spoken, private communication. Thus, ethnicity may serve not only as a guardian of diglossia (and of language maintenance based upon diglossia) but also as its potential enemy.

Table 1. U.S. population claiming non-English mother tongue, 1960 and 1970.

Language	1960 (estimated)	1970	American-born of native parentage	Second generation	First generation
Celtic	—	88,162	9,734	32,969	45,459
Norwegian	321,774	612,862	204,822	313,675	94,365
Swedish	415,597	626,102	113,119	381,575	131,408
Danish	147,619	194,462	29,089	107,155	58,218
Dutch	—	350,748	90,713	132,204	127,834
Flemish	21,613	61,889	12,064	29,024	20,801
French	1,043,220	2,598,408	1,460,130	727,698	410,580
Breton	—	32,722	7,252	15,439	10,031
German	3,145,772	6,093,054	2,488,394	2,403,125	1,201,535
Polish	2,184,936	2,437,938	670,335	1,347,691	419,912
Czech	217,771	452,818	148,944	233,165	70,703
Slovak	260,000	510,366	86,950	340,855	82,561
Hungarian	404,114	447,497	52,156	234,088	161,253
Serbo-Croatian	184,094	239,455	24,095	132,296	83,064
Slovenian	67,208	82,321	9,040	54,103	19,178
Dalmatian	—	9,802	3,038	4,748	2,016
Albanian	—	17,382	1,571	8,283	7,528
Finnish	110,168	214,168	58,124	117,754	38,290
Lithuanian	206,043	292,820	34,744	162,888	95,188
Other Baltic	—	19,748	1,231	8,309	10,208
Russian	460,834	334,615	30,665	154,673	149,277
Ukrainian	252,974	249,351	22,662	130,054	96,635
Georgian	—	757	179	157	421
Romanian	58,019	56,590	5,166	25,369	26,055
Yiddish	964,605	1,593,993	170,174	985,703	438,116
Romani (Gypsy)	—	1,588	1,252	180	156
Greek	292,031	458,699	56,839	208,115	193,745
Italian	3,673,141	4,144,315	606,625	2,512,696	1,025,994
Spanish	3,335,961	7,823,583	4,171,050	1,956,293	1,696,240
Portuguese	181,109	365,300	62,252	162,749	140,299
Basque	—	8,108	1,852	4,087	2,169
Armenian	—	100,495	13,758	48,414	38,323
Persian	—	23,923	1,555	4,037	17,329
Hebrew	—	101,686	19,691	45,883	36,112
Arabic (all)	103,908	193,520	26,734	92,045	73,657
Southern Semitic	—	1,354	380	216	758
Hamitic	—	948	445	217	286
Swahili	—	3,991	2,040	812	1,139
Libyan	—	410	265	86	59
Niger-Congo	—	6,537	1,055	1,221	4,261
Sudanic	—	2,543	336	1,347	860
Turkish	—	24,123	1,811	5,666	16,646
Other Uralic	—	15,191	765	3,016	11,410
Altaic	—	974	306	251	417
Hindi	—	26,253	1,249	2,987	22,017
Other Indo-Aryan	—	22,939	731	2,342	19,866
Dravidian	—	8,983	635	813	7,535
Korean	—	53,528	2,756	16,024	34,748
Japanese	300,000	408,504	82,886	207,528	118,090
Chinese (all dialects)	180,000	345,531	30,764	124,407	119,260
Tibetan	—	352	183	50	119
Burmese	—	1,581	248	177	1,156
Thai	—	14,416	1,178	1,543	11,695
Malay (all)	—	10,295	2,019	1,267	6,915
Tagalog	—	217,907	8,336	57,073	152,498
Polynesian	—	20,687	12,006	3,725	4,956
All native American	—	268,205	254,859	7,537	5,809
All others	—	880,779	350,126	341,483	189,170
Not reported	—	9,317,873	873,081	348,645	96,147
Total non-English[a]	19,381,786	33,175,172	11,449,410	13,900,432	7,825,330

Source: Joshua A. Fishman, *Language Loyalty in the United States* (1966; reprint, New York, 1978); National Advisory Council on Bilingual Education, *Annual Report, 1975;* U.S. Bureau of the Census, *Census of the Population, 1970* (Washington, D.C., 1973).

[a]The 1970 figures are minimal estimates which do not take into account the 9 million Americans who did not answer the mother-tongue question. The true non-English figure may thus be significantly higher.

ETHNICITY AND LANGUAGE

There is some 3,000 years of social theory concerning the relationship between language and ethnicity. Explicit and implicit views of this relationship were formulated by Hebrew prophets, Greek philosophers, Roman statesmen, spokesmen of the Western (and Eastern) church, and by medieval, renaissance, and Reformation savants and commentators. The views concerning the relationship between language and ethnicity formulated by the early fathers of modern sociology itself must also be kept in mind, as must those of most current analysts, so that the changeability of ethnicity itself can be more fully understood, as well as changeability in the language and ethnicity relationship vis-à-vis language maintenance. Only a modicum of the pertinent views and data can be presented here, the former being kept in mind as the basis of selection.

Premodern Views of Language and Ethnicity Hebraic and Greek thought were both ambivalent with respect to the evaluation of ethnicity—both their own ethnicity and that of others—viewing it as potentially perfectible but in reality regrettably imperfect. Nevertheless, its relation to language was acknowledged by both: particularly insofar as "ennobled ethnicity" was concerned, one's own ethnicity was unthinkable without one's own language. This linkage has remained in much of Hebraic and Eastern Orthodox thought, peoples (and their religious institutions) being viewed as autocephalic, characterized by their own languages and thus by their own linguistic links to God and to their perfected authenticity. The Western church inherited a more opportunistic view from the Holy Roman Empire, namely, that local ethnicities and languages were initially to be utilized as a means of influencing, controlling, and coordinating a variety of local populations, but ultimately transcended in favor of a larger, more inclusive, and more ennobling language and ethnicity.

Both East and West in premedieval Euro-Mediterranean society viewed ethnicity in basically similar terms, as an expanded, spontaneous, familylike bond to "one's own kind" and to the unique ("authentic") traditions and wisdoms associated with them. However, the East tended to view "one's own kind" as a natural and eternal unit of mankind, loss of membership in which was regarded as the ultimate punishment, whether for individuals or for collectivities, whereas the West viewed identification with "one's own kind" merely as a first step in a progression toward broader identifications, responsibilities, and opportunities. These two views continue to compete, espousing respectively narrower and broader languages, and valuing authenticities as they "naturally" are or as they ought to become in ideological or philosophical perspective.

Modern Sharpening of the Issue The Renaissance and Reformation views of language and ethnicity reflect an increasing Western recognition of local legitimacy partly as a result of the spread of Eastern views (along the Danubian route from Bulgaria into Hungary and central Europe), but primarily in consequence of local political and economic developments. In early modern times the major forces effecting the consolidation of local polities were the commercial and industrial revolutions, both of which reconcentrated mainly along the Atlantic seaboard after their earlier Mediterranean beginnings. By the time Johann Gottfried Herder's views were gaining major recognition in mid-19th-century central and eastern Europe, northern and western Europe were politically, economically, and intellectually at a different (postethnic) phase of development and inclined to far different prescriptions for the backwardness of the rest of Europe.

Herder's stress on the inviolable right and sublime value of linguistic and ethnic authenticity for every cultural collectivity—and the manifold political movements that arose in the 19th century for the political/economic liberation and defense of them—were met in the apparently consolidated and liberated West by objections from advocates for capitalism and the proletariat alike; both viewed themselves as forces on behalf of a more comprehensive level of collectivity recognition, the spokesmen for capitalism viewing claims for local language and ethnicity as disturbing barbarism, the advocates of proletarian unity denouncing such claims as a fractionating diversion. Ostensibly claiming a neutral position, modern sociology, a product of the same century, has also viewed local language and ethnicity as counterproductive, that is, as being out of place in a modern, fluid, rational, production-oriented and market-dominated *Gesellschaft*. Capitalism, Communism, and sociology alike have generally espoused social theories that have diverted American as well as international intellectual attention from the relation between language and ethnicity, at the very time that such relationships were not only omnipresent but becoming more conscious, more focused, more manipulated, and more ideologized throughout Europe, and from there throughout the colonial empires to which European social thought was exported.

The clash between the drive to safeguard natural ethnicity "as it is" and the drive to foster a higher order of aggregation "that should be," came to near-cataclysmic realization with the rise of German Nazism and Soviet Communism and with the subsequent confrontation between them. Both movements unleashed unparalleled force on behalf of their goals and against their internal and external opponents. The excesses of both have left the topics of language, language maintenance, and ethnicity under a cloud of suspicion and rejection in many enlightened American circles.

The Return to Basic Inquiry A major American difficulty in fathoming the relation between language and ethnicity derives from the common sociological bias that views ethnicity itself as a necessarily vanishing phenomenon and therefore as one to be found only on the margins of society, among the dislocated, the retrogressive, the disadvantaged, and the dissatisfied. The original Hebraic and Greek view of ethnicity as an aspect of every traditioned sociocultural aggregate, including one's own, has been lost, and as a result the concept of ethnicity has become peripheralized and trivialized, held to pertain only to marked or exceptional, decreasingly important, aggregates. The ethnic foundations of all national cultures, of most of privacy and intimacy, of much of religion, literature, and the arts, have come to be largely overlooked because dominant views of the direction of social development have no place for (or are at odds with) a vibrant, constructive, and resilient ethnicity as a component of Western life. The reluctance to view language and ethnicity as conso-

nant with modern social development has been particularly prevalent in the United States, where attention to them has been restricted to the context of immigrant dislocation and assimilation. The recent American revival of interest in ethnicity is a strong indication of that consonance.

The adoption of Herderian rhetoric by "peripheral" Slavic or non-European nationality movements had little if any influence on Western social thought in the 19th century, even though language and nationality movements were then so obviously plentiful. Similarly, it was not until the claims of ethnicity compelled official recognition and response in Great Britain, France, and the United States (as well as in Holland, Norway, and Sweden), that is, in societies that presumably had been consolidated on a supralocal basis generations or even centuries ago, did American intellectuals begin to examine ethnicity in other than dislocative and fringe-society terms. This recent development has brought together ethnicity and sociolinguistic theory and research. As a result an increasing number of social theorists have rediscovered not only ethnicity but also language—and language maintenance and language shift. The topics of societal bilingualism, language maintenance–language shift, ethnicity, and the link between language and ethnicity have come increasingly to be recognized as requiring joint treatment, if any of them are to be fully understood.

Recent work has focused on the differentiation of ethnicity from racism and on differentiating within ethnicity itself, of its being, doing, and knowing components. Although the social sciences are still a long way from understanding ethnicity—not to mention its "rebirth" during the late 60s and early 70s—it is now appreciated that it can be understood only if the basic constituents of ethnicity are recognized as pertaining to the broadest aspects of modern life itself. These components are crucial to an understanding of language maintenance and ethnicity in general and, more particularly, its manifestations in the United States.

One basic distinction within the realm of ethnicity that seems to be particularly pertinent to the study of language maintenance and language shift is that between the conscious and the unconscious. Unconscious ethnicity, prevalent among ordinary folk in small, unmobilized, static societies, involves nonideological matter-of-factness about those population characteristics—daily rounds and common beliefs—that define and distinguish sociocultural collectivities. Even so, language is widely regarded as part of ethnic "being": it issues from the body and is therefore viewed as part of the genetic continuity that stands at the heart of ethnicity. Similarly, it is recognized as part of ethnic "doing" (those behaviors that are considered authentically, often uniquely, definitive of "one's own kind") and as part of ethnic "knowing" (those beliefs and insights that are viewed as central and natural only to "one's own kind"). Consequently, when ethnicity attains a conscious level and comes to pervade the full constellation of sociocultural life, language is very naturally highlighted as a vital part of what "one's own kind" are, what they do, and what they know.

Conscious ethnicity elaborates upon all three of the recognitions and assumptions of unconscious ethnicity —including the linguistic ones—and unifies, mobilizes, and activates populations. Nationalism is just such heightened ethnicity. Elites encourage its emergence in order to gain mass support for the attainment of goals or for the solution of problems on the basis of qualities putatively inspired by authenticity, preserving of authenticity, and fostering of authenticity. The attraction of modern, conscious, mass ethnicity is mutable and manipulable—rather than "genuine" in any valid historical sense—but no more so than are the appeals of all modern mass movements. It is not its validity but its power that demands attention and response, for its power illustrates the need for a sense of authenticity, for a sense of personal identity with a specially meaningful collectivity to which one belongs deeply, fully, mysteriously, a need that even (or particularly) modern men reveal. It is the internalization of language in the subjective mystery of ethnicity that concerns us here, rather than the purely external and undifferentiating demonstration that the association between language and heightened ethnicity is mutable and manipulable by elites whose major purpose may merely be to communicate with and to control the masses for political and economic purposes. When heightened, the link between language and ethnicity becomes a cosmology, a *Weltanschauung* that clarifies the lives and purposes of masses of people. That it does so less in the United States than elsewhere is due to specific social, cultural, and historical circumstances that require special attention. Nevertheless these circumstances do not belie the phenomena themselves, much less their urgency elsewhere, nor even the possibility of their future urgency here.

CONSCIOUS AND UNCONSCIOUS ETHNICITY IN LANGUAGE MAINTENANCE

Language maintenance among bilingual American ethnic groups can be accomplished at the level of unconscious rather than conscious ethnicity. Stable, widespread multilingualism is often found throughout the world without any ideological overtones and with languages of rather small and narrow focus functioning side by side and completely unthreatened by languages of wider communication employed by millions. This is the primary mechanism of Mexican-American language maintenance in the Southwest, of Japanese-American language maintenance in Hawaii, as well as of what remains of European-derived language maintenance throughout the northeastern and central states. Ethnic newspapers, radio programs, schools, organizations, and churches are not the chief nurturers of language maintenance in the United States; all these institutions may even decrease in number without greatly influencing American non-English-language maintenance, nor its link with unconscious ethnicity. What is genuinely operative in this connection is the domain separation that intact but unconscious ethnicity maintains between the wider and the narrower languages in question. By this means certain central role relationships within the narrower circles (for example, parent-child, cleric-lay) are preserved in the original immigrant or marked language alone. These may be (and usually are) the most intimate or emotional relationships, but they can also be the more sacralized role relationships, even those that require not only speaking but reading the ethnic

tongue. This form of ethnolinguistic maintenance is particularly likely to occur among the Eastern Orthodox churches and Protestant sects. While the retained functions of the ethnic language will vary from group to group, the common crucial factors that facilitate language maintenance are the availability both of undislocated status and role relationships within the home and community and out-of-home economic or religious activity that supports those relationships, both requiring the ethnic language for membership.

Thus, English is no threat to the maintenance of hundreds of vernaculars in Africa and Asia whose speakers learn English in school, read it in inexpensive publications thereafter, hear it on the radio, on television, and at the movies, and, more rarely, use it at work. As long as there are no widespread demographic upheavals (for example, urbanization on a large scale, resulting in intermarriage across ethnic boundaries) the governmental, quasi-governmental, technological, and educational use of English in these settings are unlikely to affect the local vernaculars of home and community. The unconscious ethnicity of the latter requires no extensive network of modern media and institutions to buttress it, although some authoritative external buttressing may well be attempted. Some immigrant-derived groups in the United States have also arrived at an accommodation between their mother tongue and the host language that will enable them to maintain the ethnic mother tongue as long as a meaningful subset of their ethnically based daily rounds can be preserved and reserved for their vernaculars. Not only withdrawn or isolated nonparticipationist immigrant groups (such as Amish, Hasidim, and Hutterites) have revealed a capacity for doing just that without recourse to language ideologies. Even participationist, urbanized groups have arrived at ways of quietly preserving their own neighborhoods and central institutions and have recorded some language maintenance successes. The basic ingredient in all cases of stabilized diglossia in the United States is the preservation from dislocation of some functional part of the initial ethnic system of doings and knowings. The apparently seamless ethnic web has unconscious subsystems, and in the multicultural lives of countless ordinary people who embrace no ideological causes or political postures, one or another such subsystem appears to be sufficient for language maintenance on an unconscious ethnic (or coethnic) basis.

The consequences for language maintenance at the level of conscious ethnicity, in the United States or elsewhere, are somewhat different and require separate analysis.

LANGUAGE PLANNING PERSPECTIVE

Language planning involves authoritative allocation of resources such as funds, manpower, and governmental (or other conscious and recognized) language preference or protection in connection with specific functions. However, the basic resources that language planning allocates to language are focused attention, concern, and recognition. Language planning is a conscious enterprise and as such it easily draws upon and contributes to conscious ethnicity in the course of its efforts. Although language planning can and does also operate in ethnically unencumbered or minimally encumbered contexts (for example, language planning on behalf of English in the United States), its features are most clearly revealed when it proceeds in the context of concerns for ethnicity.

The authoritative allocation of languages to particular functions (status planning) requires a rationale for the elites and planners as well as for the target populations whose language repertoires they hope to influence. Rationales can be instrumental or sentimental; frequently they are a combination of both. Instrumental rationales of language functions stress utility, efficiency, practical advantage, and related cost-benefit notions pertaining to time, effort, and effectiveness. Sentimental rationales stress emotional attachments, obligations, historical loyalties, moral imperatives, and related concepts of uniqueness or authenticity pertaining to ethnic patrimony and commitment. There are probably limits in the extent to which either rationale can be pursued without some reinforcement from the other. Ethnicity rationales are very common in language planning—and in American ethnic-group language planning—and tend eventually to be employed even when there was no initial intention to do so.

Appeals to ethnicity seek to rally users (and potential users) to specific languages as an obligation and a privilege related to language preservation and survival. Such appeals have been utilized by all language movements (whether related to indigenous vernacular or to classical languages) and have provided them with claims upon target populations whose unification and mobilization these movements have sought to accomplish. However, when most successful, status-planning efforts and language movements are parts of larger programs of political, economic, and cultural activization that have not merely sentimental but larger, instrumental goals as well. Language-planning efforts on behalf of American minority languages lack this larger relationship. Their status is of conscious concern only to small and politically or economically naive or neutralized cultural elites who have little to offer the mass of unconscious language users whom they seek to reach.

Even though history may appear to indicate otherwise, the language and ethnicity "fit" of appeals to historical collectivities is both presented and widely experienced as natural, authentic, and eternal. The phenomenology of conscious ethnicity-language linkages is obviously more crucial because it is so often more powerful than its objective indicators.

The experience of ethnicity movements and of ethnicity-related status planning transforms populations into active and conscientious language adherents. Efforts involving advocacy of, struggle for, and conscious implementation of language in one's own behavior and in the behavior of others, justified on the bases of ethnic being, doing, and knowing, inevitably leave their mark. For those so activated, subsequent deethnification and reethnization are exceedingly difficult to accomplish (in contrast to the openness to ethnic transformation of those operating only at the level of unconscious ethnicity); their potential for language shift also becomes correspondingly circumscribed. Thus, conscious ethnicity and ethnically ideologized language consciousness are powerful bulwarks of language maintenance. That there have been few, if any, successful movements of this kind on behalf of non-English languages in the United States is due to particular circumstances—such

as the availability of unprecedented mobility via English and the ideology of incorporation—that have long characterized Anglophone power to the disadvantage of prospective language movements. Whereas the web of unconscious ethnicity of everyday English-speaking American life could easily be matched for intactness, authenticity, and personal intimacy by the remnants of unconscious ethnicity in Hispanic and other non-Anglophone communities, the conscious ideology of unlimited political and economic mobility via English has overwhelmed conscious ideologies of ethnic language maintenance in the United States. Notwithstanding the recent flurry of interest in ethnicity (which may succeed only to the extent that it is not really ideological but rather fosters unconscious patterns of daily life)— the English-anchored American dream has had more by far to deliver to the ethnic multitudes than have conscious language and ethnicity movements. As a result, the bulk of non-Anglo ethnicity is simultaneously ethnically unconscious at the nonverbal level and linguistically Anglicized; to the extent that its Anglicization is not complete it is again unconscious rather than conscious ethnicity that is its base.

Status planning usually concentrates upon formal, written, governmental functions rather than upon informal, spoken, and family ones. The former are not only more related to modern power and privilege but are basically more controllable via monitoring and sanctions. With the exception of the school years and military service, however, most members of most ethnocultural collectivities normally have meager roles to play with respect to the functions most suffused by language planning as a whole or by status planning in particular. As a result, even in nonimmigrant (host) settings fully in control of their own political and economic establishments, ethnicity-inspired status planning gains its staunchest supporters from intellectuals on the one hand, and from governmental and religious functionaries and activists on the other, with little reliable, informed support from most members of the group. Except during rare and brief stages of generally heightened ethnicity, the latter are much more influenced by the status changes in everyday life that the host population brings into being. The impact of new languages, government, education, industry, and the media upon the masses is in most cases indirect, in contrast to the direct one upon elites. The generally unconscious ethnic self-image ultimately changes as a result of stable, cross-generational implementation of new language-related statuses rather than as a result of conscious, ideological, ethnicity-encumbered formulations and convictions. This is especially true of immigrant groups in the United States. Their language ideologists simply have not been able to alter the realities of the Anglophone-related reward system; as a result they have failed to attract any mass following.

Even when their elites are ethnically ideologized, there are severe limitations to the status planning of relatively powerless immigrant minorities. Language maintenance via conscious ethnicity is rendered difficult because their elites are so limited in being able to establish and control institutions of language monitoring, language ideologization and, most particularly, language use via the establishment and control of significant political and economic bases of their own. In modern, secular settings the everyday rounds of the bulk of the immigrant population are realized largely via the language of the coterritorial power. As even home status increasingly derives from out-of-home roles involving the "other" (unmarked) language, the marked (immigrant) home language becomes increasingly difficult to maintain. Where it does exist, the conscious ethnicity of U.S. immigrant elites is as yet insufficiently linked to alternative status potentials and so can neither implant nor maintain its counterpart language within the rank and file. In addition, the processes of modernization, conducted as they are under majority auspices, are very likely to erode the unconscious immigrant ethnicity that might otherwise support minority language maintenance in home and community. In the face of such competition the ideologizing and ethnifying forces of status-planning efforts by immigrant elites are generally powerless to stem the tide of language shift. Neither programs, pronouncements, nor resolutions—nor even schools, journals, camps, theaters, and churches, not to mention U.S. government-sponsored bilingual education—can have much effect on language maintenance when they are unable to create political and economic realities that can protect at least the roles of family and everyday life from intra- and intergenerational language shift.

Thus, conscious, ethnically inspired status planning for language maintenance succeeds when the larger forces to which such status planning must relate are able to foster protective political, economic, and cultural change. Conscious ethnicity is rarely enough for immigrant language maintenance, for normally it is not pervasive or deep enough to safeguard those language functions upon which language maintenance depends. The examples of successful language maintenance—of French in the Canadian province of Québec, only recently ensured; of Hebrew by Orthodox Jews in the Diaspora, for 2,000 years; and of German by the Amish in Pennsylvania, for over 250 years—are all explicable in similar terms, namely, the ability (by different means and due to different circumstances) to go beyond conscious elitist ethnicity alone to the establishment, protection, and preservation of *mandatory* institutions of marked language use for the target population, whose ethnicity may be far less and only intermittently conscious. This is exactly what most U.S. immigrant language groups have failed to do and of which even the current ethnicity sentiment seems to be unaware. The hope of fostering non-English language maintenance through federally sponsored bilingual-education programs (or the fears of their opponents that they may do so) is groundless, for such programs are insufficiently powerful to provide the necessary support for unconscious home-based language maintenance, let alone to foster conscious language maintenance on an adequate and separate economic and political basis.

Language-maintenance efforts often wisely seek to adjust the very "body of the language" (its phonology, its lexicon, and its grammar) to the needs of the struggle for survival. However, if new nomenclatures, or new politeness/comradeship forms in the pronominal or verbal systems, or new number systems, or, indeed, new writing systems, are needed so that American immigrant languages can function more advantageously in particular modern domains, what models are to be

recognized in finding, creating, or adapting them? Very commonly, the guiding principles of such corpus planning are actually encumbered by ethnicity (purity, authenticity). Language-modernization efforts often follow rationales that seek to maximize linguistic features considered to be representative of the distinctiveness of the ethnic community, of its cultural independence, of its unique values and experiences.

The dimension of ethnicity in corpus planning interacts with language maintenance by making the very choice between linguistic alternatives a declaration of intent: to reject outside domination, to safeguard native genius, to advance autochthonous dignity, and so forth. However, the very same dependence upon elitist institutions, formality, and writing that characterizes status planning also characterizes corpus planning and, indeed, almost entirely dominates it. Thus, corpus planning for immigrant languages in the United States (on behalf of Lithuanian, Slovak, Ukrainian, Yiddish, and others) has an even more marginal impact upon the mass of immigrant-language speakers than does status planning. Finally, immigrant-language elites are even less successful with respect to corpus planning than they are with respect to status planning, both because they are less frequently either concerned with it or trained in its technical procedures. Indeed, this lack of concern and training for corpus planning often leads to ruptured relations between those immigrant-language maintenance elites who do engage in corpus planning and others who are oriented toward status planning alone. Many of the latter consider corpus planning a useless (at best) or disruptive (at worst) diversion from the main task to be pursued: the augmentation, unification, and inspiration of the beleaguered faithful. To the extent that American immigrant-language corpus planning discredits unconscious but intact usage more successfully than it provides replacements, it may well be as disruptive as some of its detractors claim. The failure of conscious corpus planning for U.S. immigrant languages is just another example of the failure of conscious language-and-ethnicity movements to work effectively on behalf of non-English languages in the U.S. setting.

CONCLUSION

An appreciation of the relationship between language maintenance and ethnicity among American ethnic groups requires a thorough familiarity with each of the foregoing topics, separately and independently of any such relationship. The study of language maintenance reveals the central importance of differentiating between various language functions (family, community, government, education, religion) and language subsystems (mother-tongue claiming, understanding, speaking, writing) in order to be able to pinpoint maintenance or shift. The study of ethnicity reveals the intimate interpenetration of language and ethnicity both in popular imagery as well as in theoretical and ideological awareness throughout the ages.

Ethnicity is manifested at both unconscious and conscious levels. The former is related most directly to informal, spontaneous, and spoken language, particularly in family and immediate community interactions; the latter is associated more specifically with formal, written, and authoritative language, particularly in high cultural interactions. In either context, ethnicity is only one of the components of the total language-maintenance matrix. The crucial question is whether a marked (minority, immigrant) language can retain its own, quite separate functions. Ethnicity can contribute to such a separate functional allocation, but it becomes increasingly difficult to do so, even at the level of mobilized, conscious ethnicity, when elites cannot provide the institutional controls and rewards necessary to the modern functional separation and maintenance of languages. Conscious language-maintenance efforts among American ethnic groups, through status planning, corpus planning, or both, commonly cannot greatly influence or control the daily life of most of the language community, and as a result can neither maintain nor expand societal functions reserved for the marked language alone.

Conscious ethnic movements in the United States are weak systems in comparison with the rival consciousness of and opportunity for gains in status via English, even in intraminority community roles. To the extent that it maintains a traditional separation between home and community roles in the ethnic mother tongue and outside roles in English, unconscious ethnicity can provide the basis of diglossic language maintenance, particularly if the separation has a strong religious or economic focus. However, it is in the very nature of modernization to render such separations between intra- and intercommunity roles difficult to maintain, particularly if substantial rewards are associated with intercommunal roles and statuses. Thus, in the long run, minority ethnicity persists in the United States, but on an increasingly Anglicized basis. Given a context of continual modernization, social change, and mobility, unconscious ethnicity as a possible support for language maintenance slowly recedes due to the difficulty of maintaining the domain separation and systemic completeness that it requires. Neither the revival of ethnic awareness in the United States during the late 1960s and early 1970s nor the bilingual-education movement of the same era seems to provide any major promise for the long-range maintenance of most language and ethnic heritage in the United States.

Bibliography
Various works by Joshua A. Fishman are a useful introduction to the relations between language and ethnicity. See particularly Fishman et al., *Language Loyalty in the United States: The Maintenance and Perpetuation of Non-English Mother Tongues by American Ethnic and Religious Groups* (1966; reprint, New York, 1978). See also his *Language and Nationalism* (Rowley, Mass., 1972); "Ethnicity and Language," in *Language and Ethnicity in Human Relations*, Howard Giles, ed. (New York, 1977); "Language and Ethnicity in Eastern Europe," in *Linguistics and Ethnicity in Eastern Europe*, Peter Sugar, ed. (Seattle, Wash., 1980); and *Never Say Die: The Sociology of Yiddish* (The Hague, Netherlands, 1980).

For case studies of the interaction between language and ethnicity, see Einar Haugen, *Language Conflict and Language Planning: The Case of Modern Norwegian* (Cambridge, Mass., 1966); Uriel Heyd, *Language Reform in Modern Turkey* (Jerusalem, 1968); and E. Glyn Lewis, *Multilingualism in the Soviet Union* (The Hague, 1972). In *Language and Community* (Dublin, Ireland, 1970), Máirtín Ó Murchú discusses the replacement of Irish and the inability of language planning to restore it as a common vernacular language.

For broad historical overviews of language shifts and the rise of ethnic consciousness, see Roman Jakobson, "The Beginnings of National Self-Determination in Europe," *Review of Politics* 7 (1945): 29–42; and E. Glyn Lewis, "Bilingualism and Bilingual Education: The Ancient World to the Renaissnce," in Joshua A. Fishman, ed., *Bilingual Education: An International Sociological Perspective* (Rowley, Mass., 1976).

Several works deal with social policy and language maintenance. See Arnold H. Leibowitz, *Educational Policy and Political Acceptance* (Arlington, Va., Center for Applied Linguistics, 1971), and two works written and edited by Joan Rubin et al., *Language Planning Processes* (The Hague, 1977), and "Language Planning in the United States," *International Journal of the Sociology of Language* no. 11 (1976). For a very recent summary of the status of various languages in the United States, see Shirley Heath and Charles A. Ferguson, eds., *Language in the U.S.A.* (Cambridge, Mass., 1979).

JOSHUA A. FISHMAN

LAOTIANS: *see* INDOCHINESE

LATIN AMERICANS: *see* CENTRAL AND SOUTH AMERICANS; CUBANS; DOMINICANS; MEXICANS; PUERTO RICANS

LATVIANS

The 1970 Census recorded 86,144 persons of Latvian origin in the United States, of whom 41,558 were foreign-born, and 44,586 were native-born of foreign or mixed parentage. The actual number in these two categories could be somewhat higher, however, since many Latvians were counted as Germans, Russians, or Scandinavians when they arrived in the United States. Some, but probably fewer, of those counted as Latvians could equally have been Latvian-born Jews, Germans, or Russians.

Latvia (Latvian Soviet Socialist Republic) is a state in northern Europe, bounded on the north by the Estonian S.S.R., on the east by the Russian S.S.R., on the south by the Lithuanian S.S.R., and on the west by the Baltic Sea. Its area of slightly less than 25,000 square miles makes it about equal in size to West Virginia. The people belong to an almost extinct group of Baltic peoples and speak a language that is most closely related to the ancient Indo-European tongues. Lithuanian is the only other language directly related to Latvian that is still spoken today. Until the end of the 19th century, however, the official language of the country was German, and since the end of World War II the official language has been Russian.

ORIGINS

In the Bronze Age the Baltic lands were known in Europe for their large deposits of amber. The Baltic peoples are believed to have arrived in the region around 2000 B.C. The four tribes that settled along the coast of the Baltic Sea established contacts with the Scandinavians, Slavs, Finnish peoples, and even the Romans. Their religion involved the worship of one true God and several minor deities. In the early Middle Ages a number of Latvian principalities were established, composed of individual farmsteads rather than villages. Lack of unity resulted in their submission to an order of German knights known as the Livonian Brothers of the Sword after intermittent warfare from 1186 to 1290. The loose Livonian Confederation established by the conquerors in Estonia and Latvia survived internal dissension, revolts of the natives, and incursions by Muscovites and by the Polish-Lithuanian Commonwealth until 1561. In that year the confederation was split up by the Poles, and the majority of the Latvians were reduced to serfdom. From 1621 to 1721 northern Latvia was a part of the kingdom of Sweden; the rest remained with Poland,

Province boundaries of the Russian Empire before 1918

Boundary of independent Latvia, 1918-1940.

except for the semi-independent Duchy of Kurland. Between 1721 and 1795 all of Latvia was gradually absorbed into the Russian Empire. Throughout these years of foreign rule and of control by German land-owning and merchant interests, the Latvian culture survived.

In the 19th century the serfs were emancipated (1817–1819), and a subsequent growing nationalist and socialist movement culminated in a revolution, beginning in 1905, throughout the Russian Empire. World War I, the Bolshevik Revolution of 1917, German defeat, and postwar unrest finally allowed the creation of the independent country of Latvia in 1918. It lasted until 1940, when Latvia was overrun first by Soviet troops, then by a German occupation, and finally by Soviet reconquest in 1945.

MIGRATION AND ARRIVAL

Latvian migration to America was intermittent at first. In 1640 a few Latvian and Estonian settlers were taken along by some Swedes to New Sweden in Delaware and Pennsylvania, and in 1687 a group of Latvian immigrants from the Couronian colony on the West Indian island of Tobago settled in Boston. Until the late 19th century, a small but steady number of Latvians settled in New York, Pennsylvania, the Midwest, and California. The 1850 U.S. Census, which counted Latvians and Lithuanians together because they spoke a similar language, indicated 3,160 Latvians and Lithuanians in the United States, 1,414 of them newcomers and 1,860 American-born; in 1870 the number had reached 4,644. Place names, such as Livonia, Mich.,

Mount Riga, N.Y., and Lake Riga and Mt. Riga, Conn., are reminders of their presence. Most were sailors or artisans, a few were missionaries.

The 1900 Census shows a total of 4,309 Latvians residing in the United States, a figure that does not include a number of stowaway Latvian sailors nor the many Latvians registered by U.S. immigration officials as Russian, German, or Scandinavian. Almost all of the immigrants found work in the large eastern and midwestern cities as construction workers, mechanics, carpenters, bricklayers, engineers, or foremen.

The second influx of Latvian immigrants came as a result of the Russian Revolution of 1905 and its aftermath. Between 1905 and 1913 approximately 5,000 Latvians entered the United States, again for the most part laborers, but this time including many well-educated socialist and nationalist leaders whose reasons for departure were largely political. Then World War I, immigration restrictions, and, finally, the Depression, slowed the pace of immigration. From 1920 to 1939 only 4,669 Latvians arrived. When Latvia was declared independent in 1918, several hundred Latvians returned to their homeland, but the great majority did not. As was the case throughout the immigration, most who came stayed. Between 1930 and 1935 only 298 Latvian Americans returned. In 1940 the U.S. Census figures indicated 34,656 persons of Latvian origin in the United States, 18,636 of them Latvian-born.

Between 1939 and 1951 over 40,000 Latvian immigrants fleeing Nazi and Soviet suppression arrived, a few after 1939, but the majority after 1945. Congress facilitated their entry by enacting laws designating them as displaced persons. The Latvian Relief, in cooperation with the National Catholic Welfare Conference, the Church World Service, the Lutheran Resettlement Service, the Legation of Latvia, and the American Latvian Society, helped transport and resettle them. Highly educated and multilingual, they carried into exile a strong national loyalty and zeal to preserve Latvian culture. Most of them had to begin their life in the United States by joining the ranks of unskilled labor, but in ten years' time the majority had either reestablished themselves in their professions or embarked upon new ones.

SETTLEMENT

When the United States first became the Latvian land of opportunity, Liepāja (Libau) was the leading port of departure and Boston the principal port of arrival. In 1888 Jacob Sieberg (1863–1963), a carpenter, landed in Boston with six other men and set about encouraging other Latvians to follow. Soon there were Latvian settlements in New York, Baltimore, Cleveland, Chicago, and in Lincoln County, Wis., the only farm community to be established.

Most of the immigrants were peasants and artisans who came to the great American urban industrial centers for better jobs, to escape service in the Russian army, or for religious reasons. They maintained ties with their relatives and friends at home, urged them to come to the United States, and provided the money for their passage. Lacking even the rudiments of English and having no industrial or entrepreneurial skills, the immigrants usually started as unskilled workers in factories, shops, packing houses, steel mills, foundries, or textile mills. Wherever they congregated they built churches and organized fraternal benefit associations to provide members and their kin financial assistance in the event of sickness or death; these associations also served as social and entertainment centers. As the Latvians became more proficient in English and in their jobs, they moved into the ranks of semiskilled and skilled workers. Many became property owners, investing their savings in land and cottages or in small retail and service businesses—boarding houses, delicatessens, funeral parlors, tailor shops, restaurants, and real-estate agencies.

Most Latvian Americans became and remained city dwellers. The 1930 Census shows 18,744 foreign-born Latvians living in urban areas, only 1,267 in rural areas. The census figures of 1940 are almost identical. The 1960 Census shows most first- and second-generation Latvians, living in the Northeast (39,839) and the north-central states (28,477); 12,331 in the West; outside of Florida and Texas, the 8,507 in the South are scattered. In 1970 the western states showed an increase, with a total of 13,771. The heaviest concentrations of Latvians are in New York, New Jersey, and Massachusetts. The major Latvian regional centers remain: in the Northeast, New York, Boston, and Philadelphia; in the Midwest, Chicago, Milwaukee, Cleveland, and Kalamazoo and Grand Rapids, Mich.; on the West Coast, Los Angeles, San Francisco, and Sacramento, Calif., and Portland, Seattle, and Tacoma, Wash.

Latvians as a rule do not live in close communities but blend into the surrounding neighborhoods, although they do tend to remain somewhat aloof. Only a few closely knit, typically Latvian communities still exist in Massachusetts and Michigan. In 1940, 25,166 of the Latvian city dwellers lived in the largest cities. They congregated in certain general areas, but not in what could be called ethnic enclaves.

Males exceeded females in the immigration, which accounts for the high percentage (about half) of marriages outside the group, usually to Scandinavians, Germans, or English. As a rule, Latvian families are small. In Washington State in 1960, 24 percent of the Latvian families had no children, 41 percent had one child, and 23 percent had two. Households often include grandparents.

In the 1890s practically all Latvian immigrants spoke their native language at home; by 1930 only 30 percent used Latvian as a family language. Among the post-World War II newcomers, 86 percent of the families used Latvian at home in 1960. But because in many cases both father and mother worked, the children did not easily learn or maintain the language unless there were grandparents at home. By the 1960s approximately 46 percent of the children spoke Latvian willingly; 31 percent fluently. Only 28 percent of the children read Latvian books willingly; 24 percent preferred books in English. Only 14 percent attended Latvian Saturday and Sunday schools.

In their patterns of living, Latvians do not differ very much from their neighbors. They prefer houses to apartments and the suburbs to the city. Parents and their adult offspring usually live in separate households but maintain close and friendly relations. Their homes are their castles, in which they invest great expense and energy. In 1958 in Milwaukee alone 43 percent of the Latvians belonged to professions; 27 percent were owners

of industrial enterprises, shops, stores, or apartment buildings; 11 percent were office workers or clerks; 14 percent were artisans; 3 percent were semiprofessionals; only 2 percent were unskilled workers. Data from Washington State generally confirm these figures.

Latvians like privacy, but they enthusiastically support ethnic organizations. Around 85 percent of Latvian Americans belong to at least one, and sometimes several, Latvian societies of one kind or another.

ORGANIZATIONS

Jacob Sieberg, Latvia's first well-documented immigrant, not only encouraged fellow Latvians to come to the United States but organized various groups to serve them when they arrived: he founded the first Latvian Evangelical Lutheran Church (1891) and the Boston Latvian Benefit Society (1889); he also published the first Latvian newspaper, *Amerikas Vēstnesis* (American Herald), between 1896 and 1920, when it merged briefly with the *Amerikas Atbalss* (Echo of America); it ceased publication in 1922. He wrote seven books, including the first Latvian handbook for the study of English, and later served as consul general for independent Latvia.

The first immigrants were Lutherans, soon followed by Baptists, who settled in Philadelphia. There they organized the first Latvian Baptist parish in 1891 and published the monthly *Amerikas Latvietis* (American Latvian) from 1902 to 1905. This was followed a number of years later by a journal, *Drauga Balss* (Voice of a Friend, 1918–1920; 1945–1948). In 1893 a socialist Latvian Workers' Association was founded in Boston, which also had its own newspaper *Amerikas Latviešu Avīze* (American Latvian Newspaper, 1898–1901) and even its own theater—the first Latvian theatrical group in the United States. In 1898 the American Latvian Social Democratic Association was founded, again in Boston, which published the first Latvian scholarly and literary monthly, *Auseklis* (Morning Star, 1898–1901), and a radical monthly, *Proletārietis* (Proletarian, 1904–1906).

World War I stimulated the first centralized Latvian-American organization. It was called the Latvian War Association (1917–1918) and later renamed the American National Latvian League (1918–1922); it received little encouragement from the government of Latvia, however, and did not last long.

Latvian-American activities were not centralized until the nationalist refugees arrived after World War II. The postwar period witnessed a proliferation of social, cultural, and professional societies organized along regional, national, and even global lines. Since 1951 the American Latvian Association (Amerikas Latviešu Apvienība) has represented the numerous smaller societies throughout the country to the American public and the U.S. government. The ALA is composed of five bureaus (education, culture, sports, information, and welfare), and its activities include supporting Latvian schools; publishing books, journals, and newsletters; and producing documentary films. The Latvian Cultural Foundation awards prizes annually for outstanding achievements in Latvian art, literature, and science.

Smaller foundations, such as the Latvian Heritage Fund (1968) and the Latvian Fund (1970), also provide support for various cultural pursuits. In addition, Latvian regional organizations have their own theatrical ensembles, Saturday and Sunday Latvian schools, and

choirs; many maintain clubhouses and halls where lectures, concerts, and other cultural activities are held. Other organizations include Daugavas Vanagi, a strongly nationalistic, politically oriented Latvian welfare group, and the Association for the Advancement of Baltic Studies (AABS, 1968), a scholarly society. Numerous other Latvian organizations represent such fields as medicine, law, architecture, and journalism. The American Latvian Relief Fund heads ten or more large credit unions. Peter Lejins (1909–), a criminologist by profession, Uldis Grava (1938–), a publisher, and Ilgvars Spilners (1925–) are among the more prominent recent organizers of the Latvian-American community.

POLITICS

Many of the Latvian immigrants who arrived in the United States after 1905 were political radicals, either socialist or Communist. They participated actively in the American labor movement and in the establishment of the Industrial Workers of the World (IWW) and the American Communist party. There were a number of factions, ranging from anarchist to moderate and nationalist.

The radical press prospered. Socialist journals, published in New York, Boston, and Philadelphia, included the newspapers *Stradnieks* (The Worker, 1906–1919), *Brīvā Tribūna* (Free Tribune, 1907–1908), *Proletārietis* (1914–1917), *Darba Balss* (The Voice of Labor, 1916–1917), and *Amerikas Cīņa* (The Struggle of America, 1926–1935), and the journal *Jaunais Prometējs* (Young Prometheus, 1919). *Brīvība* (Liberty, 1908–1911) was anarchist; the Communists published the newspapers *Rīts* (Morning, 1920–1922), *Strādnieku Rīts* (Workers' Morning, 1923–1935), *Strādnieku Cīņa* (The Struggle of Workers, 1935–1940), and *Amerikas Latvietis* (American Latvian, 1940–1975). Around 250 Latvian Communists left the United States to settle in Soviet Russia between 1917 and 1919, and a number of them eventually held responsible positions in the Bolshevik regime.

For the most part, however, Latvian political movements have been nationalist rather than left wing. Some of the nationalists eventually returned to Latvia to lead its struggle for independence; the most prominent of them was Kārlis Ulmanis (1877–1942), a former instructor at the University of Nebraska who served as the first and last prime minister of Latvia and as its last president.

The postwar refugees left their native land to escape from Nazi occupation and subsequent Soviet domination. They were ardent nationalists, and their nationalistic spirit is still apparent in the Latvian-American movement for restoration of independence for the Baltic states. The Joint Baltic American Committee (f. 1961) functions as a political liaison group between the American Baltic organizations and the U.S. government. Other organizations concerned with Baltic independence are the Committee for a Free Latvia (f. 1951), the globally organized World Association of Free Latvians (f. 1955), the Americans for Congressional Action to Free the Baltic States (f. 1962), and the Baltic Appeal to the United Nations (f. 1966). All but the Washington-based World Association are centered in New York.

Aside from their support of self-determination for the Baltic states, most of the older Latvian Americans are

politically conservative and usually vote for the Republican party. Second- and third-generation Latvian Americans are apt to be more politically moderate or liberal than their parents and grandparents.

In 1930, 60 percent of all foreign-born Latvians were already U.S. citizens, and another 10 percent had filed declarations of intention to be naturalized. Most of the Latvians who reached American shores after World War II cherished the hope, nurtured by the cold war, of eventually returning to their native country. As that hope has faded, however, they have become U.S. citizens. Between 1946 and 1964 a total of 24,699 Latvians were naturalized. By now more than 90 percent of the foreign-born Latvian Americans are citizens.

RELIGION AND CULTURAL LIFE

Most of the early Latvian immigrants were Lutheran or Baptist, but after World War II sizable numbers of Catholics came from the eastern Latvian province of Latgale. Aside from Sieberg's Boston congregation, the first Latvian Lutheran parishes in the United States were founded largely through the efforts of the Reverend Hans Rebane (1863–1911), an Estonian-Latvian missionary whose efforts were supported by the Missouri Lutheran Synod. In 1957, 80 Latvian Lutheran congregations were united in the Federation of Latvian Evangelical Lutheran Churches in America, under the leadership of Archbishop Karlis Kundzins; since 1977, they have been called the Latvian Evangelical Lutheran Church in America, under Archbishop Arnolds Lusis (1908–). There are 12 Latvian Catholic parishes, 6 Baptist congregations, and 2 Greek Orthodox congregations. According to recent statistics, 5 percent of the Latvians do not attend church services at all, 49 percent attend rarely, and 46 percent are regular churchgoers.

Despite long periods of foreign domination, the Latvians managed to maintain a distinct national culture in the homeland, which they brought with them to the United States. Latvian culture combines indigenous elements with Germanic, Scandinavian, and Slavic influences. The folk songs or *dainas*, of which more than a million original verses and variant texts have been collected, constitute its richest cultural treasure. Seemingly simple, yet poetic and richly colored, the dainas reflect Latvia through the ages. As the literary and musical expression of Latvian concepts of life, deity, mores, and events, they also have philosophical and historical value. Latvian art forms and designs, some over 3,000 years old, have been handed down from generation to generation. Latvian arts and crafts find ornamental and practical application in everyday life. The designs are mostly geometric, with a good sense of proportion and color and a rhythmic shaping of line. The Latvian national costumes reflect this sense of style.

The late 19th and early 20th century witnessed the publication of a number of Latvian-language journals, some literary or religious, others consisting of social commentary and satire, but most were short-lived. Hugo Stikhewitz (1876–1966) published seven collections of poetry under the pseudonym Hermit from 1923 to 1935; other writers were John Ozolins-Burtnieks (1894–1959) and Jūlijs Vecozols (1884–1945). The best-known modern writer is Anšlavs Eglītis (1906–), a novelist, playwright, and social satirist. Grāmatu Draugs (Friend of Books) in New York City, the most important Latvian-language publishing house in the United States, has published a semiweekly newspaper, *Laiks* (Time), since 1949. A number of magazines and journals are still published, some in English, including the *Latvian Information Bulletin* (f. 1940) and the *Journal of Baltic Studies* (f. 1970).

One of the very few university graduates among the early Latvian immigrants was Frederic Sander, who became a lecturer at Harvard University and wrote an English primer for Latvian Americans. According to data collected by the U.S. Department of State regarding the educational level of Latvians arriving after World War II, 47 percent had attended a university or college, 35 percent were high-school graduates, 5 percent had trade-school education, and 14 percent had only an elementary-school education.

This high level of education is reflected in the large number of scientists of Latvian origin. Among the earliest of them was August Krastin (1869–1942), an inventor who built one of the first American automobiles in 1896. From 1901 to 1942 his company in Cleveland manufactured gasoline and electric automobiles, refrigerators, farm machines, and electrical appliances. By now there are Latvian-American scientists and scholars in universities, colleges, and scientific institutions throughout the country.

More than 1,000 Latvian Americans are active in academic fields. The Latvian community continues to attach great importance to education and maintains 59 schools, designed to supplement regular public schooling in which instruction is in Latvian. The curriculum covers the language, literature, folklore, art, history, and ethnography of Latvia. There are a number of prominent Latvian-American architects, for example, Gunars Birkerts (1925–), and internationally known artists, including Janis Annus (1935–), Svens Lūkins (1934–), and Ivars Hirss (1931–).

There are at least 65 Latvian choirs and 30 theatrical groups in the United States, 9 ensembles that play the *kokle*, an ancient Latvian musical instrument, and 30 folk-dance groups. Since 1953 six national and ten regional song festivals have been held, each attracting up to 12,000 participants, including 1,500 singers, 600 folk dancers, and numerous other artists. Arts and crafts are exhibited, and concerts and ballets are performed.

The Latvian Americans have taken the opportunities offered by the United States for shelter and work. Although a small group, they have every reason to be proud of their contributions to the nation, particularly in various fields of science and its practical applications.

Bibliography

There are few books or articles on the Latvians in the United States. *The Latvians in America, 1640–1973: A Chronology and Fact Book* (Dobbs Ferry, N.Y., 1974), compiled by Maruta Kārklis, Liga Streips, and Laimonis Streips, is the best available. It should be supplemented by the popular *Latvians in Bicentennial America* (Waverly, Iowa, 1976), compiled by Osvalds Akmentins, and by the following articles: Edgar Anderson, "Latvians Abroad," in *Cross-Road Country Latvia*, Edgar Anderson, ed. (Waverly, Iowa, 1953); Alfreds Bilmanis, "Highlights of Latvian-American Relations," in his *Latvia as an Independent State* (Washington, D.C., 1947), and Joseph S. Roucek, "Latvians in the United States," in Francis J. Brown and Joseph S. Roucek, eds., *One America: The History, Contributions, and Present Problems of Our Racial and National Minorities* (1945; reprint, Westport, Conn., 1970).

The largest collections of materials, books, pamphlets, and primary sources on the Latvian immigration are maintained by the American

Latvian Association in Washington, D.C.; the Latvian Research Institute in New York; the Immigration History Research Center at the University of Minnesota, Minneapolis–St. Paul; Kent State University in Kent, Ohio; and the Hoover Institution on War, Revolution and Peace, Stanford University, in Stanford, Calif.

EDGAR ANDERSON

LEADERSHIP

Leaders may be defined as individuals who exercise decisive influence over others within a context of obligation or common interest. Working from such a broad definition, one can postulate that leadership, like power and authority, is a universal dimension of human society. All peoples arrange themselves into leaders and followers. Yet the importance of leadership varies enormously across the many cultures of mankind. At one end of the scale are tribes without chiefs or even councils of elders. At the other end are despotisms. In the United States leadership has tended toward the more diffuse rather than the more concentrated end of the scale. The high degree of decentralization and specialization in American society have limited the scope of leadership, while popular doubts about the legitimacy of leaders have checked their authority. The same may be said to a greater degree of American ethnic groups. Leaders have been very important at times in the consolidation and maintenance of the nation's ethnic groups, but these groups have rarely recognized any single leader or set of leaders above the local level. Effective central leadership has been a persistent problem for virtually all ethnic groups.

The essential obstacle has been the amorphous character of American society. In its larger configurations—its classes, political parties, and ethnic groups—the society does not reveal cohesive structures. Ethnic groups, with the exception of Indian tribes, lack either a legal definition or a distinct, assured territorial base. Unlike families, cities, or universities, ethnic groups have no encompassing institutional framework through which leaders can control and direct the entire body. The problem may not be acute in particular local settings, where ethnic leaders can frequently develop a stable base. When they reach out to a wider constituency, however, they must contend with the pervasive mobility and the shifting, multiple allegiances that characterize American life.

If an amorphous social structure has tended to weaken and fragment ethnic leadership, it has also given ethnic leaders a special importance. To them in large measure falls the ever-pressing task of defining the group. With certain exceptions, ethnic communities in the United States cannot take their existence for granted, so leaders must clarify what the social structure leaves indistinct or indeterminate. Leaders focus the consciousness of an ethnic group and in doing so make its identity visible.

To highlight the various ways in which ethnic leaders have coped with a fluid society, it is useful to classify them topologically, in the tradition of Kurt Lewin, by looking at the leader's location in relation both to his ethnic community and to the world outside of that community. From this point of view there are three basic situations: (1) received leadership, or leadership *over* an ethnic group, the leader deriving from preceding structures of authority a traditional claim upon the group; (2) internal leadership, or leadership that arises *within* the group and remains there, the leader being rooted in his ethnic group and addressing the external world as its representative and advocate; and (3) projective leadership, or leadership *from* an ethnic group, whereby an individual acquires a following outside of the group with which he or she is identified and thus affects its reputation without being directly subject to its control.

These different situations only begin to suggest the strains, conflicts, and opportunities that challenge those who aspire to leadership. A full account of ethnic leadership would also have to examine carefully the special limitations that massive discrimination has placed on the choices of the leaders of some groups. My emphasis is on tendencies that are generic to ethnic leadership and therefore can be found in varying degrees in groups that have not experienced severe disadvantage as well as those that have.

RECEIVED LEADERSHIP

Many American ethnic communities have been subject in some degree to received leadership during their formative years. Whenever a new ethnic community comes into being under the domination of an existing institution, at least some of the key leaders derive their authority from that institution and work primarily to realize its ends. Received leaders often failed at the outset to maintain control, but in rare instances their hegemony endured for generations.

In the colonial period many immigrants came to America in organized groups led by persons who sought a new field for exercising an authority grounded in the Old World. The tacksmen who brought large bodies of Scottish Highlanders to America in the middle decades of the 18th century provide a notable example. Tacksmen were leaseholders who collected rents and served as lieutenants for the Highland lairds. When the period of private warfare ended in Scotland and rents escalated, some of the tacksmen induced their tenants to follow them to America, hoping to reconstitute the old clan system in the New World, with themselves as chiefs. The hour was too late for that, but former tacksmen with substantial land grants were important in parts of North Carolina and New York as landlords, justices of the peace, and militia captains and in the American Revolution led their obedient followers to fight for the king.

Of the foreign entrepreneurs who brought immigrants to the United States in the 19th century, the most powerfully entrenched were the Chinese merchant-creditors who ruled San Francisco's Chinatown for many decades. Extending a form of organization that had worked well in Southeast Asia, these merchants formed companies or district associations that found jobs for arriving immigrants; from the immigrants' earnings, the merchants eventually repaid the bankers at the Chinese ports who had advanced the passage money. The district associations gained most of their members from specific regions of South China. Each association served as a benevolent society—caring for the sick, sheltering transients, and arbitrating disputes—as well as an employment agency and an all-powerful creditor. Gradually the associations federated into an umbrella organization that was popularly

known after 1862 as the Six Chinese Companies. The headmen of the Six Companies constituted an informal government, whose authority was tacitly acknowledged by civic officials. Thus, in the Chinese-American community a merchant elite acquired a social supremacy that in China itself was reserved for the landed gentry and scholar-officials.

The patterns of leadership that Scottish clansmen and Chinese merchant-creditors transplanted to America were essentially secular. Much more commonly, received leadership was religious, since the traditional institution to which most immigrants felt the deepest loyalty was their church or synagogue. Relatively few immigrants traveled under the direct guidance of a pastor and settled under his care, as did the founders of Germantown, Pa., in 1683 and the Dutch who followed their ministers to Michigan in the 1840s. Over and over again, however, people who came to the United States on their own, in search of economic opportunity, appealed for spiritual leadership to the churches they had left, as soon as they found a new home.

Early settlers necessarily relied on makeshift arrangements for their religious needs. Meeting in saloons or private homes, those who shared a common language and religion resorted to lay preachers or itinerant evangelists, or they joined an established congregation of a more or less related persuasion—but only until a properly qualified pastor arrived from their own country. Some traditional religious leaders gained an unquestioning obedience. The German pastors of the Lutheran Church's Missouri Synod, for example, acquired by the end of the 19th century the paternal authority of the proverbial shepherd over his flock. Often, however, the immigrants proved to be exceedingly indocile charges of the European clergy they had yearned to receive. A spirit of independence, nourished by the circumstances of immigrant life, made for widespread resistance to clerical efforts to impose an Old World discipline. Throughout the 19th century, Catholic laymen of various ethnic antecedents struggled to wrest financial control of their parishes from their priests and bishops. One outcome was the formation in the 1890s of the schismatic Polish National Catholic Church.

Another form of received leadership, quite rare but interesting as an extreme case, was exercised by foreign governments. For a decade before World War I, the prime minister of Hungary supervised a secret program called American Action, which operated through the Hungarian churches in the United States, Catholic and Protestant alike. By influencing ecclesiastical appointments and by subsidizing ethnic schools and newspapers, American Action sought to persuade Hungarians to retain their Hungarian citizenship and to return to their homeland. In contrast to the secrecy of the Hungarian program, the government of Japan during the same period maintained through its consuls in the United States an open control over the first generation of Japanese Americans. In this case the motive was not so much to retain the allegiance of the immigrants as to protect their reputation and status in a country that had declared them ineligible for citizenship. Accordingly, the Japanese consulate general in San Francisco in 1909 organized the Japanese Association of America, to which all resident Japanese were supposed to belong.

The association disciplined the immigrants by controlling their access to certain needed documents; it defended their property rights in American courts and ensured that the leadership of the ethnic community was acquiescent and conformist.

Thus a traditionalist foreign leadership, through economic, religious, or even political connections with the homeland, sometimes imposed itself on an emergent ethnic group. Alternatively, the group might fall under the sway of established American leaders through institutions designed to secure the group's compliance. The Indian reservations, run by government agents and Christian missionaries, are one example, as are the Negro colleges and training institutes that Yankee teachers and missionaries established through the South. Of all the institutions that imposed an external leadership on an American ethnic group, surely the most coercive was plantation slavery. For 200 years white masters wielded over black slaves a control that was both absolute and in some degree paternalistic: so absolute that the slaves could rarely challenge it openly and sufficiently paternalistic (or familylike) that many in both races accepted white leadership of blacks as the natural order.

A primary concern of the external leader was acculturation, because his relation to the ethnic group was precarious and could easily be damaged by a shift in its loyalties. He had to either resist acculturation or control it. The Americans who sought to lead an ethnic community were typically on the side of controlled acculturation. In various ways and degrees, slave owners, Indian agents, missionaries, and white teachers infused into the subordinate group selected habits and values that the host society esteemed. On the other hand, received leaders who operated from bases of authority in Europe or Asia were likely to resist acculturation outright. Fearing that Americanization would undermine religion, family values, and morality, Old World leaders reinforced and perpetuated the immigrants' traditional loyalties.

A received leadership necessarily prevailed whenever the members of an ethnic group were not free to choose their own spokesmen. When that choice existed, received leaders might nonetheless be sustained because of deference, an unquestioning submission to the great ones who had always taken for granted their own right to command. Immigrants from peasant societies often brought such attitudes with them, but habitual deference rarely survived for very long, unless the ethnic group (like the Chinese) was largely cut off from the general American predilection for independence and self-government. Received leadership was usually short-lived and ineffective in ethnic groups that were eligible for American citizenship.

INTERNAL LEADERSHIP

No sharp line separates the received leader from a second major type, the internal leader. Although the latter belonged to his ethnic group more completely, the difference was often one of degree. The internal leader might have received his training abroad, as did immigrant journalists who fled from political repression in their homeland and the many Irish priests who flowed from the seminary at Maynooth to the parishes of the New World. His first experience as a

leader might have been as the organizer of a mutual-aid society in his native village years before he brought his neighbors together in an identical institution in an American city—a sequence Josef Barton has observed widely among Czechs, Italians, and other southeastern Europeans. The continuities between American ethnic groups and their countries of origin usually permitted an internal leadership to evolve easily and imperceptibly from external initiatives.

Whatever the importance of external initiatives, the task of constituting a self-conscious, self-activating body of people fell mostly on leaders who emerged from and with the unformed group. Not every group, of course, needed to be constituted; the peoples who were already established prior to American occupation—notably the Hispanic people of the Southwest, the various Indian tribes, and the Hawaiians—lived within a web of relationships that their leaders needed only to preserve, not create. The Indians had their chiefs; Hawaiians their *alii;* Spanish-speaking peasants their *patrónes.* The vast majority of Americans, however, had been torn loose from organic societies and had to produce new leaders in order to forge new ties with one another.

Security and Services Ordinarily the first task of an internal leadership was to provide some minimal security for individuals and families. In an unstable, unfamiliar milieu the newcomers needed the assurance of familiar symbols, the solace of accustomed rituals and promises. Psychological security was best supplied by religion, and that is why religious congregations stand out so vividly as rallying points of ethnic identity. Building churches and synagogues called forth an initiative on the part of laymen that went far beyond what European circumstances permitted. Thus it was not just the clergy who rose to leadership through religion, but also the many parishioners who launched saints' societies, burial societies, sodalities, singing clubs, and so forth. Under the stimulus of American voluntarism as well as of their own need for security, immigrant congregations teemed with associative activity.

In addition to psychological security, the immigrants sought economic security, at least against the most fearful hazards, illness and death. To that end, even before they built a church, immigrant groups often formed mutual-benefit societies. Each of these societies, numbering perhaps no more than 20 or 30 people at the outset, accumulated a mutual insurance fund from the dues of its members. Often the benefit society became the nucleus for a religious congregation. Others affiliated with labor unions or political parties, but vast numbers functioned as more or less autonomous lodges where people from a particular Old World village could enjoy a continuing sociability. More than any other institution outside the family, these little societies were the infrastructure of the immigrant world in the late 19th and early 20th centuries. The profusion of mutual-benefit societies attests to abundant opportunities for immigrants, many from peasant backgrounds, to exercise leadership during the decades of ethnogenesis.

Still another route to leadership was opened by the immigrants' needs for material services that neither the church nor the benefit society could satisfy, above all for help in getting work, but also for travel arrangements, places to stay, familiar food, means of saving and sending remittances home. To meet those needs, an ethnic middle class sprang up in the immigrant districts of American cities, consisting of labor recruiters (known as *padroni* among the Italians), steamship and travel agents, boarding-house owners, realtors, saloonkeepers and grocers, immigrant bankers, and notary-interpreters. Ordinarily a single individual performed two, three, or more of these functions (he might also be the president of a mutual-benefit society). Such men were respected as the *prominenti,* the self-made men who had gained prestige and influence among their countrymen by serving as intermediaries with the outside world.

Group Solidarity One is struck by the multitude of vehicles—the church, the benefit society, the small business—that were available for gaining and exercising influence in the first phase of internal leadership. The diversity of rival mechanisms and aspirants persisted through subsequent phases as well. After the foundation of a local ethnic community was laid, the second major task of the internal leaders was to forge a group-wide solidarity. People who had thought of themselves as belonging to a particular village or province acquired a consciousness of a common national origin. But consolidation failed in almost every case to produce a unified leadership. A single individual has never succeeded in speaking for an entire nationality group; a single organization has rarely if ever gained control of a whole group. Paradoxically, however, the rivalries between competing leaders were a continual stimulus to ethnic nationalism.

The effort to build group-wide solidarity brought into being an array of new organizations. Some of these appealed exclusively to a professional and middle-class elite, while others sought a mass membership. Many of the latter were federations of local benefit societies, often reorganized as fraternal orders with elaborate costumes and rituals. The larger the membership base, the stronger and safer an order's program of benefits was likely to be, and from the 1880s to the 1920s the expanding ethnic fraternal organizations competed keenly for members. Rarely, however, did a single fraternal body gain the preeminence within its own group that B'nai B'rith (f. 1843) won among Jews. In most ethnic groups two or more federations divided the field, the divisions running along religious, political, or class lines.

No less important than the ethnic societies in stimulating group consciousness was the ethnic press; every openly organized element had its organ. The outreach of the ethnic churches, of the federations, of the labor unions, and of the principal political factions depended critically on their newspapers. Even a modest-size group such as the Swedish Americans produced altogether some 1,200 newspapers. The result was a cacophony of voices, in which appeals to group pride mingled with continual denunciations of rival spokesmen for the group. Thus the ethnic journalists had a double effect. On one hand they enlarged the circumference of their readers' loyalties and mobilized mass support for key demands. (One outstanding example was the nationwide campaign launched by Robert Vann's *Pittsburgh Courier* in 1938 for integration of the U.S. armed forces.) On the other hand the endless wrangling between competing editors advertised the divisions within ethnic groups and may have awakened in many readers a skepticism about the claims of all leaders.

Defense of Homeland The struggle to mobilize a

broadly based ethnic consciousness activated the third major task of internal leadership: defense of the homeland. In many if not most American ethnic groups no other issue stirred such passionate feeling, and different perceptions of the problem of the homeland produced especially bitter divisions within groups. Witness the furious conflict between Venizelists and Royalists in the Greek-American community in 1915–1917 and the enmity between Zionists and their opponents among American Jews in the same period. On the other hand, the cause of the homeland could lift an ethnic group to a level of unity that no other issue could. For all groups with a distinctive homeland, this issue presented the critical test of ethnic leadership.

The power of the homeland issue in moving and inspiring an immigrant people was first demonstrated on a large scale by the Irish. Their yearnings for Ireland's independence from Britain shaped the belligerent style and colored the exuberant rhetoric of Irish-American leaders throughout the 19th century. Since 1948 American Jews have taken the place of the Irish as the chief ethnic influence on American foreign policy. Having composed their earlier differences over Zionism, Jews have attained, as champions of Israel, a degree of unity and political power they never enjoyed before.

In recent years an aggressive defense of the homeland has proved highly effective for American Indian tribal leaders, and to a lesser extent it has revitalized the leadership of the Hawaiians. When such a policy runs athwart a national consensus, however, it carries heavy risks. Before U.S. entry into World War I, many German-American spokesmen championed the fatherland with a shrillness that obscured the steady erosion, through assimilation, of the German ethnic community in the United States. Thus the leaders, although unrepresentative, bore some of the responsibility for provoking the extravagant fear of divided loyalties that lashed the entire German-American community in 1917. A wave of anti-German feeling destroyed the principal ethnic federation, the National German-American Alliance, and left any national leadership among the group fatally shattered and discredited.

Group Advancement A fourth and final task of internal leadership is advancement of the group within the wider society. Like the early concern of internal leaders for establishing a secure base in the United States, group advancement has both a psychological and a material aspect. On the psychological side, advancement has meant a pursuit of status. Here the immediate gains are relatively intangible, having to do with the individual's image of himself and his group. Status goals call for attacking discrimination, widening opportunities, and attaining recognition and visibility. On the material side, group advancement has pointed toward welfare goals: the needs of deprived members of the group for better services and housing, care for the sick and aged, safe streets, and a living wage. The distinction between status goals and welfare goals, proposed by James Q. Wilson to explain the strategies of Negro leaders, may be applied to many other ethnic groups as well.

Status goals appeal especially to the most ambitious and socially mobile elements in an ethnic group. Such people take the lead in forming cultural societies that promote the more dignified aspects of an ethnic group's heritage. It is revealing, for example, that the illustrious

Milwaukee Musical Society, which was given an English name in order to attract some Yankee supporters, was founded in 1850 by a recently arrived German merchant, Theodore Wettstein, soon after he had successfully flouted the egalitarian ways of the early German community in Milwaukee by organizing a formal and exclusive ball for the more cultivated of his compatriots. Another type of cultural society that reflects the social aspirations of ethnic elites is the historical association: the American Jewish Historical Society (1892), the American Irish Historical Society (1897), the Association for the Study of Negro Life and History (1915), the American Indian Historical Society (1964), the American Italian Historical Association (1966), to name just a few. Nevertheless, status goals are not necessarily elitist, in spite of their special attraction for elites. While status claims may divide an ethnic group along class lines, they may also unify it if the entire group experiences humiliation. The unparalleled moral authority of Frederick Douglass (c. 1817–1895) in the mid-19th century and of Martin Luther King (1929–1968) a century later flowed from their espousal of a status revolution desired by every technically free black person.

For ethnic groups long dominated by native whites, throwing off the incubus of received leadership has been a crucial status objective. Among blacks even the struggle against slavery left a persisting dependence on whites: on the white philanthropists who dominated the early executive boards of the National Association for the Advancement of Colored People (NAACP, 1910), the National Urban League (1910), and other race-improvement organizations; on the white politicians who gave their black clients access to public offices, on the memory of a white hero like John Brown (1800–1859), who never consulted the blacks he tried to revolutionize. A tendency of blacks to internalize white leadership by choosing their own spokesmen from those with lighter skin suggests how deep the psychology of dependence went. It received one kind of challenge in the 1920s from Marcus Garvey's (1887–1940) flamboyant, ghetto-inspired celebration of blackness and another kind from the light-skinned intellectual W.E.B. DuBois (1868–1963), who advocated racial solidarity for American blacks under their own uncompromised leaders; he broke with the NAACP in 1934 when it refused to alter its course and structure. By the 1970s black leadership (including that of the NAACP) was, in cultural if not in phenotypical terms, effectively black.

Yet the pursuit of better status has required in all ethnic groups something more than a posture of self-respect. It has also required sufficient acculturation to participate in the wider opportunities of American life. Ethnic leaders have had to consider the needs of their people for mastery of the English language, for citizenship and civic activity, for thrifty habits, personal initiative, and suitable economic skills. The tug of these needs often raises a painful dilemma; because acculturation dilutes the ethnic heritage, will it not sooner or later obliterate the ethnic community? Some leaders have thought so and have therefore rejected the goal of success on American terms, instead choosing separate development, exodus, or resistance. Adopted by certain black radicals in times of despair, this position has probably been most strongly and continuously held

among American Indians. Ever since white authorities brought great pressure to bear on Indians to adapt to European civilization, the fundamental split among Indian leaders has been between the "friendlies" or "progressives," who accept in some measure the religions and ways of the whites, and the "hostiles" or "traditionalists," who cling to the old ways or try to resurrect them.

Indian traditionalists and the small minority of black nationalists point up by contrast the extent to which the vast majority of ethnic leaders have chosen to compromise on the dilemma of assimilation. Characteristically the internal leaders of American ethnic groups have embraced wider values and applauded American institutions while upholding a limited, nonexclusive ethnic community designed to supplement and enrich the larger society. In general the leaders have served a mediating function, weaving a web of ethnic mutuality on one hand and encouraging their people to reach beyond it on the other. The most stubborn traditionalists are likely to be found in the depressed and isolated depths of an ethnic group, not among its leaders.

The other side of group advancement, analytically distinct from aspirations of status, has to do with welfare needs. In this respect the quasi-assimilationist role of the ethnic leader may not at first stand out so clearly, because most ethnic groups have initially called upon their own resources to relieve the hardships of their neediest countrymen. In the 1840s Bishop John Hughes (1797–1864) built Catholic hospitals and asylums in New York to keep destitute immigrants out of public institutions; about the same time Jews began to create a great complex of welfare facilities. In the long run, the Jewish engagement in welfare has proved exceptional; no other immigrant or minority group has had either the wealth or the ardent philanthropic tradition necessary to manage its own welfare problems, and even the Jews felt overwhelmed by the mass immigration of the late 19th century.

Sooner or later, welfare objectives, like status objectives, have compelled ethnic leaders to turn outward to the larger society to seek accommodations. Whereas gains in status are won on diverse fronts by varied techniques, all welfare claims on the public purse must be negotiated through the medium of politics. The Irish quickly mastered local politics in the United States by a remarkable combination of organizational loyalty, belligerence, and conviviality. Well before the first Irish mayors of New York and Boston were elected in the 1880s, Irish bosses were demonstrating how the political system could yield jobs, food baskets, police protection, and a host of favors. In the 20th century, when welfare programs acquired a more systematic character, ethnic-based politicians like Alfred E. Smith (1873–1944) and Robert F. Wagner (1877–1953) played a large part in passing the legislation.

Yet modern welfare politics also offers an escape from ethnicity. Very few politicians of any stature have so homogeneous a constituency that they can afford to represent just a single group. Through welfare policies that serve broad economic categories, political leaders can generalize their appeal and modulate the clash of competing ethnic interests. Thus the path of welfare politics, perhaps even more than the roads to higher status, draws the ethnic leader toward the margins of his group—and perhaps out of it altogether.

PROJECTIVE LEADERSHIP

Movement out of the ethnic group is, in a still more obvious sense, the underlying thrust of the third type of leadership. Projective leaders are individuals who win their initial recognition outside the limits of the group that nurtured them. In some cases they may feel little identification with that group, but it canonizes them as symbols of its character and submits them as evidence of the group's "contributions" to American civilization. Such leaders are the culture-heroes of American ethnicity. They can ordinarily serve as models for the young because their deeds, while fulfilling conventional expectations, are ascribed in some stereotypical way to their ethnic heritage. Projective leaders repair the self-esteem of groups whose image of themselves has been damaged, and to groups whose culture is fading, projective leaders offer a promise of survival within the mainstream of a multiethnic United States.

Styles in projective leadership have changed. In the 19th and early 20th centuries military heroes, statesmen, businessmen, and inventors loomed large: among the Germans, John Jacob Astor (1763–1848), richest man of his time, and Carl Schurz (1829–1906), Civil War general, U.S. senator, and cabinet official; for the Irish, the consummate diplomat James Cardinal Gibbons (1834–1921) and the "Bonanza King" John Mackay (1831–1902), who parlayed a mining fortune into trans-Atlantic cables and telegraph lines; from the Indians, the peacemakers Pocahontas (1595–1617) and Hiawatha (c. 1570), and the noble warrior Chief Joseph (c. 1840–1904); among Jews, Haym Salomon (c. 1740–1785), who allegedly financed the American Revolution; for southern and eastern Europeans, the electrical inventor Nikola Tesla (1856–1943). For blacks the towering figure was Booker T. Washington (1856–1915), educator and self-made man, who translated the influence he gained among whites into a remarkable career of internal leadership as well.

In recent decades the heroes of war and business have faded, and the idols of sports, the theater, and the arts and sciences have come forward. Nobel Prize-winning physicists such as Albert Einstein (1879–1955) and Enrico Fermi (1901–1954); writers like Saul Bellow (1915–), N. Scott Momaday (1934–), and Alex Haley (1921–); musicians like Duke Ellington (1899–1974); and athletes of many origins have provided a striking proportion of the models of ethnic Americanism in the middle decades of the 20th century.

THE PROFESSIONALIZATION OF LEADERSHIP

Whatever the field of activity, however, heroes have shrunk in our time. Neither projective nor internal leaders now possess the charisma that the best of them had in the early 20th century. We have no Cardinal Gibbons, no rabbi whose voice carries like that of Stephen S. Wise (1874–1949), no Martin Luther King, perhaps the last of the charismatic leaders. Counterbalancing the decline of vivid, individual leadership is a growing professionalization and bureaucratization. The rise of professionally trained administrators within the major ethnic organizations is making leadership a more anonymous and collective function, with the leaders becoming submerged in their organizations. At the same time

this development seems likely to contribute to the stability and permanence of ethnic groups.

The professional is distinguished not by passion, though he may have that incidentally, but rather by technical competence gained through advanced education. The roots of ethnic professionalism go back to the early years of the 20th century when the National Urban League concerned itself with training black social workers and delivering welfare services in the northern ghettos. The league insisted from the outset that its local affiliates be led by paid professionals.

Professionalization has been carried furthest by American Jews, however. The rabbinate, though confined in its sphere, has been professionalized, and as the great secular apparatus of local Jewish federations, community centers, defense organizations, and educational institutions has expanded, full-time executives supervising staffs of specialists have assumed much of the initiative formerly exercised by wealthy philanthropists. A similar professionalism is spreading through organizations like the National Association of Black Social Workers (f. 1968), the Association of Arab-American University Graduates (f. 1967), and the Italian American Foundation (f. 1976). Notable also are the expanding programs of academic research and publication sponsored by the Polish Institute of Arts and Sciences of America (f. 1942) and the American Hungarian Foundation (f. 1954). More generally, one observes throughout American society the increasing prominence of nonwhites in medicine, law, and public administration.

On the whole, ethnic professionals seem to offer a relatively practical, accommodating style of leadership rather than a highly militant or ideological style. Enjoying widening success and esteem, they are little inclined to jeopardize their improving social status. In general their commitment is to provide effective services while minimizing internal conflict within their groups. In some instances (as among Puerto Ricans and blacks in New York City), a common professionalism has enabled leaders of antagonistic groups to maintain communication and avoid open hostilities. Under the leadership of such "organization men," ethnic groups may be expected more and more to conduct their affairs with the skill and calculation that govern other major interest groups in America. Possibly the distinctions between ethnic groups and other kinds of interest groups may become, in our increasingly professionalized and bureaucratized world, less and less clear.

Bibliography

John Higham, ed., *Ethnic Leadership in America* (Baltimore, 1977), contains essays on Jews by Nathan Glazer, on Afro-Americans by Nathan I. Huggins, on American Indians by Robert F. Berkhofer, Jr., on Germans by Frederick Luebke, on Japanese by Roger Daniels, on eastern and southern Europeans by Josef J. Barton, on Irish by Robert D. Cross, and on Hawaiians by John Higham. Kurt Lewin discusses "The Problem of Minority Leadership" in *Resolving Social Conflicts: Selected Papers on Group Dynamics* (New York, 1948). Gunnar Myrdal, *An American Dilemma* (New York, 1944), pt. 9, "Leadership and Concerted Action," develops in rich detail the classic distinction between protest leadership and accommodating leadership. James Q. Wilson, *Negro Politics: The Search for Leadership* (Glencoe, Ill., 1960) is a tough-minded and influential study of Chicago. Everett Carll Ladd, Jr., *Negro Political Leadership in the South* (Ithaca, N.Y., 1966), confirms and further develops Wilson's thesis in a very different setting. Melvin G. Holli and Peter d'A. Jones, eds., *The Ethnic Frontier: Essays in the History of Group Survival in Chicago and the Midwest* (Grand Rapids, Mich., 1977), contains several relevant essays, especially Victor Greene, "'Becoming American': The Role of Ethnic Leaders—Swedes, Poles, Italians, Jews." Daniel J. Elazar, *Community and Polity: The Organizational Dynamics of American Jewry* (Philadelphia, 1976), is a penetrating analysis of the structure of internal leadership. Nicholas Tavuchis, *Pastors and Immigrants: The Role of a Religious Elite in the Absorption of Norwegian Immigrants* (The Hague, 1963), is a sociological study of received leadership in the mid-19th century. Timothy L. Smith, "Lay Initiative in the Religious Life of American Immigrants, 1880–1950," in *Anonymous Americans: Explorations in Nineteenth-Century Social History*, Tamara K. Hareven, ed. (Englewood Cliffs, N.J., 1971), should be compared with Alan Graebner, *Uncertain Saints: The Laity in the Lutheran Church–Missouri Synod, 1900–1970* (Westport, Conn., 1975).

JOHN HIGHAM

LEBANESE: *see* ARABS

LEMKIANS: *see* CARPATHO-RUSYNS; UKRAINIANS

LIBYANS: *see* ARABS

LITERATURE AND ETHNICITY

THE ROOTS OF ETHNICITY: ETYMOLOGY AND DEFINITIONS

On October 9, 1854, Nathaniel Hawthorne, then serving as the American consul to Liverpool, made a curious entry in his journal: "My ancestor left England in 1635. I return in 1853. I sometimes feel as if I myself had been absent these two hundred and eighteen years." During his years in England, Hawthorne became fascinated by the idea of tracing his roots, made genealogical enquiries, and was hopeful of finding "a gravestone in one of these old churchyards, with my own name upon it; although for myself, I should wish to be buried in America. The graves are too devilish damp here."

Hawthorne's search for genealogical facts remained fruitless, but his literary curiosity was intensified by his inability to trace his real ancestors. Ready to embrace an imaginary ancestry, he was intrigued by the legend of a bloody footmark, which a 16th-century clergyman, George Marsh, had miraculously left on the stone pavement of Smithills Hall in Lancashire. When martyr Marsh was arrested, he "stamped his foot in earnest protest against the injustice with which he was treated. Blood issued from his foot, which slid along the stone pavement of the hall, leaving a long footmark printed in blood; and there it remained ever since, in spite of the scrubbings of all after generations." *The Ancestral Footstep*, one of Hawthorne's fragmentary attempts at creating an English-American romance, is an excellent image for Hawthorne's sense of what is now known as "ethnicity." It refers to a specific tradition, born out of protest against another tradition; it is as thick as blood; and it defies "scrubbing" descendants. It is embedded in myth and invites faith rather than critical scrutiny. Hawthorne reasons: "Of course, it is all humbug—a darker vein cropping up through the gray flag-stone," but concludes that "the legend is a good one."

The dark-brown stain of the footprint also defied Hawthorne's endeavors to use it as an emblematic center of a novel. Despite numerous efforts, he could not make the legend functional in the story of an American's return to his Old World roots. Hawthorne tried to make the American the "missing heir" of the English

manor house, but realized that an English title would compromise the hero's Americanness. Hawthorne then changed the plot and made the English inheritance invalid and unreal, thus making ethnicity imaginary, but again he ran into new problems. On the one hand, the English manor house represented for Hawthorne the structured social life Americans had left behind in the Old World. On the other hand, it was the doomed shell of a class structure that had left its bloody footprint on the pavement of time.

In another unfinished romance, *Septimius Felton*, Hawthorne returned to the bloody footmark, but sketched a different American protagonist with a "wild genealogy," a descendant of an old witch on one side and "an Indian prophet and powwow" on the other. This strange and exceptional man had "brooded upon the legends that clung around his line, following his ancestry, not only to the English universities, but into the wild forest, and into hell itself . . . His mind and character had a savage and fiendish strain, intermixed with its Puritan characteristics." But this multiethnic prototypical American carried Hawthorne no further than did his imaginary New England descendant of martyr Marsh. The author could not finish the tale of *The Ancestral Footstep.* Hawthorne's love-hate for his ancestors, his understanding of the "humbug" of "good" genealogical legends, and finally, his difficulties in finding a precise literary use of "ethnicity" are indicative of a persistent problem in American literature and culture. The memory of diverse pre-American pasts has instilled a pervasive sense of "ethnicity" into the minds and imaginations of American writers.

If American culture symbolizes man's entry into fragmented modernity, "ethnicity" functions as a formidable expression of a countervailing yearning for history and community. The tension between these forces is a persistent theme in American literature. Tocqueville described American society as one "which comprises all the nations of the world—English, French, German: people differing from one another in language, in beliefs, in opinions; in a word a society possessing no roots, no memories, no prejudices, no routine, no common ideas, no national character," and inquired, "What is the connecting link?" More than a century later Margaret Mead concluded that "however many generations we may actually boast of in this country, however real our lack of ties in the old world may be, we are all third generation, our European ancestry tucked away and half forgotten, the recent steps in our wanderings over America immortalized and over-emphasized." Ethnicity as a tenuous ancestry and as the interplay of different ancestries may be the most crucial aspect of the American national character.

The word "ethnicity" itself has an interesting past with etymological contexts of its own. In the modern sense of "differentiation based on nationality, race, religion, or language," "ethnicity" is an Americanism, first used in 1941 in W. Lloyd Warner's *Yankee City Series* as one category—along with age, sex, and religion—that separates "the individual from some classes of individuals and identifies him with others." In 1953 David Riesman extended the dimensions of the word "ethnicity" in a famous *American Scholar* debate about McCarthyism. Riesman suggested that the struggle between "ethnicity" and modernity was at the root of the

problem: "There is a tendency for the older 'class struggles,' rooted in clear hierarchical antagonisms, to be replaced by a new sort of warfare: the groups who, by reason of rural or small-town location, ethnicity, or other parochialism, feel threatened by the better educated upper-middle-class people (though often less wealthy and politically powerful) who follow or create the modern movements in science, art, literature, and opinion generally." Riesman furthermore argued that the shift from class to ethnicity in America created outlets for fears and hatreds of Indians, Mexicans, and other ethnic groups, but that ethnic diversity and regional and religious pluralism tended to confine the dangerous potential of a fanatical fascist leader to "his" ethnic group or section. Whereas Warner did not always include the descendants of English migrants under the term "ethnicity," Riesman applied it to *all* Americans, denying the validity of "ethnicity minus one."

"Ethnicity" is, of course, derived from the older adjective and noun, "ethnic," which in turn goes back to a Greek root comprising the word field "nation" and "heathen." The word *ethnikos* was thus used in the Greek Bible to render the Hebrew *goyim* (non-Israelites, Gentiles). In the Christianized context of the English language, the word "ethnic" (sometimes spelled "hethnic") recurred, from the 14th through the 19th centuries, in the sense of "pagan, heathen, non-Christian." Only in the mid-19th century did the more familiar meaning of "ethnic" as "peculiar to a race or nation" reemerge. However, the English language has retained the memory of "ethnic" as "heathen," often secularized in the sense of ethnic as "other," as "nonstandard," or, in the United States, as somehow "un-American." This connotation gives the opposition of "ethnic" and "American" the additional religious dimension of the contrast between "heathens" and "chosen people." Therefore, the relationship between "ethnicity" and "American identity" parallels that of "heathenish superstition" and "true religion," and it is in the sense of "heathendom" that the word ethnicity was once recorded in 1772. But this instance is described as obsolete and rare in the *Oxford English Dictionary.*

"*Ethnics*"—originally just "people"—are etymologically the "others," "they" as opposed to "us." "Ethnicity" as "otherness" refers to self-definitions of one group of people through an opposition against other groups: we are not like them, they are not like us. Puritans liked to distinguish their own religious practice from heathenish customs. In 1702 Cotton Mather wrote that the "custom of preaching at funerals may seem ethnical in origin."

The negative separation from heathens has had its counterpart in a more or less hidden envy and admiration for the "other," which reached a high point with romantic racialism in the mid-19th century. Thus, Harriet Beecher Stowe's *Uncle Tom's Cabin* (1852) expostulated that Negroes make better Christians than whites. The Anglo-Saxons, on the other hand, a "cool, logical, and practical" race, should remember that God gave the Bible "to them in the fervent language and with the glowing imagery of the more susceptible and passionate Oriental races." And in one of James Fenimore Cooper's last novels, *The Oak Openings* (1858), the Indians are "the chosen people of the Great Spirit." Frank Forrester (William H. Herbert) wrote of the slave

woman Tituba, in *The Fair Puritan, an Historical Romance of the Days of Witchcraft* (1844–1845), that there was "more of the true, the lowly, and the grateful spirit of the Christian, in that poor, overtasked, despised, scourged heathen, than in her haughty master." Similarly, in more recent times, Jack Kerouac and Norman Mailer have viewed blacks and Mexicans as more truly "American" than whites.

Ethnicity as otherness evoked disparagement and emulation in American writing. In order to attain full selfhood one has to experience otherness; and in that sense, ethnicity is not only in others but also in ourselves. Perhaps a latent fascination with the other in ourselves may account for the great popularity of autobiographical narratives of conversions from heretic to true believer, from criminal to social hero, or from ethnic to American. The affinities of ethnicity and heathendom are focused most clearly in conversion stories. Mary Antin's immigrant autobiography, *The Promised Land* (1912), begins: "I was born, I have lived, and I have been made over. Is it not time to write my life's story? I am just as much out of the way as if I were dead, for I am absolutely other than the person whose story I have to tell." It is obvious that the imagery of processive change, of a transformation from a pre-American past to an American identity—Edward Steiner's *From Alien to Citizen* (1914) or Michael Pupin's *From Immigrant to Inventor* (1923)—is patterned on the symbolism of religious conversions. There is a heathenish dimension to the past, to *any* past, in American literature; and a sacred quality to the future in America. American writers of the most diverse ancestries perceived America in religious terms, whether they sided with the saving grace of an American future ("Reborn in the Promised Land!") or with the adversary ethnicity of a "heathenish" past ("A Curse Upon Columbus!").

Horace Bushnell instructed his parishioners in 1859 that regeneration is "the naturalization of a soul in the kingdom of heaven" and thus related the process of becoming a true Christian with that of becoming an American. In 1873, Chamberlain Cummings preached that not only the "others" must be regenerated, or "naturalized," but that Jew *and* Gentile, Christian and heathen must be born again. If the completion of Cummings's metaphor means that all Americans, whether immigrant or native-born, have to be naturalized in order to become true Americans, then this expanded use of the idea of a rebirth anticipated the rhetoric of the recent ethnic "revival"; however, in the 1960s the relationship of ethnicity and American identity was inverted. Traditionally, the struggle was toward a true Christian, or later, a truly American identity; now many Americans yearn for an *ethnic* identity. Ethnicity has been transformed from a heathenish liability into a sacred asset, from a trait to be overcome in a conversion and rebirth experience to an identity to be achieved through yet another regeneration. The rhetoric of ethnicity thus comes out of the tradition of American revivalism and awakenings: American literature is a rich repository of the footprints of ethnicity. American writers from Cotton Mather to Richard Wright, from Charles Brockden Brown to Pietro di Donato, from William Faulkner to Hisaye Yamamoto have developed such a systematic religious symbolism of ethnicity and American identity that American literature as a whole can be read as the ancestral footstep or coded hieroglyph of ethnic group life of the past and ethnic tensions in the present.

In this sense, "literature and ethnicity" in America refers to nothing less than the whole range of American culture, from classics to commercials, from 17th-century migrants' letters (recently collected and edited by Everett Emerson) to 19th- and 20th-century black folk rhetoric (definitively analyzed in Lawrence Levine's *Black Culture and Black Consciousness*, 1977), from the first stage Yankee and ancestor of "Uncle Sam" in Royall Tyler's *The Contrast* (1787) to the first Ibsen productions on Scandinavian and Yiddish stages in America, from *Uncle Tom's Cabin* to Dr. Fu Man Chu serial movies; from Japanese-American detention-camp newspaper editorials to Mutt and Jeff and the Katzenjammer Kids; from T.S. Eliot to T.A. Daly; from *The Birth of a Nation* to *Roots*; from the *Bay Psalm Book* to Rhymin' Paul Simon. In his introduction to *The Uprooted* (1951), Oscar Handlin made the famous statement: "Once I thought to write a history of the immigrants in America. Then I discovered that the immigrants *were* American history." Analogously, one may say that ethnic literature *is* American literature.

Ethnicity is a pervasive theme in all American literature, whether in the shape of ethnicity as ancestry or ethnicity as diversity. The relationship of an American identity with pre-American pasts, the interaction of people with different pre-American pasts, and the emergence of an American character are among the central themes of American writing. And the very forms of American literature are also partly shaped by the forces of "ethnicity," from the first emergence of Americanized genres to the highest achievements of the American Renaissance, from the opposition of "romance" and "novel" to the rise of modernism and proletarian writing, from the growth of a mass culture to the literature of alienation and to the writings of the recent ethnic revival.

PROMISED LAND AND MELTING POT: TYPOLOGY AND ETHNICITY

The most important source of literary ethnicity in North America is in the application of biblical images to the colonists' new experiences. Biblical analogies to the drama of seafaring and settling in new worlds are common in colonial literatures; in Puritan New England, however, a systematic religious symbology was applied to the transatlantic crossing—a theme of primary importance in American literature—and to a New World consciousness. The religious thought of 17th-century New England was thus an important source of the most widespread literary treatments of American ethnicity. Especially that aspect of Protestant theology known as typology has influenced diverse ethnic literary traditions in America.

While traditional Christian typological exegesis was restricted to an interpretation of Old Testament characters and events as "types" that foreshadowed the redemptive history of the New Testament, Puritan typology related the secular history of the American colonists to biblical types. American writing from the 17th to the 20th centuries abounds with characters who, in Sacvan Bercovitch's phrase, reveal the "Puritan origins

of the American self" and who appear to be "based on fixed models, of which the most important are Adam and Christ." The events of early American history were, with the help of typology, rhetorically transformed into the biblical drama, as New Englanders interpreted their transatlantic voyage as a New Exodus, their mission as an Errand into the Wilderness, and their role as that of a New Israel. American literature is exceptionally religious in its imagery; and this is true for mainstream as well as for minority writers. These anomalous religious tendencies advanced by the literature of a modern, postrevolutionary, bourgeois culture which so often invokes the ideals of the Enlightenment were ironically reinforced by the fact of immigration.

The continuous history of immigration strengthened the typological imagination in America. Marcus Lee Hansen wrote about the "process of Puritanization" among immigrant groups when he observed how familiar the records of 17th-century Massachusetts sounded to a historian of the 19th-century immigration. The potential divisiveness of a multiethnic culture could be softened by a widespread acceptance of a modified typological framework for the American literary imagination. Roman Catholic, Jewish, and continental Protestant forms of worship had little in common with Puritan theology; yet the participants of the New Immigration, along with Afro-Americans, share a surprising concern with typology in their writings.

Among the most prevalent typological elements are the imagery of a continued exodus from Egyptian–Old World bondage to the shores of an American Promised Land, the creation of American protagonists as Adamic and Christic figures, and the related notion of the welding of an American "new man." The image of the New Exodus provides a sacral meaning to a secular migration. In the view of Puritan ministers in New England, God had carried the first settlers "by a mighty hand, and an out-stretched arm, over a sea greater than the Red Sea." Cotton Mather described both William Bradford and John Winthrop as a "new Moses"; and according to Winthrop's famous dictum, New England was the biblical "Citty vpon a Hill." Following the Book of Revelation, colonists viewed America as a typological "new Jerusalem" and a "new Canaan," an association which remained powerful and alive in New England place names as well as in American literature.

Freneau and Brackenridge's "Poem, On the Rising Glory of America" (1771) views America typologically: "A Canaan here,/Another Canaan shall excel the old." In Timothy Dwight's patriotic poem, *The Conquest of Canaan* (1785), the motif of the New World as a "last retreat for poor, oppress'd mankind" is part of a providential view of the history of America as the history of fulfillment: "And a new Moses lifts the daring wing,/Through trackless seas, an unknown flight explores,/And hails a new Canaan's promis'd shores." It is no exaggeration to say that the exodus is one of America's central symbols. When the choice of an official seal for the United States was discussed in 1776, Franklin suggested as the device "Moses lifting up his wand and dividing the Red Sea while Pharaoh was overwhelmed by its waters, with the motto, 'Rebellion to tyrants is obedience to God'"; and "Jefferson proposed the children of Israel in the wilderness 'led by a cloud by day and a pillar of fire at night.'" The eagle that was used for the seal is not just the classical emblem, but also the eagle of Revelation (12:13–17), an image of exodus and emigration.

Isaac Mitchell's novel, *The Asylum* (1811), again viewed America as a promised land and as a haven for the oppressed: "The new land is the poor man's Canaan; to him it is a land flowing with milk and honey." The belief in America as a promised land for what Emma Lazarus called the "huddled masses" and the "wretched refuse" (in her Statue of Liberty poem, "The New Colossus") may reflect the popularity of the exodus theme in the literature of non-English immigrants to America; and the association of the exodus with a deliverance from slavery may explain the widespread use of this theme in Afro-American writing. The typological adaptation of the second book of Moses to varieties of secular migrations remains a characteristic trait of American literature.

Phillis Wheatley, for example, who had been captured and enslaved in Senegal and sold to a Boston tailor in 1761, paradoxically described her own enslavement as a typological deliverance from Egypt, in the poem "To the University of Cambridge, in New England." Absorbing the American rhetoric, she also claimed a full American identity as a Christian in "On Being Brought from Africa to America" and enjoined her compatriots: "Remember, Christians, Negroes black as Cain/May be refined, and join the angelic train." Similarly, Mary Antin, in *The Promised Land*, took a position of apparent self-effacement only to proudly proclaim a sense of equality. Antin continued the portraiture of America as a New Canaan for oppressed immigrants, while leaving no doubt that the metaphor of the promised land was especially suited to Jewish immigrants, whom she all but equated with the Pilgrim Fathers in *They Who Knock at Our Gates* (1914).

The pervasive adaptation of a typological view of America also reflected a deeper need for a spiritualization of collective experiences. To see a journey as a spiritual pilgrimage was, moreover, part of the cultural background of many people who became Americans. The very titles of ethnic books often suggest their affinities to the exodus theme: Sholem Asch, *Uncle Moses* (1918); Stoyan Christowe, *My American Pilgrimage* (1947); Margaret Marchand, *Pilgrims on the Earth* (1940); Chaim Potok, *The Chosen* (1968); Mario Puzo, *The Fortunate Pilgrim* (1965); Claude Brown, *Manchild in the Promised Land* (1965); Robert Laxalt, *Sweet Promised Land* (1957), or Martin Wendell Odland, *The New Canaan* (1933).

The rhetoric of the New Exodus also permitted writers to treat the providential deliverance as a continual process. Thus, the westward movement, especially across the prairie, is often compared with the exodus; and in James Fenimore Cooper's *The Prairie* (1827) or in Ole E. Rølvaag's *Giants in the Earth* (1927), the prairie becomes a new Atlantic Ocean and a typological extension of the Red Sea. The Book of Mormon similarly extended the exodus theme westward; but the patterns established by the Puritan settlers of the 17th century found even more amazing applications to other migrations. In much black literature, the "promised land" was not Phillis Wheatley's America, but a transcendental realm of true liberty, somewhere "over Jordan" as the spiritual "Deep River" suggests. In some slave nar-

ratives, "that promised land . . . where all is peace" became equated with the North; in other stories, it could mean Canada or Africa. Following the North Star had a nautical and a messianic connotation in writings that abounded in descriptions of slaveholders as Pharaohs, or the South as Egypt. Even America's most ardent critics resorted to the exodus–promised land theme and simply inverted its use by casting the United States as Egypt. When the escaped slave, George Harris, toward the end of Harriet Beecher Stowe's *Uncle Tom's Cabin* (1852) outlines his plans for a "new enterprise," the colonization in Africa, his pioneer spirit is expressed in Winthrop's rhetoric: "As a Christian patriot . . . I go to *my country*,—my chosen, my glorious Africa!"

In *The Condition, Elevation, Emigration and Destiny of The Colored People of the United States* (1852), Martin Robison Delany, a radical 19th-century black nationalist, denounced the Liberian colonization plans in the strongest terms as an expression of white Americans "to get rid of us." Delany adapted typological rhetoric to his own plans for a black nation in Central or South America, however: "That the continent of America seems to have been designed by Providence as an asylum for all the various nations in the world, is very apparent." Facing the problem of the aboriginal Americans as owners of the land, he noted the relative "consanguinity" of Africans and Indians as opposed to Europeans and used the myth of a lost African tribe in central America—a remnant of the Carthaginian expedition—in order to justify his colonization scheme.

In the 20th century, Marcus Garvey and Elijah Muhammad adapted the chosen-people theme to an Afro-American sense of mission; Martin Luther King consciously cast himself as a Black Moses in his famous speech, "I have been to the mountain top . . . "; and even Amiri Baraka (LeRoi Jones) offered himself as a new Noah, ready to lead his chosen people out of American bondage in his New Ark (the old place name Newark recaptured in its typological dimensions). Melvin Tolson planned his volume of poetry, *Harlem Gallery* (1965), as the first of five to follow black history from 1619 to the present; the projected volumes were to be entitled "Egypt Land," "The Red Sea," "The Wilderness," and "The Promised Land."

The exodus to the promised land also meant the return to a new paradise, an enclosed garden. The paradise image goes back to the 16th-century travelers and 17th-century colonists and accounts for the notion of an enclosure and gates. Having escaped from the "wicked land" of England, the colonists wrested from the American "wilderness" the pastoral ideal of "that blest land," the American garden. In 1629 Francis Higginson reported the desire "to see our new paradise of New England." John Cotton warned of the "weeds" of religious dissent, growing so near that they might "easily creep into the Garden." In the mythic landscape of America, the "gates" often came to mean the ports through which immigrants entered; and the metaphors of closing, or guarding, or knocking at gates became commonplace in the literature of immigration and immigration restrictions. Thomas Bailey Aldrich's nativist poem, "Unguarded Gates" (1895), is typical: "Wide open and unguarded stand our gates,/And through them presses a wild motley throng . . ." The Statue of Liberty, light-

ing the way to freedom in America, yet guards the entrance to *Castle Garden.* To pass through the gates into the garden, the neophyte had to demonstrate his garden-qualities, his inner acculturation. Thomas Hooker made an important distinction between "a gracious and sanctifying knowledge, garden knowledge" that is characteristic of saints and "a wild and a common knowledge" typical of hypocrites. Much American literature is concerned with the transformation of "wild knowledge" into "garden knowledge," with the process of "civilization." And as in the case of the exodus theme, the notion of a return to the paradise has remained effective even in writers critical of America. Lincoln Steffens, for instance, in 1914 described Mexico as a paradise and Americans as the serpent. And in the American counterculture of the 1960s, Bob Dylan and Joni Mitchell sang about the gates of Eden and getting back to the garden.

Of course, there was a secular parallel to the theme of the promised land, perhaps associated with the golden calf worshiped by the people while Moses was on the mountain top. America could thus be both the new golden ark, which the Lord commanded Moses to build, and the pagan image of the land of gold, El Dorado. Columbus's hope that he had found Cathay in America and the Puritan belief that Christ's Second Coming was destined to occur in America clothed themselves in the imagery of gold. Cotton Mather's description of New England as the "golden candlestick" of Revelation, as well as Voltaire's image of the New World as a land of gold, inspired writers to sound the auric dimensions of America. The quest for gold, an obsession with European and American alchemists, could signify a spiritual search for purification and a material search for gain; and America could be seen as the philosopher's stone— which corresponded to Christ in Christian alchemy— and as the land of plenty, the location of abundant gold and of Ponce de Leon's fountain of youth. The two meanings of America's golden quality can be seen in Mark Twain's and Charles Dudley Warner's critique of *The Gilded Age* (1873) and in Van Wyck Brooks's description of the rift in American culture between Jonathan Edwards's tradition of visionaries and Benjamin Franklin's progeny of practical men. Finally, the rhetoric of America as a land of gold has also affected much metallurgical imagery in the writings concerned with the "fusion" or "welding" of a new American identity.

The pervasive sense of an *imitatio Christi* in American literature and the frequent use of melting-pot imagery may be more intimately connected than is usually assumed. Ethnicity is one source for the many Christ figures in American literature. Of course, an immediate reason for the strength of the Christic stream in the American imagination is the imagery of the garden of Eden and an American Adam; Adam and Christ are typologically related—Christ is the "new Adam"—and the connection between America and Christ is thus established. Thomas Shepard combined the motif of the transatlantic voyage with the notion of a new, Christ-like identity in New England; the migrants "passed through the waves . . . and stood many a week within six inches of death," he explained, "to see Christ here" (see Matt. 11:7–9). To the transatlantic migrants of diverse ethnic backgrounds, the New Testament references to Christ as the "new man," who has not only

united the divine with the human nature in himself, but who has broken down divisions between man and man as well, must have been significant. Christ's breaking down of the "partition wall" between us (Eph. 2:14) is explained in the Geneva Bible as making "one flocke . . . of the Iewes and the Gentiles." In order to find unity in Christ, Christians are asked to "put off the olde man and to put on Christ," the "new man," "after the image of him that created him, Where is neither Grecian nor Iewe, circumcision nor vncircumcision, Barbarian, Scythian, bonde, fre" (Col. 3:10–11). Paul's rhetoric is that of transcending segregation—symbolized by the inscriptions on the partition wall of the Temple which warned Gentiles on pain of death not to enter the inner sanctuary. It is a curious coincidence that the first occurrence of the word "ethnic" cited by the Oxford English Dictionary is in a Middle English hagiographical description—of the destruction of the Temple: "A part of It fel done & made gret distruccione Of ethnykis" (1375).

Hector St. John de Crèvecoeur's famous question, "What then is the American, this new man?" in the third of his Letters from an American Farmer (1782) alludes to Paul's "new man." Crèvecoeur's American is he who, "leaving behind him all his ancient prejudices and manners, receives new ones from the new mode of life he has embraced." America's mission continues the transethnic demands of Paul's Christianity; and, as Crèvecoeur continues, the metallurgical imagery of forging a new man is brought close to the concept of the melting pot: "He becomes an American by being received in the broad lap of our great Alma Mater. Here individuals of all nations are melted into a new race of men, whose labours and posterity will one day cause great change in the world." New York Governor De Witt Clinton made the same association when he said in 1814 that "the triumph and general adoption of the english language have been the principal means of melting us down into one people, and of extinguishing those stubborn prejudices and violent animosities which formed a wall of partition between the inhabitants of the same land."

The motif of the melting pot has persisted in American writing, from religious adaptations of Ezekiel's parable of the "seething pot" and Edward Taylor's "fining pot, and Test, and melting fire" to Crèvecoeur's new man, "melting" in the lap of an American Ceres; from Ralph Waldo Emerson's "smelting pot" to Francis Parkman's public school "crucible," Frederick Jackson Turner's frontier "crucible," and Woodrow Wilson's national "melting pot." The sociological meaning of the image is often less clear than its psychologically accurate implication of a self-renewal through a testing and refining, through a baptismal immersion, and through a rebirth. Thus, the melting pot appears not only in fictionalizations of the emergence of "the" American—sometimes from a mix of Europeans, sometimes from a fusion of all races—but also as a metaphor of the hardening of ethnic group consciousness in America.

Harriet Beecher Stowe thought that American slavery was a "furnace" for Negroes, a divine test from which they were to emerge as the best Christians of the world. In Yekl (1896) Abraham Cahan described the Lower East Side as an all-Jewish melting pot, "a seething human sea fed by streams, streamlets, and rills of immigration flowing from all the Yiddish-speaking centers of Europe." Despite the obvious differences between Cahan's realistic chapter on "The New York Ghetto" and Israel Zangwill's visionary account of the alchemical workings of the melting pot in his play called The Melting Pot (1908), the rhetoric is amazingly similar. In another ethnic tradition, Alain Locke applied Crèvecoeur's rhetoric of the "new man" to his own concept of The New Negro (1925). Locke saw Harlem as the place for an Afro-American rebirth, the Harlem Renaissance, and as the "home of the Negro's 'Zionism'"—"the first concentration in history of so many diverse elements of Negro life," and, Locke concludes, "as its elements mix and react, the laboratory of a great race-welding."

The imagery of the melting pot pervades even the essays of ardent critics of the supposed social "meaning" of the term, as Michael Novak's Rise of the Unmeltable Ethnics (1973) easily illustrates. And melting pots also appear in the often apocalyptic rhetoric of American revolutionaries. Thus, Mike Gold described the road "Towards Proletarian Art" in the classic terms of the religious and ethnic rebirth: "We cling to the old culture, and fight for it against ourselves. But it must die . . . Let us fling all we are into the cauldron of the Revolution. For out of our death shall arise glories, and out of the final corruption of this old civilization we have loved shall spring the new race—the Supermen." Zangwill's anticipation of the birth of a new Superman in America is another aspect of biblical exegesis that has been popular in the United States, culminating perhaps in Jerry Siegel's and Joe Shuster's comic-book protagonist Superman (1938), who, ironically, already is the new man, but has to disguise himself among earthlings as mild-mannered Clark Kent.

Imitatio Christi was a duty for the "Western pilgrims." Thomas à Kempis's book of instruction in the imitation of Christ was probably the only Catholic book printed in 17th-century New England. It was banned by the magistrates in 1669, but became extremely popular. It is, perhaps, the only Catholic book Cotton Mather ever admitted liking. This is not surprising since Mather struggled, throughout his writings, for a Christlike existence. "I thought, I was arrived unto the highest Pinnacle of my Happiness, if I might Represent and Exhibit, any Glory of my Lord JESUS CHRIST, unto the world," he wrote in Paterna (1699–1702). Then some "horrid people" threw anonymous libels at Mather's gate: "They drew ye Picture of a Man, hanging on ye Gallowes; They wrote my Name over it." Mather read this anonymous note as a "Token for Good" since it symbolized his own crucifixion: "Now, Now! my Soul was filled with unspeakable Joy! Now I had Gain'd all my Point! Now my Resemblance unto my Lord JESUS CHRIST, had a Glorious Addition made unto it." Cotton Mather wrote Paterna as a testament for his sons; but American literature as a whole seems to have inherited his imitation of Christ.

American protagonists are more likely than the heroes of non-American literature to be born on Christmas (as Peder in Rølvaag's Giants in the Earth) or to die on Good Friday (as Geremio in Pietro di Donato's Christ in Concrete). The hero of Charles Brockden Brown's Wieland (1798) is transformed into a "Man of Sorrows" in America; Melville's Billy Budd dies as a Christ symbol; Uncle Tom suffers contumely and mar-

tyrdom with Christic dignity; and even Conrad Dryfoos in William Dean Howells's *A Hazard of New Fortunes* (1890) bears features of Christ. The forcefulness of the Christ type is so strong that it even affected the works of the most radical nonmainstream writers. Richard Wright's "Bright and Morning Star" (1938) refers both to the star of Bethlehem and to the red star of Communism; and in Wright's *Native Son* (1940), Bigger Thomas becomes a suffering Christ who ironically feels that through his actions the people's "shame was washed away." Claude McKay was attracted to the radical journalism of *The Masses* when he saw the artistic depiction of a lynching as a crucifixion on the cover of the August 1915 issue. Martin Delany's *Blake, or the Huts* (1859–1861) was perhaps the most heretical Afro-American novel of the 19th century, both in the creation of a black protagonist who is an aristocratic hero and a revolutionary superman, and in a more or less continuous opposition to America's national symbolism. When Henry Blake sees the American flag on the slave prison in Washington, D.C., he thinks of "stars as the pride of the white man, and stripes as the emblem of power over the blacks." Yet despite his emphasis on the earthly struggle against slavery through a universal slave revolution, Blake suggests: "Let us at once drop the religion of our oppressors, and take the Scriptures for our guide and Christ as our example." One of the most radical Jewish-American novels, Mike Gold's *Jews without Money* (1930) ends with the call for a new messiah who will raze the world of inequality: "O, workers' Revolution, you brought hope to me, a lonely suicidal boy, You are the true Messiah. You will destroy the East Side when you come, and build there a garden for the human spirit."

Gold's revolutionary messianism is not Christian, but Ezra Brudno's *The Fugitive* (1904) and Edward Steiner's *The Mediator* (1907) are Jewish immigrant novels that specifically embrace Christ as the mediator and unifier of Jews and Gentiles in America, where, in Steiner's words, "a new race might be born, which should know nothing of the ancient hate and the ancient wrongs." And, for an even more astounding use of the Christian theme in American ethnic writing, Hisaye Yamamoto's story "Yoneko's Earthquake" (1951) provides the setting of a Japanese-American detention camp in World War II.

In American literature, the rebels and martyrs are likely to be Christlike. Thoreau's address to his readers in his "Plea for Captain John Brown" (1860) is typical: "You who pretend to care for Christ crucified, consider what you are about to do to him who offered himself to be the saviour of four millions of men." American ethnic writing is part of that same tradition, from the crucifixion-lynchings in Afro-American literature to David Schearl's Christlike suffering in Henry Roth's *Call It Sleep* (1934), to Studs Lonigan's death in James T. Farrell's *Judgment Day* (1935), from Casimir Pijanowski's *Passion Play of Chicago* (1924) to Piri Thomas's *Savior, Savior, Hold My Hand* (1972). America is Christ in mission and in suffering; recently, Paul Simon's "American Tune" deplored the failure of the American Dream to the tune of Paul Gerhardt's "O Haupt voll Blut und Wunden," and the "American Tune" has merged with one of the most famous Protestant songs of Christ's contumely.

William Faulkner is perhaps the most important American writer who apotheosized and transcended the typological inheritance. His novels are a comprehensive literary counterstatement to America as a promised land and to Christic ethnicity. In *Absalom, Absalom!* (1936) he created an Edenic myth and its critique; his *Light in August* (1932) is the most comprehensively Christic novel in America and, at the same time, subversive of the typological assumptions of American culture. In the former book, Faulkner made Sutpen an archetypal American "founding father" with an obsessive "design" and a sense of mission. Sutpen is the pioneer who wants to start a "house," "plant" a family; yet his progeny destroys him. Quentin Compson is the problematic heir who desperately tries to divest meaning from his cultural heritage, yet arrives at the defiantly self-destructive conclusion, "I don't hate it!" In *Light in August*, Joe Christmas is the Christic man whose ambiguous racial identity sets different actions in motion, all of which hinge on the questionable assumption that he must be black. He is loved, hated, he kills and he is lynched for his metaphoric, yet doubtful, ethnic identity. Faulkner consciously played with all the traditional Christic devices in creating Joe Christmas, who shares more than his initials with Jesus Christ. He was found on Christmas, yet Faulkner makes sure to note that he was not born on that day; he is described as 33 years old when he moves to Jefferson, not when he is crucified-killed; and he is arrested, though not lynched, on Good Friday. Faulkner realized that the Christic assumptions were so strong in American culture that his qualifiers would have to be misread. He therefore used the questionable Christic identity to buttress the theme of the doubtful ethnic identity, and the novel becomes a modernist assault on preconceptions.

RED, BLACK, AND WHITE: ETHNICITY AND HISTORY

The rhetoric of American ethnicity was derived from religious terminology and strengthened through Puritan typology. As rhetoric, the concepts of America as the golden Promised Land, as melting pot, or as Christ's kingdom, belong to the realm of ideology, not to be confused with material reality. American literary ethnicity has to be read against the histories of the various ethnic groups. One is perhaps not necessarily part of an apocalyptic tradition if one follows Cora Daniels Tappan's sarcastic statement: "A government that has for nearly a century enslaved one race (African), that proscribes another (Chinese), proposes to exterminate another (Indians), and persistently refuses to recognize the rights of one-half of its citizens (women), cannot justly be called perfect" (1869). To say that much rhetoric of ethnicity simply covered up "reality," however, is not enough. There were positive and negative sides to the capacity of ethnicity to be substituted for history, for social class, and even for sexual polarization in American literature. Of those substitutions, the use of ethnicity as would-be history in America has been the most pervasive.

In G.W.F. Hegel's *Lectures on the Philosophy of History* (1837), the United States was not yet considered part of "history" in any traditional sense. In Hegel's view, "a real State and a real Government arise only after a distinction of classes has arisen," or when "a

large portion of the people can no longer satisfy its necessities." America is "hitherto exempt from this pressure" because of the safety valve of the frontier through which "multitudes are continually streaming into the plains of the Mississippi." Despite the emigration, Europe is the place of history, America the land of the future. "Had the woods of Germany been in existence, the French Revolution would not have occurred." As a land without the pressures of history, America cannot be compared with the Old World. Louis Hartz questioned America's relationship to history in a similar way when he wondered about the possibilities of an American Enlightenment if there are no dark ages to precede it, and posed the related question concerning the lack of socialist tendencies except among recent migrants. Hartz concluded, in *The Founding of New Societies* (1964), that America was a "fragment culture" which had frozen at the historical point of detachment from the Old World, the bourgeois point, and which was equally separated from the preceding Middle Ages as cut off from the socialist "future." America's problematic relationship to history is reflected in the literary uses of ethnicity.

The achievement of a Christian and American selfhood was always part of the struggle against a heathenish, ethnic "otherness." Here more of the etymological weight of the term ethnicity becomes significant. Indian and black ethnicity were perceived —by the colonists who after about 1680 began to refer to themselves as "whites"—as that otherness which became the most important part of defining selfhood. The confrontation and cooperation with Indians and blacks inevitably changed the white colonists' outlook and confirmed their newness in a new world. As they ate corn and potatoes and smoked sotweed, as Cotton Mather used African vaccination methods in the 1721 smallpox epidemic in Boston and as Virginian participants in Bacon's Rebellion (1675) first got high on the strange "Jamestown weed," as the General Court of Massachusetts ordered 500 pairs of moccasins and as Puritans accepted, with fascination and fear, the elements of folk superstition that the Salem slave woman Tituba and her half-Indian husband introduced to the witch hunts, the settlers were becoming more American. James Kirke Paulding's *Letters from the South* (1835) merely reiterated a popular theme when they explained the phenomenon of American mobility: "The people of the United States partake, in no small degree, of the habits of their predecessors, the aborigines, who, when they have exhausted one hunting-ground, pull up stakes, and incontinently march off to another, four or five hundred miles off, where game is plenty." At least the 17th-century Narragansetts believed that the English settlers were migrating to America because they "must have burned all the firewood in their previous country and come to live where there was more."

If the Europeans became culturally Americanized through their contacts with blacks and Indians, they also saw their own mission in the conversion, education, and "civilization" of the people whom they came to think of, in the course of the 18th century, as "races." Cotton Mather's "Life of John Eliot" is an early American immigrant biography which defines Eliot not through his Old World roots, but through his New World mission. Mather calls the Atlantic a "River of

Lethe which may easily cause us to forget many of the things that happened on the other side." If England enjoyed Eliot's first breath, "it is *New-England* that with most Right can call him *hers*; his *best Breath*, and afterwards his *last Breath* was here; and here 'twas, that God bestow'd upon him *Sons and Daughters*." The drama of the American future against the Old World past finds its symbolism in the transatlantic crossing, in the disruption of parental lineage, and in the emphasis on descendants instead of ancestors. But it is in his contact with the Indians that Eliot finds his typological identity as an American evangelist. Mather's description of these contacts is torn between contempt for the Indians' barbarous way of living and admiration for their hygienic sophistication and their "extraordinary Ease in Childbirth." Mather's Eliot is ethnologist and missionary when he realizes that the first step toward Christianization had to be to learn the Indian language. Eliot, "the Anagram of whose Name was TOILE," learned to master the Algonquian language and published a translation of the Bible, *Mamusse Wunneetupanatamwe Up-Biblum God* in 1663.

It is difficult to generalize the varieties of European contacts with the varieties of Indian nations in America. But whether the Indian appeared in literature as a heathen who could be converted, as prelapsarian or postlapsarian Adamic being, or as a member of a lost tribe of Israel, a constellation emerged which increasingly associated Indians with heathendom and the past and white Americans with Christianity and the future.

Roger Williams reminded the colonists, in *Christening Make Not Christians, A Briefe Discourse Concerning that Name Heathen, Commonly Given to the Indians* (1645), that the Indians were no more "heathen" than most Europeans and wrote an interesting study of Indian culture, *A Key into the Language of America* (1643) which, ironically because of Williams's belief in typology, stayed clear of religious or cultural snobbery. Yet no easy cultural synthesis emerged. The promise of Harvard's charter of 1650 to provide education "of the English and Indian Youth of this Country" led to the establishment of the Harvard Indian College and President Henry Dunster's hope "to make Harvard the Indian Oxford as well as the New-English Cambridge." But the results of the educational and missionary efforts and the attempts at transcultural understanding remained of less importance than the continuous appropriation of Indian land, which could be rationalized most easily if the Indian could be viewed as the "other." The Indian became important for the English-American mind, according to Roy Harvey Pearce, "not for what he was in and of himself, but rather for what he showed civilized men they were not and must not be." Cotton Mather could sometimes see the Indians as part of *the* adversary and speculate that "probably the devil decoyed those miserable salvages [sic] hither" or that the devil instigated the Pequot war. With the growth of the historical imagination, however, the Indian in American literature came to stand for something else the white settlers "were not and must not be": he became the aristocrat.

American writers defined the past in European terms and were therefore looking for indigenous equivalents to Gothic castles and medieval ruins. In the course of the debate about a "native muse," Charles Brockden

Brown wrote *Wieland, or The Transformation* (1798), an early American immigration novel whose German protagonist brings sectarian Calvinist missionary zeal and Gothic horror to America. His attempts at Indian evangelization fail and the horror elements move toward the psychological sphere. One year after *Wieland,* Brown suggested in the preface to *Arthur Mervyn* that "Gothic castles and chimeras" were unnecessary for the creation of effective literature: "The incidents of Indian hostility, and the perils of the western wilderness, are far more suitable." Brown's suggestion was the reformulation of a widely accepted view of the Indians as doomed kings, a dying class of feudal lords of the land, heroic victims of the progress of bourgeois civilization. The Indians became a would-be aristocracy in American literature, and ethnicity substituted itself for history.

Aristocratic Indians were commonplace after John Smith's story of Pocahontas (1608) and could be seen on American stages as *Ponteach* (1766) or John Augustus Stone's *Metamora or The Last of the Wampanoags* (1829). "Tammany," a familiar word in the political history of immigration, was the adoption of an Indian ancestry for political clubs that were at first more social and ceremonial in function. The first American opera, Anne Kemble Hatton's *Tammany* (1794), was reputedly based on genuine Indian music and popularized the image of the Indian who became the mascot of Tammany Hall. The classic American writer who solidified the notion of the Indians as an American aristocracy was James Fenimore Cooper. Cooper disliked his popular epithet, "the American Scott," but he did, in fact, "Americanize" Walter Scott's patterns for historical romances. Cooper's figure of Chingachgook, the idealized Noble Indian, symbolizes the pervasive vision of American Indians as a doomed class as much as Magua and his tribe of "bad" Indians.

Mark Twain, the notorious note-keeper of Cooper's literary offenses, had one thing in common with his literary archenemy: the association of Indians with the European aristocracy. Counting the broken twigs in Cooper's novels, Twain did not notice the literary branch that he transplanted into his own fiction, the myth of "the" Indian as an aristocrat. Of course, Mark Twain had fewer sympathies for the aristocracy than Cooper and not only created Indians who resemble Magua but also referred to French noblemen as "Comanches." There is thus a link between "Injun Joe" in *Tom Sawyer* (1876) and the French aristocrats in "The French and the Comanches" (1879), which points to Cooper as a prototype. In *A Connecticut Yankee in King Arthur's Court* (1889), Mark Twain's problems of identifying a European feudal past with American history recall Hawthorne's difficulties with the theme of ethnicity as ancestry.

Mark Twain's blindness toward his Indian characters is all the more surprising since he made very serious attempts at creating more subtly conceived black characters in *Huckleberry Finn* (1884) and *Pudd'nhead Wilson* (1894). Although by 1700 the term "Christianity" had become linked with "complexion" and "red" and "black" were equally "heathen" and "nonwhite," the black man did not often serve as a substitute aristocrat in American literature. The tradition of the African king abducted into slavery who meets a tragic death in his quest for freedom, a story told in Sarah Wentworth Morton's poem "The African Chief" (1792) and in George Washington Cable's story of Bras-Coupé in *The Grandissimes* (1880) may perhaps live on in an aristocratic feeling about Afro-American culture which Albert Murray described so well in *The Omni-Americans* (1970). (Are Nat "King" Cole, "Count" Basie, or "Duke" Ellington merely random names for entertainers?) In American literature, however, blacks often take the position of the working class, where their quality of "endurance" is idealized. At the same time, they may be soulful and knowing, dialectically related to the American soil and to history, as well as free, often comical spirits, who know how to laugh and dance.

In William Hill Brown's *The Power of Sympathy* (1789), which is usually considered the first American novel, the confused protagonist Harrington, who has fallen in love with a woman who turns out to be his own sister, takes a trip to Carolina, unrelated to the rest of the plot. He meets a slave woman with a scar on her shoulder and learns that she was whipped because her son broke a glass, and that she accepted the guilt and punishment joyfully because she could protect her son by her own suffering. The slave woman temporarily becomes the source of inspiration for Harrington who discovers his own "soul" and "sensibility" in this instance. Black slaves, servants, and workers have provided a similarly regenerating influence upon countless characters in American literature, from *Uncle Tom's Cabin* to Sherwood Anderson's *Dark Laughter* (1925)—which Hemingway parodied by substituting an "Indian war-whoop" for the revelatory black laughter, in *The Torrents of Spring* (1926)—and from Faulkner's *The Sound and the Fury* (1929) to Jack Kerouac's *On the Road* (1957).

Sometimes the figure of the Indian as a doomed nobleman and the Afro-American as an inspiring workingman merge, as perhaps in the half-Indian, half-black character Sam Fathers in Faulkner's "The Bear." The image of the nonwhite woman as a mother figure also appears in black and Indian guise. Philip Young has traced the origin of this notion to Pocahontas, "the Mother of Us All." Powhatan's daughter who rescued John Smith and married John Rolfe, has been cast in such a way as to become identical with the land, as Hart Crane wanted her to be in "The Bridge": as "the natural body of American fertility," the land "like a woman, ripe, waiting to be taken."

The image of the Indian princess or queen as a national symbol, which goes back to Martin Waldseemüller's allegorical representation of an Indian woman on his map of America (1507), at times came close to the womb image of the melting-pot symbolism. Thus the 1787 edition of Crèvecoeur's *Letters from an American Farmer* has a frontispiece which shows the iconography of a deminude plumed Indian princess, on whose breasts the *putti*-like, reborn and rejuvenated immigrants are feeding as Romulus and Remus do on the Roman wolf. The subtitle, *Ubi panis et libertas, ibi patria,* taken from the immediate vicinity of the passage concerning the "melting" in the "lap" of the *Alma Mater,* strengthens the implications of the picture as that of an American Indian Ceres, as Mother Earth, as alchemical vessel, and as the womb symbol in which the rebirth of immigrants takes place. Vachel Lindsay's

poem "Our Mother Pocahontas" (1918) gives full expression to the Indian mother as a melting pot.

The relation of immigration to Pocahontas-Ceres is also reflected in the burlesque theater of the 19th century. John Brougham's *Pocahontas, or The Gentle Savage* (1855) was a travesty of the noble Indian drama which blatantly punned itself through the plot; more interestingly, the play is an ethnic variety show with Irish brogue and black musical interludes, and even John Rolfe is transformed into a "Dutch" immigrant who speaks with a heavy accent.

The mother image of Pocahontas, of course, allows us to conceive of an American self-creation: through the leap into the earth-womb, immigrants become their own ancestors. Neither this use of the Pocahontas tale, nor the view of the noble Indian as an aristocratic ancestor, lends itself to a vision of the melting pot as an encouragement of sexual unions across ethnic boundaries. Paradoxically, the melting pot promised a "new man" psychologically rather than genetically. Actual unions between Indians and whites and between blacks and whites appeared dangerous in American literature, and the offspring of such unions doomed. Thus Poe's half-Indian character Dirk Peters in *The Narrative of Arthur Gordon Pym* (1838) is as awesome as Hawthorne's Septimius Felton is morbid, and "mulattoes" have evoked a fairly persistent treatment as tragic figures. The cause for their tragic roles, however, is not usually assigned to social prejudice but to the original sin of miscegenation. Irish-born playwright Dion Boucicault in 1859 published *The Octoroon*, the most influential "tragic mulatto" melodrama. Interestingly, an English version of the play allowed a happy ending and a union between white lover George Peyton and "octoroon" slave girl Zoë, whereas the American version ends tragically with Zoë's suicide.

In the 1920s Sherwood Anderson and William Faulkner supposedly debated the question of whether "mixed breeds"—like mules—were infertile. But the story most central to a nervous national self-consciousness is Callender's apocryphal relation of Thomas Jefferson's slave progeny. Henry Adams quotes Irish poet Thomas Moore's allusion to the "weary statesman's" flight "From halls of council to his negro's shed,/Where, blest, he woos some black Aspasia's grace,/And dreams of freedom in his slave's embrace." William Wells Brown, the first black novelist, used Callender's story of Jefferson's reputed affair with the slave woman Sally Hemings (whom Brown baptizes "Currer") as the plot of his abolitionist novel *Clotel, or the President's Daughter* (1853). Brown's Clotel is a national symbol of the injustice that slavery perpetrates upon womanhood; she dies with arms outstretched and eyes lifted up to heaven, pursued by slave catchers onto a bridge across the Potomac, "in full view of the capitol." She dies for the national sin of slavery, but also for the president's sin of the flesh.

A taboo on sexual arrangements between white and black or white and red brings back Cooper's world in relation to Scott's. Scott's novels often mediate the historical conflicts through marriage; Cooper's Indian romances leave the opposites unreconciled. Instead of a middle ground between warring Indians and Americans, a mediating home, Cooper chooses an interesting, and culturally significant, alternative. The relationship

between white man and nonwhite woman is limited to a Pocahontas-mother myth and must apparently not be extended to a more traditional male-female opposition; the literary reflections of contacts between white women and nonwhite men are, perhaps, typically rendered by captivity narratives in the tradition of Hannah Duston, who plays the role of a leitmotif in much American literature from Hawthorne's "The Duston Family" (1836) to Thoreau's *Week on the Concord and Merrimack Rivers* (1849). Aware of the complications inherent in the relationships between white man and Indian woman or between white woman and Indian man, Cooper created an important character confrontation on ethnic rather than sexual grounds, and developed the white man—nonwhite man constellation from its tentative appearance in the narrative of Alexander Henry (1809) into a major theme of American literature.

Cooper's focus is so concentrated on the relationship between Hawkeye and Chingachgook (whose name means "big serpent" and thus led Leslie Fiedler back to the Edenic myth) that his female characters—white and Indian—become his weakest figures. The transethnic friendship of males cannot result in an offspring, but it assimilates Indian and white man to each other so that both become exceptional in their cultures. The Last of the Mohicans is as lonely as Natty Bumppo, the equally tragic pioneer for a civilization in which he will not be able to live. The mediation between white and nonwhite protagonists takes place in a middle ground of freedom that will soon be superseded by civilization. This pattern of freedom temporarily achieved through a transethnic friendship of males appears in some major works of American literature, notably in the wedding ritual of Ishmael and Queequeg in Melville's *Moby-Dick* (1851) and in Huck and Jim's experiences in Twain's *Huckleberry Finn* (1884). Leslie Fiedler has discussed the latent homosexual implications in these transethnic encounters and has delineated their recurrence from Richard Dana's *Two Years Before the Mast* (1840) to Ken Kesey's *One Flew over the Cuckoo's Nest* (1962).

Red and black ethnicity is as pervasive in minority and immigrant writing as in mainstream literature. Mike Gold describes youth gangs on Manhattan's Lower East Side in Indian terms; when the narrator of *Jews without Money* is surrounded by Italian boys who are "whooping like Indians" and who call him "Christ-killer," he views the territory of Hester and Mulberry streets as the Wild West and soon yearns for a "Messiah who would look like Buffalo Bill." In Rølvaag's *Giants in the Earth*, Norwegian settler Per Hansa has encounters with Indians which elevate his status as that of a white chieftain and patriarch. Abraham Cahan's *Yekl* interestingly depicts the protagonist's wife Gitl as a "squaw" when she arrives in America and is met by her Americanized husband Jake; being a squaw makes her a mother figure and underlines her incompatibility with her spouse. In Willibald Winckler's *Die deutschen Kleinstädter in Amerika* (1871) the heroine is abducted by the Chippewas, and in the anonymous German-American play *Die Emigranten* (1882) a German-speaking black working woman tells a recently arrived immigrant that it only takes five years for immigrants to turn black.

Occasionally, even the rhetoric of black or Indian

writers echoes these tendencies. In 1869 Frederick Douglass stated that "the negro is more like the white man than the Indian, in his tastes and tendencies, and disposition to accept civilization . . . You do not see him wearing a blanket, but coats cut in the latest European fashion." James Weldon Johnson's *Autobiography of an Ex-Colored Man* (1912), which is full of observations on the national character of different Americans and Europeans, voices the assumption that the Negro's capacity for humor saved him from going the way of the red man. Vine Deloria's essay *Custer Died for Your Sins* (1969) welcomes Black Power and speaks analogously of "Red Power," but deplores the fact that former slaves have never been treated as a *people,* an entity white Americans would negotiate with, since black people never owned reservations. And Bobby Seale's recent autobiography *A Lonely Rage* (1978) reveals the deep-seated adolescent dream of the later Black Panther to adopt an Indian name and escape to a Sioux reservation.

Perhaps the most profoundly satirical and iconoclastic cultural statement against such black and Indian stereotypes can be found in Mel Brooks's movie *Blazing Saddles* (1974). Brooks's black railroad workers are sophisticated urbanites who claim not to know the song "Camptown Races" or any Negro spirituals; when pressed by the white overseers to sing, they present a smooth version of Cole Porter's "I Get a Kick out of You." The Indian chieftain, played by Brooks himself, is quite unaristocratic, speaks Yiddish, and releases black captives with the nonchalance of a Brooklynite. By going back to the vaudeville mix of Indian, black, and immigrant lore, Brooks has inverted and exploded some important ingredients of an American ethnic myth.

"THE DIVIDED HEART":
CLASSIC ETHNIC LITERATURE AND REALISM

The Indian-black-white triangle remained a powerful basis for literary ethnicity, but became more complicated as America became more ethnically diverse. The flow of immigrants demanded recognition by imaginative writers, both among the earlier migrants and among the newcomers themselves. The responses sometimes reflected a continued substitution of ethnicity for history and expressed anxieties and fears of "otherness." The uncertainties of an American cultural identity—which was problematic within each ethnic tradition as disrupted ancestry—became even more pressing when different ancestries interacted with each other. As many studies of literary stereotypes have shown, American literature abounds with prejudices against newcomers of all backgrounds as well as animosities against older settlers and, of course, against Indians and blacks. But at times, the shared experience of Americans—having left an old identity and struggling for a new one—was understood by writers who could create literary works without fear, prejudice, or ethnocentrism.

One response was to portray German and Irish immigrants in the tradition of Indians and blacks. Some buffo roles of Negroes and Irishmen could be exchanged with ease. Similarly, Germans often assumed the pseudoaristocratic parts. In 1700 Cotton Mather delivered the sermon, "A Pillar of Gratitude" in which he described as "formidable Attempts of Satan and his Sons" the proposal that "a Colony of Irish might be sent over to check the growth of this Countrey." Mather concluded with great satisfaction that "an overwhelming blast from Heaven has defeated all those attempts." Mather's fear of an Irish colony in America reflected the Protestant feeling that "popery" held Catholics in bondage, as they had to answer to the ultimate Old World authority, the Vatican; and perhaps a similar fear of foreigners who adhere to Old World ways has been felt in American literature about Communists, German Fifth Columnists, or science-fiction androids who take orders from an "Old World" power center.

Mather's fear of the Irish resembles Benjamin Franklin's anxiety about the Germans; in 1751 Franklin asked, "Why should Pennsylvania, founded by the English, become a Colony of *Aliens,* who will shortly be so numerous as to Germanize us instead of our Anglifying them, and will never adopt our Language and Customs, any more than they can acquire our Complexion?"

Could everybody be converted to an American identity? Could a national unity be forged out of ethnic diversity? A pseudonymous "Celadon" answered these questions negatively in *The Golden Age: or Future Glory of North-America* (1785) and mapped out the United States of the future as a confederation of ethnic nation states; "Nigrania" and "Savagenia" were black and Indian states in the Southwest, and Celadon anticipated the establishment of "a French, a Spanish, a Dutch, an Irish, &c. yea, a Jewish state." In Charles Jared Ingersoll's *Inchiquin, the Jesuit's Letters* (1810), a Frenchman suggests with outrageous irony that American unity can be achieved quite easily—by making the French language and Roman Catholicism mandatory in the New World!

Emerson's notebook entry on the "smelting pot"—written in 1845 in opposition to the Native American party—attempts to define the collective process to forge a unified American identity as an equivalent to the feudal past: "as in the old burning of the Temple at Corinth, by the melting & intermixture of silver & gold & other metals, a new compound more precious than any, called the Corinthian Brass, was formed so in this Continent,—asylum of all nations, the energy of Irish, Germans, Swedes, Poles, & Cossacks, & all the European tribes,—of the Africans, & of the Polynesians, will construct a new race, a new religion, a new State, a new literature, which will be as vigorous as the new Europe which came out of the smelting pot of the Dark Ages, or that which earlier emerged from the Pelasgic & Etruscan barbarism. La Nature aime les croisements." The interplay of ethnics in American literature is generally less harmonious than in this aphorism.

Characters and themes in the literature of the 19th century reflect more ethnic concern than understanding or sympathy. Although Longfellow's *Tales of a Wayside Inn* (1886), for example, deal sympathetically with a French, Spanish, and Jewish vantage point, ethnic characters by America's major writers are often no more than stereotypes. Howard Mumford Jones observed that American literature fails to treat the "alien" equally "unless he is good and dead"; a living alien "is reduced to a subordinate role and expected to furnish comic relief." Even Washington Irving's famous Dutch characters are portrayed positively only because they are part of the past. The roles of a tragically extinct aristocratic ancestry and of an inspiring and amusing buffo

underclass remained fixed points in American literature. Cooper, who helped to create the Indian aristocrat,
also imagined many comic-relief ethnics, such as Caesar Thompson, a faithful black servant, in *The Spy*
(1821), and Elizabeth Flanagan, a stage Irishwoman who
supplies liquor for the troops, speaks with a heavy accent, and is the source of much comic relief in the same
novel.

One of Cooper's foreign admirers ironically contributed to the gradual growth of more "realism" in the picturing of ethnic characters when his works became popular in America. Eugène Sue in *Les Mystères de Paris*
(1843) promised the French readers merely an urban and
local sequel to the *Leatherstocking Tales*; instead of
Cooper's Indians, Sue presented "other barbarians, also
outside of civilization." Sue was referring to the Pari-
sian underworld of crime and poverty, where his French
"Apaches" "have customs of their own, women of their
own," and even "a language of their own . . . full of
dark images and of bloody and disgusting metaphors."
Sue's works, which became increasingly concerned
with pressing social questions, were immensely popular as they satisfied both the needs for romance—the
Cooper legacy—and for realism—the socialist leader
Daniel De Leon was among Sue's American translators.

Sue was not merely translated, he was widely copied
and adapted to American urban settings, by George Lippard and Dion Boucicault as well as by minor immigrant writers. Lippard's *The Quaker City, or Monks of
Monk Hall* (1844) transposed the picturesque argot of
Sue's Parisians into vaudeville ethnic accents of Philadelphia, including not only Negro speech but also, perhaps for the first time in American fiction, the Jewish
idiom of a character named "Gabriel Van Gelt." Ethnic
otherness is rendered no more subtly here than by
Cooper, but the attention paid to urban types and to social reformism heralds the concerns of realistic writers.
An anonymous German-American novel, *Die Geheimnisse von Philadelphia* (1850), similarly transposed
Sue's Paris to America; and Emil Klauprecht's *Cincinnati oder Geheimnisse des Westens* (1854–1855) did
not merely adapt plot elements of the city *Mysteries*,
but also of those popular novels that formed the basis of
The Octoroon, resulting in a wide spread of ethnic
types: the heroine Isabelle of French descent, Habakkuk
Maleachi the mysterious Indian herb doctor, Zenobia
the passionate octoroon girl, as well as Herrenhuter,
Italian Jesuits, and German immigrants. Klauprecht's
novel is perhaps the first immigrant novel that juxta-
poses a visionary newcomer, artist Wilhelm Steiger-
wald who remembers his heritage, with a practical
man, his thoroughly Americanized brother Carl, who
has made a successful career as a businessman and is
eager to forget or conceal his background. The tendency
toward a more realistic differentiation of ethnic
characters is palpable. Dion Boucicault moved in the
same direction. He derived his play *The Poor of New
York* (1857) from a French drama of the Sue school and
adapted it, with a change of title, to the tenement setting of many different cities. Boucicault also departed
from the stage-Irish tradition in 1860 and created more
realistic renditions of Irish life in *The Colleen Bawn*,
whose Old World Irish gentlefolk and villagers exhibit
neither burlesque nor sentimentality.

In the second half of the 19th century, the rise of
serious ethnic literature was linked with an opposition
to stereotypes and with the claims for realism and authenticity against malicious, sentimental, or careless
distortion. American writers have traditionally tried to
present their imaginative products as "truth" in order
to avoid religious, moral, or pragmatic censure. But in
the case of ethnic writing, the claim that literature represented truth meant more than that. It stood for the demand for an "inside view" of ethnicity and for a growing concern with social reform. The alliance of ethnic
realism, spokesmanship, and social criticism has remained powerful for more than a century.

The point of departure of classic ethnic literature, and
especially of writings in English, often was to blur ethnic stereotypes by presenting an inside view of ethnicity which could make "otherness" understandable
to American readers. Consciously or unconsciously,
ethnic writers often assumed the roles of pleaders, mediators, or translators who explained ethnic traits, annotated ethnic jokes and phrases, or provided glossaries
for the benefit of the reader. Afro-American writer
Charles Chesnutt, realizing that the bastion of racial
prejudice could not be taken by assault, decided to undermine it by creating a Yankee narrator who often mis-
understands the southern blacks he encounters and describes. Explaining to the imagined descendants of
Puritans and Pilgrims the uprooting, migrations, miseries, and achievements of more recent immigrants or
of ex-slaves, writers instinctively chose a language and
symbology derived from the first English migrants to
America; and this is perhaps one decisive factor in
accounting for the pervasiveness of typological elements in ethnic literature. Thus the ethnic writer as
"mediator" set out to break down the partition walls
between ethnic group and larger culture.

The mediating process is not necessarily harmonious.
Daniel Aaron delineated three typical stages in the development of "hyphenate writers," in the process from
marginal to mainstream literature. In the first phase,
the writer as "a kind of local colorist" exploits the
strangeness of his human material to win the sympathies of the unhyphenated, "but also in the hope of
humanizing the stereotyped minority and dissipating
prejudice." In the second, less conciliatory stage, the
author lashes out at political, social, and economic restrictions and the consequences of discrimination and
exploitation, risking criticism both from the larger society and from his ethnic group. In the third stage, the
writer acquires F. Scott Fitzgerald's "double vision,"
moves from marginality to the mainstream center, and
loses the sense of hyphenation while retaining a critical
relationship to society. Since Aaron's essay appeared, a
fourth stage has emerged among some writers of the
"new ethnicity," which we might call a phase of
renewed ethnic spokesmanship, social criticism, and
retrospective romanticization. In all phases ethnic writers have worked with similar themes.

There are two significant clusters of classic ethnic
themes and an interesting area where both clusters converge. The first group of themes concerns ethnicity as
ancestry; and in the treatment of these themes, minority and mainstream writing are close to each other. The
second cluster consists of themes resulting from ethnicity as diversity. The motif of the divided self marks
the area of convergence of the two main clusters. The

themes of genealogy, relationship of Old World and New, and struggle for an American identity were discussed earlier; another theme related to ethnicity as ancestry is that of generational progression and conflict. Generations often represent the Old World and the New World to each other; and generational conflicts with ethnic significance are ubiquitous in American literature, from Theodore Dreiser's *Jennie Gerhardt* (1911) to Martha Ostenso's *Wild Geese* (1925) and *O River, Remember* (1943), Joseph Pagano's *The Paesanos* (1940), Charles Driscoll's *Kansas Irish* (1943), and the classic Freudian formulation of the tensions in an immigrant family in Henry Roth's *Call It Sleep* (1934). Ethnic family sagas provide many illustrations of and variations on the return of the third generation. In such books, the first generation is non-American in origin, migrates, and gets into conflicts in the New Land. The second generation wholeheartedly absorbs the new and discards the old, repeating the antiparental and profilial gesture of its own parents. The third generation, while also future-oriented and perhaps even more intensely "American" than the second, opposes the second generation by embracing some elements of its grandparents' ethnicity that its parents repressed. There are elements of this pattern in Rølvaag's *Giants in the Earth* (1927), *Peder Victorious* (1929), and *Their Father's God* (1931); in Daniel Fuchs's *Williamsburg Trilogy* (1934–1937); in Harry Mark Petrakis's *The Odyssey of Kostas Volakis* (1963); and in Ferris Takahashi's "The Widower."

In ethnic literature, as in American literature as a whole, many protagonists are orphaned. This is, of course, especially true for the first generation, which sometimes associates the departure for the New World with the symbolic or literal death of its Old World parents. Upon the death of his mother, Abraham Cahan's David Levinsky first contemplates going to America (1917). Yet even second-generation heroes may be orphaned, or become orphans, as Paul does in Pietro di Donato's *Christ in Concrete* (1939). When the orphan theme interferes with the theme of generational progression and conflict, the result is often a mediation of generational conflicts through the uncle-nephew constellation.

Because ethnic realism sets out to overcome prejudices against the ethnic group spoken for, not to combat prejudice as such, one finds the same array of stereotypes in the literature by ethnics as in mainstream writing. It would be easy to collect, for example, anti-Semitic caricatures in minority literature, from Lars A. Stenholt's *Chicago anarkisterne* (1888) to Afro-American poetry of the 1960s. The German trickster Till Eulenspiegel became, in Pennsylvania-Dutch folklore, an "Irish pickle," and Irish buffos are as much at home in Cooper's world as they are in Charles Sealsfield's frontier novels.

The cultural conflict with the dominant society in America is the most important theme in ethnic writing and can be found in literature of childhood and adolescence, in stories of education and of ethnic politics, or in the context of religion and work. The conflicts of cultural opposition are especially exciting when they are associated with the theme of love and marriage. In Hjalmar Hjorth Boyesen's story "A Good-for-Nothing" (1875), Norwegian-born Ralph Grim, a gentleman, falls in love with the peasant girl Bertha, who tells Ralph that he must do "one manly deed" to prove his independence from the "life of idleness and vanity" the Old World class structure provided for him. A student prankster, Ralph propositions six ladies, all of whom accept him; in the ensuing scandal, Ralph emigrates to America, convinced that the New World will provide the opportunity for the manly deed that will prove him worthy of Bertha. In America, however, he associates with "high-minded and refined women"; and when he returns to marry Bertha, they discover that they have grown too far apart and that "the gulf which separates the New World from the Old . . . cannot be bridged." Interestingly, it is Bertha's complexion which signals to Ralph his alienation from the narrow past: while her face reminds him of "those pale, sweet-faced saints of Fra Angelico," "her forefinger was rough from sewing, and . . . the whiteness of her arm . . . contrasted strongly with the browned and sun-burned complexion of her hands."

A black and a Jewish writer continued Boyesen's theme by developing more full-fledged alternative figures to the values Bertha embodies. Charles Chesnutt's "The Wife of His Youth" (1898) and Abraham Cahan's *Yekl: A Tale of the New York Ghetto* (1896) show the dilemma of modernized protagonists who have to choose between two women who represent "ethnicity" and "America." Negro migrant and Jewish immigrant have changed their names (from Sam Taylor to Mr. Ryder and from Yekl to Jake) and try to be successful on the terms of their new environments. In the Blue Vein Society, Mr. Ryder has made the acquaintance of a widow, Mrs. Molly Dixon, who is much younger, lighter-complexioned, and better educated than Ryder and comes from the nation's capital. In the dancing academy, Jake makes friends with Mamie Fein, a woman with a shrewd sense of business and a strong character, who speaks better English than Jake. Suddenly, both Jake and Ryder are confronted with their past, represented, in both cases, by an ethnic wife. Both marriages were Old World arrangements: Ryder's slave marriage was not legalized after emancipation, and Jake's wedding was a parentally arranged affair lacking any consideration of "love" or "free choice."

The wife of Mr. Ryder's youth "seemed quite old; for her face was crossed and re-crossed with a hundred wrinkles, and around the edges of her bonnet could be seen protruding here and there a tuft of short grey wool . . . And she was very black,—so black that her toothless gums, revealed when she opened her mouth to speak, were not red, but blue." Jake's wife Gitl is "un-American" in appearance and conceals her hair under "a voluminous wig of pitch-black hue," which also makes her seem stouter, shorter, and older. "She was naturally dark of complexion, and the nine or ten days spent at sea had covered her face with a deep bronze, which combined with her prominent cheek bones, inky little eyes, and, above all, the smooth black wig, to lend her resemblance to a squaw." The ethnic wives are dark mother figures, represent ethnicity as ancestry (even as pseudo-Indian Pocahontas ancestry), but are antithetical to all the values of their husbands' New World.

The conclusions to these tales refer us back to the growth of urban and ethnic realism out of Cooper's and

Sue's romances. Chesnutt chooses an idealized ending and lets Mr. Ryder renounce mobility, Blue Vein status, and the attractive Molly Dixon by accepting Liza Jane, the "wife of his youth" (cf. Proverbs 5, 18–20). *Yekl*, on the other hand, concludes with the breakup of Jake's marriage and his imminent alliance with Mamie Fein. The tension between an idealized acceptance of the past and a realistic account of plausible behavior in new environments informed much ethnic literature in the period of realism. As literature, ethnic realism made more sense against the backdrop of romance, which it replaced. Boyesen, Chesnutt, and Cahan—as well as many other ethnic writers—wrote in close literary contact with William Dean Howells. If Boyesen's statement, "Howells Americanized me," is typical of his generation of ethnic writers in America, it is interesting to note that Boyesen often associated the Old World with romance and the New World with realism.

The focal point of ethnicity as ancestry and ethnicity as diversity, and perhaps one of the most fascinating themes of ethnic literature, is the experience of ethnicity by a divided self. W.E.B. DuBois's famous formulation of a "double consciousness" as "an American, a Negro" is applicable to writers who are visibly ethnic—who not only feel the tensions of "the divided heart" inwardly, but whose ethnicity is easily recognizable to others. Yet American writers have expressed anxiety concerning their identity generations and centuries after their ancestors left Old Worlds. In the quest for identity, a narcissistic tendency could ally itself with ethnicity as the literature developed a concern with that *individual* under the accidental skin or language, mask or veil. Self-division, self-pity, and self-love may be close to each other in acts of literary revelation or unmasking.

In Johan G.R. Banér's *Barr* (1926), the hyphenate makes an asset out of ethnic dualism which makes it superior to any single national identity: "You are ONE, but—I am TWO!" This attitude implies a degree of imperviousness to traditional sex roles; the human being with a double identity in literature is related to Christ and Superman rather than to average mortals and he is both Yin and Yang in himself. Characters with a divided self are less likely to find love for another person than they are to be attracted to mirrors, reflecting windows, or smooth-surfaced ponds. Confronted for the first time in his life with the ultimate slur, "Nigger, nigger, never die, Black face and shiny eye," the narrator-hero of James Weldon Johnson's *Autobiography of an Ex-Colored Man* (1912) rushes to the mirror and discovers his own beauty in black-white ambiguity: "I noticed the ivory whiteness of my skin, the beauty of my mouth, the size and liquid darkness of my eyes, and how the long, black lashes that fringed and shaded them produced an effect that was strangely fascinating even to me." And Cahan's David Levinsky feels attracted by his own new image—without side-locks and in American clothes—which he sees reflected in mirrors and shop windows.

The novels of both Johnson and Cahan can be read as an exegesis of the theme of the divided self. *The Autobiography of an Ex-Colored Man* and *The Rise of David Levinsky* (1917; first serialized in 1913 as "The Autobiography of an American Jew") are told by omnipresent first-person narrators. Though each purports to be tell-

ing his own true story, confiding his innermost secrets, the reader is aware in both narratives of an ironic voice that is closer to the author's than the narrator's point of view. Both heroes are outwardly successful at the expense of losing their inner identity, their birthright, their loyalty to kin; they are ethnic renegades. But neither Cahan nor Johnson sees ethnicity as a static factor that Americanized men should return or withdraw to; they advocate neither Jewish nor black ethnocentrism. In their works ethnicity stands for those facets of self-realization that the retrospective mind of practical men perceives as the lost potential of childhood or as the sacrifice made to America: it is the visionary quality that these characters (though not their creators) have surrendered. The ideal remained in the fusion of the legacy of childhood, folk, parish, and poverty with the experience of manhood, America, secular world, and success in the individual self's creative mind.

Cahan and Johnson describe the tensions of ethnic dualism as a tremendous artistic force, yet create their businessmen protagonists as traitors to that force, as artists *manqués*. In their moments of introspective remorse and self-pity, Levinsky and the ex-colored man wish that they had created the new American music as a synthesis of folk tradition and New World. Not persistent enough, they remain divided selves. The musical imagery, which has been part of the literature of ethnicity from melting-pot propagators like Zangwill to opponents like Horace Kallen, is here extended to the notion of the right artistic response, the truly multiethnic *form*, which might solve the dilemma of ethnic dualism.

ETHNICITY AND LITERARY FORM

It is customary to ascribe the origins of America's most characteristic art forms—jazz, musicals, and movies—to the influences of ethnic diversity. Yet attempts to relate ethnicity with literary forms are usually limited to classic ethnic realism; and in this context, "authentic" and "documentary" qualities are more highly valued than formal intricacies and innovations. The tendency to exclude writers with great formal accomplishments from the category of "ethnic" writing—Nathanael West, Eugene O'Neill, John Dos Passos, F. Scott Fitzgerald—is indicative of an enforced limitation of the scope of what we define as ethnic literature.

The development of American literature is viewed as "growth," as a process of increasing formal complexity from travelogues and letters (starting with John Smith's *True Relation* (1608), which is, perhaps, the first "America letter"), sermons, essays, and biographies, to the increasingly successful mastering of poetry, prose fiction, and drama. Analogously, we may view the development of ethnic writing as a process of growth; and again, the beginning is with immigrant and migrant letters—those collected, for example, by Everett Emerson and Charlotte Erickson for British emigrants, Alan Conway for the Welsh, Karl Larsen for the Danes, Abraham Cahan for the Jews, Thomas and Znaniecki for the Poles, and by the *Journal of Negro History* for black migrants. The literature then "grows" from nonfictional to fictional forms or from an autobiography to an autobiographic novel; from folk and popular forms to high forms, as from Uncle Remus tales to Charles Ches-

nutt's *The Conjure Woman;* from Indian folklore to N. Scott Momaday's *House Made of Dawn* or Hyemeyohsts Storm's *Seven Arrows;* or from Mexican-American popular culture to Luis Valdez's dramatic *Actos.* It grows from lower to higher degrees of literary complexity, from Dion Boucicault to Eugene O'Neill, from Abraham Cahan to Saul Bellow, or from James Weldon Johnson to Ralph Ellison. It grows finally from "parochial" marginality to "universal" significance; the American literary mainstream now consists predominantly of writers with identifiable "ethnic" backgrounds.

In many instances, this model of "growth" yields an accurate picture of literary developments against the background of an opposition between parochial ethnicity and modern movements in art and literature. In other cases, however, ethnicity and modernity do not necessarily contradict each other. Writers may adhere to "Old World" languages and yet be more "modern" than their Americanized counterparts. Ethnic writers may feel the need for "new" forms more intensely than mainstream authors. Furthermore, the rhetoric of ethnicity—as problematic ancestry and as diversity—has militated toward the "new" and thus supported the drive toward formal innovation.

Because of their close connections to another culture, American ethnic writers sometimes participated in literary innovations of other national literatures before such innovations became more widespread in America. In the beginning of the 20th century, for example, the Scandinavian, German, and especially the Yiddish stages were more "modern" than the average American theater.

Similarly, ethnic poets who used languages other than English were often more willing to work with the new forms of Whitman and the French symbolists than poets who wrote in Whitman's native tongue. The rebellious and aggressive Yiddish poets who, in 1907, formed Die Yunge (The Young Ones) and published their initial anthology, *Yugend* (Youth) by "self press," shared a common ground with the modernist rebels in Europe and America, despite the language barrier. At a time when Jewish-American writing in English showed few traces of modernist influences—only Henry Roth's *Call It Sleep* marks the breakthrough of high modernism in 1934—Die Yunge and Insichisten (Introspectivists) created a Yiddish avant-gardism in America.

When ethnic writing in languages other than English is more innovative and modern than its English-language counterpart the reason for this phenomenon lies in the problem of the audience. James Weldon Johnson, who realized that Afro-Americans do not have the option to create for exclusively black audiences, described the "Dilemma of the Negro Author" (1928) as the "problem of the double audience." Ethnic writers who use English confront a double audience of readers who are familiar with their ethnic groups and readers who are not. Imperceptibly, and sometimes involuntarily, an author may become a translator of ethnicity to ignorant, and sometimes hostile, outsiders. Such a writer may feel compelled to avoid anything that might give fuel to antiethnic sentiment among the majority audiences; and this attitude of caution and explanation may be an obstacle to the freedom of innovation. In stories written for an ethnic group and rewritten for an "American" audience—such as Abraham Cahan's "Mottke Arbel" (1891–1892), redone in English as "A Providential Match" (1895)—a distinctive and characteristic formal element of much immigrant literature appears: an omniscient narrator who explains to the reader, whose values he seems to share, aspects of the immigrant culture. This narrative voice inhibits literary experimentation and absolute freedom in the language.

The tenuous situation of writers caught between two cultures, as mediators who are alienated from both camps, however, also lends itself to a transcending "leap ahead" in literary form. Seen this way, even James Joyce's modernism was related to his Irish ethnicity, and Franz Kafka's "minority literature" was written by a German-speaking Jew in Czechoslovakia, in a situation of exaggerated ethnic alienation. The American ethnic writer could leave the weight of cultural dualism behind by taking a position of extreme individualism, by denying the adequacy of *any* existing language for his vision, and by pushing himself into linguistic innovation as an assault on those conventions, patterns, and habits that also form one basis of nativism and ethnocentrism.

Among the most interesting ethnic modernists between the wars are Jean Toomer and José García Villa. Toomer, a light-skinned Afro-American whose family had been living on both sides of the color line for generations, viewed racial as well as other "Linnaean" categories with a great sense of ironical distance. In his collection of aphorisms, *Essentials* (1931), he opposed ethnicity and all other accidental and divisive categories while advocating a Whitmanesque sense of panethnic and pansexual wholeness: "I am of no particular race. I am of the human race, a man at large in the human world, preparing a new race. I am of no specific region. I am of earth. I am of no particular class. I am of the human class, preparing a new class. I am neither male nor female nor in-between. I am of sex, with male differentiations. I am of no special field. I am of the field of being." Toomer's *Cane* (1923), a book that significantly defies genre categorization, is an experimental search for reality beyond labels, and for mankind above race and nationality. The section entitled "Bona and Paul" opposes imaginative vision to the ethnic blindness of a priori assumptions; and as Robert Bone has shown, "Toomer's central metaphor . . . is drawn from St. Paul's first epistle to the Corinthians: 'For now we see through a glass darkly; but then face to face: now I know in part; but then shall I know even as I am known.'"

If Toomer's creative thrust is directed at restoring the noumenal unity beyond the phenomenal diversity of, for example, ethnic categories, José García Villa's poetry similarly attempts to create its own formal rules and its own area of freedom and true vision. In *Have Come, Am Here* (1942), Villa—who was born in the Philippines—proudly used "a new method of rhyming, a method which has never been used in the history of English poetry, nor in any poetry," the principle of reversed consonance: "Nobody yet knows who I am,/Nor myself may;/Nor yet what I deal,/Nor yet where I lead." While ethnic literature abounds in musical imagery so that the notion of a multiethnic harmony—as in Horace Kallen's definition of American civilization as

"an orchestration of mankind"—has become a trite cliché, unusable for the subtle poet, Villa finds an adequate formal prototype for "ethnic" poetry in painting. He translates Seurat's pointillism into punctuation that blurs the sequence of lines and forces the reader to take a total view from a certain distance. Villa concludes a poem about "Christ, Oppositor,/Christ, Foeman" with the lines: "After, pure, eyes, have, peeled,/Off, skin, who, can, gaze, unburned? Who,/Can, stand, unbowed? Well, be, perceived,/And, well, perceive. Receive, be, received." Villa's comma poems may be, as Renato Poggioli claimed, an "extreme and absurd extravagance," but they indicate a radical formal response to the ethnic writer's need for a new poetic language.

Ethnicity has also been a factor in the choice of less extreme formal patterns. The belief that a new national or ethnic consciousness has to be rendered in new forms is a significant element in the criticism of works that express American themes in English forms or ethnic themes in mainstream forms. Claude McKay's work in the sonnet form has often been read as a contradiction to his themes of black pride and self-defense, as in "If We Must Die" (1919). In 1788 Nicholas Pike, the author of a mathematical textbook, was hopeful that "American arithmetic" would emerge, and in 1969 Nathan Hare similarly predicted "Black math."

One persistent literary expression in America has been the epic, which seemed suited to render the grandeur and dimensions of the new experiences and historically related to the rise of empires. The image of an American "Odyssey" is almost as popular as that of a New World exodus; and the Vergilian epic has influenced a great many American writers. Among the earliest colonial writings in America is Gaspar Pérez de Villagra's ambitious and consciously Vergilian epic, *Historia de la Nueva Mexico* (1610). Cotton Mather's famous introduction to the *Magnalia Christi Americana* (1702) begins with the Vergilian formula: "I WRITE the *Wonders* of the CHRISTIAN RELIGION, flying from the Depravations of *Europe*, to the *American Strand.*" Epic epithets are further elements which seemed especially appropriate to American subject matter.

The perception of the multiethnic character of America has often encouraged the creation of exuberant multilingual forms in which ethnic contradictions may be absorbed as in a sponge, or organized in an encylopedic and panoramic fashion. A manuscript by "the Pennsylvania Pilgrim" and founder of Germantown, Francis Daniel Pastorius, entitled "Bee-Hive or Bee-Stock" (1697; first printed in 1897), is a conglomerate of proverbs and folk wisdom, personal observations and messages for the second generation. One commentator has called it "the first American encyclopedia." Pastorius, who describes modern English as "a Minglemangle of Latin, Dutch & French" uses seven languages in his book, but mostly German, English, and Latin. The focus and central image of the book is the "bee-hive" in its literal, metaphoric, and cultural implications. The comprehensiveness of Pastorius's method makes his work a minor precursor of Melville's encyclopedic view of whales in *Moby-Dick.* Pastorius's learned and multilingual exuberance is reminiscent of Nathaniel Ward's *Simple Cobble of Aggawam* (1647) and much of Cotton Mather's work. The culmination of this rhetorical tendency (which originated perhaps merely as a baroque joy in language, but persisted in American writing) was reached in Walt Whitman's poetry; and Whitman's all-absorbing, panethnic, and future-oriented poetic consciousness has often been interpreted as peculiarly American.

Tocqueville's reflections on the question "Why American Writers and Orators Often Use an Inflated Style" (in the second volume of *Democracy in America,* 1840) have been related to an American style ranging from Whitman's poetry to Faulkner's prose; yet the opposing tendency toward a "plain style" has also been associated with American writing, from William Bradford to Ernest Hemingway. Whereas the inflated style may reflect the desire to incorporate multiethnicity into literary form, the plain style may advocate linguistic simplicity in order to reach all those new men who are in the process of forging their American identity.

Another formal tendency in American literature that can be related to ethnicity is a sense of humor or irony, which is often derived from the disparity between "sivilized" and natural behavior in the sense of Mark Twain's *Huckleberry Finn,* or from the difference between outside assumptions and inside awareness in the sense of Langston Hughes's Simple or Peter Finley Dunne's Mr. Dooley. Sometimes the irony goes so deep that any connection between assumptions about ethnic background and a literary character become tenuous. Basil Ransom in Henry James's *The Bostonians* (1886) is a cardboard Southerner perhaps because the author hesitated to use regional or ethnic characteristics as the center of character motivation. Grace Paley's "The Immigrant Story" (1975) shows even greater ironic detachment from ethnicity as a motivating force by separating a long conversation about the difficulty and dubiousness of remembering from a consciously trite ethnic memoir which begins with the classic formula: "My mother and father came from a small town in Poland. They had three sons. My father decided to go to America, to 1. stay out of the army, 2. stay out of jail, 3. save his children from everyday wars and ordinary pogroms." The "reasons" for migration ultimately say nothing about the narrator's ethnic background.

In Gertrude Stein's *The Making of Americans* (1934) the rhetoric of the New World and of ethnicity is churningly regurgitated and spewed out as a critique of the realistic and semiautobiographic novels one might expect from such a title. What could illustrate the new consciousness of earlier ethnic writers better than Mary Antin's awareness that she was "nobly related": "Undoubtedly I was a Fellow Citizen, and George Washington was another." Susannah Rowson, author of the first American bestselling novel, *Charlotte* (1791), considered American authors more fortunate than Homer who had only "barbarous chieftains" to write about, while they had "matchless Washington." The relationship to Washington is crucial to Cooper's *Spy*; in *Moby-Dick,* Melville refers to Queequeg as "George Washington cannibalistically developed." Stein's *The Making of Americans* ironically reflects the Washington rhetoric, and, at the same time, responds to the epithet "dirty" that is so often hurled against minorities. Stein writes of the immigrant boy George, who "was not named after his grandfather," that he was "strong in sport and washing. He was not foreign in his washing. Oh, no, he

was really an american." Stein continues: "It's a great question this question of washing. One never can find any one who can be satisfied with anybody else's washing. I knew a man once who never as far as any one could see ever did any washing, and yet he described another with contempt, why he is a dirty hog sir, he never does any washing. The French tell me it's the Italians who never do any washing, the French and the Italians both find the Spanish a little short in their washing, the English find all the world lax in this business of washing, and the East finds all the West a pig, which never is clean with just the little cold water washing. And so it goes." In Stein's writing—as in Toomer's or Henry Roth's—the "new style" is related to ethnicity; in the mode of "ethnic modernism" ethnicity remains palpable while the writing transcends it. "Yes, George Dehning was not at all foreign in his washing but for him, too, the old world was not altogether lost behind him."

Ironically, some American modernists who defied ethnic categories and were associated with transethnic art movements developed a pseudoethnic identity as Bohemians. Andrew Greeley once suggested that intellectuals form an "ethnic group," and Waldo Frank saw artists, in the familiar terms of ethnicity and typology, as a new "chosen people." Modernists might denounce "Puritanism" (by which they often meant Victorian moralism and nativist arrogance rather than the historical culture of 17th-century New England), but defined even their "trans-nationalism" in the rhetoric of ethnicity. Van Wyck Brooks, for example, described the "nationalism of the poets, novelists and thinkers" as "a golden world in which one finds neither Roman, Jew, Barbarian nor Greek, for the prejudices of the brazen world are left behind there." Brooks cites Frank Lloyd Wright's "open plan" in architecture as an appropriate example of melting-pot art forms because it "abolishes all the partitions that have divided room from room" in the same way the "human laboratory" of America "abolishes the barriers between man and man in the interest of a wide sociality and all-human freedom. Wright has translated Walt Whitman into architecture." And Whitman is, as Waldo Frank noted, the formal prototype of ethnic modernists, the Moses of the new chosen people, the Bohemians.

ETHNICITY IN AMERICAN LITERATURE: ROSEBUD OR MACGUFFIN?

Can American literature help define the meaning of ethnicity? Read as simple "information," not as validation of social interpretations, ethnic literature often reveals more through its cultural allusions, language, imagery, and forms than through motifs and themes. Writers have been criticized for using an assimilationist melting-pot perspective when they were creating rebirth experiences as Paul's "new man" that were somewhat more complex than much melting-pot sociology. If we look for motifs in literature we may, for example, find several occurrences of ghetto roof-top settings in Jewish-American writing; however, we miss the point if we simply read such passages as evidence that tenement houses had flat roofs on which immigrants spent time. In Cahan's *Yekl*, for example, the "housetop idyl"

is more than an incidental "realistic" setting for immigrant Jake's incipient alliance with the more Americanized Mamie Fein; as Jules Chametzky has pointed out, this scene is a symbolic battle between the Old World past and the New World future, and the sheets on the clothesline are consciously metamorphosed into the shrouds of Jake's father and the covers of Mamie's bed. In Zangwill's *Melting Pot* the final scene takes place on the tenement rooftop to allow the cosmic dimensions of the American symphony full play against the red skies of the Fourth of July and with a full view of the Statue of Liberty. David Quixano, about to marry Vera, whose father was the Russian baron responsible for the pogrom in which David's parents died, becomes the prophet of the promised melting pot; the rooftop functions as Mount Sinai. Even in Gold's *Jews without Money* the rooftop is the place of metaphoric closeness to the Old World, where the narrator's father tells Romanian folk tales. And in Roth's *Call It Sleep* the rooftop is the locus of a Joycean epiphany, a revelation of great complexity.

Few readers attempt to read ethnic literature as evidence for the existence of rooftops; but the example of what even "realistic" or "socially oriented" writers do with as simple a motif serves as a warning against reading imaginative literature as social evidence. This caution is especially necessary since reading ethnic literature is sometimes motivated by an interest to find out what it is like to be "other" and to discover the true meaning of the *Mysteries* of "ethnicity." In a situation where ethnicity is no longer merely feared as dangerous otherness but is almost worshiped as a form of inspiration, writers have been able to combine demands for authenticity and spokesmanship as they symbolically claimed to represent whole ethnic groups in addressing general American audiences. When ethnic writers maintain that they are "Speaking for Ourselves," the reader has to decide whether to interpret the pronoun "ourselves" in the sense of "ethnic groups" (as Lillian Faderman does) or in the sense of "writers" (as Herbert Gans argues); for, despite all claims of ethnic representation, writers are more usually alienated from "ethnicity" than part of it. Writers may, in fact, be once de-ethnicized and later re-ethnicized intellectuals whose relationship to the group they supposedly represent may be quite romantic—or, in any event, more problematic than they sometimes care to admit.

In "The Custom-House," Hawthorne ironically defies filiopietism as he describes himself, from the point of view of "the old trunk of the family tree, with so much venerable moss upon it" as "its topmost bough, an idler." "A writer of story books!" Hawthorne hears the gray shadow of a forefather murmur disapprovingly about his descendant's choice of a profession. "Why, the degenerate fellow might as well have been a fiddler!" The gulf that separates most writers from "their" groups and alienates them from their backgrounds is as important a factor as the cultural socialization that shaped them. The tendency to become an "ethnic" writer is offset by the literary consciousness that transcends ethnicity. When Howells tried to encourage the development of an American literature independent of British influences, he suggested the Spanish picaresque mode as a prototype, and when today's ethnic writers sometimes turn away from *the* American

tradition, they often opt for equally American literary alternatives.

Despite ethnocentrism and filiopietism on the one side, and outside ethnic prejudice on the other, there has been an amazing amount of cross-cultural, trans-ethnic literature in America. The curiosity about *How the Other Half Lives* was not limited to muckraking photojournalists. There were slummers like Carl Van Vechten and Hutchins Hapgood, who used black and Jewish ethnicity as an inspiration and as a validation for their own desires to innovate American literature; there were authors who, like Henry Harland—"Sidney Luska"—changed their names in order to write "ethnic," and there were Americans like Waldo Frank, John Howard Griffin, and, more recently, even Superman's *Lois Lane* ("I am curious black"), who become "ethnic transvestites" for a time. Since the turn of the century, many American Bohemian art movements have emerged that are essentially transethnic; ironically, some writers would consider themselves merely as writers, whereas some of their colleagues might look upon them as representatives of ethnic groups. If Philip Yordan's play *Anna Lucasta* (1944) is really a Polish immigrant play, which became only successful after it was rewritten as a black play, then this example of literary transethnicity is another indication of the structural nature of literary ethnicity: the literary interest lies less in the specific cultural emanation of one ethnic group than in the relationship of a minority to a majority—which makes it ethnically interchangeable.

What then is ethnicity, this new word? In literature, it may appear as a bloody footprint or as an adaptation of biblical lore, as wife of youth, as otherness, or as divided self. A word, a gesture, a gut reaction, a double entendre may be at the heart of ethnic consciousness. Sometimes characters in ethnic literature act like opera singers who are suddenly placed on a drama stage and have to thematize and defend their traditional form in a different medium. At other times they appear displaced in time like Rip Van Winkle who once said: "I am not myself—I'm somebody else . . . everything's changed, and I'm changed, and I can't tell what's my name, or who I am!"

The specific nature and meaning of ethnicity often remain less clear than its literary function. Alfred Hitchcock called the secret that spies are pursuing the "MacGuffin" and explained that "the logicians are wrong in trying to figure out the truth of a MacGuffin, since it's beside the point. The only thing that really matters is that . . . the plans, documents, or secrets must seem to be of vital importance to the characters. To me, the narrator, they're of no importance whatever." It may be heartless to view literary ethnicity as such a MacGuffin; yet the sum total of an experience, the pride and suffering of a specific ethnicity must be functionalized for the sake of a story—and thus ethnicity becomes a literary vehicle that may mean everything for a character, but remain general or cryptic to the reader. "Old World," "mother," "romance," "complexion," or "melting pot" are words that may be very specifically charged for different ethnic characters; yet the literary forms that have developed from such bases use the center of emotionality structurally and make felt and experienced ethnicity a MacGuffin. Perhaps the most successful literature of ethnicity, then, does not at-tempt a full and truthful initiation into the *Mysteries* of ethnicity, but stops with partial revelations and a sense of secrecy and "mystery." The word may temporarily be attached to scenic revelations—as in the confrontation with those dark mysterious mothers who pass as ethnic wives in Chesnutt and Cahan. But after such moments a sense of wonder needs to be restored. If Charles Foster Kane's last word is seen as a version of ethnicity, then it becomes apparent how "Rosebud" in *Citizen Kane* (1941) succeeds in arousing curiosity and concern because of the mystery that remains attached to the word. "Maybe Rosebud was something Kane couldn't get or something he lost, but it wouldn't have explained anything!" Thompson says in the film, and adds a remark which is as appropriate for "Rosebud" as it is for "ethnicity": "I don't think any word can explain a man's life."

If "Rosebud" cannot explain one man's life, how could "ethnicity" account for the shape of a whole nation's literature? Despite the astonishing connections that the concept of ethnicity allows us to perceive within American culture, we must remember that "ethnicity" is an abstraction, too. When Karl Marx and Friedrich Engels first developed their principles of literary realism—interestingly, in the context of a debate about Eugène Sue's *Mystères de Paris*—they reminded German Hegelians that the word "fruit," for example, was merely an abstraction, which only "the mystery of speculative construction" could place on a level superior to that of "apples," "pears," "almonds," or "raisins." This procedure allows Hegelians to maintain that "the essential qualities of these things are not to be found in their real, palpable existence, but in their essence as 'fruit'—which I first abstracted and assigned to them in my imagination" (*The Holy Family,* 1844). It may be useful to remember that the situation of the abstraction "ethnicity" is analogous to that of Marx's "fruit." No matter to what extent different literary renditions of "ethnicity" may resemble each other and be part of American patterns, "ethnicity as such" only exists as an abstraction in need of continuous concretization.

Bibliography

Among the best essays concerned with questions of ethnicity and literature are Daniel Aaron, "The Hyphenate Writer and American Letters," *Smith Alumnae Quarterly* (July 1964): 213–217; Jules Chametzky, "Our Decentralized Literature; A Consideration of Regional, Ethnic, Racial, and Sexual Factors," *Jahrbuch für Amerikastudien* 17 (1972): 56–72; Henry Pochmann, "The Mingling of Tongues," *Literary History of the United States,* ed. Robert E. Spiller, rev. ed. (New York, 1953): 676–693; and the appropriate sections in Carl Wittke, *We Who Built America: The Saga of the Immigrant* (Englewood Cliffs, N.J., 1939). A thematic survey of the literature of immigration is given by Carter Davidson, "The Immigrant Strain in Contemporary American Literature," *English Journal* 25 (December 1936): 862–868; Malcolm Cowley, "Where Writers Come From," *The Literary Situation* (New York, 1954): 152–161, raises interesting questions about ethnic, regional, and educational backgrounds of American writers; Brom Weber, "Our Multi-Ethnic Origins and American Literary Studies," *MELUS* 2 (March 1975): 5–19, is a suggestive address given at the Modern Language Association. Volume 9 of the Proceedings of the Comparative Literature Symposium at Texas Tech University is a two-part reader on *Ethnic Literature Since 1776: The Many Voices of America* (Lubbock, Tex., 1978). A "Comprehensive History of Ethnic Literatures" is being prepared by the Society for the Study of Multiethnic Literature in the United States (MELUS). Of further interest are Randolph S. Bourne, "Trans-National America," *War and the Intellectuals,* ed. Carl Resek (New York, 1964): 107–123; Van Wyck Brooks, "Transnationalism," *The Writer in America* (New York, 1953): 86–108; Howard Mumford

Jones, "American Literature and the Melting Pot," *Ideas in America* (Cambridge, Mass., 1944): 185–204; and several essays in David F. Bowers, ed., *Foreign Influences in American Life* (Princeton, N.J., 1944).

The most complete bibliography of ethnicity, arranged by ethnic groups and with many entries on literature and criticism, is *A Comprehensive Bibliography for the Study of American Minorities*, ed. Wayne Charles Miller and others, 2 vols. (New York, 1976). A more easily usable reference tool is *The Image of Pluralism in American Literature: An Annotated Bibliography on the American Experience of European Ethnic Groups* (New York, 1974) by Babette F. Inglehart and Anthony R. Mangione; it includes lists of literary works of eleven ethnic groups, brief plot summaries, and a thematic index. Further bibliographies are Joseph S. Roucek, *The Immigrant in Fiction and Biography* (New York, 1945), and Nancy S. Prichard, *A Selected Bibliography of American Ethnic Writing and Supplement* (Champaign, Ill., 1969).

Several literary anthologies contain important selections from major texts, introductory and interpretive materials, as well as bibliographic references. Katharine D. Newman, *The American Equation: Literature in a Multi-Ethnic Culture* (Boston, 1971), arranges and interprets well-selected literary works under illuminating chapter headings. Edward Ifkovic, *American Letter: Immigrant and Ethnic Writing* (Englewood Cliffs, N.J., 1975), organizes the literature, with introductions and study questions, in thematic units. Lillian Faderman and Barbara Bradshaw, *Speaking for Ourselves*, 2nd ed. (Glenview, Ill., 1975), and Wayne Miller, *A Gathering of Ghetto Writers* (New York, 1972), are arranged by ethnic groups.

WERNER SOLLORS

LITHUANIAN TATARS: *see* TATARS

LITHUANIANS

The Lithuanian-American community took shape as the result of two distinct migrations. The first began in the late 1860s and continued without major interruption until 1914, when first the outbreak of World War I and then the restrictive immigration laws of the 1920s brought the movement to a close. Most of the 300,000 or so Lithuanians who journeyed to the United States in that period had been peasants in their homeland communities; they emigrated primarily to improve their worsening socioeconomic status in eastern Europe. The second migration, occurring after World War II, was considerably smaller and was made up of a variety of social groups. These arrivals, about 30,000 in number, were often professionals and intellectuals who entered the United States as displaced persons and political exiles fleeing Soviet rule. In 1970 the number of first- and second-generation Lithuanians living in the United States was estimated at 331,000 (a figure that includes a sizable group of Jews and smaller numbers of Poles and Russians who emigrated from Lithuania), but the total number of Americans of at least partial Lithuanian descent probably exceeds 1 million.

Origins

Lithuanian immigrants of the pre-1914 period came primarily from three adjacent provinces along the western frontier of the Russian Empire: Kaunas (Kovno), Suvalkija (Suwałki), and Vilnius (Vilna). This region, together with the neighboring counties of German East Prussia, encompassed most of the Lithuanian ethnographic area in eastern Europe at the end of the 19th century. The Lithuanian peasants of East Prussia, who numbered less than 200,000 in 1900, did not figure very prominently in the emigration of this time nor in the formation of the Lithuanian-American community. Most of them belonged to the Lutheran and Reformed

Lithuania

Boundary of the Russian and German Empires before 1918

Boundaries of provinces before 1918

Boundary of the independent Lithuania, 1920-1939

200   Km.   Miles

traditions and thus felt a closer cultural kinship with their German coreligionists than with the larger, predominantly Roman Catholic, Lithuanian population living farther to the east. Because of their Old World experiences and values, the relatively small number of Lithuanian emigrants from East Prussia tended to blend into the various German Protestant groups in the United States.

The rural exodus from tsarist Lithuania, by contrast, was considerably larger and more complex. Prior to 1795 this area formed the political center of the Lithuanian Grand Duchy, a feudal state that had coalesced out of a number of pagan Baltic tribes in the 13th century. In the late 1300s, however, Grand Duke Jogaila (Jagiello), after accepting Roman Catholicism, married the heiress to the Polish throne, became king of Poland as Ladislaus II, and thereby created a common royal line for the two realms. The close dynastic and ecclesiastical ties that thus developed between Poland and Lithuania were strengthened in 1569 by the Treaty of Lublin which established a permanent constitutional union of the two states. This Polish-Lithuanian Commonwealth, a confederation known as the *Rzeczpospolita*, lasted until 1795 when most of its territories were incorporated into the Russian Empire.

It was during the period of the Rzeczpospolita that Lithuanian feudal society hardened into deeply rooted, durable forms. First, as the nobles established their political hegemony within the Lithuanian Grand Duchy in the 15th and 16th centuries, they steadily narrowed the customary privileges and legal rights of their peasant vassals until, by the late 1500s, most Lithuanian

villagers had been reduced to a permanent servile status. Second, by the middle decades of the 17th century, Roman Catholicism was firmly established as the official religion of the Lithuanian Grand Duchy; led by the Jesuits, the Counter Reformation of the late 1500s and early 1600s not only reversed the deep inroads initially made by Lutheranism and Calvinism among the Lithuanian nobility, but also destroyed many of the pagan folkways that still persisted among the peasantry. This period also witnessed the genesis of a Lithuanian literary language, as both Protestant and Catholic reformers began publishing catechisms and devotional tracts in the native vernacular. Finally, because of the close political and cultural ties that had developed with the Kingdom of Poland, most Lithuanian nobles and Catholic clergymen adopted the language and values of the Polish aristocracy as their own. Linguistic distinctions thus came to reinforce the rigid sociojuridical barriers separating the privileged from the servile: the Lithuanian dialects which remained in use among the villagers served as public symbols of their pagan and barbarous traditions and their unenviable status within the serf regime; the Polish language, by contrast, become identified in the popular mind with aristocratic valor, Christian civility, and a prestigious social position.

Only during the second half of the 19th century did these entrenched feudal values begin to erode, largely as a consequence of administrative and juridical changes gradually introduced by the new Russian rulers after 1795. The most dramatic of these was the abolition of serfdom in the 1860s; Lithuanian peasants received a greater degree of freedom in organizing their social and economic activities, and most also acquired legal title to their former serf holdings. Having thus undermined the political power of the Polish nobility and redistributed much of its landed wealth, the tsarist government next attempted to accomplish two closely related aims: the Russification of the Lithuanian peasants and their conversion from Catholicism to Orthodoxy. Between 1864 and 1904, a complete ban was placed on the publication of Lithuanian literature in the established Latin script; over the same period, Russian became the sole language of business and instruction in most administrative, judicial, and educational institutions. Existing controls on Catholic pastoral work were tightened, Catholics encountered discrimination in securing administrative positions, and their rights to acquire land were curtailed. Finally, the tsarist authorities sponsored the colonization of Russian peasants in Lithuania and encouraged Orthodox missionaries to proselytize among them. Often haphazardly executed, these repressive measures failed for the most part to change the habits or loyalties of the Lithuanian peasantry; rather, the workings of an alien and cumbersome administrative system contributed to the nascent spirit of cultural nationalism within tsarist Lithuanian society.

Although Lithuanian villagers shared a common Baltic language and a common Roman Catholic faith, the modern concept of nationalism was quite alien to most of them prior to the early 1900s. The Lithuanian ethnoreligious minority in tsarist Russia, numbering about 1.6 million in the imperial census of 1897, actually broke down into two distinctive regional folk cultures. The smaller of these, the Žemaičiai (Lowlanders), in-

habited the western districts of Kaunas province, while the Augštaičiai (Highlanders) lived to the east and south. These folk cultures contained several smaller dialect groups, the most distinctive being the Kapsai and Zanavykai in northwestern Suvalkija and the Dzukai in the eastern counties of this province and in the adjacent southwestern districts of Vilnius. Even within these smaller dialect groups, local variations of speech and circumscribed patterns of association and loyalty made each rural parish of tsarist Lithuania almost a folk culture unto itself.

Insofar as Lithuanian villagers had a more inclusive reference point of group identity, they often thought of themselves as Poles. This identification was in part territorial. For several centuries prior to 1795, the Lithuanian Grand Duchy had existed as a subordinate political unit within the larger Polish state; even after the imposition of tsarist rule, the province of Suvalkija was administered as a part of Congress (Russian) Poland. Many villagers also indentified culturally with the local Polophile elites that had traditionally dominated the social life of the Lithuanian countryside. Because the Polish language was popularly associated with superior social status, wealthier peasants and their children often adopted it as their own. The Polonization of Lithuanian villagers was further encouraged by the Catholic hierarchy. Because church leaders considered Lithuanian to be a pagan, barbarous tongue, Polish was often the sole language of worship and religious instruction in many rural parishes.

By the 1880s, however, both the Polophile traditions and the parochialism that had characterized Lithuanian rural life up to that time gradually began to give way. The shift toward a more nationalistic outlook was reflected most clearly in the emergence of a new social group, a Lithuanian intelligentsia drawn from peasant backgrounds. The young clergymen, teachers, doctors, and lawyers who made up this cosmopolitan stratum shared a broad commitment to the liberal Western ideals of religious tolerance, national autonomy, and political democracy. Although their numbers initially were quite small, the members of this nationalist underground succeeded during the 1880s and 1890s in publishing a growing body of Lithuanian literature in neighboring East Prussia. These illicit newspapers, catechisms, and political tracts were then smuggled on a massive scale into tsarist Lithuania and distributed among the villagers. Meanwhile, with the formation of a Lithuanian Social Democratic party in 1896, a more radical faction within the intelligentsia quickly coalesced and grew in importance.

The increasing popular acceptance of nationalist, liberal, and socialist values was evidenced in widespread revolutionary outbreaks throughout the Lithuanian countryside in 1905–1906 fusing economic grievances with demands for greater national autonomy. In the less repressive political climate that followed these disturbances, numerous Lithuanian schools, newspapers, and cultural and economic societies quickly established themselves. The German invasion of 1915 brought more than a century of tsarist rule to a close, and toward the end of World War I a constituent assembly meeting at Vilnius proclaimed an independent Lithuanian state. In 1945, however, the advancing Red Army once more extended Russian rule over the area and

helped establish the Communist regime that remains in power.

MIGRATION AND ARRIVAL

Small groups of Lithuanian villagers began to migrate on a regular basis in the 1860s and 1870s. Three developments served as important preconditions for this movement. First, the abolition of serfdom in the 1860s removed many of the juridical restrictions that had tended to inhibit the mobility of Lithuanian villagers in the past. Second, a state-sponsored railroad boom which began in the late 1850s and continued into the early 1870s led to an imperial railway network whose major lines transected all three provinces of tsarist Lithuania. These railroads not only facilitated travel to and from the Russian Empire and points beyond, but their construction also stimulated a regional demand for unskilled seasonal labor. Many of the earliest Lithuanian migrants began by working on those sections of the railway network that passed their native parishes. In subsequent years they would journey to seek employment as contract laborers farther along the line or on related construction projects. Finally, a severe famine disrupted the Lithuanian peasant economy in the late 1860s, compelling many landless villagers and smallholders to wander the countryside in search of work and to beg for food. Against this background of fear and despair the first groups of Lithuanian peasants made the journey to America. Migrant networks began to emerge during the 1860s and 1870s and gradually expanded over the next 40 years until, by 1914, few village communities remained completely untouched.

The continuous growth of this rural exodus after 1870 resulted primarily from the changing nature of the Lithuanian peasant economy. For one thing, the constant subdivision of small land allotments among a growing village population produced a sizable group of marginal and landless cultivators who depended almost entirely on the earnings they could make as tenants, sharecroppers, and farm laborers for the estate owners and the larger peasant landlords. The socioeconomic status of these villagers was undermined further by the worldwide agricultural depression of the 1870s and 1880s. Falling prices for cereals and flax, the two major cash crops, also sharply reduced the farm income of many peasants of average means who formed the largest stratum within Lithuanian village society; a growing number of them became caught in a vicious cycle of indebtedness from which there seemed little hope of extrication without outside earnings. The redemption payments the peasants owed for their land allotments, together with a regressive system of imperial and local taxation, drained declining farm incomes still further, and Lithuanian villagers increasingly journeyed to the developing urban industrial centers of Europe and North America in search of better economic opportunities. Although higher earnings figured as the primary consideration in the decision to move, many peasants also found in emigration an opportune means of escaping service in the tsarist army, especially after 1874 when the Russian government introduced a comprehensive system of conscription.

The patterns of Lithuanian peasant mobility that emerged between 1870 and 1914 were complex. A sizable number of Lithuanian villagers migrated only on a seasonal or temporary basis; they saw their outside cash earnings as a means of redeeming old debts, improving farm inventories, and expanding landholdings. These sojourners often traveled and worked in small labor collectives known as *artel*s. Their members would find temporary employment as agricultural laborers on the large estates in neighboring Prussia and Latvia; as factory operatives in such emerging urban industrial centers of the Russian Empire as Riga, St. Petersburg, Moscow, and Odessa; as mine laborers in the Ukraine; and as contract workers at hundreds of railroad and construction sites within tsarist Lithuania itself, in nearby Poland and Latvia, and deep in the Russian interior. In time, a growing number of migrants settled in the larger cities of eastern Europe. By 1914, according to one contemporary estimate, about 35,000 Lithuanians were to be found in Riga, 30,000 in St. Petersburg, 15,000 in Liepāja, 7,000 in Odessa, and 2,000 in Moscow.

In the 1860s and 1870s Lithuanian villagers also sought work in the major industrial centers of England and Scotland. Emigration to the British Isles was never very large, though by the early 1900s Lithuanian colonies had taken root in such cities as London, Liverpool, and Manchester and in a number of smaller mining communities in northern England and Scotland. More often, however, the British Isles served merely as a steppingstone to the United States.

Emigration to America gradually became the most important feature within the pattern of Lithuanian peasant mobility. Small groups of villagers arrived during and after the famine years of the late 1860s. Though at first relatively small, this movement continued steadily thereafter, grew during the 1880s, and became massive in the late 1890s and early 1900s. After 1870 Lithuanian villagers increasingly arrived through a process that sociologists and historians refer to as chain migration. Despite physical separation from their homeland communities, the earliest immigrants often maintained their Old World ties. As the newcomers gradually became established, many would write home to invite relatives and friends to join them and often sent back money or tickets for the trip as well. Those who crossed the Atlantic in this manner could usually also expect their American sponsors to provide them with temporary board and lodging until a job could be found or with valuable connections and information for securing employment. This pattern of informal mutual assistance within hundreds of families and villages produced, over a period of 40 years, numerous migrant chains that stretched from the dispersed peasant communities of tsarist Lithuania to the major American urban industrial centers.

Most Lithuanian immigrants were either young bachelors or married men who left their wives and children behind in the Old World. For these newcomers, the journey to America often formed one point, but by no means the terminal one, in a much larger personal history of mobility that may have begun with a summer's sojourn in Riga, in St. Petersburg, or (as in the case of Jurgis Rudkus, the hero of Upton Sinclair's novel *The Jungle*) at a railroad construction site near Smolensk. Although some immigrants quickly became involved in the economic life of a particular American city or town, many continued to be quite mobile. Without any real property or familial obligations, they could move

about easily and often from one industrial center to another, using those same extended networks of relatives and friends that had initially brought them to America. Though impossible to gauge fully, the extent of their movement is suggested by a parish census conducted in 1906 among the Lithuanian residents of Lawrence, Mass. Of the 1,324 Lithuanians who lived in Lawrence in that year, 348 had come from other industrial communities in America, chiefly from Boston and the anthracite districts of Pennsylvania, while 774 had arrived directly from tsarist Lithuania, and the remaining 202 had been born in the United States.

However, the rate of return migration was high: for every five who arrived between 1899 and 1914, one would depart. Although some of the returnees undoubtedly left America because of failure, most had probably never intended to settle there permanently in the first place. Like the seasonal migrants in the industrial centers of eastern and western Europe, the peasant sojourners who came to the United States sought only to accumulate enough cash savings to pay off old debts in their homeland communities or to expand their agricultural operations there.

Amidst this continual movement within the United States and back and forth across the Atlantic, immigrant communities gradually took root and stabilized in American cities and towns. Before 1890 most Lithuanians moved to the anthracite districts of central Pennsylvania, finding jobs as mine laborers in the many coal towns of the region (Plymouth, Freeland, Hazleton, Shenandoah, Pittston, Mahanoy City, Mount Carmel, and Scranton). At the same time, smaller groups of Lithuanians were also settling in such older urban centers as New York, Baltimore, Philadelphia, and Boston, where they tended to concentrate in the garment trades. During the late 1880s and early 1890s the nuclei of future ethnic communities formed in the bituminous districts of western Pennsylvania and southern Illinois, in many of the smaller industrial towns of Connecticut (Waterbury, New Britain, and Hartford), Massachusetts (Worcester, Brockton, and Lawrence), and New Jersey (Elizabeth and Newark), and in such midwestern cities as Pittsburgh, Cleveland, Chicago, and Detroit. Over the next three decades, smaller Lithuanian colonies appeared in virtually all the cities and most of the industrial towns of the Northeast and Midwest. By 1910 the largest immigrant communities had already coalesced in Chicago, New York, Boston, Philadelphia, and Cleveland, and these were becoming the major organizational centers of the Lithuanian-American community.

ECONOMIC LIFE

Lacking special industrial or entrepreneurial skills, Lithuanian peasant newcomers clustered at the lowest levels of the American occupational hierarchy. They usually started out as unskilled laborers in the coal mines of Pennsylvania, Illinois, and West Virginia, in the garment shops of Chicago, Rochester, N.Y., and the older cities along the Atlantic, in the textile and shoe factories of New England, in the oil refineries of New York and New Jersey, in the forest industries of Maine and Michigan, in the steel mills and foundries of Worcester, Pittsburgh, Cleveland, and Chicago, in the sugar refineries of New York, Philadelphia, and Boston, and in the packinghouses of Chicago, Omaha, Neb., and

Sioux City, Iowa. Although most immigrants would remain manual laborers for the duration of their stay in America, there was nonetheless some room for maneuver. As they developed proficiency at their jobs and learned the rudiments of the English language, a growing number slowly moved into the ranks of the semiskilled and skilled.

The immigrant families that were reunited in the United States and the new ones created there often invested their savings in lots and cottages, a purchase made easier by ethnic building and loan associations. By 1920 Lithuanian immigrants had formed about 30 of these lending agencies: 20 in Illinois alone, 4 in Pennsylvania, 3 in Maryland, 3 in New Jersey, and 1 each in Massachusetts and Ohio. By these different means, they gradually improved their status and became more closely integrated into the economic and social life of American cities and towns.

Within most Lithuanian colonies, a small group of newcomers also succeeded in establishing retail and service trades that catered primarily to the special needs of their countrymen. The most common of these enterprises was the saloon, an institution that often combined under one roof the functions of social center, boarding house, restaurant, travel agency, bank, and labor exchange. In 1909, for example, 180 of the approximately 500 Lithuanian businesses in Chicago were saloons. There and in other American cities and towns, Lithuanian immigrants also engaged in a wide variety of small enterprises that included groceries, mortuaries, barbershops, pharmacies, bakeries, printshops, and steamship and real-estate agencies. In Baltimore, Brooklyn, and Boston, a sizable number also operated small tailoring shops that did contract work for the larger clothing warehouses. Because they occupied an influential position in the social hierarchy of emerging immigrant communities, these ethnic entrepreneurs often took the lead in organizing the numerous fraternal, religious, and cultural associations that appeared in most Lithuanian colonies after 1890.

SOCIAL ORGANIZATION

The first Lithuanian immigrants did not immediately form a separate ethnic community or establish their own fraternal and religious institutions. Rather, most tended to intermingle and assimilate with their Polish Catholic coreligionists. Because of the close social and cultural ties that had traditionally existed between these two groups in eastern Europe, Lithuanian newcomers initially continued to associate Polishness with superior social status and with loyalty to Roman Catholicism, and they accepted Polish leadership; until about 1890 Polish and Polophile priests and laymen dominated most of the benefit societies and parishes that Lithuanian immigrants had helped organize and joined. In the late 1880s, however, these Old World patterns of cultural identification and deference quickly began to change. Thereafter, as the emigration from tsarist Lithuania continued to increase, Lithuanian newcomers began to organize separate fraternal and religious institutions and to draw clearer cultural boundaries between themselves and the Poles.

Two political émigrés, Jonas Šliūpas (1861–1944) and Aleksandras Burba (1854–1898), played particularly influential roles in laying the institutional and ideological

foundations of the Lithuanian-American culture that began to emerge in the late 1880s and early 1890s. Šliūpas had been a founding member of the Lithuanian intelligentsia in eastern Europe where he had helped edit *Auszra* (The Dawn), the first Lithuanian nationalist journal, published in East Prussia. In 1884, to escape arrest by the German and Russian police, Šliūpas came to New York and soon afterward began publishing *Lietuwiszkasis Balsas* (The Lithuanian Voice, 1885–1889), one of the earliest Lithuanian newspapers to appear in America. Through this journal and on periodic visits to the growing immigrant communities in the Northeast, Šliūpas constantly urged his countrymen to free themselves from the Poles and to establish separate ethnic institutions. He helped organize local fraternal and educational societies in such places as New York, Baltimore, and Shenandoah, Pa., and in 1886 initiated the first national federation of Lithuanian benefit associations, the Susiwienimas Wisu Lietuwninku Amerike (Alliance of All Lithuanians in America). By 1888, however, this alliance had dissolved, and *Lietuwiszkasis Balsas* ceased publication the following year.

Aleksandras Burba, a Catholic priest who came to America in 1889, proved to be a more effective ethnic leader. Like Šliūpas, Burba had been a prominent figure in the emerging intelligentsia of tsarist Lithuania where he had been subjected to constant harassment by the civil and ecclesiastical authorities. In the United States, by contrast, Burba found a free and fertile setting for continuing his work as a nationalist agitator and organizer. His first sermon as pastor of the Polish-Lithuanian congregation at Plymouth, Pa., provoked a riot between the two groups in 1889; shortly thereafter Burba helped his countrymen found a separate Catholic parish there. Through the early 1890s Burba traveled widely among the immigrant colonies in America, encouraging Lithuanian newcomers to shun their Polish coreligionists, form their own ethnic societies, and, where possible, organize separate Catholic congregations. Largely through Burba's sponsorship, a growing number of young nationalistic priests and seminarians arrived during the 1890s. These Catholic clergymen quickly coalesced into an ethnic leadership cadre: like Burba himself, they regularly journeyed among the dispersed immigrant settlements and worked closely with local lay leaders in establishing fraternal societies and Catholic parishes for their Lithuanian countrymen.

The Lithuanian-American community began to assume more concrete forms in the late 1880s; during the 1890s it had three overlapping levels of social organization. The first consisted of informal networks of friends and relatives originating in the village societies of tsarist Lithuania and re-created in American cities and towns through chain migration. Immigrants from the same Old World parish or region often lived together in the same boarding houses and neighborhoods, worked together in the same factories and mines, and patronized the same ethnic saloons and shops. The constant arrival of friends, wives, and sweethearts from tsarist Lithuania reinforced in American cities and towns their original ties. The personal networks around which immigrant colonies formed and grew usually reflected an extreme diversity of village origins. The 1,324 Lithuanian newcomers who lived in Lawrence, Mass., in 1906, for example, represented no less than 78 Old World

parishes, all three provinces of tsarist Lithuania, and all the major peasant folk cultures and dialect groups. A similar diversity of village origins typified most of the immigrant communities that had emerged by 1914. Even as Lithuanian peasant newcomers preserved their parochial attachments and loyalties in American urban industrial settings, they also became more aware of their common membership in a larger national group.

As Lithuanian-American communities grew in size and diversity, local immigrant leaders organized more inclusive and more tightly structured ethnic institutions. The most common voluntary associations were fraternal benefit societies. Local organizations of this type offered the Lithuanian saloonkeepers and retailers who often initiated them an opportunity to cultivate or enlarge an ethnic clientele and to institutionalize their leadership positions in the emerging community. To the members and their kin, the mutual-benefit society provided financial assistance in times of sickness and death. Finally, fraternal organizations attempted to control morals and behavior in fluid urban settings where such traditional agencies of social control as the autocratic state, the established church, and the patriarchal peasant household were absent. Benefit associations typically levied fines for such transgressions as drunk and disorderly conduct, smoking, spitting, cursing, and other types of behavior that could bring disgrace upon the society and the ethnic community. Most also required their members, under penalty of fine or expulsion, to observe their religious duties as Roman Catholics. These mutual-benefit societies in turn became the nuclei around which Lithuanian newcomers organized their Roman Catholic parishes. The same saloonkeepers and merchants who had initiated the formation of local benefit societies usually served as lay trustees of the immigrant congregations as well. Although a chronic shortage of priests and the mobility and penury of many recent arrivals often hindered the organization of Lithuanian Catholic parishes, about 30 were founded by 1900, more than 100 by 1920. Between 1890 and 1930 most of the larger Lithuanian-American communities developed extensive local networks of ethnic organizations that included educational societies, libraries, newspapers, evening and Sunday schools, women's and citizens' clubs, musical and theatrical groups, temperance and devotional societies, and professional and businessmen's associations.

National federations and centralized societies formed the third level of Lithuanian-American social organization in the 1890s. The most important of these was the Susivienijimas Lietuvių Amerikoje (Lithuanian Alliance of America, SLA). This federation was initially founded under a different name in 1886 by the Polophile clergy and laity to counteract Šliūpas's growing influence among Lithuanian newcomers. In 1890, however, Burba and his supporters gained control of the alliance, purged it of the Polophile elements, and turned it into an organization for mobilizing Lithuanian immigrants along nationalistic lines. Under the leadership of Burba and of Father Jonas Žilinskas (1870–1932), who succeeded him as president in 1894, the SLA rapidly expanded its membership and broadened its social activities. By 1900, it had almost 100 local affiliates with a combined membership of well over 2,000 and published its own newspaper, *Tėvynė* (Homeland, 1896–1901).

Though officially incorporated as a fraternal insurance association, the alliance functioned more as a Lithuanian government-in-exile. Its members sponsored anti-Russian meetings, petitions, pamphlets, and parades, provided moral and financial assistance to the nationalist underground in tsarist Lithuania and East Prussia, protested congressional bills restricting immigration, and raised funds and organized demonstrations in support of striking Lithuanian workers in the United States. At the alliance's annual convention in 1896, several delegates formed a second national federation, the Tēvynēs Mylētojų Draugija (Society of Patriots, TMD); this group sponsored the publication of Lithuanian books and pamphlets for distribution to its local affiliates as well as to people in the Old World. Finally, in 1900, the immigrant clergy formed a Catholic educational society, the Motinēlē (Little Mother), which provided scholarships for deserving Lithuanian students.

The growth of a vigorous immigrant press both reflected and contributed to the maturation of the Lithuanian-American community in the 1890s. Although five Lithuanian newspapers had appeared in the United States prior to 1890—the earliest, *Lietuwiszka Gazieta* (Lithuanian Gazette), in 1879—all of them except Šliūpas's *Balsas* were Polophile in orientation. By 1900, however, more than 20 new ethnic journals appeared; although many of them quickly folded, two weeklies, *Vienybē Lietuvninkų* (Lithuanian Unity, f. 1886) published at Plymouth, Pa., and the Chicago *Lietuva* (Lithuania, 1892–1920), acquired sizable readerships. Both journals adopted a militantly nationalistic tone, and their editors worked diligently to raise the ethnic self-consciousness of the Lithuanians. Immigrant publishers also issued reading manuals, dictionaries, astrological guides, Lithuanian short stories and plays, and a wide variety of popular tracts intended to familiarize their peasant countrymen with contemporary political, social, and scientific developments.

The federations, local societies, Catholic parishes, and publishing ventures all helped to mobilize support for the nationalist cause and to define firmer and clearer group boundaries for the growing Lithuanian minority in America. From the pulpits, at social gatherings, and in newspaper columns, the immigrants were urged to take full advantage of the opportunities for self-improvement that the host society offered: to practice thrift, to lead clean, sober lives, to seek education, and thus to find wealth and happiness.

ETHNIC POLITICS AND THE PRESS

Ethnic leaders in the 1890s sought to create an organizational and cultural unity among Lithuanian immigrants which would supplant both the Polophile traditions and the parochial outlook that had characterized the peasant communities of the Old World. As the Lithuanian-American community grew in size and complexity, however, it also began to fragment into antagonistic local factions and ideological groups. These intraethnic conflicts often stemmed from unresolved problems of authority and status. Because Catholic clergymen had traditionally enjoyed a privileged position within the hierarchical social order of the Lithuanian countryside, many immigrant priests continued to expect deference and unquestioning obedience from

their parishioners in the United States. Such Old World values, however, came into conflict with the social ambitions of those self-made laymen—the saloonkeepers, petty retailers, and ethnic publishers—who had quickly achieved leadership positions within the immigrant communities. Local conflicts between "arrogant" pastors and "presumptuous" laymen occurred with increasing frequency in the late 1890s and through the 1900s. The usually trivial initial disagreement acted as a catalyst for congregational bickering that could divide immigrant communities into antagonistic factions supporting or opposing the local pastor. In some Lithuanian parishes, the lay dissidents petitioned the diocesan authorities to transfer their priest; in others, they initiated civil suits to gain legal control of congregational property; in still others, they organized strikes and boycotts against their pastor. Mounting tensions and frustrations periodically resulted in violence. Catholic priests were sometimes assaulted, several parishes were rocked by riots in their churches, and at least two rectories were bombed. If in the end they failed to dislodge an unpopular pastor, disgruntled laymen sometimes simply organized their own schismatic parishes and invited renegade priests to minister to them. Between 1900 and 1920 about a dozen of these so-called independent or national Catholic churches could be found in such cities as Baltimore, Chicago, Worcester, Boston, Lawrence, Scranton, Pittsburgh, and Philadelphia. Most of them eventually disbanded, but the Scranton and Lawrence parishes survived into the 1970s.

Pervasive local disputes between lay leaders and the immigrant clergy also spawned the growth of secularist and anticlerical organizations. The earliest Lithuanian benefit associations usually restricted their membership to conscientious Roman Catholics, but many of the local fraternal and educational societies that formed in the late 1890s and through the 1900s completely dissociated themselves from the churches and accepted all Lithuanian newcomers without regard to their religious beliefs. In some communities lay dissidents acquired control of the older Catholic societies and used them for mobilizing opposition to their pastors. An anticlerical crusade led by Jonas Šliūpas gradually gained considerable notoriety. Although earlier he had cooperated with Father Burba in separating Lithuanian immigrants from their Polish coreligionists, Šliūpas soon turned against the Catholic church and its priests. By the early 1890s he had helped establish several local lodges of the Lietuvių Mokslo Draugija (Lithuanian Educational Society, LMD), a group that espoused the principles of materialism and free thought. The society ceased functioning by the mid-1890s, but in 1900 Šliūpas formed a second anticlerical federation, the Lietuvių Laisvamanių Susivienijimas (Lithuanian Alliance of Freethinkers, LLS). The late 1890s also witnessed the appearance of several anticlerical and atheistic newspapers that included Šliūpas's own *Nauja Gadynē* (New Age, 1894–1896) and a half-dozen short-lived weeklies and monthlies published in Baltimore, Pittsburgh, and Chicago. The older and more popular nationalist newspapers like *Vienybē Lietuvninkų* and *Lietuva* (whose editors and publishers had embroiled themselves in local parish controversies) also began to assume a more critical attitude toward the immigrant clergy in the late 1890s.

In 1901 mounting tensions between clergy and laymen split the Lithuanian Alliance of America. The immigrant priests and their lay supporters quickly established their own Susivienijimas Lietuvių Rymo Katalikų Amerikoje (Lithuanian Roman Catholic Alliance of America, SLRKA) which restricted membership to practicing Roman Catholics. The liberal nationalists, as their opponents were called, simultaneously formed a competing federation that retained the initials of the earlier alliance, SLA, and accepted all Lithuanian immigrants regardless of religious affiliation. The new SLA grew quite rapidly and by 1910 had close to 250 local affiliates and more than 10,000 members. In 1901 the liberal nationalists also organized their own educational society, Aušra (Dawn), to provide scholarships for Lithuanian students, but in 1914 this function was taken over by SLA's scholarship fund. Shortly after the outbreak of World War I, the liberals organized a political party, the Amerikos Lietuvių Tautinė Sandara (Lithuanian-American National Union). The liberal nationalist movement was supported by the SLA organ Tėvynė (Homeland, f. 1908), Lietuva, Vienybė Lietuvninkų (moved to Brooklyn in 1907), the Worcester weekly Amerikos Lietuvis (Lithuanian-American, 1912–1955), and the Cleveland weekly, Dirva (The Field, f. 1916).

The organization in 1905 of the Lietuvių Socialistų Partija Amerikoje (Lithuanian Socialist Party of America, LSPA) posed a further challenge to the status of the immigrant clergy. The Lietuvių Socialistų Sąjunga (Lithuanian Socialist Federation, LSS), the name the LSPA adopted in 1907, quickly attracted most immigrant anticlericals, many liberal nationalists, and a sizable group of left-wing émigrés who had fled to America after the tsarist authorities put down the revolutionary disturbances of 1905–1906. By 1919 the Lithuanian Socialist Federation had close to 200 local lodges and a combined membership of about 6,700. Upon affiliating with the Socialist Party of America (SPA) in 1916, it became the SPA's third largest foreign-language federation.

The Lithuanian socialist press also quickly achieved an impressive circulation among the immigrants. This was less true of the federation's official organ, Kova (The Struggle, 1905–1918), than of such independent left-wing journals as the Boston weekly, Keleivis (The Traveler, f. 1905), and the Chicago Naujienos (News, f. 1914), the first Lithuanian daily to be published in America. In many immigrant communities the socialists cooperated with liberal nationalist, anticlerical, and other progressive organizations that shared a common ideological antipathy toward the Roman Catholic Church. Indeed, in 1907 socialist supporters almost captured control of the Lithuanian Alliance of America and the Society of Patriots. Like other ethnic progressives, local socialist agitators sought to win Lithuanian newcomers away from their traditional allegiance to Roman Catholicism by organizing numerous antireligious meetings and debates and by forming their own youth clubs, evening schools, libraries, and musical and dramatic societies. Alongside the Lithuanian Socialist Federation, left-wing immigrants also established two major auxiliary groups: the Lietuvių Moterų Progresyvis Susivienijimas Amerikoje (Lithuanian-Women's Progressive Alliance of America, LMPSA) and the Amerikos Lietuvių Darbininkų Literatūros Draugija (Lithuanian-American Workers' Literary Society, ALDLD). Formed in 1908, the Women's Progressive Alliance numbered 65 lodges and 1,358 members by 1918 and published its own monthly, Moterų Balsas (Women's Voice, 1916–1921). The Workers' Literary Society, organized in 1915, sponsored the publication of Marxist literature in the Lithuanian language. In 1919 it had over 100 local discussion groups and close to 6,000 members.

By 1920, however, the Lithuanian socialist movement in the United States had lost much of its earlier momentum. After the entry of the United States into World War I and during the postwar Red Scare, a number of socialist leaders were arrested or driven into hiding and Kova was closed down by the government. In 1919 the Lithuanian Socialist Federation split into two competing groups. The supporters of the Bolshevik Revolution in Russia formed their own Lietuvių Komunistų Sąjunga (Lithuanian Communist Federation, LKS), gained control of many local socialist clubs, and quickly affiliated with the Communist Party of America. This Lithuanian Communist group published several newspapers and journals, the most prominent of which were two dailies, the Chicago Vilnis (The Wave, f. 1920) and the Brooklyn Laisvė (Freedom, f. 1911). In 1930 Communist sympathizers attempted to gain control of the Lithuanian Alliance of America. When they failed they organized their own benefit federation, the Lietuvių Darbininkų Susivienijimas (Lithuanian Workers' Alliance, LDS), which by 1939 had grown to about 8,400 members. Lithuanian Communist spokesmen supported Soviet policies and developed close political and cultural ties with the regime established in Lithuania at the end of World War II.

Faced with these problems the Lithuanian clergy in America began in the 1900s and 1910s to adopt a more democratic pastoral style, to develop a moderate program of Catholic social action modeled on the Christian democratic movements in Europe, and to erect an elaborate institutional apparatus that would reassert the church's moral authority. The major instrument of this Catholic resurgence was the Amerikos Lietuvių Rymo Katalikų Kunigų Sąjunga (Lithuanian-American Roman Catholic Priests' League), an association of immigrant clergymen formed in 1909 by Father Antanas Staniukynas (1865–1918). After his arrival in the United States in 1904, Staniukynas gradually assumed the role of informal bishop for the Lithuanian Catholic group. Largely through his efforts, a Lithuanian-American teaching order, the Sisters of St. Casimir, was founded in 1907 to staff the emerging network of parochial schools. In 1913 Staniukynas also helped the Marian Fathers, a Lithuanian missionary order, to establish a house in the United States. The Marian Fathers played an important role in strengthening the piety of Lithuanian immigrants and in reinforcing their traditional allegiance to the Roman Catholic Church. They traveled widely among troubled ethnic parishes, organized numerous missions, retreats, and catechetical classes, and published a large body of popular devotional and apologetical literature. In 1916 the Marian Fathers assumed management of Draugas (The Friend), a Chicago weekly founded in 1909 by the Priests' League, and turned it into one of the most influential

Lithuanian-American dailies. In 1914 Staniukynas also organized the Lietuvių Rymo Katalikų Labdaringoji Sąjunga (Lithuanian Roman Catholic Charity Association), which sponsored the construction of Chicago's Holy Cross Hospital and later a Lithuanian home for the elderly. Both of these philanthropic institutions were managed and staffed by the Sisters of St. Casimir.

Between 1913 and 1915 the Lithuanian-American clergy helped organize several Catholic lay federations to mobilize immigrant youths, workers, and women against the anticlerical and socialist groups in the ethnic community. The earliest of these was the Vyčiai (Knights of Lithuania), a Catholic youth organization formed in 1913. Two years later the Knights began publishing their own newspaper, *Vytis* (The Knight, f. 1915), and in the 1920s had more than 100 local affiliates with a combined membership of over 5,000. The Amerikos Lietuvių Rymo Katalikų Šv. Juozapo Darbininkų Sąjunga (Lithuanian-American Roman Catholic St. Joseph's Workers' Federation) was founded in 1915 to counter the growing influence of socialist and syndicalist views among Lithuanian immigrant workers. After a surge during the war years, membership in this federation stabilized at about 4,000 in the 1920s. It published its own newspaper, *Darbininkas* (The Worker, f. 1915), established a fund to provide economic assistance to its members during strikes, set up several local employment bureaus to help Lithuanian workers find jobs, and encouraged the formation of Lithuanian cooperative stores. The other major Catholic lay organizations founded in the early 1910s included the Lietuvių Rymo Katalikų Moksleivių Susivienijimas Amerikoje (Lithuanian Roman Catholic Students' Alliance of America); the Amerikos Lietuvių Romos Katalikų Moterų Sąjunga (Lithuanian-American Roman Catholic Women's Federation), which had about 2,500 members by 1920 and published its own journal, *Moterų Dirva* (Women's Field, f. 1916); a press association to disseminate Catholic newspapers, books, and tracts among Lithuanian immigrants; and two temperance federations. The older Lithuanian Roman Catholic Alliance of America also grew quite rapidly after 1910; in 1917 it began publishing its own organ, *Garsas* (The Sound, f. 1917), and during its peak years in the mid-1920s numbered 19,000 members.

These various Catholic assocations affiliated in turn with the Amerikos Lietuvių Rymo Katalikų Federacija (Lithuanian-American Roman Catholic Federation, ALRKF), an umbrella organization established in 1906 to provide a forum for developing a Catholic social-action program among Lithuanian immigrants and to coordinate the endeavors of the different Catholic groups and local societies. The federation, however, did not begin to function vigorously until its third congress in 1913. During World War I it created a relief fund for Lithuanian refugees, and its leaders worked diligently to mobilize American public opinion on behalf of Lithuanian independence. Through the 1920s and 1930s the federation maintained close ties with the Catholic hierarchy in the new Lithuanian state and sponsored several visitations by Lithuanian bishops among the ethnic communities in the United States. Since 1931, when it affiliated with the National Catholic Welfare Conference, the federation has received considerable financial and political assistance for its activities from the larger American Catholic community.

Perhaps the most important achievement of the Lithuanian Catholic social action program in the United States was the creation of a sizable network of parochial schools. By the early 1930s, 39 immigrant parishes had elementary schools with a combined student enrollment of about 10,000. Most were initially staffed by the Sisters of St. Casimir, but in the early 1920s two new Lithuanian-American teaching orders, the Sisters of St. Francis and the Poor Sisters of Jesus Crucified, were founded. By 1940 there were about 10 Lithuanian Catholic academies and high schools in the United States; in 1926 the Marian Fathers established a junior college and seminary near Hinsdale, Ill., and in 1931 opened Marianapolis, an accredited four-year college near Thompson, Conn. Though catering to a relatively small and privileged segment of the ethnic group, the academies and colleges founded after 1910 played an important role in nurturing a new generation of Lithuanian Catholic leaders.

RELATIONS WITH THE HOST SOCIETY

As the Lithuanian-American community grew in size and organizational strength after 1900, its members at the same time became more closely integrated into the changing economic and political structures of the host society. Local union initiatives among Lithuanian coal miners and garment workers dated from the early 1890s, but it was only after 1900 that Lithuanian immigrants in these two industries developed firm ties and loyalties to the national union movement. By the early 1900s most Lithuanian miners in the anthracite and bituminous fields of Pennsylvania and Illinois were members of the United Mine Workers of America (UMWA). After 1914 many of the Lithuanian tailors' organizations in such cities as Baltimore, New York, Philadelphia, Boston, and Chicago affiliated with the Amalgamated Clothing Workers of America (ACWA) or, to a lesser extent, with the AFL's United Garment Workers of America (UGWA). The Lithuanian locals of the ACWA were sufficiently numerous to merit their own foreign-language trade journal, *Darbas* (Work, 1919–1926). After 1910 the more radical Industrial Workers of the World (IWW) made some temporary gains among Lithuanian workers in the shoe factories and textile mills of New England and the sugar refineries of Philadelphia and New York. A Lithuanian syndicalist newspaper, *Darbininkų Balsas* (The Workers' Voice, 1914–1917), appeared in Baltimore but ceased publication when the editor was arrested by the U.S. government. Even in those industries, such as steel, meatpacking, and textiles, where strong, permanent unions did not at first take root, Lithuanian workers often fought militantly for better economic benefits; they participated in most of the major labor disputes that occurred in the United States after 1900. Striking Lithuanian workers usually received financial and moral support from the community; the major immigrant newspapers generally popularized their grievances, and benefit and cultural societies in distant cities often sent contributions for their strike funds. Despite the early successes of the UMWA and the ACWA, however, most Lithuanian

workers remained unorganized until the CIO's unionization drives of the late 1930s.

After 1890 Lithuanian newcomers also became more active in American political life. By the mid-1890s, 8 Lithuanian Republican and 3 Lithuanian Democratic associations had been formed in Chicago, and similar organizations appeared in most of the larger immigrant communities. More typical of ethnic political initiatives, however, were the independent citizens' clubs, about 50 of which were organized in New England alone. These political associations remained formally unaffiliated with either of the two major parties and concentrated primarily on helping their countrymen acquire naturalization and citizenship papers. Despite their efforts, however, as late as 1930 the Lithuanian group continued to show one of the lowest naturalization rates among the eastern and southern European immigrants. In a number of cities and towns ethnic leaders often cooperated closely with local Progressive reformers in attempting to extend better educational, health, and welfare services to their countrymen. Although the Lithuanian Socialist Federation worked actively to win the immigrants' loyalties for the SPA, by 1920 a sizable majority of Lithuanian voters (if the political preferences of the Chicago community can be generalized to the whole group) had a strong attachment to the Democratic party. The social reforms of the New Deal received broad support from ethnic leaders and undoubtedly strengthened these party loyalties.

Lithuanian Americans formed too small a group to play an influential role in national and state politics, but they controlled many public offices in small industrial communities. In the major urban centers they received appointments as municipal judges and attorneys, court interpreters, policemen, census takers, tax assessors, and, in the 1930s, as local administrators of various federal relief programs.

RELATIONS WITH THE OLD WORLD

Prior to 1914 Lithuanian immigrants in America actively supported the nationalist movement in their homeland, and during and after World War I they played an important role in the creation of an independent Lithuanian state. Through the 1890s and 1900s lay and clerical leaders nurtured the national consciousness of Lithuanian peasant newcomers by organizing numerous educational and cultural societies, by publishing newspapers, pamphlets, and books, and by staging nationalistic meetings, speeches, picnics, and parades. Most of the alliances and federations founded after 1890 maintained close ties with nationalist leaders in tsarist Lithuania and East Prussia and provided them with valuable financial and moral support in establishing clandestine newspapers and societies. In 1906 the various Lithuanian-American groups organized their first national political congress to raise funds and marshal public opinion on behalf of the revolutionary movement in their homeland. Thereafter, prominent nationalist leaders from the Old World regularly toured the ethnic communities in the United States to solicit funds for the Lithuanian schools, newspapers, and social-welfare agencies back home.

The outbreak of World War I heightened the interest of Lithuanian immigrants in the political future of their homeland. Three large national congresses met in Chicago, Brooklyn, and New York during the war years to mobilize public opinion and funds for Lithuanian autonomy and independence. The major groups, however, failed to resolve their ideological differences, and by 1915 Catholics, liberal nationalists, and socialists had formed separate national councils, central committees, and relief and fund-raising organizations to coordinate activities on behalf of the homeland. Three information bureaus were opened in Philadelphia, Washington, and New York after 1916 to disseminate English-language propaganda regarding Lithuanian political aspirations, and spokesmen for the various national councils lobbied vigorously to have Woodrow Wilson include Lithuanian independence among the Allied war aims. In 1918, after a constituent assembly met in Vilnius to proclaim an independent Lithuanian republic, ethnic leaders in America redirected their energies toward obtaining U.S. recognition for the new Baltic state. This was accomplished in 1922 when the two countries exchanged official diplomatic missions.

Lithuanian Americans contributed significantly to the economic reconstruction of their war-ravaged homeland. In 1919 a Lithuanian financial mission arrived in the United States and collected about $2 million through the sale of Lithuanian Freedom Loan bonds. The mission's delegates also helped organize ethnic businessmen in America into the Lithuanian Chamber of Commerce which worked to develop closer economic and political ties between the United States and the recently formed Lithuanian state. Finally, immigrant entrepreneurs formed a number of investment and business firms—the Lithuanian Reconstruction Corporation, the Lithuanian-American Trade Corporation, the Lithuanian Steamship Company, and two textile companies—to encourage the new republic's economic development and to expand its international trade relations.

GROUP MAINTENANCE

In the 1920s and 1930s Lithuanian-American leaders confronted the problem of maintaining group loyalty and solidarity in the face of demographic and cultural trends that portended gradual ethnic extinction. The outbreak of World War I, the restrictive immigration laws of the early 1920s, and the agrarian reforms passed by the new Lithuanian government in 1922 effectively ended the rural exodus of the prewar years. Small numbers of Lithuanian villagers continued to emigrate during the 1920s and 1930s, but their destination was usually Canada or South America. Moreover, in the immediate postwar period more than 10,000 Lithuanian immigrants returned to their homeland, including some of the more prominent ethnic leaders who now decided to apply their talents toward building a strong Lithuanian state. Given these demographic trends, the maintenance of the Lithuanian-American group depended more than ever on retaining the cultural loyalty of the American-born generation, which by 1930 accounted for more than half of all Lithuanians in the United States. The immigrants' children, however, tended to adopt more readily than their parents the language, lifestyles, and urban values of the host society,

and these increasingly lost their linguistic and social attachments to the ethnic community.

Several factors helped slow this assimilative process. The elaborate institutional apparatus erected after 1890 continued during the 1920s and 1930s to integrate sizable numbers of second-generation Lithuanians into ethnic group activities, although the older immigrant leaders were often compelled to use English in their sermons, speeches, and newspaper columns. The creation of an independent Lithuanian state and the prominent role many immigrants had played in that drama undoubtedly fostered feelings of ethnic pride in group accomplishments. Finally, various organizations and individuals on both sides of the Atlantic worked to broaden cultural contacts between Lithuanian Americans and their European countrymen. Such youth groups as the Knights of Lithuania regularly sponsored excursions to the homeland, and prominent religious, political, and intellectual figures from Lithuania frequently visited the ethnic communities in America. In 1931 the Draugija Užsienio Lietuviams Remti (Society to Aid Lithuanians in Foreign Lands) was formed in Kaunas to strengthen the ties among the emigrant groups in Europe, the United States, Canada, and South America. This society organized the first Lithuanian World Congress in 1935 where the Pasaulio Lietuvių Sąjunga (Lithuanian World Federation) was created, which later published a biweekly newspaper, *Pasaulio Lietuvis* (The World Lithuanian, 1937–1940).

The various Lithuanian-American ideological groups also responded to political developments in eastern Europe during the interwar years and World War II. After 1926, when a nationalist faction overthrew Lithuania's parliamentary government and established a more authoritarian regime, both Catholic and left-wing organizations in the United States agitated, though unsuccessfully, to liberalize the political system there. When the Poles occupied Vilnius in 1920 and threatened war in 1938, Lithuanian-American spokesmen presented petitions and memoranda to U.S. authorities and the League of Nations in support of the Lithuanian government. The Soviet occupation of Lithuania in 1940 spurred ethnic leaders in the United States to mobilize Lithuanian Americans with renewed vigor. By 1941 all the major non-Communist alliances, federations, and leagues had united to form the Amerikos Lietuvių Taryba (Lithuanian-American Council, ALTAS). The council thereafter established an information bureau in New York, disseminated anti-Soviet propaganda, and lobbied in Washington to include Lithuanian independence as part of any postwar settlement. Since 1945 it has continued to agitate for the liberation of Lithuania from Soviet rule.

The Priests' League formed the Kunigų Šalpos Fondas (Priests' Relief Fund). In 1944 it was broadened to include liberal nationalist and socialist groups and reorganized as the Bendrasis Amerikos Lietuvių Šalpos Fondas (United Lithuanian Relief Fund of America, BALFAS). BALFAS cooperated with such groups as the National Catholic Welfare Conference, the United Nations Relief and Rehabilitation Administration, and the International Relief Organization in providing assistance to Lithuanian displaced persons in the Western zones of occupied Germany. It also lobbied to improve living and health conditions in the refugee camps, to prevent the forcible repatriation of Lithuanian refugees to the U.S.S.R., and to gain congressional approval for the Displaced Persons Act of 1948. Throughout the 1950s and 1960s this organization helped support a Lithuanian high school in West Germany and sent numerous relief parcels to Lithuanian families in Poland and the Soviet Union.

THE DIPUKAI

The late 1940s and the 1950s witnessed a revitalization of the Lithuanian-American community as approximately 30,000 new immigrants entered the United States under the provisions of the Displaced Persons Act of 1948. These *dipukai*, as they were commonly called, came primarily from the Western zones of occupied Germany where about 60,000 Lithuanian refugees had found themselves after World War II. They included former concentration-camp inmates, soldiers, and laborers conscripted by the Germans during the war. Most were political exiles who had fled westward in 1944–1945 to escape Soviet rule. Many had initially hoped to return to their homeland after a satisfactory postwar settlement between the Allied powers, but growing Soviet-American tensions after 1945 made this an increasingly unrealistic expectation. About 10,000 eventually settled in West Germany. The remainder began to emigrate to Great Britain, Canada, Australia, South America, and, after 1948, the United States, where they settled primarily in the older metropolitan centers of the Northeast and Midwest.

The dipukai were generally better educated, more nationalistic, and more politicized than the peasant immigrants of the 1870–1914 period. Many had been prominent figures in the political, religious, and intellectual life of the independent Lithuanian state. Although some initially joined the older ethnic alliances, federations, and parishes, they more often established their own. The most important of these are the Vyriausias Lietuvos Išlaisvinimo Komitetas (Supreme Committee for the Liberation of Lithuania, VLIKAS) and the Pasaulio Lietuvių Bendruomenė (Lithuanian World Community, PLB). VLIKAS had been formed in 1943 by representatives of the major non-Communist political groups in Nazi-occupied Lithuania to coordinate resistance activities there. After the war, this organization was quickly revived in Germany where it encouraged Lithuanian refugees to establish their own associations. In the late 1940s VLIKAS sponsored the creation of a government-in-exile, the Lithuanian World Community, to maintain the ethnic solidarity of Lithuanian refugees in the West against the Soviets. By the mid-1950s national, regional, and local Lithuanian community organizations had been formed among the postwar immigrants in the United States, Canada, South America, Australia, and the countries of Western Europe. The Lithuanian Community, U.S.A., established two large funds to aid ethnic cultural and educational initiatives among the refugees. In cooperation with the Lithuanian Community of Canada it has sponsored numerous youth congresses, academic conferences, and choral and folk-dance festivals that attract representatives from many of the dipukai communities in North America. At the regional and local levels, Lithuanian community associations organize assemblies to commemorate Lithuanian Independence Day (February 16), to sponsor

anti-Soviet demonstrations, meetings, and petitions, and to provide financial assistance to ethnic schools, student and youth societies, folk-dance groups, radio programs, and summer camps.

In addition to global and national federations, the dipukai re-created in America many political and cultural organizations that had existed in prewar Lithuania or had formed initially in Germany. These included such youth and student groups as the Boy Scouts of Lithuania; the Catholic Ateitininkai (Futurists); the Corps Neo-Lituanica, a nationalist fraternity; and the Santaros-Šviesos Federacija (Agreement-Light Federation). In the 1950s many of the postwar refugees who had been professionals, academics, and intellectuals in Lithuania formed their own specialized ethnic associations in the United States: the Amerikos Lietuvių Inžinierių ir Architektų Sąjunga (Lithuanian-American Federation of Engineers and Architects, ALIAS), the Lietuvių Rašytojų Draugija (Lithuanian Writers' Society), the Lietuvių Žurnalistų Sąjunga (Lithuanian Journalists' Federation), the Lietuvių Profesorių Draugija Amerikoje (Society of Lithuanian Professors in America), three Lithuanian medical associations, and the Amerikos Lietuvių Dailininkų Sąjunga (Lithuanian American Artists' Federation). Finally, three Lithuanian Catholic religious orders—the Sisters of the Immaculate Conception, the Franciscans, and the Jesuits—established new centers in the United States after the war. Most of these refugee groups and associations hold regular local, regional, and national conferences, sponsor summer camps, and publish journals and bulletins. Perhaps the most influential is the cultural journal *Aidai* (Echoes, f. 1944), which has been published since 1949 by the Lithuanian Franciscan Fathers.

The dipukai placed particular emphasis on education to nurture an intense national loyalty among the younger refugees and the American-born children. Many of them had been elementary, high school, and university teachers and administrators in prewar Lithuania, so they were able quickly to initiate Saturday schools to maintain language and ethnic solidarity. In 1968 there were close to 40 of these schools with a combined student enrollment of about 3,100. The Lithuanian Community, U.S.A., helped formulate a common curriculum, published Lithuanian textbooks, and since 1967 has organized annual teachers' conventions at the Dainava Camp outside Detroit. In 1958 the Pedagoginis Lituanistikos Institutas (Lithuanian Pedagogical Institute) was established in Chicago to help train a younger generation of Saturday-school instructors. The Lietuvių Studentų Sąjunga (Lithuanian Students' Association, LSS) was formed in 1951; it publishes a scholarly English-language quarterly, *Lituanus* (f. 1954), and continues to organize ethnic student conferences as well as anti-Soviet demonstrations and petitions. Lithuanian teachers and academics in the United States also work through such ethnic professional and research associations as the Lietuvių Istorijos Draugija (Lithuanian Historical Society), the Lituanistikos Institutas (Institute of Lithuanian Studies) in New York, the Lietuvių Kalbos Draugija (Lithuanian Linguistic Society), the Lithuanian Folk-Dancing and Art Institutes in Chicago, and the Lietuvių Katalikų Mokslo Akademija (Lithuanian Catholic Academy of Sciences). These groups hold national and international conferences and exhibitions, sponsor lectures, and publish scholarly books and periodicals on Lithuanian history and culture.

The postwar immigrants often coordinated their political and cultural activities with other Eastern European refugee groups through such multiethnic associations as the Assembly of Captive European Nations, Americans for Congressional Action to Free the Baltic States, the Baltic Appeal to the United Nations, and the Association for the Advancement of Baltic Studies.

Because many refugees had already acquired educational, professional, and entrepreneurial skills in prewar Lithuania, they often adjusted to American economic life more easily than had the peasant newcomers of the 1870–1914 period. Some quickly resumed their occupations as doctors, dentists, and engineers; others opened up food stores, real-estate agencies, service stations, and bars. Although lack of proficiency in English compelled a sizable group of dipukai to accept jobs as manual laborers or low-level clerical employees, the general affluence of the 1950s and 1960s allowed even those people to acquire homes, automobiles, and a wide variety of consumer goods. They also passed on their bourgeois values to their children, many of whom are by now university-trained and are pursuing careers in management, engineering, medicine, law, and teaching.

Despite the revitalization of the Lithuanian-American communities that occurred in the 1940s and 1950s, ethnic leaders are experiencing once again the problem of maintaining group solidarity in the face of rapid acculturation and assimilation. The earliest Lithuanian benefit societies had already begun to disband in the 1920s and 1930s as their members died or moved away. The Great Depression dealt a severe economic blow to a number of Lithuanian-American organizations, even as the welfare reforms of the New Deal made their mutual-aid functions somewhat anachronistic. Except for a brief increase in the late 1940s, membership in the Lithuanian Alliance of American and the Lithuanian Roman Catholic Alliance of America dwindled steadily after 1930. The intense nationalistic and anti-Communist fervor of many of the postwar refugees does not animate their children, who have never experienced the traumas of foreign occupation, war, or exile and are therefore more likely to support a policy of détente with the U.S.S.R. Second- and third-generation Lithuanians continue to associate informally with each other, to establish ethnic families, and to participate in various ethnic activities, but the number of those who are deeply committed to preserving their language and ethnic affiliations gradually continues to decline. The most likely sources for the long-term maintenance of the Lithuanian-American community are probably the widespread popular concern for ethnic roots that was sparked by the various Afro-American movements of the 1960s and the moral and financial support that the U.S. government and various private foundations have begun to provide to ethnic-heritage programs.

Bibliography
The six-volume *Encyclopedia Lituanica* (Boston, 1970–1978) offers the most comprehensive English-language guide to Lithuanian history and culture, Lithuanian-American communities, parishes, ethnic leaders, and immigrant and refugee organizations. Alfred Senn, *The Emergence of Modern Lithuania* (1959; reprint, Westport, Conn., 1975), concentrates on the period between 1914 and 1920 but contains background information on the politics and culture of tsarist Lithuania. Anthony Kaupas, "The Lithuanians in America," *Charities* 13 (1904):

231–235, is a contemporary description of the Lithuanian-American community in the early 1900s written by a prominent clerical publicist. Antanas Kaztauskis, "From Lithuania to the Chicago Stockyards—An Autobiography," *The Independent* 57 (1904): 241–248, is an interesting personal narrative that illustrates one peasant immigrant's quick adjustment to urban industrial life in the United States. Victor R. Greene, "For God and Country: The Origins of Slavic Catholic Self-Consciousness in America," *Church History* 35 (December 1966): 446–460, includes some information on intraethnic tensions and their role in raising ethnic self-consciousness among peasant newcomers. By the same author, *Slavic Community on Strike: Immigrant Labor in Pennsylvania Anthracite* (Notre Dame, Ind., 1968) includes information on early communities in Pennsylvania and the unionization of Lithuanian coal miners in the 1890s and early 1900s. *Lituanus* (f. 1954) is a quarterly journal that publishes scholarly articles on Lithuanian and Lithuanian-American history, politics, and culture. The largest collections of materials, serials, books, pamphlets, and primary sources on the Lithuanian immigration are to be found at the World Lithuanian Archives in Chicago; the Lithuanian American Cultural Archives in Putnam, Conn.; the University of Pennsylvania Library in Philadelphia; and the New York Public Library.

ARŪNAS ALIŠAUSKAS

LOYALTIES: DUAL AND DIVIDED

Expatriation is a "natural and inherent right of all people," according to the Act of Congress of July 27, 1868. The specific purpose of the act was to protect the increasing numbers of naturalized Americans whose native countries still made claims on their allegiance, but the choice of language in the declaration was of more general significance. If every person has an inherent right of expatriation, then allegiance to a nation is a matter of individual will. A person may acquire nationality by birth, but as an adult has the right to choose the object of his allegiance. That the Congress should conceive of nationality in these terms is not remarkable; voluntary allegiance is the only possible stance for a nation of immigrants and also for a democracy, but it has not been an easy principle to live with precisely because of these factors.

Immigrant roots have left many Americans with affections and loyalties for the homeland well beyond the immigrant generation; the voluntaristic ethos of the society—its free choice, free movement, free assembly, and free expression of belief—has made it possible for people to express and act on their feelings for the ancestral country. The United States therefore has had to learn to accommodate national loyalties running both to the old country and to the new, a problem especially pressing in the 20th century when greater U.S. involvement in international affairs frequently has forced the issue to the surface of American politics.

The problem took modern shape at the outset of World War I in 1914, when the United States faced the question of whether or not to join England and France in fighting Germany. In debating the interest of the United States in relation to Europe, Americans had to consider what interests they held in common as Americans, what activities, rights, profits, hopes were important enough to the whole society to be worth the lives of young men. This meant that Americans had to confront as well the interests that divided them, particularly the differing interests of the many immigrant groups that had come to the United States during the preceding three decades. Whatever choice the United States made—even the choice of neutrality—inevitably would raise strong feelings among those of its people whose homelands might be jeopardized by its policy.

The World War I experience of divided loyalties within a system of voluntary loyalties raised questions still difficult for Americans to answer. What connections to the homeland are consistent with loyalty to the United States? In what ways is it acceptable for American ethnic groups to express and act on their sympathies for the homeland? In what circumstances? Underlying these questions are more basic ones: what is the nature of the loyalties Americans feel both for the homeland and for the United States, and, perhaps most difficult, how are the requirements of American loyalty established?

LOYALTY TO THE HOMELAND

Commitment to the interests of the homeland depends on an emotional bond sufficently strong to sustain the considerable time and energy required to express the common concerns of the group. It is a bond that has taken a variety of forms in the experience of American ethnic groups, and that has been expressed with varying degrees of intensity.

Some immigrants in some periods never completely broke ties with the homeland; their primary sense of identity remained rooted in the Old World. This form of attachment was most marked among groups that migrated to the United States without intending to stay, the sojourners who left their native lands usually under economic pressure, to find work, save money, and then return home to resume their former lives.

Many immigrants who came to the United States to seek relief from the depressed state of agriculture in the countries of eastern and southern Europe from the 1880s to 1914—Poles, Italians, Bulgarians, Hungarians, Lithuanians, Romanians, Latvians—came as sojourners and made little effort to put down roots in the United States. Rather, they moved from city to city following the best-paying jobs for unskilled labor and stayed close to other members of their group for comfort and support. Typically they learned little English but concentrated their efforts toward an eventual return to their homeland.

Census figures are inexact, but in the first quarter of the 20th century about a quarter of the Lithuanians who came to the United States, 40 percent of the Poles, and 66 percent of the Hungarians and Romanians returned to their homelands. The Turks had perhaps the highest rate of return in this period: of the 22,000 who immigrated to the United States between 1899 and 1924, 86 percent returned to Turkey. (*See* Appendix I, Table 2.) For many immigrants who stayed in the United States the option to leave remained alive and their ties to American habits, institutions, places, and friends remained tentative. Other immigrants, even some who became citizens, expressed their ultimate identification with the homeland by arranging for their bodies to be returned there for burial.

Often the decision to marry in the United States marked the turning point in national identification and created the first tangible tie to the new land. The American-born children of immigrants, far from sustaining a sojourner mentality, often reacted against the foreignness of their parents with an intensity of identification with American culture painful to the older generation.

Immigrants from the bordering countries of Canada

and Mexico frequently became commuters without settled national identification in either country. Such ambiguity could be maintained even beyond the first generation because of the ease of access to the ancestral culture and the ease of movement back and forth across the border. This pattern of migration was characteristic of the movement of French Canadians into New York and New England and of Mexicans into the Southwest. The migrants in the United States would return to farms or villages in Mexico or Canada and later remigrate to the United States, where they often formed few connections to the larger society beyond the group. The distinctiveness of the culture and language of these visitor-immigrants perpetuated their separation from other Americans; furthermore, they had less need than other immigrants to bridge this gap, for the proximity of their homelands reinforced their group identities.

Up to the outbreak of World War II, Japanese Americans also succeeded in maintaining cultural identity with the homeland beyond the first immigrant generation. A number of Japanese families in the United States followed the practice of sending at least one child to Japan to be brought up and educated by relatives. These children normally returned to the United States in adolescence and were much more likely to retain the language and customs of the homeland, especially in relation to family, than children educated in American public schools.

Unlike many European sojourners, Japanese Americans who followed this practice usually did not intend to return permanently to Japan but they faced the problem in the United States of general hostility to Asian Americans, expressed, for example, in laws restricting their landholding and eligibility for citizenship. Their bond to the homeland remained strong because legal as well as social barriers kept them from forming normal ties to the new land.

Sometimes the immigrants' unbroken ties with the homeland and their intent to return were of concern not just to themselves but to the country they left behind. The Hungarian government, alarmed at the country's large population loss to the United States at the turn of the century, operated an "American Action" program from 1904 to 1914. The program provided funds for religious and cultural activities in order to retain the loyalty of Hungarian Americans and keep alive their determination to return to the homeland. Administered by Hungarian churches in the United States, both Catholic and Protestant, the program supplied funds to support priests and ministers, to provide down payments on church buildings, to pay teachers and buy books and supplies for Saturday classes in Hungarian language and culture, to subsidize newspapers, even to lobby for health and safety legislation in areas where Hungarians formed a large part of the labor force.

The American Action program explicitly discouraged naturalization and encouraged frequent visits to the homeland, all in aid of a hoped-for repatriation after the immigrants had spent a period of wage-earning in the United States. Although it was successful in keeping the naturalization rate of Hungarians among the lowest of immigrant groups in this period, American Action predictably failed as an effort to retain the hold of the homeland over the second generation.

The government of the new Republic of Turkey, established in 1923, acted even more directly, making grants and loans available to its emigrants abroad to encourage them to return to a homeland badly in need of a work force for development.

For most ethnic groups, certainly for those beyond the first generation, the nature of their feelings for the homeland, their concern about its welfare and interests, were more complex than those of the sojourner-immigrants. Unlike the sojourners, most immigrants and the vast majority of their descendants formed a primary tie to the United States. If they felt loyalty also to the homeland of their parents, it was not because psychologically they had never left it; rather, it was because it represented something important to them despite their having left it—or, in the case of many of the American-born, in spite of their never having seen it.

For a number of American ethnic groups, the sense of connection to the homeland derived from the needs of the group in the United States. For instance, Thomas N. Brown, in *Irish-American Nationalism, 1870–1890* (1966), argues that the essential source of passionate concern for Ireland among Irish Americans in this period was their driving desire for dignity and status in the United States. Poor, despised for their ignorance, their drinking, and their priests, Irish Americans yearned for a source of pride in themselves and sought it in the fight for independence in Ireland. Brown quotes the Irish leader Michael Davitt appealing precisely to these feelings when he promised an Irish-American group in New York in 1880, "Aid us in Ireland to remove the stain of degradation from your birth and the Irish race here in America will get the respect you deserve."

The source of enthusiasm among other ethnic groups for nationalist movements in the homeland also lay in their need for self-respect and for respect from the larger society. There are a number of instances in which nationalist successes in the homeland seem to have stimulated a new interest and enthusiasm for ethnic-group activities. German-American organizations increased greatly in number and size following the unification of Germany in 1870. The success of Mussolini's regime in bringing order and prosperity to Italy in the 1920s evoked an enthusiastic response from Italian Americans who no longer had to rely on past glories as a source of pride in their heritage.

The Zionist mission, the establishment of a Jewish homeland in Palestine, evoked strong though by no means unanimous support among Jewish Americans, who saw in it not only a means for preserving the ancient religion and culture of the Jews, but also a powerful symbol with which to combat the image of weakness, helplessness, dependence on the sufferance of others that had dogged the Jews in the Diaspora. The establishment of the state of Israel in 1948 and its defense against Arab nations in the wars of 1967 and 1973 evoked a tremendous outpouring of emotion and of financial support even among Jewish Americans who were not Zionists.

For other American ethnic groups, nationalist successes in the homeland have produced an ethnic awareness, a sense of ethnic identity and pride, that previously was dormant or repressed. Belgian Americans, for example, who before 1914 considered themselves to be not Belgian but either Flemish or Walloon depending on the part of Belgium they came from, were led by the suffering and heroism of their countrymen in World

War I to assume an identity as Belgians and for the first time to designate as Belgian various cultural associations in the United States.

Conversely, immigrants to the United States from the Cape Verde Islands who had always identified themselves as Portuguese Americans responded to the independence of their homeland from Portugal in 1975 by beginning to call themselves Cape Verdeans and by setting up organizations and activities differentiating themselves from Portuguese Americans.

Arab Americans, originally immigrants from Palestine, Egypt, Lebanon, Iraq, Syria, and Jordan, rarely identified themselves as Arabs in the United States until the OPEC nations and the Arab League demonstrated to the world that Arabs were not a peripheral people with an archaic culture, but could exert control over their own affairs, compel the respect of the world, and set their own terms for dealing with it. Coincident with the development of Arab cohesiveness and power in the Middle East has been the growth among Arab Americans of interest and pride in their own ethnicity.

Perhaps most striking is the response among black Americans to the success of movements for national independence in Africa. This has ranged from an enthusiasm for African dress, hairstyles, and names for children, to the politics of militant black nationalism. Like other ethnic groups before them, Afro-Americans have translated renewed pride in their roots to renewed self-respect, confidence, and assertiveness in American society generally. African nationalism has been an important factor in the U.S. civil rights movement and in the development of cohesiveness among black Americans for the promotion of common political and cultural causes.

LOYALTY TO THE UNITED STATES

The problem for American ethnic groups in balancing and resolving a complex sense of identity is made still more difficult by the complexities surrounding the concept of national loyalty in American political history. The meaning of loyalty to the United States has been complicated from the beginning by the strong tradition of exceptionalism, the tradition of self-perception among Americans based on the conception of the United States as a nation unlike others.

Americans have considered themselves exceptional because their nation is not based as others are on common history, culture, blood, or religion, but on common allegiance to a system designed to accommodate wide differences. It is a system based, in principle, on the liberal ideal of individual freedom—on the right of individuals to follow and promote their own interests, defined by themselves in accordance with their own tastes and values. Because values and interests are the province of the individual, in this system the nation has no proper identity or interest other than the multiple interests of all its people. In the exceptionalist tradition, loyalty to the nation means loyalty to the principle of liberty, and this kind of loyalty is a bond between people and nation that, in the ideal, places no barriers between people of different countries. Americans have considered it superior to the Old World sense of nation, perceived as fostering unity within societies and hostilities among them. Further, the exceptionalist sense of nation leaves open, or even encourages, the possibil-

ity of people engaging in activities in other countries according to their own, not the nation's, interest.

Woodrow Wilson articulated this American self-perception, but also touched on a paradox within it, in a speech on May 10, 1915, to a group of newly naturalized citizens in Philadelphia. Addressing the question of national loyalty in terms which must have caused considerable bewilderment, he told his audience, "You have just taken an oath of allegiance to the United States. Of allegiance to whom? Of allegiance to no one unless it be to God . . . You have taken an oath of allegiance to a great ideal, to a great body of principles, to a great hope of the human race." To this instruction he added the "urgent advice" that as U.S. citizens they were "not only . . . to think first of America, but always, also, to think first of humanity." It is impossible, he told them, to love humanity "if you seek to divide humanity into jealous camps."

Implicit in Wilson's remarks, however, is a plea for limitation, for moderation of private demands by American citizens. He was obviously appealing to both new citizens and old not to drag the partisanships of the old country into the politics of the United States. He feared that the passions of Europe brought to the United States could push the nation into war without good cause, and also that the passionate identification of Americans with their European homelands could create divisions threatening social peace at home.

Wilson thus evoked, without examining it directly, a troubling conflict in American belief. The "great ideal" of the United States is to leave people free to express their different interests, but the open expression of dual loyalties inevitably raises problems of conflicting loyalties with the potential for causing trouble both within the United States and between the United States and other countries. Inevitably there has been tension between the principle of allegiance to the ideal of liberty and an American interest in protecting the United States against possible harm from loyalties running to other countries. The problem for Americans during World War I and since has been to try to define the point at which loyalty to the United States makes it unacceptable for ethnic groups to maintain attachments to the homeland or to promote its causes as one of the many types of privately formed interests that Americans are supposedly free to express and support.

DEFINITION OF LOYALTY: THE LAW

To a minimal extent, this point is defined by law. Congress passed major nationality laws in 1907, 1940, and 1952 mainly to codify regulations for acquiring citizenship (see Naturalization and Citizenship), but these laws also provided for deprivation of citizenship for activities that demonstrated a primary loyalty elsewhere. The first law, in 1907, defined the following grounds for loss of U.S. citizenship: naturalization in another country; taking an oath of allegiance to another country; for naturalized Americans, leaving the United States and living in the native country for two years or in any foreign country for five; and for American women, marrying an alien regardless of where they live thereafter. Loss of citizenship by marriage was repealed partially in 1922 and wholly in 1931, but otherwise the 1907 law was maintained nearly intact in the 1940 and 1952 codifications. The later acts lengthened the

amount of time naturalized Americans could live abroad without jeopardizing their U.S. citizenship, but they also specified additional types of behavior as inconsistent with allegiance to the United States.

The 1940 act provided for loss of citizenship for any person fighting in the armed forces of a foreign state if he was also a national of that state. The 1952 act and subsequent amendments dropped the condition of foreign nationality but added the provision that citizenship remain intact if the foreign armed service was authorized by the Secretary of State or Defense, with further protections of citizenship if the person in question was under 18. Under the 1940 law Americans could also lose citizenship if employed by a foreign government in positions for which only nationals were eligible. This provision was revised in the later law to apply only to Americans working for foreign governments who were also nationals of the foreign state or whose jobs required an oath of allegiance to that state. Under both the 1940 and 1952 laws an American was liable to loss of citizenship for voting in a foreign election.

The laws in the statute books (currently United States Code 8, Section 1481: Loss of Nationality) appear to provide one area of clarity, however limited, in the larger question of the meaning of loyalty, but even these apparently straightforward rules have been difficult to apply in practice because of the ever-present influence of the exceptionalist tradition. The exceptionalist emphasis on individual freedom lends strength to demands for freedom to express and act on loyalties to other nations as well as to the United States. This principle, as well as the strong interest of many Americans in maintaining connections to other countries, has been the basis for constant resistance to the limits placed by U.S. nationality laws on the exercise of dual loyalties. As a result of court challenges over the years, the laws at present have much less restrictive force than their wording would suggest.

From the beginning, administrators and courts interpreting nationality law generally followed the principle that conduct in breach of the law called for loss of citizenship only if undertaken knowingly and voluntarily. If confusion or duress were involved, it was assumed that the person was engaging in the proscribed activity not out of attachment to the foreign government, but for other reasons possibly compatible with loyalty to the United States. Judges looked for evidence of an actual, subjective transfer of allegiance to another country. If there was good evidence to the contrary, the loss of citizenship was generally not imposed.

Under this view of the law, passport officers, tax officials, other administrators, and courts had to assess not only the activities of U.S. citizens abroad, but also the state of their hearts and minds. Thus the American who voted in a Romanian election because the penalty for not voting was five years' hard labor did not lose his U.S. citizenship. Nor did the woman who married an alien thinking he was an American citizen and left him as soon as she discovered he was not. Nor ultimately did most of the hundreds of Italian and Japanese Americans who were dual nationals living abroad at the start of World War II and were drafted, without choice, into the Italian and Japanese armies. Many of the men who fought in enemy armies and sought to return to the United States after the war initially were denied passports under the 1940 law because they had served in foreign armies, but subsequent administrative and judicial reviews firmly established the principle that when the service was not voluntary the letter of the law did not apply.

More recently the Supreme Court has invalidated several parts of the law on loss of nationality as unconstitutional abridgments of the rights of citizens and has placed drastic limits on the rest of the law. In 1964 in *Schneider* v. *Rusk,* the Court found unconstitutional the law imposing loss of citizenship on naturalized Americans who lived abroad beyond a certain period because the stipulation did not apply equally to nativeborn citizens; the Court found it discriminatory to the point of denying due process to naturalized citizens. In *Afroyim* v. *Rusk* (1967) the Court declared that loss of citizenship because of voting in a foreign election was also unconstitutional. The plaintiff Afroyim was an American who had lived in Israel for ten years. When he sought an American passport to return to the United States, the passport was denied on grounds that Afroyim had voted in an Israeli election. In finding it unconstitutional to deprive a person of citizenship for this reason, the Court specifically reversed a 1958 decision (*Perez* v. *Brownell*).

The significance of the *Afroyim* decision goes beyond the issue of voting, however, for in reaching its conclusion the Court enunciated a broad new doctrine concerning the rights of citizenship. Justice Hugo Black, writing for the Court, declared that the Fourteenth Amendment citizenship clause confirmed U.S. citizenship as a right that Congress had no authority to alter. Rather, the amendment gave every citizen "a constitutional right to remain a citizen in a free country unless he voluntarily relinquishes that citizenship." Thus, the Court, acting on the libertarian premises implicit in the tradition of exceptionalism, recognized the individual and not the nation as the ultimate arbiter of his own loyalty.

Since *Afroyim,* the law on loss of nationality has stood as written in 1952, except for deletion of the sections applying to voting in foreign elections and to naturalized citizens living abroad (as well as changes in other sections not relating to dual allegiances), but the force of the law has been radically reduced. According to an attorney general's opinion interpreting *Afroyim* in 1969, loss of citizenship can be imposed for activities still specified in the law only when the U.S. citizen engaging in them *intends* by doing so to relinquish his citizenship. As a practical matter, short of formal renunciation of citizenship American citizens legally have virtually unlimited scope for the expression of dual loyalties.

DEFINITION OF LOYALTY: PUBLIC OPINION

The requirements of loyalty are no longer—if they ever were—clearly defined by law; a more potent force affecting the limits of homeland loyalties has been the pressure of public opinion. The effective line between acceptable and unacceptable connections to the homeland has been drawn largely by popular reaction, incident by incident, to various ways ethnic groups have been involved in affairs of their homelands. Sometimes appeals for the homeland have aroused positive public

enthusiasm; at other times, merely tolerance or indifference. Occasionally ethnic groups have faced public hostility and charges of disloyalty for their identification with the homeland.

The reasons for perceptions of disloyalty, when they have occurred, are extremely difficult to isolate. Sometimes there has been genuine fear that ethnic-group activities threatened the interests of the United States. However, such fears have often been mixed with tensions stemming from domestic, not international, conflicts. For an ethnic group to identify with the homeland is to emphasize foreignness, difference, and thus to arouse the always volatile fears and suspicions present in a heterogeneous society. If public opinion is the only effective measure of loyalty and disloyalty in the United States, it is also a measure that indicates the close relation between American conceptions of loyalty and American capacities for tolerance of internal differences. At some points the distinction disappears and accusations of disloyalty are clearly reflections of nothing more than the continuing force of racial and ethnic prejudice.

PRIVATE SUPPORT FOR THE HOMELAND

Among the least controversial activities of American ethnic groups has been the use of their own private resources to support causes in the homeland. Such efforts are consistent with the overriding tradition of privatism in American society and have been considered no less legitimate than those of thousands of other groups in the United States that promote causes of their own choosing. The most widely practiced form of direct support for the homeland has been that of raising funds in the United States to aid relatives abroad or more generally for organized charity in periods of special need, but also for political purposes in times of national crisis.

During World War I, eastern European groups in the United States were especially active in support of the war efforts of homeland governments, either through the purchase of their war bonds or through contributions to organizations raising funds in aid of the homeland. The Central Committee of the Serbian National Defense, founded in New York in 1914, raised over a half-million dollars for Serbia during the war; Czechs and Slovaks in the United States contributed $675,000 to the Czechoslovak National Council to finance efforts to win support for the formation of an independent Czechoslovak state after the war. Polish Americans raised a quarter-million dollars in liberty bonds to support the formation of an independent Poland. In the immediate postwar years Lithuanian Americans raised $2,000,000 through the sale of Lithuanian Freedom Loan Bonds to aid the establishment of an independent Lithuanian nation. The largest amounts of money sent from the United States during and after World War I were raised by the American Jewish Joint Distribution Committee to provide relief for the massive numbers of displaced Jews in eastern Europe and Turkey. It contributed over $16.5 million during the war and another $47.5 million from 1918 to 1922 to a network of organizations in Europe.

American ethnic groups whose homeland causes were lost during the war raised substantial amounts of money in the postwar years to help support refugees or impoverished families who remained in the homeland. The Boston-based Education of Russian Youth in Exile sent $300,000 for the education of Russian refugees in various parts of Europe in the 1920s. Carpatho-Rusyns in the United States sent millions of dollars in aid to the homeland from 1918 to 1938 when, having failed to establish its own autonomy, it was under the uneasy jurisdiction of the new state of Czechoslovakia. Ukrainian Americans raised $140,000 in the immediate postwar years for a Ukrainian government in exile and throughout the 1930s sent hundreds of thousands of dollars to support charitable, educational, and political institutions in the homeland.

For many Asian Americans in the same period, the plight of homelands threatened or occupied by Japan elicited continuing concern and financial support. Korean Americans formed various nationalist organizations and raised money throughout the period, from 1910 to 1945, of Japanese colonial rule in Korea. Chinese Americans aided the defense of China against Japan from 1937 to 1945 through the purchase of millions of dollars of Chinese war bonds.

After World War II the outpouring of private relief funds for European countries supplemented official relief and rehabilitation programs funded by the U.S. government and by international organizations. As in World War I, eastern European ethnic groups were especially energetic and successful in sending cash, clothing, food, and supplies to their homelands, although the amounts that could be sent were severely restricted in the countries that fell under the control of the Soviet Union in the late 1940s.

In the period following World War II as in the years after 1918, the single largest fund-raising effort was that of Jewish Americans, this time in support of the state of Israel, which was founded in 1948. After that event about 60 percent of the funds collected annually by federated Jewish philanthropies in the United States went to Israel, except in times of crisis when the percentage was higher. The largest amount raised in any year was the $600 million contributed by Jewish Americans in the aftermath of the 1973 war with Egypt, when the strength of the Egyptian forces had caught Israel off guard and placed it in serious jeopardy.

ARMY SERVICE

In addition to buying war bonds and sending food, clothing, and medical supplies to relieve the hardships of war, members of American ethnic groups have expressed their continued loyalty most directly by volunteering to fight for the homeland cause. This was particularly the case in World War I before the United States itself became engaged. The Serbian-American community, which had been actively involved in resistance to Austria-Hungary for several years before the war, sent thousands of young men to serve with the Serbian army when war broke out in 1914. Similarly, the Pan-Hellenic Union recruited 42,000 young Greek Americans to fight for Greece in the Balkan wars of 1912 and 1913. Before the United States entered World War I, many Polish Americans fought with European armies in the hope of promoting Polish independence.

Fighting for the homeland became more complicated after the Nationality Act of 1940 made service in a foreign army grounds for loss of citizenship, but the com-

paratively early entry of the United States into World War II made joining the homeland cause a different issue from that of the earlier war. A number of young men who fought with foreign armies in World War I were liable to loss of citizenship not for joining foreign forces, but for taking the necessary oath of allegiance to the government involved. Congress, however, in a law passed on May 9, 1918, absolved them of this forfeiture if they had fought against a country "with which the United States is now at war."

ENGAGEMENT IN HOMELAND POLITICS

In periods of intense political struggle in the homeland, the more politically active elements of American ethnic groups, often recent émigrés, engaged directly in the struggle through involvement with one of the contending factions. Fund-raising was usually an important activity of such groups, but in addition some served as long-distance analysts, advisers, and critics, guiding or even directing the efforts of their counterparts in the homeland. Often, however, the energies of American-based leaders of homeland factions have been consumed in quarrels among themselves.

Irish Americans, before the granting of Irish independence in 1921, had a long history of factional involvement in the Irish resistance to English control. As early as the 1820s Irish associations in the United States supported Daniel O'Connell's fight for Catholic Emancipation and repeal of the Act of Union which made Ireland an integral part of England. In 1857 the Irish Republican Brotherhood (the Fenians) was formed to raise funds for homeland leaders but also to organize and train forces for direct participation in the rising against England which the Fenians advocated and one faction actually attempted in 1867. The Clan na Gael, or United Brotherhood, founded in 1867 on a broader social base than the primarily working-class Fenians, joined with other nationalist groups in the 1880s in support of Charles Stewart Parnell's Home Rule movement. This group in the 1890s turned to several ventures in terrorism both in England and in the United States that divided the movement again.

In 1910, British acceptance of the principle of Home Rule reduced the direct engagement of Irish Americans in the factional politics of Ireland, but fund-raising in the United States for nationalist groups fighting for the elimination of all ties with England remained vigorous until the De Valera constitution of 1937 established the independent state of Eire. Some support from Irish Americans for the Irish Republican Army and for other groups carrying on anti-British activities in Northern Ireland never completely stopped, and increased in the 1960s with the outbreak of fighting between the Catholics and Protestants of Ulster.

In the 1970s influential Irish-American politicians, including House Speaker Thomas P. O'Neill, Jr., Senator Edward M. Kennedy of Massachusetts, and Governor Hugh L. Carey and Senator Daniel Patrick Moynihan of New York, attempted through visits and pronouncements to aid the cause of a united Ireland detached from England, while opposing private American aid for groups using violence in the fight for unity.

During World War I, eastern European and Balkan émigrés in the United States were deeply involved in the issues, choices, and strategies of political factions in the homeland. Croatian Americans formed the Croatian National Alliance in Kansas City in 1912 to organize political action against Hapsburg control and to support the establishment of a South Slav state made up of Croatia, Serbia, and Slovenia. The alliance's program included such terrorist tactics as the attempted assassination of a Hapsburg official in Zagreb in 1913, only a year before the assassination of the Archduke Franz Ferdinand in Serbia precipitated the outbreak of war.

Albanian Americans, most notably the liberal-socialist Bishop Fan Noli, played a key role through the Pan Albanian Federation of America (VATRA) in gaining backing for an independent Albania at the London Conference of 1913, convened to settle the controversies arising out of the Balkan wars. After World War I nullified the arrangements made at this conference, Noli again was instrumental in gaining the support of Woodrow Wilson, who pressed for Albanian independence at Versailles.

Perhaps the most remarkable instance of direct involvement of an American ethnic group in the politics of the homeland was the massive letter-writing campaign by Italian Americans to urge relatives and friends in Italy to vote against Communist candidates in the Italian election of April 1948. The campaign was organized through Catholic churches serving the Italian community. The clergy distributed form letters and urged in Sunday sermons that parishioners advise people in the homeland to vote for the Christian Democratic party because of its support of democracy and the church. In communities where the local church made a strong appeal, about 40 percent of the parishioners sent letters back to Italy. The deluge of letters was large enough to become a campaign issue; Socialists and Communists attacked the letters as interference and dictation in Italian affairs. The Christian Democrats, for whatever reason, won the election overwhelmingly.

RETURN TO THE HOMELAND

Another form of direct support by American ethnic groups for homeland causes—the ultimate possible commitment—is to move to the homeland to live and work. The most notable experience of return from the United States to the ancestral country has been that of Jewish American Zionists leaving the United States to take up permanent residence and citizenship in Israel.

The American Zionist movement took institutional form in 1915 with the establishment of the American Jewish Congress. It was opposed then and in subsequent years by the generally more conservative American Jewish Committee, whose position was that ethnic bonds among Jews were primarily religious and cultural and did not preclude social and political assimilation into the life of the nations of which Jews had become citizens. This was thought to be especially true of the United States with its openness and commitment to toleration. The Zionist commitment to establishment of a Jewish state in Palestine necessarily lent a secular political dimension to Jewish identity that challenged assimilationist attitudes.

The issue became more intense for the Jewish-American community with the founding of Israel, for the new state desperately needed settlers to work the land, build industries, and maintain defenses. Its need touched the conscience of Jews whether Zionist or not. The conflict

of loyalties for Jewish Americans was intensified by the Knesset's passage in 1950 of the Law of Return, which declared all Jews everywhere eligible for Israeli citizenship. Furthermore, the Israeli government attempted to make it as easy as possible for Jewish Americans to become Israeli citizens without losing U.S. citizenship. Its 1952 nationality law was designed purposely to minimize conflict with the U.S. law passed the same year. The Israeli law automatically conferred citizenship on all Jews living in Israel for a specified time without requiring a renunciation of other citizenship or an oath of allegiance to Israel, either of which would have been grounds for loss of U.S. nationality. Under these laws, levels of emigration from the United States to Israel have been steady but not high, rarely more than 500 a year in the 1950s and early 1960s. However, the number mounted to about 6,000 annually in the four years following the 1967 war.

All these private activities of American ethnic groups —whether buying Polish or Chinese war bonds, joining the Greek army, negotiating for the independence of Albania, or living in Israel for a period of years—are expressions of intense commitment to a nation other than the United States, and the intensity of such involvement might well be expected to raise questions of conflict with loyalty to the United States. Instead, such behavior, carried out within the sphere of the private actions of ethnic groups, has become so completely expected and accepted that it has scarcely been a matter of notice other than in time of war.

HOMELAND ISSUES IN AMERICAN ELECTIONS

When American ethnic groups have moved from the private to the public sphere to organize support for the homeland or otherwise to protect its interests as they are affected by the policies of the U.S. government, they have moved onto less certain ground. Efforts to relate a cause in the homeland to a more general American one necessarily invite negative reactions by other segments of the society, and at least the possibility of attack on its ethnic proponents. Some forms of political activity, however, have proved more generally acceptable than others.

One traditional means for promoting policies favorable to the homeland has been to attempt to make the desired policy an issue for candidates facing an election; this tactic has produced mixed results in terms of affecting policy, but generally has been accepted as a legitimate means of expressing ethnic-group concerns. The first to employ this tactic were the Irish Americans who began to make U.S. relations with Ireland's archenemy, England, a campaign issue as far back as the 1840s, when they attempted to exploit the dispute between Britain and the United States over the Oregon territory. In 1888 the Irish contributed to Benjamin Harrison's defeat of President Grover Cleveland when Republicans used Cleveland's attempts to sign a fisheries agreement with England to label him pro-British. The Republicans also provoked a virtual endorsement of Cleveland by the British Ambassador Sir Lionel Sackville-West on the eve of the election, which further aroused Irish indignation.

In 1897 the Senate rejected an arbitration treaty with England in the wake of heavy Irish lobbying against it. Any inclination of officials at the State Department to offer support to England during the Boer War was effectively discouraged by the combined and vocal opposition of both Irish and German Americans, a formidable constituency carefully courted by both Democratic and Republican candidates for office.

With the advent of World War I in 1914, the consequences of U.S. policy toward Old World countries became far more complex. From this point on, U.S. foreign policy inevitably affected American society generally, and seriously enough so that the demands of a particular ethnic group had to be weighed against the effect of policy on a wide range of groups or on the nation as a whole. The Irish, for example, after the Easter Rising in 1916, tried before the presidential election to gain Wilson's support for protection of the leaders of the rising. Wilson, however, necessarily concerned about the wider issue of British strength against Germany, refused to help in spite of the apparent closeness of the election.

The election of Warren Harding to the presidency in 1920 was aided by the defection of the Irish from the Democratic party because of bitterness over Wilson's failure to demand immediate independence for Ireland, as well as by the temporary defection to the Republicans of other, smaller ethnic groups—Italians, Greeks, Lithuanians, and Chinese, for example—disappointed in postwar U.S. policy toward their homelands.

The memory of the political disaster of 1920 inspired the Democrats, again facing a postwar election in 1948, to use the Nationalities Division of their campaign organization to counteract the potential defection of ethnic groups with grievances about American policies toward the homeland. Polish Americans were disappointed by the lack of effective support for non-Communist forces in Poland, as were Jewish Americans by the uncertain U.S. policy toward Palestine. Italian Americans were courted by Republicans promising to support the reestablishment of Italy's control over its former African colonies.

The Democratic appeal to these groups was cast largely in terms of domestic issues. The heavily Democratic returns from these groups were generally interpreted as crucial to Harry Truman's victory, but also as indicative of the primacy of pocketbook issues over homeland concerns in the voting habits of ethnic groups.

Whether Jewish-American voters, since 1932 predominantly liberal Democrats, would have defected to the Republicans over the issue of Palestine was never tested; Truman's immediate recognition of the state of Israel in May 1948 decisively removed the homeland cause as an election issue. The intriguing, but ultimately unanswerable, question remains whether Truman's act was motivated by the Jewish vote. Truman maintained that domestic politics played no part in his decision, that it was based on his conception of what was right and what was possible with respect to a Jewish homeland.

The raising of homeland issued at election time, both by ethnic groups seeking official attention and by candidates seeking ethnic votes, continues, as do the ritual visits of candidates to the three Is—Israel, Italy, and Ireland. However, the gravity of the factors involved in U.S. foreign policy in the years after World War II has substantially reduced both the possibility of official re-

sponse to ethnic demands as such and the expectation by ethnic groups that such response would be possible.

LOBBYING FOR A FRIENDLY HOMELAND

Although the kinds of issues raised in election years by ethnic groups have tended to be specific ones of fairly immediate concern for the homeland, a number of groups have also engaged in longer-range public campaigning designed to achieve more basic foreign-policy commitments. During World War I various groups mounted successful lobbying efforts for causes in the homeland. Eastern Europeans whose homelands had been part of the empires collapsing in the war campaigned vigorously for American backing for postwar independence. Heartened by Woodrow Wilson's proclamation of the principle of self-determination, Poles, Czechs, Slovaks, Ukrainians, Lithuanians, Armenians, Albanians, and Croats organized campaigns to convince Wilson to carry support for the homeland cause into the peace negotiations.

Some were more successful than others. The Czechs were at first dismayed by Wilson's announcement in January 1918 of a peace plan that provided some autonomy for ethnic units within Austria-Hungary but not for dissolution of the empire. They protested this plan energetically, and in May 1918 staged mass rallies across the country to bring the issue of Czech independence before the public. Tomas Masaryk, the exiled nationalist leader, traveled from rally to rally addressing the crowds. Wilson met with Masaryk and in September 1918 announced his support for an independent Czech-Slovak state, the position later adopted by the peace conference.

Albanians, Poles, and Croats also gained Wilson's support, as did the cause of an independent Armenia. The U.S. government recognized the Republic of Armenia when it was proclaimed in 1920, but was not willing to reengage in war in Europe to defend it when it was reoccupied by Russia only a few months after its founding, or when it was subsequently divided between Russia and Turkey. The initiative and persistence of the ethnic group in making the homeland cause an issue for the U.S. government contributed to the success of those that won official support, but in no case was a group successful when the promotion of its cause appeared militarily or diplomatically threatening to the United States. Loyalty to the United States requires that at some point ethnic group demands for the homeland must be subordinated to the larger interests of the country; this point has been defined by resistance from American leaders or the public generally to demands that seem too costly to the country as a whole. During World War I, for example, no amount of pressure from Irish Americans, regardless of their importance to the Democratic party, could move President Wilson to demand that the British grant immediate independence to Ireland.

Later, with the reversal suffered in World War II and afterward by most of the eastern European nations that had won their independence only 20 years earlier, American ethnic groups again organized to demand renewed guarantees from the U.S. government for the independence of their homelands, but this time without success. The United States could not contest Soviet control over the governments of eastern Europe with-

out the risk of war. Thus, in response to the pleas of American ethnic groups, the government made rhetorical gestures of protest only when the Soviet Union incorporated the nations of Latvia, Lithuania, and Estonia and imposed subservient Communist governments in Poland, East Germany, Hungary, Czechoslovakia, Romania, Bulgaria, and Albania. At the height of the Cold War in the mid-1950s, the Eisenhower administration stated a commitment in principle to the liberation of these nations—to "liberating enslaved peoples," the president said. In practical terms, however, U.S. postwar policy in Europe was one of containment of Communism within countries controlled by the Soviet Union. Even the anti-Soviet uprisings in Hungary in 1956 and Czechoslovakia in 1968 produced no greater support than official American sympathy and the admission to the United States of refugees who had managed to reach the West.

Continued lobbying for the independence of the homeland by eastern European groups, reinforced by anti-Soviet postwar immigrants, has not aroused antagonistic reactions from the public generally, partly because of shared anti-Soviet feelings, partly because the lobbying carries no risk of producing policy likely to lead to war. Willingness to encourage or even to accept official support for a homeland cause in response to pressures from an ethnic group may change abruptly, however, if the public perceives that the costs of a previously popular cause are becoming too high. This may be the case with respect to the firm policy of American support for the state of Israel, a policy ardently promoted by Jewish-American organizations since its founding in 1948.

Until the 1970s, Jewish Americans lobbying for Israel aroused little public opposition, given the general admiration for the accomplishments of the Israeli people and their courage in defending themselves. However, as the Arab countries grew in power and increased their control over their oil resources with spiraling economic impact on the West, the advantages of establishing better relations with the Arab powers became increasingly important to Americans and the public popularity of the Israeli cause began to diminish. The erosion of virtually automatic support for Israel was marked by the failure of Jewish-American leaders, despite intensive lobbying, to prevent congressional approval in the spring of 1978 of the sale of advanced jet fighters to Egypt and Saudi Arabia.

The long debate over this issue also produced increasing resentment throughout the country over the costs to the United States of maintaining support for Israel and intimations of a reaction against Jewish Americans because of it. This threat of an era of bad feeling subsided with the accord reached at the Camp David conference of September 1978 and the signing of a peace treaty between Israel and Egypt in March 1979. However, the experience illustrates the possibility that unpopular demands by an ethnic group may produce more than a negative reaction to the policy the group seeks; it may also produce some anger and resentment against the group itself—even for causes previously popular with the public.

In one case the carry-over of ancestral quarrels has created problems for American policy toward the homelands in question and thus conflict between ethnic

loyalties and the claims of U.S. national policy. Turkey's invasion of Cyprus in 1974, to aid Turkish Cypriots in their long struggle against Greek domination, provoked a move in Washington to suspend U.S. military aid to Turkey because it had violated restrictions on the use of aid for offensive purposes. This effort was strongly promoted by Greek-American organizations; the American Hellenic Institute organized a lobby in Washington to press the issue and two Greek-American congressmen, Paul Sarbannes of Maryland and John Brademas of Indiana, successfully led action to place an embargo on aid to Turkey in 1975. The embargo, and especially the Greek-American lobbying for it, caused great resentment among Turkish Americans, who mounted a countercampaign through the Federation of Turkish American Societies to have the aid to Turkey restored. The president pressed for repeal of the embargo, claiming that U.S. security required that Turkey remain militarily strong, and Congress lifted the embargo in 1978. In spite of the president's position, opposition to repeal, especially from Greek Americans, was strong enough to make the restoration of aid conditional on proof of Turkey's good faith in reducing tensions on the Cyprus issue.

FOREIGN LOBBYING

Resentment against ethnic groups lobbying for the homeland is most likely to arise when a group appears to be acting as agent for the government of the homeland rather than out of its own feelings of loyalty toward the home country. This was the situation in the 1920s and 1930s when Mussolini's government carried on extensive propaganda efforts among Italian Americans to build official good will for Italy. The deliberate nature of the campaign and the widespread enthusiasm for Mussolini among Italian Americans provoked public concern—and also conflict within the Italian-American community between supporters and opponents of Mussolini. When the United States declared war in 1941, however, Italian-American support for Mussolini ended and there was little retribution directed against Italians in the United States during the war.

Hitler's government also made attempts to organize German Americans to promote sympathy for Nazi Germany in the United States. The German-American response was slight, but the intense anti-German feelings from World War I aroused official suspicion and investigation of such organizations soon after their founding. None was able to sustain activity for more than a few years. The Friends of the New Germany, formed in 1933, collapsed in 1935 under investigation by the House Committee on Immigration and Naturalization; the German American Bund, organized in 1936, was able to stage mass rallies in 1936 and 1939 in Madison Square Garden but was weakened by the investigation by the House Un-American Activities Committee in 1938. It disbanded in 1939 when its principal organizer, Fritz Julius Kuhn, was convicted of embezzling its funds.

The government of Portugal in the early 1960s carried the appeal of the homeland to its American ethnic constituency to new lengths and aroused both public and official resentment. Portugal, which had lost its colonies in India and faced the beginnings of serious revolt in Angola, wished to promote American good will. The government of Prime Minister António de Oliveira Salazar employed a New York public-relations firm to stimulate Portuguese-American organizations to put pressure on the U.S. government to support Portuguese policies in Africa. These efforts were investigated as illegal lobbying for a foreign government by the Senate Committee on Foreign Relations in 1963.

Similarly, attempts by the government of Korea, carried out through the Korean Central Intelligence Agency, to influence U.S. policy were exposed in congressional investigations in 1977 and 1978. The exposures created a climate of suspicion and hostility potentially threatening to Korean Americans, whether they sympathized with the Korean government or not.

An unusual episode of direct appeal to the American public by foreign leaders took the form of virtual political campaigning in the United States by Egyptian President Anwar Sadat and Prime Minister Menachem Begin of Israel in the months preceding the Camp David conference of 1978. The U.S. government was acting as an unofficial mediator in the dispute, and further it could influence the bargaining process toward a peace agreement through the extension or withholding of various forms of U.S. aid to the two parties. Both leaders, therefore, sought to ensure and enlarge the favor of Washington in the negotiations, and did so partly by appealing to their respective ethnic groups and other supporters in the United States to urge the cause of the homeland directly to the American president or through congressional representatives. During this unusually direct engagement of foreign leaders with the American public, there was little evidence of resentment or recrimination directed at them or at the ethnic sympathizers to whom they appealed.

RELATIONS WITH HOSTILE OR ENEMY HOMELANDS

The difficulty of balancing dual affinities and loyalties becomes acute when relations between the ethnic homeland and the United States are tense, hostile, or worse, when the two nations are at war. Members of ethnic groups are forced to choose between hostility toward the homeland and hostility toward the United States, or to attempt against all odds to represent the homeland interest to the American public and government in the hope of changing attitudes from hostility to sympathy.

The experience of ethnic groups caught in this dilemma reveals, more than any other aspect of the experience of dual loyalty, the intensity of feeling that surrounds the question of loyalty, the strong emotional dimension of the bond between individual and nation. In times of tension and trouble, the spirit of tolerance that normally permits the open discussion of homeland interests quickly dissipates and is replaced by an aura of suspicion through which questions and differences tend to be perceived as threats and the questioners as enemies.

The response of American ethnic groups to these pressures, especially in the extreme case of war, has been to suspend their sense of connection to the homeland and to act in accordance with their primary loyalty to the United States. The number of people who have refused to support an American war effort out of loyalty to the homeland has been extremely small. It has

been more common for ethnic groups whose homelands have become unfriendly to U.S. interests to dissociate themselves from homeland policies. For example, in 1941 a group of prominent Irish Americans, incensed with Ireland's policy of neutrality in the face of full-scale European war, attempted to convince the Irish government to set aside its traditional hostility toward England and join the Allies in their fight against Nazi Germany. It was an unsuccessful effort, but noteworthy in the ordering of loyalties it expressed.

The most devastating experience of an ethnic group that tried to promote an unpopular homeland cause was that of German Americans during World War I. They attempted through their ethnic organizations to present the German point of view to Americans well beyond the time when public sympathy had turned distinctly anti-German. The major vehicle for pro-German sentiment was the National German-American Alliance (1901–1918), a cultural organization devoted before the war to such diverse causes as promoting the teaching of German and fighting Prohibition. With an impressive membership of approximately 2 million people in 1914, the alliance during the early years of the war sponsored mass demonstrations, collected German war-relief funds, lobbied for embargoes on loans and the sale of arms to England, promoted the sale of Imperial war bonds, and campaigned for the defeat of Woodrow Wilson in the presidential election of 1916. The German-American press, which included over 500 German-language publications, was also virtually unanimous in its pro-German sentiment and its insistence on American neutrality.

Joined by Irish Americans in opposition to U.S. entry into the war on the side of England and by millions of Americans without ethnic bonds to the belligerents but who opposed any American involvement in European affairs, German Americans could express antiwar sentiments in 1914 and 1915 with little fear of public resentment. Anti-German sentiment began to grow, however, as the war wore on and particularly as German attacks on merchant ships carrying civilian passengers intensified.

When the United States finally entered the war in 1917, German Americans and their organizations, churches, places of business, and cultural connections generally became the objects of furious attack. Anti-German fervor brought about the boycott of music composed by Germans, the renaming of places with German names, arrests of German Americans for unpatriotic speech, and the elimination or restriction of German-language instruction in schools. The virulence of public attitudes toward German Americans for their prewar loyalty to the homeland resulted in the rapid, often permanent, collapse of German ethnic associations. The National German-American Alliance dissolved under Senate investigation; by 1920 the number of German-language publications had dropped to half the number circulating in 1910; most local German-American organizations erased their ethnic identity.

The postwar political turbulence in Germany, followed by Hitler's attainment of power in 1933 and then World War II, made it all but impossible to express a sense of kinship with Germany. German Americans have never reestablished a strong associational life based on their ethnic bonds. Of the more than 200 German-language publications that survived World War I, only 24 remained in 1976.

Greek Americans suffered a similar fate in the aftermath of World War I. The neutrality of Greece during the war, combined with the strong German ties of the Greek royal family, created a stigma which made open expression of attachment to the homeland a rarity in the Greek-American community. In 1940, however, the resistance of the Greeks to Italy's invasion of their country made links to the homeland once more a source of pride for Greek Americans.

In the immediate postwar years, disillusion with the outcome of World War I and a general reaction against European influences in American life fed a resurgence of nativist attitudes that produced, among other things, the restrictive immigration laws of 1921 and 1924, but also acute concern about foreign subversion of U.S. politics—the Red Scare. Russian Americans, especially socialists and other radicals enthusiastic about the Bolshevik Revolution in 1917, were the primary objects of suspicion and retribution. In New York City, approximately 5,000 people were arrested in raids on the headquarters of the Union of Russian Workers in 1919 and of the Russian-dominated American Communist party in 1920. Anti-Russian feeling, first aroused by the Russian Revolution but sustained by continued hostility toward Russian Communism, has produced an assimilationist reaction among Russian Americans similar to that of German Americans since World War I. Out of fear of social or even official retribution, Russian Americans have played down their ethnic identity and allowed many of their ethnic associations to lapse.

The most repressive antiethnic reaction to the enemy status of the homeland was the internment of Japanese Americans during World War II. On February 19, 1942, two months after the Japanese attack on Pearl Harbor, Executive Order 9066 authorized the removal of "dangerous persons" from areas along the Pacific Coast and their internment in government camps in the interior. By August 1942 nearly 120,000 Japanese, 64 percent of them U.S. citizens, were moved from their homes to the camps, where most of them had to stay until the end of the war.

The military logic of the order was to counter the possibility of Japanese Americans giving secret aid to the Japanese war effort, including possibly facilitating an attack on the West Coast. There was, however, little evidence of such subversive activity or, after the outbreak of war, of the prevalence among Japanese Americans of pro-Japanese sentiments that might make military subversion a risk. Even military leaders did not agree about the need for internment as a security measure.

Pressure for the relocation of Japanese Americans came primarily from the public in California, where anti-Japanese attitudes had taken various legislative forms since the late 19th century and had been suddenly intensified by identification of the group with an actual, external enemy. In the Japanese experience, more than that of any other group, the accusation of group disloyalty was a function of prejudice, of the intolerance of difference within American society.

Similar reactions occurred in official attitudes toward Chinese Americans after the Communist revolution

had converted China from an ally to a Cold War enemy in 1949, attitudes that hardened when the Chinese entered the Korean War and became enemies on a battlefield. Concern in the mid-1950s about the illegal entry into the United States of Chinese through Hong Kong, together with suspicion about the ties and loyalties of Chinese Americans to the homeland, produced a plan for the deportation of thousands of Chinese from the United States. Intensive lobbying by the National Chinese Welfare Council forestalled the deportations, but official and public suspicion toward Chinese Americans remained alive, especially in California, and began to dissipate only with United States initiatives toward normal relations with China in the early 1970s.

Exceptions to Exceptionalism

Wilson was not alone, during the American age of innocence, in conceiving of the United States as a unique entity, as a "great ideal" that transcended and thus could unite nations. The assumption was widespread, when the United States was relatively isolated from world affairs, that Americans could be free from the old nationalisms which divided humanity into the enclaves Wilson called "jealous camps." For the new nation, the old terms of national loyalty would not apply because national divisions would be recognized as ultimately meaningless, matters of administrative convenience only. Citizens of the United States, Wilson had said, owed their first loyalty to humanity. Under this conception of the nation, problems of dual loyalty would not arise.

Although the ideal of the neutral nation, the nation without national interest and nationalist spirit, has not been fully realized since Wilson's time, neither has it been wholly irrelevant to the actual experience of the United States.

Beginning with its entry into World War I, the United States has been drawn into close, constant relations with the other centers of world power and inevitably has had to conduct these relations as a nation dealing with other nations. U.S. relations with others have been variously friendly, hostile, peaceful or warring, and the American people have responded to these conditions with traditionally patriotic attitudes of good will for friends, condemnation for enemies. Times of war or crisis have aroused in the American public much the same sentiments of national loyalty that earlier generations of Americans had deplored in the Old World. At such times the problem of dual loyalty, or suspected divided loyalty among members of an ethnic group whose homeland is hostile to the United States, has become acute—as the experience of German, Greek, Japanese, and Russian Americans illustrates.

In the absence of crisis, however, there has been a generalized tolerance, in the spirit of Wilson's ideal, for the promotion by ethnic groups in the United States of various interests important to the homeland. Continued affection for and identification with the homeland have been generally regarded as natural, and a variety of activities supporting the homeland have come to be accepted as legitimate. However, there are limits to such activities even in times of peace. While the openness of the American political system encourages a multiplicity of interests and allows groups great leeway to act on their differences, it also sets up counterpressures to

smooth out differences, even to deny them. There is greater tension in American democracy than Wilson foresaw, a greater propensity for fear of difference. As a result, American ethnic groups have experienced both extensive tolerance and extensive intolerance in reaction to their expression of their complex loyalties.

On the whole, the phenomenon of dual loyalty has not greatly influenced the relations of the United States with other nations. There has been little serious subversive activity against the United States on behalf of a group's homeland. The efforts of interested ethnic groups have had more effect instead on the establishment of friendly ties between the United States and other countries, and on the provision of U.S. aid, diplomatic or financial. However, no ethnic group has been able to promote an official policy favorable to the homeland unless it has also had a wider base of public acceptance or has carried little risk or cost to the United States.

The most serious conflict that has been created by loyalties running both to the United States and to the homeland has been the one experienced by the ethnic group itself in the process of establishing its American identity. The most important link to the homeland has been the need of each ethnic group for a source of pride and self-respect to aid it in establishing a dignified place in American society.

Bibliography

The only comprehensive book on the topic is Louis L. Gerson, *The Hyphenate in Recent American Politics and Diplomacy* (Lawrence, Kans., 1964), which provides a well-documented review of the engagement of ethnic groups in homeland issues from the late 19th century.

John Higham, *Strangers in the Land: Patterns of American Nativism, 1860–1925* (New York, 1973), is a rich and sensitive study of attitudes toward foreignness in general; chapters 8 and 9 deal with the experience of German Americans during World War I and the postwar Red Scare.

Thomas N. Brown, *Irish-American Nationalism, 1870–1890* (Philadelphia, 1966), is a perceptive examination of the sources of immigrant nationalism; his thesis is applicable to other ethnic groups as well. This connection is specifically drawn in an elegant essay by Maldwyn A. Jones, *The Old World Ties of American Ethnic Groups* (London, 1976).

Informative studies of specific ethnic-group issues of broad political significance include: Roger Daniel, *Concentration Camps U.S.A.: Japanese Americans and World War II* (New York, 1972), especially its review of the way in which the evacuation decision was made; Samuel Halperin, *The Political World of American Zionism* (Detroit, 1964), a detailed history of the movement and its opponents up to 1945; Robert Silverberg, *If I Forget Thee O Jerusalem: American Jews and the State of Israel* (New York, 1970), a detailed but undocumented journalistic account of the involvement of Jewish Americans in promoting the cause of Israel through 1969; John P. Diggin, *Mussolini and Fascism: The View from America* (Princeton, N.J., 1972), which includes two informative chapters on the reactions of Italian Americans to Fascism in Italy; and Robert G. Weisbord, *Ebony Kinship: Africa, Africans, and the Afro-American* (Westport, Conn., 1973), which traces the correspondence in attitudes black Americans have held toward Africa and toward themselves.

Mona Harrington

LUISEÑOS: *see* American Indians

LUMBEES: *see* American Indians

LUSATIAN SORBS: *see* Wends

LUXEMBOURGERS

Luxembourgers began to come to the United States in the 1840s. Most of them arrived in the two decades before 1914; only a handful have come since. It is esti-

mated that between 75,000 and 100,000 Luxembourgers and their descendants are presently living in the United States.

ORIGINS

Luxembourgers come from a duchy that has been a clearly defined territorial entity since the early Middle Ages. In 963 Siegfried, count of Ardennes, acquired the ruined Roman castle of Lucilinburhuc, near the center of what is now the city of Luxembourg. By the 14th century Luxembourg included not only the present grand duchy but also large areas of present-day eastern Belgium (province of Luxembourg), West Germany (the Eifel area around Bitburg), and northeastern France (Thionville). In the first half of the 15th century the Luxembourg dynasty ruled Bohemia, Hungary, and Brandenburg and was a powerful force in Europe. At the height of its power, the family line died out, and Luxembourg for several centuries was subject to Burgundian, Spanish, Austrian, and French domination. At the Congress of Vienna in 1815 Luxembourg was declared a grand duchy in personal union with the king of the Netherlands. Real independence came in 1839, but involved losing the province of Luxembourg to Belgium. In 1890 the crown of the grand duchy passed to the House of Nassau; since that time it has had its own reigning family.

From the 1840s until World War I Luxembourg was part of an economic union (Zollverein) with other German states, subordinate to the economic policies of Prussia. This situation did not change even after the Franco-Prussian war in 1871 which resulted in international guarantees for Luxembourg's neutrality, a neutrality that was violated by Germany in both world wars: during World War I Luxembourg was occupied, and during World War II it was annexed to Hitler's Third Reich. Subsequently, Luxembourg sought economic ties elsewhere, first with Belgium (1921) and then with Belgium and the Netherlands (1948) in a union that eventually became the basis for the European Common Market.

The Luxembourgers are linguistically and culturally related to the German people, but the recent excesses of German history have led them to stress their differences rather than their similarities. Their language, called Luxembourgish (Létzebûrgesch), belongs to the West Moselle Franconian group of German dialects, and is spoken by most of the people; the parliament, courts, church, schools, and newspapers, however, use French or German. Since the early 19th century, a Luxembourgish literature has developed, and in recent years many of its speakers have come to regard their language as a full-fledged language and not merely a dialect. More than 97 percent of the inhabitants are Roman Catholics; the rest are Jews or Protestants.

MIGRATION AND ARRIVAL

The first Luxembourger immigrants to America came with the Dutch to New Amsterdam (New York) in the 1630s. A few Luxembourger priests served the missions in the French colony of Louisiana in the early 18th century. The earliest Luxembourger immigrant is considered to be Philippe de la Noye (de Lannoy), a passenger on the *Fortune* (a sister ship of the *Mayflower*) and a direct maternal ancestor of President Franklin Delano Roosevelt. De la Noye probably belonged to the family that held the castle at Clervaux in Luxembourg.

In the 1820s several hundred Luxembourgers went to Brazil, Guatemala, and Argentina but the tropical climate, disease, and limited economic opportunities made those countries unattractive, and as population pressure encouraged further emigration they turned instead to the United States. Between 1839 and 1941 the population of Luxembourg rose 52 percent; since the country did not begin to industrialize until the last decades of the 19th century, the practice of primogeniture forced many sons of large peasant families to emigrate where land was still cheap. At mid-century a hectare (2.5 acres) of the best farmland in Luxembourg cost from 1,500 to 2,000 francs; less fertile land, from 500 to 800 francs. Comparable land in the then sparsely settled areas near Chicago and in southern Wisconsin could be had for the equivalent of 15 or 20 francs.

About 100 Luxembourgers came to the United States in the 1830s, either via New York City and moving on to rural areas along the southeastern coast of Lake Erie, or via New Orleans and moving northward to Ohio. In the 1840s larger numbers began to arrive. Official emigration statistics from the grand duchy combined with reports of Derulle-Wigreux and Sons, the agency in Luxembourg that was responsible for the majority of departures, provide a reliable body of statistical data.

The first immigration, which lasted from the 1840s to 1914, brought approximately 48,000 Luxembourgers looking for better opportunities or, sometimes, avoiding military service; this flow was interrupted by World War I. Between 1919 (when immigration resumed) and 1940 only 1,742 Luxembourgers arrived, 751 in 1920 alone. After 1920 the rise in the standard of living in

BELGIUM

Ardennes

Eifel

Clervaux

WEST GERMANY

Bastogne

Bitburg

LUXEMBOURG

Sauer

Diekirch

Echternach

LUXEMBOURG

Trier

Arlon

Luxembourg

Moselle

Esch

FRANCE

Thionville

Luxembourg

20   Km.   Miles

Luxembourg resulting from industrialization, and the Depression of the 1930s resulting in a lack of jobs in the United States, caused a decline in emigration. The only notable exception to this was the arrival in New York City between 1937 and 1940 of 200 to 300 Luxembourg Jews (some of them via France and Switzerland), fleeing the threat of Nazi persecution.

After the war Luxembourg enjoyed a period of prosperity that gave its inhabitants one of the highest standards of living in the world. As a result only about 500 have emigrated since the war, many of them women married to American servicemen stationed in nearby West Germany.

Thus, from the 1840s to the present, about 50,000 Luxembourgers have immigrated. The U.S. Census recorded 43,109 persons of Luxembourger stock in 1920 and 20,528 in 1970. The estimate of 75,000 to 100,000 for the Luxembourger community today is based on their propensity for large families. The settlement in Ozaukee County, Wis., for example (admittedly an extreme case), averaged 14 to 18 children per family in the early 1900s.

SETTLEMENT AND ECONOMIC LIFE

The settlement patterns established by Luxembourger immigrants in the 1840s have not changed greatly. Most of them headed for Chicago, settling either in the city itself, especially the northern part and its suburbs along Lake Michigan, or along Lake Michigan from Chicago to just north of Milwaukee. A secondary cluster formed around Dubuque, Iowa, on the Mississippi River. After the 1850s, some moved north from Dubuque to Rollingstone, Minneapolis–St. Paul, and St. Cloud, Minn., or west to New Ulm, Minn., or Remsen, Iowa, and several towns in western North Dakota, South Dakota, Nebraska, and Kansas, all frontier areas that offered abundant farmland.

Although the Luxembourg population in the north-central states has declined somewhat, the region in 1970 still included 61 percent of the group.

Year	Number	Percentage
1880	11,841	92
1920	36,627	85
1970	12,462	61

According to the 1920 Census, the leading Luxembourger states were Illinois (21 percent), Minnesota (16.4 percent), Iowa (16 percent), and Wisconsin (11.2 percent). About 50 percent were rural dwellers in 1920 and a strikingly high 44.7 percent in 1930.

Many Luxembourger Americans still live in Chicago and its northern and western suburbs of Des Plaines, Park Ridge, Wilmette, Evanston, Morton Grove, Skokie, and Aurora. By the early 20th century, they had monopolized the truck-gardening and greenhouse business in the Chicago area. Although urban expansion has reduced the amount of available farmland, the large number of parks in the region and several supermarket and florist businesses stem from these early Luxembourger activities. Other settlements are in Ozaukee County, Wis. (Port Washington, Fredonia, Belgium), Dubuque and Jackson counties, Iowa (Dubuque, St. Donatus, Luxemburg, Bellevue), and Sterns County, Minn. (St. Cloud, Luxembourg).

Little information is available on the economic and

social composition of the community. In 1930, 16 percent still lived on farms, and another 29 percent in rural nonfarm areas; all were probably farmers or in related industries. In Chicago they owned and operated small businesses—bakeries, construction companies, and especially taverns.

SOCIAL ORGANIZATIONS

The Luxembourger community has developed both formal and informal structures that foster interaction between members of the group. The earliest of these were the taverns that attempted to reproduce the atmosphere of the European café; patrons' conversation in the native tongue and reminiscences about the homeland were as important as the consumption of beer and wine. They also served as meeting places for the group's organizations. The last important tavern-restaurant, the Luxembourg Gardens in Chicago, served as a social center for the community until the mid-1960s.

Tavern owners and other businessmen were often group leaders as well. In Chicago in recent years Luxembourg social and cultural activity is largely in the hands of individuals like John Marsh, a construction-firm owner, Fred Pesche, a supermarket and truck-garden owner, John Thillens, a banker, and Nick Colling and Leo Eschette, restaurateurs.

The earliest organizations were founded in the 1870s. The Chicago-based Luxembourger Unterstützungs-verein (Luxembourger Benefit Society) was founded in 1870, the Létzebûrger Kranken-Ennerstétzongs Verein (Luxembourger Sick Benefit Society) in 1871, and the Luxembourger Bruderbund (Luxembourger Brotherhood) in 1887. Similar societies were set up in Milwaukee, St. Paul, and Dubuque, Iowa. All of them provided modest financial remuneration in case of the death or incapacity of their members. Of them, only the Luxembourger Brotherhood still exists; at its height it had 25 chapters; today it has 5, all in the Chicago area.

Other organizations were set up to fill specific needs. The Luxembourg Independent Club of Chicago (f. 1886) began as a political organization to collect votes for local Democratic candidates; it was led by the two Luxembourg-born city police inspectors, Dominik Welter (1839–1885) and Michael Schaack (1843–1900). It soon dropped its political activities and became a social club, but Luxembourger Americans still tend to vote Democratic as they have since the Civil War. Other groups are the Létzebûrger Sängerbond (Luxembourg Singing Society, 1900–1954); the Schwestern Verein (Sisterhood Society, f. 1901), and the Luxembourg-American Social Club (f. 1960), all in Chicago; and the Luxembourg Jewish Society, established in 1958 in New York.

RELIGION

Almost all Luxembourger Americans are Roman Catholic, but because they account for only a small percentage of U.S. Catholics, the church, with few exceptions, has not been an effective contributor to Luxembourger ethnic development in the United States. Only in a few suburbs of Chicago (High Ridge, Evanston) and in small towns like St. Nicholas, Wis., Rollingstone, Minn., and St. Donatus and Remsen, Iowa, were there at times the semblance of Luxembourger parishes. More often, Luxembourgers attended churches with neighboring Catholic immigrants, especially those

from the Eifel region of Germany and eastern Belgium. The influence of the church is reflected in a high percentage of Luxembourgers who marry other Roman Catholics and in strong local support for parochial education.

INTERGROUP RELATIONS

Throughout most of the 19th century, the larger American society thought of Luxembourgers as being Germans; some identified themselves as Germans or as Luxembourger Germans, spoke a German dialect (called Letzeburger-deitsch Sproch), and published their newspapers and organizational proceedings in German. This Germanic orientation gradually changed, however, primarily as a result of political conditions in Europe. Between 1867 and 1871, the Franco-Prussian political crisis over control of the grand duchy prompted Luxembourger immigrants to distrust the explanations of the German-language press. This led to the establishment of the first immigrant publication, the weekly *Luxemburger Gazette* (Dubuque, Iowa, 1871–1918), whose opening editorial statement made clear the Germanic cultural and linguistic allegiance of Luxembourgers, but at the same time disavowed any sympathy for Prussia.

A more profound change in attitude occurred during World War I, when the homeland was occupied by Germany. The Luxembourg Brotherhood addressed a memorandum in 1917 to President Wilson, pledging support for the U.S. war effort against Germany. The rejection of identity with Germans and an increasing sense of a distinct Luxembourger identity was prompted by Hitler's rise to power and Germany's contribution to the outbreak of World War II. Of great symbolic significance during the war were the several visits of the exiled Grand Duchess Charlotte and her son, the present Grand Duke Jean, to Luxembourger immigrant communities and the visits arranged for the royal family with another Luxembourg descendant, President Roosevelt.

CULTURE AND ETHNIC GROUP MAINTENANCE

Luxembourg culture in the United States is largely the product of the 19th-century immigration. An important figure in its development was Nicholaus Gonner (1835–1892). The editor of the *Luxemburger Gazette* from 1872 until his death 20 years later, he helped to propagate Luxembourg culture by publishing two anthologies of literature in Luxembourgish, *Onserer Lider a Gedichter* (1879) and *Prairieblummen* (1883), which included works of immigrant authors like Gonner and Nicholas Becker (b. 1842). Gonner also reprinted several Luxembourg folk tales and wrote a comprehensive history of the Luxembourg immigration.

Becker compiled a lexicon of expressions used by Luxembourgers in Ozaukee County, Wis.

Most Luxembourger publications of the early years were written in German, but after World War I the use of English became much more common. The only Luxembourger periodical in existence today is the *Luxembourg News of America* (Chicago, 1926–1965; Mt. Prospect, Ill., 1967–), the monthly organ of the Luxembourgers of America, which in addition to organizational information, carries occasional articles about the homeland. With few exceptions like the short-lived folk theater in Chicago, the Luxembourgish language was used only in everyday speech, and as a result died out with the immigrant generation, leaving its descendants without the means to maintain it.

A popular manifestation of Luxembourg culture was the annual fair (Schueberfo'er) held until the late 1960s in Chicago. This fair was first held in 1904 to bring Luxembourgers together and to advertise the products of local merchants, many of whom, then as now, were in the food business. Several other Luxembourg-born or American-born Luxembourgers are a source of pride to the community, including photographer Edward Steichen (1879–1973), biologist François Mergen (1925–), historian Arno Mayer (1926–), film star Loretta Young (1913–), and tennis player Chris Evert (1954–).

By now Luxembourger Americans lack the formal structures—schools, newspapers, theater, and literature—that make it possible to foster ethnic awareness among the younger generations, a situation only partially offset by the frequent travel to the homeland made possible by inexpensive direct flights via Icelandic Airlines and by organizations like the American-Luxembourg Society. Established in Luxembourg in 1963, this society sponsors annual tours for Luxembourgers to the United States. These contacts renew awareness of the Luxembourg heritage, but it remains to be seen if they, combined with the ethnic revival of the 1970s, will have any appreciable effect on reinvigorating ethnic identity and organizational life among Luxembourger Americans.

Bibliography
The best study of the early years of Luxembourger immigration is by Nicholaus Gonner, *Die Luxemburger in der neuen Welt* (Dubuque, Iowa, 1889). Information on community life since the 1890s is found in an historically based travel account by Roger Krieps, *Luxemburger in Amerika* (Luxembourg, 1962). An account of a single community is available in Joseph J. Lies, *Luxemburger Immigrants to Aurora* (Aurora, Ill., 1976). One of the best introductions to the Luxembourg homeland and its position between two great European cultures is Nicholas Ries, *Essai d'une psychologie du peuple luxembourgeois*, 2d ed. (Diekirch, 1920). An excellent description of contemporary conditions is the chapter on Luxembourg by Meic Stephens in *Linguistic Minorities in Western Europe* (Llandysul, Wales, 1976).

PAUL ROBERT MAGOCSI

M

MACEDONIANS

Macedonian Americans are a relatively small group with a very complicated history. It is not easy to determine who is a member of this group, and almost any discussion of Macedonians or Macedonia, the ancient kingdom of Philip and Alexander the Great, is likely to create controversy among the people who view its history from different perspectives.

Immigrants from Macedonia came to the United States in significant numbers during the early years of the 20th century. Until World War II almost all of them thought of themselves as Bulgarians and identified themselves as Bulgarians or Macedonian Bulgarians. Recently, however, for some this has begun to change. Although there are still perhaps 50,000 Macedonians who identify themselves as Bulgarians or Macedonian Bulgarians, a group of Macedonian Americans who identify themselves specifically as Macedonians is beginning to emerge as a result of developments in their Balkan homelands. (*See also* Bulgarians.)

ORIGINS

The historical region known as Macedonia is situated in the central part of the Balkan peninsula. Its frontiers have varied through the centuries, but Macedonia is generally defined as the area bounded on the east by the Rhodope Mountains and the Mesta (Nestos) River; on the south by the Aegean Sea, Mount Olympus, the Vistritsa (Aliákmon) River, and the Pindus Mountains; on the west by Lake Ohrid, the Drin River, and the Korab Mountains; and on the north by the Šar, Osogovske, and Rila Dagh mountains. In terms of current political boundaries Macedonia is divided into three parts: the Socialist Republic of Macedonia (formerly Vardar Macedonia) in Yugoslavia, Aegean or Greek Macedonia in Greece, and Pirin Macedonia or the Blagoevgrad District of Bulgaria. There are also Macedonian minorities living in other parts of Yugoslavia and in Albania.

Macedonia experienced several centuries of Roman rule, but during the 6th and 7th centuries the region was settled by Slavic tribes who soon assimilated most of the local population. In the second half of the 7th century Bulgars invaded the Balkans, and they in turn were assimilated by the Slavs. The Bulgars, or Proto-Bulgarians, established a state, usually referred to as the First Bulgarian Kingdom, which included most of Macedonia.

Christianity was introduced into the Bulgarian Kingdom during the 9th century when Saints Cyril and Methodius and their disciples converted the population and formulated for them a Slavic alphabet, Glagolitic, from which Cyrillic later developed. The Cyrillic alphabet is still used in Macedonian, which by the mid-20th century had evolved into a distinct South Slavic language closely related to Bulgarian. Most Macedonians still belong to the Eastern Orthodox Church.

During the 10th century the Bulgarian state grew weaker and split into two. The western Bulgarian King-

Macedonia

▨ Macedonian-speaking areas

75   Km.   Miles

dom with its capital in Ohrid was ruled by Tsar Samuil (997–1014), and most contemporary Macedonian historians regard this as the first Slavic Macedonian state. Samuil also created the Archbishopric of Ohrid and proclaimed its ecclesiastical independence. However, in 1018 Macedonia was conquered by the Byzantine Empire. Two centuries later it became a part of the Second Bulgarian Kingdom; for a brief period in the mid-14th century it fell under Serbian rule. Shortly thereafter the Ottoman Empire took over, and the Macedonians remained under Ottoman rule until 1912. During these centuries the Macedonians were part of the autonomous Eastern Orthodox community or millet, which was under the leadership of Greek churchmen. When the Greeks began to exert stronger influence in the late 18th and 19th centuries, the Macedonians joined the Bulgarians in an active struggle against further Hellenization. In 1870 they established an independent Bulgarian Orthodox Church that was authorized to include Macedonian territory within its jurisdiction, and the Ottoman Empire gave official recognition to Bulgarian nationality. At this time Macedonian Slavs participated in the Bulgarian national renaissance and in the armed struggle for the liberation of Bulgaria (including Macedonia) from the Ottoman Empire.

When Bulgaria finally achieved independence in 1878, Macedonia was included within its borders, but after the Treaty of Berlin was signed that year, most Macedonians found themselves again under Turkish

rule. Beginning in the 1890s, Bulgarians, Serbs, and Greeks sent armed bands into Macedonia in the hope of annexing the region. These groups attacked the Turks, fought with each other, and terrorized the local populace while their respective governments fought for the allegiance of the Macedonian Slavs.

In these unfavorable circumstances, local leaders established the Internal Macedonian Revolutionary Organization (IMRO) in an effort to unite all the ethnic groups in the region and to establish an independent Macedonian state. The IMRO leaders considered themselves Bulgarian, but they also had a strong sense of regional identity and advocated "Macedonia for Macedonians." They did not prevail, however; following the Balkan wars (1912–1913) and World War I, Macedonia remained divided among Greece, Serbia (later Yugoslavia), and Bulgaria.

Macedonian leaders began to develop a strong sense of regional identity in the 19th century, but it was not until the 20th century that some intellectuals began to argue that Macedonian Slavs were neither Bulgarian nor Serbian, nor Greek, but a separate people. The Communist party of Yugoslavia supported this idea during World War II, and in 1945 a People's (later Socialist) Republic of Macedonia was established as one of the six constituent republics of the Federal Socialist Republic of Yugoslavia. A Macedonian literary language was developed, and the idea of Macedonian nationality was encouraged. In 1958 a Macedonian Orthodox church was created, and nine years later it acquired jurisdictional independence. Neighboring Bulgaria, which has a Macedonian minority population, initially favored these developments and from 1944 to 1958 even recognized the existence of a Macedonian nationality. Since 1958, however, Bulgaria has argued that all Macedonians are Bulgarians, and this policy contributes to the discord and tension between Bulgaria and Yugoslavia. The Greek government has never recognized Macedonians as a distinct nationality.

MIGRATION AND ARRIVAL

The first immigrants who arrived in the United States from Macedonia came from the western regions near Kastoria (Kostur), Flórina (Lerin), and Bitola (Monastir). The majority were *gurbetchii* or *pechalbari*, men going abroad to seek a fortune who planned to return home after two or three years.

Macedonians were usually listed as coming from Turkey, Serbia (or Yugoslavia), Greece, and Bulgaria; in the absence of reliable statistics it can be estimated that between 1903 and 1906 about 50,000 Macedonian Bulgarians emigrated to the United States. A few thousand more came until the Balkan wars and World War I stopped the continuous flow. Approximately 20,000 remained, the rest returned to Macedonia, although years later some remigrated to the United States. About 80 percent of those who came before World War I were peasants, the remainder craftsmen, workers, and intellectuals.

Between the two world wars the majority of Macedonian/Slav immigrants to the United States were from Greece and Bulgaria. Slavs were expelled from Greek Macedonia in the early 1920s, and most of them settled in Bulgaria. Some came directly from Greece, others via Bulgaria; during these years only a handful were permit-

ted to emigrate from Yugoslavia. By the end of World War II there were an estimated 50,000 to 60,000 Macedonians in the United States.

Since 1945 most of the Macedonians have come from Yugoslavia and Greece. Only 2,000 came from Yugoslavia between the end of the war and 1960 when emigration policies were liberalized. According to Yugoslav statistics, about 40,000 Macedonians emigrated in the years from 1960 to 1977, primarily to the United States, Canada, and Australia. Some of these emigrants have been political dissidents opposed to the Yugoslav regime, but most have been seeking economic opportunity. In contrast, very few have been permitted to leave Bulgaria. The Macedonians in Greece, who are known there as Slavophones or Slavic-speaking Greeks, were expelled in 1944 and again encouraged to leave after the Greek civil war (1946–1949). As a result 70,000 have emigrated to Canada, Australia, the United States, and other European countries.

There is no way of determining the exact number of Macedonian Americans. The Matica for Macedonian Immigrants, a special institution created in the Socialist Republic of Macedonia to deal with Macedonians living abroad, estimates that there are between 120,000 and 150,000. However, this figure includes all Slavic-speaking immigrants and their descendants from the historical region and does not allow for the fact that the majority of immigrants from Macedonia and their descendants identify with the Bulgarian-American community, while many from Greece identify with the Greek-American community. Allowing for some older Macedonian-Bulgarian immigrants who have changed their ethnic orientation, in addition to the more recent immigrants from Yugoslav Macedonia who have a strong sense of Macedonian national identity, it is realistic to assume that there are between 25,000 to 30,000 Macedonian immigrants and their descendants in the United States today.

SETTLEMENT PATTERNS, ECONOMIC LIFE, AND SOCIAL ORGANIZATION

During the first decades of the 20th century, the majority of the Macedonian Bulgarians settled in the industrial centers of Ohio, Michigan, Illinois, Indiana, New York, Pennsylvania, Missouri, Wisconsin, California, and Washington; this pattern of settlement has changed little. Some community leaders claim that there are between 15,000 and 20,000 Macedonian Americans living in the Detroit area. There are other communities in Gary, Ind.; Chicago; Passaic, N.J.; Columbus, Cleveland, Lorain, Akron, Canton, Massilon, and Cincinnati, Ohio; and in New York City, Lackawanna, Buffalo, Rochester, and Syracuse, N.Y.

The early immigrants, who came from a rural, traditional, and economically and politically oppressive Ottoman society, encountered great difficulties in the industrial urban, highly competitive American environment. Most of the immigrants had to travel first to France or Germany where they spent a few days in camps before boarding the ships. Some used the Greek ports of Salonika and Piraeus as points of departure. The Macedonian peasant, who might never before have visited a large town, was almost immediately confronted with hazardous work in steel mills, foundries, mines,

and railroad construction; the complexities of city life created additional problems.

The first centers of community life were the boarding house and the coffee house. Since the majority of the immigrants were single men, individuals from the same village or region settled together and established a communal existence in which each of the participants shared in the responsibilities. The coffee house was more than a place to visit and play cards, it was a sociocultural center where the immigrants met each other, read the latest newspapers, participated in meetings of their associations, heard the latest gossip, or learned about job possibilities. In places where there were few Macedonian Bulgarians, they usually associated with other Orthodox or Slavic peoples.

The most significant institutions that gave security and some continuity to the native way of life were the fraternal, mutual-benefit, and cultural societies. Organized on the basis of place of origin, they aimed at giving moral and material support to their members in case of illness or unemployment. Moreover, they assisted humanitarian causes in their respective villages or towns in the old country. Such villages or regional societies as those of Oshchima, Tetovo, Zhelevo, Shar, Prespa, Buf, Dumbeni, Zagoricheni, Rulia, Babchor, Breznica, Pelister, and numerous others exercised a cohesive force and helped individuals overcome difficulties in adjustment to the new life. Although some of these societies still exist, their significance has decreased in the last few years. During the last two decades new mutual-benefit societies have been established.

RELIGION

The church, which satisfied spiritual needs, was also important as a social center where people from various regions could be brought together to fraternize and thus maintain ethnic awareness, language, and traditions. Over 90 percent of Macedonians are Eastern Orthodox, and in the years before World War I they played a dominant role in the creation of Bulgarian parishes in the United States. Most of the early immigrants and their descendants still belong to those Bulgarian Orthodox churches that are either under the jurisdiction of the patriarch in Bulgaria or are part of a Bulgarian diocese within the Orthodox Church in America.

With the influx of nationally conscious Macedonian immigrants from Yugoslavia after World War II, a move to establish an independent ethnic church arose during the late 1950s. A group of 90 Macedonian Americans from Gary founded a Macedonian Orthodox Church and in 1962 asked for and received recognition from the metropolitan and Holy Synod of the Macedonian Orthodox Church in Skopje, the capital of the Socialist Republic of Macedonia. Macedonian Americans in other communities followed the same pattern and established Macedonian Orthodox churches in Columbus (1965), Syracuse (1968), Passaic, Rochester, and Blasdell (Lackawanna). Other communities in Detroit, Chicago, Cincinnati, and Massilon are in the process of building their own Macedonian Orthodox churches, so that in less than 20 years Macedonian Americans have established 11 active communities centered around churches that preserve and promote distinctly Macedonian national traditions and consciousness.

Macedonian-American Orthodox churches are administered by local boards, and all but one are under the guidance of a metropolitan for the United States, Canada, and Australia. They provide a variety of social and cultural activities, and services in Macedonian and English. Each church has a community center in which women's groups play an important role. They help create a milieu in which immigrants, their children, and especially the newly arrived, all feel at home. This is achieved by means of dinners, festivals, and church bazaars organized on religious and on Macedonian and U.S. national holidays. On these occasions national specialties are served, dances held, and Macedonian food and handmade embroidered articles are sold. Through such functions, the women's groups help to preserve, transmit, and popularize Macedonian traditions, while at home women actively convey Macedonian values, language, and culture, most especially to the young. The Sunday school, at which religious instruction and the teaching of Macedonian language and culture are systematically presented, is also important.

POLITICS

Political organizations have also attempted to preserve ethnic traditions, but they are most concerned with working for the unification and independence of the Macedonian homeland. The first of these was founded in Chicago in 1902. It was followed by socialist groups in 1907, constitutional clubs in 1908, and by the Bulgarian-Macedonian People's Union in 1913. These early groups all patterned themselves after the Internal Macedonian Revolutionary Organization— they wanted to unite and free Macedonia from Ottoman Turkish rule and they generally adopted the view that Macedonians were of Bulgarian nationality.

The most important of these societies continues to be the Macedonian Political (Patriotic since 1952) Organization, founded in Fort Wayne, Ind., in 1922. This organization claims to speak for all Macedonians, and through its Bulgarian-language weekly *Makedonska tribuna/Macedonian Tribune* (Indianapolis, Ind., f. 1927) criticizes the Communist governments of Yugoslavia and Bulgaria as well as the anti-Slav-Macedonian policies of Greece. Although the Macedonian Patriotic Organization, like the older Macedonian parishes of the Bulgarian Orthodox Church, claims that Macedonians are Bulgarians, its activity is centered on Macedonia. Little is said about Bulgaria. Most of the American-born of Macedonian-Bulgarian descent have hardly any knowledge of Bulgaria and increasingly identify themselves simply as Macedonians. Few Macedonians participate actively in the two main Bulgarian political organizations in this country, the Bulgarian National Front and the Bulgarian National Committee. The purely Macedonian policies of the Macedonian Patriotic Organization have increased indirectly the Macedonianization of older, Bulgarian-oriented immigrants and their descendants.

The first organization in the United States to support the idea that Macedonians constitute a separate nationality was the Macedonian People's League. Founded during the 1930s, this leftist organization tried to persuade immigrants to join in the struggle for an independent Macedonian state within a Balkan Federation. After World War II most members of the Macedonian

People's League supported the creation of the People's Republic of Macedonia in Yugoslavia and favored the establishment of Communist regimes throughout Eastern Europe. Under its leadership immigrants sent money, clothes, and medical supplies to the new republic. The so-called "American hospital," a medical clinic in Skopje, was funded largely by immigrant dollars. Because of its pro-Communist stance, the Macedonian People's League was branded a subversive organization by the U.S. government; its activities were curtailed, and it was finally disbanded in 1948. That same year witnessed the Soviet-Yugoslav split, which had a great impact on left-wing and radical Macedonian Americans. Most of them sided with Moscow and severed their ties with the Socialist Republic of Macedonia. This development, as well as the Bulgarian government's change of attitude and refusal after 1958 to recognize the Macedonian nationality, has retarded but not stopped the Macedonianization of the immigrants.

CULTURE AND GROUP MAINTENANCE

The greatest advances in the growth of a distinct Macedonian-American community have occurred since the late 1950s. The new immigrants came from Yugoslavia's Socialist Republic of Macedonia, where since World War II they had been educated to believe that Macedonians composed a culturally and linguistically distinct nationality; the historic ties with Bulgarians in particular were deemphasized. These new immigrants not only are convinced of their own Macedonian national identity but also have been instrumental in transmitting these feelings to older Bulgarian-oriented immigrants from Macedonia.

In order to propagate these views, several new organizations have been established, such as the United Macedonians (Toronto, f. 1958) and the Macedonian Cultural Center Ilinden (Detroit, f. 1976). These organizations, as well as a number of local Macedonian-American clubs, emphasize Macedonian history and culture through publications such as Ilinden's monthly, *Makedonski zbor/Macedonian Word*; through contacts with cultural institutions in the United States and in Macedonia; and through programs in schools, sports, clubs, and churches.

Folklore and national traditions occupy an important place in the life of the Macedonian immigrants. Each community has at least one folk ensemble and orchestra and some have theater troupes as well; such groups also exist for children. These groups perform in church halls and take part in local ethnic festivals. The *vecherinka* (evening party) is a common occurrence on Sundays and holidays in Macedonian church halls, where almost all of those present participate in folk dancing. Sports clubs also foster group maintenance, especially among young people. Some soccer clubs were formed with the help of Macedonian businessmen even before the establishment of church communities. Among the better-known soccer teams are Macedonia and Vardar in the Detroit area, Red Star in Rochester, and Macedonia in Columbus. Many Macedonian communities also have one or more radio and television programs. In some places these are shared with other ethnic groups from Yugoslavia.

The institutions established by the immigrants help them preserve unity not only within the larger group as a whole but also within the family. The Macedonian-American family is still closely knit. Most of the young marry within the group, and those who marry outside usually find partners of the same faith. Furthermore, the maintenance of close ties with relatives in Macedonia intensifies group cohesiveness. Many visit the homeland and offer aid to relatives or institutions; a Macedonian from Gary, for example, established a scholarship fund at the University of Skopje.

The majority of Macedonian communities abroad maintain good relations with the Socialist Republic of Macedonia in Yugoslavia. This is especially true with regard to church affairs, which contribute most to the maintenance of Macedonian ethnic identity in the United States. Even though the immigrants and their descendants organize, build, and maintain the churches by themselves, the Macedonian mother church still provides the priests and many of the religious articles for the services. Also, the school boards and cultural institutions as well as individual immigrants deal directly with the Matica for Macedonian Immigrants.

There are other individuals and organizations which identify themselves as Macedonian but which have no relations with and may even oppose Yugoslavia's Socialist Republic of Macedonia. The St. Clement Ohridski Church in Gary holds services in Macedonian, but does not recognize the jurisdiction of the Macedonian Holy Synod and has affiliated instead with the Orthodox Church in America. Two European-based political groups, the Movement for Liberation and Unification of Macedonia and the Macedo-Thracian Revolutionary Committee, both with branches in the United States, want to see all Macedonian territories united, and as such are opposed to Yugoslav Macedonia (which they feel has given up the struggle for unification) and especially to Bulgaria and Greece because of their denial of the existence of a Macedonian nationality.

Slavophone and some Greek immigrants from Aegean Macedonia also call themselves Macedonians in the United States. The majority of these Slavophone Macedonians identify themselves as Greeks, probably for political, social, economic, or cultural reasons. Some have relatives still in Greece and are afraid that if they join a Bulgarian-Macedonian or Macedonian immigrant church or organization their relatives will suffer; others feel that they will never be permitted to visit Greece if they participate in Slav-Macedonian institutions. The Greek Macedonians have their own local fraternal, social, and cultural societies as well as a national organization, the Pan-Macedonian Association (New York, f. 1947). Although these Slavophones use Greek in their official functions, they speak Macedonian among themselves. Their traditions, dances, songs, food, and style of life are identical with those of Macedonians from Greece who may belong to Macedonian-American or Bulgarian-Macedonian-American communities. Immigrants from the same village, even the same family, may be divided and belong to Macedonian-, Bulgarian-, or Greek-American communities. Changing conditions in the family, the homeland, or the immigrant community cause some to shift their orientation from one group to another.

Political changes in the Balkans after World War II and a generally free environment in the United States

have permitted Macedonian immigrants to express themselves in a manner that was never possible in earlier times. As a result, many have asserted a sense of belonging to a distinct Macedonian ethnic group. Nonetheless, the immigrants from Macedonia and their descendants remain on the whole fragmented and concerned largely with questions of identity, local community activity, and politics.

Bibliography

There is no study that deals with Macedonian Americans. Developments among earlier immigrants from Macedonia who identify as Bulgarians are discussed in studies about Bulgarian Americans, the most useful being the reminiscences of Stoyan Christowe, *This Is My Country* (New York, 1938), *My American Pilgrimage* (Boston, 1947), and *The Eagle and the Stork: An American Memoir* (New York, 1976); and George J. Prpic, *South Slavic Immigration in America* (Boston, 1978).

All aspects of Macedonian civilization in the homeland are discussed in Mihailo Apostolski and Haralampié Polenakovich, eds., *The Socialist Republic of Macedonia* (Skopje, Yugoslavia, 1974), and in two journals, *Macedonian Review* (Skopje, f. 1971) and *Makedonija* (Skopje, f. 1954), the organ of the Matica for Macedonian Immigrants. An older study by Henry N. Brailsford, *Macedonia: Its Races and Their Future* (1906; reprint, New York, 1970), is still useful although it presents a Bulgarian viewpoint. The Greek interpretation is presented by Kariophiles Mitsakis, *Macedonia Throughout the Centuries* (Thessalonike, Greece, 1973).

MADEIRANS: *see* PORTUGUESE

MAGYARS: *see* HUNGARIANS

MAHICANS: *see* AMERICAN INDIANS

MAIDUS: *see* AMERICAN INDIANS

MAKAHS: *see* AMERICAN INDIANS

MALECITES: *see* AMERICAN INDIANS

MALTESE

For more than a century Malta's government has actively encouraged the emigration of its citizens. The minuscule size of this overpopulated island nation has dictated that policy, with the result that an estimated 70,000 Maltese immigrants and their descendants live in the United States today.

The republic of Malta consists of three islands (Malta, Gozo, and Comino), which together cover only about 122 square miles. Its 320,000 inhabitants make it one of the most densely populated areas in the world (2,600 inhabitants per square mile). Situated between Sicily and northern Africa, Malta lies in the path of the Mediterranean trade routes, and this strategic position has made it a bone of contention for hundreds of years between political forces competing for control of Mediterranean commerce.

Throughout most of its long history Malta has been ruled by whatever foreign power dominated the Mediterranean world at any given time. First came the Phoenicians, followed in turn by the Greeks, Carthaginians, Romans, Arabs, and the Normans of Sicily. In 1530 the Holy Roman Emperor Charles V bestowed the islands upon the Knights Hospitalers of St. John of Jerusalem, who, as the Knights of Malta, fortified the island and ruled it as defenders of Christianity against Islam. The French forces of Napoleon seized control for a brief

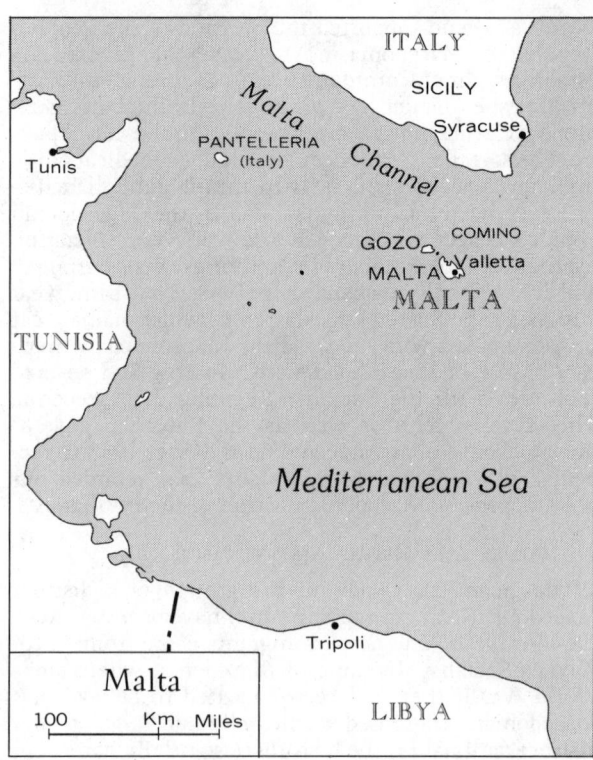

period in 1798, but within a few years the inhabitants successfully petitioned to be placed under the sovereignty of Great Britain. British rule was recognized internationally in 1814, and for the next century and a half Malta alternated between autonomy and colonial status. At the same time Malta became the base for Britain's Mediterranean fleet and, because of its strategic importance to the Allied powers, suffered severe bombing by Germany and Italy during World War II. In return for their loyalty during the war, the Maltese expected political concessions from the British; these came, although somewhat slowly, first in the form of self-government (1947) and, after further protest, in the form of independence within the framework of the British Commonwealth. In 1974 Malta was declared a republic.

The native Maltese are nearly all Roman Catholic. According to tradition they were converted to Christianity by Saint Paul when he was shipwrecked on Meletia (Malta) in the year 58. The Maltese language is of Semitic origin and akin to the Arabic spoken in northern Africa. Centuries of cultural and political contacts, however, added French, English, and especially Italian words to its vocabulary. Maltese and English are now the official languages of the country.

MIGRATION AND ARRIVAL

Malta has few natural resources, and its terrain is not well suited to agriculture; the small size of the islands and their isolation make large-scale industrialization impractical. Until the late 18th century a low rate of population growth, together with income obtained from Mediterranean trade, cotton growing, and the European estates of the Knights of St. John, provided a degree of economic prosperity. This delicate balance was

disrupted when the era of the Napoleonic wars (lucrative for the islands) was followed by an economic decline combined with a rapid increase in population. To avoid disaster, early in the 19th century authorities began urging residents to depart. The government sought to maintain the population at what it regarded as an ideal number, some 220,000 by the 20th century. To achieve this goal they set about organizing emigration to other British colonies in the Mediterranean and to the West Indies. The Maltese themselves preferred northern Africa, however, and by 1885, 36,000 had settled in Algeria, Egypt, Tunis, and Tripoli. The proximity of these areas made it easy to go home, and in some years those who returned outnumbered those who left.

An increase in the supply of cheap native labor in northern Africa finally forced the Maltese to look elsewhere, and by the last decades of the 19th century they were beginning to emigrate to Great Britain, Australia, and North America. From the 1860s until 1900 five or ten came to the United States each year. They favored New Orleans, where they found employment as market gardeners and vegetable dealers.

The largest number of Maltese came to the United States during the first decades of the 20th century, although neither U.S. nor Maltese statistics reveal exactly how many. Like Maltese emigrants throughout the world, they intended to remain for a short time and then return home; in the end, however, opportunities in the United States proved to be more attractive than the uncertainties at home, and they remained. New York by 1928 had an estimated 9,000; Detroit, 5,000 in 1920; San Francisco also had a substantial number. These cities have remained strongholds of the Maltese Americans.

Restrictions on U.S. immigration and the worldwide depression limited the number of Maltese who came to the United States in the 1920s and 1930s. After World War II the Maltese government initiated a passage assistance scheme that provided grants equivalent to 75 percent of the passage costs to Maltese willing to emigrate and remain abroad for at least two years. As a result, emigration from the islands soared; 11,447 left in 1954 alone. Under this program approximately 8,000 came to the United States between 1947 and 1977. Today the largest estimated communities are the 44,000 in Detroit, especially in the suburb of Highland Park, and the 20,000 in New York City, most of them in Astoria, Queens.

RELIGION AND ORGANIZATIONAL LIFE

Malta is officially a Roman Catholic country, and all aspects of the social structure of the islands are permeated by Catholic traditions and celebrations. The Maltese-American community is also Catholic and takes seriously its celebrations of holy days like Christmas and Easter and its annual observance of February 10—according to tradition the day Saint Paul, the patron saint of the Maltese, was shipwrecked on Malta. The Maltese for the most part worship in Catholic churches with other ethnic groups, but in Detroit they have had their own St. Paul's Maltese Church since the 1920s. That church observes worship according to traditions in the homeland and also serves as the social center for the community.

Several fraternal and social organizations have been established. (The famous Ancient and Illustrious Order of the Knights of Malta, established in 1842, is, however, not among them: this group includes only Protestant men from Great Britain who served in Malta or have been made members of this military order.) Representative of the immigrant community are groups like the Maltese-American Benevolent Society in Detroit, the Maltese Union Club (f. 1931) and the United Maltese Association of Astoria (f. 1966) in New York City, and the Maltese-American Social Club (f. 1929) in San Francisco. These and other similar organizations usually have their own clubhouses with facilities for dances, banquets, weddings, and other social affairs. Some also have libraries with material on Maltese culture. Each of the organizations publishes a newsletter or bulletin. No newspaper is published today by the Maltese community, though a *Maltese Journal* did appear between 1935 and 1945. The Detroit community has had a weekly Maltese-language radio program since 1955 and is served by the *Malta News,* published in nearby Windsor, Ontario.

Because so many Maltese emigrate, return home, and perhaps emigrate again, close ties are easily maintained with the homeland. The small but steady influx of new immigrants (since 1966 an average of 246 each year) helps reinforce a sense of identity among members of the Maltese-American community. The Maltese government also encourages the maintenance of close contacts through its embassy and consulate in Washington, D.C., its consulate and United Nations mission in New York City, and consulates in Los Angeles, San Francisco, St. Paul, Minn., and the Detroit suburb of Warren, Mich.

Bibliography
There is no study of the Maltese community in the United States. For a general introduction to the homeland, consult Harry Luke, *Malta: An Account and an Appreciation,* 2d ed. (London, 1968). Modern political history is described in Edith Dobie, *Malta's Road to Independence* (Norman, Okla., 1967). A detailed analysis of early Maltese emigration is found in Charles A. Price, *Malta and the Maltese: A Study in Nineteenth Century Migration* (Melbourne, Australia, 1954). Recent immigration figures and some data on the community in the United States appear in the annual *Malta Year Book* (St. Julian's, Malta, 1953–).

MANDANS: *see* AMERICAN INDIANS

MANX

There are perhaps 50,000 Americans who can claim to be entirely or partially Manx in origin. Either they or their ancestors emigrated to the United States from the Isle of Man in search of adventure and economic opportunity. Exact figures are not available because the Manx have never been separately enumerated in any official count.

The Isle of Man, 227 square miles in area and rising to 2,036 ft. at its highest point, sits in the Irish Sea, almost equidistant from Ireland, Scotland, England, and Wales. Slightly more than 30 miles long and 12 miles wide, it has a permanent population of approximately 60,000. Some of the present inhabitants are English or Scots who find the cost of living and the Manx tax structure to their liking; some are from Northern Ireland seeking a respite from the troubles in their country. In addition, there are always a great many tourists. The island has long been a holiday resort for residents of Liverpool,

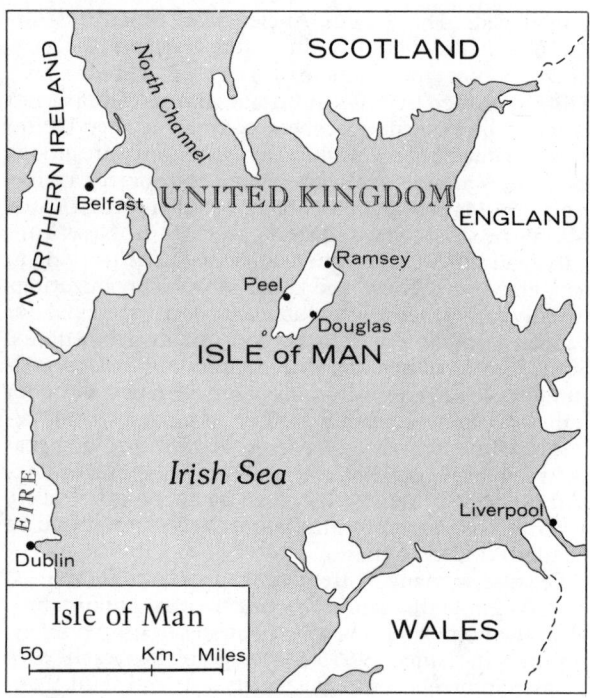

Isle of Man
50   Km. Miles

(Sodor means southern islands in Norwegian) owed allegiance to the archbishop of Canterbury. For four centuries thereafter, the control of the church was vested in the archbishop of Trondheim in Norway; it passed to the province of York in 1542. The first book to appear in Manx, a language that did not give rise to an extensive literature, was a translation of the Book of Common Prayer in 1611.

The economy of the island was originally based on agriculture, sheep raising, fishing, and the mining of lead, zinc, and silver. It is now heavily dependent on tourism, supplemented by fishing, agriculture, and light industry. Over the centuries Man has been a convenient refuge for smugglers.

Manx Americans like to claim that the first Manxman in America was Myles Standish (c. 1584–1656). It is known that Standish's family owned property in the parish of Lezayre, and it is asserted that both his first and second wives were from the island. It is better documented that the Christian brothers, William and Jonathan, and the Cottier family, also from Lezayre, left the island in 1655 and became successful planters in Virginia. However, it was not wealthy but middle- and lower-class families who established the main Manx settlements in the United States. Farmers who had suffered crop failures on the island and fishermen emigrated in the 19th century, followed by construction workers and miners.

About 200 Manx farmers and their families came to North America in 1825 and the years following and found their way via the newly opened Erie Canal to the territory then known as the Western Reserve, present-day northeastern Ohio. In 1883 it was estimated that between 3,000 and 4,000 Manx immigrants and their descendants were living in Cuyahoga County, Ohio. Today a large number of Manx Americans still live in and around Cleveland, which they refer to as the Manx capital of North America. John Gill, born in Port Erin in 1830, came to the United States in 1854 and founded a successful construction company in Cleveland that provided employment for many island artisans. There were enough Manx in Cleveland in 1851 to warrant the founding of the first benevolent society there, the Mona's Relief Society, for the aid of sick or injured countrymen. More than 125 years later the society is still in existence, now known as the Cleveland Manx Society. Membership is restricted to people of Manx birth, descent, or marriage.

At least one Manx family is numbered among the early Mormon pioneers. George Cannon and Ann Quayle made their way from Peel to Nauvoo, Ill., in 1842. Their son John Quayle Cannon (1827–1901) became the third president of the Church of Jesus Christ of Latter-day Saints, and descendants of the Cannon family, who have a strong family association, are said to number more than 2,000.

The miners, except for those attracted by the California gold rush, came from Laxey and Foxdale a few decades later as the Manx mines began to give out. They established a flourishing community near Mineral Point, Wis., where they built the Laxey Church. The names on the tombstones in the now deserted graveyard are still common names on the Isle of Man. The miners also worked with Welsh and Cornish miners in Minnesota and Colorado.

Blackpool, and the English midlands, and it is well known among fans of motorcycle racing for the yearly International Tourist Trophy Races.

Subject to Norse rule from approximately 800 to 1266, when it was ceded to Scotland, the Isle of Man was given by King Henry IV to Sir John Stanley in 1405 and ruled independently by his descendants, who became the earls of Derby, until 1765. In 1828 the island was taken over as a British crown possession and dependency. It retained a measure of local autonomy, which was enlarged and confirmed in 1866 when the island's inhabitants gained the power to choose representatives to the House of Keys, the lower chamber of their 1,000-year-old Parliament, the Tynwald. Along with the members of the Legislative Council, the upper house of the Tynwald, the Keys oversee the internal affairs of the island in concert with a lieutenant governor, who represents the crown.

The Manx people and their institutions are an intriguing blend of Celtic and Norse. The Manx language belongs to the Goidelic group of Celtic languages, an offshoot of Irish Gaelic. It was spoken by a majority of the inhabitants of the island and by the early Manx immigrants in the United States, until it was displaced by English in the middle to late 19th century. Now an extinct tongue (the last native speaker of Manx is said to have died at the age of 94 in 1974), there are presently efforts in some quarters to revive the use of Manx; 200 to 300 people on the island claim a fair degree of proficiency in the spoken language, although they lack words for many aspects of 20th-century life.

The Manx are predominantly Protestant, mainly Anglican. The island has been Christian since the days of St. Patrick, and archaelogical evidence suggests that Man was a center of Celtic Christianity. However, links with the Irish church apparently were broken in the 11th century, and the first Bishop of Sodor and Man

Today, the main link among Americans of Manx origin is the North American Manx Association, which celebrated its 50th anniversary in 1978. Founded in 1928 in Cleveland, the group, numbering less than 1,000, holds conventions biannually in various cities in the United States or Canada, or on the Isle of Man. It publishes the quarterly *Bulletin of the North American Manx Association* "to preserve whate'er is left us of ancient heritage." The Manx have a great affection for the Isle of Man and among themselves a quiet pride in their distinctive heritage.

Bibliography
The Isle of Man: A Social, Cultural and Political History (1944; reprint, Liverpool, 1975) by R.H. Kinvig is a comprehensive book on the Isle of Man. Kinvig has also written the only published account of the Manx in North America, "Manx Settlement in the United States of America," *Proceedings of the Isle of Man Natural History and Antiquarian Society*, new series, V, no. 1 (April 1942–March 1946): 436–455. The charming diary of an early settler in Ohio was first published in the *Isle of Man Examiner* in 1935 and subsequently reprinted as *Thomas Kelly and Family's Journal* (Douglas, Isle of Man, 1965). There is a chapter on the Manx language in Meic Stephens, *Linguistic Minorities in Western Europe* (Llandysul, Wales, 1976).

Manx historical materials are preserved in the Manx Museum Library in Douglas, Isle of Man; in the Mormon archives in Salt Lake City, Utah; and in the Western Reserve Historical Society Library, Cleveland.

ANN ORLOV

MARICOPAS: *see* AMERICAN INDIANS

MARONITES: *see* EASTERN CATHOLICS

MASHPEES: *see* AMERICAN INDIANS

MATTAPONIS: *see* AMERICAN INDIANS

MELKITES: *see* EASTERN CATHOLICS

MENNONITES: *see* AMISH; DUTCH; GERMANS; GERMANS FROM RUSSIA; HUTTERITES; PENNSYLVANIA GERMANS; RUSSIANS; SWISS

MENOMINEES: *see* AMERICAN INDIANS

METHODS OF ESTIMATING THE SIZE OF GROUPS: *see* APPENDIX I

MEXICANS

In 1978 the Census Bureau estimated that 7.2 million people of Mexican descent were living in the United States. The number was undoubtedly substantially higher at the end of the decade, because of the high fertility of Mexican-American families and the heavy continuing emigration from Mexico. Many analysts consider that figure to be a significant undercount, while there is an unknown but undoubtedly large number of undocumented Mexican aliens in the United States.

About 90 percent of the Mexicans reside in the southwestern states, which were formed from land that the United States seized from Mexico in the middle of the 19th century. Mexican Americans have also spread throughout the rest of the United States, particularly since World War II. In 1940 Mexicans were the most rural of the major ethnic groups in the United States, but by 1970 they were among the most strongly urbanized; 85 percent were city dwellers. The shifts from regional to national minority, from farm to city, and from field to factory have set in motion a series of other changes whose consequences are still unfolding.

No single term of self-identification is uniformly used by persons of Mexican descent in the United States. Certain terms are regional: Hispano and Spanish American in northern New Mexico and southern Colorado; Tejano, Latino, and Latin American in Texas, and Mexican in Arizona, eastern Colorado, and parts of the Midwest and Pacific Northwest. Because their origins in the area predate the emergence of the Mexican nation, some Hispanos and Tejanos do not identify with the larger group (*see* Hispanics; Spanish; Spanish-surname). However, they are included in this entry because many do consider themselves Mexican Americans and because historically they were citizens of Mexico from its independence in 1821 to the U.S. conquest in 1846. Furthermore, most of the data available on persons of Mexican origin include Hispanos and Tejanos.

The term Mexicano is most often used among Spanish-speakers. Mexican American has become common within the group and among outsiders, yet some reject this often-hyphenated term as demeaning and prefer to be known as Mexicans or Mexicanos. Chicano, a word whose roots stretch back at least to the turn of the century as an in-group term, was adopted with pride by social activists in the 1960s, although some Mexican Americans, mainly the elderly, consider it pejorative. In the 1970s the term lost most of its political overtones and pejorative connotations. Increasingly, Chicano has gained acceptance among people of Mexican descent and among the general public as a synonym for Mexican American.

Similarly, the terms Anglo-American and Anglo have come to be widely used to refer to white persons of non-Hispanic descent in the United States. These terms are used in this sense here, not as a label for Americans of British origin.

Statistics on Mexican Americans also require special caution, because the U.S. Census Bureau has never been quite sure how to categorize or count residents of Mexican ancestry. Through 1920 the census merely enumerated Mexican immigrants and their second-generation offspring. The 1930 Census attempted to include the third and later generations by treating Mexicans as a separate racial group; it recorded a total of 1.4 million in the country, one-third more than the total of the first and second generations. However, that count did not include Mexicans whom the census enumerators considered white, including most of the Hispanos or Spanish of New Mexico and Colorado. After sharp protest from Mexican Americans and the Mexican government, the designation of Mexicans as nonwhite was abandoned.

Other efforts to identify persons of Mexican descent beyond two generations have included counting persons who reported Spanish as their mother tongue—the language of their household when they were growing up—or counting those with Spanish surnames. Both methods are unreliable, because they attribute a Mexican identity to people from other Hispanic groups and fail to include people who identify as Mexican although they lack a Spanish surname or did not grow up in a Spanish-speaking household. The 1970 Census, in which respondents who received the long form were

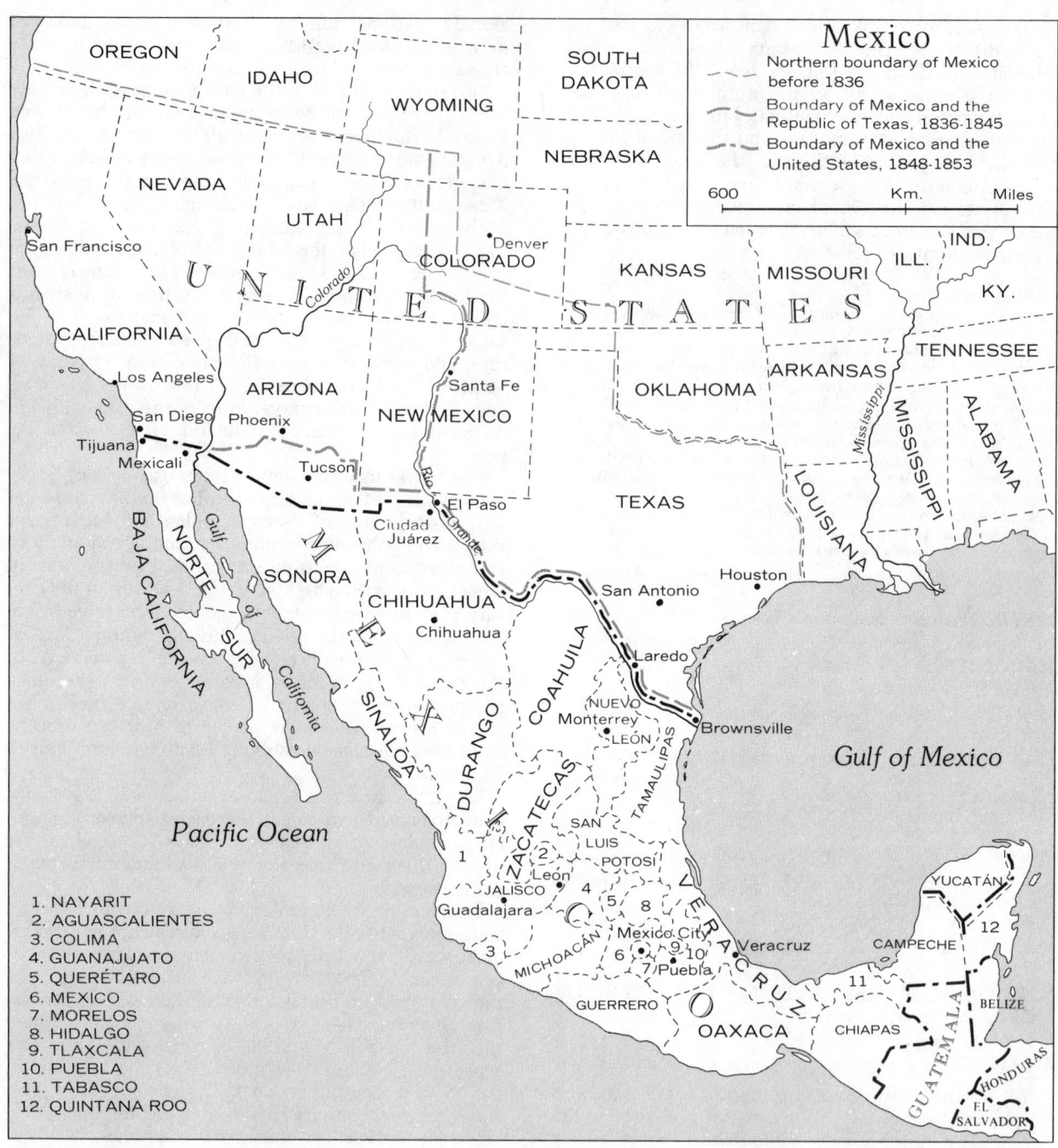

1. NAYARIT
2. AGUASCALIENTES
3. COLIMA
4. GUANAJUATO
5. QUERÉTARO
6. MEXICO
7. MORELOS
8. HIDALGO
9. TLAXCALA
10. PUEBLA
11. TABASCO
12. QUINTANA ROO

asked to indicate their national heritage, reported 2.3 million Americans of Mexican birth or parentage and 4.5 million of Mexican heritage. But these figures, too, must be regarded as rough approximations. The census routinely has difficulties in densely settled areas, the language barrier has restricted Mexican response to the census, and for obvious reasons the count does not include undocumented Mexicans. The 1980 Census has made an elaborate effort to identify the Mexican population by asking a specific question about whether respondents belong to one of five groups of Spanish "origin or descent" in addition to a general question about ancestry. Its results will be made available in 1981 or 1982.

GENERAL CHARACTERISTICS

Mexican Americans, like members of all ethnic groups, differ with respect to age, sex, racial background, physical characteristics, region, place of residence, class, education, occupation, religion, political beliefs, and experience in the United States and Mexico. They may be first generation or fourth. Yet there are certain common, although not universal, factors that characterize Mexican Americans as a group.

The first large group of Mexican Americans, some 80,000, was created through conquest and annexation following the separation of Texas and the U.S.-Mexican War. Between 1845 and 1854 the United States acquired

about half the territory formerly belonging to the Republic of Mexico, including all or part of the present states of Arizona, California, Colorado, Nevada, New Mexico, Texas, Utah, and Wyoming. The Mexican-American population of this area grew slowly until the beginning of the 20th century, when immigration from Mexico soared. With one of the highest birthrates in the nation, the group grew rapidly from natural increase as well. In the 1960s, for example, the Chicano population of the United States rose by 32 percent, some two and one-half times the rate of the U.S. population as a whole.

As the accompanying tabulation shows, Mexican immigration has been significant since the early 20th century, with the exception of the Depression era of the 1930s and the early years of World War II. However, the validity of these figures through the first quarter of the century is particularly suspect, because until the 1920s the border was generally an open frontier, and a good many more Mexicans than are indicated must have entered the United States.

Decade	Number of immigrants
1900–1909	31,200
1910–1919	185,300
1920–1929	498,900
1930–1939	32,700
1940–1949	56,200
1950–1959	273,800
1960–1969	441,800
1970–1975	364,100

A comparatively high birthrate has also contributed to the striking growth of the Chicano population. In 1969 Mexican-American women were 40 percent more fertile than Anglo-American women. In 1970 the average Mexican-American family numbered 4.5 persons, compared to 3.6 for Americans in general, 4.1 for Puerto Ricans and blacks, and 3.7 for Cuban Americans. The Chicano birthrate dropped during the 1970s, in line with the general national decline.

Mexican Americans began as an annexed regional minority and continued so throughout the 19th century. They are still concentrated heavily in the Southwest; in 1975 one of every six persons in Arizona, California, Colorado, New Mexico, and Texas was of Hispanic origin. In 1970, some 50 percent of Chicanos in the Southwest lived in California, and 34 percent lived in Texas. Los Angeles, with more than 1 million Chicanos, had more people of Mexican descent than any city in Mexico except Mexico City and Guadalajara. On the other hand, New Mexico had the highest proportion (40 percent) of people of Hispanic heritage, and these formed the majority in 15 of the state's 32 counties, primarily in the northern part of the state. Chicanos still reside mainly in the Southwest, but 20th-century immigration, migration patterns, and nationwide job opportunities have resulted in their spread throughout the United States, particularly to the Midwest and Northwest.

Although farming has traditionally been a major livelihood of Mexican Americans and many still engage in agriculture, they have moved from rural areas to the cities, attracted primarily by jobs in industry. The Great Depression and the Dust Bowl drought of the 1930s drove many to the city, particularly in New Mexico. In some cases, the city has come to Chicanos, as urban ex-

pansion and the suburban boom have often completely enveloped formerly rural *colonias*. Urbanization has been particularly rapid since World War II; in 1950 about 66 percent of all Mexican Americans were urban dwellers, and by 1970 this share had grown to 85 percent. Southern Colorado and northern New Mexico are the major large remaining rural pockets; 35 percent of all Mexicans in New Mexico are still classified as rural. Chicano occupations are less urbanized than their domiciles, indicating that many use the city as a home base but work as agricultural migrants for at least part of the year.

The average Chicano is young, Roman Catholic, speaks both English and Spanish, and was born in the United States of U.S.-born parents. In 1970 the median age of Chicanos was 20.2 years (9 years less than the national average), 46 percent were less than 18 years old (compared to 33 percent of the total white population), and less than 5 percent were over 65 (compared to 10 percent of all whites). Yet even these figures are a bit misleading, because Mexican immigrants, most of whom came as adults, raised the median age. For U.S.-born Chicanos of U.S.-born parentage, for example, the median age is only 15.8 years.

Approximately 90 percent of Chicanos belong to the Catholic church, although their attendance at mass is somewhat lower than among U.S. Catholics as a whole. English is their primary language; an estimated 80 percent also speak Spanish although they may not necessarily read it. In a 1969 survey about half of the Mexican-American respondents spoke Spanish at home.

The Mexican immigrants receive the most public attention; however, 84 percent of the Chicanos counted in the 1970 Census were born in the United States; of these, 55 percent were of U.S.-born parentage (third or later generation) and 29 percent were of foreign-born parentage (second generation). Immigrants composed only 16 percent of the total Mexican-American population, though this proportion would be substantially higher if undocumented aliens were included.

The average Chicano has had much less education than the average American, though the level of school attainment for second-generation Mexican Americans was far higher than for their immigrant parents or grandparents. For the most part, they remain a laboring people. In 1970 only one-fourth of the men with Spanish surnames held white-collar jobs, compared to more than half of Anglo men. Even in the same occupational categories Mexican Americans received lower pay than their Anglo counterparts. In the 1960s the percentage of Spanish-surname families below the poverty line declined from 35 to 25. In 1976, though, about 16 percent still had annual incomes below $4,000, twice the national average.

Possibly the most perplexing and misunderstood general characteristic of Mexican Americans is that of race. In the United States people tend to be placed in simplistic racial categories with no allowance for racially mixed individuals or multiracial groups. Chicanos are not a race, but rather a multiracial group of principally Spanish and Indian (and to a small degree, African) roots. The solution adopted by the Census Bureau in 1970—making Mexican Americans a subcategory of Caucasians—is a distortion, in view of their heavily Indian ancestry. But placing them in the Indian category

would also be incorrect, as most have some Spanish ancestry, and a few are of purely Spanish-Mexican extraction.

HISTORICAL BACKGROUND

The American Southwest as it exists today came into being between 1845 and 1854 as the result of the annexation of Texas, the conquest and annexation of northern Mexico, and the Gadsden Purchase. Before the 17th century this area had been dominated by American Indian groups, each with its own culture and society. Throughout the 16th century, periodic expeditions from central New Spain (from which the nation of Mexico later emerged) penetrated the area and developed knowledge of its geography and inhabitants. At the end of the 16th century the region that is now New Mexico became the first target for colonization, followed by the areas that are now Arizona, Texas, and California.

For the most part the colonies of northern New Spain developed in relative isolation, despite the nominal control of officials appointed by the central government. Trade and communication were irregular, although the Mexico City government made periodic efforts to increase supervision. Communications among the provinces of California, Arizona, New Mexico, and Texas were also weak. The first major northern interprovincial trade route, the Old Spanish Trail between Santa Fe, N.Mex., and Los Angeles, was established in 1829, eight years after Mexico had won its independence from Spain. Prior to Mexico's independence the northern provinces had little contact with foreigners, although a small amount of illicit international trade developed in the late 18th and early 19th centuries, particularly in the gulf region of Texas and in coastal California.

By 1821 four principal areas of settlement had developed in this region. The first and most heavily populated was New Mexico, consisting of a string of towns, ranches, and farms stretching from El Paso (now in Texas) in the south up the Rio Grande to Santa Fe and then fanning out into the canyons in the north and across the mountains to the high plains in the east. Next in size was California, consisting of missions, presidios (military fortress communities), towns, and ranches hugging the coast from San Diego to San Francisco, with a few extensions into the interior. The smaller, northeastern settlement of Texas had its center at San Antonio, and the tiny Arizona colony focused on Tucson.

The region's economy was based on agriculture and livestock. In contrast to central New Spain, colonists found little mineral wealth and few agricultural Indians for cheap labor. Most of the colonists became farmers or ranchers, either working their own land or working for other colonists. Government officials, priests, soldiers, and artisans settled in the towns, missions, or presidios. Although varying from region to region, the missions had the dual purpose of serving the colonists and of Catholicizing and Hispanicizing the local Indians. Along with the presidio, the mission became a basic northern Mexican institution. Some towns in New Mexico were created on the basis of communal land grants to groups of settlers who shared local government and natural resources.

Socially a combination class-caste system developed, although it lacked the rigidity of that in central New Spain. Most residents belonged to the lower and lower-middle classes, but some colonists arrived with or attained upper-class status, mainly through ranching or the acquisition of land grants. They were of varied backgrounds—*peninsular* (born in Spain), *criollo* (born in New Spain of pure Spanish ancestry), Indian, black, *mestizo* (of Spanish and Indian ancestry), *mulato* (of Spanish and African ancestry), and *zambo* (of Indian and African ancestry). Most colonists were of mixed racial backgrounds, and the process of *mestizaje* (racial mixture) continued in the north with the various Indian civilizations there. (*See* American Indians: The Southwest.) Racial prejudice existed, and many mestizos strove, sometimes successfully, to become identified as pure-blooded Spaniards. Racial identity affected socioeconomic mobility, with whites generally holding the major government positions and church offices and owning private lands, while mestizos and Indians were concentrated at lower levels of the social structure. However, many people with mixed blood did succeed in becoming ranch owners and leading citizens of the northern provinces, which sometimes also brought a change of ethnic identity.

Mexico's independence from Spain in 1821 diminished the traditionally weak hold of the central government over the northern provinces. In particular it led to increased trade with other countries, especially the United States. In the early 1820s Anglo-Americans developed an intensive trade with northern Mexico via the Santa Fe Trail from Independence, Mo., to Santa Fe and via clipper ships around Cape Horn to California, thus beginning the process of economic detachment from central Mexico. Santa Fe, situated at the terminus of the Chihuahua Trail from central Mexico, the Old Spanish Trail, and the Santa Fe Trail, became a hub of trade. From there sheep were sent to the south and bullion, mules, horses, beaver pelts, and buffalo robes to the east; manufactured goods and other supplies flowed in from central Mexico and particularly from the United States. Hides and tallow from California were exchanged for manufactured goods from both the United States and England. Increased trade led to increased demand for consumer goods in northern Mexico and, therefore, greater dependence on the United States as the primary source of supply.

The development of northern Mexican culture, which had begun under New Spain, continued under independent Mexico. Cultural pursuits included the composition of both religious and popular music in which the guitar was central as solo instrument or accompaniment, religious and popular poetry, and religious dramas. Popular art was widespread in New Mexico, whose inhabitants became skilled in gold and silver filigree, weaving, and silver, tin, and iron work. The carved *retablos* (religious scenes) and *santos* (saints) of the popular artists known as *santeros* (saint makers) have become collectors' items. The rodeo was a central event at which the *vaquero* (cowboy) demonstrated his skills.

Along with burgeoning economies and cultural creativity, New Mexico and California also experienced periodic revolutions, as large landowners vied for political supremacy and the Mexican government made intermittent, sometimes unpopular, efforts to tighten the reins. In contrast to politically turbulent and economi-

cally expanding New Mexico and California, Arizona's population shrank because of implacable Indian pressures. In 1846, on the eve of invasion by the United States, northern Mexico had a population of approximately 80,000 Mexicans, three-quarters of them in New Mexico.

From 1821 to 1846 northern Mexico also experienced another major change—the coming of Anglo-Americans. Anglo trappers used New Mexico as a base, and Anglo merchants settled in Santa Fe and Taos. California, too, attracted trappers and traders, who often remained to live there. In both New Mexico and southern California, many of these settlers eventually married Mexican women (usually of the local aristocracy), became Mexican citizens, and obtained land grants. In contrast, the overland pioneers who settled in the Sacramento Valley of northern California brought their families, stayed to themselves, and resisted integration into Mexican society. It was this group that ultimately rebelled in 1846 against their Mexican hosts and formed the short-lived secessionist Bear Flag Republic, nia a month later.

Texas was a special case. Whereas Anglo-Americans remained a minority in New Mexico and California, they flooded into east and south Texas and by 1835 outnumbered Mexicans six to one (30,000 to 5,000). The earliest of these Anglo-American settlers had been given a land grant by the government of New Spain in 1821. Following independence, Mexican government officials faced the dual problem of a westwardly expanding United States and their inability to convince Mexicans to settle in Texas, the sparsely populated northeastern frontier. Many Mexican leaders cautioned against the immigration of Anglo-Americans, whose loyalties to Mexico would be questionable. However, the government invited Anglos to settle in Texas, hoping to create a buffer zone between central Mexico and the United States.

In obtaining land grants in Texas, Anglo immigrants agreed to become Mexican citizens, obey Mexican laws, accept the official Catholic faith, learn Spanish, and take other steps to become fully assimilated as law-abiding citizens. However, over the years, it became clear that these settlers, now Anglo-Mexicans, were not becoming integrated into the nation and that Anglo immigration had become a problem rather that a solution. The Mexican government countered with a series of restrictions that in some respects reflected a general policy of increasing centralization and control over all the regions of Mexico and in other respects reflected a specific Texas policy.

The strains and disagreements ultimately led to the Texas Revolution in 1835. Mainly a revolt of Anglo-Mexicans who wished to secede and set up their own republic, it was also supported by some Mexican liberals who opposed centralism and wished to reinstate the federalist constitution of 1824. In this sense the Texas Revolution paralleled other anticentralist revolts that occurred in various parts of Mexico throughout the 1830s, although for the most part the Texas revolt was secessionist rather than reformist. The Mexican government attempted to quell the revolt with military force. Despite a victory at the Alamo in March 1836, the government failed. Following the final Texas triumph at San Jacinto in April of that year, the victors

formed the independent Lone Star Republic. When the republic joined the Union as the state of Texas in 1845, the remaining Mexicans (many had fled to Mexico to escape Texan rule) became the first large group of Mexican Americans.

Close on the heels of the Texas annexation came the U.S.-Mexican War of 1846–1848. Tensions between the two countries had been developing for years over the U.S. aim of expanding to the Pacific Coast. The United States had made several offers to purchase all or part of northern Mexico, which Mexico rejected. In 1842 the United States clumsily revealed that it was prepared to use force to take what money could not buy; this was made clear when the commander of the Pacific squadron, mistakenly thinking that the United States and Mexico had gone to war, prematurely invaded and captured Monterey, the capital of California, and then had to return it with apologies once the error had become clear.

On the other side, Mexico's antagonism toward the United States was exacerbated by the annexation of Texas. The Texas rebels had extracted a battlefield treaty recognizing the independence of Texas, but the Mexican government had never ratified it. To Mexico, therefore, the U.S. annexation of Texas was grand larceny.

The precipitating incident of the war came in April 1846 when small units of Mexican and U.S. soldiers clashed in disputed territory between the Nueces River and the Rio Grande, the former being the Texas boundary recognized by Mexico and the latter the one claimed by Texas. The incident merely provided a pretext for the annexation decision already made by President James K. Polk, who ordered the invasion by U.S. troops. Following early fighting in northeastern Mexico, U.S. forces occupied Veracruz and advanced overland to capture Mexico City. Simultaneously, other U.S. forces occupied the province of New Mexico and then marched to California, most of which had already come under U.S. domination as a result of a naval invasion and the Bear Flag revolt.

The initial occupations of New Mexico and California occurred with little bloodshed, but armed reactions by Mexicans ultimately broke out in both provinces. In California Mexican patriots, mainly citizen volunteers, were victorious in 1846 in battles at Los Angeles, San Pascual, and Chino Rancho, but finally had to submit to the better-trained and well-armed U.S. forces. In New Mexico, Pueblo Indians were the backbone of the revolt in January 1847 that led to the capture of Taos and other communities. However, as in California, New Mexican resistance ultimately crumbled. By early 1847 the United States had established control over northern Mexico and proceeded to admit this territory into the Union.

In central Mexico the struggle continued until late 1847. In early 1848, following the U.S. capture of Mexico City, negotiators for both sides drew up the preliminary draft of the Treaty of Guadalupe Hidalgo, which, after revision by President Polk and the U.S. Senate, was ratified by both governments later that year. It recognized U.S. possession of northern Mexico, which was about one-third of Mexico's territory, not including Texas. In return, the United States agreed to pay Mexico $15 million and to assume up to $3.25 million in

claims by U.S. citizens against the Mexican government. Among other provisions, two dealt directly with the rights of the Mexicans living in the annexed territory.

Article VIII of the treaty gave Mexicans the right to remain in U.S. territory or to remove to Mexico. Some 3,000 chose to leave their homes and return to Mexico. Those who decided to remain on their land and accept U.S. sovereignty could choose to retain Mexican citizenship or become U.S. citizens. Finally, for "property of every kind," Mexican citizens were to "enjoy with respect to it, guaranties equally ample as if the same belonged to citizens of the United States."

For those Mexicans who selected U.S. citizenship, the revised Article IX promised "the enjoyment of all rights of citizens of the United States according to the principles of the Constitution," "the free enjoyment of their liberty and property," and "the free exercise of their religion without restriction." Included in the original draft of the treaty, but eliminated by the U.S. government, was Article X, which read: "All grants of land made by the Mexican Government or by the competent authorities . . . shall be respected as valid, to the same extent that the same grants would be valid, if the said territories had remained within the limits of Mexico."

When they learned of the elimination of this important article and the radical changes in others, including Article IX, Mexican officials protested. In response U.S. representatives at the final ratification signed the Protocol of Querétaro (May 26, 1848), which stated that the changes made by the U.S. government did not annul the civil, political, and religious guarantees for the Mexican residents provided in the original treaty. However, the U.S. government later disavowed the protocol on the grounds that its representatives had not been empowered to affirm such a document.

The signing of the treaty did not bring territorial acquisition to a close. The United States soon realized that the new boundaries excluded a vital piece of real estate—the Mesilla Valley (now in southern Arizona and New Mexico), needed for the southern route of the U.S. transcontinental railway system. Financially pressured, the Mexican government sold this 30,000-square-mile strip of land to the United States for $10 million, as ratified in the Gadsden Treaty of 1854. According to Article V of the new treaty, Mexican residents in the valley were guaranteed the rights specified in the Treaty of Guadalupe Hidalgo. To their dismay, 2,000 Mexicans from the originally conquered territory who had moved to the Mesilla Valley suddenly found themselves once again annexed by the United States. Thus, with the Gadsden Purchase, another chunk of northern Mexico and another group of Mexicans were annexed by the United States.

IMMIGRATION

The 2,000-mile U.S.-Mexican boundary has played a significant role in Mexican-American history. From the Gulf of Mexico west to El Paso, Tex., the boundary is the Rio Grande. Throughout history, rivers have been convenient international dividers as well as socio-ecological systems linking life on both sides. So it has been with the Rio Grande, along which twin cities have developed, across which ranches and farms have lapped, and over which people have continually traveled back and forth. West of El Paso the boundary wanders through open land, an invitation rather than an obstacle to human movement. The barbed-wire wall, constructed in the 1950s to divide Mexican open spaces from U.S. open spaces, has had only a small impact on the natural flow of people.

Mexican immigration into the United States during the second half of the 19th century was of modest scale compared to that in the 20th century. However, the California gold rush attracted thousands of Mexican miners, principally from the state of Sonora. After working the goldfields, the miners often remained in California instead of returning to Mexico. Tucson, Ariz., also was a magnet for Mexican workers, particularly between 1850 and 1880. The economic booms in cattle, sheep, cotton, and vegetables in Texas during the last third of the 19th century attracted Mexicans not only from bordering Coahuila but also from more distant Mexican states. The 1890 Census counted over 75,000 Mexican-born immigrants in the United States, a figure that did not include either those born in the annexed areas before the conquest or U.S.-born Mexican Americans. A recent study suggests that in 1900 the total U.S.-born and foreign-born Mexican population in the United States was between 381,000 and 562,000.

Social and economic changes in both countries were setting the stage for the major migration of the early 20th century. The development of mining and industry in northern Mexico as well as the building of north-south railroad lines attracted large numbers of Mexicans to the north. The new industrial, mining, and railroad skills they learned there were useful later in the United States, and the railroad provided an easy means of travel to the north. Economic pressures were mounting; many small landowners were losing their holdings to expanding haciendas, while farm workers were increasingly and systematically trapped into peonage (servitude to their creditors) because of accumulating debts.

In 1910 political opponents of President Porfirio Díaz revolted. He was quickly overthrown, but the replacement of his government did not end the Mexican Revolution, which spread throughout the country and took on deep social and economic, as well as political, ramifications. The resulting chaos drove thousands of Mexicans north. Along with physical proximity, the United States offered jobs in industry, in mines, on railroads, and in agriculture (irrigated farming was developing throughout the Southwest) at wage levels far higher than those in Mexico. World War I further increased the demand for Mexican labor.

In the 1920s emigration from Mexico reached new heights, spurred in part by the short but violent Cristero Revolution (1926–1929), while the U.S. economy continued to expand and attract Mexican labor. Nearly 500,000 Mexicans entered the United States on permanent visas during the 1920s, some 11 percent of the total U.S. immigration of that decade. The strict immigration quotas imposed in 1921 and 1924 did not apply to immigrants from countries in the Western Hemisphere and thus did not check the entry of Mexicans. Thousands more entered informally. Even after the establishment of more stringent immigration rules and procedures, Mexicans continued to cross without legal sanction. Many of them were ignorant of the required

legal processes; others sought to avoid the head tax, the expense of a visa, and bureaucratic delays at the border. Coyotes—as the professional labor contractors and border-crossing experts were known—often received commissions from U.S. businesses; they began the industry of smuggling people and forging documents that continues to the present.

The responses of Americans to Mexican immigration varied. Most people, particularly outside of the Southwest, were either unaware or unconcerned. Social service organizations, charitable institutions, Catholic and Protestant churches, and some government agencies attempted to ease the immigrants' difficult transition. The country's industry, agriculture, and railroads generally supported open immigration from Mexico because it increased the labor pool. However, opposition to Mexican immigration grew throughout the 1920s, particularly from such groups as city chambers of commerce, local welfare agencies, nativist organizations, and labor unions. Such opposition ultimately became a part of the national debate over immigration policy. Historically, there had been few official obstacles to immigration, and the more restrictive policy that evolved after 1880 was directed mainly toward Asians and later toward Europeans. However, the establishment of the Border Patrol under the U.S. Bureau of Immigration in 1924 was a portent of things to come.

Mexican immigration began to decline in 1928, as U.S. consulates in Mexico started to apply with unprecedented rigor the literacy test legislated in 1917. The Great Depression also sharply curtailed Mexican immigration. Only 32,700 Mexicans entered the United States on permanent visas during the 1930s, down to 4 percent of total U.S. immigration. In fact, hard times in the 1930s reversed the previous trend entirely, and more Mexicans (some 500,000) left the United States than entered. The shrinking job market caused attitudes toward Mexicans in the United States to change. Previously welcomed as important contributors to an expanding agriculture and industry, Mexicans now were seen as "surplus labor," and, even worse, as a drain on public relief funds.

These changes led to the Repatriation Program, aimed at Mexican aliens who lacked documents of legal residency. In cooperation with the Mexican government, which regretted the loss of so many able workers, U.S. federal, state, county, and local officials applied pressures on Mexicans to "voluntarily" return to Mexico. At times this procedure resulted in outright deportation. Through these efforts at repatriation, about 500,000 persons were shuttled to Mexico, most of them from the Southwest, but some 10 percent from the Midwest, particularly Illinois, Michigan, Indiana, and Minnesota. Among the victims of the process were naturalized and U.S.-born husbands, wives, and children of Mexican repatriates, who had to choose between moving to Mexico or breaking up their families.

The end of the Depression and the coming of World War II reversed the migration flow again. Wartime expansion of the U.S. armed forces and war industries created a labor shortage, and Mexican workers were once again welcome. These conditions generated not only a growth of immigration, but also the Bracero Program. Initiated in 1942 by a U.S.-Mexican executive agreement, the program provided for Mexican *braceros* (laborers) to enter the United States as short-term contract workers, primarily in agriculture and transportation. Before the program ended in 1947, an estimated 200,000 braceros worked in 21 states, about half of them in California. The program was resurrected by Congress in 1951, largely because of the agricultural labor shortages created by the Korean War, and continued until 1964, peaking in 1959 when nearly 450,000 braceros entered the United States. In 1960 they formed 26 percent of the nation's seasonal agricultural labor force. Even after the program's termination, Mexican workers could enter the United States by such mechanisms as the green cards that permit temporary employment.

Immigration of Mexicans with permanent visas grew slowly in the 1940s, expanded rapidly in the 1950s, and exceeded 30,000 in every year from 1960 to the late 1970s. In 1973 Mexican immigrants with permanent visas numbered 70,141. However, changes in U.S. immigration policy have had a severe impact on permanent Mexican immigration. The 1965 Immigration and Nationality Act established annual limits of 120,000 immigrants from the Western Hemisphere and 170,000 from the Eastern Hemisphere; in 1976 Congress added a 20,000-person ceiling on immigration from any one country in the Western Hemisphere, a system that had been in effect for the Eastern Hemisphere since 1965.

But neither legal immigration nor the Bracero Program has met all U.S. labor needs, particularly in the less attractive agricultural, industrial, and service jobs, such as domestic employment. Another group of Mexican workers, referred to variously as undocumented immigrants, illegal immigrants or, more metaphorically and pejoratively, wetbacks (*mojados*), has entered to meet shortages in these areas.

Since 1946 such workers have contributed significantly to agriculture in the Southwest and have worked in other industries and services throughout the West and Midwest. Seeking to escape poverty and unemployment in Mexico and drawn by higher wages and greater economic opportunities in the United States, these workers must first avoid government border patrols and then live under the constant threat of deportation. As a result they generally have had to accept poor working conditions and low wages, because any protest might lead to their discovery and deportation.

Periodically, federal authorities have engaged in massive efforts to round up undocumented workers. From 1950 to 1955, culminating in Operation Wetback, the government expelled 3.8 million Mexicans, though many of these may have been expelled more than once. Raids on factories, restaurants, bars, and even apartments and homes in search of undocumented workers became commonplace. Among those affected have been now-elderly Mexicans who entered the United States when border crossing was more informal. Mexican Americans living near the border have been stopped on the street and asked to prove their legal right to be in the United States or have been questioned and searched at Immigration Service highway check points. Many Mexican aliens who are eligible for naturalization refuse to apply for U.S. citizenship for fear of possible deportation.

Such activities have had a dual, somewhat contradictory, impact. Some Chicanos, including many labor

leaders, have favored severe restrictions on undocumented workers on the grounds that they take jobs from Mexican Americans. They regretfully accept vigorous action by the Immigration Service, referred to sarcastically as *la migra*. Others react strongly against the actions of the Immigration Service, challenging infringements of civil rights as well as the physical violence sometimes used in search-and-seizure operations.

Undocumented Mexican workers have contributed to the U.S. economy not only by their labor, but also by their taxes. The Department of Labor estimated in 1976 that 73 percent of undocumented Mexican workers paid federal income taxes and 77 percent paid social security taxes, although few would ever receive retirement benefits. In contrast, less than 4 percent of such workers had children in U.S. schools, and only 0.5 percent received welfare benefits.

Immigrants from Mexico vary from unskilled laborers to professionals, but for the most part they have been laborers of limited education, almost no English literacy, and in many cases restricted Spanish literacy. Moreover, most have been of mixed Indian and Spanish ancestry, which is not surprising because Mexico is basically a mestizo nation. This racial factor has had a significant influence on their reception and treatment in the United States; in addition to the ethnic, cultural, and linguistic discrimination experienced by many immigrant groups, Mexicans have also experienced racial discrimination.

The Mexican immigration has historically had a high proportion of males, although the percentage of women and children increased in the 1970s, partly as a result of an admissions policy favoring family members of previous immigrants and partly owing to the increased demand for female domestics. This trend was reinforced by the 1976 immigration act, which requires that 20 percent of all immigrants from each nation be close relatives of legal U.S. residents.

Mexican immigrants have come from all the Mexican states. Not surprisingly, the northern border states of Tamaulipas, Nuevo León, Coahuila, Chihuahua, Sonora, and Baja California have contributed large numbers of immigrants—here used to include also braceros and undocumented aliens. Many of these immigrants came originally from other sections of Mexico and settled in the northern tier temporarily on their way to the United States. Northern Mexico cities like Matamoros, Ciudad Juárez, and Tijuana have become the Ellis Islands of Mexican immigrants. The chief source of Mexican immigrants, however, especially during the first heavy phase from 1910 through the 1920s, was the heavily populated and often economically depressed Mesa Central, particularly the states of Jalisco, Guanajuato, and Michoacán.

Though most of the immigrants have settled in the Southwest, employment opportunities have drawn increasing numbers elsewhere in the United States. Mexican Americans work in agriculture throughout the Northwest, Midwest, and even the East today. Industries have attracted Mexicans to such diverse locations as Chicago, Detroit, and Bethlehem, Pa. Railroads have been prime employers. Chicano *barrios* (neighborhoods) and *colonias* developed from agricultural work camps, in isolated mining towns, around railroad section houses, and near packinghouses. These communi-

ties served as magnets for later immigrants, often through the extensive informal network of families and friends throughout the Southwest and Mexico. Hostility toward Mexicans by other groups and restrictive covenants also contributed to the growth of the barrios and colonias.

The spread of Mexicans through the country has been more than the settling of new immigrants. As thousands of new immigrants went directly to areas outside of the Southwest, thousands of native-born or long-established Mexican Americans spread into the same areas. In a "push-pull" effect, the heavy immigration of Mexicans into the Southwest sometimes created a labor surplus and prompted Mexican Americans with a knowledge of English and of American customs to move on to other areas with better employment opportunities. Thousands of Tejanos, for instance, have settled in the Midwest. The average family income of Mexicans living in Detroit in 1976 was more than double that of their counterparts in Brownsville, Tex.

Mexicans have also spread throughout the United States via the process known as migrant "fallout." Thousands of Mexicans, many of them long-time U.S. residents, follow the crops from harvest to harvest in one of many migrant streams—up the Pacific Coast valleys, into the Midwest, and along the Atlantic Coast. When they complete the seasonal harvests, most return to their homes in the Southwest, but each year some decide to settle at points along the route.

While Mexican immigration bears some resemblance to the immigration of other groups, it also has some special characteristics. Mexicans, like Canadians, do not have an ocean to cross. Movement in both directions is easier, a factor that provides continuous cultural and linguistic reinforcement through family visits, travel, even the reception of Mexican radio and television broadcasts in areas near the border. Therefore, in many respects Mexican immigrants do not enter a totally foreign country, but rather a politically detached cultural homeland. They usually settle in segregated communities where the predominance of Mexican culture, social and family customs, and organizations and the widespread use of Spanish permit them to maintain cultural continuity. They can live and work without learning English or becoming involved in the mainstream society. At the same time the immigrants contribute to the continuous reinforcement of Mexican culture and society in the United States.

Compared with European immigrants, Mexicans initially entered an area of the United States that offered limited economic opportunities—the relatively undeveloped Southwest. Although there was some industry there and some Mexican immigrants settled in midwestern and eastern industrial cities, the greatest demand for their services came from agriculture, mining, and the railroads. Employment in these sectors usually led to physical isolation (as in small mining towns) or constant physical mobility (as in railroad maintenance or migratory agriculture)—situations usually without the opportunities for socioeconomic progress offered in the East. More recent Mexican immigrants entered an economy in which automation, industrial mechanization, and emphasis on skilled consumer services provided only limited opportunities for relatively uneducated and unskilled workers.

THE MEXICAN-AMERICAN EXPERIENCE: THE 19TH CENTURY

In the 19th century the major settlements in the regions acquired from Mexico continued to develop in relative isolation from each other. However, California, Arizona, New Mexico, and Texas shared certain experiences resulting from continued contact with Mexico and from the pervasive impact of Anglo-American society and institutions. In each of the annexed regions except Texas, Mexicans were a majority of the population in 1848, but by the end of the 19th century Anglo-Americans had become the majority in all except New Mexico. Texas had entered the United States with an Anglo majority. Mexicans had been a minority there even under Mexican rule. During the decade of the Lone Star Republic (1836–1845), some Mexicans fled to Mexico, and emigration from the United States swelled the Anglo-American population. About 80 percent of the early Texas Anglos came from the deep South, bearing with them racist attitudes that they applied to Mexicans as well as to blacks and Indians. Throughout the 19th century, the share of Mexican Americans in the state's population varied between 5 and 10 percent.

After the treaty with Mexico, California experienced the first major influx of Anglos because of the discovery of gold in 1848. The 13,000 Californios (preconquest Mexican Californians) soon found the territory swamped by Anglo-American migrants and foreign immigrants, including Mexicans, Chileans, and Peruvians. Overall, the Spanish-speaking population fell to 15 percent by 1850 and 4 percent by 1870. Northern California received the major thrust of the Anglo gold-rush migration, while southern California remained heavily Mexican. This ethnic contrast was one factor in the debate over the possibility of dividing California into two states, as was done in the case of New Mexico and Arizona. However, the coming of the transcontinental railroad to southern California in the 1870s spurred a land boom and the state's second major population explosion. By the 1880s Anglo settlers were numerically dominant in the south also.

Neighboring Arizona remained predominantly Mexican in population until the late 1870s, particularly Tucson, which served as a trade crossroads connecting Mexico and California to the rest of the United States. There was some mining, ranching, and farming, but Arizona's economy rested on supplying the army and maintaining the Indian reservations. In the last three decades of the century the completion of the transcontinental railroad, the final military pacification of the Indians, and the development of large-scale mining spurred Anglo migration and reversed the territory's ethnic balance.

Only New Mexico continued to have a Mexican majority throughout the 19th century. At the time of conquest it had relatively few Anglo residents and the largest Mexican population (60,000–70,000) of all of Mexico's northern territories. Nor did New Mexico immediately attract the great numbers of Anglos that California and Texas did. The sparse early migration consisted principally of bankers, lawyers, businessmen, and appointed government officials. After 1870, however, Anglo ranchers, mainly from the Lone Star State, poured into southeastern New Mexico, which became known as "Little Texas," and onto the eastern plains. This movement eroded the Hispano majority and divided New Mexico into ethnically contrasting regions—the Anglo-dominated south and the Hispano-dominated north. Centrally located Albuquerque, the state's population center, was an ethnic mosaic.

In the early postconquest period New Mexico Hispanos spread farther east onto the plains and farther north into the valleys. In 1861 Congress created the Colorado Territory and, ignoring the integrity of the extended Hispano community and the protests of New Mexico Hispanos, it slashed a geographically straight but culturally insensitive boundary across northern New Mexico. This action politically severed thousands of Hispanos, mainly those in the San Luis Valley, from their New Mexico homeland.

Politics Beginning as a population minority, the Mexicans in Texas, or Tejanos, had little statewide political power. Only in San Antonio, where substantial numbers lived, and in such Rio Grande border towns as Brownsville, Laredo, and El Paso did they have any political significance. Even so, Anglo political bosses, with economic power, control over the law enforcement system, and linkages to state government, generally dominated. Hampered also by the language barrier, Tejanos found themselves further disfranchised by such devices as "white primaries" in many Texas counties and the state poll tax, approved in 1902.

Tejanos also bore the cross of the Alamo. The memory of that carnage-filled Mexican victory and the equally bloody Texas victory at San Jacinto poisoned Anglo-Mexican relations from the beginning of the Lone Star Republic. The historical persistence of the cry, "Remember the Alamo," which Texans shouted as they killed Mexican soldiers at San Jacinto, symbolized the state's continuing interethnic conflict. Tejanos found little protection and sometimes suffered outright repression from law enforcement agencies, particularly the Texas Rangers, whom one Mexican-American state legislator labeled the Mexicans' Ku Klux Klan.

In California, in contrast, the fact of a Mexican majority contributed to a promising start for ethnic relations. Californios participated widely in the early postconquest government and provided 8 of the 48 delegates to the 1849 state constitutional convention. There they won some transitory victories, such as a provision that all state laws and regulations be translated into Spanish. In southern California, where Californios remained a majority in some places until the 1880s, they continued to be elected to local and county positions, and a few held state offices or seats in the legislature.

However, the rapid growth of a large Anglo majority quickly rendered Mexican Americans politically powerless at the state level. As a result, they could not prevent the enactment of inequitable and sometimes discriminatory laws. For example, the legislature placed the heaviest tax burden on land, an abrupt and destructive shift from the Mexican system of taxing production rather than land. Although this tax also hurt Anglo landowners, it seriously undermined Californio ranchers. The Foreign Miners' Tax of 1850, a $20 monthly fee for the right to mine, was applied not only to foreign immigrants but also to California-born conquered Mexicans, even though they had automatically become U.S. citizens. The state antivagrancy act of 1855 was so ob-

viously anti-Mexican that it became known popularly as the Greaser Law. Possibly the most blatantly anti-Mexican law was the 1855 act negating the constitutional requirement that laws be translated into Spanish. Finally, there was growing vigilantism and squatter violence against Californio landowners.

In Arizona political power rested with the Anglo immigrants, mainly ranchers from Texas and businessmen, who were anxious to disengage themselves from Hispano-dominated New Mexico. They convinced Congress to form the separate Arizona Territory in 1862 and then transferred the territorial capital from Tucson to Prescott in Anglo-dominated central Arizona, and later to the booming commercial center of Phoenix. Mexicans were in the majority into the 1870s. But unlike Hispanos in New Mexico, most of them had immigrated after the U.S.-Mexican War to work on the ranches, farms, and railroads or in the mines. They lacked economic power, political knowledge, and fluency in English and held no important territory-wide elective or appointive offices, although before 1880 they held seats in about half of the territorial legislative assemblies.

The Hispanos' political success in New Mexico contrasts with the Chicano experience in the rest of the Southwest. With their large population majority, they maintained control of the New Mexico territorial legislature and local government through most of the 19th century and generally sent Hispano territorial delegates to Congress. However, political and economic realities led to accommodation between politically astute Hispanos, particularly *ricos* (rich ones—upper-class Hispanos) and incoming Anglos. Hispanos had the numbers, local political skills, and fluency in Spanish; the Anglos brought strong political and business connections with the East as well as knowledge of the larger U.S. system. As a territory, New Mexico was subject to greater federal control than were the states, and its chief officials, including the territorial governor, were appointed in Washington. During the entire territorial period from 1848 to 1912 only one Hispano was appointed governor, Miguel Antonio Otero.

Political middlemen in the Anglo-Hispano accommodation were the *patrones,* who derived from the system that was traditional throughout colonial Mexico. The *patrón* was usually a large landowner or town leader who acted as liaison between the ranch workers (*peones*) or townspeople and the outside world. He served as political spokesman, problem-solving ombudsman, personal counselor, *compadre* (godfather) for many children, and sometimes commercial intermediary. In return he expected absolute loyalty from his followers, including their willingness to vote as he directed. Armed with this power over their ballots, the patrón could negotiate at the state level for favors for himself, his followers, and his community. In some respects the patrón system resembled the ward-boss system of eastern and midwestern urban ethnic neighborhoods.

The coming of the railroad and the movement of Anglo ranchers into southern New Mexico brought a decline, although not a disappearance, of Hispano political power by the early 20th century. By 1912 these phenomena also helped bring statehood, which had for long been held up in the crossfire of conflicting Anglo

attitudes toward Mexicans. Those who opposed statehood for too "brown," too "foreign" New Mexico, preferring Anglo control through the colonialist territorial government, clashed with those who argued that statehood would speed assimilation of the Mexicans. Some Hispano leaders saw advantages to statehood, including the right to elect the governor; others opposed it because it would threaten the dominance of traditional parochial schools and reduce federal financial support. However, faced with growing Anglo immigration, most Hispanos ultimately supported statehood in order to have a voice in the writing of the state constitution.

The 35-member Hispano bloc among the 100 delegates at the 1910 constitutional convention proved effective. The state constitution contained a number of provisions they sought, including prohibition of segregated schools, bilingual teacher education, and reaffirmation of the rights of the Treaty of Guadalupe Hidalgo. The first state legislature instituted bilingualism, making Spanish and English equal government languages.

Land   Land had been the basis of the northern Mexican socioeconomic system, but after the U.S. conquest, in spite of the theoretical protections of the Treaty of Guadalupe Hidalgo, many Mexican Americans lost their land. With some variations, the story of land loss was repeated with depressing familiarity. Holders of Spanish and Mexican land grants, most of whom were Mexican Americans, had to seek legal confirmation of their titles. Instead of automatically accepting all titles and then handling individual challenges, in line with the spirit of the treaty and as urged by some leaders, the federal government placed the burden of proof on the landowners. Already suffering from heavy taxes and generally low in capital, Mexican-American landowners had to go through the slow, expensive process of legally confirming their claims, and quite often were forced to borrow money at high interest rates to cover the costs of the legal struggle. They had to argue their cases before U.S. judges and land commissioners who were unfamiliar with the Hispanic legal principles and land tenure system upon which the grants were based. Even when they won confirmation of their grants, the Mexican Americans often found themselves personally destitute, and many had to sacrifice their land to pay the legal costs.

In Texas the destruction of Mexican landholdings began under the Lone Star Republic, where legal chicanery and physical intimidation were added to the other burdens. In Nueces County, for example, where Mexicans owned all 15 land grants at the time of Texas independence in 1836, only one Tejano holding survived by 1859. By 1860 there were only two Tejanos among the 263 Texans with over $100,000 in real property.

To adjudicate landholdings in California, Congress passed the Land Act of 1851, establishing a Board of Land Commissioners to review claims. If appealed, cases moved on to the U.S. district court and even the Supreme Court. Of the 813 claims, 549 were appealed (417 by government attorneys), some as many as six times. The board went out of business in 1856, but multiple, expensive appeals dragged out land cases to an average of 17 years.

Although the U.S. government dealt with California lands immediately after the conquest, it allowed land

titles in New Mexico to remain unresolved for decades. A surveyor-general was appointed to investigate titles in 1854, but Congress reserved for itself the power to approve them. Although over 1,000 land claims had been entered in New Mexico by 1880, the surveyor-general had sent only 150 to Congress, which in turn had ruled on only 71. Finally, 40 years after it had acted similarly in California, Congress established a Court of Private Land Claims for New Mexico, Arizona, and Colorado. Although the court completed its evaluations by 1904, confirming only 75 of 301 claims, some cases, incredibly, were still pending before the U.S. Supreme Court in the 1970s.

These delayed hearings proved disastrous for Hispanos. In addition to the usual problems prevailing elsewhere, the claims court was less receptive than the California board to arguments based on usage and custom, adhering instead to a tightly legalistic line. Moreover, the 40-year delay in establishing the court had given land companies and lawyers time to manipulate records, obtain partial rights to communal grants (often as payment for "services" rendered), and establish positions that clouded titles. Land companies often took advantage of isolated, unaware Hispano villagers who failed to register their grants in distant land offices and of Hispano subsistence farmers who were unable to pay onerous new land taxes; the land companies or Anglo businessmen would record the unregistered grants in their own names or obtain title by paying delinquent taxes. Sometimes actual fraud occurred; taxes would be increased on Hispano lands and then lowered after purchase by land companies. As a result of this process, 80 percent of New Mexico grant holders lost their lands.

Some rich Hispanos formed political or business alliances, including land companies, with Anglos; such partnerships were often based on marriage, almost always between an Anglo man and a wealthy Hispano woman. With more capital, government contracts, superior knowledge of the law, and skills at forging documents and employing legal chicanery, these land companies made inroads into community and small private landholdings at the expense of poorer, less educated, and more isolated Hispanos. The most notorious of these alliances was the Anglo-dominated Santa Fe Ring. Particularly hard hit were the communal grants of small Hispano towns, which found themselves losers in a game whose rules they did not understand. By 1930 these community lands had shrunk from an original 2 million acres to only 300,000.

The federal government also encroached upon Mexican holdings. Through the Forest Reserve Act of 1891 and subsequent decisions, the government appropriated thousands of acres for national forests, sometimes engulfing Hispano villages. Today one-eighth of New Mexico is national forest. Restricted from lands where they had traditionally grazed their sheep, cut wood, and farmed, forced to pay grazing fees for lands they once owned, poor Hispanos found themselves further hampered in their struggle for economic survival.

Socioeconomic Changes Loss of their lands throughout the Southwest was a prime factor in the relegation of Mexican Americans to the lower rungs of the socioeconomic ladder. The loss eroded their economic base, undermined their political power, and displaced ranch workers, small farmers, and residents of towns with lost or truncated communal land grants. Some managed to find work in traditional occupations. They might be vaqueros or sheep shearers, but often only on a part-time basis. Most displaced Chicanos became laborers, poorly paid and often migratory, in the expanding fruit, vegetable, and cotton commercial agriculture. Others moved to cities, where their pastoral and agricultural skills were of little use, and many found employment in railroads, mining, construction, and food processing.

Increasingly incorporated into the labor market in the 19th century as unskilled or semiskilled manual laborers, Mexican Americans experienced job displacement and in some areas downward occupational mobility. Their low levels of education and Anglo hostility limited their access to jobs in the rapidly expanding white-collar sector. They encountered obstacles to upward mobility even in occupations in which they had considerable skill and experience. Despite their long pastoral experience, Chicanos were employed on ranches only as ranch hands, while Anglos held most of the supervisory positions. Despite their mining skills and experience, many Chicanos and newly arrived Mexican immigrants were assigned manual laboring tasks in the mines, while Anglos operated the machines—a system that also prevailed in mechanized agriculture. Sometimes Chicanos received lower wages than Anglos for the same work. In some isolated mining towns and agricultural areas, a de facto debt peonage existed; workers who became indebted to the employer or the company store were unable to clear the debt because of their low wages.

Another aspect of the 19th-century economic shift was the entry of Mexican women into the labor market. As the men became occupationally disadvantaged, the women were increasingly employed as domestics, laundresses, farm laborers, and cannery and packinghouse workers. The increase in the proportion of female-headed households may have been a result of these socioeconomic stresses.

Concomitant with the Chicano economic decline was increased residential and social segregation. Some traditional Mexican towns were transformed into barrios when Anglos immigrated and established their own segregated neighborhoods or when newly established Anglo cities expanded, enveloping historic Mexican communities. Displaced Chicanos and immigrating Mexicans often established new barrios and colonias. Certain entire regions, particularly northern New Mexico, southern Colorado, and the lower Rio Grande Valley, remained predominantly Chicano because of the absence of significant Anglo immigration.

Barrios, colonias, and Chicano regions developed and survived through a combination of force and choice. In Anglo areas anti-Mexican segregation, often embodied in restrictive covenants on real estate, slammed the residential door on the vast majority, the major exceptions being Chicanos with wealth, social status, light skins, and presumed Spanish identity. On the other hand, most Chicanos and Mexican immigrants probably preferred living among people who shared their heritage, culture, and language.

Within Chicano areas the traditional extended family and community social life flourished. There were bullfights, rodeos, horse races, and various fiestas, including

the celebration of Mexican Independence Day (September 16) and Cinco de Mayo (May 5—the 1862 Mexican victory over the French at Puebla). The Catholic church provided a focus for social as well as religious life; in some cases, as in northern New Mexico, religious art and music continued to flourish. Mexican-American political, cultural, patriotic, and mutual-aid organizations began to develop but generally remained local. Chicano newspapers strengthened community cohesion and spoke out against injustices, but they were undercapitalized and were forced to engage in a constant, ultimately losing struggle for survival.

Resistance Faced with a pervasive pattern of economic dislocation, declining political influence, violence, and discrimination, Chicanos fought back. Usually they maneuvered within the system—through the courts, political channels, and newspapers—but at times they resorted to force to defend their rights.

In the Cart War of 1857, Mexican teamsters who hauled goods between San Antonio and the Texas coast had to battle marauding Anglo teamsters, who tried literally to drive them out of business. In 1859–1860 Juan Nepomuceno Cortina, a rancher, led a Chicano revolt against Anglo oppression in south Texas; he raided Brownsville, issued two major proclamations, and routed both the Brownsville militia and the Texas Rangers before the army drove him into exile in Mexico. In 1877 an Anglo land shark tried to establish a monopoly over the Guadalupe Salt Lakes near El Paso and force Mexicans to pay a fee for the salt, thereby shattering a centuries-old tradition of communal sharing. Mexicans on both sides of the Rio Grande joined in rebellion, forced the land shark and his Texas Ranger allies to surrender after a three-day gun battle, executed him after a citizens' trial, and then disbanded.

The San Diego Revolt of 1915 marked the end of the Chicanos' physical resistance to oppressive conditions in Texas. In a rebellion whose origins are still obscure, but which was connected in some respects to the Mexican Revolution and World War I, Chicanos waged a six-month guerrilla war against Texas authorities and the U.S. Army. A rebel document (the Plan of San Diego) found by U.S. authorities called for the establishment of an independent nation in the Southwest.

Even in New Mexico, where interethnic relations tended to be more benign than in other regions, violence occurred. One aspect of the oft-filmed Lincoln County War (1876–1878) was the clash between Anglo cattlemen and Hispano sheepmen. The loss of land through incomprehensible legal tangles sometimes provoked Hispanos to take direct action against what they viewed as an unfair and unresponsive system; the Mano Negra (Black Hand) and Gorras Blancas (White Caps) were secret societies that used guerrilla techniques to battle landowners and railroads. In the late 1880s and early 1890s, the Gorras Blancas destroyed ranches, telegraph lines, railroad ties, and barbed-wire fences in night raids. They disbanded in the early 1890s, and many members turned to political action through the newly formed and briefly successful local People's party.

THE MEXICAN-AMERICAN EXPERIENCE: 1900–1940

The first three decades of the 20th century saw rapid growth in the Chicano population. Between 1900 and 1930 more than 700,000 Mexicans officially entered the United States, "pushed" by the Mexican Revolution and "pulled" by the expanding U.S. economy. Over 70 percent of these immigrants identified themselves as "laborers except farm and mine." Most still settled in the Southwest, where the economic trends of the 19th century continued and accelerated. The passage of the Reclamation Act of 1902, which authorized federally funded construction of large reservoirs, fostered labor-intensive irrigated farming. Railroads, mining, and the oil industry expanded. Southwestern industrial development was generally related to agriculture and mining: food processing, packing, and shipping; textile manufacturing; and chemical production.

Texas and California were the strongest magnets. By 1930 over 40 percent of Mexican-born U.S. residents lived in Texas; over 30 percent lived in California. During World War I and the 1920s when labor was in demand, increasing numbers took advantage of agricultural, railroad, and industrial opportunities in the Northwest and Midwest—the automobile factories of Detroit; the steel mills, tanneries, and meat-packing plants of Chicago and Gary; and the steel mills of Ohio and Pennsylvania. During the 1920s the number of Mexicans in Chicago leaped from 4,000 to nearly 20,000. By 1930, 15 percent of the Mexican-born resided outside of the Southwest.

Chicanos entered nearly every occupation classified as unskilled or semiskilled. They became the bulwark of southwestern agriculture; 41 percent of the Chicano labor force was engaged in agricultural work in 1930. Thirty-five percent of the men and 20 percent of the women served as farm laborers: 10 percent of the men and 1 percent of the women were farmers or farm managers. Often entire families engaged in piece-rate harvesting, especially in Colorado and Texas.

By 1930 manufacturing (23 percent), transportation and communications (11 percent), and domestic and personal service (10 percent) had become the other major sectors of Chicano employment; mining was down to just over 3 percent. Chicanos made up 75 percent of the work force of the six major western railroads. They also held blue-collar positions in construction, food processing, textiles, automobile industries, steel production, and utilities. In California during the 1920s Chicanos constituted up to two-thirds of the work force in these industries. However, employment in these areas did not result in much further occupational mobility. In 1930, while 28 percent of Mexican-American men held unskilled nonagricultural jobs, 9 percent were in semiskilled work and less than 7 percent were in skilled positions. Less than 3 percent were managers or supervisors, and under 1 percent had professional or technical positions.

Mexican-American women participated increasingly in the labor market, but their employment patterns differed from those of the men. Nearly 45 percent were engaged in domestic and personal service. Others worked in agriculture, textiles, and food processing and packing. Nearly 5 percent had sales positions, usually in small barrio stores or in Anglo stores that catered to Chicanos. The women suffered double wage discrimination, tending to earn less than either Chicano men or Anglo women, who often received more pay for the same job.

A small middle class developed, often oriented

toward serving the Chicano population. The growth of barrios and colonias fostered the expansion of small businesses, such as grocery and dry-goods stores, restaurants, barbershops, tailor shops, and small construction firms. Some became teachers, usually in private Chicano schools or in segregated public schools.

But in general, geographical and cultural isolation reduced the opportunities for Chicanos to gain familiarity with American society through personal contact, and employers often obstructed their efforts to gain upward mobility and a greater knowledge of the system. However, numerous government agencies, religious groups, and private social-service organizations made special efforts to assist in the acculturation of Chicanos by providing instruction in English, American culture, and job skills.

Employment in migrant agriculture minimized opportunities to participate in community activities, including elections, and had a deleterious impact on the education of the workers' children. Harvesting seasons partially overlapped the academic year, and families traditionally migrated as a unit. Their children seldom spent an entire school year in their home towns. Until the 1960s government agencies and school districts made little effort to meet the special needs of migrant children, and agricultural employers were happy to have them in the fields rather than in school, a potential avenue for job mobility.

Chicanos encountered various forms of segregation, including separation of Anglo and Mexican public schools, restrictive covenants on residential property, segregated restaurants, separate "white" and "colored" sections in theaters, and special "colored" days in segregated swimming pools.

Community Life and Organization Urbanization paralleled immigration and population growth. During the 1920s, the percentage of U.S.-born Chicanos who lived in urban areas rose from 40 to 52. The proportion of Mexican immigrants living in cities climbed from 47 to 57 percent. By 1930 Chicanos made up more than half the population of El Paso, slightly less than half that of San Antonio, and one-fifth that of Los Angeles.

The dramatic increase in Mexican immigration had various effects on Chicano residential patterns. Thousands settled in older barrios, causing overcrowding and generating the construction of cheap housing to meet the sudden demand. In some barrios, immigrants attained such numerical dominance that U.S.-born Chicanos became a minority within a minority. Immigrants sometimes formed new barrios adjacent to historical Chicano areas or started new colonias as agricultural or railroad labor camps. Railroads had a special impact, because colonias were established at points along the lines. Other barrios developed in railroad centers throughout the West and Midwest, where Chicanos took up residence to work on the railroads and in agriculture, industries, and services.

The growth in size and number of Chicano communities fostered the growth of community activities. In the early 20th century there was a major increase in Chicano organizations, though some extended back to preconquest days. One of these, the Penitentes, a northern New Mexican Catholic lay society, best known for severe religious rituals reminiscent of medieval Catholicism, also provided political cohesion, social services, and emergency economic support as a type of mutual-

aid organization. Most *mutualistas* (mutual-aid societies) were established in the late 19th or the early 20th century as local organizations or as chapters of regional or national Chicano associations. Some adopted descriptive or symbolic names, such as Club Recíproco (Reciprocal Club), Sociedad Progresista Mexicana (Mexican Progressive Society), La Gran Liga Mexicana (Grand Mexican League), or La Orden de Caballeros de Texas (The Order of Knights of Texas). Others selected names of Mexican heroes, such as Sociedad Mutualista Miguel Hidalgo (the father of Mexican independence), Sociedad Mutualista Benito Juárez (the famous Mexican Liberal president), or Sociedad Ignacio Zaragosa (the victorious Texas-born general at the Battle of Puebla, 1862). Some Chicano organizations were Masonic, affiliated with the Gran Logia Masónica de México (Grand Masonic Lodge of Mexico City).

Membership varied. Some organizations were exclusively male or female, others had mixed membership. Most represented the working class, but others were essentially middle or upper class or reflected a cross section of wealth and occupations. Although each mutualista had its own goals, they all provided a focus for social life, with meetings, family gatherings, lectures, discussions, cultural presentations, and commemorations of both U.S. and Mexican holidays. Most provided services, such as assistance to families in need, emergency loans, legal services, mediation of disputes, and medical, life, and burial insurance. Some organized libraries or operated *escuelitas* (little schools), providing training in Mexican culture, Spanish, and basic school subjects to supplement the inferior education that many Chicanos felt their children received in the public schools. Mutualistas helped immigrants adapt to life in the United States, and many became involved in civil rights issues, including legal defense and struggles against residential, school, and public segregation and other forms of discrimination. Some engaged in political activism and supported candidates for public office. At times, mutualistas provided support for Chicanos on strike.

La Alianza Hispano-Americana (Hispanic-American Alliance, f. 1894) was the most extensive 19th-century Chicano organization. Established in Tucson, the Alianza spread throughout the Southwest and into midwestern and other western states. At one time it had 20,000 members. Two major statewide organizations emerged in Texas in the 1920s. La Orden de Hijos de América (The Order of Sons of America, 1921–1929) was established by a group of San Antonio leaders who were frustrated by Chicanos' lack of rights and representation in Texas. Composed of white-collar workers and professionals, the organization achieved some civil rights victories. In contrast to the short-lived Orden, the League of United Latin American Citizens (LULAC, f. 1929), formed by middle-class, Texas-born Chicanos, achieved national scope and organizational permanence. The founders of LULAC saw the need to struggle for rights and opportunities, but also emphasized Americanization and entrance into the mainstream society. LULAC has supported improved education for Chicanos, developed a college scholarship program, and brought numerous court challenges to discrimination and segregation.

No organization of equal prominence emerged in pre-Depression California, though such groups as La Liga

Protectora Latina (Latin Protective League) and the Confederación de Sociedades Mexicanas (Confederation of Mexican Societies) were established as coalitions of Chicano organizations in Los Angeles. The 35 Chicano mutualistas in the Chicago-Gary area similarly experimented for two years with a united front, La Confederación de Sociedades Mexicanas de los Estados Unidos de América (Confederation of Mexican Societies of the U.S.A.). One of the most ambitious attempts to provide organizational unity occurred in Laredo, Tex., in 1911, with the Primer Congreso Mexicanista de Texas (First Mexican Congress of Texas), out of which grew two statewide organizations—La Liga Mexicanista de Beneficiencia y Protección (Mexican Beneficent and Protective League) and La Liga Femenil Mexicanista (Mexican Women's League)—with representatives from other Texas Chicano societies. Although these attempts at long-range statewide or citywide coordination ultimately failed, during the 1920s in particular they contributed to a growing sense of community and provided notable services that Chicanos could not obtain elsewhere.

Labor Activism In addition to mutualistas, a variety of other cultural, political, service, and social organizations developed in the early 20th century. Possibly the most turbulent activity of that era was in labor, in which Mexicans played ironically conflicting roles. Because of depressed wages and unemployment in Mexico, Mexican workers could earn more in the United States, even by accepting jobs at pay levels that Anglos refused. Employers thus used Mexican labor to hold down the pay scale and often reached across the border to recruit them as strikebreakers. Because of the antipathy Mexicans generated in these roles, and also because of the biases of union leaders, local chapters of U.S. labor unions often refused to accept Chicanos as members or else required them to establish segregated locals. Unions also actively lobbied for government restrictions on Mexican immigration.

There were Mexican strikers as well as strikebreakers, though. In 1883 Chicano vaqueros were among the leaders of a successful cowboys' strike in the Texas panhandle that won improved pay from powerful cattle companies. The mining industry was another early focus of Chicano labor activism, particularly in Clifton–Morenci copper region of southeast Arizona. In 1903 Chicano miners struck over a reduction in hourly pay, but their efforts failed because of lack of support from Anglo workers, the arrest of their leaders, and a devastating flash flood that killed more than 50 Chicanos and destroyed many homes. In 1915 some 5,000 Chicanos struck over a number of issues, principally the dual-wage system. This time they were supported by a number of Anglo workers and after a five-month strike won equal pay. Chicanos and Anglos again united in strikes in 1917 and 1918, but failed because of vigilante violence and the mass deportation of hundreds of Mexican miners. Other Arizona mining walkouts occurred in Metcalf, Ray, and Bisbee.

Chicanos were also in the forefront of agricultural strikes. In 1903 more than 1,000 Mexican and Japanese sugar-beet workers carried out a successful strike near Ventura, Calif. In 1913 Mexican workers participated in a strike against degrading living conditions on the Durst hop ranch near Wheatland, Calif. Although the intervention of National Guard troops and the arrest of some 100 migrant workers broke the strike, the Wheatland events contributed to the establishment of the California Commission on Immigration and Housing and recognition of the oppressive living and working conditions of agricultural laborers.

Throughout the late 1920s and early 1930s, Mexicans led or participated in a number of agricultural strikes throughout the country, particularly in California. Mexicans struck the Imperial Valley melon fields in 1928 and 1930. In 1933 the El Monte strawberry fields, the San Joaquin Valley cotton fields and fruit orchards, the Hayward pea fields, and many other locales were affected. Strikes spread to Redlands citrus groves in 1934, to Los Angeles celery fields and Orange County citrus groves in 1936, and to Ventura County lemon groves in 1941. Mexicans also challenged the food-processing industry through strikes by lettuce packers in Salinas, Calif., in 1936; cannery workers in Stockton, Calif., in 1937; pecan shellers in San Antonio, Tex., in 1938, and others. In San Angelo, Tex., in 1934, Mexican sheepshearers struck for better pay.

During the 1920s and early 1930s, Anglo labor organizations made some efforts to recruit Chicano workers, either as members of existing unions or for special Chicano unions. The founding of the Congress of Industrial Organizations (CIO) in 1935 opened doors for Chicanos, who for the most part had not had access to craft unions. The CIO sometimes absorbed entire Chicano groups, such as the Chicano/Mexicano Texas Agricultural Workers' Organizing Committee, which in 1937 entered the CIO's United Cannery, Agricultural, Packing, and Allied Workers of America.

Chicanos created a number of their own unions, as well, mainly in California. The Confederación de Uniones Obreras Mexicanas (CUOM, Confederation of Mexican Labor Unions) was formed in 1928. Among its goals were equal pay for Mexicans and Anglos doing the same job, the termination of job discrimination against Chicano workers, and a limitation on immigration of Mexican workers. At its height, CUOM had about 20 locals and 3,000 workers.

In the early 1930s Chicanos established some 40 agricultural unions in California. The largest, the Confederación de Uniones de Campesinos y Obreros Mexicanos (CUCOM, Confederation of Mexican Farm Workers' and Laborers' Unions), created in 1933, ultimately included 50 locals and 5,000 members. Most of these unions later joined the American Federation of Labor (AFL) or the CIO. Among the unions Chicanos formed outside of California were the Sheepshearers Union of North America, under the AFL, in Arizona and Texas, and La Liga Obrera de Habla Española (The Spanish-speaking Labor League) in northern New Mexico and southern Colorado.

The Catholic Church At the time of the U.S. conquest of northern Mexico, the Mexican Catholic church had been weakened by a struggle between liberals, who wanted to reduce the church's political and economic power, and conservatives, who supported all its religious and secular pursuits. The secularization of the missions in northern Mexico—the removal of their landed holdings—and the expulsion of Spanish-born members of religious orders had reduced the presence of the church to a token by the middle of the 19th century.

After the U.S. conquest, French, Spanish, and Irish, rather than Mexican, clergy came to fill the void. The Catholic hierarchy in the United States generally viewed the remaining Mexican priests as obstacles to be removed in the process of Americanization. Padre Antonio José Martínez, the leading prelate in New Mexico and a political and community leader, was the most famous of the Mexican clerics stripped of their priestly prerogatives.

In general the church failed to adequately serve Catholics in the annexed areas. By any measure—number of priests, financial support, facilities, or parishioners per priest—the Southwest was a relatively neglected area. By 1930, for example, the combined San Diego–Los Angeles archdiocese, with 301,775 Catholics, had only 79 parochial schools, whereas Baltimore, with about the same number of Catholics, had 179 parochial schools, and St. Louis, with 440,000 Catholics, had 212. Ratios were even worse in El Paso (12 parochial schools for 119,623 Catholics) and Corpus Christi, Tex. (27 parochial schools for 247,760 Catholics). Dioceses near the Mexican border have suffered the greatest shortages of priests. As late as 1967, for example, the Brownsville diocese had a ratio of 3,012 persons per priest, six times the ratio of Baltimore.

The church's neglect was more than general for the Southwest; it was specific for Chicanos. The lack of Mexican priests lessened the church's ability to fulfill a supportive and mediating function for Chicanos. Most bishops in Texas and New Mexico were French, and they recruited French priests who were usually unfamiliar with the United States and could not speak Spanish. The 20th century increase in Mexican immigration introduced another strain in relations between Chicanos and the church. Mexican Catholicism had evolved over four centuries with a unique mixture of Spanish and Indian elements, which the U.S. hierarchy viewed with disdain. On the other hand, the heavy emphasis by American Catholics on formalism was alien and forbidding to Mexican immigrants.

These cultural tensions within the church, the paucity of Chicano priests, and the shortage of funds in the Southwest opened the way for Protestant recruitment. Presbyterians, Mormons, and various Pentecostal sects, in particular, made inroads into the Chicano community. One of the most successful approaches was through community settlement houses, which provided, along with religious conversion, various types of language and vocational training. Nonetheless, Protestant gains were limited; in 1960 less than 3 percent of Mexican Americans were Protestant.

Faced with the Protestant challenge, the Catholic Church launched a minor counterattack and began to provide English and citizenship classes, youth activities (through such means as the Catholic Youth Organization), and additional parochial schools. But seldom, until recently, did the church become involved in direct social action on behalf of its Chicano parishioners.

The Great Depression The Great Depression brought a dramatic population reversal among Mexican Americans. Tabulated immigration from Mexico fell sharply, and official figures indicate that some half-million persons of Mexican descent moved to Mexico. The Depression displaced millions of American workers, and the severe midwestern drought dispossessed hundreds of thousands more, many of whom headed for California. Chicanos not only lost their jobs in the cities along with other Americans, but also were displaced from agricultural jobs by the Dust Bowl migrants, particularly in Arizona, Colorado, and California. Prior to the Depression less than 20 percent of California migratory agricultural laborers were Anglos, but by 1936 they had increased to more than 85 percent. Texas was an exception, with Chicanos furnishing 85 percent of that state's migratory agricultural labor in 1937.

Instead of being viewed as the backbone of southwestern agriculture and as invaluable contributors to other employment sectors, Mexicans were seen as an economic liability and became the objects of resentment as recipients of scarce public relief funds. The government's solution was the Repatriation Program, which produced a sudden drop in the number of Mexicans in the United States; for example, in the 1930s the Mexican-born population of Texas declined by nearly 40 percent. Repatriation shattered families, decimated barrios and colonias, forced small businesses to close, and removed potential citizens and therefore potential voters, community leaders and, in some cases, labor organizers.

The Depression era also sharpened Chicanos' distrust of government, particularly its agents of law enforcement, an antagonism rooted in events of the 19th century. The Texas Rangers remain the foremost symbol of police mistreatment of Mexican Americans, but discrimination by the courts and abuse by law-enforcement agencies have been basic themes of Chicano history. During the Depression the use of violence to break strikes and disrupt union activities was widespread. The Repatriation Program only furthered Chicano distrust of the government.

New Mexico, the remaining bastion of major Chicano landholding, was especially hard hit by the Depression. During the 1930s some 8,000 Hispanos lost their small farms and ranches because they could not pay taxes or conservation district assessments. In addition, the small northern villages, which had always had limited economic opportunities, suffered an even greater imbalance between the small number of jobs and the growing numbers of the unemployed and those who had been dispossessed of land. These conditions forced many to become migrant agricultural workers or to seek employment in Albuquerque or Santa Fe.

THE MEXICAN-AMERICAN EXPERIENCE:
SINCE 1940

World War II marked another sharp reversal in the course of Chicano history. The Depression had left in its wake population decline, devastated communities, and shattered dreams; the war brought population growth, resurgent communities, and rising expectations.

World War II caused a tremendous drain on U.S. manpower. When the military forces called for recruits, Mexican Americans responded in great number and went on to serve with distinction. Some 350,000 Chicanos served in the armed services and won 17 medals of honor, including 5 of the 14 awarded to Texans. The war also brought industrial expansion, further aggravating the labor shortage caused by the growth of the

armed forces. Chicanos thus managed to gain entry to jobs and industries that had been virtually closed to them in the past. These new opportunities liberated many from dependence on traditional occupations, such as agriculture. The turnaround from labor surplus of the 1930s to labor shortage of the 1940s had a special impact on agriculture and transportation. For help, the United States turned to Mexico and the Bracero Program, and from 1942 until 1964, Mexican braceros were a regular part of the U.S. labor scene.

World War II brought increased tensions between Chicanos and law-enforcement agencies. Two events in Los Angeles brought this issue into focus. In the Sleepy Lagoon case of 1942–1943, 17 Chicano youths were convicted of charges ranging from assault to first-degree murder for the death of a Mexican-American boy discovered on the outskirts of the city. Throughout the trial the judge openly displayed bias against Chicanos and allowed the prosecution to bring in racial factors; further, the defendants were not permitted haircuts or changes of clothing. In 1944 the Sleepy Lagoon Defense Committee obtained a reversal of the convictions from the California District Court of Appeals, but the damage had been done. Los Angeles newspapers sensationalized the case and helped create an anti-Mexican atmosphere; police harassed Chicano youth clubs and repeatedly rounded up young Chicanos "under suspicion."

In the aftermath of the convictions and the press campaign, conflict broke out between U.S. servicemen in the area and young Mexican Americans, many dressed in the zoot suits popular during the wartime era. Soldiers and sailors attacked Chicanos on the streets, even dragging them out of theaters and public vehicles. Instead of intervening to stop the attackers, military and local police moved in afterward and arrested the Chicano victims. Spurred on by sensational, anti-Mexican press coverage of the "zoot-suit riots," these assaults spread throughout southern California and even into midwestern cities. A citizens' investigating committee appointed by the governor of California later reported that racial prejudice, discriminatory police practices, and inflammatory press coverage were among the principal causes of the riots. (The Sleepy Lagoon case and the zoot-suit affair provided the basis for Luis Valdez's Zoot Suit, which in 1979 became the first Chicano play to appear on Broadway.)

Despite such events the World War II era proved to be generally positive for Mexican Americans and is often viewed as a watershed in their history. Progress continued after the war. The G.I. Bill of Rights gave all veterans such benefits as educational subsidies and loans for business and housing; also, returning Chicano servicemen refused to accept the discriminatory practices that had been their lot. The G.I. generation furnished much of the leadership for postwar Mexican-American civil rights and political activism. Veterans were instrumental in the founding and growth of a variety of Chicano organizations, which generally were more militant than the pre-Depression assimilationist groups such as LULAC and the more service-oriented mutualistas. The American G.I. Forum developed as a reaction to discrimination in Texas, where returning Mexican-American servicemen who applied for membership in veterans' organizations were rejected or assigned to special Chicano chapters. This discrimination culminated in Corpus Christi with the refusal to bury a local Chicano war hero in the community's military cemetery. In reaction, Chicano ex-servicemen formed the G.I. Forum as their own veterans' organization. The forum has led fights against discrimination, serves as a social organization, and raises money for scholarships.

Among the heavily political organizations, the Unity Leagues and the Community Service Organization registered voters in California and supported Chicano candidates. These groups also have engaged in such diverse activities as language and citizenship education, court challenges against school segregation, and assistance to individuals in obtaining government services. More overtly political have been the Mexican American Political Association (MAPA) in California, the Political Association of Spanish-Speaking Organizations (PASSO) in Texas, and the American Coordinating Council for Political Education (ACCPE) in Arizona.

In the labor field, Chicanos demonstrated renewed activism and effectiveness. For example, in 1951 in Silver City, N.Mex., Chicano workers challenged the powerful New Jersey Zinc Corporation. A special aspect of that strike, which became the subject of a controversial feature film, Salt of the Earth, was the role of the women, who walked the picket line when a court injunction barred their husbands.

The post-Depression era brought major growth of the Chicano population and movement to cities and throughout the United States. The undependability and lack of comparability of census data make it impossible to specify the precise increase in the number of Mexican Americans. That the increase occurred is clear from both the rapid growth of Mexican immigration and the high birthrate of Mexican Americans. Documented immigration amounted to 273,800 in the 1950s and 441,-800 in the 1960s. In 1970, 85 percent of Mexican Americans lived in cities, up from 66 percent in 1950. In addition, reversing the massive exodus of the 1930s, Chicanos once again spread throughout the nation, with 10 percent outside of the Southwest, the largest number in Illinois in 1970.

Chicano progress since World War II is shown by changes in job concentrations, reflecting to some extent changes in the economy of the Southwest. Since 1940 the area has experienced a manufacturing boom and rapid growth in such areas as government, product distribution, consumer-oriented activities, and professional services, and the number of agricultural jobs has significantly declined.

In 1930, 45 percent of the men and 21 percent of the women in the Chicano labor force worked in agriculture. By 1960 the proportion had dropped to 30 percent of the men and less than 7 percent of the women, and those percentages declined to 9 and 4, respectively, by 1970. The percentage of Mexican Americans in unskilled labor positions also declined. In 1930 28 percent of Mexican-American men were classified as unskilled, but only 12 percent by 1970. The figures for women declined from 2.8 percent to 1.5 percent.

In contrast, the percentages of Mexican Americans in professional, technical, managerial, clerical, skilled craft, and semiskilled occupations have risen sharply. Between 1930 and 1970, the proportion of Mexican-American men in professional and technical occupations climbed from less than 1 percent to over 6 percent, and from 3 to nearly 8 percent for women. The

proportion of men in white-collar work of some kind almost tripled (8.3 to 21.9 percent). Men employed in skilled crafts rose from 7 percent to 21 percent, and women from less than 1 percent to over 2 percent.

There have been variations in these general trends by both state and sex. While the percentage of Mexican Americans in professional and technical occupations has increased in every southwestern state, in 1970 there was a range from 9.7 percent of the men and 10 percent of the women so employed in New Mexico, to 5.4 percent of the men and 7.4 percent of the women in Texas. In 1970 in New Mexico, 4.7 percent of the men and 0.5 percent of the women were farm laborers, and in Colorado, 4.2 percent of the men and 0.8 percent of the women. In contrast, in Arizona 9.5 percent of the men and 4.0 percent of the women were farm laborers.

Since the Depression, Mexican-American women have increasingly entered the labor market. While less than 15 percent were officially in the labor force in 1930, this rose to 21 percent in 1950, 33 percent in 1970, and 42 percent in 1975 (compared to 46 percent for all women). Mexican-American women were more highly represented than men in sales, service, and particularly clerical occupations. Men were more heavily represented than women in managerial, skilled craft, unskilled labor, and farm labor occupations.

However, Chicano socioeconomic gains did not bring full equality with other Americans. Although the percentages of Mexican Americans in professional, technical, managerial, and clerical positions have increased, they still fall far short of parity according to their population numbers. Moreover, within nearly every major occupational group, Chicanos tend to hold inferior jobs, and their earnings within the same job classification tend to be lower than those of Anglos. The 1970 Census indicated that the percentage of Mexican Americans in professional and technical positions was less than half that of the total population. People with Spanish surnames composed only 0.9 percent of the lawyers and judges, 1.1 percent of the dentists, and 3.7 percent of the physicians in the United States. Chicanos owned less than 1.0 percent of all business firms, with gross receipts less than 0.2 percent of the national figure.

On the other hand, Mexican Americans are still overrepresented in unskilled and farm labor. In 1970 Mexican-American men worked in farm labor at more than three and a half times the rate of the general U.S. male population, and Mexican-American women held such jobs at nearly five times the rate of women in the overall work force.

Income figures also reflect progress without parity. The income of Spanish-surnamed persons in the Southwest rose from slightly over 57 percent of the income of Anglo Americans in 1949 to almost 62 percent in 1959. From 1959 to 1969 the median income of families with Spanish surnames in the Southwest barely inched ahead from 62 percent to 66 percent of the median income for Anglo families. Moreover, while Spanish-surnamed families made gains in this period in four southwestern states, including a jump from 57 to 67 percent in New Mexico, in California they dropped from 79 to 73 percent of Anglo family income. In Texas they climbed from 52 percent of Anglo family income in 1959 to only 58 percent by 1969.

In 1976, Hispanic families nationally had a median income of $10,260, compared to $15,540 for all white families and $9,240 for black families. One of every four Spanish-surnamed families fell below the poverty level in that year, and 16 percent had incomes under $4,000, contrasted with 8 percent for all American families.

The unemployment rate for Chicanos has remained consistently above that for Anglos. Mexican-American women who are heads of families are at an even greater disadvantage; in 1974 their family income averaged only $4,930, whereas female-headed families nationally had an average income of $6,415. Nearly half of the families headed by Mexican-American women fell below the poverty level.

Unequal economic conditions are paralleled by low educational levels, despite progress in recent years. Before 1920 only 9 percent of Chicano men graduated from high school. By the mid-1960s the figure was 38 percent for the foreign-born and 56 percent for the second generation. Still, in 1970 Mexican Americans over 25 years old averaged less than 9 years of schooling, compared with more than 12 years for Anglo Americans. The U.S. Commission on Civil Rights reported in 1971 that in the five southwestern states 86 percent of Anglos and nearly 67 percent of blacks, but only some 60 percent of Chicanos completed high school. This gap widened at the postsecondary level, with about 24 percent of Anglos, 8 percent of blacks, and 5 percent of Chicanos graduating from college. Hispanic Americans received 254 doctorates in 1973–1974, only 1.1 percent of the national total. In 1976–1977 Chicanos made up only about 1.5 percent of first-year students in U.S. medical, dental, and American Bar Association–approved law schools.

Historically Chicanos have encountered educational segregation and deprivation. The six-volume study of Mexican Americans in education published in the early 1970s by the U.S. Commission on Civil Rights showed that Chicano schools tended to have lower expenditures per student than Anglo schools and were physically inferior, less well supplied, and less favorably staffed. Chicanos have been excessively and incorrectly assigned to classes for the mentally retarded, and they have traditionally been "tracked" into vocational rather than college preparatory programs. Part of the problem may be that Chicanos are poorly represented among teachers (only 4 percent of elementary and secondary teachers in the Southwest in 1970) in relation to their share of the student population (17 percent in 1970). Viewed from another perspective, there was a ratio of only one Chicano teacher per 120 Chicano students in the Southwest, contrasted with one black teacher per 39 black students and one Anglo teacher per 20 Anglo students.

Chicanos are also severely underrepresented among elected officials, partially because thousands of Mexican immigrants have lived in the United States for decades without obtaining U.S. citizenship. With Mexico so close, many plan to return home, although these dreams often go unfulfilled. Some immigrants, although harboring no desire to return to Mexico, have refused to surrender their Mexican citizenship. In comparison to immigrants from other countries, Mexicans have been more reluctant to become naturalized citizens. From 1959 to 1966, only 2.4 to 5.0 percent annually of those eligible became U.S. citizens, in contrast to 23 to 33 percent of other immigrants with comparable lengths of residence. Registered Mexican-

American voters do turn out at the polls about as much as other ethnic groups (over 81 percent in 1972, compared to 80 percent of black registered voters and 86 percent of Irish-American registered voters), but the high percentage of noncitizens and the comparatively low number of registered voters have sharply limited the electoral power of the group.

Other factors have contributed to Chicano electoral underrepresentation. In 1977 a California legislative committee on elections partially attributed the Chicanos' limited representation on city councils in cities with significant Chicano populations to the predominant use of citywide at-large elections instead of district elections. In 42 such cities in California, there were no Chicano council members at all. The committee argued that local at-large elections prevent "minority voters from exercising their potential political weight," since "their votes disappear in a sea of majority group votes." On the other hand, some contend that at-large elections make it less likely that candidates will write off minority votes as irrelevant, as can happen in ward-based contests.

When it comes to military service, combat decorations, and wartime casualties, Chicanos have been overrepresented in terms of population. Because of their lower educational attainment and restricted employment opportunities, many Chicanos have chosen to enter military service, and because they are underrepresented in higher education, they have not benefited from student deferments as frequently as Anglos.

The 1970 report of the U.S. Commission on Civil Rights, *Mexican Americans and the Administration of Justice in the Southwest,* documented unequal treatment by law-enforcement agencies and the judicial system. Among widespread abuses cited in this and other studies are the lack of bilingual translators in court proceedings; underrepresentation of Chicanos on grand juries, as judges, and as law-enforcement officers; unequal assignment of punishments and probation to convicted Chicanos; excessive patrolling of Chicano barrios; anti-Mexican prejudice among police and judicial officials; and wrongful use of law-enforcement agencies in the search for undocumented aliens. This negative side of the post–World War II experience provided background and impetus for the Chicano movement of the 1960s and 1970s, which has brought the most significant challenge in American history to the inequitable conditions faced by Chicanos.

Ties with the Homeland

Only Canadian immigrants share with Chicanos the experience of having the homeland as a next-door neighbor with a common border. For Chicanos this experience has meant linguistic and cultural continuity, ease of physical migration, maintenance of familial ties, and simplified commercial and labor interchange. Mexicans have constantly crossed and recrossed the U.S.-Mexican border. Along with immigrants and those who live and work temporarily in the United States, some Mexicans commute to work in the United States, and both Mexicans and Chicanos cross the border continuously to shop, visit family and friends, and tour. The obvious result has been reinforcement of the Spanish language, of Mexican culture, and of Chicano ties to Mexico.

Mexican media and publications have had a strong impact on Chicanos, particularly near the border, because radio and television stations are within receiving range. In addition, Spanish-language radio and television stations in the United States make heavy use of programs from Mexico. Mexican newspapers and magazines are distributed in the United States with little delay, and Mexican books and magazines are sold in many Spanish-language bookstores. Along with constant personal contact, the media have helped maintain ethnic consciousness and cultural cohesiveness among Chicanos.

Since the Treaty of Guadalupe Hidalgo, the Mexican government has played a significant if varying role in relation to Chicanos. Throughout the remainder of the 19th century, it made sporadic efforts to assist them in their struggles for civil and property rights, for instance, by protesting against discriminatory U.S. local, state, and federal laws and procedures. In the early 1870s a Mexican government border investigating commission issued a landmark report that publicized the repressive conditions under which Tejanos were living. In the 20th century the large-scale Mexican immigration increased pressures on the Mexican government. Mexican consulates, in particular, provided a number of services, such as facilitating movement between the two countries, cooperating with the U.S. government in the Repatriation Program of the 1930s, and supporting and sponsoring Mexican organizations and commemorations of Mexican holidays. The celebrations have sometimes reflected the periodic Mexican government policy of encouraging *Mexicanidad* (Mexican consciousness) among immigrants. Where there were no consuls, Mexican honorary commissions provided occasional services.

At times when Mexican Americans complained of abusive and unfair treatment, the Mexican government intervened decisively. Following the establishment of the Bracero Program, it protested against mistreatment of Mexicans in Texas, and, when conditions did not improve, removed Texas from the list of states eligible to hire braceros. This and other actions brought some improvement of conditions under which braceros worked and lived. But Chicanos were not always satisfied with the actions of the Mexican government or local Mexican consulates. There were charges that Mexican officials in the United States refused to respond to immigrants' complaints or acted without vigor for fear of antagonizing federal, state, or local authorities.

While the interest of the Mexican government in the welfare of Mexicans in the United States has ebbed and flowed, recent governments have demonstrated a willingness to speak out on Chicano matters. Presidents Luis Echevarría and José López Portillo invited Chicanos to Mexico to discuss how the Mexican government could strengthen ties and help support Chicano aspirations.

Chicano Culture

Language Despite the continuing impact of Mexican culture and the inevitable reflection of mainstream American influences, Chicano culture has developed its own internal dynamism, creativity, and forces of change. Intrinsic to that culture is the Spanish language. Even though English is the primary language of

Mexican Americans, the use of Spanish has persisted strongly, in part because of segregation. Isolated in barrios and colonias, older Chicanos in particular have not had to speak English. Spanish is spoken at home and in shops; services can be obtained in Spanish; newspapers, radio, and television provide news in Spanish; and Spanish-language movies provide entertainment. Mexican work crews have often been supervised in Spanish, and Spanish remains the primary language in many communities, particularly in southern Texas, northern New Mexico, and southern Colorado, and many Anglo residents there learn Spanish.

As with other foreign-rooted ethnic groups, there has been some decline in the use of the language of heritage, in particular among U.S.-born Chicanos. Increasing education, acculturation, dispersal outside of the Southwest, and exodus from barrios have contributed to the decline. For years most public schools discouraged the use of Spanish in the classroom and during recesses, although this is no longer the case. By the late 1970s the federal government was spending over $100 million a year to support Spanish bilingual education programs.

The continuation of significant immigration from Mexico has helped keep the language alive by reinforcing the use of Spanish by the American-born, expanding the number of Spanish speakers, and enlarging the Spanish-language media market. The Chicano movement of the 1960s and 1970s has also contributed to a Spanish-language renaissance. Increased pride and interest in their heritage gave Chicanos a greater desire to develop their command of Spanish. Even for those who no longer live in barrios or whose families do not speak Spanish, the language has attained a symbolic importance that encourages language maintenance. Like Spanish-speakers elsewhere in the Western Hemisphere, Chicanos have created new words and local variants. In areas where Chicanos have had considerable contact with the wider society, English words have been Hispanicized and assimilated into Spanish syntax. Although there are regional variations, the most common form of Chicano Spanish is *caló*. In sharp contrast to *caló* is the classical Spanish spoken in isolated communities of northern New Mexico and southern Colorado, which received little postconquest Mexican immigration and therefore have been less influenced by modern Mexican Spanish.

Family The family is the center of Mexican culture. In U.S. society, the term usually refers to the nuclear family—parents and children, with an occasional live-in grandparent. But among Hispanics throughout the hemisphere, including Chicanos, the *familia* has traditionally been extended—not only parents and children, but also grandparents, uncles, aunts, and cousins, by blood or by marriage. Because of their close ties, when individual members relocate, other family members may follow the migrants to their new locale to draw the family back together.

Among Chicanos extended-family gatherings are regular and frequent, sometimes every weekend. They have a strong sense of familial, rather than simply individual, identity, and individuals feel a deep sense of family obligation, including maintenance of family honor and respect. They are often committed to mutual assistance within the family, a factor that sometimes keeps Chicanos from turning to public agencies or social services for assistance. Elderly Mexicans, for instance, are rarely placed in retirement homes; in the traditional family, where older people have a special status, such a decision would be almost unthinkable.

Roles are clearly defined in the traditional Chicano family. The father has always been the acknowledged head, although his authority is often more formal and symbolic than real. More power may be in the hands of the mother, who generally controls the nurturing of the children and is the source and transmitter of cultural knowledge and traditions. The grandparents (*abuelos*) receive special love and respect for their experience and wisdom, and in turn they provide a special warmth for the grandchildren.

Time has taken its toll on these traditional characteristics, though many, perhaps even most, contemporary Mexican-American families continue to exhibit some or all of them. At least three major factors have contributed to their erosion. First, the process of acculturation to American life, including education, has drawn many Chicanos out of the tight family network, particularly the young and the American-born. Second, increasing geographical and residential mobility has disrupted the family, which depends on physical closeness and constant interaction to function in its complete traditional sense. Third, there has been increasing intermarriage with non-Chicanos, particularly among white-collar workers and the American-born.

One element of family life is the practice of *compadrazgo*, which can be translated roughly as godparentage. Traditionally godparents assume serious obligations toward their godchildren and become invitational family members thereby. On large farms and ranches, it was common for the landowner to become the compadre to many of the offspring of his workers. Like the traditional family, compadrazgo has been declining, particularly in cities, where pressures on Chicanos to acculturate are greater and where the dynamics of urban life strain traditional practices. The extended family and compadrazgo, common throughout Latin America and in many Mediterranean nations, have been brought to the United States by immigrants from these areas as well. Although these traditional structures and practices have eroded among all immigrant groups, it is likely that they have survived more widely among Mexican Americans because of their historical isolation, residential segregation, continuing immigration, geographical proximity to Mexico, and deep commitment to these social institutions.

Chicano Expression Mexican food has probably had a wider impact on American life than has any other expression of Chicano culture. Such foods as tacos, tostadas, enchiladas, carnitas, and tamales have achieved wide national popularity. The true aficionado savors the varieties of Chicano food intrinsic to different parts of the United States, as well as the distinct culinary styles adapted from the many regions of Mexico. More apparent is the nationwide explosion of Mexican fast-food outlets. While hardly the acme of Mexican cuisine, they represent one omnipresent Chicano cultural influence on mainstream American society.

Next to food, music and dance are the most popular aspects of Mexican culture in the United States. Mariachi music, which blends brass and strings, and dances such as the *jarabe tapatío* are commonly viewed as

"typical" Mexican music, although there are many Mexican regional musical forms and many varieties of Chicano music. At one end of the historical spectrum are the religious and traditional secular songs and dances of northern New Mexico. Most contemporary is *salsa,* the popular pan-Latino musical style. More restrictively Chicano is the Tex-Mex music of south Texas (also known as *música norteña*), which originated in the early 20th century from Chicano encounters with the music of German Americans, particularly in New Braunfels, Tex. Chicanos added their own instrumentation and musical variations to the German polka rhythm, and traditional Tex-Mex *polkeros* still feature the accordion and bass, while more contemporary groups use horns, drums, and electric instruments, as well as innovations from jazz, rock, and country and western music. Although Tex-Mex music began as purely instrumental, Chicanos added vocals and increasingly have used the lyrics to portray and comment on the Chicano experience.

One generic form of Chicano music is based on guitar and voice, with a wide variety of both solo guitar and accompanied vocal styles. The songs known as *corridos* have served not only as a form of popular musical expression, but also at times as a kind of oral history, capturing the exploits of Chicano heroes and the experiences of the people. As most corrido composers have not put their music and words on paper, recent efforts to tape and preserve corridos are significant steps in musical and historical maintenance.

Chicano artists, particularly in the 20th century, have worked in painting, drawing, sculpture, and lithography and in recent years have developed a full-scale art movement. Possibly the two most distinctive vehicles of contemporary Chicano art are murals and graffiti, the former harking back to the tradition of the great Mexican muralists of the postrevolution era. Mural themes include the Mexican Revolution and depictions of the Chicano experience. This form of visual expression, a true people's art oriented toward the whole community rather than the few in the art gallery, can be seen on outside walls of stores and public buildings, in public parks, and even on freeway support pillars, often blended imaginatively with architectural elements. Some barrio gangs have become involved in mural painting, at times using murals as boundary lines between their territories.

The pop-art companion to mural art as a symbol of barrio expression is Chicano graffiti. Unlike the crude or clever sayings and rhymes written on public walls, Chicano graffiti consists of purposefully conceived sets of symbols or symbolic words, notable for their careful, angular lettering. Barrio gangs generally have developed their own special symbols—*placas*—to denote their territory or their presence on the turf of other groups. Some Chicano muralists have integrated graffiti into their work, at times incorporating existing graffiti by painting around the symbols.

Along with the movement in the visual arts has come a literary one. Contemporary Chicano writers have published novels, poetry, short stories, essays, and plays. Two special characteristics are common to much of this writing: first, it generally emphasizes Mexican-American culture and experience, especially the theme of Anglo prejudice, discrimination, and exploitation;

and second, it is often bilingual, usually written primarily in English incorporating some Spanish words and phrases, though some works, particularly poetry, are entirely in Spanish.

One distinctive aspect of current Chicano expression is the *teatro* (theater). Most famous is the Teatro Campesino (Farm Workers' Theater), founded in 1965 by Luis Valdez as a component of César Chávez's United Farm Workers movement, but now an independent organization. The teatro also emphasizes themes of Anglo discrimination, Chicano resistance, and Mexican heritage. Productions blend English and Spanish and often include music. Some presentations consist of a series of brief *actos,* although the teatro also offers full-length plays. Using a style in which the players interact directly with the audience, Teatro Campesino has attained broad popularity and has inspired the creation of other teatros in barrios and universities throughout the country. Some university teatros disappeared upon the graduation of their founders and early leaders, but other groups have managed to survive despite constant financial pressures. Since 1970, grouped as Teatros Nacionales de Aztlán (TENAZ, National Theaters of Aztlán), Chicano teatros have held an annual national festival. One artistic trend has been away from the *teatro popular* toward a more professional theater and greater use of English, partially owing to increased professional training, the growth of American-born Chicano audiences, and the attempt to attract non-Chicano audiences.

Related to the literary boom has been the expansion of Chicano publications as a whole, including newspapers, magazines, and scholarly journals. Chicano newspapers have existed since the 1850s, with more than 130 established during the 19th century. However, most have had limited circulations and even more limited lifespans, primarily for two reasons: first, the Chicano population remained relatively small until the early 20th century, and the reading public was even smaller because of limited literacy; and second, the papers were plagued by undercapitalization and limited local advertising. That they achieved even a limited success, particularly during the 19th century, is a tribute to the determination of Chicano journalists.

This determination paid off in the 20th century when some Chicano newspapers, such as *La Prensa* (f. 1913) of San Antonio and *La Opinión* (f. 1926) of Los Angeles became permanent features of large urban communities. Some 250 Chicano newspapers were established from 1900 to 1960, although most did not last. The impetus of the Chicano movement in the 1960s and 1970s brought a rapid expansion of the press, and some 100 newspapers were being published in the late 1970s. The problems of undercapitalization and of educating large institutional advertisers to the potential of the Mexican-American market remain, however.

Older Chicano newspapers and those in areas with large numbers of Mexican immigrants usually include a high proportion of news from Mexico. In contrast, newspapers of recent vintage and those published in areas with a small immigrant population tend to emphasize Chicano-related news. Similarly, older newspapers are more likely to be in Spanish, and the more recently established ones tend to be either in English or in a mixture of both.

Chicanos have also established publishing enter-

prises, either privately or through universities. Their novels, short stories, and poetry, as well as literary and scholarly journals, tend to focus more on the Chicano experience and culture than on Mexico. In addition there are general-circulation magazines, such as *La Luz* (The Light), *Nuestro* (Our), *Somos* (We Are), and *Agenda*; most are in English.

Spanish is heard on a growing number of U.S. radio and television stations. During the 1970s more than 500 radio and 70 television stations broadcast partially or totally in Spanish, and the Spanish International Network (SIN) consisted of some 15 stations. In 1977, 41 southwestern radio stations devoted more than 50 percent of their air time to Spanish-language broadcasts.

The contrasting uses of Spanish and English reflect the different nature of printed and broadcast media. Chicano literature, magazines, and scholarly publications reach a more limited, educated audience throughout the country. Radio and television stations, on the other hand, focus on local populations, mainly in large urban areas of the Southwest where Spanish is a major medium of communication, at least verbally. San Antonio, Los Angeles, and San Francisco have the highest concentrations of Spanish-language stations. Most stations give considerable emphasis to local events and Chicano culture, particularly music, but they also broadcast music and programs from Mexico, especially soap operas and other serials.

The newest surge of expression has come in the field of motion pictures. Chicano filmmakers have expanded from documentaries to feature films, sometimes with the help of Mexico City studios. Los Angeles, quite naturally, has been the most active movie-making area, and several independent Chicano production companies are located there, but film enterprises have also been established in other parts of the Southwest. The 1977 annual Chicano Film Festival in San Antonio drew 7,000 people to view 55 films and videotapes.

THE CHICANO MOVEMENT AND THE FUTURE

Rising from the turbulent 1960s and drawing on the century-long foundation of Mexican-American experience, the Chicano movement has become a dynamic force for social change. The movement is not monolithic but is rather an amalgam of individuals and organizations that share a sense of pride in Mexicanidad, a dedication to the enhancement of Chicano culture, a desire to improve the Chicano socioeconomic position, and a commitment to making constructive changes in American society. A major focus has been politics. Political goals have included increasing the number of Chicano candidates, convincing non-Chicano candidates to commit themselves to the needs of the Mexican-American community, conducting broad-scale voter registration and community organization drives, working for the appointment of more Chicanos in government, and supporting the passage of legislation. Some Chicanos have chosen to work through the two major political parties or through theoretically nonpartisan organizations, such as the Mexican-American Political Association and the Political Association of Spanish-Speaking Organizations.

In 1974 two Chicanos were elected to governorships —Jerry Apodaca in New Mexico (where Chicanos won six of eight state offices) and Raul Castro in Arizona. They were the first Chicano governors since Ezequiel C. de Baca and Octaviano Larrazolo in the early years of New Mexico statehood. In the 1976 presidential election, Chicanos provided Jimmy Carter significant margins of votes in both Texas and Ohio. In Texas, which Carter won by less than 130,000 votes, Chicanos gave him a margin of more than 200,000. In Ohio, which Carter carried by some 11,000 votes, Hispanics (mainly Chicanos and Puerto Ricans) contributed a net gain of 18,000 votes. In an effort to cut into the traditionally Democratic Hispanic vote (81 percent for Carter in 1976), Republicans created a Republican National Hispanic Assembly, rivaling the Democratic National Committee's Hispanic Affairs Division.

Some Chicanos have channeled their political efforts through the Partido de la Raza Unida (PRU, United People's party). Founded in south Texas by José Angel Gutiérrez, PRU has worked to elect candidates to office in counties and communities with Chicano majorities, as well as statewide. Beginning in 1970 with a victory in the Crystal City school board elections, the party has won numerous school-board, city-council, and county positions. Chicanos have established PRUs elsewhere in the country, resulting in some school board and city council victories, but generally without the consistent success they have had in Texas.

Chicanos have given considerable attention to economic change. Goals and strategies have varied—upgrading occupations, creating more private businesses (called brown capitalism), and forming cooperative community development enterprises, for example. The most visible and dramatic aspect of the Chicano economic struggle has been the United Farm Workers movement, led by César Chávez (1927–).

Chávez has led thousands of agricultural workers, mainly Chicanos, in the struggle for better pay, improved working conditions, more favorable contracts, and the right to unionize. UFW tactics have included strikes, boycotts of targeted products, and lobbying for passage of favorable legislation. In his uphill struggle Chávez has had to contend not only with resistant agribusinesses and their legislative and law enforcement supporters, but also with the Teamsters' Union, which until 1976 challenged the UFW for the right to represent California field workers. Though California is the home base and center of UFW activities, Chávez has worked increasingly toward unionizing workers in other states. Beyond attaining financial benefits and improved conditions for farm workers, Chávez has also been a galvanizing spirit of the Chicano movement and an educational force for awakening the public to problems faced by Chicanos.

While Chávez was organizing California farm workers, Hispanos in New Mexico were organizing for a different economic goal—the recovery of communal lands lost following the U.S. conquest. This movement was led by Reies López Tijerina, founder of the Alianza Federal de Mercedes (Federal Alliance of Land Grants), which at one time claimed 20,000 members. In addition to working through the legal system and attempting to convince government officials of the validity of their cause, *aliancistas* also resorted to direct action, including attempted citizens' arrests of a local district attorney in the Tierra Amarilla courthouse and of Forest Ser-

vice rangers for trespassing on land claimed by the Alianza in Kit Carson National Forest. The latter effort resulted in a two-year imprisonment for Tijerina. The Alianza has not had the dramatic successes of either the UFW or the Texas Partido de la Raza Unida.

The public schools have long been a primary target of Mexican-American reformers. Well before the U.S. Supreme Court outlawed school segregation in the *Brown* v. *Topeka Board of Education* decision of 1954, Chicanos had challenged educational discrimination. In 1946 *Méndez* v. *Westminster School District* resulted in the banning of separate Chicano schools in California. Two years later *Delgado* v. *Bastrop Independent School District* reaffirmed this position in Texas. Yet the U.S. Civil Rights Commission pointed out that in the late 1960s two-thirds of the Chicanos in Texas and a quarter of those in California attended schools that were more than 50 percent Chicano.

Some Texas school districts responded to the outlawing of segregation by integrating Chicano and black schools, leaving Anglo schools untouched. Two Texas court decisions were at odds on this issue in the 1970s. *Cisneros* v. *Corpus Christi Independent School District* held that Mexican Americans were an identifiable ethnic minority and thereby fell under the *Brown* rubric. In contrast a Houston circuit court in *Ross* v. *Eckels* classified Mexican Americans as Caucasians and thereby accepted black-Chicano desegregation as fulfilling the letter of the law.

The Chicano movement has striven for a variety of educational goals, including reduction of school dropout rates, improvement of educational attainment, development of bilingual-bicultural programs, expansion of higher education fellowships and support services, creation of courses and programs in Chicano studies, and an increase in the number of Chicano teachers and administrators. The objectives of the traditional campaign for desegregation are not always easy to reconcile with those of the newer drive for bilingual-bicultural education. In a seeming turnabout after years of struggling for desegregation, some Mexican-American leaders recently have taken strong stands against crosstown busing in such communities as Los Angeles, fearing that dispersion of Chicano students will prevent them from participating in hard-won bilingual educational programs.

At times Chicanos have adopted traditional tactics of working quietly through existing channels or attempting to elect Chicano or pro-Chicano school-board members. Other times, out of frustration, they have turned to walkouts, sit-ins, and direct confrontation with school boards and administrations. Students have provided much of the effort toward educational reform through such organizations as the United Mexican-American Students (UMAS), Mexican American Youth Organization (MAYO), and Movimiento Estudiantil Chicano de Aztlán (MECHA, Chicano Student Movement of the Southwest). The movement has also spurred establishment of alternative schools and institutions of higher education. In 1969 the first Chicano college, Colegio Jacinto Treviño, was founded in Mission, Tex. Other colleges and universities founded in the 1970s include Colegio César Chávez (Mount Angel, Ore.), Universidad de la Tierra (Goshen, Calif.), Hispanic International University (Houston, Tex.), Univer-

sidad de Campesinos Libres (Fresno, Calif.), Juárez–Lincoln Center (Austin, Tex.), and Deganawida-Quetzalcoatl University (Davis, Calif.), the first Chicano–American Indian university.

Among other institutions affected by the Chicano movement is the Catholic church. Although historically, many priests have worked on their own with Mexican Americans, the church as an institution tended to avoid involvement in Chicano social issues. During the Repatriation Program, for example, the church generally remained silent and did little to help those affected. Although some Catholic priests and Protestant clergymen have taken their place alongside César Chávez and his followers, priests serving in strike areas have often withheld their support for the strikers so as not to alienate growers. Not until 1943 did the church even hold a conference of Catholic leaders involved with Mexican Americans. In that year the Social Action Department of the National Catholic Welfare Conference sponsored a meeting in San Antonio that ultimately led to the establishment of the Bishops' Committee for the Spanish-Speaking, under the Chicago-based American Board of Catholic Missions.

The Chicano movement generated such organizations as Católicos por la Raza (Catholics for the Chicano People), which challenged the church for pouring its money into opulent structures while neglecting social services to improve conditions for the Chicano poor. Some critics addressed the church's failure to recruit and promote Chicano priests. Although Chicanos constitute about two-thirds of the Catholic population in the Southwest and more than 20 percent of Catholics nationally, only one Chicano bishop was appointed between 1850 and 1970. Owing to the impact of the Chicano movement and the broader Hispanic movement, the church by 1977 had appointed eight Hispanic bishops in the United States—an improvement, though that is still less than 3 percent of the number of American bishops. In 1977 Hispanics made up 27 percent of U.S. Catholics, yet only 585 or slightly more than 1 percent of the 56,000 priests in the United States were Hispanics and only 185 of these were born in the United States.

Other changes have occurred within the Catholic church. In 1969 Chicano priests formed the Padres Asociados para Derechos Religiosos, Educativos y Sociales (PADRES, Priests United for Religious, Educational, and Social Rights), an activist national organization, which was followed by Las Hermanas (The Sisters), an organization of Latina nuns. In 1972, 1,100 Catholic clergy and laity gathered in Washington, D.C., for the Primer Encuentro Nacional Hispano de Pastoral. That national conference and a later meeting in 1977 made strong recommendations for church reform, including bilingual-bicultural education in parochial schools and seminaries, increased Latino representation in the church hierarchy, full amnesty for undocumented aliens, and greater efforts by the church to reach out to the people.

One of the continuing problems within the Chicano community is that of barrio gangs. Particularly for frustrated Chicano youth, these gangs have provided a strong, if transitory, sense of identity and attachment. At best, gangs provide comradeship and community services. At worst, defense of turf and honor has re-

sulted at times in violence, often against members of rival gangs. Many Chicano leaders have made special efforts to reduce gang violence and channel members' energies into constructive pursuits.

Along with politics, economics, education, and religion, the Chicano movement has generated change in many other aspects of society and has spawned an enormous number of Chicano organizations, such as the Mexican-American Legal Defense and Educational Fund, headed in the late 1970s by Vilma Martínez, which has brought court challenges, has worked to reduce anti-Chicano activities of law enforcement agencies, and has sought other reforms in the legal system. Denver's Crusade for Justice, led by Rodolfo "Corky" Gonzales, has provided legal, medical, educational, civil rights, and financial services to Chicanos and has sponsored Chicano Youth Liberation Conferences; the National Chicano Moratorium coordinated Chicano protests against the war in Vietnam. Chicanos in a wide variety of fields have formed professional organizations, such as La Raza National Lawyers' Association, the Association of Mexican-American Educators, and the Mexican-American Engineering Society.

The Mexican-American women's movement is linked to the more generalized women's liberation movement, but it also specifically seeks to free Mexican-American women from some of their traditional cultural role limitations. Yet many activist Chicanas feel that the feminist movement is at times insensitive to minority women and that its emphasis on individual fulfillment conflicts with strong Mexican familial and cooperative values. In the late 1970s some 40 independent Mexican-American women's organizations existed at the state and national levels. These groups have worked toward improving educational opportunities, raising Chicana consciousness, advocating women's rights, and providing counseling and support systems. Mexican-American women have strongly presented their positions at Latino and women's conferences and have struggled for more significant roles and positions within local and national organizations.

The Chicano movement is not the whole story of contemporary Mexican Americans, nor has it won the unanimous support of the group. Some question whether militant ethnic solidarity is the best tactic for advancement, but the movement has been a galvanizing force for change, whatever its ultimate effects prove to be.

Another trend, symbolized by the formation of the Forum of National Hispanic Organizations, is the development of a broader pan-Hispanic identity and sense of community among the numerous and diverse Latino groups in the United States. Numbers alone do not bring power, however, particularly if those numbers are not transformed into votes. In 1976 only 2.7 million of the nearly 5.0 million eligible Hispanics were registered to vote (54 percent, compared to 74 percent of Americans in general); furthermore, only 70 percent of the registered Hispanics voted, compared to 75 percent of registered Americans in general. Viewed another way, while 55 percent of all those eligible to vote cast a ballot in 1976, only 38 percent of eligible Latinos did so. The potential exists, however, for Latinos to become a more significant political force by increasing their rate of naturalization, voter registration, and voting. If Mex-

icans, Puerto Ricans, Cubans, and other Central and South Americans work toward cooperation and fulfillment of common goals, pan-Hispanic activities and efforts could have a major impact on American life.

Conditions in Mexico will continue to affect the Chicano future. The high Mexican birthrate of 3.5 children per couple could bring a doubling of Mexico's population (over 60 million in 1975) by the 21st century. Yet Mexican unemployment in the late 1970s was already extremely high, 40 percent according to some estimates. In 1975, 800,000 Mexicans entered the work force, but only 300,000 new jobs were created. Continued pressure for migration to the United States seems inevitable. U.S. interest in Mexican oil could lead to a greater willingness to accept Mexican immigrants as part of an oil exchange agreement.

Chicanos will play an increasingly significant role in the United States, if for no other reason than demography—the fact that immigration and high birthrates have made them one of the fastest growing ethnic groups in the United States. They are also moving into all occupations and areas of American life, strengthening pan-Hispanic ties, and breaking down the regional isolation that for so long separated and hampered them. With more education and experience, Chicanos are developing the skills and resources for dealing effectively with the wider society.

Bibliography
The most complete single source is Leo Grebler, Joan W. Moore, and Ralph C. Guzmán, *The Mexican American People: The Nation's Second Largest Minority* (New York, 1970). Joan W. Moore (with Harry Pachón), *Mexican Americans*, rev. ed. (Englewood Cliffs, N.J., 1976), and Ellwyn R. Stoddard, *Mexican Americans* (New York, 1973), provide more succinct sociological introductions. In *The Chicano Political Experience: Three Perspectives* (North Scituate, Mass., 1977), F. Chris García and Rudolph O. de la Garza present a brief political interpretation.

Carey McWilliams, *North from Mexico: The Spanish-Speaking People of the United States* (1948; reprint, New York, 1968) remains a classic, although somewhat dated, historical overview. Matt S. Meier and Feliciano Rivera, in *The Chicanos: A History of Mexican Americans* (New York, 1972), cover Chicano history through the 1960s; Rodolfo Acuña, *Occupied America: The Chicano's Struggle toward Liberation* (San Francisco, 1972), is a more passionate analysis. Mario Barrera, *Race and Class in the Southwest: A Theory of Racial Inequality* (Notre Dame, Ind., 1979), presents a heavily economic interpretation of Chicano history.

Anthologies and collections of documents on Chicano history include David J. Weber, *Foreigners in Their Native Land: Historical Roots of the Mexican Americans* (Albuquerque, N.Mex., 1973); Manuel P. Servín, *An Awakened Minority: The Mexican-Americans*, 2d ed. (Beverly Hills, Calif., 1974); Wayne Moquin (with Charles Van Doren), *A Documentary History of the Mexican Americans* (New York, 1971); and Renato Rosaldo, Robert A. Calvert, and Gustav L. Seligmann, *Chicano: The Evolution of a People* (Minneapolis, 1973). Two major reprint series, the 21-volume *The Mexican American* (New York, 1974), and the 55-volume *The Chicano Heritage* (New York, 1976), edited by Carlos E. Cortés, form a rich basic source. Scholarly journals devoted to Mexican Americans include *Aztlán: International Journal of Chicano Studies Research* (Los Angeles), *The Journal of Mexican American History* (Santa Barbara, Calif.), and *Atisbos: Journal of Chicano Research* (Stanford, Calif.).

Most southwestern state historical societies and university libraries, as well as a growing number outside of the Southwest, now have reasonable holdings of publications on Mexican Americans. Some libraries—such as those of the University of Texas (Austin), University of New Mexico (Albuquerque), University of California (Berkeley), and University of California (Los Angeles)—have interesting collections of Chicano primary materials. Numerous Chicano Studies programs have established their own useful libraries, often with special emphases, such as the retrospective collection of Mexican-American newspapers being developed at the University of California, Berkeley.

CARLOS E. CORTÉS

MIAMIS: *see* AMERICAN INDIANS

MICCOSUKEES: *see* AMERICAN INDIANS

MICMACS: *see* AMERICAN INDIANS

MICRONESIANS: *see* PACIFIC ISLANDERS

MISSOURIS: *see* AMERICAN INDIANS

MIWOKS: *see* AMERICAN INDIANS

MODOCS: *see* AMERICAN INDIANS

MOHAVES: *see* AMERICAN INDIANS

MOHAWKS: *see* AMERICAN INDIANS

MOHEGANS: *see* AMERICAN INDIANS

MONGOLIAN BUDDHISTS: *see* KALMYKS

MONOS: *see* AMERICAN INDIANS

MONTAUKS: *see* AMERICAN INDIANS

MONTENEGRINS: *see* SERBS

MORAVIANS: *see* CZECHS; GERMANS

MORMONS

The Mormons are perhaps the only American ethnic group whose principal migration began as an effort to move out of the United States. Moreover, this migration of the main body of Mormons from western Illinois to the Rocky Mountains in the late 1840s imprinted upon the group a self-consciousness gained through prior experience in the Midwest. The Mormons have been influenced subsequently by ritual tales of privation, wandering, and delivery under God's hand, precisely as the Jews have been influenced by their stories of the Exodus. A significant consequence of this tradition has been the development of an enduring sense of territoriality that has given a distinctive cast to Mormon group consciousness. It differentiates the Mormons from members of other sects and lends support to the judgment of sociologist Thomas F. O'Dea that the Mormons "represent the clearest example to be found in our national history of the evolution of a native and indigenously developed ethnic minority."

ORIGINS

The Mormons are the product of a religious movement begun in 1830 by Joseph Smith, Jr. (1805–1844), third son in an upstate New York farming family. Disturbed by the competing claims of various churches to divine favor, Smith in 1820 prayed for guidance. The ensuing religious experiences reported by Smith served to unify his own family and those of his friends in a new faith seen by his followers as a "restoration" of primitive Christianity in preparation for the return of the Savior. Within a short time Smith had gone beyond the millennialist and restorationist concerns of such con-

temporaries as William C. Miller and Alexander Campbell. He claimed that as part of his prophetic mission he had been instructed to restore "all things," by which he meant God's most significant communications to man from all previous Judeo-Christian revelatory epochs or "dispensations." In maintaining that Christ's earthly ministry was pivotal but not an all-encompassing or final revelatory epoch, Smith made himself a pariah among the divines of restorationist and millennialist sects.

Smith began to draw heavily from the Old Testament and over the next several years instituted the building of temples, an elaborate temple ritual, the practice of plural marriage (technically polygyny, but commonly referred to as polygamy), and a series of related doctrines and practices. He drew also from precedents in the Book of Mormon, an additional book of scriptures he claimed to have translated from records inscribed on goldlike plates provided by an angel, which described the religious history of a pre-Columbian group of New World Christians. For the rest of his life Smith endeavored to build the disparate thousands who became his followers into a unified, orderly, covenanted society. He taught that the Latter-day Saints, as they called themselves, were a people whose special relationship to God through their prophets would prepare them for a unique and critical role in the Christian eschatological scheme. Smith's early followers seemed to be seeking within the authoritarian structure and social order of the Prophet's revealed religion a haven from the chaotic and centrifugal tendencies they saw about them in Jacksonian America. Profoundly attracted to the liberal, republican ideologies of ante-bellum America, they nonetheless feared the social consequences of such ideologies and sought refuge in Mormonism.

THE MIDWEST MIGRATIONS

Smith's earliest activities as a religious leader took place near his parents' home in Manchester township, N.Y., and the home of his parents-in-law near Harmony in north-central Pennsylvania. The Book of Mormon was printed in Palmyra, N.Y., in the early spring of 1830, and on April 6 of that year Smith and a few friends formally incorporated as the Church of Christ (changed in 1838 to the Church of Jesus Christ of Latter-day Saints).

Four of Smith's disciples undertook the first major missionary journey in the fall of 1830. Traveling through newly settled farming areas in northeastern Ohio, they preached to several congregations of Alexander Campbell's followers and attracted more than 100 converts, including an important minister, Sidney Rigdon (1793–1876). Within a short time there were more followers of the new faith in Ohio than in New York. In December 1830 Smith announced a revelation commanding the New York congregations to migrate to Ohio. (Smith's revelations, often recorded verbatim, were regarded by himself and his followers as direct communications from God.) This first Mormon migration, of perhaps 70 persons, was accomplished in the early months of 1831. The region around Kirtland, Ohio, a few miles east of Cleveland, became a major center of Mormon activity for the next seven years; the Prophet himself resided there during most of the period.

Smith made it clear as early as February 1831, however, that the Ohio settlements were staging areas for a more important migration to a site he would designate as "Zion" or "The New Jerusalem," which was to be a millennial administrative center. Revelations in July 1831 named Jackson County, Mo., which encompasses present-day Kansas City, then America's westernmost frontier, as the place where the Saints were to "gather." Migration and the purchase of land in Missouri began immediately.

Mormons gathering to Missouri from all parts of the country were asked to enter into a communal order called Consecration and Stewardship. Their different social values and rapidly increasing numbers quickly caused concern among earlier, non-Mormon Missouri settlers. The Mormons—almost all New Englanders, clannish, communal, and generally opposed to slavery—threatened to take over an area previously pioneered by migrants from the hill countries of Tennessee and Kentucky. The pro-slavery earlier settlers, unsuccessful in legal attempts to dislodge the newcomers, resorted to mob action in July 1833. They destroyed the Mormon press and threatened further violence if the Saints did not leave the country. By October the mob made good its threats; 1,200 or more Mormons fled northward across the Missouri into Clay County. In 1836 they were asked to move again and reached an informal agreement that a new county, Caldwell County, would be created in which they could settle.

Mormons settled in considerable numbers in Caldwell County and built a capital city, Far West, which by 1838 had an estimated population of 5,000. Early in that year the Kirtland Saints arrived; they had fled the Ohio center because of financial difficulties and bitter feelings arising from the failure of a bank sponsored by Mormon leaders. By autumn political differences between Mormons and non-Mormons in Missouri led to mutual distrust and hostility and in October the governor ordered that the Mormons be "exterminated or driven from the state." After numerous confrontations and several dozen deaths, Smith and a few close friends were taken into custody, and mobs once again moved into Mormon settlements. This time the Saints fled northeastward into Iowa and Illinois.

Smith escaped from prison in April and found his followers in Illinois, gathering near an undeveloped tract of land called Commerce. The Mormons renamed the site Nauvoo and began immediately to build a city. Under a liberal charter and fed by a stream of immigrants converted through remarkably successful missionary efforts in England, Canada, and the United States, Nauvoo grew rapidly. In 1844 secret plans were laid for establishing a political Kingdom of God, to be governed by a Council of Fifty which would include some non-Mormons and would be responsible for civil and temporal affairs generally. Early that same year Smith, unable in conscience to support either Henry Clay or James K. Polk for the U.S. presidency, declared himself a candidate. By that time, however, dissension between Mormons and non-Mormons was rising, stirred by apostates offended by the clandestine introduction in the early 1840s of the practice of plural marriage. In June Smith was taken into custody. On June 27 an armed mob broke into the Carthage, Ill., jail where Smith was confined and killed him and his brother.

THE EXODUS

The ensuing struggle for succession led to considerable splintering, but Brigham Young (1801–1877), president of the Council of the Twelve Apostles, quickly gained the confidence of most of Smith's followers and assumed leadership of the church. However, the Prophet's death did not resolve the basic differences between Mormons and non-Mormons in western Illinois. By February 1846 relations between the two groups had become so critical that abandonment of Nauvoo could no longer be delayed. The Mormons, feeling that U.S. officials had failed to protect their constitutional rights, began to organize wagon trains and cross the Mississippi westward into Iowa.

Variously estimated at between 10,000 and 15,000 people, the group moved across Iowa, settling temporarily along the Missouri in the present Omaha and Council Bluffs area. In the spring of 1847 migration began to an area then known as Upper California in Mexican Territory. Pioneer trains arrived in the Salt Lake Valley in late July. Some months later, in February 1848, the new homesite became part of the United States through the Treaty of Guadalupe Hidalgo. Subsequent migration brought most of the refugees from the Missouri to the Great Basin by 1852. Mormon converts from Europe and North America continued to follow the same route overland until 1869, after which time they traveled by rail.

Tales of "the exodus" or "the trek" occupy a large place in Mormon folk tradition. Whether or not their ancestors were involved in the migration, most Mormons can recall stories of sacrifice and heroism associated with the experience. Although the 800-mile overland journey was arduous, the Mormons probably suffered a lower mortality than non-Mormon companies making the same trip, because from the outset their migration was well planned to minimize hazards. Brigham Young announced a revelation in January 1847 that commanded organization of the "Camps of Israel" into groups of 10, 50, and 100 wagons supervised by appointed captains at each level, a pattern paralleling that of the ancient Israelites and followed in most subsequent Mormon migrations. Farm implements, seeds, tree cuttings, and other necessities for successful colonization were included among the supplies. Poor families were distributed among the trains so that a number of the better provided would be able to share responsibility for their well-being.

Transporting the residents of the Missouri River settlements to the Great Basin severely taxed the Mormons' resources but did not prevent church leaders from setting up at the same time an elaborate system for bringing European converts to the new-found Zion. Most European immigrants sailed from Liverpool on ships chartered by the church. In the United States, Mormon agents were stationed at port cities and along the overland route to make arrangements each season for transportation of complete immigrant companies to Salt Lake City. In the late 1860s, as the transcontinental railroad extended westward, church teams were sent to the railhead to escort the immigrants to the Mormon capital. Church officials assumed responsibility for placing new immigrants in temporary homes and jobs until permanent settlement could be arranged. Comple-

tion of the railroad in 1869 eased the logistical problems of transporting immigrants to Utah and greatly changed the nature of the migration and its impact upon its participants.

Through the Perpetual Emigrating Fund the church contributed considerably to the costs as well as the logistics of migration. This revolving fund was established in 1850 and continued in use until 1887 when the federal government, during an antipolygamy campaign, revoked its charter and seized its assets. During its nearly 40 years of operation the fund directly assisted some 50,000 European immigrants. Movement from the areas of Mormon mission activity occurred in distinct phases, paralleling the general migration to the United States from those same areas. Emigration from England, Scotland, and Wales began shortly after the first Mormon mission to England in 1837 and remained fairly strong throughout the rest of the century. Scandinavian emigration began in the 1850s, reached large proportions in the 1860s, and remained strong through the 1880s. Mormon missionaries of the period traveled through most of Europe, Asia, and Oceania but were most successful in Protestant countries, especially the British Isles, Scandinavia, and Germany. Total Mormon emigration from these areas up to 1957 is estimated at some 54,000 from Great Britain, 28,041 from Scandinavia, and 13,755 from Germany. Since the 19th-century missionaries urged their European converts to gather to Zion, the resultant emigration caused local congregations to be unstable and impermanent. Most European Mormons of the period accepted fully the spirit of a contemporary Mormon hymn, "Oh Babylon, Oh Babylon, we bid thee farewell,/We're going to the mountains of Ephraim to dwell."

SETTLEMENT IN THE GREAT BASIN

To these many thousands, dwelling amidst the mountains of Ephraim was far less pleasant in fact than it had been in prospect. The Great Basin was isolated, 800 miles in either direction from the nearest settlements. The high cost of imported goods made self-sufficiency a necessary goal, but the environment did not favor such an effort. Timber was scarce, the annual rainfall averaged only 12 to 15 inches, there was little arable land, and much of the area was inhabited by Shoshonean-speaking Indians. The most promising valleys of the region stretched along the western edge of the Wasatch Mountains, which run north and south through the middle of what is now Utah. Rising abruptly several thousand feet above the valley floors, they trap winter snows and distribute them evenly during the summer along a network of small rivers and streams—a system ideally suited to irrigated agriculture.

Colonization spread from the Salt Lake Valley to low valleys lying northward as far as Brigham City and southward to the subtropical region around present-day St. George. Outlying colonies were founded in the early 1850s in San Bernardino, Calif.; Las Vegas and Carson Valley, Nev.; and on the Salmon River in Idaho. But most of these settlements faltered for various reasons; those still viable in 1857 were abandoned and their inhabitants recalled when a federal army was sent to quell an alleged uprising among the Mormons. Despite such setbacks the population grew rapidly, increasing from

11,000 in 1850 to 41,000 in 1860 and 87,000 in 1870. As the early sites filled and began to strain the resources of the immediate environment, higher mountain valleys were settled until, beginning in the 1870s, it became necessary to send colonizing missions to Arizona, Nevada, New Mexico, and Wyoming, as well as Alberta, Canada, and Sonora and Chihuahua, Mexico. The normal pattern was to found a central town under church "call" and direction that then served as a base for the settlement of satellite villages. The last church-sponsored migration, beginning in 1900, was to the Big Horn Basin in northern Wyoming.

As Mormons colonized area after area, they developed a pattern of settlement that was replicated in nearly every colonization venture through the turn of the century. When the Mormons planned a colonizing mission, church authorities "called" specific families to participate in the venture, making certain that the group included men who possessed the skills and trades necessary to the colony's success. Church and often civil government for the new location were organized before departure (the two were in fact nearly indistinguishable). Leaders planned and organized the supplies and equipment, and the whole company departed on a prearranged date from a designated staging site. Once the colonists reached the new territory, they immediately began to survey and lay out the town and the farm plots, which, following instructions Joseph Smith had given in 1833, were outside of town. Thereafter, the colonists did their private work (the plowing of individual parcels or building a home) during time left from assigned public work—the building of canals, mills, fences, churches, and schools. After this initial planting, smaller towns were founded in the vicinity on a more individualistic basis. The physiognomy of Mormon towns was remarkably uniform because of the need to find land, water, and timber nearby and because the same layout and planning procedure were used in founding both "called" and spontaneously settled towns.

The practice of living within the town and farming outside it, rarely seen in the United States outside New England and Spanish-settled areas, fostered an intense social and religious life. The strong communal sentiment of the townsfolk was reinforced by doctrines contained in Smith's revelations and by deliberate church policy. Many of these towns remained only slightly altered until the 1920s, their traditional pattern of life established and reinforced over three generations. The western Mormon towns nurtured a provincial and religious self-consciousness into an incipient ethnicity.

Almost from its initial settlement, the limited resources of any one locality encouraged further migration of those forming new families. In the 20th century, however, the direction of this movement shifted from founding new agricultural towns to further populating the urban centers of Salt Lake City, Provo, and Ogden. In the 1930s and 1940s there was also substantial migration to cities in neighboring states, especially California. Nonetheless the proportion of Mormons in Utah's population continued to grow, aided by the return migration of the 1960s and 1970s and a continuing high birthrate. Mormons made up 56 percent of the Utah population in 1920 and 72 percent in 1970.

Mormon settlement did not observe state lines. One

authority has coined the term "Deseret Mormons" for the central body of Mormons raised in those areas of the West where Mormon influence predominates—primarily Utah; much of southeastern Idaho; Star Valley, the Bear River Valley, and the Big Horn Basin in Wyoming; the San Luis Valley in Colorado; the Ramah Valley in New Mexico; the Little Colorado River Valley in northern Arizona and certain towns in the Salt and Gila river valleys; a few towns in Chihuahua and Sonora, Mexico; extensive parts of southern Alberta, Canada; and a few localities in Washington, Oregon, and California. Deseret was the Mormon name for the state planned by Brigham Young shortly after the Mormons settled in the Great Basin, an entity much larger than the present boundaries of Utah.

During the 19th century, European converts to Mormonism were expected to leave their homeland and go to Deseret, where they were utterly dependent upon the Utah church leaders for both temporal and spiritual guidance. Under these circumstances the immigrants rapidly assimilated and use of their native languages soon died out. An early Mormon apostle expressed this rapid assimilation as an avowed aim of church leaders. After visiting a settlement where ethnic differences seemed to be inhibiting the development of a native iron industry in 1852, he reported: "We found a Scotch party, a Welch party, an English party, and an American party and we turned Iron Masters and undertook to put all these parties through the furnace, and run out a party of Saints for building up the Kingdom of God."

Brigham Young, in his efforts to counter the appeal of California in the 1840s, spoke of the Great Basin as a "good place to make Saints." He referred not just to the growth of piety, but to the development of a people sufficiently distinct in values and traditions from other Americans to be regarded as a separate nation; he even went so far as to encourage the development and use of a new alphabet to facilitate written communication among Saints and widen the gulf between Deseret and the rest of America. The present distinctiveness of the Mormon core or culture region suggests that Brigham Young succeeded in this effort better than he might have expected.

In the 20th century however, rapid growth outside the Deseret area has caused some observers to suggest that Mormon distinctiveness may eventually be lost through too great a geographic diffusion. Certainly there are gradations in the degree to which members of the church are imbued with the Mormon culture, but several factors seem to favor perpetuation of Deseret influence over the entire church membership for the foreseeable future. There were almost 4 million Mormons throughout the world in 1977; of these, over 1.4 million (36 percent) were from Utah, Idaho, Wyoming, Arizona, Nevada, Colorado, and New Mexico. This substantial minority exercises a commanding influence upon the church and church members elsewhere in the world.

Deseret Mormons are almost always agents in conversion to Mormonism, a process which in most cases results in the converts' abandoning old social relations and forming new ones within the church; converts are cut off from old values and historical roots and establish new ones within the context of the newly acquired religion. Throughout this process Deseret Mormons are the dominant role models. The missionaries who en-

courage conversion, the presidents of mission areas, and the central church leaders who visit the missions periodically are for the most part Deseret Mormons. The voice of the predominantly Utah-born central church leadership—the "general authorities," as they are known to church members—seems to strike at least as strong a resonance in mission areas as it does in Deseret. The degree to which an individual participates in Mormon culture is influenced partly by length of membership in the church but is affected more strongly by the amount of interaction with other Mormons. Interaction in turn is determined primarily by commitment to the church and activity in its various programs. Non-participating Salt Lake City Mormons are often less acculturated than recent Nashville converts. Although it was formed in a particular region by particular circumstances, Mormon society is constantly being revitalized in mission areas.

Not all followers of Joseph Smith shared in the Utah experience. At the time of the founder's death several splinter groups formed, some of which still exist, most with only a few members. In the 1850s followers of several such groups began to unite as the Reorganized Church of Jesus Christ of Latter-day Saints. The Prophet's widow Emma and her family had not moved West and Smith's descendants became the leaders of the "Reorganization." As historian Jan Shipps has noted, Latter-day Saints who joined the Reorganization were attracted more by the Christian primitivism in Smith's teachings than by the neo-Judaic Christianity evidenced in temple rituals, polygamy, and the political-kingdom concept. Because they did not participate in the exodus west and escaped the traumatic experiences of the pioneer Utah period, the membership of the Reorganized church is culturally less distinctive than that of the Utah church. Now centered in Missouri, the church has over 213,000 members.

MORMON CULTURE

Rapid assimilation of ethnic groups entering the Mormon Zion has led to considerable uniformity in cultural expression. European immigrants were not moving out of their old life into relative freedom, as happened elsewhere in the American West, but rather into tightly structured, hierarchical, closely knit villages where pressures to conform were great. Anti-Mormon writers of the 19th century saw Mormon society as a form of oriental despotism, and although most Mormons, then as now, voluntarily accepted the pervasive influence of the church in their lives, critics quite rightly saw the system as alien to the more liberal and individualistic forms of social organization prevailing elsewhere in America. Most forms of creative expression were sponsored by the church, related to religion, and stressed group rather than individual achievement. Even in contemporary Mormon society there is discernibly greater emphasis on the performing arts than on the visual arts. There is widespread emphasis on group singing, in choirs and in congregations; the well-known Mormon Tabernacle Choir is a great source of local pride and the epitome of Mormon cultural expression. Musical ensembles, especially bands, have been widespread among the Mormons since the mid-19th century. The brass bands that were used to encourage members of immi-

grant trains crossing the plains became a symbol of determination and cheerfulness in the face of hardship. Musical training programs begin early in Utah public schools and are well developed in high school curriculums.

Plays and theatrical productions have also been a favorite cultural activity of the Mormons. The Salt Lake Theater, built in 1861, was long the center of drama in the Rocky Mountain West, a source of so much community pride that Salt Lake City now boasts two replicas of the original structure. The church continues to sponsor theatrical productions by the youth of each congregation and to subsidize the Promised Valley Playhouse in downtown Salt Lake City. Church members in several areas produce extravagant pageants depicting the Mormon past. The most famous is the pageant at the hill Cumorah near Palmyra, N.Y., reported by Joseph Smith as the site where he acquired the records from which the Book of Mormon was translated. Today Salt Lake City supports six professional theater companies, an impressive number for a metropolitan area of 500,000 people. Dancing has also been popular since the 19th century both as a social activity and as a form of creative expression. The city's five dance companies have made Utah a center for dance in the West. Ballet West and the Utah Repertory Dance Theater have a national reputation for excellence.

More individualistic forms of creative expression have not received the widespread support given to performing arts. Mormon painters have produced numerous portraits of church leaders, murals to decorate the interiors of temples and churches, and traveling shows to illustrate church history. Representational painting has been patronized almost to the exclusion of abstract art. There are three notable public galleries in all of Utah: the Utah Museum of Fine Arts on the University of Utah campus in Salt Lake City, the Salt Lake Art Center, and the Springville Art Museum south of Provo, a remnant of WPA activities during the Great Depression.

Both the domestic and church architecture of the Mormons are largely derivative—adaptations of styles popular in the greater United States. There is a growing emphasis in church or "meeting house" architecture upon the plain and practical over the decorative. The meeting houses demonstrate the social nature of Mormon life: in addition to a chapel for worship they always include a gymnasium with a stage for both theater and sports, numerous classrooms, a room for women's activities, a fully equipped kitchen, a library, a scout room, and a chapel for small children. Mormons have a strong tradition of landscape architecture and give considerable attention to beautifying church and public buildings with shrubs, lawns, and trees. The relative scarcity of timber in Utah, and the early teaching of Joseph Smith favoring stone or brick over frame construction have led to the widespread use of brick for houses. In the 20th century Chicago and California have been the main sources of innovation in Utah's domestic architecture.

Temples are special structures reserved to the faithful for the most sacred rituals, and as such are very different in character from the spare functionalism of the meeting houses. Mormon architects have used contemporary architectural styles in the temples, but their desire to make a significant statement in a stone structure of considerable size often gives the temples a distinctive, exotic character. Most of the 15 temples in recent use have been lavishly decorated with murals, carved woods, and ornate and costly furniture and appointments, although those designed in the 1960s and 1970s show traces of the utilitarianism that characterizes Mormon meeting houses.

Mormon writers, like Mormon painters, have worked within a fairly narrow range of acceptable forms. There are a number of excellent and powerful Mormon hymns. Periodical literature was produced in quantity at every Mormon stopping place from Missouri to Utah, and even in remote Utah towns manuscript newspapers were laboriously transcribed and circulated among the townsmen. The most important publications include the *Evening and Morning Star* (Independence, Mo., 1832–1833; Kirtland, Ohio, 1833–1834), the *Times and Seasons* (Nauvoo, Ill., 1839–1846), the *Millennial Star* (Liverpool, England, 1840–1970), the *Frontier Guardian* (Kanesville, Iowa, 1849–1852), the *Deseret News* (Salt Lake City, f. 1850), the *Woman's Exponent* (Salt Lake City, 1872–1914), and the *Improvement Era* (Salt Lake City, 1897–1970). At least 14 newspapers and as many magazines have been printed by church members as organs of the church since 1832. Most served primarily to communicate events of interest to other Mormons, church doctrine and policy, and didactic stories and messages. The first journal addressing itself to Mormon scholars was *Brigham Young University Studies* (f. 1959); in 1966 *Dialogue: A Journal of Mormon Thought* was founded in the face of strong disapproval by many in the church hierarchy. *Dialogue* was followed by the *Journal of Mormon History* (f. 1974), *Exponent II* (f. 1974), and *Sunstone* (f. 1975), the latter two serving especially Mormon women and college students. None of the scholarly journals are official organs of the church; in fact all but *Brigham Young University Studies* and the *Journal of Mormon History* are printed without official sponsoring organizations by small groups dedicated to the project. Creative writing became a Mormon literary endeavor relatively late, perhaps partially because the early church disapproved of novels. Vardis Fisher (1895–1968) is the most powerful novelist to write from a Mormon background. Many of his works, beginning with *Toilers of the Hills* (1929), are set in the Mormon West, and some, such as *Children of God* (1939), deal directly with the Mormon experience. Other novelists of Latter-day Saint background who have used Mormon themes are Samuel W. Taylor (1906–), Virginia Sorensen (1912–), and Maurine Whipple (1904–). Non-Mormons Dale L. Morgan and Wallace Stegner have also contributed significantly to the literature of Mormonism.

There is a strong tradition of folk expression in Mormon literature. Personal journals and life histories abound, many of them eloquent and compelling. Stories of persecution, migration, and deeds of the pioneers are told and retold in a form which has become almost a Mormon litany. Stories of miraculous healings, visions, and visitations—and especially of such experiences on missions—are recited often. Most of these, like the writing of hymns and the periodical literature, serve to reinforce commitment and belief among the faithful; indeed a whole genre of such stories has developed,

called by church members "faith-promoting experiences." There is also a notable collection of humorous stories and songs, some containing elements of self-ridicule, but these are not as pervasive in the folk repertoire as the more serious themes.

What Mormons may lack in creative writing they make up in technological innovation. It is paradoxical that a group that historically has been hostile to the outside world and its influences has always embraced technology fully. The arid Utah climate forced Mormons into pioneering the use of irrigated agriculture as the base of a region-wide economy. Speculators in other arid western areas pointed to Mormon accomplishments in the 1880s and 1890s as models of what could be accomplished through irrigation. The many streams flowing west from the Wasatch Mountains did not require costly large-scale dams and canals, however, and Mormon achievement rested more with evolving institutions for the control and apportionment of water than with developing the technology of surveying, designing, and constructing dams and irrigation works.

In other enterprises, however, the Mormons assiduously borrowed technologies already developed by others. In the mid-1850s, long before the sugar-beet industry was established in America, church leaders purchased machinery for a sugar factory in France, had it shipped across the Atlantic and up the Missouri, then hauled by wagon across Nebraska and Wyoming to Utah, in an unsuccessful effort to develop a native sugar industry. Similarly Mormons attempted without success to establish an iron industry in southern Utah in the 1850s. A successful paper plant was set up in 1851 and small textile mills were established in many Utah towns; some mills operated into the 20th century. Utah farmers have been quick to adopt improved farm machinery, and the state was among the first to extend electrical service to rural areas. The church uses the latest computer systems in handling population, mission, and financial data. Numerous church visitors' centers feature electronic displays as teaching and proselytizing devices. Perhaps most remarkably, parts of sacred temple rituals are now generally presented on film to participants in temple ceremonies.

ECONOMIC INSTITUTIONS

Although the Mormon church invests successfully in the markets that sustain the American economy and there is much rhetoric about devotion to free enterprise, economic institutions functioning within the church are still strongly flavored by communal laws contained in Joseph Smith's revelations. The Prophet's Law of Consecration and Stewardship stressed self-sufficiency, simplicity in living, and consumption according to need, but preserved some elements of individualism—particularly the vision of entrepreneurial activity as an engine of economic progress. It also placed capital investment in the hands of church leaders and gave particular attention to an internal system of poor relief.

Under Smith's plan, a new communicant entering the system would agree to the "consecration" of all his possessions to the church and receive in return, as a lifetime lease contingent upon faithfulness, a "stewardship" consisting of materials and property needed to pursue a chosen trade and to domicile a family. The member was to use individual initiative to improve his

stewardship during the ensuing year and report on his progress to the bishop at the end of each year. During this "stewardship interview," any surplus above the "wants, needs, and circumstances" of the family was to be defined and given voluntarily to a general fund for relief for the poor, for general church expenses, and for providing stewardships to new members and those coming of age. The system was practiced in Missouri in 1831–1833, but failed. It was replaced in the 1840s by the "lesser law" of tithing, until, as church leaders explained, the Saints could demonstrate their worthiness to live the higher law.

Though organized under consecration and stewardship for only brief periods, the church has consistently taken an interest in and considerable responsibility for the temporal as well as spiritual aspects of the lives of Mormons. Brigham Young assumed much of the burden of directing the development of Utah's economy during his lifetime. Between 1848 and 1852 the church minted gold coins and issued its own currency. Under Young's guidance the church established a large public works program to alleviate unemployment, especially for converts newly arrived in Utah who had not yet found permanent situations. It was under church call that strenuous efforts were made to develop industries in Utah in the 1850s.

Nor were the teachings of Joseph Smith forgotten in the rush to develop the newly settled land. Encouraged by some church leaders, a movement to consecrate private possessions and property to the church began in the mid-1850s. Perhaps as many as half the family heads executed deeds assigning their possessions to the church, although the church never actually took possession of the consecrated property. The cooperative movement of the late 1860s established cooperative retail stores in most Mormon towns and cooperative manufacturing establishments in many localities. Some of the retail stores lasted into the 1930s, and Zion's Cooperative Mercantile Institution (f. 1869), or ZCMI, long since shorn of its cooperative aims, is one of Utah's major department stores.

Some church leaders saw the cooperative movement as a preliminary step toward full practice of Joseph Smith's communalism. A more dramatic move in that direction took place in 1874, when the aging Brigham Young attempted to place the whole economy under the United Order of Enoch, his own version of Smith's system. In that year the economic resources of over 200 Mormon towns were organized into some form of the United Order. The aims were to combine capital, promote regional and local self-sufficiency, divide labor, equalize consumption, and generally to "unite the temporal and spiritual interests of the Saints." Although most United Orders failed almost immediately, efforts to make the system viable continued until the mid-1880s, when they were abandoned by a new church leadership less committed to communalism and under strong pressure from the U.S. government to abandon distinctive Mormon economic and social practices. Mormons have remained strongly impressed with the notion, instilled by a century of preaching and exhortation, that they are under obligation to prepare for a time when they might be asked to live the United Order again.

The most recent church-sponsored cooperative un-

dertaking, the Welfare Program, shares many aspects of the United Order. The Welfare Program was organized in 1936 as a response to the Great Depression and continues to expand. Under the plan diocesan organizations called "stakes" purchase and maintain cooperative manufacturing or farming ventures that produce essential household commodities. These products are shipped to regional or central warehouses, where they are available for bishops to draw upon for the poor within their jurisdictions. Most labor on welfare projects is voluntary, supplied through local church congregations. Welfare commodities are also drawn upon to provide relief to victims of disasters such as floods, earthquakes, or war.

Another peculiar Mormon economic practice is the contribution by church members of an amount equivalent to or greater than the cost of two meals missed in a spiritual fast on the first Sunday of each month. These "fast offerings" are used to care for the local poor. Any excess is forwarded to church headquarters to help maintain an elaborate system of social and economic welfare services. In addition, for many years all Mormons have been advised to develop a personal or family program of food storage sufficient to sustain themselves for a full year if necessary. Church leaders claim that a major purpose of these various programs, including tithing, is to teach church members sufficient selflessness to be able to live under consecration and stewardship at some future time.

ETHNIC CONSCIOUSNESS AND RELIGIOUS ORGANIZATION

A related set of doctrines has strongly influenced the development of a Mormon ethnic consciousness. Mormons have believed since the 1830s that Christ will soon return to the earth to initiate a millennial reign. Therefore, the "restoration" of the true church and authority, lost from the earth through apostasy, was accomplished expressly for the purpose of preparing a covenanted people to administer world government under Christ. The Saints were selected from the nations so that they might be trained in moral precepts and necessary administrative skills. Missionary work has always been the primary vehicle of this selection process. In the 19th century the missionaries taught that the faithful should physically remove themselves from worldly influences and gather to Zion, where, concentrated in one geographical area, they could be instructed and reinforce one another in preparing to live the Law of Consecration and Stewardship and other celestial laws. Rapid growth of church membership outside Utah in the 20th century has made physical gathering of this sort impractical, but the church still fosters a number of teachings and practices which tend to separate faithful Mormons from non-Mormons, wherever they reside.

The religious hierarchy extends into every Mormon household, even those not involved in church activity. The primary unit of church organization is the "ward" or local congregation of 300 to 600 members. A bishop oversees each ward and counsels his congregation in both religious and secular affairs. He is assisted by the Women's Relief Society, first organized by Joseph Smith in Nauvoo, and by the men and boys as members of the various priesthood quorums—high priests, seventies, and elders in the higher, or Melchizedek priest-

hood, and priests, teachers, and deacons in the lower or Aaronic priesthood. Boys enter the hierarchy at the age of 12 as deacons. Each rank has specific responsibilities; most assist in "home teaching"—making visits in pairs at least once a month to an assigned four or five families and reporting back to the bishop. Thus the ward, whether rural or urban, is like a village, with geographic boundaries (not commitment to church activity) defining membership and with considerable mutual solicitude.

Church organization ascends to the "stake" (several wards), presided over by a stake president, his two counselors, and a high council composed of twelve high priests. The next level is the region, a jurisdiction recently created in response to rapid church growth; it is presided over by a regional representative of the twelve apostles. Above the region is the churchwide level.

Those who hold high positions on a churchwide level are referred to as "general authorities." They are for faithful Mormons quite literally "general" authorities, exercising worldwide authority in ecclesiastical affairs and commanding respect and obedience when they offer advice on religious and secular matters. They include the presiding bishop of the church, the first quorum of the seventy, the patriarch, the quorum of the twelve apostles, and the three-member first presidency. The principal figure in the first presidency is the prophet or president of the church, regarded as the mouthpiece of God upon the earth.

The church organization offers responsibility and authority at some level to all members willing to accept positions. All men hold offices in the lay priesthood, and all members are subject to "calls" for staffing a wide variety of religious, cultural, social, welfare, and recreational activities for both sexes and all age groups. Demonstration of faithfulness by living according to church teachings is officially required for calls to church positions; in practice, however, different positions require different levels of faithfulness, so that almost anyone willing to accept a position is likely to be offered one. Thus members are involved in the organization through assuming responsibility for communicating general policies and teachings to others within their calling, and their involvement generates a high degree of loyalty to the broader system. It is difficult to obtain estimates on the number of "inactive" or nonengaged members—sometimes referred to as "Jack Mormons"—they probably range between 25 and 35 percent of the total church membership. Anyone baptized in the church is retained in the membership files wherever he or she goes and regardless of participation. The membership record is discontinued only upon formal request.

EDUCATION

Mormons see piety and priesthood as the main qualifications for leadership and the right to make pronouncements on doctrinal matters. There has never been a systematic rationalization of Mormon doctrines or canon of essential beliefs beyond a brief general statement by Joseph Smith in 1842. Communicants are expected to believe in Jesus Christ's redeeming mission and to accept the roles of Joseph Smith and his successors as present-day spokesmen for God. Scriptures, including the Book of Mormon and the compilation of

Smith's revelations called the *Doctrine and Covenants*, are interpreted freely and variously by church members. This amorphous lay theology has reinforced a widespread disregard for some forms of higher education among the Mormons. Yet, paradoxically, education in general is highly prized, and a favorite maxim from the *Doctrine and Covenants*, "the Glory of God is intelligence," is often used to support the contention that intellectual endeavor is divinely sanctioned. Utah has an excellent public school system; public school expenditures total more than 11 percent of the personal incomes of Utah citizens, a proportion exceeded by only two other states. In addition, the proportion of college-age youth attending college is among the highest in the nation. The church subsidizes Brigham Young University, Ricks College, and other church schools. Most college-trained Mormons tend to be involved in public education and in practical trades or professions, such as business, law, or medicine, or in applied science; general church leaders and members alike regard intellectual curiosity with suspicion unless it is directed toward a practical end or clearly infused with religious and moral perspective.

In pioneer Utah, schooling was the responsibility of the local wards, and the meeting house often served as both school and church. Mormons did not support public schools because they believed that moral and religious instruction were an integral part of a child's education and that federal influence would prevent such instruction from being part of a public school curriculum. Because of the lack of public schools, non-Mormons in Utah established private denominational schools; these were so superior to the Mormon schools that many Saints enrolled their children in them. Church officials then reversed their policy and pushed for improved free grammar schools, which the Saints could control through their numerical majority. The teaching of moral values in high school remained a concern of the church leaders, however, and in the 1870s a number of church-maintained "academies" were established in heavily Mormon localities. They proved costly and redundant, and in the 1920s were given up in favor of a program that provided religious instruction at the seminary (high school) and institute (college) levels in buildings erected and maintained by the church close to public schools. If local laws do not permit Mormon youth to attend seminary classes during the school day, the program is adapted to provide religious instruction in the early morning and late afternoon.

Mormon involvement in higher education began in Nauvoo, where a university was founded and a few classes taught in the 1840s. The University of Deseret (now the University of Utah) was founded by the Mormons in 1850 but has since become a tax-supported state institution. Brigham Young University was established as a secondary school in 1875 and has grown into a major university with a student body of more than 25,000; it is wholly owned and operated by the Mormon church.

POLITICS

In politics as in education the Mormons have had difficulty defining appropriate boundaries between religious and secular affairs. Much of the trouble encountered by the early church in Missouri and Illinois was political and arose in part from the Mormons' tendency to vote as a bloc and when possible to elect church leaders to government positions. The council of fifty, organized in Nauvoo as an instrument of secular government under church control, retained influence throughout the 19th century.

When the federal government imposed territorial status upon Utah, it set off a half-century of conflict between the Saints and federal authorities. Mormons felt that the Washington appointees did not represent local interests. Moreover, some federal officials were openly anti-Mormon; they cast aspersions on the morals of Mormons and vowed to diminish church influence in the territory. After some officials complained that the Mormons were ungovernable and disloyal, President James Buchanan in 1857 appointed a non-Mormon governor and sent a 2,500-man military force to install him. The Mormons, who had received little communication regarding the purpose of the expedition, chose to see it as an invading force and conducted guerrilla warfare against the troops, who camped on the plains of Wyoming during the winter of 1857–1858. Eventually a compromise permitted the army to establish a post in a sparsely settled area some distance southwest of Salt Lake City. Before the army was allowed to march through the city to its new quarters, the Mormons evacuated the area, filled homes and orchards with straw, and appointed men to stand by ready to fire the settlement should the army commence any hostile actions. This army was recalled at the outbreak of the Civil War. In October 1862 uncertainty as to the loyalty of the Mormons to the Union led to the establishment of Fort Douglas on the outskirts of Salt Lake City. The commander, Colonel Patrick E. Connor, encouraged publication of a virulently anti-Mormon newspaper, *The Union Vedette*, and attempted to dilute Mormon influence in the territory by fostering gold and silver mining.

Federal officials denounced the entire social system of the Mormons, including their communal activities, their hierarchical church government, and the remarkable loyalty of the general membership to church leaders. Outsiders saw the Mormons as the antithesis in almost every respect of what patriotic Americans should be and viewed the Mormon system as more akin to oriental despotism than to American democracy. This exotic image was enhanced by Mormon polygamy, practiced secretly since the 1840s and openly after 1852. Congress passed a series of antipolygamy laws between 1862 and 1887, when the Edmunds-Tucker Act provided instruments for destroying the economic and political power of the Mormon church. This act disincorporated the church and declared all church-owned property in excess of $50,000 escheat to the federal government. It dissolved the Perpetual Emigrating Fund Company in an effort to cut off the flow of Mormon converts from Europe. It undermined Mormon political strength by denying citizens of Utah the right to vote, serve on a jury, or hold public office until they had signed an oath pledging support of and obedience to all antipolygamy laws. The act further reduced Mormon political power by denying the franchise to women, who had been given the right to vote by the territorial legislature in 1870.

Initially the church avoided the full impact of the financial provisions of the Edmunds-Tucker Act by entrusting church property to individuals or associations. However, church leaders wished to challenge the law before the Supreme Court as quickly as possible; to avoid delays in lower courts they agreed to turn over to the federal receiver $800,000 in real and personal property in exchange for a promise that no more claims would be pressed against church property. Properties in downtown Salt Lake City, including even the temple block, were rented by the church from the receiver until the matter was resolved.

In the meantime church leaders, forced underground to avoid prosecution, submitted to Congress a request for statehood and prepared a constitution that outlawed polygamy and required separation of church and state. Their petition was denied in committee. Hopes for redress were dashed in May 1890 when the Supreme Court sustained the Edmunds-Tucker law. Finally, in August 1890, the church president, Wilford Woodruff, announced the "Manifesto," which recommended that Mormons no longer contract marriages contrary to federal law. After a period of adjustment the Mormons entirely abandoned polygamy. It is presently practiced only by members of what Mormons call "fundamentalist" groups, who are excommunicated by the main church when such practices are discovered.

Elections in Utah during the pioneer period featured a one-party slate with church leaders filling civil positions often analogous to their church positions. A growing non-Mormon, or Gentile, population united in the 1870s with a dissident Mormon faction to form the Liberal Party, which was countered by the pro-Mormon People's Party. In national politics the Mormons, sensitive to states' rights issues, tended to vote Democratic. So one-sided were politics in Utah that a federal commission appointed in 1882 to administer territorial elections demanded a viable two-party system as a condition of statehood; in order to achieve the recommended political balance Mormon leaders encouraged some of their followers to become Republicans. Statehood was granted in January 1896, 46 years after Brigham Young began his efforts toward that end. In the process Utah had undergone a "reconstruction" not unlike that experienced in the South after the Civil War.

Up to the end of World War II Utah residents did not consistently support any one political faction. Since that time some church leaders have outspokenly favored conservative positions on key issues, reflecting a long-standing bias against federal interference in local affairs and a protracted response to charges of un-Americanism in the late 19th century. Despite this, however, voting has for the most part followed national trends, although voting on local issues is usually conservative.

SOCIAL STRUCTURE

A conception of themselves as a "covenant people" has been reinforced by other doctrines that encourage Mormons to make the primary division in their social world between Mormon and Gentile. Mormon children grow up with a conflict between their identity as Mormons and their national identity similar to the conflict experienced by youth in ethnic minorities throughout the world. Even converts who have not been in Utah are commonly ostracized by former associates, which encourages them to develop new ties almost exclusively within the church.

The most important social stratification within Mormonism is by church office. But despite much nepotism at the higher levels, particularly in the past, the system as a whole is strongly egalitarian in character. Callings to church office are tendered on the basis of piety and diligence in church service rather than wealth or occupational status, and there is considerable rotation in all offices but those of general authorities. General church, stake, and ward offices nonetheless carry overtones connoting status within the community.

Since the mid-19th century the ward has been the fundamental social group for both urban and rural Mormons, and understanding its structure and function is necessary to an understanding of Mormon society. The ward defines the neighborhood in cities and the town in rural areas. Moreover, these ward "villages," whether in downtown Salt Lake City, suburban Dallas, or Berlin's Dahlem, are very similar. Church classes throughout the world study the same material on roughly the same schedule; the same attitudes toward the general church leadership prevail everywhere; distinctive use of particular words or phrases, or the equivalency in translation, is evident; meeting houses even have the same architecture. Although many find the uniformity stifling, newcomers to a ward usually experience an immediate sense of community approaching kinship (Mormons refer to one another as "brother" and "sister") which has distinct social and organizational advantages. Mormons feel themselves a part of an extensive family that transcends geographic and social boundaries; they are clannish and inward looking, acutely attuned to important happenings within their world, and not greatly interested in external affairs. Active Mormons have little social contact outside the ward in which they reside and even less outside the stake of which their ward is part.

FAMILY AND KINSHIP

Joseph Smith's first vision was in part a result of anxiety over division within his own family on matters of religion. Since his time Mormonism has been preoccupied with family structure and family relationships. "Sealing" or eternal marriage, initiated by Smith in Nauvoo, clearly has the function of promising to secure family unity beyond life on earth. In Mormon temple marriages partners are pronounced man and wife for all eternity rather than for just their mortal lives, with the promise that worthy parents and children will associate as a family in the hereafter. Similarly, a sealing ceremony is performed in temples for deceased families, with descendants or other Latter-day Saints assuming the names of the deceased and acting as proxies for them during the ceremony. Mormons believe that once the earthly ordinances are performed for the deceased in the temple, the dead, now residing in a spirit world where individuals still exercise free will, can decide whether or not to accept the sealings, baptisms, and other temple work performed in their interest by living persons. Such ceremonies provide the rationale for massive genealogical programs that make it a religious obligation for church members to reconstruct family his-

tory at least four generations back and further if records permit.

Implicit in the doctrine of eternal marriage is plural marriage, for several wives sealed to a man serially in this life would all be with him in the afterlife. Plural marriage was practiced secretly by Joseph Smith and a few close associates in Nauvoo. Until 1852, when the Saints were safe in Utah, church leaders issued carefully phrased denials to charges that polygamous marriages were taking place; in reality, however, polygamy was common from the early 1840s until 1890.

Although studies of Mormon polygamy have generally been based on samples overrepresenting elites, some reasonably reliable facts have emerged. Most studies indicate that 8 to 12 percent of married men had more than one wife. In one southern Utah town, however, 24 percent of the inhabitants were members of polygamous households, a figure which perhaps is more significant in understanding the importance of polygamy in the society. Census schedules for other areas suggest that this figure is not unusual. Samples of lists of polygamous families show that about 70 percent of the men had two wives, 21 percent had three, and 9 percent had four or more.

Apparently polygamy was never sufficiently widespread among the Mormons to prevent single young men from finding wives; studies indicate that there was always a reserve of unmarried persons of both sexes at all age levels. Sociologists James E. Smith and Phillip R. Kunz have concluded that because a significant number of the wives entering polygamous marriages were older than wives entering monagamous ones, they were women who had "survived" the monogamous marriage market. It is apparently not true that each polygamous union doomed some men to unwilling bachelorhood. The common practice of taking widows and spinsters into polygamous families indicates that polygamy had the effect of diminishing the importance of romantic love as a consideration in family formation. It also reduced the possibility that some women might remain involuntarily outside a family group, an important consideration, given the great stress church leaders placed on the family as the fundamental unit of an ordered society.

Polygamy was of far greater importance in shaping non-Mormon attitudes toward Mormons than the numbers involved suggest. Non-Mormon political leaders and churchmen, opposed to the Mormon system generally, were shocked by polygamy and saw it as an issue that could be used to bring about anti-Mormon feeling throughout America and destroy the movement. Thus strong attacks were launched against Mormon polygamy, especially in the 1880s. Instead of eliminating the division between the Mormon and non-Mormon worlds, these attacks increased it by causing all Mormons, polygamous or not, to unite in defense of their system.

Another aspect of Mormon preoccupation with the family is the law of adoption, begun under Joseph Smith and practiced until the 1890s. Church members without Mormon parents were "adopted" into the families of church leaders in a transaction that entailed both filial and paternal obligations and often formed the basis of lifelong associations. Modern vestiges of these concerns are evident in the prevalence of family organi-

zations and reunions among Mormons, activities strongly urged by high church leaders. Mormons are aware of and often identify others by the family or clan to which they belong.

In recent years church authorities have spent vast sums on media spots and programs to promote the teaching that stable family relationships are fundamental to a healthy society. Pornography, sexual permissiveness, gay liberation, liberal divorce laws, abortion, and women's liberation are opposed by Mormon leaders as threats to family stability. They also oppose birth control, but rather than stress that birth control devices should not be used, church leaders have consistently taught that children are a blessing and that parenthood is an essential lesson in Christian giving. Indeed, Mormons believe that the highest celestial blessings cannot be obtained outside the marriage union. In consequence, Mormon fertility remained over twice as high as American norms in the mid-1970s. In 1976 the Mormon birthrate was 29.8 per thousand, and the national average was 14.7.

The emphasis on family and family values has helped shape the response of many Mormons to the women's liberation movement, particularly the Equal Rights Amendment (ERA). The Latter-day Saint church has always been strongly patriarchal in its organizational structure and has emphasized the importance of mothers' roles as homemakers. All worthy men are ordained to the priesthood, but not women. Leadership in all church organizations except those that exclusively serve women, small children, and teenage girls is reserved to men. Surprisingly, given this fundamental aspect of church government, 19th-century Mormon women were encouraged to enter professions and take responsibilities outside the home. Apparently the pressing need for workers in a developing economy momentarily overcame the fundamental belief that women should be primarily guardians of home and family. Prominent Mormon women of the 19th century, such as Brigham Young's daughter Susa Young Gates (1856–1933) and Emmeline B. Wells (1828–1921), were active in the suffrage movement and were well acquainted with its national leadership. Utah women, who received the vote in 1870, were among the first in the nation to be given full suffrage. Twentieth-century church leaders, however, observing changes in societal values which they believe to be destructive to the family, have increasingly advised women to make nurturing children and building a family their first responsibilities in life. The leaders see the women's liberation movement generally and the ERA particularly as causes that divert women from their primary role. The position of the church has undoubtedly influenced Utah's negative response to the ERA.

INTERGROUP RELATIONS

Mormon-Gentile conflict remains a muted but real aspect of life in heavily Mormon areas, where the social world is clearly divided into Mormon and Gentile realms that have little interaction or common understanding. The tendency to regard all non-Mormons as Gentiles has diminished Mormon awareness of other ethnic groups; sizable Greek and Italian communities exist in Utah with little evidence of ethnic tension be-

yond that common in Mormon relations with all Gentile groups.

Blacks and American Indians, however, are exceptions. Until 1978 Mormons denied blacks ordination to the lay priesthood and access to temple rituals, both of which were open to males of all other races. There was no clear doctrinal rationale for this exclusion, which was applied only to Africans and not to other dark-skinned races; ironically, it apparently arose as a reaction to criticism of Mormon opposition to slavery in the 1830s.

Occasional comments by past church leaders indicated that future revelations might change the practice, a promise fulfilled in June 1978, when church president Spencer W. Kimball (1895–) announced a revelation extending the right of ordination to all worthy male members of the church. The membership responded warmly, and no significant dissent has been evident. The small number of blacks in Utah minimizes overt expression of racial tension, and it is therefore difficult to assess its effect on race relations in heavily Mormon areas. Blacks in such localities claim that exclusion was not the only expression of racial prejudice, but one sociological study has indicated that Mormons are no different in their racial attitudes from non-Mormons in the West.

Mormon doctrine teaches that American Indians are remnants of a Book of Mormon people—the Lamanites—a race descended from a migrant band of ancient Israelites with a tarnished past but great promise and a specific mission in the Mormon millennial scheme. The first major missionary effort of Mormons, in 1830, was directed toward American Indians. Strenuous efforts to "redeem" the Lamanites have continued since that time.

Indian skirmishes took place in the 1840s, 1850s, and 1860s, but Brigham Young's overriding policy was to avoid conflict and fraternize as much as possible in order to "civilize" the Indians and help them adjust to modern white society. Early Mormon settlements in areas frequented by Indians commonly set aside "Indian farms" or plots of land for their use. In the 19th century numerous efforts under church auspices to establish farms, reservations, and settled communities for local tribes were made independently of federal Indian policies. Such efforts often soured relations between Mormons and federal Indian agents but led generally to good relations between Mormons and Indians, many of whom submitted to Mormon baptism and differentiated between "Mormonee" and other whites. Mormons teach that Polynesians are likewise descendants of Book of Mormon peoples, and missionary efforts have been remarkably successful among the Maori of New Zealand and in Tonga, Samoa, Tahiti, and Hawaii. Church records indicate that in 1970 over 15 percent of all Tongans, 14 percent of all Samoans, and nearly 5 percent of all French Polynesians were Mormons. During the 1960s and 1970s members of these groups emigrated to Salt Lake City and other Mormon areas in substantial numbers.

The Mormon Indian placement program of the 20th century is clearly an extension of 19th-century efforts to change the lifestyle of the Indians and help them adapt to modern society. Under this program Indian children whose parents so decide are taken for the school year into Mormon homes, often far from the parental home, treated as family members, and sent to local public schools. Difficulties of adjustment and fear that children will be alienated from their native culture persist, but the program has been modified in an attempt to meet these problems and continues to operate. Brigham Young University has a remarkably successful record of keeping the dropout rate for first-year Indian college students far below that of other universities with sizable Indian minorities. In 1976 an Indian was elevated to the church's first quorum of the seventy, the first to become a Mormon general authority. Mormon-Indian relations have historically been fair to excellent, in contrast to the hostile relations prevailing in neighboring western states.

GROUP MAINTENANCE

Several circumstances have served to erect and maintain social boundaries between Mormons and others. Partly by design, Mormons were physically isolated from Gentiles from the earliest periods of Mormon history; where possible, the Saints lived together in separate communities. Their early difficulties resulted in part from insufficient isolation, and the choice of the Great Basin as a new settling place in 1847 was deliberate: even the waters there did not mingle with those of the outside. For a quarter-century Mormons were free to work out their own particular lifestyle. Even after 1869, when the transcontinental railroad began to bring Gentiles to Utah, the newcomers stayed for the most part in the cities or in separate mining camps. Thus the isolation continued well into the 20th century.

Social isolation has reinforced the physical isolation of Mormons. The persecutions created an initial wall of hostility and distrust; a generation later, plural marriage became an equally divisive issue that taught Mormons to regard outsiders as enemies. The desire for isolation led to Brigham Young's call in 1854 for creation of the Deseret alphabet, a phonetic system based on Pitman shorthand. Schoolbooks, newspapers, official church documents and papers, and parts of the Book of Mormon were printed in this alphabet between 1854 and 1867. One of Young's wives, Eliza R. Snow (1804–1887), designed and attempted to introduce distinctive styles of dress in order to free Mormon women from outside fashion trends. Neither the new alphabet nor the new dress styles were widely adopted or of lasting effect.

After abandoning or modifying plural marriage, communal life, and other distinctive aspects of the group character, church leaders began to place greater stress on the Word of Wisdom—the Mormon health law proscribing alcohol, tea, coffee, and tobacco. The Word of Wisdom was revealed by Joseph Smith in 1831 but was not rigidly observed until the 1920s. Now that strict adherence is required as a condition for entrance into the temple, the Word of Wisdom makes Mormons uncomfortable at cocktail parties, coffee breaks, and other such gatherings which serve the rest of American society as important occasions for social interaction. The Word of Wisdom is in some measure to 20th-century Mormons what polygamy was to those of the 19th century—a mark of peculiarity setting them apart from much of the rest of American society.

In addition Mormon youth, especially young men, are taught from childhood to prepare to fulfill a two-year mission that totally removes them from normal young adult society; they spend this time teaching and defending Mormonism, clearly an effective way of building a life-long loyalty and commitment. There is also strong pressure to marry in Mormon temples. Because only faithful Mormons can enter the temples by obtaining a certificate of worthiness from their bishop and stake president, the importance attached to temple marriage limits teenage dating and other contact with non-Mormons. Statistics for the United States are unavailable, but a recent study of Canadian Mormons reported that 80 percent of rural and 70 percent of urban youth marry other Mormons. Provision of a full range of church-sponsored social activities in each ward and the maintenance of church universities, seminaries, and institutes serve to decrease outside contact and to increase opportunities to marry within the group. In addition, ward activities permit the fully engaged Mormon little time for outside social engagements. Thus, devout Mormons have always kept considerable distance, both physically and socially, from non-Mormon society.

ACCOMMODATION AND ETHNIC COMMITMENT

In the years since the bitter decades attending resolution of the polygamy issue, Mormon accommodation to greater American society has been more apparent than real. Traits remain that caused much criticism of Mormons in the 19th century: unreserved obedience to church authority, difficulty in making distinctions between secular and religious realms, commitment to cooperative and communal activities, and devotion to the church above all other loyalties. The remarkable success of present-day general church programs depends to a considerable degree upon precisely those traits that made the system so tenacious and successful in the past. Most such programs take place within a purely religious framework, but the welfare program extends into the economic sphere and provides a model for broader expansion into the secular realm should church leaders deem it necessary. Moreover, the voluntary responsiveness of Mormons to the calls and counsel of church leaders may be even more pronounced than it was in the 19th century, and thus permits continued flexibility in the system. If the need arose, these avid proponents of capitalism and free enterprise might well lead their people into a communal life where rewards would be determined by need, and contribution by ability.

Mormon society during the first two-thirds of the 20th century was relatively outward looking and open to external influence. Since the 1960s this trend has been reversing and a more defensive attitude similar to that prevailing in the 19th century is developing, partly as a reaction to a perceived disintegration of moral values in the greater society, particularly as they relate to sexual mores and family life. Perhaps more important, however, a people committed to unity and order as prime social virtues are reacting to what they see as an increasingly chaotic outside world. Over the next few decades, the Mormons, despite an aggressive missionary program and commitment to build a world-wide church, may move toward making even sharper the boundaries dividing their world from that of the Gentiles.

Bibliography

Brief general introductions are Leonard J. Arrington and Davis Bitton, *The Mormon Experience: A History of the Latter-Day Saints* (New York, 1979), and James B. Allen and Glen M. Leonard, *The Story of the Latter-Day Saints* (Salt Lake City, 1976). Thomas F. O'Dea, *The Mormons* (Chicago, 1957), is written from a sociologist's perspective, and Leonard J. Arrington, *Great Basin Kingdom: An Economic History of the Latter-day Saints, 1830–1900* (Cambridge, Mass., 1958), adds that of an economic historian. Aspects of the early experience are discussed in David Brion Davis, "Some Themes of Counter-Subversion: An Analysis of Anti-Masonic, Anti-Catholic, and Anti-Mormon Literature," *Mississippi Valley Historical Review* 47 (September 1960): 295–324; Robert S. Flanders, "To Transform History: Early Mormon Culture and the Concept of Time and Space," *Church History* 40 (March 1971): 108–117; and Klaus J. Hansen, *Quest for Empire: The Political Kingdom of God and the Council of Fifty in Mormon History*, rev. ed. (Lincoln, Neb., 1974). The struggle between the Mormons and the federal government is described in Gustave O. Larson, *The "Americanization" of Utah for Statehood* (San Marino, Calif., 1971). Rewarding insights can be found in Austin and Alta Fife, *Saints of Sage and Saddle: Folklore among the Mormons* (Magnolia, Mass., 1956).

Aspects of the Mormon West are treated in Donald W. Meinig, "The Mormon Culture Region: Strategies and Patterns in the Geography of the American West, 1847–1964," *Annals of the Association of American Geographers* 55 (1965): 191–220; and Evon Z. Vogt and Ethel M. Albert, eds., *People of Rimrock: A Study of Values in Five Cultures* (1966; reprint, New York, 1970).

For the role of town life in Mormon society, see Charles S. Peterson, "A Mormon Village: One Man's West," *Journal of Mormon History* 3 (1976): 2–12; and Dean L. May, "The Making of Saints: The Mormon Town as Setting for the Study of Cultural Change," *Utah Historical Quarterly* 45 (Winter 1977): 75–92. See also John L. Sorenson, "Mormon World View and American Culture," *Dialogue* 8, no. 2 (1973): 17–29; Jan Shipps, "The Mormons: Looking Forward and Outward," *Christian Century*, Aug. 16–23, 1978, pp. 261–266; and Gordon C. Thomasson, "Teaching across Dispensations: A Comparative Perspective on the Challenges of Being a Worldwide Church," in *Mormonism: A Faith for all Cultures*, ed. F. LaMond Tullis (Provo, Utah, 1978).

The major collection of source materials on Mormonism is in the Latter-day Saint Church Historical Department, Salt Lake City, Utah. Other important collections are in the University of Utah, Brigham Young University, and Utah State University libraries and the Utah State Historical Society Library in Salt Lake City. Other holdings are in the Coe Collection, Yale University; the Huntington Library, San Marino, Calif.; the Bancroft Library, University of California, Berkeley; the Houghton Library, Harvard University; and the New York Public Library. An important aid is Chad J. Flake, ed., *A Mormon Bibliography, 1830–1930* (Salt Lake City, 1978).

DEAN L. MAY

MOROCCANS: *see* ARABS

MOTHER TONGUE

The term mother tongue is used routinely by the U.S. Bureau of the Census as well as by others interested in language to refer to the language that an individual first hears and first uses as a child.

A question about mother tongue was first asked in the 1910 Census, and it has been asked in almost every decennial census since, although its wording has varied slightly. Earlier in the century it was asked only of foreign-born whites. In 1980 the language question was not about mother tongue, as defined in the past, but about current language use and facility. Respondents were asked whether they spoke a language other than English at home. Those who answered yes were then asked to identify the language and to indicate the level of their English-speaking ability.

MUNSEE-CHIPPEWAS: *see* AMERICAN INDIANS

MUSLIMS

There are perhaps 200,000 to 300,000 Muslims in the United States today; it is impossible to obtain more accurate figures. They represent a variety of ethnic groups and nation states and virtually all of the major and some of the minor sects in Islam itself. (*See* Afghans; Albanians; Arabs; Azerbaijanis; Bangladeshi; Bosnian Muslims; Filipinos; Indonesians; Iranians; Kurds; North Caucasians; Pacific Islanders; Pakistanis; Tatars; Turkestanis; Turks.)

This estimate, however, does not include the 2 million Afro-Americans claimed by the Nation of Islam, founded in Detroit in 1930. The Black Muslims, a nationalist and formerly separatist religious movement, have not always been accepted by traditional Muslim groups, although there has been increased recognition and cooperation since 1975. A large number of Black Muslim centers are listed by the international Islamic Center of Washington, D.C., in a directory of mosques and Islamic organizations in the United States (1979). Nor does this estimate include Muslim students in the United States.

Muslims, approximately 17 percent of the world's population, number barely 1 percent of the U.S. population. The Muslim world stretches from North Africa—including the northern regions of sub-Saharan countries—over southwest and central Asia into the Indian subcontinent. There are large Muslim communities in Bangladesh, Indonesia, the U.S.S.R., China, and the Philippines.

Muslims recognize the oneness of God (Allah) and the role of the 7th-century Prophet Muhammed as his last prophet, superseding all earlier ones. On the plain of Arafat, near Mecca, Muhammed is believed to have received the last of the revelations that make up the 114 chapters of the Koran. Muslims live by the laws of the Koran and the Sunna. They fast during the month of Ramadan, pray to Allah five times a day, and perform, where possible, Friday prayers within their community. They undertake a pilgrimage to Mecca at least once in their lifetime.

Although the Muslim world does not comprise a homogeneous culture or society, there is a strong bond among all Muslims. Within a worldwide community of believers, cultural and political differences over 1,400 years have given rise to a variety of sects and expressions of the Islamic faith.

The large majority are Sunni Muslims—literally, those who follow the Sunna, the way of the Prophet. The Sunnis are moderates; they have attempted to avoid dogmatic extremism and sociopolitical radicalism in their interpretation of Islam. Four different schools of legal interpretation have developed within Sunni Islam: Maliki, Hanbali, Shafii, and Hanafi. The Maliki law predominates in west and northwest Africa; the Hanbalis are only in Saudi Arabia; the Shafii school is influential in East Africa. The Hanafi school of legal interpretation is perhaps the most widespread. It was the official doctrine of the Ottoman Empire and today is found almost everywhere in the Middle East and in central Asia and India.

Differences in interpretation have led to considerable violence in the past, but recent leaders have made a concerted effort to resolve them. Sunni scholars, attempting to establish the most adequate body of law for modern Islamic societies, try to combine the best from all four schools. They are least successful on the Arabian peninsula, where the Wahhabi sect has been dominant since the 18th century. Dogma is not at issue, but the Saudi Arabians differ from other Sunnis in their radical puritanism; the Hanbali legal interpretation, to which they adhere, is the most traditional and rigorous of the Sunni schools.

The second largest group of Muslims, the Shiites, number about 60 million. In Iran approximately 90 percent of the Muslim population is Shiite. There are also Shiites in the Soviet Azerbaijan Republic, in Iraq (approximately 50 percent of all Muslims), in Pakistan (25 percent), in Lebanon (20 percent), and in Turkey.

The split between the Sunnis and the Shiites, which dates back to the beginnings of Islam, was originally political. It developed from a struggle over succession to the secular rule of the Prophet. While their political ambitions were crushed, the Shiites evolved into a religious sect, holding a different concept of the role of the imam or leader of the community. They recognize 12 consecutive imams beginning with Ali, cousin and son-in-law of Muhammed, and they believe that inspired interpretation by the imams is essential for the proper understanding of Islam. Various customs and holidays have evolved differently in the Shiite community. For example, Shiites observe public mourning processions and passion plays in commemoration of the death of the second imam, Hussein, son of Ali. They have suffered much at the hands of the Sunnis, and the strong antagonism between the groups underlies and accounts for some of the bitter political differences in Turkey, Iran, and Pakistan. In the United States the antagonism is muted, but where there are sufficient numbers Shiites worship separately from Sunnis, frequently crossing national and linguistic lines to do so.

A variety of sects have developed in both groups, along political or religious lines. The Sufi orders, dating back to the 13th century, express mystic tendencies. Usually they combine the specific teachings of one master with a particular set of rituals, prayers, and dances devised to accomplish their mission. Later, orders such as the Mevlevi and Bekhtashi became identified with specific social classes, guilds, or geographic areas and took on a degree of sociopolitical importance leading to the development of still more subgroups. However, the importance of these groups has diminished in the 20th century, and they have never been as separate and independent from the larger Muslim society as the sectarian groups who differed with the Sunnis over religious doctrines. Some sects, three of which are represented in the United States, reflect extremist doctrinal tendencies within the Shiite movement.

The Ismailis split from the main body of the Shiites in the 8th century. Incorporating many neoplatonic concepts into their religious thought, they hold to a different succession of imams and believe that the living imam who guides the community today is their Aga Khan. After their initial popularity and political success, the Ismailis found themselves at the very margins of Islam, and they were soon pushed to the geo-

graphic margins of the Muslim world as well. In order to survive they had to flee to India; subsequently, many Ismailis migrated to East Africa during British colonial rule. Political developments in Uganda, Kenya, and Tanzania have forced them to migrate again, this time mainly to Alberta, Canada. Their sense of group identity is very strong; various worldwide Ismaili foundations further the education and welfare of the community in Asia and North America.

The Druse also split from the Shiites but went beyond the realm of Islam by asserting a belief in the apotheosis of one of the Fatimid Caliphs. Secretive and syncretistic, they have survived since the 12th century in the shadow of Mt. Lebanon. Some Lebanese in the United States are Druse, but virtually nothing is known about them outside their own tight circles.

The Bahais represent a further evolution of doctrine and practice. This movement originated in Iran in the mid-19th century, and set itself apart from Shiite Islam by recognizing a new prophet and absorbing other non-Islamic features. It was for a time particularly popular among the educated classes in Iran. There are no statistics about the number of Bahai in Iran or the number of Bahai Iranians in the United States. The Bahai movement, with its emphasis on the spiritual unity of mankind, has had notable missionary success in the United States.

There were very few Muslims in the United States before World War II—a few Syrians in Detroit and Toledo, some Albanians and Turks, and a group of Bosnian Muslims, who settled in Chicago. Often Muslim Arabs followed in the footsteps of the Christian Arabs who came to the United States in the late 19th and early 20th centuries. The first mosque was constructed in Cedar Rapids, Iowa, in 1934; Cedar Rapids is also the site of the Muslim National Cemetery. The early community of Cedar Rapids was largely Lebanese.

In the late 1940s and 1950s Soviet Muslims—Tatars, Azerbaijanis, North Caucasians, and Turkestanis—came to the United States as political refugees or displaced persons. The number of students from the Middle East, North Africa, India, and Pakistan gradually increased. Some eventually decided to stay permanently, but they were still relatively few in number, sharing facilities for worship in Brooklyn, N.Y., Paterson, N.J., Detroit, and a few other midwestern locations.

Muslim immigrants began to arrive in larger numbers after 1965 when immigration restrictions were removed. Some were political refugees—the Kurds and Iranians in the late 1970s, the Palestinians earlier—but the majority were well-educated men and women from Afghanistan, Bangladesh, Pakistan, and Indonesia seeking better professional and business opportunities. Typically these immigrants moved into the middle-class suburbs of major cities in California and New York, in contrast to the earliest immigrants who lived for the most part in working-class districts in Detroit, Chicago, and New York City. The newest arrivals have not had an opportunity to develop the array of ethnic institutions that characterized earlier immigrations. However, the Islamic Center in Washington, D.C., which attempts to coordinate Muslim activities in the United States, lists 316 mosques, foundations, and cultural centers in 43 states and the District of Columbia, concentrated especially in California, Illinois, Indiana, Michigan, New Jersey, New York, and Pennsylvania. Perhaps 65 of these are Black Muslim centers; another 90 cater to students, who constitute a very active part of the community in the United States. Together they attest to the growing presence of Islam in the United States.

THOMAS PHILIPP

N

NANTICOKES: *see* AMERICAN INDIANS

NARRAGANSETTS: *see* AMERICAN INDIANS

NATIVE AMERICANS: *see* AMERICAN INDIANS

NATURALIZATION AND CITIZENSHIP

Throughout the history of the United States, immigrants, blacks, American Indians, and the inhabitants of U.S. territories have been granted or denied citizenship on the basis of complicated and often contradictory legal standards and administrative procedures. At times their status before the government and the Constitution has been unequal, arbitrary, and poorly defined. To follow the historical development of United States citizenship is to follow the evolution of constitutional principles as they have shaped the boundaries of government power and individual rights, and also to follow the shifting social composition of the nation. The laws of naturalization and, later, of denaturalization would determine which aliens would be allowed to become citizens of the republic.

As the laws defining citizenship and naturalization grew more precise and more rigorously administered, a clearer conception of American nationality emerged and citizens' obligations to the federal government were prescribed more exactly. Lawmakers in the 19th century enlarged the scope of the legal and constitutional rights of U.S. citizenship and, in the 20th century, used a common citizenship and a popular naturalization process to fuse diverse ethnic groups into one nation.

THE COLONIAL PERIOD, 1600–1775

In American society admission to the political community as a citizen involves a voluntary pledge of allegiance and an agreement to follow the laws of the country's sovereign government. In return, the government confers legal, constitutional status and political privileges on its citizens. Citizenship can be acquired by *jus soli* (birth within the borders of the United States or its possessions), by *jus sanguinis* (the inheritance of the nationality of the parents), or through the process of naturalization. Citizenship by *jus soli* or *jus sanguinis* is assumed to include the same allegiance to the government as that sworn in solemn oath when a person becomes a naturalized citizen.

Citizenship in the United States has its origin in the laws of subjectship of 16th-century England, which were in turn based on feudal notions regarding natural laws governing the rulers and the ruled. Subjectship was an essential element in the natural order of the world that was perpetual and unchanging. The tie between the state and its citizens was exemplified by the bond between the king and his subject, a relationship that was itself derived from the natural principle of subjection and dominance obtaining between parent and child. The king supplied protection to the subjects, who gave service, allegiance, and obedience in return.

These reciprocal duties were indissoluble; no willful act on either side could break the ties that bound them together.

Although the idea of immutable subjectship long remained in England's constitutional law, it was influenced by new social pressures in the North American colonies. In the 17th and 18th centuries an acute need for men to till the new land opened these colonies up to newcomers from the European continent and the British Isles. English law provided for the naturalization of foreigners, and it was presumed to provide for aliens settling in the New World colonies as well, but unforeseen problems and circumstances soon arose everywhere. Colonial governments, proprietors, the Crown, and Parliament vied with each other to control the procedures for bestowing subjectship on the foreign peoples streaming into the new land. The traditional English legal strictures against property ownership and commercial enterprise by aliens seemed inappropriate in colonies where land was abundant and the economy underdeveloped, but to what sovereign power would these aliens—or native-born Englishmen, for that matter—owe their primary allegiance and loyalty? Would it be the colonial assembly, the Parliament, or the king?

Since under English law only the Crown and Parliament possessed the power to turn foreigners into British subjects, English jurists and Parliament ruled out the idea that colonial governments could perform that function for alien settlers. Aliens residing in the colonies who sought equal civil status with English subjects had to petition the king or Parliament for special naturalization, even though from the earliest days colonies such as Virginia and New York had naturalized alien newcomers. Since full civil status, political rights, and the economic privileges of the English-born could only be obtained through the imperial government, the French Huguenots, Walloons, and other immigrants of the period frequently paused in London to secure English subjectship before moving on to North America.

Parliamentary standards for the naturalization of foreigners were usually based on religious tests. In 1609 Parliament passed a sacramental-test act that excluded Catholics from eligibility for special parliamentary grants of subjectship, along with Jews and other non-Christian groups. The Crown, however, did not observe these religious restrictions in granting naturalization. After the Puritan revolution and the restoration of the monarchy, Charles II and James II practiced a generous policy of granting individual "letters patent of denization" to Jews and Catholics, and exempted the recipients from the routine alien customs charges. Jews also received extensive commercial and trade privileges from the Crown, which local authorities were not empowered to confer. When Charles II opened the dominions of the British Empire to the French Huguenot refugees driven out of France by French royal policy and promised them royal denization, hundreds of refugees flocked to England and eventually to the North American colonies. A French Huguenot refugee in Boston counseled other immigrants to "become naturalized in

London, in order to be at liberty to engage in traffic of all kinds, and to voyage among the English Islands; without this, it cannot be done." As Protestants, the Huguenots, unlike Jews and Catholics, could obtain naturalization by special act of Parliament, as well as by denization through royal letters patent.

Throughout the 17th century, Parliament resisted the Crown's requests for the establishment of a general naturalization law. It was apprehensive about competition from foreigners who would then be permitted to enter British trade. Religious intolerance and fears of foreign subversion also convinced Parliament to maintain a restrictive immigration policy.

At the beginning of the 18th century, partisan attitudes toward the issue of admitting aliens into the empire reflected the split between the Whig and Tory parties in England. The Whigs accused the "average Tory squire" of "unabashed insularity" that nourished the "belief that Whiggery itself and all it stood for was an alien growth, which would wither without the nurture it received from foreign sources." The Whigs themselves, in contrast, welcomed "the injection of foreign capital and enterprise into the English economy which Protestant refugees had already provided." They supported a general policy that would speed the development of the imperial colonies by settling industrious foreigners, and many were in favor of a more convenient naturalization law. Colonial governments and colonists, long hampered by the lack of such a law, had asked for a parliamentary grant that would empower colonial governments to naturalize foreigners. To alien and English-born colonists alike, the administration in London of the naturalization process was an inconvenience.

A turning point in English policy was almost reached in 1709 when the Whigs gained a clear majority in Parliament and passed an act that provided a simple procedure for the naturalization of foreigners. Aliens had only to swear allegiance to, and acknowledge the supremacy of, the Crown, prove that they had received a Protestant sacrament in the preceding three months, and declare in open court against the doctrine of transubstantiation. Those who could satisfy these conditions were granted the same rights and status as natural-born subjects. The fee was one shilling.

This act remained in force only three years, but even in that brief time many foreign Protestants were naturalized under its terms. Some of them, such as the German refugees from the Palatinate, eventually made their way to the American colonies. After its repeal in 1712, aliens seeking to become British subjects had once again to petition Parliament or obtain denization by royal decree.

Not until 1740 did Parliament finally enact a general naturalization law permitting foreigners in America to acquire subjectship locally. Under this law, applicants had to be residents in "any of His Majesty's Colonies in America" for at least seven years without being absent for more than two consecutive months, had to present a certificate signed by two witnesses corroborating that in the previous three months they had taken the sacrament "in some Protestant and Reformed Congregation," and had to swear allegiance to the king and profess Christian belief before a colonial judge in open court. Quakers and Jews were exempted from the sacra-

mental requirement and could swear oaths in keeping with their beliefs, but the law prohibited the naturalization of Catholics. Its most important innovation was the proviso that the rights of a person naturalized under its terms were to be honored in every dominion of the empire.

The last major British naturalization law affecting American colonists was an act of 1761 that enabled the British army to naturalize foreign Protestants who had served, or would serve, for two years in the British military in the colonies, provided they swore the necessary oaths and had received a Protestant sacrament in the preceding six months. The imperial apparatus for administering general naturalization was complete, and it was a model of enlightened toleration. Aliens naturalized under the laws of 1740 and 1761 received the same civil and political status as natural-born subjects: they could engage in trade, gain title to land, vote, and hold office.

The colonists, however, were not satisfied. From the beginning of settlement the feeling had grown that the colonies should have some authority over the admission of new members. Eager to lure settlers to develop the land, the Americans sought to establish an easy and generous naturalization policy. In the century before the 1740 law, colonists had experimented with local awards of denization. Virginia and the Carolinas established a system of naturalization through individual enrollment regulated in local courts. In New England towns, aliens were naturalized when they were admitted to freemen's status. In other colonies, proprietors and royal governors bestowed letters patent of denization, and several colonial legislatures issued special and general naturalization acts. In 1682 Pennsylvania naturalized "Strangers and Foreigners" inhabiting the lower counties of Jones, Newcastle, and Whoreskill who swore allegiance to the king and the proprietor within three months of arrival; it charged a fee of 20 shillings. In 1683 New York also naturalized all resident foreigners "professing Christianity" by administering an oath of allegiance.

The imperial government was slow to react to these colonial gestures: an order in the Privy Council did not officially terminate the practice of colonial awards of subjectship until 1700. Even then, the order allowed denization by the acts of colonial assemblies to continue so long as the new subjects received a civil status valid only in the colony granting naturalization. Colonial governments continued to pass their own naturalization laws until 1773, when the practice was permanently proscribed.

Although the naturalization laws of 1740 and 1761 provided the universal status of British subject, as opposed to the purely local subjectship granted by the colonies, and in spite of fees much higher than the two shillings charged by agents administering the imperial statute, masses of foreign immigrants continued to apply to colonial governments for naturalization, possibly because they did not care to risk waiting the seven years required for subjectship by imperial law.

The abolition of the colonial naturalization acts was part of a wider movement by the Crown and Parliament toward greater administrative control over the colonies of the empire. In 1764 the imperial government contended that foreigners who had not been naturalized

under the law of 1740 had no rights of property ownership. In 1773, after Pennsylvania and New Jersey had passed new naturalization acts, the Crown nullified the acts and instructed all colonial governors to prohibit the passing of any more local naturalization laws. To the shocked colonists this unprecedented restriction appeared as part of a sinister design to deprive them of their rights and privileges as English subjects. In the Declaration of Independence they charged George III with a tyrannical attempt to "prevent the population of these states; for that purpose obstructing the laws for the naturalization of foreigners," which, along with other grievances, gave the colonists a warrant to sever their political ties with England forever and to establish new republican governments.

Having thus freed themselves to give their allegiance to another government, the colonies formulated a new theory of contractual allegiance. It had its roots in the political ideas of the Enlightenment, particularly of the English philosopher John Locke, reinforced by a century of colonial practice that had altered the English concept of naturalization and allegiance. Since naturalization had been central to the process of forming colonial societies, the colonists began to see political allegiance as reflecting the essential character of naturalization itself and to hold that allegiance was volitional and contractual.

During the Revolution and the formation of an American government that followed, colonial statesmen recast the tradition of British subjectship. They rejected the concept that subjectship was unchanging and perpetual, asserting instead that any legitimate government rested on the principle of majority rule for which *"individual assent* is necessary, or it deserves the name of usurpation, and ought to be execrated as tyranny." Requiring the assent of the governed enabled the colonists to exchange subjectship under the British king for citizenship in the American republic. Under the new state and federal governments, every man was theoretically free to choose to be citizen or alien; his civil status was defined by an act of individual will. As a practical expedient to legitimize consent, the Continental Congress in 1776 affirmed that simply residing in a state and receiving its legal protection constituted allegiance to the new political order.

THE NEW REPUBLIC, 1776–1850

After the outbreak of the American Revolution, the new state governments quickly assumed control of naturalization policy by legislative acts, constitutional provision, and the simple exercise of executive power. New York, Pennsylvania, North Carolina, and Vermont established uniform rules for naturalization in their respective constitutions. The legislatures of Maryland, South Carolina, Virginia, and Georgia passed laws prescribing the conditions and procedures of acquiring state citizenship. South Carolina preserved the feature of graded citizenship contained in the British law of subjectship. "Free white persons" who had resided in South Carolina for one year and who swore allegiance to the state government were recognized as citizens, but they could acquire voting rights for the assembly and the city corporation of Charleston only after another year of residency; they could not be candidates for political office until they had received a special naturalization grant from the state assembly.

Although each state in the American nation developed different laws and administrative procedures for naturalization, they had a set of basic conditions in common. All required the applicant to take a public oath of allegiance to the state government. States that had passed general naturalization acts required that those persons applying for citizenship demonstrate good character through personal references, certificates, or witnesses, and nearly every state had some specified period of residency required before political privileges were granted. All states asked applicants to publicly disavow allegiance to any foreign sovereign.

The national government created by the Articles of Confederation was guided by the conviction that federal powers must be sharply delimited. The Articles gave Congress no control over naturalization or the rights of citizenship, though they did specify that each state must honor the basic civil rights of citizens of other states. The free inhabitants of a state were entitled to all privileges and immunities of citizens in the others and were permitted to come and go among them as they pleased. This clause soon stirred resentment and controversy in certain quarters. Some states complained that they were being deluged by "obnoxious aliens" who had to be given the full rights of citizenship simply because they had been naturalized by another state. James Madison urged that the Continental Congress set a uniform standard for citizenship in order to put an end to disputes among the states over naturalization policy, and eventually several states did submit plans for federal control of citizenship and naturalization to the Constitutional Convention of 1787.

All the delegates to that convention agreed that the new Constitution should empower the federal government to establish a uniform rule of naturalization. The grant of authority they designed was intended not only to produce a national standard consistent with the Constitution's comity clause, which continued the confederation's controversial principle of interstate citizenship, but to ensure that state governments would never abuse their naturalization power. The federal government's power over naturalization was construed as the authority to remove the disabilities of foreign birth, but the Constitution left to the states the authority to establish the positive rights and privileges of naturalized citizenship. As a further concession to state autonomy, it also assumed that federal or national citizenship would automatically derive from the acquisition of state citizenship.

Another critical issue dealt with at the Philadelphia convention was whether the British tradition of graded civil status should be reproduced in the United States. The need for settlers had early forced the colonists to make the terms for naturalization easy, and those generously offered rights had long since blurred the distinctions between the various legal ranks of subjects found in English law. Some delegates, including Madison, suggested a plan by which applicants would receive incremental rights as, step by step, they fulfilled the basic requirements of citizenship. They also debated limiting the vote and membership in Congress to the native-born. In the end, however, the convention agreed that the only disadvantage to be placed upon naturalized citizens would be ineligibility for the presidency of the United States. As finally drafted, the Constitution repudiated graded citizenship as well as any notion that na-

tive-born and naturalized citizens should possess different sets of rights, and confirmed the principle that U.S. citizenship, once conferred, would be uniform and complete.

Despite these clear principles, the Constitution contained ambiguities and potential areas for dispute over the nature of citizenship. It failed, for example, to define precisely what the rights and obligations of national citizenship were to be, nor did it adequately define the relationship between state and federal citizenship. The Bill of Rights added further confusion by referring to the rights of the "people," rather than of citizens. In the 19th century the Constitution's silence on these subjects posed problems in the formulation of a legal code defining the civil position of free blacks.

The framework for the naturalization process was erected in a series of statutes passed in the 1790s. The first federal naturalization law in 1790 required that an applicant be a "free white person" who had resided for two years "within the limits and under the jurisdiction of the United States." The law also granted jurisdiction over naturalization to "any common law court of record in any one of the states." To undercut the political support that aliens tended to give the Jeffersonians, the Federalist party secured the passage of a law in 1795 that raised the residency requirement for naturalization from 2 to 5 years and in 1798 to 14. When the Jeffersonian Republicans came to power in 1801, they set the basic residency requirement back to 5 years, where it has remained ever since.

The ambiguous legal position in which inhabitants of the new western territories found themselves raised the first serious question about the relation of federal to local citizenship. The Northwest Ordinance of 1787, which had established the Northwest Territories, had said nothing about the naturalization of their inhabitants. Those migrants who came from the established states farther east were still U.S. citizens in the territories by virtue of their state-derived local citizenship, though they had relinquished their state citizenship by emigration. But those newcomers who immigrated directly from a foreign country had no citizenship at all and no way of acquiring it. To provide some legal civil status for those territorial inhabitants, the Senate in 1795 gave territorial courts the authority to naturalize foreigners. Both the native-born and the naturalized residents of territories remained without state citizenship.

The civil status of American Indians was also long a source of perplexity, but in the early 19th century Indian civil-rights cases followed a trend that eventually defined their legal position. Through a gradual accumulation of judicial opinions, each Indian tribal organization came to be regarded as a "nation" to whom Indians owed their primary allegiance; thus the courts designated Indians noncitizens because, although they were born in U.S. territory, their allegiance remained to the tribe.

The first great wave of immigrants following the establishment of the republic began to arrive shortly after the War of 1812. Many of these new settlers were eager to become citizens. The law of 1802 required that applicants be free white persons and that they declare their intention of becoming citizens at least three years prior to naturalization. They could file their applications at any local court of record; they had to be residents for five years in the United States and one year in the state

to which they applied; finally, they had to swear an oath to uphold the Constitution and renounce allegiance to any foreign sovereign. In accordance with the common-law doctrine of the primacy of male citizenship, a wife and any children under 21 years of age became citizens at the time of the husband's own naturalization. These provisions were amended by Congress in 1824 to accelerate the naturalization process. The minimum time between the declaration of intention and the final award of citizenship papers was shortened to two years, and anyone residing in the country for the three years preceding the age of majority was allowed to take out both papers at once.

The easy terms for naturalization under federal statute were paralleled by the generous state laws and state constitutions of the 19th century that conferred political, commercial, and property rights on aliens. A uniform national rule for acquiring citizenship existed, but the states were left free to fix the political and civil rights of aliens. Western states, for example, manipulated the franchise to attract immigrants and absorb them into local life. In 1846 Wisconsin permitted all aliens who had filed a declaration of intention and who had resided in the state for one year to vote. Michigan in 1850 granted the right to vote to aliens who had been residents for two and a half years. Several states allowed nearly complete citizenship rights to any person who had filed a declaration of intention and who had resided in the state for a short period. All state and territorial governments placed either minimal or no restrictions on property-holding or commercial enterprise by aliens.

Natives who were eagerly promoting the development of the country, and aliens who had recently settled there, both pressured Congress to ease the federal requirements for citizenship. Citizens from New Jersey and New York urged Congress in 1824 to relax the probationary laws for naturalization. "Sundry aliens of Louisiana" asked Congress in the same year to enact federal naturalization laws that would make acquiring citizenship easier, while "sundry citizens of New York state" similarly petitioned the House of Representatives in 1835 to eliminate the declaration of intention and give aliens all the privileges of citizenship after only two years of residence.

Naturalization proceedings in the 19th century were extremely loose and casually administered. In a congressional report submitted to the Senate in 1845, based on investigations of naturalization proceedings in New York City, Philadelphia, and Baltimore, a judge of the marine court in the southern district of New York testified that only one witness was required to vouch for the character of an applicant and that the witness was never cross-examined. The judge also suspected that many of the people testifying on behalf of applicants were hired witnesses. Another justice of the marine court stated that a person could easily get several duplicate certificates of his declaration of intention which he would then distribute or sell at election time. The congressional report also described how in the New York Superior Court applicants were sworn in en masse, and their papers automatically approved. Tammany Hall organized committees that filled out application forms and affidavits for aliens and paid the required naturalization fees. The congressional report showed that the state courts, where fees were lower and standards less rigorous, naturalized many more applicants than the federal

courts did. In New York City, Philadelphia, and Baltimore, naturalization rates rose sharply during the two weeks preceding each spring and fall election.

In opposition to this liberal policy toward aliens in the mid-19th century, the Know-Nothing party—a nativist political movement that rose spectacularly in the early 1850s only to vanish just as rapidly—called for legislation curtailing alien political and civil rights. Obsessed with the notion that Catholic immigrants were taking over the country, the Know-Nothings petitioned Congress on several occasions to reform the naturalization law, extend the residency requirement, and exclude Roman Catholics from public office. The party controlled the Massachusetts legislature from 1854 to 1856 and was strong in several other states, but the Know-Nothings were unable to secure the 21-year residency requirement they sought for state citizenship, and in spite of their efforts the road to naturalization remained unobstructed.

SECTIONAL CRISIS AND RECONSTRUCTION, 1851–1890

In the first half of the 19th century, the constitutional and legal definition of American citizenship became a critical issue, as the controversy over the relation between state- and federal-government powers began to focus on the relationship between state and federal citizenship. Throughout the first half of the century, lawmakers and judges avoided making clear distinctions between the two, aware that every decision could have incalculable effects upon the delicate balance between federal and state power.

The absence of the formal distinction between the two citizenships in the Constitution challenged the ingenuity of courts and legislatures. As the nation expanded westward and newly formed states petitioned to enter the Union, the state-federal relationship became an explosive issue. The congressional debate over the admission of Missouri to the Union in 1820, which involved the future status of free blacks in Missouri, brought the matter to a head.

The issue arose over a provision in the Missouri constitution that prohibited free blacks and mulattoes from entering the state. Congressmen from the northern states contended that this provision violated the comity clause of the Constitution which bound each state to honor citizenship conferred by any other. Southern representatives repudiated this view on the grounds that free blacks were simply not citizens. In the Senate, James Burrill of Rhode Island and David L. Morril of New Hampshire pointed out that free blacks had acquired federal citizenship by satisfying the conditions prescribed by the states where they resided. Morril warned that if any state were allowed to discriminate arbitrarily against the citizens created by another state, the unraveling of federal bonds would inevitably follow. In opposing Morril, southern congressmen asserted that the rights of citizenship were derived from the municipal authority of each state; they were wholly local in their origins and, consequently, in their validity; they bestowed no right to federal immunities and privileges. Some legislators, such as Louis McLane of Delaware, held that no blacks would conform to "that description of persons contemplated by the Constitution of the United States as entitled to federal rights."

After months of debate, Congress finally admitted Missouri to the Union as a slave state, and ratified Missouri's constitution on the condition that the disputed provision could not exclude "any citizen of either of the States in this Union . . . from the enjoyment of any of the privileges and immunities to which such citizen is entitled under the Constitution of the United States," but it ignored the central issue of citizenship for free blacks and mulattoes. The debate over the admission of Missouri had split the nation, laying bare the irreconcilable ideas about the character of citizenship held by free and slave states that would be elaborated in the ensuing decades.

Southern states foresaw the undermining of their fundamental right to determine whom they would recognize as equal members of civil society. As the nonslave states that were formed out of the western territories began to admit free blacks to citizenship, the South was compelled to challenge the assumption that federal citizenship flowed from state citizenship. If southerners could not prove that state citizenship was purely local in effect and that the framers of the Constitution never intended blacks to be citizens, they faced the necessity of yielding the full rights of citizenship to free blacks —an eventuality that could lead to fundamental questions about the legal status and rights of slaves. A judge in Mississippi summed up the southern position: the state of Ohio might "confer citizenship on the chimpanzee or ourangoutang," he quipped sardonically, but no comity clause or legal, constitutional technicality could compel "states not thus demented to forget their own policy . . . and lower their own citizens."

Virginia and South Carolina were the first of several southern states to establish laws prohibiting free blacks from entering their jurisdiction, and Florida placed a clause in its state constitution of 1845 that banned their entry. Some federal officials held that those exclusionary laws violated free commerce between the states as well as the comity clause. But many, including Andrew Jackson's attorney general, John Berrien, argued that such laws were a legitimate exercise of a state's municipal police power. Congress continually debated their legality, but most of them remained in force up to the Civil War.

The Dred Scott case of 1857 produced a Supreme Court decision that heightened the legal confusion and sectional controversy over the constitutional definition of citizenship. Dred Scott was a Missouri slave who had resided in the free state of Illinois and the free territory of Minnesota, and sued for his freedom on the grounds that his residency in a free area had nullified his status as a slave. Chief Justice Roger B. Taney, who wrote the majority opinion for the Court, held that, because Scott was not a citizen of Missouri, he could not bring suit in a federal court to begin with. Furthermore, under the terms of the Constitution, no free black could ever become a citizen of the United States. He invoked the traditional distinction between state and federal citizenship, reaffirming the legal opinion that the latter derived from the former. The framers of the Constitution, he maintained, had never intended freed blacks to be admitted to the political community of citizens. Thus Taney disposed of the contention that blacks who were born free were citizens. He also decided that no black could gain citizenship by naturalization since all

the relevant statutes had mentioned only "free whites" as potential candidates. Finally, he concluded that rights granted by individual states did not confer citizenship; instead, the granting of the status of U.S. citizen conferred political and civil rights.

The Dred Scott decision underscored the ambiguities in the constitutional definition of citizenship. It upheld the notion of dual citizenship and in the process left ample room for conflict between federal and state authority in granting citizenship. It failed to determine the relative priorities of allegiance to the state and allegiance to the federal government. Finally, it ignored the need to establish who could and could not claim protection under the Constitution. The concept of citizenship that emerged from the decision reflected the ambiguous structure of political relations undergirding the federal republic. But it also reflected a halting movement toward a narrower definition of American nationality: only the descendants of those who had made the compact to form the republic in 1787 and free white aliens were eligible for citizenship under federal law.

In the first half of the 19th century, jurists and statesmen had shied away from the task of formulating a precise definition of citizenship because it would only have exacerbated growing sectional tensions. The Civil War and Reconstruction, however, brought the opportunity to clarify the relationship between state and federal government and the allegiance owed by citizens to each. The Civil Rights Act of 1866 established in federal law that "all persons born in the United States and not subject to any foreign power, excluding Indians not taxed," would receive United States citizenship. This law breached the legal wall erected by Taney that had restricted birthright citizenship to the children of free white aliens and to descendants of the citizens of the original thirteen states. The Fourteenth Amendment ratified in 1868 went a step further by incorporating the 1866 law into the Constitution. Although local courts had applied the common-law principle of citizenship by place of birth (jus soli), the Fourteenth Amendment established it as a national policy. The law of citizenship by the allegiance of parents, jus sanguinis, which Taney had invoked in extended form, was henceforth to play a minor role in the laws of naturalization.

Since the Fourteenth Amendment stated that "all persons born or naturalized in the United States, and subject to the jurisdiction thereof, are citizens of the United States and of the state wherein they reside," the allegiance of every citizen to the federal government was spelled out in precise terms. State citizens were perforce United States citizens, and no state could violate the rights of any U.S. citizen: "No state shall make or enforce any law which shall abridge the privileges or immunities of citizens of the United States; nor shall any State deprive any person of life, liberty, or property, without due process of law; nor deny to any person within its jurisdiction the equal protection of the laws." Thus, the Fourteenth Amendment asserted the primacy of federal citizenship and dissolved the former principle that it flowed ultimately from state powers.

In its first judicial review of the Fourteenth Amendment, the Slaughter-House Cases of 1873, the Supreme Court sharply circumscribed the federal government's capacity to define and safeguard the "immunities and privileges of citizens of the United States." In this case,

the right of the state of Louisiana to grant an exclusive slaughterhouse franchise to a corporation in New Orleans was upheld; the Court found that the Fourteenth Amendment did not confer to citizens privileges and immunities that they had not possessed before its adoption; that property rights, personal rights, and civil rights were matters to be fixed by state law and state action; and that the federal government could act to safeguard only those rights broadly articulated by the Constitution or that owed their existence to the character of the federal government. The Court declined to prescribe or systematically define the "immunities and privileges" of U.S. citizens; instead, it reluctantly sketched a vague outline of general rights deriving from constitutional principles. The rights of national citizenship thus remained both limited and ambiguous.

Nevertheless, after a half-century of political controversy and civil war, in the era of Reconstruction steps were taken toward establishing the dominance of the Union and the universality of federal citizenship. Radical Republicans tried to unite blacks and whites as equal citizens in a national polity and in doing so to affirm an expansive ideal of American nationality. One of them declared that the nation was "inclusive of the whole people . . . There is no difference of wealth, or race, or physical condition, that can be made the ground of exclusion from it."

Despite the optimism with which some Americans greeted Reconstruction, many policy makers continued to subscribe to a fixed and limited definition of U.S. nationality. During congressional debate on a revised naturalization law in 1870, Senator Charles Sumner of Massachusetts, a leading supporter of Reconstruction, proposed an amendment that would open naturalization to nonwhite as well as white aliens, but the measure was vehemently opposed by the western states, who were by that time intent on excluding alien Chinese from citizenship. Sumner invoked the Declaration of Independence in a Fourth of July oration to argue, "It is 'all men' and not a race or color that are placed under the protection of the Declaration, and such was the voice of our fathers . . . The word 'white' wherever it occurs as a limitation of rights, must disappear. Only in this way can you be consistent with the Declaration."

Sumner's motion was voted down 30 to 14. Shortly after, however, Congress made aliens of African descent or nativity eligible for naturalization. Under that law Arabs and Hindus from Africa, but not necessarily from Asia, could qualify for naturalization, a measure that laid the basis for future problems by mixing geographic with ethnic or racial qualifications for citizenship.

The Fourteenth Amendment assured that U.S. citizens could not be deprived of citizenship in any state, but no such law prevented a state from granting its citizenship to anyone found qualified, even if unqualified for U.S. naturalization, until a series of decisions in lower federal courts closed that possibility. In 1871 the Circuit Court of the Southern District of Alabama held that "citizenship in a state is a result of citizenship in the United States." In 1875 the Circuit Court of Appeals for the District of Minnesota ruled that "when the Constitution . . . says that Congress shall have power 'to establish a uniform rule of naturalization,' it designed these rules . . . to be the only rules by which a citizen or subject of a foreign government could become

a citizen or subject of one of the states of this union . . . and the United States." In 1893 the same court decided that a foreign-born resident who had not been naturalized according to federal law was a citizen neither of the United States nor of a state. By the late 19th century the federal courts had reached a consensus that there could be no state citizenship without federal citizenship.

NEW ALIENS AND NEW POLICIES, 1891–1940

Beginning in 1882 a series of laws suspending the entry of Chinese laborers was passed by Congress, introducing a new category into immigration laws. That category was "aliens ineligible for citizenship," and it included all Chinese immigrants. For the first time in the nation's history, a federal law prescribed that an immigrant group of a specified national origin was denied access to U.S. citizenship. Before the passage of the 1882 Chinese Exclusion Act, legislators and jurists had been plagued by the question of whether the Chinese were ineligible because they were nonwhite or because no specific law granted them this privilege.

The federal government assumed control over national immigration policy in 1891, and Congress immediately enacted the first effective law governing the deportation of illegal aliens, a law which the Supreme Court found constitutional on the grounds that deportation was an administrative, not a criminal, proceeding and therefore not subject to the due process of law guaranteed by the Fourteenth Amendment. Although a minority opinion described the deportation as a "severe and cruel" punishment inflicted upon foreigners for "no crime but that of their race and birthplace," federal officials began to establish standard procedures for deportation cases, which included arrest without warrant, detention without warrant, and denial of counsel until proceedings were well advanced. An alien could be subjected to cross-examination to determine whether his case was "inherently improbable," even if administrative officials had no evidence against him. In *Quock Ting* v. *United States* (1891), a Chinese boy who claimed to have lived in the United States for the first ten years of his life was deported because during his interrogation he did not know the names of streets of places in the area in which he claimed to have been brought up. Since the boy knew no English, an interpreter had to be used. The boy's testimony did not meet the criterion of "inherent probability." Officials were enjoined not to disregard the testimony of witnesses on racial grounds, but they were not required to give equal weight to the testimony of different races or nationalities; it was considered legally proper for officials to assume that some races were more apt to tell the truth than others.

In 1892 Congress passed the Geary Act, a comprehensive law that extended the exclusion of Chinese laborers for ten more years, denied bail to Chinese aliens in habeas corpus proceedings, ordered the immediate deportation of illegal Chinese residents, and required that all Chinese laborers carry certificates of residency. Foreign-born Chinese had to register with the Treasury Department and were subject to the police powers of the collector of internal revenue; theoretically, at least, they were placed under constant federal surveillance. They could be asked to show their residency papers at any time, and they were accountable to federal authorities for virtually all their actions.

The assassination in 1901 of President William McKinley by the immigrant anarchist Leon Czolgosz inspired a still more comprehensive deportation law. In 1903 Congress passed a law that made anarchism grounds for deportation, the first federal law to make political belief grounds for expulsion. Becoming a "public charge" and "moral turpitude," if it could be proved, could lead to summary deportation up to two years after arrival.

The Bureau of Immigration and Naturalization was established in 1906 in the Department of Commerce and Labor to administer a new naturalization law: the first major federal act since the law of 1802 that affected the naturalization process. The tangle of procedures and tests used to determine suitability for citizenship was to be codified and administered under the even-handed guidance of bureau chiefs. The naturalization process itself comprised three steps: the filing of a declaration of intention (first papers), the filing of a petition for naturalization under the applicant's signature (second papers), and a hearing on the petition which would grant or deny the certificate of naturalized citizenship (final papers). The declaration had to be submitted no less than two years and no more than seven years before a petition was filed. There was a wait of 90 days between the petition and the hearing to allow time for an investigation and to make the hearing public. The judge cross-examined in English; two witnesses had to vouch for the applicant's "moral character" and "attachment to the principles of the Constitution." The applicant was asked questions on American history and civics, and had to satisfy the court that he was neither an anarchist nor a polygamist, that he had "resided continuously within the United States five years at least, and within the State or Territory where such court is at the time held one year at least." Finally, he had to prove his ability to speak English.

To ensure that the procedures and standards for naturalization would be closely followed, the bureau stationed around the country 300 naturalization examiners supervised by 23 district directors. The federal procedure for naturalization was governed by a large administrative bureaucracy, which, it was hoped, would eliminate the frauds, corruption, and low standards for admission so characteristic of 19th-century proceedings. To discourage the abuse of naturalization for partisan political purposes, the law of 1906 banned any naturalization hearings within 30 days of any general election in a court's area of jurisdiction.

The casual system of naturalization that the state governments had followed before the Civil War was still functioning in the 1870s and 1880s. Local managers in both political parties herded recently arrived immigrants to court to see that they got naturalization papers in time to vote in the next election. Many, particularly in the large eastern cities, voted with fraudulent papers. In the early 1880s, 18 states and territories had granted voting rights to aliens who had only filed a declaration of intention.

Widespread alien suffrage and the lax administration of naturalization laws began to attract the attention of social reformers and nativists alike. They equally deplored immigrant political influence and corruption at the polls by fraud and alien suffrage. Many advocated lengthening the residency requirement; some revived the Know-Nothing demand for a minimum 21-year naturalization period.

By the end of the 19th century the movement to end alien suffrage and to raise the standards for acquiring citizenship had won powerful advocates. In several states, one critic warned, huge numbers of aliens were voting for members of Congress: eventually aliens might elect enough representatives to control the entire Congress. Another reported that in one Nebraska county the great majority of declarations were being made as a direct result of inducements from political campaigners.

The lax enforcement of the law was also discouraging naturalization, since the declaration of intention appeared to be all that one needed to exercise all the rights and privileges of citizenship. In the early 20th century several states heeded the warning that the ballot in the hands of aliens would have disastrous consequences for democracy. By the outbreak of World War I, only seven states had laws permitting alien suffrage, and those were vestiges of constitutions from earlier frontier days.

As the Congress and the courts tightened restrictions on the political activities of aliens, they also began to specify suitability for citizenship in terms of ethnic origins. The large numbers of people immigrating to the United States from the Near and Far East raised thorny problems that had originated with the law that declared the Chinese ineligible for citizenship. The combination of racial prejudice and the native worker's hostility to cheap foreign labor aroused ferocious antagonism toward the Chinese. Added to this was a general conviction that the Chinese would not adopt American habits of egalitarianism and individualism required to participate in a modern, industrializing society. Nativists saw them as unassimilable masses from an ancient and rigid civilization who were incapable of acculturation. The Chinese constantly looked back to their kinsmen, ancestral village, headman, and emperor. Californians complained that they had no interest in adopting American habits, modes of dress, and education; did not understand the sanctity of an oath; and did not even want to become citizens or perform a citizen's duties.

Policy makers struggled to find a consistent means of determining the suitability of the various ethnic groups for citizenship. A rule of thumb for doing so was derived from the amended naturalization law of 1870 which provided that only free whites and aliens of "African descent or African nativity" could apply for citizenship, but exactly what "white" meant now posed problems. In the 1870s legislatures and courts were still confused about which races would be included under the category of eligible white persons: a few Chinese on the East Coast and in western states had been naturalized before the exclusion act of 1882. Another problem was the status of children whose parents were ineligible for citizenship. Although they were obviously of the same disqualified race they had been born in the United States and thus were fully entitled by the Fourteenth Amendment to be considered U.S. citizens, a point that was affirmed by the Supreme Court in the case of the *United States* v. *Wong Kim Ark* (1898). Although the racial criterion of the naturalization law was in fundamental conflict with the Constitution, that problem was conveniently ignored.

Despite the federal law's denial of citizenship to the Chinese and the prescription that only "free whites" and those of African descent could be naturalized, the courts granted citizenship to substantial numbers of Asian immigrants. The U.S. Census of 1910 recorded 1,368 naturalized Chinese, and 420 naturalized Japanese in the United States. Misuji Miyakawa, the chief counsel for the Japanese plaintiffs in the 1906 San Francisco school desegregation case that had led to the Gentlemen's Agreement by which Japan regulated the immigration of its own laborers, was Japanese-born, naturalized, and a member of the California bar.

Judges and legislators were uncertain about the status of the brown-skinned Mexicans, but eventually developed a line of reasoning that allowed them to consider Mexicans eligible for citizenship. In 1897, a U.S. district court in Texas held that they could be classified neither as white nor as being of Asian or of African descent, but that despite their being nonwhite they could be naturalized individually because the constitution of the Republic of Texas and the laws and treaties of the United States had granted collective acts of naturalization to Mexicans when Texas entered the Union.

Because the naturalization statutes were ambiguous, the courts tended to rely on subjective considerations, popular opinion, and various, often conflicting, criteria to decide which ethnic groups could qualify for naturalization. Eventually the line between eligible and ineligible aliens was drawn by a crude definition of the nonwhite and non-African category. In 1911 the Bureau of Immigration and Naturalization ordered court clerks to reject declarations from aliens who were neither white persons nor persons of African birth or descent. In 1893 a Japanese had been rejected for naturalization because he was nonwhite, but this had been an isolated case. Between 1910 and 1920, however, Japanese applicants were consistently turned down, and finally in 1922 the Supreme Court in *Ozawa* v. *The United States* affirmed that Japanese aliens were nonwhite and hence ineligible for citizenship.

After 1911 most individuals from East Asia who applied for citizenship were refused. Burmese, Malaysian, Thai, Indian, and Korean applicants were flatly rejected by the courts as ineligible nonwhite aliens. Persons of mixed parentage could also be rejected: in 1912 a federal court turned down a "half-breed German and Japanese" and a federal court excluded a "quarter-breed Spaniard and Filipino."

Aliens from the Near East and Middle East were also subjected to close scrutiny and in several cases were denied citizenship. The 1910 U.S. Census classified Syrians, Armenians, Palestinians, Persians, and Turks as "Asiatics." These people had usually received citizenship papers, but after the directive of 1911 some of these applicants encountered difficulty in securing citizenship. A few had to resort to litigation to overturn the rulings of naturalization officers who wished to exclude them.

In the 1920s federal attorneys brought suit against a number of aliens suspected of having fraudulently acquired certificates of naturalization. In Michigan a U.S. court revoked the citizenship of an Arab from western India. The defendant claimed that his Arab ancestors had not intermarried with "the native stock of India" and "kept their Arabian blood line clear and pure," but the judge held that the Arab was disqualified on the grounds of race alone. In Oregon another revocation hearing involved a naturalized Armenian. Citing Strabo's *Geography*, Herodotus's *History*, and the testimony of a pair of well-known anthropologists, Franz Boas and Roland Dixon, this time the court found that the defendant was qualified for naturalization. It is now "judicially determined," the court remarked, "that the mere color of the skin of the individual does not afford a practical test as to whether he is eligible to American citizenship."

The Supreme Court was equally contradictory in its reasoning and criteria in determining eligibility for citizenship. In 1922 it decided that scientific tests had to be applied because misleading physical characteristics could be found "even among Anglo-Saxons," but the next year it held that a high-caste Hindu was ineligible for citizenship because, although in anthropological terms he was descended from the same stock as Europeans, he was not white by the definition of the common man.

States also used the category of "aliens ineligible for citizenship" to establish local laws restricting certain people from acquiring property and working in specified occupations. California, in particular, experimented with a variety of laws limiting the occupations that Chinese could hold, but all of them were swiftly struck down by federal courts as violating the "equal protection of the laws" guaranteed by the Fourteenth Amendment to alien and citizen alike. The phrase "equal protection of the laws," however, was then interpreted by the Court as requiring equal treatment only to those persons of a specified class. Legislation was not invalidated by the Fourteenth Amendment if it affected equally all persons placed by law in a special classification for a reasonable purpose. A state could enact laws that discriminated against all aliens or certain kinds of aliens—those who had not filed a declaration of intention or those who were ineligible for citizenship—as a class.

Several states used this qualification to erect laws prohibiting aliens ineligible for citizenship from acquiring or transferring property. A California law of 1913 raised that barrier against Asians. It was directed especially against the Japanese, who had acquired and developed sizable amounts of agricultural land by that time. The classification of aliens ineligible for citizenship was rationalized on the grounds that their allegiance was doubtful enough to warrant special treatment. In the 1930s, nine states, all but one of them (Florida) in the West, prohibited Asian aliens from purchasing real property.

Many states took the rule of equal treatment for a specified category of persons as a warrant to impose restrictions on all aliens. In the 1930s, 18 states imposed on them various restrictions on acquiring property; 15 placed limitations on both the amount of property and

Table 1. Occupations prohibited to aliens, 1941.

Occupation	States requiring citizenship
Physician	28
Attorney	26[a]
Certified public accountant	15
Pharmacist	14
Dentist	11
Optometrist	11
Teacher	10
Mine inspector, foreman	10
Engineer and land surveyor	8
Bank director	7
Architect	6
Pilot of vessels	6
Barber	5
Master plumber	4
Registered nurse	4

Source: William S. Bernard, *American Immigration Policy* (New York, 1950), p. 116.

a. Some 26 of 48 states required by law that an attorney be a citizen; in 12 others, court ruling made citizenship mandatory for admission to the bar.

the length of time it could be held. Some states also limited alien employment through the exercise of their police power. States empowered to manage natural resources and public works used that authority to discriminate legally against alien employment in the civil service and public works, and severely restricted their purchase of fishing and hunting licenses. Most states excluded aliens from practicing law and medicine and some prohibited them from dentistry, pharmacy, engineering, and optometry (see Table 1). In 1890 the Maryland legislature restricted retail liquor licenses to citizens on the grounds that they would be more concerned about social conditions and less likely to permit abuses. A Cincinnati municipal ordinance denied aliens licenses to operate poolrooms. In 1927 an alien plaintiff who challenged this law brought his case before the Supreme Court, claiming that his Fourteenth Amendment rights had been violated. The Court, in finding against the plaintiff, held that poolrooms had a strong potential for antisocial activity and that citizen proprietors were less likely than alien ones to allow their establishments to become public nuisances.

Several of these laws were struck down by federal courts on Fourteenth Amendment principles. The most radical anti-alien law, an Arizona statute requiring that 80 percent of all employees in every business employing more than five persons had to be citizens, was declared in violation of the Fourteenth Amendment in 1915 by the U.S. Supreme Court.

Laws restricting the economic activity of aliens proliferated in the early 20th century, through the authority of a state's police power and the principle of separate classification, but alien civil rights were still generally secured by the Fourteenth Amendment, which extended the due process of law and its equal protection to all "persons" whether or not they were citizens. The courts unanimously agreed that aliens were to receive protection under its terms.

A vestige of the common law of naturalization functioned as a barrier to intermarriage between male aliens and female citizens in the early 20th century. After 1855 the United States followed the doctrine that an alien wife acquired the citizenship of her American

husband. But then the converse of that principle—that any American woman who married an alien assumed the nationality of her husband—was established by a congressional act of 1907. Not only was the wife of an alien stripped of her citizenship, but she was not eligible for naturalization unless her husband was naturalized first, again on the principle that the nationality of the wife followed that of her husband.

This dependency was terminated by the Cable Act of 1922, which conferred independent citizenship on married women, after the passage of the Nineteenth Amendment granting women full political rights made the dependency of women's citizenship increasingly anomalous. Henceforth no female citizen could lose her U.S. citizenship by marriage to an alien, and no alien woman could acquire citizenship either by marriage to an American or by the naturalization of her husband. The Cable Act had been supported by those seeking to enfranchise women who had lost their citizenship through marriage, after the Nineteenth Amendment had given women the right to vote. The principle of independent citizenship would also provide protection against the political power of foreign women who had obtained citizenship, and thereby voting rights, simply by marrying U.S. citizens. Female citizens who married aliens ineligible for citizenship continued to be deprived of citizenship, however; that measure was not repealed until 1931. The laws of 1922 and 1931 on marriage and naturalization had two results. More male aliens could be assimilated through marriage to American women. The assimilation of foreign women was made to go hand in hand with the raising of standards for American citizenship; female aliens would no longer have an easy or automatic path to citizenship.

The expansion of the United States beyond its continental limits posed new problems for developing a workable concept of American nationality. The peoples inhabiting Alaska, Hawaii, the Philippines, Puerto Rico, and other territorial possessions had to be incorporated into the framework of an imperial order. Alaska, acquired by purchase in 1867, and Hawaii, annexed in 1898, became "incorporated territories" by congressional act, which meant that they were subject to the Constitution and that their inhabitants were citizens of the United States. Members of indigenous tribes were considered wards of the U.S. government.

The political and civil status of the inhabitants of the Philippines and Puerto Rico, also acquired by cession in 1898, raised more complicated problems. In the Insular Cases of 1901–1903 the Supreme Court determined that the Philippines and Puerto Rico were not incorporated by the United States, but were "appurtenant thereto as a possession"; their inhabitants were neither aliens nor citizens. For them the designation "national" was created; a national owed allegiance to the U.S. government, was permitted to enter and leave the United States at will, and was entitled to the protection of federal laws. In 1900 Congress made Puerto Rican inhabitants "citizens of Puerto Rico," and in 1902 it made Philippine inhabitants "citizens of the Philippine Islands." In 1917 it conferred American citizenship on those persons made citizens of Puerto Rico by the act of 1900, but inhabitants of other incorporated territories received different treatment. The people of the Virgin Islands were granted U.S. citizenship in 1927, but Congress chose not to define the civil status of the people of Guam, Samoa, and the Panama Canal Zone, simply considering them to be "inhabitants . . . entitled to the protection of the United States."

Racist beliefs and doubts about the assimilability of territorial peoples were again crucial factors in determining the policy that lay behind the creation of the category of national; the category placed these people in an inferior civil position and, at least in the case of Polynesian and most Filipino applicants, denied them the opportunity to become citizens through naturalization, on the grounds that they were racially ineligible for citizenship. William Howard Taft, while still civil governor of the Philippines, explained that the reason for this policy was that "tropical peoples cannot lift themselves as the Anglo-Saxons"; he firmly believed that the Filipinos were not capable of quick adaptation to self-government, an argument he used to justify the denial of independence to the islands. American citizenship was viewed as a delicate, precious handiwork; people unaccustomed to the practice and philosophy of democracy needed a long period of tutelage before they could develop the capacity to exercise its rights.

The position of the American Indians was affected by these views on the incorporation of territorial peoples. Throughout the 19th century, Indian tribes continued to be regarded as separate nations existing within the territory of the United States; as such, they were dealt with through treaties and acts of Congress. Congress had naturalized some Indians on an irregular basis through these treaties and other acts, and the Dawes Act of 1887 granted citizenship to Indians who had left the tribe for civil society; but not until 1924 did Congress grant citizenship to all Indians born within the jurisdiction of the U.S. government. At the same time their status was changed from one based on the separate-nation principle to one resembling that of inhabitants of the incorporated territories.

THE AMERICANIZATION MOVEMENT

Before World War I social reformers, legislators, and policy makers learned that the number of naturalized male adults had increased by only 7 percent from 1900 to 1910, while the number of alien adult males had increased by 73 percent. The proportion of aliens among all foreign-born adult males grew from 43 percent in 1900 to 55 percent in 1919 (see Table 2). Many policy makers feared that new immigrants from southern and eastern Europe were not making a serious effort to acquire U.S. citizenship. The U.S. Immigration Commission asserted in 1911 that there were critical differences between the old immigrants of northern and western Europe and the new eastern and southern European immigrants. The earlier immigrants had come to secure religious and political freedom and to help build a republican society, whereas the new immigrants had come only for material betterment. The recent arrivals had by and large come from countries whose government and religion were authoritarian, often even despotic; they had had no experience with democratic institutions or republican government; they had little intention of becoming citizens, and, even if they had, they were ill-prepared to exercise democratic rights.

Table 2. Aliens in the United States, 1890–1970.

Year	Total U.S. population	Number of aliens[a]	Aliens as percent of total population
1890	62,947,714	—	—
1900	75,994,575	—	—
1910	91,972,266	—	—
1920	105,710,620	7,430,809	7
1930	122,775,046	6,284,613	5
1940	131,669,275	4,314,631	3
1950	150,216,110	2,784,425	2
1960	179,325,657	—	—
1970	203,193,774		2

Year	Total foreign-born adult males	Adult male aliens[a]	Male aliens as percent of foreign-born adult males
1890	4,348,459	1,802,706	42
1900	5,010,286	2,161,479	43
1910	6,780,214	3,741,911	55
1920	7,063,594	3,743,368	53
1930	7,218,977	2,971,273	41
1940	5,969,588	1,893,381	32
1950	5,092,230	1,110,335	22
1960	4,382,844	—	—
1970	3,864,834	1,145,451	30

Year	Total foreign-born adult females	Adult female aliens[a]	Female aliens as percent of foreign-born adult females
1890	—	—	—
1900	—	—	—
1910	—	—	—
1920	5,022,799	2,724,224	54
1930	6,117,376	2,683,399	44
1940	5,323,233	2,239,797	45
1950	4,928,220	1,443,670	29
1960	4,596,680	—	—
1970	4,655,564	1,579,920	34

Source: U.S. Bureau of the Census, *Historical Statistics of the United States, Colonial Times to 1970* (Washington, D.C., 1975), p. 116.

a. Includes those aliens who had filed a declaration of intention of citizenship, and those whose nationality was not reported. The Census Bureau indicated "that much the larger proportion of those for whom no report as to citizenship was secured were aliens."

Partly in response to such concerns, Congress centralized and upgraded the naturalization procedure by forming a separate Bureau of Naturalization under the authority of a Commissioner of Naturalization in 1913. The bureau received all declarations, petitions, and naturalization approvals filed in the country; it administered the naturalization law, checked to see that only qualified applicants received citizenship, and served as a clearing-house for organized efforts to promote naturalization. The secretary of labor reported two years later that the naturalization examiners were withholding citizenship from large numbers of applicants ignorant of the American form of government, and this soon led to the organization of citizenship classes to teach petitioners for naturalization what they needed to know. The secretary estimated that 75 percent of all aliens could be transformed through citizenship classes into desirable citizenship material, and he recommended a national program to improve the quality of applicants.

In its first stages, bureau agents held conferences with public-school authorities in Chicago, St. Louis, Milwaukee, St. Paul, Minneapolis, Philadelphia, and New York in 1914 and in several other cities the next year. The delegates approved the idea of a cooperative movement between local public schools and the Bureau of Naturalization.

The bureau then conducted a national survey in 1915 to determine what efforts the public schools were making to prepare foreigners for citizenship, the nature of the citizenship courses they were offering, and the number attending their courses who were candidates for naturalization. The results showed that nearly all school systems in the larger cities offered citizenship classes for adults. New York City had the most extensive program: 1,000 classes in which 40,000 adult foreigners were enrolled. The classes taught English, basic writing, American history, and civics; attendance was often better than in the regular night-school courses. One school official saw a decided interest in the work and a determined desire to learn the English language and American customs and laws.

To aid the public schools, the Bureau of Naturalization sent the names and addresses of those who had filed first and second papers to school systems throughout the country and compiled and distributed a standardized textbook called *An Outline Course in Citizenship* (it was followed by other editions). The bureau also approached candidates for citizenship through letters exhorting them to attend citizenship courses, and it devised a "certificate of graduation," bearing signatures of bureau officials and local school authorities, which was presented to candidates when they became citizens.

Between 1913 and 1930 the Bureau of Naturalization coordinated its work with the efforts of the U.S. Bureau of Education and of citizens' organizations such as the National Americanization Committee, in order to promote and publicize the cause of naturalization. Progressive political reforms, such as the initiative and referendum, made it seem even more imperative that the foreign-born be educated in the duties of American citizenship and properly qualified for naturalization, especially those millions of newcomers from southern and eastern Europe whose notions of democracy were allegedly so underdeveloped.

Although these agencies showered immigrants with publicity and propaganda, they were aware that naturalization should not be coerced. They wanted to have as citizens only those who wanted to be citizens, who had sufficient interest in American society and politics to participate in civic life, and who possessed sufficient intelligence to make sensible political decisions. The principle underlying the movement was that the active participatory citizenship they projected as the goal of assimilation could only be secured if the naturalization process that led up to it was voluntary and popular. To compel foreigners to naturalize would be self-defeating; the indifferent, the reluctant, and the disloyal should not be encouraged. Spectacular Fourth of July celebrations, patriotic parades, and mass naturalization ceremonies were held in the major immigrant population centers to dramatize the significance of U.S. citizenship

and to involve masses of foreigners as participants in civic culture.

During the twenties and thirties social scientists began to study the naturalization rates of alien groups in an attempt to gauge how this Americanization campaign was progressing. Statistical studies of naturalization cases showed that the foreign-born with the longest residence were also the most likely to have been naturalized, and that, generally speaking, immigrants took considerably longer than the minimum five years to acquire citizenship. New immigrant groups took an average of 10.6 years, a figure that policy makers liked to interpret as confirming their theory that those people had a low degree of civic consciousness, although attempts were also made to refute that notion by showing that naturalization rates correlated better with education, occupation, and income than with ethnic background. On the other hand, whatever the reasons, one study showed that some new immigrant groups were taking an average of 20 years to acquire citizenship, although a host of government and private studies revealed that many were making an enormous effort to become naturalized.

The civic organizations of various nationality groups organized courses in English-language instruction and American history for applicants. In New Jersey in 1920 the Passaic Local of the Amalgamated Textile Workers of America, the union with the largest membership of aliens in the state, started classes in English and citizenship and planned to add courses in history, economics, and government. It was often very difficult for the immigrants to attend them, however. State bureaus of education conducted interviews that revealed over and over the serious obstacles these mostly poor and working-class people had to overcome in order to get to classes. They worked at night when the classes were held, or had to mind the children while the wife went to work, or were simply too exhausted after a hard day's factory labor. Nevertheless many managed it. The Massachusetts Department of Education reported the sacrifices involved as "both inspiring and pathetic." A Plymouth man rode ten miles after work, often without his supper, to attend his class; in Shirley, a group of Polish men went to class three nights a week, and their wives attended the other two while they looked after the children; a French Canadian resident of Melrose worked nights, and cut short his sleep to attend classes during the day. Although the average course lasted seven months and classes were held nearly every day, Cambridge reported 220 students with a 100-percent-attendance record for the whole term. In Worcester over 89 percent of those enrolled at the beginning of the term were still there at the end, and students in other towns had similar records.

These reports reflect the growing conviction on the part of many resident aliens that U.S. citizenship would give them the rights, privileges, and protections guaranteed by the federal government; they would live, vote, and secure work on the same basis as native U.S. citizens and would escape the restrictions and encumbrances of alien status. Citizenship also meant acceptance as an American: it was an unimpeachable sign that the newcomer had assimilated and had become equal as a result of possessing a set of rights that he or she had not known as an alien.

Along with this Americanization campaign, World War I had brought with it a wartime patriotism that combined nationalism, xenophobia, and constant fears about alien "subversion." In 1917 a federal law mandated deportation for any alien who at any time after his entry into the United States had advocated revolution or sabotage, and in the following year over 7,000 enemy aliens were arrested by the Justice Department, many of them German Americans; some were interned. To avoid any possibility that alien voters might gain control of local elections, in 1918 three states abolished alien suffrage.

After the war, frequent strikes and bombings by radicals aggravated the wartime mood. Using the 1917 deportation law as the basis for summary arrests and persecutions, Attorney General A. Mitchell Palmer jailed 6,000 suspects in 1920, including many citizens and many who were neither radicals, nor socialists, nor Communists; 600 aliens were actually deported. Although the attorney general repeatedly asked Congress for a general sedition law, he did not get one, and Secretary of Labor William B. Wilson at least saw to it that the deportation hearings were conducted according to the rules of evidence and fair play.

After World War I naturalization was denied by the courts to men who had been conscientious objectors, or who confessed conscientious scruples against the shedding of blood, or who lacked a clear attachment "to the principles of the Constitution." The U.S. Supreme Court denied citizenship to pacifists. Socialists, Communists, and other radicals were called into court by U.S. attorneys and their citizenship papers canceled. The Supreme Court in 1920 revoked the papers of a German American who had defended the sinking of the *Lusitania* and had "praised the attitude of Germany" during the war. Although he had filed his first papers in 1904, the Court ruled that his subsequent activities demonstrated that he had not made the declaration in "full faith," and his papers were confiscated. Throughout the 1920s courts went to extreme lengths and used questionable criteria to test for loyalty to the United States when they reviewed naturalization cases.

NATIONAL SECURITY AND LIBERALIZING NATURALIZATION, 1941 TO THE PRESENT

Notions about alien subversives persisted into the thirties, and the thousands of central European refugees fleeing fascism often received a rather cautious welcome. The strict security screening they underwent sent over 117,000 aliens back to where they had come from, many disqualified on political grounds (see Table 3). As the European situation became more tense the federal government took additional steps to protect national security and to monitor the activities of aliens. Congress passed the Alien Registration Act of 1940, which required the fingerprinting and registering of over 5 million aliens in the country. When the United States entered the war at the end of 1941, over 1 million people were classified as "enemy aliens" and had a variety of restrictions placed upon their activities; eventually they were reclassified as "aliens of enemy nationality," and many of these restrictions were abolished. Over 600,000 Italians were placed in this category, along with 35,000 Japanese and thousands of Germans.

Table 3. Aliens deported, 1892–1970.

Years	Number
1892–1900	3,127
1901–1910	11,558
1911–1920	27,912
1921–1930	92,157
1931–1940	117,086
1941–1950	110,849
1951–1960	129,887
1961–1970	96,374

Source: U.S. Bureau of the Census, *Historical Statistics of the United States, Colonial Times to 1970* (Washington, D.C., 1975), p. 114.

No further steps were taken against most Germans and Italians, but all persons of Japanese origin or ancestry, alien and citizen alike, living on the West Coast were detained in relocation camps from 1942 to 1945.

The drive for national security and wartime victory produced several changes in the naturalization law. A reorganized and combined Immigration and Naturalization Service was transferred in 1940 from the Department of Labor to the Justice Department. Under the jurisdiction of the attorney general, the service was able to coordinate its activities with those of Justice Department agents in charge of national security. Congress enacted the Nationality Act of 1940 which unified and tightened the scattered and confusing naturalization statutes enacted since 1906. The act still barred Filipinos and other Asian nationals from becoming citizens, but it opened up naturalization to indigenous territorial peoples such as the Aleuts and Eskimos. The ban on the immigration and naturalization of the Chinese was lifted in 1943 as a gesture of good will toward America's Chinese allies, and in 1946 the ban on citizenship was lifted against Filipinos and East Indians in a similar gesture of acknowledgment of their resistance to the common enemy.

After World War II the Cold War became a primary force shaping the development of federal policy toward aliens. Internal subversion and the threat of war against the Communist powers absorbed the attention of Congress, which responded with two major bills—the Internal Security Act of 1950 and the McCarran-Walter Immigration and Nationality Act of 1952. The 1950 act revived the 1940 Alien Registration Act, and required that all aliens register and report their current address to the Immigration and Naturalization Service in January of each year. It also stipulated that anyone who had ever been a Communist party member could be excluded from entry or deported.

The McCarran-Walter Act of 1952 recodified and updated the myriad immigration and naturalization statutes that had been passed in the previous half-century. This gigantic 300-page omnibus bill relaxed the restrictions on alleged ex-Communists, but enormously strengthened the federal government's deportation powers and widened its surveillance of alien residents. Aliens who became affiliated with any group or effort to oppose the U.S. government, who advocated or taught the destruction of property, who became drug addicts, or who were connected with immoral practices or an "immoral place" could be deported at any time after entry. The law gave federal officials blanket authority for prosecuting deportation cases. In the 1950s over 130,000 aliens were deported, the highest number of deportations ever ordered in a ten-year period. Many of them, however, did not come under these provisions, but were simply illegal Mexican itinerant workers. Some were the same individuals deported repeatedly.

The McCarran-Walter Act also established a new requirement that significantly raised the qualifications for citizenship: an applicant not only had to be able to speak and understand English, but he had to be able to read and write "simple words and phrases." Despite this raising of qualifications, the number of rejected petitioners was 66 percent lower in the 1950s than it had been the decade before.

The most important change in naturalization policy, however, was the abolition of all racial tests or marital qualifications for citizenship. The act declared that "the right of a person to become a naturalized citizen of the United States shall not be denied or abridged because of race or sex or because such person is married." Thus all persons were permitted for the first time by a general federal law to apply individually for naturalization and to be considered purely on the bases of merit and qualification. At one stroke the arbitrary category of "aliens ineligible for citizenship," which had consigned Asian nationalities to the inferior status of permanent-resident aliens for nearly a century, was swept away. The procedures and requirements for naturalization as a U.S. citizen remain today essentially the same as those set forth in the McCarran-Walter Act.

The composition of the foreign-born population seeking naturalization changed gradually in the next three decades. From 1900 to 1940, the vast majority of naturalized persons came from countries in Europe. In the 1970s, by contrast, a large number of naturalized citizens have come from elsewhere: some of the leading providers of naturalized immigrants have been China, Taiwan, Korea, Mexico, the Philippines, Canada, and the West Indies.

Throughout the 20th century, time of arrival and rate of return migration have been strongly correlated with naturalization patterns. In the early decades of the century, immigrants from northern and western European nations, who had resided longest in the United States, had the highest proportions of naturalized persons, while immigrants from southern and eastern European countries, more recent arrivals, had the lowest percentages of naturalized persons (see Table 4). Sixty-three percent of the English foreign-born, 69 percent of the Swedish foreign-born, and 72 percent of the German foreign-born were U.S. citizens in 1920; however, only 7 percent of the Albanian, 12 percent of the Bulgarian, 17 percent of the Greek, 28 percent of the Polish and Italian, and 29 percent of the Hungarian foreign-born were naturalized. The foreign-born from southern and eastern Europe were also those who returned in very large proportions to their home countries. When the flow of immigrants decreased after 1924, the proportion of the naturalized foreign-born from southern and eastern Europe climbed until it equaled or exceeded the proportion of naturalized newcomers from northern and western Europe. By 1950, for example, nearly 80 percent of foreign-born Italians had secured citizenship, as compared with 75 percent of immigrants from the United Kingdom. Time of arrival and rate of return migration

Table 4. Percentage of foreign-born persons naturalized, by country of origin, 1910–1970.[a]

Country	1910[b]	1920[c]	1930[c]	1950[c]	1970
All countries	45.6	48.7	58.8	67.9	63.6
England	59.4	63.1	67.0	} 74.8	
Wales	69.2	72.9	73.8		65.3
Scotland	56.5	60.9	53.5	—	
Northern Ireland	—	} 65.7	68.1	—	—
Ireland	67.8		66.1	79.7	81.8
Norway	57.1	67.3	70.9	82.4	82.5
Sweden	62.8	69.0	72.6	84.5	85.3
Denmark	61.6	} 69.2	74.9	—	82.2
Iceland	—		68.3	—	—
Netherlands	56.8	56.0	66.6	—	69.5
Belgium	43.0	49.0	65.2	—	—
Luxembourg	}	72.5	80.3	—	—
Switzerland	61.8	64.9	67.4	—	70.5
France	49.6	56.7	63.1	—	65.5
Germany	69.5	72.8	70.5	80.1	77.5[d]
Poland	—	28.0	50.5	72.0	80.2
Czechoslovakia	—	45.8	61.3	77.5	85.0
Austria	24.6	37.7	63.0	79.5	86.9
Hungary	14.3	29.1	55.7	—	83.4
Yugoslavia	—	25.1	46.3	—	71.0
Russia	26.1	} 40.2	62.2	82.7[e]	88.5
Latvia	—		60.9	—	—
Estonia	—		42.3	—	—
Lithuania	—	25.6	47.5	—	80.1
Finland	30.6	41.3	51.0	—	75.1
Romania	28.8	41.1	60.3	—	81.3
Bulgaria	—	12.1	38.3	—	—
Turkey in Europe	—	20.2	45.1	—	—
Greece	—	16.8	44.7	—	65.2
Albania	—	7.4	31.7	—	—
Italy	17.7	28.1	50.0	79.5	79.2
Spain	16.4	9.9	18.9	—	—
Portugal	24.9	16.4	18.7	—	—
Other Europe	35.6	48.0	47.8	—	61.0
Armenia	—	28.9	46.8	—	—
Palestine	—	37.5	56.5	—	—
Syria	—	28.9	50.9	—	—
Turkey in Asia	21.2	25.1	46.0	—	—
Other Asia	33.4	36.5	41.9	—	38.5
Canada, French	44.7	44.8	46.9	72.3	} 63.4
Canada, Other	} 53.9	57.9	53.4	71.0	
Newfoundland		47.4	38.8	—	—
Cuba	} 30.6	21.1	22.2	—	} 24.3
Other West Indies		34.8	45.8	—	
Mexico	10.7	5.9	23.8	26.3	38.8
Central and South America	34.8	24.1	28.8	—	—
Africa		43.6	51.1	—	—
Australia		49.5	59.3	—	—
Azores		20.7	24.4	—	—
Other Atlantic islands	} 32.3	22.2	34.7	—	—
Pacific Islands		50.1	54.2	—	—
Not specified		37.4	32.4	—	—
Born at sea		54.4	57.7	—	—

Source: U.S. Bureau of the Census, *13th Census of the United States, 1910* (Washington, D.C., 1913), I, *Population,* p. 1068; U.S. Bureau of the Census, *15th Census of the United States, 1930* (Washington, D.C., 1933), II, *Population,* pp. 406–407; U.S. Bureau of the Census, *Census of the Population, 1950* (Washington, D.C., 1954), *Special Reports,* pt. 3, ch. A, p. 130; U.S. Bureau of the Census, *Census of the Population, 1970,* I, *Characteristics of the Population* (Washington, D.C., 1973), pt. 1, p. 60u.

a. Data for 1940 and 1960 not available.
b. Percentage of foreign-born white persons 21 years and older.
c. Includes only foreign-born white persons.
d. Includes East and West Germany.
e. Excludes persons of Ukrainian origin.

turned home often; as a consequence, they have had low naturalization percentages.

In 1940 more than half the total alien population resided in the Northeast and Midwest, mainly in New York, New Jersey, Pennsylvania, Massachusetts, Michigan, and Illinois. Since that time the concentration of alien population has shifted westward with the overall distribution of the nation's population. Signifying this trend, the 1970 Census reported that California had replaced New York as the state with the largest number of resident aliens.

The highest percentage of aliens in the population was recorded in the 1920 U.S. Census and has been declining gradually ever since. In 1920, 7 percent of the population was alien; in 1940, 3 percent. In 1950 the alien population was only 2 percent of the country's population, and remained at that level up to 1970. It is important to bear in mind that these statistics refer only to those aliens enumerated in the decennial census, which do not record accurately aliens residing illegally in the country.

From 1900 the average number of aliens annually naturalized steadily increased and peaked at World War II, as a result of the large number of aliens acquiring citizenship through military service (see Table 5). The drop in the alien population after the war led to a decline in annual naturalizations. In the 1950s the number of naturalizations was 50 percent of the total from 1940 to 1950. On the annual average, more alien women than men have been naturalized each year since 1940, chiefly because the population of adult female aliens has been greater than that of male aliens since that time.

The alien population has become significantly younger since World War II. In 1944, 72 percent of the alien population was under 60 years of age; in 1970, 88 percent was under 65, and 70 percent was under 44.

The growth in the alien population spurred by the liberal Hart-Celler Immigration Act of 1965 has produced a steady rise in the number of naturalizations each year. In 1975, for example, about 142,000 persons were naturalized, 8 percent more than the approximately 132,000 naturalized the year before.

The alien population today is younger than that of 1940; ethnic groups from the Western Hemisphere and Asia are more heavily represented, and aliens are geographically more evenly distributed between the Atlan-

have also been related to the naturalization of immigrants arriving in the last two decades from Mexico, the West Indies, Central and South America, and East Asian countries. These recently arrived peoples re-

Table 5. Alien naturalization, 1907–1976.

Period	Average number of petitions for naturalization per year		Average number of naturalization certificates issued per year	
	Filed	Denied	Male	Female
1907–1910	41,000	4,425	—	—
1911–1920	138,140	11,870	—	—
1921–1930	188,430	16,550	116,620	25,520
1931–1940	163,710	4,580	96,840	55,010
1941–1950	193,810	6,480	94,150	104,550
1951–1960	123,050	2,760	50,350	68,640
1961–1970	114,300	2,360	51,350	60,680
1971–1976	140,566	2,466	63,166	71,700

Source: U.S. Department of Commerce, *Statistical Abstract of the United States, 1977* (Washington, D.C., 1977), p. 89.

tic and Pacific coasts. Recently policy makers have been concerned with the presence of a large population of illegal aliens who have migrated from Mexico across land borders to settle and work in the Southwest. Some steps have been taken to restrict their entry, to deport them, and to penalize their employers, but a systematic policy toward these aliens remains unformulated.

The development of American citizenship has been a vital ingredient in the forming of an American nation out of a multiplicity of ethnic groups. The history of citizenship has revealed the changing relationship of the individual citizen to the political structure of the nation. Citizenship was created in the American Revolution as each inhabitant placed his consent in republican government, by that voluntary act approving its sovereignty and binding his allegiance to it.

The political structure of the republic was neither securely integrated nor clearly defined in law in the first half of the 19th century. Sectional conflict between slave states and free states was mirrored in an ambiguous constitutional idea of citizenship in which competing allegiances to state and federal governments clashed.

The Civil War and Reconstruction brought a new and enduring unity to the national polity and established the primacy of the federal government. As Reconstruction amendments were passed to extend constitutional protection and national citizenship to blacks as well as whites, the status of U.S. citizenship became decisively national in scope and federal in origin. The states, however, were still accorded through Supreme Court decisions primary control over the personal, property, and civil rights of their inhabitants; the sphere of the immunities and privileges of federal citizenship were to be strictly limited to the general protections articulated in the Constitution and federal statutes.

In the late 19th and early 20th centuries the presence of aliens arriving through immigration and as a result of territorial acquisition forced open the boundaries of American nationality. A hierarchy of civil ranks—aliens ineligible for citizenship, territorial nationals, declarants for citizenship—proliferated to control the incorporation of new immigrant groups and to threaten the traditional concept of a unitary American citizenship. Naturalization had been a casual and informal process, but gradually crude racist criteria and upgraded naturalization standards were applied to admit only "suitable" aliens. The process of including new peoples was tempered by favoritism toward those thought to be more racially compatible and better prepared for civic duties. The unfamiliarity of some new immigrants with democratic government, their acquaintance with monarchical regimes and authoritarian religions, and their ignorance of English cast doubt in the minds of nativists as to their readiness for citizenship rights.

The trend toward restriction was counterbalanced by a powerful drive toward assimilation. While certain racial groups were excluded from naturalization, the vast majority of aliens continued to be accepted for citizenship. They were exposed to a widespread campaign led by government and private organizations to promote the speedy acquisition of American citizenship, especially during the Americanization drive of the World

War I era. Schools became the vehicles for the civic education of immigrants and their children which would prepare them for the responsibilities and duties of citizenship. The movement for citizenship encouraged voluntary, popular naturalization.

By the mid-20th century the racial restrictions on naturalization seemed both impolitic and impractical. Experience had shown that all ethnic groups, given time and encouragement, had the capacity to assimilate into the national civic culture, and so U.S. citizenship was opened to all.

Broader access to citizenship and expanded federal safeguards over the rights of citizens accompanied the building of a more centralized government. As the powers of the federal government grew and its jurisdiction was gradually extended to encompass more aspects of social life, every person had to be placed in a single and consistent relation to the federal authority through citizenship. Fears that ethnocultural or racial background could inhibit the proper exercise of citizenship rights were supplanted by a confidence that citizenship was a transcendent status obtainable by all individuals who shared a common membership in a democratic polity.

Bibliography

Informative legal studies on citizenship and naturalization in the United States are Frank G. Franklin, *The Legislative History of Naturalization in the United States From the Revolutionary War to 1861* (1906; reprint, New York, 1969); Luella Gettys, *The Law of Citizenship in the United States* (Chicago, 1934); John P. Roche, *The Early Development of United States Citizenship* (Ithaca, N.Y., 1949); I-Mien Tsiang, *The Question of Expatriation in America Prior to 1907* (Baltimore, 1942); Frederick Van Dyne, *A Treatise on the Law of Naturalization of the United States* (Washington, D.C., 1907); and John S. Wise, *A Treatise on American Citizenship* (Northport, N.Y., 1906). An important historical study of citizenship is James H. Kettner, *The Development of American Citizenship, 1607–1870* (Chapel Hill, N.C., 1978). Morton Keller, *Affairs of State* (Cambridge, Mass., 1977), provides an account of the impact of late-19th-century immigration and territorial acquisition on citizenship and naturalization. Also illuminating is Oscar and Mary Handlin, *The Dimensions of Liberty* (Cambridge, Mass., 1961).

The most helpful works on the status and rights of aliens are Norman Alexander, *Rights of Aliens under the Federal Constitution* (Montpelier, Vt., 1931); Max J. Kohler "Un-American Character of Race Legislation," *Annals of the American Academy* 34 (1909): 275–293; Milton R. Konvitz, *The Alien and the Asiatic in American Law* (1946; reprint, Ithaca, N.Y., 1965); and Norman MacKenzie, *The Legal Status of Aliens in Pacific Countries* (London, 1937). Racial restrictions in the naturalization law are discussed in D.O. McGovney, "American Citizenship," *Columbia Law Review* 11 (1911): 231–250, 326–347; and "Race Discrimination in Naturalization," *Iowa Law Bulletin* 8 (1923): 129–161, 211–244.

The social process of naturalization in the early 20th century is studied by William S. Bernard, "Cultural Determinants of Naturalization," *American Sociological Review* 1 (1936): 943–953; Niles Carpenter, *Immigrants and Their Children, 1920* (Washington, D.C., 1927); and John P. Gavit, *Americans by Choice* (1922; reprint, Montclair, N.J., 1971).

The most useful histories of the Americanization movement are Edward G. Hartmann, *The Movement to Americanize the Immigrant* (1948; reprint, New York, 1967); John Higham, *Strangers in the Land* (New York, 1963); and Gerd Korman, *Industrialization, Immigrants, and Americanizers* (Madison, Wis., 1967). Interesting documentary collections on immigrant naturalization are Edith Abbott, *Immigration, Select Documents and Case Records* (Chicago, 1924) and Philip Davis, ed., *Immigration and Americanization* (Boston, 1920). The rise of civic education is described in Charles E. Merriam, *Civic Education in the United States* (New York, 1934).

Philosophical commentaries on citizenship and democracy are Alexander Bickel, *The Morality of Consent* (New Haven, Conn., 1975), and Michael Walzer, *Obligations: Essays on Disobedience, War and Citizenship* (Cambridge, Mass., 1970).

REED UEDA

NAVAJOS: *see* AMERICAN INDIANS

NEGROES: *see* AFRO-AMERICANS

NESTORIANS: *see* ASSYRIANS

NETHERLANDERS: *see* DUTCH; FRISIANS

NEW ZEALANDERS: *see* AUSTRALIANS AND NEW ZEALANDERS

NEZ PERCES: *see* AMERICAN INDIANS

NICARAGUANS: *see* CENTRAL AND SOUTH AMERICANS

NIPMUCS: *see* AMERICAN INDIANS

NORDIC

Now used to designate natives of northern Europe, the term Nordic was a key concept in the racist anthropology of the early 20th century. Americans of European origin were thought to belong to one of three entirely distinct physical types: Nordic (which included Anglo-Saxon and Teutonic, or Aryan), Alpine, or Mediterranean. Nordics were viewed as superior, but their dominance was believed threatened by the mass immigration of "inferior" types from eastern and southern Europe. This theory, later entirely discredited, was the basis of the discriminatory immigration quotas enacted in the 1920s and not repealed until 1965.

NORTH CAUCASIANS

The term North Caucasian is a convenient way to refer to a variety of ethnolinguistic groups who originate north of the Caucasus Mountains within the borders of the Soviet Union. It is not a purely geographical designation, however, for the various peoples who live in the area have a well-developed sense of unity based on their Islamic faith and their common resistance to Russian domination. They are sometimes referred to as "Gortsy" or "Tavlintsy," both names that mean mountaineers, or as Circassians or Cherkess, after one of the largest of the groups in the area.

There are approximately 500 North Caucasian families in the United States, representing the largest group of Soviet Muslims in the country. They comprise three different linguistic groups. The most numerous are the Ibero-Caucasians: the Abkhazians, Adyghe, Cherkess, Kabardians, Chechen, Ingush, and the Dagestanis. Next in size is the Turkic group: the Karachais, Balkars, and Kumyks. The Iranian-speaking group is the smallest, represented only by Ossetians. With the exception of some Eastern Orthodox Ossetians and Abkhazians, all North Caucasians are Sunni Muslims.

In their homeland each group constitutes an officially recognized nationality; their languages, written in the Latin alphabet between 1929 and 1939 and in the Cyrillic since 1939, are recognized by the Soviet government as official literary languages in their eight respective national territories. These are the Abkhazian, Kabardino-Balkarian, North Ossetian, Checheno-Ingush, and Dagestan Autonomous Soviet Socialist republics, and the

Adyghei, Karachayevo-Cherkess, and (South) Ossetian autonomous oblasts. Their languages, however, are mutually unintelligible so that in order to communicate with one another the North Caucasians have long used a lingua franca. Before the Russian Revolution in 1917 their common language was classical Arabic; since 1917 it has been Azeri Turkic or Russian. At present there are more than 3 million North Caucasians in the U.S.S.R.: 80,000 Abkhazians, 280,000 Kabardians, 180,000 Karachais-Balkars, 175,000 Adyghes-Cherkess, 490,000 Ossetians, 770,000 Chechen-Ingush, and over 1 million Dagestanis.

Located along important trade routes between the Black and Caspian seas, the territory inhabited by the North Caucasians was of strategic importance to tsarist Russia, especially during its centuries of struggle with the Ottoman Empire. The Russians embarked in 1783 upon a concerted effort to conquer the territory but it was almost a century before they were successful, and as a result of the struggle half a million Circassians emigrated to Turkey during the last four years of hostilities (1861–1865). After the Russian Revolution, a united Autonomous Mountain S.S.R. was established in 1920 but it was replaced in 1924 by five individual autonomous provinces for the Kabardino-Balkars, Karachayevo-Cherkess, Chechen, Ossetians, and Ingush. During World War II the Germans occupied this territory. When the Soviets returned in 1944 they deported the Karachais, Balkars, Chechen, and Ingush and abolished or reorganized their national territories.

Political upheavals have been the primary cause of North Caucasian emigration. During the 1860s after the collapse of North Caucasian resistance to Russian rule, more than a million Circassians, Kabardians, Karachais-Balkars, and Muslim Ossetians moved to the Ottoman Empire, particularly to central and western Anatolia, Syria, and Jordan. A somewhat smaller group settled in Turkey, Germany, France, and Italy following the upheavals of the revolution and civil war in 1917–1921. A third group of emigrants is made up of individuals and families who fled during World War II or became German prisoners of war, some remaining in Germany.

The majority of North Caucasians in the United States came separately or in small groups during the late 1940s and early 1950s. Of these, 70 percent came from Germany, 20 percent from Turkey, and the remainder from other countries such as Syria, Jordan, and Italy. Most settled in the New York City area, and especially in Paterson, N.J. Some went directly to California and a small group of Karachais went to North Carolina.

The occupational profile of the North Caucasians in the countries they left behind has in the main been repeated in the United States. The former prisoners of war from Germany hold blue-collar positions, while the immigrants who came via Turkey have been teachers, technicians, engineers, and other professionals.

The North Caucasians have established two organizations, both of which are located in Paterson, N.J. The Circassian Benevolent Association was founded in 1952 by the Adyghe-Cherkess and Kabardians, and is used also by the Ossetians. The Karachais Türkleri Dini ve Kultur Derneği (Center of Religion and Culture of the Karachais Turks) was founded in 1963 and serves as a prayer house and social center for the Karachais, Balkars, and Kumyks.

In spite of the ethnic and linguistic diversity within the North Caucasian group, they have maintained unity and cohesiveness in the United States. They call themselves North Caucasians or Circassians as a designation of the larger group to which they belong. Some of the older members still speak their local languages, but Russian, Arabic, or Turkish are used by the group as a whole. Muslim religious festivals are strictly observed, and secular cultural traditions such as folk dancing are continued. Almost 90 percent of the marriages are contracted within the Muslim community, and the North Caucasians maintain familial and cultural contacts, including the exchange of publications, with the very active North Caucasian organizations in Turkey, Syria, and Jordan.

Bibliography
There is no study of North Caucasians who have come to the United States and very little written in English about their homeland. The chapter on "The North Caucasian Peoples," in Walter Kolarz, *Russia and Her Colonies* (New York, 1955), is an introduction to the subject, and there is a history of the Adyghe-Cherkess and their emigration to the Middle East in Shauket Mufti, *Heroes and Emperors in Circassian History* (Beirut, Lebanon, 1972).

ALEXANDRE BENNIGSEN

NORWEGIANS

Because of its location and its long coastline, Norway has always had its face turned to the west, toward the world beyond the sea. From the beginning, Norwegians have been seafarers, explorers, and colonizers. Before A.D. 1000 they had settled in Iceland, the Faeroe Islands, and Greenland, and had established beachheads in Normandy, Ireland, Scotland, the Isle of Man, and parts of England. Voyages from Iceland and Greenland led to the discovery of Vinland (North America) in the year 1000 by Leif Ericson, a Norseman born in Iceland. Claims of lasting Norse settlements on the east coast of North America and of penetrations as far west as Minnesota and North Dakota as early as the 13th and 14th centuries, although rejected by scholars, have been hotly debated by many Norwegian Americans because they serve as symbols of ethnic pride and identity.

MIGRATION TO THE NEW WORLD

In modern times, Norwegian migration to America started on a modest scale in the 17th century. Norwegian seamen frequently shipped out in Dutch vessels, which brought many of them to the colony of New Netherland in the present state of New York. Some settled permanently in New Amsterdam (New York City), but most of them went inland to the Rensselaerwyck colony, where Albany is now located. Descendants of these early settlers still live in Albany, Troy, and Schenectady.

In the 19th century, no other country except Ireland contributed so large a proportion of its population to the settlement of North America. Between 1820 and 1975 over 855,000 Norwegians emigrated to the United States, a number nearly equal to the total population of Norway in 1820. Most emigrants left between 1840 and 1915. During the 1860s almost 98,000 new immigrants arrived from Norway, a number that far exceeded the total over the preceding 40 years. In the 1870s the numbers fell off slightly, but in the 1880s, when immigration from all of northern Europe peaked, more than

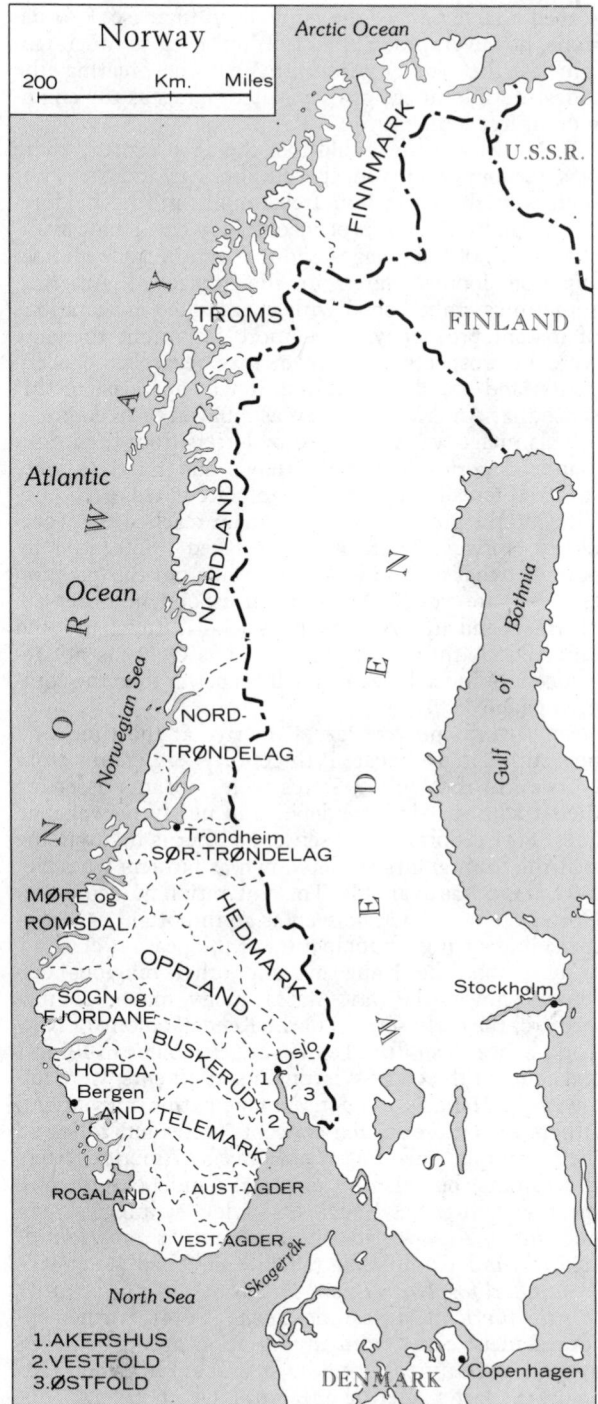

Norway

200   Km.   Miles

Arctic Ocean

U.S.S.R.

FINNMARK

TROMS   FINLAND

Atlantic

NORDLAND

Ocean

Norwegian Sea

Gulf of Bothnia

NORD-
TRØNDELAG

Trondheim
SØR-TRØNDELAG

MØRE og
ROMSDAL

HEDMARK

OPPLAND

SOGN og
FJORDANE

Stockholm

BUSKERUD   Oslo

HORDA-   1
Bergen   2   3
LAND   TELEMARK

ROGALAND   AUST-AGDER

VEST-AGDER

Skagerrak

North Sea

1.AKERSHUS
2.VESTFOLD
3.ØSTFOLD

DENMARK   Copenhagen

origin went into effect, there were almost 19,000 Norwegian immigrants, but from 1924 to 1965, Norway never filled its annual quota. The stream has continued to diminish from an average of a little more than 2,000 a year shortly after World War II to less than 400 annually in the 1970s.

THE NORWEGIAN-AMERICAN COMMUNITY

Americans of Norwegian descent are now spread over almost all of the United States and Canada. The heaviest concentrations are in the upper Midwest, particularly in Wisconsin, Minnesota, and the Dakotas. Here many settlements and communities with a predominantly Norwegian population and a distinct Norwegian flavor still exist, both in rural areas and in the cities, especially Chicago and Minneapolis. On the West Coast the greatest number of Norwegians live in Oregon, Washington, and British Columbia, with smaller concentrations in Seattle, San Francisco, and Los Angeles. The heaviest urban concentration, however, is in Brooklyn, N.Y., which with an estimated 40,000 Norwegians used to be referred to as the fourth-largest Norwegian city in the world.

The number of persons of Norwegian descent living in the United States today cannot be determined with accuracy. According to the U.S. Census, the number of foreign-born Norwegians peaked at 404,000 in 1910. An additional 609,000 second-generation Norwegian Americans brought the total to 1,013,000. By 1930 the number of foreign-born had dropped to 348,000. New arrivals were no longer keeping pace with the losses resulting partly from deaths and partly from return migration to Norway, which was particularly common among more recent immigrants. Of some 49,000 Norwegian immigrants and their American-born children who returned to Norway before World War I, almost 30,000 had arrived after 1900. On the other hand, by 1930 the number of second-generation Norwegians had increased to 752,000, making a total of 1,100,000 first- and second-generation Norwegians residing in the United States that year.

From then on there has been a steady decline in the number of first- and second-generation Norwegians living in the United States. In 1970 foreign-born Norwegians numbered 97,000, a good proportion of whom arrived after World War II. The total number of first- and second-generation Norwegians was 615,000.

These figures are of little help in determining the present size of the Norwegian ethnic group. Most immigrant groups in the United States, including the Norwegians, retain their ethnic identity beyond the second generation, in some cases into the fifth generation. Perhaps 3 million or more Americans today have partial Norwegian ancestry. But by no means all of these identify themselves as Norwegian all the time or even part of the time.

THE NORWEGIAN BACKGROUND

For at least a century prior to the Napoleonic wars, the Western world was fermenting with new and powerful ideas about liberty, human rights, and national identity and self-determination. To Norwegian peasants, these ideas conformed to old Nordic ideals. Many a battle had been fought to preserve the integrity and dignity of free men and women since Harold Fairhair

186,000 Norwegians came to the United States, almost double the number in the 1860s. There was another decline in the 1890s, but in the first decade of the 20th century, more than 190,000 migrants left Norway for the United States.

The period from 1910 to 1920 marked the end of mass migration. During the first half of the decade, Norwegian immigration dropped sharply, and during World War I it reached its lowest level in 65 years. There was an upsurge again in the early 1920s. In 1923, the year before the law establishing quotas based on national

had established the kingdom of Norway in the 9th century. In the late 14th century Norway fell under Danish rule, but the peasants maintained their rights as freeholders amidst grudging submission to Danish district officials. Toward the end of the 18th century, the old ideals were revived by a rising middle class of merchants, professionals, and intellectuals who sought political independence for Norway. The opportunity came after Napoleon's defeat, when Denmark was forced to cede Norway to the Swedish king. On May 17, 1814, a national convention declared Norway to be an independent kingdom. A brief war with Sweden brought a compromise whereby the king of Sweden was recognized as the king of Norway as well. This tenuous union was dissolved in 1905. By then, the celebration of May 17 as Norway's Independence Day was a symbol of Norwegian identity in the United States as well as in Norway.

But in the 19th century the ideals of freedom and individual integrity also manifested themselves directly through exceptionally high rates of emigration. At the beginning of that century, about 80 percent of Norway's population of less than a million belonged to the peasant class, described as *bønder*, whether they were landowning *gardfolk* (the majority) or landless *husmenn* or cotters. As in other Western countries, however, a relatively small middle class dominated the nation's political and cultural life. These were the people who occupied most of the powerful positions as *embetsmenn*, or crown officials, in the administrative bureaucracy of the young nation and to whom the peasants of Norway for generations had looked for leadership.

During the second half of the 18th century a movement began toward emancipation from this patronizing leadership, later reinforced by a pietistic religious awakening that swept the rural population of Norway during the first decades of the 19th century. Hans Nielsen Hauge (1771–1824), himself a peasant's son, was prominent in this movement. He traveled around the country organizing secret worship services that emphasized personal conversions and witnessing by lay preachers, in defiance of the law and in direct opposition to the state church. He also established cooperative business enterprises, showing the peasants the road to economic as well as religious independence. Stimulated by national-romantic ideas promulgated by the intellectual elite, the peasant movement of Norway soon blossomed into an important cultural and political force. It demanded political and economic equity for the peasants and recognition of the peasant way of life as an expression of the national "folk spirit" as opposed to the cosmopolitan lifestyle of the urban middle class.

THE IMAGE OF AMERICA

Only against this background of social and political unrest in quest of "freedom" can the extensive 19th-century Norwegian migration to America be understood. There were important economic and demographic pressures as well. The population of Norway climbed sharply in the 19th century, creating a critical situation and a higher rate of emigration from rural communities, where land for new cultivation was scarce. On the other hand, from the 1840s there was, coupled with liberal economic and social legislation, expansion of Norway's industry, commerce, shipping, and land transportation, and these developments ab-

sorbed a large part of the population increase. Few nations, however, proclaimed freedom with so much fanfare as the young American nation, creating the indestructible image of the United States as the champion of freedom.

In Norway by the middle of the 19th century there was freedom of religion, speech, thought, and trade. But there were those to whom freedom meant first and foremost equality. The prospects of free or cheap land available to all, of high wages and freedom of trade and occupation loomed large in the image of America, sometimes embellished with exaggerated expectations of instant prosperity. Even more important to many were the prospects of *social* equality, regardless of occupation and social background. It was not least in this sense that America was seen as a haven of freedom.

This image was confirmed by letters from the immigrants. America letters to friends and relatives were read and reread aloud, copied and circulated, even published in the press, until the message reached every corner of Norway. "Here it is not asked," one letter reported, "what or who was your father, but the question is, what are you?" Another correspondent observed, "Farmers and artisans are just as good as merchants and officials." A third letter stated, "The clergy is not regarded, nor indeed regards itself, as better than the common people."

Such words proved very attractive at the time, and not surprisingly most 19th-century emigrants from Norway to the United States were peasants asserting their traditional independence and newly reawakened quest for freedom in this sense. Neither is it surprising that the immigrants settled down as farmers wherever fertile land was available. The emigration movement in Norway may, in fact, be seen as an important aspect of the self-asserting emancipation of the peasant class.

Here, too, the Haugeans and other religious dissenters showed the way. A great many, maybe the majority, of the early settlers of the Kendall colony of New York, as well as of the Fox River settlement in Illinois and some of the older Wisconsin settlements, were followers of Hauge's religious emancipation movement. Others with more secular concepts of freedom followed their example, encouraged not only by America letters and rumors, but also by practical handbooks for prospective emigrants, such as Ole Rynning's *True Account of America for the Information and Help of Peasant and Commoner* (1838) and Johan Reiersen's *Pathfinder for Norwegian Emigrants to the United North-American States and Texas* (1844). Further encouragement came from immigration agents sent out by state governments, and by steamship lines and railroads, the latter offering cheap passage on special "immigrant trains" to the interior of the country. Officials in Norway offered warnings in vain, as did pastors of the Norwegian state church who had gone to the United States to serve Norwegian congregations: "It is *madness* that so many emigrate; thorn and thistle grow as abundantly here as in Norway!" The emigration fever, a contemporary observed, "spread through our country districts like a disease."

COLONIZING PROJECTS

One prominent figure in the early 19th-century Norwegian immigration was Klein Pedersen Hesthammer,

better known as Cleng Peerson (1783–1865), an independent religious dissenter who had connections with a small group of Quakers near Stavanger. In 1821 he went to America to investigate the prospects of settlement in northwestern New York. His report led to the first organized group migration from Norway. On July 4 or 5, 1825, 52 persons sailed from Stavanger in a small, 39-ton sloop, *Restauration* (Restoration). They were mostly religious dissenters from nearby rural districts; most were married couples, some with children. They had purchased the sloop for an equivalent of about $1,400 and loaded her with a cargo of iron, which they hoped to sell with the ship on arrival.

Cleng Peerson returned to the United States ahead of the group. He accompanied the settlers by steamboat up the Hudson River and through the newly opened Erie Canal to their new homes on the southern shores of Lake Ontario.

From the start, the Kendall settlement proved a near disaster. The thick forest was "almost an unsurmountable barrier," and economic problems and illness plagued the settlers. Eventually, the settlers cleared enough land to make a meager living, but many were disillusioned. In 1833 Cleng Peerson went looking for more promising opportunities. After traveling on foot across four states, he selected a site in the Fox River valley of northern Illinois and then walked back to Kendall with glowing reports of the "Promised Land." The new location was to become an important center for the further expansion of Norwegian settlements in the West.

Reportedly, Cleng Peerson's hope was to unite all Norwegians in America into one community, with all property owned in common. His contact with the Rappites (German pietists who established collectivist communes) in Pennsylvania may have stimulated the idea, and for a while in 1847 he joined the Swedish settlement at Bishop Hill in Illinois. He made several trips back to Norway but failed to attract immigrants to a settlement in Shelby County, Mo. He did succeed in establishing a small Norwegian colony in Bosque County, Tex., where the state legislature presented him with a farm in recognition of his services to immigrants. He died there at the age of 82.

Others took up the idea of creating a "New Norway" on American soil, with or without a communal organization. Hans Barlien (1772–1842), who was a self-taught peasant turned artisan, inventor, and manufacturer in Trondheim, attacked crown officials in the press and distributed freethinker pamphlets among the peasants. Elected to parliament in 1815, he became a vociferous supporter of the peasants, but in 1837, at the age of 65, frustrated by political intrigues and libel suits, he emigrated to the United States. His dream was to establish a self-sufficient Norwegian colony. In 1840 he settled at Sugar Creek in southeastern Iowa, and later that year, Cleng Peerson arrived there with a group of settlers from Norway. But Barlien died two years later with his dream still unrealized.

More famous was the project launched by the eminent Norwegian violinist Ole Bull (1810–1880). Although he was a member of a prominent family, Bull's sympathies were with the common people. In 1852 he bought, in partnership with a land speculator, 120,000 acres in Potter County, Pa., to which he later added another 20,000 acres. The project was announced in newspapers in Norway and America. The first group of 35 settlers arrived in Oleona, the "capital" of the colony of New Norway (or Oleana, as the whole colony came to be called) on September 7, 1852.

By Christmas there were about 250 people in the colony, but the settlers did not share Ole Bull's enthusiasm. They found the hilly, wooded land ill-suited for the adventure; "everybody realized that it would take a generation" to clear a farm that would adequately support a family. Bull was unable to pay the wages promised for work on roads and other projects. In February 1853 the settlers went on strike, and most decided to leave the colony for more prosperous midwestern settlements. Bull withdrew from the project, although he continued to support the remaining settlers by giving a series of concerts. Less than a year after its inauguration, the project was dead. In spite of all, Ole Bull became a folk hero to Norwegian Americans. The Norwegians of Minneapolis raised a statue of him in Loring Park, and an annual festival is held at the site of Oleana.

A NATION WITHIN A NATION

In the 1840s and 1850s Norwegian settlements had spread through southern and central Wisconsin and into northern Iowa and southern Minnesota, and in the 1860s and early 1870s large numbers of Norwegians moved into western Minnesota and the eastern fringes of the Dakota Territory. Like most immigrants of this period, the Norwegian families generally settled in groups with people of their own kind. Newly arrived immigrants usually sought out existing Norwegian settlements, where the family head often had a chance to earn money by working on an established farm, in the lead mines of Wisconsin, or in the lumber mills of Minnesota. When a family was ready to strike out on their own, they either sought land close to other Norwegians or, if that was impossible, tried to find open areas where they could establish a new Norwegian settlement. Sometimes an individual would act as a scout, seek out a suitable location, then return to an older settlement or even to his home community in Norway to guide family and friends to the chosen spot. Norwegian settlements formed in these ways dotted the map from Lake Michigan to the Dakotas and beyond, interspersed among similar settlements of other ethnic groups.

In these settlements the primary social bond was that of common background and heritage. Norwegian was spoken as a matter of course, and many peasant customs and attitudes were retained. People from the same rural community or valley in Norway often settled together and formed neighborhoods of a distinctly local flavor. In some larger settlements, or where several settlements were close together, the immigrants created their own trading centers in the form of little towns, or in some cases they eventually came to dominate a town already established. To these people, the neighborhood or community consisted of those who shared a common heritage; those who did not were outsiders, even though they might live and work in the same geographical area. Some of the towns and smaller cities developed into dual communities in which two or more ethnic groups shared a common trading center, communicating with each other in English but remaining separate in their more intimate social relations, each retaining

its own "gossip circle"—a phenomenon that still exists today.

The string of Norwegian settlements from Illinois to the Dakotas formed a nation within a nation, ambivalent, perhaps, toward the old country, but loyal to one another and with a commitment to the United States and its principles. In their own quiet way, without conscious leadership or deliberate design, the Norwegian settlers of the Midwest had realized the dream of Hans Barlien and Ole Bull.

New Horizons

Before the heavy immigration of the 1880s, relatively few Norwegians found their way to the Far West, except for the few converts who had joined the Mormons. The gold rush of 1849 attracted many more from both Norway and the midwestern settlements, and in 1857 there were enough Norwegians in San Francisco to join with Swedes and Danes in establishing a Scandinavian Society.

After the 1880s, however, new settlers had to go farther west and north, even into the Canadian provinces to find land. But new opportunities in the Far West appealed to the younger generation, the children of the immigrants. Many were farm youths who had grown up in older Norwegian settlements in the Midwest, others were craftsmen and laborers from midwestern cities; they sought new opportunities in the rapidly developing coastal areas of the Northwest, in Oregon, Washington, British Columbia, and Alaska. They were soon followed by new waves of immigrants directly from Norway, more and more of whom were from towns and cities. They were not land-hungry peasants but laborers and craftsmen, often with the additional experience and skill of seamen; or they came from Norway's northern coastal districts, where their main occupation had been ocean fishing, supplemented by small-scale dairy farming and an occasional job in a nearby town.

To these people the coastal areas of the Northwest appeared particularly attractive. "This is just like Norway!" wrote an enthusiastic settler in Puget Sound to his friends and relatives in Minnesota. Soon Norwegians had settled all along the northern coast, dominating the Puget Sound fishing industry and building towns and settlements in Alaska. Many went into the lumber industry or shipbuilding and did well. By the turn of the century, Seattle had one of the largest urban concentrations of Norwegians in the United States.

At about the same time, another urban settlement became prominent on the East Coast. In the second half of the 1870s Norwegian shipping boomed. Approximately 1,200 Norwegian ships docked annually in the port of New York during this period, and sometimes as many as 500 ships with 10,000 men aboard were in the harbor at one time. New York, known among Norwegian sailors as a seaman's El Dorado, was a popular place to go ashore, which more often than not was a euphemistic expression for jumping ship. During the period 1875–1885 an estimated 700 to 800 Norwegian seamen annually jumped ship in North American ports, mostly in New York. With excellent reputations as sailors, these men were readily accepted in American coastal and ocean-going ships, towboats, or pleasure yachts. The continuing expansion of the harbor and the building of

docks, piers, warehouses, and shipyards gave employment to many Norwegians.

The shipping traffic also attracted Norwegian ship chandlers and ship brokers. They settled in Brooklyn, creating an ethnic enclave that became increasingly self-sufficient as Norwegian merchants, artisans, business people, and professionals arrived to offer all the necessary services of a modern city. The decidedly Norwegian flavor of the settlement, nicknamed *mysostkolonien* (whey-cheese colony), has been retained and renewed over the years by a limited but continuous flow of new immigrants from Norway and by an active exchange with the homeland both in commerce and in the professions.

The Norwegian-American Church

Although Norwegian settlements were dispersed from coast to coast, only the Midwest had a sufficient population base for specifically Norwegian institutions to sprout and flourish, strengthening in turn the cohesiveness, if not always the unity, of the Norwegian Americans. Foremost among these institutions was the church, although at the outset at least, it appeared to split rather than unite the Norwegian-American community.

In the absence of a state church, the immigrants found several established churches and sects competing for their attention, and numerous itinerant preachers with a variety of interpretations of Christianity. Most of the Norwegian immigrants, however, despite their opposition to the state church and its clergy, remained loyal to their pietistic form of Lutheranism. They had a forceful leader in Elling Eielsen (1804–1883), a Haugean lay preacher from Norway. He eventually became an ordained Lutheran minister and in 1846 he organized the distinctly low-church Elling's Synod, in which the minister "wore no cassock . . . to call attention to differences in society."

Eielsen had a strong following among the Fox River, Ill., settlers, most of whom were from the Stavanger area, Norway's Bible belt. His uncompromising anti-ecclesiastical attitude, however, soon proved too much for even the staunchest Haugeans in the Muskego settlement of Wisconsin. From the 1840s onward, an increasing number of the new immigrants rejected Eielsen's revivalism. These people had a more positive attitude to the high-church ritual of the Norwegian church, and their fear of pastoral overlordship was outweighed by their desire for administrative and ritual order in church affairs and the guidance of properly trained and consecrated ministers. So they appealed for pastors of the Norwegian state church to come and "bring order out of the chaotic conditions reigning here."

In response, J.W.C. Dietrichson (1815–1883), the first ordained state church pastor from Norway, arrived in the Muskego settlement in 1844. He organized a number of Norwegian Lutheran congregations in Wisconsin. Other state church pastors followed, and in 1853 the Norwegian Evangelical Lutheran Church of America was organized, with Adolph C. Preus (1814–1878) as president or chairman (the title "bishop" was avoided). Commonly known as the Norwegian Synod, it became the high-church organization among Norwegian Americans. By 1857 a dozen pastors of the Norwegian state

church were serving congregations in Wisconsin, Iowa, and Minnesota.

Though they were widely separated, these pastors had much in common; they were well-educated members of Norway's professional elite, and their conduct and manners emphasized, for the most part unintentionally, their social distance from the rest of the immigrants. The more fiercely independent settlers felt the preachers' very presence as a threat to their newly won freedom, which led to conflicts in the congregations and a long-lasting split in Norwegian Lutheranism. Although the disagreements were overtly about doctrinal and organizational matters, underlying them was the emerging class conflict between a professional elite accustomed to assume leadership and a self-asserting peasant class.

In spite of the turbulence, the Norwegian Lutheran church has been a vital institution for the nourishment of ethnic identity among the Norwegians in the United States. The close association of church and ethnicity was a controversial issue from the start, especially among the church leaders, some of whom sensed a conflict between the ideal universal goals of the church and what they saw as the parochialism of ethnicity. The issue was hotly debated in the 1850s, when the Norwegian Synod began negotiations with the German Lutheran Missouri Synod for the use of the latter's theological school in St. Louis. Because of the Missouri Synod's reputation for rigid orthodoxy and clerical authoritarianism, the move was strongly opposed, not only by Eielsen and other low-church elements, but also by liberals within the Norwegian Synod, who argued that affiliation with the Germans would mean the end both of Norwegian national identity in the United States and of an autonomous Norwegian Lutheran church. When the affiliation took place, 4 of the 12 pastors of the Norwegian Synod returned to Norway. Eventually, leadership of the synod was taken over by Preus's cousin, Herman A. Preus (1825–1894), who leaned strongly toward the Missouri Synod.

In the 1880s, although the Norwegian Synod had by then established its own Luther Theological Seminary in Madison, Wis. (later moved to St. Paul, Minn.), the continued affiliation with the Missouri Synod led to another split. Forty pastors broke away from the Norwegian Synod and formed an Anti-Missourian Brotherhood. In 1890 they joined with other moderate Norwegian church organizations to establish a strong synodal organization called the United Norwegian Lutheran Church.

In the meantime, Elling Eielsen's extreme anticlericalism and disdain for organizational structure had alienated most of his followers. In 1876 they reorganized the synod as Hauge's Norwegian Evangelical Lutheran Synod in America, commonly know as Hauge's Synod. With the passing of time, old class differences diminished among second- and third-generation Norwegians. In 1917 the three main Norwegian Lutheran groups—the Norwegian Synod, the United Church, and Hauge's Synod—merged to form the Norwegian Lutheran Church of America. It became the third-largest Lutheran body in the United States and was by far the largest Scandinavian organization, with 492,000 members in 1922.

Three small splinter groups were not involved in the merger. A remnant of Elling's Synod, which had split off when Hauge's Synod was established continued its emphasis on lay preaching under the more proper name of the Eielsen Synod, abolishing the debasing custom of calling peasants by their first names only. At the other extreme, a hard core of the Norwegian Synod continued its affiliation with the Missouri Synod and maintained its high-church emphasis on doctrine and ritual. Also not involved in the merger was the Lutheran Free Church, which had split off from the United Church in 1897. In 1949 the Evangelical Lutheran Church had 798,045 members; the Lutheran Free Church, 54,608; the Norwegian Synod, 9,595; and the Eielsen Synod, 1,375.

Many Norwegian immigrants joined other Protestant groups, particularly the Methodists, Baptists, and Mormons. Although these denominations did not develop synodal organizations on the basis of ethnic identity, some individual congregations were organized on that basis. In the Fox River settlement a Norwegian Baptist congregation and a Norwegian Mormon society were organized in the 1840s. The Methodists were especially successful in winning converts among Scandinavian immigrants, some of whom became leaders in vigorous mission programs directed to their compatriots. The Norwegian Mission, organized in Wisconsin and Minnesota in the 1860s and 1870s, became the separate Northwest Norwegian Conference within the Methodist Church and from 1884 was known as the Norwegian-Danish conference. In 1931 the conference had 6,360 members.

These churches served as shelters of ethnic identity for the Norwegian group during difficult times, especially during and after World War I. The nativistic hysteria of this period, with its hostile propaganda against all "hyphenated" Americans cast suspicion on those who expressed any kind of loyalty other than purely American. Since denominational differentiation was an accepted fact in American life, identity could be expressed, not only in doctrine and ritual but also in social programs, such as the popular *lutefisk* dinners of the Scandinavian churches and the May 17 celebrations of Norwegian congregations.

The war hysteria deeply divided the church organizations themselves, as many members and church leaders yielded to the pressure for Americanization. Some Methodists proposed dissolving the Norwegian-Danish Conference as unpatriotic. The Norwegian Lutheran church debated whether to abandon Norwegian as its official language and change the name of the organization. In 1918 the proposal to eliminate the word "Norwegian" was adopted overwhelmingly, but the decision was reversed two years later. The issue was hotly debated for almost three decades, and it was not until World War II that these external symbols of ethnic identity were abolished. In 1943 the Norwegian-Danish Conference of the Methodist Church was dissolved, and in 1946 the Norwegian Lutheran Church of America changed its name to the Evangelical Lutheran Church.

Along with these developments, Norwegian Lutheran leaders showed a growing interest in merging with other Lutheran church bodies, stimulated by cooperation with the National Lutheran Council (from 1918) and the American Lutheran Conference (from 1930). In 1960 the Evangelical Lutheran Church joined

with German and Danish Lutherans in a giant merger that created the American Lutheran Church, which the Lutheran Free Church joined in 1962. All ethnic identity at the denominational level was abandoned, but recent surveys have shown that a Norwegian ethnic identity is still a vital element in a large number of Lutheran congregations throughout the Midwest.

EDUCATIONAL INSTITUTIONS

By the time Norwegian immigrants arrived in the Midwest, the public school system had been established, and the settlers availed themselves of it. Their churches organized either Sunday schools or summer schools to provide supplementary religious instruction, or they established a complete parochial school system as an alternative to the public schools. Generally, midwestern Norwegian congregations adopted the pattern of supplementary summer schools, where instruction was usually also given in reading and writing Norwegian.

The well-educated state church pastors of the Norwegian Synod, however, found the rough-and-tumble scene of the frontier settlements "fermenting and unsettled." In particular, they found the usual operation of schools inadequate. They were horrified by the incompetence of the teachers, the lack of discipline in the classrooms, and the general inefficiency of the schools. They therefore urged their parishioners to establish parochial schools in their congregations.

The pastors' criticism of the common school apparently touched a nerve. Born in controversy only a short generation before, the common school had become a symbol of American democracy, and attacking it was considered close to treason. Among Norwegian settlers, the dispute aroused feelings from the old but never-forgotten class conflict. There was talk of "priestly domination" inspired by the "Missouri Synod spirit." The battle raged in synodal meetings and in the Norwegian-American press for two decades, dying down after the 1870s, when it became apparent that the public school, much improved by then, was generally accepted by most Norwegian settlers.

The synod pastors were more successful in establishing institutions of higher education. By their initiative several Norwegian academies and colleges came into being, because of the need to educate ministers for the growing number of congregations in the Norwegian Synod. Use of the German Lutheran seminary of the Missouri Synod in the 1850s was meant to be only temporary, and as opposition from clergy and lay people grew, the Missouri connection became a liability to the orthodox wing of synod pastors.

The creation of a separate Norwegian university was debated again in 1861, when lay representatives outvoted the orthodox clergy, who wanted to continue the affiliation with the Missouri Synod. The obvious choice for president of the new university was Peter Laurentius Larsen (1833–1915), who held the Norwegian professorship in theology at the Missouri Synod's Concordia College and Seminary in St. Louis. He decided that the new Norwegian Lutheran School for the Education of Ministers was to be only preparatory for the seminary, which meant that those who wished to complete their education for the ministry had to study a final two or three years at Concordia. So the intended university

or seminary became Luther College, at Decorah, Iowa. Seventeen years later, in 1878, the Norwegian Synod opened Luther Theological Seminary in Madison.

St. Olaf College emerged from the common-school controversy. The initiative was taken by B.J. Muus (1832–1900), a state church pastor who served the settlement of Holden in Goodhue County, Minn., along with a number of nearby parishes. One of the sharpest critics of the common school, he had established parochial schools in several of his congregations and made an effort to staff them with competent teachers from Norway. But he also wanted to offer the sons and daughters of Norwegian settlers "a higher education than the schools of their home communities could give them." In 1869 he established Holden Academy, with a curriculum that included religion, English, Norwegian, geography, history, arithmetic, and penmanship. Financial difficulties soon caused the school to close, but in 1874 Muus organized an independent corporation to support a similar school in nearby Northfield, Minn. Named St. Olaf's School after Norway's beatified king, Olaf Haraldsson (995–1030), it remained independent of any church organization until 1899, when ownership was transferred to the United Norwegian Lutheran Church. In the meantime, the school had developed a full baccalaureate program in liberal arts, and, as St. Olaf College, later became the largest Norwegian institution of higher education in the United States.

Several other colleges, academies, and normal schools were started by Norwegians during the second half of the 19th century, some of them in collaboration with Swedes or Danes. Nearly all were church related, and some were combined with theological seminaries, since each faction of Norwegian Lutheranism wanted its own institutions. Among those that have survived are Augsburg College in Minneapolis, Minn. (established 1869), Augustana College in Sioux Falls, S.Dak. (1889), Concordia College in Moorhead, Minn. (1891), and Pacific Lutheran College in Parkland, Wash. (1894).

From their inception, these colleges were important to the Norwegian-American community as educational and cultural centers and as instruments of continued contact and exchange with Norway. Some have strong programs in Norwegian studies. They have also served as hosts for other Norwegian-American cultural institutions, such as the Norwegian-American Museum, Vesterheim, in Decorah, Iowa, begun by Luther College in 1877, and the Norwegian-American Archives and Historical Association in Northfield, Minn. The colleges have contributed significantly to the integration of Norwegian and Norwegian-American cultural traditions into the mosaic of American culture.

PRESS AND POLITICS

The Norwegian-American press provided an important link among the widely scattered Norwegian settlements. It carried news of the various settlements to every corner, along with reports from the different home communities in Norway, thus serving as a bond between the Old World and the New. At the same time, the press helped integrate the early Norwegian settlers into American society. From the outset it served as a forum for discussion of issues both of internal Norwegian-American concern and of general political interest,

with fairly wide reader participation, as shown by the many letters to the editors. Thus Norwegian settlers were introduced in their own language to American politics and conditions.

The first newspaper appealing to Norwegian Americans was *Skandinavia,* published in New York in 1847. It was Pan-Scandinavian in scope and did not last a year. In the same year the weekly *Nordlyset* (Northern Lights, 1847–1850) was launched in Muskego, Wis. In 1851 pastors of the Norwegian Synod helped establish the Scandinavian Press Association at Rock Prairie, Wis. It later moved to Madison and for many years published the newspaper *Emigranten* (1852–1892) as well as books and pamphlets in Norwegian and the church magazine *Maanedstidende* (Monthly Times), which has appeared almost continuously, under different names, from its inception in the 1850s to the present. It switched to English in the 1940s. As the years passed, one Norwegian-American newspaper or magazine followed another, and by 1914 almost 600 periodicals in the Norwegian language had been started. Most of them had a short life, and there were frequent mergers and absorptions; *Emigranten* merged with *Faedrelandet* (Fatherland) in 1868 and then both were absorbed, along with *Budstikken* (Messenger), some 25 years later by *Minneapolis Tidende* (Minneapolis Times), in turn absorbed in 1935 by *Decorah-Posten* (Decorah Post), which finally was absorbed by *Western Viking* in 1972. But at all times there have been a few Norwegian-language newspapers serving subscribers from coast to coast.

After the outbreak of World War I, the use of the Norwegian language among the immigrants declined sharply, and the number of Norwegian-language newspapers dropped correspondingly. Among those that survived, at least for several years, were *Skandinaven* (Scandinavian, 1866–1940) of Chicago; *Decorah-Posten* (1874–1972) of Decorah, Iowa; *Minneapolis Tidende* (1887–1935); *Western Viking* (f. 1889) of Seattle; and *Nordisk Tidende* (Nordic Times, f. 1891) of Brooklyn. Of more recent date is *Minnesota Posten* (Minnesota Post, f. 1956) of Minneapolis. In 1976 the last three surviving weeklies, all published partly in English, had a combined circulation of 18,840.

In Norway the peak of emigration had coincided with a period of broadening political consciousness and participation; farmers and cotters had gained self-confidence through the peasant movement and since the 1830s had plunged into political action on an increasing scale. In the 1850s an incipient labor movement was stirring among the growing urban working class under the leadership of Marcus Thrane (1817–1890), who later came to the United States and edited several short-lived Norwegian newspapers in Chicago.

The participation of Norwegians in American politics was initially limited, but with increasing mastery of the English language, their political involvement grew. Many turned into active politicians, at first in their own settlements, but successively on the state and even national level. Their political views were strongly flavored by Norwegian folk culture. They championed the "common people" and on most issues identified themselves with the "little man." They were strongly opposed to any form of "aristocratic" rule, whether it took the form of pastoral overlordship in

their own settlements or of Yankee dominance in politics and big business.

The overwhelming politcal issue of the 1850s was slavery, which most of the Norwegian immigrants regarded as a "peculiar institution" and an ugly contrast to America's promise of freedom and equality. But in their view none of the existing political parties gave a satisfactory answer to the problem. Like other immigrants, the Norwegians were repelled by the nativism of the Whigs. Although they were attracted by the Democrats' Jacksonian concern for the common man, they were dismayed by the party's tolerance of slavery. The Free Soil party attracted many Norwegians, and *Nordlyset* became their organ. But the views of many Norwegian settlers were more adequately expressed by *Frihedsbanneret* (Banner of Freedom), a short-lived Chicago weekly, which in its first issue of 1852 called for abolition. Strong antislavery articles were also published in *Maanedstidende.* When the Republican party was formed in 1854 and adopted a platform strongly opposing extension of slavery, more and more Norwegians aligned themselves with it. *Emigranten* switched its allegiance from the Democratic party to the Republican and supported Lincoln's election in 1860.

Slavery became a hot issue within the Norwegian-American community when some of the pastors of the Norwegian Synod, because of their alignment with the Missouri Synod and the Concordia Seminary in St. Louis, were suspected of favoring slavery. Challenged by the Norwegian-American press, the pastors issued a public statement saying that they did not condone the abuses of slavery, but that nothing in the Bible stamped slavery as a sin "in itself." Press and laymen then called for the termination of the Missouri connection, and it was this demand that led to the establishment of Luther College in 1861. Thus opposition to the orthodox Norwegian Synod pastors with their Missouri connection combined with antislavery sentiments to make the Norwegian settlers a solid bloc of Republican strength in the Midwest.

The progressive political leanings of Norwegian Americans were clear on many subsequent occasions as well. Knute Nelson (1843–1923), the first Norwegian governor of Minnesota (1893–1895) and later a U.S. senator (1895–1923), won the votes of his countrymen by attacking "the entire American industrial syndrome," from big banks and corporations to labor unions. In the 1880s Norwegian Americans gave moral and financial support to Johan Sverdrup (1816–1892), founder of the Liberal party of Norway, by organizing Liberal Clubs all over the Midwest. In an attempt to curb "Yankee political domination" and the growing power of industrial capitalists, they banded together in the 1880s and 1890s in Viking leagues and Scandinavian Republican leagues that denounced the "anarchistic social Darwinism" of American big business. At the end of the century, when the Republican party became increasingly identified with big business, thousands of Norwegians in Minnesota and the Dakotas joined the Farmers' Alliance and the Populist party, helping to elect a Norwegian Populist governor in South Dakota in 1897. Norwegians were also active in the cooperative movement and played a significant role in the establishment of farmers' cooperatives in the Midwest. In Wisconsin they supported Robert La Follette's progres-

sivism, particularly his efforts to introduce effective public control of the railroads and other big businesses. And when A.C. Townley created his Nonpartisan League in North Dakota in 1914, with a program that has been described as a "broad experiment in state socialism," he found staunch support among the Norwegians.

The Norwegians also had conservative elements, particularly in the old midwestern settlements where the Norwegian Synod had been a dominant influence, and this conservative element grew as Norwegians successfully entered the business world and advanced in social status. Many were motivated by party loyalty and refused to join insurgents of any persuasion. After World War I, under the pressure of the Americanization movement and with the loss of a distinctive forum in the fading Norwegian-American press, much of the special flavor of Norwegian-American politics vanished.

SOCIAL AND FRATERNAL ORGANIZATIONS

Various kinds of organizations have served over the years to strengthen the bond among Norwegians in America. They range from literary and dramatic societies to ski clubs and other athletic associations. Some have been Scandinavian rather than specifically Norwegian, especially in the early period of immigration when there were few Danes, Norwegians, or Swedes in any given locality. Also, during the 19th century, ideas of Scandinavian unity were popular both at home and among Scandinavians in the United States.

The first secular organizations of Scandinavian Americans were mutual-benefit societies, charitable organizations, or a combination of both. But whatever their stated purpose, their main function was as social clubs where Scandinavians could get together, speak their own languages, and cultivate common interests. Typically, they sprang up in the larger cities, where the need for such ethnic organizations was more strongly felt. A Scandinavian Society was organized in Philadelphia in 1768, one in New York in 1844, and one in San Francisco in 1857.

Literary societies and dramatic clubs were common among the Scandinavians in the United States during the 1860s and 1870s, not only in the cities but also in smaller towns and rural communities where there were enough Scandinavians to support them. The dramatic society in Chicago was unique because it was exclusively Norwegian. Organized in 1868 by Marcus Thrane, a labor leader who emigrated from Norway in 1863, the Norwegian Dramatic Society during its four-year existence produced 32 plays, "drawing upon the best dramatic literature of Norway, Denmark, and the European continent."

By the 1880s pan-Scandinavianism had lost its appeal, at least in the United States, and numerous specifically Norwegian organizations appeared. In Minneapolis, for example, the Scandinavian Dramatic Society, organized in 1870, existed only a few years and then was divided into separate societies for each of the Scandinavian groups.

A very popular form of association in Scandinavia in the second half of the 19th century was the male chorus or song society. Transferred to America, this institution became a conspicuous expression of Norwegian ethnic identity, particularly in urban centers, where clubs sprang up in great numbers in the 1870s and 1880s. They gave concerts and serenades for the general public and provided musical entertainment on Norwegian and American ceremonial occasions. Their repertory consisted of the four-part songs that were popular at the time in Norway, often composed for male chorus by such prominent composers as Edvard Grieg (1843–1907) or Halfdan Kjerulf (1815–1868). Sometimes, as in Scandinavia, a number of clubs held regional and national *sangerstevne* or songfests, with parades and public concerts.

In 1886 Danish, Norwegian, and Swedish male choruses formed the United Scandinavian Singers of America, which arranged biennial musical festivals. The first was held in 1887 in Philadelphia. In 1891 some 50 clubs with about 1,100 singers participated in the songfest held in Minneapolis. In 1906, however, the Swedes withdrew, probably because of the tension accompanying dissolution of the union between the kingdoms of Sweden and Norway in 1905. Eventually the Norwegians formed the Norwegian Singers' Association of America, which by the end of the 1930s had more than 40 affiliated clubs in seven states and Canada. This organization toured Norway in 1914 on the occasion of the centennial of the Norwegian constitution. Song societies still operate in Minneapolis, Chicago, Seattle, and Brooklyn.

The special loyalty of Norwegian peasants for their home district or valley found expression in the United States in the formation of *bygdelag*, social organizations for people who hailed from the same *bygd* (region) in Norway. These followed a pattern set in Norway, where similar groups existed in the larger cities. The formal organization of bygdelag throughout the Midwest and eventually the whole country was the work of the second generation. The first bygdelag, Valdres Samband (Valdres Association), named for a valley in southern Norway, was founded in 1902 by Andrew A. Veblen (1848–1932), a professor of mathematics and physics at the University of Iowa (he was the brother of economist Thorstein Veblen, 1857–1929, and father of mathematics professor Oswald Veblen, 1880–1960). Other bygdelag followed, and in 1916, 14 of them banded together, again under Veblen's leadership, to form a Joint Council, which most of the 40 or so groups then in existence eventually joined.

The bygdelag usually compiled genealogies, and some kept archives of family histories. Many published yearbooks. But their main attraction was the *stevne* (meetings), usually held in summer, where members gave speeches and listened to stories, riddles, jokes, and poetry in the time-honored vernacular of the old region. Many members dressed in the festive garb of the home district, and old-time dance music was played on the *hardingfele*, a fiddle decorated with mother-of-pearl, or the *langeleik*, a Norwegian zither.

Bygdelag activity reached a climax in 1925, when the Joint Council organized the grand celebration of the centennial of Norwegian immigration in Minneapolis. The city was decorated with Norwegian and American flags, and the four-day program of festivities included a parade, public speeches, concerts by song societies, folk dances and games, athletic competitions, and an exhibit of Norwegian-American artifacts, featuring a full-sized model of the sloop *Restauration*. Some 60,000 people

attended open-air worship services conducted in the Norwegian language, one of them led by the Bishop of Oslo, head of the Church of Norway. Other dignitaries from Norway were honored guests, and the ambassador to Washington brought a greeting from the king of Norway. President Calvin Coolidge addressed a crowd of about 100,000 persons.

One Norwegian-American organization is patterned on an American model, although it is clearly a Norwegian heritage society. Sønner av Norge (Sons of Norway), named after the opening words of a song once recognized as Norway's national anthem, was started as a mutual-insurance organization in 1895 by 18 young Norwegians in Minneapolis. After a few years, similar groups emerged in other towns, and they decided to organize, in the fashion of American fraternal orders, as secret ceremonial lodges under a supreme lodge located in Minneapolis. The organization, which only Norwegians could join, grew rapidly and by 1912 had 9,000 members and an insurance fund of $2 million. In 1974 membership exceeded 85,000 in more than 300 lodges in the United States and Canada, and the insurance fund had increased to over $115 million. The local lodges also serve as social clubs, while the supreme lodge has developed a diversified program to promote interest in and appreciation of Norwegian, as well as Norwegian-American, cultural traditions.

Other organizations devote themselves to specific aspects of the Norwegian cultural heritage. Bondeungdomslaget (The Peasant Youth League) of New York (f. 1925) sponsors a camp site and ski resort named Lake Telemark after the Telemark district in Norway, which has been called the cradle of skiing; it also arranges folk-dance festivals, as do several other organizations, including the Norwegian Folk Dance Society of Brooklyn (f. 1938). The Torskeklubb (Codfish Club) of Minneapolis–St. Paul and Chicago, whose membership is limited to men of Norwegian birth or descent, features monthly dinners of codfish flown in from Norway. Some organizations, including the Sons of Norway and the Torskeklubb, sponsor Norwegian-language camps and folk-art classes and offer scholarships for an exchange of students between the United States and Norway. Many also arrange group tours of Norway for their members. The Leif Ericson Society, with headquarters in Evanston, Ill., and branches in other states, was founded in 1963 to further research into Norse Viking exploration and colonization in America; it has also adopted a strictly American tradition and sponsors an annual Miss Viking America contest.

LITERATURE AND SCHOLARSHIP

Concern for the literary heritage of the Norwegian people in the New World began with the Scandinavian literary and dramatic societies of the 1860s and 1870s and was stimulated in the 1870s and 1880s by the Norwegian-American press, which published Norwegian poetry, short novels, and serialized novels, as well as articles about contemporary Norwegian literature. *Skandinaven* even acquired the famous Norwegian author Bjørnstjerne Bjørnson (1832–1910) as a regular correspondent. There were also special literary magazines, and some newspapers published literary supplements, such as *Ved Arnen* (By the Fireside), the magazine section of *Decorah-Posten*.

It was in these media that a specifically Norwegian-American literature began to emerge. The most popular Norwegian-American novel, *Husmandsgutten,* by H.A. Foss, was first published serially in *Ved Arnen* in 1884–1885 and is said to have brought *Decorah-Posten* 6,000 new subscribers. The first Norwegian-American writer of distinction was Hjalmar Hjorth Boyesen (1848–1895), who immigrated at the age of 20. Although he wrote in English, he professed to be writing "as a Scandinavian," and his themes were Norwegian or Norwegian-American. His early writings were strongly influenced by Bjørnson. But he failed to have a lasting impact on the Norwegian-American community, perhaps because of his increasingly negative attitude toward his Norwegian heritage.

Literary endeavors among Norwegian Americans received further stimulus when Scandinavian departments were established at American universities, usually at the instigation of Scandinavian Americans. The University of Wisconsin pioneered in this field, thanks to the efforts of Rasmus B. Anderson (1846–1936), who began teaching Norwegian and Old Norse there in 1869. Since then a Norwegian has always chaired the Scandinavian department at the university, which has become an important center of Norwegian culture and scholarship, along with Luther and St. Olaf colleges.

Literary clubs continued to bloom and fade, their life span seldom exceeding that of their charter members. Notable exceptions are Ygdrasil (f. 1896) of Madison, Wis., and Symra of Decorah, Iowa (f. 1903). Such prominent Norwegian-American writers as Johannes B. Wist (1864–1923) and Simon Johnson (1874–1964) were members of Symra, which published a literary magazine of high quality, also named *Symra.*

In January 1903 a group of Norwegian Americans met in Minneapolis and established Det norske Selskap i Amerika (the Norwegian Society of America) for the purpose of promoting a literary tradition rooted in the cultural heritage of Norway but focusing on the experience of Norwegians in the New World. A tireless promoter of the society's cause was Waldemar Ager (1869–1941), novelist, short-story writer, and editor of the Norwegian paper *Reform* in Eau Claire, Wis. In 1905 he also became editor of the Norwegian Society's *Kvartalskrift* (Quarterly) and made it a vehicle for a passionate defense of a pluralistic American society in which each ethnic group contributes to the whole by remaining faithful to its own cultural tradition.

There was an upsurge in Norwegian-American literature, painting, and sculpture as well as in historical research and writing in the first three decades of the 20th century. Ager's literary activities took place in this period, including his best-known novel, *Kristus for Pilatus: En Norsk-Amerikansk Fortaelling* (Christ Before Pilate: A Norwegian-American Story, 1910). Simon Johnson, Julius Baumann (1870–1923), and others appealed strongly to Norwegian Americans with poems and short stories of prairie and pioneer life. But the towering literary figure of the period was Norwegian-born Ole E. Rølvaag (1876–1931). As a farm hand in North Dakota, he gathered the experience of immigrant life reflected in his novels. In 1906 he began teaching Norwegian language and literature at St. Olaf College. In his book *Omkring Faedrearven* (About the Ancestral

Heritage, 1922), he declared that devotion to the heritage of the fathers was an "ethical duty" to America, whose greatest strength he saw in its rich cultural diversity. Such ideas also inspired his famous series of novels: *I de Dage* (1924), *Riket grundlaegges* (1925), *Peder Seier* (1928), and *Den signede Dag* (1931). First published in Norway, the books soon appeared in translation as *Giants in the Earth* (combining the first two volumes), *Peder Victorious*, and *Their Father's God*.

Ager and his generation had linked their hopes for a creative Norwegian-American literature to the perpetuation of the Norwegian language, which may be why they paid little attention to Boyesen's work and seem to have ignored the efforts of Martha Ostenso (1900–1963), who based her novels, such as *Wild Geese* (1925), on her experiences as an immigrant in Minnesota and South Dakota. Like Boyesen, she wrote in English and even Anglicized her name. Men like Ager did not believe that Norwegian-American identity and cultural heritage could come to full expression in the English language. It is ironic that Norwegian-American belles lettres reached a high point at a time when the use of the Norwegian language had dropped sharply among Norwegians in America. To the men of letters, this was the end of an era, and the achievements of Rølvaag, Ager, Johnson, and others, as well as the impressive display of all aspects of Norwegian-American culture during the centennial celebrations in 1925, appeared to them to be a "last rally."

It was in this atmosphere that the Norwegian-American Historical Association was founded in 1925, based on a desire to record the history of the Norwegian people in America before it vanished in the process of assimilation. Accordingly, the first works published by the association were histories of immigration, settlement, and transition, with an unconscious bow to the melting-pot ideology. The association itself, however, became an expression of ethnic identity, not only on the part of the scholarly writers and editors who put out the works, but to everybody concerned. The supporting membership, although not large (some 1,100 in the late 1970s), has been drawn from all walks of life.

CULTURAL ASSIMILATION AND ETHNIC IDENTITY

In the 19th century the peasants of Norway had fought for the right to be themselves and to be respected members of society. When the Norwegians came to the United States, whether as peasants, artisans, or professionals, most of them expected to find a land where they could be free to be what they were—Norwegians. When they found themselves under pressure to become Americanized, they fought back, challenging the notion that in order to be a loyal American, one had to be in every respect like the Yankees. So it was that the period of greatest ethnic suppression in the United States, from the 1890s until well after World War I, produced the richest flowering of Norwegian-American culture in all its aspects, from literature and the arts to folklore displayed in colorful pageantry, culminating in two centennial celebrations, one specifically Norwegian (1914) and one specifically Norwegian-American (1925).

Many Norwegians yielded to the pressure, however, and became more American than the Yankees. The loss of the struggle to retain the Norwegian language gradually undercut the foundation of the Norwegian-language press, weakened the ties of the bygdelag and similar organizations, and removed the ground for a Norwegian literature in America. The Norwegian-American churches, too, abandoned their role as catalysts of ethnic identity, at least at the denominational level, thereby removing an effective shield for ethnic identification. Yet, although fully assimilated to the wider culture, Norwegian Americans have survived as a group.

Their history since the great rally of the 1920s has not yet been written. But the fact that Norwegian ethnic identity is still a factor in the lives of many Americans was demonstrated in the mid-1970s, again by a celebration. In 1975, the 150th anniversary of the *Restauration*'s voyage was observed both in Norway and the United States. Lectures, concerts, art exhibits, and other commemorative programs were held in hundreds of cities and communities across the United States and Canada, synchronized by a national coordinating committee, with U.S. Senator Hubert Humphrey (1911–1977) as honorary chairman. Major events were staged in New York, Minneapolis, and Seattle, as well as in Stavanger, the sloop's·port of departure. King Olav of Norway visited the United States on the occasion, attended a Norwegian-American evening in Carnegie Hall, and toured the more important Norwegian-American centers.

In everyday life, Norwegian-American group identity is less conspicuous than it used to be, even in the Midwest. But it is present, and not only in the activities of the Norwegian-American Historical Association and the museum Vesterheim, institutions that by their very nature look back at what was. It is vitally present in the educational institutions established by Norwegian Americans, which continue to attract hundreds of students every year because they are Norwegian. The group is also represented by such organizations as the Sons of Norway, with its many members and their families. In large urban centers like Minneapolis and Brooklyn, business and social life often follow ethnic lines. Above all, the Norwegian-American group is present in the everyday life of midwestern settlements such as the little town in Wisconsin that displays a roadside sign wishing the traveler *Velkommen til Westby* (Welcome to Westby) and calls its shops by Norwegian names. It is present in many similar communities where the local church is still thought of as the Norwegian church. In such communities, the Norwegian language may have gone out of use, but certain phrases are often retained and exchanged as symbols of shared identity and familiarity. In many places, May 17 is celebrated annually. In other communities Norway Day and Leif Ericson festivals are regular events, and Decorah, Iowa, holds a Nordic Fest every summer. Finally, a Norwegian-American ethnic identity is present in thousands of homes where heirlooms, decorations, and cherished recipes for special occasions remind old and young of their origins.

Bibliography

The best sources concerning Norwegians in the United States are the publications of the Norwegian-American Historical Association. One of these, Theodore C. Blegen, *Norwegian Migration to America, 1825–1860* (1931; reprint, New York, 1969), is the most comprehensive history up to about 1930. Another standard work is Carlton C. Qualey,

Norwegian Settlement in the United States (Northfield, Minn., 1938). Kenneth O. Bjork, *West of the Great Divide: Norwegian Migration to the Pacific Coast, 1847–1893* (Northfield, Minn., 1958), includes an account of the Norwegian Mormons in Utah. Odd S. Lovoll, *A Folk Epic: The Bygdelag in America* (Boston, 1975), tells the story of these organizations; Arlow W. Andersen, *The Immigrant Takes His Stand: The Norwegian-American Press and Public Affairs, 1847–1872* (Northfield, Minn., 1953), and Jon Wefald, *A Voice of Protest: Norwegians in American Politics, 1890–1917* (Northfield, Minn., 1971), treat the Norwegian-language press and midwestern political activities.

Surveys of the history of the Norwegian people in the United States are Arlow W. Andersen, *The Norwegian-Americans* (Boston, 1974), which has an up-to-date bibliography, and Ingrid Semmingsen, *Norway to America: A History of the Migration* (Minneapolis, 1978). Histories of religious groups include the comprehensive work of Clifford Nelson and Eugene L. Fevold, *The Lutheran Church among Norwegian-Americans: A History of the Evangelical Lutheran Church,* 2 vols. (Minneapolis, 1960), and Arlow W. Andersen, *The Salt of the Earth: A History of Norwegian-Danish Methodism in America* (Nashville, Tenn., 1962). *Land of Their Choice: The Immigrants Write Home,* ed. Theodore C. Blegen (Minneapolis, 1955), contains translations of America letters.

Primary materials are collected in the Archives of the Norwegian-American Historical Association at St. Olaf College, Northfield, Minn.; at Luther College, Decorah, Iowa; at the Sons of Norway headquarters in Minneapolis; and at the state historical societies of Wisconsin, Minnesota, and other states.

PETER A. MUNCH

NOVA SCOTIANS: *see* CANADIANS, BRITISH

O

OJIBWAS: *see* AMERICAN INDIANS

OKINAWANS: *see* JAPANESE

OMAHAS: *see* AMERICAN INDIANS

OMANIS: *see* ARABS

ONANDAGAS: *see* AMERICAN INDIANS

ONEIDAS: *see* AMERICAN INDIANS

ORIENTAL

The Orient includes both the Near East and the Far East, and oriental is used to refer to people, objects, and institutions from Turkey to Taiwan. In the United States the term Oriental most often means a person of Chinese, Korean, Filipino, or Japanese ancestry. It is used as a synonym for Asian, but many Asian Americans consider it an outdated colonialist term and prefer to be called Asian.

ORIENTAL ORTHODOX

The Armenian Orthodox Church, the Coptic Orthodox Church, the Ethiopian Orthodox Church, the Syrian Orthodox Church of Antioch, and the Syrian Orthodox Church of India now wish to be called the Oriental Orthodox churches. In the past these five churches, all members of the World Council of Churches, have been referred to, misleadingly, as the Monophysite, Non-Chalcedonian, Pre-Chalcedonian, or Lesser Eastern churches. In 1970 they claimed a total combined membership of 22 million.

Their theological doctrine differentiates them from the Eastern (Byzantine) Orthodox. They are commonly viewed as having rejected the christology of the Council of Chalcedon (A.D. 451) and the christological teaching of the Roman Catholic Church as articulated in the *Tome of Pope Leo I* (c. A.D. 445). The Oriental Orthodox hold to the Alexandrian theological tradition declared orthodox at the Council of Ephesus (A.D. 431).

Theologians of the Oriental Orthodox churches and the Eastern Orthodox churches held their first consultation in August 1964 in Aarhus, Denmark. The patriarchs of the five Oriental Orthodox churches held a week-long conference—the first such meeting since the 5th century—in January 1965 in Addis Ababa, Ethiopia, where they adopted a number of decisions and sanctioned the appointment of various committees. The use of the term Oriental Orthodox dates from this meeting.

THOMAS E. BIRD

ORTHODOX

This term is used by two groups of Christians and a segment within Judaism. In the United States a person identifying as Orthodox may be a member of an Eastern Orthodox or Oriental Orthodox church, or an Orthodox Jew.

Eastern Orthodox refers to Christians who trace their heritage to the ancient patriarchates of Alexandria, Antioch, Constantinople, and Jerusalem; to the newer patriarchates of Bulgaria, Georgia, Romania, Russia, and Serbia; or to the autocephalous, or autonomous, churches of Albania, the Americas, Belorussia, Crete, Cyprus, Czechoslovakia, Finland, Greece, Japan, Macedonia, Poland, Serbia, or the Ukraine. In the United States, Eastern Orthodox Christians include many, though not all, Albanians, Arabs, Belorussians, Bulgarians, Carpatho-Rusyns, Estonians, Finns, Greeks, Macedonians, Romanians, Russians, Serbians, Syrians, and Ukrainians.

Oriental Orthodox refers to Christians who belong to the Armenian Orthodox Church, the Coptic Orthodox Church, the Ethiopian Orthodox Church, the Syrian Orthodox Church of Antioch, and the Syrian Orthodox Church of India. The term, formally adopted in January 1965 by a conference of the heads of these churches, distinguishes them from the Eastern Orthodox. In the United States members of these churches are found among Arabs, Armenians, Assyrians, Copts, East Indians, and Ethiopians.

Orthodox Judaism encompasses those Jews who seek to observe the 613 laws and regulations established by talmudic law, emphasizing the importance of *halakhah*, the legal portion of the Talmud, and such later Jewish literature as the Mishnah Torah and the Shulhan Arukh. The expression Orthodox Judaism came into use in the late 18th century after the American and French revolutions. It is now used to distinguish more traditional Jews from those who participate in the Reform and Conservative movements within Judaism. Orthodoxy in the United States includes such non-Hasidic groups as the Mizrachi, the Agudas Israel, and the Young Israel Movement; and such Hasidic groups as the Lubavitcher, Satmarer, Bobover, and Skverer Hasidim. (*See also* Eastern Orthodox; Jews; Oriental Orthodox; Religion.)

THOMAS E. BIRD

OSAGES: *see* AMERICAN INDIANS

OSSETIANS: *see* NORTH CAUCASIANS

OTOS: *see* AMERICAN INDIANS

OTTAWAS: *see* AMERICAN INDIANS

P

PACIFIC ISLANDERS

Migration from the Pacific Islands to the United States is a relatively new phenomenon; before 1950 very few islanders lived in the United States. By the late 1970s the number of Samoan migrants in the United States (between 40,000 and 60,000) was approximately 1.5 times the population of American Samoa, and the number of Chamorro migrants (from Guam and Saipan) in the mainland United States (30,000–50,000) about equaled the number of Chamorros estimated to reside in Guam and Saipan themselves. The number of Tongan migrants, about 10,000, was equivalent to one-tenth the population of Tonga. From a demographic perspective, the migration of Pacific Islanders to the U.S. mainland and Hawaii has important social and economic implications for their home societies.

Use of the term Pacific Islands is restricted here to the islands of Polynesia and Micronesia. Polynesians, closely related in general culture and language despite wide geographic distribution, inhabit the volcanic and coral islands of the South Pacific. Culturally far less homogeneous than the Polynesians are the Micronesian populations occupying some smaller coral atolls and

volcanic islands of the mid-Pacific and a larger chain of volcanic islands known as the Marianas, which include Guam and Saipan.

The largest migrations to the United States from the Pacific region have come from American Samoa in central Polynesia and from the Chamorro-speaking population of Guam in the Mariana Islands. Migration from Tonga, a Polynesian monarchy about 500 miles southwest of Samoa, and from Western Samoa, an independent nation of islands west of American Samoa, has also been significant. Hawaiians and part-Hawaiians are discussed elsewhere (see Hawaiians); however, migrants to the mainland are treated here even though movement between the mainland and Hawaii since 1959 is technically between states. There are also small groups of Micronesians from all six districts of the U.S. Trust Territory of the Pacific Islands (created by the United Nations in 1947) living on the West Coast and in Hawaii. Finally, groups of Tahitians and Fijians reside on the U.S. mainland, but in very small numbers compared with the other groups. There is also a small community of Fiji Indians in California, descendants of East Indians who migrated to Fiji as indentured laborers early in the 20th century and who now make up over

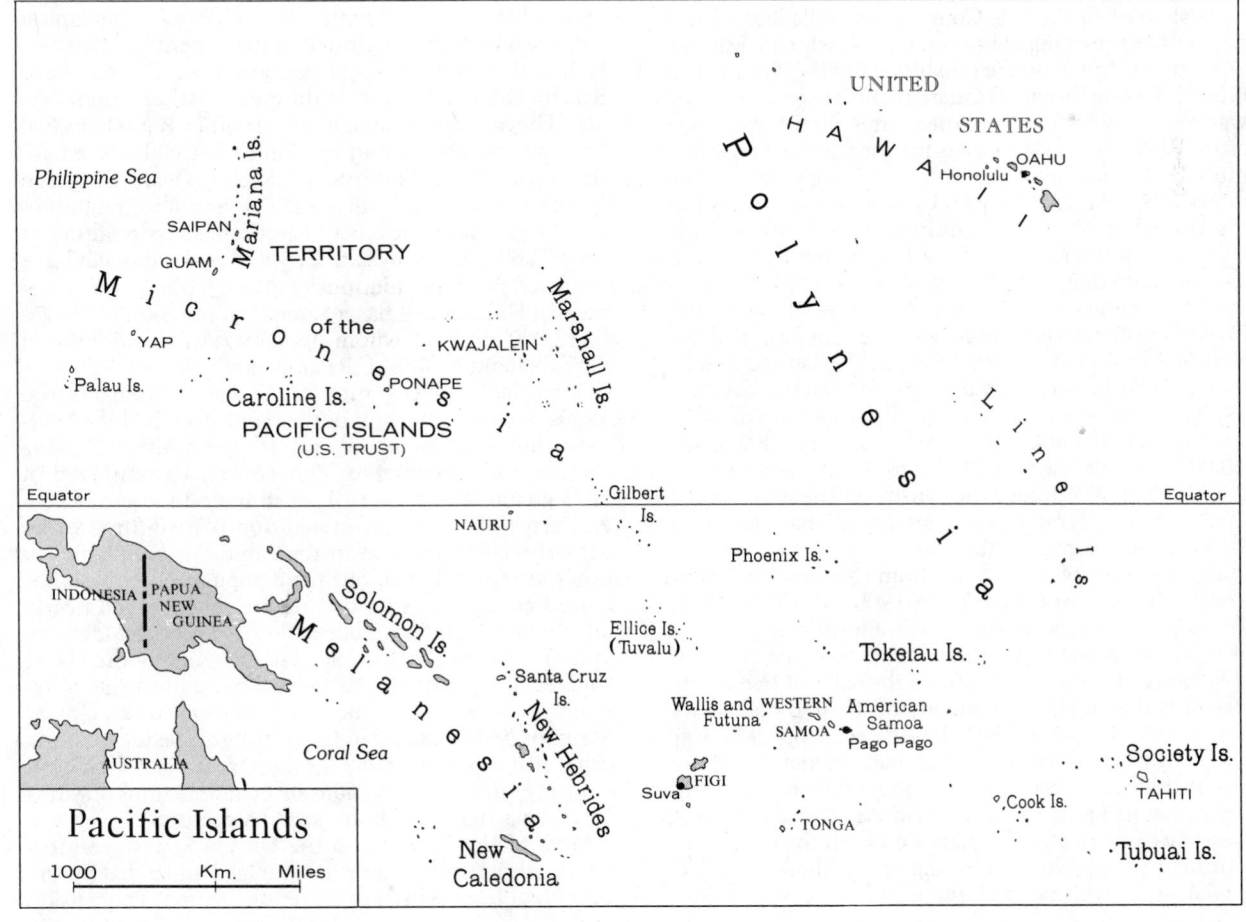

Pacific Islands

1000   Km.   Miles

half the total population of the Fiji Islands. In San Francisco they have organized the Fiji/Jamaatal Islam of America.

Published information about Pacific Island migrants to the United States is scant, and there are no reliable census data on populations or settlement patterns. More information is available about the Samoan populations than about the Chamorro or Tongan communities or the Hawaiian migrations. This information comes from the few reports available, from direct knowledge of the Samoan migrant communities, and from personal accounts by Tongan, Hawaiian, and Chamorro immigrants.

Migration of Pacific Islanders to the United States should be viewed in relation to broad patterns of migration within the Pacific region. Within both Polynesia and Micronesia there is intraregional migration from outer islands to economic centers; Guam, Saipan, Ponape, Yap, and Nauru are the centers for local migration in geographical Micronesia. Tahiti and American Samoa play an analogous role in Polynesia, attracting migrants from other, economically less important islands in the region. It is from these local centers that most of the outmigration to the metropolitan centers of New Zealand, Hawaii, and the U.S. mainland occurs; most Tongans, however, migrate directly.

MIGRATION TO THE MAINLAND

Although there has been internal migration in the Pacific during most of the 20th century, large-scale outmigration to the United States began only in the 1950s. On August 1, 1950, the U.S. Congress passed a law known popularly as the Organic Act of Guam, which conferred U.S. citizenship upon the inhabitants of the Territory of Guam. Among the rights Guamanians thereby acquired was unrestricted entry into the United States. Although citizenship was the legal basis for emigration, economic motives provided the incentive. Enlisting in the armed forces was the easiest way for Guamanian men to get to the United States and to acquire relatively high-paying jobs. U.S. Immigration and Naturalization Service figures indicate that between 1963 and 1971, 11,930 Guamanians emigrated to Hawaii and the West Coast. Community members have given estimates, perhaps high, of 50,000 Chamorros living in the United States. Most live near large naval shipyards, and concentrations have been identified in the metropolitan areas of Los Angeles (10,000), San Diego (20,000), San Francisco (10,000), Seattle-Tacoma (2,000 to 3,000), and Hawaii (2,000 to 4,000). Because the census has never recorded Guamanians separately, there are no reliable figures on their number in the United States.

The history of migration from American Samoa parallels that from Guam. From 1900 to 1951 the U.S. Territory of American Samoa was administered by the Department of the Navy. Its residents have the status of U.S. nationals, which gives them the right of free entry, although they do not have many of the political rights of U.S. citizens. Before 1951 the American naval base at Pago Pago employed many Samoans. When the base was shifted to Hawaii in 1951, the Samoan economic boom that had grown out of World War II and the naval presence came to a sudden halt. Left with the options of returning to subsistence farming or, for those who had served with the Samoan *fitafita* guard, of moving to Hawaii where they could enlist in the navy, many Samoans chose to emigrate. The stream of migrants to Hawaii increased throughout the early 1950s, encouraged by territorial authorities who saw emigration as a partial answer to rapid population expansion and a sagging agricultural economy. An increasingly unfavorable balance of trade, a sudden and severe drought, and unrealistically high expectations for a standard of material life all fueled the Samoans' desire to migrate to Hawaii.

Since 1951 American Samoa has been administered as an unincorporated territory by the U.S. Department of the Interior. Military service continued to attract Samoans, providing prestige at home, adventure abroad, education, and an American salary scale. After the early 1960s, however, other incentives began to promote Samoan migration to the United States, among them broader employment opportunities and the desire to educate children in U.S. schools. Many Samoans moved in a chain process from Hawaii to the West Coast; they helped relatives come from the home islands to the United States, and frequently also helped them find jobs and housing.

Estimates of the total current Samoan population in the United States range from 40,000 to 60,000; precise figures are lacking because American Samoans, as U.S. nationals, are not included in immigration statistics. Probably between 15 and 20 percent of the Samoans in the United States are citizens of independent Western Samoa and do not have preferential entry. Some of these Western Samoans have overstayed visitors' visas; others have become naturalized citizens. The largest concentration in the United States—perhaps 20,000—is in the Los Angeles area, mostly in Carson, Long Beach, Oceanside, and Wilmington, where there are also Tongans and Guamanians. Another 10,000–15,000 Samoans have settled in the San Francisco Bay area, for the most part in South San Francisco, Daly City, San Mateo County, and San Jose. The San Diego community is estimated at 6,000, Seattle has a population of about 2,000, and Salt Lake City and St. Louis each have attracted small populations of about 1,500 Mormon Samoans. Hawaii still has a Samoan population of 10,000 to 12,000, most of whom live on Oahu Island in Pearl City, Nanakuli, Kalihi, Palama, and Laie.

Large-scale immigration from Tonga began in the 1960s, largely as a result of the rapid growth of the Mormon church in the home islands. Again, the prevailing motives were economic. The Tongan Constitution of 1875 guarantees to every Tongan male a section of several acres of farmland, in addition to two-fifths of an acre of residential land in the capital of Nukualofa or other residential area; but rapid population growth has placed great strains on this tenure scheme, and nearly all parcels of land have been allocated. Tongan law provides for the inheritance of a father's land by the eldest son, leaving junior sons little economic incentive to remain in Tonga. Many look to migration to the United States or New Zealand in the face of increasing material expectations, an unstable local economy based on cash cropping, and the limitations on economic mobility imposed by a rigid hereditary social structure.

Most of the Tongans in the United States are Mormons, whose migration is encouraged and aided by the Church of Jesus Christ of Latter-day Saints. Tongans do

not have the right of free entry, and must apply for a quota number. Some are sponsored by parents or other close relatives who have become U.S. citizens. About 4,000 Tongans, the largest community in the country, live in the San Francisco Bay area, particularly in San Mateo County. An estimated 2,000–3,000 reside in Los Angeles in the same neighborhoods as Samoans and Chamorros; another 3,000 live in Hawaii, and about 1,000 in Salt Lake City.

In addition to the populations discussed above, a large group of Hawaiians and part-Hawaiians live on the mainland, predominantly on the West Coast. Most Hawaiians in California do not have, at least not to the same degree, the economic problems of the other Pacific Islanders. For one thing, Hawaiians have been exposed far longer than other islanders to American culture and society and are more acculturated. In fact, the pressing problem for Hawaiian migrants, voiced by community leaders, is the need to transmit their linguistic and cultural heritage to children who are in danger of losing touch with their roots.

COMMUNITY CHARACTERISTICS

There is considerable variation in the character of the different communities of Pacific Islanders in the United States. The most important variables are the particular cultural group itself, its size and residential density, the history of the original immigrant settlement of the area, and the ratio of migrants who have come alone for schooling or military service to those who are attached, through chain migration, to extended family networks. Seattle, for instance, has a relatively small and invisible population of Samoans who are spread out in different areas; many of them are temporary residents attending school. Hawaii, San Francisco, and Los Angeles have much larger and more established populations of Pacific Islanders, each community exhibiting a high degree of cohesion and cooperation. The populations of Laie (Hawaii), Salt Lake City, and St. Louis are composed almost entirely of members of the Mormon church, to which the social lives of these groups are closely linked.

Despite these variations among groups, Pacific Island migrants in general share important cultural orientations, and thus a similar set of problems in adapting to urban life in the United States. Foremost are the radical differences between the economic and social skills required for survival in the small, rural, island habitats of the Pacific and those demanded by the relatively impersonal, industrial, urban settings in which most migrants settle. Many of the farming and other subsistence skills mastered at home are of little use in America, and many migrants, including those enjoying high rank and prestige in their own societies, find employment only in unskilled and semiskilled jobs—in construction, assembly lines, as janitors or maintenance workers. Many work as night watchmen or security guards. Some never get far from the port of entry and find maintenance jobs at airports or shipyards. Faced with generally low wages, expenses swollen by large families, and constant financial obligations to the church and a large group of relatives both in America and abroad, the men often are forced to hold two jobs. Many women work, too, commonly as hotel maids, aides in hospitals and nursing homes, and in fish canneries. Although there are notable exceptions, rela-

tively few Pacific Islanders have secured white-collar jobs or are self-employed. Unemployment is high, reaching about 25 to 30 percent for adult males. No matter how difficult economic conditions are in the United States, however, they are generally brighter than in the islands.

For Pacific Islanders, identity has always been strongly local, articulated in terms of links to land, islands, local kin groups, and villages. This kind of identification becomes progressively more difficult to sustain as time passes and at such distance from the islands. Furthermore, the impersonality and the residential mobility of urban life are not conducive to a simple translation of traditional identity to American soil. Local ties are generally supplemented or replaced by links through common-interest associations like church, social, political, or sports groups. Common ethnicity eventually replaces local origins or kinship links as a focus for identity.

Despite the changes in their way of life, Samoans, Tongans, and Chamorros retain links to villages and kin in the home islands. They may also retain residual land-use rights and community political rights, both of which are strengthened and validated by continued participation in village and family affairs, if only by letters or money sent home. Contributions to relatives to help support village projects or defray expenses of funerals or weddings are a substantial part of maintaining an identity and a link with the islands. Frequent trips back to the islands by elders for political or social events provide additional continuity. For younger members of the group, particularly those born in the United States, identity becomes more complex. Immigrants from Pacific Islands remain relatively anonymous among minority groups except in areas of high concentration. In the United States, where ethnic identity has always been important, Pacific Islanders often find themselves invisible as a group, perceived as Asian Americans or misidentified as another, more visible group, such as Filipinos. Public knowledge about the Pacific Islands is so limited that islanders often find it difficult to explain who they are. Many are therefore forced to affirm their Pacific heritage mainly or only through local activities within families, churches, and other groups, but to merge their public identity and political activities with blacks, Chicanos, Filipinos, or Asians in general.

Nevertheless, in schools or places of employment with substantial numbers of Pacific Islanders, local stereotypes and ethnic identities have crystallized. Sometimes the stereotype applies to a particular island group but often different origins are lumped together into broader categories, or one group is simply perceived as another. This relative ethnic anonymity has important implications for Pacific Islanders; the stereotypes that emerge stress either a romantic image inspired by popular novels, movies, or public entertainers, or an aggressive image, usually generated by reports of barroom brawling. In either case, the image lacks the depth and subtlety that comes from real acquaintance.

On the other hand, ethnic anonymity may facilitate adaptation to urban life. Samoans, for example, are far more visible in Hawaii than on the mainland, because they concentrate in fewer but heavily populated residential communities of experimental "villages" with

traditional patterns of authority and residence. But despite apparent similarities between Hawaii and Samoa, Samoans actually adjust less successfully to life in Hawaii than they do to urban life on the mainland. It may be that adaptation and assimilation are easier in a setting that provides clear and significant contrasts to home; apparent similarities may mask more subtle but crucial differences that make adjustment difficult. Furthermore, a clear and widely disseminated stereotype for a group, such as exists for Samoans and Tongans in Hawaii, may impede adaptation. Finally, maintenance of the strong authority of chiefs, elders, and church leaders and the successful indoctrination of children to traditional values in an alien setting may create at least as many adjustment problems as they solve.

SOCIAL ORGANIZATION

Pacific Island cultures such as those of Samoa and Tonga have structured societies with explicit hierarchical authority and codes of formal deference and respect. Such systems, particularly on small islands, are strongly communal and discourage individual freedom of action; instead they encourage appropriateness of behavior to social context, obedience to age and authority, and social interdependence. All these values conflict with the American emphasis on personal independence and a strong, assertive personality. Pacific societies maintain standards of behavior through external sanctions, by fear of shame, losing face, and disgracing name and family—an effective form of social control within settings with maximal public exposure of individual behavior, a low degree of anonymity, and widely shared norms for behavior. Thus adaptation to an American urban setting poses many difficulties for Pacific Islanders, who tend to instill in their children traditional values that conflict with those of the wider society.

The economic and social opportunities that attract many Pacific Island migrants to the United States have an important impact on their lives, although the impact varies from group to group. For Samoans, migration to the United States has generally brought upward economic movement, but also a decline in social and political status. The higher cost of living in the United States does not offset the increased earning power. Thus migration often brings improved access to money and credit, with important consequences for the characteristic Polynesian economy of redistribution, where status is accrued through generosity in redistribution of valued goods, and material capital is difficult to accumulate. Traditional Polynesian societies, based on descent and family connections, did not evolve a true economic class structure. The more successful migrants, with continued access to money and material possessions, can satisfy their obligations to distribute wealth to their relatives in America and back home and still accumulate capital. This economic change has created social distinctions that have undercut traditional lines of prestige and authority and transformed both migrant and island societies.

Samoan society is characterized by a degree of political mobility and competition for status unusual in Polynesia. Titles associated with leadership of descent groups and families, control of land, and general prestige are so numerous in Samoa that almost every talented man or woman can hope to be elected a *matai* or chief. Although wealth is one avenue to power, social status for Samoans does not simply reflect material wealth. Through ability and service to chief and family, a Samoan can gain considerable prestige and power. Migration to the United States has provided avenues for individual economic mobility and personal independence, but it has considerably constricted the access of Samoans to social and political recognition within the wider society. Although many Samoan migrants still possess matai titles and are often accorded formal deference within the immigrant community, traditional chiefly status does not promote social recognition in the United States. Furthermore, most Samoans, like other Pacific Island migrants, find themselves locked within class and ethnic boundaries far less permeable than those they left behind.

The Tongan case differs from that of the Samoans, largely because of a far more rigid political and social structure that divides Tongan society into clearly defined hereditary classes of royalty, nobility, and commoners. Social status in Tonga is tied to control over land and other productive resources, and commoners have considerably less social and economic mobility than their Samoan cousins. Tongans, like Samoans, stress *alofa* or generosity and sharing, and for most, an economy emphasizing capital accumulation and individualistic competition is something new.

Hawaiians have gained both economically and socially in their move to the U.S. mainland, although they have suffered some loss of contact with their own traditions. Modern Hawaiian society is, in fact, quite clearly and uncomfortably stratified by class and ethnic group despite outward emphasis on social and racial harmony. Hawaiians share the lower rungs of the ladder with Samoans, Filipinos, and other Pacific Islanders. Whatever problems they may have on the mainland, therefore, their Hawaiian identity is probably less likely to be a social liability in the context of the greater society than it is in Hawaii itself. Many Hawaiians on the mainland also have entered the middle class.

For the Chamorros, too, economic mobility is high among the incentives for emigration. Until recently, Guamanian society shared with American Samoa a stratified salary structure, with local earnings considerably lower than those on the mainland. The loss of an agricultural subsistence economy and the impact of inflation on the cost of subsistence goods have also increased the attractiveness of migration to the mainland.

Throughout the Pacific Islands, ties of kinship and locality provide the fundamental orientations for social life. The most important social unit in these societies is the extended-family household. Brothers and their families may share a single residential compound, and the residential group may also include grandparents, widowed or unmarried sisters, adopted children, and even friends who may reside temporarily in a household where they have no kin. Household size varies considerably, but groups of 10 to 15 are not uncommon. A clear division of labor by age and sex and an explicit authority structure mark the organization of the household and make absorption of new members relatively easy. Diffuse ties of kinship throughout an island and a tradition of visiting and hospitality make the actual household composition variable at any particular time. The composition also varies over time as daughters and

sons marry and leave or establish their own household units on nearby sections. This flexible social structure provides one means of redistributing a fluctuating island population over limited resources.

In the immigrant setting, traditional social structure seems to have served equally well in radically different conditions. Despite the common assumption that extended family networks give way in urban, industrialized settings to nuclear families, this has not so far been the case with most Pacific Islanders. Samoans, Tongans, and Chamorros all maintain large local family networks as well as ties to their kin in the islands. Furthermore, most Pacific Island households in the United States maintain the same flexibility in composition and capacity to absorb newcomers that is characteristic in the islands. These strong social networks are important economically, for most adult members find employment and contribute to the maintenance of the household. A single residential group can bring in a comparatively large total income without significantly increasing household expenses except food; because everyone is expected to be productive, new household members are more of an economic asset than a liability. When housing limitations prevent the co-residence of close kin, cars and telephones provide mobility and rapid communication. Thus social ties are easily maintained in the American setting.

These extended family units also serve as socializing agents for newly arrived immigrants. Relatives usually help arrange jobs, schooling, and housing, and provide advice and important information, thus encouraging the intense social interdependence that is characteristic of island life. In some Samoan and Tongan households, the household head acts, either officially or unofficially, as a chief and collects pay packets weekly. Pocket money, food, and other necessities are redistributed as needed in Polynesian fashion. In other households, individuals control their own earnings but make regular contributions both to the household and their families in the islands.

Religious and Other Organizations

Lacking the formal political, village, and descent-group organization that defines social life in the islands, Pacific Islanders focus their collective activities in organizations that cut across traditional village and kinship ties. The church, for instance, is clearly the center of social life, particularly for Samoans and Tongans, in the United States. Particular affiliations depend largely upon which churches made missionary efforts among the island groups. Most Tongans in the United States belong to the Mormon church, although the state church in Tonga is Methodist and several Tongan Methodist congregations exist in California and Hawaii. The majority of Samoan migrants belong to various branches of the Congregational Christian church, derived from the old London Missionary Society church that is the dominant denomination in Samoa; however, throughout California and Hawaii there are Samoan Methodist, Seventh-Day Adventist, Presbyterian, and Pentecostal congregations. Catholic and Mormon Samoans in the United States joined larger congregations rather than having their own churches, but their closest social relations are with each other. There are more than 50 Samoan Protestant congregations in California,

ranging in size from 100 to 1,000 members. Most Chamorros are Catholics as a result of the early Spanish influence in the Marianas; others are Baptists and Seventh-Day Adventists. The Fijians are largely Hindu and Muslim.

In Tonga and Samoa the church is a central focus for community life; the respect accorded pastors often exceeds that given traditional chiefs. In the United States the functions of church and pastor are even more important: they must provide moral and cultural leadership in a morally ambiguous and complex urban environment. Church leaders provide their congregations with an important sense of continuity in experience between the islands and the United States. Church activities go far beyond Sunday services and include a week-long cycle of activities: Bible study, youth-group meetings, fund-raising projects, choir practice, and general social gatherings. Since services and many Sunday-school classes are conducted in Samoan or Tongan, the church also provides education in traditional language and culture to young children who might otherwise receive none.

In addition to church groups, Pacific Islanders have organized a variety of social institutions. A number of Hawaiian social and cultural organizations have spread through California; these are mainly social groups encouraging contacts among Hawaiians and providing such events as luau parties and hula exhibitions and lessons for their community members. Hawaiians have also formed several politically oriented organizations, notably the Hawaiian Interclub Council, representing all the local clubs, and Hawaiians United Incorporated (HUI). Chamorros have established a number of local organizations in California, including the Chamorro Organization, the Guamanian Organization of Long Beach, and the Sons and Daughters of Guam. Tongans have organized the American Federation of Tongans and a number of local organizations.

Samoans have the most elaborate network of organizations, including political action and welfare groups, such as the various Samoan chiefs' councils of San Francisco, Hawaii, and Los Angeles; the more broadly based Samoan Community Organization; the American Council of Samoan Communities (Los Angeles); Samoa Mo Samoa (San Francisco); the Samoan Civic Organization (Hawaii); and the United Samoan Community Organization (Hawaii). In addition, Samoans have formed several cricket teams.

Despite the number of these groups, Pacific Islanders have only recently directed their interests and skills to large-scale political and economic issues and to working with local, state, and federal government agencies to make their needs known and to develop effective social-welfare programs. In the 1970s Pacific Islanders began to form coalitions, indicating recognition that political power lies in numerical strength and that the various island groups share many problems and interests.

Many significant social and cultural transformations will inevitably take place within the U.S. communities of Pacific Islanders, and the future generations will differ radically from their relatives in the Pacific. Nonetheless, perhaps most impressive is the adaptability of the islanders' traditional institutions to an American context. In their strengths and problems alike, Pacific Island communities have a distinctive vitality and soli-

darity whose continuity in the United States depends on the maintenance of institutions associated with family and church. The relatively low incidence of outgroup marriage among all Pacific Island migrants implies the survival of community identity on their own terms as well as those imposed by their new environment. Their ties with the home islands may prove as important for their successful long-term adaptation as the transformations inevitable in the act of migration.

Bibliography

A classic introduction is Douglas Oliver, *The Pacific Islands* (Cambridge, Mass., 1961). Robert Trumbull, *Tin Roofs and Palm Trees: A Report on the New South Seas* (Seattle, 1977), gives an overview of the current situation in the Pacific Islands. Faye Untalan Munoz, "Pacific Islanders: A Perplexed, Neglected Minority," *Church and Society* (January–February 1974): 15–23, focuses on Guamanian communities in the United States and provides information on Chamorro migration. On Samoan migration and adjustment, see Gorden R. Lewthwaite, Christine Mainzer, and Patrick J. Holland, "From Polynesia to California: Samoan Migration and Its Sequel," *Journal of Pacific History* 8 (1973): 133–157; and Joan Ablon, "The Social Organization of an Urban Samoan Community," *Southwestern Journal of Anthropology* 27 (1971): 75–96, which discusses migrants in San Francisco. Cluny Macpherson, Bradd Shore, and Robert Franco, eds., *New Neighbors: Islanders in Adaptation* (Santa Cruz, Calif., 1978), contains the proceedings of a series of conferences held among Pacific migration researchers, Pacific Island community leaders, and representatives of government service agencies.

BRADD SHORE

PAIUTES: *see* AMERICAN INDIANS

PAKISTANIS

In 1979 there were approximately 20,000 Pakistanis in the United States; a few thousand were students or diplomatic personnel but most were permanent residents. The vast majority were recent arrivals, for there were very few Pakistanis in the United States before immigration restrictions were lifted in 1965 and even fewer from the area before Pakistan became an independent nation in 1947. Between 1965 and 1970 the U.S. Immigration and Naturalization Service reported a total of 2,645; but beginning in 1971 more than 2,000 Pakistanis have entered the United States each year. In 1975 there were 10,469 Pakistani resident aliens. All these figures remain only estimates, for they do not take into account the immigrants who return to Pakistan, those who enter illegally, or the students who overstay their visas.

Pakistan is officially a Muslim nation, and 75 percent of the Pakistanis in America are Sunni Muslims. Both in Pakistan and in the United States a small proportion are Shiite Muslims, Ahmadis, Hindus, Christians, Buddhists, or Zoroastrians (Parsis). Religion is the issue that led to the creation of the independent state of Pakistan after centuries of Hindu-Muslim conflict on the Indian subcontinent. And language, in addition to distance, was one of the major differences that led to the separation of the Bengali-speaking East Pakistanis (now Bangladeshi) from West Pakistan in 1971. Within present-day Pakistan there are a number of ethnic groups, each with its own language. The five major languages are Urdu, Punjabi, Sindhi, Pashto (Pushtu), and Baluchi (Bruhi). Urdu is the official language; it is a mixture of Hindi, Persian, Arabic, and Turkish, written in Persian script. English also is commonly spoken in the cities by the better educated.

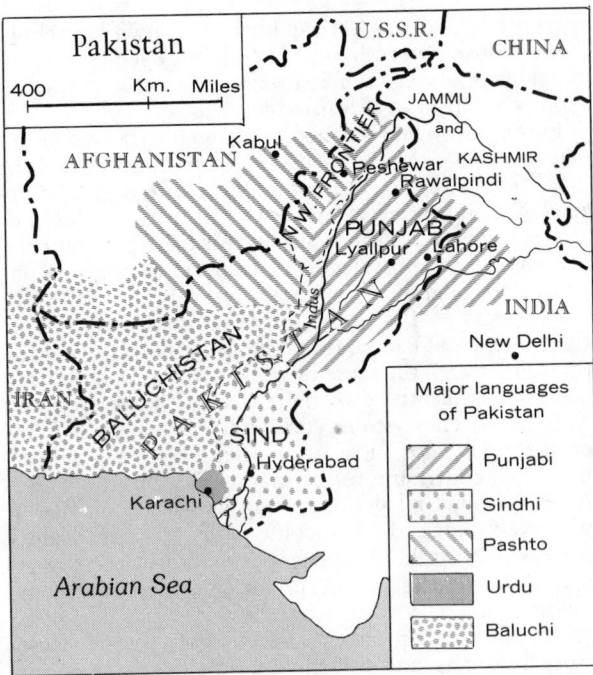

Although in Pakistan only 8 percent of the total population speak Urdu and 56 percent Punjabi, 80 percent of the Pakistanis in the United States are either Punjabi- or Urdu-speaking (50 percent Punjabi, 30 percent Urdu). They represent the groups that are most highly educated and most likely to live in urban areas. Pakistanis tend to settle in metropolitan areas that offer the job opportunities for which they have been trained. Most Pakistani male immigrants have had some university or professional education. About 10 percent are physicians, another 10 percent are engineers, and most of the rest are scientists, academics, or businessmen. They come primarily from the major cities—Karachi, Lahore, Rawalpindi, Hyderabad, Peshawar, and Faisalabad; at the time of arrival in the United States the men are typically between 25 and 39 years old, married to women a few years younger, and have one child.

Although the immigrant Pakistani is most likely to pick his closest associates from his linguistic group, ethnic-group differences characteristic of Pakistan are muted in the United States. Individuals from all linguistic backgrounds mix on every social level; the Urdu-, Punjabi-, and Gujerati-speakers, however, are likely to be most cosmopolitan; the Sindhis, Baluchis, and Pathans, who are generally less urbanized and less well educated in Pakistan, tend to keep to themselves.

The Pakistani family is the center of social life; it is hierarchically ordered and male-dominated. If two brothers, their wives, and children live in the same household, the older brother acts as the head of the household and prevails in any major decision. Most women remain in the home, confined to its management and to the upbringing of the children. Very few work outside their homes.

The family plays a major role in Pakistani immigration and settlement. When a man emigrates to the United States his entire family helps to finance the move. Once established, he is expected to help the other members of his family to join him. When a new

member arrives, the costs of education, food, and housing are met by the immigrants who came earlier. The newcomer is introduced to their acquaintances, the qualifications of the men are evaluated, and they are introduced to other Pakistanis in the community or in neighboring cities. Usually a male immigrant lives with a brother and sister-in-law and their children, but he is expected to establish his own household within a couple of years. Later he may return to Pakistan to marry, his family having arranged for a suitable wife. Although more and more marriages are arranged outside the extended family, marriages between cousins remain quite common.

Children in the Pakistani family receive a great deal of attention in the United States just as in Pakistan. Parents take their children with them wherever they go; babysitters are never used. Children usually speak their mother tongue at home until they go to school and begin to watch television; then most of them speak English exclusively, although Pakistani Sunday schools in the larger cities attempt to maintain the mother tongue as well as to teach Arabic and the tenets of Islam.

About 200 Pakistani civic and social organizations have been established in the United States; they are most active in urban centers with large Pakistani populations. The Muslim Students of America (MSA), the Pakistan Students' Association of America and Canada (PSSAA&C), and the Pakistan League of America (PLA) claim more than 1,000 members each. Their annual conventions attract Pakistanis from all over North America to attend lectures, speeches, poetry readings, recitals of passages from the Koran, seminars, variety shows, musical programs, and special programs for women and children.

Pakistani radio and television programs are broadcast each week to audiences in Chicago, San Francisco, Newark, New York, Houston, Los Angeles, Boston, and Washington, D.C. Popular songs, interviews with celebrities, and announcements about community activities are the main fare. Television programs for Pakistanis, East Indians, and Bangladeshis are broadcast from Newark, N.J., to the New York metropolitan area. Two quite popular programs are "Vision of Asia" and "Reflections." Full-length movies, news broadcasts, religious programs, commercials for Pakistani grocery and clothing stores, and reviews of important cricket matches played in Pakistan are also presented.

Occasionally Pakistani movies are shown in local school or university auditoriums; some New York and Chicago movie theaters owned by Indian and Pakistani businessmen show films from the homeland on a regular basis. Urdu poetry recitals, called mushaira, are well attended; statesmen, politicians, cabinet ministers from Pakistan, and performances by popular singers or actors from Pakistan draw enthusiastic crowds and serve to keep Pakistani culture alive in the community.

Several Pakistani periodicals are published in the United States. The largest is Pakistan Affairs, issued by the Embassy of Pakistan in Washington, D.C.; it has a national circulation of approximately 5,000. Dawn, an English-language weekly paper, provides news about recent developments in Pakistan. It also includes both news and feature articles on political, economic, literary, and social affairs in Pakistan and on Pakistanis

abroad. Jung (Struggle), published in New Jersey, is printed in both English and Urdu to keep Pakistanis informed about community events and provide articles of special interest, particularly on Pakistani politics. Pakistan Student, a monthly journal issued by the Pakistan Student Association of America, prints works of outstanding authors in the United States and Pakistan and announces events of community interest in the United States. Al-Balagh (The Communication) of Syracuse, a monthly magazine with a circulation of over 3,000, is directed toward devout Pakistani Muslims. Over 100 other Pakistani periodicals circulate regionally and nationally, important among them the New York Crescent, The Minaret of New York, and the Horizon of Indianapolis.

Community events center on religious festivals and national holidays. During the fasting month of Ramadan, travih (recitation of the Holy Koran after the regular prayers) are held every night. Eidul fitr, a celebration of the end of Ramadan, and Eidul azha, a commemoration of the pilgrimage to Mecca, are marked by prayers, social calls, poetry recitals, musical evenings, and feasts. Independence Day (August 14), Pakistan Day (March 23), and the Birthday of the Founder of the Nation (December 25) are also occasions for community festivities. All these gatherings provide cultural reinforcement for Pakistanis. Pakistani Muslims in New York and Chicago have established mosques where prayers are offered five times a day and where Sunday religious schools are run for the children. Sunnis, Shiites, and Ahmadis have their own mosques and community centers.

So far, the Pakistanis have done well in the United States; they have come well prepared for a competitive and technological society. Nevertheless they continue to face a great many adjustments and problems. Conflict is inevitable between the traditional social and moral values of the first generation and the attitudes of an American-educated second generation. On the other hand, some Pakistani immigrants have shown great adaptability to American society. A few have become millionaires, 2 percent report a family income in six digits, and some have acquired top positions in business, professional, and academic life.

However, although most Pakistanis in the United States are solidly rooted in the middle class, a small but significant minority has not been able to adjust successfully. A few blocks from Columbia University in New York City there are a few hundred who live in one-room lodgings in the slums. Among them are qualified engineers, chemists, dentists, and other professionals who have not been able to make the necessary transition to American life. They work as guards, porters, dishwashers, and in other unskilled jobs. They have found the reality of America very different from the dream, and tend to insulate themselves by socializing only with fellow Pakistanis. They keep their contacts with non-Pakistanis to a minimum, and some complain about American racism. There are similar pockets of poverty in other sections of the metropolitan New York area as well as in some parts of Chicago and Houston.

All Pakistanis are affected to some extent by conditions in Pakistan, especially with regard to intergroup relations. Ethnic, religious, tribal, and linguistic loyalties seem strong enough to supersede any sense of na-

tional identity. Sindhis, Baluchis, and Pathans respond to tensions in the homeland by associating only with others in their subgroups. They ask themselves whether they are Pakistanis first and Sindhis, Baluchis, and Pathans second, or vice versa. It is too soon to know how life in the United States will affect Pakistani ethnic identity and community life.

Bibliography

Very little has been published specifically on Pakistanis in the United States. The Government of Pakistan, *Census of 1961 and 1972* (Karachi, 1961 and 1972, respectively), is useful for background information on the social groups from which the emigrants to the United States have been drawn. The Annual Reports of the U.S. Immigration and Naturalization Service provide statistical information on the number of Pakistani immigrants and their settlement patterns. M. Arif Ghayur and J. Henry Korson, "Population and Urbanization Growth Rates as They Affect Ethnic Tensions in Pakistan," in M. Ahmed, ed., *Contemporary Pakistan: Politics, Economy and Society* (Durham, N.C., 1980), is a good background article. *Asian-Indians in America* (New York, 1980), edited by Parmatma Saran and Edwin Eames, includes several articles on various aspects of the life of East Indians in the United States, providing generalizations that can be applied, in some measure, to Pakistanis as well. Bharati Mukherjee, *Wife* (Boston, 1975), is a novel describing the social life of immigrants in the United States from the Indo-Pakistani subcontinent.

ARIF GHAYUR

PALESTINIANS: *see* ARABS

PAMUNKEYS: *see* AMERICAN INDIANS

PANAMANIANS: *see* CENTRAL AND SOUTH AMERICANS

PAPAGOS: *see* AMERICAN INDIANS

PARAGUAYANS: *see* CENTRAL AND SOUTH AMERICANS

PARSIS (PARSEES): *see* EAST INDIANS; ZOROASTRIANS

PASSAMAQUODDIES: *see* AMERICAN INDIANS

PATHANS: *see* AFGHANS; PAKISTANIS

PAUGUSETTS: *see* AMERICAN INDIANS

PAWNEES: *see* AMERICAN INDIANS

PENNSYLVANIA DUTCH: *see* PENNSYLVANIA GERMANS

PENNSYLVANIA GERMANS

The Pennsylvania Germans, frequently called Pennsylvania Dutch, are the descendants of colonial immigrants from the German-speaking lands of central Europe. Because the major center of emigration was the Electoral Palatinate (Kurpfalz), they were first called Palatines, then Dutchmen. The terms Pennsylvania Dutch and Pennsylvania German are Americanisms; Dutch is derived from an older English usage of Deutsch that denoted everyone in the area from the mouth of the Rhine to its origins in Switzerland. The 18th-century immigrants included Palatines, Swabians, Alsatians, Hessians, and Swiss, many of whom had already moved about in Europe before crossing the Atlan-

tic. A striking mixture of peoples, faiths, and ways of life could be found in the Rhineland in the 17th century, where French Huguenots and Swiss and native German elements confronted one another in the same village communities. The American experience of the colonial immigrants simply continued the unification process by which all groups merged into one comprehensive culture.

The history of the Pennsylvania Germans begins with the settlement of Germantown in 1683. Subsequent rural settlements appeared at Skippack in 1702, Oley and Conestoga in 1709, Tulpehocken in 1723, and York in 1733. By 1812 the Pennsylvania Germans had settled in eastern, central, and western Pennsylvania over an area roughly the size of Switzerland—15,000 square miles—and one-third of Pennsylvania's total area of 45,000 square miles. By the time of the Civil War there were Pennsylvania German settlements planted by migration in the South (Maryland, Virginia, North Carolina, Kentucky, and Tennessee), the North (the Genessee country in New York and Ontario in Canada), and the Midwest, where many counties in Ohio, Indiana, Illinois, Iowa, Kansas, and Nebraska were settled by Pennsylvania German farmers. In the 1970s all these areas retained cultural elements from the Pennsylvania German world.

Interethnic struggles of the colonial and federal periods—riots between the "Dutch" and the "Irish" at colonial elections and the political campaigning of "Dutch" governors against English opponents in the first half of the 19th century—sharpened Pennsylvania German ethnic consciousness. The most critical problem of the 19th century was relating to the new wave of German immigrants, particularly the politically conscious, Europe-oriented forty-eighters. Although some 19th-century immigrants settled among them, intermarried with them, and became "Dutch," the Pennsylvania Germans never culturally, ecclesiastically, or politically merged fully with the later arrivals. Eventually the Pennsylvania Germans founded their own institutions such as the Pennsylvania German Society (1891) and the Pennsylvania German Folklore Society (1935) which in 1967 merged to form the Pennsylvania German Society. Smaller groups, such as the Fereinicht Pennsylfawnish Deitsch Fulk (United Pennsylvania German People), based in Berks and Lehigh counties, and the Goschenhoppen Historians, based in Montgomery County, have since World War II launched programs for recording and preserving Pennsylvania German culture.

The Pennsylvania Germans developed a distinctive culture with attributes ranging from traditional peasant to elite forms. They produced a great many folk arts, including the *fraktur* style of manuscript decoration that flourished from about 1750 to 1850. On the elite level were such portraitists as Jacob Eichholtz and the Moravian Valentin Haidt. In the middle range were the itinerant primitivist Jacob Maentel and such genre painters as Lewis Miller. The Pennsylvania Germans had a massive repertory of secular folk songs, some brought over with the colonial immigrants, others learned from 19th-century arrivals, still others composed in Pennsylvania, like the song "Der Delamater kummt net nei" (Delamater Won't Get In), written for the Delamater-Pattison gubernatorial campaign of 1890

(Pattison won), and "Die Ford Maschin" (The Ford Car), which appeared when the first Model Ts lurched through the Dutch country around 1910. Religious folk songs were adapted from Anglo-American camp-meeting spirituals, and many Pennsylvania Germans wrote popular gospel songs after the Civil War. Chorales and organ music perpetuated the Lutheran and Reformed traditions through the church and the singing school, and Moravian choral and chamber music included both sacred and secular material. Finally, a dialect version of *H.M.S. Pinafore* played in the 1880s to packed audiences in the provincial theaters of upstate Pennsylvania.

The contributions of the Pennsylvania Germans to American culture were most widespread in folk custom and domestic economy, in agriculture and preindustrial technology, and in religious patterns. The Pennsylvania Germans contributed customs associated with the calendar; the earliest American evidence for the Christmas tree and the Easter rabbit points to Pennsylvania, although both were reinforced by 19th-century German immigrants who settled everywhere. In addition, Pennsylvania German foods (and names of foods) spread to many areas of the United States through migration: sauerkraut, smearcase, pretzels, *pannhaas* (scrapple), Lebanon bologna, *schnitz un gnepp*, hot salads, and shoofly pies.

A distinctive material culture began to develop among Pennsylvania Germans in the colonial period. By adapting techniques practiced by their British neighbors, the Pennsylvania Germans made innovations in rural technology which influenced many areas of the United States: the Conestoga wagon, documented as early as 1717, became the freight wagon of the American frontier; and the Pennsylvania rifle and Pennsylvania barn were associated with excellence when farmers and craftsmen earned the praise of foreign travelers and native historians.

In religion, the majority were members of the two main European Protestant traditions, the Lutheran and the Reformed. These churches related actively to the cultural and political environment of the Pennsylvania Germans. The minority belonged to sectarian traditions that opposed established churches, the political system, and the cultural environment. A subgroup of millennialist communitarians included the Ephrata Society, the Moravian Brethren, and the Harmonites. Revivalism produced new sects, formed as products of the First and Second Great Awakenings, and divided most of the older ecclesiastical organizations into Old Order and Progressive (that is, Americanizing) wings. The three most significant independent groups formed in this process were the United Brethren, the Evangelical Association, and the Churches of God (Winebrennerians); the first two were among the earliest native denominations established in the United States. All these ecclesiastical groups were held together by the common use of the German language in both its literary and dialect versions.

Because the Pennsylvania Germans were often the first settlers in an area of the colony and were numerous enough to be able to preserve their linguistic preferences (High German for official use in church and school, dialect for home and community use), a distinctively Pennsylvania German linguistic world took shape early in the 18th century. The Pennsylvania German dialect was a hybrid based mostly on dialects from the Palatinate and adjoining areas, with some Swiss admixture. The High German used for church, school, newspaper, and official communication gradually gave way to English, so that for a time the Pennsylvania Germans were trilingual.

One by one the key institutions of the group replaced German with English. The school was first. The advent of public schools in the 1830s sounded the death knell for German-language instruction for children, who previously had been educated in their ancestral tongue in parochial schools. Some German-language schools continued until after the Civil War, but gradually the American policy of English or nothing prevailed. The press, too, gradually shifted to English, although as late as the first decade of the 20th century several Pennsylvania newspapers such as the Lancaster *Volksfreund,* the Reading *Adler,* and the Kutztown *Journal,* were still published and edited in High German for the Pennsylvania Germans. The church was the last of the Pennsylvania German institutions to make the transition to English. In 1900 many congregations of the Lutheran and Reformed churches and of the "plain sects" continued to use German or alternated German with English. But in the 1930s the last rural Pennsylvania German churches shifted totally to English. Only the old order sectarian groups have continued to use German (or Pennsylvania High German) for worship and to a certain extent for official written communication.

The linguistic history of the Pennsylvania Germans was extremely complex, influenced as it was by Americanization (Anglicization), Germanization, and dialectization. Anglicization affected many early immigrants, particularly the upper class; before the revolution, for example, the Zimmermann family of Lancaster translated their name into Carpenter, and the Wistars of Philadelphia became Quaker and English through intermarriage. Later, the process took sharper form when community leaders attempted to root out the dialect and stifle ethnic consciousness. A Germanizing trend also took hold, so that for a time the state recorded wills in German as well as in English translation. The Lutheran pastor Justus Heinrich Christian Helmuth (1745–1820) of Philadelphia expressed the hope that Philadelphia would become a German-speaking city like Reading and Lancaster and York, and urged his fellow countrymen to teach German to their children. But as cultural ties with Germany weakened and children attended English-language public schools, in the late 19th century the German used in rural Pennsylvania became less standard, more influenced by dialect. A type of "sermon German" developed, which was preached from the pulpits into the 1930s.

In the 20th century, Pennsylvania Germans stressed the dialect as a cultural anchor. New cultural institutions after 1930 furthered its use. Among these were dialect radio and television programs, dialect theater, the dialect *Versammling,* the dialect *Grundsau Lodch* (groundhog lodge), and above all, the dialect church service. Dozens of Lutheran and United Church of Christ (formerly Reformed) congregations gave up High German, but at least once a year held a "Commemorative Service in the Language of the Fathers," that is, in dialect. In addition, dozens of dialect columnists, home-

grown Artemus Wards, appeared in upstate weekly newspapers. The earliest examples of this typically American genre of humorous writing date back to the War of 1812. The first books in Pennsylvania German appeared shortly after the Civil War. Grammars of the dialect extend from Marion Dexter Learned (1889) to Buffington-Barba (1954); the latter attempted to standardize dialect orthography by using German sound values, but the spelling of dialect is still by no means uniform.

Pennsylvania German culture is, then, essentially American. Southeastern Pennsylvania was subject to all the pressures and movements that molded Anglo-America. The historic Pennsylvania German culture contained obvious European elements, such as its south German culinary traditions; but these, like the dialect, were modified over time to yield a hybrid American form. Linguistically, ecclesiastically, and culturally the United States is different because of the presence of the Pennsylvania German element. Pennsylvania Germans today, whether in Pennsylvania, Ohio, or Ontario, may still speak the dialect, or English with a Dutch accent, or they may be completely Anglicized. What makes them different from other ethnic German enclaves in North America is their particular blend of European and American elements. (*See also* Amish; Germans; Hutterites.)

Bibliography

For general introductions see Albert B. Faust's basic work, *The German Element in the United States,* 2 vols. (1909; reprint, New York, 1969); Fredric Klees, *The Pennsylvania Dutch* (New York, 1951); and Oscar Kuhns, *The German and Swiss Settlements of Colonial Pennsylvania* (1900; reprint, New York, 1971). Phebe H. Gibbons, *"Pennsylvania Dutch" and Other Essays* (1882; reprint, New York, 1971) gives a 19th-century woman's viewpoint on many aspects of Pennsylvania German culture. Watercolor drawings by a major folk artist are found in *Lewis Miller, Sketches and Chronicles: The Reflections of a Nineteenth Century Pennsylvania German Folk Artist* (York, Pa., 1966).

Henry Glassie, *Pattern in the Material Folk Culture of the Eastern United States* (Philadelphia, 1968), and Earl F. Robacker, *Pennsylvania German Literature: Changing Trends from 1683 to 1942* (Philadelphia, 1943), document Pennsylvania German cultural and literary contributions. For the history and grammar of the Pennsylvania German dialect consult Albert F. Buffington and Preston A. Barba, *A Pennsylvania German Grammar,* rev. ed. (Allentown, Pa., 1965); and Marcus B. Lambert, *A Dictionary of the Non-English Words of the Pennsylvania German Dialect* (Lancaster, Pa., 1924).

References to specialized aspects of Pennsylvania German life and history can be found in Emil Meynen, *Bibliography on German Settlements in Colonial America, Especially on the Pennsylvania Germans and Their Descendants, 1683–1933* (Leipzig, Germany, 1937). Consult also the publications of the Pennsylvania German Society, the Pennsylvania German Folklore Society, and the Pennsylvania Folklife Society.

Principal collections of Pennsylvania German historical and ethnographic materials are found at the libraries of the Historical Society of Pennsylvania, Philadelphia; the German Society of Pennsylvania, Philadelphia; the Pennsylvania State Library, Harrisburg; the Moravian Archives, Bethlehem; the Schwenkfelder Library, Pennsburg; the seminary and college libraries of Pennsylvania German denominations; and the county historical societies of the area. Research materials on Pennsylvania German rural life can be found at the Pennsylvania Farm Museum at Landis Valley.

DON YODER

PENOBSCOTS: *see* AMERICAN INDIANS

PEORIAS: *see* AMERICAN INDIANS

PEQUOTS: *see* AMERICAN INDIANS

PERSIANS: *see* IRANIANS

PERUVIANS: *see* CENTRAL AND SOUTH AMERICANS

PILIPINOS: *see* FILIPINOS

PIMAS: *see* AMERICAN INDIANS

PIT RIVERS: *see* AMERICAN INDIANS

PLURALISM: A HUMANISTIC PERSPECTIVE

Humanists have not analyzed as closely as they should the concept of ethnicity. By and large, this task has been left to scholars in the fields of history, political science, and sociology. This essay, therefore, may appear to offer a novel view of the subject. Scholars, teachers, and writers in the fields of literature, philosophy, and theology do have resources to bring to bear upon the realities of ethnicity, not only as these have affected human life in the past, but primarily as these affect the present—and promise to affect the future—under the rubric of the "new ethnicity." These resources have not yet been fully differentiated and sharpened. Scholars in the humanities commonly work upon literary texts, public rituals and liturgies, manners, mores, and ethical practices. The empirical clarity available to social scientists is theirs only at secondhand. But what they can do—and what this essay undertakes—is to ferret out the ways by which the daily realities of ethnicity are felt and perceived in ordinary experience, and to establish the worldviews within which such experiences are daily understood.

A theory about the methods proper to the humanities may help to orient the reader. The humanities are concerned about the question, "Who?" They are concerned about the human person, the human subject, and thus about the experiencing, perceiving, imagining, understanding, judging and deciding of human persons. *Quidquid percipitur,* runs the Thomistic adage, *per modum percipientis percipitur: Whatever is perceived is perceived through the character of the one who perceives.* Who a person is (the range and quality of his or her experiences, imaginings, understandings, decidings, etc.) affects what a person perceives. The scientist is taught to operate in the mode of objectivity, discounting so much as is possible the factor of *whoness. Any* observer trained to the scientific mode should be able to replace the original observer, without loss of meaning. Subjectivity, so far as is possible, is eliminated. In the humanities, by contrast, students are trained to deepen and to enlarge their own subjectivity, to attempt to "cross over" and to enter into the subjectivity of others. They are taught that subjectivity is, in human affairs, important; that it is finally irreplaceable; and that it holds within it much that repays the effort to raise questions in order to understand more exactly. The work of scientists sometimes seems almost mystical to humanists, containing as it does measurements, lucid analytical models, mathematical invention of great brilliance, and refined and much-tested verbal clarity. Similarly, the work of humanists must seem, at times, almost mystical to scientists, with its indirect ways of eliciting almost unconscious senses of reality (myths), symbols, stories, viewpoints, sensibilities, images and imaginal structures. Necessarily, humanists must discuss ethnicity in a way unfamiliar to, and at least in

part unsatisfactory to, the scientist. Still, the work of the humanist is valuable to the scientist, if only to provoke further inquiry by turning up surprises, puzzles, anomalies, or perhaps even wholly new paradigms within which to raise further questions. For the scientist, too, and not only part time, is a human being, a *who*, trying to make sense of his own experience.

Thus, while the present essay may convey meanings not easily translatable into scientific propositions, perhaps it can succeed in expressing a plausible worldview within which to order some of our present-day experiences concerning the phenomena of ethnicity.

THE NEW ETHNICITY

Ethnicity is a baffling reality—morally ambivalent, paradoxical in experience, elusive in concept. World travelers observe that cultures differ from one another in mores and manners. Diplomats recognize that even the simplest gestures, words, or behaviors may signal multiple meanings. Nearly everyone recognizes that culture affects the subjectivity of individuals as well as their outward behavior. Culture shapes sensibility and perception, expectation and imagination, aspiration and moral striving, intellect and worldview. Yet it cannot be said that most highly educated persons are well prepared to account for the multicultural experiences available to them in the present age. Our theories about cultural differences and ethnic nuances are not as deep, broad, or subtle as our experience. Some philosophical distinctions may, therefore, be useful in charting this fascinating but treacherous terrain.

"Culture" is not an easy concept, since so many institutions, rituals, and practices contribute to its shaping. Its ramifications are sweeping, subtle, and often unarticulated. Its effects upon us often lie below the threshold of words or even of consciousness. The culture that has shaped us shapes our way of experiencing and perceiving, of imagining and speaking, so deeply that it is very difficult to think our way outside it. It teaches us what to regard as relevant and what to count as evidence; it provides our *canons* of relevance and evidence. We are not "products" of a culture in the way that objects are produced by a machine. Indeed, we must make conscious and voluntary efforts if we intend to appropriate our culture wholly, to go to its depths and to master its multiple possibilities. Cultures are freely elaborated by human beings; they lie, as the German philosophers were wont to say, in the realm of freedom, and the variety of human cultures on this planet is testimony to the capacities of human liberty over and above the necessities of nature. An individual passing over from his or her native culture into a culture quite different may experience "culture shock"; may, that is, come into a set of presuppositions, expectations, criteria for perception and evaluation and behavior so different as to undermine much that was previously taken for granted.

The concept of "ethnicity" has traditionally been seen as somewhat narrower than, although related to, the concept of culture. From earliest times, distinctive social groups found themselves living under the shaping influence of a common culture. In a sense, what made such social groups distinctive were the prior shaping influences of diverse cultures. Yet one could speak of a new overarching culture—Mesopotamian, Greek, Roman—within which the concept of ethnicity

pointed to less all-embracing cultural influences. It is useful to note that within a concept like "Western culture," for example, quite dramatic, pervasive, and persistent sources of cultural distinctiveness have remained vital. In philosophy, to choose but one example, there are quite different creative impulses, presuppositions, methods, standards and criteria manifested in different ethnic traditions: German, French, British, Italian, Spanish, American. In literature, theology, and in the arts it is possible simultaneously to discern characteristics that justify the notion both of a wider shared culture—Western culture—and of particular, original and vital sources of differentiation. Humanists have not so often used the word "ethnic" to describe these differences (until recently, the word has had a ring more proper to the social sciences). From early Latin times, the tendency has rather been to speak of *nationes* (as at the University of Paris in the 12th century), not in the modern political sense but rather in a pervasive cultural sense, signifying the existence of divergent cultural entities.

It is important, then, to recognize that any humanist wishing to work out a full theory of ethnicity may find many already cherished texts in which, under other names, a tradition of giving cultural differences their due weight has been observed. Among such texts would be Alexis de Tocqueville's *Democracy in America* (1835), Ralph Waldo Emerson's *English Traits* (1856), George Santayana's *The German Mind* (originally titled *Egotism in German Philosophy*, 1939), and many others. More recent writings include Luigi Barzini's *The Italians* (1964), Jacques Maritain's *Reflections on America* (1958), and Hedrick Smith's *The Russians* (1976).

A major watershed in our thinking about ethnicity seems to have been reached in the period after World War II. As a result of the growth of international communication and of a worldwide infrastructure of technology and commerce, human beings almost everywhere have become more aware of cultures not their own. It was long imagined that the creation of "one world" would bring with it many homogenizing tendencies, based on the imperatives of universal "reason" and science and on the standardization of technological artifacts (from Coca-Cola to Shell, from transistors to computers). It was also imagined that the managers and intellectuals who operated the new international systems would create a cadre of leaders, or even perhaps a new managerial class spread around the globe, who would be almost equally at home in the urban technical environments of London, Tokyo, New York, Berlin, Rio de Janeiro, and Calcutta. The same methods, the same problems, and (roughly) the same living conditions, it was imagined, would accompany them wherever they went. Indeed, such eventualities have come to pass, largely as expected, as a result of many homogenizing influences. Political ideals—"liberation," "equality," "national sovereignty"—have crossed virtually all the world's frontiers. So have rock music and movies, jeans and automobiles.

Simultaneously, however, the late 20th century has also been marked by a resurgence of ethnic consciousness. In the Soviet Union since about 1950 the Jewish community has become increasingly conscious of its special identity and increasingly public in its self-con-

sciousness—an attitude seen also among the ethnic Germans, Ukrainians, and other peoples of the U.S.S.R. In Great Britain, the Scots and the Welsh have demanded greater autonomy, as have the French Canadians in Canada. In Africa, Latin America, Asia and many other places throughout the world the self-consciousness of cultural bodies has been similarly heightened. There appear to be four components of this new self-consciousness, and in examining them, it is important to pause long enough to see clearly what is new in this "new ethnicity."

The new cultural self-consciousness is, first of all, post-tribal, arising in an era in which almost every culture has been obligated to become aware of many others. In contrast to the isolation of ancient times, each culture has met at least some of the others in actual experience, and many others via the media.

Secondly, the new ethnicity arises in an era of advanced technology. This technology paradoxically liberates certain energies for more intense self-consciousness, even as it binds many cultures together in standardized technical infrastructures. The communications media, for example, are neutral with respect to cultural differences. In the techniques required to operate them and in some of their internal imperatives (scientific knowledge, technical control, precision, order) they are clearly homogenizing in effect. On the other hand, the *content* of what the media express is necessarily received by audiences affected by cultural memory, cultural differences, and distinctive cultural aspirations. Communicators who had heretofore taken their own cultural identity for granted—because it was so much a part of their daily reality that they hardly needed to be aware of it—have become more sharply aware of their own distinctive tastes, needs, and hopes in using these media. They commonly find that they must become more analytical, articulate, and self-conscious about their own distinctive voice and viewpoint.

Thirdly, the new ethnicity arises in an era of intense centripetal and homogenizing forces. Great technical power has become centered in the apparatus of the state, in the central agencies of communication, and in the central distributors of technology. These new forces call into being countervailing forces, but are themselves so powerful that a wider range of diversity can be tolerated.

These new forces also generate rebellion against "mindless" and "soulless" modernism. This rebellion represents a fourth condition for the emergence of the new ethnicity—namely, a certain discrediting of the supposed moral superiority of the modern. For some generations now, high political and moral status has accrued to all things modern, enlightened, and up to date. The forces of habit, custom, and tradition have been on the defensive. Now that the fully modern type of man or woman is everywhere more visible among us, however, the secular, pragmatic style of the proponents of modernization has lost its halo and has begun to reveal serious moral flaws. In casting about for a posture that promises a higher degree of wisdom, nobility, and relevance to ordinary people, many leaders have begun to look again at the moral sources of their traditional cultures. For most, the choice is not simply dichotomous—either traditional or modern. Rather, the status of inherited wisdom has risen, while that of the modern

has slipped. In order to be evaluated, this inherited wisdom, now at last to be taken more seriously, has first to be more clearly known. Thus, the examination of "roots" has attracted both scholarly and popular attention. It is probable that a general law is here being observed: in times of moral perplexity and crisis, a reappropriation of the past, a search for renewal, gains impetus. In China there have been profound cultural cross-currents, in the United States the Bicentennial renewal, and in other cultures the drive toward cultural or national awakening; all these exhibit a strong moral dimension, fed by dissatisfaction with a merely modern morality.

In a word, peoples in every part of the world, to the surprise of those who anticipated the power only of homogenizing tendencies, are becoming both more aware of others and also more aware of their own distinctive cultural identity. A heightened cultural awareness, coupled with demands for its appropriate political expression, has made of the new ethnicity a major factor in world affairs—perhaps even one of the major sources of political energy in our era.

Revising the Liberal Tradition

In the past, tribal consciousness was with good reason considered to be a real or potential threat to liberal and rational institutions. While loyalty, fellow-feeling, and sympathy are values highly prized, they are, nevertheless, moral sentiments sometimes weakened by the propensity of human beings to limit their application to persons of their own kind. Human beings most easily grasp through shared experience, imagination, and tacit social bonding those ways of life most like their own. In his criticism of sentimental liberalism, *Moral Man and Immoral Society* (1932), Reinhold Niebuhr spelled out very clearly the limitations of such sentiments with respect to group behavior. Because of their enduring power, however, he also distrusted such counterimperatives of the modern spirit as "enlightenment" and "rationality." These were, he thought, too optimistically set in opposition to ties of kin, to "reasons of the blood," to inherited or ascribed status, and to related "nonrational" factors. The real world, he suggested, is more complex.

In his famous essay, "What is Enlightenment?" Immanuel Kant singled out two elements of great importance to the modern temper: *individuality* and *rationality*. Each individual, he argued, is an originating source of universal reason. Each individual stands equal to every other through participation in a unifying and universally distributed rationality. Kant locates reason, then, not in the group or social unit but in the individual. He holds that reason is universal in its fundamental character. In reason, persons find their individuality, their unity with all other individuals, and their dignity.

It is important in the present age to defend these basic principles of enlightenment set forth, in the language of his time, by Kant and others; the declarations of fundamental human rights embraced by the United Nations depend upon such conceptions. However, it is important, as well, to recognize that the emergence of a kind of worldwide interdependence built upon a scientific and technical base, which has been achieved since the Age of Enlightenment, has also taught us much about the diversifying impact of cultural, economic,

and political systems. Such systems affect the self-consciousness of individuals. They also affect the consciousness of whole social groups. No one would deny that there is a perfectly straightforward sense in which all human beings are members of the same human family; every human being is bound by imperatives of reasoning, justification, and communication across cultural and other boundaries; and each human being is entitled to claims of fundamental human dignity. Still, it is also widely grasped today that reason itself operates in pluralistic modes. It would be regarded as "cultural imperialism" to suggest that only one form of reasoning is valid in all matters. It would be regarded as naïve to believe that the content of human experiencing, imagining, understanding, judging, and deciding were everywhere the same. If anything, our age, perhaps, has learned too well the relativity of values and cultures, to the point of neglecting those things that unite all human beings as one.

It seems important for a liberal civilization today to thread its way philosophically between the Scylla of relativity and the Charybdis of too narrow a conception of universal reason. Bernard Lonergan in *Insight: A Study of Human Understanding* (1957) has suggested that it is of intellectual benefit to call attention to the difference between invariant human *operations* and the varying *content* upon which those operations work. In this way, he proposes to defend at one and the same time both the spiritual unity of the human race and that multiplicity of cultures that springs from human liberty.

Unlike other animals, the human being elaborates across space and time multiple forms of behaviors and practices. Cultural differentiation is a primary characteristic of human life, a direct expression of human liberty. As a source of originating agency, possessing a capacity to perceive, to intend, and to act in a self-directed manner, each individual human person stands in a certain sense alone. Yet in living in social units, in elaborating social institutions of great complexity, each individual human being is also a social creature. As a bodily organism, each is born, suffers, is hungry, loves, dies. Yet in various cultures these fundamental identities acquire distinctive symbolic meanings. On several levels of life, individual and social, intellectual and physical, certain invariant structures of experience cut across all cultures and unite all human beings in certain specific human perplexities. Daniel Bell has theorized in *The Cultural Contradictions of Capitalism* (1976) and in his Hobhouse Lecture at the London School of Economics (1977) that cultural systems are variant solutions to fundamental and common human perplexities such as birth, suffering, love, moral consciousness, and death.

In addition, according to Lonergan, certain invariant operations of human understanding also occur across cultures: every human being experiences, imagines, understands (both in flashes of insight and in conceptual expression), judges, decides. Moreover, these operations lead to one another, and depend upon one another, in certain invariant ways. Experiences raise questions for imagination. In the dark, one feels a presence and hears a sound; is it a mosquito, the effect of anxiety, or sheer restlessness? Examples posited in imagination raise questions for understanding. (What is it?) Hypotheses

conceptualized for understanding raise questions for judgment. (Is that so?) Judgments about what really is so raise questions for action. (What ought I to do?) In every culture, by every human being, such operations as these are performed daily. The manner in which they are performed, the imaginative, linguistic and conceptual equipment with which they are performed, and the content upon which they are performed vary widely. The importance attached to one or the other of these operations also varies in different cultures. The point is that we are not entirely helpless when we attempt to find our way through the disparate cultural materials we encounter in trying to understand our shared humanity. The great intellectual work of reconciling our unity to our diversity is underway. Thus, even if we have not as yet achieved adequate methods for transcultural communication and analysis; even if our present methods of trying to order the staggering cultural variety to be found upon this globe remain at a primitive level; even if international scholarship, except perhaps in elementary scientific and technical areas, remains upon deplorably parochial and ethnocentric bases—despite all this, the task of developing a truly international intellectual perspective is not in principle beyond us.

Thus, the enterprise of constructing, as it were, a new form of "universal reason" remains yet to be accomplished. It remains a valid aim for enlightened and liberal scholarship. To be sure, the discovery by each of the world's cultures of the almost immediate presence of the others has come upon the world rather suddenly, with the advent of instant communications and rapid travel since World War II. Admittedly, too, naïve and simple forms of rationality, and even the supposition that the liberal spirit itself is to be understood in one way only, have had to be modified under the pressure of the discovery of immense human variety. Still, individual human beings have been able to perform truly remarkable acts of understanding concerning cultures not their own. There is no reason to believe that the number of such explorers and interpreters will not grow.

If there was a temptation for the rationalist wing of the liberal movement (represented by Kant) to suppose a simpler and more immediate path to "universal reason" than has proved to be possible, that is no justification for refusing to embrace the possibilities of a more cosmopolitan form of the liberal spirit. If there was a temptation for the romantic wing of Western culture (Nietzsche may serve as an example) to exalt differences at the expense of the intellectual enterprise of human unity, that is no reason for conceding to despair. Different materials may be understood differently, in more than one way, by more than one method. Reasoning by way of analogy is possible. One may "cross over" from one mode of cultural experience into another, with remarkable gains in mutual understanding. It is not necessary to reduce one culture to the terms of another, invidiously or even imperialistically, in order to penetrate some, at least, of the secrets of its way of life. The way of understanding is never without trial and error. Where some explorers fail, others may do better. The enterprise of intellectual understanding and cultural sympathy stands upon firm ground and is not undercut by repeated failures.

It is a mistake, then, to hold that the new ethnic con-

sciousness is necessarily a counterrational or illiberal force. So long as the commitment to the intellectual enterprise of mutual understanding remains firm, the new cultural consciousness need not collapse into ethnic chauvinism. Insofar as the new ethnic consciousness may prove to be a post-tribal development, it would be tragic to permit it to be reduced to merely tribal intelligence. In those cases, indeed, where that reduction has taken place, the consequences are amply displayed for everyone's contempt. Indeed, the contempt we feel on such occasions is a sign that such reductionism, far from being necessary, evinces a radical human failure.

The new liberal spirit, I propose, should rest upon two pillars: a firm commitment to the laborious but rewarding enterprise of full, mutual, intellectual understanding; and a respect for differences of nuance and subtlety, particularly in the area of those diversifying "lived values" that have lain until now, in all cultures, so largely unarticulated. In this sense, the true liberal spirit is *cosmopolitan* rather than *universalist*. The connotations of those two words suggest the difference between a liberalism that expects, and desires, a certain homogenization and a liberalism that expects, and delights in, variety. Cosmopolitan liberalism is surely closer to the heart of the authentic liberal spirit. Just as Kant was eager to defend the uniqueness of individuals (despite his tendency to imagine universal and general laws), so cosmopolitan liberalism is eager to respect the individuality of cultures.

THE PLURALISTIC PERSONALITY

Culture is not only external to the individual. The individual interiorizes, appropriates, and carries culture. A culture has vitality only if it lives in the skills, disciplines, morals, and manners of individuals, only if it is carried even in the motions of the individual heart. Individuals continually re-create, modify, and enrich cultures.

In a pluralistic nation like the United States, cultural diversity plays a unique psychological role. Indeed, it appears to be bringing about the development of a unique psychological type: the pluralistic personality. Although many scores of different groups may be distinguished among the American people (the number varies with the criteria employed) this nation may not be the most linguistically and culturally diverse of nations. It is possible that the peoples of the U.S.S.R., India, China, Brazil, Canada, and other nations are at least as pluralistic as are our own. Yet, from a very early period, American society was established upon three significant principles which have led to a unique experiment in pluralistic living. These three principles have provided an important measure of a civilized reconciliation of unity and diversity, for the inspection of other nations and for any future world civilization.

First, in the United States, ethnicity has not been permitted to become an instrument of territorial sovereignty, or of political exclusion in any jurisdiction. It is not permitted to become the exclusive instrument of political organization. Political rights inhere in individuals, not in ethnic groups.

Second, individuals are free to make as much, or as little, of their ethnic belonging as they choose. No one is to be coerced into a system of ethnic identification he does not choose for himself.

Third, individuals organized together in voluntary associations are encouraged to nourish such sentiments, memories, aspirations, and practices of group life as they choose. In such matters, the state is not only neutral but positively encouraging, through favorable tax laws and other legal principles. The social dimensions of individual life are thereby recognized.

It is considered something of a sin against "the American way" for persons to be made to feel that they *must* be identified by social characteristics; for the law so to distinguish them; or for individual social groups to coerce their members into such identification. Many rituals and practices have been established, from public ceremonies of representation to such political practices as the "balanced ticket," whose purpose is symbolically to include every group of Americans within the public presence of "the American people," and to strengthen in each breast the sentiment, "We are all Americans now." In this sense, the "melting pot" has been a powerful myth and an effective practice in American life. The concept of the American people is designed to include all equally, without discrimination. On the other hand, the oath of citizenship does not require any individual to renounce his or her former cultural belonging or cultural history. In order to become a U.S. citizen, one does not have to cease living from and being nourished by the cultural traditions of one's native inheritance. In this sense, "the melting pot" does not entail the melting away of cultural differences among the American people.

The result of this special experiment in pluralism is that many Americans develop what might be called a "pluralistic personality." Each individual is, by right and by opportunity, responsible for choosing his or her own identity from among the many materials presented by the contingencies of human life. In a society like ours, an individual participates in the cultural life of more than one social group. We are each differentiated by such characteristics as age, sex, religion, biological and cultural inheritance, marriage, education, occupation, region, locality, personal exploration, and voluntary association. In at least such senses, everybody (or virtually everybody) participates in more than one social group and carries multiple associational identities. One person may be, for example, a New Yorker by birth, a professional humanist, a liberal in politics, Jewish, of parents who emigrated from eastern Europe, and by choice chiefly interested in associations and projects that establish his identity as future-oriented and assimilationist. Of some of these forms of "belonging," the individual in question may choose to make little or nothing, to pursue, as it were, a form of forgetfulness; while on others the individual may choose to focus his energy fully. Another individual of similar background might make a quite different choice.

Notwithstanding an individual's conscious choices, however, each person is also influenced by social factors over which he or she has had no control. We do not choose our grandparents, nor the basic lines of our early nurture. We do not choose (entirely) how others will regard us or what, even despite our best intentions, they may ascribe to us. Moreover, even the patterns of our conscious choices—our careers, successes, living pat-

terns, educational choices, political behaviors, and incomes—may be studied by those who quantify our age, sex, religion, ethnicity, or other group-shared characteristics. Even if we do not choose to be "ethnic," in other words, even if we consciously renounce or disregard our cultural inheritance, it can hardly surprise us that sociologists or other students of social life will notice, at least in a generalized way, materials of ethnic specificity in our outward behavior. Finally, our own conscious choices with respect to our own cultural belonging may change over time, both in extension and in intensity. Personal experiences, or changes in the world around us (the precariousness of the state of Israel, for example, or turmoil in Ireland) may conspire to alter in us our own sense of identity.

"Ethnic belonging," then, is a phenomenon of human consciousness and is subject to multiple influences and multiple transformations, in ourselves and in the eyes of others. Its importance for any individual or group may change over time. Ethnicity is not a simple phenomenon; it is not easy to define in terms that apply in precisely the same way to everyone.

In a pluralistic society like that of the United States, moreover, many persons have the opportunity to become involved in many cultural traditions not originally their own, and to appropriate music, ideas, values, and even a set of intellectual landmarks not native to their own upbringing. We find that each of us can live from many diverse spiritual sources. In this respect, too, ecumenical and multicultural activities nourish in us a pluralistic personality—a personality rooted in multiple sources of spiritual power.

In the American system, then, the ideal of ethnic belonging has a special quality. It includes not only a willingness to cooperate democratically with those nourished by other traditions, but also an openness toward learning from others. It includes a willingness to appropriate from other traditions admirable traits and purposes, and fruitful sources of insight and sensibility. The notion of a wholly closed form of ethnic belonging —entirely inward-turning and wholly resistant to others—has come to seem seriously flawed. Even those within various traditions who propose the strengthening and deepening of their own cultural traditions normally find themselves working closely with others outside their own cultural group. They feel quite honored to be cited for their services to other communities or to the nation as a whole. Thus, American life provides many inhibitions against "tribalism," both within individual groups and within the culture as a whole. Indeed, the normal worry is that homogenizing and simply ecumenical influences are, if anything, out of balance, and threaten to overwhelm the influences of differentiation and cultural continuity.

As a result, individuals in our society tend to develop a plurality of cultural roots. Those of us who are not by ancestry Anglo-American learn to assimilate the values, attitudes, and practices of—as it seems to us— one of the most liberating of the world's traditions. We gladly learn its political history, its language, and its literature. From Jewish traditions, we learn both a psychiatric and sociological sophistication, a way of looking beneath the surface of the self and of society, and a sense of the long reality of Western history as it was experienced by Jews. From black culture, Indian culture,

from the multiple Catholic cultures, from the cultures of Asia and of Latin America we appropriate other cherished values.

In the sense that all citizens share major national experiences—prosperity and depression, war and peace, great moral leadership, sad official lapses, and the assassinations of beloved figures—all of us participate in a "common culture." This common culture is built up, as well, by the tacit and powerful influences of a common language and the experience of common legal, economic, and political traditions. Yet the many cultures so united are vast, rich, and various, so that individuals do not assimilate all of them equally. In this sense, each individual lives, as well, from the particular cultures in which he or she was born and reared, and from which it has been his or her good fortune or free choice to learn. Thus, we each forge our own individual cultural identity, drawing (almost always) upon more than one tradition. In this sense, too, we each develop "a pluralistic personality," and are individually able to understand implicitly and to dwell with tacit ease in more than one cultural tradition.

A complicating factor in the attempt to sort out the many strands of actual American life as it is experienced from many standpoints—by a Filipino in Hawaii, a Polish American in Los Angeles, a Chicano in Chicago, a Georgia Baptist at Yale, a North Carolina black in New York—is the relative silence of the public media and of public discourse generally about these multiple differences. It is, perhaps, impossible to have a public language, especially for expression through media whose scope is national, which is simultaneously understandable by all and fully expressive of the nation's variety. Public communications are necessarily pitched to a kind of lowest common denominator. They reflect no specific subculture fully. In this sense, a public sort of "superculture" is imposed upon the top of the many subcultures of the land. Nearly everybody learns this national argot, which is in large measure commercial in its purposes and its utility.

"Superculture" is not precisely the same concept as "mass culture." For those forms of communication that are aimed at the national "high culture," the shared culture of national elites, are also conducted within it. The reporter or the commentator who speaks through the national media of communication is expected to exhibit a form of sophistication that is higher than that of "mass culture." In this sense, "superculture" is guarded by its own elite. But both superculture and mass culture aim at a level that is above the nation's pluralism. In order to develop a theory about the relations between the shared common culture of the American people and the particular cultural streams from which individuals draw their nourishment, it is necessary to notice how superculture and mass culture overlay, rather than grow out of, the many particular cultures that constitute our people. These overlays are probably indispensable to our system of national communication. They generate a form of ersatz culture, a sort of false consciousness, insofar as they arise from no particular culture but are constructed for broad communication.

A sign of this artificiality becomes apparent when one notices how many television shows—but also weighty generalizations about our national life and national character—actually represent no one neighbor-

hood, no single culture or region, but appear rather to represent a fictional "nowhere," a construct designed on some superficial level to represent almost everyone. It is virtually impossible to refer accurately and profoundly to everyone at once, and so this flaw in our national self-understanding is no doubt inevitable. But it does require continuous intellectual correction. When one hears sentences about "middle Americans," or "typical American values," it is usually instructive to try to visualize the actual and complex variety that such sentences attempt to cover. Such reflection often brings to one's attention materials of considerable political and moral significance. Our variety confounds our need for easy generalizations.

In self-defense, then, those who try to retain their grip on reality develop techniques of translation. We each, privately and implicitly, learn to read between the lines of public speech and to focus upon concrete realities dear to us. In this way, we often mentally cross over from one cultural horizon to another. Some, for example, inspect public generalizations for their accuracy concerning blacks, or women, or specific ethnic groups. This capacity for accepting the common idiom, while mentally translating it into one's own horizon, illustrates the pluralistic personality at work.

The pluralistic personality has, then, a quite unique historical range and liberty. Such a personality, for all its broad experience and liberty of action, is not "rootless." Under the conditions of the old ethnicity, the consciousness of many may have been essentially parochial and isolated. Under the conditions of the new ethnicity, a capacity to enter into multiple perspectives, and to see the same matter from more than one point of view seems to represent a clear gain for the human spirit. Without depending upon a kind of universal homogenization, it represents an admirable development in the liberal spirit, and a new type of social personality in human history. It is produced almost effortlessly by the sort of institutional life our pluralistic society has developed. Naturally, some individuals represent the pluralistic personality in fuller development, others in lesser. Every human being suffers from some degree of limited sympathy and limited perception. No one can claim to have a godlike capacity to understand everything about everything. The pluralistic personality discovers that learning comes by way of a certain humility, a certain hesitance to judge others too quickly, a certain generous watchfulness for possible errors in his own perceptions.

ETHNICITY AND THE SOUL

Such humility is necessary because the ways by which ethnic heritage affects an individual's inner life are subtle and complex, and mistakes of interpretation are easy. In the United States persons of Anglo-American stock have found their own heritage reinforced by the common use of English, continued close ties to the culture of Great Britain, the study of English literature, and the continuity of many institutional forms in politics and law. Those who stand directly in the line of these major cultural institutions may not be especially aware of their own cultural tradition; it forms so immediate a part of their daily reality that it may seem to them like second nature. Those Americans whose native traditions are not Anglo-American have had, by contrast, to adapt to new institutional and cultural

forms, to learn not only a new language but also a new repertoire of gestures, mores, and manners. More deeply than that, many have had to learn new ways of thinking, feeling, and imagining. Great energy was expended in the process of assimilating this rich and liberating culture. In response, America itself changed under the impact of mass immigration. The common culture was altered by being assimilated in fresh ways. Even descendants of British Americans have had to adapt to a new common culture not identical to their own. Our common culture, then, belongs to no one ethnic group, although much of it has an Anglo-American origin, and it simultaneously allows diversity to thrive, less so in national public speech but more so in living communities of thought and feeling.

Measures of external behavior then—in education, politics, occupation, income, and other areas—continue to reflect differences among individuals that are related to their cultures of origin. The social scientists note these differences well enough, but the most neglected and unexplored dimension of ethnicity lies in the fields of the humanities: how ethnicity affects the individual spirit, in its tastes, memories, aspirations, and systems of value and meaning.

There are some major intellectual difficulties blocking the way to the humanistic analysis of such materials. It is useful to mention these first. The humanistic tradition wishes, first of all, to defend the individual. Hence, one cluster of difficulties surrounds the dangers of stereotyping. Each culture, in its institutions, its religions, and its literature, celebrates a distinctive constellation of human values and upholds a distinctive set of cultural heroes, saints, and everyday models. The ideals of the French intellectual, for example, are not identical to those of the British. The folk heroes of various cultures differ; children's stories celebrate diverse values or styles. Reasons of climate or political history may have brought about the celebration of differentiated human qualities necessary for a group's survival or historical advance. The role of great originating geniuses early in the history of a culture—King Arthur, say—may have attracted the love and imitation of millions through the ages. Music, folk arts, drama, dance, games, the liturgies of church and the state, the sermonic or rhetorical forms of public discourse, and other elements of this sort may continuously have promoted certain forms of behavior and discouraged others. The arts of storytelling may have inculcated narrative expectations that celebrated cleverness, bold action, humility, creative arrogance, wit, endurance, obedience, fidelity, and so on. Finally, the economic or social order of a culture may have inculcated modes of realism—enterprise and openness, say, as opposed to a passion for security—different from those inculcated in a different economic or social system. In all these ways, culture differs from culture. In a kind of shorthand, world travelers or students of comparative culture develop brief, often anecdotal descriptions that attempt to capture the distinctive aspects of each culture. One speaks—to reduce the shorthand to adjectival dimensions—of the "phlegmatic" English, the "orderly" Germans, the "romantic" Latins, the "hotblooded" Spaniards, the "stubborn" Poles, the "melancholy" Danes, and the like. The danger of stereotyping is great.

In this respect, there is a critical difference between generalizations employed about the distinctive charac-

teristics of cultures and scientific descriptions. Scientific descriptions formulate laws based on individual behaviors. Cultures do not exercise so total a control over individuals; hence, cultural effects cannot be reduced to such descriptions. Cultures do establish distinctive ideals and perhaps even distinctive catalogues of especially abhorred sins. These then exert a kind of attraction and repulsion upon individuals born within a culture. Those who reveal in their own behavior a kind of fulfillment of the highest ideals of the culture are normally singled our for special praise and rewards, and those who do not measure up are, accordingly, less rewarded.

Generalizations about cultural characteristics must, further, observe four other conditions. First, in most complex cultures more than one set of cultural ideals is available; second, cultures are normally open to change, so that new types of cultural heroes regularly emerge; third, the function of cultural ideals is not to describe all members of a society but rather to single out, to promote, and to reward certain forms of behavior; fourth, each individual appropriates the ideals of a culture in a free and distinctive way, sometimes by rebelling against them, resisting them, muting them, or playing counterpoint against them. Without denying the force of distinctive cultural ideals upon the whole everyday life of cultures, it is important to see the wide range of liberty still exercised by individuals within them. It is a mistake to apply to individuals the generalizations that attempt to define the working ideals of a culture; this mistake is properly called stereotyping.

Nonetheless, the power of the distinctive ideals of a culture, together with the mores and manners that support them, makes entrance into a new culture difficult for refugees, emigrants, or others who move from one culture to another. The prospect of exile may hold an understandable dread for fully formed adults; they may doubt their capacity to adapt, and they may fear psychological isolation when the outer conditions of their new world will no longer supply the daily signals that they internalized as children within a different culture. On the other hand, migrants sometimes experience a release in the new culture, which rewards in them qualities of mind, heart, or action that may have been repressed in their culture of origin. Thus does the impact of a culture upon an individual affect the entire soul: every instinct, emotional response, imagination, perception, sensibility, habit of mind. "Assimilation" is often spoken of too lightly.

Generalizations about a culture are dangerous in another way. Many of the ideals or tendencies within a culture are all the more powerful for being tacit. They are most often expressed in practice not as maxims to be memorized, or as codes clearly written out. They emerge, rather, from the tacit distribution of inhibitions and rewards built into institutions, practices, and mores. To put such inhibitions into sentences is often to falsify them. Thus, for example, one may say that Americans are taught to be acquisitive. Putting matters this way, one seems to be indicting Americans for conscious and articulated motives, which many might deny holding, whereas the generalization might merely have been pointing to the unparalleled abundance of unused and unneeded things which many Americans seem to accumulate around them. Yet Jacques Maritain noted in *Reflections on America* that the imputed "ma-

terialism" of the American character, an accusation made not only by foreigners but by many Americans as well, actually represents in practice a most remarkable indifference to material things, which because so abundant are held cheap in the calculus of human purposes. In the same way, generalizations about other cultures must be examined with great care.

To put the matter in another way, such generalizations frequently make conscious materials that were in practice unconscious. When such generalizations are carefully formed, they may by that very fact seem to go beyond the materials they point to. The well-established but tacit practices they describe no longer seem to be the same when codified in propositions, for such practices do not function as conscious moral rules, ideals, or approved courses of action. Many aspects of manners, mores, and even morals, once examined and raised before consciousness in propositional form, may come into conflict with other values in the culture. Cultures are such complicated systems of multiple imperatives that they contain many internal conflicts, which are normally resolved only over long stretches of time.

Finally, it must be noted that many aspects of cultural life, just because they have been internalized in tacit and unconscious ways, are difficult to discern in one's own life. It is hard to step outside one's own culture, so as to see it whole. Even when made conscious, aspects of culture such as the distinctively American attitude toward law, for example, are often difficult to articulate in words. It is one of the functions of literature to hold up a mirror to culture in which such secrets of the inner life may be reflected, not by abstraction, but in the full concrete texture of the represented situation. Literature succeeds as an instrument of understanding, where scientific description may fail, by rendering the lived forms of life in anecdotal segments so that tacit understandings and practices may be rendered for inspection through a method different from that of abstraction.

In American life, correspondingly, both literary materials and methods of "participant observation," as employed in sociology, anthropology, and journalism, are among our best sources for understanding the impact of ethnicity upon our inner lives. Irving Howe's remarkable study *World of Our Fathers* (1976), Michael Arlen's *Passage to Ararat* (1975), Richard Gambino's *Blood of My Blood* (1974), Alex Haley's *Roots* (1976), John Gregory Dunne's *True Confessions* (1977), and many other books reveal the quite different instincts, attitudes, aspirations, and perceptions that actually motivate diverse individuals in our midst.

Ethnic identity persists among individuals, it appears, by being passed on in unconscious, tacit ways in their early nurture. The laws of such transmission are not well understood. It appears that in some families the mother and in others the father—perhaps sometimes in different respects—pass on some of the values and expectations that he or she internalized from the long line of human tradition. More study of such matters would no doubt be rewarding, for it is certain that individuals do not spring like Venus from the sea, but are social beings. The attractions and inhibitions acquired by the workings of cultures upon history are passed on through individuals. No one of us represents all the cultures of humanity, yet each of us carries so-

cial meanings and values not invented by ourselves. The reason for studying such sociality in our individual makeup is not to promote "ethnic pride," for not all that we carry forward is wholly admirable. The primary reason is to obtain self-knowledge.

Normally, our experience with central elements of culture—with a concept of God, for example—is highly colored by the culture passed on to us by our parents. Scholars do not take for granted that the images of God, and the complex of attitudes deemed appropriate for approaching God, are exactly the same in every culture, even of those which are generically Christian. Rather, in different cultures, systems of worship and liturgy, of preaching and of practice, subtly build up quite distinctive languages of the soul. In some cultures, religion is more closely identified with morality, in such a way that God is imagined rather like a great seeing eye of conscience (the "objective observer" of some Anglo-American philosophical theories, for example). In other cultures, particularly in southern and eastern Europe, religion is more closely identified with nature, in such a way that God is imagined rather as the source of unity in all things. In the former, a person who is religious but not moral may be regarded as "not really religious." In the latter, there is a distance between being religious and being moral, such that even a person who is quite moral may not be perceived as religious, and even a person of less than admirable moral practice may yet be perceived as quite religious. In some cultures history, and in other cultures nature, provides the psychological dynamism of religion. In some the individual, and in others the family or the local community, is the basic unit from which moral values are derived. Similarly, in tacit conceptions of authority and dissent, of masculinity and femininity, of social loyalty and individually defined moral principle, culture differs from culture.

The "voice" and "temperature" of cultures in the home appear also to be communicated from generation to generation to the psyches of children. The constellations within which the various passions and modes of intelligence are distributed appear to vary from culture to culture. Expression of an emotion like anger may be inhibited in some cultures, and regarded as a failure in self-control; in others, anger may be a quite familiar and uninhibited passion. Orderliness may be given high value in some cultures, and low value in others.

How often children are held in the arms, by whom, and in which emotional patterns may establish the rhythm of their own future emotional expectations. How many voices surround them and with what qualities of passion, what is encouraged in their behavior and what is inhibited, the repertoire of facial expression and gesture and information that they absorb—all these are communicated, most often, without theory and apart from conscious decision. So it goes also for the rudiments of religious, political, sexual, and other attitudes. Expectations are established, tonalities become familiar, schemes of approval and disapproval are internalized, emotions are given shape, perceptions are tutored, evil and good are identified.

The history of these transmissions from generation to generation does reflect some change and alteration within cultures, but not much. Almost always, usually through signals below the threshold of consciousness,

generation leaps across generation in cultural continuity. Even in rebellion, the sons pass on more of their fathers than they know, the daughters of their mothers. Sometimes, in generation-skipping sequences, the life of the grandfather seems to be recapitulated more in that of the grandson than of the son. Because of a long emphasis on the rational and the individual, scholars have done too little work on the patterns of transmitting culture through the generations and on the general theme of cultural continuity.

There are certain central symbolic clusters in personal life in which cultural traditions tend to be concentrated. Even in persons not aware of their own cultural indebtedness, one often finds in the patterns of their tastes, orientations, values, and repugnances clear signals from the past. Imagination and sensibility are especially affected by family culture, but so also is the pattern of perception, the way intelligence works, and desire, and aspiration. One cannot understand the dramatic success of individuals who are Jewish, both in the schools and in the world of enterprise, without understanding as well the specific strengths of the culture that nourished them both in eastern Europe and in the United States. This is particularly striking when one compares the trajectory of the individual lives of eastern European Jewish immigrants with that of those whose ancestors also came from eastern Europe, at about the same time, but who were not Jewish; or with that of other cultural groups.

Among the nodal points for cross-cultural comparison, one could single out at least eight that could illuminate a wide spectrum of other attitudes and behavior: attitudes toward the divine, the sacred, or the holy; attitudes toward nature, history, and moral striving; attitudes toward intelligence, learning, and ideas; attitudes toward the rein to be given passion and emotion, and in which respects; attitudes toward authority, the past, tradition; attitudes toward the individuality or the communality of human living, toward solitude and solidarity, self and family; attitudes toward masculinity and fathering, toward feminity and mothering; attitudes toward the power of goodness and the power of evil in human affairs. Cultures, like individuals, differ remarkably from one another in such matters. One might turn to rites of passage, to sports, to ceremonies of birth and marriage and death, and to other locations in each culture for clues as to how the above-mentioned attitudes are passed on to new generations. There are many methods for studying such attitudes. In many families, attention has for some generations now been drawn to what is "new" and "American" in the experience of individuals, rather than to what is continuous with cultures of the past. That imbalance might now be corrected.

If each of us takes a moment to reflect upon our own deepest associations with such symbols as those mentioned above, we cannot help encountering our radical and fundamental debt to the generations that have preceded us. To be sure, we are free to turn in new directions, to erase or at least to cover over the tracings of the past. We are not imprisoned by our social and cultural inheritance, but we have, in fact, felt its imprint and have been given at least nascent definition by it. Until recently, Americans have not often made explicit connection to their cultural heritage or heritages. To

have done so would have been to fly in the face of the strong emphasis in American life upon the principle that we are all individuals, responsible for re-creating ourselves anew. This principle conveys a great and important truth: each of us is responsible for creating his or her own identity. But a companion principle also conveys an important truth: each of us is a social creature, in part shaped by the others of whom we are a part; our destiny is familial as well as individual.

Discussions about values and meaning often go astray in America because the concrete contexts that give flesh and blood to our individual experience of life are left out of account. The eight symbolic clusters mentioned above focus the attention of specific cultures in diverse ways, lead each to interpret the same data within a different horizon of meaning and value, and inculcate in each different sources of attraction and repulsion. Different traditions instruct individuals differently in what power they possess to change things. In some, the tragic sense is strong, or cultural pessimism, or patience; in others, idealism and hope are very bright. The differences among us as individuals are often accounted for by phrases such as "to each his own," as though our ethical visions and choices came strictly through individual choice. Actually, it appears, there is in each individual a considerably larger range of cultural principles at work than we seem to notice. Patterns emerge. Traditions come into focus. We are not so independent or so idiosyncratic as we have been led to imagine. There is a general descriptive geography to our moral visions and choices. A kind of general "field theory" of moral symbols powerful among Americans might be developed. Anglo-American, Jewish, black, Italian, and other ethnic cultures have established significant magnetic lodes in this field, which exert contrasting forces upon large numbers of individuals.

The full cultural history of American religion has yet to be written. Accurate and detailed attention to its component historical cultures is still in its infancy. The multicultural materials of American literary history have yet to be fully explored. Particularly interesting are the ways in which a writer in one cultural tradition —a Jewish novelist, say—perceives in his work the secret springs of those who are of a different tradition. In these matters, the way people perceive each other is a valid and important subject of study.

The many divergent ways in which central cultural symbols actually function in the daily lives of Americans have not yet been mapped. The ways in which ethnicity has affected, and still does affect, the inner lives of Americans have not yet been fully explored. One hopes that in religion, philosophy, and literature, as well as in psychology and the social sciences, the materials for such a study will be assembled, and that by the time another generation passes the state of our knowlege will be considerably more concrete and exact than it is at present.

MICHAEL NOVAK

PLURALISM: A POLITICAL PERSPECTIVE

DEMOCRACY AND NATIONALISM

Most political theorists, from the time of the Greeks onward, have assumed the national or ethnic homogeneity of the communities about which they wrote. Prior to the work of Rousseau, theory was never explicitly nationalist, but the assumption of a common language, history, or religion underlay most of what was said about political practices and institutions. Hence, the only empire systematically defended in the great tradition of political theory was the Christian empire of the Middle Ages: one religious communion, it was argued, made one political community. The religiously mixed empires of ancient and modern times, by contrast, had no theoretical defenders, only publicists and apologists. Political thinking has been dominated by the Greece of Pericles, not of Alexander; by republican Rome, not the Roman empire; by Venice and Holland, not the Europe of the Hapsburgs. Even liberal writers, ready enough to acknowledge a plurality of interests, were strikingly unready for a plurality of cultures. One people made one state. The argument of the authors of *The Federalist Papers* (1787–1788) may be taken here to sum up a long tradition of thought. The Americans, John Jay wrote, were a people "descended from the same ancestors, speaking the same language, professing the same religion, attached to the same principles of government, very similar in their manners and customs." Surely a "band of brethren" so united "should never be split into a number of unsocial, jealous, and alien sovereignties."

Jay's description was only very roughly true of America in 1787, and clearly the maxim *One people, one state* has, throughout human history, been honored most often in the breach. Most often, brethren have been divided among alien sovereignties and forced to coexist with strangers under an alien sovereign. National and ethnic pluralism has been the rule, not the exception. The theoretical preference for cultural unity existed for centuries alongside dynastic and imperial institutions that made for disunity. Only in the late 18th and 19th centuries was the old assumption of homogeneity, reinforced by new democratic commitments, transformed into a practical demand for separation and independence. Underlying that demand were two powerful ideas: first, that free government was only possible under conditions of cultural unity; second, that free individuals would choose if they could to live with their own kind, that is, to join political sovereignty to national or ethnic community. No doubt these ideas could be challenged. Marx and his followers emphatically denied that they were true, arguing that conceptions of "kind" were ultimately based on class rather than ethnic distinctions. But the two ideas had the support of a long intellectual tradition, and they happily supported one another. They suggested that democracy and self-determination led to the same political arrangements that their effective exercise required: the replacement of empires by national states.

In practice, this replacement took two very different forms. The new nationalist politics was first of all expressed in the demand for the unification of peoples divided—as were the Germans, Italians, and Slavs— among the old empires and a variety of petty principalities. Nationalist leaders aimed initially at large states and at a broad (pan-German or pan-Slavic) definition of cultural homogeneity. Yugoslavia and Czechoslovakia are products of this first nationalism which, though it entailed the breakup of empires, was still a politics of composition, not of division. The Zionist "ingathering"

of Jews from Europe and the Orient has the same character. Roughly similar groups were to be welded together, on the model of the prenationalist unifications of France and Britain.

This early nation-building was hardly a failure, but the clear tendency of nationalism more recently has been to challenge not only the old empires, especially the colonial empires, but also the composite nation-states. Neither the oldest states (France, Britain) nor the newest (Pakistan, Nigeria) have been safe from such challenges. Secession rather than unification is the current theme. International society today is marked by the proliferation of states, so that "the majority of the members of the U.N.," as Eric Hobsbawm has written, "is soon likely to consist of the late-twentieth-century (republican) equivalents of Saxe-Coburg-Gotha and Schwarzburg-Sonderhausen." Important transformations of the world economy have opened the way for this process: the rules of viability have radically changed since the 19th century. But the process also represents an extraordinary triumph for the principle of self-determination—with the collective self increasingly defined in ways that reflect the actual diversity of mankind.

Confronted with this diversity, every putative nation-state is revealed as an ancient or modern composition. Self-determination looks to be a principle of endless applicability, and the appearance of new states a process of indefinite duration. If the process is to be cut short, it is unlikely to be by denying the principle—for it appears today politically undeniable—but rather by administering it in moderate doses. Thus autonomy may be an alternative to independence, loosening the bonds of the composite state, a way to avoid their fracture. Instead of sovereignty, national and ethnic groups may opt for decentralization, devolution, and federalism; these are not incompatible with self-determination, and they may be especially appropriate for groups of people who share some but not all of the characteristics of a distinct historical community and who retain a strong territorial base. Whether composite states can survive as federations is by no means certain, but it is unlikely that they can survive in any other way—not, at least, if they remain committed (even if only formally) to democratic government or to some sort of social egalitarianism.

Democracy and equality have proven to be the great solvents. In the old empires, the elites of conquered nations tended to assimilate to the dominant culture. They sent their children to be educated by their conquerors; they learned an alien language; they came to see their own culture as parochial and inferior. But ordinary men and women did not assimilate, and when they were mobilized, first for economic and then for political activity, they turned out to have deep national and ethnic loyalties. Mobilization made for conflict, not only with the dominant groups, but also with other submerged peoples. For centuries, perhaps, different nations had lived in peace, side by side, under imperial rule. Now that they had to rule themselves, they found that they could do so (peacefully) only among themselves, adjusting political lines to cultural boundaries.

So the assumptions of the theoretical tradition have proven true. Self-government has tended to produce relatively homogeneous communities and has been fully successful only within such communities. The great exception to this rule is the United States. At the same time, the Marxist argument, the most significant challenge to traditional wisdom, has proven wrong. Nowhere have class loyalties overridden the commitment to national and ethnic groups. Today, the Soviet Union resembles nothing so much as the empire of the Romanovs: a multinational state held together chiefly by force. Conceivably, if the "national question" were ever solved, if the existence and continued development of historical communities were guaranteed (as Lenin argued they should be), new patterns of alliance and cooperation might emerge. But for the moment, it must be said that politics follows nationality, wherever politics is free. Pluralism in the strong sense—*One state, many peoples*—is possible only under tyrannical regimes.

AMERICAN EXCEPTIONALISM

Except in the United States. Here too, of course, there are conquered and incorporated peoples—Indian tribes, Mexicans—who stood in the path of American expansion, and there are forcibly transported peoples—the blacks—brought to this country as slaves and subjected to a harsh and continuous repression. But the pluralist system within which these groups have only recently begun to organize and act is not primarily the product of their experience. Today, the United States can only be understood as a multiracial society. But the minority races were politically impotent and socially invisible during much of the time when American pluralism was taking shape—and the shape it took was not determined by their presence or by their repression.

In contrast to the Old World, where pluralism had its origins in conquest and dynastic alliance, pluralism in the New World originated in individual and familial migration. The largest part of the U.S. population was formed by the addition of individuals, one by one, filtered through the great port cities. Though the boundaries of the new country, like those of every other country, were determined by war and diplomacy, it was immigration that determined the character of its inhabitants—and falsified John Jay's account of their unity. The United States was not an empire; its pluralism was that of an immigrant society, and that means that nationality and ethnicity never acquired a stable territorial base. Different peoples gathered in different parts of the country, but they did so by individual choice, clustering for company, with no special tie to the land on which they lived. The Old World call for self-determination had no resonance here: the immigrants (except for the black slaves) had come voluntarily and did not have to be forced to stay (indeed, many of them returned home each year), nor did groups of immigrants have any basis for or any reason for secession. The only significant secessionist movement in U.S. history, though it involved a region with a distinctive culture, did not draw upon nationalist passions of the sort that have figured in European wars.

But if the immigrants became Americans one by one as they arrived and settled, they did so only in a political sense: they became U.S. citizens. In other respects, culturally, religiously, even for a time linguistically, they remained Germans and Swedes, Poles, Jews, and Italians. With regard to the first immigrants, the Anglo-Americans, politics still followed nationality: because

they were one people, they made one state. But with the newer immigrants, the process was reversed. Because they were citizens of one state—so it was commonly thought—they would become one people. Nationality would follow politics, as it presumably had in earlier times, when the peoples of the modern world were first formed. For a while, however, perhaps for a long while, the United States would be a country composed of many peoples, sharing residence and citizenship only, without a common history or culture.

In such circumstances, the only emotion that made for unity was patriotism. Hence the efforts of the late 19th and early 20th centuries to intensify patriotic feeling, to make a religion out of citizenship. "The voting booth is the temple of American institutions," Supreme Court Justice David Brewer wrote in 1900. "No single tribe or family is chosen to watch the sacred fires burning on its altars . . . Each of us is a priest." The rise of ethnic political machines and bloc voting, however, must have made the temple seem disturbingly like a sectarian conventicle. Few people believed politics to be a sufficient ground for national unity. Patriotism was essentially a holding action, while the country waited for the stronger solidarity of nationalism. Whether the process of Americanization was described as a gradual assimilation to Anglo-American culture or as the creation of an essentially new culture in the crucible of citizenship, its outcome was thought to be both necessary and inevitable: the immigrants would one day constitute a single people. This was the deeper meaning that the slogan *From many, one (E pluribus unum)* took on in the context of mass immigration. The only alternatives, as the history of the Old World taught, were divisiveness, turmoil, and repression.

The fear of divisiveness, or simply of difference, periodically generated outbursts of anti-immigrant feeling among the first immigrants and their descendants. Restraint of all further immigration was one goal of these "nativist" campaigns; the second goal was a more rapid Americanization of the "foreigners" already here. But what did Americanization entail? Many of the foreigners were already naturalized citizens. Now they were to be naturalized again, not politically but culturally. It is worth distinguishing this second naturalization from superficially similar campaigns in the old European empires. Russification, for example, was also a cultural program, but it was aimed at intact and rooted communities, at nations that, with the exception of the Jews, were established on lands they had occupied for many centuries. None of the peoples who were to be Russified could have been trusted with citizenship in a free Russia. Given the chance, they would have opted for secession and independence. That was why Russification was so critical: political means were required to overcome national differences. And the use of those means produced the predictable democratic response that politics should follow nationality, not oppose it. In the United States, by contrast, Americanization was aimed at peoples far more susceptible to cultural change, for they were not only uprooted; they had uprooted themselves. Whatever the pressures that had driven them to the New World, they had chosen to come, while others like themselves, in their own families, had chosen to remain. And as a reward for their choice, the immigrants had been offered citizenship, a

gift that many eagerly accepted. Though nativists feared or pretended to fear the politics of the newcomers, the fact is that the men and women who were to be Americanized were already, many of them, patriotic Americans.

Because of these differences, the response of the immigrants to cultural naturalization was very different from that of their counterparts in the Old World. They were in many cases acquiescent, ready to make themselves over, even as the nativists asked. This was especially true in the area of language: there has been no longterm or successful effort to maintain the original language of the newcomers as anything more than a second language in the United States. The vitality of Spanish in the Southwest today, though it probably results from the continued large-scale influx of Mexican immigrants, suggests a possible exception to this rule. If these immigrants do not distribute themselves around the country, as other groups have done, a state like New Mexico might provide the first arena for sustained linguistic conflict in the United States. Until now, however, in a country where many languages are spoken, there has been remarkably little conflict. English is and has always been acknowledged as the public language of the American republic, and no one has tried to make any other language the basis for regional autonomy or secession. When the immigrants did resist Americanization, struggling to hold on to old identities and old customs, their resistance took a new form. It was not a demand that politics follow nationality, but rather that politics be separated from nationality—as it was already separated from religion. It was not a demand for national liberation, but for ethnic pluralism.

THE PRACTICE OF PLURALISM

As a general intellectual tendency, pluralism in the early 20th century was above all a reaction against the doctrine of sovereignty. In its different forms—syndicalist, guild socialist, regionalist, autonomist—it was directed against the growing power and the farreaching claims of the modern state. But ethnic pluralism as it developed in the United States cannot plausibly be characterized as an antistate ideology. Its advocates did not challenge the authority of the federal government; they did not defend states' rights; they were not drawn to any of the forms of European corporatism. Their central assertion was that U.S. politics, as it was, did not require cultural homogeneity; it rested securely enough on democratic citizenship. What had previously been understood as a temporary condition was now described as if it might be permanent. The United States was, and could safely remain, a country composed of many peoples, a "nation of nationalities," as Horace Kallen called it. Indeed, this was the destiny of America: to maintain the diversity of the Old World in a single state, without persecution or repression. Not only *From many, one,* but also *Within one, many.*

Marxism was the first major challenge to the traditional argument for national homogeneity; ethnic pluralism is the second. Although the early pluralists were by no means radicals, and never advocated social transformation, there is a certain sense in which their denial of conventional wisdom goes deeper than that of the Marxists. For the Marxist argument suggests that the

future socialist state (before it withers away) will rest upon the firm base of proletarian unity. And like each previous ruling class, the proletariat is expected to produce a hegemonic culture, of which political life would be merely one expression. Pluralists, on the other hand, imagined a state unsupported by either unity or hegemony. No doubt, they were naïve not to recognize the existence of a single economic system and then of a culture reflecting dominant economic values. But their argument is far-reaching and important even if it is taken to hold only that in addition to this common culture, overlaying it, radically diversifying its impact, there is a world of ethnic multiplicity. The effect on the theory of the state is roughly the same with or without the economic understanding: politics must still create the (national) unity it was once thought merely to mirror. And it must create unity without denying or repressing multiplicity.

The early pluralist writers—theorists like Horace Kallen and Randolph Bourne, popularizers like Louis Adamic—did not produce a fully satisfying account of this creative process or of the ultimately desirable relation between the political one and the cultural many. Their arguments rarely advanced much beyond glowing description and polemical assertion. Drawing heavily upon 19th-century romanticism, they insisted upon the intrinsic value of human difference and, more plausibly and importantly, upon the deep need of human beings for historically and communally structured forms of life. Every kind of regimentation, every kind of uniformity was alien to them. They were the self-appointed guardians of a society of groups, a society resting upon stable families (despite the disruptions of the immigrant experience), tied into, bearing, and transmitting powerful cultural traditions. At the same time, their politics was little more than an unexamined liberalism. Freedom for individuals, they were certain, was all that was necessary to uphold group identification and ethnic flourishing. They had surprisingly little to say about how the different groups were to be held together in a single political order, what citizenship might mean in a pluralist society, whether state power should ever be used on behalf of groups, or what social activities should be assigned to or left to groups. The practical meaning of ethnic pluralism has been hammered out, is still being hammered out, in the various arenas of political and social life. Little theoretical justification exists for any particular outcome.

The best way to understand pluralism, then, is to look at what its protagonists have done or tried to do. Ethnic self-assertion in the United States has been the functional equivalent of national liberation in other parts of the world. What are the actual functions that it serves? There are three that seem critically important. First of all, the defense of ethnicity against cultural naturalization: Kallen's pluralism, worked out in a period of heightened nativist agitation and political persecution (see his *Culture and Democracy in the United States*, 1924), is primarily concerned with upholding the right of the new immigrants, as individuals, to form themselves into cultural communities and maintain their foreign ways. Kallen joins the early-20th-century American *kulturkampf* as the advocate of cultural permissiveness. Train citizens, but leave nationality alone! The argument, so far as it is developed, is largely negative in character, and so it fits easily into the liberal

paradigm. But Kallen is convinced that the chief product of a liberal society will not be individual selfhood but collective identity. Here surely he was right, or at least partly right. How many private wars, parallel to his intellectual campaign, have been fought on behalf of such identities—in schools, bureaucracies, corporations—against the pressures of Americanization! Most often, when individual men and women insist on "being themselves," they are in fact defending a self they share with others. Sometimes, of course, they succumb and learn to conform to standarized versions of New World behavior. Or they wait, frightened and passive, for organizational support: a league against defamation, a committee for advancement, and so on. When such organizations go to work, the pluralist form of the struggle is plain to see, even if legal and moral arguments continue to focus on individual rights.

The second function of ethnic assertiveness is more positive in character: the celebration of this or that identity. Celebration is critical to every national and ethnic movement because both foreign conquest and immigration to foreign lands work, though in different ways, to undermine communal confidence. Immigration involves a conscious rejection of the old country and then, often, of oneself as a product of the old country. A new land requires a new life, new ways of life. But in learning the new ways, the immigrant is slow, awkward, a greenhorn, quickly outpaced by his own children. He is likely to feel inferior, and his children are likely to confirm the feeling. But this sense of inferiority, so painful to him, is also a disaster for them. It cuts them adrift in a world where they are never likely to feel entirely at home. At some point, among themselves, or among their children (the second American generation), a process of recovery begins. Ethnic celebration is a feature of that process. It has a general and a particular form: the celebration of diversity itself and then of the history and culture of a particular group. The first of these, it should be stressed, would be meaningless without the second, for the first is abstract and the second concrete. Pluralism has in itself no powers of survival; it depends upon energy, enthusiasm, commitment within the component groups; it cannot outlast the particularity of cultures and creeds. From the standpoint of the liberal state, particularity is a matter of individual choice, and pluralism nothing more than toleration. From the standpoint of the individual, it is probably something else, for men and women mostly "choose" the culture and creed to which they were born —even if, after conquest and immigration, they have to be born again.

The third function of ethnic assertiveness is to build and sustain the reborn community—to create institutions, gain control of resources, and provide educational and welfare services. As with nation-building, this is hard work, but there is a difficulty peculiar to ethnic groups in a pluralist society: such groups do not have coercive authority over their members. Indeed, they do not have members in the same way that the state has citizens; they have no guaranteed population. Though they are historical communities, they must function as if they were voluntary associations. They must make ethnicity a cause, like prohibition or universal suffrage; they must persuade people to "ethnicize" rather than Americanize themselves. The advocates of religious ethnicity—German Lutherans, Irish Catholics, Jews,

and so on—have probably been most successful in doing this. But any group that hopes to survive must commit itself to the same pattern of activity—winning support, raising money, building schools, community centers, and old-age homes.

On the basis of some decades of experience, one can reasonably argue that ethnic pluralism is entirely compatible with the existence of a unified republic. Kallen would have said that it is simply the expression of democracy in the sphere of culture. It is, however, an unexpected expression: the American republic is very different from that described, for example, by Montesquieu and Rousseau. It lacks the intense political fellowship, the commitment to public affairs, that they thought necessary. "The better the constitution of a state is," wrote Rousseau, "the more do public affairs encroach on private in the minds of the citizens. Private affairs are even of much less importance, because the aggregate of the common happiness furnishes a greater proportion of that of each individual, so that there is less for him to seek in particular cares." This is an unlikely description unless ethnic culture and religious belief are closely interwoven with political activity (as Rousseau insisted they should be). It certainly misses the reality of the American republic, where both have been firmly relegated to the private sphere. The emotional life of U.S. citizens is lived mostly in private—which is not to say in solitude, but in groups considerably smaller than the community of all citizens. Americans are communal in their private affairs, individualist in their politics. Society is a collection of groups; the state is an organization of individual citizens. And society and state, though they constantly interact, are formally distinct. For support and comfort and a sense of belonging, men and women look to their groups; for freedom and mobility, they look to the state.

Still, democratic participation does bring group members into the political arena where they are likely to discover common interests. Why has this not caused radical divisiveness, as in the European empires? It certainly has made for conflict, sometimes of a frightening sort, but always within limits set by the nonterritorial and socially indeterminate character of the immigrant communities and by the sharp divorce of state and ethnicity. No single group can hope to capture the state and turn it into a nation-state. Members of the group are citizens only as Americans, not as Germans, Italians, Irishmen, or Jews. Politics forces them into alliances and coalitions; and democratic politics, because it recognizes each citizen as the equal of every other, without regard to ethnicity, fosters a unity of individuals alongside the diversity of groups. American Indians and blacks have mostly been excluded from this unity, and it is not yet clear on what terms they will be brought in. But political life is in principle open, and this openness has served to diffuse the most radical forms of ethnic competition. The result has not been a weak political order: quite the contrary. Though it has not inspired heated commitment, though politics has not become a mass religion, the republic has been remarkably stable, and state power has grown steadily over time.

TOWARD CORPORATISM?

The growth of state power sets the stage for a new kind of pluralist politics. With increasing effect, the state does for all its citizens what the various groups do or try to do for their own adherents. It defends their rights, not only against foreign invasion and domestic violence, but also against persecution, harassment, libel, and discrimination. It celebrates their collective (American) history, establishing national holidays; building monuments, memorials, and museums; supplying educational materials. It acts to sustain their communal life, collecting taxes and providing a host of welfare services. The modern state nationalizes communal activity, and the more energetically it does this, the more taxes it collects, the more services it provides, the harder it becomes for groups to act on their own. State welfare undercuts private philanthropy, much of which was organized within ethnic communities; it makes it harder to sustain private and parochial schools; it erodes the strength of cultural institutions.

All this is justified, and more than justified, by the fact that the various groups were radically unequal in strength and in their ability to provide services for their adherents. Moreover, the social coverage of the ethnic communities was uneven and incomplete. Many Americans never looked for services from any particular group, but turned instead to the state. It is not the case that state officials invaded the spheres of welfare and culture; they were invited in by disadvantaged or hardpressed or assimilated citizens. But now, it is said, pluralism cannot survive unless ethnic groups, as well as individuals, share directly in the benefits of state power. Once again, politics must follow ethnicity, recognizing and supporting communal structures.

What does this mean? First, that the state should defend collective as well as individual rights; second, that the state should expand its official celebrations, to include not only its own history but the history of all the peoples that make up the American people; third, that tax money should be fed into the ethnic communities to help in the financing of bilingual and bicultural education, and of group-oriented welfare services. And if all this is to be done, and fairly done, then it is necessary also that ethnic groups be given, as a matter of right, some sort of representation within the state agencies that do it.

These are far-reaching claims. They have not received, any more than the earlier pluralism did, a clear theoretical statement. They are the stuff of public pronouncements and political agitation. Their full significance is unclear, but the world they point to is a corporatist world, where ethnic groups no longer organize themselves like voluntary associations but have instead some political standing and some legal rights. There is, however, a major difficulty here: groups cannot be assigned rights unless they are first assigned members. There has to be a fixed population with procedures for choosing representatives before there can be representatives acting officially on behalf of that population. But ethnic groups in the United States do not have, and never have had, fixed populations (American Indian tribes are a partial exception). Historically, corporatist arrangements have only been worked out for groups that do. In fact, they have only been worked out when the fixity was guaranteed by a rigid dualism, that is, when two communities were locked into a single state: Flemings and Walloons in Belgium, Greeks and Turks in Cyprus, Christians and Muslims in Lebanon. In such cases, people not identified with one community are

virtually certain to be identified with the other. The residual category of intermarried couples and aliens will be small, especially if the two communities are anciently established and territorially based. Problems of identification are likely to arise only in the capital city. (Other sorts of problems arise more generally; these examples hardly invite emulation.)

America's immigrant communities have a radically different character. Each of them has a center of active participants, some of them men and women who have been "born-again," and a much larger periphery of individuals and families who are little more than occasional recipients of services generated at the center. They are communities without boundaries, shading off into a residual mass of people who think of themselves simply as Americans. Borders and border guards are among the first products of a successful national liberation movement, but ethnic assertiveness has no similar outcome. There is no way for the various groups to prevent or regulate individual crossings. Nor can the state do this without the most radical coercion of individuals. It cannot fix the population of the groups unless it forces each citizen to choose an ethnic identity and establishes rigid distinctions among the different identities, of a sort that pluralism by itself has not produced.

It is possible, however, to guarantee representation to ethnic groups without requiring the groups to organize and choose their own spokesmen. The alternative to internal choice is a quota system. Thus, Supreme Court appointments might be constrained by a set of quotas: a certain number of blacks, Jews, Irish and Italian Catholics, and so on, must be serving at any given time. But these men and women would stand in no political relationship to their groups; they would not be responsible agents; nor would they be bound to speak for the interests of their ethnic or religious fellows. They would represent simply by being black (Jewish, Irish) and being *there*, and the Court would be a representative body in the sense that it reflected the pluralism of the larger society in its own membership. It would not matter whether these members came from the center or the periphery of the groups, or whether the groups had clearly defined boundaries, a rich inner life, and so on.

This kind of representation depends only upon external (bureaucratic rather than political) processes, and so it can readily be extended to society at large. Quotas are easy to use in admitting candidates to colleges and professional schools and in hiring them for any sort of employment. Such candidates are not elected but selected, though here, too, there must be a fixed population from which selections can be made. In practice, efforts to identify populations and make quotas possible have been undertaken, with state support, only for oppressed groups. Men and women, marked out as victims or as the children and heirs of victims, have been assigned a right to certain advantages in the selection process; otherwise, it is said, they would not be present at all in schools, professions, and businesses. This is not the place to consider the merits of such a procedure. But it is important to point out that selection by quota functions largely to provide a kind of escape from group life for people whose identity has become a trap. Its chief purpose is to give opportunities to individuals, not a voice to groups. It serves to enhance the wealth of individuals, not necessarily the resources of the ethnic community. The community is strengthened, to be sure, if newly trained men and women return to work among its members, but only a small minority do that. Mostly, they serve, if they serve at all, as role models for other upwardly mobile men and women. When weak and hitherto passive groups mobilize themselves in order to win a place in the quota system, they do so for the sake of that mobility, and are likely to have no further raison d'être once it is achieved.

Considered more generally, there is a certain tension between quota systems and ethnic pluralism, for the administrators of any such system are bound to refuse to recognize differences among the groups. They come by their numbers through simple mathematical calculations. It would be intolerable for them to make judgments as to the character or quality of the different cultures. The tendency of their work, then, is to reproduce within every group to which quotas are applied the same educational and employment patterns. Justice is a function of the identity of the patterns among groups rather than of life chances among individuals. But it is clear that ethnic pluralism by itself would not generate any such identity. Historically specific cultures necessarily produce historically specific patterns of interest and work. This is not to say that pluralism necessarily militates against egalitarian principles, since equality might well take the form (socialists have always expected it to take the form) of roughly equal recompense for different kinds of work. It is not implausible to imagine a heterogeneous but egalitarian society: the heterogeneity, cultural and private; the equality, economic and political. Quotas point, by contrast, toward group uniformity, not individual equality. Though it would be necessary for individuals to identify themselves (or to be identified) as group members in order to receive the benefits of a quota system, these identifications would progressively lose their communal significance. The homogenization of the groups would open the way for the assimilation of their members into a prevailing or evolving national culture.

STATE AND ETHNICITY

The state can intervene in two basic ways to structure group life. It can encourage or require the groups to organize themselves in corporatist fashion, assigning a political role to the corporations in the state apparatus. This is the autonomist strategy, the nearest thing to national liberation that is possible under conditions of multiethnicity. The effect of autonomy would be to intensify and institutionalize cultural difference. Alternatively, the state can act to reduce differences among groups by establishing uniform or symmetrical achievement standards for their members. Each group would be represented, though not through any form of collective action, in roughly equal proportions in every area of political, social, and economic life. This is the integrationist strategy: it can be applied in a limited and compensatory way to particular (oppressed) groups or more generally to all groups. Applied generally, its effect would be to repress every sort of cultural specificity, turning ethnic identity into an administrative classification.

What the state cannot do is to reproduce politically the pluralist pattern that the immigrants and their children have spontaneously generated, for that pattern

is inherently fluid and indeterminate. Its existence depends upon keeping apart what nation-state and corporatist theory bring together: a state organized coercively to protect rights, a society organized on voluntarist principles to advance interests (including cultural and religious interests). State officials provide a framework within which groups can flourish but cannot guarantee their flourishing, or even their survival. The only way to provide such guarantees would be to introduce coercion into the social world, transforming the groups into something like their Old World originals and denying the whole experience of immigration, individualism, and communal rebirth. Nothing like this would appear to be on the American agenda.

The survival and flourishing of the groups depends largely upon the vitality of their centers. If that vitality cannot be sustained, pluralism will prove to be a temporary phenomenon, a way station on the road to American nationalism. The early pluralists may have been naïve in their calm assurance that ethnic vitality would have an enduring life. But they were surely right to insist that it should not artificially be kept alive, any more than it should be repressed, by state power. On the other hand, there is an argument to be made, against the early pluralists, in favor of providing some sorts of public support for ethnic activity. It is an argument familiar from economic analysis, having to do with the character of ethnicity as a collective good.

Individual mobility is the special value but also the characteristic weakness of American pluralism. It makes for loose relations between center and periphery; it generates a world without boundaries. In that world, the vitality of the center is tested by its ability to hold on to peripheral men and women and to shape their self-images and their convictions. These men and women, in turn, live off the strength of the center, which they do not have to pay for either in time or money. They are religious and cultural freeloaders, their lives enhanced by a community they do not actively support and by an identity they need not themselves cultivate. There is no way to charge them for what they receive from the center, except when they receive specific sorts of material help. But their most important gain may be nothing more than a certain sense of pride, an aura of ethnicity, otherwise unavailable. Nor is there anything unjust in their freeloading. The people at the center are not being exploited; they want to hold the periphery. Freeloading of this sort is probably inevitable in a free society.

But so long as it exists—that is, so long as ethnicity is experienced as a collective good by large numbers of people—it probably makes sense to permit collective money, taxpayers' money, to seep though the state/ethnic group (state/church) barrier. This is especially important when taxes constitute a significant portion of the national wealth and when the state has undertaken, on behalf of all its citizens, to organize education and welfare. It can be done in a variety of ways, through tax exemptions and rebates, subsidies, matching grants, certificate plans, and so on. The precise mechanisms do not matter, once it is understood that they must stop short of a corporatist system, requiring no particular form of ethnic organization and no administrative classification of members. A rough fairness in the distribution of funds is probably ensured by the normal work-ings of democratic politics in a heterogeneous society. Ticket-balancing and coalition-building will provide ethnic groups with a kind of informal representation in the allocative process. Democratic politics can be remarkably accommodating to groups, so long as it has to deal only with individuals: voters, candidates, welfare recipients, taxpayers, criminals, all without official ethnic tags. And the accommodation need not be bitterly divisive, though it is sure to generate conflict. Ethnic citizens can be remarkably loyal to a state that protects and fosters private communal life, if that is seen to be equitably done.

The question still remains whether this kind of equity, adapted to the needs of immigrant communities, can successfully be extended to the racial minorities now asserting their own group claims. Racism is the great barrier to a fully developed pluralism and as long as it exists American Indians and blacks, and perhaps Mexican Americans as well, will be tempted by (and torn between) the anti-pluralist alternatives of corporate division and state-sponsored unification. It would be presumptuous to insist that these options are foolish or unwarranted so long as opportunities for group organization and cultural expression are not equally available to all Americans. A state committed to pluralism, however, cannot do anything more than see to it that those opportunities are *available*, not that they are used, and it can only do that by ensuring that all citizens, without reference to their groups, share equally, or roughly equally, in the resources of American life.

Beyond that, distributive justice among groups is bound to be relative to the vitality of their centers and of their committed members. Short of corporatism, the state cannot help groups unable or unwilling to help themselves. It cannot save them from ultimate Americanization. Indeed, it works so as to permit individual escape (assimilation and intermarriage) as well as collective commitment. The primary function of the state, and of politics generally, is to do justice to individuals, and in a pluralist society ethnicity is simply one of the background conditions of this effort. Ethnic identification gives meaning to the lives of many men and women, but it has nothing to do with their standing as citizens. This distinction seems worth defending, even if it makes for a world in which there are no guarantees of meaning. In a culturally homogeneous society the government can foster a particular identity, deliberately merging culture and politics. This the U.S. government cannot do. Pluralism is thus still an experiment, still to be tested against the long-term historical and theoretical power of the nation-state.

MICHAEL WALZER

POLES

Polish Americans are one of the largest ethnic groups in the United States today. In 1972 the *Current Population Survey* estimated that there were 5.1 million Americans of Polish heritage, and figures of as high as 6 million have been published. Although these estimates may include some people whose ancestors belonged to minorities who lived within the territories of Poland and who assimilated in the course of time, the vast majority of Polish Americans share two characteristics: they arrived, or their forbears arrived, speaking Polish,

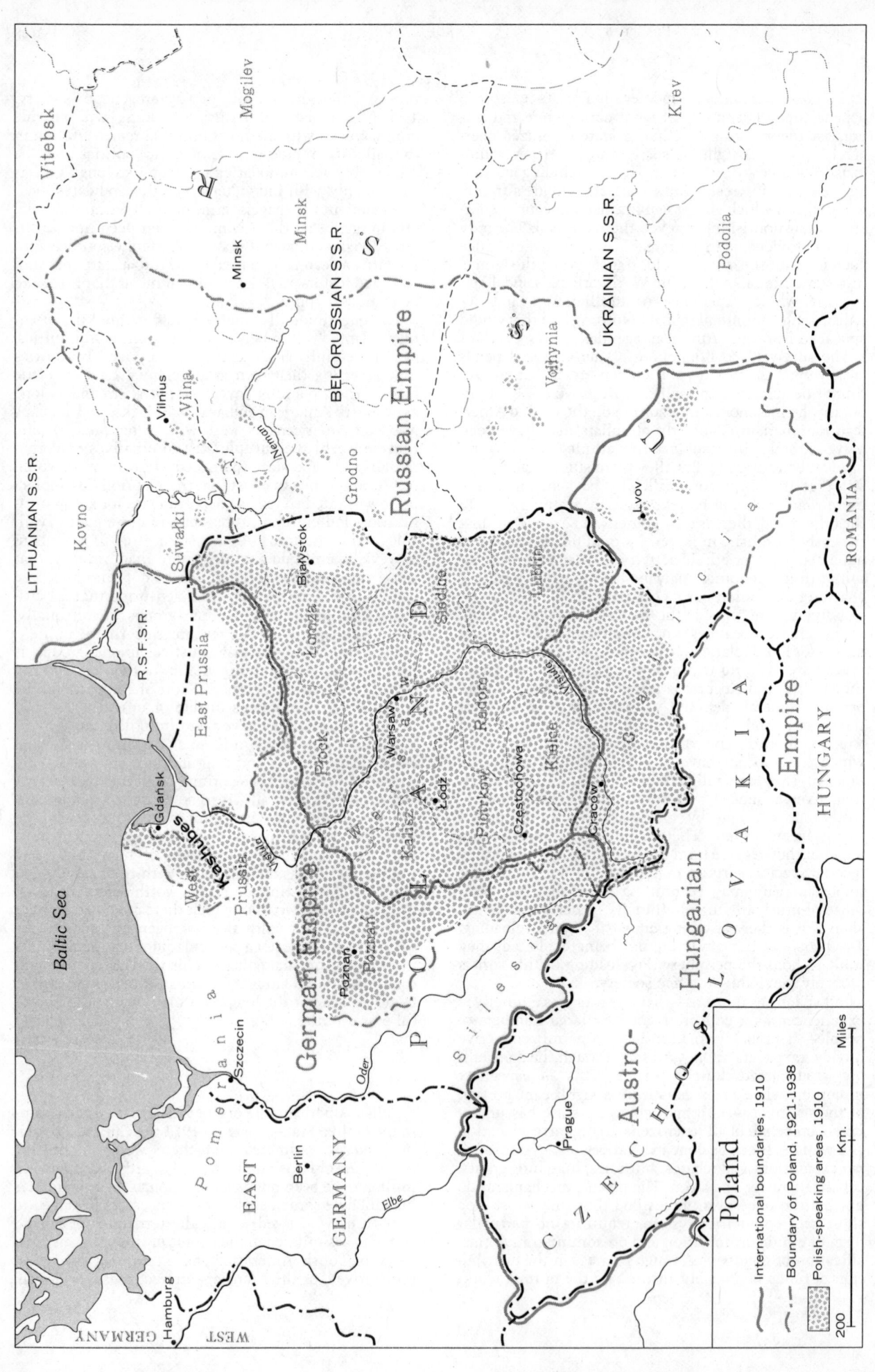

Poland

- International boundaries, 1910
- Boundary of Poland, 1921–1938
- Polish-speaking areas, 1910

Baltic Sea

WEST GERMANY

Hamburg •

EAST GERMANY

Berlin •

Szczecin •

Pomerania

Oder

Elbe

Prague •

CZECHOSLOVAKIA

Austro-Hungarian Empire

HUNGARY

ROMANIA

Vitebsk

Mogilev

Kiev

R S F S R

Minsk •

Minsk

BELORUSSIAN S.S.R.

Podolia

Russian Empire

UKRAINIAN S.S.R.

Volhynia

Vilnius •

Vilna

Neman

LITHUANIAN S.S.R.

Kovno

Lvov •

Galicia

Suwałki

East Prussia

Grodno

Białystok •

Łomża

Siedlce

Lublin

Gdańsk •

Kashubes

West Prussia

Vistula

Płock

Warsaw •

Włocławek

Vistula

POLAND

Kalisz •

Łódź •

Piotrków •

Radom

Kielce

Częstochowa •

Cracow •

Poznań •

Poznań

Silesia

German Empire

GERMANY

Km. 200

Miles

and they belonged and still belong to the Roman Catholic Church.

The Polish-American community includes within it a variety of regional subgroups, three of which—the Kashubes, the Górali, and the Mazurians—are the most distinctive. They developed regional subcultures in the homeland and have retained some of their provincial loyalties and customs in the United States. The Kashubes from Pomerania were originally not Polish at all. They lived along the Baltic coast in the 13th century and spoke their own language. A few Kashubian immigrants continue to call themselves Kashubian Poles in America, although others have been entirely absorbed into the larger Polish-American community. The Górali (Mountaineers) come from the Malopolska region in the southern districts near the Tatra Mountains. Although they were somewhat less distinctive than the Kashubes in the homeland, time seems to have increased their ethnic awareness in the United States. They possess a rich folk tradition of dance, dress, and legend, which they continue to cultivate. The Mazurians come from the northernmost lake district near the Baltic Sea in areas once known as Warmia and East Prussia. Partly Teutonic in origin, many were Germanized in the 16th century; some remained Polish but became Protestants. Finally, immigrants from certain other Polish provinces—Silesia and Galicia, for example—have also retained some, although much less, regional identity in the United States.

The origin of the Polish-speaking Catholic majority in Poland was a tribe of Western Slavs who banded together and eventually formed a political unit. They became Christian after the conversion of their king in 966. Over the next few centuries the boundaries of Poland expanded to include large parts of central and eastern Europe. Poland reached its greatest size and power after the Union of Lublin in 1569, which united the kingdom of Poland with the Grand Duchy of Lithuania. But over the next two centuries political weaknesses that arose from the vicissitudes of an elective monarchy and economic weaknesses caused by an increasingly outmoded feudal agrarian economy led to Poland's gradual decline. Surrounded on the west, east, and south by three strong powers—Prussia, Russia, and Austria—it finally succumbed. Partitioned three times in the 18th century, Poland virtually disappeared from the face of Europe until after World War I. The Russian Empire seized the largest share of the former Polish territories, and later also controlled the semiautonomous Kingdom of Poland created by the Congress of Vienna in 1815; Prussia claimed the smallest, western part; and the Austrian Empire governed the poor but populous territory of Galicia.

After World War I a reconstituted Poland arose out of the ruins of the three monarchies that had carved up its territories two centuries earlier. Although it was not as large as it had been in the 16th century, Poland in 1919 still included a varied population of Jews, Germans, Belorussians, Lithuanians, and Ukrainians as well as Poles. Its sovereignty was short-lived, however. In September 1939 Hitler's armies overran the country and six years later, driving out the Germans, the Russians established a Soviet-controlled Communist Poland with much revised borders. As a result of the war and of several forced population transfers, Poland is once again virtually as homogeneous as it was in the early Middle Ages with the result that if the Polish borders remain as they are, fewer and fewer people overseas who might once have claimed Poland as their country of origin will continue to do so. The Nazi annihilation of millions of Polish Jews and the recent anti-Zionist policy of the Polish Communist government have both reduced the number of Polish Jews and understandably weakened their loyalty to the country. The German minority in Poland has moved or been resettled outside the adjusted postwar Polish borders into territories that now belong to East and West Germany and the Soviet Union has taken away all the formerly Lithuanian, Belorussian, and Ukrainian lands to the east. In the future, then, Polish ethnicity abroad is most likely to be perpetuated by persons descended from the Polish mainstream and not from those former Polish minorities.

The history of Polish immigration to America falls into four periods. The first, from 1608 to about 1800, was one in which a small number of individuals left for personal reasons—economic, ideological, and romantic. The second, in which there were also few, was the result of particularly strong political and nationalistic sentiments and lasted from 1800 to 1860. The third period, in which there was a major wave of immigrants motivated chiefly by economic and religious considerations, took place between 1860 and 1914. In the last, the years since World War I, the immigrants have been largely refugees and émigrés, leaving Poland as a result of political or ideological differences with the government.

MIGRATION

Poles have known about America since the 17th century. There are claims that Poles came to the New World before 1600 on the ships of the Vikings or with Columbus, but the documentation for these claims is both fragmentary and suspect; hard evidence does not place a Pole in the New World until the first successful English colony at Jamestown. Although bits of information about the newly discovered wilderness did drift back, on the whole the affairs of the American colonies were not matters of common knowledge until the relations between the colonies and England began to attract attention in the mid-18th century. Those few Poles who came to the New World did so for private reasons. The American Revolution in 1775 and Benjamin Franklin's activities in Paris on behalf of the patriots aroused interest in the colonial cause all over Europe. A number of European adventurers committed to the ideas of the French Enlightenment made their way to America. The overall reaction of the Poles to the American Revolution was mixed—some supported it; others did not— but it is clear that by the time of the revolution many among the gentry (szlachta) and nobility had a surprisingly intimate knowledge of New World events.

The final partition of Poland in 1795 inaugurated the second period of Polish emigration. From 1800 to 1860 interest in America among revolutionary nationalists was great; they considered the United States to be a model liberal society, and periodically some of them found it an attractive sanctuary. Conflict had developed between the governments ruling Poland and the Polish intellectuals and lesser nobility who sought Polish in-

dependence. Both sides, aristocratic and liberal, competed for the support of the Polish peasants. In 1830 an insurrection resulting from the repressive anti-Polish measures instituted by Czar Nicholas I in the 1820s was suppressed, and the first great exodus of Polish émigrés began. Another major uprising in 1863 failed to win freedom for Poland and further added to the number of Polish émigrés who were living in Geneva, Paris, London, New York, and Chicago. Thereafter a thoroughgoing Russification policy was adopted to discourage any further ideas of Polish autonomy or nationalism. By isolating the liberals and making their movement appear to be gentry-inspired, the government limited its appeal to the peasants and destroyed the movement inside the country. However, an international network of exiles seeking the resurrection of the Polish state remained abroad.

In the latter half of the 19th century Polish emigration took on a quite different character. The new migrants were not much concerned with the reestablishment of a nation state; they were far too preoccupied with the problems of basic survival. They were called in Poland *za chlebem* (for-bread) emigrants, but no one year neatly divides the political emigration from the economic one. Many of those leaving before the 1860s no doubt did so for economic reasons, and some who left after went as political exiles. But material and religious considerations certainly played a larger role in decisions to leave the homeland after 1865 than they had before.

Eastern Europe after mid-century resembled western Europe a century earlier—an underdeveloped area with little industrialization, heavily dependent on agriculture both for subsistence and for market income. There were cities—the port towns along the Baltic, small industrial areas in Bohemia and Silesia, and inland cultural, administrative, and market centers—but most people still lived in rural areas. The Polish peasants attached particular status to the possession of land, as did the few Polish tradesmen and skilled workers. Owning property represented security; losing it meant ruin. Although the removal of feudal obligations early in the century made it legally possible for even the lowliest former serfs to acquire land, changing economic conditions made that goal less and less attainable. One of the highest birth rates in Europe, falling crop prices due to new competition from the more advanced and mechanized agriculture of western Europe and the United States, and the inability of the Polish peasants to modernize their land-holding and crop-producing practices hindered their efforts. Consequently the craving for land motivated the departure of most Polish emigrants in the late 1800s: they were looking for money to retain or purchase property. The search led them to other areas of eastern Europe, to western Europe—and to America.

While the impoverishment of the Polish peasant was general throughout most of the 19th century in Prussia, Russia, and Austria, each of these governments—and that part of Poland under its control—had particular problems of its own. The earliest large-scale overseas emigration of Poles originated in the regions under Prussian, and subsequently German, domination, particularly in Pomerania and Poznań. There, the typical conditions of overpopulation and a high birthrate were less of a problem than the new forms of agricultural organization. By mid-century the large and still expanding estates were beginning to force the less efficient and smaller farmers to look for work elsewhere. In western Pomerania, for example, less than 2 percent of the proprietors owned about 60 percent of the land by 1882; two-thirds of the peasants owned 3 percent. Unable to compete in the marketplace, the Polish peasants had to supplement their income either as agricultural laborers on these large estates or as workers in the mines and industries in nearby Silesia, Saxony, or Westphalia in western Germany. Or they had to emigrate. The German Poles were generally better educated and more enterprising than their countrymen in Russia and Austria, and the emigrating Prussian contingent included the largest percentage of skilled craftsmen. With its great need for all kinds of workers, agricultural and industrial, the United States seemed to be an obvious destination.

German imperial policy also played its role in increasing the Polish emigration of the 1870s and 1880s. The so-called Kulturkampf, or "the struggle for culture," was instituted by the German government to weaken the hold of the Roman Catholic Church in German territories. The government suppressed religious institutions, imprisoned the Polish archbishop, and placed restrictions on all Catholics. These actions encouraged Polish Catholics, especially the clergy, to move. The religious campaign ended in the late 1870s, but German efforts to reduce Polish influence in the eastern territories continued through a deliberate policy of buying up land on which to settle German colonists. The plan had some effect but Polish resistance through the establishment of cooperative land banks largely thwarted it. This experience in developing self-help associations, especially financial institutions, was helpful in the construction of the Polish-American community.

The Polish emigration from Germany began to decline after 1890, even as that from Russia and Austria increased. The economic situation of the peasant masses in Russian Poland—or Congress Poland as it was called, because its political ties to Russia had been redefined in 1815 at the Congress of Vienna—was far less happy than it had been farther west in Germany. The population had doubled from 5 million to 10 million between 1860 and 1900, for example, while agricultural production lagged, in part as a result of the excessive subdivision of farmland. Some foreign capital investment did help several Russian Polish cities, including Łódź and Warsaw, to industrialize. Land-poor or landless farmers were transformed into an army of proletarianized peasants, leaving their homes seasonally or permanently to seek employment either in these cities or those of Russia. The change was most dramatic in the northeastern provinces of Suwałki, Płock, and Łomza near the Lithuanian border. Landless peasants found jobs either as day laborers on the depopulated agrarian estates of eastern Germany, or in the rising industrial centers of their own region, or farther west in Europe, or in the United States.

The peasants in Galicia, under Austrian rule, fared the worst because there no industry developed to absorb at least some of the landless unemployed. "Galician misery" has special significance to the Poles. Under the

Hapsburgs the Galician Poles enjoyed the greatest degree of autonomy of any of the three sectors, but life was hard, and it grew harder as the 19th century drew to a close. The causes for the misery were, again, a rapidly growing population and an antiquated system of land subdivision. The average peasant holding shrank from five and a half hectares in 1850 to just over three in 1930, while the population grew from 114 to 162 per square kilometer—the highest rural density in Europe. Between 1880 and 1900 the number of inhabitants in Austrian Poland grew from 6 million to 7 million, and the Galician peasants joined the Poles in Russia in moving west. The net Polish emigration from the province between 1871 and 1913 was just over 1 million.

By the end of the century a massive migratory wave including Poles from all three sectors was in process. Most Galician and Russian Poles went abroad as temporary sojourners; they intended to return and resettle in their native districts on land bought with money earned abroad. The German Poles left as permanent settlers.

Thus, the major incentives for Polish emigration before World War I were economic and sometimes religious, but there were other considerations as well. Many young men were escaping military conscription, especially in Congress Poland and Galicia. And Polish socialists, a very small but articulate group, were fleeing the measures directed against them in the 1890s by the Russian and Austrian police. The exodus of radicals increased considerably after a series of unsuccessful labor riots and strikes in Warsaw in 1905.

The emigration after World War I was again of a different character. Although a few departed after Poland became independent in 1918 because of the stagnant economy, most left as a result of dissatisfaction with one or another of the frequent political transformations: government instability and dictatorship in the 1920s and 1930s, the German invasion and occupation from 1939 to 1945, the ensuing Russian "liberation," and the establishment of a pro-Soviet Communist regime after 1945. Polish immigrants in this period were refugees, by and large, and had no hope of returning, in contrast to the earlier peasant migrant and the political exile, both of whom expected to go home either when they had enough money or when Poland was free.

ARRIVAL AND SETTLEMENT

The very first Poles in America came to Jamestown, Virginia, in 1608; they came with Germans to help develop the colony's timber industry. Apparently no steady stream of Poles followed, although a few settled in other colonies later in the century, because sporadic news of American life drifted back to Poland. In the early 18th century a number of pietistic Protestant Poles, particularly the Socinians (precursors of the Unitarians), formed communities around Gdańsk (Danzig) in East Prussia and at other locations in the Polish lands. By the 1730s some of these dissenters, after a time in Holland and possibly in England, had joined William Penn's colony in Pennsylvania to worship unhindered, along with Polish Quakers, Moravians, Schwenkfelders, Mennonites, and others.

Beginning with the American Revolution, Polish colonists are better documented. They were still isolated individuals or small groups; there was as yet no Polish colony or settlement. Among the teachers, Indian guides, entrepreneurs, and land speculators in the Middle Colonies a few obvious Polish names can be found along with the Germans.

During the revolution about a hundred Poles came to fight with the American colonists, the most notable of whom were Count Casimir Pulaski and Thaddeus Kosciuszko. These two had been recruited by Benjamin Franklin in Paris and were both commissioned in the revolutionary army. Pulaski was a leading cavalry officer who died during the British attack on Savannah. Kosciuszko made his mark as a military engineer, but was destined to become far better known in Poland where he returned after the war to lead the Polish liberal forces against the Russians in the 1794 insurrection. Polish Americans were later to make both of them popular heroes, as many memorials around the country testify. Another group of Polish soldiers fled to the South just after the turn of the century, part of a force sent by Napoleon to suppress a slave insurrection on Santo Domingo.

It is not possible to make an accurate count of the Polish arrivals in the next half-century; it can only be said that most of those who came continued to do so largely for political reasons. Census and immigration records do list Poles, but they probably do not include the many who were officially listed as Germans or Austrians. It is also likely that then, as earlier, they came as individuals and families and not in large groups. An exception was the first party of Polish Roman Catholic priests who arrived in the early 1800s.

The refugees who came directly to the United States from the 1830–1831 insurrection in Russian Poland numbered almost 1,000. Most arrived in British ships from Prussia with Austrian help. With the aid of American supporters, they formed two societies, the Association of Poles in America, in 1842, and the Democratic Society of Polish Exiles, in 1852, both in New York. The major organizer was Henryk Kałussowski, probably the leading Polish nationalist in America in the 19th century. The U.S. Congress sympathized with their cause to the extent of offering Kałussowski and his group a land grant for a projected Polish colony, but the enterprise never materialized. After an abortive rebellion in Russian Poland in 1863 additional refugees settled in American cities as far west as San Francisco.

The exact beginning of the massive migration that followed is difficult to establish. Immigration statistics and the U.S. Census are of little help. The California gold rush and the ensuing prosperity of the 1850s attracted many immigrants to America, including some German Poles, for news of these opportunities was well publicized in eastern Europe. There is evidence of Polish peasant settlers in the United States at least as early as 1851 and a group of Polish peasant farmers from Silesia established the first Polish-American settlement and first independent Polish Catholic parish at Panna Maria, Tex., in 1854. Poles from the German area came in increasing numbers chiefly between 1850 and the early 1890s, except for a gap in the 1870s. Estimates of the number of Polish immigrants from German-controlled territory run around 434,000, with only 50,000 of these arriving between 1899 and 1914. Russian and Austrian Poles, in contrast, did not begin arriving in large numbers until after 1890.

About half of the 800,000 Galician Poles arriving before World War I came in the 1890s, and the other half between 1900 and 1914. Those from Russian Poland came last, approximately 170,000 before 1900 and 635,000 after. The total from 1870 to 1914 was more than 2 million, or 2.5 million from mid-century to the end of World War I, with a continual shift over the course of that period from west to east, that is, from German to Austrian to Russian Poland.

Most Polish immigrants who landed in America were quite well acquainted with conditions there. Even if they came alone, they were usually in touch with friends and relatives who had come earlier. Particularly helpful for the more deprived Polish contingent from Austria and Russia were the numerous migration chains, linkages that evolved at the very beginning of the large-scale Polish immigration which enabled the migrants to maintain and utilize family and local ties. Of particular importance in maintaining these bonds were letters. All Polish newcomers, particularly the early arrivals, regarded letter writing as a duty. The task frequently involved great effort since often a more literate friend or local leader had to help, but the result was a flow of practical advice. Equipped with concrete facts about life in the New World, those who had remained behind could then decide whether to follow along, how to travel, and where to go. However, the letters were also a source of the inflated claims and the widespread hyperbole about the United States.

Overseas mail was not the only source of information. From the very earliest years of the mass migration, the Polish-American press provided news as well, and eventually railroads, steamship lines, and (particularly in Germany) agents from individual states were busy disseminating propaganda to attract and then to direct the flood of migrants across the sea. Many Poles also read the advertising directed toward the Germans that touted the availability of cheap land in the American Midwest.

The Russian and Austrian Poles read their journals and listened to the letters read aloud in their villages about employment possibilities. Wage scales must have seemed particularly attractive in the depressed rural areas of eastern Europe. Agricultural workers in Galicia in 1891 were receiving 12 cents a day, while farm hands in the United States were getting eight times that much —90 cents to a dollar a day—and unskilled urban laborers were paid even more. The Russian wage was little better than the Austrian one. The immigrant letter, then, was a stimulant to emigration in its promise of comparative riches and its reminders of familial bonds even when it did not exaggerate. Virtually all Polish arrivals in 1908 told American officials at their port of entry that they had come to join family or friends.

The journey from Poland to America changed little over the years between 1880 and 1914. When an individual made the decision to leave, he bought his passage from a local transportation agent or, more likely, was sent his ticket by a contact in America. Selling personal effects, livestock, and—rarely—land, or borrowing from the local moneylender (who was often also the shipbroker) provided the necessary funds. Steamship replaced sail on the transatlantic trip after 1880, and two lines in particular, the North German Line out of Bremerhaven and the Hamburg American Line, nearly monopolized the Polish traffic. After 1900 these companies simplified the process of easing border formalities by combining overland and transatlantic passage in one price; a ticket could be purchased for the trip virtually door-to-door from Radom, say, to Wilkes-Barre, Pa.

Travel conditions were miserable for those going in steerage in the earlier decades, but after the American authorities later required transportation companies to return sick and inadmissible migrants at the shipper's expense, sanitation facilities, though still minimal, were greatly improved. By the turn of the century passengers were also being housed in fairly well maintained and protected *Auswandererhallen* (emigrant hostels) before they departed.

Few Poles were refused admission to the United States for contagious disease, indigence, or later, anarchism, or on other restrictive grounds. Immigration authorities, for example, returned less than 1 percent between 1892 and 1905. While isolated tragedies did occur—exploitation at port, sickness on board ship, denial of admission—most Polish immigrants probably fared better en route than had the Germans or Scandinavians who had arrived earlier.

The majority of Poles landed in New York—at Castle Garden before 1892 and at Ellis Island afterward. Their destination was almost always one of the already established Polish settlements. The Polish-American communities in the Northeast and Upper Midwest today still reflect these locations. The Prussian Poles who came to America in the mid-1800s either became part of German or Czech communities or established separate Polish colonies in farming areas, except for the political émigrés, most of whom remained in New York. The first truly colonizing groups established farming settlements in the Southwest and Midwest. The earliest of these was the contingent of Silesian Poles who were led to Panna Maria, Tex., in 1854 by the Reverend Leopold Moczygemba of a German Franciscan order. Two other groups arrived from Canada shortly before 1860 and settled in Wisconsin and Michigan. These pioneering ventures were small, but large enough to develop an important chain of migration. The Texas Poles drew from Europe to the New World what was to become the most influential Polish-American Catholic order, the Resurrectionists.

Since economic expansion in the United States after the Civil War was chiefly urban and industrial, the Poles who arrived in that period went to the rapidly developing cities of the Middle Atlantic and Midwest states: New York and Buffalo; Pennsylvania mining towns like Scranton, Wilkes-Barre, and Hazelton; and the steel centers of Pittsburgh and Cleveland and their surrounding towns. The mills, slaughterhouses, refineries, and foundries in midwestern cities like Cleveland and Toledo in Ohio, South Bend, Ind., Milwaukee, Wis., Minneapolis-St. Paul, Minn., Omaha, Nebr., St. Louis, Mo., and, above all, Chicago also attracted Poles seeking work. Detroit was a later, secondary destination. These communities as well as those in other smaller industrial towns first attracted individual German Polish pioneers and then after the 1880s larger contingents from Austria and Russia.

The clustering of first- and second-generation Polish Americans in the United States as of 1920 was as follows. The proportions remain essentially the same

today: Chicago, 400,000; New York, 200,000; Pittsburgh, 200,000; Buffalo, 100,000; Milwaukee, 100,000; Detroit, 100,000; Cleveland, 50,000; Philadelphia, 50,000. The high figures for New York and Pittsburgh are somewhat misleading, for the Poles there were widely scattered throughout the cities. Chicago and Buffalo, on the other hand, had centralized communities. In New England (except for Connecticut), south New Jersey, Philadelphia, and Baltimore, and in the smaller mining towns of the Far West, communities were not established until later, after 1900, and were of secondary importance in the shaping of Polish America. The overall pattern of Polish settlement has remained since 1920 bounded by the Great Lakes, the Mason-Dixon Line, and the Ohio and Missouri rivers.

Many Polish immigrants did not stay in the United States for long. Three out of every ten arrivals between 1906 and 1914, most of them Galician and Russian Poles, went home again, although some of them eventually came back and settled permanently in the United States. A rush to return to Poland, expected after the country regained its independence in 1918, in fact never materialized.

ECONOMIC, RELIGIOUS, AND SOCIAL ORGANIZATIONS

Some immigrants are likely to feel isolated and demoralized as a result of their move, but in the case of the Poles it is surprising that those who arrived first had sufficient self-confidence and initiative to establish a great variety of voluntary associations. By the 1890s later arrivals found a dense array of cooperative and self-help societies. Much of this rich organizational framework still exists today. It aided the immigrants to adjust to a new society and in time it provided the Polish-American community with a focus for its ethnic identity, since the group came to be defined largely in terms of its institutions.

This organizational structure, was, of course, common to many ethnic groups in the United States, but Polish regional and national associations were particularly strong. The assimilation of the third generation has arrested their growth, but they still represent a major aspect of ethnic life. Membership has declined in recent years, but the rate of decline has been notably slow and membership figures are not an accurate indication of the influence of these societies. Not everyone joined, particularly in the German Polish period, although almost everyone participated in at least some of their activities. It is also difficult to determine just how large the membership was, for not all the societies kept formal records and those that did might list only the dues-paying member and not his household.

The societies required organizational and managerial talent, and a surprising number of the immigrants seem to have possessed it. The early German Polish contingent had considerable intellectual and practical ability, and it was from this group that most of the early leadership was drawn. Immigrant letters recruited and guided most Polish immigrants, but the actual construction of social institutions was the work of the energetic and entrepreneurial figures already in the United States—saloonkeepers, priests, and merchants.

Anton Schermann of Chicago is an example of a model colony-builder: he is said to have "brought over" 100,000 Poles. Born in the district of Poznań in 1818, he came to Chicago with his wife and children in 1851, one of the city's first Slavic settlers, and, after working as a laborer, he opened a grocery store that soon became a social center for the city's growing Polish colony. It also sheltered the St. Stanislaus Society, which was organized to prepare for the establishment of the city's first Polish Catholic parish. For the next 40 years until his death in 1900, Schermann served the community in many capacities, as agent for other societies, and as counselor for individual group members who needed to make travel arrangements or to communicate with their Polish home districts. The Silesian Peter Kiołbassa, a friend of Schermann; Władysław Dyniewicz, the newspaper publisher from Chwalków in the Polish section of Germany; and the merchant Michael Majewski were other early leaders in Chicago. By the mid-1880s Chicago had become known as the American Warsaw. It had a population of 40,000 Poles, three-quarters of them from Germany. A tenth of them were surprisingly either skilled workers or professionals such as doctors, pharmacists, and priests.

Similar Polish-American communities resembling Chicago developed elsewhere. Wealthy businessmen Stanislaus Merlin and clothing merchant John Lemke from West Prussia helped organize the community in Detroit after their arrival in 1857 and 1858, and August Rudzinski, a former Poznań innkeeper, organized Polish Milwaukee after 1859. Organized ethnic life in all these places, even when it included the formation of a parish church, was usually directed by laymen. Only church life was in the hands of the clergy.

When a newcomer arrived, his first and most critical requirement was to find a job. His friends and relatives already established would inform him of openings. A Pennsylvania mineworker might write home that his employer needed more hands, or a company might encourage an employee to travel to Castle Garden or Ellis Island or even back to Europe to recruit friends and kin. Employers also used employment agencies to recruit laborers; most of these agencies dealt mainly in domestic service or gang labor. The community leader—the grocer or saloonkeeper—was usually a go-between, and in some cases his store or office became the labor exchange. However, the more exploitative *padrone*, or boss, system common among the Italians, Greeks, and others, had no real Polish counterpart.

The local grocer or saloonkeeper provided a clearinghouse and meeting place for a variety of other cooperative efforts as well. To guard against financial emergencies, a mutual fund was established to aid families through crises such as sickness, accident, or death; the collection was usually managed in a neighborhood saloon, grocery, or church. This early form of social insurance was later adapted to serve other ends, particularly the purchase of real estate. The grocer or innkeeper served not only as a guide and labor recruiter but also as a banker and insurance agent, steamship representative, letter writer, and dispatcher of money to Poland. His influence in the community was great. Much less frequently the local parish priest played a similar role. The most famous of the clerics, the Reverend Vincent Barzynski of the St. Stanislaus Church in Chicago, held $550,000 in deposits in 1890 and wielded great power over his parishioners.

Cooperative enterprise was not new to the Poles; it had some of its roots in their European experience, particularly in German Poland. There was considerable group cohesion evident among the Kashubes, who settled in Chicago around St. Josaphat's Church and on Jones Island in Milwaukee. The loan societies established by the German Poles to foil the anti-Polish land-buying schemes of the 1880s served as another precedent, and simple imitation of other immigrant groups was still another source of inspiration. At first, the earliest Polish immigrants often lived in German or Czech neighborhoods, where voluntary associations appropriate to the American scene had already been established. Some eventually organized separate local cooperative societies of their own; others simply never bothered and remained members of a Czech or German organization.

The purpose of these societies varied considerably. Some were designed only to ensure economic security; others to work for nationalist goals as well; still others to build a parish; a few to cultivate music and arts. Yet whatever their other objectives, almost all were working-class associations that provided social insurance and income protection.

The German period of Polish immigration produced an array of voluntary associations which, while frequently national in scope, were in fact congeries of many local associations. The major societies, then and now, were the Zjednoczenie Polskie-Rzymsko-Katolickie (Polish Roman Catholic Union) and the Związek Narodowego Polskiego (Polish National Alliance). The first was started in Detroit by the Reverend Theodore Gieryk in 1873 as a social-welfare organization, but it soon became a federation of associations dedicated to the preservation of Polish Catholic religious traditions. The Polish National Alliance was founded in 1880 as an association of 18 local nationalist clubs; many of its members were the refugees from the 1863 insurrection who had settled in cities across the country.

Another common type of association was the building-and-loan society. Most Poles, particularly those from Austria and Russia, had intended to earn enough to buy land in the Old World, but many changed their minds before long, decided to stay in the United States and began to buy homes in America instead of farms in Poland. Just when this cooperative building-and-loan society idea began among the Poles is unknown, but it certainly began early and spread everywhere. The first cooperative to be recorded was organized in 1881; by 1925, 550 societies had 400,000 members and $330 million in assets. Even these impressive statistics are low, for collections also took place informally, beyond state regulation, and there has never been a comprehensive survey. The neighborhood society was usually based on the parish. Its administration was democratic, its officers elected. The purpose was always the same: to accumulate a fund based on small, periodic contributions upon which members could draw eventually to purchase a home.

Devout Catholics at home, Polish immigrants were quick to establish parish churches in the United States. In most cities they developed from meetings of the local religious society in the local store or inn. The society was normally named for a favorite saint—Stanislaus, Adalbert, Hedwig, or Casimir—a name often given to the parish itself. The number of Polish ethnic parishes grew rapidly: from 17 in 1870 to 170 in 1890; from 390 in 1900 to 512 in 1910; from 760 in 1920 to a peak of approximately 800 in 1935, and falling to 760 in 1960.

The construction of a vast Polish Catholic institutional network based on lay cooperation in a society guided by the principle of the separation of church and state, combined with the Protestant congregational influence on laws concerning church ownership, led to strained relations between pastor and laity once parishes were under way. Especially before 1910 there was constant tension in many churches between the lay board and the priest over the control of parish holdings. This sort of controversy was new to the Poles, as priests in Europe had few administrative and money-managing duties. Only the most diplomatic pastor was able to survive the pressures of his bishop, on the one side, and his money-conscious parishioners, on the other. The tension occasionally erupted into violent disputes.

Similar conflicts between clerics and lay trustees occurred in other Catholic groups as well, but in an attenuated form. Among Poles it led a group of parishes to declare independence from the diocese—although not at first from Roman Catholicism—in 1894. Many of the dissidents were eventually excommunicated, and they retaliated by joining together in 1904 to form the independent Polish National Church. A dozen years later the Reverend Francis Hodur, the founding bishop, claimed 34 churches and 28,200 communicants. The Roman Catholic hierarchy attempted to alleviate the discontent when the Reverend Paul Rhode of Chicago was made a bishop in 1908, thus providing a measure of ethnic representation in the hierarchy. However, the Americanization policies of the hierarchy during World War I and the 1920s revived Polish clerical and lay protests. The demand for a more adequate representation of Polish Americans at top levels in the church remains a source of dispute to the present.

Despite this conflict, by 1900 Polish Catholicism had grown and matured; Polish religious institutions expanded and multiplied, especially after the founding of the two major orders. The Resurrectionist Fathers had arrived in Texas in 1866 from France. They and their first provincial superior, the Reverend Vincent Barzynski, established most of Chicago's Polish parishes before 1900, including a Polish high school, orphanage, hospital, and other institutions. An energetic Wisconsin priest, the Reverend Joseph Dąbrowski, sponsored the first order of Polish nuns, the Felician Sisters, in 1874; they staffed most of the group's parochial schools. In 1883 Father Dąbrowski organized the first Polish Catholic seminary in Detroit.

By the turn of the century the basic ethnic institutions were in place, and societies began to appear that were more ideological in character and guided by one of two philosophies—socialism on the one hand, and nationalism through physical fitness and military preparedness on the other. Similar to the German Turners and the Czech and Slovak Sokols (literally, falcons) begun in Europe and brought later to America, the original cell of Polish Falcons began within the Polish National Alliance (PNA) in 1886. By 1893 it had joined the other units to become the Związek Sokolów Polskich (Falcon Alliance) but it separated from the PNA in 1909

Table 1. Major Polish-American fraternal associations, 1873–1920.

Date organized	Name	Location
1873	Polish Roman Catholic Union	Chicago
1880	Polish National Alliance	Chicago
1888	Alliance of Polish Singers in America	Chicago
1889	Society of St. John Kanty	Philadelphia
1890	Polish Union in the United States of North America	Wilkes-Barre
1890	Polish Union	Buffalo
1890	St. Joseph Union	Pittsburgh
1893	Polish Roman Catholic Union in Bay City	Bay City, Mich.
1894	Polish Falcons of America	Chicago
1894	Polish Roman Catholic Association	Detroit
1895	Polish Association of America	Milwaukee
1896	Alliance of Polish Socialists	New York
1897	Polish Alma Mater	Chicago
1898	Polish Women's Alliance	Chicago
1903	Polish National Union of Brooklyn	Brooklyn
1908	Polish National Union	Scranton, Pa.
1920	Union of Polish Women	Philadelphia

Source: Poles of Chicago (Chicago, 1937), pp. 57–58; Miecislaus Szawleski, *Wychodztwo Polskie w Ameryce* (Lvov, 1924), chap. VII; Karol Wachtl, *Polonja w Ameryce* (Philadelphia, 1944), chap. VIII; and Lubomyr Wynar, comp., *Encyclopedic Directory of Ethnic Organizations in the United States* (Littleton, Colo., 1975), pp. 274–294.

and split into eastern and western branches. A similar nationalist body of middle-class women formed the Związek Polek (Polish Women's Alliance) in Chicago in 1898 from several clubs, the earliest of which had begun in Chicago in 1887. Originally a social insurance and nationalist organization, it was later to organize humanitarian projects in Poland, its most important function.

The socialist side was represented by the Związek Socjalistów Polskich (Alliance of Polish Socialists) organized in New York in 1896. This organization numbered no more than a few thousand, and its members were for the most part in the East, but it became more conspicuous after the 1904 revolution in Russian Poland which sent many left-wing exiles to America. The society soon split into factions, left and right, neither of which was able to agree on how to associate with non-Polish socialists in America.

Considering the apparent ease with which Poles joined together to work for their common interests, it might have been expected that they would also have organized or joined the then-burgeoning labor unions, since many needed job protection as well as social insurance. But in fact this form of collective action among Polish workers was relatively rare before the 1930s, probably because the unions also would have had to involve non-Polish workers if they were to be effective, and the U.S. labor movement was generally reluctant to organize the unskilled industries in which most of them worked. Labor leaders were not interested in recruiting non-English-speaking foreigners, and the American Federation of Labor in particular was cool to the recruitment of what it called "cheap" labor from eastern Europe and lobbied to restrict it. Several labor disputes in this period proved the militance and solidarity of Polish workers, but few American labor leaders appeared to be interested. That Polish immigrant workers could indeed be won to the union cause became

evident when efforts were made to organize them. When the United Mineworkers of America (UMW) organized the anthracite mines at the turn of the century, Polish support was an important source of UMW strength. They were also solid in demanding better conditions, occasionally even in the face of opposition by their own religious leaders, at the Bay View strike near Milwaukee in 1886, at Homestead, Pa., in 1892, in Buffalo in 1894, in Chicago in 1904, at McKees Rocks, Pa., in 1909, at Lawrence, Mass., and Paterson, N.J., in 1912–1913, and in the nationwide steel strike of 1919.

Voluntary associations among Polish professionals began to appear just before 1900. Polish doctors, lawyers, and teachers had immigrated earlier, and some had become quite prominent, but it was not until 1896 that they had the numbers to warrant an organization. In that year the Polish Medical Society was founded in Chicago; in 1908 Polish dentists formed their own society, the Association of Polish Dentists in America; in 1928 a second medical society, the Polish Medical and Dental Association of America, appeared. The lawyers organized in 1931 as the Polish Lawyers' Association.

The aims of many of the politically inspired fraternal societies began to change in the 1920s. Most continued their insurance features, which had been so important earlier, but Polish independence in 1918 led them to drop their nationalist goals and turn instead to sending aid to their homeland. The Polish National Alliance and others also began to emphasize U.S.-based activities rather than focusing on activities in Poland. The restrictive immigration legislation of the decade sharply reduced new arrivals, and the coming to adulthood of native-born Polish Americans, who took over the leadership of the associations, further encouraged a new focus.

Poles became more active in the labor unions, particularly in the automotive and steel industries which the Congress of Industrial Organizations (CIO) began to organize in the 1930s. In larger numbers than before they now began to join the ranks of organized labor. One Polish union organizer toured the mills and factories of the Midwest in the 1930s and was able to recruit many Polish Americans and enlist their support of strikes to improve conditions.

Another self-help organization in the interwar period was the regional ethnic association, a society that sought to preserve Polish culture in the United States and to aid particular Polish localities abroad. People from all the various regions of Poland had, of course, settled together in the Polish communities of America, but within these communities regional groups naturally gravitated to the same neighborhoods and churches and preserved their own traditions. In the 1920s they began to send help to their provincial friends and relatives overseas. To do so effectively, they soon discovered, they had to organize. The result was a series of nationwide federations, such as the Polish Highlanders' Alliance (f. 1927); the Alliance of Małopolski Clubs (f. 1929), which sent $550,000 to Poland in ten years; the Great Poland, Silesian, and Pomeranian Club (f. 1930); and the Polish Borderlands Educational and Protective Alliance (f. 1928). Of these, only the Małopolski Clubs are still in existence.

What impact the post–World War II political immigrants had upon the vast network of organized Polish

Table 2. Membership in selected Polish fraternal associations, 1924–1975.

Association	1924–25	1943	1955	1959	1975
Polish National Alliance (Chicago)	220,000	231,000[b]	338,000	338,000	317,352
Polish Roman Catholic Union (Chicago)	118,000	146,000[b]	175,000	170,000	129,525
Polish Women's Alliance (Chicago)	25,000	25,000	85,000	90,000	90,000
Polish National Union (Scranton, Pa.)	11,000	11,000	30,500	31,400	32,550
Polish Falcons (Pittsburgh)	12,000	10,000	20,400	22,300	28,100
Polish Union (Buffalo, N.Y.)	19,000	18,000	17,600	—	12,768
Polish Union (Wilkes-Barre, Pa.)	12,000	30,000	21,200	19,600	15,000
Polish National Alliance (Brooklyn, N.Y.)	9,000	16,000	20,700	20,000	· 15,400
Sons of Poland (Jersey City, N.J.)	—	15,000	17,200	16,900	18,000
Alliance of Poles (Cleveland)	7,000	12,000	15,000	15,800	17,000

Source: Joseph Wytrwal, *America's Polish Heritage* (Detroit, 1961), pp. 326–327; Miecislaus Haiman, *Zjednoczenie Polski Rzymsko-Katolickie w Ameryce* (Chicago, 1948), p. 541; W. Wnuk, "W Centrum Polonii," *Kronika* (Nov. 14, 1964), pp. 5–7; Lubomyr Wynar, comp., *Encyclopedic Directory of Ethnic Organizations in the United States* (Littleton, Colo., 1975), pp. 274–294.
a. 1945 figure.
b. 1941 figure.

societies is still a matter of speculation. For the most part people with considerable intellectual and occupational skills, they did not have the same need for the services of the fraternal associations as did the earlier peasant immigrants. Still, some émigrés joined these organizations simply because they provided a foothold and a culturally familiar setting. An increase in the number of upper-class members, the greater social mobility of the third generation of Polish Americans, and the recent resurgence of group consciousness among many ethnic groups all have increased the ability of these organizations to support cultural-preservation and educational projects.

Table 2 illustrates the fluctuation in membership and the assets of two of the chief societies over the years, along with the membership of several others. The salient feature is not so much the increase or decrease of members but the fact that the decline, which began in the 1950s, has been so slow. Membership has leveled off, while assets have continued to grow. Fraternalism clearly remains a vital part of Polish-American life. In 1912, for example, about 7,000 different societies totaled about 800,000 members; a short time later three-fourths of all Polish immigrants belonged to at least one organization, and even as recently as 1964 there were 4,000 Polish societies in Chicago.

FAMILY LIFE AND SOCIAL CONDITIONS

In the half-century between 1865 and World War I the Polish-American community remained strikingly homogeneous. Its social life, its working conditions, its socioeconomic level, and its spiritual needs were largely those of a working-class Roman Catholic society. Differences in regional background, a source of tension and conflict for other groups, were not disruptive enough to fragment Polish America. The values of the overwhelming majority were the same, and the Polish communities in the United States developed and prospered in similar ways, producing a rich and active cultural life. Only after World War II did the commu-

nity begin to split, because the most recent wave of middle-class immigrants had little in common with the majority of working-class Polish Americans.

Employment and Daily Life Originally the Poles were an agrarian people, ill at ease in an urban, commercial, and industrial milieu, and a good deal of this feeling has persisted. Perhaps the most fortunate immigrants were the few—between a fifth and a tenth—who were able to move directly into the countryside. But these were mainly the early-arriving German Poles who came when there was still an open frontier and a surplus of land. Later arrivals had to be content with industrial employment. Many took city jobs in order to buy a farm and some Polish-American industrial workers did manage to work their way out into the countryside. In the late 19th century there was something of a Polish exodus from cities to farms. Minnesota, Nebraska, and northern Wisconsin after 1860 and eastern Long Island and the Connecticut River Valley in the 1880s were filled with Polish immigrants looking for farm land. Some bought property outright; others first had to hire themselves out as farm laborers. The land they finally acquired was often not very productive, since the more fertile acreage had already been bought up by the earlier settlers.

The majority of Polish immigrants, however, never could leave their jobs in the factory or the mill. Instead they revised their goals, and in a sense brought the farm into the city. They purchased a small plot of ground with a house, or a lot on which to build a house, which required incredible thrift and the aid of the cooperative associations.

It was not easy for Polish immigrants without occupational skills to accumulate capital. Four-fifths of them in 1907 were unskilled laborers; the men were usually employed in the lowest-paying positions in coal mines, meatpacking factories, textile and steel mills, oil refineries, and garment-manufacturing shops. The pay was minimal, about $1.50 a day around 1900. Overall, the average annual income of the Pole was low, approximately $325 for men around 1910. The labor was

arduous; the hours long, normally ten or more daily; and the employment unsteady, at the whim of the business cycle or the season. On the whole, Polish workers enjoyed a good reputation with employers, in spite of their outside reputation as undependable, volatile, and prone to drunkenness. Employers valued their conscientiousness and stability as workers.

In the first months some kind of shelter at minimum cost was as necessary as employment. In heavily settled cities like Chicago and Detroit, Polish men without families could live initially in boarding houses run by Germans or Czechs. The Polish immigrants had their own term for the system, *trzymanie bortników* (boarder-keeping). The cost for the lodger varied in the early 1900s, from $2 to $3 a month, including laundry but excluding meals. In the more isolated areas, such as the Pennsylvania coalfields, where employers did not supply housing and there were few families, single men might occupy a common dwelling, with one of them acting as housekeeper. The boarding-house arrangement was frowned upon by many Americans as a threat to the chastity of the landlord's wife and daughters. Nonetheless, it suited both owner and tenant: one acquired additional income and influence; the other saved money.

The boarding system was most common in the early years. Once the immigrant began to consider his life in the United States as permanent he would marry, or send for his family and set up his own household. But whether single or married, his ability to save money was astonishing. In the Pennsylvania anthracite districts in 1884 the ordinary Polish mineworker was said to be saving around $135 a year. At about the same time Polish workers in South Chicago were earning about $25 a month and sending two-thirds of that back to Poland. Similar stories were reported about the Poles who lived in the farm districts of central Massachusetts about 1900.

The savings were put to a variety of purposes. The single Pole wanted to reunite his family in America. The amount of money Polish workers sent overseas eventually became so large that it worried both American and European authorities. Around 1910 it was estimated that about $40 million had been sent back to Austrian and Russian Poland from the United States. Galicia alone was supposed to be receiving $4 to $5 million per year—a sum, it was claimed, that the imperial postal system felt was a great burden to handle efficiently. And in the same period a small Russian-Polish district reported that almost $300,000 had been received. These huge remittances came to play a significant role in the economies of these hitherto impoverished provinces, and various imperial authorities openly discussed their implications. So did the United States Immigration Commission, a body appointed in 1907 to assess the impact of mass immigration. The commission, which was very unfavorably disposed toward the new immigrants, contended that the gigantic outflow of funds was weakening the American economy.

Whatever the truth of this claim, the system did help the immigrants to bring more of their countrymen to America. The number of families grew but the reassembling of kin did not terminate the intense efforts to save. Many were to comment on the anomaly of Polish families who had money in the bank but who apparently lived in dire poverty. When relatives arrived they were simply pressed into service. With an average of six children each in Chicago in 1890, the Polish immigrant family was a sizable earning and saving unit.

The pressing need for financial contributions by all its members modified, but did not transform, traditional family roles. Strong patriarchal control continued, particularly over the children and especially over the daughters. Married women worked at home to care for and supply the household needs of their husbands and offspring. When children went to work, parents made sure that the job conformed to customary family roles or was carried on close to home. Single girls were typically found in domestic service, either in private homes or in laundries, restaurants, or hotels—in other words, in work that was seen as providing practical experience for marriage. Whatever the job held by boys, girls, and the elderly, it was done near the workplace of the father so that even on the job, the working child was never far from the working parent. In the anthracite fields, young boys and older men were employed at nonmining tasks, and young women at nearby textile and garment-making factories. In the meat-packing industry in Chicago and elsewhere, girls worked near their men, either at the same plant doing the lighter, cleaner work in the packing, canning, or labeling sections, or at nearby local candy and tobacco factories. In some places Polish families were able to work as a unit, for example, as farm laborers in the Wisconsin cranberry bogs or as oyster shuckers in Baltimore.

Compensation remained minimal. Laboring under only slightly better conditions than their men, women and children earned much less money. Their average pay just before 1900 was little more than $3.00 a week, and much of the work was unsteady and seasonal. The average annual income just after 1900 for single Polish women was about $200 a year, but individual incomes fluctuated widely; many young women worked on a piecework rather than a wage basis.

The determined Polish practice of utilizing the labor of women and children antagonized reformers and union leaders, but despite substandard income it began to disappear after World War I. A 1920 survey found that less than 10 percent of the Polish families derived income from the labor of their children, and well over two-thirds were supported either by the male household head alone or by the head plus income from boarders. Wives rarely worked (most working females were unmarried), which helped maintain a stable family life. In any event, at this time the average Polish-American household income of parents and children was still low—only $1,440 a year, about $500 below what was considered the minimum necessary for an American family.

A closer look at the daily life in a Polish household shows what its economies entailed. In addition to taking in boarders, most families had a vegetable garden and even kept a cow, goat, or chickens, unless prevented by urban conditions. Their diet was simple: they ate cheap cuts of pork and beef, smoked fish, dark bread, their own vegetables, and other foods that were nutritious but scorned by others.

Their style of living did not please middle-class observers who particularly decried their habit of keeping

livestock around the house and their primitive and nondescript dwellings, but it enabled the Poles to continue to buy land and build on it. By 1887 Poles already owned about $10 million worth of real property. In 1900 the group held $500,000 worth of real estate in the heavily Polish mining town of Nanticoke, Pa., alone, and a total of $2.5 million in four towns in the region. By 1901 about one-third of the group in the United States owned real estate, with a total value of $600 million.

Furthermore, when the Polish working-class family purchased a home, it was not only a shelter but also another source of income. The structure was built or repaired in the most economical manner possible. In Milwaukee its typical form, dubbed "the Polish flat," was a small one-story frame building that over time would be raised from the ground to add living quarters for relatives, friends, or boarders. In Detroit the same sort of structure was placed at the far end of the lot so that other income-producing rooms or a front parlor could be added as funds permitted.

At the same time, however poor the immigrant household, it almost always allocated some funds to purchase a religious artifact, a homeland peasant custom. Usually it was a representation of the Black Madonna of Częstochowa, or the Holy Mother and Child, or a favorite saint. The family also willingly budgeted part of its meager income for the church itself. The contrast between the visible poverty of the parishioners and the extravagance lavished on church property often shocked non-Catholics. By 1914 the average value of each of the group's several hundred parishes, including the parish schools, was about $25,000, for a grand total of $70 million, even though most of the parishioners were common laborers. In the early 1920s about three-quarters of all Polish immigrants belonged to ethnic parishes, and most of the rest to other Catholic churches. Polish families took their spiritual obligations very seriously.

Education and Cultural Activities Because priority was given to real-estate purchases and church contributions, little money was available for educating the young, particularly in the years before 1940. It was the custom to have large families, and more children represented more wage earners, but this was a function children could not perform if they attended school. As a result most Polish parents were reluctant to see their children through high school, much less college. A basic education up to the age of confirmation was normally felt to be sufficient; the immigrant child was expected to go to work even before finishing grammar school. Although authorities probably enforced school-attendance laws more effectively after the 1930s, the practical view of education for employment persisted in most Polish families. It strained traditional family relationships, for it was difficult to remain a docile and dutiful offspring while at the same time preparing for and performing the functions of a self-reliant and independent worker.

The Poles at least did not neglect the early years of education. Almost as soon as the neighborhood was formed, the community would make arrangements for parish instruction. And in time this chiefly working-class group was supporting a sizable educational plant. By 1911 there were 300 schools in the Polish-American

parochial system; by the end of World War II the number had doubled. In addition, 15,000 students were attending Polish parochial high schools and several colleges, including St. Mary's College and SS. Cyril and Methodius Seminary at Orchard Lake, Mich., and Alliance College in Cambridge Springs, Pa. But the system existed more to perpetuate the Polish Catholic religion than for secular education. Full-time attendance was minimal, the quality of instruction was apt to be low, and many schools were overcrowded. As a result, despite the group's strong religious commitment, before World War I at most only half the Polish school-age youth attended parochial schools, about one-third in 1940, and less than a tenth by the late forties.

Limited interest in and opportunities for the education of the young were not problems unique to Polish families; before World War II formal education at the secondary and college level was rare among the children of most U.S. working-class families. Nor did the deficient Polish school system—in 1948 there were no schools in one-third of the Polish ethnic parishes—mean that opportunities for Polish cultural enrichment were lacking. Cultural activities in the Polish-American community after 1900, especially between 1920 and 1940, were numerous. The Polish press, though often utilitarian. commercial, or political in intent, nonetheless contributed to ethnic culture by encouraging the maintenance of the Polish language and by publishing literary works: the news was always accompanied by novels, short stories, and poems. The year 1863 marked the appearance of the first of the Polish newspapers, *Echo z Polski* (Echo from Poland, New York); the tradition continued with journals such as the clerical *Orzeł Polski* (Polish Eagle, Washington, Mo., f. 1870) and *Dziennik Chicagoski* (f. 1890), the nationalist *Zgoda* (Harmony; Milwaukee, Chicago, f. 1881), the fiery *Kuryer Polski* of Milwaukee (f. 1888), the very popular, independent *Ameryka-Echo* of Toledo (f. 1889), the socialist *Dziennik Ludowy* (People's Daily, Chicago, f. 1907), and the Kashubian *Wiarus* (Old Faithful, Winona, Minn., f. 1886).

These journals were often regarded as sensational and vulgar, and inferior to their European counterparts, and it is true that specifically literary periodicals among the group were both rare and invariably short-lived. Yet whatever its quality, the press was certainly popular. In 1923 when the Polish-American journals were at their height, at least 19 dailies, 67 weeklies, and 18 monthlies were in circulation. Five hundred had appeared by 1930, though after that the numbers began to decline. The newspaper was more popular than the immigrant literacy rate of about 70 percent might indicate; nonreaders could have journals read to them either at home or in the group's numerous social centers, the local tavern, a retail establishment in the smaller neighborhoods, in the community halls, or the *Dom Polski* (Polish Home) of the larger settlements. The Dom Polski was an important center of cultural activities in the metropolitan areas; the best known of them was in Buffalo. Built by Polish nationalists to propagate nationalist ideology, they usually included a library (*biblioteka*), an auditorium for lectures and dramatic productions, and sometimes a gymnasium or a bar. Musical, artistic, and dramatic clubs often presented their work in these halls.

Along with the press, the parish provided a local focus for the cultivation of the arts. The pastor and the parish organist encouraged and organized the aesthetic interests of the parishioners. The organist was the parish musician, and it was his task to train the choir, but frequently he presented concerts of secular and folk music as well. Singing ensembles emerged as early as the 1870s from the choirs of the larger Polish churches, bearing names like Harmonia, Lutnia, and Chopin. One of the first, begun in Chicago in 1879, became the national Polish Singers' Alliance ten years later; Anthony Mallek, choir director of Holy Trinity Church, was its conductor for 25 years.

In time, some of these musical groups broadened their scope to include dramatic performances, and parish theatrical companies were also organized. The first Polish amateur drama group performed in Chicago at St. Stanislaus Church in 1891. By World War I the standards of the dramatic productions were unusually high, thanks largely to the frequent visits and participation of professional actors and actresses, like the distinguished Madame Helena Modjeska, who came from the old country to tour Polish-American communities. The war itself encouraged these theatrical organizations; performances were often benefits to raise money for the homeland. Folk art was widely maintained, but outstanding formal artists were rare. The best known of the Polish professional artists was the illustrator and mask maker, Wladyslaw Benda (1872–1948).

Between 1920 and 1940 there was a decline in the quality of players, and plays became shorter and more popular. This somewhat inferior interwar theater was commercially more successful, however, so ethnic drama remained secure, with permanent companies in several larger cities, notably Chicago, Detroit, and Milwaukee. The young also began to display a marked interest in Polish-American literature. After 1920 a conscious effort to revive folk art inspired numerous folk festivals, usually sponsored by social agencies known as international institutes; these were meant to increase the appreciation of America's pluralistic cultural heritage among the general public. The Milwaukee Polish Fine Arts Club (f. 1930) grew out of one such effort. Art, music, and drama were areas of activity that new post-World War II middle- and upper-class immigrants and the older working-class immigrants could support together, and many local cultural organizations were revived through the influence of the new arrivals. A national organization, the American Council of Polish Cultural Clubs, celebrated its silver jubilee in 1973. Other agencies also fostered Polish culture in America: since 1908 the People's University movement, which has sponsored lectures and discussions about socialism; the Kosciuszko Foundation, founded in 1926 by Stefan Mierzwa with some non-Polish help; the Polish Institute of Arts and Sciences in America, founded (under a different name) in 1940; its offshoot, the Polish American Historical Association (f. 1942); the Polish Museum in Chicago; and the Pilsudski Institute.

Survival of Traditions Most of this institutional patronage has gone to the fine arts and to intellectual activities rather than to folk culture. Except for the folk fairs of the 1920s and the proliferating folk-dance troupes of more recent years, encouragement of handicrafts and the popular arts has been slight. Neverthe-

less, largely because of its intimate ties with church practice, Polish Americans have continued to preserve a few customs, especially those connected with religious and family rituals. The Christmas Eve meal, called Wigilia, has its ritual at which a wafer is broken, and Easter is an occasion for cleaning house, celebrating, and blessing a festive meal, all symbolizing renewal. Weddings, christenings, and picnics, which frequently include a good deal of drinking, dancing, and card playing, are other occasions for renewing old customs. Weddings have become more modest than the traditional three-day European celebrations; they were reduced to two days in the immigrant period, and now often take place in the bride's home or a rented hall. The polka and mazurka were, of course, the favorite dances at these affairs and at general social meetings. The polka remains popular even beyond Polish-American circles today. Funerals were occasions for emotional display in the earlier period and were not simple manifestations of grief. They, too, had their particular ostentatious ceremony, and even in recent years have become only slightly more restrained.

In the 1920s the Polish diet also began to change considerably with an increased consumption of meat, especially smoked pork sausage, along with the traditional beans, cabbage, dark bread, potatoes, barley, and oatmeal. Health, too, improved as the use of home remedies, the delivery of children by midwives, and the distrust of hospitals declined, though Poles continued to favor Polish doctors. The rude homes of the immigrant era also acquired certain amenities: indoor plumbing, carpets, and decorative furniture.

The degree to which ethnic ritual and traditions were maintained in Polish-American homes may have been surprising to observers in the 1930s, but it was likely the result of the essentially static socioeconomic condition of the group then and even down to the present. Despite the influx of recent middle- and upper-class refugees over the last half-century, the basic group profile has changed little, showing only a very modest, and recent, shift upward in occupational level. Like all the working class, the Polish-American worker is heavily dependent upon industrial prosperity, and the Depression struck him hard—many in the auto, steel, and meat-packing industries were laid off. Some survived on the income of working women and children or by leaving the city to work as farm hands. At this time many Poles hurriedly became citizens, spurred by the belief that citizenship would help them find jobs and make them eligible for public relief programs. The immigrant boarding house was also revived.

The World War II years put many Polish-American family heads back to work. A 1969 survey indicates some modest upward movement of first-, second-, and third-generation Polish Americans since then, though the majority are still just below or solidly at the middle-class level at best. Forty-five percent of Polish-American males who are working have white-collar jobs, and another quarter are skilled workers. The remaining 30 percent are either semiskilled or unskilled laborers. Almost 40 percent of Polish-American working women are in the latter category. Only 16 percent of the group has attended college. In income, Poles are clustered in the lower-middle-class bracket. Eighty percent of their incomes fall between $4,000 and $15,000, just about

the national average, and very few fall very far either below or above that range. The outlook for the 1980s is brighter; younger Polish-American generations do hold white-collar positions far more often than their predecessors did.

ETHNIC POLITICS

About 3 million Poles have come to America in the last century, and the Poles comprise one of the leading ethnic groups today. Their size and their heavy concentration in a very few urban settlements (over 80 percent of the nearly 6 million or so live in nine industrial states) might lead one to expect them to play a prominent role in American public affairs, but in fact the record shows otherwise. Until recently relatively few have been active in local politics, and even fewer have become state or federal officials. A handful have been elected to the House of Representatives, chiefly from those districts of extremely heavy group concentration, such as Chicago, Milwaukee, and Buffalo, but only in recent years. The group can claim just one senator, Edmund S. Muskie of Maine, and even his Polish affiliation is rather tenuous since he has vigorously disclaimed ethnic ties, is not married to a Pole, and speaks for a constituency in which there are very few Polish Americans. In Chicago, where they made up 12 percent of the city's population and were the largest foreign-born ethnic group in the city, they did not elect a Polish-American congressman until 1920. The first Polish-American congressman was a Milwaukee Republican in 1918.

There are several explanations for this low level of political participation. Initially language was a serious handicap and the rate of naturalization was also low, because the majority regarded themselves as sojourners rather than settlers. Then, too, they were preoccupied with private and group concerns, obtaining property, building institutions, and supporting the church. Achieving prominence in the American political system has not been a major objective, although political success is beginning to assume a place of greater importance for third- and fourth-generation Polish Americans.

The lack of success in gaining office does not mean that Polish Americans have been politically apathetic. They have been ready to exert pressure when the needs of the homeland required it. Since the late 1880s they have also supported steadfastly, although not exclusively, the Democratic party. The recent ethnic revival has led to further political mobilization in Polish communities.

Before World War I Polish Americans were concerned with the reconstruction of an independent Poland, although in the early years it was mostly political émigrés who sought to rally and enlighten the masses to build the new state. These immigrant patriots formed cells or "nests" from which they organized demonstrations for Poland on special occasions, such as the Columbian Exposition of 1893, on the centennial of the 1794 insurrection or at the unveiling of a Kosciuszko or Pulaski monument. They founded the Polish National Alliance in 1880 with that aim in mind, although those who joined did so as much for the mutual aid it offered as for the support of the nationalist cause.

Although the church and the nationalist leaders had split over nationalism around 1900, as time went on both joined to arouse the rank and file to greater national-ethnic consciousness. The appointment of the first Polish-American bishop in 1908, the 1910 unveiling of the Kosciuszko and Pulaski statues in Washington; and the formation of an all-inclusive Committee of National Defense in 1912 (it later fragmented, but clerics and nationalists remained together) did much to heal the rift. During World War I the Polish Americans demonstrated their widespread support for a new Poland by the number of their young men who enlisted in the American army, by the $250 million they lent in the form of Liberty Bonds, and by endorsing the financial and moral appeals of the pianist-patriot Ignace Paderewski, later to become independent Poland's premier in 1919.

Nonetheless, whatever the reason, Poles rarely ran for political office. In elections, whether in rural or urban areas, the Democratic party was virtually always the beneficiary of the Polish vote; a tiny minority of nationalists were the only Republicans.

The achievement of Polish independence, combined with the decline of Polish inner-city neighborhoods when many Poles began to move to the suburbs in the 1920s, left little to keep them together politically, but in 1928 they were particularly enthusiastic supporters of Al Smith, who as a Roman Catholic opposed to Prohibition was seen as a person who could be counted on to protect them from Protestant evangelism. The devastating economic effects of the Depression made them even more fervent supporters of the Democratic New Deal. But by the 1930s the Chicago-based Polish American Democratic Organization (PADO) had had enough of depending upon non-Polish officeholders, and led by Matt Szymczak and Judge Edmund K. Jarecki began to seek political recognition and power. They provided overwhelming majorities for Franklin D. Roosevelt (more than 80 percent in 1944), and were rewarded with a considerable share of federal patronage.

The invasion of Poland in 1939 by Germany and the Soviet Union renewed interest in international affairs and the homeland. Several organizations mobilized to offer aid. The fraternal associations united to form the Polish American Council. Simultaneously, the pro-Soviet American Slav Congress, largely Polish American in membership, was organized in 1942 under the leadership of the labor organizer Leo Krzycki, while a right-wing and much larger National Committee of Americans of Polish Descent soon opposed it, charging that the United States and Great Britain were violating the principles of the Atlantic Charter by accepting the Soviet Union's alteration of the Polish eastern boundary.

Polish Americans were aroused to more vigorous action after the discovery of the bodies of over 4,000 Polish officers massacred in the Katyn Forest, and the notable coolness of President Roosevelt toward the Polish government-in-exile in London. A meeting in 1944 in Buffalo led to the founding of a new federation of Polish organizations. The major aim of the Polish American Congress was to secure Polish independence in Europe; a subsidiary objective was to improve the status of Polish Americans in the United States. It began a lengthy campaign in opposition to the Yalta and Potsdam agreements that set in place the new pro-Soviet Polish Com-

munist state. The small minority of left-wing Polish-American leaders in the American Polish Labor Council and the American Slav Congress who continued to support the Soviet Union's Polish policy seemed to disappear as anti-Communist hysteria in the United States increased in the late forties and fifties.

In the 1940s Polish-American leaders again became prominent in public affairs, this time participating in a vigorous and pervasive anti-Communist campaign. In addition to its political work the Polish American Congress also helped to resettle the many Polish refugees who were fleeing the Communist regime. Lately, with the easing of the cold war and the general international recognition of the post-World War II boundaries, PAC work is emphasizing U.S. domestic issues; the organization is now trying to build up Polish-American voting power.

Polish Americans, despite their criticism of Roosevelt's actions at Yalta, seem to have retained their traditional partisan affiliation. They continue to vote heavily Democratic in national elections, although more recently as part of the party's center or right wing. Polish Americans have endorsed substantially all recent Democratic presidential candidates. John F. Kennedy's Catholic affiliation helped him win over 80 percent of their vote in 1960, and later Democratic candidates have been only slightly less popular.

GROUP MAINTENANCE AND
INTERGROUP RELATIONS

Many Americans of Polish descent have retained very little in the way of ethnic tradition, yet still regard themselves as Polish. Determining ethnic affiliation statistically is consequently difficult. One fairly reliable gauge of individual ethnic commitment is the extent to which ethnic group institutions, fraternal associations, parishes, and ethnic publications are supported. Many of those founded during the major period of Polish immigration in the late 19th and early 20th centuries still exist, so the Polish ethnic community remains an organized, viable, although transformed, subculture. Assimilation and acculturation have taken place; many among the later generations do not think of themselves as Polish any longer, and others who call themselves Polish Americans or Americans of Polish descent do so with differing ideas of what they think these terms mean. Polish ethnicity has experienced several transformations since the mid-1880s. There was first a rise of ethnic consciousness, then a period of Polish nationalism, a period of Americanization, and finally the present unstable era that combines self-doubt and group assertiveness.

Until the 1900s the ethnic consciousness of most Polish immigrants was low. In the early years they either assimilated or identified themselves according to locality or region. The few intellectuals and some of the German Poles were clearly nationalist and worked for the nationalist cause in America, but the majority had little occasion to reflect much about their affiliations. If they were anything they were Kashubes, Silesians, or Górali rather than Poles.

Living and working with non-Polish immigrants caused some people to become aware that they were different as a national group. National consciousness did not fully awaken, however, until early in the 1870s on Chicago's North Side and more dramatically in all Polish-American communities in the mid-1890s. It grew out of the tension that developed between the nationalists and the clericalists, an argument that began among the elite but quickly spread to the rank and file and frequently resulted in neighborhood violence. Before the conflict could be resolved all Polish Catholics had to decide whether they were Catholic first and Polish second, or whether their primary allegiance was nationalist or ethnic.

Fortunately the schism did not last long. When the Catholic church elevated Bishop Rhode to the hierarchy in 1908, he immediately demonstrated to Poles and non-Poles alike that he was a spirited representative of Polish nationalism in America, and satisfied many nationalists by mobilizing Polish Americans to help restore the homeland. The American Catholic hierarchy sanctioned Polish nationalism in America by allowing the ethnic community to become more nationalistic. When the new, more widespread Polish-American patriotism on behalf of Poland led to the formation in 1912 of the Committee of National Defense, this new church attitude enabled the committee to include both Catholics and nationalists.

At the same time, however, loyalty to the United States was also increasing. Although Polish speakers and writers made frequent reference to Kosciuszko and Pulaski as American as well as Polish heroes, there had been little sign of American patriotism among the Poles before 1914. During World War I Polish Americans supported Poland clearly as Americans, not as Poles, which came as something of a surprise. The substantial Polish-American funds offered to the European Poles were earmarked for relief and not for arms; the Poles endorsed the several American Liberty Loan drives with enthusiasm, and for the most part they enlisted in the U.S. Army, not the Polish Legion in Canada or in France. Moreover, the number of U.S. Poles who returned to independent Poland at the war's end and in the early 1920s was surprisingly small—tens of thousands—while millions remained in the United States. Some evidence suggests that even those who did go back did so more as Americans than as Poles; they went to rebuild the old country as a replica of the "land of Washington," to reproduce the U.S. economy and its political stability. They returned to the homeland as American missionaries.

Another indication of assimilation in the 1920s lay in the more vigorous assertions of autonomy by Polish Americans with respect to the homeland. In 1924 the group's largest fraternal association refused full membership rights to Polish citizens. Although the ethnic community assimilated more slowly than some have claimed, certainly defections occurred. The use of Polish was declining—Polish-language newspapers, for example, were beginning to have English sections. Technological innovations like the movies, radio, and the automobile helped the Americanization process. In a survey in Buffalo in the mid-1920s researchers found that social mobility and the acquisition of consumer goods were almost always accompanied by abandonment of ethnic traditions. Still, acculturation was not total, and certain customs persisted.

The Great Depression sharply limited the process of

assimilation. It blocked social mobility, especially among industrial workers. Polish Americans were no longer leaving the old working-class neighborhoods for the suburbs—in fact some suburbanites were forced back into the ethnic ghetto. The slowing of the assimilation process had an unsettling effect on families, as the gap widened between parents embittered toward the vaunted American values and children who readily accepted the new technology, the English language, and the norms of the majority culture.

Whatever the reasons for the decline in the maintenance of Polish culture in America, it has continued, as the language disappears and distinctive religious practices and folk traditions vanish. But the Polish-American community still exists—albeit with fewer, though still visible, social institutions—and people still identify themselves as ethnic-group members. They may have much in common with others of the same socioeconomic level outside the Polish community, but the feeling that they are Polish Americans still persists.

Recent sociological studies have related the assimilation of the group rather closely to generation, while still suggesting that the entire process is neither linear nor general but erratic and complex. Ethnic change among Los Angeles Poles, for example, has vacillated over three generations—children and grandchildren assimilated rapidly, but ethnic identity actually has revived among the great-grandchildren of immigrants. Even among the two "less Polish" generations, some customs have persisted. Polish Americans in Milwaukee also maintain group loyalty, although this is primarily true of older generations with ties to Poland or to Polish ethnic institutions. While preliminary findings concerning Polish-American marriage patterns suggest a high rate of marriage outside the group compared to other Catholic Americans, the partners are for the most part other east European Catholics. Evidence indicates an abandonment of certain Polish cultural habits, but for a significant number that does not mean the disappearance of ethnic-group identity.

Loss of language is another indication of assimilation, and Polish Americans seem to lose command of their mother tongue at a somewhat slower rate than most other groups. Of 23 foreign groups in the 1940–1960 period, Poles ranked eighth in language retention. In a survey of children of prominent Polish ethnic leaders, nearly 20 percent spoke Polish regularly, compared with only 9 percent of the Germans, on the one hand, and half of the Ukrainians, on the other. A major tool for language maintenance was instruction in the Polish Catholic parochial schools.

How have Polish Americans gotten along with other elements in the society? Can the persistence of their ethnicity be traced to hostility toward them? Or have relations been generally harmonious or indifferent? Arriving at an answer is difficult, partly because little research has been done on the subject and partly because contact has involved so many groups. Not the least of the problems are the emotions involved. Poles have frequently been accused of hostility toward blacks, Jews, and even other Catholics.

Over the years this largely working-class minority, suffering from all that this status entails in any middle-class society, has had occasionally hostile, frequently indifferent, and sometimes friendly relations with other groups. Certainly no specifically anti-Polish demonstrations have occurred to compare with anti-Mexican or anti-Asian riots in the Far West. Poles have been attacked in labor disputes, but more often as strikers or strikebreakers than as Poles.

On the neighborhood level the closest contacts have been with Lithuanians, Czechs, and Germans, groups with whom Poles were familiar in Europe. There were some early difficulties, but relations were usually cordial. Friction did arise with Lithuanians in Pennsylvania in the 1870s and the 1880s, when they tried to establish separate parish communities, but these were isolated instances.

Contacts with Germans and Czechs in America were surprisingly harmonious considering the tensions that characterized their relations in Europe. Since the Germans and Czechs came earlier, they helped cushion the cultural shock for many Polish immigrants, who settled in their communities and learned from them how to construct their own ethnic institutions. Another group whom the Poles knew well overseas were the east European Jews. If there was considerable anti-Semitic feelings among the Polish peasants in Europe and if it did continue in America, it did not manifest itself in any dramatic way. Jewish merchants did business in Polish-American neighborhoods and isolated examples of hostility must have occurred, but most Polish Jews melted into the larger Jewish-American community, and they did not normally compete with Catholics for jobs. Except in garment manufacturing, Poles and Jews generally labored at different tasks in different industries so their paths rarely crossed at the workplace.

Relations with the upper levels of Catholic society were more strained for Polish Americans, especially before the 1920s. Irish- and German-American church leaders occasionally sought a speedier assimilation than Polish-American leaders and clergymen would accept. However, it is an oversimplification to ascribe the rise of Polish ethnic aggressiveness and the National Catholic movement solely to such pressures.

Until recently the Poles have not been outspoken in expressing resentment toward the general low esteem in which they are held by the American majority. The stereotype widely shared by many non-Poles and given currency in "Polish" jokes is that of a group which is simple, uncultured, unintelligent, and racist.

The subject of Polish-black relations has been studied both by historians and by sociologists. No particularly Polish ethnic hostility toward nonwhites seems to exist. Poles and blacks did compete for jobs in heavy industry, and occasionally conflict resulted when blacks replaced immigrants at plants as strikebreakers. But just as often Poles viewed nonwhites as innocent pawns of employers.

Polish-black friction has erupted in the neighborhoods where, as in Chicago, Poles have been more reluctant than others to move to the suburbs. Instead they have remained in their Polish enclaves, and these are often by now surrounded by nonwhite neighborhoods. This does result in tension, but where it exists it seems to reflect the attitude of many white Americans, and has no particularly Polish content.

A reaction to the denigration of Polish Americans can be seen in the rise of ethnic spokesmen. Among the more articulate of them is Representative Barbara Mi-

kulski, a Democrat elected to Congress from Baltimore in 1976. She has condemned the melting-pot ideology that has dominated much of American life, insisting that Polish Americans along with other eastern and southern European and nonwhite groups have been the victims of economic and social discrimination, which she believes can be remedied by vigorous political action to assure a national commitment to cultural pluralism. Some pressure has been exerted to force federal policy and educational institutions to emphasize the values of diversity. Representative Mikulski and others have yet to mobilize the group politically in any major way—they do not appear to be voting as a bloc to a greater extent than they ever did. However, federal appropriations do seem to reflect the demands of these new ethnic spokesmen, and the traditional Polish organizations and group leaders are supporting their objectives more assertively.

A leading Polish congressman in the early 1970s, Representative Roman Pucinski of Chicago, with the encouragement of various ethnic group representatives, initiated and guided the passage of the Ethnic Heritage Studies Program legislation in 1974. (*See* Ethnic Heritage Studies Program.) His sponsorship suggests a new trend in Polish-American affairs as the community improves its use of communications media. Responding in part to constituent pressure, Polish leaders now appear to be doing a better job of articulating the sentiments of the group to those outside it. The election in October 1978 of a Polish pope has instilled ethnic pride among Poles worldwide. It is likely that spokesmen in politics, literature, and the arts will be expressing Polish-American attitudes more clearly than they once did, providing the wider American public with a more sensitive understanding of their needs and goals.

Bibliography
Most of the best descriptions of the Polish group appear in studies published at the end of the period of mass migration. See, for example, Felix Seroczynski, "The Poles in the United States," in the *Catholic Encyclopedia*, 15 vols. (New York, 1911), vol. 12, pp. 204–212; Paul Fox, *The Poles in America* (1922; reprint, New York, 1970); Wenceslaus Kruszka, *Historya Polska w Ameryce*, 13 vols. (Milwaukee, 1905–1908); and Mieczyslaw Szawleski, *Wychodźtwo Polskie w Stanach Zjednoczonych Ameryki* (Lvov, 1924). The most enduring perceptions about Polish immigrants come from Emily Greene Balch's classic, *Our Slavic Fellow Citizens* (1910; reprint, New York, 1969).

Attempts at synthesis are largely subjective; for example, William I. Thomas and Florian Znaniecki, *The Polish Peasant in Europe and America*, 2 vols. (Boston, 1918–1920); Joseph Wytrwal, *America's Polish Heritage* (Detroit, 1961); and Helena Z. Lopata, *Polish Americans: Status Competition in an Ethnic Community* (Englewood Cliffs, N.J., 1976).

The most reliable statistical coverage is in Walter F. Willcox, ed., *International Migrations*, 2 vols. (New York, 1929–1931), vol. 1, and Jerzy Zubrzycki, *Polish Immigrants in Britain* (The Hague, 1956). Emigrant motivation and objectives are examined in Celina Bobinska and Andrzej Pilch, eds., *Employment-Seeking Emigrations of Poles World Wide in the 19th and 20th Centuries* (Cracow, Poland, 1975), and Caroline Golab, *Immigrant Destinations* (Philadelphia, 1977).

Several other recent studies of particular segments of the Polish-American past are Victor R. Greene, *The Slavic Community on Strike: Immigrant Labor in Pennsylvania Anthracite* (Notre Dame, Ind., 1968), and *For God and Country: The Rise of Polish and Lithuanian Ethnic Consciousness in America, 1860–1910* (Madison, Wis., 1975); Daniel Buczek, *Immigrant Pastor* (Waterbury, Conn., 1974); Edward Kantowicz, *Polish-American Politics in Chicago, 1888–1940* (Chicago, 1975); Harriet Pawlowska, ed., *Merrily We Sing: 105 Polish Folksongs* (Detroit, 1961); Sula Benet, *Songs, Dance and Customs of Peasant Poland* (New York, 1951); and Neil Sandberg, *Ethnic Identity and Assimilation* (New York, 1974).

The best reference works remain Francis Bolek, ed., *Who's Who in Polish America* (1943; reprint, New York, 1970); Jan Wepsiec, *Polish American Serial Publications, 1842–1966* (Chicago, 1968); and Joseph Zurawski, *Polish American History and Culture* (Chicago, 1975). The major archives are the Polish Museum of Chicago and the Immigration History Research Center at the University of Minnesota. There are smaller collections at St. Mary's College of Orchard Lake, Mich.; the Polish National Alliance Library in Chicago; Alliance College, Cambridge Springs, Pa.; and the Kosciuszko Foundation in New York City.
                                                              VICTOR GREENE

POLISH TATARS: *see* TATARS

POLITICS

Because the United States has always been a highly diverse, pluralistic society, differences among ethnic groups have shaped much of the pattern of American political history. Voters often make political choices as part of such a group, choosing candidates who favor their group and opposing those who threaten it. Groups tend to make the same kinds of choices in one election after another; thus, group patterns form the basis of political party loyalty. Traditionally, economic class and geographic section have been considered the major factors in establishing group voting patterns; but in the last 25 years, however, historians and political scientists have begun to realize that issues arising out of ethnic, cultural, and religious values can be just as real to voters as matters based on class or section.

VOTING PATTERNS

From the 1820s and 1830s, when universal white male suffrage was established in the United States, until the Great Depression a century later, ethnic and religious differences tended to be the most important determinants of political party loyalties. Mass immigration throughout this century accentuated as well as exacerbated differences among groups; widespread suffrage gave free play to the intense emotions aroused. After the cessation of mass immigration in the 1920s, ethnic and religious differences played a diminished but still substantial role in politics. From the beginning of mass suffrage in the 1820s, ethnic groups in the United States diverged in their attitudes toward such culturally explosive issues as prohibition, sabbath observance, public schooling, immigration, slavery, and women suffrage. These issues tended to sort out groups along a political spectrum. Whether a group was pietist or dogmatist in religion, for instance, seems to have made a difference in its political stance. Pietism is a religious impulse in Protestantism that rejects formalism, elaborate ritual, and intellectualism in theology and stresses the techniques of revivalism. The religious opposites of the pietists, in both the Protestant and the Catholic traditions, emphasize formal theology, dogma, and ritual. Pietists insist upon right behavior; dogmatists right belief. In politics, the more pietistic and revivalistic a religious group, the more likely it was to vote Whig (before 1854) or Republican (since 1854). Conversely, the more dogmatic and ritualistic the religious group, the more likely it was to vote Democratic. This pietist-dogmatist dichotomy, however, fails to explain why such highly pietistic groups as Southern Methodists and Southern Baptists have been strong Democrats since the 1850s.

A slightly different interpretation is based on an in-

sider-outsider dichotomy. The closer an ethnoreligious group was to the Yankee Protestant mainstream—that is, the more "inside" it was in cultural terms—the more likely it was to vote Whig or Republican. The more alienated from the mainstream—the more "outside" a group was—the more likely it would be to vote Democratic. While this criterion helps explain the southern Democrats, who felt like outsiders during and after the Civil War crisis, it, too, admits some glaring exceptions. For example, American blacks have probably been the most oppressed outsiders in society, yet they were among the staunchest of Whig-Republican voters until the New Deal years.

Perhaps the best way to distinguish the ethnic constituencies of the two political parties is to examine each group's cultural expectations of government. Groups desiring a morally activist government, one that would intervene to impose moral standards on society, have traditionally favored the Whigs or Republicans. Groups indifferent to or threatened by a morally active government, who instead favored a laissez-faire or hands-off attitude on cultural issues, supported the Democrats. Pietist Yankee insiders therefore upheld the Whig-Republican tradition in order to advance prohibitionist, sabbatarian ideas; blacks supported the same tradition in hopes of a morally activist position on slavery and black rights. Catholics, Lutherans, and other dogmatists supported the Democrats in order to ensure a hands-off attitude on religious issues; so, too, did white Southern pietists to ensure a hands-off attitude on racial issues. A sample political spectrum of selected 19th-century groups might read as follows:

Strongly Whig-Republican:
    Blacks
    Scotch-Irish
    Quakers
    Swedish Lutherans

Moderately Whig-Republican:
    Yankees
    English
    British Canadians
    German sectarians

Moderately Democratic:
    Dutch Reformed
    German Lutheran
    German Reformed

Strongly Democratic:
    French Canadians
    German Catholics
    Irish Catholics
    Southern whites

These ethnocultural attitudes and the political loyalties they engendered remained fairly stable throughout the 19th century and at least until the Great Depression and the New Deal of the 1930s. Andrew Jackson and his followers were recognized as the secular party, the party of live-and-let-live attitudes. Jacksonian Democrats dodged and compromised on the slavery issue, they opposed local prohibition laws, they ran the federal mail trains on Sunday, they proposed no changes in the policy of unrestricted immigration, and in some states they favored voting rights for noncitizens. The Whigs were the Protestant party. Their members not only ad-

vocated moral reform causes, but they were constantly tempted by third-party and secret-society enthusiasms. In the 1840s both the antislavery Liberty party and the various native-American parties that made up the Know-Nothing movement, which was antagonistic to immigrants and Catholics, drew supporters from the Whigs.

In the 1850s three powerful cultural movements converged and reshaped the party system. A strong temperance movement took the 1851 Maine prohibition law as a model; the Know-Nothings gained strength as nativist organizations called for restrictions on the Irish and German Catholic immigrants flooding in at mid-century; and the passage of the Kansas-Nebraska Act in 1854 reopened the issue of slavery in the territories, aggravating the sectional hostility between North and South that ultimately resulted in the Civil War. These enthusiasms—temperance, nativism, and anti-Southernism—drew voters away from the Whigs into newer, fresher organizations of reform. Between 1852 and 1856 innumerable coalitions of enthusiasts fielded local political tickets under many different names—Independents, Fusionists, Americans, then finally Republicans. The new morally activist Republican party that emerged in the late 1850s retained the old Whig constituency but with some new additions and a heightened enthusiasm. The Democratic targets of these moral reformers meanwhile huddled together in their reduced but intact political haven.

After the Civil War, politics remained culturally charged. Republicans "waved the bloody shirt" at the former secessionist Democrats; they cooperated with prohibitionists at the local level. In the late 1880s, a series of school controversies energized the Democrats' constituency. The Wisconsin and Illinois legislatures passed laws requiring the use of English in all schools, public and parochial, in their states. These and similar laws in other states threatened the German parochial schools, both Lutheran and Catholic, and enraged most Catholic voters. In 1890 and 1892 the Democrats rode these cultural issues to a string of local, state, and national victories.

Their resurgence, however, was short-lived. The depression of 1893 turned attention from cultural to economic issues, and the Republicans came to power nationwide in 1896. From that year until the Great Depression of the 1930s, the Republicans remained the normal majority party. During this period, the basic ethnic constituencies of each party stayed much the same but the pattern was less clear-cut than in the 19th century. Republican prosperity attracted many normally Democratic voters, and in addition, the Republicans toned down their moralistic appeals. William McKinley, Theodore Roosevelt, and William Howard Taft avoided abrasive cultural issues and made strong ethnic appeals to Catholics. In these years William Jennings Bryan and Woodrow Wilson, as candidates for the Democrats, were identified with pietist, moralist, nativist traditions by many voters; Wilson's election in 1912 was largely a result of Theodore Roosevelt's third-party candidacy drawing support from the Republicans. Though there was no fundamental party realignment in the early 20th century, the Democrats were weaker and lost some of their traditional appeal.

Despite the stability of ethnic political loyalties in

the century from 1830 to 1930, party allegiances were not cast in concrete. Some ethnic groups changed their loyalties over time. For example, the pietistic Dutch Reformed immigrants who settled in western Michigan and in Iowa in the late 1840s and the 1850s left the Netherlands in part because they felt the established church in that country had sunk into apathy and luke-warmness. Whig politicians viewed the Dutch new-comers as prime candidates for the moral activism of their party. The Dutch, however, felt insecure and threatened in their new land; they disliked the nativist attitudes of some Whigs and feared (however incor-rectly) that Whig activism might lead to a state religion. Thus, the Dutch at first held aloof from American pie-tists; in the 1850s in both Michigan and Iowa they voted solidly for the Democratic party and its cultural laissez-faire policy. Thirty years later, the Dutch in the Midwest had prospered and no longer felt alien and threatened. Their Protestant pietism and new-found confidence turned Dutch political allegiance to the Re-publicans from the 1880s onward.

The intensity of ethnic feeling in politics also varied with time and place. Hostile feelings toward a rival group produce the most intense political reactions; and where such negative attitudes are absent, the ethnic fac-tor seems relatively weak. For instance, before the Civil War, the South was the most ethnically homogeneous section of the nation. Though there was religious diver-sity in the South, there was little hostility among the various groups. A vigorous two-party system existed in most Southern states from 1838 to 1852, but the cleav-ages were not based primarily on ethnic differences. Whigs were distinguished from Democrats by eco-nomic differences, by regional loyalties within states, and by personal loyalties to the party heroes, Henry Clay and Andrew Jackson. After the reopening of the sectional controversy in 1854, however, the two-party system withered in the South. Northern abolitionists were perceived as dangerous to the Southern way of life, and white Southerners increasingly saw themselves as a threatened regional group. Accordingly, they closed ranks behind the champions of threatened groups, the Democrats. After the Civil War and the brief interlude of Reconstruction when Northern troops protected black and other Republican voters, white Southern ad-herence to the Democratic party became nearly univer-sal and remained so until 1952. Thus, after 1854 the South falls fully within the framework of ethnic poli-tics, with white Southerners among the most strongly Democratic of groups and the few blacks allowed to vote choosing the party of Lincoln and liberation (until the 1930s).

Except in the South before 1852 cultural issues like Prohibition, nativism, abolition, and control of the schools were salient and powerful in shaping a core vote for a particular party within each ethnic group. But eco-nomic issues, the personalities of the candidates, and a host of other factors could influence a certain percent-age of each group in a given election and thus affect the outcome. If a group ordinarily voted 55 percent Demo-cratic because of that party's underlying cultural orien-tation, but an economic issue such as the protective tar-iff convinced just 6 percent of the group to switch to the Republicans, a majority of that group's vote would go to the Republicans. Swings of this sort, and even more ex-treme ones, happened frequently. For example, Polish immigrants in urban areas were among the staunchest of Democratic voters. From 1888 to 1912, the Polish vote in Chicago averaged 61 percent Democratic in presidential elections. But in 1904, when the Demo-crats nominated the lackluster, conservative judge Alton B. Parker to run against the popular "trust-busting" Teddy Roosevelt, the Polish Democratic per-centage fell to 41 percent.

At two points in American history, economic factors so overshadowed the voters' underlying ethnic loyalties that they affected many groups simultaneously and reoriented the political system. In 1894 and 1896 the politics of depression saddled Grover Cleveland and the Democrats with the blame for hard times and sold the Republican William McKinley to the voters as the "ad-vance agent of prosperity." Enough normally Demo-cratic voters were convinced, particularly groups like the German Lutherans and German Reformed who were only moderately Democratic, so that the Republi-cans became the normal majority party for almost 40 years. Again in the 1930s economic factors overrode cultural loyalties; nearly all underprivileged ethnic groups in America voted for Franklin Roosevelt in 1936, making the Democrats the majority party up to the present.

The Depression of the 1930s and the consequent Roo-sevelt revolution in politics were such profound experi-ences for Americans that they substituted an economic consciousness for an ethnic consciousness as the basic substratum of party loyalty. In 1936 even formerly Re-publican groups like the Swedes and Norwegians voted for Roosevelt. Black voters moved en masse into the Democratic party and remained there strictly on eco-nomic grounds, for the New Deal accomplished little in the civil rights field, even failing to pass an antilynch-ing law. Since the 1930s whenever the Democrats sense disaster at the polls and wish to energize their constitu-ency, they do not belabor the cultural imperialism of the Republicans as they would have in the 19th cen-tury. Instead, they campaign against the ghost of Her-bert Hoover. In the 1970 congressional elections, for ex-ample, when Richard Nixon and Spiro Agnew were using law-and-order issues in an attempt to create a Re-publican majority, the Democrats successfully retained control of Congress by conjuring up voter fears of a re-cession. Branding the Republicans as the party of hard times is the most effective way of reaching the core of Democratic voters.

Long-range changes in society have facilitated this reorientation of the political system toward economic issues. Mass immigration ceased with the passage of na-tional-quota laws in the 1920s, and ethnic conscious-ness slowly diminished with the generations since then. At the same time society has become more secu-lar, and religion has become a less potent political fac-tor. Even in the 1950s, when churchgoing increased markedly, the religious spirit remained cool. The slogan of the religious "revival" of the 1950s could be paraphrased: "Go to church this Sunday; any church will do." This is not the spirit that engenders funda-mental religious cleavages in society or politics.

Although their impact has diminished, ethnic and re-ligious issues have not become irrelevant in modern-day politics. The switch of black voters to the Demo-

crats was brought about by the Depression, but since 1948 the Democrats have solidified their appeal to blacks by championing civil-rights measures. Anti-Communism in the 1950s was a powerful cultural force that attracted many Catholic Democrats to the Republican voting column. John Kennedy's Catholicism brought these voters back to the Democrats in 1960, but alienated many Protestant voters, particularly in the usually Democratic South. Throughout the turbulent 1960s, the Republicans frequently used fears of militant blacks and unconventional youth to lure voters away from the Democrats.

In recent political history economic and ethnocultural issues seem to have reversed roles. Since the 1930s economic issues have formed the substratum of party loyalty, while ethnic, religious, and cultural fears have occasionally created a swing vote and tipped the balance. On the strength of the New Deal legacy, the Democrats have controlled Congress for all but four years since 1940, but foreign policy issues and cultural fears have allowed the Republicans to win and hold the presidency for 16 of those years. In 1952 Eisenhower and the Republicans campaigned successfully on Korea, Communism, and corruption—not one of which was an economic issue. In 1972 President Nixon was reelected by a landslide, in part because the Democratic candidate, George McGovern, was identified with culturally unconventional and radical groups. As recently as 1976, Jimmy Carter's election was jeopardized by Catholic suspicion of a "born-again" Southern Baptist. Though ethnocultural politics is no longer at the base of party allegiances, it still has important effects on electoral outcomes.

MACHINE POLITICS

Although ethnicity formed the basis of party politics through much of American history, it was most visible in the realm of big-city boss politics. Since the middle of the 19th century, the majority of immigrants to America settled in the cities, where the representative of a political machine usually introduced them to American politics.

A machine is simply a party organization: the party structure and the men who run it. But it is a particular kind of organization, one based essentially on armies of party workers kept loyal with jobs and favors. These patronage armies distinguish a political machine from a reform organization, whose canvassers are volunteers fired with idealism, or from a nonpartisan government structure without party workers. At the lowest but most fundamental level of the party machine are its cogwheels, the precinct captains, each responsible for a small district of several hundred voters. Supported by steady but undemanding jobs on the public payroll, precinct captains work nearly full time at getting to know the voters of their districts. They attend weddings and wakes, know who needs a job or a favor, and make a thorough canvass at election time persuading the voters, offering assistance, collecting IOUs.

A score or more precincts form a city ward, presided over by the party's ward committeeman or boss. He appoints the precinct captains and provides jobs for them and their constituents. He is the intermediary at city hall who obtains favors for the voters. Above him is the city boss, more a broker among the competing ward

bosses than dictator. He and the ward bosses make up the city or county executive committee, which puts together slates of candidates for office and decides on the division of the all-important jobs and favors.

From the mid-19th century until at least the 1930s, almost every major American city was governed by such a machine. Machine dominance resulted from three factors: American cities had weak governmental structures and lacked a strong municipal tradition; in the 19th century they experienced explosive growth and outgrew what government they did have; and, as they grew, they filled up with diverse ethnic groups who formed separate communities and political interests.

In the early years of the republic, cities were few and small. Their governments were not complicated or very active. The small volume of city business was handled on a part-time basis by a commercial elite who governed out of a sense of noblesse oblige or else to protect their business interests. From the 1830s on, however, the closed municipal corporation began to be battered by democratization and rapid growth. In the age of Jacksonian democracy, most municipal offices were made elective and the executive power of the mayor was strictly limited. Municipal governments were kept weak by the prevailing fear of centralized authority. At the same time, foreign immigration and country-to-city movements swelled the urban population and expanded the need for municipal services. Faced with these challenges, the part-time patrician leaders withdrew from civic politics to be replaced by full-time professional politicians. City politicians built political machines as informal agents of coordination and centralization to supplement the weak, decentralized formal machinery of government. A disciplined party machine could govern a growing, heterogeneous city, at least partially meeting its needs, whereas the weak formal government could not. If every officeholder depended on the party for advancement and every jobholder on the public payroll owed his livelihood to the party, the bosses could effectively exercise executive authority, no matter what the city charter said.

Immigration and ethnic diversity were not, strictly speaking, essential to the growth of political machines. A large, growing population of poor native-born Americans also provided the conditions for boss rule. Indeed, the Philadelphia Republican machine received much of its support from native rural migrants to the city. But in fact, most big-city machines were usually firmly rooted in a diverse immigrant constituency.

Immigrants and their children had special needs that political machines were well suited to fill. The bosses found jobs for the men, accompanied them to naturalization hearings, distributed food baskets at Christmas and buckets of coal in the winter. They deferred to each ethnic group's customs and attended festivals and holy days. For all its centralization, a machine was government with a human face. A ward boss or a precinct captain provided favors and personally asked for votes. An immigrant from the decaying feudalism of a peasant village found the city machine congenial.

Civic reformers from the displaced commercial elite or from the growing middle classes found it hard to compete with the personal favors of the bosses. Appeals for honesty and businesslike efficiency seemed remote and irrelevant; their welfare aid, when produced at all,

was, in John Boyle O'Reilly's words, "the organized charity scrimped and iced, in the name of a cautious, statistical Christ." Jane Addams, founder of Chicago's Hull House, once related that the biggest mistake she and her colleagues from the settlement house ever made was to ask the county authorities to bury an abandoned orphan girl in a pauper's grave. This action offended the moral sentiments of the girl's immigrant community. The local ward boss, Johnny Powers, on the other hand, not only frequented the neighborhood's wakes and funerals but paid the undertaker and sent a carriage if the family were too poor to pay themselves. Not surprisingly, the Hull House group had little success when they ran reform candidates for alderman against Powers's minions.

A political boss stood ready to assist immigrants at every stage of their new life. Timely advice and favors helped the men find jobs and homes for their families. If the immigrants prospered and went into business for themselves, a political friend helped them secure lucrative city contracts. If they failed and found themselves down and out, skid-row bosses like Hinky Dink Kenna and Bathhouse John Coughlin would find a place for them and other unfortunates in a flophouse, give them a free lunch and a beer, and march them to the polls like a dispirited army. Ward politics was a crude, practical form of cradle-to-grave security.

Political machines also provided recognition and advancement for both individuals and ethnic groups. For the Irish, the Poles, or the Italians, whose members usually started on the lowest rung of the occupational ladder, economic opportunity was blocked by the prejudices of the native-born or by the workers' lack of skills. Ambitious sons of immigrants, without economic security or extended education, often found politics or the rackets the only avenues out of manual labor. Sometimes there was little distinction between the two. A sharp-witted lad made friends on the streets, in gangs, and in saloons, and these friends became a political following, a little cell of dependable votes. Offering these deliverable votes to a ward boss, the aspiring politician then devoted years of hard work to the party as a precinct captain. Loyalty and luck could provide him with a career in politics.

Such political success stories had more than individual importance. When a member of a new immigrant group received a political job or was slated for office, the whole group basked in reflected glory. The ethnically balanced ticket was not only a good vote-getting device, but a psychologically sound means of making an ethnic group feel that it belonged in the wider society. Immigrants were outsiders to American institutions. When important political figures addressed their ethnic associations, sometimes haltingly uttering a few words in their own language; when local bosses helped them with jobs and favors; when their own sons entered politics and held jobs at city hall, they began to feel more like insiders. Thus American politics, under the shrewd manipulation of city bosses, served economic and psychological functions for new ethnic groups, bringing them inside the political system.

THE IRISH

Irish Catholics have been uniquely active and successful in American politics, yet a few cautions are in order lest their political prowess be exaggerated. Not all political bosses were Irish. The first Tammny Hall mayor of New York, Fernando Wood, was an old-stock American; and the notorious Tammany boss, William Marcy Tweed, was the son of Scottish immigrants. The Republican boss of Cincinnati, George B. Cox, was of English ancestry; and William Hale "Big Bill" Thompson of Chicago was a "Mayflower" American. The Irish neither invented the political machine nor did they keep an exclusive hold on it.

The Irish did not step directly off the boats and into power in the city halls of the nation. Though Irish voters and politicians began to enter Tammany Hall in the 1820s and 1830s, they did not dominate it until after Boss Tweed's downfall in 1871, when "Honest John" Kelly became the first Irish Grand Sachem. The first Irish mayor of a large city was elected in Scranton, Pa., in 1878. The voters chose an Irish mayor in New York in 1880, in Boston in 1884, and in Chicago in 1893. As a general rule, it was at least a generation after the mass migration at mid-century that the Irish came to dominate the politics of any city.

Still the Irish have shown an extraordinary flair for machine politics, and once in power they tended to stay there. Irish Tammanyites ruled New York with only occasional interruptions from the 1880s until 1934. Boston's James Michael Curley repeatedly won reelection to a number of offices over a period of 40 years, despite his reputation for squandering public funds. When the Irish belatedly consolidated their hold on the Chicago Democratic machine in the 1930s, they produced a string of mayors—Kelly, Kennelly, Daley—who ruled the city for 40 years.

Irish success in big-city machines is a product both of their old-country heritage and of the circumstances in which they found themselves after immigration. Though the Irish, fleeing headlong from famine and disease in the late 1840s, were among the most disadvantaged and miserable of immigrants economically, they had many advantages for the practice of politics. Their experience in Ireland had made them both familiar with and contemptuous of Anglo-Saxon legal and political institutions. Because oppressive English penal laws, in force in Ireland from the 17th to the 19th centuries, barred Catholics from politics, the professions, and most avenues for legal redress of grievances, Irish peasants came to rely on illegal people's courts and secret enforcement societies for justice. Thus accustomed to viewing the official government as illegitimate, the Irish were prepared to step into extralegal organizations like the political machines of American cities. Furthermore, though oppressed in Ireland, the Irish had experience in political organization. Daniel O'Connell's Catholic Association of the 1820s, aimed at the emancipation of Catholics from the civil disabilities of the penal laws, had initiated the lowliest of Irishmen into the practices of mass political action. With "monster meetings" and grassroots organization in every Irish parish, the Catholic emancipation movement was a first-rate education in the efficacy of political pressure. The Irish arrived in America with a wealth of experience that later immigrants lacked. Gregariousness and clan loyalties further suited them for the personalized politics of the machine.

Yet it is possible to overemphasize the importance of the Old World heritage in explaining Irish political

success in the New World. Typically, it was not immigrants fresh from Ireland who entered politics, but rather their American-born children. Much of the explanation lies in the circumstances in which the American-born Irish found themselves. Their parents' early arrival in America and their knowledge of the English language gave Irish Americans a head start and allowed them to get into political organizations from the ground up. Furthermore, their very poverty and lack of economic prospects in America gave them a strong incentive to explore alternative paths of mobility. The police force and the political machine offered opportunities to shrewd, strong, but unskilled sons of Irish immigrants.

A comparison of the Irish with the Germans, who arrived at the same time in America, is instructive. The Germans had a language barrier to overcome, and they lacked political experience in the fragmented German principalities they had left. On the other hand, most German settlers had more skills, larger cash reserves, and better economic prospects than the hapless famine Irish. Also, many Germans settled on farms far from the large cities and thus had neither reason nor opportunity to seek the favors of bosses or take advantage of the career possibilities offered by politics. So it was the Irish, not the Germans, who moved into the growing political machines of the mid-19th century.

Once in power, the Irish remained in control, not so much through innate natural talents as through skillful manipulation of circumstances. Numerous other immigrant groups followed the Irish into the cities around the turn of the century. None of these successor groups had the political experience of the Irish, but most were in need of alternative avenues of mobility and looked to politics for assistance. The Irish machine leaders appealed to new immigrants with the usual jobs and favors; they extended them recognition by slating them on "balanced" tickets, but reserved the most powerful and prestigious positions for themselves. So many jealous and ambitious ethnic groups were jostling for position in early 20th-century machines that the Irish could assume the role of broker and play the groups off against one another. Poles would resent a Czech being slated for ward committeeman, Poles and Czechs both would resent a Jew, and so on; but all the competing new groups would grumblingly acquiesce if an Irishman retained the position as a compromise. In 1910, for instance, the Irish had dwindled to only 15 percent of Manhattan's population, yet 26 of the 35 Democratic district leaders were still Irish. Irish machine bosses were thus able to divide and rule long after the Irish had ceased to be the most numerous ethnic group in a city.

Irish political success has not been limited to big-city wards. By 1920 numerous Irish Catholic representatives sat in Congress and a number of states had elected Irish governors. Senators David I. Walsh of Massachusetts and Thomas J. Walsh of Montana led the way for a growing number of Irishmen in the upper house of Congress. The only two Catholics to run for the presidency, Alfred E. Smith, who was defeated in 1928, and John F. Kennedy, who succeeded in 1960, were of Irish origin.

Irish-American political fortunes have always been closely tied to the Democratic party, and Irish voters have been consistently Democratic since the Jacksonian era. In the 1870s and early 1880s, as Irish nationalism developed strength in both Ireland and the United States, the Republican party made an attempt to win the Irish vote by rhetorically "twisting the lion's tail"— that is, attacking Great Britain. This policy produced a number of Irish Republican leaders and might have borne fruit in the presidential election of 1884 when the popular James G. Blaine was the Republican candidate. However, Republican hopes of capturing the Irish vote were damaged by an indiscreet Protestant minister who attacked the Democrats as the party of "Rum, Romanism, and Rebellion" a few days before the election. Faced with this and other evidence of continued Republican nativism, the Irish remained within the Democratic party. Thereafter, the only major break in Irish Democratic voting loyalty occurred in 1920 when the Irish were outraged by Woodrow Wilson's pro-British diplomacy and his refusal to include Ireland on the list of nations to benefit from self-determination after World War I. In that year, the Irish and many other ethnic groups unhappy with Wilson's treaty-making contributed heavily to Republican Warren G. Harding's landslide election.

The several faces of Irish-American politics are represented by three 20th-century political figures: The Reverend Charles E. Coughlin, the political radio-priest of the 1930s; John F. Kennedy, elected the first Catholic president in 1960; and Eugene McCarthy, former senator from Minnesota and unsuccessful presidential aspirant in 1968.

Father Coughlin, a pastor in Royal Oak, Mich., rose to prominence in the early 1930s through a weekly radio broadcast and a growing organization he called the National Union for Social Justice. Originally a proponent of papal social doctrines and a supporter of Franklin Roosevelt's New Deal, Coughlin became increasingly shrill as the Depression wore on. He broke with Roosevelt in 1935, helped organize a third-party national ticket in 1936, and began broadcasting harangues that blamed hard times on an international Communist Jewish conspiracy. Coughlin's increasingly paranoid broadcasts appealed to the working-class Irish, especially those who had not advanced much beyond the circumstances of the 19th-century immigrations and whose precarious economic state was similar to that of their countrymen in Belfast or Dublin. Irish toughs responded to the radio-priest's anti-Semitic ravings by attacking Jews in New York, Brooklyn, and Chicago.

Coughlin represents a frightening example of the politics of frustration. He provided scapegoats for Irish Americans who had not fulfilled the American dream of success. Senator Joseph McCarthy of Wisconsin appealed to the same instincts in a part of the Irish community with his anti-Communism crusade of the 1950s. This aspect of Irish politics has receded considerably, for the Irish have become since World War II one of the most middle-class of ethnic groups. Still, the violent response to racially motivated school busing in largely Irish South Boston indicates that this abrasive style of Irish politics has not completely disappeared.

Eugene McCarthy represents a variety of Irish politics quite as eccentric as Coughlin's, but in a different direction. McCarthy's cerebral, intellectual style of antiwar politics in the 1960s was deeply rooted in liberal Catholic social thought. The same papal writings from which Father Coughlin extracted quasifascist doctrines provided liberal Catholics from the city parishes and

rural monasteries of the upper Midwest with a coherent vision of a just, humane, and peaceful social order. The Benedictine Abbey of St. John's in Minnesota, where McCarthy once studied for the priesthood, was in the vanguard of American Catholic liturgical and social reform. McCarthy entered politics with a coherent ideology and an intellectual style unusual in an Irish politician. His vision and style carried him through ten years as a congressman, two terms in the U.S. Senate, and a brilliant campaign against the Vietnam war in 1968. But his clerical-intellectual politics as often baffled as dazzled his supporters, and he retired from the Senate in 1970 a lonely and disillusioned figure.

Both Coughlin and McCarthy drew upon authentic parts of the Irish heritage in America, but the mainstream of contemporary Irish politics has flowed in the direction taken by John F. Kennedy. Kennedy represented the economically successful, middle-class, post-ethnic Irish. Never more than a lukewarm Catholic in his personal life, Kennedy gave the impression that his religion had no effect whatever on his policy judgments. In a crucial campaign speech to a Protestant ministers' assembly in Houston, Tex., he decisively dissociated himself from clerical or church influences. Though his religion was inevitably an issue, and he won Catholic votes and lost Protestant ones because of it, Kennedy's political image was that of the Harvard graduate, not the Irish politician. His cool, pragmatic, opportunistic politics, though perhaps owing something to the heritage of practical ward politics, was sophisticated and urbane in a way that transcended ethnicity. The Kennedy mystique was a national, not an ethnic, phenomenon. Now that most Irish Americans are solidly middle-class in both income and status, the Kennedy style points to the future of Irish political experience in the United States.

THE POLES

The political history of Poles in the United States has been far different from that of the Irish, even though both groups have consistently supported the Democratic party. The Poles have not experienced much political success. Few have been elected to statewide offices; and only one, Senator Edmund Muskie of Maine, has become a truly national political figure. Though Polish Americans have become mayors in Detroit, Buffalo, and many smaller cities, the nation's largest Polish community, in Chicago, has never elected a Polish mayor.

The timing of Polish immigration is responsible for some of this relative lack of political success. Poles arrived in large numbers only after 1900; their peak year was 1907. Polish immigrants found the Irish well entrenched in city machines. Also, by the early 20th century, American cities had become so large and diverse that no one group could dominate them by force of numbers. In 1870 the Irish had formed roughly one-third of New York City's electorate. The Poles and other latecomers never accounted for such a large proportion of voters, except in very small cities. Unlike the Irish, the Poles lacked any experience with mass political action in the old country.

The political strategy pursued by most Polish-American leaders also limited political gains. Polish immigrants created one of the densest and most complete complexes of ethnic institutions of any group in America. Polish churches, schools, banks, fraternal societies, and cultural clubs made it possible for many Polish Americans to live their entire life in a Polish milieu. Reflecting this reality, Polish leaders played solidarity politics, organizing around in-group concerns and encouraging a bloc vote. Few attempted to build coalitions by pursuing issues of interest to other groups. As a result, they won elections only in their own ethnic enclaves and were rarely successful in city, state, or national elections where Poles were not a majority of the electorate.

Solidarity politics is a natural result of ethnic defensiveness and probably a necessary first step for any group. However, if a group is large and cohesive like the Poles, it may be tempted to retain this strategy too long and may neglect the skills of broker politics necessary for success in a pluralist society. It is not accidental that the first nationally prominent Polish politician came from the largely Yankee state of Maine. Without the bloc votes of a Polish Chicago or Hamtramck behind him, Edmund Muskie was forced to transcend solidarity politics and appeal to non-Polish voters. Most Polish leaders, however, remain today at an earlier stage of ward and district bloc politics.

Czechs, Lithuanians, Greeks, and other immigrants of the early 20th century were similar to the Poles in their Democratic tendencies, though with many local exceptions.

THE GERMANS

Polish and Irish Democrats functioned in an essentially urban milieu. The political history of Germans and Scandinavians showed the form that ethnic politics took in rural areas. Many Norwegians, Danes, and Swedes who immigrated in the 19th century settled on the land, and the Germans were about evenly divided between city and countryside. These groups clustered in the rich farmlands of the upper Midwest, from the Dakotas to Wisconsin, and from the Canadian border to the Missouri River. They were able to participate in politics sooner than immigrants in eastern cities; for in the 19th century most states of the Midwest, eager to attract new settlers, allowed aliens to vote once they had stated their intention to become citizens.

The Germans were the largest and most heterogeneous of the European immigrant groups. Church membership, or the lack of it, was the most reliable guide to German political behavior. The secular-minded forty-eighters and other freethinkers who disdained organized religion and united instead in numerous clubs and societies were most inclined to vote Republican. Members of pietist sects also tended to vote Republican, whereas Lutherans and Reformed church members leaned toward the Democrats. German Catholics were staunchly Democratic. These alignments held firm in normal political times, when underlying party loyalties were the main determinants of voting. However, when powerful ethnic issues affecting the Germans were at stake, all subgroups tended to swing one way or the other in a more unified fashion.

There has long been a myth that the German settlers in the Midwest were strong opponents of slavery and that their massed voting strength was decisive in electing Abraham Lincoln in 1860. This legend, however, is

based on little more than the statements of a few prominent German Republicans, such as Carl Schurz, who attempted to claim credit for Lincoln's election. In fact the Germans, like most white Northerners, were not in favor of slavery; but neither did they much like blacks. The whole slavery issue was rather remote from the average German settler and did not touch him personally the way Prohibition, nativism, and sabbatarianism did. For the Germans, 1860 was a normal election; and their votes divided in the usual way, probably with a slight majority for the Democrats.

The first important abnormal election for the Germans occurred in 1890. Illinois and Wisconsin had passed laws prohibiting the use of any language but English in the schools. In Nebraska and other midwestern states antiliquor agitation and a resurgent nativism appeared. All of these forces of moralistic Protestantism, centered in the Republican party, threatened the interests of Germans in the Midwest and produced heavy Democratic votes in state elections in 1890 and the presidential election of 1892. Very quickly, however, this newly united German vote switched sides. Economic depression in 1893 and Democratic fusion with agrarian radicals of the Populist party frightened many Germans; in 1896 the German vote in the presidential election moved over into the Republican column and helped elect William McKinley. With the waning of Populism and the return of prosperity in the late 1890s, German voting returned to its usual fragmented pattern.

World War I affected the German vote more powerfully than the discontents of the 1890s. The outbreak of war in 1914 and the protracted debate over American entry into the conflict produced a rising tide of superpatriotism and sharp attacks on the loyalties of ethnic groups particularly those of German Americans. Many Republicans, most notably Theodore Roosevelt, attacked American ethnic groups, but in 1916 the Democratic party took a similar stance. Furthermore, most German Americans saw clearly that President Woodrow Wilson's neutrality policy, in effect if not in intention, aided the British far more than the Germans. Consequently, the German vote in 1916 was far less Democratic than usual. Most Germans voted for the Republican, Charles Evans Hughes, while many backed the Socialist candidate, Allan Benson.

Socialists had long claimed a significant minority of German support, especially among the secular-minded Germans in the cities. Numerous small socialist groups had been formed in the late 19th century by German political émigrés, some of whom had worked with Karl Marx. After the turn of the century, Victor Berger had built a moderate social-democratic machine in the heavily German city of Milwaukee. More reformers than revolutionaries, the Milwaukee socialists first elected a mayor in 1910 and remained powerful locally for decades. In 1916, the antiwar stance of the Socialist Party of America appealed to German Americans, who desperately wanted to avoid war with their former homeland. The party also served as a neutral haven for German voters repelled by the antiethnic attitudes of the two major parties. In German wards of Milwaukee, St. Louis, and Davenport, Iowa, the Socialist Party of America won more than a third of the votes.

In the 1918 state elections the Germans continued to seek candidates not identified with superpatriotism. They favored a Democrat for governor in Iowa, a Republican in Nebraska, an independent farmer-labor candidate in Minnesota, and Socialist Emil Seidel for governor of Wisconsin. In addition, Milwaukee Germans elected Socialist Victor Berger to Congress, even though he was under indictment for antiwar activities. German politics of revenge continued in succeeding presidential elections. German voters joined the anti-Democratic landslide against the Versailles Treaty in 1920; and in 1924 they favored the third-party candidacy of Robert M. La Follette, mainly because as a senator he had voted against the declaration of war on Germany.

World War I had been traumatic for German Americans, and the ensuing years of Hitler's rise to power in the 1930s were no better. The two world wars tremendously accelerated the assimilation of Germans in America. Cultural symbols were rapidly discarded as German Americans tried to forget the past. German politics, as a visible public activity, virtually ceased with World War I. Nevertheless, underlying voter loyalties persisted. Much of the vaunted midwestern isolationism of the 1930s and 1940s can be explained by German-American votes against involvement in a war against Germany. With the replacement of Germany by Soviet Russia as the United States' enemy, however, the last trace of distinctive German political behavior disappeared.

THE SCANDINAVIANS

The Scandinavians, though divided into three different national groups, were more united in their political loyalty than the Germans. Mostly yeoman farmers, they were attracted to the party of Lincoln by the Homestead Act. Perhaps more fundamentally, the Scandinavians had strong cultural similarities with the Yankee Republicans. The established Lutheran churches of Scandinavia had been swept by repeated religious revivals in the 19th century, and many pioneer immigrants were pietistic dissenters. Scandinavians nursed a strong dislike for Roman Catholicism, and many of them also favored prohibition. The Volstead Act that put prohibition into effect in 1920 was named for Andrew Volstead, a Norwegian congressman from Minnesota. Scandinavian voters, then, were Republican from their first coming until the early decades of this century. Swedes and Norwegians quickly became officeholders in the northern tier of states where they concentrated. Norwegian-born Knute Nelson was elected the first Scandinavian governor in Minnesota in 1892. James Davidson in Wisconsin in 1906, Peter Norbeck in South Dakota in 1916, and a long string of Swedes and Norwegians in Minnesota followed Nelson into Midwest state capitols.

After 1900, however, some Midwest Scandinavians became active in agrarian, third-party movements, protesting the stranglehold of railroad and grain-elevator interests on the farmer's livelihood. Scandinavian farm communities strongly supported both the Nonpartisan League, which rose to power in North Dakota from 1915 to 1920, and the Farmer-Labor party in Minnesota from the 1920s onward. These allegiances do not belie the basic Republican tendency of the Scandinavians, but rather illustrate an important point about that persuasion. The Whig-Republican tradition embraces an

independent, antiparty spirit derived from the early Republic. The Constitution made no mention of political parties, for the founding fathers hoped that parties would never take root. Though parties soon proved necessary, the antiparty sentiment never died and often led to splinter movements and third-party action. Whigs and then Republicans preserved this tradition, often scoring the Democrats as "slaves of party."

Thus the independent spirit of politics in heavily Scandinavian Minnesota is part of the Republican tradition. The Farmer-Laborites made a strong protest showing in the 1920s and then came to power in the state from 1931 to 1939. Yet even though Farmer-Labor leaders and voters strongly supported Franklin Roosevelt in national elections, Farmer-Labor did not formally fuse with the Democrats until 1944. Minnesota Democracy was essentially an urban Irish Catholic party; and despite a seemingly natural economic alliance during the Depression, the Scandinavian Farmer-Laborites were reluctant to join with their cultural opposites.

When prosperity returned after World War II, many Scandinavian voters went back to Republican ranks, and much of the moralistic Republican spirit remains. Luther W. Youngdahl, Republican governor of Minnesota in the late 1940s, has been aptly called by his biographer "A Christian in politics." A devout Swedish Lutheran, he attacked the liquor interests, cracked down on slot machines and other forms of gambling, and championed civil rights for blacks. The social gospel politics that seem so eccentric in an Irish Catholic like Eugene McCarthy are part of a long tradition for a Swede like Youngdahl.

THE JEWS

The paradigm of ethnic voting behavior presented here, with its dichotomy between Protestant moralism and Catholic defensiveness, applies primarily to Christian ethnic groups but it can be adapted for Jewish voting as well. The tiny Jewish minority in the early Republic remembered well the restrictive laws against non-Christians in the colonial era. Thus, a natural defensiveness plus their gratitude to Jefferson, Madison, and other advocates of religious toleration led them to support the Democratic party up to 1850. The German Jews who began to arrive then, however, were a highly emancipated, secularized, and occasionally radical group. Both in Germany and in America they developed a movement called Reform Judaism, which adopted many Protestant practices like hymn singing, organ music, extended sermons, and worship on Sunday. Reform Judaism was, in many ways, a Jewish version of the Yankees' Congregational church. Confident, assimilated, German Reform Jews tended to vote Republican like their pietist Protestant counterparts, and they remained Republican until the 1930s.

Jews from eastern Europe who flooded into New York, Boston, and Chicago after 1880, were much more orthodox and ritualistic than their German coreligionists. Like Christian groups whose religious practices diverged from the Protestant mainstream, Orthodox Jews tended to feel more comfortable in the Democratic party. Two circumstances, however, produced numerous exceptions to this rule. German-Jewish Republican leadership and the strong diplomatic protests of presidents Theodore Roosevelt and William H. Taft against tsarist atrocities produced Republican majorities among Russian Jews in most presidential elections until 1916. Also, the Socialist party had strong appeal for many Jewish voters. Socialism, with its messianic and humanitarian appeals, was a kind of secularized Judaism for the working class. Jewish Socialist support was strongest on the Lower East Side of New York, where Morris Hillquit and Meyer London were local heroes; in Chicago, Socialist appeal was not much stronger among Jews than among other working-class groups. In any case, voting for Republican presidents and Socialist candidates in New York made Russian-Jewish Democratic support much less monolithic than that of the Irish and Poles.

The diversity in Jewish voting, however, ended in the 1930s. Franklin Roosevelt's social-welfare liberalism appealed to Russian Jews as more practical and concrete than Socialist theories. German Jews, who were generally more comfortable economically, were at first less drawn to the New Deal. But the candidacies of two Democrats of German-Jewish descent, Herbert Lehman and Henry Horner, for governor of New York and Illinois, respectively, together with the anti-Nazi foreign policy of the Roosevelt administration, brought German-Jewish voters into the Democratic fold by the 1936 election. Victory over Hitler in World War II and the Truman administration's support for the state of Israel in 1948 cemented the loyalty of a large majority of Jews to the Democratic party.

AFRO-AMERICANS

Along with the Jews, blacks have been the most solidly Democratic group since 1936, but in many ways the Afro-American political experience has been unique. For one thing, no other large group was systematically prevented from voting for so long. Black slaves enjoyed neither political nor civil rights, and most free blacks were also banned from voting. Before the Civil War only the five New England states and, for a time, New York allowed them the franchise. After Emancipation, despite the Fifteenth Amendment that guaranteed all blacks the right to vote, Southern states used numerous devices, such as poll taxes and all-white Democratic primaries, effectively to disfranchise them. Not until the Voting Rights Act of 1965 were all blacks, North and South, given access to the voting booth.

The Afro-American experience is different also because no other large group has changed so completely and permanently from one party allegiance to another. The few blacks permitted to vote before the Civil War overwhelmingly chose the Whigs as the morally activist, antislavery party. The administration voted into office by the Whigs' successor, the Republican party, fought the Civil War and ended slavery, thereby winning the loyalty of most former slaves. During the brief years of Reconstruction in the South, numerous freedmen served as officeholders in Republican state regimes and as Republican representatives in Congress. During the long years from the end of Reconstruction until the New Deal, blacks remained loyal to the party of Lincoln wherever they were permitted to vote; but this allegiance became increasingly vestigial, for after 1890 the Republicans ceased to take any interest in black rights. When the Depression of the 1930s struck black laborers

even more severely than whites, they were ready for a change in loyalty. In the 1936 election the black vote moved en masse into the Democratic column. The Democratic record of economic reform and civil rights legislation has kept it there ever since.

In local politics blacks have pursued a strategy similar to that of the Poles. White racism and black pride combined to produce a politics of solidarity successful only in all-black districts. Since 1960, Gary, Ind.; Newark, N.J.; Cleveland, Ohio; and Detroit, Mich., have elected black mayors, but only after blacks became a majority in those cities. Few black politicians have been able to appeal to a broad range of ethnic groups, although Thomas Bradley's election as mayor of largely white Los Angeles provides an exception.

ITALIANS AND OTHERS

The Italians, too, as a Catholic group with considerable cultural differences from American society, tended to be most comfortable with the Democrats. However, as in the case of the Jews, several circumstances created an important minority pattern of Republican voting. The small but reasonably confident and prosperous group of Northern Italians who emigrated in the 19th century gave their support to the Republican party in national elections, which often influenced the mass of Southern Italian immigrants who arrived later. Also, the Southern Italian *contadini* were restless peasants with a long tradition of seasonal migration in search of a better living. Once in the United States, they were more mobile, more geographically dispersed, and more opportunistic in pursuit of economic advancement than other contemporary immigrants. If an Italian immigrant prospered in contracting or some other business and saw an advantage in Republican party loyalties, he might well seize the opportunity. Though the majority of Italian voters have probably been Democratic adherents, some well-known Italian politicians, such as former governor of Massachusetts, John Volpe, have been Republicans.

The pattern of systematic discrimination, practiced so long against blacks, has been experienced by other nonwhite groups as well. The federal naturalization act of 1790 prevented nonwhite immigrants from becoming American citizens, and this color bar to citizenship and thus the franchise was not lifted for the Chinese until 1943 and for the Japanese and other nonwhites until 1952. The most recent Hispanic immigrants have probably tended toward the Democrats for both economic and religious reasons, but they present a new pattern in their low rates of voter participation. Though most immigrants have traditionally taken a long time to enter the political system fully, the Spanish-speaking have had distinctive reasons for nonparticipation. Innumerable Mexican immigrants have entered the United States illegally and thus keep a low profile; many others who are legal residents are migrant agricultural laborers who have difficulty establishing a voting residence. Puerto Ricans, though U.S. citizens by birth, frequently remain transients, moving back and forth between their island homeland and the U.S. mainland.

Sometimes a member of a small ethnic group seems to enjoy an advantage over politicians from a large, cohesive group like the blacks or the Poles. The Bohemian-born Anton Cermak, for example, did not fall prey to the temptations of solidarity politics as so many Polish ward bosses did. When Cermak was growing up in Chicago in the early 20th century, the Czechs were not numerous enough to attain much political influence on their own. Cermak, therefore, made himself a multiethnic spokesman on issues like Prohibition, forged important ties with many groups in Chicago, and was elected mayor of the city in 1931.

Occasionally, also, a politician from a tiny minority can serve as a neutral compromise candidate when large blocs disagree. For example, when Mayor Richard J. Daley of Chicago died in 1976, Poles and blacks formed the two largest components of the Democratic party in the city, but neither group would support a member of the other to succeed Daley. The compromise choice was Michael Bilandic, a Croat.

Throughout the history of American politics, one finds both change and continuity in ethnic allegiances. The blacks have switched party loyalties completely, the Swedes and Norwegians changed parties temporarily during the Great Depression, still others such as the Germans and the Jews have varied their political responses. Each group, too, has always had a number of nonaligned, independent voters. Nevertheless, basic group loyalties have been remarkably persistent over time. Group voting patterns often take on a life of their own and persist after the conditions that created them no longer exist. The New Deal party system was based on the economic consciousness of working-class groups. It would seem reasonable to expect that when the Irish, Poles, Italians, and Russian Jews entered the middle class and moved to the suburbs, they would shed their New Deal mentality and switch over to the Republicans. For the most part, this has not happened. Democratic voting has become a group heritage and a reflexive response for these ethnic groups, just as Republican voting was for blacks before the trauma of the Depression broke their loyalty. Both economic and ethnocultural issues make the present group patterns of politics very durable.

Bibliography

The pioneering work on ethnocultural political theory is Lee Benson, *The Concept of Jacksonian Democracy: New York as a Test Case* (Princeton, N.J., 1961). Samuel Lubell, *The Future of American Politics*, 2d ed., rev. (Garden City, N.Y., 1955), is another pathbreaking work of a more popular character. Ronald Formisano, *The Birth of Mass Political Parties: Michigan, 1827–1861* (Princeton, N.J., 1971), follows Benson's approach, as does Richard J. Jensen, *The Winning of the Midwest: Social and Political Conflict, 1888–1896* (Chicago, 1971). Two good summaries of the ethnocultural approach are Samuel T. McSeveney, "Ethnic Groups, Ethnic Conflict, and Recent Quantitative Research in American Political History," *International Migration Review* 7 (Spring 1973): 14–33, and Robert Kelley, "Ideology and Political Culture from Jefferson to Nixon," *American History Review* 82 (1977): 531–562.

A delightful introduction to boss politics is William L. Riordon, ed., *Plunkitt of Tammany Hall* (New York, 1963). Bruce Stave, ed., *Urban Bosses, Machines, and Progressive Reformers* (Lexington, Mass., 1972), is a useful collection of articles. There are numerous studies of individual bosses and machines.

Discussions of the Irish political style appear in William V. Shannon, *The American Irish*, rev. ed. (1966, reprint, 1973), and Edward M. Levine, *The Irish and Irish Politicians* (South Bend, Ind., 1966). For the Poles, see Edward R. Kantowicz, *Polish-American Politics in Chicago* (Chicago, 1975). Three works by Frederick C. Luebke discuss the Germans: *Immigrants and Politics: The Germans of Nebraska, 1880–1900* (Lincoln, Neb., 1969); *Bonds of Loyalty: German Americans and World War I* (DeKalb, Ill., 1974); *Ethnic Voters and the Election of Lincoln* (Lincoln, Neb., 1971). Information on Scandinavians in politics must be dug out of a variety of sources, for example: G. Theodore Mitau, *Politics in Minnesota*, 2d ed. (Minneapolis, 1970); and Kendric C. Babcock,

The Scandinavian Element in the United States (1914; reprint, New York, 1969). Lawrence H. Fuchs, *The Political Behavior of American Jews* (Glencoe, Ill., 1956) is a standard survey. Harold Gosnell, *Negro Politicians: The Rise of Negro Politics in Chicago* (Chicago, 1935) is a standard, older work. A useful collection of recent works on many ethnic groups, including blacks, Poles, and Jews, is Peter Jones and Melvin G. Holli, eds., *The Ethnic Frontier* (Grand Rapids, Mich., 1977).

EDWARD R. KANTOWICZ

POLYNESIANS: *see* HAWAIIANS; PACIFIC ISLANDERS

POMOS: *see* AMERICAN INDIANS

PONCAS: *see* AMERICAN INDIANS

POOSEPATUCKS: *see* AMERICAN INDIANS

PORTUGUESE

The two waves of Portuguese who have immigrated to the United States over the past century and a half have contributed to the formation of a dynamic and diversified ethnic group. Portuguese-speaking people have come from the Azores, the Madeiras, the Cape Verde Islands (now independent), continental Portugal, and China. Few Portuguese-speaking Brazilians have come to the United States; in general they live apart and are not discussed in this entry.

Until the last few years, the Portuguese Americans, a relatively small group, were modest in their aspirations, generally humble, and quite self-effacing. These characteristics were produced by the rigidly two-class society from which they originated. Settling principally in

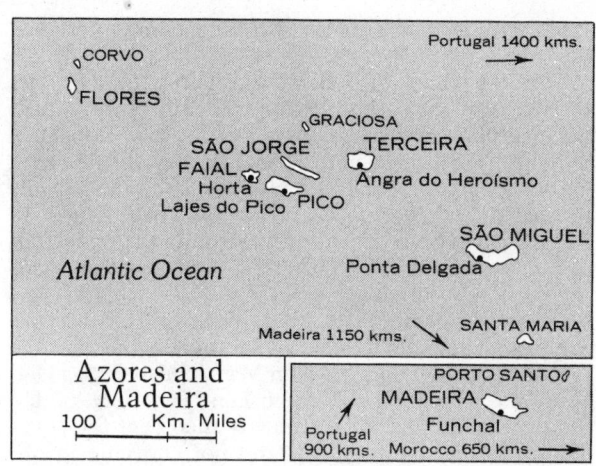

small cities and towns in southern New England and California, they have not been a major political or economic force in the United States and, in spite of their considerable influence on the three Atlantic archipelagoes, they have not had significant impact on Portugal as a European nation. However, since 1958, events in Portugal, social developments in the United States, and technological advances worldwide have dramatically transformed the Portuguese-American community. In the late 1970s the group finds itself caught in a conflict of loyalties, essentially split between the third- and fourth-generation descendants of the original immigrants and the very large number of recent arrivals.

Between 1820 and 1977 the U.S. Immigration and Naturalization Service recorded 434,837 Portuguese immigrants. Sixty-three percent of these entered over a span of 139 years; a surprising 37 percent have entered since 1958, partly as a result of the Azorean refugee acts implemented after volcanic eruptions and ensuing earthquakes on the island of Faial. This fact is strikingly important for the Portuguese-American community; although some Asian countries show even higher recent rates, the Portuguese have by far the highest percentage of new arrivals among groups of European origin. In contrast, only 26 percent of those who have immigrated to the United States from Greece have come since June 30, 1958, only 7 percent of those from Italy, 2 percent of those from Norway and Sweden, and 1 percent of those from Ireland. The experience of the recent arrivals is so different from that of the descendants of earlier Portuguese immigrants that today there are two Portuguese groups, living in close juxtaposition but not close harmony.

EARLY ARRIVALS

The annual reports of the U.S. Immigration and Naturalization Service begin the record of immigration from Portugal with 35 individuals in 1820. The early immigrants left a Portugal that was no longer on the cutting edge of European expansion as it had been in the days of Prince Henry the Navigator (1394–1460). Portugal had in 1822 just lost its major colony, Brazil, and subsequently became embroiled in a political struggle between "absolutists" and "liberals" that was to continue until the fall of the monarchy in 1910. The later arrivals, on the other hand, consisted of Portuguese brought up under a dictatorship that had indoctrinated

them with a sense of national pride lacking in the earlier group.

The 35 recorded in 1820 most certainly had a few antecedents in the second half of the 18th century, who very possibly arrived in ships belonging to or associated with the Portuguese-born Sephardic Jewish merchant Aaron Lopez, who settled in Newport, R.I., in 1752 and prospered. Early Portuguese immigrants were almost all Azorean men from the west-central and western islands of São Jorge, Pico, Faial, and Flores who signed on to fill out the crews of shorthanded American whaling vessels, often in an effort to avoid detested military service. They landed, and often settled in, the whaling ports of New Bedford and Edgartown in Massachusetts, Sag Harbor and Cold Spring Harbor on Long Island, N.Y., and Stonington, Conn. Large numbers then sent for wives and sweethearts. Those who did not continue in offshore whaling found their way to Provincetown at the end of Cape Cod, or north of Boston to Gloucester on Cape Ann, and there they and their descendants formed a permanent part of the fishing industry (witness Madeira-born Manuel in Rudyard Kipling's *Captains Courageous* of 1897).

Decade by decade the number of Portuguese immigrants, still chiefly Azoreans and virtually all Roman Catholics, rose more or less steadily until 1920 (see Table 1). The increase was particularly sharp in the 1870s—probably a reflection of economic difficulties in the Azores and the growth of direct shipping between Boston and the port of Horta on Faial. Immigration rose sharply again in the 1890s, reflecting the gradual shift in economic importance from Horta to the city of Ponta Delgada on the eastern Azores island of São Miguel (St. Michael's) and the move there of the U.S. consulate as well. Inhabitants of São Miguel, the largest and most densely populated of the nine Azores islands, and also those of nearby Santa Maria, thus had improved transportation and more precise information to aid them in emigrating to the United States.

In the first two decades of the 20th century the emigration reflected antipathy to the republican fervor in the homeland, which culminated in a revolution on October 5, 1910. The last king of Portugal fled to England and an anticlerical republic took the place of the traditional Catholic monarchy. Conservative Catholics subsequently left their homeland in large numbers; even during World War I passenger ships continued to link Lisbon, Ponta Delgada, Angra do Heroísmo on Terceira, and Horta with the United States. These Catholic emigrants moved either to the established Portuguese communities in southern New England or, in response to specific recruitment, to new centers in Connecticut and to the famous jute mills of Ludlow, Mass. The actual entry of Portugal into the war on the side of the Allies (February 1916) caused many more Portuguese both on the continent and on the islands, in accordance with an old tradition, to avoid conscription by emigrating to the United States.

These special circumstances prompting emigration were always combined with adverse social and economic conditions, and, in the case of the islanders, no doubt with the sheer boredom of midoceanic insular existence. At the other end, the rise of the great textile mills in or near the original ports of entry—New Bedford, Fall River, Lowell, and Lawrence in Massachusetts, the Blackstone Valley near Providence in Rhode Island, and elsewhere in southern New England—guaranteed employment when they arrived.

The 1900–1920 period saw the arrival of many Madeirans, as well as Azoreans. Madeirans had already been arriving in small numbers for years; the paternal grandfather of novelist John Dos Passos, for example, emigrated from the town of Ponta do Sol to Baltimore around 1830. The Madeiran immigration in the late 1840s is unusual because it stemmed from religious persecution. In 1838 a missionary of the Free Church of Scotland en route to China called at and remained in Funchal, Madeira's port city, and was soon converting Madeirans to Scotch Calvinism and colliding with the traditionally Roman Catholic local authorities, both civil and ecclesiastical. In 1845 he was replaced by another Scot who formally organized what is said to have been the first Portuguese Protestant church in history. Persecution followed, and in 1846 a large number of the converted Madeirans emigrated to Trinidad. All manner of privations followed until the American Protestant Society of New York made arrangements with the American Hemp Company of Illinois for the Madeirans to come to the Springfield–Jacksonville area of west-central Illinois. There they did well, and many descendants of these Protestant Madeirans still live in that area.

The early New England whaling ships brought many island Portuguese immigrants—Azoreans and Cape Verdeans—not only to the Northeast of the United States, but also to the Hawaiian Islands and the San Francisco Bay area of California. The gold rush of 1849 attracted a great number of Portuguese to California, although they chiefly arrived by overland trek from New England rather than by ship. Portuguese immigration to Hawaii began in earnest in 1878 with the arrival of contract laborers from Madeira, recruited—with the intervention of both the Portuguese and American governments—to work the sugar plantations (where, incidentally, they introduced the ukulele). But the competition of cheap labor from Asia and its archipelagoes made Hawaii less attractive as a destination, all the more because the ambitious and often well-trained Portuguese aspired to clerical and other white-collar positions that were rarely available there. Not only did Portuguese immigrants virtually cease going to Hawaii, but some of the Portuguese already there pulled up

Table 1. Portuguese immigration to the United States, 1820–1977.

Period	Number
1820	35
1821–1830	145
1831–1840	829
1841–1850	550
1851–1860	1,055
1861–1870	2,658
1871–1880	14,082
1881–1890	16,978
1891–1900	27,508
1901–1910	69,149
1911–1920	89,732
1921–1930	29,994
1931–1940	3,329
1941–1950	7,423
1951–1960	19,588
1961–1970	76,065
1971–1977	75,717

Source: U.S. Immigration and Naturalization Service, *Annual Report, 1976* (Washington, D.C., 1979), pp. 65–67.

stakes and went to California. Throughout this early period, in fact, there was a good deal of internal migration; the considerable Portuguese communities in the Newark–Elizabeth area of New Jersey and later in Yonkers, Mineola, and elsewhere around New York City, for example, were first settled by Portuguese who had originally lived in New England.

A small and relatively late but vital addition to the Portuguese population of California in and around San Francisco and Los Angeles was a community of Macao Portuguese. About 4,000 of them immigrated to California immediately following World War II in the wake of the troubled political situation in East Asia. Originally from the Portuguese colony of Macao dating from 1557 and located just southwest of Hong Kong, these "Luso-Sino-Americans" or "Portuguese of the Orient," as they are known, are most likely included in U.S. statistics as Chinese immigrants since many of them or their forefathers moved to Shanghai and Hong Kong and entered the United States as Chinese rather than as Portuguese. Nevertheless, they hold fast to the Portuguese elements of their heritage. They are generally well-educated and most of them have entered business and professional ranks; they have their own organization, União Macaense Americana (American Macao Union), with 646 members in San Francisco, San Mateo, San Leandro, and Los Angeles branches.

The experience of the Cape Verdeans, as differentiated from the Azoreans, Madeirans, and continental and Chinese Portuguese, has not been as happy, and their interaction with other Portuguese has not always been smooth. In contrast to the European Portuguese, the Cape Verdeans are a racially mixed group, of African as well as Portuguese heritage. The European Portuguese arrived in the United States relatively free of race prejudice, but they soon discovered that the Cape Verdeans (or Bravas, as they came to be called for one of the Cape Verdean islands) were often taken for blacks by the non-Portuguese; they encountered prejudice and discrimination, and were considered to be inferior. This began to alarm the European Portuguese, who feared that all Portuguese would be victimized. Even fellow-Catholics of southeastern New England are alleged to have said that "the Portuguese are an inferior race." And the stereotyping continues. In a history of the town of Barnstable on Cape Cod, published in 1976, one finds that the Portuguese settlers "were both black and white" and that the "early black immigrants to Cape Cod were mostly from Cape Verde or the Azores and were sometimes called Bravas after a small island." Moreover, the ethnic groups of Barnstable are listed in two alphabetical sequences—Finns, Greeks, Irish, and Jews, on the one hand, and blacks, Portuguese, and Wampanoags on the other: one is obviously white and the other nonwhite.

Thus, it is not surprising that many Portuguese Americans, especially Azoreans of the earlier generations, have reacted strongly against this manifestation of racism, which constantly recurs in American writing, for example, in Joseph C. Lincoln's novel *The Portygee* (1920) and in Donald R. Taft's sociological study of Portsmouth, Rhode Island, and Fall River entitled *Two Portuguese Communities in New England* (1923). One such American of Portuguese descent, Hawaiian-born Elvira Osorio Roll, expressed her reaction in a novel entitled *Hawaii's Kohala Breezes* (1964), an

outstanding work of Portuguese ethnic literature. In it she argued that the group's experience with racism has been no different in Hawaii (where the Portuguese and their descendants in the mid-1960s numbered some 22,000) than in southern New England. There is evidence that the Portuguese in California also suffered in like manner. As a result, some Portuguese Americans came to feel ashamed of their heritage and attempted to conceal it in various ways. The Cape Verdeans, for their part, have come full circle and now wish to deny that they are Portuguese, or at least to affirm that they are Cape Verdeans. On July 5, 1975 the former Portuguese dependency of Cape Verde became the Republic of Cape Verde. (*See* Cape Verdeans.)

It is no longer fashionable to conceal one's ancestry, but in the 19th and first half of the 20th century many Portuguese Americans changed their names—or allowed their names to be changed, da Rosa thus becoming Rogers—and some women intermarried and left the group entirely. But those who have retained surnames like Andrade, Avila, Carvalho, Costa, De Aguiar, Dias, Dos Passos, Fernandes, Fonseca, Freitas, Gomes, Medeiros, Mendonça, Monteiro, Pimentel, Pitta, Soares, Sousa, Tavares, Taveira, and Vera have not been prevented from attaining high positions in academe, agriculture, architecture, the arts, the clergy, commerce, engineering, government service, industry, law, medicine, politics, and science. A few, mostly priests and medical doctors, occasionally engineers, were professionally trained in their homeland. An infinitesimal number were high-ranking political émigrés from continental Portugal, most of whom entered the United States after the right-wing overthrow of the republic on May 28, 1926; most refugees from the left-wing revolution of April 25, 1974, went instead to Brazil.

Settlements, Organizations, and Economic Life Whether from the islands or the mainland the Portuguese immigrants had for the most part been farmers at home. The fishing industry was not well developed in the Portuguese Atlantic archipelagoes, and in continental Portugal few fishermen apparently felt the need to emigrate. The many Portuguese who became fishermen in America did not pursue a traditional vocation; they acquired a new skill upon arrival. Most of the other immigrants continued to work the soil, on small truck gardens and dairy farms in the suburbs. Some were skilled carpenters and masons and entered the building trades; others became machinists. At first the women did not work, for it was against the traditions of their culture to do so, but once factory jobs became available, many Portuguese women also entered the labor market.

In California the Portuguese became farmers and ranchers in the eastern San Francisco Bay area from San Jose north to Hayward, San Leandro, and Oakland; they were well portrayed in Jack London's novels *Martin Eden* (1909) and *The Valley of the Moon* (1913). In the San Joaquin Valley (from Sacramento down through Stockton, Modesto, and Turlock to Tulare and beyond) they became successful large-scale dairy ranchers, especially around Tulare, the officially recognized sister city of Angra do Heroísmo, as New Bedford is of Horta, and San Leandro of Ponta Delgada. In southern California, particularly around San Diego, they became fishermen and pioneered in the design of the vessels needed to catch tuna and other species. A measure of the success the Portuguese have enjoyed on the West Coast is pro-

vided by UPEC, the União Portuguesa do Estado da Califórnia (Portuguese Union of the State of California); founded in 1880 and based in San Leandro, it has 77 branches. Opposite its modern headquarters is a powerful statue commemorating the Portuguese immigrant. There is no comparable monument in the Northeast.

The periods of significant growth of many Portuguese communities are reflected in the founding dates of the Portuguese nonterritorial or so-called national Catholic parishes "erected" by Rome in many dioceses, especially in southern New England. Very few such parishes have been established since 1958, but those that originated during the first wave of immigration have prolonged their vitality, and in many cases increased it, during the second (see Table 2). Theoretically limited to immigrants and their children, these national parishes were designed to carry on the intimate and comforting work of their Old World counterparts by ministering to Portuguese families in their own language and incorporating within the church building familiar statues and patriotic symbols, including the coat of arms of Portugal. However, in some areas, especially in California and Hawaii, the Catholic bishops discouraged ethnic parishes, and instead assigned Portuguese-speaking priests to the normal territorial parishes: in Hawaii the bishops objected even to that step.

The parish of St. Peter the Apostle in Provincetown, Mass., is a good example of the way in which a territorial as opposed to a national parish functioned. Balancing the national parish of Our Lady of Good Voyage in Gloucester (f. 1889), St. Peter's was erected as a territorial parish in 1874; the church building, which still stands, was dedicated in the same year. It caters to all Catholics within its territory, but as the majority of them are of Portuguese origin it is usually staffed by priests of Portuguese descent or birth.

The nonterritorial Portuguese parishes and the territorial parishes with Portuguese priests have served as community centers for immigrants and their U.S.-born children. They sponsor traditional *festas*, with national dishes such as *lingüiça* (sausage), kale soup, and a rich assortment of breads and with colorful costumes and graceful dances. The most widely known is the Holy Ghost festival, celebrated by Azoreans at Pentecost, which includes a crowning of "imperial" or "royal" personages—possibly a folk remembrance of the marriage of Princess Leonor of Portugal to the Holy Roman Emperor Frederick III in 1452, just as the Azores were being settled by emigrants from the mainland. Other notable occasions are the Feast of the Most Blessed Sacrament, instituted in New Bedford by four Madeirans in gratitude for their salvation from shipwreck en route to the United States in 1915, and the festivities associated with the Madeiran cult of Our Lady of the Mount (a shrine on the island of Madeira).

The Portuguese have established fewer parochial schools than other Catholic groups, such as the Irish and French Canadians. The first was opened in Fall River in 1910 as an adjunct of Espírito Santo parish (f. 1904); its founder was Father John B. DeValles, a native of São Miguel, who gained fame as a brave chaplain in World War I (a public school in New Bedford was later named in his honor). The first Portuguese parish in the United States, St. John the Baptist in New Bedford (f. 1869), did not open a school until World War II; St.

Table 2. Portuguese nonterritorial parishes in the United States, by community and date of founding.

New Bedford, Mass.
 1869, St. John the Baptist
 1902, Our Lady of Mount Carmel
 1909, Our Lady of the Immaculate Conception
Boston, Mass.
 1873, St. John the Baptist (North End, suppressed 1912)
 1921, St. John the Baptist (East Boston)
Fall River, Mass.
 1876, Santo Christo
 1902, St. Michael
 1904, Espírito Santo
 1911, St. Anthony of Padua
 1915, St. Elizabeth
 1915, Our Lady of the Angels
 1924, Our Lady of Health
Providence, R.I.
 1877, Our Lady of the Rosary
Gloucester, Mass.
 1889, Our Lady of Good Voyage
Oakland, Calif.
 1892, St. Joseph (suppressed 1965)
Lowell, Mass.
 1901, St. Anthony
Cambridge, Mass.
 1902, St. Anthony
Taunton, Mass.
 1903, St. Anthony
 1905, Our Lady of Lourdes
Lawrence, Mass.
 1907, SS. Peter and Paul (a "Portuguese Mission" 1932–1976)
Sacramento, Calif.
 1909, St. Elizabeth
Bristol, R.I.
 1913, St. Elizabeth
San Jose, Calif.
 1914, Five Wounds
East Providence, R.I.
 1915, St. Francis Xavier
East Falmouth, Mass.
 1922, St. Anthony
Pawtucket, R.I.
 1923, St. Anthony
West Warwick, R.I.
 1925, St. Anthony
Newport, R.I.
 1926, Jesus Savior
Somerset, Mass.
 1928, St. John of God
Ludlow, Mass.
 1948, Our Lady of Fátima
Warren, R.I.
 1952, St. Thomas the Apostle
Cumberland, R.I.
 1953, Our Lady of Fátima (Valley Falls section)
Newark, N.J.
 1955, Our Lady of Fátima
Hartford, Conn.
 1958, Our Lady of Fátima
Bridgeport, Conn.
 1962, Our Lady of Fátima
Waterbury, Conn.
 1969, Our Lady of Fátima
Elizabeth, N.J.
 1973, Our Lady of Fátima
Peabody, Mass.
 1976, Our Lady of Fátima (a "Portuguese Mission" 1965–1976)

Mary's School two blocks away had functioned since the 1880s as the parochial school of the territorial and largely Irish St. James parish.

Closely associated with the parishes and their schools are the social clubs, folklore groups, cultural and educational associations, mutual-aid societies, credit unions, and Portuguese-language newspapers and radio programs—institutions that have helped ease the

Portuguese, like other groups, into the mainstream of American life, although in some respects they have also contributed to the maintenance of the ethnic group.

Most important for the Portuguese Americans are the fraternal benefit societies, as they are officially known. Outstanding among those still extant are the following, all of them national in scope: California's UPEC, with a membership of nearly 12,000; União Portuguesa Continental dos Estados Unidos da América (Portuguese Continental Union of the United States of America), founded in Plymouth, Mass., in 1925, now headquartered in Boston with a membership of over 9,000; United National Life Insurance Society, founded in 1957 as the result of a merger of preexisting organizations, now headquartered in San Francisco with a membership about 15,000; and, primarily for women of Portuguese descent, Sociedade Portuguesa Raínha Santa Isabel (Portuguese Society Queen St. Isabel), founded in 1898, headquartered in Oakland with a membership about 13,000. Of particular interest is the Monte Pio Luso-Americano (Portuguese American Insurance Association), founded in New Bedford in 1882; it is said that President McKinley himself gave the organization permission to fly only the Portuguese flag, exempting it from the usual requirement that the American flag be flown at the same time.

Fiercely insistent that their heritage, language, and European homeland be recognized as Portuguese and not be mistaken as Spanish, the Portuguese continue to be concerned about the ignorance most Americans display toward Portugal, in spite of the extensive contacts between their country and the United States from the 18th century to World War II. Portuguese and closely related Brazilian programs have been supported at such universities as Yale, Harvard, Stanford, Vanderbilt, Georgetown, New York University, the University of Pennsylvania, and the University of Texas, and by the offering of Portuguese as a foreign language—as distinct from bilingual education—in public schools such as New Bedford High School, where it was actually introduced in response to an interest in Brazil born during World War II. The American Portuguese Society in New York City was founded in 1959 to promote a greater understanding of Portugal in the United States; an organization of business and professional people and a few of the more affluent immigrants from Portuguese territories, it publishes a journal and a bulletin.

The first Portuguese-American newspaper appeared in the late 1870s; several others followed in the 1880s in New England, California, and Hawaii. Today, five major secular weeklies are published regularly, two of them dating from the pre-1958 period: *Jornal Português* (Portuguese Newspaper, f. 1888) in San Pablo at the northern end of San Francisco Bay, and *Luso-Americano* (Portuguese American, f. 1928) in Newark, N.J. The *Portuguese Times* (f. 1970) in New Bedford, *Jornal de Fall River* (Fall River Newspaper, f. 1975) in Fall River, and *Azorean Times* (f. 1976) in Bristol, R.I., emerged primarily to serve the immigrants of the second wave and as successors to the many Portuguese-language newspapers that had died out earlier. Most valuable as a record of the Portuguese communities in the United States was the *Diário de Notícias* (Daily News) of New Bedford, a daily which ran for over half a century but which ceased publication in 1973.

Portuguese-American newspapers, which in the early days concentrated on local news because they had no way of receiving current news from Portugal, also sought to increase the immigrants' awareness of their Portuguese heritage. All too often the Portuguese came to America vaguely acquainted only with Prince Henry the Navigator, Vasco da Gama, and the epic poet Luís de Camões (1524–1580). They were sustained by their folk culture of popular tales, folk medicine, a belief in the evil eye, and a host of superstitions and proverbial sayings. In the New World their newspapers gave them the opportunity to improve their ability to read Portuguese and even to read serialized versions of such major literary works as the novels of Eça de Queiroz (1845–1900).

The newspapers have also provided a vehicle through which community leaders can try to encourage any incipient ethnic enthusiasm. They have promoted a cult of the maritime explorer Miguel Corte-Real (lost at sea in 1502), who, they claim, left an inscription on Dighton Rock near Fall River. They have also made a hero of a soldier who fought in the American Revolution named Peter Francisco (whose ancestry is actually unknown) by declaring him Portuguese, possibly an Azorean from Pico, because Pico people are said to be large in stature and Francisco was purportedly gigantic. On the West Coast they have made an ethnic hero of navigator João Rodrigues Cabrilho, who discovered San Diego Bay in 1542 while in the service of Spain, and is consequently better known in America by his Spanish name, Juan Rodríguez Cabrillo.

Portuguese contributions to both ethnic and national culture have been numerous. Both the early and more recent immigrations have produced artists—for instance, the seascape painter Louis Sylvia (1911–), a native of New Bedford, and the Terceira-born scrimshaw artist Frank Barcelos (1926–), now active in Fall River. There are plans for a Portuguese Heritage Museum to be located in the heart of the Portuguese community of southern New England.

Family Life The Portuguese have had some success in maintaining their traditional family structure. This has been reinforced by the 1965 U.S. Immigration and Nationality Act which gives immigration priority to close relatives, who naturally tend to settle where members of their family already dwell. Unfortunately, in the cases of former New England textile centers like New Bedford–Fall River and Lowell–Lawrence this often means that they settle in economically depressed areas rather than seeking out new places where the opportunities are greater.

Gathered together in closely knit family groups, the Portuguese have avoided big cities and settle in towns where they stand a chance some day of owning a mortgage-free home. Sons and daughters are not encouraged to stay in school past the required age, but to seek gainful—although all too often underpaid—employment in the vicinity and contribute to the family's income. This stress on family welfare discourages the young people from going away to school; if they go to college at all they tend to stay in the neighborhood and attend the local community college or regional state university.

A more positive aspect of this family solidarity is the tendency of the Portuguese to care for their ill at home insofar as they can. The Portuguese are also very adept

at tracing family trees, a passion that became important to medical researchers when a genetic illness, known as Machado disease or Joseph's disease, was found among the Azoreans.

Certain other aspects of Portuguese family life, however, actually contribute to the dissolution of the group. The near tyranny that can be exercised by fathers and brothers over daughters, sisters, and even widows often prompts rebellion: women marry outside the group, and sometimes even outside the church. In the cities of southeastern New England the Portuguese are part of a cosmopolitan population. Since there are few Portuguese parochial schools, interaction with other groups often results in the marriage of Portuguese with other Catholics, with Greek Orthodox, and occasionally with Protestant ethnic groups. Portuguese were intermarrying at least as early as the mid-19th century.

Whether islanders or continentals, the immigrants were almost all coastal people, peasants farming the ocean shore; in the United States they gravitated to the coastal cities and towns. The San Joaquin Valley is as far inland as they have settled, and even there they are rarely more than a hundred or so miles from the Pacific. On the "Big Island" of Hawaii, too, they cluster at the water's edge.

The isolation and self-sufficiency of the homeland villages contributed to the splintering of the community in the United States and to a lack of cooperation among the various regional groups. The Portuguese neighborhoods of American cities and towns usually contain inhabitants not from an archipelago but from a single island: those in the South End of New Bedford come from Faial, while the North End shelters the Madeirans; those from São Miguel and Santa Maria came to Fall River; and the Terceirans have settled in Tulare, Calif. Club members often come only from specific areas—for instance, Cambridge, Mass., houses the Faialense Sport Club, the Santo Christo Center (named after a statue of Christ in a Ponta Delgada convent), and the Clube Recreio Madeirense (Madeiran Recreation Club). The Portuguese Continental Union was originally restricted to continentals.

As a result of the Portuguese pattern of settlement and family life, there are many Portuguese neighborhoods but there have never been any sizable urban Little Portugals or Portugaltowns, with the possible exception of a portion of Newark's "Ironbound" in recent years. The Portuguese are considered by others to be sober and law-abiding citizens and ideal neighbors; they have a reputation for being able to turn a dilapidated neighborhood into a showplace.

The regional accent of the Portuguese spoken by the islanders from São Miguel, Santa Maria, Madeira, and to a lesser extent from Faial, draws attention to their origins and perpetuates divisiveness. The traditional rivalry between the neighboring cities of New Bedford and Fall River, for example, is exacerbated by the tension that exists between their respective Azorean communities—the Faialese in the former, the Michaelese in the latter.

IMMIGRATION SINCE 1958

As indicated in Table 1, a total of 7,423 Portuguese immigrated into the United States in the 1940s. An additional 10,191 arrived between 1951 and June 30, 1958.

Suddenly and dramatically the number rose, bringing the total for the decade of the 1950s to 19,588. The 1960s and 1970s saw 151,782 more arrive, with the result that the Portuguese have a higher percentage of new arrivals than any other American ethnic group of European origin. The immediate explanation lies in a disaster that struck the Azores.

On September 27, 1957, a series of submarine volcanic eruptions began at the western tip of Faial and continued for several months, spreading terror among the Azoreans. Congressional representatives of Portuguese communities in the United States came to their aid in the form of Azorean refugee legislation enacted in 1958 which provided for 1,500 special nonquota immigrant visas by June 30, 1960; the number was later increased to 2,000, and the deadline to June 30, 1962. In all, 4,811 Portuguese immigrated under the provisions of the two laws, which enabled several family members to enter on a single visa.

In 1965 the U.S. Congress, influenced to some extent by the precedent of the Azorean refugee acts, decided to abolish entirely the national quota system (under which Portugal had been allowed only 440 visas per year) and adopt a system of preferences based in part on the presence in the United States of family members. This system assigned 20,000 visas annually to each eastern hemisphere country, and its immediate effect was a sudden increase in immigration from European countries with hitherto small national quotas, including Portugal.

Between 1959 and 1977 over 161,000 Portuguese were admitted to the United States, with perhaps another 10 to 20 percent entering illegally or from countries other than Portugal. Portuguese who had immigrated prior to this period—primarily Azoreans, Madeirans, Cape Verdeans, and continentals—were in general successfully settled. Although they retained a sentimental attachment to their homeland, relatives, language, and customs (in particular, food and drink), and some occasionally visited or retired there, by and large they were happy to adjust to life in the New World, influenced partly by the Americanization movement of the 1920s. After 1958, however, important changes took place in Portugal which drastically altered the nature of Portuguese-American life.

Relations with the Homeland   The head of the Portuguese government, António de Oliveira Salazar (1889–1970), who governed as a dictator from 1928 to 1968, faced a desperate situation with his "overseas provinces," especially those in Africa. Political reverses led Salazar to indoctrinate his Portuguese subjects at home and abroad, including immigrants in the United States on permanent-residence visas, to support his policies and help him retain his colonies. To do so, he made use of such networks as the school system, the press, and the church. Building on three decades of totalitarianism —his widely disseminated slogan of the 1930s was "The nation is everything, everything for the nation"— Salazar attempted to mold an emigrant who would proclaim his pride in being Portuguese and would defend Salazar's policies, however unacceptable these were to fellow residents in the adopted country.

In the United States, Salazar's supporters hired a public relations firm to disseminate pro-Portuguese propaganda, especially among Portuguese Americans, to induce them to bring pressure on the Congress and the

administration in Washington to support Salazar's African policies. When the Senate Committee on Foreign Relations exposed these activities, the contract was shifted to another firm. It was finally terminated by the revolutionary government immediately after April 25, 1974, before many members of the Portuguese-American community realized that they had been the targets of a sophisticated propaganda campaign.

After the 1974 revolution, the ends were changed greatly but the means only slightly; the goals became less political and more financial. Post-revolutionary Portugal entered a period of severe economic crisis brought on by a drop in the number of tourists from abroad, in the amount of money being sent by emigrants back to the homeland, and in the number of emigrants returning in retirement, and by the sudden swelling of the population due to the influx of Portuguese from the newly independent African colonies. The propaganda was directed toward the Portuguese Americans in general, and toward the Azoreans in particular. The personnel shifted from hired agents to officials within the central government in Lisbon (Socialist) and the newly constituted autonomous regional government of the Azores (Social Democrat). The appeal to the patriotism of the new immigrants continued, and it was successful because it could be superimposed on the indoctrination of the prior regime. One technique employed was the so-called *sessão de esclarecimento* (clarification session), in which a visiting official would expound his government's or his party's policies to a local group. What is more, a right-wing independence movement sprang up in the Azores, whose adherents exerted great pressure on Azoreans in the United States; Azorean Americans were thus the target of a three-pronged effort.

The 1970 U.S. Census was taken just as the large numbers of Portuguese immigrants of the new wave were beginning to appear, and can therefore be used to arrive at a rough estimate of the size of the overall target, newcomers as well as old, at which the Portuguese officials were aiming. The total foreign stock (immigrants and second generation) listed as being from Portugal and from the Azores was given as 318,458 (a figure viewed by ethnic leaders as much too low), distributed by state as follows:

State	Number	Portuguese as % of resident population
Massachusetts	108,919	1.91
California	98,275	0.49
Rhode Island	35,730	3.76
New Jersey	17,355	0.24
Connecticut	15,218	0.50
New York	15,126	0.08
Hawaii	6,460	0.84
Florida	3,069	0.05
Pennsylvania	2,948	0.025
Remaining states	15,358	

The recent arrivals are largely unaware of the history and traditions of the earlier group, and they tend to fill newspaper columns and radio and television programs with matters of interest only to themselves and not to the group as a whole. Air mail, jet travel, and transatlantic telephone communication have provided channels by which the old country can retain a hold over

these newcomers. Newspapers and airwaves can now easily include up-to-the-minute dispatches from continental Portugal, Madeira, and the Azores; folkloric groups and musical bands can even be flown in by jet. The media on occasion serve as conservative organs for political groups in the old country rather than as educational instruments directed at the entire Portuguese-American community.

These technological changes also encourage frequent travel between the United States and the homeland. Excursions of this sort are stimulated by the many ethnic travel agencies and the ethnic airline, Transportes Aéreos Portugueses (TAP). The prospect of retiring "back home" is nurtured by the new U.S. branches of Portuguese banks and is not discouraged by the policies of the U.S. Social Security Administration. The administration's annual publication, *Beneficiaries Residing Abroad*, gives some indication of the magnitude of this phenomenon and also reveals how the revolution in Portugal slowed the exodus of retirees from the United States. The following table shows the number of checks sent monthly to Portugal in recent years, along with their total monthly value.

Year	Number of checks sent monthly	Total monthly value
1971	5,312	$526,868
1972	5,577	666,627
1973	5,797	706,358
1974	5,825	792,744
1975	5,590	819,536
1976	5,590	877,100
1977	5,708	951,900

Group Adjustment These figures suggest the dimension of repatriation. In fact, from the earliest days of the immigration, there has been constant movement to and fro, especially between New England and the Azores; after all, Horta on Faial is the European port closest to Boston. By and large, however, the Portuguese immigrants, in spite of affirmations to the contrary by some ethnic leaders, have assimilated rapidly and have adopted the United States as their permanent homeland. They have even resisted organization as a national group.

In 1964 a movement began in Lisbon to organize Portuguese communities throughout the world. Within each country a national federation of clubs, associations, and other organizations was envisaged, all to be united in an international federation which would be based in Lisbon. The União das Comunidades de Cultura Portuguesa (Union of Communities of Portuguese Culture) was indeed formed in the Portuguese capital, but the Portuguese-American Federation organized in that same year 1964 in the United States never attained the original objective. It is today a relatively small organization of clubs and individuals chiefly active in southeastern New England. There is not now, nor has there ever been, a national organization of Portuguese Americans with officers capable of speaking for the entire group, nor have the many Portuguese national parishes ever been grouped into a national Portuguese-American diocese or archdiocese.

Some Portuguese Americans view with decidedly mixed feelings a continuing barrage of post-1974 propaganda from Lisbon suggesting that "the future of Portu-

gal is linked to the emigrants and to the communities," or, more subtly, that "the world of today is becoming one of undefined frontiers." They are becoming much more politically active than their predecessors, but, due partly to the excellent leadership of a portion of the Portuguese-language press and some radio stations, they are directing this activity toward their own problems within the United States.

The ease of modern travel, the increasingly cosmopolitan tastes of the general population, constant contact with the homeland, and ethnic-heritage, bilingual, and bicultural educational programs have encouraged a revival in ethnic cuisine among the Portuguese Americans and have reinforced their longstanding international interests. Numerous Portuguese restaurants have opened in recent years in the major areas of settlement, most of which feature the national dish known as *porco à alentejana* (pork in the manner of the Alentejo, a province south of the Tagus River), which consists of cubed pork with clams in a savory sauce, and also many of the traditional 365 ways of preparing codfish. The recent Portuguese immigrants are more attached to the homeland than the earlier arrivals had been. They are also better educated and filled with an *orgulho* (pride) carefully inculcated first by an authoritarian regime and then by a regime desperately in need of a favorable image abroad. But they are also Americans and are firmly devoted to their adopted country.

The second-wave immigrants settled into the United States just as the civil rights movement was getting under way. They soon heard about "minority groups," as opposed to European "ethnic groups," but at first did not really understand the distinction between them. Since there were economic advantages in being a "minority"—that is, in being listed with blacks, American Indians, East Asians, and Spanish-surnamed Americans —some attempted to do so, offending the sensibilities of the earlier Portuguese immigrants and their descendants.

The recent immigrants are attempting to seek real change for themselves and their families and not only to better themselves economically. Many obviously were dissatisfied with the political leadership of their native land, and some now want to have nothing more to do with its political and administrative leaders. Others concluded that their church back home had failed to respond to the needs of the times, and some of them now desire to be active in the Catholic church as it exists in America, or else have revolted altogether and joined other churches. Still others felt unfulfilled by the educational system as it existed in Portugal and want no part of bilingual education for their children, with its inevitable accompaniment of teachers and texts from the old country. A few may even desire to suppress their national origin completely and join the mainstream of American society.

Bibliography
Leo Pap has compiled a useful and thorough volume entitled *The Portuguese in the United States: A Bibliography* (Staten Island, N.Y., 1976) which gives over 800 citations, not repeated here. Pap's *Portuguese-American Speech* (New York, 1949) is a classic. The bound master file of New Bedford's daily newspaper, *Diário de Notícias* is deposited in the library of Southeastern Massachusetts University in North Dartmouth.
Social scientists are only now beginning to examine the Portuguese ethnic group. Examples are James P. Ito-Adler, *Ethnic Minorities in Cambridge, Volume One: The Portuguese* (Cambridge, Mass., 1972),

published both in a summary and an unabridged version; and three articles by M. Estellie Smith: "Portuguese Enclaves: The Invisible Minority" in Thomas K. Fitzgerald, ed., *Social and Cultural Identity* (Athens, Ga., 1974); "A Tale of Two Cities: The Reality of Historical Differences," *Urban Anthropology* 4 (Spring 1975): 61–72; and "The Portuguese Female Immigrant: 'Marginal Man' Par Excellence" in Neil Miller, ed., *Women in Portuguese Society: Proceedings of the Second Annual Symposium on the Portuguese Experience in the United States, Adelphi University, November 16, 1976* (Fall River and Cambridge, Mass., after 1976).
Recent American studies containing interesting facts, vignettes of individuals, statistical data, and bibliography are Manoel da Silveira Cardozo, comp. and ed., *The Portuguese in America, 590 B.C.–1974: A Chronology and Fact Book* (Dobbs Ferry, N.Y., 1976); two articles by Francis M. Rogers: "The Portuguese Experience in the United States: Double Melt or Minority Group?" *The Journal of the American Portuguese Society* 10 (Spring 1976): 1–16, and "The Contribution by Americans of Portuguese Descent to the U.S. Literary Scene," in Wolodymyr T. Zyla and Wendell M. Aycock, eds., *Ethnic Literatures since 1776: The Many Voices of America* (Lubbock, Tex., 1978); and Pat Amaral, *They Ploughed the Seas: Profiles of Azorean Master Mariners* (St. Petersburg, Fla., 1978). See also Carlos Almeida, *Portuguese Immigrants: The Centennial Story of the Portuguese Union of the State of California* (San Leandro, Calif., 1978) and Frederic A. Silva, *"All Our Yesterdays. . .": The Sons of Macao—Their History and Heritage* (San Francisco, Calif., 1979).
An analysis of the background culture of the majority of the Portuguese immigrants is provided in Francis M. Rogers, *Atlantic Islanders of the Azores and Madeiras* (North Quincy, Mass., 1979). Archives in the Azores are also proving to be a rich source of information on the ethnic group in America; see Maria José Lagos Trindade, "Portuguese emigration from the Azores to the United States during the 19th century," in *Portugal and America: Studies in Honor of the Bicentennial of American Independence* (Lisbon, 1976).

FRANCIS M. ROGERS

POTAWATOMIS: *see* AMERICAN INDIANS

PREJUDICE

Definitions of prejudice abound. Prejudice, one aphorism asserts, is being down on something you are not up on. Prejudice, goes another, is a vagrant opinion without visible means of support. For Voltaire, prejudice was opinion without judgment. But, like "intelligence" and other conceptions adapted from popular usage, the scientific conception of prejudice is at once both narrower and broader than its popular meanings.

Prejudice is often used to refer to bias, partiality, or a predilection; in the law, to harm and injury. None of these meanings is retained directly by social science. Instead, there has been an expansion of the popular meaning of prejudice as "an opinion for or against something without adequate basis." Notice that this conception includes both irrationality ("an opinion . . . without adequate basis") and emotional evaluation ("for or against something"). It is in these spheres of human cognition and affect, or thinking and feeling, and their links to behavior that social science has broadened its conception of prejudice into a useful tool for understanding ethnic relations.

DEFINITIONS AND CONCEPTS

There are two critical considerations for a workable definiton of prejudice. First, for the cognitive, irrational component, how can one determine what constitutes an "inadequate basis" for prejudiced attitudes? Was it "prejudice" that caused many Americans during World War II to hate Adolf Hitler and his Nazi party? If the attitudes are largely justified by "the facts," then Americans were not prejudiced. But how can "the facts" be evaluated? Obviously, no sharp distinction can be made

between an "adequate" and an "inadequate" basis for negative group attitudes. This logical problem is not as serious in practice as it first appears, thanks to the cognitive distortions that typically characterize the phenomenon. Gross overgeneralizations signal prejudice. A hatred of Nazis generalized to all of the German people regardless of their participation in the Nazi party clearly represents prejudice. Such overgeneralizations, called stereotypes, mark many, though not all, antagonistic group attitudes.

A second point concerns the affective, feeling component of prejudice. Favorable prejudice is possible as well as hostile prejudice, as illustrated by a loyal member's sympathy toward his own group. But when we fail "to love thy neighbor as thyself," to exhibit "brotherly love," to accord to outgroups what we routinely accord to our own ingroup, some degree of negative prejudice is involved. Again, no sharp demarcation can be drawn between "positive" and "negative" prejudice. But social science has limited the concept to group antipathies.

Prejudice, then, can be thought of as *irrationally based, negative attitudes against certain ethnic groups and their members*. It is clearly a value-laden concept, for it is regarded as "bad" and "wrong" to be prejudiced. Thus, prejudiced attitudes violate two basic norms, one cognitive and the other affective—"the norm of rationality" and "the norm of human-heartedness."

The norm of rationality enjoins us to seek accurate information, correct mistaken notions, make needed qualifications and differentiations—in short, to be as rational as human limitations allow. Prejudice clearly vitiates this norm with its overgeneralizations, prejudgments, and a general denial of individual differences. The norm of human-heartedness enjoins us to accept other groups and individuals in terms of their common humanity, regardless of who they are and how different they may be. Virtually all major religious and ethical traditions invoke this norm, and in secular American thought it appears in "rooting for the underdog." With its hostility toward outgroups, prejudice also vitiates this norm.

Drawing on the thought of both Gordon Allport and John Harding, a more comprehensive definition can now be advanced: Prejudice against racial and ethnic groups is an antipathy accompanied by a faulty generalization. It may be felt or expressed. It may be directed toward a group as a whole, or toward an individual because he is a member of that group. Thus, ethnic prejudice simultaneously violates two basic norms—the norm of rationality and the norm of human-heartedness.

Many other terms relate to this view of prejudice. Thus, prejudgment and intolerance each refer to just one of the critical dual aspects of prejudice. *Prejudgment* involves a premature cognitive fix on a subject prior to examining the relevant evidence; it constitutes a violation of the rationality norm. *Intolerance* represents a rejection of outgroups because of their differences from the ingroup; it constitutes a violation of the human-heartedness norm. Similarly, *bigotry* refers to a zealous ingroup devotion and consequent rejection of outgroups. *Xenophobia* goes further; it involves a fear of and aversion to all who are seen as different and strange.

Ethnocentrism is another closely related concept. It refers to the unquestioned belief in the superiority of

one's own ethnic group and the consequent inferiority of other groups. William Graham Sumner wrote that enthnocentrism is a view of one's own group as the center of everything, with all others scaled and rated with reference to it. Unlike racist notions of inborn, biological superiority, however, ethnocentric beliefs are founded upon notions of cultural superiority. In practice, however, biological and cultural explanations for group superiority and inferiority often merge, and the distinction between ethnocentrism and racism becomes blurred.

Recently, it has become fashionable in America to discuss two varieties of racism—individual and institutional. The first of these is like prejudice in that it is a phenomenon of individuals. But *individual racism* includes both prejudicial attitudes and discriminatory behavior, and is based upon the assumption of the genetic inferiority of the outgroup. Generally applied to the attitudes and behavior of white Americans toward black Americans, its superiority-inferiority claims of race can be traced back to Count Joseph Arthur de Gobineau's essay on the inequality of the human races in the mid-19th century. By contrast, *institutional racism* refers to the complex of institutional arrangements that restrict the life chances and choices of a socially defined racial group in comparison with those of the dominant group. Institutional racism refers to a society's social structure and not to individuals.

Discrimination is closely allied with this conception of institutional racism. Both operate on the societal level. Discrimination is basically an institutional process of exclusion against an outgroup, racial or cultural, based simply on who they are rather than on their knowledge or abilities. But this simple definition belies the difficulty that often arises in determining group discrimination in our society. The problem arises most sharply in realms that were not long ago considered private matters and are today under public regulation. Here personal preferences and social policy collide. Is, for example, an employer's nepotism—the granting of jobs or favors to relatives—just a family affair? Or is it an act of discrimination because it restricts the chances and choices of outgroup members who may be better qualified than the family members? A generation ago the societal answer was that it was clearly within the rights of employers to hire whomever they wished. Today, with the nation having come to realize the complexity of group discrimination, the answer is likely to be that many forms of nepotism do indeed involve group discrimination.

Prejudice and discrimination are by no means perfectly correlated; one without the other is not at all uncommon. But, obviously, the two are linked. Discrimination and institutional racism not only limit an outgroup's opportunities, but they are powerful and ever-present reminders that directly support prejudice and individual racism. Hence, anti-Irish and anti-Semitic attitudes not only led in the late 19th century to blatant discrimination against Irish and Jewish Americans, but the discrimination itself fostered negative attitudes. Prejudice does not operate in a social and institutional vacuum; it thrives in a contaminated environment of ingroup privilege and outgroup exclusion.

Prejudice, then, is distinguished by two principal components, each of which violates a widely shared

cultural norm. In terms of the intellect it violates rationality standards, and in terms of the emotions it violates human-heartedness standards. Following is a discussion of these cognitive and affective components.

COGNITIVE FACTORS IN PREJUDICE

Individuals survive psychologically in a chaotic universe, bombarded with more sensory stimulation than they can possibly process and use. They thus must strive to organize their environment and give it meaning by simplifying and packaging the incoming stimuli into readily useful information. This effort is made possible by an array of interrelated cognitive processes that usually function well. But, necessarily, in reducing the stimulus overload to manageable size, they can lead to characteristic errors in the selection, accentuation, and interpretation of sensory data. The relevance of these cognitive processes for prejudice is considerable. Rationality becomes a norm—a norm that is impossible to attain fully and consistently. The irrational distortions that comprise prejudice must therefore be viewed as grounded not in aberrant but in normal and necessary human processes.

Sensory inputs are organized basically through the use of categories—broad clusters of items that are conceptualized under a single label (furniture, people, Swedes). By classifying incoming information within our categories, we render the world meaningful. But this process typically leads us to overestimate the similarity among items *within* categories and the differences between items *across* categories. This distortion is implicated in prejudice because ethnic groups themselves, like sex, age, and social class, are salient categories for organizing what is known about people. And once individuals categorize Chicanos, Asians, and blacks, they are likely to exaggerate the commonalities within these groups and overlook the human similarities and universals that bind the groups to each other.

Individuals also make categorical differentiations within their own ethnic group, but few if any among other groups. A Scottish American may consistently employ the Highlander and Lowlander distinction to judge his fellow Scots. As a descendant of Highlanders, he can explain away unfortunate aspects of Scots by assuming that they must be of Lowland origin. But he may fail to distinguish similarly within other groups. These distortions do not in themselves constitute prejudice, but they are the foundation upon which the cognitive components of prejudice are constructed.

The ethnic organization of much of the world furthers this categorization process. Ethnic categories help individuals to understand themselves and others, as well as the culture. Furthermore, there is social support for the use of these categories, since others also use them. The mass media advance this ethnic categorization process, often in its most destructive form. Many groups objected to the *All in the Family* television series for precisely this reason.

Language and labeling also heighten this process, since ethnic labels are particularly salient and influential. Gordon Allport called them "nouns that cut slices." "Koreans," "Cubans," and other ethnic labels of primary potency obscure other human characteristics by magnifying one attribute out of proportion to its sig-

nificance. To know that a woman is an American Indian often overwhelms the equally important facts that she is also a lawyer, a resident of Chicago, and a former swimming champion. This phenomenon is enhanced further by the use of emotionally charged ethnic epithets, such as spic, chink, harp, or canuck; their use usually signals prejudice in its rawest form.

There is also a personality dimension to this categorization phenomenon. The use of dichotomous categories—the saved and the damned, the good and the bad, natives and immigrants—is particularly prone to irrational distortions leading to prejudice. Research demonstrates that prejudiced individuals of various ages are more likely to exhibit this "intolerance of ambiguity" than are equally intelligent, more tolerant individuals. This cognitive style of requiring greater definiteness is revealed by prejudiced seven-year-old children who are less willing to face uncertainty in solving problems and by prejudiced teen-agers who more often prefer structured situations and possess more rigid conceptions of sex roles. Striking evidence is provided also by an attitude item that has differentiated between the prejudiced and the tolerant in hundreds of tested samples: repeatedly, the more prejudiced tend to agree that "there are two kinds of people—the weak and the strong."

Stereotyping, a principal form of the cognitive distortions of prejudice, arises directly from these cognitive means of simplifying and rendering meaningful what our senses record. Defining stereotypes broadly as *the overgeneralization of psychological characteristics to large human groups*, the phenomenon emerges from the errors and biases of thought and perception common to everyone, rather than from any "faulty reasoning process" peculiar to prejudice.

The term "stereotype," taken from printing, was introduced in 1922 by Walter Lippmann. He thought of stereotypes as "pictures in our heads" that were acquired culturally rather than through personal experience. Social scientists have employed the concept to mean images of groups that tend to be simple, erroneous, acquired secondhand, and resistant to modification.

Blatant stereotyping is a common phenomenon. It was even more common before World War II. One famous study in the early 1930s found that Princeton University students agreed in their assignment of many traits: "Germans" were thought to be scientifically minded (72 percent) and industrious (65 percent), "Jews" shrewd (79 percent) and mercenary (49 percent), "Negroes" superstitious (84 percent) and lazy (75 percent). Many similar studies conducted throughout the world have since shown comparable results.

This prevalence of stereotyping suggests once again that this cognitive distortion is not unique to prejudice and arises from natural means of thinking and perceiving. Thus, stereotypes emerge from the process of categorization. They bring simplicity, order, and meaning by supplying packaged content to ethnic group categories. When an individual encounters a Finn, he or she can maintain cognitive order and even reinforce an erroneous image by employing the standard categorization mechanism. All Finns will be perceived as being more alike and similar to the stereotype than they actually are; simultaneously, an individual may tend to accentuate the differences between Finns and Swedes in order

to maintain differential stereotypes of the two groups. So two people of different ethnic origins but equally intelligent are likely to be perceived as differentially bright according to the stereotypes of the two ethnicities.

Stereotypes are also readily available images of social groups, images that can be triggered by nothing more than the mere mention of group membership. The distinctiveness, salience, and extremeness of stimuli all contribute to the mental availability of an image, and all three often underlie the development of stereotypes. These stimulus characteristics can establish a negative stereotype without the slightest basis in reality. In what is called "illusory correlation," the co-occurrence of two distinctive, low-probability events can lead to a sharp overestimation of the frequency with which the two rare events occur together. This pheonomenon contributes to stereotyping. Consider the publicity given by the mass media when a rare and violent crime is committed by a member of a small ethnic group. Even though there is no ethnic correlation over time with the rare crime, it is likely that an illusory correlation between the two is established in the minds of many people.

Another factor contributing to the process is that individuals tend to see outgroup members who appear to possess the accepted stereotypes as particularly representative of their group. The informational value of non-occurrences is typically overlooked. Consequently, the numerous instances of outgroup members who do not possess the stereotype are less salient, and therefore less likely to be viewed as representative. For those who believe all Italian Americans to be members of the Mafia, law-abiding Italian Americans are simply out of view.

This bias toward noticing "positive" cases and ignoring "error" cases may operate with greater force in everyday perception than in the psychological laboratory. Rarely in the "real world" is an individual privileged to know accurate baseline data about the traits of entire ethnic groups. Furthermore, differential association contributes to the bias. Individuals know their ingroup better and have more contact with its members. Thus, extreme instances among the outgroup are more salient, more available to memory, retrospectively overestimated, and more likely to be seen as representative of the outgroup. Group members who have more contact with the outgroup are therefore less likely to stereotype them. White stereotypes of blacks in Chicago, for example, become more distorted with increasing residential distance from the city's black areas. And ethnic stereotypes are used less by those English and French Canadians who have experienced the most interethnic contact. Such contact leads to a larger sampling of outgroup behaviors that acts to counter stereotypes, though the conditions of the intergroup contact are crucial.

Ethnic stereotypes also act as anchors, as initial starting points. And adjustments from these anchors are often insufficient. Bigots know that not *all* Irish are "quick tempered"; but insufficient adjustment from this anchor makes it difficult to demonstrate the opposite of a stereotypical attribute. Only a strikingly "exceptional" performance that contrasts sharply with the stereotype can keep from being assimilated to the stereotypical anchor. This process probably affects negative more than positive stereotypes, since an individual generally grants greater weight to negative than to positive characteristics in evaluations.

Contrasting traits are also involved in the particular items that are selected out to characterize a group; since contrasts provide strong stimuli, real differences between groups are likely to appear in the stereotypes each group has of the other. This tendency does not deny the possibility that stereotypes can emerge without any objective basis whatsoever. But it does make it likely that most stereotypes are exaggerations of actual differences between groups.

The objective basis of ethnic stereotypes has long been the subject of much debate but little systematic research. On the one hand, stereotypes can evolve in contradiction to the facts. Armenian-American laborers in Fresno, Calif., during the 1920s were commonly viewed as deceitful, dishonest, liars, and troublemakers; yet they appeared less often in court, applied less often for charity, and possessed credit ratings equal to those of other ethnic groups. On the other hand, widespread agreement across many groups concerning the content of ethnic stereotypes suggests that there is at least some validity for most stereotypes. Actually, a group's members generally characterize themselves in ways similar to their stereotype, though they usually place more favorable connotations on the agreed-upon traits ("sly" becomes "clever," "pushy" becomes "ambitious").

The "kernel-of-truth" possibility receives further support from the fact that two contrasting types of ethnic stereotypes emerge throughout the world in relation to the societal positions occupied by the stereotyped groups. In psychoanalytic terms, one type is rooted in superego concerns and the other in id concerns. Outgroups with superego stereotypes are seen as mercenary, ambitious, sly, and clannish. They are frequently merchants who are not native to an area—middlemen caught between the landed and the laboring classes like the medieval European Jews: the Chinese merchants of Malaysia and Indonesia are often called the "Jews of Asia," and the Muslim Indian merchants of East Africa the "Jews of Africa." Outgroups with id stereotypes are seen as superstitious, lazy, ignorant, dirty, and sexually uninhibited. They are groups found on the bottom of the social structure. In Europe, "guest-workers," Gypsies, and southern Italians are often targets; in the United States, blacks and Mexican Americans inherit the id stigma. This worldwide differentiation in ethnic stereotypes reveals some of their rationalizing function. And though often founded upon a "kernel-of-truth," stereotypes still qualify as irrational in their exaggeration, their absolutism, and their insensitivity to contrary evidence.

To achieve a stable, meaningful view of a changing world, an individual must determine the causes and implications of his or her actions and the actions of others. But in carrying out this cognitive task, another distortion is commonly created that has been called "the fundamental attribution error." Observers generally underestimate the force of situational and societal pressures and overestimate the force of a person's dispositions on his behavior. This tendency may not be purely a cognitive process, for it is probably enhanced

in a society such as ours that places particular emphasis upon values of individualism.

The fundamental attribution error is easily demonstrated. In one experiment, subjects played a quiz game with the assigned roles of "questioner" and "contestant." Though the game allowed the "questioners" the enormous advantage of generating all of the questions from their personal stores of knowledge, later ratings of "general knowledge" were higher for the questioner. This dispositional attribution was made not only by the questioners and uninvolved observers, but especially by the disadvantaged contestants themselves. Note that the powerful situational force (the quiz game's format) is minimized, dispositional characteristics of the salient person (the questioner) are causally magnified, and role requirements (of being a quiz contestant) are not fully adjusted for in the final attribution.

Analogies to these experimental results in ethnic relations come easily to mind. Groups located predominantly in one particular occupation play a limited set of social roles. But others, and even many of the group members themselves, are likely to overlook the situational and role requirements and to misattribute their behavior to some assumed personal dispositions. Ethnic cues are frequently vivid and salient, while environmental cues tend to blend into the perceptual background. Even an all-embracing institution such as slavery was generally disregarded by white Americans, and black behavior was causally attributed to peculiar qualities about blacks themselves. This widespread tendency is often described as "blaming the victim." Here we see how ethnic stereotypes and causal misattributions are components of the same cognitive process that underlies prejudice.

This fundamental attribution error is extended and accentuated in intergroup perception. It has been shown that we typically grant our spouse and close friends the benefit of the doubt in our causal perceptions. For them, we attribute positive actions to dispositional causes ("She did it because she has a good heart") and negative actions to situational causes ("He only did it because he had to under the circumstances").

Granting members of another ethnic group the benefit of the doubt, however, is not so common. In what has been labeled "the ultimate attribution error," intergroup perceptions are more likely than intragroup perceptions to assume "the worst." In explaining acts that are perceived as antisocial or undesirable, outgroup behavior is more frequently attributed to personal, dispositional causes. Often these internal causes will be seen as innate characteristics ("They have a high crime rate because they are born thieves"). But when acts are perceived as prosocial or desirable, outgroup behavior is more often "explained away" in one of four ways. We can account for the stereotype violation in situational terms with role requirements now receiving attention ("Under the circumstances, what could the cheap Scot do but pay the whole check?"). Or we can ascribe it to motivation, as opposed to innate qualities ("Jewish students make better grades, because they try so much harder"). Or we can attribute the behavior to the exceptional, even exaggerated, "special case" individual who is contrasted with her group—what Allport called "refencing" our stereotypes ("She is certainly bright and hardworking—not at all like other Chicanas"). Or we

can explain it away as simply luck ("It was just luck; they are too dumb to have won it on their own").

The human need to maintain cognitive stability and meaningfulness is the principal reason behind the natural human processes that lead to group stereotypes and misattributions. But these distortions can also rationalize our actions toward the outgroup. Stereotypes can justify categorical rejection or acceptance of an outgroup, and can even justify such systems of exploitation as slavery.

This rationalization function is not a necessary condition for stereotyping. Research subjects are willing to express stereotypes for a range of little-known ethnic groups toward whom they harbor no affective feelings whatsoever (for example, college students regarding Turks as "cruel" and Eskimos as "quaint"). However, when these cognitive distortions join with hatred to form prejudice, rationalization seems always present. Indeed, the causal order of the cognitive and affective components of prejudice is a major difference between the ways in which bigots themselves and social scientists analyze the phenomenon. Bigots regard their negative feelings as following logically from the contemptible traits of the outgroup. Social scientists believe that the negative feelings generally come first and lead to the justifying stereotypes. Evidence for the latter contention is provided by the fact that ethnic stereotypes turn either side of the coin into justification for outgroup rejection. The hated others are either too lazy or too industrious, too cold or too emotional, too stupid or too shrewd. Further evidence is supplied by reviewing the affective factors of prejudice.

AFFECTIVE FACTORS IN PREJUDICE

Many different emotions can underlie prejudice. Violating the norm of "human-heartedness" can result from fear and threat, or jealousy and envy; it can range from intense hatred to simple indifference and an absence of human sympathy. But most research on prejudice has concentrated on the single, friendly-hostile dimension.

Hostility toward outsiders is generally developed by the growing child well before the referent is learned. In an example of linguistic and affective precedence in learning, the emotional tone is acquired and attached to a label ("them," "white people," "Hungarians") before the referent of the label is learned. Allport calls this first developmental stage the period of *pregeneralization*. Later the child learns the referent for the established dislike and enters the second developmental phase of *total rejection*. All members of the designated outgroup are now repudiated; and virtually no aspects of the outgroup's stereotype are favorable. Still later the child begins to achieve adult-like differentiation. Exceptions are cited to give the appearance of reason and sympathy. These refrains are painfully familiar and usually entail the key conjunction, "but." "Some of my best friends are Jews, *but* I don't like them as a group." "I'm for everybody having a fair chance, *but* Puerto Ricans don't deserve good jobs."

Fear is often an important emotion in this developmental sequence. Children pass through particular periods of being fearful of strangers in general; parents and other socializing agents may invoke fear as a tool; and sometimes traumatic incidents link an outgroup

with fear. More commonly, symbolic transfer of fear occurs. For instance, children fearful of getting too dirty or of the night's darkness generalize this to dark skin color and subsequent dislike of dark people. Recent research has shown a pancultural preference for light over dark, presumably derived from the worldwide fear of the night together with the association of daylight with fear reduction and need satisfaction. This early light bias among children can be transformed, through general cultural and familial influences, into color and racial biases.

Further insight into the emotional components of prejudice is achieved by considering the needs of the individual that are met by social attitudes in general and prejudice in particular. Three broad classes of vital functions have been distinguished: object appraisal, social adjustment, and externalization. In *object appraisal*, attitudes aid in understanding "reality." As societies change, the social consensus as to what constitutes "reality" shifts, and attitudes may shift accordingly. This is the function of cognitive order and meaning that was previously emphasized as the dynamic underlying the cognitive components of prejudice.

In *social adjustment*, attitudes help people conform to what is expected of them. For many who harbor prejudice, attitudes against outgroups are not nearly so expressive of deep-seated personality problems as they are socially adaptive in a prejudiced milieu. The bigotry of conformity requires prejudice as "a social entrance ticket." Bigots for whom the social adjustment function is paramount possess an antipathy only for those groups that it is fashionable to dislike, not outgroups in general. They follow the path of least social resistance, for they do not need to hate so much as to be liked and accepted by people important to them. Hence, as social change proceeds and what is expected by others is altered, conforming bigots shed their prejudice with relative ease. They continue to conform but the customs and norms that guide their beliefs and actions have changed.

Attitudes can also reduce anxiety by serving an *externalization* function. This occurs when an individual senses an analogy between the object of the attitude and some unresolved inner problem. One then adopts an attitude that is a transformed version of one's way of dealing with the inner, affective problem. People project their emotional problems onto the external world through particular social attitudes. If you have sexual problems, you may regard Latins as dangerously hypersexed. If you have problems within your conflict-ridden family, you may regard Jews as dangerously clannish. Externalization theories of prejudice derive directly from psychoanalytic thought, and have received the most research attention by psychologists. The most prominent are the authoritarian personality theory and the frustration-aggression hypothesis.

The personality dynamics of anti-Semites in the United States were intensively studied during the 1940s. A syndrome of personality traits, labeled authoritarianism, was discovered that consistently differentiated highly anti-Semitic individuals from others. Central to the syndrome is anti-intraception, the refusal to look inside oneself and the lack of insight into one's own behavior and feelings. Authoritarians refuse to accept their emotions and try to deny them. As children, authoritarians may have been punished frequently by stern parents, and in turn felt intense hatred for them. Unable to express these aggressive feelings for fear of further punishment, authoritarians find them threatening and unacceptable, deny them, and begin to project them onto others. If they feel hatred for their parents, they see hatred not in themselves but in the dangerous outside world.

Consequently, authoritarians typically convey an idealized picture of their parents as near-perfect. Generalizing this unrealistic view to include other authorities, they come to view the world in good-bad, up-and-down power terms. They are outwardly submissive toward those they see as authorities with power over them, and aggressive toward those they see as beneath them in status. This hierarchical view of authority links directly with ethnic attitudes. High-status ethnic groups are respected, and authoritarians treat them with deference. But low-status ethnic groups are disparaged. Prejudice becomes for many authoritarians "a crutch upon which to limp through life." Lacking insight into their own inner feelings, they project their own unacceptable impulses onto outgroups whom they regard as beneath them.

The basic work on this personality syndrome has been extended by hundreds of research investigations conducted since the original study appeared in 1950. Fundamentally, *authoritarianism is a consistent style and orientation toward life* that permeates a range of attitudes. In addition to ethnic attitudes, it relates to political and economic orientations, traditional family ideology, nationalistic sentiments, social status concerns, even personal alienation. It also has implications for ingroup attitudes, for authoritarian Jews have been found to be strongly anti-Semitic and authoritarian blacks strongly anti-black. It also involves dichotomous thinking that leads to more rigid ethnic stereotyping.

Sweeping as this contribution is to our understanding of ethnic prejudice, some qualifications to the theory of the authoritarian personality are necessary. The enormous attention it has received has led to the neglect of the other major functions of prejudice—object appraisal and social adjustment. And analyses of prejudice emanating strictly from authoritarianism theory give virtually no attention to the critical situational and institutional contexts of ethnic relations and prejudice. Authoritarianism is closely related to breadth of social experience: the syndrome is most intense in narrowly constrained, provincial social settings.

Implications that right-wing politics and mental illness are involved with the syndrome also require qualification. The authoritarian style is often represented in far-left as well as far-right politics. Authoritarians may lack positive mental health, but they are apparently not any more likely to be hospitalized for serious mental disorders than equalitarian individuals. There is, however, an apparent difference in symptom selection: authoritarians appear more prone to paranoid symptoms, equalitarians to depression. In short, the authoritarian orientation toward life is often implicated in prejudice, but it must be understood as part of a narrowed social context and not as a reification of some particular political stance or mental health condition.

The frustration-aggression hypothesis asserts that *all aggression is preceded by frustration.* Fortunately, the converse is not true; there are sublimating alternatives to aggression for the expression of frustration. Though frustration is created by an inability to attain desired goals, aggressive behavior is frequently not directed at the agents that actually keep people from achieving their goals. Frustrating agents are usually older, stronger, more powerful, or protected by cultural traditions. So hostility often gets channeled onto approved, vulnerable objects, *scapegoats* that have little to do with the original frustration. This displacement-of-aggression principle is recognized in the adage about the boss who criticizes his employee, who in turn argues with his wife, who becomes angry with her child, who kicks the dog, who chases the cat, who finally takes it all out on an innocent mouse.

One famous study demonstrates how these mechanisms fuel prejudice. First, attitudes toward Japanese and Mexicans held by 31 young men working at a summer camp were measured. Later the men were frustrated by having to complete a series of lengthy tests when they wanted a long-awaited night out at the local theater. Then the same attitude measures were readministered. Just as expected, the camp workers as a group reported less favorable attitudes toward the Japanese and Mexicans. A control group that had not endured the same frustration did not change its attitudes. Though some hostility was directed at the researchers, the Japanese and Mexicans—completely uninvolved in the frustrating situation—bore the burden of the workers' wrath.

Compelling as these results are, it should be noted that just as frustration does not always lead to aggression, so aggression is not always displaced. Sometimes the hostility is directed at the true frustrating source, and realistic conflict rather than displaced aggression is being expressed. Nor are all scapegoats weak and vulnerable. Usually, however, scapegoats bear some symbolic relationship with the frustration.

Highly prejudiced individuals are both more susceptible to frustration and more prone to display aggression following frustration. An interview study of World War II veterans noted that the prejudiced reported more frustration during their armed service, but actually had not been exposed to objectively more harsh conditions than the less prejudiced. Another study found that highly anti-Semitic college women increased their hostility toward an innocent peer when annoyed by an experimenter, while more tolerant women actually became friendlier.

To sum up, prejudice, like attitudes in general, can serve three important functions for the individual. It can lend meaning to the world; it can help an individual to adjust socially; and it can externalize an individual's inner problems—as shown in the research on authoritarianism and frustration-aggression. Yet prejudice, in conjunction with discrimination, can also serve an additional function at the societal level. Typically, prejudice and discrimination together act in concert to protect economic and political interests. Negative group attitudes can arise from competitive fears of marginal and vulnerable groups. More often, they are manipulated to reinforce the interests of those who seek or are already in power. Anti-Semitism has long played this role in Russia, and its manipulation in Nazi Germany made this societal function of prejudice particularly notorious. In America, anti-black racism arose to protect slavery, and anti-Chinese prejudice during "the Yellow Peril" era and anti-Mexican prejudice arose to protect the exploitation of Chinese and Mexican labor. This recurrent societal phenomenon raises the question of how prejudice is related to intergroup behavior.

PREJUDICE AND BEHAVIOR

Since prejudice results from the simultaneous violation of the norms of rationality and human-heartedness, it can be understood in cognitive and emotional terms alone. But there may also be systematic implications for behavior. Is prejudice simply reflected in thoughts and feelings? Or do bigots lash out at the disliked outgroup? Here we are interested in violations of the norm of justice and fair play.

Four levels of increasingly negative intergroup behavior can be specified: verbal hostility, avoidance, individual acts of unfairness, and physical attack.

Verbal hostility is the mildest behavioral expression of group rejection. Many prejudiced people never go beyond this level; and unprejudiced people sometimes engage in this behavior rather than deviate from what is socially expected of them. Fortunately, most verbal hostility never sets off more extreme negative acts.

Even when inconvenient, many prejudiced people simply *avoid* the disliked outgroup. They "avoid a scene" and protect their prejudicial attitudes by refusing to interact. In his psychoanalytic interpretation of American racism, Joel Kovel emphasizes this behavioral consequence of anti-black prejudice and labels it "aversive racism." In contrast to "dominative racism" that "openly seeks to keep the black man down," aversive racism ignores black people, avoids contact with them, and, at best, is "polite, correct and cold in whatever dealings are necessary between the races."

In Kovel's terms, dominative racism has declined in the United States in recent decades, and aversive racism now describes more accurately much of the interracial behavior of prejudiced whites. This distinction can also be usefully applied to ethnic interaction more generally; it appears that aversive, avoidance behavior is far more common than the dominative conflict represented by the next two levels of reaction.

Typically, the aversive racist maintains a self-image of a tolerant individual, and often reveals little prejudice on a questionnaire. Some college students who report the most favorable attitudes toward blacks on a paper-and-pencil test of prejudice are more reluctant to interact with a black partner in an experimental situation than other students with moderately favorable attitudes. Their taped voices in the interracial interaction are judged colder and more condescending; they select joint tasks and chair placements that require more remote forms of interaction; and they claim to have fewer hours available for future sessions with their black partners.

Prejudice can lead to *individual acts of unfairness,* where bigots act unfairly toward members of the despised outgroup in ways they would rarely act toward ingroup members. The Los Angeles real estate agent who routinely shows Chicano clients only the poorest housing at inflated prices illustrates this acting out of prejudice. So does the rural Wisconsin gas attendant

who serves last those cars he thinks are driven by American Indians. Note that these unfair acts, while expressing the prejudicial attitudes of the actors, take place within a larger societal milieu of group discrimination. Only the extremely prejudiced, the truly dominative racists, frontally act out their hostile feelings in the face of societal sanctions against such behavior.

Unfair treatment of outgroups also includes differentially failing to provide help in situations where help is indicated. Social psychologists have studied this phenomenon by setting up field experiments in realistic situations: a black or a white man "collapses" aboard a New York subway, a black or white motorist with "car trouble" dials "the wrong number" with his or her "last dime" seeking a garage, or a black or white woman drops her packages outside a supermarket. Do bystanders differentially help these "victims"? The results generally support the view that the "subjects" in these real-life dramas often react differently according to the victim's race. In ambiguous situations, whites more readily define the situation with a black victim as one not requiring help, and consequently do not offer assistance. For example, "the wrong number" phone call may be terminated earlier for the black-voiced motorist before the relevant information can be provided. In clear situations, help is offered both black and whites, but it may be more perfunctory for the black victims. A few of the many dropped packages are picked up at the supermarket for the black shopper, rather than providing the complete help commonly granted the white shopper.

At times of heightened anger and unrest, prejudice can lead to *physical attacks* against members of a hated outgroup. Sometimes this extreme form of acting out is carried out by individuals, as in the bar fight over an ethnic slur or the lone assassin who kills the highly visible leader of the outgroup. But ethnically directed physical attack is so extreme a response, even in relatively violent America, that it generally flares up only after group mobilization has taken place first. When churches or synagogues are desecrated, or homes of "invading" outsiders are damaged in an ethnic neighborhood, the attack is almost always the work of organized groups. Although all acting out of prejudice is shaped by the social situation, physical violence especially reflects the larger societal context.

The social mobilization for interethnic violence is even more necessary for the ultimate in prejudiced frenzy—the attempted extermination of the hated outgroup. The pages of world history of even the past century record a depressing number of these tragic genocides: the anti-Jewish pogroms of Russia in the late 19th century, the Turkish massacre of the Armenians during World War I, the Jewish Holocaust of World War II. The pages of U.S. history have their own stains— massacres of Indians—as at Wounded Knee in 1890, and over 4,700 recorded lynchings of blacks since 1881.

Individual prejudice of varying intensities joins with cultural traditions to prescribe certain kinds of interaction with the outgroup and to proscribe others: this is called *social distance*. "I will buy with you, sell with you, talk with you, and so following," Shakespeare has Shylock say to Bassanio in *The Merchant of Venice*, "but I will not eat with you, drink with you, nor pray with you." Buying, selling, and talking with a Christian were within the allowable limits for Shylock, but the more intimate relations of eating, drinking, and praying violated his sense of social distance. This concept has been measured since the 1920s by a paper-and-pencil questionnaire that asks respondents if they would "willingly admit members" of various groups: "to close kinship by marriage; to my club as personal chums; to my street as neighbors; to employment in my occupation; to citizenship in my country; as visitors only to my country; would exclude from my country."

Emory Bogardus first used this measure a half century ago to gauge the attitudes of nearly 2,000 Americans throughout the country toward 40 racial, religious, and nationality groups. He found an amazingly consistent pattern of group preferences across the nation. The least social distance was accorded the British, native white Americans, and Canadians; next came the French, Germans, Swedes, and other western and northern Europeans; then the Spaniards, Italians, and Jews and other southern and eastern Europeans; and, finally, the greatest social distance was accorded blacks, Japanese, Chinese, Hindus, and Turks. This pattern varied little with the respondents' region, education, occupation, income, or even ethnicity. Lower-ranked groups shared the pattern, save for placing their own group at or near the top. It is this consistent pattern of reported social distances, together with the evidence of the authoritarian personality and the persistent group stereotypes noted earlier, that makes it useful to retain the concept of prejudice as a general factor.

The Bogardus Social Distance Scale has been employed in investigations throughout the world during the past two generations. These additional studies lend further support for the utility of the social distance concept. One study introduced for ratings the names of three fictitious groups—the Daniereans, Pireneans, and Wallonians; and the subjects who rejected most actual outgroups also tended to reject these fictitious groups as well. This finding points up the contribution of individual prejudice to the social distance phenomenon; other findings on children point up the contribution of cultural traditions. By early adolescence, American children of various ethnic backgrounds yield a social distance rank-ordering of groups that is essentially the same as that found among adults.

The importance of culture is further underlined by research on the social distance attitudes of German, Japanese, and American students. German students reported occupation as the most important single characteristic governing social distance, followed by religion, race, and nationality. For the Japanese students, the social distance ordering was occupation, race, nationality, and religion. For the American students, race —the "American dilemma"—was the most critical factor, followed by occupation, religion, and nationality. Social class, as represented by occupation, played a significant role in the responses of all three countries. Indeed, social class is intertwined with ethnicity in the stereotyped imagery of the prejudiced individual. Thus, with no class information available, many Americans assume, for example, that an "Englishman" must be upper-status and Hispanics must be poor and lower-status, and these class identifications greatly influence their group stereotypes.

Discrimination has been defined as an institutional process of outgroup exclusion on grounds of birth. So defined, discrimination operates at a different level in

ethnic relations from that of prejudice. As a social process, it is not merely the sum of all of the individually unfair acts perpetuated by bigots; prejudice and discrimination are only moderately associated, and one without the other is not at all uncommon. Clearly, one supports the other: prejudice legitimates discrimination, and discrimination breeds prejudice. Yet much discrimination is not the direct product of prejudice; it often results as an unintended result of institutional arrangements designed for other purposes. One investigation of manufacturers in Texas found no relation whatsoever between their racial attitudes and their actual practices for hiring black workers. Intended or not, however, the damage to the outgroup victims is the same.

Similarly, prejudiced people do not necessarily engage in the discriminatory process. Societal restraints and situational demands often override the impulse to act out individual prejudice. Consider a group of white steel workers in Indiana studied by D.C. Reitzes in the 1950s. These men were members of the same thoroughly interracial union and worked in interracial plants. Only 12 percent evidenced "low acceptance" of blacks in this work situation; and the deeper the involvement in union activities, the greater was their acceptance of blacks as coworkers. But neighborhood acceptance was a vastly different matter. Bolstered by a neighborhood organization that opposed desegregation, 86 percent of the white steel workers rejected the idea of allowing blacks to live near them, with those men most enmeshed in the life of the neighborhood evincing the most adamant opposition. The effects of harmonious interracial patterns in employment did not extend to housing, for no relationship existed between acceptance of blacks as fellow workers and acceptance of them as neighbors.

The key to understanding this situation is the operation of the organizations in each of the realms. Most of the steel workers conformed less to their personal prejudices than to what was expected of them in the two situations. Their inconsistency of behavior was more apparent than real, for in each instance most of the workers lived by the norms of the groups to which they referred their behavior. These reference-group norms often act in modern American society to produce what appear to be inconsistent ethnic patterns, to restrict the generalization of contact-induced attitude change from one institution to another, and to overwhelm the behavioral tendencies generated by ethnic attitudes. In this instance, prejudiced workers generally accepted blacks as coworkers along with the rest of their union, and tolerant workers generally rejected blacks as neighbors along with the rest of their coresidents.

PREJUDICE AND
CURRENT ETHNIC RELATIONS

Virtually every American ethnic group has its own story of hard times and difficulties in becoming established in the New World. Though sharpened by their retelling over the years, these stories contain considerable truth. There has, in fact, been widespread ethnic conflict throughout American history, with both prejudice and discrimination pervasive. Racial conflict has been the most severe, followed by religious conflict. These conflicts have been in full view; American society has not tended to hide or deny them. Just the reverse of Latin Americans, people in the United States often deny social class problems, but employ ethnic conflict explanations even when inappropriate.

Data collected over the last three decades, whether concerning stereotypes or social distance, point to a single conclusion: prejudice in all of its measured forms appears to have slowly receded since World War II, though considerable prejudice is still found against some groups.

Research on stereotypes that was conducted in 1933 at Princeton University was repeated in 1951 and 1967. In the later experiments many more students objected to the task, and most stereotypes had both faded in intensity and become more favorable. In 34 years, many traditional stereotypes had waned: the sly (from 29 to 6 percent), superstitious (34 to 8) Chinese; the stolid (44 to 9), scientifically minded (78 to 47) Germans; the witty (38 to 7), pugnacious (45 to 13) Irish; the musical (32 to 9), artistic (53 to 30) Italians; the shrewd (79 to 30), mercenary (49 to 15) Jews; and the lazy (75 to 26), superstitious (84 to 13) blacks. Stereotyped images remained, but often assumed a more positive cast. The grasping (34 to 17) Jewish image had evolved into an ambitious (21 to 48) one. Evidence of a similar trend for the entire adult population comes from national surveys. For example, only 42 percent of white respondents in 1942 answered "yes" to the question: "In general, do you think Negroes are as intelligent as white people?" By 1946 this figure had risen to 52 percent, and by 1956 to 77 where it has remained.

Recent American research on social distance reveals comparable shifts. While the group rankings remain similar to those of the 1920s, the amount of social distance reported for the middle-range (southern and eastern Europeans and Jews) and the lower-range nonwhite groups has declined markedly. Hence, the overall pattern is still maintained, but the differences in reported social distances between groups has significantly narrowed over recent years.

But can survey data, in an age of aversive racism, reflect "real" change? Do these data not tell more about shifts in what is considered respectable verbal behavior than shifts in prejudice itself? Of course, even shifts in verbal behavior are not unimportant and have positive implications for ethnic relations. But there are reasons to believe that these data signify more basic changes in prejudice as well. First, rapport in the survey situation is generally far closer than those unfamiliar with the technique realize. Second, the remarkable consistency of these attitude trends extends to a wide variety of groups, questions, and survey agencies. Third, predictions of the 1960 presidential election, based on a single question exploring willingness to vote for a qualified Roman Catholic for president, proved quite accurate. Finally, the most compelling reason for accepting the validity of these survey data is the fact that the diminution of prejudiced responses is consistent with the marked erosion in discrimination in U.S. society over these same years. It is consistent, too, with the reduction in ethnic stereotyping in the mass media. To be sure, there remains considerable discrimination in American life and media stereotyping continues, just as surveys still reveal considerable prejudice. But all three phenomena have receded during the past three decades in a mutually reinforcing manner.

These trends challenge the conventional wisdom about prejudice as voiced by such diverse personages as former Senator George Aiken and Frederick the Great. "If we were to wake up some morning and find that everyone was the same race, creed, and color," Aiken argued, "we would find some other causes for prejudice by noon." Frederick the Great agreed: "Drive out prejudices by the door, they will come back by the window." Are, then, these trends of recent years merely fluctuations around a persistent phenomenon? Is prejudice always to be present?

Addressing this question requires a choice between two contrasting conceptions of aggression. Sigmund Freud postulated a closed system containing a fixed amount of instinctive aggression which, if not released through one outlet, will seek and find another. According to this "steam boiler" view, society must find a way in which to channel aggression through appropriate safety valves; otherwise, the reduction of one prejudice will merely surface as an increase in another.

By contrast, Gordon Allport proposed an open-system, feedback conception. Rather than a finite force that demands release, aggression for Allport is a variable capacity whose expression is governed by both internal and external conditions. From this vantage point, present trends in group attitudes are not at all surprising. Widespread group prejudice is not inevitable; and greater tolerance of one group improves the chances for greater tolerance of others.

The evidence for choosing between these rival models is not conclusive, though Allport's open-system view receives support from both cross-cultural and laboratory research. But both the open-system conception and research on attitude change underline the importance of institutionalized group protections in American society. Indeed, the trends since World War II are products of the slow, structural process of evolving institutional safeguards that provide the necessary external conditions for the reduction of prejudice. Many of these safeguards also provide the setting for subsequent changes in the behavior of individuals. And behavior changes, in turn, produce the internal conditions for reducing prejudice.

. These protections have evolved in various ways. Sometimes they emerge dramatically, as with the Civil Rights Act of 1964. More frequently, they develop without national attention, as with the entrance of Jews into engineering and Slavs into prominent political posts. They take shape in cross-ethnic political coalitions and lowered barriers to opportunity. Taken together, these protections erode the foundation of group discrimination.

Institutional safeguards that go beyond mere restraint and prompt new intergroup behavior act to reduce prejudice directly. This process, too, contradicts conventional wisdom. It is commonly held that attitudes must change before behavior; yet social psychological research points conclusively to the opposite order of events as more common. Behavior changes first, because of new laws or other interventions; individuals then modify their ideas to fit their new acts.

The future of group prejudice in the United States cannot be foreseen apart from its social and political contexts. Although institutional safeguards developed in recent decades have been instrumental in reducing prejudice, there is no guarantee that they will be maintained, much less furthered. The retrenchment of the 1970s makes this lesson clear. But these institutional protections were largely achieved by the most self-identified races and ethnic groups, and efforts to advance them will probably be reinstated in some later, more propitious era. To be sure, ethnic loyalties themselves require group pride, even ethnocentrism; prejudice as a phenomenon will not vanish, but institutional constraints can reduce it and restrain its negative effects on American society. In this important sense, we can concur with Thoreau that "it is never too late to give up our prejudices."

Bibliography

Gordon Allport, *The Nature of Prejudice* (Reading, Mass., 1954) remains the definitive psychological treatment of the subject. More recent discussions that update Allport's analysis include: John Harding, Harold Proshansky, Bernard Kutner, and Isidor Chein, "Prejudice and Ethnic Relations," in *The Handbook of Social Psychology*, 2d ed., vol. 5, ed. Gardner Lindzey and Elliot Aronson (Reading, Mass., 1969); and Thomas Pettigrew, *Racially Separate or Together?* (New York, 1971). A modern psychoanalytic analysis of anti-black prejudice is Joel Kovel, *White Racism: A Psychohistory* (New York, 1970). Four primary sources of psychological research on prejudice are particularly noteworthy and readable: T.W. Adorno, E. Frenkel-Brunswik, D.J. Levinson, and R.N. Sanford, *The Authoritarian Personality* (New York, 1950); Judith Porter, *Black Child, White Child* (Cambridge, Mass., 1971); John Williams and J. Kenneth Morland, *Race, Color, and the Young Child* (Chapel Hill, N.C., 1976); and Phyllis Katz, ed., *Towards the Elimination of Racism* (New York, 1976).

Outstanding sociological treatments of the subject are provided in George Simpson and J. Milton Yinger, *Racial and Cultural Minorities*, 4th ed. (New York, 1972); and Robin Williams, Jr., *Strangers Next Door* (Englewood Cliffs, N.J., 1964). The classic analysis of black-white relations in the United States is Gunnar Myrdal, *An American Dilemma* (New York, 1944). A collection of recent sociological analyses of American race relations is found in Thomas F. Pettigrew, ed., *Racial Discrimination in the United States* (New York, 1975). An overview of the sociological study of race relations since 1895 is presented in Thomas F. Pettigrew, ed., *The Sociology of Race Relations: Reflection and Reform* (New York, 1980). A range of brief and authoritative articles can be found in David Sills, ed., *The International Encyclopedia of the Social Sciences* (New York, 1968); see especially articles on aggression, anti-Semitism, attitudes, attitude change, conformity, minorities, prejudice, race, race relations, social discrimination, and stereotypes.

THOMAS F. PETTIGREW

PREJUDICE AND DISCRIMINATION, HISTORY OF

Much of the history of intergroup relations in the United States is a record of prejudice and discrimination against those considered racially or culturally inferior by a dominant or majority element. The minimum qualifications for membership in the privileged majority have been a white skin and European ancestry, but these attributes by themselves usually have not been sufficient to guarantee unfettered access to the core institutions of the society. The intense Protestantism of the original British colonists helped establish a long tradition of discrimination against Roman Catholics and Jews. At times there have been efforts to make the core group not merely white and Protestant but also "Anglo-Saxon." Hence neither majorities nor minorities, neither discriminators nor their victims, can be regarded as absolute and fixed entities. The complexities of American pluralism have even made it possible for members of some groups to be "in" and "out" at the same time; "in," for example, as whites licensed to discriminate against blacks, but "out" to the extent that their religious and cultural characteristics prevented their full acceptance by an Anglo-American elite.

Prejudice and discrimination are closely related but

clearly distinguishable phenomena. Prejudice can be defined as an attitude of generalized hostility or aggression against a group of human beings who are thought to have some undesirable characteristics in common. It manifests itself in such ethnic stereotypes as the lazy Negro, the drunken Indian, the unscrupulous Jew, or the unruly Irishman. Prejudice may have its source in the personality disorders of bigoted individuals or it may be a manifestation of conformity to group norms. The latter type is of principal interest to historians and sociologists because it usually reflects an established pattern of ethnic inequality. Discrimination, on the other hand, refers to actions that serve to limit the social, political, or economic opportunities of particular groups. When such actions become institutionalized through either law or custom they result in substantial inequities in group access to wealth, social status, and political power. Discrimination may appear to be simply the acting out of prior prejudice, but there is evidence to suggest that prejudice becomes fully developed and formally sanctioned only *after* the process of differential treatment is well under way. Attitude and action tend to feed on each other, creating a vicious circle that works to enhance the power and prestige of one group at the expense of another.

Specific American minorities have experienced this vicious circle in differing ways and to varying degrees, and the historical pattern is complicated further by the changes that have occurred over time in the situation of each group. One way that the special circumstances affecting the fate of particular ethnic groups can be placed in a comparative perspective is by referring to three main variables that contemporary sociologists have found at work in all cases of "ethnic stratification." The first of these is *ethnocentrism*, a basic feeling that "we" are different from "them" in ways that make "us" better than "they" are. The intensity of ethnocentrism is determined in large part by prevailing notions of how substantial and enduring these group differences really are. To the extent that the differences are considered innate or "racial," prejudice tends to be accentuated and discrimination is likely to be more rigid and systematic. A second source of variations in attitude and treatment is the relative strength of the *incentive* for degrading and subordinating a particular group. The need for an exploitable labor force or the desire to gain an advantage in the competition for some scarce resource, such as land or industrial jobs, can be powerful motives for ethnic discrimination, but such material incentives are not constant and will vary in response to larger patterns of economic and social development. Finally there is the factor of the actual *power* differential between the groups involved. Ethnocentrism and economic interest can lead to the dominance of one group over another only to the extent that the former has the physical ability to impose its will on the latter. If group vulnerability invites oppression, any substantial increase in the material or cultural resources of a victimized group should tend in the long run to improve its social position and increase the rights and opportunities of its members.

For purposes of analysis, the principal victims of prejudice and discrimination in American history can be divided into five categories. First are the indigenous peoples conquered during the process of Euro-American colonization and territorial expansion, namely the American Indians. Next to appear on the scene as objects of domination and exploitation were the involuntary immigrants from Africa, originally imported mainly as a source of slave labor on the plantations of the colonial South. The newcomers from Asia who arrived in the West Coast during the 19th and early 20th centuries form a third category. In a unique fashion, the Chinese and Japanese shared with Afro-Americans some of the disabilities associated with race and color while at the same time retaining an integrated culture that differed substantially from that of the Euro-Americans. A Spanish-speaking or Hispanic minority was created first by the absorption of Mexicans that accompanied the westward expansion of the United States in the 19th century and then by the subsequent immigration of Mexicans, Puerto Ricans, and Cubans. The members of this fourth ethnic category have been distinguished from "Anglos" not only by language and culture but also, in some instances, by the racial characteristics resulting from a background of intermixture with Indians or blacks. The fifth and largest grouping resulted from the massive migration in the 19th and 20th centuries of Europeans with cultural and social attributes that conflicted with the Anglo-American norm. These white "ethnics" usually suffered prejudice and discrimination in more subtle and less formalized ways than Indians, Afro-Americans, Asians, or Hispanics but they were nevertheless vulnerable to some forms of economic exploitation and were, at least for a time, treated as "strangers in the land" without a full claim to the rights and privileges of those who considered themselves charter members of the United States.

There are several smaller groups that might be included by a slight stretching of each of the five categories: Eskimos, Aleuts, and Hawaiians among the indigenous peoples; black West Indians among those of slave descent; Filipinos, Koreans, and Vietnamese as part of the Asian group; South Americans of various nationalities under the Hispanic category; and Middle Eastern immigrants, especially Syrians and Lebanese, as part of the white ethnic population. But each of these groups has had its own special experience with prejudice and discrimination, and limitations of space and information preclude their inclusion in this survey.

American Indians and the Burden of White Ethnocentrism

The descriptions of American Indians available to prospective English colonists in the early 17th century provided no sure guide about how these indigenous peoples should be treated or how they might contribute to the success or failure of a European white settlement. Most voyagers and explorers had described the "savages" of the New World as living and behaving like wild beasts and had raised doubts as to whether they were fully human. But another opinion, carefully nurtured by some of the promoters of colonization, held that they were natural men, living in primal innocence, who had a gentle and tractable nature that made them obvious candidates for Christian conversion and eventual assimilation into a civilized community. If the former image implied segregation or extermination, the latter envisioned coexistence in the same society, although not necessarily on an egalitarian basis.

On the surface at least, the official ideology of the col-

onizers of Virginia and New England was strongly assimilationist. The letters patent setting up the Virginia companies of London and Plymouth in 1606 stressed the conversion and civilization of the natives as a prime motive of settlement, and missionary work was much discussed and sometimes undertaken in the early years of colonization. Considerable sums were raised for the purpose in England, and in Massachusetts there was a substantial effort to organize the red heathen into Christian communities. One need not doubt the sincerity of these endeavors to explain their failure. Seventeenth-century colonists did not give up on the Indian because they regarded him as racially inferior and innately incapable of civilization, but they did despise Indian culture and especially Indian religion, which they regarded as worship of the devil. Consequently, the Indian could become a "civilized" man only by divesting himself of everything that made him an Indian except his tawny complexion. The demand that they commit cultural suicide and subordinate themselves socially and politically to the European colonists was deeply resented by most Indians, but even more threatening was the spread of white agricultural settlement into their hunting grounds. In Virginia the Indian reaction came quickly in the form of an uprising in 1622 which wiped out approximately one-third of the colony. In Massachusetts the major explosion did not occur until 1675 when Metacom (King Philip) led a confederation of tribes in a last desperate effort to drive the Puritans into the sea. The crushing of these Indian rebellions against white encroachment and cultural imperialism brought an effective end to the assimilationist program and the hopes for Indian incorporation into the colonial communities. The new tendency to regard all Indians as permanent outsiders was manifested during King Philip's War in the unprovoked attacks by Massachusetts colonists on the "praying Indians" who had accepted Christianity and remained loyal to the whites.

It was in the wake of 17th-century Indian wars that the policy of assigning defeated or debilitated Indian tribes to a separate existence on reservations was first adumbrated. Virginia inaugurated a reservation system for tidewater tribes that were being outflanked by white settlements in 1653, nine years after a second massive Indian uprising had been suppressed. In New England the establishment of separate towns for Christianized Indians antedated King Philip's War but the policy of settling weaker tribes on small reservations was accelerated after the defeat of Metacom and his allies. The reservation system, which was to constitute the essential matrix of future relations between whites and subjugated Indians, was in part an act of mercy providing some chance for the survival of Indian communities. But it was also an act of rejection, a form of apartheid, signifying that whites preferred to isolate tribal remnants in peripheral areas rather than attempt the difficult task of intermingling whites and Indians within a single community.

Yet the very fact that Indians were not incorporated into white society probably saved them from direct economic exploitation. Red captives were sometimes enslaved in the colonial period, especially in South Carolina early in the 18th century, but the greater availability and suitability of black Africans for plantation labor brought an early end to Indian servitude. The whites wanted the Indians' land, but they neither needed nor desired his labor. Consequently, Indians as a group were not saddled with the slave stereotype of the lazy, hapless, and docile dependent.

Because of his relative isolation from white society there remained about the Indian an aura of dignified self-reliance that made it possible for some white Americans to romanticize his character. The cult of "the noble savage" may not have been transplanted in all its purity from the salons of Paris, but, beginning in the late 18th century, it did have some effect on American thinking about the real "savages" on the frontier. Intellectuals like Thomas Jefferson, responding to European attacks on the allegedly debilitating effects of the American environment, defended the Indian as a superior physical specimen. Furthermore, the Enlightenment belief in the virtues of natural man and the existence of an innate moral sense suggested that Indians might serve as exemplars of uncorrupted human nature. Yet few white Americans seriously questioned the beneficence of the westward march of "civilization." Indian virtues, it was determined, were "savage" virtues worthy of admiration, but distinctly inferior to the higher virtues of "civilization." Hence the conception of savage nobility was absorbed into a theory of social progress that posited the inevitable disappearance of precisely those qualities that gave the Indian a certain dignity. However, philanthropic opinion in the age of Jefferson did not believe that the Indian himself was necessarily doomed, even if his way of life was an inevitable casualty of social evolution. The general assumption seemed to be that a noble savage might also be an apt candidate for "civilization." Thus the massive dispossessions and removals of the tribes west of the Appalachians in the period between 1790 and the 1830s were accompanied by insistent claims that the ultimate goal of white policy was the eventual absorption of individual Indians into Euro-American society. Money was appropriated by Congress for this purpose, and government agents and missionaries cooperated in efforts to bring a combination of Christianity, literacy in English, and agricultural technology to as many of the tribes as possible. The prevailing ideology envisioned the transformation of Indians into yeoman farmers. Once they had settled down to the white man's way of farming they would no longer need hunting lands, and additional territory could be opened to white settlement without doing them any real injury. The final step was supposed to be full social and even biological assimilation.

The program failed because it was at variance with the realities of westward expansion and overestimated the willingness of Indians to abandon their traditional culture. White frontiersmen wanted land, not "civilized" Indians. And in the South, where the question of the removal of "the five civilized tribes" became a national issue in the 1820s and 1830s, state governments backed the land-grabbing ambitions of settlers and speculators, and spokesmen for white opinion made it clear that detribalized Indians left behind on farm-sized allotments would be regarded not as candidates for assimilation and citizenship but as free people of color with the same abjectly inferior status as free Negroes. Whatever the federal government and the missionaries might intend for the Indians, the common people of the South and West, who found their spokesman in Andrew Jackson, were determined to remove all Indians, civilized or

not, from their midst. When Jackson carried out mass removal of eastern tribes to the trans-Mississippi West in the 1830s, the majority of the philanthropists and missionaries did not object; they rationalized the deportations by arguing that Indians needed a new haven, free from corrupting associations with the wrong kind of whites and the constant pressure of land-hungry settlers, in order to move toward civilization at their own pace.

The story of Indian removal demonstrates the perennial gap that has existed between official rhetoric and ideology and the actual treatment of American Indians. The kind of blatant racism that rationalized the enslavement and segregation of Afro-Americans almost never appeared in official pronouncements, statements by respected political figures, or learned discourses regarding the American Indian. There were some who in the middle decades of the 19th century included the Indians as a prime example of an inferior race allegedly doomed to extinction in the face of competition from biologically superior whites. But the dominant view even then was that Indian extinction, if it occurred, would not be the result of an innate incapacity for civilization but would flow rather from a perverse refusal of the Indian to do what he was perfectly capable of doing —turn himself into a white man. The absence of a strong taboo against intermarriage between whites and Indians (racial blending was in fact positively encouraged by some advocates of the civilization program) provided the strongest evidence that, on an elite level at least, a specifically racial prejudice was not a major factor in American Indian policy. Popular attitudes, especially on the frontier, undoubtedly partook of racial feeling, and in the South particularly there was some transfer of white supremacist ideology from blacks to Indians. But it remains generally true that the Indian was more a victim of cultural than racial bias. From an early period whites have claimed red ancestry with pride and the Indian's physical appearance has often been admired. Whites, of course, have been repulsed by their image of Indian behavior—the savage cruelty of the "wild" redskin and the drunkenness of the reservation Indian. But more often than not these stereotyped defects have been attributed to environment rather than to heredity.

This peculiar situation of racial injustice without ideological racism results in part from the fact that Indians have historically existed in one of two relations with whites: as independent or semi-independent tribesmen who have inspired a combination of fear and respect, or as a conquered people who have ceased to be of any direct concern to most whites. In their first role a motive existed for their subjugation but they did not occasion the contempt that goes with powerlessness. In their second condition, degradation might inspire contempt or pity, but since there was usually no subordinate economic or social role for them to play in white society there was no need for an elaborate ideology of natural inferiority. Because Indians, unlike blacks, were rarely in a position where they represented both an inferior caste and a coerced labor force, they did not inspire the same combination of self-interest, fear, and contempt that underlay the more blatant racism directed at Afro-Americans.

Nineteenth-century Indian policy culminated in the Dawes Act of 1887 which provided for the division of communally held tribal lands into individual allotments. The professed aim, as in all previous federal Indian programs, was the destruction of aboriginal culture and the assimilation of the Indian into American life. The usual blend of white ethnocentrism and humanitarianism led to the usual disaster for the Indians. In fact the period of the allotment program, from 1887 to the 1930s, brought Indian fortunes to their lowest point. Allotment, like removal, resulted in a massive loss of Indian land. Land speculators and mining, timber, and grazing interests not only gained access to the unallotted surplus of tribal land but also succeeded in pressuring many Indians to give up their individual holdings despite safeguards in the law limiting the right of alienation. This was also the era of authoritarian paternalism in government-Indian relations. All-powerful agents and superintendents supplanted the traditional forms of tribal government on the reservations, and the education of Indian children was carried on as much as possible in government boarding schools where a brutal severing of cultural roots was attempted. Because Indians were believed by the cultural evolutionists of the day to be a "backward" people, paternalistic tutelage was deemed necessary as a prelude to acculturation and assimilation. The real injustice to the Indian, and the reason these policies can be considered discriminatory, lay in the fact that Indians were being denied the right to self-determination, the chance to decide for themselves how best to accommodate their ancestral cultures to the demands of the modern world. Hence the congressional legislation of 1924 extending rights of U.S. citizenship to all Indians did not go to the heart of the problem. It was a logical outcome of the policy of forced assimilation and ignored the special kind of collective rights that really mattered to most Indians.

The New Deal era saw a partial reversal of the traditional assimilationist policy. As a result of the Indian Reorganization Act of 1934, the allotment program was stopped and the right to communal ownership of land restored. A modified form of tribal self-government was reinstituted, official encouragement was given to efforts to preserve traditional crafts and customs, and Indians acquired greater potential control over the development of natural resources on tribal lands.

Today the position of Indians in American society is a peculiar and anomalous one. For some purposes they are individual U.S. citizens with all the legal and political rights that this status entails. But those who still live on reservations are also members of communities that enjoy a quasi-autonomous corporate existence outside the Euro-American legal and political structure. The question of what happens when tribal authorities or courts deny individual Indians some of the protections of the Bill of Rights has not yet been completely resolved. Since there is still doubt about what the fundamental rights of Indians really are, it is sometimes difficult to know exactly when they are discriminated against and their rights denied. But from an economic and educational standpoint Indians remain the most disadvantaged of all American minorities. The main source of this persistent poverty and lack of opportunity would seem to lie less in current injustices than in the relative powerlessness of Indians to exert the kind of pressure needed to remedy the legacy of past wrongs.

But one form of direct restitution for previous losses seems to be available; in recent years, tribal groups have, with some success, sued in the courts to recover lands ceded in a legally defective way. As in the case of Afro-Americans the plight of the American Indian raises the question as to whether ethnic equality requires not merely even-handedness in the present but also a retroactive compensation—reparations—for injustices that have occurred in the past.

AFRO-AMERICANS AND THE TYRANNY OF RACE

Of all American ethnic groups, Afro-Americans have carried the heaviest burden of prejudice and discrimination. Opinions differ as to how much of this oppression has resulted from an instinctive or deeply rooted color prejudice and how much from the legacy of slavery as an extreme form of social and economic degradation. But most authorities on Afro-American history would agree that both have played a role and that they have reinforced each other at crucial junctures.

Even before they arrived in the New World and began to enslave blacks, many Englishmen had developed a set of negative stereotypes about African character and behavior. Africa itself was usually pictured as the home of the most unmitigated form of "savagery," involving cannibalism, sexual promiscuity, and bizarre forms of pagan ritual. African traits were seen as the direct antithesis of those supposedly distinguishing civilized society, and its savage state had none of the aura of freshness and innocence that sometimes softened the image of the natives of the New World. Furthermore, the African's dark pigmentation conjured up all the associations of blackness with evil and filth that were firmly rooted in European culture and psychology. Finally, as a result of the 16th-century slave trade and the rise of black servitude in Spanish and Portuguese colonies, there was already a popular identification of "blackamoors" with the abject status of slavery. Ethnocentric Englishmen of the early 17th century, who rated other peoples and nationalities in descending order on the basis of how different they were from themselves in appearance, way of life, and apparent achievements, had already placed Africans at the bottom of the hierarchy.

These attitudes predictably led to some discrimination against the earliest Africans arriving in the mainland colonies of North America, most notably the handful brought to Virginia on a Dutch slaver in 1619. Yet the available evidence suggests that discrimination on specifically racial grounds developed gradually over a period of almost a century and closely paralleled the growing dependence on slavery as a system of labor. In the bellwether case of Virginia, the early pattern was one of heavy reliance on white indentured servants who were characteristically treated in a brutal and authoritarian manner until their terms of service were up. Into this labor system a few blacks were introduced before the mid-17th century, and some at least were freed, perhaps because they had fulfilled the labor obligation required of all servants who arrived without specific contracts of indenture. As early as the 1640s, however, some blacks were serving for life, and other signs of discrimination began to appear at the same time. Black women, unlike white female servants, were being used for field work, and a law requiring the arming of servants for defense against Indian attacks excluded

blacks. In the 1660s, the enslavement of blacks for life was given legal recognition, and the first law was passed to penalize interracial sex relations. Those blacks who were already freemen first became the target of special legislation in 1670 when they were denied the right to own white servants. But it was not until the early 18th century that free blacks lost the right to vote and hold office in the colony. The emergence of a formalized racial caste system by the 1720s closely paralleled the rise of plantation slavery. The official justification for excluding free blacks from the "great priviledge of a Freeman" in 1723 stressed the danger of free Negroes collaborating with slaves to threaten the security of the newly established forced-labor system.

Blacks could not so easily have been set aside for enslavement and other invidious treatment in Virginia if they had not been readily distinguishable from the rest of the population. Initially the distinction was made on religious grounds: Africans were "heathens" and white colonists were "Christians." Oppression on grounds of deviation from the true faith was a well-established and universally accepted principle in the 17th century. But the progress of Christian conversion among blacks meant that they could no longer be accorded unequal status because of their heathenism. The determination in the 1660s that conversion did not require manumission was part of a gradual shift to an overtly racial rationale for slavery and ultimately for distinctions among free people on the basis of color and ancestry.

But the simple fact of difference—religious or racial—probably is not sufficient to account for the degradation of blacks in colonial America. Blacks were also uniquely vulnerable to such treatment because they had all arrived in the colony aboard slave ships as people utterly devoid of nationality or any personal rights under international law. Unlike free immigrants, they could be legally consigned to any status that the colonial government deemed appropriate. The surprising thing is that it took so long, at least in Virginia, to decide unequivocally that this meant chattel slavery. Furthermore, white colonists had to have some practical motive or incentive to relegate blacks to servitude or caste inferiority. The greatest problem for those seeking to develop the colonies into profitable enterprises was a shortage of labor. Indians had proved unsuitable and, in any case, not enough of them were readily obtainable. White indentured servitude had met the need for a time, but as English economic conditions and population policies changed in the last half of the 17th century, the supply of "sturdy beggars" to be transported to the New World began to dry up. The increasing difficulty of obtaining white servants necessitated shorter terms and better conditions for those already in the New World and thus reduced the convenience and profitability of employing them. Furthermore, white servants eventually became free, and at certain periods, as in the Chesapeake colonies between 1660 and the 1680s, there was little land available for them to settle on as small planters. This situation raised fears among the colonial elite of a landless proletariat threatening the peace of society, fears that seemed realized in 1676 when "the giddy multitude" threw itself with enthusiasm into the insurrection known as Bacon's Rebellion and helped turn a quarrel among the Virginia elite into a virtual civil war. Black slavery was the ultimate solu-

tion to this class and labor problem, and the denial of rights also to blacks who were free helped to cement a new solidarity between the upper and lower classes of whites. When the status of freeman was reserved to whites, it tended to elevate the status of those colonists who otherwise had little stake in the established order. It proved relatively easy as time went on to convince lower-class whites that their status gain from the color caste system gave them a real interest in sustaining the dominance of slaveholding planters. Encouragement through legislation of the growing miscegenation phobia was a critical step in the certification of a privileged white caste that transcended class lines. Not only had all the English North American colonies thoroughly institutionalized slavery by the early 18th century, but most of them had also passed stringent laws against interracial marriage. Just as the freedom of whites in the plantation colonies came in the 18th century to depend to some degree upon slavery—for slavery meant that there were no servile and menial roles that whites had to perform—so the equality of whites, or at least the sense of it, came to depend in part on antimiscegenation laws and other caste legislation which stressed the fact that there were no absolute barriers to free association among whites, regardless of putative differences in their class or station. To some extent the fluidity and egalitarianism that was to become such a distinguishing feature of American society by the time of Jackson and Tocqueville was reinforced by racial proscription.

The natural-rights philosophy of the revolutionary era inspired a challenge to slavery which led to gradual emancipation in the North and some questioning of the institution in the South; but those blacks freed by state action or voluntary manumission during this period continued to suffer from most of the disabilities of a pariah class. Liberal southerners like Thomas Jefferson, who sincerely hoped for the ultimate demise of slavery, assumed that the physical differences between races and the prejudices nurtured by slavery would forever prevent whites and black freedmen from living together in peace and equality. Consequently, they coupled their tentative proposals for gradual emancipation with schemes for colonizing the freedmen outside the United States. Such ideas inspired the formation of the American Society for Colonizing Free People of Color in 1817, an organization manifesting some of the same philanthropic spirit that characterized the Indian civilization movement during the same period. But whereas the Indian civilizationists proclaimed the full incorporation of the red man into American society as their ultimate goal, the colonizationists took it for granted that free blacks were unassimilable because of their "degraded" condition and the "invincible" prejudices of the white population against them.

The abolitionists of the 1830s made the first serious attack on the prevailing practice of racial inequality. Inspired by a perfectionist humanitarianism, they not only called for the immediate abolition of slavery but also denounced the caste barrier in American society. The response of proslavery elements was to articulate the full-blown racist doctrine of inherent black inferiority, an idea that previously had existed only in rudimentary form. The notion that Afro-Americans were natural slaves because they were biologically capable of performing only the most menial and subservient roles

was soon buttressed by the science and pseudoscience of the day. A respectable contingent of biologists and ethnologists began to defend as scientific truth the proposition that blacks were created separately from whites and constituted a distinct and permanently inferior species.

In such a climate of opinion the situation of free blacks in both the North and South was bound to deteriorate even further. The basic pattern of exclusion and segregation, often called Jim Crow in the post-Reconstruction South, was implemented in both sections during the ante-bellum period. Free blacks were almost universally denied access to public facilities used by whites or were accommodated separately. Segregation or exclusion was the rule not only in theaters, hotels, taverns, steamboats, and railroad or street cars, but also in churches, prisons, orphanages, and even cemeteries. If blacks received any education at all, they obtained it in separate schools. In the 1830s free blacks were disfranchised in Pennsylvania, North Carolina, and Tennessee, three out of only a handful of states where previously they had voted on the same basis as whites. Some of the states of the Old Northwest, where blacks had never voted or exercised other civil or political rights, attempted in the late ante-bellum period to exclude free blacks entirely by barring their immigration. In the South, laws prohibiting slaves from moving about freely, assembling without white supervision, possessing firearms, or being tried in the same courts and under the same penal code as whites were also applied to free Negroes. On the eve of the Civil War some southern state legislatures were debating proposals designed to expel or enslave all free Negroes in their jurisdictions. The dominant ante-bellum attitude was the one that Chief Justice Taney, in the *Dred Scott* decision of 1857, attributed to the founding fathers—that Negroes had no rights that white men were bound to respect.

In the South the elaboration of racial caste was related to fears about the future of slavery. Not only were free blacks considered to be potential instigators of slave rebellion, but their very existence as a class in the community undermined the racial rationale for slavery. But discrimination in the North had more complex roots. Although free Negroes constituted only about 1 percent of the total population in the free states in 1860, they tended to be concentrated in a few urban areas where they came into direct economic competition with lower-class whites, especially recent immigrants. But more important than the actual competition with northern workers—an inherently unequal struggle which usually led to the rapid displacement of blacks from jobs coveted by whites—was the fear of future rivalry that might result if southern slaves were freed and migrated northward. Furthermore, the social mobility and disappearance of traditional social and political distinctions that most historians have found characteristic of the Jacksonian era bred status anxieties that could sometimes be assuaged by laying claim in some dramatic way to the automatic prestige that came from the possession of a white skin.

The political struggle that developed after 1846 over the future of slavery in the United States and eventuated in the Civil War was more a contest over the role of slaveholders in the American republic than a dis-

agreement on the basic social position of blacks. But one way to divest southern planters of their power was to take away their slaves, and this was accomplished as an act of "military necessity" during the Civil War. If the destruction of slavery did not signify a national conversion to the principle of racial equality, it did demonstrate at least that a northern majority could recognize higher priorities than the holding of Afro-Americans in abject subjugation. Nationalism was a more important force than racism when the two proved incompatible, as the story of Reconstruction demonstrates. Radical Republicans were influenced to some degree by the abolitionist argument that legalized racial caste was incompatible with American institutions, but a more pressing concern was the fear that the South would return to the Union with the old planter class still in control. Consequently, they attempted by a series of laws and constitutional amendments to create a color-blind legal and political order. Their immediate or practical objective may have been to create a "loyal" (that is, Republican) black electorate in the South, but the long-range effect of their work was to preclude overtly racial tests for national citizenship or for the enjoyment of whatever civil or political rights the courts might be willing to acknowledge as subject to federal protection.

The dominant forces of the white South resisted this program with great energy and ingenuity. As the discriminatory Black Codes passed by southern state legislatures immediately after the war revealed, there was already a well-defined niche waiting for the new freedmen in the southern social structure: they could simply be relegated to the status of ante-bellum free Negroes. Instead of being slaves of individual masters, they would now be servants of the white community in general. When this plan was overruled by the northern radicals, many southerners attempted to reestablish white supremacy by extralegal or illegal methods, intimidating or terrorizing newly enfranchised black voters and using their dominant economic and social position to enforce segregation and discrimination. When Radical Reconstruction was overthrown in the 1870s, the new rulers of the South were able to continue such practices unimpeded by federal intervention. By the 1890s the disappearance of a lingering northern concern about the rights of southern blacks and a series of Supreme Court decisions emasculating the Reconstruction amendments made it possible for southern state legislatures and constitutional conventions to begin giving legal sanction to the pattern of segregation and disfranchisement that had been developing. Between 1890 and 1910 a multitude of Jim Crow laws were passed mandating segregation in virtually all public facilities. This legislation was grounded in the "separate but equal" principle, which meant that a fictive equality in accommodations made segregation nondiscriminatory and hence constitutional—an argument that was formally accepted by the Supreme Court in *Plessy* v. *Ferguson* (1896). Blacks were also deprived of what remained of their suffrage rights by constitutional restrictions on voting that were not explicitly racial but which allowed local registrars to exclude blacks at will from the ballot box. By World War I the southern black electorate had dwindled to almost nothing and segregation in virtually all aspects of social existence from the cradle to the grave was required by law. Segregation could even reach the point of separate phone booths, separate storage facilities for school books used by white and black children, and the use of Jim Crow bibles in courtrooms.

The system of segregation in the South, which would remain virtually intact until the 1950s, was carefully constructed to symbolize the social superiority of the lowest white man to any Negro, no matter how prosperous or accomplished. This suggests that the elaborate system of racial distinctions was designed as much to heal actual or potential rifts among different classes of whites as to hold blacks in subjection. The late 19th- and early 20th-century South was characterized by a crudely exploitative economy with an agricultural system based on a form of tenancy approximating peonage and a nascent industrialization that promised to be competitive with the North only because of the cheapness of its labor. The fact that a large class of poor white farmers and industrial workers coexisted with the mass of black poor constituted both a threat and an opportunity for the dominant elements in southern life. The threat was that an interracial lower class would arise to attack the privileges of the dominant elite of landlords, merchants, and industrialists; for a time the Populist movement of the 1890s seemed to be on the verge of shaping such a coalition. The alternative was to exacerbate racial tensions between poor whites and poor blacks and to buttress the former group's loyalty to the established order by emphasizing their upper-caste position and the psychological rewards of a sense of racial superiority. If this in fact was the strategy of southern elites, it succeeded brilliantly. The implementation of Jim Crow disfranchisement not only reduced blacks to powerlessness and humiliating social inferiority, but also signalled the end of significant political and economic dissent among whites.

The establishment of the new racial order in the South and the new mood of acquiescence in the North were sustained and justified by a barrage of the most virulent racist propaganda that the nation had ever seen. The image of "the Negro as beast" (to quote the title of one of the Negrophobic tracts of the early 1900s) was promulgated in periodicals, books, pamphlets, plays, and motion pictures. Thomas W. Dixon's flagrantly racist *The Clansman* evolved from the best-selling novel of 1905 into a Broadway hit and by 1915 into the most successful of early movies (*The Birth of a Nation*). It brought the image of the vicious and subhuman black, whose lust for white women made him a suitable candidate for lynching, into the center of American consciousness. On a more refined level, scholars invoked Darwinism to legitimize the idea of a "struggle for existence" between the races which the superior whites were destined to win so long as they retained their "racial purity."

The historical development of the 20th century that most affected racial attitudes and practices was the mass migration of blacks from the rural South to the urban North beginning just before World War I. Seeking to escape grinding rural poverty and the rigors of segregation and pulled by the promise of industrial employment, hundreds of thousands of migrants poured into the poorest and most run-down neighborhoods of northern cities. What they found was not precisely what they had left behind but it was still prejudice and discrimination. The northern urban pattern was not

segregation by law but the extralegal product of concerted efforts by major institutions and interest groups to exclude blacks from the full advantages of urban and industrial life. Coalitions of white homeowners fought, sometimes with violence, to exclude blacks from their neighborhoods, and overcrowded black ghettos quickly took shape. Trade unions excluded black workers entirely or accepted them only in separate and inferior locals. Trade-union exclusiveness effectively deprived blacks of access to the best industrial jobs, and most were therefore condemned to menial and unskilled occupations. Under the pressure of such circumstances some blacks allowed themselves to be used as strikebreakers by white employers and thereby incited further animosity from white workers. Part of the background of the two great race riots of the World War I era, the East St. Louis, Ill., riot of 1917 and the one that occurred in Chicago two years later, was the familiar story of discrimination by white labor and "scabbing" by blacks. Not until the 1930s with the coming of the New Deal and the efforts of the CIO to organize black workers did Afro-Americans begin to find a secure place in the organized labor force.

Although migration to the North did not bring equality of opportunity, it did provide some sources of strength that helped reduce the powerlessness of the black community. First of all, northern blacks could vote, and by the 1930s white politicians became aware that there were now enough blacks in key industrial states to affect the outcome of elections. Second, blacks had greater opportunities than in the South to organize protest movements and air their grievances. Finally, in times of rapid economic expansion and heightened labor demand, such as existed during both the world wars, they were in a position to make some inroads into skilled and semiskilled occupations previously dominated by whites.

A relative increase in the power and resources available to the black community helps account for the growth of a national commitment to equal rights beginning in the New Deal period. No one pays much attention to the complaints of the powerless, but political leverage and organized pressure compel a response. The effectiveness of black protest between the 1940s and late 1960s also was enhanced by the fact that racist ideologies had been discredited among important elite groups in American society. Well-educated and liberal whites had become increasingly aware of the injustice and irrationality of racial prejudice and discrimination. A combination of black assertiveness and liberalized white attitudes led to a successful assault on the Southern system of segregation in the 1950s and 1960s. But the northern pattern of de facto segregation proved more resistant to change. Although palpable discrimination had certainly been a significant factor in creating this situation, black poverty and a natural tendency toward residential concentration by class and ethnicity may have played a more important role than overtly racist public policies in separating blacks from whites in schools and other local institutions. The intense desire of many whites to preserve an established pattern of white ethnic neighborhoods and schools against black intrusion has proved a powerful and, up to now, insurmountable obstacle to the full integration of northern urban communities. Whether most white resistance to open housing and to court-ordered busing to achieve racial balance in the schools should be viewed as a manifestation of racism or as a legitimate expression of the pluralist character of northern urban life remains a matter of bitter dispute.

THE ASIAN IMMIGRANT AS ULTIMATE ALIEN

No category of ethnic Americans has proved capable of arousing, at least temporarily, a more intense and unqualified antipathy than did the Asian immigrants who arrived in California between 1850 and 1908. Neither the paternalism that sometimes took the edge off Negrophobia nor the romanticization that gave the Indian a symbolic dignity were operative in this case. Because he was not white, the Chinese or Japanese newcomer was deemed biologically unassimilable. Because he possessed a culture that differed substantially from the Anglo-American norm, his way of life was denounced as utterly incompatible with American values and behavior. Hence he was simultaneously a victim of the same white-supremacist ethos that condemned blacks and Indians to inferior or marginal status and the object of a particularly virulent strain of nativism—the recurrent hostility to immigrants with cultural backgrounds considered alien to American traditions.

The treatment of recently arrived Asians in California and other western states involved much the same combination of social segregation, economic discrimination, and mob violence that was used to keep blacks "in their place" in the South after Reconstruction. But the main objective of their white enemies was not so much to create a permanent caste system as to exclude Asians entirely from American society. Consequently they not only served for a time as the western surrogate for the blacks of the South but also became the first category of immigrants to be denied free access to the United States.

The Chinese The first Asians to arrive in substantial numbers were the Chinese who emigrated to California between the 1850s and the 1880s. Welcomed by white entrepreneurs as a source of cheap contract labor for mining, railroad construction, and manufacturing, they encountered bitter hostility from white workers and small businessmen who viewed them as actual or potential competitors. The substantive complaint of these groups was that Asians were semislaves who accepted wages and working conditions which no white man would tolerate and that they consequently aided the land, railroad, and mining barons in their efforts to monopolize the sources of western wealth that once had seemed open to all enterprising migrants from the East and Europe. But such appeals to tangible white interests were heavily overlaid and sometimes even obscured by racist assaults on the Chinese as opium smokers, carriers of exotic oriental diseases, and devotees of sexual practices that threatened the health and purity of the white community. The image of the Chinese as drugaddicted, sexually depraved barbarians provoked a western equivalent of the miscegenation phobia directed toward Afro-Americans in other sections and resulted in similar forms of mob action against alleged offenders.

After the Civil War, anti-Chinese sentiment emerged as a decisive force in California politics. The Democrats used it first as a device to regain their ante-bellum dominance, but in the late 1870s a combination of economic distress and popular dissatisfaction at Democratic ac-

commodation with employers of Chinese labor provoked a strong third-party movement devoted to repression of the Chinese for the benefit of white labor. The Workingman's party of California, led by the Irish immigrant Dennis Kearney, was strongly represented at the state constitutional convention of 1878 and took the lead in enacting clauses prohibiting the employment of Chinese labor and giving local authorities carte blanche to "abate" the "Chinese menace" in any way they saw fit. Such actions were in fact mainly symbolic, for they flagrantly violated the U.S. Constitution and were overturned in federal courts. But the long-simmering California agitation for an end to all Chinese immigration bore fruit in 1882 when the Chinese Exclusion Act was passed by the U.S. Congress. This legislation reflected the fact that Sinophobia was not limited to California or the western states but had by now become part of the larger American pattern of ethnic prejudice. On a national level, as in California, spokesmen for white labor led the agitation for the first federal immigration law discriminating against a specific nationality, but it is indicative of the friendless situation of the Chinese that there was little opposition to the policy from other groups.

Hostility to the Chinese did not end with the closing of the gates but actually peaked in the mid-1880s when there was an epidemic of forced expulsions of entire Chinese communities from mining and lumbering towns all over the Far West. But the subsequent concentration of the remaining Chinese in a few virtually self-sufficient enclaves, most notably San Francisco's Chinatown, and in a few noncompetitive enterprises such as laundries and Chinese restaurants eventually resulted in a decline of active white antagonism. In the 20th century there has been a steady decrease of anti-Chinese prejudice due to such factors as the social and economic success of Sino-Americans, the projection of a more favorable image of their communal and cultural life, and—despite the notable ups and downs associated with the Communist assumption of power in mainland China and the Korean War—a general accretion of respectful attitudes toward China itself.

The Japanese Although Chinese immigration was legally ended in 1882, the door was still open to other Asians, and substantial numbers of Japanese began to arrive in California during the 1890s. Most established themselves as farm workers and then as small independent farmers, successfully employing Japanese methods of intensive agriculture. As in the case of the Chinese, white agitation for discrimination and exclusion was quick to develop. The new Asian immigrants were excoriated as the vanguard of a "yellow peril"—a tide of inferior humanity supposedly rolling out of the East and threatening to engulf the United States. Prominent in the anti-Japanese campaign were labor groups and organizations of white farmers reacting to competition from the more efficient Japanese cultivators. In 1906 the San Francisco School Board responded to the growing clamor by ordering the segregation of white and Asian children. But the emergence of Japan as a major world power at the beginning of the century made open discrimination against its nationals more difficult than the earlier mistreatment of the Chinese, whose home government had been weak and subservient to Western interests. When the imperial government issued a formal protest against school segregation in San Francisco,

President Theodore Roosevelt intervened in the controversy: in 1907 and 1908 he negotiated a withdrawal of the offending ordinance in return for a "gentlemen's agreement" from Japan to terminate emigration to the United States. But the assault on the rights of Japanese immigrants continued in California, culminating in 1913 in a law denying the right of land ownership to "aliens ineligible for citizenship" which in effect singled out the Japanese and attempted to destroy their competitive position in California agriculture. (Japanese were not considered potential citizens because the original U.S. naturalization law limiting eligibility to "free white persons" had never been amended to include Asians.)

Although association with a powerful Japanese nation provided some limited protection to Japanese-Americans in the early 20th century, the putative Japanese nationality of their descendants proved disastrous during World War II. In the most flagrant act of discrimination against any immigrant group in American history, the federal government in 1942 ordered the forced removal and internment of the entire Japanese population of the Pacific Coast, including native-born citizens of the United States. Wartime hysteria and an urge for symbolic revenge against the perpetrators of Pearl Harbor provide only part of the explanation for this unprecedented denial of civil rights. Without the century-long tradition of anti-Asian prejudice in the United States— a bias that characteristically took the form of treating Asian immigrants as the most unwelcome and unassimilable of "aliens"—such a drastic act of repression would probably have been unthinkable.

Since the end of the war there has been a dramatic decline in prejudice and discrimination against Japanese and other Asians. Special restrictions on Asian immigration have been lifted, and the prospects for upward mobility and assimilation have markedly improved for individuals of Asian descent. As far as the Japanese were concerned, this change was related to such factors as the new status of Japan as an ally of the United States, white guilt over wartime excesses, the greater geographic dispersal of the Japanese population after release from internment, and certain characteristics of Japanese-American culture that have promoted individual and collective achievement. It may be premature to claim that racial prejudice against Asians has disappeared, but the trend appears to be in the direction of according to Americans of various Asian ancestries a status roughly equivalent to that of white "ethnics." If this tendency continues, it will provide strong evidence that racism is a situational and historically determined phenomenon and not the result of some innate "consciousness of kind."

Hispanic Americans

Like the Asian minorities, Spanish-speaking Americans have been the victims of a combination of ethnocultural and racial prejudice. The social effects of such attitudes, together with the growing size of the Spanish-speaking population, have made this minority among the most conspicuous in contemporary America. Actually, it is misleading to talk about a single Hispanic group, for Mexicans, Puerto Ricans, and Cubans differ in a number of significant ways, and there are a good many other small groups from Spanish-speaking backgrounds. Their historical experiences are sufficiently

dissimilar to preclude any uniform conclusions about the sources and effects of the prejudices they have encountered in American life. By and large they were incorporated into the population of the United States at different times and through different processes. Historically they have inhabited widely removed areas of the country. Their racial make-up is different; each has established a distinctive relationship with its cultural homeland; and the position each occupies in American society accords them differential ability to protect themselves against discrimination.

The Mexicans One segment of the Mexican-American community became part of the United States through conquest in the 19th century, another through immigration, largely in the 20th century. In the 1840s and 1850s the annexation of Texas, the war with Mexico, and the Gadsden Purchase added thousands of Spanish-speaking residents to the population of the United States. Placed in the position of a conquered people, they confronted strong Anglo-American antipathies. In Texas, especially, they bore the "burden of the Alamo," the stigma of a despised alien enemy. Their concentration in established communities, their fidelity to the Roman Catholic Church, and the proximity of Mexico itself ensured that the Mexican-American population of the new Southwest maintained a cultural insularity that would continue to mark it as foreign in the eyes of ethnocentric Anglo-Americans. In the states of California and Texas as well as in the territories of Colorado, New Mexico, and Arizona, Mexicans shared the status of indigens with Indians, and like the Indians they possessed a commodity—land—that Anglo-Americans coveted. To race-conscious 19th-century Americans, particularly to the southerners who came to inhabit Texas, their mixed racial ancestry gave license for abuse. Where they remained local majorities, numbers afforded a certain protection against social slights and economic exploitation. To penetrate the most populous Spanish-speaking communities of Arizona and New Mexico, Anglo-Americans frequently had to amalgamate with the Spanish elites. But Anglo-American migration in pursuit of the profits of mining, ranching, and railroading made it inevitable that the Mexicans of the Southwest would eventually become statewide or territorial minorities. Without political influence that extended much beyond their own immediate communities, Mexican Americans became relatively powerless to repel predatory raids upon their land and assaults on their cultural inheritance. Anglo-American land commissions gradually extinguished traditional property titles, and legislatures made English the official language of government in the cause of Americanization. In Texas, many fundamental protections of the law were stripped from Mexican-Americans as from blacks by the institution of white primary elections at the turn of the century.

Immigrants from Mexico began to supplement the native-born Spanish-speaking population of the southwestern United States in the mid-19th century. Mexican miners participated in the gold rush to California during the 1840s and railroad workers passed over the international boundary in pursuit of employment as the lines of northern Mexico reached completion. In Arizona and New Mexico the newcomers reinforced the local dominance of established Spanish-American communities. But in Texas and California they swelled the ranks of a propertyless laboring class analogous to the Chinese of the Far West or to the black population of the post–Civil War South and thus invited exploitation by employers or landlords and the antipathy of native white workers.

Political disruptions associated with the Mexican Revolution and a variety of economic pressures greatly accelerated the pace of Mexican immigration to the United States in the 20th century. An open border enabled Mexican laborers to respond to employment opportunities on either side. The transient nature of some elements of the Mexican minority in the United States frequently provided Anglo-American public officials with arguments for withholding public education, welfare benefits, and political recognition from the Spanish-speaking community altogether.

Despite the clamor about the racial decay of the United States which peaked during the early 1920s, Mexicans were specifically excluded from the immigration quotas of 1921 and 1924 at the behest of southwestern employers. But by establishing the principle that only Mexicans unlikely to become a public charge were welcome to enter the United States, the national origins acts gave government officials a powerful administrative tool for adjusting the supply of immigrants to domestic economic demand. During the Great Depression this regulation was sometimes enforced with brutal efficiency. Mexican laborers were repeatedly routed from their jobs in favor of "white" Americans, and the unemployed aliens were conveyed south of the border. Substantial numbers of bona fide U.S. citizens were rounded up and threatened with expulsion because they "looked" Mexican. The Los Angeles "Zoot Suit" riots which followed during the 1940s, pitting "Anglo" servicemen against Mexican-American youth, confirmed with chilling clarity the exposure of the Hispanic community to the possibility of racial aggression and discrimination.

During the last quarter-century, Mexican Americans have become a highly visible and somewhat segregated minority. Although economic developments have transformed them from a regional to a national minority and from a largely rural population to an increasingly urban one, they remain heavily concentrated in the southwestern United States. Proximity to the Mexican border and international family ties have combined with regional concentration to encourage the preservation of a vital ethnic culture. Concentration and cultural vitality have stimulated ethnocultural bias, but they have also helped the Mexican-American community of the Southwest to organize politically in the post–Civil Rights era to protect itself from public or private discrimination.

The Immigration Act of 1965 produced a new source of anti-Mexican hostility in the United States. By establishing immigration quotas for hemispheric neighbors, the new regulations produced a much larger number of illegal, or undocumented, immigrants, many of them Mexican workers who continued to exercise their traditional liberty of crossing the border unofficially in pursuit of employment. The American economic recession of the 1970s transformed them into an emotionally charged political issue. "Illegals" were accused of stimulating the unemployment of U.S. citizens and of de-

pressing workers' wages. Other Americans express the fear that hordes of racially inferior "brown" Mexicans will undermine traditional American cultural values. Their undocumented status compounds the difficulties that Mexicans may face in the United States. By choice and circumstance, "illegals" are among the most unprotected and disadvantaged classes in the United States. Fearful of detection and expulsion, they are largely without the protection of the laws, isolated from agencies of public welfare, and in some ways at the mercy of employers. Although Mexican-American citizens are sometimes among the most vocal critics of the "illegals," the issue has embittered many Anglos against the Mexican-American community generally. Chicano political activists argue that this is evidence that Spanish-speaking minorities continue to face a malicious strain of racial prejudice in American society.

The Puerto Ricans Puerto Ricans, in contrast, have held legal status as immigrants to the continental United States since 1898, when Puerto Rico became a U.S. possession. New facilities for trans-Caribbean travel at the conclusion of World War II encouraged Puerto Ricans to escape chronic overpopulation and underemployment and seek improved economic opportunities on the mainland. This quest took them mostly to major industrial metropolitan areas, particularly New York City and Chicago. Arriving with few marketable skills or material resources, most immigrants found employment as low-paid wage laborers in manufacturing and the service industries. A high rate of fertility among this population inhibited family saving and social mobility, and the language barrier interfered with education and occupational advancement. Economic conditions condemned most Puerto Ricans to residence in decaying inner-city environments. On the whole, the Puerto Rican minority has found it even more difficult than blacks to escape the grip of urban poverty.

Puerto Ricans' ethnic identity in the United States is a compound of class, cultural, and racial distinctiveness. To some extent the ethnic group displays the characteristics of the inner-city poor generally. But their Hispanic culture makes them stand out from other working-class elements. Residential concentration and the continued accretion of newcomers from Puerto Rico reinforce cultural uniqueness in the urban environment. Although the Puerto Rican population represents many degrees of racial admixture as evidenced in a wide variety of physical types, non-Hispanic Americans have tended to lump its members together as part of a "brown" race. This classification has inhibited the amalgamation of Puerto Ricans with either blacks or whites and has consequently prevented dilution of the ethnic group's other distinguishing features.

Because of their multiple sources of group identity, Puerto Ricans have encountered a complex assortment of suspicions and prejudices in the mainland United States. Populated by a singularly poverty-stricken social class, Puerto Rican communities often strike more fortunate Americans as burdensome pockets of urban decay, welfare expense, and street crime, as well as new sources of unwelcome cultural or linguistic diversity. Working-class ethnic groups sometimes regard them as economic interlopers, stimulating unemployment and depressing wages. Detractors also charge that the social immobility that has locked much of the Puerto Rican

minority into urban barrios is encouraged by voluntary clannishness. Puerto Ricans themselves frequently insist that their economic opportunities have been hampered by a lack of education fostered by an ethnocentric language barrier. But efforts to promote bilingualism in the schools often run athwart the potent argument that it represents a dysfunctional resistance to acculturation which compounds existing economic disabilities. Because of the popular tendency to identify Puerto Ricans as nonwhites, they are open to insinuations that poverty and cultural insularity are products of innate racial proclivities and that fuller integration into American society is unlikely. Whether individual Puerto Ricans encounter racial prejudice depends in part upon personal physical features. But because the ethnic group as a whole is regarded as homogeneous, individuals may find themselves held responsible for the actions or characteristics of any other member of the minority: Puerto Rican community leaders argue that law enforcement officers often harass an entire population for the transgressions of a few.

Both poverty and prejudice have made it difficult for Puerto Ricans to get ahead in the United States. Like other ghetto dwellers, they experience the high economic costs of inner-city living which impede mobility. Racial and cultural prejudices interfere with Puerto Ricans' ability to join with other urban and working-class minorities in the pursuit of common interests. Unlike Mexican Americans, Puerto Ricans generally have not been able to make effective use of residential concentration to promote group goals or provide political protections for civil rights. As metropolitan rather than statewide or regional minorities, Puerto Ricans' political influence has been almost entirely local, making the mobilization of state and national government on their behalf more difficult.

The Cubans Cubans constitute the smallest of the three major Spanish-speaking ethnic minorities in the United States and are among the most recent arrivals. Few Cubans migrated to the United States before the 1959 revolution. The large numbers who arrived thereafter moved chiefly for political reasons. Admitted to the United States as refugees, the vast majority of immigrants were voluntary exiles from Castro's revolution. The Cuban immigration also differs from the Mexican and Puerto Rican in other important respects. Flight took Cubans to the closest point on the mainland, Miami, Fla., where for the most part they have remained, in regional isolation. This extreme concentration, together with a strong entrepreneurial ethic among the Cuban population, has produced considerable material prosperity. To a great extent, whatever prejudice the Cuban minority of south Florida has encountered has been much like that aimed at Japanese or Jewish Americans, motivated more by economic jealousy than by disrespect. The economic and political strength produced by concentration, however, has given Cuban Americans powerful weapons for warding off the potential social consequences of prejudice.

Cuban Americans have been spared much of the racial bias directed at Mexicans and Puerto Ricans largely because blacks and other dark-skinned racial mixtures were underrepresented in the movement to the mainland. Nonetheless, economic self-sufficiency, political clout, and the superpatriotism popularly associated

with the Cubans' intense anti-Communism have been at least as important as white skin in maintaining the group's freedom from the more serious expressions of prejudice and acts of discrimination faced by other Hispanics. In fact, the Cuban experience seems to demonstrate the extent to which the model of assimilation followed by many European ethnic groups remains operative and the way in which Spanish-speaking groups may be able to overcome ethnocultural and class biases without surrendering a distinctive cultural identity and community residential patterns.

Although each of the Spanish-speaking ethnic groups in the United States encounters different degrees of prejudice in American society, the fundamental sources of ethnic antipathy are similar. In the immediate future it is unlikely that prejudice against the Spanish-speaking will disappear. Despite interethnic marriages, socioeconomic advancement, and residential mobility, the size of culturally distinctive Hispanic communities continues to grow. The number of Spanish-speaking newcomers so far exceeds the numbers assimilating into the larger society that these ethnic groups are sometimes called "eternal first-generation" immigrants, for they have a constantly reinforced ethnocultural identity. Economic differences and barrio residential characteristics reinforce ethnic distinctiveness and provide outsiders with reasons or excuses for fear and disdain. Native prejudice helps sustain these conditions. Economic disabilities, in particular, bring criticism and encourage exploitation.

The relative freedom of the U.S. Cuban population from ethnic prejudice suggests that socioeconomic advancement may eventually emancipate the other Hispanic minorities from bias and exploitation. The success of the Mexican and Puerto Rican minorities depends to some extent upon their ability to take advantage of residential concentration to promote economic self-help and acquire political leverage.

EUROPEAN IMMIGRANTS AND ANGLO-AMERICAN NATIVISM

Before the English colonizers of North America had completed their assessment of blacks and Indians or begun to react to Asians or Hispanics, newcomers from Europe were challenging the ethnic homogeneity of white society itself. First as a trickle, then as a flood, the Atlantic migration introduced millions to the New World between the 17th and mid-20th centuries and deposited ethnic communities representing virtually every European nationality or would-be nationality. During times of peace, prosperity, and popular self-assurance, the United States proved remarkably receptive to this growing ethnic diversity. But in periods of crisis, colonial-stock Americans frequently singled out ethnic groups as sources of social disharmony and communal weakness. From an early date, Anglo-Americans regarded political and religious affinities as touchstones of the immigrants' potential loyalty and capacity for assimilation. Successive generations of the American-born majority—a fluid category variously labeling itself as Anglo-American, Anglo-Saxon, or Old Stock—in turn identified Roman Catholicism, Judaism, and all varieties of unrepublican "radicalism" as the principal threats to national unity and progress. Until the 20th century, American society accepted immigrants without impediment, yet popular ethnocentrism demanded that newcomers conform to the social myths, values, and traditions of old-stock Americans. The idea that American identity was accessible only to particular ethnic groups usually remained dormant. But in times of the most acute social or intellectual crisis, elements of the native majority proved themselves willing and able to redefine nationality in purely ethnic terms to keep immigrants and their children from centers of power and influence in American life and thus to maintain their own social dominance.

Colonial and Early National Periods The English settlers of 17th-century North America brought with them strong nationalist biases that affected their reception of subsequent European migrants. In the colonies, the anti-Catholic animus that was part of the contemporary Englishman's national identity vented itself not only on those who arrived under the banners of imperial rivals France and Spain but also on some of the Scots and Irish who composed part of the colonial trade in indentured servants. Roman Catholicism impressed Anglo-American colonists as a source of immorality and political unreliability; few English settlements in the New World failed to protect themselves from subversion by erecting impediments to Catholic immigration. The conditions and motives of colonization reinforced the initial disposition of Anglo-Americans to view ethnic differences in nationalistic and cultural terms. Perched on the edge of a wilderness 3,000 miles from the homeland, yet unshakably committed to remaining an identifiably English people, the colonists clung tenaciously to traditional values and prejudices. The expressly religious foundations of several colonies reinforced sectarian bigotries transported from Europe. In New England the covenantal form of community organization was utterly antithetical to cultural pluralism of any sort.

Colonial Anglo-Americans employed preponderance in numbers and an initial monopoly of political power to insist upon the acculturation of the other Europeans who came to settle among them, thrusting the most recalcitrant nonconformists to the geographical fringes of society. During the 50 years preceding the American Revolution successive waves of Scotch-Irish and German arrivals settled in disproportionate numbers along a great western arc beyond the centers of English population. There they found themselves able to retain considerable cultural distinctiveness free from Anglo-American interference. Thus, during the colonial period of American history, physical space effectively inhibited interethnic tension or at least impeded active discrimination against disapproved minorities.

Proscriptions placed by the first colonists upon the civil rights of Catholic settlers were weakened in the early 18th century in consequence of the increase of sectarian diversity among Protestants themselves. Foreign-born colonists responded so energetically to the relaxation of religious tests in politics that many traditionalists feared the eclipse of English governance and cultural predominance. Only half in jest, Benjamin Franklin suggested that future generations of Pennsylvanians school themselves in the German language lest they become strangers in their native land. In several colonies ethnocultural friction intruded into politics.

Political contention between backcountry and seacoast in the Southern colonies during the immediate prerevolutionary period frequently had an ethnic dimension. Although events leading to the Revolution itself temporarily reinvigorated anti-Catholic prejudices, the principal effect of the struggle for colonial home rule was to persuade Anglo-Americans of the fundamental loyalty of major white ethnic minorities.

During the early years of the American republic a new conviction that political culture was bound up with emerging nationalism supplanted some of the traditional distinctions that Americans had made between white ethnic groups. As Anglo-Americans came to think of themselves as a unique people, not even new arrivals from England were wholly exempt from suspicion. European challenges to the sovereignty of the fledgling United States between 1790 and 1815 provoked a temporary but widespread xenophobia exceeding the ethnocultural suspicions of the colonial era. Increasingly, Americans regarded deviations from their Protestant, bourgeois, and individualistic culture as symptomatic of antirepublican tendencies. In particular, old-stock Americans associated Roman Catholicism with monarchist leanings.

Because popular thought increasingly identified political ideology with ethnicity, public debate over U.S. foreign relations and domestic party conflict were breeding grounds for interethnic tension. Jeffersonians, despite their advertisement of the United States as a refuge for Europe's oppressed, feared that British and German immigrants might infect U.S. institutions with monarchical tendencies. Their rivals, the Federalists, expressed even greater concern at the prospect that newcomers from France and Ireland would bear the dangerous enthusiasms of the French Revolution. During the Federalist ascendancy of the 1790s, naturalization law was deliberately employed to discourage the immigration of either the Celtic Irish or the French and to keep the votes of the foreign-born out of Republican tallies. By extending the period of probationary residence for citizenship applicants from 5 to 14 years in 1798, Congress intended to protect the republic from alien subversives already on the soil. The principal targets were Irish Americans, whom Anglo-American conservatives regarded as having "red republican" leanings. Only a relative liberalization of the official treatment of immigrants accompanied the political "revolution" of 1800 which brought Thomas Jefferson to the presidency. The Democratic-Republicans, much like the Federalists, demanded total acculturation of immigrants as proof of loyalty and were prepared to manipulate naturalization laws to exclude those foreigners they found dangerous or unattractive. Although they repealed the Naturalization Act of 1798, the Democratic-Republicans responded to the hostility toward England that grew during the early years of the 19th century by placing mildly punitive conditions upon the residence of British aliens. In 1813 Congress stipulated that no British alien who had not declared an intention to become a U.S. citizen before the onset of the War of 1812 could be naturalized, a provision repealed after the war ended. Once ethnicity became entangled with American politics, simple ethnocultural differences between the native- and foreign-born lost some of their earlier salience. The Anglo-American majority increasingly fo-

cused its concern on the few immigrant groups that seemed to have either the size or the foreign connections to threaten seriously the republican system of government or the security of the nation. Late 18th- and early 19th-century ethnic antipathy, therefore, was directed primarily at French, Irish, and, to some extent, English immigrants. Perceived ideological affinities had replaced gross cultural differences as the primary stimulants of prejudice.

The Ante-Bellum Years Ethnicity remained a popular shorthand indication of political allegiance until the Civil War. Ante-bellum political adversaries proved capable of cynically manipulating anti-immigrant feeling to serve their immediate interests. Democrats denounced Illuminism, Free Masonary, and monarchism as immigrant-borne threats to the ideology of republican simplicity. Refugee forty-eighters from the German principalities, on the other hand, impressed Whigs as anarchists and moral libertines. The Irish, who began arriving in the United States in larger numbers during the 1830s, could be regarded as either the Pope's reactionary minions or as dangerous republican radicals and were alternately castigated by both Whig and Democratic politicians. It was the Whig party, however, which denounced most volubly the connection between Roman Catholicism and Old World despotism, and in time the Democrats absorbed the larger number of naturalized citizens.

Anti-Catholicism acquired a new and more highly charged meaning during the decades before the Civil War, a period when Americans were struggling to create a distinctive national identity shorn of the taints of Europe. For a people trying to discover who they were and what gave them national unity, identification of a historical enemy proved enormously useful. Accused by both native and foreign critics of excessive individualism and contentiousness, ante-bellum Americans lashed out at tangible evidence of clannishness and separatism. A popular theme in American political rhetoric during the 1820s and 1830s was opposition to secret, "subversive" organizations. Exclusivity of all kinds was denounced as antithetical to democratic notions of public openness and equality. Inevitably, ethnic fellowships—and especially the Roman Catholic Church—became targets for politicians who proclaimed them sources of disharmony in American life. The immigrants' efforts to ease the pain of transplantation and reinforce a distinctive cultural identity through mutual-aid societies and social clubs made them especially vulnerable to such charges.

The growth of the idea that the United States was destined to perform a regenerative world mission offered another kind of response to the midcentury crisis of national identity. Ante-bellum Anglo-Americans eagerly sponsored Protestant evangelical missions as part of a national crusade to bring enlightenment to the heathen and the unregenerate. Immigrant Catholics threatened this whole concept of national unification and self-justification because of their reluctance to support such popular evangelical reforms as temperance and strict sabbatarianism. Aggressive Protestant agencies like the American Home Missionary Society and the Society for the Diffusion of Christian Knowledge devoted considerable effort to counteracting what evangelistic Protestants regarded as the deleterious effects of

Romanism upon the republic. Native-born Protestants, convinced that the public schools were the proper instrument for instilling national values in youth, fiercely resisted immigrants' efforts to introduce sectarian teachings into state-supported education and attacked the creation of alternative parochial institutions of learning. The burning of the Charlestown, Mass., convent school by an enraged Protestant mob in 1834 illustrates the strength of this sentiment in some quarters.

When perfectionist reform faltered, opportunistic politicians capitalized on popular demands for a ritual national housecleaning by adopting the cause of naturalization reform. During the 1830s and 1840s Whig demagogues—and in some locales Democrats—took to the stump to persuade native-born voters that their ballots were being diluted by numbers of ill-educated and tractable foreigners, fresh off the boat, who had been brought before a partisan judge, summarily naturalized, and then marched to the polls. The proposed remedy to such corruption was an extension of the residency requirement for prospective citizens to as long as 21 years. The argument that such reforms would do much to purify U.S. politics possessed such popular appeal that when the major parties were slow to translate rhetoric into legislation, political splinter groups eagerly seized upon the program as a source of easy access to the electorate. In 1836 Samuel F.B. Morse, later to invent the telegraph, ran strongly for mayor of New York City on a pledge of naturalization reform as the candidate of the newly founded Native Democratic Association. In 1845 several of these nativist associations from the eastern states merged in Philadelphia to form a national Native American party. During the early 1850s Know-Nothings captured the governorship of Massachusetts, gained positions of influence in a handful of state legislatures, and filled a number of seats in the U.S. Congress. Recognizing the popularity of the theme of naturalization reform, the newly organized Republican party adopted the issue in some states as part of its initial campaign program. After being dropped by the Republicans because of the offense it gave to some ethnic groups which the party wished to attract, naturalization reform reemerged as part of efforts lasting through the election of 1860 to create a conservative and intersectional Unionist party that could sidestep the divisive slavery issue.

During the 1840s and 1850s the number of newcomers to the United States from Germany and Ireland grew at an unprecedented rate and tangible conflicts of interest between native- and foreign-born Americans became more acute, thus reinforcing political nativism. In northeastern seaboard cities, where the bulk of the famine-stricken Irish initially concentrated, competition between the native-born and immigrants for employment and housing exacerbated hostility to foreigners. Immigration was no longer exclusively the concern of society's moral and cultural leadership; ethnic prejudice also made considerable headway among the native-born laboring classes. The emergence of distinctive ethnic neighborhoods across the urban landscape produced cultural friction which far exceeded that of the colonial period. Fingers of Irish settlement along expanding railroad and canal routes and burgeoning German farm communities in the Northwest also produced unprecedented cultural cleavages in the rural United States. The clash of folkways, mores, and religions sometimes led only to the dissemination of humorously derisive ethnic stereotypes in American popular culture—like the brew-saturated, pot-bellied German plowman. But it also created enduring ethnic hostility toward the reputedly un-American "bog" Irish.

Interethnic competition, both material and ideological, produced considerable physical violence during the decades around mid-century. Rivalry between Anglo-American and immigrant fire companies, militia units, and street gangs resulted in murderous affrays in the streets of Baltimore, New York, and Boston. The so-called Bible Riots, which incinerated whole blocks of Philadelphia during the spring and summer of 1844, grew out of a complex of interethnic economic, political, and religious competition and criminal provocations that pitted Irish Catholics against Protestant Orangemen and Anglo-Americans. Inhabitants of Washington, D.C., came to expect an outbreak of ethnic violence every election day. The Louisville election-day riot of 1855 was so sanguinary that it became known as Bloody Monday.

Inevitably, some ante-bellum Anglo-Americans were persuaded that the failure of immigrants to be completely absorbed into American society reflected an innate inability to acculturate. As early as the 1830s there were fitful efforts to tie American national character to ethnic inheritance. The scientific theory of the plural origins of the "types of mankind," popular among some southern defenders of racial slavery, could also be extended to explain enduring "racial" differences among white Americans. During the 1840s and 1850s some observers of the nation's increasingly polyglot population worked out intricate associations between the real or imagined physical peculiarities of white ethnic stocks and their cultural, religious, and political proclivities. Parlor pseudosciences like phrenology and physiognomy groomed an entire generation of middle-class Americans to accept the idea that the smallest differences in physical form revealed important distinctions in intelligence and character.

Although the champions of naturalization reform and militant Protestantism might have found support in a racialist explanation of ethnic differences, popular theories about the degraded Celts and the noble Saxons made surprisingly little headway among the principal nativist organizations of the mid-19th century. Political nativists like the Know-Nothings remained committed to a cultural interpretation of nationality in which education and acculturation rather than birth qualified individuals for U.S. citizenship. Racialist Anglo-Saxonism surfaced primarily in the form of unflattering ethnic stereotypes—especially of the Irish—that entered into everyday American language. Undoubtedly the persistence of such images in popular culture fueled native bias against immigrants. But institutionalized "racial" discrimination against mid-century ethnic groups could not be rigorously sustained in the face of the reality that it was almost impossible to differentiate physically between Anglo-Americans and the foreign-born. The popular fiction that the peoples of Western Europe owed their origins to separate sources suffered during the Civil War years when military medical examiners had the opportunity to compare the physical characteristics of tens of thousands of citizen-soldiers. In fact, the patriotism and valorous military service of

immigrants from a variety of European backgrounds during the conflict seemed proof that the newcomers were fully capable of absorbing American values and loyalties.

The Late 19th Century Accelerating urbanization, industrialization, and changing patterns of social mobility combined during the three decades following the Civil War to give many Americans a deep sense of dislocation and anomie. Because of their concentration in urban areas and characteristic status as industrial workers, European immigrants effectively symbolized these developments and became natural targets for Americans theatened and disoriented by change. In a sense, ethnic groups became distinguished less by their particular cultural heritages than by the social and economic position they occupied in American society. Although this development eased prejudice against the German and Irish immigrants of the early 19th century (who had begun to work their way into the middle class), it made acculturation more difficult for subsequent waves of newcomers.

The rebounding economy of the immediate post–Civil War years stimulated the receptivity of American employers to accelerated European immigration. A number of states actually responded to businessmen's lobbies by passing contract-labor laws that facilitated the recruitment of workers abroad. Official encouragement of immigration sometimes extended to bounty arrangements and tax exemptions for new arrivals. Because this sanguine view of immigration possessed a fundamentally economic basis, it was repeatedly threatened and finally killed by fluctuating business conditions. The depressions of the middle 1870s, 1880s, and 1890s dampened the enthusiasm for immigration among industrialists. During these episodes of national distress, immigrants appeared a burden on already oversaturated labor markets. Second thoughts about the wisdom of unrestricted European immigration gained impetus when businessmen faced the specter of industrial strikes and labor radicalism fueled by layoffs and wage reductions.

Economic pressures also influenced the character of interethnic relations within the American working class itself during the final quarter of the 19th century. During the depression of the mid-1870s workers' organizations in several states pressured legislators to rescind the contract-labor laws of the 1860s and eliminate other inducements for immigrants. Between 1871 and 1875 violence wracked the coalfields of western Pennsylvania when Anglo-American and Irish miners fought the introduction of poorly paid Italian and eastern European immigrants into the mines. In the midst of another recession a decade later, emergent labor unions petitioned for a federal immigrant head tax to reduce the flow of new entrants to the U.S. labor pool and lobbied with individual states for legal bars to the employment of the foreign-born on public-works projects. Organized labor especially resented the use of immigrants as strikebreakers and denounced them as ignorant tools of grasping plutocrats.

While competition for employment was a powerful stimulant of interethnic hostility among working-class Americans, even more intense anti-immigrant prejudices developed among members of a U.S.-born middle class largely insulated from direct contact with foreigners. During the late 19th century these genteel na-

tivists increasingly perceived untrammeled immigration as a multifaceted threat to their traditional status and opportunities. Immigrants conveniently symbolized the problems posed by an expanding urban industrial proletariat. In immigrant ghettos middle-class Americans discerned a breeding ground for social disorder and crime. "Incurable" European poverty could thus be held responsible for the continuing deterioration of the nation's urban cores. The persistence of an economic subclass apparently trapped in poverty appeared to threaten the middle-class ideal of a mobile, homogeneous population. As the national self-confidence and self-congratulation that characterized the first years after the Civil War drained away, concern about political subversion and foreign radicalism reemerged. Labor-management strife during the Gilded Age stimulated fears of socialism, Communism, and other "European" radicalisms. Such movements not only seemed culturally alien, but also appeared to owe their existence to a growing industrial proletariat composed mainly of recent foreign arrivals. It was easy to attribute the persistence of an urban lower class to the inability of immigrants to grasp the ethic of industry, frugality, and sobriety that reputedly led to upward mobility. Ironically, at the same time that the foreign-born were denounced as fomenters of labor unrest, they were also often perceived by those in the middle ranks of society as the tools of grasping capitalists, employed to shatter a free labor market and the American dream of social mobility. Bowing to these sorts of fears, Republican conventions in Pennsylvania and Ohio endorsed federal immigration restriction in 1887.

Throughout the last quarter of the 19th century anti-Catholicism proved a useful vehicle for expressing class and ethnic insecurity. Immigrant Catholicism became a kind of identifying tag attached to the urban poor and a symbol of the social problems commonly associated with them. This identification was effectively developed by Josiah Strong in his contribution to the literature of Anglo-American nationalism, *Our Country*, published in 1885. Resurgent anti-Catholicism became endemic among rural and small-town native-born Americans. This sentiment represented their alienation from urban, industrial, cosmopolitan society and was the basis of the nativistic American Protective Asssociation founded in Clinton, Iowa, in 1887. During the late 1880s and early 1890s the APA waged a widespread lobbying campaign for public control of parochial schools. By the mid-1890s, however, the increasing secularism of American society and the inclusion of some second- and third-generation ethnics in a broadened native-born majority muted the anti-Catholic element in nativist rhetoric but did not relieve all Protestant Americans of suspicions that "Romanism" was a potential threat to the American way of life.

The unpredictability of the business cycle and the apparent hopelessness of solving the problems of urban poverty, crime, and political corruption reinforced the *fin-de-siècle* pessimism of American intellectual elites. The mood that prevailed in fashionable men's clubs and faculty lounges during the 1890s was characterized by a sense that the American people were losing their ability to cope with the developments of modern life. Contemporary jingoistic imperialism and the belief that the United States would have to be strong to make a bid for world power stimulated fears about dissipating national

vitality. Reluctant to question American institutions and the fundamental social order, native observers willingly attributed the nation's weaknesses to the alien influences of European immigrants and their U.S.-born descendants. Although natives characteristically magnified the relative dimensions of the influx, there was in fact an increasing proportion of newcomers during the 1880s and 1890s from southern and eastern Europe. Labeled as Slavs, Mediterraneans, or Semites, this component of the European immigration was accused of importing hereditary weaknesses that would undermine the American character. Urban progressives, disgruntled with the languid pace of social and political reform, easily resorted to the excuse that the foreign-born were hopelessly impoverished mentally, physically, and morally and that their presence stymied the improvement of American life.

The New Immigration and the Drive for Restriction
This interpretation of ethnic character served no set of Americans better than the Brahmin, or upper-class, intellectuals of the Northeast. Disturbed by their impotence in modern commercial and political life, they rested their waning claims to social dominance upon cultural and moral leadership. The growth of a cosmopolitan and multiethnic urban culture and the frustrations encountered by genteel urban reformers made these claims extremely shaky. It was easy for them to attribute the receding influence of their class in American life to the proportional decline of a properly appreciative population of Anglo-Saxon stock. The stereotypes of the vulgar Jewish parvenu and the shirt-sleeved Italian laborer represented all that was going awry in American life. The formation of the Immigration Restriction League in Boston in 1893 was the logical outcome of upper-class ruminations about the sources of national distress.

Jewish immigrants and their descendants, in particular, became targets upon which traditional elites, urban businessmen, and rural conservatives could focus their fears and discontents during the 1890s and later. Rather remarkable economic success in the late 19th and 20th centuries stimulated some American Jews to seek commensurate social recognition. Newly arrived Jews, first from Germany and later from eastern Europe, put their entrepreneurial talents aggressively to work, seeking both economic and social mobility. To Brahmin intellectuals these developments symbolized the collapse of a traditional social order which valued heritage, breeding, and community service above mere wealth and its display. Middle-class businessmen and professionals increasingly found themselves in direct competition with a distinctive ethnic group that displayed impressive commercial and professional talents, a competition that followed them home from office or shop once successful Jews began seeking residences in "better" neighborhoods. For small-town and rural Americans, who had little to fear in way of economic and social competition with Jewish immigrants, the Jew nonetheless conveniently represented the threat of the godless, industrial city and the control that the distant forces of the financier and the corporation appeared to be exercising over their lives.

Rather than admiring the success of members of the Jewish community in seizing on the opportunities offered by the American economic and social system, old-stock citizens seemed more inclined to believe that Jews used devious methods to warp the system for their exclusive advantage thus divesting American economic individualism of its supposed ethical restraints. The anti-Semitism that resulted produced a mottled pattern of discrimination in colleges, clubs, resorts, and hotels before the end of the century aimed at denying American Jews the fruits of their material achievement. Later, in the years just before World War I, more systematic attempts to regulate Jewish access to education and employment would deny equality of opportunity even more blatantly.

In the years around the turn of the 20th century, American nationalism became inextricably bound with a pseudoscientific "Anglo-Saxonism." The persistence of ethnic subcultures stimulated fears about the ability of American society to assimilate immigrants and about the capacity of immigrants to effectively acculturate. At the same time a heightened level of international competition raised popular questions about America's unity and strength. In this environment, the idea that only immigrants ethnically harmonious with the nation's Anglo-Saxon core could safely be welcomed into the republican polity grew more attractive. It was only a short step from defensive Anglo-Saxonism, which decried the declining dominance of traditional cultural values, to nativist racism. To the extent that immigrants failed to conform to American values and folkways, they were increasingly labeled, not merely as alien, but as biologically inferior. The belief that the United States was being flooded by the defeated members of beaten "races" fitted in neatly with contemporary social Darwinism. The same aversion to racial blending that prevented the United States from incorporating the brown inhabitants of its new Caribbean and South Seas protectorates into a unified empire at the end of the 19th century was played out at home in hostility to tawny Italians and raven-haired immigrant Jews. Southern notables in particular expressed fears that the influx of swarthy "new" immigrants might breach their region's color line, producing untold horrors.

Among federal policy makers, pseudoscientific racism made considerable headway during the last years of the 19th century and the first of the 20th. Congressional approval of a literacy-test qualification for immigrants in 1896 was the logical outgrowth of a reformism that sought "scientific" answers to social problems. The bill was vetoed by President Cleveland, but the houses of Congress periodically reconsidered the measure and finally overrode Woodrow Wilson's veto on the eve of the U.S. entry into World War I. Congress itself contributed to the popularization of racialist nativism by appointment of a blue-ribbon panel to examine the immigration "problem" in 1907. The Dillingham Commission's report of 1910 concluded that newcomers could be divided into "old" and "new" components, defined by ethnicity and geographic origins. It suggested that the "new" immigrants fitted much less readily into the American society and economy than the "old." Although the voluminous study accurately documented the shift in the national sources of immigration, it failed to take into account differences between specific ethnic groups and made unfair distinctions between the characteristics of the wave of new immigrants, still at its crest, and those of the "old" immigrants who faced examination after an extended his-

tory of acculturation and upward mobility. Intelligence tests administered by the armed forces during World War I seemed to confirm for federal officials what Madison Grant had revealed to the country in 1916 in *The Passing of a Great Race*, namely, that the moral, intellectual, and physical tone of the American people was being undermined by continued accretions of inferior "racial" stock. When immigration restriction was finally accomplished during the 1920s, it reflected these considerations. By giving strong preference to arrivals from the northwestern European sources of the "old" immigration, the legislation demonstrated the influence of a racial interpretation of ethnic differences.

The fine points of anti-immigrant racism were sufficiently complex to limit the number of its enthusiasts. But its influence among the nation's urban upper classes was paralleled by a resurgence of cultural tribalism among less sophisticated native-born Americans. Seeking a way to express their continued suspicion of urban, industrial society, country folk chastised immigrant Catholics and Jews as baleful influences upon American life. A reconstituted Ku Klux Klan merged anti-Catholicism, anti-Semitism, and Protestant fundamentalism to wage a vigorous rearguard defense of a passing American way of life. Inspired by the nationalist visions of Georgian William Simmons, the Klan took on an increasingly nativistic tone in the years after its founding in 1915 and became a genuine mass movement during the 1920s.

Ethnocultural biases grew during World War I. Resentful of imperial Germany's challenge to world order and prosperity, many Americans demanded ruthless elimination of all traces of German culture in American life. Once the United States had entered the conflict, however, the spirit of national unity that suffused the nation temporarily discouraged criticism of other ethnic groups. Wartime prosperity defused interethnic economic competition and made immigrant labor seem a valuable strategic asset. But in their zeal for a united front against the enemy, the native-born increasingly demanded the full acculturation of newcomers as proof of loyalty. The "100 percent Americanism" campaign that extended through the war years displayed the considerable intolerance of the American people for ethnic cultures and a patriotically inspired disinclination to see much virtue in cultural pluralism.

Developments in the immediate postwar world did nothing to persuade Americans to adopt a more cosmopolitan outlook on ethnic diversity. An abrupt slide into economic recession exacerbated old fears about immigration and overexpansion of the labor force. What was worse, the deteriorating economic situation was punctuated by strikes and labor unrest. Despite their relative weakness, radical labor organizations like the IWW (Industrial Workers of the World) which sought fundamental changes in the American economic system attracted excessive public attention and terrified the native-born middle class. The success of the Communist revolution in Russia and the rapid emergence of the Soviet Union as a European power reinforced the idea that an international conspiracy was afoot to undermine traditional Western liberalism. Scattered terrorist bombing incidents during 1919 encouraged the popular hysteria known as the Red Scare. Native-born Americans easily transferred their wartime hostility to Germans to central and eastern European ethnic populations in the United States, on the basis that they were propagators of radicalism and un-American ideologies. The assimilationist goal of 100 percent Americanism disappeared in the face of renewed feeling that many immigrants were incapable of understanding republican principles or of taking on the virtues of the loyal, progressive American.

When Congress passed a national origins system of immigration restriction in 1921, it was a logical culmination to the antiradical, anti-Catholic, and racialist strains of American nativism. By closing off much of the influx of immigrants from outside northwestern Europe and the British Isles, the Percentage Immigration Law met most popular demands for a solution to the the immigration question without appearing overtly xenophobic. The gates remained open to culturally and ethnically "harmonious" immigrants, preserving the idea that American society was sufficiently resilient to accept newcomers into its midst. Restriction was moved from an emergency to a permanent basis by the Johnson-Reed Act of 1924.

Since the 1920s The immediate effect of immigration restriction was to eliminate much of the excuse for contemporary excesses of ethnic bigotry. Without a clear goal to sustain it, antiforeign sentiment subsided. During the 1920s anti-Catholicism remained an effective vehicle of rural resentment against the sinful cities, merging nicely with Protestant fundamentalism and prohibitionist sentiment, a fact not without consequence in the 1928 presidential campaign of Alfred E. Smith. Likewise, anti-Semitism served to place national problems upon "foreign" shoulders. In general, however, the slower growth of American ethnic groups occasioned by immigration restriction encouraged the acculturation if not the complete assimilation of immigrants and their children. In turn, acculturation removed some of the more visible irritants to American ethnic relations. The shared trials of the Great Depression and World War II were unifying experiences in American life, and the excesses of Nazi Germany brought both racial and religious prejudice into popular disrepute. Cracks in the national-origins program of immigration admissions appeared as early as the mid-1930s when federal authorities permitted the entrance of limited numbers of nonquota European political refugees, a practice that was continued during and after the war.

Nevertheless, ethnic prejudice has not disappeared from American society in the second half of the 20th century. Clumsy forms of institutional discrimination, such as the Jewish quotas maintained by some private schools and universities before World War II, are gone; but some inhibitors to true equality of opportunity for members of American ethnic groups remain. Distinctive ethnic class and occupational characteristics in modern urban society are partly products of persistent differences in group values, goals, and economic strategies. As such, they suggest the actual limits of the acculturation and homogenization of American ethnic groups. But differential employment patterns also point to the persistence of interethnic biases that restrict the access of some citizens to a full range of occupational alternatives.

After World War II, genuine meritocracies oblivious to ethnicity took shape in some of the nation's more prestigious professions, providing new outlets for the

skills and ambitions of talented members of white ethnic groups. Immigrants and their descendants also effectively utilized postons of influence in labor unions and municipal politics to provide paths of mobility for manual and clerical workers. What were initially refuges from oppression for some ethnic groups paradoxically have become sources of power and group advancement. In fact, some ethnic leaders now assert that efforts to "reform" big-city machine politics and to impose racial quotas upon labor unions are nothing less than assaults by "WASP" Americans upon the primary avenues of ethnic social mobility and hence are ill-disguised forms of discrimination. Of all areas of American occupational life, the management hierarchies of industrial corporations have perhaps been the most difficult for white ethnic groups to enter. In corporate life, where cronyism and conformity are keys to advancement, exclusion of ethnoreligious minorities from certain kinds of clubs, lodges, and social circles has proven an impediment to occupational mobility. To a considerable extent, ethnicity has become bound with class as a social identifier in 20th-century America. The tendency of Americans to evaluate the social worth of individuals primarily in economic terms has rewarded those who are able to take advantage of available paths of social mobility, but it may also reinforce the remnants of ethnic prejudice with class bias.

CONCLUSION

For white Americans, culture has been the crux of ethnic difference, and ethnocentrism the enduring form of hostility met by ethnic minorities. Efforts to attribute the cultural proclivities of immigrants to heredity or to make fundamentally physical distinctions between white ethnic minorities have repeatedly failed. The adaptability of European immigrants to the outward forms of American life stymied attempts to prove that culture and achievement were contingent upon birth. Bolder ventures at differentiating white ethnic stocks on the basis of physical characteristics alone ran headlong into the essential similarity of Caucasian types. The elimination of even superficially distinctive physical features remained possible in the absence of effective prohibitive taboos against white ethnic amalgamation. The perception and meaning of ethnocultural differences among white Americans has been bound inextricably with the incentives for interethnic hostility. Developments in American political life, foreign relations, and intellectual or popular culture are what have invested particular ethnic characteristics with meaning. During the mid-19th century, while the American as a distinctive national type was still in the process of development, native-born Anglo-Americans regarded religion, tradition, and folkways as the determinants of nationality and heartily despised immigrants for introducing an unwanted cultural pluralism to the United States. At times in America's past when old-stock native-born citizens felt threatened by foreign enemies, they focused their concern specifically upon the elements of newcomers' political culture which could be construed as antithetical to republicanism. In periods of intense interparty political rivalry, nativist partisans emphasized the deficiencies of education, intelligence, and morality among ethnic voters.

When white ethnic groups have grown so large or locally concentrated as to challenge the economic, political, or social predominance of old-stock Americans, the motives for nativistic prejudice have been palpably transformed. Interethnic competition in the form of a conflict of material interests invests ethnocultural characteristics with primarily symbolic significance. Rather than appearing immediate threats to native values and traditions, they become mere tags to identify social competitors. Toward the end of the 19th century, ethnicity became only one of the multiple sources of American personal identity, taking its place among class, occupation, residence, and associational memberships. Old-stock Americans were especially prone to link ethnicity and social class; ethnicity had the advantage of being an optional social identity which could be selectively applied. Because few physical marks revealed the nature of white ancestry, an indelible and stigmatizing ethnicity was attributed only to Americans outside the pale of respectability—the Roman Catholic, the socialist, the urban delinquent. For members of ethnic groups who conformed to Anglo-American values and pursued an approved lifestyle, ethnicity in many cases could be dropped by choice.

Because of the permeability of ethnic boundaries within white America, it has been difficult for the native-born to institutionalize interethnic discrimination to keep immigrants and their descendants from challenging Anglo-American social predominance. Attempts to restrict the franchise to native-born citizens during the 19th century were made difficult by the invisibility of many white ethnic-group members and by intensive rivalry in American politics that made the major parties eager to attract immigrant votes. As full-fledged participants in the American political system, immigrants and their descendants acquired sufficient influence to prevent most other kinds of publicly sponsored ethnic bias. De facto discrimination against immigrants, especially in the form of residential segregation, actually had the effect of concentrating ethnic populations and giving them disproportionate political influence. Though the extraordinary convergence of nativistic prejudices during the 1920s made it impossible to halt the drive for immigration restriction, the members of ethnic groups already on American soil could expect relatively equal treatment under the laws of the United States. In the U.S. open-market economy, the value of immigrants as producers and consumers ensured that ethnic minorities could hold prosperity hostage against overzealous nativistic bias. Contemporary enthusiasm for rediscovering ethnic roots and reconstructing ethnic communities as a bulwark against the anomie of modern middle-class life illustrates the extent to which ethnic-group affiliation has now become a positive optional identity in American life.

Despite all the changes that have occurred, the situation of blacks in American society since the 18th century has been characterized by certain continuities that help set them apart from all other groups. Whereas other racially distinctive minorities, such as American Indians and Asians, have been differentiated as often by their traditional cultures as by their physical characteristics, blacks have consistently been defined solely as a racial group. Furthermore, a peculiar conception of black ethnicity dictates that an individual with any

known African ancestry is considered to be a black person, whatever his actual pigmentation or sociocultural characteristics. Hence, identification with the Afro-American community has been involuntary to a greater extent than have memberships in other ethnic groups. The taboo against miscegenation and the implied fear of "pollution" from the incorporation of anyone with black ancestry into white primary groups have remained strong despite the demise of antimiscegenation statutes. Intergroup mobility by people of mixed white-Indian or white-Asian ancestry has not, at least in recent times, raised comparable anxieties. Hence there are grounds for concern that a peculiar and exacting sense of difference, based on an implicit assumption of hereditary taint, may be an enduring element of black-white relations in the United States. But a sense of difference is only one of the preconditions for unequal treatment of blacks. Economic incentives for consigning blacks to lower-class status have proved of varying strength in different historical situations, and there is reason to believe that the transformation of most blacks from rural dependents to enfranchised competitors in the urban industrial labor market has reduced the profits of discrimination. The ability of blacks to force important concessions from the white majority has also varied over time; and the power differential, whether calculated in political or economic terms, has been greatly reduced since the Great Depression. If history is any guide, one might be inclined to predict that strong prejudices will survive so long as the black community remains an involuntary racial group rather than a voluntary ethnic community, but that elimination of the most damaging forms of discrimination is nevertheless possible within the foreseeable future.

Bibliography
A conceptual scheme for understanding the historical roots of prejudice and discrimination is suggested by Donald L. Noel, "A Theory of the Origin of Ethnic Stratification," *Social Problems* 16 (1968): 157–172. Thomas F. Gossett, *Race: The History of an Idea in America* (1963; reprint, New York, 1968), surveys a principal intellectual rationale for ethnic inequality. Many insights into how both blacks and white immigrants were viewed and treated can be found in Oscar Handlin, *Race and Nationality in American Life* (Boston, 1957). A competent overview of white attitudes toward American Indians is Robert F. Berkhofer, Jr., *The White Man's Indian* (New York, 1978). Another valuable treatment of the same subject is Roy Harvey Pearce, *The Savages of America: A Study of the Indian and the Idea of Civilization* (Baltimore, 1953). On prejudice and discrimination against blacks in early American history, see Winthrop D. Jordan's monumental *White over Black: American Attitudes toward the Negro, 1550–1812* (Chapel Hill, N.C., 1968). Two important studies that deal with the later evolution of antiblack attitudes and policies are George M. Fredrickson, *The Black Image in the White Mind: The Debate on Afro-American Character and Destiny, 1817–1914* (New York, 1971), and C. Vann Woodward, *The Strange Career of Jim Crow*, 3d rev. ed. (New York, 1974). Gunnar Myrdal, *An American Dilemma: The Negro Problem and Modern Democracy* (1944; reprint, New York, 1975), contains a vast amount of material on discrimination against Afro-Americans before World War II. On prejudice and discrimination against Asian Americans, see three recent works: Stuart Creighton Miller, *The Unwelcome Immigrant: The American Image of the Chinese, 1785–1882* (Berkeley, Calif., 1969); Alexander Saxton, *The Indispensable Enemy: Labor and the Anti-Chinese Movement in California* (Berkeley, 1971); and Roger Daniels, *The Politics of Prejudice: The Anti-Japanese Movement in California and the Struggle for Japanese Exclusion* (Berkeley, 1962). There are no major scholarly studies dealing comprehensively with the history of prejudice and discrimination against Spanish-speaking Americans, but Carey McWilliams, *North from Mexico* (1948; reprint, New York, 1968), remains valuable. The standard work on Anglo-American nativism is still John Higham, *Strangers in the Land: Patterns of American Nativism, 1860–1925* (New York, 1963). Higham's later reflections on this subject

along with a more extensive account of anti-Semitism can be found in *Send These to Me: Jews and Other Immigrants in Urban America* (New York, 1975). Oscar Handlin, *Boston's Immigrants, 1790–1880: A Study in Acculturation*, rev. ed. (New York, 1972), is the standard treatment of ethnocultural and socioeconomic conflict in the northeastern United States before the Civil War. Edward Digby Baltzell, *The Protestant Establishment: Aristocracy and Caste in America* (New York, 1964), describes recent manifestations of elite discrimination against members of white ethnic groups.

GEORGE M. FREDRICKSON AND DALE T. KNOBEL

PREJUDICE AND DISCRIMINATION, POLICY AGAINST

Prejudice and discrimination against racial and ethnic groups are major strands in the history of the American people. Another strand, initially tenuous and shaky but which has grown in the past 15 years to equal strength, is the effort of law to control or eradicate discrimination and its effects. The history of this effort is closely entwined with the history of the largest racially defined minority group in the United States: blacks. A great body of law supported their enslavement in the southern states and their civil inferiority in the North. But in the early 19th century reformers launched a countertradition of law, which attempted to assure equality for blacks. Before the Civil War this body of law was very weak and was limited to the North. The Emancipation Proclamation and the postwar constitutional amendments and Civil Rights Acts caused enormous changes in the legal position of blacks. The high point in this national effort to achieve equality was reached in 1875. Thereafter, national political reconciliation and restrictive Supreme Court judgments marked a withdrawal. Many of the achievements of the Reconstruction were lost. Aside from the historic elimination of slavery, the political, economic, and social position of blacks showed little change in the South, where the great majority lived.

There was, however, a Second Reconstruction. Its beginnings may be variously located. One was in the educational and political activities of the Negro defense organizations, principally the National Association for the Advancement of Colored People (NAACP), fighting the most outrageous of the conditions that kept blacks down—unpunished lynchings, poll taxes and other means of denying the vote, the closing of higher education opportunities to blacks in the South. In the late 1930s the Supreme Court began to erode the barriers to opportunity in higher education. The New Deal, expanding greatly the role of the federal government, and based on the rising power of second-generation immigrants and the labor movement, was another source of the Second Reconstruction. It brought to blacks in the South an awareness that federal law could improve their condition. The Second World War was a third source: waged against Nazi Germany, it embarrassed American racists and emboldened those who opposed them. The Second Reconstruction proper may be dated to the historic *Brown* decision of the Supreme Court in 1954 which struck down the "separate but equal" principle in education. It reached its climax with the black protest movement led by Martin Luther King, Jr., and the adoption of strong civil rights legislation in 1964 and 1965. In the years since, as the administration of laws against discrimination has become a major task of

federal government, there has been growing debate as to the proper character and future direction of this effort.

The Second Reconstruction has ended; three major outcomes distinguish it from the ending of the First Reconstruction. First, powerful government agencies have been established, employing thousands of people and spending hundreds of millions of dollars, whose permanent task is to fight discrimination and achieve equality for minority groups. Second, blacks and other minorities are now fully enfranchised, play a major role in government, and form a permanent support for the fight against discrimination. Third, the movement against discrimination now embraces other major ethnic groups, especially Mexican Americans, Puerto Ricans, and other Latin Americans, but also American Indians, Asians, and nonethnic groups such as women and the handicapped, augmenting its political strength even while introducing certain conflicts among all those who now benefit from antidiscrimination law.

As part of the history of discrimination, then, we must furnish some account of the efforts to overcome discrimination. This discussion focuses on the attempts to achieve equality for blacks, but those efforts were directed to a universal purpose, with the result that other groups could participate in and benefit from them. It was not blacks alone who were guaranteed "the equal protection of the laws" in various respects, just as it was not blacks alone who had suffered from their unequal application. The Chinese and Japanese in particular had been subjected to fierce discriminatory legislation. American Indians present a more complex picture. Although law was intended to preserve their special and separate status, it was also applied without their participation, in ignorance of their needs, and with a good deal of prejudice. Their special status made difficult any simple application of the principle of equal protection, for their interests also required the defense of their unique legal position.

Because the attack on discrimination emphasized the equality of races, laws designed to keep down Chinese and Japanese fell before it along with those designed to keep down blacks. The story of the legal battle against discrimination should deal with many groups besides blacks. But because this battle is integrally linked with blacks as the central concern of efforts to overcome discrimination, they are also the chief subject of this account.

The process cannot be divorced from the larger movements of American history. The American Revolution produced some reaction in the abolition of slavery in northern states, and in many of them the assumption by free Negroes of civil and political rights. But this was a weak echo. The Civil War created a much broader and more active response, even though its hopes were not fulfilled. Finally, the New Deal and World War II, with their promises of social and racial equality, began a movement of political pressure and protest and of executive, legislative, and judicial response, which has become institutionalized, and around which conflict continues. This conflict, however, is not over whether equality should prevail, but over how best to achieve it.

Before the Civil War

The social position of the Negro in the free northern states before the Civil War evoked the first organized ef-

forts to establish municipal laws prohibiting discrimination on the basis of race or descent. These states had abolished slavery by 1820 and politically opposed its expansion; civil equality there became a practical issue a half-century before the debates in Congress during Reconstruction over the rights of newly emancipated southern blacks.

The framers of the U.S. Constitution had omitted any reference to special or separate treatment of free blacks or other races, with the result that northern state policy-makers perceived no constitutional barriers to laws that imposed civil disabilities on Negroes and denied them most of the rights enjoyed by white citizens. Legislators and jurists in the North, though explicitly opposed to the form of Negro slavery practiced in the South, pursued policies of white supremacy in social and political life. They were guided by the prevailing assumption that custom and race had assigned blacks to an inferior social position which neither statute nor judicial decision could alter; a social commentator in the 1820s noted that "chains of a stronger kind manacled their limbs, from which no legislative act could free them; a mental and moral subordination and inferiority to which tyrant custom has here subjected all the sons and daughters of Africa." Democratic, Federalist, and Whig politicians passed state laws that barred blacks from the professions and skilled trades, and enforced segregation in public accommodations and transportation facilities. In New England, local school committees created separate schools for blacks; the state of New York authorized school districts to establish segregated educational facilities. Pennsylvania and Ohio required separate schools for blacks wherever accommodations could be provided for 20 or more students; and some midwestern and western states prohibited black children from attending public schools at all.

During the 1820s and 1830s, when Jacksonian Democrats were redrafting state constitutions to expand the political rights of adult white males and widen the suffrage, the political rights of blacks in northern states were drastically contracting. By 1840 the states in which over 90 percent of all northern Negroes resided had legally extinguished or practically abrogated their voting and office-holding rights. New Jersey, Pennsylvania, and Connecticut rescinded laws that had given Negroes the franchise; New York permitted them the vote only if they met specific property-holding and residency requirements that were not imposed on whites. Only in Massachusetts, Vermont, New Hampshire, and Maine, where few Negroes resided, could they exercise political rights on an equal basis with adult white males.

Most of the free northern states before the Civil War also deprived blacks, through law or practice, of fundamental judicial rights. Negro testimony in cases involving a white person was banned by Illinois, Indiana, Ohio, Iowa, and California; Oregon laws prohibited Negroes from filing lawsuits.

That northern blacks could be denied equal treatment with whites was justified constitutionally by what Andrew Jackson's attorney general, John Berrien, in 1831 called the "general right of a State to regulate persons of color within its own limits . . . recognized by the [state police-power proviso of the] tenth amendment." Many policy-makers also argued that the Constitution gave state governments sole authority to de-

fine the civil rights of state citizens and to prescribe separate sets of rights and privileges for different classes of citizens.

The growth of an organized movement to abolish slavery within the United States stimulated the first attempt to change discriminatory laws in the North. This movement was particularly successful in Massachusetts. Beginning in the early 1830s abolitionists, reformers, and Negroes repeatedly petitioned the Massachusetts legislature to repeal its law prohibiting interracial marriages, to terminate segregation in public transportation, and to create racially integrated school systems throughout the state. Their campaign began to achieve concrete results in the 1840s. A legislative committee of the state House of Representatives investigated complaints against the interracial marriage ban, and warned in 1840 that if Massachusetts continued to retain its antimiscegenation law it would "virtually assert [Negro] inequality, and justify that theory of negro slavery which represents it as a state of necessary tutelage and guardianship." Sensitive to the charge that the law was inconsistent with their opposition to slavery, Massachusetts legislators repealed it in 1843.

The strategy of abolitionists in their attack on segregated public transportation was initially to obtain a court injunction against separate facilities. Failing to achieve this, they pressed the state legislature to guarantee equal treatment of the races. A joint legislative committee found that segregation in railroad cars, steamboats, and stagecoaches violated the state constitution and recommended that segregation in public transportation on the basis of descent, sect, or color should not be permitted. This bill was defeated, but the railroads bowed to the pressure of antislavery groups and voluntarily abolished segregation in their cars and stations in the mid-1840s. Frederick Douglass (c. 1817–1895), an ex-slave who became the outstanding Negro leader of the abolitionist movement, had been a vocal critic of segregated railroad lines. He remarked in 1849 that "not a single railroad can be found in any part of Massachusetts, where a colored man is treated and esteemed in any other light than that of a man and a traveler."

The opponents of discrimination devoted greater energy to achieving equal access for Negroes to public schools, a goal which many saw as the fundamental step toward establishing a more harmonious society and fostering the social progress of blacks. Douglass, who rated equal opportunity in education as a higher priority than the achievement of full political equality, wrote: "Contact on equal terms is the best means to abolish caste. *It is caste abolished.* With Equal Suffrage, 13,675 black men come into contact [with whites] on equal terms, for ten minutes once a year, at the polls; with equal school rights, 15,778 colored children and youth come in contact on equal terms with white children and youth, three hundred days in the year, and from six to ten hours each day. And these children, in a few years, become the people of the state."

By 1845 abolitionists had secured the desegregation of the public school systems of Salem, New Bedford, Nantucket, Worcester, and Lowell. Boston's schools became the target of legal suits brought by black parents joined by the Massachusetts Anti-Slavery Society, which urged "friends of the cause" to provide Negroes with "all possible aid in securing the full and equal enjoyment of the public schools." Benjamin Roberts, whose daughter had been denied admission four times to a white primary school located in the school district where the Roberts family resided, obtained as legal counsel Charles Sumner, the anti-slavery U.S. Senator from Massachusetts, and filed a civil suit in the state Superior Court against the Boston Primary School Committee. Chief Justice Lemuel Shaw, speaking for a unanimous court, stated flatly that the school committee had discharged its responsibility to black citizens by providing their children with adequate, albeit segregated, facilities. Shaw rejected the plaintiff's contention that segregated facilities instilled in the populace the notion of black inferiority.

Negro civic leaders and parents established the Equal School Rights Committee to end segregated schools in Boston by legislation, and after five years of lobbying, public rallies, and aggressive publicity the city's committee on public instruction in 1854 recommended to the mayor and board of aldermen that the segregated schools be abolished. Before Boston could act, the state legislature in 1855 passed a law prohibiting the use of racial or religious distinctions in the admission of students to public schools in Massachusetts. The first state statute to outlaw racially discriminatory practices in a public institution was thus enacted on the eve of the Civil War. Massachusetts was also the first state to allow blacks to serve as jurors. It was not until 1860, however, after five years of intensive lobbying and publicity by abolitionists and blacks, that the first Negro jurymen were named in Worcester.

The hard-won gains of Massachusetts blacks heartened Negroes and social reformers in other free states. In 1849 Ohio bowed to the agitation of abolitionists and eliminated its ban against judicial testimony by blacks. In Rhode Island a bill prohibiting segregation in public schools missed passage by only two votes. In the 1850s Negroes brought civil suits in state courts to desegregate public schools in Ohio and Indiana, but these courts held that separate schools for blacks and whites were legitimate so long as they supplied equal educational opportunities.

CIVIL WAR AND RECONSTRUCTION

The legal principles calling for equal treatment and due process can be invoked against prejudice and discriminatory treatment independently of political power. But effective change without power is rare. In the *Dred Scott* case of 1857 the U.S. Supreme Court declared federal laws prohibiting slavery in the territories unconstitutional. This decision did not stand long, for it was one of the events that precipitated the Civil War. And with the military defeat of the South, one of the first acts of Congress was to pass the Thirteenth Amendment, prohibiting slavery.

The destruction of the power of the southern slave states set the stage for an unprecedented expansion of federal jurisdiction and the establishment of a polity anchored in a common national citizenship for blacks and whites—and, by implication, for all races. It was the task of the 39th and 40th congresses, which met from December 1865 to March 1869, to define the civil status of millions of emancipated southern blacks as well as that of blacks in the North. Clashing repeatedly with President Andrew Johnson, a Tennesseean with firm views on the inferiority of Negroes, the Republican

Congress enacted the first federal Civil Rights Act in 1866. This authorized the continued operation of the wartime Freedman's Bureau which assisted ex-slaves, declared all persons born in the United States to be American citizens, and established that all citizens "of every race and color, without regard to any previous condition of slavery or involuntary servitude," should have the same personal, property, and civil rights in every state and territory "as is enjoyed by white citizens." Moreover, any person who deprived another, on account of race or color, of civil rights enumerated in the act became guilty of a federal crime. The bill was passed over Johnson's veto.

Fearful of an adverse Supreme Court judgment on the constitutionality of the 1866 Civil Rights Act, Congress drafted the Fourteenth Amendment (ratified in 1868) which incorporated the principal elements of the 1866 legislation and extended the scope of federal protection to "citizens of the United States": no state could abridge their "privileges or immunities" or "deprive any person of life, liberty, or property, without due process of law" or "deny to any person within its jurisdiction the equal protection of the laws."

The forceful wording of the amendment affirmed a national policy of equality before the law for all races, but the degree and nature of the protection secured under federal law were subject to judicial interpretation. "What was meant by these phrases," one historian remarked, "would be the major issue in American constitutional law for the next century and more." Although the Fourteenth Amendment was a step toward expanded federal protection, it sought this objective by limiting the powers of states to interfere with broadly phrased rights rather than by positive extension of federal authority. Where federal jurisdiction ended and state jurisdiction began would be the thorniest question challenging the interpreters of the Fourteenth Amendment in the years ahead.

The Fifteenth Amendment in 1869 prohibited the federal or state governments from denying the right to vote "on account of race, color, or previous condition of servitude." Time proved, however, that discrimination in voting rights on grounds of race alone did not rule out other forms of discrimination which deprived blacks of the vote. The Fifteenth Amendment was buttressed by the Civil Rights Acts of 1870 and 1871, which made the deliberate obstruction of Negro suffrage a high federal crime punishable by a severe fine.

Although the Reconstruction congressional legislation expressed a powerful impulse to create a new and equal civil status for blacks, the motives of northern policy-makers were mixed, for many did not accept the equality of the races. Such progressive Republican leaders as Lyman Trumbull of Illinois and John Sherman of Ohio believed unquestioningly in the natural inferiority of the Negro; and many prominent congressional Republicans hoped to improve the conditions of blacks in the South chiefly in order to ward off a massive migration to the northern states. Republican support for the Civil Rights Act of 1866 rested in part on the popular view expressed by a Republican lawyer from Illinois: "It would be unwise to allow the negro to vote in Illinois and not in the South. The result of that would be to make Illinois a negro Mecca." Indeed, at the end of the Civil War, Negroes were still denied suffrage in 18 out of 25 states in the North. The majority of northern states maintained segregated public facilities and sanctioned restrictions on the residence and employment opportunities of blacks. From 1865 to 1868 voters in Connecticut, Ohio, Wisconsin, Michigan, Kansas, and Missouri rejected in popular referenda proposed amendments to their state constitutions that would have granted the franchise to Negroes.

The great majority of the states, however, chose to endorse the Fourteenth and Fifteenth amendments; the state platforms of the Republican party in the late 1860s were filled with glowing expressions of racial equality. Iowa's Republican platform stated in 1866: "The first and highest duty of our free Government is to secure to all its citizens, regardless of race, religion, or color, equality before the law, equal protection from it, equal responsibility to it." Minnesota Republicans declared that "the measure of a man's political rights should be neither his religion, his birthplace, his race, his color, nor any merely physical characteristics."

From 1865 into the 1870s a few states began to enact laws prohibiting racial discrimination. In 1865 Massachusetts became the first state to outlaw distinctions or restrictions based on race among patrons of licensed places of public accommodation. New York passed in 1874 its first civil rights law, prohibiting racial discrimination in theaters, inns, cemeteries, public conveyances, places of amusement or entertainment, and public institutions of learning. In the same year Kansas became the third state to pass an antidiscrimination law, similar to that of New York.

Black civic organizations and lobbying groups were important agents in the creation of more progressive local and national policies in the field of civil rights. State conventions of Negro civic leaders, such as the Illinois State Convention of Colored Men held in 1866, and smaller city conventions, developed surveys "to thoroughly canvass the subject of the disabilities, educational and political, that dwell on persons of color . . . and to devise and set in motion effective agencies for the permanent removal of the same." Negroes in Kansas established civil rights clubs and an equal rights association that played a major role in securing the Kansas antidiscrimination law of 1874.

The omnibus Civil Rights Act proposed by Charles Sumner in May 1870 and passed by Congress in March 1875 marked the zenith of the post-bellum movement to achieve civil rights for blacks. In its original form the bill prohibited unequal treatment of the races in "railroads, steamboats, public conveyances, hotels, licensed theatres, houses of public entertainment, common schools, and institutions of learning authorized by law, church institutions, and cemetery associations incorporated by national or state authority; also on juries in courts, national and state." The Senate Judiciary Committee refused to report the bill out. Shortly after he reintroduced it in December 1873, Sumner died. His supporters, some of them Negro members of Congress, pressed for the bill's passage. However, a significant change in rank-and-file Republican support for civil rights legislation had been developing: some feared the consequences of federally ordered school desegregation, others were offended by the inclusion of churches, and still others opposed the extension of federal control over public transportation.

The long debate over the controversial measure revealed the conception of racial equality held by proponents of the Civil Rights Act. J.H. Rainey, a black congressman from South Carolina, repeatedly denied the charge of the bill's opponents that it would produce "social equality" of the races through coercion. Rainey stressed that the bill would ensure only a common access to public facilities. "I venture to assert to my white fellow citizens," Rainey said, "that we the colored people are not in quest of social equality. For one I do not ask to be introduced into your family circles if you are not yet disposed to receive me there." Congressman Harris of Massachusetts, a supporter of the bill, emphasized that its goal was only to assure common hospitality to all races in public facilities. John Lynch, a Negro congressman from Mississippi, insisted that the bill would give rights "which should be accorded to every citizen alike," not social equality of the races. Again and again the proponents sounded the common theme that the legislation was aimed at securing equal access to public facilities and equal civil rights, not equality of social conditions between the races.

When the Civil Rights Act of 1875 finally passed, key sections of Sumner's original bill that proposed to ban segregated schools and juries were deleted. Even so, the act was still the boldest federal effort to produce civil equality between whites and Negroes. It began with phrases recalling the language of the Declaration of Independence: "Whereas, it is essential to just government we recognize the equality of all men before the law, and hold that it is the duty of government in its dealings with the people to mete out equal and exact justice to all of whatever nationality, race, color, or persuasion, religious or political." The heart of the law guaranteed all persons regardless of race "the full and equal enjoyment of the accommodations, advantages, facilities, and privileges of inns, public conveyances on land or water, theaters, and other places of public amusement."

Next came the struggle in the courts over constitutionality. During the 1870s the Supreme Court affirmed the constitutionality of the civil rights laws of 1866, 1870, and 1871. The first Supreme Court interpretation of the Fourteenth Amendment came in its review of the *Slaughter-House Cases* of 1873.

As a public health measure Louisiana had granted a monopoly to a corporation to operate stockyards, landing places, and a slaughterhouse in New Orleans, and some butchers had filed suit against the state for violating their rights under the Fourteenth Amendment. A five-to-four majority of the Court found against the butchers' contention that the state government's action was prohibited by the privileges and immunities and equal protection clauses of the Fourteenth Amendment, on the ground that the Fourteenth Amendment was intended primarily to protect the newly freed slaves. The majority also held that the amendment protected only the privileges and immunities of "citizens of the United States," that it conferred no new rights upon them, and that these rights were quite limited— for example, the right to free access to subtreasuries and land offices. The Court insisted on a distinction between rights held as a citizen of the United States and those held as a citizen of a state; to interpret the amendment otherwise would make of the Court "a perpetual

censor upon all legislation of the states, on the civil rights of their own citizens," and would produce a federal tyranny. In order to challenge state infringements on his rights, a citizen had to appeal to the state legislature or state courts. The implications for the civil rights of Negroes were tremendous, for this decision kept public education and public accommodations under state authority. With civil rights defined largely as issuing from the legislative power and judicial authority of state governments, victims of discriminatory local laws could not obtain the protection of the federal government.

A decade after the *Slaughter-House Cases* decision, the Supreme Court reviewed together seven cases which involved challenges to the constitutionality of the 1875 Civil Rights Act requiring nondiscrimination in public accommodation and facilities. The spirit of the civil rights cause had faltered by the 1880s, and the Supreme Court judgment dealt it a mortal blow. The core of the plaintiffs' arguments was that the Thirteenth Amendment had empowered Congress to pass all laws necessary for the eradication of slavery with all "its badges and incidents", and that exclusion from accommodations in public facilities amounted to the imposition of a "badge of slavery." Justice Joseph Bradley, writing for the majority, denied that refusal or denial of accommodation had no connection with involuntary servitude: "It would be running the slavery argument into the ground to make it apply to every act of discrimination which a person may see fit to make as to the guests he will entertain, or as to the people he will take into his coach or cab or car, or admit to his concert or theater." Bradley affirmed the constitutionality of the Thirteenth and Fourteenth amendments and the Civil Rights Acts of 1866, 1870, and 1871, but declared the 1875 Civil Rights Act unconstitutional. It violated the Tenth Amendment grant of authority to states for "the enforcement and vindication of all rights of life, liberty, and property" and attempted also to regulate private acts. This was only the third time in history that the Supreme Court had invalidated congressional legislation—a step it had taken in *Marbury* v. *Madison* (1803) and *Dred Scott* (1857).

Justice John Marshall Harlan wrote a vigorous dissent in which he argued that "keepers of inns, and managers of places of public amusement are agents or instrumentalities of the state, because they are charged with duties to the public, and are amenable, in respect of their duties and functions, to government regulation."

Although the Supreme Court in the late 19th century adopted an extremely narrow interpretation of the civil rights protected by the Fourteenth Amendment, it did extend to other groups the limited protections that it recognized. Chinese Americans emigrating to California in the 1850s had been subjected to discrimination by both extralegal action and positive legislation. Here the Fourteenth Amendment was held to apply to protect others besides blacks. In *Yick Wo* v. *Hopkins* (1886) the Court ruled that a municipal law prohibiting the operation of laundries in wooden buildings was unconstitutional because it discriminated without legitimate reason or cause against Chinese laundry owners as a class. Between 1885 and 1895 the Supreme Court in four separate decisions consistently affirmed that differential treatment of separate classifications of persons

could satisfy the Fourteenth Amendment's equal protection proviso only when such classification was based reasonably on substantial differences "pertinent to valid legislative objectives" and when it was applied equally to all persons in a specific classification. Even the Court's decision in *Plessy* v. *Ferguson* (1896), declaring segregation in public conveyances legal because of the authority of state governments to pass laws regulating the rights of its citizens, stressed that equality of accommodations was the sine qua non of constitutionality under the equal protection clause. What was established in *Plessy* was the constitutionality of separate but *equal* facilities.

What the majority refused to recognize, as Justice Harlan pointed out in a historic dissent, was that segregation led inevitably to *unequal* conditions, thus making Negroes an inferior caste and whites "a dominant race, a superior class of citizens." Harlan asserted that the majority decision would one day seem as "pernicious" as the *Dred Scott* ruling and would "render permanent peace impossible and . . . keep alive a conflict of races, the continuance of which must do harm to all concerned."

FROM THE END OF RECONSTRUCTION TO THE NEW DEAL

To fill the vacuum left by the retreat of the federal government, many state legislatures passed antidiscrimination statutes modeled on the ill-fated Civil Rights Act of 1875. Eighteen states in the Northeast, the Midwest, and Far West established codes by 1900 outlawing discrimination in public places for reasons of race or color. Massachusetts (1865), New York (1874), and Kansas (1874) had already done so. Connecticut, Iowa, New Jersey, and Ohio enacted similar statutes in 1884; Rhode Island, Michigan, Illinois, Indiana, Minnesota, Nebraska, and Colorado followed in 1885; and so did Washington, Wisconsin, and California in the 1890s.

The state laws were based on common principles and employed a common legal vocabulary. They stipulated that no one could be denied equal privileges and facilities in places of public accommodation on the grounds of race, color (in some states, religion), or previous condition of servitude. Not until the mid-20th century was discrimination on the basis of national origin or ancestry forbidden by state law. Most states enumerated a list of public places in which the antidiscrimination statute was operative. Violators of these laws were subject to criminal sanctions of fine or imprisonment, or civil sanctions which provided remedies to injured parties.

According to the *Slaughter-House* decision and the *Civil Rights Cases* of 1883, the state antidiscrimination laws were within the province of legitimate state police powers. But state judges often limited the application and power of these laws. Thus, on the principle that penal statutes must be strictly construed, the Nebraska Supreme Court ruled in 1889 that because a state antidiscrimination law provided for criminal penalties and ambiguously referred to "citizens" and to "persons," only citizens could claim protection under the law. A New York court in 1917 denied redress to Negroes who

sued a New York saloon because a "saloon" was not specifically mentioned among the public places listed in the state law.

In the face of strict interpretations by the courts, state legislators seeking an effective civil rights policy made the list of specifically enumerated public places exhaustive: those specified in the New York civil rights law included over 50 separately identified facilities. In 1913 New York added to its civil rights code a ban on discriminatory advertising of public facilities and accommodations; New Jersey, Maine, Massachusetts, Pennsylvania, Michigan, Wisconsin, Illinois, Colorado, Oregon, and Washington soon followed.

State civil rights laws guaranteeing equal access to public accommodations did not provide strong sanctions for enforcement. Some of the state laws in the early 20th century prescribed the same fine for damages that had been assessed in the 1880s and 1890s. In states where violation of an antidiscrimination law required a criminal trial, the plaintiffs often had to contend with juries as prejudiced as the defendants. The initiative for filing a suit and convincing a public prosecutor or grand jury to act rested with a minority-group member. And civil action required substantial resources.

The efforts of northern state legislators to fill the void left by congressional inaction and the Supreme Court's negativism were without great effect. In the South, on the other hand, the *Civil Rights Cases* decision and *Plessy* v. *Ferguson* opened the way to a massive, legal restriction of the rights of blacks. Jim Crow laws and custom separated the races in every sphere of daily life —schools, colleges and universities, government facilities, places of work, recreation, and amusement, and churches. And the separate facilities provided to blacks were uniformly inferior. Law or custom prevented blacks from voting, participating in the activities of the major (Democratic) party, holding public office, and sitting on juries.

The pattern of segregation and discrimination spread to the federal government; workers in government agencies in Washington, D.C., were segregated, beginning with the U.S. Bureau of the Census under President Taft; under Woodrow Wilson segregation extended to federal civil-service workers in Washington. The few token appointments blacks received from the federal government shrank during the Taft and Wilson administrations. In World War I the army was totally segregated (as had been the Union army in the Civil War). There were only minimal improvements under post–World War I Republican presidents.

The National Association for the Advancement of Colored People, founded in 1910, devoted itself in the 1920s principally to arousing public feeling against lynchings of blacks in the South and to securing passage of a federal antilynching law, in which it did not succeed. It was more successful in the federal courts; in 1917 the Supreme Court declared racial zoning for housing unconstitutional (*Buchanan* v. *Warley*). But other means of restricting blacks and other groups from certain areas, principally the restrictive covenant, remained intact. As early as 1924, in *Nixon* v. *Herndon*, the NAACP succeeded in having a Texas statute forbidding black participation in primaries ruled unconstitutional. But southern states had many other legal mecha-

nisms for restricting black suffrage; although many of these were struck down, legal and extralegal devices still prevented blacks from voting.

THE NEW DEAL AND WORLD WAR II

Landmarks in overcoming discrimination during the long presidency of Franklin D. Roosevelt were few. Nevertheless, the New Deal and U.S. participation in World War II undermined segregation and discriminatory treatment. A huge expansion of federal programs in aid of the poor focused specifically on the poorest part of the country with the great majority of blacks: the South. Fashioned by an administration whose electoral support included new immigrant groups, labor, and northern blacks, they were often administered in nondiscriminatory fashion. In some respects they also yielded to the apparently impregnable hold that discriminatory policies had taken on the South. But, as Gunnar Myrdal wrote in *An American Dilemma* in the early 1940s:

> Not overlooking the considerable discrimination against Negroes in the local administration of New Deal measures in the South, we must see that the New Deal has made a lasting break in Southern racial practices. It has been said that the South was once bought by the Northern capitalists, who did not care much for the Negroes and allowed the Southerners almost complete freedom in the pursuit of any kind of racial discrimination. *Now Washington is the main "buyer" of the South.* And Washington usually seeks to extend its assistance regardless of race (463–464).

The New Deal did little for blacks formally and directly. But by establishing national programs of welfare, social security, public housing, public employment, and special programs for the rural poor, it directed aid toward Negroes, North and South. Further, it indicated its sympathies by making black appointments, which had been few since Taft in Democratic and Republican administrations alike. Roosevelt's opposition to Hitler implied opposition to racist policies. Finally, important public actions came, though not without the pressure of organized blacks. In 1941, threatened with a "March on Washington" organized by black trade union leader A. Philip Randolph, the president issued an executive order banning discrimination in employment in defense industries or government, and setting up a Committee on Fair Employment Practices to enforce it. This was the first use of a major new tool, the executive order, to combat discrimination. National legislation remained impossible because of the power of southerners in Congress. The courts were cautious and slow. But the president could act independently. The model of an agency which could investigate complaints of discrimination, conduct hearings on them, and mobilize public opinion against discrimination, was established. Although the Fair Employment Practices Committee lapsed after the war, every president after Roosevelt maintained or expanded through executive order the federal obligation to ensure nondiscrimination in the federal civil service and among those who provided goods and services to the government. Under these orders the requirement of affirmative action by federal contractors eventually became in the late 1960s a powerful tool not only against

discrimination in employment but also in moving toward proportional representation of racial and ethnic groups as a test of nondiscrimination.

The armed forces in World War II would seem to have been an obvious arena in which to institute policies of nondiscrimination. There blacks had either been excluded or limited to segregated and menial tasks. Although many branches of the armed forces were for the first time opened to blacks, segregation in both training and action remained the norm. But in 1948 President Truman issued an executive order calling for a policy of equal treatment and opportunity, and by implication the end of segregation. As in the case of the executive order against discrimination in government employment and among federal contractors, the fight against discrimination and segregation in the armed forces was to be a long one, but under executive pressure during and after the Korean War the armed forces became one of the most integrated institutions in American society.

Thus the New Deal and war generated actions beyond symbolism; yet in many crucial areas there was no action at all. Education remained strictly segregated in the South and in large parts of the rest of the country. Housing, despite the provision of public housing for blacks through federally subsidized action, remained segregated, including most public housing. Although both national parties called for a permanent FEPC in 1944, although President Truman urged it, and although distinguished presidential committees called for it, Congress would not act. In the post–World War II years as in the post-Reconstruction years, northern state governments took the lead in attacking discrimination in employment and education.

STATE ACTION AGAINST DISCRIMINATION

In World War I blacks had begun to move north and west to escape southern segregation and violence and to find employment in industry. This migration continued in the 1920s, declined slightly in the 1930s, and was accelerated by World War II and the postwar mechanization of southern agriculture. The growth of Negro voting blocs in the North and West began to make blacks a significant force in national politics in the 1940s and increased their power in the states in which they had settled in substantial numbers. This migration was one of the causes of the proliferation of antidiscrimination laws in the northern states in the late 1940s. In this development blacks also had the strong support of the labor movement and of white ethnic groups, in particular Jews, who also suffered from discrimination in employment, education, and housing.

The creation of state commissions to enforce nondiscriminatory practices set an important precedent for federal programs in the 1960s. These commissions were administrative agencies whose systematic proceedings were much more effective in combating discriminatory practices than were prosecutions of isolated civil or criminal suits under existing antidiscrimination statutes. The expense of the investigation was paid by the government and speedy action was taken by special agents upon receipt of a verified complaint. The burden of proof shifted to the party suspected of discriminatory acts. No jury was involved; instead an administrative board of experts determined the extent of discrimina-

tion and damages. Their authority was sufficiently broad so that they had the right to decide when "subterfuge or evasion" within the letter of the law was practiced.

In 1945 New York established the first state commission and the first permanent governmental agency designed to eradicate racial discrimination in employment. New York had been an early leader in this cause; 13 states had passed laws before 1945 prohibiting racial discrimination in certain occupations, but New York surpassed all the others in the comprehensiveness of its laws. As early as 1909 New York banned discrimination in the certification of lawyers; in 1918 it prohibited discrimination in any form of "state employment"; in 1933 the state outlawed discriminatory hiring practices by utility companies. Discriminatory practices by a labor union were prohibited in 1940 and were outlawed the next year in firms "engaged in defense work."

A coalition of white ethnic reformers, labor unions of the CIO, and black civil rights leaders secured the passage of the Ives-Quinn Bill of 1945, which established the New York agency for the maintenance of fair employment practices. Overwhelming majorities in the state senate and assembly passed the law against strong lobbying opposition, and it became a model for other states.

The bill created a State Commission Against Discrimination to eliminate and to prevent discriminatory practices by private employers, labor organizations, and employment agencies. It declared that employment without discrimination was a fundamental civil right. The commission was empowered to investigate complaints, to persuade accused parties to end discriminatory practices voluntarily, to hold formal hearings, and to issue cease-and-desist orders enforceable by court injunction. The commission monitored patterns of employment by keeping elaborate statistical records and made regular surveys of various employment fields. It also regularly conducted educational programs and issued literature encouraging employers to maintain fair hiring practices.

The activities of the commission brought the individual decisions of hiring, promoting, or dismissing employees, formerly considered wholly private, within the domain of actions reviewable by government, and introduced the concept that the duty of government was to engage in continuous supervision, intervention, and enforcement to ensure equality of access to employment.

Other states adopted similar laws: New Jersey in 1945; Massachusetts in 1946; Connecticut in 1947; New Mexico, Oregon, Rhode Island, and Washington in 1949; Pennsylvania, Michigan, and Minnesota in 1955; Wisconsin and Colorado in 1957; Ohio, Alaska, and California in 1959; and Delaware in 1960 all established fair employment commissions which incorporated the essential features of the original New York State Commission Against Discrimination.

Opinions as to the effectiveness of these efforts differed. But thousands of complaints were filed, many individuals received satisfaction, and patterns of employment began to change. Thus, in the later 1950s and 1960s one could see blacks employed in New York and other states in white-collar jobs in banks and insurance companies, as salesclerks in downtown department stores, and in other occupations where previously blacks had not been seen. Change was definitely on the way.

In 1948 New York extended the administrative procedure for ending discrimination to the field of education. The state commissioner of education was vested with powers to enforce fair educational practices by the same procedures as the State Commission Against Discrimination—investigation, conciliation, and administrative hearings. He was given an important additional power—the right to initiate an investigation if he had "reason to believe" that an institution had exercised any form of discrimination either against a single applicant or "against applicants as a group." New Jersey again followed New York's lead. By the late 1950s four more states—Massachusetts, Oregon, Pennsylvania, and Washington—had provided similar administrative protection for equal educational opportunity.

Access to housing had been seriously restricted by racial discrimination, and it was slower to receive the protection of state law. Connecticut in 1949 placed public housing within the purview of its fair employment commission and added publicly assisted housing in 1953. In 1955 the Connecticut commission was empowered to initiate an investigation whenever it had "reason to believe" that housing discrimination had occurred. By 1957 seven other states had placed public and publicly assisted housing under the jurisdiction of administrative agencies. Several states also prohibited discrimination in housing that received financial guarantees from the Federal Housing Administration and the Veterans Administration.

The rapid proliferation of state agencies that investigated, supervised, and enforced nondiscrimination in employment, education, and housing signified a transformation of the relationship between private rights and state responsibility for the civil welfare of all races. The establishment of these agencies expressed growing acceptance of the idea that state action against discriminatory practices was a legitimate exercise of police power to protect the welfare of the people, even when that power conflicted with the private control of property, education, and employment.

COURT AND CONGRESS REENTER THE FIELD

Change in the South was barely perceptible; lynching declined, but massive segregation and the effective denial of political participation remained unbroken. But racism was no longer respectable in the aftermath of World War II, which had been fought against nations espousing racist doctrines. Anti-Semitism rapidly lost respectability. Anti-Chinese and anti-Japanese sentiment did not long survive World War II. The Chinese had been U.S. allies, and even though Japanese Americans had been interned in detention camps in World War II without regard to citizenship, and had been deprived of their property, anti-Japanese sentiment also surprisingly went into a rapid decline.

The decline in racist sentiment was evidenced in the revision of the immigration act in 1952. Asian nations, excluded by federal legislation in 1917 and 1924, now received minimal quotas. It appeared that the massive system of oppression in the South could not last, but the power of southern congressmen was great, for seniority gave them key committee chairmanships. The

presidency, particularly under Democratic tenure, was responsive to black voting power in the North and to the strong support given to antidiscrimination measures by organized labor and white ethnics. But it could not make its recommendations effective in Congress.

Under these circumstances the task of destroying the southern racial system devolved on the federal courts. Many decisions before 1954 showed the Supreme Court was moving against segregation and discrimination; it had repeatedly struck down southern state legislation which in effect denied blacks the vote. In 1948 in *Shelley* v. *Kramer* it banned racially restrictive covenants that denied blacks and other groups the right to buy property. Important decisions in the field of professional higher education opened up opportunities to blacks; and in *Brown* v. *Board of Education of Topeka, Kansas* in 1954 the Supreme Court overturned *Plessy* and declared that in public education separate was inherently unequal, thus moving in on a key area of state action previously immune to federal intervention.

Dismantling school segregation in the South was no simple task, as the Supreme Court was well aware. It called only for "deliberate speed." The Court had directed that the system by which millions of students were taught, hundreds of thousands of teachers and administrators were employed, thousands of school districts were administered, must be changed. But there was a resounding silence from President Eisenhower. Nor did Congress act, except that a large group of southern legislators declared that the Court's decision was "an unwarranted exercise of power . . . contrary to the Constitution."

Some progress was rapid. Four states (Kansas, Arizona, New Mexico, and Wyoming) had permitted racial segregation only under local option, and they quickly changed their laws. Five states—Kentucky, Maryland, Missouri, Oklahoma, and West Virginia—and the District of Columbia swiftly eliminated state laws requiring segregation. The ten states of the Deep South resisted through legal maneuvers which were struck down by the courts. The president was forced to act in 1957 when Arkansas tried to prevent integration in Little Rock, but the executive branch left it to private litigators and overburdened courts to achieve the concrete steps to desegregation. But it would be impossible for the federal courts alone to restructure southern society, even though in the wake of *Brown* they struck down segregation in action after action, in field after field. The forces of Congress and the executive would have to be brought to bear.

The legal maneuvers of the NAACP and the NAACP Legal Defense Fund were supplemented in late 1955 by the sudden explosion of grassroots black protest. A boycott of the segregated buses in Montgomery, Ala., began spontaneously in 1955. Martin Luther King, Jr., a young minister, became its spokesman, received national publicity, and emerged as a popular and charismatic leader. In 1957 for the first time since 1875 the U.S. Congress passed civil rights legislation. It was more symbolic than effective, but it created a permanent and independent Civil Rights Commission to conduct investigations and issue reports, and authorized the attorney general to act against those who deprived people of the right to vote in federal elections.

Black protest continued, and the right to vote was still denied, particularly by the discriminatory use of literacy tests. In 1960 a black student "sit-in" movement rapidly spread. The Civil Rights Act of 1960 went further: the attorney general could ask a court to find a "pattern or practice" of voting-rights denial, and if it made such a finding, any individual otherwise qualified by the state law could apply to the court to order that he be allowed to vote. This, too, was without significant effect.

When in 1960 John F. Kennedy was elected president with heavy Negro support, it was hoped and expected that the executive would be drawn more actively into the battle against segregation and discrimination, but the new administration moved cautiously. In 1962 and 1963, when the governors of Mississippi and Alabama sought to deny blacks admission to their state universities, Kennedy did act forcefully. The black protest movement continued, demanding access to public accommodations and to the vote as its chief objectives, and reaching a climax in televised acts of nonviolent protest met by southern brutality in 1963. That year President Kennedy called for comprehensive civil rights legislation to end discrimination in public facilities and segregation in public schools and to increase the power of the federal government to protect the right to vote. The year 1963, the hundredth anniversary of Lincoln's Emancipation Proclamation, seemed a fitting time finally to achieve equality for blacks. In 1964, under the shock of Kennedy's assassination and with the strong support of President Lyndon B. Johnson, Congress passed the most farreaching Civil Rights Act. It was titled "An act to enforce the constitutional right to vote, to authorize the Attorney General to institute suits to protect constitutional rights in public facilities and public education, to extend the Commission on Civil Rights, to prevent discrimination in federally assisted programs, to establish a Commission on Equal Employment Opportunity, and for other purposes."

Title I of this legislation expanded the power of the attorney general to act to guarantee the right to vote; it was rapidly superseded in 1965 by the Voting Rights Act, which suspended any literacy test or other device to prevent voting in any jurisdiction in which less than 50 percent of the voting-age population had voted or registered in the presidential election of 1964. This act covered seven southern states; without design, it turned out also to cover some counties in the North. Finally the long resistance to black exercise of the suffrage was broken, and blacks in substantial numbers began to vote in the Deep South, changing its political composition and orientation.

Title II of the Civil Rights Act of 1964 barred discrimination in places of public accommodation and gave the attorney general the right to act against such discrimination. It was remarkably and rapidly effective in the deep South. Title III desegregated all facilities maintained by public organizations; again the attorney general was empowered to support and institute suits against such practices, and segregation fell rapidly. Title IV banned segregation in public education, with similar powers given to the attorney general. Title V extended the powers of the Civil Rights Commission. Title VI prohibited discrimination in any federally assisted program. Title VII outlawed discrimination in employment on grounds of race, color, sex, or national

origin and established an Equal Employment Opportunities Commission. It could record complaints, investigate, and conciliate, but enforcement had to be referred to the attorney general.

The act was enormously effective. One of the reasons for its effectiveness was that simultaneously the federal government was expanding rapidly, providing grants to cities, states, and school districts, establishing new programs for the poor and expanding health care and higher education programs. Because almost every employer, every institution, and every branch of local and state government had become the beneficiary of federal funds, the capacity of the federal government to obtain compliance with nondiscrimination and nonsegregation through the threat of the cutting off of funds under Title VI was highly effective.

By the use of this power the long-drawn-out effort to achieve desegregation of southern schools finally succeeded. In 1968 the Supreme Court declared in *Green* v. *New Kent County* that a simple "freedom of choice" plan would not be enough to meet the mandate of *Brown* that schools be desegregated, because whites would not choose formerly black schools, and few blacks chose white schools. Using the power of Title VI of the Civil Rights Act, the Department of Health, Education, and Welfare required that specific percentages of black students in formerly white schools be reached in hundreds of southern districts. Despite the election of President Nixon, who was cool to the measures required for massive desegregation, by 1971 southern schools had become the most integrated in the United States.

But in the larger towns and cities schools were segregated wholly or in part because of black residential concentration. Nor was this a problem of the South alone; it was an even more serious problem in the North and West, where blacks were more heavily concentrated in large cities and black residential areas were much larger.

In 1971 the Supreme Court ruled unanimously in *Swann* v. *Mecklenburg County* that Charlotte, N.C., had to bus schoolchildren to overcome the vestiges of segregation. But Charlotte, like northern cities, had segregated schools because its black population was residentially concentrated and because, under the mandate of the *Brown* decision, it no longer assigned students to schools by race, but on the basis of where they lived. Such was the argument of the Charlotte school officials and of many northern districts that came under attack for school segregation.

The situation dealt with in the *Brown* decision—that in which state law required segregation and local school districts under official policy rigidly separated the races for education—had come to an end. But segregation in the schools as the result of residential concentration now came under criticism. An increasing number of plaintiffs attacking neighborhood school assignment tried to show that black concentrations in the schools were the result of local school-board actions, and thus state action, and not the result of residential concentration. When they succeeded, requirements to bus were imposed.

With the Civil Rights Act, a number of different powers became available to the federal government to fight discrimination in employment. The new Equal Employment Opportunity Commission (EEOC) turned out to have more extensive powers than the bare language of the act suggested. For example, the EEOC could issue regulations determining what was a discriminatory test of employment, and this power, within limits, was accepted by the Supreme Court in the *Griggs* case (1971). Thus, under certain circumstances the use of an intelligence test or the requirement that employees hold high-school diplomas could be considered discriminatory. The EEOC could require major corporations to adopt programs to hire given numbers of minorities and women, and to award back pay to minorities and women, by the threat of bringing action demonstrating discrimination (for example, the use of tests which it had declared discriminatory). Thus, the American Telephone and Telegraph Company accepted a consent judgment in 1972 requiring broad remedial actions to increase the number of higher-level minority and female employees. In 1972 the powers of the Equal Employment Opportunity Commission were extended, even though by that time there was widespread concern that it was requiring "reverse discrimination"—the hiring and promotion of minorities (and women, who were also protected under the Civil Rights Act of 1964) over better qualified nonminority applicants and employees. Independent of the EEOC, but with substantial powers to affect the employment and promotion policies of employers, was the Office of Federal Contract Compliance. This federal agency operated under the authority of an executive order that required "affirmative action" to overcome discrimination by federal contractors. Under its regulations federal contractors were required to set "goals" for the hiring and promotion of given numbers of minority and female employees within a given time, in order to overcome "underutilization." With the expansion of federal spending programs, more and more employers came under the category of "federal contractors." Federally supported construction projects were the first to be brought under statistical hiring requirements under affirmative action, but the practice soon was required of other federal contractors, among them universities, and was soon adopted by many states and cities for their own contractors.

In addition, federal regulatory bodies such as the Federal Communications Commission also could act against discrimination, either under statute or under their own regulations, in the industries they regulated. Individuals who encountered discrimination now had many options—state law, the civil rights act, and federal regulations; they could sue also under the old Reconstruction civil rights statutes, resuscitated by the federal courts. Overt, direct discrimination rapidly became an anachronism, and the more difficult question that replaced it was, what was discrimination? Were union seniority rules discrimination under the law? Were tests which selected different proportions of minority groups discrimination under the law? And were affirmative action plans designed to increase the proportions of minorities discrimination against whites under the law? These were the issues that began to emerge in the late 1960s and were still unsettled in the late 1970s.

THE 1970s: BEYOND DISCRIMINATION

In the middle and late 1960s, as blacks rioted in American cities, as Mexican Americans and Puerto Ricans became politically active, as American Indians

for the first time entered the arena of national politics, and as white ethnic groups also became more assertive —both in reaction to black political action, and to foster aims of their own, such as establishing the legitimacy of the maintenance of their cultures and languages—the American polity seemed to be engaged in a massive effort finally to put problems of racial and ethnic discrimination behind it. Thus, in 1965 the Hart-Celler Immigration Act swept away quotas based on race and national origin, and in 1968 a fair-housing act banned racial and ethnic discrimination.

But although segregated education by law became obsolete, and black employment rose in professional and white-collar occupations and in skilled labor, the problem of ending discrimination against racial and minority groups was not removed from the agenda of public life. Discrimination as it had been understood until the middle 1960s declined rapidly, but new issues that had not previously been considered under the heading of discrimination now emerged.

Some of these new problems arose in education and employment. Northern cities which had not thought of themselves as doing so were found by judges to have practiced segregation, enough to require the massive remedy of busing of schoolchildren so as to approximate in each school the proportions of children by race in the school district. Busing thus came to San Francisco, Boston, Denver, and other cities, generally with considerable conflict, for it infringed on the traditional neighborhood school. Whites left the cities in which black schoolchildren increased in number, and in which busing was instituted. A fierce dispute erupted over the causes of "white flight," but whatever the reasons, it was clear that blacks were becoming the majority population in more and more cities. Should then central cities be joined with suburbs to permit higher proportions of whites in urban schools? The Supreme Court denied such a solution in Detroit, permitted it in Louisville, Ky., and Wilmington, Del. Congress, which had acted so forcefully in 1964, now withdrew from defining standards of desegregation, except for the passage of occasional antibusing amendments which bound the federal bureaucracy but were without effect in the courts. The courts acted erratically; even the Supreme Court's standards became obscure, and on similar facts some federal courts imposed busing and others did not.

Behind this new, confused, and complex situation lay the reality of poor black achievement in schools. Would integration improve their scores? Would it improve them if it were imposed on unwilling whites? Could enough whites be induced to stay in the cities in which such drastic measures were adopted? While to parents the educational issues were undoubtedly paramount, to the litigants trying to prove segregation, and to the judges who accepted these proofs, it was doubtful whether the ultimate aim of improved education carried much weight against what they conceived as a moral, constitutional, and social imperative. To parents and the public at large, busing raised the contradictory picture of federal agencies requiring assignment to schools on the basis of race and ethnic group, now to achieve integration rather than segregation.

In the later 1960s and 1970s new dimensions were added to the issue of discrimination in education as Spanish-American and Asian-American groups became active. For them the problem of education was less one of segregation—to which they had also, in one degree or another, been subject—than of the attitude of public school authorities toward their language and culture. Public schools typically had ignored the foreign-language background of children; they had not taken into account the difficulties this background created for education in English. In addition, they often actively suppressed the use of foreign languages by schoolchildren. Many Mexican-American and Puerto Rican leaders wanted public schools to acknowledge that foreign-language background required special programs. Others went further: they wanted public schools to encourage the maintenance of foreign-language ability and to teach children of their ethnic group something of their group's culture. To some extent these paralleled black demands for black studies in the public schools.

But inevitably demands for special programs designed for children of a given ethnic group—whether these programs facilitated the teaching of English, or maintained language competence and cultural knowledge— conflicted with the demands for desegregation and integration. Should children of a given ethnic group be scattered, as in the pattern developing for black children, or be concentrated so that they could be educated in their own language and culture?

Even where this conflict was not severe, these new demands ran counter to what those fighting discrimination had originally set as their objective. Antidiscrimination legislation had been written under the assumption that public policy should be blind to race and ethnic group. Representatives of minority groups now demanded that public policy be responsive to the specific culture of each ethnic group. In 1968 federal legislation provided funds for bilingual programs. In 1974 this legislation was amended to expand the type and level of federal support for bilingual and bicultural education programs, including full-scale bilingual and bicultural education programs as an end in themselves rather than solely as a vehicle for easing the transition to English-only education.

Further, in 1974 the Supreme Court in its *Lau* decision upheld regulations of the Office of Civil Rights of the Department of Health, Education, and Welfare requiring bilingual programs for students of limited English-language ability. The Office of Civil Rights had interpreted the prohibition of discrimination in educational programs on grounds of national origin in the Civil Rights Act of 1964 as requiring this kind of response to language problems of students. As a result, school districts were both required to provide bilingual-bicultural education by the Office of Civil Rights, and were assisted in doing so by federal legislation. This was only one of the ways in which the long fight against discrimination shifted, in the early 1970s, to demanding public action that was conscious of, rather than blind to, color and ethnic group. (*See* Language: Issues and Legislation.)

In the field of employment, "affirmative action" became the issue. It was required under executive orders which governed contracts with federal contractors. It was demanded increasingly by the EEOC, the attorney general, and federal courts in cases where discrimination could be proved. And it was increasingly accepted by business, nonprofit, and public employers, either because they were federal contractors or because they

knew that under EEOC regulations their employment practices could be shown to be discriminatory (for example, if they used tests with disproportionate impact), even though they had not discriminated intentionally. Race and ethnicity became key factors in estimating eligibility for a job or a promotion, not in order to keep blacks and Spanish-surnamed Americans down, but to raise them up. But this meant taking account of race and ethnic background. In 1964 all sides seemed agreed that color and ethnicity should be of no account in education and employment, and it was assumed and expected that what was intended by the legislation of that day was color-blind, not color-conscious, public policy. Color consciousness, however, became the accepted public policy in the 1970s, not through congressional action—Congress on the whole still opposed it —but through the actions of permanent agencies that had been established to administer and enforce the antidiscrimination laws, and through the agreement of the courts with the way in which they carried out their mandate. In the view of many, however, these agencies were subverting the very laws they were supposed to enforce.

"Reverse discrimination" thus became the issue of the later 1970s. Strangely, it was cases in the field of higher education that brought it most prominently to public attention. First, Marco DeFunis, a Jewish applicant to the University of Washington Law School, sued the school when he was not admitted because it had a program favoring the admission of minorities. The Supreme Court refused to rule on the case, but it was clear that it was deeply divided. Then Allan Bakke, a white, filed suit because he was not admitted to the medical school of the University of California at Davis, which also had a program favoring the admission of minorities. Such practices were common in law and medical schools, where action to increase the number of minorities was widespread. The *Bakke* case spurred a passionate national debate on the problem of affirmative action and reverse discrimination. The debate divided old allies in the struggles for civil rights; the sharpest and most poignant division was between black and Jewish civil rights organizations, which had been closely allied for 30 years in achieving state and national antidiscrimination legislation. The Supreme Court in 1978 ruled on the *Bakke* case, but it was more divided than it had been for decades on a civil rights issue. Four justices would have upheld quotas, four would have rejected them under Title VI of the Civil Rights Act of 1964, and only one, writing a complex decision, permitted the Court to issue a complex and ambiguous judgment in favor of Bakke.

The decision marked a strong contrast with the unanimous ruling in *Brown* and in civil rights cases for almost 20 years following. It reflected a divided country. But it reflected, too, the end of the long history of overt discrimination against minorities as a major theme in American history. There was now a new issue: what kind of positive action in favor of minorities was to be accepted as legitimate and constitutional?

Bibliography

The most informative historical studies of state and municipal action in the 19th century are Leonard Levy and Harlan B. Phillips, "The Roberts Case: Source of the 'Separate but Equal' Doctrine," *American Historical Review* 56 (1951): 510–518, and Leon Litwack, *North of Slavery* (Chicago, 1961). Morton Keller, *Affairs of State* (Cambridge, Mass., 1977), provides a thoughtful overview of civil rights legislation and the changing status of blacks after the Civil War. J.R. Pole, *The Pursuit of Equality in American History* (Berkeley, Calif., 1978), is a survey of legal and constitutional ideas about the nature of equality in American society.

Several works by legal scholars are informative on the constitutional issues in the history of public policy against discrimination: Derrick A. Bell, Jr., *Race, Racism, and American Law* (Boston, 1973); Raoul Berger, *Government by Judiciary: The Transformation of the Fourteenth Amendment* (Cambridge, Mass., 1976); Jack Greenberg, *Race Relations and American Law* (New York, 1959); Milton Konvitz, *A Century of Civil Rights* (New York, 1961), and *The Constitution and Civil Rights* (1946; reprint, New York, 1977); and Bernard D. Reams, Jr. and Paul E. Wilson, *Segregation and the Fourteenth Amendment in the United States* (Buffalo, N.Y., 1975). Also helpful is Leon H. Mayhew, *Law and Equal Opportunity* (Cambridge, Mass., 1968).

The major work on the position of blacks at the beginning of World War II, with extensive analysis of policies imposing segregation and discriminatory treatment and the nascent efforts to counter legal and extralegal deprivation of the country's largest minority, is Gunnar Myrdal, *An American Dilemma* (New York, 1944). John Hope Franklin, *From Slavery to Freedom: A History of American Negroes* (New York, 1964), describes antidiscrimination policy in the postwar period. Albert P. Blaustein and Robert L. Zangrando, *Civil Rights and the American Negro: A Documentary History* (New York, 1968), chronicles the history of the civil rights movement and its major legal and legislative successes. Many books cover specific aspects of the legal counterattack on discrimination, among them Howard I. Kalodner and James J. Fishman, eds., *Limits of Justice: The Courts' Role in School Desegregation* (Cambridge, Mass., 1978); and Herbert Hill, *Black Labor and the American Legal System, Volume I* (Washington, D.C., 1977), which goes up to the end of World War II.

Lino A. Graglia, *Disaster by Decree: The Supreme Court Decisions on Race and the Schools* (Ithaca, N.Y., 1976), analyzes the major Supreme Court decisions and is critical of the most recent turn in favor of busing. Nathan Glazer, *Affirmative Discrimination: Ethnic Inequality and Public Policy* (New York, 1975), is also critical of this development, as well as of new developments of antidiscrimination law and regulation imposing statistical tests of nondiscrimination. The literature on "reverse discrimination" or "affirmative action" is voluminous. For a sampling see Barry Gross, ed., *Reverse Discrimination* (Buffalo, N.Y., 1977); John E. Fleming, Gerald R. Gill, and David H. Swinton, *The Case for Affirmative Action for Blacks in Higher Education* (Washington, D.C., 1978); and Allen P. Sindler, *Bakke, DeFunis and Minority Admissions: The Quest for Equal Opportunity* (New York, 1978).

NATHAN GLAZER AND REED UEDA

PUEBLOS: *see* AMERICAN INDIANS

PUERTO RICANS

According to the 1970 Census, Puerto Ricans living in the continental United States represented one-third (1,491,463) of the total Puerto Rican population; the remaining 2,712,033 lived in the Commonwealth of Puerto Rico. Slightly over half (54.8 percent) of those in the United States live in New York City, which has the largest Puerto Rican population of any city in the world —817,712 according to the 1970 Census, compared with 463,242 in San Juan, Puerto Rico's capital and largest city. Chicago has the second largest community with 78,856. Smaller settlements can be found in Philadelphia and Newark (about 26,000 each), and in other New Jersey, California, Connecticut, Massachusetts, and Ohio cities.

Puerto Ricans have been U.S. citizens since 1917 and can therefore travel freely between the island and the mainland. But because the island language and culture are foreign to most of the mainland, migration involves a cultural transition differing little from that experienced by immigrants coming from Europe or Asia. Puerto Ricans have not gone in large numbers to the Southwest, where an old and large Spanish-speaking

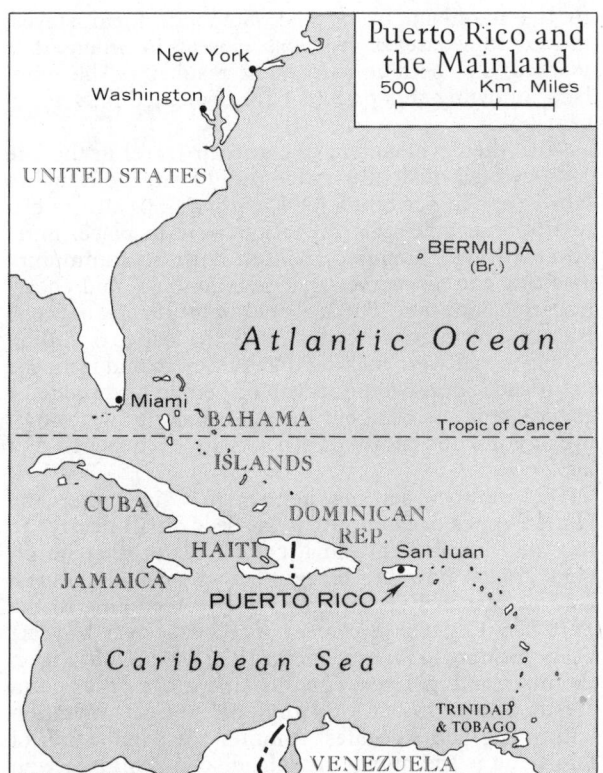

Puerto Rico and the Mainland
500   Km. Miles

UNITED STATES

Atlantic Ocean

BERMUDA (Br.)

Miami

BAHAMA ISLANDS   Tropic of Cancer

CUBA   DOMINICAN REP.

HAITI   San Juan

JAMAICA   PUERTO RICO

Caribbean Sea

TRINIDAD & TOBAGO

VENEZUELA

population is already established; their problems are those of urban-based immigrant minorities. On national issues they find themselves a minority among Spanish-speaking Americans: Mexican Americans dominate both in numbers and in influence.

ORIGINS

Puerto Rico is a Caribbean island 100 miles long and 35 miles wide situated about 1,000 miles southeast of Florida. Discovered and claimed for Spain by Columbus in 1493, it remained a Spanish colony and was used mainly as a military outpost until 1898.

When the Spanish discovered Puerto Rico, the island was inhabited by Indians called the Tainos, but they died out after the Spanish conquest. Most of them were killed or fell prey to the European diseases brought by the Spanish colonists; those few remaining were absorbed into the conquering population. Beginning in 1511 black slaves were brought from Africa to replace the Indians as laborers, and slavery remained a part of the economy until it was abolished in 1873.

The predominant features of Puerto Rico's people and culture remain those of the Spanish colonizers. Little of the Taino culture survives, although Indian physical features can still be seen on some Puerto Rican faces. Black influence has been more substantial. Intermarriage and sexual union have resulted in a varied population ranging in color from completely Caucasoid to completely Negroid, with many variations in between. But the language is Spanish, the common religion Roman Catholic, and the cultural patterns and social relations are Spanish colonial.

After the Spanish-American War, Puerto Rico was given to the United States by the terms of the Treaty of Paris (1898). After a brief period of military occupation, in 1900 the United States granted its island possession a measure of local government under the Foraker Act. This arrangement lasted until 1917 when the Jones Act, passed in reaction to pressures for independence, unilaterally declared Puerto Ricans to be citizens of the United States unless they explicitly refused it, an act widely resented by the Puerto Ricans. In 1946 the United States appointed Puerto Rico's first native-born governor, Jesus T. Piñero (1897–1952); in 1947 the Elective Governors Act authorized the popular election of a governor, and in 1948 Luis Muñoz Marín, founder of the Partido Democrático Popular (Popular Democratic party), became the first elected governor of Puerto Rico.

On July 3, 1950, the U.S. Congress passed the Puerto Rican Federal Relations Act enabling the Puerto Ricans to draft their own constitution so long as its provisions did not exceed the limitations placed on an incorporated territory of the United States—in other words, the constitution could not provide for statehood or independence. The constitution they drew up was approved by the U.S. Congress, accepted by a Puerto Rican referendum on June 4, 1951, and inaugurated on July 25, 1952. It officially designates Puerto Rico as an *estado libre asociado* (free associated state), or, in its English version, a commonwealth. Puerto Rico remains a U.S. possession subject to most federal laws, including military conscription (Puerto Ricans have fought in all American wars beginning with World War I and including Vietnam). Its citizens cannot vote in U.S. elections and have no representation, aside from an elected resident commissioner who sits with Congress but has no vote. As a result, however, they also pay no federal taxes.

The Puerto Rican political parties reflect the attitudes of Puerto Ricans toward that political status. The Popular Democratic party is committed to continuing commonwealth status; the Partido Nuevo Progresista (New Progressive party) seeks statehood; and a variety of other parties demand complete independence. The most active among the latter are the militant Partido Socialista Puertorriqueño (Puerto Rican Socialist party) and the more moderate Partido Independentista Puertorriqueño (Puerto Rican Independence party).

In 1953 the General Assembly of the United Nations categorized Puerto Rico as a possession that had already been given the right of self-determination through its commonwealth constitution and should therefore not be identified as a nonself-governing territory. The independence parties continue to challenge this decision. In the fall of 1977 all three parties came before the United Nations Committee on Decolonization to protest its limited autonomy: the Popular party because the U.S. Congress had failed to extend the island's autonomy in 1976; the Progressive party because Puerto Rico was not a state, and the independence parties because the island was not an independent nation.

MIGRATION AND ARRIVAL

The first Puerto Ricans to come to the United States in the 19th century were for the most part political exiles seeking a base in New York from which to work for the independence of the island; most prominent among them were Ramon Emeterio Betances (1827–1898), who organized Puerto Rico's first attempt at es-

tablishing an independent republic, and Eugenio Maria de Hostos (1839–1903), who struggled for Puerto Rican independence. Francisco Gonzalo (Pachin) Marín (1863–1897) moved to New York in 1891, where for a short time he published his revolutionary newspaper, *El Postillón*, after it had been suppressed twice in Puerto Rico. Santiago Iglesias (1872–1939), founder of the Socialist party in Puerto Rico, also spent time in New York, along with Luis Muñoz Rivera (1859–1916) whose son, Luis Muñoz Marín, would later become Puerto Rico's first popularly elected governor.

These first, mostly political, émigrés returned home after the island had become a U.S. possession, where they assumed the leadership of the various political movements that marked the island's later history; but they were soon replaced by other, mostly poor, islanders who came looking for work. Between 1898 and 1940 the number of Puerto Ricans who came to New York City seeking employment already constituted a substantial portion of the city's population, more than 61,000 people. From them others soon learned of economic opportunities on the mainland, and they could count on the hospitality of fellow islanders when they arrived. But their numbers were still negligible compared with the large-scale migration that followed World War II.

As a result of the sharp decline in the death rate resulting from improvements in health and sanitation on the island, the population in Puerto Rico grew from a rate of natural increase of 14.3 per thousand per year in 1899 to 28.6 per thousand per year in 1950; the island's total population doubled between 1910 (1,118,012) and 1950 (2,210,703). Had there been no migration, it would have come close to doubling again between 1950 and 1970.

The first to move were the rapidly increasing numbers of young people ready to enter the labor market in an economy unable to provide jobs for them. This migration grew rapidly when Puerto Ricans became U.S. citizens, and it grew still more rapidly during the 1920s. A hurricane in 1928 and another in 1932 devastated the coffee plantations that had been a major source of income for the island; repercussions of a worldwide depression and the accompanying drop in the price of staple crops such as tobacco and sugar made further inroads into agricultural income. High general unemployment was compounded by the seasonal nature of the major source of employment that remained—cutting sugar cane—which provided jobs for five months of the year and left the workers idle for the other seven. But in the 1930s migration was still comparatively limited because there were few jobs in the depression-struck United States, and virtually ceased when the outbreak of World War II made travel to the mainland hazardous. By 1946 a large backlog of unemployed and underemployed potential migrants were waiting for peace and prosperity to come.

Contract farm workers constituted the first postwar group to arrive. Although they had begun coming in the early forties, it took until 1947–1948 for the Department of Labor of Puerto Rico to provide them with the protection of a contract guaranteeing conditions of work, insurance, and travel and to enforce these agreements with a monitoring system. Beginning in the midforties an average of 20,000 contract farm workers came

to the mainland every year. Some of them stayed, moved to whatever city was closest to where they worked, and became permanent residents. The numbers following this pattern have decreased only in recent years.

With the development of cheap air travel in the late 1940s which made it possible to fly from the island to New York in six hours for less than $50, all the elements of a large-scale migration were in place: unrestricted travel, unemployment at home, a community awaiting the newcomers on the mainland, and cheap, fast transportation. The scale of migration and of travel back and forth grew rapidly. By 1973 close to 5 million people a year were making the journey to and from the mainland. Some were tourists or people on private or government business, but the great majority were coming or going for family or other visits or in search of a job.

The number settling permanently in either the United States or Puerto Rico has been small relative to the total number traveling; compared to other immigrant groups, however, the number who return to the island permanently is strikingly high. According to the 1970 U.S. Census, 13 percent of all those over 14 years of age residing in Puerto Rico in 1970 had been living on the mainland in 1965. The movement can best be understood in terms of a continuous internal migration within the United States. Another clear indication of this trend is the number of island schoolchildren who have attended schools on the mainland. In the 1954–1963 period New York schools had a net gain of 36,120 Puerto Rican children; this gain was down to 1,897 in the 1964–1973 period, and in the period 1969–1973, the New York City schools actually lost 12,419 more Puerto Rican children than they gained.

The return of these children is a problem for the island schools, for many of them do not know Spanish

Table 1. People of Puerto Rican origin in continental United States and New York City, 1910–1970.

Generation and year of birth	U.S. total	N.Y.C. total	Percent of U.S. total in N.Y.C.
First and second			
1910	1,513	554	36.6
1930	52,774	—	—
1940	69,967	61,462	87.8
1950	301,375	245,880	81.6
1960	887,662	612,574	69.0
1970	1,391,463	817,712	54.8
First			
1910	1,513	554	36.6
1930	52,774	—	—
1940	69,967	61,463	87.8
1950	226,110	187,420	82.9
1960	615,384	429,710	69.8
1970	810,087	473,300	58.4
Second			
1950	75,265	58,460	77.7
1960	272,278	182,964	67.2
1970	581,376	344,412	59.2

Source: U.S. Bureau of the Census, *Census of the Population, 1970*, Subject Report PC(2)-1E, *Puerto Ricans in the United States* (Washington, D.C., 1973), table 1; U.S. Bureau of the Census, *Census of the Population, 1970*, Subject Report PC(2)-1D, *Puerto Ricans in the United States, Final Report* (Washington, D.C., 1963), p. viii, table A.

well enough to be instructed in that language: in the academic year 1976–1977 as many as 45,000 children in Puerto Rico's schools were reported to be having language difficulties.

SETTLEMENT

By far the largest Puerto Rican community on the mainland is that of New York City and its environs. New York is where Puerto Ricans first settled, and it continues to be the most important and influential of the Puerto Rican settlements on the mainland, although otherwise it shares cultural and social characteristics with Puerto Rican communities in other cities.

The Puerto Ricans first came to Brooklyn and settled in the area around the Navy Yard during and after World War I. By 1930 East Harlem had become a large Puerto Rican community and had acquired the name El Barrio (the neighborhood); it is still the area of the city most clearly associated with Puerto Ricans in New York. East 116th Street, El Barrio's Main Street, and the *Marqueta* (market) on Park Avenue are both markedly Puerto Rican in atmosphere. After World War II, Puerto Ricans spread to other sections of the city, particularly the South Bronx, the Lower East Side and Upper West Side of Manhattan, and the Williamsburg section of Brooklyn.

The Puerto Rican population is extremely young; 48 percent of it was below 20 years of age in the 1970 Census. In 1974–1975, 253,000 Puerto Rican children were enrolled in the public schools of New York City, 23 percent of the total school enrollment. As these children reach marriageable age and begin to raise families— even small ones—the rapid increase in their numbers will probably make them by 1990 one of the largest ethnic groups in the city, assuming the majority of them remain there.

In New York City, as elsewhere, Puerto Ricans face problems common to most immigrant newcomers: poor housing, menial jobs, economic exploitation, unemployment, poor health, and the handicaps of language and limited education. They came to New York just as the unskilled jobs by which newcomers once sustained themselves were disappearing from the marketplace. New York City lost half a million jobs between 1970 and 1976, and large areas of the city have fallen into a state of deterioration and decay. Whole neighborhoods have been burned down, making stable residence impossible. The islanders come from a culture where color has little meaning to one where it has a great deal, and in New York they live with the largest number of blacks of any U.S. city.

Although most Puerto Ricans are Catholic, they came without their own clergy and consequently lacked the strong support that ethnic parishes gave to many earlier immigrant groups. Still, they soon emerged as a significant cultural force in the city's life, and hometown clubs and social activities have become abundant; Puerto Rican music and festivals add color to the city's urban scene; Puerto Rican associations among teachers, social workers, police, and civil servants are numerous and still increasing. These manifold activities in a new environment are helping to establish Puerto Ricans as a permanent part of New York life.

The Puerto Rican communities in Jersey City, Hobo-

ken, Newark, and Paterson, N.J., reflect an overflow from the neighborhoods of New York. Communities in Nassau and Suffolk counties in Long Island were established by contract farm workers who remained there; once established, they soon also became home for newcomers with relatives and friends. In other cities such as Elizabeth, Union City, and West New York, N.J., and the large cities of Florida, Puerto Ricans are fairly numerous but are outnumbered by Cubans. In Chicago and the West they are outnumbered by Mexican Americans.

Lorain, Ohio, is an exceptional Puerto Rican community. Puerto Ricans first came to Lorain during World War II, attracted by jobs in heavy industry nearby, especially in the steel mills and the local Ford Motor Company plant. They joined the labor unions and settled in neighborhoods of one- and two-family homes (55 percent of them now own their homes). Few families are on welfare, and this community has the lowest rate of female-headed households (7 percent) of any mainland Puerto Rican community reported by the census. A Puerto Rican Catholic parish was organized early to serve them, and a stable community formed around it. Although the educational level is much lower than that of many other Puerto Rican communities, the median family income is high, second only to that of San Francisco's Puerto Ricans. The Lorain group is an established population, and it is beginning to show political strength in both local and national elections.

More characteristic of the smaller and newer communities is that in Boston, much poorer, less stable population than in Lorain. Many are transient workers who come, work for a while, and return to Puerto Rico to buy a plot of land and settle down. It has one of the highest rates of newly arrived families of any Puerto Rican community on the mainland. Many labor at work so menial that even other unskilled workers refuse to accept it; their median family income is half that of the Puerto Ricans in Lorain. Thirty-six percent of the Boston families have a female head, and 40 percent live below the poverty level; their children have a high dropout rate from school.

In Miami the small Puerto Rican population (6,446 in 1970) is dwarfed by the large, comparatively affluent, and increasingly powerful Cuban colony. The Puerto Ricans there remain a poor and deprived minority in a Cuban world.

San Francisco with about 5,000 Puerto Ricans and Los Angeles with about 10,000 have comparatively old and well-established Puerto Rican communities, though they are far outnumbered by the Mexican Americans. These far-western communities developed during a migration many years ago to Hawaii. They show some of the more favorable socioeconomic characteristics that can be expected to develop as the eastern Puerto Rican communities mature. These communities are the only two with a population that is more than 50 percent second generation, reflecting their long residence on the mainland; they have the highest educational level and the smallest percentages living below the poverty line. In 1970 San Francisco had the highest level of income of all reported Puerto Rican populations on the mainland. Los Angeles was third (following Lorain, Ohio), but it boasted the most Puerto Rican men holding professional or managerial positions

—14 percent compared to 8 percent for New York. The benefits of stability are evident in both these communities.

ECONOMIC LIFE

Two serious and abiding problems are found in Puerto Rican communities almost everywhere: lack of education and its almost inevitable accompaniment, poverty. The Puerto Ricans as a group are the poorest in New York City. Their median family income in 1970 was $5,575, lower than the $7,150 black median, and little more than half the citywide median of $9,682. One-third of them live below poverty level—that minimum designated by the federal government as necessary for a decent standard of living. Thirty percent were receiving public assistance in New York in 1970, somewhat higher than the 25 percent receiving public assistance nationwide. Since the mid-sixties their relative income position has deteriorated: family earnings increased by 13 percent between 1959–1969, but the increase for New York families generally was 26 percent. They are also the poorest of the Hispanic groups in the United States, with a median family income in 1974 more than $1,800 below that of Mexican Americans.

Still, the situation is better than in Puerto Rico, where the median income for families in 1970 was $3,063, or $2,500 lower than on the mainland. The census reported 60 percent of all families in Puerto Rico living below the poverty level, with only 8 percent receiving public assistance, in contrast to the 25 percent on the mainland. Since the cost of living is not substantially lower in Puerto Rico than it is on the mainland, the economic pressure to come north remains formidable.

Several reasons have been suggested for this persistent poverty. Puerto Ricans come to the mainland without the skills necessary for white-collar jobs; many do not know English; their schooling leaves large numbers ill prepared; they migrate to large metropolitan eastern cities where job opportunities for unskilled labor are rapidly declining; many are victims of racial discrimination. Consequently unemployment is higher than it is among other groups. Only 48 percent of Puerto Ricans over 16 years of age were in the labor force in New York City in 1970 compared to 57 percent for the total population, partly because few Puerto Rican women over 16 years of age were in the labor force, in contrast to 40 percent of women in the total population. Puerto Rican women have more children, and earlier, than the population as a whole. In addition, many become discouraged at not finding work and eventually simply drop out of the labor force altogether. The large proportion of women (28 percent) who are heads of families, many of which include small children, rely on public welfare for a subsistence income; if they are employed, it is likely to be in a poorly paying, menial job. Family income lags even if the wife does work; in New York City a Puerto Rican couple's combined median income is comparable to that of an average non–Puerto Rican New York family with only one wage earner.

Second-generation Puerto Ricans are doing better than their parents, however. The 1970 Census reports 7 percent of second-generation men in professional and technical positions in contrast to only 3 percent in the first; 30 percent of the second-generation men are in clerical and sales in contrast to 17 percent in the first;

for women in clerical and sales employment, the advance is from 32 percent in the first generation to 66 percent in the second. This progress is not yet reflected in a higher median income, however, for only a small percentage of the second generation is old enough to be in the labor force—second-generation men represented only 13 percent of all Puerto Rican men employed in 1970.

Even at the highest occupational levels Puerto Ricans can be at a disadvantage. Those in professional and technical positions in the New York area in 1970 had median annual earnings $800 lower than those of blacks in similar positions, and $4,500 lower than the average for the total population, primarily because they are new arrivals and do not have many really high earners at those occupational levels. The Report of the United States Commission on Civil Rights of October 1976 also attributed much of these differentials to discrimination.

The issue that has elicited the most criticism of Puerto Ricans centers on the high percentage receiving public welfare assistance: 25 percent of all Puerto Rican families in 1970; 30 percent of those in New York City. Over 18 percent of second-generation families continue to receive public assistance, indicating that for many Puerto Ricans poverty and dependency span generations. Whatever economic shifts affect the lives of the poor in general affect the Puerto Ricans particularly. Because most of them are poor, large numbers in New York City make their presence very visible on the welfare rolls.

EDUCATION

Until Puerto Ricans are able to acquire the schooling for better-paying jobs, particularly white-collar jobs, or are able to continue on to college for professional training, they will have little hope of developing effective community leadership or national influence.

Puerto Ricans have a much lower educational level than the American average. According to the 1970 Census, they had completed a median of 8.6 years of schooling by age 25, compared with the norm of 12.1 years. Few ever finish college—2 percent, compared with 10 percent for the nation generally. They also have one of the highest school dropout rates of any group in the United States. In 1970, 18 percent of Puerto Rican males 18–24 years of age were still enrolled in school compared with 38 percent in the total population. The proportion of Puerto Rican college freshmen in the United States dropped from 0.6 percent of the total in 1971 to 0.4 percent in 1973.

When only second-generation Puerto Ricans are considered, the situation looks more promising. For 1970 their median of schooling was 11.5 years, almost equal to the national average. The dropout rate similarly evens out: first-generation male enrollment was 13 percent, but 33 percent of the second generation were still in school in the 18–24 group. These rates imply substantial continued improvement. Especially in New York, Puerto Ricans have begun to attend college in comparatively large numbers, thanks to the open-admissions policy of its City University. The proportion of second-generation Puerto Ricans attending adult-education classes is higher than for the country as a whole.

The Civil Rights Commission Report attributed

many of these educational difficulties to discrimination. For example, the commission reported that in New York City in the fall of 1973 there were 256,095 Puerto Rican students in the public schools, elementary through high school, accounting for almost a quarter of the student body. Almost one-fifth of these were found to have moderate to severe difficulty in English comprehension, but relatively few were receiving any special help. The poorest achievement scores in arithmetic and reading are regularly found in the school districts that are predominantly Puerto Rican. In many cities with large Puerto Rican student populations, some students were being identified as mentally retarded or slow learners even though the evident handicap was lack of English. Few teachers in the New York City school system could communicate in Spanish, in part because of tenure policies and the unavailability of Puerto Rican personnel. Efforts have been made to increase the Puerto Rican representation among the city's teachers, but progress has been slow and aggressive recruitment campaigns by the New York City Board of Education have had only limited success.

One important effort to solve these difficulties has been the introduction of bilingual programs which teach the English language but provide instruction in the other regular subjects of the curriculum in Spanish. In 1975 Aspira (Aspire), a Puerto Rican educational association, filed a class-action suit against the New York City Board of Education for failure to provide bilingual education to Puerto Rican children. The board agreed to inaugurate adequate bilingual programs by September 1975, but was later held in contempt for having failed to do so. Meanwhile courses are being taught bilingually to large numbers of children; they have been introduced too recently for their effectiveness to be evaluated, but their very existence has been a source of hope and encouragement to Puerto Rican parents and the community. (*See also* Language: Issues and Legislation.)

The most promising developments in Puerto Rican education are at the college level; in 1972 about 25,000 Puerto Ricans were enrolled as full-time college students, a substantial advance over previous years. In New York City, the percentage of Puerto Ricans in the City University increased from 4 percent in 1969 to 7.4 percent in 1974. The percentage in the senior colleges increased from 2.9 percent in 1969 to 6.3 percent in 1974.

Some of the credit for these advances can go to Antonia Pantoja, the founder of Aspira, who also established the Universidad Boricua (Puerto Rican University), in Washington, D.C., in an effort to provide advanced training for promising Puerto Rican students while involving them in significant research related to Puerto Rico. A university without walls, chartered to grant degrees in association with the Union of Experimental Colleges, it has an affiliate, the Universidad Boricua in New York City, chartered by the Board of Regents of New York State to award a junior college degree.

In other universities Puerto Ricans are becoming prominent as scholars. Frank Bonilla directs the Puerto Rican Studies Center at the City University of New York; at Fordham University Lloyd Rogler Canino holds a university professorship, the Schweitzer Chair, funded by the state of New York; Jorge Batista is a member of the New York State Board of Regents. Luis

Quero Chiesa served for many years as the chairman of the Board of Higher Education for New York City; Alfredo Matthews and Hernan La Fontaine occupy high staff positions, and one Puerto Rican, Miguel Martinez, sits on the five-member Board of Education of New York City. In 1977–1978 the New York City school system had 2 Puerto Rican district superintendents, 45 principals, and 45 assistant principals. A Puerto Rican teachers' association actively represents Puerto Rican interests; Puerto Rican studies programs exist in most of the city colleges and in many of the private colleges; Puerto Rican student associations are active and sometimes militant.

THE FAMILY

Puerto Rican families follow no single traditional pattern. Extended family households are common, but so are nuclear families, the latter often including children of former unions. There are many female-headed households. Consensual unions, relatively stable unions of men and women with no legal or religious sanction, have also been rather common at least until recent years, especially among poorer people in Puerto Rico. It is a recognized civil status there and is reported as such in the U.S. Census for Puerto Rico; consensual unions probably exist on the mainland as well, but they are not so counted.

Puerto Rican families are apt to be large—an average of 4 people compared with 3.1 for families in New York City as a whole. Puerto Rican women have an average of 2.2 children, but in 1970 one in ten Puerto Rican families had seven children or more; three-fourths had children under 18 (compared to one-half the families in the city), and 28 percent of the families with children were headed by women, slightly lower than the 33 percent of black families, but considerably higher than the 14 percent for the population as a whole or the 18 percent in Puerto Rico. The percentage of female-headed families continues to be 25 percent in the second generation.

Puerto Rican families are beset by all the problems characteristic of families suddenly thrust into an industrial society. In a traditional Puerto Rican family, the man makes the decision for the household, accepts responsibility for its support, and is granted much more freedom than the woman in the disposition of his life and his sexual behavior. That combination of bravery, or often bravado, influence over others, the quality of the *caudillo* (leader), and dominance over women, particularly sexual dominance, known as *machismo* is prominent on the island, but it has been attenuated on the mainland by the comparative availability of employment and education for women and the impact of U.S. culture generally. The relatively small number of employed wives may reflect a carry-over of Puerto Rican roles, but the increasing number of female-headed families indicates a breaking down of the island pattern. Employment and public welfare ensure the survival of women without men. Puerto Rican women on welfare in New York City leave their husbands in most cases because the union has become intolerable to them; welfare provides an alternative means of survival.

Puerto Rican women are more apt to assume a role in public life than women in the rest of Latin America: they can be found, for example, as elected mayors of Puerto Rican *municipios*, at the University of Puerto

Rico, and in appointed positions in the government. In the earlier years of the post–World War II migration, women also played a more prominent role than men in the Puerto Rican community in New York City.

Conflict between family loyalty and individual success has affected Puerto Ricans much as it affected immigrant groups in the past. The pressure to be successful and the higher level of education of successive generations often result in individual achievement at the expense of family solidarity. One indication of family loyalty among Puerto Ricans, as among Hispanics in general, has been the custom of assuming the family names of both parents as a double surname. Because this is confusing to mainland Americans, Puerto Ricans usually abandon it in the United States and adopt the custom of using only the father's surname.

One aspect of the weakening of immigrant family relationships traditionally arises from conflict between the first and second generations. The child grows up at home in one culture and becomes acculturated through school and job to another. Chaperoning the young girl comes into conflict with American dating habits; the street life of the boys is often beyond the ability of the family to handle—one reason behind the high rate of drug use and delinquency among Puerto Rican youth.

Conflict between family loyalty and individual success often appears as a theme in Puerto Rican literature and drama. Among Puerto Rican writers, Piri Thomas is the best known; his autobiography, *Down These Mean Streets* (1967), describes his early struggles with poverty and prejudice. *The Ox Cart*, by René Marqués, is a popular play depicting the struggle of a Puerto Rican mother to retain the traditional values of family life against the disruptive force of American urban society. Another play, *El Huesped* (The Guest), by Pedro Juan Soto, tells about an elderly man driven to suicide because his family tries to escape from the responsibility of caring for him.

Compadrazgo (coparenthood) is a traditional relationship that adds to the strength of the extended family. It is both an intimate and a formal relationship that is established between the parents and the godparents of children, or between a married couple and the attendants at their wedding, or, more generally, simply between old friends. People in the relationship call each other *compadres*, or "coparents." The custom is disappearing among Puerto Ricans in New York with a consequent loss of family strength, support, and stability. The Puerto Rican Family Institute, a social agency, tries to encourage families to maintain or re-create *compadrazgo* in New York as a buttress against growing family instability.

GROUP MAINTENANCE AND SOCIAL ADJUSTMENT

The American experience is changing Puerto Rican families in many ways, but by far the most significant source of change is that of marriage outside the group. The 1970 Census reported that 33 percent of second-generation Puerto Rican wives were married to non-Hispanic whites; the rate is higher for second-generation Puerto Rican husbands, and similar to that for second-generation European immigrants in New York City in the years 1908–1912, suggesting that the pattern of assimilation for Puerto Ricans is following that of earlier immigrant groups. Intermarriage correlates with higher levels of schooling: in 1970, of second-generation Puerto Rican wives who had less than 12 years of schooling, only 21 percent had married non-Hispanic whites, compared with 44 percent of those who had more than 12 years of schooling. It is clear that intermarriage will increase as the educational level rises, presumably diminishing ethnic identification as a result.

The U.S. Census continues to sort Puerto Ricans in the United States into the categories of white and Negro. Puerto Ricans have numerous terms designating gradations of color, and the general term Negro is rarely used (*negra* and *negrita* are terms of endearment for anyone of any color). The term *de color* (a colored person) is the most common. *Moreno* in Spanish-language newspapers usually describes an American black as opposed to a colored Puerto Rican. The most common term for people of in-between color is *trigueño*, *Indio* if the person has Indian features. *Grifo* refers to people with kinky hair but usually light skinned; *pelo malo* (bad hair) is more or less equivalent. The problem of discrimination in Puerto Rico centers much more on class than on color itself. Especially among the poor there is an ease of social interaction very different from the black experience in the United States. Prejudice exists, but it is not as overt and pervasive as it is on the mainland.

When Puerto Ricans come to the United States, the shock of discrimination is a major source of tension, and one for which they are not prepared. In the first place the intermediate designation of trigueño disappears; people find themselves identified simply as "white" or "black." They quickly realize that being white makes things easier. In studies of Puerto Ricans, as well as in their own writings, color is repeatedly mentioned as one of the most serious problems of adjustment they have to face. Some expect that Puerto Ricans will eventually split into two groups—those who can win acceptance as white will assimilate into the white community; those who are identified as black will join the black community—but there is as yet no evidence for this theory. Puerto Ricans themselves make a sharp distinction between Puerto Ricans who are black (de color) and American blacks. Within the ethnic group, one local study found a rather high rate (20 percent) of intermarriage between Puerto Ricans of different color, in contrast to the low rate of interracial marriage among the total United States population or between Puerto Ricans and American blacks. Considerable tension and hostility exist between the Puerto Rican and black communities. This antagonism centers largely on questions of political or community control over institutions and access to public funds, and it is related to the persistent street violence between the two groups that is common in the urban centers where both dwell.

Many Puerto Ricans arrived on the mainland when the civil-rights movement and, later, the black-power movement were in the forefront. This created problems for Puerto Ricans, for they were faced simultaneously with the fact of racial prejudice and with the ambiguities it created for them as a racially mixed group. Any representative group of Puerto Ricans has people of all

colors; they are already an integrated population and their interests hinge instead on better employment and educational opportunities. It remains to be seen whether Puerto Ricans will continue to intermingle and intermarry with people of different color. If they do, it could contribute much toward solving a major problem of mainland American life.

RELIGION

Religion has played a major role in maintaining the cohesion of many American ethnic groups. The organization of social and cultural life around the parish or congregation for Catholics, Protestants, Jews, and others provided a source of social stability, psychic satisfaction, and even political power. It is doubtful that religion can play the same role for the Puerto Ricans. They have no Puerto Rican clergy migrating with them; even on the island two-thirds of the Catholic clergy are not Puerto Rican natives. Furthermore, the Catholic hierarchy is reluctant to establish Puerto Rican parishes on the model of the ethnic parishes of, for example, the Germans or Italians because of the serious problems that beset ethnic parishes when the immigrants move on.

The Catholic faith among Puerto Ricans manifests itself as an activity of the entire community, the *pueblo*, in processions and celebrations more often than as a personal commitment to membership in a parish or fidelity to Mass and sacraments. Religious observance reflects the spontaneous and expressive practices of the Spanish and Italians and not the restrained and well-organized worship of the Irish and Germans. It is apt to include a personal relationship with the Virgin Mary or the saints, whom Hispanics look upon as friends, advocates, and compadres. They hang religious pictures in their houses, cars, and workshops, and around their necks; they pray, make promises, and light candles to them in return for favors granted. These rites can be performed quite apart from any formal worship, and they would probably continue even if the organized religious structure were entirely to disappear.

Puerto Ricans find mainland religious practices strange. The absence of the pueblo makes it difficult to transfer the traditional style of communal religious observance. The earlier immigrants shifted their sense of community to an ethnic or Spanish-language parish or congregation. But those coming later to large cities, where parishes had already been established for generations, found it more difficult to retain their traditional modes of beliefs, practice, and organization. They generally faced some form of integrated parish in which non–Puerto Rican pastors ministered to a Puerto Rican population along with older, established Irish, German, Italian, or other Catholic groups, and often as a twofold ministry—in English to earlier residents, in Spanish to newcomers. But neighborhoods changed rapidly: as Puerto Ricans moved in the older residents moved out, and many parishes became almost entirely Puerto Rican. Then other complications arose: English-speaking blacks from the United States or the Caribbean, or French- and Creole-speaking blacks from Haiti, and increasing numbers of Spanish-speaking Catholics from Cuba, the Dominican Republic, and Central and South America congregated in the same neighborhoods, creating new problems of ministering to people of different

languages or cultural backgrounds. Some parishes conduct services simultaneously in three languages, making it still more difficult for Puerto Ricans to find in their parish a foundation for community and solidarity. They seldom have the feeling that the parish is their own in the sense that the Irish, Germans, Italians, or the various Eastern Orthodox groups once did.

The dioceses of New York, Bridgeport, Boston, Brooklyn, and other cities have appointed special staffs to minister to the spiritual and religious needs of Spanish-speaking people, and the United States Catholic Conference has established a national secretariat in Washington, D.C., for a similar purpose, with regional offices around the country. Many parishes and dioceses have Spanish-speaking councils. Grass-roots pressure from Puerto Ricans and other Hispanics is beginning to be effective. In two national gatherings, Spanish-speaking people have submitted recommendations to officials of the church in the United States, and these are being given serious attention. At the first national congress of Catholics in the United States, the "Call to Action" in Detroit in October 1976, the Spanish-speaking caucus was a forceful presence. The caucus was well organized and articulate, but like most national Hispanic organizations it was dominated by the Chicanos, and the Puerto Ricans felt largely overlooked in the midst of the much larger, politically more sophisticated and experienced group.

The principal demand of the Puerto Ricans and other Hispanics is for a policy of cultural pluralism in the church that will provide for the continuation of their language and culture in their spiritual and religious life and the appointment of Puerto Ricans and other Hispanics to positions of responsibility. Six Hispanics have thus far been named bishops in the United States. New York has one of these, an assistant bishop to the cardinal of New York, but he is a Spaniard.

Among the Protestant denominations there are also organizations to deal with Spanish-speaking members, and the National Council of Churches has established a department of racial and ethnic concerns. Because most Hispanics are Catholic, the involvement of the Protestant churches is limited; Pentecostal and evangelical sects are, however, numerous. These small congregations generally operate in storefronts in the heart of the neighborhoods they serve, employing a religious style that appeals to many poor Puerto Ricans. In a world that Puerto Ricans find cold, the Pentecostal congregation provides solace as well as a familiarly emotional form of worship.

Folk religious practices continue to flourish. *Botanicas*, stores where religious articles, the paraphernalia of folk religious practices—candles, incense, charms, herbs, potions—and prayers for all occasions are sold, are scattered throughout every Puerto Rican neighborhood, sometimes three or four to a single block. Spiritualism is common. Rooted in the conviction that communication with the dead is possible, practices range from séances to folk gatherings, from manipulations of the spirit world that are often frightening to invocations of spirits that can be helpful in providing support to the bereaved, particularly to those with symptoms of severe emotional distress. The mentally ill are looked upon as being troubled by evil spirits, and this evokes compassion and support from those around them.

The role of religion among mainland Puerto Ricans in the future is unclear. In dioceses such as Manhattan and Brooklyn, more than one-third of the Catholics are from Spanish-speaking backgrounds and most of these are Puerto Ricans, but they rarely participate in organized religious worship. Despite efforts to minister to them spiritually, their needs within established religious institutions remain largely unmet. The innovations that Puerto Ricans and other Hispanics are beginning to promote, however, may in time form the basis for a religious life that can help maintain their cultural identity in the United States.

SOCIAL ORGANIZATIONS AND POLITICAL LIFE

Puerto Ricans are becoming more active politically. By 1977 the New York community had elected one congressman, two state senators, four state assemblymen, and two city councilmen. Like the poor in New York generally, Puerto Ricans are predominantly Democratic. They have a number of elected judges, and they fill an increasing number of appointed positions in the city government. Nevertheless, they are still far from entering public employment in large numbers. As of 1971 only 1 percent of the agency heads in New York City, 3 percent of the administrators, and 2 percent of the professionals were Puerto Ricans. Their leaders insist that their progress can be measured only by their presence in key positions in city government, and they are not yet there. The Commission on Civil Rights concluded that underrepresentation of Puerto Ricans in public service reflects a major discriminatory barrier. If they continue to make progress in numbers of elected officials, the numbers of appointees are also likely to grow.

In earlier years Puerto Ricans in New York were provided representation through the Office of the Commonwealth of Puerto Rico, Department of Labor, Migration Division, an agency of the government established in 1949 by Luis Muñoz Marín, then governor of Puerto Rico, to provide assistance to the numerous Puerto Ricans coming to the mainland. As the community grew, the importance of the agency decreased, and its role in any case was always complicated by its affiliation with the island government. A number of private agencies now perform many of its former functions. Aspira is still the most important and most successful of these; in addition to its bilingual-teaching campaign, it seeks out talented Puerto Rican children, counsels them, and helps find financial assistance to enable them to finish high school and go on to college. Aspira clubs exist in most of the elementary and high schools of the city. Aspira also plays a significant role in the development of local and national policies and programs to improve educational opportunities for Puerto Rican students.

The Puerto Rican Teachers Association represents Puerto Rican teachers and acts as an advocate for Puerto Rican interests within the school system by working to increase the number of Puerto Ricans in teaching and supervisory positions and to promote bilingual education. The United Bronx Parents performs a similar function on a neighborhood level. Membership is open to all parents, but the organization is most active in neighborhoods with large Puerto Rican and black populations; its founder and director is Evelina Antonetti.

The Puerto Rican Forum is another citywide, now nationwide, agency of long standing, with a broader scope than the others; it looks to the social, political, and business interests of the Puerto Ricans and represents the community on local and national issues. The major banks of Puerto Rico have more than 20 offices in the city. Only 2 percent of the Puerto Ricans owned their own business in New York in 1970 as compared with 5 percent among the general population, and almost all of those were small, family enterprises. The many Puerto Rican–run *bodegas* (neighborhood grocery stores), small cafeterias, and restaurants reflect an enterprising spirit. They are represented by the National Puerto Rican Business and Marketing Association, which provides technical assistance for the establishment and development of small businesses.

The Puerto Rican Family Institute, a citywide agency, provides a range of services to Spanish-speaking families, particularly support services that enable those with acute domestic problems to keep their children at home. It also tries to keep Spanish-speaking youths out of trouble with the law, assists new arrivals, maintains a mental-health clinic, and provides technical assistance to many other agencies in the city. The Association of Puerto Rican Social Workers is an active professional organization; the Puerto Rican Legal Defense and Education Fund undertakes class-action suits involving civil rights on behalf of Puerto Ricans throughout the nation (it provided legal assistance in the Aspira case against the New York City Board of Education). The Puerto Rican Community Development Project is a citywide agency supporting smaller agencies, and inclined toward political and community action.

A large number of agencies at the neighborhood level, many of them supported by antipoverty funds, constitute both an important local political network and a link between neighborhood residents and the city government. The most powerful of these is the Hunts Point Multi-Service Center in the Bronx, a well-funded complex of community programs; it constitutes the base of political power for its influential director, Ramon Velez, a community leader who is the object of political controversy.

The Instituto de Puerto Rico is New York's major Puerto Rican cultural organization. Under the leadership of Luis Quero Chiesa it has grown from a small institute to become a citywide organization promoting cultural events, literature, and the arts. Once a year it honors individuals who have distinguished themselves in the arts or in service to the Puerto Rican community.

CULTURAL LIFE

Achievement in the arts is a signal Puerto Rican contribution to American life. Justino Diaz and Martina Arroyo have established reputations as singers and are principals with the Metropolitan Opera; José Feliciano is a nationally recognized classical and folk guitarist; José Ferrer, Rita Moreno, and Chita Rivera have had successful careers in the theater and Raul Julia, Hector Elizondo, Priscilla Lopez, and, in ballet, Lydia Abarca are rising stars. Miriam Colon, the first lady of the Puerto Rican popular theater, established the Teatro Rodante Puertorriqueño (Puerto Rican Traveling Theater) to bring the dramatic arts to the streets and neighborhoods of the cities, and is a member of the New

York State Council on the Arts. Tina Ramirez founded the Baile Hispanico of New York as a performing company and a center for the teaching of traditional, folk, and modern dance, and most recently Julio Torres founded a similar Puerto Rican dance group.

Puerto Ricans also collaborate with other Hispanic groups in furthering the careers of Hispanic artists. Two organizations for this are the Institute of Contemporary Hispanic Arts, in which the New York Puerto Rican television personality Marife Hernandez, Chief of Protocol for New York of the U.S. Mission to the United Nations in 1979, is particularly active, and the Alliance of the Latin Arts.

An organization of long standing, the Friends of Puerto Rico, supports the development of the arts among Puerto Ricans, and, through exhibitions at its gallery, encourages many young Puerto Rican artists. In the graphic arts, El Museo del Barrio (The Neighborhood Museum) was established in 1969 as a people's museum to familiarize the community with the creative artists among them and to provide workshops and training for both children and adults in East Harlem. The Taller Boricua (Puerto Rican Studio) is another East Harlem center for Puerto Rican painters; its foremost member is Rafael Tufiño. The Teatro Intar was established by Max Ferra to encourage Puerto Rican and other Hispanic playwrights. Young poets and writers publish in the large number of magazines in Spanish and English that have been launched in recent years.

Sports have provided an avenue to success for many immigrant groups, and the Puerto Ricans are no exception. The most notable of the Puerto Rican athletes was Roberto Clemente. A national hero for his outstanding record as a professional baseball player and for his community activities, he died in a plane crash while bringing relief supplies to the earthquake victims of Nicaragua in 1973.

The direction the lives of the second generation take can well change the character of the Puerto Rican community on the mainland. They are already numerous—over half a million—but still extremely young (the median age is just under ten years). Their performance in school is much better, and their socioeconomic status when they reach adulthood will probably be higher than that of their parents. Most of them have grown up in poverty, and they are both street-wise and worldly-wise. They call themselves Neorican or Nuyorican or Rican, and cope more aggressively than their parents did with hardships and discrimination, as evidenced by the founding of the activist Young Lords party in the 1960s and the militant student demonstrations that resulted in the Puerto Rican studies programs in colleges and universities. This activism can also take violent forms—gangs such as the Ghetto Brothers and the Savage Skulls, crime, and drug abuse—or be channeled into political movements for Puerto Rican independence or for the liberation of the Third World peoples.

The Puerto Ricans arrive as immigrants who are at the same time citizens. Despite the initial advantage of citizenship they face poverty and discrimination that leaves them an underprivileged minority. Their condition in the future will be affected to some extent by whether the home island remains a commonwealth, becomes a state, or attains independence. It remains to be seen whether they will be successful in maintaining their language and culture in the United States in the face of the ambiguities of color, the lack of cohesion in their religious life, and the intricacies of their relationships with blacks and with other Hispanic groups.

Bibliography

A readily available short history of Puerto Rico and the Puerto Ricans is Kal Wagenheim, *Puerto Rico: A Profile* (New York, 1972). Federico Ribes Tovar has compiled the *Enciclopedia Puertorriqueña Ilustrada*, 3 vols. (New York, 1970), a good source in both Spanish and English for information on a wide variety of persons, events, and achievements in Puerto Rico and on the mainland. It is a hastily assembled, popular work, but is the one source for handy reference. Paquita Vivo, ed., *The Puerto Ricans: An Annotated Bibliography* (New York, 1973), is the most complete and up-to-date annotated bibliography. It includes Spanish and English titles, but the annotations are all in English. For the cultural background of Puerto Ricans, Julian Steward et al., *The People of Puerto Rico* (Champain-Urbana, Ill., 1956), a study of four distinct areas and of the top 400 families of the island, though somewhat dated, is still the best anthropological study. Federico Ribes Tovar, *Albizu Campos: Puerto Rican Revolutionary* (New York, 1971), is a conveniently available biography in English of Albizu Campos, the hero of the independence movement on the island.

A comprehensive description of Puerto Rican migration and life on the mainland can be found in Joseph P. Fitzpatrick, S.J., *Puerto Rican Americans: The Meaning of Migration to the Mainland* (Englewood Cliffs, N.J., 1971). Elena Padilla, *Up from Puerto Rico* (New York, 1958), is an anthropological study of a Puerto Rican neighborhood in New York City. Oscar Lewis, *La Vida: A Puerto Rican Family in the Culture of Poverty—San Juan and New York* (New York, 1966), is rich in detail on the daily life of people in the culture of poverty, but it ought to be used in conjunction with other books on the Puerto Rican family. Lloyd H. Rogler, *Migrant in the City: The Life of a Puerto Rican Action Group* (New York, 1972), is a study of a Puerto Rican community in a large eastern city as seen through the experience of a community-action organization.

The United States Commission on Human Rights report, *Puerto Ricans in the Continental United States: An Uncertain Future* (Washington, D.C., 1976), provides abundant and up-to-date information on Puerto Ricans on the mainland, especially employment and education. Francesco Cordasco and Eugene Bucchioni, eds., *The Puerto Rican Experience: A Sociological Sourcebook* (Totowa, N.J., 1973), presents many points of view on Puerto Rican background, migration, and education.

JOSEPH P. FITZPATRICK

PUNJABIS: *see* EAST INDIANS; PAKISTANIS

PUSHTUNS: *see* AFGHANS

PUYALLUPS: *see* AMERICAN INDIANS

Q

QATABANIANS: *see* ARABS

QUAPAWS: *see* AMERICAN INDIANS

QUECHANS (Yumas): *see* AMERICAN INDIANS

R

RACE

The term race, long highly controversial, remains so today. As used by geneticists, it refers to a group whose gene frequencies differ from those of other groups in the human species. The number of distinct races that can be distinguished by this criterion depends upon the particular genetic trait under investigation. Thus there is no single authoritative or scientific answer to the question of what are the races of mankind.

Beyond the narrow genetic usage, the concept of race has been employed in a variety of ways. The belief that mankind is divided into several biologically distinct races was widely held in the 19th and early 20th centuries, as was the belief that some races are innately superior, some innately inferior. The racist literature of that era contained many ambiguities, distortions, and contradictions. In recent decades such theories have been discredited, although some investigators still advance genetic explanations of differences among human groups that others explain in cultural and environmental terms.

Most anthropologists today reserve the term race for the three broad, physically distinctive divisions of mankind: the Caucasoid or Indo-European, the Mongoloid, and the Negroid. These conventional categories, however, do not include all the peoples of the world, and the range of variation within them is enormous. Each contains innumerable ethnic groups arising from the intersecting influence of nationality, religion, tribe, language, and region. In this usage, race is a social classification of the most general, physically different categories of humans, regardless of the cultural forms of nation, religion, or language.

In the past the U.S. Census has always included a question about race. Whites were normally distinguished from nonwhites, and the latter were divided into the categories of Negro, American Indian, Chinese, and Japanese. The term race did not appear in the official form for the 1980 Census. However, respondents were asked an open-ended question about their ancestry, "What is this person's ancestry?" and, "Is this person of Spanish/Hispanic origin or descent?" In addition, they were asked, "Is this person ———?" with 15 possible responses: White, Black or Negro, Japanese, Chinese, Filipino, Korean, Vietnamese, American Indian, Asian Indian, Hawaiian, Guamanian, Samoan, Eskimo, Aleut, Other. If the answer was American Indian, the name of the tribe was requested; if Other, the respondent was asked to specify. These categories are presumably different from ancestry or descent, but what the U.S. Bureau of the Census means by them or how they will be analyzed is uncertain.

For further discussion of the concepts of race and racism, *see* American Identity and Americanization; Concepts of Ethnicity; Prejudice; Prejudice and Discrimination, History of. *See also* Appendix I and Appendix II.

RAPPAHANNOCKS: *see* American Indians

RELIGION

In a world of cultural diversity, distinctiveness of faith and distinctiveness of people provide major historical foundations for human communities. Religion becomes a major and consequential reason for the development of ethnicity. The Armenian Orthodox, the Chinese Buddhists, the Finnish Lutherans, the German Jews, the New England Congregationalists, the Pakistani Muslims, the Scottish Presbyterians, the Sephardic Jews, the Southern Baptists, the Spanish-speaking Catholics, and the Utah Mormons are only a few of the groups in which ethnicity and religion are inextricably linked.

Religion reveals itself in a multitude of cults, sects, denominations, and churches. Ethnicity develops from the history and migration of culturally differentiated races, nations, and tribes, not to mention the unique social experiences of religious creeds. Religion and ethnicity are in many ways different and separate, yet both play an important role in all diverse societies.

The fact that ethnicity may often be religious and that religion itself may often be ethnic emphasizes their mutuality. Fifty years ago H. Richard Niebuhr wrote, "Perhaps religion is as often responsible for ethnic character as the latter is responsible for the faith." Over time, and in the course of cultural contact and migrations, the social realities of distinctive faiths and distinctive peoples emerge, overlap, and rearrange themselves, sometimes with altered labels and changing beliefs, sometimes with extraordinary persistence.

Ethnicity and religion are related in many ways. No matter how they are defined, on whatever social foundation, ethnic groups possess their own significant elements of distinctive religious character. In the earliest discussions of "ethnic peoples," as in those assembled by the *Oxford English Dictionary*, the idea of ethnicity was limited to behavior religiously different from the prevailing Christianity of Great Britain, or more broadly, Western Europe. In more modern and more neutral definitions, the idea of ethnicity is tied to a variety of cultural backgrounds, both familiar and exotic and of both historical and contemporary importance.

Similarly, in the evolution of intergroup relations, the social definitions of religious people all suggest a distinctiveness of culture and society that goes beyond the interpretations of spirituality, otherworldliness, and the divine. Distinctive faiths provide the foundation of ethnicity just as distinctive peoples offer an endowment of religious and spiritual individuality. The explanation of these two patterns lies in the cultural diversity of the larger world, the separation of historical experience in the greater society and polity in which such distinctiveness of faith or people is seen.

The religious component of ethnicity varies, however, from situation to situation and from group to group. Ethnicity may find its major foundation in religion and in essentially religious experiences, as among the Jews in diaspora, the Hutterites, the Amish, and the Mormons. For many in such groups, religion and religious culture provide the way of life and the raison

d'être of ethnicity. Alternatively, a particular ethnic group may be grounded in a relatively unique religion, but one that has a more marked association with a distinct territory or homeland, a particular language, or an evolving sense of nationality—for example, the Dutch Reformed, the Greek Orthodox, the Church of England, the Serbian Orthodox, and the Scottish Presbyterians.

More commonly, ethnicity may rest on a shared, larger religion, which itself is differentiated by numerous nationality backgrounds, languages, and even racial separations. Familiar examples include the French Canadians, Irish, Poles, Italians, Mexicans, Lithuanians, and Puerto Ricans, all within the Roman Catholic world; the Danes, Finns, Germans, Norwegians, and Swedes, among Lutherans; the German, Spanish, Russian, and Israeli backgrounds among Jews; the racial differences among black and white Southern Baptists; and the numerous tribal, sectarian, and national variations found among all of the world religions—within Islam, Buddhism, Hinduism, Judaism, Catholicism, Eastern Orthodoxy, and Protestantism. Eastern Catholicism, especially, suggests a wide array of different ethnoreligious groupings.

Finally, and least frequently, ethnicity (particularly to outsiders) may refer only minimally or marginally to any kind of distinctive religious characteristics. With the Romany people or Gypsies, and with the numerous American Indian groups, ethnicity and ethnic identity may relate more to a way of life than to a theology. At this point of the spectrum, one can even argue that ethnicity itself becomes a religion, that religious *ethos* and cultural *ethnos* are blended into a singular and cosmic world view.

In all these instances, a distinctive religious character is a greater or lesser part of a particular ethnic identity. Even in those frequent situations where the religion is known to be shared with other and differing ethnic groups, peoples develop distinctive religious practices over time. The particularities of language and history play important roles in these differentiations. By virtue of their unique cultural ethos, all ethnic peoples put their own stamps of originality on religion—in dealing with the supernatural and the unknown, and in their relation to the cosmos. Ethnic groups—peoples who are historically differentiated, culturally distinctive, and constituent elements of the larger social system—develop their own expressions and interpretations of religious matters.

On the other hand, the ethnic component of religion itself varies. All religions are not necessarily ethnic, for they may not represent constituent units within a larger society. Thus, religions are not ethnic when they are construed and represented as forces larger than society, as pannational and ecumenical expressions of humanity, as Islamic or Roman Catholic perspectives may be seen at times from the theological bases of Mecca and the Vatican, or as the Bahai and the Quakers strive to signify. Further, religions are not ethnic when they are new social movements confined to the contemporary generation of joiners and believers. Religion becomes ethnic only with the dimensions of historical memory and subsocietal scale. Illustrations abound in the American experience.

As one of the major social foundations of history and the idea of an ethnic people, religion serves in three specific ways: as a force for delimiting or defining ethnic boundaries; as a factor in narrowing or separating a traditional sense of ethnicity; and as a means of enlarging or expanding upon formerly disparate ethnic boundaries and identities. All three forms of change—of equating with ethnicity, of disengaging centrifugally, and of converging centripetally—are useful in describing the circumstances of the diverse faiths and peoples of the United States.

The equation of religion with ethnicity has been common, particularly in backgrounds with a history or a present of societal competition and conflict. Peoples such as the Irish Catholics, the Jews, the French Canadians, and the Armenian and Greek Orthodox brought the fusion of religion and ethnicity with them as immigrants to America. Their respective historical encounters with English Protestants, gentile nations, English-speaking Canadians, and Turkish Muslims facilitated these cultural equations. Other groups—the Mormons, the Jehovah's Witnesses, and the white and black Baptists of the South—created their ethnic religions on American soil. In these cases, religion has contributed to the definition of ethnic boundaries quite specifically.

Ethnic and religious disengagement as a centrifugal pattern of culture is best seen in schisms and sectarian developments. Denominationalism may be both religious and ethnic, if the splitting away persists as a separate culture over generations. Internal conflict and polarization within a cultural entity may arise because of some larger reinterpretation of basic sentiment or creed, or, just as likely, because of the constraints of modernism and political and economic adaptations. Variations on the older themes of culture helped to bring about the Reform movement in Judaism, the Polish National Catholic Church, and the numerous regional and sectarian developments within the larger world of Anglo-Saxon Protestantism.

But the most familiar, the most discussed, and the most celebrated changes of diversity in American ethnicities and religions belong to the pattern of centripetal convergence. In the expansion and enlargement of former pasts, one recognizes the various myths and interpretations of the melting pot, of assimilation, and of the anticipated directions of culture in the United States. Will Herberg's label, "the American Way of Life," in the 1950s, described a vision of an overarching Americanism filtered through one of three major American faiths: Protestantism, Catholicism, and Judaism. Based on presumed increases in marriage and close associations across ethnic lines but within religious denominators (the implications of the "triple melting pot" imagery of the sociologist Ruby Jo Reeves Kennedy), Herberg's thesis argued for a tripartite culture in broad and sweeping tones. The Herberg viewpoint was criticized for its neglect of secularism, of racial ethnicity, of alternative religious cultures, of economic differences and class situations, of empirical data, and above all, of the diversity of ethnic experiences across the breadth of the United States.

The social expansion of former ethnicities and disparate religions may, for some perspectives, also assume a new cultural identity in the shape of the melting pot, a total and singular synthesis of past cultures, in terms not unlike those presented by the author Israel Zangwill in his famous play *The Melting Pot* of 1908. A

number of treatments of this possibility emphasize an "overarching Americanism" in precisely the historical and unique symbolisms of ethnicity itself.

Centripetal convergence of past ancestries takes place, for example, at least implicitly, in Robert Bellah's conceptualization of civil religion, which does not necessarily replace historical affiliations but does exist along side of them. As a celebration of American ways, the idea of a civil religion may have all the provisions of more conventional faiths (including the idea of prophecy) and still represent a kind of panethnicity, at least in the context of the United States.

THE ETHNIC SIDE OF RELIGION

Characteristics of ethnicity, as a concept, are often taken for granted and remain submerged. But they are very prominent in the history of the United States, not only for the wide array of different groups and backgrounds, but also for both dominant and minority religions, native and immigrant peoples, and groups large and small. The dimensions of ethnicity that apply readily to religious groups are social categories (1) with a historical identification; (2) with a conception of cultural and social distinctiveness; (3) that are component units within a broader system of social relations; (4) that are larger than kinship or locality groups; (5) that have different meanings both in different social settings and for different individuals; and (6) that are emblematic—their names have symbolic meaning both for members and for analysts.

All six of these characteristics refer quite essentially to the group qualities of religion *qua* ethnicity. The first two points, on historical origins and distinctiveness, represent the idea of culture inherent in the meaning of ethnicity—a culture that develops from sources and referents in physical and racial attributes, in regional separation, in tribal and national consciousness, in linguistic differentiation, and in the religious affiliation that combines with any or all of these.

Categories three and four, pertaining to component units and spheres of interaction, show the relevance of structure in ethnicity, a structure vital for the persistence of religious bodies. The last two characteristics, on meanings and emblems, are created by ingroups and outgroups. They refer to belonging and identity, to sources of pride as well as to matters of prejudice, to the diversity of interpretations among those who share the same religious background, and to the divergent perceptions offered by observers or by those who are of different cultural experiences. These six dimensions bear a strong resemblance to the social implications of religion.

The past-oriented identification and the emphasis on origins are matters of history, and these are as applicable to the English Protestants, Dutch Calvinists, and French Catholics in early and colonial America as they are to the French Huguenots, Sephardic Jews, and the many different American Indian groups. In the social experience of all these peoples, we find the acknowledgment of a specific religious culture and group ancestry. When ethnicity thrives in intergroup contact, the group identity is projected both to the present and to the future. The past becomes a guide for contemporary and anticipated group life, the link between generations, from grandparents to grandchildren.

Further, ethnic origins, like religious myths, are putative and presumed. In the context of origins and historical identification religion takes on clear ethnic overtones during periods of conflict, and ethnicity assumes religious proportions in the same way. In sustained opposition, peoples who perceive different origins presume different gods, just as they who worship in different faiths may suppose different origins.

Catholics and Protestants in Ireland, for example, write different histories, create different religious myths, and develop different ethnic origins. Their shared physical, geographic, and national background becomes ethnicized by the force of religion, and these ethnic religions have become as much a part of American social history as they are tragically a part of contemporary Ulster. Similarly, different races or nations who share the same religion may develop their own distinctive beliefs in their myths and origins. Most blacks and whites in the history of the American South are Christian—Protestant, and mainly Baptist—but many have subscribed over time to different gospel beginnings. Their shared regional and religious culture is likewise ethnicized by the force of race, and whites and blacks have created their different biblical explanations of their respective dilemmas and status: who they are, what they are, and whence they came. Their shared religion provides different prophecies as well, with varying emphases from Moses and the Old Testament to Jesus and the New Testament.

The emphasis of the people's history and the group's origin gives ethnic meaning to the religion's collective memory and group mind. The allegory of the westward trek and the regional isolation of Utah and the Promised Land for Mormonism, the imagery of the Underground Railroad during black slavery, the persisting symbolism of diaspora and collective persecution for Armenians, Jews, and Assyrians, and the evolution of centuries of national confrontation between English-speaking Protestants and French-speaking Catholics in Canada all offer the special history that becomes a part of the ethnic religion.

The most familiar characteristics of religion and ethnicity, however, are the more visible and evident dimensions of culturally and socially distinctive behavior. Observers of American diversity who identified the English as sharers of the Protestant ethic, the Scots as thrifty Calvinists, the Irish as Romanists with large families, the Mormons as polygamists, and the Jews as peculiar in matters of worship and food, described what seemed to them some of the more salient aspects of ethnic religion.

While the descriptions of ethnic religion and corresponding cultural behavior may be made for all distinctive faiths in diverse societies, certain portraits stand out more graphically than others. These are the ethnic and religious styles of the minority and subordinate peoples—groups marked by smaller size, lower status, and less power. The religious beliefs, values, and rituals of the different immigrant populations, for example, contrast strikingly with the faiths represented among the more numerous, higher status, native-born white Americans.

Despite the racism and xenophobia of anti-Catholicism, anti-Semitism, and anti-Asian movements, and the efforts to restrict immigration in the 19th and 20th

centuries, the diversity of America has flourished and ethnic behavior as religious distinctiveness has many illustrations. The Italian *festa* for a patron saint, the Jewish *bar mitzvah*, the Irish wake, the Methodist church supper and strawberry festival, the music of black gospel, the Baptist tent revival, and the Peyotism of American Indians are only a few of the better-known examples of religion with a specifically ethnic cast. Immigration from abroad, and the migration and cultural contact of groups within America, have produced numerous instances of cultural behavior in religion which is gratifyingly familiar to the members and socially different to everybody else.

On the other hand, not all culturally distinctive behavior in religion is necessarily ethnic. Religious cults and sects, as opposed to the established denominations and churches, arise and develop their own unique rituals and assemblages to represent their values and beliefs. These often represent social movements, of a time-span of one generation. If the cults and sects persist over time, transcending generations from grandparents to grandchildren and incorporating an ethos with which they measure the world and history, they then provide their members with a sense of distinctive peoplehood as well as a quality of distinctive faith. This would yield the sentiments of ethnic religion, as the history of persecuted Quakers, Hutterites, Amish, and Mormons has shown.

Ethnic religion is clearly understood and socially meaningful in some kind of system of diversity, whether a polyglot empire, a multicultural state society, or a heterogeneous village or town. If the setting is culturally homogeneous, and if all the residents perceive that they share the same physical and racial characteristics, believe in the same divinity, speak the same language, and presume the same history and cultural origin, then ethnicity as a concept is irrelevant and inappropriate. Unless there is diversity, there is no consciousness of kind, no sensed uniformity of race, religion, speech, and history; these are all simply matters of natural existence. Under conditions of homogeneity, ethnicity and religion become synonymous with everything.

This is the key to the third characteristic, and it provides an aspect of pluralism: that the religious and ethnic groups are component units within some larger arrangement of social relations. Religion as ethnicity becomes a focus of diversity itself: numerous faiths, multiple affiliations, and a mosaic of religious backgrounds and organizations. In government and politics the American ethos is not based on formal religious and ethnic divisions, but the society has generally enhanced many local and informal instances of historic cultural pluralism. Separation of church and state has facilitated the familiar laissez-faire atmosphere of religious expression. There are numerous subcultures and subsocieties across America—in the private and public schools, in the growth of urban neighborhoods, in the rural and regional enclaves, in the voluntary associations, and in the economic system that has managed to exploit as well as to encourage ethnic and religious cohesion. The Chicano movement among agricultural workers in California and the Southwest is but the most recent familiar example in American labor history: strikes of the Spanish-speaking laborers marching under a banner of the Virgin Mary.

That ethnicity is more extensive than mere kinship and specific locality highlights the fact that ethnic religion transcends face-to-face interaction among related members. This feeling of enlarged group identity lies behind the history and sociology of diaspora, collective exile, and migration. Population movements both voluntary and involuntary, permanent and temporary, do not lead inevitably to total assimilation, to the loss and disappearance of a group's culture and religion. They are more likely to lead to evolution and the adaptation to new environments and experiences. In some instances, dislocation may even lead to increased religious activity, as illustrated by the Kalmyks, the only Mongolian Buddhists in the United States, who settled in New Jersey and Pennsylvania during the 1950s.

Persistence is most evident in the classic examples of trading peoples and in the collective situations of dispersed emigrants—the Romany people; the enduring religions of the Greeks, the Jews, and the Armenians; the networks of overseas Chinese and Irish. But it applies as well to peoples without a history or tradition of migration. Churches and religious organizations established in the United States were the meeting places and rallying points for various social needs. Wanderers, strangers, and individual migrants could reestablish connections and gain mutual aid through the agencies of ethnic religion. Kinship lines and locality relationships might be broken and changed, but knowledge of the language, familiarity with the religion, and the mention of former places could resurrect and transplant old ties or stimulate and create new ones. An ethnic consciousness would thereby develop around the social religion of Slovaks, Poles, Hungarians, Czechs, and many other peoples with little experience in dislocation.

The same pattern of transcended kinship is seen in ethnicity at the different levels of social and economic status. American Indian groups, evacuated and displaced from ancestral lands, and Afro-Americans, enslaved and divested of territory and relationships, developed similar ethnic attachments; there was an "interdependence of fate" among those who shared the same tragedies and persecutions. The pattern may be clearest in religion. In the expressions of ethnicity and the distinctiveness of a culture and history in the Peyote and Ghost Dance movements among Indians, and in the cultic, sectarian, and denominational organizations among black Christians, black Muslims, and black Jews, a strong sense of peoplehood overrides the accidents of kinship and location. Transcended kinship extends as well to the groups of higher status—for example, to the more affluent and leisured travel of ethnically dominant migrants. The diaries and memoirs of English travelers and colonists, which describe the various lands of British settlement and colonization, show their attachments to the residents who still reflect some of the shared values and symbols of Mother England.

The study of ethnicity abroad, of migrants in diaspora, is linked to this characteristic which goes beyond ascription, relation by birth, and locality of origin. Transcended kinship helps to account for the various movements of ethnic identity, of nationalism, of neonationalism, and of religious expression. These ethnic bonds are shared by individuals who remember that they once were a nation, who want to be a nation again,

or who find that, for the first time, they comprise a distinctive people, one with unique historical vision and future outlook. Such networks embrace all generations and ages, from grandparents to grandchildren, both women and men, all relevant occupational roles and necessities, and the different social classes and status backgrounds.

Social change and the vicissitudes of society, however, do account for the fact that ethnic religions themselves possess their own degree of diversity, a phenomenon that is intraethnic and within the larger consciousness of kind. Within a given background, there may be different meanings and interpretations of what it is to be a member. The influence of economic and other social forces, the variations of the environment, and the individual personality all contribute to this characteristic.

Accordingly, different denominations and sects develop over time within a larger religious body, as within Protestantism; differentiation by dialect or region or theology occurs within Judaism; regionalism influences the largely metaphorical Anglo-Saxon Protestant, with variations in New England, the South, the Middle West, and Appalachia; schismatic possibilities emerge, as in the Polish National Catholic Church or Armenian Protestantism; and, above all, contrasts evolve within the same ethnicity but in different societies as a direct result of enduring migration and settlement. The complexity within inhibits unwarranted generalizations and unqualified ethnic stereotypes.

This dynamic of ethnic religion helps to account for the social and cultural differences, not only, say, between the Irish Catholics in the Republic of Ireland and those in Ulster, England, Australia, and the United States, but also among the American Irish historically typed as the "lace curtain" middle class or as the "shanty" lower class in Boston, Chicago, or San Francisco, who were politically conservative, economically moderate, or ideologically radical. The judgments of cultural determinism, as expressed at times in racism, nativism, and ethnocentrism, invariably ignore the sociological labyrinths of ethnic life.

Lastly, the group characteristic of ethnic religion is found in the emblematic nature of cultural symbolism, which includes the levels of meaning and the constructions of ethnicity made both by the members themselves and by outsiders. Commonly, emblems are projected by outsiders, often in the form of slurs and epithets, as stereotypes and generalizations. The view of the American Indian in the United States as uncivilized or as heathen savage, the perspective of the Jew as Shylock or as Old Testament, and the interpretation of the black American as Sambo or as primitive—these were matched by emblems attributed to all migrant peoples with their own histories and ways of life.

The cross, the icon, the crescent, and the star of David are all well-known emblems of ethnic religion in mixed societies, but symbolism ranges from the familiar to the more subtle in different contexts. Such symbolism relates to gestures and body language, food and abstinence, dialect and code words, and the religious networks of the sacred and the profane. The group quality of ethnicity is communicated through all aspects of social behavior. Religious myths and ethnic origins receive concrete expression in emblems and symbolism.

These characteristics of ethnicity, particularly for the religious minority, are subject to stresses and strains in the larger society where the dominant religion is often fused with the idea and ethos of universalism and the mainstream. Religious conflict especially can be seen as the clash of symbols, of identities, of inequalities and insularities, and of cultural pasts.

The religious culture of a people, as a distinct faith, may well yield and be assimilated into some other entity—perhaps the dominant religion, perhaps another but historically different culture, and perhaps even some new synthesis. On the other hand, the religion of the ethnic people may persist despite the pressures, and different kinds of societal pluralism may emerge over time.

THE RELIGIOUS SIDE OF ETHNICITY

Ethnicity can be said to be "religious" when its social roles and purposes resemble those of a distinctive faith. Just as several points highlight the social meaning of ethnicity, so there are some basic dimensions to the larger social meaning of religion.

A number of different secular results adhere to all religions. The functions religion serves relate to the most fundamental human concerns—grief, knowledge, social control, prophecy, maturation, and identity. All religions offer systems of coping, means of support, of comfort, and of reconciliation in hard times. In moments of grief, religious association helps to minimize the tragedies and defeats and anxieties of life through emotional assistance. Religion provides a frame of reference, a perspective with which one can organize knowledge, history, and information. The teachings of religion, through cult and ceremony, help to place the past and present in a concrete and meaningful philosophy. Religion introduces a system of social control, by legitimating specific values, norms, and ethics. Socialization of individuals into proper and acceptable social behavior, as well as the handling of deviance through the expiation of guilt, are the provinces of such social control.

Prophecy offers the seeds of change, of reform, and of protest. Prophecy allows for the hope of renewal, a source of vitality in all established faiths. Finally, maturation and identity are more critical for the individual than for the group. Maturation refers to the ability of religion to aid in individual growth, through rites of passage and the age-linked cycles of human development. And identity, particularly important in culturally diverse societies, is enhanced by a religion's social characteristics. The individual receives a group identity through religion, which connects the past to the present and to the future in a changing world. These concerns are all associated with otherworldly content, yet are also connected by ethnic peoples in secular contexts.

The relevance of ethnicity for the handling of grief and uncertainty, given the vicissitudes of life and the upheavals of migration, provides a critical theme. In the American experience alone, thousands of mutual-aid societies and ethnic associations appeared, not merely to cope with specifically ceremonial needs, but to provide communal support and assistance during times of death, illness, accidents, unemployment, and loss of family. Burial societies, credit unions, savings and loan associations, and social insurance programs, were products of the different ethnic communities settled throughout the United States.

The Czech Roman Catholic Benevolent Union of Chicago, the many Jewish *landsmanshaftn* (fraternal associations), and even some labor unions such as the organization of Chicano agricultural workers under César Chávez illustrate this function of ethnicity as religion. Consider the symbolism of the celebration of the Mass in Spanish in the California fields during the famous grape strike of Mexican workers in the 1960s, with Robert Kennedy in supporting attendance: the symbolism was as ethnic as it was religious, as representative of the movement of a distinctive people as of a distinctive faith. Martin Luther King's universalistic appeals to the poorer segments of American labor were a counterpart to his inspired religious ethnicity; the symbolism of black America was indisputable in his treatment of the old "Go Tell It on the Mountain" and of the new "We Shall Overcome." Ethnicity has the potential for coping with the deprivations of poverty, with the uncertainties and inequities of the human condition.

Grief is managed ethnically in a number of other ways. Nationalism sometimes provides goals and solutions to a people's sense of grief and anxiety. The nationalism of some Puerto Ricans, black Muslims, and French Canadians corresponds broadly in this regard with the ethnic movements of minorities throughout the world.

On a more private level, death and mourning may also evoke ethnically distinctive behavior. The more secular side of the Irish wake, for example, and the jazz band funerals among blacks in New Orleans, are culturally distinctive in ethnic as well as religious terms. Both traditions dramatically convey the culture of everyday life in addition to the culture of faith. Funerals often represent the collective sentiment of a people, and in times of competition and intense conflict a funeral demonstration can become an expression of solidarity as well as a means of sustaining morale in the face of alienation; a funeral can turn into an ethnic statement.

The place of grief in ethnicity, however, is foremost and strongest in collective memory. In secular as well as in religious terms the persecution, oppression, and affliction of a people may persist for generations. Often an integrated part of a group culture and linked to historical origins in the group mind, the collective memory of persecution is the essence of grief, and there are many responses to it. The genocide suffered by Jews, Armenians, Assyrians, and others is a critical element in their ethnic heritage.

Over time, certain words develop symbolic meaning for the ethnicity of past and present cultures. Memories of oppression are invoked by the mention of Culloden for the Scots, and of Cromwell for the Irish; by the names of Dachau, Auschwitz, and Buchenwald for the Jews, the Gypsies, the Poles, and the Jehovah's Witnesses; by the mention of Wounded Knee for the Sioux, and of the Trail of Tears for the Cherokee; and by the symbolism of Selma and Attica for black Americans.

Ethnicity has the potential to offer consolation, support, and a semblance of meaning in dealing with tragedy and misfortune. The connection with knowledge and philosophy is evident. Ethnicity provides anchors and foundations for its members. Ambiguities and conflicts in human opinions may be resolved in part through the perspective of ethnic scholarship. The history of the people, despite continuing changes and rein-terpretations, is seen as a constant in the flux of the larger world.

On a smaller scale, the persisting ethnic subcultures and substructures manage to extend the knowledge and symbolism of their own experiences and histories, just as religions do. Both the formal ethnic schools, family ties, and associational attachments and the more informal networks and relationships in the community impart information and values. The socialization or acculturation of an individual to a world view sensitizes the white Southerner to the persona of Robert E. Lee, the Albanian to Scanderbeg, the Pole to Thaddeus Kosciuszko, the Irishman to Eamon de Valera, and the Hungarian to Louis Kossuth. As with different religions, world views vary with a people's history.

Ethnicity resembles religion in social control, as well, by providing a kind of morality for people. Divisive as most social parameters are in mixed societies, group boundaries imply the existence of moral codes. In religious terms, the ethical system is linked to a theology of right and wrong and to a complex understanding of variant conditions of sinfulness. In ethnic terms, the moral code lies behind the everyday life of what a people should do. Seldom are such codes consciously and deliberately enunciated. More typically, there are simply presumed understandings. Language, gestures, food, dress, and daily civility, as well as the more profound behaviors in kinship, politics, and group loyalties, comprise the substance of ethnic morality.

The presence of group boundaries in ethnicity and religion suggests a social order, more or less circumscribed. The well-known characteristics of these boundaries appear as territorial ones, membership lines drawn around some turf, some neighborhood, or some larger portion of the earth; and as familial ones, ascriptive and endogamous affiliations. Since ethnicity is a social phenomenon that transcends the accidents of place and birth, the social order is able to do so likewise. The moral code may derive a substantial part of its strength from place and birth, but the dynamics of ethnicity also foster change and the ultimate incorporation of other places and other peoples.

Ethnic boundaries (and corresponding social control) range from the close and coherent structures of immigrant generations, of separated ethnoreligious communities, and often of the minorities most excluded from the life of the larger society, all the way to the obscure borders of shifting American neighborhoods. As John Higham has pointed out, ethnic boundaries are often "vague, fluid, and indeterminate."

Despite the complexity, the function of social control in ethnicity is evident—in, for example, the daily existence of the poor in inner-city Chicago, divided as to their black, Mexican, Puerto Rican, and Italian backgrounds. A counterpart in class terms appears in the ethnically differentiated middle-class and upper-class worlds of voluntary associations, as in the parallel ways of life of the wealthy Jews, Irish Catholics, and Anglo-Saxon Protestants, who reside in contemporary West Hartford, Connecticut.

For the oppressed and the powerless, however, prophecy closely resembles religious life. The fervor of nationalism with its strong spiritual overtones emphasizes the capability of renewal, of protest, and of change. Charismatic authorities and nationalist leaders are often the principal agents of those communication

networks that are the foundations of a thriving ethnicity. Prophetic leaders may have considerably different goals, but similar visions of hope and of improvement, whether the philosophies are revolutionary, secessionist, or pluralist.

In the United States, prophecy as a meaningful function of ethnicity has been most prevalent among the poor—the American Indians, the blacks, the regionally isolated and impoverished whites of the South and of Appalachia. Out of these cultures stem many revivalist, messianic, millennial, and nativist movements. Even new peoples, such as the tri-racial isolates, have historical associations with prophetic ethnicity; these outcasts born of mixed marriages and matings among individuals of white, black, and Indian backgrounds have formed their own sense of distinctive ethnicity. (See Tri-Racial Isolates.) Prophecy arose from the experience of rejection and social separation. Specific groups came to be known in the 19th and 20th centuries as the Ben Ishmaels, the Delaware Moors, and the Jackson Whites. America's half-castes and outcasts were those people who were not integrated into the already existing ethnic groups.

Maturation and identity both pertain to individual growth, personal development, and a sense of belonging. The stages of maturation in religion are often formal and ritualized, encompassing rites of passage from birth to death. In ethnicity, such personal growth rests more on the informal and the vernacular. The socialization of an individual into an ethnic culture incorporates many nuances of membership—an appreciation of the appropriate history, heritage, language, and customs. Maturation involves both emotional and cognitive phases, and assures the security of belonging and group identity.

We must also confront the problems of excess. Just as every religion is at times a source of deep conflict, so is ethnicity. For the role that each plays in the management of grief, for example, there is the corresponding risk of too much dependence on faith and on historic culture, too little examination of the reasons for present-day alienation, which leads to the possible atrophy of resentment; there may be little concern about social problems because of excessive orthodoxy and resignation in religion or ethnicity.

A similar disposition may characterize the provision of learning and knowledge. Excessive and exclusive attention to this function may lead to provincialism, parochialism in intergroup relations, and the possible atrophy of inquiry. The corresponding excess of social control suggests still more problems within the group boundaries of ethnicity and religion: the possible exaggeration of one's own social world, the excess of rewards and punishments in the moral code, and the atrophy of tradition itself.

The prophetic role may become singularly inordinate, preceding conflict and chaos, and this may bring about an atrophy of hope for the religious and ethnic people involved. The idea of maturation may run the risk of extraordinary dependence on one's own rites of passage and informal associations, interpreted perhaps as an atrophy of individuality. And identity, viewed as attachments to distinctive faith and distinctive people, can relate to an atrophy of tolerance.

The social assets and liabilities of religion and ethnicity within the culturally heterogeneous world represent the gamut of civilization. Religion resembles ethnicity when it shares the basic characteristics of the ethnic group. Similarly, ethnicity approximates religion when it fulfills the social provisions of faiths and denominations. In both cases, ethnicity and religion fuse the elements of pride and prejudice, delineate the promise and the dissonance of diversity, and pose as cultural and structural continuities over time. The persistence of distinctive cultures, or even the idea of such, should not necessarily emphasize a history of static uniformities. Rather, the persistence is one that accommodates to change, and the American society is a clear example of these forms of cultural genesis.

Bibliography
Rather than refer to the many specific works in the separate fields of ethnicity and religion, and to particular peoples and institutions, only those studies that relate to both subjects and that use a comparative approach are noted here. Among the most important are the classic work of H. Richard Niebuhr, *The Social Sources of Denominationalism* (New York, 1929), which treats mainly European and American Protestantism, with sensitive concern for cultural diversity; the appropriate sections on religious differences in the Yankee City study of W. Lloyd Warner and Leo Srole, *The Social Systems of American Ethnic Groups* (New Haven, Conn., 1945); the chapter on the religious life of the immigrants in Oscar Handlin, *The Uprooted* (New York, 1951); and the broad-ranging statement on the changes in American religions by Will Herberg, *Protestant, Catholic, Jew: An Essay in American Religious Sociology* (Garden City, N.Y., 1955).

Historical and sociological studies began to focus more directly on ethnoreligious diversity in the last two decades. Among the former, a case study is offered by Timothy L. Smith, "Religious Denominations as Ethnic Communities," *Church History* 35 (June 1966): 207–226; an extensive history of religious movements in the United States, with much interest in diversity, is Sydney E. Ahlstrom, *A Religious History of the American People* (New Haven, Conn., 1972); and a lengthy overview, rich in material, is provided by Timothy L. Smith, "Religion and Ethnicity in America," *American Historical Review* 83 (December 1978): 1115–1185. The use of modern conceptualizations of ethnicity raises many provocative ideas for history in the work of Harry H. Stout, "Ethnicity: The Vital Center of Religion in America," *Ethnicity* 2 (June 1975): 204–224; Martin Marty, *A Nation of Believers* (Chicago, 1976); and the collection of essays in Randall M. Miller and Thomas D. Marzik, eds., *Immigrants and Religion in Urban America* (Philadelphia, 1977).

Sociological efforts in the study of ethnicity and religion have been led by Andrew M. Greeley, *Why Can't They Be Like Us?* (New York, 1971), *The Denominational Society* (Glenview, Illinois, 1972), and *Ethnicity in the United States: A Preliminary Reconnaissance* (New York, 1974). Other relevant studies include the work of Thomas F. O'Dea, *The Sociology of Religion* (Englewood Cliffs, N.J., 1966) on the functions and social provisions of the religious community; the sections on religion in Nathan Glazer and Daniel Patrick Moynihan, *Beyond the Melting Pot: The Negroes, Puerto Ricans, Jews, Italians, and Irish of New York City*, 2d ed. (Cambridge, Mass., 1970); the empirical studies of Harold J. Abramson, *Ethnic Diversity in Catholic America* (New York, 1973); an essay on contemporary religion and culture by Robert N. Bellah, *The Broken Covenant: American Civil Religion in Time of Trial* (New York, 1975); chapter reviews on the literature of religious and ethnic diversity in John Wilson, *Religion in American Society: The Effective Presence* (Englewood Cliffs, N.J., 1978); and speculative anthropology, which raises some interesting questions in A.L. Epstein, *Ethos and Identity: Three Studies in Ethnicity* (London, 1978).

In addition to the extensive bibliographic sources that can be found in many of the above citations, more complete listings are arranged under entries on religion in *A Comprehensive Bibliography for the Study of American Minorities*, ed. Wayne Charles Miller and others, 2 vols. (New York, 1976); and under racial, national, tribal, and other cultural entries in *Social Scientific Studies of Religion: A Bibliography*, ed. Morris I. Berkowitz and J. Edmund Johnson (Pittsburgh, 1967).

HAROLD J. ABRAMSON

RESOURCES AND RESEARCH CENTERS

In the past quarter-century the civil rights movement, the establishment of various bilingual and multicultural programs, and the general increase in sensitiv-

ity to American ethnic diversity have brought many changes in the political and cultural life of the United States. These changes have spurred the growth of facilities for ethnic studies and contributed to the creation of new publications, new programs, and new centers.

A score of scholarly journals devoted to immigration history and ethnic studies not only provide a forum for current research but also report on the availability of still newer resources and research centers. The *I & N Reporter* (now the *INS Reporter*) (Washington, D.C.: Immigration and Naturalization Service) was first issued in 1952; the *International Migration Review* (Staten Island, N.Y.: Center for Migration Studies) has appeared since 1964; and the *Immigration History Newsletter* (St. Paul, Minn.: Immigration History Society) began in 1968. Others reflect the renaissance of ethnic studies in the 1970s: *Journal of Ethnic Studies* (Bellingham, Wash., f. 1973); *Ethnicity* (New York, f. 1974); *Heritage Exchange* (Detroit: Michigan Ethnic Heritage Studies Center, Wayne State University, f. 1974); *Pennsylvania Ethnic Studies Newsletter* (University of Pittsburgh, f. 1975); *Spectrum* (Minneapolis: Immigration History Research Center, f. 1975); *Polyphony* (Toronto: Multicultural History Society of Ontario, f. 1977) and the theoretically oriented *Ethnic and Racial Studies* (London, f. 1978).

Another indication of the growth of ethnic studies is the bibliography edited by A. William Hoglund (to be published by the Balch Institute, Philadelphia), which lists all doctoral dissertations on immigration and assimilation written in the United States between 1899 and 1972; it reveals that half of them appeared between 1962 and 1972. This essay is a brief review of the resource and research centers currently holding materials pertaining to American ethnic groups.

UNPUBLISHED RESOURCES

The first large-scale surveys of archives and manuscript collections in the United States were initiated by the Library of Congress in the 1920s, but these early efforts lacked the necessary financial and scholarly support. Between 1935 and 1939, however, the Works Progress Administration (WPA) sponsored the Historical Records Survey. Under its auspices a great many excellent inventories of manuscript collections as well as church, town, county, state, and federal archives were prepared and published. These are listed in S.B. Child and D.P. Holmes, *Bibliography of Research Projects Reports: Check List of Historical Records Survey Publications* (Washington, D.C., 1943). The dissolution of the WPA at the end of the Depression and the advent of World War II put a stop to these efforts, dimming prospects for the immediate publication of a catalogue of unpublished historical sources.

The need to provide the growing number of historians with specific information about the location of unpublished sources intensified after 1945. Through the efforts of individuals like Herbert Keller of the American Historical Association and Philip Hamer of the National Historical Publications and Records Commission (NHPRC), several projects in the 1950s resulted in important gains for scholarship.

The first of these projects was a *Guide to Archives and Manuscripts in the United States* (New Haven,

Conn., 1961). It covered more than 8,000 separate collections in 1,300 repositories. This work is now augmented by the NHPRC guide (1978). The second project is the well-known *National Union Catalog of Manuscript Collections* (Ann Arbor, Mich., 1961), a multivolume, serially updated, guide to modern manuscripts in the United States known as NUCMC. These guides and Richard W. Hale's *Guide to Photocopied Historical Materials in the United States and Canada* (Ithaca, N.Y., 1961) are the starting points for any research into unpublished historical sources.

One of the largest collections of unpublished materials is held by the National Archives and Records Service (NARS). NARS is divided into many distinct bodies: (1) the National Archives Building in Washington; (2) the Washington National Records Center in Suitland, Md.; (3) the National Personnel Records Center in St. Louis; (4) 15 regional Federal Archives and Research Centers (FARCS), containing local, Indian affairs, and customs records; (5) the Office of Presidential Libraries, beginning with that of Herbert Hoover; (6) the Eighth Street Annex; (7) the Stock Film Library in Arlington, Va.; (8) the Office of the Federal Register; and (9) the Office of Records Management.

The core of this system, located in the National Archives Building in Washington, was founded in 1934. For administrative purposes the National Archives is divided into ten major units and contains the largest permanent concentration of ethnic-related materials in the United States. These consist of printed materials (publications, posters, charts, books, monographs) as well as nonpublished items (maps, documents, photographs, drawings, architectural plans, microfilm, and sound recordings). In the broadest terms these records include: (1) censuses of population, manufacturing, industry, and agriculture; (2) documentation relating to military and naval service and disposition of public lands; (3) immigration and naturalization reports; (4) federal agency records in the areas of labor, housing, social welfare, and relief; (5) the records of highly specialized agencies such as the War Relocation Authority; (6) Department of State records, especially diplomatic, consular instructions, and dispatches to individuals serving in the countries from which immigrants came; and (7) court records from both within and outside the District of Columbia.

Since a basic archival procedure is the observance of the principle of provenance, that is, accessioning materials with respect to the arrangement system developed by the organic body that generated the documentation, it is often impossible to isolate a specifically ethnic subject collection within the National Archives. Thus, while a general guide exists to the holdings of the National Archives (1974), only a few separate finding aids have dealt with the significance of its holdings for individual ethnic groups, among them Afro-Americans (1947, 1977), Irish (1954), Latin Americans (1974), and American Indians (1949, 1954). The important holdings of American Indian material are concentrated in Record Group 75, Records of the Bureau of Indian Affairs.

Immigrant contact with American society was not limited to governmental institutions. Religious, fraternal, and social-welfare agencies played an important role in the lives of immigrants, and their records contain much material related to the ethnic and immigrant

experience. The church, for example, was frequently the center of the ethnic community. The development of individual church archives and manuscript collections was contingent upon ecclesiastical structures and historical circumstances.

Church archives may be divided into two groups: (1) those of the church proper (structured along the lines of archdiocese, diocese, and parish); and (2) the corporate or institutional archives of religious orders (congregations), lay societies, and organizations. Some of these have been consolidated. The archives of the Vincennes, Ind., Detroit, Cincinnati, and New Orleans dioceses have been collected as the Catholic Archives of America at Notre Dame University, and the archives of the Western Province of the Society of Jesus are centralized at St. Louis University.

The materials of the Protestant Episcopal Church have been collected in several separate nondiocesan collections and seminaries in Austin, Tex.; those of the Presbyterian Church have been concentrated in Philadelphia and in Montreat, N.C.; and, finally, those of the United Methodist Church, in Lake Junaluska, N.C. Other Protestant denominations such as the Disciples of Christ, Congregationalists, Seventh-Day Adventists, and Quakers have far less centralized collections. The holdings of the Lutherans and of the American Moravians (Bethlehem, Pa.) are especially important for ethnic researchers. The Concordia Historical Institute in St. Louis serves as the archival repository for the Lutheran Church (Missouri Synod).

As a consequence of a theological doctrine which assumes the possibility of baptism by proxy, the Mormons have accumulated mountains of genealogical material from around the world. Mormon research has established methodological standards for genealogical research and has led to the preservation of vast quantities of records important for non-Mormon studies. Incorporated in 1894, the Genealogical Department of the Church of Jesus Christ of Latter-day Saints in Salt Lake City has developed an extensive collection of microfilm to supplement its large collection of printed documentation. By 1977 it had accumulated more than 930,000 rolls of microfilm; several thousand new rolls are processed each month.

Lubomyr Wynar and Lois Buttlar list more than 50 archives of fraternal organizations in their *Guide to Ethnic Museums, Libraries and Archives in the United States* (1978). The Ethnic Fraternal project of the University of Minnesota's Immigration History Research Center will attempt to survey and selectively microfilm a number of these collections. One of the largest collections of the records of welfare agencies, immigration groups, and social-improvement organizations, as well as the personal papers of individuals active in welfare reform is found at the Social Welfare Archives of the University of Minnesota. An inventory of this collection was prepared in 1970.

The records of shipping, railroad, and transport companies are also relevant. A large collection of business records is held by the Baker Library at Harvard University (f. 1927) and the Eleutherian Mills Collection in Delaware. State, local, religious, and business archives in the United States have been broadly surveyed by the Society of American Archivists. Since 1969 the annual meetings of both the Organization of American Historians and the Society of American Archivists have devoted sessions to ethnic repositories.

There are more than 5,000 historical societies in the United States. Many serve the function of state historical archives, but they also have a long-standing interest in immigrant history. Among the more important state and county collections for ethnic studies are: (1) the State Historical Society of Wisconsin (Madison); (2) the Minnesota Historical Society (St. Paul), containing especially rich holdings for Scandinavian Americans; (3) the State Historical Society of Iowa (Iowa City); (4) the Nebraska State Historical Society (Lincoln), with valuable holdings related to ethnic settlement of the Great Plains; (5) the Ohio Historical Society (Columbus); (6) the Illinois State Historical Society (Springfield); and (7) the State Historical Society of Missouri (Columbia). In addition, the Chicago Historical Society Library, Missouri Historical Society (St. Louis), and Western Reserve Historical Society (Cleveland) are important archival repositories for ethnic research. The influence of the Minnesota Historical Society is extended through its sponsorship of the Immigration History Society.

Toward the end of the 19th century many immigrant groups began to establish societies to preserve and propagate their distinctive cultural heritages. Among them were the Huguenot Historical Society (New Paltz, N.Y.), the Society for the History of the Germans in Maryland (Baltimore), the American Jewish Historical Society (Waltham, Mass.), and the American Irish Historical Society (New York). More were established in the 20th century: the Hispanic Society of America (New York), Norwegian-American Historical Association (Northfield, Minn.), Swedish Pioneer Historical Society (Chicago), Swiss-American Historical Society (Norfolk, Va.), American Jewish Archives (Hebrew Union College, Cincinnati), American Hungarian Library and Historical Society (New York), American Italian Historical Association (Staten Island, N.Y.), Chinese Historical Society of America (San Francisco), and the American Historical Society of Germans from Russia (Greeley, Colo.). These organizations gathered and preserved materials dealing with their respective national heritages; some also sponsored scholarly journals that frequently contained important bibliographical references as well as articles pertaining to archival sources.

Several major resource centers in the United States have extensive archival and library holdings dealing with several ethnic groups. The largest and oldest of these is the Immigration History Research Center at the University of Minnesota (St. Paul). Founded in 1964, the center concentrates on immigrants from eastern, central and southern Europe and the Middle East. In addition to more than 350 individual and organizational archives and manuscript collections, the center contains substantial library holdings of monographs and ethnic serials, in both original and microform copy. The Balch Institute in Philadelphia, founded in 1971, contains over 300 manuscript collections and impressive holdings of printed materials. It devotes special attention to the immigrants who settled on the East Coast, whereas the collection of the Center for Migration Studies (Staten Island) reflects its interest in immigration as a global phenomenon. All three centers pub-

lish newsletters which inform scholars of their holdings. In addition, smaller collections exist at the Program for the Study of Ethnic Publications, Kent State University (Kent, Ohio), the Bentley Library at the University of Michigan (Ann Arbor), and the Archives of Industrial Society, University of Pittsburgh.

PUBLISHED MATERIALS

The years following World War II were marked by a growing interest on the part of research libraries in the acquisition of foreign-language materials. This interest, however, rarely included foreign-language materials published by ethnic groups in the United States. Some of the larger public libraries, in Boston, Chicago, Cleveland, Detroit (Burton Historical Collection), Milwaukee, and New York, however, did acquire such foreign-language materials because of their proximity to large ethnic communities, and during the 1960s there was a marked increase in the collections of American research libraries, especially those allied with the Association of Research Libraries. The Harvard College Library, the New York Public Library, the Library of Congress, and the Yale University Library acquired substantial collections of ethnic Americana. The Library of Congress has accomplished this in part through copyright deposit and its long-standing interest in Afro-American history. The New York Public Library also has a strong interest in black history and literature (Schomburg Collection) and Judaica, in addition to having strong collections in American history and genealogy. The Harvard College Library traditionally has maintained strong collections in American history, especially in the European background of American immigration. The James Weldon Johnson Memorial Collection of Negro Arts and Letters and the archives of the American Immigration Conference Board are at Yale University.

One of the most important collections of ethnic newspapers is housed in Chicago at the Center for Research Libraries (CRL), created in 1951 for the common storage of materials. From its function as a storage facility, the center moved into the area of acquisitions by obtaining files of foreign-language serials and ethnic publications. The CRL includes institutional members throughout the United States.

Ethnic materials have often come into the collections of the great research libraries by default; other centers have made a conscious attempt to build collections emphasizing a specific group. Private research libraries such as the American Philosophical Society (Philadelphia) and the Edward E. Ayer collection of the Newberry Library (Chicago, f. 1887) are noted for their holdings of American Indian materials. The Newberry collection is also strong on railroad records and genealogical publications. The Henry E. Huntington Library (f. 1919, San Marino, Calif.) and the Hubert Howe Bancroft Library (Berkeley, Calif.) have extensive materials on Spanish Americans. The various university branches of California State University (San Jose, Los Angeles, San Diego), University of California (especially Santa Barbara), University of Texas (Austin, El Paso), and University of Miami, to name but a few, have developed extensive collections of books and manuscripts dealing with immigrants from Mexico, Latin America, and, most recently, Cuba.

In the East, the Boston University Library and the library of Holy Cross College have strong Celtic-Irish collections. Several predominantly black universities have extensive collections of Afro-Americana, for example, the Arthur B. Spingarn–Jesse E. Moorland collection at Howard University, the Heartman collection at Texas Southern University, the George Foster Peabody collection at Hampton Institute, and the Charles Chesnutt collection at Fisk University. The West Virginia University Library at Morgantown has assembled an impressive collection dealing with the people of Appalachia, as has the Frank Foster Library of the Urban Appalachian Council (Cincinnati). The G.K. Hall Company (Boston) has published catalogues of many of these publications.

Scandinavians are well known for their activities in preserving their cultural heritage in the United States. Most of these collections are located in the cultural centers of this immigration. The Honnold Library, Claremont Colleges (Claremont, Calif.); the University of North Dakota; Luther College (Decorah, Iowa); St. Olaf College (Northfield, Minn.); Johns Hopkins University (Nikulas Ottensen Collection); the University of Kentucky (Jens Christian Bay Collection); the University of Texas (Palm Collection); the Willard Fiske Icelandic collection at Cornell University; and Suomi College (Hancock, Mich.) contain resources for the study of Scandinavian groups. On the other hand, the Swedish Pioneer Historical Society (Northpark College), established in Chicago in 1948, the American Swedish Institute (Minneapolis), Grand View College (Des Moines, Iowa), and Augustana College (Rock Island, Ill.) treat only individual groups. The branches of the University of California system have impressive facilities for the study of ethnic groups strongly represented in California; among these are the ethnic collections at the Asian Studies Centers at the University of California campuses at Davis and Los Angeles, both founded within the last decade.

A significant collection on American Slavs exists at the University of Illinois at Edwardville. Of the many Slavic groups in the United States, the Poles have been the most active in preserving their cultural heritage by founding the Polish American Archives, housed at the Orchard Lakes Colleges (Orchard Lakes, Mich., and the Archives and Museum of the Polish Roman Catholic Union (Chicago). Ukrainians, Slovaks, and Hungarians have extensive archival centers in Cleveland, an active center of their respective immigrations. The famed Bakhmeteff Archives of Russian and East European culture is housed at Columbia University.

RESOURCES OUTSIDE THE UNITED STATES

The immigration of peoples from their native countries left a documentary residue not only in the national libraries and archives of these countries, but also in the collections of religious and philanthropic societies. Interest in these materials relevant to the American experience dates at least from the second half of the 19th century. By the beginning of the 20th century the Carnegie Institution in Washington made the first effort to survey manuscripts of relevance to American studies in foreign repositories. Under the leadership of C.H. van Tyne and W.G. Leland, guides to Americana in a dozen European countries were published in 23 volumes

between 1906 and 1943. This pioneering work, however, was never continued on a systematic basis, although several more recent studies have dealt with Americana in western Europe. Most often these guides have appeared under the auspices of American studies associations. Very frequently too, the publications of these organizations contain merely surveys of Americana in national libraries and archives. While the number of guides to specific ethnic materials is still small, each of the comprehensive Carnegie guides contains sections dealing with "emigration and immigration." Unfortunately, the private, nongovernmental repositories were often beyond the purview of the Carnegie guides. Thus, collections such as the Leopoldinen Stiftung (Leopold Foundation) in Vienna and the Ludwig Missionsverein (Ludwig Mission Society) in Munich, both containing letters from German-American missionaries, and private commercial archives such as the Nord Deutscher Lloyd collection, were omitted in otherwise useful guides. Some foreign national archival records of relevance to American ethnic studies have come to the United States. Thus, the archives of the Volksbund für das Deutschum im Ausland (League of Ethnic Germans Abroad) came into the custody of NARS at the end of World War II as part of the "Captured German and Related Records" (Record Group 242). As another example, the archives of the Hungarian Reformed Church (Budapest) were microfilmed by the Immigration History Research Center and are available to researchers.

In the last two decades several European nations have created research centers devoted exclusively or largely to the study of their countrymen abroad. The most important developments in this regard have taken place in Germany, Sweden, Poland, and Czechoslovakia. In Germany research is concentrated in Hamburg, Kiel (devoted especially to the Schleswig-Holesteiners in the United States), Stuttgart, and Kaiserslautern.

Sweden has several collections. The Emigrant-Institut in Växjö, conceived in 1965, was opened in 1968. The Emigrantregisteret in Karlstad is a rich repository of official documentation. The Uppsala University emigration archives (f. 1960) is located at the university library. The Danish emigrant archives in Ålborg is the richest single repository in Denmark; in Finland the Yliopisto Yleisen Historian Laitos (Institute for General History) at the University of Turko (f. 1963) is the leading institution for the study of Finnish emigration.

Central and eastern European countries also have been active in attempting to document their emigrations. In Yugoslavia each of the republics has a research center devoted to its emigrants: the Slovenska Izseljenska Matica (Slovene Emigrant Society) is located in Ljubljana; the Matica Iseljenika Srbije (Serbian Emigrant Society) in Belgrade; the Matica Iseljenika Bosnije i Hercegovine (Bosnian and Hercegovinian Emigrant Society) in Sarajevo; the Matica Iseljenika Hrvatske (Croatian Emigrant Society) and the Zavod za Migracije i Narodnosti (Institute for Peoples and Migration) both in Zagreb.

In Poland, the Society of Poles Abroad published the *Problemy Polonii Zagranicznej* (Warsaw, 1960–1975). In Czechoslovakia several organizations study Czech and Slovak emigration, among them the Naprstek Museum (Prague) and the Institute for Slovaks Abroad in Bratislava, a branch of the Matica Slovenska (Slovakian Society) in Martin. During the late 1960s the Komise pro Dějiny Čechů a Slovaků Zahranicemi (Commission on the History of Czechs and Slovaks Abroad) existed as part of the Czechoslovak Academy of Sciences. Smaller institutions exist in Italy (Centro Studi Emigrazione), Greece (the National Center for Social Research) and Malta (the Maltese Research Center, f. 1976).

CONCLUSION

The development of new social-science techniques, especially statistics and sampling, will permit researchers to go far in analyzing sources both in the United States and abroad. Now that researchers have begun to realize the extent of the available documentation on American ethnicity, an increasing amount of material will be preserved. Virtually all ethnic groups have come to acquire a sense of their own historicity. Photographs of grandparents, letters from kin in Europe, immigration and naturalization papers, old posters in the native language announcing a parish picnic, a prayer book, correspondence and calendars from fraternal insurance companies are more and more being preserved as objects of documentation for the historian and sociologist.

Bibliography
Lubomyr R. Wynar and Lois Buttlar, *Guide to Ethnic Museums, Libraries, and Archives in the United States* (Kent, Ohio, 1978), covers resources for over 70 ethnic groups, including a section for multiethnic centers. This work should be supplemented by the more than 80 ethnic and immigration collections reported in the *Directory of Archives and Manuscript Repositories in the United States* (Washington, D.C., 1978).

Walter Rundell, *In Pursuit of American History: Research and Training in the United States* (Norman, Okla., 1970) provides a good introduction to the problems of research in American history. John D. Buenker and Nicholas C. Burckel, *Immigration and Ethnicity: A Guide to Information Sources* (Detroit, 1977) is a convenient introduction to the recent secondary literature on American ethnic groups. The work edited by Francis X. Blouin, Jr. and Robert M. Warner, *Sources for the Study of Migration and Ethnicity: A Guide to Manuscripts in Finland, Ireland, Poland, The Netherlands, and the State of Michigan* (Ann Arbor, 1979) is a pioneering study of ethnic sources in Michigan and Europe.

H.G. Jones, *The Records of a Nation: Their Management, Preservation and Use* (New York, 1969), is a classic study of the general resources of the National Archives; Joseph B. Howerton, "The Resources of the National Archives for Ethnic Research," *Immigration History Newsletter* 5 (November 1973), is the sole study dealing specifically with collections of the archives for ethnic studies. Ernst Posner, *American State Archives* (Chicago, 1964), is the basic study of the organization and holdings of the American archival system on the state level.

EDWARD KASINEC

ROM: *see* GYPSIES

ROMANIANS

Romanians appeared only sporadically in the United States before the 1870s. An Orthodox priest from Transylvania, Samuel Damian, apparently had some contact with Benjamin Franklin; a few Romanians were among the forty-niners in California's gold rush; and two are recorded in the annals of the Civil War: Captain Nicolae Dunca (1827–1862) served with the 9th New York Volunteers and died in the battle of Cross Keyes, and General Gheorghe Pomutz (1828–1882) joined the 15th Iowa Volunteer Regiment, fought at Shiloh, Vicksburg, Corinth, and Atlanta, became the first and only Romanian to be raised to the rank of brigadier general, and

Romania

- Romanian-speaking areas
- Boundaries of Romania (the Regat), 1878–1913
- Boundaries of Romania, 1919–1940

300   Km.   Miles

later went to Russia where he served as U.S. consul general in St. Petersburg. Between 1870 and 1900 Romanian immigration mounted. About 18,000 immigrants listing Romania as their country of origin entered the United States during that period, although until 1895 almost all of them were Jews from Moldavia or from Romanian villages in Russian-controlled Bessarabia or Austrian-held Bukovina. After 1895 Romanian peasants began to swell the ranks; most of these were Transylvanians, although a few were Macedonian Romanians from European Turkey, northern Greece, and Albania who spoke a dialect based on Romanian with admixtures of Greek and Albanian. The first of these, from Körçe, Albania, was recorded in 1897.

By 1920 an estimated 85,000 Romanians had come to the United States and another estimated 5,400 native-born Americans were of Romanian parentage. But the basis for these statistics is tenuous at best; because over 85 percent of the Romanian immigrants were from Transylvania, Bukovina, or the Banat, territories that did not become part of the Romanian kingdom until 1918, many arrivals, though ethnically Romanian, were counted as Hungarians, Austrians, or Russians. In 1923 the "country of origin" designation used by the U.S. Census Bureau was still based on pre–World War I boundaries, which further confuses the figures. After 1895 the greatest number of Romanians came from western and central Transylvania, mainly from the regions near Făgăraş, Sibiu, Alba-Iulia, Tîrnava Mare, Satu-Mare, Sălaj, Bihor, Arad. Of the small immigration from the original kingdom of Romania, more than one-fifth came from the county of Dolj. The Macedonian Romanians came primarily from Farseroţi, Megleniţi, and Macedonia proper, while a few Dobrogeans who had previously migrated to Oltenia in southern Romania may or may not have been counted as Turks or Bulgarians when they entered the United States.

In the course of the 19th century the Romanians had thrown off foreign domination and created a united kingdom out of numerous small states and principalities that had until then been divided among the Russian, Austro-Hungarian, and Turkish empires. In 1859 the principalities of Moldavia and Walachia were united under Prince Alexandru Ioan Cuza; in 1878 the nation won its independence from the Ottoman Empire, and Carol I became its king. But even then many surrounding lands inhabited by Romanians remained under foreign rule. Until 1918 nationalist movements remained active, especially in Bukovina, Transylvania, and the Banat, seeking union with the mother country. During the same period economic and political conditions in those regions produced large-scale migrations of rural Romanians to the United States.

Motivations for leaving home were many, but they centered on the hope of escaping from the depressed economic and social position of the rural villager. More than half the landholdings in the Dual Monarchy of Austria and Hungary were smaller than 5 acres; one-third were great estates of over 250 acres. Overpopulation and the continued subdivision of land among sons of large peasant families made for a precarious future. After 1900 marginal small producers were forced out by enclosures aimed at creating capital-intensive units. A great peasant uprising in 1907 was only one manifestation of rural discontent. The Hungarian regime in Budapest, as part of the Dual Monarchy created in 1867, had been granted broad authority over Transylvania; its activities intensified the difficulties of life for Romanians by adding to agricultural exploitation an extensive and long-range policy of Magyarization in the schools, civil service, and commercial life. Its efforts to convert the subject peoples to Catholicism imposed another problem, for over 90 percent of the Romanian population were Orthodox. In the meantime American and European steamship-company agents loudly publicized not only the contents of real and imaginary letters from countrymen already in the United States—letters painting a golden picture of the wealth to be made—but also instructions on how young men could evade military service in the Austro-Hungarian army by emigrating.

ARRIVAL AND SETTLEMENT

Unlike the pre-1895 immigrants, many of whom were tradesmen or artisans and came with their families, the vast majority of the large number who came afterward were single men between the ages of 18 and 45; 97 percent were unskilled, and for the most part semiliterate, laborers. Romanians describe the period 1895–1920 with the phrase *mia şi drumul*, "a thousand dollars and home again," because so many left their wives and children behind, coming to the United States with the intention of going home after accumulating enough money to buy land and improve their economic and social status in their native villages. In the first quarter of the 20th century, two-thirds of the Romanians who came to the United States returned home. Returns were especially high after World War I when their home provinces were incorporated into the Romanian kingdom, and the postwar liberal government finally enacted land-reform measures in 1921. In the same years, however, a second wave of Romanians entered the

United States as restrictions on leaving their country eased and many hurried to reach the United States before immigration restrictions closed the door; the Immigration Act of 1924 set an annual Romanian quota of only 603.

By World War II the census showed 115,940 Romanians in the United States, and perhaps another 10,000 entered after 1945 under the Displaced Persons Act. All these figures are rough estimates. Assuming that many of the first generation had died by the 1970s, an estimate of some 90,000 first- and second-generation Romanians in the United States might be a fair approximation for the late 1970s.

The greatest numbers of Romanians settled in the industrial heartland of the mid-Atlantic and Great Lakes states. The largest concentrations and the most active communal life were in New York, Chicago, Philadelphia, Detroit, Pittsburgh, and Cleveland. Moderate-sized cities such as Youngstown, Canton, Alliance, Warren, and Akron, Ohio; Farrell, Sharon, New Castle, Ellwood City, McKeesport, Homestead, Erie, Johnstown, and Scalp Level, Pa.; and East Chicago and Gary, Ind., also developed substantial colonies. Romanians could be found in Minneapolis and South St. Paul, in Missouri, and in Montana, but for the most part they did not stray from the major industrial regions. Few settled in the Far West or the South before the 1960s, when many retired to California and some to Florida.

The first-generation immigrants were unskilled and semiskilled industrial workers, congregating in urban colonies close to the factories in which they worked and where their fellow nationals from the same region or village lived. They often would remain only a year or two in whatever city supplied their first job, then move on to another where friends or relatives would help them find employment. This second location might become a permanent home, but a third or even a fourth move before settling down was not uncommon. Conversations with surviving Romanian pioneers confirm the transitory nature of the life of these first-generation single men; once wives and families were brought over, such moving about became much rarer.

Sometimes their first housing was on city outskirts where rent was cheap, but more often Romanians congregated immediately in factory streets or boarding houses in the industrial districts. They were more apt to come from common districts than common villages; only an estimated 10 percent of the immigrant chains were village groups, with an average of five emigrants per village. The villages that produced the earliest and most numerous migrations were usually ethnically mixed; the immigrant Romanians were therefore used to living alongside Germans, Hungarians, and others, and in the United States it was common to find Romanians among Poles, Slovaks, and Russians.

Perhaps one-third of the Romanian newcomers in the larger cities were solitary migrants who had not come as part of a chain migration; these were the most likely eventually to return home. For the rest, the support provided by district and regional compatriots among their neighbors soon overrode local and village loyalties and mitigated feelings of loneliness and alienation. A common folk culture molded the conglomeration of Transylvanians into concentrated ethnic settlements based on church and club.

ECONOMIC, SOCIAL, AND POLITICAL LIFE

Although unskilled laborers continued to be the economic foundation of Romanian communities, by 1914 some immigrants had accumulated sufficient capital to become small entrepreneurs—owners of restaurants, boarding houses, saloons, pool halls, and immigrant banks. In the 1920s this petty bourgeoisie saw its sons move into the ranks of skilled labor or become white-collar workers. Romanians joined trade unions, but aside from those seriously involved in the socialist movement they were not often active members. In 1913–1914 the Federation of the Roumanian Socialist Workers of the United States affiliated with the Industrial Workers of the World and the Socialist party, and for the most part broke with the culture and society of their compatriots. Their newspaper, Deşteptarea (The Awakening), published from 1914 to 1939, was filled with bitter diatribes against the capitalist system. Despite the apprehensions aroused in other Romanians by their left-wing attitudes and their refusal to join the beneficial societies, Romanian socialists were never very numerous, and were more evolutionary than revolutionary in their socialism. Their concerns lay with cultural development and with labor questions. Most Romanians rarely questioned the capitalist system; in fact, they embraced it wholeheartedly.

Economic assimilation was rapid, and upward social movement followed economic success. Steaua Noastră (Our Star), an early newspaper, was advertising gramophones as early as 1912. By the late 1920s the traditional large families were disappearing. Fewer children, the acquisition of property, and the willingness of parents to use it to finance the education of the second generation may partially account for their early prosperity. Romanians were also more apt to send their children to public than to private or church-affiliated schools, thus increasing their exposure to the larger society. Parish schools attached to the Romanian churches were never intended to supplant the public schools, but rather to assist in the retention of Romanian language and culture without retarding assimilation. Finally, Romanians very early began to marry outside the group, even crossing religious boundaries.

In assessing the upward mobility of Romanian Americans it is necessary to distinguish among three groups. The "club and church" Romanians remained in the ethnic neighborhood through the second and third generations and continued to center their lives on factory, beneficial society, and church. Others, mostly of the second generation, began in the late 1920s and early 1930s to move away from the urban colonies into the suburbs and to detach themselves from Romanian culture. This latter group may have constituted as much as 80 or 90 percent of the ethnic population, though practically no data are available to confirm this. The existing material deals only with those who remained attached to ethnic institutions. But if structural assimilation—acceptance into the professional, social, and fraternal organizations of the dominant American culture—has taken place among Romanian Americans, it is among this group.

A third, intermediate category can also be identified: those among the second generation who continued to spend their workday in the old neighborhood and their

leisure hours and Sundays at Romanian clubs and churches but chose to live elsewhere. They made up a sizable portion of the Romanian-American working-class population by the 1950s; their third-generation children are now experiencing to a lesser degree the cultural discontinuity their parents knew in the 1920s. For most third-generation Romanians, however, English is the primary language at home, and their ethnicity is less a way of life than a subject of conversation or the reason behind a few old customs encountered at occasional weddings, funerals, or holidays. Assimilation for the third generation is nearly total: thousands of young Romanian Americans probably could not even locate Romania on a map.

ORGANIZATIONS AND THE CHURCH

Two major immigrant institutions, the boarding house and the mutual benefit society, have been credited with easing the transition between Old World and New World life. Among the early arrivals, the few men who brought their wives with them soon discovered that more money could be made by running crowded hostels for their bachelor fellow-immigrants than by laboring in a factory. Typically a two-story frame building with seven or eight rooms, the boarding house usually sheltered between 25 and 30 men. Beds were used in day and night shifts; meals were family style at long tables; food and drink often were bought cooperatively.

The boarding house provided camaraderie and helped perpetuate traditional ways. Besides singing Romanian folk songs (doine) and reciting poems and stories, the group might organize an informal musical ensemble, or at least play a shepherd's flute or two. When a group of boarders decided to move on to another house, perhaps because they had heard the cooking was better or because they had had a disagreement with the boarding-house boss, they often accompanied the move with music. Because of the reluctance of the men to use American banks, the boarding-house boss also served as custodian of the lodgers' savings, acted as agent for sending their money overseas, and purchased their steamship tickets. The Romanian boarding house was a forerunner of the later widespread and colorful combination of saloon, pool hall, steamship agency, and money-lending and savings establishment known as the immigrant bank, whose counter, office, and vault consisted of a single roll-top desk bulging with bills and receipts. The boarding house as an institution lasted well into the 1930s; by then its tenants were mainly solitary immigrants who had elected to stay in the United States but had never married.

In 1902 Romanians in Cleveland organized a mutual-benefit society known as Carpatina (The Carpathian), but the pattern for the Romanian club was not really established until the following January 1, when 29 Romanians in Homestead, Pa., founded the Societatea Române de Ajutor și Cultură (Romanian Society of Assistance and Culture), known as Vulturul (The Eagle). The frequency of industrial accidents, the need for medical and death benefits, and the example of the societies of other ethnic groups combined to encourage the rapid proliferation of societies similar to the RSAC. They were organized along the lines of a small insurance company directly controlled by the policy-holders' representatives. Each member paid a monthly fee; in addition he was assessed a given sum whenever a death occurred in the group. These sums assured each member compensation in the event of accident, and indemnity to his family should he be killed. Death benefits varied between $100 and $200 at first; later they were fixed at $700.

The societies had cultural functions as well, providing educational programs that would encourage the maintenance of the homeland culture. By 1911 there were 44 societies in a central organization called Uniunea Societăților Române de Ajutor și Cultură (Union of Romanian Beneficial and Cultural Societies, or USRA), with headquarters in Newark, Ohio. Its official organ was the newspaper America, first published in Cleveland in 1906 by the Reverend Moise Balea (1875–1942).

Not all the societies, however, joined the USRA; many remained independent until 1912 when a few intellectuals in the workers' movement federated them as the Liga de Ajutor (LSRA). Its publication was Românul, founded in Cleveland in 1905 by the Byzantine-rite Catholic priest Epaminonda Lucaciu (1877–1946). Quarreling, litigation, and sometimes even violence marked the competition between the two organizations. Not until 1928 was the breach healed with their fusion into the Uniunea și Liga Societăți Române în America (Union and League of Romanian Societies in America), commonly called the Union and League, with a total of some 6,500 members. The membership represented less than 3 percent of the Romanians in the United States in 1930, but that was the high point of Romanian benefit-society strength.

A period of consolidation during the 1930s and 1940s merged formerly rival clubs in the same cities, but the worker-intellectual split that had caused the initial rift never completely healed, and political strife in Romania during the interwar years exacerbated tensions between the two Romanian-American groups. The cleavage was reinforced when a new wave of more educated and politically conscious immigrants arrived from Romania after 1945. In 1944 membership in the Union and League was about 5,000; by 1979 an official listing for 165 societies showed 4,124 fraternal certificates still active. The Macedonian Romanian Fărșerotul Society (f. 1902), with branches in New York, Rhode Island, Connecticut, and Missouri, attempts to unite the scattered Macedonians from Albania and Romania in the United States.

The history of the Romanian Orthodox Church in the United States is one of dissension, schism, and jurisdictional controversy. For the early immigrants, a lack of trained priests delayed the regularization of religious practice. Some moved to the Byzantine-rite Catholic Church, especially after the founding of the St. Helena Greek Catholic Church in Cleveland in 1905 by Father Lucaciu. Orthodox Romanians in the early days attended whatever Greek, Serbian, or Russian Orthodox services happened to be available, or held services in boarding houses or even saloons. Upon the petition of St. Mary's, the first organized Orthodox parish in Cleveland, the Reverend Moise Balea came to America in 1905 and soon founded some 15 churches in various centers.

The building of churches kept pace with the founding of mutual-benefit societies. By 1912 a protopope (dean) of American parishes was named, who by 1934 had 32 U.S. parishes under his jurisdiction. Dissension between American- and Romanian-ordained priests, dissatisfaction with the Hungarian domination of the Metropolitanate of Sibiu, which had canonical authority over the American churches, and the refusal of many parishes to submit to the socialist-leaning protopope led to the demand for an American episcopate, but this was realized only in 1929 and the first bishop, Policarp Moruşca (1883–1958), did not arrive until 1935. Bishop Moruşca founded the diocesan paper *Solia* (The Herald) and the annual almanac *Calendarul Solia* (The Herald Calendar) in 1936.

The delay in establishing an organized local hierarchy for the Romanian Orthodox churches meant that separatist tendencies among the Romanian-American faithful remained deep-seated. The weakening of family ties and the declining interest of Romanian youth in church affairs were partially offset by the founding of what became by 1950 the American Romanian Orthodox Youth Association (AROY); it has around 450 members today. Bishop Moruşca also organized the Association of Orthodox Romanian-American Women (ARFORA). A major accomplishment was the purchase in 1937 of the Vatra Românească (Romanian Hearth), a 200-acre estate at Grass Lake, Mich., to be used as the national headquarters of the episcopate. Soon afterward Bishop Moruşca returned to Romania for a conference and was trapped there by the war; the postwar regime refused to allow him to return to the United States.

By 1950 the American churches were divided between the custodians of the Romanian Orthodox Episcopate of America (ROEA), who declared themselves autonomous in order to break with the Communist government of Romania, and a group of prelates surrounding the Akron priest Andrei Moldovan (1885–1963), who under mysterious circumstances left the United States to be ordained in Bucharest, then returned to Grass Lake in an attempt to take over the episcopate with the backing of the new Romanian government. When it became clear that Bishop Moruşca would not return, the autonomists, led by the Reverend Ioan Trutza (1895–1954) and the Episcopate Council, called the annual church congress in 1951 in Chicago. It elected Viorel B. Trifa (1914–), then editor of *Solia*, who was consecrated in Philadelphia the following year as Bishop Valerian to head the 46 parishes and 10,000 members of the ROEA.

Meanwhile some 31 parishes of the Moldovan church named themselves the Romanian Orthodox Missionary Episcopate of America (ROMEA) and accepted Victorin Ursache (1912–) as their bishop in 1966. Following separation from the Romanian Patriarchate in Bucharest, the ROEA under Valerian remained autonomous until 1960, when it affiliated with the Russian Metropolia in the United States. When the Metropolia became the Orthodox Church in America in 1970, the ROEA remained part of this self-governing American Orthodox Church; the Romanian bishop is a member of its Holy Synod. In the late 1970s ROEA included 33 churches in the United States with a membership of 6,000 dues-paying families; the number of those regularly attending church services is around 50,000. The ROMEA pres-

ently has only 10 parishes in the United States, with perhaps 500 family members and 1,500 communicants.

About 4,300 Romanians belong to the Roman Catholic Church of the Byzantine Rite, with 17 parishes from New Jersey to Illinois, under the jurisdiction of the Roman Catholic dioceses in which they are located. To promote their Catholic tradition, which stems from the introduction of Uniatism in Transylvania in 1700, the Romanian Catholics and their fraternal societies founded the Union of the Greek Catholic Romanians in Northern America in 1919. In 1948 it was reorganized in Youngstown as the Association of Romanian Catholics of America (ARCA) with some 1,500 members. It considers itself the representative of its suppressed sister church in Romania. It sponsors cultural events, has a youth section, helps Romanian refugees, and serves as an insurance company. Romanian Catholics in the United States have for years been appealing to the Vatican for their own bishop, but their request has yet to be granted. In 1975 Monsignor Octavian Bârlea was named Apostolic Visitor for Romanian Catholics in the United States, but resigned the position in 1977. In recent years an increasing number of third-generation Greek-rite Romanian Catholics have joined Roman Catholic parishes.

The first Romanian Baptist Church was established by the Reverend R.C. Igrisan in 1910 in Cincinnati, and the Romanian Baptist Association was organized three years later. By World War II there were about 20 churches and parochial schools, but today the number has fallen to 9 parishes with about 2,500 adherents. The Romanian Baptist Association of the United States continues to publish the monthly *Luminătorul* (The Enlightener) in Detroit, with a circulation of about 1,500; *Semănătorul* (The Sower) has appeared independently in Chicago since 1971, following a split between some Romanian Baptist congregations. These churches continue to hold their services in Romanian; only the sermons are in English.

In addition, there are small groups of Romanian Protestant Pentecostals, the most active of them in Dearborn, and five independent Orthodox churches in Detroit, South St. Paul, Minn., Roebling, N.J., Alliance, Ohio, and Hollywood, Fla. All Romanian religious groups have suffered losses in membership as the third and fourth generations move to other denominations, a result both of intermarriage (the Romanian partner seems the more likely to change religion) and of ignorance of the Romanian language. To counteract this, many Romanian churches now use English for at least part of the liturgy, and emphasize youth activities. Older Romanians continue to be a fairly religious and church-going people.

THE PRESS

Romanian Americans have supported an active and prolific foreign-language press. Some 37 newspapers, weeklies, and monthlies used to be published regularly in the United States, along with dozens of more ephemeral cultural and popular journals, but there is no Romanian-language daily today. The Romanian press tends to be polemical, working-class oriented, somewhat anticlerical, and to emphasize American rather than Romanian affairs. Until the LSRA merged with the USRA in

1928, *Românul* was read largely by educated immigrants, who tended to be Greek Catholics; *America* was aimed at the largely Orthodox working classes. By the 1930s those distinctions were beginning to disappear. If the Romanians read anything at all, they read *America*. It is still published today as a biweekly with a circulation of 1,800; 80 percent of it is written in English. *Steaua Noastră* was published in Romanian through its final issue in 1931. *Solia* and *Credința* (The Faith), the publications of the ROEA and ROMEA, are perhaps more widely read than *America*, and Romanian Catholics receive *Unirea* (The Union). *Cuvântul Românesc* (The Romanian Word), published in Hamilton, Ont. (1976–), has a large readership throughout the Western Hemisphere and Europe.

The most popular journal of Romanian affairs during World War II was *The New Pioneer*, published in English from 1942 to 1948 in Cleveland. The 1950s produced highly polemical newspapers attacking Communism, such as *Porunca Vremii* (Master of the Times) and *Fiii Daciei* (Sons of Dacia), a quarterly. Offsetting these was the pro-Bucharest *Românul-American*, which succeeded *Deșteptarea* in 1939 and lasted until 1968. *România*, the monthly bulletin of the Romanian National Committee in New York, has a circulation of about 2,000; many of its readers are Romanian exiles in Europe and Latin America. The monthly *Romanian Bulletin* has been distributed by the Romanian Library in New York since 1968, and it now devotes considerable space to Romanian-American affairs. *Orizont Românesc* (Romanian Horizon) is published in Los Angeles, *Micromagazin* in Astoria, N.Y., the literary quarterly *Drum* (The Path) and the scholarly *Romanian Sources* in Pittsburgh, the *Ecouri Românești* (Romanian Echoes) in Toronto, and the political *Dreptatea* (Justice) in New York. The most recent popular journal of news and culture to appear is the *American-Romanian Review* in Cleveland. Begun in 1977 by the American-Romanian Heritage Foundation, it has about 1,000 subscribers.

GROUP MAINTENANCE AND ETHNIC IDENTITY

Romanians as a group have not been intensely caught up in the ethnic revival of the past decade. With some important exceptions, such as the new heritage center at Grass Lake and the activities of communities in Cleveland and Detroit, Romanian ethnic programs have been largely confined to university and academic circles and to Romanian churches. Besides the Union and League, which sponsors two annual Romanian Days in various locations, the Iuliu Maniu Foundation in New York gives assistance to immigrants, provides some scholarship funds, and has a small folk-art collection. On a similarly modest scale are the activities of the Orthodox Brotherhood, Romanian Welfare, Inc., and the Cultural Association for Romanians and Americans of Romanian Descent. The Midwest Romanian Radio Hour in Gary, Ind., now in its 25th year, and two Romanian-hour programs in Detroit continue to have an audience. Romanian art is exhibited at the Brooklyn Museum, the Metropolitan Museum, and the Museum of Modern Art in New York; St. Dumitru's Church in New York and St. Mary's Church in Cleveland are major Romanian heritage centers, as is the University of Pittsburgh's Romanian Room. In art, literature, medicine, and athletics Romanian Americans have contributed much, from the fiction of Peter Neagoe to the Nobel Prize-winning work in medicine of George E. Palade to the studies of Mircea Eliade, one of the world's great historians of religion; in sculpture George Stănescu and Alexandru Seceni have international reputations; radiology and nuclear medicine have benefited greatly from the inventions of Traian Leucuția. Marilena Bocu and Anișoara Stan were the first Romanian-American women to become nationally known as folklorists and artists. Nicolae Novac and Vasile Posteuca are noted for their poetry, and Theodore Andrica and John Florea have central places in journalism and photography. Finally, Radu Florescu has contributed to an awareness of Transylvanian folklore. A leader of the physically handicapped is Ștefan Florescu, founder of the Rolling Romanians, a track-and-field group in Detroit.

Some 19 universities now have Romanian-language programs or area studies as part of their Romance-language, Eastern European, or—despite the status of Romanian as a Romance tongue—Slavic studies programs. The Ohio State *haiduci* dancers and Canton, Ohio's *doina* performers are well-known ensembles. A Romanian Civilization Week was held in Pittsburgh in 1976. The Romanian Studies Association of America was founded in Chicago in 1974 by several university professors; the recently reorganized Society for Romanian Studies has 150 members, but most of them are academics of non-Romanian origin. The newly begun American Romanian Academy of Arts and Sciences in Oakland, Calif., has undertaken an ambitious program of scholarly publication and conferences.

Study of Romanian-American topics remains in its infancy. The most organized archival source is the Immigration History Research Center of the University of Minnesota, but its location puts it out of touch with most of the Romanian-American community, and much documentary material remains scattered. Some oral histories are being sponsored by the Pennsylvania Ethnic Heritage Studies Center in Pittsburgh, and work on Romanian language maintenance is under way at the Center for Applied Linguistics in Washington, D.C. Purdue University has produced a teaching resource unit on Romanians in Lake County, Ind., which may serve as a prototype for ethnic profiles on Romanian communities. The opening of the elaborate Romanian-American Heritage Center in Grass Lake in 1978 is one step toward the preservation of the history and culture of Romanians in America. It was funded entirely by contributions from members of the Romanian community. Most of this activity is being carried out by a relatively small group of scholars, intellectuals, and priests.

The postwar immigrants from Romania have as often caused division as they have encouraged cohesion in Romanian-American communities. The older settlers call the newcomers the *noi-veniți* (newly arrived) and find they have little in common with them. The post-1945 arrivals tend to be better educated and far more politically aware than the earlier immigrants, who remain largely ignorant of current Romanian issues. The newly arrived are also apt not to be active in the Romanian churches, and regard the beneficial societies as mere insurance companies. Many of the refugees hold aca-

demic, journalistic, or professional positions; they take part in anti-Communist enterprises with which the earlier generations have little to do. The post–World War II Romanian community has not yet undergone the complete identification with American life that the early immigrants and their children experienced, and the Romanian-American establishment continues to exist on two distinct levels.

Most of the story of the Romanian immigrants remains unwritten. That it should be written is undoubted; it is of vital concern to the self-image and identity of the Romanian-American community. For Americans of all ethnic backgrounds there is a vital lesson to be learned in examining why and how tens of thousands of simple peasant folk removed themselves from their pastoral world and came to settle in the grime and din of America's industrial cities. It was not only for the money to be made; they were also responding to the promise of self-improvement and of freedom.

Bibliography

The best popular, though uncritical, study of an individual Romanian-American community is Mary Leuca and Peter Georgeoff, *Romanian Americans in Lake County, Indiana: Resource Guide* (Lafayette, Ind., 1977). Josef J. Barton, *Peasants and Strangers: Italians, Rumanians, and Slovaks in an American City, 1890–1950* (Cambridge, Mass., 1975), is a probing comparative analysis of the three groups in Cleveland. Christine A. Galitzi, *A Study of Assimilation among the Roumanians of the United States* (1929; reprint, New York, 1968), examines 100 Chicago families and, though dated, remains the necessary starting point. Șerban Drutu and Andrei Popovici, *Românii în America* (Bucharest, Romania, 1926), and Andrei Popovici, "Americanii de Origine Română," *Sociologie Românească* 2 (1937): 1–32, are important, if panegyrical works, as are the official 25- and 50-year histories of the Union and League: C.R. Pascu, *Istoria Uniunei și Ligei Societăților Române de Ajutor și Cultură din America, 1906–1931* (Cleveland, 1931), and Șofron S. Fekett, *Istoria Uniunii și Ligii Societăților Românești din America* (Cleveland, 1956).

The first comprehensive history of the Romanian community in Cleveland is Theodore Andrica, *Romanian Americans and Their Communities of Cleveland* (Cleveland, 1977), aimed at the general reader. Another localized study is Gerald Bobango, "Romanians in Pennsylvania," *Pennsylvania Heritage* 5 (Fall 1979): 17–21. More general in scope is Vladimir Wertsman, *The Romanians in America, 1748–1974* (Dobbs Ferry, N.Y., 1975), a chronology and fact book that reprints articles from *The New Pioneer*. The calendars published by *America*, the ROEA, and the ROMEA are sources for church and club history; the first comprehensive study of the ROEA is Gerald Bobango, *The Romanian Orthodox Episcopate of America: The First Half-Century, 1929–1979* (Jackson, Mich., 1979).

GERALD BOBANGO

ROMANSH: *see* SWISS

ROMNICHALS: *see* GYPSIES

RUMANIANS: *see* ROMANIANS

RUSINS (RUSYNS): *see* CARPATHO-RUSYNS

RUSNIAKS: *see* CARPATHO-RUSYNS

RUSSIAN GERMANS: *see* GERMANS FROM RUSSIA

RUSSIANS

Russian is often used as a generic term to describe people of widely varying ethnic and religious backgrounds who have come to the United States from lands that were once part of the Russian Empire or that are now within the borders of the U.S.S.R. Consequently, the question of who is rightly identified as an ethnic Russian in the United States, in contrast to the people who call themselves Russian because Russia or the Soviet Union is their country of origin or because they belong to the Russian Orthodox Church, is not at all simple.

At the present time less than 50 percent of the population of the Soviet Union is Russian, and in the past an even smaller percentage of immigrants arriving from Russia have been ethnic Russians. U.S. Census Bureau figures for 1910, 1920, and 1930 indicate that only 17 percent of the 1.5 million immigrants entering the United States from Russia were actually Russian, and this category has often included Belorussians and Ukrainians as well. The vast majority were Jews (58 percent), Poles (11 percent), and Germans (8 percent).

In this entry the word Russian is used to include immigrants of Russian ethnic background as well as eastern Slavs from Belorussia and the Ukraine (including a number of people from the former Hapsburg Austrian province of Galicia) who for historical and cultural reasons identify themselves as Russian. Russian Jews or individuals from other ethnic backgrounds who have played an important role in the Russian-American community are also included. The Cossacks, who regard themselves as a distinct group in the United States, are treated in a separate entry.

The Russians inhabit a large expanse of land that stretches from Leningrad (formerly St. Petersburg) on the Baltic Sea to Vladivostok on the Pacific Ocean. In the main, this territory coincides with the Russian Soviet Federated Socialist Republic of the U.S.S.R. This area was part of the Russian Empire from the time of the first immigration until the closing years of World War I. The Russians are a Slavic people whose speech, sometimes called "Great" Russian, is classified as one of the three East Slavic languages. Traditionally, Russians were adherents of the Eastern Orthodox Church, although many also belonged to dissenting groups, such as the Old Believers, Molokans, and Dukhobors.

Other Russian Americans have come from territories that are presently part of the Belorussian S.S.R. and the Ukrainian S.S.R. Before World War I these areas were part of the tsarist Russian Empire. Because the Belorussians and Ukrainians were former subjects of the tsar and belonged to the Russian Orthodox Church, and because they had a weak sense of their national identity, they often called themselves Russians. Similarly, many immigrants and their descendants from the western part of the Ukrainian S.S.R. (that is, eastern Galicia in the pre-1918 Austro-Hungarian Empire) identify themselves as Russians or Carpatho-Russians in the United States. These Galician Russians account for as much as 80 percent of the members of some Russian Orthodox churches and fraternal societies. Even among the immigrants who came after World War I, many professionals and intellectuals of Ukrainian, Jewish, Belorussian, Baltic, or other background continue to identify themselves as Russian, because Russian culture dominated the Russian Empire as it does in the Soviet successor state.

ARRIVAL AND SETTLEMENT

Unlike other eastern European immigrants, who settled chiefly in the eastern United States, the Russians

European Russia

〜〜〜 Boundary of the Russian Empire, 1910

Major concentrations of Russians

500   Km.   Miles

SWEDEN   FINLAND

Archangel

ESTONIAN S.S.R.

Leningrad

RUSSIAN S.F.S.R.

Baltic Sea

LATVIAN S.S.R.

LITHUANIAN

R.S.F.S.R.   S.S.R.

U.   S.   S.   S.   R.

Volga

Moscow

BELORUSSIAN

Warsaw

S.S.R.

POLAND

Kuibyshev (Samara)

Lvov

Kiev

CZECH.

UKRAINIAN

Galicia

Volga

HUNGARY

Dnieper

Don

KAZAKH

S.S.R.

Volgagrad

Ural

ROMANIA

Odessa

YUGOSLAVIA

Crimea

Caspian

Danube

Sea

BULGARIA

Black Sea

came first to Alaska and the West Coast. Their settlement of Alaska was part of the steady eastward expansion of the Russian Empire through the steppes and tundra of Siberia to the Pacific Coast, led by fur traders and seal hunters interested in finding pelts and skins for their Russian and European markets. In 1727 the Danish sea captain Vitus Bering, in the service of Peter the Great, discovered the straits that bear his name. In 1741 he landed on the Aleutian Islands, and by the 1760s Russian traders were hunting there. In 1784 they established the first permanent colony on Kodiak Island, just south of the Alaskan Peninsula. By the early 19th century, more than 25 settlements had been established, including Sitka and New Archangel in Alaska and the southernmost point, Fort Ross, about 100 miles north of San Francisco. These settlements were basically forts

or stockades established to protect the fur trade and to shelter missionaries bent on converting the local population to Orthodoxy. In 1861, 784 Russians were living in 43 communities; they had established 9 Orthodox churches and 35 chapels. Eventually the Russian government decided that the colony was not profitable and sold Alaska to the United States in 1867. About half the Russians returned home; many of the others moved to California.

A Russian presence in Alaska and California was preserved in the 19th century by the Russian Orthodox Diocese of Alaska and the Aleutian Islands, which had its seat first at Sitka in Alaska and, after 1872, in San Francisco. The only really large influx of Russians on the West Coast came during the first decades of the 20th century, when religious sectarians, especially Mo-

lokans, settled in California. The Molokans had rejected the precepts of the Russian Orthodox Church and in 1840 were exiled to the Transcaucasian region along the southern borders of the Russian Empire. They were pacifists, and when the Russian government threatened to induct them into the army in the early 20th century, they chose instead to emigrate. Some went to Persia (Iran), but about 5,000 came to California between 1904 and 1912 (a final group followed from Iran in the 1950s). By 1970 an estimated 20,000 Russian Molokans were living in California. Initially they settled in the industrial, multiracial, working-class neighborhood known as the Flats (Hollenbreck Heights) in Los Angeles and in San Francisco. The Molokan community in central Los Angeles subsequently dispersed, but the San Francisco group, including the Molokans from Iran, still live on Potrero Hill. Second- and third-generation Molokans have tended to move to the suburbs, while older members have retreated to rural areas like Woodburn, Ore., in an effort to preserve their tradition of simple living. For similar reasons Woodburn has also attracted dissenting groups like the Russian Old Believers. Another sect, the Dukhobors (Wrestlers of the Spirit) emigrated in large numbers to Canada. A few later came to the United States and settled temporarily in Los Angeles and San Diego, Calif., Chicago, and Detroit before moving to rural areas.

The migration of Russians to the East Coast of the United States began on an individual basis. Among the earliest known immigrants was Prince Demetrius Gallitzin (1770–1840), who arrived in Baltimore in 1792. He converted to Roman Catholicism, was ordained a priest, and served for more than forty years among the frontier settlers and Indians in western Pennsylvania. Other early immigrants during the 19th century included the radical political thinker and architect, Vladimir Stolishnikoff (d. 1907), who helped design Carnegie Hall, and Peter Demyanoff-Demens, a businessman, railroad builder, and cofounder of St. Petersburg, Fla., which he named after his birthplace.

Russians began to arrive in larger numbers during the 1880s. Between 1880 and 1914, but especially after 1905, many were impoverished peasants seeking a more prosperous life in the New World. By 1910 there were about 90,000 Russians in the United States; one-fourth were from Galicia, while many of the remainder were from the Belorussian regions of the Russian Empire.

The second period of migration, from 1920 to 1940, brought Russians who were fleeing the Soviet regime. As a result of the Bolshevik Revolution (1917) and the civil war (1918–1921), more than 2 million people fled Russia between 1920 and 1922. Most settled in France, Germany, and several east European countries, but through the help of the Red Cross, 30,000 refugees came to the United States. In the years that followed, Russians in smaller numbers continued to come from Germany, France, and eastern Europe, especially when those countries came under the sway of the Nazis in the 1930s and then were engulfed by World War II. Many of them were aristocrats, military officers, professionals, intellectuals, Orthodox churchmen, and others opposed to the Soviet regime.

In the third period (1945–1955) refugees displaced by World War II arrived in the United States. Large portions of the U.S.S.R. had been occupied by Germany in 1941–1942, and many Russians had been sent to work in the German war industry or fled when it became clear that the Soviet regime they opposed would be victorious. Between 1945 and 1955, they had lived in displaced-person camps in the Western zones of Germany and Austria until they were able to emigrate to the United States.

The most recent immigrants from Russia have arrived since 1969, when a change in Soviet policy permitted over 200,000 people to emigrate. Many of these were Jews who went to Israel, but by 1979 there were 24,000 Soviet Jews in the United States. Another 1,000 are ethnic Russians, and some, including Jews, are already playing an important role in the intellectual life of the Russian-American community.

Although it is extremely difficult to determine the actual number of Russians in the United States because of the many groups that have been called "Russian," it is reasonable to estimate on the basis of census reports and church records that by 1977 there were approximately 500,000 first-generation Russian Americans and their descendants. More than half of these can trace their roots to territories that are today ethnically Belorussian or Ukrainian.

The settlement patterns of Russians on the East Coast are similar to those of other immigrants from eastern and southern Europe. They arrived at the port of New York, occasionally Boston, and settled in nearby states where the mines and industries offered ready employment. Pennsylvania, New York, New Jersey, Connecticut, and Ohio became, and still remain, the states in which the Russians are concentrated. New York attracted immigrants both before and after World War I, and that city is still the center of the community's cultural and organizational life. There are other large communities in Chicago, Philadelphia, Boston, Pittsburgh, Cleveland, Detroit, Los Angeles, and San Francisco. In the early decades of the 20th century, each of these urban centers had one or more Russian neighborhoods, but since the 1950s these have decreased in size or have disappeared entirely as Russians moved to the suburbs. The institutional symbols—social clubs, fraternal societies, stores, and churches—often remain in the inner cities, however, and are visited on weekends and holidays by Russian-American suburbanites.

Russians also settled in rural farming areas, where they sometimes created utopian communes such as the colonies at Sicily Island, La., founded by Hermann Rosenthal (1843–1917), and at Wichita, Kan., and New Odessa, Ore., led by William Frey (Vladimir K. Gayns, d. 1870). These and many similar experiments often included Jews from Russia and other social activists; they lasted several months to a year or so at the most. More successful were agricultural colonies in southern New Jersey, Ohio, and Illinois. In 1925 an estimated 30,000 Russians were engaged in farming.

ECONOMIC LIFE AND SOCIAL ORGANIZATION

The immigrants who came to the East Coast between 1880 and 1914 were for the most part peasants or unskilled laborers. A survey conducted in 1909 found most Russians employed in coal mines, iron and steel mills, slaughterhouses, and the meat-packing industry. There were also many in the clothing industry, as Rus-

sians born in the United States turned from the hard labor in steel and coal to lighter work in the garment industry. Many others worked as bricklayers, carpenters, and house wreckers. Statistics from the Pacific Coast and Rocky Mountain states in 1909 found Russians most often employed on railroads, and in coal mining, lumber, beet-sugar refining, and canneries. Russian workers organized a Russian branch of the garment-workers' union, a Russian Polish division of the Union of Cloakmakers, the Society of Russian Bootmakers, and the Society for Russian Mechanics.

Immigrants in the second period (1920–1940) came from a higher educational and professional level, and although they may have taken on low-status jobs at first, they never entered the unskilled labor market in the large numbers that characterized their pre–World War I predecessors. Russian immigrants who have come since 1945, especially the educated among them, were in a more favorable position. Many have found their way into the teaching profession, government employment, publishing, and other jobs that reflected America's growing interest in the Soviet Union and its need for individuals who have knowledge of the Russian language and Soviet society.

Russians founded a wide variety of organizations, but these never played the central role in the life of the Russian-American community that they did for some other immigrant groups. The earliest and longest-lasting organizations were established by the immigrants from eastern Galicia, who as unskilled workers needed fraternal societies or brotherhoods to protect themselves and their families against the haphazard and often debilitating injuries of industrial labor. The brotherhoods provided modest benefits in case of injury or death. They also helped to construct and support churches, published newspapers and almanacs in a Galician variant of Russian, and sponsored social and cultural events. The oldest fraternals were all founded in the mining region of eastern Pennsylvania: Russkoe Pravoslavnoe Obshchestvo Vzaimopomoshchi (Russian Orthodox Catholic Mutual Aid Society, f. 1895, Wilkes-Barre); Obshchestvo Russkikh Bratstv (Russian Brotherhood Organization, f. 1901, Hazelton); and Russkoe Pravoslavnoe Obshchestvo "Liubov" (Russian Orthodox Fraternity Lubov, f. 1912, Jermyn). At their height in the early 1940s, all three had close to 30,000 members; by 1977 they had half as many.

The Russian immigrants of the 1920s were more active organizers. They seemed to found an organization for every social and professional group. The largest were again the working-class fraternal societies: Russkoe Ob'edinennoe Obshchestvo Vzaimopomoshchi v Amerike (The Russian Consolidated Mutual Aid Society, ROOVA, f. 1926, New York); Russkoe Nezavisimoe Obshchestvo Vzaimopomoshchi (the Russian Independent Mutual Aid Society, RNzOV, f. 1931, Chicago); and the Russkoe Narodnoe Obshchestvo Vzaimopomoshchi (the Russian National Mutual Aid Society, RNOV, f. 1927, New York) which in 1936 became the Russian branch of the International Workingmen's Association. By 1944 the three combined had 21,248 members in 150 lodges. At present, only the first two still exist, and taken together have a little over 5,000 members. Numerous professional, intellectual, aristocratic, military, and women's groups were also es-

tablished. Some sponsored publications; most were limited to social activities.

The first cultural organization was the Nauka Society, founded in 1905. During its four decades of existence it had six branches in the New York area which sponsored lectures, concerts, and social affairs, and, like the fraternal societies, provided insurance benefits. Three other cultural societies, the Fund for the Relief of Russian Writers and Scientists in Exile (f. 1918), the Obshchestvo imeni A.S. Pushkina v Amerike (Pushkin Society in America, f. 1935), and the Congress of Russian Americans (f. 1974), are also in New York. The first two give financial support to Russian writers and promote Russian culture; the third tries to preserve the Russian heritage and to present it in a favorable light to the general public. In San Francisco there is a Russian Center that houses a museum of Russian Culture (f. 1948), a library, and facilities for publishing and for social and cultural events.

Concern with the plight of the new immigrants prompted the creation of several other groups. One of the oldest is the Obshchestvo Pomoshchi Russkim Detiam za Rubezhom (Russian Children's Welfare Society Outside Russia, f. 1926, New York), which helps orphans and poor children. The most famous is the Tolstoy Foundation, set up in 1939 by Alexandra Tolstoy (1884–1979), the daughter of Count Leo Tolstoy, the famous writer. Founded by American philanthropy and in close cooperation with international relief organizations, the Tolstoy Foundation maintains branches throughout the world and has helped to settle more than 30,000 refugees from Russia in the United States. Since 1941 the foundation has operated a cultural center and an old-age home for the sick and disabled at Reed's Farm near Nyack, N.Y. In 1945 the plight of displaced persons in Germany and elsewhere who were in danger of being forcibly returned to the Soviet Union prompted Prince Serge Belosselsky-Belozersky to establish the Amerikansko-Russkii Soiuz Pomoshchi (American Russian Aid Association) with headquarters in New York City. Belosselsky subsequently donated several buildings in Glen Cove, L.I., which were transformed into a home for the aged and headquarters for several Russian professional and youth organizations.

RELIGION

Religion plays a central role in the life of Russian-American immigrants, whether they be adherents of the Eastern Orthodox Church, Old Believers, or sectarians like the Molokans. Since religion and ethnic identity have traditionally been closely related, the degree of one's Russian identity is often directly proportional to one's religious commitment.

Among the earliest settlers of the Russian colony in Alaska were Russian Orthodox priests. By 1850 the Alaskan mission included 35 churches and chapels and had converted 12,000 of the native Indians to Orthodoxy. The success of the movement was largely the achievement of the monk Saint Herman (1756–1837) and Rev. Ioann Popov-Veniaminov (1797–1879), who learned the Aleut language and published the first dictionary, grammars, Bible, and prayerbooks in that tongue. In 1840 Veniaminov assumed the name Innocent and became the first bishop of the Orthodox Dio-

cese of Kamchatka, Kurile, and the Aleutian Islands, with its seat in New Archangel, Alaska.

After Alaska was purchased by the United States in 1867, the diocese was transferred to San Francisco. Until the end of the century the Russian Orthodox establishment in the United States was very small, with only a few parishes in San Francisco (f. 1868), New Orleans (f. 1864), and New York (f. 1870). Its only notable growth came as a result of conversions of Eastern-rite (Greek) Catholic immigrants from the Austro-Hungarian Empire who had settled in the urban industrial centers of the Northeast. Between 1898 and 1907 the church was headed by Archbishop Tikhon Beliavin (1865–1925), later patriarch of Moscow, who transferred the diocesan seat from San Francisco to New York in 1903 and renamed it the Diocese of the Aleutian Islands and North America. To encourage missionary activity, the tsar's government was providing the North American Orthodox Church with almost $80,000 each year by the turn of the century, a reflection of Russia's more general campaign to undermine its Austro-Hungarian protagonist by converting to Russian Orthodoxy the Greek Catholics in eastern Galicia, northern Bukovina, and northeastern Hungary, and emigrants from those same regions who had gone to the United States. By 1914 more than 60,000 Greek Catholic immigrants had been converted to Orthodoxy.

The Russian Orthodox Church in the United States was deeply affected by the Russian Revolution and by the political associations of the post-1920 immigrants. A serious dispute arose over whether or not to recognize the hierarchy of the mother church in Moscow, which after 1917 had come under Soviet rule. This resulted in the creation of three separate churches. In 1920 the new immigrants who unequivocally rejected any association with Soviet-ruled Russia founded the Russian Orthodox Church Outside Russia. Originally based in Yugoslavia, the church's headquarters were transferred to the United States in 1950, and it became known as the Synod Abroad. Supporters of the Diocese of the Aleutian Islands and North America decided in 1924 to remain loyal to the mother church in the Soviet Union, but insisted on being given the status of an autonomous metropolitan district. It was popularly known as the Metropolia, but because the majority of its members were former Greek Catholics from the Austro-Hungarian Empire, it was renamed the Russian Orthodox Greek Catholic Church in America. Some parishes continued to express loyalty directly to Moscow, however, and in order to accommodate them a Russian Orthodox Catholic Church in America (the Patriarchal Exarchate) was established in 1933.

In 1970 the patriarchate in Moscow recognized the independence of the Metropolia and it became part of the new Orthodox Church in America. The patriarch also gave churches in the Patriarchal Exarchate that were directly under his jurisdiction the option of joining the Orthodox Church in America. Three distinct Russian Orthodox church bodies remain in the United States to this day: the multiethnic autocephalous Orthodox Church in America, with 1 million members; the patriarchal parishes of the Russian Orthodox Church in the United States and Canada under the jurisdiction of the patriarchate of Moscow, with 25,000 members; and the Russian Orthodox Church Outside Russia governed by the Synod Abroad, with 55,000 members. The last-named claims to be the legal successor of the pre-revolutionary mother church. A smaller number of Russians have joined various Baptist and Evangelical churches, and there are also a few Russian Catholic parishes in New York City, Los Angeles, San Francisco, Chicago, and Portland, Ore.

The Russian Orthodox Church has tried to maintain the culture of the Russian community through the education of its children. Both in Alaska and the United States church schools have offered instruction in Russian language and culture along with religion. The church has also sponsored publications, such as the *Russko-amerikanskii pravoslavnyi viestnik/Russian American Orthodox Messenger* (New York, f. 1896), written wholly or in part in Russian. Each of the three Russian Orthodox churches still has its own Russian-language journals and almanacs. The colorful ceremonies connected with Easter and Christmas continue to be attended by immigrants and their descendants. They are particularly reminded of their heritage on these "Russian" religious days because they observe them according to the Julian calendar, and these holidays therefore do not usually fall on the same day as their Western Christian equivalents. The Orthodox Church also fosters the Russian heritage through the Federation of Russian Orthodox Clubs (f. 1927, Wilkes-Barre, Pa.) and the Organizatsiia Rossiiskikh Pravoslavnykh Razvedchikov (Organization of Russian Orthodox Scouts), which since 1969 has sponsored an annual summer camp at Vladimirovo, near Chicago, where children receive daily instruction in Russian history, geography, and literature.

Among the Molokans and the Old Believers, religious life has played an even greater part in preserving their Russian culture. In the old country the Molokans were divided into factions, Postoianye (the steadfast or constant ones) and the Priguny (Jumpers), who expressed themselves through emotional outbursts and violent movement during religious services. The Jumpers are the more numerous in the immigration and are officially known as the Obshchestvo Dukhovnykh Khristiian Prygunov v Amerike (Society of Spiritual Christian Jumpers in America). The Old Believers were cast out of the Orthodox Church after they refused to accept certain liturgical changes instituted in official church doctrine during the 17th century. Both the Molokans and Old Believers are fundamentalists who express themselves less through external ceremony than through reading and meditating on their spiritual books. Their texts are required to be in Russian, and this encourages knowledge of the language among the young. By the 1970s the Old Believers and the other sectarians in Woodburn, Ore., were still clinging to the old traditions; Russian is now even taught as part of the federally sponsored bilingual programs in its public schools.

The church has also had a negative impact on the Russian-American community. The missionary zeal and universalist strivings of Orthodoxy have tended to diminish the Russian element within the church. The Diocese of the Aleutian Islands and North America grew during the late 19th century by including Greek, Syrian, Albanian, Serbian, Ukrainian, and Carpatho-Rusyn immigrants within its ranks. During the 1920s

the Greeks, Syrians, Ukrainians, Albanians, and Serbs founded their own churches, and this served to eliminate most of the non-Russian members from the Russian parishes. But at the same time the internal squabbling among supporters of the patriarch in Moscow, the Metropolia, and the Synod Abroad led to legal battles over the control of church properties and dissension within the community, even at the family level. As a result, many people were alienated from their religious qua Russian heritage. Since the 1960s the Metropolia has tried to remedy the situation by stressing the universal nature of Orthodoxy. The resulting Orthodox Church in America, established in 1970, includes parishes from the Metropolia, from the Patriarchal Exarchate, and from Albanian, Bulgarian, and Romanian dioceses. The Russian element has been substantially reduced; English is the dominant language of the liturgy, and the church tries actively to avoid association with any one particular ethnic group. The smaller Russian Orthodox Church Outside Russia still maintains itself as a Russian institution in both language and culture.

EDUCATION

As the Russian Orthodox Church grew in membership along the East Coast during the late 19th century, each parish tried to have its own church school. By 1916 there were 126 parish schools with 150 teachers and other staff and 6,739 pupils, where classes in religious instruction were held after regular school hours or on Saturdays. Russian language and history were also taught, and, at least until 1917, loyalty to the Russian Orthodox Church and to the Russian tsar was encouraged among the young. The Synod Abroad still operates the St. Sergius High School (f. 1959) in New York City, where most of the courses are taught in Russian.

The Russian Orthodox Church also founded seminaries where, in addition to religious subjects, students studied Russian civilization. The earliest seminary was founded in Minneapolis in 1898 and was relocated in Tenafly, N.J., between 1905 and 1912. In 1938 the Metropolia established St. Vladimir's Seminary in Manhattan, which since 1961 has been located in Crestwood, N.Y. St. Vladimir's has maintained a distinguished faculty, including a number of Russian scholars both from the homeland and from the émigré communities of western Europe—scholars such as Alexander A. Bogolepov (1886–), the Reverend Georges Florovsky (1893–1979), Nicholas O. Lossky (1870–1965), the Reverend John Meyendorff (1926–), and the Reverend Alexander Schmemann (1921–). Both the parish schools and theological seminaries have helped to foster Russian religious and secular culture.

The Russian-American community has also organized several secular schools. A grant from the Carnegie Foundation and money from other sources made possible the Russian Collegiate Institute, established in New York City in 1918 at the initiative of the eminent zoologist Alexander Petrunkevitch (1875–1947). It offered technical and academic subjects five evenings a week to Russian workers. By 1921 the average weekly attendance was 1,400. A similar school, the Russian People's University, was founded in Chicago; in 1919 it had 80 students. In 1918 a short-lived Soviet school with 300 students in New York City offered courses in Russian to working people on a wide variety of technical subjects. Students of Russian background who wanted to study in American institutions could apply for financial aid from the Russian Student Fund (f. 1921), created at the initiative of Alexis R. Wiren and supported by Boris Bakhmeteff (1880–1951) and several American philanthropists. Unlike the church schools, these technical institutes were less interested in preserving Russian culture than in teaching people how to earn a living.

The growth of American studies dealing with Russia since World War II is a result, of course, of U.S. foreign-policy interests and rivalry with the Soviet Union, but a side effect has been the opportunity it has provided Americans of Russian descent to study the heritage of their forefathers on a level of sophistication that would hardly have been possible had they been restricted to the resources of the community's own religious or secular organizations. Since the war many colleges, universities, and even some high schools have offered a variety of courses in Russian language, literature, history, political science, economics, and folklore. The first course in the Russian language was offered by Leo Wiener at Harvard University in 1896. By 1944 Russian was being taught at 62 American colleges. Inspired by the Cold War and the Soviet launching of the first satellite, Sputnik I, in 1957, Russian studies in the United States expanded in earnest during the 1960s. By 1975 more than 1,500 colleges and universities were offering at least one course, and often more, on some aspect of Russian culture.

CULTURE

The press has traditionally been the most effective medium for propagating culture within the Russian-American community, and its strength or weakness often reflects the degree to which the Russian language has survived among the immigrants and their descendants. The first newspaper was the bilingual *Svoboda/The Alaska Herald* (San Francisco, 1868–1873), published by the Ukrainian priest, Agapius Honcharenko (1832–1916). Its Russian articles informed immigrants about American life; its English articles attempted to inspire sympathy among the larger public for the anti-tsarist movement in Russia. During the 1890s a number of short-lived socialist and radical Russian newspapers appeared, such as *Znamia* (The Banner, New York, 1889–1892) and *Progress* (New York and Chicago, 1893–1894), which called for revolutionary changes in the capitalist economic system and often carried articles by leading Russian socialist thinkers. Their readership was generally limited to left-wing intellectuals, especially among Jews from Russia. The last and most successful of the socialist newspapers was the Menshevik-controlled (later Bolshevik-controlled) *Novyi mir* (New World, New York, 1911–1920). On its staff were the leading Bolshevik revolutionaries Nikolai Bukharin (1888–1939) and Leon Trotsky (1879–1940); by the time *Novyi mir* was closed down by the American authorities in 1920 it claimed 8,000 subscribers.

Working-class newspapers first appeared among the Russians from Galicia. The two best known were the Russian Orthodox Catholic Mutual Aid Society's *Svit/The Light* (Wilkes-Barre, Pa., f. 1895), edited for

many years by the Reverend Peter Kohanik (1880–1969), and the Society of Russian Brotherhoods' *Pravda/The Truth* (Philadelphia, Pa., f. 1900). They printed news about the Galician community written in a language that combined Russian with local Galician Ukrainianisms; English replaced it in the 1960s. The first lasting mass-circulating newspaper for immigrants from Russia was the daily *Russkoe slovo* (Russian Word, f. 1910), later renamed *Novoe russkoe slovo* (New Russian Word, New York, 1921–).

The 1920s were the high point for the Russian-American press; *Novoe russkoe slovo*, together with two other dailies, *Russkii golos* (Russian Voice, New York, f. 1917) and *Russkaia zhizn'* (Russian Life, San Francisco, f. 1921), had a total circulation of 75,000 copies, which included a substantial proportion of Russian-speaking Jews. At present, the total circulation of all Russian-language periodicals is about 49,000, a decline directly related to assimilation and to ignorance of the language among more recent generations.

The exodus of Russian intellectuals after the revolution resulted in the development of two distinct Russian literatures: Soviet Russian literature, whose expressive energies have often been harnessed to serve the interests of the state, and émigré literature, which flourishes in a kind of vaccum throughout the world, but which is linked to the Russian homeland through its language and often its thematic content. Émigré literature has been dominated by three themes: a nationalistic love for the motherland; the difficulty of becoming accustomed to foreign ways; and loneliness, summed up in the rhetorical query posed by the poet Iurii Ivask, "Who can be as alone as an emigrant?"

The center of Russian literature and cultural life abroad has always been Paris, though from time to time the communities in Berlin, Prague, and Belgrade were quite active. Before 1940 Russian literary activity in the United States was more limited. A few short-lived literary journals and anthologies were published in New York and San Francisco, along with books by writers such as Georgii D. Grebenshchikov-Sibiriak (1883–1964), Sergei I. Gusev-Orenburgskii (1867–1964), and Veniamin M. Levin (1892–1953).

When Paris fell to the Germans in 1940, New York temporarily replaced it as the center of Russian émigré intellectual life. A number of writers came to New York, among them Mark Aldanov (1886–1957), Vladimir Nabokov (1899–1977), and Vassily Janovsky, and critics Gleb P. Struve (1898–) and Mikhail O. Zetlin (1882–1945). Even though Nabokov began to write almost exclusively in English and others like Aldanov eventually returned to Europe, this generation of writers had a lasting impact on Russian-American literature. They established literary journals, the most influential of which was the quarterly *Novyi zhurnal* (New Journal, New York, f. 1942). It was modeled after the so-called "thick journals" of 19th century Russia, with issues numbering 300 to 400 pages and containing contributions of literary, scholarly, and journalistic content. Another was *Novosel'e* (New Home, New York, 1942–1950), edited by the poet Sophia Pregel' (1897–1972). At present, the major forums for Russian émigré literature are still the *Novyi zhurnal* and the daily newspaper *Novoe russkoe slovo*.

Russian émigré literature in the United States also produced a series of literary almanacs, *Opyty/Essays* (New York, 1953–1958) and *Vozdushnye puti* (Air Ways, New York, 1960–1967), and was encouraged by the Chekhov Publishing House in New York City, which between 1951 and 1956 published more than 150 works by Russian émigrés. Most recently, the Chekhov House has set up Khronika Press, which publishes works by Soviet dissidents (some of whom have come to the United States) in both Russian and English. Russian-American literature has also been served by the Mezhdunarodnoe Literaturnoe Sodruzhestvo (Inter-Language Literary Associates) and the Russkoe Knizhnoe Delo (Russian Book Service) of the Viktor Kamkin bookstore in Washington, D.C. Among the more prolific writers are Lidia Alekseeva (1907–), Nina Berberova (1901–), Igor Chinnov (1911–), Ivan Elagin (1918–), Boris Filipoff (1905–), and Iurii Ivask (1910–). Very few Russian writers have come to the United States since the 1960s, either from Western Europe or from the Soviet Union. Two distinguished exceptions are the poet Josef Brodsky (1940–) and the Nobel prize-winning author and anti-Soviet dissident, Alexander Solzhenitsyn (1918–).

In the performing arts Russian culture is presented through ethnic organizations as well as through professional U.S. companies. Within the community almost every church parish, especially during the 1920s and 1930s, had its own adult and children's theatrical groups that would perform simple plays with both secular and religious themes. The participation of youngsters in such performances did much to foster a lasting awareness of the heritage of their parents. Several semiprofessional Russian theatrical companies were also formed, mostly in New York City: the New Russian Theater, the Russian Free Theater, the Russkii Zarubezhnyi Teatr (Russian Émigré Theater, f. 1958), directed by Evgenii F. Evgen'ev, and the Theater of Russian Youth (f. 1968).

Music has always been an integral part of Russian-American life. The Orthodox church maintains choirs in both its local parishes and its larger cathedrals. The most famous is the Boys' Choir of New York (f. 1918), which recruits youngsters from all over the country; they live in a dormitory in New York City and perform regularly at the St. Nicholas Cathedral. Since the 1940s new liturgies have been prepared that replace Russian with English. Russian secular and religious choral music has also been spread throughout the Russian and larger American communities by professional ensembles, such as Sergei Jaroff's Don Cossack Russian Choir.

Symphonic music was propagated by a Russian symphony orchestra (f. 1904), which performed in New York City until 1919 and thereafter for several years at music festivals in the South and West. Performers from Russia have long been notable in American cultural circles where they have made known the musical and dance culture of their former homeland. Among them were leading 20th-century composers Igor Stravinsky (1882–1971) and Sergei Rachmaninoff (1873–1943), conductors Nikolai Sokoloff (1886–1965) and Serge Koussevitsky (1874–1951), cellists Gregor Piatigorsky (1903–) and Mstislav Rostropovich (1927–), the operatic bass Feodor Chaliapin (1873–1938), and the pianist Vladimir Horowitz (1904–), most of whom settled permanently in the United States. Dancers and choreog-

raphers from Russia have dominated American ballet—from Anna Pavlova (1881–1931) and Michel Fokine (1880–1942) in the earlier part of this century to George Balanchine (1904–), Rudolf Nureyev (1938–), Natalia Makarova (1940–), and Mikhail Baryshnikov (1948–) in more recent years.

Scholarship and science have also had important contributions from Russian Americans. To maintain contacts within the group, the Association of Russian-American Scholars (f. 1947) has organized several symposia and publishes a bilingual scholarly journal, *Zapiski/Transactions* (New York, f. 1967). A large number of scholars from Russia have had distinguished careers in the United States, among them Michael Florinsky, Michael M. Karpovich, Michael Rostovtzeff, Mark Slonim, Alexander A. Vasiliev, and George Vernadsky, who have written extensively on aspects of Russian civilization, and George Gamow, Wassily Leontieff, Igor Sikorsky, Pitirim Sorokin, and Vladimir Zworykin, who have made important contributions in the social and natural sciences. Whether or not these internationally known cultural figures, scholars, and scientists have played a role in Russian-American community life, they are all well known to the members of the group, who find in their achievements a great source of pride.

POLITICS

Until 1920 the Russians, including many Russian Jews, played a dominant role in the growing American socialist movement, but after 1920 with the decline of American radical socialism and the influx of the new anti-Bolshevik immigrants, Russian-American political activity turned its attention to organizations concerned with the homeland rather than with political action in the United States.

The oldest Russian-American political organization was the Russkoe Respublikanskoe Obshchestvo (Russian Republican Society, f. 1861, San Francisco), whose goals were to spread republican ideals among Russians both in America and in the Russian Empire. The increase in immigration from Russia during the 1880s, mainly of Jews, brought to the United States several socialist and Marxist thinkers, including Lev Hartmann (1849–1909), P.A. Tverskii, and Sergei Shevich, later cofounder of the American Socialist Labor party. Several organizations, among them the Russkii Rabochii Soiuz (Russian Worker's Union, f. 1888) and the Russko-Amerikanskii Klub (Russian-American Club), were short-lived clubs for intellectuals to debate their various proposals for social reform in Russia. Organizations like the Society for Aid to Political Victims of the 1905 Russian Revolution (f. 1906) and the Society for Aid to Political Exiles in Siberia (f. 1910) supported opposition to the Russian imperial regime. Of more immediate significance for the immigrants was the Russian Social-Democratic Society (f. 1891), out of which grew the Russian sections of the American Socialist party; by 1905 there were 40 of them. The revolutionary events of 1917 provided the greatest impetus for the growth of socialism, however; between 1915 and 1919 the membership in the Russian division of the American Socialist party rose from 300 to 12,000. The Russians formed the left wing of the party, and after an unsuccessful attempt to gain control of the organization in

1919, they broke away to found the American Communist party and called for radical social revolution in the United States. Other groups, such as the Obshchestvo Pomoshchi Svobodnoi Rossii (Society to Help Liberated Russia), the Soiuz Russkikh Rabochikh (Union of Russian Workers), the Mutual Aid Association of Workmen from Russia, and the Soviet mission's technical department, had similar goals. The strength of the Socialist and Communist movement was abruptly broken in 1920, when the United States government arrested several thousand members of these organizations and accused them of plotting the overthrow of the U.S. government.

In 1920 the first of more than 30,000 anti-Bolshevik immigrants began to arrive in the United States. For the most part they avoided direct participation in U.S. political life, and instead established organizations reflecting a variety of political persuasions that ideally looked forward to the restitution of a non-Communist Russia.

One faction, composed of partisans of the tsarist regime who were opposed to any kind of revolution, were the so-called "White" Russians (not to be confused with ethnic Belorussians, sometimes referred to as "White Russians" in English). Their members were primarily officers and soldiers who had fought in the counterrevolutionary "White" armies during the Russian civil war (1918–1921). The most influential was the American branch of the Russkii Obshche-Voinskii Soiuz (Russian All Soldiers' Union), founded in Paris in 1933. A few monarchist groups and publications still exist today. As a result of the Cold War between the Soviet Union and the United States, some conservatives formed anti-Communist groups. Among these are the Predstavitel'stvo Rossiiskikh Emigrantov v Ameriki (Russian Immigrant's Representative Association, f. 1956), the Obshcherossiiskii Monarkhicheskii Front (All-Russian Monarchist Front, f. 1958), and the Ob"edinenie Amerikantsev-antikommunistov Russkago Proiskhozhdeniia (Union of American Anti-Communists of Russian Descent).

Another group consisted of democrats who favored the liberal revolution that took place in February 1917 and resulted in the creation of the provisional government. This group coalesced around Boris Bakhmeteff, the provisional government's representative in the United States, and Alexander Kerensky, its last prime minister, who came to New York from Paris in 1940. In 1949 Kerensky organized a League to Fight for National Freedom that attempted to unite the socialists and liberal democrats within the Russian-American community.

Some groups still support Leninist socialism, but see it as having been violated by Stalin's totalitarian regime; others like the Mensheviks are also anticapitalist, but are critical of both Stalinist totalitarianism and Leninist socialism.

INTERGROUP RELATIONS

The Russian community's relations with the U.S. government have often been marked by serious difficulties, although these have been counterbalanced by organized aid and support from certain American philanthropic and welfare groups. The first incident that prompted the Russian community to mobilize was the U.S. Senate's ratification in 1893 of a treaty with tsarist

Russia regarding the mutual exchange of defectors. The community, at the time filled with antitsarist "revolutionaries," joined with Jews from Russia to form a Komitet Russko-Amerikanskoi Natsional'noi Ligi (Committee of the Russian-American National League). At the same time, sympathetic Americans led by Samuel Gompers and others set up in Boston a Society of Friends of Russian Liberty, but despite the protests sent by the two groups, President Grover Cleveland signed the agreement. The law was finally tested in 1908, when the tsarist government demanded extradition of a Russian immigrant, but a petition signed by 70,000 American citizens prompted President Theodore Roosevelt to free the man.

More serious encounters occurred in 1919 and 1920. The success of the Bolshevik Revolution in Russia, the postwar Communist coups in some parts of Europe, and the rapid growth of the Socialist and other left-wing parties in the United States led to the first of America's so-called Red Scares. A governmental campaign to crack down on domestic revolutionaries was soon under way, and the Russian-American community was hard hit. In New York alone one investigative committee arrested 5,000 persons during its raids on the headquarters of the Union of Russian Workers (November 1919) and the Russian-dominated American Communist party (January 1920). Of the several thousand aliens who were deported, 90 percent were returned to Russia. In the public mind, all Russian Americans were associated with Socialists, Anarchists, or Communists, and were considered dangerously un-American.

Even the apolitical Molokans suffered. Their experiences in urban Los Angeles and San Francisco threatened to destroy their traditional way of life, and having heard of revolutionary changes in Russia, they requested the United States government to permit them to return to the homeland. Their request was denied, however, because at the time Washington did not recognize the Soviet government.

The Red Scare created considerable hostility between the Russian immigrants and the rest of American society. Some tried to cover up their background and assimilate into the larger society; others simply remained hostile to the new world in which they were now forced to remain.

The anti-Bolshevik refugees who began arriving in 1920 fared somewhat better. Their political attitudes were acceptable to the American public, while their plight, especially the poverty sometimes imposed on formerly wealthy aristocrats and army officers, elicited much sympathy, particularly in American high society. Organizations were founded, like the Boston-based Committee for the Education of Russian Youth in Exile, which in its first ten years of existence (1915–1925) distributed $300,000 from American philanthropists to support the education of Russian refugees in all parts of Europe. Similar efforts were undertaken for Russian students and refugees in the United States, as money from rich Americans funded the Russian Collegiate Institute (f. 1918), the Russian Student Fund (f. 1923), and the Tolstoy Foundation (f. 1938).

Since World War II, the relations between the Russian-American community and American society have been largely determined by the changing climate of relations between the United States and the Soviet Union. During the war years the Soviet Union was considered in the American press as a brave ally in the struggle against fascism. This favorable atmosphere toward "Mother Russia" instilled pride in many segments of the Russian-American community, even those elements that were anti-Soviet. This attitude changed with the advent of the Cold War. In theory, the large anti-Soviet element in the Russian-American community should have favored America's anti-Soviet policies. In practice, however, many monarchist and some liberal Russian groups objected to them, as well as to private groups such as the American Committee for Liberation from Bolshevism (f. 1951), because they appeared to encourage independence movements of the non-Russian nationalities in the Soviet Union at the expense of a unified Russia. The goal of national liberation for Estonians, Latvians, Lithuanians, Belorussians, Ukrainians, Cossacks, and others supported in the U.S. Congress, still incurs the displeasure of large segments of the Russian-American community. Many continue to hope that a non-Bolshevik but unified Russian state within the borders of the present Soviet Union will someday come into being. These attitudes also cause estrangement between the Russian Americans and other eastern European immigrant groups in the United States, especially the Lithuanians and Ukrainians.

The Cold War produced yet another Red Scare, this time led by the Republican Senator from Wisconsin, Joseph McCarthy, which again prompted the American public to believe that anything Russian was Red and anything Red was dangerous, even treasonable. During the 1950s Americans of Russian background often maintained a low profile and some even renounced their heritage in favor of total assimilation. The enthusiasm for Russian studies in the 1960s, which popularized Russian culture through books, college courses, movies, and television programs, has removed some of the stigma of being a Russian American. Yet as recently as 1971 a Russian-American Congress was organized with the express purpose of eradicating the remnants of Russophobia in the United States which had resulted in apathy among the younger generations of Russian descent.

GROUP MAINTENANCE AND INDIVIDUAL COMMITMENT

The ability of the Russian-American community to maintain itself is threatened because of its traditional geographical and ideological fragmentation. The first period of immigration, lasting from the 1880s until 1914, consisted primarily of Belorussians and Galicians on the East Coast and sectarians like the Molokans on the West Coast. The older Belorussians have at best a passive allegiance to the Russian-American community, while the Galicians, even though they are adamant in calling themselves Russian, are isolated from what they call "real Russians," who in turn look down upon them as uneducated, lower-class working people. The Galicians no longer have newspapers in their native language and their children and grandchildren, many of whom are college-trained professionals, have either assimilated totally into American society, or, if they maintain some of their family traditions, are often confused as to whether their ethnic heritage is Russian,

Ukrainian, or something else. While the West Coast Molokans and Old Believers have instilled through religious and language training a strong sense of their Russian heritage in their children, they have virtually no contact with the Orthodox Russians on the East Coast, nor for that matter do they mix with other Russians who live nearer by.

What remains are the immigrants and their descendants who have come to this country since the 1920s. They have for the most part closed themselves off in small aristocratic, academic, or military circles that exclude any members of the Russian-American community who are not "of their kind." The Orthodox church is the only institution that includes many segments of the community (except, of course, the sectarians, and small numbers of Catholics and Protestants), but the largest church organizations are no longer Russian in character, and even those that are do not see much contact between the large number of lower-class Galician parishioners and the ethnic Russians who traditionally have held the highest positions in the hierarchy. Finally, recent immigrants from the Soviet Union cannot fit easily into existing Russian-American secular or religious organizations. The vast majority of newcomers are Jewish, while the others have little in common with the religious beliefs and political ideologies of the older immigrants.

The vast geographical, political, religious, and social differences among the various segments of the Russian-American community, combined with the restricted flow of ethnic Russians from the Soviet homeland since 1945, have resulted in a decline in the size of Russian-American organizations and of the Russian-language press. These factors, combined with the political and psychological ambiguities involved in identifying oneself as Russian, leaves the future viability of the Russian-American community in doubt.

Bibliography

A good introduction to the Russian-American group is Jaroslav Chyz and Joseph S. Rouček, "The Russians in the United States," *The Slavonic and East European Review*, vol. 17, no. 51 (1939): 638–658. For more recent developments, see Helen Kovach and Djuro J. Vrga, "The Russian Minority in America," in *Ethnic Groups in the City*, ed. Otto Feinstein (Lexington, Mass., 1971). The classic study of the pre–World War I years is Mikhail Vil'chur, *Russkie v Amerike* (New York, 1918); the interwar years are given detailed coverage in Ivan K. Okuntsov, *Russkaia èmigratsiia v Severnoi i Iuzhnoi Amerike* (Buenos Aires, 1967). The best history of the Alaska colony is by Hector Chevigny, *Russian America: The Great Alaskan Venture, 1741–1867* (New York, 1965); their short-lived presence in California is analyzed in Emil T.H. Bunje et al., *Russian California, 1805–1841* (1937; reprint, San Francisco, 1970).

The only sociological analysis is by Jerome Davis, *The Russian Immigrant* (1922; reprint, New York, 1969), which concentrates on the years immediately after World War I. The history of the church is given in Constance J. Tarasar and John H. Erickson, eds., *Orthodox America, 1794–1976* (Syosset, N.Y., 1975), and in Archimandrite Serafim, *The Quest for Orthodoxy in America: A History of the Orthodox Church in North America* (New York, 1973). The Molokan communities have received detailed attention in Pauline V. Young, *The Pilgrims of Russian Town: The Community of Spiritual Christian Jumpers in America* (1932; reprint, New York, 1967), and Willard B. Moore, *Molokan Oral Tradition* (Berkeley, 1973).

The importance of émigré literary and cultural activity is discussed in several works by Gleb Struve, with emphasis on Russian-American writers given in his "Russian Émigré Literature," in *World Literature since 1945*, ed. I. Ivask and G. von Wilpert (New York, 1973). A detailed survey is found in Nikolai P. Poltoratzky, "Russian Literature, Literary Scholarship, and Publishing in the United States," in *Ethnic Literatures since 1776: The Many Voices of America* (Lubbock, Tex., 1978) pt. 2, ed. W.T. Zyla and W.M. Aycock. The political orientations of the group in the post–World War II years are analyzed in George Fischer, ed., *Russian Émigré Politics* (New York, 1951).

There are several archives with substantial collections relevant to the Russian-American community. The most wide-ranging materials are found in Columbia University's Bakhmeteff Archive of Russian and East European History and Civilization, the Hoover Institution on War, Revolution, and Peace at Stanford University, and at the Library of Congress in Washington, D.C.. Considerable material on the development of the church in particular and on the Russian immigration in general can be found in the archives of the Orthodox Church in America, at its chancery in Syosset, L.I.

PAUL ROBERT MAGOCSI

RUTHENIANS: *see* CARPATHO-RUSYNS; UKRAINIANS

RYUKUWANS: *see* JAPANESE

SALISH: *see* AMERICAN INDIANS

SALVADOREANS: *see* CENTRAL AND SOUTH AMERICANS

SAMOANS: *see* PACIFIC ISLANDERS

SAUDI ARABIANS: *see* ARABS

SAUKS (SACS): *see* AMERICAN INDIANS

SCANDINAVIANS: *see* DANISH; FINNS; ICELANDERS; NORWEGIANS; SWEDES

SCATICOOKS: *see* AMERICAN INDIANS

SCOTCH-IRISH

The term Scotch-Irish is ambiguous; it does not refer to people of mixed Scottish and Irish ancestry, as the name might seem to imply, but to the descendants of the Presbyterians from lowland Scotland who settled in Ulster, the northernmost province of Ireland, in the 17th century and subsequently emigrated from there to America. In all, some 200,000 Scots migrated to northern Ireland and at least 2 million of their descendants made a second move across the Atlantic. Although Scotch-Irish emigration is often thought of as a phenomenon mainly of the colonial period, it did not in fact lose its impetus until the 20th century.

In the colonial period the Scotch-Irish played a significant role in the westward expansion of the frontier in Pennsylvania, Virginia, and the Carolinas. They were also largely responsible for the early development of American Presbyterianism. From the time of the Revolution onward the Scotch-Irish achieved an extraordinary degree of success in American politics. Presidents Andrew Jackson, James Buchanan, and Chester A. Arthur were all sons of Scotch-Irish immigrants, and James K. Polk, William McKinley, and Woodrow Wilson were also of Scotch-Irish descent. Other notable Americans of Scotch-Irish origin were John C. Calhoun; Thomas J. "Stonewall" Jackson; William H. McGuffey, the compiler of school readers; the composer Edward A. MacDowell; Cyrus H. McCormick, the inventor of the mechanical reaper; and Supreme Court Justice James C. McReynolds. As English-speaking Protestants, often of relatively high economic standing, the Scotch-Irish found it comparatively easy to move into the mainstream of American society. Yet their distinctive historical experience, allied with their stern Presbyterianism, nurtured strong feelings of group consciousness that were continuously renewed by immigration. Today the Scotch-Irish are widely dispersed and are not easily identifiable. But if one were to make a guess, it would be that approximately 1 in every 30 Americans —some 8 million people—have Scotch-Irish forebears.

The term Scotch-Irish is an Americanism. In the British Isles it is hardly known, though a Latin variant (Scoto-Hibernicus) was employed by Scottish universi-

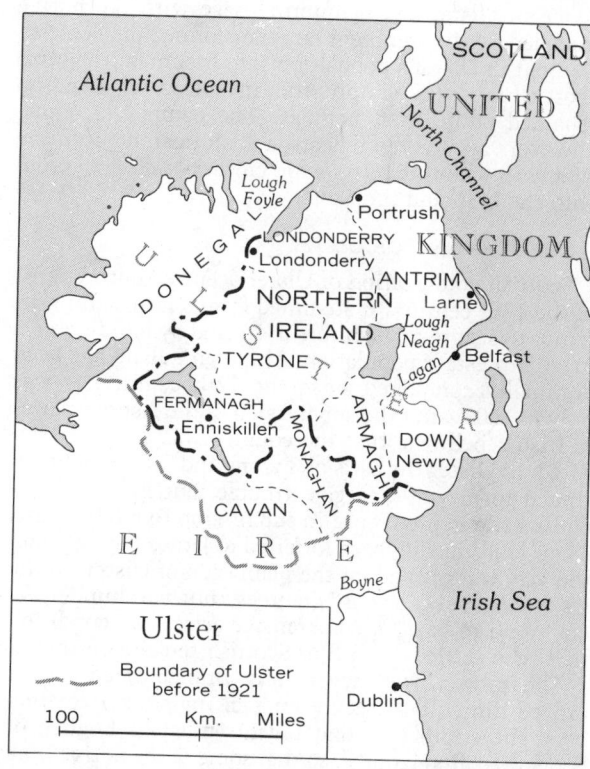

Ulster

~~~~ Boundary of Ulster before 1921

100   Km.   Miles

ties in the 17th and 18th centuries when registering students of Scottish ancestry who lived in Ireland. In Ulster itself, ethnic designations have generally been unnecessary, for nationality could readily be inferred from religion; on those occasions when an ethnic appellation is employed to describe Ulstermen of Scottish origin, the preferred term is Ulster Scots.

The first known use of the term Scotch-Irish dates from 1695 in a report by Sir Thomas Laurence, the Secretary of Maryland. A generation later, the name had become current in Pennsylvania and by the 1750s was fairly widely accepted throughout the colonies. In 1757 Edmund Burke wrote of those "who in America are generally called Scotch-Irish"; three years later, Lord Adam Gordon, a Scottish nobleman on a visit to the colonies, found Winchester, Va., inhabited by "a spurious race of mortals known by the appellation of 'Scotch-Irish.'" The Scotch-Irish themselves seem at first to have been reluctant to use the name—not surprisingly, since it was not always applied in a complimentary sense. An Irish missionary in South Carolina complained in 1711 that an English parson there had called him a "Scotch-Irish Lyllibolaro"—a taunting reference to William of Orange's Ulster supporters of 1688, for whom "Lillibolaro" had been a battlecry.

More than a century was to elapse before the Scotch-Irish showed much enthusiasm for the name. They used it to dissociate themselves from the Irish Catholic immigrants of the 1840s, whose coming had excited prejudice and hostility. By the end of the 19th century

lively controversy developed over the use of the term. Irish-American historians attacked what they called the "Scotch-Irish myth," claiming that there were no grounds for distinguishing between inhabitants of Ulster and those of other Irish provinces. A century of residence in Ulster and of intermarriage with the native Irish had, so the argument ran, transformed the Scottish element in Ulster's population into Irishmen; the term Scotch-Irish was simply the invention of a group ashamed of its Irish heritage. The compound name, however, accurately reflects a historical reality; the people to whom it refers were culturally distinct from both the Irish and the Scots.

THE PLANTING OF ULSTER

Scottish colonization of Ulster occurred during most of the 17th century. It stemmed from a far-reaching attempt to secure English rule in Ireland by building up a loyal, Protestant population. Although Ireland had been nominally conquered since the 12th century, it was only in 1603, after the suppression of the last of a series of Irish rebellions, that the country was at last subjugated. In Ulster the earls of Tyrone and Tyrconnel continued for a while to give trouble, but in 1607 they chose exile in preference to submission to English rule. Their lands having been forfeited to James I of England, the way was opened for the plantation of Ulster. In the six "escheated counties" grantees known as "undertakers" were to be allotted extensive estates on condition that they settled English or Scottish tenants on them.

The project was never fully implemented, for it proved difficult to secure enough undertakers. Moreover, the stipulation that tenants must be English or Scots was often ignored, so that some of the native Irish retained possession of their lands. Nevertheless, large numbers of settlers were introduced, Scotsmen outnumbering Englishmen. Ulster was nearer to Scotland than to England, the Scots were more poverty-stricken, and in addition they hoped to find in Ulster the religious freedom they were denied at home. Between 1608 and 1618, 30,000 to 40,000 lowland Scots, overwhelmingly Presbyterians, arrived in Ulster; 10,000 more followed in the 1630s. The plantation nearly collapsed during the Irish rebellion of 1641, but another substantial wave of Scots poured in after the Cromwellian settlement of 1652. Finally, after Protestant William of Orange had defeated James II's Catholic followers at the Battle of the Boyne in 1690, Scottish immigration reached a climax. No fewer than 50,000 Scots settled in Ulster between 1690 and 1697.

Scottish Presbyterians spread throughout Ulster. In the northern and eastern parts of the province they came to constitute a majority of the population. In time their industry and enterprise transformed a backward province into the most prosperous part of Ireland. Unlike the Cromwellian settlers in the province of Munster, who intermarried with the Irish and were ultimately absorbed by them, the Scots kept sternly aloof from the native population. They remained a distinctive group with their own independent sense of community. The Presbyterianism to which they clung was untouched by movements in 18th-century Scotland stressing freedom of religious thought and church submission to civil authority.

For this reason, and because of the peculiar conditions of life in Ulster, they developed habits of thought and conduct differentiating them from the Scots at home. Surrounded by a hostile people whom they despised, yet themselves regarded as inferior by the ruling English, the Ulster Scots became more assertive, more energetic, and less provincial than the indigenous lowland Scots. The two groups can also be distinguished by their reasons for emigrating and their patterns of settlement in America. Unlike the Scots, the Scotch-Irish did not scatter up and down the Atlantic seaboard, but formed relatively compact settlements in the interior.

17TH- AND 18TH-CENTURY EMIGRATION

Large-scale emigration from Ulster to America began only in the 18th century; it might have gotten under way several decades earlier but for a mischance. Thomas Wentworth, whom Charles I appointed Lord Deputy of Ireland in 1632, so antagonized Ulster Presbyterians by his arbitrary rule and his campaign against nonconformity that some looked to America for refuge. Late in 1636, 140 men and women, led by two deposed Presbyterian ministers, sailed from Belfast for New England in the ship *Eagle Wing*. They had received assurances of religious freedom from the governor and council of the Massachusetts Bay Colony and intended to settle near the mouth of the Merrimac River. However, halfway across the Atlantic the *Eagle Wing* ran into heavy storms and began to leak. Her captain turned back to Ireland, and the passengers abandoned the enterprise.

The renewal of religious persecution in the early 1680s once more threatened to set in motion extensive departures from Ulster. With their pulpits closed, most of the ministers in the Presbytery of Lagan were disposed to emigrate to America, but before their plans had matured, Charles II died. Most of the measures against Protestant dissenters were relaxed, but not before a number of Scotch-Irish settlements had been established in the Chesapeake Bay colonies, especially on the eastern shore of Maryland. These settlements became the cradle of the Presbyterian church in America. Although Francis Makemie (c. 1658–1708) was not the first Presbyterian minister to preach in the American colonies, he nevertheless deserves the title of father of American Presbyterianism, for he was the first to found churches of that denomination. He settled in Virginia in 1698 and soon afterward became the first dissenting minister licensed under the Toleration Act to preach in that colony. It was on his initiative that a group of ministers from Maryland, Delaware, and Pennsylvania—all but one of them from Ireland or Scotland—met at Philadelphia in 1706 to form the first presbytery in the New World.

In 1717 large-scale emigration from Ulster to the American colonies began. It was the start of a long-term movement. In the course of the next 60 years the exodus was continuous; not even wars in Europe and America could stop it altogether. There were five peak periods of emigration: 1717–1718, 1725–1729, 1740–1741, 1754–1755, and 1771–1775. Annual departures generally averaged between 3,000 and 4,000, but just before the American Revolution they rose to approximately 10,000 a year. By 1775 about 250,000 Ulster Scots had reached the American colonies.

Although Catholics, Quakers, and Anglicans were

among the emigrants from Ulster, contemporary observers agree that the great majority of them were Presbyterians of Scottish descent. That was the view, for example, of William King, archbishop of Dublin, in 1719 and also of Arthur Young, the English agricultural reformer, who visited Ireland in 1770. This observation has frequently led historians to conclude that religion was mainly responsible for their departure. But in fact it was not, even though the claim is given some weight by the fact that the first wave of Scotch-Irish emigration in 1717–1718 was planned and organized by Presbyterian ministers who were apprehensive about the religious policy of George I's Tory ministers.

It is true that Presbyterians, as dissenters from the established church, were subject to certain restrictions. For example, an act of 1704, by imposing a sacramental test, effectively excluded them from officeholding. In addition they were required to pay tithes to support the Anglican church. But many of the restrictions were not enforced. Moreover, although Presbyterians had been persecuted briefly after the Restoration of Charles II in 1660 and again after the Glorious Revolution of 1688, they had come to enjoy complete freedom of worship by the time the large-scale emigration from Ulster began. Thus they cannot properly be described as "martyrs for conscience' sake."

More of a spur to emigration than religion was economic pressure. The most potent source of discontent was the land system. Lacking any sense of social responsibility, Irish landowners looked on their estates purely as a source of revenue; they spent nothing on them and took every opportunity to raise rents. And as rents soared, tithes increased proportionally. Dean Swift may have exaggerated when he wrote in 1720 that "the screwing and racking of rents has reduced the people to worse condition than Poland," but there can be little doubt that these increased burdens were the last straw for a people already reeling under a series of crop failures.

In the late 1720s emigration reached a level high enough to alarm the Irish ruling classes and prompted government inquiries as to its causes. The replies confirmed the primacy of the economic motive. Although mention was made of the "peculiar discouragements" under which Presbyterians labored, the main emphasis was on tithes, high rents, short leases, and insecurity of tenure, coupled with the poverty and dearth resulting from a succession of bad harvests in 1725–1728. During the succeeding decades the seemingly inexorable increase in rents and the periodic visitations of famine—especially the severe famine of 1741—kept alive the spirit of emigration. Then, just before the American Revolution, an acute agrarian crisis coincided with a slump in the linen industry to produce the heaviest emigration of the century. Fifty years of rack-renting reached a climax in the early 1770s, the consequence not only of the growing demand for land but also of the system of "canting," that is, of auctioning tenancies and of the increasing tendency to lease land to middlemen. Indignation at excessive rents and at evictions produced conditions of near insurrection in Ulster; outrages against property and livestock became prevalent and there were widespread disturbances by groups of malcontents generally known as Hearts of Steel.

Exacerbating the agrarian crisis was the catastrophic collapse of the linen trade in 1772–1773, the result of a sudden decline in foreign demand. Because linen manufacture was widely dispersed throughout Ulster, the slump produced universal distress. Moreover, linen weaving was generally carried on domestically by farm tenants, and diminishing sales made it more difficult for them to pay rents that had risen to exorbitant levels. Contemporary observers insisted on the close relationship between the linen trade and emigration, and some, like Arthur Young, believed that all the 30,000 people said to have emigrated from Ulster in 1772–1773 were linen weavers.

Dissatisfaction with conditions in Ulster was sharpened by awareness of opportunity in America. Since neither emigrant guidebooks nor cheap newspapers existed in the 18th century, knowledge of the colonies depended largely on letters written by previous emigrants. The importance of these missives was recognized as early as 1729, when two Presbyterian clergymen reported that people in the north of Ireland had received "many letters from their friends and acquaintances who have already settled themselves in the American Plantations, inviting them to transport themselves thither, and promising them liberty and ease as the reward of their honest industry, with a prospect of transmitting their acquisitions and privileges safe to their posterity, without the imposition of growing rents and other burdens."

THE ULSTER EMIGRANT TRADE

Emigration was stimulated further by the recruiting activities of merchants and ship captains. Vessels going out to the colonies for flaxseed and potash—both needed in the manufacture of linen—carried less bulky cargoes on the westward voyage and were thus eager for the profits of the emigrant trade. Each of the five Ulster emigrant ports—Belfast, Londonderry, Newry, Larne, and Portrush—had a well-defined hinterland that agents combed regularly in search of passengers. In 1729 it was reported that shipowners "send agents to markets and fairs and [circulate] public advertisements through the country to assemble the people together, where they assure them that in America they can get good land to them and their posterity for little or no rent, without either paying tithes or taxes, and amuse them with such accounts of these countries as they know will be most agreeable to them."

As this account implies, deception and misrepresentation were rife. Moreover, avarice sometimes led shipowners to take more passengers than their vessels could accommodate in comfort and to neglect to carry adequate provisions. Sickness and death resulted less frequently than might have been supposed, but there were nevertheless some appalling tragedies. In 1767, for instance, fever broke out on an overcrowded vessel bound from Belfast to Charleston, S.C., and carried off more than 100 of the 450 passengers. Even when epidemics were avoided, an unduly protracted passage could result in starvation. On a voyage from Belfast to Philadelphia in 1741, 46 passengers on the *Seaflower* died from hunger and the remaining 60 survived only by resorting to cannibalism.

Reinforcing the blandishments of shipping agents were the inducements held out by land promoters.

Often natives of Ulster themselves, they were anxious to colonize tracts of land they owned or hoped to acquire. One of the earliest of these was Henry McCulloh, agent for the Granville proprietary, who planted a number of Ulster families in piedmont North Carolina in the 1730s. A more prominent figure was Arthur Dobbs, a large landowner in County Antrim and a member of the Irish Parliament, who became governor of North Carolina in 1753. Two years earlier, having purchased a part interest in 400,000 acres from the McCulloh estate —an area conforming to present-day Mecklenburg and Cabarrus counties—he had sent out his first settlers to North Carolina; others followed in 1754 and 1755. Dobbs was unusual among land promoters in that he made no attempt to stimulate emigration, held out no extravagant promises to prospective settlers, and exhibited a real concern for the welfare of those who emigrated to his American estates. The British government did not object to the Dobbs and McCulloh ventures, for the numbers involved were small. But when in the 1760s Alexander McNutt, a native of Londonderry who had settled in Virginia, started a campaign to recruit 9,000 emigrants from the north of Ireland for the estates he had been granted in Nova Scotia, the Board of Trade promptly curtailed his activities. It reasoned that "the migration from Ireland of such great numbers of his majesty's subjects must be attended with dangerous consequences for that kingdom."

Throughout the 18th century the authorities in London and Dublin generally frowned on emigration. Influenced by the prevailing mercantilism, they believed that a nation's wealth and strength depended largely on the number of its inhabitants. The Protestant landlords who dominated the Irish government had additional reasons for uneasiness. They saw an exodus consisting so overwhelmingly of Presbyterians as a threat to the Protestant ascendancy in Ireland. Besides, large-scale emigration probably would reduce competition for land and thus lower rents. In 1728 the Irish government became so alarmed that it tried to put legal obstacles in the way of emigration from Ulster. Although it shared the government's misgivings, the Privy Council in London was disinclined to impose direct restraints. After emigration had fallen off in 1729 the council feared that the threat of a ban would serve only to revive it. There was renewed alarm at the drain of Protestants when emigration soared to new peaks in the 1770s, but apart from inquiring into the reasons, the authorities took no action.

In the 18th century Ireland in general—Ulster in particular—was the most important source of bound labor for the American colonies. Those who were too poor to pay their fares to America could nevertheless get there by becoming indentured servants, that is, by signing contracts pledging their labor for a fixed term of years, usually three or four. On arrival in the colonies, captains would offer their cargoes of servants for sale in much the same way as was done with Negro slaves imported from Africa. Some nonpaying passengers preferred not to sign indentures before sailing but to go as redemptioners. This meant that on arrival in the colonies they had a brief period in which to find an employer prepared to recompense the ship's captain. Precisely what proportion of Scotch-Irish emigrants consisted of indentured servants and redemptioners can only be guessed at, but at least in the 1720s it seems to

have been high. In 1728 Archbishop Hugh Boulter of Armagh asserted that not one in ten Ulster emigrants had the means to pay their fares; the rest were compelled to accept a period of servitude in order to reach America. Until after the American Revolution virtually every vessel that advertised for emigrants in the north of Ireland indicated a readiness to take servants and redemptioners as well as paying passengers. But by the 1770s the proportion of servants appears to have declined.

In 1773 the *Belfast News Letter* remarked that whereas in the past it had been "chiefly the very meanest of the People who went off, mostly in the station of Indented Servants," the vast majority of those currently going—"People employed in the Linen Manufacture, or Farmers, and of some Property"—had paid their own fares. The paper was probably right in suggesting that indentured servants were generally poor, but they nevertheless included a substantial proportion of skilled artisans despite the ban on emigration of such persons. When the ship *Freemason* advertised in Newry for servants to go to Philadelphia in 1768, the trades specified included carpenters, tailors, shoemakers, wheelwrights, millwrights, smiths, weavers, bricklayers, plasterers, millers, coopers, barbers, bakers, milliners, cabinetmakers, hatters, turners, and tanners. Similar trades were generally mentioned when servants were offered for sale in the colonies.

Although Scotch-Irish servants could be found in all the continental colonies, there were relatively few in New England, where intensive agriculture and small holdings predominated. There were more servants in the southern colonies, but their importation declined as Negro slaves replaced whites as field hands and craftsmen. In the middle colonies, and especially in Pennsylvania, the opening up of new lands and the growth of towns created a lively demand for all types of white labor, skilled or otherwise.

Among those who emigrated from Ulster as indentured servants, a few eventually rose to fame and fortune. Charles Thomson, for instance, who left his native County Londonderry for Pennsylvania as a boy in 1729, prospered in trade in Philadelphia, entered politics, and served as secretary of the Continental Congress between 1774 and 1789. But the general lot of indentured servants, whatever their origin, seems to have been a hard one, though they were better off than the slaves, retaining whatever civil rights were not specifically denied by the terms of their indentures. At the end of their period of servitude they were free to choose their own occupations and were entitled by custom or statute to certain "freedom dues," which always denoted clothing and usually tools, seeds, and provisions. But because these dues did not normally include land, only a small proportion became independent yeomen. The majority became wage-laborers on farms or plantations, or drifted to the towns or the frontier, or in a few cases even returned to Europe.

NEW ENGLAND SETTLEMENTS

Ever since the venture of the *Eagle Wing* in the 17th century, Ulster Presbyterians had continued to think of New England as a possible refuge. Thus when large-scale emigration began in the early 18th century it turned mainly in that direction. Yet the Scotch-Irish be-

came as unpopular with New Englanders as would the famine immigrants from southern Ireland more than a century later. Initially they were welcomed, because Massachusetts, like most of the colonies, was anxious to establish frontier settlements as a shield against Indian attack. In 1718 several hundred newly arrived Scotch-Irish immigrants were sent from Boston to the frontier. Before long an arc of Scotch-Irish settlements stretched along the frontier from western Massachusetts to the coast of Maine. Many bore Ulster place-names: Belfast and Bangor on Penobscot Bay, the towns of Londonderry and Antrim and the county of Hillsboro in New Hampshire, Orange County in what would later become Vermont, and Coleraine in Massachusetts.

But even from the first there were misgivings about the new arrivals. New England in the early 18th century was as ethnically homogeneous as its name implied and was disposed to look suspiciously on strangers. The New England clergy had assumed that, because the Scotch-Irish were staunch Calvinists, there would be no doctrinal barrier to their absorption into the Congregational church. But the Scotch-Irish brought with them their own distinctive brand of Calvinism, one characterized by an elemental zeal and lacking the laxness and broad-mindedness that by then imbued New England Puritanism. To the surprise and irritation of the spiritual leaders of the Bay Colony, Scotch-Irish ministers wasted no time in denouncing New England churches for theological error, singling out their mode of baptism for particular condemnation and insisting that it would be wrong to hold communion with them. The intolerance of the newcomers seems to have reawakened that of their hosts, for in 1734 the people of Worcester tore down a newly built Scotch-Irish Presbyterian church—though the cause may have been as much reluctance to support an additional church as doctrinal disputes.

Besides religious antipathy there were other reasons for Puritan dislike of the Scotch-Irish. Although many settled on the frontier, the poor remained in Boston, adding to what was already a considerable burden of pauperism. Hence the fear expressed by the Surveyor General of the Customs at Boston in 1719 that "these confounded Irish will eat us all up." In July 1729, when a number of immigrant vessels arrived from Belfast and Londonderry, a mob prevented the passengers from landing. Even so, the Boston town records reveal that between 1729 and 1742, two-thirds of the inmates of the almshouse were Scotch-Irish. In addition to being a burden, the Scotch-Irish seemed to Bostonians to be a barbarous crew. There were frequent complaints of their drinking, blasphemy, and violence that revealed itself most graphically in the practice of biting off ears in the course of fights. Although much of the criticism of Scotch-Irish lawlessness was exaggerated and unfair, court records nevertheless confirm that the Scotch-Irish committed more than their share of crimes.

PENNSYLVANIA AND
THE SOUTHERN BACKCOUNTRY

Hostility in New England and the economic opportunities and religious freedom offered by William Penn's colony account for the wholesale diversion of the Scotch-Irish movement to Pennsylvania after about 1725. Emigration tended in any case to follow the paths of transatlantic commerce, and Ulster's colonial trade was preponderantly with Philadelphia and other Delaware River ports like New Castle and Wilmington. The earliest Scotch-Irish settlements in Pennsylvania were founded in the 1720s near Philadelphia in the present-day counties of Chester and Lancaster. But before long the direction of Scotch-Irish immigration was westward to the frontier, first up the Delaware and then beyond the Susquehanna into the rich farmlands of the Cumberland Valley. By 1750 the entire length of the Cumberland Valley was dotted with Scotch-Irish settlements, and the population had become overwhelmingly Scotch-Irish. Movement farther west was checked for a time by the Allegheny mountains, by Indian wars, and by the uncertainty of land titles; but after Pontiac's War and the Land Purchase of 1768 the Scotch-Irish played a leading role in the settlement of the trans-Allegheny region. They clustered in strength in the vicinity of the future Pittsburgh and still more numerously in southwestern Pennsylvania, which became even more of a Scotch-Irish stronghold than the Cumberland Valley.

Pennsylvania also became the main distributing center for the Scotch-Irish. In the 1730s, when the westward advance had reached the foothills of the Alleghenies, Penn's successors abandoned his liberal land policies, and more favorable opportunities developed in the southern colonies. Hence the Scotch-Irish advance was deflected southward into western Maryland and the Shenandoah Valley of Virginia and then into the backcountry of the Carolinas. By the 1750s a chain of Scotch-Irish frontier settlements dotted the 700-mile length of the Great Wagon Road that ran parallel to the Appalachians from Pennsylvania to Georgia.

Simultaneously a lesser migration occurred directly from Ulster to the Carolinas and Georgia. Whereas individual land promoters like McCulloh and Dobbs had initiated the movement to North Carolina, immigration to South Carolina owed most to official encouragement. After the near disaster of the Yamassee War of 1715, South Carolina officials were anxious to strengthen the frontier and to reduce both the danger of insurrection and the racial imbalance created by its rapidly growing slave population. Hence the colony made several attempts to attract white settlers. The first was Governor Robert Johnson's township and assisted settlement scheme in 1731, which provided Protestants who undertook to settle in townships 60 miles or so inland from Charleston free transportation from Europe, grants of land as well as provisions and tools, and a ten-year exemption from quitrents. Under the terms of the scheme several shiploads of immigrants from Belfast settled Williamsburg township on the Santee, which soon prospered through the cultivation of indigo. A similar scheme in 1761 attracted more immigrants from the north of Ireland. Georgia, whose frontier was even more exposed than South Carolina's, was eager to follow its example, but the proposals Georgia authorities made for promoting immigration were vetoed by the British government. Even so, the several hundred Scotch-Irish settlers who were brought to Georgia between 1769 and 1774 by a group of Indian traders and land speculators of Ulster origin were assisted by the Georgia authorities to establish Queensborough township on the Santee.

Although land was America's chief attraction for the Scotch-Irish, they do not appear to have been efficient frontier farmers. They were not always good judges of

soil, shunning the limestone regions favored by the Germans and choosing slate hills instead. Contemporaries frequently compared Scotch-Irish farms with those of the Germans, always to the discredit of the former. Whereas German farms were said to be models of neatness and industry, those of the Scotch-Irish were suggestive of indolence and carelessness. The Germans constructed permanent, weatherproof dwellings, but the Scotch-Irish seem to have been content with primitive log cabins, floorless and often open to the sky. A similar contrast prevailed in methods of clearing land. Before planting crops the Germans went to infinite trouble to fell trees and uproot the stumps, but the Scotch-Irish merely girdled the trees and planted their crops between the stumps. Such differences stemmed, however, more from differences in social values than from variations of skill in husbandry. If the Germans appeared more industrious and frugal, that was partly because they generally remained where they first settled. Retaining the peasant's high regard for patrimonial property, they looked on their farms as legacies to be bequeathed to their children and gave a high priority to improvement. The Scotch-Irish, on the other hand, were slow to commit themselves to particular localities. Perhaps because migration had become second nature to them, they lacked any real attachment to the soil and tended to exploit their farms ruthlessly before moving on to others.

THE FRONTIER SHIELD

Although their Ulster experience had not equipped them with the pioneering skills they needed on the American frontier, it had prepared them in other ways for the role of frontiersmen. As the occupants of lands that often had been taken forcibly from the native Irish, they knew what it was to live in a hostile environment without security for life or property. This was why colonial officials believed them to be uniquely well qualified to act as a barrier against French and Indian attack. James Logan, the Ulster-born provincial secretary of Pennsylvania, in 1720 explained his decision to grant an extensive tract of land to Scotch-Irish immigrants in Chester County, where they established the frontier township of Donegal: "At the time we were apprehensive from the Northern Indians . . . I therefore thought it prudent to plant a settlement of such men as those who formerly had so bravely defended Londonderry and Enniskillen as a frontier against any disturbance."

Nevertheless the Pennsylvanians did not welcome the Scotch-Irish unreservedly, to some extent because, as in Boston, some of them added to the poor rates; but mainly because of their aggressiveness and impatience with authority—the very qualities that made them so valuable as frontiersmen. In 1729 the same James Logan who had welcomed the Scotch-Irish to Chester County complained, "A settlement of five families from the north of Ireland gives me more trouble than fifty of any other people." He was exasperated by their "audacious and disorderly habit" of squatting on "any spot of vacant land they fancied" without bothering to obtain legal title.

The Scotch-Irish also were constantly at odds with the Germans. Their mutual antagonism produced so many disturbances, especially at election times, that in 1743 the Penns instructed their agents to sell no more land to the Scotch-Irish in the predominantly German counties of Lancaster and York and to offer those already located there generous terms to remove to the Cumberland Valley.

More disturbing still was the fact that the Scotch-Irish were "hard neighbors to the Indians." Scotch-Irish incursions into tribal lands in Pennsylvania and their general disregard for Indian rights and sensibilities threatened to undermine the Quaker policy of consideration for the Indians. Like all frontiersmen, the Scotch-Irish had no qualms about treating the Indians roughly; they regarded them simply as savages and heathens whose presence posed an obstacle to the advance of civilization. Hence in response to complaints from Philadelphia about their encroachments upon tribal territories west of the Susquehanna, the Scotch-Irish retorted that it was "against the law of God and nature that so much land should lie idle while so many Christians wanted it to labor on and raise their bread."

Situated as they were on the frontier, the Scotch-Irish bore the brunt of Indian raids. During the French and Indian War frontier settlements were pillaged and burned, and hundreds of settlers were killed. A typical experience was that of the exposed Scotch-Irish colony in the Long Canes region of the Carolina backcountry. Forewarned of an impending Cherokee attack, some 250 settlers abandoned their homes early in 1760 to seek safety in Augusta, Ga. Along the way, on February 1, 100 mounted Cherokees attacked the party and killed or captured about 40 settlers, mostly women and children. One of the slain was the grandmother of John C. Calhoun. Two days later the Cherokees similarly butchered another party of 23 women and children.

The Scotch-Irish played a large part in the military operations of the war. In 1756 a Scotch-Irish force captured Kittanning on the Allegheny River, one of the two chief Indian strongholds in Pennsylvania. Scotch-Irishmen also formed the greater part of the Pennsylvania militia who in 1758 helped British regulars capture Fort Duquesne, the key to French defenses in the Ohio Valley. During Pontiac's War in 1763–1764 it was the Scotch-Irish once more who offered the only effective resistance. In repelling Indian attacks they sometimes copied the ruthless methods of their adversaries. The most notorious example occurred in 1763, when a group of Scotch-Irish rangers descended on the peaceable Conestogas and slaughtered 20 of them because of an unsubstantiated rumor that they had been helping Pontiac's braves.

The Scotch-Irish on the Pennsylvania frontier had long harbored a grievance against the Quaker oligarchy that denied them the vote and adequate representation in the colonial assembly. They were even more resentful of the Quaker failure to protect them against Indian attacks. Their anger boiled over in 1764 when they took the lead in the march of the Paxton boys on Philadelphia.

In North Carolina, too, the Scotch-Irish were prominent in backcountry struggles against eastern political dominance. They disliked the established Anglican church and its attempts to reproduce the Old World pattern of religious conformity—it was not until 1766, for example, that Presbyterian marriages were validated in the colony. In addition to their special disabilities as

dissenters, the Scotch-Irish shared the anger of the entire backcountry population at the tyranny of tidewater officials, and in particular at the extortion which accompanied the administration of justice. It was discontent on this score which led to Scotch-Irish involvement in the disorders and rioting of the Regulator movement of 1768–1771.

In their backwoods settlements the Scotch-Irish lived the harsh, crude existence of frontiersmen generally. The wilderness environment, together with their extreme mobility, placed great strains upon kinship and marriage ties and explained the primitive quality of social organization. Regardless of exaggerations about the indolence and shiftlessness of the backcountry Scotch-Irish, there is general agreement that they were a turbulent and fiercely sectarian people whose endemic vice was an overfondness for whiskey. The absence of civilized standards, however, seems to have done little to promote frontier egalitarianism. Social distinctions persisted and democratic control failed to materialize.

RELIGION AND SOCIETY

The most distinctive characteristic of the Scotch-Irish, and the one that left the deepest mark upon them, was their Presbyterianism. It was reflected in the intensity of their religious zeal and in their violent hostility to Anglicanism and to established churches. The ability to read and interpret the Bible was fundamental to their faith and contributed to their exceptionally high literacy rate; when 319 members of an Ulster community requested permission to settle in Massachusetts in 1718, all but 13 signed their names to the petition. The Presbyterian church was the one effective Scotch-Irish social institution, the focus and center of community life. In frontier settlements the church was usually the forerunner of civil authority; the local religious court, the session, dealt not only with moral offenses but also with those concerning property rights and public order. The extent to which the clergy were acknowledged as secular as well as spiritual leaders is demonstrated by the frequency with which colonial officials appealed to them to regulate settlement and assist in the maintenance of community peace.

Like other sectarians, however, Scotch-Irish Presbyterians found it difficult to plant churches when congregations were small and scattered and communications poor. The main difficulty was the shortage of qualified clergy—that is, of ministers familiar with Latin, Greek, and Hebrew and capable of the lengthy theological discourses that were the main staple of sermons. Only a few ministers accompanied their flocks from Ulster, and although Irish and Scottish synods responded as best they could to appeals for missionaries, there were limits to what they could do. Great significance attached, therefore, to the founding of the celebrated Log College at Neshaminy, near Philadelphia, by the Reverend William Tennent, Sr. (1673–1746), a native of Antrim and a graduate of the University of Edinburgh. Established in 1726 or 1727 and surviving until 1742, this institution was the first founded by American Presbyterians to train young men for the ministry. Though in reality a classical academy rather than a college, it turned out a score of ministers. It also inspired the founding of similar schools such as Fagg's Manor Classical School and Pequea Academy, both in Pennsylvania.

Equally significant was the work of another native of Ulster, the Reverend Francis Alison (1705–1779), professor of moral philosophy at the College of Philadelphia and probably the greatest classical scholar of colonial America. Soon after emigrating to Pennsylvania in 1735, he started a school at New London, where he was Presbyterian pastor. Among the alumni of the New London Academy were John Ewing (1732–1802), second provost of the College of Philadelphia; Charles Thomson (1729–1824), secretary to the Continental Congress; and Thomas McKean (1734–1817), James Smith (1719–1806), and George Read (1733–1798), three of the signers of the Declaration of Independence.

The Scotch-Irish passion for learning—or at least for that kind of learning that was essentially religious in aim—was reflected also in the field of higher education. Some informal academies, like Samuel Blair's at Fagg's Manor, blossomed in time into true colleges. Moreover, Tennent's Log College was the seed from which the College of New Jersey (subsequently Princeton) developed in 1746. Although credit for the actual founding of Princeton must go to Scotsmen rather than to the Scotch-Irish, its early presidents included Samuel Finley (1715–1766), a Scotch-Irish graduate of the Log College. The College of New Jersey served in turn as a model for Hampden-Sydney, founded in 1776 by Presbyterians in the Virginia piedmont. In 1783 the Scotch-Irish of the Cumberland Valley established Dickinson College at Carlisle, the first denominational college in Pennsylvania and the 12th college to be founded in the United States.

Despite their efforts to secure a learned clergy, the Scotch-Irish were never able to fill all their pulpits. Many Scotch-Irish settlements, especially in frontier regions, were without church or pastor for years at a time and had to rely on the occasional visits of itinerant preachers. A proportion who did not altogether drift away from religion joined other denominations that were better equipped to supply their spiritual needs. In the southern colonies many became Baptists or Methodists and in New England, Congregationalists. At the close of the colonial period the Presbyterian church was still predominant among the Scotch-Irish, but it had been obliged, along with immigrant churches generally, to adjust to the competitive American environment. Forced to compete actively for members, it became more evangelical in tone, and more significant still, placed less emphasis on the doctrine of election which had been its distinguishing characteristic in Ulster.

THE AMERICAN REVOLUTION

The role of the Scotch-Irish in the American Revolution has been much misunderstood. It has frequently been claimed that they were on the American side almost to a man, and that their attitude stemmed from bitter memories of the wrongs they had suffered at Britain's hands in Ulster. In fact, however, the Scotch-Irish like other Americans were divided in their allegiances; there were both patriots and loyalists among them, and a substantial proportion chose to remain neutral. The existence of these divisions indicates that their attitudes were determined not by their Old World past but by local conditions.

In Pennsylvania the Scotch-Irish overwhelmingly supported independence, although the liberal and humanitarian aspects of the revolutionary movement seem to have left them cold. Fiercely intolerant themselves in matters of religion, they seem to have had scant sympathy with the ideal of religious freedom for which the Virginia patriots contended. The statute of 1779 abolishing slavery in Pennsylvania, drafted by Dublin-born George Bryan (1731–1791), was vehemently opposed by the backcountry Scotch-Irish. Nevertheless, many leaders of the Radical Whig party in Pennsylvania were Scotch-Irishmen like Thomas McKean and Joseph Reed (1741–1785). Moreover, so prominent were the Scotch-Irish in the Pennsylvania Line that General "Light-Horse" Harry Lee called it "the line of Ireland." The hostility of Scotch-Irish frontiersmen to the Quaker oligarchy in Philadelphia was largely responsible for this circumstance; in espousing the radical cause the Scotch-Irish wanted not merely to bring Pennsylvania into line with the American movement but also to overthrow the proprietary government. Yet even in Pennsylvania the Scotch-Irish were not unanimous. In 1778 Sir Henry Clinton managed to raise a loyalist regiment in Philadelphia known as the Volunteers of Ireland. Consisting of both Irish Catholics and Scotch-Irishmen, many of them deserters from the Continental Army, it fought with great distinction in Cornwallis's southern campaigns.

A similar cleavage developed among the Scotch-Irish of New England. Those on the frontier rallied to oppose General Burgoyne's advance in 1777, but two years earlier the Boston Scotch-Irish had enlisted in the Loyal Irish Volunteers. In the backcountry of the Carolinas opinion was still more divided. In North Carolina especially, the crucial factor was the resentment of small farmers about inadequate law enforcement persisting from the Regulator movement of the 1760s. Because the fight for independence was led by their old tidewater enemies, the Scotch-Irish tended to be, if not actively loyalist, then at least hostile to the patriot cause. They remained unmoved even when the Continental Congress sent two Presbyterian ministers to North Carolina to persuade them of "the rectitude of the American side of the question." Yet in the Waxhaws—the backcountry borderland between North and South Carolina —such persuasion was unnecessary. The British found the population there "universally Irish and universally disaffected," and when the Volunteers of Ireland were sent to the Waxhaws their commander, Lord Rawdon, complained that the local people used "every artifice to debauch the minds of my soldiers" and persuaded many of them to desert. But in other parts of the South Carolina backcountry, notably in the isolated frontier settlement known as Ninety-Six, there were not a few Scotch-Irish loyalists. Most of the inhabitants were recent immigrants who had received grants of land from the colonial government and feared to lose them if they joined the rebellion. One Ulster-born resident of Ninety-Six, Alexander Chesney, exemplified the prevailing confusion of loyalties: he fought for both sides in turn.

POST-REVOLUTIONARY MIGRATION

Emigration from Ulster was halted abruptly in the summer of 1775 by news of the fighting at Lexington and Concord, but resumed before the Revolution was officially over. The first emigrant ships to leave Ulster for the independent United States sailed in August 1783, a month before the peace treaty was signed at Versailles. Within a year or two the migration was much as it had been in colonial days. In the 1780s and 1790s an average of about 5,000 passengers a year left the north of Ireland for American ports. The composition of the postwar movement is difficult to ascertain, for the evidence is contradictory. In August 1783 the customs officer at Newry reported that the emigrants were "of a very inferior class": there were few propertied people among them, nearly all being "of the lower order of tradesmen, such as weavers, smiths, joiners, etc." But another observer reported at almost the same time that those leaving Ulster "in such prodigious numbers are not the refuse of the country . . . They . . . form the yeomanry of the land who take with them from £300 to £700, and the industrious, careful linen-weaver, who has scraped together a sufficiency to transport himself and his family." Whichever of these statements is closer to the truth, it is beyond question that most Scotch-Irish emigrants were now fare-paying passengers rather than indentured servants.

The decline of the Scotch-Irish servant trade had begun before the Revolution and accelerated until by 1800 it had ceased entirely. The institution of bound labor had not disappeared altogether. As yet, few Americans were disposed to question whether it was compatible with the egalitarian ideals of the Revolution. Cargoes of German redemptioners and indentured servants continued to be imported from Dutch ports until about 1819. But in Ulster ports fare-paying passengers came forward in such numbers after the Revolution that captains had less and less need to resort to the uncertain and troublesome servant trade. Moreover, the servant trade from Ulster, as from the British Isles generally, was affected by a new ban on the recruitment of skilled artisans, those who had always been most sought after as servants. In an effort to prevent the newly independent United States from developing into an industrial rival, the British Parliament adopted a measure in 1783 making it an offense to "contract with, entice, persuade, solicit or seduce a manufacturer, workman or artificer" to leave the King's dominions.

In a further effort to stop the drain of skilled manpower the Lord Lieutenant of Ireland issued a proclamation in 1795 forbidding emigrant vessels to transport artificers or manufacturers and stipulating that, before sailing, masters must hand in to the customs officers sworn statements of the names and occupations of all persons on board. But the measure proved unenforceable: as the Collector of Customs at Londonderry pointed out in 1796, agriculture and industry in the north of Ireland were so interconnected that "many of those who come under the description of farmers, and who actually are such, are also weavers." Thus it was impossible for inspecting officers to determine with any certainty whether or not prospective passengers fell within the prohibited classes.

The occupational duality of so many Ulster emigrants meant that their economic adjustment in the United States followed no single pattern. Some chose to pursue their Old World crafts. Among them were the people who flocked to the tier of New York counties that lay north of the New Jersey border on the west

bank of the Hudson—Greene, Orange, Ulster, and Sullivan—and thus made the region a stronghold of weaving and spinning. On the other hand, in 1794 when the English traveler Henry Wansey visited a newly arrived immigrant ship in New York harbor, he learned that nearly 200 passengers from the north of Ireland were "weavers of diaper and dimity" who were going to western Connecticut to take up farming. Wansey made a point of asking the newcomers why they had left Ireland and was told that "times were so hard, and everything so dear, that with all their industry, they could not live."

During the period of the French Revolution and the Napoleonic wars, political turmoil provided a further stimulus to Irish emigration. Fired by the French Revolution, Ulster radicals established the Society of United Irishmen in the early 1790s to press for political reform. By 1795 Ulster had become the center of a formidable revolutionary movement, and the United Irishmen were planning a revolt with French help. When the authorities threatened to curb their activities some of the malcontents fled to the United States. After the failure of the rebellion of 1798 larger numbers followed, including such prominent leaders as Thomas Addis Emmet (1764–1827), William Sampson (1764–1836), and William James MacNeven (1763–1841). These refugees, Catholic and Anglican as well as Presbyterian, were predominantly from the professional and business classes. According to one of their number, the Presbyterian clergyman Thomas Ledlie Birch, the United Irishmen formed "the most respectable emigration which has taken place to the United States since the settlement of the New England colonies." But there were relatively few of them, perhaps only a hundred or two, and their arrival coincided with that of a poorer element whose destitution revived earlier American apprehensions about Ulster immigration. When a vessel from Newry landed its 300 passengers at New York in 1796, the Common Council complained of the "prodigious influx of indigent foreigners" and suggested, though in vain, that poor relief should become a state rather than a municipal responsibility.

The British Passenger Act of 1803 dealt Scotch-Irish emigration a crippling blow. The first of a long series of measures regulating steerage conditions, the act severely limited the number of passengers vessels could carry, and among other things, required adequate supplies of water and provisions. Legislative action was indeed needed to remedy overcrowding and other abuses. But the British government was not motivated primarily—perhaps not at all—by humanitarian concern. It had come to regard steerage regulation as an indirect method of restricting emigration. In the event, it proved remarkably effective. Vessels that had been accustomed to carry 300 to 500 passengers were now limited by law to an average of 50. And because fares doubled or even trebled, full complements were not always forthcoming. The act's requirements could be evaded to a limited extent, either by overstating the ship's tonnage or by clandestinely taking on extra passengers after clearing customs. All the same, the act had the effect of reducing emigration from an annual average of 5,000 to a little more than 1,000. The authorities showed their hostility in other ways; thus a scarcity of food in 1811 provided a pretext for forbidding emigrant vessels in Ulster ports from laying in provisions.

Emigration was affected further by the efforts of the United States during the Napoleonic wars to force the European belligerents to respect neutral rights. The Jeffersonian embargo, imposed in December 1807 and forbidding American vessels to go abroad, produced such a shortage of emigrant shipping that in 1808 only a few hundred people could find passage. The nonintercourse policy that followed had the opposite effect, at least temporarily. When American vessels were prohibited from carrying British merchandise, they flocked to Irish ports in search of passengers. The result was that in 1811 emigration exceeded 5,000 for the first time since 1803. But even when transportation was available, emigrants could not be sure of reaching their destination. Soon after Britain and France went to war in 1793, short-handed British warships began to impress manpower on the high seas. In the 12 months before 1812, British vessels stopped at least 13 vessels en route from Ireland to the United States—generally within sight of the American coast—and impressed altogether more than 200 emigrants. Another 150 were similarly shanghaied in May 1812 from vessels lying at anchor in Moville Bay, near Londonderry. This latter group was eventually released, but only after war had been declared, so that they were unable to join their relatives in America. These events aroused intense indignation both in the north of Ireland and among the Scotch-Irish in the United States, and may well have contributed to the enthusiasm with which the Scotch-Irish greeted the news of war with Britain.

POLITICS IN THE YOUNG REPUBLIC

Despite official disapproval and the hazards of war, a total of perhaps 100,000 people left Ulster for the United States between 1783 and 1812. Many of them joined the Scotch-Irish settlements on the frontiers of Pennsylvania, Virginia, and the Carolinas; but a substantial proportion settled in the cities of the eastern seaboard, especially Philadelphia, Baltimore, and New York, as well as in the growing town of Pittsburgh, destined to become the chief Scotch-Irish stronghold in the United States. The growth of these urban Scotch-Irish colonies was a new phenomenon. It reflected the increasing proportion of artisans, businessmen, and professional men among the newcomers. It also had political repercussions, for the leaders of the exiled United Irishmen lost no time in plunging into American politics. Instinctively opposed to the Federalists as would-be aristocrats and as tools of the British, they were unanimously on the side of Thomas Jefferson and his Republican adherents, who shared their enthusiasm for revolutionary France. The rank and file were quick to follow suit, becoming prominent in Republican clubs and Republican militia units. During the agitation against Jay's Treaty in 1795 one of Philadelphia's leading merchants, the Ulster-born Blair McClenachan, led a mob to the residence of the British minister, where the treaty was ceremonially burned. Three years later Dr. James Reynolds, a United Irishman from Cookstown, County Tyrone, protested so vehemently against the Alien and Sedition Acts that he was prosecuted in Philadelphia for seditious riot.

On the frontier too the Scotch-Irish were strongly Republican. After a lengthy journey through their settlements in western Pennsylvania, the Connecticut Feder-

alist Uriah Tracy averred that "with a very few exceptions, they are United Irishmen, Free Masons, and the most God-provoking Democrats this side of Hell." Indeed, it was the enthusiastic support the Scotch-Irish gave to the Jeffersonians that convinced the Federalists of the need, as Harrison Gray Otis put it, "to prevent the indiscriminate admission of wild Irishmen and others to the right of suffrage." The Naturalization Act of 1798 implemented this conviction, and together with the Adams administration's veto of a British proposal to release several of the 1798 rebels on condition that they emigrated, transformed Scotch-Irish dislike of the Federalists into implacable opposition. The Scotch-Irish turned out in strength to vote for Thomas Jefferson in the election of 1800, and their influence, along with that of other immigrant groups, may well have been decisive in New York and thus in the nation at large.

EMIGRATION, 1815 TO THE FAMINE YEARS

Although historians of Scotch-Irish immigration have focused their attention on the colonial period, the peak of the movement came during the period between the end of the Napoleonic wars and the Great Famine. The Ulster emigration of 1815–1845, amounting to perhaps half a million people, was larger both absolutely and in proportion to the American population than it had ever been earlier or was to be subsequently. Until about 1835 Presbyterians constituted the majority of those emigrating from Ireland. Their departure meant a weakening of the Protestant element in the Irish population, and although in Ulster as a whole Protestants were still in a majority, Catholics came to predominate in three of its counties (Monaghan, Cavan, and Donegal) and to constitute a large minority in three more (Armagh, Fermanagh, and Tyrone).

The main causes of the post-1815 movement were the mounting pressures of population and of economic change. Ireland was the most densely populated country in Europe, and Ulster was the most densely populated of the four Irish provinces. Owing to the iniquitous land system, Irish agriculture had long been in decline, but after 1815 its condition worsened. The collapse of grain prices after the Napoleonic wars and the opening of the British market to Irish provisions in 1826 led to the amalgamation and clearance of estates so as to facilitate a switch from arable to pasture. This process, coupled with the growth of population, intensified the competition for land and encouraged subdivision into tiny plots too small for efficient or profitable farming. For the Ulster farmer the one mitigating feature of the land system was the custom, peculiar to the province, of tenant right. Although any improvements made to a farm by a tenant belonged in law to the landlord, tenant right meant that an outgoing lessee always in practice received monetary compensation for the improvements he had made. This practice was said to account largely for the superior condition of Ulster farmers compared with those in the rest of Ireland; moreover, it supplied them with the means to pay their fares across the Atlantic.

At the same time that the agricultural revolution was degrading and displacing those who tilled the land, the factory was ousting cottage industry, and new inventions in turn displaced the factory worker. With the linen industry in a state of continuous though fluctuat-

ing decline, independent weavers, especially from the south and west of Ulster, emigrated in large numbers. In addition the depression in the textile trade in 1826–1830 caused severe distress to Belfast cotton spinners and set in motion another stream of emigration.

The reversal of official attitudes after 1815 brought greater freedom to depart. The repeal in 1824 of the laws against the emigration of artisans had little practical effect, for they had never been properly enforced. But when the government abandoned its regulation of steerage passage, it removed what had been a serious obstacle to the departure of the poor. Alarm at the rising numbers of pauper Irish immigrants to Great Britain was responsible for this volte-face. If the Irish were not allowed to emigrate elsewhere, a Parliamentary committee warned in 1826, they would "deluge Great Britain with poverty and wretchedness." Accordingly steerage regulation was henceforth kept to a minimum, and fares fell to unprecedentedly low levels. The expansion of transatlantic commerce with the rise of the North American timber trade greatly increased the facilities for reaching America; timber ships going out from Ireland to Quebec, Saint John's, Nfld., and Halifax, N.S., offered steerage passage for as little as 30 shillings (about $7.50). Thus by the 1820s more emigrants were sailing from Ulster to British North America than to the United States. Only a small minority stayed in the British colonies; the rest proceeded overland or by sea to the United States.

The growth of the prepaid passage business, apparently pioneered by Ulster shipowners, likewise facilitated emigration. Although the prepaid system may have been established earlier, the first definite evidence of its existence dates from 1816, when Irish merchants like Malcolmson and Bell of Belfast and William McCorkell and Co. of Londonderry established branches in American ports. In 1834 two Belfast passenger brokers reported that one-third of the passages they handled were paid for in the United States. In addition they annually received drafts worth several thousand pounds, generally in small sums, from people in America on behalf of their friends at home. The remittance system, largely confined to districts of extensive emigration, was of vital significance. A Parliamentary inquiry in 1836 learned that in many parishes in Ulster, the poor would have been unable to emigrate without the help of those who had left earlier. Moreover, this tangible proof that former neighbors had prospered encouraged others to emigrate.

Although the post-1815 exodus from Ulster was as predominantly Presbyterian as in the past, contemporaries disagreed as usual as to the economic status of the emigrants. The *Londonderry Sentinel* said in 1834 that at least five-sixths of the emigrants were middle-class farmers, "the most industrious and useful classes of the community." Yet the *Londonderry Journal* claimed in the same year that "most of the emigrants are persons in very mean circumstances." Emigration was apparently making inroads into all sections of Ulster society except the very poor, who were immobilized by their poverty. The characteristic Scotch-Irish emigrant perhaps continued to be the small farmer, but there was a substantial minority of laborers and a smaller but not insignificant proportion of artisans and shopkeepers.

As emigration from the south and west of Ireland

gathered momentum in the late 1830s, Ulster's predominance in the Irish movement came to an end. In some places there was an actual decline in departures. During the depression in America set off by the panic of 1837 it was reported that in many Antrim parishes, which formerly had sent hundreds, emigration had almost ceased. Nevertheless emigration was too long-established a tradition in Ulster for the check to be more than short-lived. To be sure, the heroic period of Scotch-Irish emigration was now past. For the rest of the century attention was to be focused on the mass movement from southern Ireland. Even so, a steady stream of people continued to leave Ulster to seek their fortunes in the United States.

It is true that the Great Famine did not have the same disastrous effect on Ulster as on the rest of Ireland. Ulster was still the most densely populated of the four Irish provinces, but thanks to the growing industrialism of Belfast and the Lagan Valley, it had now developed a relatively balanced economy. Hence its population was much less dependent on agriculture and on the potato. For this reason some of the lowest emigration rates in Ireland during the famine decade were to be found in the four Ulster counties with Protestant majorities, and especially in Belfast and its hinterland. Yet, if the Scotch-Irish constituted a relatively small element—perhaps no more than 10 percent in the famine exodus, their numbers were still significant.

EMIGRATION, 1851–1899

British emigration statistics reveal that between May 1, 1851, when the records began to specify the province of origin, and December 31, 1899, Ulster, in rounded figures, accounted for 1,075,000 (or 28 percent) of the 3,797,000 emigrants who left Ireland for all destinations—more than 90 percent of them for the United States. During the period Ulster's share of the movement to the United States declined slightly, but even in the 1880s and 1890s it remained as high as 20 percent. Not all the Ulster-born emigrants were Protestants, but the presumption that most of them were seems to be borne out by the fact that the counties of heaviest emigration, Antrim and Down, were also the most heavily Protestant. As was the case with Irish emigration generally, the Ulster movement of over 1 million in the period 1851–1899 revealed a relatively even balance between the sexes: nearly 595,000 (55 percent) were male and some 480,000 (almost 45 percent) were female. The proportion of young adult emigrants, though very high, was marginally lower than from Ireland as a whole: about 76 percent compared with nearly 80 percent. Ulster, however, sent a slightly higher proportion of emigrants under the age of 15: about 14 percent in 1886, for example, compared with 10 percent from the other three Irish provinces.

ECONOMIC ADJUSTMENT

American immigration statistics do not distinguish between natives of Ulster and those of the rest of Ireland. But given that barely 10 percent of all the Irish-born settled in rural regions in the United States, it seems unlikely that a substantial proportion of the 19th-century Scotch-Irish could have taken up farming. Certainly there were no more compact rural settlements of the kind that had prevailed in colonial days.

Those who possessed industrial skills naturally became urban dwellers. Scotch-Irish weavers and spinners were to be found wherever textiles were manufactured; the Kensington district of Philadelphia in particular had large numbers of them by the 1840s. In addition many who had worked on the land at home shared the Catholic Irish experience of becoming an urban proletariat, finding employment as laborers, waiters, draymen, and in the case of young women, domestic servants. Literacy and a common language also enabled a sizable proportion to take up business or mercantile careers or to engage in journalism or teaching.

There were some spectacular success stories. Alexander T. Stewart (1803–1876) was perhaps the prototype of the merchant prince. Beginning with a small lace shop when he arrived in New York as a young man of 20, he owned the largest dry-goods establishment in the city by 1850. In 1862 he opened at Broadway and 9th Street what was then the largest retail store in the world, and after making large profits from Civil War contracts, acquired vast quantities of real estate. Two young men named John T. Pirie (1871–1940) and Samuel Carson followed a similar path. Abandoning their original intention to set up in the haberdashery business in Cookstown, County Tyrone, they went to the United States to help found the Chicago department store of Carson, Pirie, Scott. No less successful were Andrew McNally (1896–1954), founder of the publishing house of Rand, McNally, and Thomas W. Lamont (1870–1948), who became a member of the banking house of J.P. Morgan and Co. But perhaps the most striking exemplification of the rags-to-riches ideal was Thomas W. Mellon (1813–1908). Born in Mountjoy, near Omagh, he came to the United States with his parents as a boy of five. After a distinguished career in law he established a private banking house in Pittsburgh and founded a financial and philanthropic dynasty destined to become hardly less celebrated than that of the Rockefellers. His son, Andrew W. Mellon (1855–1937), secretary of the treasury in the Harding and Coolidge administrations, acquired one of the world's great art collections, which he donated to the nation together with funds to erect the National Gallery of Art.

IDENTITY WITH SCOTS AND IRISH

Given that they were twigs from the same branch, one might have expected the Scotch-Irish and the Scots to develop in America a more comprehensive Scottish identity. Affiliation with Scottish Highlanders was of course out of the question, for Highlanders were set apart by their Catholicism and their Gaelic speech. But no such barriers existed in respect of Lowlanders, whose Presbyterianism resembled that of Ulstermen. The two groups were joined in the same synods; they sent their candidates for the ministry to such colleges as Princeton. Scots-born pastors frequently ministered to Scotch-Irish congregations, the most celebrated being the Reverend Henry Patillo (1726–1801), who was a delegate to the North Carolina Provincial Congress in 1775. Moreover, when the American Presbyterian Church was rent by schism in 1837, both the Scots and the Scotch-Irish were predominantly in the conservative ranks. But otherwise there was less intermingling than might be supposed, largely because the

two groups had tended to settle in different regions. The Scotch-Irish were proud of their Scottish heritage, but they did not think of themselves simply as Scots. Thus they generally showed little interest in St. Andrew's societies or Burns suppers.

There can be little doubt that Ireland rather than Scotland was the old country to them. This was unequivocally the case until about 1830. As long as they made up the great majority of immigrants from Ireland, the Scotch-Irish were content to be known simply as Irishmen. They collaborated with the Catholic Irish in politics and shared with them membership in such benevolent organizations as the Friendly Sons of St. Patrick. For several decades after the American Revolution the name Scotch-Irish seems to have fallen into general disuse. But the influx of Catholic Irish after the Great Famine of the 1840s rekindled in a new setting the old Scotch-Irish fear of Catholic domination. At the same time as anti-Catholicism became the dominant strain in American nativism, the Scotch-Irish felt the need to insist on their own Protestant traditions as a source of identification with America. As early as the 1820s they introduced to America the Ulster practice of parading on the Twelfth of July, the anniversary of William of Orange's victory over the Catholics at the Battle of the Boyne in 1690. These annual celebrations were marked by the playing of such songs as "Boyne Water" and "Croppies Lie Down," the former being as militantly Protestant as the latter was insultingly anti-Catholic. The consequence was a series of Orange riots. One of the first occurred in 1831. "At a celebration of the Battle of the Boyne by the Gideonites or Orangemen at Philadelphia," reported *Niles' Weekly Register*, "a regular fight with swords, clubs, brickbats, etc., took place between them and the 'Catholic party,' some of the peace-officers being knocked down, and a good many of the combatants strewn on the streets, nearly murdered."

The religious prejudices of the Scotch-Irish shaped their political allegiances as well. Perhaps because Andrew Jackson was the son of Scotch-Irish immigrants from Carrickfergus, a majority of the Scotch-Irish inclined initially to the Democrats. The fact that James K. Polk and James Buchanan were also of Scotch-Irish descent exercised a similar pull later on. But a growing number were uneasy in a party in which Irish Catholic influence was strong. Even in the 1830s the Scotch-Irish of New York City were solidly Whig, and the first two Scotch-Irish governors of Ohio were Whigs also. After the Civil War their anti-Catholicism was to lead most of the Scotch-Irish into the Republican party.

ANTI-CATHOLICISM

The Scotch-Irish gave enthusiastic support to the various anti-Catholic societies that sprang up in the 1840s and 1850s. They joined the American Protestant Association in such numbers that it became known as an Orangemen's order. They were also prominently involved in outbreaks of mob violence against Catholics. The notorious anti-Catholic riots in Philadelphia in 1844, which resulted in the burning of two churches and the destruction of dozens of Catholic homes, were essentially intra-Irish affairs, at least initially. The call for the Protestant meeting that started the trouble was signed by William Craig and John McManus, men with typical Scotch-Irish names. The riots may, however, have had economic as well as religious origins. Scotch-Irish textile craftsmen were suffering from the competition of Irish Catholic millworkers. In another riot at Newark, N.J., in 1854, Scotch-Irishmen sacked a German Catholic church after an Orange procession had been stoned. But it was in New York City that sectarian passions produced the worst violence. In 1870 the annual Twelfth of July parade in the city produced a violent clash between Scotch-Irish Protestants and Irish Catholics; 8 people were killed and 13 wounded. The following year there was an even worse riot on July 12, when 2 policemen and 31 civilians were killed.

Scotch-Irish involvement in organized anti-Catholicism reached a peak in the generation after the Civil War. The campaign against Romanism received a powerful boost from the introduction to the United States of the Loyal Orange Institution. Founded in Armagh in 1795 to promote loyalty to the British Crown and maintain hostility to Catholicism, the Orange order on crossing the Atlantic abandoned its monarchism but lost none of its Protestant fervor. The first American lodge appeared in New York in 1867; others soon sprang up in places like Philadelphia and Pittsburgh. As early as 1873 the Loyal Orange Institution claimed nearly 100 lodges and 10,000 members in the United States; by 1914 it had 364 lodges and 30,000 members. Although it admitted Protestants of all nationalities, it was overwhelmingly Scotch-Irish in membership and leadership. Many of the lodges bore names from the Protestant Ulster past: the Enniskillen True Blues, the Apprentice Boys, the Walls of Derry, and the Sons of William. In 1874 Scotch-Irishmen held all but two of the offices of the American Supreme Grand Lodge.

The Orange order was closely linked with, and may even have inspired, many of the late 19th-century secret societies that sought to alert Americans to the dangers of "popery." These links were especially close with the most important anti-Catholic organization of the period, the American Protective Association, whose chief object was to curb Catholic political influence. Although the APA's membership was mixed—among its supporters were Scandinavian, Canadian, and British Protestants—Scotch-Irishmen formed the nucleus of many of its branches. During the 1890s, when the organization enjoyed an astonishing boom, many of its leaders were Orangemen. William J. Traynor, a native of Ontario who was president of the APA in 1893, had earlier been Deputy Supreme Grand Master of the Loyal Orange Institution of the United States. One of his successors as president of the APA, John Warnock Echols, had formerly been chairman of the executive committee of the Scotch-Irish Society of America.

GROUP CONSCIOUSNESS

The multiple affiliations of men like Traynor and Echols demonstrate the extent to which the Scotch-Irish were able to function as Americans without rejecting kinship with those of similar antecedents. Because they were so readily accepted by other Americans, they had less need of the distinctive social and cultural institutions that other groups developed. Yet, like other groups, they were sensitive to the question of their identity and felt a need to assert themselves in the larger society of which they were part. As a result, the

Scotch-Irish Society of America was established in 1889 to "preserve the history and perpetuate the achievements of the Scotch-Irish race in America." The founders of the organization were relatively high in social and economic status; some occupied positions of leadership in American society. They included Presbyterian clergymen like the Reverend John Hall (1829–1898), the influential pastor of the Fifth Avenue Presbyterian Church in New York City; newspaper editors and publishers like Robert Bonner (1824–1899), publisher of the *New York Ledger,* and George W. Childs (1829–1894), proprietor of the *Philadelphia Public Ledger;* and Republican politicians like A.K. McClure (1828–1909) of Pennsylvania. Some of the leaders, like Hall and Bonner, were Ulster-born; at the other extreme were individuals like the historian William Wirt Henry, grandson of Patrick Henry, whose family had been in America for several generations.

The Scotch-Irish Society of America was at pains to deny any sectarian purpose, stressing that membership was open to people of all denominations. But in the nature of things, the membership was exclusively Protestant, indeed largely Presbyterian. For a dozen years the society held an annual congress in such Scotch-Irish centers as Columbia, Tenn., and Pittsburgh. At these gatherings bands rendered Scottish and Irish airs alternately and members read lengthy papers full of extravagant and uncritical praise of the achievements of their forebears. Subsequently published in 12 volumes as the *Proceedings and Addresses of the Scotch-Irish Society of America,* these papers gave the Scotch-Irish almost exclusive credit for, among other things, the winning of the West, the triumph of the American cause during the Revolution, the adoption of a representative form of government by the Constitutional Convention of 1787, and the spread of popular education. They also compiled long lists of individuals, reputedly of Scotch-Irish descent, who had gained distinction in war and politics.

The impulse that led to these activities was soon spent. Their main justification had been that the Scotch-Irish were rapidly losing a distinctive identity and that the task of recording their contributions to America must be undertaken before assimilation went any further. By 1901 that task could be said to be completed.

THE 20TH CENTURY

By the turn of the century immigration from Ulster to the United States had lost much of its impetus. Yet right up to World War I the rate of decline was not substantially greater than for Ireland as a whole. Arrivals fell from 160,347 in the decade 1880–1889 (when they accounted for 25 percent of the total from Ireland) to 73,711 (18 percent) in the decade 1890–1899 and to 55,385 (19 percent) in the decade 1900–1909. In the years just before the war Ulster's share even increased slightly: 26,294 (25 percent) of the 104,911 arrivals from Ireland in 1910–1914 were from Ulster. This increase occurred despite the fact that Canada, which had long had a sizable Scotch-Irish population, was now beginning to attract an increasing proportion: in 1913, indeed, slightly more Ulster emigrants went there than to the United States. A decisive swing toward Canada, however, did not occur until the late 1920s, probably as

a result of the British Empire Settlement Act of 1922, which offered inducements to emigrants who settled within the empire.

The consequence was that even before the Great Depression brought immigration virtually to an end, the Ulster influx had shrunk to insignificant proportions. Between 1925 and 1930 arrivals in the United States from the 6 counties of Northern Ireland amounted to only 10,246, compared with 115,521 from the 26 counties of the Irish Free State. Nor has there been a subsequent recovery. Chronic unemployment in Northern Ireland has resulted in a steady drain of population ever since World War II. But England and Scotland have been the favored destinations; only a few have made their way to the United States.

In spite of declining immigration, Scotch-Irish organizations retained a measure of vitality for some time, especially in New York and Pennsylvania. As late as 1919 the Loyal Orange Order held a sizable Twelfth of July parade in New York City. The Ulster Irish Society of New York, founded in the 1920s, remained in existence until at least 1939. The Scotch-Irish Society of Pennsylvania has survived. Reorganized as the Scotch-Irish Society of America after World War II, it also took the lead in founding the Scotch-Irish Foundation in 1949, a Philadelphia-based organization whose purpose is to collect and preserve materials concerning the origin and history of the Scotch-Irish in Scotland, Ulster, and the United States.

Concern for Ulster's political status helped sustain Scotch-Irish identity. When the Liberal government passed the Irish Home Rule Act in 1914, Scotch-Irishmen in the United States strongly sympathized with Ulster's fierce opposition to the measure. In the years following the Easter Rising of 1916, the demands of Irish-American nationalists for an independent and united Ireland provoked vigorous Scotch-Irish reaction. Organizations like the Loyal Orange Order exerted themselves to refute the arguments of Daniel F. Cohalan's Friends of Irish Freedom. After the Twelfth of July parade in New York in 1919, the order held a meeting that adopted a series of resolutions for transmission to Senator Henry Cabot Lodge, chairman of the Senate Foreign Relations Committee, which was then conducting hearings on the Treaty of Versailles. The resolutions protested the committee's willingness to grant a hearing to representatives from the self-styled Irish Republic, accused Irish Republicans of conspiring with Germany during the war, and claimed that there was no case for independence. With turmoil persisting in Ireland during the next few years, Scotch-Irish spokesmen kept up their efforts to counter Irish-American propaganda. In October 1921 the Ulster-born magazine publisher Samuel S. McClure (1857–1949) opposed Irish independence in a Carnegie Hall debate with an Irish-American opponent. But the Anglo-Irish Treaty of 1921, which created the Irish Free State from which six Ulster counties were excluded and which granted Northern Ireland a parliament of its own, fully satisfied Scotch-Irish aspirations.

After this, Scotch-Irish absorption with the affairs of Ulster steadily diminished. During World War II, Scotch-Irishmen took comfort from the stationing of U.S. troops in Northern Ireland, a step tantamount to American endorsement of the partition of Ireland. But

since 1945, as has been the case with Irish Americans, most Scotch-Irish have grown increasingly indifferent to the old country. The sectarian strife in Northern Ireland during the past decade has not evoked any marked response; when the Reverend Ian Paisley, the fiery leader of extreme Ulster Protestantism, visited the United States in 1969 to publicize the Ulster cause, he aroused less enthusiasm among the Scotch-Irish than among conservative southern Fundamentalist churchmen, who saw him as an anti-Communist crusader.

Nevertheless, when in 1972 a subcommittee of the House of Representatives Committee on Foreign Affairs held hearings on Northern Ireland and the U.S. role there, a variety of Scotch-Irish organizations—the Scotch-Irish Foundation, the Loyal Orange Order of the United States, Ulster American Loyalists, and the Northern Ireland Service Council—appeared before it or submitted statements. Their purpose was to extol the Scotch-Irish record in America, to draw attention to Ulster's role in World War II, and to dispute allegations of discrimination against Catholics in Northern Ireland. Although such organizations do not appear to have had any substantial following, their mere existence indicates some survival of Scotch-Irish ethnic self-consciousness.

Bibliography

The most satisfactory general account, valuable for its careful background treatment, is the dispassionate study by James G. Leyburn, *The Scotch-Irish: A Social History* (Chapel Hill, N.C., 1962). A useful supplement is Edward R.R. Green, ed., *Essays in Scotch-Irish History* (London, 1969). Despite being uncritically eulogistic and excessively political, two older general works are still worth consulting: Charles A. Hanna, *The Scotch-Irish: Or, the Scot in North Britain, North Ireland and North America*, 2 vols. (1902; reprint, Baltimore, 1968); and Henry J. Ford, *The Scotch-Irish in America* (1915; reprint, Hamden, Conn., 1966). For an analysis of the Ulster background and the organization of the emigrant traffic, see Robert J. Dickson, *Ulster Emigration to Colonial America, 1718–1775* (London, 1966). Interesting material on American aspects of the 18th-century movement appears in Edward R.R. Green, "Scotch-Irish Emigration: An Imperial Problem," *Western Pennsylvania Historical Magazine* 35 (December 1952): 193–209; and Desmond Clarke, *Arthur Dobbs, Esquire, 1689–1765; Surveyor–General of Ireland, Prospector, and Governor of North Carolina* (Chapel Hill, 1957). Wayland F. Dunaway, *The Scotch-Irish of Colonial Pennsylvania* (Chapel Hill, 1944), though marred by extravagant claims, is the most detailed account of the Scotch-Irish in their favorite colony. A similar focus is employed in Guy S. Klett, *Presbyterians in Colonial Pennsylvania* (Philadelphia, 1937). A vivid picture of Scotch-Irish settlements in the Southern backcountry is to be found in Carl Bridenbaugh, *Myths and Realities: Societies of the Colonial South* (1952; reprint, New York, 1965). William F. Adams, *Ireland and the Irish Emigration from 1815 to the Famine* (New Haven, 1932), the most thorough analysis of the early 19th-century movement from Ireland, devotes much space to Ulster and the Scotch-Irish. Details of the 19th-century emigrant traffic from Londonderry may be found in Sholto Cooke, *The Maiden City and the Western Ocean* (Dublin, 1960).

The main collections of primary materials are in the Public Record Office of Northern Ireland and the Linen Hall Library, both in Belfast; the Presbyterian Historical Society and the Historical Society of Pennsylvania, both in Philadelphia; the New York Historical Society; the North Carolina State Department of Archives and History, Raleigh; the University of North Carolina Library, Chapel Hill; and the Library of Congress.

MALDWYN A. JONES

SCOTS

Scottish settlement in America began in the earliest colonial days and has continued ever since. Although immigration statistics are lacking for early periods and are imperfect for later ones, the total number of Scottish immigrants can with some confidence be said to

Scotland
Approximate division between Highlands and Lowlands
Gaelic-speaking areas
100   Km.   Miles

1 CAITHNESS
2 NAIRN
3 KINCARDINE
4 KINROSS
5 CLACKMANNAN
6 DUNBARTON
7 WEST LOTHIAN
8 MIDLOTHIAN
9 EAST LOTHIAN
10 RENFREW

have approached 1.5 million. Americans who have Scottish ancestry seldom seem to forget the fact, and the activities of numerous societies that aim at keeping alive an awareness of the Scottish heritage are a conspicuous feature of American life. A glance at place names on a map or in a gazetteer indicates the widespread nature of Scottish influence in the United States —though not always as a direct result of actual settlement. There are eight Aberdeens, eight Edinburghs, and seven Glasgows; eight places bear the name Scotland. A great many places are known by Scottish surnames—Campbell (10), Cameron (16), and Douglas (9)—though the second and third of these are place names in Scotland as well. Crawford—again both a place name and a personal name in Scotland—seems to hold the record, with about 30 appearances on the map of the United States. There are well over 100 place names beginning with "Mac" or "Mc," from McAdams, Miss., to McWilliams, Ala.

MIGRATION IN THE COLONIAL PERIOD

There have been Scots in America almost as long as Europeans have populated the continent. When the first

permanent English settlement was made in 1607, England and Scotland had for four years shared a monarch, James VI (Scotland) and I (England). In 1607–1608 full rights as nationals in both countries were granted to all Englishmen and Scotsmen born after 1603. Before this act a number of Scots had migrated to England and had been naturalized there, and at least one Scot, Thomas Henderson, was among the original settlers in Virginia. As Scots ceased to be aliens in England and in English dominions overseas, Scottish settlers began to find their way to all the English colonies.

Although Scotland and England shared a common sovereign from 1603, they continued to have separate parliaments and administrations until 1707, when they entered into a freely negotiated treaty to form the United Kingdom. It was therefore open to the Scots to plant colonies of their own in the New World, following the example not only of England but of France, Holland, and Sweden, as well as Spain and Portugal. From 1620 onward a series of proposals were made for settlement in America, and small colonies, mostly short-lived, were established in Nova Scotia (1629), East Jersey (eastern and northern New Jersey, 1683), and South Carolina (1684), as well as the better-known settlement of New Caledonia at Darién, near Panama (1698). The East Jersey and South Carolina ventures served partly as refuges for religious dissidents—in the former case Quakers, who then suffered vexatious treatment in Scotland as in England, and in the second case, Presbyterians, who were liable to prosecution because at that time the Church of Scotland had an Episcopal constitution.

However, the movement of Scots across the Atlantic was slow to gather momentum. Scots already had a long and strong tradition of migration to other European lands and throughout the Middle Ages had wandered far and wide as pilgrims, scholars, soldiers, and traders. Some Scots had been colonists within the British Isles in the later 16th and early 17th centuries; some migrated from southern Scotland to the West Highlands, the Hebrides, Orkney, and Shetland, and many more moved across to Ulster, which has been called the most successful Scottish colony of all time. Some 50,000 Scots are said to have settled there by 1650, to become the ancestors of the Scotch-Irish, who later contributed to some of the apparently Scottish aspects of American life. (See Scotch-Irish.) It was not easy, therefore, to popularize the idea of emigration to America, especially when continental wars were still offering great opportunities to those energetic Scots who felt that they had insufficient prospects in their own country and preferred to follow the old habit of taking service in foreign armies. In fact, in the early proposals for Scottish colonies across the Atlantic, much of the initiative came from somewhat unrepresentative Scots who had been to some extent Anglicized in culture and outlook and were in close touch with English colonizing enthusiasts.

A fair number of the Scots who did reach America in the 17th century did not go of their own volition but were deported as criminals, as economic failures, or as members of the losing side in civil or ecclesiastical strife. The system of deportation, then and long afterward called transportation, involved forced labor in a colony for a term of years, a recognized mode of punishment. Three times between 1648 and 1651 Scottish armies were defeated by the forces of Oliver Cromwell, and on each occasion several hundred prisoners were sent to America. The Scottish government had contemplated transportation as a form of punishment as early as about 1620 and had recourse to it after 1660 to deal with some of the recalcitrant Presbyterians as well as with criminals: in 1685, for instance, nearly 200 persons, some of them guilty of participation in a rebellion led by the Earl of Argyll, were deported from Scottish jails to East Jersey. Although this element of compulsion was an important one, other Scots did go freely to find employment in the colonies, especially to Virginia, as traders or tobacco workers. By 1700 the Scots can be said to have established a tradition of voluntary settlement in America.

In the 18th century over 1,400 Jacobites defeated in the rebellions of 1715 and 1745 and criminals were transported overseas, but from the 1730s voluntary emigration became far more significant. Very likely the parliamentary union of England and Scotland in 1707, which brought the two peoples closer together and opened up free trade between Scotland and the colonies, encouraged Scots to look to America as a land in which they had a right to settle, but economic and social factors also stimulated emigration, especially in the Highlands, which were still very much a distinct entity.

The east and south of Scotland, constituting the Lowlands, were inhabited by people partly of Teutonic origin and speaking a Teutonic tongue—the form of English that became Lowland Scots—while the Highlands of the center and west were the home of a Celtic population, speaking the Gaelic that had come from Ireland in the 6th century and was still called "Irish" by the Lowlanders. The barren Highlands had probably never been self-supporting. In earlier times their meager produce had been supplemented by armed raids on the more fertile and prosperous Lowlands, but when the extension of law and order made such raiding impossible, it became evident that the Highlands had more people than the land could sustain. Simultaneously, and partly for the same reason, the maintenance of clans as bodies of fighting men ceased to be necessary. This change depressed the status of the tacksmen, large leaseholders who served as the chiefs' lieutenants in organizing the subtenants as the military rank and file of the clans. Among the earliest Highland emigrants, therefore, were tacksmen who had in effect been driven out of business at home.

In the 1760s emigration from the Highlands increased, and the reason often given was the raising of rents. The total Scottish emigration between 1763 and 1775—the first period for which any estimate can be made—has been put at about 25,000. While a handful of the migrants went to Nova Scotia and Prince Edward Island, the great majority settled in the thirteen colonies. At the time of the American Revolution most Scottish colonists, not least the Highlanders, seem to have been loyalists. Afterward a good many of them, declining to live in a country that was no longer under the British crown, left the United States, either to settle in Canada or to return to Scotland. Even so, people of Scottish stock (some of them, however, really Scotch-Irish) still made up over 6 percent, or some 260,000 of the population of the United States in 1790.

19TH- AND 20TH-CENTURY MIGRATION

After the Revolution the main destination was Canada, which long remained the most serious competitor of the United States as a receiving area for Scottish, as indeed for other British, emigrants. Britain's war with France (1793–1815), which toward its close also involved war with the United States, caused further interruption in the outward flow from Britain. After peace was restored, however, emigration again became substantial. There was a period of economic depression, unemployment, and unrest in the Lowlands, while in the Highlands the introduction of extensive sheep farming forced a large-scale dispersal of tenants. Although at this stage few of them went directly overseas, their uprooting started a movement that ultimately often led to emigration.

The 1840s—the hungry forties—again brought difficult conditions: failure of the potato crop in the Highlands made imperative the reduction of population living on the margin of subsistence there. In the Lowlands, too, there was much distress, unemployment, and agitation. Organized migration overseas was often the remedy to these problems. The interest of emigrants, however, continued for some time to focus on Canada. The continuous official record of immigration to the United States begins in 1819 and shows that between 1820 and 1851 the number of Scots arriving very seldom reached four figures in a year and was sometimes less than 100. The total over the period was only 10,525. From 1852 onward, however, the annual number was nearly always several thousand, and the lead of Canada over the United States was much reduced. All along, it must be remembered, some immigrants to Canada later moved to the United States.

Clearly the 1850s represent a turning point in Scottish immigration to the United States. Biographical data for some 7,000 Scottish immigrants who arrived over an extended period ending in 1854 make it possible to present a sample of their origins, places of settlement, and occupations. In 5,737 cases the place of origin is reasonably certain, and no part of Scotland was unrepresented. Table 1 gives the percentages of emigrants from various areas, and for comparative purposes, the percentages of the Scottish population in each area. With allowance for counties that were partly Highland and partly Lowland, especially Dunbarton, Argyll, Perth, and Caithness, the figures represent a migration of roughly 45 percent from the Highlands and 55 percent from the Lowlands. The Highlands must therefore have produced more than their due proportion, for they contained not much more than a third of the population of the country. The proportions, of course, were not constant over the long period to which the figures relate. Most likely the majority of the 18th-century emigrants were from the Highlands, and the Lowland preponderance was due largely to emigration after 1815.

After 1852 the number of Scots entering the United States only twice fell below 1,000 a year and even in the 1850s and 1860s often totaled more than 5,000 annually. From 1870 onward the annual figures commonly exceeded 10,000 and in 1910 reached 20,000. In the half century following 1870, the ascendancy of the United States not only over Canada but over all other receiving areas was established; 53 percent of all Scottish emigrants went to the United States, though in some phases, notably at the beginning of the 20th century, Canada occasionally again received more Scots. A total of 478,224 Scots entered the United States between 1852 and 1910.

But greater emigration was still to come. An important factor in stimulating emigration had, of course, always been economic depression, and there had been decades before World War I when more than 200,000 Scots left their homeland—217,418 in 1881–1891 and 254,042 in 1901–1911. But all previous records were easily surpassed by the 391,903 Scottish emigrants in the years of severe depression between 1921 and 1931. The magnitude of the crisis is shown by the fact that this decade is the only one on record when Scotland's population dropped (by 40,000); even in the hungry forties it had increased by 270,000. As unemployment was mainly in heavy industry and textiles, most of the emigrants now came from industrialized areas. The United States continued to be the principal magnet, and in that decade (when the proportion of Scots to immigrants from other countries was higher than at any other time) more Scots than English entered the United States, although the population of England was about eight times that of Scotland. Whereas only 78,357 Scots settled in the United States between 1911 and 1920, 159,781 immigrated between 1921 and 1930.

Therefore the number of people of Scottish birth in the United States continued to rise: 233,473 in 1900; 261,034 in 1910; 254,567 in 1920; and a peak of 354,323 in 1930. In the last-named year the number of American citizens of Scottish birth or parentage was 899,591. Despite these very high figures, the Scots no longer constituted anything like their earlier proportion of Americans, owing to the vast influx of other ethnic groups. Their percentage had fallen from over 6.0 in 1790 to 3.1 in 1850, 2.4 in 1900, and only 1.9 in 1920. With the mass immigration of the 1920s, the proportion climbed to 2.5 in 1930.

After 1930 the pattern changed, and Scotland ceased to make substantial additions to the American population. In the early 1930s the Great Depression drove many Scots home again. Moreover, throughout that

Table 1. Region of origin of 5,737 Scottish settlers in the United States from colonial times through 1854.

Region	Percentage of Scottish population	Percentage of Scottish emigration
Edinburgh and Lothians	12.5	10.6
Eastern borders	4.5	4.4
Glasgow, Lanark, Renfrew, and Ayr	24.2	21.7
Southwest	7.2	8.9
Fife, etc.	6.8	4.5
Stirling and Dunbarton	4.7	3.1
Aberdeen, Kincardine, and Angus	15.0	5.5
Perth	6.9	8.7
Inverness	4.5	9.3
Ross and Cromarty	3.5	3.7
Argyll	4.9	13.9
Sutherland, Caithness, Orkney, and Shetland	5.3	3.1

Source: Donald Whyte, *Dictionary of Scottish Emigrants to the U.S.A.* (Baltimore, 1972).

decade the economic situation in Scotland was slowly improving, so that there was less incentive to emigrate. Emigration fell off sharply, to no more than 6,887 between 1931 and 1940, and it did not recover until 1946. A total of 16,131 Scots emigrated to the United States in 1941–1950, nearly all after 1945. Since 1950 emigration as a whole from Scotland has often been heavy, but relatively few Scots have gone to the United States—many have gone no farther than England. For the six years 1962–1967 the total emigration from Scotland to the United States was only 21,000, a yearly average of no more than 3,500. The number of people of Scots birth in the country dropped to 244,200 in 1950 and 170,134 in 1970, by which date the number of Americans of Scottish birth or parentage had fallen to 581,255.

SOCIAL TIES AND MIGRATION

Loyalties associated with blood relationships, tenurial links, and written or customary obligations of service had given considerable local cohesion to Scottish society. In medieval times, a great family and its following had formed a social and even a political unit, and most Scots were accustomed to look to some great man for leadership and to feel strong affinity with other members of his following. Such ties were eliminated in the Lowlands by the 17th century, but they persisted in the Highlands, where clans continued for another century and more to accept the authority of a chief or a tacksman.

Scottish emigration, therefore, was very often less of individuals than of groups. Emigration from the Highlands in particular tended to be a movement under leadership, sometimes of a chief or tacksman, but when such leadership became less relevant or was not available, the role might be assumed by a clergyman—a priest if the clan was Roman Catholic, otherwise a Presbyterian minister. The clan structure provided a ready-made unit on which organizers of emigration, or propagandists for emigration, could build. Somewhat similarly, men from certain Highland regiments, recruited from clans, sometimes settled in America after fighting there in the 18th-century wars.

A different kind of corporate action, this time in the Lowlands and on a territorial basis, came about through associations formed for the mutual help and encouragement of emigrants, the earliest of which, so far as is known, came into being at Wigtown in 1773. The weavers of Renfrew and the farmers of Stirling also formed companies or societies for the cooperative purchase of land in America. Handloom weavers in the cotton industry, once the aristocrats of Scottish artisans, were hard hit when power looms were introduced and were conspicuous among 19th-century emigrants. During the period of distress about 1820, societies were again formed, largely by weavers, to aid emigration by cooperative means; in 1826 there were upward of 30 such societies. In the hungry forties such societies were revived: in 1843 an organization of United Emigration Societies was based mainly on the textile area of Renfrew and Lanark. Weavers' societies continued to aid emigration until the 1860s. Besides the contributions of prospective emigrants and their friends, a good deal of charitable assistance came from public-spirited men

who, at a time when there was much concern about unemployment and poverty, readily thought of emigration as the obvious remedy.

From the 17th century onward the immigrants' personal letters home, telling of their success and prosperity and describing the favorable aspects of their surroundings, exerted much influence within the smallest social groups—the family, the kindred, and the circle of close acquaintances. The mere fact that education was widespread in Scotland and that so many Scots were literate may have helped to make emigration the "epidemic" kind of movement it sometimes became. It was not uncommon for a successful settler to remit funds to enable family members to follow—wife or sweetheart, brothers and sisters, and sometimes ultimately the parents as well. This feature, unlike the clan structure, persisted and was still influential in the 1920s. The fact that in that decade the numbers of male and female immigrants from Scotland were almost equal may indicate that families rather than individuals were migrating.

There was also the influence of printed propaganda, in the form of letters in the press, pamphlets, and books. Even in the days of the Nova Scotia colony of the 1620s, the promoters appealed in print to their fellow countrymen. In the 1730s when recruits were being sought for the new colony of Georgia—and were found in large numbers in the northern Highlands—Sir Robert Mountgomery wrote *A Discourse Concerning the Design'd Establishment of a New Colony to the South of Carolina, in the Most Delightful Country of the Universe.* Later in the 18th century various pamphlets encouraging emigration circulated in Scotland, and more books came in the 19th century: John Bradbury, a Scot, wrote a book to encourage immigrants to the Missouri Valley; Alexander Forbes, a Scottish merchant at Tepic, Mexico, recommended the colonization of California in 1839; and in 1852 John Regan, an Ayrshire schoolteacher who had settled in Illinois, produced *The Emigrant's Guide to the Western States of America.* Another kind of printed propaganda was the press advertisement, often by shipowners whose commercial interest lay in conveying emigrants overseas.

After the pioneering phase was over, Scots who came to the United States knew that they had a fair chance of finding fellow Scots when they arrived, and not infrequently they would obtain assistance from some of the Scottish societies (mentioned below) that had been formed in the United States partly to assist immigrants from Scotland. Knowledge that such societies existed may well have helped to focus the minds of emigrants on certain areas.

SETTLEMENT PATTERNS

In the 17th century most Scots settled in the southern and middle Atlantic states; a fair proportion also settled in New England. Much the same distribution prevailed through the 18th century. The men who were transported as rebels or as criminals went mainly to Massachusetts, New Jersey, Maryland, Virginia, and the Carolinas. The chief area of Highland settlement was the Cape Fear River and its tributaries in North Carolina; South Carolina and Georgia also received a number of Highland immigrants. Others found homes in the Mohawk Valley of New York. In 1790 Pennsylvania,

Virginia, and North Carolina had the highest proportion of Scottish stock among their inhabitants.

Secondary movement from the eastern coastal states westward began fairly early. By 1773 some Scots were in Kentucky, and by 1779 they were across the Ohio River. Some of the descendants of the North Carolina settlers pioneered in Tennessee and Missouri. As time went on, enterprising settlers from the East pressed on through Detroit to the rest of Michigan, Indiana, Illinois, and the Mississippi Valley. Scots from Canada also arrived through Detroit, especially in days when communication was easier between Canada and the United States than within Canada. Scots reached Illinois at an early stage in its growth—there were nearly 5,000 of them there in 1850—and they were among the founders of Chicago. A Scotland County was formed in Missouri in 1841; in Iowa there were 700 Scots in 1850 and 3,000 in 1860. Some Scots had settled in Texas as early as the 1820s; quite a number joined them there before Texas was admitted to the Union in 1845. Settlement in the Midwest was preceded by settlement in the South and in the Far West, in the latter case by people who made the journey by sea rather than overland. The few Scots who have been traced in California before it became part of the United States seem to have been among the first non-Spanish inhabitants of the region. The gold rush in 1849 brought more Scots to California, as it brought others.

The following list gives some indication of the pattern of settlement in the earlier phases, before the massive immigration that began in the middle of the 19th century. It gives the percentage of Scots who were residing in each of the states listed, based on some 5,000 who immigrated before 1855 and whose place of settlement can be ascertained: New York, 20.0; Pennsylvania, 12.0; Virginia, 11.5; North Carolina, 10.0; Massachusetts, 9.5; South Carolina, 7.2; Maryland, 5.7; New Jersey, 5.0; Georgia, 3.8; Ohio, 2.7; Illinois, 1.2; Louisiana, 1.1; and Connecticut, 1.0.

The pattern up to this point probably had not altered much over the generations, except for the penetration beyond the eastern seaboard. Some allowance, but possibly not enough, has been made for the fact that New York City, Philadelphia, and Boston were landing places from which immigrants dispersed, so the figures for the states of New York, Pennsylvania, and Massachusetts may be somewhat misleading. States accounting for less than 1 percent of the group are not listed. However, the residences of those 5,000 Scottish immigrants included places in every state that was in the Union in 1855, as well as a good many more in areas that were not yet states.

In the second half of the 19th century with the advent of the railways, immigrant trains crossed the continent and opened up the whole of the inland United States. Although the number of Scottish settlers in some states never became large, it is almost startling to find a place name like Leith not only in Alabama and Arkansas but in North Dakota and Nevada as well. Most of the Scots continued to be attracted to the eastern parts of the country, though the southern Atlantic states became far less important destinations than they had been earlier. The census of 1920 shows the largest numbers of people of Scottish birth or descent in the Northeast and Mid-Atlantic states; next in importance were the midwes-

tern states, especially Ohio, Illinois, and Michigan. These were followed by the Pacific coast, especially California, which had the fifth highest number of inhabitants of Scottish origin after New York, Pennsylvania, Massachusetts, and Illinois.

The great immigration between the world wars altered the pattern little: in 1940 New York had by far the largest number of persons of Scottish birth, followed by five states with almost the same figures—Michigan, New Jersey, Pennsylvania, Massachusetts, and California—and then Illinois and Ohio. In 1970 New York still had the highest number of persons of Scottish birth or parentage, but California had climbed to second place—presumably as a result of movement within the United States—followed by New Jersey, Pennsylvania, Massachusetts, Illinois, Florida, and Ohio. Every census continued to show that some Scots, however few, were still settling in every state.

OCCUPATIONAL DISTRIBUTION

In the colonial period a fair number of Scots in America were traders or merchants, some of them not permanent residents. At that stage, however, settlement on the land was the main attraction for Scottish immigrants, coming as they did from an essentially rural economy. In the late 18th and early 19th centuries, an appreciable number of the Scottish immigrants had been skilled men of one kind or another at home and found similar employment in professions and crafts across the Atlantic. An analysis of 3,624 adult male immigrants who had come to the United States by 1855 shows that 960 were the victims of transportation, all of whom had arrived by 1748 and who figure prominently in any list because they are well documented. Table 2 shows the percentages of the chief occupations of the remaining 2,664. There must be a certain distortion, in that the humbler occupations are likely to be underrepresented, and figures covering such a long period do not disclose the declining importance of rural occupations even before 1850. The listed occupations

Table 2. Occupations of 2,664 Scottish emigrants to the United States from colonial times through 1854.

Occupation	Percentage
Professionals	
Ministers	4.1
Physicians and surgeons	3.0
Teachers	1.8
Officials	1.6
Lawyers	1.0
Craftsmen	
Weavers	5.0
Construction workers	3.8
Tailors	2.4
Wrights	2.3
Smiths	1.5
Mariners	1.5
Shoemakers	1.4
Merchants	9.2
On the land	
Farmers	22.0
Planters, landowners, and "gentlemen"	6.0
Unskilled workers	
Servants (including farm servants)	11.1
Laborers	5.3

Source: Donald Whyte, *Dictionary of Scottish Emigrants to the U.S.A.* (Baltimore, 1972).

made up 83 percent of the total. In addition, a remarkable assortment of trades was represented by groups ranging in size from 23 to 1: gardeners, coopers, watchmakers, jewelers, miners, clerks, shopkeepers, printers, bakers, butchers, cooks, barbers, saddlers, and many more, including 3 wigmakers and 2 portrait painters.

Clearly the simple pattern of earlier times had already begun to alter in the first half of the 19th century, and it altered more in the second half. The determining fact was that Scotland, like Britain as a whole, had been far ahead of the United States in industrial development of almost every kind—textiles, machinery, engineering, and the exploitation of mineral resources. Therefore, as the United States began to develop its industries, it obtained both machines and skilled workers, from Britain. For a time Britain had tried to check the export of machinery and even, by an act of 1782, the export of craftsmen; but the restriction on the migration of trained men came to an end in 1825. Scotland thereafter began to export skilled workers in large numbers. The first development seems to have been in cotton manufacture, which had been expanding in Scotland since about 1780 and had become a major industry there. James Montgomery, a Scot who had become the owner of a cotton mill in New England in 1836, wrote a pamphlet to stimulate the immigration of textile workers. Table 2 indicates that the most numerous group of skilled craftsmen to immigrate before 1855 were in fact weavers, and to them we should probably add a good many female spinsters, who in those days may actually have been textile workers rather than merely unmarried women.

The movement of textile workers increased sharply after the Civil War, when cotton manufacture in Scotland slumped and the United States imposed tariffs to encourage its own production of cotton thread and cloth. Men who immigrated found the faster pace of work more difficult, but the wages were much higher than in Scotland. Scottish thread-manufacturing firms set up branches in America and staffed them with experienced workers from their factories at home: George A. Clark, from Paisley, founded works at Newark, N.J., and the more famous Paisley firm of Coats founded works at Pawtucket, R.I. Apart from cotton, Scottish woolen-cloth makers went to American factories, as did carpet weavers trained in Kilmarnock, especially in Thompsonville, Conn.

Comparable developments took place in the heavy industries at a time when the whole world was a market for British products and eager to learn British skills. Scottish engineers therefore took their experience to the American iron and steel industries; some served their apprenticeship in Scotland and then followed their trade in the United States. Scots were prominent in marine engineering and shipbuilding; in a San Francisco shipyard in 1905 there was "hardly a man . . . who did not speak with a strong Scottish accent." During depressions in Scotland, coal miners were apt to move to the United States for a season or two and could be found by the thousands in states from Maryland and Pennsylvania to Illinois and Ohio. Quarriers, too, went out: New England granite was worked by Scots who had learned their trade in Aberdeen, and the masons who followed on the heels of the quarriers established communities in Massachusetts, Maine, and New Hamp-

shire; it was remarked that Scots left their mark on American tombstones.

However, as American industry developed, the need for imported skilled men dwindled. In iron and steel manufacture the United States no longer needed Scottish guidance after about 1870; in the mining of coal and iron the turning point was about ten years later. The importance of Scottish contributions to textile processes petered out about 1900 and was probably one reason for the temporary falling-off in immigration to the United States after that point. There continued to be some specialized Scottish craftsmen outside the fields of large-scale industry, as in type founding, portrait painting, architecture, building, and engraving. Scottish gardeners, who had acquired a reputation in England in the 18th century, were highly esteemed in the United States.

The contribution of the Scots to agriculture, on the other hand, became much less significant. The 1890 Census listed only 3 percent of the immigrants from Scotland as agricultural workers. Throughout the 19th century some Scots had continued to come as farmers and had settled in New York, Illinois, Wisconsin, Iowa, Florida, Minnesota, and south-central Virginia. However, those Scots who were drawn across the Atlantic by the vision of easy possession of limitless acres of fertile land began to find the prairie country of Canada, as it was opened up, more attractive, and this may have been a factor in reducing immigration to the United States at the very end of the century. By 1920 nearly 196,000 Scottish-born Americans lived in urban areas and 58,000 in rural areas; in 1940 the round figures were 230,000 and 49,000, respectively. The percentage of Scots living in urban areas was above the national average, though they appear to have preferred moderate-sized towns to the largest cities.

In 1900 first- and second-generation Scots concentrated in the building trades, manufacturing, mining and quarrying, textiles and clerical work, with agriculture at the foot of the list. In 1950 the Scottish-born showed a higher proportion than other groups in the professions, clerical work, skilled labor, and private household service.

DISTINGUISHED SCOTS

The part that Scottish immigrants and their descendants played as men of distinction in the United States is hardly capable of statistical demonstration. Out of over 13,500 persons who qualified for inclusion in the *Dictionary of American Biography*, only 214 were of Scottish birth, though it should be noted for comparison that only 724 were of English birth. It would no doubt be possible to determine that a large number of the 13,500 Americans were of Scottish descent, but it would hardly be meaningful, for the other strands in any individual's ancestry might be more numerous and significant. The figures given earlier for the occupations of Scottish settlers down to 1855 showed that professional men made up almost precisely 10 percent, but this indication is misleading, as such men tended to be better documented than laborers, for example. Later figures show that whereas the proportion of professional men among immigrants from the British Isles was as a whole far higher (over 3 percent) than that of most other

ethnic groups, Scotland's share was actually a little less than England's.

The signatories of the Declaration of Independence included two native-born Scots, James Wilson (1742–1798) and John Witherspoon (1723–1794); the latter, a Scottish Presbyterian minister, was the only clergyman among the signatories. Of 56 members of the Continental Congress that adopted the Declaration, eleven were of Scottish extraction. Hugh Orr (1715–1798) cast guns for the American army, John Paul Jones (1747–1792) founded the navy, and James Craik (1730–1814) organized the army's medical service. Since the Revolution, over 100 men of Scottish descent have served as state governors, and of 50 justices of the U.S. Supreme Court from 1789 to 1882, at least 15 were of Scottish descent.

The contribution of Scots to education began earlier, to some extent as a by-product of the association of the churches with education. Apart from teachers at lower levels—it was said in 1773 that the Virginians imported all their tutors and schoolmasters from Scotland—the succession started with James Blair (1656–1743), founder of William and Mary College (1693). He was followed by William Smith (1727–1803), provost in 1755 of the College of Philadelphia, which was the forerunner of the University of Pennsylvania; John Blair (1720–1771), professor of theology in the Presbyterian College of New Jersey (later Princeton University); John Witherspoon, principal of that college from 1768 to 1794; Charles Nisbet (1736–1804), first president of Dickinson College (f. 1785); John Beveridge, professor at Philadelphia under Provost Smith; James McClurg (c. 1746–1823) and William Small, professors at Williamsburg; Andrew Ferrier (c. 1796–1867), minister in Pennsylvania and president of Madison College; and James McCosh (1811–1894), who became president of Princeton College in 1868.

The church, education, and other professions were all associated with the dissemination of knowledge by the printed word, and Scots were also active in printing and publishing. Among the skilled craftsmen who went out from Scotland were printers like Robert Aitken (1734–1802), a native of Dalkeith, who was a printer and publisher in Philadelphia in 1769; David Hall (c. 1714–1772), a native of Edinburgh and a skilled printer employed by Benjamin Franklin; and William Hunter, partner in the *Virginia Gazette*. In later generations George Bruce (1781–1861) introduced stereotype and Adam Ramage improved the printing press. Publishing and journalism were closely associated; John Regan, an Ayr schoolteacher, became editor and proprietor of the *Messenger* in Illinois in 1857 and James Gordon Bennett (1792–1872), from Banff, founded the *New York Daily Herald*. Booksellers and stationers operated in a humbler sphere, but it is interesting that William Adam (c. 1800–1883) served as a minister in Scotland and the United States before becoming a bookseller in Washington, D.C. Thomas Allen (1795–1826), a bookbinder and stationer in New York in association with his brother-in-law Samuel Campbell, was the first American agent for the *Encyclopaedia Britannica*. Alexander Wilson (1766–1813), a Paisley weaver who got into trouble for associating with radical agitators, emigrated in 1794; he became a schoolmaster near Philadelphia but turned to ornithology and produced the pioneering great work in American bird study, *American Ornithology* (1808–1814).

RELIGIOUS LIFE

There were various strands in the Scottish ecclesiastical tradition: a few areas in the northeast, the southwest, and the West Highlands had either retained Roman Catholicism after the Reformation or had subsequently been proselytized by missionaries from Ireland, and in the 19th century a massive immigration of Irish raised the Catholic population of Scotland tenfold. From the Reformation until 1690 the reformed church was sometimes Episcopal, sometimes Presbyterian; after 1690, when the Presbyterian system was finally established, there was still a strong Episcopal church in Scotland. In the 18th century the majority of emigrants were Presbyterians; a fair number of emigrating Highlanders were Roman Catholics, however, and Episcopal clergy went to America in some numbers at a time when their church was under certain disabilities at home. On the eve of independence there were at least 13 Scottish Episcopal ministers in Virginia; others were serving in Connecticut, South Carolina, and New York. This may explain why Samuel Seabury (1729–1796), who had been a medical student in Edinburgh, applied to the Scottish bishops for consecration as the first American bishop in 1784 and why the Protestant Episcopal Church of America adopted a communion service similar to that used in Scotland.

At first Scottish Presbyterians in America sometimes found it hard to obtain ministers (who in those days probably had better material prospects at home), but some ministers were always ready to go out to the colonies, either to settle or to serve for a time, a tradition that has continued ever since. American Presbyterianism did not derive only from Scottish immigrants; English nonconformity made its contribution, and the Scotch-Irish contributed even more, although their Presbyterianism derived from Scotland, and they always looked to the churches in Scotland as their fountainhead. Thus American Presbyterianism, whether at first or second hand, stems largely from the Scots and is apt to regard Edinburgh as its Geneva; many American divinity students go to Scotland for part of their training. Presbyterianism is strongest in Pennsylvania, New York, Ohio, Illinois, Virginia, North Carolina, Texas, and California. The general resemblance in the distribution of Presbyterianism and of Scottish influence is unmistakable.

Presbyterian schisms and secessions originating in Scotland crossed the Atlantic (sometimes by way of Ulster), and Scots in America also developed new sects of their own. The Glassites, who attempted to return to primitive and apostolic models, were known in America as Sandemanians, after Robert Sandeman (1718–1771), a son-in-law of the founder. A group called MacDonaldites, who originated in Prince Edward Island, brought their beliefs to Boston in 1895. The Campbellites, bearing the name of the clan that was the principal rival of the MacDonalds, were founded by an Ulster Scot, Alexander Campbell. And a group known as the Christian Catholic Apostolic Church in Zion was founded in San Francisco and then in Chicago by Alexander Dowie, a native of Edinburgh.

SOCIAL CHARACTERISTICS

Among Highland Presbyterians in the United States, the Gaelic language as well as religion was for a time a bond, especially as long as services in Gaelic were provided. With the passage of time, intermarriage, and general absorption into the surrounding life, however, Presbyterian churches ceased to be ethnic or linguistic enclaves, and Gaelic services died out after about 1860. Otherwise, language can have done little to maintain a sense of identity among the Scots; although in the first generation many new immigrants must have spoken strong Lowland dialects, they were no more difficult to understand than many English dialects. Lowland Scots was close enough to standard English or standard American for any awareness of linguistic identity to be eroded within a short time.

Medieval Scottish migrants to the European continent had established guilds whose corporate activity was often the endowment of an altar in a church. It was not long before Scots in America likewise founded associations, beginning, so far as is known, with the Scots Charitable Society of Boston in 1657; among others that followed within a century were those at Philadelphia, New York, and Savannah, Ga. Their purpose was partly charitable and helped to smooth the path of immigrants from Scotland, but it was also partly convivial. The first St. Andrew's Society seems to have been founded in New York in 1756, and this time-honored name is now borne by associations widely spread over the United States. Annual dinners on the festival of Scotland's patron saint (November 30) kept his memory alive when it was almost forgotten in Scotland; they are occasions when the thoughts of Scottish Americans turn to the ancestral homeland.

Some of the activities that give cohesion to Scots in the United States now are perhaps less authentic than the links of blood, faith, and language. Some popular festivities were a true part of folk tradition in Scotland, like those associated with Halloween and Hogmanay (New Year's Eve), but for a long time more attention has been focused on January 25, the birthday of Robert Burns, acclaimed as the Scottish national poet. A Burns supper was held in New York as early as 1820, only 24 years after the poet's death, and in the course of time a set of rites has gathered around such suppers, held by Burns clubs in many places.

Americans have been equally captivated by the modern cult of clans and tartans, much of which is deplorably unhistorical, especially when adopted by descendants of Lowlanders who thought the only good Highlander was a dead Highlander. An order of Scottish clans was founded in St. Louis, Mo., in 1878 but soon had its most important center in New England and the Mid-Atlantic states. The "clans" were in effect lodges that adopted the names and supposed tartans (mostly modern commercial productions) of Highland families. In addition societies bearing the names of individual clans, like the Clan Donald Society of America, had many local branches. Despite their egalitarianism, Scottish Americans always seem ready to make a fuss over a visiting peer, especially if he professes to be the head of some "clan." Highland games, another supposedly traditional aspect of Highland life, was widely taken up in Scotland in the 19th century and spread to the United States. In 1836 the Highland Society of New York held its first meeting, and within a few years the fashion had spread. There are now Gaelic clubs, Scottish country dance clubs, and bagpipe bands. The ostentatious character of Highland dress and the activities that go with it make Scottish ethnic groups conspicuous; the very ostentation creates an appeal to many who have no claim to Scottish origin.

Two traditional Scottish games were taken across the Atlantic. One was the winter sport of curling, which was well established in America by 1867, when about 30 constituent local clubs formed a Grand National Curling Club. The other was golf, which had its origins on the natural links of Scotland's east coast; it is said to have been introduced to the United States in 1818, and it flourished by the late 19th century.

The interaction of Scotland and the United States through immigrants was not a one-way traffic, although few Scots carried their enthusiasm for their native country so far as to return for more than occasional visits; it was remarked that Scotland might be the land of dreams but Pennsylvania was the land of dollars. Men of relatively humble standing in the New World doubtless sent money home to aged parents and other kinsfolk, but in addition there have been conspicuous instances of Scottish Americans making munificent gifts or bequests to their places of origin. The outstanding example was Andrew Carnegie (1835–1919), son of a Dunfermline weaver, who made a vast fortune in iron and steel and gave away hundreds of millions of dollars for educational and other purposes in Scotland. Others were Charles Bruce, who immigrated to Philadelphia before 1820, became a successful physician, and left £2,000 to the poor of his native Musselburgh; Alexander Milne (1742–1838), who immigrated in 1776, made a fortune in New Orleans and left $100,000 to create a school in his native town of Fochabers; and James Dick (1743–1828), a native of Forres, who bequeathed a part of his American fortune to benefit schoolmasters in Aberdeen, Banff, and Moray. Apart from the material benefits, such gifts served as an incentive by bringing to young Scots the knowledge of their countrymen's success overseas.

Among the characteristics of Scots overseas have been their adaptability and capacity to assimilate. In the United States, they were generally willing to identify with other Americans of British descent, and in a wider sense their obvious affinities with many of the existing inhabitants facilitated their assimilation. But it was also to their advantage that they could be remarkably tolerant of the ways of others: their egalitarianism helped them to accept peoples of varied social backgrounds, and they had some familiarity, within Scotland and within Britain, of living alongside diverse peoples. Another link lay in the sharing of religious beliefs by Protestant Scots and Protestant Americans. For a time Scots and Americans probably held in common a provincial or dependent cultural relationship with England. It was also an advantage to the Scots in their dealings with other groups that, with a broader and less insular outlook than the English, they did not regard all ways of life other than their own as backward, quaint, or barbarous. Possibly the most noticeable out-

come of the Scots' readiness to merge with other peoples is that one seldom meets Americans who claim more than a partial Scottish ancestry; they very often claim no more than one Scottish forebear, which strongly suggests that, far from associating only within their own ethnic group, many Scots intermarried with people of other origins.

Bibliography

Rowland T. Berthoff, *British Immigrants in Industrial America* (1953; reprint, New York, 1968), is a mine of information on almost all aspects of the life of immigrants. George F. Black, *Scotland's Mark on America* (1921; reprint, San Francisco, 1972), is little more than an annotated list, but a very useful one, based largely on the *Dictionary of American Biography*. Gordon Donaldson, *The Scots Overseas* (London, 1966) is a general survey, putting the Scots in America in the setting of the whole story of Scottish emigration. Ian C.C. Graham, *Colonists from Scotland: Emigration to North America, 1707–1783* (1965; reprint, Port Washington, N.Y., 1972), treats a more limited period. Duane Meyer, *The Highland Scots of North Carolina* (Chapel Hill, N.C., 1961), is a fairly intensive study of a significant group. Donald Whyte, *Dictionary of Scottish Emigrants to the U.S.A.* (Baltimore, 1972), extends to 1854; it is primarily intended for genealogists, but presents masses of useful information. All the articles in the *William and Mary Quarterly*, 3rd series (April 1954), relate to Scotland and America, mainly before 1776, and the references constitute a wide-ranging bibliography.

GORDON DONALDSON

SEMINOLES: *see* AMERICAN INDIANS

SENECAS: *see* AMERICAN INDIANS

SERBS

The Serbs are one of the national groups, along with the Croats, Slovenes, Macedonians, and others, that make up the population of modern Yugoslavia. While none of the Yugoslav groups has an absolute majority, the most recent census (1971) shows that the Serbs compose 40 percent of its total population of 20.5 million. To these might be added the 2.5 percent who indicated their nationality as Montenegrin, for the Montenegrins share a common cultural tradition with the Serbs, though in modern times they have had their own political identity. The second largest nationality, the Croats, make up 22 percent of the population.

The Serbs belong to the same vast Slavic linguistic family as the Russians, Ukrainians, Poles, Czechs, and Slovaks, but are most closely related to the other South Slavs—the Slovenes, Croats, Macedonian Slavs, and Bulgarians. The name Yugoslavia means "land of the South Slavs," and in the 19th century the Yugoslav idea of cultural and ultimately political unification included the Bulgarians as well. All the South Slavic languages are similar enough that their speakers can understand one another, though with varying degrees of difficulty. Both the Serbs and Croats speak various dialects of those languages, some of which are distinctly either Serbian or Croatian. The Croats are Roman Catholic and use the Latin alphabet modified by diacritical marks to reflect the spoken language. The Serbs are Orthodox and use the Cyrillic alphabet (as do the other Orthodox Slavs), also modified—by the Serbian lexicographer Vuk Karadžić (1787–1864)—to suit the requirements of their spoken tongue. Aside from the alphabet used, the literary language of the Serbs and the Croats is virtually identical. It is called Serbo-Croatian or Croato-Serbian.

The cultural affinities of the various Yugoslav peoples are undeniable, but circumstances have nonetheless led them to develop distinct communities both in their European homeland and in the United States. Some of the earliest immigrants, notably the Serbs and Croats, lived in close contact. The ones who came before the 1880s had lived in the same provinces along the Adriatic coast that then belonged to the Austro-Hungarian Empire, and they did not hesitate to settle in the same communities abroad. Subsequently, however, they developed separate communities, though at times, particularly before World War I, they would still cooperate in certain ventures. The first mutual-aid societies, beginning with the Slavonic Illyric Mutual and Benevolent Society of San Francisco (f. 1857) and the United Slavonian Benevolent Association in New Orleans (f. 1874), the earliest cemeteries, choral concerts, Sokol (gymnastic society) meets, anti-Austrian political rallies, and the like, were all joint endeavors. But Old World political differences eventually drove them apart. Religion, too, played a role in this estrangement. The Serbs, even though their individual religious convictions varied, wore their Orthodoxy as a badge of ethnic identification and used their church parishes as a basis for communal life in the United States. Religion consequently influenced other spheres of their organizational life—fraternal societies, choirs, literary clubs, newspapers, and sports clubs—and in the end drove them apart from their Roman Catholic neighbors, the Croats and Slovenes.

The Orthodox religion in its Serbianized form makes the Serbian ethos distinct even from the Orthodox culture of their fellow Slavic Ukrainians, Russians, Bulgarians, and Macedonian Slavs, not to mention the non-Slavic Orthodox Greeks, Romanians, or Syrians. The Serbian Church may share its dogmas and ritual and some organizational forms with the other Orthodox, but not its administration, customs, or the whole panoply of Serbian saints after whom so many Serbian churches in America have been named. Chief among these is St. Sava, the 12th-century founder of the autonomous Serbian Orthodox Church. St. Sava is to the Serbs what St. Patrick is to the Irish. Perhaps the most distinctively Serbian form of folk religion is the *slava*, or family patron-saint's day, which is inherited through the male line and symbolic of each family's ancestral conversion to Christianity.

The Cyrillic alphabet in its Serbian form is another badge of identity, though one that presents increasing difficulty for younger generations of Serbian Americans. A particular conception of the Serbian past also contributes to the special feeling of *Srpstvo*, often translated in the Serbian-American press as Serbianism. This is especially evident on such exclusively Serbian holidays as St. Sava's Day on January 27 and Vidovdan, or St. Vitus's Day, on June 28, which commemorates the Battle of Kosovo in which the Serbs were defeated by the Turks in 1389. Like the Orthodox Russians, and unlike the Greeks, Romanians, Bulgarians, and some other Orthodox groups, the Serbs still cling to the Julian or Old Style calendar in determining the date of their religious observances, though they customarily designate the day in New Style terms. In this century the difference between the two calendars is 13 days. Thus, for example, the Serbian Orthodox Church observes Christmas on January 7, which is December 25 according to

Yugoslavia

Boundary of the
Austro-Hungarian Empire, 1910
Boundary of the
Hungarian Kingdom, 1910
Boundary of the
Kingdom of Serbia, 1910

Major concentrations of Serbs

150   Km.   Miles

their calendar; St. Sava's Day is January 14 and St. Vitus's Day is June 15 in the Old Style. A feeling of distinctiveness is also assiduously promoted by Serbian organizations and the Serbian press in the United States, and is epitomized in the often repeated theme of a popular song, *Niko nema što Srbin imade* (Nobody has what the Serb has).

MIGRATION

Following the generally accepted division in American immigration history between the "old immigration" (from 1820—when immigration records were first kept—to the 1880s) and the subsequent "new immigration," clearly the great majority of Serbian immigrants belong to the latter. They came as part of the wave of southern and eastern Europeans from Austria-Hungary, Italy, and the Russian Empire. From the standpoint of the development of Serbian life in the United States, therefore, it is more useful to distinguish five periods of Serbian immigration: the earliest settlers of the old immigration (1815–1880); the first, and the largest, wave of the new immigration (1880–1914); arrivals between the two world wars (1918–1941); displaced persons from war-torn Europe (1945–1965); and the most recent immigrants from Yugoslavia (1965 to the present).

How many Serbs came in each period is impossible to

state with certainty because official U.S. immigration statistics do not distinguish Serbs from other South Slavic groups. In the records before World War I some Serbs are included in the official category of "Bulgars, Serbs, and Montenegrins," others in the category "Dalmatians, Bosnians, and Herzegovinians," along with the Croats from those provinces. Serbs may even be included in the category "Croats and Slovenes," since some Serbs from Croatia might easily have been recorded as Croats. Some Serbs and Croats were no doubt also recorded as Hungarians or Austrians, since they were subjects of the Austro-Hungarian Empire. By far the smallest number of Serbian immigrants came from the Kingdom of Serbia itself, and by far the greatest number came from the various lands of the Austro-Hungarian Empire. Many left to evade military service, consequently with false documents that gave them different nationality designations. Nor do records indicating mother tongue help, inasmuch as Serbian and Croatian are lumped together as a single language. Distinctions are even harder to make in statistics dating from after World War I, since immigrants from the newly created Kingdom of the Serbs, Croats, and Slovenes (renamed Yugoslavia in 1929) were all identified simply as Yugoslavs.

The Serbian population in the United States can only be estimated, and these estimates have varied greatly through the years. Today they range between 175,000

and 300,000 Americans of Serbian origin or extraction, including both the foreign-born and several generations of American-born descendants. For some years various Yugoslav Americans accepted the estimates of Ivan Mladineo, compiler of the *National Directory of Croat-Slovene-Serb Organizations* (1937), that there were then about 500,000 Croats, 300,000 Slovenes, and 200,000 Serbs in America. However rough those estimates were, the proportions of the three nationalities do seem to correspond to reality. The U.S. Census of 1960 gives 448,503 Americans whose country of origin was Yugoslavia. Using the 20-percent proportion for the Serbs, the figure 89,700 is obtained. The 1970 Census shows 447,273 Americans of Yugoslav origin. The same 20-percent proportion yields 89,454 Americans of Serbian origin. In both cases only the foreign-born, and American-born with at least one foreign-born parent, are counted. If third- and fourth-generation Americans whose ancestry is predominantly Serbian are added, the 1970 Census figure can easily be at least doubled.

Whatever the exact figures, the number of Serbian Americans is not large by American ethnic-group standards, though it assumes greater significance when considered in the light of distribution, both in the homeland and in the adopted country. Almost all the Serbian immigrants who came before 1914, as well as the vast majority of those who came between 1918 and 1941, and many of the postwar immigrants, did not come from Serbia proper (that is, the pre-1912 Kingdom of Serbia, plus the present Serbian Republic, minus the autonomous regions of Vojvodina and Kosovo), although those who did in recent years have had a strong influence on the Serbian-American community. The decade before World War I was the peak period of Serbian immigration to the United States. By the end of that period, on the eve of the Balkan wars of 1912–1913, the population of Serbia was about 2.9 million. In 1911 the Serbian population of Austria-Hungary had officially been estimated at 2.1 million, to which can be added about 282,000 Montenegrins from the 1907 census. Thus, of a total of about 5.3 million Serbs just before World War I, about 55 percent lived in Serbia proper, about 40 percent lived in Austria-Hungary, and a little over 5 percent lived in Montenegro. The percentage of Serbs living outside Serbia would have been even larger if the non-Serb minorities had been subtracted from the Kingdom of Serbia's population figure and if the Serbs living in the Ottoman Empire had been added to the Serbs living outside the Serbian kingdom (they were joined to Serbia in 1913, but no reliable figure exists for their numbers). The 55 percent–45 percent proportion is almost identical to that indicated by the Yugoslav census of 1971. Forty-six percent of all Serbs, including Montenegrins in Yugoslavia, still live outside Serbia proper.

The vast majority of Serbs came to the United States from Croatia (especially Lika, Banija, Kordun, Dalmatia, and Slavonia), Vojvodina, Montenegro, and Bosnia-Herzegovina. Emigration from some of these areas was so high that it had serious local consequences. Before 1912, for example, there were at least 20,000 Montenegrins in the United States. While hardly a large number in itself, it represented nearly a tenth of Montenegro's population at the time, and a much larger proportion of its able-bodied males, since most of the immigrants

were men between the ages of 19 and 24. To the obvious consequences of losing the most economically productive element in the population were added the military implications of losing its potential army conscripts, not to speak of the plight of many girls who went unmarried for want of eligible bachelors. Some girls married returning emigrants or were sent to the United States as brides in arranged marriages, but the Serbian patriarchal ethos prevented women from leaving unless they had husbands-to-be waiting for them or were being sent to previously emigrated family members. Similar problems arose in the South Slavic lands of the Austro-Hungarian Empire, notably in Bosnia-Herzegovina.

Though the overwhelming majority of Serbian immigrants before World War I were of peasant origin, they did not come to be farmers. The era of readily available, cheap farmland was over by the time most of them arrived, and in any case almost none of the post-1880 immigrants came with the idea of staying. They intended to earn money quickly in mines and factories and then to return to the homeland to pay off debts and to improve their lot. They had neither the means nor the long-term commitment required to become independent farmers, and agricultural day labor did not pay as well as jobs in mining and industry. Working on farms would also have isolated them from their fellow countrymen. On arriving in the United States, they congregated in the industrial cities of the North or the mines and lumbering areas of the North and West as far as Alaska. A few went south, largely to the port cities, especially Galveston, Tex., along the Gulf of Mexico.

When the Serbs came to the United States, they tended to converge on certain areas. Which one they chose was determined by job availability and by the location of already established colonies of compatriots— Bosnians joined Bosnians, Montenegrins joined Montenegrins, and so on. The earliest Serbian immigrants were from the region of the Bay of Kotor. They went either to New Orleans or west to the congenial climate of the California coast, both places that reminded them of home. The more venturesome and hardy among them gravitated to the mines of Nevada and Arizona. A number of Bosnians and Herzegovinians headed west along the shores of Lake Erie and Lake Michigan. The Herzegovinians in particular went on to Chicago, St. Louis, and beyond, to Butte, Mont., and Seattle. From there a northern group went to Alaska; a southern group joined the Kotor Serbs in California and the Southwest. The Montenegrins followed roughly the same paths, sometimes settling in Canada and generally scattering more widely than the others. The Serbs of Croatia (particularly from the provinces of Lika, Banija, Kordun, Dalmatia, and Slavonia) flocked to the mines and steel mills of Pennsylvania, West Virginia, Ohio, and Minnesota, with a Lika group also going west, but south of the Herzegovinians, to Kansas, Colorado, and Utah. The Serbs from Vojvodina tended to congregate in the large cities of the East or Midwest, notably Akron and Cincinnati in Ohio, Detroit, Mich., St. Louis, Mo., and St. Paul, Minn.

While the total Serbian population in the United States is not large, it is concentrated and has particular significance in certain areas. Judging by the location of Serbian Orthodox parishes and fraternal lodges, the main areas, going from east to west, are Greater New

York City (including Paterson and Elizabeth, N.J.); Greater Buffalo (including Lackawanna and Riverside-Tonawanda); eastern Pennsylvania (Philadelphia and Steelton); western Pennsylvania (especially the Pittsburgh area and Johnstown); the Youngstown-Akron-Barberton-Cleveland-Lorain area of northern Ohio; Columbus and Cincinnati; Greater Detroit; Gary and Indiana Harbor; the Chicago–South Chicago–Joliet-Waukegan area of northern Illinois; the Milwaukee-Kenosha-Racine area of Wisconsin along Lake Michigan; South St. Paul and the Mesabi Range iron-ore area of northern Minnesota, especially Duluth, Hibbing, and Chisholm; St. Louis, Mo.; Kansas City, Kan.; Omaha, Neb.; Billings and Butte, Mont.; Galveston, Tex.; Lowell, Globe, Bisbee, and Phoenix, Ariz.; Greater Los Angeles, the San Francisco Bay Area, Sacramento, and Jackson, Calif. Lists of parishes or lodges no longer include once flourishing settlements of Serbs in the mining towns of Tonopah, Nev., or Douglas, Alaska, which today have lost their importance as gold- and silver-mining centers. The steel town of Mingo Junction, Ohio, now has fewer than 5,000 inhabitants, but in 1906 it was said to have had over 3,000 Serbs alone. Most of the wage earners among them worked for a single employer—the Carnegie steel works.

Several general patterns of the group that arrived between 1880 and World War I are clear; most Serbian immigrants were of rural origin and had little, it any, formal education; the rate of return to the homeland was high; most immigrants were men in their prime working years; few were women or children. The contrast with current trends is very marked.

ARRIVAL AND SETTLEMENT

Some would like to think that there were Serbs among the Dalmatian sailors aboard the ships of Columbus in 1492, or at least aboard the ships from Dalmatia, Dubrovnik, and the Bay of Kotor that began to arrive at American ports by the late 18th and early 19th centuries, but all that is conjecture. The first Serb known to have come to America was Djordje Šagić (1795–1873), or, to use his American name, George Fisher, who came to Philadelphia in September 1815. He was born of Serbian parents in Hungary and educated in Sremski Karlovci, the seat of the Serbian Orthodox Church in the Austrian Empire. At the age of 17 he took part in the First Serbian Insurrection against the Turks (1804–1813). After the Serbian defeat he wandered from one end of Europe to the other, from Ottoman Adrianople (Edirne) to German Hamburg, where he embarked for the United States. He came as a penniless "redemptioner"—that is, one who pledged to pay for his passage by becoming a bondservant upon arrival —but when the boat docked in the mouth of the Delaware River, he and two shipmates jumped ship. He received his American name, Fisher, because bystanders who watched them row ashore referred to the three men as fishers. During Fisher's 58-year career in America he was a prominent public figure and office-holder in both Texas and California.

The earliest Serbian immigrants to come in sizable groups were the sailors, fishermen, and others from the Bay of Kotor and the adjoining maritime regions of Montenegro and Herzegovina who came to New Or-

leans beginning in the 1830s. Within ten years New Orleans had a Serbian colony, and Serbs could also be found in Biloxi, Miss., and Mobile, Ala. Along with their more numerous Croatian Dalmatian compatriots they established themselves in the fishing and oyster industry, and as fruit vendors, shopkeepers, and saloon and restaurant owners.

Many more Serbs from the southern Adriatic coast went to California, particularly to the San Francisco Bay Area. In 1847 Ilija Chielovich (Čelović) of Risan, Bay of Kotor, settled in San Francisco and opened a general store there. California's entry into the Union and the discovery of gold in 1848 caused Serbs to join the rush of immigrants that followed. They went to the goldfields of the Mother Lode region of Calaveras, Amador, El Dorado, and Placer counties along the western foothills of the Sierra Nevada. Eventually some got as far as the gold and silver mines of Nevada and Arizona. However, it was the merchants more often than the miners who found prosperity; they opened restaurants, fruit stores, hotels, saloons, and coffee houses. By the 1870s there were quite a few Serbs in San Francisco, Sacramento, the gold-mining town of Jackson, and Los Angeles, and the beginnings of a settlement in San Diego; by the 1880s there were also clusters in and around Fresno. Still others could be found in Arizona, notably in Tombstone.

Apart from the Gulf ports and the Far West, the most significant settlement before 1880 was in Chicago, where the first Serbs began to arrive in the 1870s, again mostly from the Bay of Kotor and Herzegovina. To their numbers were added the others who came to the United States in the wake of the Bosnian-Herzegovinian uprising of 1875 against the Ottoman Empire. By 1878 the Chicago Serbs had a patriotic society named Obilić (after the epic hero of the Battle of Kosovo in 1389). One of the members' first resolutions was to observe St. Sava's Day together regularly each year; the annual gatherings that resulted featured the recitation of Serbian epic poetry.

Serbian immigration altered greatly in both size and origin in the 1880s. A flood of new immigrants from Austro-Hungarian Croatia-Slavonia and Vojvodina and the hinterlands of independent Montenegro now far outnumbered the earlier immigrants from the southern Adriatic coast. The destination of most of them was not the Gulf or Pacific coast, but the industrial heartland, especially the coal mines and steel mills of Pennsylvania and the Ohio Valley, the industrial cities of the Great Lakes, and the iron, copper, lead, silver, and gold mines of Minnesota, Utah, Colorado, Nevada, Arizona, and Montana. Still, newcomers did strengthen the already existing coastal settlements; the first Serbian Orthodox church in America was built in 1893 in Jackson, Calif., and the second in 1896 in Galveston. But it was the Pittsburgh area that took the lead. In the early 20th century Carson and Sarah streets of Pittsburgh's South Side were so solidly Serbian that one could walk for blocks and hear Serbian spoken and pass Serbian saloons, grocery stores, tailor shops, and barber shops. In nearby McKeesport, in 1897, the Serbs organized the Prvo Srpsko Potporno Društvo (First Serbian Aid Society).

If the immigrants before 1880 came, in the time-honored tradition of the southern Adriatic coast, as ven-

turesome seekers after a better life, the immigrants now came as refugees from poverty, driven out of their homelands by an economic crisis brought on by over-population and the pressures of a rising capitalist economy. A growing peasant population could no longer eke out a living from constantly divided plots of land. High taxes, government neglect, lack of tools and fertilizers, a shortage of cash, and debts contracted at interest rates that were sometimes as high as 30 or 40 percent were the conditions that set in motion a general flight from the village and a quest for ready wages. As industry was either nonexistent or still underdeveloped at home, a stream of young men ventured to America. They were most apt to be from the depressed Ottoman provinces of the south—Kosovo and Macedonia—regions where the tradition of *pečalba*, or temporary sojourns abroad to earn money, was long established. Compared with the Serbs of the Ottoman Empire, of Austria-Hungary, and of Montenegro, the peasants of the fertile Serbian kingdom were relatively prosperous. Even peasants in financial difficulty were protected by law from losing their homes and garden plots. They were thus more apt to remain behind.

Serbian immigration to the United States decreased drastically during the Balkan Wars and again during World War I. Thousands of young Serbs even left the country voluntarily to fight for the Serbian cause. Though most of them had never even seen the Kingdom of Serbia, they were led by a long-nurtured love for the homeland and an epic tradition of self-sacrificing hero-ism—attitudes encouraged by recruiters sent by the embattled Serbian government. Many were killed, but even the ones who survived almost never returned to the United States. After the wars the number of Ser-bians who immigrated remained far below what it had been. The agrarian reform of 1919 and the growth of in-dustry in the newly created Kingdom of the Serbs, Croats, and Slovenes gave promise of a better life in the now free homeland. The restrictive immigration laws passed by Congress in 1921 and 1924 assigned a very low quota to Yugoslavs, including Serbs, and this fur-ther discouraged migration. The Great Depression of the 1930s was another deterrent; some older Serbs even gave up and returned home. Yet some Serbs continued to come to the United States, until World War II tempo-rarily ended Serbian immigration.

The post–World War II migration reflected a very dif-ferent situation. Thousands of Serbs were displaced per-sons—former Yugoslav army officers and soldiers who were prisoners of war or attached to the Allied forces, involuntary workers brought to Germany during the war, and refugees. Other thousands were on the losing side in a civil war that had raged during the enemy oc-cupation; they fled Yugoslavia when the Communist-led forces won out. The United States loosened its quota system to let in many thousands of Serbs, under the Displaced Persons Act of 1948 and the Refugee Re-lief Act of 1953. Of the 50,792 Yugoslavs who entered under their terms, the greatest number were Serbs and Croats, though which group was the larger is not known. By July 1974 another 31,559 Yugoslavs had been admitted under subsequent legislation, particu-larly the Immigration Act of 1965, which abolished the national-quota system altogether. Again statistics are lacking, but no one doubts that the Serbian component among the Yugoslav immigrants was large.

These most recent Serbian immigrants differed from the previous arrivals in ways that have had a major im-pact on organized Serbian life in the United States. Many of them settled in already established Serbian-American communities and in varying degrees became a part of their society of parishes, fraternal organiza-tions, cultural clubs, and the like. In cities where Serbs were numerous, such as Milwaukee, Chicago, Detroit, Cleveland, or New York, the newcomers established their own organizations and periodicals rather than simply joining the older ones. In either case they affected the whole social climate of Serbian life in America, coming as many did from urban rather than rural areas and often with extensive education and training and high social status.

Unlike the vast majority of earlier immigrants, the newcomers came more for political than for economic reasons and consequently saw the United States as a place of exile rather than as a new homeland. The more politically minded among them regarded the country as a temporary base of operations for their Serbian politi-cal activities in opposition to the Yugoslav Communist state, and some still do. They formed a variety of politi-cal organizations that reflected their differing political attitudes toward the regime and their affiliations with particular groups during World War II, including sup-porters of the monarchy and collaborators with the Ital-ian and German invaders. This array of factions bewildered many of the older immigrants and their American-born children, who were by and large un-aware of the nuances of homeland politics.

The earlier settlers had been illiterate or barely liter-ate peasants, with rarely more than four years of ele-mentary education. The postwar newcomers were often graduates of high schools, technical schools, and even universities, with urban backgrounds and training in the professions, and their literary Serbian contrasted with the peasant dialects of the earlier settlers. Some of the newcomers, oblivious to their own borrowed for-eign words, did not bother to conceal their amusement at the Anglicisms that flavored the earlier immigrants' rural Serbian. Many more of the recent immigrants were from Serbia proper, the ancestral home of the Ser-bian people. Their ways, songs, costumes, and speech became models for others to emulate. Comparing the pre-1914 editions of the largest Serbian newspaper in the United States, the *Americanski Srbobran* (Ameri-can Srbobran—the word *srbobran* means defender of the Serbs), with post-1945 editions reveals how the ear-lier *jekavian* subdialect of the Serbs outside Serbia has given way to the *ekavian* of central Serbia. Serbian radio programs, a feature of Serbian life in over a dozen metropolitan areas from Newark to San Francisco, are now often announced in ekavian, and much of the music that they play comes from Serbia proper; the ac-cordion is becoming more popular than the *tamburica*, the mandolin-like instrument so dear to the hearts of the early immigrants from Croatia-Slavonia and Vojvo-dina. Serbian dance groups in the United States today are likely to dress in the *Šumadija* costume of central Serbia, even though the parents and grandparents of many of the participants came from provinces outside.

Because the new immigrants from Serbia proper were looked up to by other Serbs, their culture soon domi-nated. Before World War II the traditions of a peasant society and the national church provided the focus for

ethnic identity. Since 1945 ethnic identity has been in part redefined in terms of a middle- and upper-class political subculture that centers on ideological questions. The earlier immigrants were conservative, working class, and bent on individual and family economic achievement. Success as they saw it depended on integration into the larger American society. Aside from pockets of organized disaffection, the majority of Serbian Americans were never affiliated with earlier American Socialist or Communist parties; they believed in the system and in their ability to rise within it. Now, in a fundamental way, the process of Americanization has been interrupted. In parishes where the American-born were beginning to take over their fathers' positions and responsibilities in community affairs, and where English was commonly used at church meetings, positions have started to go to the newcomers instead, and Serbian is again being spoken. The arrival of refugee Serbian priests from abroad has interrupted the trend toward the use of English in church services. Many of these priests have since made an effort to learn English to serve their American-born parishioners more effectively, and some will by now even venture to deliver sermons in that language, but in other ways they still nurture a Serbian cultural conservatism. The introduction of pews in church was an American innovation that could not be undone. But the very discussion of certain other innovations can provoke in many Serbian Americans suspicions of disloyalty to Serbianism. Among them might be the introduction of organ music into the service (which the Orthodox Greeks in America accomplished decades ago) and observing holy days according to the Gregorian calendar.

An undetermined number of Serbian Americans have been giving up active participation in Serbian organizations, just as the postwar Serbian immigrants have undoubtedly Serbianized organizational life. While Serbianization is generally welcomed by those Serbian Americans who derive sustenance from this kind of corporate ethnic identity, the social conservatism and the intrusion of Old World politics it carries with it alienate many others. Serbian community leaders regret this, but appear to be resigned to the process. They are committed to Serbianism in its politically conservative nationalist form, an attitude that the American cultural climate in the 1970s with its widespread preoccupation with roots and ethnics has encouraged. Foreign-born Serbs can find comfort in the propagation of a familiar Serbian environment combined with the benefits of living in the United States, and the American-born generation can appreciate their Serbian heritage and its social pleasures without being made to feel foreign.

An important new element in the postwar period has been the constant and active contact with the homeland, even among those Serbs opposed to the present government of Yugoslavia. Airmail takes less than a week, the telephone is frequently used, and low-cost air charters facilitate visits back and forth. Pensioners go "home" to live quite comfortably on social-security checks or other pensions forwarded through the American Embassy in Belgrade. Publications and phonograph records from Serbia are readily available in the larger American cities; even some people opposed to the present Yugoslav government are enthusiastic about popular Serbian music. Since Yugoslavia's borders are relatively open—over a million Yugoslavs work and live abroad—the free flow of people, goods, and ideas back and forth helps to maintain an ethnic identity for those outside. But the political subculture represented by the postwar émigrés will in its turn disappear with time. The death of the exiled Yugoslav King Peter II in 1970 has already removed an important symbol, only in part replaced by his son Alexander. The newest immigrants are less concerned than the postwar refugees were with political activities. Many of them are professionals—doctors, engineers, architects, and scientists—and they came to the United States for professional, not political, reasons. They are often successful, since unlike the politicians, lawyers, or army officers who came earlier their skills are useful to American society. The Yugoslav government actively courts its emigrants. Its Serbian association in Belgrade publishes a magazine and arranges tours, in addition to the activities of the embassy and the information and tourist offices and consulates maintained in various American cities.

ORGANIZATIONS

Serbian social life in America centers in its organizations: the Serbian Orthodox Church, fraternal societies, the Serbian Sisters Circles, the Serbian Singing Federation, and a variety of other cultural, athletic, and political clubs. Of these, the Serbian Orthodox Church provides the nucleus. Serbian Orthodoxy is and always has been at the core of Serbian ethnicity. The earliest Serbian immigrants joined other Orthodox groups to establish the first Orthodox churches, since there were too few of them to organize their own. In New Orleans the Serbs joined the Greek Holy Trinity Church that had been established by merchants there in 1864. Its parish was so cosmopolitan that its first priest was a Ukrainian, and the minutes of its meetings were kept in English because not all its officers and members knew Greek. But in 1906 an influx of Greek immigrants turned it into a Greek church, though Serbs continued to attend it. Similarly, in 1864 the Slavonic-Greek-Russian Benevolent Society of the Orthodox Catholic Eastern Church was organized in San Francisco largely by Serbs. Its president was the Russian consul (a Lutheran Finn); its two vice-presidents, Nikola Dabovich and Joko (John) Franeta, and most of its board members were Serbs. By the time a Russian priest arrived in 1868, the parish and its council had an even larger proportion of Serbs. The Serbs in Galveston joined with Greeks and Russians in the Saints Constantine and Helen parish founded by Greeks in 1862. The parish had no church until 1895, when an assembly of Serbs and Greeks built one with the help of Tsar Nicholas II's government and the Russian Holy Synod. As more and more Serbian immigrants arrived, the church eventually came under the jurisdiction of the Serbian Orthodox Church; the Greeks formed a parish of their own in 1932.

The purely Serbian churches in the United States—in Jackson, Calif. (f. 1893), McKeesport, Pa. (f. 1901), Steelton, Pa. (f. 1903), and later ones—were served by Serbian priests but were all under the jurisdiction of the Russian Orthodox Church, which had been on the North American continent (in Alaska) since the late 18th century. The first American-born Serbian Orthodox priest was the Reverend Sebastian Dabovich (1863–1940), the son of Ilija Dabovich of Sasović (Herzegovina), a pioneer Serbian American in San Francisco. Trained in the Russian seminary in San Francisco and

in Russia, Father Dabovich was appointed by Archbishop Tikhon (later Patriarch of Moscow and All Russia) in 1905 to head a Serbian mission in the United States. The Serbian immigrants respected Father Dabovich, and for that matter Russia, the traditional protector of the Orthodox Slavs, but they nonetheless wanted to replace the Russian jurisdiction with a church of their own. In 1906 Paul Radosavljevich, a parish priest in South Chicago, organized a conference of Serbian priests in Pittsburgh. It failed to found a church because the three Serbian church jurisdictions—Serbia, Austria-Hungary, and Montenegro—were unable to reach any agreement. After repeated failures, the Serbian priests in the United States met in Chicago in 1916 and, with the approval of the Russians, divided the existing 31 Serbian parishes in the United States into four districts, each headed by a protopresbyter or dean.

In 1917 a Russian-trained Montenegrin monk, the Reverend Mardary Uskokovich (d. 1935), arrived in the United States and two years later was made archimandrite and designated bishop-elect of a Serbian diocese at a Russian church assembly in Cleveland. In 1921 he persuaded the Serbian patriarchate in Belgrade to create a Serbian Orthodox Diocese of the United States and Canada under its jurisdiction; in 1926 in Belgrade he was consecrated its bishop. Earlier he had bought 31 acres of land in Libertyville, Ill., 40 miles from his residence in Chicago. In 1923 it was chartered as an orphanage; in 1927 it became the seat of the diocese, in 1931 the site of the Monastery of St. Sava, and in 1942 the site of a children's camp.

From 1936 to 1938 the diocese was administered by Bishop Irinej Djordjević of Dalmatia, in 1938–1939 by Bishop Damaskin Grdanički. He resigned and was succeeded by Bishop Dionisije Milivojević, who arrived in America in 1940 and remained as bishop until 1963. In 1945 the diocese began to publish its first English-language newspaper, the *Serbian Orthodox Herald,* and organized a makeshift seminary to train a half-dozen American-born priests. In addition to developing the property at Libertyville, the diocese built two other centers, one in Shadeland, Pa., for the East, and one in Jackson, Calif., for the West. All three centers are today used for assemblies, socials, and picnics, especially on Memorial Day, the Fourth of July, and Labor Day.

During World War II the diocese publicized the plight of the Serbs in the homeland through its book, *Martyrdom of the Serbs: Persecutions of the Serbian Orthodox Church and Massacre of the Serbian People* (Chicago, 1943), which aroused the passions of Serbian Americans. It also helped to arrange for the immigration of refugees and placed refugee priests. In 1949 the Clergy Association (Brotherhood) of the Serbian Orthodox Diocese for the United States and Canada was organized in Pittsburgh; its official organ is called *Orthodoxy.*

In 1963 a schism initiated a painful period in the history of the Serbian Church in America. It was precipitated by two events. On May 10, 1963, the Holy Synod of the Serbian Orthodox Church in Belgrade suspended Bishop Dionisije, pending an investigation into charges of misconduct filed by American and Canadian Serbs. Acting on Dionisije's own suggestion that the growing and far-flung Serbian Church in the United States and Canada needed more than one bishop, the assembly of bishops in Belgrade appointed three, all Dionisije's own

candidates, but instead of making them his auxiliaries as he had assumed they would, the assembly divided the diocese into three and placed a new bishop over each of them. Bishop Dionisije refused to accept this state of affairs and was deposed on July 27, 1963.

This touched off a conflict over the issue of the relation between the Serbian Church in America and the mother church in Communist-dominated Yugoslavia. A diocesan assembly convened by the deposed Dionisije met in Libertyville in August of 1963 to reject the decisions of the assembly of bishops and sever its ties with the mother church. A second assembly of Dionisije's supporters met again in November and proclaimed their separation from the mother church in even stronger terms. The following March the assembly of bishops defrocked Dionisije, and the three bishops designated by Belgrade—Firmilian Ocokoljich, Stefan Lastavica, and Gregory Udicki—summoned their own assembly in May, which unanimously accepted the decisions of the assembly of bishops in Belgrade. (Bishop Stefan later died and was replaced in 1967 by Bishop Sava Vukovich.)

While both sides opposed the Communist government in Yugoslavia, each had a different view of the role of the mother church. Dionisije's faction argued that they could not accept as valid the decisions of a church that was not a free, autonomous agent. The supporters of unity with the Serbian church in Belgrade argued that this was no time to abandon the mother church, that in any case Serbian Americans could continue within canonical limits to govern their own church affairs, and that the break with the mother church violated canon law. Twenty parishes and about 30 percent of the members sided with the autonomy faction; 39 parishes and about 70 percent sided with the canonical or unity church. The break was not a clean one, however; parishes and even families were split, and this resulted in a great deal of acrimony. The schism involved court battles as well as public debates, the latter at times escalating to a violence that required police intervention. In local parishes, members struggled for control over church and property; the dispossessed groups often built their own churches, increasing the number of Serbian churches to be supported. By 1977 the three canonical dioceses had 52 parishes in the United States; the autonomy faction had 39 parishes and the properties in Libertyville, Shadeland, and Jackson. The exact number of church communities belonging to each side is difficult to determine because some churches have become vacant, others have shifted allegiance, and still others are claimed by both sides. The legal battle reached its culmination on June 21, 1976, when the U.S. Supreme Court handed down its decision in the case of *Serbian Eastern Orthodox Diocese for the United States of America and Canada et al.* v. *Dionisije Milivojevich et al.* in favor of the former, but the schism continues to divide Serbian Americans in spite of this decision, and probably will for some time to come.

On June 18, 1978, the Reverend Velimir Kovacevich, a native of Galveston and a parish priest in South Chicago, was consecrated bishop in Belgrade, taking the name Christopher, and was assigned to replace Bishop Sava as head of the eastern diocese in the United States. Though not the first American to become a Serbian

bishop (Varnava Nastić preceded him), Christopher was the first native-born Serbian American to serve as a Serbian Orthodox bishop in the United States.

The Serbian Orthodox Church had early become the single most important institution in Serbian-American community life, but it was not the first. It was preceded by the fraternal mutual-aid societies, through which, like other immigrant groups, the Serbian Americans sought to find security by protecting themselves against the hazards of industrial work. The first of them, called the Srpsko Crnogorsko Literarno i Dobrotvorno Društvo (Serbian-Montenegrin Literary and Benevolent Society), was founded in San Francisco in 1880. A similar society was next founded in Chicago in 1881 and reorganized in 1894 under the name Srpsko Jedinstvo (Serbian Unity). Similar societies followed: the Serbian Benevolent Society "Obilić" in Chicago, the Serbian Independent Society "United Serbs" in New York, and the Serbian Benevolent Society "Dushan the Mighty" in Los Angeles.

These societies then began to join together in federations. (One of them, the Srpski Crnogorski Savez or Serbian Montenegrin Federation, with its headquarters in Butte, Mont., ceased to exist when it lost most of its 1,500 members as they volunteered in the Balkan Wars of 1912–1913 and World War I.) The parent organization of what was to become the largest of them, the Srpski Narodni Savez (Serb National Federation), was founded in McKeesport, Pa., in 1901, when eight Serbian lodges in the Russian Orthodox Society decided to form an organization. They were soon joined by many Serbs who had been members of Croatian societies. The original name of the new federation was the Srpski Pravoslavni Savez Srbobran (Serbian Orthodox Federation Srbobran). The organization was, and still is, based in Pittsburgh. It filled a great need for its members, largely industrial workers and miners whose jobs were both hard and dangerous. It ensured compensation in case of disabling accidents, and burial expenses and some money for families in case of death, whether accidental or, as often, premature as a result of job-induced ailments. From the start, however, the federation was far more than an insurance company. Its founder, Sava Hajdin, later remarked, "We never wished our federation to be only an association of benevolent societies. We wished it to be the matrix of Serbianism in America and the bastion of the idea of St. Sava."

In 1909, 106 delegates of four federations met in Cleveland to form the Savez Sjedinjenih Srba—Sloga (Federation of United Serbs—"Concord"). For ten years power struggles bred only discord, and the various groups within the federation split off, but in 1929 they finally got together and formed the Serb National Federation, with headquarters in Pittsburgh and a membership of 19,674. The merger was completed when the Srpski Potporni Savez Jedinstvo (Serbian Benevolent Federation Unity), based in Cleveland, brought its 1,656 members to the SNF in 1963.

The atmosphere surrounding the merger proceedings remained turbulent, with a great deal of politicking and many and passionate personal attacks. These battles absorbed so much energy that they supplied Serbian Americans with a political arena of their very own quite apart from the mainstream of American political life. The network of Serbian settlements or "colonies," as they were often called and still are by Serbian Americans, in the New World constituted a body politic within the larger American state somewhat as the Serbian community within the Austrian Empire had in the 18th and 19th centuries. The only difference was that the leaders were not great prelates, intellectuals, deputies to parliament, or army officers, but semiliterate peasant immigrants who had made good in America as saloon keepers, restaurateurs, travel agents, contractors, grocers, dairymen, and bootleggers. But as in the old country, politics was still governed by bossism and loyalty based more often on kinship and friendship than on convictions or ideals. Most of the immigrants counted for little in American life, and they found in these power struggles a way of feeling important. This was true not only for the benevolent federations but later for the church schism as well.

Yet out of its struggle the Serb National Federation became the most important single Serbian organization in the United States next to the church, largely because it could act as a bridge between the foreign-born and the later, American-born generations of Serbian Americans. In August 1978 the Serb National Federation had 173 senior-order lodges with 15,961 members, and 134 junior-order circles with 5,186 members, for a total of 21,147. This is not much more than the 19,674 members (14,486 adult and 5,188 juniors) it had in late September 1929 when Srbobran and Sloboda merged. It is also less than the 22,697 members (16,213 adult and 6,484 juniors) it had in late 1950, a decline that takes on significance when one considers that in 1977 the Serb National Federation was the only national Serbian organization in America, whereas in 1950 some 26,000 Serbs were enrolled in eight fraternal societies. It is apparent that many American-born Serbs and many post–World War II immigrants are simply not joining the SNF.

The Serb National Federation promotes cultural and athletic organizations and events, such as basketball, bowling, and golf tournaments, that can combine the Serbian ethos and the American way of life. They attract thousands of Serbian Americans from all over the country, and this in itself contributes to a sense of fellowship (and, not incidentally, to opportunities for courtships leading to proper Serbian marriages).

The Serb National Federation publishes in Pittsburgh the oldest and largest Serbian newspaper in America, the *Amerikanski Srbobran* (American Srbobran), its official organ since 1906. It comes out twice a week in Serbian and once a week in English. In October 1977 the average number of copies sold during each of the preceding 12 months was 8,600, of which 7,993 were mailed paid-subscription copies. The *American Srbobran* is by far the best equipped Serbian periodical in America, with modern presses, multilingual publishing facilities, and a salaried editor and staff. Only six other Serbian newspapers in the late 1970s had their own presses, and none employed more than one full-time paid professional. The *American Srbobran* is also rare in that its readers are not only recent immigrants, but earlier settlers and their American offspring as well. Though it certainly deals with events in Yugoslavia (and opposes the present Yugoslav government), it is not the organ of any one particular émigré political group. It is proudly American, though it also seeks to

instill in its readers some "Serbianism" and pride in Serbian heritage.

Another ubiquitous organization among Serbian Americans is the group of sisterhoods or Serbian Sisters Circles. The first of these were organized in the early years of the century, in Pittsburgh, Chicago, and Cincinnati. In 1945 the representatives of more than 30 sisterhoods met in Libertyville to form the Federation of Circles of Serbian Sisters. Raising funds through bake sales, church suppers, and picnics, the sisterhoods are active in supporting children's camps and various charities. Since they were always closely associated with the Serbian Church, they, too, have been split by the schism.

The Srpska Narodna Odbrana (Serbian National Defense) is the largest and oldest Serbian patriotic organization in the United States. It took its name from an organization formed in the Kingdom of Serbia in 1908 during the crisis created by Austria-Hungary's annexation of Bosnia-Herzegovina, and was active in the United States after the outbreak of World War I. In 1914 a central committee of the Serbian National Defense was organized in New York City, with Michael Pupin, a professor at Columbia University, as its president. It recruited thousands of volunteers to send overseas and raised over a half-million dollars for the support of the ill-fated Serbian army.

In the United States the organization fell dormant after the war, until it was revived during World War II. The leading spirit of that undertaking was the distinguished Serbian poet and diplomat-in-exile, Jovan Dučić. At a founding meeting held in the Serbian church hall in Chicago in 1941, the organization declared its loyalty to the United States and pledged support to the royalist Chetniks of Colonel Draža Mihailović who were fighting as guerrillas in Yugoslavia. The organization's first president was Mitchell Duchich, a businessman from Gary, Ind., and Jovan Dučić's cousin. In 1942 the Serbian National Defense inaugurated a radio program in Chicago, and from 1944 to 1948 published a periodical called the American Serb, which reached a circulation of 10,000.

Following the war and the collapse of the Chetnik forces, the Serbian National Defense turned to sending food and clothing to Serb refugees in various European displaced-persons camps and providing scholarships for Serbian students. Along with the Serbian Orthodox Diocese and a relief organization called Srpska Bratska Pomoć (Serbian Fraternal Aid), it brought thousands of displaced persons to America. When they arrived, President Duchich and his colleagues were disheartened to discover that the émigrés often hated one another almost as much as they did the Communists. Several attempts were made to bring unity to their ranks. In 1947 the Serbian National Defense sponsored an All-Serb Congress in Chicago which selected a Serbian Central National Committee with Constantin Fotitch, former Royal Yugoslav Ambassador to the United States, as president. In 1949 a conference in Akron formed a Serbian National Council. Bishop Nikolaj Velimirović, himself a refugee, was made honorary president, but not even his authority could inspire unity among the various Serbian émigré political groups.

After Mitchell Duchich died in 1960, the discord grew worse. The new president, Dr. Urosh Seffer (Se-

ferović), and his followers lent their support to Dionisije's autonomous Serbian church. Supporters of the canonical church thereupon organized their own American Serbian National Defense. The original organization survived the split, however, and continued to publish Sloboda (Liberty), which it had published in Chicago since 1952.

Most Serbian-language newspapers in the United States today are published by émigré political groups. Between 1870, when the Slavonian of San Francisco began to include articles in Serbian as well as in Russian and English, and World War II, some 200 Serbian periodicals were published in America; only one, the American Srbobran, has survived. Nevertheless, in the late 1970s Serbian Americans had some 25 more recently established newspapers and other periodicals to subscribe to, 20 of them published in the United States and 5 in Canada, not counting church calendars and parish bulletins. Most of them are turned out by anti-Communist émigré groups.

CULTURAL LIFE

Music plays an important role in Serbian life in America, and no single organization has done as much to promote it as the Serbian Singing Federation, founded in 1931 and led throughout most of its existence by Vladimir "Vlajko" Lugonja (1898–1977). Choirs and tamburica orchestras have been a feature of Serbian community life ever since the founding of the Gorski Vijenac (Mountain Wreath) choir in Pittsburgh in 1901 and the Branko Radičević choir in Chicago in 1906. These choirs sang at social functions; church choirs were unknown to Serbian immigrants in the early part of the century. When Lugonja founded the Serbian Singing Federation in 1931 in Chicago, 5 choirs joined. In seven years the number grew to 25. By then all of them were connected with church parishes: in fact, singing in church was a condition of their membership in the federation. Since 1935 the federation has sponsored an annual competition where both liturgical and secular music are performed. Choirs are usually named after Serbian composers.

Many of today's leaders in Serbian fraternal and church life have come from the ranks of the Serbian Singing Federation. A number of Serbian priests have organized and conducted choirs—notably Boro Petrovich and Milan Popovich of the earlier period, and George Lazich, Milan Bajich, Sava Vujkov, Milan Markovina, and Milorad Dobrota in more recent times. Among Serbian laymen Alexander Savin, for years director of Chicago's Branko Radičević, was a well-known musician. Adam Popovich, director of South Chicago's Sloboda (Liberty), is a widely admired veteran of the Serbian-American choir movement whose choir performed at the White House for Dwight D. Eisenhower's presidential inauguration.

The tamburica is a South Slavic stringed instrument, akin to the mandolin or the balalaika, especially popular with the Serbs and Croats of the former Austro-Hungarian Empire. It comes in five different sizes and musical ranges. Many Serbian parishes have tamburica orchestras and folk-dancing ensembles. The all-girl orchestra in Duluth, conducted by Nancy Dragicevich, and the Šumadija Serbian Folk Dance Ensemble of Mil-

waukee, conducted by Bob Milkovich, are notable examples. On a professional level, the Serbian orchestra of the Popovich brothers of South Chicago, especially Adam Popovich, has long been popular. The foremost and often emulated singer of Serbian folk songs and *sevdalinke* (love songs) is Vinka Ellesin, whose career spanned nearly five decades from the 1930s to the 1970s.

The chanting of epic poetry to the melancholy strains of the *gusle* is another Serbian tradition. This ancient musical instrument, about the size of a violin, is held upright and played by drawing a bow strung with horsehair across a horsehair string. Its tonal range is limited to a drone of a few notes, and it is only used to accompany this poetic chanting. Generations of Serbs have been brought up on the legends and stories of their heroic past as preserved by the *guslari* (bards). The earliest Serbian immigrants from Montenegro and Herzegovina brought the tradition with them to America. Serbian bards could be heard at public functions into the 1930s; some of them would even improvise occasional poetry to honor an event or individual. Then the custom died out, but the recent immigrants have now revived it. In the 1970s a number of guslari in major Serbian communities have held frequent picnics and other gatherings, chanting their traditional epics and composing verse commemorating everything from political events to soccer games.

Many customs that form a part of Serbian folk religion have been incorporated into the religious life of Serbian Americans as well. Unique to the Serbs is the custom of the *krsna slava* or the family patron-saint's day. It is actually pre-Christian in origin, deriving from the custom of honoring protective spirits of hearth and household, but was incorporated into the Serbian Orthodox faith as a commemoration of the family's original conversion to Christianity. The chosen day is celebrated with a church service and an open-house feast at home. The ritual involves a candle, a dish of sweetened boiled wheat, and a special round loaf of bread. Only the male head of the household may light the candle. Each guest is offered a spoonful of the cooked wheat as a memorial to the departed members of the family; the round loaf is an offering to the family's patron saint, among whom the most popular are St. George and St. Nicholas. A priest is invited to bless the house with holy water; he, the head of the household, and other family members pour wine on the loaf in a special ritual; then they break bread together, after the loaf has been turned three times by the priest and family circle during the singing of the saint's hymn. During the elaborate meal that follows, the host and hostess do not sit down with their guests; they are assumed to be too busy greeting and serving them. Most Serbian families keep an icon of the family patron saint, usually in the dining room; beneath it is a votive oil lamp that is lighted on Saturday evenings and special occasions.

The Christian holy days have their own special folk customs. Easter is celebrated with the colored eggs and lamb common to many cultures. At Epiphany priests go from house to house, blessing each one with holy water. On Palm Sunday, though some Serbian-American Orthodox churches have turned to palm fronds, pussy willows are generally still blessed instead. Many Serbian-American families have compromised with American tradition to the extent of having a Christmas tree in the house, but they still also keep the Serbian yule log (*badnjak*), the Christmas candle, the honey cake with a coin hidden in it for some lucky recipient, the straw that is spread on the floor of the dining room or even the entire house to recall the manger in which Christ was born, and the roast suckling pig for Christmas dinner. Christmas is still observed Old Style—that is, on January 7 by the Gregorian, or New Style, calendar.

Next to parents and closest kin, no one in Serbian society is as revered as the godparents—the *kum* (godfather) and *kuma* (godmother). The spiritual kinship between godchildren and their sponsors at baptism is so venerated by the Serbs that intermarriage between their families is restricted just as it is between families joined by kinship. The bond also extends to witnesses at weddings. These extremely close relationships bind families together into groups and add greatly to the cohesion of Serbian society. In the United States they connect families living in different cities and contribute to the interaction of the Serbian colonies, strengthening Serbian political and religious loyalties.

The Serbian press in the United States has devoted itself to the preservation and transmission of its own perception of Serbian cultural values and traditions. Some periodicals are addressed largely to the foreign-born: in the late 1970s five literary and historical journals were being published in Serbian in the United States. Others are also addressed to the American-born: both the canonical and the autonomous Serbian-American church publish journals—the *Path of Orthodoxy* and the *Diocesan Observer*, respectively. But the *American Srbobran* continues to reach the most Serbian Americans. All these periodicals publish articles on Serbian history, traditions, and eminent figures, and extol Serbian immigrants who have attained some status in American society. The two most frequently honored are Nikola Tesla and Michael Pupin. Tesla (1856–1943), the son of a Serbian Orthodox priest in the province of Lika, Croatia, was the inventor of more than 700 patented electrical devices. His most far-reaching discovery was the practical application of alternating current, and in 1956, as part of a worldwide observance of the centennial of Tesla's birth, the International Electrotechnical Commission named the unit of magnetic flux density a "tesla" after him. Serbian Americans take pride in the statue of Tesla that was unveiled in 1976 at the power station on Goat Island, Niagara Falls. Michael Idvorsky Pupin (1858–1935), who was born in a village in the then Hungarian Banat, also owes his fame to his work in the uses of electricity, particularly in telephone and telegraph systems and x rays. He is also well known to several generations of American readers for his autobiography, *From Immigrant to Inventor*, which won a Pulitzer Prize in 1925. At Columbia University, where Pupin was a professor most of his life, the Pupin Physics Laboratories are named after him. Tesla and Pupin are only two of the many scholars, inventors, publishers, writers, screen producers and actors, business executives, athletes, legislators, judges, and others whose Serbian ancestry is a source of pride to Serbian Americans.

The Serbian ethnic group in the United States continues to be reinforced by migration from Yugoslavia, so the precise nature of its ethnicity is difficult to foresee.

It is no longer a question simply of conserving an immigrant version of a cultural tradition; cultural and social changes in the homeland are bound to have an impact on the community in the United States. Despite attrition from increasing assimilation, the vitality of Serbian community life, as reflected in a hundred thriving Serbian centers across the United States, suggests that a core of Americans of Serbian descent will continue to be sustained by this community life—particularly insofar as it is connected with church membership—and by the cultural heritage of their Serbian forebears.

Bibliography

Robert P. Gakovich and Milan M. Radovich have compiled a helpful guide, *Serbs in the United States and Canada: A Comprehensive Bibliography* (Minneapolis, Minn., 1976); see also relevant sections of Michael B. Petrovich, *Yugoslavia: A Bibliographic Guide* (Washington, D.C., 1974).

There is still no book in English that deals solely with Serbian Americans. Even the very few booklets in Serbian on the subject—Milan Jevtić, *Mala Srbija: Srpsko Useljeništvo u Americi* (New York, 1916); Pero Slepčević, *Srbi u Americi* (Geneva, 1917); and Božidar Purić, *Naši iseljenici* (Belgrade, 1929)—are old and rare items. Most treat Yugoslav immigrants as a whole, so that it is often difficult to distinguish the Serbs from other Slavic groups. Emily Greene Balch, *Our Slavic Fellow Citizens* (1910; reprint, New York, 1969), includes useful material on Serbian Americans before 1910; a recent general treatment is Gerald Gilbert Govorchin, *Americans from Yugoslavia* (Boston, 1978). A scholarly study by Branko Mita Colakovic, *Yugoslav Migrations to America* (San Francisco, 1973), has useful statistical material.

Among regional studies are three by Adam S. Eterovich: *Croatians from Dalmatia and Montenegrin Serbs in the West and South, 1800–1900* (San Francisco, 1971); *Yugoslav Survey of California, Nevada, Arizona and the South, 1830–1900* (San Francisco, 1971); and *Yugoslavs in Nevada, 1859–1900* (San Francisco, 1973).

For historical background there is the standard work by Harold W.V. Temperley, *History of Serbia* (1917; reprint, New York, 1970). Michael B. Petrovich, *A History of Modern Serbia, 1804–1918*, 2 vols. (New York and London, 1976), is more detailed but limited to the modern period. *A Short History of Yugoslavia from Early Times to 1966* (Cambridge, 1966), ed. Stephen Clissold, with contributions by five British scholars, has the advantage of dealing not only with Serbia but with the other regions from which Serbian Americans have come.

For sociological and anthropological background, Joel M. Halpern, *A Serbian Village* (New York, 1967), is based on his observations in a central Serbian village. Joel Halpern and Barbara Kerewsky Halpern have also written *A Serbian Village in Historical Perspective* (New York, 1972).

For a sociological study on a particular aspect of recent Serbian-American life, see Djuro Jovan Vrga, *Changes and Socio-Religious Conflict in an Ethnic Minority Group: The Serbian Orthodox Church in America* (San Francisco, 1975).

Daniel Trees, *How Columbus and I Discovered America: The Life and Adventures of an Immigrant* (Grosse Pointe, Mich., 1965), is an autobiography of a Serbian immigrant who came to the United States in 1906.

MICHAEL B. PETROVICH AND JOEL HALPERN

SERRANOS: *see* AMERICAN INDIANS

SHASTAS: *see* AMERICAN INDIANS

SHAWNEES: *see* AMERICAN INDIANS

SHINNECOCKS: *see* AMERICAN INDIANS

SHOSHONES: *see* AMERICAN INDIANS

SIKHS: *see* EAST INDIANS

SILETZES: *see* AMERICAN INDIANS

SINDHIS: *see* EAST INDIANS; PAKISTANIS

SIOUX: *see* AMERICAN INDIANS

SIUSLAWS: *see* AMERICAN INDIANS

SLAVS: *see* BELORUSSIANS; BULGARIANS; CARPATHO-RUSYNS; COSSACKS; CROATIANS; CZECHS; MACEDONIANS; POLES; RUSSIANS; SERBS; SLOVAKS; SLOVENES; WENDS; UKRAINIANS

SLOVAKS

Of the Slavic groups in the United States, the Slovaks are outnumbered only by the Poles. If they remained relatively unnoticed as a group during their first three generations in this country, it was because the majority of them, peasants and agricultural laborers from Slovak villages in their native land, were for the most part industrial laborers in the United States in the late 19th and early 20th centuries. Few intellectuals immigrated during that period, and since then only rarely have individuals as gifted as inventor Jozef Murgaš (1864–1929), historian Jaroslav Pelikan (1923–), and astronaut Eugene Cernan (1934–) emerged from the group to command public attention. "Hunky Johnny" of the Whiting oil refineries, Mike Dobrejčák of the Braddock steel mills, and Ján Kulik of the Hazleton coal mines—characters from novels about a seemingly strange people from eastern Europe who made their living from manual labor—are more typical of the Slovak experience.

ORIGINS

The ancestors of today's Slovaks settled in the northern arc of the Carpathian Mountains in the 6th century of the Christian era during a migration of Western Slavic tribes. By the 9th century others from Slovakia and Moravia had joined them to form the Empire of Great Moravia, a state that at its height encompassed the territories of most of what is today Czechoslovakia, northern Hungary, and southern Poland. In 863 the Byzantine missionaries Cyril and Methodius were sent to Great Moravia where they introduced Eastern Christianity and the new Cyrillic alphabet. When Great Moravia fell to the invading Magyars in 906, its western half was incorporated into the Kingdom of Bohemia, while its eastern half, which included Slovakia, became part of the Kingdom of Hungary. The Hungarians were converted to Roman Catholicism in A.D. 1000, and helped eradicate the original Eastern Orthodoxy in that area; from then until the Reformation most Slovaks were Roman Catholic.

During the Reformation, however, much of the Hungarian kingdom turned Protestant, and despite the widespread success of the Counter Reformation during the 17th century, many Slovaks remained Lutheran or Calvinist. In the meantime, Carpatho-Rusyn shepherds who had begun to migrate across the Carpathians between the 12th and 16th centuries introduced the Byzantine Catholic rite into eastern Slovakia. As a result, by the 19th century about 80 percent of the Slovak people were Roman Catholic, 15 percent Lutheran, and the remainder either Byzantine-rite Catholic or Calvinist.

Like other nationalities living in the Hungarian kingdom, Slovaks had for centuries used their native lan-

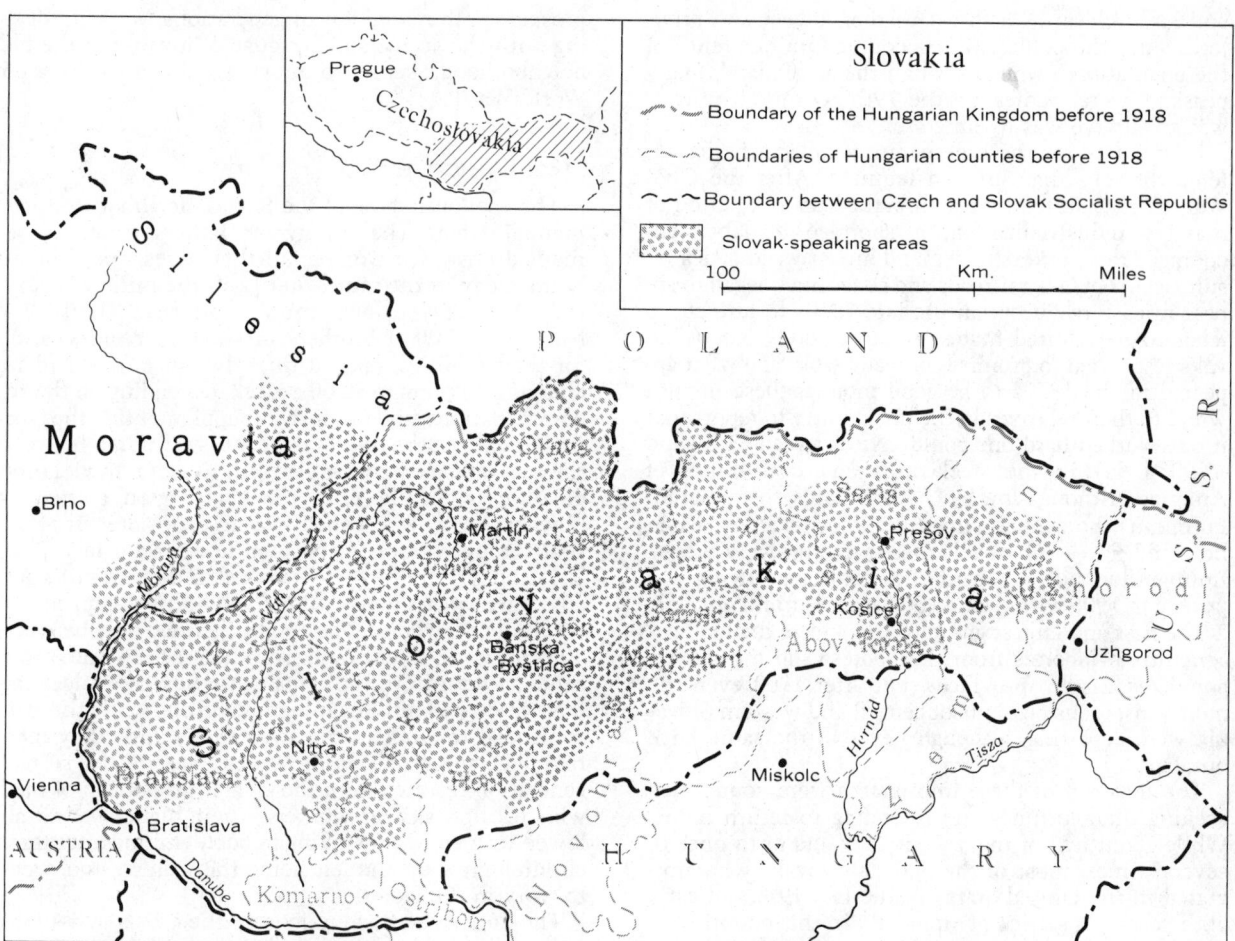

guage without any interference from the government. In 1844, however, Magyar replaced Latin as the official language of the Hungarian kingdom, and this ushered in a policy of Magyarization according to which the government tried to assimilate Slovaks and other minorities. Slovak leaders responded by forming their own national societies, by publishing books in their native tongue, and, most important, by codifying a literary language after replacing the Slovakized version of Czech (employed in writings since the 16th century) with a new standard based on the dialects of central Slovakia. This development, which took place in the 1840s, permanently established the Slovaks as a nationality distinct from the linguistically related Czechs.

The remainder of the 19th century witnessed an intensification of the government's Magyarization policy and a general weakening of Slovak national activity. A few leaders began to realize that cooperation with Czechs in the Austrian half of the Hapsburg monarchy would be the only means for national survival. This belief was also held by some Slovaks in the United States, and during World War I émigré leaders succeeded in uniting Czech and Slovak immigrant organizations behind the idea of an independent homeland. Largely as a result of these efforts, the new state of Czechoslovakia came into existence in late 1918.

Despite promises by Czech leaders, however, the Slovaks did not receive the degree of autonomy they had been led to expect, and this caused friction during the interwar period. Only after the Munich Pact in late 1938 did Slovaks gain their long-awaited autonomy. When Hitler destroyed what remained of Czechoslovakia in March 1939, the Slovaks were allowed their own state, under German protection, until the arrival of Soviet troops in the last months of World War II. When Czechoslovakia was reestablished in 1945, however, the Slovaks were once again ruled from Prague, a subordinate status that worsened after the Communist party took over leadership of the country in 1948 and imposed centralized control. Only in 1969, as a result of the "Prague Spring" led by Alexander Dubček, himself a Slovak, did Slovakia acquire status as a republic within the Czechoslovak socialist federation.

MIGRATION AND SETTLEMENT

Although a few Slovaks left their homeland in the 19th century in protest against Magyarization, the vast majority emigrated for economic reasons. Slovakia had doubled its population from 1 million in 1720 to 2.4 million in 1840. In the four eastern counties—Šariš, Spiš, Zemplín, and Abov, the regions of heaviest emigration—the population increased sevenfold. Yet Hungary neither industrialized nor instituted any land reforms to accommodate this phenomenal increase. The nobles who ruled the country resisted industrialization

and land reform as a threat to their power and privilege. Since the nobles, who accounted for one-tenth of the population, owned over half the arable land, many peasants were landless in the 19th century. The only way to survive was to emigrate.

Fortunately for these desperate people, America offered the jobs that survival required. After the Civil War, as the United States embarked upon a period of massive industrialization, a shortage of labor encouraged the workers to demand higher wages. As a result, agents of U.S. railroads and coal mines began to appear in eastern Europe in the late 1860s to lure cheap labor to the United States. Approximately 5,000 Slovaks responded to promises of ready work and what appeared in the 1870s to be good money; these in turn wrote to their relatives in the old country to report that if one worked hard one could earn between $1.50 and $2.00 a day in the steel mills and coal mines of America. Although low by U.S. standards, to an eastern European who earned only 15 to 30 cents a day, when he could find work at all, these were princely wages. Immigration picked up in the 1880s and 1890s and peaked in 1905 with over 50,000 arrivals from Slovakia.

The first and largest group to leave were the landless agricultural laborers from the poorest and most overpopulated eastern provinces, but after 1900 even the more prosperous peasants of central and western Slovakia were departing, although never in the same large numbers.

The majority of these immigrants were young men seeking their fortunes and intending to return home. While about half of them went back and forth once or several times, most of the 500,000 Slovaks who emigrated to the United States in the late 19th and early 20th centuries settled permanently in this country.

The Slovaks tended to migrate in village chains; when they arrived in America they would identify themselves in terms of their county of origin, calling themselves Šarišania, Zemplínčania, and so on. The domination of the migration by men was largely corrected after World War I, as most of those who had decided to remain in the United States sent for wives and sweethearts just before the laws were passed that restricted immigration, particularly from eastern Europe. A few lived out their lives alone in the United States, sending money to families they never saw again.

Since these Slovak immigrants had initially come to make money and then to return home, they headed for those areas that would provide ready jobs and the best wages. Thus, the vast majority settled in the industrial Northeast and Midwest with fully half in Pennsylvania and large numbers in Ohio, New Jersey, New York, Illinois, Connecticut, Indiana, and Michigan, where most of them labored in coal mines, steel mills, and oil refineries. They lived in company housing in the coal regions or in row houses around the mills and refineries, until, after a decade or so, they had saved enough money to establish their own neighborhood. They would then buy land beyond the company's holdings, erect a church, and settle near it, exhibiting the traditional peasant reverence for property by buying or building their own homes and attaching themselves to the neighborhood. The first two generations grew up in these tightly knit communities anchored by work, church, family, and lodge activities. The often more prosperous third and fourth generations, weary of dealing with the scarce and antiquated housing in the old neighborhood, began to move to the suburbs after World War II.

ECONOMIC LIFE

The economic base of the Slovak neighborhood was manual labor. The immigrant fathers generally remained unskilled workers all their lives, spending 10 hours a day in the mines and 12 in the mills well into the 1920s, and seldom earning more than $1.50 a day before World War I. Mothers, meanwhile, besides caring for their families, opened their dwellings to boarders, charging 50 cents to $2.00 a week, depending on the accommodations, and in this way supplementing the family income. At the turn of the century children between the ages of 9 and 12 were also sent to work, in violation of state laws. Those in the coal region started as "breaker boys" whose job it was to pick slate out of the coal through a rack, or breaker, under their feet. Both boys and girls in the towns worked in the silk mills and any other sweatshops willing to pool this untapped reservoir of cheap labor. The children earned only between 50 cents and 90 cents a day on the breakers and 3 to 4 cents an hour in the silk mills. As they grew older the boys graduated into the mines and mills, while the girls continued to work in the sweatshops until they married. The noticeable improvement among the second generation resulted from the greater proportion of men who became skilled workers; their higher wages allowed women to stop taking in boarders, and after their children grew up and left home the women, too, went to work in the factories.

The growth of trade unions in the 1930s and 1940s eventually enabled labor to win substantial increases in wages, shorter working hours, and many other benefits. By the 1940s second-generation men were more satisfied with their work and sometimes even proud of their skill and the part they had in building American heavy industry. The third and fourth generations, however, tried to avoid industrial work, and many became white-collar workers. Today in industrial northeastern cities the old Slovak neighborhoods still house what is left of the first two generations of blue-collar workers, but third- and fourth-generation white-collar workers have disappeared to the suburbs nearby.

Business enterprise, while quite noticeable in first-generation Slovak neighborhoods, fell off among the subsequent generations. Once a sufficient number of immigrants had settled into a community, a few began to offer goods and services vital to the neighborhood's needs. Many workers sought to forget their day's drudgery while quenching their thirst in good company, so dozens of saloonkeepers opened shop near the mines and mills. Soon the enterprising saloonkeeper began to sell steamship tickets for visits home, and the more successful ones bought safes and began to call themselves bankers. Michal Bosák (1869–1937) of Scranton, Pa., was the wealthiest and most famous of these. By 1918 he had chartered the Bosak State Bank of Scranton and had opened branches in Johnstown and Pittsburgh. With a few exceptions, however, these early businessmen did not remain successful—prohibition closed the saloons, the Depression ruined the banks;

and the chainstores stole away the trade of Slovak store-keepers who had catered to their countrymen's taste for *bryndza* (sheep's cheese) and *klobása* (garlic sausage) in their corner grocery stores and butcher shops. Only a few funeral-parlor proprietors, most of them second generation, have survived the uncertainties of the changing American economy. Compared with the large number of southern and eastern European businessmen of Jewish, Romanian, Italian, or Greek extraction, the Slovak shopkeepers remain a distinct minority.

ORGANIZATION AND LEADERSHIP

Soon after their arrival in the New World the young immigrants, congregating in the local saloon or board-ing house, would establish a fraternal benefit society. Similar organizations were familiar from the old country, but the Magyars had suppressed them. In the United States they grew partly out of a need for com-panionship and partly for insurance purposes. Since American industrialists paid virtually no workmen's compensation, disability insurance, or even death bene-fits, the lodges sought to fill this need. In the late 1880s over 40 Slovak lodges were founded in the United States, and by 1890 they had begun to consolidate into national organizations.

P.V. Rovnianek (1867–1933) wanted to unite all Slo-vaks into one national fraternal society, but his dream ran afoul of religious and secular rivalries. The majority of the early societies were formed along ethnoreligious lines, reflecting the division of Slovaks into Roman and Greek Catholics, Lutherans, and Calvinists. A few fol-lowed the example of European craft guilds and admit-ted only skilled tradesmen; some had an anticlerical bent. By the time they began to unite into national fra-ternal organizations in the 1890s, they permanently re-flected these loyalties in their names: Národný Slo-venský Spolok v Spojených Štátoch Amerických (National Slovak Society in the United States of America, f. 1890); Prvá Katolícka Slovenská Jednota v Spojených Štátoch Severnej Ameriky pod Ochranou Panny Márie, Patrónky Uhorskej Krajiny (First Catholic Slovak Union of the United States of North America under the Protection of Our Lady, Patron of Hungary), abbreviated as Catholic Union, also founded in 1890; and Slovenská Evanjelická Augsburgského Vierovyz-nania Cirkevná a v Nemoci Podporujúca Jednota v Spo-jených Štátoch Severnej Ameriky (Slovak Evangelical Augsburg Confession Church and Fraternal Benefit Union in the United States of North America), estab-lished in 1893. The first of these is today known simply as the NSS, the second as the Jednota, and the third as the Slovak Evangelical Union.

Because in the beginning these organizations ex-cluded women from membership, the women founded their own societies. To complicate the picture, in 1896 the more militant nationalist community leaders, following the Czech lead, established the Slovenská Telocvičná Jednota Sokol v Spojených Štátoch Amerických (Slovak Gymnastic Union Falcon in the United States of America) to organize a campaign against Magyar oppression of the Slovaks in Hungary. This society split in 1905 when some of its Catholic members decided it was too secular for their taste and established the Slovenská Rímsko a Gréckokatolícka Telocvičná Jednota Sokol (Slovak Roman and Greek

Catholic Gymnastic Union Falcon). The first of these is now known as Sokol U.S.A., the second as the Catholic Sokol. By 1918 over 200,000 Slovak Americans had joined 12 established national organizations as well as dozens of smaller societies; the religiously affiliated or-ganizations had a membership of over 150,000; the sec-ular organizations about 70,000.

Local lodge officers were community leaders among the first two generations, less frequently among the third and fourth. Local businessmen usually managed to win election to one (or several) lodge offices and, using this as a springboard, entered local politics. Elec-tion to lodge posts was eagerly sought, and the contests were very spirited in the early years. With the decline of ward politics and the higher educational level of the third and fourth generations, however, the importance of lodge leadership has diminished. Today, Slovak com-munity leadership stems from two sources: third-gen-eration professionals and second-generation members of the community such as Ján C. Scíranka (1902–) and Joseph C. Krajsa (1917–), editors of the influential weeklies *Katolícky Sokol* and *Jednota* and lifelong fra-ternalists.

FAMILY AND KINSHIP

Slovak family life remains for the most part closely knit, although its form has changed over time. The first two generations often lived together, as they would have done in Slovakia; in addition, their boarders were often relatives or friends from the same or a neighboring village, who ate at the family table, were cared for by the housewife, and were treated as members of the household. When the second-generation children mar-ried, they usually continued to live in the paternal home with their spouses for a few years, displacing the boarders and saving up for a place of their own. The house they eventually purchased was often located in the same neighborhood, sometimes even next door, and ties remained close. While the third and fourth genera-tions are more apt to live in the suburbs, they still maintain the ties between the old and new way of life by visiting their parents frequently.

The form of the Slovak family has changed over four generations and with it the family celebrations. Wed-dings, christenings, and funerals were once major events often involving hundreds of people. Weeks before a marriage the bride's mother cooked and baked while the father stocked up on liquor. On the appointed day the betrothed couple first formally asked their par-ents for forgiveness and a blessing, attended a high mass in a church overflowing with people, and, after the solemnization of the vows, marched in procession to the local lodge hall where folk and gypsy music, a ten-course meal, and drinking and dancing all night awaited the entire community. In lieu of the dowry that had been customary in the old country, the bride danced with male guests for a fee, collecting a respectable amount of money in the process. These early weddings could last from two days to two weeks, depending upon how much money the bride's parents were willing or able to spend. Nowadays, among the third and fourth generations, the colorful folk costumes of the old-timers have disappeared, weddings seldom last more than a day, and only a few dozen guests participate; but certain Slovak foods such as *holúbky* (stuffed cabbage)

continue to be served and polkas and *čardášes* can still be heard between renditions of "Moon River" and the latest rock hits. Today's wedding is a blend of the old and the new, but with a noticeable diminution in exuberance.

While weddings still contain elements of the original folk celebrations, christenings and funerals have lost almost all their Slovak flavor. In the first two generations a christening was every bit as exciting as a wedding, and it attracted almost as many people expecting to be wined and dined. The role the godparents played—protectors of the child should its parents die—made them exceptionally close to the family. Today, a christening involves only members of the immediate family, and the godparents' responsibility to the godchild ends with the bestowal of the sacrament. At the turn of the century, funerals similarly attracted hundreds of people. The family of the deceased provided food and drink for the mourners, and all members of the deceased's lodge had to attend the funeral in full regalia or pay a heavy fine. The funeral cortege was long and colorful. Today, only the immediate family, close friends, and one or two lodge officers attend what is usually a very brief church and burial service.

First-generation Slovaks not only married fellow Slovaks in overwhelming numbers but were also apt to marry girls from the same or neighboring Old World villages. Members of the second generation kept this practice, except that the sweethearts were usually from the same or neighboring Slovak-American communities. In the third and fourth generations, however, ethnic endogamy has declined precipitously, though religious endogamy remains, as does a preference for eastern Europeans. In these generations a Slovak Catholic is most likely to marry a fellow Catholic of Slovak, Czech, Carpatho-Rusyn, Polish, Hungarian, or Ukrainian background. Only the sons and daughters of prosperous Slovaks married outside the ethnic group in the second generation, and they preferred Irish partners, thinking that these represented the "establishment" and therefore were marriages of status.

HEALTH AND LEISURE

The first two generations suffered from frequent industrial accidents and high rates of tuberculosis, largely because they had to live and work for long hours in crowded and unsanitary surroundings. When industries began to institute safety procedures in the Progressive era, the accident rate dropped, although it would be another generation before any efforts were made to enforce regulations to clean up the polluted air in which they worked, and consequently tuberculosis continued to afflict members of the community until the 1950s.

Alcoholism also plagued many families in the first generation, when workers habitually flocked to the saloons that surrounded the mines and mills. Prohibition probably had less to do with reducing this problem among Slovaks than did the stern warning of Slovak mothers to their sons not to become drunks like their fathers. Today it has ceased to be a common problem in the community.

While the physical health of Slovak Americans has improved over four generations, their family life has suffered to some extent from their cultural adaptation.

In the first two generations divorce was practically unknown; among the third and fourth generations it has made noticeable inroads, although the Slovak divorce rate is still far below the national average. The number of children per family has also dropped, from an average of five in the first generation to between two and three in the third and fourth. This might be regarded by contemporaries as an improvement, but many old-timers would disagree. The trend from large extended families to small nuclear ones seems to be irreversible.

Leisure activities in the first two generations revolved around community institutions. Today's Slovak Americans are more inclined to find entertainment outside the neighborhood. In the early days the men would spend their evenings in the neighborhood saloon, drinking, talking, and singing about their work and the old country until late in the evening. Those who belonged to lodges spent their leisure hours at the local hall attending meetings, dances, plays, or parties well into the 1940s. The second generation became enthusiastic about American sports. They organized local athletic clubs (sometimes as a part of lodge activities), competed against other lodges and ethnic groups, and delighted in traveling around the Northeast to various competitions. Trophies of all kinds can be found in the hundreds of lodge halls across the country, testifying to their obsession with sports. For some, professional athletics provided a rewarding career. The third and fourth generations have maintained this interest in sports, but more often as spectators than as participants, although they do play such middle-class games as golf. Even bowling, the pastime of thousands of members of the second and third generations, has become less popular, again reflecting the more general decline in American participatory sports and the rise in spectator entertainment.

CULTURE AND CUSTOMS

The earliest Slovak immigrants identified themselves and their culture primarily in terms of their language and religion. The first generation continued to speak Slovak at home, in the street, at church, at lodge meetings and in saloons, and about three-quarters were literate in that language. Their children were raised to speak the language, and more than half learned to read and write it in parochial schools; they preferred to speak English among themselves, however, even though they spoke Slovak with their elders. The use of Slovak declined in the 1940s and 1950s, as many of the first generation died off. The second generation felt more comfortable speaking English and saw no advantage in teaching Slovak to their children. With few exceptions the third and fourth generations have lost the language completely.

This decline is well illustrated in Slovak publications. Since 1886 Slovak Americans have published over 200 periodicals, ranging from dailies to monthlies, in Slovak; today only one newspaper, *Slovák v Amerike* (f. 1889) still appears in that language. The other 11 surviving newspapers are either bilingual or published entirely in English. Similarly, while Slovak Americans used to issue dozens of almanacs in the vernacular, today only one is still printed entirely in Slovak, the *Kalendár Jednota*. In 1920 the Slovaks had over a dozen

major publishing houses; today two suffice, the press of the Katolícky Sokol in Passaic, N.J., and that of Jednota in Middletown, Pa.

In the early publications a minor literary tradition grew up among Slovak Americans. A few clergymen and newspaper editors tried their hand at writing, and some minor works by Father Štefan Furdek (1855–1915), Monsignor Miloš Mlynarovich (1887–1971), the Reverend Andrej Rolík (1896–), Gustáv Maršall-Petrovský (1862–1916), and Ján A. Ferienčík (1865–1925) were published. This literary tradition did not develop in the first two generations because the working-class immigrants were not equipped to foster or support it. But later generations did produce some notable writers. They wrote in English, however, and, unlike their predecessors, made their living outside the community. The first of these was Thomas Bell (originally Belejčák, 1903–1961) who, in his best novel, *Out of this Furnace* (1941), movingly captured the sufferings of his countrymen in the steel mills of Braddock, Pa. Much later Michael Novak (1933–), in *Naked I Leave* (1970), Sonya Jason (1927–), in *Concomitant Soldier* (1973), and Paul Wilkes (1938–), in various periodicals, detailed their version of growing up in "ethnic" America. All of them first established themselves as writers outside the Slovak community and only later returned to their Slovak experience.

Meanwhile, some among the second generation struggled to keep vestiges of their culture alive. Starting in the 1920s and 1930s they staged plays, minstrel shows, and Slovak days to promote group solidarity and the use of the Slovak language. They also began broadcasting radio programs in large cities during the Depression; today only a half-dozen of these survive. The Slovak days have had a minor comeback in recent years, but the plays and minstrel shows are apparently gone forever. The third and fourth generations can no longer understand the language, and in any case prefer the newer forms of entertainment: television, movies, and spectator sports.

Some folk customs, however, have survived in modified form over the four generations. On Christmas Eve the entire family still gathers in the home of parents or grandparents, and at the first sight of the evening star they begin a sumptuous meal. Straw or pine boughs are placed on the white tablecloth to symbolize the manger, and traditional dishes are served in the strict order that the mother decrees. After the father or grandfather recites a lengthy invocation, the mother directs the dipping of communion wafers in honey and smears some of it on the forehead of each person in the sign of the cross. Apples are cut: if a star-shaped design appears in the center it signifies good luck; if a cross appears it bodes ill. Then each girl breaks a walnut to see if the meat is healthy; if it is, the girl will be successful in finding a husband. Later the family dines on sauerkraut soup, fried fish or *klobása*, bean and potato salads, and finally *bobalky* (dumplings in crushed-poppyseed sauce). Mulled wine usually accompanies this meal, as do assorted poppyseed and nut pastries and a variety of fruits. At the end of the meal the family sings both English and Slovak Christmas carols, and finally the children are allowed to open their presents. Before World War II, carolers, called *jasličkári* and *betlehemci*, dressed as shepherds or the three Magi and carrying a miniature manger, used to visit each Slovak family in the neighborhood. They collected money for the church and food and drink for themselves as they made their rounds between Christmas Day and Epiphany (January 6), but the custom has now disappeared among Slovak Americans.

Easter is also a major feast day, especially for those whose ancestors hailed from eastern Slovakia. The mother prepares an elaborate Easter basket that contains *hrudka* (an imitation cheese ball made from eggs), *paska* (a sweet yeast bread with raisins), hand-painted eggs, *klobása*, ham, horseradish, and various pastries. The dairy products, meats, and pastries symbolize the fertility and renewal of the earth in the spring, while the horseradish reminds one of the bitterness and disappointments of life. The baskets are blessed by the parish priest in a special ceremony on Holy Saturday, and the contents are happily consumed on Sunday. On Easter Monday young men used to visit their sweethearts and douse them with perfumed water (some used buckets full) in a mock battle of the sexes. The sprinkling with water was supposed to promote maturity and growth. A few also braided willow whips and beat the girls about the ankles to make them "dance better." On Easter Tuesday the tables were turned as the women surprised the men by dousing them with water as they came home from work. Today, survivors of the second generation reminisce about those "good old days," but the third and fourth generations have dropped these customs. A few, however, still carry on the custom of the Easter basket and thus keep alive a remnant of a larger and older folk tradition.

Similarly, numerous Slovaks of all generations still enjoy Old World music. From the dancing in saloons in the 1880s to today's New Year's celebrations at the local lodge hall, Slovaks have danced to the tunes of polkas, waltzes, and čardášes. Some communities have even produced three generations of musicians, such as the Dadej family in Bethlehem, Pa. Today, the melodies are often interspersed with American themes, but the speed and exuberance of these dances remain and show no signs of disappearing. Indeed, the "ethnic" dance floor is one of the last places in this country where one can still see three or four generations folk dancing together.

Another strong remnant of Slovak culture can be found in its kitchen. The typical peasant food of 19th-century Slovakia consisted first of sour soups, using a base of beans, peas, or potatoes cooked in water, thickened with flour, and laced with vinegar in poor households or with sour cream in prosperous ones. Very little meat was consumed, except on special holidays when it appeared in sour-cream sauces, in sauerkraut soup, as *klobása* or *holúbky*, or as roast chicken, duck, and on very special occasions, roast goose. Potatoes, prepared in almost a hundred different ways, especially as *halušky s bryndzou* (dumplings with cottage cheese) were the more common mainstay of the peasant's dinner. Some sort of pastry typically containing crushed poppyseeds or ground nuts ended the meal. In America the sour soups gradually disappeared, as Slovak mothers took advantage of a more plentiful meat supply and made a potful of chicken or beef soup on Sundays which lasted well into the week. In the early years some households even had meat for breakfast, and meat was

combined with the traditional sauerkraut and potatoes to form a richer diet than had been available in Slovakia. The pastries appeared more regularly as well, and in greater quantities; overall, Slovaks became far better fed. Slovak Americans still treasure their homemade chicken or beef soup, their pork and sauerkraut and holúbky, and their poppyseed pastries; even third- and fourth-generation women still prepare these dishes.

RELIGION AND EDUCATION

Other strong traditions among Slovak Americans are church attendance and a devotion to the parish. By 1930 the Slovaks had built over 300 churches in the United States, 241 of them Roman Catholic, 48 Lutheran, 9 Calvinist, and the rest Greek Catholic. The parish church remains the focal point of life for all four religious groups. In the early days building a church was almost always the first major capital expense of a new community, and the people helped excavate the site and haul building materials. When they grew more prosperous this usually wooden structure would be replaced by a more substantial church of brick or stone. The Slovaks attended church services regularly; Catholics observed all the holy days, marched in processions on special feast days, and went on pilgrimages or retreats once a year. Many also sent their children to Mass every day before classes began in their parochial school.

Laymen were important in the governance of Slovak parishes in the first two generations. For the Protestants and Greek Catholics this was an old practice, but for the Roman Catholics it was something new. Since laymen built the parish church and school, they regarded these buildings as theirs, rather than the bishop's, an attitude that caused grave problems with the Irish-dominated Roman Catholic hierarchy of the United States, which never accepted the idea of lay trustees. The laymen elected their church councils and demanded control over parish finances, sometimes resorting to mob action, dynamite, or even secession from Rome in order to get their way. Problems persisted through two generations, but the third and fourth gave up the fight, and today it is no longer an issue.

Slovaks of all religious persuasions are firmly committed to their faith, and this zeal has often splintered the community along denominational lines. A typical Slovak-American neighborhood has three or four distinct churches, and there is usually a lack of communion between them. If a Catholic and Lutheran live next door to each other, they will exchange greetings on the street but seldom, if ever, attend each other's lodge or social functions. The same applies to Greek Catholic and Calvinist Slovaks, who, because they account for only about 5 percent of the total population, often worship in a parish founded jointly with another ethnic group. The Greek Catholic Slovaks most often join forces with Carpatho-Rusyn, or "Ruthenian," Greek Catholics to erect and support a parish church. While these joint efforts make good economic sense, they often lead to strained relations with those Rusyn bishops who do not recognize the existence of Slovak Greek Catholics in the United States. In addition, because such parishes stress religion over nationality, the Roman Catholic Slovaks often accuse Greek Catholics

of being "bad" Slovaks. Calvinists are the least numerous; they do have a few ethnic parishes, but more than half of them worship in Magyar-dominated churches. The Calvinists are, as a result, the furthest removed from the Slovak community and are often ostracized.

Unlike other immigrants to the United States at the turn of the century, most Slovaks displayed little interest in education. Most of them had had only a few years of elementary schooling, which had left them with bitter memories of the public school as a place where Hungarian officials had tried to Magyarize them. A deep contempt for public education made the first generation blind to its benefits. In the old country, education was thought to be a necessary part of the child's religious upbringing in preparation for the afterlife. The immigrants also thought the school should preserve the child's ethnicity. Slovak parents did not regard schools as promoters of social mobility, and they did not press for extended education. The vast majority of the second generation attended school only through the seventh or eighth grade and then left to find work and contribute to the family income. Only members of the third and fourth generations, reflecting the general American trend between the 1930s and the 1960s toward expanding high school and college education, began in growing numbers to continue their education.

While Slovaks had little interest in education in the first two generations, religion and community size did play a role in the selection of a school. Roman Catholics formed the largest contingent of any Slovak neighborhood and built parochial schools in more than half their parishes; the majority of their children attended those schools. Lutherans usually had to send their children to the local public school because there were seldom enough of them to support their own, although they did establish Saturday and summer schools where the children learned to read, write, and recite the catechism in Slovak. Greek Catholics either sent their children to a Rusyn-Slovak parochial school, to the local Slovak parochial school, or to the public schools, depending upon the size of their parish. Slovak Calvinists were so few in number that they seldom, if ever, built their own schools, relying almost exclusively on the public schools. In the case of Roman Catholic and Lutheran Slovaks, however, great care was taken to ensure that the children preserved their language and ethnicity either through parochial or through Saturday schooling. In this way the first generation fulfilled its goal of having its children raised in a "moral" Slovak atmosphere.

Children wanting to go to high school, however, could not rely on the local ethnic community to provide one. Only a few very large Slovak communities, such as those in Cleveland and Detroit, built high schools. The 20 percent among the second generation who did graduate from high school usually attended public ones. A tiny minority, principally those destined for the priesthood or religious orders, went to the Czech Benedictine College of St. Procopius in Lisle, Ill., or to Danville Academy, a school for girls, in Pennsylvania. In recent years these two institutions have become the semiexclusive preserves of the tiny Slovak upper class. The vast majority of third- and fourth-generation Slovaks attend public high schools and, in increasing numbers, public universities.

POLITICS AND NEIGHBORHOODS

In the political arena Slovak Americans have been fairly successful at the local and state levels, but their representation in the federal government has thus far been limited. A few among the first generation, chiefly businessmen and lodge leaders, tried their hand at politics in the 1890s but did not get beyond the ward level in either the Republican or Democratic organizations. The second generation, without the handicap of foreign birth and foreign accent, had more success. These ambitious sons usually inherited money, lodge offices, and their electoral aspirations from their fathers. Realizing that most Slovaks voted Democratic and that the Irish controlled the Democratic machines, they used their lodge affiliations to form political clubs and to organize the people. By the 1920s they had organized so well that they began to challenge the Irish for control of the local machine. They ran successfully at the city and state levels and produced such notables as Joseph Yasko (1903–1958) of Bethlehem, Pa., who was a state representative in the 1930s, Democratic chairman of Northampton County in the 1940s, and state senator in the 1950s. The net result of their success was their share of political patronage, and this meant more and better white-collar jobs for the community. In the 1970s they continue to hold important local and state positions, but have not elected many to national office. So far, Joseph M. Gaydos (1926–) of Pennsylvania is the only Slovak to sit in the House of Representatives in Washington. It may require another generation before the group can produce enough businessmen and professionals to mount the expensive campaigns required for election on the national level.

The Irish have played a prominent role in Slovak intergroup relations. When the Slovaks began to arrive in the United States in the 1870s their first contact with speakers of English was with the Irish, who had preceded them to the New World as unskilled laborers. The Irish saw the newcomers as a threat to their jobs, and in the early years hurled stones and epithets such as "Huns," "Hunjaks," and "Hunkies" at these former residents of Hungary who, in turn, came to fear and despise these "Americans." Once they discovered that they were both Roman Catholic the tensions declined, but the hostility has never completely disappeared.

Slovaks who still live in the old neighborhoods now often feel threatened by a new enemy; this time it is the encroaching blacks and Puerto Ricans who appear as a danger, although not so much in terms of jobs as in terms of neighborhood survival. The Slovaks pride themselves on maintaining their lawns and houses. Blacks and Puerto Ricans, it is alleged, bring with them not only rising crime rates but also a lack of concern for the neighborhood. To a people who value real estate above all, whose whole dream of social mobility is locked up in owning land, the newcomers pose a threat in the form of unscrupulous real-estate dealers and bankers engaged in "block-busting" to force the old residents to sell, so that the bankers and agents can cash in on the turnover of people and property.

While older Slovaks are usually too attached to the neighborhood, or too poor, to sell out and move elsewhere, the third and fourth generations are doing so in overwhelming numbers. They generally move to suburban ranch-style bungalows with all the modern conveniences. On the surface they have completely assimilated, and many of them actually believe that they have. A trained observer, however, will quickly notice that third- and fourth-generation Slovaks live in what are today called ethnic suburbs, such as Parma, Ohio, Columbia Heights, Minn., and northeast Bethlehem, Pa. These suburbs display the same ethnic mix that the Slovaks ostensibly left behind in the urban "ghetto"— Slovaks, Rusyns, Poles, Hungarians, and other eastern Europeans—in short, a new ethnic neighborhood composed of descendants of the old neighborhood. Ethnic churches, it is true, seldom appear here, because no one speaks the old vernacular any longer, but the parishes they attend are noticeably devoid of parishioners having English, Irish, or German forebears. The new suburbs may appear more homogenous than the old neighborhoods, but they are definitely segregated, not only by skin color but also by religion and culture. How long this will last remains to be seen. Meanwhile, these third-generation Americans still eat their traditional food, enjoy eastern European folk music, prepare their Easter baskets, raise their children in the Church, and worry about the decline of American morality and social values. They are caught between two cultures, and they are uneasy.

Unease also faces those who would like to see the Slovaks survive as an ethnic group in the United States. In the early years, preserving the culture was accomplished fairly easily through parishes, lodges, schools, and family. The persecution of the Slovaks by the Magyars in Hungary became a unifying theme that newspaper editors and nationalist priests used to bolster immigrant solidarity before World War I. After the collapse of Austria-Hungary and the founding of Czechoslovakia in 1918, however, Slovak nationalism at first seemed to lose its raison d'être. Then, with rising conflict between Czechoslovaks and Slovaks in the 1920s, Slovak Americans once again took sides, and the issue continued to divide Slovak communities, especially during the period of the Slovak Republic (1939–1945). The Protestants generally followed the Czechoslovak line, while the Catholics remained separatists. The Communist takeover of Czechoslovakia in 1948 dismayed both sides, but by then only members of the first and second generations cared. Their children in the suburbs had other interests, and many even began to cash in their 20-year fraternal-society insurance policies to help with the mortgage payments. Membership in all national fraternal societies has been on a steady decline since 1960.

Many among the second generation are concerned about the survival of the Slovaks as an ethnic group, and the ethnic revival of the late 1960s has been heartening to them. They appreciate being called Slovak now, rather than Hunky. Some have even reestablished Slovak-language classes at their old parochial schools—a subject dropped in the 1950s—and they hope that the third and fourth generations will take advantage of them. The outcome remains to be seen.

Bibliography

Good books in English on the Slovaks are few. For an analysis of the relevant literature on Slovak Americans, see Mark Stolarik, "From Field to Factory: The Historiography of Slovak Immigration to the United States," *International Migration Review* 10 (Spring 1976): 81–102. Old but still useful are Emily Greene Balch, *Our Slavic Fellow-Citizens*

(1910; reprint, New York, 1969), which deals with the Slavs on both continents and is based in part on personal observations; Konštantín Čulen, *Dejiny Slovákov v Amerike*, 2 vols. (Bratislava, 1942), a social and political history of Slovak Americans to 1914; and R.W. Seton-Watson, *A History of the Czechs and Slovaks* (1943; reprint, Hamden, Conn., 1965), still the most objective treatment of these peoples in English.

Examples of more recent scholarship are Josef J. Barton, *Peasants and Strangers: Italians, Rumanians, and Slovaks in an American City, 1890–1950* (Cambridge, Mass., 1975); František Bielik and Elo Rákoš, *Slovenské vyšťahovalectvo, Dokumenty*, 3 vols. (Bratislava, 1969–1976), containing representative documents on Slovak emigration found in the Old World; and Mark Stolarik, "Building Slovak Communities in North America," in *The Other Catholics*, ed. Keith Dyrud, Michael Novak, and Rudolph Vecoli (New York, 1978), which describes the efforts of Slovak pioneers to reestablish community life by erecting churches and establishing fraternal-benefit societies.

Examples of Slovak-American literature and culture can be found in Thomas Bell, *Out of this Furnace* (1941; reprint, Pittsburgh, 1976), a first-rate novel on Slovak family life in an American industrial town; and in Jozef Ďuris, ed., *Slovak Christmas: A Symposium of Songs, Customs and Plays* (Cleveland, 1960).

Primary source materials on Slovak Americans are scattered. The best organized and balanced collection is at the Immigration History Research Center of the University of Minnesota. A rich, but unorganized, collection is at the Slovak Institute in Cleveland. The Jankola Library in Danville, Pa., is a nicely organized and rapidly growing archive. Smaller and more parochial collections can be found at the First Catholic Slovak Union in Middletown, Pa., and the Slovak Catholic Sokol in Passaic, N.J. The Matica Slovenská in Martin, Slovakia, also houses a very large and well-organized collection of primary materials on Slovak Americans.

M. MARK STOLARIK

Slovenia

~~~~ Boundary of the Hungarian Kingdom, before 1918
- - - - Boundaries of Austrian provinces, before 1918
~~~~~ Boundary of Austro-Hungarian Empire, before 1918

[dotted box] Areas inhabited by Slovenes

100   Km.   Miles

SLOVENES

The Slovenes, or Slovenians, are a South Slav, or Yugoslav, national group who inhabit the northwestern part of modern Yugoslavia. They are both ethnically and linguistically distinct from all their immediate neighbors, the Croats, Italians, Hungarians, and German-speaking Austrians. There are also significant Slovene minorities in adjacent areas of Italy, Austria, and Hungary. The population of Slovenia—one of the republics in the Federal Republic of Yugoslavia—in 1971 was well over 1.7 million. There are an estimated 2.5 million Slovenes throughout the world, perhaps 300,000 of whom reside in the United States, if one includes both immigrants and their American-born descendants.

Slovenia has not been an independent state during the modern era. The territory inhabited by the Slovenes came into the possession of the Hapsburg dynasty by the 15th century, where it remained until the collapse of Austria-Hungary in 1918. The Hapsburg authorities did not permit the formation of a single geopolitical unit known as Slovenia; instead they distributed the Slovene regions of the monarchy among several provinces, in only two of which—Carniola and Gorizia—did Slovenes constitute a majority. Carniola, the central Slovene province, provided the large majority of Slovene immigrants to the United States. On December 1, 1918, the first independent Yugoslav state was created, and most of the Slovene lands joined it. In 1941 Germany and Italy invaded and conquered Yugoslavia, and the Slovene areas were divided between those two powers, with a small area also awarded to Hungary. After the Allied victory in 1945, Yugoslavia was reestablished under a Communist government, and the Slovene lands were combined into the Republic of Slovenia.

Slovene is a distinct South Slavic language which serves as a unifying element in both the homeland and the United States. Major regional differences in dialect have decreased in the homogenizing atmosphere of the larger Slovene settlements in the United States and with the unification after 1918 of Slovene territory in the homeland. The group that came from the Prekmurje region is an exception to this pattern. For centuries prior to 1918 Prekmurje was under the administrative control of Hungary. As a result the Prekmurje Slovenes evolved not only a very distinctive dialect, which they retained in the United States, but also an orthography that followed the Hungarian style and differed markedly from Standard Slovene. This tended to separate them from the main body of Slovene Americans.

The religious background of 95 percent of the Slovenes was and is at least nominally Roman Catholic. The largest non-Catholic group are the Evangelicals, who total about 25,000 and are concentrated in the Prekmurje region; in the United States they generally identify themselves as Lutherans. No other religious group in Slovenia has more than a few hundred adherents. A sharp cleavage did develop between those immigrants who remained loyal to the Catholic church and those calling themselves "freethinkers" or "progressives" who rejected its authority and influence. Only rarely, however, did a Slovene convert to another faith. Polemics between the pro- and antichurch groups continue to enliven many of the Slovene settlements in the United States, and on balance have served to strengthen rather than weaken ethnic identity.

MIGRATION AND ARRIVAL

Economic factors were the primary reasons behind the Slovene immigration to the United States between 1850 and 1914 and in the brief post–World War I era

(1919–1923). After 1945 and the Communist revolution in Yugoslavia, however, the thousands of Slovenes who left their homeland were motivated primarily by political considerations. Many of them, especially in the 1949–1956 period, eventually settled in the United States.

Landholding patterns in Slovenia during the century prior to 1945 were characterized by small family farms, some with as little as 2 or 3 acres of arable land; few had more than 25 acres. Families were large, and the rural overpopulation that resulted could not be absorbed by the still limited industrial development of the region. Younger sons in particular had to resort to emigration to survive. Many farm owners and eldest sons slated to inherit land found it necessary to spend a few years abroad in an effort to earn additional income.

The great majority of Slovene immigrants to the United States accordingly were poor peasants. Most of them were literate, although few had more than a basic elementary education. They migrated either because they had no choice or because they were ambitious and enterprising. Those who remained behind either had—or believed they had—a reasonably secure future or simply did not possess sufficient initiative. All the Slovene regions contributed significant numbers of immigrants to the United States, but especially large numbers came from the poorest and most overpopulated areas such as Dolenjska in southeastern Slovenia. Except for a reluctance to issue exit permits to young males who had not yet fulfilled their obligations for military service, the Hapsburg authorities made no effort to prevent or limit emigration from the Slovene lands. What halted Slovene immigration to the United States after 1914 was Austria-Hungary's involvement in World War I and then, beginning in the early 1920s, the passage by the U.S. Congress of restrictive immigration laws.

The heaviest influx of Slovenes to the United States occurred in the periods 1880–1914, 1919–1923, and 1949–1956. Unfortunately there are no reliable data on the total number who came to stay. Census and immigration records are fragmentary with respect to the Slovenes, who frequently were listed as Austrians, Germans, Yugoslavs, or were grouped with the Croats. Existing evidence indicates that in the century prior to 1945 approximately 550,000 Slovenes emigrated permanently, and that 314,000 of these left in the period 1850–1914. Because there is no doubt that most of them came to the United States, a reasonable estimate would put the total number of Slovene immigrants somewhere between 250,000 and 350,000.

Until the 1890s the Slovene immigrants usually traveled singly or in small groups. Many who settled permanently eventually sent for wives, children, and other family members. Fellow villagers who heard that an emigrant was doing well in America often decided to go too, establishing a chain migration that led many Slovene settlements in U.S. towns and cities to be composed of people from the same or neighboring villages. Gradually emigration from the Slovene lands became more organized and methodical. Growing numbers of migrants took advantage of the services provided by travel agencies representing various steamship companies. Ljubljana, the principal Slovene city, was the central base of operations. So extensive and profitable was this activity, particularly in the 1900–1914 period, that two independent travel agencies were established in Ljubljana, and the authorities had to contend with unscrupulous business practices and fraudulent agents. What motivated the emigrants most, however, was a combination of dissatisfaction with their lot in the homeland and often exaggerated expectations of the success that would be theirs in the United States.

The first coherent Slovene migration to the United States was that of Roman Catholic priests who came in the 19th century to serve as missionaries to the Indian tribes of northern Michigan, Minnesota, and the Dakotas. The most prominent of these missionary priests was the Reverend Frederick Baraga (1797–1868) (now a candidate for beatification as a saint of the Roman Catholic Church), who arrived in 1831 and remained for the rest of his life. Baraga County in Michigan is named after him. His example induced scores of fellow Slovene priests to follow him, and especially in the final third of the 19th century a sizable colony of missionaries had collected in the region. A number of them were by then ministering to the needs of lay Slovene settlers who had begun arriving in significant numbers in the 1880s to work in the copper and iron mines of Michigan's Upper Peninsula, in the Iron Range of Minnesota, and in the local lumber industry. Among the most active priests was the Reverend Joseph Buh (1833–1922), who came to the United States in 1864 and took a special interest in the Slovene immigrants in northern Minnesota. Buh sponsored the first Slovene-language newspaper in the United States, *Amerikanski Slovenec* (American Slovene), which first appeared in Chicago in 1891 and is now published in Cleveland.

Although a few Slovene immigrants had begun to arrive intermittently by the later 1700s, the total number probably did not exceed 1,000 until the early 1880s. During the three decades prior to World War I, however, what had been a sporadic trickle became a flood. When the early immigrants arrived, they often moved from one place to another in search of work—invariably the most basic requirement—usually as miners. By the 1880s there were already small groups of Slovenes scattered in many of the midwestern and western states. The first major colonies appeared in northern Michigan at Calumet and in the northern Minnesota Iron Range towns of Ely, Hibbing, and Virginia. Until the mid-1890s most Slovene immigrants appear to have settled in relatively small and isolated mining towns rather than in large urban centers. Because the mining operations in these and other areas, such as Anaconda, Mont., were relatively new, the Slovene immigrants generally found themselves in close contact with recent arrivals from other ethnic groups.

Beginning with the late 1880s and early 1890s a steadily larger proportion of Slovenes began to settle in the Cleveland and Chicago-Joliet areas, where they found employment in factories. Others came to southwestern Pennsylvania to work in the coal mines. Still others found work in the lumber industry in Davis and Thomas, W.Va. By the mid-1890s Cleveland became the most significant center of Slovene settlement in the United States, a position it retains. Because the number of arrivals was so large in the 1895–1914 period, the colony in Cleveland and its suburbs grew rapidly; by the 1920s an estimated 30,000 to 40,000 Slovenes lived

there. Many who had initially settled elsewhere moved to the city until by the beginning of this century the special role of Cleveland, particularly in Slovene cultural life, was known to the great majority of Slovenes in the United States—indeed, even to many who had never left the homeland. While heavy concentrations of Slovenes remain in northeastern Ohio, Chicago-Joliet, Milwaukee–West Allis, Wis., and in Michigan, Minnesota, and Pennsylvania, settlements have also existed for decades in most of the midwestern and western states. Until recently few Slovenes lived in the South, Southwest, or New England; since 1950, however, many have retired in Florida, Arizona, or California. A handful of the immigrant generation, totaling probably no more than several hundred, have returned to Slovenia to live out their remaining years.

ECONOMIC LIFE

Whether he arrived in the 1880s or the 1950s, the typical Slovene immigrant entered the ranks of labor at the least skilled and lowest-paid levels. A rural background and little formal education were handicaps that were compounded by lack of English and of familiarity with local customs. In addition, at least until World War II, wages in industry and mining were low and the hours long and hard. There was no real job security, and there were few employee fringe benefits. The initial expectations of most of the immigrants—in particular, the conviction that if they worked hard for a few years they would be rewarded with financial success substantial enough to allow either a prosperous return to Slovenia or a comfortable life in the new land—quickly dissipated in the face of the often harsh realities. A few did manage to accumulate considerable wealth, but most had to be content with $2 for a ten-hour day. Slovenes shared this low wage scale not only with other immigrant groups but also with many American-born workers. Over the decades some gradually worked their way up into the middle class, taking advantage of night schools to learn English and acquire various skills. But the pattern was more commonly one of hard work, frugality, and a steady improvement in wages and benefits such as pensions and health plans, as these were acquired by most blue-collar workers in the course of the 20th century.

Until the later 1890s the great majority of Slovene immigrants were young adult males. Approximately half returned home within a few years. Most of those who settled permanently sent for wives, children, or fiancées to join them. After the turn of the century many unmarried women began to immigrate on their own, usually joining family members who had arrived earlier. One avenue by which Slovene women could reach the United States was provided by Slovene tavern owners, who would pay their fare in return for their agreement to work as waitresses for a stipulated period of time. Until more sophisticated ethnic and cultural organizations were established, the tavern served as a social center for the immigrants. Because of the enormous male-female imbalance in the Slovene settlements, at least before 1914, most of the women who arrived were soon married, as the records of the various Slovene ethnic parishes reveal.

The married Slovene women frequently joined their husbands in an economic venture that was common in almost all pre-1920 ethnic settlements: the boarding house. Bachelors and men who had left their wives behind needed cheap living arrangements and preferred to live among their fellow countrymen. An enterprising Slovene couple would invest in a large house and rent rooms to boarders, occasionally as many as 10 or 12 at a time. For rates varying from $10 to $15 a month, or 20 to 25 percent of a worker's gross income, a boarder could have a bed and most of his meals. Other services, such as laundry, might be included or offered at extra charge. The living conditions were simple, not to say spartan, as were the meals. Operating a boarding house was a back breaking burden for the woman, on whom the primary responsibility fell, for she had to take care of her husband and children in addition to the boarders. Eventually, most of the boarders returned to Slovenia, or were reunited with their wives, or found spouses and established their own homes. One of the compelling goals of the Slovene immigrants, as the rapid territorial expansion of the settlements reveals, was to own a house and a piece of land. As an increasing number bought their own homes and the flow of immigrants ended in the 1920s and 1930s, the boarding houses gradually disappeared.

Although most of the immigrants spent their entire working lives either in urban-based manufacturing industries or in mining operations, a significant minority entered business for themselves. This tendency, already common by the 1890s, was especially pronounced in the large settlements such as Cleveland and in areas where the ratio of Slovenes to non-Slovenes was relatively high, as in northeastern Minnesota. The number of Slovene-owned businesses in Cleveland, for example, jumped from about 70 in 1910 to more than 400 in 1924. Not surprisingly, most of these business ventures were small and short-lived, and initially they catered exclusively or primarily to a Slovene clientele. Businessmen made a consistent effort to persuade members of the community whenever possible to patronize Slovene establishments. In any case the immigrants found it more comfortable to shop where they could use their own language rather than have to struggle with English and perhaps encounter ridicule.

Aside from the boarding house, the first Slovene business likely to appear in a settlement was the tavern. The village tavern, or *gostilna*, was a center of social life in the rural areas of the homeland. It had much the same function in the Slovene-American communities; at least during the early years. To open a tavern in pre–World War I America generally did not require much capital. Breweries were quite prepared to handle many of the practical details in return for a commitment by the proprietor to use only their product. Often the tavern owners assumed a fairly important status in the early settlements; not infrequently, for example, they served as informal bankers to immigrants reluctant to trust their money to regular savings institutions. The tavern owner would invest the money and retain the interest for himself.

As the communities grew larger and more stable, and as families began to predominate in them, it became possible for the ambitious to establish other kinds of businesses. Among these were groceries, meat markets, clothing, hardware, and furniture stores, funeral homes, and other specialized concerns. The number and variety

of these enterprises correlated closely with the population and geographic compactness of the particular Slovene community. The Slovene businessman, who was himself comparatively new to the country, its language, and its customs, was more willing to assume a business risk if he could rely on fellow Slovenes for customers than if he had to confront a non-Slovene clientele. In Cleveland, for example, St. Clair Avenue from East 30th to East 79th streets became by the 1920s so completely Slovene in character that English was the foreign language. The vast majority of Slovene businesses in Cleveland and elsewhere were small, family operations. A relative handful of these concerns have survived into the second and later generations.

CLASS STRUCTURE AND SOCIAL ORGANIZATION

Because the economic and social background of the Slovene immigrants who arrived in the United States prior to the mid-1920s was so similar, there was little class differentiation in the earliest communities. Most of the immigrants were poor and had little formal education. A small number had some vocational training, often in the construction trades, which gave them some advantage in the job market. Prior to the Communist takeover of Yugoslavia in 1945, however, there was no incentive for prosperous Slovenes, intellectuals, and professionals to emigrate. Those who left at the end of World War II and eventually made their way to the United States were compelled to abandon whatever wealth and status they had had and to begin anew.

Even among the peasant immigrants, however, some individuals soon began to display more adaptability and ambition than others. Although many in the early years did not try to learn English or to acquire U.S. citizenship, others recognized that the acquisition of both would help them get ahead in their new lives. Especially in the larger settlements, classes to teach English, citizenship, and various vocational and domestic skills were organized by Slovenes aware of their practical importance to their fellow immigrants. Eventually classes were offered under the auspices of boards of education or other appropriate public agencies.

Because systematic studies of the socioeconomic mobility of the immigrant and subsequent generations are lacking, it is not possible to do more than provide a number of brief descriptive examples of Slovene Americans who were able to distinguish themselves in economic or intellectual terms. Louis Adamic (1899–1951) was a writer who enjoyed considerable popularity in the United States during the 1930s and 1940s. Born in Slovenia, Adamic migrated to the United States in 1913. His 17 books and hundreds of articles dealt largely with the impact of the United States on its immigrants. Frank Sakser (1859–1937) immigrated in 1892 at the relatively advanced age of 33 and settled in New York City. He had been trained as a printer, and within a year of his arrival had begun a newspaper, *Glas naroda* (Voice of the People), which was published until 1963. Sakser also established a travel agency and, in 1922, the Frank Sakser State Bank. The onset of the Great Depression in 1929, however, led to the collapse of the bank. Although the depositors received most of their money, Sakser was ruined financially and spent the last few years of his life in difficult circumstances.

Anton Grdina (1874–1957) came to the United States in 1897, worked for several years in a factory, and in 1903 opened a hardware store in the heart of the Cleveland Slovene community at East 62nd and St. Clair. Later he also sold furniture, and in 1908 he established a funeral home. In 1920 Grdina and a number of associates founded the North American Bank, which specialized in home loans to Slovenes. In addition, Grdina was extremely active in various lay Roman Catholic organizations. Frank J. Kern (1887–1979) came in 1903. His original intention was to complete his studies for the priesthood at St. Paul's Seminary in St. Paul, Minn., but within a few years he had moved to Cleveland to study medicine instead; he attended Western Reserve University, graduating in 1912. In addition to his medical practice, Kern prepared an English-Slovene dictionary, which was first published in 1919.

The careers of these men were certainly not typical of the majority of Slovene immigrants; yet they serve to illustrate something of the variety of personal enterprises that emerged within the Slovene settlements. In each colony a business and intellectual elite developed. In the Cleveland St. Clair community, for example, living on certain streets, such as Bonna Avenue, represented high social status. Some prestige was also attached to residence in the St. Clair settlement itself, and some Cleveland residents sought to enhance their standing with friends and relatives elsewhere by using St. Clair as part of their address whether they lived there or not, a practice which irritated the post office.

A very important economic and social institution among the immigrant Slovenes was the mutual or fraternal insurance society. The immigrants often suffered accidents and illnesses, many of them fatal. These tragedies and their attendant economic hardships persuaded most Slovenes to join at least one of the insurance societies. They were established first on the local level, each functioning as an independent unit. A limited and volatile membership, however, left them subject to constant financial pressure, and many collapsed. By the 1890s nationally based organizations began to appear. The first, formed in 1894, was the Kranjska Slovenska Katoliška Jednota (Carniolan Slovenian Catholic Union). In 1966 its name was changed to American Slovenian Catholic Union. The KSKJ—as it is still commonly called—appealed to the actively Catholic element among the Slovene immigrants, and was established from a number of previously independent local societies. In the mid-1970s the KSKJ had 45,000 members, with lodges (chapters) in 31 states. As with the other fraternal societies, insurance benefits are paid in the event of either illness or death.

In 1904 the Slovenska Narodna Podporna Jednota (Slovene National Benefit Society) was organized. The SNPJ, which grew to become the largest institution of its kind among the Slovenes, drew its members primarily from the nonreligious and anticlerical wing of the immigration. Because of their ideological differences a marked animosity developed between the SNPJ and KSKJ, a considerable residue of which still remains. In the mid-1970s the SNPJ had over 60,000 members, including about 18,000 in the youth division. Ohio, Pennsylvania, and Illinois are the states with the largest SNPJ membership. The organization maintains its national headquarters in the Chicago suburb of Burr Ridge; KSKJ has its offices in Joliet.

Both the SNPJ and the KSKJ assumed broader roles than the mere provision of insurance to members. KSKJ was active in promoting the establishment and maintenance of Slovene Roman Catholic parishes and Catholic-oriented ethnic activities. On its part the SNPJ has consistently supported nonreligious ethnic, cultural, and educational interests. In recent decades it has also organized various kinds of sporting events, as has the KSKJ. Both organizations have sponsored Slovene-language daily newspapers, although both the SNPJ organ, *Prosveta* (Enlightenment), and the KSKJ's *Amerikanski Slovenec* have become weeklies. Since 1922 the SNPJ has published a monthly, *Mladinski List,* for the junior members of the organization; its title was changed to the English equivalent, *Voice of Youth,* in 1945. Individual lodges affiliated with each group support various local endeavors with their own funds. A third major insurance organization, especially strong in Minnesota, is the Ameriška Bratska Zveza (American Fraternal Union), with headquarters in Ely, Minn.; it had 27,000 members in the mid-1970s. The Slovenska Ženska Zveza (Slovene Women's Union) had about 12,000 members. These four societies, together with several smaller groups, retain a combined membership of about 175,000. Although membership in these organizations often overlaps, it is clear that a majority of Slovene immigrants and their American-born descendants belong to at least one of them.

RELIGION

After the fraternal insurance societies, whose practical purposes allowed them to cut across all ideological lines, the institution with the strongest hold on most Slovene immigrants was the Roman Catholic Church. Even many who were affiliated with the anticlerical SNPJ and similar organizations retained their church membership or at least their allegiance to the faith. Slovene immigrants preferred whenever possible to worship with a Slovene priest in a Slovene national parish. Invariably, when the number of Slovenes in a particular settlement grew sufficiently large, efforts would be made to establish such a national parish. If they were successful, as they often were, a parochial school would be attached to the parish, and Slovene would be one of the subjects offered. Where the parish was not large enough to support a school, Slovene-language classes for the children might be held in the church itself, along with instruction in the faith. This practice persists, and in fact the 1970s have seen an increase of interest in Slovene-language classes for adults as well as for children. In spite of this, however, Slovene-American Catholics often wonder how long it will remain possible to preserve the national parishes.

The earliest essentially Slovene churches in the United States were established in the Upper Peninsula of Michigan and Minnesota's Iron Range in the 1870s and 1880s, aided by the presence of Slovene missionary priests such as Father Buh. In 1871, for example, a log-cabin style church was built in Brockway, Minn., and in 1904 a larger brick structure was completed. Ely, a major Slovene center in the Iron Range, constructed a sizable church in 1900. Although the priests and many of the parishioners were Slovene, these churches also served numerous non-Slovene Roman Catholics,

In the larger urban settlements the parishes were spe-

cifically Slovene. In Joliet, where Slovenes began to settle in large numbers in the 1880s to work in the nearby factories, they at first had to worship in a German-language church and to be content with occasional visits from a Slovene priest. But eventually friction developed with the German parishioners, and the Slovenes petitioned the archbishop for permission to build their own church and be sent a Slovene priest. The request was granted, and Father Francis S. Šušteršič (1865–1911) was assigned to the Joliet Slovenes. In 1891 the new church was constructed and in 1895 a parochial school was opened.

Similarly, the first Slovene settlers in Cleveland in the 1880s and early 1890s who attended services in a nearby German church with additional attention from a sympathetic Slovak priest did not find this arrangement satisfactory, and petitioned their bishop to grant permission for a Slovene parish and to send them a Slovene priest. However, the bishop had no Slovene-speaking priest available and for unknown reasons did not wish to accept one from Slovenia. A compromise was reached when a young Slovene seminarian agreed to come to the United States in 1890 to complete his studies and be ordained. This occurred in 1893; in the same year St. Vitus's, the first Slovene national parish church in Cleveland, located in the heart of the St. Clair community, was established. A similar process, with variations in detail, took place in all the major Slovene settlements.

The several thousand Prekmurje Slovenes of the Lutheran faith who settled in the Lehigh Valley of eastern Pennsylvania also established their own church, St. John's Windish Lutheran Church, in 1910 in Bethlehem, Pa. This church still has more than 1,600 members. The term Windish reflected the preference of many Prekmurje Slovene immigrants, who arrived prior to the collapse of Austria-Hungary in 1918, to be identified by that name; this preference indicates the relatively low level of Slovene national consciousness in the Prekmurje area at the time of their departure as well as relatively little contact with other Slovene immigrants. The Catholic Prekmurje Slovenes in Bethlehem also established their own church, and both groups sponsored various economic and cultural organizations, all of them using the distinctive Prekmurje dialect. The dominance of the American-born generations by the 1950s and 1960s and the advanced age or death of most of the immigrant generation have made English the common language.

Although the church, Roman Catholic or Lutheran, played a central role in the lives of many—perhaps most—Slovene-American immigrants, as it had in the homeland, and of their descendants, a substantial number of them came to reject its influence and gravitated instead toward an essentially nonreligious, though still ethnic, style of living. This split between the religious and nonreligious Slovenes affected the group as a whole. The polarization that resulted led to the formation of two parallel sets of economic and cultural organizations. A Catholic Slovene, for example, would enroll in the KSKJ, while his nonreligious counterpart would gravitate to the SNPJ. Although this separation persists, it has not contributed to any lessening of Slovene ethnic identity. Each group wants to preserve the heritage its predecessors brought from the homeland and to pass it on to the next generation.

ETHNIC IDENTITY

Nowhere was the commitment to preserve Slovene ethnic consciousness more intense than in the broad realm of culture. Success depended on how early a particular settlement was formed, how large it became, and how long it remained a coherent entity. The colonies in Calumet, Mich., and Cleveland are examples of this contrast. The Calumet settlement grew rapidly in the 1880s and 1890s until it numbered 4,000 or 5,000 Slovenes. The immigrants established churches, insurance societies, a band, a singing and dramatic society, and the necessary economic institutions. Yet by the first decade of the 20th century a decline had already set in. The copper-mining industry, the principal source of employment, was depressed, leading immediately to a decrease in the number of new immigrants who settled there and to the departure of many who could no longer find work. In addition, as the American-born generation came of age its members displayed less interest in ethnic activities than their immigrant parents had shown.

One unusual facet of the Calumet Slovene community was its close association with the Croatian community, although this cooperation had its limits. Instances of multiethnic collaboration occurred within all the Slovene settlements, and still do, but as a rule the Slovenes preferred to establish their own ethnic organizations and to have no more formal contact than necessary with other ethnic groups. The larger the individual Slovene colony, the easier it was to maintain this autonomy, as can be seen by the example of Cleveland.

Because of an extensive and expanding industry requiring large amounts of unskilled and semiskilled labor, Cleveland offered many employment possibilities to Slovene immigrants, whether they arrived in the 1880s or in the 1950s. The same was true for other urban industrial areas such as Chicago and Milwaukee–West Allis, Wis. In contrast to Calumet, Cleveland witnessed a steady influx of Slovene immigrants from the 1880s into the 1920s. A revitalization came in the 1950s with the Slovene migration occasioned by the outcome of World War II. As a result the Cleveland settlement included a large number of immigrant-generation Slovenes over almost a full century, permitting not only the establishment but the perpetuation of ethnic institutions where Slovene identity could remain substantially intact. It was possible for the minority of American-born Slovenes who retained a knowledge of the language and an interest in the culture of the immigrant generation to be absorbed into the organizations founded by that group.

The Slovene language was central to the development and perpetuation of ethnic identity among the immigrants; but unlike most of the remaining immigrant generation, their American-born descendants do not generally regard competence in the language as a prerequisite for identity as Slovenes. Aside from practical organizations, such as mutual-insurance societies, shops, and the national parish, all of which responded to the basic needs of the immigrants, a wide range of purely cultural groups was also available. Singing societies formed in all large settlements and many small ones were especially popular, and remain so. In Cleveland alone, more than 40 singing groups were established, although many lasted only briefly. More than a dozen are still active, however, including several children's choruses. Bands, dramatic clubs, libraries, gymnastic groups, national homes, all appeared in Slovene colonies, the number and variety depending largely on the size of the settlement. The Cleveland Slovenes were so large and well-organized a group that for a time it was possible to perform full-scale operas on the stage of the Slovene National Home on St. Clair Avenue, in an auditorium that can accommodate 1,500 spectators. All these organizations used the Slovene language as long as it was feasible, then either disbanded or became bilingual.

The immigrant Slovenes attempted to teach the native language to their children, but generally they were not very successful. Without question most second-generation Slovene Americans acquired some familiarity with idiomatic Slovene from their parents, but they did not use it among themselves or when it was not absolutely necessary. Rarely do third- and later-generation Slovenes have any real command of the language. Exceptions do exist, of course, and especially in the 1970s there has been a resurgence of interest in the language among American-born Slovenes, with the result that several useful language manuals have been published and classes organized both in colleges and through national parishes, but these still involve only a tiny fraction of the native-born population.

The press was particularly important for the Slovenes. Publication of the *Amerikanski Slovenec* in 1891 marked the appearance of the first Slovene-language newspaper in the United States, but it did not keep its monopoly long. Since 1891 Slovene immigrants have founded more than a hundred newspapers and reviews. Many lasted for only a few issues or a few years, but others, including the *Amerikanski Slovenec* itself and *Glas naroda* (1893–1963), appeared for decades. Some were the organs of mutual-insurance societies, such as *Prosveta* for the SNPJ and *Nova doba/New Era* for the American Fraternal Union. Others were narrowly ideological, such as the Socialist publication, *Proletarec* (The Worker), published between 1906 and 1952. In the period 1910–1950 there was a Slovene-language newspaper available to suit every literary and political taste. Among the publications that catered primarily to a single settlement or special group of Slovenes was the *Amerikanszki Szlovenczov Glász* (American Slovene Voice), which appeared in Bethlehem between 1921 and 1947. Its readers were the approximately 10,000 Prekmurje Slovenes in the Lehigh Valley.

Both the variety and the sheer volume of Slovene-language newspapers and other cultural organizations provided writers, composers, and performers with ample opportunity for public exposure to develop their talents. While Louis Adamic, who soon outgrew the confines of the Slovene community, was the prime example, there were many others whose reputations remained essentially within the community. Among them were the musician and poet Ivan Zorman (1899–1957), whose works reflected an intense love for Slovenia, and the singer and choral director Anton Schubel (1899–1965). Schubel was a member of the Metropolitan Opera Company chorus from 1931 to 1945. From 1949 to 1965 he lived in Cleveland where he conducted the Glasbena Matica singing society. Among post–World War II settlers, easily the best known was Karel Mauser (1918–1977), a Catholic writer. Many immi-

grant Slovene women also distinguished themselves, including Katka Zupančič (1889–1967), a writer and dramatist, and Anna Praček-Krasna (1900–), also a writer and the last publisher of *Glas naroda*. Although the thematic concerns of Slovene immigrant writers varied widely, a common theme was the experience of the group in the United States.

Beginning in the 1930s the forms of Slovene cultural expression underwent some changes. The automobile, radio, movies, and other forms of entertainment gave the immigrant generation other options. As time went on most of the immigrants became steadily more comfortable with U.S. customs and with English and less dependent on the ethnic community. The inability of the American-born second and third generations to use Slovene led to the introduction of English into many ethnic organizations. Radio programs, for example, which remain very popular and are still broadcast in most of the larger settlements, initially were in Slovene, but in recent decades have tended to be bilingual or in English. Despite exceptions, the momentum appears to be inexorably toward English. This shift was easily accomplished in many ethnic institutions, such as the mutual-insurance societies, social organizations, and the like, but others, especially the newspapers, were decimated by it. Only one basically Slovene-language newspaper is being published more frequently than once a week: *Ameriška domovina* (American Home) in Cleveland, with a largely Roman Catholic and post–World War II immigrant readership, publishes three issues a week.

Music has provided the most effective link between the Slovene-speaking generation and its American-born, English-speaking progeny. Most settlements still have singing societies; the programs remain basically Slovene, but many listeners do not understand the words, and even some of the singers simply memorize the sounds by rote. Each year since the early 1960s at least one musical group from Slovenia or from Slovene-inhabited territory in Austria and Italy has toured the Slovene-American settlements. Slovene-American choral societies and instrumental bands also go on annual tours to Slovenia. Their performances are very popular in both countries. On a less formal level, the music performed by polka bands remains a popular form of ethnic entertainment. Easily the most famous polka performer among Slovene Americans, as well as the general American public, has been Cleveland-born Frankie Yankovic (1915–), who first became popular in the 1940s.

Contact between Slovene Americans of all generations and the homeland has been greatly encouraged since the 1950s by the availability of inexpensive group or charter flights to Slovenia and by the support for such ties shown by the government in Slovenia. A special agency, the Slovenska Izseljenska Matica (Slovene Emigrants' Society) was formed by the government in 1950 to coordinate official contacts between Slovenia and Slovene emigrants. The Matica publishes an almanac that contains numerous articles and photographs dealing with Slovenes in the United States and issues an attractive monthly magazine, *Rodna Gruda* (Native Soil), covering similar subjects. The Matica also organizes activities in Slovenia for visiting Americans, including a Fourth of July celebration—which coincides with a Slo-

vene holiday—in the picturesque town of Skofja Loka. It is attended by thousands of immigrant visitors and native Slovenes alike. Some post–World War II immigrants oppose these various contacts on political grounds, but the majority of Slovene Americans take a more moderate position toward the Communist regime. Visiting Slovenia, an experience that customarily includes becoming acquainted with relatives still living there, clearly has been a rewarding experience for many American-born Slovenes and has fortified, or even awakened, a sense of belonging.

A number of cultural and academic organizations have been formed in recent decades to promote a more systematic cultivation and preservation of the Slovene heritage in the United States. The Society for Slovene Studies brings together scholars, a majority of them Slovene Americans, involved in the study of Slovenia and Slovenes. The Slovenian-American Heritage Foundation supports cultural activities and scholarship among Slovene Americans. The League of Slovenian Americans works in the same area but focuses primarily on the post–World War II immigrant generation and the American-born of that group. The United Slovenian Society and the Slovenian Research Center, both with headquarters in the Cleveland area, have similar objectives. Membership overlaps among these groups, but occasionally they still tend to work at cross-purposes.

On special occasions Slovene Americans continue to perform Slovene dances, wear the distinctively appealing traditional national costumes, which vary widely in design from one area of the homeland to another, and cook traditional dishes. Since the 1960s the Cleveland area Slovenes have expended considerable effort on behalf of the Slovenian Home for the Aged, an 87-bed facility founded in 1962. The funds for construction, well over a half-million dollars, were raised entirely within the Slovene community, which meets some of the operating costs as well. There is another Slovene retirement home in Fontana, Calif.

POLITICAL PARTICIPATION

Political activity by immigrant Slovenes began as early as the 1870s. When the village of Red Jacket, Mich., was incorporated in 1875, a prosperous Slovene, Peter Rupe (d. 1923), was elected mayor. Especially before 1914 many Slovene immigrants believed their stay in the United States would be temporary, and this tended to discourage their acquiring citizenship and learning English; but their attitude changed as their new roots deepened. Ethnic intellectual leaders urged the immigrants to become citizens and to vote. In its issue of October 21, 1892, *Amerikanski Slovenec* gave precise information on citizenship procedure. Many immigrants attended night-school classes to prepare for naturalization. In the early 1900s a Slovene Political Democratic Club was active in Cleveland. The number of groups increased markedly with the beginning of World War I. The immigrants were deeply concerned about the fate of the Slovene lands, especially after the entry of Italy into the conflict in 1915; although many hoped for the downfall of Austria-Hungary, there was fear that Italy might annex the Slovene territory. Nevertheless, with the entry of the United States into the conflict in 1917, most immigrant Slovenes firmly

backed the U.S. war effort and President Woodrow Wilson. They hoped to see the emergence of an independent Yugoslav state in which Slovenia would be a coequal constituent, with borders that incorporated all the Slovene ethnic territory. In this they were disappointed, for substantial Slovene areas passed after 1918 into Italian and Austrian hands, a situation that was only partially rectified after World War II.

A politically active and very visible minority among immigrant Slovenes called itself socialist. Socialist clubs appeared in most of the settlements, especially in the 1900–1930 period. Many of their leaders had been members of the Austrian Social Democratic party in the homeland. The Jugoslovenska Socialistična Zveza (Yugoslav Socialist Federation), which was most active during the 1910s and 1920s, united most of these Slovene groups. The federation had separate sections for the Slovenes, Croats, and Serbs; an estimate of its membership in 1911 listed 1,850 Slovenes, 2,000 Croats, and 350 Serbs.

The fate of Slovenia during World War II again aroused Slovene Americans to action. In 1942 the Slovene-American National Council (SANS) was established in an effort to unite all Slovene Americans on behalf of a restoration of a Yugoslavia that would include an ethnic Slovenian state. The organization suffered from considerable internal friction, however, especially over the attitude to adopt toward the Partisan movement led by Josip Broz Tito. SANS chose to support the Partisans, and this alienated most of the Catholic elements. Adamic was the best known of the SANS members, and his access to the White House through Eleanor Roosevelt gave the group some influence. Anger at the role played by SANS was a major factor in preventing the majority of the strongly anti-Communist post–World War II immigrants from participating more fully in the established Slovene-American institutions not affiliated with the church.

Except for occasional success on the local level, none among the immigrant generation of Slovenes achieved political prominence, but members of the second and later generations did. Among these by far the most conspicuous is Frank J. Lausche (1895–), who was born in Cleveland and grew up in the St. Clair community. He studied law, passed his bar examination in 1920, and after several years of private practive and service as a judge, was elected mayor of Cleveland in 1940. Subsequently he won five two-year terms as governor of Ohio and in 1956 was elected to the U.S. Senate, where he served two terms (1957–1969). Five other American-born Slovenes have served in Congress, each representing a district which contained areas of Slovene settlement. John A. Blatnik (1911–) represented northeastern Minnesota, including the Iron Range, from 1947 to 1975. He was succeeded by James L. Oberstar (1934–), also of Slovene-American background. Blatnik and Oberstar are Democrats, as is Ray P. Kogovsek (1941–), elected from Colorado in 1978. Joe Skubitz (1906–), a Republican, represented a district in eastern Kansas from 1963 to 1979. The coal-mining area of southeastern Kansas, centered near the communities of Pittsburg and Frontenac, includes a number of Slovene settlements. Philip Ruppe (1927–), a Republican from Michigan, the descendant of a pioneer family in the Calumet area, served from 1967 to 1979. Hundreds of other Slo-

vene Americans have been elected to local, county, and state offices.

GROUP MAINTENANCE

Over time the great majority of immigrant Slovenes adjusted successfully to American life and came to see themselves as both Slovenes and Americans. They became loyal and patriotic citizens and acquired at least a working knowledge of English. Nevertheless, they retained a primary commitment to the cultural forms and ethnic identity they had brought from the homeland, and preserved them within their various settlements in the United States. The pluralism tolerated in America meant for the Slovenes the freedom to cultivate their own language and culture. They could publish newspapers in their native tongue and maintain as many cultural and economic organizations as they were prepared to support. Many Slovenes saw this as the most attractive feature of the country, and in the main the immigrant Slovenes took full advantage of it.

With respect to the second and later generations, however, the situation is different. Many in this group either have abandoned or never possessed a specific sense of Slovene ethnic identity. Especially with the third and subsequent generations, the impact of mixed marriages has also served to dilute Slovene ethnic identity. Accordingly, many American-born Slovenes retain only occasional connections with residual Slovene institutions, such as membership in fraternal insurance societies, national parishes, or attendance at ethnic cultural programs. Many American-born Slovenes, in addition, still have family members from the immigrant generation.

The uninterrupted presence of an appreciable number of immigrants since the 1880s and the willingness of a minority of second- and later-generation Slovene Americans actively to identify with their Slovene roots have been instrumental in preserving the group as a viable entity. Except for a brief and limited surge in the early 1950s, however, no substantial new immigration from Slovenia has occurred since the early 1920s, nor does there appear to be any realistic prospect that one will. By the final decade of this century the Slovene ethnic group in the United States probably will be composed essentially of the American-born.

In order to ensure the maintenance of the Slovene Americans as a coherent ethnic group despite the disappearance of an immigrant generation, neither a knowledge of Slovene nor even any personal experience of Slovenia, however desirable both continue to be, must be required to retain membership or even leadership within the group. A relaxation of the criteria for ethnic identity and a gradual modification of ethnic institutions are already widely apparent in the 1970s. It is possible that this relaxation, combined with intermarriage in the second and later generations, will dissipate group allegiance. The evidence as to which tendency ultimately will prevail is contradictory.

Bibliography

Gerald Gilbert Govorchin, *Americans from Yugoslavia* (Gainesville, Fla., 1961), remains the best general introduction in English, though somewhat dated. Marie Prisland, *From Slovenia—to America: Recollections and Collections* (Chicago, 1968), written in an informal style, is a useful introduction, as is George J. Prpić, *South Slavic Immigration in America* (Boston, 1978), pp. 137–173. The two best works are in Slo-

vene: J.M. Trunk, *Amerika in Amerikanci* (Celovec, Austria, 1912), is indispensable, as is Jože Zavertnik, *Ameriški Slovenci* (Chicago, 1925).

The most useful studies of the Slovene missionary experience in the United States are Sister Bernard Coleman, O.S.B., and Sister Verona LaBud, O.S.B., *Masinaigans: The Little Book. A Biography of Monsignor Joseph F. Buh, Slovenian Missionary in America, 1864–1922* (St. Paul, Minn., 1972), and Maksimilijan Jezernik, *Frederick Baraga: A Portrait of the First Bishop of Marquette Based on the Archives of the Congregatio de Propaganda Fide* (New York, 1968). Coleman and LaBud are effective in dealing with the relationship between the missionary priests and the lay Slovene settlers in Minnesota and Upper Michigan.

Mary Molek, *Immigrant Woman* (Dover, Del., 1976), is a valuable personal account of the difficulties experienced by an immigrant family in the coal-mining area of southeastern Kansas during the 1910s, 1920s, and 1930s. The writings of Louis Adamic generally include material on the Slovenes; *Laughing in the Jungle: The Autobiography of an Immigrant in America* (1932; reprint, New York, 1969), is particularly good. Also of some value are Giles Edward Gobetz and Adele Donchenko, eds., *Anthology of Slovenian American Literature, with Sixty Reproductions of Slovenian Ethnic Art* (Willoughby Hills, Ohio, 1977); and Giles Edward Gobetz and Daniel Fugger, *From Carniola to Carnegie Hall: A Biographical Study of Anton Schubel, Slovenian Immigrant Singer and Musical Pedagogue* (Willoughby Hills, 1968).

Most of the best work on Slovenes is in Slovene. The single most valuable collection appears in the annual volumes of the *Slovenski Izseljenski Koledar* (*Slovenski Koledar* since 1972) published in Ljubljana, Yugoslavia, since 1954. Each issue contains several articles dealing with Slovenes in the United States. The largest collection of materials freely available to scholars is contained in the Immigration History Research Center at the University of Minnesota, Minneapolis. In Slovenia, the best source is the National and University Library in Ljubljana.

RUDOLPH M. SUSEL

SORBS: *see* WENDS

SOUTH AFRICANS

South Africans have been coming to the United States in small but increasing numbers in the last 30 years. They represent different populations in South Africa itself and do not constitute a full-fledged ethnic group in the United States, but in various U.S. cities such as Boston, Houston, Cleveland, and New York they maintain a noticeable degree of cohesion. According to the 1970 U.S. Census, there were about 16,000 South African immigrants in the United States; in 1980 the number is likely to be in the vicinity of 30,000.

South Africa is an independent country occupying the southern tip of Africa. Originally inhabited by indigenous nomadic tribes, the area was successively settled by Bantu tribes from central and east Africa, Dutch, French Huguenot, and British settlers, and East Indian laborers, giving it a complex historical and racial pattern.

During the Napoleonic wars, the British occupied the Dutch colony at the Cape of Good Hope and held on to it to safeguard the ocean route to the East. In the 1830s farmers of Dutch descent (Boers) trekked into the interior to put themselves beyond British rule; there they established two Boer republics, the Orange Free State and the Transvaal Republic. Spectacular mineral discoveries in these republics—diamonds at Kimberley in 1870 and gold in the Witwatersrand in 1886—attracted fortune-seekers from all over the world. Conflict between the British and the Boers culminated in the Boer War (1899–1902). Britain won this struggle, annexing the Boer republics and creating the Union of South Africa (1910). English and Afrikaans, a language derived from Dutch, became its two official languages. In 1934 the Union of South Africa became a member of the British Commonwealth of Nations; in 1961 it broke away

South Africa

400   Km.   Miles

to become the independent Republic of South Africa. The estimated population in 1977 was 26,765,000: 71.2 percent black, 16.7 percent white, 9.3 percent of mixed racial heritage, and 2.8 percent Asian.

In South Africa's history, immigration into the country has been of more consequence than emigration. After the opening of the mines, many of the same streams of European immigration that entered the United States also reached South Africa, although on a much smaller scale. As the country became industrialized in the 20th century, it continued to attract both white immigrants from abroad—mainly from Britain, the Netherlands, West Germany, Belgium, Italy, Greece, and other European countries—and black migrant workers from neighboring African countries. In the 1970s whites from Rhodesia and from the former Portuguese colonies of Mozambique and Angola have moved into South Africa. Rhodesians are now coming to the United States both from South Africa and directly from Rhodesia.

Until 1950, emigration from South Africa had two different strains. One strain was a continuation of the pioneer theme—a movement from South Africa, the most established country in British Africa, to the less settled countries of Rhodesia, Namibia, Zambia, Malawi, and Kenya. The other strain reflects an opposite attraction—a movement from colony to imperial center. Even though South Africa was a colony for only a short time in this century, Western culture, particularly British, has permeated all aspects of South African life. Emigrants who left South Africa came from the only group with a cosmopolitan outlook: white English-speaking South Africans. Those who left the country were seeking a larger arena for their lives: professionals were looking for more challenging careers, artists wider audiences and sympathetic colleagues, workers in business and industry greater opportunities. Most emigrants to countries outside Africa went to Britain. Emigration to the United States was restricted by the Immigration Act of 1924; as a result, the number of immigrants entering the United States annually from 1924

to 1950 ranged from 8 to 230, averaging only 61 persons. Immigration was especially low during the Depression and World War II.

In 1948 the government of South Africa, which had previously been controlled by the English United party, passed into the hands of the Afrikaner National party. This new government represented the strongly nationalistic ideals of the Afrikaans-speaking people, descendants of the original Dutch and French settlers, but cut off by time and distance from any ties to Europe. The nationalist government transformed traditional relations between the different racial groups into a rigid system of segregation known as apartheid. The National party has remained in power since.

With the change in government and the advent of apartheid, emigrants began to leave for political reasons. Two groups can be distinguished: persons choosing to leave, and political refugees. Those who chose to leave did so out of a feeling of repugnance for the racial policies of the government, believing that sooner or later these policies would lead to a civil war between blacks and whites. Whenever racial strife has broken out, emigration has increased. This happened in 1960, after a massacre at Sharpeville where 80 blacks at a peaceful protest were shot, and again in 1976 and 1977 when protracted demonstrations against the government took place in the black townships outside Johannesburg and other cities. Again the emigrants who left voluntarily have come mostly from the white English-speaking group, although some Afrikaans-speaking professionals have chosen to emigrate, too. Other emigrants, political refugees, have fled because the government has threatened them with arrest, banning (a severe restriction on all aspects of life), or death in an effort to end their public opposition to the country's racial policies. This group consists of both blacks and whites.

Between 1951 and 1976 white emigration from South Africa was on the order of 9,000 persons per year. The majority went to Britain and Rhodesia, with a scattering to many countries in Europe and Africa, and to North America, Australia, and New Zealand. In 1975 the number of white emigrants to the United States (244) was only 2.4 percent of all white emigrants (9,797). Between 1951 and 1976 the number of white emigrants to the United States ranged from 38 to 603 per year, with an average of 280 persons. After 1976 emigration increased. Although official figures are unavailable, one estimate puts the number of South Africans entering the United States at 1,000 a year, considerably above the number in 1975. Official South African reports do not list black emigrants.

Of the 16,000 South Africans in the United States recorded by the 1970 U.S. Census, slightly less than half were foreign-born, the remainder native-born of foreign or mixed parents. In 1960, 96 percent of these South African Americans were listed as white, and 95 percent in 1970. This large percentage of white emigrants from a country in which whites constitute only 20 percent of the population reflects their monopoly of occupational skills and the wealth that enables relocation.

White immigrants to the United States have usually arrived in relatively young family units. In 1960 the ratio of men to women was about one to one, and in 1965 an age distribution of white South African immigrants showed a preponderance of persons aged 25 to 44. These data suggest that the migrating families consist of parents in the middle-income-earning years and their young children.

Many South African immigrants are professionals. A very large number are physicians attracted by the medical opportunities in the United States. They are frequently the descendants of Jewish refugees and settlers in South Africa.

White South Africans, although scattered throughout the country, are clustered in the more populous, urban parts of the United States. The states with the largest South African populations are California, New York, Massachusetts, New Jersey, and Pennsylvania. The regions of greatest South African population in 1970 were, in order, the Northeast, the West, the South, and the North Central area.

White South Africans have readily assimilated into the communities in which they live. Most white South Africans in the United States are English speaking, and the small number of Afrikaner emigrants learned English as a second language at school. Only the distinctive accents of South Africans mark their difference from Americans. It is common for families to have other South Africans as friends and acquaintances, but there are no formal associations of white South Africans. Many white South Africans in the United States still have parents and relatives in South Africa, and their incomes usually permit occasional trips home for family visits (political refugees, however, do not risk returning). Second-generation South Africans are indistinguishable from their middle-class American peers. About 40 percent of the immigrants have become naturalized. Although the remainder retain their South African citizenship, most regard their stay in the United States as permanent.

Black South Africans in the United States are mainly political refugees. Many of them entered the United States as students, either in the Southern African Student Program under the Hays-Fulbright Act (approximately 100 students over a several-year period) or in programs sponsored by individual colleges. The University of Rochester in Rochester, N.Y., Lincoln University in Jefferson City, Mo., and Howard University in Washington, D.C., have been particularly receptive. According to U.S. Census figures, there were 422 nonwhite South Africans in the United States in 1960, and 793 in 1970. The number of foreign-born nonwhites increased from 188 to 458 in this period, indicating a continued stream of new immigrants. Nearly half of all nonwhite South Africans live in New York City. There are active associations of black South African Americans. Several are U.S. branches of black South African political parties, and all aspire to racial justice and majority black rule in South Africa. They regard themselves as refugees in the United States and are planning to return home.

Racial divisions fostered by apartheid in South Africa are perpetuated among South Africans in the United States. White South African Americans are for the most part affluent and successful in their careers, whereas black South Africans struggle to live and have difficulty in finding jobs. Except for the few white South Africans who continue to work for majority rule in South Africa, the two groups have little in common.

Bibliography
Except for an occasional newspaper or journal article, there is no published material on South Africans in the United States. Useful sources on South Africa itself are Gwendolyn M. Carter, *The Politics of Inequality: South Africa Since 1948*, 3d ed. (London, 1962), and Leonard Thompson and Jeffrey Butler, eds., *Change in Contemporary South Africa* (Berkeley, 1975). For statistical data consult the following volumes published by the Union of South Africa: *Official Year Book of the Union of South Africa, Statistics of Migration,* and *Bulletin of Statistics.*

STANLEY MOSS

SOUTH AMERICANS: *see* CENTRAL AND SOUTH AMERICANS

SOUTHERNERS

If the ancestors of most present-day Southerners had had their way, there would be no question of whether they should be treated as an American ethnic group. Southern whites remained—as southern blacks became—Americans against their will, a fact that has a great deal to do with their persistence as an identifiable group.

Southerners, like members of immigrant ethnic communities, belong to a group defined by a historical experience, in which membership is ordinarily inherited but rests ultimately on a combination of individual identification and acceptance or categorization by others. Like other ethnic groups, Southerners have differed from the national norm: they have been poorer, less well educated, more rural, occupationally more specialized. They also differ culturally in important respects, and their political behavior has been distinctive. Although Southerners are not usually identifiable by name or appearance, their accent usually serves as an ethnic marker. They have been stereotyped by other Americans and, indeed, are usually willing themselves to generalize about their differences from their countrymen. The extent of discrimination against them—in the appointment of Supreme Court justices, for example—is a matter of opinion, but it is significant that it is even that.

The analogy between Southerners and immigrant ethnic groups is complicated by the fact that, for Southerners, the "old country" is part of the United States, and most still live there. Moreover, the South has always received migrants from the rest of the country and turned many of them, and more of their children, into Southerners themselves. The South has been defined in various ways, but it almost always includes the 11 former Confederate states. Most definitions would exclude parts of these states—west Texas and northern Virginia, for example, and southern Florida, if there were anywhere else to put it—and include at least parts of Kentucky and sometimes Oklahoma and the various border states. However the region is defined, though, it is clear that the term "Southerners" does not mean simply residents of the South, but refers rather to people who somehow identify themselves with the region whether they live there or not.

IDENTIFICATION

Southern identification—a sense of the South as an entity over and above the states and localities that make it up and some sense of patriotism toward it—was shaped by the sectional conflict of the early 19th century, primarily among whites from those areas where slavery and the plantation system were well established. As agriculturists, they often found their interests to be different from those of the Northeast; as residents of a biracial region with a slave system, their interests were not those of the agricultural Midwest. From the foundation of the Republic, the representatives of the southern states found themselves allied in defense of agriculture and of slavery, and regional conflict over economic and racial issues did not end with the Civil War. The war itself, with its legacy of defeat, occupation, and subordination, gave the former Confederates another common basis for identification, a distinctiveness based on history rather than current circumstances. They had not only their own flag, anthem, and holidays, but a heritage of economic—and, allegedly, cultural and moral—inferiority to set them apart from other Americans.

Even today, identification with the South appears to have something to do with ancestral, if not one's personal, sympathy with the Confederate cause. A 1971 study in North Carolina found both blacks and Appalachian whites (from areas largely pro-Union in the Civil War) less likely than other North Carolinians to regard themselves as Southerners, some explicitly rejecting the label on nationalist (that is, Unionist) grounds. Similarly, another study showed that regional identification among southern whites was strongest among those from the conventionally defined Deep South, weaker among those from Appalachia and more recently settled areas of Florida and the Southwest, and weakest of all among migrants to the South. (*See* Appalachians.) The same study found very little relation between thinking of oneself as a Southerner and support for racial segregation. The importance of ancestral commitment is underlined by the results of another study, which showed antisouthern sentiment among nonsouthern whites to be most common in New England, particularly among Republicans there.

Nevertheless, majorities of southern blacks and Appalachian whites and a substantial minority of migrants to the South do claim to be Southerners. Whether—or, rather, when and by whom—this claim is accepted as valid is another question, but it is clear that there is more to the matter of southern identification than having fought the Yankees and lost, several times. The importance of that experience seems to be diminishing: many residents of the South whose connection with the Lost Cause is complicated or nonexistent have begun to assert that they, too, are Southerners. Whether this assertion springs from a shared history of a more complex sort, from a shared cultural style, from current and future common interests, or from some combination of these, it is obvious that "Southerner" does not mean the same as "ex-Confederate."

Whatever its basis, the level of identification among Southerners is surprisingly high. Data collected in the 1960s from native-born white residents of the 11 former Confederate states show that, on a commonly used index of group identification, Southerners surpassed that of Roman Catholics with their religious group and that of union members with other unionists, and approached the levels of identification displayed by Jews and blacks.

DISTINCTIVENESS

Although Southerners retain a strong sense of themselves as different from other Americans, in some important respects they differ less than before. Census data deal with "residents of the South" rather than with soi-disant Southerners, but make it clear that with each passing decade Southerners are more and more "American" in the ways they earn their livings, in the returns from that undertaking, in the educational background they bring to it, and in the settings in which they do it.

The South was always an agricultural region, and at least after 1865, it was a poor region as well. As late as the 1930s two-thirds of its people were rural, and half were employed directly in agriculture; most of the remaining "urban" third lived in small towns and villages. Per capita income was roughly at the level used today to distinguish developed from underdeveloped countries, and the usual implications for social welfare, public health, and education followed. Since then, however, the South, like the rest of the United States, has become an urban, industrial, and comfortable (if not affluent) society. In the late 1970s two-thirds of the population was urban, and several southern cities were among the nation's largest and fastest growing. Less than a tenth of the population was employed in agriculture, and southern incomes, though still below the national average, were increasing steadily and closing the gap. Southerners in the 1970s were as likely as other Americans to have had some college education; the region's birth rate was close to the national average; a pattern of net migration from the region, established for over a century, had been reversed—more blacks and whites were moving to the South than from it. The economic and social problems that affected the region as a whole in the 1930s remained for the most part only in pockets, notably in parts of Appalachia and the old Cotton Belt. Economically and demographically the region was becoming much like the rest of the United States, and Southerners were becoming much like other Americans.

But there are other ways in which Southerners have been seen as different from other Americans. They are seen, and see themselves, as less energetic, less materialistic, more traditional and conventional, more religious and patriotic, more mannerly and hospitable, than other Americans. Many of these cultural generalizations existed in much their present form well before the Civil War, and it is interesting that Americans' stereotypes of Southerners resemble in some ways the traditional white stereotype of blacks. In general, non-Southerners' images of Southerners are about the same as Southerners' stereotypes of themselves, although the evaluation may differ. ("Easy-going" and "lazy," for example, express much the same perception.) Both see southern culture as, in many ways, simply the reverse of "American" culture. A study of southern college students, for instance, found that their image of "Northerners" was almost identical with their general image of "Americans," but their view of their own group had very little in common with either.

Perhaps not surprisingly, though, Northerners' images of Southerners seem to be less differentiated than Southerners' perceptions of their own group. One study in the urban Midwest, for instance, reported that the natives stereotyped migrants from both the Appalachian and lowland South indiscriminately as "hillbillies," ignoring a distinction that has been fairly important in the South. Similarly, a study of the "mental maps" of college students found that non-Southerners tended to regard the South as a (rather unappetizing) whole, ignoring differences that southern students perceived between, for instance, North and South Carolina, or Alabama and Mississippi.

The accuracy of the folk generalizations embodied in the common regional stereotypes remains undetermined, but large cultural differences between Southerners and other Americans seem to persist and in this respect the stereotypes appear to bear some relation to the facts. Research on this subject generally has been confined to whites, but there is little reason to suppose that regional differences are not much the same among blacks, allowing for the fact that many nonsouthern blacks are either southern-born or have southern-born parents.

A series of studies in the 1960s examined a variety of cultural questions taken from a number of national public opinion polls and compared the responses of white Americans from each of four major regions: the southern, northeastern, central, and western states. The South was by far the most distinctive of these "regions," and the differences between white Southerners and other white Americans were substantial—larger, on the average, than those between rural and urban people, Protestants and Roman Catholics, or manual and nonmanual workers, and about the same as those between blacks and whites. Some of the differences between southern respondents and others had decreased, but the average difference had not. If anything, it had increased, and appeared to be larger among young people than among older ones.

Another study found substantial differences between white Southerners and other white Americans in religious beliefs and practices (even comparing only Protestants), in attitudes toward the family and the local community, and in attitudes and reported behavior involving violence and the private use of force. (This last difference is also reflected in the historically higher rate of homicide and some other—but not all—violent crimes in the South.) In general, these differences had not decreased during the generation or so covered by the study, and they could not be explained in any obvious way by regional economic and demographic differences.

Although the racial attitudes of white Southerners are beginning to resemble those of other white Americans, in other respects their political attitudes have become even more distinctive over the past generation. Politically, Southerners have become more conservative, particularly with regard to issues concerning foreign policy and the size of the federal government, and the gap between the attitudes of Southerners and those of other Americans has widened.

There is no reason to suppose that the South's cultural distinctiveness is going the way of its economic and demographic peculiarity. The increasingly common experiences of urban life, education, travel outside the South, and exposure to the national mass media weaken some components of traditional southern culture (ethnocentrism and religious fundamentalism, for instance), and urban, educated Southerners in nonman-

ual occupations are increasingly "assimilated" in these respects. (These same middle-class elements seem also to be acquiring the postvocalic *r*, the absence of which has heretofore marked most southern accents.) But in other ways in which Southerners differ from the national mainstream—in political attitudes, some aspects of religious behavior, and attitudes toward violence, for instance—regional differences are at least as large among urban people as among rural ones, among the educated as among the uneducated, and among business and professional people as among blue-collar workers.

POLITICAL BEHAVIOR

Nowhere has Southerners' distinctiveness been more apparent than in their political behavior—most strikingly, of course, in their attempt to secede (although that attempt was opposed by many Appalachian whites, and southern blacks did not have a voice in the matter). Although 11 percent of white North Carolinians polled in the 1970s said that they would still favor an amicable secession, most southern whites since 1865 have been content to pursue what they viewed as their region's interests within the national political system.

From the end of Reconstruction until the 1960s, the Democratic "solid South" was almost a given in American political life. By disfranchising blacks (and many poor whites as well), the political leadership of the region assured the Democratic party of dependable majorities and became what seemed an indispensable part of national Democratic coalitions—first, the 19th-century one of "rum, Romanism, and rebellion"; later, Franklin D. Roosevelt's New Deal alignment. The region's strength in the party usually gave its representatives at least veto power over Democratic presidential nominations, and the combination of one-party politics and the seniority system in Congress gave southern senators and congressmen power out of proportion to their numbers.

Although this comfortable alliance showed signs of strain as early as 1928, the first major break occurred 20 years later, when many southern whites believed Harry S Truman to be insufficiently committed to racial segregation. Especially in the Deep South, voters defected to support Strom Thurmond, candidate of the States' Rights (Dixiecrat) party. In 1952 and 1956 these same voters returned to their habitual Democratic pattern (and in fact gave Adlai E. Stevenson his only majorities), but in 1964 the pattern was almost wholly reversed: the Deep South voted solidly for a Republican, Barry Goldwater, who had indicated his opposition to civil rights legislation. (As in 1952 and 1956, the loser in 1964 carried only states in the South.) In 1968 several of these same states again turned to a regional third-party candidate, George Wallace, who alleged that there was not "a dime's worth of difference" between the two major parties.

Although the states that delivered majorities for these third-party and unpopular major-party candidates were primarily in the Deep South, similar tendencies can be seen among white voters in other southern states, especially those in areas with large black populations. But for various reasons, in the states of the peripheral South, issues other than race—Al Smith's religion, Dwight Eisenhower's personal appeal, or straight economic interest—were sometimes allowed to play a part in determining elections.

The Voting Rights Act of 1965, by effectively guaranteeing the right of southern blacks to vote, has changed the face of southern politics, but it would be premature to say that those politics have been "nationalized." Although the outcome of southern elections may conform increasingly with the national pattern, the ingredients remain somewhat different. In 1976, for example, all the southern states delivered majorities for Jimmy Carter, the Democrat; but a majority of the region's white voters once again supported the loser: Carter won most southern states because of the votes of blacks. And had Carter not been a Southerner himself, his vote among southern whites presumably would have been even smaller.

RELIGION

If the political solid South is breaking up, the religious solid South—which antedates it—persists. About 90 percent of the region's whites identify themselves as Protestants; about half of these are Baptists and a sizable minority are Methodists. An even higher proportion of southern blacks are also Baptists or Methodists, the great majority of them in all-black denominations. Even these figures understate the religious homogeneity of most southern communities, since non-Protestants are geographically concentrated within the region.

The fact that most Southerners belong to low-church, evangelical Protestant denominations has affected the region's life in ways both obvious and subtle. The democratic polities and antiauthoritarian traditions of these churches, for example, may help to explain why black churches and church people were conspicuous in the struggle for black civil rights, while some white churches and church people were equally active in the opposition.

Southerners are orthodox in their religious beliefs and vigorous in support of their churches. Eighty-six percent of white southern Protestants told the Gallup Poll, for example, that they believed in the Devil, compared to 52 percent of white Protestants elsewhere. Other studies of belief show much the same pattern of regional difference. Southern white Protestants are more likely than other white Protestants to attend church, to listen to religious programs on the radio, to name a religious figure (usually Billy Graham) as the man they most admire, and to believe that regular church attendance is a necessary part of the Christian life. (They are even more likely to believe the last than Roman Catholics.)

Church attendance within the South also differs from patterns in the rest of the country. Outside the South, urban blue-collar Protestants are among the population groups least likely to attend church, much less likely to do so than relatively uneducated rural people. But in the South the urban working class is as likely to attend church as are similarly educated rural folk. Rural-to-urban migration in the South apparently has not disrupted established patterns of religious practice. Moreover, educated, urban, business and professional people are among the most churchgoing of Southerners; they are more likely to attend church services (or at least to say they do) than their white-collar employees

—a reversal of the nonsouthern pattern. The leadership of the New South, like that of the Old, apparently regards regular churchgoing as part of its role.

A few of the more distinctive correlates of southern religiosity—such as opposition to the sale of alcohol and support for Sunday blue laws—are waning, but much remains. For some time to come, Southerners will be characterized not only by religiosity but by religiosity of a distinctive kind.

LITERATURE AND MUSIC

The verbal emphasis of the southern religious tradition may help to explain the remarkable southern contribution to American literature. For reasons not clearly understood, many of America's outstanding writers in this century have been Southerners—William Faulkner, Thomas Wolfe, and Flannery O'Connor, to mention only three. A regional fascination with words may also be evident in the prominence of southern historians, literary critics, jurists, and journalists. This record has given the lie to H.L. Mencken's picture of the South as a cultural wasteland, but the absence of any remotely comparable excellence in, say, the visual arts does require an explanation, and that may lie in the South's religious tradition.

In another respect Southerners have contributed disproportionately to American cultural life: the region has been a great—probably the greatest—seedbed of American folk and popular music. The relation of jazz to New Orleans, of the blues and rock music to Memphis, and of "hillbilly" and country music to Nashville are well known, and lesser centers have also played a part. What has come to be regarded as distinctively American music has largely been southern music, created by black and white Southerners drawing on folk traditions developed and maintained, in part, in their churches.

Like Coca-Cola, Holiday Inns, and Kentucky Fried Chicken, however, the South's literary and musical contributions to American life have been adopted by the nation as a whole, and can no longer be viewed solely or even primarily as features of an ethnic "Southern" culture. Some of them, indeed, never were that: sadly, modern southern writers have usually found their publishers and most of their readers outside the region. In literature and music as in economy and demography, South and non-South are becoming more alike. But there is some question as to who is assimilating whom.

ETHNIC INSTITUTIONS

As a regional group, Southerners have developed economic, cultural, and political institutions that exist to serve residents of the region rather than ethnic Southerners, but the overlap between the two categories means that these institutions often function in a quasi-ethnic fashion, without imposing tests of loyalty or ancestry on their members or employees, and, indeed, without recognizing that they are doing so. Similarly, at the community level many local institutions operate in a distinctively southern way—a fact that would be recognized more often if there were more non-Southerners present to call attention to it. Studies have found regional differences, for example, in the values expressed by daily newspapers, Methodist clergymen, and public-school teachers. To be sure, these differences reflect the fact that most journalists, clergymen, and teachers in the South are themselves Southerners, but the point remains that the press, pulpit, and schoolroom in the South have by no means been entirely assimilated to "national" models and continue to define, interpret, and reinforce a regional culture.

Besides the institutions which the South has as an American region and which southern communities have as American communities, Southerners have a number of institutions analogous to those of other American ethnic groups. These include filiopietistic, ancestry-based organizations like the United Daughters of the Confederacy; militant ethnic defense associations, of which the Ku Klux Klan is only the best known; college fraternities, such as Kappa Alpha; and even a university (the University of the South, at Sewanee, Tenn.), which, like some other ethnic universities, never quite fulfilled its founders' expectations. Many of these organizations—the university is an exception—are devoted to a version of southern culture that includes white supremacy, at least as an implication, and many adopt the imagery and mythology of the Confederate cause, thereby effectively excluding much of the population of the South from association with them. A related development since the desegregation of southern public schools has been the growth of private "segregation academies," often under the auspices of Protestant churches whose opposition to parochial education was formerly unrelenting. These schools, too, preserve a version of Southern culture that includes (but is certainly not limited to) white racism.

A more comprehensive vision is represented by a few self-consciously sectional organizations like the Lamar Society—a progressive, "good government" organization on the model of Common Cause—that take pains to be biracial, and by some straightforwardly commercial enterprises, such as *Southern Living* magazine, that market their version of the good life without regard to the race or creed of their customers. By and large, members of white minority groups in the South—Jews and Roman Catholics, in particular—have chosen to assimilate with the dominant regional group while preserving their separate religious or ethnic identity, and they have been surprisingly successful in this maneuver. It remains to be seen to what extent southern blacks and the new wave of migrants to the South will elect, and be allowed to pursue, a similar course.

MIGRANTS TO AND FROM THE SOUTH

A particularly interesting group, but one about which little is known, is that composed of migrants to the South. It appears that many are southern-born, returning to their home region now that jobs and welfare benefits are becoming as attractive there as elsewhere. Most of these migrants have maintained ties to the South and should have few difficulties of assimilation, although their attitudes and expectations have, of course, been affected by their residence outside the South.

Migrants to the South who have never lived there before are a different matter. Their direct effect on the culture of the region is probably reduced by their concentration in the larger cities and in such "nonsouth-

ern" enclaves as Oak Ridge, Tenn. and Huntsville, Ala., where their contact with the native-born is often minimal. Although such enclaves have become a factor in the politics of some southern states, they have little effect on everyday life elsewhere in the region, nor does the regional setting greatly affect life within them. Moreover, some evidence suggests that migrants are self-selected to begin with—that is, they are more "southern," culturally, than non-Southerners who stay at home. Those who find themselves in situations where assimilation is desirable should have little trouble fitting in—as previous generations of migrants have done.

The situation of migrants from the South to other regions is similar: they are generally *less* "southern" than those who do not leave the region. (Thus their departure may contribute to the maintenance of cultural distinctiveness in the South.) Among these migrants, too, it is unlikely that regional identification persists beyond the first generation—or even that long if the regional accent, almost the only ethnic marker, is lost—unless they settle in southern enclaves outside the South.

Many of course have settled in such communities, in the urban Northeast and Midwest, and on the West Coast. Because such enclaves—especially of southern blacks and working-class whites—tend to be regarded as problems, they have been studied and analyzed. Here, it seems, the analogy between Southerners and immigrant ethnic groups is quite close: in these predominantly working-class areas, churches, clubs, and taverns play a role in sustaining group identity and cultural life, reinforced by frequent visits to relations "down home"; characteristically southern institutions, loyalties, and behavior patterns abound. Various studies have related the presence of southern migrants to the transformation of the Southern Baptist Church into a national (indeed, international) denomination, to votes for Carter in the 1976 presidential election, and to state-to-state variations in the homicide rate. Nostalgia for the South is a frequent theme in country music, and Bakersfield, Calif., is nicknamed "Nashville West"—testimony to its role in sustaining the culture of second-generation migrant Southerners.

Those who like their boundaries well defined should not attempt to talk about Southerners—a "quasi-ethnic" group that cuts across conventional ethnic distinctions, based on some ancestral or current connection with a region which is itself indeterminate, involving a sense of identification which, for many, depends largely on their immediate social setting. But, when all is said and done, this ill-defined mass of Americans has resisted and continues to resist the assimilating effects of powerful 20th-century political, economic, and social forces, and maintains, in the face of those forces, a sense of its own distinctiveness.

Bibliography
The literature on the South is vast; that on Southerners as a regional group something less, but still daunting. Arthur S. Link and Rembert W. Patrick, *Writing Southern History* (Baton Rouge, La., 1965), is a guide, somewhat outdated, to southern historiography. *The Journal of Southern History* contains yearly bibliographies of the periodical literature and reviews of books on the South. The ten-volume *History of the South*, under the general editorship of Wendell H. Stephenson and E. Merton Coulter (Baton Rouge, 1947–1967), is a monumental achievement. Rather more to the point, however, are some perceptive essays by southern historians: see, for example, George B. Tindall, *The Ethnic Southerners* (Baton Rouge, 1977); David Potter, *The South and the Sectional Conflict* (Baton Rouge, 1968); or C. Vann Woodward, *The Burden of Southern History*, rev. ed. (Baton Rouge, 1968). A good starting point for an examination of southern literature, and southern culture generally, is Louis D. Rubin, Jr., *A Bibliographical Guide to the Study of Southern Literature* (Baton Rouge, 1969). The "regionalist" school of social science at the University of North Carolina in the 1930s and 1940s produced an enormous body of literature on the South and its social problems. In some ways, Howard W. Odum, *Southern Regions of the United States* (Chapel Hill, N.C., 1936), is the epitome of this work. More recent (and more cultural) treatments by social scientists include Lewis Killian, *White Southerners* (New York, 1970); John Shelton Reed, *The Enduring South* (Chapel Hill, 1974); and Alfred O. Hero, *The Southerner and World Affairs* (Baton Rouge, 1965)—the last a broader examination of Southern culture than its title implies. The South has been the subject of a great deal of journalism, some of it brilliant: no bibliography would be complete without mention of Wilbur J. Cash, *The Mind of the South* (1941; reprint, London, 1971).

JOHN SHELTON REED

SOVIET MUSLIMS: *see* AZERBAIJANIS; NORTH CAUCASIANS; TATARS; TURKESTANIS

SPANIARDS

More than 250,000 Spaniards have come to the United States directly from Spain since U.S. authorities began keeping records in 1820. Spain was the First European power to establish an empire in the New World and to impose its language, religion, and customs upon the indigenous peoples. Apart from the contributions of the early explorers and settlers, however, direct Spanish immigration has gone virtually unnoticed on both sides of the Atlantic. American acquisition in the 19th century of formerly Spanish territories and the later mass immigration of Spanish-speaking peoples from Latin America are the two chief sources of the very large Hispanic population of the United States today. The third source—direct immigration from Spain—which has been fairly substantial in this century, is rarely recognized.

The timing of Spanish immigration to the United States is largely responsible for its relative invisibility. Half the Spaniards who have come since 1820 arrived

between 1900 and 1924 and were lost among the great waves of southern and eastern Europeans who arrived in the same period. Another third have arrived since 1950. For the most part these immigrants have been classified officially as "other persons of Spanish origin" and combined in official statistics with Argentinians, Colombians, and others from Central and South America. (*See* Central and South Americans; *see also* Cubans; Dominicans; Mexicans; Puerto Ricans; and Spanish.)

Emigration from Spain has been considerable since the 16th century, but most emigrants went to Latin America. The facts have not been of great interest to either U.S. or Spanish demographers; there is very little data on the background or motivations of these emigrants. Spain is composed of several highly diverse ethnic groups but little is known about which groups emigrated or why. Even the statistics gathered in Spain for persons leaving the ports of embarkation are not very informative. Indeed some scholars estimate that as high as 40 to 50 percent of Spanish emigration was clandestine. Usually emigrants left from Gibraltar or Bordeaux. Many took an indirect route, sojourning in Chile, Cuba, Mexico, or Puerto Rico before moving on to the United States. It is reasonable to assume, though not truly established, that the greatest proportion of Spanish emigrants to the United States originated in the Canary Islands, Galicia, Asturias, Catalonia, the Basque provinces and, to a lesser extent, New Castile and Andalusia. If so, Spaniards left home for many of the same reasons that motivated other emigrants from Europe. Rural poverty was undoubtedly a major factor. Whether the poverty stemmed from the *minifundia* system (parcelization of land—as in Galicia) or from the *latifundia* system (the concentration of land in the hands of a small, powerful elite—as in Andalusia), the rural poor provided not only a steady stream of emigrants, but also constant pressure on the urban working classes in Spain. War, which has caused many citizens to flee turmoil and political persecution, has also played a part. Spanish statistics show a significant increase in Spanish emigration after conflicts such as the 19th-century Carlist Wars and the Spanish Civil War (1936–1939). The Spaniards also seem to have participated in the more general displacement of Europeans that followed World War I.

Figures published by the U.S. Immigration and Naturalization Service show a steady, low rate of Spanish immigration to the United States through the first half of the 19th century, followed by a gradual increase in the second half. The start of the 20th century marked the beginning of a very large migration. Between 1901 and 1910 alone, three times more Spaniards entered the United States than had entered in any previous decade. In the following decade the numbers increased even more dramatically. However, just when Spanish immigration to America seemed to have developed momentum, the United States imposed its national-origin quota system in 1921; Spain was allotted only 912 immigrants per year, a figure that was further reduced to 131 immigrants per year soon after. Although exceptions were made in the case of skilled workers such as the Basque shepherds (*see* Basques), the possibility of a major direct Spanish contribution to the foreign stock of the United States was effectively precluded by the

quotas. Spanish immigration remained at almost insignificant levels until the 1950s, when it climbed to its current figure of about 4,000 immigrants per year.

Examination of the U.S. Census Bureau statistics on "total Spanish stock," including Spanish Basques but not persons of Spanish origin who did not come directly from Spain, clearly shows the effects of the national-origin quota system. In 1910 the population of first- and second-generation Spaniards was 36,575. By 1920 it had more than doubled to 80,317, and in 1930 the figure reached 110,607. However, by 1940 the total had declined to 85,133. From this point on, the statistics show a steady climb to 115,055 in 1950, 126,163 in 1960, and 155,156 in 1970 (see Table 1).

The decline in the number of Spaniards in the United States between 1930 and 1940 cannot be explained by the effects of the quota system alone. Instead it points to the relatively high rate of return to the homeland. Between 1899 and 1952 some 57 percent of all Spaniards in the United States returned to Spain or moved on to another country (usually in Latin America).

In the first quarter of the 20th century over 80 percent of the Spanish immigrants were male, the majority of them single. Compared to the average immigrant of the period, these Spaniards were fairly affluent, highly literate (85 percent of those over 14 years of age), and rather highly skilled (36 percent were either professionals or skilled craftsmen). One in four had been in the United States previously. Since World War II the profile of the immigrant from Spain has changed significantly. Although still a relatively highly skilled group (for the most part professionals, white-collar workers, and skilled craftsmen), since 1958 the male-to-female ratio has been approximately one to one, suggesting that families are now emigrating, as well as single men and women.

Until 1890 most Spaniards lived either in the vicinity of New York City (the major port of entry) or in the traditional Spanish colonial regions of California and Lou-

Table 1. Immigration from Spain to the United States, 1820–1976.

Year	Number
1820	139
1821–1830	2,477
1831–1840	2,125
1841–1850	2,209
1851–1860	9,298
1861–1870	6,697
1871–1880	5,266
1881–1890	4,419
1891–1900	8,731
1901–1910	27,935
1911–1920	68,611
1921–1930	28,958
1931–1940	3,258
1941–1950	2,898
1951–1960	7,894
1961–1970	44,659
1971	3,661
1972	4,284
1973	5,538
1974	4,704
1975	2,573
1976	2,758
Total	249,092

Source: U.S. Immigration and Naturalization Service, *Annual Report, 1976* (Washington, D.C., 1977), pp. 88–91.

isiana. Between 1890 and 1900 Florida began to emerge as a principal center for Spaniards. Attracted by the proximity of Cuba and the Cuban cigar industry, Asturians from the north of Spain started to gather in the Tampa area. By 1930 Tampa had a white Spanish community of 8,386, slightly more than 8 percent of its total population. The Tampa community drew the attention of many students of ethnicity and folklore during the 1930s and 1940s, to judge from articles in journals such as the *Southern Folklore Quarterly*. Although Tampa still boasts that it is the second largest single settlement of Spanish stock in the United States today (after New York City), it now comprises only 1.42 percent (5,227) of Tampa's 1970 population of 368,742. (*See also* Cubans.)

1901 also marked the start of a short-lived Spanish immigration to Hawaii. Between 1901 and 1910 census reports show the Spanish foreign-born population of the islands jumping from 202 to 1,622, but this increase lasted only a brief time. Most of these Spaniards were Andalusians who had been hired to work the sugar crop; by 1920 they had moved on to California, and the Spanish colony in Hawaii was reduced to 924 members. After 1910, especially during the 1920s, a new pattern developed. Relatively large numbers of Spaniards began to settle in industrial areas in states such as New York, New Jersey, Pennsylvania, Connecticut, Michigan, and Illinois; Asturian coal miners and metalworkers were attracted to West Virginia.

The fall of the Second Spanish Republic in 1939 produced a small but highly significant group of refugees and exiles. Though the U.S. government by no means encouraged them to do so, a number of Republicans, among them many leading Spanish intellectuals, followed the much earlier example of George Santayana (Jorge Augustín Nicolás de Santayana, 1863–1952) and came to the United States. The most prominent of these exiles were cellist Pablo Casals (1876–1973), biochemist Severo Ochoa (1905–), architect José Luis Sert (1902–), and scholars such as Américo Castro (1885–) and Juan Corominas (1905–). Leading Spanish writers such as Juan Ramón Jiménez, Pedro Salinas, Ramón Sender (1901–), and Jorge Guillén (1893–) also spent varying amounts of time in the United States, where they not only continued to write in Spanish, but also maintained their positions as major literary figures in their homeland.

There is little evidence that the Spaniards in the United States have ever worked to maintain a separate ethnic identity or community. This may be due to the strong Spanish tradition in parts of the United States, maintained by the large numbers of other peoples of Spanish origin, but their ethnic invisibility is also a consequence of the diversity of Spaniards themselves. Spanish immigrants to the United States have been less likely to regard themselves as Spaniards than as Galicians, Basques, Asturians, or Catalonians. They have settled in different areas, formed small regional associations, and usually have had only limited contact with Spaniards of other ethnic backgrounds. Only recently have Spanish immigrants begun to establish a collective ethnic presence. In New York City, for example, the old Asturian and Andalusian clubs have disappeared from the Lower West Side of Manhattan and the Atlantic Avenue section of Brooklyn. In their place

there are national clubs such as the Casa de España and the Spanish-American Citizens Club of Queens. The only surviving older groups seem to be the Centro Español (115 years old, formerly known as the Spanish Benevolent Society "La Nacional") and the Casa Galicia. The latter still claims to have almost 1,000 members. As the composition of immigration from Spain has diversified over the years, these organizations have added cultural functions, legal services, and employment listings to their traditional roles as social centers and mutual-aid societies. They have followed their members out of the traditional neighborhoods into the suburbs. It is claimed that in the area surrounding New York City there are approximately 14 associations for Spaniards, stretching from New Britain, Conn., to Carteret, N.J. It is not surprising that the immigrants from Spain have not functioned as a traditional ethnic group. In the areas where there are concentrations of Spaniards —in Tampa, Fla., in Idaho and Nevada, and in New York City—the expression of ethnic heritage takes the form established in Spain—the expression of one of Spain's several, not always harmonious, constituent cultures.

Bibliography
Imperfect, but by far the most important sources of information concerning Spanish immigration to and settlement in the United States are publications of the U.S. government. The ten-year reports of the U.S. Bureau of the Census and its *Historical Statistics of the United States, from Colonial Times to 1970* (Washington, D.C., 1975) are essential. So, too, are several publications of the U.S. Immigration and Naturalization Service: the annual reports, the reports to the Secretary of Labor, and the *Statistical Review of Immigration to the United States, 1820 to 1910*.

Spanish information is sketchy concerning emigration to the United States, but gives a good general impression of Spanish emigration trends. The Ministerio de Trabajo publishes *Estadisticas de migración exterior de España*. Other useful works are: Vicente Borregón Ribes, *La emigración española a América* (Vigo, 1952); Jesús García Fernández, *La emigración exterior de España* (Barcelona, 1965); and Luis Alfonso Martínez Cachero, *La emigración española a examen* (Madrid, 1969) and *La emigración española, ante el desarrollo económico y social* (Madrid, 1965).

Sources dealing specifically with Spanish immigration to the United States are very rare. The most accessible is R.A. Gómez, "Spanish Immigration to the United States," *The Americas* 19 (July 1962): 59–77. See also Miguel García de Saez, "Panorama general de la emigración española a los Estados Unidos," *Información comercial española* 409 (September 1967): 141–144.

For information concerning Spanish communities in the United States, especially Tampa, see the 1937, 1938, 1939, and 1941 issues of the *Southern Folklore Quarterly*. Prudencio de Pereda, *Windmills in Brooklyn* (New York, 1960), is a novel about the life of some Spanish immigrants in New York City. There is also an extensive assortment of books and articles on Basques who have come to the United States.

SPANISH

Among the many Spanish-speaking people in the West and Southwest of the United States (California, Texas, New Mexico, Arizona, Colorado, and Utah), the Spanish Americans constitute a minority that is distinctive by virtue of its history though not in all its cultural attributes. Known variously as Hispanos, Californios, and Tejanos, they often refer to themselves in Spanish as *Mexicanos* but usually repudiate the application of the English terms "Mexican" or "Mexican American" to themselves. They numbered about 1,000 (largely men) in 1598. They have possibly 850,000 descendants today. (*See also* Mexicans; Spaniards.)

The repudiation of the term Mexican is not semantic

niggling but reflects historical reality. Whereas the majority of the Mexicans in the United States came in large numbers after the 1910 Mexican Revolution and arrived as Mexican nationals in an alien society, Spanish Americans are the descendants of Hispanic settlers who entered northern New Spain in the 16th century as representatives of an expansive colonial power, imposing its way of life upon the lands where only Indians had lived previously. Having established their first long-term settlement in 1598 in the area that is now New Mexico, they served Crown and Church for more than two centuries. In return they received land grants and the title of *hidalgo* (landed gentry) for themselves and their posterity.

The northern frontier of New Spain, far removed from cities and courtly life, evolved a unique society that eventually became less caste-ridden and exploitative than most colonial societies of the world. Spanish Americans today have close ties with both Mexicans and Mexican Americans, whose culture they share, but because they became detached from the Mexican matrix while Mexico was still a Spanish colony and because they have been citizens of the United States for more than 130 years, they have a sense of separate and distinct group identity. (For a somewhat different view, *see* Mexicans.)

The first settlers of northern New Spain represented all the ethnic and regional diversity that characterized Spain in the 16th century and New Spain in the 16th and 17th centuries. Many made their way from Andalusia and Extremadura; others came from elsewhere on the Iberian peninsula, especially Galicia and the Basque provinces; and still others came from the Balearic and Canary Islands, as well as from Portugal, the Lowlands, and France and Greece. Current research shows that at least some of these families of Old World origin were Jews (Marranos) and some may have been Muslims. There were also some settlers of African or part-African origin.

The Mexican Indians who participated in the settling of New Mexico were those called Tlaxcalans, people of Nahua-speaking communities who had allied with Cortés in the conquest of the Aztecs, Tarascans, and Otomís. There were also *mestizos*, people of mixed Hispanic-Indian ancestry. The settlers of New Spain united with Indians in the region, as did the later settlers of Texas and California. Many different combinations resulted.

Exploration of New Mexico, Texas, and the California coast took place between 1528 and 1542 but the first efforts at colonization occurred in New Mexico. Although the failure of Coronado in 1540–1541 to conquer the Pueblo Indians discouraged further attempts for a time, later explorers reported mineral wealth in the area and the mining boom in northern Mexico provided the impetus for the next official effort. In 1598 the wealthy Zacatecan Juan de Oñate fulfilled his royal contract to lead soldiers, Franciscan missionaries, and settlers to northern New Mexico and there to claim the land in the name of God and his king.

The first phase of colonial life in New Mexico lasted from 1598 until 1680 when the Pueblo Indians rose up in a virtually unanimous revolt against colonial rule and its abuses. They killed or expelled all Spanish colonists but drew to their cause many Indians of Mexican or mixed origins, as well as Africans or part-Africans and mestizos, who remained. The colony retreated to Paso del Norte, present-day Ciudad Juárez on the southwest bank of the Rio Grande River. From there several attempts at restoring control in New Mexico were launched, but it was not until 1692, when Diego de Vargas visited the northern Pueblos and pledged his word to uphold all Indian rights, that the Pueblo leaders assented to the return of the Spanish. The Pueblos demanded an end to forced and unpaid Indian labor, the eradication of all vestiges of the *encomiendas,* and the exclusion of colonists from Pueblo villages. They further demanded that the colonial authorities abide by the Laws of the Indies. These laws, which had been created to protect the rights of indigenous populations, were widely violated in the 17th century but were enforced more seriously in the 18th century. Although the Pueblo Indians could not entirely free themselves of exploitation and abuses in the 18th century, they made increasing use of the services of their appointed legal advocate to resolve their grievances.

Under the encomienda system, colonial military leaders had lived near a Pueblo village, controlled land adjacent to it, and were authorized to exact labor and tribute from the Indians as compensation for their supposed military protection and provision of religious and temporal instruction. The end of this system altered the pattern of colonial land tenure and settlement. The colonists returned to New Mexico aware that they would have to support themselves. By the early 18th century there were three *villas* (principal towns) in New Spain: the capital Santa Fe, Santa Cruz de la Cañada in the Española Valley, and San Felipe de Neri (Albuquerque). These three centers served as administrative and religious headquarters for surrounding settlements. Although individual families continued to receive land grants during the 18th century, more grants were bestowed upon groups of families and the practice of making large community grants eventually predominated. The town grant provided one league (2.6 miles) in each direction for the founding of a single centralized community and its outlying agricultural and grazing lands. The community grant provided a much larger acreage able to support the establishment of new villages in succeeding generations. Some of the larger one-family grants also acquired the character of community grants over the years. The village became the basic unit of population.

The settlers of New Mexico were subsistence farmers and owners of livestock, principally sheep and goats. Although some families owned large herds, including cows, they were the exception. Sheep were the principal medium of exchange in an economy that was chronically short of cash. Paucity of means did not, however, extinguish the pride which settlers took in their hidalgo status and they constantly sought to improve their lot by a variety of gainful activities.

The most gainful and also the most dangerous of these activities was volunteer militia service, owed by every able-bodied man. Throughout the 18th century, settlers and their Indian allies systematically plundered their victims; booty consisted of livestock, crops, and people, with a pronounced preference for infants and women. These captives became members of the households in which they served and often married into set-

tler families. At marriage they were supposed to regain their freedom.

The life of a captive was hard, but captives were not hereditary chattel slaves. Masters were obliged to provide baptism, and a baptized person could not be sold. Usually masters served as baptismal godparents, binding themselves to a ritual kin relationship. Profit could be made from captives only if the captor was able to sell his booty prior to baptism to some chronically short-handed fellow settler. The nomadic tribes from whom captives were taken retaliated by raiding Hispanic settlements and capturing settler women and children. From time to time, captives would be exchanged, providing both the settler and the tribal communities with growing numbers of people versed in the speech and customs of the opposite group. These individuals became interpreters and mediators in intercultural relations, but it must be added that the colonists took and kept more captives than their adversaries.

The predatory side of Hispanic-Indian relations was partly offset by active trade relations. More prevalent than the occasional or annual fairs sponsored by colonial authorities was small-scale but constant unofficial barter. Small parties went out on the plains, often combining their trading search with buffalo hunting. Some traveled to the Great Basin to trade with bands of Ute Indians. Much of the trade was in contraband goods; horses which the traders had stolen from their fellow settlers were in especially great demand. *Punche* tobacco, another popular trade item, was a semidomesticated leaf which the settlers grew and traded without paying the required tariff.

Although expansion of empire was the objective of 17th-century colonization of New Mexico, a new situation early in the 18th century put pressure upon colonial authorities to hold the colony at all costs and to establish new footholds at the northern frontier. French traders and trappers had armed the Pawnees and extended their influence among the Indians of the western plains. In 1696 La Salle established a temporary post at Matagorda Bay. The Spanish government dispatched soldiers and Franciscans to build military posts and missions in the areas of San Antonio, Adaes (Nacogdoches), and Bahía (Goliad), but had little success in developing civilian settlements. In 1739 a royal decree ordered the establishment of a new colony, to be called Nuevo Santander, which would encompass the present Mexican state of Tamaulipas and the lower Rio Grande Valley of modern Texas. José de Escandón was in charge and by 1749 had succeeded in founding several settlements along both banks of the lower Rio Grande.

There was no Spanish colony in California until 1769, after Russians had established a trading settlement near San Francisco. As in Texas, initial efforts had primarily military and religious objectives. The famous Franciscan missionary Fray Junípero Serra founded 21 missions on or near the California coast. The presidio and mission of San Diego were founded in 1769 and Monterey was established the following year.

Unlike those of Texas or New Mexico, the California missions were soon thriving. The large population of coastal Indians, hitherto hunters, fisherfolk, and gatherers, readily learned the skills of irrigation agriculture and cattle herding. But although the missions prospered, the coastal Indians succumbed in large numbers to previously unknown diseases, such as smallpox and measles. Subject also to the missionaries' persistent efforts to eradicate indigenous ways and beliefs, entire tribal groups disappeared. Survivors entered the Hispanic society, usually in its lower ranks, or fled and joined the unconverted inland tribes.

Mexico won its independence from Spain in 1821. This affected Mexico's northern frontier in several ways. First and most crucial for later developments, the Spanish policy of not permitting colonies to trade with neighboring nations was replaced by the Mexican desire for active trade relations with their neighbor to the north. Hoping to defend the area from constant Indian raids by building up the population, the Mexican government invited immigrants from the United States to take up large grants of land in Texas.

The flood of immigration into Texas from the United States soon greatly exceeded that from Mexico. In 1821, before U.S. immigration to the area began, the non-Indian population of Texas was estimated at 4,000; in six years it grew to 10,000 and by 1830 it was 20,000. The Anglo-Americans heavily outnumbered the Hispanic population of Texas in 1835, when a rebellion broke out in opposition to the Mexican government's new policy of limiting the number of U.S. settlers. Texas (claiming modern-day New Mexico as far west as the Rio Grande) soon came under U.S. control, first as an independent republic and in 1845 as a state of the Union.

Most U.S. citizens saw this transition as the working of Manifest Destiny, but in Mexico it was seen as an act of savage rapine. The fledgling Mexican nation, however, was unable to hold any of the northern territories. In 1846 New Mexico, including western Colorado, Nevada, most of Utah and Arizona, and also California, fell to General Stephen W. Kearny's advancing troops. By the Treaty of Guadalupe Hidalgo, signed in 1848, all of this territory was ceded to the United States by the Mexican government, with written guarantees for the religious, civil, and property rights of the former Mexican nationals who now found themselves annexed by the United States. However, until the end of World War I the Mexican government repeatedly protested violations of this treaty involving the flagrant denial of civil and property rights. Over 130 years later, the issue of Spanish and Mexican land grants continues to be a subject of concern to Spanish Americans, who have tried repeatedly to win redress of persisting grievances.

When Texas became a state in 1845, the Spanish or Tejano settlers were a minority. In California the gold rush brought a flood of 87,000 immigrants from stateside, totally swamping 13,000 Spanish Californios and the inland Indian tribes, and in 1850 California received statehood. For generations, however, Anglos continued to be a minority in New Mexico and Arizona, which were not granted statehood until 1912. As late as 1940 the combined Hispanic-Indian population of New Mexico outnumbered the Anglo-Americans and the Spanish colonial tradition prevailed in many villages.

On the other hand, in California, Texas, Colorado, and Utah there was a substantial influx of farm workers and miners from Mexico between the wars and the Mexicans soon outnumbered the colonial Spanish Americans. It is hard though not impossible to find in those states the colonial traditions which are still apparent in New Mexico. It is in New Mexico alone that

the Penitentes—La Cofradía de Nuestro Padre Jesús Nazareno (Brotherhood of Our Father Jesus of Nazareth)—still flourish as a Catholic lay society. They are both a religious survival of the colonial period and an organization for mutual aid.

In the last 30 years Spanish Americans have settled in urban centers such as Los Angeles and San Diego, Calif., Salt Lake City and Provo, Utah, Denver and Pueblo, Colo., and other cities all over the nation, driven from their home villages in search of wage work.

Although they are consistently lumped with second- and third-generation Mexican Americans in the U.S. Census records, Hispanos, Tejanos, and Californios are generally more conservative of their traditional values of the expanded family, the Catholic faith, the Spanish language, and the home community, usually in a land-grant village, than other Spanish-speaking groups. In New Mexico, although less than 50 percent of the Hispanos now live in their home villages, the rural orientation of the city dwellers and of former New Mexicans now living in other states is still noticeable.

By 1970 two-thirds of the population of Spanish Americans resided in New Mexico, Colorado, Texas, and California; the remaining third was scattered over other states, including Alaska and Hawaii. The median age of the Spanish-American population was 19.3 years in 1970, a good deal younger than the median age of the U.S. population as a whole, which was 27.9 years. One out of eight Spanish Americans was under five years of age, suggesting a high fertility rate in the 1960s. In 1970 the average Spanish-American family of 4.2 persons was larger than the average U.S. family unit of 3.1.

Educational achievement among Spanish Americans has risen substantially since the early 20th century. One out of five Spanish Americans of high-school-completion age in 1920 graduated from high school, but by 1970 close to seven out of ten graduated; furthermore, two out of every five males and three out of ten females went on to attend college in the 1960s.

Since the colonial period, the large majority of Spanish Americans have earned their living as subsistence farmers and livestock raisers. In the early 20th century, as they began to move into the growing urban centers of the far western states, the proportion employed in agriculture declined steadily. However, the census does not record the number of part-time farmers and farm workers who supplement their income from other sources. Many Spanish Americans fall into this category.

Between 1950 and 1970 a growing proportion of Spanish Americans secured better-paying and higher-status jobs. This improvement in occupation was probably connected with the gradually rising levels of school achievement and urban residence of the population. The proportion of professionals increased from one in every thirty employed men in 1950 to one in every ten in 1970. Nearly half of employed males in 1950 worked at low-status jobs as farmers, farm laborers, and service workers, compared with only one-fourth by 1970. But the median income of Spanish-American families in 1969 was only $7,770—over $2,000 less than that of non-Spanish white families.

In the foreseeable future, Spanish Americans will probably maintain their distinctiveness within the Hispanic population of the United States, while continuing to join other Hispanic groups in the political quest for equal opportunity and recognition of their shared culture.

Bibliography
H.H. Bancroft, *History of California, 1542–1890,* 7 vols. (San Francisco, 1884–1890), *History of Texas and the North Mexican States,* 2 vols. (San Francisco, 1884–1889), and *History of New Mexico and Arizona* (San Francisco, 1889) provide historical background, but contain many outmoded interpretations. Carlos Castañeda, *Our Catholic Heritage in Texas,* 7 vols. (1936–1958; reprint, New York, 1976), and *The Mexican Side of the Texas Revolution* (1928; reprint, New York, 1976) are outstanding source books. A good treatment of issues and consequences of the Mexican-American War is Frederick Merk, *Manifest Destiny and Mission in American History* (New York, 1966). Anthropological interpretations are found in Edward H. Spicer, *Cycles of Conquest* (Tucson, Ariz., 1967), which deals with intercultural relations, and the chapter "Spanish Americans of New Mexico" in Margaret Mead, ed., *Cultural Patterns and Technical Change* (New York, 1954); also see Allan G. Harper, Kalervo Oberg, and Andrew Cordova, *Man and Resources in the Middle Rio Grande Valley* (Albuquerque, N.Mex., 1943). A sociological study dealing with Spanish Americans as something of a side issue is Leo Grebler, Joan Moore, and Ralph Guzman, *The Mexican American People* (Los Angeles, 1970). A.J. Jaffe, Ruth M. Cullen, and Thomas D. Boswell, *Spanish Americans in the United States: Changing Demographic Characteristics* (New York, Research Institute for the Study of Man, 1976) abstracts data from previous studies and from the U.S. Census up to 1970 for New Mexico.

FRANCES LEON QUINTANA

SPANISH-SURNAME

The U.S. censuses of 1950, 1960, and 1970 tabulated information about "white persons of Spanish surname" living in five southwestern states—Arizona, California, Colorado, New Mexico, and Texas. Until 1930 the census treated the Hispanic population of the Southwest in the same way it did ethnic groups of European origin. The foreign-born and their American-born children were enumerated, but members of the third and later generations were reported simply as "native whites of native parentage." The planners of the 1930 Census sought to broaden the coverage of peoples of Hispanic origin in the Southwest by adding the category "of Mexican race," and putting it within the larger rubric of "other races" along with Indians and Orientals. Hispanics with fair skin and middle- or upper-class status apparently were not enumerated as members of the "Mexican race." Protest from Mexican-American groups and the Mexican government led the Bureau of the Census to abandon the category thereafter. The Spanish-surname identification introduced in 1950 had a similar aim: to enumerate Hispanics of third and later generations in their principal area of concentration, the five southwestern states. Census coders identified "whites of Spanish surname" on the basis of a list of about 700 of the most common Spanish surnames, referring dubious cases to specialists.

The census tabulations of Spanish-surname data, though a rich source of information, have several drawbacks. They fail to distinguish a variety of different groups (*see* Central and South Americans; Cubans; Dominicans; Mexicans; Puerto Ricans; Spaniards; Spanish) and they are limited to only one region of the country. Most important, surname is a far from perfect indicator of ethnic allegiance: some Hispanics have changed their names without changing their ethnic allegiances, and the large number of ethnically mixed marriages has produced people with distinctive Hispanic names but with no sense of Hispanic identity, and vice versa. Direct questions about an individual's "ori-

gin or descent," first employed in the 1970 Census, are considerably more useful. However, analysis of the experience of Hispanic groups in the 1950s and 1960s will necessarily continue to depend heavily upon the Spanish-surname data. The 1980 Census asks respondents to specify their origin or descent and to explain whether they are Mexican American, Mexican or Chicano, Puerto Rican, Cuban, Other Spanish, or Not Spanish.

SPOKANS: *see* AMERICAN INDIANS

STOCKBRIDGES: *see* AMERICAN INDIANS

SURINAMESE: *see* CENTRAL AND SOUTH AMERICANS

SURVEY RESEARCH

Survey research on ethnicity in American society is derived from many theoretical perspectives and employs a wide array of definitions of ethnicity, few of which are entirely compatible with the others. Its results are varied and often contradictory. Ethnicity has been found to correlate with almost everything from attitudes about pain to socioeconomic achievements. Here we review mainly survey research on family, religion, social stratification, and politics, because studies in these areas predominate. Within these topical limitations, we emphasize classical survey studies that have been widely cited; studies based on nationally representative probability samples (as opposed to regional or local surveys, surveys of single ethnic groups, or surveys based on nonprobability samples); and studies that employ multivariate statistical methodologies.

Survey research means any effort to gain information about ethnic phenomena through the use of relatively standardized measuring instruments, such as questionnaires and interviews, applied to samples drawn from a population that is of theoretical interest. Surveys are thus differentiated from censuses, participant observations, ethnographic or historical studies, and journalistic accounts, and from other forms of data collection and research procedure common in the social sciences. Of these several distinctions, that between surveys and censuses is the most difficult to sustain; indeed, it may be said that censuses reveal for certain what surveys only estimate within known boundaries of error. For this reason, and because the U.S. Census has recently gathered much of its ethnic information from sample surveys rather than from enumerations of the entire population, some relevant census materials are also reviewed here. Technical aspects—sampling, probability and statistical inference, survey design, and analysis of survey data—are treated very lightly here; this review focuses on the substance rather than the methods of survey research.

DEFINING ETHNICITY

Ethnicity is one of the most elusive social science concepts. Wevolod Isajew reviewed 65 studies in sociology and anthropology and reported that only 13 defined this key term; further analysis of those 13 revealed little if any consistency in definition. Presumably authoritative sources are of equally little help. The inaugural editorial of *Ethnicity* (1974), one of relatively few journals devoted exclusively to ethnic studies, said only

that ethnicity "is social diversity that is not related to age, social class, or sex. Hence it includes diversity that arises because of race, religion, nationality, language, and even geography." That is a definition by exclusion and example, but at least the examples have reasonably precise empirical referents. Andrew Greeley in *Ethnicity in the United States* (1974) defined ethnic groups as "collectives based on presumed common origin," which apparently includes even age, sex, and social class! *Webster's New World Dictionary* tells us only that ethnicity refers to "any of the basic divisions or groups of mankind, as distinguished by customs, characteristics, language, etc."

As with many analytic social science concepts, it is far easier to point to instances of ethnic phenomena than to formulate a rigorous theoretical definition of them. Therefore we will present a brief sampling of what survey research tells us about the differences in the dimensions of family, religious practices, social stratification, and politics among groups defined by race, religion, national origin, language, and region.

MEASURING ETHNICITY

Just as there is no generally agreed-upon definition of ethnicity, there is little consensus on how to measure it, either in sample surveys or in other research situations. In sample surveys, data are obtained either by direct observation of individuals and households or through answers to questions asked of individuals. A person's or household's ethnicity is defined operationally as: what the unit appears to be to the survey interviewer (direct observation), what the individuals claim when asked about their ethnicity, or what can be inferred from respondents' reported genealogies. All three approaches involve potential measurement defects of unknown magnitudes.

Consider first the direct-observation approach. Some ethnic traits, such as race or language, are relatively visible to a survey interviewer and can be recorded directly, but many other components of ethnicity, such as religion or national origin, are not observable. Even judgments about a person's race cannot always be made reliably or validly, because genetic mixing in the United States has produced a spectrum of skin pigmentation, facial features, and hair textures, which makes the judgment regarding a person's race somewhat ambiguous, especially at the margins. Recognizing this ambiguity, most survey research organizations instruct their interviewers to record a respondent's race without asking about it, "only if there is *no* doubt in your mind." If there is some doubt, interviewers are instructed to ask, "What race do you consider yourself?" (Both these examples, taken from the National Opinion Research Center (NORC) 1977 General Social Survey, are typical of how survey organizations deal with the measurement of race.)

Perhaps the easiest approach is to ask respondents what their ethnic group is. This has some attractive features; presumably the group named is the one most likely to affect the claimant's behavior and values. The dangers are also quite clear: if one is interested in reconstructing from respondents' claimed ethnicities the racial and/or national origins of the population that the survey is sampling, the claims may be regarded as potentially biased by several measurement defects.

The quality of the resulting information depends on respondents' knowledge about their ancestry and on their resolution of the complexities of their ethnic lineage. Consider the seemingly straightforward issue of the religious denomination to which one "belongs." One person's response may be a rough assessment of the predominant denomination among many that he has attended; another's response may mean his parents' denomination; still another may be a current denominational affiliation.

Ethnicity as race or national origin poses even more complex problems. A person's lineage may be a web of considerable complexity incorporating the diverse marriages and liaisons of many lines of ancestry, doubling with each generation traced back into the past. A person who appears to be black may easily have some white ancestors. Even those first-generation immigrants who know where they migrated from may find it difficult to place their origins within the current configuration of nations because of boundary shifts, national conquests, and the like. Even when a specific national origin is known, many peoples have migrated, or been conquered in the past; although a person may know for certain that his parents migrated from Sicily, his ancestry may involve a mixture of Spanish, Norman, Schwabian, and Arab.

Although it is not likely that a researcher would be interested in the full detail of a genealogy going back more than a few generations, it is not clear whether one, two, three, four, or more generations are sufficient, and deciding on a given generational depth does not necessarily provide any degree of security. Almost all persons know about their parents, but fewer know about their grandparents, and still fewer about their great-grandparents. Anyone's recollection in detail of his lineage is bound to be selective and thus of uncertain truth value.

Surveys usually resolve this troublesome measurement problem by asking respondents to specify the predominant nationality in their ethnic background. The question on national origin in the NORC surveys reads, "From what countries or parts of the world did your ancestors come?" If respondents name more than one country, as they often do, NORC asks, "Which of these countries do you feel closer to?" Likewise, the Survey Research Center at the University of Michigan asks, "In addition to being an American, what do you consider as your *main* ethnic or nationality group?" These solutions to the measurement problem, however, result in operational definitions of ethnicity that consist of at least three distinct elements: the extent of an individual's knowledge of the objective features of his lineage; the singularity or multiplicity of origins in that lineage; and the individual's subjective identification with one of those origins. (And, as the social anthropologists have been quick to point out, a person's reported lineage in any society is somewhat of a fictional construct.) Thus, ethnicity as operationally defined in the typical sample survey taps both objective and subjective features of the concept, and the exact combination of the two is largely unknown.

The decennial U.S. Census employs a different solution to the problem of lineage complexity. The national origins of members of households are probed only one generation back from the respondent, so studies of nationality based on census data refer mainly to "foreign-born" and "persons of foreign-born stock"—those whose parents were foreign-born. The national origins of parents are known in the vast majority of cases, but some nationality groups go undetected, such as Puerto Ricans, because Puerto Rico is not a foreign nation. But the most serious problem with the census measures is that beyond the second generation all persons merge into an undifferentiated "native born of native parentage" category. Studies that purport to show how the settlement patterns of Germans, for example, change from census to census show information only on persons born in Germany or whose parents were born in that country. For nationality groups whose immigration streams have largely ceased, the census categories become increasingly irrelevant as succeeding generations are absorbed into the undifferentiated group. The main sources of information for such ethnic groups (and for religious ethnicity) have been sample surveys, which at least attempt to measure national origins regardless of the generational distance between the respondents and the immigrant generation.

Despite some very early precursors, such as W.E.B. Du Bois's classic study, *The Philadelphia Negro* (1899), large-scale surveys of ethnicity are quite recent. Modern research based on sound principles of probability sampling and survey design began with the advent of national opinion polling in the 1930s. Some of the most significant advances in the methodology were developed only after World War II. As late as 1961 Gerhard Lenski referred to the sample survey as "a new research technique." The use of statistical methods in handling large numbers of variables simultaneously (which, as we note later, is critical to the analysis of ethnicity in contemporary American society) dates largely from the utilization of computers in the mid-1960s, and some of the most promising developments have emerged only in the mid-1970s. Thus survey research on ethnicity based on sophisticated statistical methods is in its infancy.

Interest in ethnic issues was apparent even in the very first surveys and polls. The earliest Gallup Poll of which we have a record, conducted in September 1936, included background questions on respondents' race, rural-urban residence, and state. Questions about religion first appeared in the Gallup series in February 1939, and a question on national origins (of respondents and of their parents) first appeared in the poll for January 1941. Most of these items remain part of Gallup's standard data.

The first large-scale voting study conducted by the Bureau of Applied Social Research at Columbia University and reported in *The People's Choice* (1944), a study of the 1940 presidential vote in Erie County, Ohio, paid close attention to the role of ethnicity and religion in determining voting choices. Many of the findings of that early study—for example, that at all socioeconomic levels, Catholics are more likely than Protestants to vote Democratic—have been replicated in every subsequent voting study, so that many findings of *The People's Choice* seem commonplace today. In its time, however, the study provided the first valid empirical information bearing on a very loosely defined set of expectations (half hypothesis, half prejudice) about the political propensities of American ethnic groups.

Before the advent of surveys, most academic studies

of ethnicity were primarily ethnographic or historical, as many are today; usually, these studies focus on a single ethnic group in a single community. These studies constitute an invaluable part of the existing literature on American ethnicity, and many of the theoretical controversies pursued by survey researchers derive from historical or ethnographic sources. However, the following advantages of survey studies may be noted.

First, surveys provide precise quantitative information about ethnic phenomena. Questions such as, "What proportion of Jewish Americans voted for Jimmy Carter in 1976?" or "What proportion of third-generation Italian Americans are married to Italian-American spouses?" or "What is the average family size of various ethnic groups?" are essentially impossible to answer without sample survey research.

Second, properly designed sample surveys allow one to make valid inferences about characteristics of the larger population from which the survey sample was drawn. An ethnographic study of Italian-American life in the West End of Boston, such as Herbert Gans's *Urban Villagers* (1962), simply cannot provide valid quantitative information even about Italian Americans in Boston, much less in the whole nation. In contrast, sample surveys allow one to state, within known limits of error, quite precisely what is true about an ethnic group—not just what is true about the local set of subjects studied (as ethnographies can also do) but what is true in general of the population from which the sample was taken. At the same time, even a very large and well-conducted national sample survey would not allow one to say very much about Italian Americans in Boston's West End. The point, then, is not that surveys are superior to all other methods for all analytic purposes, but that surveys provide different kinds of information that are more useful for some purposes and less useful for others.

Finally, surveys facilitate comparative analysis of ethnic groups, as single-group ethnographies do not. For most analytic purposes, we are less interested in what is true about a given ethnic group (for example, that 45 percent of American Catholics attend religious services once a week or more), than in what is true about one group relative to others (although 45 percent of American Catholics attend services once a week or more, the same is true for only 27 percent of the nation's Protestants and for 14 percent of the nation's Jews). Information about one group becomes meaningful only as it is compared to similar information about other groups.

LIMITATIONS

Despite its considerable promise, survey research on ethnicity has certain recurring problems that warrant discussion. First, surveys and other studies have taught us that the various ethnic phenomena are strongly intercorrelated, often to such a degree that it is difficult to determine which component of ethnicity is primarily responsible for some empirically observed result. Consider that most Americans from British backgrounds are also Protestants, that virtually all Italian Americans are Catholics, that nearly all blacks are Protestant, that more than 80 percent of the white South is Protestant, that most Spanish-speaking Americans are Catholics, and so on. When we find that Italian-American families are typically larger than British-American families, we cannot be certain whether this difference reflects religion or national origin. When we observe some distinctive characteristic of the white South, we cannot be sure that it reflects a regional phenomenon or simply that most white Southerners are Protestant.

Similar analytic problems are posed by the correlations between ethnicity variables and certain other variables, such as social class and region. Most blacks and Hispanics are concentrated at the lower end of the socioeconomic spectrum, the white South is disproportionately working class, most Jews are middle class, and many Catholic ethnic groups (with some important exceptions discussed later) rank lower in socioeconomic achievements than certain white Protestant ethnic groups. So when we find significant differences between blacks and Jews, we are not sure whether they reflect ethnicity or socioeconomic status. As Irving Levine and Judith Herman have pointed out, "One of the reasons for the difficulty of sifting out the precise influence of ethnicity in America is that it is so often directly correlated with economic status" (*Dissent*, 1972).

Ethnicity is also correlated with geography and city size. In the 1970s Jews were heavily concentrated in New York, Los Angeles, and Miami, but elsewhere were predominantly suburban. Blacks were concentrated in the rural South and the urban North; white Southerners were disproportionately small-towners; Scandinavian Americans were most often found in the upper Midwest; Irish Americans, in the Northeast; Italian Americans in the Middle Atlantic states, and so forth.

Because of these intercorrelations, most social scientists have come to believe that American ethnicity can be properly studied only through the use of multivariate methods, that is, statistical methods that allow one to hold one (or more) variables, such as social class, constant while assessing the effects of a second variable, such as religion, on a third variable, such as the presidential vote in the last election. Without the use of multivariate methods, the causal web connecting ethnicity with other phenomena becomes so entangled that it is impossible to interpret; thus, little of substance can be concluded from the early survey literature, simply because not enough variables were controlled to make us feel confident that the results actually reflect the ethnic phenomena they are said to reflect.

A second recurring problem is that ethnic variables tend to be qualitative or nominal in nature, whereas the more advanced multivariate techniques require at least ordinal and, preferably, interval level measurements. (These distinctions, which are germane to the modern theory of measurement, cannot be fully explicated here; for additional information, see the bibliography.) The irony is that while the interrelationships among ethnic phenomena require that they be analyzed in a multivariate framework, the nature of the ethnicity variable makes this difficult to accomplish. As already noted, the statistical models apparently well suited to this task have been developed only very recently.

A final problem to note in this connection is that national surveys of the usual size (1,500 to 2,000 interviews) do not contain enough cases to provide statistically reliable information about the full range of ethnic groups. For example, the 1977 NORC General Social

Survey mentioned earlier was based on a total of 1,530 cases, about the average for national surveys of this sort. Yet among these 1,530 cases, there were only 35 Jews, 69 Italian Americans, a mere 9 Puerto Ricans, and so on. These numbers are scarcely adequate for the computation of univariate descriptive statistics (average years of education or average family size) for separate ethnic groups and are totally inadequate for more complex issues, such as generational differences in the family size of Italian Americans. The most obvious solution to this problem, greatly increasing the number of cases, is impractical because face-to-face interviews are very expensive.

Greeley has attempted to circumvent the sample-size problem by combining cases from seven separate surveys (*Ethnicity in the United States*), and yet "even with a sample of 9,593 respondents, there is an insufficient number in many American ethnic groups for any information to be provided about them." The composite data file, for example, was unable to differentiate among English, Scottish, and Welsh respondents; all three were combined into a single "British-American" category. Greeley's "Scandinavian Americans" was an amalgam of Norwegians, Swedes, Finns, and Danes; the "Spanish-speaking" included Puerto Ricans, Cubans, and even some Spaniards; and so on. These combinations, although plausible, are arbitrary and are mandated not by our understanding of American ethnicity so much as by the need to maintain adequate sample sizes in each of the analysis groups.

It should also be mentioned that the sample-size problem interacts with the problem of definition mentioned earlier. With no generally agreed-upon definition of ethnicity, survey researchers are free to define this concept more or less as they wish. The operational definition can then be made according to the optimal use of the cases available for analysis. What constitutes optimal use, varies considerably from one survey to the next, as does the operational definition of ethnicity. This greatly impedes the comparison of findings between studies and poses a distinct barrier to cumulative knowledge in this field.

RACE

Since the founding of this country, race has been a population characteristic of such consistently strong political interest that the U.S. Census has always tallied racial composition. Hence the best data on race differences come from the decennial censuses and since World War II from the Current Population Survey conducted quarterly as a sample survey by the Bureau of the Census. According to the 1970 U.S. Census, just over 87 percent of the American population are white; the remaining 13 percent are nonwhite. Afro-Americans are the largest nonwhite racial group (11.1 percent of the total 1970 population), followed by American Indians (0.39 percent), Japanese (0.29 percent), Chinese (0.21 percent), Filipinos (0.17 percent), and a small fraction of others. Of these many racial groups, only whites and blacks appear in sufficient numbers in average-size surveys to support detailed analysis; in the 1977 NORC survey, for example, only 4 respondents named China as the national origin of their ancestors (there were also 4 Filipinos and 4 Japanese). For all practical purposes

the survey literature on race in American society is focused exclusively on black–white differences. It is, nonetheless, a huge literature, the relevant studies easily numbering in the thousands.

Race and Social Stratification Inequalities between blacks and whites in education, occupation, and economic position are well documented. In the March 1974 Current Population Survey (based on about 56,000 interviews), the median years of education for whites was 12.3, and for blacks only 10.7; among whites, 13.3 percent had completed four or more years of college, while among blacks the figure was 5.9 percent. In general, the educational deficit for blacks increased with age; black–white educational differences, that is, were less pronounced among the young. Still, even among the youngest cohorts (age 25 to 29) whites were about twice as likely as blacks to have completed four years of college (16.9 percent to 7.9 percent). Half the whites (50.6 percent) but only a third of the blacks (33.0 percent) were employed in white-collar occupations; whites were almost twice as likely to hold higher-status professional, technical, and managerial positions (26.0 percent to 14.5 percent). Median income for white families was $13,356 in 1974; for blacks, $7,808. Nearly a third of all black families (31.4 percent) but only 8.9 percent of white families fell below the federal poverty line. The general patterns revealed in these and all other available survey data are unmistakable: on all relevant variables, blacks are strongly disadvantaged relative to whites.

A persistent concern of surveys on racial differences has been whether the relative socioeconomic position of American blacks is improving, worsening, or holding constant over time. Recent analyses reveal modest but significant trends toward greater black–white equality on nearly all indicators. Erdman Palmore and Frank Whittington concluded, on the basis of census and Bureau of Labor Statistics data for 1940 through 1968, that "nonwhites have made substantial, though somewhat uneven, progress toward equality in the economic areas of income, occupation, and weeks worked, as well as in education and quality of housing" (*Social Forces*, 1970). A review of data from the Current Population Surveys led Norval Glenn to conclude, "Black progress, both absolute and relative to whites, has generally accelerated since the mid-1960s" (*Social Stratification*, 1974). Glenn's projections from current trends, however, suggested that equality in occupation will not occur until the year 2004, and equality of family income, not until 2010; although change is clearly visible, it is proceeding at a slow pace. The Income Dynamics panel survey reported in James Morgan et al., *Five Thousand American Families* (1974) showed the same trend; relative to whites, "minority group members are exhibiting more rapid *rates* of economic improvement, particularly those in the middle years, ages 25 to 54." Sar Levitan and associates, in *Still a Dream* (1975), reached very similar conclusions about the rate of black gains relative to whites. Survey evidence from several sources, then, reveals significant improvements in the socioeconomic position of blacks but suggests that without further acceleration, the general pattern of inequality will persist at least for the remainder of this century.

What accounts for the generally inferior, even if improving, socioeconomic position of blacks? One com-

mon hypothesis posits a vicious cycle of poverty; poor black families lack the resources to provide good health care and quality education for their children, making it difficult or impossible for the children to rise above the economic position of their parents. However, a very sophisticated analysis of data from the Occupational Changes in a Generation survey led O. Dudley Duncan to reject this hypothesis. These data suggested, in fact, that parental socioeconomic status is less important in determining achievement for blacks than for whites. For example, even if "we could eliminate the Negro's handicap with respect to socio-economic level of the family of orientation . . . only the lesser part of the [black-white] gaps in education, occupational status, and income would be bridged." The data further suggested that even if all initial differences between blacks and whites in parental status, family size, educational attainment, and occupational position were removed, about three-eighths of the income gap would remain. On the basis of these calculations, Duncan concluded that it is not a "vicious cycle of poverty" that is responsible for the lower socioeconomic position of blacks, but rather racial discrimination. The relative disadvantage of blacks "stems largely not from the legacy of poverty but from the legacy of race."

If Duncan's analysis was substantially correct, then the trends toward greater equality noted above should be accompanied by declines in racial discrimination and improvements in white attitudes toward blacks. All available time-series survey data support this conclusion, despite periodic alarmist speculation about the white backlash. Angus Campbell's *White Attitudes toward Black People* (1971) reviewed evidence from the Survey Research Center's biannual election surveys and concluded, "It cannot be doubted that since World War II there has been a massive shift in the racial outlooks of white Americans" toward more tolerant or liberal attitudes. White racial attitudes have been continuously monitored by the National Opinion Research Center since 1944, and an analysis of the 1970s data by Garth Taylor, Paul Sheatsley, and Andrew Greeley revealed a continuation of the long-standing trend toward more positive attitudes with an extraordinary leap forward in racial tolerance between 1970 and 1972—just when the white backlash was thought to be taking effect. A similar trend is also evident in the Harris and Gallup polls as well.

Polls and general population surveys, of course, can only plot attitude trends in the general population. But the discrimination that impinges most directly on the socioeconomic life chances of blacks is that arising in decisions by corporations, government agencies, schools, and other social institutions, about which the typical sample survey reveals relatively little. One pioneering effort to study institutional discrimination through the use of surveys was that of Peter Rossi, Richard Berk, and Bettye Eidson, *The Roots of Urban Discontent* (1974).

Race and Family One of the most bitter controversies in social science in recent years has focused on the role of the black family in perpetuating relative socioeconomic disadvantage. The controversy was ignited by Daniel P. Moynihan in *The Negro Family* (1965), known universally as the Moynihan Report. Moynihan

argued that the black family "is the fundamental source of the weakness of the Negro community at the present time." At the root of the "tangle of pathology," Moynihan argued, is the strong matriarchal tendency of the black family, which "seriously retards the progress of the group as a whole." Because the father is often absent, young black males lack a role model. Absence of a father also leads to greater participation in the labor force by black women, which reduces the time they can spend caring for and socializing their children. The results of this situation are increased incidences among black youth of delinquency, crime, and other social pathologies, which also interfere with success in school and in the occupational world. Moynihan argued, "a national effort towards the problems of Negro Americans must be directed towards the question of family structure."

The available survey evidence tends to confirm Moynihan's depiction on most objective details. Every known study has shown that rates of divorce and especially separation are higher for blacks than for whites. In the 1974 Current Population Survey, 31.8 percent of all black families and only 9.9 percent of white families were headed by females. Black families are also larger than white families, meaning that lower levels of resources are spread over more people. Finally, the rate of labor-force participation is higher among black women than white women; the reverse is true for men. These data tend to sustain the notion of black matriarchy.

However, the large majority of all families, black and white, are headed by men; differences between blacks and whites in family structure are those of degree, not of kind. Moynihan argued that even in intact black families, the roles of husband and wife are often reversed, with the wife playing the dominant role, and that here too matriarchy has ultimately negative consequences for children's socioeconomic achievements. Herbert Hyman and John S. Reed reviewed several nationally representative surveys bearing on this issue in *Public Opinion Quarterly* 33 (1969), however, and found that the data did not confirm this point. Seven items dealing with relative male and female influence in the family (drawn from three separate national surveys) revealed that "the actual white pattern, contrary to expectation, is almost identical to that for Negro families." Differences between black and white families on all aspects examined were "small and inconsistent." The authors concluded, "there seems to be little evidence for any social-psychological pattern of matriarchy peculiarly characteristic of the Negro family."

Race and Religion Compared to whites, blacks are religiously a very distinct group, although this distinctiveness tends to diminish when region and social status are controlled. First, they are overwhelmingly Protestant. In the 1977 NORC General Social Survey, 87.5 percent of the black respondents (and 63.3 percent of the whites) claimed Protestant as their religious affiliation; the remainder were evenly divided between Catholic and none. (No black Jews appeared in the sample.) Further, black Protestants are heavily concentrated in a single denomination—Baptist. Slightly more than three-quarters of the black Protestants in the NORC survey listed Baptist as their religious affiliation (among white Protestants, the Baptist proportion was only

about 35 percent); most of the remaining black Protestants are Methodist, with only a few in other denominations.

Many surveys have found that blacks tend to be more devout than whites. In *The Religious Factor* (1961) Gerhard Lenski found black Protestants in Detroit slightly more likely than white Protestants to score high on doctrinal orthodoxy (belief in God and life after death, for example) and much more likely to score high on devotionalism (basically, frequency of prayer: the proportions that scored high on this measure were 68 percent for black and 29 percent for white Protestants). Several indicators from the NORC survey showed the same pattern. One question asked respondents whether their religious identification was strong or not very strong. About 53 percent of the blacks, but only 40 percent of the whites, responded "strong." A question on church attendance revealed that 62 percent of the blacks attended religious services two to three times a month or more; for whites, the figure was 42 percent. A large portion of the black distinctiveness on these measures of religiosity, however, may reflect mainly that blacks are generally less educated than whites and are disproportionately southern; statistical controls for education and region tend to diminish the differences substantially.

Perhaps the most provocative question raised by social scientists about black religiosity is whether it tends to increase or decrease the levels of black militancy, political action, and other efforts for equality by blacks. On the one hand, it has been argued that religious emphasis on salvation in the afterlife tends to depress concern for the inequities of the present (religion as opiate). On the other hand, the prominence of black religious leaders in the civil rights movement and the apparent correspondence between the ideology of the movement and the fundamental tenets of Christianity suggest an opposite relationship. Gary Marx analyzed national survey data bearing directly on this issue, and the bulk of the evidence was consistent with the first hypothesis. Blacks belonging to Protestant "sects and cults" were the least militant of all groups, followed by black Baptists, then black Methodists. The most militant blacks were those belonging to predominantly white denominations, such as Episcopalians and Presbyterians. Militancy also increased as the subjective importance of religion decreased (the most militant blacks were those who said their religion was "not at all important" to them); likewise, militance was highest among the religiously least orthodox. Both these relations held when controls for education, age, region, sex, and denomination were introduced. Further analysis revealed that even the relatively religious militants in the sample tended to have a "temporal" rather than an "other-worldly" religious outlook (that is, their religiosity was more secular than chiliastic). "The net effect of [black] religion," Marx wrote, "is clearly to inhibit attitudes of protest."

A number of more recent studies supplement Marx's findings. One of these, by Jon Alston and associates in the *Journal for the Scientific Study of Religion* (1972) reported that the relationship between religiosity and militance among blacks was generally weaker in their 1969 survey than it had been in Marx's 1964 survey;

also, among black males, blacks over 45, and Baptists, "high religiosity is clearly associated with low militancy," as Marx reported, whereas among black females, blacks under 45, and non-Baptists, the more religious respondents were "*more*, not less, likely to be militant." Thus, the relationship between religiosity and militancy seems to differ for different categories of blacks. There is also survey evidence to suggest that this relationship varies according to the kind of religious beliefs. Hart Nelson found that sect-like religious beliefs tended to decrease the level of black militancy, as Marx reported, but that more orthodox beliefs had just the opposite effect. "To the extent that beliefs affect militancy, the direction of effect depends on the character of the beliefs held."

Race and the Political Process In general, blacks are as distinct politically as they are religiously. First, they are strongly Democratic in party preference, by far the most solid bloc in the Democratic coalition. In the 1977 NORC survey roughly 80 percent of the blacks (and 55 percent of the whites) identified with the Democratic party; of those voting in 1972, 83 percent of the blacks (but only a third of the whites) voted for George McGovern; of those voting in 1976, more than 90 percent of the blacks (but only 51 percent of the whites) voted for Carter. Evidence reported by Norman Nie and others further suggested that the Democratic preference of blacks has increased somewhat in recent years.

Blacks are less likely than whites to vote in presidential elections, however, or to participate in other forms of politics. In the 1972 election only 52 percent of the eligible black population cast a vote for president, while 71 percent of eligible whites voted. Similar black–white gaps in political participation have been noted in virtually all analyses of the issue, for example, in Sidney Verba and Norman Nie, *Participation in America* (1972). However, a long-term trend (from the early 1950s to the early 1970s) toward a decline in the difference between black and white participation has been discerned in the time-series survey data reported in *The Changing American Voter* (1976), presumably reflecting the effects of civil rights legislation of the 1960s.

In political outlook, many survey analysts have noted that blacks are consistently the most liberal of the major population subgroups on virtually all political issues. Also they are usually found to be more politically alienated than whites, to feel less politically effective, and to have less trust and confidence in the political system (see James Wright, *The Dissent of the Governed*, 1976). Survey studies of young black children strongly suggest that these feelings of political alienation are part of the early political socialization of black youth.

The most comprehensive review (based on a 1967 national survey) of black participation in normal political channels, by Sidney Verba and Norman Nie, showed that although in the aggregate blacks participated less than whites, this pattern was reversed when controls for socioeconomic status were introduced. At all levels of socioeconomic status, blacks actually participated more than whites. "It is not being black *per se* but the socioeconomic conditions that usually accompany being black that lead to lower participation." The data also revealed that political participation among blacks

increased sharply with the level of "group consciousness" and that this effect was independent of socioeconomic status. Rising group consciousness among blacks over the past decade may be partly responsible for the narrowing of the black–white political participation gap.

In recent years the attention of survey researchers has turned to determinants of black participation in unconventional modes of political behavior, especially riots, protests, and sit-ins. Age and sex have consistently proved to be major predictors: young black males provide the vanguard. Interestingly, socioeconomic variables are not strongly related to riot or protest participation; several survey studies have shown no significant differences between protesters and nonprotesters in education, occupational prestige, income, or unemployment status. In general, the best predictors of unconventional political participation are attitudinal: protesters are usually found to score higher than nonprotesters on questions of race consciousness, awareness of black–white socioeconomic disparities, and political alienation, especially distrust of local government and police, as reported by Peter Rossi and associates in *The Roots of Urban Discontent*. Jeffrey Paige suggested that the attitudes most favorable to riot participation are a combination of the feeling that something can be done with the feeling that something must be done; he presented survey evidence from Newark, N.J., to support his hypothesis.

RELIGION

The U.S. Census has resisted including a question about religion in the decennial census, with the sole exception of a brief experiment in the 1957 Current Population Survey, so most of what is known about religious groupings in modern American society has been learned through survey research. The religious preference question on the 1977 NORC survey revealed that 65.9 percent of the population is Protestant, 24.5 percent Catholic, and 2.3 percent Jewish. An additional 6.1 percent stated preference for no religion, and the remaining 1.2 percent provided some other answer, such as Hindu or Muslim. Equivalent but more detailed data from the Survey Research Center's 1976 national survey are shown in Table 1. The results of these two independently conducted surveys differed by less than five-tenths of a percentage point.

The surveys on religion are dominated by Protestant–Catholic comparisons, despite widespread recognition that such comparisons are far too broad to be truly meaningful. At minimum, denominational differences among Protestants and national-origin differences among Catholics should be considered, as has been forcefully argued by Charles Glock and Rodney Stark in *Religion and Society in Tension* (1965) and by Harold Abramson in *Ethnic Diversity in Catholic America* (1973).

Among the Protestant denominations, Baptists are by far the most numerous if distinctions among the various kinds are ignored, followed by Methodists, Lutherans, Presbyterians, Episcopalians, and Pentecostalists, with the remaining Protestants widely dispersed among many minor denominations. Among Catholics, those of Irish, German, and Italian ancestry are about

Table 1. Religious affiliations of the population of the United States.

Group	Percentage
Protestant	
Methodist	10.95
Baptist	9.38
Southern Baptist	8.51
Lutheran	8.27
Presbyterian	4.36
Episcopalian	2.34
Pentecostal	2.16
Church of Christ	1.88
Primitive Baptist	1.74
Congregational	1.53
Church of God	0.73
All other[a]	10.39
Nontraditional Christian	
Latter-day Saints	1.53
All other[b]	1.40
Catholic[c]	24.80
Jewish	2.37
Other religions[d]	1.26
Agnostic, atheistic, or no religious preference	6.38

Source: 1976 Survey Research Center American National Election Study.
a. All other Protestant denominations and sects, each representing less than 1 percent of the total.
b. Includes Christian Scientists, Spiritualists, Unitarians, Jehovah's Witnesses, Quakers, and Universalists.
c. Includes Roman Catholics (N = 707) and Greek Rite Catholics (N = 4).
d. Includes Eastern Orthodox, Muslims, Buddhists, Hindus, Bahai, and others.

equally numerous, followed by Slavs, French, Polish, and Hispanics in approximately that order.

Religion and Religiosity Within each of the three major religious categories, there are sizable individual variations in the level of religiosity. The "strength of religion" question on the 1977 NORC survey revealed that substantially less than half of the American population is strongly attached to its religious preference; the proportions answering "strong" were 40 percent of Catholics, 41 percent of Protestants, and 45 percent of Jews. These data suggest extensive secularization of the population, but other data, reviewed below, do not support this depiction.

The 1977 NORC survey on attendance at religious services showed a similar pattern. For the population as a whole the average rate of attendance was about once a month, but this included some 13.9 percent who never attended and 8.1 percent who said they attended "several times a week." The survey data revealed that just over a third of the population (35.7 percent) attended their place of worship once a year or less, while just under a third (29.7 percent) attended once a week or more.

Rates of attendance at religious services vary considerably across religious groupings. Catholics are by far the most frequent attenders: almost half the Catholics (44.7 percent) attend once a week or more, and only about a fourth (24.7 percent) attend once a year or less. Protestants are next most frequent attenders: a quarter (27.2 percent) attend weekly, a third (34.5 percent) attend once a year or less. Jews are the least frequent attenders by a wide margin, with more than half (54.3 percent) attending once a year or less. These patterns have been noted by virtually every survey researcher who has inquired into the matter.

The very low attendance rates among Jews in his Detroit survey caused Lenski to wonder whether the secu-

larization of the American Jewish community was essentially complete. However, although only 12 percent of the Jews in his sample reported regular weekly attendance at religious services, all of the married Jews in the sample had Jewish spouses, some 96 percent reported that all or nearly all of their relatives were Jewish, and just over three-quarters reported that all or nearly all of their close friends were also Jewish. Lenski concluded that "while the *associational* bond is weak in the Jewish group, the *communal* bond is extremely strong." "Jew," in short, seems to be more an ethnic than a religious identification.

Andrew Greeley's *The Denominational Society* (1972) also suggested that Catholics are the most "religious" group in the society, followed in order by Protestants and Jews. Essentially all Christians (Protestant and Catholic) and about three-quarters of Jews professed to believe in God; 99 percent of the Catholics, 94 percent of the Protestants, and 70 percent of the Jews believed in prayer. The sharpest Jewish–Gentile differences, unsurprisingly, occurred on questions about Jesus Christ and beliefs in life after death; 83 percent of the Catholics, 78 percent of the Protestants, but only 17 percent of the Jews believed that there is a life after death. The sharpest Protestant-Catholic differences were not on doctrinal or belief items but on questions concerning church attendance and membership. Lenski's Detroit data, however, showed a somewhat different pattern: 62 percent of his white Catholics scored high on religious orthodoxy, against only 32 percent of the white Protestants; the comparable figures on "devotionalism" were 47 percent and 29 percent, respectively. Lenski's findings, it should be noted, may reflect the national origins of the Detroit metropolitan area population.

Charles Glock and Rodney Stark in *Religion and Society in Tension* have presented survey evidence, mostly from California, on Protestant denominational difference in religious beliefs. The most liberal, or least orthodox, of the denominations discussed by these authors were Congregationalists, Methodists, and Episcopalians; the least liberal were the Missouri Synod Lutherans, Southern Baptists, and the splinter sects. Survey data presented by N. Jay Demerath, *Social Class and American Protestantism* (1965), revealed a very similar pattern.

The most persistent debate about religious beliefs concerns the progess of secularization, which is sometimes said to be the inevitable consequence of industrialization. The survey data seem to be unclear on this issue: different analysts have found different patterns over time, depending on the kinds of questions investigated and the time points compared. Andrew Greeley's review of 1952 and 1965 survey data on religious belief revealed constancy in Gentile beliefs over 13 years but large declines in such beliefs among Jews. Questions on religious practices revealed much the same pattern, with the possible exception of an increase in church attendance and Bible reading among Gentiles over the years. Analysis of the responses by age did not show extensive secularization among youth: young Catholics held about the same beliefs as older Catholics; Protestant youth were only somewhat less orthodox than older Protestants.

Bradley Hertel and Hart Nelson reviewed survey data from 1957 and 1968 on trends in two beliefs that are central to Christian orthodoxy: belief in life after death and belief in the devil. Both these items showed the same interesting pattern over time: the proportion professing belief was virtually constant over the 11-year period, but the proportion expressing disbelief increased significantly, and the proportion saying they were uncertain showed a corresponding decrease. "These findings are not so much evidence for a decline in belief as for an increasing polarization of American opinion concerning the traditional tenets of Christianity."

Demerath discussed the many methodological problems in the time-series data, especially those deriving from official church sources, and reviewed Gallup data on church attendance from 1939 to 1965. No clear upward or downward pattern could be discerned, and the continuation of the time series to date has shown the same year-to-year fluctuations with no sharp overall trend. Demerath's review of survey questions on religious beliefs suggest "a liberalization, if not loss, of faith. And yet it is difficult to tell whether this represents a long-term trend or a reversion to an earlier state after a recrudescence of traditionalism." In sum, no clear pattern of religious change, either positive or negative, can be found in any of the available survey data; rather, one is impressed by the relative constancy across time. On these grounds alone it appears that the secularization hypothesis should be treated with skepticism.

Religion, Marriage, and Family   Lenski presented the most detailed survey evidence on the relationships between religion and family variables, although the date of the survey (1958) and the location (Detroit) make generalizations to present-day American society hazardous. Lenski reported higher divorce rates among Protestants than Catholics (Jews had the lowest rate of all); data from the 1977 NORC survey showed the same pattern, but the differences between religions were very small. Catholics also tended to come from larger families and to have larger families; again, recent data showed much smaller differences. Recent surveys of fertility revealed nearly identical patterns of contraceptive use for both Protestant and Catholic women, a substantial change over previous periods. The NORC survey also showed that white Protestants tend to marry at an earlier age than either white Catholics or Jews: the mean ages at marriage for the three groups are 21.8, 23.1, and 24.8 years, respectively. Regarding extended-kin networks, Lenski reported that 20 percent of the white Protestants in Detroit had no relatives living in Detroit other than those in the household; for Catholics, the figure was 10 percent, and for Jews, 6 percent.

Parental values for children show little consistent variation across the three major religious groups. Melvin Kohn in *Class and Conformity* (1969) reported, "a comparison of Catholics, Protestants, and Jews shows only that Jews value acting as a boy or girl should more highly than do Catholics or Protestants, and that Catholics value obedience more highly than do Protestants or Jews." Conformity values for children tended to increase with church attendance for all groups, but the pattern was weak. Lenski reported that Catholic mothers were more likely to use physical punishment to discipline children than were Protestant mothers.

Most Americans continue to practice the religious faith of their parents; in the 1977 NORC survey, 94 percent of the Protestants, 89 percent of the Catholics, and 91 percent of the Jews reported that their current religious preference was the same as the "religion in which you were raised." All other surveys have reported a similar result.

Most American marriages are religiously endogamous. In the 1977 NORC survey 84.6 percent of the married respondents were married to same-religion spouses; this varied from a high of 89.6 percent among Protestants to a low of 79.2 percent among the Jews. These figures are very close to those reported by Lenski almost two decades ago, suggesting an extremely stable pattern over time.

Early studies of religious and ethnic endogamy led to the formulation of the "triple melting pot" hypothesis, enunciated most fully in Will Herberg's *Protestant, Catholic, Jew* (1955). Comparisons of intermarriage rates for the years 1870, 1900, 1930, and 1940 in New Haven led Ruby Jo Kennedy to conclude that "while strict ethnic endogamy is loosening, religious endogamy is persisting." In short, people were marrying outside their nationality group but remaining inside their religious group. From this, Kennedy, Herberg, and others concluded that religion was replacing national origin as an organizing principle of American social life. However, a sizable body of survey data contradicts the general thrust of this prediction, especially the work of Harold Abramson and Andrew Greeley.

Generational dynamics play an important role in the triple-melting-pot thesis, according to which the children of immigrants (the second generation) are said to seek Americanization above all else and to be anxious to discard the ethnic ways of the old country. Therefore the second generation is less likely to marry endogamously, either ethnically or religiously, and less likely to continue its parents' religious practices or faith. The third generation, in contrast, is sufficiently removed from the old country that their Americanism is unquestioned; the expectation is that they and later generations will revive the culture, customs, and behaviors discarded by the second generation. The general idea that ethnoreligiosity dips in the second generation and revives in third and subsequent generations is commonly referred to as the three-generations hypothesis.

Most tests of the hypothesis have focused on church attendance as the critical dependent variable. Lenski's Detroit data did not support the expectation of a dip in the second generation: second-generation Catholics in Detroit were actually more likely to attend church regularly than first-generation Catholics; among Protestants, there was no difference. But the data did show attendance increases in third and later generations for both religious groups. Subsequent national survey data revealed essentially identical patterns, as did more recent survey data from New York City. It appears that the hypothesis of a second-generation dip in church attendance can be safely discarded.

Religion and Social Stratification Since Max Weber's famous essay on "The Protestant Ethic and the Spirit of Capitalism," it has been widely assumed that there are large socioeconomic differences among the major religious groups. Protestants are said to benefit from a value complex that is well suited to success in a capitalist economic system and thus to rise more rapidly in the various economic hierarchies of education, occupation, and income than Catholics. The position of Jews is somewhat ambiguous: their socioeconomic status depends more on their "acceptability" to the Gentile majority than on their own values; given the opportunity to compete equally, Jews tend to rise quickly into the middle and upper-middle classes.

Hadley Cantril was perhaps the first to bring national survey data to bear on this issue. The poll data he analyzed in 1943 confirmed the conventional wisdom of that time: Catholics were generally less educated and of lower social class than Protestants, especially outside the South. Other national survey data from the early-to-middle 1950s routinely showed the same general pattern, as did Lenski's Detroit data. The Detroit survey showed that white Protestants were higher in the class structure than Catholics and were more likely to be upwardly mobile if they started low. Lenski's analysis of a series of items related to work values further showed that "Protestantism is conducive to more positive attitudes toward those positions in society which are more demanding (and also more rewarding), while Catholicism is conducive to more positive attitudes toward the less demanding (and hence less rewarding) positions." Thus, value differences apparently played some role in generating the socioeconomic differences, consistent with the Protestant-ethic hypothesis.

Separate investigations by Sidney Goldstein and Galen Gockel provided information on the status allocation process intervening between religious groups and economic success. Both studies reported that income differences among the three major religious groupings virtually disappeared once educational attainment and occupation were controlled, suggesting that with rising education in all groups (and, consequently, equal competition for better-status jobs), the income differentials would ultimately disappear. Goldstein concluded "that both education and occupation play a much more crucial role than does religion itself in influencing the income levels of members of the three religious groups." However, this does not tell us why there are initial differences in education and subsequently in occupation.

The most comprehensive review of national survey data through the middle 1960s was by Norval Glenn and Ruth Hyland. Their analysis of 18 surveys conducted between 1943 and 1965, showed dramatic trends in the relative standing of Protestants and Catholics, with the early differences noted by Cantril and others disappearing, then reversing, over time. "In 1943, Protestants were well above Catholics in economic status, whereas by 1964 Catholics were clearly above Protestants." Further analysis showed, consistent with the Goldstein and Gockel findings, that the "change in relative economic status undoubtedly resulted from pronounced changes in relative occupational and educational standings." On the many points of Protestant-Catholic comparison, the only apparent lingering Protestant advantage was in a slightly greater proportion attending college. Later, even this advantage seemed to have disappeared: in the 1977 NORC survey, 8.8 percent of the Protestants and 8.7 percent of the Catholics (but 20 percent of the Jews) held bachelor's degrees, and 5.1 percent of the Protestants, 3.1 percent of the Catho-

lics, and 22.9 percent of the Jews held postgraduate degrees.

More recently, attention has turned to status differences within the Protestant and Catholic categories, especially to denominational differences among Protestants and national-origin differences among Catholics. Results from Greeley's composite sample, reported in *Ethnicity, Denomination, and Inequality* (1976), showed that among the Protestant denominations, the Episcopalians and Presbyterians ranked at the top of the hierarchies of education, occupational prestige, and income, with Methodists and Lutherans in the middle and Baptists at the bottom. Results by national origin among Catholics revealed that Irish Catholics ranked first on all measures of socioeconomic status, followed in approximate order by Germans, Poles, Italians, Slavs, French, and Spanish-speaking. (Slightly different rank-orders obtained on each major status dimension.) In terms of family income, Irish Catholics were higher than any other large religioethnic group except Jews. More recent survey data analyzed by Clark Roof showed approximately the same patterns, except that several of the higher-status Protestant denominations showed higher average incomes than Irish Catholics. Both studies make it clear, however, that Catholics as a group, and Irish Catholics in particular, have made enormous socioeconomic strides in recent decades and that many Catholics have now joined white Protestants in the nation's educational and income elite. Certainly the stereotype of the working-class Catholic should be abandoned.

Religion and Politics It is well known that Catholics and Jews are disproportionately Democratic in party preference. In the 1977 NORC survey, 67 percent of the Catholics, 71 percent of the Jews, but only 49.5 percent of the Protestants preferred the Democratic party. The Catholic vote has been heavily Democratic in every presidential election since World War II, with the exception of 1972. Of those voting in the 1972 election, 71 percent of the Jews, 45 percent of the Catholics, and 24 percent of the Protestants voted for McGovern— the lowest Democratic proportions in modern history. The 1976 votes were more characteristic: of those voting in that election, 65 percent of the Jews, 63 percent of the Catholics, and 45 percent of the Protestants voted for Carter. The strong Democratic preferences of Catholics are independent of social class, region, income, and city size; Catholics of every social description are more Democratic than Protestants, according to Richard Hamilton, in *Class and Politics in the United States* (1972).

Recently there has been speculation that Catholics may be leaving the Democratic coalition, first, because they have become more middle class in recent years and should thus be more attracted to the more conservative Republican party, and second, because as a group Catholics reject many of the policy initiatives recently undertaken by the Democratic party, especially on issues such as abortion and equal rights for blacks. The best available trend data, however, do not support this depiction. *The Changing American Voter* presented time-series data on party identification among Catholics for 1952 to 1972; these data showed a small decline in the proportion of Democrats, but also a small decline in the proportion of Republicans and a substantial increase in the proportion of independents. Focusing just on those who identify with one of the parties and omitting independents, the data showed that "if anything, the Catholic population has, compared with the rest of the public, become more distinctively Democratic over time." The data further revealed differences among Catholics according to national origin: in particular, Irish and Polish Catholics were somewhat more Democratic than other nationality groups. "But in none of the Catholic ethnic groups do we see evidence of a desertion of the Democratic party . . . In short, when it comes to party identification, there is no evidence of a shift toward the Republican party among Catholics."

Catholics also tend to participate in politics more than Protestants, even with all relevant sociodemographic variables controlled. In 1972 Catholics were about ten percentage points more likely to vote than Protestants (Jewish participation was higher still); in 1976 the Catholic edge in turnout was about five points. In the typology of the Verba-Nie survey (*Participation in America*), Protestants were overrepresented among the politically inactive and among "communalists" (those who participate in local but not national politics), while Catholics were overrepresented among the more politically active.

Most of the available survey evidence suggests that Catholics are somewhat more liberal than Protestants, again in contrast to the stereotype. Richard Hamilton reported that Catholics were more liberal than Protestants on each of a series of "economic liberalism" items, including questions on national health insurance and a guaranteed annual wage. Several investigators have reported that Catholics were also more pacifist than Protestants in their views of the wars in Korea and Vietnam. Leonard Broom and Norval Glenn reviewed seven national surveys conducted between 1953 and 1961 and reported that "in views towards racial and ethnic minorities, Jews were the most tolerant and Protestants were the least tolerant"; again, Catholics were more tolerant than Protestants. However, Angus Campbell's analysis of 1968 survey data from 15 large American cities (in *White Attitudes toward Black People*) revealed no consistent Protestant–Catholic differences on seven questions about race. In no case are the Protestant–Catholic differences in political attitudes large, but the common hypothesis that Catholics are politically more conservative than Protestants can be decisively rejected.

Religious Group Identity How salient are the categories of Protestant, Catholic, and Jew in the group identities of the American population? Angus Campbell and associates in *The American Voter* (1964) and Donald Matthews and James Prothro in *Negroes and the New Southern Politics* (1966) presented some interesting survey data on this topic. These studies constructed "group identification" scales for white Southerners, Negroes, Catholics, Jews, and union members from responses to two questions: "Would you say you feel pretty close to [Southerners, Jews, etc., depending on the category that best fits the respondent] or that you don't feel much closer to them than you do to other people?" and "How much interest would you say you have in how [Southerners, Jews, etc.] as a whole are getting along in this country—a good deal, some, or not too much?" The highest level of group identity was reg-

istered by southern Negroes (2.5 out of a possible 3), followed by nonsouthern Negroes and Jews (2.2 in both cases). White Southerners (1.9) and union members (1.8) came next, with Catholics (1.6) registering the lowest level of group identity of all groups questioned. These data thus suggest that on the whole Jews have a much higher sense of group identity than Catholics and that Catholics have little group identity. How Protestants would score on such a measure is obviously not known, but it seems unlikely that they would score higher than Catholics.

More recent and possibly more interesting national survey data on the topic are contained in Survey Research Center's 1972 presidential election study. Respondents were asked to state how close they felt to a list of groups (including Protestants, Catholics, and Jews) and to state which of the groups on the list they felt closest to. Although 72 percent of the respondents in the survey said they were Protestants, only 30 percent of the respondents felt close to Protestants, suggesting very little group cohesiveness among the Protestant community. (How many Protestants said they felt close to Protestants cannot be determined, because the original data are not available for secondary analysis as of this writing.) Group cohesiveness seemed much higher among Catholics: 25 percent of the respondents said they were Catholics, and 18 percent felt close to Catholics. The Jewish pattern was perhaps the most interesting of all: the proportion of those who felt close to Jews (7.4 percent) was higher than the proportion of Jews (2.4 percent) in the survey. All these proportions, however, dropped off sharply on the question about which group respondents felt closest to: in all, 3.3 percent mentioned Protestants, 3.0 percent mentioned Catholics, and 0.8 percent mentioned Jews as the group they felt closest to; religious group identities thus accounted for only about 7 percent of all mentions. In contrast, two groups defined by age (young people and old people) received about a quarter of all mentions, and four groups defined by social class (businessmen, poor people, middle-class people, and workingmen) received more than 40 percent. Thus age and social class, pointedly omitted from the earlier definition of ethnicity, seem substantially more important than religion in terms of subjective attachments to social groups.

NATIONAL ORIGIN

The term "ethnic group" most commonly refers to social groups based on national origin. As of the 1970 Census more than 95 percent of the American population was native-born, so "national origin" typically means the origins of one's ancestors. Some of the measurement problems posed have been discussed earlier: not everyone knows for sure where their ancestors came from, and many people have ancestors from more than one country. A related problem is that in some cases national origin is rather meaningless unless one distinguishes between British and French Canadians, Protestant and Catholic Irish, Jewish and Gentile Poles, perhaps even between northern and southern Italians. For these reasons national origin is somewhat difficult to measure in surveys. The measurement problem, plus the fact that most national-origin groups appear in very small numbers in average-size surveys, plus the com-

mon expectation that nationality differences will disappear under the combined onslaught of assimilation, Americanization, and the other homogenizing trends of modern society, have meant that the survey literature on national origin is substantially less developed than on either religion or race. The only truly comprehensive treatments are Andrew Greeley's *Ethnicity in the United States* and Harold Abramson's *Ethnic Diversity in Catholic America,* which can be consulted for additional details on virtually all topics discussed here.

The term "ethnic" is frequently used by journalists and other popular writers to refer primarily to non-English nationality groups, especially those from central or southern Europe. This usage obscures the important and frequently overlooked fact that the ancestors of every individual in the United States migrated here from somewhere else. (This is true even of American Indians, whose remote ancestors migrated from Asia to North America via the Bering Strait.) In this sense, every U.S. citizen is equally ethnic. Much of the scholarly work on national origins has focused on immigrants from central and southern Europe, and this emphasis is necessarily reflected in our review, but, it must be borne in mind that national origin is a variable upon which everyone can be located, with greater or lesser accuracy. The question of national origins has rarely been raised concerning American blacks, whose diverse origins on the African continent are apparently considered to be largely irrelevant to current concerns. In this sense there is apparent implicit agreement that American blacks have been thoroughly "assimilated."

The 1977 NORC survey asked respondents, "From what countries or part of the world did your ancestors come?" About 12 percent of the respondents were unable to name any country at all, 55 percent named only one country, and the remaining 33 percent named two or more countries. Of those naming multiple countries, about two-thirds were able to choose one as the country they felt closest to; the other third were unable to choose. Combining those who were unable to name any country and those who could not choose among several countries, we conclude that the measurement of national origin is problematic for about a fourth of the present-day U.S. population. Earlier surveys have shown nearly identical results.

Table 2 presents responses to the national-origin question from the 1977 survey and gives a relatively precise view of the remarkable diversity of the present-day U.S. population. The proportions shown in the table agree closely with all other national surveys that we have examined. People of German origin are the most numerous nationality group in the population, representing slightly more than one-fifth of the total. Given their preponderance, it is surprising that there are not more studies of German Americans, but the fact is that the Irish, Italians, and Poles have been much more commonly studied. Next to Germany, England and Wales, Ireland, and Africa are the most frequently mentioned countries of origin. Italians, Scots, and Poles are also relatively numerous; each of the other groups has less than 3 percent of the total.

Nationality: Family and Community Although there is a rich ethnographic and historiographic literature on the ethnic family among non-British nationality groups, survey investigations of this topic are rather

Table 2. National origins of the American population.

Country of origin	Percentage
Germany	22.4
England and Wales	14.7
Ireland	10.2
Africa	8.8
Italy	6.1
Scotland	3.9
Poland	3.0
Canada	2.4
Netherlands	2.4
France	2.3
Russia	2.0
Mexico	2.0
Norway	1.9
Sweden	1.8
Czechoslovakia	1.5
Austria	1.3
Denmark	1.1
Finland	1.1
Hungary	1.1
Spain	0.8
Puerto Rico	0.8
Switzerland	0.6
West Indies	0.6
Japan	0.4
Philippines	0.4
China	0.4
Greece	0.3
All others	6.0

Source: 1977 NORC General Social Survey.

rare. Greeley's composite survey data showed that among Catholic ethnic groups, Hispanics had the highest incidence of divorce and separation, and the Irish had the lowest; among Protestants, the Irish had the highest rate and the Scandinavians the lowest. In all cases the differences in divorce and separation rates across nationalities were quite small. Greeley also reported data on the average number of children for each woman who had ever married, by national origin: among Catholics, Germans and Hispanics tended to have the largest families (3.1 children for both groups) and Slavs the smallest (2.3); among Protestants, the largest families were shown for Irish and Scandinavians (2.7) and the smallest for British (2.3); Jews of all nationalities had the smallest families of all.

The most detailed investigation of nationality endogamy (marriage within the group) and related marital factors is Abramson's *Ethnic Diversity in Catholic America.* Although restricted to Catholics, the work was based on nationally representative survey data. Data were presented both for respondents in the survey and for their parents, thus giving some sense of trends over time. As might be expected from the triple-melting-pot thesis, the parental generation was substantially more endogamous than the respondent generation: in all, 80 percent of the parents' marriages were ethnically endogamous, as against 55 percent of the respondents' marriages, a relatively steep decline in one generation. In both generations the extent of endogamy was related to the time of immigration: more recent immigrant groups (Spanish-speaking and eastern European) were more endogamous than groups that immigrated earlier. In the parental generation, ethnic endogamy ranged from a high of 96 percent among the Spanish-speaking to a low of 27 percent among the British; the same rank order obtained in the respondent generation, but the rates dropped to a high of 88 percent and a low of 12 percent. In the respondent generation, there was a majority of endogamous marriages among every nationality except the British. Between generations the proportion of endogamous marriages declined for all groups—by 47 percentage points among eastern Europeans but only by 8 points among Hispanics. "The expectation of increased exogamy from parents to respondents has been clearly substantiated by the data, but the rate of change . . . varies considerably with the different ethnic backgrounds."

It should be noted that Abramson's data most likely overstated the endogamy of the parental generation, because Catholics who married and converted to another denomination and raised their children as non-Catholics were not included in his sample of Catholic respondents.

When Catholic nationality groups marry outside their group, what groups do they marry into? One might expect a pattern of homogamy to emerge, that is, marriage between nationality groups with similar cultural characteristics, but in general, Abramson's data did not strongly support this hypothesis. "Selection does not relate to homogamous considerations of cultural similarity or generational background in the United States to the degree one might have anticipated." French Canadians, Irish, and Germans showed relatively more homogamy than the other groups, and the British relatively less, but the patterns were not strong in any case. For the most part, the patterns of exogamy are about as one would expect on the basis of chance alone—roughly proportional to the size of each nationality group in the population.

Among Catholic nationality groups, endogamy is highest when the proportion of potential spouses of the same nationality is highest. Thus endogamy rates are related to region; in general, regions with the highest proportion of Catholics also show the highest Catholic endogamy rates. Endogamy is also strongly related to city size: respondents from rural areas are more endogamous than those from urban areas, even with region controlled. Further, endogamy is highest among older respondents and lowest among younger respondents and is slightly higher for females than for males, but the sex difference is not pronounced. Finally, the rate of exogamy tends to increase sharply with education. Multivariate analysis of these data reveals that generation, city size, and education are strong and consistent predictors of endogamy even with all other variables controlled.

William McCready has raised the interesting question of whether variation in certain "family values" among present-day American ethnics can be plausibly linked to family differences in the country of origin; that is, can facts about the Italian family as observed in Italy be related in any way to characteristics of the Italian-American family? Predictions regarding values such as "mother salience," "traditionalism" in the home, and so on were derived from the ethnographic and historical literature on family life in the countries of origin, then tested on national American survey data. The ethnohistorical literature tells us that the Italian family in Italy is strongly patriarchal and that the woman's role in the family is very traditionally defined; do these general patterns hold true for contemporary Italian-

American families as well? When hypotheses of this sort were tested for Italians, Irish, Poles, Jews, and blacks, the data suggested that "the ethnic factor has persisted to a greater extent than two or three generations of 'assimilation' might lead us to believe." The derived hypotheses "are supported with remarkable regularity."

At least one researcher has used surveys to study the effects of nationality on friendship preferences. Edward Laumann used data from the 1966 Detroit area survey to analyze the effects of religion and ethnicity on patterns of friendship formation. His survey asked respondents to state the religious preference, denomination (if applicable), and national origin of their three best friends. Comparing this evidence with respondents' own characteristics, he found that religion was a very strong basis for friendship selection: most of the friends of Catholics were also Catholics, most of the friends of Jews were also Jews, and so on. When friendships were formed outside of religious lines, they tended to be based on socioeconomic status. When the effects of religious group and social class are controlled for, friendships tended to be formed on the basis of similarity in religious beliefs and (in the Catholic case) national origin. The effects of national origin per se are difficult to isolate because in the Detroit study they are strongly correlated with both socioeconomic position and religious practices and beliefs; still, Laumann was able to conclude that "ethnic differences [that is, national origins] were also playing a role in channelling friendship formation."

In sum, the existing survey data show that national-origin groups tend to marry among themselves and choose one another as friends, and their family-related values are consistent with those values in the mother countries. None of these patterns is especially sharp, and there is some evidence that ethnic distinctiveness has diminished over time, but considering that the last major wave of European immigration ended more than 50 years ago, the fact that these patterns continue to exist at all is somewhat remarkable.

Nationality and Religion The most comprehensive survey analysis of the relationship between religion and national origin is again Abramson's *Ethnic Diversity in Catholic America*, although it dealt with Catholics only. Evidence on religious behavior among nationality-endogamous parental families is presented as baseline data against which changes can be measured. The assumption was that the ethnically endogamous parental generation should display more "ethnicity" in their religious behavior than mixed-nationality marriages or later generations. In the endogamous parental generation, all available indicators, such as attending Mass, receiving Communion, showed the same general pattern: the Irish, French Canadians, and Germans had the highest rates of associational involvement in Catholicism, and Italian and Hispanic Catholics had the lowest, with Poles and eastern Europeans in between. Approximately the same rank-order obtained in the data for respondents as well. The pattern was reasonably consistent under statistical controls for generation in the United States and socioeconomic status. The only control variable that made an appreciable difference was sex: women of all national origins were high in associational involvement, with only small differences by nationality. Nationality had the strongest effects on religious involvement among men. In comparing the data for respondents and respondents' parents, one is much more impressed by the similarities than the differences; the effects of national origin on religious involvement do not appear to have weakened.

Religious involvement provides another opportunity to examine the three-generations hypothesis. Following Lenski's results, data for the total Catholic sample showed that attendance at services increased regularly with generation, so again the Herberg hypothesis of a dip in the second generation was not supported. In both generations, the pattern was constant under controls for social class. The tendency for religious involvement to increase with generation, however, was not constant across all nationality groups. For German, Polish, and eastern European Catholics, attendance increased uniformly with generation, following the pattern for the total group. For Italian and Hispanic Catholics, generation seemed to be unrelated to attendance; in these two groups attendance was uniformly low, regardless of generation or social class. Among the Irish and French Canadians, however, the predicted second-generation dip occurred, but these two groups showed by far the highest levels of attendance in the parental (first) generation; thus it was essentially impossible for the second (respondent) generation to increase its attendance over the first. The pattern for these two groups may not reflect the effects of Americanization so much as a general statistical phenomenon know as regression toward the mean. In any case, Abramson's data suggest that the form and rate of Americanization are highly variable across nationality groups; not all groups become Americanized at the same pace or in the same way.

Abramson also presented detailed evidence concerning the effects of nationality exogamy on religious participation. The expectation was that exogamy would tend to "dilute" the ethnic culture and in that sense weaken the effects of nationality on religion. Data for the parental generation did not support this expectation. In the total parent sample, levels of religiosity (attendance, Communion, etc.) were about the same whether the marriage was endogamous or exogamous. This pattern varied somewhat by specific nationality group, but the variation was erratic. Only among French Canadian Catholics did a clear pattern emerge. In this group, nationality exogamy was clearly associated with a decline in religious involvement, consistent with the hypothesis. The Irish showed a similar pattern, but the effects were much weaker and less regular. Among the respondent generation, again the French Canadians and to a lesser extent the Irish became less religious as they married outside their nationality group; among Germans and Poles, marital exogamy had no apparent effect on religiosity; among Italians there was some evidence that exogamy increased attendance at religious services. The patterns noted here were generally sustained under controls for sex, generation, education, parental religiosity, and other control variables.

There is very little published data concerning the effects of nationality on aspects of religion other than formal attendance at services. Andrew Greeley in *The Denominational Society* reported scores on piety and extremism in religious beliefs for the five largest Catho-

lic ethnic groups in the United States: on piety, the Irish, Poles, and Germans scored highest and Italians lowest; on religious extremism, the Poles scored highest, followed by the French, with Italians, Irish, and Germans bunched together at the bottom. All these differences, however, were very modest and possibly insignificant. The 1977 NORC question on subjective strength of religiosity found that among Catholics, the Irish were by far the most strongly attached to their religion (65 percent responded "strong" to the question), followed by Italians (45 percent), Germans (38 percent), and Poles (36 percent), with French Canadians (30 percent) and Hispanics (20 percent) at the bottom. The same survey also provided interesting data on religious intermarriage by Catholic nationality groups. Italian respondents were the most likely to be married to a Catholic spouse (91 percent), followed closely by the French Canadians (86 percent), Hispanics (81 percent), and Poles (81 percent). The Irish (77 percent) and German (69 percent) Catholics were least likely to be married to a Catholic spouse, but the proportions were still quite large. In this survey no Catholic respondent of any of these national origins was married to a Jew.

Greeley and others have noted that national-origin differences such as those discussed here are often assumed to reflect more basic differences resulting from religion or social class; in other words, that national origin has no real effect. However, most of the studies reviewed here, which were based on Catholics only and thus hold religion constant, and still found substantial national-origin differences. Greeley in *Ethnicity in the United States* tested this by focusing on two nationality groups, Irish and Germans, with sizable proportions of both Catholics and Protestants. He reasoned that if religion were indeed more important than national origin, German Catholics would resemble Irish Catholics more than they would resemble German Protestants; alternatively, if national origin were more important, then German Catholics would be closer to German Protestants than to Irish Catholics. Comparisons among the four groups were made on 24 variables, ranging from presidential voting to marital happiness; roughly two-thirds of these comparisons showed that nationality was a better predictor than religion. The most interesting exception to the pattern was on voting turnout, in which "German Catholics are more like Irish Catholics than they are like German Protestants." But on other measures of political participation, such as, talking about politics, working for candidates, the opposite pattern obtained: "German Catholics are far more like German Protestants than they are like their Irish coreligionists." From this, Greeley inferred that "ethnicity is generally but not always more important than religion in predicting behavior."

National Origin and Social Stratification It was noted earlier that in the aggregate, Catholic and Protestant Americans are now on about the same socioeconomic plane, although this was substantially less true in the past. One implication of this trend toward diminishing Protestant-Catholic socioeconomic differences is that there are sizable differences in the rates of social mobility for various ethnic groups, with the Catholic ethnic groups "moving up" more rapidly on average than the Protestants. These trends over time confound any analysis of the effect of national origin on social stratification based on single-shot, cross-sectional survey data. The following review focuses on the few studies that provide some sense of the process of social mobility, usually by comparing results across age or generation.

Charles Nam analyzed data from the 1950 Census on nationality differences in socioeconomic achievements. These data followed patterns observed in many earlier ethnographic or single-community studies, showing that recency of migration was perhaps the single most important factor affecting the socioeconomic status of American nationality groups in the first half of the 20th century: in general, earlier-arriving groups, such as the English and Germans, ranked higher in social status than later-arriving groups, such as Italians and eastern Europeans. Even as early as 1950, however, the evidence showed that "among the foreign born, two of the 'old immigration' and one of the 'new immigration' nationalities ranked higher than the native population," and further, "among the second generation, all five of the 'old immigration' . . . nationality groups ranked higher than the natives." In short, many nationality groups, especially those that arrived in the United States earliest, had achieved socioeconomic parity with the native-born population as early as 1950. A related finding was that "the level of socio-economic status was much higher, on the whole, for the second generation than for the first," again suggesting considerable upward mobility in the span of a single generation. However, the rank-order of nationalities by economic position was the same in both generations; all groups made sizable gains relative to their parents' generation but were approximately stable in achievements relative to each other.

A more comprehensive and sophisticated analysis of nationality and stratification by Beverly Duncan and O. Dudley Duncan, based on 1962 national data from the Occupational Change in a Generation Survey, revealed "fairly substantial differences among national-origin groups (defined as foreign-born or native-born of foreign parents, i.e., first and second generation only) with respect to both educational and occupational achievement." The Russians, northwestern Europeans, and Irish showed the highest levels of achievement in both spheres, and Poles and Italians (and some residual "other" groups) showed the lowest, again suggesting recency of immigration as an important factor. As in all other studies of the topic, there were sizable differences between the respondent and parent generations. In the parent generation national origin accounted for about 11 percent of the variance in educational attainment, while among respondents, the figure was only about 3 percent; thus, the effect of nationality on educational achievement is much weaker in the respondents' generation than in the parents'. (An equivalent pattern was observed on the occupational measures.) In this sense, the Duncans concluded, "there can be little doubt that a 'melting pot' phenomenon obtains in America."

Further analysis revealed that nationality differences in occupational position diminished or disappeared once education and parental social status were controlled; the effects of nationality on occupation were indirect, in that they operated primarily through parental status and secondarily through educational attainment. Another finding of interest was "an unambiguous nar-

rowing of differences among group positions in the occupation structure between generations," providing additional evidence that the effects of nationality on socioeconomic position have weakened over time. More generally, the Duncans concluded that their findings "argue against the existence of pervasive discrimination on purely ethnic grounds. The notion of equal opportunity irrespective of national origin is a near reality."

Politics and National Origin Two main themes dominate the survey literature on politics and ethnicity. The first concerns the predicted pattern of political assimilation, the expectation being that ethnic political distinctiveness should diminish over time. The second theme, which is argued far more frequently than it is researched, is that whites of recent immigrant stock, especially Catholics, provide a bastion of political conservatism (indeed, reaction) in the American political arena.

There is no reliable evidence from any source that nationality has diminished as a force in American political life. Michael Parenti reviewed the relevant survey literature through the mid-1960s and concluded that nationality "is very much alive and with us today." The homogenizing or assimilating effects of rising education, increasing affluence, suburbanization, later generations, geographical dispersion, and exogamy have "been greatly over-estimated." Since Parenti's review all these social trends have accelerated, and yet today one is more likely to find essays on the resurgence of ethnicity than on its impending disappearance.

Are nationality groups progressive or regressive forces in American politics? The conventional wisdom, as Andrew Greeley bluntly put it, is that "white American ethnic groups are composed of bigots and hawks," but survey data from a variety of sources fail to sustain this imagery. The most comprehensive review of this evidence is in a paper by Norman Nie and associates in Greeley's *Ethnicity in the United States.* Detailed analysis of a 1967 NORC survey containing a large number of political-attitude questions showed that "far from being more conservative on race, social welfare, and the war in Vietnam, ethnic groups are more liberal than nonethnic Americans." (Nonethnic Americans were those who described their national origin as American, or Protestants of western European or mixed background.) These authors also reviewed results from other NORC surveys, from a few Harris studies, and from several Gallup polls; all data showed that "ethnics are more liberal than nonethnics on the issues of race and welfare." Ethnic liberalism on race issues appeared to result largely from the effects of region; once the South was excluded from the analysis, the ethnic edge in racial liberalism disappeared. Further, outside the South, ethnic liberalism was diminished among the relatively affluent; among the less affluent, the effect of national origin was enhanced. Thus, at higher levels of income, ethnics and nonethnics were about equally liberal on racial issues, but at lower levels of income, white ethnics were substantially more liberal than their nonethnic counterparts.

The controls for region and income, however, had little impact on the results regarding attitudes about welfare or Vietnam; recent-immigrant nationalities were more liberal than other nationalities on both issues. An addendum (by Greeley) to the analysis showed very similar results in the Survey Research Center's national election study series and in the 1972 NORC survey. This analysis was based on nine separate national surveys, each showing approximately the same result: American white ethnics are certainly no less liberal and probably are substantially more liberal than nonethnics on the entire range of political issues in the United States today.

Greeley's addendum also provided interesting evidence on political differences among recent-immigrant nationalities by comparing Irish, German, Italian, and Polish Catholics with one another and with Anglo-Saxon Protestants or "all Americans." All four of the Catholic nationality groups showed higher levels of Democratic preference and voting than the nation as a whole; among the four, the Polish Catholics consistently showed the largest Democratic majorities and German Catholics the smallest, with the Irish and Italians in between. These patterns were apparent in all presidential elections from 1952 to 1968 and in most Congressional elections from 1952 to 1970. A series of ten political-attitude questions further revealed that the Irish tended to be the most liberal of these four Catholic groups, with Italians a close second. The Germans and Poles tended to be somewhat more conservative on most issues than either Irish or Italians, but still less conservative than other groups. None of these differences was very large, but they were relatively consistent from one question to the next. These and other survey data make it quite apparent that it is not the working-class Catholic ethnic but upper-middle-class white Protestants and southern whites in general who form the backbone of political conservatism in the United States today.

Greeley has also presented the most detailed and current survey evidence on rates of political participation by nationality group. Irish Catholics registered the highest on overall political participation, followed by Scandinavian Protestants; Irish Protestants and Italian Catholics registered the lowest. All Protestant groups except the Irish scored above the grand mean; among the Catholic groups, the Irish, Germans, Slavs, and Poles scored above the mean, and the French, Italians, and Hispanics below it. The rank-ordering of groups remained approximately constant with region and social class controlled, but the difference between groups was reduced. Multivariate analysis showed that the net effect of nationality on political participation was not spurious, that, in fact, it was somewhat stronger in all comparisons than the effects of religion, region, and occupation.

Hispanics The preceding discussion has centered largely on European nationality groups. Two major nationality groups, Mexicans and Puerto Ricans, tend to be overlooked in such analyses because of their small relative size and regional concentrations. There is considerable reason to believe that both groups are underenumerated in the census, Puerto Ricans because they are citizens and therefore not foreign-born, and Mexicans because of the many migrant farm workers and the extent of illegal immigration. A recent Current Population Survey estimated the Hispanic population (Spanish speaking) at 10,577,000, about 5 percent of the U.S. population. Of these, roughly 6.3 million were of

Mexican origin, largely concentrated in the Southwest, and about 1.5 million were of Puerto Rican origin, concentrated mainly in eastern seaboard cities. The remaining Hispanics included a variety of national origins.

Hispanic groups tend to be slighted in surveys dealing with nationality, partly because the numbers in most national surveys are small and also because of language difficulties, which make these groups relatively inaccessible to sample surveys. But perhaps the most important reason is that these groups have come to public attention only within the last two decades. There is no long history of ethnographic and qualitative studies to draw upon. Although we cannot now say very much about the characteristics of Hispanic groups as derived from sample surveys, we can be quite sure that the next decade or so will add considerably to our knowledge.

Much of what is known about the characteristics of Latin Americans derives from the census and the Current Population Survey and so is restricted mainly to socioeconomic information. Useful studies on Mexicans, including many small-area and ethnographic studies, are J. Burma, *Mexican Americans in the U.S.* (1970) and R. Gomez, ed., *The Changing Mexican American* (1972). Excellent reviews of available social science data on Puerto Ricans are available in K. Wagenheim, *A Survey of Puerto Ricans on the U.S. Mainland in the 1970s* (1975), and the U.S. Commission on Civil Rights, *Puerto Ricans in the Continental U.S.* (1976). On all the Spanish groups see A.J. Jaffe, Ruth M. Cullen, and Thomas D. Boswell, *Spanish Americans in the United States—Changing Demographic Characteristics* (New York: Research Institute for the Study of Man, 1976).

REGIONAL ETHNICITY

As in many other advanced industrial nations (for example, Italy, Ireland, the Netherlands, Belgium, and France), regional differentiation continues to contribute to the pattern of American ethnicity. Of the many ethnic groups defined in whole or in part by geographical location (for example, Vermont Yankees, Appalachian whites), by far the largest and most studied are the white Southerners. As the eminent observer of the American South, W.J. Cash, once remarked, "the South is another land, sharply differentiated from the rest of the nation, and exhibiting within itself a remarkable homogeneity"—as close to the textbook definition of an ethnic group as one is likely to get.

Most of the survey literature on the white South has focused on whether that region is or is not being assimilated into the American mainstream, whether its former distinctiveness, as noted by Cash, has persisted to the present. Studies of what Milton Gordon in *Assimilation in American Life* (1964) called structural assimilation (roughly, equality in educational, occupational, and economic achievements) have generally concluded that the distinctiveness of the South is disappearing. However, studies of cultural assimilation (homogeneity with the majority culture in language, customs, politics) have tended to conclude that it is not. The white South, therefore, might constitute an important exception to Gordon's generalization that cultural assimilation is the inevitable consequence of structural assimilation.

The most compelling case for the structural assimila-

tion of the white South has been made by John McKinney and Linda Bourque, who analyzed census data over time on variables such as urbanization, industrialization, education, occupation, and income; they concluded that "in these sectors, the South has been changing more rapidly than the rest of the nation for the past 40 years and moreover is becoming increasingly indistinguishable from the rest of American society." Although the South continues to lag somewhat behind the rest of the nation in level of urbanization and in average levels of education, occupational prestige, and income, the rate of change is substantially higher in the South than outside it. If the differential in rates of change continues, the South will eventually become indistinguishable from the rest of the country. And "to the extent that the daily occupational and educational environment of the Southerner becomes similar to that of the non-Southerner, the attitudes and values of the two will also become indistinguishable." (*See* Appalachians; Southerners.)

Evidence regarding similarity in attitudes and values is much less compelling, although the former voting distinctiveness of the white South has begun to disappear. In the 1977 NORC survey essentially identical proportions of Southern and non-Southern whites identified with the Democratic party (55.7 percent and 55.1 percent, respectively); in the 1972 presidential election, the South gave proportionally more votes to the Republican candidate than any other region, and even in 1976, with a native white Southerner at the head of the Democratic ticket, the white South split nearly 50–50 between Democratic and Republican votes, much the same as the rest of the nation. In terms of national politics, then, the "solid South" apparently belongs to history.

In many other matters, however, the South remains quite distinct from the rest of the nation, with little evidence of change over time. Norval Glenn and J.L. Simons have analyzed 44 questions from 10 separate surveys, regarding issues such as religion, morals, racial and ethnic minorities, work, and political issues, comparing responses by Southerners and non-Southerners across age categories. According to the assimilationist expectation, differences would be smaller among the young than among the old, suggesting a broad pattern of value change or cultural assimilation. However, "the data fail to support the belief that regional differences have declined appreciably," and, in many areas, the differences appear to have increased; on many items, differences between Southerners and non-Southerners were actually larger among the young than among the old. Glenn and Simons concluded, "Predictions of declining interregional conflict and declining sectionalism may be too sanguine. Interregional strife may actually increase in the near future, or, at best, a great deal of it is likely to continue for many years."

In an analysis of black–white differences, Leonard Broom and Norval Glenn remarked, "in general, Negro–white differences are smaller than the differences between Southern and non-Southern whites . . . the population of the United States is apparently somewhat more divided along regional . . . than along racial lines."

Survey evidence on political attitudes does show some changes in the outlooks of white Southerners

between the 1950s and the 1970s; however, the shift was toward more conservative rather than more liberal positions (Norman Nie and associates, *The Changing American Voter*). This shift was equally apparent at all socioeconomic levels; upper-status white Southerners became more conservative on foreign policy and on the size of the federal government; lower-status white Southerners became more conservative across the board. The net result of these shifts in political outlook was that the "spread" in political conservatism between the South and the rest of the country actually widened.

By far the most comprehensive compilation of survey evidence on the persistence of white Southern ethnicity is John Shelton Reed's *The Enduring South* (1974). The analysis was based on several dozen national surveys and touched on the entire gamut of Southern distinctiveness, from preferences in food to proclivities toward violence to religious practices and beliefs.

CONCLUSIONS

The main themes of this review—socioeconomic differentials, family, marital endogamy, religiosity, political behavior, and attitudes—reflect the extent to which surveys on race, religion, and national origin have been dominated by the question whether ethnicity is one of the major lines of differentiation in our society. Some of the literature emphasizes the differences, other works stress the similarities among groups. All are concerned with the issues of assimilation, equality, and discrimination. Interethnic differences tend to be regarded ambivalently. On the one hand, some differences are deplored when they appear to reflect possible innate superordinate-subordinate qualities of the groups in question. Thus disorganization in black families may reflect negatively on that group just as conservative religious beliefs may reflect negatively on Catholics. On the other hand, interethnic differences may be regarded as evidence that such groups are still important influences on contemporary Americans, constituting a diversity to be celebrated. In general, evidence on socioeconomic assimilation is heralded as an achievement, while diversity in beliefs and values is celebrated as adding to the colorful spectrum of American pluralism.

Several fairly firm generalizations may be drawn from the survey evidence reviewed here.

First, blacks are far from socioeconomic parity with whites, even though recent decades have seen considerable gains. These socioeconomic differentials are so large that they considerably impair our ability to detect race differences that are separate from socioeconomic ones.

Second, religious denominations are distinguishable from each other in terms of the beliefs held by their members. The broad divisions of religious groups into Catholics, Protestants, and Jews also reveal important socioeconomic differences, although such differences are heavily mixed with those of region, national origins, and race. Even religious endogamy trends are obscured by the confounding factors just mentioned. Persons belonging to different denominations reflect directly corresponding differences in religious ideology and practice, but it is not at all clear that religious affiliation means anything else.

Third, nationality-group differences show a diversity of trends. The more recent immigrant groups and their descendants have moved up the socioeconomic ladder over the past three decades and are hard to distinguish now from the older immigrant groups. Some internationality differences, particularly those relating to noneconomic aspects of life, seem to persist. Nationality ethnicity clearly exists, although differences appear not to be very dramatic.

The concern of scholars and researchers with equality, discrimination, and assimilation has meant that less attention has been given to some other topics. For example, we know very little about how ethnic groups differ in food tastes, dietary practices, qualitative aspects of friendship, kinship, and marriage. Indeed, the very areas of behavior and attitudes that Americans use in identifying other people's ethnic background are the topics most neglected in sample surveys dealing with ethnicity.

Another deficiency in the sample surveys centers around measurement, as discussed at the beginning of this entry. Insufficient attention has been given to alternative ways of measuring a person's ethnic identity and clarifying the degree to which a person orients himself to others on the basis of presumed ethnic ties.

Perhaps the greatest deficiency of all is that we do not know how important race, religion, national origins, and regional location are to Americans as ways of consciously organizing their views of themselves, others, and the issues they face. The fragmentary evidence reviewed earlier suggests that ethnicity is not very important. Better evidence is needed before we can answer the critical question whether discerned ethnic differences are acquired through the implications of ancestry and the subtle effects of socialization or acquired self-consciously in striving to be like others with whom one identifies strongly.

Perhaps the most important overall generalization on the basis of the evidence reviewed here is that the effect of ethnicity has tended to diminish in the public sphere—in the occupational structure, levels of educational attainment, and economic position—but not in the private sphere. The scarce material rewards of the society are increasingly distributed more equally among ethnic groups, and in this sense, ethnicity is more and more irrelevant to the industrialized socioeconomic system. But there is no necessary connection between the decline of ethnicity in this sense and the bases upon which friendships are formed, spouses chosen, neighborhoods lived in, and so on. Americans, it appears, still gravitate toward their kind away from the marketplace. The bulk of the evidence suggests that structural, but not cultural, assimilation is the most accurate characterization of the direction of ethnicity in the contemporary United States.

Bibliography

The many relevant titles already cited above will not be repeated here. On the methods of survey research in general, a useful introduction is Earl Babbie, *Survey Research Methods* (Belmont, Calif., 1973), which discusses levels of measurement and the general logic of multivariate data analysis, as well as the more general issues of the design and conduct of survey research.

On the specific methodological problems of studying ethnicity through survey research, see Darrell Montero and Gene Levine, "Research Among Racial and Cultural Minorities: Problems, Prospects, and Pitfalls," *The Journal of Social Issues* 33:4 (Fall 1977).

Survey studies of racial differences in American society are voluminous. A useful collection of review essays is Kent S. Miller and Ralph M. Dreger, *Comparative Studies of Blacks and Whites in the United States* (New York, 1973). Much of the best data on black–white differences is found in the decennial U.S. Census and quarterly Current Population Surveys. These and other government data are found in *The Statistical Abstract of the United States*, published annually by the U.S. Department of Commerce.

JAMES D. WRIGHT, PETER H. ROSSI, AND THOMAS F. JURAVICH

SWEDES

In 1638 a Swedish mercantile company founded the colony of New Sweden at the mouth of the Delaware River and built Fort Cristina on the site of present-day Wilmington. During the Thirty Years' War, Sweden had somewhat unexpectedly become a major European power and, following the examples of England and Holland, wanted to establish itself overseas. During the next 17 years, however, only 9 ships arrived from the homeland, and New Sweden's population reached a total of about 500 people, many of whom were Dutch and Finns. In 1655 the colony fell to the Dutch and a decade later to the English. The Swedish colonial effort may have had a lasting effect on frontier America, however, for the Finns and Swedes are said to have introduced the dovetailing technique used to build the log houses of the pioneer era.

Only a few hundred Swedes arrived in America during the next century. According to a somewhat inflated estimate, about 19,000 people of Swedish descent were living in the United States in 1790, out of a total population of 3.9 million. Descendants of the Swedish colonists had significant roles during the revolutionary era. At the Continental Congress of 1776 John Morton (born Mortenson, 1724–1777) of Pennsylvania cast his delegation's deciding vote for independence. John Hanson (1715–1783) of Maryland was chief executive of the new republic in 1781–1782.

Sweden was the first neutral country to recognize the new United States, with which it signed peace and trade agreements in 1783. During the Napoleonic wars trade flourished between the two countries—both of which remained generally uninvolved—and continued to grow after the peace settlement in 1815. During the next quarter century the United States imported large quantities of Swedish iron ore and attracted a few Swedish immigrants; some 800 appeared on passenger lists before 1846, most of them adventurers, entrepreneurs, and technicians. These migrants made use of the lively ocean traffic between Gothenburg and New York, traveling "on top of the cargo," so to speak, aboard barks and brigs. Swedish immigrants gradually became much more desirable than Swedish iron: by the 1840s the United States was mining its own ore, but settlers for its vast frontier territories and labor for its developing industries were scarce.

In addition to the pull of America's labor market, hard times in Sweden in the late 1840s were a further spur for emigration. Between 1845 and 1854 some 15,000 Swedes emigrated. The steady stream of travelers grew into emigrant parties dominated by landowning farmers and artisans accompanied by their families. A prospective emigrant would sell his farm, gather together family, relatives, and even neighbors, and leave never to return, often taking considerable sums in the family's money chest. A significant number of emigrants were also fleeing religious repression, since during this period Swedes were not allowed to worship outside the state-established Lutheran church. Compared to the mass emigration from the British Isles and Germany during this period, however, this initial Swedish movement was relatively exclusive. Since it was such a new phenomenon, the participants needed a certain amount of education and some material resources. Among the many people affected by the hard times of the 1840s, the only ones who emigrated were landed farmers, skilled craftsmen, and other lower-middle-class people who had access to information about America and who could afford to finance the journey. Conditions in Sweden were not conducive to large-scale emigration until the late 1860s.

MASS EMIGRATION, 1865–1930

Despite the significant numbers of Swedes who began coming in the 1840s, Swedish immigration to the United States is largely the story of the mass movement that began in the 1860s. Of the 1.4 million Swedes who, according to official statistics, have emigrated over the past century and a half, nearly 1.2 million arrived in

Swedes

America between 1851 and 1930, when the Depression in the United States brought Swedish immigration nearly to a halt. Almost half the latter number came in 1868–1873 (103,000) and 1880–1893 (475,000). The total exodus represented about a fourth of Sweden's population in the late 19th century. Only Norway, Ireland, and possibly Iceland have surrendered a greater proportion of their population to the New World.

The emigration pattern established earlier, between 1846 and 1857, was strengthened during the mass emigration. During the entire period the poorer agrarian provinces of Halland, Småland, and Värmland showed the highest emigration intensity—an annual average of 4.5 to 5.0 per 1,000 people. These provinces had large population reserves and established traditions of migration to Denmark, Norway, and Germany. The fertile areas around Lake Mälaren in central Sweden had the nation's lowest emigration rate, largely because, in this region, Stockholm served as an alternative to America.

Until the 1870s most Swedish emigrants continued to be farmers in search of land and work; the majority journeyed to the United States with their families. In the 1880s the majority of emigrants still came from Sweden's agricultural sector, but relatively few were independent farmers. Instead, they were rural laborers who fled a countryside that could no longer support them. By the end of the century a new pattern had taken shape: single men and women now accounted for 70 percent of Swedish immigration, and a growing number were coming from the towns and the industrial working class.

Overpopulation was the single most important long-range cause of Swedish emigration. Between 1750 and 1850 the population of Sweden doubled to reach 3.5 million; by 1900 the figure was 5.1 million. This demographic increase reached its first peak in the early 1820s as a result of several factors—a lengthy peacetime period, the development of the smallpox vaccine, and the successful cultivation of potatoes. The result of this surge of growth was a dramatic increase in the number of youths looking for work 15 to 20 years later. Thus the first period of emigration began.

The burden of the population explosion in Sweden, as in Ireland, was shouldered by the agrarian population. Efforts to reform and consolidate the agricultural system, begun in the 18th century, had benefited the better-situated farmers with larger holdings and had left small homesteads to be divided and redivided among increasing numbers of children, eventually creating a landless rural proletariat. By the beginning of the era of mass emigration (1870), almost half—48 percent—of the farm population was landless. Since industrialization began late in Sweden, the economy could not absorb the many unemployed and landless agrarian workers.

A severe famine in the late 1860s—the last country-wide harvest failure in Swedish history—provoked the first truly mass migration of Swedes. The second year of the famine brought death to 22 Swedes in every 1,000. Between 1868 and 1873 some 100,000 Swedes came to the United States, where jobs made available by the boom that followed the Civil War also exercised an attraction.

It was again primarily agrarian conditions that prompted a second mass emigration from Sweden in the 1880s. European countries with economies based largely on agriculture suffered in competition with exports from newly developed American and Ukrainian grain fields. The result was the dumping of grain, low prices, unemployment, and high emigration. In 1887–1888, some 92,000 Swedes came to the United States, a record high that decreased immediately after the introduction of agricultural tariffs.

Beginning in 1879 emigration was also influenced by conditions within the industrial sector, especially in northern Sweden with its ore deposits and forest-related industries. In that year many workers lost their jobs because of crises in the lumber and iron industries precipitated by economic depression in Britain and a new tariff in Germany. These crises sparked a large-scale exodus—ten times the previous volume in the industrial province of Västernorrland.

The generating power of the emigration itself was demonstrated in the 1890s, when times were relatively good in Sweden but poor in the United States as a result of the depression of 1893–1897. Over 200,000 Swedes nonetheless left for North America in that decade. The pull from Swedish enclaves in the United States now played an important role. The network of contacts across the Atlantic increased the ordinary Swede's ability to take advantage of economic opportunities in the United States, as illustrated by record high emigration from Sweden in economically good years in America, such as the early and late 1880s, 1891–1892, and 1902–1903. Nearly a half-million people (40 percent of the transatlantic emigration) left Sweden between 1879 and 1893, although emigration was not insignificant after 1893. During the first decade of the 20th century 219,000 Swedes came to the United States, and 92,000 came in the 1920s—25,000 of them in the peak year 1923.

The objectives of the post–World War I immigrants were somewhat different from those of earlier immigrants. Since travel was easier—the Swedish American Line was established in 1915—many Swedes crossed the ocean several times in search of ever better economic opportunities. The proportion of returning migrants was 30 percent in the 1920s in contrast to 6 percent in the 1880s. After the economic crisis of 1929 and the Depression that followed, Swedish immigration virtually ceased. The number of Swedish immigrants never approached the annual quota that became effective under U.S. immigration law in the 1920s.

Over 60 percent of Swedish emigrants between 1861 and 1915 were in the prime age group of 15 to 29 years, and 56 percent of the emigrants going to non-European countries were men. The proportion of men decreased as the emigration became a mass movement: at the end of the 1890s and during World War I more women than men left Sweden. The land-owning farm families of the pioneer years gave way during the 1870s first to rural laborers and then at the end of the century to industrial workers; both the latter groups consisted mainly of young unmarried people. Whereas 68 percent of the emigrants of the 1840s migrated as family units, only 29 percent emigrated as families in the 1890s. Immediately before World War I, 33 percent of the emigrants came from manufacturing and industry as opposed to agriculture.

A number of factors besides the lack of land and jobs

motivated Swedes to emigrate, though to what extent is difficult to document. One such cause was probably discontent with employers or wages. The wave of emigrants in 1909 consisted of many people who expressed dissatisfaction with the outcome of the unsuccessful general strike of that year—at least, propaganda for emigration became especially lively after that date. Another cause was lack of a political voice; letters written by emigrants expressed bitterness about the restrictive suffrage policies in effect until 1921. Avoidance of military service prompted the departure of young men of draft age, especially after 1901 when the period of service was extended from 3 to 8 months.

THE JANSSONISTS AND RELIGIOUS REPRESSION

Religious persecution was a major factor motivating emigration before more tolerant policies became effective in 1858. Until then public worship outside the Church of Sweden was forbidden, with expatriation the ultimate punishment for repeated offenders. In the 19th century a religious upheaval shook the country, culminating sensationally in the 1840s with the Janssonist movement in north-central Sweden. This sect was led by the self-appointed "prophet" Eric Jansson, a farmer's son from Uppland, whose fierce attacks on the clergy and the established church, public burnings of Martin Luther's writings, and private communion services led to a violent confrontation with the establishment. Emigration seemed the best alternative for Jansson and some 1,200 to 1,500 followers in the period 1846–1854. This figure suggests that one of every ten Swedish emigrants in the first period of emigration left because of religious persecution.

Defenders of the state church also interfered with Baptists and Mormons and expelled members of each group. The majority of the approximately 8,000 Mormons estimated to have emigrated from 1850 to 1910, however, probably left less as a result of religious persecution than out of a desire to join their mother church in the United States.

The Janssonist emigration furnishes a good example of an important emigrant tradition. Janssonists who had been neighbors in Sweden remained neighbors after their arrival in Henry County, Ill., where they founded the Bishop Hill colony. The interest their emigration had created, the relatively long period it covered, and their ability to use letters and newspaper articles as propaganda made their settlement on the western Illinois frontier, just south of the Rock River's junction with the Mississippi, well known to thousands of their countrymen. The original immigrants arrived in family units as the first link in the tradition. Their letters from America created a second link with relatives and friends in their home provinces in north-central Sweden, ultimately bringing new immigrants to their community. In a third link, immigrants from Bishop Hill dispersed and developed new Swedish settlements in the northern Mississippi Valley.

Bishop Hill, whose name was derived from the Prophet's birthplace, is an interesting specimen of the 19th-century utopian colonies founded by revivalist immigrants in the Midwest. Shared property, work routines, meals, and worship characterized life at Bishop Hill. The Prophet's power even included family planning. On his orders, a town was built according to a grand design, with streets laid out in rectangles and lined by the highest buildings west of Chicago at that time. The colony also developed a successful collective farm system.

Catastrophe hit Bishop Hill in 1849 when cholera broke out. The following year Eric Jansson was murdered by a fellow Swede, and the colony lost the source of its religious authority. In 1853 it was reorganized on a cooperative basis, but in 1861, on the verge of bankruptcy, it was formally dissolved. Most of the former colonists remained in the Bishop Hill area and prospered as farmers. Scenes from the colony's early years and portraits of the colonists are preserved in the work of the Swedish-American primitive artist Olof Eriksson Krans (1838–1916).

SETTLEMENT AND ECONOMIC PATTERNS

Unlike many other immigrants, most Swedes could choose their place of settlement and their occupation in the New World according to their previous backgrounds and ambitions. Most farmers sought and obtained land, especially as homestead states opened up and railroads were built to the frontier. People from Swedish towns dominated by the iron industry, like Karlskoga, generally migrated to states with heavy industry, such as Massachusetts; miners from towns like Ljusnarsberg and quarry workers from the Baltic island of Öland went to the mining areas of upper Michigan; lumbermen from northern Sweden settled in the Pacific Northwest; and fishermen from Öland were attracted to San Francisco.

Until the 1890s most Swedish immigrants were farmers or rural workers who settled in the homestead states of the Midwest, especially Illinois and Minnesota, where the land had not been fully occupied by earlier immigrants from Norway and Germany. According to the censuses of 1850, 1860, and 1870, one-third of all Swedish-born residents of the United States were living in Illinois. After the Homestead Act of 1862, however, the center of Swedish-American population began to shift to the northern Mississippi Valley, to the area between the Mississippi and St. Croix rivers in Minnesota known as the Swedish Triangle.

The first Swedes in Minnesota came early, however, when the territory officially opened for colonization in 1849. Swedish pioneers from Illinois moved along the frontier, following the waterways of the Mississippi and St. Croix rivers. The story of these early immigrants is told in the series of novels written in the 1940s and 1950s by Swedish author Vilhelm Moberg and in the later films based on them, *The Emigrants* and *The New Land*. A heavy immigration to Minnesota began in 1868 and settled Chisago, Isanti, and Kanabec counties north of Minneapolis. When the Lake Superior and Mississippi railroad was built through these counties in the early 1870s, the railroad's Swedish immigration agent, Colonel Hans Mattson (1832–1893) played an important role in persuading many Swedes to settle in the area. He also worked for the St. Paul and Pacific railroad, which ran west from St. Paul and Minneapolis through Meeker and Kandiyohi counties. At the turn of the century nearly one out of every two foreign-born inhabitants of these counties was Swedish.

Despite the fact that approximately one-fifth of all Swedish immigrants came to Minnesota, the Swedes

actually dominated only a few areas. Germans and Norwegians usually had arrived earlier, cleared larger land areas, and in general had a higher birth rate. The Swedes concentrated in a few core agricultural areas and later settled in the larger cities. In 1930 first- and second-generation Swedes constituted the largest ethnic group in Minneapolis (15 percent of the city's population) and the next largest in St. Paul (9 percent) and accounted for 11 percent of the state's population, compared to 13 percent for the Germans and 10 percent for the Norwegians.

The Swedes also helped settle the prairie states. In 1855, the year after the Kansas Territory was opened, two brothers named Johnson moved from the Galesburg, Ill., area to the Blue River Valley in northeastern Kansas. They persuaded a contingent of Illinois Swedes to follow; articles in the newly established Swedish-language newspaper, *Hemlandet* (The Homeland, 1855–1914) did much to publicize their settlement. Once again a secondary migration was established.

During the famine years in Sweden, several companies were founded in Galesburg and Chicago to promote colonization in Kansas. The First Swedish Agricultural Company of Chicago, for instance, bought 14,000 acres of railroad land in the Smoky Hill River Valley and encouraged a pastor of the Swedish state church, Olof Olson, and some 100 followers to settle in the newly founded town of Lindsborg. Like Jansson, the revivalist pastor Olson dreamed of a colony built on Christian ideals. His vision came true in Lindsborg, which remains today preeminently a Swedish town. Bethany College, a small liberal-arts school, was founded there in 1881 and is still in existence today. Birger Sanzen (1871–1954), Swedish America's most famous artist, was a life-long professor at the college, where he founded an art colony that is still active.

In the 1880s Swedes from both Minnesota and the home country sought better land to the west in North and South Dakota and Nebraska. Traveling as individuals and families, rather than in groups, these people often joined established Norwegian communities. Swedes from Iowa and Illinois who followed the railroad west also settled in Nebraska.

Some enterprising individuals founded lasting colonies far from the midwestern centers. S.M. Swenson, who immigrated to Texas in 1838, brought over the first groups of Swedes to work on his ranch in 1848. After the Civil War his brother continued to import Swedish contract labor, and by 1910 over 4,000 Swedish-born people were living mainly in the Austin area. In 1930 over 14,000 Swedes and their descendants lived there.

While W.W. Thomas of Maine was consul in Gothenburg, Sweden, he decided to organize Swedish immigration to his home state and in 1870 founded the settlement New Sweden in the forested northern corner of Maine. Villages named Stockholm, Jemtland, and Westmanland grew up in the general area. This well-organized group immigration became a pattern for planned immigration to the United States. In 1930 over 4,000 Swedes were living in the colony, which still exists. The area has preserved the Swedish language and traditions and has a Swedish Museum.

In the late 19th century two trends emerged: a shift in settlement from rural areas to the cities and a shift in destination from the Midwest to the East and West coasts. These trends are related, for the coastal settlements were largely nonagrarian. While Swedish settlers in Maine, Massachusetts, and Connecticut came directly from Sweden, the first settlers in the western states often came via the Midwest. After the turn of the century, however, direct immigration increased.

Although Swedes and their descendants owned more farmland in the United States by 1920 than all the arable territory in their homeland, they had decades previously ceased to be a primarily rural ethnic group. By 1890 a third of all Swedish Americans lived in cities, and by 1910 the proportion had increased to nearly two-thirds. Since in Sweden at this time only one out of every four inhabitants lived in cities, emigrating Swedes often faced the difficult transition of moving from a rural area to a large city—a transition that frequently necessitated as great an adjustment as the emigration itself. The change in the immigrants' destination from rural areas to the cities took place as homesteading subsided and the frontier began to disappear. Twenty-six percent of the Swedes who had arrived in the United States before 1901 were described as "rural-farm" dwellers in the 1930 Census; of those who had arrived after 1925, however, only 5 percent lived on farms while 85 percent were city dwellers.

Swedes began moving to the Pacific Northwest in large numbers in the 1880s, after the Northern Pacific railroad was completed. The Swedish-born population in the state of Washington increased from 650 in 1880 to 10,000 in 1890 and 32,200 in 1910. By 1930 Washington had—and has retained—the second largest percentage of Swedes of any of the states. Lumber workers and fishermen came directly from sawmill and fishing districts in Sweden to work in similar occupations around Tacoma, Seattle, and the mouth of the Columbia River. Still other Swedes came to the Northwest en route to the Klondike gold fields. In California most Swedes chose to live in cities; the only exceptions to urban settlements were Turlock and Kingsburg in the San Joaquin Valley, where groups of Swedes from the Midwest established farming communities centered around such unfamiliar occupations as the cultivation of grapes and citrus fruits. Kingsburg remains California's "Little Sweden."

Swedish settlements in the East and Northeast were more industrial in character. Most important were Worcester, Mass., and Jamestown, N.Y., where Swedes and their descendants at various times comprised more than half the foreign population.

CHICAGO: SWEDEN'S SECOND CITY

The largest and most important urban communities of Swedes were in the Midwest—in Chicago and Minneapolis. Had it not been for Chicago, the urbanized portion of the Swedish-American population would have been much smaller. Between 1890 and 1930 about one out of every ten Swedes in America lived there. At the beginning of the 20th century, it was the second largest Swedish city in the world—second only to Stockholm. In 1900 it had 145,000 first- and second-generation Swedish residents, who made up almost 9 percent of the city's population.

The Swedish colony in Chicago was founded in October 1846 by a group of "back-sliding" Janssonists. The next two decades of settlement were characterized by a

small number of incoming Swedes, by rootlessness, and by poverty; it was during this pioneer era that the most important ethnic organizations were founded. The second period of settlement, 1868–1893, was characterized by heavy immigration, securely rooted enclaves with strong ethnic organizations, increasing home ownership, and an active social life. The third period, 1894–1920, was marked by confrontation with immigrants from southern Europe, movements to new enclaves, continued social and economic advancement, and the beginning of assimilation. In the fourth period, Chicago's Swedes became fully assimilated.

The largest of the many Swedish enclaves in Chicago was Swede Town on the Near North Side. In 1884 over 10,000 Swedes lived there, mainly around "Snuff Street" (Chicago Avenue) and formed half the population of the area. The location was within convenient walking distance of the factories along the river, but the air was polluted by chimney smoke and soot. In the long run, Swede Town was doomed to become a slum. As many Swedes became more prosperous and moved away, they sold their homes to new immigrants— Swedes at first, but at the end of the 1890s, more often to southern or eastern Europeans. The arrival of people with different customs and religion hastened the Swedes' departure. During the time of transition the area around Belmont Avenue became a new Swedish center, but the suburbs eventually proved more attractive.

A large share of the Swedish immigrants to Chicago (42 percent in 1880) were between the ages of 15 and 34—a group vital to the city's labor market. The men were from backgrounds that equipped them for occupations in the crafts and in industry. Swedes found jobs in the building, lumber, and metal trades and in clothing manufacture. They became particularly prominent in Chicago's construction industry, which was often perceived as a Swedish trade guild. According to an estimate in 1928, the Swedes had constructed 35 percent of all buildings in Chicago and 80 percent of those in Minneapolis. Studies of census data show the Swedes slowly advancing from unskilled to skilled workers, with the second generation filling white-collar jobs with increasing frequency. Many Swedes also established themselves as businessmen in Chicago's Swedish communities.

Many of the Swedish immigrants to Chicago were women. From 1860 on, single women aged 15 to 29 were attracted by opportunities in the textile industry and by the large demand for Swedish maids. In 1880 one out of every ten domestic workers in Chicago had come from Sweden. The large reserve of women of marriageable age enticed many men to stay in Chicago, and resulted in family-centered neighborhoods.

As long as the Swedes lived in enclaves, they remained segregated from other ethnic groups in the city and preserved their language and customs. Between 1850 and 1880 only 6 to 10 percent of Swedish marriages involved non-Swedish partners. The segregation was strictest toward non-Lutherans (Irish and Italians), but the barriers were less rigid toward Norwegians and Germans, who lived in the same neighborhoods as the Swedes.

The second largest Swedish urban settlement in the United States was in Minneapolis, where immigrants from Sweden formed no less than 31 percent of the foreign-born population in 1930. Their occupational distribution was similar to that of the Swedes in Chicago, with an even greater concentration in the construction industry. New York City was the home of the third largest number of Swedish city-dwellers, but here the Swedes constituted only 1.6 percent of the foreign-born population in 1930.

Concurrent with the urbanization of Swedish Americans was their increasing economic success and upward social mobility. They quickly improved upon the skills they came with or acquired new ones. Moreover, by 1900 a growing number of educated Swedes, especially engineers, began coming to the United States. A number of important inventions by Swedish Americans have contributed to the material progress of their adopted country, among them the photocopy process, developed by Chester Carlson in the 1930s.

RELIGIOUS ORGANIZATIONS

The first major Swedish settlement in the Midwest and the first substantial group migration—Bishop Hill —resulted from the mid-19th-century religious revival in Sweden. Even before they left Sweden, prospective emigrants were courted by American Protestant denominations, which continued to compete for their loyalty after their arrival. In 1845 the Methodists, for instance, established an immigrant mission in New York led by a Swede, Olof Hedstrom. His brother Jonas was the Methodist cornerstone of western Illinois. Gustaf Unonius (1810–1902), educated at the University of Uppsala, served as a Protestant Episcopal missionary among the Scandinavians before becoming rector of a church in Chicago. Mormons and Baptists also sent missionaries among the Swedes. During the hardship-plagued pioneer years the mission field could not have been more opportune for energetic ministers. Swedes were accustomed to pastors who were secular as well as spiritual leaders, and they could not imagine a society without a church and services in their mother tongue.

The first pastor from the Church of Sweden to reach the Midwest, L.P. Esbjorn (1808–1870), had been critical of the state church in the mother country. But on his arrival at Andover, Ill., in 1849, he was confronted not only by Janssonists from nearby Bishop Hill, but by Methodists and Baptists as well. Their presence caused him to abandon evangelical revivals and become a more dogmatic Lutheran. In the spring of 1850 he founded a Lutheran congregation at Andover that was to become the mother parish of the Augustana Synod. Esbjorn selected men of his liking to work with him, most often low-church Lutheran ministers from Sweden. In 1852, T.N. Hasselquist (1816–1891) immigrated to take over the congregation founded by Esbjorn at Galesburg, and in 1853 Erland Carson (1822–1893) arrived to take on the unruly field in Chicago. Esbjorn's apostle, Eric Norelius (1833–1916), was sent to Minnesota in 1855. These men were leaders of large emigrant groups just as Esbjorn had been, and their followers became charter members of new congregations. One pastor distinguished himself by becoming the agent for a railroad in Iowa and founded one of the most prosperous Swedish settlements there.

As more congregations were founded, the idea of

forming a synod jointly with Norwegian Lutherans seemed practical. The Augustana Synod was founded in 1860 with 49 midwestern congregations consisting of some 5,000 members, including Norwegians. The name of the synod derived from the Augsburg Confession of 1530, which became the main creed of the Lutheran churches. When the Norwegians left in 1870 to form their own church, the Augustana Synod became a purely Swedish institution. At the same time dissenters within its ranks, whose evangelical zeal was greater than that of the general membership, began to gain strength. These dissenters, called the "Mission Friends," came originally from a revivalist group in Sweden which was especially strong in Småland during the time of mass emigration. In 1885 this group organized the Swedish Mission Covenant Church, with some 50 congregations and several thousand members. The Mission Friends became the first revival church of Swedish background in the United States and therefore a serious rival to the Augustana congregations.

When the Norwegians withdrew in 1870, about 20 percent of the Swedish immigrants belonged to an Augustana church. During the period of mass immigration, the synod had at its disposal an excellent recruiting organization with congregations from New York to Minnesota. The poverty of the immigrants of the early part of this period compelled the pastors to serve as social workers, which also helped make recruitment successful. The largest congregation, the Immanuel Lutheran Church in Chicago, became an immigrant center; during the heavy immigration prompted by the famine of the late 1860s, the church building served as shelter, hospital, poorhouse, and school. Membership in such a congregation became an insurance policy of sorts, as well as a ticket to ethnic companionship.

During the span of a few decades, several hundred ministers and thousands of laymen built four national religious organizations covering various phases of life. Those seeking companionship among compatriots could find it among the broad social programs of the Augustana Synod, the Mission Covenant Church, and the Swedish Methodist and Baptist conferences. The oldest Swedish immigrant culture was thereby provided with religious overtones.

Church work began on a small scale with a church in the center of a pioneer settlement. Several congregations formed a district; the districts were organized into conferences, which in turn formed the national synod. The congregations had their own Swedish schools and Sunday schools. The conferences established old peoples' homes, orphanages, and in some cases, hospitals. The synod operated colleges and a theological seminary. All larger denominations supported institutions of higher learning. Educating ministers was essential for the preservation of the Swedish language and culture; without them, the church would be unacceptable to the immigrants. Augustana College and Theological Seminary was founded in 1860 and relocated at Rock Island, Ill., in 1875; it had 1,000 students by the end of the emigration era. Gustavus Adolphus College in St. Peter, Minn. (f. 1862), Bethany College in Lindsborg, Kans. (f. 1881), Upsala College in East Orange, N.J. (f. 1893), the Mission Friends' North Park College in Chicago (f. 1891), and the Baptists' Bethel Institute in St. Paul (f. 1871) are still flourishing institutions with

Swedish traditions. Swedish hospitals were built in Minneapolis, Rockford, and Seattle.

Despite the churches' impressive intellectual and social contributions, membership remained relatively modest. In 1910 no more than 20 percent of approximately 1.3 million first- and second-generation Swedish Americans were affiliated with the Augustana Synod. The next three denominations each represented a little over 3 percent of the Swedish-American population. Many Swedes, especially in the 20th century, joined non-Swedish parishes, but their number is unknown. There was a discernible division along class lines in the membership of various denominations. The Protestant Episcopal church appealed primarily to Swedes of higher social status. The evangelical churches, with their more personal religion, attracted many of the poorer and more rootless immigrants. The Mission Friend churches, especially in Chicago, became retreats for domestic workers and seamstresses, thereby establishing the first Swedish-American organization dominated by women. The Augustana people represented Swedish America's middle class of farmers, skilled workers, and small-business people and their families.

SECULAR SOCIETIES

The first Swedish secular societies were organized by educated and economically successful immigrants in the cities. These people scorned the pioneer pastor and his naïve flock with their puritan morals and conservative beliefs. They often charged the pastors with keeping their countrymen ignorant in their Swedishness, making them unable to compete in the wider society. Yet these secular leaders made use of the cities' fertile environment for ethnic organizations. As early as 1836 the Swedish Society was founded in New York and in 1859 a Scandinavian club was launched in San Francisco. Many other organizations followed on the East and West coasts. In 1857 Chicago's more prosperous Swedes founded the Svea Society, which became a prototype for hundreds of clubs and organizations in the Midwest. Svea's program was far removed from the ordinary immigrant's needs. The society started a library, subscribed to Swedish newspapers, and arranged lectures. In 1868 it formed an amateur theater group—the beginning of an 80-year-old tradition of Swedish theater in Chicago. Svea was also politically active.

The gap between the churches and the societies widened as new secular organizations were founded. Membership in a society resulted in a warning and expulsion from the church. The pastors' concern for a time seemed exaggerated; during the 1870s Chicago had only about 20 organizations, none exceeding 300 members. Furthermore, the societies' welfare programs could not compare with those of the churches.

As the industrious Swedes in the cities increased their skills and became home owners, officials, and businessmen, membership in the secular societies enhanced their status and served as a badge of success. After the early 1870s dependence on church welfare programs also decreased. The organizations simultaneously broadened their selections of activities to less sophisticated demands.

In the 1880s the Swedish societies followed the

American example of forming national fraternal orders that provided sick benefits, life insurance, and funeral funds—services that made the societies competitive as welfare institutions. In Chicago the Order of Svithiod was founded in 1880 and the Order of Vikings a decade later. Most successful was the Vasa Order founded in New Haven, Conn., in 1896; by 1928 it had 72,000 members in over 400 lodges. At their peak in the late 1920s, the Swedish-American organizations had a total of at least 100,000 adult members. In this period there were about 365,000 Swedish-American church members. Thus at the end of the emigration era, close to half of the over one million adult first- and second-generation Swedish Americans belonged to either a religious or secular ethnic organization.

As the lodges declined in membership, they shifted their focus from insurance benefits to cultural activities. They sponsored Swedish-language instruction, organized celebrations of Swedish holidays, and arranged lectures on Swedish culture. Nevertheless, they too were facing the language issue and soon, after an intense debate, most shifted to English as their official language.

As the churches and national orders shifted from Swedish to the English language in the 1920s and 1930s, smaller societies emerged whose main concern was the preservation of Swedish culture. Many were strictly local, others were affiliated with such organizations as the Swedish Cultural Society in America. Some, such as the Texas Swedish Pioneers Association (f. 1938), have sponsored primarily social and cultural activities for their members; others have focused on historical work, such as the American Swedish Historical Foundation of Philadelphia (f. 1926). Several have maintained libraries, and even though the majority closed after World War II, several still survive.

Swedish Americans have always been interested in history and take pride in the fact that the first Swedes arrived in America almost as early as the first Pilgrims. A Swedish-American historical society was founded in Chicago in 1905. In 1926 when Professor Amandus Johnson (1877–1974) initiated the idea of a Swedish-American museum to commemorate New Sweden, he received strong support. The American Swedish Museum in Philadelphia was dedicated in 1938, 300 years after the first Swedes had landed in Delaware. In 1929 the newspaper baron, S.J. Turnblad (1860–1933), donated his castlelike home in Minneapolis to be used as an ethnic center—the American Swedish Institute. In 1948 a "Swedish Pioneer Centennial" resulted in the founding of the Swedish Pioneer Society, which publishes a quarterly magazine and a yearbook. In 1973 the Swedish Council of America was founded to coordinate Swedish-American organizational activities.

THE SWEDISH-AMERICAN PRESS

Just as the churches attempted to unite the Swedish regions into a homogeneous "Swedish America" in the early years and just as the societies contributed to that end while the immigrants adapted to city life, the press served as a third force in maintaining ethnic consciousness. In connection with the American Centennial in 1876 and the 250th anniversary of New Sweden, Del., in 1888, the Swedish-language press voiced praise of Swedish immigrants. The papers' classified sections widened the circle of customers for businessmen and attracted newcomers' attention to suitable areas for settlement. The importance of the press can hardly be overestimated, especially since almost all adult Swedes could read.

The pastors were the first to realize the power of the printed word. In 1855 the Reverend Hasselquist launched the weekly *Hemlandet* from his church in Galesburg; its publication was soon transferred to Chicago as it became the voice of the Augustana Synod.

A decade later the dominance of church-oriented newspapers was broken by the publication of *Svenska Amerikanaren* (The Swedish American, 1866–1877) by the Svea Society. Although the new paper was Republican like *Hemlandet* and nearly as supportive of Swedish ethnicity, a debate about religion and morals immediately began between the two. No other source material better illustrates the intellectual dualism that existed in Swedish America. The liberal and religiously neutral *Svenska Amerikanaren* soon had the same circulation as the conservative and evangelical *Hemlandet*. In 1870 the combined circulation of the two papers was given as 9,000, an impressive number in view of the competition of many smaller papers and a Swedish-born population of 97,000 in the 1870 Census. *Svenska Amerikanaren* was absorbed by the *Svenska Tribunen* in 1877; at the same time another *Svenska Amerikanaren* appeared, which from 1936 was published as *Svenska Amerikanaren Tribunen*.

Between 1855 and 1910 nearly 1,200 Swedish newspapers and magazines were published in 29 states; every Swedish region and viewpoint had an organ. In 1910 alone there were 58 weekly and 232 monthly publications in the Swedish language; in 1915 these publications reached a combined circulation of 650,000. In the latter year the greatest number of readers subscribed to Swedish papers in Chicago; the circulation of *Svenska Tribunen Nyheter* (Swedish Tribune News) was 65,000; that of *Svenska Amerikanaren*, after it absorbed *Hemlandet*, was claimed to be 80,000; and that of the Minneapolis *Svenska Amerikanska Posten* (Swedish-American Post) was 56,000.

After 1915, however, the Swedish-American press declined. The call for 100-percent Americanism during World War I confronted immigrant cultures with unexpected difficulties from censorship commissions that scrutinized their organizations and publications. Since the Swedes were considered to be pro-German—not without reason—the Swedish-American press was hard hit by wartime pressures. *Hemlandet* ceased publication in 1914, and many others failed during the following years. By 1932 the number and combined circulation of Swedish-language publications had been reduced to about half the 1915 figures. Although the war was hard on the Swedish-American press, the deliberate change to the English language and the hard times of the Depression caused a greater number of papers to fail. By 1932 only 35 weekly or monthly papers were published in the Swedish language; their combined circulation was 309,000. Today only five Swedish-American newspapers are being published. The combined circulation probably does not exceed 15,000. During the 1920s and 1930s many papers began to be published in both English and Swedish, and the English-language press of Swedish-American organizations emerged.

SWEDISH-AMERICAN LITERATURE

In an immigrant community of several hundred thousand readers of Swedish, the demand for Swedish-language publications understandably went beyond the materials provided by newspapers and journals. To meet that demand, writers and publishers provided some 10,000 Swedish titles over the years. Religious publications were the first to appear independently; the Augustana Book Concern, founded in 1883, published an average of 25 Swedish books a year between 1891 and 1920. At its peak in the period 1911–1915, it published a total of 840,000 copies of books in Swedish, ranging from devotional literature to "moral" stories for children.

Secular literature was dominated by popular history, travel accounts, memoirs, and reprints of works by well-known Swedish authors. Frequently printed serially in newspapers, such works were sometimes bound into books later as bonuses for newspaper subscribers. Serial publication was advantageous for the many Swedish-American authors, who otherwise had to finance their own publications for the limited Swedish market. A biographical dictionary of some 300 Swedish-American poets, novelists, short-story writers, and journalists published at the beginning of the 20th century indicates the breadth and volume of their production. Relatively few of these writers were truly creative, however, especially when judged against the literature being produced in the homeland during this period. Their values were reflected most clearly in their poetry, a blend of sentimental homesickness and unrestrained praise for their adopted country. Unlike their compatriots in Sweden, they seldom used erotic or naturalist themes. Nor did they write about the everyday personal and social problems of the Swedish-American community. An exception was Arthur Landors (1888–1973), a socialist worker whose theme in two books of verse was the rootlessness of the immigrant; his social criticism gives him a unique place among Swedish-American writers.

As the second Swedish-American generation grew into adulthood, an increasing number of writers began to express themselves in English. Two became well known outside Swedish America: Joe Hill (Joel Hägglund, 1879–1915), a labor poet, and Carl Sandburg (1878–1967), a poet whose themes are universally American rather than specifically ethnic and who was a noted biographer as well. By the mid-1920s the English titles published by the Augustana Book Concern outnumbered the Swedish titles nearly three to one; by 1935 the concern published only an almanac and an annual in Swedish. In 1937 Augustana ceased producing Swedish books altogether, though it did continue to publish *Augustana*, the synod's Swedish journal, until 1956. That year *Augustana* had a circulation of 3,132, while its English counterpart, the *Lutheran Companion*, had reached 88,345.

POLITICS

The earliest Swedes in America supported the Democratic party, but their views changed as slavery became an issue. The Swedes feared that the Democrats would favor slaves over immigrants as a labor force. Moreover, the Republican party launched a program supporting homesteads, industrialization, and open immigration, and its candidate in 1860, Abraham Lincoln, embodied the immigrant dream of the poor boy who succeeds through hard work and becomes a national leader. Swedes in the Midwest overwhelmingly voted Republican in 1860.

During the Civil War, Swedish Republicanism was strengthened. About 3,000 Swedes fought for the North, an impressive figure considering that only 18,600 Swedes were living in the United States in 1860. Fifty Swedes at most fought for the Confederacy. Among approximately one hundred Swedes who were Union officers, Charles Stolbrand (1821–1894), Ernst von Vegesack (1820–1903), and John Dahlgren (1809–1870) achieved high military rank. Two Swedish inventors were instrumental in the outcome of the war. Admiral Dahlgren's canons were mounted on most Yankee ships, and John Ericsson (1803–1889) constructed the ironclad ship *Monitor*.

Participation in the Civil War contributed to the immigrants' pride in their new country and awakened their desire for a role in its politics. Outside Minnesota, however, the Swedes, usually few in number and lacking aggressive leaders, complained about political powerlessness. Even in Chicago, the capital of Swedish America, they had to be satisfied with electing an occasional judge, sheriff, alderman, or representative to the state legislature. Republican party boss Frederick Lundin (1869–1947) and Chief Justice Harry Olson (1867–1935) were Chicago's best-known Swedish politicians.

The Swedes did eventually achieve political power in cities such as Jamestown, N.Y.; Worcester, Mass.; and Rockford, Ill., where they periodically numbered about half the population. Samuel A. Carlson served as mayor of Jamestown for 30 years after his initial election in 1908. Per Holmes was elected mayor of Worcester for the period 1917–1919. In Worcester, as in many other places, it would have been abnormal for a Swede not to vote the Republican ticket, although many Republicans in that city had been socialists in Sweden. In Rockford, Swedish-born Herman Hallstrom (1888–1961) was elected mayor in 1921 on a write-in campaign by the Rockford Labor League. Hallstrom was a bricklayer, war veteran, and socialist who managed on the basis of the ethnic vote to secure the mayor's chair for five consecutive terms.

Many Swedish politicians emerged in Minnesota. The Swedish-born lawyer, John Lind (1854–1930) became the first Swede in Congress in 1886, and despite his defection to the Democrats, the first Swedish governor of Minnesota in 1898. His election helped break the Republican dominance in Minnesota and also opened the door for nine more Swedish governors. Since 1895 at least one U.S. senator from Minnesota in any term has been Scandinavian. The first Swedish senator, Magnus Johnson (1871–1936), a glassblower from Värmland and a former socialist, teamed up with the state Farmer-Labor party in 1922 and was elected to fill a vacancy, though he served only one year. He is said to have been the Senate's first blue-collar worker.

Many Swedes in Minnesota were attracted to the more radical element within the established parties and by the political alliance between workers and farmers. The Swedes' strength in Minnesota seems to have freed a radical vein that made them less politically stereo-

typed there than in other places. Even so, their radicalism seldom ventured further than solidarity with small-farm operators and blue-collar workers—that is, with the majority of Swedes. A good example is Charles A. Lindbergh, Sr. (1859–1924), father of the noted aviator, a member of Congress from Minnesota who headed the opposition to the United States' participation in World War I. Lindbergh wrote a widely read book denouncing the "money barons" and "war agitators" who were leading the country into the war. Controversy over his stand brought defeat at the polls and ended his political career. Like the populists, he attacked big business and trusts and spoke for the people who lived on farms and in small towns.

As reflected in their press during the years of World War I, Swedish Americans tended to be pro-German—they viewed Germany as the upholder of Lutheranism and later as a bulwark against communism—and strongly opposed U.S. involvement in the war. The bias of the Swedish press against big business also affected their position; many believed that all the belligerents were at fault and that the only Americans interested in entering the war were those who could make money from it, such as manufacturers of armaments. A Swedish American, Ernest Lundeen, was one of 50 members of the U.S. House of Representatives to vote against the declaration of war. Nor were Swedes who left their homeland to escape military service inclined to join voluntarily American military forces in 1917. Most Swedes in elected office did support the American war effort once it was undertaken, however; they argued that defeating the Prussian military machine was in Sweden's interest as well.

Swedish America's left wing naturally had its stronghold in industrialized regions. After the beginning of the 20th century many socialists came to America where their socialism entered a dormant stage, from which it rarely emerged until the Depression. In the early 1900s the socialists formed clubs in Chicago, Rockford, and New York and published a journal, *Svenska Socialisten* (The Swedish Socialist, Rockford and Chicago, 1905–1921).

The Great Depression caused the Swedes to reevaluate their political views. Their support of Franklin D. Roosevelt and the Democratic party in 1932 and later actually grew out of various developments over the years. In Minnesota their Republican party affiliation had weakened during the 1880s. The populist movement of the 1890s and Theodore Roosevelt's Progressives had won many Swedish sympathizers. Herbert Hoover's administration was the last nail in the coffin of uncompromising Republicanism. Since 1932 urban-dwelling Swedish Americans have voted Democratic as often as Republican. However, Swedes in rural areas, often in Republican strongholds, have adhered to tradition.

Over the years, thousands of Swedish Americans have held public office, including 26 governors (10 of them in Minnesota), 13 U.S. senators, and dozens of U.S. representatives.

MOBILITY AND IMMIGRANT TRADITIONS

The population of America's pioneer settlements was extremely mobile. In four representative midwestern farming districts hardly more than a third of the inhabitants remained after a period of ten years. These observations of frontier settlements in general differ from those in studies of Swedes who settled in Pepin and Burnett counties in Wisconsin. Here approximately half the population remained after a period of ten years. The first Swedes in Chicago also showed surprising persistence for an urban area. The much higher mobility of the general midwestern settlements as compared with the Swedish districts can be explained by the fact that the figures describe the total population, including its rather mobile "Yankee" element. Studies of the Swedish communities, however, cover a single immigrant group settling in Wisconsin to farm or in Chicago to earn a modest living. Mobility was regulated both by working conditions and home owning. The farmers who had cleared their land and had begun to farm it were naturally less inclined to move. Mobility also decreased among family providers with their own homes in Chicago. In 1930, 65 percent of all Swedish families in the United States were owners of real estate, one of the highest percentages shown by any nationality at that time.

Conditions were especially stable in rural areas with immigrant traditions. In Chisago and Kandiyohi counties, Minn., the Swedes lived in segregated districts that were in turn divided into smaller units made up of people from the same province or even the same parish in Sweden. Between 1885 and 1905 the Augustana congregations in Chisago County, for instance, had distinct "recruiting areas" resulting in a majority of members who were born in southeastern Sweden. Such parish-oriented immigrant areas proved to be strongly resistant to Americanization, as manifested by the customs, dialects, and place names that have been preserved in the Swedish regions in the Midwest.

INTERMARRIAGE AND ASSIMILATION

The Swedes were the slowest of the northern Europeans to marry outside the group, although the inclination to choose marriage partners of a different nationality increased when a region became industrialized or when the Swedish population thinned out. In 1910 both parents of 72 percent of all second-generation Swedes were born in Sweden. The majority of intermarriages were with Norwegians. In Pepin county, Wis., for instance, 8 men out of 244 married non-Swedes, and all but one of the brides came from Norway. This ethnic limitation was to a large extent the result of the desire to marry Protestants only, but a social influence could also be observed. Swedes who lived outside city enclaves and had intellectual or highly skilled occupations showed more tolerance toward intermarriage. Even today the Scandinavian-Lutheran homogeneity in the United States is noticeable.

Although the Swedes resisted intermarriage, they are believed to have assimilated faster than other ethnic groups. This apparent contradiction is a result of other social and cultural conditions. For instance, from the very beginning the Swedes had a positive attitude toward American institutions and Anglo-Saxon customs. Since the Swedes who emigrated were almost always literate in their own language, they learned English quickly. In 1930 only 1.5 percent of the Swedish-born population over ten years old could not speak English; only the Danes exceeded the Swedes in adopting

English. Most Swedes also were eager to send their children to public schools, and they had a high rate of naturalization. In 1910, 63 percent of Swedish-born men over the age of 21 had become citizens of the United States and by 1930, this figure had risen to 72 percent.

Swedes living in the cities were more likely to become Americanized than their compatriots living in the more stable rural communities. The diversity of the city made it harder to maintain the Swedish language and keep the group together; traditional customs were more quickly effaced and forgotten. Most important, urban Swedish communities, once the anchor of ethnic culture and identity, began to disintegrate—partly because Swedes were pushed out of their old neighborhoods by newcomers, partly because Swedes voluntarily departed to suburbs with higher status where housing was better. Since Swedes were largely an urban-dwelling group, the majority were susceptible to these pressures toward Americanization.

Beginning in 1910 the number of Swedish-speaking Americans diminished slowly, but as late as 1930, 615,000 Americans reported that Swedish was their mother tongue. In the United States in 1910 there were 665,000 Swedish-born people and 699,000 native-born American people with at least one Swedish-born parent; together they made up 1.5 percent of the total population. By 1920 the foreign-born generation had dropped to 633,000 and the second generation had increased to 825,000. In 1960 the two generations still totaled over a million, but a decade later they had decreased to slightly over 800,000 and represented only 0.4 percent of the total population.

"Swedish America" as an immigrant subculture reached its peak in about 1910, when there were thousands of primary settlements, usually surrounded by zones where bilingualism was common, especially in the cities. One spoke Swedish at home and at church, but English at work and in public life. Since Swedish children attending public schools began to speak English as a first language, the language question became part of a generation gap that could cause ruptures in family life. Parents identified with the Swedish language and the children avoided it as something almost shameful from the past. This second-generation complex kept many Swedish Americans aloof from ethnic fellowship and eroded ethnic cohesiveness. A reaction against that trend came, as Marcus Lee Hansen has described, with the third generation, whose members had lost all contact with their ancestral language.

As the pressures toward assimilation steadily increased, they began to affect the largest and most influential Swedish-American institution: the church. The churches, especially the Augustana Synod and the Mission Covenant, had long contended that the Swedish language was essential to their work. But when forced to choose between using the Swedish language and serving a younger generation that did not speak it, they ultimately decided in favor of the latter and were rewarded by rising memberships well into the 1930s. Despite decreasing immigration, the Augustana Synod nearly doubled in size between 1906 and 1936. The Mission Friends' strong religious relations with Sweden, however, made them especially resistant toward Americanization, and their church can still, to some degree, be considered a Swedish-American organization.

The Augustana Synod functioned as an English-speaking church on a weakening Swedish foundation up to 1962, when it merged with German, Danish, and Finnish Lutherans in the Lutheran Church of America.

Whereas the churches had resolved the language question by the end of the 1920s and shifted to English rather quickly once their decision had been made, the secular organizations adapted more slowly—or not at all—to the attitudes and interests of the younger generations. Unlike the church, whose message was not bound to the Swedish language, the secular organizations long saw their mission as the preservation of that very language and the customs and traditions associated with it. As a result, they proved far more resistant to Americanization. For example, though Vasa lodges using the English language were accepted in 1923 "where necessary," as late as 1946 only a quarter of them were officially English-speaking.

The Great Depression of the early 1930s further weakened Swedish-American institutions. To be sure, the crisis brought dispersed Swedish Americans together: since relief aid and jobs were reserved only for citizens, many immigrants had to turn to their own groups for assistance. Swedish churches and organizations collected emergency funds; in Chicago, for example, the Swedish corps of the Salvation Army aided 41,000 persons during the winter of 1931. But in general the Depression had a negative effect on Swedish ethnicity and cohesion: many Swedish-American organizations collapsed because members could not pay dues, newspapers failed for lack of subscribers, and even the churches had to limit their social services.

In the late 1930s Swedish Americans were again faced with the need to take sides in a European conflict against Germany. Though many of them had objected to the provisions of the Treaty of Versailles in 1919 and had sympathized with Germany's plight, their sympathy quickly vanished in 1940 when Hitler invaded Denmark and Norway. Swedish Americans therefore voluntarily supported the war effort, which intensified and largely completed their Americanization.

THE ETHNIC REVIVAL

Once Swedish Americans accepted the decline and even the disappearance of the Swedish language as largely inevitable but not fatal, they could turn their attention to aspects of the Swedish heritage that would interest the American-born, especially those who did not speak Swedish. Thus, Americanization did not preclude the establishment of new cultural institutions or the preservation of Swedishness at the site of old Swedish settlements. In some rural communities like Bishop Hill, Ill., Chisago County, Minn.; Lindsborg, Kans.; Kingsburg, Calif.; and New Sweden, Me., where many families still speak Swedish, Swedish homogeneity has been maintained until the present. In the 1970s that Swedishness found new expression as these communities restored 19th-century homes and shops, opened museums, and organized special cultural events. In the Bishop Hill Historic District, for instance, a dozen brick communal buildings from the mid-19th century have been restored, along with many later ones. Also in urban areas, where Swedish ethnicity had declined dramatically even before 1930, yearly festivals are held in

several neighborhoods to commemorate their Swedish past. In Chicago an attempt has been made to recreate the 19th-century atmosphere of "Andersonville," a group of Swedish shops, restaurants, and a small museum in the formerly Swedish neighborhoods around Clark Street and Foster Avenue.

The most characteristic holiday celebrated by Swedish organizations large and small, aging or rejuvenated, is St. Lucia Day (December 13). Central to a "Luciafest" —which may be held in a hospital, at a Swedish lodge, on a university campus, or at home—is the Lucia bride, dressed in a long white gown with a wreath of candles on her head. Followed by other girls in white, all carrying candles, she leads a procession to the singing of the Lucia song. For older Swedish Americans, the ceremony evokes memories of Lucia Days of earlier years. The procession is usually followed by group singing, holiday treats, and folk dancing.

The Swedish revival has been reinforced by ethnic studies programs and activities connected with the American Bicentennial. To be sure, the old Swedish-American organizations, such as Vasa, Svithiod, and the Order of Vikings, have benefited little; still oriented toward the values of the older immigrants, they have not been able to attract their Americanized grandchildren. The latter instead have enrolled in university programs in Scandinavian studies and have gone to Sweden to learn Swedish, to pursue their own family history, and to rediscover a lost heritage. In the United States special seminars for adults and summer camps for Swedish-American children are increasing in number and popularity. Between 1973 and 1977 the total enrollment in Scandinavian studies (650 courses at 87 colleges and universities) increased by 25 percent—to 4,000 students in nonlanguage subjects and 3,550 in language courses, 40 percent of whom were studying Swedish.

Interest in Swedish Americans has likewise increased in the homeland. In 1968 the Emigrantinstitutet Utvandrarnas Hus (House of Emigrants), which holds Europe's largest collection of materials on emigration history, was founded in Växjö. Vilhelm Moberg's series of novels of 1949–1959 about the Swedish emigrants to America and the two films made from them in the 1970s have added a vivid, emotional dimension to the academic research published by such American organizations as the Swedish Pioneer Historical Society and various ethnic research institutes. Increased contact with Sweden and their heritage has strengthened the ethnic consciousness of Swedish Americans and has awakened in them an interest in the experience of their immigrant forefathers and the forces that brought them to America.

Bibliography
For background information, see Franklin D. Scott, *Sweden: The Nation's History* (St. Paul, Minn., 1977). Statistical information appears in *Emigrationsutredningen* (The Emigration Commission) with 20 appendixes (Stockholm, 1908–1913). Results of Swedish research into emigration are presented by Harald Runblom and Hans Norman, eds., *From Sweden to America: A History of the Migration* (Uppsala, 1976). Allan Kastrup's encyclopedic *The Swedish Heritage in America* (St. Paul, Minn., 1975), examines the immigration and the immigrants. Arnold Barton discusses the influence of immigrant letters in his source book, *Letters from the Promised Land: Swedes in America, 1840–1914* (Minneapolis, Minn., 1975). George M. Stephenson, *The Religious Aspects of Swedish Immigration: A Study of the Immigrant Churches* (1932; re-print, New York, 1972), deals with religious conditions in Sweden and the United States.

Swedish settlements are described in detail in Helge Nelson, *The Swedes and the Swedish Settlements in North America*, 2 vols. (Lund, Sweden, 1943); vol. 2 is an atlas. Sture Lindmark, *Swedish-America, 1914–1932: Studies in Ethnicity with Emphasis on Illinois and Minnesota* (Uppsala, 1971), and Byron Nordstrom, ed., *The Swedes in Minnesota* (Minneapolis, Minn., 1976), also deal with settlements. Ulf Beijbom, *Swedes in Chicago: A Demographic and Social Study of the 1846–1880 Immigration* (Växjö, 1971), discusses the urban experience. Lars Ljungmark, *For Sale—Minnesota* (Stockholm, 1971), is about the organized promotion of immigration. Acculturation is examined by Sture Lindmark in *Swedish-America* and by Daniel M. Pearson in *The Americanization of Carl Aaron Swensson* (Davenport, Iowa, 1977). O. Fritiof Ander, *The Cultural Heritage of the Swedish Immigrant* (Rock Island, Ill., 1956), discusses Swedish-American literature and Finis H. Capps, *From Isolationism to Involvement: The Swedish Immigrant Press in America, 1914–1945* (Chicago, 1966) examines the Swedish-American press.

On immigrants and politics, see Nels M. Hokanson, *Swedish Immigrants in Lincoln's Time* (New York, 1942), and Sten Carlsson "Scandinavian Politicians in Minnesota around the Turn of the Century," *Americana Norvegica*, vol. 3 (Oslo, 1971). The scope of Swedish immigration and its impact on American life is covered by *Swedish Pioneer Historical Quarterly* (Chicago, 1950–).

Archives and libraries with immigrant materials are: the Emigrantinstitutet Utvandrarnas Hus (House of Emigrants), Växjö, Sweden; the Emigrant Register, Karlstad, Sweden; the Augustana College Library, Rock Island, Ill.; the Swedish Pioneer Historical Society, Chicago; the American Swedish Institute, Minneapolis; and the American Swedish Historical Museum, Philadelphia.

ULF BEIJBOM

SWISS

Because the Swiss are frequently taken for Germans, Dutch, French, or Italians, depending on the language or dialect they speak, they have remained largely invisible and numerically underestimated as a distinct group in the United States. According to the most reliable estimates, nearly 400,000 Swiss immigrated to the United States between 1700 and 1970; 346,468 arrived between 1820, the first year in which immigration figures were kept, and 1975, putting them in the same numerical range as immigrant groups from Denmark, the Netherlands, and Portugal. In 1970 about 218,700 Americans claimed Swiss birth or parentage (see Table 1).

ORIGINS

The unity of Swiss immigrants rests not on linguistic or religious homogeneity, but on a centuries-old tradition of political independence won through a strategic use of geopolitical advantages. The Swiss nation dates to 1291 when farmers of the Alpine valleys of Uri, Schwyz, and Unterwalden formed a league for mutual protection against the encroachments of surrounding

Table 1. Swiss stock in the United States, 1900 to 1970.

Year	Total	Swiss-born	Percent of total Swiss stock in U.S	Second generation
1900	294,284	115,593	39.3	178,691
1910	342,307	124,848	36.5	217,459
1920	376,000	118,659	31.6	257,341
1930	374,003	113,010	30.2	260,993
1940	293,973	88,293	30.0	205,680
1950	287,296	71,636	25.0	215,660
1960	263,054	61,568	23.4	201,486
1970	218,708	49,732	22.7	168,976

Source: U.S. Bureau of the Census, *Historical Statistics of the United States, Colonial Times to 1970* (Washington, D.C., 1975), I, 116–118.

Switzerland

100   Km.   Miles

French-speaking areas

German-speaking areas

Romansh-speaking areas

Italian-speaking areas

feudal lords seeking to expand their domains. The league based its strength on its control of the Alpine mountain passes that linked northern Europe to the Mediterranean world. By 1513 ten more states whose territories also controlled access routes to the central passes and whose people were also resisting external rule had joined the league. The confederacy remained relatively stable for nearly 300 years.

The political and social upheavals following in the wake of the French Revolution and the rise of industrialism led to the formation of a federal state in 1848. Local and cantonal autonomy was curtailed in order to strengthen a central government controlled by the growing entrepreneurial and managerial class. Federal centralism remained, however, somewhat limited by local differences. Linguistic diversity was, and remains, even more complex than the official divisions into German, French, Italian, and Romansch suggest. The German-speaking people, about 72 percent of the population, use a variety of regional dialects originating in Old or Middle High German. The French-speaking group (about 20 percent) also speak many local dialects showing the influence of late Latin as well as Celtic, Burgundian, and Alemannic elements. The Italian-speaking Swiss (about 6 percent) speak official Italian, a Tuscan-based dialect, and locally rooted variants. Romansch (about 1 percent) is spoken by the descendants of Romanized Celts, who retreated before the invading Ale-

manni into northeastern Switzerland in the 5th century A.D. Even they can be divided into five subgroups. Swiss emigrants have thus always had the advantage of living in a polyglot society and of having to acquire at least a rudimentary knowledge of a variety of foreign tongues. Their insistence on preserving local variations of speech and tradition has made them used to the differences found beyond the confines of their native village.

Regional and socioeconomic differences correlate only partially with linguistic diversity. The Alpine farmers and craftsmen at the center of Swiss history make up about a fifth of the population and are dispersed among all four language groups. They are often staunchly Catholic, federalist, and conservative in their outlook. Equally influential were the bourgeoisie of Zurich, Bern, Basel, Geneva, Lugano, and Chur. Except in Lugano, they were largely Protestant and pragmatic and centralist in political orientation; they closely controlled the large rural districts under their jurisdiction and engaged in mercantile, financial, and, since the mid-19th century, industrial enterprises that were international in scope. A middle position is occupied by the communities of the lowland villages, grouped around placid lakes or nestled on the slopes of wooded hills. They have been inhabited by well-to-do farmers, by tradesmen, and, since industrialization, by a working class employed in the widely dispersed industrial plants and factories of the nation. Although Catholics

and members of the traditional Protestant Reformed church predominate, Anabaptists, Pietists, and Mormons, as well as advocates of socialist doctrines, are also represented. Immigrants to the fertile agricultural regions of the United States, Canada, Brazil, and Argentina came largely from these lowland regions.

During the Reformation, Catholics retained power in the Italian-speaking and original German-speaking cantons of central Switzerland, while the Reformed faith—the interpretation of Christianity offered by Huldreich Zwingli (1484–1531)—gained ground in the major cities and their rural domains. The French- and Romansch-speaking areas were split by regional or even communal choices. The Anabaptists made inroads in several regions—most of them in the rural lowlands—but they survived the harsh repression of the established churches only in the district governed from Bern and in parts of nearby Alsace. The Brethren, as they called themselves, split in the 1690s between the Amish who followed Jacob Ammann (c. 1644–before 1730) and the Swiss Mennonites. In the United States these two groups and their descendants remained distinct; in Europe they were eventually reunited. (*See also* Amish.)

These overlapping loyalties left the Swiss tied less to their nation-state than to a specific valley or village. Multicultural coexistence was perhaps less a conscious ideal than an acceptance of necessity.

PATTERNS OF MIGRATION

Because Switzerland is small, and one-fifth of its territory is uninhabitable, population pressure is an easy explanation for the persistent emigration that has characterized its history. But a closer look at estimates for the years 1850–1914, the period both of greatest emigration and of greatest population growth, shows a nearly perfect balance between emigrants from, and immigrants to, Switzerland—410,000 Swiss departed for other countries and 409,000 foreign-born people arrived in Switzerland. In 1880, for example, 234,000 Swiss lived abroad: 38 percent of them in the United States, 29 percent in France, 13 percent in Germany, and 5 percent each in Italy and Argentina. In that same year 211,000 foreign-born people lived in Switzerland; 45 percent of them from Germany, 28 percent from France, and 20 percent from Italy. The explanation of this two-way migration pattern is that emigrants departing from the country were responding to the opening up of agricultural lands for settlement in countries such as the United States and Argentina, which provided opportunities for the Swiss who did not want to give up their independent agrarian or trade pursuits for wage labor in factories. The simultaneous movement of foreigners into the country was clearly a reflection of railroad building and industrial growth in Switzerland, which provided jobs for unemployed unskilled laborers or skilled technicians from other countries. For the departing Swiss the United States was a favorite destination. Ready land and good working conditions were attractive, and the Swiss saw the new republic as a kindred nation pursuing Swiss social and political ideals on a grand scale.

Of the 400,000 Swiss who had immigrated to America by the 1970s, an estimated 25,000 to 30,000 came in the colonial period; between 4,000 and 5,000 per decade came in the first half of the 19th century; about 250,000 arrived between 1850 and 1921 (about 82,000 of these in the 1880s); and nearly 70,000 between 1920 and 1975. The immigrants eventually settled throughout the United States—from South Carolina and Pennsylvania in the colonial era, they followed the nation's westward expansion during the 19th century. New York City and its environs and parts of Wisconsin, Ohio, California, and Oregon attracted the greatest numbers. A good many eventually returned to Switzerland, but the data available do not reveal exactly how many.

COLONIAL IMMIGRATION

Among the few Swiss who arrived in the English colonies of North America before 1710 were Diebold von Erlach (1541–1565), who perished at the hands of the Spanish, and some "Dutchmen" at Jamestown, one of whom, the "Switzer" William Henry Volda (Walder?), only narrowly escaped John Smith's vengeance for an allegedly treasonous alliance with Powhatan. In 1687 a Jean François Gignilliat from Vevey received 3,000 acres from the proprietors of South Carolina "to encourage more of the Swisse nation."

By 1700 various Swiss Mennonite families had settled in William Penn's colony. Penn began advertising for settlers in the late 1680s through pamphlets and agents, and himself undertook several journeys to Europe to recruit colonists. In 1709 the Nationalization Act granted English citizenship to all Protestants willing to take an oath of allegiance to the English king. As a result some 13,000 people moved to England, mainly from the Palatinate, the destination of numerous immigrants from Switzerland since the 1660s. The size of this influx took the government by surprise, and it seized the opportunity to stem the tide when Christopher de Graffenried (1661–1743) offered to lead some 650 Palatines and about 100 Swiss from Bernese regions to North Carolina. He founded New Bern at the confluence of the Neuse and Trent rivers, but the settlers met with hostility from the dominant Indian nation and the communities previously established under its tutelage. De Graffenried was captured and nearly killed while he was on a surveying trip in 1711, but he was released. In 1713 he returned to Switzerland; his grandson Tscharner became the progenitor of the numerous present-day de Graffenrieds.

After 1680 a movement known as Pietism swept the Swiss churches. Pietists insisted upon independent study of the scriptures, lay preaching, and the experience of conversion rather than orthodox faith and established ritual. They also rejected infant baptism. Clergymen influenced by the movement were often expelled from the Swiss Reformed church. One of these deposed ministers, Samuel Güldin (1644–1745), went to America with his large family in 1710 and became a farmer and preacher in the Oley region some 40 miles from Philadelphia. For nearly 20 years he was the only ordained German-speaking Reformed clergyman in Pennsylvania.

A group of Swiss Brethren crossed on the boat with Güldin. They became known in the United States as Mennonites, although their religious views antedated those of the Dutch Reformer Menno Simons and the affinity between them was entirely coincidental. Their

creed, formulated around Zurich in the mid-1520s, rejected established churches, the state, and infant baptism. The rapid spread of Pietism led the Reformed church to renew its pressure on the dissenting Brethren and forced their departure. In October 1710 they settled on a 10,000-acre tract at Conestoga along the Pequa Creek in Pennsylvania; some 4,000 Brethren joined them there over the next four decades. Beginning in 1738 some 200 Amish Brethren also came to Pennsylvania, but since they had split off from the Mennonites in the 1690s on doctrinal differences regarding uniform dress, footwashing, and the strict avoidance of contact with sinners and nonbelievers, they remained apart.

From the Lancaster, Pa., region the Swiss Mennonites moved to other counties and into the Shenandoah Valley. Their descendants joined the general westward movement into Ohio and Indiana in search of cheap land, at times joined by new immigrants directly from Switzerland. The Brethren did not establish villages or townships, but continued to live on widely dispersed family farms. Some 20 to 30 families formed congregations led by a lay bishop and elders. The farming methods and customs of the Amish and conservative Swiss Brethren continue to preserve features of their Swiss and Palatine origin.

Pennsylvania attracted not only Swiss Brethren and other Pietist dissenters (many of whom joined the Moravians or other religious groups) but also some 20,000 Swiss Protestants who belonged to the state Reformed church. Most of the latter were farmers or craftsmen from the cantons of Zurich, Schaffhausen, Saint Gall, and Basel. Some were well-to-do, others of more modest means; all were attracted by the accounts of returned emigrants and promoters of colonial ventures extolling the rich farmlands and freedom from taxes and services that would be theirs in the New World. In the 1730s and 1740s something of a propaganda war developed between those who praised the newly found Canaan and those who considered emigration a sure path to destruction—both could cite letters and reports to prove their point, and potential emigrants had to weigh carefully the conflicting evidence. In addition to the more obvious reasons, inducements to emigrate undoubtedly included escape from an unhappy marriage, bothersome parents, or the strict supervision by bailiffs, pastors, and neighbors. A group of Reformed ministers, licensed mainly by the governing body of the Dutch Reformed church, assumed responsibility for the welfare of the emigrating church members. The main parish organizer was Michael Schlatter (1716–1790) from Saint Gall. In 1747 a ministerial organization of the Reformed church was formed in Pennsylvania and soon after became a fully independent governing body.

In the 1730s Jean Pierre Purry (1675–1736) circulated a pamphlet inviting his countrymen to join "the Swiss now living in the New World happily and without home-sickness." Purry, a wine merchant and speculator, had already developed grand designs for founding colonies in South Africa, Indonesia, and Australia. In 1730 he submitted a plan to the British government for the founding of 12 towns along the Spanish borderlands of the Carolinas. His proposal was accepted with modifications, and Purry sailed to Charleston, S.C. Some 25 miles up the Savannah River he selected 200,000 acres

for the future town of Purrysburg. On his return to Europe he recruited some 450 people from French- and German-speaking Switzerland for his colony; about the same number emigrated on their own, enticed by his advertisements.

The reaction of the settlers varied from high praise to a bitter disappointment that included calling Purry's appeal a "booklet of lies." Nonetheless, after initial difficulties the settlement prospered, and by 1800 the Parish of St. Peter, established in 1747, counted some 1,500 parishioners. Eventually, however, the town declined and the site was given up; recurring malaria, swampy and infertile soil, and competition from nearby Savannah made survival impossible.

In 1736 Reformed minister Bartholomäus Zuberbühler (1678–1738) and the well-to-do Johannes Tobler (1696–1765), embroiled in political disputes at home and influenced by reports from Zuberbühler's son in Purry's community, led about 100 people from northeastern Switzerland to South Carolina. Tobler became a wealthy plantation owner, justice of the peace, and editor of an almanac in New Windsor, a settlement near Augusta, Ga. Zuberbühler accepted a pastorate in Charleston; the rest dispersed to various South Carolina settlements. Some Pietist families settled with their minister, Johann Ulrich Giezendanner (d. 1738), in Orangeburg, whose surviving parish records contain the names of some later arrivals as well.

The Swiss settlers blended easily into colonial society. Names were Anglicized: Gallmann became Coleman; Stauffer, Stover; and Roth, Roads. Under the pressure of frontier conditions or the influence of other immigrant groups new farming practices were adopted. In Pennsylvania the Swiss became part of the Pennsylvania German community in dress, language, and custom. The Swiss Brethren and Amish preserved many of their old ways, but they, too, blended in with Pennsylvania's "plain people."

During the American Revolution some Swiss kept aloof; others sided with England; still others criticized the crown but viewed the union between England and the colonies as binding; others supported the rebels. Pietists and Mennonites were most apt to remain uninvolved; the Reformed were about equally represented in all groups. John Joachim Zubly, a pastor in Savannah, Ga., was a delegate to the Second Continental Congress, but rejected the severing of ties with England despite his pamphlets and sermons that were harshly critical of the crown. The Reverend Abraham Blumer, in contrast, was devoted to the rebel cause. The Reverend Schlatter first joined Lord Howe's royal forces and then was neutral, but his sons fought with the rebel army. Albert Gallatin (1761–1849), who arrived from Geneva in 1780, found the emerging nation to his liking; he became a leading Jeffersonian and an outstanding American diplomat.

SETTLEMENTS, 1800–1920

The approximately 200,000 Swiss who came to the United States between 1820 and 1900 were a small segment of European expansion in general and of the westward movement of the United States in particular. (See Table 2.) About 60 percent of the 19th-century immigrants settled in rural areas. The first of several colonies established early in the century was Nouvelle Vevey

Table 2. Swiss immigration to the United States, 1821 to 1920.

Period	Number	Percentage of all immigrants
1821–1830	3,226	2.24
1831–1840	4,821	0.80
1841–1850	4,644	0.27
1851–1860	25,011	0.96
1861–1870	23,286	1.01
1871–1880	28,293	1.01
1881–1890	81,988	1.56
1891–1900	31,179	0.85
1901–1910	34,922	0.40
1911–1920	23,091	0.40
Total	260,461	0.77

Source: U.S. Immigration and Naturalization Service, Annual Report, 1975 (Washington, D.C., 1975), pp. 62–63.

(now Vevay) in Switzerland County, Ind., where Swiss settlers had come to practice viticulture; by 1810 they were producing 2,400 gallons of wine annually. Another major center of Swiss immigration, Highland in southwestern Illinois, was originally called New Switzerland. It was founded in 1831 by two well-to-do families from Sursee, in the canton of Lucerne; by 1870 some 1,500 Swiss had settled there, among them Heinrich Bosshard, who edited an emigration guide and composed the "Sempacherlied," a Swiss patriotic song.

In the second half of the 19th century about 8,000 Swiss settled around Monroe in southern Wisconsin. In 1844 communes of the valley of Glarus founded an emigration society to initiate a Glarnese settlement in the American Midwest. Nearly 200 Glarnese left in 1845; some settled in various cities, and 119 of them founded New Glarus in Green County, Wis. By 1860 over 10,000 acres were under cultivation on 149 farms with a total population of 960. In the 1870s dairying replaced wheat growing, and the region became a major dairying center. Today, street names and architectural styles commemorate the origins of New Glarus. Some older people still speak the Glarnese dialect, and various festivals, annual performances of Schiller's *William Tell*, and an outdoor "historical village" museum attract over 30,000 tourists every year. Other, smaller settlements emerged during this period in Ohio (Tell City), Kentucky (Bernstadt), West Virginia (Helvetica), and Tennessee (Grutli).

In the 19th century California was also a destination of Swiss immigrants. The pioneer was Johann August Sutter (1803–1880), who founded New Helvetia and who became famous when gold was discovered near his sawmill in 1848. Most numerous among the Swiss who came to California were Italian speakers from the Canton Ticino. The narrow mountain valleys of its northern part and the villages nestled in the forest-covered hills to the south had a long tradition of seasonal migration of craftsmen, builders, and laborers, which the emergence of industrialized economies diverted into emigration overseas. Between 1887 and 1938 approximately 17,800 of these migrant laborers went to California. Before 1900 most of them were single men, many of whom returned after a few years; after 1900 many were families who settled there permanently. The Ticinese were experienced in grape growing, dairying, and cattle raising, which they pursued in the valleys of the coastal range of California. They tended to stay in closely knit groups and to preserve their language and customs. In 1930 more than 11,000 were living in the coastal areas and about 3,000 in the Central Valley; most of the rest had settled in San Francisco.

Religious groups continued to form a part of Swiss immigration to the United States in the 19th century. The Swiss Brethren settled in Ohio and Indiana and were often joined by American-born Swiss Mennonite settlers moving westward from Pennsylvania or Virginia; in the second half of the century the farmlands of Missouri, Kansas, Iowa, and Oregon attracted Brethren immigrants. Congregations were established in the townships of Sonnenberg (1817) and Chippewa (1825) in Ohio; Berne (1838) in Indiana; Madison Township (1849) in Iowa; Whitewater (1883) in Butler County, Kansas; Tipton (1886) in Morgan and Moniteau counties, Missouri; and Silverton and Salem districts (after 1876) in Oregon.

After the Civil War many of these Swiss Brethren communities underwent significant change. The Swiss dialect was replaced first by High German, then by English. The lay ministry was superseded by professional clergymen trained in seminaries. Many children left the farms for nearby towns. The temperance, Sunday school, foreign mission, and revival movements found ready acceptance in many of these communities, and denominational schools were founded. Some communities resisted these trends, however, and kept to a life that differed little from that of the Amish.

After 1849 the Mormons recruited converts in Europe for their New Zion in Utah. Switzerland yielded a good harvest, as about 1,000 Swiss settled in Utah at Midway (Wasatch County), Santa Clara (Washington County), and Providence (Cache County) and in Idaho at Bern and Geneva (Bear Lake County) about 1870. The Swiss Mormons often had very large families, especially in the time of plural marriages, and they proved to be hardy pioneers and loyal members of the church.

Swiss Catholics also established settlements. In southern Indiana, St. Meinrad, established in 1852, started as a Benedictine monastery founded by monks from Einsiedeln, Canton Schwyz. It attracted many German-speaking settlers to the region, became an educational and pastoral center, and formed the nucleus of the Swiss-American Benedictine congregation that today embraces several foundations, including Conception (1873) in Missouri and Assumption (1899) in North Dakota. St. Meinrad's first abbot, Martin Marty (1834–1896), became the first Catholic bishop of South Dakota in 1880.

Other monastic foundations included the Order of the Precious Blood in 1853 in Seneca, Putnam, and Mercer counties, Ohio, and a Capuchin friary in Milwaukee, Wis., in 1856. Various Swiss convents established branches in the United States. The sisters from Sarnen, Canton Unterwalden, active in primary education and social service, opened a convent in Cottonwood, S.Dak.

About 40 percent of the Swiss immigrants settled in cities. Rosters for some 6,000 Swiss immigrants in New York, Chicago, Cincinnati, and Milwaukee list occupations such as carpenter, tanner, bartender, machinist, plumber, butcher, cook, and mason. The U.S. Census for 1900 shows the Swiss-born concentrated in the occupations of saloonkeeper, waiter, bartender, and in the

embroidery and silk industries. The second generation, however, showed no marked concentration in any one occupation.

America provided opportunities for many ambitious Swiss. Jacques Anton Biderman (1790–1865) became a partner in E.I. Du Pont's firm, married his daughter, and in 1837 built Winterthur near Wilmington, Del., an estate that has become a noted museum of early Americana. In 1847 Meyer Guggenheim (1828–1905), a Swiss Jew, emigrated to Philadelphia from Lengnau, Canton Aargau; he prospered as a merchant and with his sons built a large family fortune in smelting and refining. Louis Agassiz (1807–1873) found a congenial atmosphere at Harvard University and became a leading anti-Darwinian natural scientist. Martin Henni (1805–1881) entered the United States as a young theologian in 1828 and in 1843 became bishop, then archbishop (1875) of Milwaukee. Philip Schaff (1819–1893) taught for 25 years at Union Theological Seminary in New York City and was a leading Reformed theologian.

ORGANIZATIONS AND PUBLICATIONS

Most Swiss communities, especially in larger cities, established a variety of institutions adapted from the home country to assist them in time of need and to strengthen group cohesion. Before the Civil War New York had a Swiss Benevolent Society, the Helvetia Rifle Club, the Society for the Benefit of the Sick, the fraternal Helvetia Lodge, and the Helvetia Men's Choir, which held regular monthly meetings where official tasks and business and politics were discussed. Festivals connected with important dates of Swiss history acquainted the younger generation, "the real Swiss Americans, with the substance of Swissness, with its customs and rituals," as one immigrant put it. Papers were read and concerts given to raise money for charity. In 1887–1888 the Benevolent Society distributed "67 pair of shoes, 6640 pounds of bread, 55 tons of coal, 1660 dollars in cash. It helped 14 adults with 8 children to return to Switzerland and gave 527 dollars for the sick." In 1851 when the Hungarian revolutionary hero Lajos (Louis) Kossuth was given an official welcome in New York City, the Helvetia Lodge took part in the festivities with a new flag and a brass band.

A similar network of organizations grew up in the smaller cities. Dallas, Tex., in 1887 counted only 200 Swiss among its 40,000 inhabitants, but they had a Grütli Society, a library, a singing society, and a gymnasium and wrestling club. Many of these societies are still active, providing an effective link between generations and aid for newcomers.

Unity among Swiss immigrant communities was furthered in 1865 by the formation in Cincinnati of an important society of national scope, the Grütli-Bund, later renamed the North American Alliance. Its purpose was to unite all benevolent societies and, later, fraternal organizations into a federated structure patterned after the old Swiss confederacy, "to further the moral and intellectual level" of Swiss Americans. Every two years a different U.S. city was chosen Vorort, or administrative center, of the league. Despite some crises, the alliance prospered until the 1920s; in 1915 it listed over 6,000 active members dispersed throughout the United States.

The earliest exclusively Swiss newspaper in 19th-century America was Helvetia, published in German in 1859 in Cincinnati to promote the Swiss colony of Tell City in Indiana. In 1868 Conrad Bryner started the Grütlianer and its supplement Grütli in New York, but, beset by financial problems, it survived barely a year. Johann Schläpfer continued the paper under the name Helvetia (1870–1876) in Newark, N.J., until illness and insufficient subscriptions forced him to give up the venture. Johann Feierabend published the Amerikanische Schweizerzeitung as a continuation of Schläpfer's Helvetia and was more successful. The paper's name was changed to Swiss American Review in 1972; it continues to publish news items pertaining to Switzerland mainly in German and English, sometimes in French, Italian, and Romansch. The Amerikanischer Schweizer Kalender, modeled after the traditional Swiss almanac, appeared annually from 1881 until 1933. In 1876 the Courrier Suisse appeared in New York but survived hardly a year; La Croix Fédérale (1882–1885) of L. Perrelet did not last much longer. About 1880 the weekly Elvetia began to appear in San Francisco, and is still being published there. The Swiss Journal (f. 1918) is still published in German, French, Italian, and English and has a circulation of around 3,000.

Swiss immigrants fitted well into the expanding nation, sharing its ideals as well as its prejudices. The sociopolitical ideologies of the two countries were similar, as John Joachim Zubly (Züblin) had already pointed out in 1770. American colonials fought the English king in the 18th century as Swiss peasants had fought the Holy Roman emperors in the 13th; thus both nations celebrated their origins as a birth from the struggle against tyranny and oppression. The parallels in their histories were sometimes symbolized in pageants commemorating the Fourth of July or August First, the Swiss national holiday, in which William Tell would walk side by side with George Washington, and Helvetia, surrounded by the cantons, would be followed by Columbia accompanied by all the states of the Union. The Bundesbrief of 1291 would be invoked along with the Declaration of Independence.

The Swiss were active in American politics, joining parties according to personal, or sometimes regional, preference. The Swiss Mennonites of Pennsylvania were usually Republican, if they were involved in politics at all, the Brethren of Ohio were Democrats; but no national pattern of Swiss-American party affiliation can be established. In the Civil War those living in the North were loyal to the Union cause, those in the South supported the Confederacy.

The violent anti-German agitation during World War I had little impact on the German Swiss. They had never identified with the German nation, and the language they spoke did not sound much like German to the outsider. They could also rely on the tradition of friendship between Switzerland and the United States. Some Swiss Mennonites suffered hardships, but because of their radical pacifism, not their Swiss origins.

1920 TO THE PRESENT

The Immigration Act of 1924 reduced the number of Swiss coming to the United States from 3,752 in 1921 to 1,707 in 1929. But Swiss professionals continued to be admitted, and several had remarkable careers in their

adopted country. Louis Chevrolet (1878–1941) contributed significantly to the development of the combustion engine and lent his name to the automobile. Othmar Ammann (1879–1965), as chief engineer of the Port Authority of New York, built five of its major bridges, including the George Washington and the Verranzano-Narrows; William Lescaze (1896–1969) designed some of the early American skyscrapers. Adolf Meyer (1866–1950) was an important figure in American psychiatry.

Today there are four distinct groups of Swiss Americans. The descendants of the first, 18th-century, secular immigrants have fully blended into the general society and rarely show more than a passing interest in their Swiss origins. The Swiss Brethren and their offspring still constitute two-thirds of American Mennonites. Some have fully adopted American ways; others have preserved to varying degrees their Swiss and Palatine traditions; all honor their Swiss forebears as the formulators of their creed and as pure Christians. The children of 19th- and early 20th-century immigrants are fully assimilated, although some maintain ties with relatives in Switzerland and are active in organizations such as the Swiss-American Historical Society, founded in 1927 to explore the role of the Swiss in the development of the United States. Finally, the arrivals since the 1920s have been perhaps the most active in strengthening the bonds with the past and between Switzerland and the United States. They are predominantly professionals from a highly industrialized and prosperous nation, and they return frequently to the homeland. They are less immigrants than part of an often temporary exchange migration that is global in scope.

Bibliography

Bibliographies can be found in Leo Schelbert, *Swiss in North America* (Philadelphia, 1974), and, edited by the same author, *New Glarus, 1845–1970: The Making of a Swiss American Town* (Glarus, Switzerland, 1970). Demographic material on the colonial period is in Albert B. Faust and Gaius M. Brumbaugh, eds., *Lists of Swiss Emigrants in the Eighteenth Century to the American Colonies,* 2 vols. (1920–1925; reprint, Baltimore, 1968); see also corrections by Leo Schelbert, "Notes on 'Lists,'" *National Genealogical Society Quarterly* 60 (March 1972): 36–46. U.S. Census data are analyzed in John P. Grueningen, ed., *The Swiss in the United States* (Madison, Wis., 1940). The Swiss American Historical Society's publication, *Prominent Americans of Swiss Origin* (New York, 1932), is somewhat biased but provides useful detail. Leo Schelbert, "On Becoming an Emigrant: A Structural View of Eighteenth and Nineteenth Century Swiss Data," *Perspectives in American History* 7 (1974): 441–495, offers a theory of the causes of migration. His *Einführung in die schweizerische Auswanderungsgeschichte der Neuzeit* (Zurich, Switzerland, 1976), places emigration to the United States within the general Swiss migratory tradition. Delbert L. Gratz, *Bernese Anabaptists and Their American Descendants* (Scottdale, Pa., 1953), is a detailed scholarly portrait.

Robert H. Billigmeier and Fred A. Picard, eds., *The Old Land and the New: The Journals of Two Swiss Families in America in the 1820s* (Minneapolis, 1965); Heinrich Lienhard, *From St. Louis to Sutter's Fort,* eds. Erwin G. and Elisabeth K. Gudde (Norman, Okla., 1961); Heinz K. Meier, ed., *Memoirs of a Swiss Officer in the Civil War* (Bern, Switzerland, 1972); Raymond J. and Betty A. Spahn, eds., *New Switzerland in Illinois* (Edwardsville, Ill., 1977); and Leo Schelbert and Hedwig Rappolt, eds., *Alles Ist Ganz Anders Hier* (Olten, Switzerland, 1977), are all accounts of particular individuals or communities. Heinz K. Meier, *The Swiss American Historical Society, 1927–1977* (Norfolk, Va., 1977), critically examines the history of the organization.

LEO SCHELBERT

SYRIAN ARAMEANS: *see* ASSYRIANS

SYRIANS: *see* ARABS

T

TADZHIKS: *see* AFGHANS; TURKESTANIS

TAGALOGS: *see* FILIPINOS

TAMILS: *see* EAST INDIANS

TAOS (PUEBLOS): *see* AMERICAN INDIANS

TATARS

There are three groups of Tatars in the United States, the Crimean Tatars, the Kazan or Volga Tatars, and the Polish or Lithuanian Tatars. They share a strong loyalty to Islam, but each group has a distinct historical and cultural background and a different language.

CRIMEAN TATARS

The largest Tatar community in the United States is composed of the 500 to 800 families known as the Crimean Tatars. The Crimean Tatars belong to the southern (Oghuz) group of Turkic peoples and are Sunni Muslims. The Crimean Tatar language is closely related to Turkish; it was written in Arabic script until 1929, in the Latin alphabet from 1929 to 1939, and is now written in Cyrillic.

In the 15th century the ancestors of the Crimean Tatars founded the Khanate of Crimea on the peninsula that juts into the Black Sea within the present boundaries of the Soviet Union. The Crimean Khanate, which prospered on trade in slaves and other goods with the Ottoman Empire, survived until it was conquered by the Russians in 1783. Following the Russian Revolution and the civil war (1917–1920), an Autonomous Soviet Socialist Republic of Crimean Tatars was established. In 1943 Stalin accused the republic of collaboration with the invading German army and deported the Tatars en masse to Central Asia and Siberia. The Crimean Tatar republic became part of the Ukrainian Soviet Socialist Republic. After Stalin's death in 1953 the Crimean Tatars were absolved of the alleged collaboration but they were not permitted to return to their homeland, to which they still lay claim. In the last two decades the Crimean Tatars have openly demanded the right to return to the Crimea. However, the Soviet authorities deny their existence as a distinct group by not listing them in the Soviet census. Close to half a million Tatars still live in the U.S.S.R., most of them in Soviet Central Asia.

Emigration from the Crimea began after the Russian conquest in the late 18th century. More than a million

Tatar Homelands

Boundary of the Polish-Lithuanian Commonwealth, late 16th century

Crimean Tatars emigrated to the Ottoman Empire where they soon were assimilated by the Turks. During the 1917 revolution and the civil war, another group emigrated to Romania and some of these settled in Turkey after 1945. The third group, former soldiers in the Red Army and German prisoners of war, refused repatriation to the Soviet Union after World War II and chose to remain in the western zones of Germany. From there some made their way to the United States, others going to Turkey first and then emigrating to the United States in the 1960s because of the limited economic opportunities in Turkey. This Crimean Tatar emigration from Turkey to the United States has continued through the 1970s.

Crimean Tatar immigrants and their children live in and around New York City, northeastern New Jersey, and Chicago. The older immigrants, whose ancestors left the Crimea in the 19th century, and those who lived for a while in Romania, have been largely engineers, teachers, musicians, and other professionals. Most of the former prisoners of war have held blue-collar positions.

The Kirim Türkleri Amerikan Birliği (American Association of Crimean Turks) was established in Brooklyn. It serves as both a Muslim house of prayer and a meeting place for Crimean Tatars and other Soviet Muslim groups in the vicinity. Since 1963 this association has published a bimonthly bulletin in Turkish, *Kirim Türkleri Amerikan Birliği Yayin Organi-Beleten* (Bulletin-Organ of the American-Crimean Turkish Association), and it sponsors women's and youth organizations.

The Crimean Tatars are more active politically than any of the other Soviet Muslim groups; they have a very deep concern for the fate of their homeland. Usually under the direction of the Committee for the Return of Exiled Crimean Tatars to Their Homeland, they organize rallies and congresses protesting the fate of their countrymen in the Soviet Union. A Crimean Foundation, founded by the committee in 1977 and based in Commack, N.Y., publishes materials on the fate of the Crimean Tatars and dissenters in the Soviet Union.

KAZAN OR VOLGA TATARS

The Kazan Tatars are a Turkic people who live along the banks and tributaries of the middle Volga River and in the Ural Mountains. There are also communities of Kazan Tatars in Soviet Central Asia, the Caucasus, in European Russia, and in Finland. The terms Volga Tatar and Kazan Tatar are synonymous, the former suggesting geographical location, the latter alluding to the historical tradition of the Kazan Khanate. Members of the group refer to themselves simply as Tatars or Kazan Turks, less often as Bulgars. The Kazan Tatars are Sunni Muslims and speak Volga Tatar, which belongs to the northern group of Turkic languages. Volga Tatar has a literary tradition going back to the 15th century; the language was written in Arabic script until 1929, in the Latin alphabet from 1929 to 1939, and in Cyrillic letters since 1939.

The group has an old and established tradition as an independent state dating back to the Kingdom of Bulgar (10th–13th centuries) and the Khanate of Kazan (15th–16th centuries). After a period of political subjugation and cultural stagnation under Russian rule, the Kazan Tatars experienced a cultural renaissance in the 19th century. This development produced a very outspoken nationalist bourgeoisie and intelligentsia which at the time of the Russian Revolution sought to revive the Khanate of Kazan in the form of a modern pan-Islamic Idel-Ural state. Although this movement was unsuccessful, the Soviet government recognized the group as a distinct nationality and established the Tatar Autonomous Soviet Socialist Republic, or Tatarstan.

The Kazan Tatar emigration was initially the result of the military and political upheavals of the civil war that followed the Russian Revolution. The war was waged with particular ferocity in their homeland, and as a result many Tatars, especially merchants and religious teachers, followed in the wake of Aleksandr Kolchak's defeated anti-Bolshevik White Army eventually making their way to China. Here they joined forces with a smaller group of Tatar merchants who had gone to China in about 1900. After World War II the majority of Kazan Tatars left China, some going to Turkey, others to the United States. The group that came to the United States via China, and their descendants, make up about 20 percent of the Kazan Tatars in the United States today. Another 50 percent are those who have left Turkey since the 1960s for economic reasons. The remaining 30 percent are former Red Army soldiers who were German prisoners of war, and refusing repatriation to the Soviet Union, emigrated to the United States in the 1950s. A small number of Tatar women married Soviet Jews, were permitted to emigrate to Israel in the late 1960s, and have subsequently come to the United States. Among these women are artists, musicians, and writers from the highest levels of Soviet society.

By 1976 about 250 Kazan Tatar families (approximately 1,000 people) lived in the United States, most of them in New York City, northeastern New Jersey, Connecticut, Washington, D.C., and the San Francisco Bay area. In addition, there are several Bashkir families in Brooklyn. The Bashkirs are considered a separate nationality in the Soviet Union, but they are ethnically and linguistically related to, and in the United States have been virtually assimilated by, the Kazan Tatars.

The majority of Kazan Tatars are professionals— merchants, bankers, doctors, and artists. The proportion of women in the group is exceptionally high, and 90 percent have married Kazan or other Tatars in conformity with Muslim tradition. Some of the male immigrants from postwar Germany brought German or Russian wives with them.

The Kazan Tatar community in the United States is united by strong religious and cultural ties. The community uses both the Volga Tatar language and Turkish in speech and writing, and a school for the study of Volga Tatar language and literature in Arabic script functioned in New York City during the 1950s and early 1960s. The *Bulletin of the American Tatar Association* (ATA), a Volga Tatar journal printed in the Latin alphabet, has been published since 1960. Two organizations foster cultural and religious activities. The Amerikan Tatar Jemiyete (American Tatar Association) has a building in College Point, N.Y., which is used as a social center and mosque. Every April the birthday of Abdulla Tukay, the great 20th-century poet and hero of the

Tatar cultural revival, is commemorated with a program of traditional songs and dances. And the American Turko-Tatar Association of Burlingame, Calif., south of San Francisco is particularly active. Since 1968 this group has had its own mosque and social center. It sponsors a women's auxiliary and a young people's circle, and publishes a newsletter in English. Tatar identity is further maintained by the preservation of a distinct cuisine and by continuing contact and correspondence with Tatar brethren living in Turkey and Finland.

POLISH OR LITHUANIAN TATARS

The Polish Tatars are descended from a small religious community which lived in territories that were once part of the Polish-Lithuanian Commonwealth (1569–1793). The ancestors of the group were a nomadic Tatar tribe who settled along the banks of the lower Volga River and were called upon by Vitautas, grand duke of Lithuania, to help him in his struggle against the Teutonic Order. Following Vitautas's victory at the battle of Grünewald in 1410, the Tatars settled in Lithuania with the status of nobility. They married Polish, Lithuanian, and Belorussian women, and although they remained staunchly Muslim they quickly lost their Tatar language, adopting instead Lithuanian, Belorussian, and most especially Polish. The Polish Tatars were almost entirely destroyed during World War II; fewer than 5,000 survive at present in eastern Poland, the Lithuanian S.S.R., and the Belorussian S.S.R.

The Polish Tatars came to the United States in the first decade of the 20th century seeking economic improvement at a time when their homeland was part of the Russian Empire. They settled in and around New York City, northeastern New Jersey, Connecticut, and Massachusetts, and there is now a small colony in Florida. The original immigrants were mainly industrial workers and private entrepreneurs in the leather and fur businesses. The second generation includes blue-collar workers, taxi drivers, engineers, and teachers. About 70 percent of Polish Tatars have married within the group; most of the rest have married Kazan and Crimean Tatars, occasionally a non-Muslim of Polish origin.

The Polish Tatars are the only Soviet Muslim group who have entirely lost their original Turkic language. They are also abandoning Polish, which is maintained now only by the older generation. It is their Sunni Muslim faith that remains the strong basis for their ethnic identity. The Muslim religious feasts of Kurban Bairam and Ramadan are strictly observed. In 1928 the Polish Tatars built a mosque in Brooklyn, N.Y., which continues to serve as a religious and social center for their group and for other Soviet Muslims. There is also a Polish Tatar youth organization and a women's committee in Brooklyn, and from 1973 to 1975 a quarterly bulletin, *An Nur* (Light), devoted to Polish Tatar culture was published in New York City. Some members of the group still maintain the Polish cuisine and language, but in general Polish Tatars have little contact with Polish Americans, preferring to associate with their Muslim coreligionists, especially the closely related Kazan and Crimean Tatars.

Bibliography
There is no published study of the Tatars in the United States. Developments among the Crimean and Kazan Tatars in their homelands are described in Gustav Burbiel, "The Tatars and the Tatar A.S.S.R." in the *Handbook of Major Soviet Nationalities*, ed. Zev Katz (New York, 1975); in Alan W. Fisher's two works, *Russian Annexation of the Crimea, 1772–1783* (Cambridge, Mass., 1970), and *The Crimean Tatars* (Stanford, Calif., 1978); and in the chapters "Tatars" and "Crimean Tatars" in Walter Kolarz, *Russia and Her Colonies* (New York, 1955). The historical background of the Polish Tatars is discussed in Shirin Akiner, "Oriental Borrowings in the Language of the Byelorussian Tatars," *Slavonic and East European Review* 56 (1978): 224–241.
ALEXANDRE BENNIGSEN

TEJANOS: *see* SPANISH; *see also* MEXICANS

TENINOS: *see* AMERICAN INDIANS

TEUTONIC

Teutonic now refers only to Germans or to people who speak a Germanic language. In the late 19th and early 20th centuries, however, the term was used interchangeably with Nordic by racial theorists who viewed the influx of new immigrants from eastern and southern Europe with alarm, considering them genetically inferior and unassimilable. Until World War I, Anglo-Saxons were assumed to be Teutonic. The anti-German sentiment that mounted between the outbreak of the war in 1914 and U.S. entry into it in 1917 led most racial thinkers to abandon their earlier theory that the Anglo-Saxon tradition of liberty had been born in Germany, and to stress their English roots instead.

TEWAS: *see* AMERICAN INDIANS

THAI

There are more than 20,000 Thai in the United States, living for the most part in California, New York, and Illinois. Only a few were able to enter in the early 1960s, but since the middle 1970s about 5,000 immigrants from Thailand have been admitted annually.

Most Thai immigrants have been between the ages of 20 and 40 at the time of their arrival in the United States, and they have tended to come in family units. However, in the last few years women have outnumbered men three to one. Many young women have married U.S. servicemen who met them in Thailand during the Vietnam War; others are young professionals, especially nurses. Most Thai male immigrants have been professional or white-collar workers. The population of Thailand itself is largely homogeneous; the prevailing religion is Hinayana Buddhism.

TIWAS: *see* AMERICAN INDIANS

TLINGITS: *see* AMERICAN INDIANS

TOLOWAS: *see* AMERICAN INDIANS

TONGANS: *see* PACIFIC ISLANDERS

TONKAWAS: *see* AMERICAN INDIANS

TOWAS: *see* AMERICAN INDIANS

TRINIDADIANS AND TOBAGANS: *see* WEST IN-
DIANS

TRI-RACIAL ISOLATES

In the 1970s more than 200 small, almost always isolated groups apparently of combined white, black, and
American Indian ancestry lived in the United States.
Known by colorful names—the Jackson Whites, the
Brass Ankles, the Red Bones, the Melungeons, the
Ramapo Mountain People, the Turks or Moors, the Coe
Ridge Group, the Black Dutch, and the Bushwhackers
—they were for the most part ignored by the wider
world. But at least once every ten years they were discovered by journalists and anthropologists who referred
to them as mestizos, raceless people, racial orphans,
half-castes, half-breeds, local mixed groups, mixed-
blood racial islands, and tri-racial isolates.

Each group is separate and distinctive, but in virtually all instances they live in the eastern United
States, often in swamps or inaccessible mountain valleys. Frequently regarded by their neighbors as pariahs,
they are usually poor and uneducated. They keep to
themselves, and their exact numbers are impossible to
ascertain. Some have reason to avoid the law and all
government institutions. However, in a few cases, the
larger, better organized groups—of which the Lumbees
are the best known—have sought redress from state
and federal authorities and have won official recognition as American Indian tribes. In the 1950 U.S. Census
the Lumbees of Robeson County, N.C., a good many of
whom now live in Baltimore, were classified neither as
Indians nor blacks, but as "Other Non-Whites."

These isolated groups are surrounded by myth and
mystery, not the least of which is how they have maintained their continuity and cohesiveness over the years.
Some of them seem to have originated before the American Revolution; some claim to be remnants of the lost
tribes of ancient Israel, others say that they have descended from survivors of the 17th-century settlers of
Roanoke Island or from shipwrecked Portuguese or
Turks. Many probably originated from mixed groups of
Indians, adventurers, traders, runaway slaves, outlaws,
deserters, and deviants of all races. They are poor, unskilled, isolated people who absorb occasional outsiders
and marry within their group. Some groups are basically
large clans, consisting of a few families who have intermarried over several generations, and are called by a
particular family name. Similar groups, though not racially mixed, are found on the islands of Penobscot Bay,
Me., and elsewhere. Their isolation, both physical and
social, is their most conspicuous feature. When they assimilate they disappear as distinct groups by definition.
This seems to be happening to the Tennessee Melungeons but is less advanced among the Ramapo Mountain People.

Wherever they live they seem to be a third or fourth
race. Whites have not wanted to accept them; blacks
and Indians have been more receptive; but the isolates
traditionally have kept their distance from black or
Indian groups. Local governments have had great difficulty in assigning their children to schools or in
promoting attendance. Some southern state officials attempted to incorporate the children into schools for

blacks, but several groups resisted and established their
own schools. At least until the 1960s they rejected ada-
mantly all efforts to identify them as black. They have
gone so far as to avoid domestic or other service jobs
that might tend to associate them with blacks, eking
out a meager living as subsistence farmers, occasionally
as fishermen or hunters.

It is difficult to claim that the majority, if any, of the
tri-racial isolates are ethnic groups, although they perceive themselves, and are perceived by those around
them, as different. They maintain a cohesive identity
over several generations, but they retain very little European, Indian, or African language or culture. Religious
faith or religious institutions do not seem to be very
important; they generally lack communal or political
organizations. Their life in an isolated rural location
binds them together, as do kinship ties that are sometimes traced to a mythical progenitor. Their survival
and their persistence are as little understood as their
origins.

Bibliography

See Brewton Berry, *Almost White* (New York, 1963), for a useful, if
outdated, overview. See also Karen Blu, "Varieties of Ethnic Identity:
Anglo-Saxons, Blacks, Indians, and Jews in a Southern County," *Ethnicity* 4 (1977): 263–286. Also of interest are W.H. Gilbert, "Memoran-
dum Concerning the Characteristics of the Larger Mixed-Blood Racial
Islands of the Eastern United States," *Social Forces* 24 (1946): 438–447;
Calvin L. Beale, "American Triracial Isolates," *Eugenics Quarterly* 4
(1957): 187–196; David S. Cohen, *The Ramapo Mountain People* (New
Brunswick, N.J., 1974); Franklin E. Frazier, "Racial Islands," in *The
Negro Family in the United States* (1939; reprint, Chicago, 1966); Ed-
ward T. Price, "A Geographic Analysis of White-Negro-Indian Racial
Mixtures in Eastern United States," *Annals of the Association of Amer-
ican Geographers* 43 (1953): 130–155; and Calvin Trillin, "U.S. Journal:
Sumter County, S.C.—Turks," *The New Yorker* (March 8, 1969).

TÜBATULABALS: *see* AMERICAN INDIANS

TULE RIVERS: *see* AMERICAN INDIANS

TUNICAS: *see* AMERICAN INDIANS

TUNISIANS: *see* ARABS

TURKESTANIS

The Turkestanis, a term for several ethnolinguistic
groups, are Sunni Muslims from Central Asia, an area
in the Soviet Union bounded by the Caspian Sea, the
Ural Mountains, and the borders of Iran, Afghanistan,
and China. The Turkestani community in the United
States numbers about 150 families. More than 100 families are Uzbeks, 20 are Kazakhs, 10 are Tadzhiks, 6
Uigur, and 2 each Kirghiz, Turkomans, and Karakalpak.
The community is united by their common regional
origin, their Muslim faith, and their languages. Except
for the Tadzhiks, whose language is within the Iranian
group, the Turkestanis belong to the same Turkic linguistic group.

For centuries the Turkestani homeland has occupied
a strategic position on the trade routes connecting
China with the rest of Asia and with Europe. Many invaders from the East, including the Mongols, fought for
control of the region and built such rich centers of trade
and commerce as Samarkand, Bukhara, and Tashkent.
By the late 19th century the Russian advance had incor-

Turkestani Homelands

porated Turkestan in the tsarist empire; following the Russian Revolution separate Kazakh, Turkmen, Uzbek, Kirghiz, and Tadzhik Soviet Republics were established, as well as a Karakalpak autonomous region. Each of the peoples for whom these political units are named is considered a distinct nationality in the Soviet Union, and each has its own literary language (written in Arabic script before 1929, in the Latin alphabet between 1929 and 1939, and in Cyrillic letters since). Turkestanis in the homeland are uncertain whether they should indentify mainly with the smaller ethnic groups of which they are members or with Turkestan or Islam as a whole.

The Turkestanis in the United States are immigrants who came after World War II and their descendants. About half are former German prisoners of war who found themselves in displaced-persons camps; they came to the United States either directly or after a short stay in Turkey in the late 1940s and early 1950s. The others first left their Soviet-controlled homeland between 1920 and 1945, first settling in Iran and Afghanistan, then moving to Turkey and Saudi Arabia, and finally coming to the United States in the 1950s and 1960s. A small number of Uzbeks and Kazakhs are natives of eastern Turkestan (within the borders of China), while a few Turkoman and Uzbek families originate from northern Afghanistan. A few Turkestani immigrants have come more recently, mainly from Turkey and Saudi Arabia.

The Turkestanis have settled in the New York metropolitan area, Washington, D.C., and California. They are for the most part semiskilled workers and clerks; only a few are professionals. Most of the original immigrants were men; about 10 percent of them brought German or Russian wives with them; many of the rest have married Muslim women in the United States.

Within their own small groups the Turkestanis use their individual languages, but Turkish serves as a common spoken and written language. The Turkestanis have a less developed sense of national identity than the other Muslim groups from the Soviet Union (Azerbai-

janis, North Caucasians, Tatars). They have one organization in Brooklyn, N.Y., the Türkistanlilarin Amerikadaki Cemiyeti (Turkestan American Association), with many members in Boonton, N.J. For worship they share the facilities of the Polish Tatar mosque or Pakistani Islamic Center in Brooklyn.

Bibliography

There are no published studies of Turkestanis in the United States, but there are several works on their homeland. Lawrence Krader, *Peoples of Central Asia*, 3d ed. (Bloomington, Ind., 1971), and Edward Allworth, ed., *Central Asia: A Century of Russian Rule* (New York, 1967), are good introductions. See also Geoffrey Wheeler, *The Modern History of Soviet Central Asia* (1964; reprint, Westport, Conn., 1975); Elizabeth E. Bacon, *Central Asians under Russian Rule* (Ithaca, N.Y., 1966); and Alexandre Bennigsen and Chantal Lemercier-Quelquejay, *Islam in the Soviet Union* (New York, 1967).

ALEXANDRE BENNIGSEN

TURKOMANS: *see* AFGHANS; TURKESTANIS

TURKS

In the late 1970s there were less than 100,000 Turks in the United States. Reliable figures are not available, but this is a reasonable estimate. The group includes naturalized citizens, permanent residents, long-term illegal aliens, and some members of the second and third generations. In 1970 the U.S. Census reported 54,534 foreign-born and American-born people of foreign or mixed parentage from Turkey. In the same census, 24,000 listed Turkish as their mother tongue. This is virtually the extent of the statistical information that is currently available. Other data are also scarce; most figures are educated estimates at best.

The Foreign Ministry of Turkey has no precise figures for total emigration from Turkey to the United States, and Turkish consular officials in New York, Chicago, and Los Angeles base their estimate of 85,000 Turkish Americans only partially on those who are actually registered. There are two main reasons for the lack of data: the meaning of the designation Turkish or even of Turkey as a country of origin varies widely, and the Turkish-American community is not well organized. Turkish-American associations have few members and therefore cannot serve as useful sources of information.

The term Turk or Turkish designates a person born in the Ottoman Empire before 1923 or in the Turkish Republic after 1923, who is Muslim or whose family was Muslim, who was raised in a Turkish-speaking household, and who identifies as a Turk. It does not include the members of many other ethnic groups who came from Turkey (or previously from the Ottoman Empire) but consider themselves Greeks or Jews or Armenians or something other than Turkish. Ethnicity, language, and Islam together serve as effective criteria, for there have been extremely few Christian Turks in spite of missionary activities in the Ottoman Empire. The term pertains also to second- and third-generation Turkish Americans, most of whom lack proficiency in the Turkish language and are not practicing Muslims but nevertheless continue to identify with their Turkish background.

The Turkish community also encompasses to some extent the Turkic-language groups that have come to the United States from the Balkans, China, the Soviet Union, various Middle Eastern countries, and Cyprus.

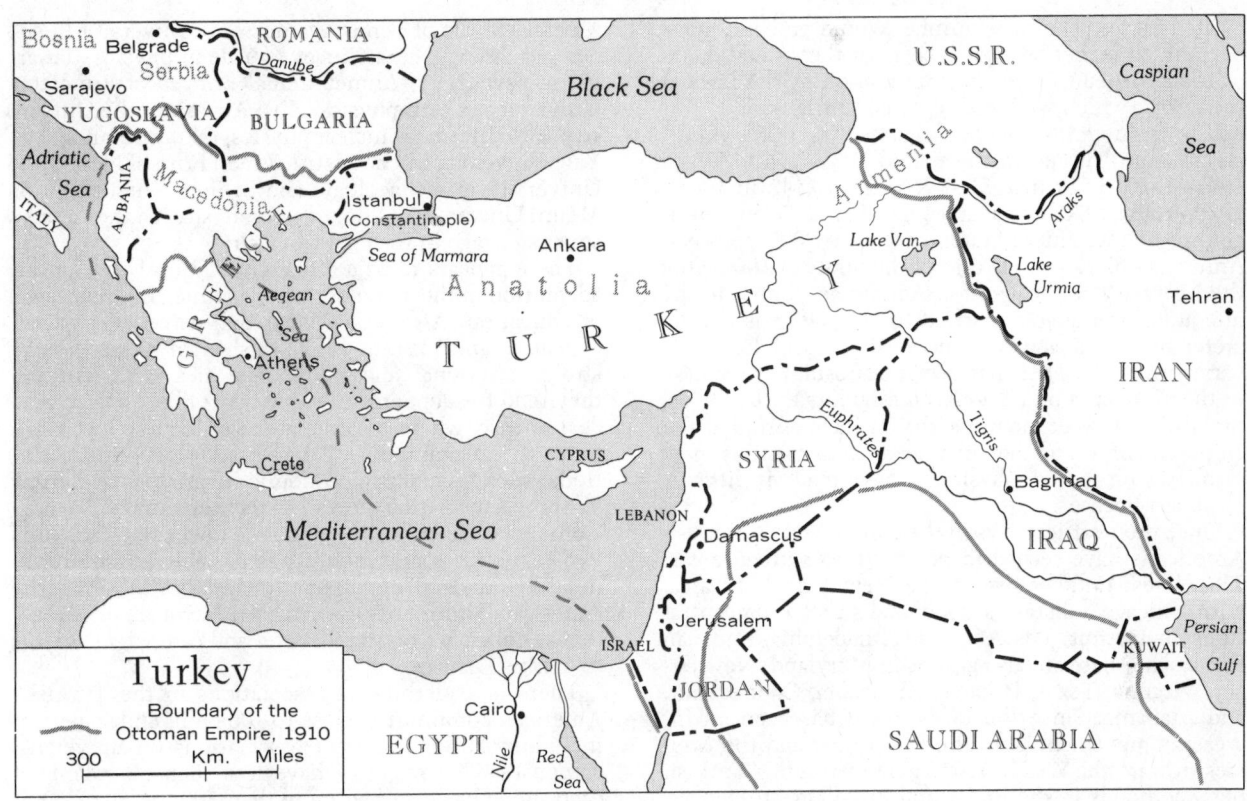

Turkey

Boundary of the
Ottoman Empire, 1910

300   Km.   Miles

Turkestanis, Azerbaijanis, and Crimean Tatars (*see* individual entries), for example, consider themselves as separate ethnic groups on some occasions and affiliate with Turks at other times.

According to official U.S. statistics, migration from the Ottoman Empire to the United States was infinitesimal between 1820 and 1860: the maximum number of registered annual arrivals was 15. Of about 360,000 immigrants from Ottoman Turkey in the period 1820–1950, probably less than 10 percent were Turks. Moreover, the rate of return migration was exceptionally high among Turks: of some 22,000 Turks who came between 1899 and 1924, an estimated 86 percent went back to Turkey. Coming from a vastly different cultural and religious background, the tiny groups of Turkish immigrants encountered profound difficulties in adjusting to American society; their numbers were never sufficient to form viable ethnic communities. The rate of return migration continued to be high throughout the 1920s, primarily for another reason: after 1923, when the Republic of Turkey was established after a long period of wars and internecine strife, its male population was critically depleted. Turks living abroad were encouraged to return home; in many cases the Turkish government made loans or outright grants to those who wanted to go back to Turkey but did not have money for the passage. In particular the well-educated Turks abroad were offered attractive incentives and job opportunities in the new republic, which was in dire need of professionals and technicians.

Of the more than 1,200,000 immigrants entering the United States in 1914, some 21 percent of all adults were listed as illiterate. The ratio among the Turks was 63 percent, but that was lower than the rate in the Otto-

man Empire. There is reason to assume that most of the literate, especially the well-educated immigrants, returned to Turkey and the vast majority of those who chose to remain were illiterates who knew very little English, and worked as unskilled laborers, often doing menial or manual work mainly in industrial plants. Although most of those who stayed had come from the rural areas and had an agricultural background, very few entered agricultural work. Their participation in U.S. life remained minimal. In the words of Oscar Handlin, they "formed lonely little cliques wherever a few gathered."

The early Turkish groups tended to maintain their linguistic and religious solidarity. They had less interest in participating in American life than in continuing their cultural traditions. Because early Turkish immigration consisted of younger males, with a minimal number of couples, families, and unmarried women, many newcomers married non-Turks. Some of them undoubtedly assimilated to the local way of life. But observers of Turkish-American communities in the 1940s and 1950s reported that most had retained their Turkish way of life without acquiring the lifestyle of their new country beyond the requirements of their jobs.

Prior to the 1930s the vast majority of Turkish immigrants were motivated by economic incentives and moved from the lower strata of Turkish society to the lower strata of American society; very few, if any, achieved prosperity. Until the 1950s no Turks attained distinction in any field in the United States, except for several wrestlers.

From the late 1940s onward, Turkish immigration has been for the most part a "brain drain"; at least 2,000 engineers and 1,500 physicians have come to the

United States. The total number would probably have been much higher had it not been for the annual quota of 100 assigned to Turkish immigration by the laws of the 1920s, which were not repealed until 1965.

U.S. Immigration Service figures list 1,065 immigrants from Turkey in the period 1931–1940, 798 in 1941–1950, 3,519 in 1951–1960, and 10,142 in 1961–1970. In the 1970s the average number of Turks immigrating to the United States exceeded 1,000 per year. Annual admissions in excess of the quota of 100 before the liberal 1965 Immigration Act are accounted for by nonquota immigrants married to U.S. citizens and by preferential arrangements accorded to specialists in a variety of fields. There has been no substantial increase in the number of professional immigrants in the 1970s, mainly because economic setbacks have curtailed the employment of foreign engineers and rigorous new standards for foreign physicians have made it difficult to obtain licenses.

Since their earliest days in the United States, Turkish Americans have settled in or near major urban areas. The largest number live in the New York City area, with Chicago a distant second, and smaller concentrations in Detroit, Los Angeles, Philadelphia, and San Francisco. There are also groups in Maryland, New Jersey, Virginia, Texas, Indiana, Minnesota, Connecticut, and Alabama. Since the 1950s there has been an increasing movement from the East Coast and the Midwest toward the West Coast. There were a few Turkish neighborhoods in the Bronx and Brooklyn, in Detroit, and in Whiting and Indianapolis in Indiana, but only one block in Brooklyn appears to have retained any visible Turkish features in the 1970s. (The so-called Turks about whom *The New Yorker* ran an article in March 1969 are a Sumter County, S.C., community of indeterminate origin, but most probably are not authentically Turkish.)

Turkish emigration after World War II was motivated by economic and professional considerations; although a number of physicians and engineers have gone back to Turkey to take advantage of an attractive opportunity or for family reasons, return migration is minimal.

Unlike the early immigrants from Turkey, the more recent arrivals have a high rate of literacy. There are a large number of university graduates, and the median income is relatively high. Very few are businessmen: most are small-scale entrepreneurs who operate shops, studios, import-export firms, and restaurants. Only a handful of Turks have successful industrial firms. The two Turkish millionaries who get the widest exposure in the U.S. media are Nesuhi and Ahmet Ertegün, who founded the Atlantic Recording Corporation in the late 1940s and now hold high positions in Warner Communications and its subsidiaries, including Atlantic; in addition they own the New York Cosmos soccer club.

The Turkish-American community has virtually no members in journalism, broadcasting, fine arts, sports, law, politics, or in the higher echelons of local or federal government. In music Arif Mardin has distinguished himself as a composer, arranger, and producer of jazz, pop, and rock-and-roll albums. Bülent Arel and İlhan Mimaroğlu are well known as electronic music composers. In the field of drama Tunç Yalman has achieved recognition as artistic director of the Milwaukee Repertory Theater and for his staging of other productions.

In science several Turks have attracted attention: Muzafer Sherif of Pennsylvania State University in social psychology, Feza Gürsey of Yale in physics; Turan İtil in psychiatry; Ahmet Cemal Eringen of Princeton University in astrophysics; Ziya Akçasu of the University of Michigan in nuclear physics; Oktay Sinanoğlu of Yale University in chemistry; Kenan Erim of New York University in archaeology; and Behram Kurşunoğlu of Miami University, Ohio, in astrophysics. Scores of physicians engage in medical research.

There appears to be a direct correlation between the adaptation of the Turks to American life and their level of education. Although a very high percentage of the educated and well-to-do Turkish Americans retain strong emotional and intellectual ties with Turkey, they tend to adopt an American way of life with a great deal of ease, whereas Turks at lower income levels are more apt to maintain a Turkish style of living. Relations among social and economic subgroups are similar to the patterns that prevail in contemporary Turkey. Contact between the upper and the lower classes is limited, although social mobility is possible for enterprising individuals. Class distinctions within the Turkish-American community are less of a factor in such matters as collective political action and campaigns for aid to Turkish causes.

There is a plethora of associations in the Turkish-American community, close to 100 clubs and societies, including Turkish student associations on university campuses. The majority have less than 50 members each; none has ever had more than 500 members. One of the oldest and most active is the American Turkish Society in New York City, which since 1949 has been the most consistently energetic and effective society of its kind. It is headed by an official in the United Nations, and there are many diplomats on its board of trustees, including Turkish and U.S. ambassadors, prominent members of the American community, and representatives of major American corporations. But the enrollment even of this society has never exceeded 250 individual members and 50 corporate members.

A number of Turkish associations are professional societies, including the Turkish-American Physicians Association, Society of Turkish Architects, Engineers and Scientists in America, and the Anadolu Club, all based in New York City. Like most other Turkish associations, these are not very active. The Association of Turkish Psychiatrists, for instance, has a membership of about 200 in the United States and Turkey, but according to its president, "not one member paid his dues in 1978."

Three Turkish clubs specialize in soccer: the Turkish Sport Club, Newark Turkish Soccer Club, and Turkish Bozkurt Soccer Club. All the other organizations, active in dozens of cities from Philadelphia to Honolulu, are essentially social clubs for Turks and friends of Turkey, offering various types of ethnic entertainment and cultural programs. Among them, the Turkish Women's League of America in New York City, the Turkish-American Cultural Alliance in Chicago, and the Turkish Cultural Alliance in Queens, N.Y., run Saturday or Sunday schools to instruct Turkish children in Turkish language, history, music, and Islamic doctrine.

The Federation of Turkish-American Societies (Türk-Amerikan Dernekleri Federasyonu), founded in 1956, includes more than 20 associations. Its basic objectives are to provide coordination and cooperation among its

constituent associations and to represent the political views of the Turkish-American community in connection with U.S. foreign policy and vis-à-vis initiatives taken by other ethnic groups, such as the Greeks on the Cyprus issue. In addition to an annual ball and various programs on national occasions, the federation frequently has coordinated campaigns for relief aid to victims of earthquakes in Turkey. Its membership includes most of the associations formed by Turkish-speaking groups from outside Turkey proper—the American Association of Crimean Turks, the Turkestan American Association, the Azerbaijan Society of America, the Turkish Cyprus Aid Society, and the Karaçay Turkish Cami Society. In the late 1970s a major rift developed within the federation as a result of personal rivalries over the presidency and disagreements about the balance between the "external" Turks (those who come from outside Turkey proper) and "internal" Turks.

Turkish-American organizations tend to be weak because of the small size and limited financial resources of the community; the ability of its potential leaders to achieve prestige and success in their own professions, which obviates the need for them to aspire to distinction in the ethnic community; and the effect of Turkey's political divisions, even fragmentation, which often deter concerted action among Turkish Americans who hold opposing political views. The issues that the Turkish community will rally around are national ones such as the Cyprus crisis or Armenian and Greek pressures, in addition to humanitarian ones like earthquake disasters. But even when unity is achieved, the activities undertaken and the funds generated fall far short of the community potential. Turks in the United States, like those in Turkey, are used to expecting initiatives and funding from their government. For many activities that other ethnic groups organize and finance on their own, the Turkish-American community tries to solicit official Turkish support. If such support does not come through, many projects are abandoned.

The Turkish-American community maintains close ties with Turkey. Most of its members tend to retain Turkish citizenship unless it becomes essential, for professional or other reasons, to become U.S. citizens. Many who are naturalized take pains to hide the fact and sound apologetic when obliged to admit it. In Turkey nationalist sentiment has attached opprobrium to change of citizenship. It is revealing that when Erol Yasin, the goalkeeper of the Cosmos soccer club, applied for a permanent-residence visa, numerous commentators in the Turkish press denounced him in harsh terms. Although many physicians have been naturalized to meet legal requirements, it is significant that five Turkish doctors who wanted to remain Turkish citizens obtained a U.S. Supreme Court decision in 1977 lifting the naturalization requirement. In general, most naturalized Turks regard themselves as primarily Turkish rather than American. In 1978 a bill allowing dual citizenship was presented to the Turkish parliament. If it becomes law, Turks who are U.S. citizens will be able to make real-estate and other investments in the homeland that are currently prohibited to citizens of foreign countries.

In the Turkish identity, language as well as Islamic background are important, but most Turkish Americans were raised and educated in the heyday of secular reforms in Kemal Atatürk's Turkey, so religious allegiance seems to be a minor factor. Any devout believers among them observe Islam's high holidays and other holy occasions in mosques or meeting places that belong mainly to Arab or Pakistani groups. There is no Turkish Muslim meeting place in the United States. Turks remain effectively secularized, and conversion of Muslim Turks to Christianity (except for the Gagauz Turks of Romania) or Judaism is almost nonexistent. The major exception, still denounced in Turkey, is the late Halouk Fikret (1895–1965), son of the prominent romantic patriotic poet Tevfik Fikret. Halouk Fikret, born a Muslim, became an engineer in the United States, married an American, and not only converted but was ordained a Presbyterian minister in the 1920s.

Cultural activities have increased in the urban areas since the late 1960s. These include public lectures, dance and drama performed by local amateur groups as well as by professionals from Turkey, panel discussions, charity balls and bazaars, art exhibits, concerts, and film showings. Some of these activities are organized by universities that offer courses in Turkish studies. Scholars of Turkish origin are frequently featured as speakers or function as sponsors of major cultural activities; among them are İlhan Başgöz of Indiana University, Halil İnalcık of the University of Chicago, Nur Yalman of Harvard University, Kemal Karpat of the University of Wisconsin, Ahmet Evin of the University of Pennsylvania, Esin Atıl of the Freer Gallery of Art, and Talat Sait Halman of Princeton University.

Many Turkish associations issue bulletins on an irregular basis, and numerous periodicals have been published in Turkish since the late 1950s. *Yankı, Türk Dünyası,* and *Anavatan* ceased publication after a few sporadic issues. The only Turkish-American periodical with a record of steady publication was *Türk Evi,* a monthly in Turkish and English, edited by Aykut Görkey. Launched in 1970, it reached a total circulation of barely 1,000 and came to an end with its 100th issue in the fall of 1978, leaving the Turkish-American community one of the few American ethnic groups without a publication of its own.

Several weekly radio programs in Turkish have been broadcast over small local stations in New York City, Chicago, and Boston since the 1950s. The most regular of these has been the "Turkish Voice," produced by Faruk Fenik on WHBI–FM in New York. Faruk Fenik also, with his wife, İnci Fenik, produced the "Turkish Hour," several series of weekly one-hour television programs, between 1975 and 1980. These programs have featured music and dance, talks and interviews, films and documentaries, and news of Turkey and of the Turkish-American community. There have also been a few Turkish television programs in the Chicago area.

For Turks living in and near New York City, the 11-story building at 46th Street and First Avenue bought in 1977 by the Turkish government is used as a very convenient center for cultural activities. It houses the Turkish Mission to the United Nations, Turkish Consulate General, Tourism and Information Office, Educational Attaché's Office, and the Federation of Turkish American Societies. It contains facilities for ceremonies, lectures, art shows, and other services.

Intergroup relations are not a significant problem for Turkish Americans, although members of the community occasionally feel that there is generally a benign

neglect of Turks and even some strong prejudice against them. The community finds itself in conflict with Armenians and Greeks. The Cyprus crisis, which erupted in late 1963 and culminated in the 1974 Turkish military intervention, exacerbated tension between Greeks and Turks in the United States. The assassinations of Mehmet Baydar, Turkish Consul General in Los Angeles, and Consul Bahadır Demir by a 77-year-old Armenian American in early 1973 and numerous Armenian demonstrations in major cities dramatizing the death of Armenians in Ottoman Turkey in 1915 have resulted in a rift between the Turks and the Armenians. There have been, however, no clashes between the respective communities.

Turkish Americans have not participated at all in national and local politics except for writing letters to congressmen or taking out political advertisements in *The New York Times*. None has ever been a candidate for public office or held any position that could even remotely influence U.S. legislation or policy. Only a few of the Turkish organizations, principally the Federation of Turkish American Societies, have sporadically undertaken initiatives to give exposure to the views of Turkish Americans. Some of these have taken the form of "antidefamation" activities to answer allegations concerning the Armenian and the Cyprus issues. The most vigorous action along these lines was the campaign mounted by the federation from 1975 onward to exert pressure on the U.S. Congress to remove the embargo on military equipment that was imposed after Turkey's decision to resume opium cultivation and especially after the Turkish intervention in Cyprus. The basic political stance of Turkish Americans is to stress the joint defense objectives and the need for strong economic ties between the United States and Turkey. When official disagreement occurs, the sentiment of the community inclines toward the Turkish government rather than toward Washington.

The young generation brought to or born in the United States since the 1950s is predominantly non-Turkish-speaking. This growing group forms a core that will exert change upon Turkish-American ethnicity through patterns of participation and achievement that have been characteristic of other ethnic groups in the United States.

Bibliography
There are no published books or articles on Turkish Americans, but there are many works on Turkey and Turkic peoples. See, for example, Geoffrey Lewis, *Turkey* (London, 1965); Bernard Lewis, *The Emergence of Modern Turkey* (London, 1966); A.J. Toynbee and K.P. Kirkwood, *Turkey* (London, 1926); and Stanford J. Shaw and Ezel Kural Shaw, *History of the Ottoman Empire and Modern Turkey: The Rise of Modern Turkey, 1808–1975* (New York, 1977).

TALAT SAIT HALMAN

TUSCARORAS: *see* AMERICAN INDIANS

U

UKRAINIANS

Ukrainians first came in large numbers to the United States as part of the great immigration from southern and eastern Europe that reached America between 1880 and 1914. They came from an ethnolinguistic territory that encompasses 288,800 square miles, the second largest of its kind on the European continent. In 1970, 41,223,000 Ukrainians were recorded. Almost all of them lived within the borders of the Soviet Union, primarily in the Ukrainian Soviet Socialist Republic; others lived in neighboring countries to the west. There are about 215,000 Ukrainians in Poland, 135,000 in Czechoslovakia, and 120,000 in Romania. Within the Ukrainian ethnolinguistic territory as a whole there have also been minority groups of Poles, Russians, Germans, Armenians, and most especially Jews, many of whom have come as immigrants to the United States. This entry, however, is devoted only to those immigrants and their descendants who in some way identify with the Ukrainian-American community.

At the time of the massive immigration (1880–1914) the Ukraine did not exist as an autonomous political entity. Ukrainian territories were split between two multinational states—the Austro-Hungarian Empire and the Russian Empire. The Austro-Hungarian, or Hapsburg, Ukrainian territories were administered within the provinces of Galicia and Bukovina in Austria and within several counties (known collectively as Carpatho-Ruthenia or Transcarpathia) of northeastern Hungary, lands that supplied roughly 85 percent of the Ukrainian immigration before 1914. The remaining 15 percent came from the Russian Empire, whose Ukrainian territory was divided into several administrative districts (guberniyas), including Volhynia, Podolia, Kiev, Poltava, Chernigov, Kharkov, Ekaterinoslav, and Kherson. After World War I, the Austro-Hungarian Ukrainian territories were divided among three states: Galicia went to a newly constituted Poland, Bukovina to Romania, and the northeastern counties of Hungary to Czechoslovakia. Within the Ukrainian homeland in the Russian Empire an independent Ukrainian state emerged, to be replaced a short time later by the Ukrainian Soviet Socialist Republic of the U.S.S.R. Most of the western Ukrainian territories were effectively united within the Soviet Ukraine only after 1945, as a result of Soviet expansion.

These political changes have more than merely administrative significance; they explain why Ukrainian immigrants often identified themselves and were identified by others, not as Ukrainians, but rather as having come from Austria, Russia, or Poland.

Ukrainians are distinguished primarily by language and religion. The dialects classified as Ukrainian are all

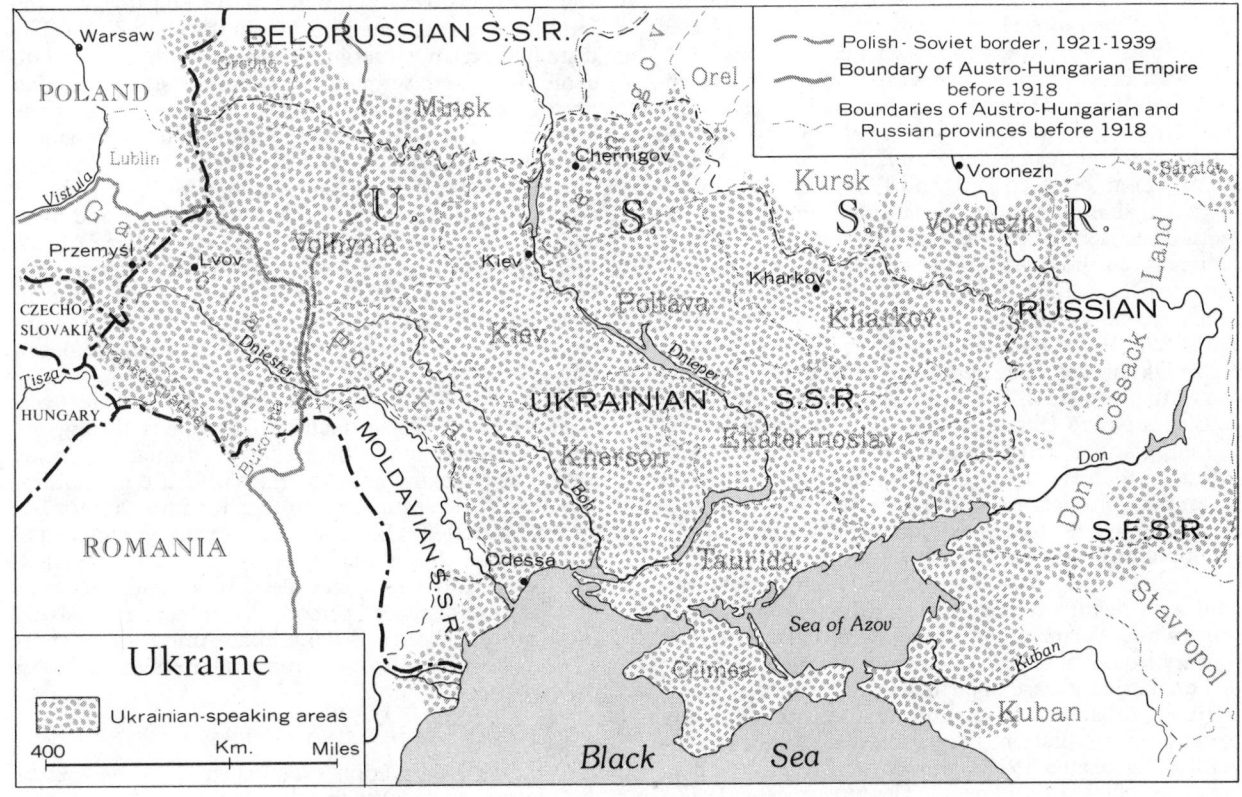

Ukraine

Ukrainian-speaking areas

400   Km.   Miles

Map legend:
Polish-Soviet border, 1921-1939
Boundary of Austro-Hungarian Empire before 1918
Boundaries of Austro-Hungarian and Russian provinces before 1918

East Slavic, and Ukrainian religious affiliations are generally split between the Ukrainian (formerly Uniate or Greek) Catholic Church and the Eastern Orthodox Church. In the past, Ukrainians have been known by various other names: the most common are Rusyn, Ruthenian, Russian, or Little Russian for the entire group; and Russniak, Carpatho-Russian, or Lemkian for regional groups. The name Ukrainian, as a national or ethnic designation, was not widely used in Europe until the second quarter of the 20th century, and most of the immigrants from Ukrainian ethnolinguistic territories arrived in the United States calling themselves something other than Ukrainian. Many have subsequently discarded the older names and adopted the name Ukrainian to indicate their ethnic awareness and national aspirations as well as their native tongue. Others, however, particularly some immigrants from Galicia, Bukovina, and the former northeastern counties of Hungary, have retained the older designations and do not consider themselves Ukrainian.

MIGRATION AND ARRIVAL

Individual Ukrainians have been coming to the New World since the beginning of the European immigrations. Ukrainian names appear in the records of New Amsterdam (New York), on the army rolls of the revolutionary war, and in the first U.S. Census (1790). Among these earliest Ukrainian immigrants were two colorful individuals. The Reverend Agapius Honcharenko (1832–1916) was an Orthodox priest and political refugee from Russia who settled first in Alaska and then in California, where he founded a Russian- and English-language newspaper, the *Alaska Herald* (1867–1872). Nicholas Sudzilovsky-Russel (1850–1930) was a physician from Kiev who came to California during the 1880s and then moved to Hawaii, where he was elected president of the first Hawaiian senate.

It was, however, the large-scale immigration of approximately 250,000 people that began in the 1880s and lasted until the outbreak of war in 1914 that created the Ukrainian-American community. A second period of immigration, between 1920 and 1939, brought another 20,000, a sharp diminution resulting from U.S. immigration restrictions imposed in 1921 and 1924. (Many emigrants in these years went elsewhere, especially to Canada.) A third period that began in 1947 brought another 85,000 Ukrainians displaced by the events of World War II and its aftermath. Since 1955 only about 5,000 Ukrainians have reached the United States because the Soviet Union and other eastern European countries where Ukrainians live do not generally permit emigration. Church records (the only reliable indicators available) suggest that an estimated 487,600 Ukrainian immigrants and their American-born descendants live in the United States today (see Table 1).

Ukrainians who came during the first two periods (1880–1914 and 1920–1939) generally left their homeland as a result of economic hardship. Rural Galicia (from which the majority came) suffered in the late 19th century from a shortage of agricultural land as a result of a dramatic increase in population. The slowly industrializing urban centers could not absorb this growing agricultural population, a situation that did not significantly change after 1917 when former Austrian Galicia was incorporated into Poland. The most recent (1947–

Table 1. Ukrainian church membership.

Church	Diocesan seat	Ukrainian membership[a]
Ukrainian Catholic Church (1916)	Philadelphia Stamford, Conn. Chicago	265,000
Ukrainian Orthodox Church of U.S.A. (1919)	South Bound Brook, N.J.	87,800
Ukrainian Orthodox Church of America—Ecumenical Patriarchate (1928)	New York	30,000
Holy Ukrainian Autocephalous Orthodox Church in Exile (1954)	New York	4,800
Protestant denominations		50,000
Roman Catholic Church		50,000
Total		487,600

Source: The Official Catholic Directory, 1978 (New York, 1978); *Yearbook of American and Canadian Churches* (Nashville, 1974); *Ukraine: A Concise Encyclopedia* (Toronto, 1971), vol. 2.

a. For Ukrainian Catholic Church the figure given is for 1978; for Ukrainian Orthodox Church of U.S.A., 1966; for Ukrainian Orthodox Church of America, 1973; for Holy Ukrainian Orthodox Church in Exile, a 1965 estimate; and for Protestants and Roman Catholics, a 1967 estimate.

1955) Ukrainian immigrants are mainly people who fled or were driven from their homes in the face of German or Soviet armies during and just after World War II. Some had settled in other European countries during the interwar years (Czechoslovakia, France, Germany); some were brought to work as forced laborers in the war industries of Hitler's Germany; others fled the advancing Soviet armies in late 1944.

The earlier two immigrations, in contrast, were largely voluntary. Agents of European and American steamship lines recruiting cheap labor during the 1880s and 1890s visited Ukrainian villages and urged young farm hands to seek their fortune in the New World. The dismal agrarian situation, together with a desire to avoid being conscripted into the Austro-Hungarian army, convinced many to leave. As was so often the case in this period, the letters these first immigrants wrote home provided a new and irresistible stimulus to others. Most of the emigrants headed for the North Sea ports of the German or Dutch shipping lines and most ended up in New York City. Family or village friends met and took care of some; others were given temporary quarters in the various homes for immigrants in New York City, sometimes sponsored by the Austro-Hungarian government or by other eastern European ethnic groups.

After World War II, economic motives were overshadowed by political factors. Ukrainians fleeing the Soviet advance found themselves in displaced-persons camps in Germany and Austria with little possibility, and often little desire, to be integrated into western European societies. Ukrainian immigrant groups, especially in the United States, organized relief programs, worked to relax U.S. quota restrictions, and sponsored thousands of displaced persons. Even more extensively than in the earlier years, Ukrainian-American relief organizations helped to find living quarters and jobs for the newcomers.

SETTLEMENT AND ECONOMIC LIFE

The first immigration established the geographical distribution of Ukrainians that has more or less pre-

vailed to the present. From the very beginning, Ukrainian immigrants settled in the industrial cities of the northeastern United States, and today over 90 percent still reside in urban areas—in contrast to the Ukrainians in Canada and South America who settled in rural areas because cheap land was still readily available. Arriving just as American industry was recovering from the depression of the early 1870s, Ukrainian and other eastern European immigrants helped to supply the expanded labor force needed for a period of rapid industrial growth and expansion in the United States. There have not been any major changes in the geographical distribution of the group since then. Sixty-one percent of the Ukrainian population in 1930 lived in New York, Pennsylvania, and New Jersey, and by 1970 this figure had declined only slightly to 54 percent; other large concentrations of Ukrainians are also for the most part in the northeastern states. However, in 1970 California had 4.4 percent of the total Ukrainian-American population, largely retired individuals (see Table 2).

In 1970 the largest concentrations of Ukrainians were found in the metropolitan areas of New York City, Philadelphia-Camden, Chicago, Detroit, Pittsburgh, Cleveland, and Newark, N.J. Other centers include Rochester and Buffalo, N.Y.; Paterson-Clifton-Passaic, N.J.; Los Angeles–Long Beach, Calif.; and Allentown-Bethlehem-Easton, Pa. Within many of these cities are several blocks that constitute a Ukrainian neighborhood, such as the Lower East Side of Manhattan between East Second and East Fourteenth streets; Franklin Street in north-central Philadelphia; Chicago Avenue, Oakley Boulevard, and Western Avenue on the northwest side of Chicago; and West Sixth to West Seventeenth streets in the lower west side of Cleveland. The immigrants who settled there established Ukrainian churches, schools, stores, and community clubs, but since the 1950s Ukrainian Americans have joined others in a flight to the suburbs, where a number of new Ukrainian communities have grown up. The city neighborhoods have diminished, replaced by renewal projects now often inhabited by blacks or Hispanics. Some Ukrainian churches and shops remain in the cities, however, and are frequented on weekends by returning suburbanites.

A small number of Ukrainians did settle in the countryside. Before 1914 Ukrainian farm communities, with their own churches, could be found in Michigan, Wisconsin, North Dakota, Virginia, Georgia, Texas, and even Hawaii. By 1936, 85 rural communities had a total population of 26,000 Ukrainians. Ukrainians also settled in the rural areas of the industrial states, areas that

have since been absorbed into the spreading urban environment. The number of surviving rural Ukrainian communities is insignificant; only the Ukrainian farming communities in North Dakota retain any ethnic cohesiveness.

U.S. immigration records show that of the total of 147,375 "Ruthenians" (Ukrainians and Carpatho-Rusyns) who came to this country between 1899 and 1910, 128,460 claimed to have had some former employment: 97.2 percent had been farmers, unskilled laborers, or servants; only 2.0 percent had been skilled workers; and a mere 0.08 percent (109 people) claimed to have been professionals or businessmen. Despite their largely agrarian background they had to go to work in mines, mills, and other industries. The anthracite-coal region of eastern Pennsylvania, the steel mills of Pittsburgh, and the factories of neighboring New York, New Jersey, and Ohio were soon filled with Ukrainian immigrants. Only in a few isolated instances did they go into business, opening grocery stores, butcher shops, or taverns. Usually operated by women, the boarding house was also a widespread business, and was the source of much-needed supplemental income.

The situation changed somewhat in the years after World War I, as many formerly unskilled workers acquired a trade, usually through their experience in industry. Statistics from that period reveal a significant number of Ukrainians in automotive manufacturing and repair, machine shops, foundries, and rope manufacturing. The number of Ukrainian businesses also increased. Grocery stores remained the most typical enterprise: 2,000 in 250 communities were recorded in 1934. Bakeries, restaurants, pharmacies, hardware stores, funeral homes, garages, and window-cleaning establishments, which in several communities seemed to have been exclusively in the hands of Ukrainians, were other common businesses.

Many of the Ukrainians who arrived after 1947 had a different socioeconomic background. Among Ukrainians living in displaced-persons camps in Germany in 1948—from which many of the new immigrants came —12.3 percent were professionals, administrators, or businessmen; 26.6 percent were skilled laborers; and 61 percent were unskilled or farm laborers. This larger proportion of better-trained people served to increase the numbers of Ukrainian professionals in the United States. The 1970 U.S. Census reported that among Ukrainian males 22.4 percent were professionals or administrators, 23.7 percent were craftsmen, 20.4 percent were skilled and semiskilled workers, 12.4 percent were sales and clerical workers, and only 11 percent were service, unskilled, and farm workers. The family median income in 1970 was a substantial $11,048 a year—12 percent above the national average; 58.4 percent of families earned more than $10,000. The large post–World War II influx of professionals and skilled workers, together with the upward social mobility of the older immigrants and their descendants, has considerably changed the socioeconomic structure of Ukrainian-American society.

RELIGION

In the European homeland, religion was an integral part of life, especially at the village level, where church-related functions were embedded in many commonplace activities and daily occupations. It is not an exag-

Table 2. Ukrainians in selected states, 1930 and 1970 (as percentage of total U.S. Ukrainian population).

State	1930	1970
New York	28.4	20.8
Pennsylvania	22.4	19.8
New Jersey	10.1	13.2
Michigan	6.7	7.3
Ohio	6.3	7.4
Illinois	5.9	7.9
Connecticut	3.5	3.8
Massachusetts	3.2	1.7
Minnesota	1.2	1.9
Rhode Island	1.0	—
California	—	4.4

Source: Compiled from the 1930 and 1970 U.S. Censuses.

geration to state that the whole life cycle of Ukrainian society was organized around the church calendar with its many holidays and traditions. Religion was, however, less a matter of conviction and belief than simply a way of life. Going to church on Sundays and holidays was almost as natural and as necessary to existence as eating or sleeping.

Ukrainian immigrants tried to re-create this religiously oriented environment in their new country. The church was one of the first buildings to be constructed, and it formed the focal point of the community. However, the subsequent history of the Ukrainian Church was marked by great difficulties, many of which were the result of: (1) the clash between the old-world, rural-based religious way of life and the urban, more secular, and culturally alien environment of American society; and (2) the internal friction between various factions of the community caused by disputes that either were brought from Europe or arose in the New World.

Ukrainians were, for the most part, members of Eastern Christian churches, either Orthodox or Eastern-rite Ukrainian (formerly Greek) Catholic. Those from Galicia were most apt to be Ukrainian Catholics, and those from Bukovina and the Russian Empire to be Orthodox. Since about 85 percent of the early Ukrainian immigration was from Galicia, Ukrainian Catholicism clearly predominated among the group in the United States. The percentage of Ukrainian Catholics was almost 85 percent during the first period of immigration; it is now only 40 percent, a decline explained partly by defections to various Russian and Ukrainian Orthodox churches, partly by the higher percentage of Orthodox Ukrainians in the most recent immigration.

The history of Ukrainian religious life in the United States has been shaped by the struggle of Ukrainian Catholics to preserve their Eastern rite and to assert their right to existence in a generally unsympathetic Latin-rite Catholic environment. At times they failed, and these failures resulted in defections to Orthodoxy and, in some cases, to Protestantism.

The experience of the first Ukrainian-immigrant priest in the United States set the tone for much of what was to follow. Lacking their own priests and Ukrainian Catholic churches, the immigrants in the 1880s usually attended the local Roman Catholic church. The initiative for their own church came from a group of Ukrainians and ethnically related Carpatho-Rusyns living in the mining districts of eastern Pennsylvania. They asked the Metropolitan of Lvov (L'viv) in Galicia, for an Eastern-rite Catholic priest. He responded by sending the Reverend Ivan Volansky (1857–1926), who arrived in Shenandoah, Pa., in 1884 to establish the first Eastern-rite Catholic parish. Volansky was greeted with open hostility by the Roman Catholic hierarchy in the vicinity. The bishop in Philadelphia refused to accept his credentials because, as was customary among the Eastern-rite Catholic clergy, Volansky was married. The Roman Catholic priests in Shenandoah denounced the plans for establishing an Eastern-rite church, and refused its supporters the right to bury their dead in the local cemetery.

In spite of all this, Volansky continued to hold services in temporary quarters until the first church, St. Michael the Archangel, was constructed in Shenandoah

in 1886. Within the next few years other parishes were established in nearby Hazelton, Olyphant, Kingston, and Wilkes-Barre, Pa., as well as in Jersey City, N.J., and Minneapolis. By 1890, ten Eastern-rite Catholic priests had arrived from Europe.

Volansky concerned himself not only with religious matters, but with community and national life as well. During his brief four-and-a-half-year stay he built the first church and organized the first fraternal society (the St. Nicholas Brotherhood), the first choir, the first reading room, the first evening school, and the first newspaper, *Ameryka* (Shenandoah, Pa., 1886–1890). He was also instrumental in establishing the first cooperative stores, and he actively supported striking coal miners in 1887–1888. His work symbolizes the vital role that the church plays in the life of Ukrainian Americans.

The period 1890–1916 was one of both growth and internal turmoil for the churches. Those years also witnessed the largest single influx of Ukrainian immigrants of any period, and this rapid increase in the size of the population, and consequently of its various factions, made the problems of organization even more acute. There were three important developments: the grudging acceptance by the Roman Catholic Church of a distinct hierarchical structure for Ukrainian Catholics; the rapid expansion of Orthodoxy as a result of defections from Catholicism; and the complete breakdown of the tenuous unity between the "Ruthenians" from Galicia (that is, Ukrainians) and those from Hungary (that is, Carpatho-Rusyns).

In 1890 and again in 1907 the Roman curia, probably as a result of pressure from the American Catholic hierarchy, issued decrees requiring that priests of the Eastern Rite were subject to the jurisdiction of the local Latin-rite Ordinary. New immigrant priests had to be celibate; married ones were recalled to Europe. Some married priests did return to Europe; others refused. The Reverend Alexis G. Toth (1853–1909), a Carpatho-Rusyn priest, was one of the latter; in 1891 he led his large Minneapolis parish into the Russian Orthodox church, which, with active support from the tsarist Russian government, was ever ready to receive new converts. Toth was sent as a missionary to Pennsylvania and other eastern states where he succeeded in bringing 13 parishes with 7,000 members into the fold of Orthodoxy. This trend continued unabated until 1916, by which time it was estimated that 163 Eastern-rite Catholic parishes with over 200,000 members had converted to Orthodoxy. About half of the converts were Ukrainians from Galicia.

Those who converted to Orthodoxy during these early years generally remained outside the mainstream of Ukrainian-American development. The Orthodox church was dominated by a Russian hierarchy, and many Ukrainians, Belorussians, and Carpatho-Rusyns who joined came to regard themselves as Russians. In an attempt to remedy this situation, a Ukrainian Orthodox Church of the United States was founded in 1919, followed in 1928 by the establishment of the Ukrainian Orthodox Church in America. The Eastern-rite Catholics who have joined these new Orthodox churches have been able to retain a Ukrainian ethnic identity.

As a result of the early conflicts within the Catholic church, combined with the proselytizing efforts of American Protestant groups, some Ukrainian Catholics

converted to Protestantism. At the beginning of the 20th century, several Ukrainian Presbyterian and Baptist churches were founded, leading in 1922 to the establishment of the Union of Ukrainian Evangelical Baptist Churches and the Ukrainian Evangelical Reformed Church.

Also between 1890 and 1916 there occurred the final separation of Eastern-rite Catholics from Galicia (Ukrainians) and those from Hungary (Carpatho-Rusyns). The first churches in the United States had included parishioners from both regions, although from the very beginning there was friction between their priests. The Galician Ukrainians accused the Carpatho-Rusyns of being pro-Hungarian, of being insufficiently conscious of their national identity, and of too often succumbing to Russian Orthodox propaganda. From their side, the Carpatho-Rusyns regarded many of the Galicians as Ukrainian "separatists" who wanted to destroy the unity of the "Russian/Rusyn" people, or as socialist and radical sympathizers seeking to undermine the fabric of society. These fears were prompted by the presence of the so-called American Circle, a group of talented and patriotic clergymen who came from Galicia during the late 1880s with the express purpose of raising the economic level and the Ukrainian national consciousness of all Eastern-rite Catholics.

The controversy between the Galician Ukrainians and the Carpatho-Rusyns, which was joined by partisan fraternal societies representing each group, came to a head in 1907, when Monsignor Soter Ortynsky (1866–1916) was appointed the first bishop for Eastern-rite Catholics. Since he was a Galician Ukrainian, he was unacceptable to Carpatho-Rusyns, and many of their clergy and laity simply refused to recognize his authority. Realizing that the controversy was more than just a clash of personalities—that it reflected deep-seated historical differences between the two groups—the Vatican decided in 1916 after Ortynsky's death to establish two separate Eastern-rite jurisdictions: one for parishes of immigrants from Galicia, the other for those from the Kingdom of Hungary. The Reverend Peter Poniatyshyn (1877–1960) was appointed the Galician administrator. This ecclesiastical division was reconfirmed in 1924 when the administrations were raised to exarchates: Bishop Constantine Bohachevsky (1884–1961) was appointed to the Ukrainian Catholic Church with its seat in Philadelphia; Bishop Basil Takach (1879–1948) was chosen to lead the Byzantine-rite Ruthenian Church with its seat in Pittsburgh.

By the 1920s this complicated early history of Ukrainian immigrant religious life had led to the creation of clearly definable Ukrainian Catholic and Ukrainian Orthodox churches, a division that still persists (see Table 1). In more general terms, religion has been both a unifying and divisive force in the life of the Ukrainian-American community.

On the positive side the churches, whether Catholic, Orthodox, or Protestant, have done much to reinforce the fabric of the Ukrainian community. Today it is still the church, with its basement or an adjacent building, that provides the facilities for dinners, wedding receptions, concerts, plays, bazaars, bingo games, and other community social occasions. It is usually the church, through its parochial-school system and Saturday schools, that provides instruction for young people in Ukrainian language and culture. The churches have also contributed to the preservation of Ukrainian culture through newspapers like the Catholic *Shliakh/The Way* (Philadelphia, f. 1940) and *Nova zoria/The New Star* (Chicago, f. 1965) or the Orthodox *Ukraïns'ke pravoslavne slovo* (The Ukrainian Orthodox Word, South Bound Brook, N.J., f. 1940); through church almanacs; and through individual books such as the Orthodox-sponsored *Ukraïna: entsyklopediia dlia molodi* (The Ukraine: An Encyclopedia for Young People, 1971).

On the negative side, the church has often been a source of discord, and this has in certain instances proved detrimental to the Ukrainian-American community, as in the defection of thousands of parishioners to the Russian Orthodox Church, where they generally became part of the Russian-American community. Similarly, the attempt of the Ukrainian Catholic church to gain control in 1911 over the largest lay organization—the Ukrainian National Association—caused dissension and the alienation or loss of many of the association's members.

The Vatican decree of 1929 further exacerbated the situation. It reaffirmed clerical celibacy and ordered church property to be turned over to the bishop. A new wave of defections to Ukrainian and Russian Orthodoxy resulted, as well as a series of court cases to determine who was to have legal control over church property—the Catholics, the Orthodox, the bishop, or the lay trustees.

The most recent controversy centers on the so-called patriarchal movement, which proposes to create one worldwide church for all Eastern-rite Catholics, to be headed by Cardinal Josyf Slipyi (1892–), the last metropolitan of the Ukrainian Catholic Church in the homeland. The Vatican, as well as a portion of the Ukrainian Catholic Church membership, opposes this plan. Supporters of the patriarchal movement, especially among the most recent immigrants, have made the issue a matter of Ukrainian national pride. Their demands have frequently led to widely publicized protests against Rome, and in some communities, such as Chicago, separate patriarchal and nonpatriarchal parishes have developed.

Faced by these various controversies, parishioners, especially young people, have often become disenchanted with the church and embarrassed by the religious squabbles that have torn the Ukrainian-American community apart. The result is a reluctance to be identified with the church and in some cases with Ukrainians at all. While the churches have done much to preserve and propagate Ukrainian traditions in the United States, they have at the same time done much to undermine the fabric of the community.

SOCIAL ORGANIZATION

Fraternal societies are the oldest Ukrainian organizations in the United States and, next to the church, the most influential force in Ukrainian-American life. In an environment in which immigrants had limited income and little savings, the need to insure themselves and their families in the event of accident or death was imperative. This led to the establishment of the fraternal societies.

The history of these organizations goes back to 1885,

when at the initiative of Reverend Ivan Volansky, the St. Nicholas Brotherhood was founded in Shenandoah, Pa. Within two years seven more fraternal societies were founded, and these were then united to form the first Spolucheniie Rus'kykh Bratstv (Union of Ruthenian Fraternal Organizations), but the union lasted only until Volansky returned to Europe in 1889. A second attempt came in 1892, when the Sojedinenije Greko-Kaftoličeskich Russkich Bratstv (Union of Greek Catholic Brotherhoods) was founded in Homestead, Pa. These earliest fraternal societies included Eastern-rite "Ruthenian" Catholics, both Ukrainians and Russophiles (i.e., those who identified themselves as Russians) from Galicia and Carpatho-Rusyns from Hungary.

Disputes within the leadership of the Union of Greek Catholic Brotherhoods over misuse of funds and the national orientation of the group prompted the Galicians to secede and to found in 1894 the Rus'kyi Narodnyi Soiuz (Ruthenian National Association). This group at first included Ukrainians and Russophiles from Galicia as well as some Carpatho-Rusyns, but during the first decade of this century the Ukrainian influence became more pronounced, leading to the resignation of the Russophiles and Carpatho-Rusyns, and the renaming of the organization in 1914 as the Ukraïns'kyi Narodnyi Soiuz (Ukrainian National Association).

These first organizations were closely allied to the Eastern-rite Catholic Church, which expected to play a dominant role in forming their policy. The result was frequent confrontation between the lay and clerical leadership and the members who supported them. For instance, in 1910 Bishop Ortynsky tried to limit the influence of the "socialistically minded" elements in the Ukrainian National Association, by changing the organization's name to Greek-Catholic and restricting its membership to the faithful of that church. This caused a crisis in the organization and resulted in the defection of some members, who established the secular and socialist-oriented Ukraïns'kyi Robitnychyi Soiuz (Ukrainian Workingmen's, recently renamed Fraternal, Association) in 1911. Members who supported the church founded the clerically oriented Provydinnia-Soiuz Ukraïntsiv Katolykiv (Providence Association of Ukrainian Catholics), in the next year. Two years later still another group, the Ukraïns'ka Narodna Pomich (Ukrainian National Aid Association), was founded, and several other smaller fraternal societies followed in subsequent years (Table 3).

The national fraternal organizations function for the Ukrainian-American community on both an economic and a spiritual or cultural level. They are still insurance companies and provide their subscribers with a variety of benefits that do not substantially differ from any standard insurance plan. As early as 1914 the Ukrainian National Association accepted (though not without protest) the modern system of assessments established by the National Fraternal Congress actuarial table, and the system was later adopted by the others.

But the Ukrainian fraternal organizations have offered much more to the community than simply insurance coverage. The founding charter of each organization states that its goal is to enlighten its members with respect to their Ukrainian heritage and to preserve Ukrainian traditions in the United States. The fraternal newspapers and annual almanacs are most useful in maintaining continual contact and cohesiveness within the community. They publish, along with announcements about their own activities, news items and feature articles on the past and present status of the homeland, announcements of births, marriages, deaths, and other events, and advertisements directing consumers to Ukrainian businesses to be patronized either in the neighborhood or through the mail.

The most important of these newspapers is the Ukrainian National Association's daily, *Svoboda* (Jersey City, N.J., f. 1894), edited by capable national leaders like Gregory Hrushka (1860–1913), Luke Myshuha (1887–1955), and Anthony Dragan (1913–). The fraternal societies have also underwritten the cost of many publications in both English and Ukrainian. The Ukrainian National Association leads in this endeavor as well, with 24 monographs to its credit, including English translations of Ukrainian histories by the distinguished scholars Mykhailo Hrushevs'kyi (1866–1934) and Dmytro Doroshenko (1882–1951), and the monumental two-volume *Ukraine: A Concise Encyclopedia* (1963–1971). The fraternal organizations also provide scholarships for their outstanding younger members, and operate two resort areas that provide an ethnic and social setting for the community: the Soyuzivka of the Ukrainian National Association near Kerhonkson, N.Y., and the Verkhovyna of the Ukrainian Fraternal Association at Glen Spey, N.Y.

In addition to the national fraternal societies, Ukrainian Americans have set up other kinds of organizations. In 1933 the Ukrainian Professional Association was born. After the arrival of large numbers of professionals in the post–World War II period, several more specialized groups were organized. Among the largest are the Ukrainian Engineers' Society (f. 1948), the Ukrainians Lawyers' Association (f. 1949), the Ukrainian Medical Association (f. 1950), the Ukrainian Journalists' Association (f. 1952), the Association of the Ukrainian Catholic Press (f. 1952), the Ukrainian American Association of University Professors (f. 1961), the Association of Ukrainian Librarians (f. 1961), and the Ukrainian Teachers' Association (f. 1966). Businessmen also have associations in those cities where there is a large Ukrainian community. Many of these groups publish journals, hold conferences, and sponsor annual dances and other social affairs that help to maintain ethnic cohesiveness.

Ukrainian women first became organized as early as 1897, when the Sisterhood of St. Olga was founded in Jersey City, N.J.; it lasted for about a decade. In 1925 a

Table 3. Selected Ukrainian fraternal societies, 1978.

Society	Headquarters	Publication	Membership
Ukrainian National Association (1894)	Jersey City, N.J.	*Svoboda*	89,000
Ukrainian Fraternal Association (1911)	Scranton, Pa.	*Narodna volia*	24,000
Providence Association of Ukrainian Catholics (1912)	Philadelphia, Pa.	*Ameryka*	18,960
Ukrainian National Aid Association (1914)	Pittsburgh, Pa.	*Narodne slovo*	8,802

Source: Encyclopedia of Associations, 13th ed. (Detroit, 1979), vol. 1.

more broadly based group, the Soiuz Ukraïnok Ameryky (Ukrainian National Women's League of America), was founded. It was led for 23 years by Helen Lotocky, and by now has over 7,000 members. It sponsors kindergartens and social and charitable activities, especially the popularization of Ukrainian folk culture (embroideries, ceramics, cuisine). Recently, the group opened the Ukrainian Museum in New York City. Other women's organizations include the philanthropic Ukrainian Gold Cross (founded in the 1930s), the World Federation of Ukrainian Women's Organizations (f. 1948), and the Union of Ukrainian Orthodox Sisterhoods.

Ukrainian youth organizations began in the interwar period with the founding of the nondenominational Ukrainian Youth League (f. 1933), the Ukrainian Catholic Youth League (f. 1933), and the Organization of Ukrainian Orthodox Youth (f. 1941). These groups emphasized sports activity and cultural education. After World War II the new immigrants set up a whole series of youth organizations devoted to Ukrainian national and political problems, the largest of which are the Ukrainian Youth Organization/Plast (a scouting group) and two politically oriented groups: the Spilka Ukraïns'koï Molodi Ameryky—SUMA (Ukrainian Youth Association of America) and the Ob'iednannia Demokratychnoï Ukraïns'koï Molodi—ODUM (Association of Democratic Ukrainian Youth). The inculcation of Ukrainian patriotism among the members is fostered through educational activity, sports rallies, and especially at summer camps. There are several Ukrainian clubs at various colleges and universities, many of which are now affiliated with the Soiuz Ukraïns'kykh Students'kykh Tovarystv Ameryky—SUSTA (Federation of Ukrainian Students Organizations), established in 1953. The Ukrainian studies program at Harvard University was funded on their initiative.

To maintain a sense of kinship Ukrainian Americans have also organized according to the specific regions from which they or their forebears came. There are clubs of former residents of cities and towns like Lvov (L'viv), Stanislav (Stanyslaviv), and Drogobych (Drohobych), as well as regional organizations made up of Podolians, Bukovinians, Lemkians, Boikians, Hutsuls, and Carpatho-Ukrainians. These regional groups, some of which have branches throughout the United States, include the Organization for the Defense of the Lemkian Region (Yonkers, N.Y), the World Federation of Lemkos (Camillus, N.Y.), the Boikian Committee (Philadelphia), the Hutsul Society (Chicago), and the Carpathian Research Center (New York City). Each organization has its own serial publication and sponsors conferences and books that deal with the regional homeland.

Veterans who fought in Ukrainian units during both world wars have their own groups as well, such as the Strilets'ka Hromada (Riflemen's Community), Sichovi Stril'tsi (Brotherhood of Ukrainian Riflemen), the Ukrainian Free Cossacks, the United Ukrainian War Veterans in America, and two associations made up of former members of the Ukrainian Insurgent Army (UPA). Ukrainian-American sports and paramilitary organizations were set up as early as World War I (Sich Organization of Ukrainians, f. 1916), which sponsored rallies and publications on physical fitness. More recent immigrants have established the Union of Ukrainian-

American Sports Clubs, which sponsors annual national tournaments. Ukrainian soccer clubs are the best known of these; the Ukrainian Nationals in Philadelphia and the Ukrainian Sports Club of New York have won national championships.

EDUCATION

Education is given high priority by Ukrainian Americans. While 55 percent of the immigrants who arrived between 1890 and 1914 were illiterate, the 1970 Census indicated that 44.5 percent had reached high school, 18.7 percent had attended college, and only 4.5 percent had had no schooling. The 1970 figures refer to both Ukrainian schools in the homeland and American public schools, and clearly attest to the improved educational standards of the group.

The first Ukrainian elementary school was set up in 1893 at the Eastern-rite Catholic parish in Shamokin, Pa., and within a year similar schools were founded in three other eastern Pennsylvania mining towns, in Pittsburgh, and in Minneapolis. By 1904 six communities had their own school buildings. This initial enthusiasm grew less from a general awareness of the value of education (although this was clearly present among the handful of intellectual leaders), than from the desire to provide instruction in the Ukrainian language and in the precepts of Eastern-rite Catholicism.

In order to maintain the social fabric of the community, the second generation had to know the Ukrainian language and religious traditions; this was the primary reason why working parents were eager to send their children to Ukrainian parish schools. For the most part, these early Ukrainian schools consisted of a few classes per week in catechism, and sometimes the native language or history, taught by the local parish cantor, who himself probably had never had more than an elementary education. Classes were held after regular school hours or on Saturdays.

As the number of schools increased, activities had to be coordinated and problems resolved, including the lack of textbooks. On the initiative of Bishop Ortynsky, an educational fund, an educational committee, and a boarding school were established in Philadelphia. In the same city a cultural congress was held in 1909, resulting in the sponsorship of the first Ukrainian-language textbooks in the United States, a project in which the Ukrainian National Association was particularly active.

Efforts to coordinate educational activities were aided during the 1920s by two new organizations: the Obiednannia Ukraïns'kykh Orhanizatsiï (United Ukrainian Organizations), which published several textbooks, and the Ridna Shkola (Native School Board), which attempted to set standards for textbooks and curricula. Both were short-lived, but the number of Ukrainian schools continued to grow, and included Catholic all-day parochial schools, 12 of which by 1940 offered some instruction in Ukrainian subjects.

The arrival of the post–World War II immigrants led to a rapid increase in the number of Ukrainian schools. Unlike the earlier immigrants, who sent their children to Ukrainian schools largely in order to maintain certain native, especially religious, traditions, the newest immigrants saw them as a mechanism for instilling in their offspring a clearly defined sense of national iden-

tity. Among the new arrivals were many teachers who could staff the growing system. The rapid expansion of Ukrainian schools led the Ukrainian Congress Committee of America to set up a Shkil'na Rada (Educational Council) in 1953 to coordinate accreditation, textbooks, and curricula.

During the 1975–1976 school year, 14,484 students were enrolled in Ukrainian schools. The largest number, 10,091 (69 percent), attend Ukrainian Catholic day schools, approximately 75 percent of which offer courses in Ukrainian language, reading, and sometimes history. The remainder attend Ukrainian Saturday schools: 3,500 (24 percent) in institutions sponsored by the Educational Council, and 893 (6 percent) in ones sponsored by the Ukrainian Orthodox Church of the United States. Ukrainian Protestant churches also operate several Saturday schools.

The Ukrainian-American community is equally concerned with higher education. As early as 1905 the Rus'ka Kolegiia (Ruthenian College) was established in Shamokin, Pa., on the model of a European gymnasium. It accepted students who had completed the equivalent of an American high school education, but it only survived one year. More successful were the Ukrainian programs at two Presbyterian institutions, Bloomfield College in Bloomfield, N.J., and the University of Dubuque in Dubuque, Iowa. Both institutions trained Protestant ministers for missionary activity among Ukrainian immigrants. Courses in Ukrainian language, literature, and history were given for a decade beginning in 1910 at Bloomfield and between 1912 and 1935 at Dubuque.

The Ukrainian Catholic Church founded two institutions that still provide courses in Ukrainian civilization. These include St. Basil's Ukrainian Catholic Seminary in Stamford, Conn., originally established in the 1930s as the basis for a Ukrainian university, and Manor Junior College in Jenkintown, Pa. As a result of the Cold War and the post-Sputnik competition between the United States and the Soviet Union, several American colleges and universities expanded or began programs in Soviet and East European studies, and a concomitant interest grew in Ukrainian affairs, especially in language. By the 1970s, about 20 American universities were offering instruction in the Ukrainian language. The most comprehensive program is now provided by Harvard University, where the funds collected from the Ukrainian-American community support three endowed chairs in Ukrainian history, Ukrainian language, and Ukrainian literature. The Harvard Ukrainian Research Institute, under the direction of Omeljan Pritsak (1919–), also undertakes research, publishing, and other scholarly activities dealing with the Ukraine.

The courses and programs at American universities do to some extent train young people from the Ukrainian community (at Harvard a summer school program is designed especially for this purpose), but equally important is their recognition that Ukrainian culture is a subject worthy of discussion and analysis in prestigious American educational institutions. This is often stressed in the Ukrainian-American press, and it has been beneficial to the self-esteem of many members of the group, even if they have not themselves participated in the programs.

Outside the universities, Ukrainian education remains closely allied with the church. In the early days, a Ukrainian education was in fact restricted to religious instruction in the mother tongue. Through the influence of the highly politicized recent immigration, Ukrainian schools have clearly become mechanisms to perpetuate national consciousness among the American-born. Despite these secular intentions, 84 percent of the Ukrainian schools are run by the Ukrainian Catholic or, to a lesser degree, Ukrainian Orthodox churches. Even among those schools sponsored by the nondenominational Education Committee, 21 of the 35 listed hold their classes in churches or church-owned buildings. In short, education, religion, and ethnic culture remain closely intertwined in the Ukrainian-American community.

CULTURE

Ukrainian-American culture is expressed primarily through traditional modes adapted to the environment of the New World. Among them, one of the most important in preserving ethnicity is language, and Ukrainian Americans have developed both informal and formal mechanisms to foster language maintenance.

The family unit contributes the most. A high percentage of young Ukrainian Americans, particularly the children of the most recent immigrants, are fluent in the mother tongue. One limited statistical analysis revealed that 86 percent of them use only Ukrainian at home. As a result of the influx of Ukrainian immigrants after 1945, the number of Ukrainian speakers in the United States more than tripled in 20 years. This represented the largest increase (202.6 percent) of 23 languages compared. In absolute figures, the number of Ukrainian speakers in this country rose from 83,600 in 1940 to 252,974 in 1960. In 1970 the U.S. Census reported 249,351 people replying that as children Ukrainian was spoken at home; 152,500 of them were born in the United States. Only 22,662 of those, however, were the children of native-born parents, suggesting a sharp decline in language maintenance among descendants of the first wave of immigrants.

Other institutions also contribute to language maintenance. Almost ninety percent of the Ukrainian Catholic and Orthodox churches hold at least one service in Ukrainian and Church Slavonic, the ancient liturgical language of the Slavic Eastern-rite churches. Ukrainian youth organizations and sports clubs also use Ukrainian to some extent, even though most, if not all, of their members speak fluent English. An extensive Ukrainian press has aided maintenance as well. In 1976, 67 Ukrainian-language newspapers and journals were published in the United States, with a total circulation of 50,000 for the newspapers and another 90,000 for magazines and journals. Modern printing technologies (offset printing, IBM Ukrainian elements) have made it comparatively easy to spread the Ukrainian word. Several publishing houses specialize in Ukrainian-language materials, such as Knyhospilka, Smoloskyp, and Prolog Research, all in New York, and the Denysiuk Publishing Company and the Ukrainian Information and Research Institute in Chicago.

Ukrainian-language radio programs are broadcast in metropolitan areas where large numbers of Ukrainian Americans live. The first of these began in the 1930s;

today at least 30 usually half-hour weekly programs are broadcast in Ukrainian throughout the nation.

Ukrainian-American literature falls into two categories: works dealing primarily with the immigration, and works that are part of the mainstream of 20th-century Ukrainian literature. Works in the first category go back to the 1890s when several poems, short stories, and short plays intended usually for production by a local amateur group were published. Among the earlier writers were Gregory Hrushka (1860–1913), Nestor Dmytriv (1863–1925), and Stephen Makar (1870–1915). Their works were dominated by themes of longing for the homeland and the hardship of immigrant life. The literary quality of these writings, as well as the subsequent patriotic works of Dmytro Zakharchuk, Stepan Musiichuk (1894–1952), and Matvii Kostyshyn (1888–1976), and the lyric realism of Ivan Tsybulsky and Nicholas Strutynsky, is not very high. Of greater interest is the poetry of Sava Chernets'kyi, Alexander Neprytsky-Granovsky (1887–1976), and most especially the talented English-language author Maria Bloch-Halun (1910–), who has written several stories for children, most of them dealing with problems of cultural adjustment and assimilation.

The situation is different among the immigrants who arrived after World War II, 150 of whom listed their profession as author. In their work immigrant themes are almost completely absent, and the style and motifs reflect either the Ukrainian literature and criticism that prevailed in Europe during the 1930s and 1940s, or the modern style of 20th-century literature generally. These writers are organized in the Association of Ukrainian Writers, which has been publishing anthologies, entitled *Slovo*, periodically since 1959.

The postwar writers can be divided into three groups. The first group, best represented by Evhen Malaniuk (1897–1968), Iurii Kosach (1909–), Vadym Lesytsch (1909–), Bohdan Krawciw (1904–1975), and Teodosii Osmachka (1895–1962), consists of writers who began their literary careers in Europe, either in the Ukraine or in émigré communities. The second group, with such writers as Ostap Tarnawsky (1917–) and Vasyl Barka (1908–), began to write during or after the immigration, either in the displaced-persons camps in Germany and Austria or in the United States. These writers have basically not departed from the literary forms that were common in the homeland when they left.

In marked contrast is the so-called New York Group, represented by the poets Bohdan Boychuk (1927–), Bohdan Rubchak (1935–), and Iurii Tarnawsky (1934–), all of whom began their literary careers in the United States and are distinguished by their urban and cosmopolitan world view. Using modern literary styles, these writers see themselves as enriching Ukrainian literature in a way that would not be possible in the homeland. Although the New York Group publishes in *Slovo*, they also have their own journal, *Novi poeziï*, and publish literary criticism in the pages of *Suchasnist'* (Munich and New York, f. 1951), a monthly edited by the distinguished scholar George Shevelov (1908–) that serves as a forum for the Ukrainian-American intelligentsia. The vitality of the New York Group has attracted to its ranks an American author, Patricia Nell Warren (1936–), who has written in Ukrainian under the pseudonym Patrytsiia Kylyna.

In painting, sculpture, and architecture, Ukrainian Americans have either continued in the styles prevalent in Europe when they left, or have adopted modern styles (with or without definable Ukrainian motifs), most of which have been outlawed since the 1930s in the Soviet Ukraine. The most renowned Ukrainian-American artist is the sculptor Alexander Archipenko (1887–1964), who before he emigrated had almost single-handedly introduced the Cubist style into sculpture. But even the cosmopolitan Archipenko reverted to the realist tradition when he created statues of national heroes for the Ukrainian-American community. Examples of these can be seen at the Ukrainian Cultural Garden in Cleveland and at the Ukrainian National Association resort near Kerhonkson, N.Y.

Since 1952 painters and sculptors have been organized in the Association of Ukrainian Artists in America. Among the established painters and graphic artists are Wolodymyr Balas, Jacques Hnizdovsky (1915–), Myroslawa Lasowska, Petro Mehyk (1899–), Michael Moroz (1904–), and Myroslav Radysh (1910–1956). A group of neo-Byzantine painters like Sviatoslav Hordynsky (1906–) and Peter Kholodny work on icons and other decorative elements in Ukrainian church interiors, while the sculptors George Bobritzky, Slava Gerulak, Mykola Holodnyk, and Alexander Hunenko (1937–) have created works in the most modern styles. Ukrainian-American architecture as expressed in church buildings is eclectic in style—for example, the neobaroque St. Nicholas Ukrainian Catholic Cathedral in Chicago (built in 1914), the Cossack-baroque Orthodox Cathedral in South Bound Brook, N.J. (built in 1964) by George Kodak, the neo-Byzantine Immaculate Conception Catholic Cathedral in Philadelphia (built in 1964) by Julian K. Jastremsky (1910–), and the Carpathian wooden churches in Hunter, N.Y. and in Glen Spey, N.Y., by Ivan Zukovsky (1910–) and Appollinaire Osadca (1916–).

At a less grand, but no less sophisticated, level are the various products of Ukrainian folk art—embroidery, rugs, Easter eggs, wood carvings, and ceramics—that continue to be produced by a host of talented craftspeople. Some of these elements, especially embroidered blouses, enjoy a recurrent vogue in American fashion.

Music, theater, and dance are forms of artistic expression that not only reflect the Ukrainian heritage but are also the basis for social occasions that help to maintain the integrity of the Ukrainian-American community. Liturgical music and folk music are the most popular, and are performed by numerous choirs and ensembles, the first of which were founded in the 1890s. The most prominent of these groups are the Ukrainian National Choir, directed by Alexander Koshyts (1875–1944), the Ukrainian Besida Choir, and the Ukrainian Youth Chorus of New York and New Jersey, all founded in the 1930s, and the more recent Dumka Choir in New York and the Kobzar Choir in Philadelphia. Ukrainian musical activity in the United States was raised to a professional level in the decade after World War I, and this was due largely to the efforts of accomplished musicians like Mychaylo Hayvoronsky (1892–1949) and Roman Prydatkewych (1895–), and to the establishment of several conservatories, the most recent being the Ukrainian Music Institute (f. 1952) in New York City. Many graduates of this Ukrainian-American mu-

sical environment have gained international reputations as performers, and as composers they often include Ukrainian themes and motifs in their works. Among the more prominent composers are Ihor Bilohrud (1916–), Nicholas Fomenko (1894–1961), Volodymyr Hrudyn (1893–), Antin Rudnytsky (1902–1975), and Ihor Sonevytsky (1924–).

Ukrainian amateur theatrical performances are often a part of ethnic programs and festivals. Several attempts have been made to establish permanent theatrical companies in New York City: the Zaporozhian Sich Society (1907–1910), the Ukrainian Theater (1923–1928), an opera group (1930s), which performed Tchaikovsky's *Mazepa* and Lysenko's *Taras Bulba*, and more recently the Theatrical Studio (later the Ukrainian Theater of America), the New Theater, and the Ukrainian Opera Company.

In addition to amateur theatrical groups, almost every Ukrainian-American community has at least one song-and-dance ensemble. The colorful costumes, tempestuous music, and Cossack-style acrobatic movements make folk dances particularly popular not only among Ukrainians, but among the general American public as well. In multiethnic programs, Ukrainian dance groups frequently make a very favorable impression, and consequently reinforce group solidarity.

The Ukrainian-American community also has a broad network of scholarly organizations. The most recent immigration has been particularly successful in recreating many of the institutions that were abolished or abandoned in Europe. In 1947, the Shevchenko Scientific Society, formerly of Lvov, was reconstituted in New York City. Three years later, the Ukrainian Academy of Arts and Sciences, whose namesake is still in Kiev, was also established in New York City. Both institutions hold conferences and publish books and journals in Ukrainian and English that deal with various aspects of Ukrainian culture in both the humanities and the natural sciences. Two other organizations have no European predecessors: the V. Lypynsky East European Institute in Philadelphia (f. 1963) and the Ukrainian Historical Society (f. 1964), both of which publish materials on Ukrainian history.

Ukrainian Americans have created several museums, archives, and libraries to preserve the group's heritage. Because the maintenance of these institutions requires funds, staff, and expertise that are often beyond the capacity of the community to provide, individuals and organizations frequently donate their materials to American institutions that already have substantial Ukrainian holdings, including Harvard University, the University of Illinois at Champaign-Urbana, Columbia University, and especially the Immigrant History Research Center at the University of Minnesota which has a special collection for the study of Ukrainian immigration.

POLITICS

Ukrainians have generally not been active in American politics. The earlier immigrants lacked the educational and political experience needed to participate effectively in what must at first have seemed a complex system of democratic government. In any event, U.S. politics did not appear useful to people who expected to stay only long enough to earn money to buy land at home. The post–World War II immigrants, many of whom had been active leaders in Europe, have also avoided U.S. politics; their political interests are confined almost exclusively to the fate of the homeland.

This concern for the homeland took time to develop. The earliest immigrants called themselves Rusyns or Ruthenians and usually had no clear idea of what "Ukraine" and "Ukrainian" meant. After the Russophile and Carpatho-Rusyn factions in the community went their separate ways, however, the remaining group did transform itself into a clearly defined Ukrainian-American community, the fraternal societies leading the way. The Ruthenian National Association was renamed the Ukrainian National Association in 1914, and three new fraternal societies were founded: the Ukrainian Workingmen's Association (f. 1911), the Providence Association of Ukrainian Catholics (f. 1912), and the Ukrainian National Aid (f. 1914).

Since that time Ukrainian Americans have closely followed events in Europe and have involved themselves by contributing both material aid and political action. The first significant sum of money was collected at the close of World War I, when an emergency fund totaling $140,000 was sent to aid the efforts of the Western Ukrainian government-in-exile. This government, originally based in the former Austrian province of Galicia, lost its effectiveness when that area was occupied by Poland in 1920. Nonetheless, the United Ukrainian Organizations continued to send aid to the region, collecting over $365,000 in the 1930s to help support charitable, educational, and political institutions in eastern Galicia. Money, food, and clothing were also sent to the autonomous Carpatho-Ukraine in 1938–1939, when many Ukrainian Americans (although not the majority of Carpatho-Rusyn Americans) hoped that the area, then part of Czechoslovakia, would become an independent Ukrainian state. The largest single amount was collected by the Zluchenyi Ukraïns'kyi Amerykans'kyi Dopomohovyi Komitet (United Ukrainian American Relief Committee), founded in Philadelphia in 1944 under the leadership of Walter Gallan (1893–1978). After 1945, when all Ukrainian lands were incorporated into the Soviet Union, direct aid to the homeland was no longer possible, and the relief committee instead directed its efforts to aid the half-million Ukrainian refugees living in displaced-persons camps in the western zones of Germany and Austria. Besides providing money, food, and clothing, the committee helped to settle over 50,000 Ukrainian refugees in the United States.

The Ukrainian-American community has also produced a number of political organizations that claim to represent the homeland or some exile government, and assume responsibility for speaking on Ukrainian problems to the U.S. government and the United Nations.

The earliest of these groups were the First Ukrainian Assembly, the pro-Austrian Ukrainian National Committee, and the anti-Austrian Federation of Ukrainians, all formed during World War I, when the rapidly changing military and political situation in Europe made it seem possible that the Ukraine could achieve political independence. Several successive short-lived Ukrainian governments were formed, but lasting independence

was not achieved, and they became governments-in-exile. In 1919–1920 the Western Ukrainian government maintained a mission in Washington, D.C., supported by the immigrant community and the Association of Friends of the Ukrainian National Republic. Subsequently, during the 1930s, a Union of Hetman's Followers, later renamed the Ukraïns'ka Hetmans'ka Orhanizatsiia (Ukrainian Hetmanate Organization) and the Orhanizatsiia Derzhavnoho Vidrodzhennia Ukraïny (Organization for the Rebirth of the Ukraine) were founded. Most of these groups are still active and view themselves as nuclei for future Ukrainian governments, whether of monarchical, nationalist, or republican persuasion.

In 1940 the Ukrainian Congress Committee of America was set up as an umbrella organization for Ukrainian-American groups. Through memorandums, pamphlets, and personal contacts, the Congress Committee, representing an anti-Soviet and anti-Nazi policy, sent observers and memorandums to the United Nations Conference in San Francisco (1945) and to the Peace Conference in Paris (1946). Since that time, its leadership, especially its president, Lev Dobriansky (1918–) of Georgetown University, has maintained close contact with U.S. congressmen and has voiced anti-Soviet viewpoints through rallies, protests, and the journal, The Ukrainian Quarterly (New York, f. 1944).

The immigrants who arrived after World War II have set up several other political organizations. The largest of these is the Orhanizatsiia Oborony Chotyriokh Svobid Ukraïny (Organization of the Defense of Four Freedoms of the Ukraine) founded in 1947. This group has its own women's organization and, in cooperation with other youth organizations (SUMA), constitutes the Ukrainian Liberation Front. Influenced by the beliefs of the World War II nationalist leader, Stephen Bandera (1909–1959), it claims to be the legal survivor of the last independent Ukrainian government proclaimed in 1941.

Ukrainian Americans have also founded several socialist groups, including the Ukrainian Progressive Organization Haidamaky (f. 1907) and the Ukrainian Workers' Party (f. 1909). Two others have directed their efforts toward the homeland, the Defense of the Ukraine and the League for the Liberation of the Homeland, both founded in the 1920s. There have also been pro-Soviet organizations, such as the Soiuz Ukraïns'kykh Robitnychykh Orhanizatsii (Union of Ukrainian Workers' Organizations), founded in 1923, and the Ukraïns'ka Liga Ameryky (Ukrainian American League), founded in 1924. Influential during the 1930s when the union had 11,000 members, today only the league remains, with a small number of members. The vast majority of Ukrainian Americans remain passionately anti-Soviet.

The relations between these political organizations and U.S. government policy makers have depended in large measure on the vacillations in Washington's relations with the Soviet Union. When the U.S.S.R. was an ally during World War II, organizations like the anti-Soviet Congress Committee were frequently an embarrassment to the American government. The Cold War made Washington more willing to listen to, and to use for its own purposes, the barrage of anti-Soviet criticism coming from Ukrainian groups. The détente of the early 1970s caused Ukrainian-American anti-Soviet protests again to be handled with caution, though they still provided rhetorical material for anti-détente elements in and out of government.

The widely based network of Ukrainian political organizations, with their factions, meetings, and publications, has largely drained the energies of those who might otherwise have entered the American political arena. In comparison with many other ethnic groups, Ukrainians are consequently poorly represented in the highest levels of government. There has never been a congressman or federal judge of Ukrainian background; candidates have never felt the need to court the Ukrainian vote in elections. At the state and local levels Ukrainian-American officeholders have appeared, and a few have had high government appointments: Joseph Charyk was Undersecretary of the Air Force from 1960 to 1963, George Kistiakowsky was special adviser to President Eisenhower for science and technology (1959–1961), and Myron Kuropas was special adviser to the president for ethnic affairs (1975–1976).

INTERGROUP RELATIONS

Relations with other groups have been determined largely by attitudes and experiences brought from Europe. As in the homeland, Ukrainians in the New World have not gotten along very well with either the Poles or the Russians, although other Americans, particularly in the early years, lumped them together under the opprobrious term "Hunkies." The causes of friction were both religious and national. Before and even after the various stages in the establishment of a Ukrainian Catholic Church in 1916 and 1924, many Ukrainians belonged to Latin-rite parishes that were predominantly Polish in membership. Since these churches wanted to hold onto their new members, they strongly opposed the establishment of the rival Eastern-rite Catholic churches. Conversions to Orthodoxy, especially in the early years of the 20th century when there was no Ukrainian Orthodox Church, similarly ran the risk that the converts would join the Russian Orthodox Church and become Russians.

The struggle between the Orthodox and Eastern-rite Catholic churches produced much hostility between Ukrainian and Russian immigrants. Closely allied was the question of national identity: in the earlier years some Polish and most Russian immigrants did not recognize Ukrainians as a separate nationality. Since World War II the Polish immigration has generally accepted the existence of Ukrainians and even respects their organizational achievements, but Russian Americans (especially Russophiles from Ukrainian territory) continue to view the Ukrainian-American community as nothing more than a politically inspired abberation devised by Ukrainians from Galicia who, like their brethren farther east, should be designated and considered "Little Russians." Relations between the Ukrainian and Carpatho-Rusyn communities have been equally strained, because Ukrainian Americans, especially the recent immigrants, refuse to recognize Carpatho-Rusyns in the United States as a distinct ethnic group.

Ukrainian Americans seem to get along much better with other East Europeans, such as the Czechs, Serbs, Latvians, and Lithuanians, with whom they have much

in common. They hold generally the same socioeconomic status in the United States, they are perceived as being similar by the larger society, and they all are opposed to the Communist regimes that rule their respective homelands.

Ukrainian Americans have also transferred to the United States the symbiotic relations with Jews that were common in Europe. In the early years of the 20th century many of the shops, travel and package-sending agencies, and local banks in Ukrainian neighborhoods were run by Jews. As they became more socially mobile, Ukrainians were apt to measure their success against the level of achievement attained by a local Jewish proprietor or a former Jewish schoolmate. In recent years, Ukrainian Americans have come to share the attitudes of many of their fellow white ethnics who view with varying degrees of scorn the less fortunate blacks and Puerto Ricans who have moved into their urban neighborhoods.

Relations with the larger society predictably vary according to the time of arrival in the United States. Those who came during the first two periods of immigration are by now largely assimilated. Third- and fourth-generation descendants operate in the larger society without any special difficulty; some are aware of their heritage only in terms of a family name or membership in an Eastern-rite church.

Many post–World War II immigrants, in contrast, seem to live their lives apart from the mainstream, displaying what might be described as a respect-disdain attitude toward American life. Like all immigrants they cannot help but be impressed by the achievements, the freedom, and the vitality of this highly industrialized society. The United States truly embraces a new world, so different from the tradition-bound, placid, even stagnant, rural or small-town environment they left behind. Change is often perceived as instability, but in America it is a way of life; this is most disconcerting to the Ukrainian psyche. Some quickly adapt and prosper, but most have found the adjustment to be too great. As a result, they have tried, and to a large degree succeeded, in creating their own world, bound by a widespread network of churches, secular organizations, and Ukrainian-language newspapers. When the mores of the larger society do not coincide with the group's own standards, the reaction is often an outward disdain that takes the form of adhering to polar opposites: in this case the Ukrainians' respect for tradition, formalized codes of conduct determined by a strict social hierarchy, the frequent use of titles (Doctor, Engineer, Magister), and patriotism toward the homeland are adopted to counter what they see as an American disregard for tradition and ritual, avoidance of titles and other social customs that clearly establish and define barriers between individuals, and pluralist or cosmopolitan attitudes, which Ukrainians interpret as being antiethnic. Thus, many post–World War II Ukrainian immigrants feel safer in their own communities and restrict contact with the larger society to a minimum.

GROUP MAINTENANCE AND INDIVIDUAL ETHNIC COMMITMENT

Several factors in Ukrainian-American life reinforce the ethnic commitment of individuals and ensure the continued viability of the group. Ukrainian Americans

have created a society within a society, particularly since World War II. All the necessary institutions—churches, schools, fraternal and professional societies, publications, social clubs, resorts, and sports teams—have been made available so that a Ukrainian American can function relatively well with only minimal contact with the mainstream of society. The Ukrainian language as spoken by members of the community is sprinkled with an assortment of abbreviated references to organizations (UNDO, Dvikari, Soiuzanka, Melnykivtsi, Banderivtsi) that carry a host of political and social connotations which only members of the community can readily grasp. The best example of this is perhaps the satirical journal, *Lys Mykyta* (The Fox, Detroit, f. 1951); to understand it requires not only a knowledge of the Ukrainian language, but also a grasp of the nuances of the immigrant social context that are available only to an insider.

Another element contributing to group maintenance is the stress that a large number of articulate immigrants place on national ideology as the basis of identity. One is a Ukrainian not only because one's forebears came from a territory that was or is now called the Ukraine, but also because one adheres to the ideals, many of them political, of the group. In a survey conducted among the youth of one Ukrainian community, 82 percent of the respondents stated that being Ukrainian carried with it the obligation to work toward a free and independent Ukraine. The larger society reinforces this attitude by regarding Ukrainians as Russians (or sometimes as Poles), obliging the Ukrainian to explain the difference, an experience that requires and thereby reinforces his or her ethnic identity.

The churches also contribute to group maintenance since, if in nothing else but name, definable Ukrainian Catholic, Orthodox, and Protestant churches do exist. Even an individual who does not come to Sunday services will find an occasion to attend a high church holiday, like Christmas or Easter, a baptism, wedding, or funeral, Saturday school, a dance group, scout or other meeting, or some other social function.

The history and structure of Ukrainian churches also strengthen the group. Unlike other Eastern-rite Catholic churches, the Ukrainian Catholic Church exists only outside the homeland. Since the mother church was suppressed by the Soviet government after 1945, many in the diaspora feel a moral imperative to assure its continued existence. The Ukrainian Orthodox churches play a similar role. Originally founded as an alternative to Russian-dominated Orthodox churches, they have been able to retain their Ukrainian character. The largest of them, the Ukrainian Orthodox Church of the U.S.A., is not a member of the Standing Conference of Orthodox Bishops; its parishioners cannot join, for marriage or other reasons, other Orthodox bodies. The distinctive features of Ukrainian churches take on a self-generating quality of their own. For instance, when the Vatican Council introduced the vernacular in the early 1960s, the Ukrainians replaced Church Slavonic with Ukrainian as well as English. Many Ukrainian-American parishes, both Catholic and Orthodox, insist on using Ukrainian even when the local priest might have liked to shift to English.

If the cohesiveness of the group can be judged from the membership patterns in ethnic institutions, then

Ukrainian-American society seems to be holding steady. After a rapid increase in the size of Ukrainian organizations during the 1950s, it leveled off and then declined slightly during the 1960s. Between 1960 and 1970 membership in Ukrainian churches dropped from 445,251 to 406,210. As a result of parental pressure at least 60 percent of all marriages continue to be between members of either the Ukrainian Catholic or Ukrainian Orthodox churches. Ukrainian fraternal societies, despite the death of older members, have registered an increase in membership—from 135,084 in 1967 to 140,060 in 1977—suggesting that many Ukrainians still prefer to receive insurance coverage and other advantages from their own ethnic organizations rather than from outside companies. A less favorable indication has been the decline in the size of the Saturday-school programs. For instance, between 1968 and 1976 the total number of students enrolled in Ukrainian Catholic day schools and in Saturday schools sponsored by the Educational Council and Ukrainian Orthodox church declined 32 percent, from 21,036 to 14,484. The decline is significant, since these schools remain the only place where Ukrainian children can receive any systematic instruction in their heritage.

The Ukrainian-American community has often been viewed by others as one of the most vital ethnic groups in the United States. Whether this reputation will continue to be deserved depends in large measure on the degree to which the many articulate new immigrants can continue to instill both in their own offspring and in the older immigrants and their descendants a sense of Ukrainian identity and awareness.

Bibliography
The best general introduction is by Vasyl Markus, "Ukrainians in the United States," in *Ukraine: A Concise Encyclopedia*, ed. Volodymyr Kubijovič (Toronto, 1971), 2: 1100–1151. This two-volume encyclopedia covers Ukrainians in the homeland and in the immigration. See also Wasyl Halich, *Ukrainians in the United States* (Chicago, 1937; reprint, New York, 1970); Yaroslav Chyz, *The Ukrainian Immigrants in the United States* (Scranton, Pa., 1959); and Myron B. Kuropas, *Ukrainians in America* (Minneapolis, 1972). The materials compiled by Vladimir Wertsman in *The Ukrainians in America, 1608–1975: A Chronology and Fact Book* (Dobbs Ferry, N.Y., 1976), and the conference proceedings, *The Ukrainian Immigrant Experience in the United States: A Symposium*, ed. Paul R. Magocsi (Cambridge, Mass., 1979), are also useful.

Iuliian Bachyns'kyi, *Ukraïns'ka immigratsiia v Z'iedynenykh Derzhavakh Ameryky* (Lvov, 1914), is a classic which still offers the best historical and sociological description of early immigrant life. More recent sociological analyses are found in a collection of articles in *Ukrainians in American and Canadian Society*, ed. Wsevolod W. Isajiw (Jersey City, N.J., 1976), and in a sociolinguistic study by Vladimir C. Nahirny and Joshua A. Fishman, "Ukrainian Language Maintenance Efforts in the United States," in *Language Loyalty in the United States*, ed. Fishman et al. (The Hague, 1966). Historical descriptions of individual communities, ethnic organizations, and group leaders are also available: Bohdan Procko, "Pennsylvania: Focal Point of Ukrainian Immigration," in *The Ethnic Experience in Pennsylvania*, ed. John J. Bodnar (Lewisburg, Pa., 1973); Alexander Lushnycky, ed., *Ukrainians in Pennsylvania* (Philadelphia, 1976); Stephan Basarab et al., *The Ukrainians of Maryland* (Baltimore, 1977); Theodore Luciw, *Father Agapius Honcharenko, First Ukrainian Priest in America* (New York, 1970); and Anthony Dragan, *Ukrainian National Association: Its Past and Present, 1896–1964* (Jersey City, N.J., 1964). Two valuable reference works are: D.M. Shtohryn, ed., *Ukrainians in America: A Biographical Directory of Noteworthy Men and Women of Ukrainian Origin in the U.S.A. and Canada* (Chicago, 1975), and Wasyl Weresh, ed., *Guide to Ukrainian-American Institutions, Professionals, and Business* (New York, 1955).

The largest collection of materials on Ukrainian immigration is the Immigration History Research Center at the University of Minnesota in Minneapolis. It includes a wide variety of serials, books, pamphlets, and archival materials. Other centers with significant collections, containing in particular the archives and libraries of leading figures in the immigration, are the Bakhmeteff Archive of Russian and East European Culture (Columbia University), the Ukraïns'kyi Muzei Arkhiv (Ukrainian Museum-Archive) in Cleveland, and the Ukraïns'ka Akademiia Nauk (Ukrainian Academy of Arts and Sciences) in New York City.

PAUL ROBERT MAGOCSI

ULSTER SCOTS: *see* SCOTCH-IRISH

UMATILLAS: *see* AMERICAN INDIANS

UMPQUAS: *see* AMERICAN INDIANS

UNIATES: *see* EASTERN CATHOLICS

URUGUAYANS: *see* CENTRAL AND SOUTH AMERICANS

UTES: *see* AMERICAN INDIANS

UZBEKS: *see* AFGHANS; TURKESTANIS

V

VANYUMES: *see* AMERICAN INDIANS

VENEZUELANS: *see* CENTRAL AND SOUTH AMERICANS

VIETNAMESE: *see* INDOCHINESE

VIRGIN ISLANDERS: *see* WEST INDIANS

VISAYANS: *see* FILIPINOS

VOLGA GERMANS: *see* GERMANS FROM RUSSIA

VOLGA TATARS: *see* TATARS

W

WALLA WALLAS: *see* AMERICAN INDIANS

WALLOONS: *see* BELGIANS

WAMPANOAGS: *see* AMERICAN INDIANS

WAPPOS: *see* AMERICAN INDIANS

WARM SPRINGS: *see* AMERICAN INDIANS

WASCOS: *see* AMERICAN INDIANS

WASHOES: *see* AMERICAN INDIANS

WEACOS: *see* AMERICAN INDIANS

WELSH

The Welsh, both in Great Britain and in America, have always stood in a special relation to their English-speaking neighbors. Descended from at least two distinct ethnic stocks—the tall, ruddy, Celtic invaders of about 500 B.C. and the earlier "Iberian" *pobl fach ddu* (little black-haired people)—the Romanized Britons were called Welsh (foreigners) by the Anglo-Saxon invaders of the 5th to 7th centuries. Perhaps most of them were eventually absorbed into the general population of England and southeastern Scotland; those *Cymry* (fellow countrymen) who held out in the mountainous west continued to speak their own Celtic language, *Cymraeg,* longer and more generally than the Gaelic-speaking Highland Scots, Irish, and Manx or their closer cousins, the Cornish. Ever since political union with England in 1536, however, *Cymru,* or Wales, has been influenced increasingly by English culture.

Anglicization of language and manners among the Welsh gentry in the 16th and 17th centuries abandoned Welsh culture to the *gwerin* (the peasantry, the folk). There, in the 18th century, it began to be recast in three new molds—religious, cultural, and economic. The evangelical revival after 1735 gradually brought most of the people into their own Independent (Congregational), Baptist, and Calvinistic Methodist chapels and taught them to read. After 1789 the medieval *eisteddfod* of poetic, musical, and scholarly contests was revived by, among others, some of the new preachers in their other guise of romanticized druids. And the Industrial Revolution that began about 1760 filled the valleys of the southeast and extreme northeast with coal mines and iron, copper, and tin works and opened slate quarries in the mountains of the northwest. As late as 1870 the industrial labor force, though partly English and Irish, was drawn mainly from the Welsh-speaking peasantry. During the era of emigration, consequently, rural and industrial Wales shared a single culture.

The social ideal that Welsh peasants implicitly followed, of self-supporting families within the culturally homogeneous, cooperative community of the gwerin, corresponded at essential points, as immigrants often sensed, to the republican doctrine of personal independence and civic virtue that the American Revolution

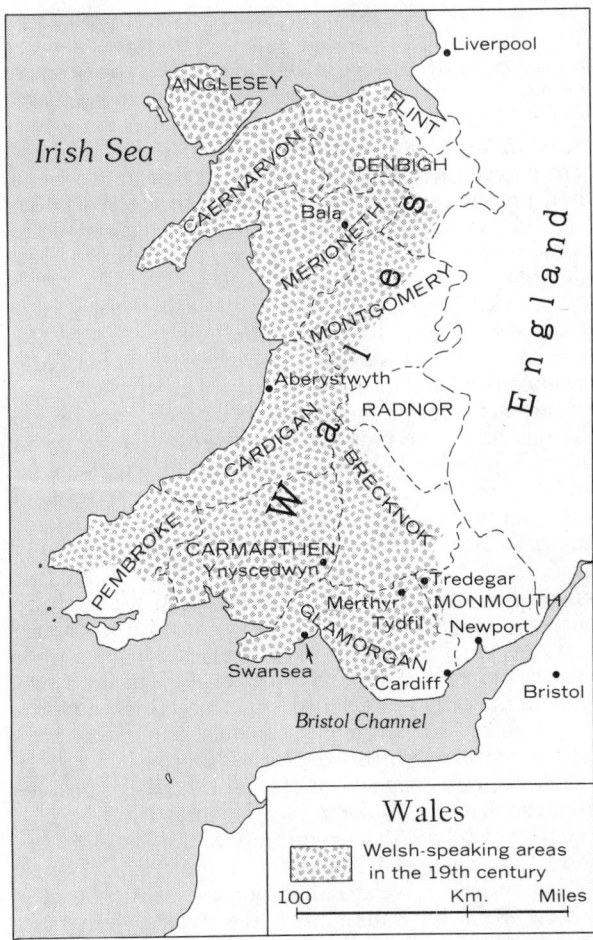

Wales

Welsh-speaking areas in the 19th century

100 Km. Miles

had made the national ideology of the United States. In the 19th century Americans nostalgically persisted in applying this old-fashioned, fundamentally static ideal to their dynamic, expansive, modern world. Welsh immigrants, attracted as they were by the antique vision of independent citizen in republican community, ultimately found that the American reality of progress through free migration and free enterprise would dissolve their distinctive culture into the modern mass society.

EMIGRATION

The first sizable emigration, 1680–1720, came well before the evangelical, cultural, and industrial revolutions and stemmed from a country with a population of only 400,000. Even earlier, 1667, a congregation of Baptists from South Wales had founded Swansea on the Plymouth–Rhode Island border. In 1681 a group of Welsh Quaker gentlemen obtained a tract of some 40,000 acres in the new colony of Pennsylvania. To what extent the few hundred farmers and servants who went there were seeking not only a Quaker refuge but also a self-governing Welsh barony—as they said, "not to entangle ourselves with Laws in an unknown

Tongue"—is uncertain. By 1685, however, they lost their separate privileges within Pennsylvania and with them any hope of excluding Welsh Anglicans, Baptists, and Presbyterians or English and German settlers. By 1720 the Welsh settled several smaller communities in southeastern Pennsylvania and in Delaware, and by mid-century established still others toward the Susquehanna frontier and in the Carolinas. Except in language, a difference that seems not to have significantly outlasted the first generation, these colonial Welsh Americans played from the start an integral part in the life of their provinces. Only a few groups like the Welsh Society of Philadelphia, founded in 1729 to assist occasional poor newcomers from Wales, continued to commemorate their ethnic origins.

The mass emigration of the 19th century was touched off by poor harvests in Wales in the 1790s. The first small groups were followed after 1817 by a fairly steady stream induced both by postwar depression and by displacement of small farmers or their sons by, on the one hand, the pressure of a two-thirds increase in the rural population between 1800 and 1850 and, on the other, consolidation of large estates, annual leases, and rising rents. Most of the uprooted went to the new industrial districts; of those who left Wales, probably more went to Liverpool, London, and other English towns than to the United States: Ocean passage and purchase of land required either the amount of capital that only a farmer might have or else assistance from relatives already settled in America. Except for a few who, in the early years, sailed from small ports in North Wales on vessels carrying slate, Welsh emigrants traveled as ordinary North Atlantic passengers.

Few came in organized parties. In 1796 the radical republican Baptist minister Morgan John Rhys (1760–1804) brought the first group from South Wales to his short-lived colony of Beulah in western Pennsylvania. As late as 1871 a Welsh emigration company promoted a new Bala in Kansas. For the typical emigrant, however, letters from family or friends in the United States were inducement enough: "The Welsh are foolish to remain under the thumb of their landlords, fighting for old, stony farms, hilly and brambly," when for a year's rent in Wales they could buy a small holding in America and live in "happy independence."

SETTLEMENT AND EMPLOYMENT

The clusters of Welsh-American rural communities were scattered, "like partridges on the mountains," according to the random circumstances of successive western frontiers. Farmers accustomed to hills and valleys evidently considered similar land in America a bargain—in the Appalachian counties of Cambria in Pennsylvania in the 1790s and especially of Oneida and Lewis in New York, where the dozen Welsh settlements were estimated to have 700 people in 1812 and 7,000 by 1838; in southwestern Ohio and in more promising spots such as Radnor, Gomer, and the "Welsh Hills" in central and northwestern Ohio in the 1830s and 1840s; and in the rough southern Ohio uplands of Jackson and Gallia counties, known as the Cardiganshire of America. People from these centers, together with farmers and land-hungry miners straight from Wales, moved west into several places in southern

Wisconsin in the 1840s; to both sides of the Iowa-Minnesota border, northern Missouri, and eastern Kansas in the 1860s and 1870s; and finally to the Pacific Northwest in the 1880s and 1890s. Because both Wales and the eastern U.S. settlements were Mormon missionary fields from 1840 to the 1870s, Utah attracted a good many Welsh converts. As towns and cities grew near these districts—Utica and Rome, N.Y.; Johnstown, Pa.; Cincinnati, Columbus, and Lima, Ohio; Racine, Milwaukee, and Oshkosh, Wis.; St. Louis; Emporia, Kans.; Salt Lake City; Seattle; and many smaller places—they too attracted people from American farms as well as directly from Wales.

Although several small iron furnaces were developed by Welsh farmers in Jackson County, Ohio, industrial towns and mining regions usually drew immigrants directly from Wales. Unlike farmers, most men with experience in old-country mines, quarries, and mills were not fleeing the prospect of outright unemployment. Short-term imbalances in demand for their skills did occur in Wales and the United States, but the generally higher American wages attracted Welsh mine and mill workers even when times were good at home. Conversely, depressions or strikes in America from time to time drove some back again.

Because Welsh industrialization had a head start of some 50 years, plenty of skilled Welsh workingmen were available for each American advance: iron puddlers and rollers after 1815, coal miners after 1830, slate quarrymen after 1840, and tin-platers as late as the 1890s. Some early employers actively recruited in Wales; in the 1830s two preachers, recently arrived among the first Welsh miners at Carbondale, Pa., were sent back to spread the word of jobs. As immigration grew, however, it became self-generating. From the familiar environment of the anthracite coal fields of northeastern Pennsylvania, Welsh colliers sent back word in the 1840s and 1850s of wages of $1.00 to $1.50 a day, or as much as $36 a month, about double the old-country level. Even an established Welsh ironworks superintendent like David Thomas (1794–1882) of Ynyscedwyn could better himself by emigrating. In 1840 Thomas built the first successful American hot-blast furnace, at Catasauqua, Pa., and, as a leading American ironmaster, became known as the father of the industry.

When a Welshman became foreman or superintendent of a mine or mill he could fill the best jobs by writing to a newspaper back home. The density of Welsh settlement in the Hyde Park section of Scranton, Pa., was largely due to the efforts of Benjamin Hughes (1824–1900), who left Nantyglo in 1848 and served as general mine superintendent for the Delaware, Lackawanna, and Western Coal Company from 1865 to 1899. At least two-thirds of the 109 miners killed in the 1869 fire at the Avondale mine near Wilkes-Barre were Welshmen, including foreman Evan Hughes, Benjamin's brother.

Welsh miners also went to the bituminous coal mines that were opened after 1840 in western Pennsylvania and Maryland, the Mahoning and Hocking valleys of Ohio, central Illinois, southern Iowa, northern Missouri, and eastern Kansas, some of them near Welsh farming communities. Iron and steel and then tin plate led to the growth of Welsh centers in Danville, Johns-

town, Pittsburgh, and Sharon, Pa.; Ironton, Portsmouth, Cleveland, Youngstown, and Warren, Ohio; Chicago; Milwaukee; and smaller places. Quarry owners as well as quarrymen in the small slate districts on the Vermont–New York line, in Maine, eastern Pennsylvania, and on the Maryland border were almost all Welsh. Welshmen also arrived in the Wisconsin lead region in the 1840s and scattered through the California and Rocky Mountain mining districts as they were opened in the following decades. Well into the 20th century, individual immigrants continued to filter into most of the 200 Welsh-American communities, both rural and industrial.

By the 1870s, however, prospects were fading. Welsh farmers were advised not to think of emigrating to the United States without £1,500. Previously, American wages had compensated the miners and mill workers for the winter overtime and summer layoffs in the coal industry, the long hours and fast pace of work in the steel mills, and the lack of safety regulations. But as American technology caught up with the British between 1880 and 1900, preferential wages for their obsolescent skills melted away. As an iron puddler from Tredegar reported from Sharon in 1887, a man could no longer "pick [h]is jobs . . . without he have friends." Some of the earlier immigrants were drawn back to Wales by the exceptional prosperity of 1880–1914, but most finished out their working years in the United States, having observed enough on visits to Wales of what now struck them as squalor and wretchedness, especially "the utter submission of the people to those in authority, and the disdain in which they in turn are held."

By comparison with Irish or even English and Scottish emigration, only a small proportion of the population of Wales—in no decade more than the 8 per 10,000 of the 1880s—went to America. And for all its industrial growth, Wales remained a small country: a half-million people in 1800; little more than 1 million in 1850; 2 million in 1900; not yet 3 million in 1970. Between 1820 and 1976 the United States officially counted only 94,854 new arrivals as Welsh, four-fifths of them after 1880. As early as 1880, however, the census found 83,302 natives of Wales in America, many of whom the immigration authorities must have listed casually as English or British. The census count of the Welsh-born reached its peak of 100,079 in 1890, followed by a steady decline to 60,205 in 1930 and only 17,014 in 1970. The census, too, may have missed a good many; in 1872 a Welsh clergyman, after a careful survey of all 200 recognizably Welsh communities in the United States, estimated their total population at 115,000, half again as many as the 1870 census figure of 74,533. He included, however, many American-born but Welsh-speaking people, especially in isolated rural settlements. By 1920 immigrants from Wales were only one-third as numerous as the second-generation Welsh; with the decline of immigration to fewer than 300 a year, by 1970 they were only one-fifth.

WELSH-AMERICAN CHARACTER

To Welshmen the 19th-century United States seemed a particularly auspicious country, where one could "make both ends meet and knot them too." The republican ethic of personal independence, ideally won and held by means of hard work, saving, and frugal living, they interpreted more literally, indeed, than most old-stock Americans. "God himself," a preacher told the Welsh Bible Society of Scranton in 1867, "belonged to this [laboring] class—He was continually working." The Welsh miners' hope was said in 1877 to be "plenty of work and good wages," which they promptly invested in decent houses. If they spent more on beer than other Americans, it was less than was so spent in Wales. The Tredegar puddler who came to Sharon in 1887 found his old acquaintances now "teatotlers and everyone owning [h]is own house." Success for them, according to an American observer, meant to "acquire a sufficient competence" to retire to "a life of ease."

The same peasant caution in the midst of progress characterized Welsh farmers among the hills of Pennsylvania, New York, Ohio, and Wisconsin. The more ambitious who pushed on to the flatter, richer soil of Minnesota and Iowa, "imbued with that sanguine enthusiasm which is the virtuous fault of our typical westerner," one of their descendants recalled in the 1890s, seemed already more American than Welsh. No longer content with 40 or 80 acres, they sometimes put off building a church for several years while they devoted themselves to acquiring property. In Kansas in 1869, on the other hand, newcomers from Wales were criticized for not being "more pushing" and for being content to "hire themselves out to other races."

Even modest success on the western prairies meant a lifetime of difficulties. In Wisconsin in the 1890s the survivors recalled the 30-year (1846–1876) "period of the wheat" (with five unsuccessful varieties) before they advanced successively through "the period of the sheep and the fleece, the period of the pig and the Indrawn [corn], the period of the cow and the milk, the period of the fast horse and the fat steers, and the period of the fine houses and the spacious barns." Welshmen were among the Iowa and Kansas farmers whose speculative optimism of the late 1860s foundered in the next decade because of inadequate capital for machinery, hired labor, taxes, and mortgage interest, as well as failure of the wheat crop, before some of them began to prosper in dairying and livestock raising.

Great wealth was more attainable in industry, even for an occasional laborer in the early years. William Johns (1805–1865) left rural Pembrokeshire at age 27 for Pennsylvania, worked as a mine laborer and then as a miner, bought a colliery at Saint Clair in 1846, and by means, it was said, of "energy, economy, and extraordinary good luck" during the Civil War, was worth $2 million, the richest man in Schuylkill County, Pa., at his death. That sort of success did not usually start with work in the mines. One "thoroughly self-made man," the Scranton mine operator, stove manufacturer, and Republican politician "Squire" Lewis Pughe (1820–1892), had come from North Wales to Carbondale, Pa., as a 22-year-old tailor and promptly won attention by giving a series of inspirational public lectures. A miner's son of the next generation, Thomas Hamer Watkins (1860–c. 1930), went through the Pittston, Pa., public schools, started his own "general market business" at 15 and failed, but prospered after 1880 as a mine operator. He sold out in 1899 to look after his investments and was appointed by President Theodore

Roosevelt as the business representative on the Anthracite Strike Commission of 1902.

The ordinary miner from South Wales was accounted a success if he rose to foreman, fire boss, weighmaster, mine superintendent, or state mine inspector, or simply saved enough in five or six years to buy a house or farm. Many of the relatives whom such men had left behind in Wales were unable to save anything for their old age. Now and then one of the immigrants slipped into helpless indigence, died of drink, or committed suicide over a business failure, but the local newspapers found their fate more remarkable than the general picture of modest success.

The miner's "pride and ambition" for his American-born sons, a Wilkes-Barre newspaper observed in 1872, were "a good common school education" and "a better position than that of a miner." Particularly after 1880, when Slavic laborers began flocking into the mines and steel mills, the second generation—as in Johnstown in 1910—either clung to supervisory positions or went into white-collar jobs, business, and the professions.

SOCIAL INSTITUTIONS

Although the immigrant peasant-workingmen were applauded for "the very elements of character that constitute the basis of good and true republican citizens," they seemed not to appreciate the other "grand American idea of the universal brotherhood of man." Precisely because they had "come from a country so full of people and society," one of their preachers observed in 1846, the indiscriminate individualism of the United States was "too much of a blow to the feelings of the Welsh." In Carbondale in the 1830s it was their "clannishness," as much as the short walk to the mine, that set Welsh Hill, with its own schoolhouse, apart from the Catholic Irish section. In the 1870s the Columbus neighborhoods of Welshburg and Jonesborough attracted people from rural Ohio settlements as well as immigrant mill workers. In spite of the Americanized manners by 1897 of the Welsh of Hyde Park, a local editor thought that they had entered not "a particle in a third of a century" into the general life of Scranton—no more than Wales itself had become part of England.

The immigrant family was one cornerstone of this ethnic identity. Many parents crossed the Atlantic with their children; when the father came alone, as many miners did, it was to save enough to bring over the rest of the family, with sometimes as many as eight children together. Some men went home to Wales for a bride. As a miner wrote in 1871, "the clean, rosy-cheeked, hard-working Welsh girls" were far preferable to novel-reading young Yankee ladies who boasted of knowing no more about cooking or baking "than a mole knows about knitting socks." Of the 75 Welshmen who were married in the Scranton area during 1886, 48 took women also born in Wales, and another 12 of the wives had Welsh parents.

Although young Welsh people were as free from parental pressure as young Americans in choosing a husband or wife, courtship was as circuitous a process as in Wales. On the way home from evening church service, it was observed in Scranton in 1877, "at first the young men walk behind, but after a while one step is quickened or the other slackened, or both, and they come together, and form lively parties until ten or

after." Welsh girls still single at 22 were "joked about being old maids." The typical immigrant farm family had six to ten children. Miners were the only modern industrial workers among whom the old rural birthrate remained high and even increased. In two small anthracite towns in 1900 the average number of children born to women of Welsh origin who had been married over 30 years was eight, though almost half the children had not survived.

The miner's wife kept the family purse and insisted that his wages be turned over to her each week; also once a week, she for her part dutifully blacked his shoes —something, so immigrants complained, women born in America refused to do. After his daily bath when he returned home from work, only the blue coal-dust scars on the miner's hands and face distinguished him from a store clerk. Families in rural Wisconsin preserved the old-country routine of breakfast, mid-morning lunch, dinner, mid-afternoon lunch, supper, and late evening meal. "The teapot was always at hand, and the loaf of bread and butter."

The preeminent 19th-century Welsh institution was the nonconformist chapel, or church, as immigrants learned to call it. Although new settlements might start with a "union church," the Baptists and Calvinistic Methodists separated from the Congregational remnant as soon as possible; furthermore, each neighborhood desired its own set of churches. The first arrivals in some new settlements organized a Welsh Sunday school—an adult Bible class—on their first Sunday. At Scranton one mine foreman was long remembered for sternly refusing the company's order to work on Saturday afternoons, his time to prepare for Sunday school. As early as 1839 there were some 46 Welsh churches in the United States, almost equally divided among the three denominations; by 1872, nearly 400, the Calvinistic Methodists and Congregationalists each having more than 150; altogether in the 1890s there were nearly 500 active churches. They all experienced the revivals that periodically swept Wales, the last in 1905.

The early churches were served by self-taught, unpaid preachers from among the local farmers or workingmen or else by itinerants who might visit three churches on a Sunday. The Calvinistic Methodists began to install regular preachers only in 1870, and in some of their churches not until 1920, although in 1878 they established a fund for students preparing for the ministry at Beloit, Ripon, and other American colleges. Welsh congregations were seldom satisfied with a single preacher. It took the annual district *gymanfa bregethu* (preaching assembly), a series of sermons that might go on for several days, to satisfy their taste for the eloquent, melodious style of preaching called *hwyl* (full sail). In Wisconsin the general "neglect of corn and hoe" during the June *cymanfaoedd* was criticized by more worldly individuals. The latter might grow richer, but the ministers were the recognized community leaders. In a Welsh description of Scranton in 1872, the name of general mine superintendent Benjamin Hughes was buried in a long list of bosses; far more space was devoted to the Reverend William Roberts (1810–1887), years afterward remembered as "the strongest pillar of the men" during the five-month strike of 1871. Accordingly, Roberts was excoriated by the company, who resolved (at least briefly) never again to take as foremen "any of his dear

fold, Deacons in his church and leaders in the riots." Hughes in his double role as boss and Welshman was distrusted by both sides at the time.

Hughes was better known as "the father of Ivorism" in the United States. Lodges of the Urdd y Gwir Iforiaid (Order of True Ivorites), the one indigenous Welsh friendly society, had spread across industrial South Wales after 1836 and first appeared in the United States at Pottsville in 1841. The American order was consolidated in 1870 with Benjamin Hughes of Teml Ifor Hael lodge, Hyde Park, as president. In the 1880s and 1890s there were more than 50 lodges, all in cities or mining towns, though never more than 2,500 members. Women's lodges were begun in 1897.

LABOR UNIONS AND POLITICS

Trade unionism in Wales began, unsuccessfully, in 1831, just when miners were starting also to emigrate. In the Pennsylvania anthracite region Welshmen were on the first strike committees, in 1849. The first sustained miners' unions began in both Wales and Pennsylvania between 1868 and 1875, and the Welsh strike of 1875 ended with establishment of a sliding scale for coal prices and wages like that demanded by the Pennsylvania miners. Welsh miners in Pennsylvania, who were said to have more money saved or invested than the Germans or Irish, were usually reluctant to risk a strike, but once committed they were the most stubborn in keeping one going. Personal independence evidently meant something more than the bank deposits, houses, and U.S. bonds for which Americans complimented them. "The most of us have left the old country to get our rights," a miner called Evans told a meeting at Pittston in 1869. When the men there hesitated to strike, their wives, led by Granny Morris and wielding broomsticks, mop handles, and stones, kept them from going to work. The strike of 1875 was attributed not only to a wage reduction but also to the companies' lack of respect for the miners' manhood in refusing to consult with them as equals.

Partly because of the longer English and Scottish experience with trade unionism and partly because of the often remarked jealousy between the clannish Welsh and the Irish, and later the Slavs, most of whom began coal mining as laborers, few men from the mines of Wales were leaders in the succession of short-lived national unions between the 1860s and 1890 or in the United Mine Workers (UMW) thereafter. The only national unions with a conspicuously Welsh leadership were the Rail Heaters, the Sons of Vulcan, and others in iron and steel in the 1870s. Although perhaps something of Welsh class-bound republicanism can be detected in the 20th-century careers of Thomas L. Lewis (1866–1939) and John L. Lewis (1880–1969) of the UMW or Iorwerth W. Abel (1908–) of the United Steel Workers, none of them ever made much of his Welsh parentage. In trades where many supervisors and even owners were Welsh, unions always had to suppress ethnic distinctions.

"Taffy, though unwilling to take much prominence in political matters, is on hand when the liberty of the citizen is at stake," a newspaper editor observed in 1856, the first election year in which Welsh immigrants were organized—almost solidly for the new free-soil, free-labor, Republican party. Democrats sometimes wondered why these emigrants from English oppression did not, like Irish Catholics, join their cause, but to the Welsh it was self-evident that "all the struggles they have ever had in their native land were but struggles to fit them to be Republicans in America." They saw perfect consistency between their evangelical theology and the old republican ideal, refurbished by the Republican party, of the independent citizen in a virtuous, homogeneous, self-regulated community. In Welsh, the Republicans were *Plaid y Gwerinwyr* or *Plaid Werinol* (party of the folk). The Welsh, who believed themselves to be "greater in our morality than anyone" and yet also worse in "tremendous thirst for intoxicating liquor," between 1856 and 1896 could readily accept the implicit unity of a cause that included "the defense of the laboring men of the country," "the honesty of the government in paying its debts in gold," and "destruction of the liquor traffic." Any doubter was suspect as an "infidel."

For a few years in the strike-torn 1870s some Welshmen deserted the Republicans as a "knownothing corporation party" and voted for local Workingmen's or Greenback-Labor tickets. The calling in of troops at Scranton during the strikes of 1871 and 1877 seemed especially unrepublican to them. Not until good times returned in the 1880s—and a suitable number of Welsh names appeared on local Republican tickets—did the Welsh forget that party leaders had called them "barbarians," "cheese-eaters," and "the nation of strikers." Thereafter, wherever the Republican party found a Welsh vote to cultivate, politicians of Welsh origin, though mostly American-born or reared, played a role. The most prominent of them, "Puddler Jim" Davis (1873–1947), who was Secretary of Labor in the 1920s and senator from Pennsylvania in the 1930s (as well as eisteddfodic Archdruid in 1940), owed his success to sustaining the party's original connection with the workingman.

CULTURE

"A nation is made up of many parts," a Welsh-American editor observed in 1898, "and each part has to be nurtured and cared for." Neither moneymaking nor politics, not even religion, was all-sufficient. Of the other facets of Welsh culture, only a few embarrassed the immigrants in the eyes of respectable Americans. Drink was one, and "bruisers" like Big John Thomas and Red Sam Morgan of Hyde Park in 1872, or the Dic Pedlar (Richard Evans) and Dai Bright (David Jones) who fought 87 rounds in the snow near Wilkes-Barre on Christmas morning in 1883, were another.

The more admirable aspects of Welsh culture were embodied in the Welsh language, and thus were less obvious to Americans. Welsh was the native tongue of most of the 19th-century immigrants—the only language of many upon arrival—and of their American-born children until they entered the public schools. In farming districts like the Welsh Hills of Ohio it was still commonly spoken in 1890, 75 years after the first settlement. In Oneida County, N.Y., in 1894 a traveler from Wales found the speech neither that of North or South Wales, but more like the literary language. As they had done with English words for centuries in

Wales, Welsh-speakers freely interpolated such common American expressions as "all right," "you know," "mortgage," and "20 percent" into their native speech.

A Welsh-language press flourished in the United States for more than a century. Each of the three sects published a monthly magazine, of which the Calvinistic Methodists' *Cyfaill o'r Hen Wlad* (Friend from the Old Country) was first and longest lived (1838–1933). Most of the 100-odd Welsh books and pamphlets printed by 1870 were hymnals, theological tracts, and memorial collections of sermons. A dozen newspapers came and went. The *Drych* (Mirror) of Utica (f. 1851) claimed a national circulation of 12,000 at its height and absorbed several competitors: *Baner America* of Scranton (1866–1877), the *Wasg* (Press) of Pittsburgh (1871–1890), and *Columbia* of Emporia, Kans., and later Chicago (1883–1894). There were also a dozen Welsh literary magazines between 1852 and 1895, but even the most successful, *Traethodydd yn America*, published in New York from 1857 to 1861 by William Roberts (subsequently the Scranton miners' champion), for the most part reprinted articles from the quarterly *Traethodydd* (Essayist) of Wales.

Ordinary workingmen were devoted to cultural improvement. Lunch hours in Illinois mines were often "gob-side parliaments," one of them later recalled, and during "the long summers with half work . . . the other half could be devoted to study." At Scranton, where some miners owned as many as 300 books, the Welsh Philosophical Society debated such topics as "The Formation of Coal," "Does Man Control Circumstances?" and "Does Intellectual Culture Promote Skepticism?" The society included members who later became mine superintendents, state mine inspectors, legislators, and judges.

The accomplishment that they, like Welshmen everywhere, most admired, however, was the ability to compose poetry either in *cynghanedd*, the ancient strict meters employing alliteration and internal rhyme, or in the modern but still only relatively free forms. Although often the result was little more than a string of nonconformist abstractions set forth in technically facile stanzas, any lack of literary quality was made up for, in America as in Wales, by the popularity and sheer quantity of versifying. Poets were known by bardic titles, such as Dewi Cwmtwrch or Bardd Coch for plain David Powell and Isaac Benjamin. Because of the narrow range of Welsh surnames (almost all patronymics), nearly every Welshman had an identifying nickname—William Davis Pontypool, Tom Metal, John Bach Alto, Thomas the Dodge—but a bardic cognomen was the most honorific. By 1870 there had been 125 identifiable bards in America and more than one lady *barddones*. Down to 1910 more than 50 bards flourished in Scranton alone, making the Hyde Park section "the great Merthyr" and "the Welsh Athens" of America.

The eisteddfod was introduced to America in the 1850s. As in Wales the original emphasis was literary: poems and essays on prescribed topics were submitted, by men and women alike, for adjudication and award of modest prizes. As the eisteddfod became a great annual secular festival, both local and national, the difficult poetry steadily gave way to competitive recitations, declamations, orations, prose translations, English elegies,

and, above all, performance of standard vocal music by soloists, trios, glee parties, and the largest choirs that different localities could muster. Handel, Haydn, and Mendelssohn were favorites for the grand choral competition; the glees ran to temperance ditties with titles like "Avoid the Cup."

The fact that working people could carry on the centuries-old Welsh tradition of part-singing fascinated 19th-century observers. There were few composers, however, among 50 Welsh-American musicians identified in 1870. Of the two of any distinction, one made his reputation before emigrating. William Aubrey Williams (Gwilym Gwent, 1838–1891), a Tredegar blacksmith and composer of popular glees, cantatas, and anthems, spent his last 20 years working at a Pennsylvania mine and conducting choirs and brass bands. A few years earlier, Joseph Parry (1841–1903), a young winner of eisteddfod prizes for canons and glees and one-time iron roller of Danville, Pa., won a scholarship to the Royal Academy of Music in London, from which he went on to professorships of music in Wales. Returning 11 times to give concerts and adjudicate at eisteddfodau in the United States, where he was regarded as "our Handel, Mozart, and Beethoven," Parry enjoyed the title of chief musician, Pencerdd America. Non-Welshmen who appreciated Parry's hymn tune "Aberystwyth" might nevertheless, at a local eisteddfod, find the phenomenon of a dozen trios or baritone soloists working over one set piece exceedingly tedious. They could only admire the animation and applause of the Welsh audience and the roars of laughter at the impromptu salutations from the bards.

The apogee of the eisteddfod in America came between 1875 and 1915. At the annual meetings of the Scranton Welsh around 1900 the audience ran to 5,000 and the mixed choral prize to $1,000. Perhaps $35 was enough for the Welsh novel and $5 for the four-line *englyn:* the nine novels submitted in 1902 were criticized for unfictional sermonizing, and all 60 englynion of 1897 for "monstrous mediocrity." The Philadelphia Bicentennial Eisteddfod in 1882 drew five 300-voice choirs from the coal regions to compete for prizes up to $1,200, and at the Chicago World's Fair in 1893 one of the two choirs from Scranton bested the Mormon Tabernacle Choir for the main prize of $5,000; a "select chorus" of 1,500 voices, accompanied by 15 harpists, also performed the cantata "Prince Llewelyn." To the Pittsburgh International Eisteddfod of 1913 came six 150-voice mixed choirs, 15 men's, 13 women's, and 27 children's choruses. By that time the local eisteddfodau were admitting almost anything that could be considered music—"Nearer, My God, to Thee" on the mouth organ or, as a solo for boys under 10, a song called "Have Courage, My Boy, to Say No"—and were giving prizes for the best love letters. A National Eisteddfod Association held large annual gatherings between 1923 and 1940, but many localities switched to less complicated Welsh Day outings where everyone could sing but the only prizes were for the oldest, tallest, and shortest Welshmen present and the like.

In Wales the eisteddfod has continued to develop as one popular Welsh-language medium, but in the United States it has survived the decline of immigration and the Welsh language only at Utica, Philadelphia, and the anthracite mining town of Edwardsville, Pa. Few poets

have ever succeeded in writing adequate *cynghanedd* in English, and the sort of eisteddfod in which, by 1910, German Liederkränze and Sängerbunde, Irish Catholic choirs, and little Polish girls could compete had ceased to be a satisfactorily Welsh festival. Since then a simpler, strictly Welsh, and exclusively Protestant musical meeting, the *gymanfa ganu* (singing assembly), which was developed in Wales after 1860 for improvement of hymn singing among the chapels of a district, has taken its place. Evangelical hymns already were virtually folk songs in the period of emigration, and with the aid of an English phonetic transcription any Welsh descendant can at least mouth "Crug-y-bar" or "Hyfrydol." Since 1929 the National Gymanfa Ganu Association has held the largest of these festivals each year.

As the second generation, especially in towns and cities, grew up speaking English, the Welsh churches lost their identity. In the 1880s and 1890s a struggle raged between those who insisted on services in Welsh —English was said to be too much "used in business and earthly bargains of all kinds, high and low"—and those who feared that their American children would reject religion preached in a "foreign" language. By 1910 most churches shifted to English, with an occasional token sermon in Welsh. In 1919 the Calvinistic Methodist general assembly merged with the Presbyterians, although the last of their regional bodies retained its identity until 1954. The looser structure of the Congregationalists and Baptists permitted some of their state associations to survive for a few years more. Of more than 600 Welsh immigrant churches, only about one-fourth still function under any name.

Adopting English gave other Welsh institutions only a temporary reprieve. The monthly *Cambrian* (1880–1919), devoted to recording the history and culture that would otherwise be lost with the language, and a weekly newspaper, the *Druid* (1907–1939), expired even before the Welsh *Drych* turned mainly to English in the 1940s. The Order of True Ivorites, though conducted in English since 1935, was reduced by 1967 to one men's and four women's lodges and disbanded in 1974.

In only a few places, either densely settled in the 19th century, notably Scranton, or quite isolated, like Oak Hill in southern Ohio, has any great sense persisted of belonging primarily to a Welsh ethnic group. For most localities a St. David's Day dinner or church service and the annual picnic or gymanfa ganu of the Cambrian or Cymrodorion society suffice. The only institutional links among the old communities are the annual National Gymanfa Ganu and the conventions of the Women's Welsh clubs; since 1911 the latter have grown to 30, mostly in Ohio and Pennsylvania. A 1975 innovation, the monthly *Ninnau* (We Ourselves), while livelier than the *Drych,* like it publicizes the brief monthly calendar of activities around the country, celebrates the past, and points out curious but mainly uncontroversial features of modern Wales.

Welsh Americans no longer share a common culture with Wales or have a significant one of their own. The revival of folk songs and dances in postevangelical Wales has gone almost unnoticed among nostalgic American hymn-singers. At the National Eisteddfod of Wales the returning *Cymry am Wasgar* (Welsh in Dispersion) sound tritely old-fashioned and look conspicu-ously foreign. The American cult of Dylan Thomas in the 1950s surprised Welsh Americans, and they have hardly noticed the 20th-century renaissance of either Welsh or Anglo-Welsh poetry. The upsurge of political nationalism in Wales since World War II has struck as little ethnic response abroad as did the socialist movement before it. Nor does what passes for Welsh culture in America offer much to anyone not already attached to his ethnic roots. Unlike the Scots, the Welsh have no authentic national costume nor any esoteric musical instrument to please the crowd. The distinctive character of the 19th-century Welsh immigrants, as a non-Welsh observer summed it up in 1897—"intensely industrious, provident, studious, religious, ambitious, musical, persistent, independent, gregarious, affectionate, grateful, and spontaneous"—has long since dissolved into the "Anglo-Saxon" generality of middle-class America.

Bibliography
The best survey of the economic and social developments that affected emigration is David Williams, *A History of Modern Wales* (London, 1950). See also R. Brinley Jones, ed., *Anatomy of Wales* (Peterston super Ely, 1972), and Brinley Thomas, "Wales and the Atlantic Economy," *Scottish Journal of Political Economy* 6 (1959): 169–192.

The only recent survey of the whole history of the Welsh in America is Edward George Hartmann, *Americans from Wales* (Boston, 1967). For 1650–1850, Arthur H. Dodd, *The Character of Early Welsh Emigration to the United States* (Cardiff, Wales, 1957), is brief but incisive. The 19th- and 20th-century Welsh are included in Rowland Berthoff, *British Immigrants in Industrial America, 1790–1950* (1953; reprint, New York, 1968). *The Dictionary of Welsh Biography down to 1940* (London, 1959) includes prominent Welsh-Americans. A good selection of immigrants' letters home, originally printed in newspapers in Wales, is translated, with introductory essays, in Alan Conway, ed., *The Welsh in America* (Minneapolis, 1961). Among the many Welsh Americans who have essayed books and articles on their history, the most reliable is Daniel Jenkins Williams, especially *One Hundred Years of Welsh Calvinistic Methodism in America* (Philadelphia, 1937).

By far the largest collection of manuscripts, newspapers, religious periodicals, and secondary works on the Welsh in America is held by the National Library of Wales, Aberystwyth. Other significant holdings are in the libraries of Harvard University and Brigham Young University.

ROWLAND BERTHOFF

WENDS

The Wends, a little-known immigrant group, settled in Texas among the Germans in the mid-19th century. An ancient Slavic people also known as Lusatian Sorbs, they had resisted assimilation in Europe for over 1,000 years, preserving their own language and customs though not their political independence.

BACKGROUND

The ancestors of the Wends were West Slavs called the Milceni and Luzici who occupied an area east of the Oder River in the early Middle Ages. The Wendish homeland is part of the territory known as Lusatia in East Germany. Approximately 50 miles southeast of Berlin, it is about 1,800 square miles in area and is bordered by Czechoslovakia on the south and Poland on the east. The Spree River flows through its two major towns, Bautzen and Cottbus. The Wends have managed to maintain their identity although they have been ruled at various times by Germans, Hungarians, Poles, and Bohemians. In both world wars they unsuccessfully sought recognition by the major powers as a nation-state.

The first of their foreign conquerors was Charles, one

Lusatia

— Boundary of Saxony and
Prussia before 1918
▒ Areas inhabited by Wends
(Sorbs)

50   Km.   Miles

of Charlemagne's sons, who defeated the Wends and burned Bautzen in 806; by the year 1100 the Wends had been subjugated. German nobles dominated the Wendish peasants and relegated the urban Wends to homes outside the walls or to restricted sections of the city. They could become active in society only through German institutions and the German language. The guilds were German, and the mercantile activity was conducted in the German manner. Under pressure, especially in the part of Lusatia under Prussian control, many Wends adopted German names and relinquished their Slavic traditions.

The Christianization of the Wends began prior to the German conquest, but it was vigorously promoted by the Germans. They also followed the Germans in the Reformation; most Wends converted to Lutheranism in 1530 after the Council of Augsburg. Martin Luther's emphasis on the vernacular encouraged the Wends to devise a written language, and in 1574 Luther's *Small Catechism* became the first work to be published in it.

There are two versions of Sorbian, also called Sorbic, Wendish, or Lusatian, corresponding to the divisions of the Lusatian region. Both versions belong to the Western Slavic group. The southern area called Upper Lusatia speaks a dialect nearer to Czech (Luther's *Catechism* was translated into Upper Sorbian); the northern area, or Lower Lusatia, a dialect nearer to Polish.

Traditionally the Wends call themselves *Srbi* in their own language, but the Germans call them *Wenden*, a term widely used both by others and by many of the Slavic Lusatians themselves, including those who migrated to foreign lands in the 19th century. In the Middle Ages, Wend was the German name for all West Slavs, however, and as a result it came to symbolize the Germanization of the Wends that began in the 9th century with the Carolingians and continued through the Weimar Republic and the Nazi period.

Although Lusatia was also ruled at times by non-German princes, it has remained under German control since the Peace of Prague in 1635. Prior to German unification in 1871 it comprised parts of the kingdoms of Prussia and Saxony—Lower Lusatia being under Prussian administration and Upper Lusatia under that of Saxony. Since World War II it has been part of the German Democratic Republic (East Germany) and divided administratively between the districts of Dresden and Cottbus. Wendish ethnic awareness has been encouraged under the German Democratic Republic, and the term Sorb has been adopted for the Slavs of Lusatia. The name is meant to reflect their Slavic heritage and at the same time to distinguish them from the Serbs of southern Europe. At present approximately 60,000 people in Lusatia call themselves Sorbs. They are served by a Sorbian cultural center (the Domowina) and a Sorbian-language newspaper, radio station, theater, folk ensemble, and publishing house. The Sorbian language is also taught in the schools.

MIGRATION AND SETTLEMENT

The Wendish migration to the United States was closely associated with that of the Germans. In 1849 some Wends settled in Austin County, Tex.; in 1853 a party of 35 Wends sailed for Texas, and the next year Pastor Jan Kilian (1811–1884) and 500 Wends landed at Galveston. Although some of the Wends had been driven there by economic hardship, especially crop failures in the 1840s and a land shortage resulting from population growth in Lusatia, the Kilian group were religious dissenters: some of them had lived under Prussian administration and left in reaction to government attempts to force the Lutherans and Calvinists to worship in a single state church; others had lived under Saxon administration and were unhappy over the doctrinal laxity in the Lutheran Church of Saxony and the impact of rationalism on the clergy. A citizen of Saxony during his early life, Kilian denounced both administrations and in 1845 contemplated emigrating to Australia. In 1848 he resigned his position in the Saxon state church and became the pastor of several small clusters of independent Lutherans who refused to worship in the Prussian church.

Although Kilian exercised religious leadership, the migration to Texas was directed by laymen living along the Prussian-Saxon border who had formed an organization to manage the emigrants and then asked Kilian to be their pastor and to serve the Wendish congregation they hoped to establish in Texas. Wends from both Saxony and Prussia joined the group, along with members of Kilian's own congregations. A few more Wends migrated before the Civil War broke out in the United States; altogether approximately 600 had arrived by 1860. Between 1865 and the end of the century another 600 came, followed by a few in the early 20th century.

But of all the groups to migrate, Kilian's remained the largest and most significant.

The Kilian party first traveled to Hamburg, from where they sailed to Hull, England. They then took the railroad to Liverpool where they waited for a ship that was scheduled to return to Texas for another cargo of cotton. Before this ship, the *Ben Nevis*, could be boarded, however, several Wends were exposed to cholera, and 73 eventually succumbed to it or to other sicknesses.

The survivors arrived at Galveston in December 1854. Most of them traveled by wagon to join the earlier Wendish immigrants at New Ulm. During the winter months their leaders purchased the Delaplain League (4,354 acres) in present-day Lee County, and there built a church and a town called Serbin. A few built homes in the village, but most of the Wends were farmers, and, like other Texans, settled on isolated farms.

The first few years in Texas were difficult for the Wends. Delays in purchasing the Delaplain League prevented early planting the first year, and two years of drought followed. Inadequate shelter and diet resulted in more sickness and death. The familiar crops of Lusatia, such as rye, wheat, and flax, did not grow well in Texas, and the Wends had to adopt the local cotton and corn economy. The Civil War brought some prosperity, when the prices for cotton rose in both the Houston and Mexican market, and many Wends turned to carting cotton across the Rio Grande. But the Wends were also confronted with the conscription laws. Not owning slaves and not interested in fighting for the Confederacy, as many as possible evaded military service, but nonetheless several of their young men lost their lives in the war.

Even in those more profitable years the Wends did not achieve the prosperity of their Texas neighbors. The agricultural censuses of 1870 and 1880 show that their farms were smaller and the productivity lower than those of the more established population. Handicapped by the low fertility of the Delaplain League, the Wends became prosperous farmers only through frugality, self-denial, and hard work.

The local German community played a significant role in Serbin's development. Many of the Wends who migrated to Texas were equally fluent in German and Sorbian, and Kilian, trained in German schools and at the University of Leipzig, preached in both languages. The church records of births, marriages, and deaths he kept in German, but the congregational minutes and obituaries he recorded in Sorbian. Some Germans had accompanied Kilian's migration, and several families had German spouses. Initially the church services were conducted in Sorbian, as was the language of the Lutheran school, taught by Kilian. However, German Lutherans also settled in the Serbin area and joined the Wendish congregation; by 1862 Kilian was preaching in German every sixth Sunday. Eventually tensions in the congregation arose over a variety of problems, and most often they were expressed in controversy about which language to use. Because of the conflict over the use of Sorbian, some Germans and "progressive" Wends left Kilian's congregation in 1870 and formed their own fellowship. Though weakened by the schism, Kilian's congregation continued construction of a larger sanctuary begun in 1866. The most significant monument to the

Texas Wends, the building was dedicated in 1871 and is still in use.

The two congregations existed side by side. In the period after the congregational division, more and more of the Wends began speaking German, and Kilian increased the use of German in his church services. Shortly before his death in 1884, Kilian began to receive assistance from his son Herman, who had graduated from the Lutheran Seminary in St. Louis. Through the diplomatic activities of the younger Kilian, the two groups renewed their friendship and, because German now predominated in the entire community, the two churches merged in 1914. Sorbian was taught in the school until 1916 and used in the pulpit from time to time until 1920, when Herman Kilian died and a replacement willing to preach in Sorbian could not be found. The new pastor, Herman Schmidt, although a Wend, used Sorbian only in private devotions and in pastoral visits. Ironically, the German culture and language that the Wends had resisted for so long in Europe finally became theirs in the United States. Just as they had made the transition, however, World War I broke out, and widespread anti-German sentiment induced the Wends to shift to English. At the end of the 1970s some older people continued to speak Sorbian, but German remained the more common second language.

The group that accompanied Kilian was interested in forming a single congregation, but the Wends who had settled earlier in Austin County did not join the settlement, and those whose occupations were suited to urban life remained in Houston. Establishing a tight, cohesive colony was complicated further by the low productivity of the land of the Delaplain League. As a result some of the Wends moved on, establishing settlements in Swiss Alp, Fedor, Warda, Manheim, and other places. Most of the Wendish immigrants who arrived after 1865 stopped at Serbin first and then continued on to one of these other Texas settlements. In more recent years the Wends have followed the general pattern of rural to urban migration by moving to Austin, Houston, Port Arthur, Corpus Christi, and San Antonio. In spite of this dispersion, however, unity among the Wends and recognition of their common heritage remain. This fellowship is maintained to an extent through membership in the Lutheran Church Missouri Synod and also, at least during the early decades of the 20th century, through the pages of the *Giddings Deutsches Volksblatt* (Giddings, Tex., 1899–1949). The Wendish Culture Club was founded in Serbin in 1971. In 1976 it was renamed the Texas Wendish Heritage Society and is now engaged in perpetuating Wendish tradition.

The folkways of the Wends are tied closely to the church calendar, especially the major festivals of Easter and Christmas, and to the personal milestones of birth, death, and marriage that are also sanctified in the church. Easter is celebrated with both religious services in church and the coloring of eggs. A particular custom observed in both Texas and Europe, and also found among other Slavic groups, is the use of "Easter water." The water dipped from a brook early on Easter morning supposedly stimulates health and beauty; in Texas it was sprinkled on sleepers' faces to awaken them. Of the personal observances, the most elaborate is the wedding, which involves both a church service and an elaborate celebration. In Europe a professional wedding

manager called a *braska* supervised practically all aspects of the celebration, but in Texas his role was limited to calling at the bride's home, leading the wedding party in songs and prayers, and directing the procession to church and back to the home. Some social gatherings in the earlier years also reflected the Wendish heritage. Feather-stripping parties, accompanied by dancing and singing, required each person to remove the soft part of the goose feathers until a cup was filled with feathers; then followed the merrymaking. In more recent years the Wendish customs have been neglected, and the celebrations of personal observances no longer reflect the Wendish heritage, but simply follow the practices of the larger Texas community.

In addition to the Texas settlement and the Wends who migrated elsewhere in the world—to Australia, Canada, South Africa—a small number went to Nebraska. Although there was some communication between a few Texas and Australian families, there was apparently none between the Texans and the small group in Sterling, Nebr., which was closely tied to the German community; at least no record of any correspondence between the Nebraska and Texas Wends remains. The Wendish poet Mato Kossyk (1853–1940), who migrated to the United States and became a Lutheran pastor, visited the Sterling group in the 1880s and communicated with them in Sorbian. But by now awareness of the Wendish heritage of some Sterling families is only a dim memory in the minds of a few of the old people.

Bibliography
The best study in English of the European Wends is Gerald Stone, *The Smallest Slavonic Nation: The Sorbs of Lusatia* (London, 1972). George C. Engerrand, *The So-Called Wends of Germany and Their Colonies in Texas and in Australia* (1934; reprint, San Francisco, 1972), also examines the European background as well as the Texas settlement. Anne Blasig, *The Wends of Texas* (San Antonio, Tex., 1954), is valuable because of its emphasis on the Serbin settlement, and Lillie Moerbe Caldwell, *Texas Wends: Their First Half Century* (Salado, Tex., 1961), adds material on the social life of the group. The most recent study is George R. Nielsen, *In Search of a Home: The Wends (Sorbs) on the Australian and Texas Frontiers* (Birmingham, England, 1977). Source materials on the Texas Wends are to be found in the Concordia Historical Institute, St. Louis, Mo., and the Texas District Archives of the Lutheran Church, Missouri Synod in Austin.

GEORGE R. NIELSEN

WEST INDIANS

Over a half-million black immigrants have moved from the British West Indies to the United States since 1820. The West Indians, descendants of African slaves imported to work on the island sugar plantations, were attracted to the United States by its growing industrial economy and its opportunities for social mobility. Their patterns of assimilation, their economic advancement, their impact on other blacks, and their leadership in political movements have revealed both the potential for individual achievement and the limits on opportunity afforded to blacks in the United States. West Indians, therefore, have attracted the attention of scholars seeking to understand the effect of racial background on social and economic progress.

British West Indians constitute the largest group of blacks who migrated voluntarily to the United States. In 1970, 78,000 West Indian–born blacks were living in the United States, and there were 52,000 second-generation residents. A 1972 estimate placed their total population at 315,000, with 222,000 residing in New York and New Jersey alone. West Indian blacks began to immigrate in the early 19th century but did not come in sizable numbers until the first quarter of the 20th century. Sixty percent of the British West Indian population in the United States are of the third or later generation and are the descendants of the first large wave of West Indian migrants.

Although they have numbered less than 1 percent of the entire black population in the United States, British West Indians have played an important role in the political and intellectual leadership of the American black community and have been disproportionately concentrated in professional, white-collar, and skilled occupations. They have achieved notable levels of home ownership and education; they have been active entrepreneurs.

THE BRITISH WEST INDIAN HOMELAND

The British West Indies are a scattered group of former British dependencies and current members of the British Commonwealth of Nations located, for the most part, in the Caribbean area. They consist of Jamaica, the Bahamas, Bermuda, the Leeward Islands (St. Kitts, Nevis, Antigua, Montserrat, and the British Virgin Islands), the Windward Islands (St. Vincent, St. Lucia, Dominica, Grenada), Barbados, Trinidad and Tobago, as well as Belize (formerly British Honduras) in Central America, and Guyana (formerly British Guiana) in South America. Trinidad and Tobago and Jamaica became independent republics in 1962, Barbados and Guyana in 1966, and the Bahamas in 1973. Several of the other islands joined together in 1967 to form the West Indies Associated States which are voluntarily associated with Great Britain. Jamaica, which had a population of 2 million in the early 1970s, is by far the most populous island, containing about half of the total British West Indian population.

Inhabited originally by Carib Indians, the West Indies received successive waves of immigrants consisting of English colonists, African slaves, Chinese and Jewish traders, Hindu laborers, and Germans, Portuguese, and Syrians. Blacks and mulattos make up 80 percent of the entire population of the British West Indies. Jamaica, St. Kitts, Antigua, and Barbados are predominantly Protestant owing to continuous British rule; Trinidad and Tobago and St. Lucia are heavily Catholic because of previous Spanish influence.

First discovered by Columbus in the 15th century, the West Indies were occupied and settled by the English in the 17th century. After unsuccessful attempts in the early 1600s to raise cotton and tobacco, the English colonists turned to sugar as a marketable crop. Because of growing European demand, sugar production rapidly returned huge profits. Great numbers of African slaves were imported to work the flourishing plantations that spread throughout the British West Indies and the black population quickly became several times larger than the white elite. Although Parliament terminated the slave trade in 1807 and abolished slavery in 1838, sugar production continued to be the major industry of the British West Indies. The newly freed black population continued to grow and by the mid-19th century outnumbered whites on some islands by 20 to 1.

British West Indies

EARLY IMMIGRATION

After 1850 a class of black freeholders began to emerge but most former slaves became tenants on the planters' estates. They and their offspring continued to serve as the principal labor force for the sugar industry, as the planters adjusted gradually to a free-labor system.

EARLY IMMIGRATION

After emancipation the annual immigration of black West Indians to the United States was fairly small. Arrivals increased slowly, rising and falling in accordance with shifting economic conditions both in the West Indies and on the mainland; the total grew from a few hundred in the mid-19th century to about 1,000 by the late 19th century. Many of the early immigrants were members of the growing mulatto middle class who sought advancement in the United States.

By the beginning of the 20th century the growth of population from natural increase and the immigration of laborers from India to help work newly opened lands led to overcrowding and heightened competition for resources on some of the islands. Especially after World War I, a trend developed toward greater consolidation of

the sugar estates and private lands in the hands of local planters, absentee landlords, and foreign corporations. In 1935, for example, half the privately owned land of St. Vincent's Island was held by only 30 plantations; in Jamaica more than half the total land was held under 1,400 titles, each averaging about 1,000 acres. The imbalance in land distribution persisted, contributing heavily to widespread rural poverty in the more densely populated islands. Diminishing opportunities in agriculture, competition from newly imported labor, increasing population, and chronic seasonal unemployment caused many black West Indians to consider emigration as a means of improving their lives.

American development of the fruit industry in the British West Indies forged new economic, transportation, and communication links between the West Indies and the United States. A series of devastating hurricanes between 1910 and 1921 severely damaged the agricultural economy of the islands, increasing the impetus to emigrate. Furthermore, entry to the United States was easy after quota limitations were imposed in 1921 and 1924. British West Indians continued to enter

as colonials under the ample British annual quota of 65,000.

From 1900 to 1930 between 80,000 and 90,000 blacks from the British West Indies entered the United States. Because steamship routes connected the islands with eastern U.S. ports, most of the immigrants entered and settled in New York, Massachusetts, Florida, and other eastern coastal states. In 1930, 90 percent of the foreign-born black population resided in New England and the Middle and South Atlantic states. New York City alone contained 65 percent of all immigrant blacks in the country. During World War I and shortly thereafter, black laborers from the British West Indies were imported to work on farms and construction projects in the South. Many of these men came from Barbados in 1919. Over 3,000 blacks from the Bahamas worked on truck farms in Florida and were employed in government construction in Charleston, S.C. Most came on a temporary basis, but many converted their status to permanent residency.

No exact figures are available for the size of the black British West Indian population in the United States in the early 20th century. The U.S. Census and the Bureau of Immigration distinguished British West Indian immigrants from Puerto Ricans and Cubans but not from the French, Dutch, and Spanish West Indians. However, the census reported that 3 percent of all foreign-born blacks over ten years of age could not speak English in 1910, and 2 percent could not in 1920 and again in 1930. Of course, many blacks from the French and Spanish West Indies had learned English, but the extremely small percentage suggests that those from the British West Indies formed a solid majority—perhaps somewhere between 80 and 90 percent—of all blacks immigrating from the West Indies. Most of the 50,480 foreign-born West Indian blacks recorded by the 1920 Census were probably from the British West Indies, as were most of the 72,138 recorded in the 1930 Census.

The U.S. Immigration and Naturalization Service recorded social characteristics of immigrants of the "West Indian race," meaning those who were chiefly of mulatto background. Unfortunately, data were not compiled for the darker-skinned Negroes from the British West Indies, who were placed in the separate category of immigrants of the "African race," which included blacks from a number of other territories and states. Those blacks were probably more numerous, less educated, and less skilled than those designated as West Indian.

From 1911 to 1924, the period of heaviest migration, 9 percent of employed West Indians were professionals, 7 percent were white-collar workers, 55 percent were skilled workers, and 31 percent were unskilled laborers; 41 percent of the immigrants were unemployed dependents. From 1911 to 1915, 126 males arrived for every 100 females, but the ratio dwindled to 96 per 100 from 1916 to 1920, and to 80 from 1921 to 1924. About 2 out of 3 West Indian men and women were unmarried when they entered the United States, and about 3 of every 4 were between 14 and 44 years of age.

Compared to other immigrant groups, an unusually large number of West Indians were literate. From 1911 to 1924, 99 percent of West Indian immigrants were able to read and write English. By contrast, one-fourth of all the immigrants arriving in these years were un-able to read or write any language, and in some groups illiterates were a majority.

British West Indians of mulatto background entered the United States in the early 20th century with considerable skills, training, and education. They were in their prime years of productive activity and were a talented, mobile population. The statistics seem to confirm impressionistic reports from that period ascribing to British West Indians notable advantages in training and schooling, especially in comparison to southern Negroes migrating to northern cities from a rural environment that had offered them few educational and employment opportunities.

ACCOMMODATION AND ASSIMILATION, 1900 TO 1940

In the 1920s British West Indians were most numerous in New York City. They probably formed 10 to 15 percent of the city's black population, and they were perceived by American-born blacks as a foreign social element. British West Indians had a distinctive English accent, worshiped as Anglicans (less frequently as Methodists or Baptists), and often expressed allegiance to the British crown.

In the island homelands British West Indians had taken for granted their membership in a majority population of blacks and mulattos; in the United States they were viewed as strangers by native-born blacks and whites, and furthermore, they became members of a distinct racial minority group. In the British West Indies mulattos were considered superior to blacks; in the United States, mulattos and blacks were usually considered to belong essentially to the same group. British West Indians struggled to adjust to the discriminatory treatment and prejudice directed toward Negroes in general, which they often found much worse in the United States than in the West Indies. Many highly skilled and educated immigrants were forced to take jobs beneath their level of training or experience; they patiently waited for the opportunity to leave jobs as elevator operators or cooks and to resume their previous occupations as teachers, lawyers, and craftsmen.

Many striving immigrants discovered that they could improve their status through small business enterprises. The West Indians seized opportunities in urban areas to open retail stores and purchase real estate, and rapidly gained a reputation for drive, ambition, thrift, and cleverness. George S. Schuyler, an American black journalist, expressed admiration for their "enterprise in business, their pushfulness." A contemporary student of British West Indian social life in the 1920s and 1930s observed that the West Indians were "legendary in Harlem for their frugalness and thrift." People who lived in Harlem began to repeat the saying that when a West Indian "got ten cents above a beggar, he opened a business." Studies in the 1930s disclosed that West Indians owned a disproportionate number of small stores in Harlem and in Columbus Hill. Another contemporary observed that they frequently formed small private companies consisting of a half-dozen investors who would pool several thousand dollars to purchase apartment buildings that they later rented out at a good profit. They also organized corporations to buy and manage larger, "elevator" apartment buildings. The An-

tillian Realty Company and another realty investment firm formed by a combine of British West Indians and native-born blacks each had holdings totaling $750,000 in this period.

James Weldon Johnson (1871–1938), a major figure in the Harlem Renaissance and a second-generation British West Indian, characterized the immigrants as "sober-minded" and as having "something of a genius for business." Johnson went on to say that they differed "almost totally" in these respects from "the average rural Negro of the South." All observers agreed that West Indians made up a disproportionately large number of black political, intellectual, professional, and business leaders. A sociologist estimated in the 1930s that in New York "as high as one-third of the Negro professional population—particularly physicians, dentists, and lawyers—is foreign-born."

The rotating credit association, a West African institution that survived in vigorous form among British West Indians, played an important role in the development of West Indian business enterprises in the United States. In this informal savings system, known by Jamaicans as "partners" and by other West Indians as *susu*, a dozen or so trusted members pooled individual contributions to form a mutual fund which was then "rotated" by lottery at regular intervals among members who used the fund to finance business activities. Some evidence suggests that the system originally was popular chiefly among the poorer British West Indian immigrants, but that middle-class immigrants quickly learned from their countrymen its usefulness as a source of capital. Women were especially active as bankers and collectors, and "threw a regular hand" for their husbands and brothers to help them finance their small businesses.

In the early 20th century students of British West Indian life consistently commented upon the cohesive strength and discipline displayed by the West Indian family in the United States. Some theorized that the pressures of immigration and acculturation in a new setting strengthened family ties and reinforced cooperation between family members. Generally the structure of the black West Indian family was patriarchal; the father, because he was the principal wage earner, was the dominant authority in the home.

POLITICAL MOVEMENTS

British West Indians arrived with a highly developed sense of class distinctions and participated eagerly in leftist political movements. Their activity in politics was fueled by their resentment at the forms of discrimination and racial prejudice they encountered. Hubert H. Harrison (1883–1927), a West Indian immigrant, became a prominent socialist leader, a trenchant critic of American society, and a defender of the "Negro's racial heritage." Other West Indians became daily political editorialists on street corners, organized tenants' unions, attempted to recruit black workers into the labor movement, and published several ephemeral Marxist periodicals. The Reverend Ethelred Brown, Richard B. Moore, and Frank R. Crosswaith—all from the British West Indies—ran as socialists or Communists for the New York City Board of Aldermen, the state Assembly, and the U.S. Congress, though none were successful.

Some political activists exhorted immigrant and American-born blacks to form a solid class alliance against the forces of racism and capitalism. The radical journal *Challenge* proclaimed, "There is no West Indian slave, no American slave. You are all slaves, base, ignoble slaves."

The political activism of the West Indians also may have stemmed in part from a history of political participation, albeit limited, in the British imperial system. Although British colonial officials had primary control over government in the late 19th and early 20th centuries, prominent businessmen and members of the middle-class population—usually mulattos—served on legislative and executive councils to the colonial governor. Council members were normally appointed, but in Jamaica, Trinidad, and Barbados, some members of the councils were elected through a limited middle-class franchise.

The career of Marcus Garvey (1887–1940), a Jamaican immigrant, was a major force shaping West Indian politics in the United States and relations between the West Indian and the Afro-American communities. After arriving in the United States in 1916, Garvey traveled across the country and recruited hundreds of thousands of native-born and West Indian blacks in 30 cities into the Universal Negro Improvement Association (UNIA). This organization spearheaded a nationalist movement to develop racial unity and organize black business enterprises. Using millions of dollars in contributions to the UNIA, Garvey established the Negro Factories Corporation, which ran cooperative grocery stores, a laundry, a restaurant, a printing plant, clothing stores, and other small businesses. Garvey also formed the Black Star Line, a steamship company to transport blacks between the United States and the West Indies, and also to Africa, where they were to help uplift their African brethren. Garvey claimed in the 1920s that the UNIA had enrolled millions of members, but the actual membership at its highest was apparently a few hundred thousand. Although some observers claimed that he attracted mainly West Indians, thousands of American Negroes, probably a greater number than the former, rallied to Garvey's leadership as active UNIA members, as stock purchasers in the Black Star Line, and as informal supporters.

Contrary to the opinion of most contemporaries and historians, Garvey never made the mass repatriation of blacks to Africa the key for solving racial problems. Instead he exalted black self-reliance and urged black achievement in enterprise: he maintained that blacks in the United States had the capacity to advance by a combination of racial solidarity and capitalistic enterprise. Garvey eschewed socialism and urged blacks to avoid unions and cooperate with white employers until they could establish their own businesses. Despite his hopeful view for black progress, a deep strain of alienation infused Garvey's ideology and was revealed in his stress on racial pride, separateness, and identification with African roots. Garvey tapped a powerful undercurrent of ambivalence among the masses of West Indian newcomers and Negro migrants from the South. It was a blend of optimism over newfound economic opportunities in northern cities and frustration over still unyielding forms of discrimination.

Contemporaries expressed views of Garvey that were

a mixture of admiration and apprehension. A black sociologist commented, "It was natural that he should appeal to the West Indians; prejudice against them was rife. They rushed to his standard. He was one of their countrymen starting a new and wonderful movement of which no American Negro ever thought." Several prominent black leaders attacked Garvey, often exaggerating his messianism and his position on African repatriation. W.E.B. Du Bois, A. Phillip Randolph, and Chandler Owen accused Garvey of charlatanism and of advocating a utopianism that would thwart the cooperative effort of all blacks to set and attain realistic goals for group progress. Du Bois admired Garvey for "tremendous vision, dynamic force, stubborn determination, and an unselfish desire to serve" but feared his "serious defects of temperament and training" and a self-pride that blinded him to hard realities. Chandler Owen was harsher, referring to Garvey in 1923 as the "mudsill of Jamaican society," a demagogue of ignorant West Indian foreigners. Many British West Indians, too, were critical of Garvey and declared that he was building a barrier that obstructed accommodation between American-born and immigrant blacks. Harlem residents contemptuously referred to the UNIA as a "West Indian movement."

During his meteoric career Marcus Garvey was placed under surveillance by federal agents as a possible threat to national security. In 1923 he was convicted of mail fraud in connection with the failing Black Star Line, and in 1927 he was deported to Jamaica, after which the UNIA movement completely collapsed. Despite the accusations of his critics, Garvey had disseminated a compelling vision of racial redemption and progress derived in part from West Indian nationalism and in part from his pained reaction to the unequal treatment of blacks in the United States.

INSTITUTIONAL AND ASSOCIATIONAL LIFE

Soon after arrival in the United States, the British West Indians developed extremely active voluntary societies for mutual benefit, social improvement, and cultural activities. All these organizations were formed with the same objectives: to serve as forums for discussion of ethnic-group affairs, to help members find employment, to provide charity and welfare assistance, to cooperate with business enterprises, and to develop improved relations both among members of the group itself and between British West Indians and American blacks and whites.

In the 1930s blacks from the British Virgin Islands, Antigua, Guiana, Dominica, Montserrat, Jamaica, Grenada, St. Lucia, and Trinidad maintained over 30 mutual benefit associations in New York City. Some societies, such as the Jamaican Progressive League, were devoted chiefly to the interests of immigrants from specific islands. However, larger umbrella organizations soon formed, such as the West Indian Federation of America, which represented the interests of all British West Indian newcomers and lobbied for self-government for the West Indies. In Boston and Cambridge, Mass., the Jamaican Associates, the Barbadian Associates, the Bermuda Overseas Club, and the West India Society fostered the continuing interest of immigrants in West Indian affairs and promoted the industrial and commercial enterprises of members. Recreational clubs

were also organized, but they tended to appeal primarily to middle-class West Indians; especially popular were literary societies, tennis clubs, and cricket clubs.

Despite the vitality of associational life and strong consciousness of ethnic-group interests, the West Indians did not develop an outstanding newspaper. The short-lived *Negro World*, the publication of Garvey's UNIA, was the only periodical devoted principally to the concerns of British West Indians. The exclusively local orientation of many immigrants interested only in news from their home island may have splintered the readership into groups too small to sustain even specialized newspapers. Many major newspapers, however, such as the New York *Amsterdam News* and the Boston *Chronicle*, both partly owned and managed by British West Indians, devoted substantial coverage to news of interest to the West Indian community.

The church was perhaps the most vital organization in West Indian group life. The majority of West Indians transferred from the Church of England to the Protestant Episcopal Church in the United States and established their own parishes. The church not only provided for the spiritual needs of West Indians but served as the focal point for social life, communication with the home islands, and the maintenance of cultural traditions. In 1935 one Harlem parish, with a membership that was 75 percent foreign-born, continued to celebrate annually the traditional West Indian Harvest Festival in which fresh produce was brought into the church itself to be distributed to the needy.

The most festive community occasions were special celebrations and programs for coronations, anniversaries, and other events connected with the British royal family. Again, the local church served as the center for these patriotic activities in which the West Indian immigrant reaffirmed his attachment to the British crown even though he was now a permanent resident if not a citizen of the United States. Several West Indian churches in Harlem held prayer services for the speedy recovery of King George V when he struggled with illness in 1928–1929. When the king died in 1936, St. Martin's Church held a massive memorial service which was attended by the British Consul General. In 1937 St. Ambrose's parish in New York City sponsored a coronation service for the new king and queen, at which the Union Jack and the flags of the West Indies flew over a gathering of 5,000 people. Once again the British Consul General was in attendance.

More than nationalistic sentiment for a colonialist regime, the expressions of attachment to the British monarchy reflected the uneasy attitude of West Indians toward both American-born blacks and prejudiced whites. Many West Indians sought to distinguish themselves from the former and to assert their superiority through association with British influences; by identifying with Great Britain they also expressed their alienation from a society that they regarded as unjust in its treatment of blacks.

NATURALIZATION

West Indian immigrants were not enthusiastic about acquiring U.S. citizenship. Those who became U.S. citizens were often criticized and scorned by their countrymen who remained loyal British subjects. More important, remaining a British subject was also a valu-

able legal protection against discriminatory practices. British West Indians frequently countered racial discrimination by proclaiming their British citizenship and threatening to appeal to the British consul. This common practice annoyed Negro leaders who complained that it kept West Indians from joining with other blacks to seek social and institutional solutions to discriminatory treatment. They also objected that West Indians were making little effort to become citizens and thereby help increase black electoral strength. As a result, in the fall of 1936 the newly organized National Negro Independent Political League of New York City initiated a campaign "to encourage citizenship among our non-citizens; encourage membership and assist them in getting citizenship papers." Major newspapers in the black community carried advertisements urging the immigrants to naturalize with all possible speed. The *Amsterdam News* in 1937 urged its readers: "*Become a Citizen—Prepare to Vote.* The Negro's strength in affairs which concern his very existence is gauged by his ballot. If you are not a citizen become one. The United States Naturalization Service has division offices at 641 Washington Street, Manhattan, Canal 6-2100."

Nevertheless, British West Indians were slow to become citizens. In 1920, only 14 percent of all foreign-born black men and 18 percent of all foreign-born black women were naturalized, compared to 49 percent of foreign-born white men and 53 percent of foreign-born white women. The lowest percentages of naturalization were among immigrant blacks in Florida, the state most accessible to the West Indian home islands.

A rising number of black British West Indians acquired citizenship in the 1930s. Many became citizens as a natural consequence of the process of social assimilation; others were inspired by the success of West Indians in politics to seek the political rights of citizenship; still others naturalized because during the Depression noncitizens did not qualify for a large number of jobs and were barred from federal employment and relief programs.

RELATIONS WITH AFRO-AMERICANS

Until World War II relations between American blacks and British West Indians were usually far from harmonious. Economic competition, cultural differences, political disagreements, and separate associational life produced obstacles to communication and mutual suspicion. Afro-Americans described British West Indians as overly aggressive, clannish, radical, and arrogant; the latter criticized native-born blacks for lack of ambition and self-confidence. In the streets of New York City, British West Indians were daily taunted by other blacks who called them "monkey-chasers," "Jew-maicans," "Garveyites," and "cockneys." National Association for the Advancement of Colored People head Walter White lamented, "We have . . . in Harlem this strange mixture of reactions not only to prejudice from without but to equally potent prejudices from within."

West Indian blacks responded to this tense situation by establishing organizations to improve relations between themselves and other blacks. They created the West Indian Reform Association, the West Indian Committee in America, and the Foreign-Born Citizens' Alliance in the 1920s to develop "cordial relations between West Indians and colored Americans." They implored the native-born to overcome their "considerable prejudice against West Indians." Radio programs discussed "Intra-Race Relations in Harlem," and the two black groups held mass discussion meetings. By the late 1930s and early 1940s intergroup tensions abated considerably, partly because in the Depression years of the 1930s and the uneasy period at the beginning of World War II, the number of arrivals from the British West Indies decreased. It is likely that by this time West Indian and American-born blacks had begun to make progress in joint political and economic enterprises.

There was a limited amount of intermarriage between American and immigrant blacks. In 1920 over 29,000 blacks (less than 0.3 percent of the total in the United States) had one foreign-born parent, and in 1930 the number had grown to nearly 40,000. The majority of these marriages consisted of a foreign-born husband and American-born wife, partly as a result of the excess number of Afro-American women.

IMMIGRATION, 1940 TO 1978

After World War II, West Indian immigration began to increase again. Approximately 20,000 Jamaicans emigrated to the United States between 1948 and 1954, most of them as contract laborers. The restrictive McCarran-Walter Immigration Act of 1952, however, barred all inhabitants of British colonial possessions from entering under the large quota of the mother country and authorized the establishment of a small annual quota of 800 for British possessions in the West Indies. A large portion of the West Indian emigration was therefore deflected to Great Britain.

The passage of the liberal Hart-Celler Immigration Act of 1965 triggered another large-scale immigration from the British West Indies. Visa quotas were abolished for those islands that had recently become independent or whose independence was imminent. Two additional factors, one internal to the Caribbean social system and the other externally produced by British Commonwealth policy, further impelled the migratory movement. First, the steady growth of population in the West Indies during the 1950s and 1960s stimulated emigration. Second, Parliament passed the Commonwealth Immigrants Act in 1962 sharply restricting West Indian migration to the United Kingdom.

Consequently, in the late 1960s, immigration from the independent countries of Jamaica, Trinidad and Tobago, Guyana, the Bahamas, and Barbados increased enormously. The number of immigrants from Jamaica alone was ten times higher in 1970 than it had been in 1962. The annual total of all British West Indian arrivals grew swiftly from 5,000 in 1962 to over 25,000 in 1970, leveling off to 20,000 per year in the mid-1970s. In the decade 1962–1971 an estimated 150,000 British West Indians entered the United States legally; thousands more came as illegal immigrants without visas. From 1962 to 1976 slightly more females than males arrived annually; immigrant males were greatly outnumbered by females in the late 1960s. Among Jamaican immigrants the ratio fell to 53 males per 100 females, probably owing to the influx of domestic workers. Throughout most of the 1960s most West Indian immigrants were between the ages of 20 and 49, and

many were unmarried; but since 1970 the number of arrivals in this age group has decreased. At the same time, the proportion of immigrants under 20 years of age began to rise sharply to as much as 50 percent of all immigrants arriving from Jamaica since 1970. A corresponding growth in the proportion of dependent family members in the 1970s suggests the development of a trend toward migration in family units and family reunion.

A substantial proportion of immigrants from the British West Indies in the 1960s continued to come from the well-educated and highly trained classes. In the first half of the decade over 50 percent of employed immigrants arriving each year from Jamaica, Barbados, Trinidad and Tobago, and the other British West Indies were professional, white-collar, and skilled workers. Only 20 percent from Jamaica and 30 percent from the other West Indies were unskilled workers. In the late 1960s the proportion of unskilled workers grew. The migration of female domestic servants, many of whom were unmarried, increased tremendously—from 1967 to 1969 they made up 39 percent of entering Jamaicans and 34 percent of Barbadians. The effect of the 1965 immigration law has been to stimulate the flow of younger, less skilled, and less educated British West Indians.

RECENT SOCIAL AND ECONOMIC PATTERNS

West Indians no longer concentrate exclusively in the urban centers of the East Coast. Sizable numbers now reside in California, Michigan, and Illinois. Nevertheless, the majority continue to live in New York City, other northeastern cities, and Miami. New York State alone contains almost two-thirds of the Jamaican blacks in the United States.

British West Indians in the United States continue to exhibit significant achievement levels in income, education, intergenerational mobility, and occupation. In 1967 their national median family income was $8,880, compared to $10,672 for a white family and $6,440 for Afro-Americans. At that time 73 percent of second-generation British West Indians had graduated from high school, in contrast with 48 percent of first-generation West Indians and 43 percent of children of black migrants from the South. In 1972 only 13 percent of first-generation British West Indian families in New York City had annual incomes of at least $15,000, compared to 30 percent of the second-generation families. The proportion of British West Indians in high-status occupations in the early 1970s was only slightly lower than that of native-born whites and distinctly higher than the proportion of American blacks (see Table 1). Recent investigations of British West Indian enterprise indicate that they own over half the black businesses in New York City and that they are especially prominent in publishing, taxi companies, real estate, advertising, banking, insurance, and retail clothing.

The heavy West Indian immigration of the past decade and the achievement of political independence by Jamaica, Guyana, Barbados, Trinidad and Tobago, and the Bahamas have strengthened ethnic ties and feelings of nationalism in the British West Indian community. A study of one area of New York City in 1962 demonstrated that little social intercourse occurred between West Indians and other black residents; 98 percent of West Indians there had friendships almost exclusively

Table 1. Occupational distribution of U.S. white population, British West Indian immigrants, U.S. black and other nonwhite population, 1973 (in percentages).

Occupation	U.S. whites	British West Indian immigrants[a]	U.S. blacks and other nonwhites
Professional, technical, managerial	25.4	19.3	14.0
Sales	6.9	2.8	2.3
Clerical	17.5	29.3	14.9
Crafts	13.9	9.7	8.9
Operative	16.3	13.0	22.2
Labor, except farm	4.6	2.4	9.7
Service, except private household	10.6	19.9	19.6
Private household	1.2	3.4	5.7
Farm labor	3.7	0.0	2.8

Source: For distribution of U.S. white population and U.S. black and other nonwhite population, see U.S. Department of Commerce, *Statistical Abstract of the United States, 1974* (Washington, D.C., 1974), p. 351. Distribution of British West Indians was obtained from a study by Thomas Sowell, director of the Ethnic Minorities Office, Urban Institute, Washington, D.C., July 1973, as given in Virginia Dominguez, *From Neighbor to Stranger: The Dilemma of Caribbean Peoples in the United States* (New Haven, 1975), pp. 108–109.

a. Percentages from the Sowell study are not exactly comparable to those from *Statistical Abstract:* the former were derived from the total adult population and have been adjusted to exclude those not in the labor force, whereas the latter are based on labor-force membership alone.

with other West Indians and some whites. A study of Barbadians in New York City in 1972 showed that 87 percent of them married other Barbadians.

West Indians usually have small families. In 1970 the average number of births was 1.8 for West Indian women, compared to 2.4 for other black women. The national average was 2.1.

West Indians and their descendants continue to be overrepresented among black intellectual, political, and cultural leaders in the United States. Roy Innes, James Farmer, Kenneth Clark, Malcolm X, Shirley Chisholm (1924–), Stokely Carmichael (1920–), and Godfrey Cambridge (1933–1977) are among those with a West Indian background.

ACHIEVEMENT AND FUTURE DIRECTION

West Indians had important advantages which southern blacks migrating to the urban centers of the North did not possess. From 1911 to 1924, 70 percent of all employed persons annually admitted (chiefly mulattos), were professional, white-collar, or skilled workers; in the mid-20th century over 50 percent of all West Indian immigrants came from these occupational classes. This large group of educated and highly trained people is the result not only of a process of migration that was selective of the West Indian middle class but also of the circumstances that produced a sizable black middle-class population in the first place. Because blacks in the British West Indies constituted over 90 percent of the area's population during much of the last century, they had to be admitted into a wide spectrum of occupations in order for the society and economy of the region to function. Accordingly, beginning in the late 19th century many blacks became government administrators, professionals, bureaucrats, white-collar personnel, proprietors, merchants, businessmen, and craftsmen. Blacks in the British West Indies thus assumed important economic, social, and political functions that were denied during the same period to Afro-Americans.

In the past decade powerful new forces have affected

the social life of British West Indians in the United States. The large number of illegal newcomers and unskilled workers has altered the economic structure of the West Indian community. Ethnic-group cohesion persisting among British West Indians and their changing social relations with Afro-Americans continue to generate controversy and debate. The independence movement in the British West Indies has undoubtedly intensified nationalist sentiments and ethnic ties among some British West Indians. Still, attachments to a separate West Indian identity and set of group interests may be substantially attenuated or even nonexistent among second-, third-, and fourth-generation West Indians, who regard themselves essentially as American blacks. Shirley Chisholm, for example, a congresswoman of West Indian descent, is a spokesperson both for American blacks and for all members of her constituency. Finally, the increase of economic opportunity for blacks, the dramatic rise of black political power, and receding social discrimination have had significant but as yet little-understood effects on the status of this important ethnic group.

Bibliography

Primary sources for British West Indians include the U.S. Census reports, the annual reports of the Commissioner-General of Immigration and the Immigration and Naturalization Service, and the special census report, *Negroes in the United States, 1920–1932* (1933; reprint, New York, 1969). Also helpful are Roy Bryce-Laporte and Delores Mortimer, *Caribbean Immigration to the United States* (Washington, D.C., 1976); and George W. Roberts and D.O. Mills, *Study of External Migration Affecting Jamaica, 1953–1955* (Jamaica, 1958).

Richard S. Dunn, *Sugar and Slaves* (Chapel Hill, N.C., 1972); Philip D. Curtin, *Two Jamaicas: The Role of Ideas in a Tropical Society, 1830–1865* (Cambridge, Mass., 1955); and Eric Williams, *The Negro in the Caribbean* (1942; reprint, New York, 1961), are important historical studies. The most useful general surveys of British West Indian immigrants are found in Nathan Glazer and Daniel P. Moynihan, *Beyond the Melting Pot*, 2d ed. (Cambridge, Mass., 1970); Gilbert Osofsky, *Harlem: The Making of a Ghetto*, 2d ed. (New York, 1971); and the pioneering monograph by Ira Reid, *The Negro Immigrant* (1939; reprint, New York, 1970). Ivan H. Light, *Ethnic Enterprise in America* (Berkeley, Calif., 1972), and Thomas Sowell, *Race and Economics* (New York, 1975), both use a comparative approach to analyze the social and economic attainments of British West Indians.

For British West Indian immigration since World War II, see the journal *Social and Economic Studies,* especially G.E. Cumper, "Working Class Emigration from Barbados to the U.K., October 1955," 6 (1957): 77–83; Margaret Katzin, "'Partners': An Informal Savings Institution in Jamaica," 8 (1959): 436–440; W.F. Maunder, "The New Jamaican Emigration," 4 (1955): 39–63; R.W. Palmer, "A Decade of West Indian Migration to the United States, 1962–1972," 23 (1974): 571–587; and G.W. Roberts, "Emigration from the Island of Barbados," 4 (1955): 245–287. Thomas Sowell's Urban Institute monograph, *American Ethnic Groups* (Washington, D.C., 1978), and "Ethnicity in a Changing America," *Daedalus* 107 (1978): 213–237, provide current statistical information. Virginia Dominguez, *From Neighbor to Stranger: The Dilemmas of Caribbean Peoples in the United States* (New Haven, 1975), furnishes comparative data on the socioeconomic position of British West Indians, whites, and American blacks.

On Marcus Garvey, see especially E. David Cronon, *Black Moses* (1955; reprint, Madison, Wis., 1969); Tony Martin, *Race First* (Westport, Conn., 1976); and Theodore G. Vincent, *Black Power and the Garvey Movement* (Berkeley, 1972). Kenneth Kusmer offers fresh insights into the Garvey movement in *A Ghetto Takes Shape: Black Cleveland, 1870–1930* (Urbana, Ill., 1976).

Harold Cruse, *The Crisis of the Negro Intellectual* (New York, 1967), and Lennox Raphael, "West Indians and Afro-Americans," *Freedomways* (Summer 1964): 438–445, discuss relations between British West Indians and Afro-Americans. Orde Coombs, "Illegal Immigrants in New York: The Invisible Subculture," *New York Magazine* (March 15, 1976): 33–41, is a compelling portrait.

REED UEDA

WHITE RUSSIANS: *see* BELORUSSIANS; RUSSIANS

WICHITAS: *see* AMERICAN INDIANS

WINDISCHES: *see* AMERICAN INDIANS

WINDISH: *see* SLOVENES

WINNEBAGOS: *see* AMERICAN INDIANS

WINTUNS: *see* AMERICAN INDIANS

WISHRAMS: *see* AMERICAN INDIANS

WIYOTS: *see* AMERICAN INDIANS

WYANDOTS: *see* AMERICAN INDIANS

Y

YANKEES

Yankee is a term occasionally applied to citizens of the United States in general, but more particularly to residents of New England, and more particularly still to descendants of the 17th-century Puritan settlers.

The origin of the word is obscure. Most early etymologists traced it to Indian sources: Washington Irving in *Knickerbocker's History of New York* (1809) imagined that it came from a word meaning "silent men"; others, including Noah Webster, guessed that it was the result of an effort by Indians to pronounce the word "English." Possibly it was of Dutch origin, derived from Janke, the diminutive of the common given name, Jan. In any case, by 1765 it was a term of derision, and by 1775 a term of pride. In the latter year, John Trumbull used it in *M'Fingal* to denote distinction.

Whatever the origins of the word, the group to which it came specifically to apply had antecedents in the Puritan settlement of New England. This migration was distinctive in form and in the broad cross section of society it embraced. Although the majority of settlers were peasants and artisans as in the other colonies, an unusually large number of learned men and gentry accompanied them for religious reasons; and they supplied substantial leadership and continuity in the first planting of Plymouth, Massachusetts, and Connecticut and in their subsequent expansion. These colonies shared distinctive forms of religious organization, and they accepted a common version of Calvinist theology. Their churches were congregational, governed not by a hierarchy of priests and bishops but by their own members, elected after having demonstrated that they had been saved by God's grace. The same men were likely to be leaders in the church, the community, and the state, and the three forms of power reinforced one another. Controls, as a result, were stricter than elsewhere in America in the 17th century and emphasized discipline, work, and the permanence of the establishment. The community was strong, incorporated in towns that maintained an oversight over individual families and successfully resisted disruption.

Almost from the start, therefore, consciousness of group identity held the region's people together. When Cotton Mather (1663–1728) wrote at the beginning of the 18th century of patriotism or love of country, he meant loyalty to New England. That sentiment endured.

The New England colonies early showed a tendency to spread out both by migration and by the absorption of strangers. A high birthrate and an aggressive commercial spirit supplied one motive, and missionary zeal to convert others supplied another. Yankees were therefore restless and quick to expand, although in an organized fashion, town by town. Already by the end of his life, William Bradford (1590–1657) deplored the fact that the original Plymouth settlers were moving away. Generation after generation repeated the experience of desertion.

The New Englanders also had the capacity to assimilate occasional outsiders. The Crowninshields, for instance, were originally German; and Scotch-Irish and Huguenot immigrants, though close to the Yankees in religion, were regarded as alien elements until they fused with the original settlers. Later, some strangers even as distinctive as the Negroes and Chinese were absorbed, as long as they were few in number.

The Yankees were heavily involved in the Revolution—so much so that the word for a while became identified with American. Yet they remained homogeneous, not in a racial but in a social and cultural sense, as when John Adams (1735–1826) confessed, on the eve of Independence, that his primary loyalty was to the people of his region—who then constituted about half the white population of the colonies. Because censuses record nativity rather than ethnicity, there is no way of estimating the number of Yankees remaining after many left ancestral New England. No doubt in the 19th century they were a diminishing proportion of the nation's population, as they felt themselves to be.

At home and away, Yankees maintained a consciousness of their identity through affiliation with the Congregational church and through communal institutions centered in the town. Along the advancing frontier, clashes with other Americans marked their distinctiveness. Continuing battles with Yorkers on the western boundary of New England lasted well into the 19th century, furnishing themes for the novels of Washington Irving and James Fenimore Cooper.

When Timothy Dwight (1752–1817) traveled through the region early in the 19th century, he still surveyed what he considered almost a separate nationality, distinctive in religion, culture, and habits. In 1832 George Ticknor (1791–1871) explained that Boston was the capital of New England because of the homogeneity of the residents' character and "the great similarity of . . . their institutions," which made them "more strictly one people, with one common centre and capital, than any other equal amount of the population of the United States."

These traits to some extent influenced the areas into which the Yankees spread. In the revolutionary era there was some movement to the south, into the great valley of Virginia and indeed as far as Georgia. But in time this region proved uncongenial. The plantation economy and the pattern of landholding did not encourage the accepted forms of New England agriculture or commerce or leave room for town communities. When the slavery issue boiled up after 1820, it became unlikely that Yankees would feel at home in the region. Individuals from New England continued to go south and some became slaveholders; but in doing so they dissolved their ties with the ancestral religion, the home region, and the ethnic group. They lost their Yankee identity and merged with the Southerners.

A more important movement took Yankees northward up the valleys of the Housatonic and the Connecticut into Vermont and New Hampshire and along the coast into the District of Maine (part of Massachusetts until 1820). After 1810, however, migration in that

direction lost popularity in the face of superior attractions elsewhere. The main line of Yankee advance turned westward along the Mohawk Valley into upper New York State and then into Pennsylvania and through the northern tier of counties of Ohio, Indiana, and Illinois. Everywhere they remained a distinctive, coherent group. By 1850 some Yankees had reached the Pacific coast in California and Oregon; and soon thereafter others pushed overland into Iowa, Kansas, and parts of Nebraska. Outside the South, the migrants long retained a sense of ethnic identity.

The westward thrust combined rural and urban elements. In the countryside the characteristic patterns of Yankee agriculture combined production for the market, efforts at improvement that would raise the value of the farm, and a willingness to speculate. In the cities Yankees clustered in commercial and professional callings. The popular image spread by P.T. Barnum (1810–1891) was that of the peddler, the shrewd trader who would swap anything and profit in the process. To that image was sometimes joined that of the inveterate tinkerer, the man of all trades and ingenious inventor, later described in Mark Twain's *Connecticut Yankee.* And indeed an army of peddlers, shopkeepers, drummers, toolmakers, and mechanics was the social reality behind the stereotype.

Less prominent but no less important was the Yankee schoolteacher, male and female, who followed in the train of other migrants. Down through the middle of the 19th century, a spell in the schoolhouse was an appropriate apprenticeship for young women awaiting marriage and for young men who thus accumulated the means to advance their professional education. Later, when teaching became more professional under the influence of Horace Mann (1796–1859) of Massachusetts and Henry Barnard (1811–1900) of Connecticut, Yankees maintained a strong position in the calling throughout the country.

Religion remained a unifying element within the group. The Congregational church and its Unitarian and Universalist offshoots were ethnic rallying points wherever Yankees were numerous. Vigorous preachers from William Ellery Channing (1780–1842) and Lyman Beecher (1775–1863) to Horace Bushnell (1802–1876) and Washington Gladden (1836–1918) reformulated the old Calvinist ideology and adjusted it to 19th-century conditions. Quakers and Baptists had been prominent in the region before the Revolution and retained their strength. In addition, Methodist and Episcopal churches spread after 1815, while entirely new sects from the Latter-day Saints (Mormons) to Christian Science drew heavily upon Yankee support. But those without the original Calvinist ingredient reached out to a wider membership and tended to lose their initial ethnic character.

The Yankees tried to develop more formal organizations as other groups did, for self-help and to maintain a sense of identity. New England societies operated in many cities through the 19th and early 20th centuries. The Society of Mayflower Descendants confined its membership to descendants of the first immigrants, to sustain their claim to a special place in the nation. Other activities in reform movements, education, and philanthropy were less visibly ethnic, yet nevertheless had a distinct Yankee character.

After the Civil War subtle tensions affected the cohesiveness of the group; inequalities gradually divided it. A would-be Brahmin aristocracy considered itself at the head of a national elite and distinguished itself from the humbler Yankees. A gradual shift to the Episcopal church reflected the desire of the uppermost social group for a more formal, hierarchical faith than that of the old meeting house. Select schools like Groton and St. Paul's, select clubs at the universities and in town, and select summer resorts reflected the wish for distance and a sense of identity of a distinct, smaller, but powerful subgroup.

The larger Yankee community preserved its cohesiveness, not least because of the need to defend its cultural heritage in a period of rapid economic change and mass immigration. Expanded protective institutions like the YMCA and an array of schools, charitable organizations, newspapers, and magazines kept alive the awareness of the group's character.

A morbid tone appeared in the consciousness of both elements. Yankees viewed their past darkly under the reflected shadows of the present. The Civil War had sapped their best energies; they knew they were declining in importance even at home; and the whole region steadily lost national influence. The more sensitive felt themselves outdistanced by vigorous competitors elsewhere in the country and blamed their own loss of vitality upon demographic changes in the area. The original sturdy Puritan farming stock, they thought, had given way to a degenerate foreign population, crowded into great cities and divorced by heredity and environment from the true sources of New England's strength. Hence the strong emphasis on the necessity for maintaining the old virtues through the discipline of strict family life and through traditional religious observances. Pride of ancestry justified social discipline. Yankees celebrated their part in the making of the nation as a means of assuring themselves of their identity as a group. Heredity was therefore exceedingly important; marriage, family life, access to voluntary societies, and other social activities revolved about it.

The 20th century subjected the Yankees to strains that ultimately snapped the ties of ethnicity. The first stages of industrialization and urbanization had strengthened the resources of the group. Influential in mercantile affairs, strongly represented in banking, its members played a prominent, though by no means an exclusive, role in accumulating the capital that went into 19th-century manufacturing. They were important also in providing the social cohesion and cultural resources which validated the general position of people of wealth at the opening of the century. It was not by accident that Newport, R.I., became the nation's effective social capital, even for families whose permanent homes were in New York and elsewhere. A cluster of educational institutions played a pivotal part in socializing and maintaining the continuity of generation to generation. Within New England, habits of thrift and the device of the trust preserved the capital and maintained the strength and cohesion of the family; and to a certain extent the same traits extended to other parts of the country. By the 1890s, however, the concern some intellectuals expressed about the declining birth rate reflected a deeper but unperceived ambiguity in the way they conceived their own identity. On the one hand, they took pride in their distinctive heritage and faith and in the family ties that sustained their position. On

the other, as spiritual heirs of John Winthrop (1588–1649) and Ralph Waldo Emerson (1803–1882) they believed that their culture had universal value for all people, at least in America. As a result, they vacillated between defensive withdrawal as a group and aggressive assertion that they represented the whole nation.

Nevertheless, financial and social power seemed secure down through the 1920s. In that decade, however, the rise to prominence of newer peoples, and especially of the Irish, eroded the political base in New England. Substantial numbers of French Canadians in New Hampshire and Maine, Italians in Connecticut and Rhode Island, and Polish Americans all along the Connecticut Valley began to assert themselves. The Yankees and the Republican party still retained strength until the effects of Depression in the 1930s and of war in the 1940s finally altered the situation. Those events undermined the fiscal and political substructure of the dominant families and called into question the cluster of values by which the group had maintained its identity. By the 1950s, in most parts of the country, under the impact of the civil rights movement, the group had blended into the general image of the WASP; and, as established religious and cultural institutions lost strength, the discipline they once imparted faded.

Bibliography

All the histories of New England perforce treat the Yankees. Although old and in some respects outdated, the most useful is still William B. Weeden, *Economic and Social History of New England, 1620–1789* (1890; reprint, New York, 1963). Dorothy Canfield Fisher, *Vermont Tradition* (Boston, 1953), is charming as well as thoughtful; and there is interesting material in Barbara M. Solomon's introduction to Timothy Dwight, *Travels in New England and New York* (Cambridge, Mass., 1969). Lois K. Matthews, *Expansion of New England* (1909; reprint, New York, 1962); L.D. Stillwell, *Migration from Vermont* (Montpelier, Vt., 1948); and Stewart H. Holbrook, *Yankee Exodus* (New York, 1950), treat internal migration.

OSCAR HANDLIN

YAQUI: *see* AMERICAN INDIANS

YAVAPAIS: *see* AMERICAN INDIANS

YEMENITES: *see* ARABS

YOKUTS: *see* AMERICAN INDIANS

YUGOSLAVS: *see* BOSNIAN MUSLIMS; CROATS; MACEDONIANS; SERBS; SLOVENES

YUROKS: *see* AMERICAN INDIANS

Z

ZOROASTRIANS

The Zoroastrians are recent arrivals in the United States. Originally a Persian (Iranian) religious group, they have evolved over the years into a community with many ethnic characteristics. Their ethnoreligious character is particularly clear in the United States and in the other western countries to which they have migrated. The approximately 2,000 Zoroastrians in the United States in the late 1970s represent a small but growing proportion of their total number—about 200,000, most of whom live in India, except for the 25,000 still in Iran.

The group is named for Zoroaster (Zarathustra, in their holy book, the *Avesta*), a prophet who in about 1000 B.C. began to advocate the worship of the deity Ahura Mazda (the Wise Lord). This religion, called by its practitioners Beh Din-e Mazda Yasnayan (the Good Religion of the Mazda Worshipers), eventually became the basis of the state church of the Sasanian Empire of Persia (A.D. 224–651), which stretched from Mesopotamia to Afghanistan. After the Islamic conquest of Persia in the 7th century, most Zoroastrians converted to Islam. The rest sought to escape Muslim pressure and discrimination by leaving Persia or retreating from the large towns. From the 10th to the 17th century, groups of Zoroastrians fled to India, where they settled in the region of Gujarat. When Bombay became an important commercial center under British rule, many moved there, mostly into the same quarter of the city. In India the Zoroastrians are called Parsis (Parsees) after their place of origin, Persia.

Those Zoroastrians who remained in Persia were tolerated as one of the three religious groups accepted by Islam, but they were kept out of public life and were called *gaber* (unclear) by the Muslims. They lived near each other in small towns and villages in central Persia, generally as peasants and weavers. For many centuries they experienced cultural and material stagnation. The Persian communities, however, always stayed in contact with the more prosperous Indian groups, which aided the poorer Persians.

As minorities within Persian and Indian society, Zoroastrians developed practices that are characteristic of similar groups. Marrying within their own community, they refused to make converts or accept outsiders into the community, and they usually gave their children names associated with their pre-Islamic Persian culture. Today they identify strongly with the non-Muslim features of Iranian culture, and many consider themselves the true heirs of the ancient Persians. The two communities have long supported mutual-aid organizations to encourage religious and secular communal activities. Most Parsis have lost Persian as a spoken language, and English is increasingly the language of communication among Zoroastrians in different parts of the world, but all religious services are held in Avestan, an extinct language distantly related to Persian.

The religion, which derives its inspiration from the *Avesta*, is founded on a dualistic principle in which the power of good (Ahura Mazda), will ultimately overcome the power of evil (Ahriman). Respect for nature and the need to prevent the pollution of the four revered elements—fire, earth, water, and air—are basic to the religion, as is the observance of strict ethical practices. Zoroastrians are not subject to any dietary restrictions. They are strictly monogomous, and divorce is rare. Because of the use of fire in their rituals, they have been mislabeled "fire worshipers."

In India and Iran, Zoroastrians live in tightly knit groups and remain distinct from the surrounding society. Socially and culturally, however, the Parsis have adopted some Indian customs, and because they were favored by the British colonial government until 1947, the community attained great wealth and influence in business. Through their self-help associations and with better access to education and travel, the Parsis have been able to pursue professional careers in other countries, including the United States. In Iran, on the other hand, Zoroastrians have gained advancement only since the 1930s, and their emigration in search of economic opportunity preceded that of the Parsis.

Among the first Iranian families to emigrate were members of the Soroushian family of Kerman who set up a retail carpet business in New York in the 1920s. One of the first Parsis to live in the United States was Baijor Wadis, an engineer, who between 1905 and 1921 worked for the Ford Motor Company in Detroit before returning to India. Until 1968, when U.S. immigration laws were liberalized, most Zoroastrians in the United States had come as students in such fields as engineering, medicine, and science. During the 1970s an increasing number brought their families with them.

As their numbers have increased, Zoroastrians have formed communities in or near large metropolitan centers where they have opportunities to practice their professions. There are associations in Chicago, New York, Boston, Los Angeles, and Philadelphia, as well as in Quebec and Toronto. The Zoroastrian Association of Greater New York (in New Rochelle) is one such organization, centered around the Darb-e Mehr (Path of Compassion), a gathering place established and funded by an Iranian Zoroastrian philanthropist, Arbab Giv, in 1977. No "fire" temples, that is, exclusively religious establishments, have been built as yet. The highest-ranking Zoroastrian religious figure is Dastur Dr. Framroze Bode of Los Angeles. The best-known Zoroastrian is Zubin Mehta, conductor of the New York Philharmonic Orchestra.

The Zoroastrian Association of Metropolitan Chicago, at Hinsdale, Ill., is the center of the North American Zoroastrian Association (NAZA) in the United States. NAZA held its first symposium in 1975 in Toronto and its second in Chicago in 1977. In addition to coordinating national activities, NAZA issues reports and newsletters. It supports Zoroastrian activities throughout the world and channels information regarding speakers, literature, and world meetings to the North American Zoroastrian communities.

Problems of assimilation and loss of identity face

Zoroastrians in the United States. Although marriage outside of the group is permitted, no outsiders, even marriage partners, may become Zoroastrians. The children of Zoroastrian fathers may elect to become members of the community at the age of 18, but children whose mothers alone are Zoroastrian may not. In India and Iran these restrictions mean little; Zoroastrians are effectively prevented from marrying outside the community because their Muslim and Hindu neighbors also prefer to marry within their own groups.

In North America, however, Zoroastrian women suffer a penalty when they marry an outsider, although the men do not. This tradition, together with the rejection of converts, has led to controversy within the group. It is feared that removing restrictions on community membership will result in the loss of ethnic identity but, on the other hand, that continuing the restrictions may lead to a decrease in membership. As a result one Zoroastrian group, the Mazda Yasnians, has split off in order to function as a purely religious group.

The Mazda Yasnians, centered in Los Angeles, recruit and welcome converts of all ethnic backgrounds. Other Zoroastrians regard the Mazda Yasnians with considerable skepticism.

Despite their small numbers and the adjustments required to adapt their traditions and practices to American life, the Zoroastrians seem willing to join together to find solutions. Their success will be based, in large part, on their long history of communal cooperation.

Bibliography

No study of the Zoroastrians in the United States has appeared in English. The following are general sources about the religion and the Zoroastrian communities in Iran and India: Mary Boyce, *History of Zoroastrianism*, 2 vols. (Leiden, Netherlands, 1975, 1979), and *A Persian Stronghold of Zoroastrianism: A Study of a Village in Iran* (Oxford, England, 1977). A book by a Parsi priest, Dastur Hormazdyar Mirza, *Outlines of Parsi History* (Bombay, 1974), contains fascinating material by a learned practitioner of the religion.

EDEN NABY

ZUNIS: *see* AMERICAN INDIANS

Appendix I

METHODS OF ESTIMATING THE SIZE OF GROUPS

In the United States and other countries in which the population consists largely of the descendants of immigrants from many countries and cultures, there has been much interest in the role of ethnicity in the life of the nation. Among the questions that provoke discussion and research is the problem of numbers—how to estimate the number of persons of a particular origin who arrived as immigrants, the number of their descendants and where they are now settled, the ways in which they differ from the descendants of other ethnic groups, and the extent to which they still identify as members of their ethnic group or maintain ethnic customs and traditions.

Some people are uneasy about probing into ethnic origins and estimating numbers and distribution; they remember the anti-Semitic persecutions of tsarist Russia and Nazi Germany, the treatment of African slaves and their descendants in the Americas, and the discriminatory immigration policies of the United States between 1882 and 1965. They fear that probing into origins may unleash unhealthy racist prejudices and foster renewed discrimination. Some even call for the abolition of all questions about race and origin in government statistics as well as in applications for jobs or college admission.

On the other hand, general interest in ethnic matters is still so great in the United States that official questions on origins remain, and some Americans press for more. At a White House seminar in June 1976 author Michael Novak urged the U.S. Bureau of the Census to devise questions that would reveal the ethnic origins and identification of the third and later generations and include religious affiliation as well. Some present-day minorities, far from fearing official questions on race and ethnicity, positively welcome them, on the grounds that attempts to abolish such questions are merely another and exceedingly skillful—because on the surface so liberal—attempt to blot out knowledge of the identity and actual size of various minorities. Recent efforts at "affirmative action," that is, giving preference in jobs, housing, or education to the disadvantaged, require estimates of group size for use in establishing targets or quotas.

In any event, masses of ethnic data have been collected by various agencies for a long time, and scholars cannot neglect them. Anyone interested in the history and development of ethnic populations must accept the fact that many relevant records were collected by governments far less sensitive about discrimination than is now the case. Concerned lest the great immigrations of the 19th century drastically change the character of the American people, they accepted biological and genetic differences as a normal means of grading peoples in terms of "assimilability"; hence all the official questions about race, race mixture, birthplace, parentage, and slavery. Although the motives and attitudes behind the statistics of bygone days are questionable, students of ethnic history can get almost nowhere without those statistics. It is important to consider some of the terms used in both historical and contemporary statistics to describe both the original immigrants and their descendants.

DEFINITIONS

Descent, Generation, Stock, Origin Descendants are normally reckoned by generations, the first generation being the original immigrants, the second generation being their children born in the new country (though some scholars include in the second generation those who arrived as infants or young children and had all their education and upbringing in the New World), the third generation being the children of the second, and so on. The U.S. censuses have long distinguished the first two generations from the rest of the population. Statistics by country of birth have been amassed for the foreign-born since 1850, after immigration rose from an annual average of 86,000 in the early 1840s to 256,000 late in the decade; statistics for natives of foreign or mixed parentage have appeared since 1870, when the numerical impact of the second generation had begun to make itself felt. Since 1910 these two generations together have sometimes been labeled "foreign stock." Until now the third, fourth, and later generations have been lumped together as "native of native parentage."

Since 1924, immigration to the United States has been relatively low; first- and second-generation Americans now constitute less than 20 percent of the total population; the U.S. Bureau of the Census has therefore abandoned the foreign-parentage category. The 1980 Census attempts to unravel the ethnic origins of the native-born by asking a question on ancestry, as it has been doing since 1969 in its Current Population Surveys. The term "ethnic origin" is used here in a very general sense to denote the group or groups to which immigrant forebears belonged when they came to the United States. Though technically the meaning is much the same, it has less distasteful associations than "national origin"; the latter was the term adopted by the 1924 immigration law for estimates of the ethnic origin of the total population, which were the basis for the discriminatory immigration quotas. The term survived the immigration debates of 1952 but was abandoned in 1965, on the grounds that it reflected undemocratic doctrines of Anglo-Saxon superiority prevalent after World War I.

Mixed Origin and Parentage An anomaly in the strict generation count arises when parents are of different generations. The census bureau has described children of one first-generation parent and one second- or later-generation parent as "native of mixed parentage" but does not distinguish children whose parents are second and third generation, and so forth. Likewise, the bureau has sometimes recorded children of mixed ethnic origin—a native-born child of a German-born father and Irish-born mother—but only when the parents are immigrants; information on mixtures in later generations has to come from special surveys. In any case, it is not always easy to allocate persons of mixed parentage

to any ethnic group, for some individuals identify with two or more groups (see below). For reasons like these, the Current Population Surveys on Ethnic Origin put all persons returning more than one origin into the general category "Other." The category is additionally ambiguous because "Other" also includes people who identify with one of the many smaller groups that are not among the choices offered respondents; it is to be hoped that the forthcoming tabulations from the 1980 Census will abandon this confusing practice, in particular because in recent surveys the "Other" category has embraced approximately half of the entire population.

Ethnic Group, People, Folk, Nation   Mixed ancestry and multiple identity raise several questions about the nature of ethnicity and ethnic origin. First, to what extent is it realistic to speak of the ethnic origin of fourth- or fifth-generation Americans, especially those of mixed origin, who may prefer to identify simply as American? (The Current Population Surveys ask further questions of those answering "American" as their origin but cannot always clarify the situation.) Second, even if descent and identification are clear, what does it mean to say "I am Macedonian," when there has been no clear-cut Macedonia since the days of Alexander the Great and much political effort in some quarters to show either that the Macedonians as a distinct people do not exist or that they have always existed? Various arguments about ethnic origin and identity stress physical characteristics, language, culture and customs, or history. As used here, the term refers more generally to a collection of families and persons who for physical, geographical, political, religious, linguistic, or other reasons consider themselves, or are considered by others, to constitute a separate people. On these grounds—though in the past Serbs, Bulgarians, and Greeks have all fiercely denied it—there has long been a distinct Macedonian people or ethnic population, now officially recognized by modern Yugoslavia with its autonomous Macedonian republic. (*See* Macedonians; *see also* Bulgarians.)

In this sense the terms "ethnic group" and "people" are almost synonymous; both terms may be used to denote not only quite large populations—Ukrainians or Welsh in Europe, Yoruba in West Africa, Karens in Burma, and so on—but also small, scattered groups such as the Gypsies or local populations with distinct dialects and customs, such as the Calabrians or Friulians of Italy. When referring to larger ethnic populations, some prefer the old English term "folk," though that has been less common since Nazi Germany's racist use of *Volk*. Others prefer "nation" or "subnation," which accords well with the original meaning of the word nation as the group into which one is born and with the language of the King James Bible. It also is in accord with the usage of the 1870 U.S. Census, which put information on country of birth under the general heading "Nativity and Nationality" and published material on certain "Special Nationalities" within the United States, such as English-Welsh, Swedish-Norwegian, British-American, and Chinese. Some Americans still use the term "nation" in this ethnographic sense, speaking of a person born and living in Scotland as a member of the Scottish nation, that is, of Scottish nationality. However, this usage can lead to confusion

(see the next section). "Ethnic group" and "people" are the least confusing terms to describe the populations under discussion.

Nationality, Citizenship, Allegiance   During the 19th century the words "nation" and "nationality" gradually became attached to the concept of state and allegiance, and they are used in that sense in both international law and the legal systems of numerous countries. For example, in British and international law a Scot is not of Scottish nationality but British, for he owes allegiance to the queen of the United Kingdom of Great Britain and Northern Ireland. The terms appear in this sense in some U.S. laws as well, for instance the Nationality Act of 1940, in which a "national of the United States" is either (1) a citizen of the United States or (2) a person who, though not a citizen, owes permanent allegiance to the United States. (This usage was repeated in the U.S. Immigration and Nationality Act of 1952.) In earlier days several classes possessed U.S. nationality but not citizenship—slaves until the Civil War, tribal American Indians until 1924, Filipinos until independence in 1935—but the distinction now pertains mainly to the indigenous population of American Samoa. Even so, in census statistics Samoans, who are actually noncitizen nationals, are listed as "citizens." Likewise, the indigenous people of the U.S. Trust Territory of the Pacific Islands are neither U.S. nationals nor citizens, but in some census statistics they, too, appear under the "Citizen" rather than the "Alien" category. Because of these ambiguities in the terms "nationality" and "citizenship," "allegiance" is used here as a more accurate description of the legal relation between a person and the state that exercises sovereignty over him; this adequately covers the inhabitants of the Trust Territory as well as nationals and citizens. It also accords with the term used by the U.S. Immigration and Naturalization Service (INS) in its statistics of persons naturalized by country or region of former allegiance. In most U.S. statistics, however, the allegiance tables are misleadingly headed "Citizenship."

THE PROBLEM OF ESTIMATION

The old saying that "there are lies, damned lies, and statistics" is particularly true for estimates of ethnic populations. Many ethnic communities want to emphasize their size and strength, especially when trying to establish ethnic radio programs or special language courses in schools and universities, and therefore use the highest estimate available. Rival groups, or those resisting their claims, look for the lowest estimate. Sometimes there are bitter exchanges between the two sides; for example, in the early 20th century some American, British, and other missionaries who supported moves for an independent Armenia estimated that there were 4 million Armenians or more (the Armenian patriarch himself went as high as 8 million), whereas the Ottoman government, determined to resist such moves, published estimates of 1 million or less. Similarly, some recent estimates of American Samoans living in the United States go as high as 60,000 (15,000 in Hawaii, about 1,000 in Seattle, and the rest mainly in California); these are based on estimates by Samoan community leaders; however, because the total native population of American Samoa has never exceeded

30,000 or so, that seems unlikely. Estimates of the Kurdish population in the Middle East today range from 7 million to more than twice that.

In some cases, enemies of an ethnic group may greatly overestimate numbers in order to frighten politicians into introducing immigration restrictions; in California in the late 19th and early 20th centuries opponents of Chinese and Japanese immigration vastly exaggerated the size of these groups; in political debates they sometimes gave estimates two or three times as high as the census results published soon afterward. In such a tangle of under- and overstatement the challenge is to find statistical sources that seem reasonably balanced and reliable.

Unfortunately, it is seldom possible to obtain exact totals for a particular ethnic group, and what totals exist often vary greatly over time. Sometimes national boundaries change by conquest, cession, or independence; this can greatly affect birthplace and allegiance statistics, and at times even origin data. Sometimes the questions change, from stress on descent, for example —as with the earlier parentage questions of the U.S. Census—to stress on identification, as with the ethnic-origin questions of the Current Population Surveys. Descent questions aim at counting everyone in the United States with, say, Italian forebears, whereas identification questions aim at counting only those claiming Italian ethnicity, thus omitting those of Italian descent who no longer identify as such. People's attitudes to questions, particularly identification questions, often change, either because of contemporary trends or because they understand better what the question really means; thus, in the short intervals between the Current Population Surveys of November 1969, March 1971, March 1972, and March 1973, the number of people giving their ethnic origin as German jumped from 19.96 million to 25.7 to 25.5 and then back to 20.5 million; similarly, the Irish figure rose from 13.3 million to 16.3, then moved to 16.4 and down again to 12.2 million. Immigration, natural increase, and sampling variation could not account for these changes (sampling variation

accounted for perhaps 500,000 in each case, but no more), nor for the changes in "Other": the number in the "Other" or "Don't Know" categories together fell from 96.6 million to 89.9 and 90.6 and then rose to 101.5 million. These statistics allow for a transfer of an estimated 9 million Scots and Welsh from "Other" to English in 1969 and keep French in "Other" all through. It is clear that in the short periods between surveys many people changed their minds about how to express their ethnic origin (see Table 1).

The only groups for which we can obtain fairly firm estimates of numbers are small groups with clear-cut conditions of membership, such as the Hutterites or Amish. Because persons who leave or are expelled no longer count as part of the ethnic community, relatively accurate totals can be derived from direct counting or sample surveys. With other ethnic groups the margins are considerably broader, and the scholar simply has to do his best with the statistics available, which vary greatly according to the purpose of the collecting agency and its efficiency, and also fluctuate widely over time. The following paragraphs briefly outline the main statistical series but make no attempt to elaborate detailed changes; these may be traced through the documents themselves with the aid of *Historical Statistics of the United States: Colonial Times to 1970* (Washington, D.C., 1975).

STATISTICS ON THE FIRST GENERATION

The main sources of data on the first generation are official counts in migration statistics, censuses, vital records (birth, death, and marriage documents), and naturalization records.

Direct Recording Occasionally ethnic totals are obtained directly, as in the U.S. immigration records for the first half of the 20th century. Beginning in 1899 officials asked immigrants sufficient questions to identify not only major countries of origin—Germany, Russia, Austria-Hungary, Turkey, and so on—but also particular ethnic groups, such as Armenians, Czechs, Slovaks, Hungarians, Lithuanians, and Scots, none of whom at

Table 1. Population by ethnic origin, in thousands.

Origin	November 1969	March 1971	March 1972	March 1973 Number	March 1973 Median age	March 1973 Males per 100 females
English[a]	19,060	31,006	29,548	25,993	28.1	90.2
French[b]	—	5,189	5,420	3,939	36.7	92.6
German	19,961	25,662	25,543	20,517	35.5	103.1
Irish	13,282	16,326	16,408	12,240	38.1	87.4
Italian	7,239	8,733	8,764	7,101	38.4	103.5
Polish	4,021	4,941	5,105	3,686	41.8	92.8
Russian	2,152	2,132	2,188	1,747	45.5	96.5
Spanish[c]	9,230	8,957	9,178	10,577	20.1	96.5
Mexican	5,073	5,023	5,254	6,293	18.8	100.9
Puerto Rican	1,454	1,450	1,518	1,548	18.8	89.7
Other[d]	105,633	84,692	85,130	97,593	21.5	92.6
Not reported[e]	17,636	15,216	17,556	22,902	30.0	96.9
Total	198,214	202,854	204,840	206,295	39.0	94.0

Source: Based on the Current Population Surveys of the United States, 1969–1973, as reported in *Statistical Abstract of the United States 1974* (Washington, D.C., 1974), p. 34.
a. English includes Scottish and Welsh from 1971 on.
b. In 1969 French were classified in "Other."
c. Spanish includes Mexican and Puerto Rican origins.
d. "Other" includes blacks and all persons reporting two or more origins.
e. "Not reported" includes "Origin unknown."

Table 2. Immigration by race or people, 1899–1952.[a]

	1899–1924				1925–1943	
	Arrivals	Departures	Net	% departures	Arrivals	Departures
Cuban	77,028	46,824	30,204	60.8	16,448	17,087
Mexican	447,065	71,074	375,991	15.9	275,824	140,609
Spanish American	41,289	15,362	25,927	37.2	30,598	26,183
West Indian	29,257	12,782	16,475	43.7	5,035	8,566
Chinese	59,079	76,332	−17,253	129.2	9,032	42,193
East Indian	8,234	3,000	5,234	36.4	423	1,843
Japanese	260,492	85,415	175,077	32.8	5,630	17,150
Korean	9,214	6,382	2,832	69.3	290	498
Armenian	76,129	11,211	64,918	14.7	7,706	619
Syrian	102,259	24,929	77,330	24.4	6,285	2,287
Turkish	22,026	19,031	2,995	86.4	1,387	1,364
Hebrew[c]	1,837,875	95,344	1,742,531	5.2	244,261	4,913
Czech (Bohemian, Moravian)	159,319	34,364	124,955	21.6	12,378	10,974
Bulgarian, Serbian (Servian), Montenegrin	165,091	148,386	16,705	89.9	6,178	12,484
Croatian, Slovenian	485,379	246,098	239,281	50.7	8,881	5,090
Dalmatian, Bosnian, Herzegovinian	52,135	16,468	35,667	31.6	1,091	3,025
Lithuanian	263,277	65,957	197,320	25.1	4,235	3,825
Hungarian (Magyar)	492,031	314,547	177,484	63.9	13,356	8,959
Polish	1,483,374	587,742	895,632	39.6	32,877	25,569
Romanian	148,251	97,861	50,390	66.0	4,042	8,858
Russian	258,983	130,840	128,143	50.5	14,521	7,257
Ruthenian	265,478	44,302	221,176	16.7	4,505	468
Slovak	536,911	298,689	238,222	55.6	19,324	9,212
Dutch, Flemish	205,910	45,486	160,424	22.1	29,885	13,097
Finnish	226,922	65,422	161,500	28.8	6,692	7,669
French	415,244	78,662	336,582	18.9	143,808	22,519
German	1,316,614	257,938	1,058,676	19.6	374,441	79,843
Scandinavian	956,308	227,620	728,688	23.8	122,825	45,923
English	1,067,659	261,295	806,364	24.5	298,183	98,672
Irish	808,762	100,108	708,654	12.4	268,345	28,409
Scottish	441,172	59,507	381,665	13.5	182,124	36,005
Welsh	43,092	5,245	37,847	12.2	11,010	2,521
Greek	500,465	241,923	258,542	48.3	27,084	27,688
Italian, North[d]	605,535	292,522	313,013	48.3	168,664	128,241
Italian, South	3,215,451	1,812,943	1,402,508	56.4		
Portuguese	186,244	60,494	125,750	32.5	9,423	19,602
Spanish	190,521	85,931	104,590	45.1	11,450	30,424
Negro	135,019	28,124	106,895	20.8	10,392	11,013
Other[e]	40,989	18,859	22,130	46.0	6,310	3,946
Total	17,636,083	6,095,019	11,541,064	34.6	2,394,943	914,605

Source: Tabulated from successive Annual Reports of the Commissioner General of Immigration, U.S. Department of Commerce and Labor, and of the Immigration and Naturalization Service, U.S. Department of Justice.

a. Filipinos were counted as U.S. nationals and not recorded until 1935. For consistency they have been excluded from this table and the totals for 1935–1952 correspondingly reduced.

b. "% departures" indicates percentage of immigrant arrivals later departing as emigrants—based on records, 1908–1952; estimated, 1899–1907. Where the % departure exceeds 100% (that is, when departures exceed arrivals in a given period), it reveals a large pool of immigrants who arrived before the period began but whose departure during that period—added to the departure of those immigrants who both arrived and departed during the period—produces a total of departures for the period that exceeds the total of arrivals for the period. This is particularly noticeable with the Chinese, who had arrived in large numbers before the restrictions of 1882–1894 and whose departure during the years 1899–1924 could not be balanced by new arrivals; likewise with the Japanese caught by the restrictions of 1924.

c. "Hebrew" ceased as a category in 1944; subsequent arrivals were listed by national origin.

d. After 1924, Italians were recorded as one group.

e. "Other" includes Pacific Islanders, shown separately until 1935 (516 arrivals in all).

the time had their own nation-state; questions also revealed major regional differences (North and South Italian) and one important ethnoreligious group, that is, the Jews (Hebrews). Such direct recording, though, was seldom followed up in the censuses or vital statistics, so this evidence indicates only how many people from these groups entered and left the country. Nor do these immigration records identify smaller ethnic groups such as the Basques or the Maltese. In other cases small groups are combined beyond recognition: in the U.S. system, for instance, the South Slav peoples were combined into three categories—Croatian, Slavonian, and Slovene; Dalmatian, Bosnian, and Herzegovinian; and Bulgarian, Serbian, and Montenegrin—which makes it difficult to undertake research specifically on Slovene or Croatian settlements. This direct recording was abandoned after the Immigration and Nationality Act

of 1952, partly, it seems, because reliable birthplace statistics were then available to form the basis of the quota restrictions, partly because some of the categories were ambiguous (for example, the overlap between Spanish Americans and West Indian), and partly because the general climate of opinion was setting firmly against any classification influenced by notions of race. The direct counts prior to 1952 employed some racial categories (East Indian, African/black, and Chinese) and were headed either "Immigration by Race or People" or "Immigration by Race or Nationality." It is not clear whether it is a distaste for racial categories or for ambiguity that has led the compilers of *Historical Statistics of the United States, Colonial Times to 1945* (and subsequent editions in 1957 and 1975) to omit all references to this particular set of immigration statistics.

Although the racial notions underlying some of the

| 1925–1943 | | 1944–1952 | | | | 1899–1952 | | | |
Net	% departures	Arrivals	Departures	Net	% departures	Arrivals	Departures	Net	% departures
-639	103.9	17,527	4,261	13,266	24.3	111,003	68,172	42,831	61.4
135,215	51.0	66,447	10,194	56,253	15.3	789,336	221,877	567,459	28.1
4,415	85.6	36,940	12,194	24,746	33.0	108,827	53,739	55,088	49.4
-3,531	170.1	12,031	1,397	10,634	11.6	46,323	22,745	23,578	49.1
-33,161	467.2	11,100	7,660	3,440	69.0	79,211	126,185	-46,974	159.3
-1,420	435.7	382	1,817	-1,435	475.7	9,039	6,660	2,379	73.7
-11,520	304.6	5,805	1,394	4,411	24.0	271,927	103,959	167,968	38.2
-208	171.7	195	186	9	95.4	9,699	7,066	2,633	72.9
7,087	8.0	4,379	313	4,066	7.2	88,214	12,143	76,071	13.8
3,998	36.4	3,572	601	2,971	16.8	112,116	27,817	84,299	24.8
23	98.3	1,116	953	163	85.4	24,529	21,348	3,181	87.0
239,348	2.0	—	—	—	—	2,082,136	100,257	1,981,879	4.8
1,404	88.7	19,637	580	19,057	3.0	191,334	45,918	145,416	24.0
-6,306	202.1	3,982	232	3,750	5.8	175,251	161,102	14,149	91.9
3,791	57.3	18,356	396	17,960	2.2	512,616	251,584	261,032	49.1
-1,934	277.3	566	129	437	22.8	53,792	19,622	34,170	36.5
410	90.3	30,119	84	30,035	0.3	297,631	69,866	227,765	23.5
4,397	67.1	22,670	348	22,322	1.5	528,057	323,854	204,203	61.3
7,308	77.8	178,640	1,466	177,174	0.8	1,694,891	614,777	1,080,114	36.3
-4,816	219.1	7,748	177	7,571	2.3	160,041	106,896	53,145	66.8
7,264	50.0	67,018	3,398	63,620	5.1	340,522	141,495	199,027	41.6
4,037	10.4	3,873	23	3,850	0.6	273,856	44,793	229,063	16.4
10,112	47.7	4,261	532	3,729	12.5	560,496	308,433	252,063	55.0
16,788	43.8	32,188	4,321	27,867	13.4	267,983	62,904	205,079	23.5
-977	114.6	3,363	602	2,761	17.9	236,977	73,693	163,284	31.1
121,289	15.7	62,338	9,126	53,212	14.6	621,390	110,307	511,083	17.8
294,598	21.3	201,096	6,474	194,622	3.2	1,892,151	344,255	1,547,896	18.2
76,902	37.4	40,428	10,079	30,349	24.9	1,119,561	283,622	835,939	25.3
199,511	33.1	178,891	28,017	150,874	15.7	1,544,733	387,984	1,156,749	25.1
239,936	10.6	74,719	4,640	70,079	6.2	1,151,826	133,157	1,018,669	11.6
146,119	19.8	53,039	5,028	48,011	9.5	676,335	100,540	575,795	14.9
8,489	22.9	5,935	596	5,339	10.0	60,037	8,362	51,675	13.9
-604	102.2	24,344	2,657	21,687	10.9	551,893	272,268	279,625	49.3
40,423	76.0	79,050	8,885	70,165	11.2	4,068,700	2,242,591	1,826,109	55.1
-10,179	208.0	9,202	3,023	6,179	32.9	204,869	83,119	121,750	40.6
-18,974	265.7	8,106	3,402	4,704	42.0	210,077	119,757	90,320	57.0
-621	106.0	13,997	4,702	9,295	33.6	159,408	43,839	115,569	27.5
2,364	62.5	93,863	29,464	64,399	31.4	141,162	52,269	88,893	37.0
1,480,388	38.2	1,396,923	169,351	1,227,572	12.1	21,427,949	7,178,975	14,248,974	33.5

statistics are debatable, the figures themselves are useful for peoples such as the Armenians, Slovaks, or Welsh, particularly when cross-classified by age, sex, country of last permanent residence, occupation, and literacy; the U.S. Immigration Commission of 1907–1910 usefully compiled much of this information. A summary of the statistics for 1899–1952 appears in Table 2.

Allegiance Designation by allegiance, common in census and migration statistics but not in vital records, is useful for reasonably coherent groups such as Italians or Germans after 1870, but is less valuable when an ethnic population is distributed over several countries. Between 1900 and 1940, for example, a Greek might emigrate with Greek, Italian, Romanian, Russian, or British nationality, depending on whether he was from Greece proper, the Dodecanese islands (Italian between the wars), Romania, the Crimea, or Cyprus. Identities are easier to determine in sovereign states retaining the notion of constituent "peoples" or "nations"; in the Ottoman Empire, for example, the Greeks in Asia Minor and Egypt were regarded as part of the Greek people even if second or third generation. Similarly, children of Russian colonists born in western or northern China usually retained their parental citizenship and arrived in the United States or Australia as Russian nationals, not as Chinese.

Allegiance, however, is too comprehensive a classification when applied to countries containing several major ethnic groups. Neither British nationality nor the more recent designation of citizenship of the United Kingdom and Colonies helps in unscrambling the English, Scottish, Irish, Welsh, Cornish, and Manx ethnic groups; nor does Yugoslav allegiance help separate out the Slovenes, Croats, Bosnian Muslims, Serbs, and Macedonians; nor Spanish allegiance, the Basques, Catalans, Galicians, and other Spaniards. In other situations, however, allegiance can be a valuable indicator, as when giving the correct ethnic classification to the many children born in the labor or refugee camps of Germany from 1942 to 1951 of parents displaced from Poland and other countries disrupted by World War II: in migration and census statistics based on birthplace, these appear under the heading German, but in the U.S. citizenship statistics they appear in their parental category of Polish, Czech, Latvian, and so on. When working with birthplace statistics to estimate the number of Poles who entered the United States from 1948 to 1952, it is necessary to include the estimates for these German-born Polish children. Conversely, when using allegiance statistics as a basis for estimating ethnic origins, it is important to include those whose countries have stripped them of citizenship and nationality and cast them, under the protection of the United Nations High

Commissioner for Refugees, into the category of "Stateless"; alternative statistics such as birthplace are necessary as a guide for reallocation to the appropriate ethnic group.

Allegiance statistics provide one measure of immigrant absorption or integration; a comparison between the census total of those born in Italy, for instance, and the total of those retaining Italian citizenship gives some indication of the speed with which first-generation Italians are severing political ties with their country of origin and forging new ones with their country of settlement. The U.S. census tables often register this trend for the major groups by presenting the totals of those naturalized as U.S. citizens, those with first papers, and those still alien. These totals can then be related to statistics given since 1923 by the Immigration and Naturalization Service, of persons naturalized by country or region of former allegiance (see Appendix II, Table 20), and since 1952 of permanent resident aliens by nationality.

Birthplace Although many countries have long asked census questions about country of birth—the United States since 1850—it is only since World War II that reliable statistics of birthplace have been produced by U.S. immigration authorities. If there is no direct recording of ethnic origin, birthplace is the most useful category available, partly because it changes only with changes in international boundaries and not, like allegiance statistics, with changes in citizenship. Furthermore, because birthplace is often given in vital records—marriage and death certificates, for instance—it enables one to link various sets of statistics together. In addition, a comparison of census and immigration birthplace statistics indicates the extent to which each ethnic group is losing population by emigration (see below).

Like allegiance, however, country-of-birth statistics do not normally distinguish ethnic groups like the French or Spanish Basques or the Croats or Serbs. This defect, however, may be overcome by more detailed census questions and analysis. In some U.S. figures, for example, Scotland, Wales, Northern Ireland, and England appear as separate birthplaces. Like allegiance, too, country of birth is sometimes irrelevant to ethnic origin. Thus, some people born in India or Indonesia are children of colonial civil servants and not East Indian or Indonesian.

Country of Last Permanent Residence Sometimes the only statistics available for assessing immigrant origins relate to the country of last permanent residence (or next residence for emigrants); since 1921 this has usually meant residence of a year or more. Country of residence is not necessarily a good guide to ethnic origin: many Armenians migrate to the Americas or Australia after spending years in Lebanon or Egypt, Russians after years in China or France, Italians or Greeks after years in West Germany or the Netherlands. Researchers of ethnic origins prefer statistics of allegiance or birthplace. Residence figures, however, can be useful in conjunction with birthplace or allegiance in assessing the character of a refugee movement, as with Vietnamese coming from Thailand or Singapore. For departures, they are useful for gauging the next stage of settlement, as with those many British migrants who spend a few years in Australia before moving on to settle in North America or New Zealand. The United

States has published statistics of immigrants by country of last (and next) permanent residence since 1906, but they are best used in conjunction with the race-or-people statistics of 1899–1952 or the birthplace statistics since 1945.

Country of Origin From 1820 to 1906, under the provisions of the U.S. Immigration Act of 1819, captains of incoming vessels were required to hand to the responsible port official a list of passengers showing sex, age, occupation, and "the country to which they severally belong." Apparently ship captains and officials interpreted this last variously as country of birth, country of allegiance, or country of last permanent residence. Consequently, although these statistics are adequate for revealing major trends, such as the shift of emigration in the 1880s from northwestern Europe to southern and eastern Europe, they cannot be used with more precision. However, they are all that are available until the race-or-people statistics of 1899, and they are summarized, with country of last residence statistics, in Appendix II, Table 3.

Naturalization Records Where census and migration statistics are not helpful for details of ethnic origin, one can turn to naturalization records, that is, the applications submitted for naturalization as distinct from the general statistics published by the Immigration and Naturalization Service on countries of former allegiance. These application records give details of both allegiance and birthplace, the latter often by township or district, which enable one to subdivide larger groupings, for example, the Spanish-born into those born in Basque country or Catalonia, or the Yugoslav-born into those born in Slovene, Croat, Serb, or Macedonian areas. These data also provide a means of access to the dialect and regional groupings of Italy or the Netherlands and to smaller ethnic communities generally. They cannot be used, however, for groups such as the Armenians or Assyrians who were driven out of their ancestral areas during World War I and scattered about the world. The naturalization records can help when there are distinctive names—as with many Armenians and Jews—but there are traps here too. Working with naturalization records is a long and tedious, though rewarding, procedure. It is much easier when the records are held centrally by federal or state authorities—as they have been in the United States by the INS since 1906.

Two Major Problems

With all statistics on the first generation—whether they be census, immigration, naturalization, or vital—two groups pose serious difficulties to establishing accurate counts.

Illegal Immigrants Illegal immigrants, often called undocumented migrants or illegal aliens, not only avoid immigration controls and arrive without permission and without record but also may avoid any official notice of their presence, even after many years in the United States. Whenever substantial penalties exist against clandestine immigration (deportation, imprisonment, or heavy fine), such people tend to avoid official recordings, whether census, vital, taxation, or social security; this is the main reason why it is difficult to estimate accurately the number of Mexicans in the United States. (*See* Mexicans.)

Amnesties can help here, though some shy and cautious illegals are suspicious that these are no more than

cunning devices to flush them into the open and then deport them. Their suspicions may be aggravated by some of the amnesty phrases to the effect that habitual lawbreakers and persons of bad character will not be protected; people accustomed to moving illegally across an international boundary often feel that amnesty authorities would certainly consider them habitual lawbreakers. Amnesties normally bring forward only a fraction of the illegal immigrants thought to be in the country. Even so, the number of those granted amnesty rights should be added to existing ethnic statistics.

Departures The other counting problem is posed by immigrants who leave the United States. Countries of settlement naturally focus on processing and recording new arrivals who are thought to be permanent additions to the society. Some of these, however, eventually decide to leave, either to return to their former country (return migration) or else to try some other country of settlement (on-migration). If such remigration is considerable—and for many years in the United States it was about one-third of immigrant arrivals—then the immigration statistics are an unreliable guide to the actual numbers of any particular ethnic group who are settling permanently. Some researchers rely on census rather than immigration totals: the decennial censuses, they argue, reveal the real growth of an ethnic population because they allow for deaths and because most of those who are likely to leave again will already have done so. Other researchers think that a census total, particularly one taken after some years of heavy immigration, may contain many persons likely to leave in the near future; also, that a proper assessment [of how the different ethnic populations are settling and integrating] should include estimates of the numbers who arrive intending permanent settlement but who later change their minds and remigrate. The U.S. Immigration Commission, for instance, estimated that for the years 1908–1910 only about one in ten Armenian, Czech, Jewish, and Irish immigrants subsequently left, compared with half or more of the Croats, Italians, Japanese, and Hungarians.

Assessing remigration can be a complex demographic exercise. There are two main methods involved: examining actual records of departures and using census totals as a basis for estimating immigrant loss. The first is possible only in countries that keep reliable departure records. Canada, which long ago gave up trying to record movement across the Canadian-American border, relies on U.S. immigration statistics. Even the United States, which for some years published ethnic details of emigrant aliens (that is, aliens who had had permanent residence in the United States and were leaving for permanent residence abroad), in recent years has done little more than publish general totals of aliens departing and passengers leaving, by port of proposed disembarkation.

The census method works in two ways. One may take, for example, the Italian-born population of the United States in 1960, subtract estimated deaths in that group for 1960–1970, add the number of Italian-born immigrants for 1960–1970, and from the total deduct the Italian-born population recorded in the 1970 Census; the difference, after allowing for Italian-born residents temporarily out of the United States and Italian-born visitors temporarily in the country at census

time, is the estimate of immigrant loss. The other method is similar but uses the census statistics of Italian-born persons by year of immigration and, after allowing for deaths and temporary movements, relates those subtotals to annual totals of Italian-born immigrants; this result gives the immigrant loss for each year of arrival.

THE LATER GENERATIONS

Direct recording of immigration and questions on allegiance or birthplace in census and vital records help mainly with the first generation and sometimes, via questions on parentage, with the second. Other questions are necessary when accounting for the third and later generations.

Paternal Line Origin For many years Canada recorded "Racial Origin," based on the ethnic origin of the paternal ancestor first arriving. This once had much value but was abandoned in the 1960s, partly because of the general reaction against "racism" and partly because increasing intermarriage had rendered it less meaningful; a person only one-sixteenth Welsh, for instance, would be recorded as Welsh simply because his parental great-great-grandfather had arrived from Wales, even though his other fifteen great-great-grandparents might have included ten who were English, two Scottish, one German, one French, and one Norwegian. Such a question has never been asked in the United States.

Surname An estimate of the ethnic origins of the U.S. population was made to establish the immigration quotas mandated by the 1924 Immigration Act. Statisticians examined surnames recorded in the 1790 Census, divided them into English, Irish, German, French, Spanish, Dutch, and other categories, and used the results to quantify the ethnic origins of the 1790 population and its descendants born in America. The surname method has been used since 1950 to identify Mexicans in the Southwest, and a mass of information is consequently available on people with Spanish surnames.

There are, however, serious problems with ethnic identification by surname. First, many names change, simply and easily as a matter of convenience, from the ethnic form to that of the dominant language—LeBlanc to White or Schmidt to Smith, for instance. Second, many people with Slavic, Greek, or other names that English-speakers sometimes find difficult to pronounce or spell may change their names—Karamourtopoulos to Paul, or Wysynski to Wise—as may those who feel that their career will be better served by an English name. Very recently there have been cases of the reverse kind—people who change their names to qualify for affirmative action. Third, some English names have exact matches in other languages: Lee is a common surname in both English and Chinese; Finger may be German or English. Last, when intermarriage is common, surnames—like paternal-line origin—can be misleading; for a person one-sixteenth Welsh in descent to be classified as Welsh solely because his surname is Lewis can be anomalous.

ETHNIC LANGUAGE

Several countries have asked census questions on ethnic language, to assess the rapidity of assimilation over the generations, to assess the language needs of the school population, or to subdivide very general birth-

place information into more meaningful ethnic categories. This last was the main aim of the U.S. Immigration Commission when it recommended that the 1910 Census ask a question on "nationality or mother tongue," beginning the series of mother-tongue questions that have appeared in later U.S. censuses (except 1950). Because of the overriding concern at that time with mass immigration from southern and eastern Europe, and the relatively small immigration from Africa, southern and eastern Asia, and the Pacific, the analysis was confined to the white population of foreign birth and, sometimes, foreign parentage. In 1960 the inquiry was extended to all foreign-born persons, and in 1970 to all generations of all origins.

Changes also occurred in the formulation of the language question. In 1910 there was confusion, with some enumerators asking immigrants about "customary" language, others asking about "ethnic stock or the ancestral language." Responsible census officers, aware that many immigrants abandoned their ethnic language within a few years of arrival, felt the original purpose could best be met by directing the question at language of upbringing; by 1930 they were framing the questions to discover the language spoken by immigrants before coming to the United States—amended in 1970 to language spoken at home as a child.

By the 1960s there was also growing interest in language retention and in comparing the mother tongue with the language usually spoken at home as an adult. The first Current Population Survey on Ethnic Origin (November 1969), besides its main question on ethnic origin or identification, asked questions both on language spoken as a child and on language usually spoken in the home. Table 3 summarizes the differences for four major groups.

Only about half of those giving Spanish, Italian, and Polish as their ethnic origin had spoken the ethnic language at home as children, and a mere quarter of the Germans. Of those with a mother tongue other than English, only 5 percent of Germans, 11 percent of Poles, and 20 percent of Italians had kept it as their usual language. Spanish-speakers, partly because they are more recent arrivals and more concentrated geographically, showed over 90 percent still using the mother tongue as their usual language. These are rough estimates; sampling variation accounts for some of the difference, and so do changes in ways of answering the questions. Unfortunately, the mother-tongue question was dropped from the 1980 Census, precluding further analysis of language retention patterns.

The statistics in Table 3 also suggest that language questions, though useful for identifying some smaller

ethnic groups (particularly long-existing, solid groups in relatively small geographic areas, such as the Pennsylvania Germans), are much less useful for long-established groups that have been steadily losing their ethnic language, unless reinforced with direct questions on ethnic origin as well. They are of almost no use for groups who arrived speaking English—the Scots, for instance—nor are they much use when tabulated in broad categories like Yugoslav, Arabic, or Chinese. The 1970 U.S. Census does quite well here, not only distinguishing Slovene from Serbo-Croatian but also giving Dalmatian, though not Macedonian (see Appendix II, Table 14). It also distinguishes Mandarin and Cantonese from other Chinese dialects and divides Arabic into Egyptian, Iraqi, Near Eastern, North African, and "Other"; although these Arabic divisions are inadequate for distinguishing the various Lebanese, Syrian, Jordanian, and Saudi Arabian ethnic communities, they nevertheless help to pinpoint areas where the ethnic community (often a Maronite, Melkite, or Druse group from Lebanon) is still maintaining its ancestral tongue. The census also distinguishes Ukrainian and Georgian from other Russian languages but, unfortunately, does not show Catalan or Maltese.

RELIGION

Though normally asked for other reasons, official questions on religious affiliation can be very useful in identifying ethnic communities, both old and new, especially in countries that do not ask questions on ethnic origin or ethnic language. Information on religion is essential to distinguish South European Jews from Slovenes and Croats (usually Catholic) and from Serbs and Macedonians (usually Orthodox), or to estimate the numbers of Orthodox Greeks, Coptic Egyptians, and Muslim Egyptians arriving from Syria and Egypt. Many countries, however, do not ask questions on religious affiliation, partly because some citizens consider them an invasion of personal privacy while others, remembering the persecution of religious bodies by some governments in the not-too-distant past, are reluctant to identify with any particular organization or faith. In Australia, Canada, and elsewhere, such feelings are acknowledged by making the question voluntary; in Australia about 90 percent answer it. The United States, with its strong tradition of separation of church and state, has never asked such a question in a decennial census. The census bureau once asked it in a voluntary sample survey, in March 1957; although 96 percent of those asked gave their religion with little hesitation, the opposition from some organizations was considerable, and the survey was not repeated.

Additionally, at intervals between 1850 and 1936 the bureau asked religious bodies to respond to a Census of Religious Organizations, which collected anonymous information on numbers of pastors, members, Sunday-school children, church buildings, and other categories, all by geographic location. Since 1936 the official *Statistical Abstract* has employed data from the *Yearbook of American and Canadian Churches* published by the National Council of Churches in New York; this also summarizes information on pastors, members, and schools. These statistics, together with the brief outlines of history and doctrine contained in the censuses of religious organizations, are particularly useful for

---

Table 3. Language retention of four major American ethnic-origin groups, in thousands, 1969.

Ethnic origin	Total	Mother tongue[a]	Percentage of total	Usual language[b]	Percentage of mother tongue
German	19,961	4,809	24	251	5
Spanish	9,230	4,878	53	4,498	92
Italian	7,239	3,147	43	631	20
Polish	4,021	1,982	49	220	11

Source: U.S. Bureau of the Census, *Current Population Report on Ethnic Origin, November 1969* (Washington, D.C., 1969).

a. Number whose mother tongue was ethnic language.

b. Number using mother tongue as usual language as adults.

smaller ethnic churches. Statistics since 1936 are less readily available for smaller churches such as the Nestorian Church of the East (Assyrian) or the Coptic Orthodox Church of Egypt.

In any case such statistics, though useful for locating particular ethnic communities, are unreliable as a basis for estimating group size, not only because individuals leave their ethnic church or change faiths but also because churches have very different ways of estimating membership. Most Protestant bodies count those who have attained full membership (usually at about age 13 though sometimes later), whereas the Roman Catholic, Lutheran, and Episcopal churches count the number of baptized persons, even infants. In addition, the membership figures omit those who have ceased participation in church services or affairs and therefore do not cover persons who, though no longer active members, would report it as their faith if asked in a census. Thus the 1957 sample survey returned 8.4 million persons aged 14 and over giving their faith as Lutheran, whereas the 1957 official Lutheran return for all members was only 6.9 million. It is clear that statistics of Lutheran membership are not a reliable guide to the number of immigrants, and their descendants, deriving from the Lutheran areas of Germany and Scandinavia. The Christian Orthodox church counts may be more accurate, for each church usually represents a clearly identifiable ethnic population (Russian, Serbian, Greek, Romanian, or Bulgarian, for example) and counts as members all those known to belong to the ethnic community. But statistics may be treacherous here too. The 1950 U.S. Census recorded 364,000 first- and second-generation persons of Greek birth; to these should be added the first- and second-generation persons born in Cyprus, Romania, Turkey, and elsewhere who identify as Greek in the United States and numbers of the third and later generations. But the Greek Orthodox membership for 1950 was given as only 300,000. Even so, the statistics are helpful as a guide to the number who maintain an important ethnic activity.

The Jews for a time were in a special position as a target population for official records. During the large-scale immigration of Jewish families—many fleeing to the United States from the Russian persecutions of the 1880s onward—some American leaders were anxious to know how many Jews were actually arriving; with no religious or ethnic question in either census or immigration records, they decided to treat Jews as a separate ethnic group. They instructed immigration officials to ask such questions on ethnicity, language, or religion as were necessary to establish Jewish identity; hence the category "Hebrew" in the race-or-people statistics of 1899 onward. At the hearings conducted by the Immigration Commission of 1907–1910, many Jews protested the practice, especially certain leaders of the Jewish communities of New York and Chicago; they contended that Jews were not a distinct race in the ethnological sense but should be counted as either of Jewish faith or of Russian, Polish, or some other country of birth. The commission, determined to have some record of Jewish immigration, rejected these contentions, and it was only in 1944 that the Immigration and Naturalization Service omitted Hebrew from the race-or-people statistics and distributed Jews according to country of birth.

Some estimates of Jewish numbers have been available from the statistics of religious bodies, which keep track of the number of Jews estimated to be in communities where synagogues have been established. Jewish officials in 1957 returned a membership count of 5.5 million, but the 1957 sample survey returned only 3.9 million aged 14 and over (compared with the 1.7 million returned by the 1970 Census for persons with Yiddish or Hebrew mother tongue). The differences among these figures raise—and reflect—the whole knotty question of Jewish ethnic identification, particularly for those men and women who consider themselves agnostics or atheists but nonetheless Jewish in some sense. This is a problem that persists all over the world, which is part of the reason for the series of surveys now being sponsored by Jewish organizations in many countries to establish more accurate totals.

RACE

Although it has been much challenged and debated in scientific and political circles, the term "race" has been an official census or migration category in some countries for many decades. In some cases, race can be a useful measure of ethnic origin, numbers, and survival. At other times it can be most misleading, notably at present with the Afro-American and, to some extent, American Indian populations.

The U.S. census recording of race illustrates the difficulty. Until 1850 censuses usually divided Afro-Americans into "Slave" and "Free Colored," sometimes including detribalized Indians with the latter. In 1850, with more precise instructions, the census schedule provided for free persons to be counted as "White," "Black," or "Mulatto"; the figures for mulattos were not published, however, and the main tables continued to designate the population as "White," "Slave," and "Free Colored." In 1860 the census distinguished "Civilized Indians" (those required to pay taxes because they were not living on reservations, some 44,000 in all) and Chinese and also gave the statistics for blacks and mulattos for 1850 and 1860: 3.23 and 3.85 million blacks and 406,000 and 588,000 mulattos. The main tables, however, retained the headings "Slave" and "Free Colored." The 1870 Census added Japanese and tried to subdivide "Civilized Indians" into "Pure Indians" and "Half-breeds"; the decision as to whether half-breeds should be "classified with respect to the superior or the inferior breed" (*A Compendium of the Ninth Census*, Washington, D.C., 1872) was left to the enumerators' evaluations on the basis of appearance and lifestyle. The 1880 Census grouped mulattos with Negroes under "Colored," avowedly on the precedent of some southern states that included in that category anyone of Negro descent, even if only one-eighth. The 1890 officials, however, disliked this crude procedure and asked questions to establish finer distinctions; 6.3 million Negroes, 957,000 mulattos, 105,000 quadroons, and 70,000 octoroons were identified. In the end, however, census authorities admitted that these divisions were valueless and for purposes of analysis put them all together with the Chinese, Japanese, and Indians under the general heading "Colored."

By 1900 the census officers, obviously influenced by current anthropological notions of race, decided to abandon all these de facto definitions and determined to

assess the U.S. population in terms of the then-presumed four great races: the Caucasian or White, Negro or Black, Mongolian or Yellow, and Indian or Red. The Chinese and Japanese appeared as subdivisions of Mongolian, and it was firmly decided to use the term Negro. How absurd, argued the report, to go on using the ambiguous term "Colored" when the 1890 Census had used it to mean all nonwhite persons, when in the West Indies it meant part-European, part-Negro, and when in the earlier censuses, in some southern states, and in some other countries it meant anyone with a Negro ancestor. It was thought appropriate to classify people of at least one-eighth Negro descent as Negro, including those of mixed Negro-Indian ancestry. The 1910 officials were slightly less definite: they reverted to "Black" (7.8 million) and "Mulatto" (2.1 million) but avoided the term "Colored"; their main divisions were "White," "Negro," "Indian," "Chinese," "Japanese," and "All Other" (including subdivisions for Hawaiians, part-Hawaiians, and other races). This set the precedent for even the most recent censuses. The Indian population was treated separately in a special census that covered both the "civilized" and those on reservations, some 266,000 in all, and provided details on tribes, languages, and areas.

It continued to be the responsibility of the enumerator to determine the race of the person and family, mainly from looks but partly from lifestyle. Mexicans were put into the "Other Races" category in 1930 but afterward were counted with whites. Filipinos appeared separately in 1920; Koreans, Hindus, Malays, Siamese, and Samoans also appeared, but only in general tables. In 1960, however, enumerators were instructed to take into account how the person or family identified itself, and in 1970 self-identification was introduced. Modern census reports hasten to explain that the term "race" has no presumed scientific exactness but is simply how the respondents identify themselves in terms of commonly held notions of race. However that may be, it is clear that anyone wishing to use racial designations as an aid to understanding American ethnic groups has to interpret the census statistics with great care and caution.

Censuses do not always make the racial distinctions sufficiently fine for comprehensive work on ethnic minorities; for instance, the published statistics of the 1970 U.S. Census, in addition to the Asian groupings, list only "White," "Negro," "Indian," and "Other," with no reference to smaller racial groups. Sometimes it is possible to use race and birthplace together to estimate an ethnic population; at other times this is impossible. The Samoan communities in Hawaii, California, and Washington State, for instance, are not identified by race or birthplace; nor do they appear in the "Other" category in the combined race/birthplace table that deals with foreign stock only, for most Samoans, deriving from a U.S. territory, do not count as foreign.

Ethnic Origin: Self-Identification The shifts in racial description are part of a more general move to self-identification, partly because this fits better with modern notions of a pluralistic democratic society and partly because it is much easier to manage when census schedules are completed by the householder instead of by an enumerator. Under the ethnic-origin category, introduced in the Current Population Survey in 1969 and included in the 1980 U.S. Census, the respondent is asked to describe his ancestry as he perceives it, whether it is based on his paternal line, culture or upbringing, the ethnic group with which he wishes to identify, or even a mixture of several origins and cultures. This approach to assessing ethnic origins is much more relevant than birthplace and parentage in a society where over 80 percent of the population belong to the third or a later generation. It is also less offensive; because they are free to refuse to answer and free to choose what origin they please, respondents—unlike many immigrants in earlier days—no longer have to accept an ethnic category imposed by officials without regard to whether they themselves think it scientifically, politically or socially unsound.

The main difficulty with this mode of distinguishing ethnic origin, apart from sampling variation, changes in respondent fashion, and the difficulties of handling ethnic mixtures, is that it is not always useful in subsequent analysis, in relating totals of ethnic origin to ethnic customs and cultures. For instance, so much of modern American social organization and values derives from the English, Scottish, German, Scandinavian, and Dutch migrations that is more difficult to relate these origins to particular cultural characteristics and family customs than is the case with smaller, more compact ethnic groups such as the Greeks, Armenians, or Japanese. But the *Current Population Reports* publish details on only eight major groups (see Table 1); only the Hispanic population, in line with the current tendency in the United States to treat Latin Americans with special sensitivity, is usefully subdivided into Mexican, Cuban, Puerto Rican, Central or South American, and Other Spanish. Other, smaller ethnic groups are included with those reporting two or more ethnic origins, and with racially distinct groups such as the Negroes or Chinese, in the large, amorphous category "Other"; this last category contains nearly half the total and is therefore useless for ethnic analysis. It is to be hoped that future censuses will offer additional, more finely subdivided, ethnic tabulations.

THE USE OF OFFICIAL STATISTICS

Census Coding and Publication It is important to realize that published tables do not necessarily provide the full number of categories available; if the census organization publishes summary tables based on much fuller but unpublished birthplace or racial tables, it is sometimes possible to obtain more detailed information from unpublished statistics on a particular ethnic grouping. If, however (as often happens), the original, detailed categories were combined at the coding stage— so that Samoans, for example, were coded with "Other" from the beginning—there is no way of obtaining the information unless the census organization permits work to be done on the original census questionnaires.

Combining the Statistics In statistical work on ethnic minorities the best results come from working with all the statistics combined. To assess the population increase of a particular grouping, say the Filipinos, one can take the 80,000 increase in Filipino-born persons in the United States between 1960 (104,843) and 1970 (184,842) and relate it to the influx of 80,000 Filipino-born immigrants during that decade; after allowing for deaths, one can conclude not only that few Filipinos

were returning home but also that some were entering in nonimmigrant categories and then staying on.

Or one might be interested in the old Yugoslav population of California, which started coming before the gold rush of 1849 and developed strong clusters in San Francisco, Santa Clara, Santa Cruz, and San Diego. The immigrants came mainly from the Croatian valleys and islands of the central Dalmatian coast, though some were from predominantly Serb (Montenegrin) districts in southern Dalmatia, notably the Konovalji running south from Dubrovnik. This Dalmatian population of California, though maintaining strong loyalties to their towns and districts (or islands) of origin, were also conscious of their common Dalmatian heritage, with its partly Italianate and Austrian culture; they were also early supporters of the South Slav, later Yugoslav, movement and early formed South Slavonic organizations—the Slavonic Illyrian Mutual Benefit Society of California dates back to 1857. Since World War II they have been overshadowed by the large refugee influx of fiercely nationalistic Croats and Serbs, but some of the older families still retain a Dalmatian identity and outlook. (See Croats; see also Serbs.)

When studying this group it is possible to obtain a general outline of the larger Slavic population involved by combining the statistics available for Dalmatians and for Bosnians and Herzegovinians (a collective category published in the race-or-people statistics from 1899 to 1952) with census information on persons born in Austria-Hungary and, later, Yugoslavia, who settled in the various counties and towns of California. Combining these results in turn with census information on those indicating Dalmatian as their mother tongue produces the information that even in 1970 some still thought of themselves as Dalmatians with a Dalmatian language. Naturalization and marriage records of more densely settled counties such as Santa Cruz reveal not only their villages or towns of origin and their occupations, but also the extent to which the Dalmatian subgroup is maintaining itself by inmarriage. Interviews with long-settled families provide additional information on the group's migration history and the extent to which members still think of themselves as Dalmatians (or as persons from one of the smaller areas such as Brač or Korčula), or as Croats or Serbs.

NONOFFICIAL ESTIMATES AND SURVEYS

Ethnic Estimates Having exhausted official statistics and records, the ethnic researcher may turn to ethnic organizations—churches, clubs, press, and radio—where, however, he often finds an anomaly. On the one hand, the estimate of ethnic numbers given by organization officers often far exceeds the researcher's estimate based on official sources; on the other hand, the organization membership lists combined give totals far lower than the researcher's estimate. Ethnic officials explain this inconsistency on the grounds that their membership lists show only interested heads of families (their wives and children are included in ethnic affairs as a matter of course) and that many heads of families are insufficiently involved to attend meetings and pay fees but are interested enough to appear at great national gatherings or festivals and to observe basic ethnic customs. Even so, their estimates of ethnic totals are often much too large: first, they include persons who

have either long since left the area or renounced all connection with ethnic matters; second, they often include persons of mixed ethnic origin who identify with another ethnic community; third, they sometimes calculate numbers of children by assuming the large family size typical of days long past. In addition, officials of ethnic organizations often display a tendency to reach for a large, nice-sounding number. Some Italians in Australia claim that the nation's population of 14 million contains 1 million of Italian descent; careful estimates, however, based on net migration and census statistics over the past 60 years and on the records of parental birthplace of children born in Australia, give no more than 500,000—and some of these are of part-Italian origin only and do not identify themselves with the Italian population. Despite frequent exaggerations, however, ethnic estimates can be very useful supplements to official statistics.

Sample Surveys The last common method of estimating ethnic numbers and delineating the boundaries of an ethnic community is the survey. Representative samples of the national population have great value. (See Survey Research.) However, their utility is limited to the very largest ethnic groups; smaller groups have too few members for reliable analyses. Surveys of local communities are an alternative. Representative samples aim at discovering whether an ethnic population is maintaining traditional customs and occupations or is becoming assimilated in terms of behavior and intermarriage. In this case the population to be examined may first be identified through membership lists of ethnic organizations, by surname counts (if ethnic surnames are distinctive) in electoral and telephone lists, and by examination of employment lists of businesses dominant in the ethnic area or, if the ethnic population is widely dispersed, dominant in traditional ethnic activities, as with the Chinese in the import-export trade with China. The questionnaire itself usually asks for other ethnic families known to the respondent; after any new names have been checked against the working list, they may be added to the sample. An alternative survey approach may sample the residential blocks in areas of ethnic concentration and establish ethnic population size and characteristics from selected households.

The main danger in these methods, apart from mistakes in sampling procedure and analysis, is that the initial population tends to be biased toward the ethnically active: those who are members of ethnic organizations, who keep their ethnic surname, or who live in the main ethnic area. Concentrating on these people means missing those who are much more assimilated to the mainstream of life in the new country or who live outside the main ethnic areas. Census statistics on birthplace or mother tongue (or religion) by district of census enumeration can be of great help in identifying areas with only a few persons of that particular origin; though these target respondents may be difficult to find, success will often follow inquiries at local churches, shops, post offices, or schools. The original sample is thus augmented with a number of people who are marginal to the main ethnic community. The influence of ethnic organizations cannot be assessed accurately without an indication of the attitudes and activities of some of these marginal families; this enables the

researcher to review the claims of ethnic leaders on the importance of ethnic festivals and customs and on the numbers attending or observing. Surveying those with only marginal ethnicity provides another check on estimates of total numbers.

CONCLUSION

This review of the sources and problems involved in estimating ethnic numbers and distribution leaves several important questions unanswered. First, who should be included? Should it be those who, if not active in ethnic affairs, at least identify as members of the ethnic grouping? Or should all those be included who, though they may no longer identify as ethnics, are descended from families who once so identified? The answer depends on the researcher's purpose; if he wants to estimate the total of those who can, if they wish, claim full membership as Jews, he will remember Jewish law and take all those known to be descended by maternal line from Jewish ancestors, regardless of whether they or their mothers or grandmothers identified as Jews. Similarly, an official of the Kuomintang required to count the number of Chinese citizens will include all those of Chinese descent whether they identify as Chinese or not. Conversely, someone seeking information on an ethnic language and culture will confine research to those who identify as ethnics and will ignore the marginal and lost. A demographer, sociologist, or political scientist will count both ways—by descent and by identification—if he wants to establish the differences between the two populations and assess whether the ethnically involved population may become active enough to reach out and affect the whole.

Second is the problem of mixed origin. Where there is some mixing, for example, between the Italians and Irish of Sydney, Australia, is it more reasonable to count the children of mixed marriages as both Italian and Irish? Or is it better to divide them between the two parent populations, or to attempt the long and complex task of discovering the culture in which the children of each family are actually reared? In Australia the answer would be based on evidence that there the children of mixed marriages normally are reared according to the mother's language and customs, particularly when, as frequently happens among Italians, there are many more male than female immigrants, and the surplus males either return home, stay single, or marry into another ethnic group and permit their children to be reared by their wives. Australian scholars lacking precise details about individual upbringing therefore count an Australian-born child with an Italian father and Irish-Australian mother as part of the Irish-Australian population, not the Italian. This practice assumes that the cases in which the Italian father's language and culture dominate are counterbalanced by cases in which an Italian mother's language and culture does not predominate. Some such assumption is necessary to avoid the anomaly of ethnic population totals that far exceed the population of the entire area or country.

On the other hand, some do not view multiple ethnic identification as an anomaly. Many third-, fourth-, or later-generation persons willingly identify with several ethnic cultures (as the *Current Population Reports* show). For instance, a person of mixed English, Scottish, German, and Ukrainian origin may belong to both a Scottish and a Ukrainian dancing group, sympathize wholeheartedly with struggles for Scottish and Ukrainian independence, yet most appreciate the cooking skills learned from a German grandmother and the quiet dignity of an English grandfather. In such a case, the personal importance of identifying with all four origins, if identification is the main interest, outweighs the contradiction that the final total of ethnic origins far exceeds the total population. Demographers to whom accurate totals are of chief importance might respond to such a situation by calculating the proportions each origin bears to the enlarged total and applying these to the actual total, thus producing a measure of the contribution each ethnic origin makes to the population. This was the method of the U.S. census officers who were asked in 1924 to calculate the national origins of the population as a basis for the immigration quotas; it took several years to estimate the ethnic origins of the 1790 U.S. population and work through to 1920, adding in the net immigration for each decade and distributing all births and deaths appropriately. The resulting general shape of the population, with respect to major origins such as English, German, Irish, Italian, Russian, and so on, did not differ significantly from the proportions produced by the recent *Current Population Reports.*

Finally, in dealing with ethnic minorities, one has to accept the reality that there is no final certainty in the matter; that estimates, no matter how well based and researched, are only estimates. In practice, those who constantly deal with the statistics and who also research the life and activities of the various ethnic groupings gradually develop a sense of when estimates are much too high or low and make adjustments accordingly. Because every group is different, there are no final rules to govern them all. The research approach adopted for a geographically concentrated and culturally homogeneous group such as the Hutterites differs greatly from that for a fragmented and dispersed people such as the Gypsies; the approach for a group with a long history of preserving a socioreligious identity against persecution (the Armenians, say) must be very different from that for a people relatively free from persecution such as the Swedish Lutherans. The complexities make it a fascinating exercise to fit the estimates all together and compare the result with the census count of total population, whether it be for a county, a metropolitan area, a state, or an entire nation. This particular exercise is rarely performed, but it is nevertheless worthwhile.

Bibliography

In addition to the sources cited in the text, see Imre Ferenczi and W.F. Willcox, *International Migrations* (National Bureau of Economic Research, New York), vol. I, *Statistics* (1929); vol. II, *Interpretations* (1931); and E.P. Hutchinson, "Notes on Immigration Statistics of the United States," *Journal of the American Statistical Association* 53 (December 1958): 963–1025. See also two articles by William Petersen, "Religious Statistics in the United States," *Journal for the Scientific Study of Religion* 1 (1965): 165–178, and "The Classification of Subnations in Hawaii," *American Sociological Review* 34 (December 1969): 863–877.

CHARLES A. PRICE

Table 1. Population, by sex and race, 1790–1970.

Source: U.S. Bureau of the Census, *Historical Statistics of the United States, Colonial Times to 1970,* Bicentennial edition (Washington, D.C., 1975). pt. 1, series A 91–104.

Year	Male							Female						
	All races	White	Negro[1]	Other races				All races	White	Negro[1]	Other races			
				Total[2]	Indian	Japanese	Chinese				Total[2]	Indian	Japanese	Chinese
	91	92	93	94	95	96	97	98	99	100	101	102	103	104
1970[3]	98,912,192	86,720,987	10,748,316	1,442,889	388,691	271,300	228,565	104,299,734	91,027,988	11,831,973	1,439,773	404,039	319,990	206,497
1960*	88,331,494	78,367,149	9,113,408	850,937	263,369	224,828	135,549	90,991,681	80,464,583	9,758,423	768,675	260,222	239,504	101,743
1960	87,864,510	78,153,040	9,105,702	605,768	255,677	124,323	115,849	90,599,726	80,301,916	9,754,415	543,395	252,998	135,736	83,109
1950	74,833,239	67,129,192	7,298,722	405,325	178,824	76,649	77,008	75,864,122	67,812,836	7,743,564	307,722	164,586	65,119	40,621
1940	66,061,592	59,448,548	6,269,038	344,006	171,427	71,967	57,389	65,607,683	58,766,322	6,596,480	244,881	162,542	54,980	20,115
1930	62,137,080	55,922,528	5,855,669	358,883	170,350	81,771	59,802	60,637,966	54,364,212	6,035,474	238,280	162,047	57,063	15,152
1920	53,900,431	48,430,655	5,209,436	260,340	125,068	72,707	53,891	51,810,189	46,390,260	5,253,695	166,234	119,369	38,303	7,748
1910	47,332,277	42,178,245	4,885,881	268,151	135,133	63,070	66,856	44,639,989	39,553,712	4,941,882	144,395	130,550	9,087	4,675
1900	38,816,448	34,201,735	4,386,547	228,166	119,484	23,341	85,341	37,178,127	32,607,461	4,447,447	123,219	117,712	985	4,522
1890	32,237,101	28,270,379	3,735,603	231,119	125,719	1,780	103,620	30,710,613	26,830,879	3,753,073	126,661	122,534	259	3,868
1880	25,518,820	22,130,900	3,253,115	134,805	33,985	134	100,686	24,636,963	21,272,070	3,327,678	37,215	32,422	14	4,779
1870	19,493,565	17,029,088	2,393,263	71,214	12,534	47	58,633	19,064,806	16,560,289	2,486,746	17,771	13,197	8	4,566
1860	16,085,204	13,811,387	2,216,744	57,073	23,924		33,149	15,358,117	13,111,150	2,225,086	21,881	20,097		1,784
1850	11,837,660	10,026,402	1,811,258					11,354,216	9,526,666	1,827,550				
1840	8,688,532	7,255,544	1,432,988					8,380,921	6,940,261	1,440,660				
1830	6,532,489	5,366,213	1,166,276					6,333,531	5,171,165	1,162,366				
1820	4,896,605	3,995,809	900,796					4,741,848	3,870,988	870,860				
1810	(5)	2,988,130	(5)					(5)	2,873,943	(5)				
1800	(5)	2,195,305	(5)					(5)	2,111,141	(5)				
1790	(5)	1,615,434	(5)					(5)	1,556,572	(5)				

* Denotes first year for which figures include Alaska and Hawaii.

1 Sex not reported before 1820. Total for both sexes: 1790—757,208; 1800—1,002,037; 1810—1,377,808. Total slave population: 1790—697,681; 1800—893,602; 1810—1,191,362; 1820—1,538,022; 1830—2,009,043; 1840—2,487,355; 1850—3,204,313; 1860—3,953,760. For slave population by sex, 1820-1860, see series A 119-134.

2 Includes races not shown separately, of which Filipinos are most numerous. Filipino males: 1910—144; 1920—5,232; 1930—42,268; 1940—39,723; 1950—46,101; 1960 (conterminous U.S.)—67,351; 1960 (including Alaska and Hawaii)—112,286; 1970—189,498. Filipino females: 1910—16; 1920—371; 1930—2,940; 1940—5,840; 1950—15,535; 1960 (conterminous U.S.)—39,075; 1960 (including Alaska and Hawaii)—64,024; 1970—153,562.

3 The population of other races (i.e., neither white nor Negro) was overstated by about 327,000 in the 1970 census. See text for series A 91-104. Excludes 23,372 persons for whom sex and race are not available. See series A 1-5, footnote 3.

4 Revisions to include adjustments for underenumeration in the Southern States show a total (both sexes) of 34,337,292 for white and 5,392,172 for Negro.

5 Data by sex not available. See series A 1-5 for total population.

Table 2. Foreign-born population, by sex and race, 1850–1970.

Source: U.S. Bureau of the Census, *Historical Statistics of the United States, Colonial Times to 1970*, Bicentennial edition (Washington, D.C., 1975), pt. 1, series A 105–118.

Year	Male							Female						
	All races	White	Negro	Other races				All races	White	Negro	Other races			
				Total [1]	Indian	Japanese	Chinese				Total [1]	Indian	Japanese	Chinese
	105	106	107	108	109	110	111	112	113	114	115	116	117	118
1970 [2]	4,403,687	3,982,797	115,406	305,484	7,153	39,375	105,907	5,215,615	4,750,973	138,052	326,590	7,335	83,125	98,325
1960 [3]*	4,760,432	4,507,502	65,952	186,978	(NA)	40,709	59,083	4,977,659	4,786,490	59,370	131,799	(NA)	60,947	34,205
1960 [3]	4,714,545	4,500,434	214,111	—	(NA)[6]	(NA)[6]	(NA)[6]	4,946,422	4,778,835	167,587	—	(NA)[6]	(NA)[6]	(NA)[6]
1950 [4]	5,258,255	5,098,370	159,885[6]	—	(NA)[6]	(NA)[6]	(NA)[6]	5,089,140	4,997,045[5]	92,095[6]	—	(NA)[6]	(NA)[6]	(NA)[6]
1940	6,121,647	6,011,015	44,488	66,144	2,463	29,651	31,687	5,473,249	5,408,123	39,453	25,673	2,028	17,654	5,555
1930	7,647,090	7,502,491	54,081	90,518	1,888	45,897	39,109	6,557,059	6,480,914	44,539	31,606	1,664	24,580	4,977
1920	7,675,435	7,528,322	42,641	104,472	3,539	57,213	40,573	6,245,257	6,184,432	31,162	29,663	2,760	24,125	2,534
1910	7,667,748	7,523,788	23,888	120,072	1,464	60,730	54,935	5,848,138	5,821,757	16,451	9,930	1,289	6,925	1,661
1900	5,630,190	5,515,285	11,829	103,076	1,207	23,185	78,684	4,711,086	4,698,532	8,507	4,047	1,006	872	2,169
1890 [7]	5,067,130	4,951,858	(8)	(8)	(8)	(8)	(8)	4,182,417	4,170,009	(8)	(8)	(8)	(8)	(8)
1880	3,630,566	3,521,635	7,758	101,173	1,002	133	100,038	3,049,377	3,038,044	6,259	5,074	818	12	4,244
1870 [9]	3,006,943	2,942,579	5,346[10]	59,018	647	46	58,325	2,560,286	2,551,133	4,299	4,854	489	8	4,357
1860	—	2,192,230	3,512[10]	33,149	—	—	—	—	1,904,523	3,499[10]	1,784	—	—	—
1850	—	1,239,434	2,015[10]	—	—	—	—	—	1,001,101	2,052[10]	—	—	—	—

* Denotes first year for which figures include Alaska and Hawaii.

NA Not available.

1 Includes races not shown separately, of which Filipinos are most numerous, of which Filipinos are most numerous. Filipino males: 1960 (including Alaska and Hawaii)—66,226; 1970—101,051; Filipino females: 1960 (including Alaska and Hawaii)—22,579; 1970—77,919.

2 15-percent sample data. These data vary in degree of comparability with data on total population by race. See text for series A 91–104.

3 25-percent sample data.

4 20-percent sample data.

5 Complete-count data: Males—5,176,390; females—4,984,778.

5 Complete-count data available only for the white population.

6 Data for specific races in the Negro and Other races grouping are based on various samples and are extremely unreliable. See *Census of Population: 1950*, vol. IV, part 3, chapter B.

7 Excludes population enumerated in the Indian Territory and on Indian reservations (totaling 325,464) which was not classified by nativity. Totals by race and sex: Males—169,221; females—156,243; white males—64,047; white females—53,321; Negro males—10,042; Negro females—8,594; Indian males—95,119; Indian females—94,328; Chinese males—13.

8 Data by sex not available. Totals for both sexes: Negro—19,979; Indian—1,235; Japanese—1,921; Chinese—104,545.

9 Excludes 1,260,078 persons for whom data on nativity are not available. See series A 1–5, footnote 3.

10 Free Negroes only. Data on nativity were not collected for slaves.

Table 3. Immigration by country, for decades 1820–1975.

Source: 1975 Annual Report: Immigration and Naturalization Service (Washington, D.C., 1976), table 13, pp. 62–64.

/From 1820-1867, figures represent alien passengers arrived; from 1868-1891 and 1895-1897, immigrant aliens arrived; from 1892-1894 and 1898 to the present time, immigrant aliens admitted. Data for years prior to 1906 relates to country whence alien came; thereafter, to country of last permanent residence. Because of changes in boundaries and changes in lists of countries, data for certain countries is not comparable throughout./

1.

Countries	1820	1821-1830	1831-1840	1841-1850	1851-1860	1861-1870	1871-1880
All countries	8,385	143,439	599,125	1,713,251	2,598,214	2,314,824	2,812,191
Europe	7,690	98,797	495,681	1,597,442	2,452,577	2,065,141	2,271,925
Austria-Hungary 2/ 5/	-	-	-	-	-	7,800	72,969
Belgium	1	27	22	5,074	4,738	6,734	7,221
Denmark	20	169	1,063	539	3,749	17,094	31,771
France	371	8,497	45,575	77,262	76,358	35,986	72,206
Germany 2/ 5/	968	6,761	152,454	434,626	951,667	787,468	718,182
Great Britain: England	1,782	14,055	7,611	32,092	247,125	222,277	437,706
Scotland	268	2,912	2,667	3,712	38,331	38,769	87,564
Wales	-	170	185	1,261	6,319	4,313	6,631
Not specified 3/ .	360	7,942	65,347	229,979	132,199	341,537	16,142
Greece	-	20	49	16	31	72	210
Ireland	3,614	50,724	207,381	780,719	914,119	435,778	436,871
Italy	30	409	2,253	1,870	9,231	11,725	55,759
Netherlands	49	1,078	1,412	8,251	10,789	9,102	16,541
Norway) 4/	3	91	1,201	13,903	20,931	(71,631)	(95,323)
Sweden)						(37,667)	(115,922)
Poland 5/	5	16	369	105	1,164	2,027	12,970
Portugal	35	145	829	550	1,055	2,658	14,082
Romania 12/	-	-	-	-	-	-	11
Spain	139	2,477	2,125	2,209	9,298	6,697	5,266
Switzerland	31	3,226	4,821	4,644	25,011	23,286	28,293
U.S.S.R. 5/ 6/	14	75	277	551	457	2,512	39,284
Other Europe	-	3	40	79	5	8	1,001
Asia	6	30	55	141	41,538	64,759	124,160
China	1	2	8	35	41,397	64,301	123,201
India	1	8	39	36	43	69	163
Japan 7/	-	-	-	-	-	186	149
Turkey	1	20	7	59	83	131	404
Other Asia	3	-	1	11	15	72	243
America	387	11,564	33,424	62,469	74,720	166,607	404,044
Canada & Newfoundland 8/	209	2,277	13,624	41,723	59,309	153,878	383,640
Mexico 9/	1	4,817	6,599	3,271	3,078	2,191	5,162
West Indies	164	3,834	12,301	13,528	10,660	9,046	13,957
Central America	2	105	44	368	449	95	157
South America	11	531	856	3,579	1,224	1,397	1,128
Africa	1	16	54	55	210	312	358
Australia & New Zealand	-	-	-	-	-	36	9,886
Pacific Islands (U.S. adm.)	-	-	-	-	-	-	1,028
Not specified	301	33,032	69,911	53,144	29,169	17,969	790

See footnotes at end of table.

Table 3 (continued)

2.

Countries	1881-1890	1891-1900	1901-1910	1911-1920	1921-1930	1931-1940	1941-1950
All countries	5,246,613	3,687,564	8,795,386	5,735,811	4,107,209	528,431	1,035,039
Europe	4,735,484	3,555,352	8,056,040	4,321,887	2,463,194	347,552	621,124
Albania 11/	-	-	-	-	-	2,040	85
Austria)				(453,649	32,868	3,563	24,860
Hungary) 2/ 5/	353,719	592,707	2,145,266	(442,693	30,680	7,861	3,469
Belgium	20,177	18,167	41,635	33,746	15,846	4,817	12,189
Bulgaria 10/	-	160	39,280	22,533	2,945	938	375
Czechoslovakia 11/	-	-	-	3,426	102,194	14,393	8,347
Denmark	88,132	50,231	65,285	41,983	32,430	2,559	5,393
Estonia	-	-	-			506	212
Finland 11/	-	-	-	756	16,691	2,146	2,503
France	50,464	30,770	73,379	61,897	49,610	12,623	38,809
Germany 2/ 5/	1,452,970	505,152	341,498	143,945	412,202	114,058	226,578
Great Britain: England	644,680	216,726	388,017	249,944	157,420	21,756	112,252
Scotland	149,869	44,188	120,469	78,357	159,781	6,887	16,131
Wales	12,640	10,557	17,464	13,107	13,012	735	3,209
Not specified 3/ ...	168	67	-	-	-	-	-
Greece	2,308	15,979	167,519	184,201	51,084	9,119	8,973
Ireland	655,482	388,416	339,065	146,181	220,591	13,167	26,967
Italy	307,309	651,893	2,045,877	1,109,524	455,315	68,028	57,661
Latvia 11/	-	-	-	-	-	1,192	361
Lithuania 11/	-	-	-	-	-	2,201	683
Luxembourg 15/	-	-	-	-	-	565	820
Netherlands	53,701	26,758	48,262	43,718	26,948	7,150	14,860
Norway 4/	176,586	95,015	190,505	66,395	68,531	4,740	10,100
Poland 5/	51,806	96,720	-	4,813	227,734	17,026	7,571
Portugal	16,978	27,508	69,149	89,732	29,994	3,329	7,423
Romania 12/	6,348	12,750	53,008	13,311	67,646	3,871	1,076
Spain	4,419	8,731	27,935	68,611	28,958	3,258	2,898
Sweden 4/	391,776	226,266	249,534	95,074	97,249	3,960	10,665
Switzerland	81,988	31,179	34,922	23,091	29,676	5,512	10,547
U.S.S.R. 5/ 6/	213,282	505,290	1,597,306	921,201	61,742	1,356	548
Yugoslavia 10/	-	-	-	1,888	49,064	5,835	1,576
Other Europe	682	122	665	8,111	22,983	2,361	3,983
Asia	69,942	74,862	323,543	247,236	112,059	16,081	32,360
China	61,711	14,799	20,605	21,278	29,907	4,928	16,709
India	269	68	4,713	2,082	1,886	496	1,761
Japan 7/	2,270	25,942	129,797	83,837	33,462	1,948	1,555
Turkey	3,782	30,425	157,369	134,066	33,824	1,065	798
Other Asia	1,910	3,628	11,059	5,973	12,980	7,644	11,537
America	426,967	38,972	361,888	1,143,671	1,516,716	160,037	354,804
Canada & Newfoundland 8/	393,304	3,311	179,226	742,185	924,515	108,527	171,718
Mexico 9/	1,913	971	49,642	219,004	459,287	22,319	60,589
West Indies	29,042	33,066	107,548	123,424	74,899	15,502	49,725
Central America	404	549	8,192	17,159	15,769	5,861	21,665
South America	2,304	1,075	17,280	41,899	42,215	7,803	21,831
Other America 13/	-	-	-	-	31	25	29,276
Africa	857	350	7,368	8,443	6,286	1,750	7,367
Australia & New Zealand	7,017	2,740	11,975	12,348	8,299	2,231	13,805
Pacific Islands (U.S. adm.) ...	5,557	1,225	1,049	1,079	427	780	5,437
Not specified 14/	789	14,063	33,523	1,147	228	-	142

See footnotes at end of table.

Table 3 (continued)

3.

Countries	1951-1960	1961-1965	1966-1970	1971	1972	1973	1974	1975	Total 156 years 1820-1975
All countries	2,515,479	1,450,312	1,871,365	370,478	384,685	400,063	394,861	386,194	47,098,919
Europe	1,325,640	528,543	594,820	91,509	86,321	91,183	80,407	72,774	35,961,083
Albania 11/	59	48	50	4	8	99	33	12	2,438
Austria 2/ 5/	67,106	6,638	13,983	1,945	2,251	1,589	669)	507)	4,312,252
Hungary 2/ 5/	36,637	2,591	2,810	488	475	1,008	897)	554)	
Belgium	18,575	5,463	3,729	577	530	438	432	437	200,575
Bulgaria 10/	104	397	222	44	40	212	131	83	67,464
Czechoslovakia 11/	918	1,005	2,268	734	1,152	910	381	267	135,995
Denmark	10,984	4,987	4,214	492	503	439	454	342	362,833
Estonia 11/	185	94	69	5	12	10	10	8	1,111
Finland 11/	4,925	2,164	2,028	331	341	283	243	215	32,626
France	51,121	24,431	20,806	2,844	2,870	2,587	2,160	1,816	742,442
Germany 2/ 5/	477,765	118,945	71,851	8,646	7,760	7,565	7,238	5,861	6,954,160
Great Britain: England	156,171	88,730	85,722	11,125	10,036	10,450	10,233	10,662	3,136,572
Scotland	32,854	19,489	10,360	740	947	790	918	1,015	817,018
Wales	2,589	1,167	885	62	85	99	85	134	94,709
Not specified 3/	3,884	696	2,979	375	453	521	425	433	803,507
Greece	47,608	19,290	66,679	15,002	10,452	10,348	10,590	9,799	629,349
Ireland	57,332	27,844	9,617	1,173	1,423	1,588	1,306	1,069	4,720,427
Italy	185,491	78,893	135,218	22,818	22,413	22,264	15,045	10,966	5,269,992
Latvia 11/	352	261	249	27	28	14	16	5	2,505
Lithuania 11/	242	344	218	20	25	18	20	11	3,782
Luxembourg 15/	684	303	253	46	26	26	45	21	2,789
Netherlands	52,277	22,218	8,388	1,092	979	966	988	755	356,282
Norway 4/	22,935	10,301	5,183	409	375	394	413	372	855,337
Poland 5/	9,985	32,889	20,650	1,928	3,770	4,136	3,492	3,482	502,658
Portugal	19,588	14,308	61,757	10,545	9,465	10,019	10,696	11,291	411,136
Romania 12/	1,039	1,158	1,373	687	354	1,106	1,184	825	165,747
Spain	7,894	16,057	28,602	3,661	4,284	5,538	4,704	2,573	246,334
Sweden 4/	21,697	10,095	7,021	648	654	597	637	507	1,269,969
Switzerland	17,675	9,921	8,532	1,066	999	704	671	673	346,468
U.S.S.R. 5/ 6/	584	872	1,464	303	400	874	921	4,713	3,354,026
Yugoslavia 10/	8,225	5,395	14,986	3,265	2,767	5,213	4,952	2,942	106,108
Other Europe	8,155	1,549	2,654	407	444	378	418	424	54,472
Asia 16/	150,106	107,032	320,739	98,062	115,978	119,984	127,003	129,196	2,274,872
China 17/	9,657	8,156	26,608	7,597	8,511	9,153	10,038	9,201	487,803
India ...	1,973	2,602	24,587	13,056	15,589	11,975	11,694	14,336	107,446
Japan 7/	46,250	19,759	20,229	4,649	5,037	6,104	5,408	4,807	391,389
Turkey ...	3,519	4,330	5,812	1,147	1,531	1,447	1,433	1,071	382,324
Other Asia	88,707	72,185	243,503	71,613	85,310	91,305	98,430	99,781	905,910
America	996,944	795,080	921,294	171,680	173,165	179,604	178,846	174,732	8,347,615
Canada and Newfoundland 8/	377,952	243,400	169,910	22,709	18,596	14,800	12,301	11,215	4,048,329
Mexico 9/	299,811	228,401	225,536	50,324	64,209	70,411	71,863	62,552	1,911,951
West Indies	123,091	119,596	350,617	66,552	60,386	62,830	61,284	66,975	1,408,027
Central America	44,751	52,182	49,148	8,870	8,407	9,125	9,431	9,800	262,533
South America	91,628	138,052	119,902	22,678	21,393	22,423	23,964	24,183	607,356
Other America 13/	59,711	13,449	6,181	547	174	15	3	7	109,419
Africa	14,092	9,631	19,323	5,844	5,472	5,537	5,227	5,868	104,421
Australia and New Zealand	11,506	8,195	11,367	2,357	2,550	2,466	1,978	1,804	110,560
Pacific Islands (U.S. adm.) 16/	4,698	848	921	158	235	176	168	198	23,984
Not specified 14/	12,493	983	2,901	868	964	1,113	1,232	1,622	276,384

1/ Since July 1, 1868, the data is for fiscal years ending June 30. Prior to fiscal year 1869, the periods covered are as follows: from 1820-1831 and 1843-1849, the years ended on September 30--1843 covers 9 months; and from 1832-1842 and 1850-1867, the years ended on December 31--1832 and 1850 cover 15 months. For 1868, the period ended on June 30 and covers 6 months.
2/ Data for Austria-Hungary was not reported until 1861. Austria and Hungary have been recorded separately since 1905. From 1938-1945, Austria is included in Germany.
3/ Great Britain not specified. From 1901-1951, included in other Europe.
4/ From 1820-1868, the figures for Norway and Sweden are combined.
5/ Poland recorded as a separate country from 1820-1898 and since 1920. From 1899-1919, Poland is included with Austria-Hungary, Germany, and Russia.
6/ From 1931-1963, the U.S.S.R. is broken down into European U.S.S.R. and Asian U.S.S.R. Since 1964 total U.S.S.R. has been reported in Europe.
7/ No record of immigration from Japan until 1861.
8/ Prior to 1920, Canada and Newfoundland are recorded as British North America. From 1820-1898, the figures include all British North American possessions.
9/ No record of immigration from Mexico from 1886-1893.
10/ Bulgaria, Serbia, and Montenegro were first reported in 1899. Bulgaria has been reported separately since 1920; also in 1920, a separate enumeration was made for the Kingdom of Serbs, Croats, and Slovenes. Since 1922, the Serbs, Croat, and Slovene Kingdom has been recorded as Yugoslavia.
11/ Countries added to the list since the beginning of World War I are included with the countries to which they belonged. Figures available since 1920 for Czechoslovakia and Finland and, since 1924, for Albania, Estonia, Latvia, and Lithuania.
12/ No record of immigration from Romania until 1880.
13/ Included with countries not specified to 1925.
14/ The figure 33,523 in column headed 1901-1910 includes 32,897 persons returning in 1906 to their homes in the United States.
15/ Figures for Luxembourg are available since 1925.
16/ Beginning with the year 1952, Asia includes the Philippines. From 1934-1951, the Philippines are included in the Pacific Islands. Prior to 1934, the Philippines are recorded in separate tables as insular travel.
17/ Beginning with the year 1957, China includes Taiwan.

Table 4. Nativities of the population, by state of residence, 1850.

Source: Superintendent of the Census, Seventh U.S. Census (Washington, D.C., 1853), table XV, p. xxxvii.

STATES.	England.	Ireland.	Scotland.	Wales.	Germany.	France.	Spain.	Portugal.	Belgium.	Holland.	Turkey.	Italy.	Austria.	Switzerland.	Russia.	Norway.	Denmark.
Maine	1,949	13,871	532	60	290	143	18	58	2	12	4	20	3	11	2	12	47
New Hampshire	1,469	8,811	467	11	147	69	8	8		1			1	9		2	3
Vermont	1,516	15,377	1,045	57	218	40	3	5		2		7		2	1	8	
Massachusetts	16,685	115,917	4,469	214	4,319	805	178	290	36	138	14	196	10	72	38	69	181
Rhode Island	4,490	15,944	988	12	230	80	14	58	2	12	1	25	1	8	1	25	15
Connecticut	5,091	26,689	1,916	111	1,671	321	12	74	2	19	2	16	20	55	5	1	16
New York	84,820	343,111	23,418	7,582	118,398	12,515	461	194	401	2,917	12	833	168	1,850	617	392	429
New Jersey	11,377	31,092	2,263	166	10,686	942	23	16	43	357		30	20	204	22	4	28
Pennsylvania	38,048	151,723	7,292	8,920	78,592	4,083	101	34	126	257	2	172	49	914	139	27	97
Delaware	952	3,513	155	17	343	73	1		1	5				22	1		1
Maryland	3,467	19,557	1,093	260	26,936	507	18	29	5	106	11	82	16	68	23	10	35
District of Columbia	682	2,373	142	20	1,404	80	20	6	14	4		74	3	36	2		6
Virginia	2,998	11,643	947	173	5,511	321	29	51	7	65		65	15	83	8	5	15
North Carolina	394	567	1,012	7	344	43	4	12	1	4		4	2	3	8		6
South Carolina	921	4,051	651	10	2,180	274	30	14		9		59	11	18	19	7	24
Georgia	679	3,292	367	13	947	177	13	5	41	11	1	33	13	38	8	6	24
Florida	390	878	142	11	307	67	70	17	4	8		40	8	7	2	17	21
Alabama	941	3,639	584	67	1,068	503	163	59	4	1	1	90	33	113	10	3	18
Mississippi	593	1,928	317	10	1,064	430	49	2	3	8		121	16	41	9	8	24
Louisiana	3,550	24,266	1,196	48	17,507	11,552	1,417	157	115	112	48	915	156	723	65	64	288
Texas	1,062	1,403	261	17	8,191	647	62	5	8	14		41	11	134	10	105	49
Arkansas	196	514	71	11	516	77	3	3	2	2		15		12	6	1	7
Tennessee	706	2,640	327	17	1,168	245	3	2	4	57		59	10	266	9		8
Kentucky	2,805	9,466	683	171	13,607	1,116	21	5	27	38		143	12	279	70	18	7
Ohio	25,660	51,562	5,232	5,849	111,257	7,355	28	7	103	348	1	174	29	3,291	84	18	53
Michigan	10,620	13,430	2,361	127	10,070	945	10	2	112	2,512	2	12	21	118	25	110	13
Indiana	5,550	12,787	1,341	169	28,584	2,279	3	6	86	43		6	17	724	6	18	10
Illinois	18,628	27,786	4,661	572	38,160	3,396	70	42	33	220		43	65	1,637	27	2,415	93
Missouri	5,359	14,734	1,049	176	44,352	2,138	46	11	58	189	7	124	71	984	29	155	55
Iowa	3,785	4,885	712	352	7,152	382	1	8	4	1,108		1	13	175	41	361	19
Wisconsin	18,952	21,043	3,527	4,319	34,519	775	4	4	45	1,157		9	61	1,244	71	8,651	146
California	3,050	2,452	883	182	2,926	1,546	220	109	12	63		228	87	177	48	124	92
TERRITORIES.																	
Minnesota	84	271	39	2	141	29	1		1	16		1	1	22	2	7	1
Oregon	207	196	106	9	155	45			11	1		5		8	1	1	2
Utah	1,056	106	232	125	50	13	1					1	3	1	1	32	2
New Mexico	43	292	29	1	215	26	8	1		2		1		11	4	2	1
Total	278,675	961,719	70,550	29,868	573,225	54,069	3,113	1,274	1,313	9,848	106	3,645	946	13,358	1,414	12,678	1,838

STATES.	Sweden.	Prussia.	Sardinia.	Greece.	China.	Asia.	Africa.	British America.	Mexico.	Central America.	South America.	West Indies.	Sandwich Islands.	Other countries.	Total foreign.	Unknown.	Aggregate.
Maine	55	27			3	5	5	14,181	2		31	61	1	51	31,456	581	583,169
New Hampshire	12	2				4	3	2,501	5		11	17	3	7	13,571	178	317,976
Vermont		6				7		14,470			3	6	4	23	32,831	322	314,120
Massachusetts	253	98	1	23	2	31	27	15,862	32	7	84	303	89	466	160,909	3,539	994,514
Rhode Island	17	5				1	9	1,024	7	21	4	57	8	52	23,111	135	147,545
Connecticut	12	42		1	5	16	72	970	4		35	192	45	57	37,473	794	370,792
New York	753	2,211			34	66	80	47,200	83	29	179	1,067	40	1,941	651,801	6,822	3,097,394
New Jersey	34	57	1	4	4	10	17	581	23	2	27	265		66	58,364	528	489,333
Pennsylvania	133	413		7	1	42	40	2,500	42	4	83	666	3	361	294,871	2,296	2,311,786
Delaware	2	28					10	21	3		3	25		35	5,211	63	89,242
Maryland	57	188			1	2	10	215	8		52	279	2	251	53,288	462	492,666
District of Columbia	5	11			1	4	2	32	9		5	15		17	22,394	585	48,000
Virginia	16	36			3	4	3	235	4	1	5	72	1	76	2,524	217	949,133
North Carolina	9	19			2		2	30	2	4	3	37		5	8,662	48	580,491
South Carolina	29	44	1		1	4	9	57	4		8	177		50	5,907	517	283,523
Georgia	11	25		1		2	13	108	8		8	95		37	2,757	58	524,503
Florida	33	17					23	97	6		3	599		116	7,638	1,109	48,135
Alabama	51	45		7			18	49	39	3	2	28	3	116	4,958	576	428,779
Mississippi	14	71				2	6	79	13	1	4	25		110	6,415	619	296,648
Louisiana	249	380	9	23	33	17	90	499	405	3	15	1,337	1	1,173	66,774	604	272,953
Texas	48	75					4	137	4,459	3	1	22	5	60	16,774	894	154,431
Arkansas	1	24					1	41	68		7			50	5,740	1,759	162,797
Tennessee	8	32	2	2		3	5	76	12		20			133	1,628	1,354	763,154
Kentucky	20	198	1	1		3	4	275	42	1	2	41		133	29,189	4,359	771,424
Ohio	55	765	15		3	6	4	5,880	26	12	41	86	1	544	218,512	1,211	1,980,427
Michigan	16	190	2	1	1	4	3	14,008	4		5	34	2	66	54,852	2,598	397,654
Indiana	16	740				4	4	1,878	31		4	12		108	54,426	3,946	988,416
Illinois	1,123	286		4	1	2	11	10,699	30		12	75	9	495	110,593	1,322	851,470
Missouri	37	697	1			3	7	1,053	94		20	50	1	954	72,474	362	594,622
Iowa	231	88				2		1,756	16		6	14		124	21,232	361	192,214
Wisconsin	88	3,545	1	1		17	1	8,277	9	11	6	20	1	191	106,695	784	305,391
California	162	158	1	9	660	117	65	834	6,454	39	877	64	319	400	22,358	629	92,597
TERRITORIES.																	
Minnesota	4	5						1,417						4	2,048	22	6,077
Oregon	2	1				2		293	1		6			57	1,159	143	13,294
Utah	1	6				1		338	7			2		12	1,990	9	11,354
New Mexico	1	14						38	1,365		1			5	2,063	223	61,547
Total	3,559	10,549	34	86	758	377	551	147,711	13,317	141	1,543	5,772	588	8,214	2,210,839	39,154	19,987,571

Table 5. Geographical distribution of the foreign-born, 1890.

Source: Department of Interior, Census Office, Eleventh U.S. Census (Washington, D.C., 1895), pt. I, p. cxl.

PRINCIPAL COUNTRIES OF BIRTH.	The United States.	GEOGRAPHICAL DIVISIONS.				
		North Atlantic.	South Atlantic.	North Central.	South Central.	Western.
	Per cent.	Per cent.	Per cent.	Per cent.	Per cent.	Per cent.
Total foreign born	100.00	100.00	100.00	100.00	100.00	100.00
North and South Americans	11.76	12.87	9.17	9.96	19.24	13.31
Canada and Newfoundland	10.61	12.61	2.59	9.89	2.33	9.79
South Americans	1.15	0.26	6.58	0.07	16.71	3.52
Great Britain and Ireland	33.76	47.80	37.62	21.23	23.71	32.11
England (a)	9.83	11.50	10.32	7.69	7.65	13.45
Scotland	2.62	3.07	3.42	2.01	2.02	3.58
Wales	1.08	1.31	0.86	0.85	0.62	1.40
Ireland	20.23	31.92	23.02	10.68	13.42	13.68
Germanic nations	33.73	25.92	41.24	42.91	41.14	19.64
Germany	30.11	23.11	39.06	38.67	35.62	15.61
Austria	1.33	1.58	1.03	0.97	3.24	1.30
Holland	0.88	0.46	0.17	1.51	0.17	0.24
Other Germanic nations	1.41	0.77	0.98	1.76	2.11	2.49
Scandinavian nations	10.09	3.06	1.48	17.47	2.46	12.17
Norway	3.49	0.41	0.32	6.99	0.56	2.63
Scandinavian nations—Continued. Sweden	5.17	2.26	0.86	8.27	1.47	6.21
Denmark	1.43	0.39	0.30	2.21	0.43	3.33
Slav nations	5.52	5.33	5.39	6.58	3.02	1.93
Russia	1.97	2.39	2.83	1.72	0.84	1.46
Hungary	0.68	1.17	0.55	0.34	0.27	0.13
Bohemia	1.28	0.31	0.82	2.45	1.15	0.12
Poland	1.59	1.46	1.19	2.07	0.76	0.22
Latin nations	3.46	4.30	4.00	1.53	8.86	6.98
France	1.22	1.05	1.20	0.95	4.47	2.19
Italy	1.98	3.05	2.35	0.54	3.83	3.23
Other Latin nations	0.26	0.29	0.45	0.04	0.56	1.56
Asiatic nations	1.23	0.23	0.45	0.10	0.53	12.68
China	1.15	0.17	0.31	0.06	0.42	12.39
Other Asiatic nations	0.08	0.06	0.14	0.04	0.11	0.29
All others	0.45	0.49	0.65	0.22	1.04	1.12

a Includes Great Britain, not specified.

Table 6. Foreign-born population, distributed according to principal countries of birth, 1850–1890.

Source: Department of Interior, Census Office, Eleventh U.S. Census (Washington, D.C., 1895), pt. I, p. cxl.

PRINCIPAL COUNTRIES OF BIRTH.	1890		1880		1870		1860		1850	
	Number.	Per cent.	Number.	Per cent.	Number.	Per cent.	Number.	Per cent.	Number.	Per cent.
Total	9,249,547	100.00	6,679,943	100.00	5,567,229	100.00	4,138,697	100.00	2,244,602	100.00
Canada and Newfoundland	980,938	10.61	717,157	10.74	493,464	8.86	249,970	6.04	147,711	6.58
Mexico	77,853	0.84	68,399	1.02	42,435	0.76	27,466	0.66	13,317	0.59
England (a)	909,092	9.83	664,160	9.94	555,046	9.97	433,494	10.47	278,675	12.42
Scotland	242,231	2.62	170,136	2.55	140,835	2.53	108,518	2.62	70,550	3.14
Wales	100,079	1.08	83,302	1.25	74,533	1.34	45,763	1.11	29,868	1.33
Ireland	1,871,509	20.23	1,854,571	27.76	1,855,827	33.34	1,611,304	38.93	961,719	42.85
Germany	2,784,894	30.11	1,966,742	29.44	1,690,533	30.37	1,276,075	30.83	583,774	26.01
Austria	123,271	1.33	38,063	0.58	30,508	0.55	25,061	0.61	946	0.04
Holland	81,828	0.88	58,090	0.87	46,802	0.84	28,281	0.68	9,848	0.44
Switzerland	104,069	1.13	88,621	1.33	75,153	1.35	53,327	1.29	13,358	0.60
Norway	322,665	3.49	181,729	2.72	114,216	2.05	43,995	1.06	12,678	0.57
Sweden	478,041	5.17	194,337	2.91	97,332	1.75	18,625	0.45	3,559	0.16
Denmark	132,543	1.43	64,196	0.96	30,107	0.54	9,962	0.24	1,838	0.08
Russia	182,644	1.97	35,722	0.54	4,644	0.08	3,160	0.08	1,414	0.06
Hungary	62,435	0.68	11,526	0.17	3,737	0.07				
Bohemia	118,106	1.28	85,361	1.28	40,289	0.72				
Poland	147,440	1.50	48,557	0.73	14,436	0.26	7,298	0.18	54,069	2.41
France	113,174	1.22	106,971	1.60	116,402	2.09	109,870	2.66	3,645	0.16
Italy	182,580	1.98	44,230	0.66	17,157	0.31	10,518	0.25	753	0.03
China	106,688	1.15	104,468	1.56	63,042	1.13	35,565	0.86		
Other countries	127,467	1.38	93,005	1.39	60,701	1.09	40,445	0.98	56,875	2.53

a Includes Great Britain, not specified.

Table 7. Foreign white stock, and foreign-born separately, by countries of origin, distributed according to mother tongues in detail, 1910.

Source: U.S. Bureau of the Census, Thirteenth U.S. Census (Washington, D.C., 1913), vol. I, table 21, pp. 992–993.

COUNTRY OF ORIGIN AND MOTHER TONGUE.	Foreign-born white: 1910	Total foreign white stock: 1910
All countries..............	13,345,545	¹32,243,382
Europe ².........	11,787,878	28,530,204
Northwestern Europe.....	6,738,554	20,491,614
Southern and Eastern Europe.....	5,046,471	8,030,688
America ³.........	1,453,186	3,271,732
All other.........	104,481	165,627
Northwestern Europe		
England.........	876,455	2,476,825
English and Celtic⁴......	855,471	2,450,744
Yiddish and Hebrew......	13,699	15,100
German......	2,660	4,456
Polish......	1,484	1,848
Russian......	598	746
Dutch and Frisian......	514	973
Lithuanian and Lettish......	503	528
French......	410	980
Italian......	397	468
Swedish......	119	158
Spanish......	73	118
Magyar......	65	79
Norwegian......	61	83
Armenian......	59	68
Roumanian......	46	48
Portuguese......	43	56
Danish......	42	69
Slovak......	35	43
Flemish......	31	50
Bohemian and Moravian......	30	67
Slovenian......	26	27
Syrian and Arabic......	20	26
All other......	69	90
Scotland.........	261,034	745,625
English and Celtic⁴......	260,043	744,226
Yiddish and Hebrew......	362	395
Lithuanian and Lettish......	198	207
German......	190	407
Polish......	74	75
Italian......	29	40
Swedish......	27	45
Russian......	27	31
All other......	84	199
Wales......	82,479	267,062
English and Celtic⁴......	82,393	266,876
Yiddish and Hebrew......	40	45
All other......	46	141
Ireland......	1,352,155	4,655,985
English and Celtic⁴......	1,351,479	4,654,633
Yiddish and Hebrew......	308	341
German......	169	519
French......	48	172
Italian......	40	86
All other......	111	234
Germany.........	2,501,181	8,430,466
German......	2,260,256	7,725,598
Polish......	190,096	513,446
Yiddish and Hebrew......	7,910	15,510
Dutch and Frisian......	6,510	21,580
Bohemian and Moravian......	6,263	17,382
Danish......	5,232	9,766
French......	3,131	8,271
Lithuanian and Lettish......	1,486	3,840
Slavic, not specified......	698	1,047
Magyar......	564	861
Russian......	552	1,002
Slovak......	488	740
English and Celtic⁴......	276	726
Italian......	245	299
Swedish......	180	340
Croatian......	152	163
Roumanian......	70	95
All other......	208	426
Unknown......	16,864	109,374
Norway......	403,858	1,012,045
Norwegian......	401,286	1,007,170
Swedish......	1,528	2,526
Finnish......	586	1,416
Danish......	204	369
German......	152	313
English and Celtic⁴......	36	66
All other......	66	185
Sweden......	665,183	1,414,945
Swedish......	662,391	1,409,228
Finnish......	1,345	3,093
German......	546	1,108
Norwegian......	340	589
Yiddish and Hebrew......	251	336
Danish......	131	230
French......	45	86
English and Celtic⁴......	41	89
Polish......	30	51
All other......	63	135

COUNTRY OF ORIGIN AND MOTHER TONGUE.	Foreign-born white: 1910	Total foreign white stock: 1910
Northwestern Europe—Con.		
Denmark.........	181,621	435,649
Danish......	179,705	431,540
German......	1,044	2,581
Swedish......	542	944
Norwegian......	130	235
English and Celtic⁴......	51	91
Dutch and Frisian......	33	82
Finnish......	23	38
French......	20	42
All other......	73	96
Netherlands......	120,053	305,846
Dutch and Frisian......	114,624	291,768
German......	4,824	12,980
Yiddish and Hebrew......	181	241
Flemish......	158	299
French......	77	194
Swedish......	50	66
Polish......	41	89
English and Celtic⁴......	37	67
All other......	61	142
Belgium......	49,397	93,633
Flemish......	25,239	43,588
French......	16,238	33,187
Dutch and Frisian......	2,765	5,952
German......	1,436	2,929
English and Celtic⁴......	109	225
Yiddish and Hebrew......	86	91
Polish......	44	64
Bohemian and Moravian......	26	59
Italian......	22	28
All other......	59	109
Unknown......	3,373	7,401
Luxemburg......	3,068	7,141
German......	2,831	6,579
French......	151	261
Dutch and Frisian......	39	110
All other......	47	191
France......	117,236	334,667
French......	110,024	320,040
German......	4,047	10,406
Italian......	1,206	1,422
Yiddish and Hebrew......	619	693
English and Celtic⁴......	419	593
Flemish......	232	464
Polish......	143	188
Spanish......	132	185
Slovak......	86	158
Russian......	74	100
Dutch and Frisian......	56	104
All other......	198	314
Switzerland......	124,834	311,725
German......	103,652	263,079
French......	11,170	25,803
Italian......	7,835	14,923
Dutch and Frisian......	85	236
Yiddish and Hebrew......	77	126
English and Celtic⁴......	54	158
All other......	110	181
Unknown......	1,851	7,219
Southern and Eastern Europe		
Portugal......	57,623	112,877
Portuguese......	57,425	112,377
Spanish......	100	253
Polish......	23	34
All other......	75	213
Spain......	21,977	35,681
Spanish......	21,657	35,070
English and Celtic⁴......	121	278
Italian......	57	69
French......	46	112
German......	34	55
Yiddish and Hebrew......	26	31
All other......	36	66
Italy......	1,343,070	2,112,961
Italian......	1,341,626	2,110,733
French......	596	936
German......	192	326
Greek......	152	257
Slovenian......	150	158
English and Celtic⁴......	73	122
Polish......	57	68
Albanian......	54	85
Yiddish and Hebrew......	35	54
Spanish......	26	57
All other......	107	165
Russia......	1,602,752	2,567,535
Yiddish and Hebrew......	838,193	1,317,157
Polish......	418,370	655,733
Lithuanian and Lettish......	137,046	204,070

COUNTRY OF ORIGIN AND MOTHER TONGUE.	Foreign-born white: 1910	Total foreign white stock: 1910
Southern and Eastern Europe—Continued		
Russia—Continued.		
German......	121,638	245,155
Russian......	40,542	65,612
Finnish......	5,865	8,861
Ruthenian......	3,402	4,798
Slovak......	1,709	2,934
Slavic, not specified......	1,658	2,217
Greek......	1,230	1,939
Armenian......	945	1,250
Bohemian and Moravian......	898	1,694
Swedish......	592	906
Magyar......	227	349
Croatian......	226	261
Roumanian......	222	403
Servian......	124	196
French......	120	255
Dutch and Frisian......	118	269
English and Celtic⁴......	104	172
Italian......	57	87
All other......	136	274
Unknown......	29,330	52,943
Finland......	129,669	213,712
Finnish......	111,985	185,532
Swedish......	16,920	26,843
Russian......	332	596
Yiddish and Hebrew......	139	208
German......	130	219
All other......	163	314
Austria......	1,174,924	2,021,860
Polish......	329,418	494,629
Bohemian and Moravian......	219,214	515,183
German......	157,917	275,002
Yiddish and Hebrew......	124,588	197,153
Slovenian......	117,740	174,943
Croatian......	64,295	81,094
Slovak......	55,766	110,829
Ruthenian......	17,169	23,793
Russian......	13,781	23,622
Servian......	11,618	13,304
Slavic, not specified......	11,196	21,821
Italian......	10,774	17,182
Dalmatian......	4,307	5,460
Roumanian......	3,399	3,706
Lithuanian and Lettish......	1,399	1,934
Greek......	839	1,497
English and Celtic⁴......	188	368
French......	157	279
Dutch and Frisian......	127	236
Bulgarian......	119	161
Montenegrin......	75	76
Magyar......	52	307
All other......	114	260
Unknown......	30,672	59,021
Hungary......	495,600	707,154
Magyar......	227,742	318,596
Slovak......	107,954	168,636
German......	73,338	99,412
Yiddish and Hebrew......	19,896	32,539
Roumanian......	15,679	16,613
Croatian......	9,034	11,140
Slavic, not specified......	6,837	9,367
Slovenian......	5,510	7,919
Servian......	5,018	5,613
Ruthenian......	4,465	6,616
Polish......	2,637	4,005
Bohemian and Moravian......	1,755	2,868
Russian......	1,400	2,315
Bulgarian......	1,352	1,947
Greek......	150	237
Lithuanian and Lettish......	134	187
Dutch and Frisian......	115	144
Italian......	70	98
All other......	140	215
Unknown......	12,374	18,687
Roumania......	65,920	89,312
Yiddish and Hebrew......	41,342	56,524
Roumanian......	22,032	29,307
German......	1,756	2,445
Magyar......	196	254
Russian......	137	204
Polish......	137	188
Bulgarian......	53	53
Servian......	50	60
All other......	217	277
Bulgaria......	11,453	11,899
Bulgarian......	10,909	11,235
Yiddish and Hebrew......	103	110
German......	81	140
Greek......	53	54
Italian......	43	44
Armenian......	40	45
Roumanian......	38	39
Servian......	27	27

¹ Includes 275,819 white persons of mixed foreign parentage, with parents born in different foreign countries but not distributed according to country of birth of either parent.
² Includes a small number of persons reported as born in Europe, country not specified.
³ Outside of the United States.
⁴ Includes persons reporting Irish, Scotch, or Welsh.

Table 7 (continued)

COUNTRY OF ORIGIN AND MOTHER TONGUE.	Foreign-born white: 1910	Total foreign white stock: 1910	COUNTRY OF ORIGIN AND MOTHER TONGUE.	Foreign-born white: 1910	Total foreign white stock: 1910	COUNTRY OF ORIGIN AND MOTHER TONGUE.	Foreign-born white: 1910	Total foreign white stock: 1910
Southern and Eastern Europe—Continued.			**Asia**—Continued.			**America**—Continued.		
Bulgaria—Continued.			Japan	198	272	South America	7,562	12,020
French	26	40	English and Celtic [1]	116	168	Spanish	2,443	4,178
Slovak	25	31	German	27	37	Italian	1,653	1,740
Slavic, not specified	22	24	Dutch and Frisian	11	12	English and Celtic [1]	847	1,740
Turkish	19	21	Swedish	9	9	German	568	887
All other	67	89	Yiddish and Hebrew	5	5	Portuguese	411	591
			All other	11	16	Yiddish and Hebrew	186	192
Servia	4,635	5,494	Unknown	19	25	French	159	283
Servian	4,321	5,122				Polish	101	112
Roumanian	67	67	India	2,078	3,948	Dutch and Frisian	44	79
Slovak	49	56	English and Celtic [1]	1,768	3,189	Russian	33	33
Croatian	45	51	German	88	163	Danish	23	24
All other	153	198	Dutch and Frisian	29	43	Slovenian	22	22
			French	11	23	All other	97	128
Montenegro	5,363	5,483	Swedish	10	14	Unknown	975	2,011
Montenegrin	3,724	3,795	All other	55	68			
Servian	1,322	1,359	Unknown	117	448	**All other**		
Slavic, not specified	130	134						
Russian	51	52	Asia, not specified	2,003	2,861	Africa	3,518	5,491
Syrian and Arabic	35	37	Syrian and Arabic	513	766	English and Celtic [1]	1,219	2,148
German	20	20	Armenian	159	192	Yiddish and Hebrew	297	328
All other	81	86	English and Celtic [1]	130	268	German	277	428
			German	93	159	Syrian and Arabic	267	425
Greece	101,264	111,161	Yiddish and Hebrew	54	77	French	246	345
Greek	100,799	110,453	Russian	46	60	Italian	198	231
Turkish	147	233	Greek	33	38	Dutch and Frisian	179	213
Italian	48	58	Turkish	29	32	Spanish	92	159
Albanian	47	51	Polish	23	44	Greek	66	86
German [1]	35	54	All other	566	631	Norwegian	46	60
English and Celtic [1]	29	38	Unknown	357	594	Armenian	41	43
Yiddish and Hebrew	19	30				Portuguese	25	35
All other	140	184	**America.** [2]			Turkish	24	25
			Canada	1,196,070	2,822,936	All other	94	145
Turkey in Europe	32,221	35,559	English and Celtic [1]	781,133	1,802,288	Unknown	447	820
Greek	12,337	12,714	French	385,083	952,456			
Bulgarian	5,807	5,852	German	17,898	39,521	Australia	8,938	15,988
Syrian and Arabic	3,582	5,057	Yiddish and Hebrew	1,434	1,541	English and Celtic [1]	8,620	15,258
Turkish	2,247	2,497	Dutch and Frisian	554	1,466	German	119	324
Albanian	1,945	1,955	Danish	520	606	Yiddish and Hebrew	31	55
Servian	808	856	Swedish	510	622	French	27	54
Yiddish and Hebrew	782	995	Polish	471	636	Danish	27	50
Armenian	572	738	Norwegian	375	501	Swedish	25	38
Roumanian	553	560	Italian	368	425	All other	89	209
Spanish	543	597	Finnish	189	204			
Slavic, not specified	241	242	Russian	147	160	Atlantic islands	15,795	30,225
German	160	225	Bohemian and Moravian	118	236	Portuguese	14,316	27,183
Montenegrin	68	71	Slovenian	106	111	English and Celtic [1]	851	1,566
English and Celtic [1]	60	127	Croatian	89	97	Spanish	117	248
Croatian	58	60	Magyar	68	77	All other	55	99
French	58	78	Slovak	48	52	Unknown	456	1,129
Italian	56	73	Syrian and Arabic	41	42			
All other	122	162	Lithuanian and Lettish	37	43	Pacific islands [4]	2,344	3,953
Unknown	2,222	2,700	Armenian	36	36	English and Celtic [1]	1,677	2,744
			Spanish	33	77	German	71	136
Europe, not specified	2,853	7,902	Flemish	30	50	Spanish	44	58
English and Celtic [1]	293	666	Roumanian	28	30	Dutch and Frisian	43	84
German	283	932	Ruthenian	27	27	French	38	65
Greek	246	272	All other	80	117	Danish	33	56
Bohemian and Moravian	148	405	Unknown	6,647	21,515	Portuguese	14	23
Slovak	124	293				Swedish	10	18
Spanish	102	164	Newfoundland	5,076	9,051	Italian	10	12
Syrian and Arabic	99	179	English and Celtic [1]	4,690	8,306	All other	20	25
Yiddish and Hebrew	82	160	French	79	110	Unknown	384	732
Polish	78	179	All other	16	33			
Magyar	41	88	Unknown	291	602	Country not specified	2,687	5,156
Slovenian	41	56				English and Celtic [1]	374	706
French	32	106	Cuba	12,869	23,701	German	341	572
Italian	30	50	Spanish	12,505	22,663	Polish	234	441
Swedish	21	49	English and Celtic [1]	232	795	Slavic, not specified	113	131
All other	106	200	French	58	138	French	67	133
Unknown	1,127	4,103	German	29	40	Greek	61	66
			All other	45	65	Yiddish and Hebrew	53	93
Asia						Spanish	40	79
			Other West Indies [3]	10,300	19,349	Lithuanian and Lettish	29	32
Turkey in Asia	59,702	79,157	English and Celtic [1]	7,533	13,656	Slovak	27	33
Syrian and Arabic	28,057	39,809	Spanish	494	771	Bohemian and Moravian	24	41
Armenian	21,893	27,382	Portuguese	262	473	Armenian	22	30
Greek	2,248	2,459	French	170	429	All other	117	157
Turkish	2,193	2,510	Danish	160	265	Unknown	1,185	2,642
Yiddish and Hebrew	834	1,044	German	92	140			
Albanian	246	246	Dutch and Frisian	61	92	Born at sea	6,885	18,013
Spanish	189	237	All other	42	52	English and Celtic [1]	1,927	4,098
German	104	140	Unknown	1,486	3,471	German	1,531	3,083
French	62	90				French	177	376
Servian	54	68	Mexico	219,802	382,647	Norwegian	167	293
Italian	50	68	Spanish	218,411	380,434	Polish	124	162
All other	316	442	English and Celtic [1]	892	1,481	Swedish	107	164
Unknown	3,456	4,662	German	207	309	Bohemian and Moravian	102	173
			French	114	218	Yiddish and Hebrew	65	76
China	333	563	Italian	68	78	Italian	52	63
English and Celtic [1]	231	401	All other	110	127	Portuguese	50	92
German	31	40				All other	202	324
Swedish	26	26	Central America	1,507	2,028	Unknown	2,381	9,109
Norwegian	10	11	Spanish	966	1,215			
French	6	6	English and Celtic [1]	173	300			
Danish	5	10	German	80	93			
Russian	5	5	French	35	50			
All other	5	9	All other	34	39			
Unknown	14	55	Unknown	219	331			

[1] Includes persons reporting Irish, Scotch, or Welsh.
[2] Outside of the United States.
[3] Except Porto Rico.
[4] Except Hawaii and Philippine Islands.

Table 8. Foreign white stock, and foreign-born white separately, by mother tongues, distributed according to countries of origin in detail, 1910.

Source: U.S. Bureau of the Census, Thirteenth U.S. Census (Washington, D.C., 1913), vol. I, table 22, pp. 994–997.

MOTHER TONGUE AND COUNTRY OF ORIGIN.	Foreign-born white: 1910	Total foreign white stock: 1910
All mother tongues	13,345,545	32,243,382
Teutonic and Celtic	7,546,799	22,126,623
All other	5,798,746	10,116,759
English and Celtic [1]	3,363,792	10,037,420
Ireland	1,351,479	4,654,633
England	855,471	2,450,744
Canada	781,133	1,802,288
Scotland	260,043	744,226
Wales	82,393	266,876
Australia	8,620	15,258
West Indies (other than Cuba and Porto Rico)	7,533	13,656
Newfoundland	4,690	8,306
At sea	1,927	4,098
India	1,768	3,189
Pacific islands	1,677	2,744
Africa	1,219	2,148
Mexico	892	1,481
Atlantic islands	851	1,566
South America	847	1,740
France	419	593
Europe, not specified	293	666
Germany	276	726
Cuba	232	795
China	231	401
Austria	188	368
Central America	173	300
Asia, not specified	130	268
Spain	121	278
Japan	116	168
Belgium	109	225
Russia	104	172
Italy	73	122
Turkey in Europe	60	127
Switzerland	54	158
Denmark	51	91
Turkey in Asia	49	120
Sweden	41	89
Netherlands	37	67
Norway	36	66
Greece	29	38
Portugal	17	69
Finland	12	30
Hungary	11	27
Bulgaria	5	6
Roumania	4	7
Montenegro	3	3
Servia	1	4
Country not specified	374	706
Mixed foreign [2]		57,777
Germanic		
German	2,759,032	8,817,271
Germany	2,260,256	7,725,598
Austria	157,917	275,002
Russia	121,638	245,155
Switzerland	103,652	263,079
Hungary	73,338	99,412
Canada	17,898	39,521
Netherlands	4,824	12,980
France	4,047	10,406
Luxemburg	2,831	6,579
England	2,660	4,456
Roumania	1,756	2,445
At sea	1,531	3,083
Belgium	1,436	2,929
Denmark	1,044	2,581
South America	568	887
Sweden	546	1,108
Europe, not specified	283	932
Africa	277	428
Mexico	207	309
Italy	192	326
Scotland	190	407
Ireland	169	519
Turkey in Europe	160	225
Norway	152	313
Finland	130	219
Australia	119	324
Turkey in Asia	104	140
Asia, not specified	93	159
West Indies (other than Cuba and Porto Rico)	92	140
India	88	163
Bulgaria	81	140
Central America	80	93
Pacific islands	71	136
Greece	35	54
Spain	34	55
China	31	40
Servia	29	43
Cuba	29	40
Japan	27	37
Montenegro	20	20
Atlantic islands	19	28
Wales	18	76
Portugal	12	20
Newfoundland	7	9
Country not specified	341	572
Mixed foreign [2]		116,083

MOTHER TONGUE AND COUNTRY OF ORIGIN.	Foreign-born white: 1910	Total foreign white stock: 1910
Germanic—Continued.		
Dutch and Frisian	126,045	324,930
Netherlands	114,624	291,768
Germany	6,510	21,580
Belgium	2,765	5,952
Canada	554	1,466
England	514	973
Africa	179	213
Austria	127	236
Russia	118	269
Hungary	115	144
Switzerland	85	236
West Indies (other than Cuba and Porto Rico)	61	92
France	56	104
South America	44	79
Pacific islands	43	84
At sea	41	84
Luxemburg	39	110
Denmark	33	82
India	29	43
Japan	11	12
Asia, not specified	11	12
Ireland	10	39
Europe, not specified	9	17
Norway	8	32
Scotland	7	18
Australia	7	11
Central America	7	9
Sweden	6	19
Mexico	6	6
Greece	4	7
Turkey in Asia	3	3
Finland	2	8
Cuba	2	6
Spain	2	4
Roumania	2	2
Wales	1	5
Atlantic islands	1	4
Turkey in Europe	1	3
Portugal	1	1
Italy	1	1
Montenegro	1	1
China	1	1
Country not specified	4	7
Mixed foreign [2]		1,187
Flemish	25,780	44,806
Belgium	25,239	43,588
France	232	464
Netherlands	158	299
Germany	35	87
England	31	50
Canada	30	50
Luxemburg	12	20
Russia	6	21
South America	6	7
At sea	5	8
Italy	5	7
Australia	5	5
Switzerland	3	7
Denmark	2	2
Mexico	1	4
Newfoundland	1	3
Cuba	1	3
Africa	1	2
Spain	1	1
Asia, not specified	1	1
Europe, not specified		16
Country not specified	5	10
Mixed foreign [2]		151
Scandinavian		
Swedish	683,218	1,445,869
Sweden	662,391	1,409,228
Finland	16,920	26,843
Norway	1,528	2,526
Russia	592	906
Denmark	542	914
Canada	510	622
Germany	180	340
England	119	158
At sea	107	164
Netherlands	50	66
Austria	28	42
Scotland	27	45
China	26	26
Australia	25	38
Europe, not specified	21	49
South America	19	28
France	16	32
Ireland	15	30
Pacific islands	10	18
India	10	14
Africa	9	12
Japan	9	9
Mexico	7	9
Turkey in Asia	7	9
Montenegro	7	7
Greece	7	7
Atlantic islands	6	14

MOTHER TONGUE AND COUNTRY OF ORIGIN.	Foreign-born white: 1910	Total foreign white stock: 1910
Scandinavian—Continued.		
Swedish—Continued.		
Belgium	5	11
Turkey in Europe	4	7
Italy	2	5
West Indies (other than Cuba and Porto Rico.)	2	4
Cuba	2	2
Hungary	1	7
Newfoundland	1	4
Asia, not specified	1	4
Wales	1	3
Roumania	1	2
Luxemburg	1	1
Bulgaria	1	1
Country not specified	8	8
Mixed foreign [2]		3,624
Norwegian	402,587	1,009,854
Norway	401,286	1,007,170
Canada	375	501
Sweden	340	589
At sea	167	293
Denmark	130	235
England	61	83
Africa	46	60
Finland	37	71
Germany	26	57
Scotland	16	25
Austria	10	30
China	10	11
Australia	8	12
Russia	7	23
Pacific islands	7	11
France	7	8
Montenegro	7	7
Ireland	6	16
West Indies (other than Cuba and Porto Rico)	5	7
Newfoundland	4	7
South America	4	4
Mexico	3	3
Greece	3	3
Netherlands	2	9
Switzerland	2	5
Belgium	2	3
Asia, not specified	2	2
Wales	1	2
Portugal	1	1
Cuba	1	1
Atlantic islands	1	1
Spain		5
Hungary		2
Country not specified	10	14
Mixed foreign [2]		583
Danish	186,345	446,473
Denmark	179,705	431,540
Germany	5,232	9,766
Canada	520	606
Norway	204	369
West Indies (other than Cuba and Porto Rico)	160	265
Sweden	131	230
At sea	49	81
England	42	69
Pacific islands	33	56
Australia	27	50
Mexico	27	27
Finland	26	45
Austria	21	38
South America	23	24
Africa	18	22
Russia	16	25
Netherlands	14	35
Scotland	13	35
France	10	16
Hungary	10	15
Belgium	8	28
Europe, not specified	8	18
Switzerland	7	16
Ireland	6	21
India	6	8
China	5	10
Cuba	4	5
Japan	4	4
Greece	3	4
Central America	3	3
Wales	2	4
Servia	2	2
Bulgaria	1	1
Country not specified	2	3
Mixed foreign [2]		3,030
Latin and Greek		
Italian	1,365,110	2,151,422
Italy	1,341,065	2,110,733
Austria	10,774	17,182
Switzerland	7,835	11,923
South America	1,653	1,710
France	1,206	1,422

[1] Includes persons reporting Irish, Scotch, or Welsh.
[2] Native whites whose parents were born in different foreign countries; for example, one parent in Ireland and the other in Scotland.

Table 8 (continued)

MOTHER TONGUE AND COUNTRY OF ORIGIN.	Foreign-born white: 1910	Total foreign white stock: 1910
Latin and Greek—Contd.		
Italian—Continued.		
England	397	468
Canada	368	425
Germany	245	299
Africa	198	231
Hungary	70	98
Mexico	68	78
Russia	57	87
Spain	57	69
Turkey in Europe	56	73
At sea	52	63
Turkey in Asia	50	68
Greece	48	58
Bulgaria	43	44
Ireland	40	86
Europe, not specified	30	50
Scotland	29	40
Roumania	29	37
Belgium	22	28
West Indies (other than Cuba and Porto Rico)	19	23
Australia	18	31
Cuba	16	26
Central America	13	14
Portugal	11	27
Atlantic islands	11	24
Sweden	10	19
Pacific islands	10	12
Finland	7	7
India	5	8
Wales	5	6
Netherlands	4	4
Servia	3	3
Montenegro	3	3
Asia, not specified	3	3
Norway	2	2
Denmark	1	1
Luxemburg	1	1
Country not specified	15	18
Mixed foreign [1]		2,888
French	528,842	1,357,169
Canada	385,083	952,456
France	110,024	320,040
Belgium	16,238	33,187
Switzerland	11,170	25,803
Germany	3,131	8,271
Italy	598	936
England	410	980
Africa	246	345
At sea	177	376
West Indies (other than Cuba and Porto Rico)	170	429
South America	159	283
Austria	157	279
Luxemburg	151	261
Russia	120	255
Mexico	114	218
Newfoundland	79	110
Netherlands	77	194
Turkey in Asia	62	90
Cuba	58	138
Turkey in Europe	58	78
Ireland	48	172
Spain	46	112
Sweden	45	86
Pacific islands	38	65
Central America	35	50
Europe, not specified	32	106
Australia	27	54
Bulgaria	26	40
Hungary	24	46
Roumania	24	33
Denmark	20	42
Scotland	18	56
Greece	18	26
Atlantic islands	15	23
Portugal	14	28
Norway	13	36
Finland	12	31
India	11	23
Wales	7	23
Asia, not specified	7	14
Montenegro	6	9
China	6	6
Japan	1	4
Country not specified	67	133
Mixed foreign [1]		11,222
Spanish	258,131	448,198
Mexico	218,411	380,431
Spain	21,657	35,070
Cuba	12,505	22,663
South America	2,443	4,178
Central America	966	1,215
Turkey in Europe	543	597
West Indies (other than Cuba and Porto Rico)	494	771
Turkey in Asia	189	237
France	132	185
Atlantic islands	117	248
Europe, not specified	102	161

MOTHER TONGUE AND COUNTRY OF ORIGIN.	Foreign-born white: 1910	Total foreign white stock: 1910
Latin and Greek—Contd.		
Spanish—Continued.		
Portugal	100	253
Africa	92	159
England	73	118
Pacific islands	44	58
At sea	34	58
Canada	33	77
Italy	26	57
Roumania	22	25
Austria	20	89
Germany	16	65
Bulgaria	13	15
Russia	11	38
Denmark	11	17
India	7	17
Belgium	5	10
Asia, not specified	5	16
Ireland	4	17
Servia	2	6
Scotland	2	5
Switzerland	2	5
Netherlands	2	4
Finland	1	10
Australia	1	7
Greece	1	5
China	1	5
Newfoundland	1	3
Japan	1	3
Norway	1	2
Montenegro	1	2
Wales		2
Hungary		8
Country not specified	40	79
Mixed foreign [1]		1,212
Portuguese	72,649	141,268
Portugal	57,425	112,377
Atlantic islands	14,316	27,183
South America	411	591
West Indies (other than Cuba and Porto Rico)	262	473
At sea	50	92
England	43	56
Africa	25	35
Canada	19	30
Pacific islands	14	23
Germany	12	21
Spain	9	20
Europe, not specified	6	6
Australia	5	32
Denmark	5	9
Italy	5	5
Austria	4	14
France	4	9
Ireland	3	6
Hungary	3	3
India	3	3
Russia	2	11
Switzerland	2	8
Belgium	2	4
Asia, not specified	2	3
Mexico	2	2
China	2	2
Turkey in Europe	1	4
Scotland	1	2
Newfoundland	1	2
Cuba	1	2
Central America	1	2
Sweden	1	1
Netherlands	1	1
Bulgaria	1	1
Turkey in Asia		1
Country not specified	5	23
Mixed foreign [1]		211
Roumanian	42,277	51,124
Roumania	22,032	29,307
Hungary	15,679	16,613
Austria	3,399	3,706
Turkey in Europe	553	560
Russia	222	403
Germany	70	95
Servia	67	67
England	46	48
Bulgaria	38	39
Turkey in Asia	37	46
France	36	61
Canada	28	30
Europe, not specified	17	23
Italy	9	15
Greece	9	9
Spain	5	5
Sweden	4	6
Ireland	3	3
South America	3	3
Scotland	2	2
At sea	1	3
Belgium	1	2
Asia, not specified	1	1
Country not specified	6	7
Mixed foreign [1]		61

MOTHER TONGUE AND COUNTRY OF ORIGIN.	Foreign-born white: 1910	Total foreign white stock: 1910
Latin and Greek—Contd.		
Greek	118,379	130,379
Greece	100,799	110,453
Turkey in Europe	12,337	12,714
Turkey in Asia	2,248	2,459
Russia	1,230	1,939
Austria	839	1,497
Europe, not specified	246	272
Italy	152	257
Hungary	150	237
Africa	66	86
Bulgaria	53	54
Roumania	41	46
Asia, not specified	33	38
Germany	30	42
Canada	19	22
England	18	26
Montenegro	11	11
Servia	8	13
Pacific islands	7	7
France	5	5
Spain	4	5
West Indies (other than Cuba and Porto Rico)	4	4
Denmark	3	4
South America	2	3
India	2	2
At sea	2	2
Ireland	1	2
Scotland	1	3
Finland	1	1
Norway	1	1
Sweden	1	1
Newfoundland	1	1
Cuba	1	1
Mexico	1	1
Australia	1	1
Country not specified	61	66
Mixed foreign [1]		101
Slavic and Lettic		
Polish	943,781	1,707,640
Russia	418,370	655,733
Austria	329,418	494,629
Germany	190,096	513,446
Hungary	2,637	4,005
England	1,484	1,848
Canada	471	636
France	143	188
Roumania	137	188
At sea	124	162
South America	101	112
Europe, not specified	78	179
Scotland	74	75
Italy	57	68
Belgium	44	64
Netherlands	41	89
Finland	37	51
Turkey in Asia	34	47
Sweden	30	51
Asia, not specified	23	44
Portugal	23	34
Switzerland	18	29
Ireland	17	32
Australia	17	28
Africa	13	14
Greece	10	12
Turkey in Europe	9	17
Denmark	8	11
Norway	7	10
Bulgaria	4	5
Servia	4	6
Mexico	3	3
Central America	3	3
Pacific islands	3	3
Wales	2	2
Luxemburg	2	2
Spain	2	2
Montenegro	2	2
Atlantic islands	1	2
Country not specified	234	441
Mixed foreign [1]		35,366
Bohemian and Moravian	228,738	539,392
Austria	219,214	515,183
Germany	6,263	17,382
Hungary	1,755	2,868
Russia	898	1,694
Europe, not specified	148	405
Canada	118	236
At sea	102	173
England	30	67
Roumania	27	38
Belgium	26	59
France	22	33
Turkey in Europe	18	20
Switzerland	16	34
Greece	11	18
Turkey in Asia	8	13
Denmark	7	13
South America	7	8
Australia	5	43
Servia	5	7

[1] Native whites whose parents were born in different foreign countries; for example, one parent in Ireland and the other in Scotland.

Table 8 (continued)

MOTHER TONGUE AND COUNTRY OF ORIGIN.	Foreign-born white: 1910	Total foreign white stock: 1910	MOTHER TONGUE AND COUNTRY OF ORIGIN.	Foreign-born white: 1910	Total foreign white stock: 1910	MOTHER TONGUE AND COUNTRY OF ORIGIN.	Foreign-born white: 1910	Total foreign white stock: 1910
Slavic and Lettic—Contd.			**Slavic and Lettic**—Contd.			**Slavic and Lettic**—Contd.		
Bohemian and Moravian—Con.			Ruthenian	25,131	35,359	Slavic, not specified—Contd.		
Norway	4	16	Austria	17,169	23,793	Belgium	6	7
Montenegro	4	4	Hungary	4,465	6,616	Roumania	5	7
India	4	4	Russia	3,402	4,798	Australia	4	11
Netherlands	3	17	Canada	27	27	England	4	5
Africa	3	10	Germany	19	27	Scotland	4	5
Ireland	3	7	England	13	13	Servia	4	4
Luxemburg	3	3	Roumania	12	12	Greece	2	6
Sweden	2	13	South America	11	11	Sweden	2	4
Bulgaria	2	3	Ireland	5	16	Ireland	2	3
Scotland	1	9	Turkey in Europe	2	2	Switzerland	2	3
Italy	1	7	Scotland	1	1	Norway	2	2
Asia, not specified	1	6	Cuba	1	1	Italy	1	2
Finland	1	5	Country not specified	4	4	Mexico	1	2
Central America	1	1	Mixed foreign [1]		38	Denmark	1	1
China	1	1				Netherlands	1	1
Spain		2	Slovenian	123,631	183,431	South America	1	1
Country not specified	21	41	Austria	117,740	174,943	India	1	1
Mixed foreign [1]		949	Hungary	5,510	7,919	Asia, not specified	1	1
Slovak	166,474	284,444	Italy	150	158	Africa	1	1
Hungary	107,954	168,636	Canada	106	111	Country not specified	113	131
Austria	55,766	110,829	Europe, not specified	41	56	Mixed foreign [1]		36
Russia	1,709	2,934	England	26	27	Lithuanian and Lettish	140,963	211,235
Germany	488	740	Servia	23	28	Russia	137,046	204,070
Europe, not specified	124	293	South America	22	22	Germany	1,486	3,840
France	86	158	At sea	3	7	Austria	1,399	1,934
Turkey in Europe	49	57	Australia	2	7	England	503	528
Servia	49	56	Denmark	2	2	Scotland	198	207
Canada	48	52	Sweden	1	3	Hungary	134	187
England	35	43	West Indies (other than Cuba and Porto Rico)		1	Canada	37	43
Bulgaria	25	31	Country not specified	5	5	Finland	21	36
Roumania	18	18	Mixed foreign [1]		142	Mexico	19	19
Italy	13	19				Netherlands	17	26
Ireland	12	15	Serbo-Croatian	105,669	129,254	Turkey in Asia	8	11
Montenegro	12	13	Austria	80,295	99,934	Bulgaria	7	12
Netherlands	11	13	Hungary	14,068	16,770	Belgium	7	11
Sweden	9	21	Montenegro	5,065	5,173	Switzerland	7	8
Turkey in Asia	8	10	Servia	4,384	5,191	France	6	16
Scotland	8	9	Turkey in Europe	934	987	Denmark	6	6
At sea	6	6	Russia	350	457	Europe, not specified	5	16
Norway	4	5	Germany	166	191	At sea	5	6
Switzerland	3	8	Canada	114	144	Sweden	3	6
South America	3	3	Turkey in Asia	102	117	Ireland	3	5
Mexico	1	3	Roumania	50	60	Greece	3	4
Atlantic islands	1	3	Bulgaria	32	32	South America	3	4
Spain	1	2	Italy	24	28	Norway	2	20
Greece	1	1	South America	15	17	Italy	2	9
Portugal	1	1	Greece	13	13	Turkey in Europe	2	2
West Indies (other than Cuba and Porto Rico)	1	1	England	12	18	Luxemburg	1	6
Asia, not specified	1	1	Denmark	6	6	Asia, not specified	1	2
Country not specified	27	33	Mexico	5	6	Portugal	1	1
Mixed foreign [1]		429	Sweden	4	4	Africa	1	1
Russian	57,926	95,137	Cuba	4	4	Australia	1	1
Russia	40,542	65,612	France	2	13	Servia		1
Austria	13,781	23,622	Central America	2	2	Country not specified	29	32
Hungary	1,400	2,315	Netherlands	1	3	Mixed foreign [1]		165
England	598	746	Australia	1	3			
Germany	552	1,002	At sea	1	3	**Unclassified and Unknown**		
Finland	332	596	Switzerland	1	1	Yiddish and Hebrew	1,051,767	1,676,762
Canada	147	160	Europe, not specified		4	Russia	838,193	1,317,157
Roumania	137	204	Country not specified	18	18	Austria	124,588	197,153
France	74	100	Mixed foreign [1]		55	Roumania	41,342	56,524
Montenegro	51	52				Hungary	19,896	32,539
Asia, not specified	46	60	Bulgarian	18,341	19,380	England	13,699	15,100
Turkey in Asia	41	49	Bulgaria	10,909	11,235	Germany	7,940	15,510
South America	33	33	Turkey in Europe	5,807	5,852	Canada	1,434	1,541
Turkey in Europe	29	38	Hungary	1,352	1,947	Turkey in Asia	834	1,044
Scotland	27	31	Austria	119	161	Turkey in Europe	782	995
Africa	17	18	Roumania	53	53	France	619	693
Sweden	16	34	Turkey in Asia	46	51	Scotland	362	395
Switzerland	16	21	Greece	15	16	Ireland	308	311
At sea	14	16	Russia	11	13	Africa	297	328
Bulgaria	13	16	Germany	5	16	Sweden	251	336
Europe, not specified	9	13	Europe, not specified	5	6	South America	186	192
Greece	8	11	France	4	4	Netherlands	181	241
Belgium	7	7	Netherlands	3	6	Finland	139	208
China	5	5	Italy	3	3	Bulgaria	103	110
Norway	3	22	Canada	2	2	Belgium	86	91
Italy	3	5	Ireland	1	1	Europe, not specified	82	160
Ireland	3	3	Servia		1	Switzerland	77	126
Japan	3	3	Country not specified	6	6	At sea	65	76
Australia	2	5	Mixed foreign [1]		7	Asia, not specified	54	77
Denmark	2	3				Wales	40	45
Mexico	2	2	Slavic, not specified	21,012	35,195	Italy	35	54
India	2	2	Austria	11,196	21,821	Australia	31	55
Portugal	1	5	Hungary	6,837	9,367	Spain	26	31
Pacific islands	1	2	Russia	1,658	2,217	Greece	19	30
Wales	1	1	Germany	698	1,047	Denmark	17	20
Spain	1	1	Turkey in Europe	241	242	Norway	16	33
Central America	1	1	Montenegro	130	134	Portugal	13	55
West Indies (other than Cuba and Porto Rico)		1	France	37	52	Servia	8	10
Country not specified	6	8	Bulgaria	22	24	Mexico	6	11
Mixed foreign [1]		312	Europe, not specified	15	31			
			Turkey in Asia	12	18			
			Canada	8	8			

[1] Native whites whose parents were born in different foreign countries; for example, one parent in Ireland and the other in Scotland.

Table 8 (continued)

MOTHER TONGUE AND COUNTRY OF ORIGIN.	Foreign-born white: 1910	Total foreign white stock: 1910	MOTHER TONGUE AND COUNTRY OF ORIGIN.	Foreign-born white: 1910	Total foreign white stock: 1910	MOTHER TONGUE AND COUNTRY OF ORIGIN.	Foreign-born white: 1910	Total foreign white stock: 1910
Unclassified and Unknown—Continued.			**Unclassified and Unknown—**Continued.			**Unclassified and Unknown—**Continued.		
Yiddish and Hebrew—Contd.			Armenian	23,938	30,021	Turkish—Continued.		
Japan	5	5	Turkey in Asia	21,893	27,382	Austria	3	5
Cuba	4	6	Russia	945	1,250	England	3	4
Central America	2	3	Turkey in Europe	572	738	Servia	2	3
Luxemburg	2	2	Asia, not specified	159	192	France	2	2
India	2	2	England	59	68	Germany	1	2
Newfoundland		2	Africa	41	43	Canada	1	2
Country not specified	53	93	Bulgaria	40	45	Scotland	1	1
Mixed foreign¹		35,368	Canada	36	36	Hungary	1	1
			Germany	23	26	Cuba	1	1
Magyar	229,094	320,893	Roumania	21	32	South America	1	1
Hungary	227,742	318,596	Italy	18	22	At sea	1	1
Germany	564	861	Europe, not specified	16	18	Country not specified	7	7
Russia	227	349	Hungary	15	17	Mixed foreign¹		1
Roumania	196	254	Ireland	14	14			
Canada	68	77	Switzerland	12	12	Albanian	2,312	2,366
England	65	79	Mexico	12	12	Turkey in Europe	1,945	1,955
Austria	52	307	Greece	11	11	Turkey in Asia	246	246
Europe, not specified	41	88	France	10	10	Italy	54	85
France	15	24	Servia	8	8	Greece	47	51
Bulgaria	15	24	Scotland	6	13	Europe, not specified	4	4
Belgium	15	18	At sea	4	5	Russia	3	11
Servia	13	13	India	1	1	Austria	3	3
At sea	13	13	Luxemburg		1	Montenegro	3	3
Asia, not specified	11	12	Spain		1	South America	2	3
Turkey in Europe	7	12	Country not specified	22	30	Canada	2	2
Switzerland	5	9	Mixed foreign¹		34	Hungary	1	1
Africa	5	8				Asia, not specified	1	1
Turkey in Asia	5	5	Syrian and Arabic	32,868	46,727	Country not specified	1	1
Finland	4	6	Turkey in Asia	28,057	39,809			
Sweden	4	4	Turkey in Europe	3,582	5,057	All other	646	790
South America	4	4	Asia, not specified	513	766	Asia, not specified	516	560
Greece	3	3	Africa	267	425	Hungary	39	51
Italy	2	4	Europe, not specified	99	179	Russia	37	63
Norway	2	3	Canada	41	42	Africa	11	42
Denmark	2	2	Montenegro	35	37	Turkey in Asia	9	9
Montenegro	2	2	Russia	31	55	India	6	8
India	2	2	Servia	23	26	Roumania	6	6
Scotland	1	8	England	20	26	Germany	5	11
Wales	1	2	France	20	24	Canada	4	4
Netherlands	1	2	Italy	18	33	South America	3	17
Portugal	1	1	Hungary	18	25	Austria	3	4
Spain	1	1	Greece	17	26	England	2	6
Country not specified	5	5	Mexico	14	14	Japan	2	2
Mixed foreign¹		95	Germany	13	18	At sea	1	3
			South America	13	14	Greece	1	1
Finnish	120,086	200,688	West Indies (other than Cuba and Porto Rico)	11	11	Servia		1
Finland	111,985	185,532	Spain	10	17	Country not specified	1	1
Russia	5,865	8,861	India	9	12	Mixed foreign¹		1
Sweden	1,345	3,093	Australia	9	9			
Norway	586	1,416	At sea	8	9	Unknown	116,272	313,044
Canada	189	204	Wales	6	6	Austria	30,672	59,021
Denmark	23	38	Roumania	5	12	Russia	29,330	52,943
Austria	19	35	Switzerland	5	5	Germany	16,864	109,374
England	17	18	Cuba	5	5	Hungary	12,374	18,687
At sea	14	19	Finland	2	11	Canada	6,647	21,515
Germany	9	26	Scotland	2	4	Turkey in Asia	3,456	4,662
Switzerland	9	10	Portugal	2	4	Belgium	3,373	7,401
Africa	6	6	Ireland	2	2	At sea	2,381	9,109
Europe, not specified	3	15	Belgium	1	2	Turkey in Europe	2,222	2,700
Australia	3	3	Norway	1	1	Switzerland	1,851	7,219
France	2	5	Netherlands	1	1	West Indies (other than Cuba and Porto Rico)	1,486	3,471
Cuba	2	2	Country not specified	8	10	Europe, not specified	1,127	4,103
Pacific islands	2	2	Mixed foreign¹		30	South America	975	2,011
Wales	1	3				Atlantic islands	456	1,129
Hungary	1	2	Turkish	4,709	5,441	Africa	447	820
Ireland	1	1	Turkey in Europe	2,247	2,497	Pacific islands	384	732
Central America	1	1	Turkey in Asia	2,193	2,510	Asia, not specified	357	594
Turkey in Asia	1	1	Greece	147	293	Newfoundland	291	602
Asia, not specified	1	1	Asia, not specified	29	32	Central America	219	331
Netherlands		20	Africa	24	25	India	117	448
Scotland		3	Bulgaria	19	21	Luxemburg	25	155
Newfoundland		2	Russia	12	14	Japan	19	25
Servia		1	Europe, not specified	9	13	China	14	55
Country not specified	1	2	India	5	5	Country not specified	1,185	2,642
Mixed foreign¹		1,366				Mixed foreign¹		3,295

¹ Native whites whose parents were born in different foreign countries; for example, one parent in Ireland and the other in Scotland.

Table 9. Country of origin of the foreign white stock, by nativity and parentage, 1890–1920. (Figures for 1920 relate to countries as constituted prior to the World War.)

Source: U.S. Bureau of the Census, Fourteenth U.S. Census (Washington, D.C., 1922), vol. II, table 1, p. 897.

1920 / 1910

COUNTRY OF ORIGIN.	Total foreign white stock.	Foreign-born white.[1]	NATIVE WHITE OF FOREIGN OR MIXED PARENTAGE.				Total foreign white stock.	Foreign-born white.[1]	NATIVE WHITE OF FOREIGN OR MIXED PARENTAGE.			
			Total.	Both parents foreign.	Father foreign.	Mother foreign.			Total.	Both parents foreign.	Father foreign.	Mother foreign.
Total	36,398,958	13,712,754	22,686,204	15,694,539	4,539,776	2,451,889	32,243,382	13,345,545	18,897,837	12,916,311	3,923,845	2,057,681
Northwestern Europe:												
England	2,307,112	824,088	1,483,024	574,499	571,560	336,965	2,322,442	876,455	1,445,987	592,285	546,215	307,487
Scotland	731,239	310,092	421,147	178,638	153,917	88,592	659,663	261,034	398,629	175,391	145,227	78,011
Wales	230,380	66,962	163,418	78,114	54,889	30,415	248,947	82,479	166,468	84,934	52,555	28,979
Ireland	4,136,395	1,164,707	2,971,688	1,966,968	573,021	431,699	4,504,360	1,352,155	3,152,205	2,141,577	603,013	407,615
Norway	1,023,225	362,051	661,174	437,623	143,314	80,237	979,099	403,858	575,241	410,951	106,805	57,485
Sweden	1,457,382	632,656	824,726	599,744	144,382	80,600	1,364,215	665,183	699,032	546,788	97,504	54,740
Denmark	467,525	191,496	276,029	170,702	73,915	31,412	400,064	181,621	218,443	147,648	49,721	21,074
Netherlands	362,318	134,229	228,089	142,547	57,301	28,241	293,574	120,053	173,521	116,331	38,199	18,991
Belgium	122,686	63,234	59,452	37,525	15,420	6,507	89,264	49,397	39,867	26,448	9,802	3,617
Luxemburg	43,109	12,837	30,272	16,263	10,847	3,162	6,945	3,068	3,877	2,381	1,244	252
Switzerland	327,797	117,270	210,527	103,452	75,315	31,760	301,650	124,834	176,816	90,669	61,244	24,903
France	333,678	124,727	208,951	90,073	86,549	32,329	292,389	117,236	175,153	78,937	73,085	23,131
Central and Eastern Europe:												
Germany	7,259,992	1,915,864	5,344,128	3,397,370	1,367,805	578,953	8,282,618	2,501,181	5,781,437	3,911,847	1,337,651	531,939
Austria	3,129,798	1,445,141	1,684,657	1,435,524	171,678	77,455	2,001,559	1,174,924	826,635	709,070	80,595	36,970
Hungary	1,110,905	598,170	512,735	472,521	29,510	10,704	700,227	495,600	204,627	191,059	10,106	3,462
Russia	3,871,109	2,020,646	1,850,463	1,671,949	135,098	43,416	2,541,649	1,602,752	938,897	873,055	51,856	13,986
Finland	296,276	150,770	145,506	130,083	9,765	5,658	211,026	129,669	81,357	76,261	3,319	1,777
Rumania	134,318	85,255	49,063	43,683	3,820	1,560	87,721	65,920	21,801	20,707	821	273
Bulgaria, Serbia, and Montenegro	43,703	32,681	11,022	9,696	1,191	135	22,685	21,451	1,234	948	239	47
Turkey in Europe	23,268	18,907	4,361	3,948	372	41	35,314	32,221	3,093	2,560	423	110
Southern Europe:												
Greece	212,342	166,786	45,556	36,990	8,287	279	109,665	101,264	8,401	5,524	2,400	477
Italy	3,336,941	1,615,180	1,721,761	1,556,065	146,304	19,392	2,098,360	1,343,070	755,290	695,187	52,947	7,156
Spain	77,947	52,686	25,261	14,973	7,972	2,316	33,134	21,977	11,157	4,387	5,364	1,406
Portugal	134,794	67,948	66,846	52,794	11,673	2,379	111,122	57,623	53,499	41,680	10,359	1,460
Europe, not specified	10,998	3,342	7,656	5,019	1,900	737	7,576	2,853	4,723	2,926	1,281	516
Asia:												
Turkey in Asia	164,480	100,843	63,637	57,915	4,827	895	78,631	59,702	18,929	17,480	1,255	194
All other countries	10,735	5,139	5,596	1,791	2,343	1,462	7,264	4,612	2,652	517	1,329	806
America:												
Canada—French	848,309	302,675	545,634	326,435	129,203	89,996	932,238	385,083	547,155	330,976	133,999	82,180
Canada—Other	1,755,519	558,775	1,196,744	343,595	467,206	385,943	1,822,377	810,987	1,011,390	307,291	387,617	316,482
Newfoundland	25,448	12,320	13,128	7,163	2,780	3,185	8,635	5,076	3,559	1,836	853	870
West Indies[2]	45,496	21,909	23,587	9,987	9,005	4,595	41,842	23,169	18,673	8,681	6,743	3,249
Mexico	725,332	473,287	252,045	178,309	45,720	28,016	382,002	219,802	162,200	107,866	34,995	19,339
Central and South America	19,487	11,782	7,705	1,424	3,595	2,686	13,510	9,069	4,441	807	2,050	1,584
All other	116,458	48,299	68,159	38,700	19,292	10,167	74,523	40,167	34,356	14,214	13,029	7,113
Of mixed foreign parentage	1,502,457	....	1,502,457	1,502,457	....	....	1,177,092	....	1,177,092	1,177,092	....	....

1900 / 1890

COUNTRY OF ORIGIN.	Total foreign white stock.	Foreign-born white.[1]	NATIVE WHITE OF FOREIGN OR MIXED PARENTAGE.				Total foreign white stock.	Foreign-born white.[1]	NATIVE WHITE OF FOREIGN OR MIXED PARENTAGE.			
			Total.	Both parents foreign.	Father foreign.	Mother foreign.			Total.	Both parents foreign.	Father foreign.	Mother foreign.
All foreign countries	25,859,834	10,213,817	15,646,017	10,632,280	3,346,652	1,667,085	20,625,542	[3]9,121,867	11,503,675	8,085,019	2,378,729	1,039,927
Northwestern Europe:												
England	2,173,741	839,830	1,333,911	565,461	494,929	273,521	1,977,595	909,092	1,068,503	488,661	386,711	193,131
Scotland	594,297	233,473	360,824	163,991	129,735	67,098	519,252	242,231	277,021	134,243	97,661	45,117
Wales	253,045	93,560	159,485	86,899	47,498	25,088	225,582	100,079	125,503	75,375	34,863	15,265
Ireland	4,826,904	1,615,232	3,211,672	2,244,241	605,987	361,444	4,795,681	1,871,509	2,924,172	2,164,397	502,155	257,620
Norway	788,758	336,379	452,379	349,220	67,649	35,510	606,316	322,665	283,651	238,679	29,883	15,089
Sweden	1,082,388	581,986	500,402	414,772	55,479	30,151	730,569	478,041	252,528	217,217	23,810	11,501
Denmark	310,127	153,644	156,483	115,173	29,514	11,796	216,995	132,543	84,452	66,196	13,677	4,579
Switzerland	257,426	115,581	141,845	74,951	48,806	18,088	(4)	(4)	(4)			
France	268,292	104,031	164,261	71,263	72,110	20,888	258,919	113,174	145,745	68,572	61,187	15,986
Central, Eastern, and Southern Europe:												
Germany	8,111,453	2,813,413	5,298,040	3,709,706	1,180,880	407,454	6,857,229	2,784,894	4,072,335	3,006,342	827,823	238,170
Austria	895,500	491,259	404,241	344,070	42,295	17,876	341,549	241,377	100,172	90,195	6,744	3,233
Hungary	218,447	145,709	72,738	66,713	4,895	1,130	77,121	62,435	14,686	13,048	1,390	248
Russia	955,918	578,072	377,846	356,249	17,719	3,878	258,583	182,644	75,939	69,802	4,962	1,175
Italy	727,844	483,963	243,881	218,750	22,442	2,689	249,544	182,580	66,964	54,742	11,096	1,126
All other:												
Canada—French	830,335	394,461	435,874	265,947	106,833	63,094	526,934	302,496	224,438	157,104	42,356	24,978
Canada—Other	1,637,603	778,399	859,204	260,471	317,988	280,745	1,255,629	[5]673,000	582,629	183,602	227,144	171,883
All other countries	871,604	454,825	416,779	268,251	101,893	46,635	1,013,774	523,107	490,667	342,574	107,267	40,826
Of mixed foreign parentage	1,056,152	....	1,056,152	1,056,152	....	....	714,270	....	714,270	714,270	....	....

[1] For 1920, according to birthplace of father; for 1910, 1900, and 1890, according to birthplace of person. (See p. 891.)

[2] Except possessions of the United States.

[3] The report for 1890 classified the foreign born by country of birth without distinction as to color or race. For the purposes of this table it is assumed that, with the exception of "Canada—Other" (see note 5), the number reported for each specified country represented white persons only. The number for "All other countries" has been obtained by deducting the sum of the items for the specified countries from the United States total, which represents foreign-born white only.

[4] Switzerland included in "All other countries" in tabulation by birthplace of parents. Number of persons born in Switzerland, 104,069, also included in "All other countries" in this table.

[5] Partly estimated; total reported for "Canada—Other" was 678,442, of whom eight-tenths of 1 per cent were estimated to be nonwhites, this proportion being based upon returns of later censuses.

Table 10. Country of origin of the foreign white stock, by nativity and parentage, 1930.

Source: U.S. Bureau of the Census, Fifteenth U.S. Census (Washington, D.C., 1933), vol. II, table 4, p. 268.

[The foreign-born white are classified by country of birth; the native white with both parents foreign or with father foreign and mother native are classified by country of birth of father; and the native white with mother foreign and father native, by country of birth of mother. Per cent not shown where less than 0.1]

COUNTRY OF ORIGIN	TOTAL FOREIGN WHITE STOCK		FOREIGN-BORN WHITE		NATIVE WHITE—FOREIGN OR MIXED PARENTAGE							
					Total		Both parents foreign		Father foreign		Mother foreign	
	Number	Per cent	Number	Per cent	Number	Per cent	Number	Per cent	Number	Per cent	Number	Per cent
All countries	38,727,593	100.0	13,366,407	100.0	25,361,186	100.0	16,999,221	100.0	5,459,530	100.0	2,902,435	100.0
Northwestern Europe:												
England	2,522,261	6.5	808,672	6.1	1,713,589	6.8	740,066	4.4	598,022	11.0	375,501	12.9
Scotland	899,591	2.3	354,323	2.7	545,268	2.2	276,483	1.6	164,673	3.0	104,112	3.6
Wales	236,667	0.6	60,205	0.5	176,462	0.7	87,710	0.5	56,644	1.0	32,108	1.1
Northern Ireland	695,999	1.8	178,832	1.3	517,167	2.0	311,652	1.8	117,431	2.2	88,084	3.0
Irish Free State	3,086,522	8.0	744,810	5.6	2,341,712	9.2	1,551,760	9.1	432,450	7.9	357,502	12.3
Norway	1,100,098	2.8	347,852	2.6	752,246	3.0	476,663	2.8	179,482	3.3	96,101	3.3
Sweden	1,562,703	4.0	595,250	4.5	967,453	3.8	676,523	4.0	191,037	3.5	99,893	3.4
Denmark	529,142	1.4	179,474	1.3	349,668	1.4	219,152	1.3	93,592	1.7	36,924	1.3
Iceland	7,413		2,764		4,649		3,177		799		673	
Netherlands	413,966	1.1	133,133	1.0	280,833	1.1	170,417	1.0	74,730	1.4	35,686	1.2
Belgium	147,091	0.4	64,194	0.5	82,897	0.3	52,484	0.3	20,883	0.4	9,530	0.3
Luxemburg	34,869	0.1	9,048	0.1	25,821	0.1	15,163	0.1	8,173	0.1	2,485	0.1
Switzerland	374,003	1.0	113,010	0.8	260,993	1.0	146,255	0.9	80,595	1.5	34,143	1.2
France	471,605	1.2	135,232	1.0	336,373	1.3	178,033	1.0	108,869	2.0	49,471	1.7
Central Europe:												
Germany	6,873,103	17.7	1,608,814	12.0	5,264,289	20.8	3,254,618	19.1	1,398,587	25.6	611,084	21.1
Poland	3,342,198	8.6	1,268,583	9.5	2,073,615	8.2	1,781,280	10.5	223,611	4.1	68,724	2.4
Czechoslovakia	1,382,079	3.6	491,638	3.7	890,441	3.5	707,384	4.2	123,363	2.3	59,694	2.1
Austria	954,648	2.5	370,914	2.8	583,734	2.3	458,177	2.7	84,443	1.5	41,114	1.4
Hungary	590,768	1.5	274,450	2.1	316,318	1.2	272,704	1.6	28,378	0.5	15,236	0.5
Yugoslavia	469,395	1.2	211,416	1.6	257,979	1.0	227,475	1.3	26,328	0.5	4,176	0.1
Eastern Europe:												
Russia	2,669,838	6.9	1,153,624	8.6	1,516,214	6.0	1,277,460	7.5	169,755	3.1	68,999	2.4
Latvia	38,091	0.1	20,673	0.2	17,418	0.1	14,645	0.1	2,132		641	
Estonia	5,317		3,550		1,767		1,417		265		85	
Lithuania	439,195	1.1	193,606	1.4	245,589	1.0	221,472	1.3	19,643	0.4	4,474	0.2
Finland	320,536	0.8	142,478	1.1	178,058	0.7	148,532	0.9	18,805	0.3	10,721	0.4
Rumania	293,453	0.8	146,393	1.1	147,060	0.6	125,479	0.7	15,351	0.3	6,230	0.2
Bulgaria	14,929		9,399	0.1	5,530		3,256		2,147		727	
Turkey in Europe	3,676		2,257		1,419		1,174		205		40	
Southern Europe:												
Greece	303,751	0.8	174,526	1.3	129,225	0.5	101,668	0.6	26,981	0.5	576	
Albania	13,223		8,814	0.1	4,409		3,700		678		31	
Italy	4,546,877	11.7	1,790,424	13.4	2,756,453	10.9	2,306,015	13.6	396,324	7.3	54,114	1.9
Spain	110,607	0.3	58,302	0.4	52,305	0.2	36,080	0.2	12,646	0.2	3,579	0.1
Portugal	167,891	0.4	69,974	0.5	97,917	0.4	75,202	0.4	17,920	0.3	4,795	0.2
Other Europe:												
Danzig	3,524		1,483		2,041		1,351		446		244	
Europe (not specified)	53,366	0.1	14,768	0.1	38,598	0.2	29,498	0.2	6,260	0.1	2,840	0.1
Asia:												
Armenia	58,037	0.1	32,166	0.2	25,871	0.1	23,230	0.1	2,440		201	
Palestine	10,446		6,135		4,311		3,356		680		275	
Syria	137,576	0.4	57,227	0.4	80,349	0.3	69,034	0.4	9,972	0.2	1,343	
Turkey in Asia	77,283	0.2	46,651	0.3	30,632	0.1	26,777	0.2	3,295	0.1	560	
China	3,675		2,279		1,396		278		642		476	
Japan	1,458		632		826		278		345		203	
India	7,095		3,300		3,795		1,018		1,596		1,181	
Other Asia	14,357		9,190	0.1	5,167		3,724		1,050		393	
America:												
Canada—French	1,106,159	2.9	370,852	2.8	735,307	2.9	389,131	2.3	198,512	3.6	147,664	5.1
Canada—Other	2,231,186	5.8	907,569	6.8	1,323,617	5.2	416,670	2.5	479,669	8.8	427,278	14.7
Newfoundland	45,733	0.1	23,971	0.2	21,762	0.1	12,794	0.1	4,005	0.1	4,963	0.2
Cuba	32,540	0.1	15,944	0.1	16,596	0.1	7,894		5,763	0.1	2,939	0.1
Other West Indies	31,108	0.1	15,482	0.1	15,626	0.1	6,546		5,490	0.1	3,590	0.1
Mexico	65,968	0.2	23,743	0.2	42,225	0.2	16,067	0.1	12,275	0.2	13,883	0.5
Central America	10,485		7,454	0.1	3,031		919		956		1,156	
South America	48,260	0.1	30,055	0.2	18,205	0.1	7,779		6,615	0.1	3,811	0.1
All other:												
Africa	13,469		7,866	0.1	5,603		2,001		2,228		1,374	
Australia	30,849	0.1	12,720	0.1	18,129	0.1	6,294		6,707	0.1	5,128	0.2
Azores	91,714	0.2	35,427	0.3	56,287	0.2	43,308	0.3	10,165	0.2	2,814	0.1
Other Atlantic Islands	9,711		4,052		5,659		3,362		1,527		770	
Pacific Islands	8,648		4,364		4,284		917		1,847		1,520	0.1
Country not specified	3,171		1,485		1,686		1,134		395		157	
Born at sea	10,270		4,958		5,312		2,585		1,708		1,019	

Table 11. Foreign-born white population by country of birth, by states, 1950.

Source: U.S. Bureau of the Census, Seventeenth U.S. Census (Washington, D.C., 1954), Special Reports, *Nativity and Parentage*, vol. IV, pt. 3, ch. A, table 12, pp. 3A–71–74.

Country of birth	United States	Alabama	Arizona	Arkansas	California	Colorado	Connecticut	Delaware	District of Columbia	Florida	Georgia	Idaho
All countries	10,158,894	13,804	45,557	9,230	985,299	59,247	297,344	13,716	39,653	122,739	16,605	19,585
EUROPE[1]												
England	554,625	1,540	2,185	650	76,145	4,160	15,390	1,080	3,325	12,770	1,645	1,790
Scotland	244,200	509	568	146	25,619	1,389	7,638	527	970	3,677	475	528
Wales	30,060	55	100	35	3,010	415	420	55	85	415	40	125
Northern Ireland	15,398	17	22	11	1,611	48	701	54	65	161	33	24
Ireland (Eire)	504,961	327	660	202	28,405	1,600	19,865	1,103	2,067	3,224	437	376
Norway	202,294	156	298	70	15,780	737	1,782	100	347	1,431	76	1,147
Sweden	324,944	302	763	175	31,067	3,893	11,304	197	545	3,511	205	1,890
Denmark	107,897	105	357	106	18,053	1,381	2,144	78	288	1,566	102	869
Netherlands	102,133	87	204	92	12,270	568	654	58	293	1,196	101	296
Belgium	52,891	85	118	70	3,766	347	439	32	165	634	86	101
Switzerland	71,515	92	260	278	15,143	663	1,456	57	390	874	90	587
France	107,924	355	363	180	18,447	802	2,591	173	1,208	2,077	373	260
Germany	984,331	1,594	1,825	1,862	70,791	5,821	17,036	1,114	3,010	11,134	2,396	1,823
Poland	861,184	422	969	657	23,776	1,773	34,530	2,151	2,346	5,203	1,113	148
Czechoslovakia	278,268	283	355	272	7,456	945	7,333	148	437	1,786	109	324
Austria	408,785	281	790	280	20,818	2,643	8,945	325	1,141	4,615	401	423
Hungary	268,022	264	570	111	13,453	692	8,685	233	558	3,483	185	105
Yugoslavia	143,956	134	540	74	13,801	1,874	566	42	199	432	50	277
Latvia	31,590	55	60	30	2,245	160	620	70	355	380	100	35
Estonia	10,085	25	5	15	895	20	340	25	60	185	35	15
Lithuania	147,765	80	234	72	3,856	217	10,081	100	467	886	125	19
Finland	95,506	47	151	19	7,467	336	2,092	103	215	1,082	79	479
Rumania	84,952	86	212	64	6,299	238	780	129	340	1,473	114	63
Bulgaria	9,615	30	45	55	1,050	190	85	...	50	10	10	35
Greece	169,083	850	600	250	14,330	1,043	3,431	374	2,087	2,849	956	306
Dodecanese Islands	1,590	10	...	...	280	10	55	...	35	10	...	...
Italy	1,427,145	1,436	1,600	670	104,215	6,329	74,270	3,031	4,422	8,087	638	633
Spain	45,565	30	420	10	10,890	168	886	46	310	3,103	66	985
Portugal	54,337	10	22	2	15,134	20	2,448	13	59	171	99	15
Iceland	2,455	...	5	...	255	15	10	...	35	25	...	5
Luxembourg	9,590	10	10	10	470	55	35	5	15	50	15	25
Albania	10,510	5	30	5	250	15	730	10	55	75	10	10
All other Europe	15,670	70	65	20	1,605	75	150	5	25	155	60	20
ASIA[1]												
Turkey	71,730	80	120	15	12,435	110	1,375	50	510	860	235	10
Lebanon	10,695	120	80	25	510	30	565	...	40	305	75	5
Syria	35,325	220	235	105	2,520	105	760	5	190	1,105	195	25
Israel	10,020	25	30	...	1,335	65	120	25	190	270	35	15
Arab Palestine	540	5	...	...	40	...	10	...	10	5	...	15
Pakistan	235	...	10	...	40	...	...	...	105	130	25	15
India	5,370	35	45	5	1,130	60	100	20	140	175	80	10
China	11,985	45	80	15	4,175	50	160	20	35	70	70	55
Japan	4,650	35	15	5	1,060	115	40	10	20	25	40	...
Korea	1,215	5	5	...	140	35	15	5	295	300	120	15
Philippine Islands	13,445	30	100	35	4,795	125	125	5	270	205	35	10
Other Asia	14,690	30	35	10	2,575	110	580	10	270	205	35	10
U.S.S.R.												
U.S.S.R.	894,844	684	1,756	330	66,552	9,306	21,180	1,193	5,994	12,585	1,553	946
NORTH AND CENTRAL AMERICA												
Canada--French	238,409	71	197	106	7,990	311	16,900	81	373	1,808	98	249
Canada--Other	796,153	866	2,707	555	102,764	3,551	14,166	580	2,557	13,184	1,345	3,565
Mexico	450,562	125	24,917	553	162,309	5,275	158	38	325	431	132	326
Guatemala	3,160	15	30	10	1,065	20	25	5	75	65	35	...
British Honduras	1,180	50	...	25	145	10	5	...	20	55	15	5
Honduras	2,700	40	...	5	550	25	5	...	35	105	10	5
Nicaragua	5,475	15	20	5	2,820	35	40	...	35	60	10	...
El Salvador	3,600	5	25	10	2,455	15	...	...	40	105	15	5
Costa Rica	2,755	5	10	...	945	5	15	10	40	210	45	10
Panama	4,605	25	20	10	1,255	25	55	...	285	7,910	205	5
Cuba	29,295	90	10	5	1,350	35	365	10	30	130	10	10
Jamaica	2,120	...	5	...	255	5	30	5	110	2,030	40	5
Other British West Indies	12,400	165	40	15	655	25	205	20	45	105	...	...
Dominican Republic	4,200	...	...	5	155	15	15	...	10	30	...	...
Haiti	1,180	...	5	...	200	10	10	5	30	115	30	...
Other West Indies[2]	2,835	15	...	...	255	...	55	...	110	175	20	10
SOUTH AMERICA												
Colombia	3,610	25	...	...	420	15	15	...	115	140	15	...
Venezuela	3,430	15	5	5	210	...	45	5	55	50	20	...
Ecuador	1,955	...	5	5	385	10	15	5	90	80	10	5
Peru	2,615	5	10	...	675	15	60	...	35	5	...	...
Bolivia	575	...	...	5	100	15	...	...	225	205	15	10
Brazil	9,680	15	40	...	1,280	50	220	20	5	10	...	...
Paraguay	450	...	...	...	110	5	...	...	25	5	...	...
Uruguay	790	5	20	...	125	15	25	...	140	40	25	15
Chile	3,005	15	40	10	675	15	45	...	150	155	10	5
Argentina	7,945	10	40	10	1,430	80	160	5	35	200	25	15
Other South America	9,405	10	25	20	1,290	75	210	5	210	235	55	25
ALL OTHER												
Africa	13,260	35	35	10	2,390	70	215	10	210	235	55	25
Azores	26,025	...	15	...	11,205	5	145	...	10	45	5	15
Other Atlantic Islands	4,595	5	10	...	640	5	165	5	25	140	15	5
Australia	19,900	85	120	75	5,890	205	285	25	270	340	125	100
New Zealand	4,965	25	30	15	2,035	35	85	...	80	80	40	40
Trust Territory of the Pacific Islands (United States administration)	145	...	...	...	60	...	...	...	...	5	...	...
Other Pacific Islands[2]	650	10	...	...	260	15	10	...	10	15	5	...
Country not specified	77,175	1,311	290	753	5,212	497	1,128	116	305	1,331	1,538	291

[1] Excluding U.S.S.R.
[2] Excluding possessions of the United States.

Table 11 (continued)

Country of birth	Illinois	Indiana	Iowa	Kansas	Kentucky	Louisiana	Maine	Maryland	Massachu-setts	Michigan	Minnesota	Missis-sippi
All countries.............	783,866	100,408	84,682	38,490	16,020	28,811	74,055	84,088	712,844	603,401	210,147	8,485
EUROPE[1]												
England....................	30,490	5,675	4,650	2,480	1,465	1,655	3,055	5,875	45,145	41,265	5,110	620
Scotland...................	14,690	2,716	1,332	755	356	418	1,225	1,920	20,559	24,937	1,824	104
Wales.....................	1,765	450	425	240	45	60	75	300	750	1,410	330	25
Northern Ireland..........	907	58	57	26	17	16	68	37	1,958	76	134	8
Ireland (Eire)............	36,075	2,352	2,066	963	667	709	2,058	2,811	81,214	9,958	2,093	173
Norway....................	15,684	553	5,531	341	53	376	381	779	4,207	4,071	33,477	55
Sweden....................	56,128	2,736	7,080	2,527	163	247	987	742	21,333	17,322	43,933	109
Denmark...................	10,425	620	7,625	649	58	213	439	521	1,884	4,219	7,374	80
Netherlands...............	8,993	1,525	6,078	262	96	263	66	520	1,723	20,215	3,512	58
Belgium...................	8,034	2,297	678	592	93	205	76	263	1,689	10,518	1,197	35
Switzerland...............	3,835	751	838	597	397	136	66	509	1,009	1,709	946	26
France....................	6,529	1,401	793	684	409	1,521	334	1,118	4,848	3,632	845	170
Germany...................	96,517	13,801	22,774	7,183	3,949	2,467	997	12,563	15,439	45,323	26,459	808
Poland....................	111,376	11,883	1,402	1,186	626	955	1,073	8,637	46,597	81,595	8,308	336
Czechoslovakia............	43,185	5,344	3,819	1,209	172	234	267	2,265	1,678	12,168	5,361	47
Austria...................	30,270	3,681	1,156	1,702	402	429	203	2,609	6,291	15,078	5,997	90
Hungary...................	19,020	6,703	319	244	318	312	87	1,518	1,175	18,818	1,508	50
Yugoslavia................	19,146	5,009	920	1,592	112	427	21	354	249	11,453	5,078	152
Latvia....................	2,665	390	455	135	135	45	105	655	2,470	1,570	830	620
Estonia...................	510	90	155	25	25	15	20	245	330	330	170	60
Lithuania.................	33,049	2,002	601	100	25	15	79	883	18,559	7,776	992	87
Finland...................	3,014	217	69	48	42	92	1,063	2,998	9,190	15,501	14,475	32
Rumania...................	6,384	1,805	132	73	113	116	31	595	1,007	6,423	1,249	34
Bulgaria..................	810	390	160	20	10	40	5	35	155	1,325	225	10
Greece....................	17,410	4,032	1,407	394	399	497	758	2,467	14,511	9,273	1,565	283
Dodecanese Islands........	130	60	10	20	...	5	10	15	45	130	85	...
Italy.....................	83,556	5,508	2,908	1,214	1,067	7,678	2,008	9,942	101,548	38,937	4,496	1,023
Spain.....................	714	475	26	50	41	388	25	262	659	890	51	23
Portugal..................	90	31	6	4	6	47	63	92	20,042	136	8	10
Iceland...................	110	10	10	...	15	5	10	45	160	50	150	10
Luxembourg................	1,555	75	330	45	5	15	15	10	70	195	475	...
Albania...................	580	120	25	15	20	...	175	5	3,280	705	20	...
All other Europe..........	660	180	35	60	65	75	25	145	210	2,840	145	35
ASIA[1]												
Turkey....................	3,130	450	120	45	65	135	240	365	10,620	5,665	80	15
Lebanon...................	215	55	60	25	30	85	105	20	1,690	785	130	130
Syria.....................	595	445	420	145	285	455	245	65	3,750	3,300	335	435
Israel....................	575	65	65	25	65	50	10	180	320	460	85	5
Arab Palestine............	55	5	10	5	...	5	...	...	10	20	5	...
Pakistan..................	10	...	...	...	...	...	...	...	10	35	5	5
India.....................	285	85	20	45	20	30	35	105	260	300	75	10
China.....................	445	145	70	70	65	60	15	145	375	325	195	25
Japan.....................	250	65	15	35	40	45	15	130	145	160	60	25
Korea.....................	80	35	...	5	...	...	5	10	60	55	20	...
Philippine Islands........	625	110	35	85	65	175	20	280	310	375	95	25
Other Asia................	1,680	210	55	95	40	55	25	165	355	1,060	70	20
U.S.S.R.												
U.S.S.R...................	59,753	3,591	2,774	4,315	1,038	1,018	1,527	13,570	52,353	30,804	8,493	456
NORTH AND CENTRAL AMERICA												
Canada--French............	3,196	598	346	226	105	173	28,329	359	69,479	15,786	2,482	39
Canada--Other.............	25,837	5,581	3,776	2,133	962	1,029	26,010	3,770	123,035	126,472	15,168	426
Mexico....................	12,463	3,222	1,253	4,204	82	1,106	40	193	324	5,235	900	259
Guatemala.................	150	20	20	20	...	235	5	45	95	110	15	30
British Honduras..........	55	5	5	...	5	170	5	15	60	45	20	20
Honduras..................	35	40	...	10	10	670	...	15	30	45	5	45
Nicaragua.................	185	20	10	20	...	475	30	40	155	85	35	15
El Salvador...............	65	20	5	...	5	85	5	20	35	35	15	15
Costa Rica................	55	15	5	10	5	150	...	35	85	20	20	15
Panama....................	100	55	60	15	25	140	15	105	130	95	10	30
Cuba......................	625	135	20	15	70	395	5	265	400	295	30	25
Jamaica...................	90	20	5	20	10	50	10	35	75	90	5	...
Other British West Indies.	170	65	50	40	35	155	40	150	485	155	30	35
Dominican Republic........	60	20	5	15	10	20	...	35	25	45	5	...
Haiti.....................	75	5	10	5	5	10	...	15	20	30	10	5
Other West Indies[2]......	65	15	...	...	...	35	...	15	125	30	15	5
SOUTH AMERICA												
Colombia..................	105	35	10	15	...	100	5	30	60	70	...	10
Venezuela.................	85	15	30	20	...	60	5	75	55	105	10	5
Ecuador...................	55	25	5	20	5	45	5	25	10	20	5	...
Peru......................	95	25	5	10	...	35	...	40	30	65	20	5
Bolivia...................	25	10	15	10	...	10	...	20	25	35	10	...
Brazil....................	520	75	25	45	25	85	10	205	800	285	45	30
Paraguay..................	10	...	...	...	...	10	...	10	5	30	10	...
Uruguay...................	65	...	...	10	5	10	...	5	20	20	...	5
Chile.....................	70	40	25	20	10	20	...	60	50	35	20	5
Argentina.................	390	45	35	60	10	60	...	110	295	220	40	...
Other South America.......	405	90	35	90	35	105	15	160	320	265	60	25
ALL OTHER												
Africa....................	705	110	90	85	30	90	40	235	520	575	195	20
Azores....................	5	10	...	...	5	10	20	30	11,460	50	15	...
Other Atlantic Islands....	75	15	...	5	...	10	20	70	1,790	70	15	10
Australia.................	880	210	180	180	125	150	60	295	500	830	265	100
New Zealand...............	135	50	40	25	10	10	30	60	160	125	35	5
Trust Territory of the Pacific Islands (United States administration).......	...	...	5	...	...	...	...	...	5	15	5	...
Other Pacific Islands[2]...	15	...	5	10	...	...	...	...	35	15	5	...
Country not specified.....	5,086	1,076	1,096	842	1,243	1,195	440	1,115	2,949	3,506	1,422	962

[1] Excluding U.S.S.R.
[2] Excluding possessions of the United States.

Table 11 (continued)

Country of birth	Missouri	Montana	Nebraska	Nevada	New Hampshire	New Jersey	New Mexico	New York	North Carolina	North Dakota	Ohio	Oklahoma
All countries	92,095	43,19?	57,192	10,419	57,742	631,058	17,296	2,500,774	1?,?43	49,23?	443,0??	18,??5
EUROPE[1]												
England	4,?15	2,850	1,990	700	2,750	34,515	81?	1?0,280	1,345	715	25,755	1,?15
Scotland	1,280	1,370	488	201	1,126	24,658	247	48,304	522	351	11,?15	464
Wales	270	225	130	25	30	1,230	50	4,725	45	30	3,045	55
Northern Ireland	60	55	34	16	139	1,419	5	4,171	24	22	399	15
Ireland (Eire)	4,131	2,003	1,058	270	2,414	33,113	202	182,581	311	417	11,146	358
Norway	325	5,228	635	148	302	5,860	107	33,073	98	13,268	,289	128
Sweden	1,713	2,731	5,449	287	1,071	8,383	187	36,747	152	3,415	4,526	356
Denmark	795	1,398	4,555	363	129	4,247	80	11,627	86	1,315	1,434	221
Netherlands	456	786	319	77	145	10,580	68	13,393	307	341	1,530	105
Belgium	668	369	333	50	369	2,420	38	7,665	83	127	1,586	146
Switzerland	1,505	458	587	253	98	5,711	87	12,276	89	143	3,617	242
France	1,285	386	271	605	340	7,405	252	28,185	352	114	3,551	408
Germany	18,337	3,025	13,276	712	1,474	75,823	957	270,661	1,878	4,195	48,528	3,202
Poland	5,922	788	2,393	115	2,817	69,404	167	254,065	704	981	41,820	724
Czechoslovakia	2,441	809	6,455	45	89	17,609	102	44,111	100	819	38,20?	899
Austria	5,250	1,370	1,159	206	381	28,713	280	149,955	295	948	23,553	484
Hungary	3,481	414	353	51	83	30,731	95	65,276	149	830	43,41?	184
Yugoslavia	2,123	1,822	519	267	34	2,646	293	10,097	80	81	26,089	7?
Latvia	275	60	385	5	70	1,675	15	7,220	530	165	1,450	145
Estonia	40	25	50	10	20	1,010	30	3,575	75	80	220	35
Lithuania	754	85	621	22	844	7,910	30	20,656	153	88	6,238	124
Finland	96	1,328	33	78	873	2,281	54	12,897	40	311	3,682	40
Rumania	1,273	196	203	35	60	3,552	28	32,270	72	481	9,167	79
Bulgaria	175	115	65	20	10	265	20	1,385	5	25	1,175	105
Greece	1,989	530	555	400	2,632	6,384	408	36,757	1,472	180	10,271	417
Dodecanese Islands	15	15	...	5	...	35	...	310	...	10	55	10
Italy	10,695	1,767	2,622	1,985	1,416	150,680	934	503,175	553	96	5?,593	805
Spain	350	38	20	815	19	3,382	117	14,705	41	4	1,141	3?
Portugal	19	6	7	41	141	3,413	8	4,256	17	3	243	7
Iceland	10	10	20	5	...	100	...	350	5	235	75	15
Luxembourg	50	70	65	...	...	170	15	670	5	90	110	15
Albania	280	25	15	5	210	230	5	1,700	70	30	415	5
All other Europe	375	35	175	...	35	565	20	3,850	60	25	795	25
ASIA[1]												
Turkey	310	75	30	40	310	3,590	45	19,520	145	45	2,130	65
Lebanon	65	60	20	...	165	275	65	1,765	220	15	890	105
Syria	385	75	185	15	195	1,815	50	6,360	240	130	2,340	435
Israel	80	10	10	5	15	400	...	4,130	50	...	280	55
Arab Palestine	15	10	20	...	...	15	...	55	...	5	5	20
Pakistan	...	...	...	...	...	...	...	50	...	...	5	...
India	80	15	40	5	10	225	10	960	35	...	185	35
China	170	20	60	10	5	340	25	1,980	140	30	445	50
Japan	40	15	55	15	20	130	10	670	35	10	175	25
Korea	25	5	10	...	...	60	...	225	5	5	25	...
Philippine Islands	225	40	45	45	20	405	40	2,095	75	10	230	60
Other Asia	105	25	15	5	40	540	10	4,205	120	5	290	45
U.S.S.R.												
U.S.S.R.	10,208	3,423	7,019	173	1,399	50,620	231	353,835	640	12,393	23,114	2,008
NORTH AND CENTRAL AMERICA												
Canada--French	329	727	178	179	24,930	2,306	50	18,254	130	634	1,713	160
Canada--Other	3,602	6,741	2,048	923	9,920	13,917	749	99,730	1,321	5,545	18,738	1,588
Mexico	2,057	693	1,673	786	34	598	9,666	4,138	96	77	1,824	1,196
Guatemala	45	10	5	...	...	50	10	415	20	...	85	25
British Honduras	15	5	...	...	10	20	...	155	...	...	30	5
Honduras	15	5	5	...	15	45	5	410	...	5	15	10
Nicaragua	15	15	10	20	10	80	...	685	10	20	75	20
El Salvador	...	...	5	...	...	10	10	320	...	...	20	20
Costa Rica	50	...	...	10	...	95	...	725	5	...	50	20
Panama	65	5	15	10	5	125	20	970	50	...	90	20
Cuba	105	5	5	10	25	945	45	13,295	135	5	250	25
Jamaica	25	...	...	5	15	120	...	760	10	...	40	35
Other British West Indies	55	15	20	10	30	745	10	5,515	55	15	120	25
Dominican Republic	...	5	5	5	...	100	...	3,265	...	...	10	5
Haiti	...	5	...	...	...	85	10	445	10	5	40	...
Other West Indies[2]	20	5	10	...	...	130	...	1,425	15	...	75	5
SOUTH AMERICA												
Colombia	10	...	5	...	5	120	...	1,775	10	5	50	75
Venezuela	25	5	10	...	15	165	...	1,925	...	...	35	45
Ecuador	5	...	...	...	...	30	...	980	10	...	30	5
Peru	40	10	...	...	...	85	5	890	15	...	30	25
Bolivia	10	...	...	...	...	15	...	125	...	...	...	10
Brazil	75	20	...	5	10	925	25	2,765	40	5	280	20
Paraguay	...	10	5	...	...	20	...	70	5	10	...	...
Uruguay	20	...	...	...	...	55	...	260	...	...	15	...
Chile	10	5	5	...	...	105	25	1,015	...	5	85	...
Argentina	55	50	25	15	20	530	25	2,710	5	30	215	20
Other South America	65	30	40	15	30	570	45	3,585	25	...	235	?0
ALL OTHER												
Africa	190	70	30	30	20	690	35	4,010	85	20	415	45
Azores	...	20	...	100	10	75	...	200	...	...	30	...
Other Atlantic Islands	10	5	5	...	35	245	10	600	...	...	35	25
Australia	275	175	85	45	50	675	65	2,165	90	25	655	1?5
New Zealand	40	15	15	20	15	80	20	415	45	10	130	30
Trust Territory of the Pacific Islands (United States administration)[2]	5	...	...	...	...	5	...	20	...	...	...	...
Other Pacific Islands[2]	5	...	5	...	5	15	...	65	5	...	30	...
Country not specified	1,761	400	634	100	233	2,783	269	10,184	1,857	250	4,815	85?

[1] Excluding U.S.S.R.
[2] Excluding possessions of the United States.

Table 11 (continued)

Country of birth	Oregon	Pennsyl-vania	Rhode Island	South Carolina	South Dakota	Tennes-see	Texas	Utah	Vermont	Vir-ginia	Washing-ton	West Virginia	Wiscon-sin	Wyoming
All countries...................	83,369	776,808	113,251	7,324	30,699	15,099	276,410	29,935	28,617	34,721	190,401	34,575	218,182	13,254
EUROPE[1]														
England..........................	5,950	42,695	14,315	815	1,015	1,485	6,745	5,520	1,290	4,230	14,565	2,335	5,735	1,120
Scotland.........................	2,635	20,231	3,754	212	265	367	1,472	780	714	1,396	5,513	795	1,750	768
Wales............................	235	6,345	100	5	110	95	320	265	185	130	900	220	580	80
Northern Ireland.................	141	1,541	184	19	20	14	59	31	18	71	159	19	79	15
Ireland (Eire)...................	2,179	44,884	8,126	202	457	328	2,384	320	627	948	3,903	393	1,808	383
Norway...........................	5,318	2,024	332	55	5,524	103	928	1,236	85	381	23,304	55	14,663	393
Sweden...........................	6,904	7,724	3,428	78	2,677	176	2,346	2,092	554	489	20,906	160	9,285	949
Denmark..........................	2,521	1,724	177	41	2,528	95	941	2,240	95	370	4,710	62	6,537	444
Netherlands......................	1,010	1,219	120	42	1,547	75	699	2,336	29	342	3,230	61	4,152	64
Belgium..........................	522	2,353	627	58	121	83	485	134	27	228	994	400	1,331	94
Switzerland......................	2,465	3,015	160	40	253	220	844	972	139	257	2,360	188	4,695	132
France...........................	838	6,550	1,601	161	109	286	1,656	248	188	808	1,458	413	1,044	297
Germany..........................	7,930	59,532	2,573	816	5,248	1,932	15,280	3,334	668	3,916	12,928	1,872	58,526	922
Poland...........................	1,312	87,947	5,336	458	381	998	3,914	148	1,010	1,737	2,922	3,250	24,446	363
Czechoslovakia...................	1,098	48,634	166	43	1,058	116	6,544	81	127	737	1,381	1,485	9,682	232
Austria..........................	2,125	60,738	1,234	142	440	297	2,748	500	144	794	3,959	1,465	12,262	854
Hungary..........................	743	32,134	193	50	151	213	932	99	149	645	770	6,006	148	
Yugoslavia.......................	1,139	21,412	42	24	98	47	479	496	17	158	2,998	1,616	7,597	604
Latvia...........................	260	1,970	70	115	335	330	330	5	60	460	670	80	680	45
Estonia..........................	160	320	10	25	40	45	140	5	15	110	260	15	145	30
Lithuania........................	299	20,432	603	53	58	113	390	24	96	444	649	521	3,136	25
Finland..........................	3,530	1,232	443	30	341	31	192	217	300	159	7,237	167	3,282	262
Rumania..........................	367	6,820	247	30	91	85	480	22	21	214	413	339	620	27
Bulgaria.........................	125	495	50	5	5	5	65	25	5	40	240	70	210	45
Greece...........................	1,230	10,474	1,050	812	222	525	1,919	1,682	180	1,717	2,392	1,724	2,476	613
Dodecanese Islands...............	10	80	25	...	10	5	45	...	...	5	35	...	...	5
Italy............................	3,581	163,359	24,380	228	202	1,552	5,059	1,750	1,766	2,087	7,566	8,557	9,663	858
Spain............................	299	1,700	100	20	5	22	604	137	269	159	232	712	55	65
Portugal.........................	74	833	6,407	2	2	3	73	5	19	89	65	44	23	9
Iceland..........................	60	35	40	5	5	25	10	45	...	20	430	5	25	...
Luxembourg.......................	85	145	15	...	160	5	45	5	10	5	100	10	255	...
Albania..........................	35	760	160	...	15	25	25	25	20	30	115	30	140	...
All other Europe.................	80	1,575	40	10	40	35	560	20	20	115	100	100	290	...
ASIA[1]														
Turkey...........................	190	3,250	2,255	85	15	65	425	55	30	400	805	190	905	25
Lebanon..........................	55	740	100	120	15	35	290	20	70	140	115	230	35	...
Syria............................	185	3,145	755	160	110	125	830	80	120	325	175	750	320	30
Israel...........................	35	410	40	10	10	20	245	25	...	35	65	10	45	20
Arab Palestine...................	25	...	5	...	5	...	40	...	...	5	35	...	5	...
Pakistan.........................	...	20	...	...	...	...	...	...	...	5	10	...	10	...
India............................	55	235	35	20	5	40	125	...	...	85	120	15	90	5
China............................	160	400	25	50	20	75	295	10	10	205	430	20	100	5
Japan............................	65	215	10	20	10	65	170	70	...	100	185	10	25	10
Korea............................	15	115	5	...	5	5	25	10	...	40	40	15	10	5
Philippine Islands...............	150	340	35	35	15	55	505	50	10	325	380	5	100	5
Other Asia.......................	50	590	65	40	5	45	170	85	...	250	95	65	110	15
U.S.S.R.														
U.S.S.R..........................	5,645	80,541	4,678	479	4,423	1,321	4,592	231	501	3,056	8,168	1,372	11,941	1,062
NORTH AND CENTRAL AMERICA														
Canada--French...................	1,171	1,114	19,163	58	213	68	524	139	12,485	280	2,508	77	1,642	69
Canada--Other....................	17,614	12,875	6,123	504	1,656	1,122	5,572	2,006	6,161	2,951	45,073	772	8,035	828
Mexico...........................	618	1,374	53	28	112	145	196,077	1,396	17	145	1,546	177	1,067	1,049
Guatemala........................	10	120	15	...	5	10	160	10	5	20	25	15	10	...
British Honduras.................	10	15	25	5	...	30	105	5	10	5	20	...	5	...
Honduras.........................	10	50	...	...	5	10	180	10	...	40	15	...	20	...
Nicaragua........................	15	70	15	5	15	10	130	5	...	30	40	...	25	...
El Salvador......................	5	55	...	...	...	30	145	5	...	30	20	...	...	...
Costa Rica.......................	5	110	...	5	...	5	65	5	...	20	20	5	...	...
Panama...........................	10	120	20	30	...	25	230	5	...	160	90	20	25	10
Cuba.............................	45	755	90	50	5	100	385	20	15	200	55	80	35	10
Jamaica..........................	40	35	25	...	...	10	50	...	5	15	20	5	10	5
Other British West Indies........	45	320	65	30	5	25	345	...	10	90	50	30	40	.10
Dominican Republic...............	20	65	10	...	...	...	60	...	...	30	50	...	15	...
Haiti............................	...	35	...	...	...	5	20	...	5	20	10	...	25	...
Other West Indies[2].............	5	130	45	...	...	15	80	...	...	20	25	5	15	5
SOUTH AMERICA														
Colombia.........................	15	115	10	10	...	20	60	...	...	20	40	5	30	...
Venezuela........................	5	70	...	...	5	...	95	...	...	20	15	5	20	...
Ecuador..........................	10	20	5	...	...	...	55	...	...	15	10	5	...	...
Peru.............................	15	45	5	5	5	5	50	...	...	30	40	10	25	...
Bolivia..........................	5	30	...	...	5	...	25	10	...	5	20	5	...	...
Brazil...........................	50	540	160	10	15	50	105	30	5	85	105	50	70	...
Paraguay.........................	25	10	5	...	5	...	10	5	...	5	45	15	...	...
Uruguay..........................	10	45	10	...	...	...	15	10	...	...	...	...	5	5
Chile............................	30	125	15	...	10	...	110	10	...	25	60	...	15	5
Argentina........................	55	355	45	...	20	10	175	25	5	40	55	35	85	20
Other South America..............	35	555	75	25	10	15	170	35	10	60	65	10	110	15
ALL OTHER														
Africa...........................	105	445	105	45	25	55	250	45	20	150	175	60	140	15
Azores...........................	60	15	2,395	...	...	5	...	...	15	15	15	...	15	5
Other Atlantic Islands...........	20	110	115	5	...	15	60	...	5	95	45	5	25	10
Australia........................	490	955	95	105	45	90	580	230	15	310	640	115	390	25
New Zealand......................	170	85	30	10	35	10	90	130	20	80	255	10	35	20
Trust Territory of the Pacific Islands (United States administration).......	5	10	...	...	...	...	5	...	...	...	...	...	...	...
Other Pacific Islands[2].........	25	15	...	...	...	...	15	15	...	...	10	...	5	5
Country not specified............	736	5,297	441	784	313	1,629	3,932	329	201	1,453	1,217	898	1,369	115

[1] Excluding U.S.S.R.
[2] Excluding possessions of the United States.

Table 12. Country of origin of the foreign stock, by nativity, color, and sex, 1960.

Source: U.S. Bureau of the Census, Eighteenth U.S. Census (Washington, D.C., 1964), vol. I: *Characteristics of the Population*, pt. I, United States summary, table 162, p. 1–366.

Country of origin	Total foreign stock			Foreign born						Native of foreign or mixed parentage					
					White			Nonwhite			White			Nonwhite	
	Total	White	Non-white	Total	Both sexes	Male	Female	Male	Female	Total	Both sexes	Male	Female	Male	Female
All countries	34,050,354	33,078,339	972,015	9,738,091	9,293,992	4,507,502	4,786,490	252,930	191,169	24,312,263	23,784,347	11,568,891	12,215,456	266,746	261,170
Europe and U.S.S.R.:															
England	1,826,825	1,820,740	6,085	528,205	526,157	217,820	308,337	807	1,241	1,298,620	1,294,583	615,258	679,325	1,916	2,121
Scotland	668,672	667,672	1,000	213,219	213,026	95,317	117,709	63	130	455,453	454,646	219,737	234,909	352	455
Wales	134,008	133,793	215	23,469	23,407	10,543	12,864	4	58	110,539	110,386	52,418	57,968	64	89
Northern Ireland	255,146	254,809	337	68,162	68,083	29,573	38,510	15	64	186,984	186,726	85,329	101,397	106	152
Ireland (Eire)	1,773,312	1,771,070	2,242	338,722	338,350	135,828	202,522	119	253	1,434,590	1,432,720	662,153	770,567	886	984
Norway	774,754	774,081	673	152,698	152,644	80,613	72,031	23	31	622,056	621,437	299,241	322,196	304	315
Sweden	1,046,942	1,045,763	1,179	214,491	214,313	111,592	102,721	82	96	832,451	831,450	401,791	429,659	419	582
Denmark	399,350	398,806	544	85,060	84,989	48,467	36,522	41	30	314,290	313,817	152,483	161,334	210	263
Netherlands	398,658	398,151	507	118,415	118,160	64,040	54,120	126	129	280,243	279,991	139,364	140,627	86	166
Belgium	140,266	140,028	238	50,294	50,210	23,320	26,890	29	55	89,972	89,818	44,729	45,089	91	63
Switzerland	263,054	262,734	320	61,568	61,490	31,444	30,046	34	44	201,486	201,244	97,244	104,000	102	140
France	351,681	349,360	2,321	111,582	110,864	42,407	68,457	346	372	240,099	238,496	110,276	128,220	822	781
Germany	4,320,664	4,312,638	8,026	989,815	986,564	441,209	545,355	1,428	1,823	3,330,849	3,326,074	1,582,588	1,743,486	2,046	2,729
Poland	2,780,026	2,778,210	1,816	747,750	747,250	368,417	378,833	253	247	2,032,276	2,030,960	1,001,315	1,029,645	445	871
Czechoslovakia	917,830	917,172	658	227,618	227,467	105,278	122,189	41	110	690,212	689,705	338,383	351,322	229	278
Austria	1,098,630	1,097,581	1,049	304,507	304,192	139,222	164,970	131	184	794,123	793,389	386,701	406,688	268	466
Hungary	701,637	700,899	738	245,252	244,945	116,797	128,148	94	213	456,385	455,954	225,210	230,744	179	252
Yugoslavia	448,503	448,142	361	165,798	165,658	90,576	75,082	68	72	282,705	282,484	140,059	142,425	84	137
Latvia	89,154	89,099	55	50,681	50,658	24,056	26,602	7	16	38,473	38,441	19,458	18,983	18	14
Estonia	19,938	19,896	42	13,991	13,974	6,677	7,297	8	9	5,947	5,922	3,052	2,870	17	8
Lithuania	402,846	402,498	348	121,475	121,349	59,107	62,242	48	78	281,371	281,149	136,066	145,083	74	148
Finland	240,827	240,525	302	67,624	67,540	29,958	37,582	37	47	173,203	172,985	82,925	90,060	122	96
Rumania	233,805	233,540	265	84,575	84,471	41,957	42,514	48	56	149,230	149,069	74,377	74,692	48	113
Bulgaria	18,913	18,787	126	8,223	8,195	5,436	2,759	15	13	10,690	10,592	5,359	5,233	47	51
Greece	378,586	377,973	613	159,167	158,894	98,632	60,262	194	79	219,419	219,079	110,401	108,678	152	188
Italy	4,543,935	4,539,692	4,243	1,256,999	1,255,812	683,081	572,731	616	571	3,286,936	3,283,880	1,638,875	1,645,005	1,236	1,820
Spain	126,163	125,167	996	44,999	44,815	27,830	16,985	101	83	81,164	80,352	39,725	40,627	417	395
Portugal	206,292	200,033	6,259	57,690	56,158	30,752	25,406	1,222	310	148,602	143,875	71,180	72,695	2,215	2,512
Iceland	9,023	9,008	15	2,780	2,769	1,012	1,757	3	8	6,243	6,239	2,846	3,393	4	...
Luxembourg	25,204	25,153	51	4,360	4,335	2,023	2,312	17	8	20,844	20,818	10,281	10,537	9	17
Albania	21,293	21,184	109	9,618	9,572	6,193	3,379	21	25	11,675	11,612	5,669	5,943	40	23
All other Europe, excl. U.S.S.R.	42,432	42,081	351	14,320	14,166	7,923	6,243	109	45	28,112	27,915	13,145	14,770	102	95
U.S.S.R.	2,290,267	2,286,986	3,281	690,598	689,462	343,340	346,122	504	632	1,599,669	1,597,524	788,563	808,961	952	1,193
Asia (excl. U.S.S.R.):															
Turkey[1]	106,225	105,790	435	52,228	51,887	27,939	23,948	188	153	53,997	53,903	26,434	27,469	34	60
Lebanon	72,640	72,417	223	22,217	22,090	11,594	10,496	73	54	50,423	50,327	25,565	24,762	39	57
Israel	29,196	28,982	214	17,724	17,560	9,635	7,925	109	55	11,472	11,422	5,864	5,558	29	21
United Arab Republic	87,076	86,357	719	25,033	24,607	13,207	11,400	309	117	62,043	61,750	30,989	30,761	150	143
Egypt	14,463	14,084	379	8,316	8,041	4,319	3,722	197	78	6,147	6,043	3,058	2,985	47	57
Syria	72,613	72,273	340	16,717	16,566	8,888	7,678	112	39	55,896	55,707	27,931	27,776	103	86
Other Southwest Asia	39,860	38,670	1,190	23,811	22,855	15,082	7,773	783	173	16,049	15,815	7,916	7,899	112	122
Pakistan	2,577	1,640	937	1,708	940	696	244	619	149	869	700	349	351	84	85
India	24,673	16,864	7,809	12,296	6,414	3,304	3,110	4,598	1,284	12,377	10,450	5,231	5,219	952	975
China	208,455	32,543	175,912	99,735	12,858	5,968	6,890	55,628	31,249	108,720	19,685	9,625	10,060	47,251	41,784
Japan	322,090	30,169	291,921	109,175	11,686	5,272	6,414	39,421	58,068	212,915	18,483	9,017	9,466	98,884	95,548
Korea	19,756	5,525	14,231	11,171	2,681	1,342	1,339	4,321	4,169	8,585	2,844	1,372	1,472	2,973	2,768
Philippine Islands	201,746	45,328	156,418	104,843	15,624	9,690	5,934	66,896	22,323	96,903	29,704	14,806	14,898	34,130	33,069
Other Asia	27,538	18,694	8,844	19,371	12,128	6,396	5,732	4,199	3,044	8,167	6,566	3,206	3,360	859	742
North and Central America:															
Canada[2]	3,181,051	3,153,514	27,537	952,500	941,906	404,918	536,988	4,251	6,343	2,228,551	2,211,608	1,077,835	1,133,773	8,363	8,580
Mexico	1,735,992	1,724,838	11,154	575,902	572,564	304,975	267,589	1,794	1,544	1,160,090	1,152,274	574,837	577,437	3,917	3,899
Guatemala	9,804	9,462	342	5,381	5,141	2,274	2,867	96	144	4,423	4,321	2,190	2,131	56	46
British Honduras	4,948	3,141	1,807	2,780	1,712	911	801	581	487	2,168	1,429	708	721	347	392
Honduras	10,782	8,306	2,476	6,503	4,977	2,253	2,724	812	714	4,279	3,329	1,785	1,544	492	458
Nicaragua	14,668	14,190	478	9,474	9,176	3,679	5,497	126	172	5,194	5,014	2,481	2,533	88	92
El Salvador	9,574	9,438	136	6,310	6,228	2,421	3,807	37	45	3,264	3,210	1,603	1,607	19	35
Costa Rica	8,773	7,957	816	5,425	4,866	2,072	2,794	227	332	3,348	3,091	1,577	1,514	166	91
Panama	22,064	12,758	9,306	13,076	6,673	2,545	4,128	2,897	3,506	8,988	6,085	3,128	2,957	1,476	1,427
Cuba	124,416	116,354	8,062	79,150	74,921	37,723	37,198	1,983	2,246	45,266	41,433	20,806	20,627	2,040	1,793
Jamaica	40,561	8,069	32,492	24,759	3,941	1,713	2,228	12,601	8,217	15,802	4,128	2,123	2,005	5,961	5,713
The West Indies (federation)	110,941	22,925	88,016	54,408	9,602	4,304	5,298	23,291	21,515	56,533	13,323	6,739	6,584	21,239	21,971
Dominican Republic	17,640	15,669	1,971	11,883	10,609	3,995	6,614	420	854	5,757	5,060	2,523	2,537	334	363
Haiti	7,324	3,508	3,816	4,816	2,106	1,021	1,085	1,218	1,492	2,508	1,402	698	704	562	544
Other West Indies[3]	45,713	13,087	32,626	18,906	4,618	2,191	2,427	8,221	6,067	26,807	8,469	4,107	4,362	8,680	9,658
South America:															
Colombia	17,192	16,758	434	12,582	12,262	5,531	6,731	149	171	4,610	4,496	2,177	2,319	71	43
Venezuela	10,544	10,035	509	6,851	6,555	3,243	3,312	181	115	3,693	3,480	1,703	1,777	82	131
Ecuador	11,081	10,396	685	7,670	7,328	3,587	3,741	227	115	3,411	3,068	1,479	1,589	164	179
Peru	11,322	10,747	575	7,102	6,657	3,608	3,049	177	268	4,220	4,090	1,984	2,106	69	61
Bolivia	2,983	2,917	66	2,168	2,133	1,121	1,012	15	20	815	784	353	431	16	15
Brazil	27,885	27,223	662	13,988	13,659	7,067	6,592	155	174	13,897	13,564	6,673	6,891	189	144
Paraguay	987	970	17	595	591	237	354	4	...	392	379	220	159	13	...
Uruguay	2,317	2,273	44	1,170	1,166	573	593	4	...	1,147	1,107	532	575	19	21
Chile	11,234	11,095	139	6,259	6,184	3,012	3,172	43	32	4,975	4,911	2,353	2,558	20	44
Argentina	28,475	28,291	184	16,579	16,467	8,592	7,875	73	39	11,896	11,824	5,894	5,930	42	30
Other South America	29,451	23,164	6,287	14,572	11,016	5,221	5,795	1,900	1,656	14,879	12,148	5,845	6,303	1,361	1,370
All other:															
Northern Africa	12,604	12,291	313	7,587	7,385	3,065	4,320	159	43	5,017	4,906	2,607	2,299	75	36
Union of South Africa	11,383	10,961	422	5,394	5,206	2,514	2,692	110	78	5,989	5,755	2,968	2,787	117	117
Other Africa	12,162	8,859	3,303	5,756	3,954	2,011	1,943	1,407	395	6,406	4,905	2,420	2,485	747	754
Azores	71,110	70,844	266	22,586	22,467	11,429	11,038	63	56	48,524	48,377	22,819	25,558	70	77
Other Atlantic Islands	21,093	13,488	7,605	8,302	4,949	2,429	2,520	1,574	1,779	12,791	8,539	4,082	4,457	1,988	2,264
Australia	54,353	53,983	370	22,209	22,060	6,862	15,198	69	80	32,144	31,923	15,821	16,102	119	102
New Zealand	13,913	13,774	139	5,826	5,741	2,136	3,605	57	28	8,087	8,033	4,049	3,984	38	16
Trust Territory of the Pacific Islands	8,680	1,446	7,234	3,650	808	331	477	1,081	1,761	5,030	638	348	290	2,323	2,069
Other Pacific Islands[3]	5,788	2,682	3,106	3,045	1,116	486	630	1,017	912	2,743	1,566	766	800	588	589
Country not specified	251,078	236,676	14,402	59,890	55,979	26,887	29,092	2,112	1,799	191,188	180,697	84,083	96,614	5,336	5,155

[1] Includes Turkey in Europe. [2] Includes Newfoundland. [3] Excluding possessions of the United States.

Table 13. Country of origin of the foreign stock, by nativity and race, 1970.

Source: U.S. Bureau of the Census, Nineteenth U.S. Census (Washington, D.C., 1973), vol. I: *Characteristics of the Population*, pt. I, United States summary—sec. 2, table 192, p. 1–598.

United States	Number						Percent distribution					
	Total foreign stock		Foreign born		Native of foreign or mixed parentage		Total foreign stock		Foreign born		Native of foreign or mixed parentage	
	Total	White	Total	White	Total	White	Total	White	Total	White	Total	White
All countries	33 575 232	31 887 935	9 619 302	8 733 770	23 955 930	23 154 165	100.0	100.0	100.0	100.0	100.0	100.0
Europe and U.S.S.R	23 552 862	23 471 607	5 712 026	5 688 153	17 840 836	17 783 454	70.1	73.6	59.4	65.1	74.5	76.8
Northwestern Europe:												
United Kingdom	2 465 050	2 451 415	686 099	681 140	1 778 951	1 770 275	7.3	7.7	7.1	7.8	7.4	7.6
England	1 637 123	1 626 104	458 114	453 867	1 179 009	1 172 237	4.9	5.1	4.8	5.2	4.9	5.1
Scotland	581 255	579 498	170 134	169 636	411 121	409 862	1.7	1.8	1.8	1.9	1.7	1.8
Wales	106 648	106 171	17 014	16 904	89 634	89 267	0.3	0.3	0.2	0.2	0.4	0.4
Northern Ireland	140 024	139 642	40 837	40 733	99 187	98 909	0.4	0.4	0.4	0.5	0.4	0.4
Ireland	1 450 220	1 445 942	251 375	250 492	1 198 845	1 195 450	4.3	4.5	2.6	2.9	5.0	5.2
Norway	614 649	613 381	97 243	96 938	517 406	516 443	1.8	1.9	1.0	1.1	2.2	2.2
Sweden	806 138	804 548	127 070	126 843	679 068	677 705	2.4	2.5	1.3	1.5	2.8	2.9
Denmark	325 561	324 577	61 410	61 307	264 151	263 270	1.0	1.0	0.6	0.7	1.1	1.1
Netherlands	383 709	381 959	110 570	109 709	273 139	272 250	1.1	1.2	1.1	1.3	1.1	1.2
Belgium	130 650	130 142	41 412	41 259	89 238	88 883	0.4	0.4	0.4	0.5	0.4	0.4
Switzerland	218 708	218 174	49 732	49 547	168 976	168 627	0.7	0.7	0.5	0.6	0.7	0.7
France	343 367	339 533	105 385	104 491	237 982	235 042	1.0	1.1	1.1	1.2	1.0	1.0
Central Europe:												
Germany	3 622 035	3 606 218	832 965	830 498	2 789 070	2 775 720	10.8	11.3	8.7	9.5	11.6	12.0
Poland	2 374 244	2 370 641	548 107	547 010	1 826 137	1 823 631	7.1	7.4	5.7	6.3	7.6	7.9
Czechoslovakia	759 527	758 110	160 899	160 672	598 628	597 438	2.3	2.4	1.7	1.8	2.5	2.6
Austria	975 325	973 488	214 014	213 501	761 311	759 987	2.9	3.1	2.2	2.4	3.2	3.3
Hungary	603 668	602 370	183 236	182 681	420 432	419 689	1.8	1.9	1.9	2.1	1.8	1.8
Yugoslavia	447 271	445 809	153 745	153 020	293 526	292 789	1.3	1.4	1.6	1.8	1.2	1.3
Eastern Europe:												
Latvia	86 413	86 144	41 707	41 558	44 706	44 586	0.3	0.3	0.4	0.5	0.2	0.2
Estonia	20 507	20 439	12 163	12 130	8 344	8 309	0.1	0.1	0.1	0.1	-	-
Lithuania	330 977	330 385	76 001	75 806	254 976	254 579	1.0	1.0	0.8	0.9	1.1	1.1
Finland	203 826	203 356	45 499	45 372	158 327	157 984	0.6	0.6	0.5	0.5	0.7	0.7
Rumania	216 803	216 255	70 687	70 364	146 116	145 891	0.6	0.7	0.7	0.8	0.6	0.6
Bulgaria	20 553	20 334	8 609	8 490	11 944	11 844	0.1	0.1	0.1	0.1	-	0.1
Southern Europe:												
Greece	434 571	432 301	177 275	176 025	257 296	256 276	1.3	1.4	1.8	2.0	1.1	1.1
Italy	4 240 779	4 231 787	1 008 533	1 005 687	3 232 246	3 226 100	12.6	13.3	10.5	11.5	13.5	13.9
Spain	155 156	152 950	57 488	56 866	97 668	96 084	0.5	0.5	0.6	0.7	0.4	0.4
Portugal	240 566	235 639	91 034	89 810	149 532	145 829	0.7	0.7	0.9	1.0	0.6	0.6
Other Europe:												
Iceland	9 768	9 733	2 895	2 868	6 873	6 865	-	-	-	-	-	-
Luxembourg	20 618	20 528	3 531	3 498	17 087	17 030	0.1	0.1	-	-	0.1	0.1
Albania	22 580	22 097	9 180	8 895	13 400	13 202	0.1	0.1	0.1	0.1	0.1	0.1
All other Europe, excluding U.S.S.R	86 428	85 321	20 700	20 232	65 728	65 089	0.3	0.3	0.2	0.2	0.3	0.3
U.S.S.R	1 943 195	1 938 031	463 462	461 444	1 479 733	1 476 587	5.8	6.1	4.8	5.3	6.2	6.4
Asia, excluding U.S.S.R	1 745 362	708 423	824 887	273 598	920 475	434 825	5.2	2.2	8.6	3.1	3.8	1.9
Turkey²	106 806	106 238	48 085	47 705	58 721	58 533	0.3	0.3	0.5	0.5	0.2	0.3
Lebanon	85 381	85 056	22 396	22 252	62 985	62 804	0.3	0.3	0.2	0.3	0.3	0.3
Israel	59 097	58 654	35 858	35 631	23 239	23 023	0.2	0.2	0.4	0.4	0.1	0.1
Syria	59 489	59 147	14 962	14 840	44 527	44 307	0.2	0.2	0.2	0.2	0.2	0.2
Other Western Asia	88 430	85 388	52 752	50 337	35 678	35 051	0.3	0.3	0.5	0.6	0.1	0.2
Pakistan	9 308	8 226	6 182	5 462	3 126	2 764	-	-	0.1	0.1	-	-
India¹	75 533	63 466	51 000	41 412	24 533	22 054	0.2	0.2	0.5	0.5	0.1	0.1
China¹	339 243	42 888	172 132	11 839	167 111	31 049	1.0	0.1	1.8	0.1	0.7	0.1
Japan	393 789	70 719	120 235	6 085	273 554	64 634	1.2	0.2	1.2	0.1	1.1	0.3
Korea⁴	70 198	16 287	38 711	2 094	31 487	14 193	0.2	0.1	0.4	-	0.1	0.1
Philippine Islands	350 082	67 513	184 842	11 187	165 240	56 326	1.0	0.2	1.9	0.1	0.7	0.2
Other Asia	108 006	44 841	77 732	24 754	30 274	20 087	0.3	0.1	0.8	0.3	0.1	0.1
North and Central America	6 507 946	6 094 576	2 361 153	2 121 722	4 146 793	3 972 854	19.4	19.1	24.5	24.3	17.3	17.2
Canada	3 034 556	2 996 437	812 421	798 782	2 222 135	2 197 655	9.0	9.4	8.4	9.1	9.3	9.5
Mexico	2 339 151	2 298 593	759 711	746 327	1 579 440	1 552 266	7.0	7.2	7.9	8.5	6.6	6.7
Guatemala	26 865	25 394	17 356	16 203	9 509	9 191	0.1	0.1	0.2	0.2	-	-
British Honduras	14 221	7 561	8 860	4 743	5 361	2 818	-	-	0.1	0.1	-	-
Honduras	31 150	23 020	19 118	13 732	12 032	9 288	0.1	0.1	0.2	0.2	0.1	-
Nicaragua	28 620	27 104	16 125	15 231	12 495	11 873	0.1	0.1	0.2	0.2	0.1	0.1
El Salvador	23 502	22 970	15 717	15 337	7 785	7 633	0.1	0.1	0.2	0.2	-	-
Costa Rica	25 840	21 645	16 691	13 593	9 149	8 052	0.1	0.1	0.2	0.2	-	-
Panama	38 196	19 807	20 046	8 293	18 150	11 514	0.1	0.1	0.2	0.1	0.1	-
Cuba	560 628	540 503	439 048	425 974	121 580	114 529	1.7	1.7	4.6	4.9	0.5	0.5
Jamaica	105 110	12 289	68 576	5 934	36 534	6 355	0.3	-	0.7	0.1	0.2	-
British West Indies	55 055	13 219	23 044	4 635	32 011	8 584	0.2	-	0.2	0.1	0.1	-
Dominican Republic	83 647	56 596	61 228	39 897	22 419	16 699	0.2	0.2	0.6	0.5	0.1	0.1
Haiti	37 469	6 757	28 026	4 160	9 443	2 597	0.1	-	0.3	-	-	-
Trinidad and Tobago	30 666	7 366	20 673	3 493	9 993	3 873	0.1	-	0.2	-	-	-
Other West Indies	73 270	15 315	34 513	5 388	38 757	9 927	0.2	-	0.4	0.1	0.2	-
South America	389 459	364 004	255 238	238 768	134 221	125 236	1.2	1.1	2.7	2.7	0.6	0.5
Colombia	84 921	82 505	63 538	61 799	21 383	20 706	0.3	0.3	0.7	0.7	0.1	0.1
Venezuela	17 321	16 292	11 348	10 663	5 973	5 629	0.1	0.1	0.1	0.1	-	-
Ecuador	49 491	47 287	36 663	34 806	12 828	12 481	0.1	0.1	0.4	0.4	0.1	0.1
Peru	35 450	33 488	21 663	20 398	13 787	13 090	0.1	0.1	0.2	0.2	0.1	0.1
Bolivia	10 187	9 916	6 872	6 709	3 315	3 207	-	-	0.1	0.1	-	-
Brazil	46 753	45 561	27 069	26 331	19 684	19 230	0.1	0.1	0.3	0.3	0.1	0.1
Uruguay	7 041	6 928	5 092	4 997	1 949	1 931	-	-	0.1	0.1	-	-
Chile	25 125	24 512	15 393	14 988	9 732	9 524	0.1	0.1	0.2	0.2	-	-
Argentina	67 364	66 874	44 803	44 494	22 561	22 380	0.2	0.2	0.5	0.5	0.1	0.1
Other South America	45 806	30 641	22 797	13 583	23 009	17 058	0.1	0.1	0.2	0.2	0.1	0.1
All other	1 379 603	1 249 325	465 998	411 529	913 605	837 796	4.1	3.9	4.8	4.7	3.8	3.6
United Arab Republic (Egypt)	31 358	30 810	20 666	20 319	10 692	10 491	0.1	0.1	0.2	0.2	-	-
Other North Africa	22 105	21 636	11 730	11 461	10 375	10 175	0.1	0.1	0.1	0.1	-	-
Union of South Africa	15 958	15 172	7 667	7 209	8 291	7 963	-	-	0.1	0.1	-	-
Other Africa	36 812	18 780	21 400	9 032	15 412	9 748	0.1	0.1	0.2	0.1	0.1	-
Azores	77 892	77 203	28 865	28 397	49 027	48 806	0.2	0.2	0.3	0.3	0.2	0.2
Other Atlantic islands	56 084	26 249	18 680	9 140	37 404	17 109	0.2	0.1	0.2	0.1	0.2	0.1
Australia	62 754	61 381	24 271	23 699	38 483	37 682	0.2	0.2	0.3	0.3	0.2	0.2
New Zealand	19 245	18 816	8 117	7 872	11 128	10 944	0.1	0.1	0.1	0.1	-	-
Trust Territory of the Pacific Islands	1 109	536	506	91	603	445	-	-	-	-	-	-
Other Pacific islands	14 810	4 984	8 364	2 479	6 446	2 505	-	-	0.1	-	-	-
Country not specified	1 041 476	973 758	315 732	291 830	725 744	681 928	3.1	3.1	3.3	3.3	3.0	2.9

¹Includes West Germany and East Germany   ²Includes Turkey in Europe.   Includes Taiwan and Mainland China.   ⁴Includes North Korea and South Korea.

Table 14. Mother tongue of the population, by nativity and parentage, 1970. (Data based on 15-percent sample.)

Source: U.S. Bureau of the Census, Nineteenth U.S. Census (Washington, D.C., 1973), Subject Reports, final report PC(2)-1A *National Origin and Language*, table 19, p. 492.

United States	Total	Native of native parentage	Foreign stock — Total	Native of foreign or mixed parentage — Total	Foreign parentage	Mixed parentage	Foreign born
Total	203 210 158	169 634 926	33 575 232	23 955 930	12 902 976	11 052 954	9 619 302
English	160 717 113	149 312 435	11 404 678	9 706 853	3 170 411	6 536 442	1 697 825
Celtic	88 162	9 734	78 428	32 969	25 655	7 314	45 459
Norwegian	612 862	204 822	408 040	313 675	191 929	121 746	94 365
Swedish	626 102	113 119	512 983	381 575	283 569	98 006	131 408
Danish	194 462	29 089	165 373	107 155	75 614	31 541	58 218
Dutch	350 748	90 713	260 035	132 201	86 463	45 738	127 834
Flemish	61 889	12 064	49 825	29 024	21 649	7 375	20 801
French	2 598 408	1 460 130	1 138 278	727 698	333 997	393 701	410 580
Breton	32 722	7 252	25 470	15 439	8 963	6 476	10 031
German	6 093 054	2 488 394	3 604 660	2 403 125	1 468 715	934 410	1 201 535
Polish	2 437 938	670 335	1 767 603	1 347 691	1 085 041	262 650	419 912
Czech	452 812	148 944	303 868	233 165	163 704	69 461	70 703
Slovak	510 366	86 950	423 416	340 855	279 203	61 652	82 561
Hungarian	447 497	52 156	395 341	234 088	195 556	38 532	161 253
Serbo-Croatian	239 455	24 095	215 360	132 296	109 262	23 034	83 064
Slovenian	82 321	9 040	73 281	54 103	47 552	6 551	19 178
Dalmatian	9 802	3 038	6 764	4 748	3 201	1 547	2 016
Albanian	17 382	1 571	15 811	8 283	6 730	1 553	7 528
Finnish	214 168	58 124	156 044	117 754	91 730	26 024	38 290
Lithuanian	292 820	34 744	258 076	162 888	143 297	19 591	95 188
Other Balto-Slavonic dialects	19 748	1 231	18 517	8 309	6 646	1 663	10 208
Russian	334 615	30 665	303 950	154 673	131 793	22 880	149 277
Ukrainian	249 351	22 662	226 689	130 054	115 982	14 072	96 635
Georgian	757	179	578	157	120	37	421
Rumanian	56 590	5 166	51 424	25 369	21 809	3 560	26 055
Yiddish	1 593 993	170 174	1 423 819	985 703	845 484	140 219	438 116
Gypsy (Romani)	1 588	1 252	336	180	79	101	156
Greek	458 699	56 839	401 860	208 115	146 897	61 218	193 745
Italian	4 144 315	605 625	3 538 690	2 512 696	1 927 001	585 695	1 025 994
Spanish	7 823 583	4 171 050	3 652 533	1 956 293	958 628	997 665	1 696 240
Portuguese	365 300	62 252	303 048	162 749	111 922	50 827	140 299
Basque	8 108	1 852	6 256	4 087	3 034	1 053	2 169
Armenian	100 495	13 758	86 737	48 414	38 930	9 484	38 323
Persian	20 553	965	19 588	3 602	1 697	1 905	15 986
Other Persian dialects	3 370	590	2 780	1 437	1 110	327	1 343
Hebrew	101 686	19 691	81 995	45 883	34 036	11 847	36 112
Arabic (n.e.c.)	123 744	14 055	109 689	52 902	38 704	14 198	56 787
Egyptian	891	33	858	79	49	30	779
Iraqi	2 413	509	1 904	758	435	323	1 146
Near Eastern Arabic dialects	66 064	10 952	55 112	40 306	31 672	8 634	14 806
North African Arabic dialects	408	217	191	52	16	36	139
Southern Semitic	1 354	380	974	216	78	138	758
Hamitic	948	445	503	217	135	82	286
Swahili	3 991	2 040	1 951	812	384	428	1 139
Libyan	410	265	145	86	29	57	59
Niger-Congo (Chari-Nile)	6 537	1 055	5 482	1 221	653	568	4 261
Eastern Sudanic	2 543	336	2 207	1 347	953	394	860
Turkish	24 123	1 811	22 312	5 666	3 826	1 840	16 646
Other Uralic	15 191	765	14 426	3 016	2 347	669	11 410
Altaic	974	306	668	251	206	45	417
Hindi (Hindustani)	26 253	1 249	25 004	2 987	1 944	1 043	22 017
Other Indo-Aryan	22 939	731	22 208	2 342	1 740	602	19 866
Dravidian	8 983	635	8 348	813	578	235	7 535
Korean	53 528	2 756	50 772	16 024	7 328	8 696	34 748
Japanese	408 504	82 886	325 618	207 528	137 373	70 155	118 090
Chinese (n.e.c.)	337 283	29 244	308 039	122 000	80 317	41 683	186 039
Mandarin	1 697	651	1 046	314	175	139	732
Cantonese	5 819	703	5 116	1 937	1 273	664	3 179
Other Chinese dialects	632	166	466	156	106	50	310
Tibetan	352	183	169	50	23	27	119
Burmese	1 581	248	1 333	177	51	126	1 156
Thai (Siamese), Lao	14 416	1 178	13 238	1 543	464	1 079	11 695
Malay (Indonesian)	6 253	826	5 427	817	311	506	4 610
Other Malayan	4 042	1 193	2 849	544	382	162	2 305
Tagalog	217 907	8 336	209 571	57 073	35 581	21 492	152 498
Polynesian	20 687	12 006	8 681	3 725	2 132	1 593	4 956
Algonquin	19 909	18 079	1 830	1 190	274	916	640
Navajo	91 860	91 092	768	648	174	474	120
Other Athapaskan	18 528	17 497	1 031	451	173	278	580
Uto-Aztecan	245	152	93	55	23	32	38
Other American Indian	137 663	128 039	9 624	5 193	1 866	3 327	4 431
All other	880 779	350 126	530 653	341 483	236 504	104 979	189 170
Not reported	9 317 873	8 873 081	444 792	348 645	177 288	171 357	96 147

Table 15. Negro population, by sex and urban and rural residence, 1970.

Source: U.S. Bureau of the Census, Nineteenth U.S. Census (Washington, D.C., 1973), Subject Reports, final report PC(2)-1B *Negro Population*, table 1, p. 1.

	Total			Urban			Rural nonfarm			Rural farm		
	Total	Male	Female	Total	Male	Female	Total	Male	Female	Total	Male	Female
United States	22 549 815	10 728 182	11 821 633	18 338 421	8 639 815	9 698 606	3 764 285	1 865 126	1 899 159	447 109	223 241	223 868
REGIONS												
Northeast	4 336 913	2 023 050	2 313 863	4 208 201	1 952 017	2 256 184	126 281	69 721	56 560	2 431	1 312	1 119
North Central	4 565 413	2 178 494	2 386 919	4 441 685	2 108 003	2 333 682	116 077	66 618	49 459	7 651	3 873	3 778
South	11 957 055	5 692 343	6 264 712	8 050 025	3 778 347	4 271 678	3 471 906	1 697 042	1 774 864	435 124	216 954	218 170
West	1 690 434	834 295	856 139	1 638 510	801 448	837 062	50 021	31 745	18 276	1 903	1 102	801
NORTHEAST												
New England	386 557	183 679	202 878	370 901	174 499	196 402	15 387	9 014	6 373	269	166	103
Middle Atlantic	3 950 356	1 839 371	2 110 985	3 837 300	1 777 518	2 059 782	110 894	60 707	50 187	2 162	1 146	1 016
NORTH CENTRAL												
East North Central	3 867 653	1 844 467	2 023 186	3 775 752	1 790 786	1 984 966	88 196	51 852	36 344	3 705	1 829	1 876
West North Central	697 760	334 027	363 733	665 933	317 217	348 716	27 881	14 766	13 115	3 946	2 044	1 902
SOUTH												
South Atlantic	6 381 843	3 047 421	3 334 422	4 236 477	1 994 587	2 241 890	1 930 208	945 422	984 786	215 158	107 412	107 746
East South Central	2 569 625	1 211 535	1 358 090	1 574 158	728 051	846 107	843 574	407 616	435 958	151 893	75 868	76 025
West South Central	3 005 587	1 433 387	1 572 200	2 239 390	1 055 709	1 183 681	698 124	344 004	354 120	68 073	33 674	34 399
WEST												
Mountain	178 416	91 671	86 745	168 918	85 664	83 254	9 070	5 788	3 282	428	219	209
Pacific	1 512 018	742 624	769 394	1 469 592	715 784	753 808	40 951	25 957	14 994	1 475	883	592
NEW ENGLAND												
Maine	2 816	1 679	1 137	2 244	1 333	911	557	340	217	15	6	9
New Hampshire	2 667	1 505	1 162	2 104	1 202	902	543	294	249	20	9	11
Vermont	684	396	288	276	159	117	390	224	166	18	13	5
Massachusetts	173 697	81 532	92 165	167 669	78 109	89 560	5 888	3 328	2 560	140	95	45
Rhode Island	25 219	12 592	12 627	23 652	11 402	12 250	1 554	1 182	372	13	8	5
Connecticut	181 474	85 975	95 499	174 956	82 294	92 662	6 455	3 646	2 809	63	35	28
MIDDLE ATLANTIC												
New York	2 164 560	999 798	1 164 762	2 126 941	978 194	1 148 747	36 706	21 127	15 579	913	477	436
New Jersey	769 245	363 587	405 658	728 277	342 616	385 661	40 184	20 530	19 654	784	441	343
Pennsylvania	1 016 551	475 986	540 565	982 082	456 708	525 374	34 004	19 050	14 954	465	228	237
EAST NORTH CENTRAL												
Ohio	970 130	460 707	509 423	941 520	445 124	496 396	27 772	15 154	12 618	838	429	409
Indiana	356 379	171 333	185 046	348 343	165 674	182 669	7 469	5 405	2 064	567	254	313
Illinois	1 422 353	671 631	750 722	1 399 692	657 729	741 963	21 396	13 257	8 139	1 265	645	620
Michigan	990 663	478 675	511 988	960 005	461 361	498 644	29 689	16 844	12 845	969	470	499
Wisconsin	128 128	62 121	66 007	126 192	60 898	65 294	1 870	1 192	678	66	31	35
WEST NORTH CENTRAL												
Minnesota	34 721	17 506	17 215	33 794	16 979	16 815	818	495	323	109	32	77
Iowa	32 542	15 856	16 686	31 721	15 475	16 246	650	284	366	171	97	74
Missouri	479 746	226 026	253 720	456 915	214 438	242 477	19 834	10 005	9 829	2 997	1 583	1 414
North Dakota	2 519	1 538	981	2 226	1 366	860	273	172	101	20	–	20
South Dakota	1 844	1 035	809	1 418	806	612	403	223	180	23	6	17
Nebraska	40 064	19 459	20 605	39 255	18 911	20 344	749	524	225	60	24	36
Kansas	106 324	52 607	53 717	100 604	49 242	51 362	5 154	3 063	2 091	566	302	264
SOUTH ATLANTIC												
Delaware	78 305	37 579	40 726	55 122	26 394	28 728	22 856	11 004	11 852	327	181	146
Maryland	698 494	336 565	361 929	576 100	273 939	302 161	115 592	58 988	56 604	6 802	3 638	3 164
District of Columbia	537 570	252 657	284 913	537 570	252 657	284 913	–	–	–			
Virginia	860 302	418 159	442 143	517 009	246 591	270 418	306 631	153 422	153 209	36 662	18 146	18 516
West Virginia	66 804	30 951	35 853	36 350	16 676	19 674	30 276	14 179	16 097	178	96	82
North Carolina	1 125 885	540 275	585 610	546 079	257 045	289 034	492 311	239 493	252 818	87 495	43 737	43 758
South Carolina	788 455	376 458	411 997	326 675	153 781	172 894	417 598	200 565	217 033	44 182	22 112	22 070
Georgia	1 184 062	556 242	627 820	781 956	359 911	422 045	372 311	181 895	190 416	29 795	14 436	15 359
Florida	1 041 966	498 535	543 431	859 616	407 593	452 023	172 633	85 876	86 757	9 717	5 066	4 651
EAST SOUTH CENTRAL												
Kentucky	230 363	111 198	119 165	182 796	86 630	96 166	39 188	20 282	18 906	8 379	4 286	4 093
Tennessee	620 636	291 105	329 531	497 029	230 516	266 513	100 642	49 175	51 467	22 965	11 414	11 551
Alabama	903 000	422 539	480 461	562 885	258 588	304 297	309 633	148 703	160 930	30 482	15 248	15 234
Mississippi	815 626	386 693	428 933	331 448	152 317	179 131	394 111	189 456	204 655	90 067	44 920	45 147
WEST SOUTH CENTRAL												
Arkansas	352 539	167 098	185 441	194 846	90 008	104 838	136 988	66 928	70 060	20 705	10 162	10 543
Louisiana	1 085 227	514 013	571 214	736 598	343 280	393 318	320 397	156 682	163 715	28 232	14 051	14 181
Oklahoma	171 216	80 944	90 272	140 944	66 005	74 939	26 239	12 972	13 267	4 033	1 967	2 066
Texas	1 396 605	671 332	725 273	1 167 002	556 416	610 586	214 500	107 422	107 078	15 103	7 494	7 609
MOUNTAIN												
Montana	1 800	1 130	670	1 457	857	600	334	273	61	9	–	9
Idaho	2 037	1 298	739	1 605	951	654	350	314	36	82	33	49
Wyoming	2 455	1 327	1 128	2 379	1 292	1 087	54	27	27	22	8	14
Colorado	66 066	33 888	32 178	64 940	33 208	31 732	1 060	642	418	66	38	28
New Mexico	19 314	9 867	9 447	18 299	9 253	9 046	947	580	367	68	34	34
Arizona	52 799	26 468	26 331	47 792	23 399	24 393	4 868	2 996	1 872	139	73	66
Utah	6 324	3 858	2 466	5 789	3 457	2 332	527	393	134	8	8	–
Nevada	27 621	13 835	13 786	26 657	13 247	13 410	930	563	367	34	25	9
PACIFIC												
Washington	70 859	37 479	33 380	67 997	35 635	32 362	2 654	1 719	935	208	125	83
Oregon	26 211	13 096	13 115	24 479	12 249	12 230	1 659	797	862	73	50	23
California	1 398 498	681 815	716 683	1 363 013	659 227	703 786	34 306	21 884	12 422	1 179	704	475
Alaska	8 860	5 188	3 672	7 085	4 063	3 022	1 760	1 121	639	15	4	11
Hawaii	7 590	5 046	2 544	7 018	4 610	2 408	572	436	136	–	–	–

Table 16. Japanese population, by sex and urban and rural residence, 1970.

Source: U.S. Bureau of the Census, Nineteenth U.S. Census (Washington, D.C., 1973), Subject Reports, final report PC(2)-1G *Japanese, Chinese, and Filipinos in the United States*, table 1, p. 1.

	Total			Urban			Rural nonfarm			Rural farm		
	Total	Male	Female	Total	Male	Female	Total	Male	Female	Total	Male	Female
United States	588 324	271 453	316 871	524 196	241 434	282 762	50 561	23 052	27 509	13 567	6 967	6 600
REGIONS												
Northeast	39 125	17 221	21 904	35 215	15 734	19 481	3 716	1 383	2 333	194	104	90
North Central	42 670	18 082	24 588	38 410	16 630	21 780	3 266	899	2 367	994	553	441
South	28 504	9 809	18 695	24 460	8 588	15 872	3 712	1 091	2 621	332	130	202
West	478 025	226 341	251 684	426 111	200 482	225 629	39 867	19 679	20 188	12 047	6 180	5 867
NORTHEAST												
New England	7 570	3 082	4 488	6 472	2 620	3 852	1 086	456	630	12	6	6
Middle Atlantic	31 555	14 139	17 416	28 743	13 114	15 629	2 630	927	1 703	182	98	84
NORTH CENTRAL												
East North Central	33 554	14 543	19 011	30 833	13 721	17 112	2 284	582	1 702	437	240	197
West North Central	9 116	3 539	5 577	7 577	2 909	4 668	982	317	665	557	313	244
SOUTH												
South Atlantic	16 412	5 517	10 895	13 976	4 844	9 132	2 288	622	1 666	148	51	97
East South Central	3 198	1 161	2 037	2 485	927	1 558	676	222	454	37	12	25
West South Central	8 894	3 131	5 763	7 999	2 817	5 182	748	247	501	147	67	80
WEST												
Mountain	20 318	9 330	10 988	16 482	7 466	9 016	2 027	912	1 115	1 809	952	857
Pacific	457 707	217 011	240 696	409 629	193 016	216 613	37 840	18 767	19 073	10 238	5 228	5 010
NEW ENGLAND												
Maine	215	98	117	165	68	97	50	30	20	–	–	–
New Hampshire	252	84	168	131	30	101	121	54	67	–	–	–
Vermont	73	27	46	9	5	4	64	22	42	–	–	–
Massachusetts	4 715	1 919	2 796	4 313	1 753	2 560	402	166	236	–	–	–
Rhode Island	744	260	484	632	201	431	112	59	53	–	–	–
Connecticut	1 571	694	877	1 222	563	659	337	125	212	12	6	6
MIDDLE ATLANTIC												
New York	19 794	9 439	10 355	18 954	9 171	9 783	794	250	544	46	18	28
New Jersey	6 344	2 582	3 762	5 371	2 221	3 150	946	344	602	27	17	10
Pennsylvania	5 417	2 118	3 299	4 418	1 722	2 696	890	333	557	109	63	46
EAST NORTH CENTRAL												
Ohio	5 896	2 105	3 791	5 370	1 960	3 410	480	125	355	46	20	26
Indiana	2 100	806	1 294	1 626	668	958	392	108	284	82	30	52
Illinois	17 645	8 371	9 274	17 041	8 172	8 869	527	140	387	77	59	18
Michigan	5 464	2 263	3 201	4 722	2 011	2 711	602	156	446	140	96	44
Wisconsin	2 449	998	1 451	2 074	910	1 164	283	53	230	92	35	57
WEST NORTH CENTRAL												
Minnesota	2 693	1 180	1 513	2 430	1 076	1 354	199	84	115	64	20	44
Iowa	773	324	449	569	239	330	156	54	102	48	31	17
Missouri	2 320	784	1 536	2 101	756	1 345	190	24	166	29	4	25
North Dakota	312	127	185	228	82	146	53	18	35	31	27	4
South Dakota	199	82	117	137	44	93	15	11	4	47	27	20
Nebraska	1 253	547	706	875	332	543	76	25	51	302	190	112
Kansas	1 566	495	1 071	1 237	380	857	293	101	192	36	14	22
SOUTH ATLANTIC												
Delaware	432	168	264	293	126	167	135	42	93	4	–	4
Maryland	3 637	1 321	2 316	3 253	1 182	2 071	352	122	230	32	17	15
District of Columbia	716	290	426	716	290	426	–	–	–	–	–	–
Virginia	3 296	1 073	2 223	2 866	931	1 935	375	132	243	55	10	45
West Virginia	266	80	186	143	68	75	123	12	111	–	–	–
North Carolina	2 088	642	1 446	1 494	517	977	561	105	456	33	20	13
South Carolina	675	219	456	487	152	335	188	67	121	–	–	–
Georgia	1 334	493	841	1 181	458	723	149	35	114	4	–	4
Florida	3 968	1 231	2 737	3 543	1 120	2 423	405	107	298	20	4	16
EAST SOUTH CENTRAL												
Kentucky	920	340	580	660	243	417	243	92	151	17	5	12
Tennessee	857	275	582	733	236	497	118	39	79	6	–	6
Alabama	1 043	386	657	850	327	523	179	52	127	14	7	7
Mississippi	378	160	218	242	121	121	136	39	97	–	–	–
WEST SOUTH CENTRAL												
Arkansas	588	252	336	443	177	266	131	65	66	14	10	4
Louisiana	876	282	594	748	258	490	113	24	89	15	–	15
Oklahoma	1 214	319	895	1 038	278	760	140	31	109	36	10	26
Texas	6 216	2 278	3 938	5 770	2 104	3 666	364	127	237	82	47	35
MOUNTAIN												
Montana	613	262	351	451	192	259	117	49	68	45	21	24
Idaho	2 012	1 009	1 003	940	483	457	374	182	192	698	344	354
Wyoming	457	189	268	311	131	180	76	25	51	70	33	37
Colorado	7 861	3 642	4 219	6 641	3 017	3 624	620	288	332	600	337	263
New Mexico	937	377	560	845	322	523	74	44	30	18	11	7
Arizona	2 530	1 025	1 505	2 204	886	1 318	238	95	143	88	44	44
Utah	4 862	2 368	2 494	4 159	2 016	2 143	434	206	228	269	146	123
Nevada	1 046	458	588	931	419	512	94	23	71	21	16	5
PACIFIC												
Washington	20 188	8 973	11 215	18 277	8 097	10 180	1 483	656	827	428	220	208
Oregon	6 213	2 752	3 461	4 857	2 160	2 697	580	195	385	776	397	379
California	213 277	100 204	113 073	199 726	93 403	106 323	7 485	3 754	3 731	6 066	3 047	3 019
Alaska	854	336	518	558	201	357	291	130	161	5	5	–
Hawaii	217 175	104 746	112 429	186 211	89 155	97 056	28 001	14 032	13 969	2 963	1 559	1 404

Table 17. Chinese population, by sex and urban and rural residence, 1970.

Source: U.S. Bureau of the Census, Nineteenth U.S. Census (Washington, D.C., 1973), Subject Reports, final report PC(2)-1G *Japanese, Chinese, and Filipinos in the United States*, table 16, p. 60.

	Total			Urban			Rural nonfarm			Rural farm		
	Total	Male	Female	Total	Male	Female	Total	Male	Female	Total	Male	Female
United States	431 583	226 733	204 850	417 032	219 258	197 774	13 671	7 013	6 658	880	462	418
REGIONS												
Northeast	115 089	61 899	53 190	111 337	60 009	51 328	3 663	1 846	1 817	89	44	45
North Central	37 811	20 559	17 252	36 554	19 885	16 669	1 159	609	550	98	65	33
South	32 462	16 929	15 533	30 032	15 746	14 286	2 425	1 178	1 247	5	5	–
West	246 221	127 346	118 875	239 109	123 618	115 491	6 424	3 380	3 044	688	348	340
NORTHEAST												
New England	17 334	9 363	7 971	16 238	8 815	7 423	1 096	548	548	–	–	–
Middle Atlantic	97 755	52 536	45 219	95 099	51 194	43 905	2 567	1 298	1 269	89	44	45
NORTH CENTRAL												
East North Central	30 388	16 377	14 011	29 492	15 884	13 608	811	434	377	85	59	26
West North Central	7 423	4 182	3 241	7 062	4 001	3 061	348	175	173	13	6	7
SOUTH												
South Atlantic	17 803	9 084	8 719	16 479	8 448	8 031	1 324	636	688	–	–	–
East South Central	3 636	1 978	1 658	3 220	1 799	1 421	416	179	237	–	–	–
West South Central	11 023	5 867	5 156	10 333	5 499	4 834	685	363	322	5	5	–
WEST												
Mountain	8 886	4 943	3 943	8 435	4 669	3 766	404	262	142	47	12	35
Pacific	237 335	122 403	114 932	230 674	118 949	111 725	6 020	3 118	2 902	641	336	305
NEW ENGLAND												
Maine	89	51	38	65	35	30	24	16	8	–	–	–
New Hampshire	268	129	139	156	77	79	112	52	60	–	–	–
Vermont	203	91	112	117	50	67	86	41	45	–	–	–
Massachusetts	14 018	7 593	6 425	13 401	7 285	6 116	617	308	309	–	–	–
Rhode Island	1 023	557	466	1 013	552	461	10	5	5	–	–	–
Connecticut	1 733	942	791	1 486	816	670	247	126	121	–	–	–
MIDDLE ATLANTIC												
New York	81 903	44 158	37 745	80 574	43 457	37 117	1 310	696	614	19	5	14
New Jersey	8 755	4 620	4 135	7 952	4 232	3 720	733	349	384	70	39	31
Pennsylvania	7 097	3 758	3 339	6 573	3 505	3 068	524	253	271	–	–	–
EAST NORTH CENTRAL												
Ohio	5 263	2 864	2 399	5 123	2 797	2 326	123	50	73	17	17	–
Indiana	1 926	969	957	1 777	894	883	145	71	74	4	4	–
Illinois	14 077	7 601	6 476	13 953	7 511	6 442	119	85	34	5	5	–
Michigan	6 611	3 521	3 090	6 223	3 294	2 929	356	210	146	32	17	15
Wisconsin	2 511	1 422	1 089	2 416	1 388	1 028	68	18	50	27	16	11
WEST NORTH CENTRAL												
Minnesota	1 992	1 118	874	1 937	1 078	859	55	40	15	–	–	–
Iowa	957	536	421	923	523	400	34	13	21	–	–	–
Missouri	2 460	1 331	1 129	2 379	1 311	1 068	81	20	61	–	–	–
North Dakota	78	27	51	45	16	29	27	5	22	6	6	–
South Dakota	285	171	114	267	153	114	18	18	–	–	–	–
Nebraska	534	340	194	525	331	194	9	9	–	–	–	–
Kansas	1 117	659	458	986	589	397	124	70	54	7	–	7
SOUTH ATLANTIC												
Delaware	508	253	255	479	240	239	29	13	16	–	–	–
Maryland	5 961	2 852	3 109	5 610	2 689	2 921	351	163	188	–	–	–
District of Columbia	2 767	1 457	1 310	2 767	1 457	1 310	–	–	–	–	–	–
Virginia	2 407	1 217	1 190	2 272	1 142	1 130	135	75	60	–	–	–
West Virginia	266	136	130	175	103	72	91	33	58	–	–	–
North Carolina	1 134	591	543	911	505	406	223	86	137	–	–	–
South Carolina	393	249	144	322	206	116	71	43	28	–	–	–
Georgia	1 327	689	638	1 175	632	543	152	57	95	–	–	–
Florida	3 040	1 640	1 400	2 768	1 474	1 294	272	166	106	–	–	–
EAST SOUTH CENTRAL												
Kentucky	565	318	247	514	305	209	51	13	38	–	–	–
Tennessee	1 429	817	612	1 366	771	595	63	46	17	–	–	–
Alabama	467	237	230	453	237	216	14	–	14	–	–	–
Mississippi	1 175	606	569	887	486	401	288	120	168	–	–	–
WEST SOUTH CENTRAL												
Arkansas	904	453	451	639	334	305	265	119	146	–	–	–
Louisiana	1 161	685	476	1 032	596	436	129	89	40	–	–	–
Oklahoma	875	458	417	850	448	402	25	10	15	–	–	–
Texas	8 083	4 271	3 812	7 812	4 121	3 691	266	145	121	5	5	–
MOUNTAIN												
Montana	264	163	101	264	163	101	–	–	–	–	–	–
Idaho	574	326	248	471	283	188	56	31	25	47	12	35
Wyoming	104	62	42	89	52	37	15	10	5	–	–	–
Colorado	1 605	877	728	1 595	872	723	10	5	5	–	–	–
New Mexico	459	298	161	417	267	150	42	31	11	–	–	–
Arizona	3 739	1 944	1 795	3 577	1 842	1 735	162	102	60	–	–	–
Utah	1 175	703	472	1 144	684	460	31	19	12	–	–	–
Nevada	966	570	396	878	506	372	88	64	24	–	–	–
PACIFIC												
Washington	9 376	4 957	4 419	9 059	4 797	4 262	301	150	151	16	10	6
Oregon	4 774	2 624	2 150	4 571	2 509	2 062	164	95	69	39	20	19
California	170 419	88 286	82 133	167 773	86 810	80 963	2 302	1 289	1 013	344	187	157
Alaska	183	124	59	137	91	46	46	33	13	–	–	–
Hawaii	52 583	26 412	26 171	49 134	24 742	24 392	3 207	1 551	1 656	242	119	123

Table 18. Filipino population, by sex and urban and rural residence, 1970.

Source: U.S. Bureau of the Census, Nineteenth U.S. Census (Washington, D.C., 1973), Subject Reports, final report PC(2)-1G *Japanese, Chinese, and Filipinos in the United States,* table 31, p. 119.

	Total			Urban			Rural nonfarm			Rural farm		
	Total	Male	Female	Total	Male	Female	Total	Male	Female	Total	Male	Female
United States	336 731	183 175	153 556	288 287	153 966	134 321	44 526	26 191	18 335	3 918	3 018	900
REGIONS												
Northeast	30 231	14 476	15 755	28 178	13 254	14 924	2 042	1 222	820	11	–	11
North Central	27 283	12 514	14 769	25 709	11 809	13 900	1 435	647	788	139	58	81
South	29 250	16 421	12 829	27 014	15 161	11 853	2 124	1 218	906	112	42	70
West	249 967	139 764	110 203	207 386	113 742	93 644	38 925	23 104	15 821	3 656	2 918	738
NORTHEAST												
New England	6 132	3 493	2 639	4 983	2 715	2 268	1 149	778	371	–	–	–
Middle Atlantic	24 099	10 983	13 116	23 195	10 539	12 656	893	444	449	11	–	11
NORTH CENTRAL												
East North Central	22 115	10 117	11 998	21 034	9 610	11 424	1 004	473	531	77	34	43
West North Central	5 168	2 397	2 771	4 675	2 199	2 476	431	174	257	62	24	38
SOUTH												
South Atlantic	22 570	13 032	9 538	20 963	12 069	8 894	1 561	950	611	46	13	33
East South Central	1 854	826	1 028	1 516	694	822	318	128	190	20	4	16
West South Central	4 826	2 563	2 263	4 535	2 398	2 137	245	140	105	46	25	21
WEST												
Mountain	4 788	2 537	2 251	4 142	2 185	1 957	583	309	274	63	43	20
Pacific	245 179	137 227	107 952	203 244	111 557	91 687	38 342	22 795	15 547	3 593	2 875	718
NEW ENGLAND												
Maine	347	218	129	269	177	92	78	41	37	–	–	–
New Hampshire	193	101	92	105	48	57	88	53	35	–	–	–
Vermont	106	39	67	49	14	35	57	25	32	–	–	–
Massachusetts	1 855	968	887	1 669	881	788	186	87	99	–	–	–
Rhode Island	1 569	1 038	531	1 243	737	506	326	301	25	–	–	–
Connecticut	2 062	1 129	933	1 648	858	790	414	271	143	–	–	–
MIDDLE ATLANTIC												
New York	14 045	6 557	7 488	13 648	6 382	7 266	392	175	217	5	–	5
New Jersey	5 323	2 376	2 947	5 052	2 221	2 831	271	155	116	–	–	–
Pennsylvania	4 731	2 050	2 681	4 495	1 936	2 559	230	114	116	6	–	6
EAST NORTH CENTRAL												
Ohio	3 732	1 676	2 056	3 472	1 568	1 904	211	85	126	49	23	26
Indiana	1 374	645	729	1 069	483	586	299	162	137	6	–	6
Illinois	12 355	5 549	6 806	12 201	5 491	6 710	136	51	85	18	7	11
Michigan	3 449	1 630	1 819	3 192	1 504	1 688	253	122	131	4	4	–
Wisconsin	1 205	617	588	1 100	564	536	105	53	52	–	–	–
WEST NORTH CENTRAL												
Minnesota	1 300	591	709	1 199	554	645	101	37	64	–	–	–
Iowa	624	265	359	527	226	301	58	15	43	39	24	15
Missouri	1 628	843	785	1 499	795	704	129	48	81	–	–	–
North Dakota	231	78	153	222	78	144	9	–	9	–	–	–
South Dakota	83	40	43	36	20	16	47	20	27	–	–	–
Nebraska	538	225	313	501	216	285	19	9	10	18	–	18
Kansas	764	355	409	691	310	381	68	45	23	5	–	5
SOUTH ATLANTIC												
Delaware	489	256	233	400	211	189	89	45	44	–	–	–
Maryland	4 833	2 795	2 038	4 220	2 337	1 883	589	445	144	24	13	11
District of Columbia	1 508	676	832	1 508	676	832	–	–	–	–	–	–
Virginia	7 218	4 382	2 836	7 078	4 299	2 779	140	83	57	–	–	–
West Virginia	704	347	357	582	289	293	122	58	64	–	–	–
North Carolina	724	332	392	504	239	265	209	93	116	11	–	11
South Carolina	1 160	655	505	1 110	638	472	39	17	22	11	–	11
Georgia	1 186	736	450	1 012	654	358	174	82	92	–	–	–
Florida	4 748	2 853	1 895	4 549	2 726	1 823	199	127	72	–	–	–
EAST SOUTH CENTRAL												
Kentucky	633	256	377	513	205	308	120	51	69	–	–	–
Tennessee	604	284	320	536	266	270	56	14	42	12	4	8
Alabama	299	131	168	267	125	142	32	6	26	–	–	–
Mississippi	318	155	163	200	98	102	110	57	53	8	–	8
WEST SOUTH CENTRAL												
Arkansas	171	64	107	120	43	77	32	11	21	19	10	9
Louisiana	937	551	386	809	483	326	122	68	54	6	–	6
Oklahoma	474	238	236	428	213	215	25	10	15	21	15	6
Texas	3 244	1 710	1 534	3 178	1 659	1 519	66	51	15	–	–	–
MOUNTAIN												
Montana	191	81	110	128	52	76	63	29	34	–	–	–
Idaho	213	117	96	126	62	64	87	55	32	–	–	–
Wyoming	118	87	31	101	87	14	17	–	17	–	–	–
Colorado	1 207	592	615	1 137	557	580	50	35	15	20	–	20
New Mexico	255	86	169	250	86	164	5	–	5	–	–	–
Arizona	1 386	824	562	1 164	662	502	179	119	60	43	43	–
Utah	484	229	255	418	208	210	66	21	45	–	–	–
Nevada	934	521	413	818	471	347	116	50	66	–	–	–
PACIFIC												
Washington	11 488	6 743	4 745	9 984	5 782	4 202	1 115	681	434	389	280	109
Oregon	1 466	779	687	1 185	624	561	254	138	116	27	17	10
California	135 248	74 798	60 450	125 960	68 198	57 762	6 948	4 549	2 399	2 340	2 051	289
Alaska	1 297	701	596	924	479	445	373	222	151	–	–	–
Hawaii	95 680	54 206	41 474	65 191	36 474	28 717	29 652	17 205	12 447	837	527	310

Table 19. Indian population of tribes, by sex, age, and whether living on identified reservations, 1970.

Source: U.S. Bureau of the Census, Nineteenth U.S. Census (Washington, D.C., 1973), Subject Reports, final report PC(2)-1F *American Indians*, table 16, p. 188.

United States	Population		Sex		Age (years)						Living on identified reservations	
	Number	Percent	Male	Female	Under 6	6 to 15	16 to 24	25 to 44	45 to 64	65 and over	Number	Percent of total
Total	763 594	100.0	375 384	388 210	111 520	199 136	130 286	174 099	104 751	43 802	213 770	28.0
Achomawi, Atsugewi, Chimariko, Pit River, and Shasta	980	0.1	494	486	152	298	128	199	138	65	46	4.7
Alaskan Athapaskans	2 125	0.3	1 117	1 008	319	616	336	513	275	66	13	0.6
Apache	22 993	3.0	11 775	11 218	3 924	6 676	4 120	5 140	2 304	829	11 735	51.0
Arapaho	2 993	0.4	1 577	1 416	475	787	538	802	296	95	1 453	48.5
Arikara	928	0.1	369	559	131	261	194	202	105	35	351	37.8
Assiniboin	2 219	0.3	1 128	1 091	299	695	322	484	299	120	1 108	49.9
Blackfeet	9 921	1.3	4 895	5 026	1 503	2 844	1 618	2 409	1 190	357	4 556	45.9
Caddo	1 207	0.2	657	550	144	420	135	357	127	24	9	0.7
Cahuilla, Luiseno, Gabrieleno, and Serrano	1 274	0.2	708	566	159	364	185	323	198	45	–	
Canadian and Latin American¹	7 282	1.0	3 697	3 585	1 209	1 913	1 132	1 897	749	382	19	0.3
Catawba, Oto, Missouri, and Iowa	2 366	0.3	1 246	1 120	310	629	339	589	364	135	8	0.3
Chehalis	1 660	0.2	766	894	314	399	287	377	172	111	511	30.8
Cherokee	66 150	8.7	32 291	33 859	6 744	13 757	10 526	16 291	12 983	5 849	3 629	5.5
Cheyenne	6 872	0.9	3 260	3 612	1 163	2 128	1 154	1 504	690	233	2 343	34.1
Chickasaw	5 616	0.7	2 786	2 830	566	1 214	812	1 199	1 190	635	43	0.8
Chinook	609	0.1	297	312	62	177	142	134	71	23	153	25.1
Chippewa	41 946	5.5	20 287	21 659	6 738	12 326	6 781	9 080	5 117	1 904	13 691	32.6
Choctaw and Houma	23 562	3.1	11 740	11 822	2 798	5 643	3 465	5 547	4 249	1 860	131	0.6
Coeur d'Alene	440	0.1	218	222	45	105	93	103	51	43	202	45.9
Columbia-Wenatchee	33	–	24	9	–	8	5	15	–	5	8	. . .
Colville and Lakes	3 180	0.4	1 504	1 676	362	891	461	769	502	195	1 360	42.8
Comanche	4 250	0.6	2 175	2 075	650	1 029	831	1 012	542	186	55	1.3
Costanoan, Washo, Yana, and Yuki	1 144	0.1	581	563	183	297	159	296	128	81	58	5.1
Cree	2 169	0.3	1 124	1 045	348	506	377	523	338	77	348	16.0
Creek, Alabama, and Coushatta	17 004	2.2	8 483	8 521	2 218	4 231	2 725	3 879	2 800	1 151	113	0.7
Crow	3 779	0.5	1 844	1 935	630	1 101	624	873	406	145	2 680	70.9
Delaware and Stockbridge	2 926	0.4	1 368	1 558	371	585	455	712	527	276	159	5.4
Flathead	3 702	0.5	1 863	1 839	526	939	662	847	477	251	2 090	56.5
Gros Ventre (Atsina)	1 519	0.2	810	709	251	481	326	309	108	44	676	44.5
Hidatsa and Mandan	1 705	0.2	792	913	224	509	285	411	197	79	642	37.7
Hupa	998	0.1	510	488	188	228	133	228	150	71	416	41.7
Iroquois	21 473	2.8	10 689	10 784	2 795	5 109	3 406	5 391	3 462	1 310	5 949	27.7
Mohawk	6 105	0.8	2 967	3 138	759	1 333	1 046	1 624	1 031	312	267	4.4
Oneida	5 673	0.7	2 836	2 837	803	1 538	895	1 340	796	301	1 552	27.4
Seneca	4 644	0.6	2 258	2 386	526	1 100	685	1 108	824	401	1 842	39.7
Onondaga, Tuscarora, Cayuga, and Wyandotte	5 051	0.7	2 628	2 423	707	1 138	780	1 319	811	296	2 288	45.3
Kalapuya	95	–	44	51	23	27	18	17	5	5		
Karok	1 406	0.2	734	672	243	334	204	305	213	107	42	3.0
Kato, Mattole, Tolowa, and Wailak	644	0.1	289	355	53	174	98	158	117	44	67	10.4
Kaw, Omaha, Osage, Ponca, and Quapaw	6 849	0.9	3 405	3 444	936	1 740	1 085	1 529	1 171	388	1 189	17.4
Kickapoo	1 249	0.2	594	655	221	357	170	269	159	73	31	2.5
Kiowa	4 337	0.6	2 099	2 238	791	1 171	856	994	427	98	116	2.7
Klamath, Modoc, Cayuse, and Molala	2 185	0.3	1 029	1 156	281	582	494	546	217	65	166	7.6
Klikitat	21		10	11	6	–	5	10	–		5	. . .
Kootenay	600	0.1	342	258	52	245	131	86	61	25	254	42.3
Lumbee	27 520	3.6	13 819	13 701	3 989	7 534	5 168	6 212	3 438	1 179		
Maidu and Miwok	2 546	0.3	1 342	1 204	323	697	392	582	408	144	30	1.2
Makah	1 482	0.2	666	816	322	297	282	305	193	83	401	27.1
Menominee	4 307	0.6	2 155	2 152	683	1 351	637	938	575	123	2 250	52.2
Miami, Piankashaw, and Wea	1 090	0.1	558	532	115	381	166	254	140	34		
Navajo	96 743	12.7	47 065	49 678	17 689	28 675	17 397	20 363	9 041	3 578	59 850	61.9
Nespelim, Okanagan, Sanpoil, and Spokane	1 675	0.2	806	869	235	455	301	397	208	79	396	23.6
New England and Long Island Algonquians	3 741	0.5	1 783	1 958	434	671	468	924	777	467	607	16.2
Nez Perce	1 987	0.3	895	1 092	369	550	332	405	253	78	949	47.8
Nooksak	505	0.1	175	330	55	174	91	78	91	16	35	6.9
Ottawa	3 533	0.5	1 644	1 889	568	781	547	791	632	214	4	0.1
Palouse and Topenish	147	–	79	68	31	29	22	26	24	15		
Papago and Pima	16 690	2.2	8 286	8 404	2 611	4 455	2 917	3 739	2 024	944	102	69.4
Pawnee	1 928	0.3	946	982	209	463	374	463	314	105	10 269	61.5
Pomo	2 626	0.3	1 268	1 358	443	668	501	638	261	115	43	2.2
Potawatomi	4 626	0.6	2 230	2 396	534	1 165	897	998	718	314	53	2.0
Powhatan	1 350	0.2	652	698	182	323	208	329	255	53	363	7.8
Pueblo	30 971	4.1	14 989	15 982	4 899	8 741	5 091	6 961	3 580	1 699	21 755	70.2
Hopi	7 236	0.9	3 473	3 763	1 169	1 997	1 381	1 440	885	364	4 380	60.5
Keresan	10 087	1.3	4 791	5 296	1 545	2 835	1 604	2 284	1 260	559	7 827	77.6
Tanoan	6 342	0.8	3 086	3 256	835	1 710	1 017	1 566	747	467	4 698	74.1
Zuni	7 306	1.0	3 639	3 667	1 350	2 199	1 089	1 671	688	309	4 850	66.4
Puget Sound Salish	2 810	0.4	1 474	1 336	305	749	502	630	409	215	549	19.5
Quileute and Chimakum	205	–	98	107	21	59	22	79	9	15		
Sac and Fox, and Mesquakie	2 182	0.3	1 022	1 160	319	687	321	496	296	63	389	17.8
Salinan and Chumash	360	–	175	185	51	91	72	61	61	24		
Seminole	5 055	0.7	2 489	2 566	679	1 347	845	1 139	809	236	575	11.4
Shawnee	2 208	0.3	1 125	1 083	287	594	323	563	342	99		
Shoshone, Northern and Southern Paiute, and Chemehuevi	14 248	1.9	6 809	7 439	1 906	3 836	2 508	3 308	1 860	830	4 083	28.7
Sioux (Dakota)	47 825	6.3	23 713	24 112	8 537	13 254	8 206	9 520	6 003	2 305	25 517	53.4
Southwest Oregon Penutians and Athapaskans	730	0.1	349	381	105	154	183	128	123	37	179	24.5
Straits Salish	2 254	0.3	1 089	1 165	329	735	382	504	221	83	778	34.5
Tillamook	139		45	94	35	50	9	31	10	4		

Includes those Canadians and Latin American tribes not elsewhere classified

Table 19 (continued)

United States	Population		Sex		Age (years)						Living on identified reservations	
	Number	Percent	Male	Female	Under 6	6 to 15	16 to 24	25 to 44	45 to 64	65 and over	Number	Percent of total
Tlingit and Haida	7 543	1.0	3 891	3 652	1 171	2 103	1 107	1 858	935	369	28	0.4
Twana	1 057	0.1	491	566	106	360	172	221	149	49	377	35.7
Umatilla	702	0.1	317	385	77	259	103	163	87	13	306	43.6
Ute	3 815	0.5	1 917	1 898	694	1 113	601	866	308	233	2 471	64.8
Walla Walla	269	–	134	135	24	56	61	72	43	13	66	24.5
Wappo and Yurok	1 852	0.2	869	983	243	593	300	480	183	53	321	17.3
Warm Springs	1 518	0.2	696	822	364	377	322	326	100	29	934	61.5
Wichita	485	0.1	241	244	76	111	39	149	85	25	–	–
Winnebago	2 832	0.4	1 432	1 400	424	716	507	651	366	168	483	17.1
Wintun	1 165	0.2	516	649	218	228	224	259	172	64	60	5.2
Wiyot	119	–	72	47	17	23	17	35	12	15	–	–
Yakima	3 856	0.5	1 857	1 999	610	1 314	566	766	468	132	1 926	49.9
Yokuts	791	0.1	324	467	111	258	109	226	53	34	13	1.6
Yuman	7 635	1.0	3 837	3 798	938	2 131	1 159	1 746	1 160	501	1 926	25.2
Other specified tribes	4 518	0.6	2 331	2 187	555	1 198	710	1 112	682	261	195	4.3
Not reported	161 543	21.2	79 092	82 451	21 220	37 534	29 308	37 978	24 298	11 205	19 062	11.8

Table 20. Persons naturalized, by country or region of former allegiance, years ended June 30, 1966–1975.

Source: 1975 Annual Report: Immigration and Naturalization Service (Washington, D.C., 1976), table 39, p. 117.

COUNTRY OF FORMER ALLEGIANCE	1966–1975	1966	1967	1968	1969	1970	1971	1972	1973	1974	1975
ALL COUNTRIES ...	1,138,349	103,059	104,902	102,726	98,709	110,399	108,407	116,215	120,740	131,655	141,537
EUROPE	516,773	62,063	61,128	57,815	51,403	48,348	45,065	44,934	47,735	48,014	50,268
ALBANIA	1,163	110	110	109	103	86	106	109	113	152	165
AUSTRIA	6,676	1,012	973	825	688	679	627	588	455	421	408
BELGIUM	2,781	334	337	330	291	358	304	235	214	188	190
BULGARIA	1,255	69	75	92	74	81	120	132	175	162	275
CZECHOSLOVAKIA	6,885	551	458	438	340	506	629	655	648	922	1,738
DENMARK	2,984	408	442	428	316	303	270	225	231	180	181
FINLAND	2,023	265	265	251	236	222	192	154	152	157	129
FRANCE	12,757	1,446	1,472	1,424	1,416	1,398	1,328	1,083	1,067	1,035	1,088
GERMANY	93,337	13,706	13,204	12,692	10,618	10,067	8,455	6,953	6,670	5,785	5,187
GREECE	40,480	3,373	3,438	3,256	3,029	2,906	2,614	4,243	5,423	5,551	6,647
HUNGARY	17,375	2,971	2,376	2,139	1,725	1,599	1,438	1,474	1,313	1,145	1,195
IRELAND	22,344	2,885	3,083	2,959	2,620	2,249	2,144	1,751	1,771	1,575	1,307
ITALY	90,207	10,981	10,572	9,379	8,773	7,892	7,637	8,375	8,902	8,898	8,798
LATVIA	2,676	388	353	403	331	250	261	219	188	142	141
LITHUANIA	2,848	393	397	360	345	272	263	217	242	188	171
NETHERLANDS	17,120	2,762	2,698	2,555	1,930	1,795	1,428	1,101	1,038	882	931
NORWAY	3,426	497	506	488	461	364	305	230	201	200	174
POLAND	34,922	3,833	4,072	3,893	3,643	3,426	3,318	3,147	3,323	3,198	3,069
PORTUGAL	22,012	2,179	2,156	1,694	1,543	1,374	1,306	2,035	2,671	3,326	3,728
ROMANIA	5,986	299	367	717	434	670	936	831	566	463	703
SPAIN	8,065	731	796	713	721	791	776	826	849	940	922
SWEDEN	3,015	327	367	359	325	299	262	218	332	332	194
SWITZERLAND	4,735	587	578	521	514	495	508	445	440	333	314
U.S.S.R.	7,509	848	874	887	767	677	850	795	740	521	550
UNITED KINGDOM	80,178	8,930	8,777	8,466	7,979	7,549	6,983	6,819	7,589	8,554	8,532
YUGOSLAVIA	20,692	1,764	1,976	2,067	1,808	1,725	1,694	1,787	2,119	2,479	3,273
OTHER EUROPE	3,322	414	406	370	373	315	311	287	303	285	258
ASIA	236,429	14,716	14,665	15,432	15,806	16,896	17,839	28,097	30,283	37,780	44,915
CHINA & TAIWAN	55,464	3,111	2,924	3,186	3,399	3,099	2,880	9,434	9,056	8,692	9,683
INDIA	8,538	224	262	303	384	325	443	1,031	1,210	1,636	2,720
INDONESIA	1,739	128	145	178	131	105	134	181	210	234	323
IRAN	4,590	357	326	334	446	416	501	569	578	562	601
IRAQ	3,029	175	164	196	214	184	235	370	578	562	601
ISRAEL	18,688	2,814	2,976	2,271	1,836	1,516	1,628	1,413	1,403	510	526
JAPAN	19,727	2,673	2,553	2,476	2,167	1,828	1,716	1,676	1,599	1,591	1,844
JORDAN	6,935	401	384	399	497	429	544	854	1,006	1,157	1,548
KOREA	26,678	1,180	1,953	1,776	1,646	1,687	2,083	2,933	3,562	4,451	1,364
LEBANON	4,417	374	351	346	338	351	345	438	504	574	6,007
PHILIPPINES	67,036	2,384	2,958	2,807	3,877	5,469	5,488	7,001	8,149	13,573	796
SYRIA	2,109	133	117	162	127	146	152	188	250	337	15,330
THAILAND	1,713	50	45	68	79	108	135	199	263	355	497
TURKEY	4,732	347	406	452	444	430	469	544	541	554	411
VIETNAM	4,540	69	72	135	159	282	366	477	675	936	545
YEMEN (SAN'A)	1,223	43	41	47	96	120	201	181	157	140	1,369
OTHER ASIA	5,271	253	288	296	296	401	519	608	665	791	197
											1,154
AFRICA	10,787	562	576	905	671	767	795	921	1,242	1,591	2,757
SOUTH AFRICA, REP.OF	1,394	111	133	134	136	130	131	130	165	139	185
EGYPT	6,072	219	252	513	334	377	355	439	637	958	1,988
OTHER AFRICA	3,321	232	191	258	201	260	309	352	440	494	584
OCEANIA	4,614	422	429	461	384	391	466	382	540	544	595
AUSTRALIA	2,533	278	295	286	247	216	267	214	248	255	227
OTHER OCEANIA	2,081	144	134	175	137	175	199	168	292	289	368
NORTH AMERICA	305,411	20,899	22,597	23,167	24,831	37,693	36,941	34,451	33,988	36,050	34,794
CANADA	59,531	8,579	8,120	6,984	6,187	6,340	5,915	4,835	4,739	4,084	3,548
MEXICO	57,866	5,677	6,044	6,134	5,111	6,195	6,361	5,850	5,507	5,206	5,781
WEST INDIES	164,733	5,031	6,670	8,109	11,219	22,675	21,944	21,283	21,170	23,940	22,692
BAHAMAS	102	–	–	–	–	–	–	–	–	50	52
BARBADOS 1/	1,722		43	112	122	122	143	169	214	347	450
CUBA	136,146	3,829	5,485	6,784	9,654	20,888	19,754	18,397	17,415	18,394	15,546
DOMINICAN REPUBLIC	7,811	333	321	363	522	538	752	930	1,104	1,430	1,518
GRENADA	22	–	–	–	–	–	–	–	–	1	21
HAITI	7,334	238	245	303	282	433	554	812	1,015	1,486	1,966
JAMAICA	8,068	519	433	429	481	479	500	606	936	1,533	2,152
TRINIDAD & TOBAGO	3,528	112	143	118	158	215	241	369	486	699	987
CENTRAL AMERICA	23,281	1,612	1,763	1,940	2,114	2,483	2,721	2,483	2,572	2,820	2,773
COSTA RICA	2,812	170	199	235	263	300	360	306	291	342	346
EL SALVADOR	2,251	119	147	140	159	200	219	265	318	342	342
GUATEMALA	2,213	125	145	184	198	208	255	249	254	287	308
HONDURAS	4,358	266	321	302	343	448	560	473	502	603	540
NICARAGUA	3,067	198	221	236	303	292	338	317	344	418	400
PANAMA	8,580	734	730	843	848	1,035	989	873	863	828	837
SOUTH AMERICA	47,877	2,538	3,065	3,081	3,758	4,679	5,713	5,837	5,905	6,579	6,722
ARGENTINA	11,583	719	820	800	1,014	1,226	1,459	1,315	1,419	1,433	1,378
BOLIVIA	2,102	103	119	145	172	182	255	302	267	273	284
BRAZIL	4,223	316	376	328	366	473	483	433	428	536	484
CHILE	3,361	200	204	224	261	334	436	481	390	441	390
COLOMBIA	10,296	481	556	587	742	970	1,182	1,290	1,303	1,486	1,699
ECUADOR	5,935	261	352	362	444	558	737	752	800	862	807
GUYANA 1/	1,991		46	69	64	132	195	226	315	420	524
PARAGUAY	510	16	30	24	35	54	74	66	69	83	59
PERU	4,723	218	298	281	365	432	537	634	591	657	710
URUGUAY	1,070	60	34	64	84	110	144	111	114	162	187
VENEZUELA	2,083	164	230	197	211	208	211	227	209	226	200
U.S. POSSESSIONS	2,872	437	476	357	285	337	353	352	169	59	47
STATELESS & NOT REPORTED	13,586	1,422	1,966	1,508	1,271	1,288	1,235	1,241	878	1,038	1,439

1/ INCLUDED IN UNITED KINGDOM PRIOR TO 1967.

Table 21. Immigrants admitted, by country or region of birth and major occupation, year ended June 30, 1975.

Source: 1975 Annual Report: Immigration and Naturalization Service (Washington, D.C., 1976), table 8, p. 44.

COUNTRY OR REGION OF BIRTH	NUMBER ADMITTED	PROFESSIONAL, TECHNICAL, & KINDRED WORKERS	MANAGERS & ADMINISTRATORS, EXCEPT FARM	SALES WORKERS	CLERICAL & KINDRED WORKERS	CRAFTSMEN & KINDRED WORKERS	OPERATIVES, EXCEPT TRANSPORT	TRANSPORT EQUIPMENT OPERATIVES	LABORERS, EXCEPT FARM	FARMERS & FARM MANAGERS	FARM LABORERS & FARM FOREMEN	SERVICE WORKERS, EXCEPT PRIVATE HOUSEHOLD	PRIVATE HOUSEHOLD WORKERS	HOUSEWIVES, CHILDREN & OTHERS WITH NO OCCUPATION REPORTED
ALL COUNTRIES ...	386,194	38,491	10,012	3,411	14,141	20,615	18,437	2,870	12,991	927	6,281	15,510	5,919	236,533
EUROPE	73,996	7,235	2,122	753	2,894	6,374	3,402	709	1,641	492	2,575	2,972	975	41,852
AUSTRIA	402	74	34	7	24	22	8	-	3	-	1	28	2	199
CZECHOSLOVAKIA	525	129	13	5	34	53	21	7	15	2	3	30	1	212
DENMARK	353	78	29	3	27	17	1	1	2	1	1	17	1	175
FRANCE	1,364	235	63	16	88	53	16	5	13	-	4	121	17	733
GERMANY	5,154	500	204	121	403	199	72	7	19	3	6	182	18	3,420
GREECE	9,984	421	242	94	157	1,223	651	133	148	72	391	679	54	5,719
HUNGARY	882	158	34	19	67	143	51	12	26	-	3	47	5	317
IRELAND	1,285	315	39	20	95	114	47	8	40	7	13	79	39	463
ITALY	11,552	420	240	52	133	1,412	738	116	429	129	404	450	121	6,903
NETHERLANDS	816	141	59	24	58	38	13	5	8	3	3	33	-	1,817
POLAND	3,941	468	71	38	160	365	296	76	194	65	167	182	42	7,375
PORTUGAL	11,845	116	139	40	216	1,031	493	141	277	180	1,084	231	522	46.
ROMANIA	1,161	323	34	11	68	116	63	16	13	1	21	32	2	1,487
SPAIN	2,549	236	71	17	49	191	110	16	56	2	120	146	48	243
SWEDEN	482	113	25	6	36	10	15	1	2	-	1	27	3	263
SWITZERLAND	538	101	34	6	38	41	5	-	1	1	1	46	3	2,446
U.S.S.R.	5,118	1,127	108	92	243	439	294	71	99	1	16	177	5	6,254
UNITED KINGDOM	10,807	1,781	574	140	843	496	247	57	78	9	16	258	54	1,986
YUGOSLAVIA	3,524	211	33	21	60	311	196	20	191	13	308	156	18	933
OTHER EUROPE	1,714	288	76	21	95	100	65	17	27	3	12	51	20	933
ASIA	132,469	23,553	4,936	1,116	4,750	4,287	2,352	605	1,448	222	966	3,816	1,436	82,982
CHINA & TAIWAN	18,536	2,621	1,447	217	941	481	623	82	619	10	130	1,312	124	9,929
HONG KONG	4,891	294	88	33	196	60	107	10	12	1	15	102	3	3,973
INDIA	15,773	6,156	481	102	414	230	193	10	52	7	99	165	41	7,763
INDONESIA	444	73	27	5	26	9	6	2	9	1	1	12	6	263
IRAN	2,337	415	132	30	86	84	43	27	30	1	3	148	5	1,333
IRAQ	2,796	182	66	28	94	215	73	25	50	1	7	61	11	1,983
ISRAEL	2,125	341	71	30	101	163	51	20	21	4	20	48	7	1,251
JAPAN	4,274	397	257	38	150	85	36	14	22	3	10	339	13	2,910
JORDAN	2,578	204	111	30	67	162	49	23	59	5	54	78	-	1,736
KOREA	28,362	3,083	894	207	854	1,255	446	186	87	24	84	506	103	20,633
LEBANON	2,075	190	88	27	61	247	67	14	22	6	12	84	5	1,252
PHILIPPINES	31,751	7,142	780	262	1,357	579	345	142	251	146	466	552	1,049	18,680
RYUKYU ISLANDS	8	1	-	-	-	-	-	-	-	-	-	-	1	6
SYRIA	1,222	183	44	13	24	169	67	6	17	4	10	27	7	651
THAILAND	4,217	572	90	6	89	59	46	4	12	-	1	124	26	3,188
TURKEY	1,592	137	49	12	77	195	63	15	16	2	8	49	4	1,015
VIETNAM	3,039	90	32	8	38	7	12	-	4	-	2	30	7	2,809
OTHER ASIA	6,449	1,472	279	68	225	230	125	25	165	7	44	179	24	3,606
AFRICA	6,729	1,521	221	94	386	341	221	42	89	1	16	209	37	3,551
EGYPT	1,707	520	43	19	65	99	35	4	11	-	1	28	5	877
OTHER AFRICA	5,022	1,001	178	75	321	242	186	38	78	1	15	181	32	2,674
OCEANIA	3,347	453	105	34	226	136	60	37	137	11	43	83	78	1,944
AUSTRALIA	1,116	275	58	12	105	26	11	1	5	-	3	29	8	583
OTHER OCEANIA	2,231	178	47	22	121	11	49	36	132	11	40	54	70	1,361
NORTH AMERICA	146,668	4,293	2,124	1,260	4,885	7,755	10,257	1,326	9,457	194	2,615	6,789	3,012	92,701
CANADA	7,308	947	309	144	384	229	116	35	137	8	19	139	22	4,819
MEXICO	62,205	612	529	242	659	2,738	3,807	485	6,061	117	1,969	3,469	650	40,467
BARBADOS	1,618	110	25	20	128	151	91	9	20	-	2	82	198	782
CUBA	25,955	710	375	519	1,427	1,224	2,556	255	2,568	7	22	1,192	67	15,033
DOMINICAN REPUBLIC .	14,066	256	241	70	264	642	1,024	185	218	44	460	475	255	9,932
HAITI	5,145	232	120	26	204	432	738	54	68	2	27	199	123	2,920
JAMAICA	11,076	503	181	78	611	929	627	147	97	10	82	395	810	6,606
TRINIDAD & TOBAGO ..	5,982	277	118	45	445	467	327	36	41	1	7	213	239	3,766
COSTA RICA	889	37	11	9	31	46	63	7	9	-	4	32	31	609
EL SALVADOR	2,416	79	39	6	149	172	241	22	36	1	3	117	179	1,372
GUATEMALA	1,859	61	26	15	75	143	255	19	31	1	4	87	66	1,076
HONDURAS	1,357	53	9	2	55	85	91	11	41	-	2	35	101	874
NICARAGUA	947	44	21	3	40	57	86	4	9	-	2	36	40	605
PANAMA	1,694	76	36	18	114	47	50	6	21	-	2	41	77	1,216
OTHER NORTH AMERICA.	4,151	296	94	63	299	395	185	51	100	3	10	277	154	2,224
SOUTH AMERICA	22,984	1,436	504	154	1,000	1,722	2,145	151	219	7	66	1,641	381	13,558
ARGENTINA	2,227	202	68	20	67	253	177	16	25	1	4	119	22	1,253
BRAZIL	1,070	99	30	8	46	47	40	7	5	-	3	50	17	725
CHILE	1,111	150	43	15	46	81	80	10	17	1	7	54	17	590
COLOMBIA	6,434	311	111	33	211	455	865	33	48	-	15	278	61	4,013
ECUADOR	4,727	89	48	13	103	360	419	34	43	1	15	712	61	2,829
GUYANA	3,169	187	77	29	320	206	177	17	21	4	12	125	138	1,856
PERU	2,256	231	56	17	96	184	243	20	32	-	9	229	33	1,106
URUGUAY	781	45	28	9	36	94	97	9	21	-	-	35	13	394
VENEZUELA	527	39	19	5	23	8	10	3	3	-	-	13	3	401
OTHER SOUTH AMERICA.	682	83	24	5	52	41	37	2	4	-	1	26	16	391
OTHER COUNTRIES	1	-	-	-	-	-	-	-	-	-	-	-	-	-

Table 22. Population of Spanish origin, by sex and type of Spanish origin, for the United States and the five southwestern states, March 1976.

Source: U.S. Bureau of the Census, *Current Population Reports* (Washington, D.C., 1977), series P-20, no. 310, table 1, p. 17.

(Numbers in thousands)

Area and origin	Total		Male		Female	
	Number	Percent	Number	Percent	Number	Percent
UNITED STATES						
Persons of Spanish origin......	11,117	100.0	5,439	100.0	5,678	100.0
Mexican.........................	6,590	59.3	3,285	60.4	3,305	58.2
Puerto Rican....................	1,753	15.8	849	15.6	904	15.9
Cuban..........................	687	6.2	315	5.8	372	6.6
Central or South American........	752	6.8	355	6.5	398	7.0
Other Spanish...................	1,335	12.0	636	11.7	700	12.3
FIVE SOUTHWESTERN STATES						
Persons of Spanish origin......	6,414	100.0	3,176	100.0	3,238	100.0
Mexican.........................	5,490	85.6	2,741	86.3	2,749	84.9
Puerto Rican....................	58	0.9	35	1.1	23	0.7
Other Spanish[1].................	866	13.5	397	12.5	466	14.4

[1] Includes Cuban, Central or South American, and other Spanish origin.

Table 23. Total and Spanish-origin population, by broad age groups, sex, and type of Spanish origin, for the United States, March 1976.

Source: U.S. Bureau of the Census, *Current Population Reports* (Washington, D.C., 1977), series P-20, no. 310, table 2, p. 17.

Sex and age	Total persons	Spanish origin					
		Total	Mexican	Puerto Rican	Cuban	Central or South American	Other Spanish
BOTH SEXES							
Median age....................years..	28.9	20.9	20.3	19.6	36.8	25.5	19.1
Percent							
Under 5 years old..................	7.4	12.8	13.3	12.5	5.6	14.1	13.7
18 years old and over..............	69.0	55.7	54.9	53.0	72.0	60.6	52.2
65 years old and over..............	10.3	3.8	3.5	2.5	9.6	2.1	4.9
MALE							
Median age....................years..	27.8	19.5	19.8	17.1	36.3	22.8	17.2
Percent							
Under 5 years old..................	7.8	13.6	13.9	13.8	7.5	14.6	14.2
18 years old and over..............	67.5	53.0	53.6	47.2	70.8	54.7	47.7
65 years old and over..............	8.7	3.3	3.1	2.3	8.0	1.5	4.6
FEMALE							
Median age....................years..	29.9	22.2	20.9	22.0	37.1	26.7	21.3
Percent							
Under 5 years old..................	7.0	12.1	12.8	11.2	4.0	13.6	13.1
18 years old and over..............	70.5	58.3	56.1	58.4	73.1	65.8	56.4
65 years old and over..............	11.7	4.2	3.9	2.6	10.9	2.6	5.3

The Harvard Encyclopedia of American Ethnic Groups *was set in Trump Medieval at Progressive Typographers, Inc., and printed web offset by The Murray Printing Company on 45-pound Thorcote manufactured by P. H. Glatfelter Company. The book was bound by The Murray Printing Company in Holliston Mills' C-1 Roxite, linen finish. Book design is by Mike Fender.*